FOCUS ON THE FAMILY

THE

Adventures
in
ODYSSEY®
BIBLE

Includes the Entire Text of the
INTERNATIONAL CHILDREN'S BIBLE

WORD 🅦 BIBLES

OLD TESTAMENT

NEW TESTAMENT

PREFACE

The Bible you're holding contains the full text of the *International Children's Bible*, the first translation ever created especially for children. This translation, unlike any other, has two important features: it is entirely for children *and* it is a full and complete translation of the Bible. No other Bible achieves this balance between faithfulness to the Word of God and appropriateness for children. With the *International Children's Bible*, children have a complete Bible translation created just for them.

A Trustworthy Translation

The *International Children's Bible* is a true translation, not a paraphrase. A team of scholars from the World Bible Translation Center worked together with twenty-one other Bible scholars to translate the text directly from the original languages. They translated this text with the same professionalism and diligence of any other full translation, putting every word through the rigors of scholarly study. You can trust that this Bible accurately represents God's Word as it came to us in the original languages.

A Children's Translation

The *International Children's Bible* is also a true children's translation, perfect for grade-school children. The translators kept sentences short and simple. They placed rigorous controls on vocabulary, sticking closely to a predetermined list prepared by experts in vocabulary choice for young readers. They used modern terms for measurements and places. And they put figures of speech and idiomatic expressions ("he rested with his fathers") in language that children would not misunderstand ("he died"). Young readers will not be lost or confused by the wording in this Bible.

An independent study confirms this. Dr. Charles K. Kinzer of Peabody College of Education at Vanderbilt University did a comparative study of the *International Children's Bible* and four other versions commonly used by children. The results showed that the *International Children's Bible* was clearly the easiest version for children to read. It was in fact the only version that could be comprehended on a third-grade level.

Until recently, children have had to choose between Bible story books and Bible translations created for adults. Now they have a third choice: a Bible translation just for them. You can be sure that every part of the *Adventures in Odyssey Bible,* including the Bible text itself, will hold your child's interest.

—*The Publisher*

THE

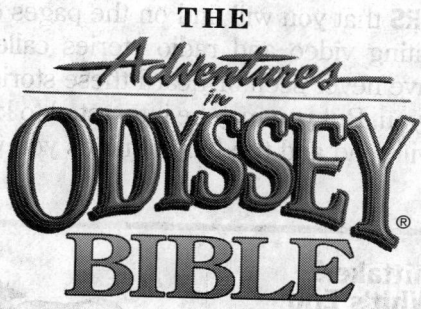

Focus on the Family and Word Publishing have joined forces to produce a Bible that will appeal to children. Many of the features take advantage of the familiar characters from the popular *Adventures in Odyssey* radio program and the best-selling *Adventures in Odyssey* animated videos. These colorful characters will introduce children to Bible stories, values, and concepts.

THE GOALS FOR THIS BIBLE INCLUDE:
- to excite the imaginations of young readers
- to stimulate creative thinking about the Bible
- to communicate godly values
- to educate with basic Bible knowledge
- to teach basic Bible study techniques
- to introduce children to the importance of applying the Bible to their lives.

The *New Century Version/International Children's Bible* is a translation using modern English. You will find an explanatory preface about the translation elsewhere in these front pages.

THE FEATURES in the *Adventures in Odyssey Bible* have been designed to make use of the interest children already have in the Odyssey radio/video characters. They direct that interest toward the truths found in God's Word.

THE CHARACTERS that you will find on the pages of your Bible are from the exciting video and radio stories called *Adventures in Odyssey*. If you have never seen or heard these stories, this Bible will still be useful for you. But you may be interested to know a little about the names you will read and the helpful notes you will find on many pages.

Who Is Mr. Whittaker? And What Is Whit's End?

Dylan Taylor is Whit's constant young visitor and helper.

Jessie Taylor is Dylan's little sister.

Mr. Whittaker has lived a long time. He is one of the oldest and wisest people in Odyssey. But he is also a teacher and friend to the kids in town. Whit owns an odd but exciting place called Whit's End. Some kids like Whit's End because it is their favorite place to get an ice cream cone or a soft drink. But Whit's End is filled with all kinds of rooms where Whit works on new inventions and scientific experiments. While the kids help Whit with his work, he teaches them about life.

When you see a picture of Mr. Whittaker on a page of your Bible, it shows you where to find a message God wants you to read. Just as he tries to do with all the kids in Odyssey, Mr. Whittaker will help you understand and learn some special lessons from the Bible.

You will see other characters from the *Adventures in Odyssey* in your Bible. They are there to point the way and to help you think about God's Word.

Sal is one of Dylan's best friends.

Carter is another close friend of Dylan.

Eugene is Mr. Whittaker's assistant. Sometimes he helps, and sometimes he makes a big mess.

Sherman

is Dylan's dog. He's one of the official mascots of Odyssey.

WHIT'S WISDOM

Whit's Wisdom notes are marked with a drawing of Mr. Whittaker. When you find him, you will have a chance to think about an important lesson in the Bible. Whit is easy to get along with. He loves your questions and will probably

IMAGINATION STATION

The Imagination Station notes are marked by a cartoon of the Imagination Station, Mr. Whittaker's one-of-a-kind time-travel contraption. If you follow these notes, you will learn some important ideas found in the Bible. When you want to find out about God's love for us, the Imagination Station notes will guide you to the places in the Bible that talk about love. These notes are organized in trips, with each note leading you to another one. Each trip includes about ten notes. So if you want to learn what God is like, for example, an Imagination Station trip can take you to ten verses and notes about God. This Bible has twenty Imagination Station trips.

Whit's Wisdom

Kids, I can't think of a better place to start than right at the beginning. That's where God started. **W**hen we start, we always start with something. If we want to make a drawing, we begin with paper and crayons. If we build a clubhouse, we start with wood and tools. And don't forget, we also need a tree! But God started with nothing! That's why we call...

get you thinking. You will learn that you fit right in with the kids from Odyssey.

God's Love for Us
PSALM 36:5-7

Think of the biggest thing you've ever seen: a mountain? A building? A whale? Whatever it is, God's love for us is much bigger. King David might have been looking at a mountain or a big body of water when he wrote these words. As he thought about how big something like an ocean or the sky is, he probably felt very small compared to it. And then he had another thought: God's love is even bigger—*much, much* bigger—than that! David was overwhelmed by God's love. Take a few minutes right now and think about how huge God's love for you really is.

To find out more about God's love for us, zoom to page 733.

STRATA-FLYER

The Strata-flyer notes are marked with a picture of Mr. Whittaker's amazing flying machine, the Strata-flyer. They are organized like Imagination Station notes. If

starbursts clarify the issues being explored and encourage children to become reflective thinkers. If you are leading one child or a group through one of the comics, stop at the starburst. Let the kids catch up by asking a question or two. Have them explore the options open to

Children Who Saw God at Work
ISAAC • GENESIS 22:2-13

Isaac knew how much his father, Abraham, loved God. Isaac loved God too and was glad to go on a trip to offer a sacrifice to God. When they sacrificed an animal, they killed it and presented it to God by burning it on an altar built of stones. God wanted his people to do this because it showed how much they loved and trusted him. But Isaac was surprised when they built their altar, and his father tied him up. Abraham didn't want to hurt Isaac, but he wanted to obey God even more. Isaac trusted that his father was doing what was right.

An angel stopped Abraham from hurting Isaac. God knew that Abraham loved him more than anything. Isaac wanted to love God, just as his father did. Do you love God more than anything else?

To meet a boy who got sold by his brothers for a few silver coins, fly to page 54.

you follow the directions, these twenty trips will take you to meet many great (and sometimes not-so-great) people, visit unusual places, discover strange creatures, and find out about some of the most important events in the Bible. For example, if you are curious about animals in the Bible, climb aboard the Strata-flyer and you will find them.

MINI COMIC INSERTS

These comics combine several important tools in communicating with kids: visual impact, thought-provoking content, humorous insight, and practical application. Make use of the starburst component of each insert to focus the thoughts of your youngsters. The

the character. Perhaps even ask them to decide which choice they think the character will make.

Once the kids catch on, make use of the starburst idea from time to time in your storytelling to introduce the extended discussion. For instance, in telling about Bartimaeus' meeting with Jesus (Luke 18:35-43) or Zacchaeus' tree climbing adventure (Luke 19:1-10), stop at a crucial point and ask: "What will Jesus do? What will Bartimaeus do? What will Zacchaeus do? What would you do?" Kids will discover that spiritual subjects are not drab and humorless.

MEMORY VERSES

Mr. Whittaker says that it is important for kids to memorize parts of the Bible. Some helpful verses are marked for you to read and memorize. Look for them and then take some time to memorize them. They really will help you!

So God created human beings in his image. In the image of God he created them. He created them male and female.
• Genesis 1:27

CHARACTER DROP-INS

From time to time you will notice one of the Odyssey characters dropping in to point out a story or verse that you ought to check out.

OTHER HELPS

In the back of this Bible you will find other helps. A memory verse checklist lets you record verses you memorize. Three indexes are provided to help locate Imagination Station notes, Strata-flyer notes, and Whit's Wisdom notes. A dictionary explains the meaning of the words that are marked with a ^{d} throughout the Bible.

When you find a word marked with an ^{n}, look for a note of explanation at the bottom of that page.

OLD TESTAMENT

Whit's Wisdom: Creation • Genesis 1 and 2

Kids, I can't think of a better place to start than right at the beginning. That's where God started.

When *we* start, we always start with something. If we want to make a drawing, we begin with paper and crayons. If we build a club house, we start with wood and tools. And don't forget, we also need a tree! But God started with nothing! That's why we call what God did *creating*. We make things, but God creates!

The first two chapters of Genesis tell us about the way God created the world. God got to choose everything: colors, shapes, and sizes. He created elephants big and grasshoppers tiny. Can you imagine a world with little elephants that could hop and huge grasshoppers that could stomp around? Think of other combinations. What would cows with humps look like? Camels with stripes? God made so many unusual and wonderful parts of creation that we can spend our whole lives looking and still not see everything.

What was the first part of God's creation? Look at the first verse of chapter 1. God started with the sky and the earth. He created a place to put everything else! Now, if you read the whole chapter, you can make a list of God's creation.

Kids, here's a question we need to learn to ask whenever we are reading the Bible: "Where do I fit?"

Of course, none of us were alive when God created the world. But can we say that he created us? Yes we can! Do you know why? Look at verses 26 to 28. God created the first family and told them to have many children. That's how we know we're part of God's creation.

This means we also have the same big job God gave to the first people-to be in charge of the earth. We are supposed to use the earth and take care of it. It will feed us as we work with it.

Do you ever have to mow the lawn at your house? Do you have a garden? Who takes care of pets that belong to your family? When you have one of these responsibilities to do, remember that you are doing more that obeying Mom or Dad. You are helping to take care of God's world.

Related Passages: Psalm 104; Hebrews 1:10-12

Teacher/Parent Hint: Younger children might enjoy drawing animals or trees they would have created. Browsing through *National Geographic* or *Smithsonian* magazine can provide good photographs of truly amazing parts of creation. For example, one article captures a photographer's quest to picture every letter of the alphabet in the natural color shapes of butterfly wings.

GENESIS

The Beginning
of All Things

The Beginning of the World

1 In the beginning God created the sky and the earth. ²The earth was empty and had no form. Darkness covered the ocean, and God's Spirit*ᵈ* was moving over the water.

³Then God said, "Let there be light!" And there was light. ⁴God saw that the light was good. So he divided the light from the darkness. ⁵God named the light "day" and the darkness "night." Evening passed, and morning came. This was the first day.

⁶Then God said, "Let there be something to divide the water in two!" ⁷So God made the air to divide the water in two. Some of the water was above the air, and some of the water was below it. ⁸God named the air "sky." Evening passed, and morning came. This was the second day.

⁹Then God said, "Let the water under the sky be gathered together so the dry land will appear." And it happened. ¹⁰God named the dry land "earth." He named the water that was gathered together "seas." God saw that this was good.

¹¹Then God said, "Let the earth produce plants. Some plants will make grain for seeds. Others will make fruit with seeds in it. Every seed will produce more of its own kind of plant." And it happened. ¹²The earth produced plants. Some plants had grain for seeds. The trees made fruit with seeds in it. Each seed grew its own kind of plant. God saw that all this was good. ¹³Evening passed, and morning came. This was the third day.

¹⁴Then God said, "Let there be lights in the sky to separate day from night. These lights will be used for signs, seasons, days and years. ¹⁵They will be in the sky to give light to the earth." And it happened.

¹⁶So God made the two large lights. He made the brighter light to rule the day. He made the smaller light to rule the night. He also made the stars. ¹⁷God put all these in the sky to shine on the earth. ¹⁸They are to rule over the day and over the night. He put them there to separate the light from the darkness. God saw that all these things were good. ¹⁹Evening passed, and morning came. This was the fourth day.

²⁰Then God said, "Let the water be filled with living things. And let birds fly in the air above the earth."

²¹So God created the large sea animals. He created every living thing that moves in the sea. The sea is filled with these living things. Each one produces more of its own kind. God also made every bird that flies. And each bird produces more of its own kind. God saw that this was good. ²²God blessed them and said, "Have many young ones and grow in number. Fill the water of the seas, and let the birds grow in number on the earth." ²³Evening passed, and morning came. This was the fifth day.

²⁴Then God said, "Let the earth be filled with animals. And let each produce more of its own kind. Let there be tame animals and small crawling animals and wild animals. And let each produce more of its kind." And it happened.

²⁵So God made the wild animals, the tame animals and all the small crawling animals to produce more of their own kind. God saw that this was good.

²⁶Then God said, "Let us make

human beings in our image and likeness. And let them rule over the fish in the sea and the birds in the sky. Let them rule over the tame animals, over all the earth and over all the small crawling animals on the earth."

27So God created human beings in his image. In the image of God he created them. He created them male and female. 28God blessed them and said, "Have many children and grow in number. Fill the earth and be its master.

So God created human beings in his image. In the image of God he created them. He created them male and female.
• Genesis 1:27

Rule over the fish in the sea and over the birds in the sky. Rule over every living thing that moves on the earth."

29God said, "Look, I have given you all the plants that have grain for seeds. And I have given you all the trees whose fruits have seeds in them. They will be food for you. 30I have given all the green plants to all the animals to eat. They will be food for every wild animal, every bird of the air and every small crawling animal." And it happened. 31God looked at everything he had made, and it was very good. Evening passed, and morning came. This was the sixth day.

The Seventh Day—Rest

2 So the sky, the earth and all that filled them were finished. 2By the seventh day God finished the work he had been doing. So on the seventh day he rested from all his work. 3God blessed the seventh day and made it a holy day. He made it holy because on that day he rested. He rested from all the work he had done in creating the world.

The First People

4This is the story of the creation of the sky and the earth. When the Lord God made the earth and the sky, 5there were no plants on the earth. Nothing was growing in the fields. The Lord God had not yet made it rain on the land. And there was no man to care for the ground. 6But a mist often rose from the earth and watered all the ground.

7Then the Lord God took dust from the ground and formed man from it. The Lord breathed the breath of life into the man's nose. And the man became a living person. 8Then the Lord God planted a garden in the East, in a place called Eden. He put the man he had formed in that garden. 9The Lord God caused every beautiful tree and every tree that was good for food to grow out of the ground. In the middle of the garden, God put the tree that gives life. And he put there the tree that gives the knowledge of good and evil.

10A river flowed through Eden and watered the garden. From that point the river was divided. It had four streams flowing into it. 11The name of the first stream is Pishon. It flows around the whole land of Havilah, where there is gold. 12That gold is good. Bdellium and onyx[n] are also there. 13The name of the second river is Gihon. It flows around the whole land of Cush. 14The name of the third river is Tigris. It flows out of Assyria toward the east. The fourth river is the Euphrates.

15The Lord God put the man in the garden of Eden to care for it and work it. 16The Lord God commanded him, "You may eat the fruit from any tree in the garden. 17But you must not eat the fruit from the tree which gives knowledge of good and evil. If you ever eat fruit from that tree, you will die!"

The First Woman

18Then the Lord God said, "It is not good for the man to be alone. I will make a helper who is right for him."

---

[n]**bdellium and onyx** Bdellium is an expensive, sweet-smelling resin like myrrh. And onyx is a gem.

¹⁹From the ground God formed every wild animal and every bird in the sky. He brought them to the man so the man could name them. Whatever the man called each living thing, that became its name. ²⁰The man gave names to all the tame animals, to the birds in the sky and to all the wild animals. But Adam[n] did not find a helper that was right for him. ²¹So the Lord God caused the man to sleep very deeply. While the man was asleep, God took one of the ribs from the man's body. Then God closed the man's skin at the place where he took the rib. ²²The Lord God used the rib from the man to make a woman. Then the Lord brought the woman to the man.

²³And the man said,

"Now, this is someone whose bones
    came from my bones.
Her body came from my body.
I will call her 'woman,'
    because she was taken out of
        man."

²⁴So a man will leave his father and mother and be united with his wife. And the two people will become one body.

²⁵The man and his wife were naked, but they were not ashamed.

The Beginning of Sin

3 Now the snake was the most clever of all the wild animals the Lord God had made. One day the snake spoke to the woman. He said, "Did God really say that you must not eat fruit from any tree in the garden?"

²The woman answered the snake, "We may eat fruit from the trees in the garden. ³But God told us, 'You must not eat fruit from the tree that is in the middle of the garden. You must not even touch it, or you will die.'"

⁴But the snake said to the woman, "You will not die. ⁵God knows that if you eat the fruit from that tree, you will learn about good and evil. Then you will be like God!"

⁶The woman saw that the tree was beautiful. She saw that its fruit was good to eat and that it would make her wise. So she took some of its fruit and ate it. She also gave some of the fruit to her husband, and he ate it.

⁷Then, it was as if the man's and the woman's eyes were opened. They realized they were naked. So they sewed fig leaves together and made something to cover themselves.

People Who Made Mistakes

ADAM AND EVE • GENESIS 3

Have you ever done anything wrong? Of course you have! Everyone makes mistakes. When God created Adam and Eve, he made them perfect and sinless. In the garden of Eden, God had only one rule, not to eat the fruit from the tree of the knowledge of good and evil. Unfortunately, Adam and Eve made a big mistake. Instead of obeying the Lord, they listened to Satan and ate the forbidden fruit. The perfect world God had made became soiled by sin.

Because of Adam and Eve's sin, each of us are born sinners. No matter who we are, what we do, or where we live, we are still sinners. We do bad things, even when we do not want to. The good news is that when we believe in Jesus Christ as our Savior, God forgives us.

To meet a man who moved to the wrong side of town, fly to page 17.

[n]**Adam** This is the name of the first man. It also means "humans," including men and women.

⁸Then they heard the Lord God walking in the garden. This was during the cool part of the day. And the man and his wife hid from the Lord God among the trees in the garden. ⁹But the Lord God called to the man. The Lord said, "Where are you?"

¹⁰The man answered, "I heard you walking in the garden. I was afraid because I was naked. So I hid."

¹¹God said to the man, "Who told you that you were naked? Did you eat fruit from that tree? I commanded you not to eat from that tree."

¹²The man said, "You gave this woman to me. She gave me fruit from the tree. So I ate it."

¹³Then the Lord God said to the woman, "What have you done?"

She answered, "The snake tricked me. So I ate the fruit."

¹⁴The Lord God said to the snake, "Because you did this,
a curse will be put on you.
You will be cursed more than any tame animal or wild animal.
You will crawl on your stomach,
and you will eat dust all the days of your life.
¹⁵I will make you and the woman enemies to each other.
Your descendants[d] and her descendants
will be enemies.
Her child will crush your head.
And you will bite his heel."

¹⁶Then God said to the woman,
"I will cause you to have much trouble when you are pregnant.
And when you give birth to children, you will have great pain.
You will greatly desire your husband, but he will rule over you."

¹⁷Then God said to the man, "You listened to what your wife said. And you ate fruit from the tree that I commanded you not to eat from.
"So I will put a curse on the ground.
You will have to work very hard for food.

Salvation
GENESIS 3:1-15

A beautiful park...a man and a woman loving one another *and* God who made them...a snake...a trick...disobedience...and all was lost.

How could that happen? How could Adam and Eve wreck the Garden of Eden? And most importantly: could anything be done to make things right again?

Genesis 3 explains what happened when Adam and Eve disobeyed God and brought sin and death into the world. This event is called the Fall. Because of what Adam and Eve did, all hope was lost until God made a way to make things right again, a way of salvation. God gave people another chance.

This passage tells about the beginning of the battle between people and Satan. Read verse 15 carefully and you will see a promise from God that someone would come and "crush" the snake's "head." That means that someone would defeat Satan and bring victory. That someone was Jesus. The Bible tells how God saved us through him.

To learn more about salvation, zoom to page 651.

In pain you will eat its food
　　all the days of your life.
18The ground will produce
　　　　thorns and weeds for you.
　And you will eat the plants of the
　　field.
19You will sweat and work hard
　　for your food.
　Later you will return to the
　　ground.
　This is because you were taken
　　from the ground.
　You are dust.
　　And when you die, you will return
　　　to the dust."

20The man named his wife Eve." This is because she is the mother of everyone who ever lived.

21The Lord God made clothes from animal skins for the man and his wife. And so the Lord dressed them. 22Then the Lord God said, "Look, the man has become like one of us. He knows good and evil. And now we must keep him from eating some of the fruit from the tree of life. If he does, he will live forever." 23So the Lord God forced the man out of the garden of Eden. He had to work the ground he was taken from. 24God forced the man out of the garden. Then God put angels on the east side of the garden. He also put a sword of fire there. It flashed around in every direction. This kept people from getting to the tree of life.

"**B**rothers and sisters sure need to be careful when they get angry! Find out what can happen if they don't in Genesis 4:1-16."

The First Family

4 Adam had sexual relations with his wife Eve. She became pregnant and gave birth to Cain." Eve said, "With the Lord's help, I have given birth to a man." 2After that, Eve gave birth to Cain's brother Abel. Abel took care of sheep. Cain became a farmer.

3Later, Cain brought a gift to God. He brought some food from the ground.

Sin
GENESIS 3:1-13

What is sin? Sin is making what we want more important than what God wants. It is saying, "I'm going to do what *I* want, no matter what anybody (including God) says." Sin happens when we do what we want, instead of doing what God wants. Sin is very serious.

The first sin happened in the Garden of Eden when Adam and Eve decided to disobey God and do what they wanted instead. This happened in several steps. First, God told them not to eat from the tree of the knowledge of good and evil. Second, the snake lied and told Eve that it was all right to eat from that tree. Third, Eve decided to believe Satan's lie. Fourth, Adam decided to do the same.

Sin is very serious. It does terrible damage to our lives and to others. Fortunately, God has a solution to the problem of sin. Read on to find out more about that.

To learn more about sin, zoom to page 379.

"**Eve**　This name sounds like the Hebrew word meaning "alive."
"**Cain**　This name sounds like the Hebrew word for "I have given birth."

⁴Abel brought the best parts of his best sheep. The Lord accepted Abel and his gift. ⁵But God did not accept Cain and his gift. Cain became very angry and looked unhappy.

⁶The Lord asked Cain, "Why are you angry? Why do you look so unhappy? ⁷If you do good, I will accept you. But if you do not do good, sin is ready to attack you. Sin wants you. But you must rule over it."

⁸Cain said to his brother Abel, "Let's go out into the field." So Cain and Abel went into the field. Then Cain attacked his brother Abel and killed him.

⁹Later, the Lord said to Cain, "Where is your brother Abel?"

Cain answered, "I don't know. Is it my job to take care of my brother?"

¹⁰Then the Lord said, "What have you done? Your brother's blood is on the ground. That blood is like a voice that tells me what happened. ¹¹And now you will be cursed in your work with the ground. It is the same ground where your brother's blood fell. Your hands killed him. ¹²You will work the ground. But it will not grow good crops for you anymore. You will wander around on the earth."

¹³Then Cain said to the Lord, "This punishment is more than I can stand! ¹⁴Look! You have forced me to stop working the ground. And now I must hide from you. I will wander around on the earth. And anyone who meets me can kill me."

¹⁵Then the Lord said to Cain, "No! If anyone kills you, I will punish that person seven times more." Then the Lord put a mark on Cain. It was a warning to anyone who met him not to kill him.

Cain's Family

¹⁶Then Cain went away from the Lord. Cain lived in the land of Nod,ⁿ east of Eden. ¹⁷Cain had sexual relations with his wife. She became pregnant and gave birth to Enoch. At that time Cain was building a city. He named it after his son Enoch. ¹⁸Enoch had a son named Irad. Irad had a son named Mehujael. Mehujael had a son named Methushael. And Methushael had a son named Lamech.

¹⁹Lamech married two women. One wife was named Adah, and the other was Zillah. ²⁰Adah gave birth to Jabal.

Feelings
GENESIS 4:2-6

When Cain found out that God was not happy with his offering, he got really mad! It only made things worse that God had accepted his brother's gift. Instead of just forgetting about the whole thing, Cain decided to hold a grudge. He ended up murdering his own brother because of his jealousy and anger. The rest of his life was spent far away from his family, and he was never able to do things that made him happy.

God doesn't expect us to feel happy and kind all the time. He knows that we will feel discouraged, angry, or jealous some times. The important thing, though, is what we do with those feelings. Instead of hurting others to make those feelings go away, we need to tell God about them. He can make us feel better!

To find out why you should show your feelings to others, zoom to page 66.

ⁿ**Nod** This name sounds like the Hebrew word for "wander."

He was the first person to live in tents and raise cattle. ²¹Jabal's brother was Jubal. Jubal was the first person to play the harp and flute. ²²Zillah gave birth to Tubal-Cain. He made tools out of bronze and iron. The sister of Tubal-Cain was Naamah.

²³Lamech said to his wives:

"Adah and Zillah, hear my voice!

You wives of Lamech, listen to what I say.

I killed a man for wounding me.

I killed a young man for hitting me.

²⁴Cain's killer may be punished 7 times.

Then Lamech's killer will be punished 77 times."

Adam and Eve Have a New Son

²⁵Adam had sexual relations with his wife Eve again. And she gave birth to a son. She named him Seth.ⁿ Eve said, "God has given me another child. He will take the place of Abel, who was

that day he blessed them and named them human beings.

³When Adam was 130 years old, he became the father of another son. He was in the likeness and image of Adam. Adam named him Seth. ⁴After Seth was born, Adam lived 800 years. During that time he had other sons and daughters. ⁵So Adam lived a total of 930 years. Then he died.

⁶When Seth was 105 years old, he had a son named Enosh. ⁷After Enosh was born, Seth lived 807 years. During that time he had other sons and daughters. ⁸So Seth lived a total of 912 years. Then he died.

⁹When Enosh was 90 years old, he had a son named Kenan. ¹⁰After Kenan was born, Enosh lived 815 years. During that time he had other sons and daughters. ¹¹So Enosh lived a total of 905 years. Then he died.

¹²When Kenan was 70 years old, he had a son named Mahalalel. ¹³After Mahalalel was born, Kenan lived 840 years.

Brothers and Sisters

CAIN AND ABEL • GENESIS 4:1-2

Cain was really jealous of his brother Abel. There were no priests or temples in those days, so each person offered sacrifices to God. Abel was a shepherd, so he brought an offering from the flocks, and that pleased God. Cain was a farmer, so he brought some of the food he grew, but that didn't please God. Instead of talking to God about it, Cain killed his brother.

Jealousy can make people bitter and angry. If you are jealous of your brother or sister, ask God to help you love instead. Jealousy only brings problems.

To meet a brother who forgave, fly to page 48.

To meet a brother who forgave, fly to page 48.

killed by Cain." ²⁶Seth also had a son. They named him Enosh. At that time people began to pray to the Lord.

Adam's Family History

5 This is the family history of Adam. When God created human beings, he made them in God's likeness. ²He created them male and female. And on

During that time he had other sons and daughters. ¹⁴So Kenan lived a total of 910 years. Then he died.

¹⁵When Mahalalel was 65 years old, he had a son named Jared. ¹⁶After Jared was born, Mahalalel lived 830 years. During that time he had other sons and daughters. ¹⁷So Mahalalel lived a total of 895 years. Then he died.

ⁿSeth   This name sounds like the Hebrew word for "to give."

[18]When Jared was 162 years old, he had a son named Enoch. [19]After Enoch was born, Jared lived 800 years. During that time he had other sons and daughters. [20]So Jared lived a total of 962 years. Then he died.

[21]When Enoch was 65 years old, he had a son named Methuselah. [22]After Methuselah was born, Enoch walked with God 300 years more. During that time he had other sons and daughters. [23]So Enoch lived a total of 365 years. [24]Enoch walked with God. One day Enoch could not be found, because God took him.

[25]When Methuselah was 187 years old, he had a son named Lamech. [26]After Lamech was born, Methuselah lived 782 years. During that time he had other sons and daughters. [27]So Methuselah lived a total of 969 years. Then he died.

[28]When Lamech was 182, he had a son. [29]Lamech named his son Noah.[n] Lamech said, "Noah will comfort us from the pain of our work. The pain is because God has cursed the ground." [30]After Noah was born, Lamech lived 595 years. During that time he had other sons and daughters. [31]So Lamech lived a total of 777 years. Then he died. [32]After Noah was 500 years old, he became the father of Shem, Ham and Japheth.

The Human Race Becomes Evil

6 The number of people on earth began to grow. Daughters were born to these people. [2]The sons of God saw that these girls were beautiful. And they married any of them they chose. [3]The Lord said, "My Spirit[d] will not remain in human beings forever. This is because they are flesh. They will live only 120 years."

[4]The Nephilim[d] were on the earth in those days and also later. That was when the sons of God had sexual relations with the daughters of men. These women gave birth to children, who became famous. They were the mighty warriors of long ago.

[5]The Lord saw that the human beings on the earth were very wicked. He also saw that their thoughts were only about evil all the time. [6]The Lord was sorry he had made human beings on the earth. His heart was filled with pain. [7]So the

Character
GENESIS 6:9

The next time you are in a crowd, notice how each person walks differently. Some shuffle their feet and some bounce happily along. Others speed-walk for exercise. They swing their arms and hips trying to get their legs to walk as fast as possible without actually running. You can try speed-walking sometime. See how fast and how far you can go!

The Bible says that people with the kind of character that pleased God "walked with God." That does not mean that God walked beside them in a body, like you walk with your friends. It means they spent time with God and talked to him and listened to him.

God wants you to walk with him, too. As you spend time with God, he will shape your character to be like him. You can please God by walking and talking with him. Read your Bible to learn about him and talk to him in prayer.

To learn more about character, zoom to page 344.

[n]**Noah** This name sounds like the Hebrew word for "rest."

Lord said, "I will destroy all human beings that I made on the earth. And I will destroy every animal and everything that crawls on the earth. I will also destroy the birds of the air. This is because I am sorry that I have made them." ⁸But Noah pleased the Lord.

Noah and the Great Flood

⁹This is the family history of Noah. Noah was a good man. He was the most innocent man of his time. He walked with God. ¹⁰Noah had three sons: Shem, Ham and Japheth.

¹¹People on earth did what God said was evil. Violence was everywhere. ¹²And God saw this evil. All people on the earth did only evil. ¹³So God said to Noah, "People have made the earth full of violence. So I will destroy all people from the earth. ¹⁴Build a boat of cypress wood for yourself. Make rooms in it and cover it inside and outside with tar. ¹⁵This is how big I want you to build the boat: 450 feet long, 75 feet wide and 45 feet high. ¹⁶Make an opening around the top of the boat. Make it 18 inches high from the edge of the roof down. Put a door in the side of the boat. Make an upper, middle and lower

deck in it. ¹⁷I will bring a flood of water on the earth. I will destroy all living things that live under the sky. This includes everything that has the breath of life. Everything on the earth will die. ¹⁸But I will make an agreement with you. You, your sons, your wife and your sons' wives will all go into the boat. ¹⁹Also, you must bring into the boat two of every living thing, male and female. Keep them alive with you. ²⁰There will be two of every kind of bird, animal and crawling thing. They will come to you to be kept alive. ²¹Also gather some of every kind of food. Store it on the boat as food for you and the animals."

²²Noah did everything that God commanded him.

The Flood Begins

7 Then the Lord said to Noah, "I have seen that you are the best man among the people of this time. So you and your family go into the boat. ²Take with you seven pairs, each male with its female, of every kind of clean*d* animal. And take one pair, each male with its female, of every kind of unclean animal. ³Take seven pairs of all the birds of the sky, each male with its female. This will allow all these animals to continue living on the earth after the flood. ⁴Seven days from now I will send rain on the

Boats with Precious Cargo
GENESIS 6:11-22

Do you know which was the biggest boat in the Bible? God designed and engineered it, and Noah built it. It was so big it could hold one-and-a-half football fields and was as high as a four-story building. Noah's boat had to carry pairs of every animal in the whole world! Considering the size of the ark, it may have carried almost 45,000 animals.

Noah, his family, and all the animals were on the ark for a whole year—so they also had to carry lots of food. God covered the entire earth with water because there was so much sin. But Noah's family and the animals were safe in the boat because Noah had obeyed God's instructions.

God tells us what to do for a good reason. We need to do what God says.

To read about the smallest boat in the Bible, fly to page 75.

earth. It will rain 40 days and 40 nights. I will destroy from the earth every living thing that I made."

[5]Noah did everything that the Lord commanded him.[6]Noah was 600 years old when the flood came. [7]He and his wife and his sons and their wives went into the boat. They went in to escape the waters of the flood. [8]The clean animals, the unclean animals, the birds and everything that crawls on the ground [9]came to Noah. They went into the boat in groups of two, male and female. This was just as God had commanded Noah. [10]Seven days later the flood started.

[11]Noah was now 600 years old. The flood started on the seventeenth day of the second month of that year. That day the underground springs split open. And the clouds in the sky poured out rain. [12]The rain fell on the earth for 40 days and 40 nights.

[13]On that same day Noah and his wife, his sons Shem, Ham and Japheth and their wives went into the boat. [14]They had every kind of wild animal and tame animal. There was every kind

---

"**I**f you're like me, you love getting wet. And unless you were in Noah's family, that is exactly what you'd be—soaked. Check out Genesis 7:1-8:22."

---

of animal that crawls on the earth. Every kind of bird was there. [15]They all came to Noah in the boat in groups of two. There was every creature that had the breath of life. [16]One male and one female of every living thing came. It was just as God had commanded Noah. Then the Lord closed the door behind them.

[17]Water flooded the earth for 40 days. As the water rose, it lifted the boat off the ground. [18]The water continued to rise, and the boat floated on the water

above the earth. [19]The water rose so much that even the highest mountains under the sky were covered by it. [20]The water continued to rise until it was more than 20 feet above the mountains.

[21]All living things that moved on the earth died. This included all the birds, tame animals, wild animals and creatures that swarm on the earth. And all human beings died. [22]So everything on dry land died. This means everything that had the breath of life in its nose. [23]So God destroyed from the earth every living thing that was on the land. This was every man, animal, crawling thing and bird of the sky. All that was left was Noah and what was with him in the boat. [24]And the waters continued to cover the earth for 150 days.

The Flood Ends

8 But God remembered Noah and all the wild animals and tame animals with him in the boat. God made a wind blow over the earth. And the water went down. [2]The underground springs stopped flowing. And the clouds in the sky stopped pouring down rain. [3-4]The water that covered the earth began to go down. After 150 days the water had gone down so much that the boat touched land again. It came to rest on one of the mountains of Ararat.[n] This was on the seventeenth day of the seventh month. [5]The water continued to go down. By the first day of the tenth month the tops of the mountains could be seen.

[6]Forty days later Noah opened the window he had made in the boat. [7]He sent out a raven. It flew here and there until the water had dried up from the earth. [8]Then Noah sent out a dove. This was to find out if the water had dried up from the ground. [9]The dove could not find a place to land because water still covered the earth. So it came back to the boat. Noah reached out his hand and took the bird. And he brought it back into the boat.

[10]After seven days Noah again sent

---

[n]**Ararat**   The ancient land of Urartu, an area in Eastern Turkey.

out the dove from the boat. ¹¹And that evening it came back to him with a fresh olive leaf in its mouth. Then Noah knew that the ground was almost dry. ¹²Seven days later he sent the dove out again. But this time it did not come back.

¹³Noah was now 601 years old. It was the first day of the first month of that year. The water was dried up from the land. Noah removed the covering of the boat and saw that the land was dry. ¹⁴By the twenty-seventh day of the second month the land was completely dry.

¹⁵Then God said to Noah, ¹⁶"You and your wife, your sons and their wives should go out of the boat. ¹⁷Bring every animal out of the boat with you—the birds, animals and everything that crawls on the earth. Let them have many young ones and let them grow in number."

¹⁸So Noah went out with his sons, his wife and his sons' wives. ¹⁹Every animal, everything that crawls on the earth and every bird went out of the boat. They left by families.

²⁰Then Noah built an altar to the Lord. Noah took some of all the clean[d] birds and animals. And he burned them on the altar as offerings to God. ²¹The Lord was pleased with these sacrifices. He said to himself, "I will never again curse the ground because of human beings. Their thoughts are evil even when they are young. But I will never again destroy every living thing on the earth as I did this time.

²²"As long as the earth continues,
    there will be planting and harvest.
Cold and hot,
    summer and winter,
    day and night
    will not stop."

The New Beginning

9 Then God blessed Noah and his sons. He said to them, "Have many children. Grow in number and fill the earth. ²Every animal on earth and every bird in the sky will respect and fear you. So will every animal that crawls on the ground and every fish in the sea respect and fear you. I have given them to you.

³"Everything that moves, everything that is alive, is yours for food. Earlier I gave you the green plants. And now I give you everything for food. ⁴But you must not eat meat that still has blood in it, because blood gives life. ⁵I will

Amazing Events That Showed God's Power

GENESIS 9:8-17

Imagine having rain all day long, every day for more than a month! Imagine so much rain falling that it floods the whole earth, covering the tops of even the highest mountains!

One time it rained like that. God allowed a flood to cover all the earth in order to destroy the evil people in the world. There was so much water that no one could escape. But God saved Noah's family and some animals.

Even though there are still floods, God promised Noah that a flood would never cover the whole earth again. God placed a rainbow in the sky as a sign of this promise. So every time you see a rainbow you can remember God's power and his promise.

To see how God destroyed two evil cities, fly to page 27.

demand your blood for your lives. That is, I will demand the life of any animal that kills a person. And I will demand the life of anyone who takes another person's life.

⁶"Whoever kills a human being
   will be killed by a human being.
This is because God made humans
   in his own image.

⁷"Noah, I want you and your family to have many children. Grow in number on the earth and become many."

⁸Then God said to Noah and his sons, ⁹"Now I am making my agreement with you and your people who will live after you. ¹⁰And I also make it with every living thing that is with you. It is with the birds, the tame animals and the wild animals. It is with all that came out of the boat with you. I make my agreement with every living thing on earth. ¹¹I make this agreement with you: I will never again destroy all living things by floodwaters. A flood will never again destroy the earth."

¹²And God said, "I am making an agreement between me and you and every living creature that is with you. It will continue from now on. This is the sign: ¹³I am putting my rainbow in the clouds. It is the sign of the agreement between me and the earth. ¹⁴When I bring clouds over the earth, a rainbow appears in the clouds. ¹⁵Then I will remember my agreement. It is between me and you and every living thing. Floodwaters will never again destroy all life on the earth. ¹⁶When the rainbow appears in the clouds, I will see it. Then I will remember the agreement that continues forever. It is between me and every living thing on the earth."

¹⁷So God said to Noah, "That rainbow is a sign. It is the sign of the agreement that I made with all living things on earth."

Noah and His Sons

¹⁸The sons of Noah came out of the boat with him. They were Shem, Ham and Japheth. (Ham was the father of Canaan.) ¹⁹These three men were Noah's sons. And all the people on earth came from these three sons.

²⁰Noah became a farmer and planted a vineyard. ²¹He drank wine made from his grapes. Then he became drunk and lay naked in his tent. ²²Ham, the father of Canaan, looked at his naked father. Ham told his brothers outside. ²³Then Shem and Japheth got a coat and carried it on both their shoulders. They walked backwards into the tent and covered their father. They turned their faces away. In this way they did not see their father without clothes.

²⁴Noah was sleeping because of the wine. Later he woke up. Then he learned what his youngest son, Ham, had done to him. ²⁵So Noah said,
"May there be a curse on Canaan!
   May he be the lowest slave to his
      brothers."
²⁶Noah also said,
"May the Lord, the God of Shem,
   be praised!
May Canaan be Shem's slave.
²⁷May God give more land to
   Japheth.
May Japheth live in Shem's tents,
   and may Canaan be their slave."

²⁸After the flood Noah lived 350 years. ²⁹He lived a total of 950 years. Then he died.

Nations Grow and Spread

10 This is the family history of the sons of Noah: Shem, Ham and Japheth. After the flood these three men had sons.

Japheth's Sons

²The sons of Japheth were Gomer, Magog, Madai, Javan, Tubal, Meshech and Tiras.

³The sons of Gomer were Ashkenaz, Riphath and Togarmah.

⁴The sons of Javan were Elishah, Tarshish, Kittim[n] and Rodanim. ⁵Those who lived in the lands around the Mediterranean Sea came from these

[n]**Kittim** His descendants were the people of Cyprus.

sons of Japheth. All the families grew and became different nations. Each nation had its own land and its own language.

Ham's Sons

6The sons of Ham were Cush, Mizraim,ⁿ Put and Canaan.

7The sons of Cush were Seba, Havilah, Sabtah, Raamah and Sabteca.

The sons of Raamah were Sheba and Dedan.

8Cush also had a descendantᵈ named Nimrod. Nimrod became a very powerful man on earth. 9He was a great hunter before the Lord. That is why people say someone is "like Nimrod, a great hunter before the Lord." 10At first Nimrod's kingdom covered Babylon, Erech, Akkad and Calneh in the land of Babylonia. 11From there he went to Assyria. There he built the cities of Nineveh, Rehoboth Ir and Calah. 12He also built Resen, the great city between Nineveh and Calah.

13Mizraim was the father of the Ludites, Anamites, Lehabites, Naphtuhites, 14Pathrusites, Casluhites and the people of Crete. (The Philistines came from the Casluhites.)

15Canaan was the father of Sidon his first son and of Heth. 16Canaan was also the father of the Jebusites, Amorites, Girgashites, 17Hivites, Arkites, Sinites, 18Arvadites, Zemarites and Hamathites. The families of the Canaanites scattered. 19The land of the Canaanites reached from Sidon to Gerar as far as Gaza. And it reached to Sodom, Gomorrah, Admah and Zeboiim, as far as Lasha.

20All these people were the sons of Ham. All these families had their own languages, their own lands and their own nations.

Shem's Sons

21Shem, Japheth's older brother, also had sons. One of his descendantsᵈ was the father of all the sons of Eber.

22The sons of Shem were Elam, Asshur, Arphaxad, Lud and Aram.

23The sons of Aram were Uz, Hul, Gether and Meshech.

24Arphaxad was the father of Shelah. Shelah was the father of Eber. 25Eber was the father of two sons. One son was named Pelegⁿ because the earth was divided during his life. Eber's other son was named Joktan.

26Joktan was the father of Almodad, Sheleph, Hazarmaveth, Jerah, 27Hadoram, Uzal, Diklah, 28Obal, Abimael, Sheba, 29Ophir, Havilah and Jobab. All these people were the sons of Joktan. 30These people lived in the area between Mesha and Sephar in the hill country in the East.

31These are the people from the family of Shem. They are arranged by families, languages, countries and nations.

32This is the list of the families from the sons of Noah. They are arranged according to their nations. From these families came all the nations who spread across the earth after the flood.

The Languages Confused

11 At this time the whole world spoke one language. Everyone used the same words. 2As people moved from the East, they found a plain in the land of Babylonia. They settled there to live.

3They said to each other, "Let's make bricks and bake them to make them hard." So they used bricks instead of stones, and tar instead of mortar. 4Then they said to each other, "Let's build for ourselves a city and a tower. And let's make the top of the tower reach high into the sky. We will become famous. If we do this, we will not be scattered over all the earth."

5The Lord came down to see the city and the tower that the people had built. 6The Lord said, "Now, these people are united. They all speak the same language. This is only the beginning of what they will do. They will be able to

ⁿ**Mizraim** This is another name for Egypt.
ⁿ**Peleg** This name sounds like the Hebrew word for "divided."

do anything they want. [7]Come, let us go down and confuse their language. Then they will not be able to understand each other."

[8]So the Lord scattered them from there over all the earth. And they stopped building the city. [9]That is where the Lord confused the language of the whole world. So the place is called Babel.[n] So the Lord caused them to spread out from there over all the whole world.

The Story of Shem's Family

[10]This is the family history of Shem. Two years after the flood, when Shem was 100 years old, his son Arphaxad was born. [11]After that, Shem lived 500 years and had other sons and daughters.

[12]When Arphaxad was 35 years old, his son Shelah was born. [13]After that, Arphaxad lived 403 years and had other sons and daughters.

[14]When Shelah was 30 years old, his son Eber was born. [15]After that, Shelah lived 403 years and had other sons and daughters.

[16]When Eber was 34 years old, his son Peleg was born. [17]After that, Eber lived 430 years and had other sons and daughters.

[18]When Peleg was 30 years old, his son Reu was born. [19]After that, Peleg lived 209 years and had other sons and daughters.

[20]When Reu was 32 years old, his son Serug was born. [21]After that, Reu lived 207 years and had other sons and daughters.

[22]When Serug was 30 years old, his son Nahor was born. [23]After that, Serug lived 200 years and had other sons and daughters.

[24]When Nahor was 29 years old, his son Terah was born. [25]After that, Nahor lived 119 years and had other sons and daughters.

[26]After Terah was 70 years old, his sons Abram, Nahor and Haran were born.

The Story of Terah's Family

[27]This is the family history of Terah.

Plans That Backfired
TOWER OF BABEL • GENESIS 11:1-9

Have you ever had a great idea that didn't turn out the way you wanted? That is what happened to the people of Babylon. Their idea was to build a big tower that would reach to the skies. The people liked themselves very much. They wanted to build a tower to show off how great they were.

But God saw them building this tower to make themselves famous, and he was very angry. He knew the people were proud they could build this tower together. So, he caused them to begin speaking in many different languages so they would stop building. The people could no longer work together because they could not understand one another. Their big plans for a tower were over.

Our plans need to be God's plans. We may have some good ideas, but we should always look for God's plans.

To learn about a man who helped the people who once tried to kill him, fly to page 65.

To learn about a man who helped the people who once tried to kill him, fly to page 65.

[n]**Babel** This name sounds like the Hebrew word for "confused."

Terah was the father of Abram, Nahor and Haran. Haran was the father of Lot. [28]Haran died while his father, Terah, was still alive. This happened in Ur in Babylonia, where he was born. [29]Abram and Nahor both married. Abram's wife was named Sarai. Nahor's wife was named Milcah. She was the daughter of Haran. Haran was the father of Milcah and Iscah. [30]Sarai was not able to have children.

[31]Terah took his son Abram, his grandson Lot (Haran's son) and his daughter-in-law Sarai (Abram's wife). They moved out of Ur of Babylonia. They had planned to go to the land of Canaan. But when they reached the city of Haran, they settled there. [32]Terah lived to be 205 years old. Then he died in Haran.

God Calls Abram[n]

12 Then the Lord said to Abram, "Leave your country, your relatives and your father's family. Go to the land I will show you.
[2]I will make you a great nation, and I will bless you.
I will make you famous.
And you will be a blessing to others.
[3]I will bless those who bless you.
I will place a curse on those who harm you.
And all the people on earth will be blessed through you."

[4]So Abram left Haran as the Lord had told him. And Lot went with him. At this time Abram was 75 years old. [5]Abram took his wife Sarai, his nephew Lot and everything they owned. They took all the servants they had gotten in Haran. They set out from Haran, planning to go to the land of Canaan. In time they arrived there.

[6]Abram traveled through that land. He went as far as the great tree of Moreh at Shechem. The Canaanites were living in the land at that time. [7]The Lord appeared to Abram. The Lord said, "I will give this land to your descendants."[d] So Abram built an altar there to the Lord, who had appeared to him. [8]Then Abram traveled from Shechem to the mountain east of Bethel. And he set up his tent there. Bethel was to the west, and Ai was to the east. There

God's Children
GENESIS 12:1-3

Think of a promise you made recently to a friend. How did your friend know you would keep it? People usually trust us to keep our promises if they know we are not likely to break them.

God's spiritual family of believers began with a promise (called the Covenant). God promised Abraham that he would start a huge family of people who would believe in God and worship him. God told Abraham that he would become famous and that all people would be blessed through his great family.

God kept his promise to Abraham. His children were the Jews, God's chosen people. And through the Jews, Jesus came. Because of Jesus, we can be God's children—the people of his covenant. Aren't you glad that God always keeps his promises?

To learn more about God's children, zoom to page 23.

[n]**Abram**   God later changed his name to Abraham.

Abram built another altar to the Lord and worshiped him. [9]After this, he traveled on toward southern Canaan.

Abram Goes to Egypt

[10]At this time there was not much food in the land. So Abram went down to Egypt to live because there was so little food. [11]Just before they arrived in Egypt, Abram said to his wife Sarai, "I know you are a very beautiful woman. [12]When the Egyptians see you, they will say, 'This woman is his wife.' Then they will kill me but let you live. [13]Tell them you are my sister. Then things will go well with me. And I may be allowed to live because of you."

[14]So Abram went into Egypt. The people of Egypt saw that Sarai was very beautiful. [15]Some of the Egyptian officers saw her also. They told the king of Egypt how beautiful she was. They took her to the king's palace. [16]The king was kind to Abram because he thought Abram was Sarai's brother. He gave Abram sheep, cattle and male and female donkeys. Abram also was given male and female servants and camels. [17]But the Lord sent terrible diseases on the king and all the people in his house. This was because of Abram's wife Sarai. [18]So the king sent for Abram. The king said, "What have you done to me? Why didn't you tell me Sarai was your wife? [19]Why did you say, 'She is my sister'? I made her my wife. But now here is your wife. Take her and leave!" [20]Then the king commanded his men to make Abram leave Egypt. So Abram and his wife left with everything they owned.

Abram and Lot Separate

13 So Abram, his wife and Lot left Egypt. They took everything they owned and traveled to southern Canaan. [2]Abram was very rich in cattle, silver and gold.

[3]He left southern Canaan and went back to Bethel. He went where he had camped before, between Bethel and Ai. [4]It was the place where Abram had built an altar before. So he worshiped the Lord there.

People Who Made Mistakes

LOT · GENESIS 13

It isn't always easy to share our things, but sometimes it is necessary. Abraham's and Lot's servants were quarreling with one another because there was not enough land and water for their animals to share. So Abraham gave Lot the first choice of all the land for him to make his home. Instead of sharing the land with his uncle Abraham, Lot chose selfishly. He picked the best land for himself, even though it was close to some wicked cities—Sodom and Gomorrah.

These cities were eventually destroyed by God because of the people's sin. When this happened, Lot was forced to run away with his wife and two daughters and leave his possessions behind. This turned out to be a costly mistake for Lot.

Are you good at sharing, or do you just try to keep all the good things for yourself?

To meet a man who got mad and hit a rock, fly to page 194.

⁵During this time Lot was traveling with Abram. Lot also had many sheep, cattle and tents. ⁶Abram and Lot had so many animals that the land could not support both of them together. ⁷Abram's herders and Lot's herders began to argue. The Canaanites and the Perizzites were living in the land at this time.

⁸So Abram said to Lot, "There should be no arguing between you and me. Your herders and mine should not argue either. We are brothers. ⁹We should separate. The whole land is there in front of you. If you go to the left, I will go to the right. If you go to the right, I will go to the left."

¹⁰Lot looked all around and saw the whole Jordan Valley. He saw that there was much water there. It was like the Lord's garden, like the land of Egypt in the direction of Zoar. (This was before the Lord destroyed Sodom and Gomorrah.) ¹¹So Lot chose to move east and live in the Jordan Valley. In this way Abram and Lot separated. ¹²Abram lived in the land of Canaan. But Lot lived among the cities in the Jordan Valley.

He moved very near to Sodom. ¹³Now the people of Sodom were very evil. They were always sinning against the Lord.

¹⁴After Lot left, the Lord said to Abram, "Look all around you. Look north and south and east and west. ¹⁵All this land that you see I will give to you and your descendants𝑑 forever. ¹⁶I will make your descendants as many as the dust of the earth. If anyone could count the dust on the earth, he could count your people. ¹⁷Get up! Walk through all this land. I am now giving it to you."

¹⁸So Abram moved his tents. He went to live near the great trees of Mamre. This was at the city of Hebron. There he built an altar to the Lord.

Lot Is Captured

14 Now Amraphel was king of Babylonia. Arioch was king of Ellasar. Kedorlaomer was king of Elam. And Tidal was king of Goiim. ²All these kings went to war against several other kings: Bera king of Sodom, Birsha king of Gomorrah, Shinab king of Admah, Shemeber king of Zeboiim and the king of Bela. (Bela is also called Zoar.)

People Who Depended on God
ABRAHAM • GENESIS 13:14-18

Abraham trusted God with his future. Abraham lived with his family in a city called Ur where there were lots of people and interesting places to visit like big cities today. But God wanted Abraham to leave his home and friends and travel to a brand new land. God wanted to start a new nation, and Abraham's family would be the first people in it! So when God told him to go to a new land, Abraham packed up his family and all their belongings and began the long journey (they had to walk!) to the land of Canaan.

God kept his promise to bless Abraham and made a new nation. God knows what is best for you. You can trust him with your future.

To read about someone who depended on God with a problem, fly to page 185.

³These kings who were attacked united their armies in the Valley of Siddim. (The Valley of Siddim is now the Dead Sea.ᵈ) ⁴These kings had served Kedorlaomer for 12 years. But in the thirteenth year, they all turned against him. ⁵Then in the fourteenth year, Kedorlaomer and the kings with him came and defeated the Rephaitesᵈ in Ashteroth Karnaim. They also defeated the Zuzites in Ham and the Emites in Shaveh Kiriathaim. ⁶And they defeated the Horites in the mountains of Edom to El Paran. (El Paran is near the desert.) ⁷Then they turned back and went to En Mishpat (that is, Kadesh). They defeated all the Amalekites. They also defeated the Amorites who lived in Hazazon Tamar.

⁸At that time the kings of Sodom, Gomorrah, Admah, Zeboiim and Bela went out to fight in the Valley of Siddim. (Bela is called Zoar.) ⁹They fought against Kedorlaomer king of Elam, Tidal king of Goiim, Amraphel king of Babylonia, and Arioch king of Ellasar. So there were four kings fighting against five. ¹⁰There were many tar pits in the Valley of Siddim. The kings of Sodom and Gomorrah and their armies ran away. Some of the soldiers fell into the tar pits. But the others ran away to the mountains.

¹¹Now Kedorlaomer and his armies took everything the people of Sodom and Gomorrah owned. They also took all their food. ¹²They took Lot, Abram's nephew who was living in Sodom. The enemy also took everything he owned. Then they left. ¹³One of the men who was not captured went to Abram, the Hebrew. He told Abram what had happened. At that time Abram was camped near the great trees of Mamre the Amorite. Mamre was a brother of Eshcol and a brother of Aner. And they had all made an agreement to help Abram.

Abram Rescues Lot

¹⁴Abram learned that Lot had been captured. So he called out his 318 trained men who had been born in his camp. Abram led the men and chased the enemy all the way to the town of

Heroes Who Trusted God
ABRAHAM • GENESIS 14:13-17

When you trust in God, you don't have to be afraid.

Abraham wasn't afraid of some bullies who lived near him. These powerful kings had united their armies to fight against each other. Abraham's nephew, Lot, got caught in the middle of their battle and was taken captive. Abraham didn't want Lot and his family to be hurt, so he gathered together his army. Do you think you would fight against a king's huge army with only 318 soldiers? But Abraham knew he was doing what was right, and he knew that God would protect him. Abraham's tiny group of men scared off the king's army, and Abraham had a great victory.

God wants you to trust him like Abraham did and not be afraid.

To learn about a man who trusted God to help him with a huge job, fly to page 256.

Dan. ¹⁵That night he divided his men into groups. And they made a surprise attack against the enemy. They chased them all the way to Hobah, north of Damascus. ¹⁶Then Abram brought back everything the enemy had stolen. Abram brought back the women and the other people. And he also brought back Lot and everything Lot owned.

¹⁷After defeating Kedorlaomer and the kings who were with him, Abram went home. As Abram was returning, the king of Sodom came out to meet him in the Valley of Shaveh. (That is now called King's Valley.)

¹⁸Melchizedek king of Salem also went to meet Abram. Melchizedek was a priest for God Most High. He brought bread and wine. ¹⁹Melchizedek blessed Abram and said,

"Abram, may God Most High give
     you blessings.
God made heaven and earth.
²⁰And we praise God Most High.
He has helped you to defeat your
     enemies."

Then Abram gave Melchizedek a tenth of everything he had brought back from the battle.

²¹Then the king of Sodom said to Abram, "You may keep all these things for yourself. Just give me my people who were captured."

²²But Abram said to the king of Sodom, "I make a promise to the Lord. He is the God Most High, who made heaven and earth. ²³I promise that I will not keep anything that is yours. I will not keep even a thread or a sandal strap. That way you cannot say, 'I made Abram rich.' ²⁴I will keep nothing but the food my young men have eaten. But give Aner, Eshcol and Mamre their share of what we won. They went with me into battle."

God's Agreement with Abram

15 After these things happened, the Lord spoke his word to Abram in a vision. God said, "Abram, don't be afraid. I will defend you. And I will give you a great reward."

²But Abram said, "Lord God, what can you give me? I have no son. So my slave Eliezer from Damascus will get everything I own after I die." ³Abram said, "Look, you have given me no son. So a slave born in my house will inherit everything I have."

⁴Then the Lord spoke his word to Abram. He said, "That slave will not be the one to inherit what you have. You will have a son of your own. And your son will inherit what you have."

⁵Then God led Abram outside. God said, "Look at the sky. There are so many stars you cannot count them. And your descendants*d* will be too many to count."

⁶Abram believed the Lord. And the Lord accepted Abram's faith, and that faith made him right with God.

⁷God said to Abram, "I am the Lord who led you out of Ur of Babylonia. I did that so I could give you this land to own."

⁸But Abram said, "Lord God, how can I be sure that I will own this land?"

⁹The Lord said to Abram, "Bring me a three-year-old cow, a three-year-old goat and a three-year-old male sheep. Also bring me a dove and a young pigeon."

¹⁰Abram brought them all to God. Then Abram killed the animals and cut each of them into two pieces. He laid each half opposite the other half. But he did not cut the birds in half. ¹¹Later, large birds flew down to eat the animals. But Abram chased them away.

¹²As the sun was going down, Abram fell into a deep sleep. While he was asleep, a very terrible darkness came. ¹³Then the Lord said to Abram, "You can be sure that your descendants will be strangers and travel in a land they don't own. The people there will make them slaves. And they will do cruel things to them for 400 years. ¹⁴But I will punish the nation where they are slaves. Then your descendants will leave that land, taking great wealth with them. ¹⁵Abram, you will live to be very old. You will die in peace and will be

buried. [16]After your great-great-grand-children are born, your people will come to this land again. It will take that long, because the Amorites are not yet evil enough to punish."

[17]The sun went down, and it was very dark. Suddenly a smoking firepot and a blazing torch passed between the halves of the dead animals.[n] [18]So on that day the Lord made an agreement with Abram. The Lord said, "I will give this land to your descendants. I will give them the land between the river of Egypt and the great river Euphrates. [19]This is the land of the Kenites, Kenizzites, Kadmonites, [20]Hittites, Perizzites, Rephaites,[d] [21]Amorites, Canaanites, Girgashites and Jebusites."

Hagar and Ishmael

16 Sarai, Abram's wife, had no children. She had a slave girl from Egypt named Hagar. [2]Sarai said to Abram, "Look, the Lord has not allowed me to have children. So have sexual relations with my slave girl. If she has a child, maybe I can have my own family through her."

Abram did what Sarai said. [3]This was after Abram lived ten years in Canaan. And Sarai gave Hagar to her husband Abram. (Hagar was her slave girl from Egypt.)

[4]Abram had sexual relations with Hagar, and she became pregnant. When Hagar learned she was pregnant, she began to treat her mistress Sarai badly. [5]Then Sarai said to Abram, "This is your fault. I gave my slave girl to you. And when she became pregnant, she began to treat me badly. Let the Lord decide who is right—you or me."

[6]But Abram said to Sarai, "You are Hagar's mistress. Do anything you want to her." Then Sarai was hard on Hagar, and Hagar ran away.

[7]The angel of the Lord found Hagar beside a spring of water in the desert. The spring was by the road to Shur. [8]The angel said, "Hagar, you are Sarai's slave girl. Where have you come from? Where are you going?"

Hagar answered, "I am running from my mistress Sarai."

Touring Bible Lands
CANAAN • GENESIS 15:18

The first stop on the tour of Bible lands is a place called Canaan, also called the Promised Land or Israel. God promised this beautiful land to all of Abraham's children and grandchildren and great-grandchildren, because Abraham believed in God! Abraham, his son Isaac, and his grandson Jacob all lived in Canaan. When Jacob was very old, a famine (a time when little rain caused no crops to grow so there was no food) came to the land. All of Jacob's family had to leave their land and go to Egypt to get food. About five hundred years later, Joshua led all of these people (the Israelites) back into Canaan. It was a land with large rivers, green valleys, and good crops. Many Jews still live in the area of Canaan.

Fly southwest from Canaan to visit the exotic land of the pharaohs on page 74.

[n]**passed . . . animals** This showed that God sealed the agreement between himself and Abram.

⁹The angel of the Lord said to her, "Go home to your mistress and obey her." ¹⁰The angel of the Lord also said, "I will give you so many descendants*d* they cannot be counted."

¹¹The angel also said to her, "You are now pregnant,

¹⁶Abram was 86 years old when Hagar gave birth to Ishmael.

Proof of the Agreement

17 When Abram was 99 years old, the Lord appeared to him. The Lord said, "I am God All-Powerful. Obey me and do what is right. ²I will make an agreement between us. I will make you the ancestor of many people."

Visiting Angels
GENESIS 16:7-10

The Bible tells about many times when God sent angels to help people and to bring them messages. In this story of Hagar, the angel of the Lord came to encourage her when she was afraid and sad. She was leaving the only home she had ever known to travel across the desert with her son. She had no one to help her.

God sent this angel to help Hagar feel better and to tell her what she should do. Hagar knew that God would protect her son Ishmael and that he would grow up to have many, many children. Hagar listened to the angel and did as she was told.

We know that God watches over us and helps us too!

To find out when an angel served a meal, fly to page 432.

and you will have a son.
You will name him Ishmael,*n*
    because the Lord has heard your cries.
¹²Ishmael will be like a wild
        donkey.
    He will be against everyone.
    And everyone will be against him.
    He will attack all his brothers."

¹³The slave girl gave a name to the Lord who spoke to her. She said to him, "You are 'God who sees me.'" This is because she said to herself, "Have I really seen God who sees me?" ¹⁴So the well there was called Beer Lahai Roi.*n* It is between Kadesh and Bered.

¹⁵Hagar gave birth to a son for Abram. And Abram named him Ishmael.

³Then Abram bowed facedown on the ground. God said to him, ⁴"I am making my agreement with you: I will make you the father of many nations. ⁵I am changing your name from Abram*n* to Abraham.*n* This is because I am making you a father of many nations. ⁶I will give you many descendants.*d* New nations will be born from you. Kings will come from you. ⁷And I will make an agreement between me and you and all your descendants from now on: I will be your God and the God of all your descendants. ⁸You live in the land of Canaan now as a stranger. But I will give you and your descendants all this land forever. And I will be the God of your descendants."

ⁿIshmael The Hebrew words for "Ishmael" and "has heard" sound similar.
ⁿBeer Lahai Roi This means "the well of the Living One who sees me."
ⁿAbram This name means "honored father."
ⁿAbraham The end of the Hebrew word for "Abraham" sounds like the beginning of the Hebrew word for "many."

[9]Then God said to Abraham, "You and your descendants must keep this agreement from now on. [10]This is my agreement with you and all your descendants: Every male among you must be circumcised.[d] You must obey this agreement. [11]Cut away the foreskin to show that you follow the agreement between me and you. [12]From now on when a baby boy is eight days old, you will circumcise him. This includes any

father. She will be the mother of many nations. Kings of nations will come from her."

[17]Abraham bowed facedown on the ground and laughed. He said to himself, "Can a man have a child when he is 100 years old? Can Sarah give birth

God's Children
GENESIS 17:1-8

How big is your family tree? No, we are not talking about a tree in your yard. A family tree is a picture that has all the people in your family written down to show how everyone is related to each other. The size of the tree depends upon how many people are in your family and how far back you go to see who is related to you.

When God made a promise to Abraham to make him the father of his chosen people, God made the biggest family tree ever. In fact, all people who have put their complete faith in God have become members of his family. That's some tree!

If you are a child of God, you can be proud to have such a huge family tree. Who can you name in your spiritual family tree?

To learn more about God's children, zoom to page 1148.

boy born among your people or any who is your slave. (He would not be one of your descendants.) [13]So circumcise every baby boy. Circumcise him whether he is born in your family or bought as a slave. Your bodies will be marked. This will show that you are part of my agreement that lasts forever. [14]Any male who is not circumcised will be separated from his people. He has broken my agreement."

Isaac—the Promised Son

[15]God said to Abraham, "I will change the name of Sarai,[n] your wife. Her new name will be Sarah.[n] [16]I will bless her. I will give her a son, and you will be the

to a child when she is 90?" [18]Then Abraham said to God, "Please let Ishmael be the son you promised."

[19]God said, "No. Sarah your wife will have a son, and you will name him Isaac.[n] I will make my agreement with him. It will be an agreement that continues forever with all his descendants.[d]

[20]"You asked me about Ishmael, and I heard you. I will bless him. I will give him many descendants. And I will cause their numbers to grow very greatly. He will be the father of 12 great leaders. I will make him into a great nation. [21]But I will make my agreement with Isaac. He is the son whom Sarah will have at this same time next year."

"**Sarai** An Aramaic name meaning "princess."
"**Sarah** A Hebrew name meaning "princess."
"**Isaac** The Hebrew words for "he laughed" (vs. 17) and "Isaac" sound the same.

²²After God finished talking with Abraham, God rose and left him.

²³Then Abraham gathered Ishmael and all the males born in his camp. He also gathered the slaves he had bought. So that day Abraham circumcised every man and boy in his camp. This was what God had told him to do. ²⁴Abraham was 99 years old when he was circumcised. ²⁵And Ishmael, his son, was 13 years old when he was circumcised. ²⁶Abraham and his son were circumcised on that same day. ²⁷Also on that day all the men in Abraham's camp were circumcised. This included all those born in his camp and all the slaves he had bought from other nations.

The Three Visitors

18 Later, the Lord again appeared to Abraham near the great trees of Mamre. At that time Abraham was sitting at the door of his tent. It was during the hottest part of the day. ²He looked up and saw three men standing near him. When Abraham saw them, he ran from his tent to meet them. He bowed facedown on the ground before them. ³Abraham said, "Sir, if you think well of me, please stay awhile with me, your servant. ⁴I will bring some water so all of you can wash your feet. You may rest under the tree. ⁵I will get some bread for you, so you can regain your strength. Then you may continue your journey."

The three men said, "That is fine. Do as you said."

⁶Abraham hurried to the tent where Sarah was. He said to her, "Hurry, prepare 20 quarts of fine flour. Make it into loaves of bread." ⁷Then Abraham ran to his cattle. He took one of his best calves and gave it to a servant. The servant hurried to kill the calf and to prepare it for food. ⁸Abraham gave the three men the calf that had been cooked. He also gave them milk curds and milk. While the three men ate, he stood under the tree near them.

⁹The men asked Abraham, "Where is your wife Sarah?"

"There, in the tent," said Abraham.

¹⁰Then the Lord said, "I will certainly return to you about this time a year from now. At that time your wife Sarah will have a son."

Sarah was listening at the entrance of the tent which was behind him. ¹¹Abraham and Sarah were very old. Sarah was past the age when women normally have children. ¹²So she laughed to herself, "My husband and I are too old to have a baby."

¹³Then the Lord said to Abraham, "Why did Sarah laugh? Why did she say, 'I am too old to have a baby'? ¹⁴Is anything too hard for the Lord? No! I will return to you at the right time a year from now. And Sarah will have a son."

¹⁵Sarah was afraid. So she lied and said, "I didn't laugh."

But the Lord said, "No. You did laugh."

¹⁶Then the men got up to leave and started out toward Sodom. Abraham walked along with them a short time to send them on their way.

Abraham's Bargain with God

¹⁷The Lord said, "Should I tell Abraham what I am going to do now? ¹⁸Abraham's children will certainly become a great and powerful nation. And all nations on earth will be blessed through him. ¹⁹I have chosen him so he would command his children and his descendants*ᵈ* to live the way the Lord wants them to. I did this so they would live right and be fair. Then I, the Lord, will give Abraham what I promised him."

²⁰Then the Lord said, "I have heard many things against the people of Sodom and Gomorrah. They are very evil. ²¹So I will go down and see if they are as bad as I have heard."

²²So the men turned and went toward Sodom. But Abraham stood there before the Lord. ²³Then Abraham approached the Lord. Abraham asked, "Lord, do you plan to destroy the good persons along with the evil persons? ²⁴What if there are 50 good people in

that city? Will you still destroy it? Surely you will save the city for the 50 good people living there. ²⁵Surely you will not destroy the good people along with the evil people. Then the good people and the evil people would be treated the same. You are the judge of all the earth. Won't you do what is right?"

²⁶Then the Lord said, "If I find 50 good people in the city of Sodom, I will save the whole city because of them."

²⁷Then Abraham said, "I am only dust and ashes. Yet I have been brave to speak to the Lord. ²⁸What if there are only 45 good people in the city? Will you destroy the whole city for the lack of 5 good people?"

The Lord said, "If I find 45 good people there, I will not destroy the city."

²⁹Again Abraham said to the Lord, "If you find only 40 good people there, will you destroy the city?"

The Lord said, "If I find 40 good people, I will not destroy the city."

³⁰Then Abraham said, "Lord, please don't be angry with me. Let me ask you this. If you find only 30 good people in the city, will you destroy it?"

The Lord said, "If I find 30 good people there, I will not destroy the city."

³¹Then Abraham said, "I have been brave to speak to the Lord. But what if there are 20 good people in the city?"

The Lord answered, "If I find 20 good people there, I will not destroy the city."

³²Then Abraham said, "Lord, please don't be angry with me. Let me bother you this one last time. What if you find 10 good people there?"

The Lord said, "If I find 10 good people there, I will not destroy it."

³³When the Lord finished speaking to Abraham, he left. And Abraham returned home.

Lot's Visitors

19 The two angels came to Sodom in the evening. Lot was sitting near the city gate and saw them. He got up and went to them and bowed face-down on the ground. ²Lot said, "Sirs, please come to my house and spend the night. There you can wash your feet. Then tomorrow you may continue your journey."

The angels answered, "No, we will spend the night in the city's public square."

³But Lot begged them to come to his house. So they agreed and went to his house. Then Lot prepared a meal for them. He baked bread without yeast, and they ate it.

⁴Before bedtime, all the men of the city surrounded Lot's house. These men were both young and old and came from every part of Sodom. ⁵They called to Lot, "Where are the two men who came to you tonight? Bring them out to us. We want to have sexual relations with them."

⁶Lot went outside to them, closing the door behind him. ⁷He said, "No, my brothers! Do not do this evil thing. ⁸Look! I have two daughters. They have never slept with a man. I will give them to you. You may do anything you want with them. But please don't do anything to these men. They have come to my house, and I must protect them."

⁹The men around the house answered, "Move out of the way!" Then they said to each other, "This man Lot came to our city as a stranger. Now he wants to tell us what to do!" They said to Lot, "We will do worse things to you than to them." So they started pushing Lot back. They were ready to break down the door.

¹⁰But the two men staying with Lot opened the door and pulled him back inside the house. Then they closed the door. ¹¹The two men struck the men outside the door with blindness. So these men, both young and old, could not find the door.

¹²The two men said to Lot, "Do you have any other relatives in this city? Do you have any sons-in-law, sons, daughters or any other relatives? If you do, tell them to leave now. ¹³We are about to destroy this city. The Lord has heard of all the evil that is here. So he has sent us to destroy it."

14So Lot went out and spoke to his future sons-in-law. They were pledged to marry his daughters. Lot said, "Hurry and leave this city! The Lord is about to destroy it!" But they thought Lot was joking.

15At dawn the next morning, the angels begged Lot to hurry. They said, "Go! Take your wife and your two daughters with you. Then you will not be destroyed when the city is punished."

16But Lot delayed. So the two men took the hands of Lot, his wife and his two daughters. The men led them safely out of the city. So the Lord was merciful to Lot and his family. 17The two men brought Lot and his family out of the city. Then one of the men said, "Run for your lives! Don't look back or stop anywhere in the valley. Run to the mountains or you will be destroyed."

18But Lot said to one of them, "Sir, please don't force me to go so far! 19You have been merciful and kind to me. You have saved my life. But I can't run to the mountains. The disaster will catch me, and I will die. 20Look, that little town over there is not too far away. Let me run there. It's really just a little town. I'll be safe there."

21The angel said to Lot, "Very well, I will allow you to do this also. I will not destroy that town. 22But run there fast. I cannot destroy Sodom until you are safely in that town." (That town is named Zoar,^{n} because it is little.)

Sodom and Gomorrah Destroyed

23The sun had already come up when Lot entered Zoar. 24The Lord sent a rain of burning sulfur down from the sky on Sodom and Gomorrah. 25So the Lord destroyed those cities. He also destroyed the whole Jordan Valley, everyone living in the cities and even all the plants.

26At that point Lot's wife looked back. When she did, she became a pillar of salt.

People Who Got Away

LOT • GENESIS 19:15-29

Lot got away just in time. Some angels warned him that God was going to destroy the evil cities near his home. The angels gave Lot very specific instructions: Lot was to run away into the mountains and never look back at the cities that would be destroyed. But Lot was afraid to go into the mountains and asked the angels if he could run to a nearby town instead. The angels agreed.

Lot and his family ran to the next town, and God began destroying the cities by fire. While he was running away, Lot could probably hear the fire burning and see the whole sky grow dark with smoke. But he remembered what the angel told him, and he did not look back to see the cities.

Lot trusted God to protect him in a dangerous situation. You can trust God to protect you too.

To read about a man who had to run from his father-in-law,
fly to page 39.

---

^{n}**Zoar**   This name sounds like the Hebrew word for "little."

²⁷Early the next morning, Abraham got up and went to the place where he had stood before the Lord. ²⁸Abraham looked down toward Sodom and Gomorrah and all the Jordan Valley. He saw smoke rising from the land. It was like smoke from a furnace.

²⁹God destroyed the cities in the valley. But he remembered what Abraham went and had sexual relations with him. But Lot did not know when she lay down or when she got up.

³⁴The next day the older daughter said to the younger, "Last night I had sexual relations with my father. Let's get him drunk again tonight. Then you can go and have sexual relations with him, too. In this way we can use our father to have children to continue our

Amazing Events That Showed God's Power

GENESIS 19:24-29

God is holy. He does not like sin. As people were born and grew up after the flood, some of them believed in God, but many did not follow God's ways. In two cities, called Sodom and Gomorrah, the people became so sinful that God decided to destroy them. He sent fire down from the sky and destroyed these two evil cities. It must have looked like an amazing fireworks display. In fact, the cities were destroyed so completely that they were never ever rebuilt.

God still does not like sin. He wants people to choose not to sin.

To find out how God's power set his people free, fly to page 88.

had asked. So God saved Lot's life. But he destroyed the city where Lot had lived.

Lot and His Daughters

³⁰Lot was afraid to continue living in Zoar. So he and his two daughters went to live in the mountains. They lived in a cave there. ³¹One day the older daughter said to the younger, "Our father is old. Everywhere on the earth women and men marry. But there are no men around here for us to marry. ³²Let's get our father drunk. Then we can have sexual relations with him. We can use our father to have children. That way we can continue our family."

³³That night the two girls got their father drunk. Then the older daughter family." ³⁵So that night they got their father drunk again. Then the younger daughter went and had sexual relations with him. Again, Lot did not know when she lay down or when she got up.

³⁶So both of Lot's daughters became pregnant by their father. ³⁷The older daughter gave birth to a son. She named him Moab. Moab is the ancestor of all the Moabite people who are still living today. ³⁸The younger daughter also gave birth to a son. She named him Ben-Ammi. He is the father of all the Ammonite people who are still living today.

Abraham and Abimelech

20 Abraham left Hebron and traveled to southern Canaan. He stayed awhile between Kadesh and Shur. Then he moved to Gerar. ²Abraham told people that his wife Sarah was his sister. Abimelech king of Gerar heard this. So he sent some servants to take her. ³But one night God spoke to Abimelech in a dream. God said, "You will die. That woman you took is married."

⁴But Abimelech had not slept with Sarah. So he said, "Lord, would you destroy an innocent nation? ⁵Abraham himself told me, 'This woman is my sister.' And she also said, 'He is my brother.' I am innocent. I did not know I was doing anything wrong."

⁶Then God said to Abimelech in the dream, "Yes, I know that you did not realize what you were doing. So I did not allow you to sin against me. I did not allow you to sleep with her. ⁷Give Abraham his wife back. He is a prophet.ᵈ He will pray for you, and you

⁹Then Abimelech called Abraham to him. Abimelech said, "What have you done to us? What wrong did I do against you? Why did you bring this trouble to my kingdom? You should not have done these things to me. ¹⁰What were you thinking that caused you to do this?"

¹¹Then Abraham answered, "I thought no one in this place respected God. I thought someone would kill me to get Sarah. ¹²And it is true that she is my sister. She is the daughter of my father. But she is not the daughter of my mother. ¹³God told me to leave my father's house and wander in many different places. When that happened, I told Sarah, 'You must do a special favor for me. Everywhere we go tell people I am your brother.'"

Honesty
GENESIS 20:1-13

Telling the truth isn't always easy. Sometimes it seems that the best way out of a bad situation is to lie. But before you tell a lie, learn a lesson from Abraham.

Genesis 20:1-13 tells how Abraham and his wife, Sarah, traveled to a foreign place called Gerar. Abraham didn't know anyone there, and he was afraid someone might hurt him in order to take Sarah away from him. So he decided to tell a lie. He said that Sarah was his sister, not his wife. It wasn't a total lie; Sarah *was* his half-sister. But it turned out to be very bad for Abimilech, king of Gerar. He almost died for taking Sarah—all because Abraham lied. In the end, it turned out OK. But Abraham's lie almost caused a lot of pain and suffering for innocent people.

Telling the truth may not be easy. But it is always the best thing to do.

To learn more about honesty, zoom to page 222.

will not die. But if you do not give Sarah back, you will die. And all your family will surely die."

⁸So early the next morning, Abimelech called all his officers. He told them everything that had happened in the dream. They were very much afraid.

¹⁴Then Abimelech gave Abraham some sheep, cattle and male and female slaves. Abimelech also gave Sarah, his wife, back to him. ¹⁵And Abimelech said, "Look around you at my land. You may live anywhere you want."

¹⁶Abimelech said to Sarah, "I gave

your brother Abraham 25 pounds of silver. I did this to make up for any wrong that people may think about you. I want everyone to know that you are innocent."

[17]Then Abraham prayed to God. And God healed Abimelech, his wife and his servant girls. Now they could have children. [18]The Lord had kept all the women in Abimelech's house from having children. This was God's punishment on Abimelech for taking Abraham's wife Sarah.

A Baby for Sarah

21 The Lord cared for Sarah as he had said. He did for her what he had promised. [2]Sarah became pregnant. And she gave birth to a son for Abraham in his old age. Everything happened at the time God had said it would. [3]Abraham named his son Isaac. Sarah gave birth to this son of Abraham. [4]Abraham circumcised[d] Isaac when he was eight days old as God had commanded.

[5]Abraham was 100 years old when his son Isaac was born. [6]And Sarah said, "God has made me laugh.[n] Everyone who hears about this will laugh with me. [7]No one thought that I would be able to have Abraham's child. But I have given Abraham a son while he is old."

Hagar and Ishmael

[8]Isaac grew and became old enough to eat food. At that time Abraham gave a great feast. [9]But Sarah saw Ishmael making fun of Isaac. (Ishmael was the son of Abraham by Hagar, Sarah's Egyptian slave.) [10]So Sarah said to Abraham, "Throw out this slave woman and her son. When we die, our son Isaac will inherit everything we have. I don't want her son to inherit any of our things."

[11]This troubled Abraham very much because Ishmael was also his son. [12]But God said to Abraham, "Don't be troubled about the boy and the slave woman. Do whatever Sarah tells you. The

descendants[d] I promised you will be from Isaac. [13]I will also make the descendants of Ishmael into a great nation. I will do this because he is your son, too."

[14]Early the next morning Abraham took some food and a leather bag full of water. He gave them to Hagar and sent her away. Hagar carried these things and her son. She went and wandered in the desert of Beersheba.

[15]Later, all the water was gone from the bag. So Hagar put her son under a bush. [16]Then she went away a short distance and sat down. Hagar thought, "My son will die. I cannot watch this happen." She sat there and began to cry.

[17]God heard the boy crying. And God's angel called to Hagar from heaven. He said, "What is wrong, Hagar? Don't be afraid! God has heard the boy crying there. [18]Help the boy up. Take him by the hand. I will make his descendants into a great nation."

[19]Then God showed Hagar a well of water. So she went to the well and filled her bag with water. Then she gave the boy a drink.

[20]God was with the boy as he grew up. Ishmael lived in the desert. He learned to shoot with a bow very well. [21]He lived in the Desert of Paran. His mother found a wife for him in Egypt.

Abraham's Bargain with Abimelech

[22]Then Abimelech came with Phicol, the commander of Abimelech's army. They said to Abraham, "God is with you in everything you do. [23]So make a promise to me here before God. Promise that you will be fair with me and my children and my descendants.[d] Be kind to me and to this land where you have lived as a stranger. Be as kind to me as I have been to you."

[24]And Abraham said, "I promise." [25]Then Abraham complained to Abimelech about Abimelech's servants. They had captured a well of water. [26]But Abimelech said, "I don't know

---

[n]**laugh** The Hebrew words for "he laughed" and "Isaac" sound the same.

who did this. You never told me about this before today."

²⁷Then Abraham gave Abimelech some sheep and cattle. And they made an agreement. ²⁸Abraham also put seven female lambs in front of Abimelech.

²⁹Abimelech asked Abraham, "Why did you put these seven female lambs by themselves?"

³⁰Abraham answered, "Accept these lambs from me. That will prove that you believe I dug this well."

³¹So that place was called Beersheba" because they made a promise to each other there.

³²So Abraham and Abimelech made an agreement at Beersheba. Then Abimelech and Phicol, the commander of his army, went back to the land of the Philistines.

³³Abraham planted a tamarisk tree at Beersheba. There Abraham prayed to the Lord, the God who lives forever. ³⁴And Abraham lived as a stranger in the land of the Philistines for a long time.

God Tests Abraham

22 After these things God tested Abraham's faith. God said to him, "Abraham!"

And he answered, "Here I am."

²Then God said, "Take your only son, Isaac, the son you love. Go to the land of Moriah. There kill him and offer him as a whole burnt offering. Do this on one of the mountains there. I will tell you which one."

³Early in the morning Abraham got up and saddled his donkey. He took Isaac and two servants with him. He cut the wood for the sacrifice. Then they went to the place God had told them to go. ⁴On the third day Abraham looked up and saw the place in the distance. ⁵He said to his servants, "Stay here with the donkey. My son and I will go over there and worship. Then we will come back to you."

⁶Abraham took the wood for the sacrifice and gave it to his son to carry.

Abraham took the knife and the fire. So Abraham and his son went on together.

⁷Isaac said to his father Abraham, "Father!"

"**R**ealize, kids, that God will ask you to do some hard things for him in your life. God asked Abraham to give up what was most important to him in Genesis 22:1-19."

Abraham answered, "Yes, my son."

Isaac said, "We have the fire and the wood. But where is the lamb we will burn as a sacrifice?"

⁸Abraham answered, "God will give us the lamb for the sacrifice, my son."

So Abraham and his son went on together. ⁹They came to the place God had told him about. There, Abraham built an altar. He laid the wood on it. Then he tied up his son Isaac. And he laid Isaac on the wood on the altar. ¹⁰Then Abraham took his knife and was about to kill his son.

¹¹But the angel of the Lord called to him from heaven. The angel said, "Abraham! Abraham!"

Abraham answered, "Yes."

¹²The angel said, "Don't kill your son or hurt him in any way. Now I can see that you respect God. I see that you have not kept your son, your only son, from me."

¹³Then Abraham looked up and saw a male sheep. Its horns were caught in a bush. So Abraham went and took the sheep and killed it. He offered it as a whole burnt offering to God. Abraham's son was saved. ¹⁴So Abraham named that place The Lord Gives. Even today people say, "On the mountain of the Lord it will be given."

"**Beersheba** This name means "well of the promise" or "well of seven."

Children Who Saw God at Work
ISAAC • GENESIS 22:2-13

Isaac knew how much his father, Abraham, loved God. Isaac loved God too and was glad to go on a trip to offer a sacrifice to God. When they sacrificed an animal, they killed it and presented it to God by burning it on an altar built of stones. God wanted his people to do this because it showed how much they loved and trusted him. But Isaac was surprised when they built their altar, and his father tied him up. Abraham didn't want to hurt Isaac, but he wanted to obey God even more. Isaac trusted that his father was doing what was right.

An angel stopped Abraham from hurting Isaac. God knew that Abraham loved him more than anything. Isaac wanted to love God, just as his father did. Do you love God more than anything else?

To meet a boy who got sold by his brothers for a few silver coins, fly to page 54.

<sup />

¹⁵The angel of the Lord called to Abraham from heaven a second time. ¹⁶The angel said, "The Lord says, 'You did not keep back your son, your only son, from me. Because you did this, I make you this promise by my own name: ¹⁷I will surely bless you and give you many descendants.ᵈ They will be as many as the stars in the sky and the sand on the seashore. And they will capture the cities of their enemies. ¹⁸Through your descendants all the nations on the earth will be blessed. This is because you obeyed me.'"

¹⁹Then Abraham returned to his servants. They all traveled back to Beersheba, and Abraham stayed there.

²⁰After these things happened, someone told Abraham: "Your brother Nahor and his wife Milcah have children now. ²¹The first son is Uz. The second son is Buz. The third son is Kemuel (the father of Aram). ²²Then there are Kesed, Hazo, Pildash, Jidlaph and Bethuel." ²³Bethuel became the father of Rebekah. Milcah was the mother of these eight sons, and Nahor was the father. Nahor was Abraham's brother. ²⁴Also Nahor had four other sons by his slave womanᵈ Reumah. Their names were Tebah, Gaham, Tahash and Maacah.

Sarah Dies

23 Sarah lived to be 127 years old. ²She died in Kiriath Arba (that is, Hebron) in the land of Canaan. Abraham was very sad and cried because of her. ³After a while Abraham got up from the side of his wife's body. And he went to talk to the Hittites. He said, ⁴"I am only a stranger and a foreigner here. Sell me some of your land so that I can bury my dead wife."

⁵The Hittites answered Abraham, ⁶"Sir, you are a great leader among us. You may have the best place we have to bury your dead. You may have any of our burying places that you want. None of us will stop you from burying your dead wife."

⁷Abraham rose and bowed to the people of the land, the Hittites. ⁸Abraham said to them, "If you truly want to help

me bury my dead wife here, speak to Ephron for me. He is the son of Zohar. ⁹Ask him to sell me the cave of Machpelah. It is at the edge of his field. I will pay him the full price. You can be the witnesses that I am buying it as a burial place."

¹⁰Ephron was sitting among the Hittites at the city gate. Ephron answered Abraham, ¹¹"No, sir. I will give you the land and the cave that is in it. I will give it to you with these people as witnesses. Bury your dead wife."

¹²Then Abraham bowed down before the Hittites. ¹³He said to Ephron before all the people, "Please let me pay you the full price for the field. Accept my money, and I will bury my dead there."

¹⁴Ephron answered Abraham, ¹⁵"Sir, the land is worth ten pounds of silver. But I won't argue with you over the price. Take the land, and bury your dead wife."

¹⁶Abraham agreed and paid Ephron in front of the Hittite witnesses. Abraham weighed out the full price: ten pounds of silver. They counted the weight as the traders normally did.

¹⁷⁻¹⁸So Ephron's field in Machpelah, east of Mamre, was sold. Abraham became the owner of the field, the cave in it and all the trees that were in the field. The sale was made at the city gate, with the Hittites as witnesses. ¹⁹After this, Abraham buried his wife Sarah in the cave. It was in that field of Machpelah, near Mamre. (Mamre was later called Hebron in the land of Canaan.) ²⁰Abraham bought the field and the cave on it from the Hittites. He used it as a burying place.

A Wife for Isaac

24 Abraham was now very old. The Lord had blessed him in every way. ²Abraham's oldest servant was in charge of everything Abraham owned. Abraham called that servant to him and said, "Put your hand under my leg.ⁿ ³Make a promise to me before the Lord, the God of heaven and earth. Don't get a wife for my son from the Canaanite girls who live around here. ⁴Instead, go back to my country, to the land of my relatives. Get a wife for my son Isaac from there."

⁵The servant said to him, "What if this woman does not want to return with me to this land? Then, should I take your son with me back to your homeland?"

⁶Abraham said to him, "No! Don't take my son back there. ⁷The Lord is the God of heaven. He brought me from the home of my father and the land of my relatives. But the Lord promised me, 'I will give this land to your descendants.'ᵈ The Lord will send his angel before you. The angel will help you get a wife for my son there. ⁸But if the girl won't come back with you, you will be free from this promise. But you must not take my son back there." ⁹So the servant put his hand under his master's leg. He made a promise to Abraham about this.

¹⁰The servant took ten of Abraham's camels and left. He carried with him many different kinds of beautiful gifts. He went to Northwest Mesopotamia to Nahor's city. ¹¹He made the camels kneel down at the well outside the city. It was in the evening when the women come out to get water.

¹²The servant said, "Lord, you are the God of my master Abraham. Allow me to find a wife for his son today. Please show this kindness to my master Abraham. ¹³Here I am, standing by the spring of water. The girls from the city are coming out to get water. ¹⁴I will say to one of the girls, 'Please put your jar down so I can drink.' Then let her say, 'Drink, and I will also give water to your camels.' If that happens, I will know she is the right one for your servant Isaac. And I will know that you have shown kindness to my master."

¹⁵Before the servant had finished praying, Rebekah came out of the city. She was the daughter of Bethuel. (Bethuel was the son of Milcah and Nahor, Abraham's brother.) Rebekah

ⁿ**Put . . . leg** This showed that a person would keep the promise.

was carrying her water jar on her shoulder. [16]She was very pretty. She was a virgin;[d] she had never had sexual relations with a man. She went down to the spring and filled her jar. Then she came back up. [17]The servant ran to her and said, "Please give me a little water from your jar."

father? Is there a place in his house for me and my men to spend the night?"

[24]Rebekah answered, "My father is Bethuel. He is the son of Milcah and Nahor." [25]Then she said, "And, yes, we have straw for your camels. We have a place for you to spend the night."

[26]The servant bowed and worshiped the Lord. [27]He said, "Blessed is the Lord, the God of my master Abraham. The

---

Words to Know: Old Testament
WELL · GENESIS 24:11

You will read about lots of **wells** in the Bible. Wells were holes dug deep in the ground to provide water. Often they were the only places where people could get water. That's why towns often grew up around wells. A person would get water from the well by dropping a clay pitcher tied to a rope down into the well and then pulling the pitcher up when it was full. Some wells were shallow, with steps down to the water so a person could walk down the steps to fill the pitchers.

Sometimes the people brought their animals to the well to give them a drink. The well was a good place to meet and talk with friends. It was a good place for Eliezer to ask God to show him the woman Isaac should marry.

To read about a handy piece of clothing, fly to page 52.

---

[18]Rebekah said, "Drink, sir." She quickly lowered the jar from her shoulder and gave him a drink. [19]After he finished drinking, Rebekah said, "I will also pour some water for your camels." [20]So she quickly poured all the water from her jar into the drinking trough for the camels. Then she kept running to the well until she had given all the camels enough to drink.

[21]The servant quietly watched her. He wanted to be sure the Lord had made his trip successful. [22]After the camels had finished drinking, he gave Rebekah a gold ring weighing one-fifth of an ounce. He also gave her two gold arm bracelets weighing about four ounces each. [23]The servant asked, "Who is your

Lord has been kind and truthful to him. He has led me to my master's relatives."

[28]Then Rebekah ran and told her mother's family about all these things. [29]She had a brother named Laban. He ran out to Abraham's servant, who was still at the spring. [30]Laban had heard what she had said. And he had seen the ring and the bracelets on his sister's arms. So he ran out to the well. And there was the man standing by the camels at the spring. [31]Laban said, "Sir, you are welcome to come in. You don't have to stand outside. I have prepared the house for you and also a place for your camels."

[32]So Abraham's servant went into the house. Laban unloaded the camels and

gave them straw and food. Then Laban gave water to Abraham's servant so he and the men with him could wash their feet. ³³Then Laban gave the servant food. But the servant said, "I will not eat until I have told you why I came."

⁴¹Then you will be free from the promise. Or if they will not give you a wife for my son, you will be free from this promise.'

⁴²"Today I came to this spring. I said, 'Lord, God of my master Abraham, please make my trip successful. ⁴³Look, I am standing by this spring of water. I will wait for a young woman to come

Women Who Trusted God

REBEKAH • GENESIS 24:15-21

Rebekah probably went to the town well every day to bring home water for her family. She would walk to the well with a large clay jar balanced on her shoulder. Then she would fill the jar by letting it down into the well and would put it back on her shoulder and carry it home. Rebekah showed a servant attitude when she willingly drew water for the stranger who rested at the well. She also drew water for his camels. A thirsty camel can drink up to twenty-five gallons of water. Eliezer had ten camels (24:10), so Rebekah had to make many trips to the well in order to give all the camels enough to drink! We should be like Rebekah—willing to serve others!

To meet a woman who ruled the nation of Israel, fly to page 292.

So Laban said, "Then tell us."

³⁴He said, "I am Abraham's servant. ³⁵The Lord has greatly blessed my master in everything. My master has become a rich man. The Lord has given him many flocks of sheep and herds of cattle. He has given Abraham silver and gold, male and female servants, camels and horses. ³⁶Sarah, my master's wife, gave birth to a son when she was old. My master has given everything he owns to that son. ³⁷My master had me make a promise to him. He said, 'Don't get a wife for my son from the Canaanite girls who live around here. ³⁸Instead you must go to my father's people and to my family. There you must get a wife for my son.' ³⁹I said to my master, 'What if the woman will not come back with me?' ⁴⁰But he said, 'I serve the Lord. He will send his angel with you and will help you. You will get a wife for my son from my family and my father's people.

out to get water. Then I will say, "Please give me water from your jar to drink." ⁴⁴Then let her say, "Drink this water. I will also get water for your camels." By this I will know the Lord has chosen her for my master's son.'

⁴⁵"Before I finished my silent prayer, Rebekah came out of the city. She had her water jar on her shoulder. She went down to the spring and got water. I said to her, 'Please give me a drink.' ⁴⁶She quickly lowered the jar from her shoulder. She said, 'Drink this. I will also get water for your camels.' So I drank, and she gave water to my camels also. ⁴⁷Then I asked her, 'Who is your father?' She answered, 'My father is Bethuel son of Milcah and Nahor.' Then I put the ring in her nose and the bracelets on her arms. ⁴⁸At that time I bowed my head and thanked the Lord. I praised the Lord, the God of my master Abraham. I thanked him because he

led me on the right road to get the granddaughter of my master's brother for his son. ⁴⁹Now, tell me, will you be kind and truthful to my master? And if not, tell me so. Then I will know what I should do."

⁵⁰Laban and Bethuel answered, "This is clearly from the Lord. We cannot change what must happen. ⁵¹Rebekah is yours. Take her and go. Let her marry your master's son as the Lord has commanded."

⁵²When Abraham's servant heard these words, he bowed facedown on the ground before the Lord. ⁵³Then the servant gave Rebekah gold and silver jewelry and clothes. He also gave expensive gifts to her brother and mother. ⁵⁴The servant and the men with him ate and drank. And they spent the night there. When they got up the next morning, the servant said, "Now let me go back to my master."

⁵⁵Rebekah's mother and her brother said, "Let Rebekah stay with us at least ten days. After that she may go."

⁵⁶But the servant said to them, "Do not make me wait. The Lord has made my trip successful. Now let me go back to my master."

⁵⁷Rebekah's brother and mother said, "We will call Rebekah and ask her what she wants to do." ⁵⁸They called her and asked her, "Do you want to go with this man now?"

She said, "Yes, I do."

⁵⁹So they allowed Rebekah and her nurse to go with Abraham's servant and his men. ⁶⁰They blessed Rebekah and said,

"Our sister, may you be the mother of
    thousands of people.
And may your descendants*ᵈ*
    capture the cities of their
      enemies."

⁶¹Then Rebekah and her servant girls got on the camels and followed the servant and his men. So the servant took Rebekah and left.

⁶²At this time Isaac had left Beer Lahai Roi. He was living in southern Canaan. ⁶³One evening he went out to the field to think. As he looked up, he saw camels coming. ⁶⁴Rebekah looked and saw Isaac. Then she jumped down from the camel. ⁶⁵She asked the servant, "Who is that man walking in the field to meet us?"

The servant answered, "That is my master." So Rebekah covered her face with her veil.

⁶⁶The servant told Isaac everything that had happened. ⁶⁷Then Isaac brought Rebekah into the tent of Sarah, his mother. And she became his wife. Isaac loved her very much. So he was comforted after his mother's death.

Abraham's Family

25 Abraham married again. His new wife was Keturah. ²She gave birth to Zimran, Jokshan, Medan, Midian, Ishbak and Shuah. ³Jokshan was the father of Sheba and Dedan. Dedan's descendants*ᵈ* were the people of Assyria, Letush and Leum. ⁴The sons of Midian were Ephah, Epher, Hanoch, Abida and Eldaah. All these were descendants of Keturah. ⁵Abraham left everything he owned to Isaac. ⁶But before Abraham died, he did give gifts to the sons of his other wives. Abraham sent them to the East to be away from Isaac.

⁷Abraham lived to be 175 years old. ⁸He breathed his last breath and died at an old age. He had lived a long and satisfying life. ⁹His sons Isaac and Ishmael buried him in the cave of Machpelah. This cave is in the field of Ephron east of Mamre. Ephron was the son of Zohar the Hittite. ¹⁰This is the same field that Abraham had bought from the Hittites. Abraham was buried there with his wife Sarah. ¹¹After Abraham died, God blessed his son Isaac. Isaac was now living at Beer Lahai Roi.

¹²This is the family history of Ishmael, Abraham's son. (Hagar, Sarah's Egyptian servant, was Ishmael's mother.) ¹³These are the names of Ishmael's sons in the order they were born. The first son was Nebaioth. Then came Kedar, Adbeel, Mibsam,

¹⁴Mishma, Dumah, Massa, ¹⁵Hadad, Tema, Jetur, Naphish and Kedemah. ¹⁶These were Ishmael's sons. And these are the names of the tribal leaders. They are listed according to their settlements and camps. ¹⁷Ishmael lived 137 years. Then he breathed his last breath and died. ¹⁸Ishmael's descendants lived from Havilah to Shur. This is east of Egypt stretching toward Assyria. Ishmael's descendants often attacked the descendants of his brothers.

struggled inside her. She asked, "Why is this happening to me?" Then she went to get an answer from the Lord.
²³The Lord said to her,

"Two nations are in your body.

Two groups of people will be taken from you.

One group will be stronger than the other.

The older will serve the younger."

Staying Away from Selfishness
GENESIS 25: 29-34

Pretend you looked inside your lunchbox one day at school and discovered that your juice had leaked all over your chips and sandwich. Soggy city! Suddenly, the person next to you at the lunch table holds up a hot, cheesy slice of her pizza and says, "Do you want it?" "YES!" you say. But just as you reach for the pizza, she quickly pulls back the slice and says, "First, what will you do for me?" She will not let you eat even one pepperoni until you do something nice for her.

That is what selfish people are like. They say: "I'll help you only if you do something for me first." And that's what Jacob said to his tired, hungry brother Esau.

Jesus doesn't want us to be like that. He wants us to do nice things for people without making them do something nice for us in return. Remember that the next time you can do something kind for someone.

To learn more ways to stay away from selfishness,
zoom to page 449.

To learn more ways to stay away from selfishness, zoom to page 449.

Isaac's Family

¹⁹This is the family history of Isaac. Abraham had a son named Isaac. ²⁰When Isaac was 40 years old, he married Rebekah. Rebekah was from Northwest Mesopotamia. She was Bethuel's daughter and the sister of Laban the Aramean. ²¹Isaac's wife could not have children. So Isaac prayed to the Lord for her. The Lord heard Isaac's prayer, and Rebekah became pregnant. ²²While she was pregnant, the babies

²⁴And when the time came, Rebekah gave birth to twins. ²⁵The first baby was born red. His skin was like a hairy robe. So he was named Esau.ⁿ ²⁶When the second baby was born, he was holding on to Esau's heel. So that baby was named Jacob.ⁿ Isaac was 60 years old when they were born.

²⁷When the boys grew up, Esau became a skilled hunter. He loved to be out in the fields. But Jacob was a quiet man. He stayed among the tents.

ⁿ**Esau** This name may mean "hairy."
ⁿ**Jacob** This name sounds like the Hebrew word for "heel." "Grabbing someone's heel" is a Hebrew saying for tricking someone.

[28]Isaac loved Esau. Esau hunted the wild animals that Isaac enjoyed eating. But Rebekah loved Jacob.

[29]One day Jacob was boiling a pot of vegetable soup. Esau came in from hunting in the fields. He was weak from hunger. [30]So Esau said to Jacob, "Let me eat some of that red soup. I am weak with hunger." (That is why people call him Edom.[n])

[31]But Jacob said, "You must sell me your rights as the firstborn son."[n]

[32]Esau said, "I am almost dead from hunger. If I die, all of my father's wealth will not help me."

[33]But Jacob said, "First, promise me that you will give it to me." So Esau made a promise to Jacob. In this way he sold his part of their father's wealth to Jacob. [34]Then Jacob gave Esau bread and vegetable soup. Esau ate and drank and then left. So Esau showed how little he cared about his rights as the firstborn son.

Isaac Lies to Abimelech

26 Once there was a time of hunger in the land. This was besides the time of hunger that happened during Abraham's life. So Isaac went to the town of Gerar. He went to see Abimelech king of the Philistines. [2]The Lord appeared to Isaac and said, "Don't go down to Egypt. Live in the land where I tell you to live. [3]Stay in this land, and I will be with you. I will bless you. I will give you and your descendants[d] all these lands. I will keep the agreement I made to Abraham your father. [4]I will give you many descendants. They will be as hard to count as the stars in the sky. And I will give them all these lands. Through your descendants all the nations on the earth will be blessed. [5]I will do this because your father Abraham obeyed me. He did what I said. He obeyed my commands, my teachings and my rules."

[6]So Isaac stayed in Gerar. [7]Isaac's wife Rebekah was very beautiful. The men of that place asked Isaac about her. Isaac said, "She is my sister." He was afraid to tell them she was his wife. He thought they might kill him so they could have her.

[8]Isaac lived there a long time. One day as Abimelech king of the Philistines looked out his window, he saw Isaac. Isaac was holding his wife Rebekah tenderly. [9]Abimelech called for Isaac and said, "This woman is your wife. Why did you say she was your sister?"

Isaac said to him, "I was afraid you would kill me so you could have her."

[10]Abimelech said, "What have you done to us? One of our men might have had sexual relations with your wife. Then we would have been guilty of a great sin."

[11]So Abimelech warned everyone. He said, "Anyone who touches this man or his wife will be put to death."

Isaac Becomes Rich

[12]Isaac planted seed in that land. And that year he gathered a great harvest. The Lord blessed him very much. [13]Isaac became rich. He gathered more wealth until he became a very rich man. [14]He had many slaves and many flocks and herds. The Philistines envied him. [15]So they stopped up all the wells the servants of Isaac's father Abraham had dug. (They had dug them when Abraham was alive.) The Philistines filled those wells with dirt. [16]And Abimelech said to Isaac, "Leave our country. You have become much more powerful than we are."

[17]So Isaac left that place. He camped in the Valley of Gerar and lived there. [18]Long before this time Abraham had dug many wells. After Abraham died, the Philistines filled them with dirt. So Isaac dug those wells again. He gave them the same names his father had given them. [19]Isaac's servants dug a well in the valley. From it a spring of

---

[n]**Edom**   This name sounds like the Hebrew word for "red."

[n]**rights . . . son**   Usually the firstborn son had a high rank in the family. The firstborn son usually became the new head of the family.

water flowed. [20]But the men who herded sheep in Gerar argued with Isaac's servants. They said, "This water is ours." So Isaac named that well Argue because they argued with him. [21]Then Isaac's servants dug another well. The people also argued about it. So Isaac named that well Fight. [22]Isaac moved from there and dug another well. No one argued about this one. So he named that well Room Enough. Isaac said, "Now the Lord has made room for us. We will be successful in this land."

[23]From there Isaac went to Beersheba. [24]The Lord appeared to Isaac that night. The Lord said, "I am the God of your father Abraham. Don't be afraid because I am with you. I will bless you and give you many descendants.[d] I will do this because of my servant Abraham." [25]So Isaac built an altar and worshiped the Lord there. He made a camp there, and his servants dug a well.

[26]Abimelech came from Gerar to see Isaac. Abimelech brought with him Ahuzzath, who advised him, and Phicol, the commander of his army. [27]Isaac asked them, "Why have you come to see me? You were my enemy. You forced me to leave your country."

[28]They answered, "Now we know that the Lord is with you. We will make a promise to you. And we would like you to make one to us. We would like to make an agreement with you. [29]We did not hurt you. So promise you will not hurt us. And we were good to you, and we sent you away in peace. Now the Lord has blessed you."

[30]So Isaac prepared food for them, and they all ate and drank. [31]Early the next morning the men made a promise to each other. Then Isaac sent them away, and they left in peace.

[32]That day Isaac's servants came and told him about the well they had dug. They said, "We found water in that well." [33]So Isaac named it Shibah[n] And that city is still called Beersheba even now.

[34]When Esau was 40 years old, he married two Hittite women. One was Judith daughter of Beeri. The other was Basemath daughter of Elon. [35]These women brought much sorrow to Isaac and Rebekah.

Jacob Tricks Isaac

27 When Isaac was old, his eyes were not good. He could not see clearly. One day he called his older son Esau to him. Isaac said, "Son."

Esau answered, "Here I am."

[2]Isaac said, "I am old. I don't know when I might die. [3]So take your bow and arrows, and go hunting in the field. Kill an animal for me to eat. [4]Prepare the tasty food that I love. Bring it to me, and I will eat. Then I will bless you before I die." [5]So Esau went out in the field to hunt.

Rebekah was listening as Isaac said this to his son Esau. [6]Rebekah said to her son Jacob, "Listen, I heard your father talking to your brother Esau. [7]Your father said, 'Kill an animal. Prepare some tasty food for me to eat. Then I will bless you before the Lord before I die.' [8]So obey me, my son. Do what I tell you. [9]Go out to our goats and bring me two fat, young ones. I will prepare them just the way your father likes them. [10]Then you will take the food to your father. And he will bless you before he dies."

[11]But Jacob said to his mother Rebekah, "My brother Esau is a hairy man. I am smooth! [12]If my father touches me, he will know I am not Esau. Then he will not bless me. He will place a curse on me because I tried to trick him."

[13]So Rebekah said to him, "If your father puts a curse on you, I will accept the blame. Just do what I said. Go and get the goats for me."

[14]So Jacob went out and got two goats and brought them to his mother. Then she cooked them in the special way Isaac enjoyed. [15]She took the best clothes of her older son Esau that were

---

[n]**Shibah**   This name sounds like the Hebrew words for "seven" and "promise."

in the house. She put them on the younger son Jacob. ¹⁶She took the skins of the goats. And she put them on Jacob's hands and neck. ¹⁷Then she gave Jacob the tasty food and the bread she had made.

¹⁸Jacob went in to his father and said, "Father."

And his father said, "Yes, my son. Who are you?"

Jacob. ²⁴Isaac asked, "Are you really my son Esau?"

Jacob answered, "Yes, I am."

²⁵Then Isaac said, "Bring me the food. I will eat it and bless you." So Jacob gave him the food, and Isaac ate. Jacob gave him wine, and he drank. ²⁶Then Isaac said to him, "My son, come near and kiss me." ²⁷So Jacob went to his father and kissed him. Isaac smelled Esau's clothes and blessed him. Isaac said,

People Who Got Away

JACOB • GENESIS 27:41-44

Jacob treated his brother Esau very badly. He cheated Esau out of a special inheritance. So Esau wanted to kill him! Jacob had to run away to Haran where his uncle lived more than 400 miles away. Jacob had to walk all that way! But Uncle Laban did not treat Jacob very well. Jacob had cheated Esau, and Uncle Laban cheated Jacob. In fact, Jacob later had to escape from his uncle (you can read about that in Genesis 31).

If you do bad things, don't be surprised if bad things happen to you. Instead, try to do good and trust God to help you.

To read about a man who escaped a murder charge, fly to page 76.

¹⁹Jacob said to him, "I am Esau, your first son. I have done what you told me. Now sit up and eat some meat of the animal I hunted for you. Then bless me."

²⁰But Isaac asked his son, "How did you find and kill the animal so quickly?"

Jacob answered, "Because the Lord your God led me to find it."

²¹Then Isaac said to Jacob, "Come near so I can touch you, my son. If I can touch you, I will know if you are really my son Esau."

²²So Jacob came near to Isaac his father. Isaac touched him and said, "Your voice sounds like Jacob's voice. But your hands are hairy like the hands of Esau." ²³Isaac did not know it was Jacob, because his hands were hairy like Esau's hands. So Isaac blessed

"The smell of my son
    is like the smell of the field
    that the Lord has blessed.
²⁸May God give you plenty of rain
    and good soil.
    Then you will have plenty of grain
    and wine.
²⁹May nations serve you.
    May peoples bow down to you.
May you be master over your
    brothers.
    May your mother's sons bow down
    to you.
May everyone who curses you be
    cursed.
    And may everyone who blesses you
    be blessed."

³⁰Isaac finished blessing Jacob. Then, just as Jacob left his father Isaac, Esau came in from hunting. ³¹Esau also

prepared some tasty food and brought it to his father. He said, "Father, rise and eat the food that your son killed for you. Then bless me."

³²Isaac asked, "Who are you?"

He answered, "I am your son—your firstborn*d* son—Esau."

³³Then Isaac trembled greatly. He said, "Then who was it that hunted the animals and brought me food before you came? I ate it, and I blessed him. And it is too late now to take back my blessing."

³⁴When Esau heard the words of his father, he let out a loud and bitter cry. He said to his father, "Bless me—me, too, my father!"

³⁵But Isaac said, "Your brother came and tricked me. He has taken your blessing."

³⁶Esau said, "Jacob*n* is the right name for him. He has tricked me these two times. He took away my share of everything I own. And now he has taken away my blessing." Then Esau asked, "Haven't you saved a blessing for me?"

³⁷Isaac answered, "I gave Jacob the power to be master over you. And all his brothers will be his servants. And I kept him strong with grain and wine. There is nothing left to give you, my son."

³⁸But Esau continued, "Do you have only one blessing, Father? Bless me, too, Father!" Then Esau began to cry out loud.

³⁹Isaac said to him,

"You will live far away from the best land,
    far from the rain.
⁴⁰You will live by using your sword
    and be a slave to your brother.
But when you struggle,
    you will break free from him."

⁴¹After that Esau hated Jacob because of the blessing from Isaac. Esau thought to himself, "My father will soon die, and I will be sad for him. After that I will kill Jacob."

⁴²Rebekah heard about Esau's plan to kill Jacob. So she sent for Jacob. She said to him, "Listen, your brother Esau is comforting himself by planning to kill you. ⁴³So, son, do what I say. My brother Laban is living in Haran. Go to him at once! ⁴⁴Stay with him for a while, until your brother is not so angry. ⁴⁵In time, your brother will not be angry. He will forget what you did to him. Then I will send a servant to bring you back. I don't want to lose both of my sons on the same day."

⁴⁶Then Rebekah said to Isaac, "I am tired of Hittite women. If Jacob marries one of these Hittite women here in this land, I want to die."

Jacob Searches for a Wife

28 Isaac called Jacob and blessed him. Then Isaac commanded him, "You must not marry a Canaanite woman. ²Go to the house of Bethuel, your mother's father, in Northwest Mesopotamia. Laban, your mother's brother, lives there. Marry one of his daughters. ³May God All-Powerful bless you and give you many children. May you become the father of many peoples. ⁴May the Lord give you and your descendants*d* the blessing of Abraham. Then you may own the land where you are now living as a stranger. This is the land God gave to Abraham." ⁵So Isaac sent Jacob to Northwest Mesopotamia. Jacob went to Laban, the brother of Rebekah. Bethuel, the Aramean, was the father of Laban and Rebekah. And Rebekah was the mother of Jacob and Esau.

⁶Esau learned that Isaac had blessed Jacob and sent him to Northwest Mesopotamia. Jacob went to find a wife there. Esau also learned that Isaac had commanded Jacob not to marry a Canaanite woman. ⁷And Esau learned that Jacob had obeyed his father and mother. He had gone to Northwest Mesopotamia. ⁸So Esau saw that his father Isaac did not want his sons to marry Canaanite women. ⁹Now Esau already had wives. But he went to Ishmael son of Abraham.

---

*ⁿ***Jacob**   This name sounds like the Hebrew word for "heel." "Grabbing someone's heel" is a Hebrew saying for tricking someone.

And he married Mahalath, Ishmael's daughter. Mahalath was the sister of Nebaioth.

Jacob's Dream at Bethel

[10]Jacob left Beersheba and set out for Haran. [11]He came to a place and spent the night there because the sun had set. He found a stone there and laid his head on it to go to sleep. [12]Jacob dreamed that there was a ladder resting on the earth and reaching up into heaven. And he saw angels of God going up and coming down the ladder. [13]And then Jacob saw the Lord standing above the ladder. The Lord said, "I am the Lord, the God of Abraham, your grandfather. And I am the God of Isaac. I will give you and your descendants[d] the land on which you are now sleeping. [14]Your descendants will be as many as the dust of the earth. They will spread west and east, north and south. All the families of the earth will be blessed through you and your descendants. [15]I am with you, and I will protect you everywhere you go. And I will bring you back to this land. I will not leave you until I have done what I have promised you."

[16]Then Jacob woke from his sleep. He said, "Surely the Lord is in this place. But I did not know it." [17]Jacob was afraid. He said, "This place frightens me! It is surely the house of God and the gate of heaven."

[18]Jacob rose early in the morning. He took the stone he had slept on and set it up on its end. Then he poured olive oil on the top of it. [19]At first, the name of that city was Luz. But Jacob named it Bethel.[n]

[20]Then Jacob made a promise. He said, "I want God to be with me and protect me on this journey. I want God to give me food to eat and clothes to wear. [21]Then I will be able to return in peace to my father's house. If the Lord does these things, he will be my God. [22]This stone which I have set up on its end

will be the house of God. And I will give God one-tenth of all he gives me."

Jacob Arrives in Northwest Mesopotamia

29 Then Jacob continued his journey. He came to the land of the people of the East. [2]He looked and saw a well in the field. Three flocks of sheep were lying nearby, because they drank water from this well. A large stone covered the mouth of the well. [3]All the flocks would gather there. The shepherds would roll the stone away from the well and water the sheep. Then they would put the stone back in its place.

[4]Jacob said to the shepherds there, "My brothers, where are you from?"

They answered, "We are from Haran."

[5]Then Jacob asked, "Do you know Laban grandson of Nahor?"

They answered, "We know him."

[6]Then Jacob asked, "How is he?"

They answered, "He is well. Look, his daughter Rachel is coming now with his sheep."

[7]Jacob said, "But look, it is still the middle part of the day. It is not time for the sheep to be gathered for the night. So give them water and let them go back into the pasture."

[8]But they said, "We cannot do that until all the flocks are gathered. Then we will roll away the stone from the mouth of the well and water the sheep."

[9]While Jacob was talking with the shepherds, Rachel came with her father's sheep. It was her job to take care of the sheep. [10]Then Jacob saw Laban's daughter Rachel and Laban's sheep. So he went to the well and rolled the stone from its mouth. Then he watered Laban's sheep. Now Laban was the brother of Rebekah, Jacob's mother. [11]Then Jacob kissed Rachel and cried. [12]He told her that he was from her father's family. He said that he was the son of Rebekah. So Rachel ran home and told her father.

[13]When Laban heard the news about

[n]**Bethel** This name means "house of God."

his sister's son Jacob, Laban ran to meet him. Laban hugged him and kissed him and brought him to his house. Jacob told Laban everything that had happened.

¹⁴Then Laban said, "You are my own flesh and blood."

Jacob Is Tricked

So Jacob stayed there a month. ¹⁵Then Laban said to Jacob, "You are my relative. But it is not right for you to keep on working for me without pay. What would you like me to pay you?"

¹⁶Now Laban had two daughters. The older was Leah, and the younger was Rachel. ¹⁷Leah had weak eyes, but Rachel was very beautiful. ¹⁸Jacob loved Rachel. So he said to Laban, "Let me marry your younger daughter Rachel. If you will, I will work seven years for you."

¹⁹Laban said, "It would be better for her to marry you than someone else. So stay here with me." ²⁰So Jacob worked for Laban seven years so he could marry Rachel. But they seemed to him like just a few days. This was because he loved Rachel very much.

²¹After seven years Jacob said to Laban, "Give me Rachel so that I may marry her. The time I promised to work for you is over."

²²So Laban gave a feast for all the people there. ²³That evening Laban brought his daughter Leah to Jacob. Jacob and Leah had sexual relations together. ²⁴(Laban gave his slave girl Zilpah to his daughter to be her servant.) ²⁵In the morning Jacob saw that he had had sexual relations with Leah! He said to Laban, "What have you done to me? I worked hard for you so that I could marry Rachel! Why did you trick me?"

²⁶Laban said, "In our country we do not allow the younger daughter to marry before the older daughter. ²⁷But complete the full week of the marriage ceremony with Leah. I will give you Rachel to marry also. But you must serve me another seven years."

²⁸So Jacob did this and completed the week with Leah. Then Laban gave him his daughter Rachel as a wife. ²⁹(Laban gave his slave girl Bilhah to his daughter Rachel to be her servant.) ³⁰So Jacob had sexual relations with Rachel also. And Jacob loved Rachel more than Leah. Jacob worked for Laban for another seven years.

Jacob's Family Grows

³¹The Lord saw that Jacob loved Rachel more than Leah. So the Lord made it possible for Leah to have children. But Rachel did not have any children. ³²Leah became pregnant and gave birth to a son. She named him Reuben,ⁿ because she said, "The Lord has seen my troubles. Surely now my husband will love me."

³³Leah became pregnant again and gave birth to another son. She named him Simeon.ⁿ She said, "The Lord has heard that I am not loved. So he gave me this son."

³⁴Leah became pregnant again and gave birth to another son. She named him Levi.ⁿ Leah said, "Now, surely my husband will be close to me. I have given him three sons."

³⁵Then Leah gave birth to another son. She named him Judah.ⁿ Leah named him this because she said, "Now I will praise the Lord." Then Leah stopped having children.

30 Rachel saw that she was not giving birth to children for Jacob. So she envied her sister Leah. Rachel said to Jacob, "Give me children, or I'll die!"

²Jacob became angry with her. He said, "Can I do what only God can do? He is the one who has kept you from having children."

³Then Rachel said, "Here is my slave

ⁿ**Reuben** This name sounds like the Hebrew word for "he has seen my troubles."
ⁿ**Simeon** This name sounds like the Hebrew word for "has heard."
ⁿ**Levi** This name sounds like the Hebrew word for "be close to."
ⁿ**Judah** This name sounds like the Hebrew word for "praise."

girl Bilhah. Have sexual relations with her so she can give birth to a child for me. Then I can have my own family through her."

⁴So Rachel gave Bilhah, her slave girl, to Jacob as a wife. And he had sexual relations with her. ⁵She became pregnant and gave Jacob a son. ⁶Rachel said, "God has declared me innocent. He has listened to my prayer and has given me a son." So Rachel named this son Dan.ⁿ

⁷Bilhah became pregnant again and gave Jacob a second son. ⁸Rachel said, "I have struggled hard with my sister. And I have won." So she named that son Naphtali.ⁿ

⁹Leah saw that she had stopped having children. So she gave her slave girl Zilpah to Jacob as a wife. ¹⁰Then Zilpah had a son. ¹¹Leah said, "I am lucky." So she named her son Gad.ⁿ ¹²Zilpah gave birth to another son. ¹³Leah said, "I am very happy! Now women will call me happy." So she named that son Asher.ⁿ

¹⁴During the wheat harvest Reuben went into the field and found some mandrakeⁿ plants. He brought them to his mother Leah. But Rachel said to Leah, "Please give me some of your son's mandrakes."

¹⁵Leah answered, "You have already taken away my husband. Now you are trying to take away my son's mandrakes."

But Rachel answered, "If you will give me your son's mandrakes, you may sleep with Jacob tonight."

¹⁶When Jacob came in from the field that night, Leah went out to meet him. She said, "You will have sexual relations with me tonight. I have paid for you with my son's mandrakes." So Jacob slept with her that night.

¹⁷Then God answered Leah's prayer,

and she became pregnant again. She gave birth to a fifth son. ¹⁸Leah said, "God has given me what I paid for, because I gave my slave girl to my husband." So Leah named her son Issachar.ⁿ

¹⁹Leah became pregnant again and gave birth to a sixth son. ²⁰She said, "God has given me a fine gift. Now surely Jacob will honor me, because I have given him six sons." So Leah named the son Zebulun.ⁿ

²¹Later Leah gave birth to a daughter. She named her Dinah.

²²Then God remembered Rachel and answered her prayer. God made it possible for her to have children. ²³She became pregnant and gave birth to a son. She said, "God has taken away my shame." ²⁴She named him Joseph.ⁿ Rachel said, "I wish the Lord would give me another son."

Jacob Tricks Laban

²⁵After the birth of Joseph, Jacob said to Laban, "Now let me go to my own home and country. ²⁶Give me my wives and my children, and let me go. I have earned them by working for you. You know that I served you well."

²⁷Laban said to him, "If I have pleased you, please stay. I know the Lord has blessed me because of you. ²⁸Tell me what I should pay you, and I will give it to you."

²⁹Jacob answered, "You know that I have worked hard for you. Your flocks have grown while I cared for them. ³⁰When I came, you had little. Now you have much. Every time I did something for you, the Lord blessed you. But when will I be able to do something for my own family?"

³¹Laban asked, "Then what should I give you?"

ⁿ**Dan**   This name means "he has declared innocent."
ⁿ**Naphtali**   This name sounds like the Hebrew word for "my struggle."
ⁿ**Gad**   This name may mean "lucky."
ⁿ**Asher**   This name may mean "happy."
ⁿ**mandrake**   A plant which was believed to cause a woman to become pregnant.
ⁿ**Issachar**   This name sounds like the Hebrew word for "paid for."
ⁿ**Zebulun**   This name sounds like the Hebrew word for "honor."
ⁿ**Joseph**   This name sounds like the Hebrew word for "he adds."

Jacob answered, "I don't want you to give me anything. Just do this one thing. Then I will come back and take care of your flocks. ³²Today let me go through all your flocks of white sheep and black goats. I will take every spotted or speckled lamb. I will take every black lamb and every spotted or speckled goat. That will be my pay. ³³In the future you can easily see if I am honest. You can come to look at my flocks. If I have any goat that isn't speckled or spotted or any sheep that isn't black, you will know I stole it."

³⁴Laban answered, "Agreed! We will do what you ask." ³⁵But that day Laban took away all the male goats that had streaks or spots. And he took all the speckled and spotted female goats (all those that had white on them). And he took all the black sheep. He told his sons to watch over them. ³⁶Laban took these animals to a place that was three days' journey away from Jacob. Jacob took care of all the animals that were left.

³⁷So Jacob cut green branches from poplar, almond and plane trees. He peeled off some of the bark so that the branches had white stripes on them. ³⁸He put the branches in front of the flocks at the watering places. When the animals came to drink, they also mated there. ³⁹So the goats mated in front of the branches. Then the young that were born were streaked, speckled or spotted. ⁴⁰Jacob separated the young animals from the others. And he made them face the streaked and dark animals in Laban's flock. Jacob kept his animals separate from Laban's. ⁴¹When the stronger animals in the flock were mating, Jacob put the branches before their eyes. This was so the animals would mate near the branches. ⁴²But when the weaker animals mated, Jacob did not put the branches there. So the animals born from the weaker animals were Laban's. And the animals born from the stronger animals were Jacob's. ⁴³In this way Jacob became very rich. He had large flocks, many male and female servants, camels and donkeys.

Jacob Runs Away

31 One day Jacob heard Laban's sons talking. They said, "Jacob has taken everything our father owned. Jacob has become rich in this way." ²Then Jacob noticed that Laban was not as friendly as he had been before. ³The Lord said to Jacob, "Go back to the land where your ancestors lived. I will be with you."

⁴So Jacob told Rachel and Leah to meet him in the field where he kept his flocks. ⁵He said to them, "I have seen that your father is not as friendly with me as he used to be. But the God of my father has been with me. ⁶You both know that I have worked as hard as I could for your father. ⁷But he cheated me. He has changed my pay ten times. But God has not allowed your father to harm me. ⁸At one time Laban said, 'You can have all the speckled goats as your pay.' After that, all the animals gave birth to speckled young ones. But then Laban said, 'You can have all the streaked goats as your pay.' After that, all the animals gave birth to streaked babies. ⁹So God has taken the animals away from your father. And God has given them to me.

¹⁰"I had a dream during the season when the animals were mating. I saw that the only male goats who were mating were streaked, speckled or spotted. ¹¹The angel of God spoke to me in that dream. He said, 'Jacob!' I answered, 'Yes!' ¹²The angel said, 'Look! Only the streaked, speckled or spotted goats are mating. I have seen all the wrong things Laban does to you. ¹³I am the God who appeared to you at Bethel. There you poured olive oil on the stone you set up on end. There you made a promise to me. Now I want you to leave here. Go back to the land where you were born.'"

¹⁴Rachel and Leah answered Jacob, "Our father has nothing to give us when he dies. ¹⁵He has treated us like strangers. He sold us to you, and then he spent all of the money you paid for

us. ¹⁶God took all this wealth from our father, and now it belongs to us and our children. So you do whatever God told you to do."

¹⁷So Jacob put his children and his wives on camels. ¹⁸Then they began their journey back to Isaac, his father. He lived in the land of Canaan. All the flocks of animals that Jacob owned walked ahead of them. He carried everything with him that he had gotten while he lived in Northwest Mesopotamia.

¹⁹Laban was gone to cut the wool from his sheep. While he was gone, Rachel stole the idols of false gods that belonged to him. ²⁰And Jacob tricked Laban the Aramean. He did not tell Laban he was leaving. ²¹Jacob and his family left quickly. They crossed the Euphrates River and traveled toward the mountains of Gilead.

²²Three days later Laban learned that Jacob had run away. ²³So Laban gathered his relatives and began to chase Jacob. After seven days Laban found him in the mountains of Gilead. ²⁴That night God came to Laban the Aramean in a dream. The Lord said, "Be careful! Do not say anything to Jacob, good or bad."

The Search for the Stolen Idols

²⁵So Laban caught up with Jacob. Now Jacob had made his camp in the mountains. So Laban and his relatives set up their camp in the mountains of Gilead. ²⁶Laban said to Jacob, "What have you done? Why did you trick me? You took my daughters as if you had captured them in a war. ²⁷Why did you run away without telling me? Why did you trick me? Why didn't you tell me? Then I could send you away with joy and singing. There would be the music of tambourines*ᵈ* and harps. ²⁸You did not even let me kiss my grandchildren and my daughters good-bye. You were very foolish to do this! ²⁹I have the power to harm you. But last night the God of your father spoke to me. He warned me not to say anything to you, good or bad. ³⁰I know you want to go

back to your home. But why did you steal my idols?"

³¹Jacob answered Laban, "I left without telling you, because I was afraid! I thought you would take your daughters away from me. ³²If you find anyone here who has taken your idols, he will be killed! Your relatives will be my witnesses. You may look for anything that belongs to you. Take anything that is yours." (Now Jacob did not know that Rachel had stolen Laban's idols.)

³³So Laban looked in Jacob's tent and in Leah's tent. He looked in the tent where the two slave women stayed. But he did not find his idols. When he left Leah's tent, he went into Rachel's tent. ³⁴Rachel had hidden the idols inside her camel's saddle. And she was sitting on them. Laban looked through the whole tent, but he did not find them.

³⁵Rachel said to her father, "Father, don't be angry with me. I am not able to stand up before you. I am having my monthly period." So Laban looked through the camp, but he did not find his idols.

³⁶Then Jacob became very angry. He said, "What wrong have I done? What law have I broken to cause you to chase me? ³⁷You have looked through everything I own. But you have found nothing that belongs to you. If you have found anything, show it to everyone. Put it in front of your relatives and my relatives. Then let them decide which one of us is right. ³⁸I have worked for you now for 20 years. During all that time none of the lambs and kids died during birth. And I have not eaten any of the male sheep from your flocks. ³⁹Any time a sheep was killed by wild animals, I did not bring it to you. I made up for the loss myself. You made me pay for any animal that was stolen during the day or night. ⁴⁰In the daytime the sun took away my strength. At night I was cold and could not sleep. ⁴¹I worked like a slave for you for 20 years. For the first 14 years I worked to get your two daughters. The last 6 years I worked to earn your animals. And dur-

ing that time you changed my pay ten times. [42]But the God of my father was with me. He is the God of Abraham and the God of Isaac. If God had not been with me, you would have sent me away with nothing. But he saw the trouble I had and the hard work I did. And last night God corrected you."

Jacob and Laban's Agreement

[43]Laban said to Jacob, "These girls are my daughters. Their children belong to me, and these animals are mine. Everything you see here belongs to me. But I can do nothing to keep my daughters and their children. [44]Let us make an agreement. Let us set up a pile of stones to remind us of our agreement."

[45]So Jacob took a large rock and set it up on its end. [46]He told his relatives to gather rocks. So they took the rocks and piled them up. Then they ate beside the pile of rocks. [47]Laban named that place in his language A Pile to Remind Us. And Jacob gave the place the same name in Hebrew.

[48]Laban said to Jacob, "This pile of rocks will remind us of the agreement between us." That is why the place was called A Pile to Remind Us. [49]It was also called Mizpah.[n] This was because Laban said, "Let the Lord watch over us while we are separated from each other. [50]Remember that God is our witness. This is true even if no one else is around us. He will know if you harm my daughters or marry other women. [51]Here is the pile of rocks that I have put between us. And here is the rock I set up on end. [52]This pile of rocks and this rock set on end will remind us of our agreement. I will never go past this pile to hurt you. And you must never come to my side of them to hurt me. [53]The God of Abraham is the God of Nahor and the God of their fathers. Let God punish either of us if we break this agreement."

So Jacob made a promise in the name of God. This was the God of his father

Isaac. [54]Then Jacob killed an animal and offered it as a sacrifice on the mountain. And he invited his relatives to share in the meal. After they finished eating, they spent the night on the mountain. [55]Early the next morning Laban kissed his grandchildren and his daughters. He blessed them, and then he left to return home.

Jacob Meets Esau

32 When Jacob also went his way, the angels of God met him. [2]When Jacob saw them, he said, "This is the camp of God!" So Jacob named that place Mahanaim.[n]

[3]Jacob's brother Esau was living in the area called Seir in the country of Edom. Jacob sent messengers to Esau. [4]Jacob told the messengers, "Give this message to my master Esau: 'This is what Jacob, your servant, says: I have lived with Laban and have remained there until now. [5]I have cattle, donkeys, flocks, and male and female servants. I send this message to you and ask you to accept us.'"

[6]The messengers returned to Jacob and said, "We went to your brother Esau. He is coming to meet you. And he has 400 men with him."

[7]Then Jacob was very afraid and worried. He divided the people who were with him into two camps. He also divided all the flocks, herds and camels into two camps. [8]Jacob thought, "Esau might come and destroy one camp. But the other camp can run away and be saved."

[9]Jacob said, "God of my father Abraham! God of my father Isaac! Lord, you told me to return to my country and my family. You said that you would do good to me. [10]I am not worthy of the kindness and continual goodness you have shown me. The first time I traveled across the Jordan River, I had only my walking stick. But now I own enough to have two camps. [11]Please save me from my brother Esau. I am

[n]**Mizpah**   This name sounds like the Hebrew word for "watch."
[n]**Mahanaim**   This name means "two camps."

afraid he will come and kill all of us, even the mothers with the children. [12]You said to me, 'I will do good to you. I will make your children as many as the sand of the seashore. There will be too many to count.'"

[13]Jacob stayed there for the night. He prepared a gift for Esau from what he had with him. [14]It was 200 female goats and 20 male goats, 200 female sheep and 20 male sheep. [15]There were 30 female camels and their young, 40 cows and 10 bulls, 20 female donkeys and 10 male donkeys. [16]Jacob gave each separate flock of animals to one of his servants. Then he said to them, "Go ahead of me and keep some space between each herd." [17]Jacob gave them their orders. To the servant with the first group of animals he said, "My brother Esau will come to you. He will ask you, 'Whose servant are you? Where are you going? Whose animals are these?' [18]Then you will answer, 'These animals belong to your servant Jacob. He sent them as a gift to you my master, Esau. And Jacob also is coming behind us.'"

[19]Jacob ordered the second servant, the third servant and all the other servants to do the same thing. He said, "Say the same thing to Esau when you meet him. [20]Say, 'Your servant Jacob is coming behind us.'" Jacob thought, "If I send this gift ahead of me, maybe Esau will forgive me. Then when I see him, perhaps he will accept me." [21]So Jacob sent the gift to Esau. But Jacob stayed that night in the camp.

Jacob Wrestles with God

[22]During the night Jacob rose and crossed the Jabbok River at the crossing. He took his 2 wives, his 2 slave girls and his 11 sons with him. [23]He sent his family and everything he had across the river. [24]But Jacob stayed behind alone. And a man came and wrestled with him until the sun came up. [25]The man saw that he could not

defeat Jacob. So he struck Jacob's hip and put it out of joint. [26]Then the man said to Jacob, "Let me go. The sun is coming up."

But Jacob said, "I will let you go if you will bless me."

[27]The man said to him, "What is your name?"

And he answered, "Jacob."

[28]Then the man said, "Your name will no longer be Jacob. Your name will now be Israel,[n] because you have wrestled with God and with men. And you have won."

[29]Then Jacob asked him, "Please tell me your name."

But the man said, "Why do you ask my name?" Then he blessed Jacob there.

[30]So Jacob named that place Peniel.[n] He said, "I have seen God face to face. But my life was saved." [31]Then the sun rose as he was leaving that place. Jacob was limping because of his leg. [32]So even today the people of Israel do not eat the muscle that is on the hip joint of animals. This is because Jacob was touched there

Jacob Shows His Bravery

33 Jacob looked up and saw Esau coming. With him were 400 men. So Jacob divided his children among Leah, Rachel and the two slave girls. [2]Jacob put the slave girls with their children first. Then he put Leah and her children behind them. And he put Rachel and Joseph last. [3]Jacob himself went out in front of them. He bowed down flat on the ground seven times as he was walking toward his brother.

[4]But Esau ran to meet Jacob. Esau put his arms around him and hugged him. Then Esau kissed him, and they both cried. [5]Esau looked up and saw the women and children. He asked, "Who are these people with you?"

Jacob answered, "These are the children God has given me. God has been good to me, your servant."

[n]**Israel** This name means "he wrestles with God."
[n]**Peniel** This name means "the face of God."

Brothers and Sisters

ESAU AND JACOB • GENESIS 33

Esau did not like his brother Jacob very much because Jacob had cheated him. As the older brother, Esau was supposed to receive a special inheritance from their father Isaac and a special blessing. The inheritance was a double amount of what would be passed on to the children after the father died. The blessing was a ceremony when the father officially gave the inheritance. But Jacob had gotten Esau's inheritance and then had tricked him out of his special blessing.

Many years later, when Jacob and Esau were about to meet again, Jacob was afraid because of what he had done to Esau. But Esau had forgiven Jacob and was living a full and happy life.

If your brother or sister has been mean to you, don't hold a grudge against that person. It is always better to forgive.

To meet some brothers who became very jealous, fly to page 53.

⁶Then the two slave girls and their children came up to Esau. They bowed down flat on the earth before him. ⁷Then Leah and her children came up to Esau. They also bowed down flat on the earth. Last of all, Joseph and Rachel came up to Esau. And they, too, bowed down flat before him.

⁸Esau said, "I saw many herds as I was coming here. Why did you bring them?"

Jacob answered, "They were to please you, my master."

⁹But Esau said, "I already have enough, my brother. Keep what you have."

¹⁰Jacob said, "No! Please! If I have pleased you, then please accept the gift I give you. I am very happy to see your face again. It is like seeing the face of God because you have accepted me. ¹¹So I beg you to accept the gift I give you. God has been very good to me. And I have more than I need." And because Jacob begged, Esau accepted the gift.

¹²Then Esau said, "Let us get going. I will travel with you."

¹³But Jacob said to him, "My master, you know that the children are weak. And I must be careful with my flocks and their young ones. If I force them to go too far in one day, all the animals will die. ¹⁴So, my master, you go on ahead of me, your servant. I will follow you slowly. I will let the animals and the children set the speed at which we travel. I will meet you, my master, in Edom."

¹⁵So Esau said, "Then let me leave some of my men with you."

"No, thank you," said Jacob. "I only want to please you, my master." ¹⁶So that day Esau started back to Edom. ¹⁷But Jacob went to Succoth. There he built a house for himself. And he made shelters for his animals. That is why the place was named Succoth.ⁿ

¹⁸Jacob left Northwest Mesopotamia. And he arrived safely at the city of Shechem in the land of Canaan. He camped east of the city. ¹⁹He bought a

ⁿ**Succoth** This name means "shelters."

part of the field where he had camped. He bought it from the sons of Hamor father of Shechem for 100 pieces of silver. ²⁰He built an altar there and named it after God, the God of Israel.

Dinah Is Attacked

34 Dinah was the daughter of Leah and Jacob. At this time Dinah went out to visit the women of that land. ²Shechem son of Hamor the Hivite, the ruler of that land, saw Dinah. He took her and forced her to have sexual relations with him. ³Shechem fell in love with Dinah, and he spoke kindly to her. ⁴He told his father, Hamor, "Please get this girl for me so I can marry her."

⁵Jacob learned how Shechem had disgraced his daughter. But Jacob's sons were out in the field with the cattle. So Jacob said nothing until they came home. ⁶And Hamor father of Shechem went to talk with Jacob.

⁷When Jacob's sons heard what had happened, they came in from the field. They were very angry, because Shechem had done such a wicked thing to Israel. It was wrong for him to have sexual relations with Jacob's daughter. A thing like this should not be done.

⁸But Hamor talked to the brothers of Dinah. He said, "My son Shechem is deeply in love with Dinah. Please let him marry her. ⁹Marry our people. Give your women to our men as wives. And take our women for your men as wives. ¹⁰You can live in the same land with us. You will be free to own land and to trade here."

¹¹Shechem also talked to Jacob and to Dinah's brothers. He said, "Please accept my offer. I will give anything you ask. ¹²Ask as much as you want for the payment for the bride. I will give it to you. Just let me marry Dinah."

¹³The sons of Jacob answered Shechem and his father with lies. They were angry because Shechem had disgraced their sister Dinah. ¹⁴The brothers said to them, "We cannot allow you to marry our sister. You are not circumcised.ᵈ That would be a disgrace

to us. ¹⁵But we will allow you to marry her if you do this one thing: Every man in your town must be circumcised like us. ¹⁶Then your men can marry our women, and our men can marry your women. Then we will live in your land and become one people. ¹⁷If you refuse to be circumcised, we will take Dinah and leave."

¹⁸What they asked seemed fair to Hamor and Shechem. ¹⁹So Shechem went quickly to be circumcised because he loved Jacob's daughter.

Now Shechem was the most respected man in his family. ²⁰So Hamor and Shechem went to the gate of their city. They spoke to the men of their city. They said, ²¹"These people want to be friends with us. So let them live in our land and trade here. There is enough land for all of us. Let us marry their women. And we can let them marry our women. ²²But our men must agree to one thing. All our men must agree to be circumcised as they are. Then they will agree to live in our land. And we will be one people. ²³If we do this, their cattle and their animals will belong to us. Let us do what they say, and they will stay in our land." ²⁴All the men who had come to the city gate heard this. And they agreed with Hamor and Shechem. And every man was circumcised.

²⁵Three days later the men who were circumcised were still in pain. Two of Jacob's sons, Simeon and Levi (Dinah's brothers), took their swords. They made a surprise attack on the city. And they killed all the men there. ²⁶Simeon and Levi killed Hamor and his son Shechem. Then they took Dinah out of Shechem's house and left. ²⁷Jacob's sons went among the dead bodies and stole everything that was in the city. This was to pay them back for what Shechem had done to their sister. ²⁸So the brothers took the flocks, herds and donkeys. And they took everything in the city and in the fields. ²⁹They took every valuable thing those people owned. They even took the

wives and children and everything that was in the houses.

[30]Then Jacob said to Simeon and Levi, "You have caused me a lot of trouble. Now the Canaanites and the Perizzites who live in the land will hate me. There are only a few of us. If they join together to attack us, my people and I will be destroyed."

[31]But the brothers said, "We will not allow our sister to be treated like a prostitute."[d]

Jacob in Bethel

35 God said to Jacob, "Go to the city of Bethel and live there. Make an altar to the God who appeared to you there. This was when you were running away from your brother Esau."

[2]So Jacob said to his family and to all who were with him, "Put away the foreign gods you have. Make yourselves clean,[d] and change your clothes. [3]We will leave here and go to Bethel. There I will build an altar to God. He has helped me during my time of trouble. He has been with me everywhere I have gone." [4]So they gave Jacob all the foreign gods they had. And they gave him the earrings they were wearing. He hid them under the great tree near the town of Shechem. [5]Then Jacob and his sons left there. But God caused the people in the nearby cities to be afraid. So they did not follow the sons of Jacob. [6]And Jacob and all the people who were with him went to Luz. It is now called Bethel. It is in the land of Canaan. [7]There Jacob built an altar. He named the place Bethel, after God, because God had appeared to him there. That was when he was running from his brother.

[8]Deborah, Rebekah's nurse, died and was buried under the oak tree at Bethel. They named that place Oak of Crying.

Jacob's New Name

[9]When Jacob came back from Northwest Mesopotamia, God appeared to him again. And God blessed him. [10]God said to him, "Your name is Jacob. But you will not be called Jacob any longer. Your new name will be Israel." So he called him Israel. [11]God said to him, "I am God All-Powerful. Have many children and grow in number as a nation. You will be the ancestor of many nations and kings. [12]I gave Abraham and Isaac land. I will give that same land to you and your descendants."[d] [13]Then God left him. [14]Jacob set up a stone on edge in that place where God had talked to him. And he poured a drink offering and olive oil on it to make it special for God. [15]And Jacob named the place Bethel.

Rachel Dies Giving Birth

[16]Jacob and his group left Bethel. Before they came to Ephrath, Rachel began giving birth to her baby. [17]But she was having much trouble with this birth. When Rachel's nurse saw this, she said, "Don't be afraid, Rachel. You are giving birth to another son." [18]Rachel gave birth to the son, but she died. As she lay dying, she named the boy Son of My Suffering. But Jacob called him Benjamin.[n]

[19]Rachel was buried on the road to Ephrath, a district of Bethlehem. [20]And Jacob set up a rock on her grave to honor her. That rock is still there today. [21]Then Israel, also called Jacob, continued his journey. He camped just south of Migdal Eder.

[22]While Israel was in that land Reuben had sexual relations with Israel's slave woman[d] Bilhah. And Israel heard about it.

The Family of Israel

Jacob had 12 sons. [23]He had 6 sons by his wife Leah. Reuben was his first son. Then Leah had Simeon, Levi, Judah, Issachar and Zebulun. [24]He had 2 sons by his wife Rachel: Joseph and Benjamin. [25]He had 2 sons by Rachel's slave girl Bilhah: Dan and Naphtali.

[n]**Benjamin**   This name means "right-hand son" or "favorite son."

26And he had 2 sons by Leah's slave girl Zilpah: Gad and Asher.

These are Jacob's sons who were born in Northwest Mesopotamia. 27Jacob went to his father Isaac at Mamre near Hebron. This is where Abraham and Isaac had lived. 28Isaac lived 180 years. 29So Isaac breathed his last breath and died when he was very old. And his sons Esau and Jacob buried him.

Esau's Family

36 This is the family history of Esau (also called Edom).
2Esau married women from the land of Canaan. He married Adah daughter of Elon the Hittite. And he married Oholibamah daughter of Anah. Anah was the son of Zibeon the Hivite. And he married 3Basemath, Ishmael's daughter, the sister of Nebaioth.

4Adah gave Esau one son, Eliphaz. Basemath gave Esau Reuel. 5And Oholibamah gave Esau Jeush, Jalam and Korah. These were Esau's sons who were born in the land of Canaan.

6Esau took his wives, his sons, his daughters and all the people who lived with him. He took his herds and other animals. And he took all the belongings he had gotten in Canaan. And he went to a land away from his brother Jacob. 7Esau's and Jacob's belongings were becoming too many for them to live in the same land. The land where they had lived could not support both of them. They had too many herds. 8So Esau lived in the mountains of Edom. (Esau is also named Edom.)

9This is the family history of Esau. He is the ancestor of the Edomites, who live in the mountains of Edom.

10Esau's sons were Eliphaz son of Adah and Esau, and Reuel son of Basemath and Esau.

11Eliphaz had five sons: Teman, Omar, Zepho, Gatam and Kenaz. 12Eliphaz also had a slave woman*d* named Timna. Timna and Eliphaz gave birth to Amalek. These were Esau's grandsons by his wife Adah.

13Reuel had four sons: Nahath, Zerah, Shammah and Mizzah. These were Esau's grandsons by his wife Basemath.

14Esau's third wife was Oholibamah. She was the daughter of Anah. (Anah was the son of Zibeon.) Esau and Oholibamah gave birth to Jeush, Jalam and Korah.

15These were the leaders that came from Esau. Esau's first son was Eliphaz. From him came these leaders: Teman, Omar, Zepho, Kenaz, 16Korah, Gatam and Amalek. These were the leaders that came from Eliphaz in the land of Edom. They were the grandsons of Adah.

17Esau's son Reuel was the father of these leaders: Nahath, Zerah, Shammah and Mizzah. These were the leaders that came from Reuel in the land of Edom. They were the grandsons of Esau's wife Basemath.

18Esau's wife Oholibamah gave birth to these leaders: Jeush, Jalam and Korah. These are the leaders that came from Esau's wife Oholibamah. She was the daughter of Anah. 19These were the sons of Esau (also called Edom), and these were their leaders.

20These were the sons of Seir the Horite, who were living in the land: Lotan, Shobal, Zibeon, Anah, 21Dishon, Ezer and Dishan. These sons of Seir were the leaders of the Horites in Edom.

22The sons of Lotan were Hori and Homam. (Timna was Lotan's sister.) 23The sons of Shobal were Alvan, Manahath, Ebal, Shepho and Onam. 24The sons of Zibeon were Aiah and Anah. Anah is the man who found the hot springs in the desert. He found them while he was caring for his father's donkeys. 25The children of Anah were Dishon and Oholibamah daughter of Anah. 26The sons of Dishon were Hemdan, Eshban, Ithran and Keran. 27The sons of Ezer were Bilhan, Zaavan and Akan. 28The sons of Dishan were Uz and Aran. 29These were the names of the Horite leaders: Lotan, Shobal, Zibeon, Anah, ³⁰Dishon, Ezer and Dishan.

These men were the leaders of the Horite families. They lived in the land of Edom.

³¹These are the kings who ruled in the land of Edom before the Israelites ever had a king.

³²Bela son of Beor was the king of Edom. He came from the city of Dinhabah.

³³When Bela died, Jobab son of Zerah became king. Jobab was from Bozrah.

³⁴When Jobab died, Husham became king. He was from the land of the Temanites.

³⁵When Husham died, Hadad son of Bedad became king. Hadad had defeated Midian in the country of Moab. Hadad was from the city of Avith.

³⁶When Hadad died, Samlah became king. He was from Masrekah.

³⁷When Samlah died, Shaul became king. He was from Rehoboth on the Euphrates River.

³⁸When Shaul died, Baal-Hanan son of Acbor became king.

³⁹When Baal-Hanan son of Acbor died, Hadad became king. He was from the city of Pau. His wife's name was Mehetabel daughter of Matred. Matred was the daughter of Me-Zahab.

⁴⁰These Edomite leaders came from Esau. They are listed by their families and regions. Their names were Timna, Alvah, Jetheth, ⁴¹Oholibamah, Elah, Pinon, ⁴²Kenaz, Teman, Mibzar, ⁴³Magdiel and Iram. These were the leaders of Edom. (Esau was the father of the Edomites.) The area where each of these families lived was named after that family.

Joseph the Dreamer

37 Jacob lived in the land of Canaan, where his father had lived. ²This is the family history of Jacob.

Joseph was a young man, 17 years old. He and his brothers cared for the flocks. His brothers were the sons of Bilhah and Zilpah, his father's wives. Joseph gave his father bad reports about his brothers. ³Joseph was born when his father Israel, also called Jacob, was old. So Israel loved Joseph more than his other sons. He made Joseph a special robe with long sleeves. ⁴Joseph's brothers saw that their father loved

Words to Know: Old Testament
ROBE • GENESIS 37:3

A robe was an important piece of clothing in Bible times. Most people did not have a lot of clothes. They only had one or two pieces. But everyone had a robe with long sleeves. The people used a robe to keep warm and also used it like a bag to wrap around things and carry them. A mother might wrap her baby in a robe to carry it, and a farmer might carry some grain tied up in his robe like a sack around his neck. When people traveled, they sometimes slept right under the stars with their robe wrapped around them or rolled up under their head for a pillow. In Bible times, if you had a special friend come to visit, you would spread out your robe for the friend to sit on.

The colorful robe that Joseph received from his father stood out from everyone else's plain robe. That is one reason his brothers were jealous of him. God doesn't want us to be jealous. He wants us to be happy for people who have more than we have.

To read about an important stick people used, fly to page 79.

Joseph more than he loved them. So they hated their brother and could not speak to him politely.

about what all these things could mean. ¹²One day Joseph's brothers went to Shechem to herd their father's sheep. ¹³Jacob said to Joseph, "Go to Shechem. Your brothers are there herding the sheep."

Joseph answered, "I will go."

Brothers and Sisters

JOSEPH AND HIS BROTHERS • GENESIS 37:4-36

Jacob had lots of sons, but he showed that one was his favorite. Jacob loved Joseph very much, and he showed his love by giving him a beautiful robe of many colors. This robe didn't make Joseph's brothers happy. Then Joseph began telling his brothers about his dreams that they would all one day bow down to him. The brothers became so angry that they decided to kill Joseph.

Joseph's brothers were hurt by their father and were angry at Joseph. But they were wrong to want to hurt their brother. God took care of Joseph, and many years later Joseph took care of his entire family—even his brothers who had been so mean to him.

To meet some brothers who sinned together, fly to page 141.

---

⁵One time Joseph had a dream. When he told his brothers about it, they hated him even more. ⁶Joseph said, "Listen to the dream I had. ⁷We were in the field tying bundles of wheat together. My bundle stood up, and your bundles of wheat gathered around mine. Your bundles bowed down to mine."

⁸His brothers said, "Do you really think you will be king over us? Do you truly think you will rule over us?" His brothers hated him even more now. They hated him because of his dreams and what he had said.

⁹Then Joseph had another dream. He told his brothers about it also. He said, "Listen, I had another dream. I saw the sun, moon and 11 stars bowing down to me."

¹⁰Joseph also told his father about this dream. But his father scolded him, saying, "What kind of dream is this? Do you really believe that your mother, your brothers and I will bow down to you?" ¹¹Joseph's brothers were jealous of him. But his father thought

¹⁴His father said, "Go and see if your brothers and the sheep are all right. Then come back and tell me." So Joseph's father sent him from the Valley of Hebron.

When Joseph came to Shechem, ¹⁵a man found him wandering in the field. He asked Joseph, "What are you looking for?"

¹⁶Joseph answered, "I am looking for my brothers. Can you tell me where they are herding the sheep?"

¹⁷The man said, "They have already gone. I heard them say they were going to Dothan." So Joseph went to look for his brothers and found them in Dothan.

Joseph Sold into Slavery

¹⁸Joseph's brothers saw him coming from far away. Before he reached them, they made a plan to kill him. ¹⁹They said to each other, "Here comes that dreamer. ²⁰Let's kill him and throw his body into one of the wells. We can tell our father that a wild animal killed him. Then we will

see what will become of his dreams."

²¹But Reuben heard their plan and saved Joseph. He said, "Let's not kill him. ²²Don't spill any blood. Throw him into this well here in the desert. But don't hurt him!" Reuben planned to save Joseph later and send him back to his father. ²³So when Joseph came to his brothers, they pulled off his robe with long sleeves. ²⁴Then they threw him into the well. It was empty. There was no water in it.

²⁵While Joseph was in the well, the brothers sat down to eat. When they looked up, they saw a group of Ishmaelites. They were traveling from Gilead to Egypt. Their camels were carrying spices, balm^d and myrrh.^{d}

²⁶Then Judah said to his brothers, "What will we gain if we kill our brother and hide his death? ²⁷Let's sell him to these Ishmaelites. Then we will not be guilty of killing our own brother. After all, he is our brother, our own flesh and blood." And the other brothers agreed. ²⁸So when the Midianite traders came by, the brothers took Joseph out of the well. They sold him to the Ishmaelites

for eight ounces of silver. And the Ishmaelites took him to Egypt.

²⁹Reuben was not with his brothers when they sold Joseph to the Ishmaelites. When Reuben came back to the well, Joseph was not there. Reuben tore his clothes to show he was sad. ³⁰Then he went back to his brothers and said, "The boy is not there! What will I do?" ³¹The brothers killed a goat and dipped Joseph's long-sleeved robe in its blood. ³²Then they brought the robe to their father. They said, "We found this robe. Look it over carefully. See if it is your son's robe."

³³Jacob looked it over and said, "It is my son's robe! Some savage animal has eaten him. My son Joseph has been torn to pieces!" ³⁴Then Jacob tore his clothes and put on rough cloth to show that he was sad. He continued to be sad about his son for a long time. ³⁵All of Jacob's sons and daughters tried to comfort him. But he could not be comforted. Jacob said, "I will be sad about my son until the day I die." So Jacob cried for his son Joseph.

³⁶Meanwhile the Midianites who had bought Joseph had taken him to Egypt. There they sold him to Potiphar. Potiphar was an officer to

Children Who Saw God at Work
JOSEPH • GENESIS 37:18-28

Joseph was terrified. He had always lived in the desert because he was a shepherd. His jealous brothers had just sold him to some traders who were on their way to a big city in Egypt. *What would these people do to him?* Joseph wondered. He didn't want to be a slave. What had he done to make his brothers so mad? Would he ever see his father again? Joseph was afraid, but God was with him. Even though Joseph didn't know where he was going and he was lonely, he knew that God would never leave him.

If you are ever afraid or lost, God promises to take care of you. He took care of Joseph in Egypt. No matter where you go, God will be with you.

To meet a boy who heard God's voice, fly to page 329.

the king of Egypt and captain of the palace guard.

Judah and Tamar

38 About that time, Judah left his brothers. He went to stay with a man named Hirah. Hirah was from the town of Adullam. [2]Judah met a Canaanite girl there and married her. Her father was named Shua. And Judah had sexual relations with her. [3]She became pregnant and gave birth to a son. Judah named him Er. [4]Later she gave birth to another son. She named him Onan. [5]Later she had another son. She named him Shelah. She was at Kezib when this third son was born.

[6]Judah chose a girl named Tamar to be the wife of his first son Er. [7]Er was Judah's oldest son. But he did what the Lord said was evil. So the Lord killed him. [8]Then Judah said to Er's brother Onan, "Go and have sexual relations with your dead brother's wife." It is your duty to provide children for your brother in this way."

[9]But Onan knew that the children would not belong to him. Onan was supposed to have sexual relations with Tamar. But he did not complete the sex act. This made it impossible for Tamar to become pregnant. So Er could not have descendants.[d] [10]The Lord was displeased by this wicked thing Onan had done. So the Lord killed Onan also. [11]Then Judah said to his daughter-in-law Tamar, "Go back to live in your father's house. And don't marry until my young son Shelah grows up." Judah was afraid that Shelah also would die like his brothers. So Tamar returned to her father's home.

[12]After a long time Judah's wife, the daughter of Shua, died. After Judah had gotten over his sorrow, he went to Timnah. He went to his men who were cutting the wool from his sheep. His friend Hirah from Adullam went with

him. [13]Tamar learned that Judah, her father-in-law, was going to Timnah to cut the wool from his sheep. [14]So she took off the clothes that showed she was a widow. Then she covered her face with a veil to hide who she was. She sat down by the gate of Enaim. It was on the road to Timnah. She did this because Judah's younger son Shelah had grown up. But Judah had not made plans for her to marry him.

[15]When Judah saw her, he thought she was a prostitute.[d] This was because she had covered her face with a veil. [16]So Judah went to her and said, "Let me have sexual relations with you." He did not know that she was Tamar, his daughter-in-law.

She asked, "What will you give me if I let you have sexual relations with me?"

[17]Judah answered, "I will send you a young goat from my flock."

She answered, "First give me something to keep as a deposit until you send the goat."

[18]Judah asked, "What do you want me to give you as a deposit?"

Tamar answered, "Give me your seal and its cord," and give me your walking stick." So Judah gave these things to her. Then Judah and Tamar had sexual relations, and Tamar became pregnant. [19]Tamar went home. She took off the veil that covered her face. And she put on the clothes that showed she was a widow.

[20]Judah sent his friend Hirah with the young goat. Judah told Hirah to find the woman and get back his seal and the walking stick he had given her. But Hirah could not find her. [21]Hirah asked some of the men at the town of Enaim, "Where is the prostitute who was here by the road?"

The men answered, "There has never been a prostitute here."

[22]So he went back to Judah and said, "I could not find the woman. The men

---

"**Go . . . wife** It was a custom in Israel that if a man died without children, one of his brothers would marry the widow. If a child was born, it would be considered the dead man's child.

"**seal . . . cord** A seal was used like a rubber stamp. People ran a string through it to tie around the neck. They wrote a contract, folded it, put wax or clay on the contract, and pressed the seal onto it as a signature.

who lived there said, 'There has never been a prostitute here.'"

²³Judah said, "Let her keep the things. I don't want people to laugh at us. I sent her the goat as I promised. But you could not find her."

²⁴About three months later someone told Judah, "Tamar, your daughter-in-law, is guilty of acting like a prostitute. Now she is pregnant."

Then Judah said, "Bring her out and let her be burned to death."

²⁵When the men went to bring Tamar out, she sent a message to her father-in-law. She said, "The man who owns

birth, there were twins in her body. ²⁸While she was giving birth, one baby put his hand out. The nurse tied a red string on his hand. She said, "This baby came out first." ²⁹But he pulled his hand back in. So the other baby was born first. The nurse said, "So you are able to break out first." And they named him Perez.ⁿ ³⁰After this, the baby with the red string on his hand was born. They named him Zerah.

Temptation
GENESIS 39:1–23

"**H**oney, don't touch these chocolate chip cookies. I baked them for the school fair."

Temptation! Whether it's a plate of warm cookies or a five dollar bill lying on a desk, temptations are all around. What do you do when you are tempted to do something wrong, but know you should do what is right?

This passage tells the story of a godly young man who faced serious temptation. Joseph, a handsome Jewish lad, was sold into slavery in Egypt. He served his Egyptian master faithfully. Then one day his master's wife tried to tempt Joseph to go into her bedroom. But he said no because he knew that was not what God would want—it would be wrong. Joseph ran away from Potiphar's wife.

When you are tempted to do the wrong thing—remember Joseph's example. Say no and get away from the temptation as quick as you can.

To learn more about temptation, zoom to page 118.

these things has made me pregnant. Look at this seal and its cord and this walking stick. Tell me whose they are."

²⁶Judah recognized them. He said, "She is more in the right than I. She did this because I did not give her to my son Shelah as I promised." And Judah did not have sexual relations with her again.

²⁷When time came for Tamar to give

Joseph Is Sold to Potiphar

39 Now Joseph had been taken down to Egypt. An Egyptian named Potiphar was an officer to the king of Egypt. He was the captain of the palace guard. He bought Joseph from the Ishmaelites who had brought him down there. ²The Lord was with Joseph, and he became a successful man. He

ⁿ**Perez**   This name means "breaking out."

lived in the house of his master, Potiphar the Egyptian.

³Potiphar saw that the Lord was with Joseph. He saw that the Lord made Joseph successful in everything he did. ⁴So Potiphar was very happy with Joseph. He allowed Joseph to be his personal servant. He put Joseph in charge of the house. Joseph was trusted with everything Potiphar owned. ⁵So Joseph was put in charge of the house. He was put in charge of everything Potiphar owned. Then the Lord blessed the people in Potiphar's house because of Joseph. And the Lord blessed everything that belonged to Potiphar, both in the house and in the field. ⁶So Potiphar put Joseph in charge of everything he owned. Potiphar was not concerned about anything, except the food he ate.

Joseph Is Put into Prison

Now Joseph was well built and handsome. ⁷After some time the wife of Joseph's master began to desire Joseph. One day she said to him, "Have sexual relations with me."

⁸But Joseph refused. He said to her, "My master trusts me with everything in his house. He has put me in charge of everything he owns. ⁹There is no one in his house greater than I. He has not kept anything from me, except you. And that is because you are his wife. How can I do such an evil thing? It is a sin against God."

¹⁰The woman talked to Joseph every day, but he refused to have sexual relations with her or even spend time with her.

¹¹One day Joseph went into the house to do his work as usual. He was the only man in the house at that time. ¹²His master's wife grabbed his coat. She said to him, "Come and have sexual relations with me." But Joseph left his coat in her hand and ran out of the house.

¹³She saw what Joseph had done. He had left his coat in her hands and had run outside. ¹⁴So she called to the servants in her house. She said, "Look!

This Hebrew slave was brought here to shame us. He came in and tried to have sexual relations with me. But I screamed. ¹⁵My scream scared him, and he ran away. But he left his coat with me." ¹⁶She kept his coat until her husband came home. ¹⁷And she told her husband the same story. She said, "This Hebrew slave you brought here came in to shame me! ¹⁸When he came near me, I screamed. He ran away, but he left his coat."

¹⁹When Joseph's master heard what his wife said Joseph had done, he became very angry. ²⁰So Potiphar arrested Joseph and put him into prison. This prison was where the king's prisoners were put. And Joseph stayed there in the prison.

²¹But the Lord was with Joseph and showed him kindness. The Lord caused the prison warden to like Joseph. ²²The prison warden chose Joseph to take care of all the prisoners. He was responsible for whatever was done in the prison. ²³The warden paid no attention to anything that was in Joseph's care. This was because the Lord was with Joseph. The Lord made Joseph successful in everything he did.

Joseph Interprets Two Dreams

40 After these things happened, two of the king's officers displeased the king. These officers were the man who served wine to the king and the king's baker. ²The king became angry with his officer who served him wine and his baker. ³So he put them in the prison of the captain of the guard. This was the same prison where Joseph was kept. ⁴The captain of the guard put the two prisoners in Joseph's care. They stayed in prison for some time.

⁵One night both the king's officer who served him wine and the baker had a dream. Each had his own dream with its own meaning. ⁶When Joseph came to them the next morning, he saw they were worried. ⁷Joseph asked the king's officers who were with him, "Why do you look so unhappy today?"

"**S**ometimes I have bad dreams and sometimes I have really fun dreams! Read about one person's dream and one person's nightmare in Genesis 40:1-23."

⁸The two men answered, "We both had dreams last night. But no one can explain the meaning of them to us."

Joseph said to them, "God is the only One who can explain the meaning of dreams. So tell me your dreams."

⁹So the man who served wine to the king told Joseph his dream. He said, "I dreamed I saw a vine. ¹⁰On the vine there were three branches. I watched the branches bud and blossom, and then the grapes ripened. ¹¹I was holding the king's cup. So I took the grapes and squeezed the juice into the cup. Then I gave it to the king."

¹²Then Joseph said, "I will explain the dream to you. The three branches stand for three days. ¹³Before the end of three days the king will free you. He will allow you to return to your work. You will serve the king his wine just as you did before. ¹⁴But when you are free, remember me. Be kind to me. Tell the king about me so that I can get out of this prison. ¹⁵I was taken by force from the land of the Hebrews. And I have done nothing here to deserve being put in prison."

¹⁶The baker saw that Joseph's explanation of the dream was good. So he said to Joseph, "I also had a dream. I dreamed there were three bread baskets on my head. ¹⁷In the top basket there were all kinds of baked food for the king. But the birds were eating this food out of the basket on my head."

¹⁸Joseph answered, "I will tell you what the dream means. The three baskets stand for three days. ¹⁹Before the end of three days, the king will cut off your head! He will hang your body on a pole. And the birds will eat your flesh."

²⁰Three days later it was the king's birthday. So he gave a feast for all his officers. In front of his officers, he let the chief officer who served his wine and the chief baker out of prison. ²¹The

Jobs in the Bible
CUPBEARER • GENESIS 40:13

In Bible times, the man who served the king his wine was called a cupbearer or butler. This was a very high position in the palace. It was not a servant or slave job. The cupbearer was an officer who had to be trustworthy. He brought the king his drinks and made sure they were not poisoned by tasting them first himself. Joseph interpreted the dream of a cupbearer who had been put in prison. Later, when the cupbearer was out of prison, he helped Joseph get out of prison too.

God has given each of us an important job too—to love him and serve him.

To read about the person who made clothing, fly to page 112.

king gave his chief officer who served wine his old position. Once again he put the king's cup of wine into the king's hand. 22But the king hanged the baker on a pole. Everything happened just as Joseph had said it would. 23But the officer who served wine did not remember Joseph. He forgot all about him.

The King's Dreams

41 Two years later the king had a dream. He dreamed he was standing on the bank of the Nile River. 2He saw seven fat and beautiful cows come up out of the river. They stood there, eating the grass. 3Then seven more cows came up out of the river. But they were thin and ugly. They stood beside the seven beautiful cows on the bank of the Nile. 4The seven thin and ugly cows ate the seven beautiful fat cows. Then the king woke up. 5The king slept again and dreamed a second time. In his dream he saw seven full and good heads of grain growing on one stalk. 6After that, seven more heads of grain sprang up. But they were thin and burned by the hot east wind. 7The thin heads of grain ate the seven full and good heads. Then the king woke up again. And he realized it was only a dream. 8The next morning the king was troubled about these dreams. So he sent for all the magicians and wise men of Egypt. The king told them his dreams. But no one could explain their meaning to him.

"**D**o you know how Joseph spent one night in prison and the next night in the palace? Read Genesis 41:1-57 to find out."

9Then the chief officer who served wine to the king said to him, "I remember something I promised to do. But I had forgotten about it. 10There was a time when you were angry with me and the baker. You put us in prison in the house of the captain of the guard. 11In prison we each had a dream on the same night. Each dream had a different meaning. 12A young Hebrew man was in the prison with us. He was a servant of the captain of the guard. We told him our dreams, and he explained their meanings to us. He told each man the meaning of his dream. 13Things happened exactly as he said they would: I was given back my old position, and the baker was hanged."

14So the king called for Joseph. The guards quickly brought him out of the prison. He shaved, put on clean clothes and went before the king.

15The king said to Joseph, "I have had a dream. But no one can explain its meaning to me. I have heard that you can explain a dream when someone tells it to you."

16Joseph answered the king, "I am not able to explain the meaning of dreams. God will do this for the king."

17Then the king said to Joseph, "In my dream I was standing on the bank of the Nile River. 18I saw seven fat and beautiful cows. They came up out of the river and ate the grass. 19Then I saw seven more cows come out of the river. They were thin and lean and ugly. They were the worst looking cows I have seen in all the land of Egypt. 20And these thin and ugly cows ate the first seven fat cows. 21But after they had eaten the seven cows, no one could tell they had eaten them. They just looked as thin and ugly as they did in the beginning. Then I woke up.

22"I had another dream. I saw seven full and good heads of grain growing on one stalk. 23Then seven more heads of grain sprang up after them. But these heads were thin and ugly. They were burned by the hot east wind. 24Then the thin heads ate the seven good heads. I told this dream to the magicians. But no one could explain its meaning to me."

Joseph Tells the Dreams' Meaning

25Then Joseph said to the king, "Both of these dreams mean the same thing. God is telling you what he is about to do. 26The seven good cows stand for seven years. And the seven good heads of grain stand for seven years. Both dreams mean the same thing. 27The seven thin and ugly cows stand for seven years. And the seven thin heads of grain burned by the hot east wind stand for seven years of hunger. 28This will happen as I told you. God is showing the king what he is about to do. 29You will have seven years of good crops and plenty to eat in all the land of Egypt. 30But after those seven years, there will come seven years of hunger. All the food that grew in the land of Egypt will be forgotten. The time of hunger will eat up the land. 31People will forget what it was like to have plenty of food. This is because the hunger that follows will be so great. 32You had two dreams which mean the same thing. This shows that God has firmly decided that this will happen. And he will make it happen soon.

33"So let the king choose a man who is very wise and understanding. Let the king set him over the land of Egypt. 34And let the king also appoint officers over the land. They should take one-fifth of all the food that is grown during the seven good years. 35They should gather all the food that is produced during the good years that are coming. Under the king's authority they should store the grain in the cities and guard it. 36That food should be saved for later. It will be used during the seven years of hunger that will come on the land of Egypt. Then the people in Egypt will not die during the seven years of hunger."

Joseph Is Made Ruler over Egypt

37This seemed like a very good idea to the king. All his officers agreed. 38And the king asked them, "Can we find a better man than Joseph to take this job? God's spirit is truly in him!"

39So the king said to Joseph, "God has shown you all this. There is no one as wise and understanding as you are. 40I will put you in charge of my palace. All the people will obey your orders. Only I will be greater than you."

41Then the king said to Joseph, "Look! I have put you in charge of all the land of Egypt." 42Then the king took off from his own finger his ring with the royal seal on it. And he put it on Joseph's finger. He gave Joseph fine linen clothes to wear. And he put a gold chain around Joseph's neck. 43The king had Joseph ride in the second royal chariot. Men walked ahead of his chariot calling, "Bow down!" By doing these things, the king put Joseph in charge of all of Egypt.

44The king said to him, "I am the king. And I say that no one in all the land of Egypt may lift a hand or a foot unless you say he may." 45The king gave Joseph the name Zaphenath-Paneah. He also gave Joseph a wife named Asenath. She was the daughter of Potiphera, priest of On. So Joseph traveled through all the land of Egypt.

46Joseph was 30 years old when he began serving the king of Egypt. And he left the king's court and traveled through all the land of Egypt. 47During the seven good years, the crops in the land grew well. 48And Joseph gathered all the food which was produced in Egypt during those seven years of good crops. He stored the food in the cities. In every city he stored grain that had been grown in the fields around that city. 49Joseph stored much grain, as much as the sand of the seashore. He stored so much grain that he could not measure it.

50Joseph's wife was Asenath daughter of Potiphera, the priest of On. Before the years of hunger came, Joseph and Asenath had two sons. 51Joseph named the first son Manasseh.ⁿ Joseph said, "God has made me forget all the troubles I have had and all my father's

ⁿ**Manasseh** This name sounds like the Hebrew word for "made me forget."

family." [52]Joseph named the second son Ephraim.[n] Joseph said, "God has given me children in the land of my troubles."

[53]The seven years of good crops came to an end in the land of Egypt. [54]Then the seven years of hunger began, just as Joseph had said. In all the lands people had nothing to eat. But in Egypt there was food. [55]The time of hunger became terrible in all of Egypt. The people cried to the king for food. He said to all the Egyptians, "Go to Joseph. Do whatever he tells you to do."

[56]The hunger was everywhere in that part of the world. And Joseph opened the storehouses and sold grain to the people of Egypt. This was because the time of hunger became terrible in Egypt. [57]And all the people in that part of the world came to Joseph in Egypt to buy grain. This was because the hunger was terrible everywhere in that part of the world.

The Dreams Come True

42 Jacob learned that there was grain in Egypt. So he said to his sons, "Why are you just sitting here looking at one another? [2]I have heard that there is grain in Egypt. Go down there and buy grain for us to eat. Then we will live and not die."

[3]So ten of Joseph's brothers went down to buy grain from Egypt. [4]But Jacob did not send Benjamin, Joseph's brother, with them. Jacob was afraid that something terrible might happen to Benjamin. [5]Along with many other people, the sons of Jacob, also called Israel, went to Egypt to buy grain. This was because the people in the land of Canaan were hungry also.

[6]Now Joseph was governor over Egypt. He was the one who sold the grain to people who came to buy it. So Joseph's brothers came to him. They bowed facedown on the ground before him. [7]When Joseph saw his brothers, he knew who they were. But he acted as if he didn't know them. He asked

unkindly, "Where do you come from?"

They answered, "We have come from the land of Canaan to buy food."

[8]Joseph knew they were his brothers. But they did not know who he was. [9]And Joseph remembered his dreams about his brothers bowing to him. He said to them, "You are spies! You came to learn where the nation is weak!"

[10]But his brothers said to him, "No, my master. We come as your servants just to buy food. [11]We are all sons of the same father. We are honest men, not spies."

[12]Then Joseph said to them, "No! You have come to learn where this nation is weak!"

[13]And they said, "We are 10 of 12 brothers. We are sons of the same father. We live in the land of Canaan. Our youngest brother is there with our father right now. And our other brother is gone."

[14]But Joseph said to them, "I can see I was right! You are spies! [15]But I will give you a way to prove you are telling the truth. As surely as the king lives, you will not leave this place until your youngest brother comes here. [16]One of you must go and get your brother. The rest of you will stay here in prison. We will see if you are telling the truth. If not, as surely as the king lives, you are spies." [17]Then Joseph put them all in prison for three days.

[18]On the third day Joseph said to them, "I am a God-fearing man. Do this thing, and I will let you live: [19]If you are honest men, let one of your brothers stay here in prison. The rest of you go and carry grain back to feed your hungry families. [20]Then bring your youngest brother back here to me. If you do this, I will know you are telling the truth. Then you will not die."

The brothers agreed to this. [21]They said to each other, "We are being punished for what we did to our brother. We saw his trouble. He begged us to save him, but we refused to listen. That is why we are in this trouble now."

---

[n]**Ephraim** This name sounds like the Hebrew word for "given me children."

²²Then Reuben said to them, "I told you not to harm the boy. But you refused to listen to me. So now we are being punished for what we did to him."

²³When Joseph talked to his brothers, he used an interpreter. So they did not know that Joseph understood what they were saying. ²⁴Then Joseph left them and cried. After a short time he went back and spoke to them. He took Simeon and tied him up while the other brothers watched. ²⁵Joseph told his servants to fill his brothers' bags with grain. They were to put the money the brothers had paid for the grain back in their bags. They were to give them things they would need for their trip back home. And the servants did this.

²⁶So the brothers put the grain on their donkeys and left. ²⁷When they stopped for the night, one of the brothers opened his sack. He was going to get food for his donkey. Then he saw his money in the top of the sack. ²⁸He said to the other brothers, "The money I paid for the grain has been put back. Here it is in my sack!"

The brothers were very frightened. They said to each other, "What has God done to us?"

The Brothers Return to Jacob

²⁹The brothers went to their father Jacob in the land of Canaan. They told him everything that had happened. ³⁰They said, "The master of that land spoke unkindly to us. He accused us of spying on his country. ³¹But we told him that we were honest men, not spies. ³²We told him that we were 10 of 12 brothers—sons of one father. We said that 1 of our brothers was gone. And we said that our youngest brother was with our father in Canaan.

³³"Then the master of the land said to us, 'Here is a way I can know you are honest men: Leave 1 of your brothers with me. Take back grain to feed your hungry families, and go. ³⁴And bring your youngest brother to me. Then I will know that you are not spies but

honest men. And I will give you back your brother whom you leave with me. And you can move about freely in our land.'"

³⁵Then the brothers emptied their sacks. And each of them found his money in his sack. When they and their father saw it, they were afraid.

³⁶Their father Jacob said to them, "You are robbing me of all my children. Joseph is gone. Simeon is gone. And now you want to take Benjamin away, too. Everything is against me."

³⁷Then Reuben said to his father, "You may put my 2 sons to death if I don't bring Benjamin back to you. Trust him to my care. I will bring him back to you."

³⁸But Jacob said, "I will not allow Benjamin to go with you. His brother is dead. He is the only son left from my wife Rachel. I am afraid something terrible might happen to him during the trip to Egypt. Then I would be sad until the day I die."

The Brothers Go Back to Egypt

43 Still no food grew in the land of Canaan. ²Jacob's family had eaten all the grain they had brought from Egypt. So Jacob said to them, "Go to Egypt again. Buy a little more grain for us to eat."

³But Judah said to Jacob, "The governor of that country strongly warned us. He said, 'Bring your brother back with you. If you don't, you will not be allowed to see me.' ⁴If you will send Benjamin with us, we will go down and buy food for you. ⁵But if you refuse to send Benjamin, we will not go. The governor of that country warned us. He said we would not see him if we didn't bring Benjamin with us."

⁶Jacob, also called Israel, said, "Why did you tell the man you had another brother? You have caused me a lot of trouble."

⁷The brothers answered, "He questioned us carefully about ourselves and our family. He asked us, 'Is your father still alive? Do you have another brother?'

We just answered his questions. How could we know he would ask us to bring our other brother to him?"

⁸Then Judah said to his father Jacob, "Send Benjamin with me. Then we will go at once. Do this so that we, you and our children may live and not die. ⁹I will guarantee you that he will be safe. I will be personally responsible for him. If I don't bring him back to you, you can blame me all my life. ¹⁰If we had not wasted all this time, we could have already made two trips."

¹¹Then their father Jacob said to them, "If it has to be that way, then do this: Take some of the best foods in our land in your packs. Give them to the man as a gift: some balm,ᵈ some honey, spices, myrrh,ᵈ pistachio nuts and almonds. ¹²Take twice as much money with you this time. Take back the money that was returned to you in your sacks last time. Maybe it was a mistake. ¹³And take Benjamin with you. Now leave and go to the man. ¹⁴I pray that God All-Powerful will cause the governor to be merciful to you. I pray that he will allow Simeon and Benjamin to come back with you. If I am robbed of my children, then I am robbed of them!"

¹⁵So the brothers took the gifts. They also took twice as much money as they had taken the first time. And they took Benjamin. They hurried down to Egypt and stood before Joseph.

¹⁶In Egypt Joseph saw Benjamin with them. Joseph said to the servant in charge of his house, "Bring those men into my house. Kill an animal and prepare a meal. Those men will eat with me today at noon." ¹⁷The servant did as Joseph told him. He brought the men to Joseph's house.

¹⁸The brothers were afraid when they were brought to Joseph's house. They thought, "We were brought here because of the money that was put in our sacks on the first trip. He wants to attack us, make us slaves and take our donkeys." ¹⁹So the brothers went to the servant in charge of Joseph's house.

They spoke to him at the door of the house. ²⁰They said, "Sir, we came here once before to buy food. ²¹While we were going home, we stopped for the night and opened our sacks. Each of us found all his money in his sack. We brought that money with us to give it back to you. ²²And we have brought more money. It is to pay for the food we want to buy this time. We don't know who put that money in our sacks."

²³But the servant answered, "It's all right. Don't be afraid. Your God, the God of your father, must have put the money in your sacks. I got the money you paid me for the grain last time." Then the servant brought Simeon out to them.

²⁴The servant led the men into Joseph's house. He gave them water, and they washed their feet. Then he gave their donkeys food to eat. ²⁵The men prepared their gift to give to Joseph when he arrived at noon. They had heard they were going to eat with him there.

²⁶When Joseph came home, the brothers gave him the gift they had brought into the house. Then they bowed down to the ground to him. ²⁷Joseph asked them how they were doing. He said, "How is your aged father you told me about? Is he still alive?" ²⁸The brothers answered, "Your servant, our father, is well. He is still alive." And they bowed low before Joseph to show him respect.

²⁹Then Joseph saw his brother Benjamin, who had the same mother as he. Joseph asked, "Is this your youngest brother you told me about?" Then Joseph said to Benjamin, "God be good to you, my son!" ³⁰Then Joseph hurried off. He had to hold back the tears when he saw his brother Benjamin. So Joseph went into his room and cried there. ³¹Then he washed his face and came out. He controlled himself and said, "Serve the meal."

³²So they served Joseph at one table. They served his brothers at another table. And they served the Egyptians

who ate with him at another table. This was because Egyptians did not like Hebrews and never ate with them. [33]Joseph's brothers were seated in front of him. They were in order of their ages, from oldest to youngest. And they looked at each other because they were so amazed. [34]Food from Joseph's table was taken to them. But Benjamin was given five times more food than the others. Joseph's brothers drank with him until they were very drunk.

Joseph Sets a Trap

44 Then Joseph gave a command to the servant in charge of his house. Joseph said, "Fill the men's sacks with as much grain as they can carry. And put each man's money into his sack with the grain. [2]Put my silver cup in the sack of the youngest brother. Also put his money for the grain in that sack." The servant did what Joseph told him.

[3]At dawn the brothers were sent away with their donkeys. [4]They were not far from the city when Joseph said to the servant in charge of his house, "Go after the men. When you catch up with them, say, 'Why have you paid back evil for good? [5]The cup you have stolen is the one my master uses for drinking. And he uses it for explaining dreams. You have done a very wicked thing!'"

[6]So the servant caught up with the brothers. He said to them what Joseph had told him to say.

[7]But the brothers said to the servant, "Why do you say these things? We would not do anything like that! [8]We brought back to you the money we found in our sacks. We brought it back from the land of Canaan. So surely we would not steal silver or gold from your master's house. [9]If you find that silver cup in the sack of one of us, then let him die. And we will be your slaves."

[10]The servant said, "We will do as you say. But only the man who has taken the cup will become my slave. The rest of you may go free."

[11]Then every brother quickly lowered his sack to the ground and opened it. [12]The servant searched the sacks, going from the oldest brother to the youngest. He found the cup in Benjamin's sack. [13]The brothers tore their clothes to show they were sad. Then they put their sacks back on the donkeys. And they returned to the city.

[14]When Judah and his brothers went back to Joseph's house, Joseph was still there. The brothers bowed facedown on the ground before him. [15]Joseph said to them, "What have you done? Didn't you know that a man like me can learn things by signs and dreams?"

[16]Judah said, "Sir, what can we say? And how can we show we are not guilty? God has uncovered our guilt. So all of us will be your slaves, not just Benjamin."

[17]But Joseph said, "I will not make you all slaves! Only the man who stole the cup will be my slave. The rest of you may go back safely to your father."

[18]Then Judah went to Joseph and said, "Sir, please let me speak plainly to you. Please don't be angry with me. I know that you are as powerful as the king of Egypt himself. [19]When we were here before, you asked us, 'Do you have a father or a brother?' [20]And we answered you, 'We have an old father. And we have a younger brother. He was born when our father was old. This youngest son's brother is dead. So he is the only one of his mother's children left alive. And our father loves him very much.' [21]Then you said to us, 'Bring that brother to me. I want to see him.' [22]And we said to you, 'That young boy cannot leave his father. If he leaves him, his father would die.' [23]But you said to us, 'You must bring your youngest brother. If you don't, you will not be allowed to see me again.' [24]So we went back to our father and told him what you had said.

[25]"Later, our father said, 'Go again. Buy us a little more food.' [26]We said to our father, 'We cannot go without our

youngest brother. Without our youngest brother, we will not be allowed to see the governor.' ²⁷Then my father said to us, 'You know that my wife Rachel gave me two sons. ²⁸One son left me. I thought, "Surely he has been torn apart by a wild animal." And I haven't seen him since. ²⁹Now you want to take this son away from me also. But something terrible might happen to him. Then I would be sad until the day I die.' ³⁰Now what will happen if we go home to our father without our youngest brother?

be your slave. And let the young boy go back home with his brothers. ³⁴I cannot go back to my father if the boy is not with me. I couldn't stand to see my father that sad."

Joseph Reveals Who He Is

45 Joseph could not control himself in front of his servants any longer. He cried out, "Have everyone leave me." When only the brothers were left with Joseph, he told them who he was. ²Joseph cried so loudly that the Egyptians heard him. And the people in the king's palace heard about it. ³He said to his brothers, "I am Joseph. Is

Plans That Backfired

JOSEPH'S BROTHERS • GENESIS 45

Sometimes there is a member of the family who always gets picked on by others. Joseph was the one who got picked on in his family. Joseph's brothers were so mean to him that they threw him into a deep well. Then they sold him to a group of people who used him as their slave. But God was with Joseph in every situation.

Eventually, Joseph ended up working for Pharaoh, the leader of Egypt. Pharaoh liked Joseph and made him a powerful ruler in Egypt. Soon there was a famine in the land nearby. Only Egypt had food, and Joseph was in charge of it. Joseph's brothers had to ask Joseph to give them something to eat. Although Joseph's brothers had meant to harm him, God used the bad things that happened to him for good. Joseph was able to save his family from starvation.

God plans to use everything that happens to us for our good. Even the bad things!

To read about a blessing that was supposed to be a curse, fly to page 197.

He is the most important thing in our father's life. ³¹When our father sees that the young boy is not with us, he will die. And it will be our fault. We will cause the great sorrow that kills our father.

³²"I gave my father a guarantee that the young boy would be safe. I said to my father, 'If I don't bring him back to you, you can blame me all my life.' ³³So now, please allow me to stay here and

my father still alive?" But the brothers could not answer him, because they were very afraid of him.

⁴So Joseph said to them, "Come close to me." So the brothers came close to him. And he said to them, "I am your brother Joseph. You sold me as a slave to go to Egypt. ⁵Now don't be worried. Don't be angry with yourselves because you sold me here. God sent me here

ahead of you to save people's lives. ⁶No food has grown on the land for two years now. And there will be five more years without planting or harvest. ⁷So God sent me here ahead of you. This was to make sure you have some descendants *d* left on earth. And it was to keep you alive in an amazing way. ⁸So it was not you who sent me here, but God. God has made me the highest officer of the king of Egypt. I am in charge of his palace. I am the master of all the land of Egypt.

⁹"So leave quickly and go to my father. Tell him, 'Your son Joseph says: God has made me master over all Egypt. Come down to me quickly. ¹⁰Live in the land of Goshen. You will be near me. Also your children, your grandchildren, your flocks and herds and all that you have will be near me. ¹¹I will care for you during the next five years of hunger. In this way, you and your family and all that you have will not starve.'

¹²"Now you can see for yourselves. The one speaking to you is really Joseph. And my brother Benjamin can see this. ¹³So tell my father about how powerful I have become in Egypt. Tell him about everything you have seen. Now hurry and bring him back to me."

¹⁴Then Joseph hugged his brother Benjamin and cried. And Benjamin cried also. ¹⁵Then Joseph kissed all his brothers. He cried as he hugged them. After this, his brothers talked with him.

¹⁶The king of Egypt and his officers learned that Joseph's brothers had come. And they were very happy about this. ¹⁷So the king said to Joseph, "Tell your brothers to load their animals and go back to the land of Canaan. ¹⁸Tell them to bring their father and their families back here to me. I will give them the best land in Egypt. And they will eat the best food we have here. ¹⁹Tell them to take some wagons from Egypt for their children and their wives. And tell them to bring their father back also. ²⁰Tell them not to worry about bringing any of their things with them. We will give them the best of what we have in Egypt."

²¹So the sons of Israel did this. Joseph gave them wagons as the king had ordered. And he gave them food for their trip. ²²He gave each brother a change of clothes. But he gave Benjamin five changes of clothes. And Joseph gave him about seven and one-half

Feelings
GENESIS 45:1-15

Joseph started out as a slave, but eventually he became one of the main rulers in all of Egypt. Even though he was one of the most powerful and important people in the whole country, he couldn't always hold back his emotions. When he saw his brother Benjamin for the first time in many years, he broke down and cried!

We all have family members and friends that we really care about. We shouldn't think that we are so big and important that we can't show those people that we love them. Tell your mom how much you appreciate it when she helps you with your homework. Let your brother or sister know that you like it when they're around. Showing and telling others that you love them will make you and them feel great!

To find out what can make you really happy, zoom to page 565.

pounds of silver. [23]Joseph also sent his father ten donkeys loaded with the best things from Egypt. And he sent ten female donkeys. They were loaded with grain, bread and other food for his father on his trip back. [24]Then Joseph told his brothers to go. As they were leaving, he said to them, "Don't quarrel on the way home."

[25]So the brothers left Egypt and went to their father Jacob in the land of Canaan. [26]They told him, "Joseph is still alive. He is the ruler over all the land of Egypt." Their father was shocked and did not believe them. [27]But the brothers told him everything Joseph had said. Then Jacob saw the wagons that Joseph had sent to carry him back to Egypt. Now Jacob felt better. [28]Jacob, also called Israel, said, "Now I believe you. My son Joseph is still alive. I will go and see him before I die."

Jacob Goes to Egypt

46 So Jacob, also called Israel, took all he had and started his trip. He went to Beersheba. There he offered sacrifices to the God of his father Isaac. [2]During the night God spoke to Israel in a vision. He said, "Jacob, Jacob."

And Jacob answered, "Here I am."

[3]Then God said, "I am God, the God of your father. Don't be afraid to go to Egypt. I will make your descendants[d] a great nation there. [4]I will go to Egypt with you. And I will bring you out of Egypt again. Joseph's own hands will close your eyes when you die."

[5]Then Jacob left Beersheba. The sons of Israel loaded their father, their children and their wives. They put them in the wagons the king of Egypt had sent. [6]They also took their farm animals and everything they had gotten in Canaan. So Jacob went to Egypt with all his descendants. [7]He took his sons and grandsons, his daughters and granddaughters. He took all his family to Egypt with him.

Jacob's Family

[8]Now these are the names of the children of Israel who went into Egypt. (They are Jacob and his descendants.[d])

Reuben was Jacob's first son. [9]Reuben's sons were Hanoch, Pallu, Hezron and Carmi.

[10]Simeon's sons were Jemuel, Jamin, Ohad, Jakin, Zohar and Shaul. (Shaul was Simeon's son by a Canaanite woman.)

[11]Levi's sons were Gershon, Kohath and Merari.

[12]Judah's sons were Er, Onan, Shelah, Perez and Zerah. (But Er and Onan had died in the land of Canaan.) Perez's sons were Hezron and Hamul.

[13]Issachar's sons were Tola, Puah, Jashub and Shimron.

[14]Zebulun's sons were Sered, Elon and Jahleei.

[15]These are the sons of Leah and Jacob born in Northwest Mesopotamia. His daughter Dinah was also born there. There were 33 persons in this part of Jacob's family.

[16]Gad's sons were Zephon, Haggi, Shuni, Ezbon, Eri, Arodi and Areli.

[17]Asher's sons were Imnah, Ishvah, Ishvi and Beriah. Their sister was Serah. Beriah's sons were Heber and Malkiel.

[18]These are Jacob's sons by Zilpah. She was the slave girl whom Laban gave to his daughter Leah. There were 16 persons in this part of Jacob's family.

[19]The sons of Jacob's wife Rachel were Joseph and Benjamin. [20]In Egypt, Joseph became the father of Manasseh and Ephraim by his wife Asenath. She was the daughter of Potiphera, priest of On.

[21]Benjamin's sons were Bela, Beker, Ashbel, Gera, Naaman, Ehi, Rosh, Muppim, Huppim and Ard.

[22]These are the sons of Jacob by his wife Rachel. There were 14 persons in this part of Jacob's family.

[23]Dan's son was Hushim.

[24]Naphtali's sons were Jahziel, Guni, Jezer and Shillem.

[25]These are Jacob's sons by Bilhah. She was the slave girl whom Laban gave to his daughter Rachel. There

were 7 persons in this part of Jacob's family.

²⁶So the total number of Jacob's direct descendants who went to Egypt was 66. (The wives of Jacob's sons were not counted in this number.) ²⁷Joseph had 2 sons born in Egypt. So the total number in the family of Jacob in Egypt was 70.

Jacob Arrives in Egypt

²⁸Jacob sent Judah ahead of him to see Joseph in Goshen. Then Jacob and his people came into the land of Goshen. ²⁹Joseph prepared his chariot and went to meet his father Israel in Goshen. As soon as Joseph saw his father, he hugged his neck. And he cried there for a long time.

³⁰Then Israel said to Joseph, "Now I am ready to die. I have seen your face. And I know that you are still alive."

³¹Joseph said to his brothers and his father's family, "I will go and tell the king you are here. I will say, 'My brothers and my father's family have left the land of Canaan. They have come here to me. ³²They are shepherds and take care of farm animals. And they have brought their flocks and their herds and everything they own with them.' ³³When the king calls you, he will ask, 'What work do you do?' ³⁴This is what you should tell him: 'We, your servants, have taken care of farm animals all our lives. Our ancestors did the same thing.' Then the king will allow you to settle in the land of Goshen. This is away from the Egyptians. They don't like to be near shepherds."

Jacob Settles in Goshen

47 Joseph went in to the king and said, "My father and my brothers have arrived from Canaan. They have their flocks and herds and everything they own with them. They are now in the land of Goshen." ²Joseph chose five of his brothers to introduce to the king.

³The king said to the brothers, "What work do you do?"

And they said to him, "We, your servants, are shepherds. Our ancestors were also shepherds." ⁴They said to the king, "We have come to live in this land. There is no grass in the land of Canaan for our animals to eat. The hunger is very terrible there. So please allow us to live in the land of Goshen."

⁵Then the king said to Joseph, "Your father and your brothers have come to you. ⁶You may choose any place in Egypt for them to live. Give your father and your brothers the best land. Let them live in the land of Goshen. And if any of them are skilled shepherds, put them in charge of my sheep and cattle."

⁷Then Joseph brought in his father Jacob and introduced him to the king. And Jacob blessed the king.

⁸Then the king said to Jacob, "How old are you?"

⁹Jacob said to him, "My life has been spent wandering from place to place. It has been short, filled with trouble. I have lived only 130 years. My ancestors lived much longer than I." ¹⁰Then Jacob blessed the king and left.

¹¹Joseph obeyed the king. He gave his father and brothers the best land in Egypt. It was near the city of Rameses. ¹²And Joseph gave his father, his brothers and everyone who lived with them the food they needed.

Joseph Buys Land for the King

¹³The hunger became worse, and there was no food anywhere in the land. The land of Egypt and the land of Canaan became very poor because of this. ¹⁴Joseph collected all the money that was to be found in Egypt and Canaan. People paid him this money for the grain they were buying. He brought that money to the king's palace. ¹⁵After some time, the people in Egypt and Canaan had no money left. So they went to Joseph and said, "Please give us food. Our money is gone. If we don't eat, we will die here in front of you."

¹⁶Joseph answered, "Since you have no money, give me your farm animals. I will give you food in return." ¹⁷So

people brought their farm animals to Joseph. And he gave them food in exchange for their horses, sheep, cattle and donkeys. So he kept them alive by trading food for their farm animals that year.

[18] The next year the people came to Joseph and said, "You know we have no money left. And all our animals belong to you. We have nothing left except our bodies and our land. [19] Surely both we and our land will die here in front of you. Buy us and our land in exchange for food. And we will be slaves to the king, together with our land. Give us seed to plant. Then we will live and not die. And the land will not become a desert."

[20] So Joseph bought all the land in Egypt for the king. Every Egyptian sold Joseph his field, because the hunger was very great. So the land became the king's. [21] And Joseph made the people slaves from one end of Egypt to the other. [22] The only land he did not buy was the land the priests owned. They did not need to sell their land because the king paid them for their work. So they had money to buy food.

[23] Joseph said to the people, "Now I have bought you and your land for the king. So I will give you seed. And you can plant your fields. [24] At harvest time you must give one-fifth to the king. You may keep four-fifths for yourselves. Use it as seed for the field and as food for yourselves, your families and your children."

[25] The people said, "You have saved our lives. If you like, we will become slaves of the king."

[26] So Joseph made a law in Egypt, which continues today: One-fifth of everything from the land belongs to the king. The only land the king did not get was the priests' land.

"Don't Bury Me in Egypt"

[27] The Israelites continued to live in the land of Goshen in Egypt. There they got possessions. They had many children and grew in number.

[28] Jacob, also called Israel, lived in Egypt 17 years. So he lived to be 147 years old. [29] Israel knew he soon would die. So he called his son Joseph to him. He said to Joseph, "If you love me, put your hand under my leg.[n] Promise me you will not bury me in Egypt. [30] When I die, carry me out of Egypt. Bury me where my ancestors are buried."

Joseph answered, "I will do as you say."

[31] Then Jacob said, "Promise me." And Joseph promised him that he would do this. Then Israel worshiped as he leaned on the top of his walking stick.

Blessings for Manasseh and Ephraim

48 Some time later Joseph learned that his father was very sick. So he took his two sons Manasseh and Ephraim and went to his father. [2] When Joseph arrived, someone told Jacob, also called Israel, "Your son Joseph has come to see you." Jacob was weak. So he used all his strength and sat up on his bed.

[3] Then Jacob said to Joseph, "God All-Powerful appeared to me at Luz in the land of Canaan. God blessed me there. [4] He said to me, 'I will give you many children. I will make you the father of many peoples. And I will give your descendants[d] this land forever.' [5] Your two sons were born here in Egypt before I came. They will be counted as my own sons. Ephraim and Manasseh will be my sons just as Reuben and Simeon are my sons. [6] But if you have other children, they will be your own. But their land will be part of the land given to Ephraim and Manasseh. [7] When I came from Northwest Mesopotamia, Rachel died in the land of Canaan. We were traveling toward Ephrath. This made me very sad. I buried her there beside the road to Ephrath." (Today Ephrath is Bethlehem.)

[8] Then Israel saw Joseph's sons. He said, "Who are these boys?"

[9] Joseph said to his father, "They are

---

[n]**put . . . leg** This showed that a person would keep a promise.

my sons. God has given them to me here in Egypt."

Israel said, "Bring your sons to me so I may bless them."

¹⁰At this time Israel's eyesight was bad because he was old. So Joseph brought the boys close to him. Israel kissed the boys and put his arms around them. ¹¹He said to Joseph, "I thought I would never see you alive again. And now God has let me see you and also your children." ¹²Then Joseph moved his sons off Israel's lap. Joseph bowed facedown to the ground. ¹³He put Ephraim on his right side and Manasseh on his left. (So Ephraim was near Israel's left hand, and Manasseh was near Israel's right hand.) Joseph brought the boys close to Israel. ¹⁴But Israel crossed his arms. He put his right hand on the head of Ephraim, who was younger. He put his left hand on the head of Manasseh. But he was the first-born^d son. ¹⁵And Israel blessed Joseph and said,

"My ancestors Abraham and Isaac
     served our God.
And like a shepherd God has led
     me all my life.
¹⁶He was the Angel who saved
     me from all my troubles.
Now I pray that he will bless these
     boys.
May my name be known through
     these boys.
And may the names of my
     ancestors Abraham and Isaac
     be known through them.
May they have many descendants^d
     on the earth."

¹⁷Joseph saw that his father put his right hand on Ephraim's head. Joseph didn't like it. So he took hold of his father's hand. He wanted to move it from Ephraim's head to Manasseh's head. ¹⁸Joseph said to his father, "You are doing it wrong, Father. Manasseh is the firstborn son. Put your right hand on his head."

¹⁹But his father refused and said, "I know, my son, I know. Manasseh will be great and have many descendants.

But his younger brother will be greater. And his descendants will be enough to make a nation."

²⁰So Israel blessed them that day. He said,

"When a blessing is given in Israel,
     they will say:
'May God make you like Ephraim
     and Manasseh.'"

In this way he made Ephraim greater than Manasseh.

²¹Then Israel said to Joseph, "Look at me. I am about to die. But God will be with you. He will take you back to the land of your fathers. ²²I have given you something that I did not give your brothers. I have given you the land of Shechem that I took from the Amorite people. I took it with my sword and my bow."

Jacob Blesses His Sons

49 Then Jacob called his sons to him. He said, "Come here to me. I will tell you what will happen to you in the future.

²"Come together and listen,
     sons of Jacob.
Listen to Israel, your father."

³"Reuben, my first son, you are
     my strength.
Your birth showed I could be a
     father.
You have the highest position
     among my sons.
You are the most powerful.
⁴But you are uncontrolled like
     water.
So you will no longer lead your
     brothers.
This is because you got into your
     father's bed.
You shamed me by having sexual
     relations with my slave girl.

⁵"Simeon and Levi are brothers.
They used their swords to do
     violence.
⁶I will not join their secret talks.
I will not meet with them to plan evil.
They killed men because they were
     angry.

And they crippled oxen just for fun.
[7]May their anger be cursed,
     because it is too violent.
May their violence be cursed,
     because it is too cruel.
I will divide them up among the
     tribes[d] of Jacob.
I will scatter them through all the
     tribes of Israel.

[8]"Judah, your brothers will
     praise you.
You will grab your enemies by the
     neck.
Your brothers will bow down to you.
[9]Judah is like a young lion.
You have returned from killing,
     my son.
Like a lion, he stretches out and lies
     down to rest.
No one is brave enough to wake
     him.
[10]Men from Judah's family will
     be kings.
Someone from Judah will always
     be on the throne.
Judah will rule until the real king
     comes.
And the nations will obey him.
[11]He ties his donkey to a
     grapevine.
He ties his young donkey to the
     best branch.
He can afford to use wine to wash his
     clothes.
He even uses grape juice to wash
     his robes.
[12]His eyes are bright from
     drinking wine.
His teeth are white from drinking
     milk.

[13]"Zebulun will live near the sea.
His shore will be a safe place for
     ships.
His land will reach as far as Sidon.

[14]"Issachar is like a strong donkey.
He lies down while carrying his
     load.
[15]He will see his resting place is
     good.
He will see how pleasant his land is.

Then he will put his back to the load.
He will become a slave.

[16]"Dan will rule his own people
     like the other tribes in Israel.
[17]Dan will be like a snake by the
     side of the road.
He will be like a dangerous snake
     lying near the path.
That snake bites a horse's leg.
And the rider is thrown off
     backward.

[18]"Lord, I wait for your salvation.

[19]"Robbers will attack Gad.
But he will defeat them and drive
     them away.

[20]"Asher's land will grow much
     good food.
He will grow food fit for a king.

[21]"Naphtali is like a female deer
     that runs free.
She has beautiful fawns.

[22]"Joseph is like a grapevine that
     produces much fruit.
He is like a healthy vine watered
     by a spring.
He is like a vine whose branches
     grow over the wall.
[23]Men attack him violently with
     arrows.
They shoot at him angrily.
[24]But he aims his bow well.
His arms are made strong.
He gets his power from the Mighty
     God of Jacob.
He gets his strength from the
     Shepherd, the Rock[d] of Israel.
[25]Your father's God helps you.
God All-Powerful blesses you.
He blesses you with rain from above.
He blesses you with water from
     springs below.
He blesses you with many babies
     born to your wives.
He blesses you with many young
     ones born to your animals.
[26]The blessings of your father are
     greater
than the blessings of the oldest
     mountains.

They are greater than the good
      things of the long-lasting hills.
May these blessings rest on the
      head of Joseph.
May they rest on the forehead of
      the one who was separated
      from his brothers.

27"Benjamin is like a hungry wolf.
In the morning he eats what he
      has caught.
In the evening he divides what he
      has taken."

28These are the 12 tribes of Israel.
And this is what their father said to
them. He gave each son the blessing
that was right for him. 29Then Israel
gave them a command. He said, "I am
about to die. Bury me with my ancestors in the cave in the field of Ephron
the Hittite. 30That cave is in the field
of Machpelah east of Mamre. It is in
the land of Canaan. Abraham bought
that field from Ephron the Hittite for a
burying place. 31Abraham and Sarah
his wife are buried there. Isaac and
Rebekah his wife are buried there. I
buried my wife Leah there. 32The field
and the cave in it were bought from
the Hittite people." 33After Jacob finished talking to his sons, he lay down.
He put his feet back on the bed, took
his last breath and died.

Jacob's Burial

50 When Jacob died, Joseph hugged
his father and cried over him and
kissed him. 2He commanded the doctors who served him to prepare his
father's body. So the doctors prepared
Jacob's body to be buried. 3It took the
doctors 40 days to prepare his body.
This was the usual time it took. And
the Egyptians had a time of sorrow for
Jacob. It lasted 70 days.

4When this time of sorrow had
ended, Joseph spoke to the king's
officers. He said, "If you think well of
me, please tell this to the king: 5'When
my father was near death, I made a
promise to him. I promised I would bury
him in a cave in the land of Canaan. This

is a burial place that he cut out for himself. So please let me go and bury my
father. Then I will return.'"
6The king answered, "Keep your
promise. Go and bury your father."
7So Joseph went to bury his father.
All the king's officers, the older leaders
and all the leading men of Egypt went
with Joseph. 8Everyone who lived with
Joseph and his brothers went with
him. And everyone who lived with his
father also went. They left only their
children, their flocks and their herds
in the land of Goshen. 9Men in chariots
and on horses also went with Joseph. It
was a very large group.
10They went to the threshing[d] floor
of Atad, east of the Jordan River. There
they cried loudly and bitterly for Jacob,
also called Israel. Joseph's time of sorrow continued for seven days. 11The
people that lived in Canaan saw the sadness at the threshing floor of Atad.
They said, "Those Egyptians are showing great sorrow!" So now that place is
named Sorrow of the Egyptians.
12So Jacob's sons did what their
father commanded. 13They carried
his body to the land of Canaan. They
buried it in the cave in the field of
Machpelah near Mamre. Abraham
had bought this cave and field from
Ephron the Hittite. He bought the
cave to use as a burial place. 14After
Joseph buried his father, he returned
to Egypt. His brothers and everyone
who had gone with him to bury his
father also returned.

The Brothers Fear Joseph

15After Jacob died, Joseph's brothers
said, "What if Joseph is still angry with
us? We did many wrong things to him.
What if he plans to pay us back?" 16So
they sent a message to Joseph. It said,
"Your father gave this command before
he died. 17He said to us, 'You have done
wrong. You have sinned and done evil
to Joseph. Tell Joseph to forgive you,
his brothers.' So now, Joseph, we beg
you to forgive our wrong. We are the
servants of the God of your father."

When Joseph received the message, he cried.

[18] And his brothers went to him and bowed low before him. They said, "We are your slaves."

[19] Then Joseph said to them, "Don't be afraid. Can I do what only God can do? [20] You meant to hurt me. But God turned your evil into good. It was to save the lives of many people. And it is being done. [21] So don't be afraid. I will take care of you and your children." So Joseph comforted his brothers and spoke kind words to them.

[22] Joseph continued to live in Egypt with all his father's family. He died when he was 110 years old. [23] During Joseph's life Ephraim had children and grand-children. And Joseph's son Manasseh had a son named Makir. Joseph accepted Makir's children as his own.

The Death of Joseph

[24] Joseph said to his brothers, "I am about to die. But God will take care of you. He will lead you out of this land. He will lead you to the land he promised to Abraham, Isaac and Jacob." [25] Then Joseph had the sons of Israel make a promise. He said, "Promise me that you will carry my bones with you out of Egypt."

[26] Joseph died when he was 110 years old. Doctors prepared his body for burial. Then they put him in a coffin in Egypt.

EXODUS
Escape from Egypt

Touring Bible Lands
EGYPT · EXODUS 1:1

When food became scarce in Canaan, sometimes the people would travel to Egypt. Both Abraham and Isaac did that. The people of Egypt had big farms and lots of sheep. The Nile River, which flows through Egypt to the Mediterranean Sea, provided water for many different crops. Food was plentiful in Egypt.

The rulers of Egypt were called pharaohs. When a pharaoh died he was buried in a huge stone building called a pyramid. A pyramid is as tall as a skyscraper! If you visit Egypt today you can still see some of the pyramids.

Fly northeast from Egypt back to Canaan and the Jews' most important city on page 372.

Jacob's Family in Egypt

1 When Jacob, also called Israel, went to Egypt, he took his sons. And each son took his own family with him. These are the names of the sons of Israel: ²Reuben, Simeon, Levi, Judah, ³Issachar, Zebulun, Benjamin, ⁴Dan, Naphtali, Gad and Asher. ⁵There was a total of 70 people who were descendants[d] of Jacob. Jacob's son Joseph was already in Egypt.

"I wonder if Moses liked being in that boat? If you want to learn how he ended up in a boat as a baby, check out Exodus 1:8–2:10."

⁶By some time later, Joseph and his brothers had died, along with all the people who had lived at that same time. ⁷But the people of Israel had many children, and their number grew greatly. They became very strong, and the country of Egypt was filled with them.

Trouble for the People of Israel

⁸Then a new king began to rule Egypt. He did not know who Joseph was. ⁹This king said to his people, "Look! The people of Israel are too many! And they are too strong for us to handle! ¹⁰We must make plans against them. If we don't, the number of their people will grow even more. Then if there is a war, they might join our enemies. Then they could fight us and escape from the country!"

¹¹So the Egyptians made life hard for the people of Israel. They put slave masters over the Israelites. The slave masters forced the Israelites to build the cities Pithom and Rameses for the king. These cities were supply centers in which the Egyptians stored things.

¹²The Egyptians forced the Israelites to work even harder. But this made the Israelites grow in number and spread more. So the Egyptians became more afraid of them. ¹³They forced the Israelites to work even harder. ¹⁴The Egyptians made life hard for the Israelites. They forced the Israelites to work very hard making bricks and mortar. They also forced them to do

than the Egyptian women. They give birth to their babies before we can get there." ²⁰God was good to the nurses. And the Hebrew people continued to grow in number. So they became even stronger. ²¹Because the nurses feared God, he gave them families of their own.

²²So the king commanded all his people: "Every time a boy is born to the Hebrews, you must throw him into the Nile River. But let all the girl babies live."

Boats with Precious Cargo
EXODUS 2:1-4

Do you know which was the smallest boat in the Bible? This boat could hold only one passenger—and that passenger was just a baby! Moses' mother made this little boat so she could hide Moses from the evil people who wanted to hurt baby boys. She took some grassy plants that grew near the river, wove them into a basket, and then made it waterproof with tar. She wrapped baby Moses in a blanket, put him in the little boat, and set the boat among the tall reeds at the river's edge. Moses' sister watched over him so he would be safe.

Because Moses' mother had risked making this little boat, Moses was kept safe. He grew up to be a great leader in Israel. God wants us to do what we know is right, even if it is not easy.

To read about a big trading ship that carried a runaway, *fly to page 1078.*

all kinds of hard work in the fields. The Egyptians were not merciful to them in all their hard work.

¹⁵There were two Hebrew nurses named Shiphrah and Puah. These nurses helped the Israelite women give birth to their babies. The king of Egypt said to the nurses, ¹⁶"When you are helping the Hebrew women give birth to their babies, watch! If the baby is a girl, let the baby live. But if it is a boy, kill it!" ¹⁷But the nurses feared God. So they did not do as the king told them. They let all the boy babies live. ¹⁸Then the king of Egypt sent for the nurses. He said, "Why did you do this? Why did you let the boys live?"

¹⁹The nurses said to him, "The Hebrew women are much stronger

Baby Moses

2 There was a man from the family of Levi. He married a woman who was also from the family of Levi. ²She became pregnant and gave birth to a son. She saw how wonderful the baby was, and she hid him for three months. ³But after three months, she was not able to hide the baby any longer. So she got a basket made of reeds and covered it with tar so that it would float. She put the baby in the basket. Then she put the basket among the tall grass at the edge of the Nile River. ⁴The baby's sister stood a short distance away. She wanted to see what would happen to him.

⁵Then the daughter of the king of

Egypt came to the river. She was going to take a bath. Her servant girls were walking beside the river. She saw the basket in the tall grass. So she sent her slave girl to get it. ⁶The king's daughter opened the basket and saw the baby boy. He was crying, and she felt sorry for him. She said, "This is one of the Hebrew babies."

One day he visited his people, the Hebrews. He saw that they were forced to work very hard. He saw an Egyptian beating a Hebrew man, one of Moses' own people. ¹²Moses looked all around and saw that no one was watching. So he killed the Egyptian and hid his body in the sand.

¹³The next day Moses returned and saw two Hebrew men fighting each other. He saw that one man was in the

People Who Got Away
MOSES • EXODUS 2:11-15

Although Moses had been raised by Pharaoh's daughter in Egypt, he knew that he was an Israelite and he loved his people. The Israelites were slaves in Egypt. One day Moses saw an Egyptian beating an Israelite. Moses defended the Israelite and killed the Egyptian. Moses had to run for his life. He ran far across the desert from Egypt to the land of Midian, leaving behind his family and friends in Egypt. During the forty years he spent in Midian, Moses became a shepherd, and God began to train him for a very important mission.

God can work through even our mistakes so that we can do what he wants us to do.

To read about a left-handed hero who escaped a wicked king, fly to page 290.

⁷Then the baby's sister asked the king's daughter, "Would you like me to find a Hebrew woman to nurse the baby for you?"

⁸The king's daughter said, "Yes, please." So the girl went and got the baby's own mother.

⁹The king's daughter said to the woman, "Take this baby and nurse him for me. I will pay you." So the woman took her baby and nursed him. ¹⁰After the child had grown older, the woman took him to the king's daughter. She adopted the baby as her own son. The king's daughter named him Moses,ⁿ because she had pulled him out of the water.

Moses Helps His People

¹¹Moses grew and became a man.

wrong. Moses said to that man, "Why are you hitting one of your own people?"

¹⁴The man answered, "Who made you our ruler and judge? Are you going to kill me as you killed the Egyptian?"

Then Moses was afraid. He thought, "Now everyone knows what I did."

¹⁵When the king heard about what Moses had done, he tried to kill Moses. But Moses ran away from the king and went to live in the land of Midian. There he sat down near a well.

Moses in Midian

¹⁶There was a priest in Midian who had seven daughters. His daughters went to that well to get water for their father's sheep. They were trying to fill the water troughs for their father's sheep. ¹⁷But some shepherds came

ⁿ**Moses** The name Moses sounds like the Hebrew word for "to pull out."

and chased the girls away. Then Moses defended the girls and watered their sheep.

[18]Then they went back to their father, Reuel, also called Jethro. He asked them, "Why have you come home early today?"

[19]The girls answered, "The shepherds chased us away. But an Egyptian defended us. He got water for us and watered our sheep.

[20]He asked his daughters, "Where is this man? Why did you leave him? Invite him to eat with us."

people of Israel, and he was concerned about them.

The Burning Bush

3 One day Moses was taking care of Jethro's sheep. Jethro was the priest of Midian and also Moses' father-in-law. Moses led the sheep to the west side of the desert. He came to Sinai, the mountain of God. [2]There the angel of the Lord appeared to Moses in flames of fire coming out of a bush. Moses saw

What God Is Like
EXODUS 3:3-14

"**M**ommy, how did we get here?"

"**G**od put us here, honey."

"**A**nd how did God get here? Who made God?"

Have you ever had a talk like that with your mother or father? Sooner or later, most of us begin to ask these questions. They are good questions, and the Bible helps us to understand them. God did put us here: the universe, our solar system, the planet earth, and everything on earth, including people. He is the creator of all there is.

But how did God get here? Did somebody create God so that he could create everything else? As hard as it may be to understand, nobody made God. He was always there, even before anything else existed. No one had to make God—he always was. That is part of what God meant when he told Moses, "I AM WHO I AM."

To learn more about what God is like, zoom to page 155.

[21]Moses agreed to stay with Jethro. And his daughter Zipporah to Moses to be his wife. [22]Zipporah gave birth to a son, and Moses named him Gershom.[n] Moses named him this because Moses was a stranger in a land that was not his own.

[23]After a long time, the king of Egypt died. The people of Israel groaned because they were forced to work very hard. They cried for help. And God heard them. [24]God heard their cries, and he remembered the agreement he had made with Abraham, Isaac and Jacob. [25]God saw the troubles of the

that the bush was on fire, but it was not burning up. [3]So Moses said, "I will go closer to this strange thing. How can a bush continue burning without burning up?"

"**D**id you know that Moses saw a burning bush that wouldn't burn up? Read what happened in Exodus 3:1-12."

[n]**Gershom** This name sounds like the Hebrew word meaning "a stranger there."

⁴The Lord saw Moses was coming to look at the bush. So God called to him from the bush, "Moses, Moses!"

And Moses said, "Here I am."

⁵Then God said, "Do not come any closer. Take off your sandals. You are standing on holy ground. ⁶I am the God of your ancestors. I am the God of Abraham, the God of Isaac and the God of Jacob." Moses covered his face because he was afraid to look at God.

⁷The Lord said, "I have seen the troubles my people have suffered in Egypt. And I have heard their cries when the Egyptian slave masters hurt them. I am concerned about their pain. ⁸I have come down to save them from the Egyptians. I will bring them out of that land. I will lead them to a good land with lots of room. This is a land where much food grows. This is the land of these people: the Canaanites, Hittites, Amorites, Perizzites, Hivites and Jebusites. ⁹I have heard the cries of the people of Israel. I have seen the way the Egyptians have made life hard for them. ¹⁰So now I am sending you to the king of Egypt. Go! Bring my people, the Israelites, out of Egypt!"

¹¹But Moses said to God, "I am not a great man! Why should I be the one to go to the king and lead the Israelites out of Egypt?"

¹²God said, "I will be with you. This will be the proof that I am sending you: You will lead the people out of Egypt. Then all of you will worship me on this mountain."

¹³Moses said to God, "When I go to the Israelites, I will say to them, 'The God of your fathers sent me to you.' What if the people say, 'What is his name?' What should I tell them?"

¹⁴Then God said to Moses, "I AM WHO I AM.ⁿ When you go to the people of Israel, tell them, 'I AM sent me to you.'"

¹⁵God also said to Moses, "This is what you should tell the people: 'The Lord is the God of your ancestors. He is the God of Abraham, the God of Isaac and the God of Jacob. And he sent me to you.' This will always be my

Worship
EXODUS 3:1-6

Some activities don't take any planning. Riding a bike, throwing a ball, jumping into a lake on a hot summer day—all that these require are a bike, a ball, or a lake, and you're ready to go. Other things, however, take a little more preparation, like studying for a test, getting ready for a music recital, or going to a worship service.

Going to a worship service? What kind of preparation does that take? As Moses found out in Exodus 3, it takes more than we might expect. God told Moses to take off his sandals while he was in God's presence as a sign of respect. He wanted Moses to understand that he should not come casually or carelessly into the presence of God. To do so is disrespectful and improper.

We don't need to be barefooted when we worship God. But we do need to be respectful, remembering that we are sinful people coming before a holy God.

To learn more about worship, zoom to page 122.

ⁿ**I . . . I AM**   The Hebrew words are like the name "YAHWEH." This Hebrew name for God, usually called "Lord," shows that God always lives and is always with his people.

name. That is how people from now on will know me.

16"Go and gather the older leaders and tell them this: 'The Lord, the God of your ancestors, has appeared to me. The God of Abraham, Isaac and Jacob spoke to me. He says: I care about you, and I have seen what has happened to you in Egypt. 17I have decided that I will take you away from the troubles you are suffering in Egypt. I will lead you to the land of the

21And I will cause the Egyptian people to think well of the people of Israel. So when you leave, they will give gifts to your people. 22Each Hebrew woman will ask her Egyptian neighbor and any Egyptian woman living in her house for gifts. Ask for silver, gold and clothing. You will put those gifts on your children when you leave Egypt. In this way you will take with you the riches of the Egyptians."

Proof for Moses

4 Then Moses answered, "What if the people of Israel do not believe

Words to Know: Old Testament
WALKING STICK • EXODUS 4:1-4

In Bible times, a **walking stick** was another important thing. Since most people walked everywhere, a walking stick gave them support. Shepherds always carried walking sticks when they took care of their flocks. The stick was a wooden rod, three to six feet long with a curved hook at the top. The shepherds used the stick to guide the sheep and to pull them out when they got stuck in tight places.

Moses became a shepherd in the land of Midian after he left Egypt. That is why he was holding a walking stick when God spoke to him from the burning bush. Later, God used Moses' ordinary walking stick to do many amazing miracles.

Remember nothing is ordinary or boring with God. He can turn the ordinary into the amazing!

To read about how a special celebration got started, fly to page 89.

To read about how a special celebration got started, fly to page 89.

Canaanites, Hittites, Amorites, Perizzites, Hivites and Jebusites. This land grows much food.'

18"The older leaders will listen to you. And then you and the older leaders of Israel will go to the king of Egypt. You will tell him, 'The Lord, the God of the Hebrews, appeared to us. Let us travel three days into the desert. There we must offer sacrifices to the Lord our God.'

19"But I know that the king of Egypt will not let you go. Only a great power will force him to let you go. 20So I will use my great power against Egypt. I will make miracles^d happen in that land. After I do this, he will let you go.

me or listen to me? What if they say, 'The Lord did not appear to you'?"

2The Lord said to him, "What is that in your hand?"

Moses answered, "It is my walking stick."

3The Lord said, "Throw it on the ground."

So Moses threw it on the ground. And it became a snake. Moses ran from the snake. 4But the Lord said to him, "Reach out and grab the snake by its tail." So Moses reached out and took hold of the snake. When he did this, it again became a stick in his hand. 5The Lord said, "When this happens, the Israelites will believe that the Lord appeared to you. I am the God of their ancestors. I am the God of Abraham, the God of Isaac and the God of Jacob."

6Then the Lord said to Moses, "Put your hand inside your coat." So Moses put his hand inside his coat. When he took his hand out, it was white with a harmful skin disease.

7Then the Lord said, "Now put your hand inside your coat again." So Moses put his hand inside his coat again. When he took it out, his hand was healthy again. It was like the rest of his skin.

made man's mouth? And who makes him deaf or not able to speak? Or who gives a man sight or makes him blind? It is I, the Lord. 12Now go! I will help you speak. I will tell you what to say."

13But Moses said, "Please, Lord, send someone else."

14The Lord became angry with Moses. He said, "Your brother Aaron, from the family of Levi, is a skilled speaker. He is already coming to meet you. And he will be happy when he sees

---

Witnessing
EXODUS 4:10-13

Imagine yourself playing a game of tag with your friends at school. "Who's 'it'?" someone asks. And what's the first thing everybody says? "NOT ME!" Nobody wants to be "it."

It was the same way with Moses when God wanted Moses to be his messenger to Pharaoh. The first thing Moses said was, "Not me!" He even had a list of excuses why he shouldn't be "it": "I can't talk right". . . "I don't know what to say". . ."Ask somebody else, anybody, but me!"

But God didn't want somebody else. He wanted Moses to tell Pharaoh about God's plan. He even promised to be with Moses to help him say all the right words. God still wants messengers to tell people about who he is today. And he gives the same promise to us that he gave to Moses.

God doesn't want somebody else to do it. He wants you. Think of how you can be God's messenger. You're "it"!

To learn more about witnessing, zoom to page 283.

8Then the Lord said, "The people may not believe you or be convinced by the first miracle.d They may believe you when you show them this second miracle. 9After these two miracles they still may not believe or listen to you. Then take some water from the Nile River. Pour it on the dry ground. The water will become blood when it touches the ground."

10But Moses said to the Lord, "But Lord, I am not a skilled speaker. I have never been able to speak well. And now, even after talking to you, I am not a good speaker. I speak slowly and can't find the best words."

11Then the Lord said to him, "Who

you. 15I will tell you what to say. Then you will tell Aaron. I will help both of you know what to say and do. 16And Aaron will speak to the people for you. You will tell him what God says. And he will speak for you. 17Take your walking stick with you. Use it to do the miracles."

Moses Returns to Egypt

18Then Moses went back to Jethro, his father-in-law. Moses said to him, "Let me go back to my people in Egypt. I want to see if they are still alive."

Jethro said to Moses, "You may go. Have a safe trip."

19While Moses was still in Midian,

the Lord said to him, "Go back to Egypt. The men who wanted to kill you are dead now."

²⁰So Moses took his wife and his sons and put them on a donkey. Then he started back to Egypt. He took with him the walking stick of God.

²¹The Lord said to Moses, "When you get back to Egypt, do all the miracles.ᵈ I have given you the power to do them. Show them to the king of Egypt. But I will make the king very stubborn. He will not let the people go. ²²Then say to the king: 'This is what the Lord says: Israel is my firstbornᵈ son. ²³And I told you to let my son go. Let him go so he may worship me. But you refused to let Israel go. So I will kill your firstborn son.'"

²⁴As Moses was on his way to Egypt, he stopped at a resting place for the night. The Lord met him there and tried to kill him. ²⁵But Zipporah took a flint knife and circumcisedᵈ her son. She took the skin and touched Moses' feet with it. Then she said to him, "You are a bridegroom of blood to me." ²⁶Zipporah said this because she had to circumcise her son. So the Lord did not kill Moses.

²⁷Meanwhile the Lord said to Aaron, "Go out into the desert to meet Moses." When Aaron went, he met Moses at Sinai, the mountain of God, and kissed him. ²⁸Moses told Aaron everything the Lord had said to him when he sent him to Egypt. And Moses told him about the miracles which the Lord had commanded him to do.

²⁹So Moses and Aaron gathered all the older leaders of the Israelites. ³⁰Aaron told them everything that the Lord had told Moses. Then Moses did the miracles for all the people to see. ³¹So the Israelites believed. They heard that the Lord was concerned about them and had seen their troubles. Then they bowed down and worshiped him.

Moses and Aaron Before the King

5 After Moses and Aaron talked to the people, they went to the king of Egypt. They said, "This is what the Lord, the God of Israel says: 'Let my people go so they may hold a feast for me in the desert.'"

²But the king of Egypt said, "Who is the Lord? Why should I obey him and let Israel go? I do not know the Lord. And I will not let Israel go."

³Then Aaron and Moses said, "The God of the Hebrews has talked with us. Now let us travel three days into the desert. There we will offer sacrifices to the Lord our God. If we don't do this, he may kill us with a disease or in war."

⁴But the king said to them, "Moses and Aaron, why are you taking the people away from their work? Go back to your hard work! ⁵There are very many Hebrews. And now you want them to quit their hard work!"

⁶That same day the king gave a command to the slave masters and foremen. ⁷He said, "Don't give the people straw to make bricks as you used to do. Let them gather their own straw. ⁸But they must still make the same number of bricks as they did before. Do not accept fewer. They have become lazy. That is why they are asking me, 'Let us go to offer sacrifices to our God.' ⁹Make these people work harder. Keep them busy. Then they will not have time to listen to the lies of Moses."

¹⁰So the slave masters and foremen went to the Israelites and said, "This is what the king says: I will no longer give you straw. ¹¹Go and get your own straw wherever you can find it. But you must make as many bricks as you made before." ¹²So the people went everywhere in Egypt looking for dry stalks to use for straw. ¹³The slave masters kept forcing the people to work harder. They said, "You must make just as many bricks as you did when you were given straw." ¹⁴The king's slave masters had chosen the Israelite foremen. They had made them responsible for the work the people did. The Egyptian slave masters beat these men and asked them, "Why aren't you making as many bricks as you made in the past?"

¹⁵Then the Israelite foremen went to

the king. They complained and said, "Why are you treating us, your servants, this way? [16]You give us no straw. But we are commanded to make bricks. Our slave masters beat us. But it is your own people's fault."

[17]The king answered, "You are lazy! You don't want to work! That is why you ask to leave here and make sacrifices to the Lord. [18]Now, go back to work! We will not give you any straw. But you must make just as many bricks as you did before."

[19]The Israelite foremen knew they were in trouble. This was because the king had told them: "You must make just as many bricks each day as you did before." [20]As they were leaving the meeting with the king, they met Moses and Aaron. Moses and Aaron were waiting for them. [21]So they said to Moses and Aaron, "May the Lord punish you. You caused the king and his officers to hate us. You have given them an excuse to kill us."

Moses Complains to God

[22]Then Moses returned to the Lord and said, "Lord, why have you brought this trouble on your people? Is this why you sent me here? [23]I went to the king and said what you told me to say. But ever since that time he has made the people suffer. And you have done nothing to save them."

6 Then the Lord said to Moses, "Now you will see what I will do to the king of Egypt. I will use my great power against him, and he will let my people go. Because of my power, he will force them out of his country."

[2]Then God said to Moses, "I am the Lord. [3]I appeared to Abraham, Isaac and Jacob by the name, God All-Powerful. But they did not know me by my name, the Lord. [4]I also made my agreement with them to give them the land of Canaan. They lived in that land, but it was not their own land. [5]Now I have heard the cries of the Israelites. The Egyptians are treating them as slaves. And I remember my agreement. [6]So tell the people of Israel that I say to them, 'I am the Lord. I will save you from the hard work the Egyptians force you to do. I will make you free. You will not be slaves to the Egyptians. I will free you by my great power. And I will punish the Egyptians terribly. [7]I will make you my own people, and I will be your God. You will know that I am the Lord your God. I am the One who saves you from the hard work the Egyptians force you to do. [8]I will lead you to the land that I promised to Abraham, Isaac and Jacob. I will give you that land to own. I am the Lord.'"

[9]So Moses told this to the people of Israel. But they would not listen to him. They were discouraged, and their slavery was hard.

[10]Then the Lord said to Moses, [11]"Go tell the king of Egypt that he must let the Israelites leave his land."

[12]But Moses answered, "The Israelites will not listen to me. So surely the king will not listen to me, either. I am not a good speaker."

[13]But the Lord told Moses and Aaron to talk to the king. He commanded them to lead the Israelites out of Egypt.

Families of Israel

[14]These are the leaders of the families of Israel:

Israel's first son, Reuben, had four sons. They were Hanoch, Pallu, Hezron and Carmi. These are the family groups of Reuben.

[15]Simeon's sons were Jemuel, Jamin, Ohad, Jakin, Zohar and Shaul. Shaul was the son of a Canaanite woman. These are the family groups of Simeon.

[16]Levi lived 137 years. These are the names of his sons according to their family history: Gershon, Kohath and Merari.

[17]Gershon had two sons, Libni and Shimei, with their families.

[18]Kohath lived 133 years. The sons of Kohath were Amram, Izhar, Hebron and Uzziel.

[19]The sons of Merari were Mahli and Mushi.

These are the family groups of Levi, according to their family history.

²⁰Amram married his father's sister Jochebed. Jochebed gave birth to Aaron and Moses. Amram lived 137 years.

²¹Izhar's sons were Korah, Nepheg and Zicri.

²²Uzziel's sons were Mishael, Elzaphan and Sithri.

²³Aaron married Elisheba. She was the daughter of Amminadab and the sister of Nahshon. Elisheba gave birth to Nadab, Abihu, Eleazar and Ithamar.

²⁴The sons of Korah were Assir, Elkanah and Abiasaph. These are the family groups of the Korahites.

²⁵Eleazar son of Aaron married a daughter of Putiel. And she gave birth to Phinehas.

These are the leaders of the family groups of the Levites.

²⁶This was the Aaron and Moses to whom the Lord spoke. He said, "Lead my people out of Israel in their divisions." ²⁷Aaron and Moses are the ones who talked to the king of Egypt. They told him to let the people of Israel leave Egypt.

God Repeats His Call to Moses

²⁸The Lord spoke to Moses in the land of Egypt. ²⁹He said, "I am the Lord. Tell the king of Egypt everything I tell you."

³⁰But Moses answered, "I am not a good speaker. The king will not listen to me."

7 The Lord said to Moses, "I have made you like God to the king of Egypt. And your brother Aaron will be like a prophet^d for you. ²Tell Aaron your brother everything that I command you. Then let him tell the king of Egypt to let the Israelites leave his country. ³But I will make the king stubborn. Then I will do many miracles^d in Egypt. ⁴But he will still refuse to listen. So then I will punish Egypt terribly. And I will lead my divisions, my people the Israelites, out of that land. ⁵I will punish Egypt with my power. And I will bring the Israelites out of that land. Then they will know I am the Lord."

⁶Moses and Aaron did just as the Lord had commanded them. ⁷Moses was 80 years old, and Aaron was 83, when they spoke to the king.

Aaron's Walking Stick Becomes a Snake

⁸The Lord said to Moses and Aaron, ⁹"The king will ask you to do a miracle.^d When he does, Moses, you tell Aaron to throw his walking stick down in front of the king. It will become a snake."

¹⁰So Moses and Aaron went to the king as the Lord had commanded. Aaron threw his walking stick down in front of the king and his officers. And it became a snake.

¹¹So the king called in his wise men and his magicians. With their tricks the Egyptian magicians were able to do the same thing. ¹²They threw their walking sticks on the ground, and their sticks became snakes. But then Aaron's stick swallowed theirs. ¹³But the king was stubborn. He refused to listen to Moses and Aaron, just as the Lord had said.

The Water Becomes Blood

¹⁴Then the Lord said to Moses, "The king is being stubborn. He refuses to let the people go. ¹⁵In the morning the king will go out to the Nile River. Go meet him by the edge of the river. Take with you the walking stick that became a snake. ¹⁶Tell him this: The Lord, the God of the Hebrews, sent me to you. He said, 'Let my people go worship me in the desert.' Until now you have not listened. ¹⁷This is what the Lord says: 'This is how you will know that I am the Lord. I will strike the water of the Nile River with this stick in my hand. And the water will change into blood. ¹⁸Then the fish in the Nile will die, and the river will begin to stink. And the Egyptians will not be able to drink the water from the Nile.'"

¹⁹The Lord said to Moses, "Tell Aaron to stretch the walking stick in his hand over the rivers, canals, ponds and pools in Egypt. The water will become blood

everywhere in Egypt. There even will be blood in the wooden buckets and stone jars."

20So Moses and Aaron did just as the Lord had commanded. Aaron raised his walking stick and struck the water in the Nile River. He did this in front of the king and his officers. So all the water in the Nile changed into blood. 21The fish in the Nile died, and the river began to stink. So the Egyptians could not drink water from it. Blood was everywhere in the land of Egypt. 22Using their tricks, their magicians of Egypt did the same thing. So the king was stubborn and refused to listen to Moses and Aaron. This happened just as the Lord had said. 23The king turned and went into his palace. He ignored what Moses and Aaron had done. 24The Egyptians could not drink the water from the Nile. So all of them dug along the bank of the river. They were looking for water to drink.

The Frogs

25Seven days passed after the Lord changed the Nile River.

8 Then the Lord told Moses, "Go to the king of Egypt and tell him, 'This is what the Lord says: Let my people go to worship me. 2If you refuse, then I will punish Egypt with frogs. 3The Nile River will be filled with frogs. They will come from the river and enter your palace. They will be in your bedroom and your bed. The frogs will enter the houses of your officers and your people. They will enter your ovens and your baking pans. 4The frogs will jump up all over you, your people and your officers.'"

5Then the Lord said to Moses, "Tell Aaron to hold his walking stick in his hand over the rivers, canals and ponds. Make frogs come up out of the water onto the land of Egypt."

6So Aaron held his hand over all the waters of Egypt. The frogs came up out of the water and covered the land of Egypt. 7The magicians used their tricks to do the same thing. So even more frogs came up onto the land of Egypt.

8So the king called for Moses and Aaron. He said, "Pray to the Lord to take the frogs away from me and my people. I will let your people go to offer sacrifices to the Lord."

9Moses said to the king, "Please set

Animals in the Bible
FROGS • EXODUS 8:1-15

Do you like to play with frogs? Or do you think they are slimy and yucky?

Could you imagine hundreds of frogs all over your house—frogs in the kitchen, frogs in the bathroom, even frogs in your bed! This actually happened to the Egyptians. God sent frogs to Egypt in order to convince Pharaoh to let the Israelites leave the country. When the frogs came, Pharaoh told Moses to get rid of them and he would let Israel go. But when the frogs died, Pharaoh broke his promise to Moses. God had to send Pharaoh and the Egyptians ten plagues before they let the Israelites leave the country.

We should always try to do what God asks us right away. Even if we don't have to worry about having frogs in our beds!

To find out about an animal that gives flying lessons, fly to page 251.

the time that I should pray for you, your people and your officers. Then the frogs will leave you and your houses. They will remain only in the Nile."

10The king answered, "Tomorrow."

Moses said, "What you want will happen. By this you will know that there is no one like the Lord our God. 11The frogs will leave you, your houses, your officers and your people. They will remain only in the Nile."

12Moses and Aaron left the king. Moses asked the Lord about the frogs he had sent to the king. 13And the Lord did as Moses asked. The frogs died in the houses, in the yards and in the fields. 14The Egyptians put them in piles. The whole country began to stink. 15When the king saw that they were free of the frogs, he became stubborn again. He did not listen to Moses and Aaron, just as the Lord had said.

The Gnats

16Then the Lord said to Moses, "Tell Aaron to raise his walking stick and strike the dust on the ground. Then everywhere in Egypt the dust will change into gnats." 17They did this. Aaron raised the walking stick that was in his hand and struck the dust on the ground. Then everywhere in Egypt the dust changed into gnats. The gnats got on the people and animals. 18Using their tricks, the magicians tried to do the same thing. But they could not make the dust change into gnats. The gnats remained on the people and animals. 19So the magicians told the king that the power of God had done this. But the king was stubborn and refused to listen to them. This happened just as the Lord had said.

The Flies

20The Lord told Moses, "Get up early in the morning. Meet the king of Egypt as he goes out to the river. Tell him, 'This is what the Lord says: Let my people go so they can worship me. 21If you don't let them go, I will send swarms of flies. I will send them into your houses. The flies will be on you,

your officers and your people. The houses of Egypt will be full of flies. And they will be all over the ground, too. 22But I will not treat the people of Israel the same as the Egyptian people. There will not be any flies in the land of Goshen, where my people live. By this you will know that I, the Lord, am in this land. 23I will treat my people differently from your people. This miracle*d* will happen tomorrow.'"

24So the Lord did as he had said. Great swarms of flies came into the king's palace and his officers' houses. All over Egypt flies were ruining the land. 25The king called for Moses and Aaron. He told them, "Offer sacrifices to your God here in this country."

26But Moses said, "It wouldn't be right to do that. The Egyptians hate the sacrifices we offer to the Lord our God. They will see us offer sacrifices they hate. Then they will throw stones at us and kill us. 27Let us make a three-day journey into the desert. We must offer sacrifices to the Lord our God there. This is what the Lord told us to do."

28The king said, "I will let you go. Then you may offer sacrifices to the Lord your God in the desert. But you must not go very far away. Now go and pray for me."

29Moses said, "I will leave and pray to the Lord. He will take the flies away from you, your officers and your people tomorrow. But do not try to trick us again. Do not stop the people from going to offer sacrifices to the Lord."

30So Moses left the king and prayed to the Lord. 31And the Lord did as Moses asked. He removed the flies from the king, his officers and his people. Not one fly was left. 32But the king became stubborn again and did not let the people go.

The Disease on the Farm Animals

9 Then the Lord told Moses, "Go to the king of Egypt. Tell him, 'This is what the Lord, the God of the Hebrews, says: Let my people go to worship me. 2You might refuse to let them go and continue to hold them. ³Then the Lord will punish you. He will send a terrible disease on all your farm animals. He will cause all of your horses, donkeys, camels, cattle and sheep to become sick. ⁴But the Lord will treat Israel's animals differently from the animals of Egypt. None of the animals that belong to the Israelites will die. ⁵The Lord has set tomorrow as the time he will do this in the land.'" ⁶The next day the Lord did as he promised. All the farm animals in Egypt died. But none of the animals belonging to Israelites died. ⁷The king sent people to see what had happened to the animals of Israel. They found that not one of them had died. But the king was still stubborn. He did not let the people go.

The Boils

⁸The Lord said to Moses and Aaron, "Fill your hands with the ashes from a furnace. Moses, throw the ashes into the air in front of the king of Egypt. ⁹The ashes will spread like dust through all the land of Egypt. The dust will cause boils to break out and become sores on the skin. These sores will be on people and animals everywhere in the land."

¹⁰So Moses and Aaron took ashes from a furnace. Then they went and stood before the king. Moses threw ashes into the air. It caused boils to break out and become sores on people and animals. ¹¹The magicians could not stand before Moses. This was because all the Egyptians had boils, even the magicians. ¹²But the Lord made the king stubborn. So he refused to listen to Moses and Aaron. This happened just as the Lord had said.

The Hail

¹³Then the Lord said to Moses, "Get up early in the morning and go to the king of Egypt. Tell him, 'This is what the Lord, the God of the Hebrews, says: Let my people go to worship me. ¹⁴If you do not do this, this time I will punish you with all my power. I will punish you, your officers and your peo-

ple. Then you will know that there is no one in the whole land like me. ¹⁵By now I could have used my power and caused a bad disease. It would have destroyed you and your people from the earth. ¹⁶But I have let you live for this reason: to show you my power. In this way my name will be talked about in all the earth. ¹⁷You are still against my people. You do not want to let them go. ¹⁸So at this time tomorrow, I will send a terrible hailstorm. It will be the worst in Egypt since it became a nation. ¹⁹Now send for your animals and whatever you have in the fields. Bring them into a safe place. The hail will fall on every person or animal that is still in the fields. If they have not been brought in, they will die.'"

²⁰Some of the king's officers respected the word of the Lord. They hurried to bring their slaves and animals inside. ²¹But others ignored the Lord's message. They left their slaves and animals in the fields.

²²The Lord told Moses, "Raise your hand toward the sky. Then the hail will start falling over all the land of Egypt. It will fall on people, animals and on everything that grows in the fields of Egypt." ²³So Moses raised his walking stick toward the sky. And the Lord sent thunder and hail. And lightning flashed down to the earth. So he caused hail to fall upon the land of Egypt. ²⁴There was hail, and there was lightning flashing as it hailed. This was the worst hailstorm in Egypt since it had become a nation. ²⁵The hail destroyed everything that was in the fields in all the land of Egypt. The hail destroyed both people and animals. It also destroyed everything that grew in the fields. It broke all the trees in the fields. ²⁶The only place it did not hail was in the land of Goshen. The people of Israel lived there.

²⁷The king sent for Moses and Aaron. He told them, "This time I have sinned. The Lord is in the right. And I and my people are in the wrong. ²⁸Pray to the Lord. We have had enough of God's thunder and hail. I will let you go. You do not have to stay here any longer."

²⁹Moses told the king, "When I leave the city, I will raise my hands to the Lord in prayer. And the thunder and hail will stop. Then you will know that the earth belongs to the Lord. ³⁰But I know that you and your officers do not yet fear the Lord God."

³¹The flax was in bloom, and the barley had ripened. So these crops were destroyed. ³²But both wheat crops ripen later. So they were not destroyed.

³³Moses left the king and went outside the city. He raised his hands to the Lord. And the thunder and hail stopped. The rain also stopped falling to the ground. ³⁴The king saw that the rain, hail and thunder had stopped. Then he sinned again. He and his officers became stubborn again. ³⁵The king became stubborn and refused to let the Israelites go. This happened just as the Lord had said through Moses.

The Locusts

10 The Lord said to Moses, "Go to the king of Egypt. I have made him and his officers stubborn. I did this so I could show them my powerful miracles.ᵈ ²I also did this so you could tell your children and your grandchildren. Tell them how I made fools of the Egyptians. Tell them about the miracles I did among them. Then all of you will know that I am the Lord."

³So Moses and Aaron went to the king. They told him, "This is what the Lord, the God of the Hebrews, says: 'How long will you refuse to be sorry for what you have done? Let my people go to worship me. ⁴If you refuse to let my people go, tomorrow I will bring locustsᵈ into your country. ⁵They will cover the land, and no one will be able to see the ground. They will eat anything that was left from the hailstorm. They will eat the leaves from every tree growing in the field. ⁶They will fill your palaces and all your officers' houses. They will fill the houses of all the Egyptian people. There will be more locusts than your fathers or ancestors have ever seen. There will be more

locusts than there have been since people began living in Egypt.'" Then Moses turned and walked away from the king.

⁷The king's officers asked him, "How long will this man make trouble for us? Let the Israelite men go to worship the Lord their God. Don't you know that Egypt is ruined?"

⁸So Moses and Aaron were brought back to the king. He said to them, "Go and worship the Lord your God. But tell me, just who is going?"

⁹Moses answered, "We will go with our young and our old people, our sons and daughters and sheep and cattle. This is because we are going to have a feast to honor the Lord."

¹⁰The king said to them, "The Lord really will have to be with you if ever I let you and all of your children leave Egypt. See, you are planning something evil. ¹¹No! Only the men may go and worship the Lord. That is what you have been asking for." Then the king forced Moses and Aaron out of his palace.

¹²The Lord told Moses, "Raise your hand over the land of Egypt, and the locusts will come. They will spread all over the land of Egypt. They will eat all the plants that the hail did not destroy."

¹³So Moses raised his walking stick over the land of Egypt. And the Lord caused a strong wind to blow from the east. It blew across the land all that day and night. When morning came, the east wind had brought the locusts. ¹⁴Swarms of locusts covered all the land of Egypt and settled everywhere. There were more locusts than ever before or after. ¹⁵The locusts covered the whole land so that it was black. They ate everything that was left after the hail. They ate every plant in the field and all the fruit on the trees. Nothing green was left on any tree or plant anywhere in Egypt.

¹⁶The king quickly called for Moses and Aaron. He said, "I have sinned against the Lord your God and against you. ¹⁷Now forgive my sin this time. Pray to the Lord your God. Ask him to stop this punishment that kills."

¹⁸Moses left the king and prayed to

the Lord. ¹⁹So the Lord changed the wind. He made a very strong wind to blow from the west. It blew the locusts away into the Red Sea.*d* Not one locust was left anywhere in Egypt. ²⁰But the Lord caused the king to be stubborn again. And he did not let the people of Israel go.

The Darkness

²¹Then the Lord told Moses, "Raise your hand toward the sky, and darkness will cover the land of Egypt. It will be so dark you will be able to feel it." ²²So Moses raised his hand toward the sky. Then total darkness was everywhere in Egypt for three days. ²³No one could see anyone else. And no one could go anywhere for three days. But the Israelites had light where they lived.

²⁴Again the king of Egypt called for Moses. He said, "All of you may go and worship the Lord. You may take your women and children with you. But you must leave your sheep and cattle here." ²⁵Moses said, "You must let us have animals to use as sacrifices and burnt offerings. We have to offer them to the Lord our God. ²⁶So we must take our animals with us. Not a hoof will be left behind. We have to use some of the animals to worship the Lord our God. We do not yet know exactly what we will need to worship the Lord. We will know when we get there."

²⁷But the Lord made the king stubborn again. So he refused to let them go. ²⁸Then he told Moses, "Get out of here! Don't come here again! The next time you see me, you will die." ²⁹Then Moses told the king, "I'll do what you say. I will not come to see you again."

The Death of the Firstborn

11 Now the Lord had told Moses, "I have one more way to punish the king and the people of Egypt. After this, the king will send all of you away from Egypt. When he does, he will force you to leave completely. ²Tell the men and women of Israel to ask their neighbors for things made of silver and gold." ³The Lord had caused the Egyptians

Amazing Events That Showed God's Power
EXODUS 10:21-29

What if it were completely dark outside for three whole days? Would you be afraid?

God made some very strange things happen in Egypt. The Egyptian people did not worship God. In fact, they made God's people their slaves. God wanted to free his people. But first he wanted to show the Egyptians that he was the only true God. So he brought ten plagues to the land. (You can read about them in Exodus 9-11.)

The Egyptians worshiped the Nile River, so God turned its water into blood. They worshiped the sun, so God sent darkness for three days. God took care of the Israelites during the plagues. God is more powerful than anything. He will help us and take care of us too!

To see what God did in a hopeless situation, fly to page 93.

to respect the Israelites. The king's officers and the Egyptian people already considered Moses to be a great man.

⁴So Moses said to the king, "This is what the Lord says: 'About midnight tonight I will go through all Egypt. ⁵Every firstborn^d son in the land of Egypt will die. The firstborn son of the king, who sits on his throne, will die. Even the firstborn of the slave girl grinding grain will die. Also the firstborn farm animals will die. ⁶There will be loud crying everywhere in Egypt. It will be worse than any time before or after this. ⁷But not even a dog will bark at the Israelites or their animals.' Then you will know that the Lord treats Israel differently from Egypt. ⁸Then all your officers will come to me. They will bow facedown to the ground before me. They will say, 'Leave and take all your people with you.' After that, I will leave." Then Moses very angrily left the king.

⁹The Lord had told Moses, "The king will not listen to you and Aaron. This is so that I may do many miracles^d in the land of Egypt." ¹⁰Moses and Aaron did all these great miracles in front of the king. But the Lord made him stubborn. And the king would not let the people of Israel leave his country.

Passover

12 The Lord spoke to Moses and Aaron in the land of Egypt: ²"This month will be the first month of the year for you. ³Both of you are to tell the whole community of Israel: On the tenth day of this month each man must get one lamb. It is for the people in his house. ⁴There may not be enough people in his house to eat a whole lamb. Then he must share it with his closest neighbor. There must be enough lamb for everyone to eat. ⁵The lamb must be a one-year-old male. It must have nothing wrong with it. This animal can be either a young sheep or a young goat. ⁶Keep the animal with you to take care of it until the fourteenth day of the month. On that day all the people of the community of Israel will kill these animals. They will do this as soon as the sun goes down. ⁷The people must take some of the blood. They must put it on the sides and tops of the doorframes. These are the doorframes of the houses where they eat the lambs. ⁸On this night they must roast the lamb over a

Words to Know: Old Testament
PASSOVER • EXODUS 12:6-11

Often the Bible tells us how God's people celebrated a festival (special party) called **Passover**. Even Jesus went to Jerusalem to celebrate this yearly festival while he was on earth. Passover began in Egypt when God freed the Israelites from slavery. The festival remembers the time when God sent the last plague on Egypt–the plague when all the firstborn sons died. The Israelites had been told to mark their front doors with blood from a lamb so God's angel would "pass over" their doors and not hurt anyone in the house. All the Israelite sons were protected from the plague.

Some Jewish people still celebrate Passover today. They eat a special meal of roast lamb served with herbs and bread.

To read about portable homes, fly to page 99.

fire. Then they must eat it with bitter herbs and bread made without yeast. [9]Do not eat the lamb raw or boiled in water. Roast the whole lamb over a fire—with its head, legs and inner organs. [10]You must not leave any of it until morning. But if any of it is left over until morning, you must burn it with fire.

[11]"This is the way you must eat it: You must be fully dressed as if you were going on a trip. You must have your sandals on, and you must have your walking stick in your hand. You must eat it in a hurry. This is the Lord's Passover.[d]

[12]"That night I will go through the land of Egypt. I will kill all the first-born[d] of animals and people in the land of Egypt. I will punish all the gods of Egypt. I am the Lord. [13]But the blood will be a sign on the houses where you are. When I see the blood, I will pass over you. Nothing terrible will hurt you when I punish the land of Egypt.

[14]"You are always to remember this day. Celebrate it with a feast to the Lord. Your descendants[d] are to honor the Lord with this feast from now on. [15]For this feast you must eat bread made without yeast for seven days. On the first day of this feast, you are to remove all the yeast from your houses. No one should eat any yeast for the full seven days of the feast. If anyone eats yeast, then that person will be separated from Israel. [16]You are to have holy meetings on the first and last days of the feast. You must not do any work on these days. The only work you may do on these days is to prepare your meals. [17]You must celebrate the Feast[d] of Unleavened Bread. Do this because on this very day I brought your divisions of people out of Egypt. So all of your descendants must celebrate this day. This is a law that will last from now on. [18]You are to eat bread made without yeast. Start this on the evening of the fourteenth day of the first month of your year. Eat this until the evening of the twenty-first day. [19]For seven days there must not be any yeast in your

houses. Anybody who eats yeast during this time must be separated from the community of Israel. This includes Israelites and non-Israelites. [20]During this feast you must not eat yeast. You must eat bread made without yeast wherever you live."

[21]Then Moses called all the older leaders of Israel together. He told them, "Get the animals for your families. Kill the animals for the Passover. [22]Take a branch of the hyssop plant and dip it into the bowl filled with blood. Wipe the blood on the sides and tops of the doorframes. No one may leave his house until morning. [23]The Lord will go through Egypt to kill the Egyptians. He will see the blood on the sides and tops of the doorframes. Then the Lord will pass over that house. He will not let the one who brings death come into your houses and kill you.

[24]"You must keep this command. This law is for you and your descendants from now on. [25]Do this when you go to the land the Lord has promised to give to you. [26]When your children ask you, 'Why are we doing these things?' [27]you will say, 'This is the Passover sacrifice to honor the Lord. When we were in Egypt, the Lord passed over the houses of Israel. The Lord killed the Egyptians, but he saved our homes.'" So now the people bowed down and worshiped the Lord. [28]They did just as the Lord commanded Moses and Aaron.

[29]At midnight the Lord killed all the firstborn sons in the land of Egypt. The firstborn of the king, who sat on the throne, died. Even the firstborn of the prisoner in jail died. Also all the firstborn farm animals died. [30]The king, his officers and all the Egyptians got up during the night. Someone had died in every house. So there was loud crying everywhere in Egypt.

Israel Leaves Egypt

[31]During the night the king called for Moses and Aaron. He said to them, "Get up and leave my people. You and

your people may do as you have asked. Go and worship the Lord. ³²Take all of your sheep and cattle as you have asked. Go. And also bless me." ³³The Egyptians also asked the Israelites to hurry and leave. They said, "If you don't leave, we will all die!"

³⁴The people of Israel took their dough before the yeast was added. They wrapped the bowls for making dough in clothing and carried them on their shoulders. ³⁵The people of Israel did what Moses told them to do. They asked their Egyptian neighbors for things made of silver and gold and for clothing. ³⁶The Lord caused the Egyptians to think well of the Israelites. So the Israelites took rich gifts from the Egyptians.

³⁷The Israelites traveled from Rameses to Succoth. There were about 600,000 men walking. This does not include the women and children. ³⁸Many other people who were not Israelites went with them. A large number of sheep, goats and cattle went with them. ³⁹The Israelites used the dough they had brought out of Egypt. They baked loaves of bread without yeast. The dough had no yeast in it because they had been rushed out of Egypt. So they had no time to get food ready for their trip.

⁴⁰The people of Israel had lived in Egypt for 430 years. ⁴¹On the day the 430 years ended, the Lord's divisions of people left Egypt. ⁴²That night the Lord kept watch to bring them out of Egypt. So on this same night the Israelites are to keep watch. They are to do this to honor the Lord from now on.

⁴³The Lord told Moses and Aaron, "Here are the rules for Passover:ᵈ No foreigner is to eat the Passover. ⁴⁴Suppose a person buys a slave and circumcisesᵈ him. Then the slave may eat the Passover. ⁴⁵But no one who lives for a short time in your country may eat it. No hired worker may eat it. ⁴⁶"The meal must be eaten inside the house. None of the meat is to be taken outside the house. Don't break any of

the bones. ⁴⁷The whole community of Israel must take part in this feast. ⁴⁸A foreigner who lives with you may share in the Lord's Passover. But first all the males in his house must be circumcised. Then, since he will be like a citizen of Israel, he may share in the meal. But a man who is not circumcised may not eat the Passover meal. ⁴⁹The same rules apply to an Israelite born in the country. And they apply to a foreigner living there."

⁵⁰So all the Israelites did just as the Lord had commanded Moses and Aaron. ⁵¹Then on that same day, the Lord led the Israelites out of Egypt. The people left by divisions.

The Law of the Firstborn

13 Then the Lord said to Moses, ²"Give every firstbornᵈ male to me. Every firstborn male among the Israelites belongs to me, whether human or animal."

³Moses said to the people, "Remember this day, the day you left Egypt. You were slaves in that land. The Lord with his great power brought you out of it. You must not eat bread made with yeast. ⁴Today, in the month of Abib,ᵈ you are leaving Egypt. ⁵The Lord made a promise to your ancestors. The Lord promised to give you the land of these people: the Canaanites, Hittites, Amorites, Hivites and Jebusites. The Lord will lead you to this land where much food grows. There you must celebrate this feast during the first month of every year. ⁶For seven days you must eat bread made without yeast. On the seventh day there will be a feast to honor the Lord. ⁷So for seven days you must not eat any bread made with yeast. There must be no bread made with yeast anywhere in your land. ⁸On that day you should tell your son: 'We are having this feast because of what the Lord did for me when I came out of Egypt.' ⁹This feast will help you remember. It will be like a mark on your hand. It will be like a reminder on your forehead. This feast will remind

you to speak the Lord's teachings. This is because the Lord used his great power to bring you out of Egypt. [10]So celebrate this feast every year at the right time.

[11]"The Lord will take you into the land of the Canaanites. He promised to give this land to you and your ancestors. [12]Then you must give him every firstborn male. And every firstborn male animal must be given to the Lord. [13]Buy back every firstborn donkey by offering a lamb. If you don't want to buy the donkey back, then break its neck. You must buy back from the Lord every firstborn of your sons.

[14]"From now on your son will ask you: 'What does this mean?' You will answer, 'With his great power, the Lord brought us out of Egypt. We were slaves in that land. [15]In Egypt the king was stubborn. He refused to let us leave. But the Lord killed every firstborn male in Egypt, both human and animal. That is why I sacrifice every firstborn male animal to the Lord. And that is why I buy back each of my firstborn sons from the Lord.' [16]This feast is like a mark on your hand. And it is like a reminder on your forehead. It will help you remember that the Lord brought us out of Egypt with his great power."

The Way Out of Egypt

[17]The king sent the people out of Egypt. God did not lead them on the road through the Philistine country. That road is the shortest way. But God said, "They might think they will have to fight. Then they might change their minds and go back to Egypt." [18]So God led them through the desert toward the Red Sea.[d] The Israelites were dressed for fighting when they left the land of Egypt.

[19]Moses carried the bones of Joseph with him. Before Joseph died, he had made the sons of Israel promise to do this. He had said, "When God saves you, remember to carry my bones with you out of Egypt."

[20]The people of Israel left Succoth and camped at Etham. Etham was on the edge of the desert. [21]The Lord showed them the way. During the day he went ahead of them in a pillar of cloud. And during the night the Lord was in a pillar of fire to give them light. They could travel during the day or night. [22]The pillar of cloud was always with them during the day. And the pillar of fire was always with them at night.

14 Then the Lord said to Moses, [2]"Tell the Israelites to turn back to Pi Hahiroth. Tell them to camp for the night between Migdol and the Red Sea. This is near Baal Zephon. [3]The king will think, 'The Israelites are lost, trapped by the desert.' [4]I will make the king stubborn again so he will chase after them. But I will defeat the king and his army. This will bring honor to me. Then the people of Egypt will know that I am the Lord." The people of Israel did just as they were told.

The King Chases the Israelites

[5]The king of Egypt was told that the people of Israel had already left. Then he and his officers changed their minds about them. They said, "What have we done? We have let the people of Israel leave. We have lost our slaves!" [6]So the king prepared his war chariot and took his army with him. [7]He took 600 of his best chariots. He also took all the other chariots of Egypt. Each chariot had an officer in it. [8]The Lord made the king of Egypt stubborn. So he chased the Israelites, who were leaving victoriously. [9]The king of Egypt came with his horses, chariot drivers and army. And they chased the Israelites. They caught up with the Israelites while they were camped by the Red Sea.[d] This was near Pi Hahiroth and Baal Zephon.

[10]The Israelites saw the king and his army coming after them. They were very frightened and cried to the Lord for help. [11]They said to Moses, "What have you done to us? Why did you bring us out of Egypt to die in the desert? There were plenty of graves for

us in Egypt. ¹²We told you in Egypt, 'Let us alone! Let us stay and serve the Egyptians.' Now we will die in the desert."

¹³But Moses answered, "Don't be afraid! Stand still and see the Lord save you today. You will never see these Egyptians again after today. ¹⁴You will only need to remain calm. The Lord will fight for you."

¹⁵Then the Lord said to Moses, "Why are you crying out to me? Command the people of Israel to start moving. ¹⁶Raise your walking stick and hold it over the sea. The sea will split. Then the people can cross the sea on dry land. ¹⁷I have made the Egyptians stubborn so they will chase the Israelites. But I will be honored when I defeat the king and all of his chariot drivers and chariots. ¹⁸I will defeat the king, his chariot drivers and chariots. Then Egypt will know that I am the Lord."

¹⁹The angel of God usually traveled in front of Israel's army. Now the angel of God moved behind them. Also, the pillar of cloud moved from in front of the people and stood behind them. ²⁰So the cloud came between the Egyptians and the people of Israel. The cloud made it dark for the Egyptians. But it gave light to the Israelites. So the cloud kept the two armies apart all night.

²¹Moses held his hand over the sea. All that night the Lord drove back the sea with a strong east wind. And so he made the sea become dry ground. The water was split. ²²And the Israelites went through the sea on dry land. A wall of water was on both sides.

²³Then all the king's horses, chariots and chariot drivers followed them into the sea. ²⁴Between two and six o'clock in the morning, the Lord looked down from the pillar of cloud and fire at the Egyptian army. He made them panic. ²⁵He kept the wheels of the chariots from turning. This made it hard to drive the chariots. The Egyptians shouted, "Let's get away from the Israelites! The Lord is fighting for them and against us Egyptians."

Amazing Events That Showed God's Power

EXODUS 14:21-22

What were the Israelites going to do? They thought they were trapped!

After escaping from Egypt, they stopped beside the Red Sea. Then Egypt's king (the Pharaoh) decided that he wanted them back. So he sent his army after them. When the Israelites saw the horses and chariots racing toward them they were afraid!

But God opened up a path for them right through the sea. Imagine the water parting and making two tall walls on each side. There were about two million Israelites, and all of them crossed over in one night. As soon as every Israelite was safely across, God closed the pathway. The walls of water fell back down and drowned the Egyptian army.

No situation is hopeless if you trust God. He has the power to help you!

To find out how somebody got an extra long day, fly to page 267.

²⁶Then the Lord told Moses, "Hold your hand over the sea. Then the water will come back over the Egyptians, their chariots and chariot drivers." ²⁷So Moses raised his hand over the sea. And at dawn the water became deep again. The Egyptians were trying to run from it. But the Lord swept them away into the sea. ²⁸The water became deep again. It covered the chariots and chariot drivers. So all the king's army that had followed the Israelites into the sea was covered. Not one of them survived.

²⁹But the people of Israel crossed the sea on dry land. There was a wall of water on their right and on their left. ³⁰So that day the Lord saved the Israelites from the Egyptians. And the Israelites saw the Egyptians lying dead on the seashore. ³¹When the people of Israel saw the great power that the Lord had used against the Egyptians, they feared the Lord. And they trusted the Lord and his servant Moses.

The Song of Moses

15 Then Moses and the Israelites sang this song to the Lord:

"I will sing to the Lord
 because he is worthy of great
   honor.
He has thrown the horse and its rider
 into the sea.
²The Lord gives me strength and
   makes me sing.
 He has saved me.
He is my God,
 and I will praise him.
He is the God of my fathers,
 and I will honor him.
³The Lord is a great warrior.
 The Lord is his name.
⁴The chariots and soldiers of the
   king of Egypt
 he has thrown into the sea.
The king's best officers
 are drowned in the Red Sea.^d
⁵The deep waters covered them.
 They sank to the bottom like a rock.
⁶Your right hand, Lord,
 is amazingly strong.
Lord, your right hand

broke the enemy into pieces.
⁷In your great victory
 you destroyed those who were
   against you.
Your anger destroyed them,
 like fire burning straw.
⁸Just a blast of your breath,
 and the waters were blown back.
The moving water stood up like a
   wall.
And the deep waters became solid
 in the middle of the sea.

⁹"The enemy bragged,
 'I'll chase them and catch them.
I'll take all their riches.
 I'll take all I want.
I'll pull out my sword,
 and my hand will destroy them.'
¹⁰But you blew on them with
   your breath
 and covered them with the sea.
They sank like lead
 in the powerful water.

¹¹"Are there any gods like you,
   Lord?
 No! There are no gods like you.
You are wonderfully holy.
You are amazingly powerful.
You do great miracles.^d
¹²You reached out with your
   right hand,
 and the earth swallowed our
   enemies.
¹³You keep your loving promise.
 You lead the people you have
   saved.
With your strength you will guide
   them
 to your holy land.

¹⁴"The other nations will hear
   this and tremble with fear.
 Terror will take hold of the
   Philistines.
¹⁵The leaders of the tribes^d of Edom
   will be very frightened.
 The powerful men of Moab will shake
   with fear.
The people of Canaan will lose all
   their courage.
¹⁶Those people will be filled with
   fear.

When they see your strength,
  they will be as still as a rock.
They will be still until your people
    pass by, Lord.
They will be still until the people
    you have bought from slavery
    pass by.
[17]You will lead your people and
    place them
  on your very own mountain.
Lord, that is the place that you made
    for yourself to live.
Lord, that is the temple that your
    hands have made.
[18]The Lord will rule forever!"

[19]The horses, chariot drivers and
chariots of the king of Egypt went into
the sea. And the Lord covered them
with water from the sea. But the Israelites walked through the sea on dry
land. [20]Then Aaron's sister Miriam, who
was a prophetess,[d] took a tambourine[d]
in her hand. All the women followed
her, playing tambourines and dancing.
[21]Miriam told them:

"Sing to the Lord
  because he is worthy of great
    honor.
He has thrown the horse and its rider
  into the sea."

The Bitter Water

[22]Moses led the people of Israel away
from the Red Sea.[d] The people went
into the Desert of Shur. They traveled
for three days in the desert but found
no water. [23]Then they came to Marah,
where there was water. But they could
not drink it because it was too bitter.
That is why the place was named
Marah.[n] [24]The people grumbled to
Moses. They asked, "What will we
drink?"

[25]Moses cried out to the Lord. So
the Lord showed him a tree. Moses
threw the tree into the water. And the
water became good to drink.

There the Lord gave the people a
rule and a law to live by. There he also
tested their loyalty to him. [26]He said,

"You must obey the Lord, your God.
You must do what the Lord said is
right. You must obey all his laws and
keep his rules. If you do these things,
I will not give you any of the sicknesses
I gave the Egyptians. I am the Lord. I
am the Lord who heals you."

[27]Then the people traveled to Elim.
At Elim there were 12 springs of water
and 70 palm trees. So the people
camped there near the water.

The People Demand Food

16 Then the whole Israelite community left Elim. They came to
the Desert of Sin. This place was
between Elim and Sinai. They came to
this place on the fifteenth day of the
second month after they had left
Egypt. [2]Then the whole Israelite community grumbled to Moses and Aaron
in the desert. [3]The Israelites said to
them, "It would have been better if the
Lord had killed us in the land of Egypt.
There we had meat to eat. We had all
the food we wanted. But you have
brought us into this desert. You will
starve us to death here."

[4]Then the Lord said to Moses, "I will
cause food to fall like rain from the sky.
This food will be for all of you. Every
day the people must go out and gather
what they need for that day. I will do
this to see if the people will do what I
teach them. [5]On the sixth day of each
week, they are to gather twice as much
as they gather on other days. Then they
are to prepare it."

[6]So Moses and Aaron said to all the
Israelites: "This evening you will know
that the Lord is the one who brought
you out of Egypt. [7]Tomorrow morning
you will see the greatness of the Lord.
He has heard you grumble against him.
We are nothing. You are not grumbling
against us, but against the Lord." [8]And
Moses said, "Each evening the Lord
will give you meat to eat. And every
morning he will give you all the bread
you want. He will do this because he
has heard you grumble against him.

---

[n]**Marah**   This name means "bitter."

You are not grumbling against Aaron and me. You are grumbling against the Lord."

⁹Then Moses said to Aaron, "Speak to the whole community of the Israelites. Say to them, 'Meet together in front of the Lord because he has heard your grumblings.'"

¹⁰So Aaron spoke to the whole community of the Israelites. While he was speaking, they looked toward the desert. There the greatness of the Lord appeared in a cloud.

¹¹The Lord said to Moses, ¹²"I have heard the grumblings of the people of Israel. So tell them, 'At twilight you will eat meat. And every morning you will eat all the bread you want. Then you will know I am the Lord, your God.'"

¹³That evening, quail came and covered the camp. And in the morning dew lay around the camp. ¹⁴When the dew was gone, thin flakes like frost were on the desert ground. ¹⁵When the Israelites saw it, they asked each other, "What is that?" They asked this question because they did not know what it was.

So Moses told them, "This is the bread the Lord has given you to eat. ¹⁶The Lord has commanded, 'Each one of you must gather what he needs. Gather about two quarts for every person in your family.'"

¹⁷So the people of Israel did this. Some people gathered much, and some gathered little. ¹⁸Then they measured it. The person who gathered more did not have too much. The person who gathered less did not have too little. Each person gathered just as much as he needed.

¹⁹Moses said to them, "Don't keep any of it to eat the next day." ²⁰But some of the people did not listen to Moses. They kept part of it to eat the next morning. But it became full of worms and began to stink. So Moses was angry with these people.

²¹Every morning each person gathered as much food as he needed. But when the sun became hot, it melted away.

²²On the sixth day the people gathered twice as much food. They gathered four quarts for every person. So all the leaders of the community came and told this to Moses. ²³Moses said to them, "This is what the Lord commanded. Tomorrow is the Sabbath,ᵈ the Lord's holy day of rest. Bake what you want to bake, and boil what you want to boil today. But save the rest of the food until tomorrow morning."

²⁴So the people saved it until the next morning, as Moses had commanded. And none of it began to stink or have worms in it. ²⁵Moses told the people, "Eat the food you gathered yesterday. Today is a Sabbath, the Lord's day of rest. So you will not find any out in the field today. ²⁶You should gather the food for six days. But the seventh day is a Sabbath day. On that day there will not be any food on the ground."

²⁷On the seventh day some of the people went out to gather food, but they couldn't find any. ²⁸Then the Lord said to Moses, "How long will all you people refuse to obey my commands and teachings? ²⁹Look, the Lord has made the Sabbath a day of rest for all of you. So on the sixth day he will give you enough food for two days. But on the Sabbath each of you must stay where you are. Do not leave your house." ³⁰So the people rested on the Sabbath.

³¹The people of Israel called the food manna.ᵈ The manna was like small white seeds. It tasted like wafers made with honey.

³²Then Moses said, "The Lord said, 'Save two quarts of this food for your descendants.ᵈ Then they can see the food that I gave you to eat. I did this in the desert when I brought you out of Egypt.'"

³³Moses told Aaron, "Take a jar and fill it with two quarts of manna. And save this manna for your descendants."

³⁴So Aaron did what the Lord had commanded Moses. Aaron put the jar of manna in front of the Boxᵈ of the Agreement. He did this so it could be kept. ³⁵The Israelites ate manna for 40

Whit's Wisdom: Complaining and Asking • Exodus 17

Traveling can be a lot of fun, don't you think? Odyssey is a wonderful place, but every year, people who live here take vacations. They enjoy going to new places and seeing strange sights. We're also glad that so many people visit Odyssey. A trip can certainly be a great adventure! But not always.

Have your parents ever heard your voice from the back seat ask, "Are we there yet?" When you are tired of sitting, or very thirsty, or you think your family may have gotten lost again, do you sometimes complain? When things don't work out, do you pout?

Now I can just hear some of my young friends saying, "But Mr. Whittaker, our car gets too hot, and sometimes it feels like we'll *never* get there!"

Well, kids, you're not the first people to complain on a long, hard trip. God's people had to travel from Egypt to their new land by walking through a desert. Along the sandy pathway there were no water fountains or fast-food restaurants. Sometimes there didn't seem to be any water at all. And do you know what the Israelites did? They complained. They even got angry. Read Exodus 17:1-7 to find out what happened.

There's a big difference between complaining and asking. Did the people of Israel ever *ask* or *tell* God they were thirsty? By complaining right away, they showed they didn't trust God to help them and that they weren't thankful for all that God had already done for them.

Sometimes we treat God just like the Israelites did a long time ago. We complain before we even ask for his help. We also do this with each other. Don't you think traveling together would be much more fun if the whole family decided: On this trip, nobody will complain! What do you think would happen if you asked nicely the next time you were thirsty or tired?

Related passages: Exodus 14:10, 11; Philippians 2:14-16.

Teacher/Parent Hint: Go on a complaint hunt with the children. Ask them to think of typical things children say when they are complaining. Make a list. Afterwards, challenge them to come up with a positive way to express each of the feelings behind the complaints. Role play a traveling family and have everyone complain until it becomes silly.

---

years. They ate it until they came to the land where they settled. They ate manna until they came to the edge of the land of Canaan. [36]The measure they used for the manna was two quarts. It was one-tenth of an ephah."

Water from a Rock

17 The whole Israelite community left the Desert of Sin. They traveled from place to place as the Lord commanded. They camped at Rephidim.

"ephah An ephah was a measure that equaled 20 quarts.

But there was no water there for the people to drink. [2]So they quarreled with Moses. They said, "Give us water to drink."

But Moses said to them, "Why do you quarrel with me? Why are you testing the Lord?"

[3]But the people were very thirsty for water. So they grumbled against Moses. They said, "Why did you bring us out of Egypt? Was it to kill us, our children and our farm animals with thirst?"

[4]So Moses cried to the Lord, "What can I do with these people? They are almost ready to kill me with stones."

[5]The Lord said to Moses, "Go ahead of the people of Israel. And take some of the older leaders of Israel with you. Carry with you the walking stick that you used to strike the Nile River. Now go! [6]I will stand in front of you on a rock at Mount Sinai. Hit that rock with the stick, and water will come out of it. Then the people can drink." Moses did these things as the older leaders of Israel watched. [7]Moses named that place Massah[n] because the Israelites tested the Lord. They asked, "Is the Lord with us or not?" He also named it Meribah[n] because they quarreled.

The Amalekites Fight Israel

[8]At Rephidim the Amalekites came and fought the Israelites. [9]So Moses said to Joshua, "Choose some men and go and fight the Amalekites. Tomorrow I will stand on the top of the hill. I will hold the stick God gave me to carry."

[10]Joshua obeyed Moses and went to fight the Amalekites. At the same time Moses, Aaron and Hur went to the top of the hill. [11]As long as Moses held his hands up, the Israelites would win the fight. But when Moses put his hands down, the Amalekites would win. [12]Later, Moses' arms became tired. So the men put a large rock under Moses, and he sat on it. Then Aaron and Hur held up Moses' hands. Aaron was on one side of Moses, and Hur was on the other side. They held his hands up like this until the sun went down. [13]So Joshua defeated the Amalekites in this battle.

[14]Then the Lord said to Moses, "Write about this battle in a book so people will remember. And be sure to tell Joshua. Tell him because I will completely destroy the Amalekites from the earth."

[15]Then Moses built an altar. He named it The Lord is my Banner. [16]Moses said, "I lifted my hands toward the Lord's throne. The Lord will fight against the Amalekites forever."

Jethro Visits Moses

18 Jethro, Moses' father-in-law, was the priest of Midian. He heard about everything that God had done for Moses and his people, the Israelites. Jethro heard how the Lord had led the Israelites out of Egypt. [2]Moses had sent his wife Zipporah to Jethro, his father-in-law. [3]Moses had also sent his two sons. The first son was named Gershom.[n] When he was born, Moses said, "I am a stranger in a foreign country." [4]The other son was named Eliezer.[n] When he was born, Moses said, "The God of my father is my help. He saved me from the king of Egypt."

[5]So Jethro, Moses' father-in-law, went to Moses. Moses was camped in the desert near Sinai, the mountain of God. Moses' wife and his two sons came with Jethro. [6]Jethro had sent a message ahead to Moses. He said, "I am Jethro, your father-in-law. I am coming to you with your wife and her two sons."

[7]So Moses went out to meet his father-in-law. Moses bowed down and then kissed him. The two men asked about each other's health. Then they went into Moses' tent. [8]Moses told his

[n]**Massah**   This name sounds like the Hebrew word for "testing."
[n]**Meribah**   This name sounds like the Hebrew word for "quarreled."
[n]**Gershom**   This name sounds like the Hebrew word for "a stranger there."
[n]**Eliezer**   This name sounds like the Hebrew word for "my help."

father-in-law everything the Lord had done to the king and the Egyptians. The Lord had done these things to help Israel. Moses told about all the problems they had faced along the way. And Moses told him how the Lord had saved them.

⁹Jethro was very happy when he heard all the good things the Lord had done for Israel. He was happy because the Lord had saved them from the Egyptians. ¹⁰Jethro said, "Praise the Lord. He has saved all of you from the Egyptians and their king. He has saved the people from the power of the Egyptians. ¹¹Now I know the Lord is greater than all gods. He did this to those who looked down on Israel."

¹²Then Jethro, Moses' father-in-law, gave a whole burnt offering and other sacrifices to God. Aaron and all the older leaders of Israel came to Moses' father-in-law. They ate the holy meal together before God.

¹³The next day Moses solved disagreements among the people. So the people stood around Moses from morning until night. ¹⁴Moses' father-in-law saw all that Moses was doing for the people. He asked, "What is all this you are doing for the people? Why are you the only one to solve disagreements? All the people are standing around you from morning until night!"

¹⁵Then Moses said to his father-in-law, "It is because the people come to me for God's help in solving their disagreements. ¹⁶When people have a disagreement, they come to me. I decide who is right. And I tell them God's laws and teachings."

¹⁷Moses' father-in-law said to him, "You are not doing this right. ¹⁸You and the people who come to you will get too tired. This is too much work for you. You can't do it by yourself. ¹⁹Now listen to me. I will give you some advice. I want God to be with you. You must talk to God for the people. You must tell him about their disagreements. ²⁰You should tell them the laws and teachings. Tell them the right way to live and what they should do. ²¹But choose some capable men from among the people. Choose men who respect God and who can be trusted. They will not change their decisions for money. Make these men officers over groups of 1,000, 100, 50 and 10 people. ²²Let these officers solve the disagreements among the people all the time. They can bring the hard cases to you. But they can decide the simple cases themselves.

Words to Know: Old Testament

TENT • EXODUS 18:7

In Bible times, not everyone lived in towns or even in houses. Shepherds and nomads (people who did not settle in one place but always moved around) lived in **tents**. Their tents looked much like tents today, but they were larger and were made of thick cloth such as goat or camel skin. This cloth helped the people to keep dry in rainy weather and cool on the hot days. The tents were large enough to be divided into rooms by hanging cloths. Animal skin rugs usually covered the ground to make a floor. Would you like to live in an interesting home like that?

To read about some important leaders in the Bible, fly to page 110.

That will make it easier for you. These men will share the work with you. 23Do this if it is what God commands. Then you will be able to do your job. And all the people will go home with their disagreements solved."

24So Moses listened to his father-in-law and did everything he said. 25He chose capable men from all the Israelites. He made them leaders over the people. They were officers over groups of 1,000, 100, 50 and 10 people. 26These officers solved disagreements among the people all the time. They brought the hard cases to Moses. But they decided the simple cases themselves.

27Then Moses let his father-in-law leave. And Jethro went back to his own home.

Israel at Sinai

19 Exactly three months after the Israelites had left Egypt, they reached the Desert of Sinai. 2They had left Rephidim and had come to the Desert of Sinai. The Israelites camped in the desert in front of Mount Sinai. 3Then Moses went up on the mountain to God. The Lord called to him from the mountain. The Lord said, "Say this to the family of Jacob. And tell this to the people of Israel: 4'Every one of you has seen what I did to the people of Egypt. You saw how I carried you out of Egypt. I did it as an eagle carries her young on her wings. And I brought you here to me. 5So now obey me and keep my agreement. Do this, and you will be my own possession, chosen from all nations. Even though the whole earth is mine, 6you will be my kingdom of priests. You will be a nation that belongs to me alone.' You must tell the Israelites these words."

7So Moses went down and called the older leaders of the people together. He told them all the words the Lord had commanded him to say. 8And all the people answered together, "We will do everything he has said." Then Moses took their answer back to the Lord.

9And the Lord said to Moses, "I will come to you in a thick cloud. I will speak to you. The people will hear me talking to you. I will do this so the people will always trust you." Then Moses told the Lord what the people had said.

10The Lord said to Moses, "Go to the people and have them spend today and tomorrow preparing themselves. They must wash their clothes 11and be ready by the day after tomorrow. On that day I, the Lord, will come down on Mount Sinai. And all the people will see me. 12But you must set a limit around the mountain. The people are not to cross it. Tell the people not to go up on the mountain. Tell them not to touch the foot of it. Anyone who touches the mountain must be put to death. 13He must be put to death with stones or shot with arrows. No one is allowed to touch him. Whether it is a person or an animal, he will not live. But the trumpet will make a long blast. Only then may the people go up on the mountain."

14So Moses went down from the mountain to the people. He made them prepare themselves for service to God. And the people washed their clothes. 15Then Moses said to the people, "Be ready in three days. Do not have sexual relations during this time."

16It was the morning of the third day. There was thunder and lightning with a thick cloud on the mountain. And there was a very loud blast from a trumpet. All the people in the camp were frightened. 17Then Moses led the people out of the camp to meet God. They stood at the foot of the mountain. 18Mount Sinai was covered with smoke. This happened because the Lord came down on it in fire. The smoke rose from the mountain like smoke from a furnace. And the whole mountain shook wildly. 19The sound from the trumpet became louder. Then Moses spoke, and the voice of God answered him.

20So the Lord came down on the top of Mount Sinai. Then he called Moses to come up to the top of the mountain.

So Moses went up. 21The Lord said to Moses, "Go down and warn the people. They must not force their way through to see me. If they do, many of them will die. 22Even the priests, who may come near me, must first prepare themselves. If they don't, I, the Lord, will punish them."

23Moses told the Lord, "The people cannot come up Mount Sinai. You yourself told us to set a limit around the mountain. We made it holy."

24The Lord said to him, "Go down and bring Aaron with you. But don't allow the priests or the people to force their way through. They must not come up to the Lord. If they do, I will punish them."

25So Moses went down to the people and told them these things.

The Ten Commandments

20 Then God spoke all these words:

2"I am the Lord your God. I brought you out of the land of Egypt where you were slaves.

3"You must not have any other gods except me.

4"You must not make for yourselves any idols. Don't make something that looks like anything in the sky above or on the earth below or in the water below the land. 5You must not worship or serve any idol. This is because I, the Lord your God, am a jealous God. A person may sin against me and hate me. I will punish his children, even his grandchildren and great-grandchildren. 6But I will be very kind to thousands who love me and obey my commands.

7"You must not use the name of the Lord your God thoughtlessly. The Lord will punish anyone who is guilty and misuses his name.

8"Remember to keep the Sabbath*d* as a holy day. 9You may work and get everything done during six days each week. 10But the seventh day is a day of rest to honor the Lord your God. On that day no one may do any work: not you, your son or daughter, or your men or women slaves. Neither your animals nor the foreigners living in your cities may work. 11The reason is that in six days the Lord made everything. He made the sky, earth, sea and everything in them. And on the seventh day, he rested. So the Lord blessed the Sabbath day and made it holy.

12"Honor your father and your mother. Then you will live a long time in the land. The Lord your God is going to give you this land.

13"You must not murder anyone.

14"You must not be guilty of adultery.*d*

15"You must not steal.

16"You must not tell lies about your neighbor in court.

17"You must not want to take your neighbor's house. You must not want his wife or his men or women slaves. You must not want his ox or his donkey. You must not want to take anything that belongs to your neighbor."

18The people heard the thunder and the trumpet. They saw the lightning on the mountain and smoke rising from the mountain. They shook with fear and stood far away from the mountain. 19Then they said to Moses, "Speak to us yourself. Then we will listen. But don't let God speak to us, or we will die."

20Then Moses said to the people, "Don't be afraid. God has come to test you. He wants you to respect him so you will not sin."

21The people stood far away from the mountain while Moses went near the dark cloud where God was. 22Then the Lord told Moses to say these things to the Israelites: "You yourselves have seen that I talked with you from heaven. 23You must not use gold or silver to make idols for yourselves. You must not worship these false gods in addition to me.

24"Make an altar of dirt for me. Offer your whole burnt offerings and fellowship offerings on this altar as a sacrifice to me. Use your sheep and your cattle to do this. Worship me in every place that I choose. Then I will come and bless you. 25You may use stones to make an altar for me. But don't use stones that you have made smooth with tools. You must not use any tools on the stones. If you do, you make them unsuitable for use in worship. 26And you must not make steps leading up to my altar. If you go up steps, people will be able to see under your clothes."

Laws for Living

21 Then God said to Moses, "These are the laws for living that you will give to the Israelites:

2"If you buy a Hebrew slave, he will serve you for six years. In the seventh year you are to set him free. And he will have to pay nothing. 3He might not be married when he becomes your slave. Then he must leave without a wife. The man might be married when he becomes your slave. Then he may take his wife with him. 4The slave's master might give him a wife, and she might give birth to sons or daughters. Then the woman and her children will belong to the master. When the slave is set free, only he may leave.

5"But the slave might say, 'I love my master, my wife and my children. I don't want to go free.' 6Then the slave's master will take him to God. The master will take him to a door or doorframe. And he will punch a hole through the slave's ear using a sharp tool. Then the slave will serve that master all his life.

7"A man might sell his daughter as a slave. There are rules for setting her free. They are different from the rules for setting the men slaves free. 8Maybe the master wanted to marry her but then decided he was not pleased with her. He must let one of her close relatives buy her back. He has no right to sell her to foreigners. This is because he has treated her unfairly. 9The man who bought her might promise to let the woman marry his son. Then he must treat her as a daughter. 10The man who bought her might marry another woman. Then he must not keep his slave woman from having food or clothing or sexual relations. 11If he does not

give her these three things, she may go free. She owes him no money.

Injuries

12"Anyone who hits a person and kills him must be put to death. 13But if a person kills someone accidentally, God allowed that to happen. So the person must go to a place I will choose. 14A person might plan and murder another person on purpose. Put him to death, even if he has run to my altar for safety.

15"Anyone who hits his father or his mother must be put to death.

16"A person might kidnap someone. Then he either sells him as a slave or still has him when he is caught. That person must be put to death.

17"Anyone who says cruel things to his father or mother must be put to death.

18"Two men might argue. And one might hit the other with a rock or with his fist. The hurt man might not be killed. But he might have to stay in bed. 19Later he might be able to get up. And he might be able to walk around outside with his walking stick. Then the one who hit him is not to be punished. But he must pay the injured man for the loss of his time. And he must support the injured man until he is completely healed.

20"A man might beat his male or female slave with a stick. And the slave might die on the spot. Then the owner must be punished. 21But the slave might get well after a day or two. Then that owner will not be punished since the slave belongs to him.

22"Two men might be fighting, and they might hit a pregnant woman so that the baby comes out. But there is no further injury. Then the man who caused the injury must pay money. He must pay what the woman's husband says and the court allows. 23But if there is further injury, then the punishment is that life must be paid for life, 24eye for eye, tooth for tooth. It is also hand for hand, foot for foot, 25burn for burn, wound for wound and bruise for bruise.

26"A man might hit his male or female slave in the eye. And the eye might be blinded. Then the man is to free the slave to pay for the eye. 27A master might knock out a tooth of his male or female slave. Then the man is to free the slave to pay for the tooth.

28"A man's bull might kill a man or woman. Then you must kill that bull with stones. You should not eat the bull. But the owner of the bull is not guilty. 29But the bull might have hurt people in the past. The owner might have been warned. If he did not keep it in a pen and then it kills a man or woman, the bull must be killed with stones. And the owner must also be put to death. 30But the family of the dead man might accept money. Then the man who owned the bull may buy back his life. But he must pay whatever is demanded. 31Use this same law if the bull kills a person's son or daughter. 32But the bull might kill a male or female slave. Then the owner must pay the master the price for a new slave. That is 12 ounces of silver. And the bull must also be killed with stones.

33"A man might take the cover off a pit. Or he might dig one and not cover it. Another man's ox or donkey might come and fall into it. 34The owner of the pit must pay the owner of the animal for his loss. The dead animal will belong to the one who pays.

35"One man's bull might kill another man's bull. Then they must sell the bull that is alive. Both men get half of the money. And both men will also get half of the bull that was killed. 36A man's bull might have hurt other animals in the past. But the owner might not have kept it in a pen. Then that owner must pay bull for bull. And the dead animal is his.

Property Laws

22 A man might steal a bull or a sheep and kill or sell it. Then he must pay back five bulls for the one bull he stole. Or he must pay back four sheep for the one sheep he stole.

2-4"The robber who is caught must pay back what he stole. He might own nothing. Then he must be sold as a slave to pay for what he stole. The stolen animal might be found alive with the robber. Then he must give the owner two animals for every animal he stole. He must pay, whether he stole a bull, donkey or sheep.

"A thief might be killed while breaking into a house at night. Then the one who killed him is not guilty of murder. But if this happens during the day, he is guilty of murder.

5"A person might let his farm animal graze in his field or vineyard. And it might wander into another person's field or vineyard. Then the owner of the animal must pay back the loss. The payment must come from the best of his crop.

6"A man might start a fire that spreads through the thornbushes to his neighbor's field. The fire might burn his neighbor's growing grain or grain that has been stacked. Or it might burn his whole field. Then the person who started the fire must pay for what was burned.

7"A man might give his neighbor money or other things to keep for him. Those things might be stolen from the neighbor's house. And the thief might be caught. Then he must pay back twice as much as he stole. 8But maybe the thief is never found. Then the owner of the house must make a promise before God. He must promise that he has not stolen his neighbor's things.

9"Two men might disagree about who owns something. It might be an ox, donkey, sheep or clothing. Or it might be something else that is lost. Each says, 'This is mine.' Each man must bring his case to God. God's judges will decide who is guilty. Then he must pay the other man twice as much as the thing is worth.

10"A man might ask his neighbor to keep his animal for him. This animal might be a donkey, ox, sheep or some other animal. And that animal might die, be hurt or be taken away. And no one saw what happened. ¹¹That neighbor must promise before the Lord that he did not harm or kill the other man's animal. The owner of the animal must accept his promise made before God. The neighbor does not have to pay the owner for the animal. ¹²But the animal might have been stolen from the neighbor. Then he must pay the owner for it. ¹³Wild animals might have killed the animal. Then the neighbor must bring the body as proof. He will not have to pay for the animal that was killed.

¹⁴"A man might borrow an animal from his neighbor. It might get hurt or die while the owner is not there. Then the one who borrowed it must pay the owner for the animal. ¹⁵The owner might be with the animal. Then the one who borrowed it does not have to pay. If the animal was rented, the rental price covers the loss.

Laws and Relationships

¹⁶"A man might find a woman who is not pledged to be married. She has never had sexual relations with a man. He might trick her into having sexual relations with him. Then he must give her family the payment to marry her. And she will be his wife. ¹⁷But her father might refuse to allow his daughter to marry him. Then the man must still give the payment for a bride. He must pay the usual charge for a woman who has never had sexual relations.

¹⁸"Put to death any woman who does evil magic.

¹⁹"Put to death anyone who has sexual relations with an animal.

²⁰"Destroy completely any person who makes a sacrifice to any god except the Lord.

²¹"Do not cheat or hurt a foreigner. Remember that you were foreigners in the land of Egypt.

²²"Do not cheat a widow or an orphan. ²³If you do, they will cry out to me for help. I certainly will hear their cry. ²⁴And I will be very angry and kill you in war. Then your wives will become widows, and your children will become orphans.

²⁵"You might lend money to one of my people who is poor. Then do not treat him as a moneylender would. Charge him nothing for using your money. ²⁶Your neighbor might give you his coat as a promise. He is promising to pay you the money he owes you. But you must give it back to him by sunset. ²⁷That coat is the only cover to keep his body warm. He has nothing else to sleep in. If he cries out to me for help, I will listen because I am merciful.

²⁸"You must not speak against God. You must not curse a leader of your people.

²⁹"Do not hold back your offering from the first of your harvest. Give me the first grain that you harvest. Give me the first wine that you make. Also, you must give me your firstborn*ᵈ* sons. ³⁰You must do the same with your bulls and your sheep. Let the firstborn males stay with their mothers for seven days. On the eighth day you must give them to me.

³¹"You are to be my holy people. You must not eat the meat of any animal that has been killed by wild animals. Instead, give it to the dogs.

Laws About Fairness

23 "You must not tell lies. You might be a witness in court. Don't help a bad person by telling lies.

²"You must not do wrong just because everyone else is doing it. You might be a witness in court. Then you must not ruin a fair trial. You must not tell lies just because everyone else is. ³A poor man might be in court. You must not take his side just because he is poor.

⁴"You might see your enemy's ox or donkey wandering away. Then you must return it to him. ⁵You might see that your enemy's donkey has fallen because its load is too heavy. You must not leave it there. You must help your enemy get the donkey back on its feet. ⁶"You must not be unfair to a poor

man when he is in court. [7]You must not lie when you accuse someone in court. Never allow an innocent or honest person to be put to death as punishment. This is because I will not treat guilty people as if they were innocent.

[8]"You must not accept money from a person who wants you to lie in court. Such money will not let you see what is right. Such money makes good people tell lies.

[9]"You must not mistreat a foreigner. You know how it feels to be a foreigner. You were foreigners in Egypt.

Laws for the Sabbath

[10]"For six years you are to plant and harvest crops on your land. [11]Then during the seventh year, do not plow or plant your land. If any food grows there, allow the poor people to have it. And let the wild animals eat what is left. You should do the same with your vineyards and your orchards of olive trees.

[12]"You should work six days a week. But on the seventh day you must rest. This lets your ox and your donkey rest. This also lets the slave born in your house and the foreigner be refreshed.

[13]"Be sure to do all that I have said to you. You must not even say the names of other gods. The names of those gods must not come out of your mouth.

Three Yearly Feasts

[14]"Three times each year you must hold a feast to honor me. [15]You must celebrate the Feast[d] of Unleavened Bread. Do this in the way I commanded you. For seven days you must eat bread that is made without yeast. You must do this at the set time during the month of Abib.[d] This is the month when you came out of Egypt. No one is to come to worship me without bringing an offering.

[16]"You must celebrate the Feast[d] of Harvest. Offer to God the first things you harvest. These are from the crops you planted in your fields.

"You must celebrate the Feast[d] of Tents in the fall. Do this when you gather all the crops from your fields.

[17]"So three times during every year all men must come to worship the Lord God.

[18]"You must not offer animal blood along with anything that has yeast in it.

"You must not save any of the fat from the sacrifice for the next day.

[19]"You must bring the best of the firstfruits[d] of your land. Bring them to the Holy Tent[n] of the Lord your God.

"You must not cook a young goat in its mother's milk.

Promises

[20]"I am sending an angel ahead of you. He will protect you as you travel. He will lead you to the place I have prepared. [21]Pay attention to the angel and obey him. Do not turn against him. He will not forgive such turning against him because my power is in him. [22]You must listen carefully to all he says. You must do everything that I tell you. If you do this, I will be an enemy to your enemies. I will fight all who fight against you. [23]My angel will go ahead of you. He will take you into the land of these people: the Amorites, Hittites, Perizzites, Canaanites, Hivites and Jebusites. And I will destroy them.

[24]"You must not bow down to their gods or worship those gods. You must not live the way those people live. You must destroy their idols. And you must break into pieces stone pillars they use in worship. [25]You must worship the Lord your God. If you do, I will bless your bread and your water. I will take away sickness from you. [26]None of your women will have her baby die before it is born. All women will have children. I will allow you to live long lives.

[27]"I will make your enemies afraid of me. I will confuse any people you fight against. I will make all your enemies run away from you. [28]I will send something like hornets ahead of you. They will force the Hivites, Canaanites and Hittites out of your way. [29]But I will not

---

[n]**Holy Tent** Literally, "house of the Lord your God." See Exodus 25:9.

force all those people out in only one year. If I did, the land would become a desert. Then the wild animals would become too many for you. ³⁰Instead, I will force those people out of your land very slowly. I will wait until there are enough of you to take over the land.

³¹"I will give you the land from the Gulf of Aqaba to the Mediterranean Sea. And I will give you the land between the desert and the Euphrates River. I will give you power over the people who now live in the land. You will force them out ahead of you. ³²You must not make an agreement with those people or with their gods. ³³You must not let them live in your land. If they live there, they will make you sin against me. If you worship their gods, you will be like someone caught in a trap."

God and Israel Make Their Agreement

24 The Lord told Moses, "You, Aaron, Nadab, Abihu and 70 of the older leaders of Israel must come up to me. You must worship me from a distance. ²Then Moses alone must come near me. The other men must not come near. And the rest of the people must not come up the mountain with Moses."

³So Moses told the people all the Lord's words and laws for living. Then all of the people answered out loud together. They said, "We will do all the things that the Lord has said." ⁴So Moses wrote down all the words of the Lord. And he got up early the next morning. He built an altar near the bottom of the mountain. He set up 12 stones, 1 stone for each of the 12 tribes^d of Israel. ⁵Then Moses sent young Israelite men to offer whole burnt offerings. They also sacrificed young bulls as fellowship offerings to the Lord. ⁶Moses took the blood of these animals. He put half of it in bowls. And he sprinkled the other half of the blood on the altar. ⁷Then Moses took the book with the agreement written in it. He read it

so the people could hear him. And they said, "We will do everything that the Lord has said. We will obey."

⁸Then Moses took the blood from the bowls. He sprinkled it on the people. He said, "This is the blood that begins the agreement. This is the agreement which the Lord has made with you about all these things."

⁹Moses, Aaron, Nadab, Abihu and 70 of the older leaders of Israel went up the mountain. ¹⁰They saw the God of Israel. Under his feet was a surface. It looked as if it were paved with blue sapphire stones. And it was as clear as the sky! ¹¹These leaders of the Israelites saw God. But God did not destroy them. Then they ate and drank together.

Moses Gets the Stone Tablets

¹²The Lord said to Moses, "Come up the mountain to me. Wait there, and I will give you two stone tablets. On these are the teachings and the commandments. I have written these to teach the people."

¹³So Moses and his helper Joshua set out. Moses went up Sinai, the mountain of God. ¹⁴Moses said to the older leaders, "Wait here for us until we come back to you. Aaron and Hur are with you. Anyone who has a disagreement with others can take it to them."

Moses Meets with God

¹⁵When Moses went up on the mountain, the cloud covered it. ¹⁶The greatness of the Lord came down on Mount Sinai. The cloud covered the mountain for six days. On the seventh day the Lord called to Moses from inside the cloud. ¹⁷The Israelites could see the greatness of the Lord. It looked like a fire burning on top of the mountain. ¹⁸Then Moses went into the cloud and went higher up the mountain. Moses was on the mountain for 40 days and 40 nights.

Gifts for the Lord

25 The Lord said to Moses, ²"Tell the Israelites to bring me gifts.

Receive for me the gifts each man wants to give. ³These are the gifts that you should receive from them: gold, silver, bronze, ⁴blue, purple and red thread, and fine linen. Receive cloth made of goat hair. ⁵Receive the male sheep skins that are dyed red. Receive fine leather, acacia wood ⁶and olive oil to burn in the lamps. And receive spices for sweet-smelling incense*d* and the special olive oil poured on a person's head to make him a priest. ⁷Also accept onyx stones and other jewels to be put on the holy vest*d* and the chest covering.

⁸"The people must build a holy place for me. Then I can live among them. ⁹Build this Holy Tent*d* and everything in it by the plan I will show you.

The Box of the Agreement

¹⁰"Use acacia wood and build a Holy Box.*d* It must be 45 inches long, 27 inches wide and 27 inches high. ¹¹Cover the Holy Box inside and out with pure gold. And put a gold strip all around it. ¹²Make four gold rings for the Holy Box. Attach the gold rings to its four feet, two rings on each side. ¹³Then make poles from acacia wood and cover them with gold. ¹⁴Put the poles through the rings on the sides of the Box. Use these poles to carry the Holy Box. ¹⁵These poles must always stay in the rings of the Holy Box. Do not take the poles out. ¹⁶Then put the two flat stones in the Holy Box. I will give you these stones on which the commands are written.

¹⁷"Then make a lid of pure gold for the Holy Box. This lid is the mercy seat.*d* Make it 45 inches long and 27 inches wide. ¹⁸Then hammer gold to make two creatures with wings. Put one on each end of the lid. ¹⁹Put one creature with wings on one end of the lid. And put the other creature with wings on the other end. Attach the creatures with wings to the lid so that they will all be one piece. ²⁰The creatures' wings should be spread out over the lid. The creatures are to face each other across the lid. ²¹Put this lid on top of the Holy Box. Also put in this Holy Box the agreement which I will make with you. ²²I will meet with you there, above the lid between the two creatures with wings. These are on the Box of the Agreement. There I will give you all my commands for the Israelites.

The Table

²³"Make a table out of acacia wood. It must be 36 inches long, 18 inches wide and 27 inches high. ²⁴Cover it with pure gold. Put a gold strip around it. ²⁵Then make a frame three inches high that stands up all around the edge. Put a gold strip around the frame. ²⁶Then make four gold rings. Attach them to the four corners of the table where the four legs are. ²⁷Put the rings close to the frame around the top of the table. These rings will hold the poles for carrying the table. ²⁸Make the poles out of acacia wood and cover them with gold. Carry the table with these poles. ²⁹Make the plates and bowls for the table out of pure gold. Make the jars and cups out of pure gold. They will be used for pouring out the drink offerings. ³⁰On this table put the bread that shows you are in my presence. It must always be there in front of me.

The Lampstand

³¹"Hammer pure gold to make a lampstand. Its base, stand, flower-like cups, buds and petals must all be joined together in one piece. ³²The lampstand must have three branches on one side and three branches on the other. ³³Each branch must have three cups shaped like almond flowers on it. Each cup must have a bud and a petal. ³⁴And there must be four more cups made like almond flowers on the lampstand itself. These cups must also have buds and petals. ³⁵Put a bud under each pair of branches that goes out from the lampstand. ³⁶The branches, buds and lampstand must be one piece of pure, hammered gold.

³⁷"Then make seven small oil lamps and put them on the lampstand. They

will give light to the area in front of the lampstand. [38]The wick trimmers and trays must be made of pure gold. [39]Use 75 pounds of pure gold to make the lampstand and everything with it. [40]Be very careful to make them by the plan I showed you on the mountain.

The Holy Tent

26 "Make the Holy Tent[d] with ten pieces of cloth. These pieces must be made of fine linen and blue, purple and red thread. Have a skilled craftsman sew designs of creatures with wings on the pieces of cloth. [2]Make each piece the same size. Each piece should be 42 feet long and 6 feet wide. [3]Sew five pieces of cloth together for one set. Sew the other pieces together for the second set. [4]Make loops of blue cloth down the edge of the end piece of each set. [5]Make 50 loops on the end piece of the first set. And make 50 loops on the end piece of the second set. These loops must be opposite each other. [6]And make 50 gold hooks. Use these to join the two sets of cloth. This will make the Holy Tent one piece.

[7]"Then make another tent that will cover the Holy Tent. Make this tent of 11 pieces of cloth made from goat hair. [8]All these pieces of cloth must be the same size. They must be 45 feet long and 6 feet wide. [9]Sew five of the pieces together into one set. Then sew the other six pieces together into the second set. Fold the sixth piece double over the front of the Tent. [10]Make 50 loops down the edge of the end piece of one set. Do the same for the end piece of the other set. [11]Then make 50 bronze hooks. Put these in the loops to join the two sets of cloth. This will make the covering one piece. [12]Let the extra half piece of cloth hang over the back of the Holy Tent. [13]There will be 18 inches hanging over the sides of the Holy Tent. This will protect the Tent. [14]Make two more coverings for the Holy Tent. One should be made from male sheep skins colored red. The outer covering should be from fine leather.

[15]"Use acacia wood to make upright frames for the Holy Tent. [16]Each frame must be 15 feet long and 27 inches wide. [17]Every frame must be made the same way. There must be two pegs side by side in each frame. [18]Make 20 frames for the south side of the Holy Tent. [19]Each frame must have 2 silver bases to go under it. A peg fits into each silver base. You must make 40 silver bases for the frames. [20]Make 20 more frames for the north side of the Holy Tent. [21]Make 40 silver bases for them. Make 2 bases for each frame. [22]You must make 6 frames for the rear or west end of the Holy Tent. [23]Make 2 frames for each corner at the rear. [24]The 2 frames at each corner are to be joined together. Hold them together from bottom to top with a metal ring. Both corner frames must be made this way. [25]So there will be a total of 8 frames at the rear of the Tent. And there will be 16 silver bases—2 bases under each frame.

[26]"Make crossbars of acacia wood to connect the upright frames of the Holy Tent. Make five crossbars to hold the frames together on one side. [27]Also make five crossbars to hold the frames together on the other side. And make crossbars to hold the frames together on the west end, at the rear. [28]The middle crossbar is to be set halfway up the frames. It is to run along the entire length of each side and rear. [29]Make gold rings on the sides of the frames. Pass the crossbars through the rings. Cover the frames and the crossbars with gold. [30]Set up the Holy Tent by the plan shown to you on the mountain.

[31]"Make a curtain of fine linen and blue, purple and red thread. Have a skilled craftsman sew designs of creatures with wings on the curtain. [32]Hang the curtain by gold hooks on four posts of acacia wood. Cover these posts with gold and set them in four silver bases. [33]Hang the curtain from the hooks in the roof. Put the Holy Box[d] containing the two flat stones behind the curtain. This curtain will separate the Holy

Place from the Most Holy Place. ³⁴Put the lid on the Holy Box in the Most Holy Place.

³⁵"Outside the curtain, put the table on the north side of the Holy Tent. And put the lampstand on the south side of the Holy Tent. This will be across from the table.

The Entrance of the Holy Tent

³⁶"Then make a curtain for the entrance of the Tent.^d Make it with fine linen and blue, purple and red thread. Someone who can sew well is to sew designs on it. ³⁷Make five posts of acacia wood covered with gold. Make five gold hooks on which to hang the curtain from the posts. And make five bronze bases for the five posts.

The Altar

27 "Make an altar for burnt offerings out of acacia wood. Make it 4½ feet high. It should be square: 7½ feet long and 7½ feet wide. ²Make each of the four corners of the altar stick out like a horn. The corners with their horns must be all one piece. Then cover the whole altar with bronze.

³"Use bronze to make all the tools and dishes that will be used on the altar. Make pots to remove the ashes. Make shovels, bowls for sprinkling blood, meat forks and pans for carrying the burning wood.

⁴"Make a large, bronze screen to hold the burning wood. And put a bronze ring at each of the four corners of the screen. ⁵Put the screen inside the altar, under its rim, halfway up from the bottom.

⁶"Make poles of acacia wood for the altar. And cover them with bronze. ⁷Put the poles through the rings on both sides of the altar to carry it. ⁸Make the altar out of boards and leave the inside hollow. Make it as you were shown on the mountain.

The Courtyard of the Holy Tent

⁹"Make a wall of curtains to form a courtyard around the Holy Tent.^d The south side should have a wall of fine linen curtains 150 feet long. ¹⁰Hang the curtain with silver hooks and bands. Put these on 20 bronze posts on 20 bronze bases. ¹¹The north side must also be 150 feet long. Hang its curtains on silver hooks and bands. Put these on 20 bronze posts on 20 bronze bases.

¹²"The west end of the courtyard must have a wall of curtains 75 feet long. It must have 10 posts and 10 bases on that wall. ¹³The east end of the courtyard must also be 75 feet long. ¹⁴On one side of the entry, there is to be a wall of curtains. It is to be 22½ feet long. It is to be held up by 3 posts on 3 bases. ¹⁵On the other side of the entry, there is to be a wall of curtains. It is to be 22½ feet long. It is to be held up by 3 posts on 3 bases.

¹⁶"The entry to the courtyard is to be a curtain 30 feet wide. It is to be made of fine linen with blue, purple and red thread. Someone who can sew well is to sew designs on it. It is to be held up by 4 posts on 4 bases. ¹⁷All the posts around the courtyard must have silver bands and hooks and bronze bases. ¹⁸The courtyard must be 150 feet long and 75 feet wide. The wall of curtains around it should be 7½ feet high. They must be made of fine linen. The bases in which the posts are set must be bronze. ¹⁹All the things used in the Holy Tent must be made of bronze. And all the tent pegs for the Holy Tent and the wall around the courtyard must be made of bronze.

Oil for the Lamp

²⁰"Command the people of Israel to bring you pure olive oil. It is to be made from pressed olives. This is to keep the lamps on the lampstand burning. ²¹Aaron and his sons must keep the lamps burning before the Lord from evening till morning. This will be in the Meeting Tent.^d It is outside the curtain which is in front of the Holy Box.^d The Israelites and their descendants^d must obey this rule from now on.

Clothes for the Priests

28 "Tell your brother Aaron to come to you. His sons Nadab, Abihu, Eleazar and Ithamar must come with him. Separate them from the other Israelites. These men must serve as priests. ²Make holy clothes for your brother Aaron to give him honor and beauty. ³Speak to all the people to whom I have given the ability to make clothes. Tell these skilled craftsmen to make the clothes for Aaron. Use these clothes to make him belong to me. Then he may serve me as a priest. ⁴These are the clothes they must

holy vest. ⁷At each top corner of this holy vest there will be a pair of shoulder straps. These are to be tied together over each shoulder.

⁸"The craftsmen will very carefully weave a belt on the holy vest. Make the belt with gold and blue, purple and red thread, and fine linen.

⁹"Take two onyx stones. Write the name of the 12 sons of Israel on these jewels. ¹⁰Write 6 names on one stone and 6 names on the other stone. Write the names in order, from the oldest son to the youngest. ¹¹Carve the names of the sons of Israel on these stones. Do this the same way a person carves words and designs on the seals.*d* Put gold around the stones to hold them on the

Words to Know: Old Testament
PRIEST • EXODUS 28:1

As you read some of the history books in the Old Testament, you will read about men who were **priests**. God's people, the nation of Israel, were supposed to worship God alone. God chose some men to become priests to help the people worship and learn about God. The priests in the Old Testament worked in the Holy Tent (and later in the temple). They offered the daily sacrifices that God wanted the people to do so they could repent of their sins. The priest taught the people God's laws and talked to God for the people.

After Jesus died on the cross and rose again, he went back to heaven to be a priest for us. We can talk to Jesus anytime we want. We don't have to be afraid!

To read about some real troublemakers, fly to page 117.

make: a chest covering, a holy vest,*d* an outer robe, a woven inner robe, a turban and a cloth belt. The craftsmen must make these holy clothes. They are for your brother Aaron and his sons. Then Aaron and his sons may serve me as priests. ⁵The craftsmen must use gold and blue, purple and red thread, and fine linen.

The Holy Vest

⁶"Use gold and blue, purple and red thread, and fine linen to make the holy vest.*d* The craftsmen are to make this

holy vest. ¹²Put the two stones on the two straps of the holy vest. These stones are reminders of the 12 sons of Israel. Aaron is to wear their names on his shoulders. They are before the Lord as reminders of the sons of Israel. ¹³Make two gold pieces to hold the stones. ¹⁴Then make two chains of pure gold. Twist them together like a rope. Attach the chains to the two gold pieces that hold the stones.

The Chest Covering

¹⁵"Make a chest covering to help in

making decisions. The craftsmen should make it as they made the holy vest.[d] They must use gold and blue, purple and red thread, and fine linen. [16]The chest covering must be square. It should be nine inches long and nine inches wide. Fold it double to make a pocket. [17]Put four rows of beautiful gems on the chest covering. The first row of jewels must have a ruby, topaz and yellow quartz. [18]The second row must have turquoise, a sapphire and an emerald. [19]The third row must have a jacinth, an agate and an amethyst. [20]The fourth row must have a chrysolite, an onyx and a jasper. Put gold around these jewels to attach them to the chest covering. [21]There must be 12 jewels on the chest covering. That is 1 jewel for each of the names of the sons of Israel. Carve the name of one of the 12 tribes[d] on each of the stones. Carve them as you would carve a seal.[d]

[22]"Make chains of pure gold for the chest covering. Twist them together like rope. [23]Make two gold rings. Put them on the two upper corners of the chest covering. [24]Attach the two gold chains to the two rings. These are at the upper corners of the chest covering. [25]Attach the other ends of the two chains to the two gold pieces on the shoulder straps. This will tie the chains to the shoulder straps in the front of the holy vest.

[26]"Make two more gold rings. Put them at the two lower corners of the chest covering. Put them on the inside edge of the chest covering next to the holy vest. [27]Make two more gold rings. Attach them to the bottom of the shoulder straps in the front of the holy vest. Put the gold rings close to the seam above the woven belt of the holy vest. [28]Join the rings of the chest covering to the rings of the holy vest with blue ribbon. This will connect it to the woven belt. In this way the chest covering will not swing out from the holy vest.

[29]"When Aaron enters the Holy Place, he will wear the names of the sons of Israel over his heart. These names are on the chest covering that helps in making decisions. This will be a continual reminder before the Lord. [30]And put the Urim and Thummim[d] inside the chest covering. These things will be on Aaron's heart when he goes before the Lord. They will help in making decisions for the Israelites. So Aaron will always carry them with him when he is before the Lord.

[31]"Make the outer robe to be worn under the holy vest, using only blue cloth. [32]Make a hole in the center for Aaron's head. And there must be a woven collar around the hole so it will not tear. [33]Make balls like pomegranates[d] of blue, purple and red thread. Hang these pomegranate balls around the bottom of the outer robe. And hang gold bells between them. [34]So all around the bottom of the outer robe there should be a gold bell and a pomegranate ball, a gold bell and a pomegranate ball. [35]Aaron must wear this robe when he serves as priest. The ringing of the bells will be heard. They will ring when he enters and leaves the Holy Place before the Lord. This way Aaron will not be killed.

[36]"Make a strip of pure gold. Carve these words on the gold strip as you would carve on a seal:[d] 'Holy to the Lord.' [37]Use blue ribbon to tie a strip of gold to the turban. Put it on the front of the turban. [38]Aaron must wear this on his forehead. In this way, he will be blamed if anything is wrong with the gifts of the Israelites. Aaron must always wear this on his head so the Lord will accept the gifts of the people.

[39]"Make the woven inner robe of fine linen. Make the turban of fine linen, also. Make the cloth belt with designs sewn on it. [40]Also make woven inner robes, cloth belts and headbands for Aaron's sons. This will give them honor and beauty. [41]Put these clothes on your brother Aaron and his sons. Then pour olive oil on their heads to appoint them as priests. Make them belong to me so they may serve me as priests.

[42]"Make for them linen underclothes

to cover them from the waist to the upper parts of the legs. ⁴³Aaron and his sons must wear these underclothes when they enter the Meeting Tent.ᵈ And they must wear these clothes anytime they come near the altar to serve as priests in the Holy Place. If they do not wear these clothes, they will be

⁵Take the clothes. Dress Aaron in the inner robe and the outer robe of the holy vest.ᵈ Then put on him the holy vest and the chest covering. Then tie the holy vest on him with its skillfully woven belt. ⁶Put the turban on his head. Put the holy crown, the strip of gold, on the turban. ⁷Take the special olive oil and pour it on his head to make him a priest.

Jobs in the Bible
WEAVER • EXODUS 28:31-39

Making cloth for clothing was the job of a weaver. In Bible times, there were no fabric stores for buying material or department stores for buying clothes. Most people had only one or two sets of clothing because cloth was expensive and took a long time to make. Weavers had to take the fibers from wool, cotton, flax, or goat's hair and make them into yarn or thread. Then this yarn or thread was woven on a big frame called a loom. If you look closely at your clothes, you'll see threads going back and forth through the material. Today big machines can do that, but in Bible times, a person had to put each of those threads in place!

Would you like to have the job of a weaver?

To read about skilled people who made beautiful objects, fly to page 116.

guilty of wrong. And they will be killed. This will be a law that will last from now on for Aaron and all his descendants.ᵈ

Appointing the Priests

29 "This is what you must do to appoint Aaron and his sons. Then they may serve me as priests. Take one young bull and two male sheep that have nothing wrong with them. ²Use fine wheat flour without yeast to make bread and cakes mixed with olive oil. Also use wheat flour without yeast to make wafers brushed with olive oil. ³Put these in one basket. Bring them in the basket along with the bull and two male sheep. ⁴Bring Aaron and his sons to the entrance of the Meeting Tent.ᵈ Then wash them with water.

⁸"Then bring his sons and put the inner robes on them. ⁹Put the headbands on their heads. Then tie cloth belts around their waists. Aaron and his descendantsᵈ will be priests in Israel. This is by a rule that will continue from now on. This is how you will appoint Aaron and his sons as priests.

¹⁰"Bring the bull to the front of the Meeting Tent. Aaron and his sons must put their hands on the bull's head. ¹¹Then kill the bull before the Lord at the entrance to the Meeting Tent. ¹²Take some of the bull's blood and go to the altar. Use your finger to put some blood on the corners of the altar. Pour the blood that is left at the bottom of the altar. ¹³Then take all the fat that covers the inner organs. Take the best

part of the liver, and take both kidneys and the fat around them. Burn these on the altar. [14]Take the bull's meat, skin and intestines. Burn these things outside the camp. This is an offering to take away sin.

[15]"Take one of the male sheep. Have Aaron and his sons put their hands on its head. [16]Then kill that male sheep. Take its blood and sprinkle it on all four sides of the altar. [17]Then cut the male sheep into pieces. Wash its inner organs and its legs. Put them with its head and its other pieces. [18]Burn the whole male sheep on the altar. It is a burnt offering made by fire to the Lord. Its smell is pleasing to the Lord.

[19]"Take the other male sheep. Have Aaron and his sons put their hands on its head. [20]Kill that male sheep and take some of its blood. Put it on the bottom of the right ears of Aaron and his sons. Also put it on the thumbs of their right hands. And put it on the big toes of their right feet. Then sprinkle the rest of the blood against all four sides of the altar. [21]Then take some of the blood from the altar. Mix it with the special oil used in appointing priests. Sprinkle this on Aaron and his clothes. And sprinkle this on his sons and their clothes. This will show that Aaron and his sons and their clothes are given to my service.

[22]"Then take the fat from the male sheep. Take the fat tail and the fat that covers the inner organs. Take the best part of the liver. Take both kidneys and the fat around them and the right thigh. This is the male sheep to be used in appointing priests.

[23]"Then take the basket of bread that you made without yeast. This is the basket you put before the Lord. From it take a loaf of bread, a cake made with olive oil and a wafer. [24]Put these in the hands of Aaron and his sons. Tell them to present these things in their hands before the Lord. This will be an offering presented to the Lord. [25]Then take them from their hands. Burn them on the altar with the whole burnt offering. This is an offering made by fire to the

Lord. Its smell is pleasing to the Lord. [26]Then take the breast of the male sheep used to appoint Aaron as priest. Present the breast of the male sheep before the Lord. It is an offering presented to the Lord. This part of the animal will be your share. [27]Then give to the service of the Lord the parts of the male sheep used to appoint them as priests. They belong to Aaron and his sons. They are the breast and the right thigh. These were presented to the Lord. [28]This is to be the regular share which the Israelites will always give to Aaron and his sons. This is the gift the Israelites must give to the Lord from their fellowship offerings.

[29]"The holy clothes made for Aaron will belong to his descendants. They must wear these clothes when they are appointed as priests. [30]Aaron's son will become high priest after Aaron. He will come to the Meeting Tent to serve in the Holy Place. He is to wear these clothes for seven days.

[31]"Take the male sheep used to appoint priests. Boil its meat in a place made holy for serving me. [32]Then Aaron and his sons must eat the meat of the male sheep. They must do that at the entrance of the Meeting Tent. And they must also eat the bread that is in the basket. [33]These offerings were used to remove their sins when they were made priests so they would belong to God. Now they should eat these offerings. But no one else is to eat these things because they are holy. [34]If any of the meat from that male sheep or any of the bread is left the next morning, it must be burned. It shall not be eaten because it is holy.

[35]"Do all these things that I commanded you to do to Aaron and his sons. You are to spend seven days appointing them. [36]Each day for seven days you are to offer a bull. This will remove the sins of Aaron and his sons so they will be given for service to the Lord. Make the altar ready for service to the Lord. Pour oil on it to make it holy. [37]Spend seven days making the

altar ready for service to God and making it holy. Then the altar will become very holy. Anything that touches it must be holy.

The Daily Sacrifices

38 "Every day from now on, offer on the altar two lambs that are one year old. 39 Offer one lamb in the morning and the other in the evening. 40 In the morning, when you offer the first lamb, offer also two quarts of fine flour. Mix it with one quart of oil from pressed olives. Pour out a quart of wine as a drink offering. 41 Offer the second lamb in the evening. Also offer the same grain offering and drink offering as you did in the morning. This is an offering by fire to the Lord. And its smell is pleasing to the Lord.

42 "You must burn these things as an offering to the Lord every day. Do this at the entrance of the Meeting Tent*d* before the Lord from now on. When you make the offering, I, the Lord, will meet you there and speak to you. 43 I will meet with the people of Israel there. And that place will be holy because of my greatness.

44 "So I will make the Meeting Tent and the altar holy. And I will make Aaron and his sons holy so they may serve me as priests. 45 I will live with the people of Israel. I will be their God. 46 And they will know that I am the Lord their God. They will know that I am the one who led them out of Egypt. I did this so I could live with them. I am the Lord their God.

The Altar for Burning Incense

30 "Make an altar out of acacia wood for burning incense.*d* 2 Make it square—18 inches long and 18 inches wide. It must be 36 inches high. Make the corners stick out like horns. These must be one piece with the altar. 3 Cover its top, its sides and its corners with pure gold. And put a gold strip all around the altar. 4 Make two gold rings beneath the gold strip on opposite sides of the altar. Slide poles through these gold rings to carry the altar. 5 Make the poles from acacia wood and cover them with gold. 6 Put the altar of incense in front of the curtain. This curtain is in front of the Box*d* of the Agreement. Put the altar in front of the lid that covers that Holy Box. There I will meet with you.

7 "Aaron must burn sweet-smelling incense on the altar every morning. He will do this when he comes to take care of the oil lamps. 8 He must burn incense again in the evening when he lights the lamps. So incense will burn before the Lord every day from now on. 9 Do not use this altar for offering any other incense or burnt offering. Do not use this altar to offer any kind of grain offering or drink offering. 10 Once a year Aaron must make the altar ready for service to God. He will do it by putting blood on its corners. This is blood of the animal offered to remove sins. He is to do this once a year from now on. This altar belongs completely to God's service."

The Tax for the Meeting Tent

11 The Lord said to Moses, 12 "Count the people of Israel. At that time every person must pay to buy back his life from the Lord. Then no terrible things will happen to the people when you number them. 13 Every person who is counted must pay one-fifth of an ounce of silver. This is set by the Holy Place measure, which weighs two-fifths of an ounce. This amount is a gift to the Lord. 14 Every person who is counted and is 20 years old or older must give this amount to the Lord. 15 A rich person must not give more than one-fifth of an ounce. And a poor person must not give less than one-fifth of an ounce. You are paying this to the Lord to buy back your lives. 16 Gather from the people of Israel this money paid to buy back their lives. Spend it to buy things for the service in the Meeting Tent.*d* This payment will remind the Lord that the Israelites' lives have been bought back."

"DYLAN and the SUPER SLAMMER 5000!"

Dylan learns that people are more important than things
A story based on Matthew 6:19-21

So, IN THE DAYS THAT FOLLOW, WITH HIS GOAL FIRM IN MIND, DYLAN SETS TO WORK ....

BASEBALL CARDS 'N' COMICS 4 SALE

ONE NIGHT....

I'M *WORRIED* ABOUT DYLAN. I THINK HE'S FOCUSING *TOO MUCH* ON THAT HOOP.

Oh, HE'LL BE ALL RIGHT. HE JUST NEEDS TO WORK THROUGH THIS FOR HIMSELF.

A FEW DAYS LATER....

WHY THE LONG FACE, SON?

JOHNNY'S DAD GOT HIM A SUPER-SLAMMER. THEY'RE SETTING IT UP RIGHT NOW!

THAT'S NICE FOR JOHNNY, ISN'T IT, DYLAN? YOU SHOULD BE *HAPPY* FOR HIM!

HAPPY?! I'M MISERABLE! WE'VE GOT A PERFECT PLACE TO PUT ONE RIGHT HERE! PLEASE, DAD, LET'S GO GET ONE!

I'M SORRY, SON, I TOLD YOU WE DON'T HAVE THE MONEY RIGHT NOW. HOW IS YOUR SAVING COMING ALONG? YOU CERTAINLY SEEM TO BE WORKING HARD AND SAVING EVERY PENNY!

I AM, DAD, BUT IT'S GOING TO TAKE *FOREVER!*

JUST STICK WITH IT, SON! IT WON'T TAKE AS LONG AS YOU THINK.

SURE, DAD.

THE NEXT DAY, DYLAN AND JESSIE ARE PASSING BY THE CHURCH'S ELEMENTARY SCHOOL...

HEY! WHAT HAPPENED TO YOUR BASKETBALL HOOP?

SOME BIG KIDS WERE HANGING ON THE RIM AND *BROKE* IT.

THAT'S TOO BAD... ...YOU SHOULD GET A HOOP LIKE THE ONE *I'M* GETTING. THEY COULDN'T BREAK THE SUPER-SLAMMER!

THAT EVENING AT FAMILY DEVOTIONS...

AS IT SAYS IN MATTHEW 6:19-21: DON'T STORE TREASURES FOR YOURSELVES HERE ON EARTH. MOTHS AND RUST WILL DESTROY TREASURES HERE ON EARTH. AND THIEVES CAN BREAK INTO YOUR HOUSE AND STEAL THE THINGS YOU HAVE."

...Uh... DYLAN?

OOPS! SORRY, DAD. I WASN'T PAYING ATTENTION. GO AHEAD, I'M LISTENING NOW!

AS I WAS SAYING...

"...SO STORE YOUR TREASURE IN *HEAVEN*. THE TREASURES IN HEAVEN CANNOT BE DESTROYED BY MOTHS OR RUST. AND THIEVES CANNOT BREAK IN AND STEAL THAT TREASURE. YOUR HEART WILL BE WHERE YOUR TREASURE IS."

DAD, IS THAT WHAT I'VE BEEN DOING WITH THIS HOOP I WANT?

Dylan realizes

...that his heart has been wrapped up in treasures on earth—the basketball goal! He has been thinking that having the goal would make him happy. But would it?

These verses could help Dylan understand what possessions are really for:

Luke 16:9
Proverbs 19:17
Luke 16:11
1 Timothy 6:18-19

FINALLY, DYLAN HAS SAVED ENOUGH MONEY, AND HIS DAD DRIVES HIM TO BUY THE HOOP...

CONGRATULATIONS, DYLAN! YOU WORKED HARD AND SAVED WELL FOR THIS HOOP!

THANKS, DAD, BUT YOU KNOW, I THINK I'D LIKE TO GIVE THE HOOP TO THE *SCHOOL*.

THAT'S A GREAT IDEA, DYLAN!

I'LL CALL THE PRINCIPAL TO MAKE SURE IT'S ALL RIGHT, THEN WE'LL SET IT UP.

SO...

I THINK THESE KIDS WILL REALLY ENJOY THE NEW HOOP, DON'T YOU, DAD?

YES, DYLAN, I'M SURE THEY WILL.

I'M REALLY *PROUD* OF YOU, SON. YOU CERTAINLY HAVE LEARNED A LOT ABOUT WHAT MONEY AND POSSESSIONS ARE REALLY FOR!

THESE KIDS WILL USE IT MORE THAN I WOULD HAVE. BESIDES, THE TEACHER SAID I COULD COME PLAY ON IT ANY TIME!

C'MON, DYLAN!

SLAM DUNK!

WAY TO GO, SAMMY!

THANKS FOR THE HOOP, DYLAN!

YOU'RE THE GREATEST!

YOU KNOW, DAD, IT'S *TRUE* WHAT THE BIBLE SAYS... IT *CAN* BE MORE FUN TO GIVE THINGS AWAY THAN IT IS TO HAVE THEM GIVEN TO YOU!

The End

The Bronze Bowl

[17]The Lord said to Moses, [18]"Make a bronze bowl for washing. Build it on a bronze stand. Put the bowl and stand between the Meeting Tent[d] and the altar. Put water in the bowl. [19]Aaron and his sons must wash their hands and feet with the water from this bowl. [20]Each time, before they enter the Meeting Tent, they must wash with water. This way they will not die. They approach the altar to serve as priests. They offer a sacrifice to the Lord by fire. [21]Each time they do this, they must wash their hands and their feet so they will not die. This is a rule which Aaron and his descendants[d] are to keep from now on."

Oil for Appointing

[22]Then the Lord said to Moses, [23]"Take the finest spices: 12 pounds of liquid myrrh,[d] half that amount (that is, 6 pounds) of sweet-smelling cinnamon, 6 pounds of sweet-smelling cane [24]and 12 pounds of cassia.[d] Weigh all these by the Holy Place measure. Also take 4 quarts of olive oil. [25]Mix all these things like a perfume to make a holy olive oil. This special oil must be put on people and things. Do this to make them ready for service to God. [26]Put this oil on the Meeting Tent[d] and the Holy Box[d] with my laws in it. [27]Put this oil on the table and all its dishes. And put this oil on the lampstand and all its tools. Put the oil on the incense[d] altar. [28]Also, put the oil on the altar for burning offerings and all its tools. Put this oil on the bowl and the stand under the bowl. Put oil on all these things to prepare them for service to God. [29]You will give these things for service to God. They will be very holy. Anything that touches these things must also be holy.

[30]"Put the oil on Aaron and his sons to make them priests. Give them for service to me. Then they may serve me as priests. [31]Tell the Israelites, 'This is to be my holy olive oil from now on. It is to be put on people and things to make them ready for service to God.

[32]Do not pour it on the bodies of ordinary people. Do not make perfume the same way you make this oil. It is holy, and you must treat it as holy. [33]Someone might make perfume like it. Or he might put it on someone who is not a priest. Then that person must be separated from his people.'"

Incense

[34]Then the Lord said to Moses, "Take these sweet-smelling spices: resin, onycha, galbanum and pure frankincense.[d] Be sure that you have equal amounts of each. [35]You must make incense[d] as a man who makes perfume would do. Add salt to it to keep it pure and holy. [36]Beat some of the incense into a fine powder. Put some of it in front of the Holy Box[d] of the Agreement in the Meeting Tent.[d] There I will meet with you. You must use this incense powder only for its very special purpose. [37]Do not make incense for yourselves the same way you make this incense. Treat it as holy to the Lord. [38]Whoever makes incense like this to use as perfume must be separated from his people."

Bezalel and Oholiab

31 Then the Lord said to Moses, [2]"See, I have chosen Bezalel son of Uri from the tribe[d] of Judah. Uri was the son of Hur. [3]I have filled Bezalel with the Spirit[d] of God. I have given him the skill, ability and knowledge to do all kinds of work. [4]He is able to design pieces to be made from gold, silver and bronze. [5]He is able to cut jewels and put them in metal. And he can carve wood. Bezalel can do all kinds of work. [6]I have also chosen Oholiab son of Ahisamach from the tribe of Dan. Oholiab will work with Bezalel. I have given skills to all skilled craftsmen. They will be able to make all these things I have commanded you: [7]the Meeting Tent,[d] the Box[d] of the Agreement, the lid that covers the Holy Box and everything in the Tent. [8]This includes the table and everything on it, the pure gold lampstand and everything with it and the altar of incense.[d]

⁹It also includes the altar for burnt offerings and everything used with it, the bowl and the stand under it. ¹⁰They will make the woven clothes and the holy clothes for Aaron and the clothes for his sons to wear when they serve as priests. ¹¹They will also make the special olive oil used in appointing people and things to the service of the Lord, and the sweet-smelling incense for the Holy Place.

"These workers will make all these things just as I have commanded you."

The Day of Rest

¹²Then the Lord said to Moses, ¹³"Tell the Israelites, 'You must keep the rules about my Sabbaths.ᵈ This is because they will be a sign between you and me from now on. In this way you will know that I, the Lord, am making you holy. ¹⁴"Make the Sabbath a holy day. If anyone treats the Sabbath like any other day, that person must be put to death. Anyone who works on the Sabbath day must be separated from his people. ¹⁵There are six days for working. But the seventh day is a day of rest. It is a day holy for the Lord.

Anyone who works during the Sabbath day must be put to death. ¹⁶The Israelites must remember the Sabbath day. It is an agreement between them and me that will continue from now on. ¹⁷The Sabbath day will be a sign between me and the Israelites forever. This is because in six days I, the Lord, made the sky and the earth. And on the seventh day I did not work. I rested.'"

¹⁸So the Lord finished speaking to Moses on Mount Sinai. Then the Lord gave him the two stone tablets with the agreement written on them. The finger of God wrote the commands on the stones.

The People Make a Gold Calf

32 The people saw that a long time had passed. And Moses had not come down from the mountain. So they gathered around Aaron. They said to him, "Moses led us out of Egypt. But we don't know what has happened to him. So make us gods who will lead us."

²Aaron said to the people, "Take off the gold earrings that your wives, sons and daughters are wearing. Bring them to me." ³So all the people took their gold earrings and brought them to Aaron. ⁴Aaron took the gold from the people. Then he melted it and made a

Jobs in the Bible

CRAFTSMAN • EXODUS 31:1-11

God used all kinds of skilled craftsmen to build his tabernacle. Two men in particular, Bezalel and Oholiab, were in charge of all the craftsmen. They made sure that the instructions were followed so that everything turned out just as God planned. There were craftsmen who designed pieces for the temple in gold, silver, and bronze. Others cut jewels and set them in metal. There were metalworkers and woodworkers, embroiders who made beautiful designs on the curtains of the tabernacle, and weavers who made the clothes for the priests.

God gives all people their abilities, and he is glad when we use our skills well and honor him.

To read about people who loved animals, fly to page 345.

statue of a calf. He finished it with a tool. Then the people said, "Israel! These are your gods who brought you out of the land of Egypt!"

⁵Aaron saw all this, and he built an altar before the calf. Then he made an announcement. He said, "Tomorrow there will be a special feast to honor the Lord." ⁶The people got up early the next morning. They offered whole burnt offerings and fellowship offerings. First the people sat down to eat and drink. Then they got up and sinned sexually.

⁷And the Lord said to Moses, "Go down from this mountain. Your people, the people you brought out of the land of Egypt, have done a terrible sin. ⁸They have quickly turned away from the things I commanded them to do. They have made for themselves a calf of melted gold. They have worshiped that calf and offered sacrifices to it. The people have said, 'Israel, these are your gods who brought you out of Egypt.'"

⁹The Lord said to Moses, "I have seen these people. I know that they are very stubborn people. ¹⁰So now do not stop me. I am so angry with them that I am going to destroy them. Then I will make you and your descendantsᵈ a great nation."

¹¹But Moses begged the Lord his God. Moses said, "Lord, don't let your anger destroy your people. You brought these people out of Egypt with your great power and strength. ¹²Don't let the people of Egypt say, 'The Lord brought the Israelites out of Egypt. But he planned to kill them in the mountains and destroy them from the earth.' So stop being angry. Don't destroy your people. ¹³Remember the men who served you—Abraham, Isaac and Israel. You promised with an oath to them. You said, 'I will make your descendants as many as the stars in the sky. I will give your descendants all this land that I have promised them. It will be theirs forever.'" ¹⁴So the Lord changed his mind. He did not destroy the people as he had said he might.

¹⁵Then Moses went down the mountain. In his hands he had the two stone tablets with the agreement on them. The commands were written on both sides of each stone, front and back.

Words to Know: Old Testament
IDOL • EXODUS 32:1-6

An **idol** is something that people worship as a god instead of the real God. The Israelites always got into trouble with idols. The first time this happened was right after they left Egypt. Aaron was supposed to serve as their priest and teach them about God. Instead, he made an idol of a golden calf for the people to worship. The people wanted a god they could see like the Egyptian idols.

Later, when the Israelites entered the promised land, they copied their neighbors and worshiped idols. This made God very sad. We may not bow down to idols today, but we can let other things such as friends, sports, or grades take the place of God. We should always put God first in our lives.

To read about an important box, fly to page 125.

16God himself had made the stones. And God himself had written the commands on the stones.

17Then Joshua heard the noise of the people shouting. He said to Moses, "It sounds like war down in the camp."

18Moses answered:

"It is not an army's shout of victory.
It is not an army's cry of defeat.
It is the sound of singing that I
    hear."

19When Moses came close to the camp, he saw the gold calf and the dancing. He became very angry. He threw down the stone tablets which he was

always ready to do wrong. 23The people said to me, 'Moses led us out of Egypt. But we don't know what has happened to him. So make us gods who will lead us.' 24So I told the people, 'Take off your gold jewelry.' So they gave me the gold. I threw it into the fire and out came this calf!"

25Moses saw that the people were acting wildly. He saw that Aaron had let them get out of control. Their enemies would laugh at them. 26So Moses stood

Temptation
EXODUS 32:1-5, 21-26

Imagine you are on your way into church. Just before you enter the building, one of your friends says, "Hey—don't go in there and worship the Lord. We took a bunch of jewelry, melted it, and made a little statue of a pig. Let's go out back and worship it!" Would you do it?

Of course not! No one with any brains would do that. And yet in this passage we read about the people of Israel doing something like that. While Moses was away meeting with God, his brother Aaron and the people made a calf out of gold and then worshiped it instead of God. As you might expect, God was very angry with the people, and he punished them for what they had done.

You will probably never be tempted to worship a gold calf or pig. But anything you put in God's place becomes an idol. It could be something or someone you like a lot. Learn from Exodus 32: don't let *anything* come between you and the Lord.

To learn more about temptation, zoom to page 653.

carrying. He broke them at the bottom of the mountain. 20Then he took the calf that the people had made. He melted it in the fire. And he ground the gold until it became powder. He threw the powder into the water. And he forced the Israelites to drink that water.

21Moses said to Aaron, "What did these people do to you? Why did you cause them to do such a terrible sin?"

22Aaron answered, "Don't be angry, master. You know that these people are

at the entrance to the camp. He said, "Let anyone who wants to follow the Lord come to me." And all the people from the family of Levi gathered around Moses.

27Then Moses said to them, "The Lord, the God of Israel, says this: 'Every man must put on his sword and go through the camp from one end to the other. Each man must kill his brother, his friend and his neighbor.'" 28The people from the family of Levi obeyed

Moses. That day about 3,000 of the people of Israel died. [29]Then Moses said, "Today you have been given for service to the Lord. You were willing to kill your own sons and brothers. And God has blessed you for this."

"I've had a few of my experiments melt down, but nothing like this. Read about some people who disrespected God in Exodus 32:1-35."

[30]The next day Moses told the people, "You have done a terrible sin. But now I will go up to the Lord. Maybe I can do something so your sins will be removed. Then you will belong to God again." [31]So Moses went back to the Lord and said, "How terrible it is! These people have sinned horribly. They have made for themselves gods from gold. [32]Now, forgive them of this sin. If you will not, then erase my name. Erase it from the book in which you have written the names of your people."

[33]But the Lord told Moses, "I will erase from my book the names of the people who sin against me. [34]So now, go. Lead the people where I have told you. My angel will lead you. When the time comes to punish, I will punish them for their sin."

[35]So the Lord caused terrible things to happen to the people. He did this because of what they did with the calf Aaron had made.

33

Then the Lord said to Moses, "You and the people you brought out of Egypt must leave this place. Go to the land that I promised with an oath to give to Abraham, Isaac and Jacob. I said, 'I will give that land to your descendants.' [2]I will send an angel to lead you. And I will force these people out of the land: the Canaanites, Amorites, Hittites, Perizzites, Hivites and Jebusites. [3]Go up to the land where much food grows.

But I will not go with you. This is because I might destroy you on the way. You are such a stubborn people."

[4]The people heard this bad news, and they became very sad. None of them put on jewelry. [5]This was because the Lord had said to Moses, "Tell the Israelites, 'You are a stubborn people. If I were to go with you even for a moment, I would destroy you. So take off all your jewelry. Then I will decide what to do with you.'" [6]So the people of Israel took off their jewelry at Mount Sinai.

The Meeting Tent

[7]Moses used to take a tent and set it up a long way outside the camp. Moses called it the "Meeting Tent."[d] A person might want to ask the Lord about something. Then he would go to the Meeting Tent outside the camp. [8]Anytime Moses went out to the Tent, all the people would rise. They stood at the entrances of their tents and watched Moses until he entered the Meeting Tent. [9]When Moses went into the Tent, the pillar of cloud would always come down. It would stay at the entrance of the Tent while the Lord spoke with Moses. [10]The people saw the pillar of cloud at the entrance of the Tent. Then they stood and worshiped, each person at the entrance of his own tent.

[11]The Lord spoke to Moses face to face as a man speaks with his friend. Then Moses would return to the camp. But Moses' young helper, Joshua son of Nun, did not leave the Tent.

[12]Moses said to the Lord, "You have told me to lead these people. But you did not say whom you would send with me. You have said to me, 'I know you very well. I am pleased with you.' [13]If I have truly pleased you, show me your plans. Then I may know you and continue to please you. Remember that this nation is your people."

[14]The Lord answered, "I myself will go with you. And I will give you victory."

[15]Then Moses said to him, "If you yourself don't go with us, then don't

send us away from this place. [16]If you don't go with us, no one will know that you are pleased with me and your people. These people and I would be no different from any other people on earth."

[17]Then the Lord said to Moses, "I will do what you ask. This is because I know you very well, and I am pleased with you."

Moses and God's Greatness

[18]Then Moses said, "Now, please show me your greatness."

[19]The Lord answered, "I will cause all

hand, and you will see my back. But my face must not be seen."

Moses Gets New Stones

34 The Lord said to Moses, "Cut two more stone tablets like the first two. I will write the same words on them that were on the first two stones which you broke. [2]Be ready tomorrow morning. Then come up on Mount Sinai. Stand before me there on the top of the mountain. [3]No one may come with you. No one should even be seen

Friendships
EXODUS 33:7-11

Do you know who wants to be your best friend? God does! In fact, he is the best person to turn to when you need a friend. He is always there, waiting to listen to you.

Just like it is important for you to spend time with your friends and family, God wants you to spend time with him. Look at Moses' example. He thought that his relationship with God was so important that he often took the time to go talk to him. He talked to God face to face, just like you talk to your friends at church or school.

Even though we can't see God when we talk to him, he is still listening. When you talk to God, be honest. Tell him all about the good and bad things happening in your life. This is a great way to become better friends with him.

To find out what to do to be a good friend to others, zoom to page 156.

my goodness to pass in front of you. I will announce my name, the Lord, so you can hear it. I will show kindness to anyone I want to show kindness. I will show mercy to anyone I want to show mercy. [20]But you cannot see my face. No one can see me and stay alive.

[21]"There is a place near me where you may stand on a rock. [22]My greatness will pass that place. I will put you in a large crack in that rock. And I will cover you with my hand until I have passed by. [23]Then I will take away my

any place on the mountain. Not even the sheep or cattle may eat grass near that mountain."

[4]So Moses cut two stone tablets like the first ones. Then early the next morning he went up Mount Sinai. He did this just as the Lord had commanded him. Moses carried the two stone tablets with him. [5]Then the Lord came down in the cloud and stood there with Moses. And the Lord called out his name, the Lord.

[6]The Lord passed in front of Moses

and said, "I am the Lord. The Lord is a God who shows mercy and is kind. The Lord doesn't become angry quickly. The Lord has great love and faithfulness. [7]The Lord is kind to thousands of people. The Lord forgives people for wrong and sin and turning against him. But the Lord does not forget to punish guilty people. The Lord will punish not only the guilty people. He will also punish their children, their grandchildren, their great-grandchildren and their great-great-grandchildren."

[8]Then Moses quickly bowed to the ground and worshiped. [9]Moses said, "Lord, if you are pleased with me, please go with us. I know that these are stubborn people. But forgive our evil and our sin. Take us as your own people."

[10]Then the Lord said, "I am making this agreement with you. I will do miracles[d] in front of all your people. These things have never before been done for any other nation on earth. The people with you will see my work. I, the Lord, will do wonderful things for you. [11]Obey the things I command you today, and I will force your enemies to leave your land. I will force out the Amorites, Canaanites, Hittites, Perizzites, Hivites and Jebusites ahead of you. [12]Be careful. Don't make any agreement with the people who live in the land where you are going. It will bring you trouble. [13]But destroy their altars. Break their stone pillars. Cut down their Asherah[d] idols. [14]Don't worship any other god. This is because I, the Lord, the Jealous One, am a jealous God.

[15]"Be careful. Don't make any agreements with the people who live in that land. They will worship their false gods. And they will invite you to join them. Then you will join them, and you will eat their sacrifices. [16]You might choose some of their daughters as wives for your sons. Those daughters worship false gods. They might lead your sons to do the same thing.

[17]"Do not make gods of melted metal.

[18]"Celebrate the Feast[d] of Unleav-ened Bread. For seven days you must eat bread made without yeast as I commanded you. Do this during the month I have chosen, the month of Abib.[d] This is because in that month you came out of Egypt.

[19]"Every firstborn[d] cow or sheep that is born to each animal belongs to me. [20]You may buy back a donkey by paying for it with a lamb. But if you don't want to buy back a donkey, you must break its neck. You must buy back all your firstborn sons.

"No one is to come before me without a gift.

[21]"You must work for six days. But on the seventh day you must rest. You must do this even during the planting season and harvest season.

[22]"Celebrate the Feast[d] of Weeks when you gather the first grain of the wheat harvest. And celebrate the Feast[d] of Harvest in the fall.

[23]"Three times each year all your men must come before the Master, the Lord, the God of Israel. [24]I will force out nations ahead of you. I will expand the borders of your land. You will go before the Lord your God three times each year. And at that time no one will try to take your land from you.

[25]"Do not offer the blood of a sacrifice to me with anything containing yeast. And do not leave any of the sacrifice of the Feast[d] of Passover. It must not be left until the next morning.

[26]"Bring the best first crops that you harvest from your ground. Bring those things to the Tent[d] of the Lord your God.

"You must not cook a young goat in its mother's milk."

[27]Then the Lord said to Moses, "Write down these words. This is because with these words I have made an agreement with you and Israel."

[28]Moses stayed there with the Lord 40 days and 40 nights. During that time he did not eat food or drink water. And Moses wrote the words of the agreement—the Ten Commandments—on the stone tablets.

The Face of Moses Shines

²⁹Then Moses came down from Mount Sinai. In his hands he was carrying the two stone tablets of the agreement. But Moses did not know that his face was shining because he had talked with the Lord. ³⁰Aaron and all the people of Israel saw that Moses' face was shining. So they were afraid to go near him. ³¹But Moses called to them. So Aaron and all the leaders of the people returned to Moses. Moses talked with them. ³²After that, all the people of Israel came near him. And he gave them all the commands that the Lord had given him on Mount Sinai.

³³When Moses finished speaking to the people, he put a covering over his face. ³⁴Anytime Moses went before the Lord to speak with him, Moses took off the covering until he came out. Then Moses would come out and tell the people of Israel the things the Lord had commanded. ³⁵The Israelites would see that Moses' face was shining. So he would cover his face again. He did this until the next time he went in to speak with the Lord.

Rules About the Sabbath

35 Moses gathered all the Israelite community together. He said to them, "These are the things the Lord has commanded you to do. ²You are to work for six days. But the seventh day will be a holy day, a Sabbath[d] of rest to honor the Lord. Anyone who works on that day must be put to death. ³On the Sabbath day you must not light a fire in any of your houses."

⁴Moses said to all the Israelites, "This is what the Lord has commanded: ⁵From what you have, take an offering for the Lord. Let everyone who is willing bring this offering to the Lord: gold, silver, bronze, ⁶blue, purple and red thread, and fine linen, goat hair ⁷and male sheep skins, colored red. And they may bring fine leather and acacia wood. ⁸They may also bring olive oil for the lamps, spices for the special olive oil used for appointing priests and for the sweet-smelling incense.[d] ⁹And they may bring onyx stones and other jewels to be put on the holy vest[d] and chest covering of the priests.

Worship
EXODUS 35:1-3

Some of God's rules for Israel in the Old Testament may sound strange. Here in Exodus 35, for example, he told them not to build a fire in their homes on the Sabbath day. We may not understand why God didn't want them to do that, but we can understand the idea behind it: God wanted his people to treat the Sabbath day *differently* from other days. He wanted it to be their day of worship.

Not building a fire in your home on the Sabbath may not be a problem—unless you live someplace cold and snowy, and the electricity goes off! But other things may keep you from worshiping God the way he wants you to. Talk to your parents about some changes your family could make that would help you to treat the Sabbath like a day of worship.

To learn more about worship, zoom to page 138.

¹⁰"Let all the skilled workers come and make everything the Lord commanded: ¹¹the Holy Tent,ᵈ its outer tent and its covering, the hooks, frames, crossbars, posts and bases; ¹²the Boxᵈ of the Agreement, its poles, lid and the curtain in front of it; ¹³the table and its poles, all the things that go with the table and the bread that shows we are in God's presence; ¹⁴the lampstand for the light and all the things that go with it, the lamps and olive oil for the light; ¹⁵the altar of incense and its poles, the special oil and the sweet-smelling incense, the curtain for the entrance of the Meeting Tent; ¹⁶the altar of burnt offering and its bronze screen, its poles and all its tools, the bronze bowl and its base; ¹⁷the curtains around the courtyard, their posts and bases, and the curtain at the entry to the courtyard; ¹⁸the pegs of the Holy Tent and of the courtyard and their ropes; ¹⁹the special clothes that the priest will wear in the Holy Place. These are the holy clothes for Aaron the priest and his sons to wear when they serve as priests."

²⁰Then all the people of Israel went away from Moses. ²¹Everyone who wanted to give came and brought a gift to the Lord. These gifts were used for making the Meeting Tent, all the things in the Tent and the special clothes. ²²All the men and women who wanted to give brought gold jewelry of all kinds. They brought pins, earrings, rings and bracelets. They all presented their gold to the Lord. ²³Everyone who had blue, purple and red thread, and fine linen came and gave it to the Lord. Anyone who had goat hair or male sheep skins colored red or fine leather brought them to the Lord. ²⁴Everyone who could give silver or bronze brought that as a gift to the Lord. Everyone who had acacia wood to be used in the work brought it. ²⁵Every skilled woman used her hands to make the blue, purple and red thread and fine linen. And they brought what they had made. ²⁶All the women who were skilled and wanted to help made thread of the goat hair. ²⁷The leaders brought onyx stones and other jewels. These stones and jewels were put on the holy vest and chest covering for the priest. ²⁸They also brought spices and olive oil. These were used for the sweet-smelling incense, the special oil and the oil to burn in the lamps. ²⁹All the men and women of Israel who wanted to help brought gifts to the Lord. They were used for all the work the Lord had commanded Moses and the people to do.

³⁰Then Moses said to the people of Israel, "Look, the Lord has chosen Bezalel. He is the son of Uri the son of Hur, from the tribeᵈ of Judah. ³¹The Lord has filled Bezalel with the Spiritᵈ of God. The Lord has given Bezalel the skill, ability and knowledge to do all kinds of work. ³²He is able to design pieces to be made of gold, silver and bronze. ³³He is able to cut stones and jewels and put them in metal. Bezalel can carve wood and do all kinds of work. ³⁴The Lord has given Bezalel and Oholiab the ability to teach others. Oholiab is the son of Ahisamach from the tribe of Dan. ³⁵The Lord has given them the skill to do all kinds of work. They are able to cut designs in metal and stone. They can plan and sew designs in the fine linen with the blue, purple and red thread. And they are also able to weave things.

36 So Bezalel, Oholiab and every skilled person will do the work the Lord has commanded. The Lord gave these people the wisdom and understanding to do all the skilled work needed to build the Holy Tent."

²Then Moses called Bezalel, Oholiab and all the other skilled people to whom the Lord had given skills. And they came because they wanted to help with the work. ³They received from Moses everything the people of Israel had brought as gifts to build the Holy Tent. The people continued to bring gifts each morning because they wanted to. ⁴So all the skilled workers left the work they were doing on the Holy Tent. And they went to speak to Moses.

They said, [5]"The people are bringing more than we need to do the work the Lord commanded."

[6]Then Moses sent this command throughout the camp: "No man or woman should make anything else as a gift for the Holy Tent." So the people were kept from giving more. [7]What they had was already more than enough to do all the work.

The Holy Tent

[8]Then the skilled workers made the Holy Tent.[d] They made the ten pieces of blue, purple and red cloth. And they sewed designs of creatures with wings on the pieces. [9]Each piece was the same size. It was 42 feet long and 6 feet wide. [10]Five of the pieces were fastened together to make one set. The other five were fastened together to make another set. [11]Then they made loops of blue cloth along the edge of the end piece on the first set of five. They did the same thing with the other set of five. [12]There were 50 loops on one piece and 50 loops on the other piece. The loops were opposite each other. [13]Then they made 50 gold hooks to join the two pieces together. So the Holy Tent was joined together as one piece.

[14]Then the workers made another tent of 11 pieces of cloth made of goat hair. This was to put over the Holy Tent. [15]All 11 pieces were the same size. They were 45 feet long and 6 feet wide. [16]The workers sewed five pieces together into one set. Then they sewed six together into another set. [17]They made 50 loops along the edge of the outside piece of one set. And they made 50 loops along the edge of the outside piece of the other set. [18]Then they made 50 bronze rings to join the two sets of cloth together and make the tent one piece. [19]Then they made two more coverings for the outer tent. One covering was made of male sheep skin colored red. The other covering was made of fine leather.

[20]Then they made upright frames of acacia wood. [21]Each board was 15 feet tall and 27 inches wide. [22]There were two pegs side by side on each frame. Every frame of the Holy Tent was made this same way. [23]They made 20 frames for the south side of the Tent. [24]Then they made 40 silver bases that went under the 20 frames. There were two bases for every frame—one for each peg of each board. [25]They also made 20 frames for the north side of the Holy Tent. [26]They made 40 silver bases—2 to go under each frame. [27]They made 6 frames for the rear or west end of the Holy Tent [28]and 2 frames for the corners at the rear of the Holy Tent. [29]These 2 frames were joined together from the bottom to the top with a metal ring. They did this for each of these corners. [30]So there were 8 frames and 16 silver bases—2 bases under each frame.

[31]Then they made crossbars of acacia wood to connect the upright frames of the Holy Tent. Five crossbars held the frames together on one side of the Tent. [32]Five crossbars held the frames together on the other side. And five crossbars held the frames together on the west end, at the rear of the Tent. [33]They made the crossbar run along the entire length of each side and rear of the Tent. It was set halfway up the frames. [34]They made gold rings on the sides of the frames. They passed the crossbars through the rings. They covered the frames and the crossbars with gold.

[35]Then they made the curtain with blue, purple and red thread, and fine linen. A skilled craftsman sewed designs of creatures with wings on it. [36]They made four posts of acacia wood and covered them with gold. Then they made gold hooks for the posts. And they made four silver bases in which to set the posts. [37]Then they made a curtain for the entrance to the Tent. They used blue, purple and red thread, and fine linen. A person who sewed well sewed designs on it. [38]Then they made five posts and hooks for it. They

covered the tops of the posts and their bands with gold. And they made five bronze bases for the posts.

The Holy Box

37 Bezalel made the Holy Box[d] of acacia wood. The Holy Box was 45 inches long, 27 inches wide and 27 inches high. [2]He covered the inside and outside of the Holy Box with pure gold. Then he put a gold strip around it. [3]He made four gold rings for it and attached them to its four feet. There were two rings on each side. [4]Then he made poles of acacia wood and covered them with gold. [5]He put the poles through the rings on each side of the Holy Box to carry it. [6]Then he made a lid of pure gold. It was 45 inches long and 27 inches wide. [7]Then Bezalel hammered gold to make two creatures with wings. He attached them to each end of the lid. [8]He made one creature with wings on one end of the lid. He made the other creature with wings on the other end. He attached them to the lid so that it would be one piece. [9]The creatures' wings were spread out over the lid. The creatures faced each other across the lid.

The Table

[10]Then he made the table of acacia wood. The table was 36 inches long, 18 inches wide and 27 inches high. [11]He covered the table with pure gold. He put a gold strip around it. [12]Then he made a frame 3 inches high that stood up all around the edge. He put a gold strip around the frame. [13]Then he made four gold rings for the table. He attached them to the four corners of the table, where the four legs were. [14]The rings were put close to the frame around the top of the table. The rings held the poles that were used to carry the table. [15]The poles for carrying the table were made of acacia wood. They were covered with gold. [16]Then he made of pure gold all the things that were used on the table: the plates, bowls, cups and jars used for pouring the drink offerings.

The Lampstand

[17]Then he made the lampstand of pure gold. He hammered out its base and stand. Its flower-like cups, buds and petals were joined together in one piece with the base and stand. [18]There were three branches on one side of the lampstand and three branches on the other. [19]Each branch had three cups

Words to Know: Old Testament

ARK OF THE AGREEMENT • EXODUS 37:1

The **Ark of the Agreement** (or Holy Box) was an important part of Israel's Holy Tent (the place where they worshiped, like a church). God told the priests how to build the Ark. It was a golden rectangular box that held the tablets of the Ten Commandments. The Ark of the Agreement was put in the most inner room of the Holy Tent where God's presence was. No one was allowed to enter that room except the high priest. He could go in only on one special day each year. The Ark of the Agreement was important to the Israelites because it was a symbol that God lived with them.

We do not need to have an Ark today. If we believe in Jesus as our Savior, God will live inside of us by the Holy Spirit.

To read about a portable church, fly to page 130.

shaped like almond flowers. Each cup had a bud and a petal. [20]There were four more cups shaped like almond flowers on the lampstand itself. Each cup had its buds and petals. [21]Three pairs of branches went out from the lampstand. A bud was under the place where each pair was attached to the lampstand. [22]The buds, branches and lampstand were all one piece of pure, hammered gold. [23]He made seven pure gold lamps for this lampstand. Then he made pure gold wick trimmers and trays. [24]He used about 75 pounds of pure gold to make the lampstand and all the things that go with it.

The Altar for Burning Incense

[25]Then he made the altar of incense[d] of acacia wood. The altar was square. It was 18 inches long, 18 inches wide and 36 inches high. Each corner stuck out like a horn. Each corner was joined into one piece with the altar. [26]He covered the top and all the sides and the corners with pure gold. Then he put gold trim around the altar. [27]He made two gold rings and put them below the trim on opposite sides of the altar. These rings held the poles for carrying the altar. [28]He made the poles of acacia wood and covered them with gold.

[29]Then he made the holy olive oil for appointing the priests. He also made the pure, sweet-smelling incense. He made them like a person who mixes perfumes.

The Altar

38 Then he built the altar for burning offerings. He made the altar of acacia wood. The altar was square. It was 7½ feet long, 7½ feet wide and 4½ feet high. [2]He made each corner stick out like a horn. The horns and the altar were joined together in one piece. Then he covered the altar with bronze. [3]He made all the tools of bronze to use on the altar: the pots, shovels, bowls for sprinkling blood, meat forks and pans for carrying the fire. [4]He made a large bronze screen to hold the burning wood

for the altar. He put the screen inside the altar, under its rim, halfway up from the bottom. [5]He made bronze rings for holding the poles for carrying the altar. He put the rings at the four corners of the screen. [6]Then he made poles of acacia wood and covered them with bronze. [7]He put the poles through the rings on both sides of the altar. They were used for carrying the altar. He made the altar of boards and left the inside hollow.

The Bronze Bowl

[8]He made the bronze bowl for washing. He built it on a bronze stand. He used the bronze of mirrors. These mirrors belonged to the women who served at the entrance to the Meeting Tent.[d]

The Courtyard of the Holy Tent

[9]Then he made a wall of curtains to form a courtyard around the Holy Tent.[d] On the south side the curtains were 150 feet long and were made of fine linen. [10]The curtains hung on silver hooks and bands. These were on 20 bronze posts on 20 bronze bases. [11]On the north side the wall of curtains was also 150 feet long. It hung on silver hooks and bands on 20 posts with 20 bronze bases.

[12]On the west side of the courtyard, the wall of curtains was 75 feet long. It was held up by silver hooks and bands on 10 posts and 10 bases. [13]The east side was 75 feet wide. [14]On one side of the entry there was a wall of curtains that was 22½ feet long. It was held up by 3 posts and 3 bases. [15]On the other side of the entry there was a wall of curtains 22½ feet long. It was held up by 3 posts and 3 bases. [16]All the curtains around the courtyard were made of fine linen. [17]The bases for the posts were made of bronze. The hooks and the bands on the posts were made of silver. The tops of the posts were covered with silver also. All the posts in the courtyard had silver bands. [18]The curtain for the entry of the

courtyard was made of blue, purple and red thread, and fine linen. It was sewn by a person who could sew well. The curtain was 30 feet long and 7½ feet high. It was the same height as the curtains around the courtyard. ¹⁹The curtain was held up by 4 posts and 4 bronze bases. The hooks and bands on the posts were made of silver. The tops on the posts were covered with silver. ²⁰All the tent pegs for the Holy Tent and for the curtains around the courtyard were made of bronze.

²¹This is a list of the metals used to make the Holy Tent. This is where the two flat stones with the Ten Commandments are kept. Moses ordered the Levites to make this list. Ithamar son of Aaron was in charge of keeping the list. ²²Bezalel son of Uri made everything the Lord commanded Moses. Uri was the son of Hur of the tribe[d] of Judah. ²³Oholiab son of Ahisamach of the tribe of Dan helped him. Oholiab could cut designs into metal and stone. He was a designer. He was also skilled at sewing the blue, purple and red thread, and fine linen.

²⁴The total amount of gold used to build the Holy Tent was presented to the Lord. It weighed over 2,000 pounds, as set by the Holy Place measure.

²⁵The silver was given by the members of the community who were counted. It weighed 7,550 pounds, as set by the Holy Place measure. ²⁶All the men 20 years old or older were counted. There were 603,550 men, and each man had to pay 1/5 ounce of silver. This is the weight as set by the Holy Place measure. ²⁷Of this silver, 7,500 pounds was used to make the 100 bases. These bases were for the Holy Tent and for the curtain. There was 75 pounds of silver in each base. ²⁸The other 50 pounds of silver was used to make the hooks for the posts. It was also used to cover the tops of the posts and to make the bands on the posts.

²⁹The bronze which was presented to the Lord weighed about 5,000 pounds. ³⁰They used the bronze to make the bases at the entrance of the Meeting Tent. They also used the bronze to make the altar and the bronze screen. And this bronze was used to make all the tools for the altar. ³¹This bronze was also used to make bases for the wall of curtains around the courtyard. It was used for the bases for the curtains at the entry to the courtyard. And this bronze was used to make the tent pegs for the Holy Tent and curtains that surrounded the courtyard.

Clothes for the Priests

39 They used blue, purple and red thread to make woven clothes for the priests. They were to wear these when they served in the Holy Place. They also made the holy clothes for Aaron as the Lord had commanded Moses.

²They made the holy vest[d] of gold and blue, purple and red thread, and fine linen. ³They hammered the gold into sheets. Then they cut the gold into long, thin strips. They worked the gold into the blue, purple and red thread, and fine linen. This was done by a skilled craftsman. ⁴They made the shoulder straps for the holy vest. These straps were attached to the top corners of the vest. Then the shoulder straps were tied together over each shoulder. ⁵The skillfully woven belt was made in the same way. It was joined to the holy vest as one piece. It was made of gold and blue, purple and red thread, and fine linen. It was made the way the Lord commanded Moses.

⁶They put gold around the onyx stones. Then they wrote the names of the sons of Israel on these gems. They did that as a person carves words and designs on a seal.[d] ⁷Then they attached the gems on the shoulder straps of the holy vest. These gems are reminders of the 12 sons of Israel. This was done the way the Lord had commanded Moses.

⁸The skilled craftsmen made the chest covering. It was made like the holy vest. It was made of gold and blue,

purple and red thread, and fine linen. ⁹The chest covering was square, nine inches long and nine inches wide. It was folded double to make a pocket. ¹⁰Then they put four rows of beautiful jewels on it. In the first row there was a ruby, a topaz and a yellow quartz. ¹¹In the second row there was a turquoise, a sapphire and an emerald. ¹²In the third row there was a jacinth, an agate and an amethyst. ¹³In the fourth row there was a chrysolite, an onyx and a jasper. Gold was put around these jewels to attach them to the chest covering. ¹⁴The names of the sons of Israel were carved on these 12 jewels as a person carves a seal. Each jewel had the name of 1 of the 12 tribes*d* of Israel.

¹⁵They made chains of pure gold for the chest covering. They were twisted together like a rope. ¹⁶The workers made two gold pieces and two gold rings. They put the two gold rings on the two upper corners of the chest covering. ¹⁷Then they put two gold chains in the two rings. These are at the ends of the chest covering. ¹⁸They fastened the other two ends of the chains to the two gold pieces. Then they attached these gold pieces to the two shoulder straps in the front of the holy vest. ¹⁹They made two more gold rings and put them at the lower corners of the chest covering. They put them on the inside edge next to the holy vest. ²⁰Then they made two more gold rings on the bottom of the shoulder straps in front of the holy vest. These rings were near the seam, just above the woven belt of the holy vest. ²¹They used a blue ribbon and tied the rings of the chest covering to the rings of the holy vest. This connected it to the woven belt. In this way the chest covering would not swing out from the holy vest. They did all these things the way the Lord commanded.

²²Then they made the outer robe to be worn under the holy vest. It was woven of blue cloth. ²³They made a hole in the center of the outer robe. A woven collar was sewn around this hole

so it would not tear. ²⁴Then they made balls like pomegranates*d* of blue, purple and red thread, and fine linen. They hung them around the bottom of the outer robe. ²⁵They also made bells of pure gold. They hung these around the bottom of the outer robe between the balls. ²⁶So around the bottom of the outer robe there was a bell and a pomegranate ball, a bell and a pomegranate ball. The priest wore this outer robe when he served as priest, just as the Lord had commanded Moses.

²⁷They wove inner robes of fine linen for Aaron and his sons. ²⁸And they made turbans and underclothes of fine linen. ²⁹Then they made the cloth belt of fine linen and blue, purple and red thread. Designs were sewn onto the cloth. These things were made as the Lord had commanded Moses.

³⁰They made a strip of pure gold, which is the holy crown. They carved these words in the gold: "Holy to the Lord." They did it as one might carve on a seal. ³¹Then they tied this flat piece to the turban with a blue ribbon. This was done as the Lord had commanded Moses.

³²So all the work on the Meeting Tent*d* was finished. The Israelites did everything just as the Lord had commanded Moses. ³³Then they brought the Holy Tent to Moses: the Tent and all its furniture, hooks, frames, crossbars, posts and bases; ³⁴the covering made of male sheep skins colored red, the covering made of fine leather and the curtain that covered the entrance to the Most Holy Place; ³⁵the Box*d* of the Agreement, its poles and lid; ³⁶the table, all its containers and the bread that showed they were in God's presence; ³⁷the pure gold lampstand with its lamps in a row, all its tools and the olive oil for the light; ³⁸the gold altar, the special olive oil used for appointing priests, the sweet-smelling incense,*d* and the curtain that covered the entrance to the Tent; ³⁹the bronze altar and its screen, its poles and all its tools, the bowl and its stand; ⁴⁰the curtains

for the courtyard with their posts and bases, the curtain that covered the entry to the courtyard, the cords, pegs and all the things in the Meeting Tent. ⁴¹They brought the clothes for the priests to wear when they served in the Holy Tent: the holy clothes for Aaron the priest and the clothes for his sons. They wore these when they served as priests.

⁴²The Israelites had done all this work just as the Lord had commanded Moses. ⁴³Moses looked closely at all the work. He saw they had done it just as the Lord had commanded. So Moses blessed them.

Setting Up the Holy Tent

40 Then the Lord said this to Moses: ²"On the first day of the first month, set up the Holy Tent,^d which is the Meeting Tent. ³Put the Box^d of the Agreement in the Meeting Tent. Hang the curtain in front of the Holy Box. ⁴Then bring in the table. Arrange everything on the table that should be there. Then bring in the lampstand and set up its lamps. ⁵Put the gold altar for burning incense^d in front of the Box of the Agreement. Then put the curtain at the entrance to the Holy Tent.

⁶"Put the altar of burnt offerings in front of the entrance of the Holy Tent, the Meeting Tent. ⁷Put the bowl between the Meeting Tent and the altar. Put water in the bowl. ⁸Set up the courtyard around the Holy Tent. Then put the curtain at the entry to the courtyard.

⁹"Use the special olive oil and pour it on the Holy Tent and everything in it. Give the Tent and all that is in it for service to the Lord. They will be holy. ¹⁰Pour the special oil on the altar for burning offerings. Pour it on all its tools. Give the altar for service to God. It will be very holy. ¹¹Then pour the special olive oil on the bowl and the base under it. When you do this, they will be given for service to God.

¹²"Bring Aaron and his sons to the entrance of the Meeting Tent. Wash them with water. ¹³Then put the holy clothes on Aaron. Pour the special oil on him, and give him for service to God. Then he may serve me as a priest. ¹⁴Bring Aaron's sons and put the inner robes on them. ¹⁵Pour the special oil on them to make them priests. Do this the same way that you appointed their father as priest. Then they may also serve me as priests. Pouring oil on them will make them a family of priests. They and their descendants^d will be priests from now on." ¹⁶Moses did everything that the Lord commanded him.

¹⁷So the Holy Tent was set up. It was the first day of the first month during the second year after they left Egypt. ¹⁸When Moses set up the Holy Tent, he put the bases in place. Then he put the frames on the bases. Next he put the crossbars through the rings of the frames and set up the posts. ¹⁹After that, Moses spread the cloth over the Holy Tent. Then he put the covering over the Tent. He did these things just as the Lord commanded.

²⁰Moses put the flat stones into the Box of the Agreement. These had God's law written on them. Moses put the poles through the rings of the Holy Box. Then he put the lid on it. ²¹Next Moses brought the Holy Box into the Tent. He hung the curtain to cover the Holy Box. Moses did these things just as the Lord commanded him.

²²Moses put the table in the Meeting Tent. He put it on the north side of the Holy Tent in front of the curtain. ²³Then he put the bread on the table before the Lord. He did this just as the Lord commanded him. ²⁴Moses put the lampstand in the Meeting Tent. He put it on the south side of the Holy Tent across from the table. ²⁵Then he put the lamps on the lampstand before the Lord. He did this just as the Lord commanded him.

²⁶Moses put the gold altar for burning incense in the Meeting Tent. He put it in front of the curtain. ²⁷Then he burned sweet-smelling incense on it, just as the Lord commanded him.

²⁸Then he hung the curtain at the entrance to the Holy Tent.

²⁹He put the altar for burning sacrifices at the entrance to the Holy Tent, the Meeting Tent. Then Moses offered a whole burnt offering and grain offerings on that altar. He did these things just as the Lord commanded him. ³⁰Moses put the bowl between the Meeting Tent and the altar for burning sacrifices. Moses put water in the bowl for washing. ³¹Moses, Aaron and Aaron's sons used this water to wash their hands and feet. ³²They washed themselves every time they entered the Meeting Tent. They also washed themselves every time they went near the altar for burning sacrifices. They did these things just as the Lord commanded Moses.

³³Then Moses set up the courtyard around the Holy Tent. He put the altar for burning sacrifices in the courtyard. Then he put up the curtain at the entry to the courtyard. So Moses finished the work.

The Cloud over the Holy Tent

³⁴Then the cloud covered the Meeting Tent.ᵈ The greatness of the Lord filled the Holy Tent. ³⁵Moses could not enter the Meeting Tent. This was because the cloud had settled on it. And this was because the greatness of the Lord filled the Holy Tent.

³⁶When the cloud rose from the Holy Tent, the Israelites would begin to travel. ³⁷But as long as the cloud stayed on the Holy Tent, the people did not travel. They stayed in that place until the cloud rose. ³⁸So the cloud of the Lord was over the Holy Tent during the day. And there was a fire in the cloud at night. So all the Israelites could see the cloud while they traveled.

Words to Know: Old Testament
HOLY TENT • EXODUS 40:34

While the Israelites traveled through the desert on their way to the promised land, God wanted them to have a place to worship. He gave them instructions for a special **Holy Tent**. It was very beautiful with lots of gold and fancy curtains. The end of the book of Exodus describes how the Holy Tent was built. It was God's home on earth. When the Israelites stopped and camped during their travels, the priests would set up the Holy Tent so the people could worship God and bring sacrifices to pay for their sins. The Tent was used for many years until King Solomon built the temple in Jerusalem.

Today we usually worship God in a church building. Could we worship God in a tent?

To read about a beautiful building, fly to page 521.

LEVITICUS

*Rules for
Worship and Living*

The Burnt Offering

1 The Lord called to Moses and spoke to him from the Meeting Tent.[d] The Lord said, [2]"Tell the people of Israel: 'When you bring an offering to the Lord, bring as your offering one of the cattle. Or you may bring one of the sheep or goats.

[3]"If anyone offers a whole burnt offering from the cattle, it must be a male. It must have nothing wrong with it. The person must take the animal to the entrance of the Meeting Tent. Then the Lord will accept the offering. [4]The person must put his hand on the animal's head. Then the Lord will accept that burnt offering. It will remove the person's sin so he will belong to God. [5]The person must kill the young bull before the Lord. Then the priests must bring its blood to the altar. They must sprinkle the blood on all sides of the altar. This is the altar at the entrance to the Meeting Tent. [6]The person will cut the skin from that animal. Then he will cut the animal into pieces. [7]The priests must put wood and fire on the altar. [8]They must lay the head, the fat and other pieces on the wood. That wood is on the fire on the altar. [9]The priest must wash the animal's inner organs and legs with water. Then the priest must burn all the animal's parts on the altar. It is a whole burnt offering, an offering made by fire. And its smell is pleasing to the Lord.

[10]"The burnt offering may be a sheep or goat. It must be a male animal that has nothing wrong with it. [11]The person must kill the animal on the north side of the altar. This is to be before the Lord. Then the priests must sprinkle its blood on the altar. They must sprinkle it on all sides. [12]The person must cut the animal into pieces. Then the priest must lay the pieces with the head and fat on the wood. The wood is on the fire on the altar. [13]The person must wash the animal's inner organs and legs with water. Then the priest must burn all its parts on the altar. It is a burnt offering, an offering made by fire. And its smell is pleasing to the Lord.

[14]"The whole burnt offering may be a bird. It must be a dove or a young pigeon. [15]The priest will bring the offering to the altar. He will pull off the bird's head. Then he will burn it on the altar. The bird's blood must be drained out on the side of the altar. [16]The priest must remove the bird's crop[n] and its contents. He must throw them on the east side of the altar. This is where they put the ashes from the altar. [17]Then the priest must tear the bird open by its wings. But he must not divide the bird into two parts. Then the priest must burn the bird on the altar. He must place it on the wood which is on the fire. It is a burnt offering, an offering made by fire. Its smell is pleasing to the Lord.

The Grain Offering

2 "When anyone offers a grain offering to the Lord, it must be made from fine flour. The person must

---

[n]**crop** A small bag inside a bird's throat. When a bird eats, its food goes into this part first. There, the food is made soft before it goes into the stomach.

pour oil on it and put incense[d] on it. [2]Then he must take it to Aaron's sons and the priests. The priest must take a handful of the fine flour, with the oil and all the incense. He must burn it on the altar as a memorial portion. It is an offering made by fire. Its smell is pleasing to the Lord. [3]The rest of the grain offering will belong to Aaron and the priests. This offering is a most holy part of the offerings made by fire to the Lord.

[4]"If you bring a grain offering that was baked in the oven, it must be made from fine flour. It may be loaves made without yeast and mixed with oil. Or it may be wafers made without yeast. They are to have oil poured over them. [5]If your grain offering is cooked on a griddle, it must be made without yeast. It must be made of fine flour mixed with oil. [6]Crumble it and pour oil over it. It is a grain offering. [7]If your grain offering is cooked in a pan, it must be made from fine flour and oil. [8]Bring the grain offering made of these things to the Lord. Give it to the priest. He will take it to the altar. [9]He will take out the memorial portion from the grain offering. He will burn it on the altar. This is an offering made by fire. Its smell is pleasing to the Lord. [10]The rest of the grain offering belongs to Aaron and the priests. It is a most holy part of the offerings made to the Lord by fire.

[11]"Every grain offering you bring to the Lord must be made without yeast. You must not burn yeast or honey in an offering made by fire to the Lord. [12]You may bring yeast and honey to the Lord as an offering from the first harvest. But yeast and honey must not be burned on the altar as a pleasing smell. [13]You must also put salt on all your grain offerings. Salt stands for your agreement with God that will last forever. Do not leave it out of your grain offering. You must add salt to all your offerings.

[14]"If you bring a grain offering from the first harvest to the Lord, bring crushed heads of new grain. They must be roasted in the fire. [15]Put oil and incense on the grain. It is a grain offering. [16]The priest will burn the memorial portion of the crushed grain and oil. It will have incense on it. It is an offering by fire to the Lord.

The Fellowship Offering

3 "'A person's fellowship offering to the Lord may be from the cattle. It may be a male or female animal. But it must have nothing wrong with it. [2]The person must put his hand on the animal's head. He must kill it at the entrance to the Meeting Tent.[d] Then the priests must sprinkle the blood on all sides of the altar. [3]This person must make a sacrifice from the fellowship offering. The sacrifice must be made by fire to the Lord. He must offer the fat of the animal's inner organs. This is both the fat that is in them and that covers them. [4]He must also offer both kidneys and the fat on them. They are near the lower back muscle. He must also offer the best part of the liver. He will remove it with the kidneys. [5]Then the priests will burn these parts on the altar. They will put them on the burnt offering that is on the wood on the fire. It is an offering made by fire. Its smell is pleasing to the Lord.

[6]"'A person's fellowship offering to the Lord may be a lamb or a goat. He may offer a male or female animal. But it must have nothing wrong with it. [7]If he offers a lamb, he must bring it before the Lord. [8]He must put his hand on its head. Then he must kill the animal in front of the Meeting Tent. The priests will sprinkle its blood on all sides of the altar. [9]Then the person must make a sacrifice from the fellowship offering. The sacrifice must be made by fire to the Lord. The person must bring the fat and the whole fat tail. The tail must be cut off close to the backbone. He must also offer the fat of the inner organs. This is both the fat that is in them and that covers them. [10]He must offer both kidneys and the fat on them. They are near the lower back muscle. And he must offer the best part of the liver. He

will remove it with the kidneys. ¹¹Then the priest will burn these parts on the altar as food. It will be an offering made by fire to the Lord.

¹²"'A person's fellowship offering may be a goat. He is to offer it before the Lord. ¹³He must put his hand on the goat's head. And he must kill it in front of the Meeting Tent. Then the priests must sprinkle its blood on all sides of the altar. ¹⁴From this fellowship offering the person must make a sacrifice. It will be an offering by fire to the Lord. The person must offer all the fat of the goat's inner organs. This is both the fat that is in them and that covers them. ¹⁵He must offer both kidneys and the fat on them. They are near the lower back muscle. And he must offer the best part of the liver. He will remove it with the kidneys. ¹⁶The priest will burn these parts on the altar as food. It is an offering made by fire. Its smell is pleasing to the Lord. All the fat belongs to the Lord.'

¹⁷"'This law will continue for people from now on, wherever you live: You must not eat fat or blood.'"

The Sin Offering

4 The Lord said to Moses, ²"Tell the people of Israel this: 'A person might sin by accident. He might do some things the Lord has commanded not to be done. If so, that person must do these things:

³"'It may be the appointed priest who has sinned. If so, he has brought guilt on the people. So he must offer a young bull to the Lord. It must have nothing wrong with it. This will be a sin offering for the sin he has done. ⁴He will bring the bull to the entrance of the Meeting Tent.ᵈ He must bring it in front of the Lord. Then he will put his hand on the bull's head. And he will kill the bull before the Lord. ⁵Then the appointed priest must bring some of the bull's blood into the Meeting Tent. ⁶The priest is to dip his finger into the blood. He must sprinkle it seven times before the Lord in front of the curtain. This

curtain is in front of the Most Holy Place. ⁷The priest must also put some of the blood on the corners of the altar of incense.ᵈ It stands before the Lord in the Meeting Tent. Then the priest must pour out the rest of the bull's blood. It must be poured at the bottom of the altar of burnt offering. That altar is at the door of the Meeting Tent. ⁸He must remove all the fat from the bull of the sin offering. He must remove the fat on and around the inner organs. ⁹He must remove both kidneys and the fat on them. They are near the lower back muscle. He must remove the best part of the liver with the kidneys. ¹⁰He must do this in the same way the fat is removed from the bull of the fellowship offering. Then the priest must burn the animal parts on the altar of burnt offering. ¹¹⁻¹²But the priest must carry out the skin of the bull and all its meat. He must take these with the rest of the bull—its head, legs, intestines and other inner organs. He must take it outside the camp to the special cleanᵈ place where the ashes are poured out. He must burn it on a wood fire on the pile of ashes.

¹³"'The whole nation of Israel might sin without knowing it. They might do something the Lord has commanded not to be done. If this happens, they are guilty. ¹⁴When they learn about the sin they have done, a young bull must be offered. It is a sin offering for the whole nation. They must bring it and give it before the Meeting Tent. ¹⁵The older leaders of the group of people must put their hands on the bull's head. It must be done before the Lord. And the bull must be killed before the Lord. ¹⁶Then the appointed priest must bring some of the bull's blood into the Meeting Tent. ¹⁷The priest will dip his finger in the blood. He must sprinkle it seven times before the Lord in front of the curtain. ¹⁸Then he must put some of the blood on the corners of the altar. The altar is before the Lord in the Meeting Tent. The priest must pour out the rest of the blood. He must pour

it at the bottom of the altar of burnt offering. That altar is at the entrance to the Meeting Tent. ¹⁹The priest must remove all the fat from the animal. And he must burn it on the altar. ²⁰He will do the same thing with this bull that he did with the first bull of the sin offering. In this way the priest removes the sins of the people so they will belong to the Lord. And the Lord will forgive them. ²¹Then the priest must carry the bull outside the camp and burn it. He must do this just as he did with the first bull. This is the sin offering for the whole community.

²²"A ruler might sin by accident. He might do something the Lord his God has commanded must not be done. If he does, he is guilty. ²³When he learns about his sin, he must bring a male goat. It must have nothing wrong with it. That will be his sin offering. ²⁴The ruler must put his hand on the goat's head and kill it. This must be done where they kill the whole burnt offering before the Lord. The goat is a sin offering. ²⁵The priest must take some of the blood of the sin offering on his finger. He must put it on the corners of the altar of burnt offering. He must pour out the rest of the blood at the bottom of the altar of burnt offering. ²⁶He must burn all the goat's fat on the altar. He must burn it in the same way he burns the fat of the fellowship offerings. In this way the priest removes the ruler's sin so he belongs to the Lord. And the Lord will forgive him.

²⁷"A person in the community might sin by accident. He might do something which the Lord has commanded must not be done. He is guilty of sin. ²⁸When the person learns about his sin, he must bring a female goat. It must have nothing wrong with it. That will be his sin offering. ²⁹He must put his hand on the animal's head. He must kill it at the place of the whole burnt offering. ³⁰Then the priest must take some of the goat's blood on his finger. He must put it on the corners of the altar of burnt offering. He must pour out the rest of

the goat's blood at the bottom of the altar. ³¹Then the priest must remove all the goat's fat. He must do it in the same way the fat is removed from the fellowship offerings. He must burn it on the altar. Its smell is pleasing to the Lord. In this way the priest will remove that person's sin so he will belong to the Lord. And the Lord will forgive him.

³²"This person may bring a lamb as his sin offering. If he does, he must bring a female. It must have nothing wrong with it. ³³The person must put his hand on the animal's head. He must kill it as a sin offering. He must kill it where they kill the whole burnt offering. ³⁴The priest must take some of the blood from the sin offering on his finger. He must put it on the corners of the altar of burnt offering. Then he must pour out the rest of the lamb's blood at the bottom of the altar. ³⁵The priest must remove all the lamb's fat. He must do it in the same way that the lamb's fat is removed from the fellowship offerings. He must burn the pieces on the altar. They go on top of the offerings made by fire for the Lord. In this way the priest will remove that person's sins so he will belong to the Lord. And the Lord will forgive him.

Special Types of Accidental Sins

5 "'These are things for which a sin offering must be made:

"'A person might be ordered to tell in court what he has seen or what he knows. If he does not tell the court, he is guilty of sin.

²"'Or someone might touch something unclean.ᵈ It might be the dead body of an unclean wild animal or an unclean farm animal or an unclean crawling animal. He might not know that he touched it. But he will still be unclean and guilty of sin.

³"'Many things come from a person which are not clean. Someone might touch one of these unclean things from a person and not know it. But when he learns about it, he will be guilty.

⁴"'Or someone might make a promise

before the Lord without thinking. He might promise to do something bad or good. The promise might be about anything. He might even make a promise before the Lord and forget about it. But when he remembers, he will be guilty.

5"'When anyone is guilty of any of these things, he must tell how he sinned. 6He must bring an offering to the Lord. It is a penalty for his sin. It must be a female lamb or goat from the flock. The priest will perform the acts to remove that person's sin so he will belong to the Lord.

7"'But perhaps the person cannot afford a lamb. Then he must bring two doves or two young pigeons to the Lord. These will be the penalty for his sin. One bird must be for a sin offering. The other must be for a burnt offering. 8He must bring them to the priest. First the priest will offer the one for the sin offering. He will pull the bird's head from its neck. But he will not pull it completely off. 9He must sprinkle the blood from the sin offering on the side of the altar. Then he must pour the rest of the blood at the bottom of the altar. It is a sin offering. 10Then the priest must offer the second bird as a burnt offering. This is what the law says. In this way the priest will remove the person's sin so he will belong to the Lord. And the Lord will forgive him.

11"'The person might not be able to afford two doves or two pigeons. If not, he must bring about two quarts of fine flour. This will be an offering for his sin. He must not put oil on the flour. And he must not put incense*d* on it, because it is a sin offering. 12He must bring the flour to the priest. The priest will take a handful of the flour as a memorial offering. He will burn it on the altar. It goes on top of the offerings made by fire to the Lord. It is a sin offering. 13In this way the priest will remove the person's sins so he will belong to the Lord. And the Lord will forgive him. What is left of the sin offering belongs to the priest. This is like the grain offering.'"

The Penalty Offering

14The Lord said to Moses, 15"A person might accidentally sin and do something against the holy things of the Lord. That person must bring a male sheep from the flock. It must have nothing wrong with it. This will be his penalty offering to the Lord. The value in silver of the male sheep must be correct. Use the proper value for silver as set by the Holy Place measure. 16That person must pay for the sin he did against the holy thing. He must add one-fifth to its value. Then he must give it all to the priest. In this way the priest will remove the person's sin so he will belong to the Lord. The priest does it by means of the male sheep of the penalty offering. And the Lord will forgive the person.

17"A person might sin and do something the Lord has commanded not to be done. It does not matter if that person knew or not. He is guilty. He is responsible for his sin. 18He must bring the priest a male sheep from the flock. It must have nothing wrong with it. It must be worth the correct amount. The male sheep will be a penalty offering. The person sinned without knowing it. But with this offering the priest will remove the sin so the person will belong to the Lord. And the Lord will forgive him. 19The person is guilty of doing wrong against the Lord. So he must give the penalty offering to the Lord."

6 The Lord said to Moses, 2"A person might sin against the Lord by doing one of these sins: He might lie about what happened to something he was taking care of for someone else. Or he might lie about a promise he made. Or he might steal something or cheat someone. 3He might find something that had been lost and then lie about it. He might make a promise before the Lord about something and not mean it. Or he might do some other sin. 4If he does any of these things, he is guilty of sin. He must bring back whatever he stole. Or he must bring back what he

took by cheating. Or he must bring back the thing he took care of for someone else. Or he must bring back what he found and lied about. [5]Or he must bring back what he made a false promise about. He must pay the full price. Then he must pay an extra one-fifth of the value of what he took. He must give the money to the true owner. This must be done on the day he brings his penalty offering. [6]He must pay a penalty to the priest. It must be a male sheep from the flock. It must not have anything wrong with it. And it must be worth the correct amount. It will be a penalty offering to the Lord. [7]Then the priest will perform the acts to remove that person's sin so he will belong to the Lord. And the Lord will forgive him for the sins that made him guilty."

The Whole Burnt Offering

[8]The Lord said to Moses, [9]"Give this command to Aaron and the priests: 'These are the teachings about the whole burnt offering. The burnt offering must stay on the altar all night until morning. The altar's fire must be kept burning. [10]The priest must put on his linen robe. He must put on linen underclothes next to his body. Then he will remove the ashes from the burnt offering on the altar. He will put these ashes beside the altar. [11]Then he must take off those clothes and put on others. He must carry the ashes outside the camp to a special clean[d] place. [12]But the fire must be kept burning on the altar. It must not be allowed to go out. The priest must put more firewood on the altar every morning. He must place the whole burnt offering on the fire. He must burn the fat of the fellowship offerings. [13]The fire must be kept burning on the altar all the time. It must not go out.

The Grain Offering

[14]"'These are the teachings about the grain offering: The priests must bring it to the Lord in front of the altar. [15]The priest must take a handful of fine flour. The oil and incense[d] must be on it. The priest must burn the grain offering on the altar. It will be a memorial offering to the Lord. Its smell is pleasing to him. [16]Aaron and the priests may eat what is left. It must be eaten without yeast in a holy place. The priests must eat it in the courtyard of the Meeting Tent.[d] [17]It must not be cooked with yeast. I have given it as their share of the offerings made to me by fire. It is most holy, like the sin offering and the penalty offering. [18]Any male descendant[d] of Aaron may eat it. It is his share of the offerings made to the Lord by fire. This will continue from now on. Whatever touches these offerings must be holy.'"

[19]The Lord said to Moses, [20]"This is the offering Aaron and the priests must bring to the Lord. They must do this on the day they appoint Aaron as high priest. They must bring two quarts of fine flour for a grain offering. They must bring half of it in the morning and half in the evening. [21]The fine flour must be mixed with oil and cooked on a griddle. Bring it when it is well mixed. You must break it into pieces. It will be a smell that is pleasing to the Lord. [22]One of the priests will be appointed to take Aaron's place as high priest. He must make the grain offering to the Lord. It is a rule forever. The grain offering must be completely burned to the Lord. [23]Every grain offering made by a priest must be completely burned. It must not be eaten."

The Sin Offering

[24]The Lord said to Moses, [25]"Tell Aaron and the priests: 'These are the teachings about the sin offering. The sin offering must be killed in front of the Lord. It must be killed in the same place the whole burnt offering is killed. It is most holy. [26]The priest who offers the sin offering must eat it. He must eat it in a holy place. It must be in the courtyard of the Meeting Tent.[d] [27]Whatever touches the meat of the sin offering must be holy. If the blood is sprinkled

on any clothes, you must wash them in a holy place. ²⁸The clay pot the meat is cooked in must be broken. If a bronze pot is used, it must be scrubbed and rinsed with water. ²⁹Any male in a priest's family may eat the offering. It is most holy. ³⁰The blood of the sin offering may be taken into the Meeting Tent. It may be used to remove sin in the Holy Place. That sin offering must be burned with fire. It must not be eaten.

The Penalty Offering

7 ¹"'These are the teachings about the penalty offering. It is most holy. ²The penalty offering must be killed where the whole burnt offering is killed. Then the priest must sprinkle its blood on all sides of the altar. ³He must offer all the fat from the penalty offering. He must offer the fat tail and the fat that covers the inner organs. ⁴He must offer both kidneys and the fat on them. They are near the lower back muscle. And he must offer the best part of the liver. This is to be removed with the kidneys. ⁵The priest must burn all these things on the altar. They will be an offering made by fire to the Lord. It is a penalty offering. ⁶Any male in a priest's family may eat it. It is most holy. So it must be eaten in a holy place.

⁷"'The penalty offering is like the sin offering. The teachings are the same for both. The priest who offers the sacrifice to remove sins will get the meat for food. ⁸The priest who offers the burnt offering may also have the skin from it. ⁹Every grain offering belongs to the priest who offers it. This includes those baked in an oven, cooked on a griddle or baked in a dish. ¹⁰The grain offerings belong to the priests. They may be dry or mixed with oil. All priests will share alike.

Fellowship Offerings

¹¹"'These are the teachings about the fellowship offering a person may offer to the Lord: ¹²He may bring the fellowship offering to show his thanks.

If he does, he should also bring loaves of bread. They must be made without yeast, mixed with oil. And he should bring wafers made without yeast. They must have oil poured over them. He should also bring loaves of fine flour mixed with oil. ¹³He must also offer loaves of bread made with yeast. These should be brought with his fellowship offering, which he gives to show thanks. ¹⁴One of each kind of offering will be for the Lord. It will be given to the priest who sprinkles the blood of the fellowship offering. ¹⁵The fellowship offering is to thank the Lord. The meat from it must be eaten the same day it is offered. None of it must be left until morning.

¹⁶"'A person might bring a fellowship offering just to give a gift to God. Or it may be done because of a special promise to God. Then, the sacrifice should be eaten the same day he offers it. If there is any left, it may be eaten the next day. ¹⁷If any meat from this sacrifice is left on the third day, it must be burned up. ¹⁸Any meat of the fellowship offering eaten on the third day will not be accepted. The Lord will not count the sacrifice for the person who offered it. It will become unclean.*d* Anyone who eats the meat will be guilty of sin.

¹⁹"'People must not eat meat that touches anything unclean. They must burn this meat with fire. But anyone who is clean may eat other meat. ²⁰But a person who is unclean might eat the meat from the fellowship offering that belongs to the Lord. If he does, he must be separated from his people.

²¹"'Someone might touch something unclean that comes from people. Or the unclean thing might be an animal or some hated thing. Touching it will make him unclean. If he then eats meat from the fellowship offering that belongs to the Lord, he must be separated from his people.'"

²²The Lord said to Moses, ²³"Tell the people of Israel: 'You must not eat any of the fat from cattle, sheep or goats. ²⁴If an animal is found dead or torn by

wild animals, you may use its fat for other things. But you must not eat it. ²⁵Someone might eat fat from an animal offering made by fire to the Lord. That person must be separated from his people. ²⁶It does not matter where you live. You must not eat blood from any bird or animal. ²⁷Anyone who eats blood must be separated from his people.'"

the fellowship offering. ³⁴I have taken the breast and the thigh of the fellowship offering. And I have given these parts to Aaron and the priests as their share from the Israelites.'"

³⁵This is the portion that belongs to

Worship
LEVITICUS 7:28-29

If a friend invited you to a birthday party and asked that you wear a green shirt with purple pants, you would probably do it. Why— because you *like* wearing green and purple together? No. You would do it because your friend asked you to, and it's *his* party.

God gave the Israelites some strict rules for worshiping him. Leviticus 7:28-38 mentions a few of them. Even though these rules may sound strange to us—and may have sounded a little strange to the people of Israel—God gave them to his people so that *they would know how to worship in a way that pleased him.* This is how God wanted them to worship, and worship is *for him.*

Talk with your pastor or Sunday school teacher about ways to worship that will please God.

To learn more about worship, zoom to page 205.

The Priests' Share

²⁸The Lord said to Moses, ²⁹"Tell the people of Israel: 'Someone may bring a fellowship offering to the Lord. He must give part of it as his sacrifice to the Lord. ³⁰He must carry that part of the gift in his own hands. It will be an offering made by fire to the Lord. He must carry the fat and the breast of the animal to the priest. The breast must be presented to the Lord as the priests' share. ³¹Then the priest must burn the fat on the altar. But the breast of the animal will belong to Aaron and the priests. ³²You must also give the right thigh from the fellowship offering to the priest as a gift. ³³It will belong to the priest who offers the blood and fat of

Aaron and his sons. It is from the offerings made by fire to the Lord. Aaron and his sons were given this share on the day they were presented to the Lord as priests. ³⁶On the day the Lord appointed the priests, he commanded Israel to give this share to them. It is to be given to the priests as their share from now on.

³⁷These are the teachings about the whole burnt offering, the grain offering, the sin offering and the penalty offering. They are the teachings about the appointment of priests. And they are the teachings about the fellowship offerings. ³⁸The Lord gave these teachings to Moses on Mount Sinai. It was on the day he commanded the Israel-

ites to bring their offerings to him in the Sinai Desert.

Aaron and His Sons Appointed

8 The Lord said to Moses, ²"Bring Aaron and his sons and their clothes. Bring the special olive oil used in appointing people and things to the service of the Lord. Also bring the bull of the sin offering and the two male sheep. And bring the basket of bread made without yeast. ³Then gather the people together at the entrance to the Meeting Tent."ᵈ ⁴Moses did as the Lord commanded him. The people met together at the entrance to the Meeting Tent.

⁵Then Moses spoke to the people. He said, "This is what the Lord has commanded to be done." ⁶Then Moses brought Aaron and his sons forward. He washed them with water. ⁷He put the inner robe on Aaron. And he tied the cloth belt around Aaron. Then he put the outer robe on him. Next he put the holy vestᵈ on Aaron. Then he tied the skillfully woven belt around him. So the holy vest was tied to Aaron. ⁸Then Moses put the chest covering on him. And he put the Urim and the Thummimᵈ in the chest covering. ⁹He also put the turban on Aaron's head. He put the strip of gold on the front of the turban. This strip of gold is the holy crown. Moses did this as the Lord commanded him to do.

¹⁰Then Moses put the special oil on the Holy Tentᵈ and everything in it. In this way Moses made them holy for the Lord. ¹¹He sprinkled some oil on the altar seven times. He sprinkled the altar and all its tools. He also sprinkled special oil on the large bowl and its base. In this way he made them holy for the Lord. ¹²Then he poured some of the special oil on Aaron's head. In this way he made Aaron holy for the Lord. ¹³Then Moses brought Aaron's sons forward. And he put the inner robes on them. He tied cloth belts around them. Then he put headbands on them. He did these things as the Lord had commanded him.

¹⁴Then Moses brought the bull for the sin offering. And Aaron and his sons put their hands on its head. ¹⁵Moses killed the bull and took some of the blood. With his finger he put some of the blood on all the corners of the altar. In this way he made the altar pure. Then he poured out the rest of the blood at the bottom of the altar. So he made it holy and ready for service to God. ¹⁶Moses took all the fat from the inner organs of the bull. He took the best part of the liver. And he took both kidneys and the fat on them. Then he burned them on the altar. ¹⁷But he took the bull's skin, its meat and its intestines outside the camp. He burned them in a fire outside the camp. Moses did all these things as the Lord had commanded him.

¹⁸Next Moses brought the male sheep of the burnt offering. Aaron and his sons put their hands on its head. ¹⁹Then Moses killed it. He sprinkled the blood on all sides of the altar. ²⁰Moses cut the male sheep into pieces. And he burned the head, the pieces and the fat. ²¹He washed the inner organs and legs with water. Then he burned the whole sheep on the altar. It was a burnt offering made by fire to the Lord. Its smell was pleasing to the Lord. Moses did these things as the Lord had commanded him.

²²Then Moses brought the other male sheep. It was used in appointing Aaron and his sons as priests. They put their hands on its head. ²³Then Moses killed the sheep. He put some of its blood on the bottom of Aaron's right ear. He put some on the thumb of Aaron's right hand. And he put some on the big toe of his right foot. ²⁴Then Moses brought Aaron's sons close to the altar. He put some of the blood on the bottom of their right ears. He put it on the thumbs of their right hands. And he put it on the big toes of their right feet. Then he sprinkled blood on all sides of the altar. ²⁵He took the fat and the fat tail from the sheep. He took all the fat on the inner organs. He took the

best part of the liver. He also took both kidneys, their fat and the right thigh. ²⁶A basket of bread made without yeast is put before the Lord each day. From the basket Moses took a loaf of bread. And he took a loaf made with oil and a wafer. He put these pieces of bread on the fat and right thigh of the male sheep. ²⁷He put all these things in the hands of Aaron and his sons. He presented the pieces as an offering before the Lord. ²⁸Then Moses took them from their hands. And he burned them on the altar on top of the burnt offering. So this was the offering for appointing Aaron and his sons as priests. It was an offering made by fire to the Lord. Its smell was pleasing to the Lord. ²⁹Moses took the breast and presented it as an offering before the Lord. It was Moses' share of the male sheep used in appointing the priests. This was as the Lord had commanded Moses.

³⁰Moses took some of the special oil and some of the blood which was on the altar. He sprinkled some of the oil on Aaron and Aaron's clothes. He also sprinkled some on Aaron's sons and their clothes. In this way Moses made Aaron, his clothes, his sons and their clothes holy for the Lord.

³¹Then Moses said to Aaron and his sons, "I gave you a command. I said, 'Aaron and his sons will eat these things.' So take the meat and basket of bread from the offering for appointing priests. Boil the meat at the door of the Meeting Tent. Eat it there with the bread. ³²If any of the meat or bread is left, burn it. ³³The time of appointing will last seven days. You must not go outside the entrance of the Meeting Tent until that time is up. Stay there until the time of your appointing is finished. ³⁴The Lord commanded the things that were done today. He commanded these things to remove your sins so you will belong to him. ³⁵You must stay at the entrance of the Meeting Tent. Stay there day and night for seven days. If you don't obey the Lord's commands, you will die! The Lord has given me these commands."

³⁶So Aaron and his sons did everything the Lord had commanded through Moses.

Aaron and His Sons Offer Sacrifices

9 On the eighth day after the time of appointing, Moses called for Aaron and his sons. He also called for the older leaders of Israel. ²He said to Aaron, "Take a bull calf and a male sheep. There must be nothing wrong with these animals. The calf will be a sin offering. And the male sheep will be a whole burnt offering. Offer these animals to the Lord. ³Tell the people of Israel, 'Take a male goat for a sin offering. And take a calf and a lamb for a whole burnt offering. The calf and the lamb must each be one year old. There must be nothing wrong with these animals. ⁴Take a bull and a male sheep for fellowship offerings. Take with these animals a grain offering mixed with oil. Offer these things to the Lord. This is because the Lord will appear to you today.'"

⁵So all the people came to the front of the Meeting Tent.^d They brought the things Moses had commanded them to bring. And they stood before the Lord. ⁶Moses said, "You have done what the Lord commanded. So you will see the Lord's glory."

⁷Then Moses told Aaron, "Go to the altar. There offer sin offerings and whole burnt offerings. Do this to remove your sins and the people's sins so you will belong to God. Offer the sacrifices for the people. And perform the acts to remove their sins for them so they will belong to the Lord. Do this as the Lord has commanded."

⁸So Aaron went to the altar. He killed the bull calf as a sin offering for himself. ⁹Then his sons brought the blood to him. Aaron dipped his finger in the blood and put it on the corners of the altar. Then he poured out the rest of the blood at the bottom of the altar. ¹⁰Aaron

took the fat, the kidneys and the best part of the liver from the sin offering. He burned these things on the altar. He did this the way the Lord had commanded Moses. ¹¹Aaron burned the meat and skin outside the camp.

¹²Then Aaron killed the animal for the whole burnt offering. Aaron's sons brought the blood to him. And he sprinkled it on all sides of the altar. ¹³Aaron's sons gave the pieces and head of the burnt offering to Aaron. And he burned them on the altar. ¹⁴Aaron also washed the inner organs and the legs of the burnt offering. And he burned them on the altar.

¹⁵Then Aaron brought the offering that was for the people. He took the goat of the people's sin offering. He killed and offered the goat of the sin offering. He did this just as he had done the first sin offering.

¹⁶Then Aaron brought the whole burnt offering and offered it. He did it as the Lord had commanded. ¹⁷He also brought the grain offering to the altar. He took a handful of the grain and burned it on the altar. This was in addition to the morning's burnt offering.

¹⁸Aaron also killed the bull and the male sheep. These were the fellowship offerings for the people. Aaron's sons brought the blood from these animals to Aaron. He sprinkled it on all sides of the altar. ¹⁹Aaron's sons also brought to Aaron the fat of the bull and the male sheep. They brought the fat tail and the fat covering the inner organs. They also brought the kidneys and the best part of the liver. ²⁰Aaron's sons put these fat parts on the breasts of the bull and sheep. Then Aaron burned these fat parts on the altar. ²¹He presented the breasts and the right thigh before the Lord as the priests' share of the offering. He did this as Moses had commanded.

²²Then Aaron lifted up his hands toward the people and blessed them. Aaron had finished offering the sin offering, the burnt offering and the fellowship offering. Then he stepped down from the altar.

²³Moses and Aaron went into the Meeting Tent. Then they came out and blessed the people. Then the Lord's glory came to all the people. ²⁴Fire came out from the Lord. It burned up the burnt offering and fat on the altar. When the people saw this, they shouted with joy. They bowed facedown on the ground.

Brothers and Sisters
NADAB AND ABIHU • LEVITICUS 10

Do you ever let your brother or sister get you into trouble? Do you sometimes do things you know you shouldn't do? Two brothers, Nadab and Abihu, were supposed to be priests serving in the Holy Tent with their father, Aaron. But Nadab and Abihu didn't take their work seriously. They didn't make the offerings the way God had told them, so God killed both of these brothers. The priests were supposed to be good examples of God's holiness to all the people. God had to punish these young men who did not obey him.

It is important to help your brother or sister do what God wants. Don't get each other into trouble by sinning against God.

To meet a brother and sister who were jealous, fly to page 184.

God Destroys Nadab and Abihu

10 Aaron's sons Nadab and Abihu took their pans for burning incense.[d] They put fire in them and added incense. But they did not use the special fire Moses had commanded them to use. ²So fire came down from the Lord and destroyed Nadab and Abihu. They died in front of the Lord. ³Then Moses said to Aaron, "This is what the Lord was speaking about when he said,

'I must be respected as holy
  by those who come near me.
Before all the people
  I must be given honor.'"

So Aaron did not say anything about the death of his sons.

⁴Aaron's uncle Uzziel had two sons named Mishael and Elzaphan. Moses said to them, "Come here. Pick up your cousins' bodies. Carry them outside the camp away from the front of the Holy Place. ⁵So Mishael and Elzaphan obeyed Moses. They carried the bodies of Nadab and Abihu outside the camp. Nadab and Abihu were still wearing the special priest's inner robes.

⁶Then Moses spoke to Aaron and his other sons, Eleazar and Ithamar. Moses told them, "Don't show any sadness. Don't tear your clothes or leave your hair uncombed. If you do those things, you will die, and the Lord will be angry with all the people. All the people of Israel are your relatives. They may cry loudly about the Lord burning Nadab and Abihu. ⁷But you must not even leave the Meeting Tent.[d] If you go out of the entrance, you will die! This is because the Lord has appointed you to his service." So Aaron, Eleazar and Ithamar obeyed Moses.

⁸Then the Lord said to Aaron, ⁹"You and your sons must not drink wine or beer when you go into the Meeting Tent. If you do, you will die! This law will continue from now on. ¹⁰You must keep what is holy separate from what is not holy. You must keep what is clean[d] separate from what is unclean. ¹¹The Lord gave his laws to Moses. And Moses gave them to the

people. You must teach the people all the laws."

¹²Moses talked to Aaron and his remaining sons, Eleazar and Ithamar. Moses said, "Some of the grain offering is left from the sacrifices offered by fire to the Lord. Eat that part of the grain offering. But do not add yeast to it. Eat it near the altar because it is most holy. ¹³The Law I gave you says this part belongs to you and your sons. But you must eat it in a holy place. It is part of the offerings made by fire to the Lord. I have been commanded to tell you this.

¹⁴"Also, you, your sons and daughters may eat the breast and thigh of the fellowship offering. They were presented to the Lord. You must eat them in a clean place. They are your share of the fellowship offerings given by the Israelites. ¹⁵The people must bring the fat from their animals. It is part of the offering made by fire. They must also bring the thigh and the breast of the fellowship offering. These will be presented to the Lord. They will be the regular share of the offerings for you and your children. The Lord has commanded it."

¹⁶Moses looked for the goat of the sin offering. But it had already been burned up. So he became very angry with Eleazar and Ithamar, Aaron's remaining sons. He said, ¹⁷"You were supposed to eat that goat in a holy place before the Lord! It is most holy! He gave it to you to take away the guilt of the people. The goat was for removing the sins of the people so they will belong to the Lord. ¹⁸You didn't bring the goat's blood inside the Holy Place. So you were supposed to eat the goat in a holy place, as I commanded!"

¹⁹But Aaron said to Moses, "Today they brought their sin offering and burnt offering before the Lord. But these terrible things have still happened to me today! Do you think the Lord would be any happier if I ate the sin offering today?" ²⁰When Moses heard this, he was satisfied.

Rules About What May Be Eaten

11 The Lord spoke to Moses and Aaron. [2]He said, "Tell the people of Israel this: 'These are the land animals you may eat: [3]You may eat any animal that has split hoofs completely divided and chews the cud.[d]

[4]"'Some animals only chew the cud or only have split hoofs. Don't eat these animals. The camel chews the cud but does not have a split hoof. It is unclean[d] for you. [5]The rock badger chews the cud but does not have a split hoof. It is unclean for you. [6]The rabbit chews the cud but does not have a split hoof. It is unclean for you. [7]Now the pig has a split hoof that is completely divided. But it does not chew the cud. It is unclean for you. [8]You must not eat the meat from these animals. Don't even touch their dead bodies. They are unclean for you.

[9]"'Some animals live in the sea or in a river. If the animal has fins and scales, you may eat it. [10]But some animals live in the sea or in a river and do not have fins and scales. This includes the things that fill the water. And it includes all other things that live in the water. You should hate them. [11]You must not eat any meat from them. Don't even touch their dead bodies. This is because you should hate them. [12]You must hate any animal in the water that does not have fins and scales.

[13]"'Also, some birds should not be eaten. They should be hated. You must not eat any of these birds: eagles, vultures, black vultures, [14]kites or any kind of falcon. [15]Don't eat any kind of raven, [16]horned owls, screech owls, sea gulls or any kind of hawk. [17]Don't eat little owls, cormorants, great owls, [18]white owls, desert owls or ospreys. [19]Don't eat storks, any kind of heron, hoopoes or bats.

[20]"'Don't eat insects that have wings and walk on all four feet. They are also to be hated.

[21]"'But you may eat certain insects that have wings and walk on four feet. You may eat those that have legs with joints above their feet so they can jump. [22]These are the insects you may eat: all kinds of locusts, winged locusts, crickets and grasshoppers. [23]But all other insects that have wings and walk on four feet are hated. [24]Those insects will make you unclean. Anyone who touches the dead body of one of these insects will become unclean until evening. [25]If someone picks up one of these dead insects, he must wash his clothes. He will be unclean until evening.

[26]"'Some animals have split hoofs. But the hoofs are not completely divided. And some animals do not chew the cud. They are unclean for you. Anyone who touches the dead body of one of these animals will become unclean. [27]Other animals do not have hoofs at all. They walk on their paws. These animals are unclean for you. Anyone who touches the dead body of one of these animals will become unclean. He will be unclean until evening. [28]Anyone who picks up their dead bodies must wash his clothes. He will be unclean until evening. These animals are unclean for you.

[29]"'These crawling animals are unclean for you: moles, rats, all kinds of great lizards, [30]geckos, crocodiles, lizards, sand reptiles and chameleons. [31]These crawling animals are unclean for you. Anyone who touches their dead bodies will be unclean until evening.

[32]"'If an unclean animal dies and falls on something, that thing will also become unclean. The animal might fall on a thing made from wood, cloth, leather or rough cloth. It does not matter what the thing was used for. Whatever the animal falls on must be washed with water. It will be unclean until evening. Then it will become clean again. [33]The dead, unclean animal might fall into a clay bowl. If it does, anything in the bowl will become unclean. And you must break the bowl. [34]If water from the unclean clay bowl gets on any food, that food will become unclean. [35]If any dead, unclean animal

falls on something, that thing becomes unclean. The animal may fall on a clay oven or a clay baking pan. If so, it must be broken into pieces. These things will be unclean. They are unclean for you. ³⁶"A spring or well that collects water will stay clean. But anyone who touches the dead body of any unclean animal will become unclean. ³⁷A dead, unclean animal might fall on a seed to be planted. That seed is still clean. ³⁸But you might put water on some seeds. If a dead, unclean animal falls on those seeds, they are unclean for you.

³⁹"Also, an animal which you use for food may die. If it does, anyone who touches its body will be unclean until evening. ⁴⁰Anyone who eats meat from this animal's dead body must wash his clothes. He will be unclean until evening. Anyone who picks up the animal's dead body must wash his clothes. He will be unclean until evening.

⁴¹"Every animal that crawls on the ground is one of the hated animals. It must not be eaten. Anyone who picks up the animal's dead body must wash his clothes. He will be unclean until evening. ⁴²You must not eat any of the animals that crawl on the ground. This includes animals that crawl on their stomachs. And it includes animals that walk on all four feet or on many feet. Those are hated animals to you. ⁴³Do not make yourself unclean by these hated animals. You must not become unclean by them. ⁴⁴I am the Lord your God. Keep yourselves holy for me because I am holy. Don't make yourselves unclean with these hated, crawling animals. ⁴⁵I am the Lord who brought you out of Egypt. I did it so I could be your God. You must be holy because I am holy.

⁴⁶"These are the teachings about all of the cattle, birds and other animals on earth. These are the teachings about the animals in the sea. And these are the teachings about the animals that crawl on the ground. ⁴⁷These teachings help people know the difference between unclean animals

and clean animals. They help people know which animals may be eaten and which ones must not be eaten.'"

Rules for New Mothers

12 The Lord said to Moses, ²"Tell the people of Israel this: 'If a woman gives birth to a son, she will become unclean*d* for 7 days. This will be like her being unclean during her monthly period. ³On the eighth day the boy must be circumcised.*d* ⁴Then it will be 33 days before she becomes clean from her loss of blood. She must not touch anything that is holy. She must not enter the holy place until her time of cleansing is finished. ⁵But a woman may give birth to a daughter. Then the mother will be unclean for 2 weeks. This is like her being unclean during her monthly period. It will be 66 days before she becomes clean from her loss of blood.

⁶"After she has a son or daughter, she must have a time of cleansing. When it is over, the new mother must bring certain sacrifices to the Meeting Tent.*d* She must give the priest at the entrance a year-old lamb for a burnt offering. And she must bring a dove or young pigeon for a sin offering. ⁷He will offer them before the Lord to make her clean so she will belong to the Lord again. Then she will be clean from her loss of blood. These are the teachings for a woman who gives birth to a boy or girl.

⁸"If she cannot afford a lamb, she is to bring two doves or two young pigeons. One bird will be for a burnt offering and one for a sin offering. In this way the priest will make her clean so she will belong to the Lord again. And she will be clean.'"

Rules About Skin Diseases

13 The Lord said to Moses and Aaron, ²"Someone might have a swelling on his skin. Or he might have a scab or a bright spot on his skin. If the sore looks like a harmful skin disease, the person must be brought to Aaron the priest. Or he must be brought to one of Aaron's sons, the priests. ³The priest must look at the sore on the person's skin. The hair in the sore may have become white. And the sore may seem deeper than the person's skin. If so, it is a harmful skin disease. When he has finished looking at the person, the priest must announce that the person is unclean.ᵈ

⁴"Sometimes there is a white spot on a person's skin, but the spot does not seem deeper than the skin. If that is true, and if the hair from the spot has not turned white, the priest must separate that person from other people for seven days. ⁵On the seventh day the priest must look at the person again. He may see that the sore has not changed. It might not have spread on the skin. Then the priest must keep the person separated for seven more days. ⁶On the seventh day the priest must look at the person again. The sore may have faded. And it may not have spread on the skin. If that is true, the priest must announce that the person is clean. The sore is only a rash. The person must wash his clothes. Then he will become clean again.

⁷"But the sore may have spread again after the priest has announced him clean. Then the person must come again to the priest. ⁸The priest must look at him. If the rash has spread on the skin, the priest must announce that person is unclean. It is a harmful skin disease.

⁹"If a person has a harmful skin disease, he must be brought to the priest. ¹⁰The priest must look at him. There might be a white swelling in the skin. And the hair may have become white. And the skin may look raw in the swelling. ¹¹If these things are true, it is a harmful skin disease. It is one that he has had for a long time. The priest must announce that the person is unclean. He will not need to separate that person from other people. This is because everyone already knows that the person is unclean.

¹²"Sometimes skin disease spreads all over a person's body. The disease covers that person's skin from his head to his feet, as far as the priest can see. Then the priest must look at the person's whole body. ¹³The priest might see that the disease covers the whole body. It might have turned all of the person's skin white. Then the priest must announce that the person is clean.

¹⁴"But when the person has an open sore, he is not clean. ¹⁵When the priest sees the open sore, he must announce that the person is unclean. The open sore is not clean. It is a harmful skin disease. ¹⁶If the open sore becomes white again, the person must come to the priest. ¹⁷The priest must look at him. If the sores have become white, the priest must announce that the person with the sores is clean. Then he will be clean.

¹⁸"Someone may have a boil on his skin, but it is healed. ¹⁹In the place where the boil was, there might be a white swelling. Or there might be a bright red spot. This place on the skin must be shown to the priest. ²⁰And the priest must look at it. The spot might seem deeper than the skin. And the hair on it might have become white. If these things are true, the priest must announce that the person is unclean. The spot is a harmful skin disease. It has broken out from inside the boil. ²¹But the priest must look at the spot. There might be no white hairs in it. The spot may not be deeper than the skin. And it may have faded. Then the priest must separate the person from other people for seven days. ²²If the spot spreads on the skin, the priest must announce that the person is unclean. It is a disease that will spread. ²³But the bright spot might not spread or change. Then it is only the scar from the old boil. Then the priest must announce that the person is clean.

²⁴"A person might get a burn on his skin. If the open sore becomes white or red, ²⁵the priest must look at it. The white spot might seem deeper than the skin. And the hair at that spot might

have become white. If these things are true, it is a harmful skin disease. The disease has broken out in the burn. Then the priest must announce that the person is unclean. It is a harmful skin disease. ²⁶But the priest must look at the spot. There might be no white hair in the bright spot. And the spot may be no deeper than the skin. It may have faded. Then the priest must separate the person from other people for seven days. ²⁷On the seventh day the priest must look at him again. If the spot has spread on the skin, the priest must announce that the person is unclean. It is a harmful skin disease. ²⁸But the bright spot may not have spread on the skin. It may have faded. Then it is the swelling from the burn. And the priest must announce that the person is clean. The spot is only a scar from the burn.

²⁹"Someone might get a sore on his scalp or on his chin. ³⁰A priest must look at the sore. It may seem to be deeper than the skin. And the hair around it may be thin and yellow. If these things are true, the priest must announce that the person is unclean. It is an itch, a harmful skin disease of the head or chin. ³¹But when the priest looks at it, the sore might not seem deeper than the skin. There might not be any black hair in it. If that is true, the priest must separate the person from other people for seven days. ³²On the seventh day the priest must look at the sore. It may not have spread. There may be no yellow hairs growing in it. And the sore may not seem deeper than the skin. ³³If these things are true, the person must shave himself. But he must not shave the sore place. The priest must separate that person from other people for seven more days. ³⁴On the seventh day the priest must look at the sore. The sore may not have spread on the skin. And it may not seem deeper than the skin. If that is true, the priest must announce that the person is clean. So the person must wash his clothes and become clean.

³⁵But the sore might spread on the skin after the person has become clean. ³⁶Then the priest must look at him again. If the sore has spread on the skin, the priest doesn't need to look for the yellowish hair. The person is unclean. ³⁷But the priest might think the sore has stopped spreading. And black hair may be growing in it. Then the sore has healed. The person is clean. And the priest must announce that he is clean.

³⁸"When a person has white spots on his skin, ³⁹a priest must look at them. If the spots on his skin are dull white, the disease is only a harmless rash. That person is clean.

⁴⁰"A man might lose hair from his head and be bald. He is clean. ⁴¹He might lose hair from the front of his head and have a bald forehead. He is clean. ⁴²But if there is a red-white sore on his scalp, it is a skin disease. ⁴³A priest must look at that person. The swelling of the sore might be red-white. It might look like a skin disease that spreads. ⁴⁴Then that person has a skin disease. He is unclean. And the priest must announce that the person is unclean because of the sore on his head.

⁴⁵"If a person has a skin disease that spreads, he must warn other people. He must shout, 'Unclean, unclean!' His clothes must be torn at the seams. He must let his hair stay uncombed. And he must cover his mouth. ⁴⁶That person will be unclean the whole time he has the disease. He is unclean. He must live alone outside the camp.

Rules About Mildew

⁴⁷"Some clothing might have mildew*d* on it. The cloth might be linen or wool. ⁴⁸It might be woven or knitted. The mildew might be on a piece of leather or on something made from leather. ⁴⁹The mildew might be in the clothing, leather or woven or knitted material. If the mildew is green or red, it is a spreading mildew. Then it must be shown to the priest. ⁵⁰The priest must look at the mildew. And he must put

that thing in a separate place for seven days. ⁵¹On the seventh day he must look at the mildew. It doesn't matter if the mildew is on leather or cloth. It doesn't matter if the cloth is woven or knitted. It doesn't matter what it was used for. If the mildew has spread, it is a mildew that destroys. ⁵²The priest must burn it. It does not matter if it is woven or knitted, wool or linen or a leather article. The mildew is spreading. The thing must be burned.

⁵³"If the priest sees that the mildew has not spread, the cloth or leather must be washed. It does not matter if it is leather or cloth, knitted or woven. It must be washed. ⁵⁴The priest must order the people to wash that piece of leather or cloth. Then he must separate the clothing for seven more days. ⁵⁵After that time the priest must look at it again. If the mildew still looks the same, that thing is unclean.ᵈ It does not matter if the mildew has not spread. You must burn that cloth or piece of leather.

⁵⁶"But when the priest looks at that piece of leather or cloth, the mildew might have faded. Then the priest must tear the mildew out of the piece of leather or cloth. It does not matter if the cloth is woven or knitted. ⁵⁷But the mildew might come back to that piece of leather or cloth. If that happens, the mildew is spreading. And that piece of leather or cloth must be burned. ⁵⁸The cloth, the woven or knitted material, or the leather may be washed. The mildew may then be gone. It must be washed again. Then it will be clean.

⁵⁹"These are the teachings about mildew on pieces of leather or cloth. It doesn't matter if the cloth is woven or knitted."

Rules for Cleansing from Skin Diseases

14 The Lord said to Moses, ²"These are the teachings for people who had a harmful skin disease and have become well. These teachings are for making that person clean.ᵈ

³"A priest must look at the person who had the skin disease. He must go to that person outside the camp. He must see if the skin disease is healed. ⁴If the person is healthy, the priest will tell him to do these things: He must get two living, clean birds. He must also get a piece of cedar wood, a piece of red cloth and a hyssop plant. These things are for cleansing the person with the skin disease.

⁵"The priest must order one bird to be killed in a clay bowl containing fresh water. ⁶Then he will take the other bird that is still alive. He will take the piece of cedar wood, the red cloth and the hyssop. He will dip the living bird and other things into the blood. (This is the blood of the bird that was killed over the fresh water.) ⁷The priest will sprinkle the blood seven times on the person who had the skin disease. He must announce that the person is clean. Then the priest must go to an open field. He must let the living bird go free.

⁸"Next, that person must wash his clothes. He must shave off all his hair. And he must wash with water. Then he will be clean and may go into the camp. But at first he must stay outside his tent for seven days. ⁹On the seventh day he must shave off all his hair. He must shave off his hair, his beard and his eyebrows. He must wash his clothes and bathe his body in water. Then he will be clean.

¹⁰"On the eighth day the person who had the skin disease must take two male lambs. They must have nothing wrong with them. He must also take a year-old female lamb. It must have nothing wrong with it. The person must take six quarts of fine flour mixed with oil. This is for a grain offering. He must also take two-thirds of a pint of olive oil. ¹¹A priest must announce that the person is clean. Then he must bring that person and his sacrifices before the Lord. This is at the entrance of the Meeting Tent.ᵈ ¹²The priest will take one of the male lambs. He will offer it and the olive oil as a guilt offering. And

he will present them before the Lord as an offering. [13]Then he will kill the male lamb in the holy place. He will kill it where they kill the sin offering and the whole burnt offering. The penalty offering is like the sin offering. It belongs to the priest. It is most holy.

[14]"The priest will take some of the blood of the penalty offering. He will put some of it on the bottom of the right ear of the person to be made clean. He will put some of it on the thumb of the person's right hand. And he will put some on the big toe of the person's right foot. [15]The priest will also take some of the oil and pour it into his own left hand. [16]Then he will dip a finger of his right hand into the oil that is in his left hand. He will use his finger to sprinkle some of the oil seven times before the Lord. [17]The priest will put some oil from his hand on the bottom of the right ear of the person to be made clean. He will put some of it on the thumb of the person's right hand. And he will put some of it on the big toe of the person's right foot. The oil will go on these places on top of the blood for the penalty offering. [18]He will put the rest of the oil that is in his left hand on the head of the person to be made clean. In this way the priest will make that person clean so he can belong to the Lord again.

[19]"Next the priest will offer the sin offering. It will make that person clean so he can belong to the Lord again. After this the priest will kill the animal for the whole burnt offering. [20]Then he will offer the burnt offering and grain offering on the altar. In this way he will make that person clean so he can belong to the Lord again.

[21]"But the person may be poor and unable to afford these offerings. Then he must take one male lamb for a penalty offering. It will be presented to the Lord so the priest can make that person clean. Then he can belong to the Lord again. The person must take two quarts of fine flour mixed with oil. It will be used for a grain offering. He must also take two-thirds of a pint of olive oil. [22]He must take two doves or two young pigeons, which he can afford. One bird will be a sin offering. The other will be a whole burnt offering. [23]On the eighth day the person will bring them to the priest at the entrance of the Meeting Tent. The gifts will be offered before the Lord. This is so the person can become clean. [24]The priest will take the lamb for the penalty offering and the oil. He will present them as an offering before the Lord. [25]Then he will kill the lamb of the penalty offering. He will take some of the blood of the penalty offering. He will put it on the bottom of the right ear of the person to be made clean. The priest will put some of this blood on the thumb of the person's right hand. And he will put some on the big toe of the person's right foot. [26]He will also pour some of the oil into his own left hand. [27]Then with a finger of his right hand, he will sprinkle some of the oil from his left hand. He will sprinkle it seven times before the Lord. [28]Then the priest will take some of the oil from his hand. He will put it on the bottom of the right ear of the person to be made clean. He will also put some of it on the thumb of the person's right hand. And he will put some on the big toe of the person's right foot. The oil will go on these places on top of the blood from the penalty offering. [29]The priest must put the rest of the oil that is in his hand on the head of the person to be made clean. In this way the priest will make the person clean so he can belong to the Lord again. [30]Then the priest will offer one of the doves or young pigeons. He must offer what the person can afford. [31]He must offer one of the birds as a sin offering. And he must offer the other bird as a whole burnt offering. He must offer them with the grain offering. In this way the priest will make the person clean so he can belong to the Lord again. The person will become clean.

[32]"These are the teachings for making a person clean. This is done after he has become well from a skin disease. These teachings are for people who cannot afford the regular sacrifices for becoming clean."

Rules for Cleaning Mildew

[33]The Lord also said to Moses and Aaron, [34]"I am giving the land of Canaan to your people. When they enter that land, I might cause mildew[d] to grow in someone's house. [35]The owner of that house must come and tell the priest. He should say, 'I have seen something like mildew in my house.' [36]Then the priest must order the people to empty the house. They must do this before he goes in to look at the mildew. This is so he will not have to say that everything in the house is unclean.[d] After the people have emptied the house, the priest will go in to look at it. [37]He will look at the mildew. The mildew on the walls of the house might be green or red. It might go into the wall's surface. [38]If these things are true, he must go out and close up the house for seven days. [39]On the seventh day the priest must come back and check the house. The mildew may have spread on the walls of the house. [40]If it has, the priest must order the people to tear out the stones with the mildew on them. They should throw the stones away. They must put the stones at a certain unclean place outside the city. [41]Then the priest must have all the inside of the house scraped. The people must throw away the plaster they scraped off the walls. They must put the plaster at a certain unclean place outside the city. [42]Then the owner must put new stones in the walls. And he must cover the walls with new clay plaster.

[43]"A person may have taken away the old stones and plaster. He may have put in new stones and plaster. But mildew may again appear in his house. [44]If it does, the priest must come back and check the house again. If the mildew has spread in the house, it is a mildew that destroys things. So the house is unclean. [45]Then the owner must tear down the house. He must remove all its stones, plaster and wood. He must take them to the unclean place outside the city. [46]Anyone who goes into that house will be unclean until evening. [47]Anyone who eats in that house or lies down there must wash his clothes.

[48]"After new stones and plaster have been put in a house, the priest must check it again. The mildew may not have spread in the house. Then the priest will announce that the house is clean. This is because the mildew is gone.

[49]"Then, to make the house clean, the priest must take two birds. He must also take a piece of cedar wood, a piece of red cloth and a hyssop plant. [50]He will kill one bird in a clay bowl containing fresh water. [51]Then he will take the other bird that is still alive. He will also take the cedar wood, the hyssop and the red cloth. He will dip the living bird and other things into the blood. (This is the blood of the bird that was killed over the fresh water.) Then the priest will sprinkle the blood on the house seven times. [52]He will use the bird's blood, the fresh water and the live bird. And he will use the cedar wood, the hyssop and the red cloth. With these things he will make the house clean. [53]The priest will go to an open field outside the city. And he will let the living bird go free. This is how the priest makes the house clean and ready for service to the Lord."

[54]These are the teachings about any kind of skin disease. [55]These are the teachings for mildew on pieces of cloth or in a house. [56]These are also the teachings for swellings, rashes or bright spots on the skin. [57]They teach when things are unclean and when they are clean. These are the teachings about all these kinds of diseases.

Rules About a Man's Body

15 The Lord also said to Moses and Aaron, ²"Say to the people of Israel: 'When a fluid comes from a man's body, he is unclean.*d* ³It doesn't matter if the fluid flows freely or if it is blocked from flowing.

⁴"'The man who discharges the body fluid may lie on a bed. If he does, that bed becomes unclean. Everything he sits on becomes unclean. ⁵Also anyone who touches his bed must wash his clothes and bathe in water. This person will be unclean until evening. ⁶Someone might sit on something that the man who discharges the fluid sat on. If he does, he must wash his clothes and bathe in water. He will be unclean until evening. ⁷Anyone who touches the man who discharges the body fluid must wash his clothes and bathe in water. The person will be unclean until evening.

⁸"'The man who discharges the body fluid might spit on a clean person. If so, the person who was clean must wash his clothes. He must bathe in water. The person will be unclean until evening. ⁹Everything on which the man who is unclean has ridden will become unclean. ¹⁰Someone might touch something that was under the man who discharges a body fluid. If he does, he will be unclean until evening. Someone might carry these things that were under the man who discharges a body fluid. This person must wash his clothes and bathe in water. He will be unclean until evening.

¹¹"'The man who discharges a body fluid may not have washed his hands in water. If he touches another person, that person must wash his clothes. That person must bathe in water. He will be unclean until evening.

¹²"'A man who discharges a body fluid may touch a clay bowl. That bowl must be broken. If he touches a wooden bowl, that bowl must be washed in water.

¹³"'A man who discharges a body fluid may be made clean. He must count seven days for himself for his cleansing. He must wash his clothes and bathe his body in fresh water. Then he will be clean. ¹⁴On the eighth day he must take two doves or two young pigeons. He must come before the Lord at the entrance of the Meeting Tent.*d* He will give the two birds to the priest. ¹⁵The priest will offer the birds. One bird is for a sin offering. The other is for a burnt offering. So the priest will make that man clean so he can belong to the Lord again.

¹⁶"'If semen*n* goes out from a man, he must bathe in water. He will be unclean until evening. ¹⁷If the fluid gets on any clothing or leather, it must be washed with water. It will be unclean until evening.

¹⁸"'If a man has sexual relations with a woman and semen comes out, both people must bathe in water. They will be unclean until evening.

Rules About a Woman's Body

¹⁹"'When a woman has her monthly period, she is unclean*d* for seven days. Anyone who touches her will be unclean until evening. ²⁰Anything she lies on during this time will be unclean. Everything she sits on during that time will be unclean. ²¹Anyone who touches her bed must wash his clothes and bathe in water. That person will be unclean until evening. ²²Anyone who touches something she has sat on must wash his clothes and bathe in water. That person will be unclean until evening. ²³It does not matter if the person touched the woman's bed or something she sat on. That person will be unclean until evening.

²⁴"'A man may have sexual relations with a woman during her monthly period. If he does, he will be unclean for seven days. Every bed he lies on will also be unclean.

²⁵"'A woman might have a loss of blood for many days. It may not be

---

ⁿsemen A man's body fluid by which he can make a woman pregnant.

during her regular monthly period. Or she may continue to have a loss of blood after her regular period. If she does, she will be unclean, as she is during her monthly period. She will be unclean for as long as she continues to bleed. 26Any bed she lies on during all the time of her bleeding will be like her bed during her regular monthly period. Everything she sits on will be unclean. It will be like during her regular monthly period.

27"If anyone touches those things, that person will be unclean. He must wash his clothes and bathe in water. He will be unclean until evening. 28When the woman becomes clean from her bleeding, she must wait seven days. After this she will be clean. 29Then on the eighth day she must take two doves or two young pigeons. She must bring them to the priest at the entrance of the Meeting Tent.d 30Then the priest must offer one bird for a sin offering. He must offer the other bird for a whole burnt offering. So the priest will make her clean so she can belong to the Lord again.

31"So you must warn the people of Israel to stay separated from things that make them unclean. If you don't warn the people, they might make my Holy Tentd unclean. And then they would have to die!'"

32These are the teachings for the man who discharges a body fluid. These are the teachings for men who become unclean from semenn coming out of their bodies. 33These are the teachings for women who become unclean from their monthly period. These are the teachings for anyone who becomes unclean by having sexual relations with another person who is unclean.

The Day of Cleansing

16 Now two of Aaron's sons had died while offering incensed to the Lord. At that time the Lord spoke to Moses. 2He said, "Talk to your brother Aaron. Tell him there are times when he cannot go behind the curtain into the Most Holy Place where the Holy Boxd is. If he goes in when I appear in a cloud over the lid on the Holy Box, he will die.

3"Aaron may enter the Most Holy Place only on the Day of Cleansing. Before he enters, he must offer a bull for a sin offering. And he must offer a male sheep for a whole burnt offering. 4He must put on these clothes. He will put on the holy linen inner robe. The linen underclothes will be next to his body. His belt will be the cloth belt. And he will wear the linen turban. These are holy clothes. So he must wash his whole body with water before he puts them on.

5"Aaron must take from the people of Israel two male goats for a sin offering. And he must take one male sheep for a burnt offering. 6Then he will offer the bull for the sin offering. This sin offering is for himself. Then he will perform the acts to remove sins from him and his family so they will belong to the Lord.

7"Next Aaron will take the two goats. He will bring them before the Lord at the entrance to the Meeting Tent.d 8Aaron will throw lotsd for the two goats. One lot will be for the Lord. The other lot will be for the goat that removes sin. 9Then Aaron will take the goat that was chosen for the Lord by throwing the lot. He must offer this goat as a sin offering. 10The other goat was chosen by lot to remove the sin. It must be brought alive before the Lord. The priest will use it to perform the acts to remove Israel's sin so they will belong to the Lord. Then this goat will be sent out into the desert.

11"Then Aaron will offer the bull as a sin offering for himself. This will remove the sins of him and his family so they will belong to the Lord. He will kill the bull for the sin offering for himself. 12Then he must take a pan full of burning coals from the altar before the

nsemen   A man's body fluid by which he can make a woman pregnant.

Lord. Aaron must take two handfuls of sweet incense that has been ground into powder. He must bring it into the room behind the curtain. ¹³He must put the incense on the fire before the Lord. Then the cloud of incense will cover the lid on the Holy Box. Then when Aaron comes in, he will not die. ¹⁴Also, Aaron must take some of the blood from the bull. He must sprinkle it with his finger on the front of the lid. Then, with his finger he will sprinkle the blood seven times in front of the lid.

¹⁵"Then Aaron must kill the goat of the sin offering for the people. He must bring this goat's blood into the room behind the curtain. He must do with the goat's blood as he did with the bull's blood. He must sprinkle the goat's blood on the lid and in front of it. ¹⁶The people in Israel have been unclean.ᵈ So Aaron will perform the acts to make the Most Holy Place ready for service to the Lord. Then it will be clean from the sins and crimes of the people of Israel. He must do this because the Meeting Tent stays in the middle of unclean people. ¹⁷When Aaron makes the Most Holy Place ready for service to the Lord, no one is allowed in the Meeting Tent. No one must go in until Aaron comes out. So Aaron will perform the acts to remove sins from himself and his family so they will belong to the Lord. Then he will remove the sins of all the people of Israel so they will belong to the Lord. ¹⁸Afterward he will go out to the altar that is before the Lord. And he will make the altar ready for service to the Lord. Aaron will take some of the bull's blood and some of the goat's blood. He will put it on the corners of the altar on all sides. ¹⁹Then he will sprinkle some of the blood with his finger. He will sprinkle it on the altar seven times. In this way Aaron will make the altar holy for the Lord. And it will be clean from all the sins of the people of Israel.

²⁰"Aaron will make the Most Holy Place, the Meeting Tent and the altar clean. Then he will bring the goat alive to the Lord. ²¹He will put both his hands on the head of the living goat. Then he will confess all the sins and crimes of Israel over the goat. In this way Aaron will put the people's sins on the goat's head. Then he will send the goat away into the desert. A man who has been appointed will lead the goat away. ²²So the goat will carry all the people's sins on itself. It will go to a lonely place in the desert. The man who leads the goat will let it loose there.

²³"Then Aaron will enter the Meeting Tent. He will take off the linen clothes. (He had put them on before he went into the Most Holy Place.) He must leave these clothes there. ²⁴He will wash his whole body with water in a holy place. Then he will put on his regular clothes. He will come out and offer the whole burnt offering for himself. And he will offer the whole burnt offering for the people. He will remove sins from himself and the people so they will belong to the Lord. ²⁵Then he will burn the fat of the sin offering on the altar.

²⁶"The person who led the goat into the desert must wash his clothes. Then he must wash his whole body with water. After that, he may come back into the camp.

²⁷"The bull and goat for the sin offerings must be taken outside the camp. The blood from these animals was brought into the Most Holy Place. It was to make the Holy Place ready for service to the Lord. The priests will burn the animals' skins, bodies and intestines in the fire. ²⁸Then the one who burns them must wash his clothes. And he must wash his whole body with water. After that, he may come back into the camp.

²⁹"This law will always continue for you: On the tenth day of the seventh month, you must not eat. You must not do any work. The travelers or foreigners living with you must not work either. ³⁰On this day the priests make you clean so you will belong to the Lord again. All your sins will be

removed. [31]This is a very important day of rest for you. And you must not eat. This law will continue forever.

[32]"So the appointed priest will perform the acts for making things ready for service to the Lord. He is the priest on whom oil was poured. He is appointed to take his father's place. That priest must put on the holy linen clothes. [33]He must make the Most Holy Place ready for service to the Lord. He must make the Meeting Tent and the altar ready for service to the Lord. He must remove the sins of himself and all the people of Israel so they will belong to the Lord. [34]That law for removing the sins of the Israelites so they will belong to the Lord will continue forever. You will do these things once a year."

So they did the things the Lord had commanded Moses.

Offering Sacrifices

17 The Lord said to Moses, [2]"Speak to Aaron, his sons and all the people of Israel. Tell them: 'This is what the Lord has commanded: [3]An Israelite might sacrifice an ox, a lamb or a goat. He might kill it inside the camp or outside it. [4]But he should have brought the animal to the entrance to the Meeting Tent.[d] He should have given the animal as a gift to the Lord. If he didn't, he is guilty of killing. He must be separated from his people. [5]This rule is so people will bring their sacrifices to the Lord. They have been sacrificing in the open fields. But they must bring those animals to the Lord at the entrance of the Meeting Tent. They must bring them to the priest and offer them as fellowship offerings. [6]Then the priest will sprinkle the blood from those animals on the Lord's altar. It is near the entrance to the Meeting Tent. And the priest will burn the fat from those animals on the altar. This smell will be pleasing to the Lord. [7]They must not offer any more sacrifices to their goat idols. They have chased after those other gods. In that way they have acted like prostitutes.[d] These rules will continue for people from now on.'

[8]"Tell the people this: 'Someone might offer a burnt offering or sacrifice. He might be a citizen of Israel. Or he might be a traveler or foreigner living with you. [9]That person must take his sacrifice to the entrance to the Meeting Tent. There he may offer it to the Lord. If he does not do this, he must be separated from his people.

[10]"'I will be against anyone who eats blood. It does not matter if it is a citizen of Israel or a foreigner living with you. I will separate that person from his people. [11]This is because the life of the body is in the blood. And I have given you rules for pouring that blood on the altar. You must do this to remove your sins so you will belong to the Lord. It is the blood that removes the sins from your life so you will belong to the Lord. [12]So I tell the people of Israel this: "None of you may eat blood. And no foreigner living among you may eat blood."

[13]"'Someone may catch a wild animal or bird that can be eaten. The person may be a citizen of Israel or a foreigner living among you. He must pour the blood on the ground and cover it with dirt. [14]This is because if blood is still in the meat, the animal's life is still in it. So I give this command to the people of Israel: "Don't eat meat that still has blood in it. Anyone who eats blood must be separated from his people."

[15]"'Someone may eat an animal that died by itself. Or he may eat an animal that was killed by another animal. The person may be a citizen of Israel or a foreigner living among you. If he eats the animal, he will be unclean until evening. He must wash his clothes and whole body with water. [16]If he does not wash his clothes and bathe his body, he will be guilty of sin.'"

Rules About Sexual Relations

18 The Lord said to Moses, [2]"Tell the people of Israel: 'I am the Lord your God. [3]In the past you lived in

Egypt. You must not do what was done in that country. And you must not do as they do in the land of Canaan where I am bringing you. Do not follow their customs. ⁴You must obey my rules and follow them. I am the Lord your God. ⁵Obey my laws and rules. A person who obeys my laws and rules will live because of them. I am the Lord.

⁶"You must never have sexual relations with your close relatives. I am the Lord.

⁷"You must not shame your father by having sexual relations with your mother. She is your mother. Do not have sexual relations with her. ⁸You must not have sexual relations with your father's wife. That would shame your father.

⁹"You must not have sexual relations with your sister. She may be the daughter of your father or your mother. It doesn't matter if she was born in your house or somewhere else.

¹⁰"You must not have sexual relations with your granddaughter. She may be your son's daughter or your daughter's daughter. That would bring shame on you.

¹¹"If your father and his wife have a daughter, she is your sister. You must not have sexual relations with her.

¹²"You must not have sexual relations with your father's sister. She is your father's close relative. ¹³You must not have sexual relations with your mother's sister. She is your mother's close relative. ¹⁴You must not have sexual relations with the wife of your father's brother. This would shame him. His wife is your aunt.

¹⁵"You must not have sexual relations with your daughter-in-law. She is your son's wife. Do not have sexual relations with her.

¹⁶"You must not have sexual relations with your brother's wife. That would shame your brother.

¹⁷"You must not have sexual relations with both a woman and her daughter. And do not have sexual relations with this woman's grand-daughter. It may be the daughter of her son or her daughter. They are her close relatives. It is evil to do this.

¹⁸"While your wife is still living, you must not take her sister as another wife. Do not have sexual relations with her.

¹⁹"You must not go near a woman to have sexual relations with her during her monthly period. She is unclean*d* during this time.

²⁰"You must not have sexual relations with your neighbor's wife and make yourself unclean with her.

²¹"You must not give any of your children to be sacrificed to Molech.*d* This will show that you do not respect your God. I am the Lord.

²²"You must not have sexual relations with a man as you would a woman. That is a hated sin.

²³"You must not have sexual relations with an animal and make yourself unclean with it. Also a woman must not have sexual relations with an animal. It is not natural.

²⁴"Don't make yourself unclean by any of these wrong things. I am forcing nations out of their countries because they did these sins. And I am giving their land to you. ²⁵The land has become unclean. So I punished it for its sins. And the land is throwing out those people who live there.

²⁶"You must obey my laws and rules. You must not do any of these hated sins. These rules are for the citizens of Israel. They are also for the people who live with you. ²⁷The people who lived in the land before you did all these hated things. So the land became unclean. ²⁸If you do these things, you will also make the land unclean. And it will throw you out as it threw out the nations before you. ²⁹Anyone who does these hated sins must be separated from his people. ³⁰The people who lived in the land before you have done these hated sins. But you must not do them. You must obey my laws. Don't make yourself unclean by these hated sins. I am the Lord your God.'"

Other Laws

19 The Lord said to Moses, ²"Tell all the people of Israel: 'I am the Lord your God. You must be holy because I am holy.

³"Each person among you must respect his mother and father. And you must keep my Sabbaths.*d* I am the Lord your God.

onto the ground, don't gather it up. ¹⁰Don't pick all the grapes in your vineyards. And don't pick up the grapes that fall to the ground. You must leave those things for poor people. You must also leave them for people traveling through your country. I am the Lord your God.

What God Is Like
LEVITICUS 19:1

Do you wonder what God is like? Is he big or small? Old or young? Nice or mean? Friendly or scary? As you read the Bible, look for words that describe God and help you know what he is like. Leviticus 19:1 gives us one important description of God: he is *holy*. That word *holy* means that God is absolutely pure and perfect in every way. He never does, says, or thinks anything wrong. Holiness is hard for us to understand, since we have never met anyone (other than Jesus) who is truly holy. But that is what God is: *holy*.

Because God is holy, you don't ever have to worry about what he is going to be like when you talk to him in prayer or worship him in church. You know that he is perfectly good, righteous, loving, and kind, and he never changes. He will be the same tomorrow as he was the day before. He is *holy*.

To learn more about what God is like, zoom to page 702.

⁴"'Do not worship idols. Do not make statues or gods for yourselves. I am the Lord your God.

⁵"'You may sacrifice a fellowship offering to the Lord. If you do, you must offer it so you will be accepted. ⁶You may eat it the same day you offer it. And you may also eat it on the next day. But if any is left on the third day, you must burn it up. ⁷If any of it is eaten on the third day, it is unclean.*d* It will not be accepted. ⁸Anyone who eats it then will be guilty of sin. This is because he did not respect the holy things that belong to the Lord. He must be separated from his people.

⁹"'You harvest your crops on your land. But do not harvest all the way to the corners of your fields. If grain falls

¹¹"'You must not steal. You must not cheat people. You must not lie to each other. ¹²You must not make a false promise by my name. If you do that, you will show that you don't respect your God. I am the Lord.

¹³"'You must not cheat your neighbor. You must not rob him. You must not keep a hired worker's salary all night until morning. ¹⁴You must not curse a deaf man. And you must not put something in front of a blind person to make him fall. But you must respect your God. I am the Lord.

¹⁵"'Be fair in your judging. You must not show special favor to poor people or great people. You must be fair when you judge your neighbor. ¹⁶You must not spread false stories against other

people. You must not do anything that would put your neighbor's life in danger. I am the Lord.

¹⁷"'You must not hate your brother in your heart. If your neighbor does something wrong, tell him about it. If you do not, you will be partly to blame. ¹⁸Forget about the wrong things people do to you. You must not try to get even. Love your neighbor as you love yourself. I am the Lord.

the sins of the man so he will belong to the Lord. Then the man will be forgiven for his sin.

²³"'In the future you will enter your country. You will plant many kinds of trees for food. After planting a tree, wait three years before using its fruit.

Friendships
LEVITICUS 19:18

"**H**ow could you do such a dumb thing?" "We don't want you to come over—we'll have more fun without you." "I could have hit that ball much farther than you did!" Words like these can hurt our feelings. Even our friends sometimes act like they don't care about us or how we feel.

When others criticize us or make us feel bad, it is natural to want to get even. But God tells us that being a true friend means loving other people, even when they are mean to us.

The next time someone in your family or one of your friends is unkind, remember God's advice. Don't try to get even. Instead of saying or doing something mean, treat that person the way you would like to be treated.

To find out what God really wants from you, zoom to page 224.

¹⁹"'Obey my laws. You must not mate two different kinds of cattle. You must not sow your field with two different kinds of seed. You must not wear clothing made from two different kinds of material mixed together.

²⁰"'A man might have sexual relations with a slave girl of another man. But this slave girl has not been bought or given her freedom. If this happens, there must be punishment. But they are not to be put to death. This is because the woman was not free. ²¹The man must bring a male sheep as his penalty offering. He must bring it to the Lord at the entrance to the Meeting Tent.ᵈ ²²The priest will offer the male sheep as a penalty offering before the Lord. It will be for the man's sin. The priest will perform the acts to remove

²⁴In the fourth year the fruit from the tree will be the Lord's. It will be a holy offering of praise to him. ²⁵Then in the fifth year, you may eat the fruit from the tree. The tree will then produce more fruit for you. I am the Lord your God.

²⁶"'You must not eat anything with the blood in it.

"'You must not try to tell the future by signs or black magic.

²⁷"'You must not cut the hair on the sides of your heads. And you must not cut the edges of your beard. ²⁸You must not cut your body to show sadness for someone who died. Do not put tattoo marks on yourselves. I am the Lord.

²⁹"'You must not make your daughter become a prostitute.ᵈ That only shows you do not respect her. If you do

this, the country will be filled with all kinds of sin.

³⁰"Obey the laws about Sabbaths. You must respect my Most Holy Place. I am the Lord.

³¹"Do not go to mediums*ᵈ* or fortune-tellers for advice. If you do, you will become unclean. I am the Lord your God.

³²"Show respect to old people. Stand up when they come into the room. Show respect also to your God. I am the Lord.

³³"Do not mistreat foreigners living in your country. ³⁴Treat them just as you treat your own citizens. Love foreigners as you love yourselves, because you were foreigners one time. That was in Egypt. I am the Lord your God.

³⁵"Be fair when you judge people. And be fair when you measure and weigh things. ³⁶Your weighing baskets should be the right size. And your jars should hold the right amount of liquid. Your weights and balances should weigh correctly. I am the Lord your God. I brought you out of the land of Egypt.

³⁷"Remember all my laws and rules, and obey them. I am the Lord.'"

Warnings About Various Sins

20 The Lord said to Moses, ²"You must also tell the people of Israel these things: 'A person in your country might give one of his children to Molech.*ᵈ* That person must be killed. It doesn't matter if he is a citizen or a foreigner living in Israel. You must throw stones at him and kill him. ³I will be against him. I will separate him from his people. This is because he gave his children to Molech. He showed that he did not respect my holy name. And he made my Holy Place unclean.*ᵈ* ⁴The people of the community might ignore that person. They might not kill the one who gave his children to Molech. ⁵But I will be against him and his family. I will separate him from his people. I will do this to anyone who is unfaithful to me and who wor-

ships Molech.

⁶"I will be against anyone who goes to mediums*ᵈ* and fortune-tellers for advice. He is being unfaithful to me. So I will separate him from his people.

⁷"Be my holy people. Be holy because I am holy. I am the Lord your God. ⁸Remember and obey my laws. I am the Lord, and I have made you holy.

⁹"Anyone who curses his father or mother must be put to death. He has cursed his father or mother. So he must be punished.

Punishments for Sexual Sins

¹⁰"A man might have sexual relations with his neighbor's wife. If he does, both the man and the woman are guilty of adultery.*ᵈ* So they must be put to death. ¹¹A man might have sexual relations with his father's wife. If he does, both the man and his father's wife must be put to death. They have brought it on themselves. That man has shamed his father.

¹²"A man might have sexual relations with his daughter-in-law. If he does, both of them must be put to death. What they have done is not natural. It must be punished.

¹³"A man might have sexual relations with another man as a man does with a woman. If he does, these two men have done a hated sin. They must be put to death. They have brought it on themselves.

¹⁴"A man might have sexual relations with both a woman and her mother. This is evil. The people must burn that man and the two women in fire. Do this so that your people will not be evil.

¹⁵"A man might have sexual relations with an animal. If he does, he must be put to death. And you must also kill the animal. ¹⁶A woman might have sexual relations with an animal. If she does, you must kill the woman and the animal. They must be put to death. They have brought it on themselves.

¹⁷"It is shameful for a brother to

marry his sister and to have sexual relations with her. In front of everyone they must both be separated from their people. The man has shamed his sister. And he is guilty of sin.

18"'A man might have sexual relations with a woman during her monthly period. If he does, both the woman and the man must be separated from their people. They sinned because they showed the source of her blood.

19"'Do not have sexual relations with your mother's sister or your father's sister. That would shame a close relative. Both of you are guilty of this sin.

20"'A man must not have sexual relations with his uncle's wife. That would shame his uncle. That man and his uncle's wife would die without children. They are guilty of sin.

21"'It is unclean for a man to marry his brother's wife. That man has shamed his brother. They would have no children.

22"'Remember all my laws and rules, and obey them. I am leading you to your own land. If you obey my laws and rules, that land will not throw you out. 23I am forcing the people who live there out of that country ahead of you. Because they did all these sins I have hated them. Do not live the way those people lived.

24"'I have told you that you will get their land. I will give it to you as your very own. It is a land where much food grows. I am the Lord your God. I have set you apart from other people and made you my own. 25So you must treat clean animals and birds differently from unclean animals. Do not make yourselves unclean by any of these unclean birds or animals or things that crawl on the ground. I have made them unclean for you. 26I have set you apart from other people. So you must be holy to me. This is because I am the Lord, and I am holy.

27"'A man or woman who is a medium*d* or a fortune-teller must be put to death. You must kill them with stones. They have brought it on themselves.'"

How Priests Must Behave

21 The Lord said to Moses, "Tell these things to Aaron's sons, the priests: 'A priest must not make himself unclean*d* by touching a dead person. 2But if the dead person was one of his close relatives, he may touch him. The priest may make himself unclean if the dead person is his mother or father, son or daughter, brother or 3unmarried sister. This sister is close to him because she has no husband. So the priest may make himself unclean for her if she dies. 4But a priest must not make himself unclean if the dead person was only related to him by marriage.

5"'Priests must not shave their heads. They must not shave off the edges of their beards. They must not cut their bodies. 6Priests must be holy to their God. They must show respect for God's name. This is because they present the offerings made by fire to the Lord. This is the food of their God. So they must be holy.

7"'A priest serves God in a special way. So he must not marry an unclean prostitute*d* or a divorced woman. 8Treat the priest in a special way. Think of him as holy. This is because he offers up the food of your God. I am the Lord. I make you holy. And I am holy.

9"'If a priest's daughter makes herself unclean by becoming a prostitute, she shames her father. She must be burned with fire.

10"'The high priest was chosen from among his brothers. The special olive oil used in appointing people and things to the service of the Lord was poured on his head. He was appointed to wear the priestly clothes. So he must not do things to show his sadness in public. He must not let his hair go uncombed. He must not tear his clothes. 11He must not go into a house where there is a dead body. He must not make himself unclean, even if it is his own father or mother. 12The high priest must not go out of the Holy Place. If he does and becomes unclean, he would make God's Holy Place unclean. The special oil used in appointing priests was poured on the high priest's head. This separated him from the rest of the people. I am the Lord.

[13] "The high priest must marry a woman who is a virgin.[d] [14]He must not marry a widow, a divorced woman or a prostitute. He must marry a virgin from his own people. [15]This is so the people will respect his children as his own. I am the Lord. I have set the high priest apart for his special job.'"

[16]The Lord said to Moses, [17]"Tell Aaron: 'Some of your descendants[d] might have something wrong with them. If they do, they must never offer the special food of their God. [18]Anyone who has something wrong with him must not serve as priest. And he must not bring sacrifices to me. These people cannot serve as priests: blind men, crippled men, men with damaged faces, deformed men, [19]men with a crippled foot or hand, [20]hunchbacks, dwarfs, men who have something wrong with their eyes, men who have an itching disease or a skin disease or men who have damaged sex glands.

[21]"'One of Aaron's descendants[d] might have something wrong with him. If he does, he cannot make the offerings made by fire to the Lord. He has something wrong with him. He cannot offer the food of his God. [22]But he is from the family of priests. So he may eat the most holy food. He may also eat the holy food. [23]But he may not go through the curtain into the Most Holy Place. He may not go near the altar. He has something wrong with him. He must not make my Holy Place unfit. I am the Lord. I make these things holy.'"

[24]So Moses told these things to Aaron, Aaron's sons and all the people of Israel.

22

The Lord said to Moses, [2]"Tell Aaron and his sons: 'The people of Israel will give offerings to me. These offerings are holy, and they are mine. So you must respect these offerings. This will show that you respect my holy name. I am the Lord. [3]The people of Israel made the offerings holy for me. One of your descendants[d] might be unclean[d] and touch the offerings. From now on, anyone who does must be separated from appearing before me. I am the Lord.

[4]"'One of Aaron's descendants might have one of the harmful skin diseases. Or he might discharge a body fluid. He cannot eat the holy offerings until he becomes clean. He can become unclean from touching a dead body or from his own semen.[n] [5]He will become unclean if he touches any unclean crawling animal. He will become unclean if he touches an unclean person. It doesn't matter what made him unclean. [6]Anyone who touches those things will become unclean until evening. That person must not eat the holy offerings. But if he washes with water, he may eat the holy offerings. [7]He will be clean only after the sun goes down. Then he may eat the holy offerings. The offerings are his food.

[8]"'A priest might find an animal that died by itself. Or he might find one that was killed by some other animal. He must not eat that dead animal. If he eats it, he will become unclean. I am the Lord.

[9]"'The priests must keep all the rules I have given. That way they will not become guilty. If they are careful, they will not die. I am the Lord. I have made them holy. [10]Only people in a priest's family may eat the holy offerings. A visitor staying with the priest must not eat it. A hired worker must not eat it. [11]But the priest might buy a slave with his own money. If he does, that slave may eat the holy offerings. Slaves who were born in the priest's house may also eat the priest's food. [12]A priest's daughter might marry a person who is not a priest. If she does, she must not eat any of the holy offerings.

---

[n]**semen**　A man's body fluid by which he can make a woman pregnant.

¹³The husband of a priest's daughter might die. Or the daughter might become divorced. She might not have children to support her. So she might go back to her father's house where she lived as a child. If this happens, she may eat some of her father's food. But only people from a priest's family may eat this food.

¹⁴"Someone might eat some of the holy offering by mistake. That person must pay back the priest for that holy food. He must also pay the priest another one-fifth of the price of that food.

¹⁵"'The people of Israel will give offerings to the Lord. These gifts become holy. So the priest must not treat these holy things as though they were not holy. ¹⁶The priests might allow someone who is not a priest to eat the holy offerings. If they do, they are treating those offerings as though they were not holy. The person who eats will become guilty. He will have to pay for it. I am the Lord. I make them holy.'"

¹⁷The Lord said to Moses, ¹⁸"Tell Aaron and his sons and all the people of Israel: 'A citizen of Israel or a foreigner living in Israel might want to bring a whole burnt offering. It might be for some special promise he has made. Or it might be a special gift he wanted to give to the Lord. ¹⁹If he does, he must bring a male animal. It must have nothing wrong with it. The gift might be a bull, a sheep or a goat. This is so it might be accepted for him. ²⁰He must not bring an animal that has something wrong with it. It will not be accepted for him.

²¹"'Someone might bring a fellowship offering to the Lord. That offering might be payment for a special promise the person made. Or it may be a special gift the person wanted to give the Lord. It might be a bull or a sheep. But it must be healthy. There must be nothing wrong with it. This is so it might be accepted for him. ²²You must not offer to the Lord any animal that is blind. It must not have broken bones or be crippled. It must not have running sores or any sort of skin disease. You must not offer any animals like these on the altar. They cannot be used as an offering by fire to the Lord.

²³"Sometimes a bull or lamb is smaller than normal. Or it may not be perfectly formed. If someone wants to give that animal as a special gift to the Lord, it will be accepted. But it will not be accepted as payment for a special promise the person made.

²⁴"'An animal might have bruised, crushed, torn or cut sex glands. If it does, you must not offer that animal to the Lord in your own land. ²⁵You must not take such animals from foreigners as sacrifices to the Lord. This is because the animals have been hurt in some way. They have something wrong with them. They will not be accepted for you.'"

²⁶The Lord said to Moses, ²⁷"When an ox, a sheep or a goat is born, it must stay seven days with its mother. But from the eighth day on, this animal will be accepted as a sacrifice. It may be offered by fire to the Lord. ²⁸But you must not kill the animal and its mother on the same day. This rule is the same for an ox or a sheep.

²⁹"You might want to offer some special offering of thanks to the Lord. But you must do it in a way that pleases the Lord. ³⁰You must eat the whole animal that same day. You must not leave any of the meat for the next morning. I am the Lord.

³¹"Remember my commands and obey them. I am the Lord. ³²Show respect for my holy name. You Israelites must remember that I am holy. I am the Lord. I have made you holy. ³³I brought you out of Egypt. I became your God. I am the Lord."

Special Holidays

23 The Lord said to Moses, ²"Tell the people of Israel: 'You will announce the Lord's appointed feasts as holy meetings. These are my special feasts.

The Sabbath

3"'There are six days for you to work. But the seventh day will be a special day of rest. It is a day for a holy meeting. You must not do any work. It is a Sabbath[d] to the Lord in all your homes.

The Passover and Unleavened Bread

4"'These are the Lord's appointed feasts. You will announce the holy meetings at the times set for them. 5The Lord's Passover[d] is on the fourteenth day of the first month. It begins at twilight. 6The Feast[d] of Unleavened Bread begins on the fifteenth day of the same month. You will eat bread made without yeast for seven days. 7On the first day of this feast you will have a holy meeting. On that day you must not do any work. 8For seven days you will bring an offering made by fire to the Lord. There will be a holy meeting on the seventh day. And on that day you must not do any regular work.'"

The Feast of Harvests

9The Lord said to Moses, 10"Tell the people of Israel: 'You will enter the land I will give you. You will gather its harvest. At that time you must bring the first bundle of grain from your harvest to the priest. 11The priest will present the bundle before the Lord. Then it will be accepted for you. He will present the bundle on the day after the Sabbath.[d]

12"'On the day when you present the bundle of grain, offer a male lamb. It must be one year old. There must be nothing wrong with it. It will be a burnt offering to the Lord. 13You must also offer a grain offering. It should be four quarts of fine flour mixed with olive oil. It is an offering made by fire to the Lord. Its smell will be pleasing to the Lord. You must also offer a quart of wine as a drink offering. 14First bring your offering to your God. Until you do this, do not eat the new grain, roasted grain or bread made from the new grain. This law will always continue for people from now on, wherever you live.

The Feast of Pentecost

15"'Count seven weeks from the morning after the Sabbath.[d] (This is the Sabbath that you bring the bundle of grain to present as an offering.) 16On the fiftieth day, you will bring a new grain offering to the Lord. This is the first day after the seventh week. 17On that day bring two loaves of bread from your homes. That bread will be presented as an offering. Use yeast and four quarts of flour to make those loaves of bread. They will be your gift to the Lord from the first wheat of your harvest.

18"'Offer one bull, two male sheep and seven male lambs. The lambs must be one year old. There must be nothing wrong with them. Offer them with their grain offerings and drink offerings. They will be a burnt offering to the Lord. They will be an offering made by fire. And the smell will be pleasing to the Lord. 19You must also offer one male goat for a sin offering. You must offer two male, one-year-old lambs as a fellowship offering.

20"'The priest will present the two lambs as an offering. He will present them with the bread from the first wheat of the harvest. They are holy to the Lord. They will belong to the priest. 21On that same day you will call a holy meeting. You must not do any work that day. This law will continue for you from now on, wherever you live.

22"'You will harvest your crops on your land. But do not harvest all the way to the corners of your field. If grain falls onto the ground, don't gather it up. Leave it for poor people and foreigners in your country. I am the Lord your God.'"

Feast of Trumpets

23Again the Lord said to Moses, 24"Tell the people of Israel: 'On the first day of the seventh month you must have a special day of rest. There will be a holy meeting. Blow the trumpet for a special time of remembering. 25Do not do any work. And bring an offering made by fire to the Lord.'"

The Day of Cleansing

26The Lord said to Moses, 27"The Day of Cleansing will be on the tenth day of the seventh month. There will be a holy meeting. You will give up eating and bring an offering made by fire to the Lord. 28Do not do any work on that day. This is because it is the Day of Cleansing. On that day the priests will go before the Lord. They will perform the acts to make you clean^d so you will belong to the Lord.

29"If anyone refuses to give up food on this day, he must be separated from his people. 30If anyone works on this day, I will destroy him from among his people. 31You must not do any work at all. This law will continue for people from now on wherever you live. 32It will be a special day of rest for you. And you must not eat. You will start this special day of rest on the evening after the ninth day of the month. It will continue from that evening until the next evening."

The Feast of Shelters

33Again the Lord said to Moses, 34"Tell the people of Israel: 'On the fifteenth day of the seventh month is the Feast^d of Shelters. This feast to the Lord will continue for seven days. 35There will be a holy meeting on the first day. Do not do any work. 36You will bring an offering made by fire to the Lord each day for seven days. On the eighth day you will have another holy meeting. And you will bring an offering made by fire to the Lord. This will be a holy meeting. Do not do any work.

37("'These are the Lord's special feasts. There will be holy meetings on these feast days. You will bring offerings made by fire to the Lord. They will be whole burnt offerings, grain offerings, sacrifices and drink offerings. You must bring these gifts at the right times. 38You must bring these offerings in addition to those for the Lord's

Sabbath^d days. You must offer them in addition to offerings you give as payment for special promises. They are also in addition to special offerings you want to give to the Lord.)

39"'So on the fifteenth day of the seventh month, celebrate the Lord's festival for seven days. By then you will have gathered in the crops of the land. You must rest on the first day and the seventh day. 40On the first day you will take good fruit from the fruit trees. And you will take branches from palm, poplars and other leafy trees. You will celebrate before the Lord your God for seven days. 41Celebrate this festival to the Lord for seven days each year. This law will continue from now on. You will celebrate it in the seventh month. 42Live in shelters for seven days. All the people born in Israel must live in shelters. 43This is so that all your descendants^d will know I made Israel live in shelters. It was during the time I brought them out of Egypt. I am the Lord your God.'"

44So Moses told the people of Israel about all of the Lord's appointed feast days.

The Lampstand and the Holy Bread

24 The Lord said to Moses, 2"Command the people of Israel to bring you pure oil from crushed olives. That oil is for the lamps. These lamps must never go out. 3Aaron will keep the lamps burning in the Meeting Tent.^d They will burn from evening until morning before the Lord. This will be in front of the curtain of the Box^d of the Agreement. This law will continue from now on. 4Aaron must always keep the lamps burning. They are on the lampstands of pure gold before the Lord.

5"Take fine flour and bake 12 loaves of bread with it. Use four quarts of flour for each loaf. 6Put them in two rows on the golden table before the Lord. Six loaves will be in each row. 7Put pure incense^d on each row. This is the memorial portion to take the place of the bread. It is an offering made by fire to the Lord. ⁸Every Sabbath*d* day Aaron will put the bread in order before the Lord. This agreement with the people of Israel will continue forever. ⁹That bread will belong to Aaron and his sons. They will eat it in a holy place. This is because it is a most holy part of the offerings made by fire to the Lord. That bread is their share forever."

The Man Who Cursed God

¹⁰Now there was a son of an Israelite woman and an Egyptian father. The son was walking among the Israelites. And a fight broke out in the camp between him and an Israelite. ¹¹The son of the Israelite woman began cursing and speaking against the Lord. So the people took him to Moses. (The mother's name was Shelomith. She was the daughter of Debri from the family of Dan.) ¹²The people held him as a prisoner. They waited for the Lord's command to be made clear to them.

¹³Then the Lord said to Moses, ¹⁴"Take the one who spoke against me outside the camp. Then bring together all the people who heard him. They must put their hands on his head.*n* Then all the people must throw stones at him and kill him. ¹⁵Tell the people of Israel this: 'If anyone curses his God, he is guilty of sin. ¹⁶Anyone who speaks against the Lord must be put to death. All the people must kill him by throwing stones at him. Foreigners must be punished just like the person born in Israel. If someone speaks against the Lord, he must be put to death.

¹⁷"'If someone kills another person, he must be put to death. ¹⁸Someone might kill an animal that belongs to another person. If he does, he must give that person another animal to take its place. ¹⁹And someone might cause an injury to his neighbor. If he does, the same kind of injury must be given

back to him. ²⁰A broken bone must be paid for a broken bone, an eye for an eye and a tooth for a tooth. In the same way someone injures another person, he must be injured in return. ²¹So anyone who kills another person's animal must give that person another animal to take its place. But the person who kills another person must be put to death.

²²"'The law will be the same for the foreigner as for those from your own country. I am the Lord your God.'"

²³Then Moses spoke to the people of Israel. And they took the person who had cursed outside the camp. Then they killed him with stones. So the people of Israel did as the Lord had commanded Moses.

The Time of Rest for the Land

25 The Lord spoke to Moses at Mount Sinai. He said, ²"Tell the people of Israel this: 'I will give you land. When you enter it, let it have a special time of rest. This will be to honor the Lord. ³You may plant seed in your field for six years. You may trim your vineyards for six years and bring in their fruits. ⁴But during the seventh year, you must let the land rest. This will be a special time to honor the Lord. You must not plant seed in your field or trim your vineyards. ⁵You must not cut the crops that grow by themselves after harvest. You must not gather the grapes from your vines that are not trimmed. The land will have a year of rest.

⁶"'You may eat whatever the land produces during that year of rest. It will be food for your men and women servants. It will be food for your hired workers and the foreigners living in your country. ⁷It will also be food for your cattle and the wild animals of your land. Whatever the land produces may be eaten.

The Year of Jubilee

⁸"'Count off seven groups of 7 years.

---

n **put . . . head** This shows that all these people were sharing in punishing the one who spoke against God.

This will be 49 years. During that time there will be 7 years of rest for the land. [9]On the Day of Cleansing,[d] you must blow the horn of a male sheep. This will be on the tenth day of the seventh month. You must blow the horn through the whole country. [10]Make the fiftieth year a special year. Announce freedom for all the people living in your country. This time will be called Jubilee.[n] Each of you will go back to his own property. And each of you will go back to his own family and family group. [11]The fiftieth year will be a special time for you to celebrate. Don't plant seeds. Don't harvest the crops that grow by themselves. Don't gather grapes from the vines that are not trimmed. [12]That year is Jubilee. It will be a holy time for you. You may eat the crops that come from the field. [13]In the year of Jubilee each person will go back to his own property.

[14]"Don't cheat your neighbor when you sell your land to him. And don't let him cheat you when you buy land from him. [15]You might want to buy your neighbor's land. If you do, count the number of years since the last Jubilee. Use that number to decide the right price. If he sells the land to you, count the number of years left for harvesting crops. Use that number to decide the right price. [16]If there are many years, the price will be high. If there are only a few years, lower the price. This is because your neighbor is really selling only a few crops to you. At the next Jubilee the land will again belong to his family. [17]You must not cheat each other. You respect your God. I am the Lord your God.

[18]"Remember my laws and rules, and obey them. Then you will live safely in the land. [19]The land will give good crops to you. You will eat as much as you want. And you will live safely in the land.

[20]"But you might ask, "If we don't plant seeds or gather crops, what will we eat the seventh year?" [21]Don't worry. I will send you a great blessing during the sixth year. That year the land will produce enough crops for 3 years. [22]When you plant in the eighth year, you will still be eating from the old crop. You will eat the old crop until the harvest of the ninth year.

Property Laws

[23]"The land really belongs to me. So you can't sell it forever. You are only foreigners and travelers living for a time on my land. [24]People might sell their land. But the family will always get its land back. [25]A person in your country might become very poor. He might be so poor that he must sell his land. So his close relatives must come and buy it back for him. [26]A person might not have a close relative to buy back his land for him. But he might get enough money to buy it back himself. [27]He must count the years since the land was sold. He must use that number to decide how much to pay for the land. Then he may buy it back. And the land will be his again. [28]But he might not find enough money to buy it back for himself. Then the one who bought it will keep it until the year of Jubilee.[d] But during that celebration, the land will go back to the first owner's family.

[29]"Someone may sell a home in a walled city. But, for a full year after he sold it, he has the right to buy it back. [30]But the owner might not buy back the house before a full year is over. If he doesn't, the house in the walled city will belong to the one who bought it. It will belong to his future sons. The house will not go back to the first owner at Jubilee. [31]But houses in small towns without walls are like open country. They can be bought back. And they must be returned to their first owner at Jubilee.

[32]"The Levites may always buy back their houses. This is true in the cities which belong to them. [33]Someone might buy a house from a Levite. But

---

[n]**Jubilee**   This word comes from the Hebrew word for a horn of a male sheep.

that house in the Levites' city will again belong to the Levites in the Jubilee. This is because houses in Levite cities belong to the people of Levi. The people of Israel gave these cities to the Levites. [34]Also the fields and pastures around the Levites' cities cannot be sold. Those fields belong to the Levites forever.

Rules for Slave Owners

[35]"'Someone from your country might become too poor to support himself. Help him to live among you as you would a stranger or foreigner. [36]Do not charge him any interest on money you loan to him. Respect your God. And let the poor man live among you. [37]Don't lend him money for interest. Don't try to make a profit from the food he buys. [38]I am the Lord your God. I brought you out of the land of Egypt. I did it to give the land of Canaan to you and to become your God.

[39]"'Someone from your country might become very poor. He might even sell himself as a slave to you. If he does, you must not make him work like a slave. [40]He will be like a hired worker. And he will be like a visitor with you until the year of Jubilee.[d] [41]Then he may leave you. He may take his children and go back to his family and the land of his ancestors. [42]This is because the Israelites are my servants. I brought them out of slavery in Egypt. They must not become slaves again. [43]You must not rule this person cruelly. You must respect your God.

[44]"'You may buy men and women slaves from other nations around you. [45]Also you may buy children as slaves. These children must come from the families of foreigners living in your land. These child slaves will belong to you. [46]You may even pass these foreign slaves on to your children after you die. You can make them slaves forever. But you must not rule cruelly over your own brothers, the Israelites.

[47]"'A foreigner or visitor among you might become rich. And someone in your country might become poor. The poor man might sell himself as a slave to a foreigner living among you. Or he might sell himself to a member of a foreigner's family. [48]The poor man has the right to be bought back and become free. One of his relatives may buy him back. [49]His uncle or his uncle's son may buy him back. One of his close relatives may buy him back. Or if he gets enough money, he may pay the money himself. Then he will be free again.

[50]"'How do you decide the price? You must count the years from the time he sold himself to the foreigner. And count up to the next year of Jubilee. Use that number to decide the price. This is because the person really only hired himself out for a certain number of years. [51]There might still be many years before the year of Jubilee. If so, the person must pay back a large part of the price. [52]There might only be a few years left until Jubilee. If so, the person must pay a small part of the first price. [53]But he will live like a hired man with the foreigner every year. Don't let the foreigner rule cruelly over him.

[54]"'That person will become free, even if no one buys him back. At the year of Jubilee, he and his children will become free. [55]This is because the people of Israel are my servants. I brought them out of slavery in Egypt. I am the Lord your God.

Rewards for Obeying God

26 "'Don't make idols for yourselves. Don't set up statues or memorials. Don't put stone statues in your land to bow down to. This is because I am the Lord your God.

[2]"'Remember my Sabbaths,[d] and respect my Holy Place. I am the Lord.

[3]"'Remember my laws and commands, and obey them. [4]If you do these things, I will give you rains at the right season. The land will produce crops. And the trees of the field will produce their fruit. [5]Your threshing[d] will continue until the grape harvest. And your grape harvest will continue until it is

time to plant. Then you will have plenty to eat. You will live safely in your land. ⁶I will give peace to your country. You will lie down in peace. No one will make you afraid. I will keep harmful animals out of your country. And armies will not pass through your country.

⁷"'You will chase your enemies and defeat them. You will kill them with your sword. ⁸Five of you will chase 100 men. And 100 of you will chase 10,000 men. You will defeat your enemies and kill them with your sword.

⁹"'Then I will show kindness to you. I will let you have many children. I will keep my agreement with you. ¹⁰You will have enough crops to last for more than a year. You will harvest the new crops. And you will have to throw out the old crops to make room for the new ones. ¹¹Also I will place my Holy Tent*d* among you. I will not turn away from you. ¹²I will walk with you and be your God. And you will be my people. ¹³I am the Lord your God. You were slaves in Egypt. You were bent low from the heavy weights you carried as slaves. But I broke the heavy weights that were on your shoulders. I let you walk proudly again.

Punishment for Not Obeying God

¹⁴"'But you must obey me. You must obey all my commands. ¹⁵If you refuse to obey all my laws and commands, you have broken our agreement. ¹⁶If you do that, I will cause terrible things to happen to you. I will cause you to have disease and fever. They will destroy your eyes and kill you. You will not have success when you plant your seed. And your enemy will eat your crops. ¹⁷I will be against you, and your enemies will defeat you. These enemies hate you. And they will rule over you. You will run away even when no one is chasing you.

¹⁸"'If you still do not obey me, I will punish you seven times more for your sins. ¹⁹And I will also break the great cities that make you proud. The skies will not give rain. The earth will not

produce crops. ²⁰You will work hard, but it will not help. Your land will not grow any crops. Your trees will not give their fruit.

²¹"'If you still turn against me and refuse to obey me, I will beat you seven times harder. The more you sin, the more you will be punished. ²²I will send wild animals to attack you. They will take your children away from you. They will destroy your cattle. They will make you so few in number the roads will be empty.

²³"'If you don't learn your lesson after all these things, and if you still turn against me, ²⁴I will also turn against you. I will punish you seven more times for your sins. ²⁵You broke my agreement, and I will punish you. I will bring armies against you. You will go into your cities for safety. But I will cause diseases to spread among you. Then your enemy will defeat you. ²⁶There will be very little bread to eat. Ten women will be able to cook all your bread in one oven. They will measure each piece of bread. You will eat, but you will still be hungry.

²⁷"'If you still refuse to listen to me, and if you still turn against me, ²⁸I will really show my anger. I will punish you seven more times for your sins. ²⁹You will eat the bodies of your sons and daughters. ³⁰I will destroy your places where false gods are worshiped. I will cut down your incense*d* altars. I will pile your dead bodies on the lifeless forms of your idols. I will hate you. ³¹I will destroy your cities. I will make your holy places empty. I will not smell the pleasing smell of your offerings. ³²I will make the land empty. Your enemies who come to live in it will be shocked at it. ³³I will scatter you among the nations. I will pull out my sword and destroy you. Your land will become empty. Your cities will become waste. ³⁴You will be taken to your enemy's country. So your land will finally get its rest. It will enjoy its time of rest all the time it lies empty. ³⁵During the time the land is empty, it

will rest. It will have the rest you should have given it while you lived in it.

36"'Those who are left alive will lose their courage in the land of their enemies. They will be frightened of everything. They will be frightened by even the sound of a leaf being blown by the wind. They will run as if someone were chasing them with a sword. They will fall even when no one is chasing them. 37They will run as if someone were chasing them with a sword. They will fall over each other, even though no one is chasing them. You will not be strong enough to stand up against your enemies. 38You will die among other nations. You will disappear in your enemies' countries. 39So those who are left alive will rot away in their enemies' countries. They will rot away because of their sins and their ancestors' sins.

There Is Always Hope

40"'But maybe the people will confess their sins and the sins of their ancestors. Maybe they will admit they turned against me and sinned against me. 41That made me turn against them. So I sent them into the land of their enemies. These disobedient people might be sorry for what they did. They might accept punishment for their sin. 42If they do, I will remember my agreement with Jacob. I will remember my agreement with Isaac and Abraham. And I will remember the land. 43The land will be empty. It will enjoy its time of rest. Then those who are left alive will accept the punishment for their sins. They will learn that they were punished because they hated my laws. And they refused to obey my rules. 44They truly sinned. But if they come to me for help, I will not turn away from them. I will listen to them even in the land of their enemies. I will not completely destroy them. I will not break my agreement with them. This is because I am the Lord their God. 45For their good I will remember the agreement with their ancestors. I brought their ancestors

out of the land of Egypt. I did it so I could become their God. The other nations saw these things. I am the Lord.'"

46These are the laws, rules and teachings the Lord gave the people of Israel. He gave these laws to the Israelites through Moses. This was at Mount Sinai.

Promises Are Important

27 The Lord said to Moses, 2"Tell the people of Israel: 'Someone might make a special promise to the Lord. He might promise to give himself or another person as a servant to the Lord. That person will then begin to serve the Lord in a special way. The priest must set a certain price for that person. That is the price that would have to be paid to free the person from his special promise to the Lord. 3The price for a man 20 to 60 years old is about 1¼ pounds of silver. (You must use the measure as set by the Holy Place.) 4The price for a woman 20 to 60 years old is about 12 ounces of silver. 5The price for a man 5 to 20 years old is about 8 ounces of silver. The price for a woman 5 to 20 years old is about 4 ounces of silver. 6The price for a baby boy 1 month to 5 years old is about 2 ounces of silver. For a baby girl the price is about 1½ ounces of silver. 7The price for a man 60 years old or older is about 6 ounces of silver. The price for a woman 60 years old or older is about 4 ounces of silver.

8"'A person might be too poor to pay the price. If he is, bring him to the priest. The priest will decide how much money the person can afford to pay.

Gifts to the Lord

9"'Some animals may be used as sacrifices to the Lord. If someone promises to bring one of these animals, it will become holy. 10That person must not try to put another animal in its place. He must not try to exchange it for something else. He must not try to exchange a good animal for a bad animal. And he must not exchange a bad animal for a good animal. If he tries to exchange animals, both animals will become holy.

11 "'Unclean*d* animals cannot be offered as sacrifices to the Lord. Someone might bring one of them to the Lord. If he does, that animal must be brought to the priest. 12 The priest will decide a price for the animal. The price will be according to whether the animal is good or bad. If the priest decides a price, that is the price for the animal. 13 If the person wants to buy back the animal, he must add an additional one-fifth to the price.

Value of a House

14 "'A person might give his house as holy to the Lord. If he does, the priest must decide its value. The price will be according to whether the house is good or bad. If the priest decides a price, that is the price for the house. 15 But the person who gives the house might want to buy it back. If he does, he must add an additional one-fifth to the price. Then the house will belong to him again.

Value of Land

16 "'A person might give part of his fields to the Lord. The value of those fields will depend on how much seed is needed to plant them. It will cost about one and one-fourth pounds of silver for each six bushels of barley seed needed. 17 The person might give his field at the year of Jubilee.*d* Then its value will be what the priest decides. 18 But he might give his field after the Jubilee. If he does, the priest must decide the exact price. He must count the number of years to the next year of Jubilee. Then he will use that number to decide the exact price. 19 The person who gave the field might want to buy it back. If he does, he must add one-fifth to that price. Then the field will belong to him again. 20 "'If he does not buy back the field,

it will always belong to the priest. If it is sold to someone else, the first person cannot buy it back. 21 But the person might not buy back the land. If he doesn't, at the year of Jubilee, it will remain holy to the Lord. It will belong to the priest forever. It will become the property of the priests.

22 "'Someone may give a field he has bought to the Lord. But it may not be a part of his family land. 23 If he gives a field, the priest must count the years to the next Jubilee. He must decide the price for the land. Then that land will belong to the Lord. 24 At the year of Jubilee, the land will go back to its first owner. It will go back to the family who sold the land.

25 "'You must use the measure as set by the Holy Place in paying these prices. It weighs two-fifths of an ounce.

Value of Animals

26 "'People may give cattle and sheep to the Lord. But if an animal is the first one born to its parent, it already belongs to the Lord. So people may not give these animals again. 27 If the animal is unclean,*d* the person must buy it back. The priest will decide the price of the animal. And the person must add one-fifth to that price. If he does not buy it back, the priest must sell it. He will sell it for the price he had decided.

28 "'There is a special kind of gift that people give to the Lord. It may be a person, animal or field from the family property. That gift cannot be bought back or sold. It is most holy to the Lord.

29 "'If a person is given for the purpose of being destroyed, he cannot be bought back. He must be put to death.

30 "'One-tenth of all crops belongs to the Lord. This includes the crops from fields and the fruit from trees. That one-tenth belongs to the Lord. 31 A person might want to get back his tenth. If he does, he must add one-fifth to its price and buy it back.

32 "'The priest will take every tenth

animal from a person's cattle or sheep. It will belong to the Lord. [33]The owner should not pick out the good animals from the bad. He should not exchange one animal for another. If he does exchange it, both animals will become holy. They cannot be bought back.'"

[34]These are the commands the Lord commanded at Mount Sinai. They are for the people of Israel.

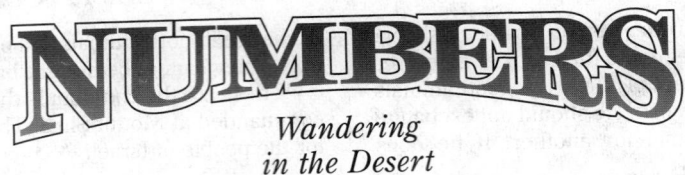

NUMBERS

Wandering in the Desert

The People of Israel Are Counted

1 The Lord spoke to Moses in the Meeting Tent.*ᵈ* This was in the Desert of Sinai. It was on the first day of the second month. This was in the second year after the people of Israel left Egypt. The Lord said to Moses: ²"Count all the people of Israel. List the name of each man with his family and family group. ³You and Aaron must count all the men of Israel 20 years old or older. They will serve in the army of Israel. List them by their divisions. ⁴One man from each tribe*ᵈ* will help you. He is to be the leader of his family. ⁵These are the names of the men who will help you:

from the tribe of Reuben—
Elizur son of Shedeur;
⁶from the tribe of Simeon—
Shelumiel son of Zurish-
addai;
⁷from the tribe of Judah—
Nahshon son of Ammin-
adab;
⁸from the tribe of Issachar—
Nethanel son of Zuar;
⁹from the tribe of Zebulun—
Eliab son of Helon;
¹⁰from the tribe of Ephraim
son of Joseph—Elishama
son of Ammihud;
from the tribe of Manasseh
son of Joseph—Gamaliel
son of Pedahzur;
¹¹from the tribe of Benjamin—
Abidan son of Gideoni;
¹²from the tribe of Dan—
Ahiezer son of Ammish-
addai;
¹³from the tribe of Asher—
Pagiel son of Ocran;
¹⁴from the tribe of Gad—
Eliasaph son of Deuel;
¹⁵from the tribe of Naphtali—
Ahira son of Enan."

¹⁶All these men were chosen by the people to be leaders of their tribes. They were the leaders of their family groups.

¹⁷Moses and Aaron took these men who had been picked. ¹⁸And Moses and Aaron called all the people of Israel together. This was the first day of the second month. Then the people were listed by their families and family groups. All the men who were 20 years old or older were listed by name. ¹⁹Moses did exactly what the Lord had commanded. Moses listed the people while they were in the Desert of Sinai.

²⁰The tribe of Reuben was counted. Reuben was the first son born to Israel. All the men 20 years old or older who were able to serve in the army were listed. They were each listed by name with their families and family groups. ²¹The tribe of Reuben totaled 46,500 men.

²²The tribe of Simeon was counted. All the men 20 years old or older who were able to serve in the army were listed. They were each listed by name with their families and family groups. ²³The tribe of Simeon totaled 59,300 men.

²⁴The tribe of Gad was counted. All the men 20 years old or older who were able to serve in the army were listed. They were listed by name with their families and family groups. ²⁵The tribe of Gad totaled 45,650 men.

²⁶The tribe of Judah was counted. All the men 20 years old or older who were able to serve in the army were

listed. They were listed by name with their families and family groups. [27]The tribe of Judah totaled 74,600 men.

[28]The tribe of Issachar was counted. All the men 20 years old or older who were able to serve in the army were listed. They were listed by name with their families and family groups. [29]The tribe of Issachar totaled 54,400 men.

[30]The tribe of Zebulun was counted. All the men 20 years old or older who were able to serve in the army were listed. They were listed by name with their families and family groups. [31]The tribe of Zebulun totaled 57,400 men.

[32]The tribe of Ephraim was counted. (Ephraim was a son of Joseph.) All the men 20 years old or older who were able to serve in the army were listed. They were listed by name with their families and family groups. [33]The tribe of Ephraim totaled 40,500 men.

[34]The tribe of Manasseh was counted. (Manasseh was also a son of Joseph.) All the men 20 years old or older who were able to serve in the army were listed. They were listed by name with their families and family groups. [35]The tribe of Manasseh totaled 32,200 men.

[36]The tribe of Benjamin was counted. All the men 20 years old or older who were able to serve in the army were listed. They were listed by name with their families and family groups. [37]The tribe of Benjamin totaled 35,400 men.

[38]The tribe of Dan was counted. All the men 20 years old or older who were able to serve in the army were listed. They were listed by name with their families and family groups. [39]The tribe of Dan totaled 62,700 men.

[40]The tribe of Asher was counted. All the men 20 years old or older who were able to serve in the army were listed. They were listed by name with their families and family groups. [41]The tribe of Asher totaled 41,500 men.

[42]The tribe of Naphtali was counted. All the men 20 years old or older who were able to serve in the army were listed. They were listed by name with

their families and family groups. [43]The tribe of Naphtali totaled 53,400 men.

[44]Moses, Aaron and the 12 leaders of Israel counted these men. There was 1 leader from each of the families. [45]Every man of Israel 20 years old or older who was able to serve in the army was counted. Each man was listed with his family. [46]The total number of men was 603,550.

[47]The families from the tribe of Levi were not listed with the others. [48]The Lord had told Moses: [49]"Do not count the tribe of Levi or include them with the other Israelites. [50]But make the Levites responsible for the Holy Tent[d] of the Agreement. They must take care of it and everything that is with it. They must carry the Holy Tent and everything in it. They must take care of it and make their camp around it. [51]Any time the Holy Tent is moved, the Levites must take it down. Any time it is set up, the Levites must do it. If anyone else goes near the Holy Tent, he will be put to death. [52]The Israelites will make their camps in separate divisions, each man near his family flag. [53]But the Levites must make their camp around the Holy Tent of the Agreement. Then I will not be angry with the Israelites. The Levites will take care of the Holy Tent of the Agreement."

[54]So the Israelites did everything the Lord commanded Moses.

The Camp Arrangement

2 The Lord said to Moses and Aaron: [2]"The Israelites should make their camps around the Meeting Tent.[d] But they should not camp too close to it. Each person should camp under the flag of his division near the banner of his family group."

[3]The camp of Judah will be on the east side, where the sun rises. They will camp by divisions there under their flag. The leader of the people of Judah is Nahshon son of Amminadab. [4]There are 74,600 men in his division.

[5]Next to them the tribe[d] of Issachar will camp. The leader of the people of

Issachar is Nethanel son of Zuar. ⁶There are 54,400 men in his division.

⁷Next is the tribe of Zebulun. The leader of the people of Zebulun is Eliab son of Helon. ⁸There are 57,400 men in his division.

⁹There are a total of 186,400 men in the camp of Judah. They are in their divisions. They will be the first to march out of camp.

¹⁰The divisions of the camp of Reuben will be south of the Holy Tent. They will camp under their flag. The leader of the people of Reuben is Elizur son of Shedeur. ¹¹There are 46,500 men in his division.

¹²Next to them the tribe of Simeon will camp. The leader of the people of Simeon is Shelumiel son of Zurishaddai. ¹³There are 59,300 men in his division.

¹⁴Next is the tribe of Gad. The leader of the people of Gad is Eliasaph son of Deuel. ¹⁵There are 45,650 men in his division.

¹⁶There are a total of 151,450 men in the camp of Reuben. They are in their divisions. They will be the second group to march out of camp.

¹⁷When the Levites move the Meeting Tent, they will be in between the other camps. The tribes will move in the same order as they camp. Each person will be with his family flag.

¹⁸The divisions of the camp of Ephraim will be on the west side. They will camp under their flag. The leader of the people of Ephraim is Elishama son of Ammihud. ¹⁹There are 40,500 men in his division.

²⁰Next to them the tribe of Manasseh will camp. The leader of the people of Manasseh is Gamaliel son of Pedahzur. ²¹There are 32,200 men in his division.

²²Next to them the tribe of Benjamin will camp. The leader of the people of Benjamin is Abidan son of Gideoni. ²³There are 35,400 men in his division.

²⁴There are a total of 108,100 men in the camp of Ephraim. They are in their divisions. They will be the third group to march out of camp.

²⁵The divisions of the camp of Dan will be on the north side. They will camp under their flag. The leader of the people of Dan is Ahiezer son of Ammishaddai. ²⁶There are 62,700 men in his division.

²⁷Next to them the tribe of Asher will camp. The leader of the people of Asher is Pagiel son of Ocran. ²⁸There are 41,500 men in his division.

²⁹Next is the tribe of Naphtali. The leader of the people of Naphtali is Ahira son of Enan. ³⁰There are 53,400 men in his division.

³¹There are 157,600 men in the camp of Dan. They will be the last to march out of camp. They will travel under their own flag.

³²These are the Israelites who were counted by families. The total number of Israelites in the camps, counted by divisions, is 603,550. ³³Moses did not count the Levites among the other people of Israel. This is what the Lord had commanded.

³⁴So the Israelites obeyed everything the Lord commanded Moses. They camped under their flags. Each person traveled with his family and family group.

Aaron's Family, the Priests

3 This is the family history of Aaron and Moses. This was at the time the Lord talked to Moses on Mount Sinai.

²Aaron had four sons. Nadab was the oldest. Then Aaron had Abihu, Eleazar and Ithamar. ³Those were the names of Aaron's sons. They were appointed to serve as priests. ⁴But Nadab and Abihu died when they sinned in the presence of the Lord. They made an offering to the Lord in the Desert of Sinai. But they used the wrong kind of fire. They had no sons. So Eleazar and Ithamar served as priests during the lifetime of their father Aaron.

⁵The Lord said to Moses, ⁶"Bring the tribe[d] of Levi to Aaron the priest. They must help him. ⁷They will help him and all the Israelites at the Meeting Tent.[d] They will do the work of the Holy Tent.

⁸The Levites must take care of everything in the Meeting Tent. They will serve the people of Israel by doing the work in the Holy Tent. ⁹Give the Levites to Aaron and his sons. Of all the Israelites, the Levites are given completely to him. ¹⁰Appoint Aaron and his sons to serve as priests. Anyone else who comes near the holy things must be put to death."

¹¹The Lord also said to Moses, ¹²"I am choosing the Levites from all the Israelites. They will take the place of all the firstborn*d* children of Israel. The Levites will be mine. ¹³All the firstborn are mine. When you were in Egypt, I killed all the firstborn children of the Egyptians. I took all the firstborn of Israel to be mine. Firstborn animals and children are mine. I am the Lord."

¹⁴The Lord again talked to Moses in the Desert of Sinai. The Lord said, ¹⁵"Count the Levites by families and family groups. Count every male one month old or older." ¹⁶So Moses obeyed the Lord and counted them all.

¹⁷Levi had three sons. Their names were Gershon, Kohath and Merari. ¹⁸The Gershonite family groups were Libni and Shimei. ¹⁹The Kohathite family groups were Amram, Izhar, Hebron and Uzziel. ²⁰The Merarite family groups were Mahli and Mushi.

These were the family groups that belonged to the Levites.

²¹The family groups of Libni and Shimei belonged to Gershon. They were all the Gershonite family groups. ²²They had 7,500 males one month or older. ²³The Gershonite family groups camped on the west side, behind the Holy Tent. ²⁴The leader of the families of Gershon was Eliasaph son of Lael. ²⁵In the Meeting Tent the Gershonites were responsible for taking care of these things: the Holy Tent, its covering, the curtain at the entrance to the Meeting Tent, ²⁶the curtains in the courtyard, the curtain at the entry to the courtyard around the Holy Tent

and the altar, the ropes and all the work connected with these things.

²⁷The family groups of Amram, Izhar, Hebron and Uzziel belonged to Kohath. They were all the Kohathite family groups. ²⁸They had 8,600 males one month old or older. They were responsible for taking care of the Holy Place. ²⁹The Kohathite family groups camped south of the Holy Tent. ³⁰The leader of the Kohathite families was Elizaphan son of Uzziel. ³¹They were responsible for the Holy Box,*d* the table, the lampstand, the altars, the tools of the holy place, the curtain and all the work connected with these things. ³²The main leader of the Levites was Eleazar son of Aaron, the priest. Eleazar was in charge of all those responsible for the Holy Place.

³³The family groups of Mahli and Mushi belonged to Merari. They were all the Merarite family groups. ³⁴They had 6,200 males one month old or older. ³⁵The leader of the Merari families was Zuriel son of Abihail. They were to camp north of the Holy Tent. ³⁶The Merarites were responsible for the frame of the Holy Tent, the braces, the posts, the bases and all the work connected with these things. ³⁷They were also responsible for the posts in the courtyard around the Holy Tent and their bases, tent pegs and ropes.

³⁸Moses, Aaron and his sons camped east of the Holy Tent. They were in front of the Meeting Tent. They were responsible for the Holy Place. They did this for the Israelites. Anyone else who came near the Holy Place was to be put to death.

³⁹Moses and Aaron counted the Levite men. The Lord commanded this. There were 22,000 males one month old or older.

Levites Take the Place of the Firstborn Sons

⁴⁰The Lord said to Moses, "Count all the firstborn*d* sons in Israel one month old or older. List their names. ⁴¹Take the Levites for me instead of the

firstborn sons of Israel. Take the animals of the Levites instead of the firstborn animals from the rest of Israel. I am the Lord."

42So Moses did what the Lord commanded. Moses counted all the firstborn sons of the Israelites. 43He listed all the firstborn sons one month old or older. There were 22,273 names.

44The Lord also said to Moses, 45"Take the Levites instead of all the firstborn sons of the Israelites. And take the animals of the Levites instead of the animals of the other people. The Levites are mine. I am the Lord. 46There are 273 more firstborn sons than Levites. 47So collect two ounces of silver for each of the 273 sons. Use the measure as set by the Holy Place. It weighs two-fifths of an ounce. 48Give the silver to Aaron and his sons. It is the payment for the 273 Israelites."

49So Moses collected the money for the people the Levites could not replace. 50Moses collected the silver from the firstborn of the Israelites. He collected 35 pounds of silver, using the measure set by the Holy Place. 51So Moses obeyed the Lord. He gave the silver to Aaron and his sons.

The Jobs of the Kohath Family

4 The Lord said to Moses and Aaron, 2"Count the Kohathites among the Levites. Count them by family groups and families. 3Count the men from 30 to 50 years old. They will serve in the Meeting Tent.d

4"They are responsible for the most holy things in the Meeting Tent. 5When the Israelites move, Aaron and his sons must go into the Holy Tent. They are to take down the curtain. Then they must cover the Holy Boxd of the Agreement with it. 6Over this they must put a covering made from fine leather. Then they must spread the solid blue cloth over it. And they must put the poles in the rings on the Holy Box.

7"Then they must spread a blue cloth over the table. This is the table for the bread that shows we are in God's presence. They must put the plates, spoons, bowls and the jars for drink offerings on the table. They must leave the bread on the table. 8Then they must put a red cloth over all of these things. They must cover everything with fine leather. Then they must put the poles in place.

9"With a blue cloth they must cover the lampstand, its lamps, its wick trimmers and trays. They must cover all the jars for the oil used in the lamps. 10Then they must wrap everything in fine leather. They must put all these things on a frame for carrying them.

11"They must spread a blue cloth over the gold altar. Then they must cover it with fine leather. They must put its poles in place.

12"They must gather everything used for serving in the Holy Place. They must wrap them in a blue cloth. Then they must cover that with fine leather. They must put these things on a frame for carrying them.

13"They must clean the ashes off the bronze altar. Then they must spread a purple cloth over it. 14They must gather all the things used for serving at the altar. These are the pans for carrying the fire, meat forks, shovels and bowls. They must put them on the bronze altar. Then they must spread a covering of fine leather over it. They must put the carrying poles in the rings on the altar.

15"When the camp is ready to move, have Aaron and his sons cover all the holy things. Then the Kohathites may go in and carry away those things. This way they won't touch the holy things and die. It is the Kohathites' job to carry the things that are in the Meeting Tent.

16"Eleazar son of Aaron, the priest, will be responsible for the Holy Tent. And he is responsible for everything in it: the oil for the lamp, the sweet-smelling incense,d the continual grain offering and the oil used to appoint priests and things to the Lord's service."

17The Lord said to Moses and Aaron,

[18]"Don't let the Kohathites be destroyed from the Levites. [19]Do this for the Kohathites. Then they may go near the Most Holy Place and not die. Aaron and his sons must go in and show each Kohathite what to do. And they must show each man what to carry. [20]The Kohathites must not enter and look at the holy things, even for a second. If they do, they will die."

The Jobs of the Gershon Family

[21]The Lord said to Moses, [22]"Count the Gershonites by families and family groups. [23]Count the men from 30 to 50 years old. Everyone has a job to do in the Meeting Tent.[d]

[24]"This is what the Gershonite family groups must do and what they must carry. [25]They must carry the pieces of cloth of the Holy Tent[d] and Meeting Tent. They must also carry its covering and the covering made from fine leather. And they must carry the curtains for the entrance to the Meeting Tent. [26]They must carry the curtains of the courtyard that goes around the Holy Tent and the altar. They must carry the curtain for the entry to the courtyard and the ropes and all the things used with the curtains. They must do everything connected with these things. [27]Aaron and his sons are in charge of what the Gershonites do or carry. You tell them what they are responsible for carrying. [28]This is the work of the Gershonite family group at the Meeting Tent. Ithamar son of Aaron, the priest, will direct their work.

The Jobs of the Merari Family

[29]"Count the Merarite families and family groups. [30]Count the men from 30 to 50 years old. They will work at the Meeting Tent.[d] [31]It is their job to carry the frame of the Meeting Tent, the crossbars, the posts and bases. [32]They must also carry the posts that go around the courtyard. They must carry the bases, tent pegs and ropes. And they must carry everything that is used with the poles around the courtyard.

Tell each man exactly what to carry. [33]This is the work the Merarites will do for the Meeting Tent. Ithamar son of Aaron, the priest, will direct their work."

The Levite Families

[34]Moses, Aaron and the leaders of Israel counted the Kohathites by families and family groups. [35]The men from 30 to 50 years old were to work at the Meeting Tent.[d] [36]The family group had 2,750 men. [37]This was the total of the Kohath family group who worked at the Meeting Tent. Moses and Aaron counted them as the Lord had commanded Moses.

[38]Also, the Gershon family group was counted by families and family groups. [39]The men from 30 to 50 years old were given work at the Meeting Tent. [40]The families and family groups had 2,630 men. [41]This was the total of the Gershon family group who worked at the Meeting Tent. Moses and Aaron counted them as the Lord had commanded.

[42]Also, the men in the families and family groups of the Merari family were counted. [43]The men from 30 to 50 years old were to work at the Meeting Tent. [44]The family group had 3,200 men. [45]This was the total of the Merari family group. Moses and Aaron counted them as the Lord had commanded Moses.

[46]So Moses, Aaron and the leaders of Israel counted all the Levites. They counted them by families and family groups. [47]The men from 30 to 50 were given work at the Meeting Tent. They also carried the Tent. [48]The total number of these men was 8,580. [49]Each man was counted as the Lord had commanded Moses. Each man was given his work and told what to carry. This was as the Lord had commanded Moses.

Rules About Cleanliness

5 The Lord said to Moses, [2]"Command the Israelites to send away from camp anyone with a harmful skin disease. Send away anyone who gives off body fluid. And send away anyone who has touched a dead body. ³Send both men and women away from camp. Then they won't spread the disease there. I am living among you." ⁴So Israel obeyed God's command. They sent those people outside the camp as the Lord had told Moses.

Paying for Doing Wrong

⁵The Lord said to Moses, ⁶"Tell the Israelites: 'When a man or woman does something wrong to another person, that is really sinning against God. That person is guilty. ⁷He must tell what he has done wrong. And he must fully pay for the wrong he has done. Then he must add one-fifth to it. And he must give it to the person he wronged. ⁸But that person may be dead. That person may not have any close relatives to receive the payment. Then the one who did wrong owes the Lord. That person must pay the priest. The priest must sacrifice a male sheep to remove the wrong so that person will belong to God. ⁹When an Israelite brings a holy gift, he should give it to the priest. ¹⁰No one has to give these holy gifts. But if someone does give them, they belong to the priest.'"

Suspicious Husbands

¹¹Then the Lord said to Moses, ¹²"Tell the Israelites: 'A man's wife might be unfaithful to him. ¹³She might have sexual relations with another man. Her sin might be kept hidden from her husband. Her husband might not know about the wrong thing she did. Perhaps no one saw it, and she wasn't caught. ¹⁴But her husband might have feelings of jealousy whether she has sinned or not. ¹⁵He then should take her to the priest. The husband must also take an offering for her. This offering will be two quarts of barley flour. He must not pour oil or incense[d] on it. This is a grain offering for jealousy. It is to find out if she is guilty.

¹⁶"'The priest will bring in the woman and make her stand before the Lord.

¹⁷He will take some holy water in a clay jar. Then he will put some dirt from the floor of the Holy Tent into the water. ¹⁸The priest will make the woman stand before the Lord. Then he will loosen her hair. And he will hand her the grain offering for jealousy. He will hold the bitter water that brings a curse on her. ¹⁹The priest will tell her what the oath says will happen to her. He will ask her, "Has another man had sexual relations with you? Have you been unfaithful to your husband? If you haven't, then this water that brings a curse won't hurt you. ²⁰But what if you have been unfaithful to your husband? What if you have had sexual relations with a man besides your husband?" ²¹The priest will tell her the curse that the oath will bring. He will say, "If you are guilty, the Lord will make the people curse you. Your stomach will get big, and you will not be able to have another baby. ²²This water that brings a curse will go inside you. Your stomach will get big, and you will not be able to have another baby."

"'The woman must say, "I agree."

²³"'The priest should write these curses on a scroll. Then he should wash the words off into the water. ²⁴Then he will make the woman drink the water that brings a curse. When she does, it may make her sick. ²⁵Then the priest will take the grain offering for jealousy from her. He will present it before the Lord. Then he will bring it to the altar. ²⁶Then the priest will take a handful of the grain. This is a memorial offering. He will burn it on the altar. After that he will make the woman drink the water. ²⁷He will make her drink it to see if she is not pure. He will know if she has sinned against her husband. When it goes into her, her stomach may get big. And she may not be able to have another baby. Her people will turn against her. ²⁸But if the woman has not sinned, she is pure. She is not guilty. She will be able to have more babies.

²⁹"'So this is the teaching about jealousy. This is what to do when a woman

is unfaithful to her husband. ³⁰It also should be done if the man gets jealous because he suspects his wife. The priest will have her stand before the Lord. Then he will do all these things. This is the teaching. ³¹If the husband is right, the woman will suffer.'"

The Nazirites

6 The Lord said to Moses, ²"Tell the Israelites: 'A man or a woman might want to promise to belong to the Lord in a special way. This person will be called a Nazirite. ³During this time, he must not drink wine or beer. He must not drink vinegar made from wine or beer. He must not even drink grape juice or eat grapes or raisins. ⁴While he is a Nazirite, he must not eat anything that comes from the grapevine. He must not even eat the seeds or the skin.

⁵"During the time he promised to belong to the Lord, he must not cut his hair. He must be holy until this special time is over. He must let his hair grow long. ⁶During his special time of belonging to the Lord, a Nazirite must not go near a dead body. ⁷Even if his own father, mother, brother or sister dies, he must not touch them. This would make him unclean.ᵈ He must still keep his promise to belong to God in a special way. ⁸While he is a Nazirite, he belongs to the Lord.

⁹"If he is next to someone who dies suddenly, his hair has been made unclean. It was part of his promise. So he must shave his head seven days later to be clean. ¹⁰Then on the eighth day, he must bring two doves or two young pigeons to the priest. The priest will be at the entrance to the Holy Tent.ᵈ ¹¹The priest will offer one as a sin offering. He will offer the other as a burnt offering. This removes sin so the man will belong to God. He had sinned because he was near a dead body. That same day he will again promise to let his hair grow for the Lord. ¹²He must give himself to the Lord for another special time. He must bring a male lamb a year old. It will be a penalty

offering. The days of the special time before don't count. This is because he became unclean during his first special time.

¹³"'This is the teaching for a Nazirite. When the promised time is over, he must go the entrance of the Meeting Tent.ᵈ ¹⁴There he will give his offerings to the Lord. He must offer a year-old male lamb as a burnt offering. It must have nothing wrong with it. He must also offer a year-old female lamb as a sin offering. There must be nothing wrong with it. And he must bring a male sheep for a fellowship offering. There must be nothing wrong with it. ¹⁵He must also bring the grain offerings and drink offerings that go with them. And he must bring a basket of bread made without yeast. There must be loaves made with fine flour mixed with oil. And there must be wafers made without yeast spread with oil.

¹⁶"'The priest will give these offerings to the Lord. He will make the sin offering and the burnt offering. ¹⁷Then he will kill the male sheep as a fellowship offering to the Lord. Along with it, he will present the basket of bread. He will also make the grain offering and the drink offering along with it.

¹⁸"'The Nazirite must go to the entrance of the Meeting Tent. There he must shave off his hair that he grew for his promise. The hair will be put in the fire that is under the sacrifice on the fellowship offering.

¹⁹"'After the Nazirite cuts off his hair, the priest will give him a boiled shoulder from the male sheep. From the basket he will also give him a loaf and a wafer. Both are made without yeast. ²⁰Then the priest will present them to the Lord. This is an offering presented before the Lord. They are holy and belong to the priest. Also, he is to present the breast and the thigh from the male sheep to the Lord. They also belong to the priest. After that, the Nazirite may drink wine.

²¹"'This is the teaching for the Nazirite promise. If a person makes the

Nazirite promise, he must give all of these gifts to the Lord. If he promised to do more, he must keep his promise. That is also the teaching of the Nazirite promise.'"

The Priests' Blessings

22The Lord said to Moses, 23"Tell Aaron and his sons, 'This is how you should bless the Israelites. Say to them:
24"May the Lord bless you and
     keep you.
25May the Lord show you his
     kindness.
  May he have mercy on you.
26May the Lord watch over you
  and give you peace."'
27"So Aaron and his sons will bless the Israelites with my name. And I will bless them."

The Holy Tent

7 When Moses finished setting up the Holy Tent,d he gave it for service to the Lord. Moses poured olive oil on the Tent and on everything used in the Tent. He also poured oil on the altar and all its tools. In this way he prepared them for service to the Lord. 2Then the leaders of Israel made offerings. These were the heads of the families and leaders of each tribe.d They were the men who counted the people. 3They brought to the Lord 6 covered carts and 12 oxen. Each leader gave an ox. Every two leaders gave a cart. They gave these to the Holy Tent.
4The Lord said to Moses, 5"Accept these gifts from the leaders. Use them in the work of the Meeting Tent. Give them to the Levites as they need them."
6So Moses accepted the carts and the oxen. He gave them to the Levites. 7He gave 2 carts and 4 oxen to the Gershonites. This is what they needed for their work. 8Then Moses gave 4 carts and 8 oxen to the Merarites. This is what they needed for their work. Ithamar son of Aaron, the priest, directed the work of all of them. 9Moses did not give any oxen or carts to the Kohathites. They were to carry the holy things on their shoulders. This was their job.
10The oil was poured on the altar. Then the leaders brought their offerings to it to give to the Lord's service. 11The Lord had already told Moses, "Each day one leader must bring his gift. The gifts will make the altar ready for service to me."
12-83Each of the 12 leaders brought these gifts. Each leader brought 1 silver plate that weighed about 3¼ pounds. And each one brought 1 silver bowl that weighed about 1¾ pounds. These weights were set by the Holy Place measure. Each bowl and plate were filled with fine flour mixed with oil. This was for a grain offering. Each leader also brought a large gold dish that weighed about 4 ounces. It was filled with incense.d

Each leader also brought 1 young bull, 1 male sheep and 1 male lamb a year old. These were for a burnt offering. Each leader also brought 1 male goat for a sin offering. Each leader brought 2 oxen, 5 male sheep, 5 male goats and 5 male lambs a year old. All of these were sacrificed for a fellowship offering.

On the first day Nahshon son of Amminadab brought his gifts. He was the leader of the tribe of Judah.

On the second day Nethanel son of Zuar brought his gifts. He was the leader of the tribe of Issachar.

On the third day Eliab son of Helon brought his gifts. He was the leader of the tribe of Zebulun.

On the fourth day Elizur son of Shedeur brought his gifts. He was the leader of the tribe of Reuben.

On the fifth day Shelumiel son of Zurishaddai brought his gifts. He was the leader of the tribe of Simeon.

On the sixth day Eliasaph son of Deuel brought his gifts. He was the leader of the tribe of Gad.

On the seventh day Elishama son of Ammihud brought his gifts. He was the leader of the tribe of Ephraim.

On the eighth day Gamaliel son of

Pedahzur brought his gifts. He was the leader of the tribe of Manasseh.

On the ninth day Abidan son of Gideoni brought his gifts. He was the leader of the tribe of Benjamin.

On the tenth day Ahiezer son of Ammishaddai brought his gifts. He was the leader of the tribe of Dan.

On the eleventh day Pagiel son of Ocran brought his gifts. He was the leader of the tribe of Asher.

On the twelfth day Ahira son of Enan brought his gifts. He was the leader of the tribe of Naphtali.

[84]So these were the gifts from the Israelite leaders. Moses poured oil on the altar. And they brought their gifts to give the altar for service to the Lord. They brought 12 silver plates, 12 silver bowls and 12 gold dishes. [85]Each silver plate weighed about 3¼ pounds. And each bowl weighed about 1¾ pounds. All the silver plates and silver bowls together weighed about 60 pounds. This weight was set by the Holy Place measure. [86]The 12 gold dishes filled with incense weighed 4 ounces each. Together the gold dishes weighed about 3 pounds. [87]The total number of animals for the burnt offering was 12 bulls, 12 male sheep and 12 male lambs a year old. There was also a grain offering. And there were 12 male goats for a sin offering. [88]The total number of animals for the fellowship offering was 24 bulls, 60 male sheep, 60 male goats and 60 male lambs a year old. All these offerings were for giving the altar to the service of the Lord. This was after Moses had poured oil on it.

[89]Moses went into the Meeting Tent to speak with the Lord. He heard the Lord speaking to him. The voice was coming from between the two gold creatures with wings. They were above the lid of the Box[d] of the Agreement. And the Lord spoke with him.

The Lampstand

8 The Lord said to Moses, [2]"Speak to Aaron. Tell him, 'Put the seven lamps where they can light the area in front of the lampstand.'"

[3]Aaron did this. He put the lamps so they lighted the area in front of the lampstand. He obeyed the command the Lord gave Moses. [4]The lampstand was made from hammered gold. It was gold from its base to the flowers. It was made exactly the way the Lord had showed Moses.

The Levites

[5]The Lord said to Moses, [6]"Take the Levites away from the other Israelites and make them clean.[d] [7]This is what you should do to make them clean. Sprinkle the cleansing water on them. Have them shave their bodies and wash their clothes. Then they will be clean. [8]They must take a young bull and the grain offering that goes with it. The grain offering will be flour mixed with oil. Then take another young bull for a sin offering. [9]Bring the Levites to the front of the Meeting Tent.[d] And gather all the Israelites around. [10]Bring the Levites before the Lord. Then the Israelites should put their hands on them.[n] [11]Aaron will present the Levites before the Lord. They will be like an offering presented from the Israelites. Then the Levites will be ready to do the work of the Lord.

[12]"The Levites will put their hands on the bulls' heads. One bull will be a sin offering to the Lord. The other will be a burnt offering. This will remove the sins of the Levites so they will belong to God. [13]Make the Levites stand in front of Aaron and his sons. Then present the Levites as an offering to the Lord. [14]In this way you must set apart the Levites from the other Israelites. The Levites will be mine.

[15]"So make the Levites pure. And present them as an offering. Then they may come to work at the Meeting Tent. [16]They will be given to me from the Israelites. I have taken them for myself. They are mine instead of the firstborn[d] son of every Israelite woman.

[n]**put . . . them**   This showed that the people had a part in giving the Levites their special work.

¹⁷Every firstborn male in Israel—man or animal—is mine. I killed all the firstborn in Egypt. So now I set them aside for myself. ¹⁸I have taken the Levites instead of all the firstborn sons in Israel. ¹⁹I have chosen the Levites from all the Israelites. And I have given them to Aaron and his sons. They will serve all the Israelites at the Meeting Tent. They will help remove the Israelites' sins so they will belong to God. Then no disaster will strike the Israelites when they approach the Holy Place."

²⁰So Moses, Aaron and all the Israelites obeyed the Lord. They did with the Levites what the Lord commanded Moses. ²¹The Levites made themselves clean and washed their clothes. Then Aaron presented them as an offering to the Lord. Aaron also removed their sins so they would be pure for the Lord. ²²After that, the Levites came to the Meeting Tent to work. Aaron and his sons told them what to do. They did with the Levites what the Lord commanded Moses.

²³The Lord said to Moses, ²⁴"This command is for the Levites. Every man 25 years old or older must come to the Meeting Tent. They all have a job to do in the work there. ²⁵At the age of 50, he must retire from his job. He doesn't have to work again. ²⁶He may help his fellow Levites with their work at the Meeting Tent. But he must not do the work himself. This is the way you are to give the Levites their jobs."

The Passover

9 The Lord spoke to Moses in the Desert of Sinai. This was in the first month of the second year after the Israelites left Egypt. He said, ²"Tell the Israelites to celebrate the Passover^d at the appointed time. ³That appointed time is the fourteenth day of this month. They should celebrate it at twilight. They must obey all the rules about it."

⁴So Moses told the Israelites to celebrate the Passover. ⁵And so they did.

It was in the Desert of Sinai at twilight. This was on the fourteenth day of the first month. The Israelites did everything just as the Lord commanded Moses.

⁶But some of the people could not celebrate the Passover on that day. They were unclean^d because of a dead body. So they went to Moses and Aaron that day. ⁷They said to Moses, "We are unclean because of a dead body. But why should we be kept from offering gifts to the Lord at this appointed time? Why can't we join the other Israelites?"

⁸Moses said to them, "Wait. I will find out what the Lord says about you."

⁹Then the Lord said to Moses, ¹⁰"Tell the Israelites this: 'You or your descendants^d might become unclean because of a dead body. Or, you might be away on a trip during the Passover. Still celebrate the Lord's Passover. ¹¹But celebrate it at twilight on the fourteenth day of the second month. Eat the lamb with bitter herbs and bread made without yeast. ¹²Don't leave any of it until the next morning. Don't break any of its bones. When you celebrate the Passover, follow all the rules. ¹³Anyone who is clean and is not away on a trip must eat the Passover. If he doesn't, he must be separated from his people. He did not give an offering to the Lord at the appointed time. He must be punished for his sin.

¹⁴"'A foreigner among you may celebrate the Lord's Passover. But he must follow all the rules. You must have the same rules for foreigners as you have for yourselves.'"

The Cloud Above the Tent

¹⁵On the day the Holy Tent^d was set up, a cloud covered it. (The Holy Tent was also called the Tent of the Agreement.) From dusk until dawn the cloud above the Tent looked like fire. ¹⁶The cloud stayed above the Tent. At night it looked like fire. ¹⁷When the cloud moved from its place over the Tent, the Israelites moved. Wherever the cloud stopped, the Israelites

camped. ¹⁸So the Israelites moved at the Lord's command. And they camped at his command. While the cloud stayed over the Tent, they stayed in place. ¹⁹Sometimes the cloud stayed over the Tent for a long time. The Israelites obeyed the Lord and did not move. ²⁰Sometimes the cloud was over it only a few days. At the Lord's command the people camped. And at his command they moved. ²¹Sometimes the cloud stayed only from dusk until dawn. When the cloud lifted the next morning, the people moved. When the cloud lifted, day or night, the people moved. ²²The cloud might stay over the Tent for two days, a month or a year. As long as it stayed, the people would camp. But when the cloud lifted, they moved. ²³At the Lord's command the people camped. And at his command they moved. They obeyed the Lord's order that he commanded through Moses.

The Silver Trumpets

10 The Lord said to Moses, ²"Make two trumpets of hammered silver. Use them to call the people together and to march out of camp. ³When both trumpets are blown, the people should gather. They should gather before you at the entrance to the Meeting Tent.ᵈ ⁴If you blow only one trumpet, the leaders should meet before you. ⁵When you blow the trumpets once, the tribesᵈ camping on the east should move. ⁶When you blow them again, the tribes camping on the south should move. The sound will tell them to move. ⁷When you want to gather the people, blow the trumpets. But don't blow them the same way.

⁸"Aaron's sons, the priests, should blow the trumpets. This is a law for you and your descendantsᵈ from now on. ⁹You might be fighting an enemy who attacks you in your own land. Blow the trumpets. The Lord your God will remember you. He will save you from your enemies. ¹⁰Also blow your trumpets at happy times. Blow them during your feasts and at New Moonᵈ festivals. Blow them over your burnt offerings and fellowship offerings. They will help you remember your God. I am the Lord your God."

The Israelites Move Camp

¹¹The cloud lifted from the Tentᵈ of the Agreement. This was on the twentieth day of the second month of the second year. ¹²So the Israelites moved from the Desert of Sinai. They moved until the cloud stopped in the Desert of Paran. ¹³This was their first time to move. They did it as the Lord had commanded Moses.

¹⁴The divisions from the camp of Judah moved first under their flag. Nahshon son of Amminadab was the commander. ¹⁵Nethanel son of Zuar was over the division of the tribeᵈ of Issachar. ¹⁶Eliab son of Helon was over the division of the tribe of Zebulun. ¹⁷Then the Meeting Tent was taken down. The Gershonites and Merarites, who carried it, moved next.

¹⁸Then came the divisions from the camp of Reuben under their flag. Elizur son of Shedeur was the commander. ¹⁹Shelumiel son of Zurishaddai was over the division of the tribe of Simeon. ²⁰Eliasaph son of Deuel was over the division of the tribe of Gad. ²¹Then came the Kohathites. They carried the holy things. The Holy Tent was to be set up before they arrived.

²²Next came the divisions from the camp of Ephraim under their flag. Elishama son of Ammihud was the commander. ²³Gamaliel son of Pedahzur was over the division of the tribe of Manasseh. ²⁴Abidan son of Gideoni was over the division of the tribe of Benjamin.

²⁵The last ones were the rear guard for all the tribes. These were the divisions from the camp of Dan under their flag. Ahiezer son of Ammishaddai was the commander. ²⁶Pagiel son of Ocran was over the division of the tribe of Asher. ²⁷Ahira son of Enan was over the division of the tribe of Naphtali. ²⁸This

was the order the Israelite divisions marched in when they moved.

29Hobab was the son of Reuel the Midianite. Reuel, who is also called Jethro, was Moses' father-in-law. Moses said to Hobab, "We are moving to the land God promised to give us. Come with us. We will be good to you. The Lord has promised good things to Israel."

30But Hobab answered, "No, I will not go. I will go back to my own land where I was born."

31But Moses said, "Please don't leave us. You know where we can camp in the desert. You can be our guide. 32Come with us. We will share with you all the good things the Lord gives us." 33So they left the mountain of the Lord. The Box[d] of the Lord's Agreement went in front of the people. For three days they looked for a place to camp. 34The Lord's cloud was over them during the day when they left their camp.

35When the Holy Box left the camp, Moses always said,

"Rise up, Lord!
   Scatter your enemies.
   Make those who are against you
      run from you."

36And when the Holy Box was set down, Moses always said,

"Return, Lord,
   to the thousands of people of Israel."

Fire from the Lord

11 The people complained to the Lord about their troubles. When he heard them, he became angry. Fire from the Lord burned among the people. It burned the edge of the camp. 2So the people cried out to Moses. He prayed to the Lord, and the fire stopped burning. 3So that place was called Taberah.[n] The people named it that because the Lord's fire had burned among them.

The 70 Older Leaders

4Some troublemakers among them wanted better food. Soon all the Israelites began complaining. They said, "We want meat! 5We remember the fish we ate for free in Egypt. We also had cucumbers, melons, leeks, onions and garlic. 6But now we have lost our appetite. We never see anything but this manna!"

7The manna was like small white seeds. 8The people would go to gather it. Then they ground it in handmills. Or they crushed it between stones. They cooked it in a pot or made cakes with it. It tasted like bread baked with olive oil. 9When the dew fell on the camp each night, so did the manna.

10Moses heard every family crying. They stood in the entrances of their tents. The Lord became very angry. And Moses got upset. 11He asked the Lord, "Why have you brought me this trouble? I'm your servant. What have I done wrong? Why did you make me responsible for all these people? 12I am not the father of all these people. I didn't give birth to them. Why do you make me carry them to the land you promised to our ancestors? Must I carry them in my arms as a nurse carries a baby? 13Where can I get meat for all these people? They keep crying to me, 'We want meat!' 14I can't take care of all these people alone. It is too much for me. 15If you are going to continue doing this to me, then kill me now. If you like me, put me to death. Then I won't have any more troubles."

16The Lord said to Moses, "Bring me 70 of Israel's older leaders. Pick men you know are leaders among the people. Bring them to the Meeting Tent.[d] Have them stand there with you. 17I will come down and speak with you there. I will take some of the Spirit[d] that is in you. And I will give it to them. They will help you care for the people. Then you will not have to care for them alone.

18"Tell the people this: 'Make yourselves holy. Tomorrow you will eat

---

nTaberah   This name means "burning."

meat. The Lord heard you cry, "We want meat! We were better off in Egypt!" So now the Lord will give you meat to eat. ¹⁹You will not eat it for just 1, 2, 5, 10 or even 20 days. ²⁰You will eat that meat for a whole month. You will eat it until it comes out your nose. You will hate it. This is because you have rejected the Lord. He is here with you. But you have cried to him. You said, "Why did we ever leave Egypt?"'"

²¹Moses said, "Lord, here are 600,000 men standing around me. And you say, 'I will give them enough meat to eat for a month!' ²²If we killed all the sheep and cattle, that would not be enough. If we caught all the fish in the sea, that would not be enough."

²³But the Lord said to Moses, "Do you think I'm weak? You will see if I can do what I say."

²⁴So Moses went out to the people. He told them what the Lord had said. Moses gathered 70 of the older leaders together. He had them stand around the Tent. ²⁵Then the Lord came down in the cloud and spoke to Moses. The Lord took some of the Spirit Moses had. And he gave it to the 70 leaders. With the Spirit in them, they prophesied,^{d} but just that one time.

²⁶Two men named Eldad and Medad were also listed as leaders. But they did not go to the Tent. They stayed in the camp. The Spirit was given to them. So they prophesied in the camp. ²⁷A young man ran to Moses. He said, "Eldad and Medad are prophesying in the camp."

²⁸Joshua son of Nun said, "Moses, my master, stop them!" (Since he was a young boy, Joshua had been Moses' assistant.)

²⁹But Moses answered, "Are you afraid for me? I wish all the Lord's people could prophesy. I wish the Lord would give his Spirit to all of them!" ³⁰Then Moses and the leaders of Israel went back to the camp.

The Quails Come

³¹The Lord sent a strong wind from the sea. It blew quail into the area all around the camp. The quail were about three feet above the ground. There were quail a day's walk in any direction. ³²The people went out and gathered quail. They gathered all that day, that night and the next day. Everyone gathered at least 60 bushels. Then they spread them around the camp. ³³But the Lord became very angry. He gave the people a terrible sickness. This came while the meat was still in their mouths. ³⁴So the people named that place Kibroth Hattaavah.^{n} They named it that because there they buried those who wanted other food.

³⁵From Kibroth Hattaavah the people went to stay at Hazeroth.

Miriam and Aaron Speak Against Moses' Wife

12 Miriam and Aaron began to talk against Moses, who had married a Cushite. ²They said to themselves, "Is Moses the only one the Lord speaks through? Doesn't he speak through us?" And the Lord heard this.

³(Now Moses was very humble. He was the least proud person on earth.)

⁴So the Lord suddenly spoke to Moses, Aaron and Miriam. He said, "All three of you come to the Meeting Tent^d now." So they went. ⁵The Lord came down in a pillar of cloud. He stood at the entrance to the Tent. He called to Aaron and Miriam, and they both came near. ⁶He said, "Listen to my words:

When a prophet^d is among you,
  I, the Lord, will show myself to
    him in visions.
  I will speak to him in dreams.
⁷But this is not true with my
    servant Moses.
  I trust him to lead all my people.
⁸I speak face to face with him.
  I speak clearly, not with hidden
    meanings.

---

^{n}**Kirbroth Hattaavah** This name in Hebrew means "graves of craving."

He has even seen the form of the
Lord.
You should be afraid
to speak against my servant Moses."
⁹The Lord was very angry with them,
but he left.

¹⁶After that, the people left Hazeroth.
And they camped in the Desert of
Paran.

The Spies Explore Canaan

13 The Lord said to Moses, ²"Send
men to explore the land of Ca-
naan. I will give that land to the Israelites. Send one leader from each tribe."ᵈ

Brothers and Sisters
MOSES, AARON, AND MIRIAM • NUMBERS 12

Do you remember the story of Moses who was put in a basket in the
Nile River to save his life while his sister, Miriam, watched out for him?
Moses was raised by Pharaoh's daughter, but later he left Egypt. God told
Moses to return to Egypt to free the Israelites. Moses didn't want to go
because he didn't think he could speak very well, so God sent his brother
Aaron to go with him.

Later, Aaron and Miriam became jealous of Moses' leadership, so they
started saying bad things about Moses. God became very angry with
them.

Sometimes when brothers and sisters disagree or argue, they say bad
things about each other. Instead of talking to someone else about this,
brothers and sisters need to apologize and talk about it to each other.
We should try to get along with everyone—especially our brothers and
sisters.

To meet a brother who tried to become a king, fly to page 400.

¹⁰The cloud lifted from the Tent.
Then Aaron turned toward Miriam. She
was as white as snow. She had a harmful skin disease. ¹¹Aaron said to Moses,
"Please, my master, forgive us for our
foolish sin. ¹²Don't let her be like a baby
who is born dead. (Sometimes a baby is
born with half of its flesh eaten away.)"
¹³So Moses cried out to the Lord,
"God, please heal her!"
¹⁴The Lord answered Moses, "If her
father had spit in her face, she would
have been shamed for seven days. So
put her outside the camp for seven
days. After that, she may come back."
¹⁵So Miriam was shut outside of the
camp for seven days. And the people
did not move on until she came back.

³So Moses obeyed the Lord's command. He sent the Israelite leaders out
from the Desert of Paran. ⁴These are
their names: from the tribe of Reuben,
Shammua son of Zaccur; ⁵from the
tribe of Simeon, Shaphat son of Hori;
⁶from the tribe of Judah, Caleb son of
Jephunneh; ⁷from the tribe of Issachar,
Igal son of Joseph; ⁸from the tribe of
Ephraim, Hoshea son of Nun; ⁹from the
tribe of Benjamin, Palti son of Raphu;
¹⁰from the tribe of Zebulun, Gaddiel
son of Sodi; ¹¹from the tribe of
Manasseh (a tribe of Joseph), Gaddi
son of Susi; ¹²from the tribe of Dan,
Ammiel son of Gamalli; ¹³from the
tribe of Asher, Sethur son of Michael;
¹⁴from the tribe of Naphtali, Nahbi son

of Vophsi; [15]from the tribe of Gad, Geuel son of Maki.

[16]These are the names of the men Moses sent to explore the land. (Moses

"**I**f you are on God's side, it doesn't matter how many are on the other side. Read about two who were right and many who were wrong in Numbers 13:1–14:25."

gave Hoshea son of Nun the new name Joshua.)

[17]Moses sent them to explore Canaan. He said, "Go through southern Canaan and then into the mountains. [18]See what the land looks like. Are the people who live there strong or weak? Are there a few or many? [19]What kind of land do they live in? Is it good or bad?

What about the towns they live in—do they have walls, or are they open like camps? [20]What about the soil? Is it fertile or poor? Are there trees there? Try to bring back some of the fruit from that land." (It was the season for the first grapes.)

[21]So they went up and explored the land. They went from the Desert of Zin all the way to Rehob by Lebo Hamath. [22]They went through the southern area to Hebron. That is where Ahiman, Sheshai and Talmai lived. They were the descendants[d] of Anak.[d] (The city of Hebron had been built seven years before Zoan in Egypt.) [23]In the Valley of Eshcol, they cut off a branch of a grapevine. It had one bunch of grapes on it. They carried that branch on a pole between two of them. They also got some pomegranates[d] and figs. [24]They call that place the Valley of Eshcol.[n] That is because the Israelites cut off the bunch of grapes there. [25]After 40 days of exploring the land, the men returned to the camp.

[26]They came back to Moses and Aaron and all the Israelites at Kadesh.

People Who Depended on God

CALEB • NUMBERS 13:26-30

Caleb trusted God to help with a huge problem. The Israelites were waiting to enter the Promised Land of Canaan after being slaves in Egypt. They knew they would have to fight all the bad people in the land. First they sent some spies there, and all the spies came back afraid. There were big cities in Canaan, powerful armies, and evil people as tall as giants. Caleb knew that God was more powerful than any army or giant, so he told the people not to be afraid but to go into the land, just as God had said.

Remember, no problem is too big for God. You can trust God with all your problems—little ones, or "giant" ones!

To read about someone who depended on God for a miracle, fly to page 259.

To read about someone who depended on God for a miracle, fly to page 259.

---

[n]**Eshcol**   This name in Hebrew means "bunch."

This was in the Desert of Paran. The men reported to them and showed everybody the fruit from the land. ²⁷They told Moses, "We went to the land where you sent us. It is a land where much food grows! Here is some of its fruit. ²⁸But the people who live there are strong. Their cities are walled and large. We even saw some Anakites there. ²⁹The Amalekites live in the southern area. The Hittites, Jebusites and Amorites live in the mountains. The Canaanites live near the sea and along the Jordan River."

³⁰Then Caleb told the people near Moses to be quiet. Caleb said, "We should go up and take the land for ourselves. We can do it."

³¹But the men who had gone with him said, "We can't attack those people. They are stronger than we are." ³²And those men gave the Israelites a bad report about the land they explored. They said, "The land would eat us up. All the people we saw are very tall. ³³We saw the Nephilim^d people there. (The Anakites come from the Nephilim people.) We felt like grasshoppers. And we looked like grasshoppers to them."

The People Complain Again

14 That night all the people in the camp began crying loudly. ²All the Israelites complained against Moses and Aaron. All the people said to them, "We should have died in Egypt. Or we should have died in the desert. ³Why is the Lord bringing us to this land? We will be killed with swords. Our wives and children will be taken away. We would be better off going back to Egypt." ⁴They said to each other, "Let's get a leader and go back to Egypt."

⁵Then Moses and Aaron bowed facedown in front of all the Israelites gathered there. ⁶Joshua son of Nun and Caleb son of Jephunneh were among those who had explored the land. They tore their clothes. ⁷They said to all of the Israelites, "The land we went to explore is very good. ⁸If the Lord is pleased with us, he will lead us into that land. He will give us that land where much food grows. ⁹Don't turn against the Lord! Don't be afraid of the people in that land! We will chew them up. They have no protection, but we have the Lord. So don't be afraid of them."

¹⁰Then all the people talked about killing them with stones. But the glory of the Lord appeared at the Meeting Tent^d to the Israelites. ¹¹The Lord said to Moses, "How long will these people ignore me? How long will it be before they believe me? I have done miracles^d

God's Love for Us
NUMBERS 14:18-19

How do you react when someone does something you don't like? It depends on who it is, and what they do, right? If the person is a friend or a family member, you may be a little more patient and forgiving. That's how God dealt with his people Israel. They continually did things that made God angry or unhappy. But instead of destroying them, he showed great love and patience. Remember that when you do something you know God doesn't want you to do: he may discipline you, but he still loves you a lot.

To find out more about God's love for us, zoom to page 667.

among them. [12]I will give them a terrible sickness. I will destroy them. But I will make you into a great nation. It will be stronger than they are."

[13]Then Moses said to the Lord, "The Egyptians will hear about it! You brought these people from there by your great power. [14]And the Egyptians will tell this to those who live in this land. They have already heard about you, Lord. They know that you are with your people. And they know you were seen face to face. They know your cloud stays over your people. They know you lead your people with that cloud during the day and with fire at night. [15]The nations have heard about your power. If you put to death your people all at once, the nations will talk. They will say, [16]'The Lord was not able to bring them into the land he promised them. So he killed them in the desert.'

[17]"So show your strength now, my Lord. Do what you said. You said: [18]'The Lord doesn't become angry quickly. The Lord has great love. The Lord forgives sin and law breaking. He has great mercy. But the Lord does not forget to punish guilty people. When parents sin, he will also punish their children. He will punish their grandchildren, great-grandchildren and great-great-grandchildren.' [19]Show your great love. Forgive these people's sin. Forgive them as you have from the time they left Egypt until now."

[20]The Lord answered, "I have forgiven them as you asked. [21]But, as surely as I live, I make this promise. As surely as my glory fills the whole earth, I make this promise. [22]All these men saw my glory. They saw the miracles I did in Egypt and in the desert. But they disobeyed me and tested me 10 times. [23]So not one will see the land I promised to their ancestors. No one who angered me will see that land. [24]But my servant Caleb has a different spirit. He follows me completely. So I will bring him into the land he has already seen. And his children will own that land. [25]The Amalekites and the Canaanites are living in the valleys. So leave tomorrow and go back. Follow the desert road toward the Gulf of Aqaba."

The Lord Punishes the People

[26]The Lord said to Moses and Aaron, [27]"How long will these evil people complain about me? I have heard these Israelites' grumbling and complaining. [28]So tell them, 'This is what the Lord says. I heard what you said. As surely as I live, I will do those things to you. [29]You will die in this desert. Every one of you who is 20 years old or older and who was counted with the people will die. You complained against me, the Lord. [30]Not one of you will enter and live in the land I promised to you. Only Caleb son of Jephunneh and Joshua son of Nun will go in. [31]You said that your children would be taken away. But I will bring them into the land. They will enjoy what you refused. [32]As for you, you will die in this desert. [33]Your children will be shepherds here for 40 years. They will suffer because you were not loyal. They will suffer until you lie dead in the desert. [34]For 40 years you will suffer for your sins. That is a year for each of the 40 days you explored the land. You will know me as your enemy.' [35]I, the Lord, have spoken. I will certainly do these things to all these evil people. They have come together against me. So they will all die here in this desert."

[36]The men Moses had sent to explore the land had returned. They had spread complaints among all the Israelites. They had given a bad report about the land. [37]They were responsible for the bad report. So the Lord killed them with a terrible sickness. [38]Only two of the men did not die. They were Joshua son of Nun and Caleb son of Jephunneh.

[39]When Moses told these things to the Israelites, they were very sad. [40]Early the next morning they started to go toward the beginning of the mountains. They said, "We have

sinned. We will go where the Lord told us."

41But Moses said, "Why are you disobeying the Lord's command? You will not win! 42Don't go. The Lord is not with you. You will be beaten by your enemies. 43You will run into the Amalekites and Canaanites. They will kill you with swords. You have turned away from the Lord. He will not be with you."

44But they were proud. They went toward the beginning of the mountains. But Moses and the Box[d] of the Agreement with the Lord did not leave the camp. 45The Amalekites and the Canaanites who lived in those mountains came down. And they attacked the Israelites. They beat them back all the way to Hormah.

Rules About Sacrifices

15 The Lord said to Moses, 2"Speak to the people of Israel. Say to them, 'You will enter a land that I am giving you as a home. 3There give the Lord offerings made by fire. These may be from your herds or flocks. And the smell will be pleasing to the Lord. These offerings may be burnt offerings or sacrifices for special promises. They may be offerings which are gifts to the Lord. Or they may be festival offerings. 4And the one who brings his offering shall also give the Lord a grain offering. It should be two quarts of fine flour mixed with one quart of olive oil. 5Each time you offer a lamb as a burnt offering or sacrifice, also prepare a quart of wine. This is a drink offering.

6"'If you are giving a male sheep, also prepare a grain offering. It should be four quarts of fine flour mixed with one and one-fourth quarts of olive oil. 7Also prepare one and one-fourth quarts of wine. This is a drink offering. Offer it to the Lord. Its smell is pleasing to him.

8"'You might prepare a young bull as a burnt offering or sacrifice. This might be for a fellowship offering or for a special promise to the Lord. 9Bring a grain offering with the bull. It should

be six quarts of fine flour mixed with two quarts of olive oil. 10Also bring two quarts of wine as a drink offering. This offering is made by fire. And its smell will be pleasing to the Lord. 11Prepare each bull or male sheep, lamb or young goat this way. 12Do this for every one of the animals you bring.

13"'All citizens must do these things in this way. And the smell of their offerings by fire will be pleasing to the Lord. 14From now on foreigners will live among you. They will make offerings by fire so the smell will be pleasing to the Lord. They must offer them the same way you do. 15The law is the same for you and for foreigners. It will be a law from now on. You and the foreigners are alike before the Lord. 16The teachings and rules are the same for you and for the foreigners among you.'"

17The Lord said to Moses, 18"Tell the Israelites: 'You are going to another land. I am taking you there. 19When you eat the food there, offer part of it to the Lord. 20Offer a loaf of bread from the first of your grain. That will be your offering from the threshing[d] floor. 21From now on offer to the Lord the first part of your grain.

22"'Now what if you forget to obey any of these commands the Lord gave Moses? 23These are the Lord's commands given to you through Moses. They began the day the Lord gave them to you. And they will continue from now on. 24But you might forget to obey one of these commands. The people might not remember the command. Then all the people must offer a young bull as a burnt offering. Its smell is pleasing to the Lord. By law you must also give the grain offering and the drink offering with it. And you must bring a male goat as a sin offering.

25"'The priest will remove that sin for all the Israelites so they will belong to God. They are forgiven. They didn't know they were sinning. For the wrong they did they brought offerings to the Lord. They brought an offering by fire and a sin offering. 26All of the people of Israel and the foreigners living among them will be forgiven. No one meant to do wrong.

27"Just one person might sin without meaning to. He must bring a year-old female goat for a sin offering. 28The priest will remove the sin of the person who sinned without meaning to. That person will belong to the Lord again. He will be forgiven. 29The same teaching is for everyone who sins without meaning to. It is the same for those born Israelites and for foreigners living among you.

30"But anyone who sins on purpose is against the Lord. That person must be separated from his people. It is the same for someone born among you or a foreigner. 31That person has turned against the Lord's word. He has not obeyed the Lord's commands. He must surely be separated from the others. He is guilty.'"

A Man Worked on the Sabbath

32This happened when the Israelites were still in the desert. They found a man gathering wood on the Sabbath[d] day. 33Those who found him gathering wood brought him to Moses and Aaron and all the people. 34They held the man under guard. They did not know what to do with him. 35Then the Lord said to Moses, "The man must die. All the people must kill him with stones outside the camp." 36So the people took him outside the camp. They killed him with stones as the Lord commanded Moses.

The Tassels

37The Lord said to Moses, 38"Speak to the Israelites. Tell them this: 'Tie several pieces of thread together. And tie them to the corners of your clothes. Put a blue thread in each one of these tassels. Wear them from now on. 39You will have these tassels to look at. They will remind you of the Lord's commands. Then you will obey them. And you won't follow what your bodies want and what your eyes

wish for. 40Remember to obey all my commands. Then you will be God's holy people. 41I am the Lord your God. I brought you out of Egypt to be your God. I am the Lord your God.'"

Korah, Dathan, Abiram and On

16 Korah, Dathan, Abiram and On turned against Moses. (Korah was the son of Izhar. Izhar was the son of Kohath, and Kohath was the son of Levi. Dathan and Abiram were brothers, the sons of Eliab. And On was the son of Peleth.) Dathan, Abiram and On were from the tribe[d] of Reuben. 2These 4 men gathered 250 other Israelite men and challenged Moses. They were well-known leaders chosen by the community. 3They came as a group to speak to Moses and Aaron. The men said, "You have gone too far. All the people are holy. Every one of them is holy. And the Lord is with them. So why do you put yourselves above all the people?"

4When Moses heard this, he bowed facedown. 5Then he said to Korah and all his followers: "Tomorrow morning the Lord will show who belongs to him. The Lord will bring the one who is holy near to him. The Lord will bring to himself the person he chooses. 6So Korah, you and all your followers do this: Get some pans for burning incense.[d] 7Tomorrow put fire and incense in them. Then take them before the Lord. He will choose the man who is holy. You Levites have gone too far."

8Moses also said to Korah, "Listen, you Levites. 9The God of Israel has separated you from the rest of the Israelites. He brought you near to himself. You do the work in the Lord's Holy Tent.[d] You stand before all the Israelites and serve them. Isn't that enough? 10The Lord has brought you and all your fellow Levites near to himself. Now you want to be priests. 11You and your followers have joined together against the Lord. Your complaint is not against Aaron."

12Then Moses called Dathan and

Abiram, the sons of Eliab. But they said, "We will not come! ¹³You have brought us out of a land where much food grows. You brought us to the desert to kill us. And now you want to order us around. ¹⁴You haven't brought us into a land where much food grows. You haven't given us any land with fields and vineyards. Will you put out the eyes of these men? No! We will not come!"

¹⁵Then Moses became very angry. He said to the Lord, "Don't accept their gifts. I have not taken anything from them, not even a donkey. I have not done wrong to any of them."

¹⁶Then Moses said to Korah, "You and all your followers must stand before the Lord tomorrow. And Aaron will stand there with you and them. ¹⁷Each of you must take your pan and put incense in it. Present these 250 pans before the Lord. You and Aaron must also present your pans." ¹⁸So each man got his pan and put burning incense in it. Then they stood with Moses and Aaron at the entrance to the Meeting Tent. ¹⁹Korah gathered all his followers who were against Moses and Aaron. And they stood at the entrance to the Meeting Tent. Then the glory of the Lord appeared to everyone.

²⁰The Lord said to Moses and Aaron, ²¹"Move away from these men. In a minute I will destroy them."

²²But Moses and Aaron bowed face-down. They cried out, "God, you are the God over the spirits of all people. Please don't be angry with this whole group. Only one man has really sinned."

²³Then the Lord said to Moses, ²⁴"Tell everyone to move away from the tents of Korah, Dathan and Abiram."

²⁵Moses stood and went to Dathan and Abiram. The older leaders of Israel followed him. ²⁶Moses warned the people, "Move away from the tents of these evil men! Don't touch anything of theirs. If you do, you will be destroyed because of their sins." ²⁷So they moved away from the tents of Korah, Dathan

and Abiram. Dathan and Abiram were standing outside their tents with their wives, children and little babies.

²⁸Then Moses said, "Now you will know that the Lord has sent me to do all these things. It was not my idea. ²⁹If these men die a normal death—the way men usually die—then the Lord did not really send me. ³⁰But if the Lord does something new, you will know they have insulted the Lord. The earth will open and swallow them. Alive, they will go to where the dead are. And everything that belongs to them will go with them."

³¹When Moses finished saying these things, the ground under the men opened up. ³²The earth seemed to open its mouth and swallow them. All their families, all Korah's men and every-thing they owned went down. ³³They were buried alive, going to where the dead are. And everything they owned went with them. Then the earth closed over them. They died and were gone from the community. ³⁴The people of Israel around them heard their screams. They ran away and said, "The earth will swallow us, too!"

³⁵Then a fire came down from the Lord. It destroyed the 250 men who had presented the incense.

³⁶The Lord said to Moses, ³⁷"Tell Eleazar son of Aaron, the priest, to take all the incense pans out of the fire. Have him scatter the coals. But the incense pans are still holy. ³⁸These men sinned and lost their lives. Take their pans and hammer them into flat sheets. Cover the altar with them. They are holy because they were presented to the Lord. It will be a sign to the Israelites."

³⁹So Eleazar the priest gathered all the bronze pans. These were the pans brought by the men who were burned up. Eleazar had the pans hammered into flat sheets to put on the altar. ⁴⁰This is what the Lord had commanded him through Moses. These sheets were to remind the Israelites that only descen-dantsᵈ of Aaron should burn incense

before the Lord. Anyone else would die like Korah and his followers.

Aaron Saves the People

41The next day all the Israelites complained against Moses and Aaron. They said, "You have killed the Lord's people."

42The people gathered to complain against Moses and Aaron. But when they turned toward the Meeting Tent,*d* the cloud covered it. The glory of the Lord appeared. 43Then Moses and Aaron went in front of the Meeting Tent.

44The Lord said to Moses, 45"Move away from these people. In a minute I am going to destroy them." So Moses and Aaron bowed facedown.

46Then Moses said to Aaron, "Get your pan. Put fire from the altar and incense*d* in it. Hurry to the people and remove their sin. The Lord is angry with them. The sickness has already started." 47So Aaron did as Moses said. He ran to the middle of all the people. The sickness had already started among them. So Aaron offered the incense to remove their sin. 48He stood between the living and the dead. And the sickness stopped there. 49But 14,700 people died from that sickness. There were also those who died because of Korah. 50Then Aaron went back to Moses at the entrance to the Meeting Tent. The terrible sickness had been stopped.

Aaron's Walking Stick Buds

17 The Lord said to Moses, 2"Speak to the people of Israel. Get 12 walking sticks from them. Get 1 from the leader of each tribe.*d* Write the name of each man on his stick. 3On the stick from Levi, write Aaron's name. There must be 1 stick for the head of each tribe. 4Put them in the Meeting Tent.*d* Place them in front of the Box*d* of the Agreement, where I meet with you. 5I will choose one man. His stick will begin to grow leaves. And I will stop the Israelites

from always complaining against you."

6So Moses spoke to the Israelites. Each of the 12 leaders gave him a walking stick. And Aaron's walking stick was among them. 7Moses put them before the Lord in the Tent of the Agreement.

8The next day Moses entered the Tent. He saw that Aaron's stick had grown leaves. (It stood for the family of Levi.) It had even budded, blossomed and produced almonds. 9So Moses brought out to the Israelites all the walking sticks from the Lord's presence. They all looked, and each man took back his stick.

10Then the Lord said to Moses, "Put Aaron's walking stick back. Put it in front of the Box of the Agreement. It will be a sign to these people who are always turning against me. This will stop their complaining against me. Now they won't die." 11So Moses obeyed what the Lord commanded him.

12The people of Israel said to Moses, "We are going to die! We are lost. We are all lost! 13Anyone who even comes near the Holy Tent of the Lord will die. Will we all die?"

The Work of the Priests and Levites

18 The Lord said to Aaron, "You, your sons and your family are now responsible for any wrongs done against the Holy Place. You and your sons are responsible for any wrongs done against the priests. 2Bring with you your fellow Levites from your tribe.*d* They will help you and your sons serve in the Tent*d* of the Agreement. 3They are under your control. They will do all the work that needs to be done in the Tent. But they must not go near the things in the Holy Place or near the altar. If they do, both you and they will die. 4They will join you. They will take care of the Meeting Tent. They must do the work at the Tent. No one else may come near you.

5"You must take care of the Holy Place and the altar. Then I won't become angry with the Israelites again. ⁶I myself chose your fellow Levites from among the Israelites. They are a gift given for you to the Lord. Their work is at the Meeting Tent. ⁷But only you and your sons may serve as priests. Only you may serve at the altar or go behind the curtain. I am giving you this gift of serving as a priest. Anyone else who comes near the Holy Place will be put to death."

⁸Then the Lord said to Aaron, "I myself make you responsible for the offerings given to me. All the holy offerings that the Israelites give to me, I give to you. They are for you and your sons as your share. They will be your continual portion. ⁹Your share of the holy offerings is that part which is not burned. The people will bring me gifts as most holy offerings. These are grain or sin or penalty offerings. These will be set apart for you and your sons. ¹⁰You must eat it in a most holy place. Any male may eat it. But you must respect it as holy.

¹¹"I also give you the offerings the Israelites present to me. I give these to you and your sons and daughters. This is your share. Anyone in your family who is cleanᵈ may eat it.

¹²"And I give you all the best olive oil and all the best new wine and grain. This is what the Israelites give to me, the Lord. These are the first things they harvest. ¹³They bring to the Lord all the first things they harvest. They will be yours. Anyone in your family who is clean may eat these things.

¹⁴"Everything in Israel that is given to the Lord is yours. ¹⁵The first one born to any family will be offered to the Lord. This is true for both men and animals. And that will be yours. But you must make a payment for every firstbornᵈ son and every firstborn animal that is unclean. ¹⁶When they are one month old, you must make a payment for them. The cost will be two ounces of silver as set by the Holy Place measure.

¹⁷"But you must not make a payment for the firstborn ox or sheep or goat. Those animals are holy. Sprinkle their blood on the altar and burn their fat. This is an offering made by fire. The smell is pleasing to the Lord. ¹⁸But the meat will be yours. Also the breast that is presented and the right thigh will be yours. ¹⁹Anything the Israelites present as holy gifts I, the Lord, give to you. It goes to you, your sons and daughters. It is your continual portion. This is a lasting promise before the Lord to you and your children forever."

²⁰The Lord also said to Aaron, "You will not inherit any of the land. And you will not own any land among the other people. I will be yours. Out of all the Israelites, only you will inherit me.

²¹"The people of Israel will give a tenth of what they make. I give that tenth to the Levites. This is their payment for the work they do serving at the Meeting Tent. ²²But the other Israelites must never go near the Meeting Tent. If they do, they will die for their sin. ²³Only the Levites should work in the Meeting Tent. They are responsible for any sins against it. This is a rule from now on. The Levites will not get any land among the other Israelites. ²⁴But the Israelites will give a tenth of everything they make to me. And I will give that tenth to the Levites. That is why I said about the Levites: 'They will not get any land among the Israelites.'"

²⁵The Lord said to Moses, ²⁶"Speak to the Levites. Tell them: 'You will receive a tenth of everything the Israelites make. I give that to you. But you must give a tenth of that back to the Lord. ²⁷I will accept your offering just as much as I accept the offerings from others. They give new grain or new wine. ²⁸In this way you will present an offering to the Lord as the other Israelites do. You will receive a tenth from the Israelites. Then you will give a tenth of that to Aaron the priest as the Lord's share. ²⁹Choose the best and holiest part from what you are given. This is the portion you must give to the Lord.'

³⁰"Say to the Levites: 'When you present the best it will be accepted as much as the grain and wine from the other people. ³¹You and your families may eat all that is left anywhere. This is your pay for your work in the Meeting Tent. ³²And if you always give the best part to the Lord, you will never be guilty. If you do not sin against the holy offerings of the Israelites, you will not die.'"

The Offering for Cleansing

19 The Lord said to Moses and Aaron, ²"These are the teachings that the Lord commanded. Tell the Israelites to get a young red cow. It must not have anything wrong with it. It must not have been worked. ³Give the cow to Eleazar the priest. He will take it outside the camp and kill it. ⁴Then Eleazar the priest must put some of the blood on his finger. He must sprinkle it seven times toward the front of the Meeting Tent.^d ⁵Then the whole cow must be burned while he watches. The skin, the meat, the blood and the intestines must all be burned. ⁶Then the priest must take a cedar stick, a hyssop branch and a red string. He must throw them onto the burning cow. ⁷Then the priest must wash himself and his clothes with water. After that, he may come back into the camp. But he will be unclean^d until evening. ⁸The man who burns the cow must wash himself and his clothes in water. He will be unclean until evening.

⁹"Then someone who is clean will collect the ashes from the cow. He will put them in a clean place outside the camp. The Israelites will use these ashes in a special ceremony to cleanse away sin. ¹⁰The man who collected the cow's ashes must wash his clothes. He will be unclean until evening. This is a lasting rule. It is for the Israelites and for the foreigners among them.

¹¹"Whoever touches a dead body will be unclean for seven days. ¹²He must wash himself with this water. He must do this on the third day and on the seventh day. Then he will be clean. But if he does not wash himself on the third day and the seventh day, he cannot be clean. ¹³Whoever touches a dead body is unclean. If he stays unclean and goes to the Lord's Holy Tent, it becomes unclean. So he must be separated from Israel. If the cleansing water is not sprinkled on him, he will stay unclean.

¹⁴"This is the teaching about someone who dies in his tent. Anyone in the tent or who enters it will be unclean for seven days. ¹⁵And every open jar or pot without a cover becomes unclean. ¹⁶If anyone touches someone who was killed by a sword or who died a natural death, he is unclean. If he touches a human bone or a grave, he is unclean. He will be unclean for seven days.

¹⁷"So you must use the ashes from the burnt offering to make that person clean again. Pour fresh water over the ashes into a jar. ¹⁸A clean person must take a hyssop branch and dip it into the water. Then he must sprinkle it over the tent and its objects. And he must sprinkle the people who were there. He must sprinkle anyone who touched a bone or the body of someone who was killed. He must sprinkle anyone who touched a dead person or a grave. ¹⁹Then someone who is clean must sprinkle this water on the unclean person. He must do this on the third day and on the seventh day. On the seventh day that person becomes clean. He must wash his clothes and take a bath. He will be clean that evening. ²⁰If anyone who is unclean does not become clean, he must be separated from the community. He was not sprinkled with the cleansing water. He stays unclean. He could make the Holy Tent unclean. ²¹This is a lasting rule. Whoever sprinkles the cleansing water must also wash his clothes. Anyone who touches the water will be unclean until evening. ²²Anyone the unclean person touches becomes unclean. And whoever touches him will be unclean until evening."

Water from the Rock

20 In the first month all the people of Israel arrived at the Desert of Zin. They stayed at Kadesh. There Miriam died and was buried. ²There was no water for the people. So they came together against Moses and Aaron. ³They argued with Moses. They said, "We should have died in front of the Lord as our brothers did. ⁴Why did you bring the Lord's people into this desert? Are we and our animals to die here? ⁵Why did you bring us from Egypt to this terrible place? It has no grain, figs or pomegranates.ᵈ And there's no water to drink!"

had said. ¹⁰He and Aaron gathered the people in front of the rock. Then Moses said, "Now listen to me, you complainers! Do you want us to bring water out of this rock?" ¹¹Then Moses lifted his hand and hit the rock twice with his stick. Water began pouring out. And the people and their animals drank it.

¹²But the Lord said to Moses and Aaron, "You did not believe me. You did not honor me as holy before the people. So you will not lead them into the land I will give them."

¹³These are the waters of Meribah.ⁿ Here the Israelites argued with the Lord. And the Lord showed them he was holy.

Edom Will Not Let Israel Pass

¹⁴From Kadesh, Moses sent messengers to the king of Edom. He said,

People Who Made Mistakes
MOSES • NUMBERS 20:1-13

Do you remember the last time you lost your temper? Did you feel like hitting something? That is what happened to Moses. God told him to speak to a rock to get water from it, but Moses was so upset at the grumbling children of Israel, that he hit the rock with his walking stick instead of speaking to it. Although several years earlier God had told Moses to hit a rock to get water out of it, this time Moses disobeyed God. Because of Moses' mistake, he was not permitted to enter the promised land with the rest of Israel.

To find out about a person who talked to a witch, fly to page 362.

⁶So Moses and Aaron left the people. Then they went to the entrance of the Meeting Tent.ᵈ They bowed facedown. And the glory of the Lord appeared to them. ⁷The Lord said to Moses, ⁸"You and your brother Aaron should gather the people. Also take your walking stick. Speak to that rock in front of them. Then water will flow from it. Give that water to the people and their animals."

⁹So Moses took the stick from in front of the Lord. He did as the Lord

"Your brothers, the Israelites, say to you: You know about all the troubles we have had. ¹⁵Our ancestors went down into Egypt. And we lived there for many years. The people of Egypt were cruel to our ancestors. ¹⁶But we cried out to the Lord. He heard us and sent us an angel to bring us out of Egypt.

"Now we are here at Kadesh, a town on the edge of your land. ¹⁷Please let us pass through your country. We will not touch any fields of grain or vineyards. We will not drink water from the wells."

ⁿ**Meribah**   This name in Hebrew means "argument."

We will travel only along the king's road. We will not turn right or left until we have passed through your country."

18But the king of Edom answered: "You may not pass through here. If you try, I will come and meet you with swords."

19The Israelites answered: "We will go along the main road. If our animals drink any of your water, we will pay for it. We only want to walk through. That's all."

20But he answered: "You may not pass through here."

Then the Edomites went out to meet the Israelites with a large and powerful army. 21The Edomites refused to let them pass through their country. So the Israelites turned back.

Aaron Dies

22All the Israelites moved from Kadesh to Mount Hor. 23It was near the border of Edom. The Lord said to Moses and Aaron, 24"Aaron will die. He will not enter the land that I'm giving to the Israelites. This is because you both acted against my command at the waters of Meribah. 25Take Aaron and his son Eleazar up on Mount Hor. 26Take off Aaron's special clothes and put them on his son Eleazar. Aaron will die there. He will join his ancestors."

27Moses obeyed the Lord's command. They climbed up Mount Hor. All the people saw them go. 28Moses took off Aaron's clothes. He put them on Aaron's son Eleazar. Then Aaron died there on top of the mountain. And Moses and Eleazar came back down the mountain. 29Then all the people learned that Aaron was dead. So everyone in Israel cried for him for 30 days.

War with the Canaanites

21 The Canaanite king of Arad lived in the southern area. He heard that the Israelites were coming on the road to Atharim. So he attacked them and captured some of them. 2Then the

Israelites made this promise to the Lord: "If you will help us defeat these people, we will completely destroy their cities." 3The Lord listened to the Israelites. And he let them defeat the Canaanites. The Israelites completely destroyed the Canaanites and their cities. So the place was named Hormah.[n]

The Bronze Snake

4The Israelites left Mount Hor and went on the road toward the Gulf of Aqaba. They did this to go around the country of Edom. But the people became impatient on the way. 5They grumbled at God and Moses. They said, "Why did you bring us out of Egypt? We will die in this desert! There is no bread! There is no water! And we hate this terrible food!"

6So the Lord sent them poisonous snakes. They bit the people, and many of the Israelites died. 7The people came to Moses and said, "We sinned when we grumbled at you and the Lord. Pray that the Lord will take away these snakes." So Moses prayed for the people.

8The Lord said to Moses, "Make a bronze snake. And put it on a pole. If anyone is bitten, he should look at it. Then he will live." 9So Moses made a bronze snake. And he put it on a pole. Then when a snake bit anyone, he looked at the bronze snake and lived.

The Journey to Moab

10The Israelites went and camped at Oboth. 11They went from Oboth to Iye Abarim. This was in the desert east of Moab. 12From there they went and camped in the Zered Valley. 13From there they went and camped across the Arnon. This was in the desert just inside the Amorite country. The Arnon is the border between the Moabites and the Amorites. 14That is why the Book of the Wars of the Lord says:

"... and Waheb in Suphah, and the ravines,

---

[n]Hormah   This name in Hebrew means "completely destroyed."

the Arnon, [15]and the slopes of the
ravines
that lead to the settlement of Ar.
These places are at the border of
Moab."

[16]The Israelites went from there to
Beer. A well is there where the Lord
said to Moses, "Gather the people. I will
give them water."

[17]Then the Israelites sang this song:
"Pour out water, well!
Sing about it.
[18]Princes dug this well.
Important men made this hole.
With their scepters[d] and poles, they
dug it."

The people went from the desert to
Mattanah. [19]From Mattanah they went
to Nahaliel and on to Bamoth. [20]From
Bamoth they went to the valley of
Moab. There the top of Mount Pisgah
looks over the desert.

Sihon and Og

[21]The people of Israel sent messengers to Sihon, king of the Amorites.
They said to him, [22]"Let us pass
through your country. We will not go
through any fields of grain or vineyards. We will not drink water from
the wells. We will travel only along
the king's road. We will stay on it until
we have passed through your country."

[23]But King Sihon would not let the
Israelites pass through his country.
He gathered his army together. They
marched out to meet Israel in the
desert. At Jahaz they fought the
Israelites. [24]Israel killed the king.
Then they captured his land from the
Arnon River to the Jabbok River. They
took the land as far as the Ammonite
border. That border was strongly
defended. [25]Israel captured all the
Amorite cities and lived in them. They
took Heshbon and all the towns
around it. [26]Heshbon was the city
where Sihon, the Amorite king, lived.
In the past he had fought with the king
of Moab. Sihon had taken all the land
as far as the Arnon.

[27]That is why the poets say:
"Come to Heshbon
and rebuild it.
Rebuild Sihon's city.
[28]A fire began in Heshbon.
Flames came from Sihon's city.
It destroyed Ar in Moab.
It burned the Arnon highlands.
[29]How terrible for you, Moab!
The people of Chemosh[d] are
ruined.
His sons ran away.
His daughters were captured
by Sihon, king of the Amorites.
[30]But we defeated those
Amorites.
We ruined their towns from
Heshbon to Dibon.
We destroyed them as far as
Nophah, near Medeba."

[31]So Israel lived in the land of the
Amorites.

[32]Moses sent spies to the town of
Jazer. Then they captured the towns
around it. They forced out the Amorites
who lived there.

[33]Then the Israelites went up the
road toward Bashan. Og, the king of
Bashan, and his army marched out to
meet the Israelites. They fought at
Edrei.

[34]The Lord said to Moses, "Don't
be afraid of him. I will hand him, his
whole army and his land over to you.
Do to him what you did to Sihon, the
Amorite king who lived in Heshbon."

[35]So the Israelites killed Og and his
sons and all his army. No one was left
alive. And they took his land.

Balaam and Balak

22 Then the people of Israel went
to the plains of Moab. They
camped near the Jordan River across
from Jericho.

[2]Balak son of Zippor saw everything
the Israelites had done to the Amorites.
[3]And Moab was scared of so many
Israelites. Truly, Moab was terrified by
them.

[4]The Moabites said to the older
leaders of Midian, "This mob will take

everything around us. It will be like an ox eating grass."

Balak son of Zippor was the king of Moab at this time. ⁵He sent messengers to Balaam son of Beor at Pethor. It was near the Euphrates River in the land of Amaw. Balak said, "A nation has come out of Egypt. They cover the land.

He sent me this message: ¹¹'A nation has come out of Egypt. They cover the land. So come and put a curse on them. Then maybe I can fight them and force them out of my land.'"

¹²But God said to Balaam, "Do not go with them. Don't put a curse on those people. I have blessed them."

¹³The next morning Balaam awoke and said to Balak's leaders, "Go back to

Plans That Backfired
KING BALAK AND BALAAM • NUMBERS 22

Can you imagine a group of thousands of men, women, and children traveling across the land? The people of Israel were traveling to the land that God had promised would be their new home. King Balak was frightened by the size of the group. He told an evil messenger, Balaam, to put a curse on them so they would leave his land.

But God told Balaam not to curse God's people. So Balaam sent a message to King Balak that he would not curse them. The king tried to offer money and riches to Balaam so he would change his mind and curse the people of Israel. But instead of cursing God's people, Balaam blessed them.

Some people will ask you to do wrong things. Don't listen to those kinds of people. It is always best to obey God instead.

To meet a really bad king of Israel, fly to page 427.

They have camped next to me. ⁶They are too powerful for me. So come and put a curse on them. Maybe then I can defeat them and make them leave the area. I know that if you bless someone, the blessings happen. And if you put a curse on someone, it happens."

⁷The leaders of Moab and Midian went with payment in their hands. They found Balaam. Then they told him what Balak had said.

⁸Balaam said to them, "Stay here for the night. I will tell you what the Lord tells me." So the Moabite leaders stayed with him.

⁹God came to Balaam and asked, "Who are these men with you?"

¹⁰Balaam said to God, "The king of Moab, Balak son of Zippor, sent them.

your own country. The Lord will not let me go with you."

¹⁴So the Moabite leaders went back to Balak. They said, "Balaam refused to come with us."

¹⁵So Balak sent other leaders. He sent more leaders this time. And they were more important. ¹⁶They went to Balaam and said, "Balak son of Zippor says this: Please don't let anything stop you from coming to me. ¹⁷I will pay you well. I will do what you say. Come and put a curse on these people for me."

¹⁸But Balaam answered Balak's servants, "King Balak could give me his palace full of silver and gold. But I cannot disobey the Lord my God in anything, great or small. ¹⁹You stay here tonight as the other men did. I

will find out what more the Lord tells me."

²⁰That night God came to Balaam. He said, "These men have come to ask you to go with them. Go. But only do what I tell you."

Balaam and His Donkey

²¹Balaam got up the next morning. He put a saddle on his donkey. Then he went with the Moabite leaders. ²²But God became angry because Balaam went. So the angel of the Lord stood in the road to stop Balaam. Balaam was riding his donkey. And he had two servants with him. ²³The donkey saw the angel of the Lord standing in the road. The angel had a sword in his hand. So the donkey left the road and went into the field. Balaam hit the donkey to force her back on the road.

²⁴Later, the angel of the Lord stood on a narrow path between two vineyards. There were walls on both sides. ²⁵Again the donkey saw the angel of the Lord. So the donkey walked close to one wall. This crushed Balaam's foot against the wall. So he hit her again.

"**W**hen Balaam's donkey talked, he wasn't horsing around! Read all about it in Numbers 22:1-35."

²⁶The angel of the Lord went ahead again. The angel stood at a narrow place. It was too narrow to turn left or right. ²⁷The donkey saw the angel of the Lord. So she lay down under Balaam. Balaam was very angry and hit her with his stick. ²⁸Then the Lord made the donkey talk. She said to Balaam, "What have I done to make you hit me three times?"

²⁹Balaam answered the donkey, "You have made me look foolish! I wish I had a sword in my hand! I would kill you right now!"

³⁰But the donkey said to Balaam, "I am your very own donkey. You have ridden me for years. Have I ever done this to you before?"

"No," Balaam said. ³¹Then the Lord let Balaam see the angel. The angel of the Lord was standing in the road with his sword drawn. Then Balaam bowed facedown on the ground.

³²The angel of the Lord asked Balaam, "Why have you hit your donkey three times? I have stood here to stop you. What you are doing is wrong. ³³The donkey saw me. She turned away from me three times. If she had not turned away, I would have killed you by now. But I would let her live."

³⁴Then Balaam said to the angel of the Lord, "I have sinned. I did not know you were standing in the road to stop me. If I am wrong, I will go back."

³⁵The angel of the Lord said to Balaam, "Go with these men. But say only what I tell you." So Balaam went with Balak's leaders.

³⁶Balak heard that Balaam was coming. So he went out to meet him at Ar in Moab. It was beside the Arnon, at the edge of his country. ³⁷Balak said to Balaam, "I had asked you before to come quickly. Why didn't you come to me? I am able to reward you well."

³⁸But Balaam answered, "I have come to you now. But I can't say just anything. I can only say what God tells me to say."

³⁹Then Balaam went with Balak to Kiriath Huzoth. ⁴⁰Balak offered cattle and sheep as a sacrifice. He gave some meat to Balaam and the leaders with him.

⁴¹The next morning Balak took Balaam to Bamoth Baal. From there he could see the edge of the Israelite camp.

Balaam's First Message

23 Balaam said, "Build me seven altars here. And prepare seven bulls and seven male sheep for me."

²Balak did what Balaam asked. Then they offered a male sheep and a bull on each of the altars.

³Then Balaam said to Balak, "Stay here beside your burnt offering. I will go. Maybe the Lord will come to me. I will tell you whatever he shows me." Then Balaam went to a higher place.

⁴God came to Balaam there. Balaam said to him, "I have prepared seven altars. And I have offered a bull and a male sheep on each altar."

⁵The Lord told Balaam what he should say. Then the Lord said, "Go back to Balak and give him this message."

⁶So Balaam went back to Balak. Balak and all the leaders of Moab were still standing beside his burnt offering. ⁷Then Balaam gave them this message:
"Balak brought me here from Aram.
The king of Moab brought me
    from the eastern mountains.
Balak said, 'Come, put a curse on
    the people of Jacob for me.
Come, wish evil on the people of
    Israel.'
⁸But God has not cursed them.
So I cannot curse them.
The Lord has not wished evil on
    them.
So I cannot wish evil on them.
⁹I see them from the mountains.
I see them from the hills.
I see a people who live alone.
    They think they are different from
    other nations.
¹⁰No one can number the people
    of Jacob.
No one can count a fourth of Israel.
Let me die like good men.
    Let me end up like them!"

¹¹Balak said to Balaam, "What have you done to me? I brought you here to curse my enemies. But you have only blessed them!"

¹²But Balaam answered, "I must say what the Lord tells me to say."

Balaam's Second Message

¹³Then Balak said to him, "Come with me to another place. There you can also see the people. But you can only see part of them, not all of them. Curse them for me from there." ¹⁴So Balak took Balaam to the field of Zophim. This was on top of Mount Pisgah. There Balak built seven altars. And he offered a bull and a male sheep on each altar.

¹⁵So Balaam said to Balak, "Stay here by your burnt offering. I will meet with God over there."

¹⁶So the Lord came to Balaam. He told Balaam what to say. Then he said, "Go back to Balak and say such and such."

¹⁷So Balaam went to Balak. Balak and the leaders of Moab were standing beside his burnt offering. Balak asked him, "What did the Lord say?"

¹⁸Then Balaam gave this message:
"Stand up, Balak, and listen.
    Hear me, son of Zippor.
¹⁹God is not a man. He will not lie.
God is not a human being. He
    does not change his mind.
What he says he will do, he does.
What he promises, he keeps.
²⁰He told me to bless them.
So I cannot change the blessing.
²¹He has found no wrong in the
    people of Jacob.
He saw no fault in Israel.
The Lord their God is with them.
    They praise their King.
²²God brought them out of Egypt.
They are as strong as a wild ox.
²³No tricks will work on the
    people of Jacob.
No magic works against Israel.
People now say this about them,
    'Look what God has done!'
²⁴The people are strong like a
    lioness.
    They get up like a lion.
Lions don't rest until they have eaten.
    They drink their enemies' blood."

²⁵Then Balak said to Balaam, "You haven't cursed these people. So at least, don't bless them!"

²⁶Balaam answered Balak, "I told you before. I can only do what the Lord tells me."

Balaam's Third Message

²⁷Then Balak said to Balaam, "Come, I will take you to another place. Maybe God will be pleased. He may let you curse them from there." ²⁸So Balak took Balaam to the top of Peor. This mountain looks over the desert.

²⁹Balaam told Balak, "Build me seven altars here. Then prepare for me seven bulls and seven male sheep." ³⁰Balak did what Balaam asked. He offered a bull and a male sheep on each altar.

24 Balaam saw that the Lord wanted to bless Israel. So Balaam did not try to use any magic. He looked toward the desert. ²Balaam saw the Israelites camped in their tribes.ᵈ Then the Spiritᵈ of God entered him. ³And Balaam gave this message:

"This is the message of Balaam son
   of Beor.
This is the message of a man who
   sees clearly.
⁴This is the message of a man
   who heard the words of
   God.
I see a vision from the All-Powerful
   One.
My eyes are open as I fall before
   him.
⁵Your tents are beautiful, people
   of Jacob!
So are your homes, Israel!
⁶Your tents spread out like valleys.
   They are like gardens beside
     a river.
They are like spices planted by
   the Lord.
They are like cedar trees growing
   by the water.
⁷Israel's water buckets will
   always be full.
Their crops will have plenty
   of water.
Their king will be greater than Agag.
   Their kingdom will be very great.
⁸God brought them out of Egypt.
   They are as strong as a wild ox.
They will defeat their enemies.
   They will break their enemies'
     bones.
   They will shoot them with arrows.

⁹Like a lion, they lie waiting to
   attack.
No one would wake a sleeping lion.
Anyone who blesses you will
   be blessed.
And anyone who curses you will
   be cursed."

¹⁰Then Balak was angry with Balaam. Balak pounded his fist. He said to Balaam, "I called you here to curse my enemies. But you have blessed them three times. ¹¹Now go home! I said I would pay you well. But the Lord has made you lose your reward."

¹²Balaam said to Balak, "You sent messengers to me. I told them, ¹³'Balak could give me his palace filled with silver and gold. But I still cannot go against the Lord's commands. I could not do anything, good or bad, on my own. I must say what the Lord says.' ¹⁴Now I am going back to my own people. But I will tell you what these people will do to your people in the future."

Balaam's Final Message

¹⁵Then Balaam gave this message:
"This is the message of Balaam son
   of Beor.
This is the message of a man who
   sees clearly.
¹⁶This is the message of a man
   who hears the words of
   God.
I know the Most High God.
I see a vision from the All-Powerful
   One.
My eyes are open as I fall before
   him.
¹⁷I see someone who will come
   some day.
I see someone who will come, but
   not soon.
A star will come from Jacob.
   A ruler will rise from Israel.
He will crush the heads of the
   Moabites.
He will smash the skulls of the
   sons of Sheth.
¹⁸Edom will be conquered.
   His enemy Edom will be
   conquered.

But Israel will grow wealthy.
[19]The descendants[d] of Jacob will
    beat them down.
The Israelites will destroy those
    left in the city."

[20]Then Balaam saw Amalek and gave
this message:
"Amalek was the most important
    nation.
But Amalek will be destroyed
    at last."

[21]Then Balaam saw the Kenites and
gave this message:
"Your home is safe.
It is like a nest on a cliff.
[22]But you Kenites will be burned
    up.
Assyria will keep you captive."

[23]Then Balaam gave this message:
"No one can live when God does this.
[24]   Ships will sail from the shores of
    Cyprus.
They will defeat Assyria and Eber.
But they will also be destroyed."

[25]Then Balaam got up and returned
home. Balak also went on his way.

Israel at Peor

25 The people of Israel were still
camped at Acacia. The men
began sinning sexually with Moabite
women. [2]The women invited them to
their sacrifices to their false gods. The
Israelites ate food there and worshiped
these gods. [3]So the Israelites began to
worship Baal[d] of Peor. And the Lord
was very angry with them.

[4]The Lord said to Moses, "Get all the
leaders of the people. Then kill them in
open daylight in the presence of the
Lord. Then the Lord will not be angry
with the people of Israel."

[5]So Moses said to Israel's judges,
"Each of you must put to death your
men who have become worshipers of
Baal of Peor."

[6]Moses and the Israelites were gathered at the entrance to the Meeting
Tent.[d] They were crying there. Then
an Israelite man brought a Midianite

woman to his brothers. This was in
plain sight of Moses and all the people.
[7]Phinehas son of Eleazar, the son of
Aaron, the priest, saw this. So he left
the meeting and got his spear. [8]He followed the Israelite into his tent. And he
drove his spear through both the
Israelite man and the Midianite woman.
Then the terrible sickness among the
Israelites stopped.
[9]This sickness had killed 24,000
people.

[10]The Lord said to Moses, [11]"Phinehas son of Eleazar, the son of Aaron,
the priest, has saved the Israelites from
my anger. He is like I am in his concern for the people. He tried to save my
honor among them. So I will not kill
them. [12]So tell Phinehas that I am making my peace agreement with him.
[13]He and all his descendants[d] will have
an agreement. They will always be
priests. This is because he had great
concern for the honor of his God. He
removed the sins of the Israelites so
they would belong to God."

[14]The Israelite man who was killed
with the Midianite woman was named
Zimri son of Salu. He was the leader of
a family in the tribe[d] of Simeon. [15]And
the name of the Midianite woman who
was put to death was Cozbi daughter of
Zur. Zur was the chief of a Midianite
family.

[16]The Lord said to Moses, [17]"The
Midianites are your enemies. You
should kill them. [18]They have already
made you their enemies. They tricked
you at Peor. Then there was Cozbi, the
daughter of a Midianite leader. She was
the woman who was killed when the
sickness came. It came because the
people were worshiping the false god
at Peor."

The People Are Counted

26 After the great sickness, the
Lord spoke to Moses and Eleazar
son of Aaron, the priest. He said,
[2]"Count all the people of Israel by families. Count all the men who are 20
years old or older. They will serve in

the army of Israel." [3]Moses and Eleazar the priest spoke to the people. They were on the plains of Moab near the Jordan River, across from Jericho. They said, [4]"Count the men 20 years old or older. This is what the Lord commanded Moses."

Here are the Israelites who came out of Egypt:

[5]The tribe[d] of Reuben was counted. Reuben was the first son born to Israel. From Hanoch came the Hanochite family group. From Pallu came the Palluite family group. [6]From Hezron came the Hezronite family group. From Carmi came the Carmite family group. [7]These were the family groups of Reuben. The total number of men was 43,730.

[8]The son of Pallu was Eliab. [9]Eliab's sons were Nemuel, Dathan and Abiram. Dathan and Abiram were the leaders who turned against Moses and Aaron. They followed Korah when he turned against the Lord. [10]The earth opened up and swallowed them and Korah. They died when the fire burned up the 250 men. This was a warning. [11]But the children of Korah did not die.

[12]These were the family groups in the tribe of Simeon. From Nemuel came the Nemuelite family group. From Jamin came the Jaminite family group. From Jakin came the Jakinite family group. [13]From Zerah came the Zerahite family group. From Shaul came the Shaulite family group. [14]These were the family groups of Simeon. The total number of men was 22,200.

[15]These were the family groups in the tribe of Gad. From Zephon came the Zephonite family group. From Haggi came the Haggite family group. From Shuni came the Shunite family group. [16]From Ozni came the Oznite family group. From Eri came the Erite family group. [17]From Arodi came the Arodite family group. From Areli came the Arelite family group. [18]These were the family groups of Gad. The total number of men was 40,500.

[19]Two of Judah's sons, Er and Onan, died in Canaan.

[20]These were the family groups in the tribe of Judah. From Shelah came the Shelanite family group. From Perez came the Perezite family group. From Zerah came the Zerahite family group. [21]These were the family groups from Perez. From Hezron came the Hezronite family group. From Hamul came the Hamulite family group. [22]These were the family groups of Judah. The total number of men was 76,500.

[23]These were the family groups in the tribe of Issachar. From Tola came the Tolaite family group. From Puah came the Puite family group. [24]From Jashub came the Jashubite family group. From Shimron came the Shimronite family group. [25]These were the family groups of Issachar. The total number of men was 64,300.

[26]These were the family groups in the tribe of Zebulun. From Sered came the Seredite family group. From Elon came the Elonite family group. From Jahleel came the Jahleelite family group. [27]These were the family groups of Zebulun. The total number of men was 60,500.

[28]These were the family groups of Joseph through Manasseh and Ephraim.

[29]These were the family groups of Manasseh. From Makir came the Makirite family group. (Makir was the father of Gilead.) From Gilead came the Gileadite family group. [30]These were the family groups that came from Gilead. From Iezer came the Iezerite family group. From Helek came the Helekite family group. [31]From Asriel came the Asrielite family group. From Shechem came the Shechemite family group. [32]From Shemida came the Shemidaite family group. From Hepher came the Hepherite family group. [33](Zelophehad son of Hepher had no sons. He had only daughters. Their names were Mahlah, Noah, Hoglah, Milcah and Tirzah.) [34]These were the

family groups of Manasseh. The total number of men was 52,700.

[35]These were the family groups in the tribe of Ephraim. From Shuthelah came the Shuthelahite family group. From Beker came the Bekerite family group. From Tahan came the Tahanite family group. [36]This was the family group from Shuthelah. From Eran came the Eranite family group. [37]These were the family groups of Ephraim. The total number of men was 32,500. These are the family groups that came from Joseph.

[38]These were the family groups in the tribe of Benjamin. From Bela came the Belaite family group. From Ashbel came the Ashbelite family group. From Ahiram came the Ahiramite family group. [39]From Shupham came the Shuphamite family group. From Hupham came the Huphamite family group. [40]These were the family groups from Bela through Ard and Naaman. From Ard came the Ardite family group. From Naaman came the Naamite family group. [41]These were the family groups of Benjamin. The total number of men was 45,600.

[42]This was the family group in the tribe of Dan. From Shuham came the Shuhamite family group. That was the family of Dan. [43]The total number of men in the Shuhamite family group of Dan was 64,400.

[44]These were the family groups in the tribe of Asher. From Imnah came the Imnite family group. From Ishvi came the Ishvite family group. From Beriah came the Beriite family group. [45]These were the family groups that came from Beriah. From Heber came the Heberite family group. From Malkiel came the Malkielite family group. [46](Asher also had a daughter named Serah.) [47]These were the family groups of Asher. The total number of men was 53,400.

[48]These were the family groups in the tribe of Naphtali. From Jahzeel came the Jahzeelite family group. From Guni came the Gunite family group.

[49]From Jezer came the Jezerite family group. From Shillem came the Shillemite family group. [50]These were the family groups of Naphtali. The total number of men was 45,400.

[51]So the total number of the men of Israel was 601,730.

[52]The Lord said to Moses, [53]"Divide the land among these people by the number of names. [54]A large tribe will get more land. And a small tribe will get less land. The amount of land each tribe gets will depend on the number of its people. [55]Divide the land by drawing lots.[d] And the land each tribe gets will be named for that tribe. [56]Divide the land by drawing lots. Divide it between large and small groups."

[57]The tribe of Levi was also counted. These were the family groups of Levi. From Gershon came the Gershonite family group. From Kohath came the Kohathite family group. From Merari came the Merarite family group. [58]These also were Levite family groups: the Libnite family group, the Hebronite family group, the Mahlite family group, the Mushite family group and the Korahite family group. (Kohath was the ancestor of Amram. [59]Amram's wife was named Jochebed. She was from the tribe of Levi. She was born in Egypt. She and Amram had two sons, Aaron and Moses, and their sister Miriam. [60]Aaron was the father of Nadab, Abihu, Eleazar and Ithamar. [61]But Nadab and Abihu died. They died because they made an offering before the Lord with the wrong kind of fire.)

[62]The total number of male Levites one month old or older was 23,000. But these men were not counted with the other Israelites. They did not receive any of the land that the Lord gave the other Israelites.

[63]Moses and Eleazar the priest counted all these people. They counted the Israelites on the plains of Moab across the Jordan River from Jericho. [64]Moses and Aaron the priest had counted the Israelites in the Desert of Sinai. But no one Moses counted on the

plains of Moab was in the first counting. [65]The Lord had told the Israelites they would all die in the desert. The only two left were Caleb son of Jephunneh and Joshua son of Nun.

Zelophehad's Daughters

27 Zelophehad was the son of Hepher. Hepher was the son of Gilead. Gilead was the son of Makir. Makir was the son of Manasseh. Zelophehad's daughters belonged to the family groups of Manasseh son of Joseph. The daughters' names were Mahlah, Noah, Hoglah, Milcah and Tirzah. [2]They went to the entrance of the Meeting Tent.[d] There they stood before Moses, Eleazar the priest, the leaders and all the people. They said, [3]"Our father died in the desert. He was not one of Korah's followers who came against the Lord. Our father died because of his own sin. But he had no sons. [4]Our father's name will die out because he had no sons. Give us property among our father's relatives."

[5]So Moses brought their case to the Lord. [6]The Lord said to him, [7]"The daughters of Zelophehad are right. They should get what their father owned. Give them property among their father's relatives.

[8]"Tell the Israelites, 'If a man dies and has no son, then everything he owned should go to his daughter. [9]If he has no daughter, then everything he owned should go to his brothers. [10]If he has no brothers, then everything he owned should go to his father's brothers. [11]If his father had no brothers, then everything he owned should go to the nearest relative in his family group. This should be a rule among the people of Israel as the Lord has given this command to Moses.'"

Joshua Is the New Leader

[12]Then the Lord said to Moses, "Climb this mountain in the Abarim Mountains. Look at the land I have given to the Israelites. [13]After you have seen it, you will die as your brother Aaron did. [14]You both acted against my command in the Desert of Zin. You did not honor me as holy before the people at the waters of Meribah." (This was at Meribah in Kadesh in the Desert of Zin.)

[15]Moses said to the Lord, [16]"The Lord is the God of the spirits of all people. May he choose a good leader for these people. [17]He must go in and out before them. He must lead them out like sheep and bring them in. The Lord's people must not be like sheep without a shepherd."

[18]So the Lord said to Moses, "Take Joshua son of Nun. My Spirit[d] is in him. Put your hand on him. [19]Have him stand before Eleazar the priest and all the people. Then give him his orders as they watch. [20]Let him share your honor. Then all the Israelites will obey him. [21]He must stand before Eleazar the priest. And Eleazar will get advice from the Lord by using the Urim.[d] At his command all the Israelites will go out. At his command they will all come in."

[22]Moses did what the Lord told him. Moses had Joshua stand before Eleazar the priest and all the people. [23]Then Moses put his hands on him and gave him orders. This was just as the Lord had told him.

Daily Offerings

28 The Lord said to Moses, [2]"Give this command to the Israelites. Tell them: 'Bring me food offerings made by fire. The smell is pleasing to me. Be sure to bring them at the right time.' [3]Say to them: 'These are the offerings you must bring to the Lord. Bring two year-old lambs as a burnt offering each day. They must have nothing wrong with them. [4]Offer one lamb in the morning and the other lamb at twilight. [5]Also bring a grain offering of two quarts of fine flour. It must be mixed with one quart of oil from pressed olives. [6]This is the daily burnt offering which began at Mount Sinai. The smell is pleasing to the Lord. [7]Offer one quart of wine with each lamb as a drink offering. Pour it out to the Lord at the Holy Place. ⁸Offer the second lamb at twilight. As in the morning, also give a grain offering and a drink offering. This offering is made by fire. Its smell is pleasing to the Lord.

Sabbath Offerings

⁹"On the Sabbath*ᵈ* day you must give two year-old lambs. They must have nothing wrong with them. Also give a drink offering and a grain offering. The grain offering must be four quarts of fine flour mixed with olive oil. ¹⁰This is the burnt offering for the Sabbath. It is in addition to the daily burnt offering and drink offering.

mixed with olive oil. This is a burnt offering. And its smell is pleasing to the Lord. ¹⁴The drink offering with each bull will be two quarts of wine. With the male sheep it will be one and one-half quarts. And with each lamb it will be one quart of wine. This is the burnt offering that must be offered each month of the year. ¹⁵Besides the daily burnt offerings and drink offerings, bring a sin offering to the Lord. It must be one male goat.

Passover

¹⁶"The Lord's Passover*ᵈ* will be on

Worship
NUMBERS 28:1-8

Your school probably has a routine schedule for classes each day. You have science class during one period, math during another, and so on. There are times when you break from that pattern for a special assembly or a field trip, but most of the time you follow the schedule.

Human beings work better when they are organized. God made us that way, and he wants us to worship him in organized ways, too. Here in Numbers 28, he tells Israel to bring offerings to him, and to "bring them at the right time." Does your family worship God regularly? The Bible makes it clear that God wants us to come together in worship at least once a week and for other special occasions. God wants us to worship "at the right time."

To learn more about worship, zoom to page 414.

Monthly Offerings

¹¹"On the first day of each month bring a burnt offering to the Lord. This will be two young bulls, one male sheep and seven male lambs a year old. They all must have nothing wrong with them. ¹²Give a grain offering with each bull. It must be six quarts of fine flour mixed with olive oil. Also give a grain offering with the male sheep. It must be four quarts of fine flour mixed with olive oil. ¹³Also give a grain offering with each lamb. It must be two quarts of fine flour

the fourteenth day of the first month. ¹⁷The Feast*ᵈ* of Unleavened Bread begins on the fifteenth day of that month. It lasts for seven days. You may eat only bread made without yeast. ¹⁸Have a holy meeting on the first day of the festival. Don't work that day. ¹⁹Bring these burnt offerings to the Lord: two young bulls, one male sheep and seven male lambs a year old. They all must have nothing wrong with them. ²⁰Also give a grain offering with each bull. It must be six quarts of fine flour mixed with olive oil. Give a grain offering with the male sheep. It must be four quarts of fine flour mixed with oil. 21Give a grain offering with each of the seven lambs. It must be two quarts of fine flour mixed with oil. 22Bring one goat as a sin offering. It will remove your sins so you will belong to God. 23Bring these offerings in addition to the burnt offerings you give every morning. 24So bring food offerings each day for seven days. The offering is made by fire. And its smell is pleasing to the Lord. Do it in addition to the daily burnt offering and its drink offering. 25On the seventh day have a holy meeting. Don't work that day.

Feast of Weeks

26"On the day of firstfruits*d* offer new grain to the Lord. This is during the Feast*d* of Weeks. Have a holy meeting. Don't work that day. 27Give this burnt offering to the Lord: two young bulls, one male sheep and seven male lambs a year old. This smell is pleasing to the Lord. 28Also give a grain offering with each bull. It must be six quarts of fine flour mixed with oil. With the male sheep, it must be four quarts of flour. 29With each of the seven lambs offer two quarts of flour. 30Offer one male goat to remove your sins so you will belong to God. 31Bring these offerings and their drink offerings. These are in addition to the daily burnt offering and its grain offering. The animals must have nothing wrong with them.

Feast of Trumpets

29 "Have a holy meeting on the first day of the seventh month. Don't work on that day. That is the day you blow the trumpets. 2Bring these burnt offerings to the Lord: one young bull, one male sheep and seven male year-old lambs. They all must have nothing wrong with them. Their smell will be pleasing to the Lord. 3Give a grain offering with the bull. It must be six quarts of fine flour mixed with oil. With the male sheep offer four quarts.

4And with each of the seven lambs offer two quarts. 5Offer one male goat for a sin offering. It will remove your sins so you will belong to God. 6These offerings are in addition to the monthly and daily burnt offerings. Their grain offerings and drink offerings must be done as you have been told. These offerings are made by fire to the Lord. And their smell is pleasing to him.

The Day of Cleansing

7"Have a holy meeting on the tenth day of the seventh month. On that day do not eat and do not work. 8Bring these burnt offerings to the Lord: one young bull, one male sheep and seven male lambs a year old. They all must have nothing wrong with them. The smell will be pleasing to the Lord. 9Give a grain offering with the bull. It must be six quarts of fine flour mixed with oil. With the male sheep it must be four quarts. 10And with each of the seven lambs it must be two quarts. 11Offer one male goat as a sin offering. This will be in addition to the sin offering which removes your sins. It will also be in addition to the daily burnt offering with its grain offering and the drink offerings.

Feast of Tents

12"Have a holy meeting on the fifteenth day of the seventh month. Do not work on that day. Celebrate a festival to the Lord for seven days. 13Give these burnt offerings to the Lord: 13 young bulls, 2 male sheep and 14 male lambs a year old. They all must have nothing wrong with them. The smell is pleasing to the Lord. 14Also offer a grain offering with each of the 13 bulls. It must be six quarts of fine flour mixed with oil. With each of the 2 male sheep it must be four quarts. 15And with each of the 14 lambs it must be two quarts. 16Offer 1 male goat as a sin offering. This must be in addition to the daily burnt offering with its grain and drink offerings.

17"On the second day of this festival give an offering. Offer 12 bulls, 2 male sheep and 14 male lambs a year old. They all must have nothing wrong with them. 18Bring the grain and drink offerings for the bulls, sheep and lambs. 19Offer 1 male goat as a sin offering. This must be in addition to the daily burnt offering with its grain and drink offerings.

20"On the third day offer 11 bulls, 2 male sheep and 14 male lambs a year old. They all must have nothing wrong with them. 21Bring the grain and drink offerings for the bulls, sheep and lambs. 22Offer 1 male goat as a sin offering. This must be in addition to the daily burnt offering with its grain and drink offerings.

23"On the fourth day offer 10 bulls, 2 male sheep and 14 male lambs a year old. They all must have nothing wrong with them. 24Bring the grain and drink offerings for the bulls, sheep and lambs. 25Offer 1 male goat as a sin offering. This must be in addition to the daily burnt offering with its grain and drink offerings.

26"On the fifth day offer 9 bulls, 2 male sheep and 14 male lambs a year old. They all must have nothing wrong with them. 27Bring the grain and drink offerings for the bulls, sheep and lambs. 28Offer 1 male goat as a sin offering. This must be in addition to the daily burnt offering with its grain and drink offerings.

29"On the sixth day offer 8 bulls, 2 male sheep and 14 male lambs a year old. They all must have nothing wrong with them. 30Bring the grain and drink offerings for the bulls, sheep and lambs. 31Offer 1 male goat as a sin offering. This must be in addition to the daily burnt offering with its grain and drink offerings.

32"On the seventh day offer 7 bulls, 2 male sheep and 14 male lambs a year old. They all must have nothing wrong with them. 33Bring the grain and drink offerings for the bulls, sheep and lambs. 34Offer 1 male goat

as a sin offering. This must be in addition to the daily burnt offering with its grain and drink offerings.

35"On the eighth day have a closing meeting. Do not work on that day. 36Bring a burnt offering. Its smell will be pleasing to the Lord. Offer 1 bull, 1 male sheep and 7 male lambs a year old. They all must have nothing wrong with them. 37Bring the grain and drink offerings for the bull, male sheep and lambs. 38Offer 1 male goat as a sin offering. This must be in addition to the daily burnt offering with its grain and drink offerings.

39"At your festivals you should bring these to the Lord: your burnt offerings, grain offerings, drink offerings and fellowship offerings. These are in addition to other promised offerings and special gifts you want to give to the Lord.'"

40Moses told the Israelites everything the Lord had commanded him.

Special Promises

30 Moses spoke with the leaders of the Israelite tribes.d He told them these commands from the Lord.

2"A person might make a promise to the Lord. He might promise to do something special. If he does, he must keep his promise. He must do what he said. 3A young woman still living at home might make a promise to the Lord. She might pledge to do something special. 4Her father might hear about the promise or pledge and say nothing. Then she must do what she promised. She must keep her pledge. 5But when her father hears about the promise or pledge, he might not allow it. Then the promise or pledge does not have to be kept. Her father would not allow them. So the Lord will free her from her promise.

6"A woman might make a pledge or a careless promise and then get married. 7Her husband might hear about it and say nothing. Then she must keep her promise or the pledge she made. 8But when her husband hears about it, he might not allow it. He cancels her pledge or the careless promise she made. The Lord will free her from keeping it.

⁹"A widow or divorced woman might make a promise. She must do whatever she promised.

¹⁰"A woman might make a promise or pledge while she was married. ¹¹When her husband hears about it, he might say nothing. He might not stop her. Then she must keep her promise or pledge. ¹²But when her husband hears about it, he might cancel it. Then she does not have to do what she said. Her husband has canceled it. The Lord will free her from it. ¹³A woman's husband may make her keep or cancel any promise or pledge she has made. ¹⁴But her husband might say nothing to her about it for several days. Then she must keep her promises. If he hears about them and says nothing, she must keep her promises. ¹⁵But he might cancel them long after he heard about them. Then he is responsible if she breaks her promise."

¹⁶These are commands that the Lord gave to Moses. They are for husbands and wives. And they are for fathers with daughters living at home.

Israel Attacks the Midianites

31 The Lord spoke to Moses. He said, ²"Pay back the Midianites for what they did to the Israelites. After that you will die."

³So Moses said to the people, "Get some men ready for war. The Lord will use them to pay back the Midianites. ⁴Send to war 1,000 men from each of the tribes𝑑 of Israel." ⁵So 12,000 men got ready for war. There were 1,000 men from each tribe. ⁶Moses sent those 1,000 men from each tribe to war. Phinehas son of Eleazar the priest was with them. He took with him the holy things and the trumpets. ⁷They fought the Midianites as the Lord had commanded Moses. And they killed every Midianite man. ⁸Among those they killed were Evi, Rekem, Zur, Hur and

Reba. They were the five kings of Midian. They also killed Balaam son of Beor with a sword.

⁹The Israelites captured the Midianite women and children. They also took all their flocks, herds and goods. ¹⁰Then they burned all the Midianite towns and camps. ¹¹They took all the people and animals and goods. ¹²Then they went back to Moses and Eleazar the priest and all the Israelites. They brought back the captives, the animals and the goods. The camp was on the plains of Moab near the Jordan River. This was across from Jericho.

¹³Moses, Eleazar the priest and all the leaders of the people went outside the camp to meet them. ¹⁴Moses was angry with the army officers who returned from war. He was angry with those commanders over 1,000 men and those over 100 men.

¹⁵He asked them, "Why did you let the women live? ¹⁶They were the ones who followed Balaam's advice. They turned the Israelites from the Lord at Peor. Then a terrible sickness struck the Lord's people. ¹⁷Kill all the Midianite boys. Kill all the Midianite women who have had sexual relations. ¹⁸But save the girls for yourselves who have not had sexual relations with a man.

¹⁹"All you men who killed anyone or touched a dead body must stay outside the camp for seven days. On the third and seventh days you and your captives must make yourselves clean.𝑑 ²⁰You must clean all your clothes. And you must clean anything made of leather, wool or wood."

²¹Then Eleazar the priest spoke to the soldiers who had gone to war. He said, "These are the teachings that the Lord gave to Moses. ²²Put any gold, silver, bronze, iron, tin or lead into the fire. ²³Put into the fire anything that will not burn. Then wash those things with the cleansing water. Then they will be clean. If something cannot stand the fire, wash it with the water. ²⁴On the seventh day wash your clothes. Then you will be clean.

After that you may come into the camp."

Dividing the Goods

25The Lord said to Moses, 26"You, Eleazar the priest and the leaders should take a count. Count the goods, the men and the animals that were taken. 27Then divide those things between the soldiers who went to war and the rest of the people. 28Tax the soldiers who went to war. The Lord's share is 1 thing out of every 500 things. This includes people, cattle, donkeys, sheep or goats. 29Take it from the soldiers' half. And give it to Eleazar the priest. It is the Lord's share. 30And from the people's half, take 1 thing out of every 50. This includes people, cattle, donkeys, sheep, goats or other animals. Give that to the Levites. They take care of the Lord's Holy Tent."d 31So Moses and Eleazar did as the Lord commanded Moses.

32There remained from what the soldiers had taken 675,000 sheep, 3372,000 cattle, 3461,000 donkeys 35and 32,000 women. These were the women who had not had sexual relations with a man. 36The soldiers who went to war got 337,500 sheep. 37They gave 675 of the sheep to the Lord. 38They got 36,000 cattle. They gave 72 of them to the Lord. 39They got 30,500 donkeys. They gave 61 of them to the Lord. 40They got 16,000 people. And they gave 32 of them to the Lord. 41Moses gave the Lord's share to Eleazar the priest. This was what the Lord had commanded him.

42Moses separated the people's half from the soldiers' half. 43The people got 337,500 sheep, 4436,000 cattle, 4530,500 donkeys 46and 16,000 people. 47From the people's half Moses took 1 thing out of every 50 for the Lord. This included the animals and the people. Then he gave them to the Levites. They took care of the Lord's Holy Tent. This was what the Lord had commanded Moses.

48Then the officers of the army came to Moses. They were the commanders of 1,000 men and commanders of 100 men. 49They told Moses, "We, your servants, have counted our soldiers under our command. Not one of them is missing. 50So we have brought the Lord a gift. We have brought the gold things that each of us found: arm bands, bracelets, signetd rings, earrings and necklaces. These are to remove our sins so we will belong to the Lord."

51So Moses and Eleazar the priest took the gold things from them. 52The commanders of 1,000 men and the commanders of 100 men gave the Lord the gold. All of it together weighed about 420 pounds. 53Each soldier had taken something for himself. 54Moses and Eleazar the priest took the gold from the commanders of 1,000 men and the commanders of 100 men. Then they put it in the Meeting Tent.d It was a memorial before the Lord for the people of Israel.

The Tribes East of the Jordan

32 The people of Reuben and Gad had many cattle. They saw that the lands of Jazer and Gilead were good for cattle. 2So they came to Moses, Eleazar the priest and the leaders of the people. 3-4They said, "We, your servants, have many cattle. The Lord has captured for the Israelites a land that is good for cattle. This is the land around Ataroth, Dibon, Jazer, Nimrah, Heshbon, Elealeh, Sebam, Nebo and Beon. 5If it pleases you, we would like this land to be given to us. Don't make us cross the Jordan River."

6Moses told the people of Gad and Reuben, "Shall your brothers go to war while you stay behind? 7You will discourage the Israelites. They will not want to go over to the land the Lord has given them. 8Your ancestors did the same thing. From Kadesh Barnea I sent them to look at the land. 9They went as far as the Valley of Eshcol. They saw the land. And they discouraged the Israelites from going into the land the Lord had given them. 10The

Lord became very angry that day. He made this promise: 11'None of the people who came from Egypt and who are 20 years old or older will see this land. I promised it to Abraham, Isaac and Jacob. But these people have not followed me completely. 12Only Caleb son of Jephunneh the Kenizzite and Joshua son of Nun followed the Lord completely.'

13"The Lord was very angry with Israel. So he made them wander in the desert for 40 years. Finally all the people who had sinned against him had died. 14And now you are acting just like your fathers! You sinful people are making the Lord even more angry with Israel. 15If you quit following the Lord, it will add to their stay in the desert. So you will destroy all these people."

16But the Reubenites and Gadites came up to Moses. They said, "We will build pens for our animals. And we will build cities for our wives and children here. 17Then our families will be in strong, walled cities. They will be safe from the people who live in this land. Then we will prepare for war. We will help the other Israelites get their land. 18We will not return home until every Israelite has received his land. 19We won't take any of the land west of the Jordan River. Our part of the land is east of the Jordan."

20So Moses told them, "You must do these things. You must go before the Lord into battle. 21You must cross the Jordan River armed. The Lord will force out the enemy. 22After the Lord helps us take the land, you may return home. You will have done your duty to the Lord and Israel. Then you may have this land as your own.

23"But if you don't do these things, you will be sinning against the Lord. And know for sure that you will be punished for your sin. 24Build cities for your wives and children and pens for your animals. But then you must do what you promised."

25The Gadites and Reubenites said to Moses, "We are your servants. We will do what you, our master, command. 26Our wives, children and all our cattle will stay in the cities of Gilead. 27But we, your servants, will prepare for battle. We will go over and fight for the Lord, as you have said."

28So Moses gave orders about them to Eleazar the priest. And he gave them to Joshua son of Nun and the leaders of the tribes*d* of Israel. 29Moses said to them, "The Gadites and Reubenites will prepare for battle. They will cross the Jordan River with you. They will go before the Lord and help you take the land. If they do that, give them the land of Gilead for their own. 30But if they do not go over armed, they will not receive it. Their land will be in Canaan with you."

31The Gadites and Reubenites answered, "We are your servants. We will do as the Lord said. 32We will cross over into Canaan. We will go before the Lord ready for battle. But our land will be east of the Jordan River."

33So Moses gave that land to the Gadites, Reubenites and the eastern half-tribe of Manasseh. (Manasseh was Joseph's son.) That land had been the kingdom of Sihon, the king of the Amorites. And it included the kingdom of Og, king of Bashan. It also included all the cities and the land around them.

34The Gadites rebuilt the cities of Dibon, Ataroth, Aroer, 35Atroth Shophan, Jazer, Jogbehah, 36Beth Nimrah and Beth Haran. These were strong, walled cities. And they built sheep pens.

37The Reubenites built Heshbon, Elealeh, Kiriathaim, 38Nebo, Baal Meon and Sibmah. They renamed Nebo and Baal Meon when they rebuilt them.

39The descendants*d* of Makir son of Manasseh went and captured Gilead. They forced out the Amorites who were there. 40So Moses gave Gilead to the family of Makir son of Manasseh. And they settled there. 41Jair son of Manasseh went out and captured the small towns there. He called them the Towns of Jair. 42Nobah went and captured Kenath and the small towns around it. Then he named it Nobah after himself.

Israel's Journey from Egypt

33 These are the places the Israelites went as Moses and Aaron led them out of Egypt in divisions. ²At the Lord's command Moses recorded the places they went. These are the places they went.

³On the fifteenth day of the first month, they left Rameses. That was the day after the Passover.ᵈ The Israelites marched out boldly in front of all the Egyptians. ⁴The Egyptians were burying their firstbornᵈ sons. The Lord had killed them. He showed that the gods of Egypt were false.

⁵The Israelites left Rameses and camped at Succoth.

⁶They left Succoth and camped at Etham. It was at the edge of the desert.

⁷They left Etham and went back to Pi Hahiroth. This was east of Baal Zephon. They camped near Migdol.

⁸They left Pi Hahiroth. They walked through the sea into the desert. After going three days through the Desert of Etham, they camped at Marah.

⁹They left Marah and went to Elim. There were 12 springs of water and 70 palm trees where they camped.

¹⁰They left Elim and camped near the Red Sea.ᵈ

¹¹They left the Red Sea and camped in the Desert of Sin.

¹²They left the Desert of Sin and camped at Dophkah.

¹³They left Dophkah and camped at Alush.

¹⁴They left Alush and camped at Rephidim. The people had no water to drink there.

¹⁵They left Rephidim and camped in the Desert of Sinai.

¹⁶They left the Desert of Sinai and camped at Kibroth Hattaavah.

¹⁷They left Kibroth Hattaavah and camped at Hazeroth.

¹⁸They left Hazeroth and camped at Rithmah.

¹⁹They left Rithmah and camped at Rimmon Perez.

²⁰They left Rimmon Perez and camped at Libnah.

²¹They left Libnah and camped at Rissah.

²²They left Rissah and camped at Kehelathah.

²³They left Kehelathah and camped at Mount Shepher.

²⁴They left Mount Shepher and camped at Haradah.

²⁵They left Haradah and camped at Makheloth.

²⁶They left Makheloth and camped at Tahath.

²⁷They left Tahath and camped at Terah.

²⁸They left Terah and camped at Mithcah.

²⁹They left Mithcah and camped at Hashmonah.

³⁰They left Hashmonah and camped at Moseroth.

³¹They left Moseroth and camped at Bene Jaakan.

³²They left Bene Jaakan and camped at Hor Haggidgad.

³³They left Hor Haggidgad and camped at Jotbathah.

³⁴They left Jotbathah and camped at Abronah.

³⁵They left Abronah and camped at Ezion Geber.

³⁶They left Ezion Geber and camped at Kadesh in the Desert of Zin.

³⁷They left Kadesh and camped at Mount Hor. This was on the border of Edom. ³⁸Aaron the priest obeyed the Lord and went up Mount Hor. There he died. He died on the first day of the fifth month. This was in the fortieth year after the Israelitesz left Egypt. ³⁹Aaron was 123 years old when he died on Mount Hor.

⁴⁰The king of Arad lived in the southern area of Canaan. He heard that the Israelites were coming.

⁴¹The people left Mount Hor and camped at Zalmonah.

⁴²They left Zalmonah and camped at Punon.

43They left Punon and camped at Oboth.

44They left Oboth and camped at Iye Abarim. This was on the border of Moab.

45They left Iye Abarim and camped at Dibon Gad.

46They left Dibon Gad and camped at Almon Diblathaim.

47They left Almon Diblathaim and camped in the mountains of Abarim, near Nebo.

48They left the mountains of Abarim and camped on the plains of Moab. This was near the Jordan River across from Jericho. 49They camped along the Jordan on the plains of Moab. Their camp went from Beth Jeshimoth to Abel Acacia.

50On the plains of Moab by the Jordan River across from Jericho, the Lord spoke to Moses. He said, 51"Speak to the Israelites. Tell them, 'Cross the Jordan River and go into Canaan. 52Force out the people who live there. Destroy all of their carved statues. Destroy their metal idols. Wreck all of their places of worship. 53Take over the land and settle there. I have given this land to you to own. 54Throw lots*d* to divide up the land by family groups. Give larger portions to larger family groups. Give smaller portions to smaller family groups. The land will be given as the lots decide. Each tribe*d* will get its own land.

55"'But if you don't force those people out of the land, they will bring you trouble. They will be like sharp hooks in your eyes. They will be like thorns in your sides. They will bring trouble to the land where you live. 56I will punish you as I had planned to punish them.'"

The Borders of Canaan

34 The Lord said to Moses, 2"Give this command to the people of Israel: 'You will soon enter Canaan. It will be yours. These shall be the borders. 3On the south you will get part of the Desert of Zin. This is near the border of Edom. On the east side your southern border will start at the south end of the Dead Sea.*d* 4It will cross south of Scorpion Pass. It will go through the Desert of Zin and south of Kadesh Barnea. Then it will go to Hazar Addar and over to Azmon. 5From Azmon it will go to the brook of Egypt. It will end at the Mediterranean Sea.

6"'Your western border will be the Mediterranean Sea.

7"'Your northern border will begin at the Mediterranean Sea and go to Mount Hor. 8From Mount Hor it will go to Lebo Hamath. Then it will go to Zedad. 9Then the border will go to Ziphron and end at Hazar Enan. This will be your northern border.

10"'Your eastern border will begin at Hazar Enan and go to Shepham. 11From Shepham the border will go east of Ain to Riblah. It will go along the hills east of Lake Galilee. 12Then the border will go down along the Jordan River. It will end at the Dead Sea.

"'These are the borders around your country.'"

13So Moses gave this command to the Israelites: "This is the land you will receive. Throw lots*d* to divide it among the nine and a half tribes.*d* The Lord commanded that it should be theirs. 14The tribes of Reuben and Gad and the eastern half-tribe of Manasseh have already received their land. 15These two and a half tribes received land east of the Jordan River. It is across from Jericho.

16Then the Lord said to Moses, 17"These are the men who will divide the land: Eleazar the priest and Joshua son of Nun. 18Also take one leader from each tribe. They will divide the land. 19These are the names of the leaders: from the tribe of Judah, Caleb son of Jephunneh; 20from the tribe of Simeon, Shemuel son of Ammihud; 21from the tribe of Benjamin, Elidad son of Kislon; 22from the tribe of Dan, Bukki son of Jogli; 23from the tribe of Manasseh son of Joseph, Hanniel son of Ephod; 24from the tribe of Ephraim son of Joseph,

Kemuel son of Shiphtan; [25]from the tribe of Zebulun, Elizaphan son of Parnach; [26]from the tribe of Issachar, Paltiel son of Azzan; [27]from the tribe of Asher, Ahihud son of Shelomi; [28]from the tribe of Naphtali, Pedahel son of Ammihud."

[29]The Lord commanded these men to divide the land of Canaan among the Israelites.

The Levites' Towns

35 The Lord spoke to Moses on the plains of Moab. This was across from Jericho by the Jordan River. He said, [2]"Command the Israelites to give the Levites cities to live in. These will be cities in the land they receive. Also give the Levites the pastureland around these cities. [3]Then the Levites will have cities where they may live. And they will have pastureland for their cattle, sheep and other animals. [4]The pastureland you give the Levites will extend 1,500 feet from the city wall. [5]Also measure 3,000 feet in each direction from the city wall. Measure 3,000 feet east of the city. Measure 3,000 feet south of the city. Measure 3,000 feet west of the city. And measure 3,000 feet north of the city. The city will be in the center. This will be pastureland for the Levites' cities.

Cities of Safety

[6]"Six of the cities you give the Levites will be cities of safety.[d] A person might accidentally kill someone. If he does, he may run to one of those cities for safety. You must also give 42 other cities to the Levites. [7]Give the Levites a total of 48 cities and their pastures. [8]The larger tribes[d] of Israel must give more cities. The smaller tribes must give fewer cities. Each tribe must give some of its cities to the Levites. The number of cities they give will depend on the size of their land."

[9]Then the Lord said to Moses, [10]"Tell the Israelites these things: 'You will cross the Jordan River and go into Canaan. [11]You must choose cities to be cities of safety. If a person accidentally kills someone, he may run to them for safety. [12]There he will be safe from the dead person's relative who has the duty of punishing the killer. He will not die before he is judged in court. [13]The six cities you give will be cities of safety. [14]Give three cities east of the Jordan River. And give three cities in Canaan as cities of safety. [15]These six cities will be places of safety for citizens of Israel. And they will be for foreigners and other people living with you. Any of these people may run to one of these cities if he accidentally kills someone.

[16]"If a person uses an iron weapon to kill someone, he is a murderer. He must be put to death. [17]A person might take a rock that could kill someone. If he kills a person with it, he is a murderer. He must be put to death. [18]A person might pick up a piece of wood that could kill someone. If he kills someone with it, he is a murderer. He must be put to death. [19]A relative of the dead person must put the murderer to death. When he finds the murderer, he must kill him. [20]A person might shove someone and kill him. Or he might throw something at someone and kill him. [21]Or he might hit someone with his hand and kill him. If he did that from hate, he is a murderer. He must be put to death. A relative of the dead person must kill the murderer when he finds him.

[22]"But a person might suddenly shove someone. He did not hate the person. Or he might accidentally throw something and hit someone. [23]Or he might drop a rock that could kill someone. It might fall on someone he did not see. And it might kill that person. He didn't plan to hurt anyone. He didn't hate the person he killed. [24]If that happens, the community must decide what to do. They must decide between the relative of the dead person and the killer. Here are the rules. [25]They must protect the killer from the dead person's relative. They must send the killer back to the city of safety that he ran to. He must stay there until the high priest

dies. The high priest had the holy oil poured on him.

26 "'That man must never go outside the limits of his city of safety. 27 If a relative of the dead person finds him outside the city, the relative may kill him. He will not be guilty of murder. 28 The killer must stay in his city of safety until the high priest dies. After the high priest dies, he may go back to his own land.

29 "'These laws are for you from now on, wherever you live.

30 "'A killer may be put to death only if he is a murderer. And there must be witnesses. No one may be put to death with only one witness.

31 "'A murderer should die. Don't take money to spare his life. He must be put to death.

32 "'A person might run to a city of safety. Don't take money to let him go back home before the high priest dies.

33 "'Don't let murder spoil your land. There is only one way to remove the sin of killing an innocent person. The murderer must be put to death. 34 I am the Lord. I live among the Israelites. I live in that land with you. So do not spoil it with murder.'"

Land for Zelophehad's Daughters

36 The leaders of Gilead's family group went to talk to Moses and the leaders of the families of Israel. (Gilead was the son of Makir. Makir was Manasseh's son, and Manasseh was Joseph's son.) 2 They said, "The Lord commanded you, our master, to give the land to the Israelites by throwing lots.*d* And the Lord commanded you to give the land of Zelophehad, our brother, to his daughters. 3 His daughters may marry men from other tribes*d*

of Israel. Then that land will leave our family. The people of the other tribes will get that land. So we will lose some of our land. 4 The time of Jubilee*d* will come for the Israelites. Then their land will go to other tribes. It will go to the tribes of the people they marry. So their land will be taken away from us. And that was land we received from our fathers."

5 Then Moses gave the Israelites this command from the Lord: "These men from the tribe of Joseph are right. 6 This is the Lord's command to Zelophehad's daughters: You may marry anyone you wish from your own tribe. 7 In this way the Israelites' land will not pass from tribe to tribe. Each Israelite will keep the land in the tribe that belonged to his ancestors. 8 A woman who inherits her father's land may marry. But she must marry someone from her own tribe. In this way every Israelite will keep the land that belonged to his ancestors. 9 The land must not pass from tribe to tribe. Each Israelite tribe will keep the land it received from its ancestors."

10 Zelophehad's daughters obeyed the Lord's command to Moses.

11 So Zelophehad's daughters—Mahlah, Tirzah, Hoglah, Milcah and Noah—married their cousins. These were their father's relatives. 12 Their husbands were from the tribe of Manasseh son of Joseph. So their land stayed in their father's family group and tribe.

13 These were the laws and commands that the Lord gave to the Israelites. He gave them through Moses. The Israelites were on the plains of Moab by the Jordan River, across from Jericho.

DEUTERONOMY

*Moses' Last
Message to Israel*

Moses Talks to the Israelites

1 This is the message Moses gave the people of Israel. They were in the desert east of the Jordan River. They were in the Jordan Valley near Suph, between Paran and the towns of Tophel, Laban, Hazeroth and Dizahab. ²(The trip from Mount Sinai to Kadesh Barnea on the Mount Edom road takes 11 days.) ³But it was now 40 years after the Israelites had left Egypt. On the first day of the eleventh month, Moses spoke to the people. He told them everything the Lord had commanded him to tell them. ⁴This was after the Lord had defeated Sihon and Og. Sihon was king of the Amorite people and lived in Heshbon. Og was king of Bashan and lived in Ashteroth and Edrei.

⁵Now the Israelites were east of the Jordan River in the land of Moab. There Moses began to explain what God had commanded. Moses said:

⁶The Lord our God spoke to us at Mount Sinai. He said, "You have stayed long enough at this mountain. ⁷Get ready. Go to the mountain country of the Amorites. Go to all the places around there—the Jordan Valley, the mountains, the western slopes, the southern area, the seacoast, the land of Canaan and Lebanon. Go as far as the great river, the Euphrates. ⁸See, I have given you this land. Go in and take it for yourselves. The Lord promised it to your ancestors—Abraham, Isaac and Jacob and their descendants."*d*

Moses Appoints Leaders

⁹At that time I said, "I am not able to take care of you by myself. ¹⁰The Lord your God has made you grow in number. There are as many of you as there are stars in the sky. ¹¹I pray that the Lord, the God of your ancestors, will give you a thousand times more people. That's what he promised. ¹²But I cannot take care of your problems, your troubles and your arguments by myself. ¹³So choose some men from each tribe.*d* Choose wise men who have understanding and experience. I will make them leaders over you."

¹⁴And you said, "That's a good thing to do."

¹⁵So I took the wise and experienced leaders of your tribes. And I made them your leaders. I appointed commanders over 1,000 people, over 100 people, over 50 people and over 10 people. I made them officers over your tribes. ¹⁶Then I told your judges, "Listen to the arguments between your people. Judge fairly between two Israelites or between an Israelite and a foreigner. ¹⁷When you judge, be fair to everyone. Don't act as if one person is more important than another. Don't be afraid of anyone, because your decision comes from God. Bring the hard cases to me. I will judge them." ¹⁸At that time I told you everything you must do.

Spies Enter the Land

¹⁹Then, as the Lord our God commanded us, we left Mount Sinai. We went toward the mountain country of the Amorite people. We went through that large and terrible desert you saw. Then we came to Kadesh Barnea. ²⁰Then I said to you, "You have now come to the mountain country of the Amorites. The Lord our God will give

us this land. ²¹Look, there it is! Go up. Take it. The Lord, the God of your ancestors, told you to do this. So don't be afraid. Don't worry."

²²Then all of you came to me. You said, "Let's send men before us to spy out the land. They can come back and tell us the way we should go. They can tell us about the cities we will find."

²³I thought that was a good idea. So I chose 12 of your men, 1 for each tribe.ᵈ ²⁴They left and went up to the mountains. They came to the Valley of Eshcol and explored it. ²⁵They took some of the fruit from that land. And they brought it down to us. They said, "It is a good land that the Lord our God is giving us."

Israel Refuses to Enter

²⁶But you refused to go. You would not obey the command of the Lord your God. ²⁷You grumbled in your tents. You said, "The Lord hates us. He brought us out of Egypt just to give us to the Amorites. They will destroy us. ²⁸Where can we go now? The spies we sent have made us afraid. They said, 'The people there are bigger and taller than we are. The cities are big. They have walls up to the sky. And we saw the Anakitesᵈ there!'"

²⁹Then I said to you, "Don't be frightened. Don't be afraid of those people. ³⁰The Lord your God will go ahead of you. He will fight for you as he did in Egypt. You saw him do it. ³¹And in the desert you saw how the Lord your God carried you. He was like a man carrying his son. And he has brought you safely all the way to this place."

³²But you still did not trust the Lord your God. ³³As you moved, he went before you. He found places for you to camp. He went before you in a fire at night and in a cloud during the day. He showed you which way to go.

³⁴When the Lord heard what you said, he was angry. He made a promise. He said, ³⁵"I promised a good land to your ancestors. But none of you evil people will see it. ³⁶Only Caleb son of Jephunneh will see it. I will give him and his descendantsᵈ the land he walked on. I will do this because he followed me completely."

³⁷Because of you, the Lord was also angry with me. He said to me, "You won't enter the land either. ³⁸But your assistant, Joshua son of Nun, will go there. Encourage Joshua, because he will lead Israel to take the land for their own."

³⁹The Lord said to us, "You said your babies would be captured. But they will go into the land. They are too young to know right from wrong. So I will give the land to them. And they will take it for their own. ⁴⁰But you must turn around. Follow the desert road toward the Gulf of Aqaba."

⁴¹Then you said to me, "We have sinned against the Lord. But now we will go up and fight, as the Lord our God commanded us." Then all of you put on weapons. You thought it would be easy to go into the mountains.

⁴²But the Lord said to me, "Tell them not to go up there and fight. I will not be with them. Their enemies will defeat them."

⁴³So I told you, but you would not listen. You would not obey the Lord's command. You were proud. So you went on up into the mountains. ⁴⁴The Amorites who lived there came out and fought you. They chased you like bees. They defeated you from Edom to Hormah. ⁴⁵So you came back and cried to the Lord. But the Lord did not hear you. He refused to listen to you. ⁴⁶So you stayed in Kadesh a long time.

Israel Wanders in the Desert

2 Then we turned around. And we traveled on the desert road toward the Gulf of Aqaba. That is what the Lord had told me to do. We traveled through the mountains of Edom for many days.

²Then the Lord said to me, ³"You have traveled through these mountains long enough. Turn north. ⁴Tell the people this: 'You will soon go through

the land of Edom. This land belongs to your relatives, the descendants[d] of Esau. They will be afraid of you. But be very careful. [5]Don't go to war against them. I am not giving you any of their land—not even a foot of it. I have given the mountains of Edom to Esau as his own. [6]You must pay them in silver for any food you eat or water you drink.'"

[7]The Lord your God has blessed everything you have done. He has protected you while you traveled through this large desert. The Lord your God has been with you for these 40 years. You have had everything you needed.

[8]So we passed by our relatives, the people of Esau who lived in Edom. We turned off the Jordan Valley road. It comes from the towns of Elath and Ezion Geber. And we traveled along the desert road of Moab.

The Land of Ar

[9]Then the Lord said to me, "Don't bother the people of Moab. Don't go to war against them. I am not giving you any of their land. I have given Ar to the descendants[d] of Lot." [10](The Emites lived in Ar before. They were strong people, and there were many of them. They were very tall, like the Anakites.[d] [11]The Emites were thought to be Rephaites,[d] like the Anakites. But the Moabite people called them Emites. [12]The Horites also lived in Edom before. But the people of Esau forced them out. They destroyed the Horites and took their place. That is also what Israel did in the land the Lord gave them as their own.)

[13]And the Lord said to me, "Now get up and cross the Zered Valley." So we crossed the valley. [14]It had been 38 years since we left Kadesh Barnea until we crossed the Zered Valley. By then, all the fighting men from that time had died. This is what the Lord had promised would happen. [15]The Lord had continued to destroy them until they were all gone from the camp. [16]Now the last of those fighting men had died.

[17]Then the Lord said to me, [18]"Today you must go by Ar, on the border of Moab. [19]When you come near the people of Ammon, don't bother them. Don't go to war against them. I am not giving you their land. I have given that land to the descendants[d] of Lot."

[20](That land was also thought to be a land of Rephaites. Those people used to live there. But the Ammonites called them Zamzummites. [21]They were strong people, and there were many of them. They were very tall, like the Anakites. The Lord went before the Ammonites and destroyed the Zamzummites. The Ammonites forced them out of the land and took their place. [22]The Lord did the same thing for the descendants of Esau. They lived in Edom. He destroyed the Horites. The Edomites forced them out of the land and took their place. And they live there to this day. [23]The Caphtorite people came from Crete. They destroyed the Avvites. The Avvites lived in towns all the way to Gaza. But the Caphtorites destroyed them and took their place.)

Fighting the Amorites

[24]The Lord said, "Get up. Cross the Arnon Ravine. See, I am giving you the power to defeat Sihon the Amorite. He is king of Heshbon. I am giving you his land. So fight against him and begin taking his land. [25]Today I will begin to make all the people in the world afraid of you. They will hear reports about you. And they will shake with fear. They will be terrified of you."

[26]I sent messengers from the desert of Kedemoth to Sihon king of Heshbon. They offered him peace. They said, [27]"Let us pass through your country. We will stay on the road. We will not turn right or left. [28]We will pay you in silver for any food we eat or water we drink. We only want to walk through your country. [29]The descendants[d] of Esau in Edom let us go through their land. So did the Moabites in Ar. We want to cross the Jordan River into the land the Lord our God has given us."

30But Sihon king of Heshbon would not let us pass. The Lord your God had made him stubborn. The Lord wanted you to defeat Sihon. And now this has happened.

31The Lord said to me, "See, I have begun to give Sihon and his country to you. Begin taking the land as your own."

32Then Sihon and all his army came out. And they fought us at Jahaz. 33But the Lord our God gave Sihon to us. We defeated him, his sons and all his army. 34We captured all his cities. We completely destroyed them, the men, women and children. We left no one alive. 35But we kept the cattle and valuable things from the cities for ourselves. 36We defeated Aroer on the edge of the Arnon Ravine. And we defeated the town in the ravine, and even Gilead. No town was too strong for us. The Lord our God gave us all of them. 37But you did not go near the land of the Ammonites. You did not go near the shores of the Jabbok River. You did not go near the towns in the mountains. This was what the Lord our God had commanded.

The Battle at Bashan

3 Then we turned and went up the road toward Bashan. Og king of Bashan and all his army came out to fight us at Edrei. 2The Lord said to me, "Don't be afraid of Og. I will hand him, his whole army and his land over to you. Do to him what you did to Sihon king of the Amorites, who ruled in Heshbon."

3So the Lord our God gave us Og king of Bashan and all his army. We defeated them and left no one alive. 4Then we captured all of Og's cities. We captured all 60 of them. We took the whole area of Argob, Og's kingdom in Bashan. 5All these were strong cities. They had high walls and gates with bars. And there were also many small towns with no walls. 6We completely destroyed them. We destroyed them just like the cities of Sihon king

of Heshbon. We killed all the men, women and children. 7But we kept all the cattle and valuable things from the cities for ourselves.

8So at that time we took the land east of the Jordan River. We took it from these two Amorite kings. It went from the Arnon Ravine to Mount Hermon. 9(Hermon is called Sirion by the Sidonian people. The Amorites call it Senir.) 10We captured all the cities on the high plain and all of Gilead. We took all of Bashan as far as Salecah and Edrei. These were towns in Og's kingdom of Bashan. 11(Only Og king of Bashan was left of the few Rephaites.d His bed was made of iron. It was more than 13 feet long and 6 feet wide! It is still in the Ammonite city of Rabbah.)

The Land Is Divided

12At that time we took this land to be our own. I gave the people of Reuben and Gad the land from Aroer by the Arnon Ravine. And I gave them half of the mountain country of Gilead and the cities in it. 13To the eastern half-tribed of Manasseh I gave the rest of Gilead. And I gave them all of Bashan, the kingdom of Og. (The area of Argob in Bashan was called the land of the Rephaites.d 14Jair, a descendantd of Manasseh, took the whole area of Argob. It went to the border of the Geshurites and Maacathites. That land was named for Jair. So even today Bashan is called the Towns of Jair.) 15I gave Gilead to Makir. 16I gave the Reubenites and the Gadites the land that begins at Gilead. It goes from the Arnon Ravine to the Jabbok River. (The middle of the Arnon is the border.) The Jabbok River is the Ammonite border. 17The border on the west was the Jordan River in the Jordan Valley. It goes from Lake Galilee to the Dead Sead west of Mount Pisgah.

18At that time I gave you this command: "The Lord your God has given you this land as your own. Now your fighting men must take their weapons. And you must lead the other Israelites across the river. ¹⁹Your wives, your young children and your cattle may stay here. I know you have many cattle. They may stay here in the cities I have given you. ²⁰Some day your Israelite relatives will also have a place to rest. They will receive the land the Lord your God has given them. It is on the other side of the Jordan River. After that, you may .

²¹Then I gave this command to Joshua: "You have seen for yourself what the Lord your God has done to these two kings. The Lord will do the same thing to all the kingdoms where you are going. ²²Don't be afraid of them. The Lord your God will fight for you."

Moses Cannot Enter the Land

²³Then I begged the Lord: ²⁴"Lord God, you have begun to show me, your servant, how great you are. You have great strength. No other god in heaven or earth can do the powerful things you do. There is no other god like you. ²⁵Please let me cross the Jordan River. I want to see the beautiful mountains and Lebanon."

²⁶But the Lord was angry with me because of you. He would not listen to me. The Lord said to me, "That's enough. Don't talk to me anymore about it. ²⁷Climb to the top of Mount Pisgah. Look west, north, south and east. You can look at the land. But you will not cross the Jordan River. ²⁸Appoint Joshua. Help him be brave and strong. He will lead the people across the river. He will give them the land that they are to inherit. You can only look at it." ²⁹So we stayed in the valley opposite Beth Peor.

Moses Tells Israel to Obey

4 Now, Israel, listen to the laws and commands I will teach you. Obey them so you will live. Then you will go over and take the land. The Lord, the God of your ancestors, is giving it to you. ²Don't add to these commands. And don't leave anything out. But obey the commands of the Lord your God that I give you.

³You have seen for yourselves what the Lord did at Baal Peor. The Lord your God destroyed everyone among you who followed Baal*ᵈ* in Peor. ⁴But you continued to follow the Lord your God. So you are still alive today.

⁵Look, I have taught you the laws and rules the Lord my God commanded me. Now you can obey the laws in the land you are entering. It is the land you will own. ⁶Obey these laws carefully. This will show the other nations that you have wisdom and understanding. They will hear about these laws. And they will say, "This great nation of Israel is wise and understanding." ⁷No other nation is as great as we are. Their gods do not come near them. But the Lord our God comes near when we pray to him. ⁸And no other nation has such good teachings and commands. I am giving them to you today.

⁹But be careful! Watch out. Don't forget the things that you have seen. Don't forget them as long as you live. Teach them to your children and grandchildren. ¹⁰Remember the day you stood before the Lord your God at Mount Sinai. He said to me, "Bring the people together to listen to what I say. Then they will respect me as long as they live in the land. And they will teach these things to their children." ¹¹Then you came and stood at the bottom of the mountain. It blazed with fire that reached to the sky. Black clouds made it very dark. ¹²Then the Lord spoke to you from the fire. You heard the sound of words. But you did not see him. There was only a voice. ¹³The Lord told you about his agreement. It was the Ten Commandments. And he told you to obey them. Then he wrote them on two stone tablets. ¹⁴Then the Lord commanded me to teach you the laws and rules. You must obey them in the land you will own when you cross the Jordan River.

Laws About Idols

¹⁵The Lord spoke to you from the fire at Mount Sinai. But you did not see him.

So watch yourselves carefully! ¹⁶Don't sin by making idols of any kind. Don't make statues of men or women. ¹⁷Don't make statues of animals on earth or birds that fly in the air. ¹⁸Don't make statues of anything that crawls on the ground. Don't make statues of fish in the water below. ¹⁹When you look up at the sky, you see the sun, moon and stars. You can see everything in the sky. But don't bow down and worship them. The Lord your God has made these things for all people everywhere. ²⁰Egypt tested you like a furnace for melting iron. The Lord brought you out of Egypt. And he made you his very own people, as you are now.

²¹The Lord was angry with me because of you. He made a strong promise that I would not cross the Jordan River. I could not go into the good land the Lord your God is giving you to own. ²²I will die here in this land. I will not cross the Jordan. But you will soon go across and take that good land. ²³Be careful. Don't forget the agreement of the Lord your God that he made with you. Don't make any idols for yourselves. The Lord your God has commanded you not to do that. ²⁴The Lord your God is a jealous God. He is like a fire that burns things up.

²⁵You will live in the land a long time. You will have children and grandchildren. Even after that, don't do evil things. Don't make any kind of idol. Don't do what the Lord says is evil. That will make him angry. ²⁶I will ask heaven and earth to speak against you that day. Then you will quickly be removed from this land. You are crossing the Jordan River to take the land. But you will not live there long after that. You will be completely destroyed. ²⁷The Lord will scatter you among the other nations. Only a few of you will be left alive. And those few will be in other nations where the Lord will send you. ²⁸There you will worship gods made by men. They will be made of wood and stone. They cannot see, hear, eat or smell. ²⁹But even there you

can look for the Lord your God. And you will find him if you look. But you must look for him with your whole being. ³⁰It will be hard when all these things happen to you. But after that you will come back to the Lord your God. You will obey him. ³¹The Lord your God is a merciful God. He will not leave you or destroy you. He will not forget the agreement he made with your ancestors. He made that agreement sure with his strong promise.

The Lord Is Great

³²Nothing like this has ever happened before! Look at the past, long before you were even born. Go all the way back to when God made man on the earth. Look from one end of heaven to the other. Nothing like this has ever been heard of! ³³No other people have ever heard God speak from a fire and still lived. But you have. ³⁴No other god has ever taken for himself one nation out of another. But the Lord your God did this for you in Egypt. He did it right before your own eyes. He did it with tests, signs, miracles,ᵈ war and great sights. He did it by his great power and strength.

³⁵He showed you things so you would know that the Lord is God. There is no other God besides him. ³⁶He spoke to you from heaven to teach you. He showed you his great fire on earth. And you heard him speak from the fire. ³⁷The Lord loved your ancestors. That is why he chose you, their descendants.ᵈ He brought you out of Egypt himself by his great strength. ³⁸He forced nations out of their land ahead of you. And these nations were bigger and stronger than you were. But the Lord brought you into their land and gave it to you to own. And this land is yours today.

³⁹Know and believe today that the Lord is God. He is God in heaven above and on the earth below. There is no other god! ⁴⁰Obey his laws and commands, which I am giving you today. Obey them so that things will go well

for you and your children. Then you will live a long time in this land. The Lord your God is giving it to you forever.

Cities of Safety

⁴¹Moses chose three cities east of the Jordan River. ⁴²A person who killed someone accidentally could go there. He did not hate the person he killed. So he could save his life by running to one of these cities. ⁴³These were the

These were the two Amorite kings east of the Jordan River. ⁴⁸This land went from Aroer to Mount Hermon. Aroer is on the edge of the Arnon Ravine. ⁴⁹It included all the Jordan Valley east of the Jordan River. And it went as far as the Dead Sea*ᵈ* below Mount Pisgah.

Get Ready, Get Set, Grow!
DEUTERONOMY 5:1

Look at pictures of yourself as a baby. You sure looked different than you do now! You're taller, heavier, and stronger. It certainly would be strange if you still looked and acted like a tiny baby.

When you first believed in Jesus as your Savior, you were like a new-born baby. You had a lot to learn about Jesus and how to serve him. That's why God wants you to grow in your faith. One way to do that is to read the Bible, God's Word, and learn what it says. In the Bible, you'll learn about how God wants you to live. Moses told God's people that they should *listen* to God's words, *learn* and remember them, and finally *obey* them.

When you read the Bible and learn about it at church, ask God to help you listen, learn, and obey.

To find out more about growing in your faith, zoom to page 829.

cities: Bezer in the desert high plain was for the Reubenites; Ramoth in Gilead was for the Gadites; Golan in Bashan was for the Manassites.

The Law Moses Gave

⁴⁴These are the teachings Moses gave to the people of Israel. ⁴⁵They are the rules, commands and laws he gave them when they came out of Egypt. ⁴⁶They were in the valley near Beth Peor. That is east of the Jordan River in the land of Sihon. Sihon was king of the Amorites. He ruled in Heshbon. He was defeated by Moses and the Israelites as they came out of Egypt. ⁴⁷The Israelites captured his land. They also took the land of Og king of Bashan.

The Ten Commandments

5 Moses called all the people of Israel together and said: Listen, Israel, to the commands and laws I give you today. Learn them and obey them carefully. ²The Lord our God made an agreement with us at Mount Sinai. ³He did not make this agreement with our ancestors. He made it with us. He made it with all of us who are alive here today. ⁴The Lord spoke to you face to face. He spoke from the fire on the mountain. ⁵(At that time I stood between you and the Lord. I told you what the Lord said. You were afraid of the fire. So you would not go up on the mountain.) The Lord said:

⁶"I am the Lord your God. I brought you out of the land of Egypt where you were slaves.

⁷"You must not have any other gods except me.

⁸"You must not make for yourselves any idols. Don't make something that looks like anything in the sky above or on the earth below or in the water below the land. ⁹You must not worship or serve any idol. This is because I, the Lord your God, am a jealous God. A person may sin against me and hate me. I will punish his children, even his grandchildren and great-grandchildren. ¹⁰But I will be very kind to thousands who love me and obey my commands.

¹¹"You must not use the name of the Lord your God thoughtlessly. The Lord will punish anyone who is guilty and misuses his name.

servants may rest as you do. ¹⁵Remember that you were slaves in Egypt. The Lord your God brought you out of Egypt by his great power and strength. So the Lord your God has commanded you to rest on the Sabbath day.

¹⁶"Honor your father and your mother. The Lord your God has commanded you to do this. Then you will live a long time. And things will go well for you in the land. The Lord your God is going to give you this land.

¹⁷"You must not murder anyone.

¹⁸"You must not be guilty of adultery.ᵈ

¹⁹"You must not steal.

²⁰"You must not tell lies about your neighbor in court.

²¹"You must not want to take your

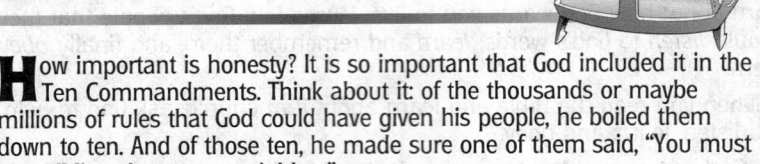

Honesty
DEUTERONOMY 5:20

How important is honesty? It is so important that God included it in the Ten Commandments. Think about it: of the thousands or maybe millions of rules that God could have given his people, he boiled them down to ten. And of those ten, he made sure one of them said, "You must not tell lies about your neighbor."

That's so simple, and yet sometimes so hard to do. What if you're mad at your teammate, or brother, or classmate? Isn't it OK to lie then? *No*, says God. Well what if the person lied about me first? *"If you want to be my child and please me,"* says the Lord, *"you must not tell lies."*

Honesty is important to God. It should be to us, too.

To learn more about honesty, zoom to page 605.

¹²"Keep the Sabbathᵈ as a holy day. The Lord your God has commanded you to do this. ¹³You may work and get everything done during six days each week. ¹⁴But the seventh day is a day of rest to honor the Lord your God. On that day no one may do any work: not you, your son or daughter, or your men or women slaves. Neither your ox, your donkey nor any of your animals may work. The foreigners living in your cities may not work. That way your

neighbor's wife. You must not want to take your neighbor's house or land. You must not want to take his men or women slaves. You must not want to take his ox or his donkey. You must not want to take anything that belongs to your neighbor."

²²The Lord gave these commands to all of you on the mountain. He spoke them in a loud voice out of the fire. He spoke from the cloud and the deep darkness. He did not say anything else.

Whit's Wisdom: The Ten Commandments • Deuteronomy 5

Odyssey has its share of thunderstorms in the summer. During one storm, some of the kids were together at my ice cream shop—a place I call Whit's End. Suddenly, there was a flash and explosion as a lightning bolt struck a tree nearby. Everybody jumped.

"Maybe God just decided to give us ten more commandments," said Carter as we all settled back down.

"What's wrong with the first ten?" I asked.

"Well, Mr. Whittaker, it doesn't seem like people are listening to them anymore," answered Carter. The other kids nodded that they thought Carter was right.

"Kids," I asked, "if your Mom or Dad warned you that you would get burned if you touched a hot pot, but you decided not to listen, what would happen?"

"I got burned!" said Dylan, making everybody laugh.

"I'm sorry you got burned, Dylan," I said, "but did that happen because your parents needed to change their warning or because you needed to listen and obey?"

The kids understood, so I went on to ask them if they even knew what the ten commandments were. Most of them could think of one or two. How many can you remember? I told them that God had included his commandments twice in the Bible: Exodus 20:1-20 and Deuteronomy 5:1-22.

I got out some Bibles, and we looked up the list in Deuteronomy, where you are right now. We also took some paper and pencils, and each of us made our own list of the ten commandments. As we listed them, we talked about what each one meant. By the time the storm was over, we were well on our way to learning some of the most important rules for living that God has put in the Bible.

As the kids were getting ready to go home I said, "Remember, knowing how God wants us to live is the first step. That's the listening part. We still have to obey."

Jessie looked at her big brother Dylan, then said, "Yeah, we don't want to get burned, do we!"

Related passages: Psalm 1, Mark 12:28-34.

Teacher/Parent Hints: Spend time memorizing the ten commandments. Be prepared for a variety of questions. Whenever possible, encourage the children to answer each other's questions.

Then he wrote them on two stone tablets. And he gave them to me.

²³You heard the voice from the darkness. The mountain was blazing with fire. Then all your older leaders and leaders of your tribes*ᵈ* came to me. ²⁴And you said, "The Lord our God has shown us his glory and majesty. We have heard his voice from the fire. Today we have seen that a person can live even if God speaks to him. ²⁵But now, we will die! This great

fire will burn us up. And we will die if we hear the Lord our God speak anymore. ²⁶No human being has ever heard the living God speaking from a fire and still lived. But we have. ²⁷Moses, you go near and listen to everything the Lord our God says. Then you tell us what the Lord our God tells you. We will listen and obey."

²⁸The Lord heard what you said to me. And he said to me, "I have heard what the people said to you. Everything they said was good. ²⁹I wish their hearts would always respect me. I wish they would always obey my commands. Then things would go well for them and their children forever!

The Command to Love God

6 These are the commands, rules and laws of the Lord your God. He told me to teach them to you. Obey them in the land you are crossing the Jordan River to own. ²You, your children and grandchildren must respect the Lord your God. You must do this as long as you live. Obey all his rules and commands I give you. Then you will live a long time. ³Listen, Israel, and carefully obey these laws. Then all will go well for you. You will become a great nation in a land where much

Friendships
DEUTERONOMY 6:5

Don't . . . Don't . . . Don't . . . . Do you ever feel that being a Christian is only about obeying a bunch of rules? Even though God does want us to obey the Bible, he is not sitting around waiting for us to goof up so he can punish us. He wants to be our friend.

The Bible is filled with a lot of rules that God wants us to follow, but Jesus told us that there is just one rule that is the most important: "Love the Lord . . . with all of your heart, all your soul, and all your strength."

When you think it is impossible to remember and obey all the rules your parents and teachers tell you, just remember one simple thing: God loves you. He wants you to obey him because you love him, too!

To find out what to do when it is hard to be a friend,
zoom to page 352.

³⁰"Go and tell the people to return to their tents. ³¹But you stay here with me. I will give you all the commands, rules and laws. Teach the people to obey them in the land I am giving them to own."

³²So be careful. Do what the Lord your God has commanded you. You must follow the commands exactly. ³³Live the way the Lord your God has commanded you. Then you will live and be successful. You will live a long time in the land you will own.

food grows. The Lord, the God of your ancestors, has promised it to you.

⁴Listen, people of Israel! The Lord is our God. He is the only Lord. ⁵Love the Lord your God with all your heart, soul and strength. ⁶Always remember these commands I give you today. ⁷Teach them to your children. Talk about them when you sit at home and walk along the road. Talk about them when you lie down and when you get up. ⁸Write them down and tie them to your hands as a sign. Tie them on your

forehead to remind you. ⁹Write them on your doors and gates.

¹⁰The Lord your God will bring you into the land. He promised it to your ancestors, to Abraham, Isaac and Jacob. He will give it to you. The land has large, growing cities you did not build. ¹¹The houses there are full of good things that you did not buy. They have wells you did not dig. There are vineyards and olive trees you did not

"**G**od wants his word to be *in* our minds and *on* our minds! Look at God's directions in Deuteronomy 6:1-25."

plant. You will eat as much as you want. ¹²But be careful! Do not forget the Lord. He brought you out of the land of Egypt where you were slaves.

¹³Respect the Lord your God. Serve only him. Make your promises in his name. ¹⁴Do not worship other gods as the people around you do. ¹⁵The Lord your God is a jealous God. He is present with you. If you worship other gods, he will become angry with you. And he will destroy you from the earth. ¹⁶Do not test the Lord your God as you did at Massah. ¹⁷Be sure to obey the commands of the Lord your God. Obey the rules and laws he has given you. ¹⁸Do what the Lord says is good and right. Then things will go well for you. Then you may go in and take the good land the Lord promised to your ancestors. ¹⁹He will force all your enemies out as you go in. This is what the Lord has said.

²⁰In the future your son will ask you, "What do the laws, commands and rules the Lord our God gave us mean?" ²¹Tell him, "We were slaves to the king of Egypt. But the Lord brought us out of Egypt by his great power. ²²The Lord showed us great and terrible signs and miracles.ᵈ He did them to

Egypt, the king and his whole family. ²³The Lord brought us out of Egypt. He led us here. And he will give us the land he promised our ancestors. ²⁴The Lord ordered us to obey all these commands. And we must respect the Lord our God. Then we will always do well and stay alive as we are today. ²⁵The right thing for us to do is this: Obey all these rules in the presence of the Lord our God. He has commanded it."

God's People

7 The Lord your God will bring you into the land. You are entering that land to own it. As you go in, he will force out these nations: the Hittites, Girgashites, Amorites, Canaanites, Perizzites, Hivites and Jebusites. These seven nations are stronger than you. ²The Lord your God will hand these nations over to you. You will defeat them. You must destroy them completely. Do not make a peace treaty with them. Do not show them any mercy. ³Do not marry any of them. Don't let your daughters marry their sons. And don't let your sons marry their daughters. ⁴Those people will turn your children away from me. Your children will begin serving other gods. The Lord will be very angry with you. And he will quickly destroy you. ⁵This is what you must do to those people: Tear down their altars. Smash their holy stone pillars. Cut down their Asherahᵈ idols and burn their idols in the fire. ⁶You are holy people. You belong to the Lord your God. He has chosen you from all the people on earth. You are his very own.

⁷The Lord did not care for you and choose you because there were many of you. You are the smallest nation of all. ⁸But the Lord chose you because he loved you. And he kept his promise to your ancestors. So he brought you out of Egypt by his great power. He brought you back from the land of slavery. He bought you back from the power of the king of Egypt. ⁹So know that the Lord your God is God. He is

the faithful God. He will keep his agreement of love for a thousand lifetimes. He does this for people who love him and obey his commands. [10]But he will pay back those people who hate him. He will destroy them. And he will not be slow to pay back those who hate him. [11]So be careful to obey the commands, rules and laws I give you today.

[12]Pay attention to these laws. Obey them carefully. Then the Lord your God will keep his agreement and show his love to you. He promised your ancestors he would. [13]He will love and bless you. He will make the number of your people grow. He will bless you with children. He will bless your fields with good crops. He will give you grain, new wine and oil. He will bless your cows with calves and your sheep with lambs. This is the way it will be in the land he promised your ancestors he would give you. [14]You will be blessed more than any other people. Every husband and wife will have children. All your cattle will have calves. [15]The Lord will take away all disease from you. You will not have the terrible diseases that were in Egypt. But he will give them to your enemies. [16]You must destroy all the people the Lord your God hands over to you. Do not feel sorry for them. Do not worship their gods. They will trap you.

[17]You might say to yourselves, "These nations are stronger than we are. We can't force them out." [18]But don't be afraid of them. Remember what the Lord your God did to all of Egypt and its king. [19]You saw for yourselves the troubles, signs and miracles[d] he did. You saw how the Lord's great power and strength brought you out of Egypt. The Lord your God will do the same thing to all the nations you now fear. [20]The Lord your God will also send hornets to attack them. Even those who are alive and hiding from you will die. [21]Don't be afraid of them. The Lord your God is with you. He is a great God and people are afraid of him. [22]The Lord your God will force those nations out of the land. They will leave little by little ahead of you. Don't destroy them all at once. Otherwise, the wild animals will grow too many in number. [23]But the Lord your God will hand those nations over to you. He will confuse them until they are destroyed. [24]The Lord will help you defeat their kings. The world will forget who they were. No one will be able to stop you. You will destroy them all. [25]Burn up their idols in the fire. Do not wish for the silver and gold on them. Don't take it for yourselves, or you will be trapped by it. The Lord your God hates it. [26]Do not bring one of those hated things into your house. If you do, you will be completely destroyed along with it. Hate and reject those things. They must be completely destroyed.

Remember the Lord

8 Carefully obey every command I give you today. Then you will live and grow in number. And you will enter and own the land the Lord promised your ancestors. [2]Remember how the Lord your God has led you in the desert for these 40 years. He took away your pride. He tested you. He wanted to know what was in your heart. He wanted to know if you would obey his commands. [3]He took away your pride. He let you get hungry. Then he fed you with manna.[d] Manna was something neither you nor your ancestors had ever seen. This was to teach you that a person does not live only by eating bread. But a person lives by everything the Lord says. [4]During these 40 years, your clothes did not wear out. And your feet did not swell. [5]Know in your heart that the Lord your God corrects you. He corrects you as a father does his son.

[6]Obey the commands of the Lord your God. Live as he has commanded you and respect him. [7]The Lord your God is bringing you into a good land. The land has rivers and pools of water. Springs flow in the valleys and

hills. [8]The land has wheat and barley, vines, fig trees, pomegranates,[d] olive oil and honey. [9]It is a land where you will have plenty of food. You will have everything you need there. The rocks are iron. You can dig copper out of the hills.

[10]You will have all you want to eat. Then praise the Lord your God. He has given you a good land. [11]Be careful not to forget the Lord your God. Do not fail to obey his commands, laws and rules. I am giving them to you today. [12]You will eat all you want. You will build nice houses and live in them. [13]Your herds of cattle and flocks of sheep will grow large. Your silver and gold will grow. You will have more of everything. [14]Then your heart will become proud. You will forget the Lord your God. He brought you out of the land of Egypt, where you were slaves. [15]He led you through the large and terrible desert. It was dry and had no water. It had poisonous snakes and stinging insects. He gave you water from a solid rock. [16]He gave you manna to eat in the desert. Manna was something your ancestors had never seen. He did this to take away your pride and to test you. He did it so things would go well for you in the end. [17]You might say to yourself, "I am rich because of my own strength and power." [18]But remember the Lord your God! It is he who gives you the power to become rich. He keeps the agreement he promised to your ancestors. So it is today.

[19]Never forget the Lord your God. Do not follow other gods. Do not worship them. Do not bow down to them. If you do, I warn you today that you will be destroyed. [20]The Lord destroyed the other nations for you. And you can be destroyed the same way if you do not obey the Lord your God.

The Lord Will Be with Israel

9 Listen, Israel. You will soon cross the Jordan River. You will go in to force out nations that are bigger and stronger than you. They have large cities with walls up to the sky. [2]The people there are Anakites.[d] They are strong and tall. You know about them. You have heard it said: "No one can stop the Anakites." [3]But today remember that the Lord your God goes in before you. He will destroy them like a fire that burns things up. He will defeat them ahead of you. And you will force them out. You will destroy them quickly. It will happen just as the Lord has said.

[4]The Lord your God will force those nations out ahead of you. After that, don't say to yourself, "The Lord brought me here. I own this land because I am so good." No! It is because these nations are evil. That is why the Lord will force them out ahead of you. [5]You are going in to own the land. But it is not because you are good and honest. It is because these nations are evil. That is why the Lord your God will force them out ahead of you. The Lord will keep his promise to your ancestors, to Abraham, Isaac and Jacob. [6]The Lord your God is giving you this good land to own. But know this: It is not because you are good. You are a stubborn people.

Remember the Lord's Anger

[7]Remember this. Do not forget it. You made the Lord your God angry in the desert. You would not obey the Lord from the day you left Egypt until you arrived here. [8]At Mount Sinai you made the Lord angry. He was angry enough to destroy you. [9]I went up on the mountain to receive the stone tablets. The tablets were the agreement the Lord had made with you. I stayed on the mountain for 40 days and 40 nights. I did not eat bread or drink water. [10]The Lord gave me two stone tablets. God had written on them with his own finger. On them were all the commands of the Lord. He gave them to you on the mountain out of the fire. This was on the day you were gathered there.

¹¹Then the 40 days and 40 nights were over. And the Lord gave me the two stone tablets. Those tablets had the agreement on them. ¹²Then the Lord told me, "Get up. Go down quickly from here. The people you brought out from Egypt are ruining themselves. They have quickly turned away from what I commanded. They have made an idol for themselves."

¹³The Lord said to me, "I have watched these people. They are very stubborn! ¹⁴Get away. I will destroy them. I will make the whole world forget who they are. Then I will make another nation from you. It will be bigger and stronger than they are."

¹⁵So I turned and came down the mountain. The mountain was burning with fire. And the two stone tablets with the agreement were in my hands. ¹⁶When I looked, I saw you had sinned against the Lord your God. You had made an idol in the shape of a calf. You had quickly turned away from what the Lord had told you to do. ¹⁷So I took the two stone tablets and threw them down. I broke them into pieces right in front of you.

¹⁸Then I again bowed facedown on the ground before the Lord. I did this for 40 days and 40 nights. I did not eat bread or drink water. You had sinned by doing what the Lord said was evil. You made him angry. ¹⁹I was afraid of the Lord's anger and rage. He was angry enough with you to destroy you. But the Lord listened to me again. ²⁰And the Lord was angry enough with Aaron to destroy him. But then I prayed for Aaron, too. ²¹I took that sinful calf idol you had made. And I burned it in the fire. I crushed it into a powder like dust. And I threw the dust into a stream that flowed down the mountain.

²²You also made the Lord angry at Taberah, Massah and Kibroth Hattaavah.

²³Then the Lord sent you away from Kadesh Barnea. He said, "Go up and take the land I have given you." But you would not obey the command of the Lord your God. You did not trust him or obey him. ²⁴You have refused to obey the Lord as long as I have known you.

²⁵The Lord had said he would destroy you. So I threw myself down in front of him for those 40 days and 40 nights. ²⁶I prayed to the Lord. I said, "Lord God, do not destroy your people. They are your own people. You freed them and brought them out of Egypt by your great power and strength. ²⁷Remember your servants Abraham, Isaac and Jacob. Don't look at how stubborn these people are. Don't look at their sin and evil. ²⁸Otherwise, Egypt will say, 'The Lord was not able to take his people into the land he promised them. He hated them. So he took them into the desert to kill them.' ²⁹But they are your people, Lord. They are your own people. You brought them out of Egypt with your great power and strength."

New Stone Tablets

10 At that time the Lord said to me, "Cut two stone tablets like the first ones. Then come up to me on the mountain. Also make a wooden box. ²I will write on the tablets the same words that were on the first tablets, which you broke. Put the new tablets in the box."

³So I made the box out of acacia wood. And I cut out two stone tablets like the first ones. Then I went up on the mountain. I had the two tablets in my hands. ⁴The Lord wrote the same things on these tablets he had written before. He wrote the Ten Commandments. He had told them to you on the mountain from the fire. This was on the day you were gathered there. And the Lord gave them to me. ⁵Then I turned and came down the mountain. I put the tablets in the box I had made. That is what the Lord had commanded. The tablets are still there in the box.

⁶(The people of Israel went from the wells of the Jaakanites to Moserah. There Aaron died and was buried. Aaron's son Eleazar became priest in Aaron's place. ⁷From Moserah they

went to Gudgodah. From Gudgodah they went to Jotbathah, a place with streams of water. [8]At that time the Lord chose the tribe[d] of Levi. They were to carry the Box[d] of the Agreement with the Lord. They were to serve the Lord. They were to bless the people in the Lord's name. They still do this today. [9]That is why the Levites did not receive any land to own. Instead, they received the Lord himself as their gift. This is what the Lord your God told them.)

[10]I stayed on the mountain 40 days and 40 nights just like the first time. And the Lord listened to me this time also. He did not want to destroy you. [11]The Lord said to me, "Go. Lead the people. They will go in and take the land I promised their ancestors."

What the Lord Wants You To Do

[12]Now, Israel, this is what the Lord wants you to do. Respect the Lord your God. Do what he has told you to do. Love him. Serve the Lord your God with your whole being. [13]And obey the Lord's commands and laws. I am giving them to you today for your own good.

[14]The Lord owns the world and everything in it. The heavens, even the highest heavens, are his. [15]But the Lord cared for and loved your ancestors. And he chose you, their descendants.[d] He chose you over all the other nations. And it is this way today. [16]Give yourselves to serving the Lord. Do not be stubborn any longer. [17]The Lord your God is God of all gods. He is the Lord of all lords. He is the great God. He is strong and wonderful. He does not take sides. And he will not be talked into doing evil. [18]He helps orphans and widows. He loves foreigners. He gives them food and clothes. [19]You also must love foreigners, because you were foreigners in Egypt. [20]Respect the Lord your God and serve him. Be loyal to him. Make your promises in his name. [21]You should praise him. He is your God. He has done great and wonderful things for you. You have seen them with your own eyes. [22]There

were only 70 of your ancestors when they went down to Egypt. Now the Lord your God has made you as many as the stars in the sky.

Great Things Israel Saw

11 Love the Lord your God. Obey his orders, rules, laws and commands. [2]Remember today it was not your children who saw and felt the correction of the Lord your God. They did not see his majesty, his power and his strength. [3]They did not see his signs and the things he did in Egypt to the king and his whole country. [4]They did not see what he did to the Egyptian army, its horses and chariots. He drowned them in the Red Sea[d] when they were chasing you. The Lord ruined them forever. [5]They did not see what he did for you in the desert until you arrived here. [6]They did not see what he did to Dathan and Abiram, the sons of Eliab the Reubenite. The ground opened up and swallowed them, their families and their tents. And it swallowed up everyone who stood with them in Israel. [7]It was you who saw all these great things the Lord has done.

[8]So obey all the commands I am giving you today. Then you will be strong. Then you can go in and take the land you are going to own. [9]Then you will live a long time in that land. The Lord promised to give it to your ancestors and their descendants.[d] It is a land where much food grows. [10]The land you are going to take is not like Egypt, where you were. There you had to plant your seed. Then you had to water it, like a vegetable garden, by using your feet. [11]But you will soon cross the Jordan River and take the land. It is a land of hills and valleys. It drinks rain from heaven. [12]It is a land the Lord your God loves. His eyes are on it continually. He watches it from the beginning of the year to the end.

[13]Carefully obey the commands I am giving you today. Love the Lord your God. Serve him with your whole being. [14]Then he will send rain on your land

at the right time, in the fall and spring. You will be able to gather your grain, new wine and oil. [15]He will put grass in the fields for your cattle. You will have plenty to eat.

[16]Be careful. Don't be fooled. Don't turn away and serve other gods. Don't worship them. [17]If you do, the Lord will become angry with you. He will shut the heavens so it will not rain. Then the land will not grow crops. And you will soon die in the good land the Lord is giving you. [18]Remember my words in your hearts and souls. Write them down and tie them to your hands as a sign. Tie them on your foreheads to remind you. [19]Teach them well to your children. Talk about them when you sit at home and walk along the road. Talk about them when you lie down and when you get up. [20]Write them on your doors and gates. [21]Then both you and your children will live a long time in the land. This is the land the Lord promised your ancestors. You will live there for as long as the skies are above the earth.

[22]Be careful to obey every command I am giving you to follow. Love the Lord your God. Do what he has told you to do. And be loyal to him. [23]Then the Lord will force all those nations out of the land ahead of you. And you will take the land from nations that are bigger and stronger than you. [24]Everywhere you step will be yours. Your land will go from the desert to Lebanon. And it will go from the Euphrates River to the Mediterranean Sea. [25]No one will be able to stop you. The Lord your God will do what he promised. He will make the people afraid everywhere you go.

[26]See, today I am letting you choose a blessing or a curse. [27]You will be blessed if you obey the commands of the Lord your God. I am giving them to you today. [28]But you will be cursed if you disobey the commands of the Lord your God. So do not disobey the commands I am giving you today. Do not worship other gods you do not know. [29]The Lord your God will bring you into the land you will own. Then you are to announce the blessings from Mount Gerizim. Announce the curses from Mount Ebal. [30]These mountains are on the other side of the Jordan River. They are west, toward the sunset. They are near the great trees of Moreh. They are in the land of the Canaanites who live in the Jordan Valley opposite Gilgal. [31]You will soon cross the Jordan River. You will enter and take the land the Lord your God is giving you. You will take it over and live there. [32]Then be careful to obey all the commands and laws I am giving you today.

The Place for Worship

12 These are the commands and laws you must carefully obey in the land the Lord your God is giving you. Obey them as long as you live in the land. [2]You will inherit the lands of these nations. You must completely destroy all the places where they serve their gods. These places are on high mountains and hills and under every green tree. [3]Tear down their altars. Smash their holy stone pillars. Burn their Asherah[d] idols. Cut down their idols. Destroy their names from those places.

[4]Don't worship the Lord your God that way. [5]But look for the place the Lord your God will choose. He will choose a place among your tribes[d] where he is to be worshiped. Go there. [6]Bring to that place your burnt offerings and sacrifices. Bring a tenth of what you gain and your special gifts. Bring what you have promised and the special gifts you want to give the Lord. And bring the first animals born to your herds and flocks.

[7]There you will be together with the Lord your God. There you and your families will eat. And you will enjoy all the good things for which you have worked. The Lord your God has blessed you.

[8]Do not worship the way we have

been doing today. Each person does what he thinks is right. ⁹You have not yet come to a resting place. The Lord your God will give you your own land. ¹⁰But you will soon cross the Jordan River. And you will live in the land the Lord your God is giving you to own. And he will give you rest from all your enemies. You will live in safety. ¹¹Then the Lord your God will choose a place where he is to be worshiped. To that place you must bring everything I tell you: your burnt offerings and sacrifices, your offerings of a tenth of what you gain, your special gifts and all your best things you promised to the Lord. ¹²There rejoice before the Lord your God. Everyone should rejoice: you, your sons and daughters, your male and female servants, and the Levites from your towns, who have no land of their own. ¹³Be careful. Don't sacrifice your burnt offerings just anywhere you please. ¹⁴Offer them only in the place the Lord will choose. He will choose a place in one of your tribes. And there you must do everything I am commanding you.

¹⁵But you may kill your animals in any of your towns. And you may eat as much of the meat as you want. Eat it as if it were a deer or a gazelle. This is the blessing the Lord your God is giving you. Anyone, clean*ᵈ* or unclean, may eat this meat. ¹⁶But do not eat the blood. Pour it out on the ground like water. ¹⁷Do not eat in your own towns what belongs to the Lord: one-tenth of your grain, new wine or oil; the first animals born to your herds or flocks; whatever you have promised to give; the special gifts you want to give to the Lord, or any other gifts. ¹⁸Eat these things when you are together with the Lord. Eat them in the place the Lord your God chooses to be worshiped. Everyone must do this: you, your sons and daughters, your male and female servants, and the Levites from your towns. Rejoice in the Lord's presence about the things you have worked for. ¹⁹Be careful not to forget the Levites as long as you live in the land.

²⁰The Lord your God will enlarge your country as he has promised. And you will want some meat. You will say, "I want some meat." Eat as much meat as you want. ²¹The Lord your God will choose a place where he is to be worshiped. But it may be too far away from you. If it is, you may kill animals from your herds and flocks. The Lord has given them to you. I have commanded that you may do this. You may eat as much of them as you want in your own towns. ²²Eat them as you would eat gazelle or deer meat. Both clean and unclean people may eat this meat. ²³But be sure you don't eat the blood. The life is in the blood. Don't eat the life with the meat. ²⁴Don't eat the blood. Pour it out on the ground like water. ²⁵Don't eat it. Then things will go well for you and your children. You will be doing what the Lord says is right.

²⁶Take your holy things and the things you have promised to give. And go to the place the Lord will choose. ²⁷Present your burnt offerings on the altar of the Lord your God. Offer both the meat and the blood. The blood of your sacrifices should be poured beside the altar. But you may eat the meat. ²⁸Be careful to obey all the rules I am giving you. Then things will always go well for you and your children. You will be doing what the Lord your God says is good and right.

²⁹You will enter the land and take it away from the nations there. The Lord your God will destroy those nations ahead of you. You will force them out and live in their land. ³⁰They will be destroyed for you. Be careful not to be trapped by asking about their gods. Don't say, "How do these nations worship? I will do the same." ³¹Don't worship the Lord your God that way. The Lord hates the evil ways they worship their gods. They even burn their sons and daughters as sacrifices to their gods! ³²Be sure to do everything I have commanded you. Do not add anything

to it. And do not take anything away from it.

False Prophets

13 A prophet[d] or someone who tells the future with dreams might come to you. He might say he will show you a miracle[d] or a sign. [2]The miracle or sign might even happen. Then he might say, "Let's serve other gods." (These are gods you have not known.) "And let's worship them." [3]But you must not listen to that prophet or dreamer. The Lord your God is testing you. He is finding out if you love him with your whole being. [4]Serve only the Lord your God. Respect him. Keep his commands and obey him. Serve him and be loyal to him. [5]That prophet or dreamer must be killed. He said you should turn against the Lord your God. The Lord brought you out of Egypt. He saved you from the land where you were slaves. That prophet tried to turn you from doing what the Lord your God commanded you to do. You must get rid of the evil among you.

[6]Some relative might try to lead you to serve other gods. It might be your brother, your son or daughter or the wife you love. Or it might be a close friend. He might say, "Let's go and worship other gods." (These are gods that neither you nor your ancestors have known. [7]They are gods of the people who live around you. Some are nearby, and some are far away. They are from one end of the land to the other.) [8]Do not give in to him. Do not listen. Do not feel sorry for him. Do not let him go free or protect him. [9]You must put him to death. You must be the first one to start to kill him. Then everyone else must join in. [10]You must throw stones at him until he dies. He tried to turn you away from the Lord your God. The Lord brought you out of the land of Egypt, where you were slaves. [11]Then everyone in Israel will hear about this. And they will be afraid. No one among you will ever do such an evil thing again.

Cities to Destroy

[12]The Lord your God is giving you cities in which to live. You might hear something about one of them. Someone might say [13]that evil men have moved in among you. And they might lead the people of that city away from God. They might say, "Let's go and worship other gods." (These are gods you have not known.) [14]Then you must ask about it. Look into the matter and check carefully. It might be true. It may be proved that a terrible thing has happened among you. [15]If it has, then you must kill with a sword everyone who lives in that city. Destroy the city completely. Kill everyone in it, as well as the animals, with a sword. [16]Gather up everything those people owned. Put it in the middle of the city square. Then completely burn the city and everything they owned. It will be a burnt offering to the Lord your God. That city should never be rebuilt. Let it be ruined forever. [17]Don't keep any of the things found in that city for yourselves. Then the Lord will not be angry anymore. He will give you mercy. He will feel sorry for you. And he will make your nation grow larger. He promised this to your ancestors. [18]You will have obeyed the Lord your God. You will be keeping all his commands. I am giving them to you today. And you will be doing what the Lord says is right.

God's Special People

14 You are the children of the Lord your God. When someone dies, do not cut yourselves or shave your heads to show your sadness. [2]You are holy people. You belong to the Lord your God. He has chosen you from all the people on earth to be his very own.

[3]Do not eat anything the Lord hates. [4]These are the animals you may eat: ox, sheep, goats, [5]deer, gazelle, roe deer, wild goats, ibex, antelope and mountain sheep. [6]You may eat any animal that has a split hoof and chews the cud.[d] [7]But you may not eat camels, rabbits or rock badgers. These animals

chew the cud, but their feet are not divided. So they are unclean[d] for you. [8]Pigs are also unclean for you. They have split hoofs, but they do not chew the cud. Do not eat their meat or touch their dead bodies.

[9]There are many things that live in the water. You may eat anything that has fins and scales. [10]But do not eat anything that does not have fins and scales. It is unclean for you.

[11]You may eat any clean bird. [12]But do not eat these birds: eagles, vultures, black vultures, [13]red kites, falcons, any kind of kite, [14]any kind of raven, [15]horned owls, screech owls, seagulls, any kind of hawk, [16]little owls, great owls, white owls, [17]desert owls, ospreys, cormorants, [18]storks, any kind of heron, the hoopoes or bats.

[19]All insects with wings are unclean for you. Do not eat them. [20]Other things with wings are clean. You may eat them.

[21]Do not eat anything you find that is already dead. You may give it to a foreigner living in your town. He may eat it. Or you may sell it to a foreigner. But you are holy people. You belong to the Lord your God.

Do not cook a baby goat in its mother's milk.

Giving One-Tenth

[22]Be sure to save one-tenth of all your crops each year. [23]Take it to the place the Lord your God will choose where he is to be worshiped. There you will be together with the Lord. There eat the tenth of your grain, new wine and oil. And eat the animals born first to your herds and flocks. Then you will learn to respect the Lord your God always. [24]But the place the Lord will choose to be worshiped might be too far away. And he may have blessed you so much you cannot carry a tenth. [25]If so, exchange your one-tenth for silver. Then take the silver with you to the place the Lord your God shall choose. [26]Use the silver to buy anything you wish. You may buy cattle, sheep, wine, beer or anything you wish. Then you and your family will eat and celebrate there before the Lord your God. [27]Do not forget the Levites in your town. They have no land of their own among you.

[28]At the end of every third year, everyone should bring one-tenth of that year's crop. Store it in your towns. [29]This is for the Levites so they may eat and be full. (They have no land of their own among you.) It is also for strangers, orphans and widows who live in your towns. All of them may eat and be full. Then the Lord your God will bless you and all the work you do.

The Special Seventh Year

15 At the end of every seven years, you must forget about collecting what people owe you. [2]This is how you must do it: Everyone who has loaned money must forget the loan. He must not make his neighbor or brother pay it back. This is the Lord's time for canceling what people owe. [3]You may make a foreigner pay what he owes you. But you must not collect what your brother owes you. [4]But there should be no poor people among you. The Lord your God will richly bless you in the land he is giving you to own. [5]He will bless you if you obey him completely. But you must be careful to obey all the commands I am giving you today. [6]The Lord your God will bless you as he promised. You will lend to other nations. But you will not need to borrow from them. You will rule over many nations. But none will rule over you.

[7]There might be a poor man among you. He might be in one of the towns of the land the Lord your God is giving you. Do not be selfish or greedy toward your poor brother. [8]But give freely to him. Freely lend him whatever he needs. [9]Beware of evil thoughts. Don't think, "The seventh year is near. It's the year to forget what people owe." You might be mean to your needy brother. You might not give him anything. Then he will complain to the Lord

about you. And the Lord will find you guilty of sin. [10]Give freely to the poor person. Do not wish that you didn't have to give. The Lord your God will bless your work and everything you touch. [11]There will always be poor people in the land. So I command you to give freely to your brothers. Give freely to the poor and needy in your land.

Letting Slaves Go Free

[12]One of your own people might sell himself to you as a slave. It may be a Hebrew man or woman. That person will serve you for six years. The seventh year you must let him go free. [13]And when you let him go, don't send him away without anything. [14]Give him some of your sheep, your grain and your wine. Give to him as the Lord has given to you. [15]Remember that you were slaves in Egypt. And the Lord your God saved you. That is why I am commanding this to you today.

[16]But your slave might say to you, "I don't want to leave you." He might love you and your family. He might have a good life with you. [17]If he does this, stick an awl[n] through his ear into the door. He will be your slave for life. Also do this to a woman slave.

[18]Do not think of it as a hard thing when you let your slave go free. After all, he served you six years. You paid him only half what a hired person would cost. The Lord your God will bless you in everything you do.

Rules About Firstborn Animals

[19]Save all the first male animals born to your herds and flocks. They are for the Lord your God. Do not work the first calf born to your oxen. And do not cut off the wool from the first lamb born to your sheep. [20]Each year you and your family are to eat these animals. Eat them in the presence of the Lord your God. Eat them in the place he will choose to be worshiped. [21]An animal might have something wrong with it. It might be crippled or blind. It

might have some other thing wrong with it. Do not sacrifice it to the Lord your God. [22]But you may eat that animal in your own town. Both clean[d] and unclean people may eat it. It would be like eating a gazelle or a deer. [23]But don't eat its blood. Pour it out on the ground like water.

The Passover

16 Celebrate the Passover[d] of the Lord your God during the month of Abib.[d] It was during Abib that he brought you out of Egypt at night. [2]Offer a sacrifice for the Passover to the Lord your God. It should be an animal from your flock or herd. Offer it at the place the Lord will choose to be worshiped. [3]Do not eat it with bread made with yeast. But for seven days eat bread made without yeast. This is the bread of suffering because you left Egypt in a hurry. So all your life you will remember the time you left Egypt. [4]There must be no yeast anywhere in your land for seven days. Offer the sacrifice on the evening of the first day. Eat all the meat before morning. Do not leave it overnight.

[5]Do not offer the Passover sacrifice in just any town the Lord your God gives you. [6]Offer it in the place he will choose to be worshiped. Offer it in the evening as the sun goes down. That is when you left Egypt. [7]Roast the meat. Then eat it at the place the Lord your God will choose. The next morning go back to your tents. [8]Eat bread made without yeast for six days. On the seventh day have a special meeting for the Lord your God. Do not work that day.

Feast of Weeks

[9]Count seven weeks from the time you begin to harvest the grain. [10]Then celebrate the Feast[d] of Weeks for the Lord your God. Bring him an offering as a special gift to him. Give to him just as he has blessed you. [11]Rejoice before the Lord your God. Rejoice at the place he will choose to be worshiped.

---

[n]**awl**   A tool like a big needle with a handle at one end.

Everybody should rejoice: you, your sons and daughters, your male and female servants, the Levites in your town, the strangers, orphans and widows living among you. [12]Remember that you were slaves in Egypt. And carefully obey all these laws.

Feast of Shelters

[13]Celebrate the Feast[d] of Shelters for seven days. Do it after you have gathered your harvest from the threshing[d] floor and winepress.[d] [14]Everybody should rejoice at your Feast: you, your sons and daughters, your male and female servants, the Levites and strangers who live in your towns, orphans and widows in your towns. [15]Celebrate the Feast to the Lord your God for seven days. Celebrate it at the place he will choose. The Lord your God will bless all your harvest. He will bless all the work you do. And you will be completely happy.

[16]All your men must come before the Lord three times a year. They must come to the place he will choose. They must come at these times: the Feast[d] of Unleavened Bread, the Feast[d] of Weeks and the Feast of Shelters. No man should come before the Lord without a gift. [17]Each of you must bring a gift. It should show how much the Lord your God has blessed you.

Judges for the People

[18]Appoint judges and officers for your tribes.[d] Appoint them in every town the Lord your God is giving you. And they must judge the people fairly. [19]Do not judge unfairly or take sides. Do not let people pay you to make wrong decisions. That kind of payment makes wise people seem blind. And it changes the words of good people. [20]Always do what is right. Then you will live and own the land the Lord your God is giving you.

God Hates Idols

[21]Do not set up a wooden Asherah[d] idol next to the altar you build for the Lord your God. [22]And do not set up holy stone pillars. The Lord your God hates them.

17 An ox or sheep might have something wrong with it. Do not offer it as a sacrifice to the Lord your God. He would hate that.

[2]A man or woman might be found doing something evil in one of the towns the Lord gave you. That man or woman is breaking his agreement. [3]That person may have served other gods. He may have bowed down to them, to the sun or moon or stars of the sky. I have commanded that should not be done. [4]If someone has told you about it, you must look into the matter. It might be true. A terrible thing may have happened in Israel. [5]If it is true, take the man or woman who has done the evil thing to the city gate. Throw stones at that person until he dies. [6]There must be two or three witnesses that he did it. Then the person should be put to death. But if there is only one witness, the person should not be put to death. [7]The witnesses must be the first to throw stones at the person. Then everyone else will follow. You must get rid of the evil among you.

Courts of Law

[8]Some cases that come before you may be too difficult to judge. It may be a case of murder, quarreling or attack. Take these cases to the place the Lord your God will choose. [9]Go to the priests who are Levites. And go to the judge who is on duty at that time. Ask them about the case, and they will decide. [10]You must follow the decision they give you. They will be at the place the Lord your God will choose. Be careful to do everything they tell you. [11]Follow the teachings they give you. Do whatever they decide. Do exactly what they tell you. [12]The person who does not show respect for the judge or priest must be put to death. They are serving the Lord your God. You must get rid of that evil from Israel. [13]Then everyone will hear about this. And they

will be afraid. They will not show disrespect anymore.

Choosing a King

¹⁴You will enter the land the Lord your God is giving you. You will take it as your own and live in it. Then you will say, "Let's appoint a king over us like the nations all around us." ¹⁵Be sure to appoint over you the king the Lord your God chooses. He must be one of your own people. Do not appoint a foreigner as your king. He is not a fellow Israelite. ¹⁶The king must not have too many horses for himself. He must not send people to Egypt to get more horses. The Lord has told you, "Don't return that way again." ¹⁷The king must not have many wives. If he does, his heart will be led away from God. He must not have too much silver and gold.

¹⁸When he becomes king, he should write a copy of the teachings on a scroll for himself. He should copy it from the priests and Levites. ¹⁹He should keep it with him all the time. He should read from it every day of his life. Then he will learn to respect the Lord his God. And he will obey all the teachings and commands. ²⁰He should not think he is better than his brothers. He must not stop obeying the law in any way. Then he and his descendants[d] will rule the kingdom for a long time.

Shares for Priests and Levites

18 The priests are from the tribe[d] of Levi. That tribe will not receive a share of the land with the Israelites. They will eat the offerings made to the Lord by fire. That is their share. ²They will not inherit any of the land like their brothers. They will inherit the Lord himself. This is what he promised them.

³When you offer a bull or sheep as a sacrifice, you must share with the priests. Give them the shoulder, the cheeks and the inner organs. ⁴Give them the first of your grain, new wine and oil. Give them the first wool you

cut from your sheep. ⁵The Lord your God has chosen the priests and their descendants[d] out of all your tribes. They are to stand and serve the Lord always.

⁶A Levite might move from one of your towns anywhere in Israel where he lives. He is sincere and comes to the place the Lord will choose. ⁷He may serve the Lord his God. He will be like his fellow Levites who serve there before the Lord. ⁸They all will have an equal share of the food. This is separate from what he has received from the sale of family possessions.

Do Not Follow Other Nations

⁹You will enter the land the Lord your God is giving you. But don't learn to do the terrible things the other nations do. ¹⁰Don't let anyone among you offer his son or daughter as a sacrifice in the fire. Don't let anyone use magic or witchcraft.[d] No one should try to explain the meaning of signs. ¹¹Don't let anyone try to control others with magic. Don't let them be mediums[d] or try to talk with the spirits of dead people. ¹²The Lord hates anyone who does these things. The other nations do these things. That is why the Lord your God will force them out of the land ahead of you. ¹³You must be innocent in the presence of the Lord your God.

The Lord's Special Prophet

¹⁴The nations you will force out listen to people who use magic and witchcraft.[d] But the Lord your God will not let you do those things. ¹⁵The Lord your God will give you a prophet[d] like me. He will be one of your own people. Listen to him. ¹⁶This is what you asked the Lord your God to do. You were gathered at Mount Sinai. You said, "Don't make us listen to the voice of the Lord our God again. Don't make us look at this terrible fire anymore. We will die."

¹⁷So the Lord said to me, "What they have said is good. ¹⁸So I will give them

a prophet like you. He will be one of their own people. I will tell him what to say. And he will tell them everything I command. [19]This prophet will speak for me. Anyone who does not listen when he speaks will answer to me. [20]But a prophet might say something I did not tell him to say. And he might say he is speaking for me. Or a prophet might speak in the name of other gods. That prophet must be killed."

[21]You might be thinking, "How can we know if a message is not from the Lord?" [22]What a prophet says in the name of the Lord might not happen. If it doesn't, it is not the Lord's message. That prophet was speaking his own ideas. Don't be afraid of him.

Cities of Safety

19 The Lord your God is giving you land that belongs to other nations. He will destroy those nations. You will force them out and live in their cities and houses. [2]Then choose three cities. They must be in the middle of the land the Lord your God is giving you to own. [3]Build roads to those cities. And divide the land the Lord is giving you into three parts. Then someone who kills another person may run to these cities.

[4]This is the rule for someone who kills another person. He may run to one of these cities to save his life. But he must have killed his neighbor without meaning to kill him. He did not hate his neighbor. [5]A man might go into the forest with his neighbor to cut wood. The man swings his ax to cut down a tree. But the ax head flies off the handle. It hits his neighbor and kills him. The man who killed him may run to one of these cities to save his life. [6]Otherwise, the dead man's relative who has the duty of punishing a murderer might be angry and chase him. And the relative might catch him if the city is far away. The relative might kill the man. But the man should not be killed because he did not mean

to kill his neighbor. [7]This is why I command you to choose these three cities.

[8-9]Carefully obey all these laws I'm giving you today. Love the Lord your God. Always do what he wants you to do. Then the Lord your God will enlarge your land as he promised your ancestors. He will give you the whole land he promised to them. After that, choose three more cities of safety. [10]This is so that innocent people will not be killed in your land. The Lord your God is giving it to you to own. By doing this you will not be guilty of murder.

[11]But a person might hate his neighbor. And he might hide and wait for him. He might attack and kill him and then run to one of these cities for safety. [12]The older leaders of his own city should send for him. They should bring him back from the city of safety. And they should hand him over to the relative who has the duty of punishing the murderer. [13]Give him no mercy. You must remove from Israel the guilt of murdering innocent people. Then things will go well for you.

[14]Do not move the stone that marks the border of your neighbor's land. People long ago set them in place. They mark what you inherit in the land the Lord your God is giving you to own.

Rules About Witnesses

[15]One witness is not enough to accuse a man of a crime or sin. A case must be proved by two or three witnesses.

[16]A witness might lie and accuse a person of a crime. [17]The two people who are arguing must stand before the Lord. They must stand before the priests and judges who are on duty. [18]The judges must check the matter carefully. The witness might be a liar. He might be lying about his fellow Israelite. [19]If so, he must be punished as he wanted his brother punished. You must get rid of the evil among you. [20]The rest of the people will hear about this and be afraid. No one among you will ever do such an evil thing again.

²¹Give him no mercy. A life must be paid for a life. It must be an eye for an eye, a tooth for a tooth, a hand for a hand, a foot for a foot.

Laws for War

20 When you go to war against your enemies, you might see horses and chariots. Their army might be bigger than yours. But don't be afraid of them. The Lord your God will be with you. He brought you out of Egypt. ²The priest must come and speak to the army before you go into battle. ³He should say, "Listen, Israel! Today you are going into battle against your enemies. Don't lose your courage or be afraid. Don't panic or be frightened. ⁴The Lord your God goes with you. He will fight for you against your enemies. And he will save you."

⁵The officers should say to the army, "Has anyone built a new house but not given it to God? He may go home. He might die in battle. Then someone else would get to give his house to God. ⁶Has anyone planted a vineyard and not begun to enjoy it? He may go home. He might die in battle. Then someone else would enjoy his vineyard. ⁷Is any man engaged to a woman and not yet married to her? He may go home. He might die in battle. Then someone else would marry her." ⁸Then the officers should also say, "Is anyone here afraid? Has anyone lost his courage? He may go home. Then he will not cause others to lose their courage, too." ⁹When the officers finish speaking to the army, they should appoint commanders to lead it.

¹⁰You will march up to attack a city. First, make them an offer of peace. ¹¹They might accept your offer and open their gates to you. If that happens, all the people of that city will become your slaves. They will work for you. ¹²But they might not make peace with you. They might fight you in battle. Then you should surround that city. ¹³The Lord your God will give you the city. Then kill all the men with

your swords. ¹⁴You may take everything else in the city for yourselves. Take the women and children and animals. And you may use these things the Lord your God gives you from your enemies. ¹⁵Do this to all the cities that are far away. They do not belong to the nations nearby.

¹⁶But leave nothing alive in the cities of the land. This is the land the Lord your God is giving you. ¹⁷Completely destroy these people: the Hittites, Amorites, Canaanites, Perizzites, Hivites and Jebusites. The Lord your God has commanded you to do this. ¹⁸Otherwise, they will teach you what they do for their gods. And if you do these terrible things, you will sin against the Lord your God.

¹⁹You might surround and attack a city for a long time, trying to capture it. But do not destroy its trees with an ax. You can eat the fruit from the trees. Do not cut them down. These trees are not the enemy. So don't make war against them. ²⁰But you may cut down trees that you know are not fruit trees. You may use them to build devices to attack the city walls. You may do this until the city is captured.

A Person Found Murdered

21 Someone might be found murdered. He might be lying in a field in the land the Lord your God is giving you to own. And no one knows who killed him. ²Your older leaders and judges should go to where he was found. And they should measure how far it is to the nearby cities. ³The older leaders of the city nearest the body are responsible. They must take a young cow that has never worked or worn a yoke.ᵈ ⁴And they must lead her down to a valley. It must never have been plowed or planted. It must have a stream flowing through it. There they must break the young cow's neck. ⁵The priests should come forward. They are the sons of Levi. They have been chosen by the Lord your God. They are to serve and give blessings in the Lord's name. And they are to decide cases of quarreling and attacks. 6Then all the older leaders of the city nearest the murdered man should wash their hands. They should do it over the young cow whose neck was broken in the valley. 7They should declare: "We did not kill this man. And we did not see it happen. 8Lord, remove this sin of your people Israel. You have saved them. Don't blame your people, the Israelites, for this innocent man's murder." And so the murder will be paid for. 9Then you will have removed from yourselves the guilt of murdering an innocent person. You will be doing what the Lord says is right.

Captive Women as Wives

10You will go to war against your enemies. The Lord will help you defeat them. You will take them captive. 11You might see a beautiful woman among the captives. And you might be attracted to her. You may take her as your wife. 12Bring her into your home. She must shave her head and cut her nails. 13She must change out of the clothes she was wearing when you captured her. And she must live in your house and cry for her parents for a month. After that, you may marry her. You will be her husband, and she will be your wife. 14But you might not be pleased with her. Then let her go anywhere she wants. You must not sell her for money. You must not make her a slave. You have taken away her honor.

The Oldest Son

15A man may have two wives. He might love one wife but not the other. Both wives might have sons by him. But the older son might be the son of the wife he does not love. 16Someday that man must will his property to his sons. But he must not give the son of the wife he loves what belongs to the older son. The older son is the son of the wife the man does not love. 17He must agree to give the older son two shares of everything he owns. The

older son is from the wife he does not love. That son was the first to prove his father could have children. So he has the rights that belong to the older son.

Sons Who Refuse to Obey

18A man might have a son who is stubborn. The son turns against his father and mother and doesn't obey them. He will not listen when they correct him. 19His parents must take him to the older leaders at the city gate. 20They will say to the leaders, "Our son is stubborn and turns against us. He will not obey us. He eats too much. And he is always drunk." 21Then all the men in his town must throw stones at him until he dies. Get rid of the evil among you. All the people of Israel will hear about this and be afraid.

Other Laws

22A man might be guilty of a sin worthy of death. He must be put to death and his body displayed on a tree. 23But don't leave his body hanging on the tree overnight. Be sure to bury him that same day. Anyone whose body is displayed on a tree is cursed by God. You must not ruin the land the Lord your God is giving you to own.

22 You might see your fellow Israelite's ox or sheep wandering away. Don't ignore it. Take it back to its owner. 2The owner might not live close to you. Or you might not know who he is. Then take the animal home with you. Keep it until the owner comes looking for it. Then give it back to him. 3Do the same thing if you find his donkey or coat or anything he lost. Don't just ignore it.

4You might see your fellow Israelite's donkey or ox fallen on the road. Don't ignore it. Help him get it up.

5A woman must not wear men's clothes. And a man must not wear women's clothes. The Lord your God hates anyone who does that.

6You might find a bird's nest by the road. It might be in a tree or on the ground. And the mother bird might be sitting on the young birds or eggs. Do not take the mother bird with the young birds. [7]You may take the young birds. But you must let the mother bird go free. Then things will go well for you. And you will live a long time.

[8]When you build a new house, build a wall around the roof.[n] Then you will not be guilty of murder if someone falls off the roof.

[9]Don't plant two different kinds of seeds in your vineyard. Otherwise, both crops will be ruined.

[10]Don't plow with an ox and a donkey tied together.

[11]Don't wear clothes made of wool and linen woven together.

[12]Tie several pieces of thread together. Then put these tassels on the four corners of your coat.

Marriage Laws

[13]A man might marry a girl and have sexual relations with her. But he might decide that he does not like her. [14]So he might lie about her and give her a bad name. He might say, "I married this woman. But when I had sexual relations with her, I did not find that she was a virgin."[d] [15]Then the girl's parents must bring proof that she was a virgin. They must bring it to the older leaders at the city gate. [16]The girl's father will say to the leaders, "I gave my daughter to this man to be his wife. But now he does not want her. [17]This man has told lies about my daughter. He has said, 'I did not find your daughter to be a virgin.' But here is the proof that my daughter was a virgin." Then her parents are to show the sheet to the city leaders. [18]Then the leaders must take the man and punish him. [19]They must make him pay about two and a half pounds of silver. The silver will go to the girl's father. This is because the man has given an Israelite girl a bad name. The girl must continue to be the man's wife. And he may not divorce her as long as he lives.

[20]But the things the husband said about his wife might be true. And there might be no proof that she was a virgin. [21]If so, the girl must be brought to the door of her father's house. Then the men of the town must put her to death by throwing stones at her. She has done a disgraceful thing in Israel. She had sexual relations before she was married. You must get rid of the evil among you.

[22]A man might be found having sexual relations with another man's wife. Both the woman and the man who had sexual relations with her must die. Get rid of this evil from Israel.

[23]A man might meet a virgin in a city and have sexual relations with her. But she might be engaged to another man. [24]You must take both of them to the city gate. Put them both to death by throwing stones at them. Kill the girl because she was in a city and did not scream for help. And kill the man for having sexual relations with another man's wife. You must get rid of the evil among you.

[25]But a man might meet a girl out in the country. He might force her to have sexual relations with him. But she might be engaged to another man. Only the man who had sexual relations with her must be put to death. [26]Don't do anything to the girl. She has not done a sin worthy of death. This is like the person who attacks and murders his neighbor. [27]The man found the engaged girl in the country. And she screamed. But no one was there to save her.

[28]A man might meet a virgin who is not engaged to be married. He might force her to have sexual relations with him. And people might find out about it. [29]The man must pay the girl's father about one and one-fourth pounds of silver. He must also marry the girl because he has dishonored her. And he may never divorce her for as long as he lives.

---

[n]**roof** In Bible times houses were built with flat roofs. The roof was used for drying things such as flax and fruit. And it was used as an extra room, as a place for worship and as a place to sleep in the summer.

[30]A man must not marry his father's wife. He must not dishonor his father in this way.

The Lord's People

23 No man who has had part of his sex organ cut off may come into the worship meeting of the Lord's people.

[2]No one born to parents who were forbidden by law to marry may come into the meeting to worship the Lord. His descendants for ten generations may not come in either.

[3]No Ammonite or Moabite may come into the meeting to worship the Lord. And none of their descendants for ten generations may come in. [4]This is because the Ammonites and Moabites did not give you bread and water when you came out of Egypt. And they hired Balaam to put a curse on you. He was the son of Beor from Pethor in Northwest Mesopotamia. [5]But the Lord your God would not listen to Balaam. He turned the curse into a blessing for you. The Lord your God loves you. [6]Don't wish for their peace or success as long as you live.

[7]Don't hate Edomites. They are your relatives. Don't hate Egyptians, because you were foreigners in their country. [8]The great-grandchildren of these two peoples may come into the meeting to worship the Lord.

Keeping the Camp Clean

[9]When you are camped in time of war, keep away from unclean[d] things. [10]A man might become unclean during the night. If he does, he must go outside the camp and not come back. [11]But when evening comes, he must wash himself. At sunset he may come back into the camp.

[12]Choose a place outside the camp where people may go to relieve themselves. [13]Carry a stick with you. When you relieve yourself, dig a hole. Cover up your dung. [14]The Lord your God moves around through your camp. He will protect you. He will help you defeat your enemies. So the camp must be holy. The Lord must not see anything unclean among you. Then he will not leave you.

Other Laws

[15]An escaped slave might come to you. Do not hand him over to his master. [16]Let the slave live with you anywhere he likes. He may live in any town he chooses. Do not mistreat him.

[17]No Israelite man or woman must ever become a temple prostitute.[d] [18]Do not bring a male or female prostitute's pay to the Temple[d] of the Lord your God to pay what you have promised to the Lord. The Lord your God hates prostitution.

[19]You may loan your fellow Israelite money or food or anything else. But don't make him pay back more than what you loaned him. [20]You may charge a foreigner, but not a fellow Israelite. Then the Lord your God will bless everything you do. He will bless you in the land you are entering to take as your own.

[21]You might make a promise to give something to the Lord your God. Do not be slow to pay it. The Lord your God demands it from you. Do not be guilty of sin. [22]But if you do not make the promise, you will not be guilty. [23]You must do whatever you say you will do. You chose to make the promise to the Lord your God.

[24]You might go into your neighbor's vineyard. You may eat as many grapes as you wish. But do not fill your basket with his grapes. [25]You might go into your neighbor's grainfield. You may pick grain with your hands. But you must not cut down his grain with your sickle.

24 A man might marry a woman. But he might decide she doesn't please him. He has found something bad about her. He writes out divorce papers for her. He gives them to her and sends her away from his house. [2]After she leaves his house, she goes and marries another man. [3]But her second husband does not like her either. So he writes out divorce papers for her. He gives them to her and sends her away from his house. Or the second husband might die. ⁴In either case, her first husband who divorced her must not marry her again. She has become unclean.ᵈ The Lord would hate this. Don't bring this sin into the land the Lord your God is giving you to own.

⁵A man who has just married must not be sent to war. And he must not be given any other duty. He should be free to stay home for a year to make his new wife happy.

⁶A man might owe you something. But do not take his two stones for grinding grain—not even the upper one—in place of what he owes. This is how he makes his living.

⁷A man might kidnap a fellow Israelite. He might make him a slave or sell him. The kidnapper must be killed. You must get rid of the evil among you.

⁸Be careful when someone has a harmful skin disease. Do exactly what the priests, the Levites, teach you. Be careful to do what I have commanded them. ⁹Remember what the Lord your God did to Miriam on your way out of Egypt.

¹⁰You might make a loan to your neighbor. But don't go into his house to get something in place of it. ¹¹Stay outside. Let the man himself go in and get what he promised you. ¹²A poor man might give you his coat to show he will pay the loan back. But don't keep his coat overnight. ¹³Give his coat back to him at sunset. He needs his coat to sleep in. He will thank you. And the Lord your God will see that you have done a good thing.

¹⁴Don't cheat a hired servant who is poor and needy. He might be a fellow Israelite. Or he might be a foreigner living in one of your towns. ¹⁵Pay him each day before sunset. He is poor and needs the money. Otherwise, he may complain to the Lord about you. And you will be guilty of sin.

¹⁶Fathers must not be put to death when their children do wrong. And children must not be put to death when their fathers do wrong. Each person must die for his own sin.

¹⁷Do not be unfair to a foreigner or an orphan. Don't take a widow's coat in place of a loan. ¹⁸Remember that you were slaves in Egypt. And the Lord your God saved you from there. That is why I am commanding you to do this.

¹⁹You might be gathering your harvest in the field. You might not see a bundle of grain. Don't go back and get it. Leave it there for foreigners, orphans and widows. Then the Lord your God can bless everything you do. ²⁰You may beat your olive trees to knock the olives off. But don't beat the trees a second time. Leave what is left for foreigners, orphans and widows. ²¹You may harvest the grapes in your vineyard. But don't pick the vines a second time. Leave what is left for foreigners, orphans and widows. ²²Remember that you were slaves in Egypt. That is why I am commanding you to do this.

25 Two people may have an argument. They should go to the court. And the judges will decide the case. They will declare one person to be right. And they will punish the one who is guilty. ²The guilty person might have to be punished with a beating. If so, the judge will make him lie down. They will beat him in front of the judge. The number of lashes should match the crime. ³But don't hit him more than 40 times. If he is beaten more than that, it would disgrace him before others.

⁴When an ox is working in the grain, do not cover its mouth to keep it from eating.

⁵Two brothers might be living together. One of them might die without having a son. His widow must not marry someone outside her husband's family. Her husband's brother must marry her. This is his duty for her as a brother-in-law. ⁶The first son she has must be named for the dead brother.

Then his name will not be forgotten in Israel.

7But a man might not want to marry his brother's widow. Then she should go to the older leaders at the town gate. And she should say, "My brother-in-law will not carry on his brother's name in Israel. He refuses to do his duty for me."

8Then the older leaders of the town must call for the man and talk to him. But he might be stubborn and say, "I don't want to marry her."

9If he does, the woman must go up to him in front of the leaders. She must take off one of his sandals. She must spit in his face and say, "This is for the man who won't continue his brother's family!" 10Then that man's family shall be known in Israel as the Family of the Unsandaled.

11Two men might be fighting. And one man's wife comes to save her husband from his attacker. And she grabs the attacker by his sex organs. 12You must cut off her hand. Give her no mercy.

13Don't carry two sets of weights with you, one heavy and one light. 14Don't have two different sets of measures in your house, one large and one small. 15You must have true and honest weights and measures. Then you will live a long time in the land the Lord your God is giving you. 16The Lord your God hates anyone who is dishonest and uses dishonest measures.

17Remember what the Amalekites did to you when you came out of Egypt. 18You were tired and worn out. And they met you on the road. They killed all those lagging behind. They were not afraid of God. 19The Lord your God will give you rest from all the enemies around you. It will be in the land he is giving you to own. Then you shall destroy any memory of the Amalekites on the earth. Do not forget!

The First Harvest

26 Soon you will go into the land the Lord your God is giving you to own. You will take it over and live in it. 2Then you must take some of the first harvest of crops. It will grow from the land the Lord your God is giving you. Put the food in a basket. Then go to the place where the Lord your God will choose to be worshiped. 3Say to the priest on duty at that time, "Today I declare this before the Lord your God. I have come into the land the Lord promised to give us. He promised this to our ancestors." 4The priest will take your basket. He will set it down in front of the altar of the Lord your God. 5Then you shall announce before the Lord your God: "My father was a wandering Aramean. He went down to Egypt. He stayed there with only a few people. But they became a great, powerful and large nation there. 6But the Egyptians were cruel to us. They made us suffer and work very hard. 7So we prayed to the Lord, the God of our ancestors. He heard us. He saw our trouble, hard work and suffering. 8Then the Lord brought us out of Egypt. He did it with his great power and strength. He used great terrors, signs and miracles.d 9Then he brought us to this place. He gave us this land where much food grows. 10Now I bring you part of the first harvest from this land. Lord, you have given me this land." Then place the basket before the Lord your God. And bow down before him. 11Then you and the Levites and foreigners among you should rejoice. The Lord your God has given good things to you and your family.

12Bring a tenth of all your harvest the third year. This is the year to give a tenth of your harvest. Give it to the Levites, foreigners, orphans and widows. Then they may eat in your towns and be full. 13Then say to the Lord your God, "I have taken out of my house the part of my harvest that belongs to God. I have given it to the Levites, foreigners, orphans and widows. I have done everything you commanded me. I have not broken your commands. And I have not forgotten any of them.

[14]I have not eaten any of the holy part while I was in sorrow. I have not removed any of it while I was unclean.[d] I have not offered it for dead people. I have obeyed you, the Lord my God. I have done everything you commanded me. [15]So look down from heaven, your holy home. Bless your people Israel. And bless the land you have given us. You promised it to our ancestors. It is a land where much food grows."

Obey the Lord's Commands

[16]Today the Lord your God commands you to obey all these rules and laws. Be careful to do them with your whole being. [17]Today you have said that the Lord is your God. You have promised to do what he wants you to do. You have promised to keep his rules, commands and laws. You have said you will obey him. [18]And today the Lord has said that you are his very own people. He has promised it. But you must obey his commands. [19]The Lord will make you greater than all the other nations he made. He will give you praise, fame and honor. And you will be a holy people to the Lord your God. This is what he said.

The Law Written on Stones

27 Moses and the older leaders of Israel commanded the people. They said, "Keep all the commands I have given you today. [2]Soon you will cross the Jordan River. You will go into the land the Lord your God is giving you. On that day set up some large stones. Cover them with plaster. [3]When you cross over, write all the words of these teachings on them. Then you may enter the land the Lord your God is giving you. It is a land where much food grows. It is just as the Lord, the God of your ancestors, promised. [4]After you have crossed the Jordan River, set up these stones. Set them on Mount Ebal as I command you today. And cover them with plaster. [5]Build an altar of stones there to the Lord your God. But don't use any iron tool to cut the stones. [6]Build the altar of the Lord your God with stones from the field. Offer burnt offerings on it to the Lord your God. [7]Offer fellowship offerings there. Eat them and rejoice before the Lord your God. [8]Then write clearly all the words of these teachings on the stones."

Curses of the Law

[9]Then Moses and the Levites, who are the priests, spoke to all Israel. They said, "Be quiet, Israel. Listen! Today you have become the people of the Lord your God. [10]Obey the Lord your God. Keep his commands and laws that I give you today."

[11]That day Moses also gave the people this command:

[12]You will cross the Jordan River. Then these tribes[d] must stand on Mount Gerizim to bless the people: Simeon, Levi, Judah, Issachar, Joseph and Benjamin. [13]And these tribes must stand on Mount Ebal to announce the curses: Reuben, Gad, Asher, Zebulun, Dan and Naphtali.

[14]The Levites will say to all the people of Israel in a loud voice:

[15]"Anyone will be cursed who makes an idol or statue and secretly sets it up. The Lord hates idols made by man."

Then all the people will say, "Amen!"
[16]"Anyone will be cursed who dishonors his father or his mother."

Then all the people will say, "Amen!"
[17]"Anyone will be cursed who moves the stone that marks his neighbor's border."

Then all the people will say, "Amen!"
[18]"Anyone will be cursed who leads a blind person away from the road."

Then all the people will say, "Amen!"
[19]"Anyone will be cursed who is unfair to foreigners, orphans or widows."

Then all the people will say, "Amen!"
[20]"A man will be cursed who has sexual relations with his father's wife. It is a dishonor to his father."

Then all the people will say, "Amen!"
[21]"Anyone will be cursed who has sexual relations with an animal."

Then all the people will say, "Amen!"

²²"A man will be cursed who has sexual relations with his sister. She may be his father's daughter or his mother's daughter."

Then all the people will say, "Amen!"

²³"A man will be cursed who has sexual relations with his mother-in-law."

Then all the people will say, "Amen!"

²⁴"Anyone will be cursed who kills his neighbor secretly."

Then all the people will say, "Amen!"

²⁵"Anyone will be cursed who takes money to murder an innocent person."

Then all the people will say, "Amen!"

²⁶"Anyone will be cursed who does not agree with the words of these teachings and does not obey them."

Then all the people will say, "Amen!"

Blessings for Obeying

28 You must completely obey the Lord your God. And you must carefully follow all his commands I am giving you today. Then the Lord your God will make you greater than any other nation on earth. ²Obey the Lord your God. Then all these blessings will come and stay with you:

³You will be blessed in the city. You will be blessed in the country.

⁴Your children will be blessed. Your crops will be blessed. Your cattle will be blessed with calves and your sheep with lambs.

⁵Your basket and your kitchen will be blessed.

⁶You will be blessed when you come in and when you go out.

⁷The Lord will let you defeat the enemies that come to fight you. They will attack you from one direction. But they will run from you in seven directions.

⁸The Lord your God will bless you with full barns. He will bless everything you do. He will bless the land he is giving you.

⁹The Lord will make you his holy people, as he promised. But you must obey his commands. You must do what he wants you to do. ¹⁰Then everyone on earth will see that you are the Lord's people. They will be afraid of you. ¹¹The Lord will make you rich. You will have many children. Your cattle will have many calves. Your land will give good crops. It is the land that the Lord promised your ancestors he would give to you.

¹²The Lord will open up his storehouse. The skies will send rain on your land at the right time. And he will bless everything you do. You will lend to other nations. But you will not need to borrow from them. ¹³The Lord will make you like the head and not like the tail. You will be on top and not on bottom. But you must obey the commands of the Lord your God that I am giving you today. Be careful to keep them. ¹⁴Do not disobey anything I command you today. Do exactly as I command. Do not follow other gods or serve them.

Curses for Disobeying

¹⁵But you might not obey the Lord your God. You might not carefully follow all his commands and laws I am giving you today. Then all these curses will come upon you and stay:

¹⁶You will be cursed in the city. You will be cursed in the country.

¹⁷Your basket and your kitchen will be cursed.

¹⁸Your children will be cursed. Your crops will be cursed. The calves of your cattle will be cursed. And the lambs of your flocks will be cursed.

¹⁹You will be cursed when you go in and when you go out.

²⁰The Lord will send you curses, confusion and punishment in everything you do. You will be destroyed. You will suddenly be ruined. You did wrong when you left him. ²¹The Lord will give you terrible diseases. He will destroy you from the land you are going to take. ²²The Lord will punish you with disease, fever, swelling, heat, no rain, plant diseases and mildew.ᵈ Then you will die. ²³The sky above will look like bronze. And the ground below will be like iron. ²⁴The Lord will turn the rain into dust

and sand. It will fall from the skies until you are destroyed.

²⁵The Lord will let your enemies defeat you. You will attack them from one direction. But you will run from them in seven directions. And you will become a thing of horror among all the kingdoms on earth. ²⁶Your dead bodies will be food for all the birds and wild animals. There will be no one to scare them away. ²⁷The Lord will punish you with boils like those the Egyptians had. You will have bad growths, sores and itches that can't be cured. ²⁸The Lord will give you madness, blindness and a confused mind. ²⁹You will have to feel around in the daylight like a blind man. You will fail in everything you do. People will hurt you and steal from you every day. There will be no one to save you.

³⁰You will be engaged to a woman. But another man will force her to have sexual relations with him. You will build a house. But you will not live in it. You will plant a vineyard. But you will not get its grapes. ³¹Your ox will be killed before your eyes. But you will not eat any of it. Your donkey will be taken away from you. And it will not be brought back. Your sheep will be given to your enemies. And no one will rescue them. ³²Your sons and daughters will be given to another nation. You will grow tired looking for them every day. But there is nothing you can do. ³³People you don't know will eat the crops your land and hard work have produced. You will be mistreated and abused all your life. ³⁴The things you see will cause you to go mad. ³⁵The Lord will give you sore boils on your knees and legs. They cannot be cured. They will go from the soles of your feet to the tops of your heads.

³⁶The Lord will send you and your king away to a nation you do not know. There you will serve other gods made of wood and stone. ³⁷You will become a hated thing to the nations where the Lord sends you. They will laugh at you and make fun of you.

³⁸You will plant much seed in your field. But your harvest will be small. Locusts*ᵈ* will eat the crop. ³⁹You will plant vineyards and work hard in them. But you will not pick the grapes or drink the wine. The worms will eat them. ⁴⁰You will have olive trees in all your land. But you will not get any olive oil. The olives will drop off the trees. ⁴¹You will have sons and daughters. But you will not be able to keep them. They will be taken captive. ⁴²Locusts will destroy all your trees and crops.

⁴³The foreigners who live among you will get stronger and stronger. And you will get weaker and weaker. ⁴⁴Foreigners will lend money to you. But you will not be able to lend to them. They will be like the head. And you will be like the tail.

⁴⁵All these curses will come upon you. They will chase you and catch you and destroy you. This will happen because you did not obey the Lord your God. You did not keep the commands and laws he gave you. ⁴⁶The curses will be signs and miracles*ᵈ* to you and your descendants*ᵈ* forever. ⁴⁷You had plenty of everything. But you did not serve the Lord your God with joy and a pure heart. ⁴⁸So you will serve the enemies the Lord sends against you. You will be hungry, thirsty, naked and poor. The Lord will put a load on you until he has destroyed you.

The Curse of an Enemy Nation

⁴⁹The Lord will bring a nation against you from far away. It will be from the end of the world. The nation will swoop down like an eagle. You won't understand their language. ⁵⁰They will look mean. They will not respect old people or feel sorry for the young. ⁵¹They will eat the calves from your cattle and the harvest of your field. And you will be destroyed. They will not leave you any grain, new wine or oil. They will not leave you any calves from your herds or lambs from your flocks. You will be ruined. ⁵²That nation will surround and attack all your cities. You trust in your

high, strong walls. But they will fall down. That nation will surround all your cities everywhere in the land the Lord your God is giving you.

⁵³Your enemy will surround you. Those people will make you starve. You will eat your own babies. You will eat the bodies of the sons and daughters the Lord gave you. ⁵⁴Even the most gentle and kind man among you will become cruel. He will be cruel to his brother, his wife whom he loves and his children who are still alive. ⁵⁵He will not even give them any of the flesh of his children he is eating. It will be all he has left. Your enemy will surround you. Those people will make you starve in all your cities. ⁵⁶The most gentle and kind woman among you will become cruel. She is so gentle and kind she would hardly even walk on the ground. But she will be cruel to her husband whom she loves. And she will be cruel to her son and daughter. ⁵⁷She will give birth to a baby. But she will plan to eat the baby and what comes after the birth itself. She will eat them while the enemy surrounds the city. Those people will make you starve in all your cities.

⁵⁸Be careful to obey everything in these teachings. They are written in this book. You must respect the glorious and wonderful name of the Lord your God. ⁵⁹The Lord will give terrible diseases to you and your descendants.ᵈ You will have long and serious diseases. You will have long and miserable sicknesses. ⁶⁰And the Lord will give you all the diseases of Egypt that you dread. And the diseases will stay with you. ⁶¹The Lord will also give you every disease and sickness not written in this Book of the Teachings. Then you will be destroyed. ⁶²You people may have outnumbered the stars. But only a few of you will be left. You did not obey the Lord your God. ⁶³Once the Lord was happy with you. He gave you good things. He made you grow in number. But now the Lord will be happy to ruin and destroy you. You will

be removed from the land you are entering to own.

⁶⁴Then the Lord will scatter you among the nations. He will scatter you from one end of the earth to the other. There you will serve other gods of wood and stone. They are gods that neither you nor your ancestors have known. ⁶⁵You will have no rest among those nations. You will have no place that is yours. The Lord will make your mind worried, your sight weak and your soul sad. ⁶⁶You will live with danger. You will be afraid night and day. You will not be sure that you will live. ⁶⁷In the morning you will say, "I wish it were evening." And in the evening you will say, "I wish it were morning." Terror will be in your heart because of the things you have seen. ⁶⁸The Lord will send you back to Egypt in ships. I, Moses, said you would never go back to Egypt. And there you will try to sell yourselves as slaves to your enemies. But no one will buy you.

The Agreement in Moab

29 The Lord commanded Moses to make an agreement with the Israelites in Moab. This agreement was in addition to the agreement he had made with them at Mount Sinai.

²Moses called all the Israelites together. And he said to them:

You have seen everything the Lord did to the king of Egypt. You saw what he did to the king's leaders and to the whole country. ³With your own eyes you saw the great troubles, signs and miracles.ᵈ ⁴But to this day the Lord has not given you a mind that understands. You don't really understand what you see with your eyes or hear with your ears. ⁵The Lord led you through the desert for 40 years. During that time neither your clothes nor sandals wore out. ⁶You ate no bread. You drank no wine or beer. This was so you would understand that he is the Lord your God.

⁷You came to this place. Then Sihon king of Heshbon and Og king of Bashan

came out to fight us. But we defeated them. [8]We captured their land. And we gave it to the Reubenites, the Gadites and the eastern half-tribe[d] of Manasseh to own.

[9]You must carefully obey everything in this agreement. Then you will succeed in everything you do. [10]Today you are all standing here before the Lord your God. Here are your leaders and important men. Your older leaders, officers and all the other men of Israel are here. [11]Here are your wives and children and the foreigners who live among you. They chop your wood and carry your water. [12]You are all here to enter into an agreement and a promise with the Lord your God. The Lord is making this agreement with you today. [13]This will make you today the Lord's own people. He will be your God. This is what he told you. He promised it to your ancestors Abraham, Isaac and Jacob. [14]But the Lord is not just making this agreement and its promises with you. [15]You are standing here before the Lord your God today. But he is also making it with those who are not here today.

[16]You know how we lived in Egypt. You know how we passed through the countries when we came here. [17]You saw their hated idols made of wood, stone, silver and gold. [18]Make sure no man, woman, family group or tribe among you leaves the Lord. Don't let them go and serve the gods of those nations. That would be like a plant that grows bitter, poisonous fruit.

[19]That kind of person might hear these curses. But he blesses himself. And he thinks, "I will be safe. I will continue doing what I want to do." That person might destroy all of your land, both wet and dry. [20]The Lord will not forgive that person. His anger will be like a burning fire against that man. All the curses written in this book will come on him. And the Lord will destroy any memory of him on the earth. [21]The Lord will separate him from all the tribes of Israel for punishment. All the curses of the agreement will happen

to him. They are written in this Book of the Teachings.

[22]Your children who will come after you will see this. And foreigners from faraway lands will see this. They will see the disasters that come to this land. And they will see the diseases the Lord will send on it. They will say, [23]"The land is nothing but burning cinders and salt. Nothing is planted. Nothing grows. Nothing blooms. It is like Sodom and Gomorrah, and Admah and Zeboiim. The Lord destroyed them because he was very angry." [24]All the other nations will ask, "Why has the Lord done this to the land? Why is he so angry?"

[25]And the answer will be, "It is because the people broke the agreement of the Lord, the God of their ancestors. He made it with them when he brought them out of Egypt. [26]They went and served other gods. They bowed down to gods they did not even know. The Lord did not allow that. [27]So the Lord became very angry at the land. And he brought all the curses on it that are written in this book. [28]The Lord became angry and furious with them. So he took them out of their land. And he put them in another land where they are today."

[29]There are some things the Lord our God has kept secret. But there are some things he has let us know. These things belong to us and our children forever. It is so we will do everything in these teachings.

The Israelites Will Return

30 All these blessings and curses I have said will happen to you. The Lord your God will send you away to other nations. There you will think about these things. [2]Then you and your children will return to the Lord your God. And you will obey him with your whole being. You will obey everything I command you today. [3]Then the Lord your God will give you back your riches. He will feel sorry for you. And he will bring you back again from the nations where he sent you. ⁴He may send you to the ends of the earth. But he will gather you. He will bring you back from there. ⁵He will bring you back to the land that belonged to your ancestors. It will be yours. He will give you success. And there will be more of you than there were of your ancestors. ⁶The Lord your God will prepare you and your descendants*d* to serve him. You will love him with your whole being. Then you will live. ⁷The Lord your God will put all these curses on your enemies. They hate you and are cruel to you. ⁸And you will again obey the Lord. You will keep all his commands that I give you today. ⁹The Lord your God will make you successful in everything you do. You will have many children. Your cattle will have many calves. Your fields will produce good crops. He will again be happy with you, just as he was with your ancestors. ¹⁰But you must obey the Lord your God. You must obey his commands and rules that are written in this Book of the Teachings. You must follow the Lord your God with your whole being.

Life or Death

¹¹This command I give you today is not too hard for you. It is not beyond what you can do. ¹²It is not up in heaven. You do not have to ask, "Who will go up to heaven and get it for us? Then we can obey it and keep it." ¹³It is not on the other side of the sea. You do not have to ask, "Who will go across the sea and get it? Who will tell it to us? Then we can keep it." ¹⁴No, the word is very near you. It is in your mouth and in your heart. So, you may obey it.

¹⁵Look, today I offer you life and success, death and destruction. ¹⁶I command you today to love the Lord your God. Do what he wants you to do. Keep his commands, his rules and his laws. Then you will live and grow in number. And the Lord your God will bless you in the land you are going to take as your own.

¹⁷But you might turn away from the Lord. You might not obey him. You might be led to bowing down and serving other gods. ¹⁸I tell you today that you will be destroyed. And you will not live long in the land you are crossing the Jordan River to enter and own.

¹⁹Today I ask heaven and earth to be witnesses. I am offering you life or death, blessings or curses. Now, choose life! Then you and your children may live. ²⁰Love the Lord your God. Obey him. Stay close to him. He is your life. And he will let you live many years in the land. This is the land he promised to give your ancestors Abraham, Isaac and Jacob.

Joshua Takes Moses' Place

31 Then Moses went and spoke these words to all the Israelites: ²"I am now 120 years old. I cannot lead you anymore. The Lord told me I would not cross the Jordan River. ³The Lord your God will lead you across himself. He will destroy those nations for you. You will take over their land. Joshua will also lead you across. This is what the Lord has said. ⁴The Lord will do to these nations what he did to Sihon and Og. They were the kings of the Amorites. He destroyed them and their land. ⁵The Lord will give those nations to you. Do to them everything I told you. ⁶Be strong and brave. Don't be afraid of them. Don't be frightened. The Lord your God will go with you. He will not leave you or forget you."

⁷Then Moses called Joshua and spoke to him in front of the people. Moses said, "Be strong and brave. Lead these people into the land the Lord promised to give their ancestors. Help the people take it as their own. ⁸The Lord himself will go before you. He will be with you. He will not leave you or forget you. Don't be afraid. Don't worry."

Moses Writes the Teachings

⁹So Moses wrote down the teachings. He gave them to the priests and all the older leaders of Israel. The priests are

the sons of Levi. They carried the Box[d] of the Agreement with the Lord. [10-11]Then Moses commanded them: "Read these teachings for all Israel to hear. Do it at the end of every seven years. That is the year to forget what people owe. Do it during the Feast[d] of Shelters. All the Israelites will come to appear before the Lord your God. They will stand at the place the Lord will choose. [12]Gather all the people: the men, women, children and foreigners living in your towns. Then they can listen and learn to respect the Lord your God. Then they can carefully obey everything in this law. [13]Their children do not know this law. They must hear it. They must learn to respect the Lord your God for as long as they live in the land. It is the land you are crossing the Jordan River to own."

The Lord Calls Moses and Joshua

[14]The Lord said to Moses, "Soon you will die. Get Joshua and come to the Meeting Tent.[d] I will command him." So Moses and Joshua went to the Meeting Tent.

[15]The Lord appeared at the Meeting Tent in a cloud. The cloud stood over the entrance of the Tent. [16]And the Lord said to Moses, "You will soon die. Then these people will not be loyal to me. They will worship the foreign gods of the land they are entering. They will leave me. And they will break the agreement I made with them. [17]Then I will become very angry at them. I will leave them. I will turn away from them. And they will be destroyed. Many terrible things will happen to them. Then they will say, 'God is not with us. That is why these terrible things are happening.' [18]I will turn away from them then. They have done wrong. They have turned to other gods.

[19]"Now write down this song. And teach it to the Israelites. Then have them sing it. It will testify against them. [20]I will bring them into the land I promised to their ancestors. It is a land where much food grows. They will

eat as much as they want and get fat. But then they will turn to other gods and serve them. They will reject me and break my agreement. [21]Then many troubles and terrible things will happen to them. And this song will testify against them. The song will not be forgotten by their descendants.[d] I know what they plan to do, even before I take them into the land I promised them." [22]So Moses wrote down the song that day. And he taught it to the Israelites.

[23]Then the Lord gave this command to Joshua son of Nun: "Be strong and brave. Lead the people of Israel to the land I promised them. And I will be with you."

[24]Moses wrote all the words of the teachings in a book. [25]Then he gave a command to the Levites. They carried the Box[d] of the Agreement with the Lord. [26]He said, "Take this Book of the Teachings. Put it beside the Box of the Agreement with the Lord your God. It must stay there as a witness against you. [27]I know how stubborn and disobedient you are. You have disobeyed the Lord while I am alive and with you. You will disobey even more after I die! [28]Gather all the older leaders of your tribes[d] and all your officers. I will say these things for them to hear. And I will ask heaven and earth to testify against them. [29]I know that after I die you will become completely evil. You will turn away from the commands I have given you. Then terrible things will happen to you in the future. You will do what the Lord says is evil. You will make him angry with the idols you have made."

Moses' Song

[30]And Moses spoke this whole song for all the people of Israel to hear:

32 Hear, heavens, and I will speak.
Listen, earth, to what I say.
[2]My teaching will drop like rain.
My words will fall like dew.
They will be like showers on the grass.

They will pour down like rain on
young plants.
³I will announce the name of the
Lord.
Praise God because he is great!
⁴He is like a rock. What he does
is perfect.
He is always fair.
He is a faithful God who does no
wrong.
He is right and fair.

He set up borders for the people.
He even numbered the Israelites.
⁹The Lord took his people as his
share.
The people of Jacob were his
very own.

¹⁰He found them in a desert.
It was a windy, empty land.
He surrounded them and brought
them up.
He guarded them as those he
loved very much.
¹¹He was like an eagle building
its nest.

Animals in the Bible
EAGLES • DEUTERONOMY 32:11

When baby eagles are learning to fly, the mother eagle gently nudges her babies out of the nest. If the baby eagles make a mistake or start to fall, the mother eagle catches them safely. She is always watching the young eagles in case they need her help. This is how the babies get used to using their wings. Soon these young eagles are old enough and strong enough to rise up in the air and soar over the trees by themselves.

The Bible says God cares for us just like the mother eagle cares for her babies. No matter how many mistakes we make, he is right there with us. God will always be there for you when you need his help.

To discover an animal that can wander off and be baaaad,
fly to page 658.

⁵They have done evil against
him.
To their shame they are no longer
his children.
They are an evil and lying people.
⁶This is not the way to repay
the Lord.
You are foolish and unwise.
He is your Father and Maker.
He made you and formed you.

⁷Remember the old days.
Think of the years already passed.
Ask your father. He will tell you.
Ask your older leaders. They will
inform you.
⁸The Most High God gave the
nations their lands.
He divided up the human race.

It flutters over its young.
It spreads its wings to catch them.
It carries them on its feathers.
¹²The Lord alone led them.
There were no foreign gods
among them.

¹³The Lord brought them to the
heights of the land.
He fed them the fruit of the fields.
He gave them honey from the rocks.
He brought oil from the solid rock.
¹⁴There were milk curds from
the cows and milk from
the sheep.
There were fat sheep and goats.
There were sheep and goats from
Bashan.

There was the best of the wheat.
You drank the juice of grapes.

15Israel grew fat and kicked.
   They were fat and full and firm.
They left the God who made them.
   They rejected the Rock*d* who
      saved them.
16They made God jealous with
      foreign gods.
   They made him angry with hated
      idols.
17They made sacrifices to
      demons,*d* not God.
   They were gods they had never
      known.
   They were new gods from nearby.
   Your ancestors did not fear them.
18You left God who is the Rock,
      your Father.
   You forgot the God who gave
      you birth.

19The Lord saw this and rejected
      them.
   His sons and daughters had made
      him angry.
20He said, "I will turn away from
      them.
   I will see what will happen to them.
They are evil people.
   They are unfaithful children.
21They used things that are not
      gods to make me jealous.
   They used worthless idols to make
      me angry.
So I will use those who are not a
      nation to make them jealous.
   I will use a nation that does not
      understand to make them
      angry.
22My anger has started a fire.
   It burns down to where the
      dead are.
It will burn up the ground and
      its crops.
   And it will set fire to the
      mountains.

23"I will pile troubles upon them.
   I will shoot my arrows at them.
24They will be starved and sick.
   They will be destroyed by terrible
      diseases.

I will send them vicious animals
   and gliding, poisonous snakes.
25In the streets the sword will
      kill.
   In their homes there will be terror.
Young men and women will die.
   So will babies and gray-haired
      men.
26I will scatter them as I said.
   And no one will remember them.
27But I didn't want their enemy
      to brag.
   Their enemy might
      misunderstand.
They might say, 'We have won!
   The Lord has done none of this.'"

28Israel has no sense.
   They do not understand.
29I wish they were wise and
      understood this.
   I wish they could see what will
      happen to them.
30One person cannot chase 1,000
      people.
   And 2 people cannot fight 10,000.
This only happens if the Lord has
      sold them.
   Their Rock would have to give
      them up.
31The rock of these people is not
      like our Rock.
   Our enemies agree to that.
32Their vine comes from Sodom.
   Their fields are like Gomorrah.
Their grapes are full of poison.
   Their bunches of grapes are bitter.
33Their wine is like snake poison,
   like the deadly poison of cobras.

34"I have been saving this.
   I have it locked in my
      storehouses.
35I will punish those who do
      wrong. I will repay them.
   Sometime their foot will slip.
Their day of trouble is near.
   And their punishment will come
      quickly."

36The Lord will defend his
      people.
   He will have mercy on his
      servants.

He will see that their strength
   is gone.
He will see that nobody is left,
   slaves or free.
37Then he will say, "Where are
   their gods?
Where is the rock they trusted?
38Who ate the fat from their
   sacrifices?
Who drank the wine of their drink
   offering?
Let those gods come to help you!
Let them protect you!

39"Now you will see that I am the
   one God!
There is no god but me.
I send life and death.
I can hurt, and I can heal.
No one can escape from me.
40I raise my hand toward heaven
   and make this promise:
As surely as I live forever,
41I will sharpen my flashing
   sword.
And I will take it in my hand
   to judge.
I will punish my enemies.
I will pay back those who hate me.
42My arrows will be covered with
   their blood.
My sword will eat their flesh.
The blood will flow from those who
   are killed and the captives.
The heads of the enemy leaders
   will be cut off."

43Be happy, nations, with his
   people.
He will repay you for the blood of
   his servants.
He will punish his enemies.
And he will remove the sin of his
   land and people.

44Moses came with Joshua son of
Nun. And they spoke all the words of
this song for the people to hear. 45When
Moses finished speaking these words
to all Israel, 46he said to them: "Pay
attention to all the words I have said to
you today. Command your children to
obey carefully everything in these
teachings. 47These should not be

unimportant words for you. They
mean life for you! By these words you
will live a long time in the land you are
crossing the Jordan River to own."

Moses Goes Up to Mount Nebo

48The Lord spoke to Moses again
that same day. He said, 49"Go up the
Abarim Mountains. Go to Mount Nebo
in the country of Moab. It is across
from Jericho. Look at the land of
Canaan. I am giving it to the Israelites
to own. 50You will die on that mountain
that you climb. This is how your
brother Aaron died on Mount Hor.
51You both sinned against me at the
waters of Meribah Kadesh. That is in
the Desert of Zin. You did not honor
me as holy there among the Israelites.
52So now you will only look at the land
from far away. You will not enter the
land I am giving the people of Israel."

Moses Blesses the People

33 Moses, the man of God, gave this
blessing to the Israelites before
he died. 2He said:

"The Lord came from Mount Sinai.
He rose like the sun from Edom.
He showed his greatness from
   Mount Paran.
He came with thousands of angels.
He came from the southern
   mountains.
3The Lord surely loves his
   people.
He takes care of all those who
   belong to him.
They bow down at his feet.
And they are taught by him.
4Moses gave us the teachings.
They belong to the people of
   Jacob.
5The Lord became king of Israel.
The leaders of the people gathered
   then.
The tribes*d* of Israel came
   together.

6"Let the people of Reuben live
   and not die.
But let the people be few."

⁷Moses said this about the people of Judah:
"Lord, listen to Judah's prayer.
  Bring them back to their people.
  They defend themselves with their hands.
  Help them fight their enemies!"

⁸Moses said this about the people of Levi:
"Lord, your Thummim and Urim[d] belong
  to Levi whom you love.
Lord, you tested him at Massah.
  You argued with him at the waters of Meribah.
⁹He said about his father and mother,
  'I don't care about them.'
He did not recognize his brothers.
  He did not know his children.
But he protected your word.
  And he guarded your agreement.
¹⁰He teaches your laws to the people of Jacob
  and your teachings to the people of Israel.
He burns incense[d] before you.
  And he makes whole burnt offerings on your altar.
¹¹Lord, make them strong.
  Be pleased with the work they do.
Defeat those who attack them.
  Don't let their enemies rise up again."

¹²Moses said this about the people of Benjamin:
"The Lord's loved ones will lie down in safety.
  The Lord protects them all day long.
  The ones the Lord loves rest with him."

¹³Moses said this about the people of Joseph:
"May the Lord bless their land with the best fruits.
  Send rain from heaven above.
  And bring the water from the springs below.
¹⁴Let the sun produce the best fruits.

Let each month bring its best fruits.
¹⁵Let the old mountains give the finest crops.
  And let the everlasting hills give the best fruits.
¹⁶Let the full earth give the best fruits.
  Let the Lord who lived in the burning bush be pleased.
May these blessings rest on the head of Joseph.
  May they rest on the forehead of the one who was separated from his brothers.
¹⁷Joseph has the majesty of a firstborn[d] bull.
  He is as strong as a wild ox.
He will stab other nations,
  even those nations far away.
These are the ten thousands of Ephraim.
  And these are the thousands of Manasseh."

¹⁸Moses said this about the people of Zebulun:
"Be happy when you go out, Zebulun.
  And be happy in your tents, Issachar.
¹⁹They will call the people to the mountain.
  And there they will offer the right sacrifices.
They will do well from all that is in the sea.
  And they will do well from the treasures hidden in the sand on the shore."

²⁰Moses said this about the people of Gad:
"Praise God who gives Gad more land!
  Gad lives there like a lion.
  He tears off arms and heads.
²¹They chose the best land for themselves.
  They received a large share, like that given to an officer.
When the leaders of the people gathered,

the people of Gad did what the
Lord said was right.
And they judged Israel fairly."

²²Moses said this about the people
of Dan:
"Dan is like a lion's cub,
who jumps out of Bashan."

²³Moses said this about the people
of Naphtali:
"Naphtali enjoys the Lord's special
kindnesses.
They are full of his blessings.
Their land goes south to Lake
Galilee."

²⁴Moses said this about the people
of Asher:
"Asher is the most blessed of the
sons.
He should be his brothers'
favorite.
Let him bathe his feet in olive oil.
²⁵Your gates will have locks of
iron and bronze.
You will be strong as long as you
live.

²⁶"There is no one like the God
of Israel.
He rides through the skies to
help you.
He rides on the clouds in his
majesty.
²⁷The everlasting God is your
place of safety.
His arms will hold you up forever.
He will force your enemy out ahead
of you.
He will say, 'Destroy the enemy!'
²⁸The people of Israel will lie
down in safety.
Jacob's spring is theirs alone.
Theirs is a land full of grain and
wine.
There the skies drop their dew.
²⁹Israel, you are blessed!
No one else is like you.
You are a people saved by
the Lord.
He is your shield and helper.

He is your glorious sword.
Your enemies will be afraid of you.
You will walk all over their holy
places."

Moses Dies

34 Then Moses climbed up Mount
Nebo. He went from the plains
of Moab to the top of Mount Pisgah. It
is across from Jericho. From there the
Lord showed him all the land. He could
see from Gilead to Dan. ²He could see
all of Naphtali and the lands of Ephraim
and Manasseh. He could see all the
land of Judah as far as the Mediterranean Sea. ³He could see the southern
desert and the whole Valley of Jericho
up to Zoar. Jericho is called the city of
palm trees. ⁴Then the Lord said to
Moses, "This is the land I promised to
Abraham, Isaac and Jacob. I said to
them, 'I will give this land to your
descendants.'ᵈ I have let you look at it,
Moses. But you will not cross over
there."

⁵Then Moses, the servant of the
Lord, died there in Moab. It was as the
Lord had said. ⁶The Lord buried
Moses in Moab in the valley opposite
Beth Peor. But even today no one
knows where his grave is. ⁷Moses was
120 years old when he died. His eyes
were not weak. And he was still strong.
⁸The Israelites cried for Moses for 30
days. They stayed in the plains of Moab
until the time of sadness was over.

⁹Joshua son of Nun was then filled
with wisdom. Moses had put his
hands on Joshua. So the Israelites listened to Joshua. And they did what
the Lord had commanded Moses.

¹⁰There has never been another
prophetᵈ like Moses. The Lord knew
Moses face to face. ¹¹The Lord sent
Moses to do signs and miraclesᵈ in
Egypt. He did them to the king, to all
his officers and to the whole land of
Egypt. ¹²Moses had great power. He
did wonderful things for all the
Israelites to see.

JOSHUA
Israel Conquers the Promised Land

God's Command to Joshua

1 Moses was the servant of the Lord. Joshua son of Nun was Moses' assistant. After Moses died, the Lord said to Joshua: ²"My servant Moses is dead. Now you and all these people go across the Jordan River. Go into the land I am giving to the people of Israel. ³I promised Moses I would give you this land. So I will give you every place you go in the land. ⁴All the land from the desert in the south to Lebanon in the north will be yours. All the land from the great river, the Euphrates, in the east, to the Mediterranean Sea in the west will be yours. This includes the land of the Hittites. ⁵Just as I was with Moses, so I will be with you. No one will be able to stop you all your life. I will not leave you. I will never leave you alone.

⁶"Joshua, be strong and brave! You must lead these people so they can take their land. This is the land I promised their fathers I would give them. ⁷Be strong and brave. Be sure to obey all the teachings my servant Moses gave you. If you follow them exactly, you will be successful in everything you do. ⁸Always remember what is written in the Book of the Teachings. Study it day and night. Then you will be sure to obey everything that is written there. If you do this, you will be wise and successful in everything. ⁹Remember that I commanded you to be strong and brave. So don't be afraid. The Lord your God will be with you everywhere you go."

Heroes Who Trusted God
JOSHUA • JOSHUA 1:6-11

Joshua had a big job to do. Moses, Israel's leader, was going to die soon, and Joshua was going to be the next leader. Joshua would lead the people into the land that God had promised them. But the people would have to fight the evil people of the land first.

Joshua may have been a little afraid because there were two million people in Israel. That was a lot of people to lead. But God told Joshua that if he continued to obey, he would always be successful.

You may not become a president or leader of a nation, but you will have lots of important jobs in life. God wants you to stay close to him and do what he says. He will help you to be successful too!

To learn about a woman who trusted God and helped some spies, *fly to page 258.*

Joshua's Orders to the People

[10]So Joshua gave orders to the officers of the people. He said, [11]"Go through the camp and tell the people, 'Get your supplies ready. Three days from now you will cross the Jordan River. You will go and take the land the Lord your God is giving you.'"

Remember that I commanded you to be strong and brave. So don't be afraid. The Lord your God will be with you everywhere you go.
• Joshua 1:9

---

[12]Then Joshua spoke to the people of Reuben, Gad and the eastern half-tribe[d] of Manasseh. Joshua said, [13]"Remember what Moses, the servant of the Lord, told you. He said the Lord your God would give you rest. And he said the Lord would give you this land. [14]Now the Lord has given you this land east of the Jordan River. Your wives, your children and your animals may stay here. But your fighting men

"**D**o you play at being brave? Joshua had to be brave even though he was quite young. Read some of his story in Joshua 1:1-18."

must dress for war and cross the Jordan River ahead of your brothers. You must help your brothers. [15]The Lord has given you a place to rest. He will do the same for your brothers. But you must help them until they take the land. This is the land the Lord their God is giving them. Then you may return to your own land east of the Jordan River. That is the land that Moses, the servant of the Lord, gave you."

[16]Then the people answered Joshua, "Anything you command us to do, we will do. Any place you send us, we will go. [17]Just as we fully obeyed Moses, we will obey you. We ask only that the Lord your God be with you just as he was with Moses. [18]Then, if anyone refuses to obey your commands or turns against you, he will be put to death. Just be strong and brave!"

Spies Sent to Jericho

2 Joshua son of Nun secretly sent out two spies from Acacia. Joshua said to them, "Go and look at the land. Look closely at the city of Jericho."

So the men went to Jericho. They went to the house of a prostitute[d] and stayed there. This woman's name was Rahab.

[2]Someone told the king of Jericho, "Some men from Israel have come here tonight. They are spying out the land."

[3]So the king of Jericho sent this message to Rahab: "Bring out the men who came to you and entered your house. They have come to spy out our whole land."

[4]Now the woman had hidden the two men. She said, "They did come here. But I didn't know where they came from. [5]In the evening, when it was time to close the city gate, they left. I don't know where they went. Go quickly. Maybe you can catch them." [6](But the woman had taken the men up to the roof.[n] She had hidden them there under stalks of flax.[d] She had spread the flax out there to dry.) [7]So the king's men went out looking for the spies from Israel. They went to the places where people cross the Jordan River. The city gate was closed just after the king's men left the city.

[8]The spies were ready to sleep for the night. So Rahab went to the roof and talked to them. [9]She said, "I know

---

[n]**roof** In Bible times houses were built with flat roofs. The roof was used for drying things such as flax and fruit. And it was used as an extra room, as a place for worship and as a place to sleep in the summer.

the Lord has given this land to your people. You frighten us very much. Everyone living in this land is terribly afraid of you. ¹⁰We are afraid because we have heard how the Lord helped you. We heard how he dried up the Red Sea*d* when you came out of Egypt. We heard how you destroyed Sihon and Og. They were the two Amorite kings who lived east of the Jordan. ¹¹When we heard this, we became very frightened. Now our men are afraid to fight you.

the Lord gives us our land, we will be kind to you. You may trust us."

¹⁵The house Rahab lived in was built on the city wall. So she used a rope to let the men down through a window. ¹⁶She said to them, "Go into the hills. The king's men will not find you there. Hide there for three days. After the king's men return, you may go on your way."

¹⁷The men said to her, "You must do as we say. If not, we cannot be responsible for keeping our promise. ¹⁸You are using a red rope to help us escape. When we return to this land, you must

Heroes Who Trusted God
RAHAB • JOSHUA 2:8-15

Did you know that one time a woman saved the lives of some spies from Israel? Rahab lived in Jericho. Like most cities in ancient times, Jericho had a high, thick stone wall around it. The wall kept the city safe from armies that might want to fight against it.

Rahab's house had a window on the city wall, so when Israel's spies needed to get out of Jericho at night without being seen, they went down a rope out her window. Rahab did this because she wanted to learn more about the true God. Later, when the Israelites conquered Jericho, they kept Rahab and her family safe.

God took care of Rahab because she did what was right. God always wants us to do what is right and to trust him to take care of us.

To learn about a woman who trusted God to help her lead an army, fly to page 291.

This is because the Lord your God rules the heavens above and the earth below! ¹²So now, make me a promise before the Lord. Promise that you will show kindness to my family just as I showed you kindness. Give me some proof that you will do this. ¹³Promise me you will allow my family to live. Save my father, mother, brothers, sisters and all of their families from death."

¹⁴The men agreed. They said, "We will trade our lives for your lives. Don't tell anyone what we are doing. When

tie it in the window through which you let us down. Bring your father, mother, brothers and all your family into your house. ¹⁹We can keep everyone safe who stays in this house. If anyone in your house is hurt, we will be responsible. If anyone goes out of your house and is killed, it is his own fault. We cannot be responsible for him. ²⁰But you must not tell anyone about this agreement. If you do, we are free from it."

²¹Rahab answered, "I agree to this." So she sent them away, and they left.

Then she tied the red rope in the window.

²²The men left and went into the hills. There they stayed for three days. The king's men looked for them all along the road. But after three days, the king's men returned to the city without finding them. ²³Then the two men started back to Joshua. They left the hills and crossed the river. They went to Joshua son of Nun and told him everything that had happened to them. ²⁴They said to Joshua, "The Lord surely has given us all of the land. All the people in that land are terribly afraid of us."

Crossing the Jordan

3 Early the next morning Joshua and all the people of Israel left Acacia. They traveled to the Jordan River and camped there before crossing it. ²After three days the officers went through the camp. ³They gave orders to the people. They said, "You will see the priests and Levites carrying the Box*ᵈ* of the Agreement with the Lord your God. Then you should leave where you are and follow it. ⁴That way you will know which way to go. You have never traveled this way before. But do not follow too closely. Stay about a thousand yards behind the Box of the Agreement."

⁵Then Joshua told the people, "Make yourselves holy for the Lord. Tomorrow the Lord will do amazing things among you."

⁶Joshua said to the priests, "Take the Box of the Agreement. Cross over the river ahead of the people." So the priests lifted the Holy Box and carried it ahead of the people.

⁷Then the Lord said to Joshua, "Today I will begin to make you a great man to all the Israelites. So the people will know I am with you just as I was with Moses. ⁸The priests will carry the Box of the Agreement. Tell them this: 'Go to the edge of the Jordan River and stand in the water.'"

⁹Then Joshua said to the people of Israel, "Come here. Listen to the words of the Lord your God. ¹⁰Here is proof that the living God is with you. Here is proof that he will drive out the Canaanites, Hittites, Hivites, Perizzites, Girgashites, Amorites and the Jebusites. ¹¹This is the proof: The Box of the Agreement will go ahead of you into the Jordan River. It is the Agreement with

People Who Depended on God

JOSHUA • JOSHUA 3:5-17

Joshua did what God told him to do. God told Joshua to lead the people into the Promised Land of Canaan. But there was a problem. The entire nation (about two million people) had to cross over the Jordan River. The Jordan River was wide and deep. There were no bridges, and the people couldn't swim with all their children, animals, and baggage. But that didn't stop Joshua. Instead, he trusted that somehow God would help the nation cross the river. Sure enough, just as God had parted the waters of the Red Sea, he also parted the waters of the Jordan River.

Do what God tells you to do and trust him to help you get it done. He might even do a miracle!

To read about someone who depended on God with the impossible, *fly to page 471.*

the Lord of the whole world. 12Now choose 12 men from among you. Choose 1 from each of the 12 tribes*d* of Israel. 13The priests will carry the Holy Box of the Lord, the Master of the whole world. They will carry it into the Jordan ahead of you. When they enter the water, the river will stop flowing. The water will be stopped. It will stand up in a heap as if a dam were there."

14So the priests carried the Box of the Agreement. And the people left the place where they had camped. Then they started across the Jordan River. 15During harvest the Jordan is flooded. So the river was at its fullest. The priests who were carrying the Holy Box came to the edge of the river. And they stepped into the water. 16Just at that moment, the water stopped flowing. It stood up in a heap a great distance away at Adam. This is a town near Zarethan. The water flowing down to the Sea of Arabah (the Dead Sea*d*) was completely cut off. So the people crossed the river near Jericho. 17The ground there became dry. The priests carried the Box of the Agreement with the Lord to the middle of the river and stopped. They waited there while all the people of Israel walked across. They crossed the Jordan River on dry land.

Rocks to Remind the People

4 All the people finished crossing the Jordan. Then the Lord said to Joshua, 2"Choose 12 men from among the people. Choose 1 from each tribe.*d* 3Tell the men to get 12 large rocks from the middle of the river. Take them from where the priests stood. Carry the rocks and put them down where you stay tonight."

4So Joshua chose 1 man from each tribe. Then he called the 12 men together. 5He said to them, "Go out into the river where the Holy Box*d* of the Lord your God is. Each of you should find 1 large rock. There will be 1 rock for each tribe of Israel. Carry the rock on your

you. In the future your children will ask you, 'What do these rocks mean?' 7Tell them the Lord stopped the water from flowing in the Jordan. When the Holy Box of the Agreement with the Lord crossed the river, the water was stopped. These rocks will help the Israelites remember this forever."

8So the Israelites obeyed Joshua. They carried 12 rocks from the middle of the Jordan River. There was 1 rock for each of the 12 tribes of Israel. They did this the way the Lord had commanded Joshua. They carried the rocks with them. And they put them down where they made their camp. 9Joshua also put 12 rocks in the middle of the Jordan River. He put them where the priests had stood while carrying the Holy Box of the Lord. These rocks are still there today.

10The Lord had commanded Joshua to tell the people what to do. It was what Moses had said Joshua must do. So the priests carrying the Holy Box continued standing in the middle of the river until everything was done. And the people hurried across the river. 11The people finished crossing the river. Then the priests carried the Holy Box of the Lord to the other side. As they carried it, the people watched. 12The men from the tribes of Reuben, Gad and the eastern half-tribe of Manasseh obeyed what Moses had told them. They were prepared for war. So they crossed the river ahead of the other people. 13About 40,000 soldiers were prepared for war. They passed before the Lord as they marched across the river. Then they went toward the plains of Jericho to go to war.

14That day the Lord made Joshua a great man to all the Israelites. They respected Joshua all his life, just as they had respected Moses.

15Then the Lord spoke to Joshua. 16He said, "Command the priests to bring the Box of the Agreement out of the river."

17So Joshua commanded the priests, "Come up out of the Jordan."

[18]So the priests carried the Box of the Agreement with the Lord out of the river. As soon as their feet touched dry land, the water began flowing again. The river again overflowed its banks. It was just as it had been before they crossed.

[19]The people crossed the Jordan on the tenth day of the first month. They camped at Gilgal, east of Jericho. [20]They carried with them the 12 rocks taken from the Jordan. And Joshua set them up at Gilgal. [21]Then he spoke to the Israelites. He said, "In the future your children will ask you, 'What do these rocks mean?' [22]Tell them, 'Israel crossed the Jordan River on dry land. [23]The Lord your God caused the water to stop flowing. The river was dry until the people finished crossing it. The Lord did the same thing for us at the Jordan that he did for the people at the Red Sea.[d] Remember that he stopped the water at the Red Sea so we could cross. [24]The Lord did this so all people would know he has great power. Then they will always respect the Lord your God.'"

5 So the Lord dried up the Jordan River until the Israelites had crossed it. Now all the kings of the Amorites west of the Jordan heard about it. And the Canaanite kings living by the Mediterranean Sea heard about it. They were very scared. After that they were too afraid to face the Israelites.

The Israelites Are Circumcised

[2]At that time the Lord spoke to Joshua. He said, "Make knives from flint stones. Circumcise[d] the Israelites again." [3]So Joshua made knives from flint stones. Then he circumcised the Israelites at Gibeath Haaraloth.

[4]This is why Joshua circumcised the men: After the Israelites left Egypt, all the men old enough to serve in the army died. They died in the desert on the way out of Egypt. [5]The men who had come out of Egypt had been circumcised. But many were born in the desert on the trip from Egypt. They had not been circumcised. [6]The Israelites had moved about in the desert for 40 years. During that time all the fighting men who had left Egypt had died. This was because they had not obeyed the Lord. So the Lord swore they would not see the land. This was the land he had promised their ancestors to give them. It was a land where much food grows. [7]So their sons took their places. But none of the sons born on the trip from Egypt had been circumcised. So Joshua circumcised them. [8]After all the Israelites had been circumcised, they stayed in camp until they were healed.

[9]Then the Lord said to Joshua, "As slaves in Egypt you were ashamed. But today I have removed that shame." So Joshua named that place Gilgal. And it is still named Gilgal today.

[10]The people of Israel were still camped at Gilgal on the plains of Jericho. It was there, on the evening of the fourteenth day of the month, they celebrated the Passover[d] Feast. [11]The next day after the Passover, the people ate some of the food grown on that land: bread made without yeast and roasted grain. [12]The day they ate this food, the manna[d] stopped coming. The Israelites no longer got the manna from heaven. They ate the food grown in the land of Canaan that year.

[13]Joshua was near Jericho. He looked up and saw a man standing in front of him. The man had a sword in his hand. Joshua went to him and asked, "Are you a friend or an enemy?"

[14]The man answered, "I am neither one. I have come as the commander of the Lord's army."

Then Joshua bowed facedown on the ground. He asked, "Does my master have a command for me, his servant?"

[15]The commander of the Lord's army answered, "Take off your sandals. The place where you are standing is holy." So Joshua did.

The Fall of Jericho

6 Now the people of Jericho were afraid because the Israelites were near. So they closed the city gates and guarded them. No one went into the city. And no one came out.

²Then the Lord spoke to Joshua. He said, "Look, I have given you Jericho, its king and all its fighting men. ³March around the city with your army one time every day. Do this for six days. ⁴Have seven priests carry trumpets made from horns of male sheep. Tell them to march in front of the Holy Box.ᵈ On the seventh day march around the city seven times. On that day tell the priests to blow the trumpets as they march. ⁵They will make one long blast on the trumpets. When you hear that sound, have all the people give a loud shout. Then the walls of the city will fall. And the people will go straight into the city."

⁶So Joshua son of Nun called the priests together. He said to them, "Carry the Box of the Agreement with the Lord. Tell seven priests to carry trumpets and march in front of it." ⁷Then Joshua ordered the people, "Now go! March around the city. The soldiers with weapons should march in front of the Box of the Agreement with the Lord."

⁸So Joshua finished speaking to the people. Then the seven priests began marching before the Lord. They carried the seven trumpets and blew them as they marched. The priests carrying the Box of the Agreement with the Lord followed them. ⁹The soldiers with weapons marched in front of the priests. And armed men walked behind the Holy Box. They were blowing their trumpets. ¹⁰But Joshua had told the people not to give a war cry. He said, "Don't shout. Don't say a word until the day I tell you. Then shout!" ¹¹So Joshua had the Holy Box of the Lord carried around the city one time. Then they went back to camp for the night.

¹²Early the next morning Joshua got up. And the priests carried the Holy Box of the Lord again. ¹³The seven priests carried the seven trumpets. They marched in front of the Holy Box of the Lord, blowing their trumpets. The soldiers with weapons marched in front of them. Other soldiers walked behind the Holy Box of the Lord. All this time the priests were blowing their trumpets. ¹⁴So on the second day they marched around the city one time. Then they went back to camp. They did this every day for six days.

¹⁵On the seventh day they got up at dawn. They marched around the city seven times. They marched just as they had on the days before. But on that day they marched around the city seven times. ¹⁶The seventh time around the priests blew their trumpets. Then Joshua gave the command: "Now, shout! The Lord has given you this city! ¹⁷The city and everything in it are to be destroyed as an offering to the Lord. Only Rahab the prostituteᵈ and everyone in her house should remain alive. They must not be killed. This is because Rahab hid the two spies we sent out. ¹⁸Don't take any of the things that are to be destroyed as an offering to the Lord. If you take them and bring them into our camp, then you yourselves will be destroyed. You will also bring trouble to all of Israel. ¹⁹All the silver and gold and things made from bronze and iron belong to the Lord. They must be saved for him."

²⁰When the priests blew the trumpets, the people shouted. At the sound of the trumpets and the people's shout, the walls fell. And everyone ran straight into the city. So the Israelites defeated that city. ²¹They completely destroyed every living thing in the city. They killed men and women, young and old. They killed cattle, sheep and donkeys.

²²Joshua spoke to the two men who had spied out the land. Joshua said, "Go into the prostitute's house. Bring her out. And bring out all the people who are with her. Do this because of the promise you made to her." ²³So the two men went into the house and brought

263

out Rahab. They also brought out her father, mother, brothers and all those with her. They put all of her family in a safe place outside the camp of Israel.

²⁴Then Israel burned the whole city and everything in it. But they did not burn the things made from silver, gold, bronze and iron. These were saved for the Lord. ²⁵Joshua saved Rahab the prostitute, her family and all who were with her. He let them live. This was

"**A** storm made our club house look pretty bad. Maybe Jericho looked like that." Read about it in Joshua 6:1-23.

because Rahab had helped the men he had sent to spy out Jericho. Rahab still lives among the Israelites today.

²⁶Then Joshua made this important promise. He said:
"Anyone who tries to rebuild this
 city of Jericho
will be punished by a curse from
 the Lord.
The man who lays the foundation of
 this city
will lose his oldest son.
The man who sets up the gates
will lose his youngest son."

²⁷So the Lord was with Joshua. And Joshua became famous through all the land.

The Sin of Achan

7 But the people of Israel did not obey the Lord. There was a man from the tribe^d of Judah named Achan. (He was the son of Carmi and grandson of Zimri. And Zimri was the son of Zerah.) Achan kept some of the things that were to be given to the Lord. So the Lord became very angry at the Israelites.

²Joshua sent some men from Jericho to Ai. (Ai was near Beth Aven, east of Bethel.) He told them, "Go to Ai and spy out the area." So the men went to spy on Ai.

³Later they came back to Joshua. They said, "There are only a few men in Ai to fight against us. So we will not need all our people to defeat them. Send 2,000 or 3,000 men to fight there. There is no need to send all of our people." ⁴So about 3,000 men went to Ai. But the people of Ai beat them badly. ⁵The people of Ai chased the Israelites. They chased them from the city gate all the way to where stones were cut from the ground. They killed about 36 Israelites as they went down the hill. When the Israelites saw this, they became very afraid.

⁶Then Joshua tore his clothes to show how upset he was. He bowed facedown on the ground before the Box^d of the Lord. And he stayed there until evening. The leaders of Israel did the same thing. They also threw dirt on their heads to show they were upset. ⁷Then Joshua said, "Lord God, you brought our people across the Jordan River. Why did you bring us this far and then let the Amorites destroy us? We should have been happy to stay on the other side of the Jordan. ⁸Lord, there is nothing I can say now. Israel has been beaten by the enemy. ⁹The Canaanites and all the other people in this country will hear about this. They will surround and kill all of us! Then what will you do for your own great name?"

¹⁰The Lord said to Joshua, "Stand up! Why are you down on your face? ¹¹The Israelites have sinned. They have broken the agreement I commanded them to obey. They took some of the things I commanded them to destroy. They have stolen from me. They have lied. They have taken those things for themselves. ¹²That is why the Israelites cannot face their enemies. They turn away from the fight and run. I have commanded that they be destroyed. You must destroy everything I commanded you to destroy. I will not

help you anymore unless you do this. [13]"Now go! Have the people make themselves holy for me. Tell them, 'Set yourselves apart to the Lord for tomorrow. The Lord, the God of Israel, says some of you are keeping things he commanded you to destroy. You will never defeat your enemies until you throw away these things.

[14]"'Tomorrow morning you must all stand before the Lord. All the tribes will stand before him. The Lord will choose one tribe. And that tribe must stand alone before him. Then the Lord will choose one family group from that tribe. And that family group must stand alone before him. Then the Lord will choose one family from that family group. And it must stand alone before him. Then the Lord will look at that family man by man. [15]The man who is keeping what should have been destroyed will himself be destroyed by fire. And everything he owns will be destroyed with him. He has broken the agreement with the Lord. He has done a disgraceful thing among the people of Israel!'"

[16]Early the next morning Joshua led all of Israel before the Lord. All of the tribes stood before him. And the Lord chose the tribe of Judah. [17]So all the family groups of Judah stood before the Lord. The Lord then chose the family group of Zerah. And all the families of Zerah stood before the Lord. Then the family of Zimri was chosen. [18]And Joshua told all the men in that family to come before the Lord. The Lord chose Achan son of Carmi. (Carmi was the son of Zimri. And Zimri was the son of Zerah.)

[19]Then Joshua said to Achan, "My son, you should tell the truth. Confess to the Lord, the God of Israel. Tell me what you did. Don't try to hide anything from me."

[20]Achan answered, "It is true! I have sinned against the Lord, the God of Israel. This is what I did: [21]Among the things I saw was a beautiful coat from Babylonia. And I saw about five pounds of silver and more than one and one-

quarter pounds of gold. I wanted these things very much for myself. So I took them. You will find them buried in the ground under my tent. The silver is under the coat."

[22]So Joshua sent some men to the tent. They ran to the tent and found the things hidden there. The silver was under the coat. [23]The men brought them out of the tent. Then they took them to Joshua and all the Israelites. They spread them out on the ground before the Lord. [24]Then Joshua and all the people led Achan son of Zerah to the Valley of Trouble. They also took the silver, the coat and the gold. They took Achan's sons, daughters, cattle, donkeys, sheep, tent and everything he owned. [25]Joshua said, "I don't know why you caused so much trouble for us. But now the Lord will bring trouble to you." Then all the people threw stones at Achan until he died. They also killed his family with stones. Then the people burned them. [26]They piled rocks over Achan's body. And those rocks are still there today. That is why it is called the Valley of Trouble. After this the Lord was no longer angry.

Ai Is Destroyed

8 Then the Lord said to Joshua, "Don't be afraid. Don't give up. Lead all your fighting men to Ai. I will help you defeat the king of Ai. I am giving you his people, his city and his land. [2]You will do to Ai and its king what you did to Jericho and its king. Only this time you may take all the wealth. You may keep it for yourselves. Now tell some of your soldiers to set up an ambush behind the city."

[3]So Joshua led his whole army toward Ai. Then he chose 30,000 of his best fighting men. He sent these men out at night. [4]Joshua gave them these orders: "Listen carefully. You must set up an ambush behind the city. Don't go far from it. Continue to watch and be ready. [5]I and the men who are with me will march toward the city. The men in the city will come out to fight us. Then

we will turn and run away from them as we did before. ⁶They will chase us away from the city. They will think we are running away from them as we did before. When we run away, ⁷come out from your ambush and take the city. The Lord your God will give you the power to win. ⁸After you take the city, burn it. See to it! You have your orders."

⁹Then Joshua sent them to their place of ambush to wait. They went to a place between Bethel and Ai, to the west of Ai. But Joshua stayed the night with his people.

¹⁰Early the next morning Joshua gathered his men together. He and the older leaders of Israel led them to Ai. ¹¹All of the soldiers who were with Joshua marched to Ai. They stopped in front of the city and made camp north of Ai. There was a valley between them and the city. ¹²Then Joshua chose about 5,000 men. He set them in ambush in the area west of the city between Bethel and Ai. ¹³So the people took their positions. The main camp was north of the city. The other men were hiding to the west. That night Joshua went down into the valley.

¹⁴Now the king of Ai saw the army of Israel. So he and his people got up early the next morning and hurried out to fight them. They went out to a place east of the city. The king did not know soldiers were waiting in ambush behind the city. ¹⁵Joshua and all the men of Israel let the army of Ai push them back. Then they ran east toward the desert. ¹⁶The men in Ai were called to chase Joshua and his men. So they left the city and went after them. ¹⁷All the men of Ai and Bethel chased the army of Israel. The city was left open. Not a man stayed to protect it.

¹⁸Then the Lord said to Joshua, "Hold your spear toward Ai. I will give you that city." So Joshua held his spear toward the city of Ai. ¹⁹The men of Israel who were in ambush saw this. They quickly came out of their hiding place and hurried toward the city. They entered the city and took control of it.

Then they quickly set it on fire.

²⁰When the men of Ai looked back, they saw smoke rising from their city. At the same time the men of Israel stopped running. They turned against the men of Ai. The men of Ai could not escape in any direction. ²¹Joshua and all his men saw that the army had taken control of the city. They saw the smoke rising from it. So they stopped running and turned to fight the men of Ai. ²²The men who were in ambush also came out of the city to help with the fight. The men of Ai were caught between the armies of Israel. The Israelites fought until not one of the men of Ai was left alive. None of the enemy escaped. ²³But the king of Ai was left alive. And Joshua's men brought him to Joshua.

A Review of the Fighting

²⁴During the fighting the army of Israel chased the men of Ai into the fields and desert. So the Israelites killed all of them in the fields and desert. Then they went back to Ai and killed everyone there. ²⁵All the people of Ai died that day, 12,000 men and women. ²⁶Joshua had held his spear toward Ai. It was a sign to his people to destroy the city. And Joshua held out his spear until all the people of Ai were destroyed. ²⁷The people of Israel kept the animals for themselves. They also kept the other things the people of Ai had owned. This is what the Lord told them to do when he gave Joshua the commands.

²⁸Then Joshua burned the city of Ai. It became an empty pile of ruins. And it is still like that today. ²⁹Joshua hung the king of Ai on a tree. He left him hanging there until evening. At sunset Joshua told his men to take the king's body down from the tree. He told them to throw it down at the city gate. Then they covered it with rocks. That pile of rocks is still there today.

³⁰Then Joshua built an altar for the Lord, the God of Israel. He built it on Mount Ebal, as ³¹Moses, the Lord's servant, had commanded. Joshua built the

altar as it was explained in the Book of the Teachings of Moses. The altar was made from stones that were not cut. No tool was ever used on them. The Israelites offered burnt offerings to the Lord on that altar. They also offered fellowship offerings. ³²There Joshua wrote the teachings of Moses on stones. He did this for all the people of Israel to see. ³³The older leaders, officers, judges and all the Israelites were there. They were standing around the Box*d* of the Agreement with the Lord. They stood before the priests, the Levites who had carried the Holy Box. Israelites and non-Israelites were all standing there. Half of the people stood in front of Mount Ebal. The other half stood in front of Mount Gerizim. This was the way the Lord's servant Moses had earlier commanded the people to be blessed.

³⁴Then Joshua read all the words of the teachings. He read the blessings and the curses. He read it exactly as they were written in the Book of the Teachings. ³⁵All the Israelites were gathered together. All the women and children were there. All the non-Israelites living with the Israelites were there. Joshua read every command that Moses had given.

The Gibeonite Trickery

9 All the kings west of the Jordan River heard about these things. These were the kings of the Hittites, Amorites, Canaanites, Perizzites, Hivites and Jebusites. They lived in the mountains and on the western mountain slopes. They also lived along the whole Mediterranean Sea coast. ²All these kings gathered to fight Joshua and the Israelites.

³The people of Gibeon heard how Joshua had defeated Jericho and Ai. ⁴So they decided to trick the Israelites. They gathered old leather wine bags that were cracked and mended. They put them on the backs of their donkeys. They also put old sacks on their

their feet and wore old clothes. They took some dry, moldy bread. ⁶Then they went to Joshua in the camp near Gilgal.

The men spoke to Joshua and the men of Israel. They said, "We have traveled from a faraway country. Make a peace agreement with us."

⁷The men of Israel said to these Hivites, "Maybe you live near us. How can we make a peace agreement with you?"

⁸The Hivites said to Joshua, "We are your servants."

But Joshua asked, "Who are you? Where do you come from?"

⁹The men answered, "We are your servants. We have come from a far country. We came because we heard of the fame of the Lord your God. We heard about what he has done. We heard about everything he did in Egypt. ¹⁰We heard that he defeated the two kings of the Amorites. They were from the east side of the Jordan River: Sihon king of Heshbon and Og king of Bashan who was king in Ashtaroth. ¹¹So our older leaders and our people spoke to us. They said, 'Take food for your journey. Go and meet the Israelites. Tell them, "We are your servants. Make a peace agreement with us."'

¹²"Look at our bread. When we left home it was warm and fresh. But now it is dry and moldy. ¹³Look at our leather winebags. When we left home they were new and filled with wine. Now they are cracked and old. Look at our clothes and sandals. The long journey has almost destroyed them."

¹⁴The men of Israel tasted the bread. But they did not ask the Lord what to do. ¹⁵So Joshua agreed to make peace with the Gibeonites. He agreed to let them live. The leaders of the Israelites made a promise to keep the agreement.

¹⁶Three days later the Israelites learned that the Gibeonites lived nearby. ¹⁷So the Israelites went to where they lived. On the third day the Israel-

ites came to their cities. The cities were Gibeon, Kephirah, Beeroth and Kiriath Jearim. 18But the Israelites did not attack those cities. They had made a promise to them before the Lord, the God of Israel.

All the Israelites grumbled against the leaders who had made the agreement. 19But the leaders answered, "We have given our promise before the Lord, the God of Israel. We cannot attack them now. 20This is what we must do. We must let them live. We cannot hurt them, or God's anger will be against us. We would be breaking the promise we made to them. 21So let them live. But they will cut wood and carry water for our people." So the leaders kept their promise of peace to them.

22Joshua called for the Gibeonites. He said, "Why did you lie to us? Your land was near our camp. But you told us you were from a far country. 23Now, you will be placed under a curse. You will be our slaves. You will have to cut wood and carry water for the people of the house of God."

24The Gibeonites answered Joshua, "We lied to you because we were afraid you would kill us. We heard that God commanded his servant Moses to give you all of this land. And God told you to kill all the people who lived in the land. That is why we did this. 25Now you can decide what to do with us. You can do anything to us that you think is right."

26So Joshua saved their lives. He did not allow the Israelites to kill them. 27But Joshua made the Gibeonites slaves to the Israelites. They cut wood and carried water for the Israelites. And they did it for the altar of the Lord—wherever he chose it to be. They are still doing this today.

The Sun Stands Still

10 At this time Adoni-Zedek was the king of Jerusalem. He heard that Joshua had defeated Ai and completely destroyed it. He learned that Joshua had done the same thing to Jericho and its king. The king also learned that the Gibeonites had made a peace agreement with Israel. And they lived very near Jerusalem. 2So Adoni-Zedek and his people were very afraid because of this.

Amazing Events That Showed God's Power

JOSHUA 10:12-14

Did you ever wish that the sun wouldn't go down so you could stay up longer and play?

Once a man did pray for the sun to stay up. Joshua, Israel's leader, prayed that the sun would stay up so the Israelites could finish their battle. Five kings combined their armies to fight against Israel. But God had promised their land to Israel. He told the Israelites to fight all the evil people and take the land. Although Israel was outnumbered against these armies, God gave the Israelites the victory.

Do you ever feel like you're facing a problem that is too big for you? Remember that God is on your side. He controls the sun, and he can help you with your problem.

To read about an amazing form of transportation, fly to page 442.

Gibeon was not a little town like Ai. It was a large city. It was as big as a city that had a king. All its men were good fighters. ³So Adoni-Zedek king of Jerusalem sent a message to Hoham king of Hebron. He also sent it to Piram king of Jarmuth, Japhia king of Lachish, and Debir king of Eglon. The king of Jerusalem begged these men, ⁴"Come with me and help me attack Gibeon. Gibeon has made a peace agreement with Joshua and the Israelites."

⁵Then these five Amorite kings joined their armies. They were the kings of Jerusalem, Hebron, Jarmuth, Lachish and Eglon. These armies went to Gibeon, surrounded it and attacked it.

⁶The Gibeonites sent a message to Joshua in his camp at Gilgal. The message said: "We are your servants. Don't let us be destroyed. Come quickly and help us! Save us! All the Amorite kings from the mountains have joined their armies. They are fighting against us."

⁷So Joshua marched out of Gilgal with his whole army. His best fighting men were with him. ⁸The Lord said to Joshua, "Don't be afraid of those armies. I will allow you to defeat them. None of them will be able to defeat you."

⁹Joshua and his army marched all night to Gibeon. So Joshua surprised them when he attacked. ¹⁰The Lord confused those armies when Israel attacked. So Israel defeated them in a great victory. They chased them from Gibeon on the road going to Beth Horon. The army of Israel killed men all the way to Azekah and Makkedah. ¹¹They chased the enemy down the road from Beth Horon to Azekah. While they were chasing them, the Lord threw large hailstones on them from the sky. Many of the enemy were killed by the hailstones. More men were killed by the hailstones than the Israelites killed with their swords.

¹²That day the Lord allowed the Israelites to defeat the Amorites. And that day Joshua stood before all the people of Israel and said to the Lord: "Sun, stand still over Gibeon.

Moon, stand still over the Valley of Aijalon."

¹³So the sun stood still.
And the moon stopped
until the people defeated their
enemies.

These words are written in the Book of Jashar.

The sun stopped in the middle of the sky. It waited to go down for a full day. ¹⁴That has never happened at any time before that day or since. That was the day the Lord listened to a man. Truly the Lord was fighting for Israel!

¹⁵After this, Joshua and his army went back to the camp at Gilgal.

¹⁶During the fight the five kings ran away. They hid in a cave near Makkedah. ¹⁷But someone found them hiding in the cave and told Joshua. ¹⁸So he said, "Cover the opening to the cave with large rocks. Put some men there to guard it. ¹⁹But don't stay there yourselves. Continue chasing the enemy. Continue attacking them from behind. Don't let them get to their cities safely. The Lord your God has given you the victory over them."

²⁰So Joshua and the Israelites killed the enemy. But a few were able to get back to their strong, walled cities. ²¹After the fighting, Joshua's men came back safely to him at Makkedah. No one was brave enough to say a word against the Israelites.

²²Joshua said, "Move the rocks that are covering the opening to the cave. Bring those five kings out to me." ²³So Joshua's men brought the five kings out of the cave. They were the kings of Jerusalem, Hebron, Jarmuth, Lachish and Eglon. ²⁴They brought the five kings out to Joshua. He called all his men to come to that place. He said to the commanders of his army, "Come here! Put your feet on the necks of these kings." So they came close and put their feet on their necks.

²⁵Then Joshua said to his men, "Be strong and brave! Don't be afraid. I will show you what the Lord will do to the enemies you will fight in the future." ²⁶Then Joshua killed the five kings. He hung their bodies on five trees. And he left them hanging on the trees until evening.

²⁷At sunset Joshua told his men to take the bodies down from the trees. Then they threw their bodies into the same cave where they had been hiding. They covered the opening to the cave with large rocks. They are still there today.

²⁸That day Joshua defeated Makkedah. He killed the king and completely destroyed all the people in that city. He killed them as an offering to the Lord. There was no one left alive. He did the same thing to the king of Makkedah as he had done to the king of Jericho.

Defeating Southern Cities

²⁹Then Joshua and all the Israelites traveled from Makkedah. They went to Libnah and attacked it. ³⁰The Lord allowed them to defeat it and its king. They killed every person in the city. No one was left alive. And they did the same thing to that king as they had done to the king of Jericho.

³¹Then Joshua and all the Israelites left Libnah and went to Lachish. They camped around Lachish and attacked it. ³²The Lord allowed them to defeat Lachish. On the second day Joshua defeated it. The Israelites killed everyone in that city. This was the same thing they had done to Libnah. ³³During this same time Horam king of Gezer came to help Lachish. But Joshua also defeated him and his army. There was no one left alive.

³⁴Then Joshua and all the Israelites went from Lachish to Eglon. They camped around Eglon and attacked it. ³⁵That day they captured Eglon. They killed all its people and completely destroyed everything in it as an offering to the Lord. This is the same thing they had done to Lachish.

³⁶Then Joshua and the Israelites went from Eglon to Hebron and attacked it. ³⁷They captured it and all the little towns near it. The Israelites killed everyone in Hebron. No one was left alive there. This was the same thing they had done to Eglon. They completely destroyed the city and all its people as an offering to the Lord.

³⁸Then Joshua and the Israelites went back to Debir and attacked it. ³⁹They captured that city, its king and all the little towns near it. They completely destroyed everyone in Debir as an offering to the Lord. No one was left alive there. Israel did to Debir and its king the same thing they had done to Libnah and its king. This was what they had done to Hebron.

⁴⁰So Joshua defeated all the kings of the cities of these areas: the mountains, southern Canaan, the western mountain slopes and the eastern mountain slopes. The Lord, the God of Israel, had told Joshua to completely destroy all the people as an offering to the Lord. So he left no one alive in those places. ⁴¹Joshua captured all the cities from Kadesh Barnea to Gaza. And he captured all the cities from Goshen to Gibeon. ⁴²He captured all these cities and their kings on one trip. He did it because the Lord, the God of Israel, was fighting for Israel.

⁴³Then Joshua and all the Israelites returned to their camp at Gilgal.

Defeating Northern Kings

11 Jabin king of Hazor heard about all that had happened. He sent messages to Jobab king of Madon, to the king of Shimron and to the king of Acshaph. ²He sent one to the kings in the northern mountains. Jabin also sent a message to the kings in the Jordan Valley south of Lake Galilee and in the western mountain slopes. He sent a message to the king of Naphoth Dor in the west. ³Jabin also sent one to the kings of the Canaanites in the east and in the west. He sent messages to the Amorites, Hittites, Perizzites and Jebusites in the mountains. Jabin also sent one to the Hivites. They lived below Mount Hermon in the area of Mizpah. ⁴So the armies of all these kings came together. There were many fighting men, horses and chariots. It was a huge army. It looked like there were as many men as grains of sand on the seashore.

⁵All of these kings met together at the Waters of Merom. They joined their armies together into one camp. They made plans to fight against the Israelites.

⁶Then the Lord said to Joshua, "Don't be afraid of them. At this time tomorrow I will allow you to defeat them. You will kill all of them. You will cripple their horses and burn all their chariots."

⁷So Joshua and his whole army surprised the enemy. They attacked them at the Waters of Merom. ⁸The Lord allowed Israel to defeat them. They chased them to Greater Sidon, Misrephoth Maim and the Valley of Mizpah in the east. Israel fought until none of the enemy was left alive. ⁹Joshua did what the Lord said to do. He cut the legs of their horses and burned their chariots.

¹⁰Then Joshua went back and captured the city of Hazor. He killed the king of Hazor. (Hazor had been the leader of all the kingdoms that fought against Israel.) ¹¹Israel killed everyone in Hazor. They completely destroyed them. There was nothing left alive. Then they burned Hazor itself.

¹²Joshua captured all of these cities. He killed all of their kings. He completely destroyed everything in these cities. He did this the way Moses, the servant of the Lord, had commanded. ¹³But the Israelites did not burn any cities that were built on their hills, except Hazor. That city alone was burned by Joshua. ¹⁴The people of Israel kept for themselves everything they found in the cities. They kept all the animals they found. But they killed all the people there. They did not leave anyone alive. ¹⁵Long ago the Lord had commanded his servant Moses to do this. Then Moses had commanded Joshua to do it. So Joshua obeyed God. He did everything the Lord had commanded Moses.

¹⁶So Joshua defeated all the people in the land. He had control of the mountains and the area of southern Canaan. He controlled all the areas of Goshen, the western mountain slopes and the Jordan Valley. He controlled the mountains of Israel and all the hills near them. ¹⁷Joshua controlled all the land from Mount Halak near Edom to Baal Gad. Baal Gad was in the Valley of Lebanon, below Mount Hermon. Joshua captured all the kings in the land and killed them. ¹⁸He fought against them for many years. ¹⁹The people of only one city in all the land had made a peace agreement with Israel. They were the Hivites living in Gibeon. All the other cities were defeated in war. ²⁰The Lord made those people stubborn so they would fight against Israel. This way he could completely destroy them without mercy. This is what the Lord had commanded Moses to do.

²¹Now Joshua fought the Anakites*d* who lived in the mountains of Hebron, Debir, Anab, Judah and Israel. And he completely destroyed them and their towns. ²²There were no Anakites left living in the land of the Israelites. Only a few Anakites were left in Gaza, Gath and Ashdod. ²³Joshua took control of all the land of Israel. This was what the Lord had told Moses to do long ago. He gave the land to Israel because he had promised it to them. Then Joshua divided the land among the tribes*d* of Israel. The fighting had finally ended. And there was peace in the land.

Kings Defeated by Israel

12 The Israelites took control of the land east of the Jordan River. They now had all the land from the

Arnon Ravine to Mount Hermon. And they had all the land along the eastern side of the Jordan Valley. Here are all the kings the Israelites defeated to take this land:

²Sihon was the king of the Amorites. He lived in the city of Heshbon. He ruled the land from Aroer at the Arnon Ravine to the Jabbok River. His land started in the middle of the ravine. This was their border with the Ammonites. Sihon ruled over half the land of Gilead. ³He also ruled over the eastern side of the Jordan Valley from Lake Galilee to the Dead Sea.ᵈ And he ruled from Beth Jeshimoth south to the hills of Pisgah.

⁴Og king of Bashan was one of the last of the Rephaites.ᵈ He ruled the land in Ashtaroth and Edrei. ⁵He ruled over Mount Hermon, Salecah and all the area of Bashan. His land ended where the people of Geshur and Maacah lived. Og also ruled half the land of Gilead. It stopped at the border of Sihon king of Heshbon.

⁶The Lord's servant Moses and the Israelites defeated all these kings. And Moses gave that land to the tribesᵈ of Reuben and Gad and to the eastern half-tribe of Manasseh. This land was to be their own.

⁷The Israelites also defeated kings in the land that was west of the Jordan River. Joshua led the people in this land. He gave the people this land and divided it among the 12 tribes. This was the land that was promised to them. It was between Baal Gad in the Valley of Lebanon and Mount Halak near Edom. ⁸This included the mountains, the western mountain slopes and the Jordan Valley. It also included the eastern mountain slopes, the desert and southern Canaan. This was the land where the Hittites, Amorites, Canaanites, Perizzites, Hivites and Jebusites had lived. The people of Israel defeated the king of each of the following cities: ⁹Jericho, Ai (near Bethel), ¹⁰Jerusalem, Hebron, ¹¹Jarmuth, Lachish, ¹²Eglon, Gezer, ¹³Debir, Geder, ¹⁴Hormah, Arad,

¹⁵Libnah, Adullam, ¹⁶Makkedah, Bethel, ¹⁷Tappuah, Hepher, ¹⁸Aphek, Lasharon, ¹⁹Madon, Hazor, ²⁰Shimron Meron, Acshaph, ²¹Taanach, Megiddo, ²²Kedesh, Jokneam in Carmel, ²³Dor (in Naphoth Dor), Goyim in Gilgal, and ²⁴Tirzah.

The total number of kings was 31.

Land Still to Be Taken

13 When Joshua was very old, the Lord spoke to him. He said, "Joshua, you have grown old. But there is still much land for you to take. ²You have not yet taken the land of Geshur and the land of the Philistines. ³You have not yet taken the area from the Shihor River at the border of Egypt to Ekron in the north. That belongs to the Canaanites. You must still defeat the five Philistine leaders. They are at Gaza, Ashdod, Ashkelon, Gath and Ekron. You must also defeat the Avvites. ⁴They live south of the Canaanite land. ⁵You have not yet defeated the Gebalites. And there is also the area of Lebanon east of Baal Gad below Mount Hermon to Lebo Hamath.

⁶"The Sidonians are living in the hill country from Lebanon to Misrephoth Maim. But I will force out all of them ahead of the Israelites. Be sure to remember this land when you divide the land among the Israelites. Do this as I told you.

⁷"Now divide the land among the nine tribesᵈ and the western half-tribe of Manasseh."

Dividing the Land

⁸The eastern half-tribeᵈ of Manasseh and the tribes of Reuben and Gad had received their land. The Lord's servant Moses gave them the land east of the Jordan River. ⁹Their land started at Aroer at the Arnon Ravine. It continued to the town in the middle of the ravine. And it included the whole plain from Medeba to Dibon. ¹⁰All the towns that Sihon king of the Amorites ruled were in that land. He ruled in the city of Heshbon. The land continued to the

area where the Ammonites lived. [11]Gilead was also there. And the area where the people of Geshur and Maacah lived was in that land. All of Mount Hermon and all of Bashan as far as Salecah was included. [12]All the kingdom of Og king of Bashan was in the land. In the past he ruled in Ashtaroth and Edrei. Og was one of the last of the Rephaites.[d] In the past Moses had defeated them and had taken their land. [13]The Israelites did not force out the people of Geshur and Maacah. They still live among the Israelites today.

[14]The tribe of Levi was the only one that did not get any land. Instead, they were to be given all the burned sacrifices made to the Lord, the God of Israel. That is what the Lord had promised them.

[15]Moses had given each family group from the tribe of Reuben some land. This is the land they were given: [16]It was the land from Aroer near the Arnon Ravine to the town of Medeba. This included the whole plain and the town in the middle of the ravine. [17]The land continued to Heshbon. It included all the towns on the plain. These towns were Dibon, Bamoth Baal and Beth Baal Meon. [18]They included Jahaz, Kedemoth, Mephaath, [19]Kiriathaim, Sibmah and Zereth Shahar on the hill in the valley. [20]They also included Beth Peor, the hills of Pisgah and Beth Jeshimoth. [21]So that land included all the towns on the plain and all the area that Sihon the king of the Amorites had ruled. He ruled from the town of Heshbon. But Moses had defeated him and the leaders of the Midianites. Those leaders included Evi, Rekem, Zur, Hur and Reba. All these leaders fought together with Sihon. And they lived in that country. [22]The Israelites killed many people during the fighting. They also killed Balaam of Beor. He tried to use magic to tell the future. [23]The land given to Reuben stopped at the shore of the Jordan River. So the land given to the family groups of Reuben included all these towns and their fields that were listed.

[24]This is the land Moses gave to the tribe of Gad. He gave it to all the family groups: [25]He gave them the land of Jazar and all the towns of Gilead. He also gave them half the land of the Ammonites. It went as far as Aroer near Rabbah. [26]It included the area from Heshbon to Ramath Mizpah and Betonim. It included the area from Mahanaim to the land of Debir. [27]The land included the valley, Beth Haram, Beth Nimrah, Succoth and Zaphon. All the other land Sihon king of Heshbon had ruled was also included in it. This is the land on the east side of the Jordan River. It continued to the end of Lake Galilee. [28]All this is the land Moses gave to the tribe of Gad. It included all the towns that were listed. Moses gave it to all the family groups.

[29]This is the land Moses had given to the eastern half-tribe of Manasseh. Half of all the family groups in the tribe of Manasseh were given this land: [30]The land started at Mahanaim. It included all of Bashan and the land ruled by Og king of Bashan. It also included all the Towns of Jair in Bashan. There were 60 cities in all. [31]It also included half of Gilead, Ashtaroth and Edrei. (These were the cities where Og king of Bashan had ruled.) All this land had been given to the family of Makir son of Manasseh. Half of all his sons had been given this land.

[32]Moses had given this land to these tribes on the plains of Moab. It was across the Jordan River east of Jericho. [33]But Moses had given no land to the tribe of Levi. The Lord, the God of Israel, promised that he himself would be the gift for the Levites.

14 Eleazar the priest, Joshua son of Nun and the leaders of all the tribes of Israel decided what land to give to the people. [2]The Lord had commanded Moses long ago how he wanted the people to choose their land. The people of the nine-and-a-half tribes threw lots[d] to decide which land they would receive. ³Moses had already given the two-and-a-half tribes their land east of the Jordan River. But the tribe of Levi was not given any land like the others. ⁴The sons of Joseph had divided into two tribes—Manasseh and Ephraim. The tribe of Levi was not given any land. It was given only some towns in which to live. It was also given pastures for its animals. ⁵The Lord had told Moses how to give the land to the tribes of Israel. The Israelites divided the land as the Lord had commanded.

Caleb's Land

⁶One day some men from the tribe*ᵈ* of Judah went to Joshua at Gilgal. One of those men was Caleb son of Jephunneh the Kenizzite. He said to Joshua, "You remember what the Lord said at Kadesh Barnea. He was speaking to the prophet Moses about you and me. ⁷Moses, the Lord's servant, sent me to look at the land where we were going. I was 40 years old then. When I came back, I told Moses what I thought about the land. ⁸The other men who went with me told the people things that made them afraid. But I fully believed the Lord would allow us to take the land. ⁹So that day Moses promised me, 'The land where you went will become your land. Your children will own it forever. I will give you that land because you fully believed in the Lord, my God.'

¹⁰"Now then, the Lord has kept his promise. He has kept me alive for 45 years from the time he said this to Moses. During that time we all wandered in the desert. Now here I am, 85 years old. ¹¹I am still as strong today as I was the day Moses sent me out. I am just as ready to fight now as I was then. ¹²So give me the mountain country the Lord promised me that day long ago. Back then you heard that the Anakite*ᵈ* people lived there. And the cities were large and well protected. But now with the Lord helping me, I will force them out, just as the Lord said."

¹³Joshua blessed Caleb son of Jephunneh. He gave him the city of Hebron as his own. ¹⁴And Hebron still belongs to the family of Caleb son of Jephunneh the Kenizzite. It still belongs to his people because he had faith. He obeyed the Lord, the God of Israel. ¹⁵(In the past it was called Kiriath Arba. It was named for the greatest man among the Anakites. He was named Arba.)

After this there was peace in the land.

Land for Judah

15 The land that was given to the tribe*ᵈ* of Judah was divided among all the family groups. It went all the way to the Desert of Zin in the far south, at the border of Edom.

²The southern border of Judah's land started at the south end of the Dead Sea.*ᵈ* ³It went south of Scorpion Pass to Zin. From there it passed to the south of Kadesh Barnea. It continued past Hezron to Addar. From Addar it turned and went to Karka. ⁴It continued to Azmon, the brook of Egypt and then to the Mediterranean Sea. This was the southern border.

⁵The eastern border was the shore of the Dead Sea. It went as far as the area where the Jordan River flowed into the sea.

The northern border started at the area where the Jordan River flowed into the Dead Sea. ⁶Then it went to Beth Hoglah and continued north of Beth Arabah. It continued to the stone of Bohan. Bohan was the son of Reuben. ⁷Then the northern border went through the Valley of Achor to Debir. There it turned toward the north and went to Gilgal. Gilgal is across from the road that goes through the mountain of Adummim. It is on the south side of the ravine. The border continued along the waters of En Shemesh. It stopped at En Rogel. ⁸Then it went through the Valley of Ben Hinnom. This is next to the southern side of the Jebusite city. (That city was called Jerusalem.) There the border went to the top of the hill on the west side of Hinnom Valley. This was at the northern end of the Valley of Giants. [9]From there it went to the spring of the Waters of Nephtoah. Then it went to the cities near Mount Ephron. There it turned and went toward Baalah. (Baalah is also called Kiriath Jearim.) [10]At Baalah the border turned west and went toward Mount Edom. It continued along the north side of Mount Jearim (also called Kesalon) and came to Beth Shemesh. From there it went past Timnah. [11]Then it went to the hill north of Ekron. From there it turned toward Shikkeron and went past Mount Baalah. It continued on to Jabneel and ended at the sea.

[12]The Mediterranean Sea was the western border. Inside these borders lived the family groups of Judah.

[13]The Lord had commanded Joshua to give Caleb son of Jephunneh part of the land in Judah. So he gave Caleb the land God had commanded. He gave him the town of Kiriath Arba, also called Hebron. (Arba was the father of Anak.[d]) [14]Caleb forced out the three Anakite families living in Hebron. Those families were Sheshai, Ahiman and Talmai. They were descendants[d] of Anak. [15]Then he fought against the people living in Debir. (In the past Debir had been called Kiriath Sepher.) [16]Caleb said, "I want a man to attack and capture Kiriath Sepher. I will give him Acsah, my daughter, as a wife." [17]Othniel son of Kenaz defeated the city. So Caleb gave his daughter Acsah to Othniel to be his wife. [18]Acsah wanted Othniel to ask her father Caleb for more land.

So Acsah went to her father. When she got off her donkey, Caleb asked her, "What do you want?"

[19]Acsah answered, "I would like a special favor. The land you gave me is very dry. So also give me land with springs of water on it."

So Caleb gave her land with springs of water on the upper and lower part of it.

[20]The tribe of Judah got the land God had promised them. Each family group got part of the land.

[21]The tribe of Judah got all the towns in the southern part of Canaan. These towns were near the border of Edom. Here is a list of the towns: Kabzeel, Eder, Jagur, [22]Kinah, Dimonah, Adadah, [23]Kedesh, Hazor and Ithnan; [24]Ziph, Telem, Bealoth, [25]Hazor Hadattah and Kerioth Hezron (also called Hazor); [26]Amam, Shema, Moladah, [27]Hazar Gaddah, Heshmon and Beth Pelet; [28]Hazar Shual, Beersheba, Biziothiah, [29]Baalah, Iim, Ezem, [30]Eltolad, Kesil and Hormah; [31]Ziklag, Madmannah, Sansannah, [32]Lebaoth, Shilhim, Ain and Rimmon. There were 29 towns and all their fields.

[33]The tribe of Judah got these towns in the western mountain slopes: Eshtaol, Zorah, Ashnah, [34]Zanoah, En Gannim, Tappuah and Enam; [35]Jarmuth, Adullam, Socoh, Azekah, [36]Shaaraim, Adithaim and Gederah (also called Gederothaim). There were 14 towns and all their fields.

[37]Judah was also given these towns in the western mountain slopes: Zenan, Hadashah, Migdal Gad, [38]Dilean, Mizpah, Joktheel, [39]Lachish, Bozkath and Eglon; [40]Cabbon, Lahmas, Kitlish, [41]Gederoth, Beth Dagon, Naamah and Makkedah. There were 16 towns and all their fields.

[42]Judah was also given these towns in the western mountain slopes: Libnah, Ether, Ashan, [43]Iphtah, Ashnah, Nezib, [44]Keilah, Aczib and Mareshah. There were nine towns and all their fields.

[45]The tribe of Judah also got the town of Ekron and all the small towns and fields near it. [46]They also got the area west of Ekron and all the fields and towns near Ashdod. [47]Ashdod and all the small towns around it were part of the land of Judah. They also got the fields and towns around Gaza. Their land continued to the brook of Egypt. And it went on along the coast of the Mediterranean Sea.

⁴⁸The tribe of Judah was also given these towns in the mountains: Shamir, Jattir, Socoh, ⁴⁹Dannah and Kiriath Sannah (also called Debir); ⁵⁰Anab, Eshtemoh, Anim, ⁵¹Goshen, Holon and Giloh. There were 11 towns and all their fields.

⁵²They were also given these towns in the mountains: Arab, Dumah, Eshan, ⁵³Janim, Beth Tappuah and Aphekah; ⁵⁴Humtah, Kiriath Arba (also called Hebron) and Zior. There were 9 towns and all their fields.

⁵⁵Judah was also given these towns in the mountains: Maon, Carmel, Ziph, Juttah, ⁵⁶Jezreel, Jokdeam, Zanoah, ⁵⁷Kain, Gibeah and Timnah. There were 10 towns and all their fields.

⁵⁸They were also given these towns in the mountains: Halhul, Beth Zur, Gedor, ⁵⁹Maarath, Beth Anoth and Eltekon. There were 6 towns and all their fields.

⁶⁰The people of Judah were also given the 2 towns of Rabbah and Kiriath Baal (also called Kiriath Jearim).

⁶¹Judah was given towns in the desert. Here are those towns: Beth Arabah, Middin, Secacah, ⁶²Nibshan, the City of Salt and En Gedi. There were 6 towns and all their fields.

⁶³The army of Judah was not able to force out the Jebusites living in Jerusalem. So the Jebusites still live among the people of Judah in Jerusalem to this day.

Land for Ephraim and Manasseh

16 This is the land the tribe*d* of Joseph received. It started at the Jordan River near Jericho. It continued to the waters of Jericho, just east of the city. The border went up from Jericho to the mountains of Bethel. ²Then it continued from Bethel (also called Luz) to the Arkite border at Ataroth. ³From there it went west to the border of the Japhletites. It continued to the area of the Lower Beth Horon. Then it went to Gezer and ended at the sea.

⁴So Manasseh and Ephraim received their land. They were sons of Joseph.

⁵This is the land that was given to the family groups of Ephraim: Their border started at Ataroth Addar in the east. It went to Upper Beth Horon ⁶and then to the sea. From Micmethath it turned eastward toward Taanath Shiloh and continued eastward to Janoah. ⁷Then it went down from Janoah to Ataroth and to Naarah. It continued until it touched Jericho and stopped at the Jordan River. ⁸The border went from Tappuah west to Kanah Ravine and went to the sea. This is all the land that was given to the Ephraimites. Each family group in the tribe got a part of this land. ⁹Many of the border towns of Ephraim were actually within Manasseh's borders. But the people of Ephraim got those towns and their fields. ¹⁰The Ephraimites could not force the Canaanites to leave Gezer. So the Canaanites still live among the Ephraimites today. But they became slaves of the Ephraimites.

17 Then land was given to the tribe of Manasseh. He was Joseph's first son. Manasseh's first son was Makir, the father of Gilead. Makir was a great soldier. So the lands of Gilead and Bashan were given to his family. ²Land was also given to the other family groups of Manasseh. They were Abiezer, Helek, Asriel, Shechem, Hepher and Shemida. These were all the other sons of Manasseh son of Joseph.

³Zelophehad was the son of Hepher. Hepher was the son of Gilead. Gilead was the son of Makir, and Makir was the son of Manasseh. But Zelophehad had no sons. He had five daughters. The daughters were named Mahlah, Noah, Hoglah, Milcah and Tirzah. ⁴The daughters went to Eleazar the priest. They also went to Joshua son of Nun and all the leaders. They said, "The Lord told Moses to give us land like the men received." So Eleazar obeyed the Lord and gave the daughters some land. These daughters received land just as the brothers of their father

did. ⁵So the tribe of Manasseh had ten sections of land west of the Jordan River. They also had two more sections, Gilead and Bashan. These sections were on the other side of the Jordan River. ⁶The daughters of Manasseh got land just as the sons did. Gilead was given to the rest of the families of Manasseh.

⁷The lands of Manasseh were in the area between Asher and Micmethath. This is near Shechem. The border went south to the En Tappuah area. ⁸The land of Tappuah belonged to Manasseh. But the town of Tappuah did not. It was along the border of Manasseh's land and belonged to the sons of Ephraim. ⁹The border of Manasseh continued south to Kanah Ravine. The cities in this area of Manasseh belonged to Ephraim. Manasseh's border was on the north side of the ravine and went to the sea. ¹⁰The land to the south belonged to Ephraim. And the land to the north belonged to Manasseh. The Mediterranean Sea was the western border. The border touched Asher's land on the north. And it touched Issachar's land on the east.

¹¹In the areas of Issachar and Asher, the people of Manasseh owned Beth Shan and its small towns. They also owned Ibleam and its small towns. And they owned all the people who lived in Dor and its small towns. They owned the people in Naphoth Dor and its small towns. And they owned all the people who lived in Taanach and its small towns. Manasseh also owned the people in Megiddo and its small towns. ¹²Manasseh was not able to defeat those cities. So the Canaanites continued to live there. ¹³But the Israelites grew strong. When this happened, they forced the Canaanites to work for them. But they did not force them to leave the land.

¹⁴The people from the tribes of Joseph spoke to Joshua. They said, "You gave us only one area of land. But we are many people. Why did you give us only one part of all the land the Lord gave his people?"

¹⁵And Joshua answered them, "You have many people. Go up to the forest. Make a place for yourselves to live there. This is in the land of the Perizzites and the Rephaites.ᵈ The mountain country of Ephraim is too small for you."

¹⁶The people of Joseph said, "It is true. The mountain country of Ephraim is not enough for us. But the land where the Canaanites live is dangerous. They are skilled fighters. They have powerful weapons in Beth Shan and all the small towns in that area. And they are also in the Valley of Jezreel."

¹⁷Then Joshua spoke to the people of Joseph—to Ephraim and to Manasseh. He said, "But there are many of you. And you have great power. You should be given more than one share of land. ¹⁸You also will have the mountain country. It is a forest. But you can cut down the trees and make it a good place to live. And you will own all of it. You will force the Canaanites to leave the land. You can defeat them even though they have powerful weapons and are strong."

The Rest of the Land Divided

18 All of the Israelites gathered together at Shiloh. There they set up the Meeting Tent.ᵈ The Israelites controlled that country. They had defeated all the enemies there. ²But there were still seven tribesᵈ of Israel that had not yet received the land God had promised them.

³So Joshua said to the Israelites: "Why do you wait so long to take your land? The Lord, the God of your fathers, has given this land to you. ⁴So each tribe should choose three men. I will send them out to study the land. They will describe in writing the land their tribe wants as its share. Then they will come back to me. ⁵They will divide the land into seven parts. The people of Judah will keep their land in the south. The people of Joseph will keep their land in the north. ⁶But you should

divide the land into seven parts. Describe the seven parts in writing. Then bring what you have written to me. We will let the Lord our God decide which tribe will get which land. [7]But the Levites do not get any part of these lands. They are priests, and their work is to serve the Lord. Gad, Reuben and the eastern half-tribe of Manasseh have received the land promised to them. They are on the east side of the Jordan River. Moses, the servant of the Lord, gave it to them."

[8]So the men who were chosen started into the land. Their plan was to describe it in writing and take it back to Joshua. Joshua told them, "Go and study the land. Describe it in writing. Then come back to me. Then I will ask the Lord to choose the land you should get. We will do this here in Shiloh." [9]So the men left and went into the land. They studied it and described it in writing for Joshua. They studied each town. They saw that the land had seven parts. They described it in writing and then came back to Joshua. He was still at the camp at Shiloh. [10]Then Joshua asked the Lord to help. He threw lots[d] to choose the lands that should be given to each tribe.

Land for Benjamin

[11]The first part of the land was given to the tribe[d] of Benjamin. Each family group in the tribe of Benjamin received some land. They were given the land between the land of Judah and the land of Joseph. This is the land chosen for Benjamin:

[12]The northern border started at the Jordan River. It went along the northern edge of Jericho. Then it went west into the mountains. That boundary continued until it was just east of Beth Aven. [13]From there it went south to Luz (also called Bethel). Then it went down to Ataroth Addar. Ataroth Addar is on the hill south of Lower Beth Horon. [14]There is a hill to the south of Beth Horon. At this hill the border turned and went south near the western side

of the hill. It went to Kiriath Baal (also called Kiriath Jearim). This is a town where people of Judah lived. It was the western border.

[15]The southern border started near Kiriath Jearim and went to the Waters of Nephtoah. [16]Then it went down to the bottom of the hill. This was near the Valley of Ben Hinnom. It was the north side of the Valley of Rephaim. The border continued down the Hinnom Valley just south of the Jebusite city to En Rogel. [17]There it turned north and went to En Shemesh. It continued to Geliloth near the Adummim Pass in the mountains. Then it went down to the great Stone of Bohan. Bohan was the son of Reuben. [18]The border continued to the northern part of Beth Arabah. Then it went down into the Jordan Valley. [19]From there it went to the northern part of Beth Hoglah. It ended at the north shore of the Dead Sea.[d] This is where the Jordan River flows into the sea. This was the southern border.

[20]The Jordan River was the border on the eastern side. So this was the land given to the family groups of Benjamin. These were the borders on all sides.

[21]Each family group of Benjamin received some of this land. And these are the cities they owned: Jericho, Beth Hoglah, Emek Keziz, [22]Beth Arabah, Zemaraim and Bethel; [23]Avvim, Parah, Ophrah, [24]Kephar Ammoni, Ophni and Geba. There were 12 towns and all their villages.

[25]The tribe of Benjamin also owned Gibeon, Ramah and Beeroth. [26]They owned Mizpah, Kephirah, Mozah, [27]Rekem, Irpeel and Taralah. [28]They also owned Zelah, Haeleph, the Jebusite city (Jerusalem), Gibeah and Kiriath. There were 14 towns and all their villages. All these areas are the lands the tribe of Benjamin was given.

Land for Simeon

19 The second part of the land was given to the tribe[d] of Simeon. Each family group received some of the land. It was inside the area of Judah. [2]They received Beersheba (also called Sheba), Moladah, [3]Hazar Shual, Balah, Ezem, [4]Eltolad, Bethul and Hormah. [5]They also received Ziklag, Beth Marcaboth, Hazar Susah, [6]Beth Lebaoth and Sharuhen. There were 13 towns and all their fields.

[7]They also received the towns of Ain, Rimmon, Ether and Ashan. There were 4 towns and all their fields. [8]They also received all the very small areas with people living in them as far as Baalath Beer. (This is the same as Ramah in southern Canaan.) So these were the lands given to the tribe of Simeon. Each family group received some of the land. [9]The land of the Simeonites was taken from part of the land of Judah. Judah had much more land than they needed. So the Simeonites received part of their land.

Land for Zebulun

[10]The third part of the land was given to the tribe[d] of Zebulun. Each family group of Zebulun received some of the land. The border of Zebulun went as far as Sarid. [11]Then it went west to Maralah and came near Dabbesheth. Then it went near Jokneam. [12]Then it turned to the east. It went from Sarid to the area of Kisloth Tabor. From there it went on to Daberath and to Japhia. [13]It continued eastward to Gath Hepher and Eth Kazin. Then it ended at Rimmon. Then the border turned and went toward Neah. [14]At Neah it turned again and went to the north. It went to Hannathon and continued to the Valley of Iphtah El. [15]Inside this border were the cities of Kattath, Nahalal, Shimron, Idalah and Bethlehem. There were 12 towns and all their fields.

[16]So these are the towns and the areas that were given to Zebulun. Each family group received some of the land.

Land for Issachar

[17]The fourth part of the land was given to the tribe[d] of Issachar. Each family group of Issachar received some of the land. [18]Their land included Jezreel, Kesulloth, Shunem, [19]Hapharaim, Shion and Anaharath; [20]Rabbith, Kishion, Ebez, [21]Remeth, En Gannim, En Haddah and Beth Pazzez.

[22]The border of their land touched the area called Tabor, Shahazumah and Beth Shemesh. It stopped at the Jordan River. There were 16 towns and their fields.

[23]These cities and towns were part of the land that was given to the tribe of Issachar. Each family group received part of this land.

Land for Asher

[24]The fifth part of the land was given to the tribe[d] of Asher. Each family group of Asher received some of the land. [25]Their land included Helkath, Hali, Beten, Acshaph, [26]Allammelech, Amad and Mishal.

The western border touched Mount Carmel and Shihor Libnath. [27]Then it turned toward the east. It went to Beth Dagon. It touched Zebulun and the Valley of Iphtah El. Then it went north of Beth Emek and Neiel. It passed north to Cabul. [28]Then it went to Abdon, Rehob, Hammon and Kanah. It continued to Greater Sidon. [29]Then the border went back south toward Ramah. It continued to the strong, walled city of Tyre. Then it turned and went toward Hosah. It ended at the sea. This was in the area of Aczib, [30]Ummah, Aphek and Rehob. There were 22 towns and their fields.

[31]These cities and their fields were part of the land that was given to the tribe of Asher. Each family group in that tribe received some of this land.

Land for Naphtali

[32]The sixth part of the land was given to the tribe[d] of Naphtali. Each family group of Naphtali received some of the land. [33]The border of their land started at the large tree in the area of Zaanannim. This is near Heleph. Then it went through Adami Nekeb and Jabneel. It continued to the area of

Lakkum and ended at the Jordan River. [34]Then it went to the west through Aznoth Tabor. It stopped at Hukkok. It went to the area of Zebulun on the south. And it went to the area of Asher on the west. It went to Judah, at the Jordan River, on the east. [35]There were some strong, walled cities inside these borders. Those cities were Ziddim, Zer, Hammath, Rakkath and Kinnereth; [36]Adamah, Ramah, Hazor, [37]Kedesh, Edrei and En Hazor; [38]Iron, Migdal El, Horem, Beth Anath and Beth Shemesh. There were 19 towns and all their fields.

[39]The cities and the towns around them were in the land that was given to the tribe of Naphtali. Each family group in that tribe got some of this land.

Land for Dan

[40]The seventh part of the land was given to the tribe[d] of Dan. Each family group of Dan received some of the land. [41]Their land included Zorah, Eshtaol, Ir Shemesh, [42]Shaalabbin, Aijalon and Ithlah; [43]Elon, Timnah, Ekron, [44]Eltekeh, Gibbethon, Baalath, [45]Jehud, Bene Berak and Gath Rimmon; [46]Me Jarkon, Rakkon and the area near Joppa.

[47](But the Danites had trouble taking their land. There were strong enemies there. And the Danites could not easily defeat them. So the Danites went and fought against Leshem. They defeated Leshem and killed the people who lived there. So the Danites lived in the town of Leshem. They changed its name to Dan because he was the father of their tribe.) [48]All of these cities and towns were given to the tribe of Dan. Each family group got part of this land.

Land for Joshua

[49]So the Israelite leaders finished dividing the land and giving it to the different tribes.[d] After they finished, all the Israelites decided to give Joshua son of Nun some land, too. This was land that had been promised to him. [50]The Lord had commanded that he be given

this land. So they gave Joshua the town of Timnath Serah in the mountains of Ephraim. This was the town that Joshua told them he wanted. So he built up the town and lived there.

[51]So all of these lands were given to the different tribes of Israel. Eleazar the priest, Joshua son of Nun and the leaders of each tribe worked together. They divided up the land while they were at Shiloh. They met before the Lord at the entrance to the Meeting Tent[d] to do this. Now they had finished dividing the land.

Cities of Safety

20 Then the Lord said to Joshua: [2]"Tell the Israelites to choose the special cities of safety.[d] This is what I had Moses command you to do. [3]A person might kill someone accidentally and without meaning to kill him. He may go to a city of safety to hide. There he will be safe from the relative who has the duty of punishing a murderer.

[4]"This is what he must do. When he runs to one of those cities, he must stop at the entrance gate. He must stand there and tell the leaders of the people what happened. Then they will allow him to enter the city. They will give him a place to live among them. [5]But the one who is chasing him might follow him to that city. If this happens, the leaders of the city must not give him up. They must protect the person who came to them for safety. They must protect him because he killed that person accidentally. He was not angry and did not decide ahead of time to kill the person. [6]He should stay in the city until he has been judged by the court there. And he should stay until the high priest dies. Then he may go back to his own home in the town from which he ran away."

[7]So the Israelites chose some cities to be cities of safety. These cities were: Kedesh in Galilee in the mountains of Naphtali; Shechem in the mountains of Ephraim; Kiriath Arba (also called Hebron) in the mountains of Judah;

8Bezer on the east side of the Jordan River near Jericho in the desert in the land of Reuben; Ramoth in Gilead in the land of Gad; and Golan in Bashan in the land of Manasseh. 9Any Israelite or anyone living among them who killed someone accidentally was included. He was to be allowed to run to one of these cities of safety. Then he could be safe there and would not be killed by the relative who had the duty of punishing a murderer. He would be judged by the court in that city.

Towns for the Levites

21 The heads of the Levite families went to talk to Eleazar the priest. They also talked to Joshua son of Nun and to the heads of the families of all the tribes*d* of Israel. 2This happened at the town of Shiloh in the land of Canaan. The heads of the Levite families said to them, "The Lord commanded Moses that you give us towns where we may live. And he commanded that you give us pastures." 3So the Israelites obeyed this commandment of the Lord. They gave the Levite people these towns and pastures: 4The Kohath family groups were part of the tribe of Levi. Some of the Levites in the Kohath family groups were from the family of Aaron the priest. To these Levites were given 13 towns. These towns were in the areas that belonged to Judah, Simeon and Benjamin. 5The other family groups of Kohath were given 10 towns. These 10 towns were in the areas of Ephraim, Dan and West Manasseh.

6The people from the Gershon groups were given 13 towns. They were in the land that belonged to Issachar, Asher, Naphtali and the eastern half-tribe of Manasseh in Bashan.

7The family groups of Merari were given 12 towns. These 12 towns were in the area that belonged to Reuben, Gad and Zebulun.

8So the Israelites gave the Levites these towns and the pastures around them. They did this to obey the commandment that the Lord had given Moses.

9These are the names of the towns that came from the lands of Judah and Simeon. 10The first choice of towns was given to the Kohath family groups of the Levites. 11They gave them Kiriath Arba (also called Hebron) and all its pastures. This was in the mountains of Judah. (Arba was the father of Anak.*d*) 12But the fields and the small towns around the city of Kiriath Arba had been given to Caleb son of Jephunneh.

13So they gave the city of Hebron to the descendants*d* of Aaron. (Hebron was a city of safety.*d*) They also gave them these towns: Libnah, 14Jattir, Eshtemoa, 15Holon, Debir, 16Ain, Juttah and Beth Shemesh. They also gave them all the pastures that were around these towns. There were 9 towns given to these two groups.

17They also gave the people of Aaron cities that belonged to the tribe of Benjamin. These cities were Gibeon, Geba, 18Anathoth and Almon. They gave them these 4 towns and all the pastures around them.

19So these towns were given to the priests. These priests were from the family of Aaron. The total number of towns with their pastures was 13.

20The other Kohathite family groups of the Levites were given these towns from the tribe of Ephraim: 21They gave them the city of Shechem from the mountains of Ephraim. (Shechem was a city of safety.) They also gave them Gezer, 22Kibzaim and Beth Horon. There were 4 towns and their pastures.

23The tribe of Dan gave them Eltekeh, Gibbethon, 24Aijalon and Gath Rimmon. There were 4 towns and their pastures.

25The western half-tribe of Manasseh gave them Taanach and Gath Rimmon. They were also given all the pastures around these 2 towns.

26So this was 10 more towns and all the pastures around the towns. These were given to the rest of the Kohathite family groups.

^{27}The Gershonite family groups of the Levite tribe were given these towns: The eastern half-tribe of Manasseh gave them Golan in Bashan. (Golan was a city of safety.) Manasseh also gave them Be Eshtarah. All the pastures around these two towns were also given to the Gershonites.

^{28}The tribe of Issachar gave them Kishion, Daberath, ^{29}Jarmuth and En Gannim. Issachar also gave them all the pastures around these 4 towns.

^{30}The tribe of Asher gave them Mishal, Abdon, ^{31}Helkath and Rehob. All the pastures around these 4 towns were also given to them.

^{32}The tribe of Naphtali gave them Kedesh in Galilee. (Kedesh was a city of safety.) Naphtali also gave them Hammoth Dor and Kartan. All the pastures around these 2 towns were also given to the Gershonites.

^{33}So the Gershonite family groups received 13 towns. They also received all the pastures around these towns.

^{34}The Merarite family groups (the rest of the Levites) were given these towns: The tribe of Zebulun gave them Jokneam, Kartah, ^{35}Dimnah and Nahalal. All the pastures around these 4 towns were also given to the Merarites.

^{36}The tribe of Reuben gave them Bezer, Jahaz, ^{37}Kedemoth and Mephaath. All the pastures around these 4 towns were also given to the Merarites.

^{38}The tribe of Gad gave them Ramoth in Gilead. (Ramoth was a city of safety.) They also gave them Mahanaim, ^{39}Heshbon and Jazer. Gad also gave them all the pastures around these 4 towns.

^{40}So the total number of towns given to the Merarite family groups was 12.

^{41}A total of 48 towns with their pastures were given to the Levites. All these towns were in the land controlled by the Israelites. ^{42}Each town had pastures around it.

^{43}So the Lord kept the promise he had made to the Israelites. He gave the people all the land he had promised. The people took the land and lived there. ^{44}The Lord allowed them to have peace on all sides of their land. This is what he had promised to their people who lived long ago. None of their enemies defeated them. The Lord allowed the Israelites to defeat every enemy. ^{45}He kept every promise he had made to the Israelites. No promises failed. Each one came true.

Three Tribes Go Home

22 Then Joshua called a meeting of all the people from the tribes^d of Reuben, Gad and the eastern half-tribe of Manasseh. ^{2}He said to them, "You have obeyed everything Moses told you to do. He was a servant of the Lord. And also, you have obeyed all my commands. ^{3}All this time you have supported all the other Israelites. You have been careful to obey all the commands the Lord your God gave you. ^{4}The Lord your God promised to give the Israelites peace. Now he has kept his promise. Now you may go back to your homes. You may go to the land that Moses, the Lord's servant, gave you. It is the land on the east side of the Jordan River. ^{5}But continue to obey the teachings Moses gave you. That law is to love the Lord your God and obey his commands. Continue to follow him and serve him the very best you can."

^{6}Then Joshua said good-bye to them, and they left. They went away to their homes. ^{7}Moses had given the land of Bashan to the eastern half-tribe of Manasseh. Joshua gave land on the west side of the Jordan River to the western half-tribe of Manasseh. And he sent them to their homes. He blessed them. ^{8}He said, "Go back to your homes and your riches. You have many animals, silver, gold, bronze and iron. And you have many beautiful clothes. Also, you have taken many things from your enemies. You should divide these among yourselves."

^{9}So the people from the tribes of Reuben, Gad and the eastern half-tribe of Manasseh left the other Israelites. They left Shiloh in Canaan and went back towards Gilead. This was their own land. Moses gave it to them as the Lord had commanded.

10The people of Reuben, Gad and the eastern half-tribe of Manasseh traveled to Geliloth. This was near the Jordan River in the land of Canaan. There they built a beautiful altar. 11But the other Israelites still at Shiloh heard about the altar these three tribes had built. They heard that the altar was at the border of Canaan at Geliloth. It was near the Jordan River on Israel's side. 12All the Israelites became very angry at these three tribes. They met together and decided to fight them.

13So the Israelites sent some men to talk to the people of Reuben, Gad and the eastern half-tribe of Manasseh. The leader of these men was Phinehas son of Eleazar the priest. 14They also sent one leader of each of the ten tribes at Shiloh. Each of these men was a leader of his family group of Israelites.

15So these men went to Gilead. They went to talk to the people of Reuben, Gad and the eastern half-tribe of Manasseh. The men said to them: 16"All the Israelites ask you: 'Why did you turn against the God of Israel? Why did you build an altar for yourselves? You know that this is against God's law. 17Remember what happened at Peor? We still suffer today because of that sin. Because of it, God caused many of the Israelites to become very sick. 18And now are you doing the same thing? Are you turning against the Lord? Will you refuse to follow the Lord?

"'If you don't stop what you're doing, the Lord will be angry with everyone in Israel. 19Your land may not be a good enough place to worship. If not, come over into our land. The Lord's Tent is in our land. You may have some of our land and live there. But don't turn against the Lord by building another altar. We already have the altar of the Lord our God. 20Remember Achan son

of Zerah. He refused to obey the command about what must be completely destroyed. That one man broke God's law, but all the Israelites were punished. Achan died because of his sin. But many other people also died.'"

21The people from Reuben, Gad and the eastern half-tribe of Manasseh answered them. They said: 22"The Lord is our God! Again we say that the Lord is our God! God knows why we did this. We want you to know also. You can judge what we did. If you believe we have done something wrong, you may kill us. 23If we broke God's law, we ask the Lord himself to punish us. Do you think we built this altar to offer burnt offerings? And did we build it to use for offerings of grain and fellowship?

24"No! We did not build it for that reason. We feared that some day your people would not accept us as part of your nation. Then they might say, 'You cannot worship the Lord, the God of Israel. 25God gave you land on the other side of the Jordan River. It separates us from you people of Reuben and Gad. You cannot worship the Lord.' So we feared that your children might make our children stop worshiping the Lord.

26"So we decided to build this altar. But we did not plan to use it for burning sacrifices and making offerings. 27It was really to show our people that we worship the same God as you. This altar is proof to you and us. And it will prove to all our children who will come after us that we worship the Lord. We give our whole burnt offerings, grain and fellowship offerings to the Lord. This was to keep your children from saying that our children could not worship the Lord.

28"In the future your children might say that we do not belong to Israel. Then our children could say, 'Look! Our fathers who lived before us made an altar. It is exactly like the Lord's altar. We do not use it for sacrifices. This altar shows that we are part of Israel.'

29"Truly, we don't want to be against the Lord. We don't want to stop following him. We know the only true altar is the one in front of the Holy Tent.*d* It belongs to the Lord our God."

³⁰Phinehas the priest and the ten leaders heard these things. They listened to the people of Reuben, Gad and Manasseh. And they were pleased. ³¹So Phinehas, son of Eleazar the priest, spoke. He said, "Now we know the Lord is with us. And we know you didn't turn against him. We're happy that the Israelites will not be punished by the Lord."

³²Then Phinehas and the leaders went home. They left the people of Reuben and Gad in Gilead. And they went back to Canaan. There they told the Israelites what had happened. ³³They were also pleased. They were happy and thanked God. And they decided not to fight against the people of Reuben and Gad. They decided not to destroy those lands.

³⁴And the people of Reuben and Gad gave the altar a name. They called it Proof that We Believe that the Lord Is God.

Joshua Says Good-bye

23 The Lord gave Israel peace from their enemies around them. He made Israel safe. Many years passed, and Joshua became very old. ²So he called a meeting of all the older leaders, heads of families, judges and officers of the Israelites. He said, "I am now very old. ³You have seen what the Lord has done to our enemies. He did it to help us. The Lord your God fought for you. ⁴Remember that your people have been given their land. It's the land between the Jordan River and the Mediterranean Sea in the west. It's the land I promised to give you. But you don't control that land yet. ⁵The Lord your God will make the people living there leave. You will enter the land. And the Lord will force them out ahead of you. He has promised you this.

⁶"Be strong. You must be careful to obey everything the Lord has commanded. Obey everything written in

Witnessing
JOSHUA 22:34

At the scene of a fire, how can you tell who the firefighters are? They're the ones holding the hose and wearing funny-looking hats. In a football game, how can you tell who the quarterback is? He's the one who takes the ball from center and throws it. The quarterback doesn't have to say to the cheering crowd, "Hey! Just thought I'd let you know I'm the quarterback!" We know who these people are by what they do. They don't have to tell us.

When you want to tell other people about God, sometimes you don't have to say anything. You can *do* something that shows everyone around you that you love God. That's what the people in this passage did. They built an altar and named it, "Proof that we believe that the Lord is God". They gave a message about God to everyone who saw the altar. They didn't have to say one word. What is something you can "say" to your friends about God, without even opening your mouth?

To learn more about witnessing, zoom to page 776.

the Book of the Teachings of Moses. Do exactly as it says. ⁷There are still some people living among us who are not Israelites. They worship their own gods. Don't become friends with them. Don't serve or worship their gods. ⁸You must continue to follow the Lord your God. You have done this in the past. And you must continue to do it.

⁹"The Lord has helped you defeat many great and powerful nations. He has forced them to leave ahead of you. No nation has been able to defeat you. ¹⁰With his help, one Israelite could defeat a thousand enemies. This is because the Lord your God fights for you, as he promised to do. ¹¹So you must be careful to love the Lord your God.

¹²"Don't turn away from the way of the Lord. Don't become friends with these people who are not part of Israel. Don't marry them. If you do become their friends, ¹³the Lord your God will not help you defeat your enemies. So they will become like traps for you. They will cause you pain like a whip on your back and thorns in your eyes. And none of you will be left in this good land the Lord your God has given you.

¹⁴"It's almost time for me to die. You know and fully believe that the Lord has done great things for you. You know that he has not failed in any of his promises. He has kept every promise he has given. ¹⁵Every good promise that the Lord your God made has come true. And in the same way, his other promises will come true. He promised that evil will come to you. He will destroy you from this good land that he gave you. ¹⁶This will happen if you don't keep your agreement with the Lord your God. You will lose this land if you go and serve other gods. You must not worship them. If you do, the Lord will become very angry with you. Then none of you will be left in this good land he has given you."

24 Then all the tribes*d* of Israel met together at Shechem. Joshua called them all together there. Then he called the older leaders, heads of families, judges and officers of Israel. These men stood before God.

²Then Joshua spoke to all the people. He said, "Here's what the Lord, the God of Israel, says to you: 'A long time ago your ancestors lived on the other side of the Euphrates River. I am talking about men like Terah, the father of Abraham and Nahor. They worshiped other gods. ³But I, the Lord, took your ancestor Abraham out of the land on the other side of the river. I led him through the land of Canaan. And I gave him many children. I gave him his son Isaac. ⁴And I gave Isaac two sons named Jacob and Esau. I gave the land around the mountains of Edom to Esau. But Jacob and his sons went down to Egypt. ⁵Then I sent Moses and Aaron to Egypt. I caused many terrible things to happen to the Egyptians. Then I brought you people out. ⁶When I brought your fathers out of Egypt, they came to the Red Sea.*d* And the Egyptians chased them. There were chariots and men on horses. ⁷So the people asked me, the Lord, for help. And I caused great trouble to come to the Egyptians. I caused the sea to cover them. You yourselves saw what I did to the army of Egypt. After that, you lived in the desert for a long time.

⁸"'Then I brought you to the land of the Amorites. This was east of the Jordan River. They fought against you, but I gave you the power to defeat them. I destroyed them before you. Then you took control of that land. ⁹But the king of Moab, Balak son of Zippor, prepared to fight against the Israelites. The king sent for Balaam son of Beor to curse you. ¹⁰But I, the Lord, refused to listen to Balaam. So he asked for good things to happen to you! He blessed you many times. I saved you and brought you out of his power.

¹¹"'Then you traveled across the Jordan River and came to Jericho. The people in the city of Jericho fought against you. Also, the Amorites,

Perizzites, Canaanites, Hittites, Girgashites, Hivites and Jebusites fought against you. But I allowed you to defeat them all. [12]While your army traveled forward, I sent hornets ahead of them. These hornets made the people leave before you came. So you took the land without using your swords and bows. [13]It was I, the Lord, who gave you that land. I gave you land where you did not have to work. I gave you cities that you did not have to build. And now you live in that land and in those cities. You eat from vineyards and olive trees. But you did not have to plant them.'"

[14]Then Joshua spoke to the people. He said, "Now you have heard the Lord's words. So you must respect the Lord and serve him fully and sincerely. Throw away the false gods that your people worshiped. That happened on the other side of the Euphrates River and in Egypt. Now you must serve the Lord. [15]But maybe you don't want to serve the Lord. You must choose for yourselves today. You must decide whom you will serve. You may serve the gods that your people worshiped when they lived on the other side of the Euphrates River. Or you may serve the gods of the Amorites who lived in this land. As for me and my family, we will serve the Lord."

[16]Then the people answered, "No! We will never stop following the Lord. We will never serve other gods! [17]We know it was the Lord our God who brought our people out of Egypt. We were slaves in that land. But the Lord did great things for us there. He brought us out. He protected us while we traveled through other lands. [18]Then he helped us defeat the people living in these lands. He helped us defeat the Amorites who lived here. So we will continue to serve the Lord because he is our God."

[19]Then Joshua said, "You will not be able to serve the Lord well enough. He is a holy God. And he is a jealous God. If you turn against him and sin, he will not forgive you. [20]If you leave the Lord

and serve other gods, he will cause great trouble to come to you. The Lord has been good to you. But if you turn against him, he will destroy you."

[21]But the people said to Joshua, "No! We will serve the Lord."

[22]Then Joshua said, "Look around at yourselves and the people with you here. Do you all know and agree that you have chosen to serve the Lord? Are you all witnesses to this?"

The people answered, "Yes, it's true! We all see that we have chosen to serve the Lord."

[23]Then Joshua said, "Now throw away the false gods that you have among you. Love the Lord, the God of Israel, with all your heart."

[24]Then the people said to Joshua, "We will serve the Lord our God. We will obey him."

[25]On that day Joshua made an agreement for the people. He made the agreement a law for them to follow. This happened at Shechem. [26]Joshua wrote these things in the Book of the Teachings of God. Then he found a large stone. He put the stone under the oak tree near the Lord's Holy Tent.[d]

[27]Then Joshua said to all the people, "See this stone! It will help you remember what we did today. It was here when the Lord was speaking to us today. It will help you remember what happened. It will stop you from turning against your God."

Joshua Dies

[28]Then Joshua told the people to go back to their homes. And everyone went back to his own land.

[29]After that, Joshua son of Nun died. He was 110 years old. [30]And they buried him in his own land at Timnath Serah. This was in the mountains of Ephraim, north of Mount Gaash.

[31]The Israelites had served the Lord during the time Joshua was living. And after he died, they continued to serve the Lord. They continued to serve him while their older leaders were still alive. These were the leaders who had seen

what the Lord had done for the Israelites.

Joseph Comes Home

[32]When the Israelites left Egypt, they carried the bones of Joseph with them. They buried them at Shechem, in the land Jacob had bought from the sons of Hamor. (Hamor was the father of Shechem.) Jacob had bought the land for 100 pieces of silver. This land belonged to Joseph's children.

[33]And Eleazar son of Aaron died. He was buried at Gibeah in the mountains of Ephraim. Gibeah had been given to Eleazar's son Phinehas.

JUDGES

Great Leaders Rescue Israel

The Men of Judah Fight the Canaanites

1 Joshua died. Then the people of Israel prayed to the Lord. They said, "Who will be first to go and fight for us against the Canaanite people?"

²The Lord said to them, "The tribe*d* of Judah will go. I have given them the power to take this land."

³The men of Judah asked for help from the men of Simeon, their relatives. The men of Judah said, "Come and help us fight the Canaanites for our land. If you do, we will go and help you fight for your land." So the men of Simeon went with them.

⁴The Lord gave the men of Judah the victory over the Canaanites and the Perizzites. The men of Judah defeated 10,000 men at the city of Bezek. ⁵There they found Adoni-Bezek, the ruler of the city, and fought him. The men of Judah defeated the Canaanites and the Perizzites. ⁶So Adoni-Bezek ran away. But the men of Judah chased him. When they caught him, they cut off his thumbs and big toes.

⁷Then Adoni-Bezek said, "I cut off the thumbs and big toes of 70 kings. And those kings had to eat scraps that fell from my table. Now God has paid me back for what I did to them." The men of Judah took Adoni-Bezek to Jerusalem, and he died there.

⁸Then the men of Judah fought against Jerusalem and captured it. They used their swords to kill the people of Jerusalem. And they burned the city.

⁹Later, they went down to fight against more of the Canaanites. Some of the Canaanites lived in the mountains. Others lived in the dry country to the south. And still others lived in the western mountain slopes. ¹⁰Then the men of Judah went to fight against the Canaanites in the city of Hebron. (Hebron used to be called Kiriath Arba.) The men of Judah defeated the descendants*d* of Sheshai, Ahiman and Talmai.

Caleb and His Daughter

¹¹Then the men of Judah left Hebron. They went to the city of Debir to fight against the people there. (Debir used to be called Kiriath Sepher.) ¹²Before attacking the city, Caleb said, "I want a man to attack and capture the city of Kiriath Sepher. I will give him Acsah, my daughter, as a wife." ¹³Caleb had a younger brother named Kenaz. Kenaz had a son named Othniel. Othniel captured the city of Kiriath Sepher. So Caleb gave his daughter Acsah to Othniel to be his wife. ¹⁴When Acsah came to Othniel, he told her to ask her father for some land. So she got down from her donkey, and Caleb said, "What do you want?"

¹⁵Acsah answered Caleb, "Do me a favor. You have put me in the dry land of southern Judah. Give me some land with springs of water." So Caleb gave her the upper and lower springs of water.

Fights with the Canaanites

¹⁶The Kenite people left Jericho, the city of palm trees. They went with the men of Judah. The Kenites went to the Desert of Judah to live with the people there. This was in southern Judah near the city of Arad. (The Kenites were from the family of Moses' father-in-law.)

17Some Canaanite people also lived in the city of Zephath. So the men of Judah and the men of Simeon, their relatives, defeated those Canaanites. They completely destroyed the city. So they called the city Hormah.*n* 18The men of Judah captured Gaza, Ashkelon and Ekron and all the lands around them.

19The Lord was on the side of the men of Judah. They took the land in the mountains. But they could not force out the people living on the plain. This was because those people had iron chariots. 20As Moses had promised, Hebron was given to Caleb. Caleb forced out the three sons of Anak.*d* 21But the people of Benjamin could not make the Jebusite people leave Jerusalem. Since that time the Jebusites have lived with the Benjaminites in Jerusalem.

22The men of Joseph went to fight against the city of Bethel. The Lord was on their side. 23They sent some spies to Bethel. (Bethel used to be called Luz.) 24The spies saw a man coming out of the city. They said to him, "Show us a way into the city. If you help us, we will be kind to you." 25The man showed the spies the way into the city. The men of Joseph killed the people in Bethel. But the man who helped them and his family were allowed to go free. 26He went to the land where the Hittite people lived, and he built a city. He named the city Luz, and it is called that today.

27There were Canaanites living in the cities of Beth Shan, Taanach, Dor, Ibleam, Megiddo and the small towns around them. The people of Manasseh did not force those people out of their towns. The Canaanites were determined to stay there. 28Later, the people of Israel grew strong. They forced the Canaanites to work as slaves for them. But the Israelites did not make all the Canaanites leave their land. 29There were Canaanites living in Gezer. And the people of Ephraim did not make all of those Canaanites leave their land. So the Canaanite people continued to live in Gezer with the people of Ephraim. 30Some Canaanites lived in the cities of Kitron and Nahalol. The people of Zebulun did not make them leave their land. They stayed and lived with the people of Zebulun. But Zebulun made them work as slaves.

31The people of Asher did not make the Canaanites leave the cities of Acco, Sidon, Ahlab, Aczib, Helbah, Aphek and Rehob. 32The people of Asher did not make them leave their land. So the Canaanites continued to live with the people of Asher. 33The people of Naphtali did not make the people leave the cities of Beth Shemesh and Beth Anath. So the people of Naphtali continued to live with the Canaanites in those cities. Those people worked as slaves for the people of Naphtali. 34The Amorites forced the Danites back into the mountains. The Amorites would not let them come down to live in the plain. 35The Amorites were determined to stay in Mount Heres, Aijalon and Shaalbim. But the Israelites grew stronger. Then they made the Amorites work as slaves for them. 36The land of the Amorites was from Scorpion Pass to Sela and beyond it.

The Angel of the Lord at Bokim

2 The angel of the Lord went up from Gilgal to Bokim. He spoke to the people of Israel there and said: "I brought you up from Egypt. I led you to the land I promised to give to your ancestors. I said, 'I will never break my agreement with you. 2But in return, you must not make an agreement with the people who live in this land. You must destroy their altars.' But you did not obey me. How could you do this? 3Now I will tell you this: 'I will not force out the people in this land. They will become your enemies. Their gods will become a trap for you.'"

4After the angel gave Israel this message from the Lord, they cried loudly.

---

*n***Hormah** Hormah sounds like the Hebrew word meaning "to destroy completely."

[5]So they named the place Bokim.[n] There they offered sacrifices to the Lord.

Joshua Dies

[6]Then Joshua told the people they could go home. So each one went to take his own share of the land. [7]The people of Israel served the Lord as long as Joshua was alive. They continued serving the Lord during the lifetimes of the older leaders who lived on after Joshua. These men had seen all the great things the Lord had done for Israel. [8]Joshua son of Nun was the servant of the Lord. Joshua died at the age of 110. [9]So the Israelites buried him in the land he had been given. That land was at Timnath Heres. It was in the mountains of Ephraim, north of Mount Gaash.

The People Disobey

[10]After those people had died, their children grew up. They did not know the Lord or what he had done for Israel. [11]So they did evil and worshiped the Baal[d] idols. They did what the Lord said was wrong. [12]The Lord had brought the people of Israel out of Egypt. And the ancestors of these people had worshiped the Lord. But the Israelites quit following the Lord. They began to worship the gods of the people who lived around them. That made the Lord angry. [13]The Israelites quit following the Lord and worshiped Baal and Ashtoreth.[d] [14]The Lord was angry with the people of Israel. So he let robbers attack them and take their possessions. He let their enemies who lived around them defeat them. They could not protect themselves from their enemies. [15]When the Israelites went out to fight, they always lost. They lost because the Lord was not on their side. The Lord had sworn to them this would happen. So the Israelites suffered very much.

God Chooses Judges

[16]Then the Lord chose leaders called judges.[n] These leaders saved the people of Israel from the robbers. [17]But the Israelites did not listen to their judges. They were not faithful to God. They followed other gods instead. In the past the people of Israel obeyed the Lord's commands. But now the Israelites stopped obeying the Lord. [18]Many times the enemies of Israel hurt the Israelites. So the Israelites would cry for help. And each time the Lord felt sorry for them. Each time he sent a judge to save them from their enemies. The Lord was with those judges. [19]But when each judge died, the Israelites again sinned and worshiped the false gods. They became worse than their ancestors. The Israelites were very stubborn; they refused to change their evil ways.

[20]So the Lord became angry with the Israelites. He said, "These people have broken the agreement I made with their ancestors. They have not listened to me. [21]So I will no longer defeat the nations who were left when Joshua died. [22]I will use those nations to test Israel. I will see if Israel keeps the Lord's commands as their ancestors did." [23]In the past the Lord had permitted those nations to stay in the land. He did not quickly force them out. He did not help Joshua's army defeat them.

3 These are the nations the Lord did not force to leave. He wanted to test the Israelites who had not fought in the wars to take Canaan. [2]The only reason the Lord left those nations in the land was to teach the descendants[d] of the Israelites. He wanted to teach the people who had not fought in those wars how to fight. [3]These are the nations: the five rulers of the Philistines, all the Canaanites, the people of Sidon and the Hivites. The Hivites lived in the Lebanon mountains from Mount Baal

---

[n]**Bokim**   This name means "crying."
[n]**judges**   They were not judges in courts of law, but leaders of the people in times of emergency.

Hermon to Lebo Hamath. ⁴Those nations were in the land to test the Israelites. The Lord wanted to see if Israel would obey the commands he had given to their ancestors by Moses.

⁵The people of Israel lived with the Canaanites, Hittites, Amorites, Perizzites, Hivites and Jebusites. ⁶The Israelites began to marry the daughters of those people. And the Israelites allowed their daughters to marry the sons of those people. Israel served the gods of those people.

of Kenaz. (Kenaz was Caleb's younger brother.) Othniel saved the Israelites. ¹⁰The Spirit*d* of the Lord entered Othniel. And he became Israel's judge and went to war. The Lord helped him to defeat Cushan-Rishathaim king of Northwest Mesopotamia. ¹¹So the land was at peace for 40 years. Then Othniel son of Kenaz died.

Ehud, the Judge

¹²Again the people of Israel did what the Lord said was wrong. So the Lord gave Eglon king of Moab power to defeat Israel. This was because of the evil Israel did. ¹³Eglon got the Ammonite people and the Amalekite people to

People Who Got Away

EHUD • JUDGES 3:15-26

The nation of Moab was one of Israel's worst enemies. King Eglon of Moab conquered Israel. For eighteen years the Moabites made life hard for the Israelites, forcing them to pay a lot of money to Moab. God called Ehud to be Israel's leader (judge) and to free the nation from Moab. Ehud was left-handed, which was considered a handicap. But because Eglon did not expect Ehud to use his left hand, Ehud surprised the evil king, killed him, and escaped. By the time the Moabites realized what had happened, Ehud had gathered an army of Israelites to fight for their freedom. Israel won the battle. Ehud's victory gave Israel eighty years of peace.

When God wants to use you, trust him to turn even your "handicaps" into tools that can be used for him!

To read about a young man who escaped a wicked brother, fly to page 301.

Othniel, the First Judge

⁷The people of Israel did what the Lord said was wrong. They forgot about the Lord their God. Instead, they served the idols of Baal*d* and Asherah.*d* ⁸The Lord was angry with Israel. He allowed Cushan-Rishathaim king of Northwest Mesopotamia to rule over the Israelites. They were under that king's rule for eight years. ⁹Then Israel cried to the Lord. So the Lord sent a man to save them. He was Othniel son

join him. Then he attacked Israel and took Jericho, the city of palm trees. ¹⁴The people of Israel were under the rule of Eglon king of Moab for 18 years.

¹⁵So the people cried to the Lord. And he sent a man to save them. That man was Ehud, who was left-handed. Ehud was the son of Gera from the people of Benjamin. Israel sent Ehud to give Eglon king of Moab the payment he demanded. ¹⁶Ehud made a

sword for himself. The sword had two edges and was about 18 inches long. He tied the sword to his right upper leg under his clothes. 17So Ehud came to Eglon king of Moab and gave him the payment he demanded. Eglon was a very fat man. 18After he had given Eglon the payment, Ehud sent home the men who had carried it. 19When he passed the statues near the city Gilgal, he turned around. Ehud said to Eglon, "I have a secret message for you, King Eglon."

The king said, "Be quiet!" Then he sent all of his servants out of the room. 20Ehud went to King Eglon. Eglon was now sitting alone in the room on top of his summer palace.

The king's fat covered the whole sword. So Ehud left the sword in Eglon. 23He went out of the room and closed and locked the doors behind him.

24The servants returned just after Ehud left. They found the doors to the room locked. So they thought the king was relieving himself. 25They waited for a long time. Finally they became worried because he still had not opened the doors. So they got the key and unlocked them. When they entered, they saw their king lying dead on the floor!

26While the servants were waiting, Ehud had escaped. He passed by the statues and went to Seirah. 27When he arrived there, he blew a trumpet in the mountains of Ephraim. The people of Israel heard it and went down from the hills with Ehud leading them.

Heroes Who Trusted God
DEBORAH • JUDGES 4:4-10

The book of Judges tells about some people God chose to help Israel defeat its enemies. One was a woman named Deborah. She trusted God and helped people know what was right to do. She also was very courageous, for she led the Israelites into battle against a mighty king and his army. Deborah was not afraid. She knew that God would help her lead the army and win the battle. While Deborah led the army, another woman named Jael killed the leader of the enemy army.

Because these women believed in God, the Israelites were once again set free from their enemies so they could worship God. Would you trust God to help you lead an army?

To learn about a man who trusted in God for victory instead of a big army, fly to page 298.

Ehud said, "I have a message from God for you." As the king stood up from his chair, 21Ehud reached with his left hand. He took out the sword that was tied to his right upper leg. Then he stabbed the sword deep into the king's belly! 22The sword went into Eglon's belly so far that even the handle sank in. And the blade came out his back.

28He said to them, "Follow me! The Lord has helped us to defeat our enemies, the people of Moab." So Israel followed Ehud. They took control of the places where the Jordan River could easily be crossed. Israel did not allow the Moabites to come across the Jordan River. 29Israel killed about 10,000 strong and able men from

Moab. Not one Moabite man escaped. [30]So that day Moab was forced to be under the rule of Israel. And there was peace in the land for 80 years.

Shamgar, the Judge

[31]After Ehud, another man saved Israel. His name was Shamgar son of Anath. Shamgar killed 600 Philistines with a sharp stick used to guide oxen.

Deborah, the Woman Judge

4 After Ehud died, the people of Israel again did what the Lord said was wrong. [2]So he let Jabin, a king of Canaan, defeat Israel. Jabin ruled in the city of Hazor. Sisera was the commander of Jabin's army. Sisera lived in Harosheth Haggoyim. [3]He had 900 iron chariots and was very cruel to the people of Israel for 20 years. So they cried to the Lord for help.

[4]There was a prophetess[d] named Deborah. She was the wife of Lappidoth. She was judge of Israel at that time. [5]Deborah would sit under the Palm Tree of Deborah. This was between the cities of Ramah and Bethel, in the mountains of Ephraim. And the people of Israel would come to her to settle their arguments.

[6]Deborah sent a message to a man named Barak. He was the son of Abinoam. Barak lived in the city of Kedesh, which is in the area of Naphtali. Deborah said to Barak, "The Lord, the God of Israel, commands you: 'Go and gather 10,000 men of Naphtali and Zebulun. Lead them to Mount Tabor. [7]I will make Sisera, the commander of Jabin's army, come to you. Sisera, his chariots and his army will meet you at the Kishon River. I will help you to defeat Sisera there.'"

[8]Then Barak said to Deborah, "I will go if you will go with me. But if you will not go with me, I won't go."

[9]"Of course I will go with you," Deborah answered. "But you will not get credit for the victory. The Lord will let a woman defeat Sisera." So Deborah

Women Who Trusted God

DEBORAH • JUDGES 5:31

Deborah was the only woman who served as one of Israel's judges. A judge was a leader chosen by God to help Israel. The book of Judges tells how God's people kept turning away from God and not worshiping him. When they disobeyed, some of their enemies would take over their land and hurt them. When that happened, they prayed for God to help. God always heard their prayers and sent a leader, called a judge, to help them defeat their enemies. The judge was also supposed to help the people begin worshiping God again.

Some judges did a good job. Deborah was one of those. Usually women did not become leaders, but Deborah was a strong leader and she depended on God. When she led Israel to a great victory, she did not take the credit, she thanked God.

Whatever job God leads you to do, trust him to help you do it well and remember to give him the credit.

To meet a woman who thought of others first, fly to page 320.

went with Barak to Kedesh. ¹⁰At Kedesh, Barak called the people of Zebulun and Naphtali together. From them, he gathered 10,000 men to follow him. Deborah went with Barak also.

¹¹Now Heber the Kenite had left the other Kenite people. (The Kenites were descendants^d of Hobab, Moses' brother-in-law.) Heber had put up his tent by the great tree in Zaanannim. This is near Kedesh.

¹²Then Sisera was told that Barak son of Abinoam had gone up to Mount Tabor. ¹³So Sisera gathered his 900 iron chariots and all the men with him. They went from Harosheth Haggoyim to the Kishon River.

"**S**ometimes bullies really get what's coming to them! God knows how to handle them. Read about one in Judges 4:1-16."

¹⁴Then Deborah said to Barak, "Get up! Today is the day the Lord will help you defeat Sisera. You know the Lord has already cleared the way for you." So Barak led 10,000 men down from Mount Tabor. ¹⁵He and his men attacked Sisera and his men. During the battle the Lord confused Sisera and his army and chariots. So Barak and his men used their swords to defeat Sisera's army. But Sisera left his chariot and ran away on foot. ¹⁶Barak and his men chased Sisera's chariots and army to Harosheth Haggoyim. They used their swords to kill all of Sisera's men. Not one of them was left alive.

¹⁷But Sisera himself ran away. He came to the tent where Jael lived. She was the wife of Heber, one of the Kenite family groups. Heber's family was at peace with Jabin king of Hazor. ¹⁸Jael went out to meet Sisera. She said to him, "Come into my tent, master!

Come in. Don't be afraid." So Sisera went into Jael's tent, and she covered him with a rug.

¹⁹Sisera said to Jael, "I am thirsty. Please give me some water to drink." So she opened a leather bag in which she kept milk and gave him a drink. Then she covered him up.

²⁰Then Sisera said to Jael, "Go stand at the entrance to the tent. If anyone comes and asks you, 'Is anyone here?' say, 'No.'"

²¹But Jael, the wife of Heber, took a tent peg and a hammer. She quietly went to Sisera. Since he was very tired, he was sleeping. She hammered the tent peg through the side of Sisera's head and into the ground! And so Sisera died.

²²Then Barak came by Jael's tent, chasing Sisera. Jael went out to meet him and said, "Come. I will show you the man you are looking for." So Barak entered her tent. There Sisera lay dead, with the tent peg in his head.

²³On that day God defeated Jabin king of Canaan in the sight of Israel.

²⁴Israel became stronger and stronger against Jabin king of Canaan. Finally, they destroyed him.

The Song of Deborah

5 On that day Deborah and Barak son of Abinoam sang this song:

²"The leaders led Israel.
    The people volunteered to go
        to battle.
    Praise the Lord!
³Listen, kings.
    Pay attention, rulers!
I myself will sing to the Lord.
    I will make music to the Lord, the
        God of Israel.

⁴"Lord, in the past you came
        from Edom.
    You marched from the land
        of Edom,
and the earth shook.
    The skies rained,
        and the clouds dropped water.
⁵The mountains shook before

the Lord, the God of
Mount Sinai.
They shook before the Lord, the
God of Israel!

6"In the days of Shamgar son
of Anath,
in the days of Jael, the main roads
were empty.
Travelers went on the back roads.
7There were no warriors in Israel
until I, Deborah, arose.
I arose to be a mother to Israel.
8At that time they chose to
follow new gods.
Because of this, enemies fought us
at our city gates.
No one could find a shield or a spear
among the 40,000 men of Israel.
9My heart is with the
commanders of Israel.
They volunteered freely from
among the people.
Praise the Lord!

10"You who ride on white donkeys
and sit on saddle blankets, listen!
And you who walk along the road,
listen!
11Listen to the sound of the
singers
at the watering holes.
There they tell about the victories of
the Lord.
They tell about the victories of the
Lord's warriors in Israel.
Then the Lord's people went down
to the city gates.

12"Wake up, wake up, Deborah!
Wake up, wake up, sing a song!
Get up, Barak!
Go capture your enemies, son
of Abinoam!

13"Then the men who were left
came down to the
important leaders.
The Lord's people came down to
me with strong men.
14They came from Ephraim in
the mountains of Amalek.
Benjamin was among the people
who followed you.

From the family group of Makir in
West Manasseh, the
commanders came down.
And from Zebulun came those
men who lead with an officer's
staff.
15The princes of Issachar were
with Deborah.
The people of Issachar were loyal
to Barak.
They followed him into the valley.
The Reubenites thought hard
about what they would do.
16Why did you stay by the
sheepfold?
Was it to hear the music played for
your sheep?
The Reubenites thought hard
about what they would do.
17The people of Gilead stayed
east of the Jordan River.
People of Dan, why did you stay by
the ships?
The people of Asher stayed at the
seashore.
They stayed at their safe harbors.
18But the people of Zebulun
risked their lives.
So did the people of Naphtali on
the battlefield.

19"The kings came, and they
fought.
At that time the kings of Canaan
fought
at Taanach, by the waters of
Megiddo.
But they took away no silver or
possessions of Israel.
20The stars fought from heaven.
From their paths, they fought
Sisera.
21The Kishon River swept
Sisera's men away,
that old river, the Kishon River.
March on, my soul, with strength!
22Then the horses' hoofs beat the
ground.
Galloping, galloping go Sisera's
mighty horses.
23'May the town of Meroz be
cursed,' said the angel of
the Lord.

'Bitterly curse its people,
because they did not come to help
the Lord.
They did not fight the strong
enemy.'

24"May Jael, the wife of Heber
the Kenite,
be blessed above all women who
live in tents.
25Sisera asked for water,
but Jael gave him milk.
In a bowl fit for a ruler,
she brought him cream.
26Jael reached out and took the
tent peg.
Her right hand reached for the
workman's hammer.
And she hit Sisera! She smashed
his head!
She crushed and pierced the side
of his head!
27At Jael's feet he sank.
He fell, and he lay there.
At her feet he sank. He fell.
Where Sisera sank, there he fell,
dead!

28"Sisera's mother looked out
through the window.
She looked through the curtains.
She asked, 'Why is Sisera's chariot
so late in coming?
Why are sounds of his chariots'
horses delayed?'
29The wisest of her servant ladies
answer her.
And Sisera's mother says to herself,
30'Surely they are taking the
possessions of the people
they defeated!
Surely they are dividing those
things among themselves!
A girl or two is being given to each
soldier.
Maybe Sisera is taking pieces of
dyed cloth.
Maybe they are even taking
pieces of dyed, embroidered cloth
for the necks of the victors!'

31"Let all your enemies die this
way, Lord!
But let all the people who love you
be powerful like the rising sun!"

So there was peace in the land for 40
years.

The Midianites Attack Israel

6 Again the people of Israel did what the Lord said was wrong. So for seven years the Lord let the people of Midian rule Israel. 2The Midianites were very powerful and were cruel to the Israelites. So the Israelites made hiding places in the mountains. They also hid in caves and safe places. 3Whenever the Israelites planted crops, the Midianites, Amalekites and other peoples from the east would come and attack them. 4These people camped in the land. And they destroyed the crops that the Israelites had planted. They did this as far as the land near Gaza. The people left nothing for Israel to eat. They left them no sheep, cattle or donkeys. 5The Midianites came up and camped in the land. They brought their tents and their animals with them. They were like swarms of locusts!d There were so many people and camels they could not be counted. These people came into the land to ruin it. 6Israel became very poor because of the Midianites. So the Israelites cried out to the Lord for help.

7The Israelites cried out to the Lord for help against the Midianites. 8So the Lord sent a prophetd to them. The prophet said, "This is what the Lord, the God of Israel, says: I brought you out of Egypt, the land of slavery. 9I saved you from the people of Egypt. And I saved you from all the people of Canaan. I forced them out of their land. And I gave it to you. 10Then I said to you, 'I am the Lord your God. You will live in the land of the Amorites, but you must not worship their gods.' But you did not obey me."

The Angel of the Lord Visits Gideon

11The angel of the Lord came and sat down under an oak tree at Ophrah.

The oak tree belonged to Joash, who was one of the Abiezrite people. Joash was the father of Gideon. Gideon was separating some wheat from the chaff[d] in a winepress.[d] Gideon did this to keep the wheat from the Midianites. [12]The angel of the Lord appeared to Gideon and said, "The Lord is with you, mighty warrior!"

[13]Then Gideon said, "Pardon me, sir. If the Lord is with us, why are we having so many troubles? Our ancestors told us he did miracles.[d] They told us the Lord brought them out of Egypt. But now he has left us. He has allowed the Midianites to defeat us."

[14]The Lord turned to Gideon and said, "You have the strength to save the people of Israel. Go and save them from the Midianites. I am the one who is sending you."

[15]But Gideon answered, "Pardon me, Lord. How can I save Israel? My family group is the weakest in Manasseh. And I am the least important member of my family."

[16]The Lord answered him, "I will be with you. It will seem as if you are fighting only one man."

[17]Then Gideon said to the Lord, "If you are pleased with me, give me proof. Show me that it is really you talking with me. [18]Please wait here. Do not go away until I come back to you. Let me bring my offering and set it in front of you."

And the Lord said, "I will wait until you come back."

[19]So Gideon went in and cooked a young goat. He also took about 20 quarts of flour and made bread without yeast. Then he put the meat into a basket. And he put the broth from the boiled meat into a pot. He brought out the meat, the bread and the bread without yeast. He brought the food to the angel of the Lord. Gideon gave it to him under the oak tree.

[20]The angel of God said to Gideon, "Put the meat and the bread without yeast on that rock over there. Then pour the broth on them." And Gideon did as he was told. [21]The angel of the Lord had a stick in his hand. He touched the meat and the bread with the end of the stick. Then fire jumped up from the rock! The meat and the bread were completely burned up! And the angel of the Lord disappeared! [22]Then Gideon understood he had been talking to the angel of the Lord. So Gideon cried, "Lord God! I have seen the angel of the Lord face to face!"

[23]But the Lord said to Gideon, "Calm down! Don't be afraid! You will not die!"

[24]So Gideon built an altar there to worship the Lord. Gideon named the altar The Lord Is Peace. It still stands at Ophrah, where the Abiezrites live.

Gideon Tears Down the Altar of Baal

[25]That same night the Lord spoke to Gideon. The Lord said, "Take the bull that belongs to your father and a second bull seven years old. Pull down your father's altar to Baal.[d] Cut down the Asherah[d] idol beside it. [26]Then build an altar to the Lord your God. Build it on this high ground. Lay its stones in the right order. Then kill and burn the bull on this altar. Use the wood from the Asherah idol to burn your offering."

[27]So Gideon got ten of his servants. And he did what the Lord had told him to do. But Gideon was afraid that his family and the men of the city might see him. So he did it at night, not in the daytime.

[28]The men of the city got up the next morning. They saw that the altar for Baal had been destroyed! And they saw that the Asherah idol beside it had been cut down! They also saw the altar Gideon had built. And they saw the bull that had been sacrificed on it. [29]The men of the city looked at each other and asked, "Who did this?" They asked many questions and looked for the person who had done those things.

Someone told them, "Gideon son of Joash did this."

³⁰So they said to Joash, "Bring your son out. He has pulled down the altar of Baal. He has cut down the Asherah idol beside it. So your son must die!"

³¹But Joash spoke to the angry crowd around him. He said, "Are you going to take Baal's side? Are you going to defend Baal? Anyone who takes Baal's side will be killed by morning! If Baal is a god, let him fight for himself. It's his altar that has been

entered Gideon! Gideon blew a trumpet to call the Abiezrites to follow him. ³⁵He sent messengers to all of Manasseh. The people of Manasseh were called to follow Gideon. Gideon also sent messengers to the people of Asher, Zebulun and Naphtali. They also went up to meet Gideon and his men.

³⁶Then Gideon said to God, "You said you would help me save Israel. ³⁷I will put some wool on the threshing*d* floor. Let there be dew only on the wool. But let all of the ground be dry. Then I will know what you said is true. I will know that you will use me to save

Miracles from God

JUDGES 6:36-40

Gideon had a hard time believing God would help him to conquer his enemies. Gideon knew he could never win against his enemies without God's help. He did something very unusual to make sure God would be with him.

Gideon laid a piece of material on the ground overnight. He asked God to make only the material wet and the ground around it dry. This would prove to Gideon that God was really going to help him win the battle against his enemies. Gideon checked the material the next day. It was wet and the ground was perfectly dry! God did the same thing with the material the next night, only this time the material remained dry and the ground around it was wet. Gideon knew God would indeed be with him in the battle.

We do not have to ask God to prove that he will help us. He says in the Bible that he will be with us in every situation. We know what he says is always true.

To find the contest where 3000 players died, fly to page 430.

pulled down." ³²So on that day Gideon got the name Jerub-Baal. The name means "let Baal fight against him." They named him this because Gideon pulled down Baal's altar.

Gideon Defeats Midian

³³All the Midianites, the Amalekites and other peoples from the east joined together. They came across the Jordan River and camped in the Valley of Jezreel. ³⁴But the Spirit*d* of the Lord

Israel." ³⁸And that is just what happened. Gideon got up early the next morning and squeezed the wool. He got a full bowl of water from the wool.

³⁹Then Gideon said to God, "Don't be angry with me. Let me ask just one more thing. Please let me make one more test. Let the wool be dry while the ground around it gets wet with dew." ⁴⁰That night God did that very thing. Just the wool was dry, but the ground around it was wet with dew.

7 Early in the morning Jerub-Baal and all his men set up their camp at the spring of Harod. (Jerub-Baal is also called Gideon.) The Midianites were camped north of them. The Midianites were camped in the valley at the bottom of the hill called Moreh. [2]Then the Lord said to Gideon, "You have too many men to defeat the Midianites. I don't want the Israelites to brag that they saved themselves. [3]So now, announce to the people, 'Anyone who is afraid may leave Mount Gilead. He may go back home.'" And 22,000 men went back home. But 10,000 remained.

[4]Then the Lord said to Gideon, "There are still too many men. Take the men down to the water, and I will test them for you there. If I say, 'This man will go with you,' he will go. But if I say, 'That one will not go with you,' he will not go."

[5]So Gideon led the men down to the water. There the Lord said to him, "Separate them. Those who drink water by lapping it up like a dog will be in one group. Those who bend down to drink will be in the other group." [6]There were 300 men who used their hands to bring water to their mouths. They lapped it as a dog does. All the rest got down on their knees to drink.

[7]Then the Lord said to Gideon, "I will save you, using the 300 men who lapped the water. And I will allow you to defeat Midian. Let all the other men go to their homes." [8]So Gideon sent the rest of Israel to their homes. But he kept 300 men. He took the jars and the trumpets of those who went home.

Now the camp of Midian was in the valley below Gideon. [9]That night the Lord spoke to Gideon. He said, "Get up. Go down and attack the camp of the Midianites. I will allow you to defeat them. [10]But if you are afraid to go down, take your servant Purah with you. [11]When you come to the camp of Midian, you will hear what they are saying. Then you will not be afraid to attack the camp."

Gideon Is Encouraged

So Gideon and his servant Purah went down to the edge of the enemy camp. [12]The Midianites, the Amalekites and all the peoples from the east were camped in that valley. There were so many of them they seemed like locusts.[d] They had so many camels no one could count them.

Heroes Who Trusted God
GIDEON • JUDGES 7:19-22

God wants us to count on him for help. Gideon was getting ready to lead Israel in a battle against the Midianites. He had 32,000 soldiers in his army. In fact, he had so many that God told him not to take them all. Wow! That doesn't seem to make any sense. But God wanted to show Gideon and Israel that they would win the battle because of God's power, not because of their big army. So God only let Gideon keep 300 soldiers, and they defeated the entire Midianite army!

You won't have to fight a big army, but you might need God's help with other things, like being afraid or worried. He wants to help you.

To learn about a prisoner who trusted God to defeat his captors, *fly to page 312.*

There were as many as there are grains of sand on the seashore!

[13] When Gideon came to the enemy camp, he heard a man talking. That man was telling his friend about a dream. He was saying, "Listen, I dreamed that a loaf of barley bread rolled into the camp of Midian. It hit the tent so hard that the tent turned over and fell flat!"

[14] The man's friend said, "Your dream is about the sword of Gideon son of Joash, a man of Israel. God will let Gideon defeat Midian and the whole army!"

[15] When Gideon heard about the dream and what it meant, he worshiped God. Then Gideon went back to the camp of Israel. He called out to them, "Get up! The Lord has defeated the army of Midian for you!" [16] Then Gideon divided the 300 men into three groups. He gave each man a trumpet and an empty jar. A burning torch was inside each jar.

[17] Gideon told the men, "Watch me and do what I do. When I get to the edge of the camp, do what I do. [18] Surround the enemy camp. I and everyone with me will blow our trumpets. When we blow our trumpets, you blow your trumpets, too. Then shout, 'For the Lord and for Gideon!'"

"**M**om, would you let me pretend to be one of Gideon's men? They got to break their jars in Judges 7:1-22. I wonder if their moms got upset?"

Midian Is Defeated

[19] So Gideon and the 100 men with him came to the edge of the enemy camp. They came just after the enemy had changed guards. It was during the middle watch of the night. Then Gideon and his men blew their trumpets and smashed their jars. [20] All three groups of Gideon's men blew their trumpets and smashed their jars. They held the torches in their left hands and the trumpets in their right hands. Then they shouted, "A sword for the Lord and for Gideon!" [21] Each of Gideon's men stayed in his place around the camp. But inside the camp, the men of Midian began shouting and running away.

[22] When Gideon's 300 men blew their trumpets, the Lord caused all the men of Midian to fight each other with their swords! The enemy army ran away to the city of Beth Shittah. It is toward Zererah. They ran as far as the border of the city of Abel Meholah. It is near the city of Tabbath. [23] Then men of Israel from Naphtali, Asher and all of Manasseh were called out to chase the Midianites. [24] Gideon sent messengers through all the mountains of Ephraim. They said, "Come down and attack the Midianites. Take control of the Jordan River as far as Beth Barah. Do this before the Midianites can get to the river and cross it."

So they called out all the men of Ephraim. They took control of the Jordan River as far as Beth Barah. [25] The men of Ephraim captured two princes of Midian named Oreb and Zeeb. The men of Ephraim killed Oreb at the rock of Oreb. They killed Zeeb at the winepress[d] of Zeeb. And they continued chasing the Midianites. They cut off the heads of Oreb and Zeeb and took them to Gideon. He was now east of the Jordan River.

8 The men of Ephraim asked Gideon, Why did you treat us this way? Why didn't you call us when you went to fight against Midian?" They were very angry at Gideon.

[2] But he answered them, "I have not done as well as you! The small part you did was better than all that my people of Abiezer did. [3] God allowed you to capture Oreb and Zeeb, the princes of Midian. How can I compare what I did with what you did?" When

the men of Ephraim heard Gideon's answer, they were not as angry anymore.

Gideon Captures Two Kings

⁴Then Gideon and his 300 men came to the Jordan River. They were tired, but they chased the enemy across to the other side. ⁵Gideon said to the men of Succoth, "Please give my soldiers some bread. They are very tired. I am chasing Zebah and Zalmunna, the kings of Midian."

⁶But the leaders of Succoth said, "Why should we give your soldiers bread? You haven't caught Zebah and Zalmunna yet."

⁷Then Gideon said, "The Lord will help me capture Zebah and Zalmunna. After that, I will whip your skin with thorns and briers from the desert."

⁸Gideon left Succoth and went to the city of Peniel. He asked the men there for food. It was just as he had asked the men of Succoth. And the men of Peniel gave him the same answer as the men of Succoth. ⁹So Gideon said to the men of Peniel, "After I win the victory, I will come back here. And I will pull down this tower."

¹⁰Zebah and Zalmunna and their army were in the city of Karkor. Their army had about 15,000 men. They were all who were left of the army of the peoples of the east. Already 120,000 soldiers of that army had been killed. ¹¹Gideon used the road of those who live in tents. This road is east of Nobah and Jogbehah. Gideon attacked the enemy army when they did not expect it. ¹²Zebah and Zalmunna, the kings of Midian, ran away. But Gideon chased and captured them. Gideon and his men defeated the enemy army.

¹³Then Gideon son of Joash returned from the battle. He and his men returned by the Pass of Heres. ¹⁴Gideon captured a young man from Succoth and asked him some questions. The young man wrote down for Gideon the names of 77 men. They were the officers and older leaders of Succoth.

Gideon Punishes Succoth

¹⁵Then Gideon came to Succoth. He said to the men of that city, "Here are Zebah and Zalmunna. You made fun of me by saying, 'Why should we give bread to your tired men? You have not caught Zebah and Zalmunna yet.'" ¹⁶So Gideon took the older leaders of the city. He punished them with thorns and briers from the desert. ¹⁷He also pulled down the tower of Peniel. Then he killed the men in that city.

¹⁸Gideon spoke to Zebah and Zalmunna. He said, "You killed some men on Mount Tabor. What were those men like?"

Zebah and Zalmunna answered, "They were like you. Each one of them seemed like a prince."

¹⁹Gideon said, "Those were my brothers, my mother's sons. As surely as the Lord lives, I would not kill you if you had spared them." ²⁰Then Gideon turned to Jether, his oldest son. Gideon said to him, "Kill them." But Jether was only a boy and was afraid. So he did not take out his sword.

²¹Then Zebah and Zalmunna said to Gideon, "Come on. Kill us yourself. As the saying goes, 'It takes a man to do a man's job.'" So Gideon got up and killed Zebah and Zalmunna. Then he took the decorations off their camels' necks.

Gideon Makes an Idol

²²The people of Israel said to Gideon, "You saved us from the Midianites. So now, rule over us. We want you, your son and your grandson to rule over us."

²³But Gideon told them, "The Lord will be your ruler. I will not rule over you. And my son will not rule over you." ²⁴He said, "I want you to do this one thing for me. I want each of you to give me a gold earring from the things you took in the fighting." (The Ishmaelite men wore gold earrings. And some Ishmaelites had been defeated in the battle.)

²⁵So the people of Israel said to Gideon, "We will gladly give you what you want." So they put a coat down on

the ground. Each man threw an earring onto the coat. ²⁶The gold earrings weighed about 43 pounds. This did not count the weight of the other gifts the people gave to Gideon. They gave him decorations, necklaces and purple robes. These were things that the kings of Midian had worn. The people also gave him chains from the camels of the kings of Midian. ²⁷Gideon used the gold to make an idol. He put the idol in his hometown of Ophrah. All the people of Israel were unfaithful to God and worshiped the idol. It became a trap that caused Gideon and his family to sin.

The Death of Gideon

²⁸So Midian was forced to be under the rule of Israel. Midian did not cause trouble anymore. And the land had peace for 40 years, as long as Gideon was alive.

also had a son by her. He named that son Abimelech. ³²So Gideon son of Joash died at a good old age. He was buried in the tomb of Joash, his father. That tomb is in Ophrah, where the Abiezrites live.

³³As soon as Gideon died, the people of Israel were again unfaithful to God. They followed the Baal^d gods. They made Baal-of-the-Agreement their god. ³⁴The Israelites did not remember the Lord their God. He had saved them from all their enemies who were living all around them. ³⁵And Jerub-Baal, also called Gideon, had done many good things for Israel. But Israel was not kind to the family of Gideon for these things.

Abimelech Becomes King

9 Abimelech son of Jerub-Baal, also called Gideon, went to his uncles. They lived in the city of Shechem. He said to his uncles and all of his mother's family group, ²"Ask the leaders of Shechem this question: 'Is it better for

People Who Got Away
JOTHAM • JUDGES 9:1-21

Abimelech wanted to become king over Israel. His father Gideon had been Israel's leader, a judge. Abimilech was determined, and he was also evil. After his father died, he killed all his brothers so he could become king. But one brother, Jotham, escaped. Jotham told the people that they should not choose someone like Abimelech to be their leader, because he was a very bad person and did not follow God. Soon pride and selfishness brought Abimelech down. Eventually, the people understood that Jotham had been telling them the truth about Abimelech.

You should always be faithful to tell God's truth whether people listen and agree with you or not.

To find out why David had a statue in his bed, fly to page 351.

²⁹Gideon son of Joash went to his home to live. ³⁰He had 70 sons of his own. He had many sons because he had many wives. ³¹Gideon had a slave woman^d who lived in Shechem. He

you to be ruled by the 70 sons of Jerub-Baal or to be ruled by only 1 man?' Remember, I am your relative."

³Abimelech's uncles spoke to all the leaders of Shechem. They asked them

that question. All the leaders decided to follow Abimelech. They said, "He is our brother." [4]So the leaders of Shechem gave Abimelech about one and three-fourths pounds of silver. The silver was from the temple of the god Baal[d]-of-the-Agreement. Abimelech used the silver to hire some worthless, reckless men. They followed Abimelech wherever he went. [5]Abimelech went to Ophrah, the hometown of his father. There Abimelech murdered his 70 brothers. They were the sons of Abimelech's father, Gideon. He killed them all on one stone. But Gideon's youngest son, Jotham, hid from Abimelech and escaped. [6]Then all of the leaders of Shechem and Beth Millo came together. They gathered beside the great tree at the stone pillar in Shechem. There they made Abimelech their king.

Jotham's Story

[7]When Jotham heard this, he went and stood on the top of Mount Gerizim. Jotham shouted to the people: "Listen to me, you leaders of Shechem. Then God may listen to you! [8]One day the trees decided to appoint a king to rule over them. They said to the olive tree, 'You be king over us!'

[9]"But the olive tree said, 'Men and gods are honored by my oil. Should I stop making it just to go and sway over the other trees?'

[10]"Then the trees said to the fig tree, 'Come and be our king!'

[11]"But the fig tree answered, 'Should I stop making my sweet and good fruit? Should I stop just to go and sway over the other trees?'

[12]"Then the trees said to the vine, 'Come and be our king!'

[13]"But the vine answered, 'My wine makes men and gods happy. Should I stop making it just to go and sway over the trees?'

[14]"Then all the trees said to the thornbush, 'Come and be our king.'

[15]"But the thornbush said to the trees, 'If you really want to appoint me king over you, come and find shelter in my shade! But if you do not want to do this, let fire come out of the thornbush. Let the fire burn up the cedars of Lebanon!'

[16]"Now, were you completely honest and sincere when you made Abimelech king? Have you been fair to Gideon and his family? Have you treated Gideon as you should? [17]Remember, my father fought for you. He risked his life to save you from the power of the Midianites. [18]But now you have turned against my father's family. You have killed my father's 70 sons on one stone. You have made Abimelech king over the people of Shechem. He is the son of my father's slave girl! You have made Abimelech king just because he is your relative. [19]So then, if you have been honest and sincere to Gideon and his family today, be happy with Abimelech as your king. And may he be happy with you! [20]But if you have not acted right, may fire come out of Abimelech! May that fire completely burn you leaders of Shechem and Beth Millo! Also may fire come out of the leaders of Shechem and burn up Abimelech!"

[21]Then Jotham ran away. He escaped to the city of Beer. He lived there because he was afraid of his brother Abimelech.

Abimelech Fights Against Shechem

[22]Abimelech ruled Israel for three years. [23]Then God sent an evil spirit to make trouble between Abimelech and the leaders of Shechem. So the leaders of Shechem turned against him. [24]Abimelech had killed Gideon's 70 sons. They were Abimelech's own brothers. And the leaders of Shechem had helped him kill them. So God sent the evil spirit to punish them. [25]The leaders of Shechem were against Abimelech then. They put men on the hilltops. These men attacked and robbed everyone who went by. Abimelech was told about these attacks.

26A man named Gaal and his brothers moved into Shechem. He was the son of Ebed. The leaders of Shechem decided to trust and follow Gaal. 27The people of Shechem went out to the vineyards to pick grapes. They walked on the grapes to make wine. Then they had a feast in the temple of their god. The people ate and drank and cursed Abimelech. 28Then Gaal son of Ebed said, "We are the men of Shechem. Why should we obey Abimelech? Who does he think he is? Isn't Abimelech one of Gideon's sons? Didn't Abimelech make Zebul his officer? We should not obey Abimelech! We should obey the men of Hamor, Shechem's father. Why should we obey Abimelech? 29If you made me commander of these people, I would get rid of Abimelech! I would say to him, 'Get your army ready and come out to battle!'"

30Now Zebul was the ruler of Shechem. He heard what Gaal son of Ebed said. And Zebul became very angry. 31He sent messengers to Abimelech in the city of Arumah. The message said, "Gaal son of Ebed and Gaal's brothers have come to Shechem. Gaal is turning the city against you! 32So now you and your men should get up in the night. Then go lie in the fields outside the city. 33When the sun comes up in the morning, attack the city. Gaal and his men will come out to fight you. Then do what you can to them."

34So Abimelech and all his soldiers got up during the night. They went near Shechem and separated into four groups. There they hid. 35Gaal son of Ebed went out and was standing at the entrance to the city gate. As he was standing there, Abimelech and his soldiers came out of their hiding places.

36When Gaal saw the soldiers, he said to Zebul, "Look! There are people coming down from the mountains!"

But Zebul said, "You are seeing the shadows of the mountains. The shadows just look like people."

37But again Gaal said, "Look, there are people coming down from the center of the land. And there is a group coming from the fortune-tellers' tree!"

38Zebul said to Gaal, "Where is your bragging now? You said, 'Who is Abimelech? Why should we obey him?' You made fun of these men. Now go out and fight them."

39So Gaal led the men of Shechem out to fight Abimelech. 40Abimelech and his men chased them. Many of Gaal's men were killed before they could get back to the city gate. 41Then Abimelech stayed at Arumah. Zebul forced Gaal and his brothers to leave Shechem.

42The next day the people of Shechem went out to the fields. Abimelech was told about it. 43So he separated his men into three groups. And he hid them in the fields. When he saw the people coming out of the city, he jumped up and attacked them. 44Abimelech and his group ran to the entrance gate to the city. The other two groups ran out to the people in the fields and killed them. 45Abimelech and his men fought the city of Shechem all day. They captured it and killed its people. Then Abimelech tore down the city. And he threw salt*n* over the ruins so nothing would ever grow there.

The Tower of Shechem

46The people who lived at the nearby Tower of Shechem heard what had happened to Shechem. So the leaders gathered in the safest room of the temple of the god Baal*d*-of-the-Agreement. 47Abimelech heard that all the leaders of the Tower of Shechem had gathered there. 48So he and all his men went up to Mount Zalmon, near Shechem. Abimelech took an ax and cut some branches. Then he put them on his shoulders. He said to all his men with him, "Hurry! Do what I have done!" 49So all those men cut branches and followed Abimelech. They piled the

---

*n***salt**   The salt would keep crops from growing there.

branches against the safest room of the temple. Then they set them on fire and burned the people in the room. So all the people who lived at the Tower of Shechem also died. There were about 1,000 men and women.

Abimelech's Death

⁵⁰Then Abimelech went to the city of Thebez. He surrounded the city, attacked it and captured it. ⁵¹But inside the city was a strong tower. All the men and women of that city ran to the tower. When they got inside, they locked the door behind them. Then they climbed up to the roof of the tower. ⁵²Abimelech came to the tower and attacked it. He went up to the door of the tower to set it on fire. ⁵³As Abimelech came near, a woman dropped a large stone for grinding grain on his head. The stone crushed Abimelech's skull.

⁵⁴He quickly called to the officer who carried his armor. He said, "Take out your sword and kill me. I don't want people to say, 'A woman killed Abimelech.'" So the officer stabbed Abimelech, and he died. ⁵⁵When the people of Israel saw Abimelech was dead, they all returned home.

⁵⁶In that way God punished Abimelech for all the evil he had done. Abimelech had sinned against his own father by killing his 70 brothers. ⁵⁷God also punished the men of Shechem for the evil they had done. So the curse Jotham had spoken came true. (Jotham was the youngest son of Gideon.)

Tola, the Judge

10 After Abimelech died, another judge came to save the people of Israel. He was Tola son of Puah. (Puah was the son of Dodo.) Tola was from the people of Issachar. He lived in the city of Shamir in the mountains of Ephraim. ²Tola was a judge for Israel for 23 years. Then he died and was buried in Shamir.

Jair, the Judge

³After Tola died, Jair became judge. He lived in the region of Gilead. He was a judge for Israel for 22 years. ⁴Jair had 30 sons, who rode 30 donkeys. These 30 sons controlled 30 towns in Gilead. These towns are called the Towns of Jair to this day. ⁵Jair died and was buried in the city of Kamon.

The Ammonites Trouble Israel

⁶Again the Israelites did what the Lord said was wrong. They worshiped the Baal[d] and Ashtoreth[d] idols. They also worshiped the gods of the peoples of Aram, Sidon, Moab and Ammon. And they worshiped the gods of the Philistines. The Israelites left the Lord and stopped serving him. ⁷So the Lord became angry with them. He allowed the Philistines and the Ammonites to defeat them. ⁸In the same year those people destroyed the Israelites who lived east of the Jordan River. This is in the region of Gilead, where the Amorites lived. The Israelites suffered for 18 years. ⁹The Ammonites then crossed the Jordan River to fight the people of Judah, Benjamin and Ephraim. The Ammonites caused much trouble to the people of Israel. ¹⁰So the Israelites cried out to the Lord, "We have sinned against you. We left our God and worshiped the Baal idols."

¹¹The Lord answered the Israelites, "You cried to me when the Egyptians, the Amorites, the Ammonites and the Philistines hurt you. I saved you from these people. ¹²You cried to me when the Sidonians, Amalekites and Maonites hurt you. I also saved you from those people. ¹³But you have left me. You have worshiped other gods. So I refuse to save you again! ¹⁴You have chosen those gods. So go call to them for help. Let them save you when you are in trouble!"

¹⁵But the people of Israel said to the Lord, "We have sinned. Do to us whatever you want, but please save us today!" ¹⁶Then the Israelites threw away the foreign gods among them. And they worshiped the Lord again. So he felt sorry for them when he saw their suffering.

17The Ammonite people gathered for war and camped in Gilead. The Israelites gathered and camped at Mizpah. 18The leaders of the people of Gilead said, "Who will lead us to attack the people of Ammon? He will become the head of all those who live in Gilead."

Jephthah Is Chosen as Leader

11 Jephthah was from the people of Gilead. He was a strong soldier. His father was named Gilead, and his mother was a prostitute.d 2Gilead's wife had several sons. When they grew up, they forced Jephthah to leave his home. They said to him, "You will not get any of our father's property. You are the son of another woman." 3So Jephthah ran away from his brothers. He lived in the land of Tob. There some worthless men began to follow Jephthah.

4After a time the Ammonite people fought against Israel. 5The Ammonites made war against Israel. At that time the older leaders of Gilead came to Jephthah. They wanted him to come back to Gilead. 6They said to him, "Come and lead our army so we can fight the Ammonites."

7But Jephthah said to them, "Didn't you hate me? You forced me to leave my father's house! Why are you coming to me now that you are in trouble?"

8The older leaders of Gilead said to Jephthah, "That is the reason we come to you now. Please come with us and fight against the Ammonites! You will be the ruler over everyone who lives in Gilead."

9Then Jephthah answered, "Suppose you take me back to Gilead to fight the Ammonites. If the Lord helps me win, I will be your ruler."

10The older leaders of Gilead said to him, "The Lord is listening to everything we are saying. We promise to do all that you tell us to do." 11So Jephthah went with the older leaders of Gilead. The people made him their leader and commander of their army. Jephthah repeated all of his words in front of the Lord at Mizpah.

Jephthah Sends Messengers to the Ammonite King

12Jephthah sent messengers to the king of the Ammonites. The messengers asked the king, "What have you got against Israel? Why have you come to attack our land?"

13The king of the Ammonites answered the messengers of Jephthah. He said, "We are fighting Israel because you took our land when you came up from Egypt. You took our land from the Arnon River to the Jabbok River to the Jordan River. Now tell the people of Israel to give our land back to us in peace."

14Jephthah sent the messengers to the Ammonite king again. 15They took this message:

"This is what Jephthah says: Israel did not take the land of the people of Moab or Ammon. 16When the people of Israel came out of Egypt, they went into the desert. They went to the Gulf of Aqaba and then to Kadesh. 17Israel sent messengers to the king of Edom. They asked, 'Let the people of Israel go across your land.' But the king of Edom didn't let us. We sent the same message to the king of Moab. But he would not let us go across his land either. So the Israelites stayed at Kadesh.

18"Then the Israelites went into the desert. They went around the borders of the lands of Edom and Moab. Israel walked east of the land of Moab. They camped on the other side of the Arnon River. It was the border of the land of Moab. They did not cross it to go into the land of Moab.

19"Then Israel sent messengers to Sihon king of the Amorites. Sihon was the king of the city of Heshbon. The messengers asked Sihon, 'Let the people of Israel pass through your land. We want to go to our land.' 20But Sihon would not let the Israelites cross his land. He gathered all of his people and camped at Jahaz. Then the Amorites fought with Israel.

²¹"But the Lord, the God of Israel, helped the Israelites to defeat Sihon and his army. All the land of the Amorites became the property of Israel. ²²So Israel took all the land of the Amorites. It went from the Arnon River to the Jabbok River. It also went from the desert to the Jordan River.

²³"It was the Lord, the God of Israel, who forced out the Amorites ahead of the people of Israel. So do you think you can make the people of Israel leave this land? ²⁴Surely you can live in the land which your god Chemosh[d] has given you. So we will live in the land the Lord our God has given us!

²⁵"Are you any better than Balak son of Zippor? He was the king of Moab. Did he ever quarrel or fight with the people of Israel? ²⁶For 300 years the Israelites have lived in Heshbon and Aroer and the towns around them. They have lived for 300 years in all the cities along the Arnon River. Why have you not taken these cities back in all that time? ²⁷I have not sinned against you. But you are sinning against me by making war on me! May the Lord, the Judge, decide whether the Israelites or Ammonites are right."

²⁸But the king of the Ammonites ignored this message from Jephthah.

Jephthah's Promise

²⁹Then the Spirit[d] of the Lord entered Jephthah. Jephthah passed through Gilead and Manasseh. He came to the city of Mizpah in Gilead. From there, Jephthah passed through to the land of the Ammonites. ³⁰Jephthah made a promise to the Lord. He said, "If you will let me defeat the Ammonites, ³¹I will give you a burnt offering. I will sacrifice the first thing that comes out of my house to meet me when I return from the victory. It will be the Lord's."

³²Then Jephthah went over to fight the Ammonites. The Lord helped him defeat them. ³³Jephthah defeated

them from the city of Aroer to the area of Minnith. He defeated them as far as the city of Abel Keramim. He defeated 20 cities in this area. The defeat was great. So the Ammonites were defeated by the Israelites.

³⁴When Jephthah returned home to Mizpah, his daughter came out to meet him. She was playing a tambourine[d] and dancing. She was his only child. Jephthah did not have any other sons or daughters. ³⁵When Jephthah saw his daughter, he tore his clothes to show how upset he was. He said, "My daughter! You have made me so sad! This is because I have made a promise to the Lord, and I cannot break it!"

³⁶Then his daughter said, "Father, you made a promise to the Lord. So do to me just what you promised. The Lord helped you defeat your enemies, the Ammonites." ³⁷Then she said, "But let me do one thing. Let me be alone for two months to go to the mountains. I will never marry. So let me and my friends go and cry together."

³⁸Jephthah said, "Go." He sent her away for two months. She and her friends stayed in the mountains. There they cried for her because she would never marry. ³⁹After two months she returned to her father. Jephthah did to her what he promised to the Lord. Now Jephthah's daughter had never had a husband.

So this became a custom in Israel. ⁴⁰Every year the women of Israel would go out for four days. They did this to remember the daughter of Jephthah from Gilead.

Jephthah and Ephraim

12 The men of Ephraim called all their soldiers together. Then they crossed the river to the town of Zaphon. They said to Jephthah, "Why didn't you call us to help you fight the Ammonites? We will burn your house down with you in it!"

²Jephthah answered them, "My people and I fought a great battle against

"The Greatest Bike On Earth"

Dylan learns about sharing
A story based on **Acts 20:35**

Saturday....

WOW, DYLAN! AWESOME BIKE!

I'VE NEVER SEEN A GARGUZZI BEFORE!

CAN I TAKE IT FOR A QUICK RIDE AROUND THE BLOCK?

LET'S RACE!

MAYBE ...NEXT SATURDAY....

At the end of the day...

I'D BETTER PUT THIS IN A SAFE PLACE. GOOD...NO ONE'S WATCHING!

I DON'T WANT ANYONE BORROWING IT. I'LL LOCK IT UP HERE BEHIND ALL THIS JUNK.

the Ammonites. I called you, but you didn't come to help me. ³I saw that you would not help me. So I risked my own life! I went over to fight against the Ammonites. The Lord helped me to defeat them. Now why have you come to fight against me today?"

⁴Then Jephthah called the men of Gilead together. They fought the men of Ephraim. The men of Gilead attacked them because the Ephraimites had insulted them. They had said, "You men of Gilead are nothing but deserters from Ephraim and Manasseh." ⁵The men of Gilead captured the crossing places of the Jordan River. Those places led to the country of Ephraim. A man from Ephraim trying to escape would say, "Let me cross the river." Then the men of Gilead would ask him, "Are you from Ephraim?" If he said, "No," ⁶they would say to him, "Say the word 'Shibboleth.'" The men of Ephraim could not say that word correctly. They pronounced it "Sibboleth." If the man from Ephraim said, "Sibboleth," the men of Gilead would kill him at the crossing place. So 42,000 men from Ephraim were killed at that time.

⁷Jephthah was a judge for the people of Israel for six years. Then Jephthah, the man from Gilead, died. He was buried in a town in Gilead.

Ibzan, the Judge

⁸After Jephthah died, Ibzan was a judge for Israel. He was from Bethlehem. ⁹He had 30 sons and 30 daughters. He let his daughters marry men who were not in his family group. And he brought 30 women who were not in his tribe to be wives for his sons. Ibzan judged Israel for seven years. ¹⁰Then he died and was buried in Bethlehem.

Elon, the Judge

¹¹After Ibzan died, Elon was a judge for Israel. He was from the tribe*d* of Zebulun. He judged Israel for ten years. ¹²Then Elon, the man of Zebulun,

died. He was buried in the city of Aijalon in the land of Zebulun.

Abdon, the Judge

¹³After Elon died, Abdon was a judge for Israel. He was the son of Hillel. Abdon was from the city of Pirathon. ¹⁴He had 40 sons and 30 grandsons, who rode on 70 donkeys. He judged Israel for eight years. ¹⁵Then Abdon son of Hillel died. He was buried in Pirathon in the land of Ephraim. This is in the mountains where the Amalekites lived.

The Birth of Samson

13 Again the people of Israel did what the Lord said was wrong. So he let the Philistines rule over them for 40 years.

²There was a man named Manoah from the city of Zorah. Manoah was from the tribe*d* of Dan. He had a wife, but she could not have children. ³The angel of the Lord appeared to Manoah's wife. He said, "You have not been able to have children. But you will become pregnant and have a son! ⁴Don't drink wine or beer. Don't eat anything that is unclean.*d* ⁵You will become pregnant and have a son. You must never cut his hair because he will be a Nazirite.*d* He will be given to God from birth. He will begin the work of saving Israel from the power of the Philistines."

⁶Then Manoah's wife went to him and told him what had happened. She said, "A man from God came to me. He looked like an angel from God. His appearance was frightening. I didn't ask him where he was from. And he didn't tell me his name. ⁷But he said to me, 'You will be pregnant and will have a son. Don't drink wine or beer. Don't eat anything that is unclean. The reason is that the boy will be a Nazirite to God. He will be that from his birth until the day of his death.'"

⁸Then Manoah said a prayer to the Lord: "Lord, I beg you to let the man of God come to us again. Let him

teach us what we should do for the boy who will be born to us."

9God heard Manoah's prayer. The angel of God came to Manoah's wife again. This was while she was sitting in a field. But her husband Manoah was not with her. 10So she ran to tell him, "He is here! The man who appeared to me the other day is here!" 11Manoah got up and followed his wife. When he came to the man, he said, "Are you the man who spoke to my wife?"

The man said, "I am."

12So Manoah asked, "When what you say happens, what kind of life should the boy live? What should he do?"

13The angel of the Lord said, "Your wife must do everything I told her to do. 14She must not eat anything that grows on a grapevine. She must not drink any wine or beer. She must not eat anything that is unclean. She must do everything I have commanded her to do."

15Manoah said to the angel of the Lord, "We would like you to stay awhile. We want to cook a young goat for you."

16The angel of the Lord answered, "Even if I stay awhile, I would not eat your food. But if you want to prepare something, offer a burnt offering to the Lord." (Manoah did not understand that the man was really the angel of the Lord.)

17Then Manoah asked the angel of the Lord, "What is your name? We want to know. Then we may honor you when what you have said really happens."

18The angel of the Lord said, "Why do you ask my name? It is too wonderful for you to understand." 19Then Manoah sacrificed a young goat on a rock. He also offered some grain as a gift to the Lord. The Lord did an amazing thing. Manoah and his wife watched what happened. 20The flames went up to the sky from the altar. As the fire burned, the angel of the Lord

went up to heaven in the fire! When Manoah and his wife saw that, they bowed facedown on the ground. 21The angel of the Lord did not appear to them again. Then Manoah understood that the man was really the angel of the Lord. 22Manoah said, "We have seen God! Surely we will die because of this!"

23But his wife said to him, "The Lord does not want to kill us. If he wanted to kill us, he would not have accepted our burnt offering or grain offering. He would not have shown us all these things. And he would not have told us all this."

24So the woman gave birth to a boy. She named him Samson. Samson grew, and the Lord blessed him. 25The Spirit*d* of the Lord began to work in Samson. This was while he was in the city of Mahaneh Dan. It is between the cities of Zorah and Eshtaol.

Samson's Marriage

14 Samson went down to the city of Timnah. There he saw a young Philistine woman. 2When he returned home, he said to his father and mother, "I saw a Philistine woman in Timnah. I want you to get her for me. I want to marry her."

3His father and mother answered, "Surely there is a woman from Israel you can marry. Do you have to marry a woman from the Philistines? The Philistines are not even circumcised."*d*

But Samson said, "Get that woman for me! She is the one I want!" 4(Samson's parents did not know that the Lord wanted this to happen. He was looking for a way to start a fight with the Philistines. They were ruling over Israel at this time.) 5Samson went down with his father and mother to Timnah. They went as far as the vineyard near there. Suddenly, a young lion came roaring toward Samson! 6The Spirit*d* of the Lord entered Samson with great power. Samson tore the lion apart with his bare hands. For him it was as easy as tearing apart a young goat. But Samson did not tell his father or mother what he had done. [7]Then he went down to the city. There he talked to the Philistine woman, and he liked her.

[8]Several days later Samson went back to marry her. On his way he went over to look at the body of the dead lion. He found a swarm of bees in it. They had made some honey. [9]Samson got some of the honey with his hands. He walked along eating it. When he came to his parents, he gave some to them. They ate it, too. But Samson did not tell them he had taken the honey from the body of the dead lion.

[10]Samson's father went down to see the Philistine woman. The custom was for the bridegroom to give a feast. So Samson gave a feast. [11]When the people saw him, they sent 30 men to be with him.

Samson's Riddle

[12]Then Samson said to the 30 men, "Let me tell you a riddle. This feast will last for seven days. Try to find the answer during that time. If you can, I will give you 30 linen shirts. I will also give you 30 changes of clothes. [13]But if you can't tell me the answer, you must pay me. You must give me 30 linen shirts and 30 changes of clothes."

So they said, "Tell us your riddle. We want to hear it."

[14]Samson said,

"Out of the eater comes something
    to eat.
Out of the strong comes
    something sweet."

The 30 men tried for three days to figure it out. But they could not find the answer.

[15]On the fourth[n] day, they came to Samson's wife. They said, "Did you invite us here to make us poor? Trick your husband into telling us the answer to the riddle. If you don't, we will burn you and everyone in your father's house!"

[16]So Samson's wife went to him and began crying. She said, "You hate me! You don't really love me! You told my people a riddle, but you won't tell me the answer."

Samson said, "I haven't even told my father or mother. Why should I tell you?"

[17]Samson's wife cried for the rest of the seven days of the feast. So he finally gave her the answer on the seventh day. He told her because she kept bothering him. Then she told her people the answer to the riddle.

[18]Before sunset on the seventh day of the feast, the Philistine men had the answer. They came to Samson and said,

"What is sweeter than honey?
  What is stronger than a lion?"

Then Samson said to them,

"If you had not plowed with my
    little cow,
  you would not have solved my
    riddle!"

[19]The Spirit[d] of the Lord entered Samson and gave him great power. Samson went down to the city of Ashkelon. He killed 30 of their men and took all their clothes and property. He gave those clothes to the men who had answered his riddle. Then he went to his father's house very angry. [20]And Samson's wife was given to his best man at the wedding.

Samson Troubles the Philistines

15 At the time of the wheat harvest, Samson went to visit his wife. He took a young goat with him. He said, "I'm going to my wife's room." But her father would not let Samson go in.

[2]He said to Samson, "I thought you really hated your wife. So I gave her to the best man from the wedding. Her younger sister is more beautiful. Take her."

[3]But Samson said to him, "Now I have a good reason to hurt you Philistines. No one will blame me!" [4]So

---

[n]**fourth**   The Hebrew word is "seventh." Some old translations say "fourth," which fits the order of events better.

Samson went out and caught 300 foxes. He took 2 foxes at a time and tied their tails together. Then he tied a torch to the tails of each pair of foxes. ⁵Samson lit the torches. Then he let the foxes loose in the grainfields of the Philistines. In this way he burned up their standing grain and the piles of grain. He also burned up their vineyards and their olive trees.

⁶The Philistines asked, "Who did this?"

Someone told them, "Samson, the son-in-law of the man from Timnah, did. He did this because his father-in-law gave his wife to his best man."

So the Philistines burned Samson's wife and her father to death. ⁷Then Samson said to the Philistines, "Since you did this, I will hurt you, too! I won't stop until I pay you back!" ⁸Samson attacked the Philistines and killed many of them. Then he went down and stayed in a cave. It was in the rock of Etam.

⁹Then the Philistines went up and camped in the land of Judah. They stopped near a place named Lehi. ¹⁰The men of Judah asked them, "Why have you come here to fight us?"

They answered, "We have come to make Samson our prisoner. We want to pay him back for what he did to our people."

¹¹Then 3,000 men of Judah went to the cave in the rock of Etam. They said to Samson, "What have you done to us? Don't you know that the Philistines rule over us?"

Samson answered, "I only paid them back for what they did to me!"

¹²Then they said to him, "We have come to tie you up. We will give you to the Philistines."

Samson said to them, "Promise me you will not hurt me yourselves."

¹³The men from Judah said, "We agree. We will just tie you up and give you to the Philistines. We will not kill you." So they tied Samson with two new ropes. Then they led him up from the cave in the rock. ¹⁴When Samson came to the place named Lehi, the Philistines came to meet him. They were shouting for joy. Then the Spirit*d* of the Lord entered Samson and gave him great power. The ropes on him became weak like strings that had been burned. They fell off his hands! ¹⁵Samson found a jawbone of a donkey that had just died. He took it and killed 1,000 men with it!

¹⁶Then Samson said,

"With a donkey's jawbone
 I have made donkeys out of them.
With a donkey's jawbone
 I have killed 1,000 men!"

¹⁷When he finished speaking, he threw away the jawbone. So that place was named Ramath Lehi.*ⁿ*

¹⁸Samson was very thirsty. So he cried out to the Lord. He said, "I am your servant. You gave me this great victory. Do I have to die of thirst now? Do I have to be captured by people who are not circumcised?"*d* ¹⁹Then God opened up a hole in the ground at Lehi, and water came out. When Samson drank that water, he felt better. He felt strong again. So he named that spring Caller's Spring. It is still there in Lehi to this day.

²⁰So Samson judged Israel for 20 years. That was in the days of the Philistines.

Samson Goes to the City of Gaza

16 One day Samson went to Gaza. He saw a prostitute*d* there. He went in to spend the night with her. ²Someone told the people of Gaza, "Samson has come here!" So they surrounded the place and hid and waited for him. Remaining very quiet, they stayed near the city gate all night. They said to each other, "When dawn comes, we will kill Samson!"

³But Samson only stayed with the prostitute until midnight. Then he got up and took hold of the doors and the two posts of the city gate. He tore them loose, along with the bar. Then he put

ⁿRamath Lehi   This name means Jawbone Hill.

them on his shoulders. And he carried them to the top of the hill that faces the city of Hebron!

Samson and Delilah

⁴After this, Samson fell in love with a woman named Delilah. She lived in the Valley of Sorek. ⁵The kings of the Philistines went to Delilah. They said, "Try to find out what makes Samson so strong. Try to trick him into telling you. Find out how we could capture him and tie him up. Then we will be able to control him. If you do this, each one of us will give you 28 pounds of silver."

⁶So Delilah said to Samson, "Tell me why you are so strong. How could someone tie you up and take control of you?"

⁷Samson answered, "Someone would have to tie me up. He would have to use seven new bowstrings that have not been dried. If he did that, I would be as weak as any other man."

⁸Then the kings of the Philistines brought seven new bowstrings to Delilah. They had not been dried. She tied Samson with them. ⁹Some men were hiding in another room. Delilah said to Samson, "Samson, the Philistines are about to capture you!" But Samson easily broke the bowstrings. They broke like pieces of string burned in a fire. So the Philistines did not find out the secret of Samson's strength.

¹⁰Then Delilah said to Samson, "You've made me look foolish. You lied to me. Please tell me. How could someone tie you up?"

¹¹Samson said, "They would have to tie me with new ropes that have not been used before. Then I would become as weak as any other man."

¹²So Delilah took new ropes and tied Samson. Some men were hiding in another room. Then she called out to him, "Samson, the Philistines are about to capture you!" But he broke the ropes as easily as if they were threads.

¹³Then Delilah said to Samson, "Until now, you have made me look foolish. You have lied to me. Tell me how someone could tie you up."

He said, "Use the loom.ⁿ Weave the seven braids of my hair into the cloth. Tighten it with a pin. Then I will become as weak as any other man."

Then Samson went to sleep. So Delilah wove the seven braids of his hair into the cloth. ¹⁴Then she fastened it with a pin.

Again she called out to him, "Samson, the Philistines are about to capture you!" Samson woke up and pulled up the pin and the loom with the cloth.

¹⁵Then Delilah said to him, "How can you say, 'I love you,' when you don't even trust me? This is the third time you have made me look foolish. You haven't told me the secret of your great strength." ¹⁶She kept bothering Samson about his secret day after day. He became so tired of it he felt he was going to die!

¹⁷So he told her everything. He said, "I have never had my hair cut. I have been set apart to God as a Nazirite*ᵈ* since I was born. If someone shaved my head, then I would lose my strength. I would become as weak as any other man."

¹⁸Delilah saw that he had told her everything sincerely. So she sent a message to the kings of the Philistines. She said, "Come back one more time. He has told me everything." So the kings of the Philistines came back to Delilah. They brought the silver they had promised to give her. ¹⁹Delilah got Samson to go to sleep. He was lying in her lap. Then she called in a man to shave off the seven braids of Samson's hair. In this way she began to make him weak. And Samson's strength left him.

²⁰Then she called out to him, "Samson, the Philistines are about to capture you!"

He woke up and thought, "I'll get loose as I did before and shake myself

---

ⁿ**loom**   A machine for making cloth from thread.

free." But he did not know that the Lord had left him.

²¹Then the Philistines captured Samson. They tore out his eyes. And they took him down to Gaza. They put bronze chains on him. They put him in prison and made him grind grain. ²²But his hair began to grow again.

²⁵The people were having a good time at the celebration. They said, "Bring Samson out to perform for us." So they brought Samson from the prison. He performed for them. They made him stand between the pillars of the temple of Dagon. ²⁶A servant was holding his hand. Samson said to him, "Let me feel the pillars that hold up the temple. I want to lean against them." ²⁷Now the temple was full of men and women. All the kings of the Philistines

Heroes Who Trusted God

SAMSON • JUDGES 16:23-30

God gave Samson incredible physical strength. Samson once killed a thousand men by himself. Another time, Samson was attacked by a fierce lion. But he tore the lion apart with his bare hands. No problem! The secret of Samson's strength was his long hair. He never cut it. But the Philistines, Samson's enemies, found out Samson's secret and planned to cut his hair.

When Samson lost his hair, he lost his strength too. He became the prisoner of the Philistines. They tore out his eyes and put him in chains. But Samson trusted God. One day the kings and leaders of the Philistines had a party in the temple to celebrate their victory over Samson. Samson prayed and asked God to give him strength one more time so he could kill the Philistines. Samson pushed on the tall pillars that held the roof of the temple so the temple fell down and killed everyone inside.

We can trust God to answer our prayers. You can count on God to hear you cry for help anytime.

To learn about two men who trusted God to help them defeat an enemy army, fly to page 340.

Samson Dies

²³The kings of the Philistines gathered to celebrate. They were going to offer a great sacrifice to their god Dagon.ᵈ They said, "Our god has given us Samson our enemy." ²⁴When they saw him, they praised their god. They said,

"This man destroyed our country.
    He killed many of us!
But our god helped us
    capture our enemy."

were there. There were about 3,000 men and women on the roof.ⁿ They watched Samson perform. ²⁸Then Samson prayed to the Lord. He said, "Lord God, remember me. God, please give me strength one more time. Let me pay these Philistines back for putting out my two eyes!" ²⁹Then Samson held the two center pillars of the temple. These two pillars supported the whole temple. He braced himself

---

ⁿ**roof** In Bible times houses were built with flat roofs. The roof was used for drying things such as flax and fruit. And it was used as an extra room, as a place for worship and as a place to sleep in the summer.

between the two pillars. His right hand was on one, and his left hand was on the other. [30]Samson said, "Let me die with these Philistines!" Then he pushed as hard as he could. And the temple fell on the kings and all the people in it. So Samson killed more of the Philistines when he died than when he was alive.

"I've made messes in the lab before, but they don't compare to the one Samson made!" Read about it in Judges 16:23-31.

[31]Samson's brothers and his whole family went down to get his body. They brought him back and buried him in the tomb of Manoah, his father. That tomb is between the cities of Zorah and Eshtaol. Samson was a judge for the people of Israel for 20 years.

Micah's Idols

17 There was a man named Micah. He lived in the mountains of Ephraim. [2]He said to his mother, "You remember the 28 pounds of silver that were taken from you. I heard you say a curse about it. I have the silver with me. I took it."

His mother said, "The Lord bless you, my son!"

[3]Micah gave the 28 pounds of silver to his mother. Then she said, "I will give this silver to the Lord. I will have my son make a carved idol and an idol of melted silver. So I will give the silver back to you."

[4]So he gave the silver back to his mother. She took about 5 pounds of the silver and gave it to a silversmith. He used it to make a carved idol and an idol of melted silver. The idols were put in Micah's house. [5]Micah had a

temple for worshiping idols. He made a vest[d] for a priest and some household idols. Then Micah chose one of his sons to be his priest. [6]At that time the Israelites did not have a king. So everyone did what he thought was right.

[7]There was a young man who was a Levite.[n] He was from the city of Bethlehem in the land of Judah. He had been living with the people of Judah. [8]He left Bethlehem to look for another place to live. On his way he came to Micah's house. It was in the mountains of Ephraim. [9]Micah asked him, "Where have you come from?"

He answered, "I'm a Levite from Bethlehem in Judah. I'm looking for a place to live."

[10]Then Micah said to him, "Live with me. Be my father and my priest. I will give you 4 ounces of silver each year. I will also give you clothes and food." So the Levite went in. [11]The young Levite agreed to live with Micah. He became like one of Micah's own sons. [12]Micah made him a priest. And he lived in Micah's house. [13]Then Micah said, "Now I know the Lord will be good to me. I know this because I have a Levite as my priest!"

Dan's Family Captures Laish

18 At that time the Israelites did not have a king. The people of Dan were still looking for a land where they could live. They wanted a land of their own. The other tribes[d] of Israel already had their own lands. But the Danites did not yet have their own land. [2]So they chose five soldiers from all their family groups. These five men were from the cities of Zorah and Eshtaol. They sent the men to spy out and explore the land. They were told, "Go, explore the land."

So they came to the mountains of Ephraim. They came to Micah's house, where they spent the night. [3]When they came near Micah's house, they recognized the voice of the young Levite.[n] So they stopped at Micah's

---

[n]**Levite** The Levites were the only ones God had appointed as priests.

house. They asked the young Levite, "Who brought you to this place? What are you doing here? Why are you here?"

[4]He told them what Micah had done for him. "He has hired me. I am his priest."

[5]They said to him, "Please ask God something for us. Will our search for a place to live be successful?"

[6]The priest said to them, "Go in peace. The Lord is pleased with your journey."

[7]So the five men left. They came to the city of Laish. They saw that the people there lived in safety. They were like the people of Sidon. They lived in peace and were not afraid of others. They had plenty of everything. They lived a long way from the Sidonians. And they had no dealings with anyone else.

[8]The five men went back to Zorah and Eshtaol. Their relatives asked them, "What did you find?"

[9]They answered, "We have seen the land. And it is very good. We should attack them. Aren't you going to do something? Don't wait! Let's go and take that land! [10]When you go, you will see there is plenty of land. There is plenty of everything! The people are not expecting an attack. Surely God has given that land to us!"

[11]So 600 men of Dan left Zorah and Eshtaol. They were ready for war. [12]On their way they stopped near the city of Kiriath Jearim in Judah. They set up camp there. That is why the place is named Mahaneh Dan[n] to this very day. It is west of Kiriath Jearim. [13]From there they traveled on to the mountains of Ephraim. Then they came to Micah's house.

[14]So the five men who had explored the land around Laish spoke. They said to their relatives, "There is a vest[d] for a priest in one of these houses. And there are household gods in these houses. There are also a carved idol and an idol of melted silver in these houses. You know what to do."

[15]So they stopped at the Levite's house. This was also Micah's house. And they greeted the Levite. [16]The 600 men of Dan stood at the gate entrance. They wore their weapons of war. [17]The five spies went into the house. They took the carved idol, the vest for a priest, the household idols and the silver idol. The priest and the 600 men ready for war stood by the gate entrance.

[18]When the spies went into Micah's house and took the carved image, the vest for a priest, the household idols and the silver idol, the priest asked them, "What are you doing?"

[19]They answered, "Be quiet! Don't say a word. Come with us. Be our father and our priest. Is it better for you to be a priest for the people in one man's house? Or is it better for you to be a priest for a tribe[d] and family group in Israel?" [20]This made the Levite happy. So he took the vest for a priest, the household idols and the carved idol. And he went with the men of Dan. [21]They left Micah's house. They put their little children, their animals and everything they owned in front of them.

[22]The men of Dan went a long way from Micah's house. Then the men who lived near Micah were called out. They chased the men of Dan and caught up with them. [23]The men with Micah shouted at the men of Dan. The men of Dan turned around. They said to Micah, "What's the matter with you? Why have you called out your men to fight?"

[24]Micah answered, "You took my idols! I made those idols. You have also taken my priest. What do I have left? How can you ask me, 'What's the matter?'"

[25]The men of Dan answered, "You should not argue with us. Some of our men have hot tempers. If you shout at us, they might attack you. You and your family might be killed." [26]Then the men of Dan went on their way.

[n]**Mahaneh Dan**   This name means "the camp of Dan."

Micah knew they were too strong for him. So he turned and went back home. ²⁷So the men of Dan took what Micah had made. They also took his priest and went on to Laish. They attacked those peaceful people. The people of Laish had not expected an attack. The men of Dan killed them with their swords. Then they burned the city. ²⁸There was no one to save the people of Laish. They lived too far from Sidon. And they had no dealings with anyone else. Laish was in a valley near Beth Rehob.

The people of Dan rebuilt the city in that place. And they lived there. ²⁹They changed the name of Laish to Dan. They named it after their ancestor Dan. He was one of the sons of Israel. ³⁰The people of Dan set up the idols in the city of Dan. They made Jonathan son of Gershom their priest. Gershom was the son of Moses. Jonathan and his sons were priests for the tribe of Dan. They served as priests until the Israelites were taken captive. ³¹The people of Dan worshiped the idols Micah had made. They worshiped them as long as the Holy Tent[d] of God was in Shiloh.

A Levite and His Servant

19 At that time the people of Israel did not have a king.

There was a Levite who lived in the faraway part of the mountains of Ephraim. He had taken a slave woman.[d] She was from the city of Bethlehem in the land of Judah. ²But she was unfaithful to him. She left him and went back to her father's house. It was in Bethlehem in Judah. She stayed there for four months. ³Then her husband went to ask her to come back to him. He took with him his servant and two donkeys. The Levite came to her father's house. And she invited the Levite to come in. Her father was happy to see him. ⁴The father-in-law, the young woman's father, asked him to stay. So he stayed for three days. He ate, drank and slept there.

⁵On the fourth day they got up early in the morning. The Levite was getting ready to leave. But the woman's father said to his son-in-law, "Refresh yourself by eating something. Then you may go." ⁶So the two men sat down to eat and drink together. After that, the father said to him, "Please stay tonight. Relax and enjoy yourself." ⁷When the man got up to go, his father-in-law asked him to stay. So he stayed again that night. ⁸On the fifth day the man got up early in the morning to leave. The woman's father said, "Refresh yourself. Wait until this afternoon." So the two men ate together.

⁹Then the Levite, his slave woman and his servant got up to leave. His father-in-law, the young woman's father, said, "It's almost night. The day is almost gone. So spend the night here and enjoy yourself. Tomorrow morning you may get up early and go on your way home." ¹⁰But the Levite did not want to stay another night. He took his two saddled donkeys and his slave woman. He traveled toward the city of Jebus. (Jebus is another name for Jerusalem.)

¹¹The day was almost over. They were near Jebus. So the servant said to his master, "Let's stop at this city. It's the city of the Jebusite people. Let's spend the night here."

¹²But his master said, "No. We won't go inside a strange city. Those people are not Israelites. We will go on to the city of Gibeah." ¹³Then he said, "Come on. Let's try to make it to Gibeah or Ramah. We can spend the night in one of those cities." ¹⁴So they went on. And the sun went down as they came near Gibeah. Gibeah belongs to the tribe[d] of Benjamin. ¹⁵So they stopped there to spend the night. They came to the public square in the middle of the city and sat down. But no one invited them home to spend the night.

¹⁶That evening an old man came into the city from his work in the fields. His home was in the mountains of Ephraim. But now he was living in

Gibeah. (The men of Gibeah were from the tribe of Benjamin.) [17]He saw the traveler, the Levite, in the public square. He asked, "Where are you going? Where did you come from?"

[18]The Levite answered, "We are traveling from Bethlehem in Judah. We're going to my home. I'm from a faraway part of the mountains of Ephraim. I have been to Bethlehem in Judah. Now I am going to the Holy Tent[d] of the Lord. No one has invited me to stay in his house. [19]We already have straw and food for our donkeys. There is bread and wine for me, the young woman and my servant. We don't need anything."

[20]The old man said, "You are welcome to stay at my house. Let me give you anything you need. But don't spend the night in the public square." [21]So the old man took the Levite into his house. He fed their donkeys, and they washed their feet. Then he gave them something to eat and drink.

[22]While they were enjoying themselves, some wicked men of the city surrounded the house. They beat on the door. They shouted to the old man who owned the house. They said, "Bring out the man who came to your house. We want to have sexual relations with him."

[23]The owner of the house went outside. And he said to them, "No, my friends. Don't be so evil. This man is a guest in my house. Don't do this terrible thing! [24]Look, here is my daughter. She has never had sexual relations before. And here is the man's slave woman. I will bring them out to you now. Do anything you want with them. But don't do such a terrible thing to this man."

[25]But the men would not listen to him. So the Levite took his slave woman and sent her outside to them. They had sexual relations with her even though she didn't want to. They treated her very badly all night long.

Then, at dawn, they let her go. [26]She came back to the house where her master was staying. She fell down at the door and lay there until daylight.

[27]In the morning the Levite got up. He opened the door of the house. He went outside to go on his way. But there lay his slave woman. She had fallen down at the doorway of the house. Her hands were on the doorsill. [28]Then the Levite said to her, "Get up; let's go." But she did not answer. So he put her on his donkey and went home.

[29]When the Levite got home, he took a knife and cut his slave woman into 12 parts. Then he sent a part to each of the areas where the people of Israel lived. [30]Everyone who saw this said, "Nothing like this has ever happened before. It has never happened since the people of Israel came out of Egypt. Think about it. Tell us what to do."

The War Between Israel and Benjamin

20 So all the Israelites joined together. They came to stand before the Lord in the city of Mizpah. They came from as far away as the cities of Dan and Beersheba.[n] Even the Israelites from the land of Gilead were there. [2]The leaders of all the tribes[d] of Israel were there. They took their places in the meeting of the people of God. There were 400,000 soldiers with swords. [3](The people of Benjamin heard that the Israelites had gone up to Mizpah.) Then the Israelites said to the Levite, "Tell us how this evil thing happened."

[4]So the husband of the murdered woman answered: "My slave woman[d] and I came to Gibeah in Benjamin to spend the night. [5]During the night the men of Gibeah came after me. They surrounded the house and wanted to kill me. They had sexual relations with my slave woman even though she didn't want to. And she died! [6]So I took her

---

[n]**Dan . . . Beersheba** Dan was the city farthest north in Israel. Beersheba was the city farthest south. So this means all the people of Israel.

and cut her into parts. Then I sent one part to each area of Israel's land. I did it because the people of Benjamin have done this wicked and terrible thing in Israel. [7]Now, all you men of Israel, speak up. Tell what you have decided we should do."

[8]Then all the people stood up at the same time. They said, "None of us will go home. Not one of us will go back to his house! [9]Now this is what we will do to Gibeah. We will throw lots[d] so that God can show us what to do. [10]We will choose 10 men from each 100 men. They will be from all the tribes of Israel. And we will choose 100 men from each 1,000. We will choose 1,000 men from each 10,000. These men will find supplies for the army. Then the army will go to the city of Gibeah of Benjamin. They will repay those people for the terrible thing they have done in Israel." [11]So all the men of Israel gathered against the city. They all agreed about what they were doing.

[12]The tribes of Israel sent men to all the family groups of Benjamin with a message. They said, "What is this evil thing some of your men have done? [13]Give up the evil men in Gibeah so that we can put them to death. We must remove this evil from Israel."

But the Benjaminites would not listen to their relatives, the people of Israel. [14]The Benjaminites left their own cities and met at Gibeah. They went to fight against the Israelites. [15]In only one day the Benjaminites got 26,000 soldiers together. These soldiers were trained with swords. They also had 700 chosen men from Gibeah. [16]Seven hundred of these trained soldiers were left-handed. Each of these left-handed soldiers could sling a stone at a hair and not miss!

[17]The Israelites, except for the Benjaminites, gathered 400,000 fighting men. These 400,000 men used swords and were trained soldiers.

[18]The Israelites went up to the city of Bethel. They asked God, "Which tribe shall be first to attack the Benjaminites?"

The Lord answered, "Judah shall go first."

[19]The next morning the Israelites got up. They made a camp near Gibeah. [20]Then the men of Israel went out to fight the Benjaminites. The Israelites got into battle position at Gibeah. [21]Then the Benjaminites came out of Gibeah. They killed 22,000 Israelites during the battle that day. [22-23]The Israelites went before the Lord. They cried until evening. They asked the Lord, "Shall we go to fight our relatives, the Benjaminites, again?"

The Lord answered, "Go up and fight them." The men of Israel encouraged each other. So they took the same battle positions they had taken the first day.

[24]The Israelites brought their battle lines against the Benjaminites the second day. [25]The Benjaminites came out of Gibeah to attack the Israelites. This time, the Benjaminites killed 18,000 Israelites. All of these Israelites had been trained with swords.

[26]Then the Israelites went up to Bethel. There they sat down and cried to the Lord. They went without food all day until evening. They also brought burnt offerings and fellowship offerings to the Lord. [27]The Israelites asked the Lord a question. (In those days the Box[d] of the Agreement with God was there at Bethel. [28]A priest named Phinehas served before the Box of the Agreement. He was the son of Eleazar, who was the son of Aaron.) The people of Israel asked, "Shall we again go to fight against our relatives the Benjaminites? Or shall we stop fighting?"

The Lord answered, "Go, because tomorrow I will help you defeat them."

[29]Then the Israelites hid some men all around Gibeah. [30]They went to fight against the Benjaminites at Gibeah on the third day. They got into position for battle, as they had done before. [31]Then the Benjaminites came

out of the city to fight them. The Israelites backed up and led the Benjaminites away from the city. The Benjaminites began to kill some of the Israelites as they had done before. About 30 men from Israel were killed. Some of them were killed in the fields and some on the roads. One road led to Bethel. Another road led to Gibeah.

³²The Benjaminites said, "We are winning as before!"

But the Israelites said, "Let's run. Let's trick them into going farther away from their city and onto the roads."

³³All the men of Israel moved from their places. They got into battle positions at a place named Baal Tamar. Then the Israelites ran out from their hiding places west of Gibeah. ³⁴Ten thousand of the best trained soldiers from the army of Israel attacked Gibeah. The battle was very hard. The Benjaminites did not know disaster was about to come to them. ³⁵The Lord used the Israelites to defeat the Benjaminites. On that day the Israelites killed 25,100 Benjaminites. All these men were armed with swords. ³⁶Then the Benjaminites saw that they were defeated.

The men of Israel had moved back. They backed up because they were depending on the surprise attack. They had set it up near Gibeah. ³⁷The men in hiding rushed into Gibeah. They spread out and killed everyone in the city with their swords. ³⁸Now the men of Israel had made a plan with the men in hiding. The men in the surprise attack were to send up a signal. It was to be a big cloud of smoke from the city. ³⁹So the army of Israel turned around in the battle.

The Benjaminites had killed about 30 Israelites. They were saying, "We are winning, as in the first battle!" ⁴⁰But then the big cloud of smoke began to rise from the city. The Benjaminites turned around and saw it. The whole city was full of smoke that went up into the sky. ⁴¹Then the

Israelites turned and began to fight. The Benjaminites were terrified. Now they knew that disaster was coming to them. ⁴²So the Benjaminites ran away from the Israelites. They ran toward the desert. But they could not escape the battle. And the Israelites who came out of the cities killed them. ⁴³They surrounded the Benjaminites and chased them. They caught them in the area east of Gibeah. ⁴⁴So 18,000 brave and strong Benjaminite fighters were killed. ⁴⁵The Benjaminites ran toward the desert. They ran to a place called the rock of Rimmon. But the Israelites killed 5,000 Benjaminites along the roads. They kept chasing them as far as a place named Gidom. And they killed 2,000 more Benjaminites there.

⁴⁶On that day 25,000 Benjaminites were killed. All of them had fought bravely with swords. ⁴⁷But 600 Benjaminites ran to the rock of Rimmon in the desert. They stayed there for four months. ⁴⁸Then the men of Israel went back to the land of Benjamin. They killed the people in every city. They also killed the animals. They destroyed everything they could find. And they burned every city they found.

Wives for the Men of Benjamin

21 At Mizpah the men of Israel had made a promise. This was their promise: "Not one of us will let his daughter marry a man from the tribe*d* of Benjamin."

²The people went to the city of Bethel. There they sat before God until evening, crying loudly. ³They said, "Lord, you are the God of Israel. Why has this terrible thing happened to us? Why has one tribe of Israel been taken away?"

⁴Early the next day the people built an altar. They put burnt offerings and fellowship offerings to God on it.

⁵Then the Israelites asked, "Did any tribe of Israel not come here to meet with us before the Lord?" They asked this question because they had made

a great promise. They had promised that anyone who did not meet with them at Mizpah would be killed.

6The Israelites felt sorry for their relatives, the Benjaminites. They said, "Today one tribe has been separated from Israel. 7We made a promise before the Lord. We will not allow our daughters to marry a Benjaminite. How can we make sure that the men of Benjamin will have wives?" 8Then they asked, "Which one of the tribes of Israel did not come here to Mizpah?" They found that no one from the city of Jabesh Gilead was there. 9The people of Israel counted everyone, but no one from Jabesh Gilead was there.

10So the whole group of Israelites sent 12,000 soldiers to Jabesh Gilead. They told the soldiers to kill the people in Jabesh Gilead with their swords. Even the women and children were to be killed.

11"This is what you must do: Kill every man in Jabesh Gilead. Also kill every woman who has had sexual relations with a man." 12The soldiers found 400 young women in Jabesh Gilead who had never had sexual relations with a man. They brought these women to the camp at Shiloh in Canaan.

13Then the whole group of Israelites sent a message to the men of Benjamin. They offered to make peace with them. The men of Benjamin were at the rock of Rimmon. 14So the men of Benjamin came back at that time. The Israelites gave them the women from Jabesh Gilead who had not been killed. But there were not enough women for all of them.

15The people of Israel felt sorry for the Benjaminites. This was because the Lord had separated the tribes of Israel. 16The older leaders of the Israelites spoke. They said, "The women of Benjamin have been killed. Where can we get wives for the men of Benjamin who are still alive? 17These men must have children to continue their families. This is so a tribe in Israel will not die out. 18But we cannot allow our daughters to marry them. We have made this promise: 'Anyone who gives a wife to a man of Benjamin is cursed.' 19We have an idea! There is a yearly festival of the Lord at Shiloh. Shiloh is north of the city of Bethel. It is east of the road that goes from Bethel to Shechem. And it is south of the city of Lebonah."

20So the older leaders told the men of Benjamin about their idea. They said, "Go and hide in the vineyards. 21Watch for the young women from Shiloh to come out. They will come to join the dancing. Then run out from the vineyards. Each of you take one of the young Shiloh women and go to the land of Benjamin. 22The fathers or brothers of those young women will come to us. They will complain, but we will say: 'Be kind to the men of Benjamin. We did not get wives for Benjamin during the war. And you did not give the women to the men from Benjamin. So you are not guilty.'"

23So that is what the Benjaminites did. While the young women were dancing, each man caught one of them. They took them away and married them. Then they went back to the land God had given them. They rebuilt their cities and lived there.

24Then the Israelites went home. They went to their own tribes and family groups. They went to their own land that God had given them.

25In those days the Israelites did not have a king. Everyone did what he thought was right.

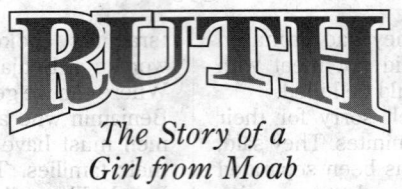

RUTH

The Story of a Girl from Moab

1 **1-2**Long ago the judges[n] ruled Israel. During their rule, there was a time in the land when there was not enough food to eat. A man named Elimelech left Bethlehem in Judah and moved to the country of Moab. He took his wife and his two sons with him. His wife was named Naomi, and his two sons were named Mahlon and Kilion. These people were from the Ephrathah district around Bethlehem in Judah. The family traveled to Moab and lived there.

was Ruth. Naomi and her sons lived in Moab about ten years. **5**Then Mahlon and Kilion also died. So Naomi was left alone without her husband or her two sons.

6While Naomi was in Moab, she heard that the Lord had taken care of his people. He had given food to them in Judah. So Naomi got ready to leave Moab and go back home. The wives of Naomi's sons also got ready to go with her. **7**So they left the place where they had lived. And they started back on the way to the land of Judah. **8**But Naomi said to her two daughters-in-law, "Go back home. Each of you go to

Women Who Trusted God
NAOMI • RUTH 1:8

Naomi showed great love for her daughters-in-law. Naomi's husband had died, leaving her a widow. Then her two sons died, leaving their wives as widows. Being a widow was very difficult in Bible times because a widow did not have any way to earn money to take care of herself. Naomi could have insisted that her daughters-in-law stay with her, but instead she let them choose to go home if they wanted to.

Naomi thought of other people first. God is pleased when we don't always put ourselves first but think about others and try to do what is best for them.

To meet a woman who helped her mother-in-law, fly to page 322.

3Later, Naomi's husband, Elimelech, died. So only Naomi and her two sons were left. **4**These sons married women from Moab. The name of one wife was Orpah. The name of the other wife

your own mother's house. You have been very kind to me and to my sons who are now dead. I hope the Lord will also be kind to you in the same way. **9**I hope the Lord will give you

---

[n]judges   They were not judges in courts of law, but leaders of the people in times of emergency.

another home and a new husband."

Then Naomi kissed the women. And they began to cry out loud. [10]Her daughters-in-law said to her, "No. We will go with you to your people."

[11]But Naomi said, "My daughters, go back to your own homes. Why do you want to go with me? I cannot give birth to more sons to give you new husbands. [12]So go back to your own homes. I am too old to have another husband. But even if I had another husband tonight and if I had more sons, it wouldn't help! [13]Would you wait until the babies were grown into men? Would you live for so many years without husbands? Don't do this thing. My life is much too sad for you to share. This is because the Lord is against me!"

[14]The women cried together again. Then Orpah kissed Naomi good-bye, but Ruth held on to her.

[15]Naomi said, "Look, your sister-in-law is going back to her own people and her own gods. Go back with her."

Ruth Stays with Naomi

[16]But Ruth said, "Don't ask me to leave you! Don't beg me not to follow you! Every place you go, I will go. Every place you live, I will live. Your people will be my people. Your God will be my God. [17]And where you die, I will die. And there I will be buried. I ask the Lord to punish me terribly if I do not keep this promise: Only death will separate us."

[18]Naomi saw that Ruth had made up her mind to go with her. So Naomi stopped arguing with her. [19]Naomi and Ruth went on until they came to the town of Bethlehem. When the two women entered Bethlehem, all the people became very excited. The women of the town said, "Is this Naomi?"

[20]But Naomi told the people, "Don't call me Naomi.[n] Call me Mara,[n] because God All-Powerful has made my life very sad. [21]When I left, I had all

I wanted. But now, the Lord has brought me home with nothing. So why should you call me Naomi when the Lord has spoken against me? God All-Powerful has given me much trouble."

[22]So Naomi and her daughter-in-law Ruth, the woman from Moab, came back from Moab. They came to Bethlehem at the beginning of the barley harvest.

Ruth Meets Boaz

2 Now there was a rich man living in Bethlehem whose name was Boaz. Boaz was one of Naomi's close relatives from Elimelech's family.

[2]One day Ruth, the woman from Moab, said to Naomi, "Let me go to the fields. Maybe someone will be kind and let me gather the grain he leaves in his field."

Naomi said, "Go, my daughter."

[3]So Ruth went to the fields. She followed the workers who were cutting the grain. And she gathered the grain that they had left. It just so happened that the field belonged to Boaz. He was a close relative from Elimelech's family.

[4]When Boaz came from Bethlehem, he spoke to his workers: "The Lord be with you!"

And the workers answered, "May the Lord bless you!"

[5]Then Boaz spoke to his servant who was in charge of the workers. He asked, "Whose girl is that?"

[6]The servant answered, "She is the Moabite woman who came with Naomi from the country of Moab. [7]She said, 'Please let me follow the workers and gather the grain that they leave on the ground.' She came and has remained here. From morning until just now, she has stopped only a few moments to rest in the shelter."

[8]Then Boaz said to Ruth, "Listen, my daughter. Stay here in my field to gather grain for yourself. Do not go to any other person's field. Continue following behind my women workers.

---

[n]**Naomi** This name means "happy" or "pleasant."
[n]**Mara** This name means "bitter" or "sad."

9Watch to see which fields they go to and follow them. I have warned the young men not to bother you. When you are thirsty, you may go and drink. Take water from the water jugs that the servants have filled."

10Then Ruth bowed low with her face to the ground. She said to Boaz, "I am a stranger. Why have you been so kind to notice me?"

here! Eat some of our bread. Here, dip your bread in our vinegar."

So Ruth sat down with the workers. Boaz gave her some roasted grain. Ruth ate until she was full, and there was some food left over. 15Ruth rose and went back to work. Then Boaz told his servants, "Let her gather even around the bundles of grain. Don't tell her to go away. 16Drop some full heads of grain for her. Let her gather that grain, and don't tell her to stop."

17So Ruth gathered grain in the field

Women Who Trusted God
RUTH • RUTH 2:11-12

Although Ruth could have returned to her home when her mother-in-law offered, she decided that she wanted to stay with Naomi. She loved Naomi very much, and so the two of them traveled back to Israel from Moab. Ruth went to work gathering grain in the fields. God's law said that poor people could gather the grain that the harvesters left behind. That was how Naomi and Ruth gathered food to eat.

Even though Ruth was sad about losing her husband and had to work in the fields to get food, she worked very hard and did not feel sorry for herself. If you feel sad, be like Ruth and trust God to help you. Then continue to do your best at school and at home. God will be pleased.

To meet a woman who kept a promise, fly to page 325.

11Boaz answered her, "I know about all the help you have given to Naomi, your mother-in-law. You helped her even after your husband died. You left your father and mother and your own country. You came to this nation where you did not know anyone. 12The Lord will reward you for all you have done. You will be paid in full by the Lord, the God of Israel. You have come to him as a little bird finds shelter under the wings of its mother."

13Then Ruth said, "You are very kind to me, sir. You have said kind words to me, your servant. You have given me hope. And I am not even good enough to be one of your servants."

14At mealtime Boaz told Ruth, "Come

until evening. Then she separated the grain from the chaff.*d* There was about one-half bushel of barley. 18Ruth carried the grain into town. And her mother-in-law saw what she had gathered. Ruth also gave her the food that was left over from lunch.

19Naomi asked her, "Where did you gather all this grain today? Where did you work? Blessed be the man who noticed you!"

Ruth told her about whose field she had worked in. She said, "The man I worked with today is named Boaz."

20Naomi told her daughter-in-law, "The Lord bless him! The Lord still continues to be kind to all people—the living and the dead!" Then Naomi told

Ruth, "Boaz is one of our close relatives,[n] one who will take care of us."

²¹Then Ruth said, "Boaz also told me to come back and continue working. He said, 'Keep close by my servants until they have finished the harvest.'"

²²Then Naomi said to her daughter-in-law Ruth, "It is good for you to continue working with his women servants. If you work in another field, someone might hurt you." ²³So Ruth continued working closely with the women servants of Boaz. She gathered grain until the barley harvest was finished. She also worked there through the end of the wheat harvest. And Ruth continued to live with Naomi, her mother-in-law.

Naomi's Plan

3 Then Naomi, Ruth's mother-in-law, said to her, "My daughter, I must find a suitable home for you. That would be good for you. ²Now Boaz is our close relative.[n] You worked with his women servants. Tonight he will be working at the threshing[d] floor. ³Go wash yourself and put on perfume. Change your clothes, and go down to the threshing floor. But don't let him see you until he has finished eating and drinking. ⁴Then he will lie down. Watch him so you will know the place where he lies down. Go there and lift the cover off his feet[n] and lie down. He will tell you what you should do."

⁵Then Ruth answered, "I will do everything you say."

⁶So Ruth went down to the threshing floor. She did all her mother-in-law told her to do. ⁷After eating and drinking, Boaz was feeling good. He went to lie down beside the pile of grain. Then Ruth went to him quietly. She lifted the cover from his feet and lay down.

⁸About midnight Boaz woke up suddenly and rolled over. He was startled! There was a woman lying near his feet! ⁹Boaz asked, "Who are you?"

She said, "I am Ruth, your servant girl. Spread your cover over me because you are the one who is to take care of me."

¹⁰Then Boaz said, "The Lord bless you, my daughter. Your kindness to me is greater than the kindness you showed to Naomi in the beginning. You didn't look for a young man to marry, either rich or poor. ¹¹Now, my daughter, don't be afraid. I will do everything you ask. All the people in our town know you are a very good woman. ¹²And it is true, I am a relative who is to take care of you. But there is a man who is a closer relative to you than I. ¹³But stay here tonight. In the morning we will see if he will take care of you. If he decides to take care of you, that is fine. If he refuses to take care of you, I myself will marry you. Then I will buy back Elimelech's land for you. As surely as the Lord lives, I promise to do this. So lie here until morning."

¹⁴So Ruth lay near his feet until the morning. She rose while it was still too dark to be recognized. Boaz said to his servants, "Don't tell anyone that the woman came here to the threshing[d] floor." ¹⁵Then Boaz said to Ruth, "Bring me your shawl. Now, hold it open."

So Ruth held her shawl open, and Boaz poured six portions of barley into it. Boaz then put it on her back, and she went to the city.

¹⁶Ruth went to the home of her mother-in-law. And Naomi asked, "How did you do, my daughter?"

So Ruth told Naomi everything that Boaz did for her. ¹⁷She said, "Boaz gave me these six portions of barley. He said, 'You must not go home without a gift for your mother-in-law.'"

¹⁸Naomi answered, "Ruth, my daughter, wait until you hear what happens. Boaz will not rest until he has finished doing what he should do this day."

---

[n]**close relatives** In Bible times the closest relative could marry a widow without children so she could have children. He would care for this family, but they and their property would not belong to him. They would belong to the dead husband.
[n]**lift . . . feet** This showed Ruth was asking him to be her husband.

Boaz Marries Ruth

4 Boaz went to the city gate. He sat there until the close relative he had mentioned passed by. Boaz called to him, "Come here, friend! Sit down here!" So the man came over and sat down. [2]Boaz gathered ten of the old men who were leaders of the city. He told them, "Sit down here!" So they sat down.

[3]Then Boaz spoke to the close relative. He said, "Naomi has come back from the country of Moab. She wants to sell the piece of land that belonged to our relative Elimelech. [4]So I decided to say this to you: If you want to buy back the land, then buy it! Buy it in front of the people who live here and in front of the older leaders of my people. If you don't want to buy it, tell me. I am the only person after you who can buy back the land. If you don't buy it back, I will."

And the close relative said, "I will buy back the land."

[5]Then Boaz said, "When you buy the land from Naomi, you must marry Ruth, the dead man's wife. She is the woman from Moab. That way, the land will stay in her dead husband's family."

[6]The close relative answered, "Then I can't buy back the land. If I did, I might lose what I can pass on to my own sons. I cannot buy the land back. So you buy it yourself."

[7]Long ago in Israel when people traded or bought back something, one person took off his sandal and gave it to the other person. This was their proof of purchase.

[8]So the close relative said, "Buy the land yourself." And then he took off his sandal.

[9]Then Boaz spoke to the older leaders and to all the people. He said, "You are witnesses today of what I am buying from Naomi. I am buying everything that belonged to Elimelech and Kilion and Mahlon. [10]I am also taking Ruth as

my wife. She is the Moabite who was the wife of Mahlon. I am doing this so her dead husband's property will stay with his family. This way, his name will not be separated from his family and his land. You are witnesses this day."

[11]So all the people and older leaders who were at the city gate said, "We are witnesses. This woman will be coming into your home. We hope the Lord will make her like Rachel and Leah. They had many children. So the people of Israel grew in number. May you become powerful in the district of Ephrathah. May you become famous in Bethlehem! [12]Tamar gave birth to Judah's son Perez.[n] In the same way, may the Lord give you many children through Ruth. And may your family be great like his."

[13]So Boaz took Ruth and married her. The Lord let her become pregnant, and she gave birth to a son. [14]The women told Naomi, "Praise the Lord who gave you this grandson. And may he become famous in Israel. [15]He will give you new life. And he will take care of you in your old age. This happened because of your daughter-in-law. She loves you. And she is better for you than seven sons. She has given birth to your grandson."

[16]Naomi took the boy, held him in her arms and cared for him. [17]The neighbors gave the boy his name. These women said, "This boy was born for Naomi." The neighbors named him Obed. Obed was Jesse's father. And Jesse was the father of David.

[18]This is the family history of Perez. Perez was the father of Hezron. [19]Hezron was the father of Ram. Ram was the father of Amminadab. [20]Amminadab was the father of Nahshon. Nahshon was the father of Salmon. [21]Salmon was the father of Boaz. Boaz was the father of Obed. [22]Obed was the father of Jesse, and Jesse was the father of David.

[n]**Perez**   One of Boaz's ancestors.

1 SAMUEL

Samuel
and King Saul

Samuel's Birth

1 There was a man named Elkanah son of Jeroham. He was from Ramathaim in the mountains of Ephraim. Elkanah was from the family of Zuph. (Jeroham was Elihu's son. Elihu was Tohu's son. And Tohu was the son of Zuph from the family group of Ephraim.) ²Elkanah had two wives. One was named Hannah, and the other was named Peninnah. Peninnah had children, but Hannah had none.

³Every year Elkanah left his town Ramah and went up to Shiloh. There he worshiped the Lord of heaven's armies and offered sacrifices to him. Shiloh was where Hophni and Phinehas served as priests of the Lord. They were the sons of Eli. ⁴When Elkanah offered sacrifices, he always gave a share of the meat to his wife Peninnah. He also gave shares of the meat to her sons and daughters. ⁵But Elkanah always gave a special share of the meat to Hannah. He did this because he loved Hannah and because the Lord had made Hannah unable to have children. ⁶Peninnah would upset Hannah and make her feel bad. She did this because the Lord had made Hannah unable to have children.

Women Who Trusted God
HANNAH • 1 SAMUEL 1:9-11

Hannah wanted to have a baby very much. But she had been married for many years and still did not have any children. One day when she and her husband traveled to worship God at the Tent of the Lord, she prayed to God for a baby. She promised God that if she had a baby boy, she would bring the boy to the Tent so he could grow up there and be trained to serve God as a priest.

God answered Hannah's prayer for a son, and Hannah kept her promise. When Samuel was about three years old, Hannah brought him to the Tent of the Lord to be dedicated to serving God all his life. Hannah visited Samuel every year. She loved him very much, but she kept her promise to God.

Do you keep your promises to other people and to God? Be like Hannah and keep your promises.

To meet a woman who waited all of her life to see the Messiah,
fly to page 1222.

[7]This happened every year when they went up to the Tent[d] of the Lord at Shiloh. Peninnah would upset Hannah until Hannah would cry and not eat anything. [8]Her husband Elkanah would say to her, "Hannah, why are you crying? Why won't you eat? Why are you sad? Don't I mean more to you than ten sons?"

[9]Once, after they had eaten their meal in Shiloh, Hannah got up. Now Eli the priest was sitting on a chair near the entrance to the Lord's Holy Tent. [10]Hannah was very sad. She cried much and prayed to the Lord. [11]She made a promise. She said, "Lord of heaven's armies, see how bad I feel. Remember me! Don't forget me. If you will give me a son, I will give him back to you all his life. And no one will ever use a razor to cut his hair."[n]

[12]While Hannah kept praying, Eli watched her mouth. [13]She was praying in her heart. Her lips moved, but her voice was not heard. So Eli thought she was drunk. [14]He said to her, "Stop getting drunk! Throw away your wine!"

[15]Hannah answered, "No, master, I have not drunk any wine or beer. I am a woman who is deeply troubled. I was telling the Lord about all my problems. [16]Don't think of me as an evil woman. I have been praying because of my many troubles and much sadness."

[17]Eli answered, "Go in peace. May the God of Israel give you what you asked of him."

[18]Hannah said, "I want to be pleasing to you always." Then she left and ate something. She was not sad anymore.

[19]Early the next morning Elkanah's family got up and worshiped the Lord. Then they went back home to Ramah. Elkanah had sexual relations with his wife Hannah. And the Lord remembered her. [20]So Hannah became pregnant, and in time she gave birth to a son. She named him Samuel.[n] She said, "His name is Samuel because I asked the Lord for him."

Hannah Gives Samuel to God

[21]Every year Elkanah went to Shiloh to offer sacrifices. He went to keep the promise he had made to God. He brought his whole family with him. So once again he went up to Shiloh. [22]But Hannah did not go with him. She told him, "When the boy is old enough to eat solid food, I will take him to Shiloh. Then I will give him to the Lord. He will become a Nazirite.[d] He will always live there at Shiloh."

[23]Elkanah, Hannah's husband, said to her, "Do what you think is best. You may stay home until the boy is old enough to eat. May the Lord do what you have said." So Hannah stayed at home to nurse her son until he was old enough to eat.

"**K**ids, making promises to God is very serious. Read how Hannah kept her promise in 1 Samuel 1:1–2:26."

[24]When Samuel was old enough to eat, Hannah took him to the Tent[d] of the Lord at Shiloh. She also took a three-year-old bull, one-half bushel of flour and a leather bag filled with wine. [25]They killed the bull for the sacrifice. Then Hannah brought Samuel to Eli. [26]She said to Eli, "As surely as you live, my master, I am the same woman who stood near you praying to the Lord. [27]I prayed for this child. The Lord answered my prayer and gave him to me. [28]Now I give him back to the Lord. He will belong to the Lord all his life." And he worshiped the Lord there.

---

[n]**And . . . hair** People who made special promises not to cut their hair or to drink wine or beer were called Nazirites. These people gave their lives to the Lord. See Numbers 6:1-5.
[n]**Samuel** This name sounds like the Hebrew word for "God heard."

Hannah Gives Thanks

2 Hannah said:

"The Lord has filled my heart with
    joy.
I feel very strong in the Lord.
I can laugh at my enemies.
I am glad because you have helped
    me!

2"There is no one holy like the
    Lord.
    There is no God but you.
    There is no Rock[d] like our God.

3"Don't continue bragging.
    Don't speak proud words.
The Lord is a God who knows
    everything.
    He judges what people do.

4"The bows of warriors break,
    but weak people become strong.
5Those who once had plenty of
    food now must work for
    food.
But people who once were hungry
    now grow fat on food.
The woman who was unable to have
    children now has had seven.
But the woman who had many
    sons now is sad.

6"The Lord causes people to die,
    and he causes them to live.
He brings people down to where the
    dead are,
    and he raises them to life
    again.
7The Lord makes people poor,
    and he makes people rich.
He makes people humble,
    and he makes people great.
8The Lord raises the poor up
    from the dust.
And he picks needy people up
    from the ashes.
He lets the poor sit with princes.
    He lets them sit on a throne of
    honor.

"The foundations of the earth
    belong to the Lord.
The Lord set the world upon them.
9He protects his holy people.

But those who do evil will be
    silenced in darkness.
Their power will not help them
    win.
10The Lord destroys his enemies.
    He will thunder in heaven against
    them.
The Lord will judge all the earth.
    He will give power to his king.
    He will make his appointed king
    strong."

Eli's Evil Sons

11Then Elkanah went home to Ramah. But the boy continued to serve the Lord under Eli the priest.

12Now Eli's sons were evil men. They did not care about the Lord. 13This is what the priests would do to the people: Every time someone brought a sacrifice, the meat would be cooked in a pot. The priest's servant would then come with a fork in his hand. The fork had three prongs. 14He would plunge the fork into the pot or the kettle. Whatever the fork brought out of the pot belonged to the priest. This is how they treated all the Israelites who came to Shiloh to offer sacrifices. 15But even before the fat was burned, the priest's servant would come to the person offering sacrifices. The servant would say, "Give the priest some meat to roast. The priest won't accept boiled meat from you. He will only accept raw meat."

16But the man who offered the sacrifice might say, "Let the fat be burned up first as usual. Then you may take anything you want."

If so, the priest's servant would answer, "No, give me the meat now. If you don't, I'll take it by force."

17The Lord saw that the sin of the servants was very great. They did not show respect for the offerings made to the Lord.

Samuel Grows Up

18But Samuel obeyed the Lord. He wore a linen holy vest.[d] 19Every year Samuel's mother would make a little coat for him. She would take it to him when she went to Shiloh. She went there with her husband for the sacrifice. [20]Eli would bless Elkanah and his wife. Eli would say, "May the Lord repay you with children through Hannah. They will take the place of the boy Hannah prayed for and gave back to the Lord." Then Elkanah and Hannah would go home. [21]The Lord was kind to Hannah. She became the mother of three sons and two daughters. And the boy Samuel grew up serving the Lord.

[22]Now Eli was very old. He heard about everything his sons were doing to all the Israelites. He also heard about how his sons had sexual relations with the women who served at the entrance to the Meeting Tent.[d] [23]Eli said to his sons, "The people here tell me about the evil you do. Why do you do these evil things? [24]No, my sons. The Lord's people are saying bad things about you. [25]If someone sins against another person, God can help him. But if he sins against the Lord himself, no one can help him!" But Eli's sons would not listen to him. This was because the Lord had decided to put them to death.

[26]The boy Samuel kept growing. He pleased God and the people.

[27]A man of God came to Eli. He said, "This is what the Lord says: 'I clearly showed myself to the family of your ancestor Aaron. This was when they were slaves to the king of Egypt. [28]I chose them from all the tribes[d] of Israel to be my priests. I wanted them to go up to my altar, to burn incense[d] and to wear the holy vest. I also let the family of your ancestor have part of all the offerings sacrificed by the Israelites. [29]So why don't you respect the sacrifices and gifts? You honor your sons more than me. You become fat on the best parts of the meat the Israelites bring to me.'

[30]"Here's what the Lord, the God of Israel, says: 'I promised that your family and your ancestor's family would serve me forever.' But now the Lord says this: 'That will never be! I will honor those who honor me. But I will take honor away from those who do not honor me. [31]The time is coming when I will destroy the descendants[d] of both you and your ancestors. No man will grow old in your family. [32]You will see trouble in my house. Good things will be done to Israel. But there will never be an old man in your family. [33]I will save one man to serve as priest at my altar. He will wear out his eyes and use up his strength. The rest of your descendants will die by the sword.

[34]"'I will give you a sign. Both your sons, Hophni and Phinehas, will die on the same day. [35]I will choose a loyal priest for myself. He will listen to me and do what I want. I will make his family strong. He will always serve before my appointed king. [36]Then everyone left in your family will come and bow down before him. They will beg for a little money or a little food. They will say, "Please give me a job as priest so I can have food to eat."'"

God Calls Samuel

3 The boy Samuel served the Lord under Eli. In those days the Lord did not speak directly to people very often. There were very few visions.

[2]Eli's eyes were so weak he was almost blind. One night he was lying in bed. [3]Samuel was also in bed in the Lord's Holy Tent.[d] The Box[d] of the Agreement was in the Holy Tent. God's lamp was still burning.

[4]Then the Lord called Samuel. Samuel answered, "I am here!" [5]He ran to Eli and said, "I am here. You called me."

But Eli said, "I didn't call you. Go back to bed." So Samuel went back to bed.

[6]The Lord called again, "Samuel!"

Samuel again went to Eli and said, "I am here. You called me."

Again Eli said, "I didn't call you. Go back to bed."

⁷Samuel did not yet know the Lord. The Lord had not spoken directly to him yet.

Eli I would punish his family forever. I will do it because Eli knew his sons were evil. They spoke against me, but he did not control them. ¹⁴So here is what I promised Eli's family: 'Your guilt will never be removed by sacrifice or offering.'"

Children Who Saw God at Work
SAMUEL • 1 SAMUEL 3:1-10

Imagine if you lived in your church! Samuel did. He lived in Israel's "church," which was called the Holy Tent or tabernacle. Samuel helped Eli, the priest, in the tabernacle. The priest taught the people about God and made sacrifices to God for them. Samuel's mother had dedicated Samuel to God. He lived in the tabernacle because he was going to grow up and be a priest. Even when Samuel was a young boy, he helped in the tabernacle by sweeping floors and doing other jobs.

One night, God spoke to Samuel. At first, Samuel didn't know who it was. But when he found out it was God, he listened and did exactly what God told him to do. When Samuel grew up, he kept listening to God and doing what God wanted. He taught other people to listen to God, too. God wants you to listen to him and do what he says.

To meet a boy who had a giant problem, fly to page 346.

⁸The Lord called Samuel for the third time. Samuel got up and went to Eli. He said, "I am here. You called me."

Then Eli realized the Lord was calling the boy. ⁹So he told Samuel, "Go to bed. If he calls you again, say, 'Speak, Lord. I am your servant, and I am listening.'" So Samuel went and lay down in bed.

¹⁰The Lord came and stood there. He called as he had before. He said, "Samuel, Samuel!"

Samuel said, "Speak, Lord. I am your servant, and I am listening."

¹¹The Lord said to Samuel, "See, I am going to do something in Israel. It will shock those who hear about it. ¹²At that time I will do to Eli and his family everything I promised. I will not stop until I have finished. ¹³I told

¹⁵Samuel lay down until morning. Then he opened the doors of the Tentᵈ of the Lord. He was afraid to tell Eli about the vision. ¹⁶But Eli said to him, "Samuel, my son!"

Samuel answered, "I am here."

¹⁷Eli asked, "What did the Lord say to you? Don't hide it from me. May God punish you terribly if you hide from me anything he said to you." ¹⁸So Samuel told Eli everything. He did not hide anything from him. Then Eli said, "He is the Lord. Let him do what he thinks is best."

¹⁹The Lord was with Samuel as he grew up. He did not let any of Samuel's messages fail to come true. ²⁰Then all Israel, from Dan to Beersheba,ⁿ knew Samuel was a prophetᵈ of the Lord. ²¹And the Lord continued to show

ⁿ**Dan to Beersheba** Dan was the city farthest north in Israel. Beersheba was the city farthest south. So this means all the people of Israel.

himself to Samuel at Shiloh. He also showed himself to Samuel through his word.

"**L**ord, help me to listen for all the ways you may speak to me. Help me to obey like Samuel did." Read about Samuel when he was a kid in 1 Samuel 3:1-21.

4 News about Samuel spread through all of Israel.

The Philistines Capture the Box of the Agreement

At that time the Israelites went out to fight the Philistines. The Israelites camped at Ebenezer, and the Philistines camped at Aphek. ²The Philistines went to meet the Israelites in battle. And as the battle spread, the Philistines defeated the Israelites. They killed about 4,000 soldiers of the Israelite army. ³Then some Israelite soldiers went back to their camp. The older leaders of Israel asked, "Why did the Lord let the Philistines defeat us? Let's bring the Box*d* of the Agreement with the Lord here from Shiloh. In this way God will go with us into battle. He will save us from our enemies."

⁴So the people sent men to Shiloh. They brought back the Box of the Agreement with the Lord of heaven's armies. Eli's two sons, Hophni and Phinehas, were there with the Holy Box.

⁵The Box of the Agreement with the Lord came into the camp. And all the Israelites gave a great shout of joy. It made the ground shake. ⁶The Philistines heard Israel's shout. They asked, "What's all this shouting in the Hebrew camp?"

Then the Philistines found out that the Holy Box of the Lord had come into the Hebrew camp. ⁷They were afraid and said, "A god has come into the Hebrew camp! We're in trouble! This has never happened before! ⁸How terrible it will be for us! Who can save us from these powerful gods? They are the ones who struck the Egyptians with all kinds of disasters in the desert. ⁹Be brave, Philistines! Fight like men! In the past they were our slaves. So fight like men, or you will become their slaves."

¹⁰So the Philistines fought hard and defeated the Israelites. Every Israelite soldier ran away to his own home. It was a great defeat for Israel, because 30,000 Israelite soldiers were killed. ¹¹The Holy Box of God was taken by the Philistines. And Eli's two sons, Hophni and Phinehas, were killed.

¹²That same day a man from the tribe*d* of Benjamin ran from the battle. He tore his clothes and put dust on his head to show his great sadness. ¹³When he arrived in Shiloh, Eli was by the side of the road. Eli was sitting there in a chair, watching. He was worried about the Holy Box of God. When the Benjaminite entered Shiloh, he told the bad news. Then all the people in town cried loudly. ¹⁴Eli heard the crying and asked, "What's all this noise?"

The Benjaminite ran to Eli and told him what had happened. ¹⁵Eli was now 98 years old, and he was blind. ¹⁶The Benjaminite told him, "I have come from the battle. I ran all the way here today."

Eli asked, "What happened, my son?"

¹⁷The Benjaminite answered, "Israel ran away from the Philistines. The Israelite army has lost many soldiers. Your two sons are both dead. And the Philistines have taken the Holy Box of God."

¹⁸When he mentioned the Holy Box of God, Eli fell backward off his chair. He fell beside the gate and broke his neck, because he was old and fat. And Eli died. He had led Israel for 40 years.

The Glory Is Gone

[19]Eli's daughter-in-law, the wife of Phinehas, was pregnant. It was nearly time for her baby to be born. She heard the news that the Holy Box[d] of God had been taken. She heard also that Eli, her father-in-law, and Phinehas, her husband, were both dead. So she began to give birth to her child. The child was born, but the mother had much trouble in giving birth. [20]As she was dying, the women who helped her give birth said, "Don't worry! You've given birth to a son!" But she did not answer or pay attention. She named the baby Ichabod.[n] [21]She named him Ichabod and said, "Israel's glory is gone." She said this because the Holy Box of God had been taken. It was also because her father-in-law and husband were dead. [22]She said, "Israel's glory is gone, because the Holy Box of God has been taken away."

Trouble for the Philistines

5 After the Philistines had captured the Holy Box[d] of God, they took it from Ebenezer to Ashdod. [2]They carried it into Dagon's[d] temple and put it next to Dagon. [3]The people of Ashdod rose early the next morning. They found that Dagon had fallen on his face on the ground. He was lying before the Holy Box of the Lord. So the people of Ashdod put Dagon back in his place. [4]The next morning the people of Ashdod rose from sleep. And again they found Dagon on the ground! He had fallen down before the Holy Box of the Lord. His head and hands had broken off and were lying in the doorway. Only his body was still in one piece. [5]So, even today, Dagon's priests and others who enter his temple at Ashdod refuse to step on the doorsill.

[6]The Lord punished the people of Ashdod and their neighbors. He gave them much trouble. He gave them growths on their skin. [7]The people of Ashdod saw what was happening. They said, "The Holy Box of the God of Israel can't stay with us. God is punishing us and Dagon our god." [8]The people of Ashdod called all five Philistine kings together. They asked them, "What should we do with the Holy Box of the God of Israel?"

The rulers answered, "Move the Holy Box of the God of Israel to Gath." So the Philistines moved it to Gath.

[9]But after they had moved it to Gath, the Lord punished that city also. He made the people very afraid. God troubled both old and young people in Gath. He caused them to have growths on their skin. [10]Then the Philistines sent the Holy Box of God to Ekron.

But when it came into Ekron, the people of Ekron yelled. They said, "Why are you bringing the Holy Box of the God of Israel to our city? Do you want to kill us and our people?" [11]The people of Ekron called all the kings of the Philistines together. They said to the kings, "Send the Holy Box of the God of Israel back to its place. Do it before it kills us and our people!" They were very afraid. God's punishment was very terrible there. [12]The people who did not die were troubled with growths on their skin. So the people of Ekron cried loudly to heaven.

The Holy Box of God Is Sent Home

6 The Philistines kept the Holy Box[d] of God in their land seven months. [2]Then they called for their priests and magicians. They said, "What should we do with the Holy Box of the Lord? Tell us how to send it back home!"

[3]The priests and magicians answered them. They said, "If you send back the Holy Box of the God of Israel, don't send it away empty. You must offer a penalty offering so the God of Israel will forgive your sins. Then you will be healed. When God has forgiven you, he will stop punishing you."

[4]The Philistines asked, "What kind

[n]**Ichabod** This name means "where is the glory?"

of penalty offering should we send to Israel's God?"

The priests and magicians answered, "Make five gold models of the growths on your skin. Also make five gold models of rats. The number of models must be the same as the number of Philistine kings. This is because the same sickness has come on you and your kings. ⁵Make models of the growths and the rats that are ruining the country. Give them to Israel's God and honor him. Then maybe Israel's God will stop punishing you, your gods and your land. ⁶Don't be stubborn like the king of Egypt and the Egyptians. God punished them terribly. That is why the Egyptians let the Israelites leave Egypt.

⁷"You must build a new cart. And get two cows that have just had calves. These must be cows that have never had yokes^d on their necks. Then hitch the cows to the cart. Take the calves home. Don't let them follow their mothers. ⁸Put the Holy Box of the Lord on the cart. And put the gold models in a box beside the Holy Box. They are your penalty offerings for God to forgive your sins. Send the cart straight on its way. ⁹Watch the cart. It may go toward Beth Shemesh in Israel's own land. If so, the Lord has given us this great sickness. But it may not go toward Beth Shemesh. Then we will know that Israel's God has not punished us. We will know that our sickness just happened by chance."

¹⁰The Philistines did what the priests and magicians said. They took two cows that had just had calves. They hitched them to the cart. But they kept their calves at home. ¹¹They put the Holy Box of the Lord on the cart. And they put the box with the gold rats and models of growths on the cart. ¹²Then the cows went straight toward Beth Shemesh. They stayed on the road, mooing all the way. They did not turn right or left. The Philistine kings followed the cows as far as the border of Beth Shemesh.

¹³Now the people of Beth Shemesh were harvesting their wheat in the valley. They looked up and saw the Holy Box of the Lord. They were very happy to see it again. ¹⁴The cart came to the field belonging to Joshua of Beth Shemesh. The cart stopped in this field near a large rock. The people of Beth Shemesh chopped up the wood of the cart. Then they killed the cows and sacrificed them to the Lord. ¹⁵The Levites took down the Holy Box of the Lord. They also took down the box that had the gold models. They put both on the large rock. That day the people of Beth Shemesh offered whole burnt offerings and made sacrifices to the Lord. ¹⁶The five Philistine kings watched them do all these things. Then they went back to Ekron the same day.

¹⁷The Philistines sent these gold models of the growths. They were penalty offerings to the Lord for their sins. They sent one model for each Philistine town. These towns were Ashdod, Gaza, Ashkelon, Gath and Ekron. ¹⁸And the Philistines also sent gold models of rats. The number of rats was the same as the number of towns belonging to the Philistine kings. These towns included strong, walled cities and country villages. The large rock on which they put the Holy Box of the Lord is still there. It is in the field of Joshua of Beth Shemesh.

¹⁹But some of the men of Beth Shemesh looked into the Holy Box of the Lord. So God killed 70 of them. The people of Beth Shemesh cried because the Lord had punished them so terribly. ²⁰They said, "Who can stand before the Lord, this holy God? Where can the Holy Box go from here?"

²¹Then they sent messengers to the people of Kiriath Jearim. The messengers said, "The Philistines have brought back the Holy Box of the Lord. Come down and take it to your city."

7 The men of Kiriath Jearim came and took the Holy Box of the Lord. They took it to Abinadab's house on a hill. There they made Abinadab's son Eleazar holy for the Lord so he could guard the Holy Box.

The Lord Saves the Israelites

²The Holy Box*d* stayed at Kiriath Jearim a long time—20 years in all. And the people of Israel began to follow the Lord again. ³Samuel spoke to the whole group of Israel. He said, "If you're turning back to the Lord with all your hearts, you must remove your foreign gods. You must remove your idols of Ashtoreth.*d* You must give yourselves fully to the Lord and serve only him. Then he will save you from the Philistines."

⁴So the Israelites put away their idols of Baal*d* and Ashtoreth. And they served only the Lord.

⁵Samuel said, "All Israel must meet at Mizpah. I will pray to the Lord for you." ⁶So the Israelites met together at Mizpah. They drew water from the ground and poured it out before the Lord. They did not eat that day. They confessed, "We have sinned against the Lord." And Samuel served as judge of Israel at Mizpah.

⁷The Philistines heard the Israelites were meeting at Mizpah. So the Philistine kings came up to attack them. When the Israelites heard they were coming, they were afraid. ⁸They said to Samuel, "Don't stop praying to the Lord our God for us! Ask the Lord to save us from the Philistines!" ⁹Then Samuel took a baby lamb. He offered the lamb to the Lord as a whole burnt offering. He called to the Lord for Israel's sake. And the Lord answered him.

¹⁰While Samuel was burning the offering, the Philistines came near. They were going to attack Israel. But the Lord thundered against the Philistines with loud thunder. They were so frightened they became confused. So the Israelites defeated the Philistines in battle. ¹¹The men of Israel ran out of Mizpah and chased

the Philistines. They went almost to Beth Car, killing the Philistines along the way.

Peace Comes to Israel

¹²After this happened Samuel took a stone. He set it up between Mizpah and Shen. He named the stone Ebenezer.*n* Samuel said, "The Lord has helped us to this point." ¹³So the Philistines were defeated. They did not enter the Israelites' land again.

The Lord was against the Philistines all Samuel's life. ¹⁴Earlier the Philistines had taken towns from the Israelites. But the Israelites won them back, from Ekron to Gath. They also took back from the Philistines the neighboring lands of these towns. There was peace also between Israel and the Amorites.

¹⁵Samuel continued as judge of Israel all his life. ¹⁶Every year he went from Bethel to Gilgal to Mizpah. He judged the Israelites in all these towns. ¹⁷But Samuel always went back to Ramah, where his home was. He also judged Israel there. And there he built an altar to the Lord.

Israel Asks for a King

8 When Samuel became old, he made his sons judges for Israel. ²His first son was named Joel, and his second son was named Abijah. Joel and Abijah were judges in Beersheba. ³But Samuel's sons did not live as he did. They tried to get money dishonestly. They took money secretly to be dishonest in their judging.

⁴So all the older leaders came together and met Samuel at Ramah. ⁵They said to him, "You're old, and your sons don't live as you do. Give us a king to rule over us like all the other nations."

⁶When the older leaders said that, Samuel was not pleased. He prayed to the Lord. ⁷The Lord told Samuel, "Listen to whatever the people say to you. They have not rejected you. They

*n***Ebenezer**   This name means "stone of help."

have rejected me from being their king. ⁸They are doing as they have always done. When I took them out of Egypt, they left me. They served other gods. They are doing the same to you. ⁹Now listen to the people. But give them a warning. Tell them what the king who rules over them will do."

¹⁰Samuel answered those who had asked him for a king. He told them all the words of the Lord. ¹¹Samuel said, "If you have a king ruling over you, this is what he will do: He will take your sons. He will make them serve with his chariots and his horses. They will run in front of the king's chariot. ¹²The king will make some of your sons commanders over 1,000 men or over 50 men. He will make some of your other sons plow his ground and reap his harvest. He will take others to make weapons of war and equipment for his chariots. ¹³This king will take your daughters. Some of your daughters will make perfume. Others will cook and bake for him. ¹⁴He will take your best fields, vineyards and olive groves. He will give them to his servants. ¹⁵He will take one-tenth of your grain and grapes and give it to his officers and servants. ¹⁶He will take your men servants and girl servants. He will take your best cattle and your donkeys. He will use them all for his own work. ¹⁷He will take one-tenth of your flocks. And you yourselves will become his slaves. ¹⁸When that time comes, you will cry out because of the king you chose. The Lord will not answer you then."

¹⁹But the people would not listen to Samuel. They said, "No! We want a king to rule over us. ²⁰Then we will be the same as all the other nations. Our king will judge us. He will go with us and fight our battles."

²¹Samuel heard all that the people said. Then he repeated all their words to the Lord. ²²The Lord answered, "You must listen to them. Give them a king."

Then Samuel told the people of Israel, "Everyone go back to his town."

Saul Looks for His Father's Donkeys

9 Kish son of Abiel was from the tribe*ᵈ* of Benjamin. He was an important man. (Abiel was the son of Zeror. And Zeror was the son of Becorath. He was the son of Aphiah of Benjamin.) ²Kish had a son named Saul. Saul was a fine young man. There was no Israelite better than he. Saul stood a head taller than any other man in Israel.

³Now the donkeys of Saul's father, Kish, were lost. So Kish said to Saul, his son, "Take one of the servants. Go and look for the donkeys." ⁴Saul went through the mountains of Ephraim. And he went through the land of Shalisha. But he and the servant could not find the donkeys. They went into the land of Shaalim, but the donkeys were not there. They went through the land of Benjamin. But they still did not find the donkeys. ⁵They arrived in the area of Zuph. Saul said to his servant, "Let's go back. My father will stop thinking about the donkeys. He will start worrying about us."

⁶But the servant answered, "A man of God is in this town. People respect him because everything he says comes true. Let's go into the town now. Maybe he can tell us something about the journey we have taken."

⁷Saul said to his servant, "If we go into the town, what can we give him? The food in our bags is gone. We have no gift to give him. Do we have anything at all to give him?"

⁸Again the servant answered Saul. "Look, I have one-tenth of an ounce of silver. Give it to the man of God. Then he will tell us about our journey." ⁹(In the past, someone in Israel might want to ask something from God. If so, he would say, "Let's go to the seer."*ᵈ* We call the person a man of God today. But in the past he was called a "seer.")

¹⁰Saul said to his servant, "That is a good idea. Come, let's go." So they went toward the town where the man of God was.

[11]Saul and the servant were going up the hill to the town. On the way they met some young women coming out to get water. Saul and the servant asked them, "Is the seer here?"

[12]The young women answered, "Yes, he's here. He's ahead of you. Hurry now. He has just come to our town today. This is because the people will offer a sacrifice at the place of worship. [13]When you enter the town, you will find him. He will be there before he goes up to the place of worship to eat. The people will not begin eating until the seer comes. He must bless the sacrifice. After that, the guests will eat. Go now, and you should find him."

Saul Meets Samuel

[14]Saul and the servant went up to the town. Just as they entered the town, they saw Samuel. He was on his way up to the place of worship. So he was coming out of the city toward them.

[15]The day before Saul came, the Lord had told Samuel: [16]"About this time tomorrow I will send you a man. He will be from Benjamin. You must appoint him as leader over my people Israel. He will save my people from the Philistines. I have seen the suffering of my people. I have listened to their cry."

[17]When Samuel first saw Saul, the Lord spoke to Samuel. He said, "This is the man I told you about. He will rule my people."

[18]Saul came near Samuel at the gate. Saul said, "Please tell me where the seer's[d] house is."

[19]Samuel answered, "I am the seer. Go ahead of me to the place of worship. Today you and your servant are to eat with me. Tomorrow morning I will send you home. And I will answer all your questions. [20]Don't worry about the donkeys you lost three days ago. They have been found. Israel now wants you and all your father's family."

[21]Saul answered, "But I am from the tribe[d] of Benjamin. It's the smallest tribe in Israel. And my family group is the smallest in the tribe of Benjamin. Why do you say Israel wants me?"

[22]Then Samuel took Saul and his servant into a large room. He gave them a chief place at the table. About 30 guests were there. [23]Samuel said to the cook, "Bring the meat I gave you. It's the portion I told you to set aside."

[24]So the cook took the thigh and put it on the table in front of Saul. Samuel said, "This is the meat saved for you. Eat it because it was set aside for you for this special time. As I said, 'I have invited the people.'" So Saul ate with Samuel that day.

[25]After they finished eating, they came down from the place of worship. They went to the town. Then Samuel talked with Saul on the roof[n] of his house. [26]At dawn they got up, and Samuel called to Saul on the roof. He said, "Get up, and I will send you on your way." So Saul got up. He went out of the house with Samuel. [27]Saul, his servant and Samuel were getting near the edge of the city. Samuel said to Saul, "Tell the servant to go on ahead of us. I have a message from God for you."

Samuel Appoints Saul

10 Samuel took a jar of olive oil. He poured the oil on Saul's head. He kissed Saul and said, "The Lord has appointed you to be leader of his people Israel. You will rule over the people of the Lord. You will save them from their enemies all around. This will be the sign that the Lord has appointed you as leader of his people. [2]After you leave me today, you will meet two men. They will be near Rachel's tomb on the border of Benjamin at Zelzah. They will say to you, 'The donkeys you were looking for have been found. But now your father has stopped thinking about his donkeys. He is worrying about you. He is asking, "What will I do about my son?"'

[3]Then you will go on until you reach the great tree at Tabor. There

---

[n]**roof** In Bible times houses were built with flat roofs. The roof was used for drying things such as flax and fruit. And it was used as an extra room, as a place for worship and as a place to sleep in the summer.

three men will meet you. They will be on their way to worship God at Bethel. One man will be carrying three young goats. The second man will be carrying three loaves of bread. And the third one will have a leather bag full of wine. [4]They will greet you and offer you two loaves of bread. You will accept the bread from them. [5]Then you will go to Gibeah of God. There is a Philistine camp there. When you come near this town, a group of prophets[d] will come out. They will be coming from the place of worship. And they will be playing harps, tambourines,[d] flutes and lyres.[d] And they will be prophesying. [6]The Spirit[d] of the Lord will enter you with power. You will prophesy with these prophets. You will be changed into a different man. [7]After these signs happen, do whatever you find to do. God will help you.

[8]"Go ahead of me to Gilgal. I will come down to you. Then I will offer whole burnt offerings and fellowship offerings. But you must wait seven days. Then I will come and tell you what to do."

Saul Made King

[9]When Saul turned to leave Samuel, God changed Saul's heart. All these signs came true that day. [10]When Saul and his servant arrived at Gibeah, Saul met a group of prophets.[d] The Spirit[d] of God entered him. And he prophesied with the prophets. [11]People who had known Saul before saw him prophesying with the prophets. They asked each other, "What has happened to Kish's son? Is even Saul one of the prophets?"

[12]A man who lived there said, "Who is the father of these prophets?" This became a famous saying: "Is even Saul one of the prophets?" [13]When Saul finished prophesying, he went to the place of worship.

[14]Saul's uncle asked him and his servant, "Where have you been?"

Saul said, "We were looking for the donkeys. When we couldn't find them, we went to talk to Samuel."

[15]Saul's uncle asked, "Please tell me. What did Samuel say to you?"

[16]Saul answered, "He told us the donkeys had already been found." But Saul did not tell his uncle what Samuel had said about his becoming king.

[17]Samuel called all the people of Israel to meet with the Lord at Mizpah. [18]He said, "This is what the Lord, the God of Israel, says: 'I led Israel out of Egypt. I saved you from Egypt's control. And I saved you from other kingdoms that were troubling you.' [19]But now you have rejected your God. He saves you from all your troubles and problems. But you said, 'No! We want a king to rule over us.' Now come, stand before the Lord in your tribes[d] and family groups."

[20]Samuel brought all the tribes of Israel near. And the tribe of Benjamin was chosen. [21]Samuel had them pass by in family groups, and Matri's family was chosen. Then he had each man of Matri's family pass by. And Saul son of Kish was chosen. But when they looked for Saul, they could not find him. [22]Then they asked the Lord, "Has Saul come here yet?"

The Lord said, "Yes. He's hiding behind the baggage."

[23]So they ran and brought him out. When Saul stood among the people, he was a head taller than anyone else. [24]Then Samuel said to the people, "See the man the Lord has chosen. There is no one like him among all the people."

Then the people shouted, "Long live the king!"

[25]Samuel explained the rights and duties of the king. He wrote the rules in a book and put the book before the Lord. Then he told the people to go to their homes.

[26]Saul also went to his home in Gibeah. God touched the hearts of certain brave men who went along with him. [27]But some troublemakers said, "How can this man save us?" They

hated Saul and refused to bring gifts to him. But Saul kept quiet.

Nahash Troubles Jabesh Gilead

11 About a month later Nahash the Ammonite and his army surrounded the city of Jabesh in Gilead. All the people of Jabesh said to Nahash, "Make a treaty with us. And we will serve you."

[2]But he answered, "I will make a treaty with you. But I will only do it if I'm allowed to tear out the right eye of each of you. Then all Israel will be ashamed!"

[3]The older leaders of Jabesh said to Nahash, "Let us have seven days. We will send messengers through all Israel. If no one comes to help us, we will give ourselves up to you."

[4]The messengers came to Gibeah where Saul lived. When they told the people the news, the people cried loudly. [5]Saul had finished plowing in the fields with his oxen. He was coming home when he heard the people crying. He asked, "What's wrong with the people? Why are they crying?" Then they told Saul what the messengers from Jabesh had said. [6]When Saul heard their words, God's Spirit[d] entered him with power. Saul became very angry. [7]So he took a pair of oxen and cut them into pieces. Then he gave the pieces of the oxen to messengers. He ordered them to carry the pieces through all the land of Israel.

The messengers made an announcement to the people. They said, "This is what will happen to the oxen of anyone who does not follow Saul and Samuel." So the people became very afraid of the Lord. They all came together as if they were one person. [8]Saul gathered the people together at Bezek. There were 300,000 men from Israel and 30,000 men from Judah.

[9]They spoke to the messengers who had come. They said, "Tell the people at Jabesh Gilead this: 'Before the day becomes hot tomorrow, you will be saved.'" So the messengers went and reported this to the people at Jabesh. They were very happy. [10]The people said to Nahash the Ammonite, "Tomorrow we will give ourselves up to you. Then you can do anything you want to us."

[11]The next morning Saul divided his soldiers into three groups. At dawn they entered the Ammonite camp. And they defeated the Ammonites before the heat of the day. The Ammonites who were left alive were scattered. Not even two of them were still together.

[12]Then the people said to Samuel, "Who was it that didn't want Saul as king? Bring them here, and we will kill them!"

[13]But Saul said, "No! No one will be put to death today. The Lord has saved Israel today!"

[14]Then Samuel said to the people, "Come, let's go to Gilgal. At Gilgal we will again promise to obey the king." [15]All the people went to Gilgal. And there, before the Lord, the people made Saul king. They offered fellowship offerings to the Lord. Saul and all the Israelites had a great celebration.

Samuel's Farewell Speech

12 Samuel said to all Israel, "I have done everything you wanted me to do. I have put a king over you. [2]Now you have a king to lead you. I am old and gray, and my sons are here with you. I have been your leader since I was young. [3]Here I am. If I have done anything wrong, you must testify against me. Do this before the Lord and his appointed king. Did I steal anyone's ox or donkey? Did I hurt or cheat anyone? Did I ever secretly take money to pretend not to see something wrong? If I did any of these things, I will make it right."

[4]The Israelites answered, "You have not cheated us. You have not hurt us. You have not taken anything unfairly from anyone."

[5]Samuel said to them, "The Lord is a witness to what you have said. His appointed king is also a witness today.

They are both witnesses that you did not find anything wrong in me."

"He is our witness," they said.

6Then Samuel said to the people, "The Lord is our witness. He chose Moses and Aaron. He brought your ancestors out of Egypt. 7Now, stand there. And I will talk with you about all the good things the Lord did for you and your ancestors.

8"After Jacob entered Egypt, his descendants*d* cried to the Lord for help. So the Lord sent Moses and Aaron. They took your ancestors out of Egypt and brought them to live in this place.

9"But they forgot the Lord their God. So he let them become the slaves of Sisera. He was the commander of the army of Hazor. The Lord let them become the slaves of the Philistines and the king of Moab. They all fought against your ancestors. 10Then your ancestors cried to the Lord. They said, 'We have sinned. We have left the Lord. We served the Baals*d* and the Ashtoreths.*d* But now save us from our enemies, and we will serve you.' 11The Lord sent Gideon, who is also called Jerub-Baal. And he sent Barak, Jephthah and Samuel. Then he saved you from your enemies around you. And you lived in safety. 12But then you saw Nahash king of the Ammonites coming against you. You said, 'No! We want a king to rule over us!' 13Now here is the king you chose. The Lord has put him over you. 14You must honor the Lord and serve him. You must obey his commands. Both you and the king ruling over you must follow the Lord your God. If you do, it will be well with you. 15But if you don't obey the Lord, and if you fight against his commands, he will be against you. He will do to you what he did to your ancestors.

16"Now stand still and see the great thing the Lord will do before your eyes.

17It is now the time of the wheat harvest.*n* I will pray for the Lord to send thunder and rain. Then you will know what an evil thing you did against the Lord when you asked for a king."

18Then Samuel prayed to the Lord. That same day the Lord sent thunder and rain. And the people became very afraid of the Lord and Samuel. 19They said to Samuel, "Pray to the Lord your God for us, your servants! Don't let us die! We've added to all our sins the evil of asking for a king."

But you must honor the Lord. You must always serve him with all your heart. Remember the wonderful things he did for you!
• 1 Samuel 12:24

20Samuel answered, "Don't be afraid. It's true that you did wrong. But don't turn away from the Lord. Serve the Lord with all your heart. 21Idols are of no use. So don't worship them. They can't help you or save you. They are useless! 22For his own sake, the Lord won't leave his people. Instead, he was pleased to make you his own people. 23I will surely not stop praying for you. If I did, I would be sinning against the Lord. I will teach you what is good and right. 24But you must honor the Lord. You must always serve him with all your heart. Remember the wonderful things he did for you! 25But if you are stubborn and do evil, God will sweep you and your king away."

13 Saul was 30 years old when he became king. He was king over Israel 42 years.*n* 2Saul chose 3,000 men from Israel. There were 2,000 men who stayed with him at Micmash in the mountains of Bethel. And 1,000 men stayed with Jonathan at Gibeah

---

*n***time . . . harvest** This was a dry time in the summer when no rains fell.
*n***Saul . . . years** This is how the verse is worded in some early Greek copies. The Hebrew is not clear here.

in Benjamin. Saul sent the other men in the army back home.

³Jonathan attacked the Philistine camp in Geba. And the other Philistines heard about it. Saul said, "Let the Hebrew people hear what happened." So he told the men to blow trumpets through all the land of Israel. ⁴All the Israelites heard the news. The men said, "Saul has defeated the Philistine camp. Now the Philistines really hate us!" Then the Israelites were called to join Saul at Gilgal.

⁵The Philistines gathered to fight Israel. They had 3,000ⁿ chariots and 6,000 men to ride in the chariots. Their soldiers were many in number, like the grains of sand on the seashore. The Philistines went and camped at Micmash which is east of Beth Aven. ⁶The Israelites saw that they were in trouble. So they went to hide in caves and bushes. They also hid among the rocks and in pits and wells. ⁷Some Hebrews even went across the Jordan River to the land of Gad and Gilead.

But Saul stayed at Gilgal. All the men in his army were shaking with fear. ⁸Saul waited seven days, because Samuel had said he would meet him then. But Samuel did not come to Gilgal. And the soldiers began to leave. ⁹So Saul said, "Bring me the whole burnt offering and the fellowship offerings." Then Saul offered the whole burnt offering. ¹⁰Just as he finished, Samuel arrived. Saul went to meet him.

¹¹Samuel asked, "What have you done?"

Saul answered, "I saw the soldiers leaving me, and you were not here. The Philistines were gathering at Micmash. ¹²Then I thought, 'The Philistines will come against me at Gilgal. And I haven't asked for the Lord's approval.' So I forced myself to offer the whole burnt offering."

¹³Samuel said, "You acted foolishly! You haven't obeyed God's command. If you had obeyed him, God would make

your kingdom continue in Israel forever. ¹⁴But now your kingdom will not continue. The Lord has looked for the kind of man he wants. The Lord has appointed him to become ruler of his people. He is doing this because you haven't obeyed his command."

¹⁵Then Samuel left Gilgal and went to Gibeah in Benjamin. The rest of the army followed Saul into battle. Saul counted the men still with him, and there were about 600.

Hard Times for Israel

¹⁶Saul and his son Jonathan stayed in Geba in the land of Benjamin. The soldiers with them also stayed there. The Philistines made their camp at Micmash. ¹⁷Three groups went out from their camp to attack. One group went on the Ophrah road in the land of Shual. ¹⁸The second group went on the Beth Horon road. And the third group went on the border road. It overlooked the Valley of Zeboim toward the desert.

¹⁹The whole land of Israel had no blacksmith. This is because the Philistines had said, "The Hebrews might make swords and spears." ²⁰So all the Israelites went down to the Philistines. They went to have their plows, hoes, axes and sickles sharpened. ²¹The Philistine blacksmiths charged about one-fourth of an ounce of silver for sharpening plows and hoes. And they charged one-eighth of an ounce of silver for sharpening picks, axes and the sticks used to guide oxen.

²²So when the battle came, the soldiers with Saul and Jonathan had no swords or spears. Only Saul and his son Jonathan had them.

Israel Defeats the Philistines

²³A group from the Philistine army had gone out to the mountain pass at Micmash.

14 One day Jonathan, Saul's son, spoke to the officer who carried his armor. Jonathan said, "Come, let's

---

ⁿ**3,000** Some Greek copies say 3,000. The Hebrew copies say 30,000.

go over to the Philistine camp on the other side." But Jonathan did not tell his father.

²Saul was sitting under a pomegranate[d] tree at the threshing[d] floor near Gibeah. He had about 600 men with him. ³One man was Ahijah, who was a son of Ichabod's brother Ahitub. Ichabod was the son of Phinehas, Eli's son. Eli was the Lord's priest in Shiloh. He wore the holy vest.[d] No one knew Jonathan had left.

camp of those men who are not circumcised.[d] Maybe the Lord will help us. It doesn't matter if we have many people, or just a few. Nothing can keep the Lord from giving us victory."

⁷The officer who carried Jonathan's armor said to him, "Do whatever you think is best. Go ahead. I'm with you."

⁸Jonathan said, "Then come. We will cross over to the Philistines. We will let them see us. ⁹They may say to us, 'Stay there until we come to you.' If they do, we will stay where we are. We won't go up to them. ¹⁰But they may say, 'Come up to us.' If so, we will climb up. And

Heroes Who Trusted God

JONATHAN • 1 SAMUEL 14:1-23

When have you been brave in a scary situation?

The Israelite army was in a battle against the Philistines. The Israelites were scared to fight the Philistines because the Philistines had so many more men in their army. The leader of the Israelite army, King Saul, decided the army should hide from the Philistines. But Jonathan was brave because he believed God could defeat the Philistines anyway.

Jonathan left the place where the Israelites were hiding and crept into the Philistine camp. With God's help, Jonathan and his bodyguard surprised the Philistine army. The Philistines were so confused they started fighting each other! The others in the Israelite army were encouraged because of Jonathan. The Israelite army was able to chase the Philistines away and win the battle.

Jonathan was brave because he knew God was with him. We can be brave in any situation because God promises to help us.

To learn about a woman who trusted God and stopped a battle, *fly to page 359.*

⁴There was a steep slope on each side of the pass. Jonathan planned to go through the pass to the Philistine camp. The cliff on one side was named Bozez. The other cliff was named Seneh. ⁵One cliff faced north toward Micmash. The other faced south toward Geba.

⁶Jonathan said to his officer who carried his armor, "Come. Let's go to the

the Lord will allow us to defeat them. This will be the sign for us."

¹¹Both Jonathan and his officer let the Philistines see them. The Philistines said, "Look! The Hebrews are crawling out of the holes they were hiding in!" ¹²The Philistines in the camp shouted to Jonathan and his officer, "Come up to us. We'll teach you a lesson!"

Jonathan said to his officer, "Climb up behind me. The Lord has given the Philistines to Israel!" ¹³So Jonathan climbed up, using his hands and feet. His officer climbed just behind him. Jonathan cut down the Philistines as he went. And his officer killed them as he followed behind Jonathan. ¹⁴In that first fight Jonathan and his officer killed about 20 Philistines.

¹⁵All the Philistine soldiers panicked. Those in the camp and those in the raiding party were frightened. The ground itself shook! God caused the panic.

¹⁶Saul's guards were at Gibeah in the land of Benjamin. They saw the Philistine soldiers running in every direction. ¹⁷Saul said to his army, "Check and find who has left our camp." When they checked, they learned that Jonathan and his officer were gone.

¹⁸So Saul said to Ahijah the priest, "Bring the Holy Box[d] of God." (At that time it was with the Israelites.) ¹⁹While Saul was talking to the priest, the confusion in the Philistine camp was growing. Then Saul said to Ahijah, "Stop. There's not time to pray now!"

²⁰Then Saul and the army with him gathered and entered the battle. They found the Philistines confused, even striking each other with their swords! ²¹Earlier, there were Hebrews who had served the Philistines and had stayed in their camp. They now joined the Israelites with Saul and Jonathan. ²²All the Israelites hidden in the mountains of Ephraim heard that the Philistine soldiers were running away. They too joined the battle and chased the Philistines. ²³So the Lord saved the Israelites that day. And the battle moved on past Beth Aven.

Saul Makes Another Mistake

²⁴The men of Israel were miserable that day. This was because Saul had made an oath for all of them. He had said, "No one should eat food before evening and before I finish defeating my enemies. If he does, he will be cursed!" So no Israelite soldier ate food.

²⁵Now the army went into the woods. There was some honey on the ground. ²⁶They came to where the honey was. But no one took any because they were afraid of the oath. ²⁷But Jonathan had not heard the oath Saul had put on the people. So Jonathan dipped the end of his stick into the honey. He pulled out the honey and ate it. Then he felt better. ²⁸So one of the soldiers told Jonathan, "Your father made an oath for all the soldiers. He said any man who eats today will be cursed! That's why they are weak."

²⁹Jonathan said, "My father has made trouble for the land! See how much better I feel after just tasting a little of this honey! ³⁰It would have been much better for the men to eat the food they took from their enemies today. We could have killed many more Philistines!"

³¹That day the Israelites defeated the Philistines from Micmash to Aijalon. After they did this, they were very tired. ³²They had taken sheep, cattle and calves from the Philistines. Now they were so hungry they killed the animals on the ground and ate them. But the blood was still in the animals! ³³Someone said to Saul, "Look! The men are sinning against the Lord. They're eating meat that still has blood in it!"

Saul said, "You have sinned! Roll a large stone over here now!" ³⁴Then he said, "Go to the men. Tell them that each person must bring his ox and sheep to me. They must kill and eat their ox and sheep here. Don't sin against the Lord. Don't eat meat with the blood still in it."

That night everyone brought his animals and killed them there. ³⁵Then Saul built an altar to the Lord. It was the first altar Saul had built to the Lord.

³⁶Saul said, "Let's go after the Philistines tonight. Let's take what they own. We won't let any of them live!"

The men answered, "Do whatever you think is best."

But the priest said, "Let's ask God." 37So Saul asked God, "Should I chase the Philistines? Will you let us defeat them?" But that day God did not answer Saul. 38That is why Saul said to all the leaders of his army, "Come here. Let's find what sin has been done today. 39As surely as the Lord lives, even if my son Jonathan did the sin, he must die." But no one in the army answered.

40Then Saul said to all the Israelites, "You stand on this side. I and my son Jonathan will stand on the other side."

The men answered, "Do whatever you think is best."

41Then Saul prayed to the Lord, the God of Israel, "Give me the right answer."

And Saul and Jonathan were chosen by throwing lots.*d* The other men went free. 42Saul said, "Throw the lot. It will show if it is I or Jonathan my son who is guilty." And Jonathan was chosen.

43Saul said to Jonathan, "Tell me what you have done."

So Jonathan told Saul, "I only tasted a little honey from the end of my stick. And must I die now?"

44Saul said, "Jonathan, if you don't die, may God punish me terribly."

45But the soldiers said to Saul, "Must Jonathan die? Never! He is responsible for saving Israel today! As surely as the Lord lives, not even a hair of his head will fall to the ground! Today Jonathan fought against the Philistines with God's help!" So the army saved Jonathan, and he did not die.

46Then Saul stopped chasing the Philistines. And they went back to their own land.

Saul Fights Israel's Enemies

47When Saul became king over Israel, he fought against Israel's enemies all around. He fought Moab, the Ammonites, Edom, the king of Zobah and the Philistines. Everywhere Saul went he defeated Israel's enemies. 48He became strong. He fought bravely and defeated the Amalekites. He saved Israel from the enemies who had taken what the Israelites owned.

49Saul's sons were Jonathan, Ishvi and Malki-Shua. His older daughter was named Merab. His younger daughter was named Michal. 50Saul's wife was Ahinoam daughter of Ahimaaz. The commander of his army was Abner son of Ner. Ner was Saul's uncle. 51Saul's father Kish and Abner's father Ner were sons of Abiel.

52All Saul's life he fought hard against the Philistines. When he saw strong or brave men, he took them into his army.

Saul Rejected as King

15 Samuel said to Saul, "The Lord sent me to appoint you king over Israel. Now listen to his message. 2This is what the Lord of heaven's armies says: 'The Israelites came out of Egypt. But the Amalekites tried to stop them from going to Canaan. I saw what they did. 3Now go, attack the Amalekites. Destroy everything that belongs to them as an offering to the Lord. Don't let anything live. Put to death men and women, children and small babies. Kill the cattle and sheep, camels and donkeys.'"

4So Saul called the army together at Telaim. There were 200,000 soldiers and 10,000 men from Judah. 5Then Saul went to the city of Amalek and set up an ambush in the ravine. 6He said to the Kenites, "Go away. Leave the Amalekites so that I won't destroy you with them. You showed kindness to the Israelites when they came out of Egypt." So the Kenites moved away from the Amalekites.

7Then Saul defeated the Amalekites. He fought them all the way from Havilah to Shur, at the border of Egypt. 8He took Agag king of the Amalekites alive. But he killed all of Agag's army with the sword. 9But Saul and the army let Agag live. They also let the best sheep, fat cattle and lambs live. They let every good animal live. They did not want to destroy them. But when they found an animal that was weak or useless, they killed it.

¹⁰Then the Lord spoke his word to Samuel: ¹¹"Saul has stopped following me. And I am sorry I made him king. He has not obeyed my commands." Samuel was upset, and he cried out to the Lord all night long.

Saul answered, "Tell me."

¹⁷Samuel said, "Once you didn't think much of yourself. But now you have become the leader of the tribes^d of Israel. The Lord appointed you to be king over Israel. ¹⁸And he told you to do something. He said, 'Go and destroy those evil people, the Amalekites. Make war on them until all of them are dead.' ¹⁹Why didn't you obey the Lord? Why did you take the best things? Why did you do what the Lord said was wrong?"

Good Kings and Bad Kings

SAUL • 1 SAMUEL 15:17-26

Saul was the very first king of Israel. God chose him to lead the nation, but Saul did not choose to follow God. When Saul obeyed, he only obeyed half way. He always had excuses for what he did.

The prophet Samuel was teaching the people about God during Saul's reign. Samuel did not let Saul get away with disobeying God. Samuel told Saul that because he only did good things in order to look good and did not obey God with all his heart, God would take his kingdom from him.

Sometimes do you try to get away with only obeying God part way? Do you make lots of excuses? Remember Saul, and ask God to help you obey him.

To meet a wise king who didn't act very wisely, fly to page 417.

¹²Early the next morning Samuel got up and went to meet Saul. But the people told Samuel, "Saul has gone to Carmel. He has put up a monument in his own honor. Now he has gone down to Gilgal."

¹³Then Samuel came to Saul. And Saul said, "May the Lord bless you! I have obeyed the Lord's commands."

¹⁴But Samuel said, "Then why do I hear cattle mooing and sheep bleating?"

¹⁵Saul answered, "The soldiers took them from the Amalekites. They saved the best sheep and cattle to offer as sacrifices to the Lord your God. But we destroyed all the other animals."

¹⁶Samuel said to Saul, "Stop! Let me tell you what the Lord said to me last night."

²⁰Saul said, "But I did obey the Lord. I did what the Lord told me to do. I destroyed all the Amalekites. And I brought back Agag their king. ²¹The soldiers took the best sheep and cattle to sacrifice to the Lord your God at Gilgal."

²²But Samuel answered,

"What pleases the Lord more:
burnt offerings and sacrifices or
obedience?
It is better to obey God than to offer
a sacrifice.
It is better to listen to God than to
offer the fat of male sheep.
²³Refusing to obey is as bad as
the sin of sorcery.^d
Being stubborn is as bad as the sin
of worshiping idols.

You have rejected the Lord's command.

For this reason, he now rejects you as king."

²⁴Then Saul said to Samuel, "I have sinned. I didn't obey the Lord's commands. I didn't do what you told me. I was afraid of the people, and I did what they said. ²⁵Now I beg you, forgive my sin. Come back with me so I may worship the Lord."

²⁶But Samuel said to Saul, "I won't go back with you. You refused the Lord's command. And now he rejects you as king of Israel."

²⁷As Samuel turned to leave, Saul caught his robe, and it tore. ²⁸Samuel said to him, "The Lord has torn the kingdom of Israel from you today. He has given it to one of your neighbors. He has given it to one better than you. ²⁹The Lord is the Eternal One of Israel. He does not lie or change his mind. He is not a man. So he does not change his mind as men do."

³⁰Saul answered, "I have sinned. But please honor me in front of my people's older leaders. Please honor me in front of the Israelites. Come back with me so that I may worship the Lord your God." ³¹So Samuel went back with Saul, and Saul worshiped the Lord.

³²Then Samuel said, "Bring me Agag king of the Amalekites."

Agag came to Samuel in chains. Yet Agag thought, "Surely the threat of death has passed."

³³Samuel said to him, "Your sword caused mothers to be without their children. Now your mother will have no children." And Samuel cut Agag to pieces before the Lord at Gilgal.

³⁴Then Samuel left and went to Ramah. But Saul went up to his home in Gibeah. ³⁵And Samuel never saw Saul again all the rest of his life. But he was sorry for Saul. And the Lord was very sorry he had made Saul king of Israel.

Samuel Goes to Bethlehem

16 The Lord said to Samuel, "How long will you continue to feel sorry for Saul? I have rejected him as

Character
1 SAMUEL 16:7

If you could change anything about your body, what would you change? Would you change your height, your weight, your hair, the color of your eyes? Most of us have at least one or two things we would like to change if we could. But what about your *character*—the person you are inside? Things like honesty, loyalty, kindness, and a willingness to work show what we are like inside. Would you change any of those?

We give a lot of importance to how we look on the outside. Everyone wants to be good looking. It's OK to want that, but God tells us in this verse that what a person is like on the *inside* is much more important than the *outside*. Our bodies will eventually grow old and wear out. But the person we are inside—our *character*—can continue to grow better and stronger all our lives.

It's great to look nice on the outside, but it's even more important to look good on the inside.

To learn more about character, zoom to page 507.

king of Israel. Fill your container with olive oil and go. I am sending you to Jesse who lives in Bethlehem. I have chosen one of his sons to be king."

²But Samuel said, "If I go, Saul will hear the news. And he will try to kill me."

The Lord said, "Take a young calf with you. Say, 'I have come to offer a sacrifice to the Lord.' ³Invite Jesse to the sacrifice. Then I will show you what to do. You must appoint the one I show you."

⁶When they arrived, Samuel saw Eliab. Samuel thought, "Surely the Lord has appointed this person standing here before him."

⁷But the Lord said to Samuel, "Don't look at how handsome Eliab is. Don't look at how tall he is. I have not chosen him. God does not see the same way people see. People look at the outside of a person, but the Lord looks at the heart."

⁸Then Jesse called Abinadab and told him to pass by Samuel. But Samuel said, "The Lord has not chosen this man either." ⁹Then Jesse had Shammah pass by. But Samuel said,

Jobs in the Bible

SHEPHERD • 1 SAMUEL 16:11

One of the most common jobs in the Bible was being a shepherd. This was hard work because a shepherd often had to take care of a flock of a hundred or more sheep. He watched over the sheep and protected them from wild animals. He led them to pastures with grass and water, and then at night he took them safely back to their sheepfold (a walled area so the sheep could not wander away and wild animals could not get in). A good shepherd knew each of his sheep, even by name! He cared for the sheep so much that he would risk his life for them.

David was a shepherd for many years before he became king of Israel. As the king, David loved his people. He cared for them and protected them, just as he had cared for his father's sheep. Jesus is like a shepherd to us. He cares for us and protects us.

To read about people whose job was making music,
fly to page 489.

⁴Samuel did what the Lord told him to do. When he arrived at Bethlehem, the older leaders of Bethlehem shook with fear. They met him and asked, "Are you coming in peace?"

⁵Samuel answered, "Yes, I come in peace. I have come to make a sacrifice to the Lord. Make yourselves holy for the Lord and come to the sacrifice with me." Then he made Jesse and his sons holy for the Lord. And he invited them to come to the sacrifice.

"No, the Lord has not chosen this one." ¹⁰Jesse had seven of his sons pass by Samuel. But Samuel said to him, "The Lord has not chosen any of these."

¹¹Then he asked Jesse, "Are these all the sons you have?"

Jesse answered, "I still have the youngest son. He is out taking care of the sheep."

Samuel said, "Send for him. We will not sit down to eat until he arrives."

¹²So Jesse sent and had his youngest son brought in. He was a fine boy, tanned and handsome.

The Lord said to Samuel, "Go! Appoint him. He is the one."

¹³So Samuel took the container of olive oil. Then he poured oil on Jesse's youngest son to appoint him in front of his brothers. From that day on, the Lord's Spirit[d] entered David with power. Samuel then went back to Ramah.

David Serves Saul

¹⁴But the Lord's Spirit[d] had gone out of Saul. And an evil spirit from the Lord troubled him.

¹⁵Saul's servants said to him, "See, an evil spirit from God is troubling you. ¹⁶Give us the command. We will look for someone who can play the harp. When the evil spirit from the Lord enters you, he will play. Then the evil spirit will leave you alone. And you will feel better."

¹⁷So Saul said to his servants, "Find someone. If he plays well, bring him to me."

¹⁸One of the servants said, "Jesse of Bethlehem has a son who plays the harp. I have seen him play it. He is a brave man and fights well. He is a good speaker and handsome. And the Lord is with him."

¹⁹Then Saul sent messengers to Jesse. The message said, "Send me your son David, who is with the sheep." ²⁰So Jesse loaded a donkey with bread and a leather bag full of wine. He also took a young goat. He sent them all with his son David to Saul.

²¹When David came to Saul, he began to serve him. Saul loved David very much. And David became the officer who carried Saul's armor. ²²Saul sent a message to Jesse. He said, "Let David stay and serve me. I like him."

²³When the evil spirit from God entered Saul, David would take his harp and play. Then the evil spirit would go out of him. And Saul would feel relief. He would feel better again.

David and Goliath

17 The Philistines gathered their armies for war. They met at Socoh in Judah. Their camp was at

Children Who Saw God at Work
DAVID • 1 SAMUEL 17:1-50

The Israelites and Philistines were bitter enemies. The Philistines were big bullies. They picked on Israel and made fun of God. They had a bigger army and better weapons. They also had a giant—Goliath—who was nine feet tall. He could win any battle, so he challenged the Israelites to fight him. Goliath wasn't afraid of anyone, not even God.

David was not a soldier. He was a shepherd boy. But David was not afraid of Goliath. He had courage because he trusted in God. When David shot a stone at Goliath from his slingshot, God made it hit Goliath right between the eyes and knock him out.

You may not have to fight a nine-foot-tall bully, but you will have other "giant" problems. When they challenge you, you won't have to worry because you'll know that God is with you.

To meet an unselfish little girl, fly to page 448.

Ephes Dammim between Socoh and Azekah. ²Saul and the Israelites gathered in the Valley of Elah. And they camped there. They took their positions to fight the Philistines. ³The Philistines controlled one hill. The Israelites controlled another. The valley was between them.

⁴The Philistines had a champion fighter named Goliath. He was from Gath. He was about nine feet four inches tall. He came out of the Philistine camp. ⁵He had a bronze helmet on his head. And he wore a coat of scale armor. It was made of bronze and weighed about 125 pounds. ⁶He wore bronze protectors on his legs. And he had a small spear of bronze tied on his back. ⁷The wooden part of his larger spear was like a weaver's rod. And its blade weighed about 15 pounds. The officer who carried his shield walked in front of him.

⁸Goliath stood and shouted to the Israelite soldiers, "Why have you taken positions for battle? I am a Philistine, and you are Saul's servants! Choose a man and send him to fight me. ⁹If he can fight and kill me, we will become your servants. But if I defeat and kill him, you will become our servants." ¹⁰Then he said, "Today I stand and dare the army of Israel! Send one of your men to fight me!" ¹¹When Saul and the Israelites heard the Philistine's words, they were very afraid.

¹²Now David was the son of Jesse, an Ephrathite. Jesse was from Bethlehem in Judah. He had eight sons. In Saul's time Jesse was an old man. ¹³His three oldest sons followed Saul to the war. The first son was Eliab. The second son was Abinadab. And the third son was Shammah. ¹⁴David was the youngest son. Jesse's three oldest sons followed Saul. ¹⁵But David went back and forth from Saul to Bethlehem. There he took care of his father's sheep.

¹⁶The Philistine Goliath came out every morning and evening. He stood before the Israelite army. This continued for 40 days.

¹⁷Now Jesse said to his son David, "Take this half bushel of cooked grain. And take ten loaves of bread. Take them to your brothers in the camp. ¹⁸Also take ten pieces of cheese. Give them to the commander of your brothers' group of 1,000 soldiers. See how your brothers are. Bring back something to show me they are all right. ¹⁹Your brothers are with Saul and the army in the Valley of Elah. They are fighting against the Philistines."

²⁰Early in the morning David left the sheep with another shepherd. He took the food and left as Jesse had told him. When David arrived at the camp, the army was leaving. They were going out to their battle positions. The soldiers were shouting their war cry. ²¹The Israelites and Philistines were lining up their men to face each other in battle.

²²David left the food with the man who kept the supplies. Then he ran to the battle line and talked to his brothers. ²³While he was talking with them, Goliath came out. He was the Philistine champion from Gath. He shouted things against Israel as usual, and David heard it. ²⁴When the Israelites saw Goliath, they were very much afraid and ran away.

²⁵They said, "Look at this man Goliath. He keeps coming out to speak against Israel. The king will give much money to the man who kills Goliath. He will also give his daughter in marriage to whoever kills him. And his father's family will not have to pay taxes in Israel."

²⁶David asked the men who stood near him, "What will be done to reward the man who kills this Philistine? What will be done for whoever takes away the shame from Israel? Goliath is a Philistine. He is not circumcised.ᵈ Why does he think he can speak against the armies of the living God?"

²⁷The Israelites told David what they had been saying. They said, "This is what will be done for the man who kills Goliath."

28David's oldest brother Eliab heard David talking with the soldiers. He became angry with David. He asked David, "Why did you come here? Who's taking care of those few sheep of yours in the desert? I know you are proud. Your attitude is very bad. You came down here just to watch the battle!"

29David asked, "Now what have I done wrong? Can't I even talk?" 30He then turned to other people and asked the same questions. And they gave him the same answer as before. 31Some men heard what David said and told Saul. Then Saul ordered David to be sent to him.

32David said to Saul, "Don't let anyone be discouraged. I, your servant, will go and fight this Philistine!"

33Saul answered, "You can't go out against this Philistine and fight him. You're only a boy. Goliath has been a warrior since he was a young man."

34But David said to Saul, "I, your servant, have been keeping my father's sheep. When a lion or bear came and took a sheep from the flock, 35I would chase it. I would attack it and save the sheep from its mouth. When it attacked me, I caught it by its fur. I would hit it and kill it. 36I, your servant, have killed both a lion and a bear! Goliath, the Philistine who is not circumcised, will be like the lion or bear I killed. He will die because he has stood against the armies of the living God. 37The Lord saved me from a lion and a bear. He will also save me from this Philistine."

Saul said to David, "Go, and may the Lord be with you." 38Saul put his own clothes on David. He put a bronze helmet on David's head and armor on his body. 39David put on Saul's sword and tried to walk around. But he was not used to all the armor Saul had put on him.

He said to Saul, "I can't go in this. I'm not used to it." Then David took it all off. 40He took his stick in his hand. And he chose five smooth stones from a stream. He put them in his pouch and held his sling in his hand. Then he went to meet Goliath.

41At the same time, the Philistine was coming closer to David. The man who held his shield walked in front of him. 42Goliath looked at David. He saw that David was only a boy, tanned and handsome. He looked down at David with disgust. 43He said, "Do you think I am a dog, that you come at me with a stick?" He used his gods' names to curse David. 44He said to David, "Come here. I'll feed your body to the birds of the air and the wild animals!"

45But David said to him, "You come to me using a sword, a large spear and a small spear. But I come to you in the name of the Lord of heaven's armies. He's the God of the armies of Israel! You have spoken out against him. 46Today the Lord will give you to me. I'll kill you, and I'll cut off your head. Today I'll feed the bodies of the Philistine soldiers to the birds of the air and the wild animals. Then all the world will know there is a God in Israel! 47Everyone gathered here will know the Lord does not need swords or spears to save people. The battle belongs to him! And he will help us defeat all of you."

48As Goliath came near to attack him, David ran quickly to meet him. 49He took a stone from his pouch. He put it into his sling and slung it. The stone hit the Philistine on his forehead and sank into it. Goliath fell facedown on the ground.

50So David defeated the Philistine with only a sling and a stone! He hit him and killed him. He did not even have a sword in his hand. 51David ran and stood beside the Philistine. He took Goliath's sword out of its holder and killed him. Then he cut off Goliath's head.

When the Philistines saw that their champion was dead, they turned and ran. 52The men of Israel and Judah shouted and started chasing the Philistines. They chased them all the way to the entrance to the city of Gath.

And they chased them to the gates of Ekron.

Many of the Philistines died. Their bodies lay on the Shaaraim road as far as Gath and Ekron. ⁵³The Israelites returned after chasing the Philistines. Then they took many things from the Philistine camp. ⁵⁴David took Goliath's head to Jerusalem. He also put Goliath's weapons in his own tent.

⁵⁵Saul had watched David go out to meet Goliath. Saul spoke to Abner, commander of the army. He said, "Abner, who is that young man's father?"

Abner answered, "As surely as you live, my king, I don't know."

⁵⁶The king said, "Find out whose son he is."

⁵⁷When David came back from killing Goliath, Abner brought him to Saul. David still held Goliath's head.

⁵⁸Saul asked him, "Young man, who is your father?"

David answered, "I am the son of your servant Jesse of Bethlehem."

Saul Fears David

18 When David finished talking with Saul, Jonathan felt very close to David. He loved David as much as he loved himself. ²Saul kept David with him from that day on. He did not let David go home to his father's house. ³Jonathan made an agreement with David. He did this because he loved David as much as himself. ⁴He took off his coat and gave it to David. He also gave David his uniform, including his sword, bow and belt.

⁵Saul sent David to fight in different battles. And David was very successful. Then Saul put David over the soldiers. When he did this, Saul's officers and all the other people were pleased.

⁶After David had killed the Philistine, he and the men returned home. Women came out from all the towns of Israel to meet King Saul. They sang songs of joy, danced and played tambourines*ᵈ* and stringed instruments. ⁷As they played, they sang,

"Saul has killed thousands of his enemies.
But David has killed tens of thousands!"

⁸The women's song upset Saul, and he became very angry. He thought, "The women say David has killed tens of thousands of enemies. But they say I killed only thousands of enemies. The only thing left for him to have is the kingdom!" ⁹So Saul watched David closely from then on. He was jealous of him.

¹⁰The next day an evil spirit from God entered Saul with power. And he prophesied*ᵈ* in his house. David was playing the harp as he usually did. But Saul had a spear in his hand. ¹¹He raised the spear and thought, "I'll pin David to the wall." But David got away from him two times.

¹²The Lord was with David but had left Saul. So Saul was afraid of David. ¹³He sent David away from him. He made David commander of 1,000 soldiers. So David led them in battle. ¹⁴He had great success in everything he did because the Lord was with him. ¹⁵Saul saw that David was very successful. And he became even more afraid of David. ¹⁶But all the people of Israel and Judah loved David. This was because he led them well in battle.

Saul's Daughter and David

¹⁷Saul said to David, "You're a brave soldier. And you fight the Lord's battles. Here is my older daughter Merab. I will let you marry her." Saul had decided, "I won't have to kill David. The Philistines will do that!"

¹⁸But David said, "I am not good enough for this honor. And my family is not important enough for me to become the king's son-in-law." ¹⁹So when the time came for Saul's daughter Merab to marry David, Saul gave her instead to Adriel of Meholah.

²⁰Now Saul's other daughter Michal loved David. When they told Saul about Michal loving David, he was

pleased. ²¹He thought, "I will let Michal marry David. Then she will become a trap for him. And the Philistines will defeat him." So Saul said to David a second time, "You may become my son-in-law."

²²And Saul gave an order to his servants. He told them, "Speak to David in private. Say, 'Look, the king is pleased with you. His servants like you. You should become his son-in-law.'"

²³Saul's servants said these words to David. But David answered, "Do you think it is easy to become the king's son-in-law? I'm only a poor man. Nobody knows me."

²⁴Then Saul's servants told him what David had said. ²⁵Saul said, "Say to David, 'The king doesn't want you to pay a large price for the bride. All he wants is 100 Philistine foreskins. Then he will be even with his enemies.'" Saul planned to let the Philistines kill David.

²⁶Saul's servants told David these words. David was pleased that he could become the king's son-in-law. ²⁷So he and his men went out and killed 200 Philistines. David took all their foreskins and brought them to Saul. He wanted to become the king's son-in-law. Then Saul gave him his daughter Michal for his wife. ²⁸Saul saw that the Lord was with David. He also saw that his daughter Michal loved David. ²⁹So he became even more afraid of David. And he was David's enemy all his life.

³⁰The Philistine commanders continued to go out to fight the Israelites. But every time, David defeated them. He had more success than Saul's officers. And he became famous.

Saul Plans to Kill David

19 Saul told his son Jonathan and all his servants to kill David. But Jonathan cared very much for David. ²So he warned David, "My father Saul is looking for a chance to kill you. Watch out in the morning. Hide in a secret place. ³I will go out and stand with my father in the field where you are hiding. I'll talk to him about you. Then I'll let you know what I find out."

⁴Jonathan talked to Saul his father. He said good things about David. Jonathan said, "You are the king. Don't do wrong to your servant David. He did nothing wrong to you. What he did has helped you greatly. ⁵David risked his life when he killed Goliath the Philistine. The Lord won a great victory for all Israel. You saw it, and you were happy. Why would you do wrong against David? He's innocent. There's no reason to kill him!"

⁶Saul listened to Jonathan. Then he made this promise: "As surely as the Lord lives, David won't be put to death."

⁷So Jonathan called to David. He told David everything that had been said. And he brought David to Saul. So David was with Saul as before.

⁸When war broke out again, David went out to fight the Philistines. He defeated them, and they ran away from him.

⁹But once again an evil spirit from the Lord entered Saul. He was sitting in his house, and he had his spear in his hand. David was playing the harp. ¹⁰Saul tried to pin David to the wall with his spear. But David moved away from him. So Saul's spear went into the wall. And David ran away that night.

¹¹Saul sent men to David's house. They watched it, wanting to kill him in the morning. But Michal, David's wife, warned him. She said, "Tonight you must run away to save your own life. If you don't, you will be killed tomorrow morning." ¹²Then she let David down out of a window. So he ran away and escaped. ¹³Then Michal took an idol and laid it on the bed. She covered it with clothes and put goats' hair at its head.

¹⁴Saul sent messengers to take David prisoner. But Michal said, "He is sick."

¹⁵The men went and told Saul, but he sent them back to see David. He

told them, "Bring him to me on his bed so I can kill him."

¹⁶But when the messengers entered David's house, they found it was just an idol on the bed. Its hair was goats' hair.

¹⁷Saul said to Michal, "Why did you trick me this way? You let my enemy go. He has run away!"

Michal answered Saul, "David told me if I did not help him escape, he would kill me."

Spirit*ᵈ* of God entered Saul's men, and they also prophesied.

²¹Saul heard the news. So he sent other men, but they also prophesied. Then he sent men a third time, but they also prophesied. ²²Finally, Saul himself went to Ramah. He came to the well at Secu. He asked, "Where are Samuel and David?"

The people answered, "In Naioth at Ramah."

²³Then Saul went to Naioth at Ramah. But the Spirit of God also entered him. And he walked on, prophesying until he came to Naioth

People Who Got Away

DAVID • 1 SAMUEL 19:13

Saul had tried and tried to kill David . . . but each time David had escaped. This time, it seemed there was no way out. Saul's men had surrounded David's house. David's wife, Michal, was very frightened. But she and David came up with a plan.

Saul's guards came into the house and went to David's room. It looked like David was covered up on the bed asleep. But when the guards tried to get David out of his bed, they discovered he was not there at all! They had been tricked!

Before the guards came, Michal had helped David escape through a window. David ran away without anyone noticing. Then Michal got a statue, put it under the covers of David's bed, and put goat hair on top of the statue's head so it would look like David was asleep! But David was long gone!

God will always protect us. We need to be brave and trust him even when we are afraid.

To read about an army of soldiers who became blind for a day, fly to page 450.

¹⁸After David had escaped from Saul, he went to Samuel at Ramah. He told Samuel everything Saul had done to him. Then David and Samuel went to Naioth and stayed there. ¹⁹Saul heard that David was in Naioth at Ramah. ²⁰So he sent men to capture him. But they met a group of prophets*ᵈ* prophesying. Samuel was leading this group and was standing there. The

at Ramah. ²⁴He took off his robes and prophesied in front of Samuel. He lay that way all day and all night. That is why people ask, "Is even Saul one of the prophets?"

David and Jonathan

20 Then David ran away from Naioth in Ramah. He went to Jonathan and asked, "What have I done? What is my crime? How have I sinned against your father so that he's trying to kill me?"

²Jonathan answered, "No! You won't die! See, my father doesn't do anything without first telling me. It doesn't matter if it is very important or just a small thing. Why would he refuse to tell me he wants to kill you? No, it's not true!"

³But David took an oath. He said, "Your father knows very well that I'm your friend. He has said to himself, 'Jonathan must not know about it. If he knows, he will tell David.' But as surely as the Lord lives and as you live, I am very close to death!"

⁴Jonathan said to David, "I'll do anything you want me to do."

wants to hurt me. ⁸Jonathan, be kind to me, your servant. You have made an agreement with me before the Lord. If I am guilty, you may kill me yourself! Why hand me over to your father?"

⁹Jonathan answered, "No, never! If I learn that my father plans to harm you, I will warn you!"

¹⁰David asked, "Who will let me know if your father answers you unkindly?"

¹¹Then Jonathan said, "Come, let's go out into the field." So Jonathan and David went together into the field.

¹²Jonathan said to David, "I promise this before the Lord, the God of Israel:

Friendships
1 SAMUEL 20:1-13

A good friend is someone who helps others, even when it hurts.

Jonathan was the closest friend David ever had. Probably one of the main reasons that David liked Jonathan so much was that he knew he could depend on Jonathan, even in the hard times. In this story, David found himself in hot water. The king was so mad at him that he wanted to kill him! Who did David turn to? His good friend, Jonathan. Jonathan helped David, even when it could have gotten him in deep trouble.

What kind of friend are you? Do you help out your friends only when it's convenient and easy for you? Or do you stick by your friends, even when it hurts?

To find out how to deal with people who get on your nerves , *zoom to page 1132.*

⁵So David said, "Look, tomorrow is the New Moon^d festival. I am supposed to eat with the king. But let me hide in the field until the third evening. ⁶Your father may notice I am gone. If he does, tell him, 'David begged me to let him go to his hometown of Bethlehem. Every year at this time, his family group offers a sacrifice.' ⁷If your father says, 'Fine,' I am safe. But if he becomes angry, you can believe he

At this same time day after tomorrow, I will find out how my father feels. If he feels good toward you, I'll send word to you. I'll let you know. ¹³But my father may mean to hurt you. If so, I will let you know and send you away safely. May the Lord punish me terribly if I don't do this. And may the Lord be with you as he has been with my father. ¹⁴But show me the kindness of the Lord as long as I live. Do this so that I may not die. [15]You must not stop showing your kindness to my family. Don't do this, even when the Lord has destroyed all your enemies from the earth."

"I hope I can be just as good a friend to Dylan as Jonathan was to David. Read about their friendship in 1 Samuel 20:1-42."

[16]So Jonathan made an agreement with David. He said, "May the Lord punish David's enemies." [17]And Jonathan asked David to repeat his promise of love for him. He did this because he loved David as much as he loved himself.

[18]Jonathan said to David, "Tomorrow is the New Moon festival. Your seat will be empty. So my father will notice you're gone. [19]On the third day go to the place where you hid when this trouble began. Wait by the rock Ezel. [20]On the third day I will shoot three arrows to the side of the rock. I will shoot as if I am shooting at a target. [21]Then I will send a boy and tell him to go find the arrows. I may say to him, 'Look, the arrows are on this side of you. Bring them here.' If so, you may come out of hiding. You may do this as surely as the Lord lives because you are safe. There is no danger. [22]But I may say to the boy, 'Look, the arrows are beyond you.' If I do, you must go, because the Lord has sent you away. [23]Remember what we talked about. The Lord is a witness between you and me forever."

[24]So David hid in the field. And when the New Moon festival came, the king sat down to eat. [25]He sat where he always sat, near the wall. Jonathan sat across from him, and Abner sat next to him. But David's place was empty. [26]That day Saul said nothing. He thought, "Maybe something has happened to David so that he is unclean."[d] [27]But the next day was the second day of the month. And David's place was empty again. So Saul said to Jonathan, "Why hasn't the son of Jesse come to the festival yesterday or today?"

[28]Jonathan answered, "David begged me to let him go to Bethlehem. [29]He said, 'Let me go, because our family has a sacrifice in the town. And my brother has ordered me to be there. Now if I am your friend, please let me go and see my brothers.' That is why he has not come to the king's table."

[30]Then Saul became very angry with Jonathan. He said, "You son of an evil and disobedient woman! I know you are on the side of David son of Jesse! You bring shame on yourself and on your mother who gave birth to you. [31]As long as Jesse's son lives, you'll never be king or have a kingdom. Now send for David and bring him to me. He must die!"

[32]Jonathan asked his father, "Why should David be killed? What wrong has he done?" [33]Then Saul threw his spear at Jonathan, trying to kill him. So Jonathan knew that his father really wanted to kill David. [34]Jonathan was very angry and left the table. That second day of the month he refused to eat. He was upset about what his father wanted to do to David.

[35]The next morning Jonathan went out to the field. He went to meet David as they had agreed. He had a young boy with him. [36]Jonathan said to the boy, "Run and find the arrows I shoot." When he ran, Jonathan shot an arrow beyond him. [37]The boy ran to the place where Jonathan's arrow fell. But Jonathan called, "The arrow is beyond you!" [38]Then he shouted, "Hurry! Go quickly! Don't stop!" The boy picked up the arrow and brought it back to his master. [39](The boy knew nothing about what this meant. Only Jonathan and David knew.) [40]Then Jonathan gave his weapons to the boy. He told him, "Go back to town."

⁴¹When the boy left, David came out from the south side of the rock. He bowed facedown on the ground before Jonathan. He did this three times. Then David and Jonathan kissed each other. They cried together, but David cried the most.

⁴²Jonathan said to David, "Go in peace. We have promised by the Lord that we will be friends. We said, 'The Lord will be a witness between you and me, and between our descendants*ᵈ* forever.'" Then David left, and Jonathan went back to town.

David Goes to See Ahimelech

21 David went to Nob to see Ahimelech the priest. Ahimelech shook with fear when he saw David. He asked David, "Why are you alone? Why is no one with you?"

²David answered him, "The king gave me a special order. He told me, 'No one must know about the work I am sending you to do. And no one must know what I told you to do.' I told my men where to meet me. ³Now, what food do you have with you? Give me five loaves of bread or anything you find."

⁴The priest said to David, "I don't have any plain bread here. But I do have some holy bread*ⁿ* here. You may eat it if your men have kept themselves from women."

⁵David answered, "Women have been kept from us. My men always keep their bodies holy, even when we do ordinary work. And this is especially true when the work is holy."

⁶There was no bread except the bread made holy for the Lord. So the priest gave David the bread that showed the people were in the presence of God. This was the bread the priests had taken from the holy table before the Lord. Each day they took this bread away and put hot bread in its place.

⁷Now one of Saul's servants was there that day. He had been held there before the Lord. He was Doeg the Edomite, the chief of Saul's shepherds.

⁸David asked Ahimelech, "Do you have a spear or sword here? The king's business was very important. I had to leave quickly, and I didn't bring my sword or any other weapon."

⁹The priest answered, "The sword of Goliath the Philistine is here. He is the one you killed in the Valley of Elah. His sword is wrapped in a cloth. It is behind the holy vest.*ᵈ* If you want it, you may take it. There's no other sword here but that one."

David said, "There is no other sword like Goliath's. Give it to me."

David Goes to Gath

¹⁰That day David ran away from Saul. He went to Achish king of Gath. ¹¹But the servants of Achish said to him, "This is David king of the Israelites. He's the man the Israelite women sing about when they dance. They sing:

'Saul has killed thousands of his
    enemies.
  But David has killed tens of
    thousands.'"

¹²David paid attention to these words. And he was very much afraid of Achish king of Gath. ¹³So he pretended to be insane in front of Achish and his servants. While he was with them, he acted like a madman. He made marks on the doors of the gate. He let spit run down his beard.

¹⁴Achish said to his servants, "Look at the man! He's insane! Why do you bring him to me? ¹⁵I have enough madmen. I don't need you to bring him here to act like this in front of me! Don't leave him in my house!"

David at Adullam and Mizpah

22 David left Gath and escaped to the cave of Adullam. His brothers and other relatives heard that he

---

*ⁿ***holy bread** This was the bread that showed the people were in the presence of God. Normally only the priests should eat this bread.

was there. And they went to see him. ²Many people joined David. All those who were in trouble, who owed money or who were unsatisfied gathered around him. And he became their leader. He had about 400 men with him.

³From there David went to Mizpah in Moab. He spoke to the king of Moab. He said, "Please let my father and mother come and stay with you. Let them stay until I learn what God is going to do for me." ⁴So he left them with the king of Moab. And they stayed with the king as long as David was hiding in the protected place.

⁵But the prophet*d* Gad said to David, "Don't stay in the protected place. Go to the land of Judah." So David left and went to the forest of Hereth.

Saul Destroys Ahimelech's Family

⁶Saul heard that David and his men had been seen. He sat under the tamarisk tree on the hill at Gibeah. All his officers were standing around him. He had a spear in his hand. ⁷Saul said to them, "Listen, men of Benjamin! Do you think the son of Jesse will give all of you fields and vineyards? Will David make you commanders over thousands of men or hundreds of men? ⁸You have all made plans against me! No one tells me when my son makes an agreement with the son of Jesse! No one cares about me! No one tells me my son has encouraged my servant to ambush me! And David is doing this now!"

⁹Doeg the Edomite was standing there with Saul's officers. He said, "I saw the son of Jesse. He came to see Ahimelech son of Ahitub at Nob. ¹⁰Ahimelech prayed to the Lord for David. He also gave him food. And he gave him the sword of Goliath the Philistine."

¹¹Then the king sent for the priest Ahimelech son of Ahitub. He sent for all of Ahimelech's relatives who were priests at Nob. And they all came to the king. ¹²Saul said to Ahimelech, "Listen now, son of Ahitub."

Ahimelech answered, "Yes, master."

¹³Saul said, "Why have you and Jesse's son made plans against me? You gave him bread and a sword! You prayed to God for him. David is waiting to attack me. He is doing this now!"

¹⁴Ahimelech answered, "David is very loyal to you. You have no other servant who is as loyal as David. He is your own son-in-law and captain of your bodyguards. All the people in your house respect him. ¹⁵That was not the first time I prayed to God for David. Not at all! Don't blame me or any of my relatives. We are your servants. I know nothing about what is going on."

¹⁶But the king said, "Ahimelech, you and all your relatives must die!" ¹⁷Then he told the guards at his side, "Go and kill the priests of the Lord. Do this because they are on David's side. They knew he was running away, but they didn't tell me!"

But the king's officers refused to hurt the priests of the Lord.

¹⁸Then the king ordered Doeg, "Go and kill the priests." So Doeg the Edomite went and killed the priests. That day he killed 85 men who wore the linen holy vest.*d* ¹⁹He also killed the people of Nob, the city of the priests. With the sword he killed men, women, children and small babies. And he killed cattle, donkeys and sheep.

²⁰But Abiathar escaped. He was a son of Ahimelech, who was the son of Ahitub. Abiathar ran away and joined David. ²¹He told David that Saul had killed the Lord's priests. ²²Then David told him, "Doeg the Edomite was there at Nob that day. I knew he would surely tell Saul. So I am responsible for the death of all your father's family. ²³The man who wants to kill you also wants to kill me. Stay with me. Don't be afraid. You will be safe with me."

David at Keilah

23 Someone told David, "Look, the Philistines are fighting against Keilah. They are robbing grain from the threshing[d] floors."

[2]David asked the Lord, "Should I go and fight these Philistines?"

The Lord answered him, "Go. Attack them, and save Keilah."

[3]But David's men said to him, "We're afraid here in Judah. We will be much more afraid if we go to Keilah where the Philistine army is."

Saul Chases David

[7]Someone told Saul that David was now at Keilah. Saul said, "God has given David to me! He has trapped himself because he has entered a town with gates and bars." [8]Saul called all his army together for battle. They prepared to go down to Keilah to attack David and his men.

[9]David learned Saul was making evil plans against him. So he said to

Helping Others
1 SAMUEL 23:15-18

How far would you go to help a friend?

Would you give a friend money? Stick up for her when someone puts her down? Listen to all his problems? Of course you would. Friends do that for each other. But would you risk your life for your friend? 1 Samuel 23:15-18 tells about a friendship so strong that one man risked his life for his friend.

Jonathan was the son of Saul, the king of Israel. He was in line to become king after his father. But God had chosen David to be king, and Jonathan and David were close friends. Saul hated David and even tried to kill him. Anyone who helped David risked facing Saul's anger, which could mean death. Regardless, Jonathan went to David to "strengthen his faith in God." That's a good friend!

How far would you go for a friend? You may never have to risk your life, but it may cost you in other ways. Be a good friend, like Jonathan.

To learn more about helping others, zoom to page 753.

[4]David again asked the Lord. And the Lord answered, "Go down to Keilah. I will help you defeat the Philistines." [5]So David and his men went to Keilah. They fought the Philistines and took their cattle. David killed many Philistines and saved the people of Keilah. [6](Now Abiathar son of Ahimelech had brought the holy vest[d] with him. He brought it when he came to David at Keilah.)

Abiathar the priest, "Bring the holy vest."[d] [10]David prayed, "Lord, God of Israel, I have heard about Saul's plans. He is coming to Keilah to destroy the town because of me. [11]Will the people of Keilah give me to Saul? Will Saul come to Keilah, as I heard? Lord, God of Israel, tell me, your servant!"

The Lord answered, "Saul will come down."

[12]Again David asked, "Will the people

of Keilah give me and my men to Saul?"

The Lord answered, "They will."

13So David and his men left Keilah. There were about 600 men who went with him. And they kept moving from place to place. When Saul found that David had escaped from Keilah, he did not go there.

14David stayed in the protected places in the desert. He also stayed in the hills of the Desert of Ziph. Every day Saul looked for David. But the Lord did not let him take David.

15David was at Horesh in the Desert of Ziph. He was afraid because Saul was coming to kill him. 16But Saul's son Jonathan went to David at Horesh. He helped David have stronger faith in God. 17Jonathan told him, "Don't be afraid. My father won't touch you. You will become king of Israel, and I will be second to you. Even my father Saul knows this." 18The two of them made an agreement before the Lord. Then Jonathan went home. But David stayed at Horesh.

19The people from Ziph went to Saul at Gibeah. They told him, "David is hiding in our land. He's at the protected places of Horesh. They are on the hill of Hakilah, south of Jeshimon. 20Now, our king, come down anytime you want. It's our duty to give David to you."

21Saul answered, "The Lord bless you for helping me. 22Go and learn more about him. Find out where he is staying. Find out who has seen him there. I have heard that he is clever. 23Find all the hiding places he uses. And come back and tell me everything. Then I'll go with you. If David is in the area, I will find him. I will track him down among all the families in Judah."

24So they went back to Ziph ahead of Saul. David and his men were in the Desert of Maon.ⁿ This was in the desert area south of Jeshimon. 25Saul and his men went to look for David. But people warned David that Saul

was looking for him. David then went down to a rock and stayed in the Desert of Maon. Saul heard that David had gone there. So he went after him into the Desert of Maon.

26Saul was going along one side of the mountain. David and his men were on the other side. They were hurrying to get away from Saul. Saul and his soldiers were closing in on David and his men. 27But a messenger came to Saul. He said, "Come quickly! The Philistines are attacking our land!" 28So Saul stopped chasing David and went to fight the Philistines. That is why people call this place Rock of Parting. 29David left the Desert of Maon and lived in the protected places of En Gedi.

David Shames Saul

24 Now Saul had chased the Philis -tines away. Then he was told, "David is in the Desert of En Gedi." 2So he chose 3,000 men from all Israel. He took these men and began looking for David and his men. They looked near the Rocks of the Wild Goats.

3Saul came to the sheep pens beside the road. A cave was there, and he went in to relieve himself. Now David and his men were hiding far back in the cave. 4The men said to David, "Today is the day the Lord talked about! The Lord told you, 'I will give your enemy to you. You can do anything you want with him.'"

Then David crawled near Saul. He cut off a corner of Saul's robe. But Saul did not notice him. 5Later David felt guilty because he had cut off a corner of Saul's robe. 6He said to his men, "May the Lord keep me from doing such a thing to my master! Saul is the Lord's appointed king. I should not do anything against him, because he is the Lord's appointed king!" 7David used these words to stop his men. He did not let them attack Saul. Then Saul left the cave and went his way.

8When David came out of the cave,

ⁿ**Maon**   Some early Greek copies say "Maon." The Hebrew copies say "Paran."

he shouted to Saul, "My master and king!" Saul looked back, and David bowed facedown on the ground. [9]He said to Saul, "Why do you listen when people say, 'David plans to harm you'? [10]You have seen something with your own eyes today. You have seen how the Lord put you in my power in the cave. But I refused to kill you. I was merciful to you. I said, 'I won't harm my master, because he is the Lord's appointed king.' [11]My father, look at this piece of your robe in my hand! I cut off the corner of your robe, but I didn't kill you. Now understand and know I am not planning any evil against you. I did nothing wrong to you, but you are hunting me to kill me. [12]May the Lord judge between us. And may he punish you for the wrong you have done to me! But I won't fight you. [13]There is an old saying: 'Evil things come from evil people.' So I won't hurt you. [14]Whom is the king of Israel coming out against? Whom are you chasing? You're not chasing someone who will hurt you! It's as if you are chasing a dead dog or a flea. [15]May the Lord be our judge and decide between you and me. May the Lord support me and show that I am right. May he save me from you!"

[16]David finished saying these words. Then Saul asked, "Is that your voice, David my son?" And he cried loudly. [17]He said, "You are right, and I am wrong. You have been good to me. But I have done wrong to you. [18]You told me what good things you did. The Lord brought me to you, but you did not kill me. [19]If a man finds his enemy, he won't send him away with goodness, will he? May the Lord reward you because you were good to me today. [20]I know you will surely be king. You will rule the kingdom of Israel. [21]Now make a promise to me. Promise in the name of the Lord that you will not kill my descendants.[d] Promise me that you won't wipe out my name from my father's family."

[22]So David made the promise to Saul. Then Saul went back home. David and his men went up to the protected place.

David and Nabal

25 Now Samuel died. All the Israelites met and had a time of sadness for him. They buried him at his home in Ramah.

Then David moved to the Desert of Maon.[n] [2]A man in Maon who had land at Carmel was very rich. He had 3,000 sheep and 1,000 goats. He was cutting the wool off his sheep at Carmel. [3]His name was Nabal, and he was a descendant[d] of Caleb. His wife was named Abigail. She was a wise and beautiful woman. But Nabal was cruel and mean.

[4]David was in the desert. He heard that Nabal was cutting the wool from his sheep. [5]So he sent ten young men. He told them, "Go to Nabal at Carmel. Greet him for me. [6]Say to Nabal, 'May you and your family have good health! And may all who belong to you have good health. [7]I have heard that you are cutting the wool from your sheep. When your shepherds were with us, we did nothing wrong to them. All the time your shepherds were at Carmel, we stole nothing from them. [8]Ask your servants, and they will tell you. We come at a happy time. So for this reason, be kind to my young men. Please give them anything you can find for them. Please do this for your son David.'"

[9]When the men arrived, they gave the message to Nabal. But Nabal insulted them. [10]He answered them, "Who is David? Who is this son of Jesse? Many slaves are running away from their masters today! [11]I have bread and water. And I have meat that I killed for my servants who cut the wool. But I won't give it to men I don't know."

[12]David's men went back and told him all Nabal had said. [13]Then David said to them, "Put on your swords!" So they put on their swords, and David

---

[n]**Maon**   Some early Greek copies say "Maon." The Hebrew copies say "Paran."

put on his also. About 400 men went with David. But 200 men stayed with the supplies.

She put all these on donkeys. ¹⁹Then she told her servants, "Go on. I'll follow you." But she did not tell her husband.

²⁰Abigail rode her donkey and came down into the mountain ravine. There

Heroes Who Trusted God

ABIGAIL • 1 SAMUEL 25:23-28

Saying you are sorry might be the most important words you say.

Nabal had been very rude to King David and the king's men. This made King David angry, and he decided to fight Nabal and his servants. But Nabal would not apologize to David. Nabal's wife, Abigail, knew Nabal had been wrong to insult David. So, she prepared a huge amount of food and brought it to King David's men. She wanted to show how sorry Nabal was for insulting David and his men.

It was very dangerous for Abigail to go to David's men. They could have killed her. But God honored her for apologizing to David. David promised not to kill Abigail's husband.

Don't be afraid to say you are sorry.

To learn about a queen who risked her life to talk to the king,
fly to page 598.

¹⁴One of Nabal's servants spoke to Abigail, Nabal's wife. He said, "David sent messengers from the desert to greet our master. But Nabal insulted them. ¹⁵These men were very good to us. They did nothing wrong to us. They stole nothing from us during all the time we were out in the field with them. ¹⁶Night and day they protected us. They were like a wall around us while we were with them caring for the sheep. ¹⁷Now think about it, and decide what you can do. Terrible trouble is coming to our master and all his family. Nabal is such a wicked man that no one can even talk to him."

¹⁸Abigail hurried. She took 200 loaves of bread, 2 leather bags full of wine and 5 cooked sheep. She took about a bushel of cooked grain, 100 cakes of raisins and 200 cakes of pressed figs.

she met David and his men coming down toward her.

²¹David had just said, "It's been useless! I watched over Nabal's property in the desert. I made sure none of his sheep were missing. I did good to him, but he has paid me back with evil. ²²May God punish me terribly if I let just one of Nabal's family live until tomorrow."

²³When Abigail saw David, she quickly got off her donkey. She bowed facedown on the ground before David. ²⁴She lay at David's feet. She said, "My master, let the blame be on me! Please let me talk to you! Listen to what I say. ²⁵My master, don't pay attention to this worthless man Nabal. He is the same as his name. His name means 'fool,' and he is truly foolish. But I, your servant, didn't see the men you sent. ²⁶The Lord has kept you from

killing and punishing people yourself. As surely as the Lord lives and as surely as you live, may your enemies become like Nabal! [27]I have brought a gift to you. Please give it to the men who follow you. [28]Please forgive my wrong. The Lord will certainly let your family have many kings. He will do this because you fight his battles. As long as you live, people will find nothing bad in you. [29]A man might chase you to kill you. But the Lord your God will keep you alive. He will throw away your enemies' lives as he would throw a stone from a sling. [30]The Lord will keep all his promises about good things for you. He will make you leader over Israel. [31]Then you won't feel guilty. You won't have problems about killing innocent people and punishing them yourself. Please remember me when the Lord brings you success."

[32]David answered Abigail, "Praise the Lord, the God of Israel. He sent you to meet me. [33]May you be blessed for your wisdom. You have kept me from killing or punishing people today. [34]As surely as the Lord, the God of Israel, lives, he has kept me from hurting you. If you hadn't come quickly to meet me, no one belonging to Nabal would have lived until tomorrow."

[35]Then David accepted Abigail's gifts. He told her, "Go home in peace. I have heard your words, and I will do what you have asked."

Nabal's Death

[36]When Abigail went back to Nabal, he was in the house. He was eating like a king. He was very drunk and in a good mood. So she told him nothing until the next morning. [37]In the morning he was not drunk. Then his wife told him everything. His heart failed him, and he became like a stone. [38]About ten days later the Lord struck Nabal and caused him to die.

[39]When David heard that Nabal was dead, he said, "Praise the Lord! Nabal insulted me, but the Lord has supported me! He has kept me from doing wrong. And the Lord caused Nabal to die because he did wrong."

Then David sent a message to Abigail. He asked her to become his wife. [40]His servants went to Carmel and spoke to Abigail. They said, "David sent us to take you so you can become his wife."

[41]Abigail bowed facedown on the ground. She said, "I am your servant. I'm ready to serve you. I'm ready to wash the feet of my master's servants." [42]Abigail quickly got on a donkey and went with David's messengers. She had five maids following her. And she became David's wife.

[43]David also had married Ahinoam of Jezreel. So they were both David's wives. [44]Saul's daughter Michal was also David's wife. But Saul had given her to Paltiel son of Laish. Paltiel was from Gallim.

David Shames Saul Again

26 The people of Ziph went to see Saul at Gibeah. They said to him, "David is hiding on the hill of Hakilah opposite Jeshimon."

[2]So Saul went down to the Desert of Ziph. His 3,000 chosen men of Israel went with him. They looked for David in the Desert of Ziph. [3]Saul made his camp on the hill of Hakilah, beside the road opposite Jeshimon. But David stayed in the desert. He heard Saul had followed him. [4]So David sent out spies and learned that Saul had come to Hakilah.

[5]Then David went to the place where Saul had camped. He saw where Saul and Abner son of Ner were sleeping. Abner was the commander of Saul's army. Saul was sleeping in the middle of the camp with all the army around him.

[6]David talkexd to Ahimelech the Hittite and Abishai son of Zeruiah. Abishai was Joab's brother. He asked them, "Who will go down into Saul's camp with me?"

Abishai answered, "I'll go with you." [7]So that night David and Abishai went into Saul's camp. Saul was asleep in the middle of the camp. His spear was stuck in the ground near his head. Abner and the army were sleeping around Saul. [8]Abishai said to David, "Today God has let you defeat your enemy! Let me pin Saul to the ground with the spear. I'll only do it once! I won't hit him twice."

[9]But David said to Abishai, "Don't kill Saul! No one can harm the Lord's appointed king and still be innocent! [10]As surely as the Lord lives, the Lord himself will punish Saul. Maybe Saul will die naturally. Or maybe he will go into battle and be killed. [11]But may the Lord keep me from harming his appointed king! Now pick up the spear and water jug that are near Saul's head. Then let's go."

[12]So David took the spear and water jug that were near Saul's head. They left, and no one saw them. No one knew about it or woke up. The Lord had made them stay asleep.

[13]David crossed over to the other side of the hill. He stood on top of the mountain far from Saul's camp. David's and Saul's camps were far apart. [14]David shouted to the army and to Abner son of Ner, "Answer me, Abner!"

Abner answered, "Who is calling for the king? Who are you?"

[15]David said, "You're the greatest man in Israel. Isn't that true? Then why didn't you guard your master the king? Someone came into your camp to kill your master the king! [16]What you have done is not good. As surely as the Lord lives, you and your men should die. You haven't guarded your master, the Lord's appointed king. Look! Where are the king's spear and water jug that were near his head?"

[17]Saul knew David's voice. He said, "Is that your voice, David my son?"

David answered, "Yes, it is, my master and king." [18]David also said, "Why are you chasing me, my master? What wrong have I done? What evil am I guilty of? [19]My master and king, listen to me. If the Lord caused you to be angry with me, let him accept an offering. But if men caused you to be angry with me, let the Lord curse them! They have made me leave the land the Lord gave me. They have told me, 'Go and serve other gods.' [20]Now don't let me die far away from the Lord's presence. The king of Israel has come out looking for a flea! You're like a man hunting a partridge bird in the mountains!"

[21]Then Saul said, "I have sinned. Come back, David my son. Today you respected my life. So I will not try to hurt you. I have acted foolishly. I have made a big mistake."

[22]David answered, "Here is your spear. Let one of your young men come here and get it. [23]The Lord rewards every man for the things he does right and for his loyalty to him. The Lord put you into my power today. But I wouldn't harm the Lord's appointed king. [24]I respected your life today. Surely, in the same way, the Lord will respect my life. Surely he will save me from all trouble."

[25]Then Saul said to David, "You are blessed, my son David. You will do great things and succeed."

So David went on his way, and Saul went back home.

David and the Philistines

27 But David thought to himself, "Saul will catch me someday. The best thing I can do is escape to the land of the Philistines. Then he will give up looking for me in Israel. That way I can get away from him."

[2]So David and his 600 men left Israel. They went to Achish son of Maoch. Achish was king of Gath. [3]David, his men and their families made their home in Gath with Achish. David had his two wives with him. Their names were Ahinoam of Jezreel and Abigail of Carmel. Abigail was the widow of Nabal. [4]Now Saul was told that David had run away to Gath. So he stopped looking for him.

[5]Then David said to Achish, "If you

are pleased with me, give me a place in one of the country towns. I can live there. I don't need to live in the royal city with you."

now hate David very much. So David will serve me forever."

Saul and the Witch of Endor

28 Later, the Philistines gathered their armies to fight against Israel. Achish said to David, "You

People Who Made Mistakes
KING SAUL • 1 SAMUEL 28

Have you ever been in trouble? King Saul was in big trouble because he had to fight a bad army. Instead of trusting the Lord, Saul went to talk to a witch. In those days, witches didn't look like the cartoon witches we have on Halloween, with brooms and black cats. This witch served Satan. Because Saul went to her for help, God punished him. The next day in battle, Saul and his sons were killed, and his army was defeated.

When we get into trouble, we should always go to the Lord for help. He will lead us and show us what to do.

To find a man who gave in to peer pressure, fly to page 1308.

⁶That day Achish gave David the town of Ziklag. That is why Ziklag has belonged to the kings of Judah ever since. ⁷David lived in the Philistine land a year and four months.

⁸David and his men went to raid the people of Geshur, Girzi and Amalek. (These people had lived for a long time in the land that reached to Shur and Egypt.) ⁹When David fought them, he killed all the men and women. He took sheep, cattle, donkeys, camels and clothes. Then he returned to Achish.

¹⁰Many times Achish would ask David, "Where did you go raiding today?" And David would tell him that he had gone to the southern part of Judah. Or he would say he had gone to the territory of the Jerahmeelites or of the Kenites. ¹¹David never brought a man or woman alive to Gath. He thought, "If we bring anyone alive, he may tell Achish, 'This is what David really did.'" David did this all the time he lived in the Philistine land. ¹²Achish trusted David. He said to himself, "David's own people, the Israelites,

understand that you and your men must join with me in my army."

²David answered, "Certainly! Then you can see for yourself what I, your servant, can do!"

Achish said, "Fine, I'll make you my bodyguard for life."

³Now Samuel was dead, and all the Israelites had shown their sadness for him. They had buried Samuel in his hometown of Ramah.

And Saul had forced out the mediums*d* and fortune-tellers from the land of Israel.

⁴The Philistines came together and made camp at Shunem. Saul gathered all the Israelites and made camp at Gilboa. ⁵When he saw the Philistine army, he was afraid. His heart pounded with fear. ⁶He prayed to the Lord, but the Lord did not answer him through dreams, Urim*d* or prophets.*d* ⁷Then Saul said to his servants, "Find me a woman who is a medium. I'll go and ask her what will happen."

His servants answered, "There is a medium in Endor."

⁸Then Saul put on other clothes so no one would know who he was. At night Saul and two of his men went to see the woman. Saul said to her, "Talk to a spirit for me. Call up the person I name."

God does not want his children to be interested in evil and the occult. Trying to get help from Satan never works out right. Look at what happened to King Saul in 1 Samuel 28:1-25."

⁹But the woman said to him, "Surely you know what Saul has done. He has forced the mediums and fortune-tellers out from the land of Israel. You are trying to trap me and kill me."

¹⁰Saul made a promise to the woman in the name of the Lord. He said, "As surely as the Lord lives, you won't be punished for doing this."

¹¹The woman asked, "Whom do you want me to bring up for you?"

He answered, "Bring up Samuel."

¹²When the woman saw Samuel, she screamed loudly. She said, "Why have you tricked me? You are Saul!"

¹³The king said to the woman, "Don't be afraid! What do you see?"

The woman said, "I see a spirit coming up out of the ground."

¹⁴Saul asked, "What does he look like?"

The woman answered, "An old man wearing a coat is coming up."

Then Saul knew it was Samuel, and he bowed facedown on the ground.

¹⁵Samuel asked Saul, "Why have you disturbed me by bringing me up?"

Saul said, "I am greatly troubled. The Philistines are fighting against me. God has left me. He won't answer me anymore, either by prophets or in dreams. That's why I called you. I want you to tell me what to do."

¹⁶Samuel said, "The Lord has left you. He has become your enemy. So why do you call on me? ¹⁷He has done

what he said he would do. He said these things through me. He has torn the kingdom out of your hands. He has given it to one of your neighbors, David. ¹⁸You did not obey the Lord. You did not show the Amalekites how angry he was with them. That's why he has done this to you today. ¹⁹The Lord will give both Israel and you to the Philistines. Tomorrow you and your sons will be with me. The Lord will let the Philistines defeat the army of Israel."

²⁰Saul quickly fell to the ground and lay there. He was afraid because of what Samuel had said. He was also very weak because he had eaten nothing all that day and night.

²¹Then the woman came to Saul. She saw that he was really frightened. She said, "Look, I, your servant, have obeyed you. I have risked my life and done what you told me to do. ²²Now please listen to me. Let me give you some food. Then you may eat and have enough strength to go on your way."

²³But Saul refused. He said, "I won't eat."

His servants joined the woman in asking him to eat. And he listened to them. So he got up from the ground and sat on the bed.

²⁴The woman had a fat calf at the house. She quickly killed it. She took some flour and mixed dough with her hands. Then she baked some bread without yeast. ²⁵She put the food before them, and they ate. Then that same night they got up and left.

David Goes Back to Ziklag

29 The Philistines gathered all their soldiers at Aphek. Israel camped by the spring at Jezreel. ²The Philistine kings were marching with their groups of 100 and 1,000 men. David and his men were marching at the back with Achish. ³The Philistine commanders asked, "What are these Hebrews doing here?"

Achish told them, "This is David. He was an officer to Saul king of Israel.

But he has been with me for over a year now. I have found nothing wrong in David since the time he left Saul and came to me."

⁴But the Philistine commanders were angry with Achish. They said, "Send David back! He must go back to the city you gave him. He can't go with us into battle. If he's here, we'll have an enemy in our own camp. He would please his king by killing our own men. ⁵David is the one the Israelites sing about in their dances:

'Saul has killed thousands of his
      enemies.
But David has killed tens of
      thousands.'"

⁶So Achish called David. He said to him, "As surely as the Lord lives, you are loyal. I would be pleased to have you serve in my army. Since the day you came to me, I have found no wrong in you. But the Philistine kings don't trust you. ⁷Go back in peace. Don't do anything to displease the Philistine kings."

⁸David asked, "What wrong have I done? What evil have you found in me from the day I came to you until now? Why won't you allow me to fight your enemies, my lord and king?"

⁹Achish answered, "I know you are as pleasing to me as an angel from God. But the Philistine commanders have said, 'David can't go with us into battle.' ¹⁰Early in the morning you and your master's servants, the Israelites, should go back. Go back to the city I gave you. Leave as soon as the sun comes up."

¹¹So David and his men got up early in the morning. They went back to the country of the Philistines. And the Philistines went up to Jezreel.

David's War with the Amalekites

30 On the third day David and his men arrived at Ziklag. The Amalekites had raided southern Judah and Ziklag. They had attacked Ziklag and burned it. ²They took the women and everyone in Ziklag as prisoners, both young and old. But they did not kill any of the people. They only took them away.

³When David and his men came to Ziklag, they found the town had been burned. Their wives, sons and daughters had been taken as prisoners. ⁴Then David and his army cried loudly until they were too weak to cry anymore. ⁵David's two wives had also been taken. They were Ahinoam of Jezreel and Abigail the widow of Nabal from Carmel. ⁶The men in the army were threatening to kill David with stones. This upset David very much. Each man was sad and angry because his sons and daughters had been taken as prisoners. But David found strength in the Lord his God. ⁷David said to Abiathar the priest, "Bring me the holy vest."ᵈ

⁸Then David prayed to the Lord. He said, "Should I chase the people who took our families? Will I catch them?"

The Lord answered, "Chase them. You will catch them. You will succeed in saving your families."

⁹David and the 600 men with him came to the Besor Ravine. Some of the men stayed there. ¹⁰David and 400 men kept up the chase. The other 200 men stayed behind because they were too tired and weak to cross the ravine.

¹¹David's men found an Egyptian in a field. They took him to David. They gave the Egyptian some water to drink and some food to eat. ¹²They gave him a piece of a fig cake and two clusters of raisins. He felt better after eating. He had not eaten any food or drunk any water for three days and nights.

¹³David asked him, "Who is your master? Where do you come from?"

He answered, "I'm an Egyptian. I'm the slave of an Amalekite. Three days ago my master left me, because I became sick. ¹⁴We attacked the southern area of the Kerethites. We attacked the land of Judah and the southern area belonging to Caleb. We burned Ziklag, as well."

[15]David asked him, "Will you lead me to the people who took our families?"

He answered, "Yes, if you will make a promise to me before God. Promise that you won't kill me or give me back to my master. Then I will take you to them."

[16]So the Egyptian led David to the Amalekites. They were lying around on the ground, eating and drinking. They were celebrating with the things they had taken from the land of the Philistines and from Judah. [17]David fought them from sunset until evening the next day. None of them escaped, except 400 young men who rode off on their camels. [18]David got his two wives back. He also got back everything the Amalekites had taken. [19]Nothing was missing. David brought back everything: the young and old people, the sons and daughters, the valuable things and everything the Amalekites had taken. [20]David took all the sheep and cattle. His men made these animals go in front. They said, "They are David's prize."

[21]Then David came to the 200 men who had been too tired and weak to follow him. He had made them stay at the Besor Ravine. They came out to meet David and the army with him. When he came near, the men at the ravine greeted David and his army. [22]But there were evil men and troublemakers in the group that followed David. They said, "These 200 men didn't go with us. So we won't give them any of the things we took. But each man may take his wife and children and go."

[23]David answered, "No, my brothers. Don't do that after what the Lord has given us. He has given us the enemy who attacked us. [24]Who will listen to what you say? The share will be the same for the man who stayed with the supplies as for the man who went into battle. All will share alike." [25]David made this an order and rule for Israel. This order and rule continues even today.

[26]David arrived in Ziklag. Then he sent some of the things he had taken from the Amalekites to his friends, the leaders of Judah. He said, "Here is a present for you from the things we took from the Lord's enemies."

[27]David sent some things from the Amalekites to the leaders in Bethel, Ramoth in the southern part of Judah, Jattir, [28]Aroer, Siphmoth, Eshtemoa [29]and Racal. He also sent some to the leaders of the cities of the Jerahmeelites and the Kenites, [30]to Hormah, Bor Ashan, Athach [31]and Hebron. He sent some things to the people in all the other places where he and his men had been.

The Death of Saul

31 The Philistines fought against Israel, and the Israelites ran away from them. Many Israelites were killed at Mount Gilboa. [2]The Philistines fought hard against Saul and his sons. They killed his sons Jonathan, Abinadab and Malki-Shua. [3]The fighting became bad around Saul. When the archers shot at him, he was badly wounded. [4]He said to the officer who carried his armor, "Pull out your sword and kill me. Then those uncircumcised[d] men won't make fun of me and kill me." But Saul's officer refused, because he was afraid. So Saul took his own sword and threw himself on it. [5]The officer saw that Saul was dead. So he threw himself on his own sword. And he died with Saul. [6]So Saul, his three sons and the officer who carried his armor died together that day.

[7]Now there were Israelites who lived on the other side of Jezreel Valley. And some lived across the Jordan River. They saw how the Israelite army had run away. And they saw that Saul and his sons were dead. So they left their cities and ran away. Then the Philistines came and lived there.

[8]The next day the Philistines came to take all the valuable things from the dead soldiers. They found Saul and his three sons dead on Mount Gilboa.

⁹They cut off Saul's head and took off his armor. Then they sent men to tell the news through all the land of the Philistines. They told it in the temple of their idols and to their people. ¹⁰They put Saul's armor in the temple of the Ashtoreths.ᵈ They also hung his body on the wall of Beth Shan.

¹¹The people living in Jabesh Gilead heard what the Philistines had done to Saul. ¹²So the brave soldiers of Jabesh marched all night and came to Beth Shan. They took the bodies of Saul and his sons off the wall of Beth Shan. Then they took them to Jabesh. There the people of Jabesh burned the bodies. ¹³They took their bones and buried them under the tamarisk tree in Jabesh. Then the people of Jabesh gave up eating for seven days.

2 SAMUEL

David,
the Greatest King

David Learns About Saul's Death

1 Now Saul was dead. And after David had defeated the Amalekites, he returned to Ziklag. He stayed there two days. ²On the third day a young man came to Ziklag. He came from Saul's camp. To show his sadness his clothes were torn, and he had dirt on his head. He came and bowed face-down on the ground before David.

³David asked him, "Where did you come from?"

The man answered him, "I escaped from the Israelite camp."

⁴David asked him, "What happened? Please tell me!"

The man answered, "The people have run away from the battle. Many of them have fallen dead. Saul and his son Jonathan are dead also."

⁵David said to him, "How do you know Saul and his son Jonathan are dead?"

⁶The young man answered, "I happened to be on Mount Gilboa. There I saw Saul leaning on his spear. The Philistine chariots and the men riding in them were coming closer to Saul. ⁷When he looked back and saw me, he called to me. I answered him, 'Here I am!'

⁸"Then Saul asked me, 'Who are you?'

"I told him, 'I am an Amalekite.'

⁹"Then Saul said to me, 'Please come here and kill me. I am badly hurt and am almost dead already.'

¹⁰"So I went over and killed him. He had been hurt so badly I knew he couldn't live. Then I took the crown from his head and the bracelet from his arm. I have brought them here to you, my master."

¹¹Then David tore his clothes to show his sorrow. And all the men with him did also. ¹²They were very sad and cried. They did not eat until evening. They cried for Saul and his son Jonathan. And they cried for the Israelites who had been killed with swords.

David Orders the Amalekite Killed

¹³David asked the young man who brought the report, "Where are you from?"

The young man answered, "I am the son of a foreigner. I am an Amalekite."

¹⁴David asked him, "Why were you not afraid to kill the Lord's appointed king?"

¹⁵Then David called one of his men. David told him, "Go! Kill the Amalekite!" So the Israelite killed the Amalekite. ¹⁶David had said to the Amalekite, "You are responsible for your own death. You have spoken against yourself! You said, 'I have killed the Lord's appointed king.' "

David's Song About Saul and Jonathan

¹⁷David sang a funeral song about Saul and his son Jonathan. ¹⁸David ordered that the people of Judah be taught this song. It is called "The Bow." This song is written in the Book of Jashar:

¹⁹"Israel, your leaders have been
    killed on the hills.
How the mighty men have fallen
    in battle!
²⁰Don't tell it in Gath.
    Don't announce it in the streets of
    Ashkelon.

If you do, the daughters of the
    Philistines will be happy.
The daughters of the Philistines
    will rejoice.

21"May there be no dew or rain
    on the mountains of
    Gilboa.
May their fields produce no grain.
This is because there the mighty
    warrior's shield was
    dishonored.
Saul's shield was no longer rubbed
    with oil.
22Jonathan's bow killed its share
    of enemies.
And Saul's sword killed its share,
    too.
Their weapons are stained with the
    blood of dead men.
Their weapons have stabbed the
    flesh of strong men.

23"We loved Saul and Jonathan.
    We enjoyed them while they lived.
Saul and Jonathan are together
    even in death.
They were faster than eagles.
They were stronger than lions.

24"You daughters of Israel, cry
    for Saul.
Saul clothed you with red dresses.
He put gold decorations on your
    dresses.

25"How the mighty men have
    fallen in battle!
Jonathan is dead on Gilboa's hills.
26I cry for you, my brother
    Jonathan.
I enjoyed your friendship so much.
Your love to me was wonderful,
    more wonderful than the love of
    women.

27"How the mighty men have
    fallen in battle!
The weapons of war are gone."

David Is Made King of Judah

2 Later, David prayed to the Lord.
David said, "Should I go up to any
of the cities of Judah?"
    The Lord said to David, "Go."

David asked, "Where should I go?"
The Lord answered, "To Hebron."
2So David went up to Hebron with
his two wives. One was Ahinoam from
Jezreel. The other was Abigail, the
widow of Nabal in Carmel. 3David also
brought his men and their families.
They all made their homes in the cities
of Hebron. 4Then the men of Judah
came to Hebron. They appointed David
king over Judah.
    They told David that the men of
Jabesh Gilead had buried Saul. 5So
David sent messengers to the men of
Jabesh Gilead. They told David's message to the men in Jabesh: "The Lord
bless you. You have shown kindness
to your master Saul by burying him.
6May the Lord now be kind and true to
you. I will also be kind to you because
you have done this. 7Now be strong
and brave. Saul your master is dead.
The people of Judah have appointed
me their king."

War Between Judah and Israel

8Now Abner son of Ner was the
commander of Saul's army. Abner took
Saul's son Ish-Bosheth to Mahanaim.
9There Abner made him king of Gilead,
Ashuri, Jezreel, Ephraim, Benjamin
and all Israel. 10Saul's son Ish-Bosheth
was 40 years old when he became
king over Israel. He ruled two years.
But the people of Judah followed
David. 11David was king in Hebron for
seven years and six months.
    12Abner son of Ner and the servants
of Ish-Bosheth son of Saul left Mahanaim. They went to Gibeon. 13Joab son
of Zeruiah and David's men also went
there. They met Abner and Ish-
Bosheth's men at the pool of Gibeon.
Abner's group sat on one side of the
pool. Joab's group sat on the other side.
    14Abner said to Joab, "Let's have the
young men get up and have a contest
here."
    Joab said, "Yes, let them have a
contest."
    15Then the young men got up. The
two groups counted their men for the

contest. Twelve men were chosen from the people of Benjamin for Ish-Bosheth son of Saul. Twelve men were chosen from David's men. [16]Each man grabbed his enemy's head. Then he stabbed his enemy's side with a knife. And the men fell down together. So that place in Gibeon is called The Field of the Sharp Knives. [17]That day the contest became a terrible battle. And David's men defeated Abner and the Israelites.

Abner Kills Asahel

[18]Zeruiah's three sons, Joab, Abishai and Asahel, were there. Now Asahel was a fast runner. He was as fast as a deer in the field. [19]Asahel chased Abner, going straight toward him. [20]Abner looked back and asked, "Are you Asahel?"

Asahel said, "Yes, I am."

[21]Then Abner said to Asahel, "Turn to your right or left. Catch one of the young men and take his armor." But Asahel refused to stop chasing him.

[22]Abner again said to Asahel, "Stop chasing me! If you don't stop, I'll have to kill you! Then I won't be able to face your brother Joab again!"

[23]But Asahel refused to stop chasing Abner. So Abner used the back end of his spear. He stabbed it into Asahel's stomach, and the spear came out of his back. Asahel died right there. Everyone stopped when they came to the place where Asahel's body lay.

[24]But Joab and Abishai continued chasing Abner. The sun was going down when they arrived at the hill of Ammah. This is near Giah on the way to the empty land near Gibeon. [25]The men of Benjamin came to Abner. They all stood together at the top of the hill.

[26]Abner shouted to Joab, "Must the sword kill forever? Surely you must know this will only end in sadness! Tell the people to stop chasing their own brothers!"

[27]Then Joab said, "If you had not said anything, the people would have chased their brothers until morning. This is as sure as God is alive." [28]Then

Joab blew a trumpet, and his people stopped chasing the Israelites. They did not try to fight them anymore.

[29]Abner and his men marched all night through the Jordan Valley. They crossed the Jordan River. After marching all day, they arrived at Mahanaim.

[30]Joab came back after he had stopped chasing Abner. Then Joab gathered the people together. Asahel and 19 of David's men were missing. [31]But David's men had killed 360 Benjaminites who had followed Abner. [32]David's men took Asahel and buried him. They put him in the tomb of his father at Bethlehem. Then Joab and his men marched all night. The sun came up as they reached Hebron.

3 There was a long war between the people who supported Saul's family and those who supported David's family. The supporters of David's family became stronger and stronger. And the supporters of Saul's family became weaker and weaker.

David's Sons

[2]Sons were born to David at Hebron. The first son was Amnon. Amnon's mother was Ahinoam from Jezreel. [3]The second son was Kileab. Kileab's mother was Abigail, the widow of Nabal from Carmel. The third son was Absalom. Absalom's mother was Maacah daughter of Talmai. Talmai was king of Geshur. [4]The fourth son was Adonijah. His mother was Haggith. The fifth son was Shephatiah. His mother was Abital. [5]The sixth son was Ithream. His mother was Eglah, David's wife. These sons were born to David at Hebron.

Abner Joins David

[6]Abner made himself a main leader among the supporters of Saul. He did this during the war between the supporters of Saul's family and the supporters of David's family.

[7]Now Saul had once had a slave woman[d] named Rizpah. She was the daughter of Aiah. Ish-Bosheth said to

Abner, "Why did you have sexual relations with my father's slave woman?"

[8] Abner was very angry because of what Ish-Bosheth said. Abner said, "I have been loyal to Saul and his family and friends! I didn't hand you over to David. I am not a traitor working for Judah! But now you are saying I did something wrong with this woman! [9] May God punish me terribly if I don't help David. I will make sure that what God promised does happen! [10] I will take the kingdom from the family of Saul. I will make David king of Israel and Judah! He will rule from Dan to Beersheba."[n]

[11] Ish-Bosheth couldn't say anything to Abner. He was too afraid of Abner.

[12] Then Abner sent messengers to David. Abner said, "Who is going to rule the land? Make an agreement with me, and I will help you become the king of all Israel."

[13] David answered, "Good! I will make an agreement with you. But I ask you one thing. I will not meet with you unless you bring Saul's daughter Michal to me." [14] Then David sent messengers to Saul's son Ish-Bosheth. David said, "Give me my wife Michal. She was promised to me. I killed 100 Philistines to get her."

[15] So Ish-Bosheth sent men to take Michal from her husband. He was Paltiel son of Laish. [16] Michal's husband went with her, crying as he followed her to Bahurim. But Abner said to Paltiel, "Go back home." So he went home.

[17] Abner sent a message to the older leaders of Israel. He said, "You have been wanting to make David your king. [18] Now do it! The Lord has spoken about David. The Lord said, 'I will save my people the Israelites. I will save them from the Philistines and all their enemies. I will do this through my servant David.' "

[19] Abner also said these things to the people of Benjamin. He then went to Hebron to tell David what the Benjaminites and Israel wanted to do. [20] Abner came with 20 men to David at Hebron. There David prepared a feast for them. [21] Then Abner said to David, "My master and king, I will go and bring all the Israelites to you. Then they will make an agreement with you. You will rule over all Israel as you wanted." So David let Abner go, and he left in peace.

Abner's Death

[22] Just then Joab and David's men came from a battle. They had many valuable things they had taken from the enemy. David had let Abner leave in peace. So he was not with David at Hebron. [23] Joab and all his army arrived at Hebron. The army said to Joab, "Abner son of Ner came to King David. And David let him leave in peace."

[24] Joab came to the king and said, "What have you done? Abner came to you. Why did you let him go? Now he's gone. [25] You know Abner son of Ner! He came to trick you! He came to learn about everything you are doing!"

[26] Then Joab left David and sent messengers after Abner. They brought Abner back from the well of Sirah. But David did not know this. [27] When Abner arrived at Hebron, Joab took him aside into the gateway. Joab acted as though he wanted to talk with him in private. But Joab stabbed Abner in the stomach, and Abner died. Abner had killed Joab's brother Asahel. So Joab killed Abner to pay him back.

[28] Later David heard the news. He said, "My kingdom and I are innocent forever. We did not kill Abner son of Ner. The Lord knows this. [29] Joab and his family are responsible for this. I hope many troubles will come to his family. May his family always have someone with sores or with a harmful skin disease. May they always have someone who must lean on a crutch. May some of his family be killed in war. May they always have someone without food to eat."

---

[n] **Dan to Beersheba** Dan was the city farthest north in Israel. Beersheba was the city farthest south. So this means all the people of Israel.

[30] (Joab and his brother Abishai had killed Abner, because he had killed their brother Asahel. This was in the battle at Gibeon.)

[31] Then David spoke to Joab and to all the people with Joab. He said, "Tear your clothes and put on rough cloth to show how sad you are. Cry for Abner." King David himself followed behind the body of Abner. [32] So they buried Abner in Hebron. David and all the people cried at Abner's grave.

[33] King David sang this funeral song for Abner.

"Did Abner die like a foolish man?
[34]   His hands were not tied.
   His feet were not in chains.
He fell as a person falls before evil
   men."

Then all the people cried again for Abner. [35] They came to encourage David to eat while it was still day. But he made a promise. He said, "May God punish me terribly if I eat bread or any other food before the sun sets!"

[36] All the people saw what happened. They agreed with what the king was doing. [37] That day all the people of Judah and all the Israelites understood. They knew it was not David who had killed Abner son of Ner.

[38] David said to his officers, "You know that a very important leader died today in Israel. [39] Even though I am the appointed king, I am weak today. These sons of Zeruiah are too strong for me. May the Lord give them the punishment they should have."

Ish-Bosheth's Death

4 Ish-Bosheth son of Saul heard that Abner had died at Hebron. Then Ish-Bosheth and all Israel became very frightened. [2] Two men who were captains in Saul's army came to Ish-Bosheth. One man was named Baanah, and the other was named Recab. They were the sons of Rimmon of Beeroth, who was a Benjaminite. (The town Beeroth belonged to the tribe[d] of Benjamin.) [3] The people of Beeroth ran away to Gittaim. And they still live there today.

[4] (Now Jonathan son of Saul had a son who was crippled in both feet. His name was Mephibosheth. He was five years old when the news came from Jezreel that Saul and Jonathan were dead. Mephibosheth's nurse picked him up and ran away. But as she hurried to leave, he fell and became crippled.)

[5] Recab and Baanah, sons of Rimmon, were from Beeroth. They went to Ish-Bosheth's house at noon. [6-7] They came into the middle of the house. Recab and Baanah came as if they were going to get some wheat. Ish-Bosheth was lying on his bed in his bedroom. Recab and Baanah stabbed him in the stomach. Then they cut off his head and took it with them. They traveled all night through the Jordan Valley. [8] When they arrived at Hebron, they gave his head to David. They said to the king, "Here is the head of Ish-Bosheth son of Saul. He was your enemy. He tried to kill you! Today the Lord has paid back Saul and his family for what they did to you!"

[9] David answered Recab and his brother Baanah sons of Rimmon of Beeroth. David said, "As surely as the Lord lives, he has saved me from all trouble! [10] Once a man thought he was bringing me good news. He told me, 'Look! Saul is dead!' But I took hold of him and killed him at Ziklag. That was the reward I gave him for his news! [11] So even more I must require your death. This is because evil men have killed an innocent man. And he was on his own bed in his own house!"

[12] So David commanded his men to kill Recab and Baanah. Then they cut off the hands and feet of Recab and Baanah. They hung their hands and feet over the pool of Hebron. Then they took Ish-Bosheth's head and buried it in Abner's tomb at Hebron.

David Is Made King of Israel

5 Then all the tribes[d] of Israel came to David at Hebron. They said to him, "Look, we are your own family.

²In the past Saul was king over us. But you were the one leading us in battle for Israel. The Lord said to you, 'You will be like a shepherd for my people, the Israelites. You will become their ruler.'"

³All the older leaders of Israel came to King David at Hebron. Then he made an agreement with them in Hebron in front of the Lord. Then they poured oil on David to make him king over Israel.

⁴David was 30 years old when he became king. He ruled 40 years. ⁵He was king over Judah in Hebron for 7 years and 6 months. And he was king over all Israel and Judah in Jerusalem for 33 years.

enter their city. ⁷But David did take the city of Jerusalem with its strong walls. It became the City of David.

⁸That day David said to his men, "To defeat the Jebusites you must go through the water tunnel. Then you can reach those 'crippled' and 'blind' enemies. This is why people say, 'The blind and the crippled cannot enter the palace.'"

⁹So David lived in the city with its strong walls. He called it the City of David. David built more buildings around it. He began where the land was filled in on the east side of the city. He also built more buildings inside the city. ¹⁰He became stronger and stronger, because the Lord of heaven's armies was with him.

¹¹Hiram king of the city of Tyre sent messengers to David. He also sent cedar logs, carpenters and men to cut

Touring Bible Lands

JERUSALEM • 2 SAMUEL 5:6-7

Jerusalem is the most famous city in the Bible. It was built on three hills with large walls on all sides for protection. The city of Jerusalem became Israel's capital when David was the king. Later, David's son Solomon built the temple there. Jerusalem is also called the City of David or Zion.

When Jesus was on earth he often visited this city. When he went to the temple there, he drove out the greedy merchants. The leaders in Jerusalem wanted to kill Jesus. He was crucified on a hill outside the city and was buried in a tomb. He rose from the dead and later went back to heaven from the Mount of Olives, just east of Jerusalem.

Jesus' disciples formed the first church in Jerusalem. From there other churches grew up all over the world as more and more people believed in Jesus. Can you see why Jerusalem is such a famous city?

Fly northeast from Jerusalem to a city where lots of people were believing in Jesus as their Savior on page 466.

⁶The king and his men went to Jerusalem to attack the Jebusites who lived there. The Jebusites said to David, "You can't come into our city. Even our people who are blind and crippled can stop you." They said this because they thought David could not

stone. They built a palace for David. ¹²Then David knew the Lord really had made him king of Israel. And he knew the Lord had made his kingdom very important. This was because the Lord loved his people, the Israelites.

¹³In Jerusalem David took for himself

more slave women[d] and wives. This was after he moved there from Hebron. More sons and daughters were born to David. [14]These are the names of the sons born to David in Jerusalem: Shammua, Shobab, Nathan, Solomon, [15]Ibhar, Elishua, Nepheg, Japhia, [16]Elishama, Eliada and Eliphelet.

David Defeats the Philistines

[17]Now the Philistines heard that David had been made king over Israel. So all the Philistines went to look for him. But when David heard the news, he went down to a safe place. [18]So the Philistines came and camped in the Valley of Rephaim. David asked the Lord, "Should I attack the Philistines? Will you help me defeat them?"

[19]The Lord said to David, "Go! I will certainly help you defeat them."

[20]So David went to Baal Perazim and defeated the Philistines there. David said, "Like a flood of water, the Lord has broken through my enemies." So David named the place Baal Perazim.[n] [21]The Philistines left their idols behind at Baal Perazim. And David and his men carried these idols away.

[22]Once again the Philistines came and camped at the Valley of Rephaim. [23]David prayed to the Lord. This time the Lord told David, "Don't attack the Philistines from the front. Instead, go around them. Attack them opposite the balsam trees. [24]You will hear the sound of marching in the tops of the balsam trees. Then you must act quickly. I, the Lord, will have gone ahead of you and defeated the Philistine army." [25]So David did what the Lord commanded. He defeated the Philistines and chased them all the way from Gibeon to Gezer.

The Holy Box Is Brought to Jerusalem

6 David again gathered all the chosen men of Israel. There were 30,000 of them. [2]Then David and all his people went to Baalah in Judah.[n]

They took the Holy Box[d] of God from Baalah in Judah and moved it to Jerusalem. The Holy Box is called by the Name, the name of the Lord of heaven's armies. His throne is between the gold creatures with wings that are on the Holy Box. [3]David's men put the Holy Box of God on a new cart. Then they brought the Holy Box out of Abinadab's house on the hill. Uzzah and Ahio, sons of Abinadab, led the new cart. [4]This cart had the Holy Box of God on it. Ahio was walking in front of it. [5]David and all the Israelites were playing all kinds of musical instruments before the Lord. They were made of pine wood. There were lyres,[d] harps, tambourines,[d] rattles and cymbals.

[6]When David's men came to the threshing[d] floor of Nacon, the oxen stumbled. The Holy Box of God began to fall off the cart. So Uzzah reached out and took hold of it. [7]The Lord was angry with Uzzah and killed him. Uzzah had not honored God when he touched the Holy Box. So Uzzah died there beside it. [8]David was angry because the Lord had killed Uzzah. So that place is called The Punishment of Uzzah even today.

[9]David was afraid of the Lord that day. He said, "How can the Holy Box of the Lord come to me now?" [10]So David would not move the Holy Box of the Lord to be with him in Jerusalem. Instead, he took it to the house of Obed-Edom, a man from Gath. [11]The Holy Box of the Lord stayed in Obed-Edom's house for three months. And the Lord blessed Obed-Edom and all his family.

[12]The people told David, "The Lord has blessed the family of Obed-Edom. And all his things are blessed. This is because the Holy Box of God is there." So David went and brought it up from Obed-Edom's house to Jerusalem with joy. [13]When the men carrying the Holy Box of the Lord had walked six steps, David sacrificed a bull and a fat calf. [14]Then David danced with all his might before the Lord. He had on a holy linen

---

[n]**Baal Perazim**   This name means "The Lord breaks through."
[n]**Baalah in Judah**   Another name for Kiriath Jearim.

vest.*d* 15David and all the Israelites shouted with joy. They blew the trumpets as they brought the Holy Box of the Lord to the city.

16Saul's daughter Michal was looking out the window. She watched as the Holy Box of the Lord came into the city. When she saw David jumping and dancing before the Lord, she hated him.

17David put up a tent for the Holy Box. Then the Israelites put it in its place inside the tent. David offered whole burnt offerings and fellowship offerings before the Lord. 18When David finished offering the whole burnt offerings and the fellowship offerings, he blessed the people in the name of the Lord of heaven's armies. 19David gave a loaf of bread, a cake of dates and a cake of raisins to everyone. He gave them to all the Israelites, both men and women. Then all the people went home.

20David went back to bless the people in his home. But Saul's daughter Michal came out to meet him. She said, "The king of Israel did not honor himself today! You took off your clothes in front of the servant girls of your officers. You were like a foolish man who takes off his clothes without shame!"

21Then David said to Michal, "I did it before the Lord. The Lord chose me, not your father. He didn't choose anyone from Saul's family. The Lord appointed me to be leader of his people, the Israelites. So I will celebrate in front of the Lord. 22Maybe I will lose even more honor. And you may think little of me. But the girls you talk about will honor me!"

23And Saul's daughter Michal had no children to the day she died.

David Wants to Build a Temple

7 King David was living in his palace. And the Lord gave him peace from all his enemies around him. 2David said to Nathan the prophet,*d* "Look, I am living in a palace made of cedar wood. But the Holy Box*d* of God is still kept in a tent!"

3Nathan said to the king, "Go and do what you really want to do. The Lord is with you."

4But that night the Lord spoke his word to Nathan. The Lord said, 5"Go and tell my servant David, 'This is what the Lord says: You are not the person to build a house for me to live in. 6I did not live in a house when I brought the Israelites out of Egypt. I have been moving around all this time with a tent as my home. 7I have continued to move with the tribes*d* of Israel. But I have never asked their leaders who take care of them to build me a house of cedar wood.'

8"You must tell my servant David, 'This is what the Lord of heaven's armies says: I took you from the pasture when you were following the sheep. I took you to become leader of my people, the Israelites. 9I have been with you everywhere you have gone. I have defeated your enemies for you. I will make you as famous as any of the great men on the earth. 10Also I will choose a place for my people, the Israelites. I will plant them so they can live in their own home. They will not be bothered anymore. Wicked people will no longer make them suffer as they have in the past. 11Wicked people continued to do this even when I appointed judges. But I will give you peace from all your enemies. I also tell you that I will make your descendants*d* kings of Israel after you.

12" 'Your days will come to an end, and you will die. At that time I will make one of your sons the next king. 13He will build a temple*d* for me. I will make his kingdom strong forever. 14I will be his father, and he will be my son. When he sins, I will use other people to punish him. They will be my whips. 15But I will not stop loving him. I took away my love and kindness from Saul. I removed Saul when I turned to you. 16But your family and your kingdom will continue forever before me. Your rule will last forever.'"

17Nathan told David everything he had heard.

David Prays to God

¹⁸Then King David went in the tent and sat in front of the Lord. David said, "Lord God, why have you made me so important to you? Why have you made my family important? ¹⁹But that was not enough for you, Lord God. You have also said these kind things about my future family. I am your servant. Lord God, this is not the usual way you talk to people.

²⁰"What more can I say to you? Lord God, you love me, your servant, so much! ²¹You have done this wonderful thing because you said you would. You have done it because you wanted to. And you have decided to let me know all these great things. ²²This is why you are great, Lord God! There is no one like you. There is no God except you. We have heard all this ourselves! ²³And there are no others like your people, the Israelites. They are the one nation on earth that God chose to be his people. You used them to make your name well-known. You did great and wonderful miracles^d for them. You went ahead of them and forced other nations and their gods out of the land. You freed your people from slavery in Egypt. ²⁴You made the people of Israel your very own people forever. And, Lord, you became their God.

²⁵"Now, Lord God, keep the promise you made about my family and me, your servant. Do what you have promised. ²⁶Then you will be honored forever. And people will say, 'The Lord of heaven's armies is God over Israel!' And the family of your servant David will continue before you.

²⁷"Lord of heaven's armies, the God of Israel, you have shown things to me. You have said, 'I will make your family great.' So I, your servant, am brave enough to pray to you. ²⁸Lord God, you are God, and your words are true. And you have promised these good things to me, your servant. ²⁹Please, bless my family. Let it continue before you forever. Lord God, you have said these wonderful things. With your blessing let my family be blessed forever."

David Wins Many Wars

8 Later, David defeated the Philistines. And he took control of their capital city.

²He also defeated the people of Moab. He forced them to lie on the ground. Then he used a rope to measure them. When two men were measured, David ordered them killed. But every third man was allowed to live. So the people of Moab became servants of David. They gave him the payments he demanded.

³As David went to take control again at the Euphrates River, he defeated Hadadezer. Hadadezer son of Rehob was king of Zobah. ⁴David took from Hadadezer 1,700 men who rode in his chariots. He also captured 20,000 foot soldiers. David crippled all but 100 of the chariot horses. He saved those horses to pull chariots.

⁵Arameans from Damascus came to help Hadadezer king of Zobah. But David defeated those 22,000 Arameans. ⁶Then David put groups of soldiers in Damascus in Aram. The Arameans became David's servants and gave him the payments he demanded. The Lord gave David victory everywhere he went.

⁷David took the shields of gold that had belonged to Hadadezer's officers. He brought them to Jerusalem. ⁸David also took many things made of bronze from Tebah and Berothai. (They were cities that had belonged to Hadadezer.)

⁹Toi king of Hamath heard that David had defeated all the army of Hadadezer. ¹⁰So Toi sent his son Joram to greet and congratulate King David. Joram congratulated David for defeating Hadadezer. (Hadadezer had fought wars against Toi before.) Joram brought things made of silver, gold and bronze. ¹¹David took these things and gave them to the Lord. He also had given other silver and gold to the Lord. He had taken it from the nations he had defeated. ¹²These

nations were Edom, Moab, Ammon, Philistia and Amalek. David also defeated the king of Zobah who was Hadadezer son of Rehob.

[13]David was famous after he returned from the Valley of Salt. There he had defeated 18,000 Arameans. [14]David put groups of soldiers through all the land of Edom. All the people of Edom became servants for him. The Lord gave David victory everywhere he went.

[15]David was king over all Israel. His decisions were fair and right for all his people. [16]Joab son of Zeruiah was commander over the army. Jehoshaphat son of Ahilud was the recorder. [17]Zadok son of Ahitub and Ahimelech son of Abiathar were priests. Seraiah was the royal assistant. [18]Benaiah son of Jehoiada was over the Kerethites and Pelethites, the king's bodyguards. And David's sons were important leaders.

David Helps Saul's Family

9 David asked, "Is there anyone still left in Saul's family? I want to show kindness to this person for Jonathan's sake!"

[2]Now there was a servant named Ziba from Saul's family. So David's servants called Ziba to him. King David said to him, "Are you Ziba?"

He answered, "Yes, I am Ziba, your servant."

[3]The king asked, "Is there anyone left in Saul's family? I want to show God's kindness to this person."

Ziba answered the king, "Jonathan has a son still living. He is crippled in both feet."

[4]The king asked Ziba, "Where is this son?"

Ziba answered, "He is at the house of Makir son of Ammiel in Lo Debar."

[5]Then King David had servants bring Jonathan's son from the house of Makir son of Ammiel in Lo Debar. [6]Mephibosheth, Jonathan's son, came before David and bowed facedown on the floor.

David said, "Mephibosheth!"

Mephibosheth said, "I am your servant."

[7]David said to him, "Don't be afraid. I will be kind to you for your father Jonathan's sake. I will give you back all the land of your grandfather Saul. And you will always be able to eat at my table."

[8]Mephibosheth bowed to David again. Mephibosheth said, "You are being very kind to me, your servant! And I am no better than a dead dog!"

[9]Then King David called Saul's servant Ziba. David said to him, "I have given your master's grandson everything that belonged to Saul and his family. [10]You, your sons and your servants will farm the land for Mephibosheth. You will harvest the crops. Then your master's grandson will have food to eat. But Mephibosheth, your master's grandson, will always be able to eat at my table."

(Now Ziba had 15 sons and 20 servants.) [11]Ziba said to King David, "I am your servant. I will do everything my master, the king, commands me."

So Mephibosheth ate at David's table as if he were one of the king's sons. [12]Mephibosheth had a young son named Mica. Everyone in Ziba's family became Mephibosheth's servants. [13]Mephibosheth was crippled in both feet. He lived in Jerusalem and always ate at the king's table.

War with the Ammonites and Arameans

10 Later Nahash king of the Ammonites died. His son Hanun became king after him. [2]David said, "Nahash was kind to me. So I will be kind to his son Hanun." So David sent his officers to comfort Hanun about his father's death.

David's servants went to the land of the Ammonites. [3]But the important men of Ammon spoke to Hanun, their master. They said, "Do you think David wants to honor your father by sending men to comfort you? No! David sent them to study the city and to spy it out. They plan to capture it!" [4]So Hanun took David's officers and shaved off half their beards to shame them. He cut their clothes off at the hips to insult them. Then he sent them away.

⁵When the people told David, he sent messengers to meet his officers. He did this because these men were very ashamed. King David said, "Wait at Jericho until your beards have grown out. Then come back to Jerusalem."

⁶Now the Ammonites saw that they had become David's enemies. So they hired 20,000 Aramean foot soldiers from Beth Rehob and Zobah. They also hired the king of Maacah with 1,000 men. And they hired 12,000 men from Tob.

⁷David heard about this. So he sent Joab with the whole army of warriors. ⁸The Ammonites came out and got ready for the battle. They stood at the city gate. The Arameans from Zobah and Rehob and the men from Tob and Maacah were out in the field. They were standing away from the Ammonites.

⁹Joab saw that there were enemies both in front of him and behind him. So he chose some of the best men from the Israelites. He got them ready for battle against the Arameans. ¹⁰Then Joab gave the other men to his brother Abishai to lead against the Ammonites. ¹¹Joab said to Abishai, "If the Arameans are too strong for me, come help me. If the Ammonites are too strong for you, I will come and help you. ¹²Be strong. Let us fight bravely for our people and for the cities of our God. The Lord will do what he decides is right."

¹³Then Joab and his men attacked the Arameans, and they ran away. ¹⁴The Ammonites saw that the Arameans were running away. So they ran away from Abishai and went back to their city. So Joab returned from the battle with the Ammonites and came to Jerusalem.

¹⁵The Arameans saw that the Israelites had defeated them. So they came together into one big army. ¹⁶Hadadezer sent messengers to bring the Arameans who lived on the other side of the Euphrates River. These Arameans went to Helam. Their leader was Shobach, the commander of Hadadezer's army.

¹⁷When David heard about this, he gathered all the Israelites together. They crossed over the Jordan River and went to Helam. There the Arameans prepared for battle and attacked. ¹⁸But David defeated the Arameans, and they ran away from the Israelites. David killed 700 Aramean chariot drivers and 40,000 Aramean horsemen. He also killed Shobach, the commander of the Aramean army.

¹⁹The kings who served Hadadezer saw that the Israelites had defeated them. So they made peace with the Israelites and served them. And the Arameans were afraid to help the Ammonites again.

David and Bathsheba

11 In the spring the kings would go out to war. So in the spring David sent out Joab, his servants and all the Israelites. They destroyed the Ammonites and attacked the city of Rabbah. But David stayed in Jerusalem. ²One evening David got up from his bed. He walked around on the roof[n] of his palace. While he was on the roof, he saw a woman bathing. She was very beautiful. ³So David sent his servants to find out who she was. A servant answered, "That woman is Bathsheba daughter of Eliam. She is the wife of Uriah the Hittite." ⁴David sent messengers to bring Bathsheba to him. When she came to him, he had sexual relations with her. (Now Bathsheba had purified herself from her monthly period.) Then she went back to her house. ⁵But Bathsheba became pregnant. She sent word to David, saying, "I am pregnant."

⁶So David sent this message to Joab:

---

[n]**roof** In Bible times houses were built with flat roofs. The roof was used for drying things such as flax and fruit. And it was used as an extra room, as a place for worship and as a place to sleep in the summer.

"Send Uriah the Hittite to me." So Joab sent Uriah to David. [7]Uriah came to David. And David asked him how Joab was, how the soldiers were and how the war was going. [8]Then David said to Uriah, "Go home and rest."

So Uriah left the palace. The king also sent a gift to him. [9]But Uriah did not go home. He slept outside the door of the palace. He slept there as all the king's officers did.

[10]The officers told David, "Uriah did not go home."

Then David said to Uriah, "You came from a long trip. Why didn't you go home?"

[11]Uriah said to him, "The Holy Box[d] and the soldiers of Israel and Judah are staying in tents. My master Joab and his officers are camping out in the fields. It isn't right for me to go home to eat and drink and have sexual relations with my wife!"

[12]David said to Uriah, "Stay here today. Tomorrow I'll send you back to the battle." So Uriah stayed in Jerusalem that day and the next. [13]Then David called Uriah to come to see him. Uriah ate and drank with David. David made Uriah drunk, but he still did not go home. That evening Uriah went to sleep with the king's officers outside the king's door.

[14]The next morning David wrote a letter to Joab and sent it by Uriah. [15]In the letter David wrote, "Put Uriah on the front lines where the fighting is worst. Then leave him there alone. Let him be killed in battle."

[16]Joab watched the city and saw where its strongest defenders were. He put Uriah there. [17]The men of the city came out to fight against Joab. Some of David's men were killed. And Uriah the Hittite was one of them.

[18]Then Joab sent a report to David about everything that had happened in the war. [19]Joab told the messenger, "Tell King David what happened in the war. [20]After you finish, the king may become angry. He may ask you, 'Why did you go so near the city to fight? Didn't you know they would shoot arrows from the city wall? [21]Do you remember who killed Abimelech son of Jerub-Besheth?[n] It was a woman on the city wall. She threw a large stone for grinding grain on Abimelech. She killed him there in Thebez. Why did you go so near the wall?' If King David asks that, you must answer, 'Your servant Uriah the Hittite also died.'"

[22]The messenger went in and told David everything Joab had told him to say. [23]The messenger told David, "The men of Ammon were winning. They came out and attacked us in the field. But we fought them back to the city gate. [24]The men on the city wall shot arrows at your servants. Some of your men were killed. Your servant Uriah the Hittite also died."

[25]David said to the messenger, "Say this to Joab: 'Don't be upset about this. The sword kills everyone the same. Make a stronger attack against the city and capture it.' Encourage Joab with these words."

[26]When Bathsheba heard that her husband was dead, she cried for him. [27]After she finished her time of sadness, David sent servants to bring her to his house. She became David's wife and gave birth to his son. But the Lord did not like what David had done.

David's Son Dies

12 The Lord sent Nathan to David. When Nathan came to David, Nathan said, "There were two men in a city. One man was rich, but the other was poor. [2]The rich man had very many sheep and cattle. [3]But the poor man had nothing except one little female lamb he had bought. The poor man fed the lamb. It grew up with him and his children. It shared his food and drank from his cup. It slept in his arms. The lamb was like a daughter to him.

[4]"Then a traveler stopped to visit the rich man. The rich man wanted to give food to the traveler. But he didn't want

---

[n]**Jerub-Besheth**   Another name for Gideon.

to take one of his own sheep or cattle to feed the traveler. Instead, he took the lamb from the poor man. The rich man killed the lamb and cooked it for his visitor."

your wives from you. And I will give them to someone who is very close to you. He will have sexual relations with

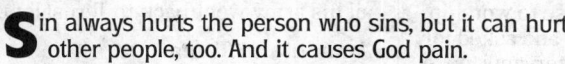

Sin
2 SAMUEL 12:1-13

Sin always hurts the person who sins, but it can hurt other people, too. And it causes God pain.

King David sinned by marrying another man's wife. Then he made plans to have her husband killed. David's sins were terrible, and he caused many people to suffer. But when he finally admitted that he had done wrong, he first said, "I have sinned against the Lord."

If you have sinned against another person, you need to say that you are sorry and try to make it right. But even before you do that, you need to tell God about your sin and ask him to forgive you. He is the first person your sins have hurt. He is also ready to forgive when you ask.

To learn more about sin, zoom to page 398.

⁵David became very angry at the rich man. He said to Nathan, "As surely as the Lord lives, the man who did this should die! ⁶He must pay for the lamb four times for doing such a thing. He had no mercy!"

⁷Then Nathan said to David, "You are the man! This is what the Lord, the God of Israel, says: 'I appointed you king of Israel. I saved you from Saul. ⁸I gave you his kingdom and his wives. And I made you king of Israel and Judah. And if that had not been enough, I would have given you even more. ⁹So why did you ignore the Lord's command? Why did you do what he says is wrong? You killed Uriah the Hittite with the sword of the Ammonites! And you took his wife to become your wife! ¹⁰So there will always be people in your family who will be killed by a sword. This is because you showed that you did not respect me! And you took the wife of Uriah the Hittite!'

¹¹"This is what the Lord says: 'I am bringing trouble to you from your own family. While you watch, I will take

your wives, and everyone will know it. ¹²You had sexual relations with Bathsheba in secret. But I will do this so all the people of Israel can see it.'"

¹³Then David said to Nathan, "I have sinned against the Lord."

Nathan answered, "The Lord has taken away your sin. You will not die. ¹⁴But what you did caused the Lord's enemies to lose all respect for him. For this reason the son who was born to you will die."

¹⁵Then Nathan went home. And the Lord caused the son of David and Bathsheba, Uriah's widow, to become very sick. ¹⁶David prayed to God for the baby. David refused to eat or drink. He went into his house and stayed there. He lay on the ground all night. ¹⁷The older leaders of David's family came to him. They tried to pull him up from the ground. But he refused to get up. And he refused to eat food with them.

¹⁸On the seventh day the baby died. David's servants were afraid to tell him that the baby was dead. They said, "Look, we tried to talk to David while

the baby was alive. But he refused to listen to us. If we tell him the baby is dead, he may harm himself."

[19] But David saw his servants whispering. Then he understood that the baby was dead. So he asked them, "Is the baby dead?"

They answered, "Yes, he is dead."

[20] Then David got up from the floor. He washed himself, put lotions on himself and changed his clothes. Then he went into the Lord's house to worship. After that, he went home and asked for something to eat. His servants gave him some food, and he ate.

[21] David's servants said to him, "Why are you doing this? When the baby was still alive, you refused to eat. You cried. But when the baby died, you got up and ate food."

[22] David said, "While the baby was still alive, I refused to eat, and I cried. I thought, 'Who knows? Maybe the Lord will feel sorry for me and let the baby live.' [23] But now the baby is dead. So why should I go without food? I can't bring him back to life. Some day I will go to him. But he cannot come back to me."

[24] Then David comforted Bathsheba his wife. He slept with her and had sexual relations with her. She became pregnant again and had another son. David named the boy Solomon. The Lord loved Solomon. [25] The Lord sent word through Nathan the prophet[d] to name the baby Jedidiah.[n] This was because the Lord loved the child.

David Captures Rabbah

[26] Now Joab fought against Rabbah, a city of the Ammonites. And he was about to capture the royal city. [27] Joab sent messengers to David and said, "I have fought against Rabbah. I have captured its water supply. [28] Now bring the other soldiers together and attack this city. Capture it before I capture it myself. If I capture this city, it will be called by my name!"

[29] So David gathered all the army and went to Rabbah. He fought against Rabbah and captured it. [30] David took the crown off their king's head. It was gold and weighed about 75 pounds. It also had gems in it. They put the crown on David's head. And David took many valuable things out of the city. [31] He also brought out the people of the city. He made them work with saws, iron picks and axes. He also forced them to build with bricks. David did this to all the Ammonite cities. Then David and all his army went back to Jerusalem.

Amnon and Tamar

13 Now David had a son named Absalom and a son named Amnon. Absalom had a beautiful sister named Tamar. And Amnon loved her. [2] Tamar was a virgin.[d] Amnon did not think he should do anything bad to her. But he wanted her very much. He made himself sick just thinking about her.

[3] Amnon had a friend named Jonadab son of Shimeah. (Shimeah was David's brother.) Jonadab was a very clever man. [4] He asked Amnon, "Why do you look so sad day after day? You are the king's son! Tell me what's wrong!"

Amnon told him, "I love Tamar. But she is the sister of my half-brother Absalom."

[5] Jonadab said to Amnon, "Go to bed. Act as if you are sick. Then your father will come to see you. Tell him, 'Please let my sister Tamar come in and give me food to eat. Let her make the food in front of me. Then I will see it and eat it from her hand.'"

[6] So Amnon lay down in bed and acted as if he were sick. King David came in to see him. Amnon said to him, "Please let my sister Tamar come in. Let her make two of her special cakes for me while I watch. Then I will eat them from her hands."

[7] David sent messengers to Tamar in the palace. They told her, "Go to your brother Amnon's house and make some food for him." [8] So Tamar went to her brother Amnon's house. He was in bed. Tamar took some dough and pressed

[n] **Jedidiah** This name means "loved by the Lord."

it together with her hands. She made some special cakes while Amnon watched. Then she baked them. ⁹Next she took the pan and took out the cakes for Amnon. But he refused to eat.

He said to his servants, "All of you, leave me alone!" So all his servants left the room. ¹⁰Amnon said to Tamar, "Bring the food into the inner room. Then I'll eat from your hand."

Tamar took the cakes she had made. And she brought them to her brother Amnon in the inner room. ¹¹She went to him so he could eat from her hands. But Amnon grabbed her. He said, "Sister, come and have sexual relations with me."

¹²Tamar said to him, "No, brother! Don't force me! This should never be done in Israel! Don't do this shameful thing! ¹³I could never get rid of my shame! And you will become like the shameful fools in Israel! Please talk with the king. He will let you marry me."

¹⁴But Amnon refused to listen to her. He was stronger than she was. So he forced her to have sexual relations with him. ¹⁵After that, Amnon hated Tamar. He hated her much more than he had loved her before. Amnon said to her, "Get up and leave!"

¹⁶Tamar said to him, "No! Sending me away would be an even greater evil. That would be worse than what you've already done!"

But he refused to listen to her. ¹⁷He called his young servant back in. Amnon said, "Get this girl out of here right now! Lock the door after her." ¹⁸So his servant led her out of the room. And he bolted the door after her. Now Tamar was wearing a special robe with long sleeves. The king's virgin daughters wore this kind of robe. ¹⁹To show how upset she was Tamar took ashes and put them on her head. She tore her special robe. And she put her hand on her head. Then she went away, crying loudly.

²⁰Absalom, Tamar's brother, said to her, "Has Amnon, that brother of yours, forced you to have sexual relations with him? He is your brother. So for now, sister, be quiet. Don't let this upset you so much!" So Tamar lived in her brother Absalom's house. She was sad and lonely.

²¹When King David heard the news, he was very angry. ²²Absalom did not say a word, good or bad, to Amnon. He hated Amnon for forcing his sister Tamar to have sexual relations with him.

Absalom's Revenge

²³Two years later Absalom had some men come to Baal Hazor, near Ephraim. They were to cut the wool from his sheep. Absalom invited all the king's sons to come also. ²⁴Absalom went to the king and said, "I have men coming to cut the wool. Please come with your officers and join me."

²⁵King David said to Absalom, "No, my son. We won't all go. It would be too much trouble for you." Absalom begged David to go. David did not go, but he did give his blessing.

²⁶Absalom said, "If you don't want to go, then please let my brother Amnon go with me."

King David asked Absalom, "Why should he go with you?"

²⁷Absalom kept begging David. Finally, David let Amnon and all the king's sons go with Absalom.

²⁸Then Absalom gave a command to his servants. He said, "Watch Amnon. When he is drunk, I will tell you, 'Kill Amnon.' Right then, kill him! Don't be afraid. I have commanded you! Be strong and brave!" ²⁹So Absalom's young men killed Amnon as Absalom commanded. But all of David's other sons got on their mules and escaped.

³⁰While the king's sons were on their way, the news came to David. The message was, "Absalom has killed all of the king's sons! Not one of them is left alive!" ³¹King David tore his clothes and lay on the ground to show his sadness. All his servants standing nearby tore their clothes also.

³²Jonadab was the son of Shimeah, David's brother. Jonadab said to David,

"Don't think all the young men, your sons, are killed. No, only Amnon is dead! Absalom planned this because Amnon forced his sister Tamar to have sexual relations with him. 33My master and king, don't think that all of the king's sons are dead. Only Amnon is dead!"

34In the meantime Absalom had run away.

There was a guard standing on the city wall. He saw many people coming from the other side of the hill. 35So Jonadab said to King David, "Look, I was right! The king's sons are coming!"

36As soon as Jonadab had said this, the king's sons arrived. They were crying loudly. David and all his servants began crying also. They all cried very much. 37David cried for his son every day.

But Absalom ran away to Talmai[n] son of Ammihud. Talmai was king of Geshur. 38After Absalom ran away to Geshur, he stayed there for three years. 39When King David got over Amnon's death, he missed Absalom greatly.

Joab Sends a Wise Woman to David

14 Joab son of Zeruiah knew that King David missed Absalom very much. 2So Joab sent messengers to Tekoa to bring a wise woman from there. Joab said to her, "Please pretend to be very sad for someone. Put on clothes to show your sadness. Don't put lotion on yourself. Act like a woman who has been crying many days for someone who died. 3Go to the king. Talk to him using the words that I tell you." Then Joab told the wise woman what to say.

4So the woman from Tekoa talked to the king. She bowed facedown on the ground to show respect. She said, "My king, help me!"

5King David asked her, "What is the matter?"

The woman said, "I am a widow. My husband is dead. 6I had two sons. They were out in the field fighting. No one was there to stop them. So one son killed the other son. 7Now all the family group is against me. They said to me, 'Bring the son who killed his brother. Then we will kill him for killing his brother. That way we will also get rid of the one who would receive what belonged to his father. My son is like the last spark of a fire. He is all I have left. If they kill him, my husband's name and property will be gone from the earth."

8Then the king said to the woman, "Go home. I will take care of this for you."

9The woman of Tekoa said to him, "Let the blame be on me. My father's family and I are to blame, my master and king. But you and your throne are innocent."

10King David said, "Bring me anyone who says anything bad to you. Then he won't bother you again."

11The woman said, "Please promise in the name of the Lord your God. Then my relative who has the duty of punishing a murderer won't add to the destruction. And he won't kill my son."

David said, "As surely as the Lord lives, no one will hurt your son. Not even one hair from your son's head will fall to the ground."

12The woman said, "Let me say something to you, my master and king."

The king said, "Speak."

13Then the woman said, "Why have you planned this? It is against the people of God. When you say this, you show that you are guilty. You have not brought back your son whom you forced to leave home. 14We will all die some day. We're like water spilled on the ground. No one can gather it back. But God doesn't take away life. Instead, he plans ways that those who have been sent away will not have to stay away from him! 15My master and king, I came to say this to you because the people have made me afraid! I thought, 'Let me talk to the king. Maybe he will

---

[n]**Talmai** He was Absalom's grandfather.

do what I ask. [16]Maybe he will listen. Perhaps he will save me from the man who wants to kill both me and my son. That man is trying to keep us from getting what God gave us.'

[17]"Now I say, 'May the words of my master the king give me rest. Like an angel of God, you know what is good and what is bad. May the Lord your God be with you!'"

[18]Then King David said, "You must answer the question I will ask you."

The woman said, "My master the king, please ask your question."

[19]The king said, "Did Joab tell you to say all these things?"

The woman answered, "As you live, my master the king, you are right. Your servant Joab did tell me to say these things. [20]Joab did it so you would see things differently. My master, you are wise like an angel of God. You know everything that happens on earth."

Absalom Returns to Jerusalem

[21]The king said to Joab, "Look, I will do what I promised. Now please bring back the young man Absalom."

[22]Joab bowed facedown on the ground. He blessed the king. Then he said, "Today I know you are pleased with me. I know because you have done what I asked."

[23]Then Joab got up and went to Geshur. And he brought Absalom back to Jerusalem. [24]But King David said, "Absalom must go to his own house. He may not come to see me." So Absalom went to his own house. He did not go to see the king.

[25]Now Absalom was greatly praised for his handsome appearance. No man in Israel was as handsome as Absalom. No blemish was on him from his head to his foot. [26]At the end of every year, Absalom would cut the hair on his head. He cut it because it became too heavy. He would weigh it, and it would weigh about five pounds by the royal measure.

[27]Absalom had three sons and one daughter. His daughter's name was Tamar. She was a beautiful woman.

[28]So Absalom lived in Jerusalem for two full years without seeing King David. [29]Then Absalom sent for Joab. Absalom wanted to send Joab to the king. But Joab would not come. Absalom sent a message a second time. But Joab still refused to come. [30]Then Absalom said to his servants, "Look, Joab's field is next to mine. He has barley growing there. Go burn it." So Absalom's servants set fire to Joab's field.

[31]Then Joab went to Absalom's house. Joab said to him, "Why did your servants burn my field?"

[32]Absalom said to Joab, "I sent a message to you, asking you to come here. I wanted to send you to the king. I wanted you to ask him why he brought me home from Geshur. It would have been better for me to stay there! Now let me see the king. If I have sinned, he can kill me!"

[33]So Joab went to the king and told him Absalom's words. The king called for Absalom, and Absalom came. He bowed facedown on the ground before the king. And the king kissed him.

Absalom Plans to Take David's Kingdom

15 After this, Absalom got a chariot and horses for himself. He got 50 men to run before him. [2]Absalom would get up early and stand near the city gate.[n] If anyone had a problem he wanted the king to settle, he would come here. When he came, Absalom would call to the man. Absalom would say, "What city are you from?"

The man would answer, "I'm from one of the tribes[d] of Israel."

[3]Then Absalom would say to him, "Look, your claims are right. But the king has no one to listen to you." [4]Absalom would also say, "I wish someone would make me judge in this land! Then I could help everyone who comes with a problem. I could help him get a fair decision for his problem!"

[n]**city gate** People came here to conduct business. Public meetings and court cases were also held here.

⁵People would come near Absalom to bow to him. When they did, Absalom would reach out his hand and take hold of them. Then he would kiss them. ⁶Absalom did that to all the Israelites who came to King David for decisions. In this way, Absalom won the hearts of all Israel.

⁷After four years Absalom said to King David, "Please let me go to Hebron. I want to carry out my promise that I made to the Lord. ⁸I made it while I was living in Geshur in Aram. I said, 'If the Lord takes me back to Jerusalem, I will worship him in Hebron.'"

⁹The king said, "Go in peace."

So Absalom went to Hebron. ¹⁰But he sent secret messengers through all the tribes of Israel. They told the people, "When you hear the trumpets, say this: 'Absalom has become the king at Hebron!'"

¹¹Absalom had invited 200 men to go with him. So they went from Jerusalem with him. But they didn't know what he was planning. ¹²Ahithophel was one of the people who advised David. He was from the town of Giloh. While Absalom was offering sacrifices, he called Ahithophel to come from his hometown of Giloh. So Absalom's plans were working very well. More and more people began to support him.

¹³A man came in to tell the news to David. The man said, "The Israelites are beginning to follow Absalom."

¹⁴Then David spoke to all his officers who were with him in Jerusalem. He said, "We must leave quickly! If we don't, we won't be able to get away from Absalom. We must hurry before he catches us. He would destroy us and kill the people of Jerusalem."

¹⁵The king's officers said to him, "We will do anything you say."

¹⁶The king set out with everyone in his house. But he left ten slave women*d* to take care of the palace. ¹⁷The king left with all his people following him. They stopped at the last house. ¹⁸All the king's servants passed by him. All the Kerethites and Pelethites, the king's bodyguards, passed by him. All those from Gath, the 600 men who had followed him, passed by him.

¹⁹The king spoke to Ittai, a man from Gath. He said, "Why are you also going with us? Turn back and stay with King Absalom. You are a foreigner. This is not your homeland. ²⁰Only a short time ago you came to join me. Today should I make you go with us to other places? I don't even know where I'm going. Turn back, and take your brothers with you. May kindness and loyalty be shown to you."

²¹But Ittai said to the king, "As surely as the Lord lives and as you live, I will stay with you. I'll be with you wherever you are. I'll be with you whether it means life or death."

²²David said to Ittai, "Go, march on." So Ittai from Gath and all his people with their children marched on. ²³All the people cried loudly as everyone passed by. King David also crossed the Kidron Valley. Then all the people went on to the desert. ²⁴Zadok and all the Levites with him were carrying the Box*d* of the Agreement with God. They set down the Holy Box. And Abiathar offered sacrifices until all the people had left the city.

²⁵The king said to Zadok, "Take the Holy Box of God back into the city. If the Lord is pleased with me, he will bring me back. He will let me see both it and Jerusalem again. ²⁶But if the Lord says he is not pleased with me, I am ready. He can do what he wants with me."

²⁷The king also said to Zadok the priest, "You are a seer.*d* Go back to the city in peace. Take your son Ahimaaz and Abiathar's son Jonathan with you. ²⁸I will wait near the crossings into the desert until I hear from you." ²⁹So Zadok and Abiathar took the Holy Box of God back to Jerusalem and stayed there.

³⁰David went up the Mount of Olives*d* crying as he went. He covered his head and went barefoot. All the people with David covered their heads

also. And they were crying as they went. ³¹Someone told David, "Ahithophel is one of the people with Absalom who made secret plans against you."

So David prayed, "Lord, please make Ahithophel's advice foolish."

³²David came to the top of the mountain. This was where he used to worship God. Hushai the Arkite came to meet him. Hushai's coat was torn, and there was dirt on his head to show how sad he was. ³³David said to Hushai, "If you go with me, you will be just one more person to take care of. ³⁴But if you return to the city, you can make Ahithophel's advice useless. Tell Absalom, 'I am your servant, my king. In the past I served your father. But now I will serve you.' ³⁵The priests Zadok and Abiathar will be with you. You must tell them everything you hear in the king's palace. ³⁶Zadok's son Ahimaaz and Abiathar's son Jonathan are with them. Send them to tell me everything you hear." ³⁷So David's friend Hushai entered Jerusalem. About that time, Absalom also arrived there.

Ziba Meets David

16 David passed a short way over the top of the Mount of Olives.^d There Ziba, Mephibosheth's servant, met David. Ziba had two donkeys with saddles on them. They carried 200 loaves of bread, 100 cakes of raisins and 100 cakes of figs. They also carried leather bags full of wine. ²The king asked Ziba, "What are these things for?"

Ziba answered, "The donkeys are for your family to ride. The bread and cakes of figs are for the servants to eat. And the wine is for anyone to drink who becomes weak in the desert."

³The king asked, "Where is Mephibosheth?"

Ziba answered him, "Mephibosheth is staying in Jerusalem. He thinks, 'Today the Israelites will give my father's kingdom back to me!'"

⁴Then the king said to Ziba, "All right. Everything that belonged to Mephibosheth, I now give to you!"

Ziba said, "I bow to you. I hope I will always be able to please you."

Shimei Curses David

⁵As King David came to Bahurim, a man came out from there. He was from Saul's family group. His name was Shimei son of Gera. Shimei came out, cursing David as he came. ⁶He began throwing stones at David and his officers. But the people and soldiers gathered all around David. ⁷Shimei cursed David. He said, "Get out, get out, you murderer, you troublemaker. ⁸The Lord is punishing you for the people in Saul's family you killed! You took Saul's place as king! But now the Lord has given the kingdom to your son Absalom! Now you are ruined because you are a murderer!"

⁹Abishai son of Zeruiah said to the king, "Why should this dead dog curse you, the king? Let me go over and cut off his head!"

¹⁰But the king answered, "This does not concern you, sons of Zeruiah! If he is cursing me because the Lord told him to, who can question him?"

¹¹David also said to Abishai and all his officers, "My own son is trying to kill me! This man is a Benjaminite and has more right to kill me! Leave him alone. Let him curse me. The Lord told him to do this. ¹²Maybe the Lord will see my misery. Then maybe he will repay me with something good for the curses Shimei says today!"

¹³So David and his men went on down the road. But Shimei kept following David. Shimei walked on the hillside on the other side of the road. He kept cursing David and throwing stones and dirt at him. ¹⁴The king and all his people arrived at the Jordan. They were very tired. So they rested there.

¹⁵Meanwhile, Absalom, Ahithophel and all the men of Israel arrived at Jerusalem. ¹⁶David's friend Hushai the Arkite came to Absalom. He said to Absalom, "Long live the king! Long live the king!"

[17] Absalom asked, "Why are you not loyal to your friend David? Why didn't you leave Jerusalem with your friend?"

[18] Hushai said, "I belong to the one chosen by the Lord and by these people and all the men of Israel. I will stay with you. [19] In the past I served your father. So whom should I serve now? David's son! I will serve you."

Ahithophel's Advice

[20] Absalom said to Ahithophel, "Please tell us what we should do."

[21] Ahithophel said, "Your father left behind some of his slave women[d] who give birth to his children. He left them here to take care of the palace. Have sexual relations with them. Then all the Israelites will hear that your father is your enemy. And all your people will be encouraged to give you more support." [22] So they put up a tent for Absalom on the flat roof[n] of the palace. Everyone in Israel could see it. And Absalom had sexual relations with his father's slave women.

[23] At that time people thought Ahithophel's advice was as reliable as God's own word. Both David and Absalom thought it was that reliable.

17

Ahithophel said to Absalom, "Let me choose 12,000 men. I'll chase David tonight. [2] I'll catch him while he is tired and weak. I'll frighten him so all his people will run away. But I'll kill only King David. [3] Then I'll bring everyone back to you. If the man you are looking for is dead, everyone else will return safely." [4] This plan seemed good to Absalom and to all the leaders of Israel.

[5] But Absalom said, "Now call Hushai the Arkite. I also want to hear what he says." [6] So Hushai came to Absalom. Absalom said to him, "This is the plan Ahithophel gave. Should we follow it? If not, tell us."

[7] Hushai said to Absalom, "Ahithophel's advice is not good this time." [8] Hushai added, "You know your father and his men are strong. They are as angry as a bear that is robbed of its babies. Your father is a skilled fighter. He won't stay all night with the people. [9] He is probably already hiding in a cave or some other place. If your father attacks your men first, people will hear the news. And they will think, 'Absalom's followers are losing!' [10] Then even the men who are as brave as a lion will become frightened. This is because all the Israelites know your father is a fighter. They know his men are brave!

[11] "This is what I suggest: Gather all the Israelites from Dan to Beersheba.[n] There will be as many people as grains of sand by the sea. Then you yourself must go into the battle. [12] We will catch David where he is hiding. We will fall on him as dew falls on the ground. We will kill him and all of his men. No one will be left alive. [13] What if David escapes into a city? Then all the Israelites will bring ropes to that city. We'll pull that city into the valley. There won't be even a small stone left there!"

[14] Absalom and all the Israelites said, "The advice of Hushai the Arkite is better than that of Ahithophel." They said this because the Lord had planned to destroy the good advice of Ahithophel. In this way the Lord could bring disaster on Absalom.

[15] Hushai told these things to Zadok and Abiathar, the priests. He told them what Ahithophel had suggested to Absalom and the older leaders of Israel. He also reported to them what he himself had suggested. Hushai said, [16] "Quickly! Send a message to David. Tell him not to stay tonight at the crossings into the desert. Tell him to cross over the Jordan River at once. If he crosses the river, he and all his people won't be caught."

[n] **roof** In Bible times houses were built with flat roofs. The roof was used for drying things such as flax and fruit. And it was used as an extra room, as a place for worship and as a place to sleep in the summer.
[n] **Dan to Beersheba** Dan was the city farthest north in Israel. And Beersheba was the city farthest south. So this means all the people of Israel.

¹⁷Jonathan and Ahimaaz were waiting at En Rogel. They did not want to be seen going into the town. So a servant girl would go out to them and give them messages. Then Jonathan and Ahimaaz would go and tell King David. ¹⁸But a boy saw Jonathan and Ahimaaz and told Absalom. So Jonathan and Ahimaaz ran away quickly. They went to a man's house in Bahurim. He had a well in his courtyard, and they climbed down into it. ¹⁹The man's wife spread a sheet over the opening of the well. Then she covered it with grain. No one could tell that Jonathan and Ahimaaz were hiding there.

²⁰Absalom's servants came to the woman at the house. They asked, "Where are Ahimaaz and Jonathan?"

She said to them, "They have already crossed the brook."

Absalom's servants then went to look for Jonathan and Ahimaaz. But they could not find them. So they went back to Jerusalem.

²¹After Absalom's servants had left, Jonathan and Ahimaaz climbed out of the well. Then they went to tell King David. They said, "Hurry, cross over the river! Ahithophel has said these things against you!" ²²So David and all his people crossed the Jordan River. By dawn, everyone had crossed the Jordan.

²³Now Ahithophel saw that the Israelites did not accept his advice. So he saddled his donkey and went to his hometown. He gave orders for his family and property. Then he hung himself. After Ahithophel died, he was buried in his father's tomb.

War Between David and Absalom

²⁴David arrived at Mahanaim. And Absalom and all his Israelites crossed over the Jordan River. ²⁵Now Absalom had made Amasa captain of the army instead of Joab. Amasa was the son of a man named Jether the Ishmaelite. Amasa's mother was Abigail daughter of Nahash and sister of Zeruiah. Zeruiah was Joab's mother. ²⁶Absalom and the Israelites camped in the land of Gilead.

²⁷Shobi, Makir and Barzillai were at Mahanaim when David arrived. Shobi son of Nahash was from the Ammonite town of Rabbah. Makir son of Ammiel was from Lo Debar. And Barzillai was from Rogelim in Gilead. ²⁸They brought beds, bowls and clay pots. They brought wheat, barley, flour, roasted grain, beans and small peas. ²⁹They also brought honey and milk curds, sheep, and cheese made from cows' milk. They brought these things for David and his people. They had said, "The people have become hungry and tired and thirsty in the desert."

18 David counted his men. He chose commanders over groups of 1,000 and commanders over groups of 100. ²He sent the troops out in three groups. Joab commanded one-third of the men. Joab's brother Abishai son of Zeruiah commanded another third. And Ittai from Gath commanded the last third. King David said to them, "I will also go with you."

³But the men said, "No! You must not go with us! If we run away in the battle, Absalom's men won't care. Even if half of us are killed, Absalom's men won't care. But you're worth 10,000 of us! It is better for you to stay in the city. Then, if we need help, you can send it."

⁴The king said to his people, "I will do what you think is best." So the king stood at the side of the gate as the army went out. They went out in groups of 100 and 1,000.

⁵The king gave a command to Joab, Abishai and Ittai. He said, "Be gentle with young Absalom for my sake." Everyone heard the king's orders about Absalom to the commanders.

⁶David's army went out into the field against Absalom's Israelites. They fought in the forest of Ephraim. ⁷There David's army defeated the Israelites. Many died that day—20,000 men. ⁸The battle spread through all the country. But that day more men died in the forest than in the fighting.

Absalom Dies

9Then Absalom happened to meet David's troops. As Absalom was riding his mule, it went under a large oak tree. The branches were thick, and Absalom's head got caught in the tree. His mule ran out from under him. So Absalom was left hanging above the ground.

10When one of the men saw it happen, he told Joab. He said, "I saw Absalom hanging in an oak tree!"

11Joab said to him, "You saw him? Why didn't you kill him and let him fall to the ground? I would have given you a belt and four ounces of silver!"

12The man answered, "I wouldn't try to hurt the king's son. I wouldn't even if you gave me 25 pounds of silver. We heard the king's command to you, Abishai and Ittai. The king said, 'Be careful not to hurt young Absalom.' 13If I had killed him, the king would have found out. And you would not have protected me!"

14Joab said, "I won't waste time here with you!" Now Absalom was still alive in the oak tree. So Joab took three spears and stabbed him in the heart. 15Ten young men who carried Joab's armor also gathered around Absalom. They struck him and killed him.

16Then Joab blew the trumpet. So the troops stopped chasing Absalom's Israelites. 17Then Joab's men took Absalom's body. They threw it into a large pit in the forest. Then they filled the pit with many stones. All the Israelites who followed Absalom ran away and went home.

18When Absalom was alive, he had put up a pillar in the King's Valley. It was a monument to himself. He said, "I have no son to keep my name alive." So he named the pillar after himself. That pillar is called Absalom's Monument even today.

19Ahimaaz son of Zadok spoke to Joab. He said, "Let me run and take the news to King David. I'll tell him the Lord has destroyed the enemy for him."

20Joab answered Ahimaaz, "No, you are not the one to take the news today. You may do it another time. But do not take it today, because the king's son is dead."

21Then Joab said to a man from Cush, "Go. Tell the king what you have seen." The Cushite bowed to Joab and ran to tell David.

22But Ahimaaz son of Zadok begged Joab again. He said, "No matter what happens, please let me go, along with the Cushite!"

Joab said, "Son, why do you want to carry the news? You won't get any reward for the news you bring!"

23Ahimaaz answered, "No matter what happens, I will run."

So Joab said to Ahimaaz, "Run!" Then Ahimaaz ran by way of the Jordan Valley and passed the Cushite.

24Now David was sitting between the inner and outer gates of the city. The watchman went up to the roof by the gate walls. As he looked up, he saw a man running alone. 25He shouted to tell King David.

The king said, "If he is alone, he is bringing good news!"

The man came nearer and nearer to the city. 26Then the watchman saw another man running. The watchman called to the gatekeeper, "Look! Another man is running alone!"

The king said, "He is also bringing good news!"

27The watchman said, "I think the first man runs like Ahimaaz son of Zadok."

The king said, "Ahimaaz is a good man. He must be bringing good news!"

28Then Ahimaaz called a greeting to the king. He bowed facedown on the ground to the king. He said, "Praise the Lord your God! The Lord has defeated the men who were against you, my king."

29The king asked, "Is young Absalom all right?"

Ahimaaz answered, "When Joab sent me, I saw some great excitement. But I don't know what it was."

30Then the king said, "Step over here

and wait." So Ahimaaz stepped aside and stood there.

³¹Then the Cushite arrived. He said, "Master and king, hear the good news! Today the Lord has punished the people who were against you!"

³²The king asked the Cushite, "Is young Absalom all right?"

The Cushite answered, "May your enemies be like that young man. May all who come to hurt you be like that young man!"

³³Then the king knew Absalom was dead. He was very upset. He went to the room over the city gate and cried. As he went, he cried out, "My son Absalom, my son Absalom! I wish I had died for you. Absalom, my son, my son!"

Joab Scolds David

19 People told Joab, "Look, the king is crying. He is very sad because of Absalom." ²David's army had won the battle that day. But it became a very sad day for all the people. This was because they heard, "The king is very sad for his son." ³The people came into the city quietly. They were like people who had been defeated in battle and had run away. ⁴The king covered his face and cried loudly, "My son Absalom! Absalom, my son, my son!"

⁵Then Joab went into the king's house. He said to the king, "Today you have shamed all your men. They saved your life today! They saved the lives of your sons, daughters, wives and slave women.ᵈ ⁶You have shamed them because you love those who hate you. And you hate those people who love you. Today you've made it clear that your commanders and men mean nothing to you. What if Absalom had lived and all of us were dead? I can see you would be very pleased. ⁷Now go out and encourage your servants. I swear by the Lord that if you don't go out, no man will be left with you by tonight! That will be worse than all the troubles you have had from your youth until today."

⁸So the king went to the city gate.ⁿ The news spread that the king was at the gate. So everyone came to see him.

David Goes Back to Jerusalem

All the Israelites who had followed Absalom had run away to their homes. ⁹People in all the tribesᵈ of Israel began to argue. They said, "The king saved us from the Philistines and our other enemies. But he left the country because of Absalom. ¹⁰We appointed Absalom to rule us, but now he has died in battle. We should make David the king again."

¹¹King David sent a message to Zadok and Abiathar, the priests. David said, "Speak to the older leaders of Judah. Say, 'Even in my house I have heard what all the Israelites are saying. So why are you the last tribe to bring the king back to his palace? ¹²You are my brothers, my own family. Then why are you the last tribe to bring back the king?' ¹³And say to Amasa, 'You are part of my own family. May God punish me terribly if I don't make you commander of the army in Joab's place!'"

¹⁴David touched the hearts of all the people of Judah. They agreed as if they were one man. They sent a message to the king. They said, "Return with all your men." ¹⁵Then the king returned as far as the Jordan River. The men of Judah came to Gilgal to meet him. They wanted to bring the king across the Jordan River.

¹⁶Shimei son of Gera was a Benjaminite. He lived in Bahurim. He hurried down with the men of Judah to meet King David. ¹⁷With Shimei came 1,000 Benjaminites. Ziba, the servant from Saul's family, also came. He brought his 15 sons and 20 servants with him. They all hurried to the Jordan River to meet the king. ¹⁸The people went across the Jordan River to help bring the king's family back to Judah. They did whatever the king wanted. As the king was about to cross

ⁿ**city gate**   People came here to conduct business. Public meetings and court cases were also held here.

the river, Shimei son of Gera came to him. Shimei bowed facedown on the ground in front of the king. ¹⁹He said to the king, "My master, don't hold me guilty. Don't remember the wrong things I did when you left Jerusalem! Don't hold it against me. ²⁰I know I have sinned. That is why I am the first person from Joseph's family to come down and meet you today, my master and king!"

²¹But Abishai son of Zeruiah said, "Shimei should die. He cursed you, the Lord's appointed king!"

²²David said, "This does not concern you, sons of Zeruiah! Today you're against me! No one will be put to death in Israel today. Today I know I am king over Israel!" ²³Then the king said to Shimei, "You won't die." The king made this promise to Shimei.

²⁴Mephibosheth, Saul's grandson, also went down to meet King David. Mephibosheth had not cared for his feet, cut his beard or washed his clothes while David was gone. He had not done this from the time the king had left Jerusalem until he returned safely. ²⁵Mephibosheth came from Jerusalem to meet the king. The king asked him, "Mephibosheth, why didn't you go with me?"

²⁶He answered, "My master, my servant Ziba tricked me! I said to Ziba, 'I am crippled. So saddle a donkey. Then I will ride it so I can go with the king.' ²⁷But he lied about me to you. You, my master and king, are like an angel from God. Do what you think is good. ²⁸You could have killed all my grandfather's family. Instead, you put me with the people who eat at your own table. So I don't have a right to ask anything more from the king!"

²⁹The king said to him, "Don't say anything more. I have decided that you and Ziba may divide the land."

³⁰Mephibosheth said to the king, "Let Ziba take all the land. I'm just happy that my master the king has arrived in peace at his own house."

³¹Barzillai of Gilead came down from Rogelim to cross the Jordan River with the king. ³²Now Barzillai was a very old man. He was 80 years old. He had taken care of the king when David was staying at Mahanaim. Barzillai could do this, because he was a very rich man. ³³David said to Barzillai, "Cross the river with me. Come with me to Jerusalem, and I will take care of you."

³⁴But Barzillai answered the king, "Do you know how old I am? Do you think I can go with you to Jerusalem? ³⁵I am 80 years old! I am too old to taste what I eat or drink. I am too old to hear the voices of men and women singers. Why should you be bothered with me? ³⁶I am not worthy of a reward from you. But I will cross the Jordan River with you. ³⁷Then please let me go back so I may die in my own city. Let me die near the grave of my father and mother. But here is Kimham. Let him go with you, my master and king. Do with him whatever you want."

³⁸The king answered, "Kimham will go with me. I will do for him anything you wish. And I will do anything for you that you wish." ³⁹The king kissed Barzillai and blessed him. Then Barzillai returned home. And the king and all the people crossed the Jordan.

⁴⁰When the king crossed the Jordan to Gilgal, Kimham went with him. All the troops of Judah and half the troops of Israel led David across the river.

⁴¹Soon all the men of Israel came to the king. They said to him, "Our brothers, the men of Judah, stole you away. They brought you and your family across the Jordan River with your men! Why did they do this?"

⁴²All the men of Judah answered the Israelites, "We did this because the king is our close relative. Why are you angry about it? We have not eaten food at the king's expense! He did not give us any gifts!"

⁴³The men of Israel answered the people of Judah, "We have ten tribes in the kingdom. So we have more right to David than you do! But you ignored

us! We were the first ones to talk about bringing our king back!"

But the men of Judah spoke even more unkindly than the men of Israel.

Sheba Leads Israel Away from David

20 It happened that a troublemaker named Sheba son of Bicri was there. Sheba was from the tribe[d] of Benjamin. He blew the trumpet and said:

"We have no share in David!
We have no part in the son of Jesse!
People of Israel, let's go to our own homes!"

²So all the Israelites left David and followed Sheba son of Bicri. But the men of Judah stayed with their king all the way from the Jordan River to Jerusalem.

³David came to his palace in Jerusalem. Earlier he had left there ten of his slave women[d] who gave birth to his children. He had left them there to take care of the palace. Now he put them in a house where they would be guarded. They were kept there for the rest of their lives. David gave them food, but he did not have sexual relations with them. They lived like widows until they died.

⁴The king said to Amasa, "Tell the men of Judah to meet with me in three days. And you must also be here." ⁵So Amasa went to call the men of Judah together. But he took longer than the time the king had told him.

⁶David said to Abishai, "Sheba son of Bicri is more dangerous to us than Absalom was. Take my men and chase him. Hurry before he finds strong, walled cities. If he gets there, he will escape from us." ⁷So Joab's men, the Kerethites and the Pelethites, who were the king's bodyguards, and all the soldiers went with Abishai. They went out from Jerusalem to chase Sheba son of Bicri.

⁸When Joab and the army came to the great rock at Gibeon, Amasa came out to meet them. Joab was wearing his uniform. At his waist he wore a belt. It held his sword in its case. As Joab stepped forward, his sword fell out of its case. ⁹Joab asked Amasa, "Brother, is everything all right with you?" Then with his right hand he took Amasa by the beard to kiss him. ¹⁰Amasa did not guard against the sword that was in Joab's hand. So Joab pushed the sword into Amasa's stomach. This caused Amasa's insides to spill on the ground. Joab did not have to stab Amasa again. He was already dead. Then Joab and his brother Abishai continued to chase Sheba son of Bicri.

¹¹One of Joab's young men stood by Amasa's body. The young man said, "Everyone who is for Joab and David should follow Joab!" ¹²Amasa lay in the middle of the road, covered with his own blood. The young man saw that everyone was stopping to look at the body. So he dragged Amasa's body from the road and laid it in a field. Then he put a cloth over it. ¹³After Amasa's body was taken off the road, all the men followed Joab. They went with him to chase Sheba son of Bicri.

¹⁴Sheba went through all the tribes of Israel to Abel Beth Maacah. All the Berites also came together and followed him. ¹⁵So Joab and his men came to Abel Beth Maacah and surrounded it. They piled dirt up against the city wall so they could attack it. And they began digging under the city walls to make them fall down.

¹⁶But a wise woman shouted out from the city. She said, "Listen! Listen! Tell Joab to come here. I want to talk to him!"

¹⁷So Joab came near her. She asked him, "Are you Joab?"

He answered, "Yes, I am."

Then she said, "Listen to what I say!"

Joab said, "I'm listening."

¹⁸Then the woman said, "In the past people would say, 'Ask for advice at Abel.' Then the problem would be solved. ¹⁹I am one of the peaceful, loyal

people of Israel. You are trying to destroy an important city of Israel. Why must you destroy what belongs to the Lord?"

²⁰Joab answered, "May I not destroy or ruin anything. ²¹That is not what I want. But there is a man here from the mountains of Ephraim. He is named Sheba son of Bicri. He has turned against King David. If you will bring him to me, I will leave the city alone."

The woman said to Joab, "His head will be thrown over the wall to you."

²²Then the woman spoke very wisely to all the people of the city. They cut off the head of Sheba son of Bicri. Then they threw it over the wall to Joab. So he blew the trumpet, and the army left the city. Every man returned home. And Joab went back to the king in Jerusalem.

²³Joab was commander of all the army of Israel. Benaiah son of Jehoiada led the Kerethites and Pelethites, the king's bodyguards. ²⁴Adoniram led the men who were forced to do hard work. Jehoshaphat son of Ahilud was the recorder. ²⁵Sheba was the royal assistant. Zadok and Abiathar were the priests. ²⁶And Ira the Jairite was David's priest.

The Gibeonites Punish Saul's Family

21 During the time David was king, there was a time of hunger. It continued for three years. So David prayed to the Lord.

The Lord answered, "Saul and his family of murderers are the reason for this time of hunger. It has come because Saul killed the Gibeonites." ²(Now the Gibeonites were not Israelites. They were a group of Amorites who were left alive. The Israelites had promised not to hurt the Gibeonites. But Saul was very eager to help the people of Israel and Judah. So he tried to kill all the Gibeonites.)

King David called the Gibeonites together and talked to them. ³He asked them, "What can I do for you? What can I do to take away Israel's sin so you can bless the Lord's people?"

⁴The Gibeonites said to David, "Saul and his family don't have enough silver and gold to pay for what they did! And we don't have the right to kill anyone in Israel."

Then David asked, "What do you want me to do for you?"

⁵The Gibeonites said to him, "Saul made plans against us. He tried to destroy all our people who are left in the land of Israel. ⁶Saul was the Lord's chosen king. So bring seven of his sons to us. Then we will kill them and hang them on stakes. We will put them in front of the Lord at Gibeah, Saul's hometown."

The king said, "I will give them to you." ⁷But the king protected Jonathan's son Mephibosheth. (Jonathan was Saul's son.) David did this because of the promise he had made to Jonathan in the Lord's name. So the king did not let them hurt Mephibosheth. ⁸But the king did take Armoni and Mephibosheth,ⁿ sons of Rizpah and Saul. (Rizpah was the daughter of Aiah.) And the king took the five sons of Saul's daughter Merab. Adriel was the father of Merab's five sons. (Adriel was the son of Barzillai the Meholathite.) ⁹David gave these seven sons to the Gibeonites. Then the Gibeonites killed them and hung them on stakes on a hill before the Lord. All seven sons died together. They were put to death during the first days of the harvest season. (The barley harvest was just beginning.)

¹⁰Aiah's daughter Rizpah took the rough cloth that was worn to show sadness. Then she put it on a rock for herself. She stayed there from the beginning of the harvest until the rain fell on her sons' bodies. During the day she did not let the birds of the sky touch her sons' bodies. At night she did not let the wild animals touch them.

¹¹People told David what Aiah's

ⁿ**Mephibosheth** This is not Jonathan's son but another man with the same name.

daughter Rizpah, Saul's slave woman,[d] was doing. [12]Then David took the bones of Saul and Jonathan from the men of Jabesh Gilead. (They had taken these bones secretly from the public square of Beth Shan. The Philistines had hung the bodies of Saul and Jonathan there after they had killed Saul at Gilboa.) [13]David brought the bones of Saul and his son Jonathan from Gilead. Then the people gathered the bodies of Saul's seven sons who were hanged on stakes. [14]The people buried the bones of Saul and his son Jonathan at Zela in Benjamin. They buried them in the tomb of Saul's father Kish. The people did everything the king commanded.

Then God answered the prayers of the people in the land.

Wars with the Philistines

[15]Again there was war between the Philistines and Israel. David and his men went out to fight the Philistines. But David became tired and weak. [16]Ishbi-Benob was one of the sons of Rapha.[d] His bronze spearhead weighed about seven and a half pounds. Ishbi-Benob had a new sword, and he planned to kill David. [17]But Abishai son of Zeruiah killed the Philistine. So he saved David's life.

Then David's men made a promise to David. They said, "Never again will you go out with us to battle. If you were killed, Israel would lose its greatest leader."

[18]Later, at Gob, there was another battle with the Philistines. Sibbecai the Hushathite killed Saph, another one of the sons of Rapha.

[19]Later, there was another battle at Gob with the Philistines. Elhanan son of Jaare-Oregim from Bethlehem killed Goliath[n] from Gath. Goliath's spear was as large as a weaver's rod.

[20]At Gath another battle took place. A very large man was there. He had 6 fingers on each hand. And he had 6 toes on each foot. He had 24 fingers and toes in all. This man also was one of the sons of Rapha. [21]When he challenged Israel, Jonathan killed him. Jonathan was the son of Shimeah, David's brother.

[22]These four men were sons of Rapha from Gath. They all were killed by David and his men.

People Who Spoke God's Words
DAVID · 2 SAMUEL 22

David killed a giant when he was just a young boy. Later he became Israel's greatest king. He was also a prophet, a person who spoke for God. Prophets came from lots of different occupations. Some prophets were even musicians. They sang God's praises and told his message through songs. This is one of those songs. You can also read it in Psalm 18. David wrote many songs that are in the book of Psalms. The songs describe David's feelings and tell about how much he loved and trusted God.

Next time you sing in church, listen to the words and think about what you are singing. You are praising God in your song!

To meet a prophet who asked for great power, fly to page 441.

---

[n]**Goliath**   In 1 Chronicles 20:5 he is called Lahmi brother of Goliath.

David's Song of Praise

22 David sang this song to the Lord. He sang it when the Lord had saved him from Saul and all his other enemies. ²He said:

"The Lord is my rock, my place of
    safety, my Savior.
³My God is my rock.
    I can run to him for safety.
He is my shield and my saving
    strength.
    The Lord is my high tower and my
        place of safety.
    The Lord saves me from those
        who want to harm me.
⁴I will call to the Lord.
    He is worthy of praise.
    And I will be saved from my
        enemies.

⁵"The waves of death came
    around me.
    The deadly rivers overwhelmed me.
⁶The ropes of death wrapped
    around me.
    The traps of death were before me.
⁷In my trouble I called to the
    Lord.
    I cried out to my God.
From his temple he heard my voice.
    My call for help reached his ears.

⁸"The earth trembled and shook.
    The foundations of heaven began
        to shake.
    They shook because the Lord
        was angry.
⁹Smoke came out of his nose.
    Burning fire came out of his
        mouth.
    Burning coals went before him.
¹⁰He tore open the sky and came
    down.
    Dark clouds were under his feet.
¹¹He rode a creature with wings
    and flew.
    He flew on the wings of the wind.
¹²He made darkness his shelter
    around him,
    surrounded by fog and clouds.
¹Out of the brightness of his
    presence
came flashes of lightning.
¹⁴The Lord thundered from
    heaven.
    The Most High God raised his
        voice.
¹⁵He shot his arrows and
    scattered his enemies.
    His bolts of lightning confused
        them with fear.
¹⁶The Lord spoke strongly.
    The wind blew from his nose.
    The valleys of the sea appeared.
    The foundations of the earth
        were seen.

¹⁷"The Lord reached down from
    above and took me.
    He pulled me from the deep water.
¹⁸He saved me from my powerful
    enemies.
    Those who hated me were too
        strong for me.
¹⁹They attacked me at my time of
    trouble.
    But the Lord supported me.
²⁰He took me to a safe place.
    Because he delights in me, he
        saved me.

²¹"The Lord spared me because I
    did what was right.
    Because I have not done evil, he
        has rescued me.
²²I have followed the ways of the
    Lord.
    I have not done evil by turning
        from my God.
²³I remember all his laws.
    I have not broken his rules.
²⁴I have kept myself innocent
    before him.
    I have kept myself from doing evil.
²⁵The Lord rescued me because I
    did what was right.
    I did what the Lord said was right.

²⁶"Lord, you are loyal to those
    who are loyal.
    You are good to those who
        are good.
²⁷You are pure to those who
    are pure.
    But you are against those who
        are bad.

²⁸You save those who are not
　　proud.
　　But you make humble those who
　　　are proud.
²⁹Lord, you give light to my
　　lamp.
　　The Lord brightens the darkness
　　　around me.
³⁰With your help, I can attack an
　　army.
　　With God's help, I can jump over
　　　a wall.

³¹"The ways of God are without
　　fault.
　　The Lord's words are pure.
　He is a shield to those who trust
　　　him.
³²Who is God? Only the Lord.
　　Who is the Rock?ᵈ Only our God.
³³God is my protection.
　　He makes my way free from fault.
³⁴He makes me like a deer,
　　which does not stumble.
　　He helps me stand on the steep
　　　mountains.
³⁵He trains my hands for battle.
　　So my arms can bend a bronze
　　　bow.
³⁶You protect me with your
　　saving shield.
　　You have stooped to make me
　　　great.
³⁷You give me a better way to
　　live.
　　So I live as you want me to.
³⁸I chased my enemies and
　　destroyed them.
　　I did not quit till they were
　　　destroyed.
³⁹I destroyed and crushed them,
　　so they couldn't rise up again.
　　They fell beneath my feet.
⁴⁰You gave me strength in battle.
　　You made my enemies bow before
　　　me.
⁴¹You made my enemies turn
　　back.
　　I destroyed those who hated me.
⁴²They called for help,
　　but no one came to save them.
　　They called to the Lord,
　　but he did not answer them.

⁴³I beat my enemies into pieces.
　　They were like dust on the
　　　ground.
　I pounded them out and walked
　　　on them
　　like mud in the streets.

⁴⁴"You saved me when my
　　people attacked me.
　　You kept me as the leader of
　　　nations.
　People I never knew serve me.
⁴⁵Foreigners obey me.
　　As soon as they hear me, they
　　　obey me.
⁴⁶They all become afraid.
　　They tremble in their hiding
　　　places.

⁴⁷"The Lord lives!
　　May my Rock be praised!
　　Praise God, the Rock, who saves
　　　me!
⁴⁸God gives me victory over my
　　enemies.
　　He brings people under my rule.
⁴⁹He frees me from my enemies.

　"You set me over those who hate
　　me.
　　You saved me from cruel men.
⁵⁰So I will praise you, Lord,
　　among the nations.
　　I will sing praises to your name.
⁵¹The Lord gives great victories
　　to his king.
　　He is loyal to his appointed king,
　　to David and his descendantsᵈ
　　　forever."

David's Last Words

23 These are the last words of
　　David.

　This is the message of David son of
　　　Jesse.
　　The man made great by the Most
　　　High God speaks.
　He is the appointed king of the God
　　　of Jacob.
　　He is the sweet singer of Israel.

²"The Lord's Spiritᵈ spoke
　　through me.
　　His word was on my tongue.

³The God of Israel spoke.
    The Rock^d of Israel said to me:
'The person who rules fairly over
    people,
  the person who rules with respect
    for God,
⁴he is like the morning light at
    dawn.
He is like a morning without
    clouds.
He is like sunshine after a rain.
The sunshine makes the tender
    grass grow out of the ground.'

⁵"This is how God has cared for
    my family.
God made a lasting agreement
    with me,
  good in every way and strong.
This agreement is my salvation.
This agreement is all I want.
  Truly, the Lord will make it grow.

⁶"But all evil people will be
    thrown away like thorns.
  People cannot hold on to thorns.
⁷Anyone who touches them
  uses a tool of iron or a spear.
They will be thrown in the fire and
    burned where they lie."

David's Army

⁸These are the names of David's
warriors:
  Josheb-Basshebeth, the Tahkemo-
nite, was head of the Three.ⁿ He killed
800 men at one time.
  ⁹Next there was Eleazar son of Dodai
the Ahohite. Eleazar was one of the
three soldiers who were with David
when they challenged the Philistines.
The Philistines were gathered for battle, and the Israelites drew back. ¹⁰But
Eleazar stayed where he was. He
fought the Philistines until he was so
tired he could not let go of his sword.
The Lord gave a great victory for the
Israelites that day. The people came
back after Eleazar had won the battle.
But they came only to take weapons
and armor from the enemy.
  ¹¹Next there was Shammah son of

Agee the Hararite. The Philistines came
together to fight. They stood where
there was a field full of small peas.
Israel's troops ran away from the
Philistines. ¹²But Shammah stood in
the middle of the field. He fought for
the field and killed the Philistines.
And the Lord gave a great victory.

  ¹³Once, three of the Thirty, David's
chief soldiers, came down to him during harvest. Now David was at the
cave of Adullam. The Philistine army
had camped in the Valley of Rephaim.
¹⁴At that time David was in a protected
place. And some of the Philistine soldiers were in Bethlehem.
  ¹⁵David had a strong desire for some
water. He said, "Oh, I wish someone
would get me water from the well near
the city gate of Bethlehem!" ¹⁶So the
three warriors broke through the
Philistine army. They took water out
of the well near the city gate of
Bethlehem. Then they took it to David.
But he refused to drink it. He poured
it out on the ground before the Lord.
¹⁷David said, "Lord, I can't drink this!
It would be like drinking the blood of
the men who risked their lives!" So
David refused to drink the water. These
were the brave things that the three
warriors did.
  ¹⁸Abishai was the brother of Joab son
of Zeruiah. He was captain of the Three.
Abishai used his spear against 300
enemies and killed them. He became
as famous as the Three. ¹⁹Abishai
received even more honor than the
Three. He became their commander.
But he was not a member of them.
  ²⁰Benaiah son of Jehoiada was a brave
fighter from Kabzeel. He did many
brave things. He killed two of the best
soldiers from Moab. He also went down
into a pit when it was snowing. There
he killed a lion. ²¹Benaiah killed a big
Egyptian. The Egyptian had a spear in
his hand. But Benaiah only had a club.
Benaiah grabbed the spear from the
Egyptian's hand. Then Benaiah killed
him with his own spear. ²²These were

ⁿ**Three** These were David's most powerful soldiers. See 1 Chronicles 11:11.

the brave things that Benaiah son of Jehoiada did. He was as famous as the Three. [23]He received more honor than the Thirty. But he did not become a member of the Three. David made him leader of his bodyguard.

The Thirty Chief Soldiers

[24]The following men were among the Thirty:

Asahel the brother of Joab;
Elhanan son of Dodo from Bethlehem;
[25]Shammah the Harodite;
Elika the Harodite;
[26]Helez the Paltite;
Ira son of Ikkesh (from Tekoa);
[27]Abiezer the Anathothite;
Mebunnai the Hushathite;
[28]Zalmon the Ahohite;
Maharai the Netophathite;
[29]Heled son of Baanah the Netophathite;
Ithai son of Ribai from Gibeah of the land of Benjamin;
[30]Benaiah the Pirathonite;
Hiddai from the ravines of Gaash;
[31]Abi-Albon the Arbathite;
Azmaveth the Barhumite;
[32]Eliahba the Shaalbonite;
the sons of Jashen;
Jonathan [33]son of Shammah the Hararite;
Ahiam son of Sharar the Hararite;
[34]Eliphelet son of Ahasbai the Maacathite;
Eliam son of Ahithophel the Gilonite;
[35]Hezro the Carmelite;
Paarai the Arbite;
[36]Igal son of Nathan of Zobah;
the son of Hagri;
[37]Zelek the Ammonite;
Naharai the Beerothite, who carried the armor of Joab son of Zeruiah;
[38]Ira the Ithrite;

Gareb the Ithrite
[39]and Uriah the Hittite.

There were 37 in all.

David Counts His Army

24 The Lord was angry with Israel again. He caused David to turn against the Israelites. David said, "Go, count the people of Israel and Judah."

[2]King David spoke to Joab, the commander of the army. David said, "Go through all the tribes[d] of Israel. Go from Dan to Beersheba[n] and count the people. Then I will know how many there are."

[3]But Joab said to the king, "May the Lord your God give you 100 times more people. And may you live to see this happen. But why do you want to do this?"

[4]But the king very strongly commanded Joab and the commanders of the army. So they left the king to count the people of Israel.

[5]After crossing the Jordan River, they camped near Aroer. They camped on the south side of the city in the ravine. They went through Gad and on to Jazer. [6]Then they went to Gilead and the land of Tahtim Hodshi. Next they went to Dan Jaan and around to Sidon. [7]They went to the strong, walled city of Tyre. They also went to all the cities of the Hivites and Canaanites. Finally, they went to southern Judah, to Beersheba. [8]After 9 months and 20 days, they had gone through all the land. Then they came back to Jerusalem.

[9]Joab gave the list of the people to the king. There were 800,000 men in Israel who could use the sword. And there were 500,000 men in Judah.

[10]David felt ashamed after he had counted the people. He said to the Lord, "I have sinned greatly in what I have done! Lord, I beg you, forgive my sin! I have been very foolish."

[11]Before David got up in the morning, the Lord spoke his word to Gad. He was a prophet[d] and David's seer.[d] [12]The

[n]**Dan to Beersheba** Dan was the city farthest north in Israel. Beersheba was the city farthest south. So this means all the people of Israel.

Lord told Gad, "Go and tell David, 'This is what the Lord says: I offer you three choices. Choose one for me to do to you.'"

13Gad went to David and told him. Gad said, "Choose one of these three things. Should three years of hunger come to you and your land? Or should your enemies chase you for three months? Or should there be three days of disease in your country? Think about it. Then decide which of these things I should tell the Lord who sent me."

17David saw the angel that killed the people. Then he said to the Lord, "I've sinned! I've done wrong! But these people only followed me like sheep! They did nothing wrong! Please let your punishment be against me and my father's family!"

18That day Gad came to David. Gad told him, "Go and build an altar to the Lord. Build it on the threshing floor of Araunah the Jebusite." 19So David did

Sin
2 SAMUEL 24:10-15

Have you ever broken a vase or carved your initials in a tree? If so, your parents (or whoever owned the vase or tree) were probably unhappy with you. Later on, they forgave you and got over their anger. They may have even repaired the damage, at least to the vase. Even so, the cracks in the vase and the scars on the tree were still there for everyone to see.

Sin is like that. Even after you have admitted that what you did was wrong and have been forgiven, the scars can remain. Maybe you hurt your friend's feelings by saying something unkind. Your friend got over it, and you became friends again, but the hurt was still there. Or maybe you got mad at your sister and broke her favorite doll. She forgave you, but the doll was still broken.

God forgives our sins, but that doesn't mean there won't be any bad results.

To learn more about sin, zoom to page 677.

14David said to Gad, "I am really in trouble. But the Lord is very merciful. So let the Lord punish us. Don't let my punishment come from people!"

15So the Lord sent disease on Israel. It began in the morning. And it continued until the chosen time to stop. From Dan to Beersheba 70,000 people died. 16The angel raised his arm toward Jerusalem to destroy it also. But the Lord felt very sorry about the terrible things that had happened. He said to the angel who was destroying the people, "That's enough! Put down your arm!" At this time the angel of the Lord was by the threshing[d] floor of Araunah the Jebusite.

what Gad told him to do. He obeyed the Lord's command and went to see Araunah.

20Araunah looked and saw the king and his servants coming to him. So he went out and bowed facedown on the ground. 21He said, "Why has my master the king come to me?"

David answered, "To buy the threshing floor from you. I want to build an altar to the Lord. Then the disease will stop."

22Araunah said to David, "My master and king, you may take anything you want for a sacrifice. Here are some oxen for the whole burnt offering. Here are the threshing boards and the yokes[d] for the wood! 23My king, I give everything to you!" Araunah also said to the king, "May the Lord your God be pleased with you!"

24But the king answered Araunah, "No. I will pay you for the land. I won't offer to the Lord my God burnt offerings which cost me nothing!"

So David bought the threshing floor and the oxen for one and one-fourth pounds of silver. 25Then he built an altar to the Lord there. And he offered whole burnt offerings and fellowship offerings. Then the Lord answered his prayer for the country. And the disease in Israel stopped.

1 KINGS

The Kingdom Is Divided

Adonijah Tries to Become King

1 At this time King David was very old. His servants covered him with blankets, but he could not keep warm. ²So they said to him, "We will find a young woman to care for you. She will lie close to you and keep you warm." ³So the king's servants looked everywhere in Israel for a beautiful young woman. They found a girl named Abishag from the Shunammite people. They brought her to the king. ⁴The girl was very beautiful. She cared for the king and served him. But King David did not have sexual relations with her.

man. He said, "I will be the king." So he got chariots and horses for himself. And he got 50 men to run ahead of him. Now David had never interfered with him by questioning what he did.

⁷Adonijah talked with Joab son of Zeruiah. He also talked with Abiathar the priest. They told him they would help him. ⁸But several men did not join Adonijah. These men were Zadok the priest, Benaiah son of Jehoiada, Nathan the prophet,*d* Shimei, Rei and King David's special guard.

⁹Then Adonijah killed some sheep, cows and fat calves for sacrifices. He made these sacrifices at the Stone of Zoheleth near the spring, En Rogel. He invited all his brothers, the other sons of King David, to come. He invited all the rulers and leaders of Judah also.

Brothers and Sisters
ADONIJAH AND SOLOMON • 1 KINGS 1:5-30

Adonijah wanted to be king of Israel. His father David was going to die soon, and Adonijah thought he deserved to be the next king. So he got some people to agree with him and had himself crowned king. But God had told David that his son Solomon would be Israel's next king. Adonijah had to give up his crown and ask Solomon for forgiveness. He looked pretty foolish.

Sometimes we want something very much, but our brother or sister gets it. Maybe it is good looks or popularity or a room of our own. Instead of fighting and looking foolish or being angry and pouting, we should ask God to help us be happy for our brother or sister.

To meet some brothers who had to learn to serve, fly to page 1202.

5-6Adonijah was King David and Haggith's son. He was born next after Absalom. He was a very handsome

¹⁰But Adonijah did not invite Nathan the prophet, Benaiah, his father's special guard or his brother Solomon.

[11]When Nathan heard about this, he went to Bathsheba. She was the mother of Solomon. Nathan asked her, "Have you heard what Adonijah, Haggith's son, is doing? He has made himself king. And our real king, David, does not know it. [12]Your life and the life of your son Solomon may be in danger. But I will tell you how to save yourselves. [13]Go to King David and say to him, 'My master and king, you made a promise to me. You promised that my son Solomon would be the king after you. You said he would rule on your throne. So why has Adonijah become king?' [14]While you are still talking to him, I will come in. I will tell the king that what you have said about Adonijah is true."

[15]So Bathsheba went in to see the king in his bedroom. He was now very old. Abishag, the girl from Shunam, was caring for him there. [16]Bathsheba bowed down before the king.

He asked, "What do you want?"

[17]She answered, "My master, you made a promise to me in the name of the Lord your God. You said, 'Your son Solomon will become king after me. He will rule on my throne.' [18]But now Adonijah has become king. And you did not know it. [19]Adonijah has killed many cows, fat calves and sheep for sacrifices. And he has invited all your sons. He also has invited Abiathar the priest and Joab the commander of your army. But he did not invite Solomon, your son who serves you. [20]My master and king, all the people of Israel are watching you. They are waiting for you to decide who will be king after you. [21]As soon as you die, Solomon and I will be treated as criminals."

[22]While Bathsheba was still talking with the king, Nathan the prophet arrived. [23]The servants told the king, "Nathan the prophet is here." So Nathan went to the king and bowed facedown on the ground before him.

[24]Then Nathan said, "My master and king, have you said that Adonijah will be the king after you? Have you

decided he will rule on your throne after you? [25]Today he has sacrificed many cows, fat calves and sheep. And he has invited all your other sons, the commanders of the army and Abiathar the priest. Right now they are eating and drinking with him. They are saying, 'Long live King Adonijah!' [26]But he did not invite me, Zadok the priest, Benaiah son of Jehoiada or your son Solomon. [27]Did you do this? We are your servants. Why didn't you tell us whom you chose to be the king after you?"

David Makes Solomon King

[28]Then King David said, "Tell Bathsheba to come in!" So she came in and stood before the king.

[29]Then the king said, "The Lord has saved me from all trouble. As surely as he lives, I make this promise to you. [30]Today I will do what I promised you in the past. I made that promise in the name of the Lord, the God of Israel. I promised that your son Solomon would be king after me. I promised he would rule on my throne after me."

[31]Then Bathsheba bowed facedown on the ground before the king. She said, "Long live my master King David!"

[32]Then King David said, "Tell Zadok the priest, Nathan the prophet[d] and Benaiah son of Jehoiada to come in here." So they came before the king. [33]Then the king said to them, "Take my servants with you and put my son Solomon on my own mule. Take him down to the spring called Gihon. [34]There Zadok the priest and Nathan the prophet should pour olive oil on him and make him king over Israel. Blow the trumpet and shout, 'Long live King Solomon!' [35]Then come back here with him. He will sit on my throne and rule in my place. I have chosen him to be the ruler over Israel and Judah."

[36]Benaiah son of Jehoiada answered the king, "This is good! And may your God make it happen. [37]The Lord has

always helped you, our king. Let the Lord also help Solomon. And let King Solomon be an even greater king than you."

38So Zadok the priest, Nathan the prophet and Benaiah son of Jehoiada went down. The Kerethites and Pelethites, the king's bodyguards, went with them. They put Solomon on King David's mule and went with him to the spring called Gihon. 39Zadok the priest took with him the container of olive oil from the Holy Tent.*d* He poured the olive oil on Solomon's head to show he was the king. Then they blew the trumpet. And all the people shouted, "Long live King Solomon!" 40All the people followed Solomon into the city. They were playing flutes and shouting for joy. They made so much noise the ground shook.

41At this time Adonijah and all the guests with him were finishing their meal. They heard the sound from the trumpet. Joab asked, "What does all that noise from the city mean?"

42While Joab was speaking, Jonathan son of Abiathar the priest arrived. Adonijah said, "Come in! You are an important man. So you must be bringing good news."

43But Jonathan answered, "No! Our master King David has made Solomon the new king. 44King David sent Zadok the priest, Nathan the prophet, Benaiah son of Jehoiada and all the king's bodyguards with him. They put Solomon on the king's own mule. 45And Zadok the priest and Nathan the prophet poured olive oil on Solomon at Gihon to make him king. Then they went into the city, shouting with joy. Now the whole city is excited. That is the noise you hear. 46Solomon has now become the king. 47All the king's officers have come to tell King David that he has done a good thing. They are saying, 'May your God make Solomon even more famous than you. And may your God make Solomon an even

greater king than you.'" Jonathan continued, "And King David bowed down on his bed to worship God. 48He said, 'Praise the Lord, the God of Israel. Today he has made one of my sons the king and allowed me to see it.'"

49Then all of Adonijah's guests were afraid, and they left quickly. 50Adonijah was also afraid of Solomon. So he went and took hold of the corners of the altar.*n* 51Then someone told Solomon, "Adonijah is afraid of you. He is at the altar, holding on to its corners. He says, 'Tell King Solomon to promise me today that he will not kill me.'"

52So Solomon answered, "Adonijah must show that he is a man of honor. If he does, I promise that he will not lose even a hair from his head. But if he does anything wrong, he will die." 53Then King Solomon sent some men to get Adonijah. They brought him to King Solomon. So Adonijah came before King Solomon and bowed down. Then Solomon said, "Go home."

The Death of David

2 It was almost time for David to die. So he talked to Solomon and gave him his last commands. 2David said, "My time to die is near. Be a good and strong leader. 3Obey everything that the Lord commands. Follow the commands he has given us. Obey all his laws, and do what he told us. Obey what is written in the teachings of Moses. If you do these things, you will be successful in all you do and wherever you go. 4And if you obey the Lord, he will keep the promise he made to me. He promised: 'Your descendants*d* must live as I tell them. They must have complete faith in me. If they do this, then a man from your family will always be king over the people of Israel.'

5"Also, you remember what Joab son of Zeruiah did to me. He killed the two commanders of Israel's armies. He killed Abner son of Ner and Amasa

---

*n***corners of the altar** If a person were innocent of a crime, he could run into the Holy Place. If he held on to the corners of the altar there, he would not be punished. The corners looked like horns.

son of Jether. He killed them as if he and they were at war. But this was in a time of peace. He killed innocent men. And their blood got on his belt and sandals. [6]You should punish him in the way you think is wisest. (But do not let him die peacefully of old age.) [7]"Be kind to the children of Barzillai of Gilead. Allow them to eat at your table. They helped me when I ran away from your brother Absalom.

[8]"And remember, Shimei son of Gera is here with you. He is from the people of Benjamin in Bahurim. Remember he cursed me the day I went to Mahanaim. Then he came down to meet me at the Jordan River. I promised him before the Lord, 'Shimei, I will not kill you.' [9]But you should not leave him unpunished. You are a wise man. You will know what to do to him. But you must be sure he is killed."

[10]Then David died and was buried with his ancestors in Jerusalem. [11]He had ruled over Israel 40 years. Seven years were in Hebron, and 33 years were in Jerusalem.

Solomon Takes Control as King

[12]Now Solomon became king after David, his father. And he was in control of his kingdom.

[13]At this time Adonijah son of Haggith went to Bathsheba, Solomon's mother. Bathsheba asked, "Do you come in peace?"

Adonijah answered, "Yes. This is a peaceful visit. [14]I have something to say to you."

"You may speak," she said.

[15]Adonijah said, "You remember that at one time the kingdom was mine. All the people of Israel thought I was their king. But things changed. Now my brother is the king because the Lord chose him. [16]So now I have one thing to ask you. Please do not refuse me."

Bathsheba answered, "What do you want?"

[17]Adonijah said, "I know King Solomon will do anything you ask him. So please ask him to give me Abishag the Shunammite woman to be my wife."

[18]"Very well," she answered. "I will speak to the king for you."

[19]So Bathsheba went to King Solomon to talk to him for Adonijah. When Solomon saw her, he stood up to meet her. Then he bowed down to her and sat on the throne. He told some servants to bring another throne for his mother. Then she sat down at his right side.

[20]Bathsheba said to him, "I have one small thing to ask you. Please do not refuse me."

The king answered, "Ask, mother. I will not refuse you."

[21]So she said, "Allow Abishag the Shunammite woman to marry your brother Adonijah."

[22]King Solomon answered his mother, "Why do you ask me to give him Abishag? Why don't you ask for him to become the king also since he is my older brother? Abiathar the priest and Joab son of Zeruiah will support him!"

[23]Then King Solomon made a promise in the name of the Lord. He said, "I promise Adonijah will pay for asking me this! May God punish me terribly if it doesn't cost Adonijah his life! [24]The Lord has given me the throne that belonged to my father David. The Lord has kept his promise and given the kingdom to me and my people. As surely as the Lord lives, Adonijah will die today!" [25]So King Solomon gave orders to Benaiah son of Jehoiada. And he went out and killed Adonijah.

[26]Then King Solomon said to Abiathar the priest, "I should kill you. But I will allow you to go back to your home in Anathoth. I will not kill you now because you helped to carry the Holy Box[d] of the Lord God while marching with my father David. And I know you shared in all of the hard times with my father." [27]So Solomon removed Abiathar from being a priest to the Lord. This happened as the Lord had said it would. He had said

this about the priest Eli and his family in Shiloh.

[28]When Joab heard about this, he was afraid. He had supported Adonijah, but not Absalom. So Joab ran to the Tent[d] of the Lord and took hold of the corners of the altar.[n] [29]Someone told King Solomon that Joab had run to the Tent of the Lord and was beside the altar. So Solomon ordered Benaiah to go and kill him.

[30]Benaiah went into the Tent of the Lord and said to Joab, "The king says, 'Come out!'"

But Joab answered, "No, I will die here."

So Benaiah went back to the king and told him what Joab had said. [31]Then the king commanded Benaiah, "Do as he says! Kill him there and bury him. Then my family and I will be free of the guilt of Joab. Joab is guilty of killing innocent people. [32]He killed two men who were much better than he was. They were Abner son of Ner and Amasa son of Jether. Abner was the commander of Israel's army, and Amasa was the commander of Judah's army. My father David did not know that he killed them. So the Lord will pay him back for those men he killed. [33]He and his family will be forever guilty for their deaths. But there will be peace from God for David, his descendants,[d] his family and his rule forever."

[34]So Benaiah son of Jehoiada killed Joab. And he was buried near his home in the desert. [35]Solomon then made Benaiah son of Jehoiada commander of the army in Joab's place. Solomon also made Zadok the new high priest in Abiathar's place.

[36]Next the king sent for Shimei. The king said to him, "Build a house for yourself here in Jerusalem. Live in the house, and don't leave the city. [37]If you leave and go past Kidron Valley, someone will kill you. And it will be your own fault."

[38]So Shimei answered the king, "What you have said is good. I will obey you, my master and king." So Shimei lived in Jerusalem for a long time.

[39]But three years later two of Shimei's slaves ran away. They went to Achish king of Gath. He was the son of Maacah. Shimei heard that his slaves were in Gath. [40]So he put his saddle on his donkey and left. He went to Achish at Gath to find his slaves. When he found them there, he brought them back to his home.

[41]Someone told Solomon that Shimei had gone from Jerusalem to Gath and had returned. [42]So Solomon sent for Shimei. Solomon said, "I made you promise in the name of the Lord not to leave Jerusalem. I warned you that if you went anywhere else you would die. And you agreed to what I said. You said you would obey me. [43]Why did you break your promise to the Lord? Why did you not obey my command? [44]You know the many wrong things you did against my father David. Now the Lord will punish you for those wrongs. [45]But the Lord will bless me. He will make the rule of David safe before the Lord forever."

[46]Then the king ordered Benaiah to kill Shimei, and he did. Now Solomon was in full control of his kingdom.

Solomon Asks for Wisdom

3 Solomon made an agreement with the king of Egypt by marrying his daughter. Solomon brought her to Jerusalem. At this time Solomon was still building his palace and the Temple[d] of the Lord. He was also building a wall around Jerusalem. [2]The Temple had not yet been finished. So people were still offering animal sacrifices at altars in many places of worship. [3]Solomon showed that he loved the Lord. He did this by following the commands his father David had given him. But Solomon still used the many places of worship to offer sacrifices and to burn incense.[d]

---

[n]**corners of the altar** If a person were innocent of a crime, he could run into the Holy Place. If he held on to the corners of the altar there, he would not be punished. The corners looked like horns.

⁴King Solomon went to Gibeon to offer a sacrifice. He went there because it was the most important place of worship. He offered 1,000 burnt offerings on that altar. ⁵While he was at Gibeon, the Lord came to him in a dream during the night. God said, "Ask for anything you want. I will give it to you."

⁶Solomon answered, "You were very kind to your servant, my father David. He obeyed you. He was honest and lived right. And you showed great kindness to him when you allowed his son to be king after him. ⁷Lord my God, you have allowed me to be king in my father's place. But I am like a little child. I do not have the wisdom I need to do what I must do. ⁸I, your servant, am here among your chosen people. There are too many of them to count. ⁹So I ask that you give me wisdom. Then I can rule the people in the right way. Then I will know the difference between right and wrong. Without wisdom, it is impossible to rule this great people of yours."

¹⁰The Lord was pleased that Solomon had asked him for this. ¹¹So God said to him, "You did not ask for a long life. And you did not ask for riches for yourself. You did not ask for the death of your enemies. Since you asked for wisdom to make the right decisions, ¹²I will give you what you asked. I will give you wisdom and understanding. Your wisdom will be greater than anyone has had in the past. And there will never be anyone in the future like you. ¹³Also, I will give you what you did not ask for. You will have riches and honor. During your life no other king will be as great as you. ¹⁴I ask you to follow me and obey my laws and commands. Do this as your father David did. If you do, I will also give you a long life."

¹⁵Then Solomon woke up. He knew that God had talked to him in the dream. Then he went to Jerusalem and stood before the Box*d* of the Agreement with the Lord. There he gave burnt offerings and fellowship offerings to the Lord. After that, he gave a feast for all of his leaders and officers.

Solomon Makes a Wise Decision

¹⁶One day two women who were prostitutes*d* came to Solomon. They stood before him. ¹⁷One of the women said, "My master, this woman and I live in the same house. I gave birth to a baby while she was there with me. ¹⁸Three days later this woman also gave birth to a baby. No one else was in the house with us. There were only the two of us. ¹⁹One night this woman rolled over on her baby, and it died. ²⁰So during the night she took my son from my bed while I was asleep. She carried him to her bed. Then she put the dead baby in my bed. ²¹The next morning I got up to feed my baby. But I saw that he was dead! Then I looked at him more closely. I saw that he was not my son."

²²But the other woman said, "No! The living baby is my son. The dead baby is yours!"

But the first woman said, "No! The dead baby is yours, and the living one is mine!" So the two women argued before the king.

²³Then King Solomon said, "Each of you says the living baby is your own. And each of you says the dead baby belongs to the other woman."

²⁴Then King Solomon sent his servants to get a sword. When they brought it to him, ²⁵he said, "Cut the living baby into two pieces. Give each woman half of the baby."

²⁶The real mother of the living child was full of love for her son. She said to the king, "Please, my master, don't kill him! Give the baby to her!"

But the other woman said, "Neither of us will have him. Cut him into two pieces!"

²⁷Then King Solomon said, "Give the baby to the first woman. Don't kill him. She is the real mother."

²⁸When the people of Israel heard about King Solomon's decision, they respected him very much. They saw

he had wisdom from God to make the right decisions.

Solomon's Officers

4 King Solomon ruled over all Israel. [2]These are the names of his leading officers:

Azariah son of Zadok was the priest;

[3]Elihoreph and Ahijah, sons of Shisha, recorded what happened in the courts;

Jehoshaphat son of Ahilud recorded the history of the people;

[4]Benaiah son of Jehoiada was commander of the army;

Zadok and Abiathar were priests;

[5]Azariah son of Nathan was in charge of the district governors;

Zabud son of Nathan was a priest and adviser to the king;

[6]Ahishar was responsible for everything in the palace;

Adoniram son of Abda was in charge of the slaves.

[7]Solomon placed 12 governors over the districts of Israel. They had to gather food from their districts. Then they were to give it to the king and his family. Each governor was responsible for giving food to the king one month of each year. [8]These are the names of the 12 governors:

Ben-Hur was governor over the mountain country of Ephraim.

[9]Ben-Deker was governor over Makaz, Shaalbim, Beth Shemesh and Elon Bethhanan.

[10]Ben-Hesed was governor over Arubboth, Socoh and Hepher.

[11]Ben-Abinadab was governor over Naphoth Dor. (He was married to Taphath daughter of Solomon.)

[12]Baana son of Ahilud was governor over Taanach, Megiddo and all of Beth Shan next to Zarethan. (This was below Jezreel from Beth Shan to Abel Meholah across Jokmeam.)

[13]Ben-Geber was governor over Ramoth in Gilead. (He was governor over all the Towns of Jair in Gilead. Jair was the son of Manasseh. Ben-Geber was also over the district of Argob in Bashan. It had 60 large, walled cities with bronze bars on their gates.)

[14]Ahinadab son of Iddo was governor over Mahanaim.

[15]Ahimaaz was governor over Naphtali. (He was married to Basemath daughter of Solomon.)

[16]Baana son of Hushai was governor over Asher and Aloth.

[17]Jehoshaphat son of Paruah was governor over Issachar.

[18]Shimei son of Ela was governor over Benjamin.

[19]Geber son of Uri was governor over Gilead. (Gilead was the country where Sihon king of the Amorite people lived. Og king of Bashan also lived there.) But Geber was the only governor over the district.

Solomon's Kingdom

[20]There were many people in Judah and Israel. There were as many people as there were grains of sand on the seashore. The people ate, drank and were happy. [21]Solomon ruled over all the kingdoms from the Euphrates River to the land of the Philistine people. His kingdom went as far as the border of Egypt. These countries brought Solomon the payments he demanded. And they obeyed him all his life.

[22]Solomon needed much food each day to feed himself and all the people who ate at his table. It took 185 bushels of fine flour and 375 bushels of meal. [23]It also took 10 cows that were fed good grain, 20 cows that were raised in the fields and 100 sheep. And it took 3 different kinds of deer and fat birds.

[24]Solomon ruled over all the countries west of the Euphrates River. This was the land from Tiphsah to Gaza. And Solomon had peace on all sides of his kingdom. [25]During Solomon's life Judah and Israel, from Dan to Beersheba,[n] lived in peace. Each man was

---

[n]**Dan to Beersheba** Dan was the city farthest north in Israel. Beersheba was the city farthest south. So this means all the people of Israel.

able to sit under his own fig trees and grapevines.

²⁶Solomon had 4,000 stalls for his chariot horses. And he had 12,000 chariot soldiers. ²⁷Each month one of the district governors gave King Solomon all the food he needed. This was enough for every person who ate at the king's table. The governors made sure he had everything he needed. ²⁸They also gave the king enough barley and straw for the chariot and work horses. Each person brought this grain to the required places.

Solomon's Wisdom

²⁹God gave great wisdom to Solomon. Solomon could understand many things. His wisdom was as hard to measure as the sand on the seashore. ³⁰His wisdom was greater than the wisdom of all the men in the East. And his wisdom was greater than all the wisdom of the men in Egypt. ³¹He was wiser than any other man on earth. He was even wiser than Ethan the Ezrahite. He was wiser than Heman, Calcol and Darda. They were the sons of Mahol. King Solomon became famous in all the countries around Israel and Judah. ³²During his life King Solomon spoke 3,000 wise teachings. He also knew 1,005 songs. ³³He taught about many different kinds of plants. He taught about everything from the great cedar trees of Lebanon to the hyssop that grows out of the walls. He also taught about animals, birds, crawling things and fish. ³⁴People from all nations came to listen to King Solomon's wisdom. The kings of all nations sent them to listen to him. These kings had heard of Solomon's wisdom.

Solomon Prepares to Build the Temple

5 Now King Hiram was the king of Tyre. He had always been a friend of David. Hiram heard that Solomon had been made king in David's place. So he sent his messengers to Solomon. ²Then Solomon sent this message back to King Hiram: ³"You remember that my father David had to fight many wars with the countries around him. So he was never able to build a temple for worship to the Lord his God. David was waiting until the Lord allowed him to defeat all his enemies. ⁴But now the Lord my God has given me peace. There is peace on all sides of my country. I have no enemies now. My people are in no danger.

⁵"The Lord made a promise to my father David. The Lord said, 'I will make your son king after you. And he will build a temple for worship to me.' Now, I plan to build that temple for worship to the Lord my God. ⁶And so I ask for your help. Send your men to cut down cedar trees for me from Lebanon. My servants will work with yours. I will pay your servants whatever wages you decide. We don't have anyone who can cut down trees as well as the people of Sidon can."

⁷When Hiram heard what Solomon asked, he was very happy. He said, "I thank the Lord today! He has given David a wise son to rule over this great nation!" ⁸Then Hiram sent back this message to Solomon: "I received the message you sent. I will give you all the cedar and pine trees you want. ⁹My servants will bring them down from Lebanon to the sea. There I will tie them together. Then I will float them down the shore to the place you choose. There I will separate the logs, and you can take them away. In return you will give food to all those who live with me." ¹⁰So Hiram gave Solomon as much cedar and pine as he wanted. ¹¹And Solomon gave Hiram about 125,000 bushels of wheat each year. It was to feed all those who lived with Hiram. And Solomon gave him about 115,000 gallons of pure olive oil every year.

¹²The Lord gave wisdom to Solomon as he had promised. And there was peace between Hiram and Solomon. These two kings made a treaty between themselves.

[13]King Solomon forced 30,000 men of Israel to help in this work. [14]He put a man named Adoniram over them. Solomon sent a group of 10,000 men each month to Lebanon. So each group worked in Lebanon one month. Then it went home for two months. [15]Solomon forced 80,000 men to work in the hill country, cutting stone. And he had 70,000 men to carry the stones. [16]There were also 3,300 men who directed the workers. [17]King Solomon commanded them to cut large blocks of fine stone. These were to be used for the foundation of the Temple.[d] [18]Solomon's and Hiram's builders and the men from Byblos carved the stones. They prepared the stones and the logs for building the Temple.

Solomon Builds the Temple

6 So Solomon began to build the Temple.[d] This was 480 years after the people of Israel had left Egypt. (This was the fourth year of King Solomon's rule over Israel.) It was the second month, the month of Ziv.

[2]The Temple was 90 feet long and 30 feet wide. It was 45 feet high. [3]The porch in front of the main room of the Temple was 15 feet deep and 30 feet wide. The room ran along the front of the Temple itself. Its width was equal to the width of the Temple. [4]There were narrow windows in the Temple. These windows were narrow on the outside and larger on the inside. [5]Then Solomon built some side rooms against the walls of the main room of the Temple. These rooms were built on top of each other. [6]The rooms on the bottom floor were 7½ feet wide. The rooms on the middle floor were 9 feet wide. The rooms above that were 10½ feet wide. The Temple wall which made the side of each room was thinner than the wall in the room below. The rooms were pushed against the wall but did not have their main beams built into the wall.

[7]The stones were prepared at the same place they were cut from the ground. Only these stones were used to build the Temple. So there was no noise of hammers, axes or any other iron tools at the Temple.

[8]The entrance to the bottom rooms built beside the Temple was on the south side. From there, stairs went up to the second floor rooms. And from there, they went on to the third floor rooms. [9]Solomon put a roof made from beams and cedar boards on the Temple. So he finished building the Temple. [10]He also finished building the bottom floor that was beside the Temple. It was 7½ feet high. It was attached to the Temple by cedar beams.

[11]The Lord spoke his word to Solomon: [12]"Obey all my laws and commands. If you do, I will do for you what I promised your father David. [13]And I will live among the children of Israel in this Temple you are building. I will never leave the people of Israel."

[14]So Solomon finished building the Temple. [15]The inside walls were covered from floor to ceiling with cedar boards. The floor was made from pine boards. [16]A room 30 feet long was built in the back part of the Temple. It was divided from the rest of the Temple by cedar boards reaching from floor to ceiling. It was called the Most Holy Place. [17]The main room, the room in front of the Most Holy Place, was 60 feet long. [18]Inside the Temple was cedar. It was carved with pictures of flowers and plants. Everything inside was covered with cedar. So a person could not see the stones of the wall.

[19]He prepared the inner room at the back of the Temple to keep the Box[d] of the Agreement with the Lord. [20]This inner room was 30 feet long, 30 feet wide and 30 feet high. Solomon covered this room with pure gold. He built an altar of cedar and covered it also. [21]He covered the inside of the Temple with pure gold. And he placed gold chains across the front of the inner room. It was covered with gold. [22]So all the inside of the Temple was covered

with gold. Also the altar in the Most Holy Place was covered with gold.

23Solomon made two creatures with wings from olive wood. Each creature was 15 feet tall. They were put in the Most Holy Place. 24Each creature had two wings. Each wing was 7½ feet long. So it was 15 feet from the end of one wing to the end of the other wing. 25The creatures were the same size and shape. 26And each was 15 feet tall. 27These creatures were put beside each other in the Most Holy Place. Their wings were spread out. So one creature's wing touched one wall. The other creature's wing touched the other wall. And their wings touched each other in the middle of the room. 28The two creatures were covered with gold.

29All the walls around the Temple were carved. They were carved with pictures of creatures with wings, palm trees and flowers. This was true for both the main room and the inner room. 30The floors of both rooms were covered with gold.

31Doors made from olive wood were put at the entrance to the Most Holy Place. The doors were made to fit into an area with five sides. 32Creatures with wings, palm trees and flowers were carved on the two olive wood doors. Then the doors were covered with gold. And the creatures and the palm trees were covered with gold. 33At the entrance to the main room there was a door frame. It was square and was made of olive wood. 34Two doors were made from pine. Each door had two parts so that the doors folded. 35The doors were covered with pictures of creatures with wings, palm trees and flowers. And all of the carvings were covered with gold. The gold was smoothed over the carvings.

36The inner courtyard was built and enclosed with walls. The walls were made of three rows of cut stones and one row of cedar boards.

37Work began on the Temple in Ziv, the second month. This was during the fourth year Solomon ruled over Israel. 38The Temple was finished during the eleventh year Solomon ruled. It was finished in the eighth month, the month of Bul. It was finished exactly as it was planned. Solomon had worked seven years to build the Temple.

Solomon's Palace

7 King Solomon also built a palace for himself. It took him 13 years to finish building it. 2He built the Palace of the Forest of Lebanon. It was 150 feet long, 75 feet wide and 45 feet high. It had four rows of cedar columns. They supported the cedar beams. 3The ceiling was covered with cedar above the beams. There were 45 beams on the roof, with 15 beams in each row. 4Windows were placed in three rows facing each other. 5All the doors were square. The three doors at each end faced each other.

6Solomon also built the porch of pillars. It was 75 feet long and 45 feet wide. Along the front of the porch, there was a covering supported by pillars.

7Solomon also built a throne room where he judged people. He called this the Hall of Justice. The room was covered with cedar from the floor to the ceiling. 8The palace where Solomon was to live was behind the Hall of Justice. And it was built like the Hall of Justice. Solomon also built the same kind of palace for his wife. She was the daughter of the king of Egypt.

9All these buildings were made with blocks of carefully cut fine stone. Then they were trimmed with a saw in the front and back. These fine stones went from the foundations of the buildings to the top of the walls. Even the courtyard was made with blocks of stone. 10The foundations were made with large blocks of fine stone. Some of the stones were 15 feet long. Others were 12 feet long. 11On top of those stones there were other cut blocks of fine stone and cedar beams. 12The palace courtyard, the courtyard inside the Temple[d] and the porch to the Temple were surrounded by walls. All of these walls had three rows of cut stone blocks and one row of cedar beams.

The Temple Is Completed Inside

¹³King Solomon sent to Tyre and had Huram brought to him. ¹⁴Huram's mother was a widow from the tribe[d] of Naphtali. His father was from Tyre and had been skilled in making things from bronze. Huram was also very skilled and experienced in bronze work. So he came to King Solomon. And he did all the bronze work Solomon wanted.

¹⁵He made two bronze pillars. Each one was 27 feet tall and 18 feet around. ¹⁶He also made two bronze capitals[d] that were 7½ feet tall. He put them on top of the pillars. ¹⁷Then he made a net of seven chains for each capital. They covered the capitals on top of the two pillars. ¹⁸Then he made two rows of bronze pomegranates[d] to go on the nets. They were to cover the capitals at the top of the pillars. ¹⁹The capitals on top of the pillars in the porch were shaped like lilies. They were 6 feet tall. ²⁰The capitals were on top of both pillars. They were above the bowl-shaped section and next to the nets. At that place there were 200 pomegranates in rows all around the capitals. ²¹Huram put these two bronze pillars at the porch of the Temple.[d] He named the south pillar He Establishes. And he named the north pillar In Him Is Strength. ²²The capitals on top of the pillars were shaped like lilies. So the work on the pillars was finished.

²³Then Huram made a large round bowl from bronze, which was called the Sea. It was 45 feet around. It was 15 feet across and 7½ feet deep. ²⁴There was a rim around the outer edge of the bowl. Under this rim there were two rows of bronze plants surrounding the bowl. There were ten plants in every 18 inches. They were made in one piece with the bowl. ²⁵The bowl rested on the backs of 12 bronze

bulls. They faced outward from the center of the bowl. Three bulls faced north, 3 faced east, 3 faced south and 3 faced west. ²⁶The sides of the bowl were 4 inches thick. The rim was like the rim of a cup or like a lily blossom. The bowl held about 11,000 gallons.

²⁷Then Huram made ten bronze stands. Each one was 6 feet long, 6 feet wide and 4½ feet high. ²⁸The stands were made from square sides, which were put on frames. ²⁹On the sides were bronze lions, bulls and creatures with wings. On the frames above and below the lions and bulls there were designs of flowers hammered into the bronze. ³⁰Each stand had four bronze wheels with bronze axles. At the corners there were bronze supports for a large bowl. The supports had designs of flowers. ³¹There was a frame on top of the bowls. It was 18 inches high above the bowls. The opening of the bowl was round, 27 inches deep. There were designs carved into the bronze on the frame. The frame was square, not round. ³²The four wheels were under the frame. They were 27 inches high. The axles between the wheels were made as one piece with the stand. ³³The wheels were like a chariot's wheels. Everything on the wheels was made of bronze. The axles, rims, spokes and hubs were made of bronze.

³⁴The four supports were on the four corners of each stand. They were made as one piece with the stand. ³⁵There was a strip of bronze around the top of each stand. It was 9 inches deep. It was made as one piece with the stand. ³⁶The sides of the stand and the frames were totally covered with carvings. They were carved with pictures of creatures with wings, lions and palm trees. There were also flowers carved all around. ³⁷So this is the way Huram made the ten stands. The bronze for each stand was melted and poured into a mold. So all of the stands were the same size and shape.

³⁸Huram also made ten bronze bowls. There was one bowl for each of

the ten stands. Each bowl was six feet across and could hold about 230 gallons. ³⁹Huram put five of the stands on the south side of the Temple. And he put the other five stands on the north side. He put the large bowl in the southeast corner of the Temple. ⁴⁰Huram also made bowls, shovels and small bowls.

So Huram finished making everything King Solomon wanted him to make. Here is a list of what Huram made for the Temple of the Lord:

⁴¹two pillars;

two large bowls for the capitals on top of the pillars;

two nets to cover the two large bowls for the capitals on top of the pillars;

⁴²400 pomegranates for the two nets (there were two rows of pomegranates for each net covering the bowls for the capitals on top of the pillars);

⁴³ten stands with a bowl on each stand;

⁴⁴the large bowl with 12 bulls under it;

⁴⁵the pots, shovels, small bowls and all the dishes for the Temple of the Lord.

Huram made everything King Solomon wanted. They were all made from polished bronze. ⁴⁶The king ordered these things to be made near the Jordan River between Succoth and Zarethan. They were made by melting and pouring bronze into clay molds. ⁴⁷Solomon never weighed the bronze used to make these things. There was too much to weigh. So the total weight of all the bronze was never known.

⁴⁸Solomon also commanded that many things be made of gold for the Temple:

the golden altar;

the golden table which held the bread that shows God's people are in his presence;

⁴⁹the lampstands of pure gold (five on the right side and

five on the left side in front of the Most Holy Place);

the gold flowers, lamps and tongs;

⁵⁰the pure gold bowls, wick trimmers, small bowls, pans and dishes used to carry coals;

the hinges for the doors of the Most Holy Place and the main room of the Temple.

⁵¹So the work King Solomon did for the Temple of the Lord was finished. David, Solomon's father, had saved silver, gold and other articles for the Temple. So Solomon brought these things into the Temple. And he put them into the treasuries of the Temple of the Lord.

The Holy Box Is Brought into the Temple

8 Then King Solomon called for all the leaders of Israel to come to him in Jerusalem. He called for the older leaders, the heads of the tribes^d and the leaders of the families. He wanted them to bring the Box^d of the Agreement with the Lord from the older part of the city. ²So all the men of Israel came together with King Solomon. This was during a festival in the month of Ethanim. That is the seventh month.

³All of the older leaders of Israel arrived. Then the priests took up the Holy Box. ⁴They carried the Holy Box of the Lord, the Meeting Tent^d and the holy things in it. The Levites helped the priests carry these things. ⁵King Solomon and all the people of Israel gathered before the Box of the Agreement. They sacrificed so many sheep and cattle no one could count them all. ⁶Then the priests put the Box of the Agreement with the Lord in its right place. This was inside the Most Holy Place in the Temple.^d The Box of the Agreement was put under the wings of the golden creatures. ⁷The wings of the creatures were spread out over the place of the Holy Box. So

they covered it and its carrying poles. [8]The carrying poles were very long. Anyone standing in the Holy Place in front of the Most Holy Place could see the ends of the poles. But no one could see them from outside the Holy Place. The poles are still there today. [9]The only things inside the Holy Box were two stone tablets.[n] Moses had put them in the Holy Box at Mount Sinai. That was where the Lord made his agreement with the Israelites after they came out of Egypt.

[10]When the priests left the Holy Place, the cloud filled the Temple of the Lord. [11]The priests could not continue their work. This was because the Temple was filled with the glory of the Lord.

Solomon Speaks to the People

[12]Then Solomon said, "The Lord said he would live in a dark cloud. [13]Lord, I have truly built a wonderful Temple[d] for you. It is a place for you to live forever."

[14]While all the people of Israel were standing there, King Solomon turned to them and blessed them.

[15]Then he prayed: "Praise the Lord, the God of Israel. He himself has done what he promised to my father David. The Lord told my father, [16]'I brought my people Israel out of Egypt. But I have not yet chosen a city in any tribe[d] of Israel where a temple will be built for worshiping me. But I have chosen David to rule over my people Israel.'

[17]"My father David wanted to build a temple for worshiping the Lord, the God of Israel. [18]But the Lord said to my father David, 'I know you want to build a temple for worshiping me. And this is good. [19]But you are not the one to build the temple. It will be your son, who comes from your own body. He is the one who will build my temple.'

[20]"So the Lord has kept the promise that he gave. I am the king now in place of David my father. Now I rule Israel as the Lord promised. And I have built

the Temple for worshiping the Lord, the God of Israel. [21]I have made a place in the Temple for the Holy Box. Inside that Box is the agreement the Lord made with our ancestors. He made that agreement when he brought them out of Egypt."

Solomon's Prayer

[22]Then Solomon stood facing the Lord's altar. All of the people of Israel were standing behind him. He spread out his hands and looked toward the sky. [23]He said:

"Lord, God of Israel, there is no god like you. There is no god like you in heaven above or on the earth below. You make agreements with your people because you love them. And you keep your agreements with those who truly follow you. [24]You have kept the promise you made to your servant David, my father. You made that promise with your own mouth. And with your great power you have made it come true today. [25]Now Lord, God of Israel, keep the other promises you made to your servant David, my father. You said, 'Your sons must be careful to obey me as you have obeyed me. If they do this, there will always be someone from your family ruling Israel.' [26]Again, Lord, God of Israel, I ask you. Please continue to keep that promise you made to my father.

[27]"But, God, can you really live here on the earth? Even the sky and the highest place in heaven cannot contain you. Certainly this house which I have built cannot contain you either. [28]But please listen to my prayer and my request. I am your servant, and you are the Lord my God. Hear this prayer I am praying to you today. [29]In the past you said, 'I will be worshiped there.' So please watch over this Temple[d] night and day. Hear the prayer I pray to you here. [30]Hear my prayers and the prayers of your people Israel. Please hear us when we pray facing this place. Hear us from

[n]**stone tablets**   They were the two tablets on which God wrote the Ten Commandments.

your home in heaven. And when you hear us, forgive us.

³¹"If a person does something wrong against someone else, he will be brought to the altar in this Temple. If he swears an oath that he is not guilty, ³²then hear in heaven. Judge the man. Punish the guilty person for what he has done. And declare that the innocent person is not guilty.

³³"Sometimes your people of Israel will sin against you. Because of this their enemies will defeat them. Then the people will come back to you and praise you. They will pray to you in this Temple. ³⁴Please hear them in heaven. Forgive the sins of your people Israel. Allow them to have their land again. This is the land you gave to their ancestors.

³⁵"Sometimes when they sin against you, you will stop the rain from falling on their land. Then they will pray, facing this place. They will praise you. They will stop sinning when you make them suffer. ³⁶When this happens, please hear their prayer in heaven. Then forgive the sins of your servant. And forgive the sins of the people of Israel. Teach them to do what is right. Then please send rain to this land you gave them.

³⁷"At times the land will become so dry that no food will grow. Or, a great sickness will spread among the people. Sometimes all the crops will be destroyed by locusts*d* or grasshoppers. Your people will be attacked in their cities by their enemies. Your people will become sick. ³⁸When any of these things happen, the people will become truly sorry. If anyone of your people Israel spreads his hands in prayer toward this Temple, ³⁹please hear his prayer. Hear it from your home in heaven. Then forgive the people and help them. Only you know what people are really thinking. So judge each person, and do to him what is right. ⁴⁰Do this so your people will respect you all the time they live in this land. This is the land you gave to our ancestors.

⁴¹⁻⁴²"People who are not Israelites, who come from other lands, will hear about your greatness and power. They will come from far away to pray at this Temple. ⁴³Please hear their prayers from your home in heaven. Please do whatever they ask you. Then people everywhere will know you and respect you, as your people in Israel do. Then everyone will know I built this Temple for worship to you.

⁴⁴"Sometimes you will command your people to go and fight against their enemies. Then your people will pray to you facing this city which you have chosen. They will pray facing the Temple I have built for your worship. ⁴⁵When they pray, hear their prayers from your home in heaven. Then help them.

⁴⁶"Everyone sins. So your people will also sin against you. And you will become angry with your people. You will let their enemies defeat them. Their enemies will make them prisoners and carry them away to their own countries. ⁴⁷Your people might be sorry for their sins when they are held as prisoners in another country. Perhaps they will be sorry and pray to you in the land where they are held as prisoners. They might say, 'We have sinned and done wrong.' ⁴⁸They may truly turn back to you in the land of their enemies. Perhaps they will pray to you, facing this land you gave their fathers. They may pray to you, facing this city you have chosen. They may face this Temple I have built for your worship. ⁴⁹If they do, then please hear them from your home in heaven. Hear their prayers and do what is right. ⁵⁰Forgive your people of all their sins. And forgive them for turning against you. Make those who have taken them as prisoners show them mercy. ⁵¹Remember that they are your people. Remember that you brought them out of Egypt. It was as if you pulled them out of a blazing furnace!

⁵²"Please give your attention to my prayers. And please give your attention

to the prayers of your people Israel. Listen to their prayers anytime they ask you for help. ⁵³You chose them from all the nations on earth to be your very own people. This is what you promised through Moses your servant. You promised it when you brought our ancestors out of Egypt, Lord God."

prayer. I pray that he will help his servant and his people Israel. I pray he will help us every day as we need it. ⁶⁰Then all the people of the world will know the Lord is the only true God. ⁶¹So you must fully obey the Lord our

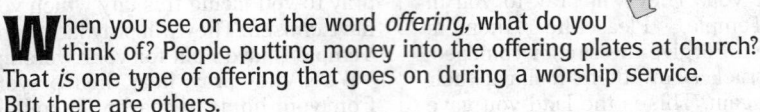

Worship
1 KINGS 8:62-66

When you see or hear the word *offering*, what do you think of? People putting money into the offering plates at church? That *is* one type of offering that goes on during a worship service. But there are others.

Did you know that other things you do in the service can also be an offering to God? Do you sing the songs or just mumble along? Do you pray sincerely, or just close your eyes and daydream? Do you pay attention and try to learn, or do you mess around with your friends? In what ways have you let God know that you're happy just to be in his presence?

Read 1 Kings 8:62-66 and see what a spectacular offering Solomon and the people gave to God as they dedicated the Temple. You probably can't match that, but you can still please God with *your* "offerings" throughout the service . . . if you want to!

To learn more about worship, zoom to page 656.

⁵⁴Solomon prayed this prayer to the Lord. He had been kneeling in front of the altar. And his arms had been raised toward heaven. When Solomon finished praying, he stood up. ⁵⁵Then, in a loud voice, he blessed all the people of Israel. Solomon said: ⁵⁶"Praise the Lord! He promised he would give rest to his people Israel. And he has given us rest! The Lord has kept all the good promises he gave through his servant Moses. ⁵⁷I ask that the Lord our God be with us. May he be with us as he was with our ancestors. May he never leave us. ⁵⁸May he cause us to turn to him and follow him. May we obey all the laws and commands he gave our ancestors. ⁵⁹I ask that the Lord our God always remember this

God. You must follow all his laws and commands. You must continue to obey in the future as you do now."

Sacrifices Are Offered

⁶²Then King Solomon and all Israel with him offered sacrifices to the Lord. ⁶³Solomon killed 22,000 cattle and 120,000 sheep. These were fellowship offerings. In this way the king and the Israelites showed they had given the Temple*ᵈ* to the Lord.

⁶⁴Also that day King Solomon made the courtyard before the Temple holy. He offered whole burnt sacrifices and grain offerings. He also offered the fat from the fellowship offerings. He had to make these offerings in the courtyard. This was because the bronze

altar before the Lord was too small. It could not hold all the offerings.

65So King Solomon and all the people of Israel also celebrated the other festival that came at that time. People came from as far away as Lebo Hamath in the north. And they came from as far as the brook of Egypt in the south. A great many people were there. They ate, drank and rejoiced before the Lord for a total of 14 days. 66On the following day Solomon sent the people home. So they blessed the king and went home. They were happy because of all the good things the Lord had done for his servant David and for his people, Israel.

The Lord Appears to Solomon Again

9 So Solomon finished building the Temple*d* of the Lord and his royal palace. Solomon finished building everything he wanted to build. 2Then the Lord appeared to him again. This was just as he had done before, in Gibeon. 3The Lord said to him: "I have heard your prayer. I have heard what you asked me to do. You built this Temple. And I have made it a holy place. So I will be worshiped there forever. I will watch over it and protect it always.

4"But you must serve me as your father David did. He was fair and sincere. You must obey my laws and do everything I command. 5If you do these things, I will allow your family to rule Israel forever. I made this promise to your father David. I told him that someone from his family would always be king over Israel.

6"But you and your children must follow me. You must obey the laws and commands I have given you. You must not go off to serve or worship other gods. 7If you do, I will force Israel to leave the land I have given them. I made the Temple holy for people to worship me there. But if you don't obey me, I will tear it down. Then Israel will become a bad example, a joke, to other people. 8If the Temple is destroyed, everyone who sees it will be shocked. They will make fun of you and ask, 'Why did the Lord do this? Why did he do this terrible thing to this land and this Temple?' 9Other people will answer, 'This happened because they left the Lord their God. He brought their ancestors out of Egypt. But they decided to follow other gods. They worshiped and served those gods. That is why the Lord brought all this disaster to them.'"

Solomon's Other Activities

10By the end of 20 years, King Solomon had built the Temple*d* of the Lord. And he had built the royal palace. 11At that time King Solomon gave 20 towns in Galilee to Hiram king of Tyre. Solomon did this because Hiram had helped with the buildings. Hiram had given him all the cedar, pine and gold he wanted. 12So Hiram traveled from Tyre to see the towns Solomon had given him. When Hiram saw them, he was not pleased. 13He asked, "What are these towns you have given me, my brother?" So he named that land the Land of Cabul.*n* And it is still called that today. 14Hiram had sent to King Solomon about 9,000 pounds of gold.

15King Solomon had forced slaves to build the Temple and the palace. Then he had them fill in the land on the east side of the city. And he had them build the wall around Jerusalem. He also had them rebuild the cities of Hazor, Megiddo and Gezer. 16(In the past the king of Egypt had attacked Gezer and captured it. He had burned it and killed the Canaanites who lived there. Then he gave it to his daughter as a wedding present. His daughter married Solomon. 17So Solomon rebuilt it.) He also built the cities of Lower Beth Horon, 18Baalath and Tadmor, which is in the Judean desert. 19King Solomon also built cities where he

*n***Cabul** This name sounds like the Hebrew word for "worthless."

could store grain and supplies. And he built cities for his chariots and chariot soldiers. Solomon built whatever he wanted in Jerusalem, Lebanon and everywhere he ruled.

20There were people in the land who were not Israelites. There were some Amorites, Hittites, Perizzites, Hivites and Jebusites. 21The Israelites had not been able to destroy them from the land. So Solomon forced them to work for him as slaves. And they are still slaves today. 22But Solomon did not force any Israelites to be his slaves. The Israelites were his soldiers, government leaders, officers, captains and chariot commanders and drivers.

23There were 550 supervisors over Solomon's projects. They were supervisors over the men who did the work.

24The daughter of the king of Egypt moved from the old part of Jerusalem to the palace. This was the palace Solomon had built for her. Then Solomon filled in the land on the east side of the city.

25Three times each year Solomon offered whole burnt offerings and fellowship offerings on the altar. This is the altar he had built for the Lord. Solomon also burned incense[d] before the Lord. So he finished the work on the Temple.

26Solomon also built ships at Ezion Geber. This town is near Elath. It is on the shore of the Gulf of Aqaba, in the land of Edom. 27King Hiram had sailors who knew much about the sea. So he sent them to serve in Solomon's ships with Solomon's men. 28Solomon's ships sailed to Ophir. From there they brought back about 32,000 pounds of gold to King Solomon.

The Queen of Sheba Visits Solomon

10 Now the queen of Sheba heard about Solomon's fame. So she came to test him with hard questions. 2She traveled to Jerusalem with a very large group of servants. There were many camels carrying spices, jewels and much gold. She came to Solomon and talked with him about all that she had in mind. 3Solomon answered all her questions. Nothing was too hard for him to explain to her. 4The queen of Sheba learned that Solomon was very wise. She saw the palace he had built. 5She saw his many officers and the food on his table. She saw the palace servants and their good clothes. She was shown the servants who served him at feasts. And she was shown the whole burnt offerings he made in the Temple[d] of the Lord. All these things amazed her.

6So she said to King Solomon, "I heard in my own country about your achievements and wisdom. And all of it is true. 7I could not believe it then. But now I have come and seen it with my own eyes. I was not told even half of it! Your wisdom and wealth are much greater than I had heard. 8Your men and officers are very lucky! In always serving you, they are able to hear your wisdom! 9Praise the Lord your God! He was pleased to make you king of Israel. The Lord has constant love for Israel. So he made you king to keep justice and to rule fairly."

10Then the queen of Sheba gave the king about 9,000 pounds of gold. She also gave him many spices and jewels. No one since that time has brought more spices into Israel than the queen of Sheba gave King Solomon.

11(Hiram's ships brought gold from Ophir. They also brought from there very much juniper wood and jewels. 12Solomon used the juniper wood to build supports for the Temple of the Lord and the palace. He also used it to make harps and lyres[d] for the musicians. Such fine juniper wood has not been brought in or seen since that time.)

13King Solomon gave the queen of Sheba many gifts. He gave her gifts that a king would give to another ruler. Then he gave her whatever else she wanted and asked for. After this, she and her servants went back to her own country.

Solomon's Wealth

[14] Every year King Solomon received about 50,000 pounds of gold. [15] Besides that he also received gold from the traders and merchants. And he received gold from the kings of Arabia and governors of the land.

[21] All of Solomon's drinking cups were made of gold. All of the dishes in the Palace of the Forest of Lebanon were pure gold. Nothing was made from silver. In Solomon's time people did not think silver was valuable.

[22] King Solomon also had many trading ships at sea, along with Hiram's ships. Every three years the ships returned. They brought back gold, silver, ivory, apes and baboons.

Good Kings and Bad Kings

SOLOMON • 1 KINGS 11:1-13

David's son Solomon had lots of privileges. He was a prince in Israel and was very rich. His father had made peace with all of Israel's enemies, and he was supposed to be Israel's next king. David had followed God and worshiped him. Solomon knew that in order to be a good king he needed to follow God too. Solomon started out being a good king, but then he married some foreign women who worshiped other gods. Solomon started worshiping those gods too. He began to sin and to do evil things.

It is important to follow God always and to have friends (and eventually a husband or wife) who follow him too. Do you have friends who love God, or do your friends try to make you do bad things?

To meet a king who should have taken good advice, fly to page 420.

[16] King Solomon made 200 large shields of hammered gold. Each shield contained about seven and one-half pounds of gold. [17] He also made 300 smaller shields of hammered gold. They each contained about three and three-fourths pounds of gold. The king put them in the Palace of the Forest of Lebanon.

[18] Then King Solomon built a large throne of ivory. And he covered it with pure gold. [19] There were six steps leading up to the throne. The back of the throne was round at the top. There were armrests on both sides of the chair. And beside each armrest was a statue of a lion. [20] Twelve lions stood on the six steps. There was one lion at each end of each step. Nothing like this had ever been made for any other

[23] So Solomon had more riches and wisdom than all the other kings on earth. [24] People everywhere wanted to see King Solomon. They wanted to hear the wisdom God had given him. [25] Every year everyone who came brought a gift. They brought things made of gold and silver, along with clothes, weapons, spices, horses and mules.

[26] So Solomon had many chariots and horses. He had 1,400 chariots and 12,000 chariot soldiers. He kept some in special cities for the chariots. And he kept some with him in Jerusalem. [27] In Jerusalem silver was as common as stones while Solomon was king. Cedar trees were as common as the fig trees growing on the mountain slopes. [28] Solomon brought in horses

from Egypt and Kue. His traders bought them in Kue and brought them to Israel. [29]A chariot from Egypt cost about 15 pounds of silver. And a horse cost about 3¾ pounds of silver. The traders also sold horses and chariots to the kings of the Hittites and the Arameans.

Solomon's Many Wives

11 But King Solomon loved many women who were not from Israel. He loved the daughter of the king of Egypt. He also loved women of the Moabites, Ammonites, Edomites, Sidonians and Hittites. [2]The Lord had told the Israelites, "You must not marry people of other nations. If you do, they will cause you to follow their gods." But Solomon fell in love with these women. [3]He had 700 wives who were from royal families. He also had 300 slave women[d] who gave birth to his children. His wives caused him to turn away from God. [4]As Solomon grew old, his wives caused him to follow other gods. He did not follow the Lord completely as his father David had done. [5]Solomon worshiped Ashtoreth,[d] the goddess of the people of Sidon. And he worshiped Molech,[d] the hated god of the Ammonites. [6]So Solomon did what the Lord said was wrong. He did not follow the Lord completely as his father David had done.

[7]On a hill east of Jerusalem, Solomon built two places for worship. He built a place to worship Chemosh,[d] the hated god of the Moabites. And he built a place to worship Molech, the hated god of the Ammonites. [8]Solomon did the same thing for all of his foreign wives. So they burned incense[d] and gave sacrifices to their gods.

[9]The Lord had appeared to Solomon twice. But Solomon turned away from following the Lord, the God of Israel. So the Lord was angry with him. [10]The Lord had commanded Solomon not to follow other gods. But Solomon did not obey the Lord's command. [11]So the Lord said to Solomon, "You have chosen to break your agreement with me. You have not obeyed my commands. So I promise I will tear your kingdom away from you. I will give it to one of your officers. [12]But I will not take it away while you are alive. This is because of my love for your father David. I will tear it away from your son when he becomes king. [13]But I will not tear away all the kingdom from him. I will leave him one tribe[d] to rule. I will do this because of David, my servant. And I will do it because of Jerusalem, the city I have chosen."

Solomon's Enemies

[14]Now Hadad was a member of the family of the king of Edom. And the Lord caused Hadad the Edomite to become Solomon's enemy. [15]Earlier, David had defeated Edom. Joab, the commander of David's army, went into Edom to bury the dead. While he was there, he killed all the males. [16]Joab and all the Israelites stayed in Edom for six months. During that time they killed every male in Edom. [17]But at that time Hadad was only a young boy. So he ran away to Egypt with some of his father's officers. [18]They left Midian and went to Paran. In Paran other men joined them. Then they all went to Egypt to see the king. He gave Hadad a house, some land and food to eat.

[19]The king liked Hadad so much he gave Hadad a wife. She was the sister of Tahpenes, the king's wife. [20]They had a son named Genubath. Queen Tahpenes allowed him to grow up in the royal palace. So he grew up with the king's own children.

[21]While he was in Egypt, Hadad heard that David had died. He also heard that Joab, the commander of the army, was dead. So Hadad said to the king, "Let me go home. Let me return to my own country."

[22]But the king said, "Why do you want to go back to your own country? What haven't I given you here?"

Hadad answered, "Nothing. But please, let me go."

²³God also caused another man to be an enemy to Solomon. This man was Rezon son of Eliada. Rezon had run away from his master, Hadadezer king of Zobah. ²⁴After David defeated the army of Zobah, Rezon gathered some men. He became the leader of a small army. They went to Damascus and settled there. And Rezon became king of Damascus. ²⁵Rezon ruled Aram, and he hated Israel. So he was an enemy of Israel all the time Solomon was alive. Rezon and Hadad caused some trouble for Israel.

²⁶Jeroboam son of Nebat was one of Solomon's officers. Jeroboam was one of the Ephraimite people. He was from the town of Zeredah. His mother was a widow named Zeruah. He turned against the king.

²⁷This is the story of how Jeroboam turned against the king. Solomon was filling in the land on the east side of Jerusalem. He was also repairing the wall of Jerusalem. It was the city of David, his ancestor. ²⁸Jeroboam was a capable man. Solomon saw that this young man was a good worker. So Solomon put him over all the workers from the tribes*d* of Ephraim and Manasseh.

²⁹One day Jeroboam was leaving Jerusalem. Ahijah, the prophet*d* from Shiloh, met him on the road. Ahijah was wearing a new coat. The two men were alone out in the country. ³⁰Ahijah took his new coat and tore it into 12 pieces. ³¹Then he said to Jeroboam, "Take 10 pieces of this coat for yourself. The Lord, the God of Israel, says: 'I will tear the kingdom away from Solomon. Then I will give you 10 tribes. ³²But I will allow the family of David to control 1 tribe. I will do this for my servant David and for Jerusalem. Jerusalem is the city I have chosen from all the tribes of Israel. ³³I will do this because Solomon has stopped following me. He worships the Sidonian god Ashtoreth*d* and the Moabite god Chemosh.*d* He also worships Molech,*d* the Ammonite god. Solomon has not

obeyed me. He has not done what I said is right. He has not obeyed my laws and commands. He is not living the way his father David lived.

³⁴"'But I will not take all the kingdom away from Solomon. I will let him rule all his life. I will do this because of my servant David. I chose David, and he obeyed all my commands and laws. ³⁵But I will take the kingdom away from his son. Jeroboam, I will allow you to rule over the 10 tribes. ³⁶I will allow Solomon's son to continue to rule over 1 tribe. I will do this so that David, my servant, will always have a king before me in Jerusalem. It is the city where I chose to be worshiped. ³⁷But I will make you rule over everything you want. You will rule over all of Israel. ³⁸I will always be with you if you do what I say is right. You must obey all my commands. If you obey my laws and commands as David did, I will be with you. I will make your family a family of kings, as I did for David. I will give Israel to you. ³⁹I will punish David's children because of this. But I will not punish them forever.'"

Solomon's Death

⁴⁰Solomon tried to kill Jeroboam. But Jeroboam ran away to Egypt. He went to Shishak king of Egypt. And Jeroboam stayed there until Solomon died.

⁴¹Everything else Solomon did is written down. He showed much wisdom. It is written in the book of the history of Solomon. ⁴²Solomon ruled in Jerusalem over all Israel for 40 years. ⁴³Then he died and was buried in Jerusalem, the city of David, his father. And his son Rehoboam became king after him.

Israel Turns Against Rehoboam

12 Rehoboam went to Shechem because all the Israelites had gone there to make him king. ²Jeroboam son of Nebat was still in Egypt. He had gone there to escape from Solomon. When Jeroboam heard about

Rehoboam being made king, Jeroboam returned from Egypt. ³So the people sent for him. Then he and the people went to Rehoboam. They said to Rehoboam, ⁴"Your father forced us to work very hard. Now, make it easier for us. Don't make us work as hard as your father did. Then we will serve you."

said, "The people said, 'Don't make us work as hard as your father did.' How do you think I should answer them? What is your advice?"

¹⁰The young men answered, "Those people came to you and said, 'Your father forced us to work very hard. Now make our work easier.' So you should tell them, 'My little finger is bigger than my father's whole body. ¹¹My father forced you to work hard. But I will make you work even harder!

Good Kings and Bad Kings
REHOBOAM • 1 KINGS 12:1-17

Rehoboam watched his father, Solomon, make mistakes. So he should have realized that if he wanted to succeed, he needed to follow God. But Rehoboam didn't follow God, nor did he know how to get good advice. At the very beginning of his reign as king, he had a choice to make. The older men advised him to be kind and understanding to people. All his young friends advised him to be tough. Rehoboam followed his young friends' advice, so the people got angry with him and divided the kingdom.

Wise people get advice and then know which advice is best. It's good to listen to people who are older than you, rather than just listen to friends your own age. Older people have experience that helps them know what is best.

To meet a king who should have chosen better friends, fly to page 537.

⁵Rehoboam answered, "Come back to me in three days. Then I will answer you." So the people left.

⁶Some of the older leaders had helped Solomon make decisions during his lifetime. So King Rehoboam asked them what he should do. He said, "How do you think I should answer these people?"

⁷They answered, "You should be like a servant to them today. Serve them, and give them a kind answer. If you do, they will serve you always."

⁸But Rehoboam did not listen to this advice. He asked the young men who had grown up with him. They advised him in making decisions. ⁹Rehoboam

My father beat you with whips. But I will beat you with whips that have sharp points.'"

¹²Rehoboam had told the people, "Come back to me in three days." So after three days all the people returned to Rehoboam. ¹³At that time King Rehoboam spoke cruel words to them. He did not listen to the advice that the older leaders had given him. ¹⁴He did what the young men had told him to do. Rehoboam said, "My father forced you to work hard. So I will give you even more work. My father beat you with whips. But I will beat you with whips that have sharp points." ¹⁵So the king did not do what the people

wanted. The Lord caused this to happen. He did this to keep the promise he had made to Jeroboam son of Nebat. He had made this promise through Ahijah, the prophet[d] from Shiloh.

16All the people of Israel saw that the new king refused to listen to them. So they said to the king,

"We have no share in David!
We have no part in the son of Jesse!
People of Israel, let's go to our own homes!
Let David's son rule his own people!"

So the Israelites went home. 17But Rehoboam still ruled over the Israelites who lived in the towns of Judah.

18Adoniram was in charge of the people who were forced to work. King Rehoboam sent him to the people. But they threw stones at him until he died. But King Rehoboam ran to his chariot and escaped to Jerusalem. 19Since then, Israel has been against the family of David.

20All the Israelites heard that Jeroboam had returned. So they called him to a meeting. And they made him king over all Israel. But the tribe[d] of Judah continued to follow the family of David.

21When Rehoboam arrived in Jerusalem, he gathered the tribes of Judah and Benjamin. This was an army of 180,000 men. Rehoboam wanted to fight against the people of Israel. He wanted to take back his kingdom.

22But God spoke his word to Shemaiah, a man of God. The Lord said, 23"Talk to Solomon's son Rehoboam, the king of Judah. Talk also to all the people of Judah and Benjamin and to the rest of the people. 24Say to them, 'The Lord says you must not go to war against your brothers, the Israelites. Every one of you should go home. I made all these things happen!'" So the men in Rehoboam's army obeyed the Lord's command. They all went home as the Lord had commanded.

25Then Jeroboam made Shechem a very strong city. It is in the mountains of Ephraim. And Jeroboam lived there. He also went to the city of Peniel and made it stronger.

Jeroboam Builds Golden Calves

26Jeroboam said to himself, "The kingdom will probably go back to David's family. 27The people will continue going to the Temple[d] of the Lord in Jerusalem. If they do, they will want to be ruled again by Rehoboam. Then they will kill me and follow Rehoboam king of Judah.

28King Jeroboam asked his men for advice. So he made two golden calves. He said to the people, "It is too hard for you to go to Jerusalem to worship. Israel, here are your gods who brought you out of Egypt." 29King Jeroboam put one golden calf in the city of Bethel. And he put the other in the city of Dan. 30And this became a very great sin. The people traveled as far as Dan to worship the calf there.

31Jeroboam built temples on the places of worship. He chose priests from all the people. (He did not choose priests only from the tribe of Levi.) 32And he started a new festival. It was the fifteenth day of the eighth month. This was like the festival in Judah. During that time the king offered sacrifices on the altar. He offered sacrifices to the calves in Bethel he had made. He also chose priests in Bethel to serve at the places of worship he had made. 33So Jeroboam chose his own time for a festival for the Israelites. It was the fifteenth day of the eighth month. During that time he offered sacrifices on the altar he had built in Bethel. So he set up a festival for the Israelites. And he offered sacrifices on the altar.

The Man of God Speaks Against Bethel

13 The Lord commanded a man of God from Judah to go to Bethel. When he arrived, Jeroboam was standing by the altar to offer a sacrifice. ²The Lord had commanded the man of God to speak against the altar. The man said, "Altar, the Lord says to you: 'David's family will have a son named Josiah. He will kill the priests of the places of worship. They now make their sacrifices on you. But Josiah will sacrifice those priests on you. Human bones will be burned on you.'" ³The man of God gave proof that these things would happen. He said, "This is God's sign that this will happen. This altar will break apart. And the ashes on it will fall onto the ground."

⁴King Jeroboam heard what the man of God said about the altar in Bethel. So Jeroboam raised his hand from the altar and pointed at the man. "Capture him!" he said. But when the king said this, his arm became paralyzed. He could not move it. ⁵Also, the altar broke into pieces. All its ashes fell onto the ground. This was the sign the Lord had told the man of God to give.

⁶Then the king said to the man of God, "Please pray to the Lord your God for me. Ask him to heal my arm."

So the man of God prayed to the Lord. And the king's arm was healed. It became as it was before.

⁷Then the king said to the man of God, "Please come home and eat with me. I will give you a gift."

⁸But the man of God answered the king, "I will not go home with you! Even if you gave me half of your kingdom, I would not go! I will not eat or drink anything in this place. ⁹The Lord commanded me not to eat or drink anything. He also commanded me not to return on the same road by which I came." ¹⁰So he traveled on a different road. He did not return on the same road by which he had come to Bethel.

¹¹Now there was an old prophet*ᵈ* living in Bethel. His sons came and told him what the man of God had done there that day. They told their father what he had said to King Jeroboam. ¹²The father asked, "Which road did he use when he left?" So his sons showed him which road the man of God from Judah had taken. ¹³The prophet told his sons to put a saddle on his donkey. So they saddled the donkey, and he left.

¹⁴He went after the man of God. He found the man sitting under an oak tree. The prophet asked, "Are you the man of God who came from Judah?"

The man answered, "Yes, I am."

¹⁵So the prophet said, "Please come home and eat with me."

¹⁶But the man of God answered, "I can't go home with you. I can't eat or drink with you in this place. ¹⁷The Lord said to me, 'You must not eat or drink anything there. And you must not return on the same road by which you came.'"

¹⁸Then the old prophet said, "But I also am a prophet like you." Then he told a lie. He said, "An angel from the Lord came to me. He told me to bring you to my home. He said you should eat and drink with me." ¹⁹So the man of God went to the old prophet's house. And he ate and drank with him there.

²⁰While they were sitting at the table, the Lord spoke his word to the old prophet. ²¹The old prophet cried out to the man of God from Judah. He said, "The Lord said you did not obey him! He said you did not do what the Lord your God commanded you. ²²The Lord commanded you not to eat or drink anything in this place. But you came back and ate and drank. So your body will not be buried in your family grave."

²³The man of God finished eating. Then the prophet put a saddle on his donkey for him. And the man left. ²⁴As he was traveling on the road home, a lion attacked and killed him. His body lay on the road. The donkey and the lion stood near it. ²⁵Some men were traveling on that road. They saw the body and the lion standing near it. So they went to the city where the old prophet lived. And they told what they had seen.

[26]The old prophet who had brought the man of God back heard about what had happened. He said, "It is the man of God who did not obey the Lord's command. So the Lord sent a lion to kill him. The Lord said he would do this."

[27]Then the prophet said to his sons, "Put a saddle on my donkey." So they did. [28]The old prophet went out and found the body lying on the road. The donkey and the lion were still standing near it. The lion had not eaten the body. And it had not hurt the donkey. [29]So the prophet put the body on his donkey. And he carried it back to the city. There he would have a time of sadness for him and bury him. [30]The prophet buried the body in his own family grave. And he was sad for the man of God. He said, "Oh, my brother."

[31]So the prophet buried the body. Then he said to his sons, "When I die, bury me in this same grave. Put my bones next to his. [32]Through him the Lord spoke against the altar at Bethel. And he spoke against the places of worship in the towns of Samaria. And what the Lord spoke through him will certainly come true."

[33]But King Jeroboam did not stop doing evil things. He continued to choose priests for the places of worship from all the people. Anyone who wanted to be a priest for the places of worship was allowed. [34]In this way the kingdom of Jeroboam sinned. And that sin caused its ruin and destruction from the earth.

Jeroboam's Son Dies

14 At that time Jeroboam's son Abijah became very sick. [2]So Jeroboam said to his wife, "Go to Shiloh. Go to see the prophet[d] Ahijah. He is the one who said I would become king of Israel. But dress yourself so people won't know you are my wife. [3]Give the prophet ten loaves of bread, some cakes and a jar of honey. Then ask him what will happen to our son. And he will tell you." [4]So the king's wife did as he said. She went to Ahijah's home in Shiloh.

Now Ahijah was very old and had become blind. [5]But the Lord had said to him, "Jeroboam's son is sick. So Jeroboam's wife is coming to ask you about him. When she arrives, she will pretend to be someone else." Then the Lord told Ahijah what to say.

[6]When Ahijah heard her walking to the door, he said, "Come in, wife of Jeroboam. Why are you pretending to be someone else? I have bad news for you. [7]Go back and tell Jeroboam that this is what the Lord, the God of Israel, says: 'Jeroboam, I chose you from among all the people of Israel. I made you the leader of my people. [8]I took the kingdom away from David's family. And I gave it to you. But you are not like my servant David. He always obeyed my commands. He followed me with all his heart. He did only the things I said were right. [9]But you have done more evil things than anyone who ruled before you. You have quit following me. You have made other gods and idols of metal. This has made me very angry. [10]So I will bring disaster to the family of Jeroboam. I will kill all of the men in your family, both slaves and free men. I will destroy your family as completely as fire burns up manure. [11]Anyone from your family who dies in the city will be eaten by dogs. And anyone from your family who dies in the fields will be eaten by the birds. The Lord has spoken!'"

[12]Then Ahijah said to Jeroboam's wife, "Now go home. When you enter your city gate, your son will die. [13]All Israel will be sad for him and bury him. He will be the only one of Jeroboam's family who will be buried. This is because he is the only one in Jeroboam's family who pleased the Lord, the God of Israel.

[14]"The Lord will put a new king over Israel. That king will destroy Jeroboam's family. This will happen soon. [15]Then the Lord will punish Israel. The people of Israel will be like grass

moving in the water. The Lord will pull up Israel from this good land. This is the land he gave their ancestors. But he will scatter Israel beyond the Euphrates River. This will happen because the Lord is angry with the people. They made him angry when they made idols to worship Asherah.[d] [16]Jeroboam sinned, and then he made the people of Israel sin. So the Lord will let the people of Israel be defeated."

[17]Then Jeroboam's wife traveled back to Tirzah. When she entered her home, the boy died. [18]They buried him. And all Israel had a time of sadness for him. This happened as the Lord said it would. The Lord had said these things through his servant, the prophet Ahijah.

[19]Everything else Jeroboam did is written down. He fought wars and continued to rule the people. It is all written in the book of the history of the kings of Israel. [20]Jeroboam ruled as king for 22 years. Then he died, and his son Nadab became king in his place.

The Death of Rehoboam

[21]Solomon's son Rehoboam was 41 years old when he became king of Judah. His mother was Naamah from the land of Ammon. Rehoboam ruled in Jerusalem for 17 years. (The Lord had chosen that city from all the land of Israel. He chose to be worshiped there.)

[22]The people of Judah did what the Lord said was wrong. The people's sins made the Lord very angry at them. They made the Lord even more angry than their ancestors had done. [23]The people built stone pillars and places to worship false gods and Asherah[d] idols. They built them on every high hill and under every green tree. [24]There were even male prostitutes[d] at the places of worship to the gods. The people who had lived in the land before the Israelites had done many evil things. And God had taken the land away from them. Now the people of Judah were doing the same evil things.

[25]During the fifth year Rehoboam was king, Shishak attacked Jerusalem. Shishak was king of Egypt. [26]He took the treasures from the Temple[d] of the Lord and the king's palace. He took everything, even the gold shields Solomon had made. [27]So King Rehoboam made bronze shields to put in their place. He gave them to the men who were guarding the palace gates. [28]Whenever the king went to the Temple of the Lord, the guards carried the shields. After they were finished, they put the shields back in the guardroom.

[29]Everything else King Rehoboam did is written down. It is in the book of the history of the kings of Judah. [30]Rehoboam and Jeroboam were always fighting a war with each other. [31]Rehoboam died and was buried with his ancestors in Jerusalem. His mother was Naamah from Ammon. And Rehoboam's son Abijah became king in his place.

Abijah King of Judah

15 Abijah became king of Judah. This was during the eighteenth year Jeroboam son of Nebat ruled Israel. [2]And Abijah ruled in Jerusalem for three years. His mother was Maacah daughter of Abishalom. [3]He did all the same sins his father before him had done. Abijah was not faithful to the Lord his God. In this way he was not like David, his great-grandfather. [4]Because the Lord had loved David, the Lord gave Abijah a kingdom in Jerusalem. And the Lord allowed him to have a son to be king after him. The Lord also kept Jerusalem safe. [5]David had always done what the Lord said was right. All his life he had always obeyed the Lord's commands. There was only one time David did not obey the Lord. This was when he sinned against Uriah the Hittite.

[6]Now there was war between Abijah and Jeroboam during Abijah's lifetime. [7]Everything else Abijah did is written down. It is in the book of the history of

the kings of Judah. During the time Abijah ruled, there was war between Abijah and Jeroboam. [8]And Abijah died and was buried in Jerusalem. Abijah's son Asa became king in his place.

Asa King of Judah

[9]During the twentieth year Jeroboam was king of Israel, Asa became king of Judah. [10]Asa ruled in Jerusalem for 41 years. His grandmother's name was Maacah. She was the daughter of Abishalom.

[11]Asa did what the Lord said was right. This was as his ancestor David had done. [12]There were male prostitutes[d] at the places where false gods were worshiped. Asa forced them to leave the country. He also took away the idols that his ancestors had made. [13]His grandmother Maacah had made a terrible Asherah[d] idol. So Asa removed her from being queen. He cut down this idol and burned it in the Kidron Valley. [14]Asa was faithful to the Lord all his life. But he did not destroy the places where false gods were worshiped. [15]Asa and his father had given some things to God. They had given gifts of gold, silver and other objects. Asa put all these things in the Temple.[d]

[16]There was war between Asa and Baasha king of Israel. [17]Baasha fought against Judah. He wanted to stop people from leaving or entering Asa's country, Judah. So he made the city of Ramah very strong.

[18]Then Asa took all the silver and gold from the treasuries of the Temple of the Lord and his own palace. He gave it to his officers. And he sent them to Ben-Hadad king of Aram. (Ben-Hadad was the son of Tabrimmon. And he was the son of Hezion.) Ben-Hadad was ruling in the city of Damascus. [19]Asa sent this message: "My father and your father had a peace agreement. I am sending you a gift of gold and silver. Break your treaty with Baasha king of Israel so that he will leave my land."

[20]Ben-Hadad agreed with King Asa. So he sent his army to fight against the towns of Israel. He defeated the towns of Ijon, Dan and Abel Bethmaacah. And he defeated all the land near Lake Galilee and the area of Naphtali. [21]Baasha heard about these attacks. So he stopped building up Ramah and returned to Tirzah. [22]Then King Asa gave an order to all the people of Judah. Everyone had to help. They carried away all the stones and wood Baasha had been using in Ramah. King Asa used those things to build up Geba and Mizpah. (Geba was in the land of Benjamin.)

[23]Everything else Asa did is written down. His victories and the cities he built are written down. They are in the book of the history of the kings of Judah. When he became old, he got a disease in his feet. [24]Then Asa died. And he was buried with his ancestors in Jerusalem. It was the city of David, his ancestor. Then Jehoshaphat, Asa's son, became king in his place.

Nadab King of Israel

[25]Nadab son of Jeroboam became king of Israel. This was during the second year Asa was king of Judah. And Nadab was king of Israel for two years. [26]He did what the Lord said was wrong. Jeroboam had caused the people of Israel to sin. Nadab sinned in the same way his father Jeroboam had sinned.

[27]Baasha son of Ahijah was from the tribe[d] of Issachar. He made plans to kill Nadab. Nadab and all Israel were attacking the Philistine town of Gibbethon. So Baasha killed Nadab there. [28]This happened during Asa's third year as king of Judah. And Baasha became the next king of Israel.

Baasha King of Israel

[29]As soon as Baasha became king, he killed all of Jeroboam's family. He left no one in Jeroboam's family alive. This happened as the Lord had said it would. The Lord had said this through his servant Ahijah from Shiloh. [30]This

happened because King Jeroboam had sinned very much. And he had caused the people of Israel to sin. Jeroboam had made the Lord, the God of Israel, very angry.

³¹Everything else Nadab did is written down. It is in the book of the history of the kings of Israel. ³²There was war between Asa king of Judah and Baasha king of Israel all the time they were kings.

³³Baasha son of Ahijah became king of Israel. This was during Asa's third year as king of Judah. And Baasha ruled in Tirzah for 24 years. ³⁴But Baasha did what the Lord said was wrong. Jeroboam had caused the people of Israel to sin. And Baasha sinned in the same way Jeroboam had sinned.

16 Then Jehu son of Hanani spoke the word of the Lord against King Baasha. ²The Lord said, "You were nothing. Then I took you and made you a leader over my people Israel. But you have followed the ways of Jeroboam. You have caused my people Israel to sin. Their sins have made me angry. ³So, Baasha, I will destroy you and your family. I will do to you what I did to the family of Jeroboam son of Nebat. ⁴Anyone from your family who dies in the city will be eaten by dogs. And anyone from your family who dies in the fields will be eaten by birds."

⁵Everything else Baasha did and all his victories are written down. They are in the book of the history of the kings of Israel. ⁶So Baasha died and was buried in Tirzah. His son Elah became king in his place.

⁷The Lord spoke his word through the prophet[d] Jehu son of Hanani. The Lord's message was against Baasha and his family. Baasha had done many things the Lord said were wrong. This made the Lord very angry. Baasha did the same things that Jeroboam's family had done before him. The Lord was also angry because Baasha killed all of Jeroboam's family.

Elah King of Israel

⁸Elah son of Baasha became king of Israel. This was during Asa's twenty-sixth year as king of Judah. And Elah ruled in Tirzah for two years.

⁹Zimri was one of Elah's officers. He commanded half of Elah's chariots. But Zimri made plans against Elah.

Elah was in Tirzah, getting drunk at Arza's home. (Arza was the man in charge of the palace at Tirzah.) ¹⁰So Zimri went into Arza's house and killed Elah. This was during Asa's twenty-seventh year as king of Judah. Then Zimri became king of Israel in Elah's place.

Zimri King of Israel

¹¹As soon as Zimri became king, he killed all of Baasha's family. He did not let any man of Baasha's family or friends live. ¹²So Zimri destroyed all of Baasha's family. This happened as the Lord had said it would. The Lord had spoken this against Baasha through the prophet[d] Jehu. ¹³This happened because of all the sins of Baasha and his son Elah. They sinned and caused the people of Israel to sin. They also made the Lord, the God of Israel, angry because they had made worthless idols.

¹⁴Everything else Elah did is written down. It is in the book of the history of the kings of Israel.

¹⁵So Zimri became king of Israel. This was during Asa's twenty-seventh year as king of Judah. Zimri ruled in Tirzah seven days. This is what happened:

The army of Israel was camped near Gibbethon, a Philistine town. ¹⁶The men in the camp heard that Zimri had made secret plans against the king. And they heard that Zimri had killed him. So that day in the camp they made Omri king over Israel. (Omri was commander of the army.) ¹⁷So Omri and all the Israelites left Gibbethon and attacked Tirzah. ¹⁸Zimri saw that the city had been captured. So he went into the palace and set it on fire.

He burned the palace and himself with it. ¹⁹So Zimri died because he had sinned. He did what the Lord said was wrong. Jeroboam had caused the people of Israel to sin. And Zimri sinned in the same way Jeroboam had sinned.

²⁰Everything else Zimri did is written down. It is in the book of the history of the kings of Israel. The story of how Zimri turned against King Elah is also written there.

Israel for 12 years. Six of those years he ruled in the town of Tirzah. ²⁴Omri bought the hill of Samaria from Shemer. He paid about 150 pounds of silver for it. Omri built a city on that hill. And he called it Samaria after the name of its earlier owner, Shemer.

²⁵But Omri did what the Lord said was wrong. He did more evil than all the kings who were before him. ²⁶Jeroboam son of Nebat had caused the people of Israel to sin. And Omri sinned in the same way Jeroboam had sinned. So the Israelites made the Lord, the God of

Plans That Backfired

AHAB • 1 KINGS 16:29–17:1

Ahab was one of the worst kings that Israel ever had! He didn't care about God at all. He prayed to statues of wood and stone, and whenever God sent him a message, he wouldn't even listen.

Ahab had no use for God. He couldn't stand God's messengers (prophets) because they always pointed out how bad he was. Ahab did whatever he wanted, and he planned to get away with it.

However, Ahab's evil deeds did not go unnoticed by God. In fact, God punished him and caused his kingdom to go without rain for many years. This caused all the plants to die. It was a great hardship for all the people. God also put a curse on Ahab's family that would punish them for many years.

The evil in one person's life can cause many people to suffer. This makes us sad, and it makes God sad. Smart people stay away from people like Ahab.

To meet Ahab's wicked wife, Jezebel, fly to page 435.

Omri King of Israel

²¹The people of Israel were divided into two groups. Half of the people wanted Tibni to be king. He was the son of Ginath. The other half of the people wanted Omri. ²²But Omri's followers were stronger than the followers of Tibni son of Ginath. So Tibni died, and Omri became king.

²³Omri became king of Israel. This was during the thirty-first year Asa was king of Judah. And Omri ruled

Israel, very angry. He was angry because they worshiped worthless idols.

²⁷Everything else Omri did and all his successes are written down. They are all in the book of the history of the kings of Israel. ²⁸So Omri died and was buried in Samaria. His son Ahab became king in his place.

Ahab King of Israel

²⁹So Ahab son of Omri became king of Israel. This was during Asa's thirty-eighth year as king of Judah. Ahab

ruled Israel in the town of Samaria for 22 years. [30]Ahab did many things that the Lord said were wrong. He did more evil than any of the kings before him. [31]He sinned in the same ways that Jeroboam son of Nebat had sinned. But he did even worse things. He married Jezebel daughter of Ethbaal. (Ethbaal was king of the city of Sidon.) Then Ahab began to serve Baal[d] and worship him. [32]He built a temple in Samaria for worshiping Baal. And he put an altar there for Baal. [33]Ahab also made an idol for worshiping Asherah.[d] He did more things to make the Lord, the God of Israel, angry than all the other kings before him.

[34]During the time of Ahab, Hiel from Bethel rebuilt the town of Jericho. It cost Hiel the life of Abiram, his oldest son, to begin work on the city. And it cost the life of Segub, his youngest son, to build the city gates. The Lord had said, through Joshua, that this would happen.[n] (Joshua was the son of Nun.)

Elijah Stops the Rain

17 Now Elijah was a prophet[d] from the town of Tishbe in Gilead. Elijah said to King Ahab, "I serve the Lord, the God of Israel. As surely as the Lord lives, I tell you the truth. No rain or dew will fall during the next few years unless I command it."

[2]Then the Lord spoke his word to Elijah: [3]"Leave this place. Go east and hide near Kerith Ravine. It is east of the Jordan River. [4]You may drink from the brook. And I have commanded ravens to bring you food there." [5]So Elijah did what the Lord told him to do. He went to Kerith Ravine, east of the Jordan, and lived there. [6]The birds brought Elijah bread and meat every morning and every evening. And he drank water from the brook.

[7]After a while the brook dried up because there was no rain. [8]Then the Lord spoke his word to Elijah, [9]"Go to Zarephath in Sidon. Live there. I have commanded a widow there to take care of you."

[10]So Elijah went to Zarephath. When he reached the town gate, he saw a widow there. She was gathering wood for a fire. Elijah asked her, "Would you bring me a little water in a cup? I would like to have a drink." [11]As she was going to get his water, Elijah said, "Please bring me a piece of bread, too."

[12]The woman answered, "As surely as the Lord your God lives, I tell you the truth. I have no bread. I have only a handful of flour in a jar. And I have only a little olive oil in a jug. I came here to gather some wood. I will take it home and cook our last meal. My son and I will eat it and then die from hunger."

[13]Elijah said to her, "Don't worry. Go home and cook your food as you have said. But first make a small loaf of bread from the flour you have. Bring it to me. Then cook something for yourself and your son. [14]The Lord, the God of Israel, says, 'That jar of flour will never become empty. The jug will always have oil in it. This will continue until the day the Lord sends rain to the land.'"

[15]So the woman went home. And she did what Elijah told her to do. So Elijah, the woman and her son had enough food every day. [16]The jar of flour and the jug of oil were never empty. This happened just as the Lord, through Elijah, said it would.

Elijah Brings a Boy Back to Life

[17]Some time later the son of the woman who owned the house became sick. He grew worse and worse. Finally he stopped breathing. [18]So the woman said to Elijah, "You are a man of God. What have you done to me? Did you come here to remind me of my sin? Did you come here to kill my son?"

[19]Elijah said to her, "Give me your son." So Elijah took the boy from her and carried him upstairs. Elijah laid

---

[n] **The Lord . . . happen** When Joshua destroyed Jericho, he said whoever rebuilt the city would lose his oldest and youngest sons. See Joshua 6:26.

the boy on the bed in the room where he was staying. [20]Then he prayed to the Lord. He said, "Lord my God, this widow is letting me stay in her house. Why have you done this terrible thing to her? Why have you caused her son to die?" [21]Then Elijah lay on top of the boy three times. Elijah prayed to the Lord, "Lord my God, let this boy live again!"

[22]The Lord answered Elijah's prayer. The boy began breathing again, and he was alive. [23]Elijah carried the boy downstairs. He gave the boy to his mother and said, "See! Your son is alive!"

[24]The woman said to Elijah, "Now I know you really are a man from God. I know that the Lord truly speaks through you!"

Elijah and the Prophets of Baal

18 During the third year without rain, the Lord spoke his word to Elijah. The Lord said, "Go and meet King Ahab. I will soon send rain." [2]So Elijah went to meet Ahab.

By this time there was no food in Samaria. [3]So King Ahab sent for Obadiah. Obadiah was in charge of the king's palace. (Obadiah was a true follower of the Lord. [4]One time Jezebel was killing all the Lord's prophets.[d] So Obadiah took 100 of them and hid them in two caves. He put 50 in one cave and 50 in another cave. And he brought them food and water.) [5]King Ahab said to Obadiah, "Let's look at every spring and valley in the land. Maybe we can find enough grass to keep our horses and mules alive. Then we will not have to kill our animals." [6]So each one chose a part of the country to search. Ahab went in one direction. Obadiah went in another direction.

[7]While Obadiah was walking along, Elijah met him. Obadiah knew who Elijah was. So he bowed down to the ground before Elijah. He said, "Elijah? Is it really you, master?"

[8]Elijah answered, "Yes. Go tell your master the king that I am here."

[9]Then Obadiah said, "If I tell Ahab that, he will kill me! I have done nothing wrong that I should be killed! [10]As surely as the Lord your God lives, the king has looked everywhere for you! He has sent people to every country to look for you. If the ruler said you were not there, that was not enough. Ahab then forced the ruler to swear you could not be found in his country. [11]Now you want me to go to my master and tell him, 'Elijah is here'? [12]The Spirit[d] of the Lord may carry you to some other place after I leave. If I go tell King Ahab you are here, he will come. If he doesn't find you, he will kill me! I have followed the Lord since I was a boy. [13]Haven't you heard what I did? When Jezebel was killing the Lord's prophets, I hid 100 of them. I put 50 prophets in one cave and 50 prophets in another cave. I brought them food and water. [14]Now you want me to go and tell the king you are here. He will kill me!"

[15]Elijah answered, "I serve the Lord of heaven's armies. As surely as the Lord lives, I will stand before Ahab today."

[16]So Obadiah went to Ahab and told him where Elijah was. Then Ahab went to meet Elijah.

[17]When he saw Elijah, he said, "Is it you—the biggest troublemaker in Israel?"

[18]Elijah answered, "I have not caused trouble in Israel. You and your father's family have caused all this trouble. You have not obeyed the Lord's commands. You have followed the Baals.[d] [19]Now tell all Israel to meet me at Mount Carmel. Also bring the 450 prophets of Baal there. And bring the 400 prophets of Asherah,[d] who eat at Jezebel's table."

[20]So Ahab called all the Israelites and those prophets to Mount Carmel. [21]Elijah stood before the people. He said, "How long will you try to serve both Baal and the Lord? If the Lord is the true God, follow him. But if Baal is the true God, follow him!"

But the people said nothing.

[22]Elijah said, "I am the only prophet of the Lord here. But there are 450 prophets of Baal. [23]So bring two bulls. Let the prophets of Baal choose one bull. Let them kill it and cut it into pieces. Then let them put the meat on the wood. But they are not to set fire to it. Then I will do the same with the other bull. And I will put it on the wood. But I will not set fire to it. [24]You prophets of Baal, pray to your god. And I will pray to the Lord. The god who answers the prayer will set fire to his wood. He is the true God."

was no sound. No one answered. They danced around the altar they had built.

[27]At noon Elijah began to make fun of them. He said, "Pray louder! If Baal really is a god, maybe he is thinking. Or maybe he is busy or traveling! Maybe he is sleeping so you will have to wake him!" [28]So the prophets prayed louder. They cut themselves with swords and spears until their blood flowed. (This was the way they worshiped.) [29]The afternoon passed, and the prophets continued to act wildly. They continued until it was time for the evening sacrifice. But no voice was heard. Baal did not answer. No one paid attention.

[30]Then Elijah said to all the people, "Now come to me." So they gathered

Miracles from God
1 KINGS 18:16-46

Do you ever play, "let's pretend" with your friends? It is fun to use your imagination to pretend when you play. But the prophet Elijah had to tell the Israelites to stop pretending about God. They believed that a god made from wood, metal, and stone (an idol) was just as powerful as the true God who created the heavens and the earth.

So, Elijah had a contest with the priests of Baal. Baal was an idol that the Israelites were worshiping. The contest was that whoever's god was real would make fire come down from heaven. Then they could see who was pretending. Of course God won the contest because nothing is more powerful than God. He sent fire down to burn up the sacrifice.

Our God is real and not pretend. He has the power to take care of us if we trust in him.

To find the oil that poured and poured, fly to page 444.

All the people agreed that this was a good idea.

[25]Then Elijah said to the prophets of Baal, "There are many of you. So you go first. Choose a bull and prepare it. Pray to your god, but don't start the fire."

[26]So they took the bull that was given to them and prepared it. They prayed to Baal from morning until noon. They shouted, "Baal, answer us!" But there

around him. Elijah rebuilt the altar of the Lord because it had been torn down. [31]He took 12 stones. He took 1 stone for each of the 12 tribes.[d] These 12 tribes were named for the 12 sons of Jacob. (Jacob was the man the Lord had called Israel.) [32]Elijah used these stones to rebuild the altar in honor of the Lord. Then he dug a small ditch around it. It was big enough to hold about 13 quarts of seed. [33]Elijah put the wood on the altar. He cut the bull into pieces and laid them on the wood. Then he said, "Fill four jars with water. Put the water on the meat and on the wood."

³⁴Then Elijah said, "Do it again." And they did it again.

Then he said, "Do it a third time." And they did it the third time. ³⁵So the water ran off of the altar and filled the ditch.

³⁶It was time for the evening sacrifice. So the prophet Elijah went near the altar. He prayed, "Lord, you are the God of Abraham, Isaac and Israel. I ask you now to prove that you are the God of Israel. And prove that I am your servant. Show these people that you commanded me to do all these things. ³⁷Lord, answer my prayer. Show these people that you, Lord, are God. Then the people will know that you are bringing them back to you."

"**W**hen my dad can't get his charcoal to light, he needs the same kind of lighter fluid that Elijah had! Read about it in 1 Kings 18:1-39."

³⁸Then fire from the Lord came down. It burned the sacrifice, the wood, the stones and the ground around the altar. It also dried up the water in the ditch. ³⁹When all the people saw this, they fell down to the ground. They cried, "The Lord is God! The Lord is God!"

⁴⁰Then Elijah said, "Capture the prophets of Baal! Don't let any of them run away!" So the people captured all the prophets. Then Elijah led them down to Kishon Valley. There he killed all the prophets.

The Rain Comes Again

⁴¹Then Elijah said to Ahab, "Now, go, eat and drink. A heavy rain is coming."

⁴²So King Ahab went to eat and drink. At the same time Elijah climbed to the top of Mount Carmel. There he bent down to the ground with his head between his knees.

⁴³Then Elijah said to his servant, "Go and look toward the sea."

The servant went and looked. He said, "I see nothing."

Elijah told him to go and look again. This happened seven times. ⁴⁴The seventh time, the servant said, "I see a small cloud. It's the size of a man's fist. It's coming from the sea."

Elijah told the servant, "Go to Ahab. Tell him to get his chariot ready and to go home now. If he doesn't leave now, the rain will stop him."

⁴⁵After a short time the sky was covered with dark clouds. The wind began to blow. Then a heavy rain began to fall. Ahab got in his chariot and started back to Jezreel. ⁴⁶The Lord gave his power to Elijah. Elijah tightened his clothes around him. Then he ran ahead of King Ahab all the way to Jezreel.

Elijah at Mount Sinai

19 King Ahab told Jezebel everything Elijah had done. Ahab told her how Elijah had killed all the prophets[d] with a sword. ²So Jezebel sent a messenger to Elijah. Jezebel said, "By this time tomorrow I will kill you. I will kill you as you killed those prophets. If I don't succeed, may the gods punish me terribly."

³When Elijah heard this, he was afraid. So he ran away to save his life. He took his servant with him. When they came to Beersheba in Judah, Elijah left his servant there. ⁴Then Elijah walked for a whole day into the desert. He sat down under a bush and asked to die. Elijah prayed, "I have had enough, Lord. Let me die. I am no better than my ancestors." ⁵Then Elijah lay down under the tree and slept.

Suddenly an angel came to him and touched him. The angel said, "Get up and eat." ⁶Elijah saw near his head a loaf baked over coals and a jar of water. So he ate and drank. Then he went back to sleep.

⁷Later the Lord's angel came to him a second time. The angel touched him and said, "Get up and eat. If you don't, the journey will be too hard for you." ⁸So Elijah got up and ate and drank. The food made him strong enough to walk for 40 days and nights. He walked to Mount Sinai, the mountain of God. ⁹There Elijah went into a cave and stayed all night.

break apart. It broke apart large rocks in front of the Lord. But the Lord was not in the wind. After the wind, there was an earthquake. But the Lord was not in the earthquake. ¹²After the earthquake, there was a fire. But the Lord was not in the fire. After the fire, there was a quiet, gentle voice. ¹³When Elijah heard it, he covered his face with his coat. He went out and stood at the entrance to the cave.

Then a voice said to him, "Elijah! Why are you here?"

¹⁴Elijah answered, "Lord, God of heaven's armies, I have always served you the best I could. But the people of Israel have broken their agreement

Visiting Angels

1 KINGS 19:5-7

Sometimes angels came to serve people. Elijah was a good man who spoke for God and told people what God wanted them to do. He was a prophet. But King Ahab and Queen Jezebel did not like Elijah. They wanted to kill him. So Elijah ran far away. He was so sad and tired that he wanted to die. But God still had work for Elijah to do. Elijah fell asleep, but an angel woke him up and gave him food to eat to make him strong. The angel told Elijah what he must do to continue to serve God. The food gave Elijah strength to travel another forty days!

Elijah did as the angel said and obeyed God. He served as a prophet for many more years. Can you think of ways that you can serve God?

To read about an angel who tamed some lions, fly to page 1039.

Then the Lord spoke his word to him: "Elijah! Why are you here?"

¹⁰Elijah answered, "Lord, God of heaven's armies, I have always served you the best I could. But the people of Israel have broken their agreement with you. They have destroyed your altars. They have killed your prophets with swords. I am the only prophet left. And now they are trying to kill me, too!"

¹¹Then the Lord said to Elijah, "Go. Stand in front of me on the mountain. I will pass by you." Then a very strong wind blew. It caused the mountains to

with you. They have destroyed your altars. They have killed your prophets with swords. I am the only prophet left. And now they are trying to kill me, too."

¹⁵The Lord said to him, "Go back on the road that leads to the desert around Damascus. Enter that city. There pour olive oil on Hazael to make him king over Aram. ¹⁶Then pour oil on Jehu son of Nimshi to make him king over Israel. Next, pour oil on Elisha son of Shaphat from Abel Meholah. He will be a prophet in your place. ¹⁷Jehu will kill anyone who escapes from Hazael's

sword. And Elisha will kill anyone who escapes from Jehu's sword. [18]But I have left 7,000 people living in Israel. Those 7,000 have never bowed down before Baal.[d] Their mouths have never kissed his idol."

Elisha Becomes a Prophet

[19]So Elijah left there and found Elisha son of Shaphat. He was plowing a field with a team of oxen. There were 11 teams ahead of him. Elisha was plowing with the twelfth team of oxen. Elijah came up to Elisha. Elijah took off his coat and put it on Elisha. [20]Then Elisha left his oxen and ran to follow Elijah. Elisha said, "Let me kiss my father and my mother good-bye. Then I will go with you."

Elijah answered, "That is fine. Go back. I won't stop you."

[21]So Elisha went back. He took his pair of oxen and killed them. He used the wooden yoke[d] for the fire. Then he cooked the meat and gave it to the people. And they ate it. Then Elisha went and followed Elijah and became his helper.

Ben-Hadad and Ahab Go to War

20 Now Ben-Hadad was king of Aram. He gathered together all his army. There were 32 kings with their horses and chariots. They went with him and surrounded Samaria and attacked it. [2]The king sent messengers into the city to Ahab king of Israel. [3]This was his message: "Ben-Hadad says, 'You must give me your silver and gold and the best of your wives and children.'"

[4]Ahab king of Israel answered, "My master and king, I agree to what you say. I and everything I have belongs to you."

[5]Then the messengers came to Ahab again. They said, "Ben-Hadad says, 'I told you before that you must give me your silver and gold, your wives and your children. [6]About this time tomorrow I am going to send my men to you. They are to search everywhere in your palace. And they are to search the homes of the men who rule under you. My men will take anything they want.'"

[7]So Ahab called a meeting of all the older leaders of his country. He said, "Ben-Hadad is looking for trouble. First he said I had to give him my wives, my children, my silver and my gold. I agreed to that."

[8]But the older leaders and all the people said, "Pay no attention to him. Don't do what he says."

[9]So Ahab said to Ben-Hadad's messengers, "Tell my master the king this: 'I will do what you said at first. But I will not obey your second command.'" So King Ben-Hadad's men carried the message back to him.

[10]Then Ben-Hadad sent another message to Ahab: "I will completely destroy Samaria. There won't be even enough left for each of my men to get a handful of dust. May the gods punish me terribly if I don't do this!"

[11]Ahab answered, "Tell Ben-Hadad this: 'The man who puts on his armor should not brag too soon. It's the man who lives long enough to take it off who has the right to brag.'"

[12]Now Ben-Hadad was drinking in his tent with the other rulers. The messengers came and gave him the message from Ahab. Ben-Hadad commanded his men to prepare to attack the city. So they moved into their places for the battle.

[13]At the same time a prophet[d] came to Ahab, king of Israel. The prophet said, "Ahab, the Lord says to you, 'Do you see that big army? I will let you defeat it today. Then you will know I am the Lord.'"

[14]Ahab said, "Who will you use to defeat them?"

The prophet answered, "The Lord says, 'The young officers of the district governors will defeat them.'"

Then the king asked, "Who will command the main army?"

The prophet answered, "You will."

[15]So Ahab gathered the young officers of the district governors. There

were 232 of them. Then he called together the army of Israel. There were 7,000 of them.

¹⁶At noon Ben-Hadad and the 32 rulers helping him were getting drunk in their tents. At this time Ahab attacked them. ¹⁷The young officers of the district governors attacked first.

Ben-Hadad's scouts told him that soldiers were coming from Samaria. ¹⁸So Ben-Hadad said, "They may be coming to fight. Or they may be coming to ask for peace. In either case capture them alive."

¹⁹The young officers of the district governors led the attack. The army of Israel followed them. ²⁰Then each officer of Israel killed the man who came against him. So the men from Aram ran away as Israel chased them. But Ben-Hadad king of Aram escaped on a horse with some of his horsemen. ²¹Ahab king of Israel led the army. He captured the Arameans' horses and chariots. So King Ahab caused a great defeat of the Aramean army.

²²Then the prophet went to Ahab king of Israel and said, "The king of Aram will attack you again next spring. So you should go home now and make your army stronger. Make plans to defend yourself."

²³The officers of Ben-Hadad king of Aram said to him, "The gods of Israel are mountain gods. Since we fought in a mountain area, Israel won. So let's fight them on the flat land. Then we will win. ²⁴This is what you should do. Don't allow the 32 rulers to command the armies. Put commanders in their places. ²⁵Gather an army like the one that was destroyed. Gather as many horses and chariots as it had. We will fight the Israelites on flat land. Then we will win." Ben-Hadad agreed with their advice and did what they said.

²⁶The next spring Ben-Hadad gathered the people of Aram. He went to Aphek to fight against Israel. ²⁷The Israelites also prepared for war. They marched out to meet the Arameans and camped opposite them.

They looked like two small groups of goats. But the Arameans covered the area.

²⁸A man of God came to the king of Israel with this message: "The Lord says, 'The people of Aram say that I, the Lord, am a god of the mountains. They think I am not a god of the valleys. So I will allow you to defeat this big army. Then you will know I am the Lord.'"

²⁹The armies were camped across from each other for seven days. On the seventh day the battle began. The Israelites killed 100,000 Aramean soldiers in one day. ³⁰The rest of them ran away to the city of Aphek. There a city wall fell on 27,000 of them. Ben-Hadad also ran away to the city and hid in a room.

³¹His officers said to him, "We have heard that the kings of Israel are merciful. Let's dress in rough cloth to show our sadness. And let's wear ropes on our heads as a sign of surrender. Then let's go to the king of Israel. Maybe he will let you live."

³²So they dressed in rough cloth and wore ropes on their heads. Then they went to the king of Israel. They said, "Your servant Ben-Hadad says, 'Please let me live.'"

Ahab answered, "Is he still alive? He is my brother."

³³Now Ben-Hadad's men had wanted a sign from Ahab. They wanted to know he would not kill Ben-Hadad. So when Ahab called Ben-Hadad his brother, they quickly said, "Yes! Ben-Hadad is your brother."

Ahab said, "Bring him to me." When Ben-Hadad came, Ahab asked him to join him in the chariot.

³⁴Ben-Hadad said to him, "Ahab, I will give you back the towns my father took from your father. And you may put shops in Damascus, as my father did in Samaria."

Ahab said, "If you agree to this, I will allow you to go free." So the two kings made a peace agreement. Then Ahab let Ben-Hadad go free.

A Prophet Speaks Against Ahab

[35]One of the prophets[d] told another prophet, "Hit me!" He told him to do this because the Lord had commanded it. But the other prophet refused. [36]So the first prophet said, "You did not obey the Lord's command. So a lion will kill you as soon as you leave me." When the second prophet left, a lion found him and killed him.

[37]The first prophet went to another man and said, "Hit me, please!" So the man hit him and hurt him. [38]Then the prophet wrapped his face in a cloth. This way no one could tell who he was. Then he went and waited by the road for the king. [39]As Ahab king of Israel passed by, the prophet called out to him. The prophet said, "I went to fight in the battle. One of our men brought an enemy soldier to me. Our man said, 'Guard this man. If he runs away, you will have to give your life in his place. Or, you will have to pay a fine of 75 pounds of silver.' [40]But I became busy doing other things. So the man ran away."

The king of Israel answered, "You have said what the punishment is. You must do what the man said."

[41]Then the prophet quickly took the cloth from his face. When the king of Israel saw him, he knew he was one of the prophets. [42]Then the prophet said to the king, "This is what the Lord says: 'You set free the man I said should die. So your life will be taken in his place. And the lives of your people will be taken in place of the lives of his people.'"

[43]Then the king went back to his palace in Samaria. He was angry and upset.

Plans That Backfired

JEZEBEL • 1 KINGS 21

Sugar and spice and everything nice–that's what little girls are supposedly made of.

Somewhere along the way, Jezebel lost every bit of sugar and every ounce of spice and replaced them with poison and weeds and everything rude. She gets the prize for being the most evil woman in the Bible.

Like her husband, Ahab, Jezebel prayed to statues of wood and stone. She worked hard to get everyone else to do bad things like she did. She tried to kill anyone who wanted to stop her or who prayed to the one true God. Sadly, she had the power to do this because she was the queen. For years she tried to have the prophet Elijah killed. But God made sure her plan to kill Elijah did not succeed. Instead, Jezebel was killed by another one of God's messengers.

Do you know anyone as bad as Jezebel? Such people do not make God happy, and they are not happy either.

To meet a king's friend with a king-sized bad attitude, fly to page 600.

Naboth's Vineyard

21 A man named Naboth owned a vineyard. It was in Jezreel, near the palace of Ahab king of Israel. [2]One day Ahab said to Naboth, "Give me your vineyard. It is near my palace. I want to make it into a vegetable garden. I will give you a better vineyard in its place. Or, if you prefer, I will pay you what it is worth."

³Naboth answered, "May the Lord keep me from ever giving my land to you. It belongs to my family."

⁴So Ahab went home, angry and upset. He did not like what Naboth from Jezreel had said. (Naboth had said, "I will not give you my family's land.") So Ahab lay down on his bed. He turned his face to the wall and refused to eat.

⁵His wife, Jezebel, came in. She asked him, "Why are you upset? Why do you refuse to eat?"

⁶Ahab answered, "I talked to Naboth, the man from Jezreel. I said, 'Sell me your vineyard. Or, if you prefer, I will give you another vineyard for it.' But Naboth refused."

⁷Jezebel answered, "Is this how you rule as king over Israel? Get out of bed. Eat something. Cheer up. I will get Naboth's vineyard for you."

⁸So Jezebel wrote some letters and signed Ahab's name to them. And she used his own seal*d* to seal them. Then she sent them to the older leaders and important men who lived in Naboth's town. ⁹The letter she wrote said: "Declare a day during which the people are to give up eating. Call the people together. And give Naboth a place of honor among them. ¹⁰Seat two troublemakers across from him. Have them say they heard Naboth speak against God and the king. Then take Naboth out of the city and kill him with stones."

¹¹So the older leaders and important men of Jezreel obeyed Jezebel's command. ¹²They declared a special day. On that day the people were to give up eating. They called the people together. And they put Naboth in a place of honor before the people. ¹³Then two troublemakers sat across from Naboth. They said they had heard Naboth speak against God and the king. So the people carried Naboth out of the city. And they killed him with stones. ¹⁴Then the leaders sent a message to Jezebel. It said, "Naboth has been killed."

¹⁵When Jezebel heard that Naboth had been killed, she told Ahab. She said, "Naboth of Jezreel is dead. Now you may go and take for yourself his vineyard you wanted." ¹⁶When Ahab heard that Naboth was dead, he left. He went to the vineyard to take it for his own.

¹⁷At this time the Lord spoke his word to Elijah. (Elijah was the prophet*d* from Tishbe.) The Lord said, ¹⁸"Go to Ahab king of Israel, who rules in Samaria. He is at Naboth's vineyard to take it as his own. ¹⁹Tell Ahab that I, the Lord, say to him, 'Ahab! You have murdered Naboth and have taken his land. So I tell you this! In the same place that Naboth died, you will also die. The dogs that licked up Naboth's blood will lick up your blood in the same place!'"

²⁰When Ahab saw Elijah, he said, "So you have found me, my enemy!"

Elijah answered, "Yes, I have found you. You have always chosen to do what the Lord says is wrong. ²¹So the Lord says to you, 'I will destroy you. I will kill you and every male in your family, both slave and free. ²²Your family will be like the family of King Jeroboam son of Nebat. And it will be like the family of King Baasha son of Ahijah. Both of these families were completely destroyed. I will do this to you because you have made me angry. And you have caused the people of Israel to sin.'

²³"And the Lord also says, 'Dogs will eat the body of Jezebel in the city of Jezreel.'

²⁴"Anyone in your family who dies in the city will be eaten by dogs. Anyone who dies in the fields will be eaten by birds."

²⁵There was no one like Ahab. No one had so often chosen to do what the Lord said was wrong. His wife Jezebel

influenced him to do evil. [26]Ahab sinned terribly by worshiping idols. This was the same thing the Amorite people did. So the Lord took their land away from them. And he gave it to the people of Israel.

[27]After Elijah finished speaking, Ahab tore his clothes. He put on rough cloth and refused to eat. He even slept in the rough cloth. He did this to show how sad and upset he was.

[28]The Lord spoke his word to Elijah from Tishbe: [29]"I see that Ahab is now sorry for what he has done. So I will not cause the trouble to come to him during his life. I will wait until his son is king. Then I will bring this trouble to Ahab's family."

The Death of Ahab

22 For three years there was peace between Israel and Aram. [2]During the third year Jehoshaphat king of Judah went to visit Ahab king of Israel.

[3]At this same time Ahab asked his officers, "Remember that the king of Aram took Ramoth in Gilead from us? Why have we done nothing to get it back?" [4]So Ahab asked King Jehoshaphat, "Will you go with us? Will you fight against the army of Aram at Ramoth in Gilead?"

Jehoshaphat answered, "I will go with you. My soldiers and my horses are ready to join with your army. [5]But first we should ask the Lord to guide us."

[6]So Ahab called the prophets[d] together. There were about 400 men. He asked them, "Should I go to war against the army of Aram at Ramoth in Gilead? Or should I wait?"

The prophets answered, "Go, because the Lord will let you defeat them."

[7]But Jehoshaphat asked, "Isn't there a prophet of the Lord here? Let's ask him what we should do."

[8]King Ahab answered, "There is one other prophet. We could ask the Lord through him. But I hate him. When he prophesies, he never says anything good about me. He always says something bad. He is Micaiah, Imlah's son."

Jehoshaphat said, "King Ahab, you shouldn't say that!"

[9]So Ahab king of Israel told one of his officers to bring Micaiah to him at once.

[10]Ahab king of Israel and Jehoshaphat king of Judah had on their royal robes. They were sitting on their thrones at the threshing[d] floor. This was near the entrance to the gate of Samaria. All the prophets were standing before them, speaking messages from the Lord. [11]One of the prophets was Zedekiah son of Kenaanah. He had made some iron horns. He said to Ahab, "This is what the Lord says, 'You will use these horns to fight the Arameans. And you will destroy them.'"

[12]All the other prophets said the same thing. They said, "Attack Ramoth in Gilead and win. The Lord will let you defeat the Arameans."

[13]The messenger who had gone to get Micaiah found him. He said to Micaiah, "All the other prophets are saying the king will succeed. You should agree with them. Give the king a good answer."

[14]But Micaiah answered, "As surely as the Lord lives, I can tell him only what the Lord tells me."

[15]Then Micaiah came to Ahab. The king asked him, "Micaiah, should we attack Ramoth in Gilead or not?"

Micaiah answered, "Attack and win! The Lord will let you defeat them."

[16]But Ahab said to Micaiah, "Tell me only the truth in the name of the Lord. How many times do I have to tell you this?"

[17]So Micaiah answered, "I saw the army of Israel. They were scattered over the hills like sheep without a shepherd. The Lord said, 'They have no leader. They should go home and not fight.'"

[18]Then Ahab king of Israel said to Jehoshaphat, "I told you! This prophet never says anything good about me.

He only says bad things about me."

¹⁹But Micaiah continued to speak. He said, "Hear the message from the Lord: I saw the Lord sitting on his throne. His heavenly army was standing near him on his right and on his left. ²⁰The Lord said, 'Who will trick Ahab into attacking Ramoth in Gilead? Do this so he will go and be killed.'

"The spirits did not agree about what they should do. ²¹Then one spirit came and stood before the Lord. He said, 'I will trick him.'

²²"The Lord asked, 'How will you trick Ahab?'

"The spirit answered, 'I will go to Ahab's prophets. I will make them tell lies.'

"So the Lord said, 'You will succeed in tricking him. Go and do it.'"

²³Micaiah said, "Ahab, this has now happened. The Lord has caused your prophets to lie to you. The Lord has decided that great trouble should come to you."

²⁴Then Zedekiah son of Kenaanah went up to Micaiah. And he hit Micaiah in the face. Zedekiah said, "Do you really believe the Lord's spirit has left me and is now speaking through you?"

²⁵Micaiah answered, "You will find out on the day you go to hide in an inside room."

²⁶Then Ahab king of Israel ordered, "Take Micaiah. Send him to Amon, the governor of the city, and to Joash, the king's son. ²⁷Tell them I said to put Micaiah in prison. Give him only bread and water for food. Keep him there until I come home from the battle."

²⁸Micaiah said, "Ahab, if you come back safely from battle, the Lord has not spoken through me. Remember my words, all you people."

²⁹So Ahab king of Israel and Jehoshaphat king of Judah went to Ramoth in Gilead. ³⁰Ahab said to Jehoshaphat, "I will go into battle. But I will change my appearance so that no one will recognize me. But you wear your royal clothes." So Ahab changed his appearance and went into battle.

³¹The king of Aram had 32 chariot commanders. He ordered them, "Don't fight with anyone but the king of Israel. It doesn't matter if they are important or unimportant." ³²When these commanders saw Jehoshaphat, they thought he was the king of Israel. So they turned to attack him. But Jehoshaphat began shouting. ³³Then the commanders saw he was not Ahab. So they stopped chasing him. ³⁴A soldier shot an arrow without aiming at anyone. But he hit Ahab king of Israel. The arrow hit him in a place not covered by his armor. King Ahab said to his chariot driver, "Turn the chariot around. Take me out of the battle. I am hurt!" ³⁵The battle continued all day. King Ahab was in his chariot, leaning against it to hold himself up. He was facing the Arameans. His blood flowed down and covered the bottom of the chariot. That evening he died. ³⁶Near sunset a cry went out through the army of Israel: "Each man go back to his own country and city."

³⁷So in that way King Ahab died. His body was carried to Samaria and buried there. ³⁸The men cleaned Ahab's chariot at a pool in Samaria. This was a pool where prostitutes*ᵈ* bathed. And the dogs licked King Ahab's blood from the chariot. These things happened as the Lord had said they would.

³⁹Everything else Ahab did is written down. It is in the book of the history of the kings of Israel. That book also tells about the palace Ahab built and decorated with ivory. And it tells about the cities he built. ⁴⁰So Ahab died, and his son Ahaziah became king in his place.

Jehoshaphat King of Judah

⁴¹Jehoshaphat son of Asa became king of Judah. This was during Ahab's fourth year as king over Israel. ⁴²Jehoshaphat was 35 years old when he became king. And he ruled in Jerusalem for 25 years. His mother was the daughter of Shilhi. She was named

Azubah. [43]Jehoshaphat was good like his father before him. He did what the Lord said was right. But Jehoshaphat did not destroy the places where false gods were worshiped. So the people continued offering sacrifices and burning incense[d] there. [44]Jehoshaphat was at peace with the king of Israel. [45]Jehoshaphat fought many wars. These wars and his successes are written down. They are in the book of the history of the kings of Judah. [46]There were prostitutes[d] in the places where false gods were worshiped. Jehoshaphat's father, Asa, had not forced all of them out. But Jehoshaphat forced the rest of them to leave.

[47]During this time the land of Edom had no king. It was ruled by a governor.

[48]King Jehoshaphat built trading ships to sale to Ophir for gold. But the ships were destroyed at Ezion Geber. So they never set sail. [49]Ahaziah son of Ahab went to help Jehoshaphat.

Ahaziah said he would give Jehoshaphat some men to sail with his men. But Jehoshaphat refused.

[50]Jehoshaphat died and was buried with his ancestors. He was buried in Jerusalem, the city of David, his ancestor. And his son Jehoram became king.

Ahaziah King of Israel

[51]Ahaziah son of Ahab became king of Israel in Samaria. This was during Jehoshaphat's seventeenth year as king over Judah. Ahaziah ruled Israel for two years. [52]Ahaziah did what the Lord said was wrong. He did the same things his father Ahab, his mother Jezebel and Jeroboam son of Nebat had done. All these rulers led the people of Israel into more sin. [53]Ahaziah worshiped and served the god Baal.[d] So Ahaziah made the Lord, the God of Israel, very angry. In these ways Ahaziah did what his father had done.

2 KINGS

Two Kingdoms
Are Destroyed

Elijah and King Ahaziah

1 After Ahab died, Moab broke away from Israel's rule. ²Ahaziah fell down through the wooden bars in his upstairs room in Samaria. He was badly hurt. He sent messengers and told them, "Go. Ask Baal-Zebub god of Ekron if I will get well from my injuries."

³But the Lord's angel said to Elijah the Tishbite, "Get up. Go meet the messengers sent by the king of Samaria. Say to them, 'Why are you going to ask questions of Baal-Zebub god of Ekron? Is it because you think there is no God in Israel?' ⁴So this is what the Lord says: 'You will not get up from the bed you are lying on. You will die.'" Then Elijah left.

⁵The messengers came back to Ahaziah. He asked them, "Why have you come back?"

⁶They said, "A man came to meet us. He said, 'Go back to the king who sent you. Tell him what the Lord says: "Why do you send men to ask questions of Baal-Zebub god of Ekron? Is it because you think there is no God in Israel? This is why you will not get up from your bed. You will die."'"

⁷Ahaziah asked them, "What did the man look like who met you and told you this?"

⁸They answered, "He wore a hairy coat and a leather belt around his waist."

Ahaziah said, "It was Elijah the Tishbite."

⁹Then he sent a captain with his 50 men to Elijah. The captain went to Elijah, who was sitting on top of the hill. He said to Elijah, "Man of God, the king says, 'Come down!'"

¹⁰Elijah answered the captain, "I am a man of God. So let fire come down from heaven and burn up you and your 50 men." Then fire came down from heaven. It burned up the captain and his 50 men.

¹¹Ahaziah sent another captain and 50 men to Elijah. The captain said to him, "Man of God, this is what the king says: 'Come down quickly!'"

¹²Elijah answered, "I am a man of God. So let fire come down from heaven and burn up you and your 50 men!" Then fire came down from heaven. It burned up the captain and his 50 men.

¹³Ahaziah sent a third captain with his 50 men. The third captain came and fell down on his knees before Elijah. He begged Elijah, "Man of God, I ask you. Please let my life and the lives of your 50 servants be valuable to you! ¹⁴See, fire came down from heaven. It burned up the first two captains of 50 with all their men. But now, let my life be valuable to you."

¹⁵The Lord's angel said to Elijah, "Go with him. Don't be afraid of him." So Elijah got up and went with him to see the king.

¹⁶Elijah told Ahaziah, "This is what the Lord says: 'You have sent messengers to ask questions of Baal-Zebub god of Ekron. Is it because you think there is no God in Israel to ask? Because of this, you will not get up from your bed. You will die.'" ¹⁷So he died, just as the Lord, through Elijah, had said he would.

Joram became king in Ahaziah's place. This was during the second year Jehoram son of Jehoshaphat was king of Judah. Joram ruled because Ahaziah had no son to take his place. ¹⁸The other things Ahaziah did are written down. They are in the book of the history of the kings of Israel.

Elijah Is Taken to Heaven

2 It was near the time for the Lord to take Elijah. He was going to take him by a whirlwind up into heaven. Elijah and Elisha were at Gilgal. ²Elijah said to Elisha, "Please stay here. The Lord has told me to go to Bethel."

But Elisha said, "As the Lord lives, and as you live, I won't leave you." So they went down to Bethel. ³A group of the prophets[d] at Bethel came to Elisha. They said to him, "Do you know the Lord will take your master away from you today?"

Elisha said, "Yes, I know. But don't talk about it."

⁴Elijah said to him, "Stay here, because the Lord has sent me to Jericho."

But Elisha said, "As the Lord lives, and as you live, I won't leave you."

So they went to Jericho. ⁵A group of the prophets at Jericho came to Elisha. They said, "Do you know that the Lord will take your master away from you today?"

Elisha answered, "Yes, I know. But don't talk about it."

⁶Elijah said to Elisha, "Stay here. The Lord has sent me to the Jordan River."

Elisha answered, "As the Lord lives, and as you live, I won't leave you."

So the two of them went on. ⁷Fifty men from a group of the prophets came. They stood far from where Elijah and Elisha were by the Jordan. ⁸Elijah took off his coat. Then he rolled it up and hit the water. The water divided to the right and to the left. Then Elijah and Elisha crossed over on dry ground.

⁹After they had crossed over, Elijah said to Elisha, "What can I do for you before I am taken from you?"

Elisha said, "Leave me a double share of your spirit."[n]

¹⁰Elijah said, "You have asked a hard thing. But if you see me when I am taken from you, it will be yours. If you don't, it won't happen."

¹¹Elijah and Elisha were still walking and talking. Then a chariot and horses of fire appeared. The chariot and horses of fire separated Elijah from Elisha.

People Who Spoke God's Words

ELISHA • 2 KINGS 2:9

Elisha became the main prophet to Israel after Elijah died. But before Elijah died, Elisha asked him for a "double share" of his spirit. Elisha was asking to be filled with twice as much of God's power as Elijah had. Elisha received his request because he wanted to do more work for God. He did not want to use the power for himself. We don't need to be afraid to ask great things of God. Elisha did indeed serve God well in the evil nation of Israel.

When God has a big job for you to do, he will give you everything you need to do it!

To meet a prophet who wasn't always popular, fly to page 807.

---

[n]**Leave . . . spirit** By law, the first son in a family would inherit a double share of his father's possessions. Elisha is asking to inherit a share of his master's power. He is not asking for twice as much power as Elijah had.

Then Elijah went up to heaven in a whirlwind. ¹²Elisha saw it and shouted, "My father! My father! The chariots of Israel and their horsemen!" Elisha did not see him anymore. Elisha grabbed his own clothes and tore them to show how sad he was.

"I asked my dad how his car compared with the chariot that Elijah rode in. Read all about it in 2 Kings 2:1-14."

¹³He picked up Elijah's coat that had fallen from him. Then Elisha returned and stood on the bank of the Jordan. ¹⁴Elisha hit the water with Elijah's coat. He said, "Where is the Lord, the God of Elijah?" When he hit the water, it divided to the right and to the left. Then Elisha crossed over.

¹⁵A group of the prophets at Jericho were watching. They said, "Elisha now has the spirit Elijah had." They came to meet him. And they bowed down to the ground before him. ¹⁶They said to him, "There are 50 strong men with us! Please let them go and look for your master. Maybe the Spirit^d of the Lord has taken Elijah up and set him down. He may be on some mountain or in some valley."

But Elisha answered, "No. Don't send them."

¹⁷The group of prophets begged Elisha until he hated to refuse them anymore. Then he said, "Send them." So they sent 50 men who looked for three days. But they could not find Elijah. ¹⁸Then they came back to Elisha at Jericho where he was staying. He said to them, "I told you not to go, didn't I?"

Elisha Makes the Water Pure

¹⁹The men of the city said to Elisha, "Look, master, this city is a nice place to live. You can see that. But the water is bad. That's why the land cannot grow crops."

Amazing Events That Showed God's Power

2 KINGS 2:11

Did you know that there were two people who went straight to heaven without dying? One was a man named Enoch (see Genesis 5:21-24). We don't know what happened because the Bible only tells us that "Enoch walked with God; one day Enoch could not be found, because God took him."

Elijah the prophet also went to heaven without dying. He spoke to the people for God and taught them God's truth. The man who helped him was Elisha. One day when he was walking with Elijah, Elisha saw a chariot and horses of fire take Elijah to heaven in a great whirlwind.

God's power will take us to heaven one day, too, if we believe in Jesus. But probably not in a chariot!

To find out how God's power made the sun go backwards, fly to page 472.

²⁰Elisha said, "Bring me a new bowl and put salt in it." So they brought it to him.

²¹Then Elisha went out to the spring of water and threw the salt in it. He said, "This is what the Lord says: 'I have healed this water. From now on it won't cause death. And it won't keep the land from growing crops.'" ²²The water was healed. It is still good today. It happened just as Elisha had said.

Young People Make Fun of Elisha

²³From there Elisha went up to Bethel. On the way some young men came out of the city. They made fun of Elisha. They said to him, "Go up, you baldhead! Go up, you baldhead!" ²⁴Elisha turned around and looked at them. He put a curse on them in the name of the Lord. Then two female bears came out of the woods. They tore to pieces 42 of the young men. ²⁵Then Elisha left and went on to Mount Carmel. From there he went back to Samaria.

War Between Israel and Moab

3 Joram son of Ahab became king over Israel at Samaria. He began to rule in Jehoshaphat's eighteenth year as king of Judah. Joram ruled 12 years. ²Joram did what the Lord said was wrong. But he was not like his father and mother. He removed the stone pillars his father had made for Baal.ᵈ ³But he continued to do the same sins Jeroboam son of Nebat had done. Jeroboam had caused the people of Israel to sin. And Joram did not stop doing these same sins.

⁴Mesha king of Moab raised sheep. He had to give 100,000 lambs and the wool of 100,000 male sheep to the king of Israel. ⁵But when Ahab died, the king of Moab turned against the king of Israel. ⁶So King Joram went out from Samaria and gathered all Israel. ⁷He sent messengers to Jehoshaphat king of Judah. He said, "The king of Moab has turned against me. Will you go with me against Moab in battle?"

Jehoshaphat said, "I will go with you. I am ready to join you. My soldiers and my horses are ready to join with your army."

⁸Jehoshaphat asked, "Which way should we go to attack?"

Joram answered, "Through the Desert of Edom."

⁹So the king of Israel went with the king of Judah and the king of Edom. They marched seven days. There was no more water for the army or for their animals that were with them. ¹⁰The king of Israel said, "How terrible this is! Has the Lord called us three kings together so the Moabites can defeat us?"

¹¹But Jehoshaphat asked, "Is there a prophetᵈ of the Lord here? We can ask the Lord through a prophet."

An officer of the king of Israel answered, "Elisha son of Shaphat is here. He was Elijah's servant."

¹²Jehoshaphat said, "He speaks the Lord's truth." So the king of Israel and Jehoshaphat and the king of Edom went down to see Elisha.

¹³Elisha spoke to the king of Israel. He said, "I have nothing to do with you! Go to the prophets of your father and to the prophets of your mother!"

The king of Israel said to Elisha, "No. The Lord has called us three kings together to let the Moabites defeat us."

¹⁴Elisha said, "I serve the Lord of heaven's armies. As surely as he lives, I tell you the truth. I wouldn't even look at you or notice you if Jehoshaphat king of Judah were not here. I respect him! ¹⁵Now bring me someone who plays the harp."

While the harp was being played, the Lord gave Elisha power. ¹⁶Then Elisha said, "The Lord says to dig holes in the valley. ¹⁷He says that you won't see wind or rain. But the valley will be filled with water. Then you, your cattle and other animals will drink. ¹⁸This is easy for the Lord to do. He will also let you defeat Moab. ¹⁹You will destroy every strong, walled city and every important town. You will cut down every good tree. You will stop up all springs of water. You will ruin every good field with rocks."

²⁰The next morning, about the time the sacrifice was offered, there was water! It came from the direction of Edom and filled the valley.

²¹All the Moabites had heard that the kings had come up to fight against them. They gathered everyone old enough to put on armor. And they waited at the border. ²²But when the Moabites got up early in the morning, the sun was shining on the water. They saw the water across from them. It looked as red as blood. ²³The Moabites said, "This is blood! Surely the kings have fought and killed each other! Come, Moabites, let's take what is valuable from the dead bodies!"

²⁴The Moabites came to the camp of the Israelites. But the Israelites came out and fought them until they ran away. The Israelites went on into the land to fight the Moabites. ²⁵They tore down the cities. They threw rocks on every good field and filled it. They stopped up all the springs of water.

And they cut down all the good trees. Kir Hareseth was the only city with its stones still in place. But the men with slings surrounded Kir Hareseth and conquered it, too.

²⁶The king of Moab saw that the battle was too strong for him. So he took 700 men with swords to break through to the king of Edom. But they could not break through. ²⁷Then the king of Moab took his oldest son, who would have become king after him. And he offered his son as a burnt offering on the wall. So there was great anger against the Israelites. They left and went back to their own land.

A Widow Asks Elisha for Help

4 The wife of a man from a group of the prophets*ᵈ* came to Elisha. She said, "Your servant, my husband, is dead! You know he honored the Lord. But now the man he owes money to is coming to take my two boys. He will make them his slaves!"

²Elisha answered, "How can I help you? Tell me, what do you have in your house?"

The woman said, "I don't have anything there except a pot of oil."

³Then Elisha said, "Go and get empty jars from all your neighbors. Don't ask for just a few. ⁴Then you

Miracles from God

2 KINGS 4:1-7

How would you like it if your parents had a big bill they couldn't pay and they had to sell you as a slave? When the Old Testament was written, people sometimes had to sell their children if there was no other way for them to pay their bills. This almost happened to a widow until she trusted God and asked Elisha for help.

Like the widow with the never-ending jar of oil, when we have faith in God, even the impossible can happen. When we trust the Lord, anything is possible.

To find out how no one went home hungry even when they had no food, fly to page 1153.

must go into your house and close the door. Only you and your sons will be there. Then pour oil into all the jars. Set the full ones to one side."

"**G**od has always made a lot with a little. He did it in a special way for a widow who needed help. Check out 2 Kings 4:1-7."

⁵She left Elisha and shut the door. Only she and her sons were in the house. As they brought the jars to her, she poured the oil. ⁶When the jars were all full, she said to her son, "Bring me another jar."

But he said, "There are no more jars." Then the oil stopped flowing.

⁷She went and told Elisha. Elisha said to her, "Go. Sell the oil and pay what you owe. You and your sons can live on what is left."

The Shunammite Woman

⁸One day Elisha went to Shunem. An important woman lived there. She begged Elisha to stay and eat. So every time Elisha passed by, he stopped there to eat. ⁹The woman said to her husband, "I know that Elisha is a holy man of God. He passes by our house all the time. ¹⁰Let's make a small room on the roof.ⁿ Let's put a bed in the room for Elisha. And we can put a table, a chair and a lampstand there. Then when he comes by, he can stay there."

¹¹One day Elisha came to the woman's house. He went to his room and rested. ¹²He said to his servant Gehazi, "Call the Shunammite."

When the servant called her, she stood in front of him. ¹³Elisha told his servant, "Now say to her, 'You have gone to all this trouble for us. What can I do for you? Do you want me to speak

to the king or the commander of the army for you?'"

The woman answered, "I live among my own people."

¹⁴Elisha said, "But what can we do for her?"

Gehazi answered, "She has no son, and her husband is old."

¹⁵Then Elisha said, "Call her." So he called her, and she stood in the doorway. ¹⁶Then Elisha said, "About this time next year, you will hold a son in your arms."

The woman said, "No, master, man of God. Don't lie to me!"

¹⁷But the woman became pregnant. And she gave birth to a son at that time the next year as Elisha had told her.

¹⁸The child grew. One day he went out to his father, who was with the men harvesting grain. ¹⁹The boy said to his father, "My head! My head!"

The father said to his servant, "Carry him to his mother!" ²⁰The servant took him to his mother. He lay on his mother's lap until noon. Then he died. ²¹She took him up and laid him on Elisha's bed. Then she shut the door and went out.

²²She called to her husband. She said, "Send me one of the servants and one of the donkeys. Then I can go quickly to the man of God and come back."

²³The woman's husband said, "Why do you want to go to him today? It isn't the New Moonᵈ or the Sabbathᵈ day."

She said, "It will be all right."

²⁴Then she saddled the donkey and said to her servant, "Lead on. Don't slow down for me unless I tell you." ²⁵So she went to Elisha at Mount Carmel.

He saw her coming from far away. So he said to his servant Gehazi, "Look, there's the Shunammite woman! ²⁶Run to meet her! Say to her, 'Are you all right? Is your husband all right? Is the child all right?'"

She answered, "Everything is all right."

ⁿ**roof** In Bible times houses were built with flat roofs. The roof was used for drying things such as flax and fruit. And it was used as an extra room, as a place for worship and as a place to sleep in the summer.

²⁷Then she came to Elisha at the hill. She caught hold of his feet. Gehazi came near to pull her away. But Elisha said to him, "Let her alone. She's very upset, and the Lord has not told me about it. He has hidden it from me."

²⁸She said, "Master, I didn't tell you I wanted a son. I told you, 'Don't fool me.'"

²⁹Then Elisha said to Gehazi, "Get ready. Take my walking stick in your hand and go quickly. If you meet anyone, don't greet him. If anyone greets you, don't answer him. Lay my walking stick on the face of the boy."

³⁰But the child's mother said, "As surely as the Lord lives and as you live, I won't leave you!" So he got up and followed her.

³¹Gehazi went on ahead. He laid the walking stick on the child's face. But the child did not talk or move. Then Gehazi went back to meet Elisha. He told Elisha, "The child has not awakened."

³²Elisha came into the house. There was the child, lying dead on his bed. ³³When Elisha entered the room, he shut the door. Only he and the child were in the room. Then Elisha prayed to the Lord. ³⁴He went to the bed and lay on the child. He put his mouth on the child's mouth. He put his eyes on the child's eyes and his hands on the child's hands. He stretched himself out on top of the child. Then the child's skin became warm. ³⁵Elisha turned away and walked around the room. Then he went back and put himself on the child again. Then the child sneezed seven times and opened his eyes.

³⁶Elisha called Gehazi and said, "Call the Shunammite!" And he did. When she came, Elisha said, "Pick up your son." ³⁷She came in and fell at Elisha's feet. She bowed facedown to the floor. Then she picked up her son and went out.

Elisha and the Poison

³⁸Elisha came to Gilgal again. There was a time of hunger in the land. A group of prophets*ᵈ* was sitting in front of him. He said to his servant, "Put the large pot on the fire. Boil some stew for these men."

³⁹One of them went out into the field to gather plants. He found a wild vine. He picked fruit from the vine and filled his robe with it. Then he came and cut up the fruit into the pot. But they did not know what kind of fruit it was. ⁴⁰Then they poured out the stew for the men to eat. But when they began to eat it, they shouted out, "Man of God! There's death in the pot!" They could not eat it.

⁴¹Elisha told them to bring some flour. Then he threw it into the pot. He said, "Pour it out for the people to eat." And there was nothing harmful in the pot.

Elisha Multiplies Bread

⁴²A man from Baal Shalishah came to Elisha. He brought 20 loaves of barley bread from the first harvest to Elisha. He also brought fresh grain in his sack. Then Elisha said, "Give it to the people to eat."

⁴³Elisha's servant said, "How can I feed 100 men with so little?"

But Elisha said, "Give the bread to the people to eat. This is what the Lord says: 'They will eat and will have food left over.'" ⁴⁴Then he gave it to them. The people ate and had food left over, as the Lord had said.

Naaman Is Healed

5 Naaman was commander of the army of the king of Aram. He was a great man to his master. He had much honor because the Lord had used him to give victory to Aram. He was a mighty and brave man. But he had a harmful skin disease.

²The Arameans had gone out to steal from the Israelites. And they had taken a little girl as a captive from Israel. This little girl served Naaman's wife. ³She said to her mistress, "I wish that my master would meet the prophet*ᵈ* who

Whit's Wisdom: Parents Need God • 2 Kings 5

Most of the time, children learn from their parents. But sometimes, parents learn from their children. As I've watched moms and dads in Odyssey over the years, I've noticed that kids really can teach us older folks some valuable lessons. For instance, not too long ago my young friend Dylan Taylor stopped by Whit's End, my ice cream shop and inventors' hang out.

"**M**r. Whittaker, I'm worried about my dad," he said. "He's been sick a lot and won't go to the doctor. Mom has asked him over and over. I don't know what to do."

As I listened, it sounded like he and his mother *did* have something to be concerned about. His dad might be very sick. "Dylan," I said, "your problem reminds me of a Bible story." I handed him a Bible and had him look up 2 Kings 5:1-14. Why don't you read it like Dylan did.

After Dylan read the passage, he said, "My dad is acting a little like this guy Naaman. I guess he doesn't want to go to the doctor because he thinks he won't like what the doctor will tell him."

"**T**hat could be true, Dylan," I said. "But remember, as I always ask, where do you fit in this story?"

"**I** guess I'm like the girl who told about God's prophet," he said.

"**T**hat's right, Dylan. That little girl reminded those adults that they needed to turn to God for help. And that they needed to see the right person, too."

"**S**o, if I tell Dad to see the doctor, will that mean everything will be OK?" asked Dylan.

"**I** can't say that for sure, Dylan. God has his own plans. But he does want us to trust him. I think if you remind your dad about God, you may help him decide to see a doctor." Well, you know what? Dylan went home and told his dad he was worried too. He prayed for his dad that night before supper. And he kept on praying. And his dad did see a doctor. It turned out to be a simple problem he could fix with some medicine.

Dylan's dad dropped by Whit's End a few days later. He told me that hearing his son pray for him made him realize how important it was to take care of himself. "And then Dylan showed me this Bible story about Naaman and asked me where I thought I fit. Boy, did that open my eyes!"

See, I told you. Sometimes parents *do* learn from kids.

Related passages: Deuteronomy 6:1-9; Mark 10:13-16; 1 Corinthians 1:26-31.

Teacher/Parent Hint: Encourage children to pray for their parents. Pray with them. Discuss different ways parents need children's prayers for work, marriage, health, etc.

lives in Samaria. He would heal Naaman of his disease."

that you tore your clothes? Let Naaman come to me. Then he will know there is a prophet in Israel!" ⁹So Naaman went with his horses and chariots

Children Who Saw God at Work

NAAMAN'S SLAVE • 2 KINGS 5:1-5

This little girl became a slave when the soldiers of Assyria invaded her country of Israel. She was taken away from her family and had to serve in the home of Naaman, a commander in the Assyrian army. She missed her family and probably didn't like Naaman very much for taking her away from them.

But Naaman had a skin disease called leprosy. This disease was so bad that no one could cure it. The little girl knew about a man in Israel, a prophet, who loved God and could heal people by God's power. She told Naaman's wife about him. When Naaman went to see the prophet, he did what the prophet said, and the disease went away.

Are there people you don't like? Have some people been mean to you? God still wants you to be kind to them because he loves them.

To meet the youngest king of Judah, fly to page 542.

⁴Naaman went to the king. He told him what the girl from Israel had said. ⁵The king of Aram said, "Go now. And I will send a letter to the king of Israel." So Naaman left and took about 750 pounds of silver. He also took about 150 pounds of gold and ten changes of clothes with him. ⁶He brought the letter to the king of Israel. It read, "I am sending my servant Naaman to you. I'm sending him so you can heal him of his skin disease."

⁷The king of Israel read the letter. Then he tore his clothes to show how upset he was. He said, "I'm not God! I can't kill and make alive again! Why does this man send someone with a harmful skin disease for me to heal? You can see that the king of Aram is trying to start trouble with me!"

⁸Elisha, the man of God, heard that the king of Israel had torn his clothes. So he sent a message to the king. It said, "Why have you become so upset

to Elisha's house. And he stood outside the door.

¹⁰Elisha sent a messenger to Naaman. The messenger said, "Go and wash in the Jordan River seven times. Then your skin will be healed, and you will be clean."

¹¹Naaman became angry and left. He said, "I thought Elisha would surely come out and stand before me. I thought he would call on the name of the Lord his God. I thought he would wave his hand over the place and heal the disease! ¹²Abana and Pharpar, the rivers of Damascus, are better than all the waters of Israel! Why can't I wash in them and become clean?" So Naaman went away very angry.

¹³But Naaman's servants came near and talked to him. They said, "My father, if the prophet had told you to do some great thing, wouldn't you have done it? Doesn't it make more sense just to do it? After all, he only told you,

'Wash, and you will be clean.'" ¹⁴So Naaman went down and dipped in the Jordan seven times. He did just as Elisha had said. Then Naaman's skin became new again. It was like the skin of a little boy. And Naaman was clean!

¹⁵Naaman and all his group came back to Elisha. He stood before Elisha and said, "Look. I now know there is no God in all the earth except in Israel! Now please accept a gift from me."

¹⁶But Elisha said, "I serve the Lord. As surely as the Lord lives, I won't accept anything." Naaman urged him to take the gift, but he refused.

¹⁷Then Naaman said, "If you won't take the gift, then please give me some dirt. Give me as much as two of my mules can carry. From now on I'll not offer any burnt offering or sacrifice to any other gods. I'll only offer sacrifices to the Lord. ¹⁸But let the Lord pardon me for this: My master goes into the temple of Rimmon* to worship. When he goes, he will lean on my arm. Then I must bow in that temple. May the Lord pardon me when I do that."

¹⁹Elisha said to him, "Go in peace."

Naaman left Elisha and went a short way. ²⁰Gehazi was the servant of Elisha the man of God. Gehazi thought, "My master has not accepted what Naaman the Aramean brought. As surely as the Lord lives, I'll run after him. I'll get something from him." ²¹So he went after him.

Naaman saw someone running after him. So he got off the chariot to meet Gehazi. He said, "Is everything all right?"

²²Gehazi said, "Everything is all right. My master has sent me. He said, 'Two young men just came to me. They are from the group of the prophets in the mountains of Ephraim. Please give them 75 pounds of silver and two changes of clothes.'"

²³Naaman said, "Please take 150 pounds." He urged Gehazi to take it. He tied 150 pounds of silver in two bags with two changes of clothes. Then

Staying Away from Selfishness
2 KINGS 5:20-27

What is the most popular toy or game around right now? You can usually find out by watching television to see how many commercials advertise that product. A lot of those commercials make you feel as though you must have everything you see.

Gehazi did not have a television to watch, but he did see an opportunity right before his eyes to get exactly what he wanted. In fact, he was so determined to get riches and fine clothes from Naaman that he lied to get them. Poor Gehazi. His selfishness cost him more than he had planned.

Be careful about deciding that you *must* have something you see. Ask God to help you make good choices about the things you want.

To learn more ways to stay away from selfishness,
zoom to page 452.

*temple of Rimmon The place where the Aramean people worshiped the false god Rimmon.

he gave them to two of his servants. They carried them for Gehazi. ²⁴When they came to the hill, Gehazi took these things from Naaman's servants. And he put them in the house. He let Naaman's servants go, and they left.

²⁵Then he came in and stood before his master. Elisha said to him, "Where have you been, Gehazi?"

Gehazi said, "I didn't go anywhere."

²⁶But Elisha said to him, "My spirit was with you. I knew when the man turned from his chariot to meet you. This isn't a time to receive money, clothes, olives and grapes. It isn't a time to receive sheep, oxen, male servants and female servants. ²⁷Naaman's skin disease will come on you and your children forever." When Gehazi left Elisha, he had the disease. He was as white as snow.

An Axhead Floats

6 The group of the prophets[d] said to Elisha, "The place where we meet with you is too small for us. ²Let's go to the Jordan River. There every man can get a pole. And let's build a place there to live."

Elisha said, "Go."

³One of them said, "Please go with us."

Elisha said, "I will go." ⁴So he went with them. When they arrived at the Jordan, they cut down some trees. ⁵As one man was cutting down a tree, the head of his ax fell into the water. He yelled, "Oh, my master! I borrowed that ax!"

⁶Elisha asked, "Where did it fall?" The man showed Elisha the place. Then Elisha cut down a stick and threw it into the water. It made the iron head float. ⁷Elisha said, "Pick up the axhead." Then the man reached out and took it.

Elisha and the Blinded Arameans

⁸The king of Aram was at war with Israel. He had a council meeting with his officers. He said, "I will set up my camp in this place."

People Who Got Away

THE ARAMEAN ARMY • 2 KINGS 6:8-23

Can you imagine a fight between one man and an entire army? That is not fair! The king of Aram sent his army to kill Elisha, God's messenger. Elisha was outnumbered by several hundred men. But he prayed and asked God to make the soldiers in the army blind so they could not see where they were going. And God did!

The army stumbled along, bumping into one another, not knowing where they were going. Then Elisha went out to greet them. He knew they could not see who he was. He told the army they were on the wrong road and in the wrong city. He had the army follow him to the city of their enemy—the king of Israel. The Aramean army was trapped! But Elisha told the king of Israel not to kill the Aramean army. Instead, Elisha said to feed the Arameans and send them home unharmed. Elisha let the Arameans get away, and they never came back!

If someone tries to hurt you, you do not have to hurt them too. The Bible tells us to love everyone—even our enemies.

To read about a man who escaped in a basket, fly to page 1331.

⁹But Elisha sent a message to the king of Israel. It said, "Be careful! Don't pass that place. The Arameans are going down there!"

"I've discovered you can't watch where you're going if your eyes are closed!" 2 Kings 6:8-23 is the story about soldiers who lost their sight.

¹⁰The king of Israel checked the place about which Elisha had warned him. Elisha warned him several times. So the king added guards in those places.

¹¹The king of Aram was angry about this. He called his officers together. He said to them, "Tell me who of us is working for the king of Israel."

¹²One of the officers of the king of Aram said, "No, my master and king. It's Elisha, the prophet[d] from Israel. He can tell you what you speak in your bedroom."

¹³The king said, "Go and find him. Then I can send men and catch him." The servants came back and reported, "He is in Dothan."

¹⁴Then the king sent horses, chariots and a large army to Dothan. They arrived at night and surrounded the city.

¹⁵The servant of Elisha got up early. When he went out, he saw an army with horses and chariots all around the city. The servant said to Elisha, "Oh, my master, what can we do?"

¹⁶Elisha said, "Don't be afraid. The army that fights for us is larger than the one against us."

¹⁷Then Elisha prayed, "Lord, open my servant's eyes. Let him see." The Lord opened the eyes of the young man. And he saw that the mountain was full of horses and chariots of fire all around Elisha.

¹⁸As the enemy came down toward Elisha, he prayed to the Lord. He said,

"Make these people blind." So the Lord made the Aramean army blind, as Elisha had asked.

¹⁹Elisha said to them, "This is not the right road. This is not the right city. Follow me. I'll take you to the man you are looking for." Then Elisha led them to Samaria.

²⁰After they entered Samaria, Elisha said, "Lord, open these men's eyes so they can see." So the Lord opened their eyes. And the Aramean army saw that they were inside the city of Samaria!

²¹The king of Israel saw the Aramean army. He said to Elisha, "My father, should I kill them? Should I kill them?"

²²Elisha answered, "Don't kill them. You wouldn't kill people whom you captured with your sword and bow. Give them food and water. And let them eat and drink. Then let them go home to their master." ²³So he prepared a great feast for the Aramean army. They ate and drank. Then the king sent them away. They went home to their master. The soldiers of Aram did not come anymore into the land of Israel.

A Time of Hunger

²⁴Later, Ben-Hadad king of Aram gathered all his army. He went to surround and attack Samaria. ²⁵There was a time of terrible hunger in Samaria. It was so bad that a donkey's head was sold for about two pounds of silver. Half of a pint of dove's dung sold for about two ounces of silver.

²⁶The king of Israel was passing by on the wall. A woman yelled out to him, "Help me, my master and king!"

²⁷The king said, "If the Lord doesn't help you, how can I? Can I get help from the threshing[d] floor or from the winepress?"[d] ²⁸Then the king said to her, "What is your trouble?"

She answered, "This woman said to me, 'Give up your son so we can eat him today. Then we will eat my son tomorrow.' ²⁹So we boiled my son and ate him. Then the next day I said to her, 'Give up your son so we can eat him.' But she had hidden him."

³⁰When the king heard the woman's words, he tore his clothes to show how upset he was. He walked along the wall. The people looked and saw he had on rough cloth under his clothes. This was to show his sadness. ³¹He said, "The head of Elisha son of Shaphat will be taken from his body today! May God punish me terribly if this doesn't happen!"

³²The king sent a messenger to Elisha. Elisha was sitting in his house. And the older leaders were sitting with him. But before the messenger arrived, Elisha spoke to them. He said, "See, this murderer is sending men to take off my head. When the messenger arrives, shut the door. Hold it and don't let him in. The sound of his master's feet is behind him."

³³While Elisha was still talking with the leaders, the king came. He said, "This trouble has come from the Lord. Why should I wait for the Lord any longer?"

7 Elisha said, "Listen to the Lord's word. This is what he says: 'About this time tomorrow 7 quarts of fine flour will be sold for two-fifths of an ounce of silver. And 13 quarts of barley will be sold for two-fifths of an ounce of silver. This will happen at the gate of Samaria.'"

²Then the officer who was close to the king answered Elisha. He said, "Even if the Lord opened windows in heaven, that couldn't happen."

Elisha said, "Because you have said that, you will see it with your eyes. But you will not eat any of it."

³There were four men with a harmful skin disease at the entrance to the city gate. They said to each other, "Why do we sit here until we die? ⁴A time of hunger is in the city. So if we go into the city, we will die there. If we stay here, we will die. So let's go to the

Staying Away from Selfishness
2 KINGS 7:3-9

Wow! You found a million dollars buried in your backyard. What will you do with it?

Buy a new bike for each day of the year? Buy your own video game store? If those kinds of things jump to your mind when you think of spending a million dollars, that's pretty normal. But there's more to life than being normal!

At first, the guys in this story wanted to keep all the food and riches they found to themselves. But they changed their minds and decided to share with others. With a million dollars you could help pay for a new hospital for sick kids, or you could buy supplies for a village in a poor country, or you could feed a lot of hungry people.

Most kids probably wouldn't think of doing anything like that with the money. But God wants you to be better than most. He wants you to be unselfish with everything he has given you.

To learn more ways to stay away from selfishness,
zoom to page 775.

Aramean camp. If they let us live, we will live. If they kill us, then we die."

⁵So they got up at twilight. And they went to the Aramean camp. But when they arrived, no one was there. ⁶The Lord had caused the Aramean army to hear the sound of chariots, horses and a large army. They had said to each other, "The king of Israel has hired the Hittite and Egyptian kings to attack us!" ⁷So they ran away in the twilight. They left their tents, horses and donkeys. They left the camp standing and ran for their lives.

⁸The men with the skin disease came to the edge of the camp. Then they went into one of the tents. They ate and drank. They carried silver, gold and clothes out of the camp and hid them. Then they came back and entered another tent. They carried things from this tent and hid them, also. ⁹Then they said to each other, "We're doing wrong. Today we have good news, but we are silent. If we wait until the sun comes up, we'll be punished. Let's go now and tell the people in the king's palace."

¹⁰So they went and called to the gate-keepers of the city. They said, "We went to the Aramean camp. But no one is there. We didn't hear anyone. The horses and donkeys were still tied up, and the tents were still standing." ¹¹Then the gatekeepers shouted out and told the people in the palace.

¹²So the king got up in the night. He said to his officers, "I'll tell you what the Arameans are doing to us. They know we are hungry. They have gone out of the camp to hide in the field. They're saying, 'When the Israelites come out of the city, we'll capture them alive. Then we'll enter the city.'"

¹³One of his officers answered, "Let some men take five horses still left in the city. These men are like all the Israelites who are left. They are also about to die. Let's send them to see what has happened."

¹⁴So the men took two chariots with horses. The king sent them after the Aramean army. He told them, "Go and see what has happened." ¹⁵The men followed the Aramean army as far as the Jordan River. The road was full of clothes and equipment. The Arameans had thrown these things away as they had hurried away. So the messengers came back and told the king. ¹⁶Then the people went out and took valuable things from the Aramean camp. So 7 quarts of fine flour were sold for two-fifths of an ounce of silver. And 13 quarts of barley were sold for two-fifths of an ounce of silver. It happened just as the Lord had said.

¹⁷The king chose the officer who was close to him to guard the gate. But the people ran over the officer so that he died. This happened just as the man of God had told the king. Elisha had said it when the king came to his house. ¹⁸He had said, "Thirteen quarts of barley and 7 quarts of fine flour will each sell for two-fifths of an ounce of silver. It will happen about this time tomorrow at the gate of Samaria."

¹⁹But the officer had answered, "Even if the Lord opened windows in heaven, that couldn't happen." And Elisha had told him, "Because you have said that, you will see it with your eyes. But you won't eat any of it." ²⁰It happened to the officer just that way. The people ran over him in the gate, and he died.

The Shunammite Regains Her Land

8 Elisha talked to the woman whose son he had brought back to life. He said, "Get up and go with your family. Stay any place you can. This is because the Lord has called for a time of hunger. It will last seven years." ²So the woman got up and did as the man of God said. She left with her family. And they stayed in the land of the Philistines for seven years. ³After seven years she came back from the land of the Philistines. She went to beg the king for her house and land back. ⁴The king was talking with Gehazi. He was the servant of the man of God. The king had said to Gehazi, "Please tell me all the great things Elisha has done." ⁵Now Gehazi was telling the king how Elisha had brought a dead person back to life. Just then the woman whose son Elisha had brought back to life came and begged the king for her house and land.

Gehazi said, "My master and king, this is the woman. And this is the son Elisha brought back to life."

⁶The king asked the woman, and she told him about it. Then the king chose an officer to help her. The king said, "Give the woman everything that is hers. Give her all the money made from her land from the day she left until now."

Ben-Hadad Is Killed

⁷Elisha went to Damascus. Now Ben-Hadad king of Aram was sick. Someone told him, "The man of God has come here."

⁸Then the king said to Hazael, "Take a gift in your hand and go meet him. Ask the Lord through him if I will get well from my sickness."

⁹So Hazael went to meet Elisha. He took with him a gift. It was 40 camels loaded with every good thing in Damascus. He came and stood before Elisha. Hazael said, "Your son Ben-Hadad king of Aram sent me to you. He asks if he will get well from his sickness."

¹⁰Then Elisha said to Hazael, "Go and tell Ben-Hadad, 'You will surely get well.' But the Lord has told me he will really die." ¹¹Elisha stared at Hazael until Hazael felt ashamed. Then Elisha cried.

¹²Hazael asked, "Why are you crying, master?"

Elisha answered, "Because I know what evil you will do to the Israelites. You will burn their strong, walled cities with fire. You will kill their young men with swords. You will throw their babies to the ground. You will split open their pregnant women."

¹³Hazael said, "I, your servant, am only a dog. How could I do such things?"

Elisha answered, "The Lord has shown me that you will be king over Aram."

¹⁴Then Hazael left Elisha and came to his master. Ben-Hadad said to Hazael, "What did Elisha say to you?"

Hazael answered, "He told me that you will surely get well." ¹⁵But the next day Hazael took a blanket and dipped it in water. Then he put it over Ben-Hadad's face, and he died. So Hazael became king in Ben-Hadad's place.

Jehoram King of Judah

¹⁶Jehoram son of Jehoshaphat became king of Judah. This was during Joram's fifth year as king of Israel. Joram was the son of Ahab. ¹⁷Jehoram was 32 years old when he began to rule. He ruled eight years in Jerusalem. ¹⁸But Jehoram followed the ways of the kings of Israel. This was just as the family of Ahab had done. It was because Ahab's daughter was Jehoram's wife. Jehoram did what the Lord said was wrong. ¹⁹But the Lord would not destroy Judah because of his servant David. The Lord had promised that David and his children would always have a kingdom.

²⁰In Jehoram's time Edom broke away from Judah's rule. The people of Edom chose their own king. ²¹So Jehoram and all his chariots went to Zair. At night the Edomites came around him and his chariot commanders. Jehoram got up and attacked the Edomites. But his army ran away to their tents. ²²So the Edomites broke away from the rule of Judah. And they are still separate today. At the same time Libnah also broke away from Judah's rule.

²³The other acts of Jehoram and all the things he did are written down. They are in the book of the history of the kings of Judah. ²⁴Jehoram died and was buried with his ancestors in Jerusalem. Jehoram's son Ahaziah ruled in his place.

²⁵Ahaziah son of Jehoram became king of Judah. This was during Joram's twelfth year as king of Israel. Joram was the son of Ahab. ²⁶Ahaziah was 22 years old when he became king. He ruled one year in Jerusalem. His

mother's name was Athaliah. She was a granddaughter of Omri king of Israel. [27]Ahaziah followed the ways of Ahab's family. He did what the Lord said was wrong, as Ahab's family had done. He did this because he was a son-in-law in Ahab's family.

[28]Ahaziah went with Joram son of Ahab to Ramoth in Gilead. There they fought against Hazael king of Aram. The Arameans wounded Joram. [29]So King Joram returned to Jezreel to heal from the injuries. (He had been wounded by the Arameans at Ramoth. This was when he fought Hazael king of Aram.) And Ahaziah son of Jehoram king of Judah went down to see Joram. He went to see Joram son of Ahab at Jezreel because he had been wounded.

Jehu Is Chosen King

9 Elisha called a man from the group of the prophets.[d] Elisha said, "Tighten your clothes around you. And take this small bottle of olive oil in your hand. Go to Ramoth in Gilead. [2]When you arrive, find Jehu son of Jehoshaphat. Jehoshaphat is the son of Nimshi. Go in and make Jehu get up from among his brothers. Take him to an inner room. [3]Take the bottle and pour the oil on Jehu's head. Say, 'This is what the Lord says: I have appointed you king over Israel.' Then open the door and run away. Don't wait!"

[4]So the young man, the prophet, went to Ramoth in Gilead. [5]When he arrived, he saw the officers of the army sitting together. He said, "Commander, I have a message for you."

Jehu asked, "For which one of us?"

The young man said, "For you, commander."

[6]Jehu got up and went into the house. Then the young prophet poured the olive oil on Jehu's head. He said to Jehu, "This is what the Lord of Israel says: 'I have appointed you king over the Lord's people, Israel. [7]You must destroy the family of Ahab your master. I will punish Jezebel for the deaths of my servants the prophets. And I will

punish her for all the Lord's servants who were murdered. [8]So all Ahab's family will die. I will not let any male child in Ahab's family live in Israel. It does not matter if he is a slave or a free person. [9]I will make Ahab's family like the family of Jeroboam son of Nebat. They will be like the family of Baasha son of Ahijah. [10]The dogs will eat Jezebel in the portion of land at Jezreel. And no one will bury her.'"

Then the young prophet opened the door and ran away.

[11]Jehu went back to his master's officers. One of them said to Jehu, "Is everything all right? Why did this crazy man come to you?"

Jehu answered, "You know the man and how he talks."

[12]They answered, "That's not true! Tell us."

Jehu said, "He said, 'This is what the Lord says: I have appointed you to be king over Israel.'"

[13]Then the officers hurried. Each man took off his own coat. They put them on the stairs for Jehu. Then they blew the trumpet. They said, "Jehu is king!"

Joram and Ahaziah Are Killed

[14]So Jehu son of Jehoshaphat made plans against Joram. (Jehoshaphat was the son of Nimshi.) Now Joram and all Israel had been defending Ramoth in Gilead from Hazael king of Aram. [15]But King Joram had to return to Israel to heal from the injuries the Arameans had given him. He received these injuries when he fought against Hazael king of Aram.

Jehu said, "If you agree with this, don't let anyone leave the city. They might tell the news in Jezreel." [16]Then he got into his chariot and set out for Jezreel. Joram was resting there. And Ahaziah king of Judah had gone down to see him.

[17]The lookout was standing on the watchtower in Jezreel. He saw Jehu's troops coming. He said, "I see some soldiers!"

Joram said, "Take a horseman and send him to meet them. Tell him to ask, 'Do you bring good news?'"

[18]So the horseman rode out to meet Jehu. The horseman said, "This is what the king says: 'Do you bring good news?'"

Jehu said, "That's none of your business! Come along behind me."

The lookout reported, "The messenger reached them. But he is not coming back."

[19]So Joram sent out a second horseman. This rider came to Jehu's group and said, "This is what the king says: 'Do you bring good news?'"

Jehu answered, "That's none of your business! Come along behind me."

[20]The lookout reported, "The second man reached them. But he is not coming back. The man in the chariot is driving like Jehu son of Nimshi. He drives as if he were crazy!"

[21]Joram said, "Get my chariot ready." Then the servant got Joram's chariot ready. Joram and Ahaziah king of Judah went out. Each king went in his own chariot to meet Jehu. And they met him at the property of Naboth the Jezreelite.

[22]When Joram saw Jehu, he said, "Do you bring good news, Jehu?"

Jehu answered, "There will never be any good news as long as your mother Jezebel worships idols and uses witchcraft."[d]

[23]Joram turned the horses to run away. He yelled to Ahaziah, "It's a trick, Ahaziah!"

[24]Then Jehu drew his bow and shot Joram between his shoulders. The arrow went through Joram's heart. And he fell down in his chariot.

[25]Jehu ordered Bidkar, his chariot officer, "Pick up Joram's body. Throw it into the field of Naboth the Jezreelite. Remember when you and I rode together with Joram's father Ahab. The Lord made this prophecy[d] against him: [26]'Yesterday I saw the blood of Naboth and his sons, says the Lord. So I will punish Ahab in his field, says the Lord.' So take Joram's body and throw it into the field, as the Lord has said."

[27]When Ahaziah king of Judah saw this, he ran away toward Beth Haggan. Jehu chased him, saying, "Shoot Ahaziah, too!" Ahaziah was wounded in his chariot on the way up to Gur near Ibleam. Ahaziah got as far as Megiddo but died there. [28]His servants carried his body in a chariot to Jerusalem. They buried him with his ancestors in his tomb in Jerusalem. [29](Ahaziah had become king over Judah in Joram's eleventh year as king. Joram was the son of Ahab.)

Death of Jezebel

[30]When Jehu came to Jezreel, Jezebel heard about it. She put paint on her eyes and fixed her hair. Then she looked out the window. [31]Jehu entered the city gate. And Jezebel said, "Have you come in peace, you Zimri,[n] you who killed your master?"

[32]Jehu looked up at the window. He said, "Who is on my side? Who?" Two or three eunuchs[d] looked out from the window at Jehu. [33]Jehu said to them, "Throw her down!" So they threw Jezebel down. And the horses ran over her body. Some of her blood splashed on the wall and on the horses.

[34]Jehu went into the house and ate and drank. Then he said, "Now see about this cursed woman. Bury her, because she is a king's daughter."

[35]The men went to bury Jezebel. But they could not find her body. They could only find the skull, feet and palms of her hands. [36]So they came back and told Jehu. Then Jehu said, "The Lord said this through his servant Elijah the Tishbite: 'The dogs will eat the body of Jezebel in the portion of land at Jezreel. [37]Her body will be like manure on the field in the land at Jezreel. Then people cannot say that the body is Jezebel.'"

[n]Zimri He was the man who killed Elah and the family of Baasha. Read 1 Kings 16:8-12.

Families of Ahab and Ahaziah Killed

10 Ahab's family had 70 sons in Samaria. Jehu wrote letters and sent them to Samaria. He sent them to the officers and older leaders of Jezreel. He also sent them to the guardians of the sons of Ahab. Jehu said, ²"You have chariots, horses and a city with strong walls. You also have weapons. When you get this letter, ³choose the best and most worthy person among your master's sons. Make him king. Then fight for your master's family."

⁴But the officers and older leaders of Jezreel were very frightened. They said, "The two kings could not stop Jehu. So, surely we can't either."

⁵The palace manager, the city governor, the older leaders and the guardians sent a message to Jehu. They said, "We are your servants. We will do everything you tell us to do. We won't make any man king. Do whatever you think is best."

⁶Then Jehu wrote a second letter. It said, "If you are on my side and will obey me, cut off the heads of your master's sons. And come to me at Jezreel tomorrow about this time."

Now there were 70 sons of the king's family. They were with the leading men of the city who were their guardians. ⁷The leaders received the letter. Then they took the king's sons and killed all 70 of them. They put their heads in baskets. And they sent them to Jehu at Jezreel. ⁸The messenger came to Jehu. He told Jehu, "They have brought the heads of the king's sons!"

Then Jehu said, "Lay the heads in two piles at the city gate until morning."

⁹In the morning, Jehu went out and stood before the people. He said to them, "You are innocent. Look, I made plans against my master. I killed him. But who killed all these? ¹⁰You should know that nothing the Lord said will fail. Everything the Lord said about Ahab's family will come true. The Lord has spoken through his servant Elijah. And the Lord has done what he said."

¹¹So Jehu killed everyone of Ahab's family in Jezreel who was still alive. He also killed all Ahab's leading men, close friends and priests. No one was left alive who had helped Ahab.

¹²Then Jehu left and went to Samaria. He went on the road to Beth Eked of the Shepherds. ¹³There Jehu met some relatives of Ahaziah king of Judah. Jehu said, "Who are you?"

They answered, "We are relatives of Ahaziah. We have come down to visit the families of the king and the king's mother."

¹⁴Then Jehu said, "Take them alive!" So they captured Ahaziah's relatives alive. But they killed them at the well near Beth Eked. There were 42 of them. Jehu did not leave anyone alive.

¹⁵After Jehu left there, he met Jehonadab son of Recab. He was also on his way to meet Jehu. Jehu greeted him and said, "Are you as good a friend to me as I am to you?"

Jehonadab answered, "Yes, I am."

Jehu said, "If you are, then give me your hand." So Jehonadab gave him his hand, and Jehu pulled him into the chariot. ¹⁶Jehu said, "Come with me. You can see how strong my feelings are for the Lord." So Jehu had Jehonadab ride in his chariot.

¹⁷When Jehu came to Samaria, he killed all of Ahab's family. He did this until he had destroyed all of those who were left. Jehu did what the Lord had told Elijah would happen.

Baal Worshipers Killed

¹⁸Then Jehu gathered all the people together. He said to them, "Ahab served Baal[d] a little. But Jehu will serve Baal much. ¹⁹Now call for me all Baal's prophets and priests. Call all the people who worship Baal. Don't let anyone miss this meeting. I have a great sacrifice for Baal. Anyone who is not there will not remain alive." But Jehu was tricking them so he could destroy the worshipers of Baal. ²⁰He said, "Prepare a holy meeting for Baal." So they announced the meeting. ²¹Then Jehu

sent word through all Israel. All the worshipers of Baal came. Not one stayed home. They came into the temple of Baal. The temple was filled from one side to the other.

22Jehu spoke to the man who kept the robes. He said, "Bring out robes for all the worshipers of Baal." So he brought out robes for them. 23Then Jehu and Jehonadab son of Recab went into the temple of Baal. Jehu said to the worshipers of Baal, "Look around. Be sure there are no servants of the Lord with you. Be sure there are only people here who worship Baal." 24So the worshipers of Baal went in to offer sacrifices and burnt offerings.

But Jehu had 80 men waiting outside. He told them, "Don't let anyone escape. If you let anyone escape, you must pay with your own life."

25Jehu finished offering the burnt offering. Then he spoke to the guards and the captains. He said, "Go in and kill the worshipers of Baal! Don't let anyone come out." So the guards and captains killed the worshipers of Baal with the sword. They threw the bodies of the worshipers of Baal out. Then they went to the inner rooms of the temple. 26They brought out the pillars of the temple of Baal and burned them. 27Then they tore down the stone pillar of Baal. They also tore down the temple of Baal. They made it into a sewage pit, and it is still true today.

28So Jehu destroyed Baal worship in Israel. 29But he did not stop doing the sins Jeroboam son of Nebat had done. Jeroboam had caused Israel to sin. They worshiped the golden calves in Bethel and Dan.

30The Lord said to Jehu, "You have done well. You have done what I said was right. You have done to the family of Ahab as I wanted. Your descendants*d* as far as your great-great-grandchildren will be kings of Israel." 31But Jehu was not careful to keep the teachings of the Lord with all his heart. He did not stop doing the same sins Jeroboam had done. Jeroboam had caused Israel to sin.

32At that time the Lord began to make Israel smaller. Hazael defeated the Israelites in all the land of Israel. 33He took all the land on the east side of the Jordan. This was the land of Gilead. (It was the region of Gad, Reuben and Manasseh.) He took land from Aroer by the Arnon Ravine through Gilead to Bashan.

34The other things Jehu did are written down. Everything he did and all his victories are recorded. They are in the book of the history of the kings of Israel. 35Jehu died and was buried in Samaria. Jehu's son Jehoahaz became king in his place. 36Jehu was king over Israel in Samaria for 28 years.

Athaliah and Joash

11 Now Ahaziah's mother, Athaliah, saw that her son was dead. Then she killed all the royal family. 2But Jehosheba took Joash, Ahaziah's son. She stole him from among the other sons of the king who were about to be murdered. (Jehosheba was King Jehoram's daughter and Ahaziah's sister.) She put Joash and his nurse in a bedroom. She hid Joash from Athaliah. So he was not killed. 3He was hidden with her in the Temple*d* of the Lord for six years. During that time Athaliah ruled the land.

4In the seventh year Jehoiada sent for the commanders of groups of 100 men. He sent for guards and the Carites, the royal bodyguards. He brought them together in the Temple of the Lord. Then he made an agreement with them. There, in the Temple of the Lord, he made them promise loyalty. Then he showed them the king's son. 5He commanded them, "This is what you must do. A third of you who come in on the Sabbath*d* will guard the king's palace. 6Another third of you will be at the Sur Gate. And another third will be at the gate behind the guard. This way you will guard the Temple. 7Two groups will go off duty on the Sabbath. They must protect the Temple of the Lord for the king. 8All of you must stand around the king. Each man must have his weapon in his hand. If anyone comes near, kill him. Stay close to the king when he goes out and when he comes in."

⁹The commanders over 100 men obeyed everything Jehoiada the priest had commanded. Each one took his men who were beginning their Sabbath duty. Each one also took those who were ending their Sabbath duty. Both groups came to Jehoiada the priest. ¹⁰And he gave spears and shields to the commanders. They used to belong to King David. They were kept in the Temple of the Lord.

Joash Becomes King

¹¹Then each of the guards took his place. Each man had his weapon in his hand. There were guards from the south side of the Temple*d* to the north side. They stood by the altar and the Temple and around the king. ¹²Jehoiada brought out the king's son. He put the crown on Joash. Then he gave Joash a copy of the Agreement with the Lord. They appointed him king and poured olive oil on him. They clapped their hands and said, "Long live the king!"

¹³Athaliah heard the noise of the guards and the people. So she came to the people at the Temple of the Lord. ¹⁴She looked, and there was the king. He was standing by the pillar, as the custom was. The officers and trumpeters were standing beside him. All the people of the land were very happy and were blowing trumpets. Then Athaliah tore her clothes to show how upset she was. She screamed, "Traitors! Traitors!"

¹⁵Jehoiada the priest gave orders to the commanders of 100 men who led the army. He said, "Surround her with soldiers. Kill with a sword anyone who follows her." He said this because he had said, "Don't put Athaliah to death in the Temple of the Lord." ¹⁶So they caught her when she came to where the horses enter the palace grounds. There she was put to death.

¹⁷Then Jehoiada made an agreement. It was between the Lord and the king and the people. They agreed to be the Lord's special people. He also made an agreement between the king and the people. ¹⁸All the people of the land went to the temple of Baal*d* and tore it down. They smashed the altars and idols into small pieces. And they killed Mattan, the priest of Baal, in front of the altars.

Then Jehoiada the priest placed guards at the Temple of the Lord. ¹⁹He took with him the commanders of 100 men and the Carites, the royal bodyguards. He took the guards and all the people of the land. Together they took the king out of the Temple of the Lord. They went into the palace through the gate of the guards. Then the king sat on the royal throne. ²⁰So all the people of Judah were very happy. And Jerusalem had peace because Athaliah had been put to death with the sword at the palace.

²¹Joash was seven years old when he became king.

12 Joash became king of Judah in Jehu's seventh year as king of Israel. Joash ruled for 40 years in Jerusalem. His mother's name was Zibiah. She was from Beersheba. ²Joash did what the Lord said was right all the time Jehoiada the priest taught him. ³But the places where false gods were worshiped were not removed. The people still made sacrifices and burned incense*d* there.

The Temple to Be Repaired

⁴Joash said to the priests, "Take all the money brought as offerings to the Temple*d* of the Lord. This includes the money each person owes in taxes. It also includes the money each person promises or brings to the Lord because he wants to. ⁵Each priest must take the money from the people he serves. Then the priests must repair any damage they find in the Temple."

⁶But by the twenty-third year of Joash the priests still had not repaired the Temple. ⁷So King Joash called for Jehoiada the priest and the other

priests. He said to them, "Why are you not repairing the damage of the Temple? Don't take any more money from the people you serve. But hand over the money for the repair of the Temple." ⁸The priests agreed not to take any more money from the people. And they agreed not to repair the Temple themselves.

⁹But Jehoiada the priest took a box and made a hole in the top of it. Then he put it by the altar. It was on the right side as the people came into the Temple of the Lord. The priests guarding the doorway put all the money brought to the Temple of the Lord into the box.

¹⁰Each time the priests saw that the box was full of money, the king's royal assistant and the high priest came. They counted the money that had been brought to the Temple of the Lord. Then they put it into bags. ¹¹Next they weighed the money. They gave it to the men who were in charge of the work on the Temple. With it they paid the carpenters and the builders who worked on the Temple of the Lord. ¹²They also paid the stoneworkers and stonecutters. They used the money to buy timber and cut stone. The money was used to repair the damage of the Temple of the Lord. It paid for everything.

¹³The money brought into the Temple of the Lord was not used to make silver cups. It was not used for wick trimmers, bowls or trumpets. And it wasn't used for any gold or silver vessels. ¹⁴They paid the money to the workers. And the workers used it to repair the Temple of the Lord. ¹⁵They did not make the men tell how the money was spent. This was because the men were honest. ¹⁶The money from the penalty offerings and sin offerings was not brought into the Temple of the Lord. It belonged to the priests.

Joash Saves Jerusalem

¹⁷About this time Hazael king of Aram attacked Gath and captured it. Then he went to attack Jerusalem. ¹⁸But Joash king of Judah took all the holy things his ancestors had given. His ancestors were the kings of Judah— Jehoshaphat, Jehoram and Ahaziah. He also took his own holy things. He took the gold that was found in the treasuries of the Temple^d of the Lord. And he took the gold from the palace. Joash sent all this treasure to Hazael king of Aram. Then Hazael turned away from Jerusalem.

¹⁹Everything else Joash did is written down. It is in the book of the history of the kings of Judah. ²⁰His officers made plans against him. They killed him at Beth Millo on the road to Silla. ²¹The officers who killed him were Jozabad son of Shimeath and Jehozabad son of Shomer. Joash was buried with his ancestors in Jerusalem. And Amaziah, his son, became king in his place.

Jehoahaz King of Israel

13 Jehoahaz son of Jehu became king over Israel in Samaria. This was during Joash's twenty-third year as king of Judah. Joash was the son of Ahaziah. And Jehoahaz ruled 17 years. ²He did what the Lord said was wrong. Jehoahaz did the same sins Jeroboam son of Nebat had done. Jeroboam had caused Israel to sin. And Jehoahaz did not stop doing these same sins. ³So the Lord was angry with Israel. And he gave them into the power of Hazael king of Aram and his son Ben-Hadad.

⁴Then Jehoahaz begged the Lord, and the Lord listened to him. The Lord had seen the troubles of Israel. He saw how terribly the king of Aram was treating the Israelites. ⁵So he gave Israel a man to save them. And they escaped from the Arameans. So the Israelites lived in their own homes as they had before. ⁶But the Israelites still did not stop doing the same sins that the family of Jeroboam had done. He had caused Israel to sin. They continued doing those sins. The Asherah^d idol also was left standing in Samaria. ⁷Nothing was left of Jehoahaz's army

except 50 horsemen, 10 chariots and 10,000 foot soldiers. The king of Aram had destroyed them. He had made them like dust at the time of threshing.[d]

[8]Everything else Jehoahaz did and all his victories are written down. They are in the book of history of the kings of Israel. [9]Jehoahaz died and was buried in Samaria. His son Jehoash became king in his place.

Jehoash King of Israel

[10]Jehoash son of Jehoahaz became king of Israel in Samaria. This was during Joash's thirty-seventh year as king of Judah. Jehoash ruled 16 years. [11]He did what the Lord said was wrong. He did not stop doing the same sins Jeroboam son of Nebat had done. Jeroboam had caused Israel to sin. And Jehoash continued to do the same thing. [12]Everything else he did and all his victories are written down. This includes his war against Amaziah king of Judah. All this is written in the book of the history of the kings of Israel. [13]Jehoash died, and Jeroboam took his place on the throne. Jehoash was buried in Samaria with the kings of Israel.

The Death of Elisha

[14]At this time Elisha became sick. (Later, he died from this illness.) Jehoash king of Israel went to Elisha and cried for him. Jehoash said, "My father, my father! The chariots of Israel and their horsemen!"

[15]Elisha said to Jehoash, "Take a bow and arrows." So he took a bow and arrows. [16]Then Elisha said to him, "Put your hand on the bow." So Jehoash put his hand on the bow. Then Elisha put his hands on the king's hands. [17]Elisha said, "Open the east window." So Jehoash opened the window. Then Elisha said, "Shoot," and Jehoash shot. Elisha said, "The Lord's arrow of victory over Aram! You will defeat the Arameans at Aphek until you destroy them."

[18]Elisha said, "Take the arrows." So Jehoash took them. Then Elisha said to him, "Hit the ground." So Jehoash hit the ground three times. Then he stopped. [19]The man of God was angry with him. Elisha said, "You should have hit five or six times! Then you would have defeated Aram until you had completely destroyed it! But now you will defeat it only three times."

[20]So Elisha died and was buried.

At that time groups of Moabites would rob the land in the springtime. [21]Once the Israelites were burying a man. Suddenly they saw a group of Moabites coming. The Israelites threw the dead man into Elisha's grave. When the man touched Elisha's bones, the man came back to life. And he stood up on his feet.

War with Aram

[22]During all the days Jehoahaz was king, Hazael king of Aram troubled Israel. [23]But the Lord was kind to the Israelites. He had mercy on them. And he helped them because of his agreement with Abraham, Isaac and Jacob. He did not destroy them or reject them.

[24]Hazael king of Aram died. And his son Ben-Hadad became king in his place. [25]During a war Hazael had taken some cities from Jehoahaz, Jehoash's father. But now Jehoash took back those cities from Hazael's son Ben-Hadad. He defeated Ben-Hadad three times and took back the cities of Israel.

Amaziah King of Judah

14 Amaziah son of Joash became king of Judah. This was during the second year Jehoash son of Jehoahaz was king of Israel. [2]Amaziah was 25 years old when he became king. He ruled 29 years in Jerusalem. His mother was Jehoaddin. She was from Jerusalem. [3]Amaziah did what the Lord said was right. Amaziah did everything his father Joash had done. But he did not do as David his ancestor had done. [4]The places where false gods were worshiped were not removed. The people still sacrificed and burned incense[d] there.

⁵Amaziah took strong control of the kingdom. Then he put the officers to death who had killed his father the king. ⁶But he did not put to death the children of the murderers. This is because of the rule written in the Book of the Teachings of Moses. The Lord had commanded: "Fathers must not be put to death when their children do wrong. And children must not be put to death when their fathers do wrong. Each person must die for his own sins."ⁿ

⁷Amaziah killed 10,000 Edomites in the Valley of Salt. In a battle Amaziah took the city of Sela. He called it Joktheel, and it is still called that today.

⁸Amaziah sent messengers to Jehoash son of Jehoahaz. (Jehoahaz was the son of Jehu, king of Israel.) The message read, "Come, let's meet face to face in battle."

⁹Then Jehoash king of Israel answered Amaziah king of Judah. Jehoash said, "A little thornbush in Lebanon sent a message to a big cedar tree in Lebanon. It said, 'Let your daughter marry my son.' But then a wild animal from Lebanon came by. It walked on and crushed the thornbush. ¹⁰Yes, you have defeated Edom. But you have become proud because of your victory over Edom. Stay at home and brag! Don't ask for trouble by fighting me. If you do, you and Judah will be defeated."

¹¹But Amaziah would not listen. So Jehoash king of Israel went to attack. He and Amaziah king of Judah faced each other in battle at Beth Shemesh in Judah. ¹²Israel defeated Judah. Every man of Judah ran away to his home. ¹³At Beth Shemesh Jehoash king of Israel captured Amaziah king of Judah. Amaziah was the son of Joash, who was the son of Ahaziah. Then Jehoash went to Jerusalem. He broke down the wall of Jerusalem from the Gate of Ephraim to the Corner Gate. This part of the wall was about 600 feet long. ¹⁴Then he took all the gold and silver and everything in the Tem‍pleᵈ of the Lord. And he took the treasuries of the palace. He also took some hostages and returned to Samaria.

¹⁵The other acts of Jehoash and his victories are written down. This includes his war against Amaziah king of Judah. All this is in the book of the history of the kings of Israel. ¹⁶Jehoash died and was buried in Samaria with the kings of Israel. And his son Jeroboam became king in his place.

¹⁷Amaziah son of Joash was king of Judah. He lived 15 years after Jehoash king of Israel died. Jehoash was the son of Jehoahaz. ¹⁸The other things Amaziah did as king are written down. They are in the book of the history of the kings of Judah. ¹⁹The people made plans in Jerusalem against Amaziah. So he ran away to the town of Lachish. But they sent men after him to Lachish and killed him. ²⁰They brought his body back on horses. And he was buried with his ancestors in Jerusalem, the city of David.

²¹Then all the people of Judah chose Azariahⁿ to be king. He became king in place of his father Amaziah. Azariah was 16 years old. ²²He rebuilt the town of Elath and made it part of Judah again. He did this after Amaziah died.

Jeroboam King of Israel

²³Jeroboam son of Jehoash became king of Israel in Samaria. This was during the fifteenth year Amaziah was king of Judah. (Amaziah was the son of Joash.) And Jeroboam ruled 41 years. ²⁴He did what the Lord said was wrong. Jeroboam son of Nebat had caused Israel to sin. And Jeroboam son of Jehoash did not stop doing the same sins. ²⁵Jeroboam won back Israel's border from Lebo Hamath to the Dead Sea.ᵈ This happened as the Lord of Israel had said. He said it through his servant Jonah son of Amittai. He was the prophetᵈ from Gath Hepher. ²⁶The Lord had seen how the Israelites, both slave and free, were suffering terribly.

ⁿ**"Fathers . . . sins."** See Deuteronomy 24:16.
ⁿ**Azariah** Also called Uzziah in 2 Chronicles.

No one was left who could help Israel. [27]But the Lord had not said that he would completely destroy Israel from the world. So he saved the Israelites through Jeroboam son of Jehoash.

[28]Everything else Jeroboam did is written down. All his victories are recorded. He won back Damascus and Hamath for Israel. (They had belonged to Judah.) All this is written in the book of the history of the kings of Israel. [29]Jeroboam died and was buried with his ancestors, the kings of Israel. Jeroboam's son Zechariah became king in his place.

Azariah King of Judah

15 Azariah[n] son of Amaziah became king of Judah. This was during Jeroboam's twenty-seventh year as king of Israel. [2]Azariah was 16 years old when he became king. He ruled 52 years in Jerusalem. His mother was named Jecoliah, and she was from Jerusalem. [3]He did what the Lord said was right. He obeyed God just as his father Amaziah had done. [4]But the places where false gods were worshiped were not removed. So the people still made sacrifices and burned incense[d] there.

[5]The Lord struck Azariah with a harmful skin disease. He had this disease until the day he died. He lived in a separate house. Jotham, the king's son, was in charge of the palace. He governed the people of the land.

[6]All the other things Azariah did are written down. They are in the book of the history of the kings of Judah. [7]Azariah died and was buried near his ancestors in Jerusalem. And his son Jotham became king in his place.

Zechariah King of Israel

[8]Zechariah son of Jeroboam was king over Israel in Samaria. He ruled for six months. This was during Azariah's thirty-eighth year as king of Judah. [9]Zechariah did what the Lord said was wrong. He did just as his ancestors had done. Jeroboam son of Nebat had caused the people of Israel to sin. And Zechariah did not stop doing the same sins.

[10]Shallum son of Jabesh made plans against Zechariah. He killed Zechariah in Ibleam. And Shallum became king in Zechariah's place. [11]The other acts of Zechariah are written down. They are in the book of the history of the kings of Israel. [12]Now the Lord had told Jehu: "Your sons down to your great-great-grandchildren will be kings of Israel." And the Lord's word came true.

Shallum King of Israel

[13]Then Shallum son of Jabesh became king. This was during Uzziah's thirty-ninth year as king of Judah. Shallum ruled for a month in Samaria. [14]Then Menahem son of Gadi came up from Tirzah to Samaria. He attacked Shallum son of Jabesh in Samaria. He killed him and became king in Shallum's place.

[15]The other acts of Shallum and his secret plans are written down. They are in the book of the history of the kings of Israel.

Menahem King of Israel

[16]Menahem started out from Tirzah and attacked Tiphsah. He destroyed the city and the area nearby. This was because the people had refused to open the city gate for him. So he defeated them and ripped open all their pregnant women.

[17]Menahem son of Gadi became king over Israel. This was during Azariah's thirty-ninth year as king of Judah. And Menahem ruled ten years in Samaria. [18]He did what the Lord said was wrong. Jeroboam son of Nebat had caused Israel to sin. And all the time Menahem was king, he did not stop doing the same sins.

[19]Pul king of Assyria came to attack the land. Menahem gave him about 74,000 pounds of silver. This was so Pul would support Menahem and make his hold on the kingdom stronger.

[n]**Azariah**   Also called Uzziah in 2 Chronicles.

[20]Menahem raised the money by taxing all the rich men of Israel. He taxed each man about 1¼ pounds of silver. Then he gave the money to the king of Assyria. So the king of Assyria left and did not stay in the land.

[21]Everything else Menahem did is written down. It is in the book of the history of the kings of Israel. [22]Then Menahem died. And his son Pekahiah became king in his place.

Pekahiah King of Israel

[23]Pekahiah son of Menahem became king over Israel in Samaria. This was during Azariah's fiftieth year as king of Judah. Pekahiah ruled two years. [24]He did what the Lord said was wrong. Jeroboam son of Nebat had caused Israel to sin. And Pekahiah did not stop doing the same sins.

[25]Pekah son of Remaliah was one of Pekahiah's captains. He made plans against Pekahiah. He took 50 men of Gilead with him and killed Pekahiah. They killed him, Argob and Arieh in the palace at Samaria. Then Pekah became king in Pekahiah's place.

[26]Everything else Pekahiah did is written down. It is in the book of the history of the kings of Israel.

Pekah King of Israel

[27]Pekah son of Remaliah became king over Israel in Samaria. This was during Azariah's fifty-second year as king of Judah. And Pekah ruled 20 years. [28]He did what the Lord said was wrong. Jeroboam son of Nebat had caused Israel to sin. And Pekah did not stop doing the same sins.

[29]Tiglath-Pileser, also called Pul, was king of Assyria. He attacked while Pekah was king of Israel. Tiglath-Pileser captured the cities of Ijon, Abel Beth Maacah, Janoah, Kedesh and Hazor. He also captured Gilead and Galilee. And he captured all the land of Naphtali. He sent the people from these places away to Assyria. [30]Then Hoshea son of Elah made plans against Pekah son of Remaliah. Hoshea attacked and killed Pekah. Then he became king in Pekah's place. This was during the twentieth year Jotham son of Uzziah was king.

[31]Everything else Pekah did is written down. It is in the book of the history of the kings of Israel.

Jotham King of Judah

[32]Then Jotham son of Uzziah became king of Judah. This was during the second year Pekah son of Remaliah was king of Israel. [33]Jotham was 25 years old when he became king. He ruled 16 years in Jerusalem. His mother's name was Jerusha daughter of Zadok. [34]Jotham did what the Lord said was right. He obeyed God just as his father Uzziah had done. [35]But the places where false gods were worshiped were not removed. And the people still made sacrifices and burned incense[d] there. Jotham rebuilt the Upper Gate of the Temple[d] of the Lord.

[36]The other things Jotham did while he was king are written down. They are in the book of the history of the kings of Judah. [37]At that time the Lord began to send Rezin king of Aram against Judah. He also sent Pekah son of Remaliah against them. [38]Jotham died and was buried with his ancestors in Jerusalem. It was the city of David, his ancestor. And Jotham's son Ahaz became king in his place.

Ahaz King of Judah

16 Ahaz was the son of Jotham king of Judah. Ahaz became king of Judah in the seventeenth year Pekah was king of Israel. Pekah was the son of Remaliah. [2]Ahaz was 20 years old when he became king. He ruled 16 years in Jerusalem. He was not like his ancestor David. He did not do what the Lord his God said was right. [3]Ahaz did the same things the kings of Israel had done. He even sacrificed his sons by burning them in the fire. He did the same hated sins as the other nations had done. And the Lord had forced these nations out of the land ahead of the Israelites. ⁴Ahaz offered sacrifices and burned incense^d at the places where false gods were worshiped. And he did this on the hills and under every green tree.

⁵Rezin king of Aram and Pekah king of Israel came up to Jerusalem to attack it. (Pekah was the son of Remaliah.) They surrounded Ahaz but could not defeat him. ⁶At that time Rezin king of Aram took back the city of Elath for Aram. He forced out all the people of Judah. Then Edomites moved into Elath. And they still live there today.

⁷Ahaz sent messengers to Tiglath-Pileser king of Assyria. Ahaz said, "I am your servant. Come and save me from the king of Aram and the king of Israel. They are attacking me." ⁸Ahaz took the silver and gold that was in the Temple^d of the Lord. He also took the treasuries of the palace. He sent these as a gift to the king of Assyria. ⁹So the king of Assyria listened to Ahaz. He attacked Damascus and captured it. Then he sent all the people of Damascus to Kir. And he killed Rezin.

¹⁰Then King Ahaz went to Damascus to meet Tiglath-Pileser king of Assyria. Ahaz saw an altar at Damascus. He sent plans and a pattern of this altar to Uriah the priest. ¹¹So Uriah the priest built an altar. It was just like the plans King Ahaz had sent him from Damascus. Uriah finished the altar before King Ahaz came back from Damascus. ¹²When the king arrived from Damascus, he saw the altar. He went near and offered sacrifices on it. ¹³He burned his burnt offerings and grain offerings. He poured out his drink offering. He also sprinkled the blood of his fellowship offerings on the altar.

¹⁴Ahaz moved the bronze altar that was before the Lord at the front of the Temple. It was between Ahaz's altar and the Temple of the Lord. He put it on the north side of his altar. ¹⁵King Ahaz gave a command to Uriah the priest. Ahaz said, "Burn the morning burnt offering and the evening grain offering on the large altar. Also offer

the king's burnt offering and his grain offering. Offer the whole burnt offering for all the people of the land. And offer their grain offering and drink offering. Sprinkle on the altar all the blood of the burnt offering and of the sacrifice. But I will use the bronze altar to ask questions of God." ¹⁶Uriah the priest did everything King Ahaz commanded him to do.

¹⁷Then King Ahaz took off the side panels from the bases. He took the washing bowls off the top of the bases. He also took the large bowl, which was called the Sea, off the bronze bulls that held it up. And he put it on a stone base. ¹⁸Ahaz took away the platform for the royal throne. It had been built at the Temple. He also took away the outside entrance for the king. He did these things because of the king of Assyria.

¹⁹The other things Ahaz did as king are written down. They are in the book of the history of the kings of Judah. ²⁰Ahaz died and was buried with his ancestors in Jerusalem. Ahaz's son Hezekiah became king in his place.

Hoshea, Last King of Israel

17 Hoshea son of Elah became king over Israel. This was during Ahaz's twelfth year as king of Judah. Hoshea ruled in Samaria nine years. ²He did what the Lord said was wrong. But he was not as bad as the kings of Israel who had ruled before him.

³Shalmaneser king of Assyria came to attack Hoshea. Hoshea had been Shalmaneser's servant. He had made the payments to Shalmaneser that he had demanded. ⁴But the king of Assyria found out that Hoshea had made plans against him. Hoshea had sent messengers to So, the king of Egypt. And Hoshea had quit giving Shalmaneser the payments he demanded. In the past Hoshea had paid him every year. So the king put Hoshea in prison. ⁵Then the king of Assyria came and attacked all the land of Israel. He surrounded Samaria and attacked it for three years.

⁶He defeated Samaria in the ninth year Hoshea was king. He took the Israelites away to Assyria. He settled some of them in Halah. Some were made to settle in Gozan on the Habor River. Others were settled in the cities of the Medes.

Israelites Punished for Sin

⁷All these things happened because the Israelites had sinned against the Lord their God. He had brought them out of Egypt. He had rescued them from the power of the king of Egypt. But the Israelites had honored other gods. ⁸They lived like the nations the Lord had forced out of the land ahead of them. They also lived as the evil kings had shown them. ⁹They secretly sinned against the Lord their God. They built places in all their cities where false gods were worshiped. They built them everywhere from the watchtower to the strong, walled city.

¹⁰They put up stone pillars for worshiping false gods. And they put up Asherah^d idols on every high hill and under every green tree. ¹¹The Israelites burned incense^d everywhere false gods were worshiped. The nations who lived there before them had done this. And the Lord had forced them out of the land. The Israelites did wicked things that made the Lord angry. ¹²They served idols. And the Lord had said, "You must not do this." ¹³The Lord used every prophet^d and seer^d to warn Israel and Judah. He said, "Stop your evil ways. Obey my commands and laws. Follow all the teachings that I commanded your ancestors to obey. I sent you this law through my servants the prophets."

¹⁴But the people would not listen. They were stubborn, just as their ancestors had been. Their ancestors did not believe in the Lord their God. ¹⁵They rejected the Lord's laws and the agreement he had made with their ancestors. And they refused to listen to his warnings. They worshiped useless

Touring Bible Lands
NINEVAH • 2 KINGS 17:1-6

Ninevah is one of the oldest cities in the world. It was first built by Noah's great-grandson Nimrod on the banks of the Tigris River. Ninevah became the capital of the Assyrian Empire. An empire was a nation that controlled a lot of land by conquering other nations.

Everyone was afraid of Assyria. If you became a slave there, you were treated very badly. That's part of the reason Jonah didn't want to go to Nineveh to tell the people about God. He didn't want the Assyrians to be saved because of all the bad things they had done to the country. But after he got out of the whale, Jonah went to Ninevah and the people turned to God.

If you were in Jonah's place, would you rather walk to Ninevah or be swallowed by a whale?

Fly south from Ninevah to the capital city of another great empire on page 480.

idols and became useless themselves. They did what the nations around them did. And the Lord had warned them not to do this.

¹⁶The people disobeyed all the commands of the Lord their God. They made statues of two calves from melted metal. And they made an Asherah idol. They worshiped all the stars of heaven and served Baal.ᵈ ¹⁷They sacrificed their sons and daughters in the fire. And they tried to find out the future by magic and witchcraft.ᵈ They always chose to do what the Lord said was wrong. And this made him angry. ¹⁸So he was very angry with the people of Israel. He removed them from his presence. Only the tribeᵈ of Judah was left.

Judah Is Also Guilty

¹⁹But even Judah did not obey the commands of the Lord their God. They did what the Israelites had done. ²⁰So the Lord rejected all the people of Israel. He punished them and let people destroy them. He threw them out of his presence. ²¹The Lord separated them from the family of David. And the Israelites made Jeroboam son of Nebat their king. Jeroboam led the Israelites away from following the Lord. He caused them to sin greatly. ²²So they continued to do all the sins Jeroboam did. They did not stop doing these sins ²³until the Lord removed the people from his presence. This was just as he had said he would do. He had said this through all his servants the prophets.ᵈ So the Israelites were taken out of their land to Assyria. And they have been there to this day.

The Beginning of the Samaritan People

²⁴The king of Assyria brought people from Babylon, Cuthah, Avva, Hamath and Sepharvaim. He put them in the cities of Samaria to replace the Israelites. These people took over Samaria and lived in the cities. ²⁵At first they did not worship the Lord. So he sent lions among them. The lions killed some of them. ²⁶The king of Assyria was told this. It was said, "You sent foreigners into the cities of Samaria. They do not know the law of the god of the land. This is why that land's god has sent lions among them. The lions are killing them because they don't know what the god wants."

²⁷Then the king of Assyria gave a command. He said, "You took Samaria's priests away. Send back one of the priests to live there. Let him teach them what the god wants." ²⁸So one of the priests who had been carried away from Samaria returned. He came to live in Bethel. And he taught the people how to worship the Lord.

²⁹But each nation made gods of its own. They put them in the cities where they lived. They put them in the temples where false gods were worshiped. These temples had been made by the Samaritans. ³⁰The men from Babylon made Succoth Benoth their god. The men from Cuthah worshiped Nergal. The men of Hamath worshiped Ashima. ³¹The Avvites worshiped Nibhaz and Tartak. And the Sepharvites burned their children in the fire. They sacrificed them to Adrammelech and Anammelech, the gods of Sepharvaim. ³²They also worshiped the Lord. But they chose priests for the places where false gods were worshiped. The priests were chosen from among themselves. And they made sacrifices for the people. ³³The people worshiped the Lord but also served their own gods. They served their gods as the nations did from which they had been brought. ³⁴Even today they do as they did in the past. They do not worship the Lord. They do not obey his rules and commands. They do not obey the teachings or the commands of the Lord. He gave these commands to the children of Jacob, whom the Lord had named Israel. ³⁵The Lord had made an agreement with them. He had commanded them, "Do not worship other gods. Do not bow down to them or serve them.

Do not give sacrifices to them. [36]Worship the Lord who brought you up out of the land of Egypt. He did it with great power and strength. Bow to the Lord and make sacrifices to him. [37]Obey the rules, orders and the teachings. Obey the commands the Lord wrote for you. Obey and always do them. Do not worship other gods. [38]Do not forget the agreement I made with you. And do not worship other gods. [39]Instead worship the Lord your God. He will save you from all your enemies."

[40]But the Israelites did not listen. They kept on doing the same things they had done before. [41]So these nations worshiped the Lord but served their idols. And their children and grandchildren still do as their ancestors did.

Hezekiah King of Judah

18 Hezekiah son of Ahaz king of Judah became king. This was during the third year Hoshea son of Elah was king of Israel. [2]Hezekiah was 25 years old when he became king. And he ruled 29 years in Jerusalem. His mother's name was Abijah daughter of Zechariah. [3]Hezekiah did what the Lord said was right. He did just as his ancestor David had done. [4]He removed the places where false gods were worshiped. He broke the stone pillars they worshiped. He cut down the Asherah[d] idols. Also the Israelites had been burning incense[d] to the bronze snake made by Moses. (It was called Nehushtan.) But Hezekiah broke it into pieces.

[5]Hezekiah trusted in the Lord, the God of Israel. There was no one like him among all the kings of Judah. There was no king like him, before him or after him. [6]Hezekiah was loyal to the Lord. He did not stop following the Lord. He obeyed the commands the Lord had given Moses. [7]And the Lord was with Hezekiah. He had success in everything he did. He turned against the king of Assyria and stopped serving him. [8]Hezekiah defeated the Philistines all the way to Gaza and its borders.

He defeated them everywhere, from the watchtower to the strong, walled city.

The Assyrians Capture Samaria

[9]Shalmaneser king of Assyria surrounded Samaria and attacked it. This was in the fourth year Hezekiah was king. And it was the seventh year Hoshea son of Elah was king of Israel. [10]After three years the Assyrians captured Samaria. This was in the sixth year Hezekiah was king. And it was Hoshea's ninth year as king of Israel. [11]The king of Assyria took the Israelites away to Assyria. He put them in Halah and in Gozan on the Habor River. He also put them in the cities of the Medes. [12]This happened because they did not obey the Lord their God. They broke his agreement. They did not obey all that Moses, the Lord's servant, had commanded. They would not listen to the commands or do them.

Assyria Attacks Judah

[13]During Hezekiah's fourteenth year as king, Sennacherib king of Assyria attacked Judah. He attacked all the strong, walled cities of Judah and defeated them. [14]Then Hezekiah king of Judah sent a message to the king of Assyria at Lachish. He said, "I have done wrong. Leave me alone. Then I will pay anything you demand of me." So the king of Assyria told Hezekiah how much to pay. It was about 22,000 pounds of silver and 2,000 pounds of gold. [15]Hezekiah gave him all the silver that was in the Temple[d] of the Lord. And he gave him all the silver in the palace treasuries. [16]Hezekiah cut off all the gold that covered the doors of the Temple of the Lord. He also removed the gold from the doorposts. Hezekiah had put gold on these doors himself. He gave it all to the king of Assyria.

Assyria Troubles Hezekiah

[17]The king of Assyria sent out his supreme commander, his chief officer and his field commander. They went with a large army from Lachish to King

Hezekiah in Jerusalem. When they came near the waterway from the upper pool, they stopped. The upper pool is on the road to the Washerman's Field. [18]They called for the king. So Eliakim, Shebna and Joah went out to meet them. Eliakim son of Hilkiah was the palace manager. Shebna was the royal assistant. And Joah son of Asaph was the recorder.

[19]The field commander said to them, "Tell Hezekiah this:

"'The great king, the king of Assyria, says: You have nothing to trust in to help you. [20]You say you have battle plans and power for war. But your words mean nothing. Whom are you trusting for help so that you turn against me? [21]Look, you are depending on Egypt to help you. Egypt is like a splintered walking stick. If you lean on it for help, it will stab you and hurt you. The king of Egypt will hurt those who depend on him. [22]You might say, "We are depending on the Lord our God." But Hezekiah destroyed the Lord's altars and the places of worship. Hezekiah told Judah and Jerusalem, "You must worship only at this one altar in Jerusalem."

[23]"'Now make an agreement with my master, the king of Assyria: I will give you 2,000 horses if you can find enough men to ride them. [24]You cannot defeat one of my master's least important officers. So why do you depend on Egypt to give you chariots and horsemen? [25]I have not come to attack and destroy this place without an order from the Lord. The Lord himself told me to come to this country and destroy it.'"

[26]Then Eliakim son of Hilkiah, Shebna and Joah spoke to the field commander. They said, "Please speak to us in the Aramaic language. We understand it. Don't speak to us in Hebrew because the people on the city wall can hear you."

[27]But the commander said, "No. My master did not send me to tell these things only to you and your king. My master sent me to tell them also to those people sitting on the wall. They will have to eat their own dung and drink their own urine like you."

[28]Then the commander stood and shouted loudly in the Hebrew language. He said, "Listen to the word from the great king, the king of Assyria! [29]The king says you should not let Hezekiah fool you. Hezekiah can't save you from my power. [30]Don't let Hezekiah talk you into trusting the Lord. Hezekiah says, 'The Lord will surely save us. This city won't be given over to the king of Assyria.'

[31]"Don't listen to Hezekiah. The king of Assyria says, 'Make peace with me. Come out of the city to me. Then everyone will be free to eat the fruit from his own grapevine and fig tree. Everyone will be free to drink water from his own well. [32]Then I will come and take you to a land like your own. It is a land with grain and new wine. It has bread and vineyards. It is a land of olives and honey. Then you can choose to live and not to die!'

"Don't listen to Hezekiah. He is fooling you when he says, 'The Lord will save us.' [33]The god of any other nation has not saved his people from the power of the king of Assyria. [34]Where are the gods of Hamath and Arpad? Where are the gods of Sepharvaim, Hena and Ivvah? They did not save Samaria from my power. [35]Not one of all the gods of these countries has saved his people from me. Then the Lord cannot save Jerusalem from my power."

[36]The people were silent. They didn't answer the commander at all. This was because King Hezekiah had ordered, "Don't answer him."

[37]Then Eliakim, Shebna and Joah tore their clothes to show how upset they were. (Eliakim son of Hilkiah was the palace manager. Shebna was the royal assistant. And Joah son of Asaph was the recorder.) The three men went to Hezekiah and told him what the field commander had said.

Jerusalem Will Be Saved

19 When King Hezekiah heard the message, he tore his clothes. And he put on rough cloth to show how sad he was. Then he went into the Temple[d] of the Lord. [2]Hezekiah sent Eliakim, Shebna and the older priests to Isaiah. Eliakim was the palace manager, and Shebna was the royal assistant. The men were all wearing the rough cloth when they came to Isaiah. He was a prophet,[d] the son of Amoz. [3]These men told Isaiah, "This is what Hezekiah says: Today is a day of sorrow and punishment and disgrace. It is sad, as when a child should be born, but the mother is not strong enough to give birth to it. [4]The king of Assyria sent his field commander to make fun of the living God. Maybe the Lord your God will hear what the commander said. Maybe the Lord your God will punish him for what he said. So pray for the few people of Israel who are left alive."

[5]When Hezekiah's officers came to Isaiah, [6]he said to them, "Tell your master this: The Lord says, 'Don't be afraid of what you have heard. Don't be frightened by the words the servants of the king of Assyria said against me. [7]Listen! I am going to put a spirit in the king of Assyria. He will hear a report that will make him return to his own country. And I will cause him to die by the sword there.'"

[8]The field commander heard that the king of Assyria had left Lachish. So the commander left and found the king fighting against the city of Libnah. [9]The king received a report that Tirhakah was coming to attack him. Tirhakah was the Cushite king of Egypt. When the king of Assyria heard this, he sent messengers to Hezekiah. The king said: [10]"Say this to Hezekiah king of Judah: Don't be fooled by the god you trust. Don't believe him when he says Jerusalem will not be defeated by the king of Assyria. [11]You have heard what the kings of Assyria have done. They have completely defeated every country. Do not think you will be saved.

[12]The gods of those people did not save them. My ancestors destroyed them. My ancestors defeated the cities of Gozan, Haran and Rezeph. They defeated the people of Eden living in Tel Assar. [13]Where are the kings of Hamath and Arpad? Where is the king of the city of Sepharvaim? Where are the kings of Hena and Ivvah?"

Hezekiah Prays to the Lord

[14]Hezekiah received the letter from the messengers and read it. Then he went up to the Temple[d] of the Lord. Hezekiah spread the letter out before the Lord. [15]And he prayed to the Lord: "Lord, God of Israel, your throne is between the gold creatures with wings! Only you are God of all the kingdoms of the earth. You made the heavens and the earth. [16]Hear, Lord, and listen. Open your eyes, Lord, and see. Listen to the word Sennacherib has said to insult the living God. [17]It is true, Lord. The kings of Assyria have destroyed these countries and their lands. [18]These kings have thrown the gods of these nations into the fire. But they were only wood and rock statues that men made. So the kings have destroyed them. [19]Now, Lord our God, save us from the king's power. Then all the kingdoms of the earth will know that you, Lord, are the only God."

God Answers Hezekiah

[20]Then Isaiah son of Amoz sent a message to Hezekiah. Isaiah said, "The Lord, the God of Israel, says this: I have heard your prayer to me about Sennacherib king of Assyria. [21]So this is what the Lord has said against Sennacherib:

'The people of Jerusalem
  hate you and make fun of you.
The people of Jerusalem
  laugh at you as you run away.
[22]You have insulted me and spoken
    against me.
  You have raised your voice against
    me.
  You have a proud look on your face.

You disobey me, the Holy One of
Israel!
23You have used your messengers to
insult the Lord.
You have said, "I have many
chariots.
With them I have gone to the tops
of the mountains.
I have climbed the highest
mountains of Lebanon.

I allowed you to turn those strong,
walled cities
into piles of rocks.
26"The people living in those cities were
weak.
They were frightened and put to
shame.
They were like grass in the field.
They were like tender, young grass.
They were like grass that grows on
the housetop.
It is burned by the wind before it
can grow.

People Who Depended on God

HEZEKIAH • 2 KINGS 19:14-19

Hezekiah trusted God to do something that seemed impossible.
Hezekiah was a king of Judah, the southern kingdom of Israel. (Israel
was divided into two kingdoms.) The northern kingdom had already been
defeated by a big army led by king Sennacherib. This king did not love
God. In fact, he told Hezekiah that God could not protect Judah.
Sennacherib thought he was more powerful than God.

Hezekiah's army was not as big or powerful as Sennacherib's army,
but he knew that God could protect Judah. Hezekiah prayed that God
would give Judah victory. God helped Judah conquer the army and sent
Sennacherib back home where he was killed.

We can be sure that with God on our side, nothing is impossible!

*To read about someone who depended on God for a construction
project, fly to page 568.*

I have cut down its tallest cedars.
I have cut down its best pine trees.
I have reached its farthest places.
I have gone to its best forests.
24I have dug wells in foreign countries.
I have drunk water there.
By the soles of my feet,
I have dried up all the rivers of
Egypt."

25"'King of Assyria, surely you have
heard.
Long ago I, the Lord, planned
these things.
Long ago I planned them.
Now I have made them happen.

27"'I know when you rest and when
you come and go.
I know how you speak against me.
28You speak strongly against me.
And I have heard your proud words.
So I will put my hook in your nose.
And I will put my bit in your mouth.
Then I will force you to leave my
country
the same way that you came.'

29"Then the Lord said, 'Hezekiah, I
will give you this sign:
This year you will eat the grain that
grows wild.
And the second year you will eat

what grows wild from that.
But in the third year, plant grain and
harvest it.
Plant vineyards and eat their fruit.
30 Some of the people in the family of
Judah
will be saved.
Like plants that take root,
they will grow strong and have
many children.
31 A few people will come out of
Jerusalem alive.
There will be a few from Mount
Zion[d] who will live.
The strong love of the Lord of
heaven's armies
will cause this to happen.'

32 "So this is what the Lord says about
the king of Assyria:
'He will not enter this city.
He will not even shoot an arrow here.
He will not fight against it with
shields.
He will not build a ramp to attack
the city walls.
33 He will return to his country the
same way he came.
He will not enter this city,'
says the Lord.
34 The Lord says, 'I will defend and save
this city.
I will do this for myself and for
David, my servant.'"

35 That night the angel of the Lord
went out. He killed 185,000 men in the
Assyrian camp. The people got up
early the next morning. And they saw
all the dead bodies! 36 So Sennacherib
king of Assyria left. He went back to
Nineveh and stayed there.

37 One day Sennacherib was worshiping in the temple of his god Nisroch.
While he was there, his sons Adrammelech and Sharezer killed him with a
sword. Then they escaped to the land
of Ararat. So Sennacherib's son Esarhaddon became king of Assyria.

Hezekiah's Illness

20 At that time Hezekiah became
very sick. He was almost dead.
The prophet[d] Isaiah son of Amoz went
to see him. Isaiah told him, "This is
what the Lord says: You are going to
die. So you should give your last orders

Amazing Events That Showed God's Power

2 KINGS 20:1-11

Hezekiah was a good king who obeyed God. Once he became very ill and
almost died. God told Hezekiah that he would get better and promised
a miracle to prove this would happen. So Hezekiah asked to see God's power
on the stairway of Ahaz. This stairway was a sundial. People could tell time
by where the shadows were on the steps. The shadows would go forward on
the steps as it got later in the day. As a sign of God's power, Hezekiah asked
God to make the shadows go *backward* on the steps. God showed that he
controlled the forces of nature by doing what Hezekiah asked.

We probably won't ask God to make shadows go backward, but we can
bring important requests to him. God wants to hear our prayers and will
show his power to us in many ways.

To read about another amazing event in the sky, fly to page 1123.

to everyone. You will not get well."

²Hezekiah turned toward the wall and prayed to the Lord. He said, ³"Lord, please remember that I have always obeyed you. I have given myself completely to you. I have done what you said was right." And Hezekiah cried loudly.

⁴Before Isaiah had left the middle courtyard, the Lord spoke his word to Isaiah: ⁵"Go back and tell Hezekiah, the leader of my people: 'This is what the Lord, the God of your ancestor David, says: I have heard your prayer. And I have seen your tears. So I will heal you. Three days from now you will go up to the Temple^d of the Lord. ⁶I will add 15 years to your life. I will save you and this

⁹Isaiah said, "The Lord will do what he says. This is the sign from the Lord to show you: Do you want the shadow to go forward ten steps? Or do you want it to go back ten steps?"

¹⁰Hezekiah answered, "It's easy for the shadow to go forward ten steps. Instead, let it go back ten steps."

¹¹Then Isaiah the prophet called to the Lord. And the Lord brought the shadow back ten steps. It went back up the stairway of Ahaz that it had gone down.

Prayer
2 KINGS 20:1-11

You wake up in the darkness. You are sweating, and your stomach aches. You feel terrible. Even though it's the middle of the night and they are sound asleep, you know who will come to your aid: your parents. "Mom! Dad! Come quickly—I'm sick," you call out.

That's what King Hezekiah did. He wasn't just sick. He was dying, and he knew it. So he called out to the one person he knew loved him and could help him: God, his heavenly father. God heard Hezekiah's prayer and granted his request. He healed Hezekiah and gave him fifteen more years to live.

God doesn't always answer our prayers the way we want him to. Many people pray for healing or for other important needs. Sometimes God says, "No." But when you are in need, no matter how big the problem is, remember to do what Hezekiah did. Take your needs to your loving heavenly father.

To learn more about prayer, zoom to page 709.

To learn more about prayer, zoom to page 709.

city from the king of Assyria. And I will protect the city for myself and for my servant David.'"

⁷Then Isaiah said, "Make a paste from figs." So they made it and put it on Hezekiah's boil. And he got well.

⁸Hezekiah asked Isaiah, "What will be the sign that the Lord will heal me? What is the sign that I will go up to the Temple^d of the Lord on the third day?"

Messengers from Babylon

¹²At that time Merodach-Baladan, son of Baladan, was king of Babylon. He sent letters and a gift to Hezekiah. He did this because he had heard that Hezekiah had been sick. ¹³Hezekiah was happy to see the messengers. So he showed them what was in his storehouses: the silver, gold, spices and expensive perfumes. He showed them

his swords and shields. He showed them all his wealth. He showed them everything in his palace and his kingdom.

¹⁴Then Isaiah the prophet*ᵈ* went to King Hezekiah. Isaiah asked him, "What did these men say? Where did they come from?"

Hezekiah said, "They came from a faraway country. They came to me from Babylon."

¹⁵So Isaiah asked him, "What did they see in your palace?"

Hezekiah said, "They saw everything in my palace. I showed them all my wealth."

¹⁶Then Isaiah said to Hezekiah, "Listen to the words of the Lord: ¹⁷'In the future everything in your palace will be taken away to Babylon. Everything your ancestors have stored up until this day will be taken away. Nothing will be left,' says the Lord. ¹⁸'Some of your own children will be taken away. Those who will be born to you will be taken away. And they will become eunuchs*ᵈ* in the palace of the king of Babylon.'"

¹⁹Hezekiah told Isaiah, "These words from the Lord are good." He said this because he thought, "There will be peace and security while I am king."

²⁰Everything else Hezekiah did is written down. All his victories and his work on the pool are written down. And his work on the tunnel to bring water into the city is recorded. They are all written in the book of the history of the kings of Judah. ²¹Then Hezekiah died. And his son Manasseh became king in his place.

Manasseh King of Judah

21 Manasseh was 12 years old when he became king. And he was king 55 years in Jerusalem. His mother's name was Hephzibah. ²He did what the Lord said was wrong. He did the hated things the other nations had done. And the Lord had forced these nations out of the land ahead of the Israelites. ³Manasseh's father, Hezekiah, had destroyed the places where false gods were worshiped. But Manasseh rebuilt them. He built altars for Baal.*ᵈ* And he made an Asherah*ᵈ* idol as Ahab king of Israel had done. Manasseh worshiped all the stars of heaven and served them. ⁴The Lord had said about the Temple,*ᵈ* "I will be worshiped in Jerusalem." But Manasseh built altars in the Temple of the Lord. ⁵He built altars to worship the stars in the two courtyards of the Temple of the Lord. ⁶He burned his own son as a sacrifice. He practiced magic and told the future by explaining signs and dreams. He got advice from mediums*ᵈ* and fortune-tellers. He did many things that the Lord said were wrong. And this made the Lord angry.

⁷Manasseh carved an Asherah idol and put it in the Temple. The Lord had spoken to David and his son Solomon about the Temple. He had said, "I will be worshiped in this Temple and in Jerusalem forever. I have chosen Jerusalem from all the tribes*ᵈ* of Israel. ⁸I will never again make the Israelites wander out of the land I gave their ancestors. But they must obey everything I have commanded them. And they must obey all the teachings my servant Moses gave them." ⁹But the people did not listen. Manasseh led them to do wrong. They did more evil than the nations the Lord had destroyed ahead of the Israelites.

¹⁰The Lord spoke through his servants the prophets.*ᵈ* He said, ¹¹"Manasseh king of Judah has done these hated things. He has done more evil than the Amorites before him. Manasseh also has caused Judah to sin with his idols. ¹²So this is what the Lord, the God of Israel, says: 'I will bring much trouble on Jerusalem and Judah. Anyone who hears about it will be shocked. ¹³I will stretch the measuring line of Samaria over Jerusalem. And the plumb line*ᵈ* used against Ahab's family will be used on Jerusalem. I will wipe out Jerusalem as a man wipes a dish. He wipes it and turns it upside down. ¹⁴I will go away from the rest of my people who are left.

I will give them to their enemies. They will be robbed by all their enemies. [15]My people did what I said was wrong. They have made me angry from the day their ancestors left Egypt until now.'"

[16]Manasseh also killed many innocent people. He filled Jerusalem from one end to the other with their blood. This was besides the sin he caused Judah to do. He caused Judah to do what the Lord said was wrong.

[17]The other things Manasseh did as king are written down, even the sin he did. They are in the book of the history of the kings of Judah. [18]Manasseh died and was buried in the garden of his own palace. It is the garden of Uzza. Then Manasseh's son Amon became king in his place.

Amon King of Judah

[19]Amon was 22 years old when he became king. He was king for two years in Jerusalem. His mother's name was Meshullemeth daughter of Haruz. She was from Jotbah. [20]Amon did what the Lord said was wrong. He did as his father Manasseh had done. [21]Amon lived in the same way his father had lived. He worshiped the idols his father had worshiped. And he bowed down before them. [22]Amon rejected the Lord, the God of his ancestors. He did not follow the ways of the Lord.

[23]Amon's officers made plans against him and killed him in his palace. [24]Then the people of Judah killed all those who had made plans to kill King Amon. And they made his son Josiah king in his place.

[25]Everything else Amon did is written down. It is in the book of the history of the kings of Judah. [26]He was buried in his grave in the garden of Uzza. And his son Josiah became king in his place.

Josiah King of Judah

22 Josiah was eight years old when he became king. He ruled 31 years in Jerusalem. His mother's name was Jedidah daughter of Adaiah. Adaiah was from Bozkath. [2]Josiah did what the Lord said was right. He did good things as his ancestor David had done. Josiah did not stop doing what was right.

[3]In Josiah's eighteenth year as king, he sent Shaphan to the Temple[d] of the Lord. Shaphan was the son of Azaliah, who was the son of Meshullam. Shaphan was the royal assistant. Josiah said, [4]"Go up to Hilkiah the high priest. Have him empty out the money the gatekeepers have gathered from the people. This is the money they have brought into the Temple of the Lord. [5]Have him give the money to the supervisors of the work on the Temple. They must pay the men who work to repair the Temple of the Lord. [6]The workers are carpenters, builders and stoneworkers. Also use the money to buy timber and cut stone to repair the Temple. [7]They do not need to report how they use the money given to them. They are working honestly."

The Book of the Law Is Found

[8]Hilkiah the high priest said to Shaphan the royal assistant, "I've found the Book of the Teachings. It was in the Temple[d] of the Lord." He gave it to Shaphan, who read it.

[9]Then Shaphan the royal assistant went to the king and reported to Josiah, "Your officers have paid out the money that was in the Temple of the Lord. They have given it to the workers and supervisors at the Temple." [10]Then Shaphan the royal assistant told the king, "Hilkiah the priest has given me a book." And Shaphan read from the book to the king.

[11]The king heard the words of the Book of the Teachings. Then he tore his clothes to show how upset he was. [12]He gave these orders to Hilkiah the priest and Ahikam son of Shaphan. He also gave them to Acbor son of Micaiah, Shaphan and Asaiah. Shaphan was the royal assistant. And Asaiah was the king's servant. These were the orders: [13]"Go and ask the Lord about the words in the book that has been found. Ask for me and for all the people and for all

Judah. The Lord's anger is burning against us because our ancestors did not obey the words of this book. They did not do all the things written for us to do!"

"**C**an you imagine what it would be like not to have a Bible you could read? Look in 2 Kings 22:1–23:3 to discover what happened when God's word was lost for a long time."

¹⁴So Hilkiah the priest, Ahikam, Acbor, Shaphan and Asaiah left. They went to talk to Huldah the prophetess.ᵈ She was the wife of Shallum son of Tikvah, the son of Harhas. Harhas took care of the king's clothes. Huldah lived in Jerusalem, in the new area of the city.

¹⁵She said to them, "This is what the Lord, the God of Israel, says: Tell the man who sent you to me, ¹⁶'This is what the Lord says: I will bring trouble to this place and to the people living here. It is in the words of the book which the king of Judah has read. ¹⁷The people of Judah have left me. They have burned incenseᵈ to other gods. They have made me angry by all the idols they have made. My anger burns against this place like a fire. It will not be put out.' ¹⁸Tell the king of Judah, who sent you to ask the Lord, 'This is what the Lord, the God of Israel, says about the words you heard: ¹⁹You heard my words against this place and its people. You became sorry in the Lord's presence for what you had done. I said they would become cursed and would be destroyed. Then you tore your clothes to show how upset you were. And you cried in my presence. This is why I have heard you, says the Lord. ²⁰So I will cause you to die. You will be buried in peace. You

won't see all the trouble I will bring to this place.'"

So they took her message back to the king.

The People Hear the Law

23 Then the king gathered all the older leaders of Judah and Jerusalem together. ²He went up to the Templeᵈ of the Lord. All the men from Judah and Jerusalem went with him. The priests, prophetsᵈ and all the people—from the least important to the most important—went with him. He read to them all the words of the Book of the Agreement. That book was found in the Temple of the Lord. ³The king stood by the pillar. He made an agreement in the presence of the Lord. He agreed to follow the Lord and obey his commands, rules and laws with his whole being. He agreed to do what was written in this book. Then all the people promised to obey the agreement.

Josiah Destroys the Places for Idol Worship

⁴The king gave a command to Hilkiah the high priest. He also gave it to the priests of the next rank and the gatekeepers. He told them to bring out of the Temple of the Lord everything made for Baal,ᵈ Asherahᵈ and all the stars of heaven. Then Josiah burned them outside Jerusalem in the fields of the Kidron Valley. And he carried the ashes to Bethel. ⁵The kings of Judah had chosen priests for these gods. These priests burned incenseᵈ on the places where false gods were worshiped. These places were in the cities of Judah and the towns around Jerusalem. The priests burned incense to Baal, the sun and the moon. And they burned incense to the planets and all the stars of heaven. But Josiah took those priests away. ⁶He removed the Asherah idol from the Temple of the Lord. He took it outside Jerusalem to the Kidron Valley. There he burned it and beat it into dust. And he threw the dust on the graves of the common people. ⁷Then he tore

down the houses of the male prostitutes[d] who were in the Temple of the Lord. This was where the women did weaving for Asherah.

[8]King Josiah brought all the false priests from the cities of Judah. He made the places where false gods were worshiped impure. This is where the priests had burned incense. These places of worship were everywhere, from Geba to Beersheba. He destroyed the places of worship at the entrance to the Gate of Joshua. (Joshua was the ruler of the city.) This gate was on the left side of the city gate. [9]The priests at the places where false gods were worshiped were not allowed to serve at the Lord's altar in Jerusalem. But they could eat bread made without yeast with their brothers.

[10]Topheth was in the Valley of Ben Hinnom. Josiah made it impure so no one could sacrifice his son or daughter to Molech.[d] [11]Judah's kings had placed horses at the front door of the Temple of the Lord. This was in the courtyard near the room of Nathan-Melech, an officer. These horses were for the worship of the sun. But Josiah removed them. Then he burned the chariots that were for sun worship.

[12]The kings of Judah had also built altars on the roof[n] of the upstairs room of Ahaz. Josiah broke down these altars. He also broke down the altars Manasseh had made. These were in the two courtyards of the Temple of the Lord. He smashed them to pieces. Then he threw their dust into the Kidron Valley. [13]King Josiah made impure the places east of Jerusalem where false gods were worshiped. These were south of the Mount of Olives.[n] Solomon king of Israel had built these places. One was for Ashtoreth,[d] the hated goddess of the Sidonians. One was for Chemosh,[d] the hated god of Moab. And one was for Molech, the hated god of the Ammonites. [14]Josiah smashed into pieces

the stone pillars they worshiped. He cut down the Asherah idols. And he covered the places with human bones.

[15]Josiah also broke down the altar at Bethel. This was the place of worship Jeroboam son of Nebat had made. Jeroboam had caused Israel to sin. Josiah burned that place. He broke the stones of the altar to pieces. Then he beat them into dust. And he burned the Asherah idol. [16]When he turned around, he saw the graves on the mountain. He had the bones taken from the graves. Then he burned the bones on the altar to make it impure. This happened as the Lord had said it would through the man of God.

[17]Josiah asked, "What is that monument to the dead I see?"

The people of the city answered, "It's the grave of the man of God who came from Judah. This prophet announced the things you have done against the altar of Bethel."

[18]Josiah said, "Leave the grave alone. No person may move this man's bones." So they left his bones. And they left the bones of the prophet who had come from Samaria.

[19]The kings of Israel had built temples for worshiping false gods in the cities of Samaria. That had caused the Lord to be angry. Josiah removed all those temples. He did the same things as he had done at Bethel. [20]Josiah killed all the priests of those places of worship. He killed them on the altars. And he burned human bones on the altars. Then he went back to Jerusalem.

The Passover Is Brought Back

[21]The king gave a command to all the people. He said, "Celebrate the Passover[d] to the Lord your God. Do it as it is written in this Book of the Agreement." [22]No Passover like this one had been celebrated since the judges led Israel. Nor had one like it happened while there were kings of

---

[n]**roof** In Bible times houses were built with flat roofs. The roof was used for drying things such as flax and fruit. And it was used as an extra room, as a place for worship and as a place to sleep in the summer.
[n]**Mount of Olives** Literally, "The Mountain of Ruin."

Israel and kings of Judah. ²³This Passover was celebrated to the Lord in Jerusalem. It was the eighteenth year of King Josiah's rule.

²⁴Josiah destroyed the mediums,ᵈ fortune-tellers, house gods and idols. He destroyed all the hated gods seen in the land of Judah and Jerusalem. He did this to obey the words of the teachings. They were written in the book Hilkiah the priest had found in the Templeᵈ of the Lord.

²⁵There was no king like Josiah before or after him. He obeyed the Lord with all his heart, soul and strength. He followed all the Teachings of Moses.

²⁶Even so, the Lord did not stop his strong and terrible anger. His anger burned against Judah. It was because of all that Manasseh had done to make him angry. ²⁷The Lord said, "I have taken Israel away. I will do the same to Judah. I will take them out of my sight. I will reject Jerusalem which I chose. I will take away the Temple about which I said, 'I will be honored there.'"

²⁸Everything else Josiah did is written down. It is in the book of the history of the kings of Judah.

²⁹While Josiah was king, Neco king of Egypt went to help the king of Assyria. Neco was at the Euphrates River. King Josiah marched out to fight against Neco. But at Megiddo, Neco faced Josiah and killed him. ³⁰Josiah's servants carried his body in a chariot from Megiddo. They brought him to Jerusalem and buried him in his own grave. Then the people of Judah chose Josiah's son Jehoahaz. They poured olive oil on him to appoint him king in his father's place.

Jehoahaz King of Judah

³¹Jehoahaz was 23 years old when he became king. And he was king in Jerusalem for three months. His mother's name was Hamutal. She was the daughter of Jeremiah from Libnah. ³²Jehoahaz did what the Lord said was wrong. He did just as his ancestors had done.

³³King Neco took Jehoahaz prisoner at Riblah in the land of Hamath. He did this so Jehoahaz could not rule in Jerusalem. Neco made the people of Judah pay about 7,500 pounds of silver and about 75 pounds of gold.

³⁴King Neco made Josiah's son Eliakim the king in place of Josiah his father. Then Neco changed Eliakim's name to Jehoiakim. But Neco took Jehoahaz to Egypt, and he died there. ³⁵Jehoiakim gave King Neco the silver and gold he demanded. But Jehoiakim taxed the land so he could pay the king. He took silver and gold from the people of the land. The amount he took from each person depended on how much he had.

Jehoiakim King of Judah

³⁶Jehoiakim was 25 years old when he became king. He was king in Jerusalem for 11 years. His mother's name was Zebidah daughter of Pedaiah. She was from Rumah. ³⁷Jehoiakim did what the Lord said was wrong, just as his ancestors had done.

24 While Jehoiakim was king, Nebuchadnezzar king of Babylon attacked the land of Judah. So Jehoiakim became Nebuchadnezzar's servant for three years. Then Jehoiakim turned against Nebuchadnezzar. And he broke away from his rule. ²The Lord sent men from Babylon, Aram, Moab and Ammon against Jehoiakim. He sent them to destroy Judah. This happened the way the Lord had said it would through his servants the prophets.ᵈ

³The Lord commanded this to happen to the people of Judah. He did it to remove them from his presence. This was because of all the sins Manasseh had done. ⁴He had killed many innocent people. He had filled Jerusalem with their blood. And the Lord would not forgive these sins.

⁵The other things that happened while Jehoiakim was king and all he did are written down. They are in the book of the history of the kings of Judah.

[6]Jehoiakim died, and his son Jehoiachin became king in his place.

[7]The king of Egypt did not come out of his land again. This was because of the king of Babylon. He had captured all that belonged to the king of Egypt. He took all the land from the brook of Egypt to the Euphrates River.

Jehoiachin King of Judah

[8]Jehoiachin was 18 years old when he became king. He was king three months in Jerusalem. His mother's name was Nehushta daughter of Elnathan. She was from Jerusalem. [9]Jehoiachin did what the Lord said was wrong, just as his father had done.

[10]At that time the officers of Nebuchadnezzar king of Babylon came up to Jerusalem. They surrounded the city and attacked it. [11]Nebuchadnezzar himself came to the city while his officers were attacking it. [12]Jehoiachin king of Judah surrendered to the king of Babylon. Jehoiachin's mother, servants, leaders and officers also surrendered. Then the king of Babylon made Jehoiachin a prisoner. This was in the eighth year Nebuchadnezzar was king. [13]Nebuchadnezzar took all the treasures from the Temple[d] of the Lord. He also removed the treasures from the palace. He took all the gold objects Solomon king of Israel had made for the Temple. This happened as the Lord had said it would. [14]Nebuchadnezzar took away all the people of Jerusalem. This included all the leaders and all the wealthy people. He also took all the craftsmen and metal workers. There were 10,000 prisoners in all. Only the poorest people in the land were left. [15]Nebuchadnezzar carried away Jehoiachin to Babylon. He took the king's mother and his wives. He also took the officers and leading men of the land. They were taken captive from Jerusalem to Babylon. [16]The king of Babylon also took all 7,000 soldiers. These men were all strong and able to fight in war. And 1,000 craftsmen and metal workers were taken, too. Nebuchadnezzar took them as prisoners to Babylon. [17]He made Mattaniah king in Jehoiachin's place. Mattaniah was Jehoiachin's uncle. He also changed Mattaniah's name to Zedekiah.

Zedekiah King of Judah

[18]Zedekiah was 21 years old when he became king. And he was king in Jerusalem for 11 years. His mother's name was Hamutal daughter of Jeremiah.[n] She was from Libnah. [19]Zedekiah did what the Lord said was wrong, just as Jehoiakim had done. [20]All this happened in Jerusalem and Judah because the Lord was angry with them. Finally, he threw them out of his presence.

The Fall of Jerusalem

Zedekiah turned against the king of Babylon.

25 Then Nebuchadnezzar king of Babylon marched against Jerusalem with his whole army. This happened during Zedekiah's ninth year, tenth month and tenth day as king. He made a camp around the city. Then he built devices all around the city walls to attack it. [2]The city was under attack until Zedekiah's eleventh year as king. [3]By the ninth day of the fourth month, the hunger was terrible in the city. There was no food for the people to eat. [4]Then the city wall was broken through. And the whole army ran away at night. They went through the gate between the two walls by the king's garden. The Babylonians were still surrounding the city. Zedekiah and his men ran toward the Jordan Valley. [5]But the Babylonian army chased King Zedekiah. They caught up with him in the plains of Jericho. All of his army was scattered from him. [6]So they captured Zedekiah and took him to the king of Babylon at Riblah. There he passed sentence on Zedekiah. [7]They killed Zedekiah's sons as he watched. Then they put out his eyes. They put bronze chains on him and took him to Babylon.

[n]**Jeremiah** This is not the prophet Jeremiah, but a different man with the same name.

⁸Nebuzaradan was the commander of the king's special guards. This officer of the king of Babylon came to Jerusalem. This was on the seventh day of the fifth month. This was in Nebuchadnezzar's nineteenth year as king of Babylon. ⁹Nebuzaradan set fire to the Temple^d of the Lord and the palace. He also set fire to all the houses of Jerusalem. Every important building was burned.

¹³The Babylonians broke up the bronze pillars, the bronze stands and the large bronze bowl, which was called the Sea. These were in the Temple of the Lord. Then they carried the bronze to Babylon. ¹⁴They also took the pots, shovels, wick trimmers, dishes and all the bronze objects. These were used to serve in the Temple. ¹⁵The commander of the king's special guards took away the pans for carrying hot coals. He also took the bowls and everything made of pure gold or silver. ¹⁶There was so

Touring Bible Lands
BABYLON • 2 KINGS 25:1-21

One of the most beautiful cities of ancient Bible times was Babylon, the capital of the Babylonian empire. Babylon was an enormous city built around palm trees and flower gardens. It was an important center of trade and travel for camel caravans. One of the kings of the Babylonian Empire was Nebuchadnezzar. He lived in a huge palace made of beautiful blue brick.

Nebuchadnezzar sent his army to fight against God's people in Judah. He took many of the people as slaves back to Babylon. Daniel (who survived the lion's den) and Shadrach, Meshach, and Abednego (who survived the fiery furnace) were among the young men who were taken back to Babylon as slaves.

Babylon was a beautiful city, but it was also very wicked. Yet even in that faraway place God cared for his people. Wherever you go, God will care for you.

Fly southwest from Babylon back across the great desert, to a tiny town in Israel where a very important baby would be born on page 1086.

¹⁰The whole Babylonian army broke down the walls around Jerusalem. That army was led by the commander of the king's special guards. ¹¹Nebuzaradan, the commander of the guards, took captive the people left in Jerusalem. And he took captive those who had surrendered to the king of Babylon. The rest of the people were also taken away. ¹²But the commander left behind some of the poorest people of the land. They were to take care of the vineyards and fields.

much bronze that it could not be weighed. There were two pillars and the large bronze bowl. There were also the movable stands which Solomon had made for the Temple of the Lord. ¹⁷Each pillar was about 27 feet high. The bronze capital^d on top of the pillar was about 4½ feet high. It was decorated with a net design and bronze pomegranates^d all around it. The other pillar also had a net design. It was like the first pillar.

Judah Is Taken Prisoner

[18]The commander of the guards took some prisoners. He took Seraiah the chief priest, Zephaniah the priest next in rank, and the three doorkeepers. [19]The commander also took other people who were still in the city. He took the officer in charge of the fighting men. He also took five people who advised the king. And he took the royal assistant who selected people for the army. And he took 60 other men who were in the city. [20]Nebuzaradan, the commander, took all these people. And he brought them to the king of Babylon at Riblah. [21]There at Riblah, in the land of Hamath, the king had them killed. So the people of Judah were led away from their country as captives.

Gedaliah Becomes Governor

[22]Nebuchadnezzar king of Babylon left some people in the land of Judah. He appointed Gedaliah son of Ahikam as governor. (Ahikam was the son of Shaphan.)

[23]The army captains and their men heard that the king of Babylon had made Gedaliah governor. So they all came to Gedaliah at Mizpah. They were Ishmael son of Nethaniah and Johanan son of Kareah. Also there were Seraiah son of Tanhumeth the Netophathite, Jaazaniah son of the Maacathite and

their men. [24]Then Gedaliah made promises to these army captains and their men. He said, "Don't be afraid of the Babylonian officers. Live in the land and serve the king of Babylon. Then everything will go well for you."

[25]Ishmael was the son of Nethaniah. Nethaniah was the son of Elishama from the king's family. In the seventh month Ishmael came with ten men and killed Gedaliah. They also killed the men of Judah and Babylon who were with Gedaliah at Mizpah. [26]Then all the people, from the least important to the most important, ran away to Egypt. The army leaders also went. This was because they were afraid of the Babylonians.

Jehoiachin Is Set Free

[27]Jehoiachin king of Judah was held in Babylon for 37 years. In the thirty-seventh year Evil-Merodach became king of Babylon. He let Jehoiachin out of prison on the twenty-seventh day of the twelfth month. [28]Evil-Merodach spoke kindly to Jehoiachin. He gave Jehoiachin a seat of honor. It was above the seats of the other kings who were with him in Babylon. [29]So Jehoiachin put away his prison clothes. For the rest of his life, he ate at the king's table. [30]Every day the king gave Jehoiachin an allowance. This lasted as long as he lived.

1 CHRONICLES

Israel's History
from Adam to David

From Adam to Abraham

1 Adam was the father of Seth. Seth was the father of Enosh. Enosh was the father of Kenan. ²Kenan was the father of Mahalalel. Mahalalel was the father of Jared. Jared was the father of Enoch. ³Enoch was the father of Methuselah. Methuselah was the father of Lamech. And he was the father of Noah.

⁴The sons of Noah were Shem, Ham and Japheth.

⁵Japheth's sons were Gomer, Magog, Madai, Javan, Tubal, Meshech and Tiras.

⁶Gomer's sons were Ashkenaz, Riphath and Togarmah.

⁷Javan's sons were Elishah, Tarshish, Kittim*ⁿ* and Rodanim.

⁸Ham's sons were Cush, Mizraim,*ⁿ* Put and Canaan.

⁹Cush's sons were Seba, Havilah, Sabta, Raamah and Sabteca.

Raamah's sons were Sheba and Dedan.

¹⁰Cush was the father of Nimrod. Nimrod grew up to become a mighty warrior on the earth.

¹¹Mizraim was the father of the people living in Lud, Anam, Lehab and Naphtuh.

¹²Mizraim was also the father of the people living in Pathrus, Casluh and Crete. (The Philistine people came from Casluh.)

¹³Canaan's first child was Sidon. Canaan was also the father of the Hittites, ¹⁴Jebusites, Amorites and the Girgashites. ¹⁵He was the father of the Hivites, Arkites, Sinites, ¹⁶Arvadites, Zemarites and the Hamathites.

¹⁷Shem's sons were Elam, Asshur, Arphaxad, Lud and Aram.

Aram's sons were Uz, Hul, Gether and Meshech.

¹⁸Arphaxad was the father of Shelah. Shelah was the father of Eber.

¹⁹Eber had two sons. One son was named Peleg.*ⁿ* He was named this because the people on the earth were divided into different languages during his life. Peleg's brother was named Joktan.

²⁰Joktan was the father of Almodad, Sheleph, Hazarmaveth, Jerah, ²¹Hadoram, Uzal and Diklah. ²²He was also the father of Obal, Abimael, Sheba, ²³Ophir, Havilah and Jobab. All these were Joktan's sons. ²⁴The family line went from Shem to Abraham. It included Shem, Arphaxad, Shelah, ²⁵Eber, Peleg, Reu, ²⁶Serug, Nahor, Terah ²⁷and Abram, who is called Abraham.

Abraham's Family

²⁸Abraham's sons were Isaac and Ishmael.

²⁹These were the sons of Isaac and Ishmael. Ishmael's first son was Nebaioth. Ishmael's other sons were Kedar, Adbeel, Mibsam, ³⁰Mishma, Dumah, Massa, Hadad, Tema, ³¹Jetur, Naphish and Kedemah. These were Ishmael's sons. ³²Keturah was Abraham's slave woman.*ᵈ* She gave birth to Zimran, Jokshan, Medan, Midian, Ishbak and Shuah.

---

*ⁿ***Kittim** His descendants were the people of Cyprus.
*ⁿ***Mizraim** This is another name for Egypt.
*ⁿ***Peleg** This name sounds like the Hebrew word for "divided."

Jokshan's sons were Sheba and Dedan.

³³Midian's sons were Ephah, Epher, Hanoch, Abida and Eldaah. All these people were descendants^d of Keturah.

³⁴Abraham was the father of Isaac. Isaac's sons were Esau and Israel.

³⁵Esau's sons were Eliphaz, Reuel, Jeush, Jalam and Korah.

³⁶Eliphaz's sons were Teman, Omar, Zepho, Gatam, Kenaz, Timna and Amalek.

³⁷Reuel's sons were Nahath, Zerah, Shammah and Mizzah.

The Edomites from Seir

³⁸Seir's sons were Lotan, Shobal, Zibeon, Anah, Dishon, Ezer and Dishan.

³⁹Lotan's sons were Hori and Homam. Lotan had a sister named Timna.

⁴⁰Shobal's sons were Alvan, Manahath, Ebal, Shepho and Onam.

Zibeon's sons were Aiah and Anah.

⁴¹Anah's son was Dishon.

Dishon's sons were Hemdan, Eshban, Ithran and Keran.

⁴²Ezer's sons were Bilhan, Zaavan and Akan.

Dishan's sons were Uz and Aran.

The Kings of Edom

⁴³There were kings ruling in Edom before there were kings in Israel. Bela son of Beor was king of Edom. Bela's city was named Dinhabah.

⁴⁴When Bela died, Jobab son of Zerah became king. Jobab was from Bozrah.

⁴⁵When Jobab died, Husham became king. He was from Teman.

⁴⁶When Husham died, Hadad son of Bedad became king. Hadad's city was named Avith. Hadad defeated Midian in the country of Moab.

⁴⁷When Hadad died, Samlah became king. He was from Masrekah.

⁴⁸When Samlah died, Shaul became king. He was from Rehoboth by the River.

⁴⁹When Shaul died, Baal-Hanan son of Acbor became king.

⁵⁰When Baal-Hanan died, Hadad became king. Hadad's city was named Pau. Hadad's wife was named Mehetabel, and she was Matred's daughter. Matred was the daughter of Me-Zahab. ⁵¹Then Hadad died.

The leaders of the family groups of Edom were Timna, Alvah, Jetheth, ⁵²Oholibamah, Elah, Pinon, ⁵³Kenaz, Teman, Mibzar, ⁵⁴Magdiel and Iram. These were the leaders of Edom.

Israel's Family

2 The sons of Israel, also called Jacob, were Reuben, Simeon, Levi, Judah, Issachar, Zebulun, ²Dan, Joseph, Benjamin, Naphtali, Gad and Asher.

Judah's Family

³Judah's sons were Er, Onan and Shelah. A Canaanite woman, the daughter of Shua, was their mother. Judah's first son, Er, did what the Lord said was wicked. So the Lord put him to death. ⁴Judah's daughter-in-law Tamar gave birth to Perez and Zerah. Judah was the father. So Judah had five sons.

⁵Perez's sons were Hezron and Hamul.

⁶Zerah had five sons. They were Zimri, Ethan, Heman, Calcol and Darda.

⁷Carmi's son was Achan. He caused trouble for Israel because he took things that had been given to the Lord to be destroyed.

⁸Ethan's son was Azariah.

⁹Hezron's sons were Jerahmeel, Ram and Caleb.

¹⁰Ram was Amminadab's father. And Amminadab was Nashon's father. Nahshon was the leader of the people of Judah. ¹¹Nahshon was the father of Salmon. Salmon was the father of Boaz. ¹²Boaz was the father of Obed. Obed was the father of Jesse.

¹³Jesse's first son was Eliab. His second son was Abinadab. His third son was Shimea. ¹⁴His fourth son was Nethanel. His fifth son was Raddai. ¹⁵Jesse's sixth son was Ozem, and his seventh son was David. ¹⁶Their sisters were Zeruiah and Abigail. Zeruiah's

three sons were Abishai, Joab and Asahel. [17]Abigail was the mother of Amasa. Amasa's father was an Ishmaelite named Jether.

Caleb's Family

[18]Caleb son of Hezron had children by his wife Azubah and by Jerioth. Caleb and Azubah's sons were Jesher, Shobab and Ardon. [19]When Azubah died, Caleb married Ephrath. They had a son named Hur. [20]Hur was the father of Uri. Uri was the father of Bezalel.

[21]Later, when Hezron was 60 years old, he married the daughter of Makir. Makir was Gilead's father. Hezron had sexual relations with Makir's daughter, and she had a son named Segub. [22]Segub was the father of Jair. Jair controlled 23 cities in the country of Gilead. [23](But Geshur and Aram captured the Towns of Jair. They also captured Kenath and the small towns around it. There were 60 towns in all.) All these were descendants[d] of Makir, the father of Gilead.

[24]After Hezron died in Caleb Ephrathah, his wife Abijah had his son. He was named Ashur. Ashur became the father of Tekoa.

Jerahmeel's Family

[25]Jerahmeel was Hezron's first son. Jerahmeel's sons were Ram, Bunah, Oren, Ozem and Ahijah. Ram was Jerahmeel's first son. [26]Jerahmeel had another wife, who was named Atarah. She was the mother of Onam. [27]Jerahmeel's first son, Ram, had sons. They were Maaz, Jamin and Eker. [28]Onam's sons were Shammai and Jada. Shammai's sons were Nadab and Abishur. [29]Abishur's wife was named Abihail. Abishur and Abihail's sons were Ahban and Molid. [30]Nadab's sons were Seled and Appaim. Seled died without having children. [31]Appaim's son was Ishi. Ishi was the father of Sheshan.

Sheshan was the father of Ahlai.

[32]Jada was Shammai's brother. Jada's sons were Jether and Jonathan. Jether died without having children.

[33]Jonathan's sons were Peleth and Zaza.

These were Jerahmeel's descendants.[d]

[34]Sheshan did not have any sons, only daughters. He had a servant from Egypt named Jarha. [35]Sheshan let his daughter marry his servant Jarha. Then she had a son named Attai.

[36]Attai was the father of Nathan. Nathan was the father of Zabad. [37]Zabad was the father of Ephlal. Ephlal was the father of Obed. [38]Obed was the father of Jehu. Jehu was the father of Azariah. [39]Azariah was the father of Helez. Helez was the father of Eleasah. [40]Eleasah was the father of Sismai. Sismai was the father of Shallum. [41]Shallum was the father of Jekamiah. And Jekamiah was the father of Elishama.

Caleb's Family

[42]Caleb was Jerahmeel's brother. Caleb's first son was Mesha. Mesha was the father of Ziph. And his son Mareshah was the father of Hebron.

[43]Hebron's sons were Korah, Tappuah, Rekem and Shema. [44]Shema was the father of Raham. Raham was the father of Jorkeam. Rekem was the father of Shammai. [45]Shammai's son was Maon. Maon was the father of Beth Zur.

[46]Caleb's slave woman[d] was named Ephah. She was the mother of Haran, Moza and Gazez. Haran was the father of Gazez.

[47]Jahdai's sons were Regem, Jotham, Geshan, Pelet, Ephah and Shaaph.

[48]Caleb had another slave woman named Maacah. She was the mother of Sheber and Tirhanah. [49]She was also the mother of Shaaph and Sheva. Shaaph was the father of Madmannah. Sheva was the father of Macbenah and Gibea. Caleb's daughter was Acsah.

[50-51]These were Caleb's descendants:[d]

Caleb's son Hur was the first son of his mother Ephrathah. Hur's sons were Shobal, Salma and Hareph. Shobal was the father of Kiriath Jearim. Salma was the father of Bethlehem. And Hareph was the father of Beth Gader.

52Shobal was the father of Kiriath Jearim. These were Shobal's descendants: Haroeh, half the Manahathites, 53and the family groups of Kiriath Jearim. Shobal was also the ancestor of the Ithrites, Puthites, Shumathites and the Mishraites. The Zorathites and the Eshtaolites came from the Mishraite people.

54Salma's descendants were Bethlehem, the Netophathites, Atroth Beth Joab, half the Manahathites and the Zorites. 55His descendants were also the families who lived at Jabez. These were the people who wrote and copied important papers. These people were the Tirathites, Shimeathites and Sucathites. They were from the Kenite family group who came from Hammath. He was the father of the people living in Recab.

David's Family

3 These are David's sons who were born in Hebron. David's first son was Amnon. Amnon's mother was Ahinoam from the town of Jezreel. David's second son was Daniel. His mother was Abigail from Carmel. 2David's third son was Absalom. His mother was Maacah, the daughter of Talmai king of Geshur. David's fourth son was Adonijah. His mother was Haggith. 3David's fifth son was Shephatiah. His mother was Abital. David's sixth son was Ithream. David's wife Eglah was his mother. 4These six sons of David were born to him in Hebron. David ruled there 7 years and 6 months.

David ruled in Jerusalem 33 years. 5These were David's children who were born in Jerusalem: David and Bathsheba, Ammiel's daughter, had four children. They were Shammua, Shobab, Nathan and Solomon. 6-8David's other nine children were Ibhar,

Elishua, Eliphelet, Nogah, Nepheg, Japhia, Elishama, Eliada and Eliphelet. 9Those are all of David's sons, except for those born to his slave women.d David also had a daughter named Tamar.

The Kings of Judah

10Solomon's son was Rehoboam. Rehoboam's son was Abijah. Abijah's son was Asa. Asa's son was Jehoshaphat. 11Jehoshaphat's son was Jehoram. Jehoram's son was Ahaziah. Ahaziah's son was Joash. 12Joash's son was Amaziah. Amaziah's son was Azariah. Azariah's son was Jotham. 13Jotham's son was Ahaz. Ahaz's son was Hezekiah. Hezekiah's son was Manasseh. 14Manasseh's son was Amon. Amon's son was Josiah.

15These were Josiah's sons: Josiah's first son was Johanan. His second son was Jehoiakim. His third son was Zedekiah. His fourth son was Shallum.

16Jehoiakim was followed by Jehoiachin. Jehoiachin was followed by Zedekiah.

David's Descendants After the Babylonian Captivity

17Jehoiachin was taken as a prisoner. His sons were Shealtiel, 18Malkiram, Pedaiah, Shenazzar, Jekamiah, Hoshama and Nedabiah.

19Pedaiah's sons were Zerubbabel and Shimei.

Zerubbabel's sons were Meshullam and Hananiah. Their sister was Shelomith. 20Zerubbabel also had five other sons. Their names were Hashubah, Ohel, Berekiah, Hasadiah and Jushab-Hesed.

21Hananiah's descendantsd were Pelatiah and Jeshaiah, and the sons of Rephaiah, Arnan, Obadiah and Shecaniah.

22Shecaniah's son was Shemaiah. Shemaiah's sons were Hattush, Igal, Bariah, Neariah and Shaphat. There were six in all.

23Neariah had three sons. They were Elioenai, Hizkiah and Azrikam.

24Elioenai had seven sons. They were

Hodaviah, Eliashib, Pelaiah, Akkub, Johanan, Delaiah and Anani.

Other Family Groups of Judah

4 Judah's descendants[d] were Perez, Hezron, Carmi, Hur and Shobal.
[2]Reaiah was Shobal's son. Reaiah was the father of Jahath. Jahath was the father of Ahumai and Lahad. They were the family groups of the Zorathite people.

[3-4]Hur was the oldest son of Caleb and his wife Ephrath. Hur was the leader of Bethlehem. Hur's three sons were Etam, Penuel and Ezer. Etam's sons were Jezreel, Ishma and Idbash. They had a sister named Hazzelelponi. Penuel was the father of Gedor. Ezer was the father of Hushah.

[5]Tekoa's father was Ashhur. Ashhur had two wives named Helah and Naarah.

[6]The sons of Ashhur and Naarah were Ahuzzam, Hepher, Temeni and Haahashtari. These were the descendants of Naarah.

[7]Helah's sons were Zereth, Zohar, Ethnan [8]and Koz. Koz was the father of Anub and Hazzobebah. He was also the father of the Aharhel family group. Aharhel was the son of Harum.

[9]There was a man named Jabez. He was respected more than his brothers. His mother named him Jabez[n] because she said, "I was in much pain when I gave birth to him." [10]Jabez prayed to the God of Israel. Jabez said, "Please do good things for me. Please give me more land. Stay with me, and don't let anyone hurt me. Then I won't have any pain." And God did what Jabez had asked.

[11]Kelub was Shuhah's brother. Kelub was the father of Mehir. Mehir was the father of Eshton. [12]Eshton was the father of Beth Rapha, Paseah and Tehinnah. Tehinnah was the father of the people from the town of Nahash. These people were from Recah.

[13]The sons of Kenaz were Othniel and Seraiah.

Othniel's sons were Hathath and Meonothai. [14]Meonothai was the father of Ophrah.

Seraiah was the father of Joab. Joab was the ancestor of the people from Craftsmen's Valley. It is called Craftsmen's Valley because the people living there were craftsmen.

[15]Caleb was Jephunneh's son. Caleb's sons were Iru, Elah and Naam. Elah's son was Kenaz.

[16]Jehallelel's sons were Ziph, Ziphah, Tiria and Asarel.

[17-18]Ezrah's sons were Jether, Mered, Epher and Jalon. Mered married Bithiah, the daughter of the king of Egypt. The children of Mered and Bithiah were Miriam, Shammai and Ishbah. Ishbah was the father of Eshtemoa. Mered also had a wife from Judah. She gave birth to Jered, Heber and Jekuthiel. Jered became the father of Gedor. Heber became the father of Soco. And Jekuthiel became the father of Zanoah.

[19]Hodiah's wife was Naham's sister. The sons of Hodiah's wife were Eshtemoa and the father of Keilah. Keilah was from the Garmite people. And Eshtemoa was from the Maacathite people.

[20]Shimon's sons were Amnon, Rinnah, Ben-Hanan and Tilon.

Ishi's sons were Zoheth and Ben-Zoheth.

[21-22]Shelah was Judah's son. Shelah's sons were Er, Laadah, Jokim, the men from Cozeba, Joash and Saraph. Er was the father of Lecah. Laadah was the father of Mareshah and the family groups of linen workers at Beth Ashbea. Joash and Saraph ruled in Moab and Jashubi Lehem. The writings about this family are very old. [23]These sons of Shelah made things from clay. They lived in Netaim and Gederah. They stayed there and worked for the king.

Simeon's Children

[24]Simeon's sons were Nemuel, Jamin, Jarib, Zerah and Shaul. [25]Shaul's son was Shallum. Shallum's son was

---

[n]**Jabez**   This name in Hebrew sounds like the word for "pain."

Mibsam. Mibsam's son was Mishma. [26]Mishma's son was Hammuel. Hammuel's son was Zaccur. Zaccur's son was Shimei. [27]Shimei had 16 sons and 6 daughters. But his brothers did not have many children. So there were not as many people in their family group as there were in Judah.

[28]Shimei's children lived in Beersheba, Moladah, Hazar Shual, [29]Bilhah, Ezem and Tolad. [30]They also lived in Bethuel, Hormah, Ziklag, [31]Beth Marcaboth, Hazar Susim, Beth Biri and Shaaraim. They lived in these cities until David became king. [32]The five villages near these cities were Etam, Ain, Rimmon, Token and Ashan. [33]There were also other villages as far away as Baalath. This is where they lived. And they wrote the history of their family.

[34-38]This is the list of men who were leaders of their family groups. There were Meshobab, Jamlech, Joshah son of Amaziah, Joel and Jehu son of Joshibiah. (Joshibiah was the son of Seraiah, who was the son of Asiel.) There were also Elioenai, Jaakobah, Jeshohaiah, Asaiah, Adiel, Jesimiel, Benaiah and Ziza. (Ziza was the son of Shiphi, who was the son of Allon. Allon was the son of Jedaiah, who was the son of Shimri. And Shimri was the son of Shemaiah.)

These men's families grew to be very large. [39]They went to the area outside the city of Gedor to the east side of the valley. They went there to look for pasture for their sheep. [40]They found good pastures with plenty of grass. The land was open country and peaceful and quiet. Ham's descendants[d] had lived there in the past.

[41]These men listed above came to Gedor while Hezekiah was king of Judah. They fought against the Hamite people and destroyed their tents. They also fought against the Meunite people who lived there and completely destroyed them. So there are no Meunites there even today. Then these men began to live there, because there was pasture for their sheep. [42]Ishi's sons, Pelatiah, Neariah, Rephaiah and

Uzziel, led 500 of the Simeonite people. They attacked the people living in the mountains of Edom. [43]They killed the few Amalekite people who were still alive. From that time until now these Simeonites have lived in Edom.

Reuben's Children

5 Reuben was Israel's first son. Reuben should have received the special privileges of the oldest son. But he had sexual relations with his father's slave woman.[d] So those special privileges were given to Joseph's sons. (Joseph was a son of Israel.) In the family history Reuben's name is not listed as the first son. [2]Judah became stronger than his brothers. And a leader came from his family. But Joseph's family received the privileges that belonged to the oldest son. [3]Reuben was the first son born to Israel. Reuben's sons were Hanoch, Pallu, Hezron and Carmi.

[4]These were the children of Joel: Shemaiah was Joel's son. Gog was Shemaiah's son. Shimei was Gog's son. [5]Micah was Shimei's son. Reaiah was Micah's son. Baal was Reaiah's son. [6]Beerah was Baal's son. Beerah was a leader of the tribe[d] of Reuben. Tiglath-Pileser king of Assyria captured Beerah and took him away.

[7]Joel's brothers and all his family groups are listed just as they are written in their family histories: Jeiel was the first, then Zechariah [8]and Bela. (Bela was the son of Azaz. Azaz was Shema's son. Shema was Joel's son.) They lived in the area of Aroer all the way to Nebo and Baal Meon. [9]Bela's people lived to the east. Their land went as far as the edge of the desert, which is beside the Euphrates River. They lived there because they had too many cattle for the land of Gilead.

[10]When Saul was king, Bela's people fought a war against the Hagrite people. And they defeated the Hagrites. Then Bela's people lived in the tents that had belonged to the Hagrites. They lived in all the area east of Gilead.

Gad's Children

[11]The people from the tribe[d] of Gad lived near the Reubenite people. The Gadites lived in the area of Bashan all the way to Salecah. [12]Joel was the main leader in Bashan. Shapham was the second leader. Then Janai and Shaphat were leaders.

[13]The seven relatives in their families were Michael, Meshullam, Sheba, Jorai, Jacan, Zia and Eber. [14]They were the descendants[d] of Abihail. Abihail was Huri's son. Huri was Jaroah's son. Jaroah was Gilead's son. Gilead was Michael's son. Michael was Jeshishai's son. Jeshishai was Jahdo's son. Jahdo was the son of Buz. [15]Ahi was Abdiel's son. Abdiel was Guni's son. Ahi was the leader of their family.

[16]The Gadite people lived in Gilead, Bashan and in the small towns around Bashan. They also lived on all the pasturelands in the Plain of Sharon all the way to the borders.

[17]All these people's names were written in the family history of Gad. This was done during the time Jotham was king of Judah and Jeroboam was king of Israel.

Soldiers Skilled in War

[18]There were 44,760 fighters from the tribes[d] of Reuben and Gad and the eastern half-tribe of Manasseh. They were brave men who could use shields and swords. They could use their bows well. They were skilled in war. [19]They started a war against the Hagrites and the people of Jetur, Naphish and Nodab. [20]The men from the tribes of Manasseh, Reuben and Gad prayed to God in the war. They asked God to help them. So he helped them because they trusted him. He allowed them to defeat the Hagrites. And they also defeated all those who were with the Hagrites. [21]They took the animals that belonged to the Hagrites. They took 50,000 camels, 250,000 sheep and 2,000 donkeys. They also captured 100,000 people. [22]Many Hagrites were killed. This is because God helped the people of Reuben, Gad and Manasseh. Then they lived there until Babylon captured them and took them away.

The Eastern Half-Tribe of Manasseh

[23]There were many people in the eastern half-tribe[d] of Manasseh. They lived in the area of Bashan all the way to Baal Hermon, Senir and Mount Hermon. [24]These were the family leaders: Epher, Ishi, Eliel, Azriel, Jeremiah, Hodaviah and Jahdiel. They were all strong, brave and famous men. And they were leaders in their families. [25]But they sinned against the God that their ancestors had worshiped. They began worshiping the gods of the people in that land. And those were the people God was destroying. [26]So the God of Israel made Pul king of Assyria want to go to war. Pul was also called Tiglath-Pileser. He captured the people of Reuben, Gad and the eastern half-tribe of Manasseh. And he took them away to Halah, Habor, Hara and near the Gozan River. And they have lived there from that time until this day.

Levi's Children

6 Levi's sons were Gershon, Kohath and Merari.

[2]Kohath's sons were Amram, Izhar, Hebron and Uzziel.

[3]Amram's children were Aaron, Moses and Miriam.

Aaron's sons were Nadab, Abihu, Eleazar and Ithamar. [4]Eleazar was the father of Phinehas. Phinehas was the father of Abishua. [5]Abishua was the father of Bukki. Bukki was the father of Uzzi. [6]Uzzi was the father of Zerahiah. Zerahiah was the father of Meraioth. [7]Meraioth was the father of Amariah. Amariah was the father of Ahitub. [8]Ahitub was the father of Zadok. Zadok was the father of Ahimaaz. [9]Ahimaaz was the father of Azariah. Azariah was the father of Johanan. [10]Johanan was the father of Azariah. (Azariah was a priest in the Temple[d] Solomon built in Jerusalem.)

¹¹Azariah was the father of Amariah. Amariah was the father of Ahitub. ¹²Ahitub was the father of Zadok. Zadok was the father of Shallum. ¹³Shallum was the father of Hilkiah. Hilkiah was the father of Azariah. ¹⁴Azariah was the father of Seraiah. Seraiah was the father of Jehozadak.

¹⁵Jehozadak was forced to leave his home when the Lord sent Judah and Jerusalem into captivity. That was when Nebuchadnezzar captured them and took them away.

¹⁶Levi's sons were Gershon, Kohath and Merari.

¹⁷The names of Gershon's sons were Libni and Shimei.

¹⁸Kohath's sons were Amram, Izhar, Hebron and Uzziel.

¹⁹Merari's sons were Mahli and Mushi.

This is a list of the family groups of Levi. They are listed by the name of the father of each group.

²⁰Gershon's son was Libni. Libni's son was Jehath. Jehath's son was Zimmah. ²¹Zimmah's son was Joah. Joah's son was Iddo. Iddo's son was Zerah. And Zerah's son was Jeatherai.

²²Kohath's son was Amminadab. Amminadab's son was Korah. Korah's son was Assir. ²³Assir's son was Elkanah. Elkanah's son was Ebiasaph. Ebiasaph's son was Assir. ²⁴Assir's son was Tahath. Tahath's son was Uriel. Uriel's son was Uzziah, and Uzziah's son was Shaul.

²⁵Elkanah's sons were Amasai and Ahimoth. ²⁶Ahimoth's son was Elkanah. Elkanah's son was Zophai. Zophai's son was Nahath. ²⁷Nahath's son was Eliab. Eliab's son was Jeroham. Jeroham's son was Elkanah, and Elkanah's son was Samuel.

²⁸Samuel's sons were Joel, the first son, and Abijah, the second son.

²⁹Merari's son was Mahli. Mahli's son was Libni. Libni's son was Shimei. Shimei's son was Uzzah. ³⁰Uzzah's son was Shimea. Shimea's son was Haggiah, and Haggiah's son was Asaiah.

The Temple Musicians

³¹David chose some men to be in charge of the music in the house of the Lord. They began their work after the Box^d of the Agreement was put there. ³²They served by making music at the Holy Tent.^d (It is also called the Meeting Tent.) And they served until Solomon built the Temple^d of the Lord in Jerusalem. They followed the rules for their work.

³³These are the musicians and their sons:

Jobs in the Bible

MUSICIAN • 1 CHRONICLES 6:31-46

Singing was an important part of Israel's worship, just as it probably is in your church. Singing is a way to tell God how much we love him, and it was no different in Bible times. When King David was planning how to build the temple, he also planned who would work there. He got certain people to lead songs and other people to sing in a choir. Some musicians played harps and lyres (instruments with strings that were strummed). Others played tambourines and cymbals. David divided the musicians into groups to play at different times so there would always be music during temple worship. God enjoys for his people to sing praises to him!

To read about the people who made the pots and pans, fly to page 907.

From Kohath's family there was Heman the singer. Heman was Joel's son. Joel was Samuel's son. ³⁴Samuel was Elkanah's son. Elkanah was Jeroham's son. Jeroham was Eliel's son. Eliel was Toah's son. ³⁵Toah was Zuph's son. Zuph was Elkanah's son. Elkanah was Mahath's son. Mahath was Amasai's son. ³⁶Amasai was Elkanah's son. Elkanah was Joel's son. Joel was Azariah's son. Azariah was Zephaniah's son. ³⁷Zephaniah was Tahath's son. Tahath was Assir's son. Assir was Ebiasaph's son. Ebiasaph was Korah's son. ³⁸Korah was Izhar's son. Izhar was Kohath's son. Kohath was Levi's son. Levi was Israel's son.

³⁹There was Heman's helper Asaph. Asaph's group stood by Heman's right side. Asaph was Berekiah's son. Berekiah was Shimea's son. ⁴⁰Shimea was Michael's son. Michael was Baaseiah's son. Baaseiah was Malkijah's son. ⁴¹Malkijah was Ethni's son. Ethni was Zerah's son. Zerah was Adaiah's son. ⁴²Adaiah was Ethan's son. Ethan was Zimmah's son. Zimmah was Shimei's son. ⁴³Shimei was Jahath's son. Jahath was Gershon's son. Gershon was Levi's son.

⁴⁴Merari's family were the helpers of Heman and Asaph. Merari's family stood by Heman's left side. In this group was Ethan son of Kishi. Kishi was Abdi's son. Abdi was Malluch's son. ⁴⁵Malluch was Hashabiah's son. Hashabiah was Amaziah's son. Amaziah was Hilkiah's son. ⁴⁶Hilkiah was Amzi's son. Amzi was Bani's son. Bani was Shemer's son. ⁴⁷Shemer was Mahli's son. Mahli was Mushi's son. Mushi was Merari's son. Merari was Levi's son.

⁴⁸The other Levites served by doing their own special work in the Holy Tent. It is the house of God. ⁴⁹Aaron and his descendants*d* offered the sacrifices on the altar of burnt offering. They also burned the incense on the altar of incense. They offered the sacrifices that removed the Israelites' sins so

they could belong to God. They did all the work in the Most Holy Place. They followed all the laws that Moses, God's servant, had commanded.

⁵⁰These were Aaron's sons: Eleazar was Aaron's son. Phinehas was Eleazar's son. Abishua was Phinehas' son. ⁵¹Bukki was Abishua's son. Uzzi was Bukki's son. Zerahiah was Uzzi's son. ⁵²Meraioth was Zerahiah's son. Amariah was Meraioth's son. Ahitub was Amariah's son. ⁵³Zadok was Ahitub's son. Ahimaaz was Zadok's son.

Land for the Levites

⁵⁴These are the places where Aaron's descendants*d* lived. Aaron's descendants from the Kohath family group were given this land to live in. They received the first share of the land that was given to the Levites.

⁵⁵They were given the city of Hebron in Judah and the pastures around it. ⁵⁶But the fields farther from the city were given to Caleb son of Jephunneh. And the villages near Hebron were given to Caleb. ⁵⁷So the descendants of Aaron were given Hebron. It was one of the cities of safety.*n* They also received the cities of Libnah, Jattir, Eshtemoa, ⁵⁸Hilen, Debir, ⁵⁹Ashan, Juttah and Beth Shemesh. They received all these cities and the pastures around them. ⁶⁰They also received cities from the tribe of Benjamin. They received Gibeon, Geba, Alemeth, Anathoth and their pastures.

The Kohath family groups received a total of 13 cities.

⁶¹The rest of the Kohath family group was given 10 cities. These cities were from the family groups of the western half-tribe*d* of Manasseh. The cities were chosen by throwing lots.*d*

⁶²The Gershon family group received 13 cities. They were from the tribes of Issachar, Asher, Naphtali and the part of Manasseh living in Bashan.

⁶³The Merari family group received 12 cities from the tribes of Reuben,

---

*n***cities of safety** A person who had accidentally killed someone could go to one of the six cities of safety. There he would receive protection and a fair trial.

Gad and Zebulun. Those cities were chosen by throwing lots.

⁶⁴So the Israelites gave these cities and their pastures to the Levites. ⁶⁵The cities from the tribes of Judah, Simeon and Benjamin were chosen by throwing lots. They are the cities named above.

⁶⁶Some of the Kohath family groups received cities and pastures from the tribe of Ephraim. ⁶⁷They received Shechem in the mountains of Ephraim. It was one of the cities of safety. They also received the cities of Gezer, ⁶⁸Jokmeam, Beth Horon, ⁶⁹Aijalon and Gath Rimmon. They received the cities and the pastures around them.

⁷⁰The rest of the people in the Kohath family group received cities from the western half-tribe of Manasseh. They received the cities of Aner and Bileam and their pastures.

⁷¹From the eastern half-tribe of Manasseh, the Gershon family received towns and pastures. They received Golan in Bashan, Ashtaroth and the pastures around them.

⁷²⁻⁷³From the tribe of Issachar, the Gershon family received towns and pastures. They received Kedesh, Daberath, Ramoth, Anem and their pastures.

⁷⁴⁻⁷⁵From the tribe of Asher, the Gershon family received towns and pastures. They received Mashal, Abdon, Hukok, Rehob and their pastures.

⁷⁶From the tribe of Naphtali, the Gershon family received towns and pastures. They received Kedesh in Galilee, Hammon, Kiriathaim and their pastures.

⁷⁷The rest of the Levites, the people from the Merari family, also received towns and pastures. They received Jokneam, Kartah, Rimmono and Tabor from the tribe of Zebulun. They also received the pastures around those cities.

⁷⁸⁻⁷⁹From the tribe of Reuben, the Merari family received towns and pastures. They received Bezer in the desert, Jahzah, Kedemoth, Mephaath and their pastures. (The tribe of Reuben lived east of the Jordan River, across from Jericho.)

⁸⁰⁻⁸¹From the tribe of Gad, the Merari family received towns and pastures. They received Ramoth in Gilead, Mahanaim, Heshbon, Jazer and their pastures.

Issachar's Children

7 Issachar had four sons. Their names were Tola, Puah, Jashub and Shimron.

²Tola's sons were Uzzi, Rephaiah, Jeriel, Jahmai, Ibsam and Samuel. They were leaders of their families. In the family history of Tola's descendants,[d] 22,600 men were listed as fighting men. This was during the time David was king.

³Uzzi's son was Izrahiah.

Izrahiah's sons were Michael, Obadiah, Joel and Isshiah. All five of them were leaders. ⁴Their family history shows they had 36,000 men ready to serve in the army. This was because they had many women and children.

⁵The records of the family groups of Issachar show there were 87,000 fighting men.

Benjamin's Children

⁶Benjamin had three sons. Their names were Bela, Beker and Jediael.

⁷Bela had five sons. Their names were Ezbon, Uzzi, Uzziel, Jerimoth and Iri. They were leaders of their families. Their family history shows they had 22,034 fighting men.

⁸Beker's sons were Zemirah, Joash, Eliezer, Elioenai, Omri, Jeremoth, Abijah, Anathoth and Alemeth. They all were Beker's sons. ⁹Their family history listed the family leaders and 20,200 fighting men.

¹⁰Jediael's son was Bilhan.

Bilhan's sons were Jeush, Benjamin, Ehud, Kenaanah, Zethan, Tarshish and Ahishahar. ¹¹All these sons of Jediael were leaders of their families. They had 17,200 fighting men ready to serve in the army.

¹²The Shuppites and Huppites were descendants[d] of Ir. And the Hushites were descendants of Aher.

Naphtali's Children

[13] Naphtali's sons were Jahziel, Guni, Jezer and Shillem. They were Bilhah's grandsons.

Manasseh's Children

[14] These are Manasseh's descendants:[d] Manasseh had an Aramean slave woman.[d] She was the mother of Asriel and Makir. Makir was Gilead's father. [15] Makir took a wife from the Huppites and Shuppites. His sister was named Maacah. His second son was named Zelophehad. Zelophehad had only daughters. [16] Makir's wife Maacah had a son whom she named Peresh. Peresh's brother was named Sheresh. Sheresh's sons were Ulam and Rakem.

[17] Ulam's son was Bedan.

These were the sons of Gilead. Gilead was Makir's son. Makir was Manasseh's son. [18] Makir's sister Hammoleketh gave birth to Ishhod, Abiezer and Mahlah.

[19] The sons of Shemida were Ahian, Shechem, Likhi and Aniam.

Ephraim's Children

[20] These are the names of Ephraim's descendants.[d] Ephraim's son was Shuthelah. Shuthelah's son was Bered. Bered's son was Tahath. Tahath's son was Eleadah. Eleadah's son was Tahath. [21] Tahath's son was Zabad. Zabad's son was Shuthelah.

Ezer and Elead went to Gath to steal the people's cows and sheep. So some men who grew up in that city killed Ezer and Elead. [22] Their father Ephraim cried for them many days. And his family came to comfort him. [23] Then he had sexual relations with his wife again. She became pregnant and gave birth to a son. Ephraim named his son Beriah[n] because of the bad things that had happened to his family. [24] Ephraim's daughter was Sheerah. She built Lower Beth Horon and Upper Beth Horon and Uzzen Sheerah.

[25] Rephah was Ephraim's son. Resheph was Rephah's son. Telah was Resheph's son. Tahan was Telah's son. [26] Ladan was Tahan's son. Ammihud was Ladan's son. Elishama was Ammihud's son. [27] Nun was Elishama's son. Joshua was the son of Nun.

[28] Ephraim's descendants lived in these lands and cities: Bethel and the villages near it, Naaran on the east, Gezer and the villages near it on the west, and Shechem and the villages near it. These villages went all the way to Ayyah and its villages. [29] Along the borders of Manasseh's land were the towns of Beth Shan, Taanach, Megiddo and Dor. There were also villages near them. The descendants of Joseph son of Israel lived in these towns.

Asher's Children

[30] Asher's sons were Imnah, Ishvah, Ishvi and Beriah. Their sister was Serah.

[31] Beriah's sons were Heber and Malkiel. Malkiel was Birzaith's father. [32] Heber was the father of Japhlet, Shomer and Hotham and their sister Shua.

[33] Japhlet's sons were Pasach, Bimhal and Ashvath. They were Japhlet's children.

[34] Japhlet's brother was Shomer. Shomer's sons were Rohgah, Hubbah and Aram.

[35] Shomer's brother was Hotham. Hotham's sons were Zophah, Imna, Shelesh and Amal.

[36] Zophah's sons were Suah, Harnepher, Shual, Beri, Imrah, [37] Bezer, Hod, Shamma, Shilshah, Ithran and Beera.

[38] Jether's sons were Jephunneh, Pispah and Ara.

[39] Ulla's sons were Arah, Hanniel and Rizia.

[40] All these men were descendants of Asher. They were leaders of their families. They were powerful warriors and outstanding leaders. Their family history lists that they had 26,000 soldiers ready to serve in the army.

---

[n] **Beriah** This name sounds like the Hebrew word for "trouble."

The Family History of King Saul

8 Benjamin was the father of Bela. Bela was Benjamin's first son. Ashbel was his second son. Aharah was his third son. ²Nohah was Benjamin's fourth son, and Rapha was his fifth son.

³Bela's sons were Addar, Gera, Abihud, ⁴Abishua, Naaman, Ahoah, ⁵Gera, Shephuphan and Huram.

⁶These were the descendants^d of Ehud. They were leaders of their families in Geba. They were forced to leave their homes and move to Manahath. ⁷Ehud's descendants were Naaman, Ahijah and Gera. Gera forced them to leave their homes. He was the father of Uzza and Ahihud.

⁸⁻¹¹Shaharaim and his wife Hushim had sons named Abitub and Elpaal. In Moab Shaharaim divorced his wives Hushim and Baara. Shaharaim and his wife Hodesh had these children: Jobab, Zibia, Mesha, Malcam, Jeuz, Sakia and Mirmah. These sons were leaders of their families.

¹²⁻¹³Elpaal's sons were Eber, Misham, Shemed, Beriah and Shema. Shemed built the towns of Ono and Lod and the villages around them. Beriah and Shema were leaders of the families living in Aijalon. These sons forced the people who lived in Gath to leave.

¹⁴Beriah's sons were Ahio, Shashak, Jeremoth, ¹⁵Zebadiah, Arad, Eder, ¹⁶Michael, Ishpah and Joha.

¹⁷Elpaal's sons were Zebadiah, Meshullam, Hizki, Heber, ¹⁸Ishmerai, Izliah and Jobab.

¹⁹Shimei's sons were Jakim, Zicri, Zabdi, ²⁰Elienai, Zillethai, Eliel, ²¹Adaiah, Beraiah and Shimrath.

²²Shashak's sons were Ishpan, Eber, Eliel, ²³Abdon, Zicri, Hanan, ²⁴Hananiah, Elam, Anthothijah, ²⁵Iphdeiah and Penuel.

²⁶Jeroham's sons were Shamsherai, Shehariah, Athaliah, ²⁷Jaareshiah, Elijah and Zicri.

²⁸The family histories show that all these men were leaders of their families. They lived in Jerusalem.

²⁹Jeiel lived in the town of Gibeon, where he was the leader. His wife was named Maacah. ³⁰Jeiel's first son was Abdon. His other sons were Zur, Kish, Baal, Ner, Nadab, ³¹Gedor, Ahio, Zeker ³²and Mikloth. Mikloth was the father of Shimeah. These sons also lived near their relatives in Jerusalem.

³³Ner was the father of Kish. Kish was the father of Saul. And Saul was the father of Jonathan, Malki-Shua, Abinadab and Esh-Baal.

³⁴Jonathan's son was Merib-Baal. Merib-Baal was Micah's father.

³⁵Micah's sons were Pithon, Melech, Tarea and Ahaz. ³⁶Ahaz was the father of Jehoaddah. Jehoaddah was the father of Alemeth, Azmaveth and Zimri. Zimri was the father of Moza. ³⁷Moza was the father of Binea. Raphah was Binea's son. Eleasah was Raphah's son. And Azel was Eleasah's son.

³⁸Azel had six sons. Their names were Azrikam, Bokeru, Ishmael, Sheariah, Obadiah and Hanan. All these were Azel's sons.

³⁹Azel's brother was Eshek. Eshek's first son was Ulam. Jeush was his second son, and Eliphelet was his third son. ⁴⁰Ulam's sons were mighty warriors who could use a bow and arrow well. They had many sons and grandsons. There were 150 of them in all.

All these men were Benjamin's descendants.

9 The names of all the people of Israel were listed in their family histories. Those family histories were put in the book of the kings of Israel.

The People in Jerusalem

The people of Judah were captured and forced to go to Babylon. This is because they were not faithful to God. ²The first people to come back and live in their own lands and towns were some Israelites, priests, Levites and Temple^d servants.

³People from the tribes^d of Judah, Benjamin, Ephraim and Manasseh lived in Jerusalem. This is a list of those people.

⁴There was Uthai son of Ammihud.

(Ammihud was Omri's son. Omri was Imri's son. Imri was Bani's son. Bani was a descendant[d] of Perez. Perez was Judah's son.)

[5]Of the Shilonite people there were Asaiah and his sons. Asaiah was the oldest son in his family.

[6]Of the Zerahite people there were Jeuel and other relatives of Zerah. There were 690 of them in all.

[7]From the tribe of Benjamin there was Sallu son of Meshullam. (Meshullam was Hodaviah's son. Hodaviah was Hassenuah's son.) [8]There was also Ibneiah son of Jeroham and Elah son of Uzzi. (Uzzi was Micri's son.) And there was Meshullam son of Shephatiah. (Shephatiah was Reuel's son, and Reuel was Ibnijah's son.) [9]The family history of Benjamin lists 956 people living in Jerusalem. All these men were leaders of their families.

[10]Of the priests there were Jedaiah, Jehoiarib, Jakin and [11]Azariah son of Hilkiah. (Hilkiah was Meshullam's son. Meshullam was Zadok's son. Zadok was Meraioth's son. Meraioth was Ahitub's son. Ahitub was the officer who was responsible for the Temple of God.) [12]Also there was Adaiah son of Jeroham. (Jeroham was Pashhur's son, and Pashhur was Malkijah's son.) And there was Maasai son of Adiel. (Adiel was Jahzerah's son. Jahzerah was Meshullam's son. Meshullam was Meshillemith's son, and Meshillemith was Immer's son.) [13]There were 1,760 priests. They were leaders of their families. They were responsible for serving in the Temple of God.

[14]Of the Levites there was Semaiah son of Hasshub. (Hasshub was Azrikam's son. Azrikam was Hashabiah's son. Hashabiah was from the family of Merari.) [15]There were also Bakbakkar, Heresh, Galal and Mattaniah son of Mica. (Mica was Zicri's son. Zicri was Asaph's son.) [16]There was also Obadiah son of Shemaiah. (Shemaiah was Galal's son, and Galal was Jeduthun's son.) And there was Berekiah son of Asa. (Asa was Elkanah's son. Elkanah lived in the villages of the Netophathite people.)

[17]Of the gatekeepers there were Shallum, Akkub, Talmon, Ahiman and their relatives. Shallum was their leader. [18]These gatekeepers from the tribe of Levi still stand next to the King's Gate on the east side of the city. [19]Shallum was Kore's son. Kore was Ebiasaph's son. Ebiasaph was Korah's son. Shallum and his relatives from the family of Korah were gatekeepers. They were responsible for guarding the gates of the Temple. Their ancestors had also been responsible for guarding the entrance to the Temple. [20]In the past Phinehas was in charge of the gatekeepers. He was Eleazar's son. The Lord was with Phinehas. [21]Zechariah was the gatekeeper at the entrance to the Temple. He was the son of Meshelemiah.

[22]In all, 212 men were chosen to guard the gates. Their names were written in their family histories in their villages. David and Samuel the seer[d] chose these men because they were dependable. [23]The gatekeepers and their descendants had the responsibility of guarding the gates of the Temple of the Lord. (The Temple took the place of the Holy Tent.[d]) [24]There were gatekeepers on all four sides of the Temple: east, west, north and south. [25]The gatekeepers' relatives who lived in the villages had to come and help them at certain times. Each time they came they helped the gatekeepers for seven days. [26]Because they were dependable, four gatekeepers were made the leaders of all the gatekeepers. They were Levites. They were responsible for the rooms and treasures in the Temple of God. [27]They stayed up all night guarding the Temple of God. And they opened it every morning.

[28]Some of the gatekeepers were responsible for the tools and dishes used in the Temple services. They counted these tools and dishes when people took them out. And they counted them when people brought them back.

²⁹Other gatekeepers were chosen to take care of the things in the Holy Place. They also took care of the flour, wine, oil, incense^d and spices. ³⁰But some of the priests took care of mixing the spices. ³¹There was a Levite named Mattithiah. Because he was dependable, he had the job of baking the bread used for the offerings. He was Shallum's first son. Shallum was from the family of Korah. ³²Some of the gatekeepers had the job of preparing the special bread. This was the bread that was put on the table every Sabbath.^d These people were from the Kohath family.

³³Some of the Levites were musicians in the Temple. The leaders of these families stayed in the rooms of the Temple. They were on duty day and night. So they did not do other work in the Temple.

³⁴These are the leaders of the Levite families. Their names were listed in their family histories. They lived in Jerusalem.

The Family History of King Saul

³⁵Jeiel lived in the town of Gibeon, where he was the leader. His wife was named Maacah. ³⁶Jeiel's first son was Abdon. His other sons were Zur, Kish, Baal, Ner, Nadab, ³⁷Gedor, Ahio, Zechariah and Mikloth. ³⁸Mikloth was Shimeam's father. Jeiel's family lived near their relatives in Jerusalem.

³⁹Ner was Kish's father. Kish was Saul's father. And Saul was the father of Jonathan, Malki-Shua, Abinadab and Esh-Baal.

⁴⁰Jonathan's son was Merib-Baal. Merib-Baal was Micah's father.

⁴¹Micah's sons were Pithon, Melech, Tahrea and Ahaz. ⁴²Ahaz was Jadah's father. Jadah was the father of Alemeth, Azmaveth and Zimri. Zimri was Moza's father. ⁴³Moza was Binea's father. Rephaiah was Binea's son. Eleasah was Rephaiah's son, and Azel was Eleasah's son.

⁴⁴Azel had six sons. Their names were Azrikam, Bokeru, Ishmael, Sheariah, Obadiah and Hanan. They were Azel's sons.

The Death of King Saul

10 The Philistine people fought against the people of Israel. The Israelites ran away from them. And many Israelites were killed on Mount Gilboa. ²The Philistines continued chasing Saul and his sons. And they killed Saul's sons Jonathan, Abinadab and Malki-Shua. ³The fighting became heavy around Saul. The archers shot him with their arrows and wounded him.

⁴Then Saul said to the officer who carried his armor, "Pull out your sword and kill me. If you don't, these men who are not circumcised will come and hurt me." But the officer was afraid. So he refused to kill Saul. Then Saul took his own sword and fell on it. ⁵The officer saw that Saul was dead. So he fell on his own sword and died. ⁶So Saul and three of his sons died. All his family died together.

⁷The Israelites living in the valley saw that their army had run away. And they saw that Saul and his sons were dead. So they left their towns and ran away. Then the Philistines came and lived in those towns.

⁸The next day the Philistines came to take valuable things from the dead bodies. On Mount Gilboa they found the bodies of Saul and his sons. ⁹The Philistines stripped Saul's body. And they took his head and his armor. They sent messengers through all their country to tell the news to their idols and their people. ¹⁰The Philistines put Saul's armor in the temple of their idols. And they hung his head in the temple of Dagon.^d

¹¹All the people living in Jabesh Gilead heard what the Philistines had done to Saul. ¹²So all the brave men from Jabesh Gilead went and got the bodies of Saul and his sons. They brought them to Jabesh Gilead. Then they buried the bones of Saul and his sons under the large tree in Jabesh. And they gave up eating for seven days.

¹³Saul died because he was not faithful to the Lord. He did not obey the Lord. He even went to a medium^d and

asked her for advice. [14]He did this instead of asking the Lord for help. This is why the Lord put Saul to death and gave the kingdom to Jesse's son David.

David Becomes King

11 All the people of Israel came to David at the town of Hebron. They said, "We are your people. [2]Even when Saul was king, you were the man who led Israel in battle. The Lord your God spoke to you. He said, 'David, you will be the shepherd of my people, the people of Israel. You will become their leader.'"

[3]All the leaders of Israel came to King David at Hebron. He made an agreement with them before the Lord in Hebron. The leaders poured olive oil on David to appoint him king over Israel. The Lord had promised this would happen. He had made this promise through Samuel.

David Defeats Jerusalem

[4]David and all the Israelites went to the city of Jerusalem. At that time Jerusalem was called Jebus. The people living there were named Jebusites. [5]They said to David, "You can't get inside our city." But David captured their strong city of Jerusalem, the City of David.

[6]David had said, "The person who leads the attack against the Jebusites will become the commander over all my army." Joab son of Zeruiah led the attack. So he became the commander of the army.

[7]Then David made his home in the strong, walled city. That is why it was named the City of David. [8]David rebuilt the city. He started where the land was filled in and went to the wall that was around the city. Joab repaired the other parts of the city. [9]David became more and more powerful. And the Lord of heaven's armies was with him.

David's Mighty Warriors

[10]This is a list of the leaders over David's warriors. These warriors helped make David's kingdom strong. All the people of Israel also supported David's kingdom. These heroes and all the people of Israel made David king. This happened as the Lord had promised.

[11]This is a list of David's warriors:
Jashobeam was from the Hacmonite people. He was the leader of the Three,[n] David's most powerful soldiers. He used his spear to fight 300 men at one time. And he killed them all.

[12]Next was Eleazar. He was one of the Three. Eleazar was Dodai's son. Dodai was from the Ahohite people. [13]Eleazar was with David at Pas-Dammim. The Philistines came there to fight the Israelites. There was a field of barley at that place. The Israelites ran away from the Philistines. [14]But they stopped in the middle of that field and fought the Philistines. And they killed the Philistines. The Lord gave Israel a great victory.

[15]Three of the 30 leaders went to David. He was at the rock by the cave near Adullam. At the same time a group from the Philistine army was camped in the Valley of Rephaim. [16]David was in a protected place at that time. The Philistine army was staying in the town of Bethlehem. [17]David had a strong desire for some water. He said, "Oh, I wish someone would get me water from the well near the city gate of Bethlehem!" [18]So the Three fought their way through the Philistine army. And they took water out of the well near the city gate in Bethlehem. Then they took it back to David. But he refused to drink it. He poured it out before the Lord. [19]David said, "May God keep me from drinking this water! It would be like drinking the blood of the men who risked their lives to bring me this water." So David refused to drink it.

These were the brave things the Three did.

[20]Abishai brother of Joab was the leader of the Three. Abishai fought 300 men with his spear and killed them. He became as famous as the Three. [21]He

---

[n]**Three** Or maybe "Thirty." These were David's most powerful soldiers. See 2 Samuel 23:8.

was more honored than the Three. He became their commander even though he was not one of them.

[22] Benaiah son of Jehoiada was a brave fighter from Kabzeel. Benaiah did many brave things. He killed two of the best warriors from Moab. He also went down into a pit when it was snowing. There he killed a lion. [23] Benaiah also killed an Egyptian who was about seven and a half feet tall. The Egyptian had a spear as large as a weaver's rod. Benaiah had a club. But he grabbed the spear from the Egyptian's hand. And he used the Egyptian's own spear to kill him. [24] These were the things Benaiah son of Jehoiada did. Benaiah became as famous as the Three. [25] He received more honor than the Thirty, David's most powerful soldiers. But he did not become a member of the Three. David chose Benaiah to be the leader of his bodyguards.

[26] These were also mighty warriors:

Asahel brother of Joab;

Elhanan son of Dodo from Bethlehem;

[27] Shammoth from the Harorites;

Helez from the Pelonites;

[28] Ira son of Ikkesh from Tekoa;

Abiezer from the Anathothites;

[29] Sibbecai from the Hushathites;

Ilai from the Ahohites;

[30] Maharai from the Netophathites;

Heled son of Baanah from the Netophathites;

[31] Ithai son of Ribai from Gibeah in Benjamin.

Benaiah from the Pirathonites;

[32] Hurai from the ravines of Gaash;

Abiel from the Arbathites;

[33] Azmaveth from the Baharumites;

Eliahba from the Shaalbonites;

[34] the sons of Hashem from the Gizonites;

Jonathan son of Shagee from the Hararites;

[35] Ahiam son of Sacar from the Hararites;

Eliphal son of Ur;

[36] Hepher from the Mekerathites;

Ahijah from the Pelonites;

[37] Hezro from the Carmelites;

Naarai son of Ezbai;

[38] Joel brother of Nathan;

Mibhar son of Hagri;

[39] Zelek from the Ammonites;

Naharai, from the Berothites, the officer who carried the armor for Joab son of Zeruiah;

[40] Ira from the Ithrites;

Gareb from the Ithrites;

[41] Uriah from the Hittites;

Zabad son of Ahlai;

[42] Adina son of Shiza the Reubenite, who was the leader of the Reubenites, and his 30 soldiers;

[43] Hanan son of Maacah;

Joshaphat from the Mithnites;

[44] Uzzia from the Ashterathites;

Shama and Jeiel sons of Hotham from the Aroer;

[45] Jediael son of Shimri;

Joha, Jediael's brother, from the Tizites;

[46] Eliel from the Mahavites;

Jeribai and Joshaviah, Elnaam's sons;

Ithmah from the Moabites;

[47] Eliel, Obed and Jaasiel from the Mezobaites.

Warriors Join David

12 These were the men who came to David at Ziklag. David was hiding from Saul son of Kish at that time. These were the men who helped David in battle. [2] They came with bows for weapons. They could use either their right or left hands to shoot arrows or to sling rocks. They were Saul's relatives from the tribe[d] of Benjamin. [3] Ahiezer was their leader. And there was Joash. (Ahiezer and Joash were Shemaah's sons. He was from the town of Gibeah.) There were also Jeziel and Pelet the sons of Azmaveth. There were Beracah and Jehu from the town of Anathoth. [4] And there was Ishmaiah from the town of Gibeon. Ishmaiah was one of the Thirty. In fact, he was the leader of the Thirty. There were Jeremiah, Jahaziel, Johanan and Jozabad from Gederah. ⁵There were Eluzai, Jerimoth, Bealiah and Shemariah. There was Shephatiah from Haruph. ⁶There were Elkanah, Isshiah, Azarel, Joezer and Jashobeam. They were from the family group of Korah. ⁷And there were Joelah and Zebadiah the sons of Jeroham. They were from the town of Gedor.

⁸Part of the people of Gad joined David at his protected place in the desert. They were brave warriors trained for war. They were skilled with shields and spears. They were as fierce as lions. And they could run as fast as gazelles*d* over the hills.

⁹Ezer was the leader of Gad's army. Obadiah was second in command. Eliab was third. ¹⁰Mishmannah was fourth, and Jeremiah was fifth. ¹¹Attai was sixth, and Eliel was seventh. ¹²Johanan was eighth, and Elzabad was ninth. ¹³Jeremiah was tenth, and Macbannai was eleventh in command.

¹⁴They were the commanders of the army from Gad. The weakest of these leaders was in charge of 100 soldiers. The strongest was in charge of 1,000 soldiers. ¹⁵They crossed the Jordan River and chased away the people living in the valleys. They chased them to the east and to the west. This happened in the first month of the year when the Jordan floods the valley.

¹⁶Other people from the tribes*d* of Benjamin and Judah also came to David at his protected place. ¹⁷David went out to meet them. He said to them, "If you have come peacefully to help me, I welcome you. Join me. But you might have come to turn me over to my enemies, even though I have done nothing wrong. If you do this, the God of our fathers will see this and punish you."

¹⁸Then the Spirit*d* entered Amasai, the leader of the Thirty. Amasai said:

"We belong to you, David.
We are with you, son of Jesse.
Success, success to you.
Success to those who help you,
because your God helps you."

So David welcomed these men. He made them leaders of his army.

¹⁹Some of the men from Manasseh also joined David. They joined him when he went with the Philistines to fight Saul. But David and his men did not really help the Philistines. After talking about it, the Philistine leaders decided to send David away. They said, "If David goes back to his master Saul, we will be killed!" ²⁰The men from Manasseh joined David when he went to Ziklag. These were the men: Adnah, Jozabad, Jediael, Michael, Jozabad, Elihu and Zillethai. Each of these men was a leader of a thousand men from Manasseh. ²¹All these men of Manasseh were brave soldiers. They helped David fight against groups of men who went around the country robbing people. These soldiers became commanders in David's army. ²²Every day more men joined David. So his army became large. It was like the army of God.

Others Join David at Hebron

²³These are the numbers of the men who joined David at Hebron. They came ready for battle. They came to help turn the kingdom of Saul over to David. The Lord had said this would happen.

²⁴There were 6,800 men with their weapons from the people of Judah. They carried shields and spears.

²⁵There were 7,100 men from the people of Simeon. They were warriors ready for war.

²⁶There were 4,600 men from the people of Levi. ²⁷Jehoiada, a leader from Aaron's family, was in that group. There were 3,700 with him. ²⁸Zadok was also in that group. He was a strong young warrior. He came with 22 leaders from his family.

²⁹There were 3,000 men from the people of Benjamin. They were Saul's relatives. And most of them had remained loyal to Saul's family until then.

³⁰There were 20,800 men from the

Adventures in ODYSSEY BIBLE

"PARTY to CONFUSION!"

Dylan learns the meaning of friendship
A story based on I Corinthians 13:4–7

HEY, WERE YOU INVITED TO SAL'S PARTY?

YEAH! SOUNDS GREAT! CLOWNS, RIDES IN THE STRATA FLYER, AND ALL YOU CAN EAT AT WHIT'S ICE CREAM PARLOR!

WHAT'S GOING ON?

SAL'S THROWING THE MOST EXCELLENT PARTY EVER! DIDN'T YOU GET AN INVITATION?

YEAH... Uh, SURE I DID. IT'S AT MY HOUSE.

MOM, DID I GET ANY MAIL?

NO, HONEY, I DIDN'T SEE ANYTHING.

Aw... I'M GOING UP TO MY ROOM....

WOW! SAL'S PARTY IS GOING TO BE TOTALLY RADICAL!

YEAH, I CAN'T WAIT!

Oh BOY, DYLAN, ISN'T THIS PARTY GOING TO BE GREAT?! I'VE GOT TO THINK OF A REAL COOL PRESENT FOR SAL. WHAT ARE YOU GETTING FOR HIM?

GET OUT OF MY ROOM, JESSIE! GO TO YOUR OWN ROOM!

YEAH, I'LL GIVE HIM A PRESENT, ALL RIGHT! I THOUGHT SAL WAS MY FRIEND, BUT I GUESS I KNOW BETTER NOW. I'M GONNA THINK OF SOMETHING TO FIX HIM BUT GOOD!

THE NEXT DAY, DYLAN VISITS WHIT'S END....

...SAL LEFT ME OUT, SO I'M GOING TO GET HIM BACK!

WHOA, THERE, DYLAN! I THOUGHT SAL WAS YOUR *FRIEND!*

YEAH, SO DID *I!*

THEN DON'T YOU THINK YOU OUGHT TO GIVE SAL THE BENEFIT OF THE DOUBT? I'M SURE THERE'S A GOOD EXPLANATION WHY YOU DIDN'T GET AN INVITATION.

THE LOVE OF FRIENDSHIP FORMS A SPECIAL *BOND* BETWEEN PEOPLE. THERE'S A BIBLE PASSAGE THAT TALKS ABOUT THAT. I CORINTHIANS 13:4-7 SAYS THAT LOVE DOES NOT COUNT UP WRONGS THAT HAVE BEEN DONE BUT ALWAYS *TRUSTS, HOPES,* AND REMAINS *STRONG.* PERHAPS YOU SHOULD THINK THIS OVER BEFORE YOU RUSH OUT AND DO SOMETHING TO SAL THAT YOU BOTH MIGHT *REGRET* LATER ON.

LATER, AT THE TAYLOR HOME....

ding dong!

I'LL GET IT!

THAT'S SAL WITH MY INVITATION! HE FINALLY CAME TO HIS SENSES!

HELLO, DYLAN!

SAL'S PARENTS! Uh, HI!

WE THOUGHT SINCE YOU'RE SUCH A GOOD FRIEND OF SAL'S YOU MIGHT HELP US OUT...

...WOULD YOU LIKE TO WRAP AND HIDE THIS *SCOOTER* WE'RE GIVING TO SAL? IT'S A SURPRISE YOU CAN BRING TO THE PARTY!

Oh, WHAT A GREAT IDEA! WOULDN'T THAT BE FUN, DYLAN?

YEAH... *LOTSA* FUN....

SURE, I'LL BE *HAPPY* TO HELP "SURPRISE" OL' SAL... HEH, HEH....

Dylan's feelings have been terribly hurt by not being invited to Sal's party. He can't understand why his friend Sal would leave him out. Now, he has an opportunity to get revenge on Sal by messing up the scooter, or ruining the surprise at the party. What should Dylan do? These verses could help you decide what you could tell him:

1 Corinthians 10:24 + 33
2 Timothy 2:10
James 1:19

THAT NIGHT....

DYLAN, WOULD YOU READ TO ME BEFORE I GO TO BED?

Uh, SURE, JESSIE, OF COURSE. I'M SORRY I TOLD YOU TO GET OUT OF MY ROOM BEFORE.

WERE YOU *UPSET* ABOUT SOMETHING, DYLAN? YOU ACTED LIKE YOU WERE *MAD* AT ME.

NO, I WASN'T MAD AT YOU. DON'T WORRY, IT'LL BE ALL RIGHT.

SO, WHAT DO YOU WANT ME TO READ?

I DON'T KNOW. *YOU* PICK OUT SOMETHING.

Hmm... LET'S SEE... MR. WHITTAKER WAS TELLING ME ABOUT A VERSE TODAY... Oh, HERE IT IS ...

"... LOVE IS PATIENT AND KIND. LOVE IS NOT JEALOUS, IT DOES NOT BRAG, AND IS NOT *PROUD*. LOVE IS NOT RUDE, IS NOT SELF-ISH, AND DOES NOT BECOME ANGRY EASILY. LOVE DOES NOT REMEMBER WRONGS DONE AGAINST IT. LOVE IS NOT HAPPY WITH EVIL, BUT IS HAPPY WITH THE *TRUTH*. LOVE PATIENTLY *ACCEPTS* ALL THINGS. IT ALWAYS *TRUSTS*, ALWAYS *HOPES*, AND ALWAYS CONTINUES *STRONG*."

THANKS, DYLAN. GOOD NIGHT!

THAT'S OKAY, JESSIE, I NEEDED TO READ THAT, TOO.

THE NEXT MORNING....

HEY, DYLAN, WHERE ARE YOU GOING WITH ALL THAT STUFF?

I'VE GOT TO DO SOMETHING *SPECIAL* FOR A FRIEND, DAD.

HAPPY BDAY SAL!

PAINT

WHEN HE'S FINISHED WRAPPING THE PRESENT, DYLAN CLEANS UP THE TRASH AND TAKES IT OUT TO THE GARBAGE....

HEY! WHAT'S *THIS?!*

SAL *DIDN'T* LEAVE ME OUT!

PARTY TIME!

DYLAN! SLOW DOWN!

I'VE GOT TO GET CLEANED UP! I'M GOING TO BE LATE FOR THE PARTY!

WOW, THANKS EVERYBODY! WHAT A GREAT PARTY!

THANK DYLAN! HE HID YOUR PRESENT AND DECORATED IT.

THANKS, BUDDY!

DYLAN, YOU DID A *FINE* JOB ON THAT SCOOTER. AND YOU DID A GOOD THING TO HELP OUT SAL AND HIS PARENTS. I'M *PROUD* OF YOU, BOY!

THANKS, MISTER WHITTAKER!

IT WAS A LOT EASIER ONCE I READ ABOUT LOVING YOUR FRIENDS IN THE BIBLE VERSE YOU TOLD ME ABOUT!

The End

people of Ephraim. They were brave warriors. They were famous men in their own family groups.

³¹There were 18,000 men from the western half-tribe of Manasseh. Each man was especially chosen to make David king.

³²There were 200 leaders from the family of Issachar. They knew what Israel should do. And they knew the right time to do it. Their relatives were with them and under their command.

³³There were 50,000 men from the people of Zebulun. They were trained soldiers. They were trained to use every kind of weapon of war. They followed David completely.

³⁴There were 1,000 officers from the people of Naphtali. They had 37,000 men with them who carried shields and spears.

³⁵There were 28,600 men from the people of Dan. They were ready for war.

³⁶There were 40,000 trained soldiers from the people of Asher. They were ready for war.

³⁷There were 120,000 men from the east side of the Jordan River. They were from the people of Reuben, Gad and the eastern half-tribe of Manasseh. They had every kind of weapon.

³⁸All these fighting men were ready to go to war. They came to Hebron fully agreed to make David king of all Israel. All the other Israelites also agreed to make David king. ³⁹The men spent three days there with David. They ate and drank, because their relatives had prepared food for them. ⁴⁰Also, their neighbors brought food. They came from as far as the areas belonging to Issachar, Zebulun and Naphtali. They brought food on donkeys, camels, mules and oxen. They brought much flour, fig cakes, raisins, wine, oil, cows and sheep. This was because the people of Israel were very happy.

Bringing Back the Holy Box

13 David talked with all the officers of his army. He talked with the commanders of 100 men and the commanders of 1,000 men. ²Then David called the people of Israel together. He said, "If you think it is a good idea, and if it is what the Lord our God wants, let's send a message. Let's send it to our fellow Israelites in all the areas of Israel. Let's also send it to the priests and Levites living with them in their towns and pastures. Tell them to come and join us. ³Let's bring the Holy Box^d of our God back to us. We did not use it to ask God for help while Saul was king." ⁴So all the people agreed with David. They all thought it was the right thing to do.

⁵So David gathered all the Israelites from the Shihor River in Egypt to Lebo Hamath. They were to bring the Holy Box of God back from the town of Kiriath Jearim. ⁶David and all the Israelites with him went to Baalah of Judah. (Baalah is another name for Kiriath Jearim.) They went there to get the Holy Box of God the Lord. His throne is between the golden creatures with wings on the Holy Box. It is called by the Lord's name.

⁷The people moved the Holy Box of God from Abinadab's house. They put it on a new cart. And Uzzah and Ahio guided the cart. ⁸David and all the Israelites were celebrating with all their strength before God. They were singing and playing harps, lyres,^d tambourines,^d cymbals and trumpets.

⁹They came to the threshing^d floor of Kidon. The oxen pulling the cart stumbled. And Uzzah reached out his hand to steady the Holy Box. ¹⁰The Lord became very angry with Uzzah. And he killed Uzzah because Uzzah had touched the Holy Box. So Uzzah died there in the presence of God.

¹¹David became angry because the Lord had punished Uzzah in his anger. So even today that place is called the Punishment of Uzzah.

¹²David was afraid of God that day. David asked, "How can I bring the Holy Box of God home to me?" ¹³So David did not take the Holy Box with him to Jerusalem. Instead, he took it to the house of Obed-Edom of Gath.

[14]The Holy Box of God stayed with Obed-Edom's family in his house for three months. And the Lord blessed Obed-Edom's family and everything he owned.

David's Kingdom Grows

14 Hiram king of the city of Tyre sent messengers to David. He also sent cedar logs, stonecutters and carpenters. He sent them to build a palace for David. [2]Then David knew that the Lord really had made him king of Israel. And he knew the Lord had made his kingdom very important. The Lord did this because he loved his people, the Israelites.

[3]David married more women in Jerusalem. And he had more sons and daughters. [4]These are the names of David's children born in Jerusalem: Shammua, Shobab, Nathan, Solomon, [5]Ibhar, Elishua, Elpelet, [6]Nogah, Nepheg, Japhia, [7]Elishama, Beeliada and Eliphelet.

David Defeats the Philistines

[8]The Philistine people heard that David had been appointed king of all Israel. So all the Philistines went to look for him. When David heard about it, he went out to fight them. [9]The Philistines had attacked and robbed the people in the Valley of Rephaim. [10]David asked God, "Should I go and attack the Philistines? Will you let me defeat them?"

The Lord answered him, "Go. I will let you defeat them."

[11]So David and his men went up to the town of Baal Perazim. There he defeated the Philistines. David said, "Like a flood of water, God has broken through my enemies. He has done this through me." So that place was named Baal Perazim.[n] [12]The Philistines had left their idols there. So David ordered his men to burn them.

[13]Soon the Philistines attacked the people in the valley again. [14]So David prayed to God again, and God answered him. God said, "Don't attack the Philistines from the front. Instead, go around them. Attack them in front of the balsam trees. [15]You will hear the sound of marching in the tops of the balsam trees. Then quickly attack the Philistines. I, God, will have gone out before you to defeat the Philistine army." [16]David did what God commanded him to do. So David and his men defeated the Philistine army. They killed the Philistines all the way from Gibeon to Gezer.

[17]So David became famous in all the countries. And the Lord made all nations afraid of David.

The Holy Box Is Brought to Jerusalem

15 David built houses for himself in Jerusalem. Then he built a place for the Holy Box[d] of God. And he set up a tent for it. [2]Then David said, "Only the Levites may carry the Holy Box of God. The Lord chose them to carry the Holy Box of the Lord. He chose them to serve him forever."

[3]David called all the people of Israel to come to Jerusalem. He wanted to bring the Holy Box of the Lord to the place he had made for it. [4]David called together the descendants[d] of Aaron and the Levites. [5]There were 120 people from Kohath's family group. Uriel was their leader. [6]There were 220 people from Merari's family group. Asaiah was their leader. [7]There were 130 people from Gershon's family group. Joel was their leader. [8]There were 200 people from Elizaphan's family group. Shemaiah was their leader. [9]There were 80 people from Hebron's family group. Eliel was their leader. [10]There were 112 people from Uzziel's family group. Amminadab was their leader.

[11]Then David asked the priests Zadok and Abiathar to come to him. He also asked these Levites to come: Uriel, Asaiah, Joel, Shemaiah, Eliel and Amminadab. [12]David said to them, "You are the leaders of the families of Levi.

---

[n]**Baal Perazim**   This name means "the Lord breaks through."

You and the other Levites must give yourselves for service to the Lord. Then bring up the Holy Box of the Lord, the God of Israel. Bring it to the place I have made for it. [13]The last time we did not ask the Lord how to carry it. You Levites didn't carry it. So the Lord our God punished us."

[14]Then the priests and Levites prepared themselves for service to the Lord. They did this so they could carry the Holy Box of the Lord, the God of Israel. [15]The Levites used special poles to carry the Holy Box of God on their shoulders. This was the way Moses had commanded. They carried it just as the Lord had said they should.

[16]David told the leaders of the Levites to appoint their brothers as singers. The singers were to play their lyres,[d] harps and cymbals. And they were to sing happy songs.

[17]So the Levites appointed Heman and his relatives Asaph and Ethan. Heman was Joel's son. Asaph was Berekiah's son. And Ethan, from the Merari family group, was Kushaiah's son. [18]There was also a second group of Levites. They were Zechariah, Jaaziel, Shemiramoth, Jehiel, Unni, Eliab, Benaiah, Maaseiah, Mattithiah, Eliphelehu, Mikneiah, Obed-Edom and Jeiel. They were the Levite guards.

[19]The singers Heman, Asaph and Ethan played bronze cymbals. [20]Zechariah, Jaaziel, Shemiramoth, Jehiel, Unni, Eliab, Maaseiah and Benaiah played the high-pitched lyres. [21]Mattithiah, Eliphelehu, Mikneiah, Obed-Edom, Jeiel and Azaziah played the low-pitched harps. [22]The Levite leader Kenaniah was in charge of the singing. He had this job because he was very good at singing.

[23]Berekiah and Elkanah were two of the guards for the Box of the Agreement. [24]The priests Shebaniah, Joshaphat, Nethanel, Amasai, Zechariah, Benaiah and Eliezer had the job of blowing trumpets. They did this in front of the Box of the Agreement. Obed-Edom and Jehiah were also guards for the Box of the Agreement.

[25]David, the leaders of Israel, and the commanders went to get the Box of the Agreement with the Lord. Each of the commanders was over a group of 1,000 soldiers. They all went to bring the Holy Box from Obed-Edom's house. And they were very happy. [26]God helped the Levites who carried the Box of the Agreement with the Lord. So they sacrificed seven bulls and seven male sheep. [27]All the Levites who carried the Holy Box wore robes of fine linen. Kenaniah, the man in charge of the singing, and all the singers wore robes of fine linen. David wore a robe of fine linen. And he also wore a holy vest[d] of fine linen. [28]So all the people of Israel brought up the Box of the Agreement with the Lord. They shouted and blew sheep horns and trumpets. They played cymbals, lyres, and harps.

[29]So the Box of the Agreement with the Lord entered Jerusalem. As it entered, Saul's daughter Michal watched from a window. When she saw King David dancing and celebrating, she hated him.

16

They brought the Holy Box of God and put it inside the tent. This was the tent David had set up for it. Then they offered burnt offerings and fellowship offerings to God. [2]David finished giving the burnt offerings and fellowship offerings. Then he used the Lord's name to bless the people. [3]He gave a loaf of bread, some dates and raisins to every Israelite man and woman.

[4]Then David appointed some of the Levites to serve before the Holy Box of the Lord. They had the job of leading the worship. They gave thanks and praise to the Lord, the God of Israel. [5]Asaph was the leader. He played the cymbals. Zechariah was second to him. The other Levites were Jaaziel, Shemiramoth, Jehiel, Mattithiah, Eliab, Benaiah, Obed-Edom and Jeiel. They played the lyres and harps. [6]Benaiah and Jahaziel were priests. They blew

the trumpets regularly before the Box of the Agreement with God. ⁷That day David first gave Asaph and his relatives the job of singing praises to the Lord.

David's Song of Thanks

⁸Give thanks to the Lord and pray to him.
Tell the nations what he has done.
⁹Sing to him. Sing praises to him.
Tell about all the wonderful things he has done.
¹⁰Be glad that you are his.
Let those who ask the Lord for help be happy.
¹¹Depend on the Lord and his strength.
Always go to him for help.
¹²Remember the wonderful things he has done.
Remember his miracles*ᵈ* and his decisions.
¹³You are the descendants*ᵈ* of Israel, the Lord's servant.
You are the children of Jacob, his chosen people.

¹⁴He is the Lord our God.
His laws are for all the world.
¹⁵He will keep his agreement forever.
He will keep his promises always.

¹⁶He will keep the agreement he made with Abraham.
He will keep the promise he made to Isaac.
¹⁷The Lord made it a law for the people of Jacob.
He made it an agreement with Israel to last forever.
¹⁸The Lord said, "I will give you the land of Canaan. The promised land will belong to you."

¹⁹Then God's people were few in number.
They were strangers in the land.
²⁰They went from one nation to another.
They went from one kingdom to another.
²¹But the Lord did not let anyone hurt them.
He warned kings not to harm them.
²²He said, "Don't hurt my chosen people.
Don't harm my prophets."*ᵈ*

²³Sing to the Lord, all the earth.
Every day tell how he saves us.

Thankfulness
1 CHRONICLES 16:8

What is your favorite story—the one you like to read or have someone tell you over and over again? People of all ages love to hear stories.

Back in the time when this verse was written, telling stories was a popular way for God's people to give thanks to him. They would tell stories to other people about what God had done for them. They were so thankful that they wrote and told stories to anyone who would listen.

They didn't say a quiet "thank you" to God, hoping no one would hear. They gave God a loud "THANK YOU" in front of all kinds of people in all sorts of places. What stories can you tell to others about what God has done for you?

To learn more about thankfulness, zoom to page 707.

²⁴Tell the nations about the Lord's
glory.
Tell all peoples about his
wonderful works.
²⁵The Lord is great; he should be
praised.
He should be honored more than
all the gods.
²⁶All the gods of the nations are
only idols.
But the Lord made the skies.
²⁷The Lord has glory and majesty.
He has power and joy in his
Temple.ᵈ

²⁸Praise the Lord, all nations on earth.
Praise the Lord's glory and power.

**Praise the Lord for the
glory of his name. Bring
your offering to him.
Worship the Lord
because he is holy.
• 1 Chronicles 16:8**

²⁹   Praise the Lord for the glory of his
name.
Bring your offering to him.
Worship the Lord because he is
holy.
³⁰The whole earth should tremble
before the Lord.
The earth is set, and it cannot
be moved.
³¹Let the skies rejoice and the earth
be glad.
Let people everywhere say, "The
Lord is king!"
³²Let the sea and everything in
it shout.
Let the fields and everything in
them show their joy.
³³Then the trees of the forest will sing.
They will sing with joy before
the Lord.
They will sing because the Lord is
coming to judge the world.
³⁴Thank the Lord because he is good.
His love continues forever.
³⁵Say to him, "Save us, God our
Savior.

Bring us back and save us from
the nations.
Then we will thank you.
Then we will gladly praise you."
³⁶Praise the Lord, the God of Israel,
forever and forever.

All the people said, "Amen" and
"Praise the Lord."

³⁷Then David left Asaph and the
other Levites there in front of the Boxᵈ
of the Agreement with the Lord. They
were to serve there every day. ³⁸David
also left Obed-Edom and 68 other
Levites to serve with them. Hosah and
Obed-Edom son of Jeduthun were
guards.

³⁹David left Zadok the priest and the
other priests who served with him in
front of the Tent of the Lord. This was at
the place of worship in Gibeon. ⁴⁰Every
morning and evening they offered burnt
offerings on the altar of burnt offerings.
They did this to follow the rules written in the Teachings of the Lord. These
were the Teachings he had given Israel.
⁴¹With them were Heman and Jeduthun
and other Levites. They were chosen by
name to sing praises to the Lord because the Lord's love continues forever. ⁴²Heman and Jeduthun also had the
job of playing the trumpets and cymbals.
They also played other musical instruments when songs were sung to God.
Jeduthun's sons guarded the gates.

⁴³Then all the people left. Each person went to his own home. And David
also went home to bless his family.

God's Promise to David

17 David moved into his palace.
Then he said to Nathan the
prophet, "Look, I am living in a palace
made of cedar. But the Boxᵈ of the
Agreement with the Lord sits in a tent."
²Nathan answered David, "Do what
you want to do. God is with you."

³But that night God spoke his word
to Nathan. God said, ⁴"Go and tell my
servant David: 'This is what the Lord
says: David, you are not the person to
build a house for me to live in. ⁵From
the time I brought Israel out of Egypt

until now I have not lived in a house. I have moved from one tent site to another. I have gone from one place to another. ⁶I have moved with the Israelites to different places. I commanded leaders to take care of my people. I never said to any of those leaders, "Why haven't you built me a house of cedar?"'

⁷"Now, tell my servant David: 'The Lord of heaven's armies says: I took you from the pasture and from tending the sheep. I made you king of my people Israel. ⁸I have been with you everywhere you have gone. I have killed your enemies for you. Now I will make you one of the most famous men on earth. ⁹I will give this place to my people Israel. I will settle them here. Then they will have a home of their own. They won't be bothered anymore. Evil people won't hurt them as they have done since the first. ¹⁰Evil people have hurt them since I chose leaders for my people Israel. I will also defeat all your enemies.

"'I tell you that the Lord will make your descendants[d] kings of Israel after you. ¹¹When you die and join your ancestors, I will let your child be the new king. He will be one of your own sons. And I will make his kingdom strong. ¹²He will build a house for me. And I will let his family rule forever. ¹³I will be his father, and he will be my son. I took away my love from Saul, who ruled before you. But I will never stop loving your son. ¹⁴I will put him in charge of my house and kingdom forever. His family will rule forever.'"

¹⁵Nathan told David everything God had said in this vision.

David's Prayer

¹⁶Then King David went in and sat in front of the Lord. David said, "Lord God, why have you made me so important to you? Why have you made my family important? ¹⁷But that was not enough for you, God. You have also said these kind things about my future family. I am your servant. Lord God, you have treated me like a very important man.

¹⁸"What more can I say to you? You have done so much for me, your servant. You love me so much. ¹⁹Lord, you have done this wonderful thing for me for my sake. And you have done it because you wanted to. You have let me know all these great promises.

²⁰"There is no one like you, Lord. There is no God except you. We have heard all this ourselves. ²¹There is no one like your people, the Israelites. It is the one nation on earth that God chose to be his people. You used them to make your name well-known. You did great and wonderful things for them. You went ahead of them and forced other nations out of the land. You freed your people from slavery in Egypt. ²²You made the people of Israel your very own people forever. And, Lord, you became their God.

²³"Lord, you made this promise about my family and me, your servant. Now, keep your promise forever. Do what you have promised. ²⁴Then people will know you and honor you forever. And people will say, 'The Lord of heaven's armies, the God over Israel, is Israel's God!' And the family of your servant David will continue before you.

²⁵"My God, you have told me that you would make my family great. So I, your servant, am brave enough to pray to you. ²⁶Lord, you are God. You have promised these good things to me, your servant. ²⁷You have chosen to bless my family. Let it continue before you forever. Lord, you have blessed my family. So it will be blessed forever."

David Defeats Nations

18 Later, David attacked the Philistine people and defeated them. He took Gath and the small towns around it from the Philistines.

²Then David defeated the country of Moab. So the Moabites became David's servants. And they brought the payments he demanded from them.

³David also fought against Hadadezer king of Zobah. David fought Hadadezer's army all the way to the town of

Hamath. He did this because Hadadezer tried to spread his kingdom all the way to the Euphrates River. [4]David took from Hadadezer 1,000 chariots and 7,000 chariot drivers. And he took 20,000 soldiers on foot. David also crippled most of Hadadezer's horses used for pulling chariots. He saved only 100 of the chariot horses.

[5]The Aramean people from Damascus came to help Hadadezer king of Zobah. But David killed 22,000 of them. [6]Then David put camps of troops in Damascus in Aram. The Arameans became David's servants and brought him the payments he demanded. So the Lord gave David victory everywhere he went.

[7]David took the gold shields from Hadadezer's army leaders. And he brought them to Jerusalem. [8]David also took much bronze from the towns of Tebah and Cun. These towns belonged to Hadadezer. Later, Solomon used this bronze to make things for the Temple:[d] the large bronze bowl, which was called the Sea, the pillars and other bronze things.

[9]Toi was king of the city of Hamath. He heard that David had defeated the whole army of Hadadezer king of Zobah. [10]So Toi sent his son Hadoram to greet King David. Hadoram also congratulated David for fighting and defeating Hadadezer. Hadadezer had been at war with Toi before. Hadoram gave David all kinds of things made of gold, silver and bronze. [11]King David gave these things to the Lord. David had done the same thing with the silver and gold he had taken from these nations: Edom, Moab, the Ammonites, the Philistines and Amalek.

[12]Abishai son of Zeruiah killed 18,000 Edomite people in the Valley of Salt. [13]Abishai also put camps of troops in Edom. And all the Edomites became David's servants. The Lord gave David victory everywhere he went.

David's Important Officers

[14]David was king over all of Israel. He did what was right and fair for everyone. [15]Joab son of Zeruiah was commander of David's army. Jehoshaphat son of Ahilud was the recorder. [16]Zadok son of Ahitub and Ahimelech son of Abiathar were priests. Shavsha was the royal assistant. [17]Benaiah was responsible for leading the Kerethites and Pelethites, the king's bodyguards. Benaiah was Jehoiada's son. And David's sons were important officers. They served at King David's side.

David Fights the Ammonites

19 Nahash was king of the Ammonite people. When Nahash died, his son became the king. [2]David said, "Nahash was kind to me. So I will be kind to Hanun son of Nahash." Then David sent a group to comfort Hanun about the death of his father.

David's men went to comfort Hanun in the country of Ammon. [3]But the Ammonite leaders said to Hanun, "Don't be fooled. David didn't send these men to comfort you. They are not here to honor your dead father. David sent his men to spy on you and your land. He wants to destroy your country." [4]So Hanun arrested David's men. To shame them he cut off their beards and cut off their clothes at the hips. Then he sent them away.

[5]David's men were too ashamed to go home. Some people came to David and told him what had happened to his men. So he sent messengers to meet them. He said, "Stay in Jericho until your beards have grown back. Then come home."

[6]The Ammonite people saw they had caused David to hate them. So Hanun and the Ammonites sent about 74,000 pounds of silver to hire chariots and chariot drivers. They hired Arameans from Northwest Mesopotamia, Aram Maacah and Zobah. [7]The Ammonites hired 32,000 chariots and chariot drivers. They also hired the king of Maacah and his army. So he and his army came and set up camp near the town of Medeba. The Ammonites

themselves came out of their towns and got ready for battle.

[8] David heard about this. So he sent out Joab and the whole army of Israel. [9] The Ammonites came out and got ready for battle. They were near the city gate. The kings who had come to help stayed out in the fields by themselves. [10] Joab saw that there were enemy troops in front of him and behind him. So Joab chose some of the best soldiers of Israel. And he sent them out to fight the Arameans. [11] Joab put the rest of the army of Israel under the command of Abishai, his brother. Then they went out to fight the Ammonites. [12] Joab said to Abishai, "The Arameans may be too strong for me. If they are, then you must help me. Or, the Ammonites may be too strong for you. If they are, then I will help you. [13] Let's be strong. We must fight bravely for our people and the cities of our God. The Lord will do what he thinks is right."

[14] Then Joab and the army with him went to attack the Arameans. And the Arameans ran away from them. [15] The Ammonite army saw that the Arameans were running away. So they also ran away from Abishai and his army. The Ammonites went back inside their city. And Joab went back to Jerusalem.

[16] The Arameans saw that Israel had defeated them. So they sent messengers to bring other Arameans from east of the Euphrates River. Shophach the commander of Hadadezer's army led them.

[17] When David heard about this, he gathered all the Israelites. And he led them across the Jordan River. He lined them up for battle, facing the Arameans. And they attacked the Arameans. [18] But the Arameans ran away from the Israelites. David and his army killed 7,000 Aramean chariot drivers. And they killed 40,000 Aramean foot soldiers. They also killed Shophach, the commander of the Aramean army.

[19] Hadadezer's officers saw that Israel had defeated them. So they made peace with David. They became his servants. So the Arameans refused to help the Ammonites again.

Joab Destroys the Ammonites

20 In the spring Joab led the army of Israel out to battle. This was the time of year when kings went out to battle. But David stayed in Jerusalem. The army of Israel destroyed the land of Ammon. Then they went to the city of Rabbah. They surrounded it and attacked it until they destroyed it. [2] David took the crown from the head of their king.[n] That gold crown weighed about 75 pounds. And it had valuable gems in it. The crown was put on David's head. Then David took many valuable things from the city. [3] David brought out the people from Rabbah. And he forced them to work with saws, iron picks and axes. David did the same thing to all the Ammonite towns. Then David and all the army returned to Jerusalem.

Philistine Giants Are Killed

[4] Later, war broke out between Israel and the Philistines at Gezer. At this time Sibbecai from Hushah killed Sippai. Sippai was one of the descendants[d] of the Rephaites.[d] So those Philistines were defeated.

[5] Another time, the Israelites again fought the Philistines. Elhanan son of Jair killed Lahmi, the brother of Goliath. Goliath was from the town of Gath. Lahmi's spear was as large as a weaver's rod.

[6] Later, the Israelites fought another war with the Philistines at Gath. In this town there was a very large man. He had 6 fingers on each hand and 6 toes on each foot. So he had 24 fingers and toes in all. He also was a descendant of Rapha.[d] [7] When he made fun of Israel, Jonathan killed him. Jonathan was the son of Shimea, David's brother.

[8] These Philistines were descendants of Rapha from Gath. David and his men killed them.

---

[n] **king** Or, "Milcom," the god of the Ammonite people.

David Counts Israel

21 Satan was against Israel. He encouraged David to count the people of Israel. ²So David gave an order to Joab and the commanders of the troops. He said, "Go and count all the Israelites. Count everyone from Beersheba to Dan.ⁿ Then tell me so I will know how many people there are."

³But Joab answered, "May the Lord make the nation 100 times as large. My master the king, all the Israelites are your servants. Why do you want to do this, my master? You will make Israel guilty of sin."

them because he didn't like King David's order. ⁷David had done something God had said was wrong. So God punished Israel.

⁸Then David said to God, "I have done something very foolish. It was a terrible sin. Now, I beg you to forgive me, your servant."

⁹Gad was David's seer.ᵈ The Lord said to Gad, ¹⁰"Go and tell David: 'This is what the Lord says: I am going to give you three choices. Choose one, and I will punish you in that way.'"

Character
1 CHRONICLES 21:8

"**U**h-oh—I blew it!"

Those are hard words to say. We don't like to admit we have made a mistake. It's much easier to pretend we didn't, or to blame someone else for our errors. But we all make mistakes, and when we do, it is best to admit it. This helps us become a good person on the inside.

David was a person like that. David made lots of mistakes—some of them huge. This chapter tells the story of one of those blunders. It was so big that God was going to punish all of Israel for it. What would you have done if you were David? Try to cover up your mistake? David didn't. He admitted his sin and asked God to forgive him. God still punished Israel, but he forgave David and eventually turned his anger away from the people.

When you sin or make a mess of things, be like David. Admit you did wrong and ask God to forgive you. He will!

To learn more about character, zoom to page 660.

⁴But King David made Joab follow his order. So Joab left and went through all Israel, counting the people. Then he returned to Jerusalem. ⁵He told David how many people there were. In Israel there were 1,100,000 men who could use a sword. And there were 470,000 men in Judah who could use a sword. ⁶But Joab did not count the tribesᵈ of Levi and Benjamin. He didn't count

¹¹So Gad went to David and said to him, "This is what the Lord says: 'Choose which punishment you want. ¹²You may choose three years without enough food for the nation. Or choose three months of running from your enemies as they chase you with their swords. Or choose three days of punishment from the Lord. A terrible disease will spread through the country.

ⁿ**Beersheba to Dan** Beersheba was the city farthest south in Israel. Dan was the city farthest north. So this means all the people of Israel.

The angel of the Lord will go through Israel destroying the people.' Now, David, decide which answer I will give to the Lord, who sent me."

¹³David said to Gad, "I am in trouble. I don't want some man to punish me. The Lord is very merciful. So let the Lord punish me."

¹⁴So the Lord sent a terrible disease on Israel, and 70,000 people died. ¹⁵God sent an angel to destroy Jerusalem. But when the angel started to destroy it, the Lord saw it and felt sorry. So he said to the angel who was destroying, "That is enough! Stop!" The angel of the Lord was then standing at the threshing*d* floor of Araunah the Jebusite.

¹⁶David looked up and saw the angel of the Lord in the sky. The angel was holding his sword over Jerusalem. Then David and the older leaders bowed facedown on the ground. They were wearing rough cloth to show their sadness. ¹⁷David said to God, "I am the one who sinned. I gave the order for the people to be counted. I have done wrong. These people are only sheep. What wrong have they done? Lord my God, punish me and my family. But stop the terrible disease that is killing your people."

¹⁸Then the angel of the Lord gave an order to Gad. He told Gad to tell David to build an altar to worship the Lord. It was to be at the threshing floor of Araunah the Jebusite. ¹⁹Gad told David these things from the Lord. So David went to Araunah's threshing floor.

²⁰Araunah was separating the straw from the wheat. When he turned around, he saw the angel. Araunah's four sons who were with him hid. ²¹David went to Araunah. When Araunah saw David, he left the threshing floor. He bowed facedown on the ground before David.

²²David said to him, "Sell me your threshing floor. Then I can build an altar to worship the Lord here. Then the terrible disease will be stopped. Sell it to me for the full price."

²³Araunah said to David, "Take this threshing floor. You are my master the king. Do anything you want. Look, I will also give you oxen for the burnt offering. I will give you boards as wood for the fire. And I will give the wheat for the grain offering. I will give all this to you."

²⁴But King David answered Araunah, "No, I must pay the full price. I won't take anything that is yours and give it to the Lord. I won't give an offering that costs me nothing."

²⁵So David paid Araunah about 15 pounds of gold for the place. ²⁶David built an altar to worship the Lord there. He offered burnt offerings and fellowship offerings. David prayed to the Lord. And the Lord answered him by sending down fire from heaven. It came down on the altar of burnt offering. ²⁷Then the Lord commanded the angel to put his sword back into its holder.

²⁸David saw that the Lord had answered him on the threshing floor of Araunah. So he offered sacrifices to the Lord there. ²⁹The Holy Tent*d* and the altar of burnt offerings were in Gibeon. They were at the place of worship there. Moses had made the Holy Tent while the Israelites were in the desert. ³⁰But David could not go to the Holy Tent to speak with God. He was afraid of the angel of the Lord and his sword.

22 David said, "The Temple*d* of the Lord God will be built here. And the altar for burnt offerings for Israel will be built here."

David Makes Plans for the Temple

²So David gave an order for all foreigners living in Israel to be gathered together. From that group David chose stonecutters. Their job was to cut stones to be used in building the Temple*d* of God. ³David supplied a large amount of iron. It was used for making nails and hinges for the gate doors. He also supplied more bronze than could be weighed. ⁴And he supplied more cedar

logs than could be counted. Much of the cedar had been brought to David by the people from Sidon and Tyre.

[5]David said, "We should build a great Temple for the Lord. It should be famous everywhere for its greatness and beauty. But my son Solomon is young. He hasn't yet learned what he needs to know. So I will prepare for the building of it." So David got many of the materials ready before he died.

[6]Then David called for his son Solomon. He told Solomon to build the Temple for the Lord, the God of Israel. [7]David said to him, "My son, I wanted to build a temple for worshiping the Lord my God. [8]But the Lord spoke his word to me, 'David, you have killed too many people. You have fought too many wars. So you cannot build a temple for worship to me. You have killed too many people. [9]But, you will have a son. He will be a man of peace and rest. I will give him rest from all his enemies around him. His name will be Solomon.[n] And I will give Israel peace and quiet while he is king. [10]Solomon will build a temple for worship to me. He will be my son, and I will be his father. I will make his kingdom strong. Someone from his family will rule Israel forever.'"

[11]David also said, "Now, my son, may the Lord be with you. May you build a temple for the Lord your God, as he said you would. [12]The Lord will make you the king of Israel. May the Lord give you wisdom and understanding. Then you will be able to obey the teachings of the Lord your God. [13]Be careful to obey the rules and laws the Lord gave Moses for Israel. If you obey them, you will have success. Be strong and brave. Don't be afraid or discouraged.

[14]"Solomon, I have worked hard getting many of the materials for building the Temple of the Lord. I have supplied about seven and a half million pounds of gold. And I have supplied about seventy-five million pounds of silver. I have supplied so much bronze

and iron it cannot be weighed. And I have supplied wood and stone. And you may add to them. [15]You have many workmen. You have stonecutters, stoneworkers and carpenters. You have men skilled in every kind of work. [16]They are skilled in working with gold, silver, bronze and iron. You have more craftsmen than can be counted. Now begin the work. And may the Lord be with you."

[17]Then David ordered all the leaders of Israel to help his son Solomon. [18]David said to them, "The Lord your God is with you. He has given you rest from our enemies. He helped me to defeat the people living around us. The Lord and his people are in control of this land. [19]Now give yourself completely to obeying the Lord your God. Build the holy place of the Lord God. Build the Temple for worship to the Lord. Then bring the Box[d] of the Agreement with the Lord into the Temple. And bring in the holy things that belong to God."

The Levites

23 David had lived long and was old. Then he made his son Solomon the new king of Israel. [2]David gathered all the leaders of Israel, along with the priests and Levites. [3]David counted the Levites who were 30 years old and older. In all, there were 38,000 Levites. [4]David said, "Of these, 24,000 Levites will direct the work of the Temple[d] of the Lord. And 6,000 Levites will be officers and judges. [5]And 4,000 Levites will be gatekeepers. And 4,000 Levites will praise the Lord with musical instruments. I made these instruments for them to use for praise."

[6]David separated the Levites into three groups. These groups were led by Levi's three sons: Gershon, Kohath and Merari.

The People of Gershon

[7]From the people of Gershon, there were Ladan and Shimei.

---

[n]**Solomon** This name sounds like the Hebrew word for "peace."

⁸Ladan had three sons. His first son was Jehiel. His other sons were Zetham and Joel.

⁹Shimei's sons were Shelomoth, Haziel and Haran. These three sons were leaders of Ladan's families. ¹⁰Shimei had four sons. They were Jahath, Ziza, Jeush and Beriah. ¹¹Jahath was the first son, and Ziza was the second son. But Jeush and Beriah did not have many children. So they were counted as if they were one family.

The People of Kohath

¹²Kohath had four sons. They were Amram, Izhar, Hebron and Uzziel.

¹³Amram's sons were Aaron and Moses. Aaron and his descendants*d* were chosen to be special forever. They were chosen to prepare the holy things for the Lord's service. They were to offer sacrifices before the Lord. They were to serve him as priests. They were to give blessings in the Lord's name forever.

¹⁴Moses was the man of God. Moses' sons were counted as part of the tribe*d* of Levi. ¹⁵Moses' sons were Gershom and Eliezer. ¹⁶Gershom's first son was Shubael. ¹⁷Eliezer's first son was Rehabiah. Eliezer had no other sons, but Rehabiah had many sons.

¹⁸Izhar's first son was Shelomith.

¹⁹Hebron's first son was Jeriah. His second son was Amariah. Jahaziel was the third son. And Jekameam was the fourth son.

²⁰Uzziel's first son was Micah. And Isshiah was his second son.

The People of Merari

²¹Merari's sons were Mahli and Mushi. Mahli's sons were Eleazar and Kish. ²²Eleazar died without having sons. He had only daughters. Eleazar's daughters married their cousins, the sons of Kish. ²³Mushi's three sons were Mahli, Eder and Jerimoth.

The Levites' Work

²⁴These were Levi's descendants*d* listed by their families. They were the leaders of families. Each person who was 20 years old or older was listed. They served in the Lord's Temple.*d*

²⁵David had said, "The Lord is the God of Israel. He has given rest to his people. He has come to live in Jerusalem forever. ²⁶So the Levites don't need to carry the Holy Tent.*d* They don't need to carry any of the things used in its services anymore." ²⁷David's last instructions were to count the Levites. All who were 20 years old and older were counted.

²⁸The Levites had the job of helping Aaron's descendants. They helped in the service of the Temple of the Lord. They cared for the Temple courtyard and side rooms. They had the job of making all the holy things pure. Their job was to serve in the Temple of God. ²⁹They were responsible for putting the holy bread on the table. They also were responsible for the flour in the grain offerings. And they were responsible for the bread made without yeast. They were also responsible for the baking and mixing. And they did all the measuring. ³⁰The Levites also stood every morning and gave thanks and praise to the Lord. They also did this every evening. ³¹The Levites offered all the burnt offerings to the Lord on the special days of rest. And they offered them at the New Moon*d* festivals and at all appointed feasts. They served before the Lord every day. They were to follow the rules for how many Levites should serve each time. ³²So the Levites took care of the Meeting Tent. They also took care of the Holy Place. And they helped their relatives, Aaron's descendants, with the services at the Temple of the Lord.

The Groups of the Priests

24 These were the groups of Aaron's sons:

Aaron's sons were Nadab, Abihu, Eleazar and Ithamar. ²But Nadab and Abihu died before their father did. And they had no sons. So Eleazar and Ithamar served as the priests. ³David separated the family groups of Eleazar and Ithamar into two different groups. Each group had certain duties it had been given. Zadok and Ahimelech helped David. Zadok was a descendant[d] of Eleazar. And Ahimelech was a descendant of Ithamar. [4]There were more leaders from Eleazar's family than from Ithamar's. There were 16 leaders from Eleazar's family. And there were 8 leaders from Ithamar's family. [5]Men were chosen from Eleazar's and Ithamar's families by throwing lots.[d] Some men from each family were chosen to be in charge of the Holy Place. And some men from each family were chosen to serve as priests.

[6]Shemaiah son of Nethanel was the secretary. He was from the tribe[d] of Levi. Shemaiah recorded the names of those descendants in front of King David and these officers: Zadok the priest, Ahimelech son of Abiathar, and the leaders of the families of the priests and Levites. The work was divided by lots among the families of Eleazar and Ithamar. The following men with their groups were chosen.

[7]The first one chosen was Jehoiarib. The second was Jedaiah. [8]The third was Harim. The fourth was Seorim. [9]The fifth was Malkijah. The sixth was Mijamin. [10]The seventh was Hakkoz. The eighth was Abijah. [11]The ninth was Jeshua. The tenth was Shecaniah. [12]The eleventh was Eliashib. The twelfth was Jakim. [13]The thirteenth was Huppah. The fourteenth was Jeshebeab. [14]The fifteenth was Bilgah. The sixteenth was Immer. [15]The seventeenth was Hezir. The eighteenth was Happizzez. [16]The nineteenth was Pethahiah. The twentieth was Jehezkel. [17]The twenty-first was Jakin. The twenty-second was Gamul. [18]The twenty-third was Delaiah. The twenty-fourth was Maaziah.

[19]These were the groups chosen to serve in the Temple of the Lord. They obeyed the rules Aaron had given them. The Lord, the God of Israel, had given those rules to Aaron.

The Other Levites

[20]These are the names of the rest of Levi's descendants:[d]

Shubael was a descendant of Amram. And Jehdeiah was a descendant of Shubael.

[21]Isshiah was the first son of Rehabiah.

[22]From the Izhar family group, there was Shelomoth. And Jahath was a descendant of Shelomoth.

[23]Hebron's first son was Jeriah. Amariah was his second son. Jahaziel was his third son, and Jekameam was his fourth.

[24]Uzziel's son was Micah. Micah's son was Shamir. [25]Isshiah was Micah's brother. Isshiah's son was Zechariah.

[26]Merari's descendants were Mahli and Mushi. Merari's son was Jaaziah. [27]Jaaziah son of Merari had sons named Shoham, Zaccur and Ibri. [28]Mahli's son was Eleazar. But Eleazar did not have any sons.

[29]Kish's son was Jerahmeel.

[30]Mushi's sons were Mahli, Eder and Jerimoth.

These are the Levites, listed by their families. [31]They were chosen for special jobs by throwing lots.[d] They did this just as their relatives, the priests, had done. The priests were Aaron's descendants. They threw lots in front of King David, Zadok and Ahimelech. The leaders of the families of the priests and Levites were also there. The families of the oldest brother and the youngest brother were treated the same.

The Music Groups

25 David and the commanders of the army chose some men to preach. They chose some of the sons of Asaph, Heman and Jeduthun. They were to preach God's message and play harps, lyres[d] and cymbals. Here is a list of the men who served in this way:

[2]Asaph's sons who served were Zaccur, Joseph, Nethaniah and Asarelah. King David chose Asaph to preach. And Asaph directed his sons.

[3]Jeduthun's sons who served were Gedaliah, Zeri, Jeshaiah, Shimei, Hashabiah and Mattithiah. There were six of them, and Jeduthun directed them. He preached. And he used a harp to give thanks and praise to the Lord.

[4]Heman's sons who served were Bukkiah, Mattaniah, Uzziel, Shubael and Jerimoth. There were also Hananiah, Hanani, Eliathah, Giddalti and Romamti-Ezer. And there were Joshbekashah, Mallothi, Hothir and Mahazioth. [5]All these men were sons of Heman, David's seer.[d] God promised to make Heman strong. So Heman had many sons. God gave him 14 sons and 3 daughters. [6]Heman directed all his sons in making music for the Temple[d] of the Lord. They used cymbals, lyres and harps. That was their way of serving in the Temple of God. And King David was in charge of Asaph, Jeduthun and Heman. [7]These men and their relatives from the Levites were trained in music. They were skilled in making music for the Lord. There were 288 of them. [8]Everyone threw lots[d] to choose the time his family was to serve at the Temple. The young and the old had to throw lots. The teacher and the student had to throw lots.

[9]First, 12 men were chosen from Joseph, his sons and relatives. Joseph was from the family of Asaph.

Second, 12 men were chosen from Gedaliah, his sons and relatives.

[10]Third, 12 men were chosen from Zaccur, his sons and relatives.

[11]Fourth, 12 men were chosen from Izri, his sons and relatives.

[12]Fifth, 12 men were chosen from Nethaniah, his sons and relatives.

[13]Sixth, 12 men were chosen from Bukkiah, his sons and relatives.

[14]Seventh, 12 men were chosen from Jesarelah, his sons and relatives.

[15]Eighth, 12 men were chosen from Jeshaiah, his sons and relatives.

[16]Ninth, 12 men were chosen from Mattaniah, his sons and relatives.

[17]Tenth, 12 men were chosen from Shimei, his sons and relatives.

[18]Eleventh, 12 men were chosen from Azarel, his sons and relatives.

[19]Twelfth, 12 men were chosen from Hashabiah, his sons and relatives.

[20]Thirteenth, 12 men were chosen from Shubael, his sons and relatives.

[21]Fourteenth, 12 men were chosen from Mattithiah, his sons and relatives.

[22]Fifteenth, 12 men were chosen from Jerimoth, his sons and relatives.

[23]Sixteenth, 12 men were chosen from Hananiah, his sons and relatives.

[24]Seventeenth, 12 men were chosen from Joshbekashah, his sons and relatives.

[25]Eighteenth, 12 men were chosen from Hanani, his sons and relatives.

[26]Nineteenth, 12 men were chosen from Mallothi, his sons and relatives.

[27]Twentieth, 12 men were chosen from Eliathah, his sons and relatives.

[28]Twenty-first, 12 men were chosen from Hothir, his sons and relatives.

[29]Twenty-second, 12 men were chosen from Giddalti, his sons and relatives.

[30]Twenty-third, 12 men were chosen from Mahazioth, his sons and relatives.

[31]Twenty-fourth, 12 men were chosen from Romamti-Ezer, his sons and relatives.

The Gatekeepers

26 These are the groups of the gatekeepers.

From the family of Korah, there was Meshelemiah and his sons. (Meshelemiah son of Kore was from Asaph's family.) [2]Meshelemiah had sons. Zechariah was his first son. Jediael was his second son. Zebadiah was his third son. Jathniel was his fourth son. [3]Elam was his fifth son. Jehohanan was his sixth son, and Eliehoenai was his seventh son.

[4]There were also Obed-Edom and his sons. Obed-Edom's first son was Shemaiah. Jehozabad was his second son. Joah was his third son. Sacar was his fourth son. Nethanel was his fifth

son. [5]Ammiel was his sixth son. Issachar was his seventh son, and Peullethai was his eighth son. God had blessed Obed-Edom with children.

[6]Obed-Edom's son Shemaiah also had sons. They were leaders in their father's family because they were capable men. [7]Shemaiah's sons were Othni, Rephael, Obed, Elzabad, Elihu and Semakiah. Elihu and Semakiah were skilled workers. [8]All these men were Obed-Edom's descendants.[d] They and their sons and relatives were capable men. They were strong enough to do the work. Obed-Edom had 62 descendants in all.

[9]Meshelemiah had sons and relatives. They were skilled workers. In all, there were 18 sons and relatives.

[10]These are the gatekeepers from the Merari family. Hosah had sons. Shimri was chosen to be in charge. He was not the oldest son, but his father chose him to be in charge. [11]Hilkiah was his second son. Tabaliah was his third son, and Zechariah was his fourth son. In all, Hosah had 13 sons and relatives.

[12]These were the leaders of the groups of the gatekeepers. They had jobs for serving in the Temple[d] of the Lord. Their relatives also had jobs in the Temple. [13]Each family was given a gate to guard. They were chosen by throwing lots.[d] Young and old threw lots.

[14]Meshelemiah was chosen by lot to guard the East Gate. Then lots were thrown for Meshelemiah's son Zechariah. He was a wise counselor. He was chosen for the North Gate. [15]Obed-Edom was chosen for the South Gate. And Obed-Edom's sons were chosen to guard the storehouse. [16]Shuppim and Hosah were chosen for the West Gate. They also were to guard the Shalleketh Gate on the upper road.

Guards stood side by side with guards. [17]Six Levites stood guard every day at the East Gate. Four Levites stood guard every day at the North Gate. Four Levites stood guard every day at the South Gate. And two Levites at a time guarded the storehouse. [18]There were two guards at the western court. And there were four guards on the road to the court.

[19]These were the groups of the gatekeepers. They were from the families of Korah and Merari.

Other Leaders

[20]Other Levites were responsible for taking care of the treasuries of the Temple[d] of God. They were also responsible for the places where the holy things were kept.

[21]Ladan was Gershon's son. Ladan was the ancestor of several family groups. Jehiel was a leader of one of the family groups. [22]Jehiel's sons were Zetham and his brother Joel. They were responsible for the treasuries of the Temple of the Lord.

[23]Other leaders were chosen from the family groups of Amram, Izhar, Hebron and Uzziel. [24]Shubael was the leader responsible for the treasuries of the Temple of the Lord. Shubael was the descendant[d] of Gershom, who was Moses' son. [25]These were Shubael's relatives from Eliezer: Eliezer's son Rehabiah, Rehabiah's son Jeshaiah, Jeshaiah's son Joram, Joram's son Zicri and Zicri's son Shelomith. [26]Shelomith and his relatives were responsible for everything that had been collected for the Temple. Things had been collected by King David and the heads of families. They had been collected by commanders of 1,000 men and of 100 men and other army commanders. [27]They also gave some of the things they had taken in wars. They gave them to be used in repairing the Temple of the Lord. [28]Shelomith and his relatives took care of all the holy things. Some had been given by Samuel the seer[d] and Saul son of Kish. Some had been given by Abner son of Ner and Joab son of Zeruiah.

[29]Kenaniah was from the Izhar family. He and his sons worked outside the Temple. They worked as officers and judges in different places in Israel.

[30]Hashabiah was from the Hebron family. He and his relatives were responsible for the Lord's work and the king's business in Israel west of the Jordan River. There were 1,700 skilled men in Hashabiah's group. [31]The history of the Hebron family shows that Jeriah was their leader. In David's fortieth year as king, the records were searched. Some capable men of the Hebron family were found living at Jazer in Gilead. [32]Jeriah had 2,700 relatives who were skilled men. They were leaders of families. King David gave them the responsibility of directing the tribes[d] of Reuben, Gad and the eastern half-tribe of Manasseh. They took care of the Lord's work and the king's business for them.

Army Divisions

27 This is the list of the Israelite people who served the king in the army. Each division was on duty one month each year. There were leaders of families, commanders of 100 men, commanders of 1,000 men and other officers. Each division had 24,000 men. [2]Jashobeam son of Zabdiel was in charge of the first division for the first month. There were 24,000 men in his division. [3]He was one of the descendants[d] of Perez. Jashobeam was leader of all the army officers for the first month.

[4]Dodai was in charge of the division for the second month. He was from the Ahohites. Mikloth was a leader in the division. There were 24,000 men in Dodai's division.

[5]The third commander was Benaiah son of Jehoiada the priest. He was the commander for the third month. There were 24,000 men in Benaiah's division. [6]He was the Benaiah who was one of the Thirty[n] soldiers. Benaiah was a brave warrior who led those men. Benaiah's son Ammizabad was in charge of Benaiah's division.

[7]The fourth commander was Asahel, the brother of Joab. He was the com-

mander for the fourth month. Later, Asahel's son Zebadiah took his place as commander. There were 24,000 men in his division.

[8]The fifth commander was Shamhuth, from Izrah's family. He was the commander for the fifth month. There were 24,000 men in his division.

[9]The sixth commander was Ira son of Ikkesh. He was the commander for the sixth month. He was from the town of Tekoa. There were 24,000 men in his division.

[10]The seventh commander was Helez. He was the commander for the seventh month. He was from the Pelonites and a descendant of Ephraim. There were 24,000 men in his division.

[11]The eighth commander was Sibbecai. He was the commander for the eighth month. He was from Hushah and was from Zerah's family. There were 24,000 men in his division.

[12]The ninth commander was Abiezer, from the town of Anathoth. He was the commander for the ninth month. He was from the tribe[d] of Benjamin. There were 24,000 men in his division.

[13]The tenth commander was Maharai. He was the commander for the tenth month. He was from Netophah and was from Zerah's family. There were 24,000 men in his division.

[14]The eleventh commander was Benaiah. He was the commander for the eleventh month. He was from Pirathon and was from the tribe of Ephraim. There were 24,000 men in his division.

[15]The twelfth commander was Heldai. He was the commander for the twelfth month. He was from Netophah and was from Othniel's family. There were 24,000 men in his division.

Leaders of the Tribes

[16]These were the leaders of the tribes[d] of Israel. Eliezer son of Zicri was over the tribe of Reuben. Shephatiah son of Maacah was over the tribe of Simeon. [17]Hashabiah son of Kemuel was over the tribe of Levi. Zadok was

[n]**Thirty**   These were David's most powerful soldiers. See 2 Samuel 23:28.

over the people of Aaron. [18]Elihu, one of David's brothers, was over the tribe of Judah. Omri son of Michael was over the tribe of Issachar. [19]Ishmaiah son of Obadiah was over the tribe of Zebulun. Jerimoth son of Azriel was over the tribe of Naphtali. [20]Hoshea son of Azaziah was over the tribe of Ephraim. Joel son of Pedaiah was over the western half-tribe of Manasseh. [21]Iddo son of Zechariah was over the eastern half-tribe of Manasseh. Jaasiel son of Abner was over the tribe of Benjamin. [22]Azarel son of Jeroham was over the tribe of Dan.

These were the leaders of the tribes of Israel.

[23]The Lord had promised to make the Israelites as many as the stars in the sky. So David only counted the men who were 20 years old and older. [24]Joab son of Zeruiah began to count the people. But he did not finish. God became angry with Israel for counting the people. So the number of the people was not put in the history book about King David's rule.

The King's Directors

[25]Azmaveth son of Adiel was in charge of the royal storehouses.

Jonathan was in charge of the storehouses in the towns, villages and towers. He was the son of Uzziah.

[26]Ezri son of Kelub was in charge of the field workers. They farmed the land.

[27]Shimei was in charge of the vineyards. He was from the town of Ramah.

Zabdi was in charge of storing the wine that came from the vineyards. Zabdi was from Shepham.

[28]Baal-Hanan was in charge of the olive trees and sycamore trees in the western mountain slopes. He was from Geder.

Joash was in charge of storing the olive oil.

[29]Shitrai was in charge of the cows that fed in the Plain of Sharon. He was from Sharon.

Shaphat son of Adlai was in charge of the cows in the valleys.

[30]Obil was in charge of the camels. He was an Ishmaelite.

Jehdeiah was in charge of the donkeys. He was from Meronoth.

[31]Jaziz was in charge of the sheep. He was from the Hagrites.

All these men were the officers who took care of King David's property.

[32]Jonathan was David's uncle. He advised David. Jonathan was a wise man and a teacher of the law. Jehiel son of Hacmoni took care of the king's sons. [33]Ahithophel advised the king. Hushai was the king's friend. He was from the Arkite people. [34]Jehoiada and Abiathar later took Ahithophel's place in advising the king. Jehoiada was Benaiah's son. Joab was the commander of the king's army.

David's Plans for the Temple

28 David commanded all the leaders of Israel to come to Jerusalem. There were the leaders of the tribes[d] and the commanders of the divisions serving the king. There were the commanders of 1000 men and of 100 men. There were the leaders who took care of the property and animals that belonged to the king and his sons. There were the men over the palace, the powerful men and all the brave warriors.

[2]King David stood up and said, "Listen to me, my relatives and my people. I wanted to build a place to keep the Box[d] of the Agreement with the Lord. I wanted it to be God's footstool. And I made plans to build a temple for worship to God. [3]But God said to me, 'You must not build a temple for worship to me. You must not do that because you are a soldier. You have killed many men.'

[4]"But the Lord, the God of Israel, chose me from my whole family. He chose me to be king of Israel forever. The Lord chose the tribe of Judah to be a leader. And from the people of Judah, he chose my father's family. And from that family God was pleased to make me king of Israel. [5]The Lord

has given me many sons. And from those sons he has chosen Solomon. Solomon will be the new king of Israel. Israel is the Lord's kingdom. [6]The Lord said to me, 'Your son Solomon will build my Temple.[d] And he will build the area around it. This is because I have chosen Solomon to be my son. And I will be his father. [7]He is obeying my laws and commands now. If he continues to obey them, I will make his kingdom strong forever.'"

[8]David said, "Now, in front of all Israel and God, I tell you these things: Be careful to obey all the commands of the Lord your God. Then you may keep this good land. And you may pass it on to your descendants[d] forever.

[9]"And you, my son Solomon, accept the God of your father. Serve him completely. Be happy to serve him. Do this because the Lord knows what is in every person's mind. He understands everything you think. If you go to him for help, you will get an answer. But if you turn away from the Lord, he will leave you forever. [10]Solomon, you must understand this. The Lord has chosen you to build the Temple as his holy place. Be strong and finish the job."

[11]Then David gave his son Solomon the plans for building the Temple. Those plans were also for the porch around the Temple. They were for its buildings, its storerooms, its upper rooms and its inside rooms. They also were the plans for the place where the people's sins were removed. [12]David gave him plans for everything he had in mind. David gave him plans for the courtyards around the Lord's Temple and all the rooms around it. He gave him plans for the Temple treasuries. And he gave him plans for the treasuries of the holy things used in the Temple. [13]David gave Solomon directions for the groups of the priests and Levites. David told him about all the work of serving in the Temple of the Lord. He told him about the things to be used in the Temple service. [14]Many things made of gold or silver would be

used in the Temple. David told Solomon how much gold or silver should be used to make each thing. [15]David told him how much gold to use for each gold lampstand and its lamps. He told him how much silver to use for each silver lampstand and its lamps. The different lampstands were to be used where needed. [16]David told how much gold should be used for each table that held the holy bread. And he told how much silver should be used for the silver tables. [17]He told how much pure gold should be used to make the forks, bowls and pitchers. He told how much gold should be used to make each gold dish. He told how much silver should be used to make each silver dish. [18]David told how much pure gold should be used for the altar of incense.[d] He also gave Solomon the plans for the chariot. This is where the golden creatures spread their wings over the Box[d] of the Agreement with the Lord.

[19]David said, "All these plans were written with the Lord guiding me. He helped me understand everything in the plans."

[20]David also said to his son Solomon, "Be strong and brave. Do the work. Don't be afraid or discouraged. The Lord God, my God, is with you. He will help you until all the work is finished. He will not leave you. You will build the Temple of the Lord. [21]The groups of the priests and Levites are ready for all the work on the Temple of God. Every skilled worker is ready to help you with all the work. The leaders and all the people will obey every command you give."

Gifts for Building the Temple

29 King David spoke to all the Israelites who were gathered. He said, "God chose my son Solomon. Solomon is young and hasn't yet learned what he needs to know. But the work is important. This palace is not for people. It is for the Lord God. [2]I have done my best to prepare for building the Temple[d] of God. I have given gold for the things made of gold. I have given silver for the things made of silver. I have given bronze for the things made of bronze. I have given iron for the things made of iron. I have given wood for the things made of wood. I have given onyx for the settings and turquoise. I have given gems of many different colors. I have given valuable stones and white marble. I have given much of all these things. [3]I have already given this for the Temple. But now I am also giving my own treasures of gold and silver. I am doing this because I really want the Temple of my God to be built. [4]I have given about 220,000 pounds of pure gold from Ophir. And I have given about 520,000 pounds of pure silver. They will be used to cover the walls of the buildings. [5]They will also be used for all the gold and silver work. Skilled men may use the gold and silver to make things for the Temple. Now, who is ready to give himself to the service of the Lord today?"

[6]The family leaders and the leaders of the tribes of Israel gave their valuable things. The commanders of 1,000 men and of 100 men gave their valuable things. And the leaders responsible for the king's work gave their valuable things. [7]These are the things they gave for the Temple of God: about 380,000 pounds of gold, about 750,000 pounds of silver, about 1,350,000 pounds of bronze and about 7,500,000 pounds of iron. [8]People who had valuable gems gave them to the treasury of the Temple of the Lord. Jehiel, from the Gershon family, took care of the valuable gems. [9]The leaders gave freely and completely to the Lord. The people were happy to see their leaders give so gladly. King David was also very happy.

David's Prayer

[10]David praised the Lord in front of all of the people who were gathered. He said:

"We praise you, Lord.
  You are the God of our father
    Israel.
  We praise you forever and ever.
[11]Lord, you are great and powerful.
  You have glory, victory and honor.
  Everything in heaven and on earth
    belongs to you.
  The kingdom belongs to you, Lord.
  You are the ruler over everything.
[12]Riches and honor come from you.
  You rule everything.
  You have the power and strength
    to make anyone great and strong.
[13]Now, our God, we thank you.
  And we praise your glorious name.

[14]"These things did not really come
    from me and my people.
  Everything comes from you.
  We have given you back what you
    gave us.
[15]We are like foreigners and strangers.
  All our ancestors were also
    foreigners and strangers.
  Our time on earth is like a shadow.
  There is no hope.
[16]Lord our God, we have gathered all
    this to build your Temple.
  We will build it for worship to you.
  But everything has come from you.
  Everything belongs to you.
[17]I know, my God, that you test
    people's hearts.
  You are happy when people do
    what is right.
  I was happy to give all these things.
  I gave with an honest heart.
  Your people gathered here are
    happy to give to you.
  I am happy to see their giving.
[18]Lord, you are the God of our
    ancestors.
  You are the God of Abraham, Isaac
    and Jacob.
  Please help your people to want to
    serve you always.
  And help them to want to obey
    you always.
[19]Give my son Solomon a strong
    desire to serve you.
  Help him always obey your
    commands, laws and rules.

Help him build the Temple
for which I have prepared."

20 Then David said to all the people who were gathered, "Praise the Lord your God." So they all praised the Lord, the God their ancestors worshiped. They bowed to the ground to give honor to the Lord and the king.

Solomon Becomes King

21 The next day the people made sacrifices to the Lord. They offered burnt offerings to him. They offered 1,000 bulls, 1,000 male sheep and 1,000 male lambs. They also brought drink offerings. Many sacrifices were made for all the people of Israel. 22 That day the people ate and drank with much joy. And the Lord was with them.

And they made David's son Solomon king for the second time. They poured olive oil on Solomon to appoint him king. And they poured oil on Zadok to appoint him as priest. They did this in the presence of the Lord. 23 Then Solomon sat on the Lord's throne as king. He took his father David's place. Solomon was very successful. And all the people of Israel obeyed him. 24 All the leaders and soldiers and King David's sons accepted Solomon as king. They promised to obey him. 25 The Lord made Solomon great before all the Israelites. The Lord gave Solomon much honor. No king of Israel before Solomon had such honor.

David's Death

26 David son of Jesse was king over all Israel. 27 He was king for 40 years. He ruled in the city of Hebron for 7 years. And he ruled in Jerusalem for 33 years. 28 David died when he was old. He had lived a good, long life. He had received many riches and honors. And David's son Solomon became king after him.

29 Everything King David did as king, from beginning to end, is recorded. Those things are written in the records of Samuel the seer.[d] And they are in the records of Nathan the prophet and the records of Gad the seer. 30 Those writings tell what David did as king of Israel. They tell about his power and all that happened to him. And they tell what happened to Israel and all the kingdoms around them.

2 CHRONICLES

Israel's History from Solomon to the Captivity

Solomon Asks for Wisdom

1 Solomon was David's son, and he became a powerful king. This was because the Lord his God was with him. The Lord made Solomon very great.

² Solomon spoke to all the people of Israel. He spoke to the commanders of 100 men and of 1,000 men. He spoke to the judges, to every leader in all Israel and to the leaders of the families. ³ Then Solomon and all the people gathered with him went to the place of worship. This was at the town of Gibeon. God's Meeting Tent*d* was there. Moses, the Lord's servant, had made that Tent in the desert. ⁴ David had brought the Box*d* of the Agreement with God from Kiriath Jearim to Jerusalem. David had made a place for it there. He had set up a tent for it in Jerusalem. ⁵ Bezalel was Uri's son, and Uri was Hur's son. Bezalel had made a bronze altar. It was in Gibeon in front of the Holy Tent. So Solomon and the people worshiped the Lord there. ⁶ Solomon went up to the bronze altar before the Lord at the Meeting Tent. He offered 1,000 burnt offerings on the altar.

⁷ That night God appeared to Solomon. God said, "Solomon, ask for whatever you want me to give you."

⁸ Solomon answered, "You have been very kind to my father David. You have chosen me to be the king in his place. ⁹ Now, Lord God, may your promise to my father David come true. You have made me king of a very large nation. There are so many of them they are like the dust of the earth. ¹⁰ Now give me wisdom and knowledge so I can lead these people in the right way. No one can rule them without your help."

¹¹ God said to Solomon, "What you want is good. I have chosen you to be king of these people. You have not asked for wealth or riches or honor. You have not asked for your enemies to be killed. You have not asked for a long life. But you have asked for wisdom and knowledge to lead my people. ¹² So I will give you wisdom and knowledge. I will also give you more wealth, riches and honor than any king who has lived before you. And the kings who will live after you will not have as much."

¹³ Then Solomon left the place of worship at Gibeon. He left the Meeting Tent and went back to Jerusalem. There King Solomon ruled over Israel.

Solomon's Wealth

¹⁴ Solomon gathered horses and chariots. He had 1,400 chariots and 12,000 horses. He put some horses and chariots in the cities where the chariots were kept. And he kept some with him in Jerusalem. ¹⁵ In Jerusalem, Solomon gathered much silver and gold. He got so much it was as common as rocks. He also gathered much cedar wood. It became as plentiful as the sycamore trees on the western mountain slopes. ¹⁶ Solomon imported horses from Egypt and Kue. The king's traders bought the horses in Kue. ¹⁷ They imported a chariot from Egypt for about 15 pounds of silver. And they imported a horse for nearly 4 pounds of silver. Then they sold the horses and chariots to all the kings of the Hittites and the Arameans.

Solomon Prepares for the Temple

2 Solomon decided to build a temple[d] as a place to worship the Lord. He also decided to build a palace for himself. [2]He chose 70,000 men to carry things. He chose 80,000 men to cut stone in the mountains. And he chose 3,600 men to direct the workers.

[3]Then Solomon sent a message to Hiram king of the city of Tyre. Solomon said:

Help me as you helped my father David. You sent him cedar logs so he could build himself a palace to live in. [4]I will build a temple as a place to worship the Lord my God. And I will give this temple to the Lord. There we will burn sweet-smelling spices in his presence. We will set out the bread that shows we are in God's presence. And we will burn sacrifices every morning and evening. We will worship him on Sabbath[d] days and New Moons.[d] And we will worship him on the other feast days the Lord our God has commanded us to celebrate. This is a rule for Israel to obey forever.

[5]The temple I build will be great. This is because our God is greater than all gods. [6]But no one can really build a house for our God. Not even the highest of heavens can hold God. How then can I build a temple for him? I can only build a place to burn sacrifices to God.

[7]Now send me a man skilled in working with gold, silver, bronze and iron. He must know how to work with purple, red and blue thread. He must know how to make engravings. He will work with my skilled craftsmen in Judah and Jerusalem. These are the men my father David chose.

[8]Also send me cedar, pine and juniper logs from Lebanon. I know your servants are experienced at cutting down the trees in Lebanon. My servants will help them. [9]Send me a lot of wood. The temple I am going to build will be large and wonderful. [10]I will give your servants who cut the wood 125,000 bushels of wheat. And I will give them 125,000 bushels of barley, 115,000 gallons of wine and 115,000 gallons of oil.

[11]Then Hiram king of Tyre answered Solomon with this letter:

Solomon, the Lord loves his people. That is why he chose you to be their king.

[12]Hiram also said:

Praise the Lord, the God of Israel! He made heaven and earth! He gave King David a wise son. Solomon, you have wisdom and understanding. You will build a temple for the Lord and a palace for yourself.

[13]I will send you a skilled and wise man named Huram-Abi. [14]His mother was from the people of Dan. And his father was from Tyre. Huram-Abi has skill in working with gold, silver, bronze, iron, stone and wood. He has skill in working with purple, blue and red thread and expensive linen. And he is skilled in making engravings. He can make any design you show him. He will help your craftsmen and the craftsmen of your father David.

[15]Now send my servants the wheat, barley, oil and wine you promised. [16]We will cut as much wood from Lebanon as you need. We will use rafts to carry it by sea to Joppa. Then you may carry it to Jerusalem.

[17]Solomon counted all the foreigners living in Israel. This was after the time his father David had counted the people. There were 153,600 foreigners in the country. [18]Solomon chose 70,000 of them to carry things. He chose 80,000 of them to cut stone in the mountains. And he chose 3,600 of them to direct the workers. They were to keep the people working.

Solomon Builds the Temple

3 Solomon began to build the Temple[d] of the Lord. He built it in Jerusalem on Mount Moriah. This was where the Lord had appeared to David, Solomon's father. Solomon built the Temple on the place David had prepared. This place was the threshing[d] floor of Araunah the Jebusite. ²Solomon began building in the second month of the fourth year he ruled Israel.

³Solomon used these measurements for building the Temple of God. It was 90 feet long and 30 feet wide. (Solomon used the old measurement.) ⁴The porch in front of the Temple was 30 feet long and 30 feet high.

chains in the gold. ⁶He put gems in the Temple for beauty. And he used gold from Parvaim.[n] ⁷Solomon put gold on the Temple's ceiling beams, doorposts, walls and doors. And he carved creatures with wings on the walls.

⁸Then Solomon made the Most Holy Place. It was 30 feet long and 30 feet wide. It was as wide as the Temple. He covered its walls with about 46,000 pounds of pure gold. ⁹The gold nails weighed over a pound. Solomon also covered the upper rooms with gold.

¹⁰He made two creatures with wings for the Most Holy Place. He made them out of hot liquid gold. ¹¹The wings of the gold creatures were spread out. Together, they were 30 feet across. One wing of one creature touched the Temple wall. The wing was 7½ feet long. The creature's other wing touched a wing of the second

Words to Know: Old Testament
TEMPLE • 2 CHRONICLES 3:13-14

King David's son, Solomon, was given the privilege of building the **Temple** of the Lord in the city of Jerusalem. It took seven years to build this beautiful place of worship. Cedar wood was brought from a country far to the north. All the stones were carved miles away and brought to the temple site so that no sound of a hammer could be heard there. This showed reverence and respect for God's temple.

The temple that Solomon built was destroyed when King Nebuchadnezzar of Babylon conquered the nation of Judah and burned Jerusalem. Later, Zerubbabel built a smaller temple (you can read about that in the book of Ezra). The temple in Jesus' day had been rebuilt and made larger by King Herod. That temple was destroyed by the Romans and was never rebuilt. All that remains of the temple today is one wall in Jerusalem where many Jews still pray.

Do you go to church to worship God? What is your church like?

Solomon covered the inside of the porch with pure gold. ⁵He put panels of pine on the walls of the main room. Then he covered them with pure gold. And he put designs of palm trees and

creature. This wing was also 7½ feet long. ¹²One wing of the second creature touched the other side of the room. It was also 7½ feet long. The second creature's other wing touched

[n]**Parvaim** There was much gold there. It may have been in the country of Ophir.

the first creature's wing. This wing was also 7½ feet long. ¹³Together, the creatures' wings were 30 feet across. The creatures stood on their feet. They looked inside toward the main room.

¹⁴Solomon made the curtain of blue, purple and red thread and expensive linen. And he put designs of creatures with wings in it.

¹⁵Solomon made two pillars to stand in front of the Temple. They were about 52 feet tall. The capital*d* of each pillar was over 7 feet tall. ¹⁶Solomon made a net of chains. He put them on the tops of the pillars. He made 100 pomegranates*d* and put them on the chains. ¹⁷Then Solomon put the pillars up in front of the Temple. One pillar stood on the south side. The other stood on the north. He named the south pillar He Establishes. And he named the north pillar In Him Is Strength.

Things for the Temple

4 Solomon made a bronze altar. It was 30 feet long, 30 feet wide and 15 feet tall. ²Then Solomon used melted bronze to make a large bowl, which was called the Sea. It was round and measured 15 feet across from edge to edge. It was over 7 feet tall, and it measured 45 feet around. ³There were carvings of bulls under the rim of the bowl. There were 10 bulls in every 1½ feet. They were put in two rows around the bowl when it was made.

⁴The bowl rested on 12 statues of bulls. Three bulls faced north, 3 faced west, 3 faced south and 3 faced east. The bowl was on top of them. They faced outward from the center of the bowl. ⁵The bowl was 3 inches thick. Its rim was like the rim of a cup. It looked like a lily blossom. It could hold about 17,500 gallons.

⁶Solomon made 10 smaller bowls. He put 5 of them on the south side. And he put 5 of them on the north. They were to be used to wash the animals for the burnt offerings. But the large bowl was to be used by the priests for washing.

⁷Solomon made 10 lampstands of gold, following the plans for them. He put them in the Temple.*d* He put 5 on the south side and 5 on the north.

⁸Solomon made 10 tables and put them in the Temple. He put 5 on the south side and 5 on the north. And he used gold to make 100 other bowls.

⁹Solomon also made the priests' courtyard and the large courtyard. He made the doors that opened to the courtyard and covered them with bronze. ¹⁰Then he put the large bowl on the south side. He put it in the Temple's southeast corner.

¹¹He made the pots, shovels and bowls. So Huram finished his work for King Solomon on the Temple of God. He had made these things:

¹²two pillars;

two large bowls for the capitals on top of the pillars;

two nets to cover the two large bowls for the capitals on top of the pillars;

¹³400 pomegranates*d* for the two nets (there were two rows of pomegranates for each net covering the bowls for the capitals on top of the pillars);

¹⁴the stands with a bowl on each stand;

¹⁵the large bowl with 12 bulls under it;

¹⁶the pots, shovels, forks and all the things to go with them.

All the things Huram-Abi made King Solomon for the Temple of the Lord were made of polished bronze. ¹⁷King Solomon first had these things poured into clay molds. The molds were made in the plain of the Jordan between Succoth and Zarethan. ¹⁸Solomon had so many things made no one even tried to weigh all the bronze used.

¹⁹Solomon also made all the things for God's Temple. He made the gold altar. He made tables to hold the bread that shows we are in God's presence. ²⁰He made the lampstands and their

lamps of pure gold. They were to burn in front of the Most Holy Place as planned. [21]Solomon used pure gold to make the flowers, lamps and tongs. [22]He used pure gold to make the wick trimmers. He used pure gold for the bowls, pans and dishes used to carry coals. He used pure gold to make the doors for the Temple. And he used pure gold for the inside doors for the Most Holy Place and the doors for the main room.

5 Then all the work Solomon had done for the Temple of the Lord was finished. He brought in everything his father David had given for the Temple. He brought in all the silver and gold and all the furniture. And he put everything in the treasuries of God's Temple.

The Holy Box Is Carried into the Temple

[2]Then Solomon called for all the leaders of Israel. He asked them to come to him in Jerusalem. He called for all the older leaders, the heads of the tribes[d] and the leaders of the families. He wanted them to bring the Box[d] of the Agreement with the Lord from the older part of the city. [3]All the men of Israel came together with King Solomon. This was during the festival that was held in the seventh month.

[4]All the older leaders of Israel arrived. Then the Levites picked up the Holy Box. [5]The priests and the Levites carried the Box of the Agreement. They also carried the Meeting Tent[d] and the holy things in it. [6]King Solomon and all the Israelites met in front of the Box of the Agreement. They sacrificed so many sheep and bulls no one could count them.

[7]Then the priests put the Box of the Agreement with the Lord in its place. This was inside the Most Holy Place in the Temple.[d] They put it under the wings of the gold creatures. [8]The wings of the creatures were spread out over the place for the Holy Box. They covered it and its carrying poles. [9]The carrying poles were very long. Anyone standing in the Holy Place in front of the Most Holy Place could see the ends of the poles. But no one could see the poles from outside the Holy Place. The poles are still there today. [10]The only things inside the Holy Box were two stone tablets.[n] Moses had put them in the Holy Box at Mount Sinai. That was where the Lord made an agreement with the Israelites after they came out of Egypt.

[11]Then all the priests left the Holy Place. All the priests from each group made themselves ready to serve the Lord. [12]All the Levite musicians stood on the east side of the altar. They were Asaph, Heman, Jeduthun and all their sons and relatives. They were dressed in white linen and played cymbals, lyres[d] and harps. With them were 120 priests who blew trumpets. [13]Those who blew the trumpets and those who sang together sounded like one person. They praised and thanked the Lord. They sang as they played their trumpets, cymbals and other instruments. They praised the Lord with this song:

"The Lord is good.
    His love continues forever."

Then the Temple of the Lord was filled with a cloud. [14]The priests could not continue their work because of the cloud. This was because the Lord's glory filled the Temple of God.

6 Then Solomon said, "The Lord said he would live in the dark cloud. [2]I have built a great Temple for you, Lord. It is a place for you to live forever."

Solomon's Speech

[3]King Solomon turned around and blessed all the Israelites gathered in front of him. [4]He said, "Praise the Lord, the God of Israel. He has done what he promised my father David. The Lord said, [5]'I brought my people out of

---

[n]**stone tablets** They were the two stone tablets on which God wrote the Ten Commandments.

Egypt. But I have not yet chosen a city in any tribe[d] of Israel for my temple.[d] This is where I have chosen to be worshiped. I have not chosen a man to lead my people, the Israelites. [6]But now I have chosen Jerusalem as the place I am to be worshiped. And I have chosen David to lead my people Israel.'

[7]"My father David wanted to build a temple as a place to worship the Lord, the God of Israel. [8]But the Lord said to my father, 'David, it was good that you wanted to build a temple as a place to worship me. [9]But you are not the one who will build the temple. Your own son will build my temple.'

[10]"Now the Lord has kept his promise. I have taken my father David's place. Now I am Israel's king. This is what the Lord promised. And I have built the Temple where the Lord, the God of Israel, will be worshiped. [11]I have put the Box[d] of the Agreement there. The agreement that the Lord made with the people of Israel is kept in the Holy Box."

Solomon's Prayer

[12]Solomon stood in front of the Lord's altar. He was standing before all the people gathered there. Then he spread his arms out. [13]He had made a bronze platform. It was 7½ feet long, 7½ feet wide and 7½ feet high. And he had placed it in the middle of the outer courtyard. Solomon stood on the platform. Then he kneeled in front of all the people of Israel who were gathered there. Solomon spread his hands out toward the sky. [14]He said, "Lord, God of Israel, there is no god like you in heaven or on earth. You keep your agreement of love with your servants who completely obey you. [15]You have kept your promise to my father David, your servant. With your words you made a promise. And with the work of your hands, you have made that promise come true today.

[16]"Now, Lord, God of Israel, also keep this promise you made to my father David, your servant. You said, 'David, you will always have someone from your family rule Israel. But this will happen only if they are careful to obey my teachings in everything they do. They must obey my teachings just as you have.' [17]Now, Lord, God of Israel, keep your promise. Let this promise to your servant David come true.

[18]"But, God, can you really live here on the earth with people? Not even the highest of heavens can hold you. And this Temple[d] I built cannot hold you. [19]But pay attention to my prayer and my cry for mercy. Lord my God, listen to my cry. Listen to the prayer I, your servant, pray to you. [20]I pray that you will watch over this Temple day and night. You said you would make this the place to worship you. I pray that you will hear my prayers when I pray facing this Temple. [21]Hear my prayers and the prayers of your people Israel. Hear us when we pray facing this Temple. Hear from your home in heaven. And when you hear our prayers, forgive us.

[22]"A person might do something wrong against someone else. The person who did the wrong will have to swear he is innocent. He will come to swear this before your altar in the Temple. [23]When he does this, listen from heaven and act. Judge your servants. Punish the one who did wrong. Make him suffer the same things he made others suffer. Prove that the person who has done right is innocent.

[24]"An enemy might defeat your people Israel because they have sinned against you. Then the people of Israel will return to you and say you are God. They will pray and beg you for help in this Temple. [25]When this happens, listen from heaven. Forgive the sin of your people, the Israelites. Bring them back into the land you gave to them and their ancestors.

[26]"The sky might not let it rain because your people have sinned against you. Then they will pray, facing this Temple. They will say you are

God. They will stop doing their sin because you are punishing them. [27]When that happens, then listen from heaven. Forgive the sins of your servants, the Israelites. Then teach them the right way to live. And send rain on your land. This is the land you gave your people as their own.

[28]"There might be a time without food in the land. Or there might be terrible sicknesses, disease in the crops, mildew,[d] locusts[d] or grasshoppers. Or enemies might attack Israel's cities. There might be a disaster in Israel. [29]Then one of your people, an Israelite, will pray or cry for help. Each person knows his own trouble and pain. He will spread his arms out, facing this Temple. [30]When that happens, then listen from heaven, your home. Forgive and treat each person as he should be treated. You know what is in his heart. (Only you know what is in a person's heart.) [31]Then the people will fear and obey you as long as they live in this land. This is the land you gave our ancestors.

[32]"A foreigner might come here from a country far away. He is not one of your people, the people of Israel. But he will come because he has heard about your greatness and power. He knows about the things you have done. When he comes and prays, facing this Temple, [33]then listen. Listen from heaven, your home. And do what he asks you to do. Then all the peoples of the earth will know you and respect you, just as your people Israel do. And they will know that this Temple I built is for worshiping you.

[34]"You might send your people to fight their enemies. They will pray to you, facing this city you chose and the Temple I built for worshiping you. [35]If they do, then listen from heaven to their prayer. Listen to their cry and help them.

[36]"People will sin against you. There is not a person who does not sin. And you will become angry with them. You will let an enemy defeat them. The enemy will capture them and take them away. It may be to a land far away or near. [37]But then they will be sorry for what they have done. As captives in that land, they will cry out to you. They will say, 'We have sinned. We have done wrong and acted wickedly.' [38]In the land where they are captives, they will come back to you. They will want to obey you completely. They will pray, facing their land, the land you gave their ancestors. They will pray, facing the city you chose and the Temple I built for you. [39]When this happens, listen from your home in heaven. Listen to their cries and help them. Forgive your people who have sinned against you.

[40]"Now, my God, look at us. Listen to the prayers we will pray in this place.
[41]Now, rise, Lord God, and come to
    your resting place.
Come with the Box[d] of the
    Agreement that shows your
    strength.
Let your priests receive your
    salvation, Lord God.
And may your holy people be happy
    because of your goodness.
[42]Lord God, do not reject your
    appointed one.
Remember your love for your
    servant David."

The Temple Is Given to the Lord

7 When Solomon finished praying, fire came down from the sky. It burned up the burnt offering and the sacrifices. The Lord's glory filled the Temple.[d] [2]The priests could not enter the Temple of the Lord because the Lord's glory filled it. [3]All the people of Israel saw the fire come down from heaven. They also saw the Lord's glory on the Temple. Then they bowed down on the pavement with their faces to the ground. They worshiped and thanked the Lord. They said,

"The Lord is good.
    His love continues forever."

[4]Then King Solomon and all the Israelites offered sacrifices before the

Lord. 5King Solomon offered a sacrifice of 22,000 cattle and 120,000 sheep. So the king and all the people gave the Temple for the worship of God. 6The priests stood ready to do their work. The Levites also stood with the instruments of the Lord's music. King David had made these instruments for praising the Lord. The priests and Levites were saying, "The Lord's love continues forever." The priests, who stood across from the Levites, blew their trumpets. And all the Israelites were standing.

7Solomon made the middle part of the courtyard holy for the Lord. That courtyard is in front of the Temple of the Lord. There Solomon offered burnt offerings and the fat of the fellowship offerings. He used the middle of the courtyard because the bronze altar he had made could not hold everything. It couldn't hold the burnt offerings, grain offerings and fat.

8Solomon and all the Israelites celebrated the festival for seven days. There were many people. They came from as far away as Lebo Hamath. And they came all the way from the brook of Egypt. 9They had given the altar for the worship of the Lord. And they celebrated that for seven days. Then they celebrated the festival for seven days. On the eighth day they had a meeting. 10On the twenty-third day of the seventh month Solomon sent the people home. They were full of joy. They were happy because the Lord had been so good to David, Solomon and his people the Israelites.

The Lord Appears to Solomon

11Solomon finished the Temple*d* of the Lord and the king's palace. He had success in doing everything he planned in the Temple of the Lord and his own palace. 12Then the Lord appeared to Solomon at night. The Lord said, "Solomon, I have heard your prayer. And I have chosen this place for myself to be a Temple for sacrifices.

13"I may stop the sky from sending rain. I may command the locusts*d* to destroy the land. I may send sicknesses to my people. 14Then my people, who are called by my name, will be sorry for what they have done. They will pray and obey me and stop their evil ways. If they do, I will hear them from heaven. I will forgive their sin, and I will heal their land. 15Now I will see them. And I will listen to the prayers prayed in this place. 16I have chosen this Temple and made it holy. So I will be worshiped here forever. Yes, I will always watch over it and love it.

17"Solomon, obey me as your father David did. Obey all I have commanded. Obey my laws and rules. 18If you do, I will make your kingdom strong. This is the agreement I made with your father David. I told him, 'David, someone from your family will always be king in Israel.'

19"But you must not turn away from me. You must not stop obeying the laws and commands I gave you. You must not serve and worship other gods. 20If you do, I will take the Israelites out of my land, the land I gave them. And I will leave this Temple that I have made holy. All the nations will make fun of it and speak evil about it. 21This Temple is honored now. But then, everyone who passes by will be surprised. They will say, 'Why has the Lord done this terrible thing to this land and this Temple?' 22Then people will answer, 'It's because the Israelites left the Lord, the God their ancestors obeyed. He is the God who led them out of Egypt. But they accepted other gods and worshiped and served them. That is why the Lord brought this disaster on them.'"

Solomon's Other Achievements

8 It took Solomon 20 years to build the Temple*d* of the Lord and his own palace. 2Then Solomon rebuilt the towns that Hiram had given him. And Solomon sent Israelites to live in them.

³Then he went to Hamath Zobah and captured it. ⁴Solomon also built the town of Tadmor in the desert. He built all the towns in Hamath as towns for storing things. ⁵He rebuilt the towns of Upper Beth Horon and Lower Beth Horon. He made them protected towns with strong walls, gates and bars in the gates. ⁶He also rebuilt the town of Baalath. And he built all the other towns where he stored things. He built all the cities where the chariots and horses were kept. Solomon built all he wanted in Jerusalem, Lebanon and in all the country he ruled.

⁷⁻⁸Many people who were not Israelites were left living in the country. These people were the Hittites, Amorites, Perizzites, Hivites and Jebusites. They were descendants*d* of the people that the Israelites had not destroyed. Solomon forced all of them to be slave workers. This is still true today. ⁹But Solomon did not force any of the Israelites to be slave workers. They were his fighting men. They were the commanders of his army officers, his chariots and his chariot drivers. ¹⁰Some of them were his most important officers. There were 250 of them to direct the people.

¹¹Solomon brought the daughter of the king of Egypt from the older part of Jerusalem. He brought her to the palace he had built for her. Solomon said, "My wife must not live in King David's palace. This is because the places where the Box*d* of the Agreement has been are holy places."

¹²Then Solomon offered burnt offerings to the Lord on the Lord's altar. Solomon built that altar in front of the Temple porch. ¹³He offered sacrifices every day as Moses had commanded. Sacrifices were to be offered on the Sabbath*d* days, New Moons*d* and the three yearly feasts. The three yearly feasts were the Feast*d* of Unleavened Bread, the Feast of Weeks and the Feast of Shelters. ¹⁴Solomon followed his father David's instructions. Solomon chose the groups of priests for their service. He chose the Levites to lead the praise. And they were to help the priests do their daily work. And he chose the gatekeepers by their groups to serve at each gate. This is what David, the man of God, had commanded. ¹⁵They obeyed all of Solomon's commands to the priests and Levites. And they obeyed his commands about the treasuries.

¹⁶All Solomon's work was done. Everything was done as he had said from the day the Temple of the Lord was begun until it was finished. So the Temple was finished.

¹⁷Then Solomon went to the towns of Ezion Geber and Elath. They were near the Red Sea*d* in the country of Edom. ¹⁸Hiram sent to Solomon ships commanded by his own men. They were skilled sailors. Hiram's men went with Solomon's men to Ophir. And they brought back about 34,000 pounds of gold to King Solomon.

The Queen of Sheba Visits Solomon

9 The queen of Sheba heard about Solomon's fame. So she came to Jerusalem to test him with hard questions. She had a very large group of people with her. She had camels that carried spices, much gold and many gems. She came to Solomon and talked with him about all her questions. ²And Solomon answered all her questions. Nothing was too hard for him to explain to her. ³The queen of Sheba saw that Solomon was very wise. She also saw the palace he had built. ⁴She saw the food on his table and his many officers. She saw the palace servants and their good clothes. She saw the servants who served Solomon his wine. And she saw their good clothes. She saw the burnt offerings he made in the Temple*d* of the Lord. All these things amazed her. ⁵So she said to King Solomon, "I heard in my own country about your achievements and wisdom. And all of it is true. ⁶I did not believe it then. But now I have come and seen it with my own eyes. Not even half of your great wisdom was told to me! You are much greater than I had heard. [7]Your men and officers are very lucky! Since they are always serving you, they are able to hear your wisdom! [8]Praise the Lord your God! He was pleased to make you king. He has put you on his throne to rule for the Lord your God. Your God loves Israel and supports Israel forever. So the Lord has made you king of Israel to keep law and order and to rule fairly."

[9]Then the queen of Sheba gave King Solomon about 9,000 pounds of gold. She also gave him many spices and gems. No one had ever given such fine spices as she gave to King Solomon.

[10]Hiram's men and Solomon's men brought in gold from Ophir. They also brought in juniper wood and gems. [11]King Solomon used the juniper wood to make steps for the Temple of the Lord and the palace. He also used it to make lyres[d] and harps for the singers. No one in Judah had ever seen such beautiful things as these.

[12]King Solomon gave the queen of Sheba everything she wanted and asked for. He gave her more than she had brought to him. Then she and her servants left and returned to their own country.

Solomon's Great Wealth

[13]The amount of gold that Solomon received in one year weighed about 50,000 pounds. [14]Besides that, he also received gold from merchants and traders. All the kings of Arabia and the rulers of the land also brought gold and silver to Solomon.

[15]King Solomon made 200 large shields from hammered gold. Each shield contained about 7½ pounds of hammered gold. [16]Solomon also made 300 small shields of hammered gold. Each shield contained about 4 pounds of gold. King Solomon put them in the Palace of the Forest of Lebanon.

[17]Then he built a large throne of ivory. And he covered it with pure gold. [18]The throne had six steps on it. And it had a gold footstool on it. There were armrests on both sides of the chair. And beside each armrest was a statue of a lion. [19]Twelve lions stood on the six steps. There was one lion at each end of each step. Nothing like this had ever been made for any other kingdom. [20]All King Solomon's drinking cups were made of gold. All of the dishes in the Palace of the Forest of Lebanon were pure gold. In Solomon's time people did not think silver was valuable. So nothing was made of silver. [21]King Solomon had many ships that he sent out to trade. Hiram's men sailed Solomon's ships. Every three years the ships returned. They brought back gold, silver, ivory, apes and baboons.

[22]King Solomon had more riches and wisdom than all the other kings on earth. [23]All the kings of the earth came to see Solomon. They wanted to hear the wisdom God had given him. [24]Every year everyone who came brought a gift. They brought things made of silver and gold, clothes, weapons, spices, horses and mules.

[25]Solomon had 4,000 stalls to hold his horses and chariots. He had 12,000 horses. He kept them in special cities for the chariots. And he kept some with him in Jerusalem. [26]Solomon was king over all the kings from the Euphrates River to the Philistine country to the border of Egypt. [27]In Jerusalem silver was as common as stones while Solomon was king. Cedar trees were as common as the fig trees growing on the western mountain slopes. [28]Solomon imported horses from Egypt and all other countries.

Solomon's Death

[29]The other things Solomon did as king, from the beginning to the end, are written down. They are in the writings of Nathan the prophet.[d] And they are in the prophecy of Ahijah and the visions of Iddo. Ahijah was from Shiloh.

2 CHRONICLES 10

Iddo was a seer[d] who wrote about Jeroboam, Nebat's son. ³⁰Solomon was king in Jerusalem over all Israel for 40 years. ³¹Then Solomon died and was buried in Jerusalem. This was the city of his father David. And Solomon's son Rehoboam became king in his place.

Rehoboam Acts Foolishly

10 Rehoboam went to Shechem because all the Israelites had gone there to make him king. ²Jeroboam son of Nebat was in Egypt. He had gone there to run away from King Solomon. Jeroboam heard that Rehoboam was going to be the new king. So he returned from Egypt. ³The people sent for Jeroboam. Then he and the people went to Rehoboam. They said to Rehoboam, ⁴"Your father forced us to work very hard. Now, make it easier for us. Don't make us work as hard as your father did. Then we will serve you."

⁵Rehoboam answered, "Come back to me in three days." So the people left.

⁶There were some older leaders who had helped Solomon make decisions during his lifetime. So King Rehoboam asked them what he should do. He said, "How do you think I should answer these people?"

⁷They answered, "Be kind to these people. Please them and give them a kind answer. If you do, they will serve you always."

⁸But Rehoboam did not listen to the advice the older leaders gave him. He talked with the young men who had grown up with him. They advised him in making decisions. ⁹Rehoboam asked them, "What is your advice? How should we answer these people? They said, 'Don't make us work as hard as your father did.'"

¹⁰Then the young men who had grown up with him said, "The people said to you, 'Your father forced us to work very hard. Now make our work easier.' But you should tell those people, 'My little finger is thicker than my father's waist. ¹¹My father forced you to work hard. But I will make you work even harder. My father beat you with whips. But I will beat you with whips that have sharp points.'"

¹²King Rehoboam had told the people, "Come back to me in three days." So three days later Jeroboam and all the people returned to Rehoboam. ¹³Then King Rehoboam spoke to them in a cruel way. He did not take the advice of the older leaders. ¹⁴He followed the advice of the young men. He said, "My father forced you to work hard. But I will give you even more work. My father beat you with whips. But I will beat you with whips that have sharp points." ¹⁵So King Rehoboam did not do what the people wanted. God caused this to happen. He did this so the Lord could keep his promise to Jeroboam son of Nebat. The Lord had made this promise through Ahijah, a prophet[d] from Shiloh.

¹⁶The people of Israel saw that King Rehoboam did not listen to them. So they said to the king,

"We have no share in David.
We have no part in the son of Jesse.
People of Israel, let's go to our own homes!
Let David's son rule his own people."

So all the Israelites went home. ¹⁷But Rehoboam still ruled over the Israelites who lived in the towns of Judah.

¹⁸Adoniram was in charge of the people who were forced to work. Rehoboam sent him to the people. But they threw stones at Adoniram until he died. But King Rehoboam was able to run to his chariot and escape to Jerusalem. ¹⁹Since then, Israel has always turned against the family of David.

11 When Rehoboam came to Jerusalem, he gathered 180,000 of the best soldiers. They were from the people of Judah and Benjamin. He gathered them to fight Israel. He wanted to bring the kingdom back under his control. ²But the Lord spoke his word to Shemaiah, the man of God. The Lord said, [3]"Shemaiah, talk to Solomon's son Rehoboam, the king of Judah. Talk also to all the Israelites living in Judah and Benjamin. Say to them, [4]'The Lord says you must not go to war against your brothers. Every one of you should go home. I made all these things happen.'" So King Rehoboam and his army obeyed the Lord's command. They turned back and did not attack Jeroboam.

Rehoboam Makes Judah Strong

[5]Rehoboam lived in Jerusalem. He built strong cities in Judah to defend it against attacks. [6]He built up the cities of Bethlehem, Etam, Tekoa, [7]Beth Zur, Soco, Adullam, [8]Gath, Mareshah, Ziph, [9]Adoraim, Lachish, Azekah, [10]Zorah, Aijalon and Hebron. These were strong, walled cities in Judah and Benjamin. [11]When Rehoboam made those cities strong, he put commanders in them. He also put supplies of food, oil and wine in them. [12]Also, Rehoboam put shields and spears in all the cities. So he made them very strong. Rehoboam kept the peoples and cities of Judah and Benjamin under his control.

[13]The priests and the Levites from all over Israel joined Rehoboam. [14]The Levites even left their pasturelands and fields and came to Judah and Jerusalem. They did this because Jeroboam and his sons refused to let them serve as priests to the Lord. [15]Jeroboam chose his own priests to serve in the places of worship. He chose his own priests for the goat and calf idols he had made. [16]There were people from all the tribes[d] of Israel who wanted to obey the Lord, the God of Israel. They went to Jerusalem with the Levites. They went to sacrifice to the Lord, the God of their fathers. [17]These people made the kingdom of Judah strong. And they supported Solomon's son Rehoboam for three years. During this time they lived the way David and Solomon had lived.

Rehoboam's Family

[18]Rehoboam married Mahalath. She was the daughter of Jerimoth and Abihail. Jerimoth was David's son. Abihail was Eliab's daughter, and Eliab was Jesse's son. [19]Mahalath gave Rehoboam these sons: Jeush, Shemariah and Zaham. [20]Then Rehoboam married Absalom's daughter Maacah. And she gave Rehoboam these children: Abijah, Attai, Ziza and Shelomith. [21]Rehoboam loved Maacah more than his other wives and slave women.[d] Rehoboam had 18 wives and 60 slave women. He was the father of 28 sons and 60 daughters.

[22]Rehoboam chose Abijah to be the leader of his own brothers. He did this because he planned to make Abijah king. [23]Rehoboam acted wisely. He spread his sons through all the areas of Judah and Benjamin. He sent them to every strong, walled city. And he gave plenty of supplies to his sons. He also found wives for them.

Shishak Attacks Jerusalem

12 Rehoboam became a strong king. He also made his kingdom strong. Then he and the people of Judah stopped obeying the teachings of the Lord. [2]Shishak was the king of Egypt. He attacked Jerusalem in the fifth year Rehoboam was king. This happened because Rehoboam and the people were unfaithful to the Lord. [3]Shishak had 1,200 chariots and 60,000 horsemen. He brought troops of Libyans, Sukkites and Cushites from Egypt with him. There were so many they couldn't be counted. [4]Shishak captured the strong, walled cities of Judah. And he came as far as Jerusalem.

[5]Then Shemaiah the prophet[d] came to Rehoboam and the leaders of Judah. They had gathered in Jerusalem because they were afraid of Shishak. Shemaiah said to them, "This is what the Lord says: 'You have left me. So now I will leave you to face Shishak alone.'"

[6]Then the leaders of Judah and King Rehoboam were sorry for what they

had done. They said, "The Lord does what is right."

⁷The Lord saw that they were sorry for what they had done. So the Lord spoke his word to Shemaiah. The Lord said, "The king and the leaders are sorry. So I will not destroy them but will save them soon. I will not use Shishak to punish Jerusalem in my anger. ⁸But the people of Jerusalem will become Shishak's servants. Then they may learn that serving me is different than serving the kings of other nations."

⁹Shishak king of Egypt attacked Jerusalem. He took the treasures from the Temple*ᵈ* of the Lord and from the king's palace. He took everything, even the gold shields Solomon had made. ¹⁰So King Rehoboam made bronze shields to take their place. He gave them to the commanders of the guards for the entrance to the king's palace. ¹¹Whenever the king entered the Temple of the Lord, the guards went with him. They would carry the shields. Later, they would put them back in the guard room.

¹²When Rehoboam was sorry for what he had done, the Lord held his anger back. So the Lord did not fully destroy Rehoboam. There was some good in Judah.

¹³King Rehoboam made himself a strong king in Jerusalem. He was 41 years old when he became king. And he was king in Jerusalem for 17 years. Jerusalem is the city that the Lord chose from all the tribes*ᵈ* of Israel. He chose to be worshiped in Jerusalem. Rehoboam's mother was Naamah from the country of Ammon. ¹⁴Rehoboam did evil things because he did not want to ask the Lord for help.

¹⁵The things Rehoboam did as king, from the beginning to the end, are written down. They are in the records of Shemaiah the prophet. And they are in the records of Iddo the seer.*ᵈ* These men wrote family histories. There were wars between Rehoboam and Jeroboam all the time they ruled.

¹⁶Rehoboam died and was buried in Jerusalem. Then Rehoboam's son Abijah became king.

Abijah King of Judah

13 Abijah became the king of Judah. This was during the eighteenth year Jeroboam was king of Israel. ²Abijah was king in Jerusalem for three years. Abijah's mother was Maacah daughter of Uriel. Uriel was from the town of Gibeah.

And there was war between Abijah and Jeroboam. ³Abijah led an army of 400,000 capable soldiers into battle. And Jeroboam prepared to fight him with 800,000 capable soldiers.

⁴Abijah stood on Mount Zemaraim in the mountains of Ephraim. He said, "Jeroboam and all Israel, listen to me! ⁵You should know this: The Lord, the God of Israel, gave David and his sons the right to be king over Israel forever. God gave this right to David with an agreement which will last forever. ⁶But Jeroboam turned against his master. Jeroboam was the son of Nebat, one of Solomon's officers. Solomon was David's son. ⁷Then worthless, evil men became friends with Jeroboam. They were against Rehoboam, Solomon's son. Rehoboam was young and didn't know what to do. So he could not stop them.

⁸"Now you people are making plans against the Lord's kingdom. The Lord's kingdom belongs to David's sons! There are many of you. And you have the gold calves Jeroboam made for you as gods. ⁹You have thrown out the Lord's priests and the Levites. The priests are Aaron's sons. You have chosen your own priests as people in other countries do. Anyone who comes to make himself ready to serve the Lord with a young bull and seven male sheep can become a priest. He may become a priest of idols that are not gods.

¹⁰"But as for us, the Lord is our God. We have not left him. The priests who serve the Lord are Aaron's sons. And

the Levites help the priests serve the Lord. [11]They offer burnt offerings and sweet-smelling incense[d] to the Lord every morning and evening. They also put the bread on the special table in the Temple.[d] And they light the lamps on the gold lampstand every evening. We obey the command of the Lord our God. But you have left the Lord. [12]God himself is with us. He is our ruler, and his priests are with us. The priests blow the trumpet to call us to war against you. Men of Israel, don't fight against the Lord because you won't succeed. He is the God of your ancestors."

[13]But Jeroboam had sent some troops to sneak behind Abijah's army. So while Jeroboam was in front of Abijah's army, Jeroboam's soldiers were behind them. [14]The soldiers in Abijah's army looked around. Then they saw Jeroboam's army attacking both in front and back. They cried out to the Lord. And the priests blew the trumpets. [15]Then the men of Judah gave a battle cry. When they shouted, God defeated Jeroboam and the army of Israel. They ran away from Abijah and the army of Judah. [16]The men of Israel ran away from the men of Judah. God let the army from Judah defeat them. [17]Abijah's army killed many of Israel's men. Of Israel's best men 500,000 were killed. [18]So at that time the people of Israel were defeated. And the people of Judah won. They won because they depended on the Lord, the God of their ancestors.

[19]Abijah's army chased Jeroboam's army. Abijah's army captured from Jeroboam the towns of Bethel, Jeshanah and Ephron. They also captured the small villages near these towns. [20]Jeroboam never became strong again while Abijah was alive. The Lord struck Jeroboam, and he died.

[21]But Abijah became strong. He married 14 women. And he was the father of 22 sons and 16 daughters. [22]All the other things Abijah did as king are written down. What he said

and did are recorded in what the prophet Iddo has written.

14 Abijah died and was buried in Jerusalem. Then Abijah's son Asa became king in his place. There was peace in the country for 10 years in Asa's time.

Asa King of Judah

[2]Asa did what the Lord said was good and right. [3]He removed the foreign altars used for idol worship. He removed the places where false gods were worshiped. He smashed the stone pillars that honored false gods. And he tore down the Asherah[d] idols. [4]Asa commanded the people of Judah to obey the Lord, the God their ancestors followed. Asa commanded them to obey the Lord's teachings and commandments. [5]He also removed the places where false gods were worshiped and the incense altars from every town in Judah. So the kingdom had peace while Asa was king. [6]Asa built strong, walled cities in Judah during the time of peace. He had no war in these years because the Lord gave him peace.

[7]Asa said to the people of Judah, "Let's build up these towns and put walls around them. Let's make towers, gates and bars in the gates. This country is ours because we have obeyed the Lord our God. We have tried to obey him, and he has given us peace all around." So they built and had success.

[8]Asa had an army of 300,000 men from the people of Judah. And he had 280,000 men from the people of Benjamin. The men from Judah carried large shields and spears. The men from Benjamin carried small shields and bows and arrows. All these men were brave fighting men.

[9]Then Zerah from Cush came out to fight Asa's army. Zerah had a large army and 300 chariots. They came as far as the town of Mareshah. [10]Asa went out to fight Zerah. Asa's army prepared for battle in the Valley of Zephathah at Mareshah.

[11]Asa called out to the Lord his God. He said, "Lord, only you can help weak people against the strong. Help us, Lord our God. We depend on you. We fight against this large army in your name. Lord, you are our God. Don't let anyone win against you."

[12]Then the Lord defeated the Cushites when Asa's army from Judah attacked them. And the Cushites ran away. [13]Asa's army chased them as far as the town of Gerar. So many Cushites were killed that the army could not fight again. They were crushed by the Lord and his army. Asa and his army carried many valuable things away from the enemy. [14]They destroyed all the towns near Gerar. The people living in these towns were afraid of the Lord. These towns had many valuable things. So Asa's army took these things away. [15]Asa's army also attacked the camps where the shepherds lived. And they took many sheep and camels. Then they went back to Jerusalem.

Asa's Changes

15 The Spirit[d] of God entered Azariah son of Oded. [2]Azariah went to meet Asa. Azariah said, "Listen to me, Asa and all you people of Judah and Benjamin. The Lord is with you when you are with him. If you obey the Lord, you will find him. But if you leave him, he will leave you. [3]For a long time Israel was without the true God. And they were without a priest to teach them and without the teachings. [4]But when they were in trouble, they turned to the Lord again. He is the God of Israel. They looked for the Lord and found him. [5]In those days no one could travel safely. There was much trouble in all the nations. [6]One nation would destroy another nation. And one city would destroy another city. This happened because God troubled them with all kinds of trouble. [7]But you should be strong. Don't give up, because you will get a reward for your good work."

[8]Asa felt brave when he heard these words and the message from Azariah. Azariah was the son of Oded the prophet.[d] So he removed the hated idols from all of Judah and Benjamin. And he removed them from the towns he had captured in the hills of Ephraim. He repaired the Lord's altar that was in front of the porch of the Temple[d] of the Lord.

[9]Then Asa gathered all the people from Judah and Benjamin. He also gathered the people of the tribes[d] of Ephraim, Manasseh and Simeon who were living in Judah. Many people came to Asa from Israel. They came because they saw that the Lord, Asa's God, was with him.

[10]Asa and these people gathered in Jerusalem. This was in the third month of the fifteenth year of Asa's rule. [11]At that time they sacrificed to the Lord 700 bulls and 7,000 sheep and goats. Asa's army had taken these animals and other valuable things from their enemies. [12]Then they made an agreement. They promised to obey the Lord with their whole being. He is the God their ancestors served. [13]Anyone who refused to obey the Lord, the God of Israel, was to be killed. It did not matter if that person was important or unimportant. It did not matter if that person was a man or woman. [14]Then Asa and the people made a promise before the Lord. They shouted with a loud voice. They also blew on trumpets and sheep's horns. [15]All the people of Judah were happy about the promise. They had promised with all their heart. They looked for God and found him. So the Lord gave them peace in all the country.

[16]King Asa also removed Maacah, his mother, from being queen mother. He did this because she had made an Asherah[d] idol, which the Lord hated. Asa cut down that idol and smashed it into pieces. Then he burned it in the Kidron Valley. [17]The places of worship to false gods were not removed from Judah. Asa desired very much to obey the Lord all his life.

¹⁸And Asa put the holy gifts that he and his father had given into the Temple of God. These things were made of silver and gold.

¹⁹There was no more war until the thirty-fifth year of Asa's rule.

Asa's Last Years

16 In the thirty-sixth year of Asa's rule, Baasha king of Israel attacked Judah. He went to the town of Ramah and made it strong. He used it to keep people from going in or out of the country of Judah.

²Asa took silver and gold out of the treasuries of the Temple*d* of the Lord. And he took silver and gold out of his own palace. Then he sent it with messengers to Ben-Hadad king of Aram. Ben-Hadad was living in Damascus. Asa's message said: ³"Let's make an agreement between you and me. Let's make it like the agreement between your father and mine. See, I am sending you silver and gold. Now break your agreement with Baasha king of Israel. Then he will take his army away from my country."

⁴Ben-Hadad agreed with King Asa. So Ben-Hadad sent the commanders of his armies to attack the towns of Israel. These commanders defeated the towns of Ijon, Dan and Abel Beth Maacah. They also defeated all the towns in Naphtali where treasures were stored. ⁵When Baasha heard about this, he stopped building Ramah. He left his work. ⁶Then King Asa called all the men of Judah together. They went to Ramah and took away the rocks and wood that Baasha had used. And they used the rocks and wood to build up Geba and Mizpah.

⁷At that time Hanani the seer*d* came to Asa king of Judah. Hanani said to him, "You depended on the king of Aram to help you. You did not depend on the Lord your God. So the king of Aram's army escaped from you. ⁸The Cushites and Libyans had a large and powerful army. They had many chariots

and horsemen. But you depended on the Lord to help you. So he let you defeat them. ⁹The Lord searches all the earth for people who have given themselves completely to him. He wants to make them strong. Asa, you did a foolish thing. From now on you will have wars."

¹⁰Asa was angry with Hanani the seer because of what he had said. Asa was so angry that he put Hanani in prison. Asa was cruel with some of the people at that same time.

¹¹The things Asa did as king, from the beginning to the end, are written down. They are in the book of the kings of Judah and Israel. ¹²In the thirty-ninth year of his rule, Asa got a disease in his feet. His disease was very bad. But he did not ask for help from the Lord. He only asked for help from the doctors. ¹³Then Asa died in the forty-first year of his rule. ¹⁴The people buried Asa in the tomb he had made for himself in Jerusalem. They laid him on a bed. It was filled with spices and different kinds of mixed perfumes. And they made a large fire to honor Asa.

Jehoshaphat King of Judah

17 Jehoshaphat, Asa's son, became king of Judah in Asa's place. Jehoshaphat made Judah strong so they could fight against Israel. ²He put troops in all the strong, walled cities of Judah. And he put troops in Judah and in the towns of Ephraim his father Asa had captured.

³The Lord was with Jehoshaphat because he did good things. He lived as his father Asa did when he first became king. Jehoshaphat did not ask for help from the Baal*d* idols. ⁴He asked for help from the God his father had followed. He obeyed God's commands. He did not live as the people of Israel lived. ⁵The Lord made Jehoshaphat a strong king over Judah. All the people of Judah brought gifts to Jehoshaphat. So he had much wealth and honor. ⁶He wanted very much to obey

the Lord. He also removed the places for worshiping false gods and the Asherah[d] idols from Judah.

[7]Jehoshaphat sent his officers to teach in the towns of Judah. This happened in the third year of his rule. These officers were Ben-Hail, Obadiah, Zechariah, Nethanel and Micaiah. [8]Jehoshaphat sent with them these Levites: Shemaiah, Nethaniah, Zebadiah, Asahel, Shemiramoth, Jehonathan, Adonijah, Tobijah and Tob-Adonijah. He also sent the priests Elishama and Jehoram. [9]These leaders, Levites and priests taught the people in Judah. They took the Book of the Teachings of the Lord with them. And they went through all the towns of Judah and taught the people.

[12]Jehoshaphat became more and more powerful. He built strong, walled cities and storage towns in Judah. [13]He kept many supplies in the towns of Judah. And he kept trained soldiers in Jerusalem. [14]These soldiers were listed by families.

From the families of Judah, these were the commanders of groups of 1,000 men: Adnah was the commander of 300,000 soldiers. [15]Jehohanan was the commander of 280,000 soldiers. [16]And Amasiah was the commander of 200,000 soldiers. Amasiah son of Zicri had volunteered to serve the Lord.

[17]These were the commanders from the families of Benjamin: Eliada had

The Bible
2 CHRONICLES 17:9

You're sitting in church. The pastor stands up in the pulpit and says, "Our Scripture reading this morning is ...." Do you snap to attention or do you start daydreaming?

If we're honest, we have to admit that sometimes our minds wander when we hear someone reading the Bible. But it wasn't always that way for God's people. To be sure, they went through periods when they did not give God's word proper respect and attention. But sometimes, as in this passage, they understood how important God's word was to them. King Jehoshaphat thought it was so important that he sent his own officials around to the various towns of Judah to teach the people from the Bible.

No government official will be sent to read the Bible to you. But when your pastor (or Sunday school teacher, or whoever) does, remember how important God's word is to his people. Including you!

To learn more about the Bible, zoom to page 558.

[10]The nations near Judah were afraid of the Lord. So they did not start a war against Jehoshaphat. [11]Some of the Philistines brought gifts and silver to Jehoshaphat as forced payments. Some Arabs brought him flocks. They brought him 7,700 male sheep and 7,700 goats.

200,000 soldiers who used bows and shields. Eliada was a brave soldier. [18]And Jehozabad had 180,000 men armed for war.

[19]All these soldiers served King Jehoshaphat. The king also put other men in the strong, walled cities through all of Judah.

Micaiah Warns King Ahab

18 Jehoshaphat had much wealth and honor. He made an agreement with King Ahab through marriage.[n] [2] A few years later Jehoshaphat visited Ahab in Samaria. Ahab sacrificed many sheep and cattle as a great feast to honor Jehoshaphat and the people with him. He encouraged Jehoshaphat to attack Ramoth in Gilead. [3] Ahab king of Israel asked Jehoshaphat king of Judah, "Will you go with me to attack Ramoth in Gilead?"

Jehoshaphat answered, "I will be with you. And my soldiers will be like your own soldiers. We will join you in the battle." [4] Jehoshaphat also said to Ahab, "But first we should ask the Lord to guide us."

[5] So King Ahab called a meeting of the prophets.[d] There were 400 men. Ahab asked them, "Should we go to war against Ramoth in Gilead or not?"

They answered, "Go, because God will let you defeat it."

[6] But Jehoshaphat asked, "Is there a prophet of the Lord here? If there is, let's ask him what we should do."

[7] Then King Ahab said to Jehoshaphat, "There is one other prophet. We could ask the Lord through him. But I hate him. When he prophesies, he never says anything good about me. He always says something bad. He is Micaiah, Imlah's son."

Jehoshaphat said, "King Ahab, you shouldn't say that."

[8] So King Ahab told one of his officers to bring Micaiah to him at once.

[9] King Ahab of Israel and King Jehoshaphat of Judah had on their royal robes. They were sitting on their thrones at the threshing[d] floor. This was near the entrance to the gate of Samaria. All the prophets were speaking messages in front of the two kings. [10] One of the prophets was Zedekiah son of Kenaanah. He had made some iron horns. He said to Ahab, "This is what the Lord says: 'You will use these horns to fight the Arameans. And you will destroy them.'"

[11] All the other prophets said the same thing. They said, "Attack Ramoth in Gilead and win. The Lord will let you defeat the Arameans."

[12] The messenger who had gone to get Micaiah found him. He said to Micaiah, "All the other prophets are saying the same thing. They are saying that King Ahab will win against the Arameans. You had better agree with them. Give the king a good answer."

[13] But Micaiah said, "As surely as the Lord lives, I can tell him only what my God says."

[14] Then Micaiah came to King Ahab. The king asked him, "Micaiah, should we attack Ramoth in Gilead or not?"

Micaiah answered, "Attack and win. You will defeat it."

[15] King Ahab said to Micaiah, "Tell me only the truth by the power of the Lord. How many times do I have to tell you this?"

[16] Then Micaiah answered, "I saw the army of Israel. They were scattered over the hills like sheep without a shepherd. The Lord said, 'They have no leaders. Let each one go home and not fight.'"

[17] Then King Ahab of Israel said to Jehoshaphat, "I told you! This prophet never says anything good about me. He only says bad things about me."

[18] But Micaiah continued to speak. He said, "Hear the message from the Lord: I saw the Lord sitting on his throne. His heavenly army was standing on his right and on his left. [19] The Lord said, 'Who will trick King Ahab of Israel into attacking Ramoth in Gilead? Do this so he will go and be killed.' The spirits did not agree about what they should do. [20] Then a spirit came and stood before the Lord. He said, 'I will trick him.' The Lord asked, 'How will you do it?' [21] The spirit answered,

---

[n] **agreement . . . through marriage** Jehoshaphat's son Jehoram married Athaliah, Ahab's daughter.
See 2 Chronicles 21:6.

'I will go to Ahab's prophets. I will make them tell lies.' So the Lord said, 'You will succeed in tricking him. Go and do it.'"

²²Micaiah said, "Ahab, this has now happened. The Lord has caused your prophets to lie to you. The Lord has decided that great trouble should come to you."

²⁷Micaiah said, "Ahab, if you come back safely from the battle, the Lord has not spoken through me. Remember my words, all you people!"

Ahab Is Killed

²⁸So Ahab king of Israel and Jehoshaphat king of Judah went to Ramoth in Gilead. ²⁹King Ahab said to Jehoshaphat, "I will go into battle. But I will wear other clothes so no one will know who I am. But you wear your royal

Good Kings and Bad Kings
JEHOSHAPHAT • 2 CHRONICLES 19:1-3

Jehoshaphat should have known better. He was a good king who reigned over the southern kingdom of Judah. He loved God and tried to follow him, but he made one big mistake. He made an alliance with wicked king Ahab. An alliance meant that he would work with Ahab and that the two kings would go to battle together. The problem was that Ahab was the most evil king who ever reigned over the northern kingdom of Israel. Ahab did not care about God and did not want to listen to any of God's prophets. Jehoshaphat did care about God and wanted to obey him. There was no way for Jehoshaphat to be able to serve God and also be friends with evil Ahab.

Be sure that the people you want as your closest friends are people who also love God. Otherwise you will have to choose between your friends and God.

To meet a king who served God even though his father didn't, fly to page 553.

²³Then Zedekiah son of Kenaanah went up to Micaiah. And he slapped Micaiah in the face. Zedekiah said, "Do you really believe that the Lord's Spirit[d] has left me and is now speaking through you?"

²⁴Micaiah answered, "You will find out on the day you go to hide in an inside room."

²⁵Then King Ahab ordered, "Take Micaiah. Send him to Amon, the governor of the city, and to Joash, the king's son. ²⁶Tell them I said to put Micaiah in prison. Give him only bread and water. Keep him there until I come back safely from the battle."

clothes." So King Ahab of Israel wore other clothes and went into battle.

³⁰The king of Aram gave an order to his chariot commanders. He said, "Don't fight with anyone but the king of Israel. It doesn't matter if they are important or unimportant." ³¹When these commanders saw Jehoshaphat, they thought he was the king of Israel. So they turned to attack him. But Jehoshaphat called out, and the Lord helped him. God made the chariot commanders turn away from Jehoshaphat. ³²When they saw he was not King Ahab, they stopped chasing him.

[33]By chance, a soldier shot an arrow. And it hit Ahab king of Israel. The arrow went in between the pieces of his armor. King Ahab said to his chariot driver, "Turn around and get me out of the battle. I've been wounded." [34]The battle went on all day. King Ahab held himself up in his chariot. He faced the Arameans until evening. Then Ahab died at sunset.

19 Jehoshaphat king of Judah came back safely to his palace in Jerusalem. [2]Jehu son of Hanani went out to meet him. Jehu was a seer.[d] He said to King Jehoshaphat, "Why did you help evil people? Why do you love those who hate the Lord? That is the reason the Lord is angry with you. [3]But there is some good in you. You took the Asherah[d] idols out of this country. And you have wanted to obey God."

Jehoshaphat Chooses Judges

[4]Jehoshaphat lived in Jerusalem. He went out again to be with the people. He went from Beersheba to the mountains of Ephraim. He brought these people back to the Lord, the God their ancestors followed. [5]Jehoshaphat appointed judges in all the land. He appointed judges for each of the strong, walled cities of Judah. [6]Jehoshaphat said to them, "Be careful in what you do. This is because you are not judging for people but for the Lord. He will be with you when you make a decision. [7]Now let each of you fear the Lord. Be careful in what you do because the Lord our God wants people to be fair. He wants all people to be treated the same. And he doesn't want people to accept money to change their judgments."

[8]And in Jerusalem Jehoshaphat appointed some of the Levites, priests and leaders of Israelite families to be judges. They were to decide cases about the law of the Lord. And they were to settle problems between the people who lived in Jerusalem. [9]Jehoshaphat gave them commands. He said, "You must always serve the Lord completely. You must fear him. [10]You will have cases about killing, about the teachings, commands, rules or some other law. These cases will come from your people living in the cities. In all these cases you must warn the people not to sin against the Lord. If you don't, the Lord will be angry with you and your people. But if you warn them, you won't be guilty. [11]"Amariah is the leading priest. He will be over you in all cases about the Lord. Zebadiah son of Ishmael is a leader in the tribe[d] of Judah. He will be over you in all cases about the king. Also, the Levites will serve as officers for you. Have courage. May the Lord be with those who do what is right."

Jehoshaphat Faces War

20 Later some people came to start a war with Jehoshaphat. They were the Moabites, Ammonites and some Meunites. [2]Some men came and told Jehoshaphat, "A large army is coming against you from Edom. They are coming from the other side of the Dead Sea.[d] They are already in Hazazon Tamar!" (Hazazon Tamar is also called En Gedi.) [3]Jehoshaphat was afraid. So he decided to ask the Lord what to do. He announced that no one in Judah should eat during this special time of prayer to God. [4]The people of Judah came together to ask the Lord for help. They came from every town in Judah to ask for his help.

[5]The people of Judah and Jerusalem met in front of the new courtyard in the Temple[d] of the Lord. Then Jehoshaphat stood up before them. [6]He said, "Lord, you are the God of our ancestors. You are the God in heaven. You rule over all the kingdoms of the nations. You have power and strength. No one can stand against you. [7]Our God, you forced out the people who lived in this land. You forced them out as your people Israel moved in. And you gave this land forever to the descendants[d] of your friend Abraham. [8]They lived in this land and built a

Temple for worshiping you. They said, [9]"Trouble may come to us. It may be war, punishment, sickness or a time of hunger. If it comes, we will stand before you and before this Temple where you have chosen to be worshiped. We will cry out to you when we are in trouble. Then you will hear and save us.'

[10]"But now here are men from Ammon, Moab and Edom. You wouldn't let the Israelites enter their lands when the Israelites came from Egypt. So the Israelites turned away and did not destroy them. [11]But see how they repay us for not destroying them! They have come to force us out of your land. And you gave us this land as our own. [12]Our God, punish those people. We have no power against this large army that is attacking us. We don't know what to do. So we look to you for help."

[13]All the men of Judah stood before the Lord. Their babies, wives and children were with them. [14]Then the Spirit[d] of the Lord entered Jahaziel. (Jahaziel was Zechariah's son. Zechariah was Benaiah's son. Benaiah was Jeiel's son, and Jeiel was Mattaniah's son.) Jahaziel was a Levite and a descendant of Asaph. He stood up in the meeting. [15]And he said: "Listen to me, King Jehoshaphat! Listen, all you people living in Judah and Jerusalem! The Lord says this to you: 'Don't be afraid or discouraged because of this large army. The battle is not your battle. It is God's battle. [16]Tomorrow go down there and fight those people. They will come up through the Pass of Ziz. You will find them at the end of the ravine that leads to the Desert of Jeruel. [17]You won't need to fight in this battle. Just stand strong in your places. You will see the Lord save you. Judah and Jerusalem, don't be afraid. Don't be discouraged. The Lord is with you. So go out against those people tomorrow!'"

[18]Jehoshaphat bowed facedown on the ground. All the people of Judah and Jerusalem bowed down before the Lord. And they worshiped him. [19]Then some Levites from the Kohathite and Korahite people stood up and praised the Lord. They praised the God of Israel with very loud voices.

[20]Jehoshaphat's army went out into the Desert of Tekoa early in the morning. As they were starting out, Jehoshaphat stood and said, "Listen to me, people of Judah and Jerusalem! Have faith in the Lord your God. Then you will stand strong. Have faith in the Lord's prophets.[d] Then you will succeed." [21]Jehoshaphat listened to the people's advice. Then he chose men to be singers to the Lord. They were to praise the Lord because he is holy and wonderful. They marched in front of the army. They said,

"Thank the Lord.

His love continues forever."

[22]As they began to sing and praise God, the Lord set ambushes. He set them for the people of Ammon, Moab and Edom. They were the ones who came to attack Judah. And they were defeated. [23]The men of Ammon and Moab started to attack the men from Edom. They killed and destroyed them. After they had killed the men from Edom, they killed each other.

[24]The men from Judah came to a place where they could see the desert. They looked at the enemy's large army. But they only saw dead bodies lying on the ground. No one had escaped. [25]Jehoshaphat and his army came to take valuable things from the dead bodies. They found many supplies, much clothing, and other valuable things. There was more than they could carry away. There was so much it took three days to gather it all. [26]On the fourth day Jehoshaphat and his army met in the Valley of Beracah. There they praised the Lord. That is why that place has been called the Valley of Beracah[n] to this day.

[27]Then Jehoshaphat led all the men from Judah and Jerusalem back to

[n]**Beracah**　This name means "blessing or praise."

Jerusalem. The Lord had made them happy because their enemies were defeated. ²⁸They entered Jerusalem with lyres,ᵈ harps and trumpets and went to the Temple of the Lord.

²⁹All the kingdoms of the lands around them heard how the Lord had fought Israel's enemies. So they feared the Lord. ³⁰So Jehoshaphat's kingdom was not at war. His God gave him peace from all the countries around him.

Jehoshaphat's Rule Ends

³¹Jehoshaphat ruled over the country of Judah. He was 35 years old when he began to rule. And he ruled 25 years in Jerusalem. His mother's name was Azubah daughter of Shilhi. ³²Jehoshaphat lived as his father Asa had lived. He followed what Asa had done. He did what the Lord said was right. ³³But the places where false gods were worshiped were not removed. And the people did not strongly desire to follow the God their ancestors had followed.

³⁴The other things Jehoshaphat did as king, from the beginning to the end, are written down. They are in the writings of Jehu son of Hanani. These writings are in the book of the kings of Israel.

³⁵Later, Jehoshaphat king of Judah made an agreement with Ahaziah king of Israel. It was wrong for him to do this. ³⁶Jehoshaphat agreed with Ahaziah to build trading ships. They built them in the town of Ezion Geber. ³⁷Then Eliezer son of Dodavahu spoke against Jehoshaphat. Eliezer was from the town of Mareshah. He said, "Jehoshaphat, because you joined with Ahaziah, the Lord will destroy what you have made." The ships were wrecked. So Jehoshaphat and Ahaziah could not send them out to trade.

21 Then Jehoshaphat died and was buried with his ancestors in Jerusalem. Jehoshaphat's son Jehoram became king in his place. ²Jehoram's brothers were Azariah, Jehiel, Zechariah, Azariahu, Michael and Shephatiah.

They were the sons of Jehoshaphat king of Judah. ³Jehoshaphat gave his sons many gifts of silver, gold and valuable things. He also gave them strong, walled cities in Judah. But Jehoshaphat gave the kingdom to Jehoram because he was the first son.

Jehoram King of Judah

⁴Jehoram took control of his father's kingdom. Then he killed all his brothers with a sword. He also killed some of the leaders of Israel. ⁵He was 32 years old when he began to rule. And he ruled eight years in Jerusalem. ⁶He lived as the kings of Israel had lived. He lived as Ahab's family had lived. This was because he married Ahab's daughter. Jehoram did what the Lord said was wrong. ⁷But the Lord would not destroy David's family. This was because of the agreement he had made with David. The Lord had promised that one of David's descendantsᵈ would always rule.

⁸While Jehoram was king, Edom turned against Judah's rule. The people of Edom chose their own king. ⁹So Jehoram went to Edom with all his commanders and chariots. The Edomite army surrounded Jehoram and his chariot commanders. But Jehoram fought his way out at night. ¹⁰From then until now the country of Edom has fought against Judah.

At the same time the people of Libnah also turned against Jehoram. This happened because Jehoram left the Lord, the God his ancestors followed. ¹¹Jehoram also had built places to worship false gods on the hills in Judah. He had led the people of Jerusalem into sinning. And he had led the people of Judah away from the Lord. ¹²Jehoram received a letter from Elijah the prophet. The letter said:

This is what the Lord says. He is the God your father David followed. The Lord says, "Jehoram, you have not lived as your father Jehoshaphat lived. You have not lived as Asa king of Judah lived. ¹³But you have lived as the kings of Israel lived. You have led the people of Judah and Jerusalem into sinning against God. That is what Ahab and his family did. You have killed your brothers. And they were better than you. ¹⁴So now the Lord is about to punish your people terribly. He will punish your children, wives and everything you own. ¹⁵You will have a terrible disease in your intestines. It will become worse every day. Finally it will cause your intestines to come out."

¹⁶The Lord caused the Philistines and the Arabs to be angry with Jehoram. They lived near the Cushites. ¹⁷So the Philistines and Arabs attacked Judah. They took away all the wealth of Jehoram's palace, as well as his sons and wives. Only Jehoram's youngest son, Ahaziah, was left.

¹⁸After these things happened, the Lord gave Jehoram a disease in his intestines. It could not be cured. ¹⁹After he was sick for two years, Jehoram's intestines fell out because of the disease. He died in terrible pain. The people did not make a large fire to honor Jehoram as they had done for his ancestors.

²⁰Jehoram was 32 years old when he became king. And he ruled eight years in Jerusalem. No one was sad when he died. He was buried in Jerusalem, but not in the graves for the kings.

Ahaziah King of Judah

22 The people of Jerusalem chose Ahaziah to be king in Jehoram's place. Ahaziah was Jehoram's youngest son. The robbers who had come with the Arabs to attack Jehoram's camp had killed all of Jehoram's older sons. So Ahaziah began to rule Judah. ²He was 22 years old when he began to rule. And he ruled one year in Jerusalem. His mother's name was Athaliah, a granddaughter of Omri. ³Ahaziah also lived as Ahab's family had lived. This was because his mother encouraged him to do wrong things. ⁴Ahaziah did

what the Lord said was wrong. That is what Ahab's family had done. And they gave advice to Ahaziah after his father died. Their bad advice led to his death. ⁵Ahaziah followed their advice when he went to fight King Hazael of Aram. King Joram of Israel, Ahab's son, went with him. They met Hazael at the town of Ramoth in Gilead. The Arameans wounded Joram in battle. ⁶So Joram returned to the town of Jezreel to get well. He was wounded at Ramoth when he fought Hazael king of Aram.

Then King Ahaziah of Judah, son of Jehoram, went to Jezreel. He went there to visit Joram son of Ahab because he was wounded.

⁷God caused Ahaziah's death when he went to visit Joram. Ahaziah arrived and went out with Joram to meet Jehu son of Nimshi. The Lord had appointed Jehu to destroy Ahab's family. ⁸While Jehu was punishing Ahab's family, he found the leaders of Judah. He also found Ahaziah's relatives who served Ahaziah. Jehu killed them all. ⁹Then Jehu looked for Ahaziah. Jehu's men caught him hiding in Samaria. So they brought him to Jehu. Then they killed and buried him. They said, "Ahaziah is a descendant*d* of Jehoshaphat. And Jehoshaphat obeyed the Lord with all his heart." No one in Ahaziah's family had the power to take control of the kingdom of Judah.

Athaliah Queen of Judah

¹⁰Now Ahaziah's mother, Athaliah, saw that her son was dead. Then she killed all the royal family in Judah. ¹¹But Jehosheba took Joash, Ahaziah's son. She stole him from among the other sons of the king. Those sons were going to be murdered. She put Joash and his nurse in a bedroom. Jehosheba was King Jehoram's daughter and Ahaziah's sister. She was also the wife of Jehoiada the priest. She hid Joash so Athaliah could not kill him. ¹²Joash was hidden with them in the Temple*d* of God for six years. During that time Athaliah ruled the land.

23 In the seventh year Jehoiada decided to do something. He made an agreement with the commanders of the groups of 100 men. These were the commanders: Azariah son of Jeroham, Ishmael son of Jehohanan, Azariah son of Obed, Maaseiah son of Adaiah, and Elishaphat son of Zicri. ²They went around in Judah and gathered the Levites from all the towns. They also gathered the leaders of the families of Israel. Then they went to Jerusalem. ³All the people together made an agreement with the king in the Temple of God.

the Temple of the Lord. ⁶Don't let anyone come into the Temple of the Lord. Only the priests and Levites who serve may come in. They may come because they have been made ready to serve the Lord. But all the other men must do the job the Lord has given them. ⁷The Levites must stay near the king. Every man must have his sword with him. If anyone tries to enter the Temple, kill him. You must stay with the king everywhere he goes."

⁸The Levites and all the people of Judah obeyed everything Jehoiada the priest had commanded. He did not excuse anyone from the groups of the priests. So each commander took the men who came on duty on the Sabbath

Children Who Saw God at Work

JOASH • 2 CHRONICLES 23:1-11

What would you do if someone crowned you king or queen? That's what happened to seven-year-old Joash. When his father died, Joash was supposed to be the next king. But Athaliah hoped to kill Joash because she wanted to be queen. So Joash's aunt and uncle hid him in the temple of God for six years.

Athaliah was a very evil queen. She worshiped idols (stone or wood carvings) instead of God. Joash was safe in the temple of God because Athaliah never went there; she went to her own temples to worship idols. This made God angry. The people who still worshiped God decided to crown the young Prince Joash, even though he was only seven.

Being king was a big job for a little boy, but the priests and other people who loved God helped him. Do you have a big job to do? God wants to help you, and other people can help you too. Don't be afraid to ask.

To meet a little girl who came back from the dead, fly to page 1191.

Jehoiada said to them, "The king's son will rule. That is what the Lord promised about David's descendants.ᵈ ⁴Now this is what you must do: You priests and Levites go on duty on the Sabbath.ᵈ A third of you will guard the doors. ⁵A third of you will be at the king's palace. And a third of you will be at the Foundation Gate. All the other people will stay in the courtyards of

with those who went off duty on the Sabbath. ⁹Jehoiada gave the commanders of the groups of 100 men spears and the large and small shields. They had belonged to King David. They were kept in the Temple of God. ¹⁰Then Jehoiada told the men where to stand. Every man had his weapon in his hand. They stood around the king, near the altar and the Temple. They stood from the south side of the Temple to the north side.

[11]Jehoiada and his sons brought out the king's son. And they put the crown on him. They gave him a copy of the law. Then they appointed him king and poured olive oil on him. Then they shouted, "Long live the king!"

[12]Athaliah heard the noise of the people running and praising the king. So she went to them at the Temple of the Lord. [13]She looked and saw the king standing by his pillar at the entrance. The officers and the men who blew trumpets were near him. All the people of the land were happy and blowing trumpets. The singers were playing musical instruments and leading praises. Then Athaliah tore her clothes to show how upset she was. She shouted, "Traitors! Traitors!"

[14]Jehoiada the priest sent out the commanders of 100 men who led the army. He said to them, "Surround her with soldiers and take her out of the Temple area. Kill with a sword anyone who follows her." He had said, "Don't put Athaliah to death in the Temple of the Lord." [15]So they caught her when she came to the entrance of the Horse Gate near the palace. And they put her to death there.

[16]Then Jehoiada made an agreement with the people and the king. They agreed that they would be the Lord's special people. [17]All the people went to the temple of Baal[d] and tore it down. They smashed the altars and idols there. And they killed Mattan the priest of Baal in front of the altars.

[18]Then Jehoiada chose the priests to be responsible for the Temple of the Lord. These priests were Levites. David had given them duties in the Temple of the Lord. They were to offer the burnt offerings to the Lord as the Teachings of Moses commanded. They offered the sacrifices with much joy and singing as David had commanded. [19]Jehoiada put guards at the gates of the Temple of the Lord. Then anyone who was unclean[d] in any way could not enter the Temple.

[20]Jehoiada took with him the commanders of 100 men, the important men, the rulers of the people and all the people of the land. They brought the king down from the Temple of the Lord. They went through the Upper Gate into the palace. Then they seated the king on the throne. [21]All the people of Judah were very happy. And Jerusalem had peace because Athaliah had been put to death with the sword.

Joash Rebuilds the Temple

24 Joash was seven years old when he became king. And he ruled 40 years in Jerusalem. His mother's name was Zibiah. She was from Beersheba. [2]Joash did what the Lord said was right as long as Jehoiada the priest was alive. [3]Jehoiada chose two wives for Joash. And Joash had sons and daughters.

[4]Later, Joash decided to repair the Temple[d] of the Lord. [5]He called the priests and the Levites together. He said to them, "Go to the towns of Judah. Gather the money all the Israelites have to pay every year. Use it to repair the Temple of your God. Do this now." But the Levites did not hurry.

[6]So King Joash called Jehoiada the leading priest. Joash said to him, "Why haven't you made the Levites bring in the tax money from Judah and Jerusalem? Moses the Lord's servant and the people of Israel used that money for the Holy Tent."[d]

[7]In the past the sons of wicked Athaliah had broken into the Temple of God. They had used its holy things for worshiping the Baal[d] idols.

[8]King Joash commanded that a box for contributions be made. It was to be put outside, at the gate of the Temple of the Lord. [9]Then the Levites made an announcement in Judah and Jerusalem. They told the people to bring the tax money to the Lord. Moses the servant of God had made the Israelites give it while they were in the desert. [10]All the officers and people were happy

to give their money. They put it in the box until the box was full. [11]Then the Levites would take the box to the king's officers. They would see that it was full of money. Then the king's royal assistant and the leading priest's officer would come and take out the money. Then they would take the box back to its place. They did this often and gathered much money. [12]King Joash and Jehoiada gave the money to the people who worked on the Temple of the Lord. And they hired stoneworkers and carpenters to repair the Temple of the Lord. They also hired people to work with iron and bronze to repair the Temple.

[13]The people worked hard. And the work to repair the Temple went well. They rebuilt the Temple of God to be as it was before. And they made it stronger. [14]When the workers finished, they brought the money that was left to King Joash and Jehoiada. They used that money to make things for the Temple of the Lord. They made things for the service in the Temple and for the burnt offerings. They also made bowls and other things from gold and silver. Burnt offerings were given every day in the Temple of the Lord while Jehoiada was alive.

[15]Jehoiada grew old. He had lived many years. Then he died when he was 130 years old. [16]Jehoiada was buried in Jerusalem with the kings. He was buried there because he had done much good in Israel for God and his Temple.

Joash Does Evil

[17]After Jehoiada died, the officers of Judah came and bowed down to King Joash. The king listened to them. [18]The king and these leaders stopped worshiping in the Temple[d] of the Lord. He is the God their ancestors obeyed. The king and the officers began to worship the Asherah[d] idols and other idols. Because they did wrong, God was angry with the people of Judah and Jerusalem. [19]The Lord sent prophets[d]

to the people to turn them back to him. The prophets warned them, but the people refused to listen.

[20]Then the Spirit[d] of God entered Zechariah son of Jehoiada the priest. Zechariah stood before the people and said, "This is what God says: 'Why do you disobey the Lord's commands? You will not be successful. You have left the Lord. So the Lord has also left you.'"

[21]But the king and his officers made plans against Zechariah. The king commanded them to kill Zechariah. So they threw stones at him in the Temple courtyard until he died. [22]King Joash did not remember Jehoiada's kindness to him. So Joash killed Zechariah, Jehoiada's son. Before Zechariah died, he said, "May the Lord see what you are doing and punish you."

[23]At the end of the year, the Aramean army came against Joash. They attacked Judah and Jerusalem and killed all the leaders of the people. Then they sent all the valuable things to their king in Damascus. [24]The Aramean army came with only a small group of men. But the Lord let them defeat a very large army from Judah. He did this because the people of Judah had left the Lord. He is the God their ancestors followed. So Joash was punished. [25]When the Arameans left, Joash was badly wounded. His own officers made plans against him. They did this because he had killed Zechariah son of Jehoiada the priest. So they killed Joash in his own bed. He died and was buried in Jerusalem. But he was not buried in the graves of the kings.

[26]The officers who made plans against Joash were Jozabad and Jehozabad. Jozabad was the son of Shimeath, a woman from Ammon. And Jehozabad was the son of Shimrith, a woman from Moab. [27]The story of Joash's sons, the great prophecies[d] against him, and how he rebuilt the Temple of God are written down. They are in the book of the kings. Joash's son Amaziah became king in his place.

Amaziah King of Judah

25 Amaziah was 25 years old when he became king. He ruled for 29 years in Jerusalem. His mother's name was Jehoaddin. She was from Jerusalem. [2]Amaziah did what the Lord said was right. But he did not really want to obey the Lord. [3]Amaziah took strong control of the kingdom. Then he put to death the officers who had murdered his father the king. [4]But Amaziah did not put their children to death. He obeyed what was written in the Book of Moses. There the Lord commanded, "Fathers must not be put to death when their children do wrong. And children must not be put to death when their fathers do wrong. Each person must die for his own sins."[n]

[5]Amaziah gathered the people of Judah together. He grouped all the people of Judah and Benjamin by families. And he put commanders over groups of 1,000 and over groups of 100. He counted the men who were 20 years old and older. In all there were 300,000 soldiers ready to fight. They were skilled with spears and shields. [6]Amaziah also hired 100,000 soldiers from Israel. He paid about 7,500 pounds of silver for them. [7]But a man of God came to Amaziah and said, "My king, don't let the army of Israel go with you. The Lord is not with Israel. He is not with the people from the tribes[d] of Israel. [8]You can make yourself strong for war. But God will defeat you. He has the power to help you or to defeat you."

[9]Amaziah said to the man of God, "But what about the 7,500 pounds of silver I paid to the Israelite army?"

The man of God answered, "The Lord can give you much more than that!"

[10]So Amaziah sent the Israelite army back home to Israel. They were very angry with the people of Judah. And they went home angry.

[11]Then Amaziah became very brave and led his army to the Valley of Salt. It is in the country of Edom. There Amaziah's army killed 10,000 men from Edom. [12]The army of Judah also captured 10,000 men. They took those men to the top of a cliff and threw them off. And they were broken to pieces.

[13]At the same time the Israelite army was robbing some towns in Judah. These were troops that Amaziah had not let fight in the war. They robbed towns from Samaria to Beth Horon. They killed 3,000 people and took many valuable things.

[14]Amaziah came home after he had defeated the Edomites. He brought back the idols they worshiped. And he started to worship them also. He bowed down to them and offered sacrifices to them. [15]The Lord was very angry with Amaziah. The Lord sent a prophet[d] to him. The prophet said, "Why have you asked their gods for help? They could not even save their own people from you!"

[16]As the prophet spoke, Amaziah said to him, "We never gave you the job of advising the king! Stop, or you will be killed."

The prophet stopped speaking. Then he said, "I know that God has decided to destroy you because you have done this. You did not listen to my advice."

[17]Amaziah king of Judah talked with his men who gave him advice. Then he sent a message to Jehoash son of Jehoahaz. (Jehoahaz was the son of Jehu king of Israel.) Amaziah said to Jehoash, "Come, let's meet face to face in battle."

[18]Then Jehoash king of Israel answered Amaziah king of Judah. Jehoash said, "A little thornbush in Lebanon sent a message to a big cedar tree in Lebanon. It said, 'Let your daughter marry my son.' But then a wild animal from Lebanon came by. It walked on and crushed the thornbush. [19]You say to yourself that you have defeated Edom. You are proud, and you brag.

---

[n]"Fathers . . . sins."   See Deuteronomy 24:16.

But you stay at home! Don't ask for trouble by fighting me. If you do, you and Judah will be defeated."

[20]But Amaziah would not listen. God caused this to happen. He planned to let Jehoash of Israel defeat Judah. This was because Judah asked for help from the gods of Edom. [21]So Jehoash king of Israel went to attack. He and Amaziah king of Judah faced each other in battle at Beth Shemesh in Judah. [22]Israel defeated Judah. Every man of Judah ran away to his home. [23]At Beth Shemesh Jehoash king of Israel captured Amaziah king of Judah. (Amaziah was the son of Joash, who was the son of Ahaziah.) Then Jehoash brought him to Jerusalem. Jehoash broke down the wall of Jerusalem from the Gate of Ephraim to the Corner Gate. This part of the wall was about 600 feet long. [24]Then he took all the gold and silver and everything in the Temple[d] of God. Obed-Edom had taken care of these things. Jehoash also took the treasures from the king's palace. Then he took some hostages and returned to Samaria.

[25]Amaziah son of Joash was king of Judah. He lived 15 years after Jehoash king of Israel died. Jehoash was the son of Jehoahaz. [26]The other things Amaziah did as king, from the beginning to the end, are written down. They are in the book of the kings of Judah and Israel. [27]When Amaziah stopped obeying the Lord, the people in Jerusalem made plans against him. So he ran away to the town of Lachish. But they sent men after him to Lachish and killed him there. [28]They brought his body back on horses. And he was buried with his ancestors in Jerusalem.

Uzziah King of Judah

26 Then all the people of Judah chose Uzziah[n] to be king. He became king in place of Amaziah, his father. Uzziah was 16 years old. [2]He rebuilt the town of Elath and made it part of Judah again. He did this after Amaziah died.

[3]Uzziah was 16 years old when he became king. And he ruled 52 years in Jerusalem. His mother's name was Jecoliah, and she was from Jerusalem. [4]He did what the Lord said was right. He obeyed God just as his father Amaziah had done. [5]Uzziah obeyed God while Zechariah was alive. Zechariah taught Uzziah how to respect and obey God. As long as Uzziah obeyed the Lord, God gave him success.

[6]Uzziah fought a war against the Philistine people. He tore down the walls around their towns of Gath, Jabneh and Ashdod. He built new towns near Ashdod and in other places among the Philistines. [7]God helped Uzziah fight the Philistines, the Arabs living in Gur Baal and the Meunites. [8]The Ammonites made payments Uzziah demanded. Uzziah was very powerful. So his name became famous all the way to the border of Egypt.

[9]Uzziah built towers in Jerusalem and made them strong. He built them at the Corner Gate, the Valley Gate and where the wall turned. [10]He also built towers in the desert and dug many wells. He had many cattle on the western mountain slopes and in the plains. He had people who worked his fields and vineyards. They worked in the hills and in the fertile lands. Uzziah loved the land.

[11]He had an army of trained soldiers. They were counted and put in groups by Jeiel the royal assistant and Maaseiah the officer. Hananiah, one of the king's commanders, was their leader. [12]There were 2,600 leaders over the soldiers. [13]They were in charge of an army of 307,500 men. The army fought with great power. And they helped the king against the enemy. [14]Uzziah gave his army shields, spears, helmets, armor, bows and stones for their slings. [15]In Jerusalem Uzziah made devices that were invented by clever

men. These devices were put on the towers and corners of the city walls. They were used to shoot arrows and large rocks. So Uzziah became famous in faraway places. He had much help until he became powerful.

[16] But when Uzziah became strong, his pride caused him to be destroyed. He was unfaithful to the Lord his God. He went into the Temple[d] of the Lord to burn incense[d] on the altar for incense. [17] Azariah and 80 other brave priests who served the Lord followed Uzziah into the Temple. [18] They told Uzziah he was wrong. They said to him, "You don't have the right to burn incense to the Lord. Only the priests, Aaron's descendants,[d] should burn the incense. They have been made holy for the Lord to do this special duty. Leave this holy place. You have been unfaithful to God. The Lord God will not honor you for this."

[19] Uzziah was standing beside the altar for incense in the Temple of the Lord. He had in his hand a pan for burning incense. He was very angry with the priests. As he was standing in front of the priests, a harmful skin disease broke out on his forehead. [20] Azariah the leading priest and all the other priests looked at him. They could see the harmful skin disease on his forehead. So they hurried him out of the Temple. Uzziah rushed out, because the Lord had punished him. [21] So King Uzziah had the skin disease until the day he died. He had to live in a separate house. He could not enter the Temple of the Lord. His son Jotham was in charge of the palace. He governed the people of the land.

[22] The other things Uzziah did as king were written down by the prophet Isaiah. Isaiah son of Amoz wrote about Uzziah's rule from beginning to end. [23] Uzziah died and was buried near his ancestors in a graveyard that belonged to the kings. This was because people said, "He had a harmful skin disease." And his son Jotham became king in his place.

Jotham King of Judah

27 Jotham was 25 years old when he became king. He ruled 16 years in Jerusalem. His mother's name was Jerusha daughter of Zadok. [2] Jotham did what the Lord said was right. He obeyed God just as his father Uzziah had done. But Jotham did not enter the Temple[d] of the Lord to burn incense[d] as his father had. But the people continued doing wrong. [3] Jotham rebuilt the Upper Gate of the Temple of the Lord. He did much building on the wall at the place named Ophel. [4] He also built towns in the hill country of Judah. And he built walled cities and towers in the forests.

[5] Jotham also fought the king of the Ammonite people. And Jotham defeated the Ammonites. So each year for three years they gave Jotham about 7,500 pounds of silver. They also gave him about 62,000 bushels of wheat and about 62,000 bushels of barley. [6] Jotham became powerful because he always obeyed the Lord his God.

[7] The other things Jotham did while he was king and all his wars are written down. They are in the book of the kings of Israel and Judah. [8] Jotham was 25 years old when he became king. And he ruled 16 years in Jerusalem. [9] Jotham died and was buried in Jerusalem. And Jotham's son Ahaz became king in his place.

Ahaz King of Judah

28 Ahaz was 20 years old when he became king. And he ruled 16 years in Jerusalem. He was not like his ancestor David. He did not do what the Lord said was right. [2] Ahaz did the same things the kings of Israel had done. He made metal idols to worship Baal.[d] [3] He burned incense[d] in the Valley of Ben Hinnom. He sacrificed his own sons by burning them in the fire. He did the same terrible sins as the other nations had done. And the Lord had forced these nations out of the land ahead of the Israelites. [4] Ahaz offered sacrifices and burned incense at the places where false gods were worshiped. And he did this on the hills and under every green tree.

⁵So the Lord his God let the king of Aram defeat Ahaz. The Arameans defeated Ahaz and took many people of Judah as prisoners. The Arameans took them to Damascus.

The Lord also let Pekah king of Israel defeat Ahaz. Pekah's army killed many soldiers of Ahaz. ⁶Pekah was the son of Remaliah. Pekah's army killed 120,000 brave soldiers from Judah in one day. Pekah defeated them because they had left the Lord. He is the God their ancestors obeyed. ⁷Zicri was a warrior from Ephraim. He killed King Ahaz's son Maaseiah. He also killed Azrikam, the officer in charge of the palace and Elkanah, second in command to the king. ⁸The Israelite army captured 200,000 of their own relatives. They took women, sons and daughters and many valuable things from Judah. Then they carried them back to Samaria. ⁹But a prophet*d* of the Lord named Oded was there. He met the Israelite army when it returned to Samaria. He said to them, "The Lord is the God your ancestors obeyed. He let you defeat Judah because he was angry with those people. But God has seen the cruel way you killed them. ¹⁰Now you plan to make the people of Judah and Jerusalem your slaves. But you also have sinned against the Lord your God. ¹¹Now listen to me. Send back your brothers and sisters whom you captured. Do this because the Lord is very angry with you."

¹²Then some of the leaders in Israel met the Israelite soldiers coming home from war. These leaders were Azariah son of Jehohanan, Berekiah son of Meshillemoth, Jehizkiah son of Shallum and Amasa son of Hadlai. ¹³They warned the soldiers, "Don't bring the prisoners from Judah here. If you do, we will be guilty of sin. That will make our sin and guilt even worse. And our guilt is already so much that the Lord is angry with Israel."

¹⁴So the soldiers left the prisoners and valuable things in front of the officers and people there. ¹⁵The leaders who were named took the prisoners. These four men got the clothes that the Israelite army had taken. And they gave them to these people who were naked. They gave the prisoners clothes, sandals, food, drink and medicine. They put the weak prisoners on donkeys. Then they took them back to their families in Jericho, the city of palm trees. Then they returned home to Samaria.

¹⁶⁻¹⁷At that same time the Edomites came again. They attacked Judah and carried away prisoners. So King Ahaz asked the king of Assyria for help. ¹⁸The Philistines also robbed the towns in the western mountain slopes and in southern Judah. They captured the towns of Beth Shemesh, Aijalon, Gederoth, Soco, Timnah and Gimzo. They also captured the villages around them. Then the Philistines lived in those towns. ¹⁹The Lord brought trouble on Judah because of Ahaz their king. Ahaz had caused the people of Judah to sin. And he had been unfaithful to the Lord. ²⁰Tiglath-Pileser king of Assyria came to Ahaz. But he gave Ahaz trouble instead of help. ²¹Ahaz took some valuable things from the Temple*d* of the Lord. He also took some from the king's palace and from the princes. Ahaz gave them to the king of Assyria, but it did not help.

²²In Ahaz's troubles he was even more unfaithful to the Lord. ²³He offered sacrifices to the gods the people of Damascus worshiped. These people had defeated him. So he thought, "The gods of the kings of Aram helped them. If I offer sacrifices to them, they will help me also." But this brought ruin to Ahaz and all Israel.

²⁴Ahaz gathered the things from the Temple of God and broke them into pieces. Then he closed the doors of the Temple of the Lord. He made altars and put them on every street corner in Jerusalem. ²⁵In every town in Judah,

Ahaz made places for burning sacrifices to worship other gods. He made the Lord, the God his ancestors worshiped, very angry.

26The other things Ahaz did as king, from the beginning to the end, are written down. They are in the book of the kings of Judah and Israel. 27Ahaz died and was buried in the city of Jerusalem. But he was not buried in the graves of the kings of Israel. Ahaz's son Hezekiah became king in his place.

Hezekiah Purifies the Temple

29 Hezekiah was 25 years old when he became king. And he ruled 29 years in Jerusalem. His mother's name was Abijah daughter of Zechariah. 2Hezekiah did what the Lord said was right. He did just as his ancestor David had done.

3Hezekiah opened the doors of the Temple[d] of the Lord and repaired them. He did this in the first month of the first year he was king. 4Hezekiah brought the priests and Levites together in a group. He met with them in the courtyard on the east side of the Temple. 5Hezekiah said, "Listen to me, Levites! Make yourselves ready for the Lord's service. And make the Temple of the Lord holy. He is the God your ancestors obeyed. Remove from the Temple the things that make it impure. 6Our ancestors were unfaithful to God. They did what the Lord said was wrong. They left the Lord. They stopped worshiping at the Temple where he lives. They rejected him. 7They shut the doors of the porch of the Temple. They let the fire go out in the lamps. They stopped burning incense[d] and offering burnt offerings in the holy place to the God of Israel. 8So the Lord became very angry with the people of Judah and Jerusalem. And he punished them. Other peoples are frightened and shocked by what the Lord did to Judah and Jerusalem. They insult the people of Judah. You know these things are true. 9That is

why our ancestors were killed in battle. That is why our sons, daughters and wives were taken prisoner. 10So now I, Hezekiah, have decided to make an agreement with the Lord, the God of Israel. Then he will not be angry with us anymore. 11My sons, don't waste any more time. The Lord chose you to serve him. You should serve him and burn incense to him."

12These are the Levites who started to work. From the Kohathite family there were Mahath son of Amasai and Joel son of Azariah. From the Merarite family there were Kish son of Abdi and Azariah son of Jehallelel. From the Gershonite family there were Joah son of Zimmah and Eden son of Joah. 13From Elizaphan's family there were Shimri and Jeiel. From Asaph's family there were Zechariah and Mattaniah. 14From Heman's family there were Jehiel and Shimei. From Jeduthun's family there were Shemaiah and Uzziel.

15These Levites gathered their brothers together. Then they made themselves holy for service in the Temple. They obeyed the king's command that had come from the Lord. They went into the Temple of the Lord to purify it. 16The priests went into the Temple of the Lord to purify it. They took out all the unclean[d] things they found in the Temple of the Lord. And they put them in the Temple courtyard. Then the Levites took these things out to the Kidron Valley. 17They made the Temple holy for the Lord's service. They began on the first day of the first month. On the eighth day of the month, they came to the porch of the Temple. For eight more days they made the Temple of the Lord holy. They finished on the sixteenth day of the first month.

18Then they went to King Hezekiah. They said to him, "We have purified all the Temple of the Lord. We have purified the altar for burnt offerings and its things. We have purified the table for the holy bread and all its things.

¹⁹When Ahaz was king, he was unfaithful to God. He removed some things from the Temple. But we have put them back and made them holy for the Lord. They are now in front of the Lord's altar."

²⁰Early the next morning King Hezekiah gathered the leaders of the city. They went up to the Temple of the Lord. ²¹They brought seven bulls, seven male sheep, seven male lambs and seven male goats. These animals were an offering to remove the sin of the people and the kingdom of Judah. And this offering made the Temple ready for service to God. King Hezekiah commanded the priests to offer these animals on the Lord's altar. The priests were from the family of Aaron. ²²So the priests killed the bulls. Then they sprinkled the bulls' blood on the altar. They killed the male sheep and sprinkled their blood on the altar. Then they killed the lambs. And they sprinkled the lambs' blood on the altar. ²³Then the priests brought the male goats before the king and the people there. The goats were for the sin offering. The king and the people put their hands on the goats. ²⁴Then the priests killed the goats. They made a sin offering with the goats' blood on the altar. They did this to remove the sins of the Israelites so they would belong to the Lord. The king had said that the burnt offering and sin offering should be made for all Israel.

²⁵King Hezekiah put the Levites in the Temple of the Lord with cymbals, harps and lyres.ᵈ He did this as David, Gad and Nathan had commanded. (Gad was the king's seer,ᵈ and Nathan was a prophet.ᵈ) This command came from the Lord through his prophets. ²⁶So the Levites stood ready with David's instruments of music. And the priests stood ready with their trumpets. ²⁷Then Hezekiah gave the order to sacrifice the burnt offering on the altar. When the burnt offering began, the singing to the Lord also began. The trumpets were blown. And the musical instruments of David king of Israel were played. ²⁸All the people worshiped, the singers sang, and the trumpet players blew their trumpets. They did this until the burnt offering was finished.

²⁹When the sacrifices were finished, King Hezekiah and everyone with him bowed down and worshiped. ³⁰King Hezekiah and his officers ordered the Levites to praise the Lord. They were to use the words David and Asaph the seer used. They praised God with joy. And they bowed down and worshiped.

³¹Then Hezekiah said, "Now you people of Judah have given yourselves to the Lord. Come near to the Temple of the Lord. Bring sacrifices and offerings to show thanks to the Lord." So the people brought sacrifices and offerings to show thanks to the Lord. Anyone who wanted to also brought burnt offerings. ³²For burnt offerings they brought a total of 70 bulls, 100 male sheep and 200 lambs. All these animals were sacrificed as burnt offerings to the Lord. ³³The offerings made holy for the Lord totaled 600 bulls and 3,000 sheep and goats. ³⁴There were not enough priests to skin all the animals for the burnt offerings. So their relatives the Levites helped them. They helped until the work was finished and other priests could be made holy for the Lord's service. The Levites had been more careful to make themselves holy for the Lord's service than the priests. ³⁵There were many burnt offerings. With them were the fat of fellowship offerings and drink offerings. So the service in the Temple of the Lord began again. ³⁶And Hezekiah and the people were very happy. They were happy that God had made it happen so quickly for his people.

Hezekiah Celebrates the Passover

30 King Hezekiah sent messages to all the people of Israel and Judah. He also wrote letters to the people of Ephraim and Manasseh. Hezekiah invited all these people to come to the Temple[d] of the Lord in Jerusalem. There they could celebrate the Passover[d] for the Lord, the God of Israel. [2]King Hezekiah, his officers and all the people in Jerusalem agreed to celebrate the Passover in the second month. [3]They could not celebrate it at the normal time. This was because not enough priests had made themselves ready to serve the Lord. And the people had not gathered yet in Jerusalem. [4]This plan satisfied King Hezekiah and all the people. [5]So they made an announcement everywhere in Israel, from Beersheba to Dan.[n] They told the people to come to Jerusalem. There they would celebrate the Passover for the Lord, the God of Israel. For a long time most of the people had not celebrated the Passover as the law commanded. [6]So the messengers took letters from the king and his officers all through Israel and Judah. This is what the letters said:

People of Israel, come back to obeying the Lord. He is the God that Abraham, Isaac and Israel obeyed. Then God will come back to you who are still alive. You have escaped from the kings of Assyria. [7]Don't be like your ancestors or your relatives. They turned against the Lord, the God their fathers obeyed. So the Lord caused other people to be disgusted with them. You know this is true. [8]Don't be stubborn as your ancestors were. Obey the Lord willingly. Come to the Temple, which the Lord has made holy for his service forever. Serve the Lord your God. Then he will not be angry with you. [9]Come back and obey the Lord. Then the people who captured your relatives and children will be kind to them. They will let them return to this land. The Lord your God is kind and merciful. He will not turn away from you if you come back to him.

[10]The messengers went to every town in Ephraim and Manasseh. They went all the way to Zebulun. But the people laughed at the messengers and made fun of them. [11]But some men from Asher, Manasseh and Zebulun were sorry for what they had done and went to Jerusalem. [12]And God caused all the people of Judah to agree to obey King Hezekiah and his officers. Their command had come from the Lord.

[13]A large crowd came together in Jerusalem to celebrate the Feast[d] of Unleavened Bread. This was in the second month. [14]The people removed the altars and incense[d] altars to false gods in Jerusalem. And they threw them into the Kidron Valley.

[15]They killed the Passover lamb on the fourteenth day of the second month. The priests and the Levites were ashamed. So they made themselves holy for the Lord. They brought burnt offerings into the Temple of the Lord. [16]They took their regular places in the Temple as the Teachings of Moses the man of God commanded. The Levites gave the blood of the sacrifices to the priests. Then the priests sprinkled the blood on the altar. [17]Many people in the crowd had not made themselves holy for the Lord. So they were not permitted to kill the Passover lambs. So the Levites were responsible for killing the Passover lambs for everyone who was not clean.[d] The Levites made each lamb holy for the Lord. [18-19]Many people from Ephraim, Manasseh, Issachar and Zebulun had not purified themselves for the feast. But they ate the Passover even though it was against the law. So Hezekiah prayed for them. He said, "Lord, you are good. You are the Lord, the God our ancestors obeyed. Please forgive everyone who tries to obey you. Forgive them even if they did not make themselves clean as the rules of the Temple command." [20]The Lord listened to Hezekiah's

prayer, and he healed the people. [21]The Israelites in Jerusalem celebrated the Feast of Unleavened Bread for seven days. And they were very happy. The Levites and priests praised the Lord every day with loud music. [22]Some of the Levites understood well how to do their service for the Lord. And Hezekiah encouraged them. The people ate the feast for seven days. And they offered fellowship offerings. They praised the Lord, the God their ancestors worshiped.

[23]Then all the people agreed to stay seven more days. So they celebrated the Passover with joy for seven more days. [24]Hezekiah king of Judah gave 1,000 bulls and 7,000 sheep to the people. The officers gave 1,000 bulls and 10,000 sheep to the people. Many priests made themselves holy for the Lord. [25]All the people of Judah, the priests, the Levites, those who came from Israel, the foreigners from Israel and the foreigners living in Judah were very happy. [26]There was much joy in Jerusalem. There had not been a celebration like this since Solomon's time. He was the son of David and king of Israel. [27]The priests and Levites stood up and blessed the people. And God heard them because their prayer reached heaven, which is his holy home.

The Collection for the Priests

31 The Passover[d] celebration was finished. All the Israelites in Jerusalem went out to the towns of Judah. There they smashed the stone pillars used to worship false gods. They cut down the Asherah[d] idols. They destroyed the altars and places for worshiping false gods. They destroyed all of them in the areas of Judah, Benjamin, Ephraim and Manasseh. They destroyed everything used for worshiping the false gods. Then all the Israelites returned to their own towns and homes.

[2]King Hezekiah appointed groups of priests and Levites for their special duties. They were to offer burnt offerings and fellowship offerings. They were to worship and to give thanks and praise at the gates where the Lord lives. [3]Hezekiah gave some of his own animals for the burnt offerings. Burnt offerings were given every morning and evening. They were also given on Sabbath[d] days and during New Moons[d] and other feasts commanded by the Lord's Teachings.

[4]Hezekiah commanded the people living in Jerusalem to give the priests and Levites the portion that belonged to them. Then the priests and Levites could give all their time to the Lord's Teachings. [5]Soon the king's command went out to the Israelites. And they gave quickly and freely. They gave the first portion of their grain, wine, oil and honey. They gave the first portion of everything they grew in their fields. They brought a large amount, one-tenth of everything. [6]The men of Israel and Judah who lived in Judah also gave. They brought one-tenth of their cattle and sheep. And they brought one-tenth of the holy things that were given to the Lord their God. They put all these things in piles. [7]The people began bringing their things in the third month. And they finished in the seventh month. [8]Hezekiah and his officers came and saw the piles. Then they praised the Lord and his people, the people of Israel. [9]Hezekiah asked the priests and Levites about the piles. [10]Azariah was the leading priest from Zadok's family. He answered Hezekiah, "Since the people began to bring their offerings to the Temple[d] of the Lord, we have had plenty to eat. We have had plenty left over. The Lord has blessed his people. So we have all this left over."

[11]Then Hezekiah commanded the priests to prepare the storerooms in the Temple of the Lord. So this was done. [12]Then the priests brought the offerings and the things given to the Lord. They also brought the tenth of everything the people had given. All these things were put in the storerooms.

Conaniah the Levite was in charge of these things. Conaniah's brother Shimei was second to him. ¹³Conaniah and his brother Shimei were over these supervisors: Jehiel, Azaziah, Nahath, Asahel, Jerimoth, Jozabad, Eliel, Ismakiah, Mahath and Benaiah. King Hezekiah and Azariah the officer in charge of the Temple of God chose those men.

the Lord for their daily service. Each group had its own responsibilities. ¹⁷The priests were given their part of the collection. This was done by families, as listed in the family histories. The Levites 20 years old and older were given their part of the collection. This was done by their responsibilities and by their groups. ¹⁸The Levites' babies, wives, sons and daughters also got part of the collection. This was done for all the Levites who were listed in the family histories. This was

Good Kings and Bad Kings
HEZEKIAH • 2 CHRONICLES 31:20-21

Hezekiah served God well as king of Judah, the southern kingdom. Hezekiah's father, Ahaz, had not been a good king. In fact, he had been very evil and had led the people of his nation into worshiping idols instead of God. He even closed up the temple (where the people worshiped God) so that no one could worship there! But when Hezekiah became king, he opened up the temple and repaired it so that all the people could come and worship God again. Even though his father had been a bad example, Hezekiah was a good king who pleased God.

If your mom and dad don't believe in Jesus or if they don't always do good things, you can still follow Jesus. He can use you to do great things for him!

To meet the most evil king of the southern kingdom, fly to page 556.

¹⁴Kore was in charge of the special gifts the people wanted to give to God. He was responsible for giving out the contributions made to the Lord and the holy gifts. Kore was the son of Imnah the Levite. Kore was the guard at the East Gate. ¹⁵Eden, Miniamin, Jeshua, Shemaiah, Amariah and Shecaniah helped Kore. They served well in the towns where the priests lived. They gave from what was collected to the other groups of priests. They gave both to the young and the old.

¹⁶These men also gave from what was collected to the males 3 years old and older. These were males who had their names in the Levite family histories. They were to enter the Temple of

because the Levites always kept themselves ready to serve the Lord.

¹⁹Some of Aaron's descendants,ᵈ the priests, lived on the farmland near the towns. Some also lived in the towns. Men were chosen by name to give part of the collection to these priests. All the males and those named in the family histories of the Levites received part of the collection.

²⁰This is what King Hezekiah did in Judah. He did what was good and right and obedient before the Lord his God. ²¹Hezekiah tried to obey God in his service of the Temple of God. He tried to obey God's teachings and commands. He gave himself fully to his work for God. So he had success.

Assyria Troubles Hezekiah

32 Hezekiah did all these things to serve the Lord. Sennacherib king of Assyria came to attack Judah. He and his army surrounded and attacked the strong, walled cities. He wanted to take them for himself. ²Hezekiah knew that Sennacherib had come to Jerusalem to attack it. ³So Hezekiah talked to his officers and army commanders. They decided to cut off the waters from the springs outside the city. So the officers and commanders helped Hezekiah. ⁴Many people came to help. They cut off all the springs and the stream that flowed through the land. They said, "The king of Assyria will not find much water when he comes here." ⁵Then Hezekiah made Jerusalem stronger. He rebuilt all the broken parts of the wall. And he built towers on the wall. He also built another wall outside the first one. And he made the area that was filled in on the east side of the old part of Jerusalem stronger. He made many weapons and shields.

⁶Hezekiah put army commanders over the people. He met with these commanders at the open place near the city gate. Hezekiah encouraged them, saying, ⁷"Be strong and brave. Don't be afraid or worried because of the king of Assyria or his large army. There is a greater power with us than with him. ⁸He only has men, but we have the Lord our God. He will help us. He will fight our battles." The people were encouraged by the words of Hezekiah king of Judah.

⁹King Sennacherib of Assyria and all his army surrounded and attacked Lachish. Then he sent his officers to Jerusalem with a message. The message was for King Hezekiah of Judah and all the people of Judah in Jerusalem. This was the message:

¹⁰Sennacherib king of Assyria says this: "You have nothing to trust in to help you. It is no use for you to stay in Jerusalem under attack. ¹¹Hezekiah says to you, 'The Lord our God will save us from the king of Assyria.' But he is fooling you. If you stay in Jerusalem, you will die from hunger and thirst. ¹²Hezekiah himself removed your Lord's places of worship and altars. He told you people of Judah and Jerusalem that you must worship and burn incense*d* on only one altar.

¹³"You know what my ancestors and I have done to all the people in other nations. The gods of those nations could not save their people from my power. ¹⁴My ancestors destroyed those nations. None of their gods could save them from me. So your god cannot save you from my power. ¹⁵Do not let Hezekiah fool you or trick you. Do not believe him. No god of any nation or kingdom has been able to save his people from me or my ancestors. Your god is even less able to save you from me."

¹⁶Sennacherib's officers said worse things against the Lord God and his servant Hezekiah. ¹⁷King Sennacherib also wrote letters insulting the Lord, the God of Israel. This is what his letters said: "The gods of the other nations could not save their people from me. In the same way Hezekiah's god won't be able to save his people from me." ¹⁸Then the king's officers shouted out in Hebrew. They called out to the people of Jerusalem who were on the city wall. The officers wanted to scare the people away so they could capture Jerusalem. ¹⁹They said evil things about the gods the people of the world worshiped. They are only things people have made with their hands. In the same way the officers said evil things about the God of Jerusalem.

²⁰King Hezekiah and the prophet*d* Isaiah son of Amoz prayed to heaven about this. ²¹Then the Lord sent an angel to the king of Assyria's camp. That angel killed all the soldiers, lead-

ers and officers of the Assyrian army. So the king of Assyria returned to his own country in disgrace. He went into the temple of his god. There some of his own sons killed him with a sword.

²²So the Lord saved Hezekiah and the people in Jerusalem. He saved them from Sennacherib king of Assyria and from all other people. The Lord took care of Hezekiah and the people of Jerusalem. ²³Many people brought gifts for the Lord to Jerusalem. They also brought valuable gifts to King Hezekiah of Judah. From then on all the nations respected Hezekiah.

stopped being proud. So the Lord did not punish them while Hezekiah was alive.

²⁷Hezekiah had many riches and much honor. He made treasuries for his silver, gold, gems, spices, shields and other valuable things. ²⁸Hezekiah built storage buildings for grain, new wine and oil. He built stalls for all the cattle and pens for the sheep. ²⁹He also built many towns. He had many flocks of sheep and herds of cattle. God gave Hezekiah much wealth.

Humility
2 CHRONICLES 32:24-26

Throughout the Bible, we meet people who are called *proud* or *humble.* Proud people think they are great and take all the credit. Humble people give the credit to God. God doesn't like a proud attitude. He wants us to have a humble attitude.

King Hezekiah was very sick and was dying. He asked God to let him live, and God did. But Hezekiah was *proud,* and he did not thank God for making him well. So God became angry with Hezekiah and with the people, and he let them know it. When Hezekiah realized that his pride was causing big problems, he *humbled* himself. Because he did this, God was no longer angry.

Whenever you have a choice between taking credit for something or giving that credit to God, remember: he rewards those who are humble and punishes those who are proud. Always give *God* the credit, and let him give *you* his blessing.

To learn more about humility, zoom to page 648.

Hezekiah Dies

²⁴At that time Hezekiah became very sick. He was almost dead. He prayed to the Lord. And the Lord spoke to him and gave him a sign.ⁿ ²⁵But Hezekiah was proud. So he did not thank God for his kindness. So the Lord was angry with him and the people of Judah and Jerusalem. ²⁶But later Hezekiah and the people of Jerusalem were sorry and

³⁰It was Hezekiah who cut off the upper pool of the Gihon spring. He made those waters flow straight down on the west side of the older part of Jerusalem. And Hezekiah was successful in everything he did. ³¹But one time the leaders of Babylon sent messengers to Hezekiah. They asked him about a strange signⁿ that had happened in the land. When they came,

ⁿ**sign** See Isaiah 38:1-8. It tells the story about the sign and how the Lord gave Hezekiah 15 more years to live.

God left Hezekiah alone to test him. He wanted to know everything that was in Hezekiah's heart.[n]

[32] Hezekiah's love for the Lord and the other things he did as king are recorded. They are written in the vision of the prophet[d] Isaiah son of Amoz. This is in the book of the kings of Judah and Israel. [33] Hezekiah died and was buried on a hill. It is where the graves of David's ancestors are. All the people of Judah and Jerusalem honored Hezekiah when he died. And Hezekiah's son Manasseh became king in his place.

Manasseh also built altars for the Baal[d] gods and made Asherah[d] idols. He bowed down to the stars and worshiped them. [4] The Lord had said about the Temple,[d] "I will be worshiped in Jerusalem forever." But Manasseh built altars for false gods in the Temple of the Lord. [5] He built altars to worship the stars in the two courtyards of the Temple of the Lord. [6] He burned his sons as sacrifices in the Valley of Ben Hinnom. He practiced magic and witchcraft.[d] He told the future by explaining signs and dreams. He got advice from mediums[d] and fortune-tellers. He did many things the Lord said were wrong. And this made the Lord angry.

Good Kings and Bad Kings
MANASSEH • 2 CHRONICLES 33:12-13

Manasseh became king when he was only twelve years old. His father was Hezekiah, a good king who had helped the people worship God. But Manasseh was very bad. He worshiped idols and even put an idol inside God's temple. This made God angry because Manasseh led all the people to do bad things too. So God punished him. Manasseh became sorry for all his sins and asked God to forgive him. God did forgive him. Manasseh took the idol out of the temple and worshiped God.

If you have done bad things, God wants to forgive you. Just tell him you're sorry and stop doing those bad things.

To meet a good king who repented of his sins, fly to page 676.

Manasseh King of Judah

33 Manasseh was 12 years old when he became king of Judah. And he was king for 55 years in Jerusalem. [2] He did what the Lord said was wrong. He did the hated things the other nations had done. And the Lord had forced these nations out of the land ahead of Israel. [3] Manasseh's father, Hezekiah, had torn down the places where false gods were worshiped. But Manasseh rebuilt them.

[7] He carved an idol and put it in the Temple of God. God had spoken to David and his son Solomon about the Temple. He had said, "I will be worshiped in this Temple and in Jerusalem forever. I have chosen Jerusalem from all the tribes[d] of Israel. [8] I will never again make the Israelites leave the land I gave to their ancestors. But they must obey everything I commanded them. They must obey all the teachings, rules and commands I gave them through Moses." [9] But Manasseh

[n] **God . . . heart**   See 2 Kings 20:12-19.

led the people of Judah and Jerusalem to do wrong. They did more evil than the nations the Lord had destroyed ahead of the Israelites.

[10]The Lord spoke to Manasseh and his people, but they did not listen. [11]So the Lord brought the king of Assyria's army commanders to attack Judah. They captured Manasseh and put hooks in him. They put bronze chains on his hands. They made him their prisoner and took him to Babylon. [12]As Manasseh suffered, he begged the Lord his God for help. He became very sorry for what he had done before the God of his ancestors. [13]When Manasseh prayed, the Lord heard him and had pity for him. So the Lord let him return to Jerusalem and to his kingdom. Then Manasseh knew that the Lord is the true God.

[14]After that happened, Manasseh rebuilt the outer wall for Jerusalem. It was in the valley on the west side of the Gihon spring. It went to the entrance of the Fish Gate and around the hill of Ophel. He also made the wall higher. Then he put commanders in all the strong, walled cities in Judah.

[15]Manasseh removed the idols of other nations. And he took the idol out of the Temple of the Lord. He removed all the altars he had built on the Temple hill and in Jerusalem. And he threw them out of the city. [16]Then he set up the Lord's altar. And he sacrificed on it fellowship offerings and offerings to show thanks to the Lord. Manasseh commanded all the people of Judah to serve the Lord, the God of Israel. [17]The people continued to offer sacrifices at the places of worship. But their sacrifices were only to the Lord their God. [18]The other things Manasseh did as king are written down. His prayer to his God is recorded. And what the seers[d] said to him in the name of the Lord, the God of Israel, is recorded. They are all in the book of the history of the kings of Israel. [19]Manasseh's prayer and God's pity for him are written down. Also all of Manasseh's sins

and how he was unfaithful to the Lord are recorded. The places he built for worshiping false gods and for the Asherah[d] idols are recorded. He did all these things but later became sorry for them. They are all in the book of the seers. [20]Manasseh died and was buried in his palace. Then Manasseh's son Amon became king in his place.

Amon King of Judah

[21]Amon was 22 years old when he became king. And he was king for two years in Jerusalem. [22]He did what the Lord said was wrong. He did as his father Manasseh had done. Amon worshiped and offered sacrifices to all the carved idols Manasseh had made. [23]Amon was not sorry for what he did wrong before the Lord. He was not sorry as his father Manasseh had been. Instead, Amon sinned even more.

[24]Amon's officers made plans against him and killed him in his palace. [25]But the people of Judah killed all those who had made plans to kill King Amon. And they made his son Josiah to be king in his place.

Josiah King of Judah

34 Josiah was eight years old when he became king. He ruled 31 years in Jerusalem. [2]He did what the Lord said was right. He did good things as his ancestor David had done. Josiah did not stop doing what was right.

[3]In his eighth year as king, Josiah began to obey the God his ancestor David had followed. This was while Josiah was still young. In his twelfth year as king, Josiah began to remove the false gods from Judah and Jerusalem. He destroyed the places for worshiping false gods. He removed the Asherah[d] idols and the wooden and metal idols. [4]The people tore down the altars for the Baal[d] gods as Josiah directed. Then Josiah cut down the incense[d] altars that were above them. He broke up the Asherah idols and the wooden and metal idols. He beat them into powder. Then he sprin-

kled the powder on the graves of the people who had offered sacrifices to these gods. [5]He burned the bones of their priests on their own altars. So Josiah removed idol worship from Judah and Jerusalem. [6]He did the same for the towns in the areas of Manasseh, Ephraim and Simeon. He did this all the way to Naphtali. And he did the same for the ruins near these towns. [7]Josiah broke down the altars and Asherah idols. Then he beat the idols into powder. He cut down all the incense altars in all of Israel. Then he went back to Jerusalem.

people of Judah, Benjamin and Jerusalem. [10]Then the Levites gave it to the men who directed the work on the Temple of the Lord. And these supervisors paid the workers that rebuilt and repaired the Temple. [11]They gave money to carpenters and builders to buy cut rocks and wood. The wood was used to rebuild the buildings and to make beams for them. The kings of Judah had let the buildings become ruins. [12]The men did their work well. Their supervisors were Jahath, Oba-

The Bible
2 CHRONICLES 34:14-21

Many families have a Bible. It sits in a bookcase, or maybe on a mantle above a fireplace. It looks important, with its heavy black cover and gold-edged pages. But in many homes, it also has a layer of dust on it, which makes it look plain and ordinary. The dust also shows that no one has read it for a while. But a Bible that isn't read doesn't do any good.

The people of Judah had done something like that. They had ignored the word of God for so long that they had actually lost it and didn't know where it was. These verses tell what happened when they found it and read it again after all those years. It was a sad day for King Josiah and the people because they realized that they had not been obeying God's laws.

Don't make that mistake! Blow the dust off that Bible, *read* it, *study* it, and *obey* it.

To learn more about the Bible, zoom to page 725.

[8]In Josiah's eighteenth year as king, he made Judah and the Temple[d] pure again. He sent Shaphan son of Azaliah, Maaseiah the city leader and Joah son of Joahaz the recorder. They were to repair the Temple of the Lord, the God of Josiah. [9]These men went to Hilkiah the high priest. They gave him the money the people had given for the Temple of God. The Levite doorkeepers had collected this money from the people of Manasseh, Ephraim and all the Israelites who were left alive. They also collected this money from all the

diah, Zechariah and Meshullam. Jahath and Obadiah were Levites from the family of Merari. Zechariah and Meshullam were from the family of Kohath. These Levites were all skilled musicians. [13]They were in charge of the workers who carried things and all the other workers. Some Levites worked as secretaries, officers and doorkeepers.

The Law Is Found

[14]The Levites brought out the money that was in the Temple[d] of the Lord. As they were doing this, Hilkiah the

priest found the Book of the Lord's Teachings. These teachings had been given through Moses. [15]Hilkiah said to Shaphan the royal assistant, "I've found the Book of the Teachings. It was in the Temple of the Lord!" He gave it to Shaphan.

[16]Then Shaphan took the book to the king and reported to Josiah: "Your officers are doing everything you told them to do. [17]They have paid out the money that was in the Temple of the Lord. They have given it to the supervisors and the workers." [18]Then Shaphan the royal assistant told the king, "Hilkiah the priest has given me a book." And Shaphan read from the book to the king.

[19]The king heard the words of the Teachings. Then he tore his clothes to show how upset he was. [20]He gave these orders to Hilkiah, Ahikam son of Shaphan. He also gave them to Acbor son of Micaiah, Shaphan and Asaiah. Shaphan was the royal assistant. And Asaiah was the king's servant. These were the orders: [21]"Go and ask the Lord about the words in the book that was found. Ask for me and for the people who are left alive in Israel and Judah. The Lord is very angry with us because our ancestors did not obey the Lord's word. They did not do everything this book says to do."

[22]So Hilkiah and those the king sent with him left. They went to talk to Huldah the prophetess.[d] She was the wife of Shallum son of Tikvah, the son of Harhas. Harhas took care of the king's clothes. Huldah lived in Jerusalem, in the new area of the city. [23]She said to them, "This is what the Lord, the God of Israel, says: Tell the man who sent you to me, [24]'This is what the Lord says: I will bring trouble to this place and to the people living here. I will bring all the curses that are written in the book that was read to the king of Judah. [25]The people of Judah have left me. They have burned incense[d] to other gods. They have made me angry by all the bad things they have made.

So I will punish them in my anger. My anger will not be stopped.' [26]Tell the king of Judah who sent you to ask the Lord, 'This is what the Lord, the God of Israel, says about the words you heard: [27]You heard my words against this place and its people. And you became sorry for what you had done. You became sorry in my presence. You tore your clothes to show how upset you were. And you cried in my presence. This is why I have heard you, says the Lord. [28]So I will let you die. You will be buried in peace. You won't see all the trouble that I will bring to this place and the people living here.'"

So they took her message back to the king.

[29]Then the king gathered all the older leaders of Judah and Jerusalem together. [30]He went up to the Temple of the Lord. All the men from Judah and the people from Jerusalem went with him. The priests and the Levites and all the people—from the most important to the least important—went with him. He read to them all the words in the Book of the Agreement. That book was found in the Temple of the Lord. [31]Then the king stood by his pillar. He made an agreement in the presence of the Lord. He agreed to follow the Lord and to obey his commands, rules and laws with his whole being. And he agreed to obey the words of the agreement written in this book. [32]Then Josiah made all the people in Jerusalem and Benjamin promise to accept the agreement. The people of Jerusalem obeyed the agreement of God, the God their ancestors obeyed.

[33]And Josiah threw out the hated idols from all the land that belonged to the Israelites. He led everyone in Israel to serve the Lord their God. While Josiah lived, the people obeyed the Lord, the God their ancestors obeyed.

Josiah Celebrates the Passover

35 King Josiah celebrated the Passover[d] to the Lord in Jerusalem. The Passover lamb was killed on the fourteenth day of the first month. [2]Josiah chose the priests to do their duties. And he encouraged them as they served in the Temple[d] of the Lord. [3]The Levites taught the Israelites and were made holy for service to the Lord. Josiah said to them: "When David's son Solomon was king of Israel, he built the Temple. Put the Holy Box[d] in that Temple. Do not carry it from place to place on your shoulders anymore. Now serve the Lord your God and his people the Israelites. [4]Prepare yourselves by your family groups for service. Do the jobs that King David and his son Solomon gave you to do.

[5]"Stand in the holy place with a group of the Levites. Do this for each family group of the people so you may help them. [6]Kill the Passover lambs. Make yourselves holy to the Lord. And prepare the lambs for your relatives, the people of Israel. Do everything the Lord through Moses commanded us to do."

[7]Josiah gave the Israelites 30,000 sheep and goats to kill for the Passover sacrifices. He also gave them 3,000 cattle. They were all King Josiah's own animals.

[8]Josiah's officers also gave willingly to the people, the priests and the Levites. Hilkiah, Zechariah and Jehiel were the officers in charge of the Temple. They gave the priests 2,600 lambs and goats and 300 cattle for Passover sacrifices. [9]Also Conaniah, his brothers Shemaiah and Nethanel, and Hashabiah, Jeiel and Jozabad gave the Levites animals. They gave 5,000 sheep and goats and 500 cattle for Passover sacrifices. These men were leaders of the Levites.

[10]When everything was ready for the Passover service, the priests and Levites went to their places. This is what the king had commanded. [11]The Passover lambs were killed. Then the Levites skinned the animals and gave the blood to the priests. The priests sprinkled the blood on the altar. [12]Then they gave the animals for the burnt offerings to the different family groups. This was done so the burnt offerings could be offered to the Lord as the Law of Moses taught. They also did this with the cattle. [13]The Levites roasted the Passover sacrifices over the fire as they were commanded. And they boiled the holy offerings in pots, kettles and pans. Then they quickly gave the meat to the people. [14]After this was finished, the Levites prepared meat for themselves and for the priests. The priests were the descendants[d] of Aaron. The priests worked until night, offering the burnt offerings and burning the fat of the sacrifices.

[15]The Levite singers were from Asaph's family. They stood in the places King David had chosen for them. They were Asaph, Heman and Jeduthun, the king's seer.[d] The gatekeepers at each gate did not have to leave their places. This was because their fellow Levites had prepared everything for them for the Passover.

[16]So everything was done that day for the worship of the Lord. And it was done as King Josiah commanded. The Passover was celebrated, and the burnt offerings were offered on the Lord's altar. [17]The Israelites who were there celebrated the Passover and the Feast[d] of Unleavened Bread for seven days. [18]The Passover had not been celebrated like this in Israel since the prophet[d] Samuel was alive. None of the kings of Israel had ever celebrated a Passover like this. King Josiah, the priests and the Levites celebrated it. And the people of Judah and Israel who were there with the people of Jerusalem celebrated it. [19]This Passover was celebrated in the eighteenth year Josiah was king.

The Death of Josiah

[20]So Josiah did all this for the Temple.[d] After this, King Neco of Egypt led an army to attack Carchemish. It was a town on the Euphrates River. And Josiah marched out to fight against Neco. [21]But Neco sent messengers to Josiah. They said, "King Josiah, there

should not be war between us. I did not come to fight you, but my enemies. God told me to hurry, and he is on my side. So don't fight God, or he will destroy you."

²²But Josiah did not go away. He wore different clothes so no one would know who he was. He refused to listen to what Neco said at God's command. So Josiah went to fight on the plain of Megiddo. ²³In the battle King Josiah was shot by arrows. He told his servants, "Take me away. I am badly wounded." ²⁴So they took him out of his chariot. And they put him in another chariot he had brought to the battle. Then they took him to Jerusalem where he died. He was buried in the graves where his ancestors were buried. All the people of Judah and Jerusalem were very sad because he was dead.

²⁵Jeremiah wrote some sad songs about Josiah. Even to this day all the men and women singers remember and honor Josiah with these songs. It became a custom in Israel to sing these songs. They are written in the collection of sad songs.

²⁶⁻²⁷The other things Josiah did as king, from the beginning to the end, are written down. They are in the book of the kings of Israel and Judah. It tells how he loved the Lord and obeyed the Lord's teachings.

Jehoahaz King of Judah

36 The people of Judah chose Josiah's son Jehoahaz. They made him king in Jerusalem in his father's place.

²Jehoahaz was 23 years old when he became king. And he was king in Jerusalem for three months. ³Then King Neco of Egypt made Jehoahaz no longer a king in Jerusalem. Neco made the people of Judah pay about 7,500 pounds of silver and about 75 pounds of gold. ⁴The king of Egypt made Jehoahaz's brother Eliakim the king of Judah and Jerusalem. Then Neco changed Eliakim's name to Jehoiakim.

But Neco took Eliakim's brother Jehoahaz to Egypt.

Jehoiakim King of Judah

⁵Jehoiakim was 25 years old when he became king. And he was king in Jerusalem for 11 years. He did what the Lord his God said was wrong. ⁶King Nebuchadnezzar of Babylon attacked Judah. He captured Jehoiakim and put bronze chains on him. Then Nebuchadnezzar took him to Babylon. ⁷Nebuchadnezzar took some of the things from the Temple[d] of the Lord. And he took them to Babylon and put them in his own palace.

⁸The other things Jehoiakim did as king are written down. The hated things he did and everything he was guilty of doing are recorded. They are in the book of the kings of Israel and Judah. Jehoiakim's son Jehoiachin became king in his place.

Jehoiachin King of Judah

⁹Jehoiachin was 18 years old when he became king of Judah. And he was king in Jerusalem for three months and ten days. He did what the Lord said was wrong. ¹⁰In the spring King Nebuchadnezzar sent some servants to get Jehoiachin. They took him and some valuable treasures from the Temple[d] of the Lord to Babylon. Then Nebuchadnezzar made Jehoiachin's relative Zedekiah the king of Judah and Jerusalem.

Zedekiah King of Judah

¹¹Zedekiah was 21 years old when he became king of Judah. And he was king in Jerusalem for 11 years. ¹²Zedekiah did what the Lord his God said was wrong. The prophet[d] Jeremiah spoke messages from the Lord. But Zedekiah did not obey.

Jerusalem Is Destroyed

¹³Zedekiah turned against King Nebuchadnezzar. Nebuchadnezzar had forced Zedekiah to promise to be loyal to him. And Zedekiah had promised,

using God's name. But Zedekiah became stubborn. He refused to obey the Lord, the God of Israel. [14]Also, all the leaders of the priests and the people of Judah became more wicked. They followed the evil example of the other nations. The Lord had made the Temple[d] in Jerusalem holy. But the leaders made the Temple unholy.

The Fall of Jerusalem

[15]The Lord, the God of their ancestors, sent prophets[d] again and again to warn his people. He did this because he had pity for them and for his Temple. [16]But they made fun of God's prophets. They hated God's messages. So they refused to listen to the prophets. Finally God became so angry with his people that he could not be stopped. [17]So God brought the king of Babylon to attack them. The king killed the young men even when they were in the Temple. He did not have mercy on the people. He killed both young men and women. He even killed the old men and those who were sick. God permitted Nebuchadnezzar to punish the people of Judah and Jerusalem. [18]Nebuchadnezzar carried away to Babylon all the things from the Temple of God, both large and small. He took all the treasures from the Temple of the Lord and from the king and his officers. [19]Nebuchadnezzar and his army set fire to God's Temple. They broke down Jerusalem's wall. And they burned all the palaces. They took or destroyed every valuable thing in Jerusalem.

[20]Nebuchadnezzar took captive to Babylon the people who were left alive. And he forced them to be slaves for him and his descendants.[d] They remained there as slaves until the Persian kingdom defeated Babylon. [21]And so what the Lord had told Israel through the prophet Jeremiah happened. The Lord had said that place would be an empty wasteland for 70 years. This happened to make up for the years of Sabbath rests[n] that the people had not kept.

[22]It was the first year Cyrus was king of Persia. The Lord caused Cyrus to write an announcement and send it everywhere in his kingdom. This happened so the Lord's message spoken by Jeremiah would come true.

[23]This is what Cyrus king of Persia says:

"The Lord, the God of heaven, has given all the kingdoms of the earth to me. And he has appointed me to build a Temple for him at Jerusalem in Judah. Now all of you who are God's people are free to go to Jerusalem. May the Lord your God be with you."

---

[n]**Sabbath rests**   The Law said that every seventh year the land was not to be farmed. See Leviticus 25:1-7.

The Return from Captivity

Cyrus Helps the Captives Return

1 It was the first year Cyrus was king of Persia. The Lord caused Cyrus to write an announcement and send it everywhere in his kingdom. And he also put it in writing. This happened so the Lord's message spoken by Jeremiah would come true. The announcement said:

²This is what Cyrus king of Persia says:

The Lord, the God of heaven, has given all the kingdoms of the earth to me. And he has appointed me to build a Temple*d* for him at Jerusalem in Judah. ³Now all of you who are God's people are free to go to Jerusalem. May your God be with you. And you may build the Temple of the Lord. He is the God of Israel, who is in Jerusalem. ⁴Those who stay behind should support anyone who wants to go. Give them silver and gold, supplies and cattle. And give them special gifts for the Temple of God in Jerusalem.

⁵Then the family leaders of Judah and Benjamin got ready to go to Jerusalem. So did the priests and the Levites. They were going to Jerusalem to build the Temple of the Lord. God made all these people want to go. ⁶All their neighbors helped them. They gave them things made of silver and gold, along with supplies, cattle and valuable gifts. And they gave them the special gifts for the Temple. ⁷Also, King Cyrus brought out the bowls and pans that belonged in the Temple of the Lord. Nebuchadnezzar had taken them from Jerusalem. And he had put them in the temple of his own god. ⁸Cyrus king of Persia had Mithredath the treasurer get them out. So he made a list of the things for Sheshbazzar the prince of Judah.

⁹There were 30 gold dishes, 1,000 silver dishes, 29 silver pans, ¹⁰30 gold bowls, 410 matching silver bowls and 1,000 other pieces.

¹¹There was a total of 5,400 pieces of gold and silver. Sheshbazzar brought all these things along when the captives went from Babylon to Jerusalem.

The Captives Who Returned

2 These are the people of the area who returned from captivity. Nebuchadnezzar king of Babylon had taken them captive to Babylon. Now they returned to Jerusalem and Judah. Each one went back to his own town. ²These people returned with Zerubbabel, Jeshua, Nehemiah, Seraiah, Reelaiah, Mordecai, Bilshan, Mispar, Bigvai, Rehum and Baanah.

These are the men from Israel: ³the descendants*d* of Parosh—2,172; ⁴the descendants of Shephatiah—372; ⁵the descendants of Arah—775; ⁶the descendants of Pahath-Moab (through the family of Jeshua and Joab)—2,812; ⁷the descendants of Elam—1,254; ⁸the descendants of Zattu—945; ⁹the descendants of Zaccai—760; ¹⁰the descendants of Bani—642; ¹¹the descendants of Bebai—623; ¹²the descendants of Azgad—1,222; ¹³the descendants of Adonikam—666; ¹⁴the descendants of Bigvai—2,056; ¹⁵the descendants of Adin—454; ¹⁶the descendants of Ater (through the family of Hezekiah)—98; ¹⁷the descendants of Bezai—323; ¹⁸the descendants of Jorah—112; ¹⁹the descendants of Hashum—

223; ²⁰the descendants of Gibbar—95.

²¹These are the men from the town of Bethlehem—123; ²²from Netophah—56; ²³from Anathoth—128; ²⁴from Azmaveth—42; ²⁵from Kiriath Jearim, Kephirah and Beeroth—743; ²⁶from Ramah and Geba—621; ²⁷from Micmash—122; ²⁸from Bethel and Ai—223; ²⁹from Nebo—52; ³⁰from Magbish—156; ³¹from the other town of Elam—1,254; ³²from Harim—320; ³³from Lod, Hadid and Ono—725; ³⁴from Jericho—345; ³⁵from Senaah—3,630.

³⁶These are the priests: the descendants of Jedaiah (through the family of Jeshua)—973; ³⁷the descendants of Immer—1,052; ³⁸the descendants of Pashhur—1,247; ³⁹the descendants of Harim—1,017.

⁴⁰These are the Levites: the descendants of Jeshua and Kadmiel (through the family of Hodaviah)—74.

⁴¹These are the singers: the descendants of Asaph—128.

⁴²These are the gatekeepers of the Temple:^d the descendants of Shallum, Ater, Talmon, Akkub, Hatita and Shobai—139.

⁴³These are the Temple servants: the descendants of Ziha, Hasupha, Tabbaoth, ⁴⁴Keros, Siaha, Padon, ⁴⁵Lebanah, Hagabah, Akkub, ⁴⁶Hagab, Shalmai, Hanan, ⁴⁷Giddel, Gahar, Reaiah, ⁴⁸Rezin, Nekoda, Gazzam, ⁴⁹Uzza, Paseah, Besai, ⁵⁰Asnah, Meunim, Nephussim, ⁵¹Bakbuk, Hakupha, Harhur, ⁵²Bazluth, Mehida, Harsha, ⁵³Barkos, Sisera, Temah, ⁵⁴Neziah and Hatipha.

⁵⁵These are the descendants of the servants of Solomon: the descendants of Sotai, Hassophereth, Peruda, ⁵⁶Jaala, Darkon, Giddel, ⁵⁷Shephatiah, Hattil, Pokereth-Hazzebaim and Ami.

⁵⁸The Temple servants and the descendants of the servants of Solomon numbered 392.

⁵⁹Some people came to Jerusalem from these towns: Tel Melah, Tel Harsha, Kerub, Addon and Immer. But they could not prove that their families came from the family of Israel.

Here are their names and their number: ⁶⁰the descendants of Delaiah, Tobiah and Nekoda—652.

⁶¹And these priests could not prove that their families came from Israel: the descendants of Hobaiah, Hakkoz and Barzillai. (He had married a daughter of Barzillai from Gilead and was called by her family name.)

⁶²These people searched for their family records. But they could not find them. So they could not be priests because they were thought to be unclean.^d ⁶³The governor ordered them not to eat any of the food offered to God. First a priest had to settle this matter by using the Urim and Thummim.^d

⁶⁴The total number of those who returned was 42,360. ⁶⁵This is not counting their 7,337 male and female servants. They also had 200 men and women singers with them. ⁶⁶They had 736 horses, 245 mules, ⁶⁷435 camels and 6,720 donkeys.

⁶⁸That group arrived at the Temple of the Lord in Jerusalem. Some of the leaders of families gave special offerings. Those offerings were given to rebuild the Temple of God. It would be on the same site as before. ⁶⁹Those people gave as much as they could to the treasury. It was to rebuild the Temple. They gave about 1,100 pounds of gold, about 6,000 pounds of silver and 100 pieces of clothing for the priests.

⁷⁰All the Israelites settled in their hometowns. The priests, Levites, singers, gatekeepers and temple servants, along with some of the other people, settled in their own towns.

Rebuilding the Altar

3 By the seventh month, the Israelites were settled in their hometowns. They met together in Jerusalem. ²Then Jeshua son of Jozadak and his fellow priests joined Zerubbabel son of Shealtiel. They began to build the altar of the God of Israel. That's where they offered burnt offerings just as it is written in the Teachings of Moses. Moses was the man of God. ³They were afraid of the people living around them. But they still built the altar where it had been before. They offered burnt offerings on it to the Lord morning and evening. ⁴Then, to obey what was written, they celebrated the Feast*ᵈ* of Shelters. They offered the right number of sacrifices for each day of the festival. ⁵After the Feast of Shelters, they had regular sacrifices every day. They had sacrifices for the New Moon*ᵈ* and all the festivals commanded by the Lord. Also there were special offerings brought as gifts to the Lord. ⁶On the first

arrival at the Temple*ᵈ* of God in Jerusalem. In the second month Zerubbabel and Jeshua began the work. So did the rest of their fellow priests and Levites. And all who had returned from captivity to Jerusalem began to work. They chose Levites 20 years old and older to be in charge of the building of the Temple of the Lord. ⁹These men were in charge of the work of building the Temple of God: Jeshua and his sons

Feelings
EZRA 3:13

After many years of being held captive by their enemies, God finally brought the Israelites back to their homes. Because their enemies had destroyed many of their buildings, they had the big job of fixing everything up again.

The most important building they worked on was the Temple of the Lord, the place where they worshiped God. When the foundation of the Temple was finally built, the people were filled with strong feeling. They had mixed feelings: some cried and others shouted for joy. They made so much noise it could be heard far away!

When we go to church, we should also show our true feelings. Sometimes you may feel sad because you realize you have done something wrong that has disappointed God. Other times you may want to shout and sing when you think of how good God is. God wants us to worship him with all of our feelings.

To find out why things can't make you truly happy, zoom to page 584.

day of the seventh month they began to bring burnt offerings to the Lord. But the foundation of the Lord's Temple*ᵈ* had not yet been laid.

Rebuilding the Temple

⁷Then they gave money to the stoneworkers and carpenters. They also gave food, wine and oil to the cities of Sidon and Tyre. This was so they would float cedar logs from Lebanon to the seacoast town of Joppa. Cyrus king of Persia had given permission for this.

⁸It was in the second year after their

and brothers; Kadmiel and his sons who were the descendants of Hodaviah; and the sons of Henadad and their sons and brothers. They were all Levites.

¹⁰The builders finished laying the foundation of the Temple of the Lord. Then the priests, dressed in their robes, got trumpets. And the Levites, the sons of Asaph, had cymbals. They all took their places. They praised the Lord just as David king of Israel had said to do. ¹¹With praise and thanksgiving, they sang to the Lord:

"He is good;

his love for Israel continues forever." And then all the people shouted loudly, "Praise the Lord! The foundation of his Temple has been laid." ¹²But many of the older priests, Levites and family leaders cried aloud. They had seen the first Temple. Now they saw the foundation of this Temple. But most of the other people were shouting with joy. ¹³The people made so much noise no one could tell the difference between the joyful shouting and the sad crying. It could be heard far away.

Enemies of the Rebuilding

4 The people of Judah and Benjamin had enemies. They heard that the returned captives were building a Temple*ᵈ* for the Lord, the God of Israel. ²So the enemies came to Zerubbabel and the leaders of the families. The enemies said, "Let us help you build. We are like you. We want to worship your God. We have been offering sacrifices to him since the time of Esarhaddon. He was king of Assyria, and he brought us here."

³But Zerubbabel, Jeshua and the leaders of Israel answered, "No. You people will not help us build a Temple to our God. We will build it ourselves. It is for the Lord, the God of Israel. This is what King Cyrus, the king of Persia, commanded us to do."

⁴Then the people around them tried to discourage the people of Judah. They tried to make them afraid to build. ⁵Their enemies hired others to delay the building plans. This went on during the time Cyrus was king of Persia. And it continued to the time Darius was king of Persia.

More Problems for the Builders

⁶When Xerxes became king, those enemies wrote a letter against the people of Judah and Jerusalem.

⁷Later Artaxerxes became king of Persia. Then Bishlam, Mithredath, Tabeel and those with them wrote a letter to Artaxerxes. The letter was written in the Aramaic language.

⁸Also Rehum the governor and Shimshai the governor's assistant wrote a letter. It was to Artaxerxes the king. And it was against Jerusalem. It said:

⁹This letter is from Rehum the governor, Shimshai the assistant and others. They are judges and important officers. They are over the men who came from Tripolis, Persia, Erech and Babylon. They are over the Elamite people of Susa. ¹⁰And they are over those whom the great and honorable Ashurbanipal forced out of their countries. He forced them to move and settle in the city of Samaria. And he forced them to settle in other places west of the Euphrates River.

¹¹(This is a copy of the letter they sent to Artaxerxes:)

To King Artaxerxes.
From your servants who live west of the Euphrates River.

¹²King Artaxerxes, you remember the Jews who came to us from you. You should know they have gone to Jerusalem. They are rebuilding that evil city that refuses to obey. They are fixing the walls and repairing the foundations of the buildings. ¹³Now, King Artaxerxes, you should know what could happen. If Jerusalem is built and its walls are fixed, Jerusalem will pay no taxes of any kind. Then the amount of money your government collects will be less. ¹⁴Since we must be loyal to the government, we don't want to see the king dishonored. So we are writing to let the king know. ¹⁵We suggest you search the records of the kings who ruled before you. You will find out that the city of Jerusalem refuses to obey. It makes trouble for kings and areas controlled by Persia. Since long ago it has been a place where disobedience started. That is why it was destroyed. ¹⁶We want you to know this, King Artaxerxes.

This city should not be rebuilt and its walls fixed. If it is, you will be left with nothing west of the Euphrates River.

[17]King Artaxerxes sent this answer:

To Rehum the governor and Shimshai the assistant. To all the people with them living in Samaria. And to those in other places west of the Euphrates.

Greetings.

[18]The letter you sent to us has been translated and read to me. [19]I ordered the records to be searched, and it was done. We found that Jerusalem has a long history of disobedience to kings. It has been a place of problems and trouble. [20]Jerusalem has had powerful kings. They have ruled over the whole area west of the Euphrates. Taxes of all kinds have been paid to them. [21]Now, give an order for those men to stop work. The city of Jerusalem will not be rebuilt until I say so. [22]Make sure you do this. If it continues, it will hurt the government.

[23]A copy of the letter that King Artaxerxes sent was read. It was read to Rehum and Shimshai the assistant and the others. Then they quickly went to the Jews in Jerusalem. They forced them to stop building.

[24]So the work on the Temple[d] of God in Jerusalem stopped. It stopped until the second year Darius was king of Persia.

Tattenai's Letter to Darius

5 Haggai and Zechariah son of Iddo were prophets.[d] They prophesied to the Jews in Judah and Jerusalem. They prophesied in the name of the God of Israel. [2]Then Zerubbabel son of Shealtiel and Jeshua son of Jozadak started working again. They worked to rebuild the Temple[d] of God in Jerusalem. The prophets of God were there, helping them.

[3]At that time Tattenai was the governor west of the Euphrates. He and Shethar-Bozenai and others went to the Jews. They asked, "Who gave you permission to rebuild this Temple and fix these walls?" [4]They also asked, "What are the names of these men working on this building?" [5]But their God was watching over the older leaders of the Jews. The builders were not stopped until a report could go to King Darius. And then his written answer had to be received.

[6]This is a copy of the letter that Tattenai, Shethar-Bozenai and the others sent to King Darius. Tattenai was governor west of the Euphrates River. The other people were important officers west of the Euphrates. [7]This is what the report they sent to him said:

To King Darius.

Greetings. May you have peace. [8]King Darius, you should know that we went to the district of Judah. That is where the Temple of the great God is. The people there are building that Temple with large stones. They are putting timbers in the walls. The people are working very hard. And they are building very fast.

[9]We asked their older leaders, "Who gave you permission to rebuild this Temple and these walls?" [10]We also asked for their names. We wrote down the names of their leaders so you would know who they are.

[11]This is the answer they gave to us: "We are the servants of the God of heaven and earth. We are rebuilding the Temple that a great king of Israel built. He finished it many years ago. [12]But our ancestors made the God of heaven angry. So God let them be defeated by Nebuchadnezzar king of Babylon. He destroyed this Temple. And he took the people to Babylon as captives.

[13]"Later, Cyrus was in his first year as king of Babylon. He gave a special order for this Temple to be rebuilt. [14]And Cyrus brought out things from the temple in Babylon.

They were the gold and silver bowls and pans that came from the Temple of God. Nebuchadnezzar had taken them from the Temple in Jerusalem. And he had put them in the temple in Babylon.

"Then King Cyrus gave them to Sheshbazzar. He had appointed Sheshbazzar as governor. [15]Cyrus said to him, 'Take these gold and silver bowls and pans. Put them back in the Temple in Jerusalem. And rebuild the Temple of God where it was.' [16]So Sheshbazzar came. He laid the foundations of the Temple of God in Jerusalem. From that day until now the work has been going on. But it is not yet finished."

[17]Now, if the king wishes, let a search be made. Search the royal records of Babylon to see if King Cyrus gave such an order. See if he gave an order to rebuild this Temple in Jerusalem. Then let the king write us and tell us what he has decided.

The Order of Darius

6 So King Darius gave an order to search the records. They were kept in the treasury in Babylon. [2]A scroll was found in the capital city, Ecbatana. It is in the area of Media. This is what was written on it:

Note:

[3]King Cyrus gave an order about the Temple[d] of God in Jerusalem. This was in the first year he was king. This was the order:

'Let the Temple be rebuilt. It will be a place to present sacrifices. Let its foundations be laid. The Temple should be 90 feet high and 90 feet wide. [4]It must have three layers of large stones, then one layer of timbers. The costs should be paid from the king's treasury. [5]The gold and silver things from the Temple of God should be put back in their places. Nebuchadnezzar took those things from the Temple in Jerusalem. And he brought them to Babylon. They are to be put back in the Temple of God in Jerusalem.'

People Who Depended on God
ZERUBBABEL • EZRA 6:15-18

Zerubbabel trusted God even though a lot of people tried to stop his work. Zerubbabel's family had been taken from Judah to be prisoners in Persia. When they were allowed to return to Judah, Zerubbabel led about fifty thousand Israelites from Persia back to Jerusalem. One of their jobs was to rebuild the temple so they could worship God. But some enemies who lived in Israel tried to stop them. They sent letters to the king of Persia and lied about Zerubbabel. They tried to make the people stop rebuilding.

Zerubabbel trusted God and told the people to keep working. When they finished the temple, they had a wonderful time of worship as they thanked God for protecting them.

People may try to make you stop obeying God, but you must trust and serve him, no matter what.

To read about someone who depended on God even though he was afraid, fly to page 577.

[6]Now then, I, Darius, give this order to you, Tattenai, governor west of the Euphrates. And I give it to Shethar-Bozenai and all the officers of that area. Stay away from there. [7]Do not bother or interrupt the work on that Temple of God. Let the governor of the Jews and the older Jewish leaders rebuild this Temple. Let them build it where it was before.

[8]Also, I order you to do this for those older leaders of the Jews. They are building this Temple. The cost of the building is to be fully paid from the royal treasury. The money will come from taxes collected west of the Euphrates River. Do this so the work will not stop. [9]Give those people anything they need. Give them young bulls, male sheep or male lambs for burnt offerings to the God of heaven. Give them wheat, salt, wine or olive oil. Give the priests in Jerusalem anything they ask for. Give it every day without fail. [10]Then they may offer sacrifices pleasing to the God of heaven. And they can pray for the life of the king and his sons.

[11]Also, I give this order: If anyone changes this order, a wood beam is to be pulled from his house. Drive one end of the beam through his body. And because he did this crime, make his house a pile of ruins. [12]God has chosen Jerusalem as the place he is to be worshiped. May he defeat any king or person who tries to change this order. May God destroy anyone who tries to destroy this Temple.

I, Darius, have given this order. Let it be obeyed quickly and carefully.

Completion of the Temple

[13]So, Tattenai, the governor west of the Euphrates, Shethar-Bozenai and the others obeyed. They carried out King Darius' order quickly and carefully. [14]So the older Jewish leaders continued to build. And they were successful because of the preaching of Haggai the prophet[d] and Zechariah son of Iddo. They finished building the Temple[d] as the God of Israel had said. It was also done to obey the kings Cyrus, Darius and Artaxerxes of Persia. [15]The Temple was finished on the third day of the month Adar. It was the sixth year that Darius was king.

[16]Then the people of Israel celebrated. They gave the Temple to God to honor him. Everybody was happy: the priests, the Levites and the rest of the Jews who had returned from captivity. [17]This is how they gave the Temple to God for worshiping him: They offered 100 bulls, 200 male sheep and 400 male lambs as sacrifices. And as an offering to forgive the sins of all Israel, they offered 12 male goats. That is 1 goat for each tribe[d] in Israel. [18]Then they put the priests and the Levites into their separate groups. Each group had a certain time to serve God in the Temple at Jerusalem. This was done just as it is written in the Book of Moses.

The Passover

[19]The Jews who returned from captivity celebrated the Passover.[d] This was on the fourteenth day of the first month. [20]The priests and Levites had made themselves clean.[d] The Levites killed the Passover lambs for all the Jews who had returned from captivity. They also did it for their relatives the priests and for themselves. [21]So all the people of Israel who returned from captivity ate the Passover lamb. So did those who had given up the unclean ways of their non-Jewish neighbors. They worshiped the Lord, the God of Israel. [22]For seven days they celebrated the Feast[d] of Unleavened Bread in a very joyful way. The Lord had made them happy by changing the mind of the King of Assyria. So the king had helped them in the work on the Temple of the God of Israel.

Ezra Comes to Jerusalem

7 After these things[n] during the rule of Artaxerxes king of Persia, Ezra came up from Babylon. Ezra was the

---

[n]**After these things**   There is a time period of about 60 years between chapters six and seven.

son of Seraiah. Seraiah was the son of Azariah. Azariah was the son of Hilkiah. [2]Hilkiah was the son of Shallum. Shallum was the son of Zadok. Zadok was the son of Ahitub. [3]Ahitub was the son of Amariah. Amariah was the son of Azariah. Azariah was the son of Meraioth. [4]Meraioth was the son of Zerahiah. Zerahiah was the son of Uzzi. Uzzi was the son of Bukki. [5]Bukki was the son of Abishua. Abishua was the son of

he arrived in Jerusalem on the first day of the fifth month. God was helping Ezra. [10]Ezra had worked hard to know and obey the Teachings of the Lord. He also taught the rules and commands of the Lord to the Israelites.

Artaxerxes' Letter to Ezra

[11]King Artaxerxes had given a letter to Ezra. Ezra was a priest and teacher. He taught about the commands and laws the Lord gave Israel. This is a copy of the letter:

[12]From Artaxerxes, king of kings.

Unsung Heroes

EZRA • EZRA 7:8-10

After the Israelites were allowed to return to their homeland, many of them made the long journey from Persia to Jerusalem. The city had been destroyed by enemy armies, so the people had to rebuild it. A man named Zerubbabel led the people back to Jerusalem, and they rebuilt the temple. Then Ezra returned with another group of people.

Ezra was a scribe. He studied God's word and taught it to the people. Ezra had taught the people in Persia, and when he returned to Jerusalem he continued to teach them about God. Ezra was not an important general or king, but he did an important work. He helped the people rebuild their nation by helping them to obey God.

To read about a hero who took care of an orphan, fly to page 595.

Phinehas. Phinehas was the son of Eleazar. Eleazar was the son of Aaron the high priest. [6]This Ezra came to Jerusalem from Babylon. He was a teacher. He knew the Teachings of Moses well. The Teachings had been given by the Lord, the God of Israel. Ezra received everything he asked for from the king. This was because the Lord his God was helping him. [7]In the seventh year of King Artaxerxes more Israelites came to Jerusalem. Among them were priests, Levites, singers, gatekeepers and Temple[d] servants.

[8]Ezra also arrived in Jerusalem. It was the fifth month of Artaxerxes' seventh year as king. [9]Ezra had left Babylon on the first day of the first month. And

To Ezra the priest, a teacher of the Law of the God of heaven.
Greetings.
[13]Now I give this order: Any Israelite in my kingdom who wishes may go with you to Jerusalem. This includes priests and Levites. [14]Ezra, you are sent by the king and the seven people who advise him. You are to ask about how Judah and Jerusalem are obeying the Law of your God, which you are carrying with you. [15]Also take with you the silver and gold the king and those who advise him have given freely. It's for the God of Israel, whose Temple[d] is in Jerusalem. [16]Also take the silver and gold you receive from the area

of Babylon. And take the offerings the Israelites and their priests have given as gifts to the Lord. They are for the Temple of their God in Jerusalem. ¹⁷With this money buy bulls, male sheep and male lambs. Buy the grain offerings and drink offerings that go with those sacrifices. Then sacrifice them on the altar in the Temple of your God in Jerusalem.

¹⁸Then you and your fellow Jews may spend the silver and gold left over. Use it as you want and as God wishes. ¹⁹Take to the God of Jerusalem all the things put in your care. They are for the worship in the Temple of your God. ²⁰And you may get anything else you need for the Temple of your God. Pay for it from the royal treasury.

²¹Now I, King Artaxerxes, give this order to all the men in charge of the treasury west of the Euphrates: Give Ezra anything he asks for right away. Ezra is a priest and a teacher of the Law of the God of heaven. ²²Give him up to 7,500 pounds of silver, 600 bushels of wheat, 600 gallons of wine and 600 gallons of olive oil. And give him as much salt as he wants. ²³Carefully give him whatever the God of heaven wants. Do it for the Temple of the God of heaven. We do not want God to be angry with the king and his sons. ²⁴Remember, you must not make these people pay taxes of any kind: priests, Levites, singers, gatekeepers, Temple servants and other workers in this Temple of God.

²⁵And you, Ezra, use the wisdom you have from your God. Choose judges and lawmakers to rule the Jews west of the Euphrates. They know the laws of your God. And teach anyone who does not know them. ²⁶Whoever does not obey the law of your God or of the king must be punished. He will be killed or sent away. He will have his property taken away or be put in jail.

²⁷Praise the Lord, the God of our ancestors. He caused the king to want to honor the Temple of the Lord in Jerusalem. ²⁸The Lord has shown me, Ezra, his love. He did this before the king, those who advise the king and the royal officers. The Lord my God was helping me. So I had courage. I gathered the leaders of Israel to return with me.

Leaders Who Returned with Ezra

8 These are the leaders of the family groups who returned with me. And it is a listing of those who were with them. They came back from Babylon during the rule of King Artaxerxes.

²From the descendants^d of Phinehas, there was Gershom.

From the descendants of Ithamar, there was Daniel.

From the descendants of David, there was Hattush ³of the descendants of Shecaniah.

From the descendants of Parosh, there was Zechariah. And 150 men came with him.

⁴From the descendants of Pahath-Moab, there was Eliehoenai son of Zerahiah, with 200 men.

⁵From the descendants of Zattu, there was Shecaniah son of Jahaziel, with 300 men.

⁶From the descendants of Adin, there was Ebed son of Jonathan, with 50 men.

⁷From the descendants of Elam, there was Jeshaiah son of Athaliah, with 70 men.

⁸From the descendants of Shephatiah, there was Zebadiah son of Michael, with 80 men.

⁹From the descendants of Joab, there was Obadiah son of Jehiel, with 218 men.

¹⁰From the descendants of Bani, there was Shelomith son of Josiphiah, with 160 men.

¹¹From the descendants of Bebai, there was Zechariah son of Bebai, with 28 men.

¹²From the descendants of Azgad,

there was Johanan son of Hakkatan, with 110 men.

[13]From the descendants of Adonikam, these were the last ones: Eliphelet, Jeuel and Shemaiah. With them were 60 men.

[14]From the descendants of Bigvai, there were Uthai and Zaccur, with 70 men.

The Return to Jerusalem

[15]I, Ezra, called all those people together at the canal. It flows toward Ahava. We camped there for three days. I checked all the people and the priests. But I did not find any Levites. [16]So I called these leaders: Eliezer, Ariel, Shemaiah, Elnathan, Jarib, Elnathan, Nathan, Zechariah and Meshullam. And I called Joiarib and Elnathan, who were teachers. [17]I sent those men to Iddo, the leader at Casiphia. I told them what to say to Iddo and his relatives, who are the Temple[d] servants in Casiphia. I sent them to bring servants to us for the Temple[d] of our God. [18]Our God was helping us. So Iddo's relatives gave us Sherebiah, a wise man from the descendants of Mahli. Mahli was the son of Levi. And Levi was the son of Israel. And they brought Sherebiah's sons and brothers. In all there were 18 men. [19]And they brought to us Hashabiah and Jeshaiah from the descendants of Merari. And they also brought his brothers and nephews. In all there were 20 men. [20]They also brought 220 of the Temple servants. This is a group David and the officers had set up to help the Levites. All of those men were listed by name.

[21]There by the Ahava Canal, I announced we would all give up eating. We would make ourselves humble before our God. And we would ask God for a safe trip for ourselves, our children and all our possessions. [22]I was ashamed to ask the king for soldiers and horsemen. They could have protected us from enemies on the road. But we had said to the king, "Our God helps everyone who obeys him. But

God is very angry with all who reject him." [23]So we gave up eating and prayed to our God about our trip. He answered our prayers.

[24]Then I chose 12 of the priests who were leaders. They were Sherebiah and Hashabiah and 10 of their relatives. [25]I weighed the offering of silver and gold. And I weighed the things given for the Temple of our God. I gave them to the 12 priests I had chosen. The king, the people who advised him, his officers and all the Israelites there with us had given these things for the Temple. [26]I weighed out and gave them about 50,000 pounds of silver, about 7,500 pounds of silver objects and about 7,500 pounds of gold. [27]I gave them 20 gold bowls that weighed about 19 pounds. And I gave them 2 fine pieces of polished bronze that were as valuable as gold.

[28]Then I said to the priests, "You and these things belong to the Lord for his service. The silver and gold are gifts to the Lord, the God of your ancestors. [29]Guard these things carefully. In Jerusalem, weigh them in front of the leading priests, Levites and the leaders of the family groups of Israel. Do this in the rooms of the Temple of the Lord." [30]So the priests and Levites took the silver, the gold and the special things that had been weighed out. They were to take them to the Temple of our God in Jerusalem.

[31]On the twelfth day of the first month we left the Ahava Canal. We started toward Jerusalem. Our God helped us. He protected us from enemies and robbers along the way. [32]Then we arrived in Jerusalem. We rested there three days.

[33]On the fourth day we weighed out the silver, the gold and the special things in the Temple of our God. We handed them to the priest Meremoth son of Uriah. Eleazar son of Phinehas was with Meremoth. Also the Levites Jozabad son of Jeshua and Noadiah son of Binnui were with them. [34]We checked everything by number and by

weight. And the total weight was written down at that time.

35Then the captives who returned made burnt offerings to the God of Israel. They sacrificed 12 bulls for all Israel, 96 male sheep and 77 male lambs. All these animals were burned as sacrifices to the Lord. For a sin offering to the Lord there were 12 male goats. 36They took King Artaxerxes' orders to the royal officers and to the governors west of the Euphrates. Then these men gave help to the people and the Temple of God.

Ezra's Prayer

9 After these things had been done, the leaders came to me. They said, "Ezra, the Israelites, including the priests and Levites, have not kept themselves separate from the people around us. Those neighbors do evil things as the Canaanites, Hittites, Perizzites, Jebusites, Ammonites, Moabites, Egyptians and Amorites did. 2The Israelite men and their sons have married the women of these non-Jewish people. They have mixed the people who belong to God with the people around them. The leaders and officers of Israel did this first. And they caused the rest of the Israelites to do this unfaithful thing."

3When I heard this, I angrily tore my robe and coat. I pulled hair from my head and beard and sat down in shock. 4Then everyone who trembled in fear at the word of the God of Israel gathered around me. This was because of the unfaithfulness of the captives who had returned. I sat there in shock until the evening sacrifice.

5Then, at the evening sacrifice, I got up from where I had shown my disgrace. My inner robe and coat were torn. And I fell on my knees with my hands spread out to the Lord my God. 6I prayed,

"My God, I am too ashamed and embarrassed to lift up my face to you. I am in disgrace because our sins are so many they are higher than our heads. Our sins even reach up to the sky.

7From the days of our ancestors until now, we have been very guilty. Because of our sins, we, our kings and priests have suffered punishment. We have been punished by the sword and captivity. Foreign kings have taken away our things and shamed us. It is that way today.

8"But now, for a short time, the Lord our God has been kind to us. He has let some of us come back from captivity. He has let us live in safety in his holy place. And so our God gives us hope and a little relief from our slavery. 9Even though we are slaves, our God has not left us. He caused the kings of Persia to be kind to us. He has given us new life. So we can rebuild the Temple*d* and repair its ruins. And he has given us a wall to protect us in Judah and Jerusalem.

10"But now, our God, what can we say after you have done all this? We have disobeyed your commands. 11You gave these commands through your servants the prophets.*d* You said, 'The land you are entering to own is ruined. The people living there have spoiled it by the evil they do. Their evil filled the land with uncleanness*d* from one end to the other. 12So do not let your daughters marry their sons. And do not let their daughters marry your sons. Do not wish for their peace or success. Then you may be strong and eat the good things of the land. And then you can leave this land to your descendants*d* forever.'

13"What has happened to us is our own fault. We have done evil things. Our guilt is great. But you, our God, have punished us less than we deserve. You have left a few of us alive. 14We should not again break your commands by allowing marriages with these wicked people. If we did, you would get angry enough to destroy us. Then none of us would be left alive. 15Lord, God of Israel, by your goodness a few of us are left alive today. We admit that we are guilty. None of us should be allowed to stand before you."

The People Confess Sin

10 Ezra was praying and confessing. He was crying and throwing himself down in front of the Temple.[d] A large group of Israelite men, women and children gathered around him. They were also crying loudly. [2]Then Shecaniah son of Jehiel the Elamite spoke to Ezra. Shecaniah said, "We have been unfaithful to our God. We have been marrying women from the peoples around us. But even so, there is still hope for Israel. [3]Now let us make an agreement before our God. We will send away all these women and their children. This is your advice. It is also the advice of those who respect the commands of our God. Let it be done to obey his Teachings. [4]Get up, Ezra. You are in charge. But we will support you. So have courage and do it."

[5]So Ezra got up. He made these people make a promise: the priests, the Levites and all the people of Israel. They promised to do what was suggested. [6]Then Ezra left the Temple. He went to the room of Jehohanan son of Eliashib. While Ezra was there, he did not eat or drink. He was still sad about the unfaithfulness of the captives who had returned.

[7]Then an order was sent everywhere in Judah and Jerusalem. All the captives who had returned had to meet together in Jerusalem. [8]Whoever did not come to Jerusalem within three days would lose his property. And he would no longer be a member of the community of the returned captives. That was the decision of the officers and older leaders.

[9]So within three days all the men of Judah and Benjamin gathered in Jerusalem. It was the twentieth day of the ninth month. All the people were sitting in the open place in front of the Temple. They were upset because of the meeting and because it was raining. [10]Then Ezra the priest stood up and said to them, "You have been unfaithful. You have married non-Jewish women. You have made Israel more guilty. [11]Now, confess it to the Lord, the God of your ancestors. Do the Lord's will. Separate yourselves from the people living around you and from your non-Jewish wives."

[12]Then the whole group answered Ezra. They shouted, "Ezra, you're right! We must do what you say. [13]But there are many people here. It's the rainy season. We can't stand outside. Also, this problem can't be solved in a day or two. We have sinned badly. [14]Let our officers make a decision for the whole group. Then let everyone in our towns who has married a non-Jewish woman meet with the older leaders and judges of each town. Let them meet at a planned time. Then the hot anger of our God will turn away from us." [15]Only these men were against the plan: Jonathan son of Asahel, Jahzeiah son of Tikvah, Meshullam and Shabbethai the Levite.

[16]So the returned captives did what was suggested. Ezra the priest chose men who were leaders of the family groups. He named one from each family division. On the first day of the tenth month they sat down to study each case. [17]By the first day of the first month, they had finished. They had dealt with all the men who had married non-Jewish women.

Those Guilty of Marrying Non-Jewish Women

[18]These are the descendants[d] of the priests who had married foreign women:

From the descendants of Jeshua son of Jozadak and Jeshua's brothers, there were Maaseiah, Eliezer, Jarib and Gedaliah. [19](They all promised to divorce their wives. Then each one brought a male sheep from the flock as a penalty offering.)

[20]From the descendants of Immer, there were Hanani and Zebadiah.

[21]From the descendants of Harim, there were Maaseiah, Elijah, Shemaiah, Jehiel and Uzziah.

[22]From the descendants of Pashhur, there were Elioenai, Maaseiah, Ishmael, Nethanel, Jozabad and Elasah.

23Among the Levites, there were Jozabad, Shimei, Kelaiah (also called Kelita), Pethahiah, Judah and Eliezer.

24Among the singers, there was Eliashib.

Among the gatekeepers, there were Shallum, Telem and Uri.

25And among the other Israelites, these married non-Jewish women:

From the descendants of Parosh, there were Ramiah, Izziah, Malkijah, Mijamin, Eleazar, Malkijah and Benaiah.

26From the descendants of Elam, there were Mattaniah, Zechariah, Jehiel, Abdi, Jeremoth and Elijah.

27From the descendants of Zattu, there were Elioenai, Eliashib, Mattaniah, Jeremoth, Zabad and Aziza.

28From the descendants of Bebai, there were Jehohanan, Hananiah, Zabbai and Athlai.

29From the descendants of Bani, there were Meshullam, Malluch, Adaiah, Jashub, Sheal and Jeremoth.

30From the descendants of Pahath-Moab, there were Adna, Kelal, Benaiah, Maaseiah, Mattaniah, Bezalel, Binnui and Manasseh.

31From the descendants of Harim, there were Eliezer, Ishijah, Malkijah, Shemaiah, Shimeon, 32Benjamin, Malluch and Shemariah.

33From the descendants of Hashum, there were Mattenai, Mattattah, Zabad, Eliphelet, Jeremai, Manasseh and Shimei.

34From the descendants of Bani, there were Maadai, Amram, Uel, 35Benaiah, Bedeiah, Keluhi, 36Vaniah, Meremoth, Eliashib, 37Mattaniah, Mattenai and Jaasu.

38From the descendants of Binnui, there were Shimei, 39Shelemiah, Nathan, Adaiah, 40Macnadebai, Shashai, Sharai, 41Azarel, Shelemiah, Shemariah, 42Shallum, Amariah and Joseph.

43From the descendants of Nebo, there were Jeiel, Mattithiah, Zabad, Zebina, Jaddai, Joel and Benaiah.

44All these men had married non-Jewish women. And some of them had children by these wives.

NEHEMIAH

Rebuilding the Walls of Jerusalem

Nehemiah's Prayer

1 These are the words of Nehemiah son of Hacaliah.

I, Nehemiah, was in the capital city of Susa. It was in the month of Kislev. This was in the twentieth year.[n] ²One of my brothers named Hanani came from Judah. Some other men were with him. I asked them about the Jews who lived through the captivity. And I also asked about Jerusalem.

³They answered, "Nehemiah, those who are left from the captivity are back in the area of Judah. But they are in much trouble and are full of shame. The wall around Jerusalem is broken down. And its gates have been burned."

⁴When I heard these things, I sat down and cried for several days. I was sad and did not eat food. I prayed to the God of heaven. ⁵I said, "Lord, God of heaven, you are the great God who is to be respected. You keep your agreement of love with those who love you and obey your commands. ⁶Listen carefully. Look at me. Hear the prayer your servant is praying to you day and night. I am praying for your servants, the people of Israel. I confess the sins we Israelites have done against you. My father's family and I have sinned against you. ⁷We have been wicked toward you. We have not obeyed the commands, rules and laws you gave your servant Moses.

⁸"Remember what you taught your servant Moses. You said, 'If you are unfaithful, I will scatter you among the nations. ⁹But if you come back to me and obey my commands, I will gather your people. I will gather them from the far ends of the earth. And I will bring them from captivity to where I have chosen to be worshiped.'

¹⁰"They are your servants and your people. You have saved them with your great strength and power. ¹¹Lord, listen carefully to my prayer. I am your servant. And listen to the prayers of your servants who love to honor you. Give me, your servant, success today. Allow this king to show kindness to me."

I was the one who served wine to the king.

Nehemiah Is Sent to Jerusalem

2 It was the month of Nisan. It was in the twentieth year King Artaxerxes was king. He wanted some wine. So I took some and gave it to the king. I had not been sad in his presence before. ²So the king said, "Why does your face look sad? You are not sick. Your heart must be sad."

Then I was very afraid. ³I said to the king, "May the king live forever! My face is sad because the city where my ancestors are buried lies in ruins. And its gates have been destroyed by fire."

⁴Then the king said to me, "What do you want?"

First I prayed to the God of heaven. ⁵Then I answered the king, "Send me to the city in Judah where my ancestors are buried. I will rebuild it. Do this if you are willing and if I have pleased you."

⁶The queen was sitting next to the king. He asked me, "How long will your trip take? When will you get back?" It pleased the king to send me. So I set a time.

---

[n]**twentieth year**   This is probably referring to the twentieth year King Artaxerxes I ruled Persia.

People Who Depended on God

NEHEMIAH • NEHEMIAH 2:1-9

Nehemiah trusted God even though he was afraid. Nehemiah's family had been taken as captives from Judah. Nehemiah served the King of Persia as his cupbearer. He served food to the king and had to taste it to make sure it wasn't poisoned.

Many Israelites had already returned to Jerusalem and had rebuilt the temple. But the walls around the city were still broken down. The city had no protection from enemy attacks. This made Nehemiah very sad, and one day the king noticed that he was sad. That was dangerous. The king could have killed Nehemiah for looking sad when he served the food. But Nehemiah prayed for courage and asked the king if he could go back to Jerusalem to rebuild the walls. The king did not kill him. The king said yes!

To read about three men who depended on God even though they might die, fly to page 1032.

To read about three men who depended on God even though they might die, fly to page 1032.

⁷I also said to him, "If you are willing, give me letters for the governors west of the Euphrates River. Tell them to let me pass safely through their lands on my way to Judah. ⁸And may I have a letter for Asaph? He is the keeper of the king's forest. Tell him to give me timber. I will need it to make boards for the gates of the palace. It is by the Temple.ᵈ The wood is also for the city wall and the house I will live in." So the king gave me the letters. This was because God was showing kindness to me. ⁹So I went to the governors west of the Euphrates River. I gave them the king's letters. The king had also sent army officers and soldiers on horses with me.

¹⁰Sanballat the Horonite and Tobiah the Ammonite leader heard about this. They were upset that someone had come to help the Israelites.

Nehemiah Inspects Jerusalem

¹¹I went to Jerusalem and stayed there three days. ¹²Then at night I started out with a few men. I had not told anyone what God had caused me to do for Jerusalem. There were no animals with me except the one I was riding.

¹³It was night. I went out through the Valley Gate. I rode toward the Dragon Well and the Trash Gate. I was inspecting the walls of Jerusalem. They had been broken down. And the gates had been destroyed by fire. ¹⁴Then I rode on toward the Fountain Gate and the King's Pool. But there was not enough room for the animal I was riding to get through. ¹⁵So I went up the valley at night. I was inspecting the wall. Finally, I turned and went back in through the Valley Gate. ¹⁶The officers did not know where I had gone or what I was doing. I had not yet said anything to the Jews, the priests, the important men or the officers. I had not said anything to any of the others who would do the work.

¹⁷Then I said to them, "You can see the trouble we have here. Jerusalem is a pile of ruins. And its gates have been

burned. Come, let's rebuild the wall of Jerusalem. Then we won't be full of shame any longer." [18]I also told them how God had been kind to me. And I told them what the king had said to me.

Then they answered, "Let's start rebuilding." So they began to work hard.

[19]But Sanballat the Horonite, Tobiah the Ammonite leader and Geshem the Arab heard about it. They made fun of us and laughed at us. They said, "What are you doing? Are you turning against the king?"

[20]But I answered them, "The God of heaven will give us success. We are God's servants. We will start rebuilding. But you have no share in Jerusalem. You have no claim or past right to it."

Builders of the Wall

3 Eliashib the high priest and his fellow priests went to work. They rebuilt the Sheep Gate. They gave it to the Lord's service and set its doors in place. They worked as far as the Tower of the Hundred, and they gave it to the Lord's service. Then they went on to the Tower of Hananel. [2]The men of Jericho built the part of the wall next to the priests. And Zaccur son of Imri built next to them.

[3]The sons of Hassenaah rebuilt the Fish Gate. They set the boards in place. And they put its doors, bolts and bars in place. [4]Meremoth son of Uriah made repairs next to them. (Uriah was the son of Hakkoz.) Meshullam son of Berekiah worked next to Meremoth. (Berekiah was the son of Meshezabel.) And Zadok son of Baana worked next to Meshullam. [5]The men from Tekoa made repairs next to them. But the leading men of Tekoa would not work under their supervisors.

[6]Joiada son of Paseah and Meshullam son of Besodeiah repaired the Old Gate. They set its boards in place. And they put its doors, bolts and bars in place. [7]Next to them, men from Gibeon and Mizpah made repairs. Melatiah was

from Gibeon, and Jadon was from Meronoth. These places were ruled by the governor west of the Euphrates River. [8]Next to them, Uzziel son of Harhaiah made repairs. He was a goldsmith. And next to him, Hananiah made repairs. He was one of the people who made perfume. These men rebuilt Jerusalem as far as the Broad Wall. [9]The next part of the wall was repaired by Rephaiah son of Hur. He was ruler of half of the district of Jerusalem. [10]Next to him, Jedaiah son of Harumaph made repairs. He worked opposite his own house. And next to him, Hattush son of Hashabneiah made repairs. [11]Malkijah son of Harim and Hasshub son of Pahath-Moab repaired another part of the wall. And they repaired the Tower of the Ovens. [12]Next to them, Shallum son of Hallohesh made repairs. He was ruler of half of the district of Jerusalem. His daughters helped him.

[13]Hanun and the people of Zanoah repaired the Valley Gate. They rebuilt it and put its doors, bolts and bars in place. They also repaired the 500 yards of the wall to the Trash Gate.

[14]Malkijah son of Recab repaired the Trash Gate. He was ruler of the district of Beth Hakkerem. He rebuilt that gate and put its doors, bolts and bars in place.

[15]Shallun son of Col-Hozeh repaired the Fountain Gate. He was ruler of the district of Mizpah. He rebuilt it and put a roof over it. And he put its doors, bolts and bars in place. He also repaired the wall of the Pool of Siloam. It is next to the King's Garden. He repaired the wall all the way to the steps. They went down from the older part of the city. [16]Next to Shallun, Nehemiah[n] son of Azbuk made repairs. He was ruler of half of the district of Beth Zur. He made repairs up to a place opposite the tombs of David. He made repairs as far as the man-made pool and the House of the Heroes.

[17]Next to him, the Levites made repairs. Some worked under Rehum son of Bani. Next to him, Hashabiah

made repairs for his district. He was ruler of half of the district of Keilah. [18]Next to him, Binnui son of Henadad and his Levites made repairs. Binnui was the ruler of the other half of the district of Keilah. [19]Next to them, Ezer son of Jeshua worked. He was ruler of Mizpah. He repaired another part of the wall. He worked across from the way up to the storehouse for weapons. And he worked to the place where the wall turns. [20]Next to him, Baruch son of Zabbai worked very hard to repair another part of the wall. It went from the place where the wall turns to the entrance of the house of Eliashib. He was the high priest. [21]Next to him, Meremoth son of Uriah worked. (Uriah was the son of Hakkoz.) He repaired another part of the wall. It went from the entrance to Eliashib's house to the far end of it.

[22]Next to him worked the priests from the surrounding area. [23]Next to them, Benjamin and Hasshub made repairs in front of their own house. Next to them, Azariah son of Maaseiah made repairs beside his own house. (Maaseiah was the son of Ananiah.) [24]Next to him, Binnui son of Henadad repaired another part of the wall. It went from Azariah's house to the place where the wall turned. And it went to the corner. [25]Palal son of Uzai worked across from the place where the wall turned. And he worked by the tower on the upper palace. That is near the courtyard of the king's guard. Next to Palal, Pedaiah son of Parosh made repairs. [26]The Temple[d] servants lived on the hill of Ophel. They made repairs as far as a point opposite the Water Gate. They worked toward the east and the tower that extends from the palace. [27]Next to them, the men of Tekoa made repairs. They worked on the wall from the great tower that extends from the palace to the wall of Ophel.

[28]The priests made repairs above the Horse Gate. Each worked in front of his own house. [29]Next to them, Zadok son of Immer made repairs across from his own house. Next to him, Shemaiah son of Shecaniah made repairs. He was the guard of the East Gate. [30]Next to him, Hananiah son of Shelemiah and Hanun, the sixth son of Zalaph, made repairs. They worked on another part of the wall. Next to them, Meshullam son of Berekiah made repairs. It was across from where he lived. [31]Next to him, Malkijah made repairs. He was one of the goldsmiths. He worked as far as the house of the Temple servants and the traders. That is across from the Inspection Gate. And he worked as far as the room above the corner of the wall. [32]The goldsmiths and the traders made repairs on another part of the wall. It was between the room above the corner of the wall and the Sheep Gate.

Those Against the Rebuilding

4 Sanballat heard we were rebuilding the wall. He was very angry, even furious. He made fun of the Jews. [2]He said to his friends and the army of Samaria, "What are these weak Jews doing? They think they can rebuild the wall. They think they will offer sacrifices. Maybe they think they can finish rebuilding it in only one day. They can't bring stones back to life. These are piles of trash and ashes."

[3]Tobiah the Ammonite was next to Sanballat. Tobiah said, "A fox could climb up on what they are building. Even it could break down their stone wall."

[4]I prayed, "Hear us, our God. We are hated. Turn the insults of Sanballat and Tobiah back on their own heads. Let them be captured and taken away like valuables that are stolen. [5]Do not hide their guilt. Do not take away their sins so you can't see them. The builders have seen them make you angry."

[6]So we rebuilt the wall until all of it went halfway up. The people were willing to work hard.

[7]But Sanballat, Tobiah, the Arabs, the Ammonites and the men from Ashdod were very angry. They heard that the

repairs to Jerusalem's walls were continuing. And they heard that the holes in the wall were being closed. [8]So they all made plans against Jerusalem. They planned to come and fight and stir up trouble. [9]But we prayed to our God. And we appointed guards to watch for them day and night.

[10]The people of Judah said, "The workers are getting tired. There is too much dirt and trash. We cannot rebuild the wall."

[11]And our enemies said, "The Jews won't know it or see us. But we will come among them and kill them. We will stop the work."

[12]Then the Jews who lived near our enemies came. They told us ten times, "Everywhere you turn, the enemy will attack us." [13]So I put some of the people behind the lowest places along the wall. And I put some at the open places. I put families together with their swords, spears and bows. [14]Then I looked around. I stood up and spoke to the important men, the leaders and the rest of the people. I said, "Don't be afraid of them. Remember the Lord. He is great and others are afraid of him. And fight for your brothers, your sons and daughters, your wives and your homes."

[15]Then our enemies heard that we knew about their plans. God had ruined their plans. So we all went back to the wall. Each person went back to his own work.

[16]From that day on, half my men worked on the wall. The other half was ready with spears, shields, bows and armor. The officers stood in back of the people of Judah [17]who were building the wall. Those who carried materials did their work with one hand. They carried a weapon in the other hand. [18]Each builder wore his sword at his side as he worked. The man who blew the trumpet to warn the people stayed next to me.

[19]Then I spoke to the important men, the leaders and the rest of the people. I said, "This is a very big job. We are spreading out along the wall. We are far apart. [20]So wherever you hear the sound of the trumpet, assemble there. Our God will fight for us."

[21]So we continued to work. Half the men held spears. We worked from sunrise till the stars came out. [22]At that time I also said to the people, "Let every man and his helper stay inside Jerusalem at night. They can be our guards at night. And they can be workmen during the day." [23]Neither I, my brothers, my men nor the guards with me ever took off our clothes. Each person carried his weapon even when he went for water.

Nehemiah Helps Poor People

5 The men and their wives complained loudly against their fellow Jews. [2]Some of them were saying, "We have many sons and daughters in our families. To eat and stay alive, we need grain."

[3]Others were saying, "We are borrowing money to get grain. There is not much food. We might not be able to pay back the money we've borrowed. Then we will have to pay with our fields, vineyards and homes."

[4]And still others were saying, "We are having to borrow money. We have to pay the king's tax on our fields and vineyards. [5]We are just like our fellow Jews. Our sons are like their sons. But we have to sell our sons and daughters as slaves. Some of our daughters have already been sold. But there is nothing we can do. Our fields and vineyards already belong to other people."

[6]When I heard their complaints about these things, I was very angry. [7]I thought about it. Then I accused the important people and the leaders. I told them, "You are charging your own brothers too much interest." So I called a large meeting to deal with them. [8]I said to them, "Our fellow Jews had been sold to non-Jewish nations. But, as much as possible, we have bought them back. Now you are making your fellow Jews sell themselves to us!" The leaders were quiet. They had nothing to say.

⁹Then I said, "What you are doing is not right. You should live in fear of God. Don't let our non-Jewish enemies shame us. ¹⁰I, my brothers and my men are also lending money and grain to the people. But stop charging them too much for this! ¹¹Give back their fields, vineyards, olive trees and houses right now. Also give them back the extra amount you charged them. That is the hundredth part of the money, grain, new wine and oil."

¹²They said, "We will give it back. And we will not demand anything more from them. We will do as you say."

Then I called for the priests. And I made the important men and leaders promise to do what they had said. ¹³Also I shook out the folds of my robe. I said, "In this way may God shake out every man who does not keep his promise. May God shake him out of his house. And may he shake him out of the things that are his. Let that man be shaken out and emptied!"

Then the whole group said, "Amen." And they praised the Lord. So the people did what they had promised.

¹⁴I was appointed governor in the land of Judah. This was in the twentieth year of King Artaxerxes' rule. I was governor till his thirty-second year. So I was governor of Judah for 12 years. During that time neither my brothers nor I ate the food that was allowed for the governor. ¹⁵But the governors before me placed a heavy load on the people. They took about one pound of silver from each person. And they took food and wine. The governors' helpers before me also controlled the people. But I did not do that because I feared God. ¹⁶I worked on the wall. So did all my men who were gathered there. We did not buy any fields.

¹⁷Also, I fed 150 Jews and officers at my table. And I fed those who came from the nations around us. ¹⁸This is what was prepared every day for me and those who ate with me: one ox, six good sheep, and birds. And every ten days there were all kinds of wine. But I never demanded the food that was allowed for the governor. This was because the people were already working very hard.

¹⁹Remember, my God, to be kind to me. Remember all the good I have done for these people.

More Problems for Nehemiah

6 Then Sanballat, Tobiah, Geshem the Arab and our other enemies heard that I had rebuilt the wall. There was not one gap in it. But I had not yet set the doors in the gates. ²So Sanballat and Geshem sent me this message: "Come, Nehemiah, let's meet together in Kephirim on the plain of Ono."

But they were planning to harm me. ³So I sent messengers to them with this answer: "I am doing a great work. I can't come down. I don't want the work to stop while I leave to meet you." ⁴Sanballat and Geshem sent the same message to me four times. And I sent back the same answer each time.

⁵The fifth time Sanballat sent his helper to me with the message. And in his hand was an unsealed letter. ⁶This is what was written:

A report is going around to all the nations. And Geshem says it is true. It says you and the Jews are planning to turn against the king. That's why you are rebuilding the wall. They say you are going to be their king. ⁷They say you have appointed prophets*d* to announce in Jerusalem: "There is a king of Judah!" The king will hear about this. So come, let's discuss this together.

⁸So I sent him back this answer: "Nothing you are saying is really happening. You are just making it up in your own mind."

⁹Our enemies were trying to scare us. They were thinking, "They will get too weak to work. Then the wall will not be finished."

But I prayed, "God, make me strong."

¹⁰One day I went to the house of Shemaiah son of Delaiah. Delaiah was

the son of Mehetabel. Shemaiah had to stay at home. He said, "Nehemiah, let's meet in the Temple[d] of God. Let's go inside the Temple and close the doors. Men are coming at night to kill you."

[11]But I said, "Should a man like me run away? Should I run into the Temple to save my life? I will not go." [12]I knew that God had not sent him. Tobiah and Sanballat had paid him to prophesy against me. [13]They paid him to frighten me so I would do this and sin. Then they could give me a bad name to shame me.

[14]I prayed, "Remember Tobiah and Sanballat, my God. Remember what they have done. Also remember the prophetess Noadiah and the other prophets who have been trying to frighten me."

The Wall Is Finished

[15]So the wall of Jerusalem was completed. It was on the twenty-fifth day of the month of Elul. It took 52 days to rebuild. [16]Then all our enemies heard about it. And all the nations around us saw it. So they were shamed. They understood that the work had been done with the help of our God.

[17]Also in those days the important men of Judah sent many letters to Tobiah. And Tobiah answered them. [18]Many Jews had promised to be faithful to Tobiah. This was because Tobiah was the son-in-law of Shecaniah son of Arah. And Tobiah's son Jehohanan had married the daughter of Meshullam son of Berekiah. [19]Those important men kept telling me about the good things Tobiah was doing. Then they would tell Tobiah what I said about him. So Tobiah sent letters to frighten me.

7 After the wall had been rebuilt, I had set the doors in place. Then the gatekeepers, singers and Levites were chosen. [2]I put my brother Hanani, along with Hananiah, in charge of Jerusalem. Hananiah was commander of the palace. He was honest, and he feared God more than most men. [3]I said to them, "The gates of Jerusalem

should not be opened until the sun is hot. While the gatekeepers are still on duty, have them shut and bolt the doors. Appoint people who live in Jerusalem as guards. Put some at guard posts and some near their own houses."

The Captives Who Returned

[4]The city was large and full of room. But there were few people in it. And the houses had not yet been rebuilt. [5]So my God caused me to gather the people. I gathered the important men, the leaders and the common people. This was so I could register them by families. I found the family history of those who had returned first. This is what I found written there:

[6]These are the people of the area who returned from captivity. Nebuchadnezzar king of Babylon had taken them captive. Now they returned to Jerusalem and Judah. Each one went back to his own town. [7]These people returned with Zerubbabel, Jeshua, Nehemiah, Azariah, Raamiah, Nahamani, Mordecai, Bilshan, Mispereth, Bigvai, Nehum and Baanah.

These are the men from Israel: [8]the descendants[d] of Parosh—2,172; [9]the descendants of Shephatiah—372; [10]the descendants of Arah—652; [11]the descendants of Pahath-Moab (through the family of Jeshua and Joab)—2,818; [12]the descendants of Elam—1,254; [13]the descendants of Zattu—845; [14]the descendants of Zaccai—760; [15]the descendants of Binnui—648; [16]the descendants of Bebai—628; [17]the descendants of Azgad—2,322; [18]the descendants of Adonikam—667; [19]the descendants of Bigvai—2,067; [20]the descendants of Adin—655; [21]the descendants of Ater (through Hezekiah)—98; [22]the descendants of Hashum—328; [23]the descendants of Bezai—324; [24]the descendants of Hariph—112; [25]the descendants of Gibeon—95.

[26]These are the men from the towns of Bethlehem and Netophah—188; [27]the men from Anathoth—128; [28]the

men from Beth Azmaveth—42; [29]the men from Kiriath Jearim, Kephirah and Beeroth—743; [30]the men from Ramah and Geba—621; [31]the men from Micmash—122; [32]the men from Bethel and Ai—123; [33]the men from the other Nebo—52; [34]the men from the other Elam—1,254; [35]the men from Harim—320; [36]the men from Jericho—345; [37]the men from Lod, Hadid and Ono—721; [38]the men from Senaah—3,930.

[39]These are the priests: the descendants of Jedaiah (through the family of Jeshua)—973; [40]the descendants of Immer—1,052; [41]the descendants of Pashhur—1,247; [42]the descendants of Harim—1,017.

[43]These are the Levites: the descendants of Jeshua (through Kadmiel through the family of Hodaviah)—74.

[44]These are the singers: the descendants of Asaph—148.

[45]These are the gatekeepers: the descendants of Shallum, Ater, Talmon, Akkub, Hatita and Shobai—138.

[46]These are the Temple[d] servants: the descendants of Ziha, Hasupha, Tabbaoth, [47]Keros, Sia, Padon, [48]Lebana, Hagaba, Shalmai, [49]Hanan, Giddel, Gahar, [50]Reaiah, Rezin, Nekoda, [51]Gazzam, Uzza, Paseah, [52]Besai, Meunim, Nephussim, [53]Bakbuk, Hakupha, Harhur, [54]Bazluth, Mehida, Harsha, [55]Barkos, Sisera, Temah, [56]Neziah and Hatipha.

[57]These are the descendants of the servants of Solomon: the descendants of Sotai, Sophereth, Perida, [58]Jaala, Darkon, Giddel, [59]Shephatiah, Hattil, Pokereth-Hazzebaim and Amon.

[60]The Temple servants and the descendants of the servants of Solomon totaled 392 people.

[61]Some people came to Jerusalem from these towns: Tel Melah, Tel Harsha, Kerub, Addon and Immer. But they could not prove that their families came from the family of Israel. Here are their names and their number: [62]the descendants of Delaiah, Tobiah and Nekoda—642.

[63]And these priests could not prove that their families came from Israel: the descendants of Hobaiah, Hakkoz and Barzillai. (He had married a daughter of Barzillai from Gilead and was called by her family name.)

[64]These people searched for their family records. But they could not find them. So they could not be priests because they were thought to be unclean.[d] [65]So the governor ordered them not to eat any of the food offered to God. First a priest had to settle this matter by using the Urim and Thummim.[d]

[66]The total number of those who returned was 42,360. [67]This is not counting their 7,337 male and female servants. They also had 245 men and women singers with them. [68]They had 736 horses, 245 mules, [69]435 camels and 6,720 donkeys.

[70]Some of the family leaders gave to the work. The governor gave to the treasury about 19 pounds of gold. He also gave 50 bowls and 530 pieces of clothing for the priests. [71]Some of the family leaders gave about 375 pounds of gold to the treasury for the work. They also gave about 2,660 pounds of silver. [72]This is the total of what the other people gave: about 375 pounds of gold, about 2,250 pounds of silver and 67 pieces of clothing for the priests. [73]So these people all settled in their own towns: the priests, the Levites, the gatekeepers, the singers, the Temple servants and all the other people of Israel.

Ezra Reads the Teachings

By the seventh month the Israelites were settled in their own towns.

8 All the people of Israel gathered together in the square by the Water Gate. They asked Ezra the teacher to bring out the Book of the Teachings of Moses. These are the Teachings the Lord had given to Israel.

[2]So Ezra the priest brought out the Teachings for the crowd. This was on the first day of the seventh month. Men, women and all who could listen and understand had gathered. [3]Ezra

read the Teachings out loud. He read from early morning until noon. He was facing the square by the Water Gate. He read to the men, women and everyone who could listen and understand. All the people listened carefully to the Book of the Teachings.

"**H**ow much attention do you pay when someone reads the Bible out loud? We need to listen like the people did in Nehemiah 8:1-12."

⁴Ezra the teacher stood on a high wooden platform. It had been built just for this time. On his right were Mattithiah, Shema, Anaiah, Uriah, Hilkiah and Maaseiah. And on his left were Pedaiah, Mishael, Malkijah, Hashum, Hashbaddanah, Zechariah and Meshullam.

⁵Ezra opened the book. All the people could see him because he was above them. As he opened it, all the people stood up. ⁶Ezra praised the Lord, the great God. And all the people held up their hands and said, "Amen! Amen!" Then they bowed down and worshiped the Lord with their faces to the ground.

⁷These Levites taught the people the Teachings as they stood there: Jeshua, Bani, Sherebiah, Jamin, Akkub, Shabbethai, Hodiah, Maaseiah, Kelita, Azariah, Jozabad, Hanan and Pelaiah. ⁸They read the Book of the Teachings of God. They read so the people could understand. And they explained what it meant. Then the people understood what was being read.

⁹Then Nehemiah the governor and Ezra the priest and teacher spoke up. And the Levites who were teaching spoke up. They said to all the people, "This is a holy day to the Lord your God. Don't be sad or cry." All the people had been crying as they listened to the words of the Teachings.

¹⁰Nehemiah said, "Go and enjoy good food and sweet drinks. Send some to people who have none. Today is a holy day to the Lord. Don't be sad. The joy of the Lord will make you strong."

¹¹The Levites helped calm the people. They said, "Be quiet. This is a holy day. Don't be sad."

Feelings
NEHEMIAH 8:12

What usually makes you happy? A double-scoop, chocolate-chip ice-cream cone . . . opening presents on Christmas morning . . . a hot, sunny day at the pool? God gives us a lot of great things that bring us happiness.

The one gift from God that made the people of Israel happy in this story was the Bible! When Ezra read Scripture and the other leaders explained it to them, the people were overwhelmed with joy. They had a big celebration—they ate special foods and gave each other presents just because they were so excited about hearing God's word.

The Bible is one of the best gifts God has ever given us. Let's tell God how happy we are to have it!

To find why you shouldn't bottle up your feelings inside, zoom to page 606.

¹²Then all the people went away to eat and drink. They sent some of their food to others. And they celebrated with great joy. They finally understood what they had been taught.

¹³On the second day of the month, the leaders of all the families met with Ezra the teacher. The priests and Levites also met with him. They gathered to study the words of the Teachings. ¹⁴This is what they found written in the Teachings: The Lord had commanded through Moses that the people of Israel were to live in shelters. This was during the feast of the seventh month. ¹⁵The people were supposed to preach this message. They were to spread it through all of their towns and in Jerusalem: "Go out into the mountains. Bring back branches from olive and wild olive trees, myrtle trees, palms and shade trees. Make shelters with them. It is written in the Law."

¹⁶So the people went out and got tree branches. They built shelters on their roofs[n] and in their courtyards. They built shelters in the courtyards of the Temple.[d] And they built them in the square by the Water Gate and the square next to the Gate of Ephraim. ¹⁷The whole group that had come back from captivity built shelters. And they lived in them. The Israelites had not done this since the time of Joshua son of Nun. And they were very happy.

¹⁸Ezra read to them from the Book of the Teachings. He read every day, from the first day to the last. The people of Israel celebrated the feast for seven days. Then on the eighth day the people gathered as the law said.

Israel Confesses Sins

9 It was on the twenty-fourth day of that same month. The people of Israel gathered together. They did not eat. And they put on rough cloth and put dust on their heads. This was to show their sadness. ²Those people whose ancestors were from Israel had sepa-

rated themselves from all foreigners. They stood and confessed their sins and their ancestors' sins. ³For a fourth of the day they stood where they were. And they read from the Book of the Teachings of the Lord their God. Then they spent another fourth of the day confessing their sins. And they worshiped the Lord their God. ⁴These Levites were standing on the stairs: Jeshua, Bani, Kadmiel, Shebaniah, Bunni, Sherebiah, Bani and Kanani. They called out to the Lord their God with loud voices. ⁵And these Levites spoke: Jeshua, Kadmiel, Bani, Hashabneiah, Sherebiah, Hodiah, Shebaniah and Pethahiah. They said, "Stand up and praise the Lord your God. He lives forever and ever."

The People's Prayer

"Blessed be your wonderful name.
  It is more wonderful than all
    blessing and praise.
⁶You are the only Lord.
  You made the heavens, even the
    highest heavens.
  You made all the stars.
  You made the earth and everything
    that is on it.
  You made the seas and everything
    that is in them.
  You give life to everything.
  The heavenly army worships you.

⁷"You are the Lord God.
  You chose Abram.
  You brought him out of Ur of the
    Babylonians.
  You named him Abraham.
⁸You found that he was faithful to you.
  So you made an agreement with
    him.
  You promised to give his
    descendants[d] the land of the
    Canaanites,
  Hittites, Amorites,
  Perizzites, Jebusites and
    Girgashites.
  You have kept your promise.
  You are fair.

---

[n]roofs In Bible times houses were built with flat roofs. The roof was used for drying things such as flax and fruit. And it was used as an extra room, as a place for worship and as a place to sleep in the summer.

⁹"You saw our ancestors suffering in
  Egypt.
  You heard them cry out at the Red
    Sea.ᵈ
¹⁰You did signs and miraclesᵈ against
  the king of Egypt.
  And you did them against all his
    officers and all the people of
    Egypt.
  You knew how proud they were.
  You made everyone know your name.
  And it is still known today.
¹¹You divided the sea in front of our
  ancestors.
  They walked through it on dry
    ground.
  But you threw the people chasing
    them into the deep water.
  They were like a stone being
    thrown into mighty waters.
¹²You led our ancestors with a pillar
  of cloud in the daytime.
  And you led them with a pillar of
    fire at night.
  It lit the way
  they were supposed to go.
¹³You came down to Mount Sinai.
  You talked to our ancestors from
    heaven.
  You gave them fair rules and true
    teachings.
  You gave them good orders and
    commands.
¹⁴You told them about your holy
  Sabbath.ᵈ
  You gave commands, orders and
    teachings to them
  through your servant Moses.
¹⁵When they were hungry, you gave
  them bread from heaven.
  When they were thirsty, you
    brought them water from the
    rock.
  You told them to go into the land
    and take it over.
  You had promised to give it to them.

¹⁶"But our ancestors were proud and
  stubborn.
  They did not obey your commands.
¹⁷They refused to listen.
  They forgot the miraclesᵈ you did
    for them.

They became stubborn and turned
  against you.
  They chose a leader to lead them
    back to their slavery.
But you are a forgiving God.
  You are kind and full of mercy.
  You do not become angry quickly.
    And you have great love.
  So you did not leave them.
¹⁸Our ancestors even made an idol of
  a calf for themselves.
  They said, 'This is your god, Israel.
  It brought you up out of Egypt.'
  They spoke against you.

¹⁹"You have great mercy.
  So you did not leave them in the
    desert.
  During the day the pillar of cloud
    guided them on their way.
  And the pillar of fire led them at
    night.
  It lit the way they were supposed
    to go.
²⁰You gave your good Spiritᵈ to teach
  them.
  You gave them mannaᵈ to eat.
  And you gave them water when
    they were thirsty.
²¹You took care of them for 40 years
  in the desert.
  They needed nothing.
  Their clothes did not wear out.
  And their feet did not swell.

²²"You gave them kingdoms and
  nations.
  You gave them more land.
  They took over the country of Sihon
    king of Heshbon.
  And they took over the country of
    Og king of Bashan.
²³You made their children as many as
  the stars in the sky.
  And you brought them into the
    land.
  This was where you had told their
    fathers to enter and take over.
²⁴So their children went into the land
  and took over.
  The Canaanites lived there.
  But you defeated them for our
    ancestors.

You handed over to them the
    Canaanites, their kings and
    the people of the land.
Our ancestors could do what they
    wanted with them.
25Our ancestors captured strong,
    walled cities and fertile land.
They took over houses full of good
    things.
They took over wells that were
    already dug.
They took vineyards, olive trees
    and many fruit trees.
They ate until they were full and
    became fat.
They enjoyed your great goodness.

26"But they were disobedient and
    turned against you.
They ignored your teachings.
Your prophetsᵈ warned them to come
    back to you.
But they killed those prophets.
And they spoke against you.
27So you allowed their enemies to
    defeat them.
Their enemies treated them badly.
But in this time of trouble our
    ancestors cried out to you.
And you heard from heaven.
You had great mercy.
You gave them saviors who saved
    them from the power of their
    enemies.
28But as soon as they had rest,
they again did what was evil.
So you left them to their enemies
    who ruled over them.
But they cried out to you again.
And you heard from heaven.
Because of your mercy, you saved
    them again and again.
29You warned them to return to
    obeying your teachings.
But they were proud. They did not
    obey your commands.
If a man obeys your laws, he will live.
But they sinned against your laws.
They were stubborn and
    disobedient.
They would not listen.
30You were patient with them for many
    years.

You warned them by your Spirit
    through the prophets.
But they did not pay attention.
So you allowed them to be
    defeated by other countries.
31But because your mercy is great,
    you did not kill them all.
You did not leave them.
You are a kind and merciful God.

32"And so, our God, you are the great
    and mighty and wonderful
    God.
You keep your agreement of love.
Do not let all our trouble seem
    unimportant in your eyes.
This trouble has come to us, to our
    kings and to our leaders.
It has come to our priests and
    prophets.
It has come to our ancestors and
    all your people.
This trouble has come to us since
    the days of the kings of Assyria.
And it has lasted until today.
33You have been fair in everything
    that has happened to us.
You have been loyal, but we have
    been wicked.
34Our kings, leaders, priests and
    ancestors did not obey your
    teachings.
They did not pay attention to the
    commands and warnings you
    gave them.
35Even when our ancestors were
    living in their kingdom,
    they did not serve you.
They were enjoying all the good
    things you had given them.
They were enjoying the land that
    was fertile and full of room.
But they did not stop their evil
    ways.

36"Look, we are slaves today
in the land you gave our ancestors.
They were to enjoy its fruit and its
    good things.
But look, we are slaves here.
37The land's great harvest belongs to
    the kings you have put over us.
This is because of our sins.

Those kings rule over us and our cattle as they please.

And we are in much trouble.

The People's Agreement

38"Because of all this, we are making an agreement in writing. Our leaders, Levites and priests are putting their seals[d] on it."

10 These are the men who sealed the agreement:

Nehemiah the governor, son of Hacaliah, sealed it.

These men also sealed it: Zedekiah, 2Seraiah, Azariah, Jeremiah, 3Pashhur, Amariah, Malkijah, 4Hattush, Shebaniah, Malluch, 5Harim, Meremoth, Obadiah, 6Daniel, Ginnethon, Baruch, 7Meshullam, Abijah, Mijamin, 8Maaziah, Bilgai and Shemaiah. These are the priests.

9These are the Levites who sealed it: Jeshua son of Azaniah, Binnui of the sons of Henadad, Kadmiel, 10and their fellow Levites: Shebaniah, Hodiah, Kelita, Pelaiah, Hanan, 11Mica, Rehob, Hashabiah, 12Zaccur, Sherebiah, Shebaniah, 13Hodiah, Bani and Beninu.

14These are the leaders of the people who sealed the agreement: Parosh, Pahath-Moab, Elam, Zattu, Bani, 15Bunni, Azgad, Bebai, 16Adonijah, Bigvai, Adin, 17Ater, Hezekiah, Azzur, 18Hodiah, Hashum, Bezai, 19Hariph, Anathoth, Nebai, 20Magpiash, Meshullam, Hezir, 21Meshezabel, Zadok, Jaddua, 22Pelatiah, Hanan, Anaiah, 23Hoshea, Hananiah, Hasshub, 24Hallohesh, Pilha, Shobek, 25Rehum, Hashabnah, Maaseiah, 26Ahiah, Hanan, Anan, 27Malluch, Harim and Baanah.

28The rest of the people took an oath. They were the priests, Levites, gatekeepers, singers and Temple[d] servants. And they were all those who separated themselves from foreigners to keep the Teachings of God. It was also their wives and their sons and daughters who could understand. 29They joined their fellow Israelites and their leading men. They took an oath, which was tied to a curse in case they broke the oath.

They promised to follow the Teachings of God, which they had been given through Moses the servant of God. These people also promised to obey all the commands, rules and laws of the Lord our Master.

30They said:

We promise not to let our daughters marry foreigners. And we promise not to let our sons marry their daughters. 31The foreigners might bring goods or grain to sell on the Sabbath.[d] But we will not buy on the Sabbath day or any holy day. Every seventh year we will not plant. And that year we will forget all that people owe us.

32We will be responsible for obeying the commands. We will pay for the service of the Temple of our God. We will give an eighth of an ounce of silver each year. 33It is to pay for the bread that is set out on the table. It is to pay for the regular grain offerings and burnt offerings. It is for the offerings on the Sabbaths, New Moon[d] festivals and special feasts. It is for the holy offerings. And it is for the offerings to remove the sins of the Israelites so they will belong to God. It is for the work of the Temple of our God.

34We are the priests, the Levites and the people. We have thrown lots[d] to decide when each family must bring wood to the Temple. This is to be done at certain times each year. The wood is for burning on the altar of the Lord our God. We will do this as it is written in the Teachings.

35We also will bring the first fruits from our crops. And we will bring the first fruits of every tree to the Temple each year.

36We will bring our firstborn[d] sons and cattle to the Temple. We will bring the firstborn of our herds and flocks. We will do this as it is written in the Teachings. We will bring them to the priests who are serving in the Temple.

³⁷We will bring things to the priests at the storerooms of the Temple. We will bring the first of our ground meal, our offerings, the fruit from all our trees and our new wine and oil. And we will bring a tenth of our crops to the Levites. The Levites will collect these things in all the towns where we work. ³⁸A priest of Aaron's family must be with the Levites when they receive the tenth of the people's crops. The Levites must bring a tenth of all they receive to the Temple of our God. Then they will put it in the storerooms of the treasury. ³⁹The people of Israel and the Levites are to bring their gifts to the storerooms. These are the gifts of grain, new wine and oil. The things for the Temple are kept in the storerooms. It is also where the priests, who are serving, the gatekeepers and singers stay.

We will not ignore the Temple of our God.

New People Move into Jerusalem

11 The leaders of Israel lived in Jerusalem. The rest of the people threw lots.^d One person out of every ten was to come and live in Jerusalem. It was the holy city. The other nine could stay in their own cities. ²The people blessed those who volunteered to live in Jerusalem.

³These are the area leaders who lived in Jerusalem. (Some people lived on their own land in the cities of Judah. These included Israelites, priests, Levites, Temple servants and descendants^d of Solomon's servants. ⁴Others from the families of Judah and Benjamin lived in Jerusalem.)

These are descendants of Judah who moved into Jerusalem. There was Athaiah son of Uzziah. (Uzziah was the son of Zechariah, who was the son of Amariah. Amariah was the son of Shephatiah, who was the son of Mahalalel. Mahalalel was a descendant of Perez.) ⁵There was also Masseiah son of Baruch. (Baruch was the son of Col-

Hozeh, who was the son of Hazaiah. Hazaiah was the son of Adaiah, who was the son of Joiarib. Joiarib was the son of Zechariah, who was a descendant of Shelah.) ⁶All the descendants of Perez who lived in Jerusalem totaled 468 men. They were soldiers.

⁷These are descendants of Benjamin who moved into Jerusalem. There was Sallu son of Meshullam. (Meshullam was the son of Joed, who was the son of Pedaiah. Pedaiah was the son of Kolaiah, who was the son of Maaseiah. Maaseiah was the son of Ithiel, who was the son of Jeshaiah.) ⁸Following him were Gabbai and Sallai. All together there were 928 men. ⁹Joel son of Zicri was appointed over them. And Judah son of Hassenuah was second in charge of the new area of the city.

¹⁰These are the priests who moved into Jerusalem. There was Jedaiah son of Joiarib, Jakin ¹¹and Seraiah son of Hilkiah. (Hilkiah was the son of Meshullam, who was the son of Zadok. Zadok was the son of Meraioth, who was the son of Ahitub. Seraiah was the supervisor in the Temple.) ¹²And there were others with them who did the work for the Temple. All together there were 822 men. Also there was Adaiah son of Jeroham. (Jeroham was the son of Pelaliah, who was the son of Amzi. Amzi was the son of Zechariah, who was the son of Pashhur. Pashhur was the son of Malkijah.) ¹³And there were family heads with him. All together there were 242 men. Also there was Amashsai son of Azarel. (Azarel was the son of Ahzai, who was the son of Meshillemoth. Meshillemoth was the son of Immer.) ¹⁴And there were brave men with Amashsai. All together there were 128 men. Zabdiel son of Haggedolim was appointed over them.

¹⁵These are the Levites who moved into Jerusalem. There was Shemaiah son of Hasshub. (Hasshub was the son of Azrikam, who was the son of Hashabiah. Hashabiah was the son of Bunni.) ¹⁶And there were Shabbethai and Jozabad. They were two of the

leaders of the Levites. They were in charge of the work outside the Temple. [17]There was Mattaniah son of Mica. (Mica was the son of Zabdi, who was the son of Asaph.) Mattaniah was the director. He led the people in thanksgiving and prayer. There was Bakbukiah, who was second in charge over his fellow Levites. And there was Abda son of Shammua. (Shammua was the son of Galal, who was the son of Jeduthun.) [18]All together 284 Levites lived in the holy city of Jerusalem.

[19]These are the gatekeepers who moved into Jerusalem. There were Akkub, Talmon and others with them. There was a total of 172 men. They guarded the city gates.

[20]The other Israelites, priests and Levites lived on their own land. They were in all the cities of Judah.

[21]The Temple servants lived on the hill of Ophel. Ziha and Gishpa were in charge of them.

[22]Uzzi son of Bani was appointed over the Levites in Jerusalem. (Bani was the son of Hashabiah, who was the son of Mattaniah. Mattaniah was the son of Mica.) Uzzi was one of Asaph's descendants. They were the singers. They were responsible for the service of the Temple. [23]The singers took orders from the king. Those orders told the singers what to do each day.

[24]Pethahiah son of Meshezabel was the king's spokesman. Meshezabel was a descendant of Zerah, the son of Judah.

[25]Some of the people of Judah lived in villages with their surrounding fields. Some lived in Kiriath Arba and its surroundings. Some lived in Dibon and its surroundings. Some lived in Jekabzeel and its surroundings. [26]Others lived in Jeshua, Moladah, Beth Pelet, [27]Hazar Shual, Beersheba and its surroundings. [28]Others were in Ziklag and Meconah and its surroundings. [29]Some people lived in En Rimmon, Zorah, Jarmuth, [30]Zanoah, Adullam and their villages. Some were in Lachish and the fields around it. Some lived in Azekah and its surroundings. So they settled from Beersheba all the way to the Valley of Hinnom.

[31]The descendants of the Benjaminites from Geba lived in Micmash, Aija, Bethel and its surroundings, [32]They lived in Anathoth, Nob, Ananiah, [33]Hazor, Ramah and Gittaim. [34]They lived in Hadid, Zeboim, Neballat, [35]Lod, Ono and in the Valley of the Craftsmen. [36]Some groups of the Levites from Judah settled in the land of Benjamin.

Priests and Levites

12 These are the priests and Levites who returned with Zerubbabel son of Shealtiel and with Jeshua. There were Seraiah, Jeremiah, Ezra, [2]Amariah, Malluch, Hattush, [3]Shecaniah, Rehum, Meremoth, [4]Iddo, Ginnethon, Abijah, [5]Mijamin, Moadiah, Bilgah, [6]Shemaiah, Joiarib, Jedaiah, [7]Sallu, Amok, Hilkiah and Jedaiah. They were the leaders of the priests and their relatives. This was in the days of Jeshua.

[8]The Levites were Jeshua, Binnui, Kadmiel, Sherebiah, Judah and also Mattaniah. He and his relatives were in charge of the songs of thanksgiving. [9]Bakbukiah and Unni, their relatives, stood across from them in the services.

[10]Jeshua was the father of Joiakim. Joiakim was the father of Eliashib. Eliashib was the father of Joiada. [11]Joiada was the father of Jonathan. And Jonathan was the father of Jaddua.

[12]In the days of Joiakim, these priests were the leaders of the families of priests. Meraiah was over Seraiah's family. Hananiah was over Jeremiah's family. [13]Meshullam was over Ezra's family. Jehohanan was over Amariah's family. [14]Jonathan was over Malluch's family. Joseph was over Shecaniah's family. [15]Adna was over Harim's family. Helkai was over Meremoth's family. [16]Zechariah was over Iddo's family. Meshullam was over Ginnethon's family. [17]Zicri was over Abijah's family. Piltai was over Miniamin's and Moadiah's families. [18]Shammua was over Bilgah's family. Jehonathan was over Shemaiah's family. [19]Mattenai was over Joiarib's

family. Uzzi was over Jedaiah's family. [20]Kallai was over Sallu's family. Eber was over Amok's family. [21]Hashabiah was over Hilkiah's family. Nethanel was over Jedaiah's family.

[22]The leaders of the families of the Levites and the priests were written down. This was in the days of Eliashib, Joiada, Johanan and Jaddua. They were written down while Darius the Persian was king. [23]The family leaders among the Levites were written down in the history book. These were only up to the time of Johanan son of Eliashib. [24]The leaders of the Levites were Hashabiah, Sherebiah, Jeshua son of Kadmiel and their relatives. Their relatives stood across from them. They gave praise and thanksgiving to God. One group answered the other group. That is what David, the man of God, had commanded.

[25]These were the gatekeepers who guarded the storerooms next to the gates: Mattaniah, Bakbukiah, Obadiah, Meshullam, Talmon and Akkub. [26]They served in the days of Joiakim son of Jeshua. (Jeshua was the son of Jozadak.) They also served in the days of Nehemiah the governor and Ezra the priest and teacher.

Giving of the Wall of Jerusalem

[27]The wall of Jerusalem was offered as a gift to God. The Levites were found in the places where they lived. And they were brought to Jerusalem to celebrate with joy the giving of the wall. They were to celebrate with songs of thanksgiving and with the music of cymbals, harps and lyres.[d] [28]They also brought together singers. They came from all around Jerusalem and from the Netophathite villages. [29]They came from Beth Gilgal and the areas of Geba and Azmaveth. The singers had built villages for themselves around Jerusalem. [30]The priests and Levites made themselves pure. They also made the people, the gates and the wall of Jerusalem pure.

[31]I had the leaders of Judah go up on top of the wall. I appointed two large

choruses to give thanks. One chorus went to the right on top of the wall. This was toward the Trash Gate. [32]Behind them went Hoshaiah and half the leaders of Judah. [33]Azariah, Ezra, Meshullam, [34]Judah, Benjamin, Shemaiah and Jeremiah also went. [35]Some priests with trumpets also went, along with Zechariah son of Jonathan. (Jonathan was the son of Shemaiah, who was the son of Mattaniah. Mattaniah was the son of Micaiah, who was the son of Zaccur. Zaccur was the son of Asaph.) [36]Zechariah's relatives also went. They were Shemaiah, Azarel, Milalai, Gilalai, Maai, Nethanel, Judah and Hanani. These men played the musical instruments of David, the man of God. Ezra the teacher walked in front of them. [37]They went from the Fountain Gate straight up the steps to the older part of the city. They went on to the slope of the wall. They went above the house of David to the Water Gate on the east.

[38]The second chorus went to the left. I followed them on top of the wall. Half the people were with me. We went from the Tower of the Ovens to the Broad Wall. [39]We went over the Gate of Ephraim to the Old Gate and the Fish Gate. We went to the Tower of Hananel and the Tower of the Hundred. We went as far as the Sheep Gate. We stopped at the Gate of the Guard.

[40]The two choruses took their places at the Temple.[d] Half of the leaders and I did also. [41]These priests were there with their trumpets: Eliakim, Maaseiah, Miniamin, Micaiah, Elioenai, Zechariah and Hananiah. [42]These people were also there: Maaseiah, Shemaiah, Eleazar, Uzzi, Jehohanan, Malkijah, Elam and Ezer. The choruses sang, led by Jezrahiah. [43]The people offered many sacrifices that day. They were happy because God made them very happy. The women and children were happy. The sound of happiness in Jerusalem could be heard far away.

[44]At that time the leaders appointed men to be in charge of the storerooms.

These rooms were for the gifts, the first fruits and a tenth of what the people gained. The Teachings said they should bring a share for the priests and Levites. These were to come from the fields around the towns. The people of Judah were happy to do this for the priests and Levites who served. ⁴⁵They performed the service of their God. They had the service of purifying things. The singers and gatekeepers also did their jobs as David had commanded his son Solomon. ⁴⁶Earlier, in the time of David and Asaph, there was a leader of the singers. There were songs of praise and thanksgiving to God. ⁴⁷So it was in the days of Zerubbabel and Nehemiah. All the people of Israel gave something to the singers and gatekeepers. They also set aside things for the Levites. The Levites set aside things for the descendants*d* of Aaron.

Foreign People Are Sent Away

13 On that day they read the Book of Moses to the people. They found that it said no Ammonite or Moabite should ever be allowed in the meeting to worship. ²The Ammonites and Moabites had not welcomed the Israelites with food and water. Instead, they hired Balaam to put a curse on Israel. (But our God turned the curse into a blessing.) ³The people heard this teaching. So they separated all foreigners from Israel.

Nehemiah Returns to Jerusalem

⁴Before that happened, Eliashib the priest was in charge of the Temple*d* storerooms. He was friendly with Tobiah. ⁵Eliashib let Tobiah use one of the large storerooms. That storeroom had been used for grain offerings, incense*d* and other things for the Temple. It was also used for the tenth offerings of grain, new wine and olive oil. These belonged to the Levites, singers and gatekeepers. It had also been used for gifts for the priests. ⁶I was not in Jerusalem when this

happened. I had gone back to Artaxerxes king of Babylon. I went back in the thirty-second year he was king. Finally I asked the king to let me leave. ⁷I came to Jerusalem. Then I found out the evil thing Eliashib had done. He had let Tobiah have a room in the Temple courtyard. ⁸I was very upset at this. I threw all of Tobiah's goods out of the room. ⁹I ordered the rooms to be purified. And I brought back the things for God's Temple, the grain offerings and the incense.*d*

¹⁰Then I found out the people were not giving the Levites their shares. So the Levites and singers who served had gone to their own farms. ¹¹So I argued with the officers. I said, "Why haven't you taken care of the Temple?" Then I gathered the Levites and singers. I put them back at their places.

¹²Then all the people of Judah brought a tenth of what they had gained in grain, new wine and olive oil. And they brought it to the storerooms. ¹³I put these men in charge of the storerooms: Shelemiah the priest, Zadok the teacher and Pedaiah a Levite. I made Hanan son of Zaccur their helper. (Zaccur was the son of Mattaniah.) Everyone knew they were honest men. They gave out the portions that went to their relatives.

¹⁴Remember me, my God, for this. Do not ignore my love for the Temple and its service.

¹⁵In those days I saw people in Judah working in the winepresses*d* on the Sabbath*d* day. People were bringing in grain and loading it on donkeys on the Sabbath day. People were bringing loads of wine, grapes and figs into Jerusalem on the Sabbath day. I warned them about selling food on that day. ¹⁶Men from the city of Tyre were living in Jerusalem. They brought in fish and other things. They sold them in Jerusalem on the Sabbath day to the people of Judah. ¹⁷I argued with the important men of Judah. I said to them, "What is this evil thing you are doing? You are ruining the Sabbath day. ¹⁸This

is just what your ancestors did. So our God did terrible things to us and this city. Now you are making him even more angry at Israel. You are ruining the Sabbath day."

[19] So I ordered the doors shut at sunset before the Sabbath. The gates were not to be opened until the Sabbath was over. I put my servants at the gates. So no load could come in on the Sabbath. [20] Once or twice traders and sellers of all kinds of goods spent the night outside Jerusalem. [21] So I warned them. I said, "Why are you spending the night by the wall? If you do it again, I will force you away." After that, they did not come back on the Sabbath. [22] Then I ordered the Levites to purify themselves. I told them to go and guard the city gates. They were to make sure the Sabbath remained holy.

Remember me, my God, for this. Have mercy on me because of your great love.

[23] In those days I saw men of Judah who had married women from Ashdod, Ammon and Moab. [24] Half their children were speaking the language of Ashdod or some other place. They couldn't speak the language of Judah. [25] I argued with those people. I put curses on them. I hit some of them and pulled out their hair. I forced them to make a promise to God. I said, "Do not let your daughters marry the sons of foreigners. Do not take the daughters of foreigners as wives for your sons or yourselves. [26] Foreign women made King Solomon of Israel sin. There was never a king like him in any of the nations. God loved Solomon. God made him king over all Israel. But foreign women made Solomon sin. [27] And now you are not obedient when you do this evil thing. You are unfaithful to our God when you marry foreign wives."

[28] Joiada was the son of Eliashib the high priest. One of Joiada's sons married a daughter of Sanballat the Horonite, who was not a Jew. So I forced Joiada's son away from me.

[29] Remember them, my God. They made the priesthood unclean.[d] They made the agreement of the priests and Levites unclean.

[30] So I purified them of everything that was foreign. I appointed duties for the priests and Levites. Each man had his own job. [31] I also made sure wood was brought for the altar at regular times. And I made sure the first fruits were brought.

Remember, my God, to be kind to me.

ESTHER

*Esther Saves
Her People*

Queen Vashti Disobeys the King

1 This is what happened during the time of King Xerxes. He was the king who ruled the 127 areas from India to Cush. ²In those days King Xerxes ruled from his capital city of Susa. ³In the third year of his rule, he gave a banquet. It was for all his important men and royal officers. The army leaders from the countries of Persia and Media were there. And the important men from all Xerxes' empire were there.

⁴The banquet lasted 180 days. All during that time King Xerxes was showing off the great wealth of his kingdom. And he was showing his own honor and greatness. ⁵When the 180 days were over, the king gave another banquet. It was held in the courtyard of the palace garden for 7 days. It was for everybody in the palace at Susa, from the greatest to the least important. ⁶The courtyard had fine white curtains and purple drapes. These were tied to silver rings on marble pillars by white and purple cords. And there were gold and silver couches. These were on a floor set with tiles of white marble, shells and gems. ⁷Wine was served in gold cups of various kinds. And there was plenty of the king's wine because he was very generous. ⁸The king commanded that each guest be permitted to drink as much as he wished. He had told the wine servers to serve each man what he wanted.

⁹Queen Vashti also gave a banquet. It was for the women in the royal palace of King Xerxes.

¹⁰On the seventh day of the banquet, King Xerxes was very happy because he had been drinking much wine. He gave a command to the seven eunuchs*ᵈ*

who served him. They were Mehuman, Biztha, Harbona, Bigtha, Abagtha, Zethar and Carcas. ¹¹He commanded them to bring him Queen Vashti, wearing her royal crown. She was to come to show her beauty to the people and important men. She was very beautiful. ¹²The eunuchs told Queen Vashti about the king's command. But she refused to come. Then the king became very angry. His anger was like a burning fire.

¹³It was a custom for the king to ask advice from experts about law and order. So King Xerxes spoke with the wise men. They would know the right thing to do. ¹⁴The wise men the king usually talked to were Carshena, Shethar, Admatha, Tarshish, Meres, Marsena and Memucan. They were seven of the important men of Persia and Media. These seven had special privileges to see the king. They had the highest rank in the kingdom.

¹⁵The king asked those men, "What does the law say must be done to Queen Vashti? She has not obeyed the command of King Xerxes, which the eunuchs took to her."

¹⁶Then Memucan spoke to the king and the other important men. He said, "Queen Vashti has not done wrong to the king alone. She has also done wrong to all the important men and all the people in all the empire of King Xerxes. ¹⁷All the wives of the important men of Persia and Media will hear about the queen's actions. Then they will no longer honor their husbands. They will say, 'King Xerxes commanded Queen Vashti to be brought to him. But she refused to come.' ¹⁸Today the wives of the important men of Persia and

Media have heard about the queen's actions. And they will speak in the same way to their husbands. And there will be no end to disrespect and anger.

¹⁹"So, our king, if it pleases you, give a royal order. And let it be written in the laws of Persia and Media, which cannot be changed. The law should say Vashti is never again to enter the presence of King Xerxes. Also let the king give her place as queen to someone who is better than she is. ²⁰And let the king's order be announced everywhere in his large kingdom. Then all the women will respect their husbands, from the greatest to the least important."

²¹The king and his important men were happy with this advice. So King Xerxes did as Memucan suggested. ²²He sent letters to all the areas of the kingdom. A letter was sent to each area, written in its own form of writing. And a letter was sent to each group of people, written in their own language. These letters announced that each man was to be the ruler of his own family. Also, each family was to speak the language of the man.

Esther Is Made Queen

2 Later, King Xerxes was not so angry. Then he remembered Vashti and what she had done. And he remembered his order about her. ²Then the king's personal servants had a suggestion. They said, "Let a search be made for beautiful young virgins*d* for the king. ³Let the king choose supervisors in every area of his kingdom. Let them bring every beautiful young virgin to the palace at Susa. These women should be taken to the women's quarters and put under the care of Hegai. He is the king's eunuch*d* in charge of the women. And let beauty treatments be given to them. ⁴Then let the girl who most pleases the king become queen in place of Vashti." The king liked this advice. So he did as they said.

⁵Now there was a Jewish man in the palace of Susa. His name was Mordecai son of Jair. Jair was the son of Shimei. And Shimei was the son of Kish. Mordecai was from the tribe*d* of Benjamin. ⁶Mordecai had been taken captive from Jerusalem by Nebuchadnezzar king of Babylon. Mordecai was part of the group taken into captivity with Jehoiachin king of Judah. ⁷Mordecai had a cousin named Hadassah, who had no father or mother. So Mordecai took

Unsung Heroes
MORDECAI • ESTHER 2:5-7

Mordecai was a Jewish man who lived in the Persian city of Susa. He served the King of Persia, but he served God first. Mordecai had a cousin called Esther. Her parents had died when she was young, so Mordecai raised her as his own daughter. He taught her to love and serve God.

One day, Esther became the Queen of Persia. Mordecai helped her and reminded her to serve God. She was able to save all the Jews from an evil leader who wanted to kill them. Esther learned to love God from her cousin Mordecai. The lessons you are learning about God now will help you to obey him and serve him when you grow up.

To read about a hero who helped a prophet, fly to page 933.

care of her. Hadassah was also called Esther, and she had a very pretty figure and face. Mordecai had adopted her as his own daughter when her father and mother died.

⁸The king's command and order had been heard. And many girls had been brought to the palace in Susa. They had been put under the care of Hegai. When this happened, Esther was also taken to the king's palace. She was put into the care of Hegai, who was in charge of the women. ⁹Esther pleased Hegai, and he liked her. So Hegai quickly began giving Esther her beauty treatments and special food. He gave her seven servant girls chosen from the king's palace. Then Hegai moved Esther and her seven servant girls to the best part of the women's quarters.

¹⁰Esther did not tell anyone about her family or who her people were. Mordecai had told her not to. ¹¹Every day Mordecai walked back and forth near the courtyard. This was where the king's women lived. He wanted to find out how Esther was and what was happening to her.

¹²Before a girl could take her turn with King Xerxes, she had to complete 12 months of beauty treatments. These were ordered for the women. For 6 months she was treated with oil and myrrh.ᵈ And she spent 6 months with perfumes and cosmetics. ¹³Then she was ready to go to the king. Anything she asked for was given to her. She could take it with her from the women's quarters to the king's palace. ¹⁴In the evening she would go to the king's palace. And in the morning she would return to another part of the women's quarters. There she would be placed under the care of a man named Shaashgaz. Shaashgaz was the king's eunuch in charge of the slave women.ᵈ The girl would not go back to the king again unless he was pleased with her. Then he would call her by name to come back to him.

¹⁵Esther daughter of Abihail, Mordecai's uncle, had been adopted by Mordecai. The time came for Esther to go to the king. She asked for only what Hegai suggested she should take. (Hegai was the king's eunuch who was in charge of the women.) And everyone who saw Esther liked her. ¹⁶So Esther was taken to King Xerxes in the royal palace. This happened in the tenth month, the month of Tebeth. It was in Xerxes' seventh year as king.

¹⁷And the king was pleased with Esther more than with any of the other girls. And he liked her more than any of the other virgins. So King Xerxes put a royal crown on Esther's head. And he made her queen in place of Vashti. ¹⁸Then the king gave a great banquet for Esther. He invited all his important men and royal officers. He announced a holiday in all the empire. And he was generous and gave everyone a gift.

Mordecai Discovers an Evil Plan

¹⁹Now Mordecai was sitting at the king's gate. This was when the virginsᵈ were gathered the second time. ²⁰And Esther had still not told anyone about her family or who her people were. That is what Mordecai had told her to do. She still obeyed Mordecai just as she had done when he was bringing her up.

²¹Now Bigthana and Teresh were two of the king's officers who guarded the doorway. While Mordecai was sitting at the king's gate, Bigthana and Teresh became angry at the king. And they began to make plans to kill King Xerxes. ²²But Mordecai found out about their plans and told Queen Esther. Then Queen Esther told the king. She also told him that Mordecai had found out about the evil plan. ²³When the report was investigated, it was found to be true. The two officers who had planned to kill the king were hanged. And all this was written down in the daily court record in the king's presence.

Haman Plans to Destroy the Jews

3 After these things happened, King Xerxes honored Haman son of Hammedatha the Agagite. He gave

Haman a new rank that was higher than all the important men. ²And all the royal officers at the king's gate would bow down and kneel before Haman. This was what the king had ordered. But Mordecai would not bow down, and he did not kneel.

³Then the royal officers at the king's gate asked Mordecai, "Why don't you obey the king's command?" ⁴And they said this to him every day. When he did not listen to them, they told Haman about it. They wanted to see if Haman would accept Mordecai's behavior because Mordecai had told them that he was a Jew.

⁵Then Haman saw that Mordecai would not bow down to him or kneel before him. And he became very angry. ⁶He had been told who the people of Mordecai were. And he thought of himself as too important to try to kill only Mordecai. So he looked for a way to destroy all of Mordecai's people, the Jews, in all of Xerxes' kingdom.

⁷It was in the first month of the twelfth year of King Xerxes' rule. That is the month of Nisan. Pur (that is, the lot^d) was thrown before Haman. The lot was used to choose a day and a month. So the twelfth month, the month of Adar, was chosen.

⁸Then Haman said to King Xerxes, "There is a certain group of people in all the areas of your kingdom. They are scattered among the other people. They keep themselves separate. Their customs are different from those of all the other people. And they do not obey the king's laws. It is not right for you to allow them to continue living in your kingdom. ⁹If it pleases the king, let an order be given to destroy those people. Then I will pay 375 tons of silver to those who do the king's business. They will put it into the royal treasury."

¹⁰So the king took his signet^d ring off and gave it to Haman. Haman son of Hammedatha, the Agagite, was the enemy of the Jews. ¹¹Then the king said to Haman, "The money and the people are yours. Do with them as you please."

¹²On the thirteenth day of the first month, the royal secretaries were called. They wrote out all of Haman's orders. They wrote to the king's governors and to the captains of the soldiers in each area. And they wrote to the important men of each group of people. The orders were written to each area in its own form of writing. And they were written to each group of people in their own language. They were written in the name of King Xerxes and sealed with his signet ring. ¹³Letters were sent by messengers to all the king's empire. They stated the king's order to destroy, kill and completely wipe out all the Jews. That meant young and old, women and little children, too. The order said to kill all the Jews on a single day. That was to be the thirteenth day of the twelfth month, which was Adar. And it said to take all the things that belonged to the Jews. ¹⁴A copy of the order was to be given out as a law in every area. It was to be made known to all the people so that they would be ready for that day.

¹⁵The messengers set out, hurried by the king's command. At the same time the order was given in the palace at Susa. And the king and Haman sat down to drink. But the city of Susa was in confusion.

Mordecai Asks Esther to Help

4 Now Mordecai heard about all that had been done. To show how upset he was, he tore his clothes. Then he put on rough cloth and ashes. And he went out into the city crying loudly and very sadly. ²But Mordecai went only as far

"**I** wonder what Esther was like? Because of her, many people were kept alive. Read about her courageous action in Esther 4:1-17."

as the king's gate. This was because no one was allowed to enter that gate dressed in rough cloth. ³The king's order reached every area. And there was great sadness and loud crying among the Jews. They gave up eating and cried out loudly. Many Jews lay down on rough cloth and ashes to show how sad they were.

to him. And he told Hathach about the amount of money Haman had promised to pay into the king's treasury for the killing of the Jews. ⁸Mordecai also gave him a copy of the order to kill the Jews, which had been given in Susa. He wanted Hathach to show it to Esther and to tell her about it. And Mordecai told him to order Esther to go into the king's presence. He wanted ed her to beg for mercy and to plead with him for her people.

Heroes Who Trusted God
ESTHER • ESTHER 4:15-16

It was not easy to visit King Xerxes. People could not visit the king unless he invited them. If a person came to the king anyway, that person would be killed. Even though Esther was the king's wife, she could not visit the king unless he asked her to come see him. But Esther had to talk with the king about something important. She could not wait for an invitation to see him.

An evil ruler in the king's court did not like the Jews. This ruler had tricked the king so he would order all the Jews to be murdered. Esther was a Jew. She had to ask the king to help save her and her people. She prayed and asked God to protect her before she talked to the king. God answered her prayer. Esther was not killed when she went to see the king. Instead, the king protected Esther and the Jews and punished the evil ruler who had tricked him.

Sometimes doing the right thing takes a lot of courage. But we can trust God to give us the courage we need to obey him.

To learn about a young woman who trusted God and obeyed him, *fly to page 1219.*

⁴Esther's servant girls and eunuchs*ᵈ* came to her and told her about Mordecai. Esther was very upset and afraid. She sent clothes for Mordecai to put on instead of the rough cloth. But he would not wear them. ⁵Then Esther called for Hathach. He was one of the king's eunuchs chosen by the king to serve her. Esther ordered him to find out what was bothering Mordecai and why. ⁶So Hathach went to Mordecai. Mordecai was in the city square in front of the king's gate. ⁷Then Mordecai told Hathach everything that had happened

⁹Hathach went back and reported to Esther everything Mordecai had said. ¹⁰Then Esther told Hathach to say to Mordecai, ¹¹"All the royal officers and people of the royal areas know this: No man or woman may go to the king in the inner courtyard without being called. There is only one law about this. Anyone who enters must be put to death. But if the king holds out his gold scepter,*ᵈ* that person may live. And I have not been called to go to the king for 30 days."
¹²And Esther's message was given to

Mordecai. ¹³Then Mordecai gave orders to say to Esther: "Just because you live in the king's palace, don't think that out of all the Jews you alone will escape. ¹⁴You might keep quiet at this time. Then someone else will help and save the Jews. But you and your father's family will all die. And who knows, you may have been chosen queen for just such a time as this."

¹⁵Then Esther sent this answer to Mordecai: ¹⁶"Go and get all the Jews in Susa together. For my sake, give up eating. Do not eat or drink for three days, night and day. I and my servant girls will also give up eating. Then I will go to the king, even though it is against the law. And if I die, I die."

¹⁷So Mordecai went away. He did everything Esther had told him to do.

Esther Speaks to the King

5 On the third day Esther put on her royal robes. Then she stood in the inner courtyard of the king's palace, facing the king's hall. The king was sitting on his royal throne in the hall, facing the doorway. ²The king saw Queen Esther standing in the courtyard. When he saw her, he was very pleased. He held out to her the gold scepter*d* that was in his hand. So Esther went up to him and touched the end of the scepter.

³Then the king asked, "What is it, Queen Esther? What do you want to ask me? I will give you as much as half of my kingdom."

⁴Esther answered, "My king, if it pleases you, come today with Haman to a banquet. I have prepared it for him."

⁵Then the king said, "Bring Haman quickly so we may do what Esther asks."

So the king and Haman went to the banquet Esther had prepared for them. ⁶As they were drinking wine, the king said to Esther, "Now, Esther, what are you asking for? I will give it to you. What is it you want? I will give you as much as half of my kingdom."

⁷Esther answered, "This is what I want and ask for. ⁸My king, I hope you are pleased with me. If it pleases you, give me what I ask for and do what I want. Come with Haman tomorrow to the banquet I will prepare for you. Then I will answer your question about what I want."

Haman's Plans Against Mordecai

⁹Haman left the king's palace that day happy and content. Then he saw Mordecai at the king's gate. And he saw that Mordecai did not stand up nor did he tremble with fear before him. So Haman became very angry with Mordecai. ¹⁰But he controlled his anger and went home.

Then Haman called his friends and Zeresh, his wife, together. ¹¹And he told them about how wealthy he was and how many sons he had. He also told them about all the ways the king had honored him. And he told them how the king had placed him higher than his important men and his royal officers. ¹²"And that's not all," Haman added. "I'm the only person Queen Esther invited to come with the king to the banquet she gave. And tomorrow also the queen has asked me to be her guest with the king. ¹³But all this does not really make me happy. I'm not happy as long as I see that Jew Mordecai sitting at the king's gate."

¹⁴Then Haman's wife Zeresh and all his friends said, "Have a platform built to hang someone. Build it 75 feet high. And in the morning ask the king to have Mordecai hanged on it. Then go to the banquet with the king and be happy." Haman liked this suggestion. So he ordered the platform to be built.

Mordecai Is Honored

6 That same night the king could not sleep. So he gave an order for the daily court record to be brought in and read to him. ²And it was found recorded that Mordecai had warned the king about Bigthana and Teresh. These men had planned to kill the king. They were two of the king's officers who guarded the doorway.

³Then the king asked, "What honor and reward have been given to Mordecai for this?"

The king's personal servants answered, "Nothing has been done for Mordecai."

⁴The king said, "Who is in the courtyard?" Now Haman had just entered the outer court of the king's palace. He had come to ask the king about hanging Mordecai on the platform he had prepared.

⁵The king's personal servants said, "Haman is standing in the courtyard."

So the king said, "Bring him in."

⁶So Haman came in. And the king asked him, "What should be done for a man that the king wants very much to honor?"

And Haman thought to himself, "Whom would the king want to honor more than me?" ⁷So he answered the king, "This is what you could do for the man you want very much to honor. ⁸Have the servants bring a royal robe that the king himself has worn. And also bring a horse with a royal crown on its head. The horse should be one the king himself has ridden. ⁹Then let the robe and the horse be given to one of the king's most important men. Let the servants put the robe on the man the king wants very much to honor. And let them lead him on the horse through the city streets. As they are leading him, let them announce: 'This is what is done for the man the king wants very much to honor!'"

¹⁰The king commanded Haman, "Go quickly. Take the robe and the horse just as you have said. And do all this for Mordecai the Jew who sits at the king's gate. Do not leave out anything that you have suggested."

¹¹So Haman took the robe and the horse. And he put the robe on Mordecai. Then he led him on horseback through the city streets. Haman announced before Mordecai: "This is what is done

Plans That Backfired
HAMAN • ESTHER 7

King Xerxes honored his friend Haman as the highest ranking official in his kingdom. The king also commanded all the royal officers to bow down to Haman. Haman thought he was hot stuff. That is until one of the officers, a Jew named Mordecai, refused to bow.

Haman was angry and offended by this one officer. He planned to kill Mordecai and all of the Jews in the kingdom. Anxious to get rid of Mordecai, Haman built a special platform for hanging him. However, these plans backfired when the king realized that Haman was really evil. King Xerxes kept Mordecai and the Jews safe and decided to hang Haman instead. Haman died on the platform he had built to hang Mordecai.

Sometimes people will hurt us by the things they do or say. It is never wise to plan to hurt someone else. We may end up hurting ourselves instead.

To meet a king who thought someone was always out to get him,
fly to page 1125.

for the man the king wants very much to honor!"

¹²Then Mordecai went back to the king's gate. But Haman hurried home with his head covered. He was embarrassed and ashamed. ¹³He told his wife Zeresh and all his friends everything that had happened to him.

Haman's wife and the men who gave him advice said, "You are starting to lose power to Mordecai. Since he is a Jew, you cannot win against him. You will surely be ruined." ¹⁴While they were still talking, the king's eunuchs*ᵈ* came to Haman's house. They made Haman hurry to the banquet Esther had prepared.

Haman Is Hanged

7 So the king and Haman went in to eat with Queen Esther. ²They were drinking wine. And the king said to Esther on this second day also, "What are you asking for? I will give it to you. What is it you want? I will give you as much as half of my kingdom."

³Then Queen Esther answered, "My king, I hope you are pleased with me. If it pleases you, let me live. This is what I ask. And let my people live, too. This is what I want. ⁴I ask this because my people and I have been sold to be destroyed. We are to be killed and completely wiped out. If we had been sold as male and female slaves, I would have kept quiet. That would not be enough of a problem to bother the king."

⁵Then King Xerxes asked Queen Esther, "Who is he? Where is he? Who has done such a thing?"

⁶Esther said, "A man who is against us! Our enemy is this wicked Haman!"

Then Haman was filled with terror before the king and queen. ⁷The king was very angry. He got up, left his wine and went out into the palace garden. But Haman stayed inside to beg Queen Esther to save his life. He could see that the king had already decided to kill him.

⁸The king came back from the palace garden to the banquet hall. And he saw Haman falling on the couch where Esther was lying. The king said, "Will he even attack the queen while I am in the house?"

As soon as the king said that, servants came in and covered Haman's face. ⁹Harbona was one of the eunuchs*ᵈ* there serving the king. He said, "Look, a platform for hanging people stands near Haman's house. It is 75 feet high. This is the one Haman had prepared for Mordecai, who gave the warning that saved the king."

The king said, "Hang Haman on it!" ¹⁰So they hanged Haman on the platform he had prepared for Mordecai. Then the king was not so angry anymore.

The King Helps the Jews

8 That same day King Xerxes gave Queen Esther everything Haman had left when he died. Haman had been the enemy of the Jews. And Mordecai came in to see the king. He came because Esther had told the king how he was related to her. ²Then the king took off his signet*ᵈ* ring, which he had taken back from Haman. And he gave it to Mordecai. Then Esther put Mordecai in charge of everything Haman had left when he died.

³Once again Esther spoke to the king. She fell at the king's feet and cried. She begged the king to stop the evil plan of Haman the Agagite. Haman had thought up the plan against the Jews. ⁴The king held out the gold scepter*ᵈ* to Esther. Esther got up and stood in front of the king.

⁵She said, "My king, I hope you are pleased with me. And maybe it will please you to do this. You might think it is the right thing to do. And maybe you are happy with me. If so, let an order be written to cancel the letters Haman wrote. ⁶I could not stand to see that terrible thing happen to my people. I could not stand to see my family killed."

⁷King Xerxes answered Queen Esther and Mordecai the Jew. He said, "Because Haman was against the Jews,

I have given his things to Esther. And my soldiers have hanged him. [8]Now write another order in the king's name. Write it to the Jews as it seems best to you. Then seal the order with the king's signet[d] ring. No letter written in the king's name and sealed with his signet ring can be canceled."

[9]At that time the king's secretaries were called. This was done on the twenty-third day of the third month, which is Sivan. The secretaries wrote out all of Mordecai's orders. They wrote to the Jews and to the governors and to the captains of the soldiers in each area. And they wrote to the important men of the 127 areas which reached from India to Cush. They wrote to each area in its own form of writing. And they wrote to each group of people in their own language. They also wrote to the Jews in their own form of writing and their own language. [10]Mordecai wrote orders in the name of King Xerxes. And he sealed the letters with the king's signet ring. Then he sent the king's orders by messengers on horses. The messengers rode fast horses, which were raised just for the king.

[11]These were the king's orders: The Jews in every city have the right to gather together to protect themselves. They have the right to destroy, kill and completely wipe out the army of any area or people who attack them. And they are to do the same to the women and children of that army. The Jews also have the right to take by force the property of the enemies. [12]The one day set for the Jews to do this was the thirteenth day of the twelfth month. This was the month of Adar. They were allowed to do this in all the empire of King Xerxes. [13]A copy of the king's order was to be sent out as a law in every area. It was to be made known to the people of every nation living in the kingdom. This was so the Jews would be ready on that set day. The Jews would be allowed to pay back their enemies.

[14]The messengers hurried out, riding on the royal horses. The king commanded those messengers to hurry. And the order was also given in the palace at Susa.

[15]Mordecai left the king's presence wearing royal clothes. They were blue and white. And he had on a large gold crown. He also had a purple robe made of the best linen. And the people of Susa shouted for joy. [16]It was a time of happiness, joy, gladness and honor for the Jews. [17]The king's order went to every area and city. And there was joy and gladness among the Jews. This happened in every area and city to which the king's order went. The Jews were having feasts and celebrating. And many people through all the empire became Jews. They did that because they were afraid of the Jews.

Victory for the Jews

9 The order the king had commanded was to be done on the thirteenth day of the twelfth month. That was the month of Adar. That was the day the enemies of the Jews had hoped to defeat them. But that was changed. So the Jews themselves defeated those who hated them. [2]The Jews met in their cities in all the empire of King Xerxes. They met in order to attack those who wanted to harm them. And no one was strong enough to fight against them. This was because all the other people living in the empire were afraid of the Jews. [3]And all the important men of the areas, the governors, captains of the soldiers, and the king's officers helped the Jews. They helped because they were afraid of Mordecai. [4]Mordecai was very important in the king's palace. He was famous in all the empire. This was because he was becoming a leader of more and more people.

[5]And, with their swords, the Jews defeated all their enemies, killing and destroying them. And the Jews did what they wanted with those people who hated them. [6]In the palace at Susa, they killed and destroyed 500 men. [7]They also killed these men:

Parshandatha, Dalphon, Aspatha, [8]Poratha, Adalia, Aridatha, [9]Parmashta, Arisai, Aridai and Vaizatha. [10]They were the ten sons of Haman, son of Hammedatha, the enemy of the Jews. But the Jews did not take their belongings.

[11]And on that day the number of the men killed in the palace at Susa was reported to the king. [12]The king said to Queen Esther, "The Jews have killed and destroyed 500 men in the palace at Susa. And they have also killed Haman's ten sons. What have they done in the rest of the king's empire! Now what else are you asking? I will do it! And what else do you want? It will be done."

[13]Esther answered, "If it pleases the king, give the Jews who are in Susa permission to do this. Let them do again tomorrow what the king ordered for today. And let the bodies of Haman's ten sons be hanged on the platform built for hanging people to death."

[14]So the king ordered that it be done. A law was given in Susa, and the bodies of the ten sons of Haman were hanged. [15]The Jews in Susa came together. It was on the fourteenth day of the month of Adar. And they killed 300 men in Susa. But they did not take their belongings.

[16]At that same time, the other Jews in the king's empire also met. They met in order to protect themselves and get rid of their enemies. And they killed 75,000 of those who hated them. But they did not take their belongings. [17]This happened on the thirteenth day of the month of Adar. And on the fourteenth day the Jews rested. They made it a day of joyful feasting.

The Feast of Purim

[18]But the Jews in Susa met on the thirteenth and fourteenth days of the month of Adar. Then they rested on the fifteenth day. They made it a day of joyful feasting.

[19]This is why the Jews who live in the country and small villages celebrate on the fourteenth day. They keep the four-

teenth day of the month of Adar as a day of joyful feasting. And it is also a day for giving presents to each other.

[20]Mordecai wrote down everything that had happened. Then he sent letters to all the Jews in all the empire of King Xerxes. He sent letters to places far and near. [21]Mordecai did this to have the Jews celebrate every year. They were to celebrate on the fourteenth and fifteenth days of the month of Adar. [22]It was to celebrate a time when the Jews got rid of their enemies. They were also to celebrate it as the month their sadness was turned to joy. It was the month when their crying for the dead was turned into celebration. Mordecai wrote letters to all the Jews. He wrote to tell them to celebrate those days as days of joyful feasting. It was to be a time of giving food to each other. And it was a time of giving presents to the poor.

[23]So the Jews agreed to do what Mordecai had written to them. And they agreed to hold the celebration every year. [24]Haman son of Hammedatha, the Agagite, was the enemy of all the Jews. He had made an evil plan against the Jews to destroy them. And Haman had thrown the pur (that is, the lot[d]) to choose a day to ruin and destroy the Jews. [25]But when the king learned of the evil plan, he sent out written orders. This was so the evil plans Haman had made against the Jews would be used against him. And those orders said that Haman and his sons should be hanged on the platform for hanging. [26]So these days were called Purim. The name Purim comes from the word "pur" (the lot). [27]And so the Jews set up this custom. They and their descendants[d] would celebrate these two days every year. The Jews and all those who join them are to celebrate these two days. They should do it without fail every year. They should do it in the right way and at the time Mordecai had ordered them in the letter. [28]These two days should be remembered and celebrated from now on in every family. And they

must be celebrated in every area and every city. These days of Purim should never stop being celebrated by the Jews. And the descendants of the Jews should always remember to celebrate these two days of Purim.

[29]So Queen Esther daughter of Abihail, along with Mordecai the Jew, wrote this second letter about Purim. Using the power they had, they wrote to prove the first letter was true. [30]And Mordecai sent letters to all the Jews in the 127 areas of the kingdom of Xerxes. Mordecai wrote a message of peace and truth. [31]He wrote to set up these days of Purim. They are to be celebrated at their chosen times. Mordecai the Jew and Queen Esther had sent out the order for the Jews. They had set up for themselves and their descendants these two days. They set them up so the Jews would give up eating and cry loudly. [32]Esther's letter showed that these practices about Purim were correct. They were written down in the records.

The Greatness of Mordecai

10 King Xerxes made people pay taxes. Even the cities far away on the seacoast had to pay taxes. [2]And all the great things that Xerxes did are written down. They tell of his power and strength. They are written in the record books of the kings of Media and Persia. Also written in those record books are all the things that Mordecai did. The king had made Mordecai a great man. [3]Mordecai the Jew was second in importance to King Xerxes. He was the most important man among the Jews. And his fellow Jews respected him very much. They respected Mordecai because he worked for the good of his people. And they respected him because he spoke up for the safety of all the Jews.

JOB

A Good Man Suffers

Job, the Good Man

1 A man named Job lived in the land of Uz. He was an honest man and innocent of any wrong. He honored God and stayed away from evil. ²Job had seven sons and three daughters. ³He owned 7,000 sheep, 3,000 camels, 500 pairs of oxen and 500 female donkeys. And he had a large number of servants. He was the greatest man among all the people of the East.

⁴Job's sons took turns holding feasts in their homes. And they invited their sisters to eat and drink with them. ⁵After a feast was over, Job would send and have them made clean.*d* Early in the morning Job would offer a burnt offering for each of them. He thought, "My children may have sinned and cursed God in their hearts." Job did this every time.

Satan Appears Before God

⁶One day the angels came to show themselves before the Lord. Satan also came with them. ⁷The Lord said to Satan, "Where have you come from?"

Satan answered the Lord, "I have been wandering around the earth. I have been going back and forth in it."

⁸Then the Lord said to Satan, "Have you noticed my servant Job? No one else on earth is like him. He is an honest man and innocent of any wrong. He honors God and stays away from evil."

⁹But Satan answered God, "Job honors God for a good reason. ¹⁰You have put a wall around him, his family and everything he owns. You have blessed the things he has done. So his flocks of sheep and herds of cattle are large.

Honesty
JOB 1:1

When you're not around, would you like people to say that you are nice, smart, or funny? Those kinds of compliments are great, but what about saying that you are honest?

That's what we learn about Job. He lived long ago in a place called Uz, and the first thing written about him in this book of the Bible is that he was honest. What a reputation to have! We learn a lot more about Job throughout the forty-two chapters in his book, but the first impression we get of him is how honest he was.

You may not always look great or be able to make people laugh, but you can always be honest.

To learn more about honesty, zoom to page 754.

They almost cover the land. ¹¹But reach out your hand and destroy everything he has. Then he will curse you to your face."

¹²The Lord said to Satan, "All right, then. Everything Job has is in your power. But you must not touch Job

swept down and stole your camels. They killed the servants. And I am the only one who escaped to tell you!"

¹⁸The third messenger was still

Feelings
JOB 1:20-22

Job went from having it all to having nothing! He lost his money, his beautiful houses, his children, and his health.

What did he do? He sure didn't hide his feelings from God! He spoke openly to God about how he felt. He had not given up on God. He was just upset about all the bad things that had happened.

God gave us our feelings and emotions. He doesn't want us to keep them bottled up inside. In fact, it is much better to pour out our feelings to God than to let them explode in mean words and actions towards our friends and family. Tell God how you feel, even when you are mad, disappointed, or frustrated. He helped Job through the hard times. He will help you, too!

To discover how to get help when you feel down, zoom to page 758.

himself." Then Satan left the Lord's presence.

¹³One day Job's sons and daughters were eating and drinking wine together. They were at the oldest brother's house. ¹⁴A messenger came to Job and said, "The oxen were plowing. And the donkeys were eating grass nearby. ¹⁵And the Sabeans attacked and carried them away. They killed the servants with swords. And I am the only one who escaped to tell you!"

¹⁶The messenger was still speaking when another messenger came in. He said, "Lightning from God fell from the sky. It burned up the sheep and the servants. And I am the only one who escaped to tell you!"

¹⁷The second messenger was still speaking when another messenger came in. He said, "The Babylonians sent three groups of attackers. They

speaking when another messenger came in. He said, "Your sons and daughters were eating and drinking wine together. They were at the oldest brother's house. ¹⁹Suddenly a great wind came in from the desert. It struck all four corners of the house at once. The house fell in on your sons and daughters. And they are all dead. I am the only one who escaped to tell you!"

"**S**ometimes bad and hurtful things happen that we can't understand. We have to keep trusting God just like Job did. Look at what happened to him in Job 1:1-22."

²⁰When Job heard this, he got up. To show how sad he was he tore his robe and shaved his head. Then he bowed down to the ground to worship God. ²¹He said:

"I was naked when I was born.
And I will be naked when I die.
The Lord gave these things to me.
     And he has taken them away.
Praise the name of the Lord."

²²In all this Job did not sin. He did not blame God.

Satan Appears Before God Again

2 On another day the angels came to show themselves before the Lord. And Satan also came with them. ²The Lord said to Satan, "Where have you come from?"

Satan answered the Lord, "I have been wandering around the earth. I have been going back and forth in it."

³Then the Lord said to Satan, "Have you noticed my servant Job? No one else on earth is like him. He is an honest man, innocent of any wrong. He honors God and stays away from evil. You caused me to ruin him for no good reason. But he continues to be without blame."

⁴"One skin for another!" Satan answered. "A man will give all he has to save his own life. ⁵But reach out your hand and destroy his own flesh and bones. Then he will curse you to your face."

⁶The Lord said to Satan, "All right, then. Job is in your power. But you must let him live."

⁷So Satan left the Lord's presence. And he put painful sores all over Job's body. They went from the top of his head to the soles of his feet. ⁸Then Job took a piece of broken pottery. And he used it to scrape himself. He sat in ashes to show how upset he was.

⁹Job's wife said to him, "Are you still trying to stay innocent? You should just curse God and die!"

¹⁰Job answered, "You are talking like a foolish woman. Should we take only good things from God and not trouble?"

In all this Job did not sin in what he said.

Job's Three Friends

¹¹Now Job had three friends. They were Eliphaz the Temanite, Bildad the Shuhite and Zophar the Naamathite. These friends heard about the troubles that had happened to Job. So they agreed to meet and go see Job. They wanted to show him they were upset for him, too. And they wanted to comfort him. ¹²They saw Job from far away. But he looked so different they almost didn't recognize him. They began to cry loudly. They tore their robes and put dirt on their heads to show how sad they were. ¹³Then they sat on the ground with Job seven days and seven nights. No one said a word to him. This was because they saw how much he was suffering.

Job Curses His Birth

3 After seven days Job spoke. He cursed the day he had been born. ²Job said:

³"Let the day I was born be destroyed.
     And destroy the night when it was
          said, 'A boy is born!'
⁴Let that day turn to darkness.
     Let God not even care about it.
     Don't let light shine on that day.
⁵Let darkness and gloom have that
          day.
     Let a cloud hide that day.
     Let darkness cover its light.
⁶Let thick darkness capture that night.
     Don't count it among the days of
          the year.
     Don't put it in any of the months.
⁷Let that night be empty.
     Let no shout of joy be heard in it.
⁸Let the people who curse days
          curse that day.
     They know how to wake up the sea
          monster Leviathan.ᵈ
⁹Let that day's morning stars
          become dark.
     Let it wait for daylight, but don't let
          it come.
     Don't let it see the first light of
          dawn.

¹⁰This is because it allowed me to be born.
That day did not hide trouble from my eyes.

¹¹"Why didn't I die as soon as I was born?
Why didn't I die when I came out of the womb?
¹²Why did my mother's knees receive me?
Why did my mother's breasts feed me?
¹³If they had not been there, I would be lying dead in peace.
I would be asleep and at rest.
¹⁴I would be asleep with kings and wise men of the earth.
They built places for themselves that are now ruined.
¹⁵I would be asleep with rulers who had gold.
They filled their houses with silver!
¹⁶Or why was I not buried like a child born dead?
I wish I were like a baby who never saw the light of day.
¹⁷In the grave the wicked stop causing trouble.
And people who are tired are at rest.
¹⁸In the grave there is rest for the captives.
They no longer hear the shout of the slave driver.
¹⁹People great and small are in the grave.
And the slave is freed from his master.

²⁰"Why is life given to those who are in misery?
Why is it given to those who are so unhappy?
²¹Some people want to die, but death does not come.
They search for death more than for hidden treasure.
²²They are very happy when they get to the grave.
²³Life shouldn't be given to a man who doesn't know what will happen to him.

It shouldn't be given to a man who feels trapped by God.
²⁴I make sad sounds as I eat.
My groans pour out like water.
²⁵The thing I was afraid of has happened to me.
And the thing I dreaded has happened.
²⁶I have no peace. I have no quietness.
I have no rest. I only have trouble."

Eliphaz Speaks

4 Then Eliphaz the Temanite answered:

²"If someone tried to speak with you, would you be upset?
I cannot keep from speaking.
³Think about how many people you have taught.
Think about how you have made weak hands strong.
⁴Your words have comforted those who fell.
And you have given strength to those who could not stand.
⁵But now trouble comes to you. And you are discouraged.
Trouble hits you, and you are terrified.
⁶You should trust in your respect for God.
You should have hope because you are innocent.

⁷"Think about this now: A person who has not done wrong will not die.
Honest people were never destroyed.
⁸I have noticed that people who plow evil
and plant trouble harvest it.
⁹God's breath destroys them.
A blast of his anger kills them.
¹⁰The lions roar and growl.
But the teeth of great lions are broken.
¹¹The lion dies because he can't find an animal to eat.
So the cubs of the female lion are scattered.

¹²"A word was brought to me in secret.
My ears heard a whisper of it.

¹³It was during troublesome dreams
 in the night
when men are in deep sleep.
¹⁴I was shaking with fear.
 All my bones were shaking.
¹⁵A spirit glided past my face.
 The hair on my body stood up in
 fear.
¹⁶The spirit stopped,
 but I could not see what it was.
 A shape stood before my eyes.
 And I heard a quiet voice.
¹⁷It said, 'Can a man be holy in the
 presence of God?
 Can a man be pure before the one
 who made him?
¹⁸God does not trust his servants.
 He even blames his angels for
 mistakes.
¹⁹So he puts even more blame on
 people who live in clay houses.ⁿ
 The foundations of these houses
 are made of dust.
 They can be crushed more easily
 than a moth.
²⁰Between dawn and sunset they are
 broken to pieces.
 They are not noticed. They die and
 are gone forever.
²¹The ropes of their tents are pulled up.
 And they die without wisdom.'

5 "Call if you want to, but no one will
 answer you.
 You can't turn to any of the holy
 ones.
²Foolish anger kills a person.
 And jealousy kills a weak-minded
 person.
³I have seen a fool have success like
 a tree taking root.
 But suddenly his home was
 destroyed.
⁴His children are far away from safety.
 They are crushed in court with no
 one to defend them.
⁵Hungry people eat this fool's harvest.
 They even take what grew up
 among the thorns.
 And thirsty people want his
 wealth.

⁶Hard times do not come up from the
 ground.
 And trouble does not grow from the
 earth.
⁷But man is born to have trouble
 as surely as sparks fly upward.

⁸"But if I were you, I would call on God.
 I would bring my problem before
 him.
⁹God does wonderful things that
 cannot be understood.
 He does so many miraclesᵈ they
 cannot be counted.
¹⁰God gives rain to the earth.
 He sends water on the fields.
¹¹God makes the humble person
 important.
 He lifts to places of safety those
 who are sad.
¹²God ruins the plans of those who
 trick others.
 Then they have no success.
¹³He catches wise men in their own
 clever traps.
 And the plans of those who try to
 trick others are swept away.
¹⁴Darkness covers them up in the
 daytime.
 At noon they feel around in the dark.
¹⁵God saves needy people from their
 lies.
 He saves them from the harm
 done by powerful people.
¹⁶So the poor people have hope.
 And those who are unfair are
 silenced.

¹⁷"The person whom God corrects is
 happy.
 So do not hate being corrected by
 God All-Powerful.
¹⁸God hurts, but he also bandages up.
 He injures, but his hands also heal.
¹⁹He will save you from six troubles.
 Even seven troubles will not harm
 you.
²⁰God will buy you back from death in
 times of hunger.
 And in battle he will save you from
 death by the sword.

ⁿ**clay houses**   This is probably talking about people's bodies.

²¹You will be hidden from the tongue
that hits like a whip.
You will not need to be afraid when
destruction comes.
²²You will laugh at destruction and
hunger.
You do not need to fear the wild
animals.
²³This is because you will have an
agreement with the animals
born in the wild.
And the wild animals will be at
peace with you.
²⁴You will know that your tent is safe.
You will check the things you own
and find nothing missing.
²⁵You will know that you will have
many children.
Your descendants*d* will be as many
as the blades of grass on the
earth.
²⁶You will come to the grave with all
your strength.
You will be like bundles of grain
gathered at the right time.
²⁷"We have checked this, and it is true.
So hear it and decide what it means
to you."

Job Answers Eliphaz

6 Then Job answered:
²"I wish my suffering could be
weighed.
And I wish my misery could be put
on the scales.
³My sadness would be heavier than
the sand of the seas.
No wonder my words seem
careless.
⁴The arrows of God All-Powerful are
in me.
My spirit drinks in their poison.
God's terrors are gathered against
me.
⁵A wild donkey does not bray when it
has grass to eat.
An ox is quiet when it has feed.
⁶Tasteless food is not eaten without salt.
There is no flavor in the white part
of an egg.
⁷I refuse to touch it.

Such food makes me sick.
⁸"How I wish I might have what I ask
for.
How I wish God would give me
what I hope for.
⁹I wish God would be willing to
crush me
and reach out his hand to destroy
me.
¹⁰Then I would have this comfort.
I would be glad even in this
unending pain.
I would know I did not reject the
words of the Holy One.

¹¹"I do not have the strength to wait.
There is nothing to hope for so how
can I be patient?
¹²I do not have the strength of stone.
My flesh is not bronze.
¹³I have no power to help myself.
This is because success has been
taken away from me.

¹⁴"They say, 'A man's friends should
be kind to him when he is in
trouble.
This should be done even if he
stops fearing God All-
Powerful.'
¹⁵But my brothers cannot be counted
on.
They are like streams that do not
flow regularly,
streams that sometimes run over.
¹⁶They are like streams made dark by
melting ice,
that rise with melting snow.
¹⁷But they stop flowing when it is the
dry season.
They go away when it is hot.
¹⁸Groups of travelers turn away from
their paths.
They go into the desert and die.
¹⁹The groups of travelers from Tema
look for water.
The traders of Sheba who travel
look hopefully.
²⁰They are upset because they had
been sure.
But when they arrive, they are
disappointed.
²¹You also have been no help.

You see something terrible, and
you are afraid.
²²I have never said, 'Give me a gift.
Use your wealth to pay my debt.
²³Save me from the enemy's power.
Buy me back from the clutches of
cruel people.'

²⁴"Teach me, and I will be quiet.
Show me where I have been wrong.
²⁵Honest words are painful!
But your arguments prove nothing.
²⁶Do you mean to correct what I say?
Will you treat the words of a
troubled man as if they were
only wind?
²⁷You would even throw lots*d* for orphans.
And you would trade away your
friend.

²⁸"But now please look at me.
I would not lie to your face.
²⁹Change your mind. Do not be unfair.
Think again, because my innocence
is being questioned.
³⁰What I am saying is not wicked.
I can tell the difference between
right and wrong.

7 "Man has a hard task on earth.
His days are like those of a hired
man.
²Man is like a slave wishing for the
evening shadows.
Or he is like a hired man who wants
his pay.
³But I am given months that are empty.
Nights of misery have been given
to me.
⁴When I lie down, I think, 'How long
is it until I get up?'
The night is long, and I toss until
dawn.
⁵My body is covered with worms and
scabs.
My skin is broken and full of
running sores.

⁶"My days go by faster than a weaver
moves his tool.
And they come to an end without
hope.
⁷Remember, God, that my life is only
as long as a breath.

My eyes will never see happy times
again.
⁸Those who see me now will see me
no more.
You will look for me, but I will be
gone.
⁹A cloud disappears and is gone.
In the same way, a person who goes
where the dead are does not
return.
¹⁰He will never come back to his house
again.
His place will not know him
anymore.

¹¹"So I will not stay quiet.
I will speak out in the suffering of
my spirit.
I will complain because I am so
unhappy.
¹²I am not the sea or the sea monster.
So why have you set a guard over
me?
¹³Sometimes I think my bed will
comfort me.
Or I think my couch will stop my
complaint.
¹⁴Then you frighten me with dreams.
You terrify me with visions.
¹⁵My throat prefers to be choked.
My bones welcome death.
¹⁶I hate my life. I don't want to live
forever.
Let me alone. My days have no
meaning.

¹⁷"Why do you make man so important?
Why do you give him so much
attention?
¹⁸Will you examine him every morning?
Why do you test him every moment?
¹⁹Will you never look away from me?
Will you not let me alone even
long enough to swallow?
²⁰If I have sinned, what have I done to
you,
you watcher of men?
Why have you made me your
target?
Have I become a heavy load for
you?
²¹Why don't you pardon my wrongs
and forgive my sins?

I will soon lie down in the dust and
die.
You will search for me, but I will be
no more."

Bildad Speaks to Job

8 Then Bildad the Shuhite answered:
² "How long will you say such
things?
Your words are no more than a
strong wind.
³ God does not twist fairness.
God All-Powerful does not make
wrong what is right.
⁴ Your children sinned against God.
And he punished them for their sins.
⁵ But you should ask God for help.
Pray to God All-Powerful for mercy.
⁶ You must be good and honest.
Then he will start doing something
for you.
And he will bring you back where
you belong.
⁷ The place you began will seem
unimportant
because your future will be so
successful.

⁸ "Ask old people
and find out what their ancestors
learned.
⁹ We were only born yesterday and
know nothing.
Our days on earth are like only a
shadow.
¹⁰ Those people will teach you and tell
you.
They will tell you what they know.
¹¹ Papyrus*d* plants cannot grow tall
where there is no wet land.
Reeds cannot grow tall without
water.
¹² While they are still growing and not
yet cut,
they will dry up more quickly than
grass.
¹³ That is what will happen to everyone
who forgets God.
The hope of the person without
God will be gone.
¹⁴ What he trusts in is easily broken.
It is as easily broken as a spider's web.

¹⁵ He leans on the spider's web, but it
breaks.
He holds on to it, but it does not
hold him up.
¹⁶ He is like a well-watered plant in the
sunshine.
The plant spreads its roots all
through the garden.
¹⁷ It wraps its roots around a pile of rocks.
And it looks for a place among the
stones.
¹⁸ But the plant may be torn from its
place.
Then that place rejects it and says,
'I never saw you.'
¹⁹ Then its life dries up.
And other plants grow up from the
dirt in its place.

²⁰ "Surely God does not reject innocent
men.
He does not give strength to those
who do evil.
²¹ God will yet fill your mouth with
laughter.
And he will fill your lips with shouts
of joy.
²² Your enemies will be covered in
shame.
And the tents of the wicked will be
gone."

Job Answers Bildad

9 Then Job answered:
² "Yes, I know that this is true.
But how can man be right in the
presence of God?
³ A person might want to argue with
God.
But he could not answer God one
time out of a thousand.
⁴ God's wisdom is deep, and his
power is great.
No one can fight God without being
hurt.
⁵ God moves mountains without
anyone knowing it.
He turns mountains over when he is
angry.
⁶ God shakes the earth out of its place.
And he makes the earth's
foundations shake.

7God commands the sun not to shine.
   He shuts off the light of the stars.
8God alone stretches out the skies.
   And he walks on the waves of the
      sea.
9It is God who made the Bear, Orion
      and the Pleiades[n]
   and the groups of stars in the
      southern sky.
10God does wonderful things that
      people cannot understand.
   He does so many miracles[d] they
      cannot be counted.
11When he passes me, I cannot see
      him.
   When he goes by me, I cannot
      recognize him.
12If God snatches something away, no
      one can stop him.
   No one can say to him, 'What are
      you doing?'
13God will not hold back his anger.
   Even the helpers of the monster
      Rahab[d] lie at God's feet in fear.
14So how can I argue with God?
   I cannot find words to argue with
      him.
15Even if I was right, I could not answer
      him.
   I could only beg God, my Judge, for
      mercy.
16I might call to him. But even if he
      answered,
   I still would not believe he would
      listen to me.
17God would crush me with a storm.
   He would multiply my hurts for no
      reason.
18He would not let me catch my breath.
   He would overwhelm me with
      misery.
19When it comes to strength, God is
      stronger than I.
   And when it comes to justice, no one
      can accuse him!
20Even if I were right, my own mouth
      would say I was wrong.
   If I were innocent, my mouth
      would say I was guilty.
21"I am innocent.

But I don't think about myself.
   I hate my own life.
22It is all the same. That is why I say,
   'God destroys both the innocent
      and the evil people.'
23A whip may bring sudden death.
   And God will laugh when good
      people suffer.
24When land falls into the hands of evil
      people,
   God covers the judges' faces so they
      can't see it.
   If it is not God who does this, then
      who is it?

25"My days go by faster than a runner.
   They fly away without my seeing
      even a little joy.
26They glide past like boats made of
      papyrus[d] plants.
   My days are like eagles that swoop
      down on animals they attack.
27I might say, 'I will forget my
      complaint.
   I will change the look on my face,
      and smile.'
28But I will still dread all my suffering.
   I know you will hold me guilty.
29I have already been found guilty.
   So why should I struggle for no
      reason?
30I might wash myself with soap.
   And I might even wash my hands
      with strong soap.
31But you would push me into a dirty
      pit.
   And even my clothes would hate
      me.

32"God is not a man like me. So I
      cannot answer him.
   We cannot meet each other in
      court.
33I wish there was someone to make
      peace between us.
   I wish someone could decide our
      case.
34I wish someone could remove God's
      punishment from me.
   Then his terror would not frighten
      me anymore.

[n]**Bear . . . Pleiades**   Names of well-known groups of stars.

³⁵Then I could speak up without
   being afraid of God.
But I am not able to do that.

10

"I hate my own life.
So I will complain without
   holding back.
And I will speak because I am so
   unhappy.
²I will say to God: Do not hold me
   guilty.
But tell me what you have against
   me.
³Does it make you happy to trouble
   me?
Don't you care about me, the work
   of your own hands?
Are you happy with the plans of
   evil people?
⁴Do you have human eyes?
Do you see as a man sees?
⁵Are your days like the days of man?
Are your years like the years of a
   man?
⁶You look for evil I have done
   and search for my sin.
⁷But you know I am not guilty.
And you know no one can save me
   from your power.

⁸"Your hands shaped me and made me.
But now you turn around and
   destroy me.
⁹Remember that you molded me like
   a piece of clay.
Now will you turn me back into
   dust?
¹⁰You formed me in my mother's womb
   as cheese is formed from milk.
¹¹You put skin and flesh on me like
   clothing.
You sewed me together with bones
   and muscles.
¹²You gave me life and showed me
   kindness.
And in your care you watched over
   my life.
¹³"But in your heart you hid other
   plans.
I know this is what was in your
   mind:
¹⁴If I sinned, you would be watching
   me.

You would not let my sin go
   unpunished.
¹⁵How terrible it will be for me if I am
   guilty!
But even if I am right, I cannot lift
   my head.
I am full of shame.
It is as if I am drowning in my pain.
¹⁶If I hold up my head, you hunt me
   like a lion.
And again you show your terrible
   power against me.
¹⁷You bring new witnesses against me.
You increase your anger against me.
Your armies come against me like
   waves of the sea.

¹⁸"So why did you allow me to be born?
I wish I had died before anyone
   saw me.
¹⁹I wish I had never been born.
Or I wish I had been carried
   straight from birth to the grave!
²⁰My few days of life are almost over.
Leave me alone so I can have a
   moment of joy.
²¹Soon I will leave and not return.
I will go to the land of darkness
   and gloom.
²²It is the land of darkest night.
It is the land of gloom and
   confusion.
Even the light is darkness there."

Zophar Speaks to Job

11

Then Zophar the Naamathite answered:

²"All these words should not go
   without an answer.
Is this talker to be judged as right?
³Your talk should not make people
   be quiet.
People should shame you when
   you make fun of God.
⁴You say to God, 'My teachings are
   right.
And I am clean*ᵈ* in God's sight.'
⁵I wish God would speak.
I wish he would open his lips to
   speak against you.
⁶I wish he would tell you the secrets
   of wisdom.

This is because wisdom has
  two sides.
Know this: God has even forgotten
  some of your sin.

⁷"Can you understand the secrets
  of God?
Can you search the limits of the
  God All-Powerful?
⁸God's limits are higher than the
  heavens. You cannot reach
  them!
They are deeper than where the
  dead are. You cannot know
  them!
⁹His limits are longer than the earth
  and wider than the sea.
¹⁰"God might come along and put you
  in prison.
If he calls you into court, no one can
  stop him.
¹¹God knows which men are evil.
And when he sees evil, he notices it.
¹²A stupid person cannot become wise.
That is as impossible as a wild
  donkey being born tame.

¹³"You must give your whole heart
  to him.
You must hold out your hands to
  him for help.
¹⁴Put away the sin that is in your hand.
Let no evil live in your tent.
¹⁵Then you can lift up your face
  without shame.
You can stand strong without fear.
¹⁶You will forget your trouble.
You will remember your troubles
  only as water that has passed by.
¹⁷Your life will be as bright as the
  noonday sun.
And darkness will seem like
  morning.
¹⁸You will feel safe because there
  is hope.
You will look around and rest
  in safety.
¹⁹You will lie down, and no one will
  make you afraid.
Many people will want favor
  from you.
²⁰But the wicked people will not be
  able to see.

So they will not be able to find the
  way to escape.
Their only hope will be to die."

Job Answers Zophar

12 Then Job answered:
²"You really think you are the
  only wise people.
You think when you die wisdom
  will die with you.
³But my mind is as good as yours.
You are not better than I am.
Everyone knows all these things.
⁴My friends all laugh at me
when I call on God and expect him
  to answer me.
They laugh at me even though I am
  right and innocent!
⁵People who are comfortable don't
  care that others have trouble.
They think that people who are in
  trouble should have more
  troubles.
⁶The tents of robbers are not bothered.
Those who make God angry are safe.
They have their god in their pocket.

⁷"But ask the animals, and they will
  teach you.
Or ask the birds of the air, and they
  will tell you.
⁸Speak to the earth, and it will
  teach you.
Or let the fish of the sea tell you.
⁹Every one of these knows
  that the hand of the Lord has
  done this.
¹⁰The life of every creature
  and the breath of all people are in
  God's hand.
¹¹The ear tests words
  as the tongue tastes food.
¹²Older people are supposed to be wise.
Long life is supposed to bring
  understanding.

¹³"But God has wisdom and power.
He has good advice and
  understanding.
¹⁴What God tears down cannot be
  rebuilt.
The man God puts in prison
  cannot be let out.

15If God holds back the waters, there
is a time without rain.
But if he lets the waters go, they
flood the land.
16God is strong and victorious.
Both the person who fools others
and the one who is fooled
belong to him.
17God leads wise men away as captives.
He turns wise judges into fools.
18God takes the royal belt off of kings.
And he dresses them like prisoners
with only a cloth around their
waist.
19He leads priests away as captives.
He destroys the power of those who
have been powerful.
20God makes trusted people be silent.
And he takes away the wisdom of
older leaders.
21God brings disgrace on important
people.
And he takes away the weapons of
the strong.
22God uncovers the deep things of
darkness.
He brings dark shadows into the
light.
23He makes nations great, and he
destroys them.
He makes nations large, and he
scatters them.
24He takes understanding away from
the leaders of the earth.
He makes them wander through a
desert with no paths.
25They feel around in darkness with
no light.
God makes them stumble around
like drunken people.

13 "My eyes have seen all this.
My ears have heard and
understood it.
2What you know, I also know.
You are not better than I am.
3But I want to speak to God All-
Powerful.
I want to argue my case with God.
4But you smear me with lies.
You are worthless doctors, all of you!

5I wish you would just stop talking.
Then you would really be wise!
6Listen to my argument.
Hear my lips begging.
7You should not speak for God by
saying evil things.
You cannot speak God's truth by
telling lies.
8You should not unfairly choose his
side against mine.
You should not argue the case
for God.
9You will not do well if he examines
you.
You cannot fool God as you might
fool men.
10God would surely scold you
if you unfairly took one person's
side.
11His bright glory would scare you.
You would be very much afraid
of him.
12Your wise sayings are worth no
more than ashes.
Your arguments are as weak as clay.

13"Be quiet and let me speak.
Then let things happen to me as
they will.
14I will put myself in danger
and take my life in my own hands.
15He will kill me. I have no hope."
But I still will defend my ways to
his face.
16This might really save me,
because a wicked man would not be
brave enough to come before
him.
17Listen carefully to what I say.
Let your ears hear what I say.
18See now, I have prepared my case.
I know I will be proved right.
19No one can blame me for doing
wrong.
If someone can, I will be quiet
and die.
20"God, please just give me these two
things.
Then I will not hide from you.
21Take your punishment away from me.

"He . . . hope   Or "Even if God kills me, I will still put my hope in him."

And stop frightening me with your
terrors.
²²Then call me, and I will answer.
Or let me speak and you answer.
²³How many evil things and sins have
I done?
Show me my wrong and my sin.
²⁴Don't hide your face from me.
Don't think of me as your enemy.
²⁵Don't punish a leaf that is blown by
the wind.
Don't chase after dry chaff.ᵈ
²⁶You write down cruel things against
me.
You make me suffer for sins I did
when I was young.
²⁷You put my feet in chains.
You keep close watch on
everywhere I go.
And you mark the soles of my feet.
²⁸So man wears out like something
rotten.
He is like clothing that has been
eaten by moths.

14 "All of us born to women
live only a few days and have a
lot of trouble.
²We grow up like flowers and then
dry up and go away.
We are like a passing shadow that
does not last.
³Lord, do you need to watch
someone like this?
Do you need to bring him before
you to be judged?
⁴I wish something cleanᵈ could come
from something unclean.
But it never can!
⁵Our time is limited.
You have given us only so many
months to live.
You have set limits we cannot go
beyond.
⁶So look away from us and leave us
alone.
Leave us alone until we put in our
time like a hired man.

⁷"There is hope for a tree.
If you cut it down, it will grow again.
It will keep sending out new
branches.

⁸Its roots may grow old in the ground.
And its stump may die in the dirt.
⁹But at the smell of water it will bud.
It will put out new shoots like a
plant.
¹⁰But we die, and our bodies are laid
in the ground.
We take our last breath and are
gone.
¹¹Water disappears from a lake.
And a river loses its water and
dries up.
¹²In the same way we lie down and do
not rise again.
We will not get up or be awakened
until the heavens disappear.

¹³"I wish you would hide me where the
dead are.
Hide me until your anger is gone.
I wish you would set a time
and then remember me!
¹⁴If a man dies, will he live again?
I will wait, struggling hard
until things change for me.
¹⁵You will call, and I will answer you.
You will desire the creature your
hands have made.
¹⁶Then you will count my steps.
But you will not keep track of
my sin.
¹⁷My wrongs will be closed up in a bag.
And you will cover up my sin.

¹⁸"A mountain washes away and
crumbles.
And a rock can be moved from its
place.
¹⁹Water washes over stones and
wears them down.
And rushing waters wash away
the dirt.
In the same way, you destroy
my hope.
²⁰You defeat man forever, and he
is gone.
You change his appearance and
send him away.
²¹His sons are honored, but he does
not know it.
His sons are disgraced, but he
does not see it.
²²He only feels the pain of his body.

And he feels sorry only for himself."

Eliphaz Answers Job

15 Then Eliphaz the Temanite answered:

2"A wise man would not answer with empty words.
He would not fill his stomach with hot, east wind.
3He would not argue with useless words.
He would not make speeches that have no value.
4But you even break down the worship of God.
You stand in the way of those who pray to him.
5Your sin teaches your mouth what to say.
You use the same words as people who trick others.
6It is your own mouth, not mine, that shows you are wicked.
Your own lips speak as a witness against you.

7"You are not the first man ever born.
You were not born before the hills were made.
8You cannot listen in on God's secret advice.
You cannot limit wisdom to yourself.
9You don't know any more than we know.
You don't understand any more than we understand.
10Old people with gray hair are on our side.
They are men even older than your father.
11The comfort God gives you is not enough for you,
even when words are spoken gently to you.
12Your heart has carried you away from God.
Your eyes flash with anger.
13You speak out your anger against God.
And these words pour out of your mouth.

14"How can man be pure?
How can a person born to a woman be good?
15God places no trust in his holy ones.
Even the heavens are not pure in his eyes.
16And man is even less than they are.
He is terrible and rotten.
He drinks up evil as if it were water!

17"Job, listen to me, and I will tell you about it.
I will tell you what I have seen.
18These are things wise men have told.
Their fathers told them these things, and they have hidden nothing.
19(The land was given to their fathers only.
No foreigner lived among them.)
20The evil man suffers pain all his life.
The cruel man suffers during all the years saved up for him.
21Terrible sounds fill his ears.
When things seem to be going well, robbers attack him.
22The evil person gives up trying to escape from the darkness.
It has been decided that he will die by the sword.
23He wanders around. He will become food for vultures.
He knows death will soon come.
24Worry and suffering terrify him.
They overwhelm him. They seem like a king ready to attack.
25This is because he shakes his fist at God.
He tries to get his own way against God All-Powerful.
26He stubbornly charges at God with a thick, strong shield.

27"The evil person's face is covered with fat.
His waist is fat with flesh.
28He will live in towns that are ruined.
He will live in houses where no one lives.
They are houses that are crumbling into ruins.
29The evil person will no longer get rich. And the riches he has will not last.

The things he owns will no longer
   spread over the land.
³⁰He will not escape the darkness.
   A flame will dry up his branches.
   God's breath will carry that evil
      person away.
³¹The evil person should not fool
      himself by trusting what is
      useless.
   If he does, he will get nothing in
      return.
³²His branch will dry up before it
      finishes growing.
   It will not even become green.
³³He will be like a vine whose grapes
      are pulled off before they
      are ripe.
   He will be like an olive tree that
      loses its blossoms.
³⁴People without God can produce
      nothing.
   Fire will destroy the tents of people
      who take money to do evil.
³⁵They plan trouble and give birth
      to evil.
   Their hearts plan ways to trick
      people."

Job Answers Eliphaz

16 Then Job answered:
   ²"I have heard many things
      like these.
   You are all painful comforters!
³Will your long, useless speeches
      never end?
   What makes you keep on arguing?
⁴I also could speak as you do
      if you were in my place.
   I could make great speeches against
      you.
   And I could shake my head at you.
⁵But, instead, my words would
      encourage you.
   I would speak words of comfort to
      bring you relief.

⁶"But if I speak, my pain does not
      become less.
   And if I don't speak, it still does not
      go away.
⁷God, you have surely taken away
      my strength.

You have destroyed my whole
   family.
⁸You have made me thin and weak.
   And people feel that this shows I
      have done wrong.
⁹God attacks me and tears me with
      anger.
   He grinds his teeth at me.
   My enemy stares at me with his
      angry eyes.
¹⁰People open their mouths to make
      fun of me.
   They hit my cheeks to insult me.
   They join together against me.
¹¹God has turned me over to evil men.
   He has thrown me into the clutches
      of the wicked.
¹²Everything was fine with me.
   But then God broke me into pieces.
   He held me by the neck and
      crushed me.
   He has made me his target.
¹³ God's archers surround me.
   He stabs my kidneys and has no
      mercy.
   He spills my blood on the ground.
¹⁴Again and again God attacks me.
   He runs at me like a soldier.

¹⁵"I have sewed rough cloth over my
      skin to show my sadness.
   I have buried my face in the dust.
¹⁶My face is red from crying.
   I have dark circles around my eyes.
¹⁷And yet my hands have never done
      anything cruel.
   And my prayer is pure.

¹⁸"Earth, please do not cover up my
      blood.
   Don't let my cry ever stop being
      heard!
¹⁹Even now I have one who speaks for
      me in heaven.
   The one who is on my side is high
      above.
²⁰The one who speaks for me is my
      friend.
   While he does this, my eyes pour
      out tears to God.
²¹He begs God on behalf of a man
      as a man begs for his friend.

²²"Only a few years will pass

before I go on the journey from
which I cannot return.

17 My spirit is broken.
The days of my life are almost
gone.
The grave is waiting for me.
²Those who laugh at me surround me.
I watch them insult me.

³"God, make me a promise.
No one else will make a promise
for me.
⁴You have closed the minds of my
friends so they do not
understand.
So you will not let them win over me.
⁵A man might speak against his
friends for money.
But if he does, the eyes of his
children go blind.

⁶"God has caused people to use my
name as a curse word.
People spit in my face.
⁷My sight has grown weak because
of my sadness.
My body is so thin it's like a shadow.
⁸Honest people are upset about this.
Innocent people are upset with
people who do wrong.
⁹But people who do right will
continue to do right.
And those whose hands are not
dirty with sin will grow
stronger.

¹⁰"But, all of you, come and try again!
I do not find a wise man among you!
¹¹My days are gone, and my plans have
been destroyed.
The desires of my heart are also
destroyed.
¹²These men think night is day.
When it is dark, they say, 'Light is
near.'
¹³It might be that the only home I
hope for is where the dead are.
I might spread out my bed in
darkness.
¹⁴I might say to the grave, 'You are
my father.'
And I might say to the worm, 'You
are my mother' or 'You are my
sister.'

¹⁵If these things are true, I have no
hope.
No one can see any hope for me.
¹⁶Hope will go down to the gates of
death.
We will go down together into the
dust."

Bildad Answers Job

18 Then Bildad the Shuhite answered:

²"When will you stop these speeches?
Be sensible, and then we can talk.
³You think of us as only cattle.
You think we are stupid.
⁴You tear yourself to pieces in your
anger.
Does everyone have to leave the
earth just for you?
Do the rocks have to be moved
from their place for you?

⁵"The lamp of the wicked person will
be put out.
The flame in his lamp will stop
burning.
⁶The light in his tent will become
dark.
The lamp by his side will go out.
⁷His footsteps will become weak and
lose their strength.
He will fall into his own evil trap.
⁸His feet are caught in a net
when he walks into its web.
⁹A trap will catch him by the heel.
And it will hold him tight.
¹⁰A trap for him is hidden on the
ground.
It lies in his path.
¹¹Terrible things startle him from
every side.
They chase him at every step.
¹²Hunger takes away his strength.
Disaster is at his side.
¹³Disease eats away parts of his skin.
The signs of death begin to eat
away at his arms and legs.
¹⁴The evil person is torn from the
safety of his tent.
He is dragged off to Death, the
King of Terrors.
¹⁵His tent is set on fire.

Burning sulfur is scattered over
his home.
¹⁶His roots dry up below ground,
and his branches above ground die.
¹⁷People on earth will not remember
him.
His name will be forgotten in
the land.
¹⁸He will be driven from the light into
darkness.
He will be chased out of the world.
¹⁹He has no children or descendants*d*
among his people.
No one will be left alive where he
once lived.
²⁰People of the west are shocked at
what has happened to him.
People of the east are very
frightened.
²¹This is surely what will happen to
the home of an evil person.
This is the place of one who does
not know God."

Job Answers Bildad

19 Then Job answered:

²"How long will you hurt me
and crush me with your words?
³You have insulted me ten times now.
You attack me without shame.
⁴If I have sinned,
it is my worry alone.
⁵Maybe you want to make yourselves
look better than I do
so you can blame me for my
suffering.
⁶Then know that God has wronged me.
He has pulled his net around me.

⁷"I shout, 'I have been wronged!'
But I get no answer.
I call loudly for help,
but I receive no justice.
⁸God has blocked my way so I
cannot pass.
He has covered my paths with
darkness.
⁹He has taken away my honor.
He has removed the crown from
my head.
¹⁰He beats me down on every side until
I am gone.

He pulls up my hope as a tree is
pulled up by its roots.
¹¹His anger burns against me.
And he treats me as one of his
enemies.
¹²His armies gather.
They prepare a way to attack me.
They camp around my tent.

¹³"God has made my brothers my
enemies.
My friends have become complete
strangers.
¹⁴My relatives have gone away.
My friends have forgotten me.
¹⁵My guests and my women servants
think of me as a stranger.
They look at me as if I were a
foreigner.
¹⁶I call for my servant, but he does
not answer.
I even beg him with my own mouth.
¹⁷My wife hates my breath.
My own family hates me.
¹⁸Even the little boys hate me.
When I leave, they talk about me.
¹⁹All my close friends hate me.
Even those I love have turned
against me.
²⁰I am nothing but skin and bones.
I have escaped with only the skin
of my teeth.
²¹Pity me, my friends. Pity me!
The hand of God has hit me.
²²Why do you chase me as God does?
Haven't you had enough of hurting
my body?

²³"How I wish my words were written
down.
I wish they were written on a scroll.
²⁴I wish they were carved with an iron
pen into lead,
or carved into stone forever!
²⁵I know that my Defender lives.
And in the end he will come to
show that I am right.
²⁶Even after my skin has been
destroyed,
in my flesh I will still see God.
²⁷I will see him myself.
I myself will see him with my own
eyes.

How my heart wants that to happen!

28 "You may say, 'We will continue to trouble Job.
The problem lies with him.'
29 But you should be afraid of the sword yourselves.
God's anger will bring punishment by the sword.
Then you will know that there is judgment."

Zophar Answers

20 Then Zophar the Naamathite answered:

2 "My troubled thoughts cause me to answer.
I am very upset.
3 I hear you criticize, and I am insulted.
But I understand how to answer you.

4 "You know how it has been for a long time.
It has been this way since man was put on the earth.
5 The happiness of an evil person is very short.
The joy of a person without God lasts only a moment.
6 His pride may be as high as the heavens.
His head may touch the clouds.
7 But he will be gone forever, like his own dung.
People who knew him will say, 'Where is he?'
8 He will fly away like a dream.
He will not be found again.
He will be chased away like a vision in the night.
9 Those who saw him will not see him again.
The place where he lived will see him no more.
10 His children will have to make up for how he mistreated the poor.
He will have to give his wealth back with his own hands.
11 He has the strength of his youth in his bones.
But it will lie with him in the dust of death.

12 "Evil may taste sweet in the evil person's mouth.
He may hide it under his tongue.
13 He cannot stand to let go of it.
So he keeps it in his mouth.
14 But his food will turn sour in his stomach.
It will be like the poison of a snake inside him.
15 He has swallowed riches, but he will spit them out.
God will make the evil person's stomach vomit them up.
16 He will suck the poison of snakes.
The snake's poisonous fangs will kill him.
17 He will not admire the sparkling streams
or the rivers flowing with honey and cream.
18 He must give back what he worked for without eating it.
He will not enjoy the money he made from his trading.
19 This is because he has troubled the poor people and left them with nothing.
He has taken houses he did not build.

20 "The evil person has no rest from his desire.
Nothing escapes his selfishness.
21 But nothing will be left for him to eat.
His riches will not continue.
22 When he still has plenty, trouble will catch up to him.
Great misery will come down on him.
23 The evil person may eat until his stomach is full.
But then God will send his burning anger against him.
God will send blows of punishment down on him like rain.
24 The evil person may run away from an iron weapon.
But then a bronze arrow will stab him.
25 He will pull the arrow out of his back.
He will pull its point out of his liver.
Terrors will come over him.
26 Total darkness waits for his treasure.

A fire not fanned by people will
destroy him.
That fire will burn up what is left
of his tent.
²⁷The heavens will show his guilt.
The earth will rise up against him.
²⁸A flood will carry his house away.
The rushing waters will come on
the day of God's anger.
²⁹This is what God plans for evil people.
This is what he has decided they
will receive."

Job Answers Zophar

21Then Job answered:

²"Listen carefully to my words.
Let this be the way you comfort me.
³Be patient while I speak.
After I have finished, you may
continue to make fun of me if
you wish.

⁴"My complaint is not just against
people.
I have reason to be impatient.
⁵Look at me then and be shocked.
Put your hand over your mouth in
shock.
⁶When I think about this, I am
terribly afraid.
My body shakes!
⁷Why do evil people live a long time?
They grow old and become more
powerful.
⁸They see their children become
strong around them.
They watch their children grow up.
⁹Their homes are safe and without fear.
God does not punish them.
¹⁰Their bulls never fail to mate.
Their cows have healthy calves.
¹¹Their children run and play like
flocks of lambs.
Their little ones dance about.
¹²They sing to the music of
tambourines*ᵈ* and harps.
The sound of the flute makes
them happy.
¹³Evil people enjoy success during
their lives.
Then they go down in peace to
where the dead are.

¹⁴But they say to God, 'Leave us alone!
We don't want to know your ways.
¹⁵Who is God All-Powerful that we
should serve him?
We would gain nothing by praying
to him.'
¹⁶But the wicked think they succeed
by their own strength.
Their way of thinking is not godly.
¹⁷Yet how often is the lamp of evil
people turned off?
How often does trouble come to
them?
How often do they suffer the
punishment God plans in his
anger?
¹⁸How often are they like straw in the
wind
or like chaff*ᵈ* that is blown away by
a storm?
¹⁹It is said, 'God saves up a man's
punishment for the man's
children.'
God should punish the evil person
himself so he will know it.
²⁰His eyes should see his own
destruction.
He should suffer the anger of God
All-Powerful.
²¹He does not care about the family he
leaves behind
when his life has come to an end.

²²"No one can teach knowledge to God.
He is the one who judges even the
most important people.
²³One man dies while he still has all
his strength.
He feels completely safe and
comfortable.
²⁴His body was well fed.
And his bones were strong and
healthy.
²⁵But another man dies with an
unhappy heart.
He never had any happiness.
²⁶These two men are buried next to
each other.
And worms cover both of them.

²⁷"I know very well what you are
thinking.
I know your plans to do wrong to me.

²⁸You say about me, 'Now where is
　　this great man's house?
　　And where are the tents where the
　　　evil men lived?'
²⁹You have never asked those who
　　travel.
　　You have not listened to their
　　　stories.
³⁰On the day of God's anger and
　　punishment,
　　it is the evil man who is spared.
³¹Who will accuse him to his face?
　　No one pays him back for the evil
　　　he has done.
³²He is carried to his grave.
　　And someone keeps watch over
　　　his tomb.
³³The dirt in the valley will seem sweet
　　to him.
　　Everybody follows after him.
　　Many people go before him.

³⁴"So you cannot comfort me with this
　　nonsense.
　　Your answers are still only lies!"

Eliphaz Answers

22 Then Eliphaz the Temanite an-
　　swered:

²"A man cannot be of any real use to
　　God.
　　Even a wise man does him no good.
³It does not help God All-Powerful
　　for you to be good.
　　He gains nothing if you are
　　　innocent.
⁴God does not punish you for
　　respecting him.
　　He does not bring you into court
　　　for this.
⁵No! It is because your evil is without
　　limits.
　　And your sins have no end.
⁶You took your brothers' things to
　　pay a debt they didn't owe.
　　You took clothes from people and
　　　left them naked.
⁷You did not give water to tired people.
　　And you kept food away from the
　　　hungry.
⁸You were a powerful man who
　　owned land.

You were honored and lived in the
　　land.
⁹But you sent widows away without
　　giving them anything.
　　You even mistreated orphans.
¹⁰That is why traps are all around you.
　　That is why sudden danger
　　　frightens you.
¹¹That is why it is so dark you cannot
　　see.
　　And that is why a flood of water
　　　covers you.

¹²"God is in the highest part of heaven.
　　See how high the highest stars are!
¹³But you say, 'God knows nothing.
　　He cannot judge us through the
　　　dark clouds.
¹⁴Thick clouds cover him so he cannot
　　see us.
　　He walks around high up in the
　　　sky.'
¹⁵Are you going to stay on the old path
　　where evil people walk?
¹⁶They were carried away before their
　　time was up.
　　Their foundations were washed
　　　away by a flood.
¹⁷They said to God, 'Leave us alone!
　　God All-Powerful can do nothing
　　　to us.'
¹⁸But it was God who filled their
　　houses with good things.
　　He did this even though their way
　　　of thinking was not godly.

¹⁹"Good people can watch and be glad.
　　Innocent people can laugh at them
　　　and say,
²⁰'Surely our enemies are destroyed.
　　And fire burns up their wealth.'

²¹"Obey God, and then you will be at
　　peace with him.
　　This way you can be happy.
²²Accept teaching from his mouth.
　　Keep his words in your heart.
²³If you return to God All-Powerful,
　　you will be blessed again.
　　Remove evil from your house.
²⁴Throw your gold nuggets into the
　　dust.
　　Throw your fine gold to the rocks
　　　in the ravines.

²⁵Then God All-Powerful will be
  your gold.
He will be the best silver for you.
²⁶You will find pleasure in God All-
  Powerful.
And you will look up to him.
²⁷You will pray to him, and he will
  hear you.
And you will keep your promises
  to him.
²⁸Anything you decide will be done.
And light will shine on your ways.
²⁹When terrible things happen to
  people, you will say, 'Have
  courage.'
Then those who are humble will
  be saved.
³⁰Even the guilty will escape.
They will be saved because your
  hands are clean."ᵈ

Job Answers

23 Then Job answered:

²"My complaint is still strong
  today.
God's hand is heavy against me
  even though I am groaning.
³I wish I knew where to find God.
I wish I could go to where he lives.
⁴I would present my case before him.
I would fill my mouth with
  arguments.
⁵I would know the words of his answer.
And I would think about what he
  would say.
⁶He would not come against me with
  great power.
He would really listen to me.
⁷Then an honest person could
  present his case to God.
And I would be saved forever from
  my judge.

⁸"If I go to the east, God is not there.
And if I go to the west, I do not see
  him there.
⁹When he is at work in the north, I
  catch no sight of him.
And when he turns to the south, I
  cannot see him.
¹⁰But God knows the way that I take.
When he has tested me, I will

come out pure as gold.
¹¹My feet have closely followed his
  steps.
I have stayed in his way without
  turning aside.
¹²I have never left the commands he
  has spoken.
I have treasured his words more
  than my food.

¹³"But he is the only God.
No one can come against him.
He does anything he wants.
¹⁴He will do to me what he said he
  would do.
And he has many plans like this.
¹⁵That is why I am so afraid before
  him.
When I think of all this, I am afraid
  of him.
¹⁶God has made me afraid.
God All-Powerful has made me
  terribly afraid.
¹⁷But I am not cut off by the darkness,
  by the thick darkness that covers
  my face.

24 "I wish God All-Powerful would
  set a time for judging.
People who know God look for such
  a day, but they do not see it.
²Wicked people take other people's
  land.
They steal flocks of sheep and take
  them to new pastures.
³They chase away the orphan's donkey.
And they take the widow's ox when
  she cannot pay what she owes.
⁴They push needy people off the path.
So all the poor people of the land
  hide from them.
⁵The poor become like wild donkeys
  in the desert.
They go about their job of finding
  food.
The desert gives them food for
  their children.
⁶They gather hay and straw in
  the fields.
And they pick up leftover grapes
  from the evil man's vineyard.
⁷They spend the night naked,
  because they have no clothes.

They have nothing to cover
    themselves in the cold.
⁸They are soaked from mountain rains.
    They stay near the large rocks
        because they have no shelter.
⁹The child who has no father is grabbed
        from its mother's breast.
    They take a poor mother's baby to
        pay for what she owes.
¹⁰So the poor go around naked
        because they have no clothes.
    They carry bundles of grain for evil
        people, but they still go hungry.
¹¹They crush olives to get oil.
    And they crush grapes in the
        winepresses,ᵈ but they still are
        thirsty.
¹²Dying people groan in the city.
    People who are injured cry out
        for help.
    But God accuses no one of doing
        wrong.

¹³"There are people who fight against
        the light.
    God's ways are strange to them.
    And they do not stay in the lighted
        path.
¹⁴When the light of day is gone, the
        murderer gets up.
    He kills poor and needy people.
    At night he goes about like a thief.
¹⁵The person who is guilty of adulteryᵈ
        watches for the night.
    He thinks, 'No one will see me.'
    And he keeps his face covered.
¹⁶In the dark, evil people break into
        houses.
    But in the daytime they shut
        themselves up in their own
        houses.
    They want nothing to do with the
        light.
¹⁷Darkness is like morning to all these
        evil people.
    They make friends with the terrors
        of darkness.

¹⁸"They are like foam floating on the
        water.
    Their part of the land is cursed.
    No one uses the road that goes by
        their vineyards.

¹⁹Heat and dryness quickly take away
        the melted snow.
    In the same way, the place for the
        dead quickly takes away those
        who have sinned.
²⁰The evil person's mother will even
        forget him.
    The worms will eat his body.
    He will no longer be remembered.
    So wickedness is broken in pieces
        like a stick.
²¹These evil men are unfair to women
        who cannot have children.
    And they show no kindness to
        widows.
²²God drags away strong men by his
        power.
    But even though they seem strong,
        they do not know how long
        they will live.
²³God may let these evil people feel
        safe.
    But he is watching their ways.
²⁴For a little while they are important,
        and then they are gone.
    They are made unimportant and
        gathered up like everyone else.
    They are cut off like the tops of
        stalks of grain.
²⁵If this is not true, who can prove I
        am wrong?
    And who can show that my words
        are worth nothing?"

Bildad Answers

25 Then Bildad the Shuhite an-
    swered:

²"God rules and must be honored.
    He set up order in his high heaven.
³No one can count God's armies.
    His light shines on all people.
⁴So no man can be good in the
        presence of God.
    No one born to a woman can be
        pure.
⁵Even the moon is not bright,
    and the stars are not pure in
        his eyes.
⁶Man is much less! He is like
        an insect.
    He is only a worm!"

Job Answers Bildad

26 Then Job answered:

[2] "You are no help to a person
who has no strength!
You have given no help to one
whose arm is weak!
[3] You have given advice to me as if I
had no wisdom!
This is not great wisdom you have
shown!
[4] Who has helped you say these words?
And where did you get these words
you speak?

[5] "The spirits of the dead beneath the
waters shake.
And so do those that live in the
waters.
[6] Death is naked before God.
Destruction is uncovered before
him.
[7] God stretches the northern sky out
over empty space.
And he hangs the earth on nothing.
[8] God wraps up the waters in his
thick clouds.
But the clouds do not break under
the weight of the water.
[9] God covers the face of the full moon.
He spreads his clouds over it.
[10] God draws the horizon like a circle
on the water
at the place where light and
darkness meet.
[11] Heaven's foundations shake
when he thunders at them.
[12] God's power controls the sea.
By his wisdom he destroyed
Rahab,[d] the sea monster.
[13] God breathes, and the sky becomes
clear.
God's hand stabs the gliding snake.
[14] And these are only a small part of
God's works.
We only hear a small whisper of
him.
So who can understand God's
thundering power?"

27 And Job continued speaking:

[2] "As surely as God lives, he has
taken away my rights.

God All-Powerful has made me
unhappy.
[3] As long as I am alive
and God's breath of life is in
my nose,
[4] My lips will not speak evil.
And my tongue will not tell a lie.
[5] I will never agree you are right.
Until I die, I will never stop saying
I was innocent.
[6] I will hold tightly to the right things
I said.
My sense of right and wrong does
not bother me at all.

[7] "Let my enemies be like evil people.
Let them be like those who are not
fair!
[8] What hope does a wicked person
have when he dies?
He has no hope when God takes his
life away.
[9] God will not listen to his cry
when trouble comes to him.
[10] He will not find joy in God All-
Powerful,
even though he calls out to God all
the time.

[11] "I will teach you about the power
of God.
I will not hide the ways of God All-
Powerful.
[12] You have all seen this yourselves.
So why are we having all this talk
that means nothing?

[13] "Here is what God has planned for
evil people.
This is what cruel people will get
from God All-Powerful:
[14] They may have many children, but
the sword will kill them.
The children who are left will never
have enough to eat.
[15] Then they will die and be buried.
And the widows will not even cry
for them.
[16] The evil person may heap up silver
like piles of dirt.
He may have so many clothes they
are like piles of clay.
[17] But good people will wear what the
evil person has gathered.

And those who are not guilty of
wrong will divide up his silver.
¹⁸The house the evil person builds is
like a spider's web.
It is like a hut that a guard builds.
¹⁹The evil person is rich when he goes
to bed, but he is rich for the last
time.
When he opens his eyes,
everything is gone.
²⁰Fears come over him like a flood.
A storm snatches him away in
the night.
²¹The east wind will carry him away,
and then he is gone.
It sweeps him out of his place.
²²The wind will hit the evil person
without mercy
as he tries to run away from its
power.
²³It will be as if the wind is clapping
its hands at him.
It will whistle at him as he runs
from his place.

28 "There are mines where people
dig silver.
And there are places where gold is
made pure.
²Iron is taken out of the ground.
And copper is melted out of rocks.
³Miners bring light into the mines.
They search even the deepest parts
of the mines.
They look for metal in places of
thick darkness.
⁴Miners dig a tunnel far away from
where people live.
They dig it where people never go.
They work far away from people,
swinging and swaying from
ropes.
⁵Food grows on top of the earth.
But below ground things are
changed as if by fire.
⁶Sapphires are found in rocks.
And the dust of the earth contains
gold.
⁷No hawk knows the path.
The falcon has not seen it.
⁸Proud animals have not walked on
this path.
And no lions cross over it.

⁹Men hit the rocks of flint.
They dig away at the bottom of the
mountains.
¹⁰Miners cut tunnels through the rock.
They see all the treasures there.
¹¹They search the places where rivers
begin.
And they bring things hidden there
out into the light.

¹²"But where can wisdom be found.
Where does understanding live?
¹³People do not understand the value
of wisdom.
It cannot be found among living
people.
¹⁴The deep ocean says, 'It's not in me.'
The sea says, 'It's not in me.'
¹⁵Wisdom cannot be bought with the
best gold.
Its cost cannot be weighed in silver.
¹⁶Wisdom cannot be bought with fine
gold.
It cannot be bought with valuable
onyx or sapphire gems.
¹⁷Gold and crystal are not as valuable
as wisdom.
And you cannot buy it with jewels
of gold.
¹⁸Coral and jasper are not even worth
talking about.
The price of wisdom is much
greater than rubies.
¹⁹The topaz from Cush cannot compare
to wisdom.
It cannot even be bought with the
purest gold.

²⁰"So from where does wisdom come?
And where does understanding live?
²¹It is hidden from the eyes of every
living thing.
It is hidden even from the birds of
the air.
²²The places of destruction and death
say,
'We have only heard reports about
it.'
²³God understands the way to wisdom.
And he is the only one who knows
where it lives.
²⁴This is because God sees to the
farthest parts of the earth.

And he sees everything under the heavens.

²⁵Wisdom began when God gave power to the wind.

It was when he measured the water and put limits on it.

²⁶It was when God made rules for the rain.

And he set a path for a thunderstorm to follow.

²⁷Then God looked at wisdom and decided its worth.

He set wisdom up and tested it.

²⁸Then he said to man,

'The fear of the Lord is wisdom, and to stay away from evil is understanding.'"

Job Continues

29 Job continued to speak:

²"How I wish for the months that have passed.

I wish for the days when God watched over me.

³I wish for the days when God's lamp shined on my head.

And I wish for the time I walked through darkness by his light.

⁴I wish for the days when I was at my strongest,

when God's close friendship blessed my house.

⁵That was when my children were all around me.

And God All-Powerful was still with me.

⁶Life was so good. It was as if my path were covered with cream.

It was as if even the rocks poured out streams of olive oil for me.

⁷I would go to the city gate and sit in the public square.

⁸When the young men saw me, they would step out of my way.

And the old men would stand up in respect for me.

⁹The leading men stopped speaking and covered their mouths with their hands.

¹⁰The voices of the important men were quiet.

It was as if each man's tongue stuck to the roof of his mouth.

¹¹Anyone who heard me said good things about me.

And those who saw me praised me.

¹²This was because I saved the poor who cried for help.

And I saved the orphan who had no one to help him.

¹³The dying person blessed me.

And I made the widow's heart sing.

¹⁴I put on right living as if it were clothing.

I wore fairness as if it were my robe and my turban.

¹⁵I tried to be eyes for the blind.

And I tried to be feet for those who were crippled.

¹⁶I was like a father to needy people.

And I took the side of strangers when they were in trouble.

¹⁷I broke the fangs of evil people.

And I snatched from their teeth the people they wanted to hurt.

¹⁸"I thought, 'I will live for as many days as there are grains of sand.

And I will die in my own house.

¹⁹I will be like a tree whose roots reach down to the water.

The dew will lie on the branches all night.

²⁰New honors will come to me continually.

I will always have great strength.'

²¹"People listened to me carefully.

They waited quietly for my advice.

²²After I finished speaking, they spoke no more.

My words fell very gently on their ears.

²³They waited for me as they would for rain.

They drank in my words as if they were spring rain.

²⁴I smiled at them when they doubted.

And my approval was important to them.

²⁵I chose the right way for them and was their leader.

I lived like a king among his army.

I was like a person who gives comfort to sad people.

30 "But now men who are younger than I
make fun of me.
I would not have even let their fathers
sit with my sheep dogs.
[2] Their hands had no strength to
help me.
They had even lost their strength
to work.
[3] They were thin from being hungry
and in need.
They wandered through the dry
and ruined land at night.
[4] They gathered desert plants by the
brush for food.
They even ate the root of the
broom tree.
[5] They were forced to live away from
other people.
People shouted at them as if they
were thieves.
[6] These young men had to live in
dried up streambeds.
They lived in caves and among
the rocks.
[7] They howled like animals out
among the bushes.
And they huddled together in
the brush.
[8] They are worthless people without
names.
They were forced to leave the land.

[9] "Now they make fun of me with songs.
My name has become a joke among
them.
[10] They hate me and stay far away
from me.
But they do not mind spitting in
my face.
[11] God has taken away my strength and
made me suffer.
So they attack me with all their
anger.
[12] On my right side they attack me like
a mob.
They lay traps for my feet.
They prepare to attack me.
[13] They break up my road.
They work to destroy me
without anyone stopping them.
[14] They go forward as if through a hole
in the wall.

They roll in among the ruins.
[15] Great fears overwhelm me.
They blow my honor away as if by
a great wind.
My safety disappears like a cloud.

[16] "Now my life is almost over.
My days are full of suffering.
[17] At night my bones ache.
Gnawing pains never stop.
[18] In his great power God grabs hold of
my clothing.
He chokes me with the collar of
my coat.
[19] He throws me into the mud.
And I become like dirt and ashes.

[20] "I cry out to you, God, but you do not
answer.
I stand up, but you just look at me.
[21] You turn on me without mercy.
You attack me with your powerful
hand.
[22] You snatch me up and throw me into
the wind.
You toss me about in the storm.
[23] I know you will bring me down to
death.
You will bring me to the place
where all living people must go.

[24] "Surely no one would hurt a ruined
man
when he cries for help in his time
of trouble.
[25] I have cried for those who are in
trouble.
My soul has been very sad for poor
people.
[26] But when I hoped for good, only evil
came to me.
When I looked for light, darkness
came.
[27] I never stop being upset inside.
Days of suffering are ahead of me.
[28] I have become black, but not by
the sun.
I stand up in public and cry for help.
[29] It is as if I have become a brother to
wild dogs
and a friend to ostriches.
[30] My skin becomes black and peels
off.
My body burns with fever.

³¹My harp is tuned for singing a sad
        song.
    And my flute is tuned for the sound
        of loud crying.

31

"But I made an agreement with
    my eyes
    not to look with desire at a girl.
²What has God above promised
        those who do this?
    What has God All-Powerful on high
        planned for them?
³It is ruin for the evil people.
    It is disaster for those who do wrong.
⁴God sees my ways,
    and he counts every step I take.

⁵"I have not been a dishonest person.
    I have not lied to others.
⁶Let God weigh me on honest scales.
    Then he will know I have done
        nothing wrong.
⁷I have not turned away from doing
        what is right.
    My heart has not been led by my
        eyes to do wrong.
    My hands have not been made
        unclean.ᵈ
⁸If I have done these things, then let
        other people eat what I have
        planted.
    And let my crops be plowed up.

⁹"I have not desired another woman.
    I have never waited at my
        neighbor's door to have sexual
        relations with his wife.
¹⁰If I have done these things, then let
        my wife grind another man's
        grain.
    And let other men have sexual
        relations with her.
¹¹Sexual sin is shameful.
    It is a sin which must be punished.
¹²It is like a fire that burns and
        destroys forever.
    It would destroy all I have.

¹³"I have been fair to my male and
        female slaves
    when they had a complaint against
        me.
¹⁴If I have not, how could I tell God
        what I did?

What will I answer when God asks
        me to explain what I've done?
¹⁵God made me in my mother's womb,
        and he also made them.
    The same God formed both of us
        in our mothers' wombs.

¹⁶"I have never refused anything the
        poor wanted.
    I have never let widows give up
        hope while looking for help.
¹⁷I have not kept my food to myself.
    I have also given it to the orphans.
¹⁸Since I was young, I have been like
        a father to the orphans.
    And from my birth I guided the
        widows.
¹⁹I have not let a person die because
        he had no clothes.
    I have not let a needy person go
        without a coat.
²⁰That person's heart blessed me.
    This was because I warmed him
        with the wool of my sheep.
²¹I have never hurt an orphan
    even when I knew I could win in
        court.
²²If I have, then let my arm fall off
        my shoulder.
    Let it be broken at the joint.
²³This is because I dread destruction
        from God.
    I could not do such things because
        I fear his majesty.

²⁴"I have not put my trust in gold.
    I have not said to pure gold, 'You
        are my safety.'
²⁵I have not celebrated my great wealth.
    I have not celebrated that my
        hands had gained riches.
²⁶I have not thought about worshiping
        the sun in its brightness.
    I have not admired the moon
        moving in glory
²⁷so that my heart was pulled away
        from God.
    My hand has never offered the sun
        and moon a kiss of worship.
²⁸If I had, these also would have been
        sins to be punished.
    I would have been unfaithful to
        God if I had done these things.

29"I have not been happy when my
    enemy was ruined.
I have not laughed when he had
    trouble.
30I have not let my mouth sin
    by cursing my enemy's life.
31The men of my house have always
    said,
'Everyone has eaten all he wants of
    Job's food.'
32No stranger ever had to spend the
    night in the street.
I always let the traveler stay in my
    home.
33I have not hidden my sin as other
    men do.
I did not hide my guilt in my heart.
34I was not so afraid of the crowd.
I did not keep quiet and stay inside
    because I feared being hated by
    other families.

35("How I wish a court would hear my
    case!
Here I sign my name to show I have
    told the truth.
Now let God All-Powerful answer me.
Let the one who is against me write
    down what he accuses me of.
36I would surely wear the writing on
    my shoulder.
I would put it on like a crown.
37I would explain to God every step
    I took.
I would come near to God like a
    prince.)

38"My land did not cry out against me.
Its plowed rows were not wet with
    tears.
39I did not take the land's harvest
    without paying.
I did not break the spirit of those
    who took care of the land.
40If I did, then let thorns come up
    instead of wheat.
And let weeds come up instead of
    barley."

The words of Job are finished.

Elihu Speaks

32 These three men stopped answering Job. This is because Job
was so sure he was right. 2But Elihu
son of Barakel the Buzite became very
angry with Job. (Elihu was from the
family of Ram.) He was angry because
Job claimed he was right instead of
God. 3Elihu was also angry with Job's
three friends. They had no answer to
show that Job was wrong. And yet they
continued to blame him. 4Now Elihu
had waited before speaking to Job. This
is because the three friends were older
than he was. 5But when Elihu saw that
the three men had nothing more to say,
he became very angry.

6So Elihu son of Barakel the Buzite
said this:

"I am young,
    and you are old.
That is why I was afraid
    to tell you what I know.
7I thought, 'Older people should speak.
    Those who have lived many years
        should teach wisdom.'
8But it is the spirit in a person that
    gives him understanding.
It is the breath of God All-Powerful
    in him.
9It is not just older people who are wise.
    Older people are not the only ones
        who understand what is right.
10So I say, listen to me!
    I will also tell you what I know.
11I waited while you spoke.
    I listened to your explanations.
I waited while you looked for words
    to use.
12   I paid close attention to you.
But not one of you has proved Job
    wrong.
    Not one of you has answered his
        arguments.
13Don't you say, 'We have found
    wisdom.
    Only God will show Job to be
        wrong, not people.'
14Job has not spoken his words against
    me.
    So I will not use your arguments to
        answer Job.

15"These three friends are defeated
    and have no more to say.

Words have failed them.

¹⁶Now they are standing there with no
answer for Job.

Now that they are quiet, must I wait
to speak?

¹⁷No, I also will speak.

I will also tell what I know.

¹⁸I am full of words.

And the spirit in me causes me
to speak.

¹⁹I am like wine that has been
bottled up.

I am ready to burst like a new
leather bag for holding wine.

²⁰I must speak. Then I will feel relief.

I must open my mouth and answer.

²¹I will be fair to everyone.

I will not flatter anyone.

²²I don't know how to flatter.

If I did, God, my Maker, would
quickly take me away.

33
"But now, Job, listen to my
words.

Pay attention to everything I say.

²I open my mouth.

I am ready to speak.

³My words come from an honest heart.

I am sincere when I speak what
I know.

⁴The Spirit*ᵈ* of God created me.

The breath of God All-Powerful
gave me life.

⁵Answer me if you can.

Get yourself ready and stand
before me.

⁶I am just like you before God.

I was also made out of clay.

⁷Don't be afraid of me.

I will not be hard on you.

⁸"But I heard what you have said.

I heard every word.

⁹You said, 'I am pure and without sin.

I am innocent and free from guilt.

¹⁰But God has found fault with me.

He considers me his enemy.

¹¹He locks my feet in chains.

He closely watches everywhere I go.'

¹²"But I tell you, you are not right in
saying this.

God is greater than we are!

¹³Why do you accuse God

of not answering man's complaints?

¹⁴God does speak—sometimes one
way and sometimes another.

He speaks even though men may
not understand it.

¹⁵God may speak in a dream or a vision
of the night.

This is when men are in a deep
sleep

and lying in their beds.

¹⁶He may speak in their ears
and frighten them with warnings.

¹⁷He warns them to turn away from
doing wrong.

And he warns them not to be proud.

¹⁸God does this to save a man's soul
from death.

He does it to keep him from dying.

¹⁹A man may be corrected while on
his bed in great pain.

He may have continual pain in his
very bones.

²⁰He may be in such pain that he even
hates food.

He may hate even the very best
meal.

²¹His body becomes so thin there is
almost nothing left of it.

And his bones that were hidden by
flesh now stick out.

²²His soul is near the place of death.

His life is almost over.

²³"But there may be an angel on
his side.

The angel may be one out of a
thousand who will speak for
the man.

He will tell the man what he
should do.

²⁴The angel will beg for mercy and say:
'Save this man from the place of
death.

I have found a way to pay for his
life.'

²⁵Then his body is made new like a
child's body.

It will be returned to the way it was
when he was young.

²⁶That person will pray to God, and
God will listen to him.

He will see God's face and will
shout with happiness.

And God will set things right for
    him again.
27 Then the man will say to other
    people,
  'I sinned and twisted what was right.
  But I did not receive the
    punishment I should have
    received.
28 God bought back my life from death.
  And I will continue to enjoy life.'

29 "God does all these things to a man.
  He does them two times or even
    three.
30 He does them so a person won't die
    as punishment for his sins.
  He does it so the man may still
    enjoy life.

31 "Job, pay attention and listen to me.
  Be quiet, and I will speak.
32 If you have anything to say, answer
    me.
  Speak up, because I want you to be
    shown as right.
33 But if you have nothing to say, then
    listen to me.
  Be quiet, and I will teach you
    wisdom."

34 Then Elihu said:

2 "Hear my words, you men who
    think you are wise.
  Listen to me, you men who think
    you know a lot.
3 The ear tests words
  as the tongue tastes food.
4 Let's decide for ourselves what is
    right.
  And let's learn together what is
    good.

5 "Job says, 'I am not guilty.
  But God has refused me a fair
    trial.
6 Instead of getting a fair trial,
  I am called a liar.
 I have been seriously hurt,
  even though I have not sinned.'
7 There is no other man like Job.
  He takes insults as if he were
    drinking water.
8 He is around people who do evil.
  He spends time with wicked men.

9 This is because he says, 'It does not
    help a man
  to try and please God.'

10 "So listen to me, you who can
    understand.
  God All-Powerful can never do
    wrong!
  It is impossible for God to do evil.
11 God pays a person back for what he
    has done.
  God gives him what his actions
    deserve.
12 Truly God will never do wrong!
  God All-Powerful will never twist
    what is right.
13 No one chose God to rule over
    the earth.
  No one put him in charge of the
    whole world.
14 God could decide
  to take away his spirit and breath.
15 If he did, all people would die
    together.
  And they would all turn back
    into dust.

16 "If you can understand, hear this.
  Listen to what I have to say.
17 Can anyone govern who hates what
    is right?
  How can you blame God who is
    both fair and powerful?
18 God is the one who says to kings,
  'You are worth nothing.'
  And he says to important people,
  'You are evil.'
19 God is not better to princes than
    other people.
  He is not better to rich people than
    poor people.
  This is because he made them all
    with his own hands.
20 They can die in a moment, in the
    middle of the night.
  The rich are struck down, and then
    they pass away.
  Powerful people die without man's
    help.

21 "God watches where people go.
  He sees every step they take.
22 There is no dark place or deep
    shadow

where those who do evil can hide from God.

²³God does not need to watch people more closely.

He does not need for men to come before him for judging.

²⁴Without asking questions, God breaks powerful people into pieces.

And he puts other people in their place.

²⁵This is because God knows what people do.

He defeats them in the night, and they are crushed.

²⁶He punishes them for the evil things they do.

He does it so that everyone else can watch.

²⁷This is because they stopped following God.

They did not care about any of his ways.

²⁸God lets the cry of poor people reach him.

He hears the cry of the needy.

²⁹But if God keeps quiet, who can blame him?

If he hides his face, no one can see him.

But God still rules over both men and nations.

³⁰ He still keeps wicked men from ruling.

And he keeps them from trapping others.

³¹"But suppose such a man says to God, 'I am guilty, but I will not sin anymore.

³²Teach me what I cannot see.

If I have done wrong, I will not do it again.'

³³So, Job, should God reward you the way you want

when you will not change your heart and life?

You must decide, not I.

So tell me what you know.

³⁴"Men who understand speak.

And wise men who hear me say,

³⁵'Job speaks without knowing what is true.

His words show he does not understand.'

³⁶I wish Job would be tested completely because he answered like an evil man!

³⁷Job has sinned, and now he turns against God.

He claps his hands as an insult.

And he speaks more and more against God."

35 Then Elihu said:

²"Do you think this is fair?

You say, 'God will show that I am right.'

³But you say to him, 'What good is it to me?

I don't gain anything by not sinning.'

⁴"I would like to answer you.

And I want to answer your friends who are with you.

⁵Look up at the sky and see.

Look at the clouds so high above you.

⁶If you sin, it does nothing to God.

Even if your sins are many, they do nothing to God.

⁷If you are good, you give nothing to God.

He receives nothing from your hand.

⁸Your evil ways only hurt a man like yourself.

And the good you do only helps other human beings.

⁹"People cry out for help when they are in trouble.

They beg for relief from powerful people.

¹⁰But no one asks, 'Where is God, my Maker?

He gives us songs in the night.

¹¹He makes us more clever than the animals of the earth.

He makes us wiser than the birds of the air.'

¹²God does not answer evil people when they cry for help.

This is because they are too proud.

¹³He does not listen to their useless begging.

God All-Powerful pays no attention
to them.
¹⁴He will listen to you even less
when you say you do not see him.
He will not listen when you say your
case is before him
and you must wait for him.
¹⁵He will not listen when you say his
anger never punishes
and that he doesn't notice evil.
¹⁶So Job is only speaking useless words.
He says many words without
knowing what is true."

Elihu's Speech Continues

36 Elihu continued:

²"Listen to me a little longer.
Then I will show you
that there is more to be said for
God's side.
³What I know comes from far away.
I will show that God, my Maker, is
right.
⁴You can be sure that my words are
not false.
One who really knows is with you.

⁵"God is powerful, but he does not
hate people.
He is powerful and sure of what he
wants to do.
⁶God will not keep evil people alive.
But he gives troubled people their
rights.
⁷God does not stop watching over
those who do right.
He sets them on thrones with kings.
And he lifts them up on high forever.
⁸People may be bound in chains.
Or trouble may tie them up like
ropes around them.
⁹But then God tells them what they
have done.
He tells them they have sinned by
being too proud.
¹⁰God makes them listen to his
warning.
He commands them to change from
doing evil.
¹¹If they obey and serve him,
the rest of their lives will be
successful.

And the rest of their years will be
happy.
¹²But if they do not listen,
they will die by the sword.
And they will die without knowing
better.

¹³"People who have wicked hearts hold
on to anger.
Even when God ties them down
with trouble, they do not cry
for help.
¹⁴They die while they are still young.
They die among the male
prostitutes*d* at the places of
worship.
¹⁵But God will save suffering people by
their suffering.
He gets them to listen through their
pain.

¹⁶"God is gently calling you from the
jaws of trouble.
He is calling you to an open place
of freedom.
There he has set your table full of
the best food.
¹⁷But now you are given the
punishment evil people should
have.
Now you are being punished.
¹⁸Be careful! Don't be led away from
God by riches.
Don't let a promise of much
money turn you away.
¹⁹Neither your wealth nor all your
great strength
will keep you out of trouble.
²⁰Don't wish for the night.
That is when people are taken
from their homes.
²¹Be careful not to turn to evil,
which you seem to want more than
suffering.

²²"God does great things by his power.
No other teacher is like him.
²³No one has planned his ways for him.
No one has said to God, 'You have
done wrong.'
²⁴Remember to praise his work.
Men sing about it.
²⁵Everybody has seen it.
People look at it from far off.

²⁶God is so great! He is greater than we can understand!

No one can discover how many years he has been alive.

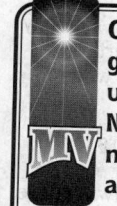

God is so great! He is greater than we can understand!
No one can discover how many years he has been alive.
• Job 36:26

²⁷"God takes up the drops of water from the earth.

And he turns them into drops of rain.

²⁸Then the rain pours down from the clouds.

And showers fall on people.

²⁹No one understands how God spreads out the clouds.

No one understands how he thunders from where he lives.

³⁰Watch how God scatters his lightning around him.

It even lights up the deepest parts of the sea.

³¹This is the way God governs the nations.

This is how he gives us enough food.

³²God fills his hands with lightning.

And he commands it to strike its target.

³³His thunder announces that a storm is coming.

Even the cattle show that the storm is coming.

37 "At the sound of his thunder, my heart pounds.

It is as if my heart will jump out of my chest.

²Listen! Listen to the thunder of God's voice.

Listen to the rumbling that comes from his mouth.

³He turns his lightning loose under the whole sky.

And he sends it to the farthest parts of the earth.

⁴After that you can hear the roar when he thunders with a great sound.

He does not hold back the flashing when his voice is heard.

⁵God's voice thunders in wonderful ways.

He does great things we cannot understand.

⁶God says to the snow, 'Fall on the earth.'

And he says to the rain shower, 'Be a heavy rain.'

⁷With it, God stops everyone from working.

That way, everyone knows it is the work of God.

⁸The animals take cover from the rain. They stay in their dens.

⁹The storm comes from where it was stored.

The cold comes from the strong winds.

¹⁰The breath of God makes ice.

And the wide waters become frozen.

¹¹God fills the clouds up with water.

And he scatters his lightning through them.

¹²At God's command they swirl around over the whole earth.

They do whatever he commands.

¹³God uses the clouds to punish people or to water his earth and show his love.

¹⁴"Job, listen to this.

Stop and notice God's miracles.ᵈ

¹⁵Do you know how God controls the clouds

and makes his lightning flash?

¹⁶Do you know how the clouds hang in the sky?

They are the miracles of God, who knows everything.

¹⁷You suffer in your clothes

when the land is made quiet by the hot, south wind.

¹⁸You cannot stretch out the sky like God

and make it look as hard as polished bronze.

¹⁹Tell us what we should say to God.

We cannot get our arguments ready

because we do not have
enough understanding.
20Should God be told that I want to
speak?
A man might try to speak to God,
but he would surely be
swallowed up.
21No one can look at the sun
when it is bright in the sky
after the wind has blown all the
clouds away.
22God comes out of the north in golden
light.
He comes in overwhelming
greatness.
23God All-Powerful is too high for us
to reach.
He has great strength.
He is always right and never
punishes unfairly.
24That is why people honor God.
He does not respect those who say
they are wise."

The Lord Questions Job

38 Then the Lord answered Job
from the storm. He said:

2"Who is this that makes my purpose
unclear
by saying things that are not true?
3Be strong like a man.
I will ask you questions,
and you must answer me.
4Where were you when I made the
earth's foundation?
Tell me, if you understand.
5Who marked off how big it should be?
Surely you know!
6What were the earth's foundations
set on?
Or who put its cornerstone[d] in
place?
7Who did all this while the morning
stars sang together?
Who did this while the angels
shouted with joy?
8"Who shut the doors to keep the sea in
when it broke through and was
born?
9This was when I made the clouds
like a coat for the sea.

And I wrapped the sea in dark
clouds.
10It was when I put limits on the sea.
And I put its doors and bars in
place.
11It was when I said to the sea, 'You may
come this far, but no farther.
This is where your proud waves
must stop.'

12"Have you ever given orders for
morning to begin?
Or have you shown the dawn where
its place was?
13The dawn takes hold of earth by
its edges
and shakes evil people out of it.
14At dawn the earth changes like clay
being pressed by a seal.[d]
The hills and valleys stand out like
folds in a coat.
15Light is not given to evil people.
Their arm is raised to do harm, but
it is broken.

16"Have you ever gone to where the sea
begins?
Or have you walked in the valleys
under the sea?
17Have the gates of death been opened
to you?
Or have you seen the gates of the
deep darkness?
18Do you understand the great width
of the earth?
Tell me, if you know all these things.

19"What is the path to light's home?
And where does darkness live?
20Can you take them to their places?
Do you know the way to their homes?
21Surely you know, if you were already
born when all this happened!
Have you lived that many years?

22"Have you ever gone into the
storehouse where snow is kept?
Or have you seen the storehouses
for hail?
23I save the snow and hail for times of
trouble.
I save them for days of war and battle.
24How do you get to the place where
light comes from?

Or where is the place from which the east winds are scattered over the earth?

25 Who cuts a waterway for the heavy rains?

And who sets a path for the thunderstorm to follow?

26 Who waters the land where no one lives?

Who waters the desert that has no one in it?

27 Who sends rain to satisfy the empty land

so the grass begins to grow?

28 Does the rain have a father?

Who is father to the drops of dew?

29 Who is the mother of the ice?

Who gives birth to the frost from the sky?

30 The waters become hard as stone.

Even the surface of the deep ocean is frozen.

31 "Can you tie up the stars of the Pleiades?

Can you loosen the ropes of the stars in Orion?

32 Can you bring out the stars at the right times?

Or can you lead out the stars of the Bear with its cubs?

33 Do you know the laws of the sky?

Can you understand their rule over the earth?

34 "Can you shout an order to the clouds and cover yourself with a flood of water?

35 Can you send lightning bolts on their way?

Do the flashes of lightning report to you and say, 'Here we are'?

36 Who put wisdom inside the mind?

Or who put understanding in the heart?

37 Who has the wisdom to count the clouds?

Who can pour water from the jars of heaven?

38 Who can do this when the dust becomes hard

and the clumps of dirt stick together?

39 "Do you hunt food for the female lion to satisfy the hunger of the young lions?

40 Do you hunt for them while they lie in their dens

or hide in the bushes waiting to attack?

41 Who gives food to the birds

when their young cry out to God?

And who gives them food when they wander about without any?

39

"Do you know when the mountain goats give birth?

Do you watch when the deer gives birth to her fawn?

2 Do you count the months until they give birth?

Do you know when the time is right for them to give birth?

3 They lie down, and their young are born.

Then the pain of giving birth is over.

4 Their young ones grow and become strong in the wild country.

Then they leave their homes and do not come back.

5 "Who let the wild donkey go free?

Who untied his ropes?

6 I am the one who gave the donkey the desert as his home.

I gave him the desert lands as a place to live.

7 The wild donkey laughs at the confusion in the city.

He does not hear the drivers shout.

8 He roams the hills looking for pasture.

And he looks for anything green to eat.

9 "Will the wild ox agree to serve you?

Will he stay by your feeding box at night?

10 Can you hold him to the plowed row with a harness?

Will he plow the valleys for you?

11 Will you depend on the wild ox for his great strength?

Will you leave your heavy work for him to do?

12 Can you trust the ox to bring in your grain?

Will he gather it to your threshing[d]
   floor?

¹³"The wings of the ostrich flap happily.
   But the ostrich's wings are not as
     beautiful as the feathers of the
     stork.
¹⁴The ostrich lays her eggs on the
   ground
   and lets them warm in the sand.
¹⁵She does not stop to think that a foot
    might step on them and crush
    them.
   She does not care that some animal
    might walk on them.
¹⁶The ostrich is cruel to her young, as
    if they were not even hers.
   She does not care that her work is
    for nothing.
¹⁷This is because God did not give the
    ostrich wisdom.
   God did not give her a share of
    good sense.
¹⁸But when the ostrich gets up to run,
    she is so fast
   that she laughs at the horse and its
    rider.

¹⁹"Job, are you the one who gives the
    horse his strength?
   Or do you put a flowing mane on
    his neck?
²⁰Do you make the horse jump like a
    locust?[d]
   He scares people with his proud
    snorting.
²¹He paws wildly, enjoying his strength.
   And he charges into the battle.
²²He laughs at fear and is afraid of
    nothing.
   He will not run away from the
    sword.
²³The bag of arrows rattles against
    the horse's side.
   It is there with the flashing spears.
²⁴With great excitement, the horse
    races over the ground.
   He cannot stand still when he hears
    the trumpet.
²⁵When the trumpet blows, the horse
    snorts, 'Aha!'
   He smells the battle from far away.
   He hears the thunder of

commanders and the shouts of
   battle.

²⁶"Is it through your wisdom that the
    hawk flies?
   Is this why he spreads his wings
    toward the south?
²⁷Are you the one that commands the
    eagle to fly
   and build his nest so high?
²⁸The eagle lives on a high cliff and
    stays there at night.
   The rocky peak is his protected
    place.
²⁹From there he looks for his food.
   His eyes can see it from far away.
³⁰His young eat blood.
   And where there is something
    dead, the eagle is there."

40 The Lord said to Job:
²"Will the person who argues
   with God All-Powerful correct
   him?
   Let the person who accuses God
    answer him!"

³Then Job answered the Lord:
⁴"I am not worthy. I cannot answer
    you anything.
   I will put my hand over my mouth.
⁵I spoke one time, but I will not
    answer again.
   I even spoke two times, but I will
    say nothing more."

⁶Then the Lord spoke to Job from
the storm:
⁷"Be strong, like a man.
   I will ask you questions.
   And you must answer me.
⁸Would you say that I am unfair?
   Would you blame me to make
    yourself look right?
⁹Are you as strong as God?
   And can your voice thunder like his?
¹⁰If so, then decorate yourself with
    glory and beauty.
   And put on honor and greatness as
    if they were clothing.
¹¹Let your great anger punish.
   Look at everyone who is proud and
    make him feel unimportant.
¹²Look at everyone who is proud and

Whit's Wisdom: Patience and Suffering • Job 40–42

"**M**r. Whittaker, why is there such a long Bible book about work?" asked Holly one day when I bumped into her on Main Street in Odyssey.

"**W**ell, Holly," I answered, "I know the Bible tells us many things about work, but I don't recall any books about work."

"**W**hat about that book just before Psalms called Job?" she asked. When she said Job she said the word like "Bob" instead of like "robe."

I couldn't help myself. I just had to chuckle. I gave her a hug and told her how to say the book name correctly. I told her I was glad she was reading the Bible on her own.

"**S**o, Mr. Whittaker, if Job isn't about work, then what *is* the book about?" she asked.

I told her that was an excellent question. Job is the story of a man who trusted God and then had to learn to trust God even more. Holly wanted to know what I meant.

"**L**et me put it this way," I started. "God allowed Job to have many good things like a big family, a beautiful house, and many possessions. Job loved God and thanked him. Then God allowed Job to lose everything. His children were killed and his possessions were ruined or stolen. Job even got a terrible skin desease.

"**T**hat's awful!" Holly said. "What did he do next?"

"**H**e still trusted God," I told her.

"**J**ob's friends came to help him. They tried to figure out whose fault it was that all this happened. They couldn't understand what was happening, so they said it was all Job's fault—God was punishing him. Job didn't agree with his friends, but he couldn't explain what went wrong either. So he told God he wanted an explanation."

"**S**o did God explain?"

"**N**o, Holly, God didn't explain. And God won't explain everything that will happen in your life or mine. God did show Job that there are many things about life that we can't understand. He showed Job that all of us must trust God even when we don't understand why things happen the way they do."

Read some of the things God said to Job in Job 38:1–41:34. What has happened in your life that you don't understand? You need to keep trusting God. If you read the end of Job's story, you will find out it that turned out all right.

Related passages: Isaiah 55:6-13; John 9; Romans 8:28.

Teacher/Parent Hint: Suffering is a difficult concept for children to understand. Although they generally accept their own suffering better than we adults, they struggle with the suffering of others. Comforting their hurts and assuring them of God's faithfulness will probably be more helpful than explanations.

bring him under your control.
Crush the wicked wherever they
      are.
¹³Bury them all in the dirt together.
Cover their faces in the grave.
¹⁴If you can do that, then I myself will
      praise you
because you are strong enough to
      save yourself.

¹⁵"Look at the behemoth."ⁿ
I made him just as I made you.
He eats grass like an ox.
¹⁶Look at the strength he has in
      his body.
The muscles of his stomach are
      powerful!
¹⁷His tail extends like a cedar tree.
The muscles of his thighs are
      woven together.
¹⁸His bones are like tubes of bronze
      metal.
His legs are like bars of iron.
¹⁹He is one of the first of God's works.
But God, his Maker, can destroy
      him.
²⁰The hills, where the wild animals
      play,
provide food for him.
²¹He lies under the lotus plants
hidden by the tall grass in the
      swamp.
²²The lotus plants hide him in their
      shadow.
The poplar trees by the streams
      surround him.
²³If the river floods, he will not be
      afraid.
He is not afraid even if the Jordan
      River rushes to his mouth.
²⁴Can anyone blind his eyes and
      capture him?
Can anyone put hooks in his nose?

41 "Can you catch the leviathan"ⁿ on
      a fishhook?
Or can you tie his tongue down with
      a rope?
²Can you put a cord through his nose
or put a hook in his jaw?
³Will he keep begging you for mercy?

Will he speak to you with gentle
      words?
⁴Will he make an agreement with you?
Will he let you take him as your
      slave for life?
⁵Can you make a pet of the leviathan
as you would a bird?
Or can you put him on a leash for
      your girls?
⁶Will traders try to bargain with you
for him?
Will they divide him up among the
      traders?
⁷Can you stick him with darts until
his skin is full of them?
Or can you fill his head with fishing
      spears?
⁸If you put one hand on him,
you will never forget the battle.
And you will never do it again!
⁹There is no hope of defeating him.
Just seeing him overwhelms people.
¹⁰No one is brave enough to make him
      angry.
So who would be able to stand up
      against me?
¹¹No one has ever given me anything
that I must pay back.
Everything under heaven belongs
      to me.

¹²"I can silence his bragging.
I can silence his brave words and
      powerful arguments.
¹³No one can tear off his outer hide.
No one can poke through his
      double armor.
¹⁴No one can force open his great jaws.
There are frightening teeth all
      around his jaws.
¹⁵He has rows of shields on his back.
They are tightly sealed together.
¹⁶Each shield is so close to the next one
that no air can go between them.
¹⁷They are joined strongly to one
      another.
They hold on to each other and
      cannot be broken apart.
¹⁸When he snorts, flashes of light are
      thrown out.

ⁿ**behemoth**   A large land animal. It could refer to the hippopotamus, the elephant or a monster.
ⁿ**leviathan**   Possibly a crocodile or a sea monster.

His eyes look like the light at dawn.
[19]Flames blaze from his mouth.
  Sparks of fire shoot out.
[20]Smoke pours out of his nose
  as if coming from a large pot over a
    hot fire.
[21]His breath sets coals on fire.
  And flames come out of his mouth.
[22]There is great strength in his neck.
  People are afraid and run away
    from him.
[23]The folds of his skin are tightly
    joined.
  They are set and cannot be moved.
[24]His chest is as hard as a rock.
  It is as hard as a stone used to grind
    grain.
[25]Powerful creatures fear his terrible
    looks.
  They draw back in fear as he
    moves.
[26]The sword that hits him does not
    hurt him.
  The darts and spears, small and
    large, do not hurt him.
[27]He treats iron as if it were straw.
  And he treats bronze metal as if it
    were rotten wood.
[28]He does not run away from arrows.
  Stones from slings are like chaff[d]
    to him.
[29]Clubs feel like pieces of straw to him.
  And he laughs when they shake a
    spear at him.
[30]The underside of his body is like
    broken pieces of pottery.
  It leaves a trail in the mud like a
    threshing[d] board.
[31]He makes the deep sea bubble like
    a boiling pot.
  And he stirs up the sea like a pot
    of oil.
[32]When he swims, he leaves a shining
    path in the water.
  It makes the sea look as if it had
    white hair.
[33]Nothing else on earth is equal to him.
  He is a creature without fear.
[34]He looks down on all those who are
    too proud.
  He is king over all proud
    creatures."

Job Answers the Lord

42 Then Job answered the Lord:
[2]"I know that you can do all
    things.
  No plan of yours can be ruined.
[3]You asked, 'Who is this that made
    my purpose unclear by saying
    things that are not true?'
  Surely I talked about things I did
    not understand.
  I spoke of things too wonderful for
    me to know.

[4]You said, 'Listen now, and I will speak.
  I will ask you questions.
  And you must answer me.'
[5]My ears had heard of you before.
  But now my eyes have seen you.
[6]So now I hate myself.
  I will change my heart and life and
    sit in the dust and ashes."

End of the Story

[7]After the Lord had said these things
to Job, he spoke to Eliphaz the Temanite. The Lord said to him, "I am angry
with you and your two friends. This is
because you have not said what is right
about me. But my servant Job did. [8]So
now take seven bulls and seven male
sheep. Go to my servant Job. And offer
a burnt offering for yourselves. My servant Job will pray for you. And I will listen to his prayer. Then I will not punish
you for being foolish. You have not said
what is right about me. But my servant
Job did." [9]So Eliphaz the Temanite did
as the Lord told him to do. Bildad the
Shuhite and Zophar the Naamathite
also did as the Lord said. And the Lord
listened to Job's prayer.

[10]After Job had prayed for his
friends, God gave him success again.
God gave Job twice as much as he had
owned before. [11]Job's brothers and
sisters came to his house. Everyone
who had known him before came to
his house. And they all ate with him
there. They comforted Job and spoke
kindly to him. They made him feel
better about the trouble the Lord
brought on him. And each one gave

Job a piece of silver and a gold ring.

¹²The Lord blessed the last part of Job's life even more than the first part. Job had 14,000 sheep and 6,000 camels. He had 1,000 pairs of oxen and 1,000 female donkeys. ¹³Job also had seven sons and three daughters. ¹⁴He named the first daughter Jemimah. The second daughter he named Keziah. And his third daughter he named Keren-Happuch. ¹⁵There were no other women in all the land as beautiful as Job's daughters. And their father Job gave them land to own along with their brothers.

¹⁶After this, Job lived 140 years. He lived to see his children, grandchildren, great-grandchildren and great-great-grandchildren. ¹⁷Then Job died. He was old and had lived many years.

PSALMS

The Songbook of Israel

Book 1

Two Ways to Live

1 Happy is the person who doesn't listen to the wicked.
He doesn't go where sinners go.
He doesn't do what bad people do.
[2] He loves the Lord's teachings.
He thinks about those teachings day and night.
[3] He is strong, like a tree planted by a river.
It produces fruit in season.
Its leaves don't die.
Everything he does will succeed.

[4] But wicked people are not like that.
They are like useless chaff[d]
that the wind blows away.
[5] So the wicked will not escape God's punishment.
Sinners will not worship God with good people.
[6] This is because the Lord protects good people.
But the wicked will be destroyed.

This is because the Lord protects good people. But the wicked will be destroyed.
• Psalm 1:6

God's Chosen King

2 Why are the nations so angry?
Why are the people making useless plans?
[2] The kings of the earth prepare to fight.
Their leaders make plans together against the Lord

and his appointed king.
[3] "Let's break the chains that hold us prisoners.
Let's throw off the ropes that tie us," the nations say.

[4] But the Lord in heaven laughs.
He makes fun of them.
[5] Then the Lord warns them.
He frightens them with his anger.
[6] He says, "I have appointed my own king!
He will rule in Jerusalem on my holy mountain."

[7] Now I will tell you what the Lord has declared:
He said to me, "You are my son.
Today I have become your father.
[8] If you ask me, I will give you the nations.
All the people on earth will be yours.
[9] You will make them obey you by punishing them with an iron rod.
You will break them into pieces like pottery."

[10] So, kings, be wise.
Rulers, learn this lesson.
[11] Obey the Lord with great fear.
Be happy, but tremble.
[12] Show that you are loyal to his son.
Otherwise you will be destroyed.
He can quickly become angry.
But happy are those who trust him for protection.

A Morning Prayer

David sang this when he ran away from his son Absalom.

3 Lord, I have many enemies!
Many people have turned against me.

2Many people are talking about me.
They say, "God won't rescue him."
Selah[d]

3But, Lord, you are my shield.
You are my wonderful God who
gives me courage.
4I will pray to the Lord.
And he will answer me from his
holy mountain.   *Selah*

5I can lie down and go to sleep.
And I will wake up again
because the Lord protects me.
6Thousands of enemies may
surround me.
But I am not afraid.

7Lord, rise up!
My God, come save me!
You have hit my enemies on the
cheek.
You have broken the teeth of the
wicked.
8The Lord can save his people.
Lord, bless your people.   *Selah*

An Evening Prayer

For the director of music. With stringed
instruments. A song of David.

4 Answer me when I pray to you,
my God who does what is right.
Lift the load that I carry.
Be kind to me and hear my prayer.

2People, how long will you turn my
honor into shame?
You love what is false, and you
look for new lies.   *Selah*[d]
3You know that the Lord has chosen
for himself those who are loyal
to him.
The Lord listens when I pray to him.
4When you are angry, do not sin.
Think about these things quietly
as you go to bed.   *Selah*
5Do what is right as a sacrifice to the
Lord.
And trust the Lord.

6Many people ask,
"Who will give us anything good?
Lord, be kind to us."
7But you have made me very happy.

I am happier than they are,
even with all their grain and wine.
8I go to bed and sleep in peace.
Lord, only you keep me safe.

A Morning Prayer for Protection

For the director of music. For flutes.
A song of David.

5 Lord, listen to my words.
Understand what I am thinking.
2Listen to my cry for help.
My king and my God, I pray to you.
3Lord, every morning you hear my
voice.
Every morning, I tell you what I
need.
And I wait for your answer.

4You are not a God who is pleased
with what is wicked.
You do not live with those who do
evil.
5Those people who make fun of you
cannot stand before you.
You hate all those who do wrong.
6You destroy liars.
The Lord hates those who kill and
trick others.

7Because of your great love,
I can come into your Temple.[d]
Because I fear and respect you,
I can worship in your holy Temple.
8Lord, since I have many enemies,
show me the right thing to do.
Show me clearly how you want me
to live.

9With their mouths my enemies do
not tell the truth.
In their hearts they want to
destroy people.
Their throats are like open graves.
They use their tongues for telling
lies.
10God, declare them guilty!
Let them fall into their own traps.
Send them away because their sins
are many.
They have turned against you.

11But let everyone who trusts you be
happy.
Let them sing glad songs forever.

Protect those who love you.
They are happy because
of you.
¹²Lord, you bless those who do what
is right.
You protect them like a soldier's
shield.

A Prayer for Mercy in Troubled Times

For the director of music. With stringed
instruments. By the sheminith.ᵈ A song
of David.

6 Lord, don't correct me when you
are angry.
Don't punish me when you are
very angry.
²Lord, be kind to me because I am
weak.
Heal me, Lord, because my bones
ache.
³I am very upset.
Lord, how long will it be?

⁴Lord, return and save me.
Save me because of your
kindness.
⁵Dead people don't remember
you.
Those in the grave don't praise
you.

⁶I am tired of crying to you.
Every night my bed is wet with
tears.
My bed is soaked from my
crying.
⁷My eyes are weak from so much
crying.
They are weak from crying about
my enemies.

⁸Get away from me, all you who do
evil.
The Lord has heard my crying.
⁹The Lord has heard my cry for
help.
The Lord will answer my
prayer.
¹⁰All my enemies will be ashamed
and troubled.
They will turn and suddenly leave
in shame.

A Prayer for Fairness

A shiggaionᵈ of David which he sang to
the Lord about Cush, from the tribe
of Benjamin.

7 Lord my God, I trust in you for
protection.
Save me and rescue me
from those who are chasing me.
²Otherwise, they will tear me apart
like a lion.
They will rip me to pieces, and no
one can save me.

³Lord my God, what have I done?
Have my hands done something
wrong?
⁴Have I done wrong to my friend?
Have I stolen from my enemy?
⁵If I have, let my enemy chase me
and capture me.
Let him trample me into the dust.
Let him bury me in the ground.
Selahᵈ

⁶Lord, rise up in your anger.
Stand up against my enemies'
anger.
Get up and demand fairness.
⁷Gather the nations around you,
and rule them from above.
⁸Lord, judge the people.
Lord, defend me.
Prove that I am right.
Show that I have done no wrong,
God Most High.
⁹God, you do what is right.
You know our thoughts and
feelings.
Stop those wicked actions done by
evil people.
And help those who do what is
right.

¹⁰God Most High protects me like a
shield.
He saves those whose hearts are
right.
¹¹God judges by what is right.
And God is always ready to punish
the wicked.
¹²If they do not change their lives,
God will sharpen his sword.
He will string his bow and take aim.

¹³He has prepared his deadly
    weapons.
  He has made his flaming arrows.

¹⁴There are people who think up evil.
  They plan trouble and tell lies.
¹⁵They dig a hole to trap other people.
  But they will fall into it themselves.

This is because of your enemies.
And so you silence your enemies
  and destroy those who try to get
  even.

Humility
PSALM 8:3-5

If you stand outside on a clear night and look at all the
stars, you will see thousands of them twinkle in the night sky like dia-
monds on a black blanket. When you do this, you may feel very small and
unimportant compared to such an amazing display.

That is how David felt when he wrote Psalm 8:3-5. He was amazed that
God, who made the moon, the stars, and the heavens, also made human
beings. Why would such a great God even bother with little creatures like
us? It is even more amazing that this same powerful, creative God made
us just a little lower than himself!

This helps us understand two facts: *one*, we are very small and weak
compared to God. This should keep us from thinking too highly of ourselves. *Two*, we are made by God in his image, second only to him in all
of his creation. That should make us thankful, and keep us from feeling
like we don't really matter.

To learn more about humility, zoom to page 806.

¹⁶They themselves will get into
    trouble.
  The violence they cause will hurt
    only themselves.

¹⁷I praise the Lord because he does
    what is right.
  I sing praises to the name of the
    Lord Most High.

God's Greatness and Man's Worth

For the director of music. By the gittith.ᵈ
A song of David.

8 Lord our Master,
  your name is the most wonderful
    name in all the earth!
  It brings you praise in heaven
    above.
²You have taught children and
    babies
  to sing praises to you.

³I look at the heavens,
  which you made with your hands.
  I see the moon and stars,
  which you created.
⁴But why is man important to you?
  Why do you take care of human
    beings?
⁵You made man a little lower than
    the angels.
  And you crowned him with glory
    and honor.

"I'm watching the
stars like King
David did. It sure is
neat to think God
made all of this
and cares for us!
That is what it says
in Psalm 8:1-9."

⁶You put him in charge of everything
you made.
You put all things under his control:
⁷all the sheep, the cattle
and the wild animals,
⁸the birds in the sky,
the fish in the sea,
and everything that lives under
water.
⁹Lord our Master,
your name is the most wonderful
name in all the earth!

Thanksgiving for Victory

For the director of music. To the tune of
"The Death of the Son." A song
of David.

9 I will praise you, Lord, with all my
heart.
I will tell all the miracles *d* you have
done.
²I will be happy because of you.
God Most High, I will sing praises
to your name.

³My enemies turn back.
They are overwhelmed and die
because of you.
⁴You have heard what I complained
to you about.
You sat on your throne and judged
by what was right.
⁵You spoke strongly against the
foreign nations
and destroyed the wicked
people.
You wiped out their names forever
and ever.
⁶The enemy is gone forever.
You destroyed their cities.
No one even remembers them.

⁷But the Lord rules forever.
He sits on his throne to judge.
⁸The Lord will judge the world by
what is right.
He will decide what is fair for the
nations.
⁹The Lord defends those who suffer.
He protects them in times of
trouble.
¹⁰Those who know the Lord trust
him.

He will not leave those who come
to him.
¹¹Sing praises to the Lord who is king
on Mount Zion.*d*
Tell the nations what he has done.
¹²He remembers who the murderers
are.
He will not forget the cries of
those who suffer.
¹³Lord, be kind to me.
See how my enemies hurt me.
Do not let me go through the
gates of death.
¹⁴Then, at the gates of Jerusalem, I
will praise you.
I will rejoice because you saved
me.

¹⁵The nations have fallen into the pit
they dug.
Their feet are caught in the nets
they laid.
¹⁶The Lord has made himself known
by his fair decisions.
The wicked get trapped by what
they do.   *Higgaion.ᵈ Selahᵈ*
¹⁷Wicked people will go to the grave.
So will all those who forget God.
¹⁸Those who have troubles will not be
forgotten.
The hopes of the poor will not die.

¹⁹Lord, rise up and judge the nations.
Don't let humans think they are
strong.
²⁰Teach them to fear you, Lord.
The nations must learn that they
are only human.   *Selah*

A Complaint About Evil People

10 Lord, why are you so far away?
Why do you hide when there is
trouble?
²Proudly the wicked chase down
those who suffer.
The wicked set traps to catch
them.
³They brag about the things they
want.
They bless the greedy but hate the
Lord.
⁴The wicked people are too proud.
They do not look for God.

There is no room for God in their
    thoughts.
⁵They always succeed.
  They are far from keeping your
    laws.
  They make fun of their enemies.
⁶They say to themselves, "Nothing
    bad will ever happen to me.
  I will never be ruined."
⁷Their mouths are full of curses, lies
    and threats.
  They use their tongues for sin and
    evil.
⁸They hide near the villages.
  They look for innocent people to
    kill.
  They watch in secret for the
    helpless.
⁹They wait in hiding like a lion.
  They wait to catch poor people.
  They catch the poor in nets.
¹⁰The poor are thrown down and
    crushed.
  They are defeated because the
    others are stronger.
¹¹The wicked think,
  "God has forgotten us.
  He doesn't see what is happening."

¹²Lord, rise up and punish the
    wicked.
  Don't forget those who need help.
¹³Why do wicked people hate God?
  They say to themselves, "God
    won't punish us."
¹⁴Lord, surely you see these cruel
    and evil things.
  Look at them and do something.
  People in trouble look to you for
    help.
  You are the one who helps the
    orphans.
¹⁵Break the power of wicked men.
  Punish them for the evil they have
    done.

¹⁶The Lord is King forever and ever.
  Remove from your land those
    nations that do not worship
    you.
¹⁷Lord, you have heard what the poor
    people want.
  Do what they ask. Listen to them.

¹⁸Protect the orphans. Put an end to
    suffering.
  Then they will no longer be afraid
    of evil people.

A Statement About Trust in God

For the director of music. Of David.

11 I trust in the Lord for protection.
  So why do you say to me,
  "Fly like a bird to your mountain.
²Like hunters, the wicked string
    their bows.
  They set their arrows on the
    bowstrings.
  They shoot from dark places
  at those who are honest.
³When all that is good falls apart,
  what can good people do?"

⁴The Lord is in his holy temple.
  The Lord sits on his throne in
    heaven.
  And he sees what people do.
  He keeps his eye on them.
⁵The Lord tests those who do right.
  But he hates the wicked and those
    who love to hurt others.
⁶He will send hot coals on the wicked.
  Burning sulfur and a whirlwind is
    what they will get.
⁷The Lord does what is right, and he
    loves justice.
  So honest people will see his face.

A Prayer Against Liars

For the director of music. By the shemi-
nith.ᵈ A song of David.

12 Save me, Lord, because the good
  people are all gone.
  No true believers are left on earth.
²Everyone lies to his neighbors.
  They say one thing and mean
    another.

³The Lord will stop those lying lips.
  He will cut off those bragging
    tongues.
⁴They say, "Our tongues will help us
    win.
  We can say what we wish. No one
    is our master."

⁵But the Lord says,

"I will now rise up
because the poor are being hurt.
Because of the moans of the helpless,
I will give them the help they want."
⁶The Lord's words are pure.
They are like silver purified by fire,
like silver purified seven times over.

⁷Lord, keep us safe.
Always protect us from such people.
⁸The wicked are all around us.
Everyone loves what is wrong.

A Prayer for God to Be Near

*For the director of music. A song
of David.*

13 How long will you forget me,
Lord?
How long will you hide from me?
Forever?
²How long must I worry?
How long must I feel sad in my
heart?
How long will my enemy win over
me?
³Lord, look at me.
Answer me, my God.
Tell me, or I will die.
⁴Otherwise my enemy will say, "I
have won!"

Those against me will rejoice that
I've been defeated.

⁵I trust in your love.
My heart is happy because you
saved me.
⁶I sing to the Lord
because he has taken care of me.

The Unbelieving Fool

For the director of music. Of David.

14 A wicked fool says to himself,
"There is no God."
Fools are evil. They do terrible
things.
None of them does anything good.

²The Lord looked down from heaven
at all the people.
He looked to see if anyone was
wise,
if anyone was looking to God for
help.
³But all have turned away.
Together, everyone has become
evil.
None of them does anything good.

⁴Don't the wicked understand?

Salvation
PSALM 14:1-3

Are you a good person?

Most people would probably say, "Yes. I try to do the right things (most of the time), and I try not to hurt other people." Someone might say, "Well, I'm no angel, but I'm as good as anybody else." Would you be surprised to learn that the Bible says, *"Wrong!"*?

In these verses, God says that nobody is good. This means that sin has hurt all of us and made us guilty. That is why God made a way to save us from our sins. He did that through Jesus.

We cannot be truly good without God. Salvation comes when we admit this, and then we ask God to forgive us and to make us good in his sight.

To learn more about salvation, zoom to page 683.

They destroy my people as if they
were eating bread.
They do not ask the Lord for help.
[5]But the wicked are filled with terror
because God is with those who do
what is right.
[6]The wicked upset the plans of the
poor.
But the Lord will protect the poor.

[7]I pray that victory will come to
Israel from Mount Zion![d]
May the Lord give them back their
riches.
Then the people of Jacob will
rejoice.
And the people of Israel will be
glad.

What God Demands

A song of David.

15 Lord, who may enter your Holy
Tent?[d]
Who may live on your holy
mountain?

[2]Only a person who is innocent
and who does what is right.
He must speak the truth from his
heart.
[3] He must not tell lies about others.
He must do no wrong to his
neighbors.
He must not gossip.
[4]He must not respect hateful people.
He must honor those who honor
the Lord.
He must keep his promises to his
neighbor,
even when it hurts.
[5]He must not charge interest on
money he lends.
And he must not take money to
hurt innocent people.

Whoever does all these things will
never be destroyed.

The Lord Takes Care of His People

A miktam[d] of David.

16 Protect me, God,
because I trust in you.

[2]I said to the Lord, "You are my Lord.
Every good thing I have comes
from you."
[3]There are godly people in the
world.
I enjoy them.
[4]But those who turn to idols will
have much pain.
I will not offer blood to those idols.
I won't even speak their names.

[5]No, the Lord is all I need.
He takes care of me.
[6]My share in life has been pleasant.
My part has been beautiful.
[7]I praise the Lord because he guides
me.
Even at night, I feel his leading.
[8]I keep the Lord before me always.
Because he is close by my side
I will not be hurt.
[9]So I rejoice, and I am glad.
Even my body has hope.
[10]This is because you will not leave
me in the grave.
You will not let your holy one rot.
[11]You will teach me God's way to live.
Being with you will fill me with joy.
At your right hand I will find
pleasure forever.

A Prayer for Protection

A prayer of David.

17 Lord, hear me begging for fair-
ness.
Listen to my cry for help.
Pay attention to my prayer.
I speak the truth.
[2]You will judge that I am right.
Your eyes can see what is true.
[3]You have examined my heart.
You have tested me all night.
You questioned me without finding
anything wrong.
I did not plan any evil.
[4]I have obeyed your commands.
I have not done what evil
people do.
[5]I have done what you told me to do.
I have not failed.
[6]I call to you, God,

and you answer me.
Listen to me now.
Hear what I say.
7Your love is wonderful.
By your power you save
from their enemies those who
trust you.
8Protect me as you would protect
your own eye.
Protect me as a bird hides her
young under her wings.
9Keep me from the wicked who
attack me.
Protect me from my enemies who
surround me.
10They are selfish.
They brag about themselves.
11They have chased me.
Now they surround me.
They plan to throw me to the
ground.
12They are like lions ready to kill.
Like lions, they sit in hiding.

13Lord, rise up and face the enemy.
Throw them down.
Save me from the wicked
with your sword.
14Lord, save me from them by your
power.
Their reward is in this life.
They have plenty of food.

They have many sons.
They leave money to their children.

15Because I have lived right, I will see
your face.
When I wake up, I will see your
likeness and be satisfied.

A Song of Victory

For the director of music. By the Lord's
servant, David. David sang this song to
the Lord. He sang it when the Lord had
saved him from Saul and all his
other enemies.

18 I love you, Lord. You are my
strength.

2The Lord is my rock, my protection,
my Savior.
My God is my rock.
I can run to him for safety.
He is my shield and my saving
strength, my high tower.
3I will call to the Lord.
He is worthy of praise.
And I will be saved from my
enemies.

4The ropes of death bound me.
The deadly rivers overwhelmed me.

Temptation
PSALM 18:6

David was surrounded by his enemies and was afraid
he might die, but God rescued him. Because of this, David wrote this
song that thanks God for helping him when he asked.

Sometimes we can feel as though we are surrounded by temptations.
In fact, every choice seems to be wrong. At other times, a temptation
might feel very strong. We don't think we can hold out but may give in.
That's when we need to call out to God for help like David did. God loves
and hears us. He will show us what to do and will give us the power and
courage to do it.

When you are in trouble or tempted to do something wrong, remember to do what David did. Don't *give* up, *look* up.

To learn more about temptation, zoom to page 741.

⁵The ropes of death wrapped around
    me.
  The traps of death were before me.
⁶In my trouble I called to the Lord.
  I cried out to my God for help.
 From his temple he heard
    my voice.
  My call for help reached his ears.

⁷The earth trembled and shook.
  The foundations of the mountains
    began to shake.
  They shook because the Lord was
    angry.
⁸Smoke came out of his nose.
  Burning fire came out of his mouth.
  Burning coals went before him.
⁹He tore open the sky and came
    down.
  Dark clouds were under his feet.
¹⁰He rode a creature with wings and
    flew.
  He flew on the wings of the wind.
¹¹He made darkness his covering, his
    shelter around him,
  surrounded by fog and clouds.
¹²Out of the brightness of his
    presence came clouds.
  They came with hail and lightning.
¹³The Lord thundered from heaven.
  God Most High raised his voice.
  And there was hail and lightning.
¹⁴He shot his arrows and scattered
    his enemies.
  His many bolts of lightning
    confused them with fear.
¹⁵Lord, you spoke strongly.
  The wind blew from your nose.
  The valleys of the sea appeared.
  The foundations of the earth were
    seen.

¹⁶The Lord reached down from above
    and took me.
  He pulled me from the deep water.
¹⁷He saved me from my powerful
    enemies.
  Those who hated me were too
    strong for me.
¹⁸They attacked me at my time of
    trouble.
  But the Lord supported me.
¹⁹He took me to a safe place.

Because he delights in me, he
    saved me.
²⁰The Lord spared me because I did
    what was right.
  Because I have not done evil, he
    has rewarded me.
²¹I have followed the ways of the Lord.
  I have not done evil by turning
    away from my God.
²²I remember all his laws.
  I have not broken his rules.
²³I am innocent before him.
  I have kept myself from doing evil.
²⁴The Lord rewarded me because I
    did what was right.
  I did what the Lord said was right.

²⁵Lord, you are loyal to those who are
    loyal.
  You are good to those who are
    good.
²⁶You are pure to those who are pure.
  But you are against those who are
    bad.
²⁷You save those who are not proud.
  But you make humble those who
    are proud.
²⁸Lord, you give light to my lamp.
  My God brightens the darkness
    around me.
²⁹With your help I can attack an army.
  With God's help I can jump over a
    wall.

³⁰The ways of God are without fault.
  The Lord's words are pure.
  He is a shield to those who trust him.
³¹Who is God? Only the Lord.
  Who is the Rock?^d Only our God.
³²God is my protection.
  He makes my way free from fault.
³³He makes me like a deer, which
    does not stumble.
  He helps me stand on the steep
    mountains.
³⁴He trains my hands for battle.
  So my arms can bend a bronze bow.
³⁵You protect me with your saving
    shield.
  You support me with your right
    hand.
  You have stooped to make me
    great.

³⁶You give me a wide path on which
　　to walk.
　My feet have not slipped.
³⁷I chased my enemies and caught
　　them.
　I did not quit till they were
　　destroyed.
³⁸I crushed them so they couldn't rise
　up again.
　They fell beneath my feet.
³⁹You gave me strength in battle.
　You made my enemies bow before
　　me.
⁴⁰You made my enemies turn back.
　I destroyed those who hated me.
⁴¹They called for help,
　but no one came to save them.
　They called to the Lord,
　but he did not answer them.
⁴²I beat my enemies into pieces.
　They were like dust in the wind.
　I poured them out like mud in the
　　streets.

⁴³You saved me when the people
　　attacked me.
　You made me the leader of
　　nations.
　People I never knew serve me.
⁴⁴As soon as they hear me, they obey
　　me.
　Foreigners obey me.
⁴⁵They all become afraid.
　They tremble in their hiding
　　places.

⁴⁶The Lord lives!
　May my Rock be praised.
　Praise the God who saves me!
⁴⁷God gives me victory over my
　　enemies.
　He brings people under my rule.
⁴⁸He saves me from my enemies.

　You set me over those who hate me.
　You saved me from cruel men.
⁴⁹So I will praise you, Lord, among
　　the nations.
　I will sing praises to your name.
⁵⁰The Lord gives great victories to his
　　king.
　He is loyal to his appointed king,
　to David and his descendants^d
　　forever.

God's Works and Word

For the director of music. A song
of David.

19 The heavens tell the glory of
　God.
　And the skies announce what his
　　hands have made.
²Day after day they tell the story.
　Night after night they tell it again.
³They have no speech or words.
　They don't make any sound to be
　　heard.
⁴But their message goes out through
　　all the world.
　It goes everywhere on earth.
　The sky is like a home for the sun.
⁵　The sun comes out like a
　　　bridegroom from his
　　　bedroom.
　It rejoices like an athlete eager to
　　run a race.
⁶The sun rises at one end of the sky,
　and it follows its path to the other
　　end.
　Nothing hides from its heat.

⁷The Lord's teachings are perfect.
　They give new strength.
　The Lord's rules can be trusted.
　They make plain people wise.
⁸The Lord's orders are right.
　They make people happy.
　The Lord's commands are pure.
　They light up the way.
⁹It is good to respect the Lord.
　That respect will last forever.
　The Lord's judgments are true.
　They are completely right.
¹⁰They are worth more than gold,
　even the purest gold.
　They are sweeter than honey,
　even the finest honey.
¹¹They tell your servant what to do.
　Keeping them brings great reward.

¹²No one can see all his own mistakes.
　Forgive me for my secret sins.
¹³Keep me from the sins that I want
　　to do.
　Don't let them rule me.
　Then I can be pure
　and free from the greatest of sins.

Worship
PSALM 19:1-6

"**G**randpa, do you believe in God?" asked eight-year-old Johnny.

"**Y**es, I do," replied the old man. "Why do you ask?"

"**C**ause I'd like to believe in God, too, Grandpa, but it sure would be easier if I could *see* him."

"**W**hy," said Grandpa, "I sometimes wonder if there's anywhere I *can't* see him!"

Johnny's grandpa was saying that he sees signs of God in this world wherever he looks. The never-changing path of the sun from east to west, the seasons following in their pattern, the love of a mother for her baby, the yearly event of birds flying south for the winter . . . all these are the fingerprints of God. We can see God everywhere, if we look for him. And when we see God's work, we have a good reason to praise him.

As you read Psalm 19, see how many of God's fingerprints you can find.

To learn more about worship, zoom to page 805.

To learn more about worship, zoom to page 805.

---

¹⁴I hope my words and thoughts
please you.
Lord, you are my Rock,ᵈ the one
who saves me.

A Prayer for the King

For the director of music. A song of David.

20 May the Lord answer you in times of trouble.
May the God of Jacob protect you.
²May he send you help from his
Temple.ᵈ
May he support you from Mount
Zion.ᵈ
³May he remember all your
offerings.
May he accept all your sacrifices.
Selahᵈ
⁴May he give you what you want.
May all your plans succeed.
⁵We will shout for joy when you
succeed.

We will raise a flag in the name of
our God.
May the Lord give you all that you
ask for.
⁶Now I know the Lord helps his
appointed king.
He answers him from his holy
heaven.
He saves him with his strong right
hand.
⁷Some trust in chariots, others in
horses.
But we trust the Lord our God.
⁸They are overwhelmed and defeated.
But we march forward and win.
⁹Lord, save the king!
Answer us when we call for help.

Thanksgiving for the King

For the director of music. A song of David.

21 Lord, the king rejoices because of your strength.

He is so happy when you save him!
²You gave the king what he wanted.
You did not refuse what he asked
for.   *Selah*^d
³You put good things before him.
You placed a gold crown on his
head.
⁴He asked you for life.
And you gave it to him.
His years go on and on.
⁵He has great glory because you
gave him victories.
You gave him honor and praise.
⁶You always gave him blessings.
You made him glad because you
were with him.
⁷The king truly trusts the Lord.
Because God Most High always
loves him,
he will not be overwhelmed.
⁸Your hand is against all your
enemies.
Those who hate you will feel your
power.
⁹When you appear, you will burn
them like wood in a furnace.
In your anger you will eat them up.
Your fire will burn them up.
¹⁰You will destroy their families from
the earth.
Their children will not live.
¹¹They made evil plans against you.
But their traps won't work.
¹²You will make them turn their backs
when you aim your arrows at them.
¹³Be supreme, Lord, in your power.
We sing and praise your greatness.

The Prayer of a Suffering Man

For the director of music. To the tune of
"The Doe of Dawn." A song of David.

22 My God, my God, why have you
left me alone?
You are too far away to save me.
You are too far away to hear my
moans.
²My God, I call to you during the day.
But you do not answer.
And I call at night.
I am not silent.
³You sit as the Holy One.

The praises of Israel are your
throne.
⁴Our ancestors trusted you.
They trusted you, and you saved
them.
⁵They called to you for help.
And they were rescued.
They trusted you.
And they were not disappointed.
⁶But I am like a worm instead of a
man.
Men make fun of me.
They look down on me.
⁷Everyone who looks at me laughs.
They stick out their tongues.
They shake their heads.
⁸They say, "Turn to the Lord for help.
Maybe he will save you.
If he likes you,
maybe he will rescue you."
⁹You had my mother give birth to me.
You made me trust you
while I was just a baby.
¹⁰I have leaned on you since the day I
was born.
You have been my God since my
mother gave birth to me.
¹¹So don't be far away from me.
Now trouble is near,
and there is no one to help.
¹²Men have surrounded me like
angry bulls.
The strong bulls of Bashan are on
every side.
¹³Like hungry, roaring lions
they open their jaws at me.
¹⁴My strength is gone
like water poured out onto the
ground.
All my bones are out of joint.
My heart is like wax.
It has melted inside me.
¹⁵My strength has dried up like a
piece of a broken pot.
My tongue sticks to the top of my
mouth.
You laid me in the dust of death.
¹⁶Evil men have surrounded me.
Like dogs they have trapped me.
They have bitten my arms and legs.
¹⁷I can count all my bones.

People look and stare at me.
¹⁸They divided my clothes among
    them,
  and they threw lots^d for my
    clothing.

¹⁹But, Lord, don't be far away.
  You are my power. Hurry to help
    me.
²⁰Save me from the sword.
  Save my life from the dogs.
²¹Rescue me from the lion's mouth.
  Save me from the horns of the
    bulls.

²²Then I will tell my fellow Israelites
    about you.
  I will praise you when your people
    meet to worship you.
²³Praise the Lord, all you who
    worship him.
  All you descendants^d of Jacob,
    honor him.
  Fear him, all you Israelites.
²⁴The Lord does not ignore
    the one who is in trouble.
  He doesn't hide from him.
  He listens when the one in trouble
    calls out to him.
²⁵Lord, I praise you in the great
    meeting of your people.

These worshipers will see me do
    what I promised.
²⁶Poor people will eat until they are
    full.
  Those who look to the Lord will
    praise him.
  May your hearts live forever!
²⁷People everywhere will remember
    and will turn to the Lord.
  All the families of the nations
    will worship him.
²⁸This is because the Lord is King.
  He rules the nations.

²⁹All the powerful people on earth
    will eat and worship.
  Everyone will bow down to him.
³⁰The people in the future will serve
    him.
  They will always be told about the
    Lord.
³¹They will tell that he does what is
    right.
  People who are not yet born
    will hear what God has done.

The Lord the Shepherd

A song of David.

23 The Lord is my shepherd.
    I have everything I need.
²He gives me rest in green pastures.
  He leads me to calm water.
³ He gives me new strength.

Animals in the Bible

SHEEP • PSALM 23

If you could be any animal in the whole world, what would you be?

In the Bible, God's people are often called sheep. This is because sheep are not able to take care of themselves very well. They need a shepherd to guide them and keep them safe. It is so easy for sheep to wander off and get lost. If the shepherd doesn't find them quickly, they can be eaten by a wild animal.

Jesus is like a shepherd to us. He wants to guide us and take care of us. But we must follow him.

To discover an animal who can be stubborn, fly to page 664.

"You know, this chapter is just about a kid in sheep's clothing! Read Psalm 23 to find out what I mean."

For the good of his name,
  he leads me on paths that are
    right.
[4]Even if I walk
  through a very dark valley,
I will not be afraid
  because you are with me.
Your rod and your walking stick[n]
  comfort me.
[5]You prepare a meal for me
  in front of my enemies.
You pour oil on my head.[n]
  You give me more than I can hold.
[6]Surely your goodness and love will
    be with me
all my life.
And I will live in the house of the
    Lord forever.

A Welcome for God into the Temple

A song of David.

24 The earth and everything in it
  belong to the Lord.
The world and all its people belong
  to him.
[2]He built it on the waters.
  He set it on the rivers.

[3]Who may go up on the mountain of
    the Lord?
Who may stand in his holy
    Temple?[d]
[4]Only those with clean hands and
    pure hearts.
They must not have worshiped
    idols.
They must not have made
    promises in the name of a false
    god.

[5]It is they who will receive a blessing
    from the Lord.
The God who saves them will
    declare them right.
[6]They try to follow God.
  They look to the God of Jacob for
    help.   Selah[d]

[7]Gates, open all the way.
  Open wide, aged doors.
Then the glorious king will come in.
[8]Who is this glorious king?
  The Lord, strong and mighty.
  The Lord, the powerful warrior.

The Lord is my shepherd. I have everything I need.
• Psalm 23:1

[9]Gates, open all the way.
  Open wide, aged doors.
Then the glorious king will come in.
[10]Who is this glorious king?
  The Lord of heaven's armies—
  he is the glorious king.   Selah

A Prayer for God to Guide

Of David.

25 Lord, I give myself to you.
[2] My God, I trust you.
Do not let me be disgraced.
  Do not let my enemies laugh at me.
[3]No one who trusts you will be
    disgraced.
But those who sin without excuse
    will be disgraced.

[4]Lord, tell me your ways.
  Show me how to live.
[5]Guide me in your truth.
  Teach me, my God, my Savior.
  I trust you all day long.
[6]Lord, remember your mercy and
    love.
You have shown them since long
    ago.

---

[n]**walking stick** The stick a shepherd uses to guide and protect his sheep.
[n]**pour oil . . . head** This can mean that God gave him great wealth and blessed him.

⁷Do not remember the sins
   and wrong things I did when I was
      young.
But remember to love me always
   because you are good, Lord.

⁸The Lord is good and right.
   He points sinners to the right way.
⁹He shows those who are not proud
      how to do right.
   He teaches them his ways.
¹⁰All the Lord's ways are loving and
      true
   for those who follow the demands
      of his agreement.
¹¹For the sake of your name, Lord,
   forgive my many sins.
¹²Is there someone who worships the
      Lord?
   The Lord will point him to the best
      way.
¹³He will enjoy a good life.
   His children will inherit the land.
¹⁴The Lord tells his secrets to those
      who respect him.
   He tells them about his
      agreement.
¹⁵My eyes are always looking to the
      Lord for help.
   He will keep me from any traps.

¹⁶Turn to me and be kind to me.
   I am lonely and hurting.
¹⁷My troubles have grown larger.
   Free me from my problems.
¹⁸Look at my suffering and troubles.
   Take away all my sins.
¹⁹Look at how many enemies I have!
   See how much they hate me!
²⁰Protect me and save me.
   I trust you.
   Do not let me be disgraced.
²¹My hope is in you.
   So may goodness and honesty
      guard me.
²²God, save Israel from all their
      troubles!

The Prayer of an Innocent Man

Of David.

26 Lord, defend me.
   I have lived an innocent life.
I trusted the Lord and never doubted.
²Lord, try me and test me.
   Look closely into my heart and
      mind.
³I see your love.
   I live by your truth.

Character
PSALM 25:21

"**W**hat do you want to be when you grow up?"

Has anyone ever asked you that question? How did you answer? Maybe you said you wanted to be a policeman, a doctor, a teacher, a nurse, or a ballerina—someone you admire. It is natural to want to be like someone you look up to.

In this verse David says that he puts his hope and trust in the Lord. He asks God to help him by letting goodness and honesty guard him. David wanted to be like God, honest and good.

Be careful who you look up to. You may become like that person. David was wise to want God's goodness and honesty to guard him. You can ask God to help you be good and honest in your life, too.

To learn more about character, zoom to page 761.

⁴I do not spend time with liars.
I do not make friends with people
who hide their sin.
⁵I hate the company of evil
people.
I won't sit with the wicked.
⁶I wash my hands to show I am
innocent.
I come to your altar, Lord.
⁷I raise my voice in praise.
I tell of all the miracles*d* you have
done.
⁸Lord, I love the Temple*d* where you
live.
It is where your greatness is.
⁹Do not kill me with those sinners.
Do not take my life with those
murderers.
¹⁰Evil is in their hands.
They do wrong for money.
¹¹But I have lived an innocent life.
So save me and be kind to me.
¹²I stand in a safe place.
Lord, I praise you in the great
meeting.

A Song of Trust in God

Of David.

27 The Lord is my light and the one
who saves me.
I fear no one.
The Lord protects my life.
I am afraid of no one.

**The Lord is my light
and the one who saves
me. I fear no one.
The Lord protects my life.
I am afraid of no one.**
• **Psalm 27:1**

²Evil people may try to destroy my
body.
My enemies and those who hate
me attack me.
But they are overwhelmed and
defeated.
³If an army surrounds me,
I will not be afraid.
If war breaks out,
I will trust the Lord.

⁴I ask only one thing from the Lord.
This is what I want:
Let me live in the Lord's house
all my life.
Let me see the Lord's beauty.
Let me look around in his Temple.*d*
⁵During danger he will keep me safe
in his shelter.
He will hide me in his Holy Tent.*d*
Or he will keep me safe on a high
mountain.
⁶My head is higher
than my enemies around me.
I will offer joyful sacrifices in his
Holy Tent.
I will sing and praise the Lord.

⁷Lord, hear me when I call.
Be kind and answer me.
⁸My heart said of you, "Go, worship
him."
So I come to worship you, Lord.
⁹Do not turn away from me.
Do not turn your servant away in
anger.
You have helped me.
Do not push me away or leave me
alone,
God, my Savior.
¹⁰If my father and mother leave me,
the Lord will take me in.
¹¹Lord, teach me your ways.
Guide me to do what is right
because I have enemies.
¹²Do not let my enemies defeat me.
They tell lies about me.
They say they will hurt me.

¹³I truly believe
I will live to see the Lord's
goodness.
¹⁴Wait for the Lord's help.
Be strong and brave
and wait for the Lord's help.

A Prayer in Troubled Times

Of David.

28 Lord, my Rock,*d* I call out to you
for help.
Do not be deaf to me.
If you are silent,
I will be like those in the grave.
²Hear the sound of my prayer,

when I cry out to you for help.
I raise my hands
toward your Most Holy Place.
³Don't drag me away with the wicked,
with those who do evil.
They say, "Peace" to their neighbors.
But evil is in their hearts.
⁴Pay them back for what they have
done.
They have done evil.
Pay them back for what they have
done.
Give them their reward.
⁵They don't understand what the
Lord has done
or what he has made.
So he will knock them down
and not lift them up.

⁶Praise the Lord.
He heard my prayer for help.
⁷The Lord is my strength and shield.
I trust him, and he helps me.
I am very happy.
And I praise him with my song.
⁸The Lord is powerful.
He gives power and victory to his
chosen one.
⁹Save your people.
Bless those who are your own.
Be their shepherd and carry them
forever.

God in the Thunderstorm

A song of David.

29 Praise the Lord, you angels.
Praise the Lord's glory and
power.
²Praise the Lord for the glory of his
name.
Worship the Lord because he is
holy.

³The Lord's voice is heard over the
sea.
The glorious God thunders.
The Lord thunders over the great
ocean.
⁴The Lord's voice is powerful.
The Lord's voice is majestic.
⁵The Lord's voice breaks the trees.
The Lord breaks the cedars of
Lebanon.

⁶He makes the land of Lebanon
dance like a calf.
He makes Mount Hermon jump
like a baby bull.
⁷The Lord's voice makes the
lightning flash.
⁸The Lord's voice shakes the desert.
The Lord shakes the Desert of
Kadesh.
⁹The Lord's voice shakes the oaks.
The leaves fall off the trees.
In his Temple^d everyone says,
"Glory to God!"

¹⁰The Lord controls the flood.
The Lord will be King forever.
¹¹The Lord gives strength to his
people.
The Lord blesses his people with
peace.

Thanksgiving for Escaping Death

A song of David. A song for giving the
Temple^d to the Lord.

30 I will praise you, Lord,
because you rescued me.
You did not let my enemies laugh
at me.
²Lord, my God, I prayed to you.
And you healed me.
³You lifted me out of the grave.
You spared me from going down
where the dead are.

⁴Sing praises to the Lord, you who
belong to him.
Praise his holy name.
⁵His anger lasts only a moment.
But his kindness lasts for a
lifetime.
Crying may last for a night.
But joy comes in the morning.

⁶When I felt safe, I said,
"I will never fail."
⁷Lord, in your kindness you made
my mountain safe.
But when you turned away, I was
frightened.

⁸I called to you, Lord.
I asked you to have mercy on me.
⁹I said, "What good will it do if I die
or if I go down to the grave?

Dust cannot praise you.
  It cannot speak about your truth.
¹⁰Lord, hear me and be merciful to
    me.
  Lord, help me."

¹¹You changed my sorrow into dancing.
  You took away my rough cloth,
    which shows sadness, and
    clothed me in happiness.
¹²I will sing to you and not be silent.
  Lord, my God, I will praise you
    forever.

A Prayer of Faith in Troubled Times

*For the director of music. A song
of David.*

31 Lord, I trust in you.
     Let me never be disgraced.
  Save me because you do what is
    right.
²Listen to me.
  Save me quickly.
  Be my rock of protection,
  a strong city to save me.
³You are my rock and my protection.
  For the good of your name, lead
    me and guide me.
⁴Set me free from the trap they set
    for me.
  You are my protection.
⁵I give you my life.
  Save me, Lord, God of truth.

⁶I hate those who worship false gods.
  I trust only in the Lord.
⁷I will be glad because of your love.
  You saw my suffering.
  You knew my troubles.
⁸You have not let my enemies defeat
    me.
  You have set me in a safe place.

⁹Lord, have mercy. I am in misery.
  My eyes are weak from so much
    crying.
  My whole being is tired from grief.
¹⁰My life is ending in sadness.
  My years are spent in crying.
  My troubles are using up my
    strength.
  My bones are getting weaker.

¹¹Because of all my troubles, my
    enemies hate me.
  Even my neighbors look down on
    me.
  When my friends see me,
    they are afraid and run.
¹²I am like a piece of a broken pot.
  I am forgotten as if I were dead.
¹³I have heard many insults.
  Terror is all around me.
  They make plans against me.
  They want to kill me.

¹⁴Lord, I trust you.
  I have said, "You are my God."
¹⁵My life is in your hands.
  Save me from my enemies' grasp.
  Save me from those who are
    chasing me.
¹⁶Show your kindness to me, your
    servant.
  Save me because of your love.
¹⁷Lord, I called to you.
  So do not let me be disgraced.
  Let the wicked be disgraced.
  Let them lie silent in the grave.
¹⁸With pride and hatred
    they speak against the righteous.
  So shut their lying lips.

¹⁹How great is your goodness!
  You have stored it up for those
    who fear you.
  You do good things for those who
    trust you.
  You do this for all to see.
²⁰You protect them by your presence
    from what people plan against them.
  You keep them safe in your shelter
    from evil words.
²¹Praise the Lord.
  His love to me was wonderful
    when my city was attacked.
²²In my distress, I said,
    "God cannot see me!"
  But you heard my prayer
    when I cried out to you for help.
²³Love the Lord, all you who belong
    to him.
  The Lord protects those who truly
    believe.
  But he punishes the proud as
    much as they have sinned.

²⁴All you who put your hope in the
    Lord
  be strong and brave.

It Is Better to Confess Sin

A maskil[d] of David.

32 Happy is the person
    whose sins are forgiven,
  whose wrongs are pardoned.
²Happy is the person
  whom the Lord does not consider
    guilty.
  In that person there is nothing
    false.

Animals in the Bible

DONKEYS • PSALM 32:9

Today when we travel, we use cars and trucks, or airplanes or trains. In Bible times, people often traveled on donkeys. Donkeys are good workers. They can carry heavy loads and can walk for a long distance without getting tired.

But sometimes donkeys get stubborn and refuse to do what their masters tell them. The Bible warns us not to be stubborn like donkeys. God wants to teach us and make us wise. But we must follow him obediently.

To read about an animal that lives in a rock house, fly to page 778.

---

³When I kept things to myself,
  I felt weak deep inside me.
  I moaned all day long.
⁴Day and night
  you punished me.
  My strength was gone
    as in the summer heat.   *Selah[d]*
⁵Then I confessed my sins to you.
  I didn't hide my guilt.
  I said, "I will confess my sins to the
    Lord."
  And you forgave my guilt.   *Selah*

⁶For this reason, all who obey you
    should pray to you while they still
    can.
  When troubles rise like a flood,
    they will not reach them.

⁷You are my hiding place.
  You protect me from my troubles.
  You fill me with songs of salvation.
                                Selah

⁸The Lord says, "I will make you wise.
  I will show you where to go.
  I will guide you and watch over you.
⁹So don't be like a horse or donkey.
  They don't understand.
  They must be led with bits and reins,
    or they will not come near you."

¹⁰Wicked people have many troubles.
  But the Lord's love surrounds
    those who trust him.
¹¹Good people, rejoice and be happy
    in the Lord.
  All you whose hearts are right, sing.

Praise God Who Creates and Saves

33 Sing to the Lord, you who do
    what is right.

  Honest people should praise him.
²Praise the Lord on the harp.
  Make music for him on the ten-
    stringed lyre.[d]
³Sing a new song to him.
  Play well and joyfully.

⁴God's word is true.
  Everything he does is right.
⁵He loves what is right and fair.
  The Lord's love fills the earth.
⁶The sky was made at the Lord's
    command.

By the breath from his mouth, he
made all the stars.
7He gathered the water in the sea
into a heap.
He made the great ocean stay in
its place.
8All the earth should worship the
Lord.
The whole world should fear him.
9He spoke, and it happened.
He commanded, and it appeared.
10The Lord upsets the plans of nations.
He ruins all their plans.
11But the Lord's plans will stand
forever.
His ideas will last from now on.
12Happy is the nation whose God is
the Lord.
Happy are the people he chose for
his very own.
13The Lord looks down from heaven.
He sees every person.
14From his throne he watches
everyone who lives on earth.
15He made their hearts.
He understands everything they do.
16No king is saved by his great army.
No warrior escapes by his great
strength.
17Horses can't bring victory.
They can't save by their strength.
18But the Lord looks after those who
fear him.
He watches over those who put
their hope in his love.
19He saves them from death.
He spares their lives in times of
hunger.
20So our hope is in the Lord.
He is our help, our shield to
protect us.
21We rejoice in him.
We trust his holy name.
22Lord, show your love to us
as we put our hope in you.

Praise God Who Judges and Saves

David's song from the time he acted
crazy so Abimelech would send him
away. And David did leave.

34 I will praise the Lord at all times.
His praise is always on my lips.

2My whole being praises the Lord.
The poor will hear and be glad.
3Tell the greatness of the Lord
with me.
Let us praise his name together.

4I asked the Lord for help, and he
answered me.
He saved me from all that I feared.
5Those who go to him for help are
happy.
They are never disgraced.
6This poor man called, and the Lord
heard him.
The Lord saved him from all his
troubles.
7The Lord saves those who fear him.
His angel camps around them.

8Examine and see how good the
Lord is.
Happy is the person who trusts
the Lord.
9People who belong to the Lord, fear
him!
Those who fear him will have
everything they need.
10Even lions may become weak and
hungry.
But those people who go to the
Lord for help will have every
good thing.
11Children, come and listen to me.
I will teach you to worship the
Lord.
12You must do these things
to enjoy life and have many happy
days.
13You must not say evil things.
You must not tell lies.
14Stop doing evil and do good.
Look for peace and work for it.

15The Lord sees the good people.
He listens to their prayers.
16But the Lord is against those who
do evil.
He makes the world forget them.
17The Lord hears good people when
they cry out to him.
He saves them from all their
troubles.
18The Lord is close to the
brokenhearted.

He saves those whose spirits have been crushed.

19People who do what is right may have many problems.
But the Lord will solve them all.
20He will protect their very bones.
Not one of them will be broken.
21Evil will kill the wicked people.
Those who hate good people will be judged guilty.
22But the Lord saves his servants' lives.
No one who trusts him will be judged guilty.

A Prayer for Help

Of David.

35 Lord, battle with those who battle with me.
Fight against those who fight against me.
2Pick up the shield and armor.
Rise up and help me.
3Lift up your spears, both large and small,
against those who chase me.
Tell me, "I will save you."

4Make those who want to kill me be ashamed and disgraced.
Make those who plan to harm me turn back and run away.
5Make them like chaff*d* blown by the wind.
Let the angel of the Lord chase them away.
6Let their road be dark and slippery as the angel of the Lord chases them.
7For no reason they spread out their net to trap me.
For no reason they dug a pit for me.
8So let ruin strike them suddenly.
Let them be caught in their own nets.
Let them fall into the pit and die.
9Then I will rejoice in the Lord.
I will be happy when he saves me.
10Even my bones will say,
"Lord, who is like you?
You save the weak from the strong.
You save the weak and poor from robbers."

11Men without mercy stand up to testify.
They ask me things I do not know.
12They repay me with evil for the good I have done.
They make me very sad.
13Yet when they were sick, I put on rough cloth to show my sadness.
I showed my sorrow by going without food.
But my prayers were not answered.
14 I acted as if they were my friends or brothers.
I bowed in sadness as if I were crying for my mother.
15But when I was in trouble, they gathered and laughed.
They gathered to attack before I knew it.
They insulted me without stopping.
16They made fun of me and were cruel to me.
They ground their teeth at me in anger.
17Lord, how long will you watch this happen?
Save my life from their attacks.
Save me from these people who are like lions.
18I will praise you in the great meeting.
I will praise you among crowds of people.
19Do not let my enemies laugh at me.
They hate me for no reason.
Do not let them make fun of me.
They have no reason to hate me.
20Their words are not friendly.
They think up lies about peace-loving people.
21They speak against me.
They say, "Aha! We saw what you did!"

22Lord, you have been watching. Do not keep quiet.
Lord, do not leave me alone.
23Wake up! Come and defend me!
My God and Lord, fight for me!
24Lord my God, defend me with your justice.
Don't let them laugh at me.

²⁵Don't let them think, "Aha! We got
what we wanted!"
Don't let them say, "We destroyed
him."
²⁶Let them be ashamed and
embarrassed.
They were happy when I hurt.
Cover them with shame and
disgrace.
They thought they were better
than I was.
²⁷May my friends sing and shout for
joy.
May they always say, "Praise the
greatness of the Lord.
He loves to see his servants do
well."
²⁸I will tell of your goodness.
I will praise you every day.

Wicked Men and a Good God

For the director of music. Of David, the
servant of the Lord.

36 Sin speaks to the wicked man in
his heart.
He has no fear of or respect for
God.

He doesn't refuse things that are
evil.
⁵Lord, your love reaches to the
heavens.
Your loyalty goes to the skies.
⁶Your goodness is as high as the
mountains.
Your justice is as deep as the great
ocean.
Lord, you protect both men and
animals.
⁷God, your love is so precious!
You protect people as a bird
protects her young under
her wings.
⁸They eat the rich food in your
house.
You let them drink from your river
of pleasure.
⁹You are the giver of life.
Your light lets us enjoy life.
¹⁰Continue to love those who know
you.

God's Love for Us
PSALM 36:5-7

Think of the biggest thing you've ever seen: a
mountain? A building? A whale? Whatever it is, God's love for us is
much bigger. King David might have been looking at a mountain or a big
body of water when he wrote these words. As he thought about how big
something like an ocean or the sky is, he probably felt very small compared
to it. And then he had another thought: God's love is even bigger—*much,
much* bigger—than that! David was overwhelmed by God's love. Take a few
minutes right now and think about how huge God's love for you really is.

To find out more about God's love for us, zoom to page 733.

²He thinks too much of himself.
He doesn't see his sin and
hate it.
³His words are wicked lies.
He is no longer wise or good.
⁴At night he makes evil plans.
What he does leads to nothing
good.

And continue to do good to those
who are good.
¹¹Don't let proud people attack me.
Don't let the wicked force me away.
¹²Those who do evil have been
defeated.
They are overwhelmed; they
cannot do evil any longer.

God Will Reward Fairly

Of David.

37 Don't be upset because of evil people.
Don't be jealous of those who do wrong.

2Like the grass, they will soon dry up.
Like green plants, they will soon die away.

3Trust the Lord and do good.
Live in the land and enjoy its safety.
4Enjoy serving the Lord.
And he will give you what you want.
5Depend on the Lord.
Trust him, and he will take care of you.
6Then your goodness will shine like the sun.
Your fairness will shine like the noonday sun.

7Wait and trust the Lord.
Don't be upset when others get rich or when someone else's plans succeed.
8Don't get angry.
Don't be upset; it only leads to trouble.
9Evil people will be sent away.
But people who trust the Lord will inherit the land.
10In a little while there will be no more wicked people.
You may look for them, but they will be gone.
11People who are not proud will inherit the land.
They will enjoy complete peace.

12The wicked make evil plans against good people.
They grind their teeth at them in anger.
13But the Lord laughs at the wicked.
He sees that their day is coming.
14The wicked draw their swords.
They bend their bows.
They try to kill the poor and helpless.
They want to kill those who are honest.
15But their swords will stab their own hearts.

Their bows will break.
16It's better to have little and be right than to have much and be wrong.
17The power of the wicked will be broken.
But the Lord supports those who do right.
18The Lord watches over the lives of the innocent.
Their reward will last forever.
19They will not be ashamed when trouble comes.
They will be full in times of hunger.
20But the wicked will die.
The Lord's enemies will be like the flowers of the fields.
They will disappear like smoke.
21The wicked people borrow but don't pay back.
But those who do right give freely to others.
22Those people the Lord blesses will inherit the land.
But those he curses will be sent away.

23When a man's steps follow the Lord, God is pleased with his ways.
24If he stumbles, he will not fall, because the Lord holds his hand.

25I was young, and now I am old.
But I have never seen the Lord leave good people helpless.
I have never seen their children begging for food.
26Good people always lend freely to others.
And their children are a blessing.

27Stop doing evil and do good.
Then you will live forever.
28The Lord loves justice.
He will not leave those who worship him.
He will always protect them.
But the children of the wicked will die.
29Good people will inherit the land.
They will live in it forever.

30A good person speaks with wisdom.
He says what is fair.

³¹The teachings of his God are in his
heart.
He does not fail to keep them.
³²The wicked watch for good people.
They want to kill them.
³³The Lord will not take away his
protection.
He will not judge good people guilty.

³⁴Wait for the Lord's help
and follow him.
He will honor you and give you the
land.
And you will see the wicked
people sent away.

³⁵I saw a wicked and cruel man.
He looked strong like a healthy
tree in good soil.
³⁶But he died and was gone.
I looked for him, but he couldn't
be found.

³⁷Think of the innocent person.
Watch the honest one.
The man who has peace
will have children to live after him.
³⁸But sinners will be destroyed.
In the end the wicked will die.

³⁹The Lord saves good people.
He is their strong city in times of
trouble.
⁴⁰The Lord helps them and saves them.
He saves them from the wicked
because they trust in him for
protection.

A Prayer in Time of Sickness

A song of David to remember.

38 Lord, don't correct me when
you are angry.
Don't punish me when you are
very angry.
²Your arrows have wounded me.
Your hand has come down on me.
³My body is sick from your
punishment.
Even my bones are not healthy
because of my sin.
⁴My guilt has overwhelmed me.
Like a load it weighs me down.

⁵My sores stink and become infected
because I was foolish.
⁶I am bent over and bowed down.
I am sad all day long.
⁷I am burning with fever.
My whole body is sore.
⁸I am weak and faint.
I moan from the pain I feel.

⁹Lord, you know everything I want.
My cries are not hidden from you.
¹⁰My heart pounds, and my strength
is gone.
I am losing my sight.
¹¹Because of my wounds, my friends
and neighbors leave me alone.
My relatives stay far away.
¹²Some people set traps to kill me.
Those who want to hurt me plan
trouble.
All day long they think up lies.

¹³I am like a deaf man; I cannot hear.
Like a mute, I cannot speak.
¹⁴I am like a person who does not
hear.
I have no answer to give.
¹⁵I trust you, Lord.
You will answer, my God and Lord.
¹⁶I said, "Don't let them laugh at me.
Don't let them brag when I am
defeated."
¹⁷I am about to die.
I cannot forget my pain.
¹⁸I confess my guilt.
I am troubled by my sin.
¹⁹My enemies are strong and healthy.
Many people hate me for no
reason.
²⁰They repay me with evil for the
good I did.
They lie about me because I try to
do good.

²¹Lord, don't leave me.
My God, don't go away.
²²Quickly come and help me,
my Lord and Savior.

Life Is Short

*For the director of music. For Jeduthun.
A song of David.*

39 I said, "I will be careful how I act.
I will not sin by what I say.

I will be careful what I say
around wicked people."
²So I kept very quiet.
I didn't even say anything good.
But I became even more upset.
³I became very angry inside.
And the more I thought about it,
the angrier I became.
So I spoke:
⁴"Lord, tell me when the end will come.
How long will I live?
Let me know how long I have.
⁵You have given me only a short life.
My lifetime is like nothing to you.
Everyone's life is only a breath.

Selah^d

⁶A person is like a shadow moving
about.
All his work is for nothing.
He collects things, but he doesn't
know who will get them.

⁷"So, Lord, what hope do I have?
You are my hope.
⁸Save me from all my sins.
Don't let wicked fools make fun
of me.
⁹I am quiet. I do not open my mouth.
You are the one who has done this.
¹⁰Quit punishing me.
Your beating is about to kill me.
¹¹You correct and punish people for
their sins.
Like a moth, you destroy what
they love.
Everyone's life is only a breath.

Selah

¹²"Lord, hear my prayer.
Listen to my cry.
Do not ignore my tears.
I am like a visitor with you.
Like my ancestors, I'm only here a
short time.
¹³Leave me alone so I can be happy.
Soon I will leave and be no more."

Praise and Prayer for Help

For the director of music. A song
of David.

40 I waited patiently for the Lord.
He turned to me and heard my
cry.

²He lifted me out of the pit of
destruction,
out of the sticky mud.
He stood me on a rock.
He made my feet steady.
³He put a new song in my mouth.
It was a song of praise to our God.
Many people will see this and
worship him.
Then they will trust the Lord.

⁴Happy is the person
who trusts the Lord.
He doesn't turn to those who are
proud,
to those who worship false gods.
⁵Lord our God, you have done many
miracles.^d
Your plans for us are many.
If I tried to tell them all,
there would be too many to count.

⁶You do not want sacrifices and
offerings.
But you have made a hole in my ear
to show that my body and life are
yours.
You do not ask for burnt offerings
and offerings to take away sins.
⁷Then I said, "Look, I have come.
It is written about me in the book.
⁸My God, I want to do what you want.
Your teachings are in my heart."

**My God, I want to do
what you want.
Your teachings are
in my heart.
• Psalm 40:8**

⁹I will tell about your goodness in the
great meeting of your people.
Lord, you know my lips are not
silent.
¹⁰I do not hide your goodness in my
heart.
I speak about your loyalty and
salvation.
I do not hide your love and truth
from the people in the great
meeting.

[11] Lord, do not hold back your mercy
  from me.
  Let your love and truth always
    protect me.
[12] Troubles have gathered around me.
  There are too many to count.
  My sins have caught me.
  I cannot see a way to escape.
  I have more sins than hairs on my
    head.
  I have lost my courage.
[13] Please, Lord, save me.
  Hurry, Lord, to help me.
[14] People are trying to kill me.
  Shame them and disgrace them.
  People want to hurt me.
  Let them run away in disgrace.
[15] People are making fun of me.
  Let them be shamed into silence.
[16] But let those who follow you
  be happy and glad.
  They love you for saving them.
  May they always say, "Praise the
    Lord!"

[17] Lord, I am poor and helpless.
  But please remember me.
  You are my helper and savior.
  My God, do not wait.

A Prayer in Time of Sickness

For the director of music. A song
of David.

41 Happy is the person who thinks
  about the poor.
  When trouble comes, the Lord will
    save him.
[2] The Lord will protect him and spare
    his life.
  The Lord will bless him in the land.
  The Lord will not let his enemies
    take him.
[3] The Lord will give him strength
    when he is sick.
  The Lord will make him well again.

[4] I said, "Lord, be kind to me.
  Heal me because I have sinned
    against you."
[5] My enemies are saying bad things
    about me.
  They say, "When will he die and
    be forgotten?"

[6] Some people come to see me.
  But they lie.
  They just come to get bad news.
  Then they go and gossip.
[7] All my enemies whisper about me.
  They think the worst about me.
[8] They say, "He has a terrible disease.
  He will never get out of bed again."
[9] My best and truest friend ate at my
    table.
  Now even he has turned against me.

[10] Lord, have mercy on me.
  Give me strength so I can pay
    them back.
[11] My enemies do not defeat me.
  That's how I know you are pleased
    with me.
[12] Because I am innocent, you support
    me.
  You will let me be with you forever.

[13] Praise the Lord, the God of Israel.
  He has always been,
  and he will always be.
    Amen and amen.

Book 2

Wishing to Be near God

For the director of music. A maskil[d]
of the sons of Korah.

42 A deer thirsts for a stream of
  water.
  In the same way, I thirst for you,
    God.
[2] I thirst for the living God.
  When can I go to meet with him?
[3] Day and night, my tears have been
    my food.
  People are always saying,
    "Where is your God?"
[4] When I remember these things,
  I speak with a broken heart.
  I used to walk with the crowd.
  I led the happy crowd to God's
    Temple,[d]
  with songs of praise.

[5] Why am I so sad?
  Why am I so upset?
  I should put my hope in God.
  I should keep praising him,

My Savior and [6]my God.

I am very sad.
So I remember you while I am in
the land where the Jordan
River begins.
I will remember you while I am near
the Hermon mountains
and on the mountain of Mizar.
[7]Troubles have come again and again.
They sound like waterfalls.
Your waves are crashing
all around me.
[8]The Lord shows his true love every
day.
At night I have a song,
and I pray to my living God.
[9]I say to God, my Rock,[d]
"Why have you forgotten me?
Why am I sad
and troubled by my enemies?"
[10]My enemies' insults make me feel
as if my bones were broken.
They are always saying,
"Where is your God?"

[11]Why am I so sad?
Why am I so upset?
I should put my hope in God.
I should keep praising him,
my Savior and my God.

A Prayer for Protection

43 God, defend me.
Argue my case against those
who don't follow you.
Save me from liars and those who
do evil.
[2]God, you are my strength.
Why have you rejected me?
Why am I sad
and troubled by my enemies?
[3]Send me your light and truth.
They will guide me.
Lead me to your holy mountain.
Lead me to where you live.
[4]I will go to the altar of God,
to God who is my joy and happiness.
I will praise you with a harp,
God, my God.

[5]Why am I so sad?
Why am I so upset?
I should put my hope in God.

I should keep praising him,
my Savior and my God.

A Prayer for Help

For the director of music. A maskil[d]
of the sons of Korah.

44 God, we have heard about you.
Our ancestors told us
what you did in their days,
in days long ago.
[2]With your power you forced the
nations out of the land.
You placed our ancestors here.
You destroyed those other nations.
But you made our ancestors grow
strong.
[3]It wasn't their swords that took the
land.
It wasn't their power that gave
them victory.
But it was your great power and
strength.
You were with them because you
loved them.

[4]My God, you are my King.
Your commands led Jacob's people
to victory.
[5]With your help we pushed back our
enemies.
In your name we walked on those
who came against us.
[6]I don't trust my bow to help me.
My sword can't save me.
[7]You saved us from Egypt.
You made our enemies ashamed.
[8]We will praise God every day.
We will praise your name forever.
Selah[d]

[9]But you have rejected us and
shamed us.
You don't march with our armies
anymore.
[10]You let our enemies push us back.
Our enemies have taken our wealth.
[11]You gave us away like sheep to be
eaten.
You scattered us among the nations.
[12]You sold your people for nothing.
You made no profit on the sale.
[13]You made us a joke to our neighbors.

The community laughs and makes
    fun of us.
[14] You made us a joke to the other
    nations.
    People shake their heads.
[15] I am always in disgrace.
    I am covered with shame.
[16] My enemy is getting even
    with insults and curses.

[17] All these things have happened to us,
    but we have not forgotten you.
    We have kept our agreement with
    you.
[18] Our hearts haven't turned away
    from you.
    We haven't stopped following you.
[19] But you crushed us in this place
    where wild dogs live.
    You covered us with deep darkness.

[20] We did not forget our God.
    We did not lift our hands in prayer
    to foreign gods.
[21] God would have known if we had.
    He knows what is in our hearts.
[22] But for you we are in danger of
    death all the time.
    People think we are worth no
    more than sheep to be killed.

[23] Wake up, Lord! Why are you
    sleeping?
    Get up! Don't reject us forever.
[24] Why are you hidden from us?
    Have you forgotten our pain and
    troubles?

[25] We have been pushed down into the
    dirt.
    We are flat on the ground.
[26] Get up and help us.
    Because of your love, save us.

A Song for the King's Wedding

For the director of music. To the tune of
"Lilies." A maskil.[d] A love song of the
sons of Korah.

45 Beautiful words fill my mind.
    I am speaking of royal things.
    My tongue is like the pen of a
    skilled writer.

[2] You are more handsome than anyone.
    You are a very good speaker.

God has blessed you forever.
[3] Put on your sword, powerful warrior.
    Show your glory and majesty.
[4] In your majesty win the victory.
    Defend what is true and right.
    Your power will do amazing things.
[5] Your sharp arrows will enter
    the hearts of the king's enemies.
    Nations will be defeated before you.
[6] God, your throne will last forever
    and ever.
    You will rule your kingdom with
    fairness.
[7] You love right and hate evil.
    So God has chosen you to rule
    those with you.
    Your God has given you much joy.
[8] Your clothes smell like myrrh,[d]
    aloes[d] and cassia.[d]
    From palaces of ivory
    music comes to make you happy.
[9] Kings' daughters are among your
    honored women.
    Your bride stands at your right side
    wearing gold from Ophir.

[10] Listen to me, daughter. Look and
    pay attention.
    Forget your people and your
    father's family.
[11] The king loves your beauty.
    Because he is your master, you
    should obey him.
[12] People from the city of Tyre have
    brought a gift.
    Wealthy people will want to
    meet you.

[13] The princess is very beautiful.
    Her gown is woven with gold.
[14] In her beautiful clothes she is
    brought to the king.
    Her bridesmaids follow behind
    her.
    And they are also brought to him.
[15] They come with happiness and joy.
    They enter the king's palace.

[16] You will have sons to take the place
    of your ancestors.
    You will make them rulers
    through all the land.
[17] I will make your name famous from
    now on.

People will praise you forever and
ever.

God Protects His People

For the director of music. By alamoth.[d]
A song of the sons of Korah.

46 God is our protection and our
strength.
He always helps in times of
trouble.

"**E**ver been in trouble? I mean really big trouble?" Check out a promise Eugene should read here in Psalm 46:1-3.

[2]So we will not be afraid if the earth
shakes,
or if the mountains fall into the sea.
[3]We will not fear even if the oceans
roar and foam,
or if the mountains shake at the
raging sea. *Selah[d]*

[4]There is a river which brings joy to
the city of God.
This is the holy place where God
Most High lives.
[5]God is in that city, and so it will not
be shaken.
God will help her at dawn.
[6]Nations tremble, and kingdoms
shake.
God shouts, and the earth
crumbles.
[7]The Lord of heaven's armies is
with us.
The God of Jacob is our
protection. *Selah*
[8]Come and see what the Lord has
done.
He has done amazing things on
the earth.
[9]He stops wars everywhere on the
earth.
He breaks all bows and spears

and burns up the chariots
with fire.
[10]God says, "Be quiet and know that I
am God.
I will be supreme over all the
nations.
I will be supreme in the earth."
[11]The Lord of heaven's armies is
with us.
The God of Jacob is our
protection. *Selah*

God, the King of the World

For the director of music. A song of the
sons of Korah.

47 Clap your hands, all you people.
Shout to God with joy.
[2]The Lord Most High is wonderful.
He is the great King over all the
earth!
[3]He defeated nations for us
and put them under our control.
[4]He chose the land we would inherit.
We are the children of Jacob,
whom he loved. *Selah[d]*

[5]God has risen with a shout of joy.
The Lord has risen as the
trumpets sounded.
[6]Sing praises to God. Sing praises.
Sing praises to our King. Sing
praises.
[7]God is King of all the earth.
So sing a song of praise to him.
[8]God is King over the nations.
God sits on his holy throne.
[9]The leaders of the nations meet
with the people of the God of
Abraham.
Even the leaders of the earth
belong to God.
He is supreme.

Jerusalem, the City of God

A song of the sons of Korah.

48 The Lord is great; he should be
praised
in the city of our God, on his holy
mountain.
[2]It is high and beautiful.
It brings joy to the whole world.

Mount Zion[d] is like the high
    mountains of the north.
It is the city of the Great King.
[3]God is within its palaces.
    He is known as its protection.
[4]Kings joined together
    and came together to attack the city.
[5]But when they saw it, they were
    amazed.
    They ran away in fear.
[6]Fear took hold of them.
    They hurt like a woman having a
    baby.
[7]You destroyed the large trading ships
    with an east wind.

[8]First we heard.
    And now we have seen that
God will always keep his city safe.
It is the city of the Lord of
    heaven's armies,
    the city of our God.   *Selah[d]*

[9]God, we come into your Temple.[d]
    There we think about your love.
[10]God, your name is known
    everywhere.
    Everywhere on earth people
    praise you.
    Your right hand is full of goodness.
[11]Mount Zion is happy.
    All the towns of Judah rejoice
because your decisions are fair.

[12]Walk around Jerusalem
    and count its towers.
[13]Notice how strong they are. Look at
    the palaces.
    Then you will be able to tell your
    children about them.
[14]This God is our God forever and ever.
    He will guide us from now on.

Trusting Money Is Foolish

For the director of music. A song of the
sons of Korah.

49 Listen to this, all you nations.
    Listen, all you who live on earth.
[2]Listen, both great and small,
    rich and poor together.
[3]What I say is wise.
    My heart speaks with
    understanding.

[4]I will pay attention to a wise saying.
    I will explain my riddle on the harp.

[5]Why should I be afraid of bad days?
    Why should I fear when evil men
    surround me?
[6]They trust in their money.
    They brag about their riches.
[7]No one can buy back the life of
    another person.
    No one can pay God for his own life.
[8]The price of a life is high.
    No payment is ever enough.
[9]Do people live forever?
    Don't they all face death?

[10]See, even wise men die.
    Fools and stupid people also die.
    They leave their wealth to others.
[11]Their graves will always be their
    homes.
    They will live there from now on,
    even though they named places
    after themselves.
[12]Even rich people do not live forever.
    Like the animals, people die.

[13]This is what will happen to people
    who trust in themselves.
    And this will happen to their
    followers who believe them.
         Selah[d]

[14]Like sheep, they must die.
    And death will be their shepherd.
Honest people will rule over them
    in the morning.
    Their bodies will rot in a grave far
    from home.
[15]But God will save my life.
    He will take me from the grave.
         Selah

[16]Don't be afraid of a rich man
    because his house is more beautiful.
[17]He won't take anything to the grave.
    His wealth won't die with him.
[18]He was praised when he was alive.
    (And people may praise you when
    you succeed.)
[19]But he will go to where his
    ancestors are.
    He will never see light again.
[20]Rich people with no understanding
    are just like animals that die.

God Wants True Worship

A song of Asaph.

50 The God of gods, the Lord, speaks.
He calls the earth from the rising
to the setting sun.
²God shines from Jerusalem,
whose beauty is perfect.
³Our God comes, and he will not be
silent.
A fire burns in front of him,
and a storm surrounds him.
⁴He calls to the sky and to the earth
to see him judge his people.
⁵He says, "You who worship me,
gather around.
You have made an agreement with
me, using a sacrifice."
⁶God is the judge.
Even the skies say he is right.

Selah[d]

⁷God says, "My people, listen to me.
Israel, I will testify against you.
I am God, your God.
⁸I do not scold you for your sacrifices.
You always bring me your burnt
offerings.
⁹But I do not need the bulls from
your stalls

or the goats from your pens.
¹⁰Every animal of the forest is already
mine.
The cattle on a thousand hills are
mine.
¹¹I know every bird on the mountains.
Every living thing in the fields is
mine.
¹²If I were hungry, I would not tell you.
The earth and everything on it are
mine.
¹³I don't eat the meat of bulls
or drink the blood of goats.

¹⁴Give an offering to show thanks to
God.
Give God Most High what you
have promised.
¹⁵Call to me in times of trouble.
I will save you, and you will honor
me."

¹⁶But God says to the wicked people,
"Why do you talk about my laws?
Why do you mention my
agreement?
¹⁷You hate my teachings.
You turn your back on what I say.
¹⁸When you see a thief, you join him.
You take part in adultery.[d]
¹⁹You don't stop your mouth from
speaking evil.
Your tongue makes up lies.
²⁰You speak against your brother.

Good Kings and Bad Kings

DAVID • PSALM 51

Although he was a good king, David made mistakes. He wrote this psalm
when he realized that he had sinned. God showed David what he had
done wrong. Even though David was punished for his sin, he told God how
sorry he was and asked God to forgive him. David is known as a king who
truly loved God, even though he made some pretty big mistakes.

When we sin, God wants us to pray to him and ask him to forgive us.
Don't ever think that because you're a Christian, you won't sin anymore.
You will sin, but you can ask God to forgive you and to help you stop
sinning.

To meet a king who was named in a prophecy, fly to page 854.

Sin
PSALM 51:1-10

Imagine that you and some friends are on the school playground. One of your buddies says, "Hey—watch me hit the telephone pole with this rock." *Whoosh!* He fires it at the pole . . . and just misses. "Let me show you how to do it," you say, and before you know it, you're all throwing rocks at the pole. Suddenly—*CRASH!* Someone hits the windshield of a car parked nearby.

As the group sits in front of the principal, you try this excuse: "Well, sir, I'm sorry we broke that windshield, but it wasn't *your* car . . . so may we go now?" He will probably explain that it may not have been his car, but it *is* his school. Therefore, you have to answer to him *and* the car's owner for what you did.

Sometimes our sins involve other people. So we need to say that we're sorry and make everything right, if possible. But our sins *always* involve God. We should remember to apologize to him first.

To learn more about sin, zoom to page 1131.

You lie about your mother's son.
²¹I have kept quiet while you did
   these things.
So you thought I was just like you.
But I will scold you.
I will accuse you to your face.

²²"Think about this, you people who
      forget God.
Otherwise, I will tear you apart,
   and no one will save you.
²³Those people honor me
   who give me offerings to show
      thanks.
And I, God, will save those who do
   that."

A Prayer for Forgiveness

For the director of music. A song
of David when the prophet*ᵈ* Nathan
came to David after David's sin
with Bathsheba.

51 God, be merciful to me
      because you are loving.
Because you are always ready to be
   merciful,
wipe out all my wrongs.

²Wash away all my guilt
   and make me clean again.
³I know about my wrongs.
   I can't forget my sin.
⁴You are the one I have sinned against.
   I have done what you say is wrong.
So you are right when you speak.
   You are fair when you judge me.
⁵I was brought into this world in sin.
   In sin my mother gave birth to me.

⁶You want me to be completely
      truthful.
   So teach me wisdom.
⁷Take away my sin, and I will be clean.
   Wash me, and I will be whiter than
      snow.
⁸Make me hear sounds of joy and
      gladness.
   Let the bones you crushed be
      happy again.
⁹Turn your face from my sins.
   Wipe out all my guilt.

¹⁰Create in me a pure heart, God.
   Make my spirit right again.
¹¹Do not send me away from you.

Do not take your Holy Spirit[d] away
   from me.
12Give me back the joy that comes
   when you save me.
Keep me strong by giving me a
   willing spirit.
13Then I will teach your ways to those
   who do wrong.
And sinners will turn back to you.

14God, save me from the guilt of
   murder.
God, you are the one who saves me.
I will sing about your goodness.
15Lord, let me speak
   so I may praise you.
16You are not pleased by sacrifices.
Otherwise, I would give them.
You don't want burnt offerings.
17The sacrifice God wants is a willing
   spirit.
God, you will not reject
   a heart that is broken and sorry
   for its sin.

18Do whatever good you wish for
   Jerusalem.
Rebuild the walls of Jerusalem.
19Then you will be pleased with right
   sacrifices and whole burnt
   offerings.
And bulls will be offered on your
   altar.

God Will Punish the Proud

For the director of music. A maskil[d]
of David. When Doeg the Edomite came
to Saul and said to him, "David is in
Ahimelech's house."

52 Mighty warrior, why do you brag
about the evil you do?
God's love will continue forever.
2You think up evil plans.
Your tongue is like a sharp razor,
   making up lies.
3You love wrong more than right
and lies more than truth.   *Selah*[d]
4You love words that bite
and tongues that lie.

5But God will ruin you forever.
He will grab you and throw you
   out of your tent.

He will tear you away from the
   land of the living.   *Selah*
6Those who do right will see this and
   fear God.
They will laugh at you and say,
7"Look what happened to the man
   who did not depend on God.
Instead, he depended on his money.
He grew strong by his evil plans."

8But I am like an olive tree
   growing in God's Temple.[d]
I trust God's love
   forever and ever.
9God, I will thank you forever for
   what you have done.
With those who worship you, I will
   trust you because you are good.

The Unbelieving Fool

For the director of music. By mahalath.[d]
A maskil[d] of David.

53 A wicked fool says to himself,
"There is no God."
Fools are evil. They do terrible
   things.
None of them does anything good.

2God looked down from heaven at all
   the people.
He looked to see if anyone was
   wise,
if anyone was looking to God for
   help.
3But everyone has turned away.
Together, everyone has become
   evil.
None of them does anything good.

4Don't the wicked understand?
They destroy my people as if they
   were eating bread.
They have not asked God for help.
5The wicked became filled with
   terror
where there had been nothing to
   be terrified of.
God will scatter the bones of your
   enemies.
You will defeat them,
   because God has rejected them.

6I pray that victory will come to
   Israel from Mount Zion![d]

May God give them back their riches.
Then the people of Jacob will rejoice.
And the people of Israel will be glad.

A Prayer for Help

For the director of music. With stringed instruments. A maskil[d] of David when the Ziphites went to Saul and said, "We think David is hiding among our people."

54 God, save me because of who you are.
By your strength show that I am innocent.
[2] Hear my prayer, God.
Listen to what I say.
[3] Strangers turn against me.
Cruel men want to kill me.
They do not care about God.   *Selah*[d]

[4] See, God will help me.
The Lord will spare my life.
[5] Let my enemies be punished with their own evil.
Destroy them because you are loyal to me.

[6] I will offer a sacrifice as a special gift to you.
I will thank you, Lord, because you are good.
[7] You have saved me from all my troubles.
I have seen my enemies defeated.

A Prayer About a False Friend

For the director of music. With stringed instruments. A maskil[d] of David.

55 God, listen to my prayer.
Do not ignore my prayer.
[2] Pay attention to me and answer me.
I am troubled and upset
[3] by what the enemy says
and how the wicked look at me.
They bring troubles down on me.
In anger they attack me.

[4] I am frightened inside.
The terror of death has attacked me.
[5] I am scared and shaking.
Terror grips me.

[6] I said, "I wish I had wings like a dove.
Then I would fly away and rest.
[7] I would wander far away.
I would stay in the desert.   *Selah*[d]
[8] I would hurry to my place of escape, far away from the wind and storm."

[9] Lord, destroy and confuse their words.
I see violence and fighting in the city.
[10] Day and night they are all around its walls.
Evil and trouble are everywhere inside.
[11] Destruction is everywhere in the city.
Trouble and lying never leave its streets.

[12] It was not an enemy insulting me.
I could stand that.
It was not someone who hated me.
I could hide from him.
[13] But it is you, a person like me.
You were my companion and good friend.
[14] We had a good friendship.
We went together to God's Temple.[d]

[15] Let death take away my enemies.
Let them die while they are still young
because evil lives with them.
[16] But I will call to God for help.
And the Lord will save me.
[17] Morning, noon and night I am troubled and upset.
But he will listen to me.
[18] Many are against me.
But he keeps me safe in battle.
[19] God who lives forever
will hear me and punish them.
But they will not change.
They do not fear God.   *Selah*

[20] The one who was my friend attacks his friends.
He breaks his promises.
[21] His words are slippery like butter.
But war is in his heart.
His words are smoother than oil,

but they cut like knives.

22Give your worries to the Lord.
  He will take care of you.
  He will never let good people
    down.
23But, God, you will bring down
    the wicked to the grave.
  Murderers and liars will live
    only half a lifetime.
  But I will trust in you.

Trusting God for Help

For the director of music. To the tune of
"The Dove in the Distant Oak." A miktam*d* of David when the Philistines captured him in Gath.

56 God, be merciful to me because
    people are chasing me.
  The battle has pressed me all day
    long.
2My enemies have chased me all day.
  There are many of them fighting me.
3When I am afraid,
  I will trust you.
4I praise God for his word.
  I trust God. So I am not afraid.
  What can human beings do to me?

5All day long they twist my words.
  All their evil plans are against me.
6They wait. They hide.
  They watch my steps.
  They hope to kill me.
7God, do not let them escape.
  Punish the foreign nations in your
    anger.
8You have recorded my troubles.
  You have kept a list of my tears.
  Aren't they in your records?

9On the day I call for help, my
    enemies will be defeated.
  I know that God is on my side.
10I praise God for his word to me.
  I praise the Lord for his word.
11I trust in God. I will not be afraid.
  What can people do to me?

12God, I must keep my promises to
    you.
  I will give you my offerings to
    thank you.
13You have saved me from death.

You have kept me from being
    defeated.
  So I will walk with God
    in light among the living.

A Prayer in Troubled Times

For the director of music. To the tune of
"Do Not Destroy." A miktam*d* of David
when he escaped from Saul in a cave.

57 Be merciful to me, God. Be mer-
    ciful to me
  because I come to you for
    protection.
  I will come to you as a bird comes
    for protection under its
    mother's wings
  until the trouble has passed.

2I cry out to God Most High,
  to the God who does everything
    for me.
3He sends help from heaven and
    saves me.
  He punishes those who attack me.
                              *Selah*d
  God sends me his love and truth.

4Enemies are like lions all
    around me.
  I must lie down among them.
  Their teeth are like spears and
    arrows.
    Their tongues are as sharp as
      swords.

5God is supreme over the skies.
  His greatness covers the earth.

6They set a trap for me.
  I am very worried.
  They dug a pit in my path.
    But they fell into it themselves.
                              Selah

7My heart is right, God. My heart is
    right.
  I will sing and praise you.
8Wake up, my soul.
  Wake up, harp and lyre!*d*
  I will wake up the dawn.
9Lord, I will praise you among the
    nations.
  I will sing songs of praise about
    you to all the nations.

¹⁰Your love is so great it reaches to
the skies.
Your truth reaches to the clouds.
¹¹God, you are supreme over the
skies.
Let your glory be over all the
earth.

Unfair Judges

For the director of music. To the tune of
"Do Not Destroy." A miktam*ᵈ* of David.

58 Do you rulers really say what is
right?
Do you judge people fairly?
²No, in your heart you plan evil.
You think up violent crimes in the
land.
³From birth evil men start doing bad
things.
They tell lies and do wrong as
soon as they are born.
⁴They are like poisonous snakes,
like deaf cobras that can't hear.
⁵They cannot hear the music of the
snake charmer
no matter how well he plays for
them.

⁶God, break the teeth out of their
mouths!
Tear out the fangs of those lions,
Lord!
⁷Let them disappear like water that
flows away.
Let them be cut short like a
broken arrow.
⁸Let them be like snails that melt as
they move.
Let them be like a child born dead
who never saw the sun.
⁹His anger will blow them away alive.
It will happen faster than burning
thorns can heat a pot.
¹⁰Good people will be glad when they
see him get even.
They will wash their feet in the
blood of the wicked.
¹¹Then people will say,
"There really are rewards for
doing what is right.
There really is a God who judges
the world."

A Prayer for Protection

For the director of music. To the tune of
"Do Not Destroy." A miktam*ᵈ* of David
when Saul sent men to watch David's
house to kill him.

59 God, save me from my enemies.
Protect me from those who
come against me.
²Save me from those who do evil.
Save me from murderers.

³Look, men are waiting to attack me.
Cruel men attack me.
But I have not sinned or done
wrong, Lord.
⁴I have done nothing wrong, but
they are ready to attack me.
Wake up to help me and look.
⁵You are the Lord God of heaven's
armies, the God of Israel.
Come and punish those people.
Do not give those traitors any
mercy.   *Selahᵈ*

⁶They come back at night.
Like dogs they growl and roam
around the city.
⁷Notice what comes from their
mouths.
Insults come from their lips.
They say, "Who's listening?"
⁸But, Lord, you laugh at them.
You make fun of all of them.

⁹God, my strength, I wait for you.
God, you are my protection.
¹⁰My God loves me, and he will be
with me.
He will help me defeat my enemies.
¹¹Lord, our protector, do not kill them.
If you do, my people will forget.
With your power scatter them
and defeat them.
¹²They sin by what they say.
They sin with their words.
They curse and tell lies.
So let their pride trap them.
¹³Destroy them in your anger.
Destroy them completely!
Then they will know
that God rules over Israel
and to the ends of the earth.   *Selah*

¹⁴They come back at night.

Like dogs they growl
and roam around the city.
¹⁵They wander about looking for food.
And they howl if they do not find
enough.
¹⁶But I will sing about your strength.
In the morning I will sing about
your love.
You are my protection,
my place of safety in times of
trouble.
¹⁷God, my strength, I will sing praises
to you.
God, my protection, you are the
God who loves me.

A Prayer After a Defeat

For the director of music. To the tune of
"Lily of the Agreement." A miktam[d]
of David. For teaching. When David
fought the Arameans of Northwest
Mesopotamia and Zobah, and when Joab
returned and defeated 12,000 Edomites
at the Valley of Salt.

60 God, you have rejected us and
scattered us.
You have been angry, but please
come back to us.
²You made the earth shake and crack.
Fix its breaks because it is shaking.
³You have given your people trouble.
You made us unable to walk
straight, like people drunk
with wine.
⁴You have raised a banner to gather
those who fear you.
Now they can escape the enemy.
                    Selah[d]
⁵Answer us and save us by your power.
Then the people you love will be
rescued.

⁶God has said from his Temple,[d]
"When I win, I will divide Shechem
and cut up the Valley of Succoth.
⁷Gilead and Manasseh are mine.
Ephraim is like my helmet.
Judah holds my royal scepter.[d]
⁸Moab is like my washbowl.
I throw my sandals at Edom.
I shout at Philistia."

⁹Who will bring me to the strong,
walled city?

Who will lead me to Edom?
¹⁰God, surely you have rejected us.
You do not go out with our armies.
¹¹Help us fight the enemy.
Human help is useless.
¹²But we can win with God's help.
He will defeat our enemies.

A Prayer for Protection

For the director of music. With stringed
instruments. Of David.

61 God, hear my cry.
Listen to my prayer.
²I call to you from the ends of the
earth.
I am afraid.
Carry me away to a high mountain.
³You have been my protection,
like a strong tower against my
enemies.
⁴Let me live in your Holy Tent[d]
forever.
Protect me as a bird protects its
young under its wings.   Selah[d]
⁵God, you have heard my promises.
You have given me the things that
belong to those who fear you.

⁶Give the king a long life.
Let him live many years.
⁷Let him rule in the presence of God
forever.
Protect him with your love and
truth.
⁸Then I will praise your name forever.
And every day I will keep my
promises.

Trust Only in God

For the director of music. For Jeduthun.
A song of David.

62 I wait patiently for God.
Only he can save me.
²He is my rock, who saves me.
He protects me like a strong,
walled city.
I will not be defeated.

³How long will you attack me?
Will all of you throw me down?
I am like a leaning wall, like a
fence ready to fall.

Salvation
PSALM 62:1-2

If you were hanging over the edge of a cliff and a pair of big, strong hands reached over to pull you up to safety, would you let them rescue you? Or would you hang around to see if anybody else would come along?

Because you're smart, you would let the first pair of hands save you. You wouldn't know whether you would ever get a second chance. The Bible says that only God can save us from our sins. Only he can pull us up to safety. There is nothing we can do to save ourselves. In Jesus, God has offered to rescue us from sin. The Bible tells us that only Jesus is able and willing to do this. Will you let him save you? Choose life in Christ!

To learn more about salvation, zoom to page 808.

---

⁴You are planning to make me fall.
   You enjoy telling lies about me.
With your mouth you bless me.
   But in your heart you curse me.
                  Selahᵈ

⁵I wait patiently for God to save me.
   Only he gives me hope.
⁶He is my rock, who saves me.
   He protects me like a strong,
      walled city.
   I will not be defeated.
⁷My honor and salvation come from
      God.
   He is my mighty rock and my
      protection.

⁸People, trust God all the time.
   Tell him all your problems.
   God is our protection.   *Selah*

⁹People are only a breath.
   Even the greatest men are just a lie.
On the scales, they weigh nothing.
   Together they are only a breath.
¹⁰Do not trust in force.
   Stealing is of no use.
Even if you gain more riches,
   don't put your trust in them.

¹¹God has said this,
   and I have heard it over and over:
   God, you are strong.
¹²Lord, you are loving.
   You reward a person for what he
      does.

Wishing to Be near God

A song of David when he was in the desert of Judah.

63 God, you are my God.
   I want to follow you.
My whole being
   thirsts for you,
like a man in a dry, empty land
   where there is no water.
²I have seen you in the Temple.ᵈ
   I have seen your strength and glory.
³Your love is better than life.
   I will praise you.
⁴I will praise you as long as I live.
   I will lift up my hands in prayer to
      your name.
⁵I will be content as if I had eaten the
      best foods.
   My lips will sing. My mouth will
      praise you.

⁶I remember you while I'm lying in
      bed.

I think about you through the night.
⁷You are my help.

Because of your protection, I sing.
⁸I stay close to you.

You support me with your right
    hand.

⁹Some people are trying to kill me.
    But they will go down to the grave.
¹⁰They will be killed with swords.
    They will be eaten by wild dogs.
¹¹But the king will rejoice in his God.
    All who make promises in his
        name will praise him.
    But the mouths of liars will be shut.

A Prayer Against Enemies

For the director of music. A song
of David.

64 God, listen to my complaint.
    I am afraid of my enemies.
    Protect my life from them.
²Hide me from those wicked people,
    from that gang who does evil.
³They sharpen their tongues like
        swords.
    They shoot bitter words like arrows.
⁴They hide and shoot at innocent
        people.
    They shoot suddenly and are not
        afraid.
⁵They encourage each other to do
        wrong.
    They talk about setting traps.
    They think no one will see them.
⁶They plan wicked things and say,
    "We have a perfect plan."
    The mind of man is hard to
        understand.

⁷But God will shoot them with arrows.
    They will suddenly be struck down.
⁸Their own words will be used
        against them.
    All who see them will shake their
        heads.
⁹Then everyone will fear God.
    They will tell what God has done.
    They will learn from what he has
        done.
¹⁰Good people will be happy in the
        Lord.
    They will find protection in him.

Let everyone who is honest praise
    the Lord.

A Hymn of Thanksgiving

For the director of music. A song
of David.

65 God, you will be praised in Jeru-
    salem.
    We will keep our promises to you.
²You hear our prayers.
    All people will come to you.
³Our guilt overwhelms us.
    But you forgive our sins.
⁴Happy are the people you choose.
    You have them stay in your
        courtyards.
    We are filled with good things in
        your house,
    your holy Temple.ᵈ

⁵You answer us in amazing ways,
    God our Savior.
People everywhere on the earth
    and beyond the sea trust you.
⁶You made the mountains by your
        strength.
    You have great power.
⁷You stopped the roaring seas,
    the roaring waves and the uproar
        of the nations.
⁸Even those people at the ends of the
        earth fear your miracles.ᵈ
    You are praised from where the
        sun rises to where it sets.

⁹You take care of the land and water it.
    You make it very fertile.
The rivers of God are full of water.
    Grain grows because you make it
        grow.
¹⁰You cause rain to fall on the plowed
        fields.
    You soak them with water.
    You soften the ground with rain.
    And then you bless it.
¹¹You give the year a good harvest.
    You load the wagons with many
        crops.
¹²The desert is covered with grass.
    The hills are covered with
        happiness.
¹³The pastures are full of sheep.
    The valleys are covered with grain.

Everything shouts and sings for
joy.

Praise God for Answering Prayers

*For the director of music. A song
of praise.*

66 Everything on earth, shout with
joy to God!
2Sing about his glory!
Make his praise glorious!
3Say to God, "Your works are
amazing!
Your power is great.
Your enemies fall before you.
4All the earth worships you.
They sing praises to you.
They sing praises to your name."
Selah^d

5Come and see what God has done.
See what amazing things he has
done for people.
6He turned the sea into dry land.
The people crossed the river on
foot.
So let us rejoice because of what
he did.
7He rules forever with his power.
He keeps his eye on the nations.
So people should not turn against
him.　　　*Selah*

8You people, praise our God.
Loudly sing his praise.
9He protects our lives
and does not let us be defeated.
10God, you have tested us.
You have purified us like silver.
11You let us be trapped.
You put a heavy load on us.
12You let our enemies walk on our
heads.
We went through fire and flood.
But you brought us to a place with
good things.

13I will come to your Temple^d with
burnt offerings.
I will give you what I promised.
14I promised to give you these things
when I was in trouble.
15I will bring you offerings of fat
animals.

And I will offer male sheep, bulls
and goats.　　　*Selah*

16All of you who fear God, come and
listen.
I will tell you what he has done
for me.
17I cried out to him with my mouth.
I praised him with my tongue.
18If I had known of any sin in my heart,
the Lord would not have listened
to me.
19But God has listened.
He has heard my prayer.
20Praise God.
He did not ignore my prayer.
He did not hold back his love
from me.

Everyone Should Praise God

*For the director of music. With stringed
instruments. A song of praise.*

67 God, have mercy on us and bless
us.
Show your kindness to us.　　*Selah^d*
2Then the world will learn your ways.
All nations will learn that you can
save.

3God, the people should praise you.
All people should praise you.
4The nations should be glad and sing
because you judge people fairly.
You guide all the nations on earth.
Selah
5God, the people should praise you.
All people should praise you.

6The land has given its crops.
God, our God, blesses us.
7God blesses us
so people to the ends of the earth
will fear him.

Praise God Who Saved the Nation

*For the director of music. A song of
David.*

68 Let God come and scatter his
enemies.
Let those who hate him run away.
2Blow them away as smoke
is driven away by the wind.

As wax melts before a fire,
 let the wicked be destroyed before
   God.
[3] But those who do right should be
   glad.
 They should rejoice before God.
 They should be happy and glad.

[4] Sing to God. Sing praises to his name.
 Prepare the way for him
   who rides through the desert.
 His name is the Lord.
 Rejoice before him.
[5] God is in his holy Temple.[d]
 He is a father to orphans.
 He defends the widows.
[6] God gives the lonely a home.
 He leads prisoners out with joy.
 But those who turn against God
   will live in a dry land.

[7] God, you led your people out.
 You marched through the desert.
                          Selah[d]
[8] The ground shook,
   and the sky poured down rain
 before God, the God of Mount Sinai,
 before God, the God of Israel.
[9] God, you sent much rain.
 You refreshed your tired land.
[10] Your people settled there.
 God, in your goodness
   you took care of the poor.

[11] The Lord gave the command.
 And a great army told the news:
[12] "Kings and their armies run away.
 The women at home divide the
   wealth taken in war."
[13] Those who stayed behind by the
   sheepfold
 will get the riches taken in battle.
[14] God scattered kings
 like snow on Mount Zalmon.

[15] The mountains of Bashan are great
   mountains.
 Mount Bashan has many peaks.
[16] Why do you mountains with many
   peaks look down
 on Mount Zion,[d] which God chose
   for his home?
 The Lord will live there forever.
[17] God comes with millions of chariots.

The Lord comes from Mount Sinai
 to his holy place.
[18] He went up to the heights.
 He led a parade of captives.
 He received the payment he
   demanded from the people,
 even from those who turned
   against him.
 And the Lord God will live there.

[19] Praise the Lord, day by day.
 God our Savior helps us.   *Selah*
[20] Our God is a God who saves us.
 The Lord God saves us from death.

[21] God will crush his enemies' heads,
 the hairy skulls of those who
   continue to sin.
[22] The Lord said, "I will bring the
   enemy back from Bashan.
 I will bring them back from the
   depths of the sea.
[23] Then you can stick your feet in their
   blood.
 And your dogs can lick their share."

[24] God, people have seen your victory
   march.
 God my King marched into the
   holy place.
[25] The singers are in front, and the
   instruments are behind.
 In the middle are the girls with the
   tambourines.[d]
[26] Praise God in the meeting place.
 Praise the Lord in the gathering of
   Israel.
[27] There is the smallest tribe,[d]
   Benjamin, leading them.
 And there are the leaders of Judah
   with their group.
 There also are the leaders of
   Zebulun and of Naphtali.

[28] God, order up your power.
 Show the mighty power you have
   used for us before.
[29] Kings will bring their wealth to you,
 to your Temple in Jerusalem.
[30] Punish Egypt, the beast among the
   tall grass along the river.
 Punish the leaders of nations,
   those bulls among the cows.
 Then they will bring you their silver.

Scatter those nations that love war.
³¹Messengers will come from Egypt
with forced payment.
The people of Cush will pray to God.

³²Kingdoms of the earth, sing to God.
Sing praises to the Lord.   *Selah*
³³Sing to the one who rides through
the skies, which are from long
ago.
He speaks with a thundering voice.
³⁴Announce that God is powerful.
He rules over Israel.
His power is in the skies.
³⁵God, you are wonderful in your
Temple.
The God of Israel gives his people
strength and power.

Praise God!

A Cry for Help

For the director of music. To the tune of
"Lilies." A song of David.

69 God, save me.
The water has risen to my neck.
²I'm sinking down into the mud.
There is nothing to stand on.
I am in deep water.
The flood covers me.
³I am tired from calling for help.
My throat is sore.
My eyes are tired from waiting
for God to help me.
⁴There are more people who hate me
for no reason
than hairs on my head.
Those who want to destroy me are
powerful.
My enemies are liars.
They make me pay back
what I did not steal.

⁵God, you know what I have done
wrong.
I cannot hide my guilt from you.
⁶Master, the Lord of heaven's armies,
do not let those who hope in you
be ashamed because of me.
God of Israel,
do not let your worshipers
be disgraced because of me.
⁷For you, I carry this shame.

My face is covered with disgrace.
⁸I am like a stranger to my brothers.
I am like a foreigner to my
mother's sons.
⁹My strong love for your Temple*d*
completely controls me.
When people insult you, it hurts me.
¹⁰When I cry and go without food,
they make fun of me.
¹¹When I wear rough cloth to show
my sadness,
they joke about me.
¹²They make fun of me in public places.
The drunkards make up songs
about me.

¹³But I pray to you, Lord.
I pray that you will accept me.
God, because of your great love,
answer me.
You are truly able to save.
¹⁴Pull me from the mud.
Do not let me sink.
Save me from those who hate me
and from the deep water.
¹⁵Do not let the flood drown me.
Do not let the deep water swallow
me.
Do not let the grave close its
mouth over me.
¹⁶Lord, answer me because your love
is so good.
Because of your great kindness,
turn to me.
¹⁷Do not hide from me, your servant.
I am in trouble. Hurry to help me!
¹⁸Come near and save me.
Rescue me from my enemies.

¹⁹You see my shame and disgrace.
You know all my enemies and
what they have said.
²⁰Insults have broken my heart.
I am weak.
I looked for sympathy, but there
was none.
I found no one to comfort me.
²¹They put poison in my food.
They gave me vinegar to drink.

²²Let their own feasts cause their
ruin.
Let their feasts trap them and pay
them back.

²³Let their eyes be closed so they
cannot see.
Let their backs be forever weak
from troubles.
²⁴Pour your anger out on them.
Show them how angry you are.
²⁵May their place be empty.
Leave no one to live in their tents.
²⁶They chase after those you have hurt.
They talk about the pain of those
you have wounded.
²⁷Charge them with crime after crime.
Do not let them have anything good.
²⁸Wipe their names from the book of
life.
Do not list them with those who
do what is right.

²⁹I am sad and hurting.
God, save me and protect me.

³⁰I will praise God in a song.
I will honor him by giving thanks.
³¹That will please the Lord more than
offering him cattle.
It will please him more than the
sacrifice of a bull with horns
and hoofs.
³²People who are not proud will see
this and be glad.
Be encouraged, you who worship
God.
³³The Lord listens to those in need.
He does not look down on captives.

³⁴Heaven and earth should praise him.
The seas and everything in them
should also.
³⁵God will save Jerusalem.
He will rebuild the cities of Judah.
Then people will live there and
own the land.
³⁶ The descendants*d* of his servants
will inherit that land.
Those who love him will live there.

A Cry for God to Help Quickly

For the director of music. A song
of David. To help people remember.

70 God, save me.
Lord, hurry to help me.
²People are trying to kill me.
Shame them and disgrace them.

People want to hurt me.
Let them run away in disgrace.
³People make fun of me.
Stop them and make them
ashamed.
⁴But let all the people who worship
you
rejoice and be glad.
Let the people who love your
salvation
always say, "Praise the greatness
of God."
⁵I am poor and helpless.
God, hurry to me.
You help me and save me.
Lord, do not wait.

An Old Person's Prayer

71 In you, Lord, is my protection.
Never let me be ashamed.
²Because you do what is right, save
and rescue me.
Listen to me and save me.
³Be my place of safety
where I can always come.
Give the command to save me.
You are my rock and my strong,
walled city.
⁴My God, save me from the power of
the wicked.
Save me from the hold of evil and
cruel people.
⁵Lord God, you are my hope.
I have trusted you since I was
young.
⁶I have depended on you since I was
born.
You have been my help from the
day I was born.
I will always praise you.

⁷I am an example to many people.
You are my strong protection.
⁸I am always praising you.
All day long I honor you.
⁹Do not reject me when I am old.
Do not leave me when my
strength is gone.
¹⁰My enemies have made plans
against me.
They meet together to kill me.
¹¹They say, "God has left him.
Go after him and take him.

No one will save him."

¹²God, don't be far off.
　My God, hurry to help me.
¹³Let them be ashamed.
　Destroy those who accuse me.
　They are trying to hurt me.
　　Cover them with shame and
　　　disgrace.
¹⁴But I will always have hope.
　And I will praise you more and
　　more.
¹⁵I will tell about how you do what is
　　right.
　I will tell about your salvation all
　　day long,
　　even though it is more than I can
　　　tell.
¹⁶I will come and tell about your
　　powerful works, Lord God.
　I will tell only about you and how
　　you do what is right.

¹⁷God, you have taught me since I
　　was young.
　Even until today I tell about the
　　miracles*d* you do.
¹⁸Even though I am old and gray,
　　do not leave me, God.
　I will tell the children about your
　　power.
　I will tell those who will live after
　　me about your might.

¹⁹God, your justice reaches to the skies.
　You have done great things.
　God, there is no one like you.
²⁰You have given me many troubles
　　and bad times.
　But you will give me life again.
　When I am almost dead,
　　you will keep me alive.
²¹You will make me greater than ever.
　And you will comfort me again.

²²I will praise you with the harp.
　I trust you, my God.
　I will sing to you with the lyre.*d*
　You are the Holy One of Israel.
²³I will shout for joy when I sing
　　praises to you.
　You have saved me.
²⁴I will tell about your justice all day
　　long.

And those who want to hurt me
　will be ashamed and disgraced.

A Prayer for the King

Of Solomon.

72 God, give the king your good
　　judgment
　and the king's son your goodness.
²Help him judge your people fairly.
　Help him decide what is right for
　　the poor.
³Let there be peace on the mountains
　and goodness on the hills.
⁴Help him be fair to the poor.
　Help him save the needy
　and punish those who hurt them.

⁵Help him live as long as the sun
　　shines.
　Help him rule as long as the moon
　　glows.
　Let him be king from now on!
⁶Let him be like rain on the grass,
　like showers that water the earth.
⁷Let goodness be plentiful while he
　　lives.
　Let peace continue as long as
　　there is a moon.

⁸Let his kingdom go from sea to sea,
　and from the Euphrates River to
　　the ends of the earth.
⁹Let the people of the desert bow
　　down to him.
　And make his enemies lick the
　　dust.
¹⁰Let the kings of Tarshish and the
　　faraway lands
　bring him gifts.
　Let the kings of Sheba and Seba
　bring their presents to him.
¹¹Let all kings bow down to him.
　Let all nations serve him.

¹²He will help the poor when they cry
　　for help.
　He will help the needy when no
　　one else will help them.
¹³He will be kind to the weak and poor.
　He will save their lives.
¹⁴He will save them from cruel people
　　who try to hurt them.
　Their lives are precious to him.

¹⁵Long live the king!
　　Let him receive gold from Sheba.
　　Let people always pray for him.
　　Let them bless him all day long.
¹⁶Let the fields grow plenty of grain.
　　Let the hills be covered with crops.
　　Let the land be as fertile as Lebanon.
　　Let the cities grow like the grass
　　　in a field.
¹⁷Let the king be famous forever.
　　Let him be remembered as long as
　　　the sun shines.
　　Let the nations be blessed because
　　　of him.
　　And may they all bless him.

¹⁸Praise the Lord God, the God of
　　Israel.
　　Only he does such miracles.ᵈ
¹⁹Praise his glorious name forever.
　　Let his glory fill the whole world.
　　　Amen and amen.

²⁰This ends the prayers of David son
of Jesse.

Book 3

Should the Wicked Be Rich?

A song of Asaph.

73 God is truly good to Israel,
　　to those who have pure hearts.
²But I had almost stopped believing
　　this truth.
　　I had almost lost my faith
³because I was jealous of proud
　　people.
　　I saw wicked people doing well.

⁴They are not suffering.
　　They are healthy and strong.
⁵They don't have troubles like the
　　rest of us.
　　They don't have problems like
　　　other people.
⁶So they wear pride like a necklace.
　　They put on violence as their
　　　clothing.
⁷They are looking for profits.
　　They do not control their selfish
　　　desires.
⁸They make fun of others and speak
　　evil.

　　Proudly they speak of hurting
　　　others.
⁹They brag to the sky.
　　Their mouths gossip on the earth.
¹⁰So their people turn to them
　　and give them whatever they want.
¹¹They say, "How can God know?
　　What does God Most High know?"
¹²These people are wicked,
　　always at ease and getting richer.
¹³So why have I kept my heart pure?
　　Why have I kept my hands from
　　　doing wrong?
¹⁴I have suffered all day long.
　　I have been punished every
　　　morning.

¹⁵God, if I had decided to talk about
　　this,
　　I would have let your people down.
¹⁶I tried to understand all this.
　　But it was too hard for me to see
¹⁷until I went to the Templeᵈ of God.
　　Then I understood what will
　　　happen to them.
¹⁸You have put them in danger.
　　You cause them to be destroyed.
¹⁹They are destroyed in a moment.
　　They are swept away by terrors.
²⁰It will be like waking from a dream.
　　Lord, when you come, they will
　　　disappear.

²¹When my heart was sad and
　　I was angry,
²²I was senseless and stupid.
　　I acted like an animal toward you.
²³But I am always with you.
　　You have held my hand.
²⁴You guide me with your advice.
　　And later you will receive me in
　　　honor.
²⁵I have no one in heaven but you.
　　I want nothing on earth besides you.
²⁶My mind and my body may become
　　weak.
　　But God is my strength.
　　He is mine forever.

²⁷Those who are far from God will die.
　　You destroy those who are
　　　unfaithful.
²⁸But I am close to God, and that is
　　good.

Adventures in ODYSSEY BIBLE

"THE MELON PATCH!"

The kids learn about taking care of God's world
A story based on *Luke 19:13-17*

WE HOPE YOU HAVE A GOOD TIME ON YOUR *VACATION,* MISTER WHITTAKER!

THANKS FOR COMING TO SEE ME OFF, KIDS!

WHILE I'M GONE, IF YOU'LL ALL TAKE CARE OF MY WATERMELON PATCH, WE'LL HAVE A BIG MELON PARTY WHEN I RETURN.

YAY! A PARTY!

TO CARE FOR THE MELONS, YOU NEED TO WATER, HOE AND WEED. HERE ARE SOME *INSTRUCTIONS* TO HELP YOU THROUGH IT.

BYE, MISTER WHITTAKER!

HAVE A GOOD TRIP!

THIS IS GOING TO BE A *SNAP!* THESE MELONS WILL GROW ALL BY THEM-SELVES!

WE'LL JUST COME BACK AND CHECK ON THEM LATER!

AND WHEN MR. WHITTAKER GETS BACK, WE'LL HAVE A *PARTY!*

WHIT'S E

As the days of summer go by, Dylan, Jessie, Sal and Holly are having too much fun to think about the melon patch....

Dylan and the other kids have really dropped the ball and now, they are in danger of letting Whit down. Because of their lack of care the melons are being ruined. Reading the following verses will help you decide what Dylan and his friends should do:

Proverbs 10:4-5
Proverbs 20:4
Matthew 25:14-28
Luke 19:13-17

THE NEXT DAY, A MEETING IS CALLED....

YOU KNOW, MR. WHITTAKER *TRUSTED* US TO TAKE CARE OF HIS MELONS AND WE *MESSED UP.* WE HAVEN'T SPENT ANY TIME AT ALL ATTENDING TO THEM AND NOW THEY'RE IN *REAL BAD SHAPE.*

YEAH, AND IF WE WANT THAT MELON PARTY, WE'D BETTER GET BUSY STRAIGHTENING OUT THIS *PATCH!*

SURE, IT WOULD BE TOO BAD NOT TO HAVE THE PARTY, BUT I'D FEEL WORSE ABOUT LETTING MISTER WHITTAKER DOWN.

HERE ARE THE INSTRUCTIONS MISTER WHITTAKER LEFT TO HELP US OUT. LET'S GET STARTED!

HEY, SAL, HOLD ON! I'VE GOT SOME MORE WEEDS YOU CAN DUMP OUT!

HOLLY, COULD YOU BRING SOME OF THAT FERTILIZER OVER HERE?

SURE, DYLAN!

MISTER WHITTAKER SAYS TO *SOAK* IT GOOD!

LOOK, I CAN SEE A *RAIN-BOW!*

The Lord God is my protection.
I will tell all that you have done.

A Nation in Trouble Prays

A maskil[d] of Asaph.

74 God, why have you rejected us
for so long?
Why are you angry with us, the
sheep of your pasture?
[2]Remember the people you bought
long ago.
You saved us. We are your very
own.
You live on Mount Zion.[d]
[3]Make your way through these old
ruins.
The enemy wrecked everything in
the Temple.[d]

[4]Those who were against you
shouted in your meeting place.
They raised their flags there.
[5]They came with axes raised
as if to cut down a forest of trees.
[6]They smashed the carved panels
with their axes and hatchets.
[7]They burned your Temple to the
ground.
They have made the place where
you live unclean.[d]
[8]They thought, "We will completely
crush them!"
They burned every place where
God was worshiped in the land.
[9]We do not see any signs.
There are no more prophets.
And no one knows how long this
will last.
[10]God, how much longer will the
enemy make fun of you?
Will they insult you forever?
[11]Why do you hold back your power?
Bring your power out in the open
and destroy them!

[12]God, you have been our king for a
long time.
You have saved this country.
[13]You split open the sea by your power.
You broke the heads of the sea
monster.
[14]You smashed the heads of the
monster Leviathan.[d]

You gave him to the desert
creatures as food.
[15]You opened up the springs and
streams.
And you made the rivers run dry.
[16]Both the day and the night are yours.
You made the sun and the moon.
[17]You made all the limits on the earth.
You created summer and winter.

[18]Lord, remember how the enemy
insulted you.
Remember how those foolish
people turned away from you.
[19]Do not give us, your doves, to those
wild animals.
Never forget your poor people.
[20]Remember the agreement you
made with us
because violence fills every dark
corner of this land.
[21]Do not let your suffering people be
disgraced.
The poor and helpless people
praise you.

[22]God, come and defend yourself.
Remember the insults that come
from those foolish people all
day long.
[23]Don't forget what your enemies said.
Don't forget their roar as they rise
against you always.

God the Judge

For the director of music. To the tune of
"Do Not Destroy." A song of Asaph.

75 God, we thank you.
We thank you because you are
near.
We tell about the wonderful things
you do.

[2]You say, "I set the time for trial.
I will judge fairly.
[3]The earth with all its people may
shake.
I am the one who holds it steady.
Selah[d]
[4]I say to those who are proud, 'Don't
brag.'
I say to the wicked, 'Don't show
your power.

⁵Don't try to use your power against
    heaven.
    Don't be stubborn.'"

⁶No one from the east or the west
    or the desert can judge you.
⁷God is the judge.
    He judges one person as guilty,
        and another as innocent.
⁸The Lord holds a cup of anger in his
    hand.
    It is full of wine mixed with spices.
    He pours it out even to the last
        drop.
    And the wicked drink it all.

⁹I will tell about this forever.
    I will sing praise to the God of
        Jacob.
¹⁰He will take all power away from the
    wicked.
    But the power of good people will
        grow.

The God Who Always Wins

For the director of music. With stringed
instruments. A song of Asaph.

76 People in Judah know God.
    People in Israel know he is great.
²He lives in Jerusalem.
    His home is on Mount Zion.ᵈ
³There God broke the flaming arrows,
    the shields and swords of war.
                       *Selah*ᵈ

⁴God, how wonderful you are!
    You are more wonderful than the
        hills full of animals.
⁵The brave soldiers were stripped
    as they lay asleep in death.
    Not one warrior
        had the strength to stop it.
⁶God of Jacob, when you spoke
        strongly,
    horses and riders fell dead.
⁷You should be feared.
    Who can stand against you when
        you are angry?
⁸From heaven you gave the decision.
    And the earth was afraid and silent.
⁹God, you stood up to judge
    and to save the people of the earth
        who were not proud.   *Selah*

¹⁰People praise you for your anger
    against evil.
    Those who live through your
        anger are stopped from doing
        more evil.

¹¹Keep your promises to the Lord
    your God.
    From all around gifts should come
        to the God we worship.
¹²God defeats great leaders.
    The kings on earth fear him.

Remembering God's Help

For the director of music. For Jeduthun.
A song of Asaph.

77 I cry out loud to God.
    I call to God, and he will hear
        me.
²I looked for the Lord on the day of
    trouble.
    All night long I reached out my
        hands.
    I cannot be comforted.
³When I remember God, I become
    upset.
    When I think, I become afraid.
                     *Selah*ᵈ

⁴You keep my eyes from closing.
    I am too upset to say anything.
⁵I keep thinking about the old days,
    the years of long ago.
⁶At night I remember my songs.
    I think, and I ask myself:
⁷"Will the Lord reject us forever?
    Will he never be kind to us again?
⁸Is his love gone forever?
    Has he stopped speaking for all
        time?
⁹Has God forgotten mercy?
    Is he too angry to pity us?"   *Selah*
¹⁰Then I said, "This is what makes
    me sad:
    For years the power of God Most
        High was with us."

¹¹I remember what the Lord did.
    I remember the miraclesᵈ you did
        long ago.
¹²I think about all the things you did.
    I think about what you have done.

¹³God, your ways are holy.

No god is as great as our God.

[14] You are the God who did miracles.
You showed people your power.

[15] By your power you have saved your
people,
the descendants[d] of Jacob and
Joseph. *Selah*

[16] God, the waters saw you.
They saw you and became afraid.
The deep waters shook with fear.

[17] The clouds poured down their rain.
The sky thundered.
Your lightning flashed back and
forth.

[18] Your thunder sounded in the
whirlwind.
Lightning lit up the world.
The earth trembled and shook.

[19] You made a way through the sea
and paths through the deep waters.
But your footprints were not seen.

[20] You led your people like a flock of
sheep.
You led them by using Moses and
Aaron.

God Saved Israel from Egypt

A maskil[d] of Asaph.

78 My people, listen to my teaching.
Listen to what I say.

[2] I will speak using stories.
I will tell things that have been
secret since long ago.

[3] We have heard them and know them.
Our fathers told them to us.

[4] We will not keep them from our
children.
We will tell those who come later
about the praises of the Lord.
We will tell about his power
and the miracles[d] he has done.

[5] The Lord made an agreement with
Jacob.
He gave the teachings to Israel.
And he commanded our ancestors
to teach them to their children.

[6] Then their children would know
them,
even their children not yet born.
And they would tell their children.

[7] So they would all trust God.

They would not forget what God
had done.
Instead, they would obey his
commands.

[8] They would not be like their
ancestors
who were stubborn and
disobedient.
Their hearts were not loyal to God.
They were not true to him.

[9] The men of Ephraim had bows for
weapons.
But they ran away on the day of
battle.

[10] They didn't keep their agreement
with God.
They refused to live by his
teachings.

[11] They forgot what he had done
and the miracles he had shown
them.

[12] He did miracles while their
ancestors watched,
in the fields of Zoan in Egypt.

[13] He divided the Red Sea[d] and led
them through.
He made the water stand up like a
wall.

[14] He led them with a cloud by day.
And he led them at night by the
light of a fire.

[15] He split the rocks in the desert.
And he gave them much water, as
if it were from the deep ocean.

[16] He brought streams out of the rock.
The water flowed down like rivers.

[17] But the people continued to sin
against him.
In the desert they turned against
God Most High.

[18] They decided to test God
by asking for the food they wanted.

[19] Then they spoke against God.
They said, "Can God prepare food
in the desert?

[20] When he hit the rock, water poured
out.
Rivers flowed down.
But can he give us bread also?
Will he provide his people with
meat?"

²¹When the Lord heard them, he was
very angry.
His anger was like fire to the
people of Jacob.
His anger grew against the people
of Israel.
²²They had not believed God.
They had not trusted him to save
them.
²³But he gave a command to the
clouds above.
The doors of heaven opened.
²⁴He rained manna[d] down on them to
eat.
He gave them grain from heaven.
²⁵So they ate the bread of angels.
He sent them all the food they
could eat.
²⁶He sent the east wind from
heaven.
He led the south wind by his
power.
²⁷He rained meat on them like dust.
The birds were as many as the
sand of the sea.
²⁸He made the birds fall inside the
camp,
all around the tents.
²⁹So the people ate and became very
full.
God had given them what they
wanted.
³⁰While they were still eating,
and while the food was still in their
mouths,
³¹God became angry with them.
He killed some of the healthiest of
them.
He struck down the best young
men of Israel.
³²But they kept on sinning.
They did not believe even with the
miracles.
³³So he ended their days without
meaning
and their years in terror.
³⁴Anytime he killed them, some
would look to him for help.
They would come back to God and
follow him.
³⁵They would remember that God
was their Rock,[d]

that God Most High had saved
them.
³⁶But their words were false.
Their tongues lied to him.
³⁷Their hearts were not really loyal to
God.
They did not keep his agreement.
³⁸Still God was merciful.
He forgave their sins.
He did not destroy them.
Many times he held back his anger.
He did not stir up all his anger.
³⁹He remembered that they were only
human.
They were like a wind that blows
and does not come back.

⁴⁰They turned against God so often in
the desert!
There they made him very sad.
⁴¹Again and again they tested God.
They brought pain to the Holy
One of Israel.
⁴²They did not remember his power
or the time he saved them from
the enemy.
⁴³They forgot the signs he did in
Egypt
and his miracles in the fields of
Zoan.
⁴⁴He turned the rivers to blood.
So no one could drink the water.
⁴⁵He sent flies that bit the people.
He sent frogs that destroyed
them.
⁴⁶He gave their crops to grasshoppers
and what they worked for to
locusts.[d]
⁴⁷He destroyed their vines with hail
and their sycamore trees with
sleet.
⁴⁸He killed their animals with hail
and their cattle with lightning.
⁴⁹He showed them his hot anger.
He sent his strong anger against
them.
He sent his destroying angels.
⁵⁰He found a way to show his anger.
He did not keep them from dying.
He let them die by a terrible
disease.
⁵¹God killed all the firstborn[d] sons in
Egypt,

the oldest son of each family of
Ham.[n]
[52]But God led out his people like sheep.
He guided them like a flock
through the desert.
[53]He led them to safety. They had
nothing to fear.
But their enemies drowned in the
sea.
[54]So God brought them to his holy
land.
He brought them to the mountain
country he took with his own
power.
[55]He forced out the other nations.
And he had his people inherit the
land.
He let the tribes[d] of Israel settle
there in tents.

[56]But they tested God
and turned against the Most High.
They did not keep his rules.
[57]They turned away and sinned just
like their ancestors.
They were like a crooked bow that
does not shoot straight.
[58]They made God angry by building
places to worship false gods.
They made him jealous with their
idols.
[59]When God heard them, he became
very angry.
And he rejected the people of
Israel completely.
[60]He left his dwelling at Shiloh,
the tent where he lived among men.
[61]He let his Holy Box[d] be captured.
He let the Holy Box, which was his
glory, be taken by enemies.
[62]He let his people be killed.
He was very angry with his
children.
[63]The young men died by fire.
The young women had no one to
marry.
[64]Their priests fell by the sword.
But their widows were not allowed
to cry.

[65]Then the Lord got up as if he had
been asleep.

He awoke like a man who was
drunk with wine.
[66]He struck down his enemies.
He disgraced them forever.
[67]But God rejected the family of
Joseph.
He did not choose the tribe of
Ephraim.
[68]Instead, he chose the tribe of Judah
and Mount Zion,[d] which he loves.
[69]And he built his Temple[d] high like
the mountains.
Like the earth, he built it to last
forever.
[70]He chose David to be his servant.
He took him from the sheep pens.
[71]He brought him from tending the
sheep
so he could lead the flock, the
people of Jacob.
This flock was his own people, the
people of Israel.
[72]And David led them with an
innocent heart.
He guided them with skillful
hands.

The Nation Cries for Jerusalem

A song of Asaph.

79 God, nations have come against
your people.
They have ruined your holy
Temple.[d]
They have turned Jerusalem into
ruins.
[2]They have given the bodies of your
servants
as food to the wild birds.
They have given the bodies of those
who worship you
to the wild animals.
[3]They have spilled blood like water
all around Jerusalem.
No one was left to bury the dead.
[4]We are a bad joke to the other nations.
They laugh and make fun of us.

[5]Lord, how long will this last? Will
you be angry forever?
How long will your jealousy burn
like a fire?

[n]**Ham**   The people in Egypt were descendants of Ham, one of Noah's sons. See Genesis 10:6.

⁶Be angry with the nations that do
　　not know you.
　Be angry with the kingdoms that
　　do not honor you.
⁷They have destroyed the people of
　　Jacob.
　Those nations have destroyed the
　　people's land.
⁸Don't punish us for the sins of our
　　ancestors.
　Show your mercy to us soon.
　We are helpless!
⁹God our Savior, help us
　　so people will praise you.
　Save us and forgive our sins
　　so people will honor you.
¹⁰Why should the nations say,
　　"Where is their God?"
　Tell the other nations in our
　　presence
　　that you punish those who kill
　　　your servants.
¹¹Hear the moans of the prisoners.
　Use your great power
　　to save those sentenced to die.

¹²Repay those around us seven times
　　over
　　for their insults to you, Lord.
¹³We are your people, the sheep of
　　your flock.
　We will thank you always.
　Forever and ever we will praise you.

A Prayer to Bring Israel Back

For the director of music. To the tune of
"Lilies of the Agreement." A song
of Asaph.

80 Shepherd of Israel, listen to us.
You lead the people of Joseph
like a flock.
You sit on your throne between the
　gold creatures with wings.
　Show your greatness
²to the people of Ephraim, Benjamin
　　and Manasseh.
　Use your strength.
　Come and save us.

³God, take us back.
　Show us your kindness so we can
　　be saved.

⁴Lord God of heaven's armies,

how long will you be angry
　at the prayers of your people?
⁵You have fed your people tears.
　You have made them drink many
　　tears.
⁶You made those around us fight
　　over us.
　Our enemies make fun of us.

⁷God of heaven's armies, take us back.
　Show us your kindness so we can
　　be saved.

⁸You brought us out of Egypt as if we
　　were a vine.
　You forced out other nations and
　　planted us in the land.
⁹You cleared the land for us.
　Like a vine, we took root and filled
　　the land.
¹⁰We covered the mountains with our
　　shade.
　We had limbs like the mighty
　　cedar tree.
¹¹Our branches reached the
　　Mediterranean Sea.
　And our shoots went to the
　　Euphrates River.

¹²So why did you pull down our walls?
　Now everyone who passes by
　　steals from us.
¹³Like wild pigs they walk over us.
　Like wild animals they feed on us.

¹⁴God of heaven's armies, come back.
　Look down from heaven and see.
　Take care of us, your vine.
15 　You planted this shoot with your
　　own hands.
　You raised and strengthened this
　　child.
¹⁶Now it is cut down and burned with
　　fire.
　You destroyed us by your angry
　　looks.
¹⁷Help the man you have chosen.
　Make this human being strong for
　　your service.
¹⁸Then we will not turn away from you.
　Give us life again, and we will call
　　to you for help.

¹⁹Lord God of heaven's armies, take
　　us back.

Show us your kindness so we can
be saved.

A Song for a Holiday

For the director of music. By the gittith.[d]
A song of Asaph.

81 Sing for joy to God, our strength.
Shout out loud to the God of
Jacob.
[2]Begin the music. Play the
tambourines.[d]
Play pleasant music on the harps
and lyres.[d]
[3]Blow the sheep's horn at the time of
the New Moon.[d]
Blow it when the moon is full,
when our feast begins.
[4]This is the law for Israel.
It is God's command to the people
of Jacob.
[5]He made this agreement with the
people of Joseph
when they went out of the land of
Egypt.

I heard a language I did not know,
saying:
[6]"I took the load off your shoulders.
I let you put down your baskets.
[7]When you were in trouble, you
called, and I saved you.
I answered you with thunder.
I tested you at the waters of
Meribah.   Selah[d]
[8]My people, listen. I am warning you.
Israel, please listen to me!
[9]You must not have foreign gods
among you.
You must not worship any false
god.
[10]I, the Lord, am your God.
I brought you out of Egypt.
Open your mouth, and I will feed
you.

[11]"But my people did not listen to me.
Israel did not want me.
[12]So I let them go their stubborn way.
They followed their own advice.
[13]I wish my people would listen to me.
I wish Israel would live my way.
[14]Then I would quickly defeat their
enemies.

I would turn my hand against
those who are against them.
[15]Those who hate the Lord would
bow before him.
Their punishment would continue
forever.
[16]But I would give you the finest wheat.
I would fill you with honey from
the rocks."

God Judges the Judges

A song of Asaph.

82 God is in charge of the great
meeting of his people.
He judges the judges.
[2]He says, "How long will you defend
evil people?
How long will you show greater
kindness to the wicked? Selah[d]
[3]Defend the orphans and the weak.
Defend the rights of the poor and
suffering.
[4]Save the weak and helpless
from the power of the wicked.

[5]"You know nothing. You don't
understand.
You walk in the dark,
while the world is falling apart.
[6]I said, 'You are gods.
You are all sons of the Most High
God.'
[7]But you will die like any other person.
You will die like all the leaders."

[8]God, come and judge the earth.
You own all the nations.

A Prayer Against the Enemies

A song of Asaph.

83 God, do not keep quiet.
God, do not be silent or still.
[2]Your enemies are making plans.
Those who hate you are getting
ready to attack.
[3]They are making plans against your
people.
They plan to hurt those you love.
[4]They say, "Come, let's destroy them
as a nation.
Then no one will remember the
name 'Israel' anymore."

⁵They are united in their plan.
These have made an agreement
against you:
⁶the families of Edom and the
Ishmaelites,
Moab and the Hagrites,
⁷the people of Byblos, Ammon,
Amalek,
Philistia and Tyre.
⁸Even Assyria has joined them
to help Ammon and Moab, the
descendants*d* of Lot.   *Selah*d

⁹God, do to them what you did to
Midian.
Do what you did to Sisera and
Jabin at the Kishon River.
¹⁰They died at Endor.
Their bodies rotted on the ground.
¹¹Do to their important leaders what
you did to Oreb and Zeeb.
Do to their princes what you did to
Zebah and Zalmunna.
¹²They said, "Let's take for ourselves
the pasturelands that belong to
God."
¹³My God, make them like the
tumbleweed,
like chaff*d* blown away by the wind.
¹⁴Be like a fire that burns a forest
or like flames that blaze through
the hills.
¹⁵Chase them with your storm.
Frighten them with your wind.
¹⁶Cover them with shame.
Then people will look for you, Lord.
¹⁷Make them afraid and ashamed
forever.
Disgrace them and destroy them.
¹⁸Then they will know that you are
the Lord.
They will know that only you are
God Most High over all the
earth.

Wishing to Be in the Temple

For the director of music. By the gittith.*d*
A song of the sons of Korah.

84 Lord of heaven's armies,
how lovely is your Temple!*d*
²I want to be in
the courtyards of the Lord's Temple.

My whole being wants
to be with the living God.
³The sparrows have found a home.
And the swallows have nests.
They raise their young near your
altars,
Lord of heaven's armies, my King
and my God.
⁴Happy are the people who live at
your Temple.
They are always praising you.*Selah*d

⁵Happy are those whose strength
comes from you.
They want to travel to Jerusalem.
⁶As they pass through the Valley of
Baca,
they make it like a spring.
The autumn rains fill it with pools
of water.
⁷The people get stronger as they go.
And everyone meets with God in
Jerusalem.

⁸Lord God of heaven's armies, hear
my prayer.
God of Jacob, listen to me.   *Selah*
⁹God, look at our shield.
Be kind to your appointed king.
¹⁰One day in the courtyards of your
Temple is better
than a thousand days anywhere
else.
I would rather be a doorkeeper in
the Temple of my God
than live in the homes of the
wicked.
¹¹The Lord God is like our sun and
shield.
The Lord gives us kindness and
glory.
He does not hold back anything good
from those whose life is innocent.
¹²Lord of heaven's armies,
happy are the people who trust
you!

A Prayer for the Nation

For the director of music. A song of the
sons of Korah.

85 Lord, you have been kind to
your land.

You gave the people of Jacob back
their riches.
²You forgave the guilt of the people.
You covered all their sins.   *Selah*ᵈ
³You stopped all your anger.
You stopped your strong anger.

⁴God our Savior, bring us back again.
Stop being angry with us.
⁵Will you be angry with us forever?
Will you stay angry from now on?
⁶Won't you give us life again?
Your people would rejoice in you.
⁷Lord, show us your love.
Save us.

⁸I will listen to God the Lord.
He has ordered peace for his
people who worship him.
Don't let them go back to
foolishness.
⁹God will soon save those who
respect him.
And his greatness will be seen in
our land.
¹⁰Love and truth will belong to God's
people.
Goodness and peace will be theirs.
¹¹On earth people will be loyal to God.
And God's goodness will shine
down from heaven.
¹²The Lord will give his goodness.
And the land will give its crops.
¹³Goodness will go before God
and prepare the way for him.

A Cry for Help

A prayer of David.

86 Lord, listen to me and answer
me.
I am poor and helpless.
²Protect me, because I worship you.
My God, save me, your servant.
I trust in you.
³Lord, be merciful to me.
I have called to you all day.
⁴Give happiness to me, your servant.
Lord, I give my life to you.
⁵Lord, you are kind and forgiving.
You have great love for those who
call to you.
⁶Lord, hear my prayer.
Listen when I ask for mercy.

⁷I call to you in times of trouble.
You certainly will answer me.
⁸Lord, there is no god like you.
There are no works like yours.
⁹Lord, all the nations you have made
will come and worship you.
They will honor you.
¹⁰You are great, and you do miracles.ᵈ
Only you are God.

¹¹Lord, teach me what you want me
to do.
And I will live by your truth.
Teach me to respect you completely.
¹²Lord, my God, I will praise you with
all my heart.
I will honor your name forever.
¹³You have great love for me.
You have saved me from death.

¹⁴God, proud men turn against me.
A gang of cruel men are trying to
kill me.
They do not respect you.
¹⁵But Lord, you are a God who shows
mercy and is kind.
You don't become angry quickly.
You have great love and
faithfulness.
¹⁶Turn to me and be merciful.
Give me, your servant, strength.
Save me, the son of your female
servant.
¹⁷Show me a sign of your goodness.
When my enemies look, they will
be ashamed.
You, Lord, have helped me and
comforted me.

God Loves Jerusalem

A song of the sons of Korah.

87 The Lord built Jerusalem on the
holy mountain.
² He loves its gates
more than any other place in
Israel.
³City of God,
wonderful things are said about
you.   *Selah*ᵈ
⁴God says, "I will put Egypt and
Babylonia
on the list of nations that know me.

People from Philistia, Tyre and Cush
  will be born there."

⁵They will say about Jerusalem,
  "This one and that one were born
    there.
  God Most High will strengthen
    her."
⁶The Lord will keep a list of the
    nations.
  He will note, "This person was
    born there."   *Selah*
⁷They will dance and sing,
  "All good things come from
    Jerusalem."

A Sad Complaint

A song of the sons of Korah. For the
director of music. By the mahalath lean-
noth.ᵈ A maskilᵈ of Heman the Ezrahite.

88 Lord, you are the God who
  saves me.
  I cry out to you day and night.
²Accept my prayer.
  Listen to my cry.

³My life is full of troubles.
  I am nearly dead.
⁴They think I am on the way to my
    grave.
  I am like a man with no strength.
⁵I have been left as dead,
  like a body lying in a grave.
  You don't remember dead people.
  They are cut off from your care.
⁶You have brought me close to death.
  I am almost in the dark place of
    the dead.
⁷You have been very angry with me.
  All your waves crush me.   *Selah*ᵈ
⁸You have taken my friends away
    from me.
  You have made them hate me.
  I am trapped and cannot escape.
⁹ My eyes are weak from crying.
  Lord, I have prayed to you every day.
  I have lifted my hands in prayer to
    you.

¹⁰Do you show your miraclesᵈ for the
    dead?
  Do their spirits rise up and praise
    you?   *Selah*
¹¹Will your love be told in the grave?

Will your loyalty be told in the
    place of death?
¹²Will your miracles be known in the
    dark grave?
  Will your goodness be known in
    the land where the dead are
    forgotten?

¹³But, Lord, I have called out to you
    for help.
  Every morning I pray to you.
¹⁴Lord, why do you reject me?
  Why do you hide from me?
¹⁵I have been weak and dying since I
    was young.
  I suffer from your terrors, and I
    am helpless.
¹⁶You have been angry with me.
  Your terrors have destroyed me.
¹⁷They surround me daily like a flood.
  They are all around me.
¹⁸You have taken away my loved ones
    and friends.
  Darkness is my only friend.

A Song About God's Loyalty

A maskilᵈ of Ethan the Ezrahite.

89 I will always sing about the
  Lord's love.
  I will tell of his loyalty from now on.
²I will say, "Your love continues
    forever.
  Your loyalty goes on and on like
    the sky."
³You said, "I made an agreement
    with the man of my choice.
  I made a promise to my servant
    David.
⁴I told him, 'I will make your family
    continue forever.
  Your kingdom will continue from
    now on.'"   *Selah*ᵈ

⁵Lord, the heavens praise you for
    your miraclesᵈ
  and for your loyalty in the meeting
    of your holy ones.
⁶Who in heaven is equal to the Lord?
  None of the angels is like the Lord.
⁷When the holy ones meet, it is God
    they fear.
  He is more frightening than all
    who surround him.

8Lord God of heaven's armies, who
      is like you?
   Lord, you are powerful and
      completely to be trusted.
9You rule the mighty sea.
   You calm the stormy waves.
10You crushed the sea monster
      Rahab.*d*
   By your power you scattered your
      enemies.

11The skies and the earth belong to
      you.
   You made the world and
      everything in it.
12You created the north and the south.
   Mount Tabor and Mount Hermon
      sing for joy at your name.
13Your arm has great power.
   Your hand is strong. Your right
      hand is lifted up.
14Your kingdom is built on what is
      right and fair.
   Love and truth are in all you do.

15Happy are the people who know
      how to praise you.
   Lord, let them live in the light of
      your presence.
16In your name they rejoice all the
      time.
   They praise your goodness.
17You are their glorious strength.
   In your kindness you honor our
      king.
18Our king, our shield, belongs to the
      Lord.
   Our king belongs to the Holy One
      of Israel.

19Once, in a vision, you spoke
   to those who worship you.
   You said, "I have given strength to a
      warrior.
   I have selected a young man from
      my people.
20I have found my servant David.
   I appointed him by pouring holy
      oil on him.
21I will steady him with my hand.
   I will strengthen him with my arm.
22No enemy will make him give
      forced payments.
   Wicked people will not defeat him.

23I will crush his enemies in front of
      him.
   I will defeat those who hate him.
24My loyalty and love will be with him.
   Through me he will be strong.
25I will give him power over the sea
      and control over the rivers.
26He will say to me, 'You are my father,
      my God, the Rock,*d* the one who
      saves me.'
27I will make him my firstborn*d* son.
   He will be the greatest king on
      earth.
28My love will watch over him forever.
   My agreement with him will never
      end.
29I will make his family continue.
   His kingdom will last as long as
      the skies.

30"But his descendants*d* might reject
      my teachings
   and not follow my rules.
31They might break my laws
   and disobey my commands.
32Then I will punish their sins with a
      rod
   and their wrongs with a whip.
33But I will not hold back my love
      from David.
   I will not stop being loyal.
34I will not break my agreement.
   I will not change what I have said.
35It is certain that I am a holy God.
   So it is certain I will not lie to David.
36His family will continue forever.
   His kingdom will continue before
      me like the sun.
37It will last forever, like the moon,
   like a lasting witness in the sky."

                                          Selah

38But now, you have rejected your
      appointed king.
   You have been angry with him.
39You have broken the agreement
      with your servant.
   You threw his crown to the ground.
40You have torn down all the city walls.
   You have turned his strong, walled
      cities into ruins.
41Everyone who passes by steals
      from him.

His neighbors insult him.
42You have given strength to his
    enemies.
You have made them all happy.
43You have made his sword useless.
    You did not help him stand in
    battle.
44You have kept him from winning.
    You threw his throne to the
    ground.
45You have cut his life short.
    You have covered him with shame.
                                    Selah

46Lord, how long will this go on?
    Will you ignore us forever?
    How long will your anger burn like
    a fire?
47Remember how short my life is.
    Why did you create us anyway?
48What man alive will not die?
    Can he escape the grave?   *Selah*

49Lord, where is your love from times
    past?
    With loyalty you promised it to
    David.
50Lord, remember how they insulted
    your servant.
    Remember how I have suffered
    the insults of the nations.
51Lord, remember how your enemies
    insulted you.

Remember how they insulted your
    appointed king wherever he
    went.

52Praise the Lord forever!
    Amen and amen.

Book 4

God Is Eternal, and We Are Not

A prayer of Moses, the man of God.

90 Lord, you have been our home
    since the beginning.
2Before the mountains were born,
    and before you created the earth
        and the world,
    you are God.
    You have always been, and you will
        always be.

3You turn people back into dust.
    You say, "Go back into dust,
        human beings."
4To you, a thousand years
    is like the passing of a day.
    It passes like an hour in the night.
5While people sleep, you take their
        lives.
    They are like weeds that grow in
        the morning.

What God Is Like
PSALM 90:2

Have you ever gotten your way or won an argument by saying, "I was here first!"? Maybe you had a fight with your brother or sister over who was going to sit in the front seat of the car next to Mom or Dad. Whoever got there first usually got his or her way.

Psalm 90 tells us again that God was here first. He was here before the mountains and the rest of the world, and he will be here when they are gone. That is what *eternal* means: God always was, and he always will be. He had no beginning, and he will have no end. And even though God never has to worry about winning arguments, he will have his way in the end. It should make you feel safe and secure knowing that God, who is eternal, is watching over you.

To learn more about what God is like, zoom to page 710.

⁶In the morning they are fresh and
    new.
    But by evening they dry up and die.

⁷We are destroyed by your anger.
    We are terrified by your hot anger.
⁸You have put the evil we have done
    right in front of you.
    You clearly see our secret sins.
⁹All our days pass while you are
    angry.
    Our years end with a moan.
¹⁰Our lifetime is 70 years.
    If we are strong, we may live to be
    80.
    But the years are full of hard work
    and pain.
    They pass quickly, and then we
    are gone.

¹¹Who knows the full power of your
    anger?
    Your anger is as great as our fear
    of you should be.
¹²Teach us how short our lives really
    are
    so that we may be wise.

¹³Lord, how long before you return
    and show kindness to your
    servants?
¹⁴Fill us with your love every
    morning.
    Then we will sing and rejoice all
    our lives.
¹⁵We have seen years of trouble.
    Now give us joy as you gave us
    sorrow.
¹⁶Show your servants the wonderful
    things you do.
    Show your greatness to their
    children.
¹⁷Lord our God, be pleased with us.
    Give us success in what we do.
    Yes, give us success in what we do.

Safe in the Lord

91 Those who go to God Most
    High for safety
    will be protected by God All-
    Powerful.
²I will say to the Lord, "You are my
    place of safety and protection.
    You are my God, and I trust you."

³God will save you from hidden traps
    and from deadly diseases.
⁴He will protect you like a bird
    spreading its wings over its young.
    His truth will be like your armor
    and shield.
⁵You will not fear any danger by night
    or an arrow during the day.
⁶You will not be afraid of diseases
    that come in the dark
    or sickness that strikes at noon.
⁷At your side 1,000 people may die,
    or even 10,000 right beside you.
    But you will not be hurt.
⁸You will only watch what happens.
    You will see the wicked punished.

⁹The Lord is your protection.
    You have made God Most High
    your place of safety.
¹⁰Nothing bad will happen to you.
    No disaster will come to your home.
¹¹He has put his angels in charge of
    you.
    They will watch over you wherever
    you go.
¹²They will catch you with their hands.
    And you will not hit your foot on a
    rock.
¹³You will walk on lions and cobras.
    You will step on strong lions and
    snakes.

¹⁴The Lord says, "If someone loves
    me, I will save him.
    I will protect those who know me.
¹⁵They will call to me, and I will
    answer them.
    I will be with them in trouble.
    I will rescue them and honor them.
¹⁶I will give them a long, full life.
    They will see how I can save."

Thanksgiving for God's Goodness

A song for the Sabbath[d] day.

92 It is good to praise the Lord,
    to sing praises to God Most
    High.
²It is good to tell of your love in the
    morning
    and of your loyalty at night.
³It is good to praise you with the ten-
    stringed lyre[d]

and with the soft-sounding harp.

⁴Lord, you have made me happy by
    what you have done.
I will sing for joy about what your
    hands have done.
⁵Lord, you have done such great
    things!
How deep are your thoughts!
⁶Stupid people don't know these
    things.
Fools don't understand.
⁷Wicked people grow like the grass.
Evil people seem to do well.
But they will be destroyed forever.
⁸But, Lord, you will be honored
    forever.

⁹Lord, surely your enemies,
    surely your enemies will be
    destroyed.
All who do evil will be scattered.
¹⁰But you have made me as strong as
    a wild ox.
You have poured fine oils on me.
¹¹When I looked, I saw my enemies.
I heard the cries of those who are
    against me.

¹²But good people will grow like palm
    trees.
They will be tall like the cedar
    trees of Lebanon.
¹³They will be like trees planted in the
    courtyards of the Lord.
They will grow strong in the
    courtyards of our God.
¹⁴When they are old, they will still
    produce fruit.
They will be healthy and fresh.
¹⁵They will say that the Lord is good.
He is my Rock,^d and there is no
    wrong in him.

The Majesty of God

93 The Lord is king. He is clothed
    with majesty.
The Lord is clothed in majesty
and armed with strength.
The world is set,
and it cannot be moved.
²Lord, your kingdom was set up long
    ago.
You are everlasting.

³Lord, the seas rise up.
The seas raise their voice.
The seas lift up their pounding
    waves.
⁴The sound of the water is loud.
The ocean waves are powerful.
But the Lord above is much greater.
⁵Lord, your laws will stand forever.
Your Temple^d will be holy
    forevermore.

God Will Pay Back His Enemies

94 The Lord is a God who gives
    people what they should get.
God, show your greatness and
    punish!
²Rise up, Judge of the earth.
Give the proud what they should
    get.
³How long will the wicked be happy?
How long, Lord?

⁴They are full of proud words.
Those who do evil brag about what
    they have done.
⁵Lord, they crush your people.
They make your children suffer.
⁶They kill widows and foreigners.
They murder orphans.
⁷They say, "The Lord doesn't see.
The God of Jacob doesn't notice."

⁸You stupid ones among the people,
    pay attention.
You fools, when will you
    understand?
⁹Can't the creator of ears hear?
Can't the maker of eyes see?
¹⁰Won't the one who corrects nations
    punish you?
Doesn't the teacher of men know
    everything?
¹¹The Lord knows what people think.
He knows they are just a puff of
    wind.

¹²Lord, those you correct are happy.
You give them your teachings.
¹³You give them rest from times of
    trouble
until a grave is dug for the wicked.
¹⁴The Lord won't leave his people.
He will not give up his children.

¹⁵Judgment will again be fair.
  And all who are honest will follow it.

¹⁶Who will help me fight against the
    wicked?
  Who will stand with me against
    those who do evil?
¹⁷If the Lord had not helped me,
  I would have died soon.
¹⁸I said, "I am about to be
    overwhelmed."
  But, Lord, your love kept me safe.
¹⁹I was very worried.
  But you comforted me and made
    me happy.

²⁰Crooked leaders cannot be your
    friends.
  They use the law to cause
    suffering.
²¹They join forces against people who
    do right.
  They sentence to death the
    innocent.
²²But the Lord protects me like a
    strong, walled city.
  My God is the rock of my
    protection.
²³God will pay them back for their sins.
  He will destroy them for their evil.
  The Lord our God will destroy
    them.

A Call to Praise and Obedience

95 Come, let's sing for joy to the
    Lord.
  Let's shout praises to the Rock[d]
    who saves us.
²Let's come to him with thanksgiving.
  Let's sing songs to him.
³The Lord is the great God.
  He is the great King over all gods.
⁴The deepest places on earth are his.
  And the highest mountains belong
    to him.
⁵The sea is his because he made it.
  He created the land with his own
    hands.

⁶Come, let's bow down and worship
    him.
  Let's kneel before the Lord who
    made us.
⁷He is our God.

And we are the people he takes
    care of
  and the sheep that he tends.

Today listen to what he says:
⁸ "Do not be stubborn, as your
    ancestors were at Meribah,
  as they were that day at Massah in
    the desert.
⁹There your ancestors tested me.
  They put me to the test even
    though they saw what I did.
¹⁰I was angry with those people for 40
    years.
  I said, 'They are not loyal to me.
  They have not understood my
    ways.'
¹¹I was angry and made a promise,
  'They will never enter my land of
    rest.'"

Praise for God's Glory

96 Sing to the Lord a new song.
  Sing to the Lord, all the earth.
²Sing to the Lord and praise his
    name.
  Every day tell how he saves us.
³Tell the nations of his glory.
  Tell all peoples the miracles[d] he
    does.

⁴The Lord is great; he should be
    praised.
  He should be honored more than
    all the gods.
⁵All the gods of the nations are only
    idols.
  But the Lord made the skies.
⁶The Lord has glory and majesty.
  He has power and beauty in his
    Temple.[d]

⁷Praise the Lord, all nations on earth.
  Praise the Lord's glory and power.
⁸Praise the glory of the Lord's name.
  Bring an offering and come into
    his Temple courtyards.
⁹Worship the Lord because he is holy.
  The whole earth should tremble
    before the Lord.
¹⁰Tell the nations, "The Lord is king."
  The earth is set, and it cannot be
    moved.
  He will judge the people fairly.

[11]Let the skies rejoice and the earth
be glad.
Let the sea and everything in it
shout.
[12]Let the fields and everything in
them show their joy.
Then all the trees of the forest will
sing for joy.
[13] They will sing before the Lord
because he is coming.
He is coming to judge the world.
He will judge the world with fairness
and the nations with truth.

A Hymn About God's Power

97 The Lord is king. Let the earth
rejoice.
Faraway lands should be glad.
[2]Thick, dark clouds surround him.
His kingdom is built on what is
right and fair.
[3]A fire goes before him
and burns up his enemies all
around.
[4]His lightning flashes in the sky.
When the people see it, they
tremble.
[5]The mountains melt like wax before
the Lord.
He is Lord of all the earth.
[6]The skies tell about his goodness.
And all the people see his glory.

[7]Those who worship idols should be
ashamed.
They brag about their false gods.
All the gods should worship the
Lord.
[8]When Jerusalem hears this, she is
glad.
The towns of Judah rejoice.
They are happy because of your
judgments, Lord.
[9]You are the Lord Most High over all
the earth.
You are supreme over all gods.

[10]People who love the Lord should
hate evil.
The Lord watches over those who
follow him.
He frees them from the power of
the wicked.

[11]Light shines on those who do right.
Joy belongs to those who are
honest.
[12]Rejoice in the Lord, you who do
right.
Praise his holy name.

The God of Power and Justice

A song.

98 Sing to the Lord a new song
because he has done miracles.[d]
By his right hand and holy arm
he has won the victory.
[2]The Lord has told about his power
to save.
He has shown the other nations
his victory for his people.
[3]He has remembered his love
and his loyalty to the people of
Israel.
All the ends of the earth have seen
God's power to save.

[4]Shout with joy to the Lord, all the
earth.
Burst into songs and praise.
[5]Make music to the Lord with harps,
with harps and the sound of
singing.
[6]Blow the trumpets and the sheep's
horns.
Shout for joy to the Lord the King.

[7]Let the sea and everything in it
shout.
Let the world and everyone on it
sing.
[8]Let the rivers clap their hands.
Let the mountains sing together
for joy.
[9]Let them sing before the Lord
because he is coming to judge the
world.
He will judge the world fairly.
He will judge the nations with
fairness.

God the Fair and Holy King

99 The Lord is king.
Let the nations shake with fear.
He sits between the gold creatures
with wings.
Let the earth shake.

Thankfulness
PSALM 100:4

Have you ever given anyone a "just because"?
That's when you hug a friend or say, "I love you," for no special reason. You do it because you care.

When the Bible says to give thanks to God, it doesn't mean you have to wait until God does something extra special for you. You can give him a "just because" anytime by thanking him just because you care about him.

Although there will always be reasons to give God thanks, try to mix in a "just because" thank-you now and then. Like the writer of this psalm, you can be creative and sing it or you can just say it. It doesn't matter why you thank him or how. God just loves to hear it.

To learn more about thankfulness, zoom to page 714.

²The Lord in Jerusalem is great.
He is supreme over all the nations.
³Let them praise your name.
It is great, holy and to be feared.

⁴The King is powerful and loves justice.
Lord, you made things fair.
You have done what is fair and right
for the people of Jacob.
⁵Praise the Lord our God.
Worship at the Temple,ᵈ his
footstool.
He is holy.

⁶Moses and Aaron were among his
priests.
And Samuel was among his
worshipers.
They called to the Lord,
and he answered them.
⁷He spoke to them from the pillar of
cloud.
They kept the rules and laws he
gave them.

⁸Lord our God, you answered them.
You showed them that you are a
forgiving God.
But you punished them for their
wrongs.

⁹Praise the Lord our God.
Worship at his holy mountain.
The Lord our God is holy.

A Call to Praise God

A song of thanks.

100 Shout to the Lord, all the
earth.
² Serve the Lord with joy.
Come before him with singing.
³Know that the Lord is God.
He made us, and we belong to him.
We are his people, the sheep he
tends.

⁴Come into his city with songs of
thanksgiving.
Come into his courtyards with
songs of praise.
Thank him, and praise his name.
⁵The Lord is good. His love
continues forever.
His loyalty continues from now on.

A Promise to Rule Well

A song of David.

101 I will sing of love and fairness.
Lord, I will sing praises to you.

²I will be careful to live an innocent
life.
When will you come to me?

I will live an innocent life in my
house.
³ I will not look at anything wicked.
I hate those who turn against you.
They will not be found near me.
⁴Let those who want to do wrong
stay away from me.
I will have nothing to do with evil.
⁵If anyone secretly says things
against his neighbor,
I will stop him.
I will not allow people
to be proud and look down on
others.

⁶I will look for trustworthy people
so I can live with them in the land.
Only those who live innocent lives
will be my servants.
⁷No one who is dishonest will live in
my house.
No liars will stay around me.
⁸Every morning I will destroy
the wicked in the land.
I will rid the Lord's city
of people who do evil.

A Cry for Help

*A prayer of a person who is suffering
when he is discouraged and tells the
Lord his complaints.*

102 Lord, listen to my prayer.
Let my cry for help come to
you.
²Do not hide from me
in my time of trouble.
Pay attention to me.
When I cry for help, answer me
quickly.

³My life is passing away like smoke.
My bones are burned up with fire.
⁴My heart is like grass
that has been cut and dried.
I forget to eat.
⁵Because of my grief,
my skin hangs on my bones.
⁶I am like a desert owl.
I am like an owl living among the
ruins.

⁷I lie awake.
I am like a lonely bird on a
housetop.
⁸All day long enemies insult me.
Those who make fun of me use my
name as a curse.
⁹I eat ashes as my food.
My tears fall into my drinks.
¹⁰Because of your great anger,
you have picked me up and
thrown me away.
¹¹My days are like a passing shadow.
I am like dried grass.

¹²But, Lord, you rule forever.
Your fame continues from now on.
¹³You will come and have mercy on
Jerusalem.
The time has now come to be kind
to her.
¹⁴Your servants love even her stones.
They even care about her dust.
¹⁵Nations will fear the name of the
Lord.
All the kings on earth will honor
him.
¹⁶The Lord will rebuild Jerusalem.
There his glory will be seen.
¹⁷He will answer the prayers of the
needy.
He will not reject their prayers.

¹⁸Write these things for the future.
Then people who are not yet born
will praise the Lord.
¹⁹The Lord looked down from his
holy place above.
From heaven he looked down at
the earth.
²⁰He heard the moans of the
prisoners.
And he freed those sentenced to
die.
²¹The name of the Lord will be heard
in Jerusalem.
His praise will be heard in
Jerusalem.
²²People will come together.
Kingdoms will serve the Lord.

²³God has made me tired of living.
He has cut short my life.
²⁴So I said, "My God, do not take me
in the middle of my life.

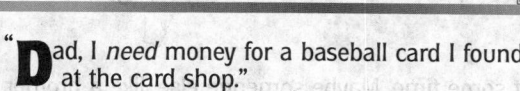

Prayer
PSALM 102:17

"**D**ad, I *need* money for a baseball card I found at the card shop."

"**B**ut Mom, I *need* to go to Suzy's party Friday!"

We use that word *need* in lots of different ways. We say we *need* something when we really *want* it. Wise parents know the difference between what their children need, like food and clothes, and what they want, like candy and toys. Parents try to give their children what they need. But they may not always give them what they want.

God is a good parent. He knows what his children need and what they want. This verse tells us that he always listens to the needy. He also knows what everyone wants, and like any good parent, he enjoys giving those things . . . sometimes. There are other times when what a person wants is not what is best, and God says no. But we can always trust him to do what is right for us.

It is great to know we can take our needs and wants to God in prayer, and that he will do what is right.

To learn more about prayer, zoom to page 1134.

Your years go on and on.
²⁵In the beginning you made the earth.
And your hands made the skies.
²⁶They will be destroyed, but you will remain.
They will all wear out like clothes.
And, like clothes, you will change them.
And they will be thrown away.
²⁷But you never change.
And your life will never end.
²⁸Our children will live in your presence.
And their children will remain with you."

Praise to the God of Love

Of David.

103 My whole being, praise the Lord.
All my being, praise his holy name.
²My whole being, praise the Lord.
Do not forget all his kindnesses.
³The Lord forgives me for all my sins.
He heals all my diseases.
⁴He saves my life from the grave.
He loads me with love and mercy.
⁵He satisfies me with good things.
He makes me young again, like the eagle.
⁶The Lord does what is right and fair for all who are wronged by others.
⁷He showed his ways to Moses and his miracles*ᵈ* to the people of Israel.
⁸The Lord shows mercy and is kind.
He does not become angry quickly, and he has great love.
⁹He will not always scold us.
He will not be angry forever.
¹⁰He has not punished us as our sins should be punished.

What God Is Like
PSALM 103:8-13

"**T**hat's not fair!"

Everyone has felt that at some time. Maybe someone else, like a brother or sister or classmate, got something you wanted. Or possibly you got in trouble for what another person did. However it happened, you felt that the other person got an unfair reward, or you got an unjust punishment, and so you said: "It's not fair!"

But have you ever been the one who got more than you should have, or got off easy instead of being punished? Did you think *that* was unfair? Probably not. And that is what God has done for us. He has not punished us as severely as our sins deserved, and he has rewarded us more for our goodness than he needed to. That is why King David says in this psalm that God is *merciful.* He is kind to us beyond what he has to be. And no one can complain about that!

To learn more about what God is like, zoom to page 727.

He has not repaid us for the evil
   we have done.
11As high as the sky is above the earth,
   so great is his love for those who
   respect him.
12He has taken our sins away from us
   as far as the east is from west.
13The Lord has mercy on those who
   fear him,
   as a father has mercy on his
   children.
14He knows how we were made.
   He remembers that we are dust.

15Human life is like grass.
   We grow like a flower in the field.
16After the wind blows, the flower is
   gone.
   There is no sign of where it was.
17But the Lord's love for those who
   fear him
   continues forever and ever.
   And his goodness continues to
   their grandchildren
18and to those who keep his
   agreement
   and who remember to obey his
   orders.

19The Lord has set his throne in
   heaven.
   And his kingdom rules over
   everything.
20You who are his angels, praise the
   Lord.
   You are the mighty warriors who
   do what he says.
   Listen to what he says.
21You, his armies, praise the Lord.
   You are his servants who do what
   he wants.
22Everything the Lord has made
   should praise him in all the places
   he rules.
   My whole being, praise the Lord.

Praise to God Who Made the World

104 My whole being, praise the Lord.
   Lord my God, you are very great.
You are clothed with glory and
   majesty.
2   You wear light like a robe.
   You stretch out the skies like a
   tent.

3 You build your room above the
    clouds.
You make the clouds your chariot.
    You ride on the wings of the wind.
4 You make the winds your
    messengers.
    Flames of fire are your servants.

5 You built the earth on its
    foundations.
    So it can never be moved.
6 You covered the earth with oceans.
    The water was above the
        mountains.
7 But at your command, the water
    rushed away.
    When you gave your orders like
        thunder, it hurried away.
8 The mountains rose.
    The valleys sank.
    The water went to the places you
        made for it.
9 You set borders for the seas that
    they cannot cross.
    The water will never cover the
        earth again.

10 You make springs pour into the
    ravines.
    They flow between the mountains.
11 They water all the wild animals.
    The wild donkeys come there to
        drink.
12 Wild birds make nests by the water.
    They sing among the tree
        branches.
13 You water the mountains from above.
    The earth is full of the things you
        made.
14 You make the grass for cattle
    and vegetables for the use of man.
    You make food grow from the
        earth.
15 You give us wine that makes happy
    hearts.
    And you give us olive oil that
        makes our faces shine.
    You give us bread that gives us
        strength.
16 The Lord's trees have plenty of water.
    They are the cedar trees of
        Lebanon, which he planted.
17 The birds make their nests there.

The stork's home is in the fir
    trees.
18 The high mountains belong to the
    wild goats.
    The rocks are hiding places for the
        badgers.

19 You made the moon to mark the
    seasons.
    And the sun always knows when to
        set.
20 You make it dark, and it becomes
    night.
    Then all the wild animals creep
        around.
21 The lions roar as they attack.
    They look to God for food.
22 When the sun rises, they leave.
    They go back to their dens to lie
        down.
23 Then people go to work.
    And they work until evening.

24 Lord, you have made many things.
    With your wisdom you made them
        all.
    The earth is full of your riches.
25 Look at the sea, so big and wide.
    Its creatures large and small
        cannot be counted.
26 Ships travel over the ocean.
    And there is the sea monster
        Leviathan,*d*
    which you made to play there.

27 All these things depend on you
    to give them their food at the right
        time.
28 When you give it to them,
    they gather it up.
    When you open your hand, they are
        filled with good food.
29 When you turn away from them,
    they become frightened.
    When you take away their breath,
        they die and turn into dust.
30 When you breathe on them,
    they are created.
    You make the land new again.

31 May the glory of the Lord be
    forever.
    May the Lord enjoy what he has
        made.

³²He just looks at the earth, and it
      shakes.
   He touches the mountains, and
      they smoke.

³³I will sing to the Lord all my life.
   I will sing praises to my God as
      long as I live.
³⁴May my thoughts please him.
   I am happy in the Lord.
³⁵Let sinners be destroyed from the
      earth.
   Let the wicked people live no
      longer.

   My whole being, praise the Lord.
   Praise the Lord.

God's Love for Israel

105 Give thanks to the Lord and
      pray to him.
   Tell the nations what he has done.
²Sing to him. Sing praises to him.
   Tell about all the wonderful things
      he has done.
³Be glad that you are his.
   Let those who ask the Lord for
      help be happy.
⁴Depend on the Lord and his strength.
   Always go to him for help.
⁵Remember the wonderful things he
      has done.
   Remember his miracles[d] and his
      decisions.
⁶You are descendants[d] of his servant
      Abraham,
   the children of Jacob, his chosen
      people.
⁷He is the Lord our God.
   His laws are for all the world.

⁸He will keep his agreement forever.
   He will keep his promises always.
⁹He will keep his agreement he
      made with Abraham.
   He will keep the promise he made
      to Isaac.
¹⁰He made it a law for the people of
      Jacob.
   He made it an agreement with
      Israel to last forever.

¹¹The Lord said, "I will give you the
      land of Canaan.
   The promised land will belong to
      you."

¹²Then God's people were few in
      number.
   They were strangers in the land.
¹³They went from one nation to
      another.
   They went from one kingdom to
      another.
¹⁴But the Lord did not let anyone hurt
      them.
   He warned kings not to harm
      them.
¹⁵He said, "Don't hurt my chosen
      people.
   Don't harm my prophets."[d]

¹⁶God ordered a time of hunger in the
      land.
   And he destroyed all the food.
¹⁷Then he sent a man ahead of them.
   It was Joseph, who was sold as a
      slave.
¹⁸They put chains around his feet
   and an iron ring around his neck.
¹⁹Then the time he had spoken of
      came.
   The Lord's words proved that
      Joseph was right.
²⁰The king of Egypt sent for Joseph
      and freed him.
   The ruler of the people set him
      free.
²¹He made him the master of his
      house.
   Joseph was in charge of his riches.
²²He could order the princes as he
      wished.
   He taught the older men to be
      wise.
²³Then his father Israel came to
      Egypt.
   Jacob, also called Israel, lived in
      Egypt.[n]
²⁴The Lord made his people grow in
      number.
   He made them stronger than their
      enemies.

---

[n]**Egypt** Literally, "the land of Ham." Also in verse 27. The people in Egypt were descendants of Ham,
one of Noah's sons. See Genesis 10:6.

25And he caused the Egyptians to
hate his people.
They made plans against the
Lord's servants.
26Then he sent his servant Moses,
and Aaron, whom he had chosen.
27They did many signs among the
Egyptians.
They worked miracles in Egypt.
28The Lord sent darkness and made
the land dark.
But the Egyptians turned against
what he said.
29So he changed their water into blood
and made their fish die.
30Then their country was filled with
frogs.
They were even in the bedrooms
of their rulers.
31The Lord spoke, and flies came.
Gnats were everywhere in the
country.
32He made hail fall like rain.
And he sent lightning through
their land.
33He struck down their grapevines
and fig trees.
He destroyed every tree in the
country.
34He spoke, and grasshoppers came.
The locusts*d* were too many to
count.
35They ate all the plants in the land.
They ate what the earth produced.
36The Lord also killed all the
firstborn*d* sons in the land,
the oldest son of each family.
37Then he brought his people out,
and they carried with them silver
and gold.
Not one of his people stumbled.
38The Egyptians were glad when they
left
because the Egyptians were afraid
of them.
39The Lord covered them with a
cloud
and lit up the night with fire.
40When they asked, he brought them
quail.
He filled them with bread from
heaven.

41God split the rock, and water flowed
out.
It ran like a river through the
desert.
42He remembered his holy promise
to his servant Abraham.
43So God brought his people out with
joy.
He brought out his chosen ones
with singing.
44He gave them lands that belonged
to other nations.
They received what others had
worked for.
45This was so they would keep his
orders
and obey his teachings.

Praise the Lord!

Israel's Failure to Trust God

106 Praise the Lord!
Thank the Lord because he
is good.
His love continues forever.
2No one can tell all the mighty things
the Lord has done.
No one can speak all his praise.
3Happy are those people who are fair,
who do what is right at all times.

4Lord, remember me when you are
kind to your people.
Help me when you save them.
5Let me see the good things you do
for your chosen people.
Let me be happy along with your
happy nation.
Let me join your own people in
praising you.

6We have sinned just as our
ancestors did.
We have done wrong. We have
done evil.
7Our ancestors in Egypt
did not learn from your miracles.*d*
They did not remember all your
kindnesses.
So they turned against you at the
Red Sea.*d*
8But the Lord saved them for his own
sake,

Thankfulness
PSALM 106:1

When does forever begin? How do we get to the end of it? The answer to both questions is, never. It never begins and it never ends, because it has always been and always will be. That is why *forever* is a perfect way to describe God's love for us. His love is forever.

So, when do we get to the end of his love? Never.

That kind of love deserves a big thank-you. But wait, there's more. The God who loves us forever is also forever good. So, when do we get to the end of his goodness? You've got it now: never!

No wonder the writer of this psalm wanted to say thank you. Stop right now and thank God too.

To learn more about thankfulness, zoom to page 716.

to show his great power.

9He commanded the Red Sea, and it
dried up.
He led them through the deep sea
as if it were a desert.
10He saved them from those who
hated them.
He saved them from their
enemies.
11And the water covered their
enemies.
Not one of them escaped.
12Then the people believed what the
Lord said.
They sang praises to him.

13But they quickly forgot what he had
done.
They did not wait for his advice.
14They became greedy for food in the
desert.
And they tested God there.
15So he gave them what they wanted.
But he also sent a terrible disease
among them.

16The people in the camp became
jealous of Moses

and of Aaron, the holy priest of the
Lord.
17Then the ground opened up and
swallowed Dathan.
It closed over Abiram's group.
18Then a fire burned among their
followers.
Flames burned up the wicked
people.

19The people made a gold calf at
Mount Sinai.
They worshiped a metal statue.
20They exchanged their glorious
God
for a statue of a bull, which eats
grass.
21They forgot the God who saved
them,
who had done great things in
Egypt.
22He did miracles in Egypt.*n*
He did amazing things by the Red
Sea.
23So God said he would destroy them.
But Moses, his chosen one, stood
before him.

*n*Egypt   Literally, "the land of Ham." The people in Egypt were descendants of Ham, one of Noah's
sons. See Genesis 10:6.

He stopped God's anger from
destroying them.

24Then they refused to go into the
beautiful land of Canaan.
They did not believe what God
promised.
25They grumbled in their tents
and did not obey the Lord.
26So he swore to them
that they would die in the desert.
27He said their children would be
killed by other nations
and that they would be scattered
among other countries.

28They joined in worshiping Baal[d] at
Peor.
They ate meat that had been
sacrificed to lifeless statues.
29They made the Lord angry by what
they did.
So many people became sick with
a terrible disease.
30But Phinehas prayed to the Lord,
and the disease stopped.
31The Lord will remember that
Phinehas did what was right.
And God will remember this from
now on.

32The people also made the Lord
angry at Meribah.
And Moses was in trouble because
of them.
33The people turned against the
Spirit[d] of God.
So Moses spoke without stopping
to think.

34The people did not destroy the
other nations
as the Lord had told them to do.
35Instead, they mixed with the other
nations.
And they learned their customs.
36They worshiped other nations' idols.
And they were trapped by them.
37They even killed their sons and
daughters
as sacrifices to demons.[d]
38They killed innocent people.
They killed their own sons and
daughters

as sacrifices to the idols of Canaan.
So the land was made unholy by
their blood.
39The people became unholy by their
sins.
They were unfaithful to God in
what they did.

40So the Lord became angry with his
people.
He hated his own children.
41He let other nations defeat them.
He let their enemies rule over
them.
42Their enemies were cruel to them.
Their enemies kept them under
their power.
43The Lord saved his people many
times.
But they continued to turn against
him.
So they became even more wicked.

44But God saw their misery.
He heard their cry.
45He remembered his agreement
with them.
And he felt sorry for them because
of his great love.
46He caused them to be pitied
by those who held them captive.

47Lord our God, save us.
Bring us back from other nations.
Then we will thank you.
Then we will gladly praise you.

48Praise the Lord, the God of Israel.
He always was and always will be.
Let all the people say, "Amen!"

Praise the Lord!

Book 5

God Saves from Many Dangers

107 Thank the Lord because he
is good.
His love continues forever.
2That is what the people the Lord
has saved should say.
They are the ones he has saved
from the enemy.
3He has gathered them from other
lands,

from east and west, north and south.

⁴Some people had wandered in the desert lands.
  They found no city to live in.
⁵They were hungry and thirsty.
  They were discouraged.
⁶In their misery they cried out to the Lord.
  And he saved them from their troubles.
⁷He led them on a straight road
  to a city where they could live.
⁸Let them give thanks to the Lord for his love
  and for the miracles^d he does for people.
⁹He satisfies the thirsty.
  He fills up the hungry.

¹⁰Some sat in gloom and darkness.
  They were prisoners suffering in chains.
¹¹They had turned against the words of God.
  They had refused the advice of God Most High.
¹²So he broke their pride by hard work.
  They stumbled, and no one helped.

¹³In their misery they cried out to the Lord.
  And he saved them from their troubles.
¹⁴He brought them out of their gloom and darkness.
  He broke their chains.
¹⁵Let them give thanks to the Lord for his love
  and for the miracles he does for people.
¹⁶He breaks down bronze gates.
  And he cuts apart iron bars.

¹⁷Some became fools who turned against God.
  They suffered for the evil they did.
¹⁸They refused to eat anything.
  So they almost died.
¹⁹In their misery they cried out to the Lord.
  And he saved them from their troubles.
²⁰God gave the command and healed them.
  So they were saved from dying.
²¹Let them give thanks to the Lord for his love

Thankfulness
PSALM 107:8

What is your favorite *Odyssey* episode?
You've probably enjoyed it over and over. But you never get tired of it. Although we don't know who wrote this particular psalm, we can see that one of the author's favorite things to do was to give thanks to the Lord. He said it over and over and over, and he didn't get tired of it.

In the same way, the Lord never gets tired of hearing people thank him. There are so many things to thank him for we could never run out of words. Look at the rest of this psalm and see how many times you can find where the author repeats this same verse.

How can you thank the Lord for his love and for all that he has done for you? God never gets tired of hearing you thank him. You can say it over and over.

To learn more about thankfulness, zoom to page 1038.

and for the miracles he does for people.

²²Let them offer sacrifices to thank him.
With joy they should tell what he has done.

²³Others went out to sea in ships.
They did business on the great oceans.

²⁴They saw what the Lord could do.
They saw the miracles he did.

²⁵He spoke, and a storm came up.
It blew up high waves.

²⁶The ships tossed as high as the sky and fell low in the waves.
The storm was so bad the men lost their courage.

²⁷They stumbled and fell like men who were drunk.
They did not know what to do.

²⁸In their misery they cried out to the Lord.
And he saved them from their troubles.

²⁹He made the storm be still.
He calmed the waves.

³⁰They were happy that it was quiet.
And God guided them to the port they wanted.

³¹Let them give thanks to the Lord for his love
and for the miracles he does for people.

³²Let them praise his greatness in the meeting of the people.
They should praise him in the meeting of the older leaders.

³³He changed rivers into a desert,
and springs of water into dry ground.

³⁴He made fertile land salty
because the people there did evil.

³⁵He changed the desert into pools of water
and dry ground into springs of water.

³⁶He had the hungry settle there.
They built a city to live in.

³⁷They planted seeds in the fields and vineyards.
And they had a good harvest.

³⁸God blessed them, and they grew in number.
Their cattle did not become fewer.

³⁹Because of disaster, troubles and sadness,
their families grew smaller and weaker.

⁴⁰He showed he was displeased with their important men.
He made them wander in a pathless desert.

⁴¹But he lifted the poor out of their suffering.
And he made their families grow like flocks of sheep.

⁴²Good people see this and are happy.
But the wicked say nothing.

⁴³Whoever is wise will remember these things.
He will think about the love of the Lord.

A Prayer for Victory

A song of David.

108

God, my heart is right.
I will sing and praise you with all my being.

²Wake up, harp and lyre!^d
I will wake up the dawn.

³Lord, I will praise you among the nations.
I will sing songs of praise about you to all the nations.

⁴Your love is so great that it is higher than the skies.
Your truth reaches to the clouds.

⁵God, you are supreme over the skies.
Let your glory be over all the earth.

⁶Answer us and save us by your power.
Then the people you love will be rescued.

⁷God has said from his Temple,^d
"When I win, I will divide Shechem and cut up the Valley of Succoth.

⁸Gilead and Manasseh are mine.
Ephraim is like my helmet.
Judah holds my royal scepter.^d

⁹Moab is like my washbowl.

I throw my sandals at Edom.
I shout at Philistia."

¹⁰Who will bring me to the strong,
        walled city?
Who will lead me to Edom?
¹¹God, surely you have rejected us.
You do not go out with our armies.
¹²Help us fight the enemy.
Human help is useless.
¹³But we can win with God's help.
He will defeat our enemies.

A Prayer Against an Enemy

For the director of music. A song
of David.

109 God, I praise you.
Do not be silent.
²Wicked people and liars have
        spoken against me.
They have told lies about me.
³They have said hateful things about
        me.
They attack me for no reason.
⁴They attacked me, even though I
        loved them
and prayed for them.
⁵I was good to them, but they repay
        me with evil.
I loved them, but they hate me in
        return.

⁶They say about me, "Have the Evil
        One work against him.
Let the devil accuse him.
⁷When he is judged, let him be found
        guilty.
Let even his prayers show that he
        is guilty.
⁸Let his life be cut short.
Let another man replace him as
        leader.
⁹Let his children become orphans.
Let his wife become a widow.
¹⁰Make his children wander around,
        begging for food.
Let them be forced out of the ruins
        they live in.
¹¹Let the people he owes money to
        take everything he owns.
Let strangers steal everything he
        has worked for.
¹²Let no one show him love.

Let no one have mercy on his
        children.
¹³Let all his descendants[d] die.
Let him be forgotten by people
        who live after him.
¹⁴Let the Lord remember how wicked
        his ancestors were.
Don't let the sins of his mother be
        wiped out.
¹⁵Let the Lord always remember their
        sins.
Then he will make people forget
        about them completely.

¹⁶"He did not remember to be loving.
He hurt the poor, the needy and
        those who were sad
until they were nearly dead.
¹⁷He loved to put curses on others.
So let those same curses fall on
        him.
He did not like to bless others.
So do not let good things happen
        to him.
¹⁸He cursed others as often as he
        wore clothes.
Cursing others filled his body and
        his life,
like drinking water and using olive
        oil.
¹⁹So let curses cover him like
        clothes.
Let them wrap around him like a
        belt."
²⁰May the Lord do these things to
        those who accuse me,
to those who speak evil against me.

²¹But you, Lord God,
        be kind to me so others will know
        you are good.
Because your love is good, save me.
²²I am poor and helpless.
And I am very sad.
²³I am dying like an evening shadow.
I am shaken off like a locust.[d]
²⁴My knees are weak from hunger.
I have become thin.
²⁵My enemies insult me.
They look at me and shake their
        heads.

²⁶Lord my God, help me.
Because you are loving, save me.

²⁷Then they will know that you have
    saved me.
  They will know it was your power,
    Lord.
²⁸They may curse me, but you bless
    me.
  They may attack me, but they will
    be disgraced.
  Then I, your servant, will be glad.
²⁹Let those who accuse me be
    disgraced.
  Let them be covered with shame
    like a coat.

³⁰I will thank the Lord very much.
  I will praise him in front of many
    people.
³¹He defends the helpless.
  He saved me from those who
    accuse me.

The Lord Appoints a King

A song of David.

110 The Lord said to my Master,
    "Sit by me at my right side
  until I put your enemies under
    your control."
²The Lord will make you king in
    Jerusalem over all nations.
  And you will rule your enemies in
    their own countries.
³Your people will join you on the day
    you come to power.
  You have been dressed in holiness
    from birth.
  You have the freshness of a child.

⁴The Lord has made a promise
  and will not change his mind.
  He said, "You are a priest forever,
  a priest like Melchizedek."

⁵The Lord is beside you to help you.
  When he becomes angry, he will
    crush kings.
⁶He will judge those nations, filling
    them with dead bodies.
  He will defeat rulers all over the
    world.
⁷The king will drink from the brook
    on the way.
  Then he will be strengthened and
    win the battle.

Praise for God's Goodness

111 Praise the Lord!
    I will thank the Lord with all
    my heart
  in the meeting of his good people.
²The Lord does great things.
  Those people who love them think
    about them.
³What he does is glorious and
    splendid.
  His goodness continues forever.
⁴His miracles*d* are unforgettable.
  The Lord is kind and merciful.
⁵He gives food to those who fear him.
  He remembers his agreement
    forever.
⁶He has shown his people his power
  when he gave them the lands of
    other nations.

⁷Everything he does is good and fair.
  All his orders can be trusted.
⁸They will continue forever.
  They were made true and right.
⁹He sets his people free.
  He made his agreement
    everlasting.
  He is holy and wonderful.

¹⁰Wisdom begins with respect for the
    Lord.
  Those who obey his orders have
    good understanding.
  He should be praised forever.

**Wisdom begins with
respect for the Lord.
Those who obey his
orders have good
understanding. He
should be praised forever.**
• Psalm 111:10

Honest People Are Blessed

112 Praise the Lord!
    Happy is the person who
  fears the Lord.
  He loves what the Lord commands.
²His descendants*d* will be powerful in
    the land.

The children of honest people will
be blessed.
³His house will be full of wealth and
riches.

His goodness will continue forever.

⁴A light shines in the dark for honest
people.

It shines for those who are good
and kind and merciful.
⁵It is good to be kind and generous.

Whoever is fair in his business
⁶will never be defeated.

A good person will be remembered
from now on.
⁷He won't be afraid of bad news.

He is safe because he trusts the
Lord.
⁸That person is confident. He will not
be afraid.

He will look down on his enemies.
⁹He gives freely to the poor.

The things he does are right and
will continue forever.

He will be given great honor.

¹⁰The wicked will see this and
become angry.

They will grind their teeth in
anger and then disappear.

The wishes of the wicked will
come to nothing.

Praise for God's Kindness

113 Praise the Lord!

Praise him, you servants of
the Lord.

Praise the name of the Lord.
²The Lord's name should be praised
now and forever.
³The Lord's name should be praised
from where the sun rises to where
it sets.
⁴The Lord is supreme over all the
nations.

His glory reaches to the skies.

⁵No one is like the Lord our God.

He rules from heaven.
⁶He bends down to look

at the skies and the earth.
⁷The Lord lifts the poor from the
dirt.

He takes the helpless from the
ashes.
⁸And he seats them with princes,
the princes of his people.
⁹He gives children to the woman
who has none.

He makes her a happy mother.

Praise the Lord!

God Brought Israel from Egypt

114 The Israelites went out of
Egypt.

The people of Jacob left that
foreign country.
²Then Judah became God's holy
place.

Israel became the land he ruled.

³The Red Sea*ᵈ* looked and ran away.

The Jordan River turned back.
⁴The mountains danced like sheep
and the hills like little lambs.
⁵Sea, why did you run away?

Jordan, why did you turn back?
⁶Mountains, why did you dance like
sheep?

Hills, why did you dance like little
lambs?

⁷Earth, shake with fear before the
Lord.

Tremble in the presence of the
God of Jacob.
⁸He turned a rock into a pool of water.

He changed a hard rock into a
spring of water.

The One True God

115 It does not belong to us, Lord.
The praise belongs to you
because of your love and loyalty.

²Why do the nations ask,
"Where is their God?"
³Our God is in heaven.

He does what he wants.
⁴Their idols are made of silver and
gold.

They are made by human hands.
⁵They have mouths, but they cannot
speak.

They have eyes, but they cannot
see.

6They have ears, but they cannot hear.
They have noses, but they cannot
smell.
7They have hands, but they cannot
feel.
They have feet, but they cannot
walk.
And no sounds come from their
throats.
8The people who make idols and
trust them
are all like them.

9Family of Israel, trust the Lord.
He is your helper and your
protection.
10Family of Aaron, trust the Lord.
He is your helper and your
protection.
11You people who fear the Lord
should trust him.
He is your helper and your
protection.

12The Lord remembers us and will
bless us.
He will bless the family of Israel.
He will bless the family of Aaron.
13The Lord will bless those who fear
him,
from the smallest to the greatest.

14May the Lord give you many
children.
And may he give them children
also.
15May the Lord bless you.
He made heaven and earth.

16Heaven belongs to the Lord.
But he gave the earth to people.
17Dead people do not praise the Lord.
Those in the grave are silent.
18But we will praise the Lord
now and forever.

Praise the Lord!

Thanksgiving for Escaping Death

116 I love the Lord because he listens
to my prayers for help.
2He paid attention to me.
So I will call to him for help as
long as I live.

3The ropes of death bound me.
The fear of death took hold of me.
I was troubled and sad.
4Then I called out the name of the
Lord.
I said, "Please, Lord, save me!"

5The Lord is kind and does what is
right.
Our God is merciful.
6The Lord watches over the foolish.
When I was helpless, he saved me.
7I said to myself, "Relax,
because the Lord takes care of you."
8Lord, you have saved me from death.
You have stopped my eyes from
crying.
You have kept me from being
defeated.
9So I will walk with the Lord
in the land of the living.
10I believed, so I said,
"I am completely ruined."
11In my distress I said,
"All people are liars."

12What can I give the Lord
for all the good things he has
given to me?
13I will give him a drink offering for
saving me.
And I will pray to the Lord.
14In front of all his people,
I will give the Lord what I
promised.

15The death of one that belongs to him
is precious to the Lord.
16Lord, I am your servant.
I am your servant and the son of
your female servant.
You have freed me from my
chains.
17I will give an offering to show
thanks to you.
And I will worship the Lord.
18In front of all his people,
I will give the Lord what I
promised.
19I will do this in the Temple[d]
courtyards
in Jerusalem.

Praise the Lord!

A Hymn of Praise

117 All you nations, praise the Lord.
All you people, praise him.
2The Lord loves us very much.
His truth is everlasting.

Praise the Lord!

Thanksgiving for Victory

118 Thank the Lord because he is good.
His love continues forever.
2Let the people of Israel say,
"His love continues forever."
3Let the family of Aaron say,
"His love continues forever."
4Let those who fear the Lord say,
"His love continues forever."

5I was in trouble. So I called to the Lord.
The Lord answered me and set me free.
6I will not be afraid because the Lord is with me.
People can't do anything to me.
7The Lord is with me to help me.
I will see my enemies defeated.
8It is better to trust the Lord
than to trust people.
9It is better to trust the Lord
than to trust princes.

10All the nations surrounded me.
But I defeated them in the name of the Lord.
11They surrounded me on every side.
But with the Lord's power, I defeated them.
12They surrounded me like a swarm of bees.
But they died as quickly as thorns burn.
By the Lord's power, I defeated them.
13They chased me until I was almost defeated.
But the Lord helped me.
14The Lord gives me strength and makes me sing.
He has saved me.

15Shouts of joy and victory

come from the tents of those who do right:
"The Lord has done powerful things."
16The power of the Lord has won the victory.
With his power the Lord has done mighty things.

17I will not die, but live.
And I will tell what the Lord has done.
18The Lord has taught me a hard lesson.
But he did not let me die.

19Open for me the Temple*d* gates.
Then I will come in and thank the Lord.
20This is the Lord's gate.
Only those who are good may enter it.
21Lord, I thank you for answering me.
You have saved me.

22The stone that the builders did not want
became the cornerstone.*d*
23The Lord did this,
and it is wonderful to us.
24This is the day that the Lord has made.
Let us rejoice and be glad today!

25Please, Lord, save us.
Please, Lord, give us success.
26God bless the one who comes in the name of the Lord.
We bless all of you from the Temple of the Lord.
27The Lord is God.
And he has shown kindness to us.
With branches in your hands, join the feast.
Come to the corners of the altar.

28You are my God, and I will thank you.
You are my God, and I will praise your greatness.

29Thank the Lord because he is good.
His love continues forever.

The Word of God

119 Happy are the people who live pure lives.

They follow the Lord's teachings.
²Happy are the people who keep his rules.

They ask him for help with their whole heart.
³They don't do what is wrong.
They follow his ways.
⁴Lord, you gave your orders
to be followed completely.
⁵I wish I were more loyal
in meeting your demands.
⁶Then I would not be ashamed
when I think of your commands.
⁷When I learned that your laws are fair,

I praised you with an honest heart.
⁸I will meet your demands.
So please don't ever leave me.

⁹How can a young person live a pure life?

He can do it by obeying your word.

"**A**ll I need is a little soap and water to get my body clean. But to keep a life clean, you need something much stronger. Read Psalm 119:9-16 to find out what you need."

¹⁰With all my heart I try to obey you, God.

Don't let me break your commands.
¹¹I have taken your words to heart
so I would not sin against you.
¹²Lord, you should be praised.
Teach me your demands.
¹³My lips will tell about
all the laws you have spoken.
¹⁴I enjoy living by your rules
as people enjoy great riches.
¹⁵I think about your orders
and study your ways.
¹⁶I enjoy obeying your demands.
And I will not forget your word.

¹⁷Do good to me, your servant, so I can live,

so I can obey your word.
¹⁸Open my eyes to see the wonderful things
in your teachings.
¹⁹I am a stranger on earth.
Do not hide your commands from me.
²⁰I want to study
your laws all the time.
²¹You scold proud people.
Those who ignore your commands are cursed.
²²Don't let me be insulted and hated
because I obey your rules.
²³Even if princes speak against me,
I, your servant, will think about your demands.
²⁴Your rules give me pleasure.
They give me good advice.

²⁵I am about to die.
Give me life, as you have promised.
²⁶I told you about my life, and you answered me.
Teach me your demands.
²⁷Help me understand your orders.
Then I will think about your miracles.ᵈ
²⁸I am sad and tired.
Make me strong again as you have promised.
²⁹Don't let me be dishonest.
Be kind to me by helping me obey your teachings.
³⁰I have chosen to obey you.
I have obeyed your laws.
³¹I hold on to your rules.
Lord, do not let me be disgraced.
³²I will obey your commands
because you have made me happy.

³³Lord, teach me your demands.
Then I will obey them until the end.
³⁴Help me understand, so I can obey your teachings.
I will obey them with all my heart.
³⁵Help me obey your commands
because that makes me happy.
³⁶Help me want to obey your rules
instead of selfishly wanting riches.
³⁷Keep me from looking at worthless things.
Let me live by your word.

38Keep your promise to me, your
    servant,
  so you will be feared.
39Take away the shame I fear.
  Your laws are good.
40How I want to follow your orders.
  Give me life because of your
    goodness.

41Lord, show me your love.
  Save me as you have promised.
42Then I will have an answer for
    people who insult me.
  I trust what you say.
43Never keep me from speaking your
    truth.
  I depend on your fair laws.
44I will obey your teachings
  forever and ever.
45So I will live in freedom
  because I want to follow your
    orders.
46I will discuss your rules with kings.
  And I will not be ashamed.
47I enjoy obeying your commands.
  I love them.
48I praise your commands, which I love.
  And I think about your demands.

49Remember your promise to me,
    your servant.
  It gives me hope.
50When I suffer, this comforts me:
  Your promise gives me life.
51Proud people make fun of me all the
    time.
  But I do not reject your teachings.
52I remember your laws from long ago.
  They comfort me, Lord.
53I become angry with wicked people.
  They have not kept your
    teachings.
54I sing about your demands
  wherever I live.
55Lord, I remember you at night.
  I will obey your teachings.
56This is what I do:
  I follow your orders.

57Lord, you are my share in life.
  I have promised to obey your words.
58I prayed to you with all my heart.
  Be kind to me as you have
    promised.

59I thought about my life,
  and I decided to obey your rules.
60I hurried and did not wait
  to obey your commands.
61Wicked people have surrounded me.
  But I have not forgotten your
    teachings.
62In the middle of the night, I get up
    to thank you
  because your laws are right.
63I am a friend to everyone who fears
    you.
  I am a friend to anyone who
    follows your orders.
64Lord, your love fills the earth.
  Teach me your demands.

65You have done good things for me,
    your servant,
  as you have promised, Lord.
66Teach me wisdom and knowledge
  because I trust your commands.
67Before I suffered, I did wrong.
  But now I obey your word.
68You are good, and you do what is
    good.
  Teach me your demands.
69Proud people have made up lies
    about me.
  But I will follow your orders with
    all my heart.
70Those people have no feelings,
  but I love your teachings.
71It was good for me to suffer
  so I would learn your demands.
72Your teachings are worth more to me
  than thousands of pieces of gold
    and silver.

73You made me and formed me with
    your hands.
  Give me understanding so I can
    learn your commands.
74Let those who fear you rejoice when
    they see me
  because I put my hope in your word.
75Lord, I know that your laws are right.
  And it was right for you to punish
    me.
76Comfort me with your love,
  as you promised me, your servant.
77Have mercy on me so that I may
    live.

I love your teachings.

78 Make the proud people ashamed
  because they lied about me.
But I will think about your orders.
79 Let those who fear you come to me.
  They know your rules.
80 Let me obey your demands perfectly.
  Then I will not be ashamed.

81 I am weak from waiting for you to
  save me.
But I trust your word.
82 My eyes are tired from looking for
  your promise.
When will you comfort me?
83 Even though I am like a leather
  wine bag going up in smoke,
I do not forget your demands.
84 How long will I live?
When will you judge those who
  are hurting me?
85 Proud people have dug pits to trap
  me.
They have nothing to do with your
  teachings.
86 All of your commands can be
  trusted.

Liars are hurting me. Help me!
87 They have almost put me in the
  grave.
But I have not rejected your orders.
88 Give me life by your love
  so I can obey your rules.

89 Lord, your word is everlasting.
  It continues forever in heaven.
90 Your loyalty will continue from now
  on.
You made the earth, and it still
  stands.
91 All things continue to this day
  because of your laws.
All things serve you.
92 If I had not loved your teachings,
  I would have died from my
  sufferings.
93 I will never forget your orders
  because you have given me life by
  them.
94 I am yours. Save me.
I have wanted to know your orders.

The Bible
PSALM 119:97-100

Want to be a wise-guy?

Your parents or a teacher would tell you that being a wise-guy does not mean being smart or intelligent. It means someone who is a smart-aleck or is rude to those in authority. When these verses talk about being a wise person, they mean something totally different. Here, wisdom means knowing what the Bible says about what pleases God and what displeases him. It also means having the courage to live according to what the Bible says.

This is how you can be wiser than your enemies, your teachers, and those older than you. They may know more about the world and may be very intelligent. But if they don't know God's word and live according to it, they are not wise.

You don't want to known as a wise-guy. But if you know God and obey his commandments, you will be a wise person.

To learn more about the Bible, zoom to page 726.

The Bible
PSALM 119:105

Imagine yourself lost in a thick jungle at night. It is so dark, you can't tell whether you're moving forward, sideways, or in a circle. As you push a vine away from your face, you suddenly see in front of you a powerful flashlight. Its beam cuts a line through the blackness. Great! Now you can find your way home. But instead of using that flashlight, you say to yourself, "Only weak people use lights to find their way through the jungle. I'd rather stumble around in the darkness some more." Would that make you *brave*, or *foolish*?

Hopefully you'll never be in that situation. But life can be like a jungle sometimes, dark and confusing. That's when you should remember that the Bible is "like a lamp for [your] feet and a light for [your] path." It will help you find your way out of the "jungle." Even better, it will keep you from getting lost in the first place!

To learn more about the Bible, zoom to page 1130.

95Wicked people are waiting to
       destroy me.
   But I will think about your rules.
96Everything I see has its limits.
   But your commands have none.

97How I love your teachings!
   I think about them all day long.
98Your commands make me wiser
       than my enemies
   because they are mine forever.
99I am wiser than all my teachers
   because I think about your rules.
100I have more understanding than
       the older leaders
   because I follow your orders.
101I have avoided every evil way
   so I could obey your word.
102I haven't stopped obeying your laws
   because you yourself are my
       teacher.
103Your promises are so sweet to me.
   They are like honey to my mouth!
104Your orders give me
       understanding.
   So I hate lying ways.

105Your word is like a lamp for my feet
   and a light for my way.
106I will do what I have promised
   and obey your fair laws.
107I have suffered for a long time.
   Lord, give me life by your word.
108Lord, accept my willing praise.
   And teach me your laws.
109My life is always in danger.
   But I haven't forgotten your
       teachings.
110Wicked people have set a trap for
       me.
   But I haven't disobeyed your
       orders.
111I will follow your rules forever.
   They make me happy.
112I will try to do what you demand
   forever, until the end.
113I hate people who are not
       completely loyal to you.
   But I love your teachings.
114You are my hiding place and my
       shield.
   I trust your word.
115Get away from me, you people who
       do evil,
   so I can keep my God's commands.

[116]Support me as you promised so I
     can live.
  Don't let me be embarrassed
     because of my hopes.
[117]Help me, and I will be saved.
  I will always respect your
     demands.
[118]You reject everyone who ignores
     your demands.
  Their lies mislead them.
[119]You throw away the wicked of the
     world like trash.
  So I will love your rules.
[120]I shake in fear of you.
  I fear your laws.

[121]I have done what is fair and right.
  Don't leave me to my enemies.
[122]Promise that you will help me, your
     servant.
  Don't let proud people hurt me.
[123]My eyes are tired from looking for
     your salvation
  and for your good promise.
[124]Show your love to me, your servant.
  Teach me your demands.
[125]I am your servant. Give me wisdom
  so I can understand your rules.
[126]Lord, it is time for you to do
     something.
  People have disobeyed your
     teachings.

[127]I love your commands
  more than the purest gold.
[128]I respect all your orders.
  So I hate lying ways.

[129]Your rules are wonderful.
  That is why I obey them.
[130]Learning your words gives wisdom
  and understanding for the foolish.
[131]I want to learn your commands.
  I am like a person breathing hard
     and waiting impatiently.
[132]Look at me and have mercy on me
  as you do for those who love you.
[133]Guide my steps as you promised.
  Don't let any sin control me.
[134]Save me from harmful people.
  Then I will obey your orders.
[135]Show your kindness to me, your
     servant.
  Teach me your demands.
[136]Tears stream from my eyes
  because people do not obey your
     teachings.

[137]Lord, you do what is right.
  And your laws are fair.
[138]The rules you commanded are
     right
  and completely trustworthy.

What God Is Like
PSALM 119:137

Maybe you've seen this happen, or even had it happen to you: two teams play their hearts out against each other, the score is tied right down to the last few seconds, when . . . *"TWEET!"* The referee's whistle blows, and the game is decided by his call. The winning team is overjoyed, while the losers walk away stunned, their heads hanging down. And whenever this happens, there is bound to be an argument: was the call right? Did the referee play favorites?

God's rules and decisions are always right. He never plays favorites. His laws tell every person to do what is right and to avoid what is wrong. You can trust that his Word and his laws always point you in the right direction . . . even if you don't win every time.

To learn more about what God is like, zoom to page 849.

139 I am so upset I am worn out.
This is because my enemies have
forgotten your words.
140 Your promises are proven.
I, your servant, love them.
141 I am unimportant and hated.
But I have not forgotten your
orders.
142 Your goodness continues forever.
And your teachings are true.
143 I have had troubles and misery.
But I love your commands.
144 Your rules are good forever.
Help me understand so I can live.

145 Lord, I call to you with all my heart.
Answer me,
and I will keep your demands.
146 I call to you. Save me
so I can obey your rules.
147 I wake up early in the morning and
cry out.
I trust your word.
148 I stay awake all night
so I can think about your promises.
149 Listen to me because of your love.
Lord, give me life by your laws.
150 Those who love evil are near.
They are far from your teachings.
151 But, Lord, you are also near.
And all your commands are true.
152 Long ago I learned from your rules
that you made them to continue
forever.

153 See my suffering and save me
because I have not forgotten your
teachings.
154 Argue my case and save me.
Let me live by your promises.
155 Wicked people are far from being
saved
because they do not want to obey
your demands.
156 Lord, you are very kind.
Give me life by your laws.
157 Many enemies are after me.
But I have not rejected your rules.
158 I see those traitors, and I hate them
because they do not obey what
you say.
159 See how I love your orders.
Lord, give me life by your love.

160 Your words are true from the start.
And all your laws will be fair
forever.

161 Leaders attack me for no reason.
But I fear your law in my heart.
162 I am as happy over your promises
as if I had found a great treasure.
163 I hate and despise lies.
But I love your teachings.
164 Seven times a day I praise you
for your fair laws.
165 Those who love your teachings will
find true peace.
Nothing will defeat them.
166 I am waiting for you to save me,
Lord.
I will obey your commands.
167 I keep your rules.
I love them very much.
168 I keep your orders and rules.
You know everything I do.

169 Hear my cry to you, Lord.
Let your word help me
understand.
170 Listen to my prayer.
Save me as you promised.
171 Let me speak your praise.
You have taught me your
demands.
172 Let me sing about your promises.
All your commands are fair.
173 Always be ready to help me
because I have chosen to obey
your commands.
174 I want you to save me, Lord.
I love your teachings.
175 Let me live so I can praise you.
Your laws will help me.
176 I have wandered like a lost sheep.
Look for your servant because I
have not forgotten your
commands.

A Prayer of Someone Far from Home

A song for going up to worship.

120 When I was in trouble, I
called to the Lord.
And he answered me.
2 Lord, save me from liars
and from those who plan evil.

[3]You who plan evil, what will God do
to you?
How will he punish you?
[4]He will punish you with the sharp
arrows of a warrior
and with burning coals of wood.

[5]How terrible it is to live in the land
of Meshech.
I have to live among the people of
Kedar.
[6]I have lived too long
with people who hate peace.
[7]I want peace and try to talk peace,
but they want war.

The Lord Guards His People

A song for going up to worship.

121 I look up to the hills.
But where does my help
come from?
[2]My help comes from the Lord.
He made heaven and earth.

[3]He will not let you be defeated.
He who guards you never sleeps.
[4]He who guards Israel
never rests or sleeps.
[5]The Lord guards you.
The Lord protects you as the shade
protects you from the sun.
[6]The sun cannot hurt you during the
day.
And the moon cannot hurt you at
night.
[7]The Lord will guard you from all
dangers.
He will guard your life.
[8]The Lord will guard you as you
come and go,
both now and forever.

Happy People in Jerusalem

A song for going up to worship.
Of David.

122 I was happy when they said
to me,
"Let's go to the Temple[d] of the
Lord."
[2]Jerusalem, we are standing
at your gates.
[3]Jerusalem is built as a city

where friends can come together.
[4]The people from the tribes[d] go up
there.
The tribes belong to the Lord.
It is the rule to praise
the Lord at Jerusalem.
[5]There the descendants[d] of David
set their thrones to judge the
people.

[6]Pray for peace in Jerusalem:
"May those who love her be safe.
[7]May there be peace within her walls
and safety within her strong
towers."
[8]To help my relatives and friends,
I repeat, "Let Jerusalem have
peace."
[9]For the sake of the Temple of the
Lord our God,
I wish good for her.

A Prayer for Mercy

A song for going up to worship.

123 Lord, I look up to you.
You live in heaven.
[2]Slaves depend on their masters.
And a female servant depends on
her mistress.
In the same way, we depend on our
God.
We wait for him to show us mercy.

[3]Be kind to us, Lord. Be kind to us
because we have been insulted.
[4]We have suffered many insults from
lazy people
and much cruelty from the proud.

The Lord Saves His People

A song for going up to worship.
Of David.

124 What if the Lord had not been
on our side?
(Let Israel repeat this.)
[2]What if the Lord had not been on
our side
when men attacked us?
[3]When they were angry with us,
they would have swallowed us
alive.
[4]They would have been like a flood
drowning us.

They would have poured over us
like a river.
5 They would have swept us away
like a mighty stream.

6Praise the Lord.
He did not let them chew us up.
7We have escaped like a bird
from the hunter's trap.
The trap has been broken,
and we have escaped.
8Our help comes from the Lord,
who made heaven and earth.

God Protects Those Who Trust Him

A song for going up to worship.

125 Those who trust the Lord are
like Mount Zion.*d*
It sits unmoved forever.
2The mountains surround Jerusalem.
And the Lord surrounds his people
now and forever.

3The wicked will not rule
over those who do right.
If they did, the people who do right
might use their power to do evil.

4Lord, be good to those who are
good,
whose hearts are honest.
5But, Lord, when you punish those
who do evil,
also punish those who stop
following you.

Let there be peace in Israel.

Lord, Give Our Riches Back

A song for going up to worship.

126 When the Lord gave the riches back to Jerusalem,
it seemed as if we were dreaming.
2Then we were filled with laughter,
and we sang happy songs.
Then the other nations said,
"The Lord has done great things
for them."
3The Lord has done great things
for us,
and we are very glad.

4Lord, give us back our riches again.

Do this as you bring streams to
the desert.
5Those who cry as they plant crops
will sing at harvesttime.
6Those who cry
as they carry out the seeds
will return singing
and carrying bundles of grain.

All Good Things Come from God

A song for going up to worship.
Of Solomon.

127 If the Lord doesn't build the
house,
the builders are working for
nothing.
If the Lord doesn't guard the city,
the guards are watching for
nothing.
2It is no use for you to get up early
and stay up late,
working for a living.
The Lord gives sleep to those he
loves.
3Children are a gift from the Lord.
Babies are a reward.
4Sons who are born to a young man
are like arrows in the hand of a
warrior.
5Happy is the man
who has his bag full of arrows.
They will not be defeated
when they fight their enemies in
court.

The Happy Home

A song for going up to worship.

128 Happy are those who respect
the Lord
and obey him.
2You will enjoy what you work for.
You will be blessed with good
things.
3Your wife will give you many
children.
She will be like a vine that
produces a lot of fruit.
Your children will bring you much
good.
They will be like olive branches
that produce many olives.

[4]This is how the man who respects
the Lord
will be blessed.
[5]May the Lord bless you from Mount
Zion.[d]

May you enjoy the good things of
Jerusalem all your life.
[6]May you see your grandchildren.

Let there be peace in Israel.

A Prayer Against the Enemies

A song for going up to worship.

129 They have treated me badly
all my life.
(Let Israel repeat this.)
[2]They have treated me badly all my
life.
But they have not defeated me.
[3]Like farmers plowing, they plowed
over my back,
making long wounds.
[4]But the Lord does what is right.
He has set me free from those
wicked people.

[5]Let those who hate Jerusalem
be turned back in shame.
[6]Let them be like the grass on the
roof.
It dries up before it has grown.
[7]There is not enough of it to fill a
man's hand
or to make into a bundle to fill his
arms.
[8]Let those who pass by them not say,
"May the Lord bless you.
We bless you by the power of the
Lord."

A Prayer for Mercy

A song for going up to worship.

130 Lord, I am in great trouble.
So I call out to you for help.
[2]Lord, hear my voice.
Listen to my prayer for help.
[3]Lord, if you punished people for all
their sins,
no one would be left.
[4]But you forgive us.
So you are respected.

[5]I wait for the Lord to help me.

I trust his word.
[6]I wait for the Lord to help me
more than night watchmen wait
for the dawn,
more than night watchmen wait
for the dawn.

[7]People of Israel, put your hope in
the Lord
because he is loving
and able to save.
[8]He will save Israel
from all their sins.

Childlike Trust in God

A song for going up to worship.
Of David.

131 Lord, my heart is not proud.
I don't look down on others.
I don't do great things,
and I can't do miracles.[d]
[2]But I am calm and quiet.
I am like a baby with its mother.
I am at peace, like a baby with its
mother.

[3]People of Israel, put your hope in
the Lord
now and forever.

In Praise of the Temple

A song for going up to worship.

132 Lord, remember David
and all his suffering.
[2]He made a promise to the Lord.
He made a promise to the Mighty
God of Jacob.
[3]He said, "I will not go home to my
house.
I will not lie down on my bed.
[4]I will not close my eyes
or let myself sleep
[5]until I find a place for the Lord.
I want to provide a home for the
Mighty God of Jacob."

[6]We heard about the Box[d] of the
Agreement in Bethlehem.
We found it at Kiriath Jearim.
[7]Let's go to the Lord's house.
Let's worship at his footstool.
[8]Rise, Lord, and come to your
resting place.

Come with the Holy Box that
  shows your strength.
⁹May your priests do what is right.
  May your people sing for joy.

¹⁰For the sake of your servant David,
  do not reject your appointed king.
¹¹The Lord made a promise to David.
  It was a sure promise that he will
    not take back.
  He promised, "I will make one of
    your descendants^d
  rule as king after you.
¹²But your sons must keep my
    agreement
  and the rules that I teach them.
  Then their sons after them will rule
    on your throne forever and ever."

¹³The Lord has chosen Jerusalem.
  He wants it for his home.
¹⁴He says, "This is my resting place
    forever.
  Here is where I want to stay.
¹⁵I will bless her with plenty of food.
  I will fill her poor with food.
¹⁶I will let her priests receive
    salvation.
  And those who worship me will
    really sing for joy.

¹⁷"I will make a king come from the
    family of David.
  I will provide my appointed one
    descendants^d to rule after him.
¹⁸I will cover his enemies with shame.
  But his crown will shine."

The Love of God's People

A song for going up to worship.
Of David.

133 It is good and pleasant
  when God's people live
    together in peace!
²It is like having perfumed oil
    poured on the priest's head
  and running down his beard.
  It ran down Aaron's beard
    and on to the collar of his robes.
³It is like the dew of Mount Hermon
    falling on the hills of Jerusalem.
  There the Lord gives his blessing
    of life forever.

Temple Guards, Praise the Lord

A song for going up to worship.

134 Praise the Lord, all you servants of the Lord.
You serve at night in the Temple^d
  of the Lord.
²Raise your hands in the Temple
  and praise the Lord.

³May the Lord bless you from Mount
  Zion.^d
  He made heaven and earth.

God Saves, Idols Do Not

135 Praise the Lord!
  Praise the name of the Lord.
  Praise him, you servants of the
    Lord.
²Praise him, you who stand in the
    Lord's Temple^d
  and in the Temple courtyards.
³Praise the Lord, because he is good.
  Sing praises to him, because it is
    pleasant.

⁴The Lord has chosen the people of
    Jacob for himself.
  He has chosen the people of Israel
    for his very own.
⁵I know that the Lord is great.
  Our Lord is greater than all the
    gods.
⁶The Lord does what he wants,
  in heaven and on earth,
  in the seas and the deep oceans.
⁷He brings the clouds from the ends
    of the earth.
  He sends the lightning with the
    rain.
  He brings out the wind from his
    storehouses.

⁸He destroyed the firstborn^d sons in
    Egypt,
  the firstborn of both men and
    animals.
⁹He did many signs and miracles^d in
    Egypt.
  He did amazing things to the king
    and his servants.
¹⁰He defeated many nations
  and killed powerful kings:

God's Love for Us
PSALM 136:1, 23-25

It's easy to believe God loves us when things are going great. But what about when times get tough? Maybe you've had a fight with your best friend . . . your parents are getting a divorce . . . you broke your arm doing something you shouldn't have . . . your family is moving to another city. What about *those* times? Does God still care about you in times like that?

Good news—he does! God does not abandon you when the tough times come. The people of Israel had been in terrible trouble: they had lost their homes, their country, their possessions, and many of their loved ones. They wondered whether God still cared about them, too. The writer of Psalm 136 answered them by repeating over and over, "His love continues forever." Even when they were in trouble and living as slaves, God never forgot about them, and he never stopped loving them.

No matter what your situation is, God's love for you *never* fails.

To find out more about God's love for us, zoom to page 1090.

11 Sihon king of the Amorites,
    Og king of Bashan
    and all the kings of Canaan.
12 Then he gave their land as a gift.
    It was a gift to his people, the
      Israelites.

13 Lord, your name is everlasting.
    Lord, you will be remembered
      from now on.
14 You defend your people.
    You have mercy on your servants.

15 The idols of other nations are made
      of silver and gold.
    They are made by human hands.
16 They have mouths, but they cannot
      speak.
    They have eyes, but they cannot
      see.
17 They have ears, but they cannot hear.
    They have no breath in their
      mouths.
18 The people who make idols and
      trust them
    are all like them.

19 Family of Israel, praise the Lord.

Family of Aaron, praise the Lord.
20 Family of Levi, praise the Lord.
    You people who fear the Lord
      should praise him.
21 You people of Jerusalem, praise the
      Lord on Mount Zion.[d]
Praise the Lord!

God's Love Continues Forever

136 Give thanks to the Lord because he is good.
    His love continues forever.
2 Give thanks to the God over all gods.
    His love continues forever.
3 Give thanks to the Lord of all lords.
    His love continues forever.

4 Only he can do great miracles.[d]
    His love continues forever.
5 With his wisdom he made the skies.
    His love continues forever.
6 He spread out the earth on the seas.
    His love continues forever.
7 He made the sun and the moon.
    His love continues forever.
8 He made the sun to rule the day.
    His love continues forever.

⁹He made the moon and stars to rule
    the night.
  His love continues forever.

¹⁰He killed the firstborn*d* sons of the
    Egyptians.
  His love continues forever.
¹¹He brought the people of Israel out
    of Egypt.
  His love continues forever.
¹²He did it with his great power and
    strength.
  His love continues forever.
¹³He parted the water of the Red Sea.*d*
  His love continues forever.
¹⁴He brought the Israelites through
    the middle of it.
  His love continues forever.
¹⁵But the king of Egypt and his army
    drowned in the Red Sea.
  His love continues forever.

¹⁶He led his people through the desert.
  His love continues forever.
¹⁷He defeated great kings.
  His love continues forever.
¹⁸He killed powerful kings.
  His love continues forever.
¹⁹He defeated Sihon king of the
    Amorites.
  His love continues forever.
²⁰He defeated Og king of Bashan.
  His love continues forever.
²¹He gave their land as a gift.
  His love continues forever.
²²It was a gift to his servants, the
    Israelites.
  His love continues forever.

²³He remembered us when we were
    in trouble.
  His love continues forever.
²⁴He freed us from our enemies.
  His love continues forever.
²⁵He gives food to every living
    creature.
  His love continues forever.

²⁶Give thanks to the God of heaven.
  His love continues forever.

Israelites in Captivity

137 By the rivers in Babylon we
    sat and cried

when we remembered Jerusalem.
²On the poplar trees nearby
  we hung our harps.
³Those who captured us asked us to
    sing.
  Our enemies wanted happy
    songs.
  They said, "Sing us a Temple*d*
    song from Jerusalem!"

⁴But we cannot sing songs about the
    Lord
  while we are in this foreign
    country!
⁵Jerusalem, if I forget you,
  let my right hand lose its skill.
⁶Let my tongue stick to the roof of
    my mouth
  if I do not remember you.
  Let these things happen if I do not
    think about Jerusalem
  as my greatest joy.

⁷Lord, remember what the Edomites
    did
  on the day Jerusalem fell.
  They said, "Tear it down!
  Tear it down to its foundations!"

⁸People of Babylon, you will be
    destroyed.
  The people who pay you back will
    be happy.
  They will punish you for what you
    did to us.
⁹They will grab your babies
  and throw them against the rocks.

A Hymn of Thanksgiving

A song of David.

138 Lord, I will thank you with all
    my heart.
  I will sing to you before the false
    gods.
²I will bow down facing your holy
    Temple.*d*
  And I will thank you for your love
    and loyalty.
  You have made your name and your
    word
  greater than anything.
³On the day I called to you, you
    answered me.

You made me strong and brave.

⁴Lord, let all the kings of the earth
    praise you.
  They have heard the words you
    speak.
⁵They will sing about what the Lord
    has done
  because the Lord's glory is great.

⁶Though the Lord is supreme
  he takes care of those who are not
    proud.
  But he stays away from those who
    are proud.
⁷Lord, even when I have trouble all
    around me,
  you will keep me alive.
  When my enemies are angry,
    you will reach down and save me
    by your power.
⁸Lord, you do everything for me.
  Lord, your love continues forever.
  You made us. Do not leave us.

God Knows Everything

For the director of music. A song
of David.

139
Lord, you have examined me.
  You know all about me.
²You know when I sit down and
    when I get up.
  You know my thoughts before I
    think them.
³You know where I go and where I
    lie down.
  You know well everything I do.
⁴Lord, even before I say a word,
  you already know what I am going
    to say.
⁵You are all around me—in front and
    in back.
  You have put your hand on me.
⁶Your knowledge is amazing to me.
  It is more than I can understand.

⁷Where can I go to get away from
    your Spirit?ᵈ
  Where can I run from you?
⁸If I go up to the skies, you are there.
  If I lie down where the dead are,
    you are there.
⁹If I rise with the sun in the east,

and settle in the west beyond the
    sea,
¹⁰even there you would guide me.
  With your right hand you would
    hold me.

¹¹I could say, "The darkness will hide
    me.
  The light around me will turn into
    night."
¹²But even the darkness is not dark to
    you.
  The night is as light as the day.
  Darkness and light are the same to
    you.

¹³You made my whole being.
  You formed me in my mother's
    body.
¹⁴I praise you because you made me
    in an amazing and wonderful
    way.
  What you have done is wonderful.
  I know this very well.
¹⁵You saw my bones being formed
  as I took shape in my mother's
    body.
  When I was put together there,
¹⁶ you saw my body as it was formed.
  All the days planned for me
  were written in your book
  before I was one day old.

¹⁷God, your thoughts are precious to
    me.
  They are so many!
¹⁸If I could count them,
  they would be more than all the
    grains of sand.
  When I wake up,
  I am still with you.

¹⁹God, I wish you would kill the
    wicked!
  Get away from me, you
    murderers!
²⁰These men say evil things about you.
  Your enemies use your name
    thoughtlessly.
²¹Lord, I hate those who hate you.
  I hate those who rise up against you.
²²I feel only hate for them.
  They are my enemies.

²³God, examine me and know my heart.

Test me and know my thoughts.
24See if there is any bad thing in me.
Lead me in the way you set long
ago.

A Prayer for Protection

For the director of music. A song
of David.

140 Lord, rescue me from evil
people.
Save me from cruel men.
2They make evil plans.
They always start fights.
3They make their tongues sharp as a
snake's.
Their words are like snake poison.
*Selah*ᵈ

4Lord, guard me from the power of
wicked people.
Save me from cruel men
who plan to trip me up.
5Proud men have hidden a trap for
me.
They have spread out a net beside
the road.
They have set traps for me.   *Selah*

6I said to the Lord, "You are my God."
Lord, listen to my prayer for help.
7Lord God, my mighty savior,
you protect me in battle.
8Lord, do not give the wicked what
they want.
Don't let their plans succeed,
or they will become proud.   *Selah*

9Those around me have planned
trouble.
Now let it come to them.
10Let burning coals fall on them.
Throw them into the fire
or into pits from which they
cannot escape.
11Don't let liars settle in the land.
Let evil quickly hunt down cruel
men.

12I know the Lord will get justice for
the poor.
He will defend the needy in court.
13Good people will praise his name.
Honest people will live in his
presence.

A Prayer Not to Sin

A song of David.

141 Lord, I call to you. Come
quickly.
Listen to me when I call to you.
2Let my prayer be like incenseᵈ
placed before you.
Let my praise be like the evening
sacrifice.

3Lord, help me control my tongue.
Help me be careful about what I say.
4Don't let me want to do evil
or join others in doing wrong.
Don't let me eat
with those who do evil.

5If a good man punished me, that
would be kind.
If he corrected me,
that would be like having
perfumed oil on my head.
I shouldn't refuse it.
But I pray against those who do evil.
6 Let their leaders be thrown down
the cliffs.
Then people will know that I have
spoken the truth:
7"The ground is plowed and broken
up.
In the same way, our bones have
been scattered at the grave."

8Lord God, I look to you for help.
I trust in you. Don't let me die.
9Protect me from the traps they set
for me
and from the net evil people have
spread.
10Let the wicked fall into their own pits.
And let me pass by safely.

A Prayer for Safety

A maskilᵈ of David when he was
in the cave. A prayer.

142 I cry out to the Lord.
I pray to the Lord for mercy.
2I pour out my problems to him.
I tell him my troubles.
3When I am afraid,
you, Lord, know the way out.
In the path where I walk,
a trap is hidden for me.

⁴Look around me and see.
  No one cares about me.
I have no place of safety.
  No one cares if I live.

⁵Lord, I cry out to you.
  I say, "You are my protection.
  You are all I want in this life."
⁶Listen to my cry
  because I am helpless.
Save me from those who are
    chasing me.
  They are too strong for me.
⁷Free me from my prison.
  Then I will praise your name.
Then the good people will surround
    me
  because you have taken care of me.

A Prayer Not to Be Killed

A song of David.

143 Lord, hear my prayer.
  Listen to my cry for mercy.
Come to help me
  because you are loyal and good.
²Don't judge me, your servant,
  because no one alive is right
    before you.
³My enemies are chasing me.
  They have crushed me to the
    ground.
They have made me live in darkness
  like those who are long dead.
⁴I am afraid.
  My courage is gone.

⁵I remember what happened long ago.
  I recall everything you have done.
  I think about all you have made.
⁶I lift my hands to you in prayer.
  As a dry land needs rain, I thirst
    for you.   *Selahᵈ*

⁷Lord, answer me quickly.
  I am getting weak.
Don't turn away from me,
  or I will be like those who are dead.
⁸Tell me in the morning about your
    love.
  I trust you.
Show me what I should do
  because my prayers go up to you.
⁹Lord, save me from my enemies.

I come to you for safety.
¹⁰Teach me to do what you want,
  because you are my God.
Let your good Spiritᵈ
  lead me on level ground.

¹¹Lord, let me live
  so people will praise you.
In your goodness
  save me from my troubles.
¹²In your love defeat my enemies.
  Destroy all those who trouble me
  because I am your servant.

A Prayer for Victory

Of David.

144 Praise the Lord, my Rock.ᵈ
  He trains me for war.
  He trains me for battle.
²He gives me love and protects me
  like a strong, walled city.
  He is my place of safety and my
    Savior.
He is my shield and my protection.
  He helps me rule my people.

³Lord, why is man important to you?
  Why do you even think about a
    human being?
⁴A man is like a breath.
  His life is like a passing shadow.

⁵Lord, tear open the sky and come
    down.
  Touch the mountains so they will
    smoke.
⁶Send the lightning and scatter my
    enemies.
  Shoot your arrows and force them
    away.
⁷Reach down from above.
  Pull me out of this sea of enemies.
  Rescue me from these foreigners.
⁸They are liars.
  They are dishonest.

⁹God, I will sing a new song to you.
  I will play to you on the ten-
    stringed harp.
¹⁰You give victory to kings.
  You save your servant David from
    cruel swords.
¹¹Save me, rescue me from these
    foreigners.

They are liars.
They are dishonest.

¹²Let our sons in their youth
grow like strong trees.
Let our daughters be
like the decorated stones in the
Temple.ᵈ
¹³Let our barns be filled
with crops of all kinds.
Let our sheep in the fields have
thousands and thousands of lambs.
¹⁴ Let our cattle be strong.
Let no one break in.
Let there be no war.
Let there be no screams in our
streets.

¹⁵Happy are those who are like this.
Happy are the people whose God
is the Lord.

Praise to God the King

A song of praise. Of David.

145 I praise your greatness, my
God the King.
I will praise you forever and ever.
²I will praise you every day.
I will praise you forever and ever.
³The Lord is great. He is worthy of
our praise.
No one can understand how great
he is.

⁴Parents will tell their children what
you have done.
They will retell your mighty acts,
⁵wonderful majesty and glory.
And I will think about your
miracles.ᵈ
⁶They will tell about the amazing
things you do.
I will tell how great you are.
⁷They will remember your great
goodness.
They will sing about your fairness.

⁸The Lord is kind and shows mercy.
He does not become angry quickly
but is full of love.
⁹The Lord is good to everyone.
He is merciful to all he has made.
¹⁰Lord, everything you have made
will praise you.

Those who belong to you will
bless you.
¹¹They will tell about the glory of
your kingdom.
They will speak about your power.
¹²Then everyone will know what
powerful things you do.
They will know about the glory
and majesty of your kingdom.
¹³Your kingdom will continue forever.
And you will be King from now on.

The Lord will keep his promises.
With love he takes care of all he
has made.
¹⁴The Lord helps those who have
been defeated.
He takes care of those who are in
trouble.
¹⁵All living things look to you for food.
And you give it to them at the right
time.
¹⁶You open your hand,
and you satisfy all living things.

¹⁷Everything the Lord does is right.
With love he takes care of all he
has made.
¹⁸The Lord is close to everyone who
prays to him,
to all who truly pray to him.
¹⁹He gives those who fear him what
they want.
He listens when they cry, and he
saves them.
²⁰The Lord protects everyone who
loves him.
But he will destroy the wicked.

²¹I will praise the Lord.
Let everyone praise his holy name
forever.

Praise God Who Helps the Weak

146 Praise the Lord!
My whole being, praise the
Lord.
²I will praise the Lord all my life.
I will sing praises to my God as
long as I live.

³Do not put your trust in princes
or other people, who cannot save
you.

⁴When people die, they are buried.
  Then all of their plans come to an
    end.
⁵Happy are those who are helped by
    the God of Jacob.
  Their hope is in the Lord their God.
⁶He made heaven and earth,
  the sea and everything in it.
  He remains loyal forever.
⁷The Lord does what is fair for those
    who have been wronged.
  He gives food to the hungry.
  The Lord sets the prisoners free.
⁸ The Lord gives sight to the blind.
  The Lord lifts up people who are in
    trouble.
  The Lord loves those who do right.
⁹The Lord protects the foreigners.
  He defends the orphans and
    widows.
  But he overthrows the wicked.

¹⁰The Lord will be King forever.
  Jerusalem, your God is everlasting.

Praise the Lord!

Praise God Who Helps His People

147 Praise the Lord!
    It is good to sing praises to
  our God.
  It is good and pleasant to praise
    him.
²The Lord rebuilds Jerusalem.
  He brings back the scattered
    Israelites who were taken
    captive.
³He heals the brokenhearted.
  He bandages their wounds.
⁴He counts the stars
  and names each one.
⁵Our Lord is great and very powerful.
  There is no limit to what he knows.
⁶The Lord defends those who are not
    proud.
  But he throws the wicked to the
    ground.
⁷Sing praises to the Lord.
  Praise our God with harps.
⁸He fills the sky with clouds.
  He sends rain to the earth.

He makes grass grow on the hills.
⁹He gives food to cattle
  and to the little birds that call.
¹⁰He is not pleased by the strength of
    a horse
  or the power of a man.
¹¹The Lord is pleased with those who
    fear him,
  with those who trust his love.

¹²Jerusalem, praise the Lord.
  Jerusalem, praise your God.
¹³He makes your city gates strong.
  He blesses the people inside.
¹⁴He brings peace to your country.
  He fills you with the finest grain.

¹⁵He gives a command to the earth,
  and it quickly obeys him.
¹⁶He spreads the snow like wool.
  He scatters the frost like ashes.
¹⁷He throws down hail like rocks.
  No one can stand the cold he
    sends.
¹⁸Then he gives a command, and it
    melts.
  He sends the breezes, and the
    waters flow.

¹⁹He gave his word to Jacob.
  He gave his laws and demands to
    Israel.
²⁰He didn't do this for any other nation.
  They don't know his laws.

Praise the Lord!

The World Should Praise the Lord

148 Praise the Lord!
    Praise the Lord from the
  heavens.
  Praise him high above the earth.
²Praise him, all you angels.
  Praise him, all you armies of
    heaven.
³Praise him, sun and moon.
  Praise him, all you shining stars.
⁴Praise him, highest heavens
  and you waters above the sky.
⁵Let them praise the Lord
  because they were created by his
    command.

⁶He set them in place forever and ever.
   He made a law that will never end.

⁷Praise the Lord from the earth.
   Praise him, you large sea animals
      and all the oceans.
⁸Praise him, lightning and hail, snow
      and clouds,
   and stormy winds that obey him.
⁹Praise him, mountains and all hills,
   fruit trees and all cedar trees.
¹⁰Praise him, you wild animals and all
      cattle,
   small crawling animals and birds.
¹¹Praise him, you kings of the earth
      and all nations,
   princes and all rulers of the earth.
¹²Praise him, you young men and
      women,
   old people and children.

¹³Praise the Lord.
   He alone is great.
   He is greater than heaven and
      earth.
¹⁴God has given his people a king.
   He should be praised by all who
      belong to him.
   He should be praised by the
      Israelites, the people closest to
      his heart.

   Praise the Lord!

Praise the God of Israel

149 Praise the Lord!
         Sing a new song to the Lord.
   Sing his praise in the meeting of
      his people.

²Let the Israelites be happy because
      of God, their Maker.
   Let the people of Jerusalem rejoice
      because of their King.

³They should praise him with
      dancing.
   They should praise him with
      tambourines[d] and harps.
⁴The Lord is pleased with his people.
   He saves those who are not proud.
⁵Let those who worship him rejoice
      in his glory.
   Let them sing for joy even in bed!

⁶Let them shout his praise
   with their two-edged swords in
      their hands.
⁷They will punish the nations.
   They will defeat the people.
⁸They will put those kings in chains
   and those important men in iron
      bands.
⁹They will punish them as God has
      written.
   God is honored by all who worship
      him.

   Praise the Lord!

Praise the Lord with Music

150 Praise the Lord!
         Praise God in his Temple.[d]
   Praise him in his mighty heaven.
²Praise him for his strength.
   Praise him for his greatness.
³Praise him with trumpet blasts.
   Praise him with harps and lyres.[d]
⁴Praise him with tambourines[d] and
      dancing.
   Praise him with stringed
      instruments and flutes.
⁵Praise him with loud cymbals.
   Praise him with crashing cymbals.
⁶Let everything that breathes praise
      the Lord.

   Praise the Lord!

PROVERBS

*Wise Teachings
for God's People*

Why Proverbs Is Important

1 These are the wise words of Solomon son of David. Solomon was king of Israel.

²They teach wisdom and self-control.
They give understanding.
³They will teach you how to be wise and self-controlled.
They will teach you what is honest and fair and right.
⁴They give the ability to think to those with little knowledge.
They give knowledge and good sense to the young.
⁵Wise people should also listen to them and learn even more.
Even smart people will find wise advice in these words.

⁶Then they will be able to understand wise words and stories.
They will understand the words of wise men and their riddles.

⁷Knowledge begins with respect for the Lord.
But foolish people hate wisdom and self-control.

Warnings Against Evil

⁸My child, listen to your father's teaching.
And do not forget your mother's advice.
⁹Their teaching will beautify your life.
It will be like flowers in your hair or a chain around your neck.

Temptation
PROVERBS 1:10

Have you ever played "follow the leader"? It's a fun game, especially if you and your friends think of crazy ways to walk. But if the leader begins to do something dangerous or wrong, it's time to stop the game. It's not worth getting someone hurt.

King Solomon gives the same advice in this verse. Solomon understood that we follow leaders in life, too. Everyone wants to be liked and to be part of the group. Just like the game, though, it is time to stop following when we are being led or pushed into doing something wrong or unwise. It is not worth the damage we can do to ourselves or someone else.

It's OK to be part of a group. It's fine to want to do things with our friends. But Proverbs warns us to draw the line at following others into sin or foolish actions.

To learn more about temptation, zoom to page 1266.

¹⁰My child, sinners will try to lead you
into sin.
But do not follow them.
¹¹They might say, "Come with us.
Let's ambush and kill someone.
Let's attack some harmless person
just for fun.
¹²Let's swallow them alive, as death
does.
Let's swallow them whole, as the
grave does.
¹³We will take all kinds of valuable
things.
We will fill our houses with what
we steal.
¹⁴Come join us,
and we will share with you what we
steal."
¹⁵My child, do not go along with them.
Do not do what they do.
¹⁶They run to do evil.
They are quick to kill.
¹⁷It is useless to spread out a net
right where the birds can see it!
¹⁸These men are setting their own
trap.
They will only catch themselves!
¹⁹All greedy people end up this way.
Greed takes away the life of the
greedy person.

Wisdom Speaks

²⁰Wisdom is like a good woman who
shouts in the street.
She raises her voice in the city
squares.
²¹She cries out in the noisy street.
She makes her speech at the city
gates:
²²"You foolish people! How long do
you want to stay foolish?
How long will you make fun of
wisdom?
How long will you hate knowledge?
²³Listen when I correct you.
I will tell you what's in my heart.
I will tell you what I am thinking.
²⁴I called, but you refused to listen.
I held out my hand, but you paid
no attention.
²⁵You did not follow my advice.
You did not want me to correct you.

²⁶So I will laugh when you are in
trouble.
I will make fun when disaster
happens to you.
²⁷Disaster will come over you like a
storm.
Trouble will strike you like a
whirlwind.
Pain and trouble will overwhelm you.

²⁸"Then you will call out to me.
But I will not answer.
You will look for me.
But you will not find me.
²⁹You rejected knowledge.
You did not choose to respect the
Lord.
³⁰You did not accept my advice.
You rejected my correction.
³¹So you will get what you deserve.
You will get what you planned for
others.
³²Fools wander away and get killed.
They are destroyed because they
do not care.
³³But those who listen to me will live
in safety.
They will be safe, without fear of
being hurt."

Rewards of Wisdom

2 My child, believe what I say.
And remember what I command
you.
²Listen to wisdom.
Try with all your heart to gain
understanding.
³Cry out for wisdom.
Beg for understanding.
⁴Search for it as you would for silver.
Hunt for it like hidden treasure.
⁵Then you will understand what it
means to respect the Lord.
Then you will begin to know God.
⁶Only the Lord gives wisdom.
Knowledge and understanding
come from him.
⁷He stores up wisdom for those who
are honest.
Like a shield he protects those who
are innocent.
⁸He guards those who are fair to others.

Whit's Wisdom: Wisdom • Proverbs 2

I guess my white hair tells you I've been around for a few years, kids. I've learned a lot, but I certainly haven't learned everything. In fact, every day I learn something new. God made this world so wonderful that there's always more to discover. That's one reason I like to live in Odyssey. The name of our town means *journey, adventure,* or *quest.* I'll tell you about my odyssey: I'm having a great adventure discovering wisdom! And I'm so glad to have you traveling with me. The best time to start becoming wise is when you are young! The best place to find wisdom is in the Bible, God's Word.

This note from me is located in one of the places where the Bible speaks a lot about wisdom. Read Proverbs 2:1-8. How many times can you find the word *wisdom* in these eight verses? Who gives us wisdom (look at verse 6)? How are we supposed to look for wisdom (look at verse 4)?

Now I know some of you are asking, "But Mr. Whittaker, what *is* wisdom? How will I know when I have found some?"

That's a good question. It shows that you're already on the treasure hunt for wisdom. You want to know what you're looking for. Here's the answer: A wise person is someone who has learned to live the way God wants us to live. Wisdom, then, is knowing and understanding God.

Gaining wisdom is a lot like putting on a special pair of sunglasses. When you look through colored lenses, they change everything you see. The more wisdom you have, the more you will see life differently. God wants you to see everything the way he sees it! That's why gaining wisdom is so important and so exciting. Never, ever stop looking for God's wisdom!

Related passages: Proverbs 3:5-8; James 3:13-18.

Teacher/Parent Hint: Challenge your students/children to read through Proverbs during a month. Have them write down at least one memorable proverb from each chapter. One grandparent offered his grandchildren a token financial reward for each time they read through Proverbs. That challenge worked!

Create a treasure hunt for the children by hiding written proverbs all around the room. Have them "search for them like silver."

He protects those who are loyal to him.
⁹Then you will understand what is honest and fair and right.
You will understand what is good to do.
¹⁰You will have wisdom in your heart.

And knowledge will be pleasing to you.
¹¹Good sense will protect you.
Understanding will guard you.
¹²It will keep you from doing evil.
It will save you from people whose words are bad.

¹³Such people do not do what is right.
  They do what is evil.
¹⁴They enjoy doing wrong.
  They are happy to do what is
    crooked and evil.
¹⁵What they do is wrong.
  Their ways are dishonest.

¹⁶It will save you from the unfaithful
    wife
  who tries to lead you into adultery*d*
    with pleasing words.
¹⁷Such women leave the husbands they
    married when they were young.
  They forget the promise they made
    before God.
¹⁸If you go to her house, you are on
    your way to death.
  What she does leads to death.
¹⁹No one who goes to her comes back.
  He will not continue to live.

²⁰But wisdom will help you be a good
    person.
  It will help you do what is right.
²¹Those who are honest will stay in
    the land.
  Those who are innocent will remain
    in it.
²²But evil people will be removed from
    the land.
  The unfaithful will be thrown out
    of it.

Advice to Children

3 My child, do not forget my teaching.
    Keep my commands in mind.
²Then you will live a long time.
  And your life will be successful.

³Don't ever stop being kind and
    truthful.
  Let kindness and truth show in all
    you do.
  Write them down in your mind as
    if on a tablet.
⁴Then you will be respected
  and pleasing to both God and men.

⁵Trust the Lord with all your heart.
  Don't depend on your own
    understanding.
⁶Remember the Lord in everything
    you do.

**Trust the Lord with all
your heart.
Don't depend on your
own understanding.**
• Proverbs 3:5

And he will give you success.

⁷Don't depend on your own wisdom.
  Respect the Lord and refuse to do
    wrong.
⁸Then your body will be healthy.
  And your bones will be strong.

⁹Honor the Lord by giving him part
    of your wealth.
  Give him the firstfruits*d* from all
    your crops.
¹⁰Then your barns will be full.
  And your wine barrels will overflow
    with new wine.

¹¹My child, do not reject the Lord's
    discipline.
  And don't become angry when he
    corrects you.
¹²The Lord corrects those he loves,
  just as a father corrects the child
    that he likes.

¹³Happy is the person who finds
    wisdom.
  And happy is the person who gets
    understanding.
¹⁴Wisdom is worth more than silver.
  It brings more profit than gold.
¹⁵Wisdom is more precious than rubies.
  Nothing you want is equal to it.
¹⁶With her right hand wisdom offers
    you a long life.
  With her left hand she gives you
    riches and honor.
¹⁷Wisdom will make your life pleasant.
  It will bring you peace.
¹⁸As a tree makes fruit, wisdom gives
    life to those who use it.
  Everyone who uses wisdom will
    be happy.
¹⁹Using his wisdom, the Lord made
    the earth.

Using his understanding, he set the
     sky in place.
20Using his knowledge, he made rivers
     flow from underground springs.
And he made the clouds drop rain
     on the earth.

21My child, hold on to wisdom and
     reason.
Don't let them out of your sight!
22They will give you life.
     Like a necklace, they will beautify
     your life.
23Then you will go on your way in
     safety.
And you will not get hurt.
24You won't need to be afraid when you
     lie down.
When you lie down, your sleep will
     be peaceful.
25You won't need to be afraid of trouble
     coming suddenly.
You won't need to fear the ruin
     that comes to the wicked.
26The Lord will keep you safe.
He will keep you from being trapped.

27Whenever you are able,
     do good to people who need help.
28If you have what your neighbor
     asks for,
     don't say to him,
"Come back later. I will give it to
     you tomorrow."
29Don't make plans to hurt your
     neighbor.
He lives nearby and trusts you.
30Don't accuse a man for no good
     reason.
Don't accuse him if he has not
     harmed you.
31Don't be jealous of men who use
     violence.
And don't choose to be like them.
32The Lord hates those who do wrong.
But he is a friend to those who are
     honest.
33The Lord will put a curse on the evil
     person's house.
But he will bless the home of people
     who do what is right.
34The Lord laughs at those who laugh
     at him.

But he is kind to those who are not
     proud.
35Wise people will receive honor.
But foolish people will be disgraced.

Wisdom Is Important

4 My children, listen to your father's
     teaching.
Pay attention so you will understand.
2What I am telling you is good.
Do not forget what I teach you.
3I was once a young boy in my
     father's house.
I was like an only child to my mother.
4And my father taught me and said,
"Hold on to my words with all
     your heart.
Keep my commands and you
     will live.

"It takes a lot
more than growing
a beard to become
a wise person. Just
read Proverbs 4:1-9
to find out what is
really important."

5Get wisdom and understanding.
Don't forget or ignore my words.
6Use wisdom, and it will take care of
     you.
Love wisdom, and it will keep you
     safe.
7Wisdom is the most important
     thing. So get wisdom.
If it costs everything you have, get
     understanding.
8Believe in the value of wisdom, and it
     will make you great.
Use it, and it will bring honor to you.
9Like flowers in your hair, it will
     beautify your life.
Like a crown, it will make you look
     beautiful."

10My child, listen and accept what I say.
Then you will have a long life.
11I am guiding you in wisdom.
And I am leading you to do what is
     right.

¹²Nothing will hold you back.
You will not be overwhelmed.
¹³Always remember what you have
been taught.
Don't let go of it.
Keep safe all that you have learned.
It is the most important thing in
your life.
¹⁴Don't follow the ways of the wicked.
Don't do what evil people do.
¹⁵Avoid their ways. Don't go near
what they do.
Stay away from them and keep on
going.
¹⁶They cannot sleep until they do evil.
They cannot rest until they hurt
someone.
¹⁷They fill themselves with
wickedness and cruelty
as if they were eating bread and
drinking wine.

¹⁸The way of the good person is like
the light of dawn.
It grows brighter and brighter until
it is full daylight.
¹⁹But the wicked are like those who
stumble in the dark.
They can't even see what has hurt
them.

²⁰My child, pay attention to my
words.
Listen closely to what I say.
²¹Don't ever forget my words.
Keep them deep within your heart.
²²These words are the secret to life
for those who find them.
They bring health to the whole
body.
²³Be very careful about what you think.
Your thoughts run your life.
²⁴Don't use your mouth to tell lies.
Don't ever say things that are
not true.
²⁵Keep your eyes focused on what
is right.
Keep looking straight ahead to what
is good.
²⁶Be careful what you do.
Always do what is right.
²⁷Do not do anything unless it is right.
Stay away from evil.

Warning About Adultery

5 My son, pay attention to my wisdom.
Listen to my words of
understanding.
²Be careful to use good sense.
Watch what you say.
³The words of another man's wife
may seem sweet as honey.
Her words may be as pleasant as
olive oil.
⁴But in the end she will bring you
sorrow. She will cause you
pain like a two-edged sword.
⁵She is on the way to death.
Her steps are headed straight to
the grave.
⁶She gives no thought to life.
She does not know that her ways
are wrong.

⁷Now, my sons, listen to me.
Don't ignore what I say.
⁸Stay away from such a woman.
Don't even go near the door of
her house.
⁹If you do, you will give your riches
to others.
And the best years of your life will
be given to someone who
is cruel.
¹⁰Strangers will enjoy your wealth.
And what you worked so hard for
will go to someone else.
¹¹You will groan at the end of your life.
Then your health will be gone.
¹²Then you will say, "I hated self-
control!
I would not listen when I was
corrected!
¹³I would not listen to my teachers.
I paid no attention to what they
taught me.
¹⁴I have come very close to being
completely ruined
in front of a whole group of people."

¹⁵Be faithful to your own wife.
She is like your own well of water
from which you drink.
¹⁶You wouldn't drink from streams
flowing in the city streets or
squares.
So be satisfied with your wife,

not those outside your home.

¹⁷These things are yours alone.
Don't share them with strangers.

¹⁸Be happy with the wife
you married when you were young.
She gives you joys
as your fountain gives you water.

¹⁹She is as lovely and graceful as
a deer.
Let her love always make you happy.
Let her love always hold you
captive.

²⁰My son, don't be held captive by a
woman who takes part in
adultery.^d
Don't hold another man's wife.

²¹The Lord sees everything you do.
He watches where you go.

²²An evil man will be caught in his evil
ways.
He will be tied up by his sins as if
they were ropes.

²³He will die because he does not
control himself.
He will be held captive by his own
foolishness.

Dangers of Being Foolish

6 My child, be careful about giving a
guarantee for somebody else.
Be careful about promising to pay
what someone else owes.

²You might get trapped by what you
say.
You might be caught by your own
words.

³My child, you might do this and be
under somebody's control.
Then here is how to get free.
Go to your neighbor and don't be
proud.
Beg him to free you from your
promise.

⁴Don't go to sleep.
Don't even rest your eyes.

⁵But free yourself like a deer running
from a hunter.
Free yourself like a bird flying away
from a trapper.

⁶Go watch the ants, you lazy person.
Watch what they do and be wise.

⁷Ants have no commander.
They have no leader or ruler.

⁸But they store up food in the summer.
They gather their supplies at
harvest.

⁹How long will you lie there, you lazy
person?
When will you get up from
sleeping?

¹⁰You sleep a little; you take a nap.
You fold your hands and rest.

¹¹So you will be as poor as if you had
been robbed.
You will have as little as if you had
been held up.

¹²Some people are wicked and no
good.
They go around telling lies.

¹³They wink with their eyes and signal
with their feet.
They make signs with their fingers.

¹⁴They make evil plans in their hearts.
They are always causing trouble.

¹⁵So trouble will strike them in an
instant.
Suddenly they will be hurt beyond
cure.

¹⁶There are six things the Lord hates.
There are seven things he cannot
stand:

¹⁷   a proud look,
a lying tongue,
hands that kill innocent people,

¹⁸   a mind that thinks up evil plans,
feet that are quick to do evil,

¹⁹   a witness who tells lies
and a man who causes trouble
among brothers.

Warning About Adultery

²⁰My son, keep your father's
commands.
Don't forget your mother's teaching.

²¹Remember their words forever.
Let it be as if they were tied around
your neck.

²²They will guide you when you walk.
They will guard you while you
sleep.
They will speak to you when you
are awake.

23Their commands are like a lamp.
Their teaching is like a light.
And the correction that comes
from them
helps you have life.
24Such teaching will keep you from
sinful women
and from the pleasing words of
another man's unfaithful wife.
25Don't want her because she is
beautiful.
Don't let her capture you by the
way she looks at you.
26A prostitute*d* may leave you with only
a loaf of bread.
And a woman who takes part in
adultery*d* may cost you your life.
27You cannot carry hot coals against
your chest
without burning your clothes.
28And you cannot walk on hot coals
without burning your feet.
29The same thing happens if you have
sexual relations with another
man's wife.
Anyone who does so will be
punished.

30People do not hate a thief
when he steals because he is
hungry.
31But if he is caught, he must pay back
seven times what he stole.
It may cost him everything he owns.
32A man who takes part in adultery
doesn't have any sense.
He will destroy himself.
33He will be beaten up and disgraced.
And his shame will never go away.
34Jealousy makes a husband very
angry.
He will have no mercy when he
gets even.
35He will accept no payment for the
wrong.
He will take no money, no matter
how much it is.

The Woman of Adultery

7 My son, remember what I say.
Treasure my commands.
2Obey my commands, and you will
live.

Protect my teachings as you would
your own eyes.
3Remind yourself of them.
Write them down in your mind as
if on a tablet.
4Be good to wisdom as if she were
your sister.
Make understanding your closest
friend.
5Wisdom and understanding will
keep you away from adultery.*d*
They will keep you away from the
unfaithful wife and her pleasing
words.

6I once was standing at the window
of my house.
I looked out through the shutters.
7I saw some foolish, young men.
I noticed one of them who had no
wisdom.
8He was walking down the street
near the corner.
He was on the road leading to her
house.
9It was the twilight of the evening.
The darkness of the night was just
beginning.
10Then the woman approached him.
She was dressed like a prostitute*d*
and was planning to trick him.
11She was a loud and stubborn woman.
She never stayed at home.
12She was always out in the streets or
in the city squares.
She was always waiting around on
the street corners.
13She grabbed him and kissed him.
Without shame she said to him,
14"I made my fellowship offering and
have the meat at home.
I have kept my special promises.
15So I have come out to meet you.
I have been looking for you and
have found you!
16I have covered my bed
with colored sheets from Egypt.
17I have made my bed smell sweet
with myrrh,*d* aloes*d* and cinnamon.
18Come, let's make love until morning.
Let's enjoy each other's love!
19My husband is not home.
He has gone on a long trip.

²⁰He took a lot of money with him.
  And he won't be home for weeks."
²¹By her clever words she made him
    give in.
  By her pleasing words she led him
    into doing wrong.
²²All at once he followed her.
  He was like an ox being led to the
    butcher.
  He was like a deer caught in a trap.
²³ But quickly an arrow shot through
    his liver.
  He was like a bird caught in a trap.
  He didn't know what he did would
    kill him.

²⁴Now, my sons, listen to me.
  Pay attention to what I say.
²⁵Don't let yourself be tricked by the
    woman who is guilty of
    adultery.
  Don't join her in her evil actions.
²⁶She has ruined many good men.
  Many have died because of her.
²⁷Going to her house is like taking the
    road to death.
  That road leads down to where the
    dead are.

Listen to Wisdom

8 Like a person, wisdom calls out to
    you.
  Understanding raises her voice.
²On the hilltops along the road
  and at the crossroads, she stands
    calling.
³She stands beside the city gates.
  At the entrances into the city, she
    calls out:
⁴"People, I'm calling out to you.
  I am shouting to all people.
⁵You who do not know better, get
    the ability to think.
  You who are foolish, get
    understanding.
⁶Listen. I have important things to say.
  What I tell you is right.
⁷What I say is true.
  I hate it when people speak evil.
⁸Everything I say is honest.
  Nothing I say is crooked or false.
⁹People with good sense know that
    what I say is true.

People with knowledge know that
    my words are right.
¹⁰Choose my teachings instead of
    silver.
  Choose knowledge rather than the
    finest gold.
¹¹Wisdom is more precious than
    rubies.
  Nothing you want is equal to it.

¹²"I am wisdom, and I have the ability
    to think.
  I also have knowledge and good
    sense.
¹³If you respect the Lord, you also will
    hate evil.
  It is wise to hate pride and
    bragging,
  evil ways and lies.
¹⁴I have good sense and advice.
  I have understanding and power.
¹⁵Kings use me to govern.
  And rulers use me to make fair
    laws.
¹⁶Princes use me to lead.
  So do important men and all good
    judges.
¹⁷I love those who love me.
  Those who want me find me.
¹⁸Riches and honor are mine.
  So are wealth and lasting success.
¹⁹What I give is better than the finest
    gold.
  What I give is better than pure
    silver.
²⁰I do what is right.
  I do what is fair.
²¹I give wealth to those who love me.
  I fill them with treasures.

²²"I, wisdom, was with God when he
    began his work.
  This was before he made anything
    else long ago.
²³I was appointed in the very
    beginning,
  even before the world began.
²⁴I began before there were oceans.
  There were no springs overflowing
    with water.
²⁵I began before the hills were there.
  The mountains had not even been
    put in place.

26God still had not made the earth or
fields.
He had not even made the first dust
of the earth.
27I was there when God put the skies
in place,
when he stretched the horizon over
the oceans.
28I was there when he made the clouds
above.
I was there when he put the
fountains in the oceans.
29I was there when he ordered the sea
not to go beyond the borders he
had set for it.
I was there when he laid the earth's
foundation.
30 I was like a child by his side.
I was happy every day
and enjoyed being in his presence.
31I enjoyed the whole world.
And I was happy with all its people.

32"Now, my children, listen to me.
Those who follow my ways are
happy.
33Listen to my teaching, and you will
be wise.
Do not ignore it.
34Those who listen to me are happy.
They stand watching at my door
every day.
They are at my open doorway,
wanting to be with me.
35Whoever finds me finds life.
And the Lord will be pleased with
him.
36Whoever does not find me hurts
himself.
Those who hate me love death."

Being Wise or Foolish

9 Wisdom has built her house.
She has made its seven columns.
2She has prepared her food and wine.
She has set her table.
3She has sent out her servant girls.
She calls out from the highest place
in the city.
4She says to those who are not wise,
"Come in here, you foolish people!
5Come and eat my food.
And drink the wine I have prepared.

6Stop your foolish ways, and you
will live.
Be a person of understanding.

7"If you correct someone who makes
fun of wisdom, you will get
insulted.
If you correct an evil person, you
will get hurt.
8Do not correct someone who makes
fun of wisdom, or he will hate
you.
But correct a wise man, and he will
love you.
9Teach a wise man, and he will
become even wiser.
Teach a good man, and he will learn
even more.

10"Wisdom begins with respect for the
Lord.
And understanding begins with
knowing God, the Holy One.
11If you live wisely, you will live a long
time.
Wisdom will add years to your life.
12The wise person is rewarded by his
wisdom.
But a person who makes fun of
wisdom will suffer for it."

13Foolishness is like a loud woman.
She does not have wisdom or
knowledge.
14She sits at the door of her house.
It is at the highest place in the city.
15She calls out to those who are
passing by.
They are minding their own
business.
16She says to those who are not wise,
"Come in here, you foolish people!
17Stolen water is sweeter.
Stolen food tastes better."
18But these people don't know that
everyone dies who goes there.
They don't realize that her guests
are deep in the grave.

The Proverbs of Solomon

10 These are the wise words of
Solomon:

A wise son makes his father happy.

But a foolish son makes his mother sad.

2 Riches gotten by doing wrong have no value.
But right living will save you from death.

3 The Lord does not let people who live right go hungry.
But he does not let evil people get what they hunger for.

4 A lazy person will end up poor.
But a hard worker will become rich.

5 A son who gathers crops when they are ready is wise.
But the son who sleeps through the harvest is a disgrace.

6 People who do what is right will have rich blessings.
But the wicked will be overwhelmed by violence.

7 Good people will be remembered as a blessing.
But evil people will soon be forgotten.

8 A wise person does what he is told.
But a talkative fool will be ruined.

9 The honest person will live safely.
But the one who is dishonest will be caught.

10 A wink may get you into trouble.
And foolish talk will lead to your ruin.

11 Like a fountain of water, the words of a good person give life.
But the words of the wicked contain nothing but violence.

12 Hatred stirs up trouble.
But love forgives all wrongs.

13 You can expect smart people to speak wisely.
But people without wisdom can expect to be punished.

14 Wise people don't tell everything they know.
But a foolish person talks too much and is ruined.

15 Having lots of money protects the rich.
But having no money destroys the poor.

16 Good people are rewarded with life.
But evil people are paid back with punishment.

17 The person who accepts correction is on the way to life.
But the person who ignores correction will be ruined.

18 Whoever hides his hate is a liar.
Whoever tells lies is a fool.

19 If you talk a lot, you are sure to sin.
If you are wise, you will keep quiet.

20 The words of a good person are like pure silver.
But an evil person's thoughts are worth little.

21 A good person's words will help many others.
But a foolish person dies because he doesn't have wisdom.

22 The Lord's blessing brings wealth.
And with it comes no sorrow.

23 A foolish person enjoys doing wrong.
But a person with understanding enjoys doing what is wise.

24 An evil person will get what he fears most.
But a good person will receive what he wants most.

25 A storm will blow the evil person away.
But a good person will always be safe.

26 A lazy person brings trouble to the one he works for.
He bothers others like vinegar on the teeth or smoke in the eyes.

27 Whoever respects the Lord will have a long life.
But an evil person will have his life cut short.

28 A good person can look forward to happiness.

But an evil person can expect
  nothing.

29The Lord will protect good people.
  But he will ruin those who do evil.

30Good people will always be safe.
  But evil people will not remain in
  the land.

31A good person says wise things.
  But a liar's tongue will be stopped.

32Good people say the right thing.
  But the wicked tell lies.

11 The Lord hates dishonest scales.
  But he is pleased with correct
  weights.

2Pride leads only to shame.
  It is wise not to be proud.

3Good people will be guided by
  honesty.
  But dishonesty will destroy those
  who are not trustworthy.

4Riches will not help when it's time
  to die.
  But doing what is right will save
  you from dying too soon.

5The goodness of an innocent person
  makes his life easier.
  But a wicked person will be
  destroyed by his wickedness.

6Doing what is right brings freedom
  to honest people.
  But those who are not trustworthy
  will be caught by their own
  desires.

7When a wicked person dies, his
  hope is gone.
  The hopes he placed in his riches
  will come to nothing.

8The good man is saved from trouble.
  It comes to the wicked instead.

9By his words an evil person can
  destroy his neighbor.
  But a good person will escape by
  being smart.

10When good people succeed, the city
  is happy.

When evil people die, there are
  shouts of joy.

11The influence of good people makes
  a city great.
  But the wicked can destroy it with
  their words.

12A person without good sense finds
  fault with his neighbor.
  But a person with understanding
  keeps quiet.

13A person who gossips can't keep
  secrets.
  But a trustworthy person can keep
  a secret.

14Without leadership a nation will be
  defeated.
  But when many people give advice,
  it will be safe.

15Whoever guarantees to pay what
  somebody else owes will suffer.
  It is safer to avoid such promises.

16A kind woman is respected.
  But cruel men get wealth.

17A kind person is doing himself a
  favor.
  But a cruel person brings trouble
  on himself.

18An evil person really gains nothing
  from what he earns.
  But a good person will surely be
  rewarded.

19Those who are truly good will live.
  But those who chase after evil will
  die.

20The Lord hates those with evil hearts.
  But he is pleased with those who
  are innocent.

21You can be sure that evil people will
  be punished.
  But those who do what is right will
  not be punished.

22A beautiful woman without good
  sense
  is like a gold ring in a pig's snout.

23The wishes of those who do right will
  come true.

But the hopes of the wicked will
    be defeated by God's anger.

24Some people give much but get back
    even more.
But others don't give what they
    should, and they end up poor.
25A person who gives to others will
    get richer.
Whoever helps others will himself
    be helped.

30As a tree makes fruit, a good person
    gives life to others.
The wise person shows others how
    to be wise.

31Good people will be rewarded on
    earth.
So the wicked and the sinners will
    also be punished.

Helping Others
PROVERBS 11:25

Which kind of person do you want as your friend:
one who is stingy and selfish with what she has, or one who loves to
share her things with others? Of course you would want the second kind
of person. But which kind of person would other people say *you* are?

There's an old saying: "To *have* a friend, you must *be* a friend." That
applies to how we treat others, too. If you want people to be helpful and
kind to you, you must be helpful and kind to them. This verse says that
people who are kind and unselfish are treated that way in return. If you
give to others when they need you, they are much more likely to help
you when you need them.

Be the kind of person who loves to help others.

To learn more about helping others, zoom to page 1144.

26People curse someone who keeps
    all the grain for himself.
But they bless a person who is
    willing to sell it.

27Whoever looks for good will find
    kindness.
But whoever looks for evil will find
    trouble.

28Those who trust in riches will be
    ruined.
But a good person will be as healthy
    as a green leaf.

29Whoever brings trouble to his family
    will be left with nothing but
    the wind.
And a foolish person will become a
    servant to the wise.

12 Anyone who loves learning accepts being corrected.
But a person who hates being
    corrected is stupid.

2The Lord is pleased with a good
    person.

**Anyone who loves
learning accepts being
corrected.
But a person who hates
being corrected is stupid.**
• **Proverbs 12:1**

But he will punish anyone who
    plans evil.

³Doing evil brings a person no safety at all.
But a good person has safety and security.

⁴A good wife is like a crown for her husband.
But a disgraceful wife is like a disease in his bones.

⁵The plans that good people make are fair.
But the advice of the wicked will trick you.

⁶The wicked talk of killing people.
But the words of good people will save them.

⁷Wicked people die and leave nothing behind.
But a good man's family goes on.

⁸A wise person is praised.
But a stupid person is not respected.

⁹A person might not be important but still have a servant.
He is better off than someone who acts important but has no food.

¹⁰A good man takes care of his animals.
But even the kindest acts of the wicked are cruel.

¹¹The person who works his land will have plenty of food.
But the one who chases useless dreams isn't wise.

¹²Evil people want what other evil people have stolen.
But good people want to give to others.

¹³Evil people are trapped by their evil talk.
But good people stay out of trouble.

¹⁴A person will be rewarded for what he says.
And he will also be rewarded for what he does.

¹⁵A foolish person thinks he is doing right.
But a wise person listens to advice.

¹⁶A foolish person quickly shows that he is upset.
But a wise person ignores an insult.

¹⁷An honest witness tells the truth.
But a dishonest witness tells lies.

Honesty
PROVERBS 12:17, 19, 20, 22

Which is better: telling the truth or telling a lie?

Everyone knows it's better to tell the truth. Right? Then why do we tell lies? Part of the answer is that we are sinners, so we naturally disobey God's laws. If you don't believe this, watch someone who's been caught doing something wrong. Often, that person will say *anything* to keep from getting punished. But being a sinner does not excuse lying.

Often we lie to get out of trouble or to get ahead. That's when we should remember Proverbs 12:19: "Truth will continue forever, but lies are only for a moment."

It may seem like a lie will help you right now. But in God's eyes, truth stands strong long after a lie has hurt you.

To learn more about honesty, zoom to page 764.

¹⁸Careless words stab like a sword.
But wise words bring healing.

¹⁹Truth will last forever.
But lies last only a moment.

²⁰Those who plan evil mean to lie.
But those who plan peace will be
happy.

²¹No harm comes to a good person.
But an evil person's life is full of
trouble.

²²The Lord hates those who tell lies.
But he is pleased with those who do
what they promise.

²³A wise person keeps what he knows
to himself.
But a foolish person shows how
foolish he is.

²⁴Hard workers will become leaders.
But those who are lazy will be slaves.

²⁵Worry makes a person feel as if he is
carrying a heavy load.
But a kind word cheers up a person.

²⁶A good person takes advice from his
friends.
But an evil person is easily led to do
wrong.

²⁷A lazy person catches no food to
cook.
But a hard worker will have great
wealth.

²⁸Doing what is right is the way to life.
But there is another way that leads
to death.

13 A wise son takes his father's
advice.
But a person who makes fun of
wisdom won't listen to
correction.

²A person will be rewarded for what
he says.
But those who can't be trusted want
only violence.

³Whoever is careful about what he says
protects his life.
But anyone who speaks without
thinking will be ruined.

**A wise son takes his
father's advice.
But a person who makes
fun of wisdom won't
listen to correction.**
• **Proverbs 13:1**

⁴The lazy person will not get what he
wants.
But a hard worker gets everything
he wants.

⁵Good people hate what is false.
But wicked people do shameful and
disgraceful things.

⁶Doing what is right protects the
honest person.
But evil ruins the sinner.

⁷Some people pretend to be rich but
really have nothing.
Other people pretend to be poor but
really are wealthy.

⁸A rich man may have to pay a
ransom for his life.
But a poor person will never have to
face such a danger.

⁹Good people will live long like
bright flames.
But the wicked will die like a flame
going out.

¹⁰Pride leads to arguments.
But those who take advice are
wise.

¹¹Money that comes easily disappears
quickly.
But money that is gathered little by
little will slowly grow.

¹²It is sad when you don't get what you
hoped for.
But when wishes come true, it's like
eating fruit from the tree of life.

¹³Whoever rejects what he is taught
will pay for it.
But whoever does what he is told
will be rewarded.

¹⁴The teaching of a wise person gives
life.
It is like a fountain of water that can
save people from death.

¹⁵People with good understanding will
be liked.
But the lives of those who are not
trustworthy are hard.

¹⁶Every wise person acts with good
sense.
But a foolish person shows how
foolish he is.

¹⁷A wicked messenger brings nothing
but trouble.
But a trustworthy one makes
everything right.

¹⁸A person who refuses correction will
end up poor and disgraced.
But a person who accepts
correction will be honored.

¹⁹It is so good when wishes come true.
But foolish people still refuse to
stop doing evil.

²⁰Whoever spends time with wise
people will become wise.
But whoever makes friends with
fools will suffer.

²¹Trouble always comes to sinners.
But good people enjoy success.

²²Good people's wealth will be
inherited by their
grandchildren.
And a sinner's wealth will be saved
for good people.

²³A poor man's field might have plenty
of food.
But unfair people steal it from him.

²⁴If a person does not punish his
children, he does not love them.
But the person who loves his
children is careful to correct
them.

²⁵Good people have enough to eat.
But the wicked will go hungry.

14 A wise woman strengthens her
family.

But a foolish woman destroys hers
by what she does.

²People who live good lives show
respect for the Lord.
But those who live evil lives show
no respect for him.

³A foolish person will be punished
for his proud words.
But a wise person's words will
protect him.

⁴When there are no oxen, there is no
food in the barn.
But with the strength of an ox,
much grain can be grown.

⁵A truthful witness does not lie.
But a false witness tells nothing but
lies.

⁶Those who make fun of wisdom
look for it but do not find it.
But the person with understanding
easily finds knowledge.

⁷Stay away from a foolish person.
You won't learn anything from him.

⁸What makes a person wise is
understanding what to do.
But what makes a person foolish is
dishonesty.

⁹Foolish people don't care if they sin.
But honest people work at being
right with others.

¹⁰No one else can know your sadness.
Strangers cannot share your joy.

¹¹The wicked person's house will be
destroyed.
But a good person's tent will still be
standing.

¹²Some people think they are doing
what's right.
But what they are doing will really
kill them.

¹³When someone is laughing, he may
be sad inside.
And when the laughter is over,
there is sorrow.

¹⁴Evil people will be paid back for their
evil ways.

And good people will be rewarded for their good ones.

15 A foolish person will believe anything.
But a wise person thinks about what he does.

16 A wise person is careful and stays out of trouble.
But a foolish person is quick to act and careless.

17 A person who quickly loses his temper does foolish things.
But a person with understanding remains calm.

18 Foolish people get nothing for their work but more foolishness.
But wise people are rewarded with knowledge.

19 Evil people will have to bow down to good people.
The wicked will bow down at the door of those who do right.

20 The poor are rejected, even by their neighbors.
But rich people have many friends.

21 It is a sin to hate your neighbor.
But being kind to the needy brings happiness.

22 Those who make evil plans will be ruined.
But people love and trust those who plan to do good.

23 Those who work hard make a profit.
But those who only talk will be poor.

24 Wise people are rewarded with wealth.
But foolish people will only be rewarded with more foolishness.

25 A truthful witness saves lives.
But a false witness is a traitor.

26 A person who respects the Lord will have security.
And his children will be protected.

27 Respect for the Lord gives life.

It is like a fountain of water that can save people from death.

28 A king is honored when he has many people to rule.
But a prince is ruined if he has none.

29 A person who does not quickly get angry shows that he has understanding.
But a person who quickly loses his temper shows his foolishness.

30 Peace of mind means a healthy body.
But jealousy will rot your bones.

31 Whoever is cruel to the poor insults their Maker.
But anyone who is kind to the needy honors God.

32 The wicked are ruined by their own evil.
But those who do what is right are protected by their honesty.

33 The person who has understanding has wisdom.
And even fools recognize it.

34 Doing what is right makes a nation great.
But sin will bring disgrace to any people.

35 A king is pleased with a wise servant.
But he will become angry with one who causes him shame.

"**H**as someone ever been really angry at you? Have they yelled at you? What can you do? Start by reading Proverbs 15:1."

15 A gentle answer will calm a person's anger.
But an unkind answer will cause more anger.

2 Wise people use knowledge when they speak.

But fools speak only foolishness.

³The Lord's eyes see everything that happens.
He watches both evil and good people.

⁴As a tree gives us fruit, healing words give us life.
But evil words crush the spirit.

But he loves those who do what is right.

¹⁰The person who quits doing what is right will really be punished.
The one who hates to be corrected will die.

Feelings
PROVERBS 15:13

Did you know that your face is like a window? Others can usually tell how you feel by looking into the "window" of your eyes.

This proverb says that our faces show our true feelings. It is pretty hard to act happy when you feel rotten inside. Your dad and mom are probably especially good at knowing when you feel bad.

It's OK to show others your real feelings. Your family and friends love you and want to help you when you feel down. If you pretend to be happy when you are really unhappy, others can't even try to cheer you up.

Let your parents and friends know when you need their help. Even if they can't make your problems go away, it always helps to have a friend to talk to!

To discover what the wisest person in the world learned about happiness, zoom to page 781.

⁵A foolish person rejects his father's correction.
But anyone who accepts correction is wise.

⁶There is much wealth in the houses of good people.
But evil people are paid only with trouble.

⁷With their words wise people spread knowledge.
But there is no knowledge in the thoughts of the foolish.

⁸The Lord hates the sacrifice that the wicked person offers.
But he is pleased with an honest person's prayer.

⁹The Lord hates what evil people do.

¹¹The Lord knows what is happening where the dead people are.
So he can surely know what living people are thinking.

¹²A person who laughs at wisdom does not like to be corrected.
He will not ask advice from the wise.

¹³Happiness makes a person smile.
But sadness breaks a person's spirit.

¹⁴Smart people want more knowledge.
But a foolish person just wants more foolishness.

¹⁵Every day is hard for those who suffer.
But a happy heart makes it like a continual feast.

16It is better to be poor and respect the
Lord
  than to be wealthy and have much
  trouble.

17It is better to eat vegetables with
  those who love you
  than to eat meat with those who
  hate you.

18A person who quickly gets angry
  causes trouble.
  But a person who controls his
  temper stops a quarrel.

19A lazy person's life is as difficult as
  walking through a patch of
  thorns.
  But an honest person's life is as
  easy as walking down a smooth
  highway.

20A wise son makes his father happy.
  But a foolish person hates his
  mother.

21A man without wisdom enjoys being
  foolish.
  But a man with understanding does
  what is right.

22Plans fail without good advice.
  But plans succeed when you get
  advice from many others.

23People enjoy giving good answers!
  Saying the right word at the right
  time is so pleasing!

24A wise person does things that will
  make his life better.
  He avoids whatever would cause his
  death.

25The Lord will tear down the proud
  person's house.
  But he will protect the property of
  a widow.

26The Lord hates evil thoughts.
  But he is pleased with kind
  words.

27A greedy person brings trouble to
  his family.
  But the person who can't be paid to
  do wrong will live.

28Good people think before they
  answer.
  But the wicked simply give evil
  answers.

29The Lord does not listen to the
  wicked.
  But he hears the prayers of those
  who do right.

30Good news makes you feel better.
  Your happiness will show in your
  eyes.

31A wise person pays attention to
  correction
  that will improve his life.

32A person who refuses correction
  hates himself.
  But a person who accepts
  correction gains understanding.

33Respect for the Lord will teach you
  wisdom.
  If you want to be honored, you must
  not be proud.

16 People make plans in their hearts.
But only the Lord can make
those plans come true.

2A person may believe he is doing
  right.
  But the Lord will judge his reasons.

3Depend on the Lord in whatever
  you do.
  Then your plans will succeed.

4The Lord makes everything work
  the way he wants it.
  He even has a day of disaster for
  evil people.

5The Lord hates those who are proud.
  You can be sure that they will be
  punished.

6Love and truth bring forgiveness of
  sin.
  By respecting the Lord you will
  avoid evil.

7A person should live so that he
  pleases the Lord.
  If he does, even his enemies will
  make peace with him.

⁸It is better to be poor and do what is
   right
   than to be wealthy and be unfair.

⁹A person may think up plans.
   But the Lord decides what he will
   do.

¹⁰The words of a king are like a
   message from God.
   So his decisions should be fair.

¹¹The Lord wants honest balances and
   scales to be used.
   He wants all weights to be honest.

¹²Kings hate those who do wrong
   because governments only last if
   they are fair.

¹³Kings are pleased with those who
   speak honest words.
   They value a person who speaks the
   truth.

¹⁴If a king becomes angry, he may put
   someone to death.
   So a wise man will try to keep peace.

¹⁵A king's kindness can give people
   life.
   His kindness is like a spring
   shower.

¹⁶It is better to get wisdom than gold.
   It is better to choose understanding
   than silver!

¹⁷A good person stays away from evil.
   A person who watches what he
   does protects his life.

¹⁸Pride will destroy a person.
   A proud attitude leads to ruin.

¹⁹It is better not to be proud and to be
   with those who suffer
   than to share stolen property with
   proud people.

²⁰Whoever pays attention to what he
   is taught will succeed.
   And whoever trusts the Lord will
   be happy.

²¹A wise person is known for his
   understanding.
   He wins people to his side with
   pleasant words.

Whoever pays attention
to what he is taught
will succeed.
And whoever trusts the
Lord will be happy.
• Proverbs 16:20

²²Understanding is like a fountain of
   water which gives life to those
   who use it.
   But foolishness will cause foolish
   people to be punished.

²³A wise person's mind tells him what
   to say.
   This helps him to teach others better.

²⁴Pleasant words are like a honeycomb.
   They make a person happy and
   healthy.

²⁵Some people think they are doing
   what's right.
   But in the end it causes them to die.

²⁶The worker's hunger helps him.
   His desire to eat makes him work.

²⁷An evil person makes evil plans.
   And his words are like a burning
   fire.

²⁸An evil person causes trouble.
   And a person who gossips ruins
   friendships.

²⁹A cruel man tricks his neighbor.
   He leads him to do wrong.

³⁰Someone who winks at you is
   planning evil.
   And the one who grins at you is
   about to do something wrong.

³¹Gray hair is like a crown of honor.
   You earn it by living a good life.

³²Patience is better than strength.
   Controlling your temper is better
   than capturing a city.

³³People throw lotsᵈ to make a decision.
   But the answer comes from the
   Lord.

17 It is better to eat a dry crust of bread in peace
than to have a feast where there is quarreling.

²A wise servant will rule over his master's disgraceful son.
And he will even inherit a share of what the master leaves his sons.

³A hot furnace tests silver and gold.
In the same way, the Lord tests a person's heart.

⁴An evil person listens to evil words.
A liar pays attention to cruel words.

⁵If you make fun of the poor,
you insult God, who made them.
If you laugh at someone's trouble,
you will be punished.

⁶Grandchildren are the reward of old people.
And children are proud of their parents.

⁷Foolish people should not be proud.
And rulers should not be liars!

⁸A person might think he can pay people and they will do anything he asks.
He thinks it will succeed every time.

⁹Whoever forgives someone's sin makes a friend.
But the one who tells about the sin breaks up friendships.

¹⁰A wise man will learn more from a warning
than a foolish person will learn from 100 lashings.

¹¹A disobedient person is only looking for trouble.
So a cruel messenger will be sent against him.

¹²It is better to meet a bear robbed of her cubs
than to meet a foolish person doing foolish things.

¹³If a person gives evil in return for good,
his house will always be full of trouble.

Character
PROVERBS 17:17

Imagine that you went to school one day and announced, "Hey everybody, I'm going to Disney World this weekend. Anybody who wants to can come along, and I'll pay for everything!" Who would respond to your invitation? Everyone! People you don't even know would try to go on the trip.

Now imagine that you went to school another time. This time you said, "I'm in real trouble, and I need help. It may be difficult and may cost a lot of money, but I need someone to help me out of this problem." Who would stand by you then? Whoever would help you in a time like that is a real friend. That's what this verse teaches.

It's easy to be someone's friend when things are going great. But it takes someone with good inner qualities to help a friend who is having problems. Do you have a friend like that? Would *you* be a friend like that?

To learn more about character, zoom to page 1133.

¹⁴Starting a quarrel is like a leak in a
    dam.
  So stop the quarrel before a fight
    breaks out.

¹⁵The Lord hates both these things:
  letting guilty people go free and
    punishing those who are not
    guilty.

¹⁶It won't do a fool any good to try to
    buy wisdom.
  He doesn't really want to be wise.

¹⁷A friend loves you all the time.
  A brother is always there to help
    you.

¹⁸It is not wise to promise
  to pay what your neighbor owes.

¹⁹Whoever loves to quarrel loves to sin.
  Whoever is proud is asking for
    trouble.

²⁰A person with an evil heart will find
    no success.
  And the person whose words are
    evil will get into trouble.

²¹It is sad to have a foolish son.
  There is no joy in being the father
    of a fool.

²²A happy heart is like good medicine.
  But a broken spirit drains your
    strength.

²³A wicked person secretly accepts
    money to do wrong.
  Then there will be no fairness.

²⁴The person with understanding
    looks for wisdom.
  But a foolish person lets his mind
    wander everywhere.

²⁵A foolish son makes his father sad.
  And he causes his mother great
    sorrow.

²⁶It is not good to punish those who
    have done what is right.
  Nor is it good to punish leaders for
    being honest.

²⁷The person who has knowledge says
    very little.

And a person with understanding
    stays calm.

²⁸Even a foolish person seems to be
    wise if he keeps quiet.
  He appears to have understanding
    if he doesn't speak.

18 An unfriendly person cares only
    about himself.
  He makes fun of all wisdom.

²A foolish person does not want to
    understand anything.
  He only enjoys telling others what
    he thinks.

³Do something evil, and people won't
    like you.
  Do something shameful, and they
    will make fun of you.

⁴Understanding people's words is as
    hard as getting water out of a
    deep well.
  But understanding wisdom is as
    easy as getting water from a
    flowing stream.

⁵It is not good to honor the wicked.
  Nor is it good to be unfair to the
    innocent.

⁶A fool's words start quarrels.
  They make people want to give him
    a beating.

⁷A fool's words will ruin him.
  He will be trapped by his own words.

⁸The words of a gossip are like tasty
    bits of food.
  People take them all in.

⁹A person who doesn't work hard
  is just like a person who destroys
    things.

¹⁰The Lord is like a strong tower.
  Those who do what is right can run
    to him for safety.

¹¹Rich people trust their wealth to
    protect them.
  They think it is like the high walls
    of a city.

¹²People who are proud will be
    ruined.

But those who are not proud will be honored.

¹³A person who answers without listening is foolish and disgraceful.

¹⁴The will to live can get you through sickness.
But no one can live with a broken spirit.

¹⁵The mind of a smart person is ready to get knowledge.
The wise person listens to learn more.

¹⁶Taking a gift to an important person will help get you in to see him.

¹⁷The first person to tell his side of a story seems right.
But that may change when somebody comes and asks him questions.

¹⁸Throwing lots*d* settles arguments.
It keeps the two sides from fighting.

¹⁹A brother who has been insulted is harder to win back than a walled city.
And arguments separate people like the barred gates of a palace.

²⁰What you say affects how you live.
You will be rewarded by how you speak.

²¹What you say can mean life or death.
Those who love to talk will be rewarded for what they say.

²²A man who finds a wife finds something good.
She shows that the Lord is pleased with him.

²³Poor people beg for mercy.
Rich people give rude answers.

²⁴Some friends may ruin you.
But a real friend will be more loyal than a brother.

19 It is better to be poor and honest than to be foolish and tell lies.

²Enthusiasm without knowledge is not good.

Some friends may ruin you. But a real friend will be more loyal than a brother.
• Proverbs 18:24

If you act too quickly, you might make a mistake.

³A person's own foolishness ruins his life.
But in his mind he blames the Lord for it.

⁴Wealthy people are always finding more friends.
But the poor lose their friends.

⁵A witness who lies will be punished.
An untruthful person will not be left unpunished.

⁶Many people want to please a leader.
And everyone is friends with those who give gifts.

⁷A poor person's relatives avoid him.
Even his friends stay far away!
He runs after them, begging.
But they are gone.

⁸The person who gets wisdom is good to himself.
And the one who has understanding will succeed.

⁹A witness who lies will be punished.
An untruthful person will die.

¹⁰No foolish person should live in luxury.
No slave should rule over princes!

¹¹A wise person is patient.
He will be honored if he ignores a wrong done against him.

¹²A king's anger scares people like the roar of a lion.
But his kindness is as pleasant as the dew on the grass.

¹³A foolish son will ruin his father.

And a quarreling wife is as
    bothersome as dripping water.

¹⁴Houses and wealth are inherited
    from parents.
  But a wise wife is a gift from the
    Lord.

¹⁵Lazy people sleep a lot.
  Idle people will go hungry.

¹⁶Whoever obeys the commands
    protects his life.
  Whoever is careless in what he
    does will die.

¹⁷Being kind to the poor is like lending
    to the Lord.
  The Lord will reward you for what
    you have done.

¹⁸Correct your son while there is
    still hope.
  Do not help him destroy himself.

¹⁹A person who is always getting angry
    will pay for it.
  If you help him, you will have to do
    it again and again.

²⁰Listen to advice and accept
    correction.
  Then in the end you will be wise.

²¹People can make many different
    plans.
  But only the Lord's plan will happen.

²²People want others to be loyal.
  So it is better to be poor than to be
    a liar.

²³Those who respect the Lord will live
    and be content, unbothered by
    trouble.

²⁴The lazy person may put his hand in
    the dish,
  but he won't lift the food to his
    mouth!

²⁵Whip a person who makes fun of
    wisdom, and then foolish
    people will learn how to think.
  Just correct a smart man, and he
    will gain knowledge.

²⁶A son who robs his father and sends
    away his mother
  brings shame and disgrace on
    himself.

²⁷Don't stop listening to correction, my
    child.
  If you do, you will not obey what you
    have already learned.

²⁸An evil witness makes fun of fairness.
  And wicked people love what is evil.

²⁹People who make fun of wisdom will
    be punished.

Honesty
PROVERBS 19:22

A good friend likes the things you like, listens to your problems, laughs at your jokes, and keeps your secrets. One thing is for sure: you don't become friends with someone who lies *to* you or *about* you. You can't build a friendship on dishonesty.

That's why this verse says that it is better to be poor than to be a liar. While we might not want to be poor, there is nothing wrong with not having money. It is wrong, however, not to be honest.

People who tell the truth to others and about others are considered loyal friends. That is worth more than money any time.

To learn more about honesty, zoom to page 1252.

And the backs of foolish people will be beaten.

20 Wine and beer make people loud and uncontrolled.
It is not wise to get drunk on them.

²A king's anger is like the roar of a lion.
Making him angry may cost you your life.

³Foolish people are always getting into quarrels.
But avoiding quarrels will bring you honor.

⁴A lazy farmer doesn't plow when he should.
So at harvest time he has no crop.

⁵Understanding a person's thoughts is as hard as getting water from a deep well.
But someone with understanding can find the wisdom there.

⁶Many people claim to be loyal.
But it is hard to find someone who really can be trusted.

⁷The good person who lives an honest life
is a blessing to his children.

⁸A king sits on his throne and judges people.
He knows evil when he sees it.

⁹No one can say, "I am innocent.
I have never done anything wrong."

¹⁰The Lord hates both these things: dishonest weights and dishonest measures.

¹¹Even a child is known by his behavior.
His actions show if he is innocent and good.

¹²The Lord has made both these things:
Ears that can hear and eyes that can see.

¹³If you love to sleep, you will be poor.
If you stay awake, you will have plenty of food.

¹⁴The buyer says, "This is bad. It's no good."
Then he goes away and brags about what he bought.

¹⁵There is plenty of gold, and there are many rubies.
But there are only a few people who speak with knowledge.

¹⁶Take the coat of someone who promises to pay what a stranger owes.
Keep it until he pays the stranger's bills.

¹⁷When a person gets food dishonestly, it may taste sweet at first.
But later he will feel as if he has a mouth full of gravel.

¹⁸Get advice if you want your plans to work.
If you go to war, get the advice of others.

¹⁹Gossips can't keep secrets.
So avoid people who talk too much.

²⁰Whoever curses his father or mother will die like a light going out in darkness.

²¹Wealth that is gotten quickly in the beginning
will do you no good in the end.

²²Don't say, "I'll pay you back for the evil you did."
Wait for the Lord. He will make things right.

²³The Lord hates dishonest weights.
And dishonest scales do not please him.

²⁴The Lord decides what a person does.
So no one can understand what his life is all about.

²⁵It's dangerous to promise something to God too quickly.
After you've thought about it, it may be too late.

²⁶A wise king finds out who the evil people are.
Then he punishes them.

²⁷The Lord looks into a person's
feelings.
He searches through a person's
thoughts.

²⁸Loyalty and truth keep a king in power.
He continues to rule if he is loyal.

²⁹Young men are admired for their
strength.
Old men are honored for their
experience.

³⁰Hard punishment will get rid of evil.
Whippings can change the evil
person's heart.

21 The Lord can control a king's
mind as easily as he controls a
river.
He can direct it as he pleases.

²A person may believe he is doing right.
But the Lord judges his reasons.

³Do what is right and fair.
That is more important to the Lord
than animal sacrifices.

⁴Proud looks, proud thoughts
and evil actions are sin.

⁵Those who plan and work hard earn
a profit.
But those who act too quickly
become poor.

⁶Wealth that comes from telling lies
vanishes like a mist and leads to
death.

⁷The violence of the wicked will
destroy them
because they refuse to do what is
right.

⁸Guilty people live dishonest lives.
But honest people do what is right.

⁹It is better to live in a corner on
the roof[n]
than inside the house with a
quarreling wife.

¹⁰An evil person only wants to harm
others.

His neighbor will get no mercy
from him.

¹¹Punish a person who makes fun of
wisdom, and he will become
wise.
But just teach a wise person, and he
will get knowledge.

¹²God, who is always right, sees the
house of the wicked.
And he brings about the ruin of every
evil person.

¹³If you ignore the poor when they cry
for help,
you also will cry for help and not be
answered.

¹⁴A gift given secretly will calm an
angry man.
A present given in secrecy will calm
even great anger.

¹⁵When things are done fairly, good
people are happy,
but evil people are frightened.

¹⁶A person who does not use
understanding
will join the dead.

¹⁷Whoever loves pleasure will become
poor.
Whoever loves wine and rich food
will never be wealthy.

¹⁸Wicked people will suffer instead of
good people.
And those who cannot be trusted will
suffer instead of those who can.

¹⁹It is better to live alone in the
desert
than with a quarreling and
complaining wife.

²⁰Wise people store up the best foods
and olive oil.
But a foolish person eats up
everything he has.

²¹A person who tries to live right and
be loyal
finds life, success and honor.

ⁿ**roof** In Bible times houses were built with flat roofs. The roof was used for drying things such as flax and
fruit. And it was used as an extra room, as a place for worship and as a place to sleep in the summer.

²²A wise person can defeat a city full of
strong men.
　He can tear down the defenses they
　trust.

²³A person who is careful about what
he says
　keeps himself out of trouble.

²⁴People who act with stubborn pride
are called "proud" and "bragger."

²⁵The lazy person's desire for sleep
will kill him
　because he refuses to work.
²⁶All day long the lazy person wishes
for more.
　But the good person gives without
　holding back.

²⁷The Lord hates sacrifices made by
evil people,
　particularly when they make them
　for the wrong reasons.

²⁸The words of a lying witness
will die.
　But the words of an obedient man
　will always be remembered.

²⁹A wicked person is stubborn.
　But an honest person thinks
　carefully about what he does.

³⁰There is no wisdom, understanding
or advice
　that can succeed against the Lord.

³¹You can get the horses ready for
battle.
　But it is the Lord who gives the
　victory.

22 Being respected is more important than having great riches.
To be well thought of is better than
　owning silver or gold.

²The rich and the poor are alike
in that the Lord made them all.

³When a wise person sees danger
ahead, he avoids it.
　But a foolish person keeps going
　and gets into trouble.

⁴Respecting the Lord and not being
proud

will bring you wealth, honor and
life.

⁵The lives of evil people are like paths
covered with thorns and traps.
　People who protect themselves
　don't have such problems.

⁶Train a child how to live the right way.
　Then even when he is old, he will
　still live that way.

⁷The rich rule over the poor.
　And borrowers become servants to
　those who lend.

⁸A person who does evil things will
receive trouble in return.
　Then he won't be cruel to others
　any longer.

⁹A generous person will be blessed
because he shares his food with the
poor.

¹⁰Get rid of the person who makes fun
of wisdom.
　Then fighting, quarrels and insults
　will stop.

¹¹A person who loves innocent
thoughts and kind words
　will have even the king as a friend.

¹²The Lord protects knowledge from
being lost.
　But he destroys false words.

¹³The lazy person says, "There's a lion
outside!
　I might get killed out in the street!"

¹⁴The words of an unfaithful wife are
like a deep trap.
　Those who make the Lord angry
　will get caught by them.

¹⁵Every child is full of foolishness.
　But punishment can get rid of it.

¹⁶The one who gets rich by being cruel
to the poor will become poor.
　And so will the one who gives
　presents to the wealthy.

Other Wise Sayings

¹⁷Pay attention and listen to what wise
people say.

Remember what I am teaching you.
¹⁸It will be good to keep these things
   in mind.
Be prepared to repeat them.
¹⁹I am teaching them to you now
   so that you will put your trust in the
   Lord.
²⁰I have written down 30 sayings for
   you.
They give knowledge and good
   advice.
²¹I am teaching you true and reliable
   words.
Then you can give true answers to
   anyone who asks.

²²Do not abuse poor people because
   they are poor.
And do not take away the rights of
   the needy in court.
²³The Lord will defend them in court.
And he will take the life of those
   who take away their rights.

²⁴Don't make friends with someone
   who easily gets angry.
Don't spend time with someone
   who has a bad temper.
²⁵If you do, you may learn to be like
   him.
Then you will be in real danger.

²⁶Don't promise to pay what someone
   else owes.
And don't give guarantees that you
   will pay what he owes.
²⁷If you cannot pay what he owes,
   your own bed will be taken and sold.

²⁸Don't move an old stone that shows
   where a person's land is.
These stones were set up by your
   ancestors.

²⁹Do you see a man skilled in his work?
That man will work for kings.
He won't have to work for ordinary
   people.

23 If you sit down to eat with a ruler,
   notice the food that is in front of
   you.
²Control yourself
   if you have a big appetite.
³Don't be greedy for his fine foods.

He might use that rich food to trick
   you.
⁴Don't wear yourself out trying to get
   rich.
Be wise enough to control yourself.
⁵Wealth can vanish in the wink of an
   eye.
It seems to grow wings
   and fly away like an eagle in the sky.

⁶Don't eat the food of a selfish person.
Don't be greedy for his fine foods.
⁷A selfish person is always worrying
   about how much the food costs.
He tells you, "Eat and drink."
But he doesn't really mean it.
⁸So you will feel like throwing up the
   little bit you have eaten.
And you will have wasted your kind
   words.

⁹Don't speak to a foolish person.
He will only ignore your wise
   words.

¹⁰Don't move an old stone that shows
   where somebody's land is.
And don't take fields that belong to
   orphans.
¹¹God, their defender, is strong.
He will take their side against you.

¹²Remember what you are taught.
And listen carefully to words of
   knowledge.

¹³Don't fail to punish a child.
If you spank him, you will keep him
   from dying.
¹⁴If you punish him with a spanking,
   you will save him from a fool's
   death.

¹⁵My child, if you are wise,
   then I will be happy.
¹⁶I will be so pleased
   if you speak what is right.

¹⁷Don't envy sinners.
But always respect the Lord.
¹⁸If you do, you will have hope for the
   future.
Your wishes will come true.

¹⁹Listen, my child, and be wise.
Keep your mind on what is right.

²⁰Don't be one of those who drink too
much wine
or who eat too much food.
²¹Those who drink too much and eat
too much become poor.
They sleep too much and end up
wearing rags.
²²Listen to your father, who gave you
life.
And do not forget your mother
when she is old.

**Listen to your father,
who gave you life.
And do not forget your
mother when she is old.**
• Proverbs 23:22

²³Learn the truth and never reject it.
Get wisdom, self-control and
understanding.
²⁴The father of a good child is very
happy.
The person who has a wise son is
glad because of him.
²⁵Make your father and mother happy.
Give your mother a reason to be
glad.

²⁶My son, pay attention to me.
And watch closely what I do.
²⁷A prostitute^d is as dangerous as a
deep pit.
And an unfaithful wife is like a
narrow well.
²⁸They ambush you like robbers.
And they cause many men to be
unfaithful to their wives.

²⁹⁻³⁰Some people drink too much wine.
They try out all the different kinds
of drinks.
So they have trouble. They are sad.
They fight. They complain.
They have unnecessary bruises.
They have bloodshot eyes.
³¹Don't stare at the wine's pretty, red
color.
It may sparkle in the cup.
It may go down your throat smoothly.

³²But later it bites like a snake.
Like a snake, it poisons you.
³³Your eyes will see strange sights.
And your mind will be confused.
³⁴You will feel dizzy, as if you're out on
the stormy ocean.
You will feel as if you're on top of a
ship's sails.
³⁵You will think, "They hit me, but
I'm not hurt!
They have beaten me up, but I don't
remember it.
I wish I could wake up.
Then I would get another drink."

24 Don't envy evil people.
Don't try to be friends with them.
²In their minds they plan cruel things.
And they always talk about making
trouble.

³It takes wisdom to have a good family.
It takes understanding to make it
strong.
⁴It takes knowledge to fill a home
with rare and beautiful treasures.

⁵A wise man has great power.
And a man who has knowledge is
very strong.
⁶So you need the advice of others
when you go to war.
If you have many people to give
advice, you will win.

⁷A foolish person cannot understand
wisdom.
He has nothing to say in court.

⁸Whoever makes evil plans
will be known as a troublemaker.
⁹Making foolish plans is sinful.
And making fun of others is hateful.

¹⁰If you give up when trouble comes,
it shows that you have very little
strength.

¹¹Save those who are being led to their
death.
Rescue those who are about to be
killed.
¹²You may say, "We don't know
anything about this."
But God knows what is in your
mind, and he will notice.

He is watching you, and he will
    know.
He will pay each person back for
    what he has done.

13My child, eat honey because it is
    good.
Honey from the honeycomb tastes
    sweet.
14In the same way, wisdom is pleasing
    to you.
If you find it, you have hope for the
    future.
Your wishes will come true.

15Don't be like the wicked and attack
    a good man's house.
Don't rob the place where he lives.
16A good man may be bothered by
    trouble seven times, but he
    does not give up.
But the wicked are overwhelmed
    by trouble.

17Don't be happy when your enemy is
    defeated.
Don't be glad when he is
    overwhelmed.
18The Lord will notice and be
    displeased.
Then the Lord may not be angry
    with him anymore.

19Don't envy evil people.
And don't be jealous of the wicked.
20An evil person has nothing to hope
    for.
The wicked will die like a flame that
    is put out.

21My child, respect the Lord and the
    king.
Don't join those people who refuse
    to obey them.
22The Lord and the king will quickly
    destroy such people.
Those two can cause great trouble!

More Words of Wisdom

23These are also wise sayings:

It is not good to take sides when
    you are the judge.
24Don't say that the wicked have done
    right.

People will curse you, and nations
    will hate you.
25But things will go well for judges
    who punish the guilty.
And they will receive good things
    from God.

26An honest answer is as pleasing
    as a kiss on the lips.

27First, you should work outside
    and prepare your fields.
After that, you can start having your
    family.

28Don't testify against your neighbor
    for no good reason.
Don't say things that are false.
29Don't say, "I'll get even with that
    man.
I'll do to him what he did to me."

30I passed by a lazy person's field.
I went by the vineyard of a man who
    had no sense.
31Thorns had grown up everywhere.
The ground was covered with
    weeds.
And the stone walls had fallen
    down.
32I thought about what I had seen.
I learned this lesson from what I
    saw.
33You sleep a little; you take a nap.
You fold your hands and rest.
34Soon you will be poor, as if you had
    been robbed.
You will have as little as if you had
    been held up.

More Wise Sayings of Solomon

25 These are more wise sayings of
Solomon. They were copied by
the men of Hezekiah king of Judah.

2God is honored for what he keeps
    secret.
Kings are honored for what they
    can discover.

3No one can measure the height of
    the skies or the depth of the
    earth.
So also no one can understand the
    mind of a king.

⁴Remove the scum from the silver.
  Then the silver can be used by the
    silversmith.
⁵Remove wicked people from the
    king's presence.
  Then his government will be honest
    and last a long time.

⁶Don't brag to the king.
  Don't act as if you are a great man.
⁷It is better for him to promote you
    to a higher job
  than to give you a less important
    position.

Because of something you have seen,
⁸ do not quickly take someone to
    court.
  What will you do later
    when your neighbor proves you are
    wrong?

⁹If you have an argument with your
    neighbor,
  don't tell other people what was
    said.
¹⁰Whoever hears it might say bad
    things about you.
  And you might not ever be
    respected again.

¹¹The right word spoken at the
    right time
  is as beautiful as gold apples in a
    silver bowl.

¹²The warning of a wise person is
    valuable to someone who will
    listen.
  It is worth as much as gold earrings
    or fine gold jewelry.

¹³A trustworthy messenger refreshes
    those who send him.
  He is like the coolness of snow in
    the summertime.

¹⁴People who brag about gifts they
    never give
  are like clouds and wind that give
    no rain.

¹⁵With patience you can convince a
    ruler.

And a gentle word can get through
    to the hard-headed.

¹⁶If you find honey, don't eat too much.
  Too much of it will make you sick.
¹⁷Don't go to your neighbor's house too
    often.
  Too much of you will make him hate
    you.

¹⁸Anyone who lies about his neighbor
    hurts him as a club, a sword or a
    sharp arrow would.

¹⁹Don't trust unfaithful people when
    you are in trouble.
  It's like eating with a broken tooth
    or walking with a crippled foot.

²⁰Don't sing songs to someone who
    is sad.
  It's like taking off a coat on a
    cold day
  or pouring vinegar on soda.

²¹If your enemy is hungry, feed him.
  If he is thirsty, give him a drink.
²²Doing this will be like pouring
    burning coals on his head.
  And the Lord will reward you.

²³The north wind brings rain.
  In the same way, telling gossip
    brings angry looks.

²⁴It is better to live in a corner on the
    roof[n]
  than inside the house with a
    quarreling wife.

²⁵Hearing good news from a faraway
    place
  is like having a cool drink when you
    are tired.

²⁶A good person who gives in to evil
  is like a muddy spring or a dirty
    well.

²⁷It is not good to eat too much honey.
  In the same way, it is not good to
    brag about yourself.

²⁸A person who does not control
    himself

---

[n] **roof** In Bible times houses were built with flat roofs. The roof was used for drying things such as flax and fruit. And it was used as an extra room, as a place for worship and as a place to sleep in the summer.

is like a city whose walls have been broken down.

26 It shouldn't snow in summer or rain at harvest.
Neither should a foolish person ever be honored.

2Curses will not harm someone who is innocent.
They are like sparrows or swallows that fly around and never land.

3A whip is used to guide a horse, and a harness is used for a donkey.
In the same way, a paddle is used on a foolish person to guide him.

4Don't give a foolish person a foolish answer.
If you do, you will be just like him.

5But answer a foolish person as he should be answered.
If you don't, he will think he is really wise.

6Don't send a message by a foolish person.
That would be like cutting off your feet or drinking poison.

7A wise saying spoken by a fool does no good.
It is like the legs of a crippled person.

8Giving honor to a foolish person does no good.
It is like tying a stone in a slingshot.

9A wise saying spoken by a fool is like a thorn stuck in the hand of a drunk.

10Someone might employ a foolish person or anyone just passing by.
That employer is like an archer who shoots at anything he sees.

11A dog eats what it throws up.

And a foolish person repeats his foolishness.

12Some people think they are wise.
There is more hope for a foolish person than for them.

13The lazy person says, "There's a lion in the road.
There's a lion in the streets!"

14The lazy person is like a door that turns back and forth on its hinges.
He stays in bed and turns over and over.

15The lazy person may put his hand in the dish.
But he's too tired to lift the food to his mouth.

16The lazy person thinks he is wiser than seven people who give sensible answers.

17To grab a dog by the ears is asking for trouble.
So is interfering in someone else's quarrel if you're just passing by.

18-19A person shouldn't trick his neighbor and then say, "I was just joking!"
That is like a madman shooting deadly, burning arrows.

20Without wood, a fire will go out.
And without gossip, quarreling will stop.

21Charcoal and wood keep a fire going.
In the same way, a quarrelsome person keeps an argument going.

22The words of a gossip are like tasty bits of food.
People take them all in.

23Kind words from a wicked mind are like a shiny coating on a clay pot.

24A person who hates you may fool you with his words.
But in his mind he is planning evil.
25His words are kind, but don't believe him.
His mind is full of evil thoughts.
26He hides his hate with lies.
But his evil will be plain to everyone.

27Whoever digs a deep trap for others will fall into it himself.
Whoever tries to roll a boulder over others will be crushed by it.

²⁸A liar hates the people he hurts.
And false praise can ruin others.

27 Don't brag about what will happen tomorrow.
You don't really know what will happen then.

²Don't praise yourself. Let someone else do it.
Let the praise come from a stranger and not from your own mouth.

³Stone is heavy, and sand is hard to carry.
But the complaining of a foolish person causes more trouble than either.

⁴Anger is cruel. It destroys like a flood.
But who can put up with jealousy!

⁵It is better to correct someone openly than to love him and not show it.

⁶The slap of a friend can be trusted to help you.
But the kisses of an enemy are nothing but lies.

⁷When someone is full, not even honey tastes good.
But when he is hungry, even something bitter tastes sweet.

⁸A man who leaves his home is like a bird that leaves its nest.

⁹Perfume and oils make you happy.
And good advice from a friend is sweet.

¹⁰Don't forget your friend or your father's friend.
Don't always go to your brother for help when trouble comes.
A neighbor close by is better than a brother far away.

¹¹Be wise, my child, and you will make me happy.
Then I can respond to any insult.

¹²When a wise person sees danger ahead, he avoids it.
But a foolish person keeps going and gets into trouble.

¹³Take the coat of someone who promises to pay what a stranger owes.
Keep it until he pays the stranger's bills.

¹⁴Don't greet your neighbor loudly early in the morning.
He will think of it as a curse.

¹⁵A quarreling wife is as bothersome as a continual dripping on a rainy day.

¹⁶Stopping her is like stopping the wind.
It's like trying to grab oil in your hand.

¹⁷Iron can sharpen iron.
In the same way, people can help each other.

¹⁸The person who tends a fig tree will eat its fruit.
And the person who takes care of his master will be honored.

¹⁹As water shows you your face,
so your mind shows you what kind of person you are.

²⁰People will never stop dying and being destroyed.
In the same way, people will never stop wanting more than they have.

²¹A hot furnace tests silver and gold.
And people are tested by the praise they receive.

²²Even if you ground up a foolish person like grain in a bowl,
you couldn't remove his foolishness.

²³Be sure you know how your sheep are doing.
Pay close attention to the condition of your cattle.

²⁴Riches will not continue forever.
Nor do governments continue forever.

²⁵Bring in the hay. Let the new grass appear.
Gather the grass from the hills.

²⁶Make clothes from the lambs' wool.
Sell some goats to buy a field.

²⁷There will be plenty of goat milk

to feed you and your family.
It will make your servant girls
healthy.

28 Evil people run even though no
one is chasing them.
But good people are as brave as a
lion.

2 When a country is disobedient, it
has one ruler after another.
But when it is led by a man with
understanding and knowledge,
it continues strong.

3 Rulers who are cruel to the poor
are like a hard rain that destroys the
crops.

4 People who disobey what they have
been taught praise the wicked.
But those who obey what they have
been taught are against the
wicked.

5 Evil people do not understand fairness.
But those who follow the Lord
understand it completely.

6 It is better to be poor and innocent
than to be rich and wicked.

7 The son who obeys what he has
been taught
shows he is smart.
But the son who makes friends with
those who have no self-control
disgraces his father.

8 Some people get rich by
overcharging others.
But their wealth will be given to
those who are kind to the poor.

9 If you refuse to obey what you have
been taught,
your prayers will not be heard.

10 Those who lead honest people to
do wrong
will be ruined by their own evil.
But the innocent will be rewarded
with good things.

11 A rich man may think he is wise.
But a poor man who has understanding knows the rich man
is wrong.

12 When good people win, there is great
happiness.
But when the wicked get power,
everybody hides.

13 If you hide your sins, you will not
succeed.
If you confess and reject them, you
will receive mercy.

14 Those who always respect the Lord
will be happy.
But those who are stubborn will
get into trouble.

15 A wicked ruler is as dangerous to
poor people
as a roaring lion or a charging
bear.

16 A ruler who is cruel does not have
wisdom.
But the one who hates money taken
dishonestly will live a long time.

17 A man who is guilty of murder
will run until he dies.
So do not stop him.

18 Innocent people will be kept safe.
But those who are dishonest will
suddenly be ruined.

19 The person who works his land will
have plenty of food.
But the one who chases useless
dreams instead will end up very
poor.

20 A truthful man will have many
blessings.
But those eager to get rich will be
punished.

21 It is not good for a judge to take sides.
But some will sin for just a piece of
bread.

22 A selfish person is in a hurry to get
rich.
He does not realize his selfishness
will make him poor.

23 Those who correct others will later
be liked
more than those who give false
praise.

²⁴Some people rob their fathers or
      mothers
   and say, "It's not wrong."
   Such people are just like those who
      destroy things.

But when evil people rule,
   everyone groans.

Staying Away from Selfishness
PROVERBS 28:22

"**I** want it NOW!" Those seem like the magic words today.
   If we are hungry, we can zap a whole meal in the microwave in less than two minutes. If we want to see a movie, we just have to go down to the videostore. But if you often find yourself saying "get it now" or "give it to me," watch out. You will sound like you are only concerned about yourself.

Practicing patience is a good way to fight against selfishness. Don't be in a hurry to get the things you want: money, friends, the hottest shoes, or the latest games. Be patient. God will give you the things you need. Ask God to show you the difference between what you need and what you want.

To learn more more ways to stay away from selfishness, zoom to page 1161.

---

²⁵A greedy person causes trouble.
   But the one who trusts the Lord will
      succeed.

²⁶The person who trusts in himself is
      foolish.
   But the person who lives wisely will
      be kept safe.

²⁷The person who gives to the poor
      will have everything he needs.
   But the one who ignores the poor
      will have many curses put on
      him.
²⁸When the wicked get power,
      everybody hides.
   But when the wicked die, the good
      people do well.

29 Some people are still stubborn
      after they have been corrected
      many times.
   But they will suddenly be hurt
      beyond cure.

²When good people do well,
      everyone is happy.

³Whoever loves wisdom makes his
      father happy.
   But the one who makes friends
      with prostitutes^d wastes his
      money.

⁴If a king is fair, he makes his
      country strong.
   But if he takes money dishonestly,
      he tears his country down.

⁵Anyone who gives false praise to his
      neighbor
   is setting a trap for him.

⁶An evil person is trapped by his
      own sin.
   But a good person can sing and
      be happy.

⁷Good people are concerned that the
      poor are treated fairly.
   But the wicked don't care.

⁸People who make fun of others
      cause trouble in a city.
   But wise people calm anger down.

9A wise man should not take a
    foolish person to court.
  The fool will only shout or laugh at
    him. There will be no peace.

10Murderers hate honest people.
  But those who do right try to
    protect them.
11A foolish person loses his temper.

But those who do right will see
    them destroyed.

17Correct your child, and you will be
    proud of him.
  He will give you pleasure.

18Where there is no word from God,
    people are uncontrolled.

Witnessing
PROVERBS 29:25

Have you ever been really, really scared, and then
someone said, "Why are you scared? There's nothing to
be afraid of." Maybe you felt like saying, "That's easy for you to say!" And
you kept on being scared.

Maybe that's how you feel when you think about telling other people
about God. Maybe you are afraid of how your friends might act if you
told them about how great he is. The Bible says here that we shouldn't
fear people; instead, we should trust God. "Sure, that's easy for God to
say," you may think, "He's God!"

But think about this: What if there really is nothing to be afraid of?
Nothing in the dark to make you afraid. Nothing in your closet, or even
under your bed, to make you afraid. And nothing that people might say
to you when you tell them about God to make you afraid. What would
you do differently?

To learn more about witnessing, zoom to page 909.

But a wise person controls his
    anger.

12If a ruler pays attention to lies,
    then all his officers will become
    wicked.

13The poor person and the cruel
    person are alike in this way:
  The Lord gave eyes to both of them.

14A king should judge poor people fairly.
  Then his government will continue
    forever.

15Punishment and correction make a
    child wise.
  If he is left to do as he pleases, he
    will disgrace his mother.

16When there are many wicked people,
    there is much sin.

But those who obey what they have
    been taught are happy.

19Words alone cannot correct a servant.
  Even if he understands, he won't
    respond.

20Sometimes you see people who speak
    too quickly.
  There is more hope for a foolish
    person than for them.

21Don't spoil your servant when he is
    young.
  If you do, he will bring you grief
    later on.

22An angry person causes trouble.
  A person who easily gets angry sins
    a lot.

23A man's pride will ruin him.

But a person who is humble will be honored.

24The partner of a thief is his own worst enemy.
He has to testify in court, but he is afraid to say anything.

25Being afraid of people can get you into trouble.
But if you trust the Lord, you will be safe.

26Many people want to be heard by a ruler.
But fairness comes from the Lord.

27Good people hate those who are dishonest.
And the wicked hate those who are honest.

Wise Words from Agur

30 These are the words of Agur son of Jakeh.

This is his message to Ithiel and Ucal:

2"I am the most stupid person there is.
I have no understanding.
3I have not learned to be wise.
And I don't know much about God, the Holy One.
4Who has gone up to heaven and come back down?
Who can hold the wind in his hand?
Who can gather up the waters in his coat?
Who has decided where the ends of the earth will be?
What is his name? And what is his son's name?
Surely, you know!

5"Every word of God can be trusted.
He protects those who come to him for safety.
6Do not add to his words.
If you do, he will correct you and prove that you are a liar.

7"I ask two things from you, Lord.
Don't refuse me before I die.
8Keep me from lying and being dishonest.

And don't make me either rich or poor.
Just give me enough food for each day.
9If I have too much, I might reject you.
I might say, 'I don't know the Lord.'
If I am poor, I might steal.
Then I would disgrace the name of my God.

10"Do not say bad things about a servant to his master.
If you do, he will curse you, and you will suffer for it.

11"Some people curse their fathers.
And they do not bless their mothers.
12Some people think they are pure.
But they are not really free from evil.
13Some people have such a proud look!
They look down on others.
14Some people have teeth like swords.
It is as if their jaws are full of knives.
They want to remove the poor people from the earth.
They want to get rid of the needy.

15"Greed has two daughters.
Their names are 'Give me. Give me.'
There are three things that are never satisfied.
There are really four that never say, 'I've had enough!'
16These things are the cemetery, the childless mother,
the land that never gets enough rain,
and fire that never says, 'I've had enough!'

17"Don't make fun of your father.
Don't refuse to obey your mother.
If you do, your eye will be pecked out by the birds of the valley.
You will be eaten by hawks.

18"There are three things that are too hard for me.
There are really four that I don't understand:
19the way an eagle flies in the sky,
the way a snake slides over a rock,
the way a ship sails on the sea
and the way a man acts with a girl.

²⁰"This is the way a woman who takes
     part in adultery^d acts:
She sins and doesn't care.
She says, 'I haven't done anything
     wrong.'
²¹"There are three things that make
     the earth tremble.
There are really four that it cannot
     stand:
²²a servant who becomes a king,
     a foolish person who has plenty to
     eat,

²⁷Locusts^d have no king.
But they all go out in formation.
²⁸And lizards can be caught in the
     hand.
But they are found even in kings'
     palaces.

²⁹"There are three things that strut
     proudly.
There are really four that walk as if
     they are important:
³⁰Lions are the proudest animals.
They are strong and run from
     nothing.
³¹Roosters and male goats strut proudly.
And so does a king when his army
     is around him.

Animals in the Bible

BADGERS • PROVERBS 30:24-26

Do any of your friends have a pet guinea pig? Maybe you have seen one in a pet shop. The badger that is mentioned in the Bible is furry and small like a guinea pig. But you could not keep a wild badger as a pet!

The badger is called wise because it makes its home in the rocks to protect itself. The Bible mentions the badger as an example of a smart animal that knows a good place to hide. Badgers live around cliffs and hillsides where the ground is rocky. These kinds of badgers are also called cliff badgers or rock badgers. They have special pads on their feet to help them climb over sharp rocks with ease. You can read more about badgers in Psalm 104:18.

We don't have to hide somewhere when we want to feel safe. We are protected by our heavenly father. He will guard us and help us feel safe.

To read about an animal who can drink twenty-five gallons of water in ten minutes, fly to page 1115.

²³a hateful woman who gets married
     and a maid who replaces her
     mistress.
²⁴"There are four things on earth that
     are small.
But they are very wise:
²⁵Ants are not very strong.
But they store up food in the
     summer.
²⁶Rock badgers are not powerful
     animals.
But they can live among the rocks.

³²"You may have been foolish and
     proud.
If you planned evil, cover your mouth.
³³Stirring milk makes butter.
Twisting noses makes them bleed.
And stirring up anger makes
     trouble."

Wise Words of King Lemuel

31 These are the words of King
Lemuel. This is the message his
mother taught him:

2"My son, I gave birth to you.
You are the son I prayed for.
3Don't waste your strength on women.
Don't waste your time on those who
ruin kings.

4"Kings should not drink wine, Lemuel.
Rulers should not desire beer.
5If they drink, they might forget the law.
They might keep the needy from
getting their rights.
6Give beer to people who are dying.
And give wine to those who are sad.
7Let them drink and forget their need.
Then they won't remember their
misery anymore.

8"Speak up for those who cannot
speak for themselves.
Defend the rights of all those who
have nothing.
9Speak up and judge fairly.
Defend the rights of the poor and
needy."

The Good Wife

10It is hard to find an excellent wife.
She is worth more than rubies.
11Her husband trusts her completely.
With her, he has everything he
needs.
12She does him good and not harm
for as long as she lives.
13She looks for wool and linen.
She likes to work with her hands.
14She is like a trader's ship.
She goes far to get food.
15She gets up while it is still dark.
She prepares food for her family.
She also feeds her servant girls.
16She looks at a field and buys it.
With money she has earned, she
plants a vineyard.
17She does her work with energy.

Her arms are strong.
18She makes sure that what she makes
is good.
She works by her lamp late into the
night.
19She makes thread with her hands
and weaves her own cloth.
20She welcomes the poor.
She helps the needy.
21She does not worry about her family
when it snows.
They all have fine clothes to keep
them warm.
22She makes coverings for her bed.
Her clothes are made of linen and
other expensive material.
23Her husband is recognized at the city
meetings.
He makes decisions as one of the
leaders of the land.
24She makes linen clothes and sells
them.
She provides belts to the merchants.
25She is strong and is respected by the
people.
She looks forward to the future with
joy.
26She speaks wise words.
And she teaches others to be kind.
27She watches over her family.
And she is always busy.
28Her children bless her.
Her husband also praises her.
29He says, "There are many excellent
wives,
but you are better than all of them."
30Charm can fool you, and beauty can
trick you.
But a woman who respects the
Lord should be praised.
31Give her the reward she has earned.
She should be openly praised for
what she has done.

ECCLESIASTES

A Wise Man
Believes in God

1 These are the words of the Teacher. He is a son of David, king in Jerusalem.

² The Teacher says,
"Useless! Useless!
Completely useless!
All things are useless."

³ What do people really gain
from all the hard work they do
here on earth?

Things Never Change

⁴ People live, and people die.
But the earth continues forever.
⁵ The sun rises, and the sun sets.
Then it hurries back to the place
where it rises again.
⁶ The wind blows to the south.
Then it blows to the north.
It blows from one direction and
then another.
Then it turns around and repeats
the same pattern, going
nowhere.
⁷ All the rivers flow to the sea.
But the sea never becomes full.
⁸ Everything is boring.
It makes you so tired you don't
even want to talk about it.
Words come again and again to
our ears.
But we never can hear enough.
Nor can we ever really see all we
want to see.
⁹ All things continue the way they
have been since the beginning.
The same things will be done that
have always been done.
There is nothing new here on earth.
¹⁰ A person might say,
"Look, this is new!"
But really it has always been here.

It was here before we were!
¹¹ People don't remember what
happened long ago.
In the future, people will not
remember what happens now.
And later, other people will not
remember what was done
before them.

Does Wisdom Bring Happiness?

¹² I, the Teacher, was king over Israel in Jerusalem. ¹³ I decided to use my wisdom. I wanted to learn about everything that happens here on earth. I learned that God has given us terrible things to face here on earth. ¹⁴ I looked at everything done here on earth. I saw that it is all a waste of time. It is like chasing the wind.

¹⁵ If something is crooked,
you can't make it straight.
If something is missing,
you can't say it is there.

¹⁶ I said to myself, "I have become very wise. I am now wiser than anyone who ruled Jerusalem before me. I know what wisdom and knowledge really are." ¹⁷ So I decided to find out how wisdom and knowledge are better than foolish thinking. But I learned that trying to become wise is also like chasing the wind.

¹⁸ With much wisdom comes much
disappointment.
The person who gains more
knowledge also gains more
sorrow.

Does "Having Fun" Bring Happiness?

2 I said to myself, "I will try having fun. I will enjoy myself." But I found that this is also useless. ²It is foolish to laugh all the time. Having fun gets nothing done. ³I decided to cheer myself up with wine. At the same time my mind was still thinking wisely. I wanted to find a way to enjoy myself. I wanted to see what was good for people to do during their few days of life.

Does Hard Work Bring Happiness?

⁴Then I did great things. I built houses, and I planted vineyards for myself. ⁵I planted gardens, and I made parks.

wisdom helped me in all this.

¹⁰Anything I saw and wanted, I got
 for myself.
 I did not miss any pleasure I
 desired.
 I was pleased with everything I did.
 And this pleasure was the reward
 for all my hard work.
¹¹But then I looked at what I had done.
 I thought about all the hard work.
 Suddenly I realized it was just a

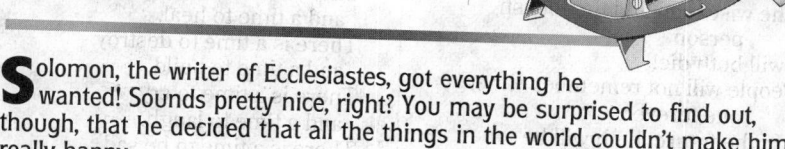

Feelings
ECCLESIASTES 2:10-11

Solomon, the writer of Ecclesiastes, got everything he wanted! Sounds pretty nice, right? You may be surprised to find out, though, that he decided that all the things in the world couldn't make him really happy.

Some of your friends may think that cool clothes, the newest video games, and the fastest bikes will bring them happiness. But they will only be disappointed. All of these things are fun, but eventually they break or get worn out. Sometimes we even get tired of them long before they wear out!

God is the only one who can bring you happiness that lasts forever! Instead of always trying to get more and more things, depend on God to bring you joy. He is much better at making you happy than all of the latest toys and clothes at the mall.

To find out what you can learn from the shortest verse in the Bible,
zoom to page 1296.

I planted all kinds of fruit trees in them. ⁶I made pools of water for myself. And I used them to water my growing trees. ⁷I bought men and women slaves. Slaves were also born in my house. I had large herds of cattle and flocks of sheep. I had more than anyone in Jerusalem before me. ⁸I also gathered silver and gold for myself. I took treasures from kings and other areas. I had men and women singers. I had all the wives a man could ever want. ⁹I became very famous. I was greater than anyone who had lived in Jerusalem before me. My

waste of time, like chasing
 the wind!
 There is nothing to gain from
 anything we do here on earth.

Maybe Wisdom Is the Answer

¹²Then I began to think again about
 being wise.
 And I thought also about being
 foolish and doing crazy things.
 But after all, what more can any
 king do?
 He can only do what some other
 king has already done.

13I saw that being wise is certainly
        better than being foolish,
    just as light is better than
        darkness.
14A wise man sees where he is going.
    But a foolish person is like
        someone walking around in
        the dark.
    Yet I saw that
        both the foolish person and the
        wise man end the same way.

15I thought to myself,
    "What happens to a foolish person
        will happen to me, too.
    So what do I get for being so wise?"
    I said to myself,
        "Being wise is also useless."
16The wise man and the foolish
        person
    will both die!
    People will not remember either
        one forever.
    In the future, both will be
        forgotten.

Is There Real Happiness in Life?

17So I hated life. It made me sad to
think that everything here on earth is
useless. It is like chasing the wind. 18I
hated all the things I had worked for
here on earth. I hated them because I
must leave them to someone who will
live after me. 19Someone else will control everything for which I worked so
hard here on earth. And I don't know
if he will be wise or foolish. This is also
useless. 20So I became sad about all the
hard work I had done here on earth. 21A
person can work hard using all his wisdom, knowledge and skill. But he will
die, and other people will get the things
he worked for. They did not do the
work, but they will get everything. This
is also unfair and useless. 22What does
a person get for all his work and struggling here on earth? 23All his life his
work is full of pain and sorrow. Even
at night his mind doesn't rest. This is
also useless.

24The best a person can do is eat,
drink and enjoy his work. I saw that
even this comes from God. 25No one

can eat or enjoy life without God. 26If a
person pleases God, God will give him
wisdom, knowledge and joy. But the
sinner will get only the work of gathering and storing wealth. Then he will
have to give it to the one who pleases
God. So all his work is useless. It is like
chasing the wind.

There Is a Time for Everything

3 There is a right time for everything.
Everything on earth has its
        special season.
2There is a time to be born
    and a time to die.
There is a time to plant
    and a time to pull up plants.
3There is a time to kill
    and a time to heal.
There is a time to destroy
    and a time to build.
4There is a time to cry
    and a time to laugh.
There is a time to be sad
    and a time to dance.
5There is a time to throw away stones
    and a time to gather them.
There is a time to hug
    and a time not to hug.
6There is a time to look for something
    and a time to stop looking for it.
There is a time to keep things
    and a time to throw things away.
7There is a time to tear apart
    and a time to sew together.
There is a time to be silent
    and a time to speak.
8There is a time to love
    and a time to hate.
There is a time for war
    and a time for peace.

God Controls His World

9Does a person really gain anything
from his work? 10I saw the hard work
God has given us to do. 11God has also
given us a desire to know the future.
God certainly does everything at just
the right time. But we can never completely understand what he is doing.
12So I realize that the best thing for people is to be happy. They should enjoy

themselves as long as they live. [13]God wants everyone to eat and drink and be happy in his work. These are gifts from God. [14]I know anything God does will continue forever. People cannot add anything to what God has done. And they cannot take anything away from it. God does it this way to cause people to honor him.

[15]What happens now has also
    happened in the past.
Things that will happen in the
    future have also happened
    before.
God makes the same things
    happen again and again.

God Allows Unfairness

[16]I also saw this here on earth:
Where there should have been
    justice, there was evil.
Where there should have been
    fairness, there was
    wickedness.
[17]I certainly believe that
God has planned a time for every
    thing and every action.
He will judge both good people
    and bad people.

[18]But I decided that God leaves it the way it is to test people. He wants to show them they are just like animals. [19]The same thing happens to animals and to people. They both have the same breath. So they both die. People are no better off than the animals. The lives of both are soon gone. [20]Both end up the same way. Both came from dust. And both will go back to dust. [21]Who can be sure that the spirit of man goes up to God? Or who can be sure that the spirit of an animal goes down into the ground? [22]So I saw the best thing a person can do is to enjoy his work. That is all he has. No one can help a person see what will happen in the future.

Is It Better to Be Dead?

4 Again I saw all the people who were treated badly here on earth.
I saw their tears.

I saw that they had no one to
    comfort them.
Cruel people had all the power.
There was no one to comfort the
    people they hurt.
[2]I decided that the dead
are better off than the living.
[3]But those who have never been born
are better off still.
They have not seen the evil
    that is done here on earth.

Why Work So Hard?

[4]I realized the reason people work hard and try to succeed: They are jealous of each other. This, too, is useless. It is like chasing the wind.

[5]Some say that it is foolish to fold
    your hands and do nothing.
You will starve to death!
[6]Maybe so, but I say it is better to
    be content
with what little you have.
Otherwise, you will always be
    struggling for more.
That is like chasing the wind.

[7]Again I saw something here on
    earth that was senseless:
[8]I saw a person who had no family.
He had no son or brother.
He always worked hard.
But he was never satisfied with
    what he had.
He never asked himself, "For whom
    am I working so hard?
Why don't I let myself enjoy life?"
This also is very sad and senseless.

Friends and Family Give Strength

[9]Two people are better than one.
They get more done by working
    together.
[10]If one person falls,
    the other can help him up.
But it is bad for the person who is
    alone when he falls.
No one is there to help him.
[11]If two lie down together, they will
    be warm.
But a person alone will not
    be warm.

¹²An enemy might defeat one person,
   but two people together can
      defend themselves.
A rope that has three parts wrapped
   together
is hard to break.

Fame and Power Are Useless

¹³A young person may be poor but
wise. He is better than a foolish, old
king who doesn't listen to advice. ¹⁴I
saw such a young person become king.
He had been born poor in the kingdom.
He had even gone to prison before
becoming king. ¹⁵I watched some of the
people who live on earth follow him.
They made him their king. ¹⁶Yes, a great
many people followed him at first. But
later, they did not like him, either. So
fame and power are shown to be useless. They are like chasing the wind.

Be Careful About Making Promises

5 Be careful when you go to worship
at the Temple.*ᵈ* It is better to listen
than to offer foolish sacrifices. People
who do this don't even know they are
doing wrong.

²Think before you speak.
   Be careful about what you promise
      to God.
God is in heaven,
   and you are on the earth.
So say only a few words to God.
³The saying is true: Bad dreams
      come from too much
      worrying.
So too many words come from
      foolish people.

⁴If you make a promise to God, don't
be slow to keep it. God is not happy with
foolish people. Give God what you
promised. ⁵It is better not to promise
anything than to promise something
and not do it. ⁶So don't let your words
cause you to sin. Also, don't say to the
priest at the Temple, "I didn't mean
what I promised!" If you do, God will
become angry with your words. He will
destroy everything you have worked

for. ⁷Many empty promises are like
many foolish dreams. They mean nothing. You should honor God.

Officers Cheat Each Other

⁸In some countries you will see poor
people treated badly. They are not treated fairly or given their rights. Don't be
surprised! One officer is cheated by a
higher officer. They in turn are cheated
by even higher officers. ⁹The wealth of
the country is divided up among them
all. Even the king makes sure he gets
his share of the profits.

Wealth Cannot Buy Happiness

¹⁰The person who loves money
   will never have all the money
      he wants.
The person who loves wealth
   will not be satisfied when he gets it.
This is also useless.
¹¹The more wealth a person has,
   the more friends he has to help
      him spend it.
So what does he really gain?
   He gains nothing except to look at
      his riches.
¹²A man who works hard sleeps
   in peace.
It is not important if he has little
   or much to eat.
But a rich person worries about
   his wealth.
He cannot sleep.

¹³I have seen something unfair here
   on earth:
A person suffers harm from saving
   up his money.
¹⁴ Then he loses it all in a bad deal.
So he has nothing
   to give to his son.
¹⁵A person comes into this world
   with nothing.
And when he dies, he leaves
   with nothing.
In spite of all his hard work,
   he leaves exactly as he came.
¹⁶This, too, is unfair:
He leaves exactly as he came.
   So what does he gain from chasing
      the wind?

[17]All he gets are days filled with
    sadness and sorrow.
  He ends up sick, defeated and
    angry.

Enjoy Your Life's Work

[18]I have seen what is best for a person to do here on earth. He should eat and drink and enjoy his work. This is because the life God has given him on earth is short. [19]God gives some people the ability to enjoy the wealth and property he gives them. He also gives them the ability to accept their state in life and enjoy their work. [20]Such people do not worry much about how short life is. This is because God keeps them busy with the things they love to do.

6 I have seen something else unfair here on earth. It causes serious problems for people. [2]God gives some people great wealth, riches and honor. They have everything they want. But God does not let them enjoy such things. Someone else enjoys them instead. This is unfair and senseless. [3]It is sad when a person can't enjoy the good things God gives him. Such a person might have 100 children. He might live a long time. But what good is it if he can't enjoy the good God gives him? I say a baby who is born dead is better off than he is. [4]It is useless for such a baby to be born. It ends up in the darkness of the grave without even a name. [5]That baby never saw the sun. It never knew anything. But it finds more rest than the person who never gets to enjoy the good things God gives him. [6]Even if he lives 2,000 years, it is sad if a person can't enjoy the good things God gives him. After all, both he and the baby born dead go to the same place—the grave.

[7]A person works just to feed himself.
  But he never seems to get enough
    to eat.
[8]In this way a wise man
  is no better off than a foolish person.
  Then, too, it does a poor man
    little good
  to know how to get along in life.

[9]So it is better to be happy with what
    you have
  than always to be wanting more.
  Always wanting more is useless—
    like chasing the wind.

Who Can Understand God's Plan?

[10]Everything that happens was
    planned long ago.
  A man is only what he was created
    to be.
  It is useless to argue with God
    about it.
  This is because God is more
    powerful than man is.
[11]The more you argue,
  the more useless it is.
  You gain nothing at all by
    arguing.

[12]A person has only a few days of life on the earth. His short life passes like a shadow. And who knows what is best for him while he lives? Who can tell him what will happen after his time on earth?

Some Benefits of Serious Thinking

7 It is better to have respect than good perfume.
  The day a person dies is better
    than the day he was born.
[2]It is better to go to a funeral
  than to a party.
  We all must die.
  Everyone living should think
    about this.
[3]Sorrow is better than laughter.
  Sadness has a good influence
    on you.
[4]A wise man thinks about death,
  but a foolish person thinks only
    about having a good time.
[5]It is better to be criticized by a
    wise man
  than to be praised by a foolish
    person.
[6]The laughter of foolish people is
    useless.
  It is like heating a pot by
    burning straw.
  There is a lot of fire but no heat.

⁷Even a wise man will become foolish
if he lets money change his thinking.

⁸It is better to finish something
than to start it.
It is better to be patient
than to be proud.
⁹Don't become mad quickly,
because getting angry is foolish.
¹⁰Don't ask, "Why was life better in the 'good old days'?"
It is not wise to ask such questions.

¹¹Wisdom is as good to have as inheriting property.
It helps people see what to do.
¹²Wisdom is like money.
They both help a person.
But wisdom is better than money,
because it can save a person's life.

¹³Stop and think about everything that God causes to happen.
You cannot change a thing,
even if you think it is wrong.
¹⁴When life is good, enjoy it.
But when life is hard, remember:
God gives us good times and hard times.
And no one knows what tomorrow will bring.

It Is Impossible to Be Truly Good

¹⁵In my short life I have seen both of these:
I have seen good men die being good.
And I have seen evil men living a long time.
¹⁶Don't try to be too right all the time.
Don't try to be too wise, either.
Why should you destroy yourself this way?
¹⁷Don't be too wicked.
And don't be a foolish person.
You will die young if you do so.
¹⁸Try to avoid going too far in doing anything.
Those who honor God will avoid doing too much of anything.

¹⁹Wisdom gives a person strength.
One wise man is stronger than ten leaders in a city.

²⁰Surely there is not a good man on earth
who always does good and never sins.

²¹Don't listen to everything people say.
You might hear your servant insulting you.
²²You know that many times
you also have insulted others.

²³I used wisdom to test all these things.
I wanted to be wise,
but it was too hard for me.
²⁴I cannot understand why things are as they are.
It is too hard for anyone to understand.
²⁵I studied and tried very hard to find wisdom.
I tried to find some meaning for everything.
I learned that it is foolish to be evil.
And it is crazy to act like a fool.

²⁶I found that some women are worse than death.
They are as dangerous as traps.
Their love is like a net.
Their arms hold men like chains.
A man who follows God will run away from them.
But a sinner will be caught by them.

²⁷The Teacher says, "This is what I learned:
I added all these things together
to see if I could find some meaning for everything.
²⁸I am still looking for it,
but I have not found it.
But I did discover that truly good people are hard to find.
Such people are one in a million!
²⁹One thing I have learned:
God made people good.
But people have found all kinds of ways to be bad."

Obey the King

8 No one is like the wise man.
He can understand what things
mean.
His wisdom makes him happy.
It makes his sad face happy.

²I advise you always to obey the king's command. Do this because you made a promise to God. ³Don't be too quick to quit the job the king gave you. But don't support something that is wrong. Remember, the king does whatever he pleases. ⁴The king is the highest power. No one can tell him what to do.

⁵A person will be safe if he obeys the
king's command.
A wise man knows how to do the
right thing at the right time.
⁶And there is a right time and a right
way for everything.
Yet people often have many
troubles.
⁷They do not know what the future
holds.
No one can tell them what
will happen.
⁸No one has the power to keep the
wind from blowing.
No one has the power to stop his
own death.
During war a soldier cannot go
home.
So also, the person who does evil
will not get away free.

Justice, Rewards and Punishment

⁹I saw all of this as I studied. I considered all that is done here on earth. And I saw men rule others and hurt them. ¹⁰I saw evil people being buried. They used to go in and out of the holy place. Good things were said about them in the same towns where they had done evil. This is senseless, too.

¹¹Sometimes people are not punished right away for the bad things they do. That makes other people want to do bad things, too. ¹²A sinner might do a hundred evil things. And he might live a long time. Even so, I know it will be better for those who honor God. They

fear him, and he sees it. ¹³And I also know it will not go well for evil people. Their lives will be like a brief shadow. They will not live very long. ¹⁴But sometimes something senseless happens on earth. Bad things happen to good people. Good things happen to bad people. This is truly senseless. ¹⁵So I decided it was more important to enjoy life. The best that people can do here on earth is to eat, drink and enjoy life. These joys will help people do the hard work God gives them here on earth.

We Cannot Understand All God Does

¹⁶I used my mind to learn about all that happens on earth. I saw how busy people are. They work day and night and hardly ever sleep. ¹⁷I also saw all that God has done. Nobody can understand what God does here on earth. No matter how hard a person tries to understand it, he cannot. Even if a wise man says he understands, he really cannot. No one at all can really understand it.

Is Death Fair?

9 I thought about something else and tried hard to understand it. I saw that God takes care of both good people and wise people and what they do. But no one knows if he will see good or bad times.

²Both good and bad things happen
to everyone.
They happen to those who are fair
and to those who are wicked.
They happen to those who are good
and to those who are evil.
They happen to those who
sacrifice and to those who
do not.
The same things happen to a good
person
as happen to a sinner.
The same things happen to a person
who makes promises to God
as to one who does not.

³This is something unfair that happens here on earth. The same things

happen to everyone. So men's minds are full of evil and foolish thoughts while they live. After that, they join the dead. [4]But anyone still alive has hope. Even a live dog is better off than a dead lion!

[5]The living know they will die.
But the dead no longer think about
such things.
Dead people have no more reward.
People forget them.
[6]After a person is dead,
he can no longer show love or hate
or jealousy.
And he will never again share
in the things that happen here
on earth.

Enjoy Life While You Can

[7]So go eat your food and enjoy it.
Drink your wine and be happy.
It is all right with God
if you do this.
[8]Put on nice clothes
and make yourself look good.

[9]Enjoy life with the wife you love. Enjoy all the days of this short life God has given you here on earth. It is all you have. So enjoy the work you have to do here on earth. [10]Whatever work you do, do your best. This is because you are going to the grave. There is no working, no planning, no knowledge and no wisdom there.

Time and Chance

[11]I also realized something else here
on earth that is senseless:
The fast runner does not always win
the race.
The strong army does not always
win the battle.
The wise man does not always
have food.
The smart man does not always
become wealthy.
And the man with special skills
does not always receive praise.
Bad things happen to everyone.
[12]A person never knows what will
happen to him next.
He is like a fish caught in a cruel net.

He is like a bird caught in a trap.
In the same way, a person is
trapped by bad things
that suddenly happen to him.

Wisdom Does Not Always Win

[13]I also saw something wise happen here on earth. And it was very impressive to me. [14]There was a small town with only a few people in it. A great king fought against it and put his armies all around it. [15]Now there was a wise man in the town. He was poor, but he used his wisdom to save his town. But later on, everyone forgot about him. [16]I still think wisdom is better than strength. But those people forgot about the poor man's wisdom. And they stopped listening to what he said.

[17]The quiet words of a wise man are
better
than the shouts of a foolish ruler.
[18]Wisdom is better than weapons
of war.
But one sinner can destroy much
good.

10 Dead flies will make even perfume
smell bad.
In the same way, a little
foolishness can ruin
a wise man's fame for wisdom.
[2]A wise man's heart leads him in the
right way.
But the heart of a foolish person
leads him in the wrong way.
[3]A foolish person is not wise.
It shows in everything he does.
Even as he walks along the road,
he shows everyone how stupid
he is.
[4]Don't leave your job
just because the ruler is angry
with you.
Remain calm.
It will help correct your mistakes.

[5]Here is something else unfair that
happens here on earth.
It is the kind of mistake rulers
make:
[6]Foolish people are given important
positions

while rich people are given less
important ones.

[7]I have seen servants ride on horses
while princes walk beside them
on foot.

[8]Anyone who digs a pit might fall
into it.
Anyone who knocks down a wall
might be bitten by a snake.

[9]Anyone who moves large stones
might be hurt by them.
And anyone who cuts logs might
get hurt while doing it.

[10]Cutting logs with a dull ax
makes you work harder.
A wise man will sharpen his ax.
In the same way, wisdom can
make any job easier.

[11]Someone might know how to
control snakes.
But what good is such wisdom if
the snake has already bitten
him?

[12]A wise man's words bring him praise.
But a foolish person's words will
destroy him.

[13]A foolish person begins by saying
something foolish.
In the end he is saying even
crazier things.

[14]A foolish person talks too much
about what he will do.
No one knows the future.
No one can tell him what will
happen after he dies.

[15]A foolish person doesn't know even
the most obvious things.
He can't even find his way back
to town.
So he has to wear himself out
working.

The Value of Work

[16]How terrible it will be for a country
if its king is a child.
How terrible it will be for that country
if its leaders have parties all
the time.

[17]A country is well off
if its king comes from a good family.

It is good for a country
if its leaders control their eating
and drinking.
They should eat and drink for
strength,
not to get drunk.

[18]If a person is lazy and doesn't repair
the roof,
it will begin to fall.
If he refuses to fix it,
the house will leak.

[19]A party makes you feel good.
And wine makes you feel happy.
But both cost you a lot of money.

[20]Don't say or think bad things about
the king.
And don't say bad things about
rich people even alone in your
bedroom.
A little bird might report it
to others.
A bird might fly to them and tell all
you said.

Boldly Face the Future

11 Do good things everywhere you
go.*
After a while the good you do will
return to help you.

[2]Invest what you have in several
different businesses.
You don't know what bad things
might happen on earth.

[3]If clouds are full of rain,
they will pour water on the earth.
A tree can fall to the north or south.
But it will stay where it falls.

[4]If a person waits for perfect weather,
he will never plant his seeds.
And if he is afraid that every cloud
will bring rain,
he will never harvest his crops.

[5]You don't know where the wind will
blow.
And you don't know how a baby
grows in its mother's body.
In the same way, God certainly
made all things.

*Do good . . . go   Literally, "Throw your bread upon the water."

But you can't understand what he
is doing.
⁶Begin planting early in the morning,
and don't stop working until evening.
This is because you don't know
which things you do will
succeed.
It is even possible that everything
you do will succeed.

Serve God While You Are Young

⁷It is good to be alive
to enjoy the light of day.
⁸A person ought to enjoy every day
of his life.
This is true no matter how long
he lives.
But he should also remember this:
You will be dead much longer than
you live.
After you are dead, you
accomplish nothing.
⁹Young people, enjoy yourselves
while you are young.
Be happy while you are young.
Do whatever your heart desires.
Do whatever you want to do.
But remember that God will
judge you
for everything you do.
¹⁰So avoid sorrow and sadness.
Forget about all the bad things
that happen to you.
This is because the joys of youth
pass quickly away.

"**M**y grandpa
showed me these
verses and he said
this is all true about
getting old. That's
why it's so impor-
tant to get to know
God now. Take a
look at Ecclesiastes
12:1-14."

The Problems of Old Age

12 Remember your Creator
while you are young.
Your old age is coming

when you will have many
troubles.
When that time comes,
you won't have much to enjoy.
²When you become old,
the light from the sun, moon and
stars will seem dark to you.
It will seem as if the rain clouds
never go away.
³At that time your arms will lose
their strength.
Your strong legs will become weak
and bent.
Your teeth will fall out so you
cannot chew.
Your eyes will not see clearly.
⁴Your ears will be deaf to the noise in
the streets.
You will barely hear singing.
The sound of the millstone grinding
your grain will seem
very quiet.
But you'll wake up when a bird
first starts singing!
⁵You will fear high places.
And you will be afraid to go for a
walk because you may fall.
Your hair will become white like the
flowers on an almond tree.
You will limp along like a
grasshopper when you walk.
Your desires will be gone.
Then you will go to your everlasting
home.
And people will go to your
funeral.
⁶Remember God before your life is
snapped like a silver chain.
Remember God before your life is
broken like a golden bowl.
It will be as useless as a broken
bucket at the spring.
It will be no good, like a broken
wheel at a water well.
⁷Your body will become part of the
dust of the earth again.
But your spirit will return to God
who gave it.

⁸Everything is useless!
The Teacher says that everything
is useless.

Conclusion

⁹The Teacher was very wise. He taught the people what he knew. The Teacher very carefully thought about, studied and set in order many wise teachings. ¹⁰The Teacher looked for just the right words. He wrote teachings that are dependable and true.

¹¹Words from wise men are like sharp sticks used to guide animals. These words are like nails that have been driven in firmly. They are wise teachings that come from God the Shepherd. ¹²So be careful, my son, about other teach-ings. People are always writing books. And too much study will make you very tired.

¹³Now, everything has been heard.
Here is my final advice:
Honor God and obey his
commands.
This is the most important thing
people can do.
¹⁴God knows everything people do,
even the things done in secret.
He knows all the good and all
the bad.
He will judge everything people do.

SONG OF SOLOMON

A Love Song

1 Solomon's Greatest Song.

The Woman Speaks to the Man She Loves

2Kiss me with the kisses of your
mouth!
Your love is better than wine.
3The smell of your perfume is pleasant.
Your name is pleasant like
expensive perfume!
That's why the young women
love you.
4Take me with you; let's run.
The king takes me into his rooms.

Friends Speak to the Man

We will rejoice and be happy with
you.
We praise your love more than
wine.

The Woman Speaks

With good reason, the young
women love you, my lover.
5I'm dark but lovely,
women of Jerusalem.
I'm dark like the tents of Kedar,
like the curtains of Solomon.
6Don't look at how dark I am,
at how dark the sun has made me.
My brothers were angry with me.
They made me tend the vineyards.
So I haven't tended my own
vineyard!
7Tell me, you whom I love,
where do you feed your sheep?
Where do you make them rest at
noon?
Why should I look for you near your
friend's sheep?

Am I like a woman who wears a
veil?[n]

The Man Speaks to the Woman

8You are the most beautiful of women.
Surely you know to follow the
sheep.
Feed your young goats
near the shepherds' tents.
9My darling, you are like a mare
that pulls the king's chariots.
10Your cheeks are beautiful with
ornaments.
Your neck is beautiful with jewels.
11We will make for you gold earrings
with silver hooks.

The Woman Speaks

12The smell of my perfume spreads
out
to the king on his couch.
13My lover is like a bag of myrrh[d]
that lies all night between my
breasts.
14My lover is like a bunch of flowers
from the vineyards at En Gedi.

The Man Speaks

15My darling, you are beautiful!
Oh, you are beautiful!
Your eyes are like doves!

The Woman Answers the Man

16You are so handsome, my lover.
You are so pleasant!
Our bed is the grass.
17The boards of our house are
cedar trees.
And the wood of our ceiling is
juniper trees.

[n]veil This was the way a prostitute usually dressed.

The Woman Speaks Again

2 I am a rose in the Plain of Sharon.
I am a lily in the valleys.

The Man Speaks Again

²Among the young women, my darling
is like a lily among thorns!

The Woman Answers

³Among young men, my lover
is like an apple tree among the
trees in the woods!
I enjoy sitting in his shadow.
His fruit is sweet to my taste.
⁴He brought me to the banquet room.
His banner over me is love.
⁵Strengthen me with raisins.
Refresh me with apples,
because I am weak with love.
⁶My lover's left hand is under my
head.
And his right arm holds me tight!

The Woman Speaks to the Friends

⁷Women of Jerusalem, promise me
by the gazelles*ᵈ* and the deer.
Promise not to wake love.
Don't excite my feelings of love
until I'm ready.

The Woman Speaks Again

⁸I hear my lover's voice.
He comes jumping across the
mountains.
He comes skipping over the hills!
⁹My lover is like a gazelle*ᵈ* or a
young deer.
Look, he stands behind our wall.
He stares in through the windows,
looking through the blinds.
¹⁰My lover spoke. He said to me,
"Get up, my darling.
Let's go away, my beautiful one.
¹¹Look, the winter is past.
The rains are over and gone.
¹²Blossoms appear through all the
land.
The time has come to sing.
The cooing of doves is heard in
our land.
¹³There are young figs on the fig trees.

The blossoms on the vines smell
sweet.
Get up, my darling.
Let's go away, my beautiful
one."

The Man Speaks

¹⁴My beloved is like a dove that hides
in the cracks of the rock.
She hides in the secret places of
the cliff.
Show me your face.
Let me hear your voice.
Your voice is very sweet,
and your face is lovely.
¹⁵Catch the foxes for us—
the little foxes that ruin the
vineyards.
Our vineyards are in blossom.

The Woman Speaks

¹⁶My lover is mine, and I am his.
He feeds among the lilies
¹⁷until the day dawns
and the shadows disappear.
Turn, my lover.
Be like a gazelle*ᵈ* or a young
deer
on the rugged mountains.

The Woman Dreams

3 At night on my bed,
I looked for the one I love.
I looked for him, but I could not
find him.
²I will get up now. I will go around
the city,
in the streets and squares.
I will look for the one I love.
I looked for him, but I could not
find him.
³The watchmen found me as they
patrolled the city.
I asked, "Have you seen the one
I love?"
⁴As soon as I had left them
I found the one I love.
I held him. I would not let him go
until I had brought him to my
mother's house.
I brought him into the room where
I was born.

The Woman Speaks to the Friends

⁵Women of Jerusalem, promise me
by the gazelles[d] and the deer.
Promise not to wake love.
Don't excite my feelings of love
until I'm ready.
⁶Who is this coming out of the desert
like a cloud of smoke?
Who is this that smells like myrrh,[d]
incense[d]
and other spices?
⁷Look, it's Solomon's couch[n]
with 60 soldiers around it.
They are the finest soldiers of
Israel.
⁸These soldiers all carry swords.
They have been trained in war.
Every man wears his sword at his
side.
He is ready for the dangers of the
night.
⁹King Solomon had a couch made for
himself.
It is made of wood from Lebanon.
¹⁰He made its posts of silver
and its braces of gold.
The seat was covered with purple
cloth.
The women of Jerusalem wove it
with love.
¹¹Women of Jerusalem, go out and
see King Solomon.
He is wearing the crown his
mother put on his head.
It was his wedding day,
when his heart was happy!

The Man Speaks to the Woman

4 How beautiful you are, my darling!
Oh, you are beautiful!
Your eyes behind your veil are like
doves.
Your hair is like a flock of goats
streaming down Mount Gilead.
²Your teeth are white like newly-
sheared sheep
just coming from their bath.
Each one has a twin.
None of them is alone.
³Your lips are like red silk thread.

Your mouth is lovely.
Your cheeks behind your veil
are like slices of a pomegranate.[d]
⁴Your neck looks like David's tower.
The tower was built with rows of
stones.
A thousand shields hang on its
walls.
Each shield belongs to a strong
soldier.
⁵Your breasts are like two fawns.
They are like twins of a gazelle,[d]
eating among the lilies.
⁶Until the day dawns
and the shadows disappear,
I will go to that mountain of myrrh.[d]
And I will go to that hill of
incense.[d]
⁷My darling, everything about you is
beautiful.
There is nothing at all wrong with
you.
⁸Come with me from Lebanon, my
bride.
Come with me from Lebanon.
Come from the top of Mount
Amana,
from the tops of Mount Senir and
Mount Hermon.
Come from the lions' dens
and from the leopards' hills.
⁹My sister, my bride,
you have thrilled my heart.
You have thrilled my heart
with a glance of your eyes,
with one jewel from your necklace.
¹⁰Your love is so sweet, my sister, my
bride!
Your love is better than wine.
Your perfume smells better than
any spice.
¹¹My bride, your lips drip honey.
Honey and milk are under your
tongue.
Your clothes smell like the cedars
of Lebanon.
¹²My sister, my bride, you are like a
garden locked up.
You are like a spring with a wall
around it, a fountain that is
closed.

---

[n]**couch**   Something like a bed carried by slaves on which the king lay or sat while traveling.

¹³Your limbs are like an orchard
of pomegranates and all the best
fruit.
It is filled with flowers and nard.*d*
¹⁴It also has saffron,*d* calamus*d* and
cinnamon.
It is filled with trees of incense,
myrrh and aloes*d*—
all the best spices.
¹⁵You are like a garden fountain—
a well of fresh water
flowing down from the mountains
of Lebanon.

The Woman Speaks

¹⁶Awake, north wind!
Come, you south wind!
Blow on my garden.
Let its sweet smells flow out.
Let my lover enter the garden.
And let him eat its best fruits.

The Man Speaks

5 I have entered my garden, my sister, my bride.
I have gathered my myrrh*d* with
my spice.
I have eaten my honeycomb and my
honey.
I have drunk my wine and my
milk.

The Friends Speak

Eat, friends, and drink.
Yes, drink deeply, lovers.

The Woman Dreams

²I sleep, but my heart is awake.
I hear my lover knocking.
"Open to me, my sister, my darling,
my dove, my perfect one.
My head is wet with dew.
And my hair is wet with the
dampness of the night."
³I have taken off my garment.
I don't want to put it on again!
I have washed my feet.
I don't want to get them dirty
again!
⁴My lover put his hand through the
door opening.
I felt excited inside.

⁵I got up to open the door for my
lover.
Myrrh*d* was dripping from my
hands.
Myrrh was flowing from my fingers,
onto the handles of the lock.
⁶I opened the door for my lover.
But my lover had left. He was
gone.
When he had spoken, he had
taken my breath away.
I looked for him, but I could not
find him.
I called for him, but he did not
answer me.
⁷The watchmen found me
as they patrolled the city.
They hit me; they hurt me.
The guards on the wall took away
my coat.
⁸I tell you, women of Jerusalem,
if you find my lover,
tell him I am weak with love.

The Friends Answer the Woman

⁹Is your lover better than other
lovers,
you, the most beautiful of women?
Is your lover better than other
lovers?
Is that why you talk like this?

The Woman Answers the Friends

¹⁰My lover is clean and tanned.
He's the best of 10,000 men.
¹¹His head is like the finest gold.
His hair is wavy and black like a
raven.
¹²His eyes are like doves
by springs of water.
They seem to be bathed in cream.
They are set like jewels.
¹³His cheeks are like garden beds of
spices.
They smell like mounds of
perfume.
His lips are like lilies
flowing with myrrh.*d*
¹⁴His hands are like gold hinges,
filled with jewels.
His body is like smooth ivory
covered with sapphires.

[15]His legs are like large marble posts,
standing on bases of fine gold.
He is tall like a cedar of Lebanon—
like the best cedar trees.
[16]His mouth is sweet to kiss.
I desire him very much.
Yes, daughters of Jerusalem,
this is my lover.
This is my friend.

The Friends Speak to the Woman

6 Where has your lover gone,
most beautiful of women?
Which way did your lover turn?
We will look for him with you.

The Woman Answers the Friends

[2]My lover has gone down to his
garden.
He has gone to the garden beds
of spices
to feed in the gardens
and to gather lilies.
[3]I belong to my lover.
And my lover belongs to me.
He feeds among the lilies.

The Man Speaks to the Woman

[4]My darling, you are as beautiful as
the city of Tirzah.
You are as lovely as the city of
Jerusalem.
You are as wonderful as an army
flying flags.
[5]Turn your eyes from me.
They excite me too much!
Your hair is like a flock of goats
streaming down Mount Gilead.
[6]Your teeth are white like sheep
just coming from their bath.
Each one has a twin.
None of them is alone.
[7]Your cheeks behind your veil
are like slices of a pomegranate.[d]
[8]There may be 60 queens and 80
slave women[d]
and so many girls you cannot
count them.
[9]But there is only one like my dove,
my perfect one.
She is her mother's only
daughter,

the brightest of the one who gave
her birth.
The young women saw her and
called her happy.
The queens and the slave women
also praised her.

The Young Women Praise the Woman

[10]Who is that young woman?
She shines out like the dawn.
She's as pretty as the moon.
She's as bright as the sun.
And she's as wonderful
as an army flying flags.

The Man Speaks

[11]I went down into the orchard of
nut trees.
I went to see the blossoms of the
valley.
I went to look for buds on the vines,
to see if the pomegranate[d] trees
had bloomed.
[12]My desire for you makes me feel
like a prince in a chariot.

The Friends Call to the Woman

[13]Come back, come back, woman of
Shulam.
Come back, come back,
so we may look at you!

The Woman Answers the Friends

Why do you want to look at the
woman of Shulam
as you would at the dance of two
groups?

The Man Speaks to the Woman

7 Your feet are beautiful in sandals,
you daughter of a prince.
Your round thighs are like jewels
shaped by an artist.
[2]Your navel is like a round drinking
cup
always filled with wine.
Your stomach is like a pile of wheat
with lilies around it like a fence.
[3]Your breasts are like two fawns.
They are like twins of a gazelle.[d]
[4]Your neck is like an ivory tower.

Your eyes are like the pools in
Heshbon
near the gate of Bath Rabbim.
Your nose is like a tower of Lebanon
which looks toward Damascus.
5Your head is like Mount Carmel.
And your hair is like purple cloth.
The king is captured in its folds.
6You are beautiful.
You are very pleasant.
My love, you are full of delights!
7You are tall like a palm tree.
Your breasts are like its bunches
of fruit.
8I said, "I will climb up the palm tree.
I will take hold of its fruit."
Let your breasts be like bunches of
grapes.
Let the smell of your breath be
like apples.
9 And let your mouth be like the
best wine.

The Woman Speaks to the Man

Let this wine go down sweetly for
my lover.
May it flow gently past the lips and
teeth.
10I belong to my lover,
and he desires only me.
11Come, my lover.
Let's go out into the country.
Let's spend the night in the fields.
12Let's go early to the vineyards.
Let's see if the buds are on the
vines.
Let's see if the blossoms have
already opened
and if the pomegranates*d* have
bloomed.
There I will give you my love.
13The mandrake flowers give their
sweet smell.
And at our gates there are all the
best fruits.
I have saved them for you, my lover,
the old delights and the new.

8 I wish you were like my brother
who was fed at my mother's
breasts!
If I found you outside,
I would kiss you.

And no one would look down on
me.
2I would lead you and bring you
to my mother's house.
She is the one who has taught me.
I would give you a drink of spiced
wine
from my pomegranates.

The Woman Speaks to the Friends

3My lover's left hand is under my head.
And his right arm holds me tight!
4Women of Jerusalem, promise me.
Promise not to wake love.
Don't excite my feelings of love
until I'm ready.

The Friends Speak

5Who is this coming out of the desert,
leaning on her lover?

The Man Speaks to the Woman

I woke you under the apple tree.
It was there that you were born.
There your mother gave birth to you.
6Put me like a seal on your heart,
like a seal on your arm.
Love is as strong as death.
Desire is as strong as the grave.
Love bursts into flames.
It burns like a very hot fire.
7Even much water cannot put out the
flame of love.
Floods cannot drown love.
If a man offered everything in his
house for love,
people would totally reject it.

The Woman's Brothers Speak

8We have a little sister,
and her breasts are not yet grown.
What should we do for our sister
on the day she becomes engaged?
9If she is a wall,
we will put silver towers on her.
If she is a door,
we will protect her with cedar
boards.

The Woman Speaks

10I am a wall,
and my breasts are like towers.

So I was to him,
as one who brings happiness.
[11]Solomon had a vineyard at Baal
Hamon.
He rented the vineyards for others
to tend.
Everyone who rented had to pay
25 pounds of silver for the fruit.
[12]But my own vineyard is mine to give.
Solomon, the 25 pounds of silver
are for you.
And 5 pounds are for those who
tend the fruit.

The Man Speaks to the Woman

[13]You who live in the gardens,
my friends are listening for your
voice.
Let me hear it!

The Woman Speaks to the Man

[14]Hurry, my lover.
Be like a gazelle[d]
or a young deer
on the mountains where spices
grow.

ISAIAH

God's Message
in Troubled Times

1 This is the vision Isaiah son of Amoz saw. God showed Isaiah what would happen to Judah and Jerusalem. Isaiah saw these things while Uzziah, Jotham, Ahaz and Hezekiah were kings of Judah.

God Finds Fault with His People

2 Heaven and earth, listen,
  because the Lord is speaking:
"I raised my children and helped
  them grow.
But they have turned against me.
3 An ox knows its master.
And a donkey knows where its
  owner feeds it.
But the people of Israel do not know
  me.
My people do not understand."

4 Terrible times are coming for Israel,
  a nation of sin.
The people are loaded down with
  guilt.
They are like a group of children
  doing evil.
They are full of evil.
They have left the Lord.
They hate God, the Holy One of
  Israel.
They have turned away from him.

5 Why should you continue to be
  punished?
Why do you continue to turn
  against him?
Your whole head is hurt.
And your whole heart is sick.
6 There is no healthy spot
  from the bottom of your foot to the
  top of your head.
You are covered with wounds,
  hurts and open sores.

Your wounds are not cleaned and
  covered.
No medicine takes away the pain.
7 Your land is ruined.
Your cities have been burned with
  fire.
While you watch,
  your enemies are stealing
  everything from your land.
Your land is ruined like a country
  destroyed by enemies.
8 Jerusalem is left alone
  like an empty shelter in a vineyard.
It is like a hut left in a field of
  melons.
It is like a city surrounded by
  enemies.
9 The Lord of heaven's armies
  allowed a few of our people to live.
Otherwise we would have been
  completely destroyed
like the cities of Sodom and
  Gomorrah.

10 Jerusalem, your rulers are like
  those of Sodom.
Your people are like those of
  Gomorrah.
Hear the word of the Lord.
Listen to the teachings of our God!
11 The Lord says,
"I do not want all these sacrifices
  you give me.
I have had enough of your sacrifices
  of male sheep and fat from fine
  animals.
I am not pleased
  by the blood of bulls, sheep and
  goats.
12 You come to meet with me.
But who asked you to do
all this running in and out?

¹³Don't continue bringing me
worthless sacrifices!
I hate the incense^d you burn.
I can't stand your New Moons,^d
Sabbaths^d and other feast days.
I can't stand the evil you do in
holding your holy meetings.
¹⁴I hate your New Moon feasts
and your other yearly feasts.
They have become like heavy
weights on me.
I am tired of carrying them.
¹⁵You will raise your arms in prayer
to me.
But I will refuse to look at you.
Even if you say many prayers,
I will not listen to you.
It's because your hands are full of
blood.
¹⁶Wash yourselves and make
yourselves clean.^d
Stop doing the evil things I see
you do.
Stop doing wrong!
¹⁷ Learn to do good.
Be fair to other people.
Punish those who hurt others.
Help the orphans.
Stand up for the rights of widows."

¹⁸The Lord says,
"Come, we will talk these things
over.
Your sins are red like deep red
cloth.
But they can be as white as snow.
Your sins are bright red.
But you can be white like wool.
¹⁹If you will obey me,
you will eat good crops from the
land.
²⁰But if you refuse to obey and if you
turn against me,
you will be destroyed by your
enemies' swords."
The Lord himself said these things.

Jerusalem Is Not Loyal to God

²¹The city of Jerusalem once followed
the Lord.
But she is no longer loyal to the
Lord.
She used to be filled with fairness.

People there lived the way God
wanted.
But now, murderers live there.
²²Jerusalem, you have become like the
scum left when silver is purified.
You are like wine mixed with water.
²³Your rulers are rebels.
They are friends of thieves.
They all accept money for doing
wrong things.
They are paid to cheat people.
They don't try to help the orphans.
And they don't listen to the
widows' needs.
²⁴The Master, the Lord of heaven's
armies,
the Mighty One of Israel, says:
"You, my enemies, will not cause
me any more trouble.
I will pay you back for what you did.
²⁵I will turn against you.
I will clean away all your wrongs
as if with soap.
I will take all the worthless things
out of you.
²⁶I will bring back judges as you had
long ago.
Your counselors will be like the
ones you had in the beginning.
Then you will be called the City
That Is Right with God.
You will be called the Loyal City."

²⁷Because the Lord does what is fair,
he will rescue Jerusalem.
Because the Lord does what is right,
he will save her people who come
back to him.
²⁸But sinners and those who turn
against him will be destroyed.
Those who have left the Lord will
die.

²⁹"You will be ashamed
because you have worshiped false
gods under the oak trees.
You will be disgraced
because you have worshiped idols
in your gardens.
³⁰You will be like an oak whose leaves
are dying.
You will be like a garden without
water.

31Powerful people will be like small,
  dry pieces of wood.
And what they do will be like
  sparks.
The people and what they do will
  burn together.
And no one will be able to stop
  that fire."

The Message About Jerusalem

2 Isaiah son of Amoz saw this message about Judah and Jerusalem.
2In the last days
the mountain on which the Lord's
  Temple*d* stands
will become the most important of
  all mountains.
It will be raised above the hills.
And people from all nations will
  come streaming to it.
3Many nations will come and say,
"Come, let us go up to the
  mountain of the Lord.
Let us go to the Temple of the God
  of Jacob.
Then God will teach us his ways.
And we will obey his teachings."
The Lord's teachings will go out
  from Jerusalem.
The Lord's message will go out
  from Jerusalem.
4Then the Lord will settle arguments
  among many nations.
He will make decisions for strong
  nations that are far away.
Then the nations will make their
  swords into plows.
They will make their spears into
  hooks for trimming trees.
Nations will no longer fight other
  nations.
They will not even train for war
  anymore.

5Come, family of Jacob.
We should follow the way of the
  Lord.

A Terrible Day Is Coming

6Lord, you have left your people,
  the family of Jacob.
They have become filled with wrong
  ideas from people in the East.

Your people try to tell the future
  like the Philistines.
They have completely accepted
  those foreign ideas.
7Their land has been filled with
  silver and gold.
There are a great many treasures
  there.
Their land has been filled with horses.
There are many chariots there.
8Their land is full of idols.
The people worship these idols
  that they made with their own
  hands.
They worship statues shaped by
  their fingers.
9People will not be proud any longer.
They will bow low with shame.
God, do not forgive them.

10Go into the caves of the cliffs.
Dig holes and hide in the ground.
Hide from the anger of the Lord
  and from his great power!
11Proud people will stop being proud.
They will bow low with shame.
At that time only the Lord will still
  be praised.

12The Lord of heaven's armies has a
  certain day planned.
On that day he will punish the
  proud and those who brag.
They will no longer be important.
13He will bring down the tall cedar
  trees from Lebanon.
He will destroy the great oak trees
  of Bashan.
14He will destroy all the tall mountains
  and the high hills.
15He will knock down every tall tower
  and every high, strong wall.
16He will sink all the trading ships.
And he will destroy the beautiful
  ships.
17At that time proud people will stop
  being proud.
They will bow low with shame.
And at that time only the Lord will
  be praised.
18 But all the idols will be gone.

19People will run to caves in the rocky
  cliffs.

They will dig holes and hide in the
ground.
They will hide from the anger of the
Lord
and his great power.
They will do this when the Lord
stands to shake the earth.
20At that time people will throw away
their gold and silver idols.
They made these idols for
themselves to worship.
But they will throw them away to
the bats and moles.
21Then the people will hide in caves
and cracks in the rocks.
They will hide from the anger of the
Lord
and his great power.
They will do this when the Lord
stands to shake the earth.

22You should stop trusting in people
to save you.
People are only human.
They aren't able to help you.

God Will Punish Judah and Jerusalem

3 Understand what I am telling you.
The Master, the Lord of heaven's
armies,
will take away everything Judah and
Jerusalem need.
He will take away all the food and
water.
2He will take away all the heroes and
great soldiers.
He will take away all the judges,
prophets,[d]
people who do magic and older
leaders.
3He will take away the military leaders
and government leaders.
He will take away the counselors,
the skilled craftsmen and
those who try to tell the future.
4The Lord says, "I will cause young
boys to be your leaders.
Foolish children will rule over you.
5Everyone will be against everyone
else.
Young people will not respect
older people.

Common people will not respect
important people."
6At that time a man will grab one of
his brothers
from his own family and say,
"You have a coat. So you will be our
leader.
You will be the leader over all
these ruins."
7But that brother will stand up and
say,
"I cannot help you.
I do not have food or clothes in my
house.
You will not make me your
leader."
8This will happen because Jerusalem
has stumbled
and Judah has fallen.
The things they say and do are
against the Lord.
They sin openly against the Lord.
9The look on their faces shows they
are guilty of doing wrong.
Like the people of Sodom, they are
proud of their sin.
They don't care who sees it.
How terrible it will be for them!
They have brought much trouble
to themselves.

10Tell the good people that good
things will happen to them.
They will receive a reward for the
good they do.
11But how terrible it will be for
wicked people!
They will be punished for all the
wrong they have done.
12Children treat my people cruelly.
Women rule over them.
My people, your guides lead you in
the wrong way.
They turn you away from what is
right.

13The Lord takes his place in court.
He stands to judge the people.
14The Lord presents his case
against the older leaders and other
leaders of his people.
He says, "You have burned my
vineyard.

Your houses are full of what you
took from the poor.
[15] What gives you the right to crush
my people?
How can you grind the faces of the
poor into the dirt?"
The Master, the Lord of heaven's
armies, said this.

A Warning to Women of Jerusalem

[16] The Lord says,
"The women of Jerusalem are proud.
They walk around with their heads
held high.
They flirt with their eyes.
They take quick, short steps,
making noise with their ankle
bracelets."
[17] So the Lord will put sores on the
heads of those women in
Jerusalem.
He will make them lose all their
hair.

[18] At that time the Lord will take away
everything that makes them proud. He
will take away their beautiful ankle
bracelets, their headbands and their
necklaces shaped like the moon. [19] He
will take away their earrings, bracelets
and veils. [20] He will take away their
scarves, ankle chains, the cloth belts
worn around their waists, their bottles
of perfume and charms. [21] He will take
away their signet[d] rings, nose rings,
[22] their fine robes, capes, shawls and
purses. [23] And he will take away their
mirrors, linen dresses, turbans and
long shawls.

[24] Instead of having sweet-smelling
perfume, they will stink.
Instead of fine cloth belts, they will
have ropes of captives to wear.
Instead of having their hair fixed in
fancy ways, they will be bald.
Instead of fine clothes, they will
have rough clothes of sadness.
Instead of having beauty, they will
have the brand of a captive.
[25] At that time your men will be killed
with swords.

Your heroes will die in war.
[26] There will be crying and sadness in
the meeting places near the
city gates.
Jerusalem will be like a woman
who has lost everything and
sits on the ground.

4 At that time seven women
will grab one man.
They will say, "We will make our
own bread.
And we will make our own clothes.
But please marry us!
Please, take away our shame."

The Branch of the Lord

[2] At that time the Lord's branch will
be very beautiful and great. The people still living in Israel will be proud of
what the land grows. [3] All the people
who are still living in Jerusalem will be
called holy. This will be all the people
whose names are recorded among the
living in Jerusalem. [4] The Lord will wash
away the filth from the women of Jerusalem. He will wash the bloodstains
out of Jerusalem. He will clean Jerusalem with the spirit of fairness and the
spirit of fire. [5] As he did when Israel left
Egypt, the Lord will cover them with a
cloud of smoke during the day. And he
will cover them with a bright, flaming
fire at night. These proofs will be over
Mount Zion.[d] They will be over every
meeting of the people there. There will
be a covering over every person. [6] This
covering will be a place of safety. It will
protect the people from the heat of the
sun. It will be a safe place to hide from
the storm and rain.

Israel, God's Special Field

5 Now I will sing a song to my friend.
This song is about his vineyard.
My friend had a vineyard
on a hill with very rich soil.
[2] He dug and cleared the field of
stones.
He planted the best grapevines
there.
And he built a tower in the middle
of it.

He cut out a winepress[d] as well.
He hoped good grapes would grow
    there.
But only bad grapes grew.

3My friend says, "You people living
    in Jerusalem,
and you men of Judah,
judge between me and my vineyard.
4What more could I have done for
    my vineyard?
I did everything I could.
I hoped for good grapes to grow.
But why were there only bad
    grapes?
5Now I will tell you
    what I will do to my vineyard:
I will remove the hedge,
    and it will be burned.
I will break down the stone wall,
    and it will be walked on.
6I will ruin my field.
It will not be trimmed or hoed.
Weeds and thorns will grow there.
I will command the clouds
    not to rain on it."

7The vineyard belonging to the Lord
    of heaven's armies
    is the nation of Israel.
The garden that the Lord loves
    is the men of Judah.
The Lord looked for justice, but
    there was only killing.
The Lord hoped for right living, but
    there were only cries of pain.

8How terrible it will be for you who add
    more houses to your houses
and more fields to your fields.
Finally there is no room left for
    other people.
Then you are left alone in the land.

9The Lord of heaven's armies said
this to me:
"The fine houses will be destroyed.
The large and beautiful houses will
    be left empty.
10At that time a ten-acre vineyard will
    make only six gallons of wine.
And ten bushels of seed will grow
    only half a bushel of grain."

11How terrible it will be for people

who rise early in the morning
    to look for strong drink.
They stay awake late at night,
    becoming drunk with wine.
12At their parties they have lyres,[d]
    harps,
    tambourines,[d] flutes and wine.
They don't see what the Lord has
    done.
They don't notice the work of his
    hands.
13So my people will be captured and
    taken away
    because they don't really know me.
All the great men will die of hunger.
The common people will die of
    thirst.
14So the place where the dead are
    wants more and more people.
It opens its mouth wide.
Jerusalem's important men will go
    down into it.
And the common people will go
    down into it.
15So the common people and the
    great people will be humbled.
Those who are proud will be
    humbled.
16The Lord of heaven's armies will
    receive glory by judging fairly.
The holy God will show himself
    holy by doing what is right.
17Then the sheep will go anywhere
    they want.
Lambs will feed on the land that
    rich people once owned.

18How terrible it will be for those
    people!
They pull their guilt and sins
    behind them
as people pull wagons with ropes.
19They say, "Let's see God hurry.
Let's see him do his work soon.
We want to see it.
Let's see the plan of the Holy One of
    Israel happen soon.
Then we would know what it
    really is."

20How terrible it will be for people
    who call good things bad
and bad things good.

They think darkness is light
  and light is darkness.
They think sour is sweet
  and sweet is sour.

21 How terrible it will be for people
    who think they are wise.
  They think they are clever.

22 How terrible it will be for people who
    are famous for drinking wine.
  They are champions at mixing
    drinks.
23 They take money to set the guilty
    free.
  But they don't allow good people
    to be judged fairly.
24 They will be destroyed
    just as fire burns straw or dry grass.
  They will be destroyed
    like a plant whose roots rot
    and whose flower dies and blows
      away like dust.
  They have refused to obey the
    teachings of the Lord of
    heaven's armies.
  They hated the message from the
    Holy God of Israel.
25 So the Lord has become very angry
    with his people.

And he has raised his hand to
    punish them.
Even the mountains are frightened.
  Dead bodies lie in the streets like
    garbage.

But the Lord is still angry.
  His hand is still raised to strike
    down the people.

26 God raises a banner for the nations
    far away.
  He is whistling to call those people.
  The enemy comes quickly!
27 Not one of them becomes tired or
    falls down.
  Not one of them gets sleepy and
    falls asleep.
  Their weapons are close at hand.
  Their sandal straps are not
    broken.
28 Their arrows are sharp.
  All of their bows are ready to shoot.
  The horses' hoofs are hard as rock.
  Their chariot wheels move like a
    whirlwind.
29 Their shout is like the roar of a lion.
  It is loud like a young lion.

Worship
ISAIAH 6:1-7

Have you ever been frightened during a
worship service? Not scared because you got caught fooling around
or hitting your sister, but because of what was going on in *worship*. Most
people would answer no, but not Isaiah. Isaiah 6 tells about when Isaiah
was frightened right down to his toenails as he was worshiping God.

Isaiah was scared because he saw God sitting on his throne, surrounded by heavenly creatures. When he saw how pure and holy God was,
Isaiah felt small and sinful. He was afraid that God would destroy him
because he was so bad.

Worship isn't supposed to scare us to death. In fact, we should leave a
service feeling encouraged, happy, comforted, or thoughtful. But every
now and then, we should leave church feeling wonder at God's holiness
and purity.

To learn more about worship, zoom to page 1279.

Humility
ISAIAH 6:1-7

Do you ever compare yourself to your friends? You may take pride in being taller or stronger or more athletic than others. That is, until someone *else* even taller, stronger, or whatever comes along—then you don't feel so great!

One time Isaiah had a meeting with God that left him feeling anything but tall and strong. Isaiah was one of God's finest, most faithful people in all Israel. If he had compared himself to other people, he might have thought he was better than they were. But one day he saw God in all his greatness and glory, and Isaiah saw himself for what he was: a small, weak, sinful human being in the presence of a holy God. Isaiah felt terrible! No wonder he said, "Oh, no!"

Understanding God's holiness helps us understand our sinfulness. The good news is that God is willing to make us clean and to use our lives.

To learn more about humility, zoom to page 1088.

To learn more about humility, zoom to page 1088.

The enemy growls as they grab
their captives.
There is no one to stop them from
taking their captives away.
30 On that day they will roar
like the waves of the sea.
And when people look at the land,
they will see only darkness and
pain.
All light will become dark in this
thick cloud.

Isaiah Becomes a Prophet

6 In the year that King Uzziah died, I saw the Lord. He was sitting on a very high throne. His long robe filled the Temple.*d* 2Burning heavenly creatures stood above him. Each creature had six wings. They used two wings to cover their faces. They used two wings to cover their feet. And they used two wings for flying. 3Each creature was calling to the others:

"Holy, holy, holy is the Lord of
heaven's armies."
His glory fills the whole earth."

4Their voices caused the frame around the door to shake. The Temple filled with smoke.

5I said, "Oh, no! I will be destroyed. I am not pure. And I live among people who are not pure. But I have seen the King, the Lord of heaven's armies."

"**C**an you imagine seeing what Isaiah saw? What would you say if God wanted you for special duty? Would you say what Isaiah said? Look at Isaiah 6:1-10."

6On the altar there was a fire. One of the burning heavenly creatures used a pair of tongs to take a hot coal from the fire. Then he flew to me with the hot coal in his hand. 7The creature touched my mouth with the hot coal. Then he said, "Look. Your guilt is taken away because this hot coal has touched your lips. Your sin is taken away."

[8]Then I heard the Lord's voice. He said, "Whom can I send? Who will go for us?"

So I said, "Here I am. Send me!"

[9]Then the Lord said, "Go and tell this to the people:

'You will listen and listen, but you will not understand.
You will look and look, but you will not learn.'

"Do this until the cities are destroyed
and the people are gone.
Do this until there are no people left living in the houses.
Do this until the land is destroyed and left empty.

[12]I will send the people far away.
And the land will be left empty.

[13]One-tenth of the people will be left in the land.
But the land will be destroyed again.
These people will be like an oak tree.

People Who Spoke God's Words

ISAIAH • ISAIAH 6:8

Isaiah is considered one of the greatest prophets. He wrote one of the biggest books of prophecy in the Bible. Isaiah did not plan to be a prophet, but when God called him, Isaiah was available for God to use. Isaiah spoke God's words to the southern kingdom of Judah during the reigns of five kings. If a prophet was truly from God, all his messages would come true. Many of Isaiah's prophecies have already come true because he told how Jesus would come and die for sin. Some of the things he predicted are yet to happen. Most of the time, the kings and people did not listen to Isaiah's words. God had already warned him of that. But Isaiah did not stop speaking for God.

If God calls you to a job, could you answer by saying "Send me"?

To meet a prophet who was sad about his nation's sins, fly to page 964.

[10]Make these people stubborn.
Make them not able to understand what they hear and see.
Otherwise, they might really understand
what they see with their eyes and hear with their ears.
They might really understand in their minds.
If they did this, they would come back to me and be forgiven."

[11]Then I asked, "Lord, how long should I do this?"
He answered,

When the tree is chopped down, a stump is left.
The people who remain will be like a stump that will sprout again."

Trouble with Aram

7 Now Ahaz was the son of Jotham, who was the son of Uzziah. When Ahaz was king of Judah, Rezin and Pekah went up to Jerusalem to fight against it. Rezin was king of Aram. And Pekah son of Remaliah was king of Israel. But they were not able to defeat the city.

Salvation
ISAIAH 7:14

Imagine that you are hiking through a forest and have gotten lost. Whatever way you look, you cannot see a way out. Then you hear footsteps coming toward you. Out of the trees appears . . . a forest ranger! Whew. The ranger gives you three choices. He can *tell* you how to find your way home; he can give you a map that *points* the way; or he can *go with you* and lead you out. Which one would you choose?

God has done something like that for us. We were lost in our sins. God *told* us in his Word how we could be saved. He *pointed* the way through his prophets and other people. Then, as we read in these verses, he gave the greatest sign of all: a special baby named *Immanuel* who would save people from their sins. In the New Testament we discover that this baby is Jesus.

God sent Jesus, his only Son, to lead us to salvation. Will you follow him?

To learn more about salvation, zoom to page 1121.

To learn more about salvation, zoom to page 1121.

[2]A message was told to Ahaz king of Judah. It said, "The armies of Aram and Israel*n* have joined together."

When Ahaz heard this, he and the people became very frightened. They shook with fear like trees of the forest blown by the wind.

[3]Then the Lord told Isaiah, "You and your son Shear-Jashub should go out and talk to Ahaz. Go to the place where the water flows into the upper pool. This is on the road to the Washerman's Field. [4]Tell Ahaz, 'Be careful. Be calm, and don't be afraid. Don't let those two men, Rezin and Remaliah's son Pekah, scare you. Don't be afraid of their anger and Aram's anger. Those two men are as weak as two barely burning sticks that are ready to go out. [5]They have made plans against you. They said, [6]"Let's fight against Judah and tear it apart. We will divide Judah for ourselves. We will make the son of Tabeel the new king of Judah." [7]But I, the Lord God, say,

Their plan will not succeed.
  It will not happen.
[8]That is because Aram is led by the
  city of Damascus.
And Damascus is led by its weak
  king, Rezin.
Within 65 years Israel will no longer
  be a nation.
[9]Israel is led by the city of
  Samaria,
  and Samaria is led by its weak
  king, the son of Remaliah.
If your faith is not strong,
  then you will not have strength to
  last.'"

Immanuel—God Is with Us

[10]Then the Lord spoke to Ahaz again. [11]The Lord said, "Ask for a sign to prove to yourself that these things are true. It may be a sign from as deep as the place where the dead are or as high as the heavens."

[12]But Ahaz said, "I will not ask for a sign. I will not test the Lord."

*n*Israel Literally, "Ephraim." Isaiah often uses "Ephraim" to mean all of Israel.

¹³Then Isaiah said, "Ahaz, descendant[d] of David, listen very carefully! Isn't it bad enough that you wear out the patience of people? Do you have to wear out the patience of my God also? ¹⁴But the Lord himself will give you a sign: The virgin[n] will be pregnant. She will have a son, and she will name him Immanuel.[n] ¹⁵He will be eating milk curds and honey when he learns to reject what is evil and to choose what is good. ¹⁶You are afraid of the kings of Israel and Aram now. But before the child learns what is good and what is evil, the lands of Israel and Aram will be empty. ¹⁷The Lord will bring some troubled times to you. Those troubles will come to your people and to the people of your father's family. The Lord will bring the king of Assyria to fight against you.

¹⁸"At that time the Lord will whistle to call for the Egyptians. And they will come like flies from the streams of Egypt. The Lord will call for the Assyrians. And they will come like bees from the land of Assyria. ¹⁹These enemies will camp in the deep ravines and in the cliffs. They will camp by the thornbushes and watering holes. ²⁰The Lord will use Assyria to punish Judah. Assyria will be hired and used like a razor. It will be as if the Lord is shaving the hair from Judah's head and legs and is shaving off Judah's beard.

²¹"At that time a person will be able to keep only one young cow and two sheep alive. ²²There will be only enough milk for that person to eat milk curds. All who remain in the land will go back to eating only milk curds and honey. ²³In this land there are now vineyards that have 1,000 grapevines. These grapevines are worth about 25 pounds of silver. But these fields will become full of weeds and thorns. ²⁴The land will become wild and useful only as a hunting ground. ²⁵People once worked and grew food on these hills. But at that time people will not go there. The land will be filled with weeds and thorns. Only sheep and cattle will go to those places."

Assyria Will Come Soon

8 The Lord told me, "Take a large scroll on which to write. Use a pen to write these words: 'Maher-Shalal-Hash-Baz.'[n] ²I will gather some men to be reliable witnesses. They will be Uriah the priest and Zechariah son of Jeberekiah."

³Then I went to the prophetess.[d] She became pregnant and had a son. Then the Lord told me, "Name the boy Maher-Shalal-Hash-Baz. ⁴The king of Assyria will take away all the wealth and possessions of Damascus and Samaria. This will happen before the boy learns to say 'my father' or 'my mother.'"

⁵Again the Lord spoke to me. ⁶He said,

"These people refuse to accept
    the slow-moving waters of the pool
    of Shiloah.
These people are terrified of Rezin
    and Remaliah's son Pekah.
⁷So I, the Lord, will bring
    the king of Assyria and all his
    power against them.
They will come like a powerful
    flood of water from the
    Euphrates River.
The Assyrians will be like water
    rising over the banks of the
    river,
flowing over the land.
⁸That water will flow into Judah and
    pass through it.
It will rise to Judah's throat.
Immanuel, this army will spread its
    wings like a bird
until it covers your whole country."

⁹Be broken, all you nations.
Be smashed to pieces.
Listen, all you faraway countries.

ⁿ**virgin** The Hebrew word means "a young woman." Often this meant a girl who was not married and had not yet had sexual relations with anyone.
ⁿ**Immanuel** This name means "God is with us."
ⁿ**Maher-Shalal-Hash-Baz** This name means "there will soon be looting and stealing."

Prepare for battle and be smashed
  to pieces!
Prepare for battle and be smashed
  to pieces!
[10]Make your plans for the fight.
  But your plans will be defeated.
  Give orders to your armies.
  But your orders will be useless.
  This is because God is with us.

Warnings to Isaiah

[11]The Lord spoke to me with his great
power. He warned me not to follow
the lead of the rest of the people. The
Lord said,
[12]"People are saying that others make
    plans against them.
  You should not believe those
    things.
  Don't be afraid of the things they
    fear.
  Do not dread those things.
[13]But remember that the Lord of
    heaven's armies is holy.
  He is the one you should fear.
  He is the one you should dread.
[14]Then he would be a place of safety
    for you.
  But for the two families of Israel,
  he will be like a stone that causes
    people to stumble.
  He will be like a rock that makes
    them fall.
  He will be like a trap for the people
    of Jerusalem.
  He will catch them in his trap.
[15]Many people will fall over this rock.
  They will fall and be broken.
  They will be trapped and caught."

[16]Make an agreement.
  Seal up the teaching while my
    followers are watching.
[17]I will wait for the Lord to help us.
  The Lord is ashamed of the family
    of Israel.
  I will trust the Lord.

[18]I am here. And with me are the children the Lord has given me. We are
signs and proofs for the people of Israel.
We have been sent by the Lord of heav-
en's armies. He lives on Mount Zion.[d]

[19]Some people say, "Ask the mediums[d] and fortune-tellers what to do.
They whisper and mutter and ask dead
people what to do." But I tell you that
people should ask their God for help.
Why should people who are still alive
ask something from the dead? [20]You
should follow the teachings and the
agreement with the Lord. The mediums and fortune-tellers do not speak
the word of the Lord. Their words are
worth nothing.
[21]People will wander through the
land troubled and hungry. When they
become hungry, they will become
angry. Then they will look up and curse
their king and their God. [22]They will
look around them at their land. And
they will see only trouble and darkness
and awful gloom. And they will be
forced into the darkness.

A New Day Is Coming

9 But suddenly there will be no more
gloom for the land that suffered.
In the past God made the lands of Zebulun and Naphtali hang their heads in
shame. But in the future that land will
be made great. That land stretches
from the way along the Mediterranean
Sea to the land along the Jordan River.
And it goes north to Galilee where the
people who are not Israelites live.

[2]Now those people live in darkness.
  But they will see a great light.
  They live in a place that is very dark.
  But a light will shine on them.
[3]God, you will cause the nation to grow.
  You will make the people happy.
  And they will show their happiness
    to you.
  It will be like the joy during
    harvest time.
  It will be like the joy of people
    taking what they have won in war.
[4]Like the time you defeated Midian,
  you will take away their heavy load.
  You will take away the heavy pole
    from their backs.
  You will take away the rod the
    enemy uses to punish your
    people.

⁵Every boot that marched in battle
   will be destroyed.
Every uniform stained with blood
   will be destroyed.
They will be thrown into the fire.
⁶A child will be born to us.
God will give a son to us.
He will be responsible for leading
   the people.
His name will be Wonderful
   Counselor, Powerful God,
Father Who Lives Forever, Prince
   of Peace.
⁷Power and peace will be in his
   kingdom.
It will continue to grow.
He will rule as king on David's throne
   and over David's kingdom.
He will make it strong,
   by ruling with goodness and fair
   judgment.
He will rule it forever and ever.
The Lord of heaven's armies will do
   this
   because of his strong love for his
   people.

God Will Punish Israel

⁸The Lord sent a message against
   the people of Jacob.
That message says that God will
   judge Israel.
⁹Then everyone in Israel, even the
   leaders in Samaria,
will know that God punished them.
Those people, who are proud and
   who brag now, say this:
¹⁰"These bricks have fallen,
   but we will build again with cut
   stones.
These small trees have been
   chopped down.
But we will put great cedars there."
¹¹But the Lord will make the enemies
   of Rezin strong against them.
He will stir up their enemies
   against them.
¹²The Arameans come from the east
   and the Philistines from the west.
They will eat up Israel with their
   armies.

But the Lord is still angry.

His hand is still raised to punish
   the people.

¹³But the people do not return to the
   one who struck them.
They do not follow the Lord of
   heaven's armies.
¹⁴So the Lord will cut off Israel's head
   and tail.
He will take away both the branch
   and stalk in one day.
¹⁵The older leaders and important
   men are the head.
The prophets*d* who speak lies are
   the tail.
¹⁶Those who lead the people lead
   them in the wrong direction.
And those who follow them will be
   destroyed.
¹⁷So the Lord is not happy with the
   young men.
He will not show mercy to the
   widows and orphans.
All the people are separated from
   God and are very evil.
They all speak lies.

But the Lord is still angry.
His hand is still raised to strike
   down the people.

¹⁸Evil is like a small fire.
First, it burns weeds and thorns.
Next, it burns the larger bushes in
   the forest.
They all go up in a column of smoke.
¹⁹The Lord of heaven's armies is angry.
So the land will be burned.
All the people will be burned in that
   fire.
No one will try to save his brother.
²⁰People will grab something on the
   right,
   but they will still be hungry.
They will eat something on the left,
   but they will not be filled.
Then each person will turn and eat
   his own children.
²¹The people of Manasseh will fight
   against the people of Ephraim.
And Ephraim will fight against
   Manasseh.
Then both of them will turn
   against Judah.

But the Lord is still angry.
His hand is still raised to strike
down the people.

10 How terrible it will be for the law-
makers who write evil laws.
They write laws that make life
hard for people.
²They are not fair to the poor.
They rob my people of their rights.
They allow people to steal from
widows
and to take from orphans what
they should get.
³Lawmakers, how will you explain
the things you have done?
What will you do when your destruction comes from far away?
Where will you run for help?
Where will you hide your money
and your riches then?
⁴You will have to bow down among
the captives.
You will fall down among the dead
bodies.

But the Lord is still angry.
His hand is still raised to strike
down the people.

God Will Punish Assyria

⁵God says, "How terrible it will be for
the king of Assyria.
I use him like a stick.
In anger I use Assyria like a club.
⁶I send it to fight against a nation
that is separated from God.
I am angry with those people.
So I command Assyria to fight
against them.
Assyria will take their wealth from
them.
Judah will become like dirt for
them to walk on in the streets.
⁷But Assyria's king doesn't understand that I am using him.
He doesn't know he is a tool for me.
He only wants to destroy other
people.
He plans to destroy many nations.
⁸The king of Assyria says to himself,
'All of my commanders are like
kings.

⁹The city Calno is like the city
Carchemish.
And the city Hamath is like the
city Arpad.
The city Samaria is like the city
Damascus.
¹⁰I defeated those kingdoms that
worship idols.
And those idols were more than
the idols of Jerusalem and
Samaria.
¹¹I defeated Samaria and her idols.
So I will also defeat Jerusalem and
her idols.'"

¹²The Lord will finish doing what he
planned to Mount Zion*d* and Jerusalem.
Then he will punish Assyria. The king
of Assyria is very proud. His pride
made him do these bad things. So God
will punish him. ¹³The king of Assyria
says this:
"By my own power I have done
these things.
By my wisdom I have defeated
many nations.
I have taken their wealth.
And like a mighty one, I have
taken their people.
¹⁴I have taken the riches of all these
people,
like one who reaches into a bird's
nest.
I have taken these nations,
like a person taking eggs.
No one raised a hand against me.
No one opened his mouth to
stop me."

¹⁵An ax is not better than the person
who swings it.
A saw is not better than the person
who uses it.
A stick cannot control the person
who picks it up.
A club cannot pick up the
person!
¹⁶So the Master, the Lord of heaven's
armies,
will send a terrible disease against
Assyria's soldiers.
The strength of Assyria will be
burned up.

It will be like a fire burning until
   everything is gone.
17God, the Light of Israel, will be like
   a fire.
The Holy One will be like a flame.
He will be like a fire
   that suddenly burns the weeds and
     thorns.
18The fire burns away the great trees
   and rich farmlands.
It will destroy everything.
Things will be like a sick man who
   wastes away.
19Only a few trees will be left standing.
There will be so few even a child
   will be able to count them.

20At that time some people will be left
   alive in Israel
from the family of Jacob.
They will not continue to depend
   on the person who defeated
     them.
They will learn truly to depend on
   the Lord,
the Holy One of Israel.
21The people who are left alive in
   Jacob's family
will again follow the powerful
   God.
22Israel, your people are very many.
They are like the grains of sand by
   the sea.
But only a few of them will be left
   alive to return to the Lord.
God has announced that he will
   destroy the land
completely and fairly.
23The Master, the Lord of heaven's
   armies, will certainly destroy
     this land.
He will destroy it as he has
   announced.

24This is what the Master, the Lord
of heaven's armies, says:
"My people living in Jerusalem,
   don't be afraid of the Assyrians.
They beat you with a rod.
   They raise a stick to hurt you, as
     Egypt did.
25But after a short time my anger
   will stop.

Then I will turn my anger to
   destroying them."

26Then the Lord of heaven's armies
   will beat the Assyrians with a
     whip.
He will defeat them as he defeated
   Midian at the rock of Oreb.
He will raise his stick over the
   waters
as he did in Egypt.
27Then the troubles that Assyria puts
   on you
will be removed.
The load they make you carry
   will be taken away.

Assyria Invades Israel

28The army of Assyria will enter near
   Aiath.
They will walk through Migron.
They will store their food in
   Micmash.
29The army will go over the pass.
They will sleep at Geba.
The people of Ramah will be afraid.
The people at Gibeah of Saul will
   run away.
30Cry out, Bath Gallim!
Laishah, listen!
Poor Anathoth!
31The people of Madmenah are
   running away.
The people of Gebim are hiding.
32This day the army will stop at Nob.
And the army will shake their fist
   at Mount Zion,ᵈ
at the hill of Jerusalem.

33Watch! The Master, the Lord of
   heaven's armies,
will chop them down like a great
   tree.
He will do this with his great power.
Those who are great will be cut
   down.
Those who are important will fall
   to the ground.
34The Lord will cut them down
   as a forest is cut down with an ax.
And the great trees of Lebanon
   will fall by the power of the Mighty
     One.

The King of Peace Is Coming

11 A branch will grow
from a stump of a tree that was
cut down.
So a new king will come
from the family of Jesse.[n]
[2]The Spirit[d] of the Lord will rest
upon that king.
The Spirit gives him wisdom,
understanding, guidance and
power.
And the Spirit teaches him to
know and respect the Lord.
[3]This king will be glad to obey the
Lord.
He will not judge by the way things
look.
He will not judge by what people
say.
[4]He will judge the poor honestly.
He will be fair in his decisions for
the poor people of the land.
At his command evil people will be
punished.
By his words the wicked will be
put to death.
[5]Goodness and fairness will give him
strength.
They will be like a belt around his
waist.

[6]Then wolves will live in peace with
lambs.
And leopards will lie down to rest
with goats.
Calves, lions and young bulls will
eat together.
And a little child will lead them.
[7]Cows and bears will eat together in
peace.
Their young will lie down together.
Lions will eat hay as oxen do.
[8]A baby will be able to play near a
cobra's hole.
A child will be able to put his hand
into the nest of a poisonous
snake.
[9]They will not hurt or destroy each
other
on all my holy mountain.

The earth will be full of the
knowledge of the Lord,
as the sea is full of water.

[10]At that time the new king from the
family of Jesse will stand as a banner
for the people. The nations will come
together around him. And the place
where he lives will be filled with glory.
[11]At that time the Lord will again reach
out and take his people who are left
alive. These are God's people who are
left alive in Assyria, North Egypt, South
Egypt, Cush, Elam, Babylonia, Hamath
and all the islands of the sea.

[12]God will raise a banner as a sign for
all people.
He will gather the people of Israel
who were forced from their
country.
He will gather the scattered people
of Judah
from all parts of the earth.
[13]At that time Israel will not be
jealous anymore.
Judah will have no enemies left.
Israel will not be jealous of Judah.
And Judah will not hate Israel.
[14]But Israel and Judah will attack the
Philistines on the west.
Together they will take the riches
from the people of the east.
They will conquer Edom and Moab.
And the people of Ammon will be
under their control.
[15]The Lord will dry up
the Red Sea[d] of Egypt.
He will wave his arm over the
Euphrates River.
He will dry it up with a scorching
wind.
He will divide it into seven small
rivers.
And people will be able to walk
across them with their sandals
on.
[16]So God's people who are left alive
will have a way to leave Assyria.
It will be like the time the Israelites
went out of Egypt.

[n]**Jesse**   King David's father.

A Song of Praise to God

12 At that time you will say:
"I praise you, Lord!
You were angry with me.
But you are not angry with me now!
You have comforted me.
²God is the one who saves me.
I trust him. I am not afraid.
The Lord, the Lord, gives me
strength and makes me sing.
He has saved me."
³You will receive your salvation with
joy.
You will take it as you would draw
water from a well.

⁴At that time you will say,
"Praise the Lord, and worship him.
Tell everyone what he has done.
Tell them how great he is.
⁵Sing praise to the Lord, because he
has done great things.
Let all the world know what he has
done.
⁶Shout and sing for joy, you people of
Jerusalem.
The Holy One of Israel does great
things before your eyes."

God's Message to Babylon

13 God showed Isaiah son of Amoz
this message about Babylon:
²Raise a flag on the bare mountain.
Call out to the men.
Raise your hand to signal them.
Tell them to enter through the
gates for important people.
³I myself have commanded those
people
whom I have separated as mine.
I have called those warriors to carry
out my anger.
They rejoice and are glad to do my
will.

⁴Listen to the loud noise in the
mountains.
It sounds like many people.
Listen to the noise among the
kingdoms.
Nations are gathering together.
The Lord of heaven's armies is
calling

his army together for battle.
⁵This army is coming from a faraway
land.
It is coming from the edge of the
horizon.
In anger the Lord is using this army
like a weapon.
And it will destroy the whole
country.
⁶Cry, because the Lord's day of
judging is near.
God All-Powerful is sending
destruction.
⁷People will be weak with fear.
Their courage will melt away.
⁸Everyone will be afraid.
Pain and hurt will grab them.
They will hurt like a woman giving
birth to a baby.
They will look at each other in fear.
Their faces will become red like
fire.

⁹Look, the Lord's day of judging is
coming.
It will be a terrible day. God will be
very angry,
and he will destroy the country.
God will destroy the sinners who
live in the land.
¹⁰The stars will not show their light.
The skies will be dark.
The sun will grow dark as it rises.
And the moon will not give its light.

¹¹The Lord says, "I will punish the
world for its evil.
I will punish wicked people for
their sins.
I will cause the proud people to lose
their pride.
I will destroy the pride of those
who are cruel to others.
¹²People will be harder to find than
pure gold.
There will be fewer people than
there is fine gold in Ophir.
¹³I will make the sky shake.
And the earth will be moved from
its place.
The Lord of heaven's armies will be
very angry.
His anger will burn at that time.

14"Then the people from Babylon will
    run away like hunted deer.
They will run like sheep who have
    no shepherd.
Everyone will turn back to his own
    people.
Each will run back to his own land.
15Anyone who is captured will be killed.
Everyone who is caught will be
    killed with a sword.
16Their little children will be beaten to
    death as their parents watch.
Everything in their houses will be
    stolen.
And their wives will be raped.
17Look, I will cause the armies of
    Media to attack Babylon.
They do not care about silver.
They do not delight in gold.
18Their soldiers will shoot the young
    men with arrows.
The soldiers will show no mercy
    on the children.
They will not feel sorry for the
    little boys.
19Babylon is the most beautiful of all
    kingdoms.
The Babylonians are very proud of it.
But God will destroy it
like Sodom and Gomorrah.
20No one will ever live there.
No one will settle there again.
No Arab will put his tent there.
No shepherd will bring his sheep
    there.
21Only animals from the desert will
    live there.
The houses of Babylon will be full
    of wild dogs.
Owls will live there.
Wild goats will leap about in the
    houses.
22Wolves will howl within the strong
    walls.
Wild dogs will bark in the beautiful
    buildings.
The end of Babylon is near.
Its time is almost over."

Israel Will Return Home

14 The Lord will again show mercy
to the people of Jacob. The Lord
will again choose the people of Israel.
He will settle them in their own land.
Then non-Israelite people will join the
Israelites. The non-Israelite people will
become a part of the family of Jacob.
2Nations will take the Israelites back to
their land. Those men and women from
the other nations will become slaves to
Israel. In the past the Israelites were
their slaves. But now the Israelites will
defeat those nations and rule over them.

The King of Babylon Will Fall

3The Lord will take away the Israelites' hard work, and he will comfort
them. They will no longer have to work
as slaves. 4On that day Israel will sing
this song about the king of Babylon:
The cruel king who ruled us is
    finished.
    His rule is finished!
5The Lord breaks the scepter*d* of evil
    rulers.
He takes away their power.
6The king of Babylon beat people in
    anger.
He beat them again and again.
He ruled the people in anger.
He kept on doing terrible things to
    the people.
7But now, the whole land rests and is
    quiet.
Now the people begin to sing.
8Even the pine trees are happy.
And the cedar trees of Lebanon
    rejoice.
They say, "The king has fallen.
No one will ever cut us down again."

9The place of the dead is excited
    to meet you when you come.
It wakes the spirits of the dead to
    greet you.
They were the leaders of the world.
It makes dead kings stand up from
    their thrones to greet you.
They were rulers of nations.
10All these leaders will make fun of you.
They will say,
"Now you are weak, as we are.
Now you are just like us."
11Your pride has been sent down to
    where the dead are.

The music from your harps goes
with it.
Flies are spread out like your bed
beneath you.
And worms cover your body like a
blanket.

12King of Babylon, morning star, you
have fallen from heaven,
even though you were as bright as
the rising sun!
In the past all the nations on earth
bowed down before you.
But now you have been cut down.
13You told yourself,
"I will go up to heaven.
I will put my throne
above God's stars.
I will sit on the mountain of the gods.
I will sit on the slopes of the
sacred mountain.
14I will go up above the tops of the
clouds.
I will be like God Most High."
15But you were brought down to the
grave.
You were brought down to the deep
places where the dead are.

16Those who see you stare at you.
They think about what has
happened to you.
They say, "Is this the same man who
caused great fear on earth?
Is he the one who shook the
kingdoms?
17Is this the man who turned the land
into a desert?
Is he the one who destroyed its
cities?
Is he the one who captured people
in war
and would not let them go home?"
18Every king of the earth has been
buried with honor.
Every king has his own grave.
19But you are thrown out of your grave,
like an unwanted branch is cut
from a tree and thrown away.
You are covered by bodies
that died in battle.
You have been thrown into a rocky
pit.

And other soldiers walk on you.
20 You will not be buried like other
people.
This is because you ruined your
own country.
And you killed your own people.
So your children will never
be mentioned again.

21Prepare to kill his children.
Kill them because their father is
guilty.
They will never again take control
of the earth.
They will never again fill the world
with their cities.

22The Lord of heaven's armies says
this:
"I will fight against those people.
I will destroy Babylon and its people.
I will destroy its people and their
descendants,"d says the Lord.
23"I will make Babylon fit only for owls.
It will become a swamp.
I will sweep Babylon as with a
broom of destruction,"
says the Lord of heaven's armies.

God Will Punish Assyria

24The Lord of heaven's armies has
made this promise:
"These things will happen exactly
as I planned them.
These things will happen exactly
as I set them up.
25I will destroy the king of Assyria in
my country.
I will trample him on my
mountains.
He put a heavy load on my people.
But that weight will be removed.

26"This is what I plan to do against all
the earth.
I will raise my hand to strike down
all nations."
27When the Lord of heaven's armies
makes a plan,
no one can stop it.
When the Lord raises his hand to
punish people,
no one can stop him.

God's Message to Philistia

28This message was given the year King Ahaz died:

29Country of Philistia, don't be so happy.

The king who beat you is now dead.
But he is like a snake that will give birth to another dangerous snake.

The new king will be like a quick, dangerous snake to bite you.

30Even the poorest of my people will be able to eat safely.

People in need will be able to lie down in safety.

But I will kill your family with hunger.
And all your people who are left will die.

31People near the city gates, cry out!
Philistines, be frightened!

A cloud of dust comes from the north.
It is an army, full of men ready to fight.

32What shall we tell the messengers from Philistia?

Say that the Lord has made Jerusalem strong.

Say that his poor people will go there for safety.

God's Message to Moab

15 This is a message about Moab:
In one night armies took the wealth from Ar in Moab.

That night the city was destroyed.
In one night armies took the wealth from Kir in Moab.

That night the city was destroyed.

2The people of Dibon go to the places of worship to cry.

The people of Moab cry for the cities of Nebo and Medeba.

Everyone has shaved his head and beard to show how sad he is.

3In the streets at Moab they wear rough cloth to show their sadness.

On the roofs" and in the public squares,

they are crying loudly.

4People in the cities Heshbon and Elealeh cry out loud.

You can hear their voices far away in the city Jahaz.

Even the soldiers are frightened.
They are shaking from fear.

5My heart cries with sorrow for Moab.
Its people run away to Zoar for safety.

They run to Eglath Shelishiyah.
People are going up the mountain road to Luhith.

They are crying as they go.
People are going on the road to Horonaim.

They cry out loud over their destruction.

6But the water of Nimrim has dried up.
The grass has dried up.

All the plants are dead.
Nothing green is left.

7So the people gather up what they have saved.

They carry those things and cross the Ravine of the Poplars.

8Crying is heard everywhere in Moab.
Their crying is heard as far away as the city Eglaim.

Their crying is heard as far away as Beer Elim.

9The water of the city Dibon is full of blood.

And I, the Lord, will bring even more troubles to Dibon.

A few people living in Moab have escaped the enemy.

But I will send lions to kill them.

16 Send the king of the land the payment he demands.
Send a lamb from Sela through the desert

to the mountain of Jerusalem.

2The women of Moab
try to cross the river Arnon.

They are like little birds
that have fallen from their nest.

3They say: "Help us.

"**roofs** In Bible times houses were built with flat roofs. The roof was used for drying things such as flax and fruit. And it was used as an extra room, as a place for worship and as a place to sleep in the summer.

Tell us what to do.
Protect us from our enemies
as shade protects us from the
noon sun.
Hide us because we are running for
safety!
Don't give us to our enemies.
⁴Let those of us who were forced out
of Moab live in your land.
Hide us from our enemies."

The robbing of Moab will stop.
The enemy will be defeated.
The men who hurt others will
disappear from the land.
⁵Then a new loyal king will come.
This faithful king will be from the
family of David.
He will judge fairly.
He wants to do what is right.

⁶We have heard that the people of
Moab are proud
and very conceited.
They are very proud and angry.
But their bragging means nothing.
⁷So the people of Moab will cry.
They will all be sad.
They will moan and groan
for the raisin cakes they had in Kir
Hareseth.
⁸But the fields of Heshbon and the
vines of Sibmah cannot grow
grapes.
Foreign rulers have destroyed the
grapevines.
The grapevines once spread as far
as the city of Jazer and into the
desert.
They had spread as far as the sea.
⁹I cry with the people of Jazer
for the grapevines of Sibmah.
I will cry with the people of
Heshbon and Elealeh.
There will be no shouts of joy,
because there will be no harvest or
ripe fruit.
¹⁰There will be no joy and happiness
in the orchards.
There will be no songs or shouts
of joy in the vineyards.
No one makes wine in the
winepresses.ᵈ

I have put an end to shouts of joy.
¹¹My heart cries for Moab like a harp
playing a funeral song.
I am very sad for Kir Hareseth.
¹²The people of Moab will go to their
places of worship.
They will try to pray.
But when they go to their temple to
pray,
they will not be able.

¹³The Lord said these things about
Moab before. ¹⁴And now the Lord says,
"In three years all those people and
what they are proud of will be hated.
(This is three years as a hired helper
would count time.) There will be a few
people left, but they will be weak."

God's Message to Aram

17 This is the message for Damascus:
"The city of Damascus will be
destroyed.
Only ruins will be left there.
²People will leave the cities of Aroer.
Flocks of sheep will wander freely
in those empty towns.
There will be no one to bother
them.
³The strong, walled cities of Israel
will be destroyed.
The government in Damascus will
end.
Those left alive of Aram will be
like the glory of Israel," says the
Lord of heaven's armies.

⁴"At that time Israel's wealth will all
be gone.
Israel will be like a man who has
lost much weight from
sickness.
⁵That time will be like the grain
harvest in the Valley of
Rephaim.
The workers cut the wheat.
Then they cut the heads of grain
from the plants.
And they collect the grain.
⁶That time will also be like the olive
harvest,
when a few olives are left.

Two or three olives are left in the
top branches.
Four or five olives are left on full
branches," says the Lord, the
God of Israel.

7At that time people will look to God,
their Maker.
Their eyes will see the Holy One
of Israel.
8They will not trust the altars they
have made.
They will not trust what their
hands have made.
They will not respect the Asherah[d]
idols
and altars they have made.

9In that day all their strong cities will
be empty. They will be like the cities
that the Hivites and the Amorites left.
They left their cities when the Israelites
came to take the land. Everything will
be ruined.

10You have forgotten the God who
saves you.
You have not remembered that
God is your place of safety.
You plant the finest grapevines.
You plant grapevines from faraway
places.
11You will plant your grapevines one
day and try to make them
grow.
The next day they will begin to
grow.
But at harvest time everything will
be dead.
A sickness will kill all the plants.

12Listen to the many people!
They are crying loud like the noise
from the sea.
Listen to the noise!
The crying is like the crashing of
great waves.
13The people roar like those waves.
But when God speaks harshly to
them, they will run away.
They will be like chaff[d] on the hills
being blown by the wind.
They will be like tumbleweeds
blown away by a storm.

14At night the people will be very
frightened.
Before morning, no one will be left.
So our enemies will come to our land,
but they will become nothing.

God's Message to Cush

18 How terrible it will be for the
land beyond the rivers of Cush.
It is filled with the sound of wings.
2That land sends people across the sea.
They go on the water in boats
made of reeds.

Quick messengers, go
to the people who are tall and
smooth-skinned.
They are feared everywhere.
They are a powerful nation with
strange speech.
They defeat the other nations.
Their land is divided by rivers.

3All you people of the world, look!
Everyone who lives in the world,
look!
You will see a banner raised on a
mountain.
You will hear a trumpet sound.
4The Lord said to me,
"I will quietly watch from where I
live.
I will be like heat in the sunshine.
I will be like the dew in the heat of
harvest time."
5The time will be after the flowers
have bloomed and before the
harvest.
The new grapes will be budding
and growing.
Then the enemy will cut the plants
with knives.
He will cut down the vines and
take them away.
6They will be left for the birds of the
mountains to eat.
They will be left for the wild
animals to eat.
Birds will feed on them all summer.
And that winter wild animals will
eat them."

7At that time gifts will be brought to
the Lord of heaven's armies.

They will come from the people
who are tall and smooth-
skinned.
They are feared everywhere.
They are a powerful nation with
strange speech.
Their land is divided by rivers.
These gifts will be brought to the
place of the Lord of heaven's
armies.
They will be brought to Mount
Zion.[d]

God's Message to Egypt

19 The message about Egypt:
Look, the Lord is coming on a
fast cloud.
He will enter Egypt.
And the idols of Egypt will tremble
before him.
Egypt's courage will melt away.

2The Lord says, "I will cause the
Egyptians to fight against
themselves.
Men will fight with their brothers.
Neighbors will fight neighbors.
Cities will fight cities.
Kingdoms will fight kingdoms.
3The Egyptians will be afraid.
I will ruin their plans.
They will ask their idols and spirits of
the dead what they should do.
They will ask their mediums[d] and
fortune-tellers."
4The Master, the Lord of heaven's
armies, says,
"I will give Egypt to a hard master.
A powerful king will rule over
them."

5The sea will become dry.
The water will disappear from the
Nile River.
6The canals will stink.
The streams of Egypt will
decrease and dry up.
All the water plants will rot.
7 All the plants along the banks of
the Nile will die.
Even the planted fields by the Nile
will dry up, blow away and
disappear.

8The fishermen, all those who catch
fish from the Nile,
will groan and cry.
Those who depend on the Nile for
food will be sad.
9All the people who make cloth from
flax will be sad.
Those who weave linen will lose
hope.
10Those who weave cloth will be
broken.
All those who work for money will
be sad.

11The officers of the city of Zoan are
fools.
The wise men who advise the king
of Egypt give wrong advice.
How can they say to him they are
wise?
How can they say they are from
the old family of the kings?
12Egypt, where are your wise men?
Let them show you
what the Lord of heaven's armies
has planned for Egypt.
13The officers of Zoan have been
fooled.
The leaders of Memphis have
believed false things.
So the leaders of Egypt
lead her the wrong way.
14The Lord has made the leaders
confused.
They wander and lead Egypt in the
wrong ways.
They are like drunk people
stumbling in their own vomit.
15There is nothing Egypt can do.
No one in Egypt can help.

16In that day the people of Egypt will
be like frightened women. They will be
afraid of the Lord of heaven's armies.
He will raise his hand to strike them
down. 17The land of Judah will bring fear
to the people in Egypt. Anyone in Egypt
who hears the name Judah will be afraid.
This will happen because the Lord of
heaven's armies has planned terrible
things for Egypt. 18At that time five
cities in Egypt will speak Hebrew, the
language of Canaan. They will promise

to be loyal to the Lord of heaven's armies. One of these cities will be named the City of Destruction. ¹⁹At that time there will be an altar for the Lord in the middle of Egypt. At the border of Egypt there will be a monument to the Lord. ²⁰This will be a sign. It will show that the Lord of heaven's armies is powerful. When the people cry to the Lord for help, he will send help. He will send someone to save and defend the people. He will rescue them from those who hurt them.

²¹So the Lord will show himself to the Egyptians. Then they will say he is the Lord. They will serve God and offer many sacrifices. They will make promises to the Lord, and they will keep them. ²²The Lord will punish the Egyptians. Then he will heal them. They will come back to the Lord. He will listen to their prayers and heal them.

²³At that time there will be a highway from Egypt to Assyria. Then people from Assyria will go to Egypt. And the Egyptians will go to Assyria. The Egyptians and Assyrians will worship God together. ²⁴At that time Israel, Assyria and Egypt will join together. This will be a blessing for the earth. ²⁵The Lord of heaven's armies will bless them. He will say, "Egypt, you are my people. Assyria, I made you. Israel, I own you. You are all blessed!"

Assyria Will Defeat Egypt and Cush

20 Sargon was the king of Assyria. He sent a military commander to Ashdod to attack that city. So the commander attacked and captured it. ²Then the Lord spoke through Isaiah son of Amoz. The Lord said, "Take the rough cloth off your body. Take your sandals off your feet." So Isaiah obeyed the Lord. He walked around without his clothes of rough cloth or his sandals.

³Then the Lord said, "Isaiah my servant has walked around without his clothes of rough cloth or his sandals for three years. This is a sign for Egypt

and Cush. ⁴The king of Assyria will defeat Egypt and Cush. Assyria will take prisoners and lead them away from their countries. The old people and young people will be led away naked. They will go without clothes and without sandals. So the Egyptians will be shamed. ⁵People who looked to Cush for help will be afraid. People who were amazed by Egypt's glory will be shamed. ⁶Those people who live near the sea will say, 'We trusted those countries to help us. We ran to them so they would save us from the king of Assyria. But look at them. They have been captured. So how will we be able to escape?'"

God's Message to Babylon

21 The message about the Desert by the Sea:ⁿ
Disaster is coming from the desert.
  It is coming like wind blowing in the south.
  It is coming from a terrible country.
²I have seen a terrible vision.
  I see traitors turning against you.
  I see people taking your wealth.

Elam, attack the people!
  Media, surround the city and attack it!
  I will bring an end to the pain the city causes.

³I saw those terrible things, and now I am in pain.
  My pains are like the pains of giving birth.
What I hear makes me very afraid.
  What I see causes me to shake with fear.
⁴I am worried,
  and I am shaking with fear.
My pleasant evening
  has become a night of fear.

⁵They set the table.
  They spread the rugs.
  They eat and drink!
Leaders, stand up.
  Prepare the shields for battle!

⁶The Lord said to me,

ⁿ**Desert by the Sea** Probably Babylon.

"Go. Have a man be a lookout for
    the city.
Have him report what he sees.
[7] If he sees chariots and teams of
        horses,
    donkeys or camels,
he should pay very close attention."

[8] Then the lookout called out,
"My Master, each day I stand in the
        watchtower watching.
Every night I have been on guard.
[9] Look. I see a man coming in a chariot
    with a team of horses."
The man gives back the answer,
"Babylon has fallen. It has fallen!
All the statues of her gods
    lie broken on the ground."

[10] My people are crushed like grain on
    the threshing[d] floor.
My people, I tell you what I have
    heard from the Lord.
He is the Lord of heaven's armies,
    the God of Israel.

God's Message to Edom

[11] The message about Dumah:[n]
Someone calls to me from Edom.
He says, "Watchman, how much
    of the night is left?
Watchman, how much longer will
    it be night?"
[12] The watchman answered,
"Morning is coming, but then
    night will come again.
If you have something to ask,
    then come back and ask."

God's Message to Arabia

[13] The message about Arabia:
A group of traders from Dedan
    spent the night near some trees in
    Arabia.
[14]   They gave water to thirsty travelers.
The people of Tema gave food
    to those who were escaping.
[15] They were running from swords.
The swords were ready to kill.

They were running from bows
    ready to shoot.
They were running from a hard
    battle.

[16] This is what the Lord said to me:
"In one year all the glory of the country
of Kedar will be gone. (This is a year
as a hired helper counts time.) [17] At that
time only a few of the archers will be
left. Only a few of the soldiers of Kedar
will be left alive." The Lord, the God of
Israel, has spoken.

God's Message to Jerusalem

22 The message about the Valley
        of Vision:[n]
What is wrong with you people?
Why are you on your roofs?[n]
[2] This city was a very busy city.
It was full of noise and wild parties.
But your people have been killed,
    but not with swords.
They did not die in battle.
[3] All your leaders ran away together.
But they all have been captured
    without using a bow.
All you who were captured
    tried to run away before the
    enemy came near.
[4] So I say, "Don't look at me.
Let me cry loudly.
Don't hurry to comfort me
    about the destruction of
    Jerusalem."
[5] The Master, the Lord of heaven's
    armies, has chosen a special
    day.
There will be riots and confusion.
People will trample each other in
    the Valley of Vision.
The city walls will be knocked down.
The people will cry out to the
    mountain.
[6] The soldiers from Elam will take
    their bags of arrows.
Men in chariots and on horses will
    attack.
Kir will prepare their shields.

[n]**Dumah**   Another name for Edom.
[n]**Valley of Vision**   This probably means a valley near Jerusalem.
[n]**roofs**   In Bible times houses were built with flat roofs. The roof was used for drying things such as flax
    and fruit. And it was used as an extra room, as a place for worship and as a place to sleep in the summer.

⁷Your nicest valleys will be filled with
    chariots.
  Horsemen will be ordered to
    guard the gates of the city.
⁸ The walls protecting Judah will fall.

At that time the people of Jerusalem
    depended on
  the weapons kept at the Palace of
    the Forest.
⁹You saw that the walls of Jerusalem
  had many cracks that needed
    repairing.
  You stored up water in the lower
    pool.
¹⁰You counted the houses of
    Jerusalem.
  You tore them down to fix the
    walls with their stones.
¹¹You made a pool between the two
    walls.
  It was to save water from the old
    pool.
  But you did not trust the God who
    made these things.
  You did not respect the One who
    planned them long ago.

¹²The Master, the Lord of heaven's
    armies, told the people
  to cry and be sad.
  He told them to shave their heads
    and wear rough cloth.
¹³But look. The people are happy.
  There are wild parties.
  They kill the cattle and the sheep.
  They eat the food and drink the
    wine.
  They say, "Let us eat and drink,
    because tomorrow we will die."

¹⁴The Lord of heaven's armies said
to me: "You people will die before this
guilt is forgiven." The Master, the Lord
of heaven's armies, said this.

God's Message to Shebna

¹⁵This is what the Master, the Lord
of heaven's armies, says:

"Go to this servant Shebna.
  He is the manager of the palace.
¹⁶Say to him, 'What are you doing here?
  Who said you could cut out a tomb
    for yourself here?

Why are you preparing your tomb
    in a high place?
  Why are you carving out a tomb
    from the rock?
¹⁷Look, mighty man! The Lord will
    throw you away.
  He will take firm hold of you.
¹⁸He will roll you tightly into a ball
  and throw you into another country.
  There you will die.
  Your fine chariots will remain there.
  You are a disgrace to your
    master's house.
¹⁹I will force you out of your
    important job here.
  You will be thrown down from
    your important place.'

²⁰"At that time I will call for my servant Eliakim son of Hilkiah. ²¹I will take
your robe and put it on him. I will give
him your belt. I will give him the important job you have. He will be like a
father to the people of Jerusalem and
the family of Judah. ²²I will put the key
to the house of David around his neck.
If he opens a door, no one will be able
to close it. If he closes a door, no one
will be able to open it. ²³He will be like
an honored chair in his father's house.
I will make him strong like a peg that
is hammered into a strong board. ²⁴All
the honored and important things of
his family will depend on him. All the
adults and little children will depend on
him. They will be like bowls and jars
hanging on him.

²⁵"At that time," says the Lord of
heaven's armies, "the peg hammered
into the strong board will weaken. It will
break and fall. And everything hanging on it will be destroyed." The Lord
says this.

God's Message to Lebanon

23 The message about Tyre:
    You ships of Tarshish, cry!
  The houses and harbor of Tyre are
    destroyed.
  This news came to the ships
    from the land of Cyprus.
²Be silent, you who live on the island
    of Tyre.

You merchants of Sidon, be silent.
Seamen have made you rich.
³They traveled the sea to bring grain
from Egypt.
The men of Tyre brought grain
from the Nile Valley
and sold it to other nations.

⁴Sidon, be ashamed.
Strong city of the sea, be ashamed.
The sea says:
"I have not felt the pain of giving
birth.
I have not reared young men or
women."
⁵Egypt will hear the news about Tyre.
And it will make Egypt hurt with
sorrow.

⁶You ships should return to Tarshish.
You people living near the sea
should be sad.
⁷Look at your once happy city!
Look at your old, old city!
People from that city have traveled
far away to live.
⁸Who planned Tyre's destruction?
Tyre made others rich.
Her merchants were treated like
princes.
Her traders were greatly respected.
⁹It was the Lord of heaven's armies
who planned this!
He decided to make these proud
men unimportant.
He decided to disgrace those who
were greatly respected.
¹⁰Go through your land,
Tarshish, like the Nile goes
through Egypt.
There is no harbor for you now!
¹¹The Lord has stretched his hand
over the sea.
He makes its kingdoms tremble.
He commands that Canaan's
places of safety be destroyed.
¹²The Lord said, "Sidon, you will not
rejoice any longer.
You are destroyed.
Even if you cross the sea to Cyprus,
you will not find a place to rest."
¹³Look at the land of the Babylonians.
Babylonia is not a country now.

Assyria has made it a place for wild
animals.
Assyria built towers to attack it.
The soldiers took all the treasures
from its cities.
They turned it into ruins.
¹⁴So be sad, you trading ships.
Your place of safety is destroyed.
¹⁵At that time people will forget about
Tyre for 70 years. That is the length of
a king's life. After 70 years, Tyre will be
like the prostitute*ᵈ* in this song:

¹⁶"Oh woman, you are forgotten.
Take your harp and walk through
the city.
Play your harp well. Sing your song
often.
Then people will remember you."

¹⁷After 70 years the Lord will deal
with Tyre. Tyre will again have trade. It
will be like a prostitute for all the nations
of the earth. ¹⁸The profits will be saved
for the Lord. Tyre will not keep the
money she earns. It will give them to
the people who serve the Lord. So they
will have plenty of food and nice clothes.

God Will Punish the World

24 Look! The Lord will destroy the
earth and leave it empty.
He will ruin the surface of the land
and scatter its people.
²At that time the same thing will
happen to everyone:
to common people and priests,
to slaves and masters,
to women slaves and their women
masters,
to buyers and sellers,
to those who borrow and those
who lend,
and to bankers and those who owe
the bank.
³The earth will be completely empty.
The wealth will all be taken.
This will happen because the Lord
commanded it.
⁴The earth will dry up and die.
The world will grow weak and die.
The great leaders in this land will
become weak.

⁵The people of the earth have ruined
it.
They do not follow God's teachings.
They do not obey God's laws.
They break their agreement with
God that was to last forever.
⁶A curse will destroy the earth.
The people of the world are guilty.
So they will be burned up.
Only a few will be left.
⁷The new wine will be bad, and the
grapevines will die.
People who were happy will be sad.
⁸The happy music of the
tambourines*d* will end.
The happy sounds of wild parties
will stop.
The joyful music from the harps
will end.
⁹People will no longer sing while
they drink their wine.
The beer will taste bitter to those
who drink it.
¹⁰The ruined city will be empty.
People will hide behind closed
doors.
¹¹People in the streets will ask for
wine.
But joy will have turned to sadness.
All the happiness will have left.
¹²The city will be left in ruins.
Its gates will be smashed to pieces.
¹³This is what will happen all over the
earth.
This will happen to all the nations.
The earth will be like an olive tree
after the harvest.
It will be like the few grapes left on
a vine after harvest.

¹⁴The people shout for joy.
From the west they praise the
greatness of the Lord.
¹⁵People in the east, praise the Lord.
People in the islands of the sea,
praise the name of the Lord, the
God of Israel.
¹⁶We hear songs from every part of
the earth.
These songs praise God, the
Righteous One.

But I said, "I am dying! I am dying!

How terrible it will be for me!
Traitors turn against people.
With their dishonesty, they turn
against people."
¹⁷There are terrors, holes and traps
for the people of the earth.
¹⁸Anyone who tries to escape from
the sound of terror
will fall into a hole.
Anyone who climbs out of the hole
will be caught in a trap.
The clouds in the sky will pour out
rain.
The foundations of the earth will
shake.
¹⁹The earth will be broken up.
And the earth will split open.
The earth will shake violently.
²⁰The earth will stumble around like a
man who is drunk.
It will shake like a hut in a storm.
Its sin is like a heavy weight on its
back.
The earth will fall and never rise
again.

²¹At that time the Lord will punish
the powers in the sky above
and the rulers on earth below.
²²They will be gathered together.
They will be thrown into a pit as
prisoners.
They will be shut up in prison.
After much time they will be
punished.
²³The moon will be embarrassed.
The sun will be ashamed.
This will happen because the Lord
of heaven's armies will rule as
king
on Mount Zion*d* in Jerusalem.
Jerusalem's leaders will see his
greatness.

A Song of Praise to God

25 Lord, you are my God.
I honor you and praise you.
You have done amazing things.
You have always done what you
said you would.
You have done what you planned
long ago.
²You have made the city a pile of rocks.

You have destroyed her walls.
The city our enemies built with
strong walls is gone.
It will never be built again.
³People from powerful nations will
honor you.
Cruel people from strong cities
will fear you.
⁴You help the poor people.
You help the helpless when they
are in danger.
You are like a shelter from storms.
You are like shade that protects
them from the heat.
The cruel people attack
like a rainstorm beating against
the wall.
⁵ The cruel people burn like the
heat in the desert.
But you, God, stop their violent
attack.
As a cloud cools a hot day,
Lord, you silence the songs of
those who have no mercy.

God's Banquet for His Servants

⁶The Lord of heaven's armies will
give a feast.
It will be on this mountain for all
people.
It will be a feast with the best food
and wine.
The meat and wine will be the
finest.
⁷On this mountain God will destroy
the veil that covers all nations.
This veil, called "death," covers all
peoples.
⁸But God will destroy death forever.
The Lord God will wipe away
every tear from every face.
God will take away the shame
of his people from the earth.
The Lord has spoken.

⁹At that time people will say,
"Our God is doing this!
We have trusted in him, and he has
come to save us.
We have been trusting our Lord.
So we will rejoice and be happy
when he saves us."
¹⁰The Lord will protect Jerusalem.

But the Lord will crush our enemy
Moab.
Moab will be like straw that is
trampled down in the manure.
¹¹They will spread their arms in it
like a person who is swimming.
The Lord will bring down their pride.
All the clever things they have
made will mean nothing.
¹²Moab's high walls protect them.
But the Lord will destroy these
walls.
The Lord will throw them down on
the ground.
The stones will lie in the dust.

A Song of Praise to God

26 At that time people will sing this
song in Judah:
We have a strong city.
God protects us with its strong
walls and defenses.
²Open the gates,
and the good people will enter.
They follow God's good way of
living.
³You, Lord, give true peace.
You give peace to those who
depend on you.
You give peace to those who trust
you.
⁴So, trust the Lord always.
Trust the Lord because he is our
Rock*ᵈ* forever.
⁵But the Lord will destroy the proud
city.
And he will punish the people
living there.
He will bring that high city down to
the ground.
He throws it down into the dust.
⁶Then those who were hurt by the
city will walk on its ruins.
Those who were made poor by the
city will trample it under their
feet.

⁷The path of life of the people who
are right with God is level.
Lord, you make the way of life
smooth for those people.
⁸But, Lord, we are waiting
for your way of justice.

Our souls want to remember
you and your name.
⁹My soul wants to be with you at night.
And my spirit wants to be with you
at the dawn of every day.
When your way of justice comes to
the land,
people of the world will learn the
right way of living.
¹⁰An evil person will not learn to do
good
even if you show him kindness.
He will continue doing evil, even if
he lives in a good world.
He never sees the Lord's greatness.
¹¹Lord, you are ready to punish those
people.
But they do not see that.
Lord, show them your strong love
for your people.
Then the evil people will be
ashamed.
Burn them in the fire
you have prepared for your
enemies.
¹²Lord, all our success is because of
what you have done.
So give us peace.
¹³Lord, our God, other masters
besides you have ruled us.
But we honor only you.
¹⁴Those masters are now dead.
Their ghosts will not rise from
death.
You decided to destroy them.
And you destroyed any memory of
them.
¹⁵Lord, you multiplied the number of
your people.
You multiplied them and brought
honor to yourself.
You made the borders of the land
wide.
¹⁶Lord, people remember you when
they are in trouble.
They say quiet prayers to you
when you punish them.
¹⁷Lord, when we are with you,
we are like a woman giving birth
to a baby.
She cries and has pain from the
birth.

¹⁸In the same way, we had pain.
We gave birth, but only to wind.
We don't bring salvation to the
land.
We don't make new people for the
world.
¹⁹Your people have died, but they will
live again.
Their bodies will rise from death.
Dead people in the ground,
get up and be happy!
The dew covering you is like the
dew of a new day.
The ground will give birth to the
dead buried in it.

Judgment: Reward or Punishment

²⁰My people, go into your rooms.
Shut your doors behind you.
Hide in your rooms for a short
time.
Hide until God's anger is finished.
²¹The Lord will leave his place.
He will punish the people of the
world for their sins.
The earth will show the blood of the
people who have been killed.
It will not cover the dead any
longer.

27 At that time the Lord will judge
Leviathan,ᵈ the gliding snake.
He will punish Leviathan, the
coiled snake.
The Lord will use his great sword,
his hard and powerful sword.
He will kill the monster in the sea.

²In that day
people will sing about the pleasant
vineyard.
³"I, the Lord, will care for that
vineyard.
I will water it at the right time.
No one will hurt it.
I will guard it day and night.
⁴I am not angry.
If anyone builds a wall of
thornbushes in war,
I will march to it and burn it.
⁵But if anyone comes to me for safety
and wants to make peace with me,
he should come and make peace
with me."

Get Ready, Get Set, Grow!
ISAIAH 27:2-6

Have you ever picked a rose and put it in a glass of water? It didn't last very long, did it? It died because it wasn't getting the nourishment it needed from the rose bush.

God wants you to grow as a Christian, but you can't do that unless you're connected to God like a rose to the bush. You can't grow if you don't get the "nourishment" you need from going to church, reading your Bible, and praying. If you stay close to God, then he stays close to you, just as God cared for the vineyard in this story. Jesus says, "I am the true vine. . . . Remain in me, and I will remain in you" (John 15:1, 4). If you want to grow in your faith, stay close to God. He has what you need to grow.

To find out more about growing in your faith, zoom to page 1061.

To find out more about growing in your faith, zoom to page 1061.

6In the days to come, the people of
 Jacob will be like a plant with
 good roots.
Israel will grow like a plant
 beginning to bloom.
Then the world will be filled with
 their children.

God "Divorces" Israel

7The Lord has not hurt his people as
 he hurt their enemies.
His people have not been killed like
 those who tried to kill them.
8The Lord will settle his argument
 with Israel by sending it far
 away.
Like a hot desert wind, he will
 drive Israel away.
9This is how Israel's guilt will be
 forgiven.
This is how its sins will be taken
 away.
Israel will crush the rocks of the
 altar to dust.
No statues or altars will be left
 standing for the Asherah[d]
 idols.
10At that time the strong, walled city
 will be empty.

It will be like a desert.
Calves will eat grass there.
 They will lie down there.
 They will eat leaves from the
 branches.
11The limbs will become dry and
 break off.
Women will use them for firewood.
The people refuse to understand.
 So God will not comfort them.
 Their Maker will not be kind to
 them.
12At that time the Lord will begin gathering his people one by one. He will gather all his people from the Euphrates River to the brook of Egypt. He will separate them from others as grain is separated from chaff.[d] 13Many of my people are now lost in Assyria. Some of my people have run away to Egypt. But at that time a great trumpet will be blown. And all those people will come back to Jerusalem. They will bow down before the Lord on that holy mountain.

Warnings to North Israel

28 How terrible it will be for Sam͏ia, the pride of Israel's dr͏ people!

That beautiful crown of flowers is
    just a dying plant.
It sits on a hill above a rich valley
    where drunkards live.
²Look, the Lord has someone who is
    strong and full of power.
That person will come like a storm
    of hail and strong wind.
He will come like a sudden flood of
    water pouring over the country.
He will throw Samaria down to the
    ground.
³That city, the pride of Israel's
    drunken people,
will be trampled underfoot.
⁴That beautiful crown of flowers is
    just a dying plant.
It sits on a hill above a rich valley.
That city will be like the first fig of
    summer.
When a person sees it,
    he quickly picks it and eats it.

⁵At that time the Lord of heaven's
    armies
will be like a beautiful crown.
He will be like a wonderful crown of
    flowers
    for his people who are left alive.
⁶Then the Lord will give wisdom
    to the judges who rule his people.
The Lord will give strength
    to those who battle at the city gate.
⁷But now those leaders are drunk
    with wine.
They stumble from drinking too
    much beer.
The priests and prophets*d* are drunk
    with beer.
They are filled with wine.
They stumble from too much beer.
The prophets are drunk when they
    see their visions.
The judges stumble when they
    make their decisions.
⁸Every table is covered with vomit.
    There is not a clean place anywhere.

⁹The Lord is trying to teach the
    people a lesson.
He is trying to make them
    understand his teachings.
But the people are like little babies.

They are like babies who just
    nursed at their mother's breast.
¹⁰So they make fun of the Lord's
    prophet and say:
"A command here, a command
    there.
A rule here, a rule there.
A lesson here, a lesson there."
¹¹So the Lord will use strange words
    and foreign languages
    to speak to these people.
¹²God said to them,
"Here is a place of rest.
Let the tired people come and rest.
This is the place of peace."
But the people would not listen.
¹³So the words of the Lord will be,
"A command here, a command
    there.
A rule here, a rule there.
A lesson here, a lesson there."
They will fall back and will be
    defeated.
They will be trapped and captured.

¹⁴You who brag should listen to the
    Lord's message.
Pay attention, you leaders in
    Jerusalem.
¹⁵You say, "We have made an
    agreement with death.
We have a contract with death.
When punishment passes by,
    it won't hurt us.
We will be safe with our lies.
We will hide behind our tricks."

¹⁶Because of these things, this is
what the Lord God says:
"I will put a stone in the ground in
    Jerusalem.
This will be a tested stone.
Everything will be built on this
    important and precious rock.
Anyone who trusts in it will never
    be disappointed.
¹⁷I will use justice as a measuring
    line.
I will use goodness to measure by.
The lies you hide behind will be
    destroyed as if by hail.
They will be washed away as if in a
    flood.

¹⁸Your agreement with death will be
    erased.
Your contract with death will not
    help you.
When punishment comes,
    you will be crushed by it.
¹⁹Whenever punishment comes, it
    will take you away.
It will come morning after morning.
It will defeat you by day and by
    night.
Those who hear of this punishment
    will be terrified."
²⁰You will be like the man who tried
    to sleep
on a bed that was too short for him.
And his blanket was too narrow
    to wrap around himself.
²¹The Lord will fight as he did at
    Mount Perazim.
He will be angry as he was in the
    Valley of Gibeon.
Then the Lord will do his work, his
    strange work.
He will finish his job, his strange job.
²²Now, you must not make fun of
    these things.
If you do, the ropes around you
    will become tighter.
The Lord of heaven's armies has
    told me these things.
He has told me how the whole
    earth will be destroyed.

The Lord Punishes Fairly

²³Listen closely to what I tell you.
Listen carefully to what I say.
²⁴A farmer does not plow his field all
    the time.
He does not go on working the soil.
²⁵He prepares the ground.
Then he plants the dill seed and
    scatters the cummin seed.
He plants the wheat in rows.
He plants barley in its special place,
    and other wheat in its own field.
²⁶His God teaches him
    and shows him the right way.
²⁷A farmer doesn't use heavy boards
    to crush dill.
He doesn't use a wagon to crush
    cummin.

He uses a small stick to break open
    the dill.
With a stick he opens the cummin.
²⁸The grain is ground to make bread.
People do not ruin it by crushing it
    forever.
The farmer separates the wheat
    from the chaff^d with his cart.
But he does not let his horses
    grind it.
²⁹This lesson comes from the Lord of
    heaven's armies.
He gives wonderful advice. He is
    very wise.

Warnings to Jerusalem

29 How terrible it will be for you,
    Jerusalem.
You are the city where David
    camped.
Her festivals have continued
    year after year.
²I will attack Jerusalem.
That city will be filled with sadness
    and crying.
It will be like an altar to me.
³I will put armies all around you,
    Jerusalem.
I will surround you with towers.
I will build devices around you to
    attack you.
⁴You will be pulled down and will
    speak from the ground.
I will hear your voice rising from
    the ground.
It will sound like the voice of a ghost.
Your words will come like a
    whisper from the dirt.

⁵Your many enemies will become
    like fine dust.
The groups of cruel people will be
    like chaff^d that is blown away.
Everything will happen very quickly.
⁶ The Lord of heaven's armies will
    come.
He will come with thunder,
    earthquakes and great noises.
He will come with storms, strong
    winds and a fire that destroys.
⁷Then all the nations that fight
    against Jerusalem
will be like a dream.

All the nations that surround and
    attack her
  will be like a vision in the night.
[8]They will be like a hungry man who
    dreams he is eating.
  But when he wakes up, he is still
    hungry.
  They will be like a thirsty man who
    dreams he is drinking.
  But when he wakes up, he is still
    weak and thirsty.
  It will be the same way with all the
    nations
  who fight against Mount Zion.[d]

[9]Be surprised and amazed.
  Blind yourselves so that you
    cannot see.
  Become drunk, but not from wine.
  Trip and fall, but not from beer.
[10]The Lord has made you go into a
    deep sleep.
  He has closed your eyes. (The
    prophets are your eyes.)
  He has covered your heads. (The
    seers[d] are your heads.)

[11]This vision is like the words of a
book that is closed and sealed. You may
give the book to someone who can read.
And you may tell that person to read
it. But he will say, "I can't read the book.
It is closed, and I can't open it." [12]Or
you may give the book to someone who
cannot read. You may tell him to read
the book. But he will say, "I can't read
it because I don't know how to read."

[13]The Lord says:
"These people say they love me.
  They show honor to me with
    words.
  But their hearts are far from me.
  The honor they show me
  is nothing but human rules they
    have memorized.
[14]So I will continue to amaze these
    people
  by doing more and more miracles.[d]
  Their wise men will lose their
    wisdom.
  Their wise men will not be able to
    understand."

Warnings About Other Nations

[15]How terrible it will be for those who
    try
  to hide things from the Lord.
  How terrible it will be for those who
    do their work in darkness.
  They think no one will see them or
    know what they do.
[16]You are confused.
  You think the clay is equal to the
    potter.
  You think that an object can tell the
    person who made it,
  "You didn't make me."
  This is like a pot telling its maker,
  "You don't know anything."

A Better Time Is Coming

[17]In a very short time, Lebanon will
    become rich farmland.
  And the rich farmland will seem
    like a forest.
[18]At that time the deaf will hear the
    words in a book.
  Instead of having darkness and
    gloom, the blind will see.
[19]The Lord will make the poor people
    happy.
  They will rejoice in the Holy One
    of Israel.
[20]Then the people without mercy will
    come to an end.
  Those who do not respect God will
    disappear.
  Those who enjoy doing evil will be
    gone.
[21]Those who lie about others in court
    will be gone.
  Those who trap people in court
    will be gone.
  Those who lie and take justice
    from innocent people in court
    will be gone.

[22]The Lord set Abraham free. This
Lord speaks to the family of Jacob.
"Now the people of Jacob will not be
    ashamed.
  They will not be disgraced any
    longer.
[23]They will see all their children,
  the children I made with my hands.

And they will say my name is holy.
The people will agree that the
Holy One of Jacob is holy.
They will respect the God of Israel.
24People who do wrong will now
understand.
Those who complain will accept
being taught."

Warnings to the Stubborn Nation

30 The Lord said,
"How terrible it will be for
these stubborn children.
They make plans, but they don't ask
me to help them.
They make agreements with other
nations, without asking my
Spirit.*d*
They are adding more and more
sins to themselves.
2They go down to Egypt for help,
but they didn't ask me about it
first.
They hope they will be saved by the
king of Egypt.
They want Egypt to protect them.
3But hiding in Egypt will bring you
only shame.
Egypt's protection will only
disappoint you.
4Your officers have gone to Zoan.
Your messengers have gone to
Hanes.
5But they will be put to shame,
because Egypt is useless to them.
Egypt will give no help and be of no
use.
It will cause them only shame and
embarrassment."

God's Message to Judah

6This is the message about the animals in southern Judah:
Southern Judah is a dangerous place.
It is full of lions and lionesses,
poisonous snakes and darting
snakes.
The messengers travel through
there with their wealth on
donkeys' backs.
They have put their treasure on
the backs of camels.

They carry them to a nation that
cannot help them.
7 They go to Egypt whose help is
useless.
So I call that country Rahab*d* the Do-
Nothing.

8Now write this on a sign for the
people.
Write this on a scroll.
Write these things for the days to
come.
Write them so they will last
forever.
9These people are like children who
lie and refuse to obey.
They refuse to listen to the Lord's
teachings.
10They tell the seers,*d*
"Don't see any more visions!"
They say to the prophets,*d*
"Don't tell us the truth!
Say things that will make us feel
good.
See only good things for us.
11Stop blocking our path.
Get out of our way.
Stop telling us
about God, the Holy One of Israel."

12So this is what the Holy One of
Israel says:
"You people have refused to accept
this message from the Lord.
You depended on cruelty and lies
to help you.
13You are guilty of these things.
So you are like a high wall with
cracks in it.
It will fall suddenly and break into
small pieces.
14You will be like a clay jar that breaks.
It breaks into many pieces.
Those pieces will be too small
to take coals from the fire
or to get water from a well."

15This is what the Lord God, the Holy
One of Israel, says:
"If you come back to me and trust
me, you will be saved.
If you will be calm and trust me,
you will be strong."
But you don't want to do that.

[16]You say, "No, we need horses to run away on."

So you will run away on horses.
You say, "We will ride away on fast horses."
So those who chase you will be fast.
[17]One enemy will make threats,
and 1,000 of your men will run away.
Five enemies will make threats,
and all of you will run from them.
You will be left alone like a flagpole on a hilltop.
You will be like a banner on a hill.
[18]The Lord wants to show his mercy to you.
He wants to rise and comfort you.
The Lord is a fair God.
And everyone who waits for his help will be happy.

God Will Help His People

[19]You people who live on Mount Zion[d] in Jerusalem will not cry anymore. The Lord will hear your crying, and he will comfort you. The Lord will hear you, and he will help you. [20]The Lord has given you sorrow and hurt. It was like the bread and water you ate every day. But he is your teacher, and he will not continue to hide from you. You will see your teacher with your own eyes. [21]If you go the wrong way—to the right or to the left—you will hear a voice behind you. It will say, "This is the right way. You should go this way." [22]You have statues covered with silver and gold. But you will ruin them for further use. You will throw them away like filthy rags. You will say, "Go away!"

[23]At that time the Lord will send rain for you. You will plant seeds in the ground, and the ground will grow food for you. The harvest will be very great. You will have plenty of food in the fields for your animals. There will be large fields for your sheep. [24]Your oxen and donkeys will work the soil. They will have all the food they need. You will have to use shovels and pitchforks to spread all the food for your animals to eat. [25]Every mountain and hill will have streams filled with water. These things will happen after many people are killed and the towers are pulled down. [26]At that time the light from the moon will be bright like the sun. The light from the sun will be seven times brighter than now. The light from the sun in one day will be like a full week. These things will happen when the Lord bandages his broken people and heals the hurts he gave them.

[27]Look! The Lord comes from far away.
His anger is like a fire with thick clouds of smoke.
His mouth is filled with anger,
and his tongue is like a burning fire.
[28]The Lord's breath is like a rushing river.
It rises until it reaches the throat.
He will judge the nations as if he is sifting them through the strainer of destruction.
He will place in their mouths a bit that will lead them the wrong way.
[29]You will sing happy songs
as on the nights you begin a festival.
You will be happy as people listening to flutes
as they go to the mountain of the Lord.
The Lord is the Rock[d] of Israel.
[30]The Lord will cause all people to hear his great voice.
He will cause them to see his powerful arm come down.
It will come with anger like a great fire that burns everything.
It will be like a great storm with much rain and hail.
[31]Assyria will be afraid when it hears the voice of the Lord.
The Lord will beat Assyria with a rod.
[32]The Lord will punish Assyria with a rod.
He will beat them to the music of tambourines[d] and harps.
The Lord will fight against them with his mighty weapons.

[33]Topheth[n] has been made ready for a
  long time.
It is ready for the king.
It was made deep and wide.
There is much wood and fire there.
And the Lord's breath will come
  like a stream of burning sulfur and
  burn it.

Warnings About Relying on Egypt

31 How terrible it will be for those
people who go down to Egypt for
help.
They think horses will save them.
They think their many chariots
  and strong horsemen will save them.
They don't trust God, the Holy One
  of Israel.
They don't ask the Lord for help.
[2]But it is the Lord who is wise and
  who can bring them trouble.
He does not change his warnings.
He will rise up and fight against the
  evil people.
And he will fight against those
  who try to help evil people.
[3]The Egyptians are only people and
  are not God.
Their horses are only animals and
  are not spirit.
The Lord will stretch out his arm,
  and the one who helps will
  stumble.
The people who wanted help will
  fall.
All of them will be destroyed
  together.

[4]The Lord says this to me:
"When a lion or a lion's cub kills an
  animal to eat,
it stands over the dead animal and
  roars.
A band of shepherds
  may be assembled against it.
But the lion will not be afraid of
  their yelling.
It will not be upset by their noise.
So the Lord of heaven's armies will
  come down

to fight on Mount Zion[d] and on its
  hill.
[5]The Lord of heaven's armies will
  defend Jerusalem.
He will defend it like birds flying
  over their nests.
He will defend and save it.
He will 'pass over' and save
  Jerusalem."

[6]You children of Israel, come back to
the God that you fought against. [7]The
time is coming when each of you will
stop worshiping the idols of gold and
silver that you made. You truly sinned
when you made them.

[8]"Assyria will be defeated by a sword,
  but not the sword of a man.
Assyria will be destroyed, but not
  by a man's sword.
Assyria will run away from the
  sword of God.
But their young men will be
  caught and made slaves.
[9]They will panic, and their place of
  safety will be destroyed.
Their commanders will be terrified
  when they see God's battle
  flag."
The Lord said all these things.
The Lord's fire is in Jerusalem.
His furnace is in Jerusalem.

A Good Kingdom Is Coming

32 A king will rule in a way that
brings justice.
Leaders will make fair decisions.
[2]Then each ruler will be like a
  shelter from the wind.
He will be like a safe place in a
  storm.
He will be like streams of water in a
  dry land.
He will be like a cool shadow from
  a large rock in a hot land.

[3]People will look to the king for
  help.
And they will truly listen to what
  he says.

---

[n]**Topheth** Gehenna; the Valley of Hinnom. Here people burned the bodies of criminals and animals,
along with garbage.

⁴People who are now worried will be
able to understand.

Those who cannot speak clearly
now will then be able to speak
clearly and quickly.

⁵Fools will not be called great men.

People will not respect wicked
men.

⁶A fool says foolish things.

And in his mind he plans to do evil
things.

A fool wants to do things that are
wrong.

He says wrong things about the
Lord.

A fool does not feed the hungry.

He does not let thirsty people
drink water.

⁷The wicked man uses evil like a tool.

He plans ways to take everything
from poor people.

He destroys the poor with lies,
even when the poor man is in the
right.

⁸But a good leader plans good things
to do.

And those good things make him a
good leader.

Hard Times Are Coming

⁹You women who are calm now,
stand up and listen to me.

You women who feel safe now,
hear what I say.

¹⁰You women feel safe now,
but after one year you will be afraid.

There will be no grape harvest.

There will not be any summer fruit
to gather.

¹¹Women, you are calm now, but you
should shake with fear.

Women, you feel safe now, but you
should tremble.

Take off your nice clothes.

Then put rough cloth around your
waist to show your sadness.

¹²Beat your breasts in grief because
the fields that were pleasant
are now empty.

Cry because the vines that once had
fruit now have no more grapes.

¹³Cry for the land of my people.

Cry because only thorns and
weeds grow there now.

Cry for the city that once was happy.

And cry for all the houses that
once were filled with joy.

¹⁴The palace will be empty.

People will leave the noisy city.

Strong cities and towers will be
empty.

Wild donkeys will love to live there.

Sheep will go there to eat.

Things Will Get Better

¹⁵This will continue until God puts his
Spirit[d] from above into us.

Then the desert will be like a
fertile field.

And the fertile field will be like a
forest.

¹⁶Justice will be found even in the
desert.

And fairness will be found in the
fertile fields.

¹⁷That fairness will bring peace.

And fairness will bring calm and
safety forever.

¹⁸My people will live in peaceful
places.

They will have safe homes.

They will live in calm places of rest.

¹⁹Hail will destroy the forest.

And the city will be completely
destroyed.

²⁰But you will be happy as you plant
seeds near every stream.

You will let your cattle and
donkeys wander freely.

Warnings to Assyria and Promises to God's People

33 How terrible it will be for you
who destroy others.

But you have not been destroyed
yet.

How terrible it will be for you,
traitor.

But no one has turned against you
yet.

When you stop destroying,
others will destroy you.

When you stop turning against
others,

they will turn against you.

²Lord, be kind to us.
We have waited for your help.
Lord, give us strength every
morning.
Save us when we are in trouble.
³Your powerful voice makes people
run away in fear.
Your greatness causes the nations
to run away.
⁴Like locusts,^d your enemies will take
away the things you stole in
war.
Like locusts rushing about, they
will take your wealth.
⁵The Lord is very great. He lives in a
high place.
He fills Jerusalem with fairness
and justice.
⁶The Lord will be your safety.
He is full of salvation, wisdom and
knowledge.
Respect for the Lord is the
greatest treasure.

⁷See, brave men are crying out in the
streets.
Those who tried to bring peace are
crying loudly.
⁸There is no one on the roads.
No one is walking in the paths.
People have broken the agreements
they made.
People refuse to believe the proof
from witnesses.
No one respects other people.
⁹The land is sick and dying.
Lebanon is ashamed and dying.
The Plain of Sharon is dry like the
desert.
The trees of Bashan and Carmel
are dying.

¹⁰The Lord says, "Now, I will stand up
and show my greatness.
Now, I will become important to
the people.
¹¹You people do useless things.
These things are like hay and straw.
A destructive wind will burn you
like fire.
¹²People will be burned until their
bones become like lime.

They will burn quickly like dry
thornbushes."

¹³You people in faraway lands, hear
what I have done.
You people who are near me, learn
about my power.
¹⁴The sinners in Jerusalem are afraid.
The people who are separated
from God shake with fear.
They say, "Can any of us live
through this fire that destroys?
Who can live near this fire that
burns on and on?"
¹⁵A person might do what is right.
He might speak what is right.
He might refuse to take money
unfairly.
He might refuse to take money to
hurt others.
He might not listen to plans of
murder.
He might refuse to think about
evil.
¹⁶This is the kind of person who will
be safe.
He will be protected as he would
be in a high, walled city.
He will always have bread,
and he will not run out of water.
¹⁷Your eyes will see the king in his
beauty.
You will see the land that stretches
far away.
¹⁸You will think about the terror of
the past.
You will think, "Where is that
officer?
Where is the one who collected
the taxes?
Where is the officer in charge of
our defense towers?"
¹⁹You will not see those proud people
from other countries anymore.
No more will you hear their
strange language
that you couldn't understand.

God Will Protect Jerusalem

²⁰Look at Jerusalem, the city of our
festivals.
Look at Jerusalem, that beautiful
place of rest.

It is like a tent that will never be
moved.
The pegs that hold her in place
will never be moved.
Her ropes will never be broken.
21There the Lord will be our Mighty
One.
That land is a place with streams
and wide rivers.
But there will be no enemy boats on
those rivers.
No powerful ship will sail on those
rivers.
22This is because the Lord is our judge.
The Lord makes our laws.
The Lord is our king.
He will save us.
23You sailors from other lands, hear:
The ropes on your boats hang loose.
The mast is not held firm.
The sails are not spread open.
The Lord will give us your wealth.
There will be so much wealth even
the crippled people will carry
off a share.
24No one living in Jerusalem will say,
"I am sick."
The people who live there will
have their sins forgiven.

God Will Punish His Enemies

34 All you nations, come near and
listen.
Pay attention, you peoples!
The earth and all the people in it
should listen.
The world and everything in it
should listen.
2The Lord is angry with all the nations.
He is angry with their armies.
He will destroy them and kill them
all.
3Their bodies will be thrown outside.
The stink will rise from the bodies,
and the blood will flow down the
mountains.
4The sun, moon and stars will dissolve.
The sky will be rolled up like a
scroll.
The stars will fall
like dead leaves from a vine
or dried-up figs from a fig tree.

5The Lord's sword in the sky is
covered with blood.
It will cut through Edom.
He will destroy these people as an
offering to the Lord.
6The Lord's sword will be covered
with blood.
It will be covered with fat.
It is the blood from lambs and goats.
It is the fat from the kidneys of
male sheep.
This is because the Lord decided
there will be a sacrifice in
Bozrah.
He has decided there will be much
killing in Edom.
7The oxen will be killed.
And the cattle and the strong bulls
will be killed.
The land will be filled with their
blood.
The dirt will be covered with their
fat.

8The Lord has chosen a time for
punishment.
He has chosen a year when people
must pay for the wrongs they
did to Jerusalem.
9Edom's rivers will be like hot tar.
The dirt of Edom will be like
burning sulfur.
The land of Edom will be like
burning tar.
10The fires will burn night and day.
The smoke will rise from Edom
forever.
Year after year that land will be
empty.
No one will ever travel through
that land again.
11Birds and small animals will own
that land.
Owls and ravens will live there.
God will make it an empty wasteland.
It will have nothing left in it.
12The important men will have no one
left to rule them.
The leaders will all be gone.
13Thorns will take over the strong
towers.
Wild bushes will grow in the
walled cities.

Wild dogs will live there.
Owls will live in those homes.
¹⁴Desert animals will live with the
    hyenas there.
And wild goats will call to their
    friends.
Night animals will live there.
They will find a place of rest there.
¹⁵Owls will nest there and lay eggs.
When the eggs open, the owls will
    gather their young under their
    wings.
Hawks will gather
with their own kind.

¹⁶Look at the Lord's scroll. Read what
is written there:
None of these will be missing.
Every one will have its mate.
God said he will gather them
    together.
So his Spirit[d] will gather them
    together.
¹⁷God has divided the land among
    them.
And he has given them each their
    land.
So they will own that land forever.
They will live there year after year.

God Will Comfort His People

35 The desert and dry land will
become happy.
The desert will be glad and will
    produce flowers.
Like a flower, ²it will have many
    blooms.
It will show its happiness, as if it is
    shouting with joy.
It will be beautiful like the forest of
    Lebanon.
It will be as beautiful as the hill of
    Carmel and the Plain of Sharon.
All people will see the glory of the
    Lord.
They will see the splendor of our
    God.

³Make the weak hands strong.
Make the weak knees strong.
⁴Say to people who are afraid and
    confused,
"Be strong. Don't be afraid.

Look, your God will come,
and he will punish your enemies.
He will make them pay for the
    wrongs they did.
He will come and save you."

⁵Then the blind people will see again.
Then the deaf will hear.
⁶Crippled people will jump like deer.
And those who can't talk now will
    shout with joy.
Springs of water will flow in the
    desert.
Streams will flow in the dry land.
⁷The burning desert will have pools
    of water.
The dry ground will have springs.
Where wild dogs once lived,
grass and water plants will grow.
⁸A road will be there.
This highway will be called "The
    Road to Being Holy."
Evil people will not be allowed to
    walk on that road.
Only good people will walk on that
    road.
No fools will go on it.
⁹No lions will be there.
No dangerous animals will be on
    that road.
They will not be found there.
That road will be for the people God
    saves.
¹⁰ The people the Lord has freed will
    return there.
They will enter Jerusalem with joy.
Their happiness will last forever.
Their gladness and joy will fill them
    completely.
Sorrow and sadness will go far away.

The Assyrians Invade Judah

36 During Hezekiah's fourteenth
year as king, Sennacherib king
of Assyria attacked Judah. He attacked
all the strong, walled cities of Judah
and defeated them. ²The king of Assyria
sent out his field commander. He went
with a large army from Lachish to King
Hezekiah in Jerusalem. When the commander came near the waterway from
the upper pool, he stopped. The upper
pool is on the road to the Washerman's

Field. ³Eliakim, Shebna and Joah went out to meet him. Eliakim son of Hilkiah was the palace manager. Shebna was the royal assistant. And Joah son of Asaph was the recorder.

⁴The field commander said to them, "Tell Hezekiah this:

"'The great king, the king of Assyria, says: You have nothing to trust in to help you. ⁵You say you have battle plans and power for war. But your words mean nothing. Whom are you trusting for help so that you turn against me? ⁶Look, you are depending on Egypt to help you. Egypt is like a splintered walking stick. If you lean on it for help, it will stab you and hurt you. The king of Egypt will hurt those who depend on him. ⁷You might say, "We are depending on the Lord our God." But Hezekiah destroyed the Lord's altars and the places of worship. Hezekiah told Judah and Jerusalem, "You must worship only at this one altar."

⁸"'Now make an agreement with my master, the king of Assyria: I will give you 2,000 horses if you can find enough men to ride them. ⁹You cannot defeat one of my master's least important officers. So why do you depend on Egypt to give you chariots and horsemen? ¹⁰I have not come to attack and destroy this country without an order from the Lord. The Lord himself told me to come to this country and destroy it.'"

¹¹Then Eliakim, Shebna and Joah spoke to the field commander. They said, "Please speak to us in the Aramaic language. We understand it. Don't speak to us in Hebrew because the people on the city wall can hear you."

¹²But the commander said, "No. My master did not send me to tell these things only to you and your king. My master sent me to tell them also to those people sitting on the wall. They will have to eat their own dung and drink their own urine like you."

¹³Then the commander stood and shouted loudly in the Hebrew language. He said, "Listen to the words from the great king, the king of Assyria! ¹⁴The

king says you should not let Hezekiah fool you. Hezekiah can't save you. ¹⁵Don't let Hezekiah talk you into trusting the Lord. Hezekiah says, 'The Lord will surely save us. This city won't be given over to the king of Assyria.'

¹⁶"Don't listen to Hezekiah. The king of Assyria says, 'Make peace with me. Come out of the city to me. Then everyone will be free to eat the fruit from his own grapevine and fig tree. Everyone will be free to drink water from his own well. ¹⁷Then I will come and take you to a land like your own. It is a land with grain and new wine. It has bread and vineyards.'

¹⁸"Don't let Hezekiah fool you. He says, 'The Lord will save us.' The god of any other nation has not saved his people from the power of the king of Assyria. ¹⁹Where are the gods of Hamath and Arpad? Where are the gods of Sepharvaim? They did not save Samaria from my power. ²⁰Not one of all the gods of these countries has saved his people from me. Then the Lord cannot save Jerusalem from my power."

²¹The people were silent. They didn't answer the commander at all. This was because King Hezekiah had ordered, "Don't answer him."

²²Then Eliakim, Shebna and Joah tore their clothes to show how upset they were. (Eliakim son of Hilkiah was the palace manager. Shebna was the royal assistant. And Joah son of Asaph was the recorder.) The three men went to Hezekiah and told him what the field commander had said.

Hezekiah Asks God to Help

37 When King Hezekiah heard the message, he tore his clothes. And he put on rough cloth to show how sad he was. Then he went into the Temple*d* of the Lord. ²Hezekiah sent Eliakim, Shebna and the older priests to Isaiah. Eliakim was the palace manager, and Shebna was the royal assistant. The men were all wearing the rough cloth when they came to Isaiah. He was a prophet,*d* the son of Amoz. ³These men told Isaiah, "This is what Hezekiah says: Today is a day of sorrow and punishment and disgrace. It is sad, as when a child should be born, but the mother is not strong enough to give birth to it. [4]The king of Assyria sent his field commander to make fun of the living God. Maybe the Lord your God will hear what the commander said. Maybe the Lord your God will punish him for what he said. So pray for the few people of Israel who are left alive."

[5]When Hezekiah's officers came to Isaiah, [6]he said to them, "Tell your master this: The Lord says, 'Don't be afraid of what you have heard. Don't be frightened by the words the servants of the king of Assyria said against me. [7]Listen! I am going to put a spirit in the king of Assyria. He will hear a report that will make him return to his own country. And I will cause him to die by the sword there.'"

[8]The field commander heard that the king of Assyria had left Lachish. So the commander left and found the king fighting against the city of Libnah. [9]The king received a report that Tirhakah was coming to attack him. Tirhakah was the Cushite king of Egypt. When the king of Assyria heard this, he sent messengers to Hezekiah. The king said: [10]"Say this to Hezekiah king of Judah: Don't be fooled by the god you trust. Don't believe him when he says Jerusalem will not be defeated by the king of Assyria. [11]You have heard what the kings of Assyria have done. They have completely defeated every country. Do not think you will be saved. [12]The gods of those people did not save them. My ancestors destroyed them. My ancestors defeated the cities of Gozan, Haran and Rezeph. They defeated the people of Eden living in Tel Assar. [13]Where are the kings of Hamath and Arpad? Where is the king of the city of Sepharvaim? Where are the kings of Hena and Ivvah?"

Hezekiah Prays to the Lord

[14]Hezekiah received the letter from the messengers and read it. Then he went up to the Temple[d] of the Lord. Hezekiah spread the letter out before the Lord. [15]And he prayed to the Lord: [16]"Lord of heaven's armies, you are the God of Israel. Your throne is between the gold creatures with wings. Only you are the God of all the kingdoms of the earth. You made the heavens and the earth. [17]Hear, Lord, and listen. Open your eyes, Lord, and see. Listen to all the words Sennacherib has said to insult the living God.

[18]"It is true, Lord. The kings of Assyria have destroyed all these countries and their lands. [19]These kings have thrown the gods of these nations into the fire. But they were only wood and rock statues that men made. So the kings have destroyed them. [20]Now, Lord our God, save us from the king's power. Then all the kingdoms of the earth will know that you, Lord, are the only God."

God Answers Hezekiah

[21]Then Isaiah son of Amoz sent a message to Hezekiah. Isaiah said, "The Lord, the God of Israel, says this: 'You prayed to me about Sennacherib king of Assyria. [22]So this is what the Lord has said against Sennacherib:

The people of Jerusalem
   hate you and make fun of you.
The people of Jerusalem
   laugh at you as you run away.
[23]You have insulted me and spoken
      against me.
   You have raised your voice against
      me.
   You have a proud look on your face.
   You disobey me, the Holy One of
      Israel!
[24]You have used your messengers to
      insult the Lord.
   You have said, "I have many
      chariots.
With them I have gone to the tops
      of the mountains.
   I have climbed the highest
      mountains of Lebanon.
I have cut down its tallest cedars.

I have cut down its best pine trees.
I have gone to its greatest heights.
I have gone to its best forests.
25 I have dug wells in foreign countries.
I have drunk water there.
By the soles of my feet,
I have dried up all the rivers of
　Egypt."

26 "'King of Assyria, surely you have
　heard.
Long ago I, the Lord, planned
　these things.
Long ago I planned them.
Now I have made them happen.
I allowed you to turn those strong,
　walled cities
into piles of rocks.
27 The people living in those cities
　were weak.
They were frightened and put to
　shame.
They were like grass in the field.
They were like tender, young grass.
They were like grass that grows on
　the housetop.
It is burned by the wind before it
　can grow.

28 "'I know when you rest and when
　you come and go.
I know how you speak against me.
29 You speak strongly against me.
And I have heard your proud words.
So I will put my hook in your nose.
And I will put my bit in your
　mouth.
Then I will force you to leave my
　country
the same way that you came.'

30 "Then the Lord said, 'Hezekiah, I
will give you this sign:
This year you will eat the grain that
　grows wild.
And the second year you will eat
　what grows wild from that.
But in the third year, plant grain
　and harvest it.
Plant vineyards and eat their fruit.
31 The people left alive in the family of
　Judah
will be saved.
Like plants that take root,

they will grow strong and have
　many children.
32 A few people will come out of
　Jerusalem alive.
There will be a few from Mount
　Zion[d] who will live.
The strong love of the Lord of
　heaven's armies
will cause this to happen.'

33 "So this is what the Lord says about
the king of Assyria:
'He will not enter this city.
He will not even shoot an arrow
　here.
He will not fight against it with
　shields.
He will not build a ramp to attack
　the city walls.
34 He will return to his country the
　same way he came.
He will not enter this city,'
says the Lord.
35 The Lord says, 'I will defend and
　save this city.
I will do this for myself and for
　David, my servant.'"

36 Then the angel of the Lord went
out. He killed 185,000 men in the Assyrian camp. When the people got up
early the next morning, they saw all
the dead bodies! 37 So Sennacherib king
of Assyria left. He went back to Nineveh and stayed there.

38 One day Sennacherib was worshiping in the temple of his god Nisroch.
While he was there, his sons Adrammelech and Sharezer killed him with a
sword. Then they escaped to the land
of Ararat. So Sennacherib's son Esarhaddon became king of Assyria.

Hezekiah's Illness

38 At that time Hezekiah became
very sick. He was almost dead.
The prophet[d] Isaiah son of Amoz went
to see him. Isaiah told him, "This is
what the Lord says: You are going to
die. So you should give your last orders
to everyone. You will not get well."
2 Hezekiah turned toward the wall
and prayed to the Lord. 3 He said, "Lord,

please remember that I have always obeyed you. I have given myself completely to you. I have done what you said was right." And Hezekiah cried loudly.

[4]Then the Lord spoke his word to Isaiah: [5]"Go to Hezekiah and tell him: 'This is what the Lord, the God of your ancestor David, says: I have heard your prayer. And I have seen your tears. I will add 15 years to your life. [6]I will save you and this city from the king of Assyria. I will defend this city.'"

[21n] Then Isaiah said, "Make a paste from figs. Put it on Hezekiah's boil. Then he will get well."

[22]Hezekiah asked Isaiah, "What will be the sign? What will show that I will go up to the Temple[d] of the Lord?"

[7]Isaiah said, "The Lord will do what he says. This is the sign from the Lord to show you: [8]The sun has made a shadow go down the stairway of Ahaz. I will make it go back ten steps." So the shadow made by the sun went back up the ten steps it had gone down.

[9]After Hezekiah king of Judah got well, he wrote this song:
[10]I said, "I am in the middle of my life.
Do I have to go through the gates
where the dead are now?
Will I have the rest of my life taken
away from me?"
[11]I said, "I will not see the Lord
in the land of the living again.
I will not again see the people
who live on the earth.
[12]Like a shepherd's tent,
my home has been pulled down
and taken from me.
I am finished like the cloth
a weaver rolls up and cuts from the
loom.[n]
In one day you brought me to this
end.
[13]All night I cried loudly.
Like a lion, he crushed all my bones.
In one day you brought me to this
end.

[14]I cried like a bird.
I moaned like a dove.
My eyes became tired as I looked to
the heavens.
Lord, I have troubles. Please help
me."

[15]What can I say?
The Lord told me what would
happen and then made it
happen.
I have had these troubles in my soul.
So now I will be humble all my life.
[16]Lord, because of you, men live.
Because of you, my spirit also lives.
You made me well and let me live.
[17]It was for my own good
that I had such troubles.
Because you love me very much,
you did not let me die.
You threw my sins
far away.
[18]People in the place where the dead
are cannot praise you.
Those who have died cannot sing
praises to you.
Those who die don't trust you
to help them.
[19]The people who are alive are the
ones who praise you.
They praise you as I praise you
today.
A father should tell his children
that you provide help.

[20]The Lord saved me.
So we will sing and play songs.
We will make music in the Temple
of the Lord
all the days of our lives.

Messengers from Babylon

39 At that time Merodach-Baladan son of Baladan was king of Babylon. He sent letters and a gift to Hezekiah. He did this because he had heard that Hezekiah had been sick and was now well. [2]Hezekiah was happy to see the messengers. So he showed them what was in his storehouses: the silver,

---

[n]**Verses 21-22** These verses are generally found at the end of chapter 38. But the same story in 2 Kings 20:6-9 shows the events happened in this order.
[n]**loom** A machine for making cloth from thread.

gold, spices and expensive perfumes. He showed them his swords and shields. He showed them all his wealth. He showed them everything in his palace and in his kingdom.

[3] Then Isaiah the prophet[d] went to King Hezekiah. He asked Hezekiah, "What did these men say? Where did they come from?"

Hezekiah said, "They came from a faraway country. They came to me from Babylon."

[4] So Isaiah asked him, "What did they see in your palace?"

Hezekiah said, "They saw everything in my palace. I showed them all my wealth."

[5] Then Isaiah said to Hezekiah: "Listen to the words of the Lord of heaven's armies: [6] 'In the future everything in your palace will be taken away to Babylon. Everything your ancestors have stored up until this day will be taken away. Nothing will be left,' says the Lord. [7] Some of your own children will be taken away. Those who will be born to you will be taken away. And they will become eunuchs[d] in the palace of the king of Babylon."

[8] Hezekiah told Isaiah, "These words from the Lord are good." He said this because he thought, "There will be peace and security while I am king."

Israel's Punishment Will End

40 Your God says,
Comfort, comfort my people.
[2] Speak kindly to the people of
Jerusalem.
Tell them
that their time of service is finished.
Tell them that they have paid for
their sins.
Tell them that the Lord has
punished Jerusalem
twice for every sin they did."

[3] This is the voice of a man who
calls out:
"Prepare in the desert
the way for the Lord.
Make the road in the dry lands
straight for our God.

[4] Every valley should be raised up.
Every mountain and hill should be
made flat.
The rough ground should be made
level.
The rugged ground should be
made smooth.
[5] Then the glory of the Lord will be
shown.
All people together will see it.
The Lord himself said these things."

[6] A voice says, "Cry out!"
Then I said, "What shall I cry out?"

"Say all people are like the grass.
And all their strength is like the
flowers of the field.
[7] The grass dies, and the flowers fall.
This is because the breath of the
Lord blows on them.
Surely the people are like grass.
[8] The grass dies, and the flowers fall.
But the word of our God will live
forever."

The grass dies, and the flowers fall. But the word of our God will live forever.
• Isaiah 40:8

[9] Jerusalem, you have good news to
tell.
Go up on a high mountain.
Jerusalem, you have good news to
tell.
Shout out loud the good news.
Shout it out and don't be afraid.
Say to the towns of Judah,
"Here is your God."
[10] Look, the Lord God is coming with
power.
He will use his power to rule all
the people.
Look, he will bring reward for his
people.
He will have their payment with
him.
[11] The Lord takes care of his people
like a shepherd.

He gathers the people like lambs
in his arms.
He carries them close to him.
He gently leads the mothers of the
lambs.

God Is Supreme

¹²Who has measured the oceans in
the palm of his hand?
Who has used his hand to
measure the sky?
Who has used a bowl to measure all
the dust of the earth?
Who has used scales to weigh the
mountains and hills?
¹³Who has known the mind of the
Lord?
Who has been able to give the
Lord advice?
¹⁴Whom did the Lord ask for help?
Who taught him the right way?
Who taught the Lord
knowledge?
Who showed him the way to
understanding?
¹⁵The nations are like one small drop
in a bucket.
They are no more than the dust on
his measuring scales.
To him the islands are no more
than fine dust on his scales.
¹⁶All the trees in Lebanon are not
enough for the altar fires.
And all the animals in Lebanon are
not enough for burnt offerings.
¹⁷Compared to the Lord all the
nations are worth nothing.
To him they are less than
nothing.
¹⁸Can you compare God to
anything?
Can you compare him to an image
of anything?
¹⁹An idol is formed by a man.
And another man covers it with
gold.
And he makes silver chains for it.
²⁰A poor man cannot buy those
expensive statues.
So he finds a tree that will not rot.
And he finds a skilled workman

to make it into an idol that will not
fall over.

²¹Surely you know. Surely you have
heard.
Surely in the beginning someone
told you.
Surely you understand how the
earth was created.
²²God sits on his throne above the
circle of the earth.
And compared to him, people are
like grasshoppers.
He stretches out the skies like a
piece of cloth.
He spreads them out like a tent to
sit under.
²³He makes rulers unimportant.
He makes the judges of this world
worth nothing.
²⁴They are like plants that are placed
in the ground.
They are like seeds that are planted.
As soon as they begin to grow
strong,
he blows on them and they die.
The wind blows them away like
chaff.ᵈ

²⁵God, the Holy One, says, "Can you
compare me to anyone?
Is anyone equal to me?
²⁶Look up to the skies.
Who created all these stars?
He leads out all the army of heaven
one by one.
He calls all the stars by name.
He is very strong and full of power.
So not one of them is missing.

²⁷People of Jacob, why do you
complain?
People of Israel, why do you say,
"The Lord does not see what
happens to me.
He does not care if I am treated
fairly"?
²⁸Surely you know.
Surely you have heard.
The Lord is the God who lives
forever.
He created all the world.
He does not become tired or need
to rest.

No one can understand how great
his wisdom is.

²⁹The Lord gives strength to those
who are tired.

He gives more power to those who
are weak.

³⁰Even boys become tired and need
to rest.

Even young men trip and fall.

³¹But the people who trust the Lord
will become strong again.

They will be able to rise up as an
eagle in the sky.

They will run without needing rest.

They will walk without becoming
tired.

The Lord Will Help Israel

41 The Lord says, "Faraway countries, listen to me.

Let the nations become strong.

Come to me and speak.

We will meet together to decide
who is right.

²"Who caused the man to come from
the east?

Who gives the man victories
everywhere he goes?

The one who brought him gives
nations over to him.

He defeats kings for him.

The man uses his sword, and the
kings become like dust.

He uses his bow, and they are
blown away like chaff.^d

³He chases them and is never hurt.

He goes places where he has
never been before.

⁴Who caused this to happen?

Who has controlled history since
the beginning?

I, the Lord, am the one. I was here
at the beginning.

And I will be here when all things
are finished."

⁵All you faraway places, look and be
afraid.

All you places far away on the
earth, shake with fear.

Come close and listen to me.

⁶ The workers help each other.

They say to each other, "Be strong!"

⁷The man who carves wood
encourages the man who
works with gold.

The workman who smooths the
metal with a hammer
encourages the man who
shapes the metal.

This last workman says, "This metal
work is good."

He nails the statue to a base so it
can't fall over.

Only the Lord Can Save Us

⁸The Lord says, "People of Israel,
you are my servants.

People of Jacob, I chose you.

You are from the family of my friend
Abraham.

⁹You were far away on the earth.

I called you from a faraway country.

I said, 'You are my servants.'

I have chosen you, and I have not
turned against you.

¹⁰So don't worry, because I am with
you.

Don't be afraid, because I am your
God.

I will make you strong and will help
you.

I will support you with my right
hand that saves you.

¹¹"All those people who are angry
with you
will be ashamed and disgraced.

Those who are against you
will disappear and be lost.

¹²You will look for your enemies.

But you will not find them.

Those who fought against you
will vanish completely.

¹³I am the Lord your God.

I am holding your right hand.

And I tell you, 'Don't be afraid.

I will help you.'

¹⁴You few people of Israel who are left,
do not be afraid even though you
are weak as a worm.

I myself will help you," says the Lord.

"I am the one who saves you, the
Holy One of Israel.

¹⁵Look, I have made you like a
    threshing[d] board.
  You are new, with many sharp
    teeth.
  So you will walk on mountains and
    crush them.
  You will make the hills like chaff.[d]
¹⁶You will throw them into the air.
    And the wind will carry them
    away.
  A windstorm will scatter them.
  Then you will be happy in the Lord.
  You will be proud of the Holy One
    of Israel.

¹⁷"The poor and needy people look
    for water.
  But they can't find any.
  Their tongues are dry with thirst.
  But I, the Lord, will answer their
    prayers.
  I, the God of Israel, will not leave
    them to die.
¹⁸I will make rivers flow on the dry
    hills.
  I will make springs of water flow
    through the valleys.
  I will change the desert into a lake
    of water.
  I will change the dry land into
    springs of water.
¹⁹I will make trees grow in the desert.
  There will be cedars, acacia,
    myrtle and olive trees.
  I will put pine, fir and cypress trees
    growing together in the desert.
²⁰People will see these things and
    understand.
  Together they will think carefully
    about these things.
  They will know that the Lord's
    power did this.
  They will know that the Holy One
    of Israel made these things."

The Lord Challenges False Gods

²¹The Lord says, "Present your case."
  The Lord, the King of Jacob, says,
    "Tell me your arguments.
²²Bring in your idols to tell us
  what is going to happen.

  Have them tell us what happened in
    the beginning.
  Then we will think about these
    things.
  Then we will know how they will
    turn out.
  Tell us what will happen in the future.
²³ Tell us what is coming next.
  Then we will believe that you are
    gods.
  Do something, whether it is good or
    bad.
  Make us afraid of you.
²⁴You false gods are less than nothing.
  You can't do anything.
  Those who worship you should be
    hated."

²⁵"I have brought someone to come
    out of the north.[n]
  I have called by name a man from
    the east, and he knows me.
  He walks on kings as if they were
    mud.
  He walks on them as a potter
    walks on the clay.
²⁶Who told us about this before it
    happened?
  Who told us ahead of time so we
    could say, 'He was right'?
  None of you told us anything.
  None of you told us before it
    happened.
  No one heard you tell about it.
²⁷I, the Lord, was the first one to tell
    Jerusalem that the people
    were coming home.
  I sent a messenger to Jerusalem
    with the good news.
²⁸I look at the idols, but there is not
    one that can answer.
  None of them can give advice.
  None of them can answer my
    questions.
²⁹Look, all these idols are false gods.
  They cannot do anything.
  They are worth nothing.

The Lord's Special Servant

42 "Here is my servant, the one I
  support.

---

[n]**someone . . . north**   This probably means Cyrus, a king of Persia.

He is the one I chose, and I am
    pleased with him.
I will put my Spirit*d* in him.
    And he will bring justice to all
    nations.
²He will not cry out or yell.
    He will not speak loudly in the
    streets.
³He will not break a crushed blade of
    grass.
    He will not put out even a weak
    flame.
    He will bring justice and find what
    is true.
⁴ He will not lose hope or give up
until he brings justice to the
    world.
    And people far away will trust his
    teachings."

⁵God, the Lord, said these things.
He created the skies and stretched
    them out.
    He spread out the earth and
    everything on it.
He gives life to all people on earth.
    He gives life to everyone who
    walks on the earth.
⁶The Lord says, "I called you to do
    right.
    And I will hold your hand.
I will protect you.
    You will be the sign of my
    agreement with the people.
    You will be a light to shine for all
    people.
⁷You will help the blind to see.
    You will free those who are in
    prison.
    You will lead those who live in
    darkness out of their prison.

⁸"I am the Lord. That is my name.
    I will not give my glory to
    another.
    I will not let idols take the praise
    that should be mine.
⁹The things I said would happen
    have happened.
    And now I tell you about new
    things.
Before those things happen,
    I tell you about them.

A Song of Praise to the Lord

¹⁰Sing a new song to the Lord.
    Sing his praise everywhere on the
    earth.
    Praise him, you people who sail on
    the seas and you animals who
    live in them.
    Praise him, you people living in
    faraway places.
¹¹The deserts and their cities should
    praise him.
    The settlements of Kedar should
    praise him.
    The people living in Sela should
    sing for joy.
    They should sing from the
    mountaintops.
¹²They should give glory to the Lord.
    People in faraway lands should
    praise him.
¹³The Lord will march out like a
    strong soldier.
    He will be excited like a man ready
    to fight a war.
    He will shout out the battle cry.
    And he will defeat his enemies.

¹⁴The Lord says, "For a long time I
    have said nothing.
    I have been quiet and held myself
    back.
    But now I will cry out.
    I will strain like a woman giving
    birth to a child.
¹⁵I will destroy the hills and mountains.
    I will dry up all the plants that
    grow there.
    I will make the rivers become dry
    land.
    I will dry up the pools of water.
¹⁶Then I will lead the blind along a
    way they never knew.
    I will guide them along paths they
    have not known.
    I will make the darkness become
    light for them.
    And I will make the rough ground
    smooth.
    These are the things I will do.
    I will not leave my people.
¹⁷But some people trust in idols.
    They say to their statues,

'You are our gods.'
Those people will be rejected in
disgrace.

Israel Refused to Listen to God

18"You who are deaf, hear me.
You who are blind, look and see.
19No one is more blind than my
servant Israel.
The messenger I send is the most
deaf.
No one is more blind than the
person I own.
No one is more blind than the
servant of the Lord.
20Israel, you have seen much, but you
have not obeyed.
You have heard, but you refuse to
listen."
21The Lord made his teachings
wonderful.
He did this because he is good.
22These people have been defeated
and robbed.
They are trapped in pits.
They are locked up in prison.
Like robbers, enemies have taken
them away.
There is no one to save them.
Enemies carried them off.

And no one said, "Bring them
back."
23Will any of you listen to this?
Will you listen carefully in the
future?
24Who let the people of Jacob be
carried off?
Who let robbers take Israel away?
The Lord allowed this to happen
because we sinned against him.
We did not live the way the Lord
wanted us to live.
We did not obey his teaching.
25So the Lord became very angry with
us.
He brought terrible wars against
us.
It was as if the people of Israel had
fire all around them.
But they didn't know what was
happening.
It was as if they were burning.
But they didn't pay any attention.

God Is Always with His People

43 Now this is what the Lord says.
He created you, people of
Jacob.

What God Is Like
ISAIAH 43:1-3

Imagine that you are in the middle of a very busy
intersection with cars roaring by you at high speeds from all directions. You
want to get safely out of the intersection and over to the sidewalk, but you
are afraid to move. What if the cars don't see you, or just won't stop? What
if you get hit? You need somebody to help you, somebody with the power to
make the traffic stop and get you to safety—somebody like a traffic policeman!

There are times when life will seem that way—dangerous and out of
control, with no one to help you get through it. At times like that, it is
good to know what Isaiah wrote in Isaiah 43:1-3: God is in control. He
will do what he plans, and his plans are for your good. He is much more
than a traffic policeman, but he doesn't mind helping you out of a tough
situation.

To learn more about what God is like, zoom to page 852.

He formed you, people of Israel.
He says, "Don't be afraid, because I
have saved you.
I have called you by name, and you
are mine.
²When you pass through the waters,
I will be with you.
When you cross rivers, you will
not drown.
When you walk through fire, you
will not be burned.
The flames will not hurt you.
³This is because I, the Lord, am your
God.
I, the Holy One of Israel, am your
Savior.
I gave Egypt to pay for you.
I gave Cush and Seba to make you
mine.
⁴You are precious to me.
I give you honor, and I love you.
So I will give other people in your
place.
I will give other nations to save
your life.
⁵So don't be afraid. I am with you.
I will gather your children from
the east.
I will gather you from the west.
⁶I will tell the north: Give my people
to me.
I will tell the south: Don't keep my
people in prison.
Bring my sons from far away.
Bring my daughters from faraway
places.
⁷Bring to me all the people who are
mine.
I made them for my glory.
I formed them; I made them."

Judah Is God's Witness

⁸Bring out the people who have eyes
but don't see.
Bring out those who have ears but
don't hear.
⁹All the nations should gather
together.
All the people should come
together.
Which of their gods said that this
would happen?

Which of their gods can tell what
happened in the beginning?
They should bring their witnesses
to prove they were right.
Then others will say, "It is true."
¹⁰The Lord says, "You are my
witnesses.
You are the servant I chose.
I chose you so you would know and
believe me.
I chose you so you would
understand that I am the true
God.
There was no God before me,
and there will be no God after me.
¹¹I myself am the Lord.
I am the only Savior.
¹²I myself have spoken to you, saved
you and told you these things.
It was not some foreign god
among you.
You are my witnesses, and I am God,"
says the Lord.
¹³ "I have always been God.
No one can save people from my
power.
When I do something, no one can
change it."

¹⁴This is what the Lord says.
He is the Holy One of Israel who
saves you.
He says, "I will send armies to
Babylon for you.
All the Babylonians will be
captured.
They will be taken away in their
ships they are proud of.
¹⁵I am the Lord, your Holy One.
I made Israel. I am your king."

God Will Save His People Again

¹⁶This is what the Lord says.
He is the one who made a road
through the sea.
Even through rough waters he
made a path for his people.
¹⁷He is the one who defeated the
chariots and horses.
He defeated the mighty armies.
They fell together, and they will
never rise again.

They were destroyed as a flame is
    put out.
[18]The Lord says, "Forget what
    happened before.
Do not think about the past.
[19]Look at the new thing I am going to
    do.
It is already happening. Don't you
    see it?
I will make a road in the desert.
I will make rivers in the dry land.
[20]Even the wild animals will be
    thankful to me.
The wild dogs and owls will honor
    me.
They will honor me when I put
    water in the desert.
They will honor me when I make
    rivers in the dry land.
I will do this to give water to my
    people, the ones I chose.
[21]   These are the people I made.
And they will sing songs to praise
    me.

[22]"People of Jacob, you have not
    called to me.
People of Israel, you have become
    tired of me.
[23]You have not brought your
    sacrifices of sheep to me.
You have not honored me by
    bringing sacrifices to me.
I did not force you to give sacrifices
    to me.
I did not force you to burn incense[d]
    until you became tired.
[24]So you did not buy incense for me.
You did not freely bring fat from
    your sacrifices to me.
Instead you have weighed me down
    with your many sins.
You have made me tired of your
    many wrongs.

[25]"I, I am the One who forgives all
    your sins.
I do this to please myself.
I will not remember your sins.
[26]But you should remind me.
Let's meet and decide what is right.
Tell what you have done and show
    you are right.

[27]Your first father sinned.
And your leaders have turned
    against me.
[28]So I will make your holy rulers not
    holy.
And I will bring destruction on the
    people of Jacob.
And I will let Israel be insulted."

The Lord Is the Only God

44 The Lord says, "People of Jacob,
you are my servants. Listen to
me!
    People of Israel, I chose you."
[2]This is what the Lord says. He
    made you.
He formed you when you were in
    your mother's body.
And he will help you.
The Lord says, "People of Jacob, my
    servants, don't be afraid.
Israel, I chose you.
[3]I will pour out water for the thirsty
    land.
I will make streams flow on dry
    land.
I will put my Spirit[d] into your
    children.
My blessing will be like a stream
    of water flowing over your
    family.
[4]Your children will grow like a tree
    in the grass.
They will be like poplar trees
    growing beside streams of
    water.
[5]One person will say, 'I belong to the
    Lord.'
Another will use the name Jacob.
Another will sign his name 'I am the
    Lord's.'
And another will use the name
    Israel."

[6]The Lord is the king of Israel.
The Lord of heaven's armies saves
    Israel.
The Lord says, "I am the beginning
    and the end.
I am the only God.
[7]There is no other God like me.
If there is, then that god should
    come and prove it.

What God Is Like
ISAIAH 44:6-7

Sooner or later, you may meet someone who belongs to another religion. What he or she believes and what you believe may be very different. Does it make any difference to God?

The Bible clearly teaches that our God is the *only* God. If that is true, then other religions are off the mark. That may be hard to understand, but that is what the Bible says in places like Isaiah 44:6-7. God is *unique*–there are no other Gods. Try to think about it this way.

If the Bible is true, then God is the only God. There are no others. It is not possible for Christianity to be true and other religions to be true, too. So we must choose whom we will believe: our God, some other god, or no one. If we listen to what God tells us in the Bible, we won't go wrong.

Put your faith in the one *true* God.

To learn more about what God is like, zoom to page 1251.

Who has announced coming events
    from the beginning?
He should tell what will happen in
    the future.
⁸Don't be afraid! Don't worry!
    I have always told you what will
        happen.
You are my witnesses.
    There is no other God.
I know of no other Rock.*ᵈ* I am the
    only One."

False Gods Are Useless

⁹Some people make idols, but they
    are worth nothing.
People love them, but they are
    useless.
Those people are witnesses for the
    statues. But those people
    cannot see.
They know nothing. They don't
    know enough to be ashamed.
¹⁰Who made these false gods?
    Who made these useless idols?
¹¹The workmen who made those
    gods will be ashamed!
Those workmen are only human.

If they all would come together,
    they would all be ashamed and
    afraid.

¹²One workman uses tools to heat
    iron.
He works over hot coals.
He uses his hammer to beat the
    metal and make a statue.
He uses his powerful arms.
But when he becomes hungry, he
    loses his power.
If he does not drink water, he
    becomes tired.

¹³Another workman uses a line and a
    compass
    to draw lines on the wood.
Then he uses his chisels to cut a
    statue from wood.
He uses his calipers to measure
    the statue.
This way, the workman makes the
    wood look exactly like a man.
And this statue of a man sits in the
    house.
¹⁴A man cuts down cedar
    or gets cypress or oak trees.

Those trees grew by their own
power in the forest.
Or he plants a pine tree, and the
rain makes it grow.
¹⁵Then he burns the tree.
He uses some of the wood for a
fire to keep himself warm.
He also starts a fire to bake his
bread.
But he uses part of the wood to make
a god. Then he worships it!
He makes the idol and bows down
to it!
¹⁶The man burns half of the wood in
the fire.
He uses the fire to cook his meat.
And he eats the meat until he is full.
He burns the wood to keep himself
warm. He says,
"Good! Now I am warm. I can see
because of the fire's light."
¹⁷But the man makes a statue from
the wood that is left. He calls it
his god.
He bows down to it and worships it.
He prays to it and says,
"You are my god. Save me!"
¹⁸Those people don't know what they
are doing. They don't
understand!
It is as if their eyes are covered so
they can't see.
Their minds don't understand.
¹⁹They have not thought about these
things.
They don't understand.
They have never thought to
themselves,
"I burned half of the wood in the
fire.
I used the hot coals to bake my
bread.
I cooked and ate my meat.
And I used the wood that was left to
make this hated thing.
I am worshiping a block of wood!"
²⁰He doesn't know what he is doing.
His confused mind leads him the
wrong way.
He cannot save himself.
He cannot say, "This statue I am
holding is a false god."

The Lord Is the True God

²¹The Lord says, "People of Jacob,
remember these things!
People of Israel, remember you
are my servants.
I made you. You are my servants.
So Israel, I will not forget you.
²²I have swept away your sins like a
big cloud.
I have removed your sins like a
cloud that disappears into the
air.
Come back to me because I saved
you."

²³Skies, sing for joy because the Lord
did great things!
Earth, shout for joy, even in your
deepest parts!
Sing, you mountains, with thanks to
God.
Sing, too, you trees in the forest!
The Lord saved the people of Jacob!
The Lord showed his greatness
when he saved Israel.
²⁴The Lord saved you.
He formed you while you were still
in your mother's body.
The Lord says, "I, the Lord, made
everything!
I alone stretched out the skies.
I spread out the earth by myself.
²⁵I show that the lying prophets'ᵈ
signs are false.
I make fools of those who do
magic.
I confuse even wise men.
They think they know much, but I
make them look foolish.
²⁶I make the messages of my servants
come true.
I make the advice of my
messengers come true.
I say to Jerusalem,
'People will live in you again!'
I say to the towns of Judah,
'You will be built again!'
I say to Jerusalem's ruins,
'I will repair you.'
²⁷I tell the deep waters, 'Become dry!
I will make your streams become
dry!'

Good Kings and Bad Kings

CYRUS • ISAIAH 44:28

God is in control of the world. About 150 years before Cyrus became the king of the Persian empire, the prophet Isaiah wrote his name in a prophecy that told about the future of God's people. God's people in Judah were taken into captivity by the Babylonians. They were taken back to Babylonia to live, and their country became part of the empire. But later the Babylonians were conquered by the Medes and Persians. While Cyrus was king, he allowed all the Jewish people to return and rebuild their country. That is exactly what Isaiah wrote about here—that Cyrus would allow the people to return and rebuild Jerusalem and its temple.

God knows what will happen in each person's life. He knows your future. Trust him to help you do what he wants.

To meet a king who got too proud, fly to page 1035.

---

²⁸I say of Cyrus,ⁿ 'He is my shepherd.
  He will do all that I want him
    to do.
  He will say to Jerusalem, "You will
    be built again!"
  He will tell the Temple,^d "Your
    foundations will be rebuilt."'"

God Chooses Cyrus to Free Israel

45 This is what the Lord says to Cyrus, his appointed king:
"I hold your right hand.
I will help you defeat nations.
I will help you take other kings'
    power away.
I will open doors for you
  so city gates will not stop you.
²I will go before you.
  And I will make the mountains flat.
I will break down the bronze gates
    of the cities.
I will cut through the iron bars on
    the gates.
³I will give you the wealth that is
    stored away.
  And I will give you hidden riches.

I will do this so you will know I am
    the Lord.
  I, the God of Israel, call you by name.
⁴I do these things for my servants,
    the people of Jacob.
  I do these things for my chosen
    people, the Israelites.
Cyrus, I call you by name.
  I give you a title of honor even
    though you don't know me.
⁵I am the Lord. There is no other God.
  I am the only God.
I will make you strong
  even though you don't know me.
⁶I do these things so everyone will
    know
  there is no other God.
From the east to the west they will
    know
  I alone am the Lord.
⁷I made the light and the darkness.
  I bring peace, and I cause troubles.
  I, the Lord, do all these things.

⁸"Sky above, make victory fall like
    rain.
  Clouds, pour down victory.

ⁿ**Cyrus** A king of Persia. He ruled from about 550-530 B.C.

May the earth receive it.
May salvation grow.
May victory grow with it.
I, the Lord, have created it.

9"How terrible it will be for those
    who argue with the God who
    made them.
They are like one piece of broken
    pottery among many pieces.
The clay does not ask the potter,
  'What are you doing?'
The thing that is made doesn't say
    to its maker,
  'You have no hands.'
10How terrible it will be for the child
    who says to his father,
  'Why are you giving me life?'
How terrible it will be for the child
    who says to his mother,
  'Why are you giving birth to me?'"

11The Lord is the Holy One of Israel,
    and its Maker.
He says this:
"You ask me about what will happen.
You question me about my
    children.
You give me orders about what I
    have made.
12I made the earth.
And I made all the people living on
    it.
With my own hands I stretched out
    the skies.
I command all the armies in the
    sky.
13I will bring Cyrus to do good things.
And I will make his work easy.
Cyrus will rebuild my city,
    and he will set my people free.
Cyrus has not been paid to do these
    things.
The Lord of heaven's armies says
    this."

14The Lord says,
"The things made in Egypt and Cush
    and the tall people of Seba
will come to you.
They will become yours.
The Sabeans will walk behind you.
They will come along in chains.
They will bow down before you.

They will pray to you, saying,
  'God is with you.
And there is no other God.'"

15You are a God that people cannot
    see.
You are the God and Savior of
    Israel.
16All the people who make idols will
    be put to great shame.
They will go off together in
    disgrace.
17But Israel will be saved by the Lord.
That salvation will continue forever.
Never again will Israel be put to
    shame.

18The Lord created the heavens.
He is the God
who formed the earth.
He made the earth.
But he did not want it to be empty.
He wanted life to be on the earth.
This is what the Lord says:
"I am the Lord. There is no other
    God.
19I did not speak in secret.
I did not hide my words
    somewhere in a dark place.
I did not tell the family of Jacob
    to look for me in empty places.
I am the Lord, and I speak the truth.
I say what is right.

20"You people have escaped from
    other nations.
So gather together and come
    before me.
Come near together.
People who carry idols of wood don't
    know what they are doing.
They pray to a god who cannot
    save them.
21Tell these people to come to me.
Let them talk about these things
    together.
Who told you long ago that this
    would happen?
Who told about it long ago?
I, the Lord, said these things.
There is no other God besides me.
I am the only good God. I am the
    Savior.
There is no other God.

²²"All people everywhere,
follow me and be saved.
I am God. There is no other God.
²³I will make a promise by my own
power.
And my promise is true.
What I say will not be changed.
I promise that everyone will bow
before me.
Everyone will promise to follow me.
²⁴People will say, 'Goodness and power
come only from the Lord.'"
Everyone who has been angry with
the Lord
will come to him and be ashamed.
²⁵But with the Lord's help, the people
of Israel
will be found to be good.
And they will praise him.

False Gods Are Useless

46 Bel[d] and Nebo[d] bow down.
Their idols are carried by
animals.
The statues are only heavy loads
that must be carried.
They only make people tired.
²These false gods will all bow down.
They cannot save themselves.
They will all be carried away like
prisoners.

³"Family of Jacob, listen to me!
All you people from Israel who are
still alive, listen!
I have carried you since you were
born.
I have taken care of you from your
birth.
⁴Even when you are old, I will take
care of you.
Even when your hair has turned
gray, I will take care of you.
I made you and will take care of you.
I will carry you, and I will save you.

⁵"Can you compare me to anyone?
No one is equal to me or like me.
⁶Some people are rich with gold.
They weigh their silver on the
scales.
They hire a goldsmith, and he
makes it into a god.
Then they bow down and worship
it.
⁷They put it on their shoulders and
carry it.
They set it in its place, and there it
stands.
It cannot move from its place.
People may yell at it, but it cannot
answer.
It cannot save people from their
troubles.

⁸"Remember this, and do not forget it!
Think about these things, you who
turn against God.
⁹Remember what happened long ago.
Remember that I am God. There is
no other God.
I am God. There is no one like me.
¹⁰From the beginning I told you what
would happen in the end.
A long time ago I told you things
that have not yet happened.
When I plan something, it happens.
I do the things I want to do.
¹¹I am calling a man from the east to
carry out my plan.
He will come like a hawk from a
country far away.
I will make what I have said come
true.
I will do what I have planned.
¹²Listen to me, you stubborn people.
You are far from what is right.
¹³I will soon do the things that are right.
I will bring salvation soon.
I will save Jerusalem.
And I will bring glory to Israel."

God Will Destroy Babylon

47 The Lord says, "City of Babylon,
go down and sit in the dirt.
People of Babylon, sit on the ground.
You are no longer the ruler.
You will no longer be called
tender or beautiful.
² You must use large stones to grind
grain into flour.
Remove your veil and your nice
skirts.
Uncover your legs and cross the
rivers.
³Men will see your nakedness.

They will see your shame.
I will punish you.
I will punish every one of you."

4Our Savior is named the Lord of
heaven's armies.
He is the Holy One of Israel.

5"Babylon, sit in darkness and say
nothing.
You will no longer be called the
queen of kingdoms.
6I was angry with my people.
So I rejected those people who
belonged to me.
I gave them to you,
but you showed them no mercy.
You even made the old people
work very hard.
7You said, 'I will live forever.
I will always be the queen.'
You did not think about these things.
You did not think about what
would happen.

8"Now, listen, you lover of pleasure.
You think you are safe.
You tell yourself,
'I am the only important person.
I will never be a widow.
I will never lose my children.'
9Two things will happen to you
suddenly in a single day.
You will lose your children and
your husband.
These things will truly happen to you.
All your magic and powerful tricks
will not save you.
10You do evil things, but you feel safe.
You say, 'No one sees what I do.'
Your wisdom and knowledge
have fooled you.
You say to yourself,
'I am God. No one is equal to me.'
11But troubles will come to you.
You will not know how to stop them.
Disaster will fall on you.
And you will not be able to keep it
away.
You will be destroyed quickly.
You will not even see it coming.
12"Keep on using your tricks.
Continue doing all your magic.

You have done these things since
you were young.
Maybe they will help you.
Maybe you will be able to scare
someone.
13You are tired of the advice you have
received.
So let those who study the sky
come.
They tell the future by looking at
the stars.
So let them save you from what is
about to happen to you.
14But they are like straw.
Fire will quickly burn them up.
They cannot save themselves
from the power of the fire.
They are not like coals that give
warmth.
They are not like a fire you may sit
beside.
15You have worked with these people.
They have been with you since
you were young.
But they will not be able to help
you.
Everyone will go his own way.
And there will be no one left to
save you."

God Controls the Future

48 The Lord says, "Family of Jacob,
listen to me.
You are called Israel.
You come from the family of Judah.
You use the Lord's name to make
promises.
You praise the God of Israel,
but you are not honest or sincere.
2You call yourselves people of the
holy city.
You depend on the God of Israel.
He is named the Lord of heaven's
armies.
3Long ago I told you what would
happen.
I said these things and made them
known.
Suddenly I acted, and these things
happened.
4I did that because I knew you were
stubborn.

Your neck was like an iron muscle.
It was as if your head were made
   of bronze.
5So a long time ago I told you about
   these things.
I told you about them before they
   happened.
I did this so you couldn't say, 'My
   idols did this.
My wooden and metal statues
   made these things happen.'

6"You heard and saw all the things
   that happened.
So you should tell this news to
   others.
Now I will tell you about new things.
These are hidden things that you
   don't know yet.
7These things are happening now,
   not long ago.
You have not heard about them
   before today.
So you cannot say, 'We already
   knew about that.'
8But you have not heard me. You
   have not understood.
Even long ago you did not listen to
   me.
I knew you would surely turn
   against me.
You have fought against me since
   you were born.
9But for my own sake I will be patient.
People will praise me for not
   becoming angry
and destroying you.
10I have made you pure, but not by
   fire, as silver is made pure.
I have purified you by giving you
   troubles.
11I do this for myself, for my own sake.
I will not let people speak evil
   against me.
I will not let some false god take
   my glory.

Israel Will Be Free

12"People of Jacob, listen to me.
People of Israel, I have called you
   to be my people.

I am God.
I am the beginning and the end.
13I made the earth with my own hands.
With my right hand I spread out
   the skies.
When I call them,
they come together before me.

14"All of you, come together and listen.
None of the false gods said these
   things would happen.
I, the Lord, have chosen someone
to attack the Babylonians.
He will carry out my wishes
   against Babylon.
15I have spoken. I have called him.[n]
I have brought him, and I will
   make him successful.
16Come to me and listen to this.
From the beginning I have spoken
   openly.
From the time it began, I was
   there."

Now, the Lord God
has sent me with his Spirit.[d]

17The Lord is your close relative who
   saves you, the Holy One of
   Israel.
The Lord says,
"I am the Lord your God.
I teach you to do what is good.
I lead you in the way you should go.
18If you had obeyed me,
you would have had peace like a
   full-flowing river.
Good things would have flowed to
   you like the waves of the sea.
19You would have had many children.
They would have been as many as
   the grains of sand.
They would never have died out.
They would not have been
   destroyed."

20My people, leave Babylon!
Run from the Babylonians!
Tell this news with shouts of joy to
   the people.
Spread it everywhere on earth.
Say, "The Lord has saved
his servants, the people of Jacob."

[n]**him**   This probably refers to Cyrus king of Persia.

²¹They did not become thirsty when he
led them through the deserts.
He made water flow from a rock
for them.
He split the rock,
and water flowed out.

²²"There is no peace for evil people,"
says the Lord.

God Calls His Special Servant

49 All of you people in faraway
places, listen to me.
Listen, all you nations far away.
Before I was born, the Lord called
me to serve him.
The Lord named me while I was
still in my mother's body.
²The Lord made my tongue like a
sharp sword.
He hid me in the shadow of his
hand.
The Lord made me like a sharp
arrow.
He hid me in the holder for his
arrows.
³The Lord told me, "Israel, you are
my servant.
I will show my glory through you."
⁴But I said, "I have worked hard for
nothing.
I have used all my power, but I did
nothing useful.
But the Lord will decide what my
work is worth.
God will decide my reward."
⁵The Lord made me in the body of
my mother
so I would be his servant.
He made me to lead the people of
Jacob back to him.
He made me so that Israel might
be gathered to him.
The Lord will honor me.
I will get my strength from my God.
⁶The Lord told me,
"You are an important servant to me.
You will bring back the tribes^d of
Jacob.
You will bring back the people of
Israel who are left alive.
But, more importantly, I will make
you a light for all nations.

You will show people all over the
world the way to be saved."
⁷The Lord is your close relative who
saves you.
He is the Holy One of Israel.
He speaks to the one who is hated
by the people.
He speaks to the servant of rulers.
The Lord says, "Kings will see you
and stand to honor you.
Great leaders will bow down
before you.
This is because the Lord can be
trusted.
He is the Holy One of Israel, who
has chosen you."

The Day of Salvation

⁸This is what the Lord says:
"At the right time I will hear your
prayers.
On the day of salvation I will help
you.
I will protect you.
And you will be the sign of my
agreement with the people.
You will bring back the people to
the land.
You will give the land that is now
ruined back to its owners.
⁹You will tell the prisoners, 'Come
out of your prison.'
You will tell those in darkness,
'Come into the light.'
The people will eat beside the
roads.
They will find food even on bare
hills.
¹⁰They will not be hungry or thirsty.
Neither the hot sun nor the desert
wind will hurt them.
The God who comforts them will
lead them.
He will lead them by springs of
water.
¹¹I will make my mountains into roads
for my people.
And the roads will be raised up.
¹²Look, people are coming to me from
far away.
They are coming from the north
and from the west.

They are coming from Aswan in
southern Egypt."

13Heavens and earth, be happy.
Mountains, shout with joy.
Be happy because the Lord
comforts his people.
He will comfort those who suffer.

Jerusalem and Her Children

14But Jerusalem said, "The Lord has
left me.
The Lord has forgotten me."

15The Lord answers, "Can a woman
forget the baby she nurses?
Can she feel no kindness for the
child she gave birth to?
Even if she could forget her children,
I will not forget you.
16See, I have written your name on
my hand.
Jerusalem, I always think about
your walls.
17Your children will soon return to
you.
And the people who defeated you
and destroyed you will leave.
18Look up and look around you.
All your children are gathering to
return to you."
The Lord says, "As surely as I live,
your children will be like jewels.
You will be as proud of them as a
bride is of her jewels.

19"You were destroyed and defeated.
Your land was made useless.
But now you will have more people
than the land can hold.
And those people who destroyed
you will be far away.
20Children were born to you while you
were sad.
But they will say to you,
'This place is too small for us.
Give us a bigger place to live.'
21Then you will say to yourself,
'Who gave me all these children?
I was sad and lonely.
I was defeated and away from my
people.
So who reared these children?
I was left all alone.

Where did all these children come
from?'"

22This is what the Lord God says:
"See, I will lift my hand to signal the
nations.
I will raise my banner for all
people to see.
Then they will bring your sons back
to you in their arms.
They will carry your daughters on
their shoulders.
23Kings will teach your children.
Daughters of kings will take care
of those children.
They will bow down before you.
They will kiss the dirt at your
feet.
Then you will know I am the Lord.
Anyone who trusts in me will not
be disappointed."

24Can the wealth a soldier wins in war
be taken away from him?
Can a prisoner be freed from a
powerful soldier?
25But this is what the Lord says:
"The prisoners will be taken from
the strong soldiers.
What the soldiers have taken will
be saved.
I will fight your enemies.
I will save your children.
26I will force those who trouble you to
eat their own flesh.
Their own blood will be the wine
that makes them drunk.
Then everyone will know
I, the Lord, am the One who saves
you.
I am the Powerful One of Jacob
who saves you."

Israel Was Punished for Its Sin

50 This is what the Lord says:
"People of Israel, you say I
divorced your mother.
Then where is the paper that
proves it?
Or do you think I sold you to pay a
debt?
No! It was because of the evil things
you did that I sold you.

It was because of the times she
turned against me that your
mother was sent away.
[2]I came home and found no one there.
I called, but no one answered.
Do you think I am not able to save
you?
Do I not have the power to save
you?
Look, I need only to shout, and the
sea becomes dry.
I change rivers into a desert.
Their fish rot because there is no
water.
The fish die of thirst.
[3]I can make the skies dark.
I can make them black like clothes
of sadness."

God's Servant Obeys

[4]The Lord God gave me the ability to
teach.
He has taught me what to say to
make the weak strong.
Every morning he wakes me.
He teaches me to listen like a
student.
[5]The Lord God helps me learn.
And I have not turned against him.
I have not stopped following
him.
[6]I offered my back to those who beat
me.
I offered my cheeks to those who
pulled my beard.
I won't hide my face from them
when they make fun of me and spit
at me.
[7]The Lord God helps me.
So I will not be ashamed.
I will be determined.
I know I will not be disgraced.
[8]The Lord shows that I am innocent,
and he is close to me.
So who can accuse me?
If there is someone, let us go to
court together.
If someone wants to prove I have
done wrong,
he should come and tell me.
[9]It is the Lord God who helps me.
So who can prove me guilty?

All those who try will become
useless like old clothes.
Moths will eat them.

[10]Who among you fears the Lord
and obeys his servant?
That person may walk in the dark
and have no light.
Then let him trust in the Lord.
Let him depend on his God.
[11]But instead, some of you want to
light your own fires.
You want to make your own light.
So, go, walk in the light of your fires.
Trust your own light to guide you.
But this is what you will receive
from me:
You will lie down in a place of pain.

Jerusalem Will Be Saved

51 The Lord says, "Listen to me,
those of you who try to live
right and follow the Lord.
Look at the rock from which you
were cut.
Look at the stone quarry from
which you were dug.
[2]Look at Abraham, your ancestor.
Look at Sarah, who gave birth to
your ancestors.
Abraham had no children when I
called him.
But I blessed him and gave him
many descendants.[d]
[3]So the Lord will comfort
Jerusalem.
He will show mercy to those who
live in her ruins.
He will change her deserts into a
garden like Eden.
He will make her empty lands like
the garden of the Lord.
People there will be very happy.
They will give thanks and sing
songs.

[4]"My people, listen to me.
My nation, pay attention to me.
I will give the people my teachings.
And my decisions will be like a
light to all people.
[5]I will soon show I do what is right.
I will soon save you.

I will use my power and judge all
   nations.
All the faraway places are waiting
   for me.
They wait for my power to help
   them.
⁶Look up to the heavens.
   Look around you at the earth below.
The skies will disappear like clouds
   of smoke.
The earth will become useless like
   old clothes.
Its people will die like flies.
But my salvation will continue
   forever.
   My goodness will never end.

⁷"You people who know what is right
   should listen to me.
   You people who follow my teachings
      should hear what I say.
Don't be afraid of the evil things
   people say.
   Don't be upset by their insults.
⁸Moths will eat those people as if
   they were clothes.
   Worms will eat them as if they
      were wool.
But my goodness will continue
   forever.
   My salvation will continue from
      now on."

⁹Wake up, wake up, and use your
   strength,
      powerful Lord.
Wake up as you did in the old times.
   Wake up as you did a long time ago.
With your own power, you cut
   Rahab*d* into pieces.
   You killed that sea monster.
¹⁰You caused the sea to become dry.
   You dried the waters of the deep
      ocean.
   You made the deepest parts of the
      sea into a road.
      Your people crossed over on that
         road and were saved.
¹¹The people the Lord has freed will
   return.
   They will enter Jerusalem with joy.
   Their happiness will last forever.
   They will have joy and gladness.

All sadness and sorrow will be
   gone far away.

¹²The Lord says, "I am the one who
   comforts you.
   So why should you be afraid of
      people, who die?
   Why should you fear people who
      die like the grass?
¹³Have you forgotten that the Lord
   made you?
   He stretched out the skies.
   He made the earth.
Why are you always afraid
   of those angry people who trouble
      you?
   They want to destroy.
   But where are those angry people
      now?
¹⁴   People in prison will soon be set
   free.
   They will not die in prison.
   They will have enough food.
¹⁵This is because I am the Lord your
   God.
   I stir the sea and make the waves
      roar.
   My name is the Lord of heaven's
      armies.
¹⁶I will give you the words I want you
   to say.
   I will cover you with my hands and
      protect you.
I made the heavens and the earth.
   And I say to Jerusalem, 'You are
      my people.'"

God Punished Israel

¹⁷The Lord was very angry with you.
   Your punishment was like wine in
      a cup.
   The Lord made you drink that
      wine
   until you stumbled.
¹⁸Jerusalem had many people.
   But there was not a person to lead
      her.
   Of all the people who grew up there,
      no one was there to guide her.
¹⁹Troubles came to you in groups of
   two.
   No one will feel sorry for you.

There was ruin and disaster, great
    hunger and fighting.
No one can comfort you.
20Your people have become weak.
    They fall down and lie on every
      street corner.
They are like animals caught in a
    net.
They have felt the full anger of the
    Lord.
They have heard God's angry shout.

21So listen to me, poor Jerusalem,
    you who are drunk but not from
      wine.
22Your God will fight for his people.
    This is what the Lord your God
      says:
"The punishment I gave you is like
    a cup of wine.
You drank it and could not walk
    straight.
I am taking that cup of my anger
    away from you.
You will never be punished by my
    anger again.
23I will now give that cup of punishment
    to those who gave you pain.
They told you,
    'Bow down so we can walk over
      you.'
They made your back like dirt for
    them to walk on.
You were like a street for them to
    travel on."

Jerusalem Will Be Saved

52 Wake up, wake up, Jerusalem!
    Become strong!
Be beautiful again,
    holy city of Jerusalem.
The people who do not worship God
    and who are not pure
will not enter you again.
2Jerusalem, you once were a prisoner.
    Now shake off the dust and stand
      up.
Jerusalem, you once were a prisoner.
    But now free yourself from the
      chains around your neck.
3This is what the Lord says:
"You were not sold for a price.
    So you will be saved without cost."

4This is what the Lord God says:
"First my people went down to
    Egypt to live.
Later Assyria made them slaves.

5"Now see what has happened," says
    the Lord.
"Another nation has taken away my
    people for nothing.
This nation who rules them makes
    fun of me," says the Lord.
"All day long they speak against me.
6But this has happened so my people
    will know who I am.
They will know I am God.
And they will know that I am the
    one speaking to them."

7How beautiful is the person
    who comes over the mountains to
      bring good news.
How beautiful is the one who
    announces peace.
He brings good news
and announces salvation.
How beautiful are the feet of the
    one who says to Jerusalem,
    "Your God is king."
8Listen! Your guards are shouting.
    They are all shouting for joy!
They all will see with their own eyes
    when the Lord returns to
      Jerusalem.
9Jerusalem, your buildings are
    destroyed now.
But shout and rejoice together.
You can rejoice because the Lord
    has comforted his people.
He has saved Jerusalem.
10The Lord will show his holy power
    to all the nations.
Then everyone on earth
    will see the salvation of our God.

11You people, leave, leave; get out of
    Babylon!
Touch nothing that is unclean.*d*
You men who carry the things used
    in worship,
    leave there and make yourselves
      pure.
12You will not be forced to leave
    Babylon quickly.
You will not be forced to run away.

The Lord will go before you.
And the God of Israel will guard
you from behind.

God's Suffering Servant

13The Lord says, "See, my servant will
act wisely.
People will greatly honor and
respect him.
14Many people were shocked when
they saw him.
His appearance was so changed he
did not look like a man.
His form was changed so much
they could barely tell he was
human.
15But now he will sprinkle many
people.
Kings will be amazed and shut
their mouths.
They will see the things they had not
been told about my servant.
They will understand the things
they had not heard."

53 Who would have believed what
we heard?
Who saw the Lord's power in this?
2He grew up like a small plant before
the Lord.
He was like a root growing in a dry
land.
He had no special beauty or form to
make us notice him.
There was nothing in his appearance to make us desire him.
3He was hated and rejected by people.
He had much pain and suffering.
People would not even look at him.
He was hated, and we didn't even
notice him.

4But he took our suffering on him
and felt our pain for us.
We saw his suffering.
We thought God was punishing
him.
5But he was wounded for the wrong
things we did.
He was crushed for the evil things
we did.
The punishment, which made us
well, was given to him.

And we are healed because of his
wounds.
6We all have wandered away like
sheep.
Each of us has gone his own way.
But the Lord has put on him the
punishment
for all the evil we have done.

We all have wandered
away like sheep. Each of
us has gone his own
way. But the Lord has
put on him the punish-
ment for all the evil we
have done.
• Isaiah 53:6

7He was beaten down and punished.
But he didn't say a word.
He was like a lamb being led to be
killed.
He was quiet, as a sheep is quiet
while its wool is being cut.
He never opened his mouth.
8Men took him away roughly and
unfairly.
He died without children to
continue his family.
He was put to death.
He was punished for the sins of
my people.
9He was buried with wicked men.
He died with the rich.
He had done nothing wrong.
He had never lied.

10But it was the Lord who decided
to crush him and make him suffer.
So the Lord made his life a penalty
offering.
But he will see his descendants[d]
and live a long life.
He will complete the things the
Lord wants him to do.
11He will suffer many things in his soul.
But then he will see life and be
satisfied.
My good servant will make many
people right with God.
He carried away their sins.

[12]For this reason I will make him a
    great man among people.
He will share in all things with
    those who are strong.
He willingly gave his life.
He was treated like a criminal.
But he carried away the sins of
    many people.
And he asked forgiveness for
    those who sinned.

People Will Return to Jerusalem

54 The Lord says, "Sing, Jerusalem.
    You are like a woman who
    never gave birth to children.
Start singing and shout for joy.
You never felt the pain of giving
    birth.
But you will have more children
    than the woman who has a husband.
[2]Make your tent bigger.
    Stretch it out and make it wider.
    Do not hold back.
Make the ropes longer.
    Make its stakes stronger.
[3]Do this because you will begin
    growing very much.
Your children will take over other
    nations.
And they will again live in cities
    that once were destroyed.

[4]"Don't be afraid because you will
    not be ashamed.
Don't be embarrassed because
    you will not be disgraced.
You will forget the shame you felt
    earlier.
You will not remember the shame
    you felt when you lost your
    husband.
[5]This is because the God who made
    you is like your husband.
His name is the Lord of heaven's
    armies.
The Holy One of Israel is the one
    who saves you.
He is called the God of all the earth.
[6]You were like a woman whose
    husband left her.
And you were very sad.
You were like a wife who married
    young

and then her husband left her.
But the Lord called you to be his,"
    says your God.
[7]God says, "I left you, but only for a
    short time.
But with great kindness I will
    bring you back again.
[8]I became very angry
    and hid from you for a short time.
But I will show you mercy with
    kindness forever,"
    says the Lord your close relative
    who saves you.

[9]The Lord says, "This is like the time
    of Noah.
I promised then
    that I would never flood the world
    again.
In the same way, I promise
    I will not be angry with you or
    punish you again.
[10]The mountains may disappear,
    and the hills may come to an end.
But my love will never disappear.
My promise of peace will not come
    to an end,"
    says the Lord who shows mercy to
    you.

[11]"You poor city. Storms have hurt you,
    and you have not been
    comforted.
But I will rebuild you using
    turquoise stones.
I will build your foundations with
    sapphires.
[12]I will use rubies to build your walls.
I will use shining jewels for the
    gates.
I will build all your outer walls
    from precious jewels.
[13]All your children will be taught by
    the Lord.
And they will have much peace.
[14]I will build you using fairness.
You will be safe from those who
    would hurt you.
So you will have nothing to fear.
Nothing will come to make you
    afraid.
[15]I will not send anyone to attack
    you.

And you will defeat those who do
attack you.

16"See, I made the blacksmith.
He fans the fire to make it hotter.
And he makes the kind of tool he
wants.
In the same way I have made the
destroyer to destroy.
17 So no weapon that is used against
you will defeat you.
You will show that those who
speak against you are wrong.
These are the good things my
servants receive.
Their victory comes from me,"
says the Lord.

God Gives What Is Good

55 The Lord says, "All you who are
thirsty,
come and drink.
Those of you who do not have
money,
come, buy and eat!
Come buy wine and milk.
You don't need money; it will cost
you nothing.
2Why spend your money on something that is not real food?
Why work for something that
doesn't really satisfy you?
Listen closely to me, and you will
eat what is good.
You will enjoy the food that
satisfies your soul.
3Come to me and listen.
Listen to me so you may live.
I will make an agreement with you
that will last forever.
I will give you the blessings I
promised to David.
4I made David a witness of my power
for all nations.
I made him a ruler and
commander of many nations.
5You will call for nations that you
don't yet know.
And these nations will run to you.
This will happen because of the
Lord your God.
The Holy One of Israel honors
you."

6So you should look for the Lord
before it is too late.
You should call to him while he is
near.
7Evil people should stop being evil.
They should stop thinking bad
thoughts.
They should return to the Lord, and
he will have mercy on them.
They should come to our God,
because he will freely forgive
them.

8The Lord says, "Your thoughts are
not like my thoughts.
Your ways are not like my ways.
9Just as the heavens are higher than
the earth,
so are my ways higher than your
ways.
And my thoughts are higher than
your thoughts.
10Rain and snow fall from the sky.
They don't return without
watering the ground.
They cause the plants to sprout and
grow.
And the plants make seeds for the
farmer.
And from these seeds people have
bread to eat.
11The words I say do the same
thing.
They will not return to me empty.
They make the things happen that I
want to happen.
They succeed in doing what I send
them to do.

12"So you will go out with joy.
You will be led out in peace.
The mountains and hills will burst
into song before you.
All the trees in the fields will clap
their hands.
13Large cypress trees will grow where
thornbushes were.
Myrtle trees will grow where
weeds were.
These things will be a reminder of
the Lord's promise.
And this reminder will never be
destroyed."

All Nations Will Obey the Lord

56 This is what the Lord says:
"Give justice to all people.
Do what is right.
Do this because my salvation will
come to you soon.
Soon everyone will know that I do
what is right.
[2]The person who obeys the law
about the Sabbath[d]
will be blessed.
And the person who does no evil
will be blessed."

[3]Foreigners have joined the Lord.
They should not say,
"The Lord will not accept me with
his people."
The eunuch[d] should not say,
"Because I cannot have children
the Lord will not accept me."
[4]This is what the Lord says:
"The eunuchs should obey the law
about the Sabbath.
They should do what I want.
They should keep my
agreement.
[5]If they do, I will make their names
remembered
within my Temple[d] and its walls.
It will be better for them than
children.
I will give them a name that will last
forever.
It will never be forgotten.
[6]Foreigners will join the Lord to
serve him.
They will worship and love him.
They will worship him.
They will obey the law about the
Sabbath.
They will keep the agreement with
the Lord.
[7]I will bring these people to my holy
mountain.
I will give them joy in my house of
prayer.
The offerings and sacrifices
they place on my altar will please
me.
This is because my Temple will be
called

a house for prayer for people from
all nations."
[8]The Lord gathers the Israelites who
were forced to leave their
country.
This is what the Lord God says,
"I will bring other people to those
who are already gathered."

Israel's Leaders Are Evil

[9]All you animals of the field, come to
eat.
All you animals of the forest, come
to eat.
[10]The leaders who are to guard the
people are blind.
They don't know what they are
doing.
All of them are like quiet dogs.
They don't know how to bark.
They lie down and dream.
They love to sleep.
[11]They are like hungry dogs.
They are never satisfied.
They are like shepherds
who don't know what they are
doing.
They each have gone their
own way.
All they want to do is satisfy
themselves.
[12]They say, "Come, let's drink some
wine.
Let's drink all the beer we want.
And tomorrow we will do this
again.
Or, maybe we will have even a
better time."

Israel Does Not Follow God

57 Those right with God may die,
but no one pays attention.
Good people are taken away,
but no one understands.
The people who do right are being
taken away because of evil.
[2] But they are given peace.
The people who live the way God
wants them to
find rest in death.

[3]"Come here, you magicians!

Come here, you sons of
    prostitutes[d] and those who
    take part in adultery![d]
4Whom are you making fun of?
    Whom are you insulting?
    At whom do you stick out your
    tongue?
You turn against God,
    and you are liars.
5You have sexual relations under
    every green tree
to worship your false gods.
You kill children in the ravines
    and sacrifice them in the rocky
    places.
6You take the smooth rocks from the
    ravines.
    They are your portion.
You pour drink offerings on them to
    worship them.
    You give grain offerings to them.
    Do you think this makes me want
    to forgive you?
7You make your bed on every hill
    and mountain.
    And there you offer sacrifices.
8You have hidden your idols
    behind your doors and doorposts.
You have left me, and you have
    uncovered yourself.
You have pulled back the covers
    and climbed into bed.
You have made an agreement with
    the ones whose beds you love.
And you have looked at their
    nakedness.
9You use your oils and perfumes
    to look nice for Molech.[d]
You have sent your messengers to
    faraway lands.
    You even tried to send them to
    where the dead are.
10You have worked hard to do these
    things.
    But you never gave up.
You found new strength.
    So you did not quit.

11"Whom were you so afraid of
    that you lied to me?
You have not remembered me
    or even thought about me.
I have been quiet for a long time.

Is that why you are not afraid of me?
12I will tell about your 'goodness' and
    what you do.
And those things will do you no
    good.
13When you cry out for help,
    let the false gods you have
    gathered help you.
The wind will blow them all away.
    Just a puff of wind will take them
    away.
But the person who depends on me
    will receive the land.
He will have my holy mountain."

The Lord Will Save His People

14The Lord says, "Build a road! Build
    a road! Prepare the way!
    Make the way clear for my people."
15God lives forever and is holy.
    He is high and lifted up, and he
    says,
"I live in a high and holy place.
    But I also live with people who are
    sad and humble.
I give new life to those who are
    humble.
    I give new life to those whose
    hearts are broken.
16I will not accuse forever.
    I will not always be angry.
If I continued to be angry, man's life
    would grow weak.
    Man, whom I created, would die.
17I was angry because they were dis-
    honest in order to make money.
    I punished them and turned away
    from them in anger.
But they continued to do evil.
18I have seen what they have done,
    but I will heal them.
I will guide them and comfort them.
    And those who were sad will
    praise me.
19I will give peace, real peace, to
    those far and near.
    And I will heal them," says the Lord.
20But evil people are like the angry sea.
    It cannot rest.
    Its waves toss up waste and mud.
21"There is no peace for evil people,"
    says my God.

How to Honor God

58 The Lord says, "Shout out loud.
Don't hold back.
Shout out loud like a trumpet.
Tell the people about the things
they have done against God.
Tell the family of Jacob about their
sins.
[2]Then they will come every day
looking for me.
And they will want to learn my
ways.
They will become a nation that does
what is right.
They will obey the commands of
their God.
They will ask me to judge them fairly.
They will want God to be near them.
[3]They say, 'To honor you we had
special days when we gave up
eating.
But you didn't see.
We humbled ourselves to honor you.
But you didn't notice.'"

But the Lord says, "You do what
pleases yourselves on these
special days.
And you are unfair to your workers.
[4]On these special days when you do
not eat, you argue and fight.
You hit each other with your fists.
You cannot do these things as you
do now
and believe I will listen to your
prayers.
[5]This kind of special day is not what
I want.
This is not the way I want people
to be sorry for what they have
done.
I don't want people just to bow their
heads like a plant.
I don't want them to wear rough
cloth and lie in ashes to show
their sadness.
This is what you do on your special
days when you do not eat.
But do you think this is what the
Lord wants?
[6]"I will tell you the kind of special
day I want.

I want you to free the people you
have put in prison unfairly.
Undo their chains.
Free those to whom you are unfair.
Free them from their hard labor.
[7]I want you to share your food with
hungry people.
I want you to bring poor, homeless
people into your own homes.
When you see someone who has no
clothes, give him yours.
Don't refuse to help your own
relatives.
[8]If you do these things, your light
will shine like the dawn.
Then your wounds will quickly heal.
Your God will walk before you,
and the glory of the Lord will
protect you from behind.
[9]Then you will call to the Lord, and
the Lord will answer you.
You will cry out to the Lord, and
he will say, 'Here I am.'

"You should stop making trouble
for others.
You should stop using cruel words
and pointing your finger at
others.
[10]You should feed those who are
hungry.
You should take care of the needs
of those who are troubled.
Then your light will shine in the
darkness.
And you will be bright like
sunshine at noon.
[11]The Lord will always lead you.
He will satisfy your needs in dry
lands.
He will give strength to your bones.
You will be like a garden that has
much water.
You will be like a spring that never
runs dry.
[12]Your people will rebuild the old
cities that are now in ruins.
You will rebuild the foundations of
these ancient cities.
You will be known for repairing the
broken places.
You will be known for rebuilding
the roads and houses.

¹³"You must obey God's law about the Sabbath.^d

You must not do what pleases yourselves on that holy day.

You should call the Sabbath a joyful day.

You should honor the Lord's holy day.

You should honor it by not doing whatever you please on that day.

You should not say whatever you please on that day.

¹⁴Then you will find joy in the Lord.

And I, the Lord, will carry you to the high places above the earth.

I will let you eat the crops of the land your ancestor Jacob had."

The Lord has said these things.

The Evil That People Do

59 Surely the Lord's power is enough to save you.

He can hear you when you ask him for help.

²It is your evil that has separated you from your God.

Your sins cause him to turn away from you.

And then he does not hear you.

³With your hands you have killed others.

Your fingers are covered with blood from killing people.

With your lips you have lied.

With your tongue you say evil things.

⁴People take each other to court unfairly.

No one tells the truth in arguing his case.

They accuse each other falsely and tell lies.

They cause trouble and create more evil.

⁵They hatch evil like eggs from poisonous snakes.

If you eat one of those eggs, you will die.

And if you break one open, a poisonous snake comes out.

People tell lies as they would spin a spider's web.

⁶ The webs they make cannot be used for clothes.

You can't cover yourself with those webs.

The things they do are evil.

They use their hands to hurt others.

⁷They eagerly run to do evil.

They are always ready to kill innocent people.

They think evil thoughts.

Everywhere they go they cause ruin and destruction.

⁸They don't know how to live in peace.

There is no fairness in their lives.

They are dishonest.

Anyone who lives as they live will never have peace.

Israel's Sin Brings Trouble

⁹Fairness has gone far away.

Goodness is nowhere to be found.

We wait for the light, but there is only darkness now.

We hope for a bright light, but all we have is darkness.

¹⁰We are like blind people feeling our way along a wall.

We have to feel our way as if we had no eyes.

In the brightness of day we trip as if it were night.

We are like dead men among the strong.

¹¹All of us growl like the bears.

We call out sadly like the doves.

We look for justice, but there isn't any.

We want to be saved, but salvation is far away.

¹²We have done many wrong things against our God.

Our sins show we are wrong.

We know we have turned against God.

We know the evil things we have done.

¹³We have sinned and turned against the Lord.

We have turned away from our God.

We have planned to hurt others and
to disobey God.
We have planned and spoken lies.
[14] We have driven away justice.
We have kept away from what is
right.
Truth is not spoken in the streets.
What is honest is not allowed to
enter the city.
[15] Truth cannot be found anywhere.
And people who refuse to do evil
are attacked.

The Lord looked and could not find
any justice.
And he was displeased.
[16] He could not find anyone to help the
people.
He was surprised that there was
no one to help.
So the Lord used his own power to
save the people.
His own goodness gave him
strength.
[17] The Lord covered himself with
goodness like armor.
He put on the helmet of salvation.
He put on the clothes of punishment.
And he put on the coat of his
strong love.
[18] The Lord will pay back his enemies
for what they have done.
He will show his anger to those
who were against him.
He will punish the people in faraway
places.
He will give them the punishment
they should have.
[19] Then people from the west will fear
the Lord.
People in the east will fear his glory.
The Lord will come quickly like a
fast-flowing river,
driven by the breath of the Lord.

[20] "Then a close relative who will save
you will come to Jerusalem.
He will come to the people of
Jacob who sinned but turned
back to God,"
says the Lord.

[21] The Lord says, "I will make an
agreement with these people. I promise

that my Spirit[d] and my words that I
give you will never leave you. They will
be with your children and your grandchildren. They will be with you now
and forever."

Jerusalem Will Be Great

60 "Jerusalem, get up and shine.
Your light has come.
The glory of the Lord shines on you.
[2] Darkness now covers the earth.
Deep darkness covers her people.
But the Lord shines on you,
and people see his glory around
you.
[3] Nations will come to your light.
Kings will come to the brightness
of your sunrise.

[4] "Look around you.
People are gathering and coming
to you.
They are your sons coming from far
away.
And your daughters are coming
with them.
[5] When you see them, you will shine
with happiness.
You will be excited and full of joy.
The wealth of the nations across the
seas will be given to you.
The riches of the nations will come
to you.
[6] Herds of camels will cover your land.
Young camels will come from
Midian and Ephah.
People will come from Sheba
bringing gold and incense.[d]
And they will sing praises to the
Lord.
[7] All the sheep from Kedar will be
given to you.
The male sheep from Nebaioth
will be brought to you.
They will be pleasing sacrifices on
my altar.
And I will make my beautiful
Temple[d] more beautiful.

[8] "The people are returning to you
like clouds.
They are like doves flying to their
nests.

⁹People in faraway lands are waiting
    for me.
  The great trading ships will come
    first.
  They are bringing your children
    from faraway lands.
  And with them they bring silver
    and gold.
  This will happen to honor the Lord
    your God.
  He is the Holy One of Israel.
  And he does wonderful things for
    you.

¹⁰"Jerusalem, foreigners will rebuild
    your walls.
  Their kings will serve you.
  When I was angry, I hurt you.
  But now I want to be kind to you
    and comfort you.
¹¹Your gates will always be open.
  They will not be closed day or night
 so the nations can bring their
    wealth to you.
  And their kings will be led to you.
¹²If a nation or kingdom doesn't serve
    you,
  it will be destroyed.
  It will be completely ruined.

¹³"The great trees of Lebanon will be
    given to you.
  Its pine, fir and cypress trees will
    come to you.
  You will use these trees to make my
    Temple beautiful.
  And I will give much honor to this
    place where I rest my feet.
¹⁴The people who have hurt you will
    bow down to you.
  Those who hated you will bow
    down at your feet.
  They will call you The City of the
    Lord.
  They will call you Jerusalem, city
    of the Holy One of Israel.

¹⁵"You have been hated and left empty.
  No one has even passed through.
  But I will make you great from now
    on.
  You will be a place of happiness
    forever and ever.
¹⁶Nations will give you what you need.

It will be like a child drinking milk
    from its mother.
  Then you will know that it is I, the
    Lord, who saves you.
  You will know that the Powerful
    One of Jacob protects you.
¹⁷I will bring you gold in place of
    bronze.
  I will bring you silver in place of
    iron.
  I will bring you bronze in place of
    wood.
  I will bring you iron in place of
    rocks.
  I will change your punishment into
    peace.
  And you will be ruled by what is
    right.
¹⁸There will be no more violence in
    your country.
  It will not be ruined or destroyed.
  You will name your walls Salvation.
  And you will name your gates
    Praise.
¹⁹The sun will no longer be your light
    during the day.
  The light from the moon will no
    longer be your light.
  This is because the Lord will be
    your light forever.
  Your God will be your glory.
²⁰Your sun will never set again.
  Your moon will never be dark again.
  This is because the Lord will be
    your light forever.
  And your time of sadness will end.
²¹All of your people will do what is right.
  They will receive the earth forever.
  They are the plant I have planted.
  I made them with my own hands
    to show my greatness.
²²The smallest family will grow to a
    thousand.
  The least important of you will
    become a powerful nation.
  I am the Lord,
  and when it is time, I will make
    these things happen quickly."

The Lord's Message of Freedom

61 The Lord God has put his Spirit^d
     in me.

This is because he has appointed
me to tell the good news to the
poor.
He has sent me to comfort those
whose hearts are broken.
He has sent me to tell the captives
they are free.
He has sent me to tell the prisoners
that they are released.
²He has sent me to announce the
time when the Lord will show
his kindness
and the time when our God will
punish evil people.
He has sent me to comfort all those
who are sad.
³He has sent me to the sorrowing
people of Jerusalem.
I will give them a crown to replace
their ashes.
I will give them the oil of gladness
to replace their sorrow.
I will give them clothes of praise to
replace their spirit of sadness.
Then they will be called Trees of
Goodness.
They will be like trees planted by
the Lord and will show his
greatness.

⁴They will rebuild the old ruins.
They will build up the places
destroyed long ago.
They will repair the ruined cities
that were destroyed for so long.

⁵My people, foreigners will come to
tend your sheep.
People from other countries will
tend your vineyards.
⁶You will be called priests of the Lord.
You will be named the servants of
our God.
You will have riches from all the
nations on earth.
And you will take pride in them.
⁷Instead of being ashamed, you will
receive twice as much wealth.
Instead of being disgraced, you
will be happy because of what
you receive.
You will receive a double share of
the land.

So your happiness will continue
forever.
⁸The Lord says, "I love justice.
I hate stealing and everything that
is wrong.
I will be fair and give my people
what they should have.
I will make an agreement with
them that will continue
forever.
⁹Everyone in all nations will know
the children of my people.
And their children will be known
among the nations.
Anyone who sees them will know
that the Lord blesses them."

¹⁰The Lord makes me very happy.
All that I am rejoices in my God.
The Lord has covered me with
clothes of salvation.
He has covered me with a coat of
goodness.
I am like a bridegroom dressed for
his wedding.
I am like a bride dressed in jewels.
¹¹The earth causes plants to grow.
And a garden causes the seeds
planted there to grow.
In the same way the Lord God will
make grow what is right.
He will make praise come from all
the nations.

New Jerusalem

62 Because I love Jerusalem, I will
continue to speak for her.
For Jerusalem's sake I will not
stop speaking.
I will speak until her goodness
shines like a bright light.
I will speak until her salvation
burns bright like a flame.
²Jerusalem, the nations will see your
goodness.
All kings will see your honor.
Then you will have a new name.
The Lord himself will give you that
new name.
³You will be like a beautiful crown in
the Lord's hand.
You will be like a king's crown in
your God's hand.

⁴You will never again be called the
People that God Left.
Your land will never again be called
the Land that God Destroyed.
You will be called the People God
Loves.
Your land will be called the Bride
of God.
This is because the Lord loves you.
And your land will belong to him as
a bride belongs to her husband.
⁵As a young man marries a woman,
so your children will marry your
land.
As a man is very happy about his
new wife,
so your God will be happy with you.

⁶Jerusalem, I have put guards on the
walls to watch.
They must not be silent day or
night.
You people who remind the Lord
should never be quiet.
⁷You should not stop praying to the
Lord until he builds up
Jerusalem.
Don't stop until he makes Jerusalem
a city all people will praise.

⁸The Lord has made a promise.
And by his power he will keep his
promise.
He said, "I will never again give
your grain
as food to your enemies.
I will not let your enemies drink the
wine
that you have worked to make.
⁹The person who gathers food will
eat it.
And he will praise the Lord.
The person who gathers the grapes
will drink the wine
in the courts of my Temple."ᵈ

¹⁰Go through, go through the gates!
Make the way ready for the people.
Build up, build up the road!
Move all the stones off the road.
Raise the banner as a sign for the
people.
¹¹The Lord is speaking

to all the faraway lands:
"Tell the people of Jerusalem,
'Look, your Savior is coming.
He is bringing your reward to you.
He is bringing his payment with
him.'"
¹²His people will be called the Holy
People.
They will be called the Saved
People of the Lord.
And Jerusalem will be called the
City God Wants.
It will be named the City God Has
Not Rejected.

The Lord Judges His People

63 Who is this coming from Edom?
He comes from the city of
Bozrah dressed in red.
Who is this dressed in fine clothes?
He marches forward with his great
power.

He says, "I, the Lord, speak what is
right.
I have the power to save you."

²Why are your clothes bright red
as if you had walked on the grapes
to make wine?

³The Lord answers, "I have walked
in the winepressᵈ alone.
No one among the nations helped
me.
I was angry and walked on the
nations.
I crushed them because of my
anger.
Blood splashed on my clothes.
I stained all my clothing.
⁴I chose a time to punish people.
And the time has come for me to
save my people.
⁵I looked around, but I saw no one to
help me.
I was surprised that no one
supported me.
So I used my own power to save my
people.
My own anger supported me.
⁶While I was angry, I walked on the
nations.
In my anger I punished them

and poured their blood on the
ground."

The Lord's Kindness to His People

[7]I will tell about the Lord's kindness.
And I will praise him for what he
has done.
He has given many good things
to us.
He has been very good to the
people of Israel.
The Lord has shown mercy to us.
And he has been kind to us.
[8]The Lord said, "These are my people.
My children will not lie to me."
So the Lord saved them.
[9]When they suffered, he suffered also.
He sent his own angel to save them.
Because of his love and kindness,
the Lord saved them.
Since long ago he has picked them
up and carried them.
[10]But they turned against the Lord.
They made his Holy Spirit[d] very
sad.
So the Lord became their enemy.
And he fought against them.

[11]But then his people remembered
what happened long ago.
They remembered Moses.
Where is the Lord who brought the
people through the sea?
Where is the one who brought
them with the leaders of his
people?
Where is the one
who put his Holy Spirit among
them?
[12]The Lord led Moses by the right
hand.
The Lord led him by his wonderful
power.
The Lord divided the water before
them so the people could walk
through the sea.
And by this the Lord made his
name famous forever.
[13]The Lord led the people through
the deep waters.
Like a horse walking through a
desert,

the people did not stumble.
[14]Like cattle that go down to the
valley,
the Spirit of the Lord led the
people to a place of rest.
Lord, that is the way you led your
people.
And by this you made your name
wonderful.

A Prayer for Help

[15]Lord, look down from the heavens
and see.
Look at us from your wonderful
holy home in heaven.
Where is your strong love and
power?
Why are you keeping your love
and mercy from us?
[16]You are our father.
Abraham doesn't know we are his
children.
Israel doesn't know who we are.
Lord, you are our father.
You are called "the one who has
always saved us."
[17]Lord, why are you making us
wander from your ways?
Why do you make us stubborn so
that we don't honor you?
For our sake come back to us.
We are your servants, and we
belong to you.
[18]Your people had your Temple[d] for a
while.
But now our enemies have walked
on your holy place and
crushed it.
[19]You have never ruled over some
people.
They have never worn your name.
And we have become like those
people.

64 Tear open the skies and come
down to earth.
The mountains would tremble
before you.
[2]Be like a fire that burns twigs.
Be like a fire that makes water
boil.
Do this so that your enemies will
know who you are.

Then all nations will shake with
fear when they see you.
3You have done amazing things that
we did not expect.
You came down, and the mountains
trembled before you.
4From long ago no one has ever
heard of a God like you.
No one has ever seen a God
besides you.
You help the people who trust you.
5You help those who enjoy doing good.
You help those who remember
how you want them to live.
But you were angry because we
sinned.
For a long time we disobeyed.
How will we be saved?
6All of us are dirty with sin.
All the right things we have done
are like filthy pieces of cloth.
All of us are like dead leaves.
Like the wind our sins have
carried us away.
7No one worships you.
No one even asks you to help us.
So you have turned away from us.
And we are destroyed because of
our sins.

8But Lord, you are our father.
We are like clay, and you are the
potter.
Your hands made us all.
9Lord, don't continue to be angry
with us.
Don't remember our sins forever.
Please, look at us
because we are your people.
10Your holy cities are empty like the
desert.
Jerusalem is like a desert;
Jerusalem is destroyed.
11Our ancestors worshiped you
in our holy and wonderful Temple.
But now it has been burned with fire.
All our precious things have been
destroyed.
12When you see these things, will you
hold yourself back from
helping us, Lord?
Will you be silent and punish us
beyond what we can stand?

All People Will Learn About God

65 The Lord says, "I made myself
known to people who were not
looking for me.
I was found by those who were not
asking me for help.
I spoke to a nation that was not
praying to me.
I said, 'Here I am. Here I am.'
2All day long I stood ready to accept
people who turned against me.
But the way they continue to live is
not good.
They do anything they want to do.
3Right in front of me they continue
to do things that make me angry.
They offer sacrifices to their false
gods in their gardens.
They burn incense^d on altars of
brick.
4They sit among the graves.
They spend their nights waiting to
get messages from the dead.
They eat the meat of pigs.
Their pots are full of soup made
from meat that is wrong to eat.
5But they tell others, 'Stay away.
Don't come near me.
I am too holy for you.'
These people are like smoke in my
nose.
Like a fire that burns all the time,
they continue to make me
angry.

6"Look, it is written here before me.
I will not be quiet. Instead, I will
repay you in full.
I will punish you for what you have
done.
7I will punish you for your sins and
your ancestors' sins,"
says the Lord.
"They burned incense to false gods
on the mountains.
They shamed me on those hills.
So I will punish them as they should
be punished
for what they did."

8This is what the Lord says:
"When there is juice left in the
grapes,

people do not destroy them.
They know there is good left in
them.
I will do the same thing to my
servants.
I will not completely destroy them.
⁹I will leave some of the children of
Jacob.
Some of the people of Judah will
receive my mountain.
I will choose the people who will
live there.
My servants will live there.
¹⁰Then the Plain of Sharon will be a
field for sheep.
The Valley of Achor will be a place
for cattle to rest.
They will be for the people who
want to follow me.

¹¹"But you who left the Lord will be
punished.
You forgot about my holy mountain.
You worship the false god Luck.
You hold religious feasts for the
false god Fate.
¹²But I decide your fate, and I will
punish you with my sword.
You will all be killed.
This is because I called you, but you
refused to answer.
I spoke to you, but you wouldn't
listen.
You did the things I said were evil.
You chose to do things that
displease me."

¹³So the Lord God said these things:
"My servants will eat.
But you evil people will be hungry.
My servants will drink.
But you evil people will be thirsty.
My servants will be happy.
But you evil people will be shamed.
¹⁴My servants will shout for joy
because of the goodness of their
hearts.
But you evil people will cry,
because you will be sad.
You will cry loudly because your
spirits will be broken.
¹⁵Your names will be like curses to
my servants.

And the Lord God will put you to
death.
But he will call his servants by
another name.
¹⁶People in the land who ask for
blessings
will ask for them from the faithful
God.
People in the land who make a
promise
will promise in the name of the
faithful God.
This is because the troubles of the
past will be forgotten.
I will make those troubles go away.

A New Time Is Coming

¹⁷"Look, I will make new heavens and
a new earth.
And people will not remember the
past.
They will not think about those
things.
¹⁸My people will be happy forever
because of the things I will make.
I will make a Jerusalem that is full of
joy.
And I will make her people a
delight.
¹⁹Then I will rejoice over Jerusalem.
I will be delighted with my
people.
There will never again be
crying and sadness in that city.
²⁰There will never be a baby from that
city
who lives only a few days.
And there will never be an older
person
who doesn't have a long life.
A person who lives 100 years will be
called young.
And the person who dies before he
is 100 will be thought of as a
sinner.
²¹In that city the person who builds a
house will live there.
The person who plants vineyards
will get to eat grapes.
²²No more will one person build a
house and someone else live
there.

One person will not plant a
  garden and someone else
  eat its fruit.
My people will live a long time
  as trees live long.
My chosen people will live there
  and enjoy the things they make.
23 People will never again work for
  nothing.
  They will never again give birth to
    children who die young.
  All my people will be blessed by the
    Lord.
  My people and their children will
    be blessed.
24 I will provide for their needs before
  they ask.
  I will help them while they are still
    asking for help.
25 Wolves and lambs will eat together
  in peace.
  Lions will eat hay like oxen.
  A snake on the ground will not hurt
    anyone.
  They will not hurt or destroy each
    other
  on all my holy mountain,"
says the Lord.

God Will Judge All Nations

66 This is what the Lord says:
    "The skies are my throne.
  The earth is my footstool.
So do you think you can build a
  house for me?
  There is no place where I need to
    rest.
2 My hand made all things.
  All things are here because I made
    them,"
says the Lord.

"These are the people I am pleased
  with.
  They are those who are not proud
    or stubborn.
  They fear me and obey me.
3 But those people who kill bulls as a
  sacrifice to me
  are like those who kill men.

Those who kill sheep as a sacrifice
  to me
  are like those who break the necks
    of dogs.
Those who give me grain offerings
  are like those who offer me the
    blood of pigs.[n]
Those who burn incense[d]
  are like those who worship idols.
These people choose their own
  ways—not mine.
  They love the terrible things they
    do.
4 So I will punish them.
  I will punish them using what they
    fear most.
I called to them, but they did not
  listen.
  I spoke to them, but they did not
    hear me.
They did things I said were evil.
  They chose to do things I did not
    like."

5 You people who obey the words of
  the Lord,
  listen to what he says:
"Your brothers hated you.
  They turned against you because
    you followed me.
Your brothers said, 'When the Lord
  is honored,
  we will come back and rejoice with
    you.'
But they will be punished.
6 Listen to the loud noise coming
  from the city.
  Hear the noise from the Temple.[d]
It is the Lord punishing his
  enemies.
  He is giving them the punishment
    they should have.

7 "A woman does not give birth
  before she feels the pain.
  She does not give birth to a son
    before she feels the pain of
    birth.
8 No one has ever heard of that
  happening.
  No one has ever seen that happen.

---

[n] **dogs . . . pigs** God did not want his people to offer dogs and pigs as sacrifices because they were unclean animals.

In the same way no one ever saw a
country begin in one day.
No one has ever heard of a new
nation beginning in one day.
But Jerusalem will give birth to her
children
just as soon as she feels the birth
pains.
⁹In the same way I will not cause
pain
without allowing something new to
be born," says the Lord.
"If I cause you the pain,
I will not stop you from giving birth
to your new nation," says your
God.
¹⁰"Jerusalem, rejoice.
All you people who love Jerusalem,
be happy.
Those of you who felt sad for
Jerusalem
should now feel happy with her.
¹¹You will enjoy her good things and
be satisfied
as a child is nursed by its mother.
You will receive her good things
and enjoy her wealth."

¹²This is what the Lord says:

"I will give her peace that will flow
to her like a river.
The wealth of the nations will
come flowing to her.
Like babies you will be nursed and
held in my arms.
You will be bounced on my knees.
¹³I will comfort you
as a mother comforts her child.
You will be comforted in
Jerusalem."

¹⁴When you see these things, you will
be happy.
You will grow like the grass.
The Lord's servants will see his
power.
But the Lord's enemies will see his
anger.
¹⁵Look, the Lord is coming with fire.
The Lord's armies are coming with
clouds of dust.
He will punish those people with his
anger.

He will punish them with flames of
fire.
¹⁶The Lord will judge the people with
fire.
He will destroy many people with
his sword.
He will kill many people.

¹⁷"These people make themselves
holy and pure to go to worship their
false gods in their gardens. They follow
each other into their special gardens.
They eat the meat of pigs and rats and
other hated things. But they will all be
destroyed together," says the Lord.

¹⁸"I know they have evil thoughts and
do evil things. So I am coming to punish them. I will gather all nations and
all people. All people will come together and see my glory.

¹⁹"I will put a mark on some of the
people. And I will send some of these
saved people to the nations. I will
send them to Tarshish, Libya, Lud (the land
of archers), Tubal, Greece and all the
faraway lands. These people have never
heard about what I have done. They
have never seen my glory. So the saved
people will tell the nations about my
glory. ²⁰And they will bring all your
fellow Israelites from all nations. They
will bring them to my holy mountain
in Jerusalem. Your fellow Israelites will
come on horses, donkeys, camels and
in chariots and wagons. They will be
like the grain offerings that the people
bring in clean containers to the Temple," says the Lord. ²¹"And I will choose
some of these people to be priests and
Levites," says the Lord.

²²"I will make new heavens and the
new earth. And they will last forever,"
says the Lord. "In the same way, your
names and your children will always
be with me. ²³All people will come to
worship me. They will come to worship
me every Sabbath*d* and every New
Moon,"*d* says the Lord. ²⁴"They will go
out and see the dead bodies of the people who sinned against me. The worms
that eat them will never die. The fires
that burn them will never stop. And
everyone will hate to see those bodies."

JEREMIAH

A Warning About Captivity

1 These are the words of Jeremiah son of Hilkiah. He belonged to the family of priests who lived in the town of Anathoth. That town is in the land that belongs to the tribe*d* of Benjamin. ²The Lord spoke his word to Jeremiah. This happened during the thirteenth year that Josiah son of Amon was king of Judah. ³The Lord also spoke to Jeremiah while Jehoiakim son of Josiah was king of Judah. And the Lord spoke to Jeremiah during the 11 years and 5 months Zedekiah son of Josiah was king of Judah. After that, the people who lived in Jerusalem were taken away as captives out of their country.

God Calls Jeremiah

⁴The Lord spoke these words to me:
⁵"Before I made you in your
    mother's womb, I
    chose you.
Before you were born, I set you
    apart for a special work.
I appointed you as a prophet*d* to
    the nations."

⁶Then I said, "But Lord God, I don't know how to speak. I am only a boy."

⁷But the Lord said to me, "Don't say, 'I am only a boy.' You must go everywhere that I send you. You must say everything I tell you to say. ⁸Don't be afraid of anyone, because I am with you. I will protect you," says the Lord.

⁹Then the Lord reached out with his hand and touched my mouth. He said to me, "See, I am putting my words in your mouth. ¹⁰Today I have put you in charge of nations and kingdoms. You will pull up and tear down, destroy and overthrow. You will build up and plant."

Two Visions

¹¹The Lord spoke this word to me: "Jeremiah, what do you see?"

I answered the Lord and said, "I see a stick of almond wood."

¹²The Lord said to me, "You have seen correctly! And I am watching to make sure my words come true."

¹³The Lord spoke his word to me again: "Jeremiah, what do you see?"

I answered the Lord and said, "I see a pot of boiling water. It is tipping over from the north!"

¹⁴The Lord said to me, "Disaster will come from the north. It will happen to all the people who live in this country. ¹⁵In a short time I will call all of the people in the northern kingdoms," said the Lord.

"Those kings will come and set up
    their thrones
near the entrance of the gates of
    Jerusalem.
They will attack the city walls
    around Jerusalem.
They will attack all the cities
    in Judah.
¹⁶And I will announce my judgments
    against my people.
I will do this because of their evil
    in turning away from me.
They offered sacrifices to other gods.
And they worshiped idols they had
    made with their own hands.

¹⁷"Jeremiah, get ready. Stand up and speak to the people. Tell them everything I tell you to say. Don't be afraid of the people. If you are afraid of them, I will give you good reason to be afraid of them. ¹⁸Today I am going to make you a strong city, an iron pillar, a bronze

Whit's Wisdom: Responsibility • Jeremiah 1

"**M**r. Whittaker, what's a *responsibility*?" asked Jessie one day when we were cleaning up the basement at Whit's End. That's where I have a little inventor's hangout. We were trying to invent some instant ice cream, but we only managed to make an instant mess.

"**W**ell, Jessie, when someone counts on you to do something, they call that a responsibility. We messed up this place trying to make an invention, so it's our responsibility to clean it up," I answered.

"**Y**ou mean when Dad says that keeping my room picked up is my responsibility, I'm really supposed to do it? That's going to be hard," she said.

"**M**ost responsibilities aren't easy, Jessie. But they do help us grow up."

"**H**ow do they do that, Mr. Whittaker?"

"**R**esponsibilities are jobs we do even when we don't feel like doing them. One reason God tells us to obey our parents is because he wants us to learn responsibility. He has some important things for each of us to do. Which reminds me of a young man in the Bible who got some important responsibilities from God," I said.

Jessie was interested, so I had her open a Bible to the same page you're on right now. I told her to read Jeremiah 1:4-8. Why don't you take a minute to read it yourself?

I told Jessie that it's OK to be a kid. That's how we all start out. I reminded her that her dad was once her age. But, just like Jeremiah, God doesn't want us to call ourselves "only a kid." We may not be able to handle big responsibilities when we are still young, but we can start to be responsible with little jobs.

Did you notice what else God told Jeremiah? Verse 5 says that God had a special work for Jeremiah to do. The same is true for you. Ask God to help you do what he wants you to do.

Related Passages: Ephesians 6:1-3; Colossians 3:17

Parent/Teacher Hint: Have children brainstorm a list of the responsibilities they have already been given. Point out that the more they are faithful with their present duties, the more they will be able to handle later.

wall. You will be able to stand against everyone in the land: Judah's kings, officers, priests and the people of the land. ¹⁹They will fight against you. But they will not defeat you. This is because I am with you, and I will save you!" says the Lord.

Israel Turns from God

2 The Lord spoke this word to me: ²"Go and speak to the people of Jerusalem. Say to them: This is what the Lord says:

'When you were a young nation,
    you were faithful to me.
You loved me like a young bride.
You followed me through the
    desert.
    It was a land that had never been
    planted.
³The people of Israel were holy to
    the Lord.
    They were like the first fruits from
    his harvest.
Those who tried to hurt Israel were
    judged guilty.
Disasters happened to them,'"
    says the Lord.

⁴Hear the word of the Lord, family of
    Jacob.
    Hear the message, all you family
    groups of Israel.
⁵This is what the Lord says:
"I was fair to your ancestors.
    Why did they turn away from me?
Your ancestors worshiped useless
    idols.
    And they became useless
    themselves.
⁶Your ancestors didn't say,
    'The Lord brought us out of Egypt.
He led us through the desert.
    He led us through a dry and rocky
    land.
    He led us through a dark and
    dangerous land.
    He led us where no one travels
    or lives.
But where is he now?'
⁷I brought you into a fertile land.
    I did this so you could eat its fruit
    and produce.

But you came and made my land
    unclean.ᵈ
    You made it a hated place.
⁸The priests didn't ask,
    'Where is the Lord?'
The people who know the teachings
    didn't know me.
The leaders turned against me.
The prophetsᵈ prophesied in the
    name of Baal.ᵈ
    They worshiped useless idols.

⁹"So now I will again tell what I have
    against you," says the Lord.
    "And I will tell what I have against
    your grandchildren.
¹⁰Go across the sea to the island of
    Cyprus and see.
    Send someone to the land of
    Kedar to look closely.
    See if there has ever been
    anything like this!
¹¹Has a nation ever exchanged their
    old gods for new ones?
    (Of course, their gods are not
    really gods at all.)
But my people have exchanged
    their glorious God
    for idols worth nothing!
¹²Skies, be shocked at the things that
    have happened.
    Shake with great fear!" says
    the Lord.
¹³"My people have done two sins.
    They have turned away from me.
    And I am the spring of living water.
And they have dug their own wells.
    But they are broken wells that
    cannot hold water.
¹⁴Have the people of Israel become
    slaves?
    Have they become like someone
    who was born a slave?
Why was their wealth stolen?
¹⁵Enemies roar like lions at Israel.
    They growl at Israel.
They have destroyed the land of
    Israel.
    The cities of Israel have been
    burned,
    and all the people have left.
¹⁶The men from the Egyptian cities of
    Memphis and Tahpanhes

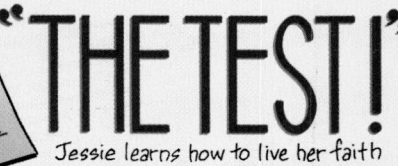

Adventures in ODYSSEY BIBLE

"THE TEST!"

Jessie learns how to live her faith
A story based on 1 Timothy 4:12

JESSIE, YOU HAD A **FEVER** LAST NIGHT AND I WANT TO GET YOU TO THE DOCTOR THIS MORNING.

BUT MOM, I HAVE A **TEST** I CAN'T MISS!

I CALLED YOUR TEACHER AND EXPLAINED THE SITUATION TO HER. WE'LL GET A NOTE FROM THE DOCTOR AND YOU CAN TAKE THE TEST LATER.

THE NEXT DAY, JESSIE RETURNS TO SCHOOL...

STOP

HOW DO YOU DID ON THE TEST? WAS IT **HARD**?

YEAH, IT WAS **REAL** HARD...

...THERE WERE THREE PROBLEMS ON ADDING UP LONG LISTS OF FIGURES AND THERE WERE A COUPLE WHERE YOU HAD TO SUBTRACT ONE NUMBER FROM ANOTHER, THEN SUBTRACT ANOTHER NUMBER FROM YOUR ANSWER, AND THEN....

FRAN! DON'T TELL ME ABOUT IT! I JUST ASKED IF YOU THOUGHT IT WAS HARD!

SEE FOR YOURSELF. WHEN THE TEACHER PASSED OUT TESTS YESTERDAY, I **KEPT** ONE!

HERE, YOU CAN **HAVE** IT IF YOU WANT....

NO WAY! THAT WOULD BE CHEATING!

NO, THAT WOULD BE **SMART**! IT'S A PERFECT CHANCE FOR YOU TO MAKE AN EASY "A"!

I CAN'T **BELIEVE** YOU WOULDN'T WANT TO TAKE IT!

AND **I** CAN'T BELIEVE YOU WOULD WANT ME TO DO IT! IT'S NOT **FAIR** AND IT'S **NOT RIGHT!**

HEY, CALM DOWN. I WAS... JUST **KIDDING**. I WASN'T GOING TO GIVE YOU THE TEST ANYWAY. I WAS JUST SEEING IF YOU WERE REALLY A GOOD CHRISTIAN.

COME ON, GIRLS, LET'S GO TO CLASS. SEE YOU LATER, JESSIE!

*T*HAT NIGHT, JESSIE TALKS WITH HER MOM....

YOU DID THE RIGHT THING, JESSIE. I'M VERY **PROUD** OF YOU.

I KNOW, BUT HOW CAN I TELL THOSE GIRLS ABOUT **GOD**?

IN A WAY, YOU ALREADY **DID**. YOU SHOWED THEM AN EXAMPLE OF HOW A CHRISTIAN HANDLES TEMPTATION.

MAYBE SO, BUT I STILL DIDN'T REALLY TELL THEM ABOUT **JESUS**.

IT'S IMPORTANT FOR YOUR FRIENDS TO SEE THAT YOU ARE **HONEST**. SOMETIMES THAT WILL MAKE THEM **CURIOUS** ABOUT WHY YOU MAKE THE CHOICES YOU DO. THEN YOU CAN TALK TO THEM ABOUT **WHY** YOU ARE HONEST AND HOW THEY CAN BE TOO.

BUT FRAN WAS SO **EMBARRASSED**, I'M AFRAID I'LL **NEVER** BE ABLE TO TALK TO HER AGAIN!

SOON, BACK AT THE LEMONADE STAND...

The End

have disgraced you by shaving the
top of your head.
¹⁷You have brought this on yourselves.
You turned away from me, the
Lord your God,
when I led you in the way.
¹⁸It did not help to go to Egypt
and drink from the Shihor River.
It did not help to go to Assyria
and drink from the Euphrates River.
¹⁹Your evil will bring punishment
to you.
The wrong you have done will
teach you a lesson.
Think about it and understand.
It is a terrible evil to turn away from
the Lord your God.
It is wrong not to fear me,"
says the Lord, the Lord of heaven's
armies.

²⁰"A long time ago you refused to obey
me as an ox breaks its yoke.^d
You broke the ropes I used to hold
you to me.
You said to me, 'I will not serve you!'
In fact, on every high hill
and under every green tree
you lay down as a prostitute.^d
²¹I planted you as a special vine.
You were like very good seed.
How then did you turn
into a wild vine that grows bad fruit?
²²You might wash yourself with
cleanser.
And you might use much soap.
But I can still see the stain of your
guilt," says the Lord God.
²³"How can you say to me, 'I am not
guilty.
I have not worshiped the Baal^d
idols'?
Think about the things you did in
the valley.
Think about what you have done.
You are like a she-camel in mating
season
that runs from place to place.
²⁴You are like a wild donkey that lives
in the desert.
At mating time she sniffs the wind.
At that time no one can hold her
back.

Any male who chases her will easily
catch her.
At mating time, it is easy to find her.
²⁵Don't run until your feet are bare
or until your throat is dry.
But you say, 'It's no use!
I love those other gods.
I must worship them!'

²⁶"A thief is ashamed when someone
catches him stealing.
In the same way the family of
Israel is ashamed.
The kings and the officers,
the priests and the prophets are
ashamed.
²⁷They say to things of wood, 'You are
my father.'
They say to idols of stone, 'You
gave birth to me.'
Those people won't look at me.
They have turned their backs
to me.
But when they get into trouble,
they say,
'Come and save us!'
²⁸Where are the idols you have made
for yourselves?
Let them come and save you
when you are in trouble!
People of Judah, you have as
many idols
as you have towns!

²⁹"Why do you accuse me?
All of you have turned against me,"
says the Lord.
³⁰"I punished your people, but it did
not help.
They didn't come back when they
were punished.
You killed with your swords the
prophets who came to you.
You were like a dangerous lion.

³¹"People of Judah, pay attention to
the word of the Lord:
Have I been like a desert to the
people of Israel?
Have I been like a dark and
dangerous land to them?
Why do my people say, 'We are free
to wander.
We won't come to you anymore'?

³²A young woman does not forget
  her jewelry.
  A bride does not forget the
    decorations for her dress.
  But my people have forgotten me
    for more days than can be counted!
³³You really know how to chase
    after love.
  Even the worst women can learn
    evil ways from you.
³⁴You have blood on your clothes.
  It is the blood of the poor and
    innocent people.
  You killed them,
    but they weren't thieves you had
      caught breaking in.
  You do all these things,
³⁵ but you say, 'I am innocent.
    God is not angry with me.'
  But I will judge you guilty of lying.
  It is because you say, 'I have not
    sinned.'
³⁶It is so easy for you to change your
    mind.
  Assyria let you down.
  And Egypt will let you down, too.
³⁷You will eventually leave that place.
  And, like captives, your hands will
    be on your head.
  You trusted those countries.
  But you will not be helped by them.
  This is because the Lord has
    rejected them.

Judah Is Unfaithful

3 "Now a man might divorce his wife.
   And she might leave him and
     marry another man.
  Should her first husband come back
    to her again?
  If he went back to her, the land
    would become completely
    unclean.ᵈ
  But you have acted like a prostituteᵈ
    with many lovers.
  And now you want to come back to
    me?" says the Lord.
²"Look up to the bare hilltops, Judah.
  Is there any place where you have
    not been a prostitute?
  You have sat by the road waiting
    for lovers.

You sat there like an Arab in the
    desert.
  You made the land unclean.
  This was because you did evil and
    were like a prostitute.
³So the rain has not come.
  There have not been any spring
    rains.
  But your face still looks like the face
    of a prostitute.
  You refuse even to be ashamed of
    what you did.
⁴But now you are calling to me.
  You say, 'My father, you have been
    my friend since I was young.
⁵Will you always be angry at me?
  Will your anger last forever?'
  Judah, you say this,
    but you do as much evil as you can!"

Judah and Israel Are like Sisters

⁶When King Josiah was ruling Judah,
the Lord spoke to me. He said: "Jeremiah, you saw what unfaithful Israel
did. She was guilty of adultery.ᵈ She
had idols on every hill and under every
green tree. ⁷I said to myself, 'Israel will
come back to me after she does this
evil.' But she didn't come back to me.
And Israel's wicked sister Judah saw
what Israel did. ⁸Unfaithful Israel knew
that I divorced her because of her adultery. But that didn't make her wicked
sister Judah afraid. She also went out
and acted like a prostitute!ᵈ ⁹And she
didn't care that she was acting like a
prostitute. So she made her country un-
clean.ᵈ She was guilty of adultery. This
was because she worshiped idols made
of stone and wood. ¹⁰Israel's wicked
sister didn't come back to me with her
whole heart. She only pretended to
come back to me," says the Lord.

¹¹The Lord said to me, "Unfaithful
Israel had a better excuse than wicked
Judah. ¹²Go and speak this message
toward the north:
  'Come back, unfaithful people of
    Israel,' says the Lord.
  'I will stop frowning at you.
  I am full of mercy,' says the Lord.
  'I will not be angry with you forever.

¹³All you have to do is admit your sin.
  You turned against the Lord
    your God.
You worshiped the false gods of
    other nations.
You worshiped them under every
    green tree.
You didn't obey me,'" says the Lord.

¹⁴"Come back to me, you unfaithful
people," says the Lord. "I am your husband. I will take one person from every
city. And I will take two people from
every family group. And I will bring you
to Jerusalem. ¹⁵Then I will give you new
rulers. They will be faithful to me. They
will lead you with knowledge and understanding. ¹⁶In those days there will be
many of you in the land," says the Lord.
"At that time people will no longer say,
'I remember the Box^d of the Agreement.' They won't even think about the
Holy Box anymore. They won't even
remember or miss it or make another
one. ¹⁷At that time Jerusalem will be
called The Throne of the Lord. All
nations will come together in Jerusalem
to show respect to the Lord. They will
not follow their stubborn, evil hearts
anymore. ¹⁸In those days the family of
Judah will join the family of Israel. They
will come together from a land in the
north. They will come to the land I gave
to their ancestors.

¹⁹"I, the Lord, said,
'How happy I would be to treat you
    as sons!
  I would be glad to give you a
    pleasant land.
  It's a land more beautiful than that
    of any other nation.'
I thought you would call me 'Father'
    and not turn away from me.
²⁰But like a woman who is unfaithful
    to her husband,
  family of Israel, you have been un-
    faithful to me," says the Lord.

²¹You can hear crying on the bare
    hilltops.
  The people of Israel are crying and
    praying for mercy.
  They have become very evil.

They have forgotten the Lord
    their God.
²²"Come back to me, you unfaithful
    people of Israel.
  Come back, and I will forgive you
    for being unfaithful."

"Yes, we will come to you.
  You are the Lord our God.
²³It was foolish to worship idols on
    the hills.
  All the loud noises on the
    mountains were a lie.
  Surely the salvation of Israel
    comes from the Lord our God.
²⁴Since we were young, shameful
    gods have eaten up in sacrifice
everything our fathers worked for.
  The shameful gods have taken our
    fathers' sheep and cattle.
  They have taken our fathers' sons
    and daughters.
²⁵Let us lie down in our shame.
  And let our shame cover us like
    a blanket.
  We have sinned against the Lord
    our God.
  Both we and our fathers have
    sinned.
Since we were children and until now,
  we have not obeyed the Lord our
    God."

4 "If you will come back, Israel,
   then come back to me," says
     the Lord.
"Throw away your idols that I hate.
  Don't wander away from me.
²Then you may say when you make
    a promise,
  'As surely as the Lord lives.'
  And you can say it in a truthful,
    honest and right way.
Then the nations will be blessed by
    the Lord.
  And they will praise the Lord for
    what he has done."

³This is what the Lord says to the
men of Judah and Jerusalem:
"Plow your unplowed fields.
  Don't plant seeds among the thorns.
⁴Give yourselves to the service of the
    Lord.

Decide to obey him.
Do this, men of Judah and people
of Jerusalem.
If you don't, my anger will spread
among you like a fire.
No one will be able to put it out
because of the evil you have done.

Trouble from the North

⁵"Announce this message to Judah
and say it in Jerusalem:
'Blow the trumpet throughout
the country!'
Shout out loud and say,
'Come together!
Let's all escape to the strong,
walled cities!'
⁶Raise the signal flag toward
Jerusalem!
Run for your lives! And don't wait!
Do this because I am bringing
disaster from the north.
It will be terrible destruction."

⁷A lion has come out of his den.
A destroyer of nations has begun
to march.
He has left his home
to destroy your land.
Your towns will be destroyed.
There will be no people left to live
in them.
⁸So put on rough cloth,
show how sad you are and cry
loudly.
The terrible anger of the Lord
has not turned away from us.

⁹"When this happens," says the Lord,
"the king and officers will lose
their courage.
The priests will be terribly afraid.
And the prophets*d* will be shocked!"

¹⁰Then I, Jeremiah, said, "Lord God,
you have tricked the people of Judah
and Jerusalem. You said, 'You will have
peace.' But now the sword is pointing
at our throats!"

¹¹At that time this message will be
given to Judah and Jerusalem: "A hot
wind blows from the bare hilltops. It
comes out of the desert toward the
Lord's people. It is not like the gentle
wind farmers use to separate grain from
chaff.*d* ¹²It's a stronger wind than that.
And it comes from the Lord. Now he
will announce his judgment against the
people of Judah."

¹³Look! The enemy rises up like a
cloud.
His chariots come like a windstorm.
His horses are faster than eagles.
How terrible it will be for us! We
are ruined!
¹⁴People of Jerusalem, clean the evil
from your hearts and be saved.
Don't continue making evil plans.
¹⁵A voice from Dan makes an
announcement.
From the mountains of Ephraim
someone brings bad news.
¹⁶"Report this to the nations.
Spread this news in Jerusalem:
'Enemies are coming from a
faraway country.
They are shouting words of war
against the cities of Judah.
¹⁷The enemy has surrounded
Jerusalem as men guard a field.
This is because Judah turned
against me,'" says the Lord.
¹⁸"The way you have lived and acted
has brought this trouble to you.
This is your punishment.
How terrible it is!
The pain stabs your heart!"

Jeremiah's Cry

¹⁹Oh, how I hurt! How I hurt!
I am bent over in pain.
Oh, the torture in my heart!
My heart is pounding inside me.
I cannot keep quiet.
This is because I have heard the
sound of the trumpet.
I have heard the words of war.
²⁰Disaster follows disaster.
The whole country has been
destroyed.
My tents are destroyed in only a
moment.
My curtains are torn down quickly.
²¹How long must I look at the war flag?
How long must I listen to the war
trumpets?

22The Lord says, "My people are
  foolish.
They do not know me.
They are stupid children.
They don't understand.
They are skillful at doing evil.
They don't know how to do good."

Disaster Is Coming

23I looked at the earth.
  It was empty and had no shape!
I looked at the sky.
  And its light was gone.
24I looked at the mountains,
  and they were shaking!
All the hills were trembling.
25I looked, and there were no people!
Every bird in the sky had flown
  away.
26I looked, and the good, rich land
  had become a desert!
All its towns had been destroyed.
The Lord and his great anger has
  caused this.

27This is what the Lord says:
"All the land will be ruined.
But I will not completely destroy it.
28So the people in the land will cry
  loudly.
And the sky will grow dark.
This is because I have spoken and
  will not change my mind.
I have made a decision, and I will
  not change it."

29The towns will hear the sound of
  the horsemen and soldiers
  with bows.
All the people will run away.
Some of them will hide in the thick
  bushes.
Some will climb up into the rocks.
All of the cities of Judah are empty.
No one lives in them.
30Judah, you destroyed nation, what
  are you doing?
Why do you put on your finest
  dress?
Why do you put on your gold
  jewelry?
Why do you put on your eye
  shadow?

You make yourself beautiful, but it
  is all useless.
Your lovers hate you.
  They want to kill you.

31I hear a cry like a woman having
  a baby.
It is a cry like a woman having her
  first child.
It is the voice of Jerusalem gasping
  for breath.
She lifts her hands in prayer
  and says,
"Oh! I am about to faint.
They are about to murder me!"

No One Is Right

5 The Lord says, "Walk up and down
  the streets of Jerusalem.
Look around and think about
  these things.
Search the public squares of
  the city.
See if you can find one person who
  does honest things.
Find just one who searches for
  the truth.
If you can, I will forgive this city.
2The people say, 'As surely as the
  Lord lives!'
But they don't really mean it."

3Lord, don't you look for truth in
  people?
You hit the people of Judah.
  But they didn't feel any pain.
You crushed them,
  but they refused to learn what is
  right.
They became more stubborn than a
  rock.
They refused to turn back to God.
4But I thought,
"These are only the poor, foolish
  people.
They have not learned the way of
  the Lord.
They do not know what their God
  wants them to do.
5So I will go to the leaders of Judah.
I will talk to them.
Surely they understand the way of
  the Lord.

They know what God wants them
   to do."
But the leaders had all joined
   together to break away from
   the Lord.
They broke their ties with him.
⁶So a lion from the forest will attack
   them.
A wolf from the desert will kill them.
A leopard is hiding and waiting for
   them near their towns.
It will tear to pieces anyone who
   comes out of the city.
This will happen because the people
   of Judah have sinned greatly.
They have wandered away from
   the Lord many times.

⁷The Lord said, "Tell me why I
   should forgive you.
Your children have left me.
They have made promises to idols
   that are not gods at all.
I gave your children everything
   they needed.
But they still were like an unfaithful
   wife to me.
They spent much time in houses
   of prostitutes.*ᵈ*
⁸They are like well-fed, male horses
   filled with sexual desire.
Each one wants another man's wife.
⁹Shouldn't I punish the people of
   Judah for doing these things?"
   says the Lord.
"I should give a nation such as this
   the punishment it deserves.

¹⁰"Go along and cut down Judah's
   vineyards.
But do not completely destroy them.
Cut off all her people as if they were
   branches.
Do it because they do not belong
   to the Lord.
¹¹The families of Israel and Judah
   have been completely unfaithful to
   me," says the Lord!

¹²Those people have lied about the
   Lord.
They have said, "The Lord will not
   do anything to us!
Nothing bad will happen to us.

We will never see war or hunger.
¹³The prophets*ᵈ* are like an empty wind.
The word of God is not in them.
Let these bad things they say
   happen to them."

¹⁴So this is what the Lord of heaven's
armies says:
"The people said I would not punish
   them.
So, Jeremiah, the words I give you
   will be like fire.
And these people will be like wood
   the fire burns up.
¹⁵Listen, family of Israel," says
   the Lord.
"I will soon bring a nation from far
   away to attack you.
It is an old nation that has lasted a
   long time.
The people there speak a language
   you do not know.
You cannot understand what
   they say.
¹⁶Their arrows bring death.
All their men are strong warriors.
¹⁷They will eat your crops and your
   food.
They will eat your sons and
   daughters.
They will eat your flocks and herds.
They will eat your grapes and figs.
They will destroy with their swords
   the strong, walled cities you trust in!

¹⁸"Yet even then," says the Lord, "I
will not destroy you completely. ¹⁹The
people of Judah will ask, 'Why has the
Lord our God done this terrible thing
to us?' Give them this answer: 'You have
left the Lord. You have served foreign
idols in your own land. So now you will
serve foreigners in a land that does not
belong to you!'

²⁰"Announce this message to the
   family of Jacob.
And tell it to the nation of Judah:
²¹Hear this message, you foolish
   people who have no sense.
You have eyes, but you don't really
   see.
You have ears, but you don't really
   listen.

22Surely you are afraid of me," says the Lord.

"You should shake with fear in my presence.
I am the one who made the beaches to be a border for the sea.
They keep the water in its place forever.
The waves may pound the beach, but they can't win over it.
The waves may roar, but they cannot go beyond it.
23But the people of Judah are stubborn and have turned against me.
They have turned aside and gone away from me.
24They do not say to themselves, 'We should fear the Lord our God.
He gives us autumn and spring rains in their seasons.
He makes sure we have the harvest at the right time.'
25But your evil has kept away both rain and harvest.
Your sins have kept you from enjoying good things.
26There are wicked men among my people.
They are like men who make nets for catching birds.
But they set their traps to catch men instead of birds.
27Like cages full of birds, their houses are full of lies.
They have become rich and powerful.
28 They have grown big and fat.
There is no end to the evil things they do.
They won't plead the case of the orphan.
They won't help the poor be judged fairly.
29Shouldn't I punish the people of Judah for doing these things?" says the Lord.

"I should give a nation such as this the punishment it deserves.

30"A terrible and shocking thing has happened in the land of Judah:
31The prophets tell lies.
The priests take power into their own hands.

And my people love it this way.
But what will you do when the end comes?

Jerusalem Is Surrounded

6 "Run for your lives, people of Benjamin!
Run away from Jerusalem!
Blow the war trumpet in the town of Tekoa!
Raise the warning flag over the town of Beth Hakkerem!
Disaster is coming from the north.
Terrible destruction is coming to you.
2Jerusalem, I will destroy you.
You are fragile and gentle.
3Shepherds with their flocks will come against Jerusalem.
They will set up their tents all around her.
Each shepherd will take care of his own section."
4They say, "Get ready to fight against Jerusalem!
Get up! We will attack at noon!
But it is already getting late.
The evening shadows are growing long.
5So get up! We will attack at night.
We will destroy the strong towers of Jerusalem!"

6This is what the Lord of heaven's armies says:

"Cut down the trees around Jerusalem.
Build an attack ramp to the top of Jerusalem's walls.
This city must be punished!
Inside this city is nothing but slavery.
7Jerusalem pours out her evil as a well pours out its water.
The sounds of violence and destruction are heard within her.
I can see the sickness and hurts of Jerusalem.
8Listen to this warning, Jerusalem.
If you don't listen, I will turn my back on you.
I will make your land an empty desert.

No one will be able to live there!"

⁹This is what the Lord of heaven's armies says:
"Gather the few people of Israel
    who are left alive.
Gather them as you would the last
    grapes on a grapevine.
Check each vine again,
    like someone who gathers grapes."

¹⁰To whom can I speak? Whom can
    I warn?
Who will listen to me?
The people of Israel have closed ears!
    So they cannot hear my warnings.
They don't like the word of the Lord.
    They don't want to listen to it!
¹¹But I am full of the anger of the Lord.
    I am tired of holding it in.

"Pour out the Lord's anger on the
    children who play in the street.
Pour it out on the young men
    gathered together.
A husband and his wife will both be
    caught in his anger.
The very old people will be caught
    in it.
¹²Their houses will be turned over
    to others.
Their fields and wives will be
    given away.
I will raise my hand
    and punish the people of Judah,"
    says the Lord.
¹³"Everyone, from the least important
    to the greatest,
is greedy for money.
Even the prophets*ᵈ* and priests
    all tell lies.
¹⁴They try to heal my people's serious
    injuries
as if they were small wounds.
They say, 'It's all right, it's all right!'
    But really, it is not all right.
¹⁵They should be ashamed of the
    terrible way they act.
But they are not ashamed at all.
They don't even know how to
    blush about their sins.
So they will fall, along with
    everyone else.
They will be thrown to the ground

when I punish them," says
    the Lord.

¹⁶This is what the Lord says:
"Stand where the roads cross and
    look.
Ask where the old way is.
Ask where the good way is, and
    walk on it.
If you do, you will find rest for
    yourselves.
But you have said, 'We will not
    walk on the good way!'
¹⁷I chose watchmen to watch over you.
I told you, 'Listen for the sound of
    the war trumpet!'
But you said, 'We will not listen.'
¹⁸So listen, all you nations.
Pay attention, you witnesses.
Watch what I will do to the people
    of Judah.
¹⁹Hear this, people of the earth:
I am going to bring disaster to the
    people of Judah!
It will happen because of the evil
    they plan.
They have not listened to my
    messages.
They have rejected my teachings.
²⁰Why do you bring me offerings of
    incense*ᵈ* from the land of
    Sheba?
Why do you bring me sweet-
    smelling cane from a faraway
    land?
Your burnt offerings will not
    be accepted.
Your sacrifices do not please me."

²¹So this is what the Lord says:
"I will put problems in front of Judah.
Fathers and sons will stumble
    over them.
Neighbors and friends will die."

²²This is what the Lord says:
"Look, an army is coming
    from the land of the north.
A great nation is coming
    from the far sides of the earth.
²³The soldiers carry bows and spears.
    They are cruel and show no mercy.
They sound like the roaring ocean
    when they ride their horses.

That army is coming lined up for
battle.
It is coming to attack you,
Jerusalem."

²⁴We have heard the news about
that army.
We are helpless from fear.
We feel trapped by our troubles.
We are in pain like a woman
having a baby.
²⁵Don't go out into the fields.
Don't walk down the roads!
This is because the enemy has
swords.
There is terror on every side.
²⁶My people, put on rough cloth
and roll in the ashes to show how
sad you are.
Cry loudly for those who are dead.
Cry as if your only son had died.
Do it because the destroyer
will soon come against us.

²⁷"Jeremiah, I have made you like a
worker who tests metal.
And my people are like the ore for
the metal.
You must observe their ways.
And you must test them.
²⁸My people have turned against me
and are stubborn.
They go around telling lies about
people.
They are like bronze and iron,
that became covered with rust.
²⁹The fire is fanned to make it
hotter.
But the lead does not melt.
The pure silver does not come out.
And the evil is not removed from
my people.
³⁰My people will be called rejected
silver.
They will be given that name
because the Lord has
rejected them."

Jeremiah's Temple Sermon

7 This is the word that the Lord
spoke to Jeremiah: ²"Stand at the
gate of the Temple.ᵈ Preach this message there:

"'Hear the word of the Lord, all you
people of the nation of Judah! All you
who come through these gates to worship the Lord, listen to this message!
³This is what the Lord of heaven's armies, the God of Israel, says: Change
your lives and do what is right! If you
do, I will let you live in this place. ⁴Don't
trust the lies that some people say! They
say, "This is the Temple of the Lord.
This is the Temple of the Lord. This is
the Temple of the Lord!" ⁵You must
change your lives and do what is right.
You must be fair to each other. ⁶You
must not be hard on the strangers, the
orphans and widows. Don't kill innocent people in this place! Don't follow
other gods, or they will ruin your lives.
⁷If you do these things, I will let you
live in this land. This is the land I gave
to your ancestors to keep forever.

⁸"'But look! You are trusting lies.
Such trust is useless. ⁹Will you steal
and murder? Will you be guilty of adultery?ᵈ Will you falsely accuse other people? Will you worship the false god
Baal?ᵈ And will you follow other gods
you have not known? ¹⁰If you do that,
do you think you can come before me?
Can you stand in this place where I
have chosen to be worshiped? Do you
think you can say, "We are safe!" Are
you safe to do all these hated things?
¹¹This is the place where I have chosen
to be worshiped. Is it nothing more to
you than a hideout for robbers? I have
been watching you, says the Lord!

¹²"'You people of Judah, go now to
the town of Shiloh. It was there that I
first made a place to be worshiped. Go
there and see what I did because of the
evil things they had done. ¹³You people of Israel were doing all these evil
things, says the Lord. I spoke to you
again and again. But you did not listen
to me. I called you, but you did not answer. ¹⁴So I will destroy the place where
I have chosen to be worshiped in Jerusalem. You trust in that place. I gave it
to you and your ancestors. But I will destroy it just as I destroyed Shiloh. ¹⁵I
will push you away from me. I will do

it just as I pushed away your brothers, the people of Israel!'

¹⁶"As for you, Jeremiah, don't pray for these people. Don't cry out for them or ask anything for them. Don't beg me to help them. I will not listen to you. ¹⁷Don't you see what they are doing in the towns of Judah? Don't you see what they are doing in the streets of Jerusalem? ¹⁸This is what the people of Judah are doing: The children gather wood. The fathers use the wood to make a fire. The women make the dough for cakes of bread. And they offer them to the Queen Goddess.*ᵈ* They pour out drink offerings to worship other gods. They do this to make me angry. ¹⁹But I am not the one the people of Judah are really hurting, says the Lord. They are only hurting themselves. They are bringing shame upon themselves.

²⁰"So this is what the Lord says: I will pour out my anger on this place. I will pour it out on man and animal. I will pour out my anger on the trees in the field. And I will pour it out on the crops in the ground. My anger will be like a hot fire. And no one will be able to put it out.

Obedience Is More than Sacrifice

²¹"This is what the Lord of heaven's armies, the God of Israel, says: Go and offer as many burnt offerings and sacrifices as you want! Eat the meat of those sacrifices yourselves! ²²I brought your ancestors out of Egypt. I spoke to them. But I did not give them commands only about burnt offerings and sacrifices. ²³I also gave them this command: Obey me, and I will be your God and you will be my people. Do all that I command, and good things will happen to you. ²⁴But your ancestors did not listen or pay attention to me. They were stubborn and did whatever their evil hearts wanted. They went backward, not forward. ²⁵Since the day your ancestors left Egypt, I have sent you my servants, the prophets.*ᵈ* I sent them to you again and again. ²⁶But your ancestors did not listen or pay attention to me. They were

very stubborn. And they did more evil than their ancestors.'

²⁷"Jeremiah, you will tell these things to the people of Judah. But they will not listen to you! You will call to them, but they will not answer you. ²⁸So say to them, 'This is the nation that has not obeyed the Lord its God. These people do nothing when I correct them. They do not tell the truth. It has disappeared from their lips.

The Valley of Killing

²⁹"Cut off your hair and throw it away. Go up to the bare hilltop and cry. Do it because I, the Lord, have rejected these people. I have turned my back on them. And in my anger I will punish them! ³⁰The people of Judah have done what I said was evil, says the Lord. They have set up their hated idols in the place where I have chosen to be worshiped. They have made it unclean!*ᵈ* ³¹The people of Judah have built places of worship at Topheth in the Valley of Ben Hinnom. There the people offered their own sons and daughters as sacrifices. This is something I never commanded. It never even entered my mind! ³²So, I warn you. The days are coming, says the Lord, when people will not call this place Topheth. They will not call it the Valley of Ben Hinnom anymore. They will call it the Valley of Killing. They will bury dead people in Topheth until there is no room to bury anyone else! ³³Then the bodies of the dead will lie on top of the ground. They will become food for the birds of the sky. Wild animals will eat the bodies. There will be no one left alive to chase the birds or animals away. ³⁴I will end the happy sounds of the bride and bridegroom. There will be no happy sounds in Judah or in the streets of Jerusalem. The land will become an empty desert!

8 "'The Lord says: At that time the bones will be removed from the tombs. The bones of Judah's kings and officers, priests and prophets*ᵈ* and the people of Jerusalem will be removed. ²The bones will be spread on the ground under the sun, moon and stars the people loved and served. They went after these gods, searched them out and worshiped them. No one will gather up the bones and bury them. So they will be like dung thrown on the ground. ³I will force the people of Judah to leave their homes and their land. Those of this evil family who are not dead will wish they were dead, says the Lord.'

Sin and Punishment

⁴"Say to the people of Judah: 'This is what the Lord says:
When a man falls down, doesn't he
    get up again?
And when a man goes the wrong
    way, doesn't he come back
    again?
⁵Why, then, have the people of Judah
    gone the wrong way?
And why do the people of
    Jerusalem not turn back?
They believe their own lies.
They refuse to turn around and
    come back.
⁶I have listened to them very carefully.
But they do not say what is right.
They do not feel sorry about their
    wicked ways.
The people don't think about the
    bad things they have done.
Each person goes his own way.
He is like a horse charging into
    a battle.
⁷Even the birds in the sky
know the right times to do things.
The storks, doves, swifts and
    thrushes
know when it is time to migrate.
But my people don't know
what the Lord wants them to do!

⁸"You keep saying, "We are wise.
This is because we have the
    teachings of the Lord."
But actually, those who copy the
    Scriptures
have written lies with their pens.
⁹These wise men refused to listen to
    the word of the Lord.
So they are not really wise at all.
They will be ashamed.

They will be shocked and trapped.
¹⁰So I will give their wives to other
    men.
I will give their fields to new
    owners.
Everyone, from the least important
    to the greatest,
is greedy for money.
Even the prophets^d and priests
all tell lies.
¹¹They try to heal my people's serious
    injuries
as if they were small wounds.
They say, "It's all right, it's all right!"
But really, it is not all right.
¹²They should be ashamed of the
    terrible way they act.
But they are not ashamed at all.
They don't even know how to
    blush about their sins.
So they will fall, along with
    everyone else.
They will be thrown to the ground
    when I punish them, says
    the Lord.

¹³"'I will take away their crops, says
    the Lord.
There will be no grapes on the vine.
There will be no figs on the fig tree.
Even the leaves will dry up and die.
I will take away what I gave them!'"

¹⁴"Why are we just sitting here?
Let's get together!
We have sinned against the Lord.
So he has given us poisoned water
    to drink.
Come, let's run to the strong, walled
    cities.
The Lord our God has decided
    that we must die.
So let's die there.
¹⁵We hoped to have peace.
But nothing good has come.
We hoped for a time when he would
    heal us.
But only disaster has come!
¹⁶From the land of the tribe^d of Dan,
the snorting of the enemy's horses
    is heard.
The ground shakes from the
    neighing of their large horses.

They have come to destroy
   the land and everything in it.
They have come to destroy
   the city and all the people who live
   there."

17"Look! I am sending poisonous
   snakes to attack you.
These snakes cannot be charmed.
   They will bite you," says the Lord.

Jeremiah's Sadness

18God, you are my comfort when I am
   very sad.
   You are my comfort when I'm
   afraid.
19Listen to my people!
   They are crying for help from a
   faraway land.
   They say, "Is the Lord still in
   Jerusalem?
   Is Jerusalem's king still there?"

But God says, "Why did the people
   make me angry by worshiping
   idols?
   They worshiped their useless
   foreign idols."

20And the people say, "Harvest time
   is over.
   Summer has ended.
   And we have not been saved."

21My people are crushed. So I am
   crushed.
   I cry loudly, and I am afraid for
   them.
22Surely there is a balm^d in the land of
   Gilead.
   Surely there is a doctor there.
So why aren't the hurts of my
   people healed?

9 I wish my head were like a spring
   of water.
   And I wish my eyes were a
   fountain of tears!
   Then I could cry day and night
   for my people who have been killed.
2I wish I had a place in the desert—
   a house where travelers spend
   the night.
   Then I could leave my people.
   I could go away from them.

This is because they are all
   unfaithful to God.
   They are all turning against him.

Judah's Failures

3"They use their tongues like a bow.
   They shoot lies from their mouths
   like arrows.
Lies, not truth,
   have grown strong in the land.
They go from one evil thing to
   another.
   They do not know who I am," says
   the Lord.
4"Watch your friends.
   Don't trust your own brothers.
This is because every brother is a
   cheater.
   And every friend tells lies about you.
5Everyone lies to his friend.
   No one speaks the truth.
The people of Judah have taught
   their tongues to lie.
   They become tired from sinning.
6Jeremiah, you live in the middle
   of evil.
   And lies follow lies.
The people have refused to know
   me," says the Lord.

7So this is what the Lord of heaven's
armies says:
"I will test the people of Judah as a
   person tests metal in a fire.
   I have no other choice.
   My people have sinned.
8Their tongues are like sharp arrows.
   Their mouths speak lies.
Everyone speaks nicely to his
   neighbor.
   But he is secretly planning to
   attack him.
9Shouldn't I punish the people for
   doing this?" says the Lord.
"Shouldn't I give them the
   punishment they deserve?"

10I, Jeremiah, will cry loudly for the
   mountains.
   I will sing a funeral song for the
   empty fields.
   They are empty, and no one passes
   through.

The mooing of cattle cannot be
    heard.
The birds have flown away,
    and the animals are gone.

¹¹"I, the Lord, will make the city of
    Jerusalem a heap of ruins.
It will become a home for wild
    dogs.
I will destroy the cities in the land of
    Judah
so no one can live there."

¹²What man is wise enough to understand these things? Is there someone
who has been taught by the Lord who
can explain them? Why was the land
ruined? Why has it been made like an
empty desert where no one goes?
¹³The Lord answered, "It is because
Judah quit following my teachings that
I gave them. They have not obeyed me.
They have not done what I told them
to do. ¹⁴Instead, the people of Judah
were stubborn. They followed the false
god Baal.ᵈ Their fathers taught them
to do this!" ¹⁵So this is what the Lord
of heaven's armies, God of Israel, says:
"I will soon make the people of Judah
eat bitter food. I will make them drink
poisoned water. ¹⁶I will scatter them
through other nations. They will live in
strange nations that they and their ancestors never knew about. I will chase
the people of Judah with the sword until
they are all killed."

¹⁷This is what the Lord of heaven's
armies says:
"Now, think about these things!
    Call for the women who cry at
        funerals.
    Send for those women who are
        good at that job.
¹⁸Let them come quickly
    and cry loudly for us.
Then our eyes will fill with tears.
    And streams of water will come
        out of our eyes.
¹⁹The sound of loud crying is heard
    from Jerusalem:
'We are truly ruined!
We are truly ashamed!
We must leave our land,

because our houses are in ruins.'"

²⁰Now, women of Judah, listen to the
    word of the Lord.
Open your ears to hear the words
    of his mouth.
Teach your daughters how to cry
    loudly.
Teach one another a funeral song!
²¹Death has climbed in through our
    windows.
It has entered our strong cities.
Death has taken away our children
    who play in the streets.
It has taken the young men who
    meet in the city squares.

²²Say, "This is what the Lord says:
'The dead bodies of men will lie
    in the open field like dung.
They will lie on the ground like
    grain a farmer has cut.
But there will be no one to gather
    them.'"

²³This is what the Lord says:
"Wise men must not brag about
    their wisdom.
Strong men must not brag about
    their strength.
Rich men must not brag about
    their money.

"**D**id you know that
there's one thing
the Bible says we
can brag about?
Read in Jeremiah
9:23-24 about that
and the three kinds
of bragging most
people do that God
does not want."

²⁴But if someone wants to brag, let
    him brag about this:
Let him brag that he understands
    and knows me.
Let him brag that I am the Lord.
    Let him brag that I am kind and fair.
Let him brag that I do things that
    are right on earth.
This kind of bragging pleases me,"
    says the Lord.

²⁵The Lord says, "The time is coming when I will punish all those who are circumcised[d] only in the flesh. ²⁶That is the people of Egypt, Judah, Edom, Ammon and Moab. I will also punish the desert people who cut their hair short. The men in all those countries have not given themselves to serving me. And the men of Israel do not give themselves to serving me."

The Lord and the Idols

10 Family of Israel, listen to what the Lord says to you. ²This is what he says:

"Don't live like the people from other nations.
Don't be afraid of special signs in the sky,
even though the other nations are afraid of them.
³The customs of other people are worth nothing.
Their idols are nothing but wood from the forest.
They are made by a worker with his chisel.
⁴They decorate their idols with silver and gold.
With hammers and nails they fasten them down.
That keeps them from falling over.
⁵Their idols are like scarecrows in melon fields.
They cannot talk.
They cannot walk.
They must be carried.
Do not be afraid of those idols.
They can't hurt you.
And they can't help you either!"

⁶Lord, there is no one like you.
You are great.
Your name is great and powerful.
⁷Everyone should respect you, King of all nations.
You deserve their respect.
There are many wise men among the nations.
And there are wise men in all the kingdoms.
But none of them are as wise as you.

⁸Those wise men are stupid and foolish.
Their teachings come from worthless wooden idols.
⁹They use silver from Tarshish and gold from Uphaz.
Their idols are made by craftsmen and goldsmiths.
They put blue and purple clothes on the idols.
All these things are made by skilled workers.
¹⁰But the Lord is the only true God.
He is the only living God, King forever.
The earth shakes when he is angry.
The nations cannot stand up to his anger.

¹¹"Tell them this message: 'These false gods did not make heaven and earth. But they will be destroyed and disappear from heaven and earth.'"

¹²God made the earth by his power.
He used his wisdom to build the world.
He used his understanding to stretch out the skies.
¹³When he thunders, the waters in the skies roar.
He makes clouds rise in the sky all over the earth.
He sends lightning with the rain.
He brings out the wind from his storehouses.

¹⁴People are so stupid and know so little.
Goldsmiths are made ashamed by their idols.
Those statues are only false gods.
They have no breath in them.
¹⁵They are worth nothing.
People make fun of them.
When they are judged, they will be destroyed.
¹⁶But God, who is Jacob's Portion,[d] is not like the idols.
God made everything.
And he made Israel to be his special people.
The Lord of heaven's armies is his name.

Destruction Is Coming

¹⁷Get everything you own and
　　prepare to leave.
　You people of Judah are trapped in
　　the city by your enemies.
¹⁸This is what the Lord says:
　"At this time I will throw out the
　　people of Judah who live in
　　this land.
　I will bring pain and trouble to them.
　And they will really feel it."
¹⁹How terrible it will be for me
　　because of my injury.
　I am injured and cannot be healed.
　Yet I told myself,
　"This is my sickness; I must suffer
　　through it."
²⁰My tent is ruined.
　All its ropes are broken.
　My children have gone away and
　　left me.
　No one is left to put up my tent.
　No one is left to set up a shelter
　　for me.
²¹The shepherds are stupid.
　They don't ask the Lord.
　So they do not have success.
　Their flocks are scattered and lost.
²²Listen! The news is coming.
　The loud noise is coming from
　　the north.
　It will make the towns of Judah an
　　empty desert.
　They will become a home for
　　wild dogs!

Jeremiah's Prayer

²³Lord, I know that a person's life
　　doesn't really belong to him.
　No one can control his own life.
²⁴Lord, correct me, but be fair.
　Don't punish me in anger.
　If you do, you will destroy me.
²⁵Pour out your anger on other
　　nations.
　They do not know you.
　They do not pray to you.
　Those nations have destroyed
　　Jacob's family.
　They have eaten him up.
　They destroyed his homeland.

The Agreement Is Broken

11 These are the words that the Lord spoke to Jeremiah: ²"Listen to the words of this agreement. Tell the people of Judah about it. Tell it to those living in Jerusalem. ³Tell them this is what the Lord, the God of Israel, says: 'Trouble will come to anyone who does not obey this agreement. ⁴I am talking about the agreement I made with your ancestors. I made it with them when I brought them out of Egypt. Egypt was like a furnace for melting iron!' I told them, 'Obey me and do everything I command you. If you do this, you will be my people. And I will be your God. ⁵Then I will keep the promise I made to your ancestors. I promised to give them a land where much food grows.' And you are living in that country today!"

I, Jeremiah, answered, "Amen, Lord."

⁶The Lord said this to me: "Prophesy[d] this message in the towns of Judah and in the streets of Jerusalem: 'Listen to the words of this agreement. Then obey them! ⁷I warned your ancestors to obey me when I brought them out of Egypt. I have warned them again and again to this very day! ⁸But your ancestors did not listen to me. They were stubborn and did what their own evil hearts wanted. The agreement says curses will come upon them if they don't obey it. So I made all those curses come upon them! I commanded them to obey the agreement, but they did not.'"

⁹Then the Lord said to me, "I know the people of Judah and those living in Jerusalem have made secret plans. ¹⁰They are doing the same sins their ancestors did! Their ancestors refused to listen to my message. They followed and worshiped other gods. The families of Israel and Judah have broken the agreement I made with their ancestors. ¹¹So this is what the Lord says: 'I will soon bring a disaster on the people of Judah. They will not be able to escape! And they will cry to me for help. But I will not listen to them! ¹²The people living in the towns of Judah and the

city of Jerusalem will pray to their idols for help. They will burn incense[d] to their idols. But those idols will not be able to help when that terrible time comes! [13]The people of Judah have as many idols as there are towns in Judah. They have built many altars for worshiping that shameful god Baal.[d] There are as many altars as there are streets in Jerusalem!'

[14]"As for you, Jeremiah, don't pray for these people. Don't cry out for them or ask anything for them. I will not listen when they call to me in the time of their trouble.

[15]"What is my lover, Judah, doing in
　　my Temple?[d]
　She makes many evil plans.
　Does she think animal sacrifices
　　will stop her punishment?
　When you do your evil, then you
　　are happy."
[16]The Lord called you "a leafy olive
　　tree,
　with beautiful fruit to look at."
　But with a strong storm
　　the Lord will set that tree on fire.
　And its branches will be burned
　　up.

[17]The Lord of heaven's armies planted you. And he has announced that disaster will come to you. This is because the families of Israel and Judah have done evil things. They have made him angry by offering sacrifices to Baal.

Evil Plans Against Jeremiah

[18]The Lord showed me that men were making plans against me. The Lord showed me what they were doing. So I knew they were against me. [19]Before this, I was like a gentle lamb waiting to be butchered. I did not know they had made plans against me. They said:
　"Let us destroy the tree and its fruit!
　Let's kill him!
　Then people will forget him!"
[20]But, Lord of heaven's armies, you
　　are a fair judge.
　You know how to test peoples'
　　hearts and minds.

I will tell you what I have against
　　them.
　And I will let you give them the
　　punishment they should have!

[21]So the Lord speaks about the men from Anathoth who were planning to kill Jeremiah. Those men say, "Don't prophesy[d] in the name of the Lord. If you do, we will kill you!" [22]So this is what the Lord of heaven's armies says: "I will soon punish the men from Anathoth. Their young men will die in war. Their sons and daughters will die from hunger. [23]No one from the city of Anathoth will be left alive. I will cause a disaster to happen to them that year."

Jeremiah's First Complaint

12 Lord, if I complain to you,
　　you are always right.
　But I want to ask you about the
　　justice you give.
　Why are evil people successful?
　Why do dishonest people have
　　such easy lives?
[2]You have put the evil people here.
　They are like plants with strong
　　roots.
　They grow and produce fruit.
　With their mouths they speak well
　　of you.
　But their hearts are really far away
　　from you.
[3]But you know my heart, Lord.
　You see me and test my mind.
　Drag the evil people away like
　　sheep to be butchered.
　Set them aside for the day of killing.
[4]How much longer will the land stay
　　dried up?
　How long will the grass in every
　　field be dead?
　The animals and birds in the land
　　have died.
　And it is because the people are
　　evil.
　Yet, they are saying,
　　"God does not see what happens
　　to us!"

God's Answer to Jeremiah

[5]"If you get tired racing against men,

how can you race against horses?
You stumble in a country that
is safe.
What will you do in the thick thornbushes along the Jordan River?
⁶These men are your own brothers.
Members of your own family are
making plans against you.
People from your own family are
crying out against you.
Don't trust them,
even when they speak to you like
friends!

⁷"I have left Israel.
I have left my people.
I have given the people I love
to their enemies.
⁸My people have become
like a lion in the forest to me.
They roar at me.
So I hate them.
⁹My people have become to me
like a speckled bird attacked by
hawks.
Go, gather the wild animals!
Bring them to get something to eat.
¹⁰Many shepherds will ruin my
vineyards.
They will walk on the plants in my
field.
They will turn my beautiful field
into an empty desert.
¹¹They will turn my field into a desert.
It will be wilted and dead.
The whole country is an empty desert.
This is because no one who lives
there cares.
¹²Many soldiers will march over
those barren hills.
The Lord will use the armies to
punish that land.
People from one end of the land to
the other will be punished.
No one will be safe.
¹³The people will plant wheat.
But they will harvest only thorns.
They will work hard until they are
very tired.
But they will get nothing for all
their work.
You will be ashamed of your poor
harvest.

The Lord's terrible anger has
caused this."

¹⁴This is what the Lord said to me:
"Here is what I will do to those wicked
people who take the land I gave my people, the Israelites. I will pull them up
and throw them out of their land. And
I will pull up the people of Judah from
among them. ¹⁵But after I pull them
up, I will feel sorry for them. I will bring
each person back to his own property.
And I will bring him back to his own
land. ¹⁶I want them to learn their lessons
well. In the past they taught my people to use Baal'sᵈ name to make promises. Now I want them to learn to use
my name! I want them to say, 'As surely as the Lord lives . . .' If they do, I will
allow them to be successful. And I will
let them live among my people. ¹⁷But
a nation might not listen to my message. If it doesn't, I will pull it up completely and destroy it," says the Lord.

Jeremiah's Linen Belt

13 This is what the Lord said to me:
"Go and buy a linen belt. Then
put it around your waist. Don't let the
belt get wet."

²So I bought a linen belt, just as the
Lord told me. And I put it around my
waist. ³Then the Lord spoke his word
to me a second time: ⁴"Take the belt
you bought and are wearing. Go to Perath. Hide the belt there in a crack in
the rocks." ⁵So I went to Perath and hid
the belt there, just as the Lord told me.

⁶Many days later the Lord said to me,
"Now go to Perath. Get the belt that I
told you to hide there." ⁷So I went to
Perath and dug up the belt. I took it
from where I had hidden it. But now it
was ruined. It was good for nothing.

⁸Then the Lord spoke his word to me.
⁹This is what the Lord said: "In the
same way I will ruin the pride of the
people of Judah and the great pride of
Jerusalem. ¹⁰These evil people refuse
to listen to my warnings. They stubbornly do only what they want to do.
They follow other gods to serve and
worship them. So they will become like

this linen belt. They will be good for nothing. ¹¹A belt is wrapped tightly around a man's waist. In the same way I wrapped the families of Israel and Judah around me," says the Lord. "I did that so they would be my people. Then they would bring fame, praise and honor to me. But my people would not listen to me.

Warnings About Leather Wine Bags

¹²"Say to them: 'This is what the Lord, the God of Israel, says: All leather bags for holding wine should be filled with wine.' People will say to you: 'Of course, we know all wine bags should be filled with wine.' ¹³Then you will say to them, 'This is what the Lord says: I will make everyone in this land like a drunken man. I am talking about the kings who sit on David's throne. I am also talking about the priests and the prophets.ᵈ I am talking about all the people who live in Jerusalem. ¹⁴I will make the people of Judah stumble and fall into one another. Fathers and sons will fall into one another, says the Lord. I will not feel sorry or have pity for them. My mercy will not stop me from destroying them!'"

Threat of Slavery

¹⁵Listen and pay attention.
    Don't be too proud.
    The Lord has spoken to you.
¹⁶Honor the Lord your God.
    Give him glory before he brings
        darkness.
Praise him before you fall
    on the dark hills.
You hope for light.
    But the Lord will turn it into thick
        darkness.
    He will change it into deep gloom.
¹⁷If you don't listen to the Lord,
    I will cry secretly.
    Your pride will cause me to cry.
I will cry painfully.
    My eyes will overflow with tears.
    This is because the Lord's people
        will be captured.
¹⁸Tell this to the king and queen
    mother:

"Come down from your thrones.
Your beautiful crowns
    have fallen from your heads."
¹⁹The cities in the desert of southern
        Judah are shut up.
    No one can open them.
All Judah will be taken as captives
    to a foreign land.
    They will be carried away
        completely.

²⁰Jerusalem, look up and see.
    Someone comes from the north.
Where is the flock God gave to you
    to care for?
    It is the flock you bragged about.
²¹What will you say when they
        appoint as your heads
    those you had thought were your
        friends?
Won't you have much pain and
        trouble?
    Your pain will be like that of a
        woman having a baby.
²²You might ask yourself,
    "Why has this happened to me?"
    It happened because of your many
        sins.
    Because of your sins, your skirt
        was torn off
    and your body has been treated
        badly.
²³A black man from Cush cannot
        change the color of his skin.
    A leopard cannot change his spots.
In the same way, Jerusalem, you
        cannot change and do good.
    You always do evil.

²⁴"I will scatter you like chaffᵈ that is
        blown away by the desert wind.
²⁵This is what will happen to you.
    This is your part in my plans," says
        the Lord.
    "This will happen because you
        forgot me.
    You have trusted in false gods.
²⁶Jerusalem, I will pull your skirts up
        over your face.
    Everyone will see you, and you will
        be ashamed.
²⁷I have seen the terrible things you
        have done.

I know your acts of adultery[d] and
  your snorting.
I have seen you acting like a
  prostitute.[d]
I have seen your hated acts
  on the hills and in the fields.
How terrible it will be for you,
  Jerusalem.
How long will you continue being
  unclean?"[d]

A Time Without Rain

14 These are the words that the
Lord spoke to Jeremiah about the
time when there was no rain:
[2]"The nation of Judah cries.
  Her cities are dying.
They cry out for the land.
  A cry goes up to God from
    Jerusalem.
[3]The important men send their
  servants to get water.
  The servants go to the wells,
  but they find no water.
So they return with empty jars.
  They are ashamed and
    embarrassed.
  They cover their heads in shame.
[4]The ground is dry and cracked open
  because no rain falls on the land.
The farmers are upset and sad.
  So they cover their heads in
    shame.
[5]Even the mother deer in the field
  leaves her fawn.
  She does this because there is no
    grass.
[6]Wild donkeys stand on the bare hills.
  They sniff the wind like wild dogs.
But their eyes are dull because
  there is no food."

[7]We know that we suffer because of
  our sins.
  Lord, do something to help us for
    the good of your name.
We have left you many times.
  We have sinned against you.
[8]God, you are the Hope of Israel.
  You have saved Israel in times of
    trouble.
But now you are like a stranger in
  the land.
You are like a traveler who only
  stays one night.
[9]You seem like a man who has been
  attacked by surprise.
  You seem like a warrior who is not
    able to save anyone.
But you are among us, Lord.
  And we are called by your name.
  So don't leave us without help!

[10]This is what the Lord says about
the people of Judah:
"They really love to wander from me.
  They don't stop themselves from
    leaving me.
So now I, the Lord, will not accept
  them.
I will now remember the evil
  they do.
  I will punish them for their sins."

[11]Then the Lord said this to me:
"Don't pray for good things to happen
to the people of Judah. [12]Even if they
give up eating, I will not listen to their
prayers. Even if they offer burnt offerings and grain offerings to me, I will
not accept them. I will destroy the people of Judah with war, hunger and terrible diseases."

[13]But I said, "Oh! Lord God, the false
prophets[d] keep telling the people
something different! They are saying,
'You will not suffer from an enemy's
sword. You will never suffer from hunger. The Lord will give you peace in
this land.'"

[14]Then the Lord said to me, "Those
prophets are prophesying lies in my
name. I did not send them. I did not
appoint them or speak to them. They
have been prophesying false visions,
idolatries and worthless magic. And
they have been prophesying their own
wishful thinking. [15]So this is what I say
about the prophets who are prophesying in my name. I did not send them.
They said, 'No enemy with swords will
ever attack this country. There will
never be hunger in this land.' Those
prophets will die from hunger. And an
enemy's sword will kill them. [16]And
the people the prophets spoke to will

be thrown into the streets of Jerusalem. They will die from hunger and from an enemy's sword. No one will be there to bury them. And no one will bury their wives, their sons or their daughters. I will punish them.

17"Speak this message to the people of Judah:

'Let my eyes be filled with tears.
  I will cry night and day, without
    stopping.
I will cry for my people.
  They have received a terrible blow.
  They have been hurt very badly.
18If I go into the country,
  I see people killed by swords.
If I go into the city,
  I see much sickness because the
    people have no food.
Both the priests and the prophets
  have been taken to a foreign land.'"

19Lord, have you completely rejected
    the nation of Judah?
  Do you hate Jerusalem?
Why have you hurt us so badly
  that we cannot be made well again?
We hoped for peace,
  but nothing good has come.
We looked for a time of healing,
  but only terror came.
20Lord, we admit that we are very
    wicked.
  We admit that our ancestors did
    evil things.
  We have sinned against you.
21For your sake, do not hate us.
  Do not take away the honor from
    your glorious throne.
  Remember your agreement with us.
  Do not break it.
22Do foreign idols have the power to
    bring rain?
  Does the sky itself have the power
    to send down showers of rain?
No, it is you, Lord our God.
  You are our only hope.
  You are the one who made all
    these things.

15 The Lord said to me: "I would not feel sorry for the people of Judah even if Moses and Samuel prayed for

them. Send the people away from me! Tell them to go! 2They might ask you, 'Where will we go?' You tell them this: 'This is what the Lord says:

Some people are meant to die.
  And they will die.
Some are meant to die in war.
  And they will die in war.
Some are meant to die from hunger.
  And they will die from hunger.
Some are meant to be taken as
    slaves to a foreign country.
  And they will become slaves in
    that foreign country.'

3"I will send four kinds of destroyers against them," says the Lord. "I will send war to kill. I will send dogs to drag the bodies away. I will send birds of the air and wild animals. They will eat and destroy the bodies. 4I will make the people of Judah hated by everyone on earth. I will do this because of what Manasseh did in Jerusalem. (Manasseh son of Hezekiah was king of the nation of Judah.)

5"Who will feel sorry for you,
    Jerusalem?
  Who will be sad and cry for you?
  Who will go out of his way to ask
    how you are?
6Jerusalem, you have left me," says
    the Lord.
  "You keep going farther and
    farther away.
So I will take hold of you and
    destroy you.
  I am tired of holding back my
    anger.
7I will separate the people of Judah
    with my pitchfork.
  I will scatter them at the city gates
    of the land.
My people haven't changed their
    ways.
  So I will destroy them.
  I will take away their children.
8Many women will lose their
    husbands.
  There will be more widows than
    the sand of the sea.
  I will bring a destroyer at noontime

against the mothers of the young
men of Judah.
I will suddenly bring pain and fear
on the people of Judah.
⁹The enemy will attack.
I will still hand over to the killers
those who are left alive from
Judah.
A woman might have seven sons,
but they will all die.
She will cry until she becomes
weak and unable to breathe.
She will be upset and confused.
Her bright day will become dark
from sadness!" says the Lord.

Jeremiah's Second Complaint

¹⁰Mother, I am sorry that you gave
birth to me.
I am the one who must accuse and
criticize the whole land.
I have not loaned or borrowed
anything.
But everyone curses me.
¹¹The Lord said,
"I will save you for a good reason.
I will make your enemies beg you
in times of disaster and trouble.
¹²No one can smash a piece of iron
or bronze.
I mean the kind of iron and bronze
that comes from the north.
¹³The people of Judah have wealth
and treasures.
But I will freely give those riches
to others.
This is because the people of Judah
have sinned
throughout the country.
¹⁴I will make you slaves to your
enemies.
You will be slaves in a land that
you have never known.
My anger is like a hot fire.
And it will burn against you."

¹⁵Lord, you understand.
Remember me and take care
of me.
Punish for me the people who are
hurting me.
Don't destroy me while you remain
patient with them.

Think about the pain I suffer for
you, Lord.
¹⁶Your words came to me, and I
listened carefully to them.
Your words made me very happy.
I was happy because I am called by
your name.
Your name is the Lord God of
heaven's armies.
¹⁷I never sat with the crowd
as they laughed and had fun.
I sat by myself because you were
there.
You filled me with anger at the evil
around me.
¹⁸I don't understand why my pain has
no end.
I don't understand why my injury
is not cured or healed!
Lord, will you be like a brook that
goes dry?
Will you be like a spring whose
water stops flowing?

¹⁹So this is what the Lord says:
"If you change your heart and come
back to me, I will take you back.
Then you may serve me.
You must speak things that have
worth.
You must not speak useless words.
Then you may speak for me.
Let the people of Judah turn to you.
But you must not change and be
like them.
²⁰I will make you as strong as a wall
to this people.
You will be as strong as a wall of
bronze.
They will fight against you.
But they will not defeat you.
This is because I am with you.
I will rescue you and save you,"
says the Lord.
²¹"I will save you from these evil people.
I will save you from these cruel
people."

The Day of Disaster

16 Then the Lord spoke his word to
me: ²"You must not get married.
You must not have sons or daughters
in this place."

³The Lord says this about the sons and daughters born in this land. And he says this about the mothers and fathers of those children: ⁴"They will die of terrible diseases. No one will cry for them. No one will bury them. Their bodies will lie on the ground like dung. They will die in war, or they will starve to death. Their dead bodies will be food for the birds of the sky. And they will be food for the wild animals."

⁵So this is what the Lord says: "Jeremiah, do not go into a house where there is a funeral meal. Do not go there to cry for the dead or to show your sorrow. Do not do this because I have taken back my blessing, my love and my pity from these people," says the Lord. ⁶"Important people and common people will die in the land of Judah. No one will bury them or cry for them. No one will cut himself for them. And no one will shave his head to show sorrow for them. ⁷No one will bring food to the people who are crying for the dead. No one will comfort one whose mother or father has died. No one will offer a drink to comfort them.

⁸"Do not go into a house where the people are having a feast. Do not go there and sit down to eat and drink. ⁹This is what the Lord of heaven's armies, the God of Israel, says: I will soon stop the sounds of joy and gladness in this place! I will stop the happy sounds of brides and bridegrooms! This will happen during your lifetime.

¹⁰"You will tell the people of Judah these things. And they will ask you, 'Why has the Lord said these terrible things to us? What have we done wrong? What sin have we done against the Lord our God?' ¹¹"Then say to them: 'This is because your ancestors quit following me,' says the Lord. 'And they began to follow other gods. They served and worshiped other gods. Your ancestors left me. And they quit obeying my teaching. ¹²But you have done even more evil than your ancestors. You are very stubborn. You do only what you want to do. You have

not obeyed me. ¹³So I will throw you out of this country. You will go to a land that you and your ancestors never knew. There you can serve false gods day and night. I will not help you or show you any favors.'

¹⁴"People say, 'As surely as the Lord lives, who brought the people of Israel out of Egypt . . .' But the time is coming," says the Lord, "when people will not say this anymore. ¹⁵They will say instead, 'As surely as the Lord lives, who brought the Israelites from the northern land and from all the countries where he had sent them . . .' And I will bring them back to the land I gave to their ancestors.

¹⁶"I will soon send for many fishermen to come to this land," says the Lord. "The fishermen will catch the people of Judah. After that, I will send for many hunters to come to this land. Those hunters will hunt the people of Judah on every mountain and hill. And they will hunt Judah in the cracks of the rocks. ¹⁷I see everything they do. They cannot hide the things they do from me. Their sin is not hidden from my eyes! ¹⁸I will pay back the people of Judah for the evil they have done. I will punish them two times for every one of their sins. I will do this because they have made my land unclean.ᵈ They have done it with their hated idols. They have filled my country with them!"

¹⁹Lord, you are my strength and my
    protection.
  You are a safe place for me to run
    to in times of trouble.
  The nations will come to you from
    all over the world.
  They will say, "Our fathers had
    only false gods.
  They worshiped useless idols that
    didn't help them.
²⁰Can people make gods for
    themselves?
  They will not really be gods!"

²¹The Lord says, "So I will teach
    those who make idols.
  Right now I will teach them

about my power and my
strength.
Then they will know
that my name is the Lord.

Judah's Guilty Heart

17 " The sin of the people of Judah
is written with an iron tool.
Their sins were cut into stone with
a hard point.
That stone is their hearts.
Their sins were cut into the
corners of their altars.
[2] Even their children remember
their altars to idols and their
Asherah[d] idols.
They remember the altars under
the green trees
and on the high hills.
[3] They remember the altars on my
mountain and in the open
country.
I will give your wealth and
treasures
to other people.
And they will destroy the places of
worship in your country.
You sinned by worshiping at those
places.
[4] You will lose the land I gave you.
And it is your own fault.
I will let your enemies take you as
their slaves.
You will be slaves in a land you
have never known.
This is because you have made my
anger burn like a hot fire.
And it will burn forever."

Trusting in Man or God

[5] This is what the Lord says:
"A curse will be placed on those
who trust other people.
It will happen to those who depend
on people for strength.
Those are the ones who have
stopped trusting the Lord.
[6] They are like a bush in a desert.
It grows in a land where no one
lives.
It is in a hot and dry land with bad
soil.

They don't know about the good
things that God can give.
[7] "But the person who trusts in the
Lord will be blessed.
The Lord will show him that he
can be trusted.
[8] He will be strong, like a tree planted
near water.
That tree has large roots that find
the water.
It is not afraid when the days are
hot.
Its leaves are always green.
It does not worry in a year when no
rain comes.
That tree always produces fruit."

[9] "More than anything else, a
person's mind is evil.
It cannot be healed.
No one truly understands it.
[10] But I am the Lord, and I can look
into a person's heart.
I can test a person's mind.
So I can decide what each one
deserves.
I can give each one the right
payment for what he
does."

[11] Sometimes a bird will hatch an egg
that it did not lay.
That bird is like the man who gets
rich by cheating.
When that man's life is half
finished, he will lose his
riches.
At the end of his life, it will be
clear he was a fool.

[12] From the beginning, our Temple[d]
has been honored
as a glorious throne for God.
[13] Lord, you are the hope of Israel.
Those who leave you will be
shamed.
A person who quits following the
Lord will be like a name
written in the dust.
That is because he has left the
Lord.
The Lord is the spring of living
water.

Jeremiah's Third Complaint

14Lord, heal me, and I will truly be
    healed.
  Save me, and I will truly be saved.
  Lord, you are the one I praise.
15The people of Judah keep asking me,
  "Where is the word from the Lord?
  Let's see that message come true!"

16Lord, I didn't run away from being
    the shepherd you wanted.
  I didn't want the terrible day to
    come.
  You know everything I have said.
  You see all that is happening.
17Lord, don't bring terror to me.
  I run to you for safety in times of
    trouble.
18Make those who are hurting me be
    ashamed.
  But don't bring shame to me.
  Let them be terrified,
    but keep me from terror.
  Bring the day of disaster on my
    enemies.
  Destroy them, and destroy them
    again.

Keeping the Sabbath Holy

19This is what the Lord said to me:
"Go and stand at the People's Gate of
Jerusalem. This is where the kings of
Judah go in and out. And then go to all
the other gates of Jerusalem. 20Say to
them there: 'Hear the word of the Lord.
Listen, kings of Judah. Listen, all you
people of Judah and all who come
through these gates into Jerusalem!
21This is what the Lord says: Be careful not to carry a load on the Sabbath*d*
day. And don't bring it through the
gates of Jerusalem on the Sabbath.
22Don't take a load out of your houses
on the Sabbath. Don't do any work on
that day. Keep the Sabbath as a holy
day. I gave this same command to your
ancestors. 23But your ancestors did not
listen. They did not pay attention to
me. They were very stubborn. I punished them, but it didn't do any good.
They did not listen to me. 24But you
must be careful to obey me, says the
Lord. You must not bring a load
through the gates of Jerusalem on the
Sabbath. You must keep the Sabbath
as a holy day. You must not do any
work on that day.
25"If you obey this command, this
is what will happen: Kings who sit on
David's throne will come through the
gates of Jerusalem with their officers.
They will come riding in chariots and
on horses. The people of Judah and Jerusalem will be with them. And the city
of Jerusalem will have people living in
it forever! 26People will come to Jerusalem from the villages around it and
from the towns of Judah. They will
come from the land of Benjamin. They
will come from the western mountain
slopes and from the mountains. And
they will come from southern Judah.
They will all bring burnt offerings, sacrifices, grain offerings, incense*d* and offerings to show thanks to God. They
will bring these to the Temple*d* of the
Lord. 27But you must obey me and keep
the Sabbath day as a holy day. You must
not carry any loads into Jerusalem on
the Sabbath. If you do, I will start a fire
that cannot be put out. It will start at
the gates of Jerusalem. And it will burn
until it burns even the strong towers!'"

The Potter and the Clay

18 This is the word the Lord spoke
to Jeremiah: 2"Go down to the
potter's house. I will give you my message there." 3So I went down to the potter's house. I saw him working at the
potter's wheel. 4He was making a pot
from clay. But something went wrong
with it. So the potter used that clay to
make another pot. He used his hands
to shape the pot the way that he wanted it to be.

5Then the Lord spoke his word to me:
6"Family of Israel, can't I do the same
thing with you?" says the Lord. "You
are like the clay in the potter's hands.
7There may come a time when I will
speak about a nation or a kingdom. I
might say I will pull that nation up by
its roots. Or I might say I will pull that

Jobs in the Bible
POTTER • JEREMIAH 18:1-4

Potters were busy people. They put a piece of clay on a flat round surface that they spun around like a wheel. As the round surface spun, the potter used his hands to form the clay into a pot, pan, or jar. When it was set to dry, the clay would turn hard like stone. No one had pots and pans made out of metal or glass. Almost everything used for cooking or for storing food or for carrying water was made out of clay. People carried clay jars to the well for water and small clay dishes held oil and a wick for lamps. Even plates and "glasses" were made from clay.

Being a potter was not easy. The potter had to work carefully in order to make the dish turn out just right. Jesus is like a potter. He is working in our lives to help us turn out just right!

To read about people who supplied lots of food to Israel,
fly to page 1126.

nation down and destroy it. ⁸But if the people of that nation are sorry for the evil they have done, I would change my mind. I would not carry out my plans to bring disaster to them. ⁹There may come another time when I will speak about a nation. I might say that I will build up and plant that nation. ¹⁰But if I see it doing evil by not obeying me, I would change my mind. I would not carry out my plans to do good for them.

¹¹"So, say this to the people of Judah and those who live in Jerusalem: 'This is what the Lord says: I am preparing disaster for you right now. I am making plans against you. So stop doing the evil you are doing. Change your ways and do what is right.' ¹²But the people of Judah will answer, 'It won't do any good to try! We will continue to do what we want. Each of us will do what his stubborn, evil heart wants!'"

¹³So this is what the Lord says:
"Ask the people in other nations
    this question:
'Have you ever heard anything like
    this?'

The people of Israel have done a
    horrible thing.
¹⁴The snow on the mountains of
    Lebanon
never melts from the rocks.
Its cool, flowing streams
do not dry up.
¹⁵But my people have forgotten me.
They make offerings to worthless
    idols.
This makes them stumble in what
    they do.
They stumble about in the old
    ways of their ancestors.
They walk along back roads
and on poor highways.
¹⁶So Judah's country will become an
    empty desert.
People will not stop making fun of it.
They will shake their heads as they
    pass by.
They will be shocked at how the
    country was destroyed.
¹⁷I will scatter them before their
    enemies
as a strong east wind blows things
    away.

At that awful time they will not see
  me coming to help them.
They will see me leaving."

Jeremiah's Fourth Complaint

18Then the people said, "Come, let's
make plans against Jeremiah. Surely
the teaching of the law by the priest will
not be lost. And the advice from the wise
men will still be with us. We will still
have the words of the prophets.[d] So let's
ruin him by telling lies about him! We
won't pay attention to anything he says."

19Lord, listen to me.
  Listen to what my accusers are
    saying!
20Good should not be paid back with
    evil.
  But they have dug a pit in order to
    kill me.
  Lord, remember that I stood before
    you
  and asked you to do good things
    for these people.
  I asked you to turn your anger
    away from them.
21So now, let their children starve.
  Let their enemies defeat them with
    swords.
  Let their wives lose their children
    and husbands.
  Let the men from Judah be put to
    death.
  Let the young men be killed in
    battle.
22Let them cry out in their houses.
  Bring an enemy against them
    suddenly.
  Let all this happen because my ene-
    mies have dug a pit to trap me.
  And they have hidden traps for me
    to step in.
23Lord, you know
  about their plans to kill me.
  Don't forgive their crimes.
  Don't erase their sins.
  Make them fall from their places.
  Punish them while you are angry.

The Broken Jar

19 This is what the Lord said to me:
"Go and buy a clay jar from a potter. 2Go out to the Valley of Ben Hinnom. Go near the front of the Potsherd
Gate. Take some of the older leaders of
the people and priests with you. There
speak the words I tell you. 3Say, 'King
of Judah and people of Jerusalem, listen
to this message from the Lord. This is
what the Lord of heaven's armies, the
God of Israel, says: I will soon bring a
disaster on this place! Everyone who
hears about it will be amazed and full
of fear. 4I will do this because the people
of Judah have quit following me. They
have made this a place for foreign gods.
They have burned sacrifices to other
gods. They did not worship these gods
long ago! Their ancestors didn't worship these gods. The kings of Judah
filled this place with the blood of the
innocent people. 5The kings of Judah
have built places to worship Baal.[d] There
they burn their sons in the fire to Baal.
I did not speak about it or tell them to
do that. I never even thought of such
a thing. 6Now people call this place
the Valley of Ben Hinnom or Topheth.
But watch out! The days are coming,
says the Lord, when people will call this
place the Valley of Killing.

7"'At this place I will ruin the plans
of the people of Judah and Jerusalem.
The enemy will chase them. And I will
let the people of Judah be killed with
swords. I will make their dead bodies
food for the birds and wild animals. 8I
will completely destroy this city. People
will make fun of it and hiss at it. And
they will shake their heads when they
pass by Jerusalem. They will be shocked
when they see how the city was destroyed. 9An enemy army will surround
the city. They will not let anyone go out
to get food. The people will become so
hungry they will eat the bodies of their
own sons and daughters. And then they
will begin to eat each other.'"

10The Lord said, "While the people
with you are watching, break that jar.
11Then say this: 'The Lord of heaven's
armies says: I will break this nation and
this city just as someone breaks a clay
jar. It cannot be put back together

again. The dead people will be buried here in Topheth. We will bury bodies until there is no more room. ¹²This is what I will do to these people and to this place, says the Lord. I will make this city like Topheth. ¹³The houses in Jerusalem and the king's palaces will become as unclean*d* as this place, Topheth. This is because the people worshiped false gods on the roofs*ⁿ* of their houses. They worshiped the stars and burned incense*d* to honor them. They gave drink offerings to false gods.'"

¹⁴Then Jeremiah left Topheth where the Lord had told him to prophesy.*d* He went to the Lord's Temple,*d* stood in the courtyard and said to all the people: ¹⁵"This is what the Lord of heaven's armies, the God of Israel, says: 'I said I would bring disaster to Jerusalem and the villages around it. I will make it happen soon! This is because the people are very stubborn. They do not listen at all to what I say.'"

Jeremiah and Pashhur

20 Pashhur son of Immer was a priest. He was the highest officer in the Temple*d* of the Lord. He heard Jeremiah prophesying*d* in the Temple courtyard. ²So he had Jeremiah the prophet beaten. And he had Jeremiah's hands and feet locked between large blocks of wood. This was at the Upper Gate of Benjamin of the Lord's Temple. ³The next day Pashhur took Jeremiah out from between the blocks of wood. Then Jeremiah said to him, "The Lord's name for you is not Pashhur. Now the Lord's name for you is Terror on Every Side. ⁴That is your name because this is what the Lord says: 'I will soon make you a terror to yourself and to all your friends. You will watch enemies killing your friends with swords. And I will give all the people of Judah to the king of Babylon. He will take them away as captives to Babylon. Then his army will kill them with swords. ⁵I will give all the wealth of this city to its enemies. I will give them its goods and its valuables. I will give the treasures of the kings of Judah to their enemies. The enemies will carry Judah and all its valuables off to Babylon. ⁶And Pashhur, you and everyone in your house will be taken

Witnessing
JEREMIAH 20:7-9

Have you ever been asked to keep a big, BIG secret? Well? Did you keep the secret until you just couldn't stand it anymore? Or did you tell it to the first person you saw? There is something about knowing important information that makes it hard to keep it to ourselves.

That's how it was with Jeremiah. Some of the people he told about God made fun of him. So, he told God he wouldn't be his witness anymore. But the important information about who God is and what he wants people to do was hard for Jeremiah to keep inside. The things Jeremiah knew God wanted people to hear were so BIG that Jeremiah thought he might burst if he didn't tell everyone.

What God has done for us and the way we feel about him isn't a secret. In fact, it's something so important we're *supposed* to tell everyone we can. Who can you tell?

To learn more about witnessing, zoom to page 1080.

away. You will be forced to go as a captive to Babylon. You will die and be buried there. Your friends you have prophesied lies to will also die and be buried in Babylon!'"

Jeremiah's Fifth Complaint

7Lord, you tricked me, and I was fooled.
  You are stronger than I am. So you won.
I have become a joke.
  Everyone makes fun of me all day long.
8Every time I speak, I shout.
  I am always shouting about violence and destruction.
I tell the people about the message I received from the Lord.
  But this only brings me insults.
  The people make fun of me all day long.
9Sometimes I say to myself,
  "I will forget about the Lord.
  I will not speak anymore in his name."
But then the Lord's message becomes like a burning fire inside me.
  It feels like it burns deep within my bones.
I get tired of trying to hold the Lord's message inside of me.
  And finally, I cannot hold it in.
10I hear many people whispering about me:
  "Terror on every side!
  Let's tell the rulers about him."
My friends are all just waiting for me to make some mistake.
  They are saying,
"Maybe we can trick Jeremiah.
  Then we can defeat him.
  Then we can pay him back."

11But the Lord is with me like a strong warrior.
  So those who are chasing me will trip and fall.
  They will not defeat me.
They will be very disappointed and ashamed.
  Their shame will never be forgotten.

12Lord of heaven's armies, you test good people.
  You look deeply into the heart and mind of a person.
I have told you my arguments against these people.
  So let me see you give them the punishment they deserve.

13Sing to the Lord!
  Praise the Lord!
He saves the life of the poor.
  He saves them from the power of wicked people.

Jeremiah's Sixth Complaint

14Let there be a curse on the day I was born.
  Let there be no blessing on the day when my mother gave birth to me.
15Let there be a curse on the man who brought my father the news:
  "You have a son!"
  This made my father glad.
16Let that man be like the towns the Lord destroyed without pity.
  Let that man hear loud crying in the morning.
  And let him hear battle cries at noon.
17This is because he did not kill me before I was born.
  Then my mother would have been my grave.
  I would never have been born.
18Why did I have to come out of my mother's body?
  All I have known is trouble and sorrow.
  And my life will end in shame.

God Rejects King Zedekiah's Request

21 This is the word that the Lord spoke to Jeremiah. It came when Zedekiah king of Judah sent Pashhur son of Malkijah to Jeremiah. He also sent the priest Zephaniah son of Maaseiah. 2They said, "Ask the Lord for us what will happen. We want to know because Nebuchadnezzar king of Babylon is attacking us. Maybe the Lord will do

... did in the past. Nebuchadnezzar will leave."

... answered them, "Tell ...: "Here is what the ... Israel, says: You have ... your hands. You are ... defend yourselves ... of Babylon and the ... I will make those ... The army from Baby... the outside of the city ... bring that army into ... the city. ⁵I myself will ... you with my great power ... I am very angry with you. ... fight against you with my own ... arm. I will fight very hard ... against you in my very great anger. ⁶I will kill everything living in Jerusalem— both people and animals. They will die from terrible diseases. ⁷Then, says the Lord, I'll give Zedekiah king of Judah to Nebuchadnezzar king of Babylon. I will also give Zedekiah's officers to Nebuchadnezzar. Some of the people in Jerusalem will not die from the terrible diseases. Some will not die in battle or from hunger. I will give them also to Nebuchadnezzar king of Babylon. I will let those win who want to kill the people of Judah. So the people of Judah and Jerusalem will be killed in war. Nebuchadnezzar will not show any mercy or pity or feel sorry for them!'

⁸"Also tell this to the people of Jerusalem: 'This is what the Lord says: I will let you choose to live or die. ⁹Anyone who stays in Jerusalem will die. He will die in war or from hunger or from a terrible disease. But anyone who goes out of Jerusalem and surrenders to the Babylonians who are around the city will live. Anyone who leaves the city will save his life. ¹⁰I have decided to make trouble for this city and not to help it, says the Lord. I will give it to the king of Babylon. He will burn it with fire.'

¹¹"Tell these things to Judah's royal family: 'Hear the word of the Lord! ¹²Family of David, the Lord says these things:

You must judge people fairly every day.
Protect from criminals
the person who has been robbed.
If you don't do that, I will become very angry.
My anger will be like a fire that no one can put out.
This will happen because you have done evil things.

¹³"'Jerusalem, I am against you.
You sit on top of the mountain.
You sit over this valley, says the Lord.
You say, "No one can attack us.
No one can come into our strong city."
¹⁴But I will give you the punishment you deserve, says the Lord.
I will start a fire in your forests.
It will burn up everything around you!'"

Judgment Against Evil Kings

22 This is what the Lord says: "Go down to the palace of the king of Judah. Prophesy*ᵈ* this message there: ²'Hear the word of the Lord, king of Judah. You rule from David's throne. You and your officers, listen well! All of your people who come through these gates, listen! ³This is what the Lord says: Do what is fair and right. Protect those who have been robbed from those who robbed them. Don't do any wrong to the orphans or widows. Don't hurt them. Don't kill innocent people here. ⁴If you carefully obey these commands, this is what will happen: Kings who sit on David's throne will come through the gates of this palace. They will come with their officers and people. They will all come riding in chariots and on horses. ⁵But if you don't obey these commands, this is what the Lord says: I promise in my own name that this king's palace will become a ruin.'"

⁶This is what the Lord says about the palace where the king of Judah lives:

"This palace is tall like the forests of Gilead.

It is high like the mountains of
    Lebanon.
But I will truly make it like a desert.
It will be empty like towns where
    no one lives.
⁷I will send men to destroy the palace.
    Each man will have his weapons
      with him.
They will cut up your strong,
    beautiful cedar beams.
And they will throw them into the
    fire.

⁸"People from many nations will pass
by this city. They will ask each other,
'Why has the Lord done such a terrible thing to Jerusalem? This was such
a great city.' ⁹And the answer will be:
'It was because the people of Judah
quit following the agreement with the
Lord their God. They worshiped and
served other gods.'"

Judgment Against Jehoahaz

¹⁰Don't cry for the king who has died.
    Don't cry loudly for him.
But cry painfully for the king who
    is being taken away from here.
Cry for him because he will never
    come back again.
He will never see his homeland
    again.

¹¹This is what the Lord says about
Jehoahaz son of Josiah. Jehoahaz became king of Judah after his father died.
He has left this place. The Lord says,
"He will never come back again. ¹²He
will die where those who captured him
have taken him. He will not see this
land again."

Judgment Against Jehoiakim

¹³"How terrible it will be for him who
    builds his palace by doing evil.
He cheats people so he can build
    its upper rooms.
He is making his own people work
    for nothing.
He is not paying them for their work.
¹⁴He says, 'I will build a great palace
    for myself.
I will have large upper rooms.'

So he builds th...
    windows. ...with large
He uses cedar woo...
And he paints it re... walls.
¹⁵"Does having a lot of c...
    house
make you a great king?
Your father was satisfied ...
    food and drink.
He did what was right and ...
So everything went well for ...
¹⁶He helped those who were poo...
    needy.
So everything went well for him...
That's what it means to know God...
    says the Lord.
¹⁷"But your eyes only look for what
    you can get dishonestly.
You are always thinking about
    getting more for yourself.
You are even willing to kill innocent
    people to get it.
You are making it hard for people.
You even steal things from them."
¹⁸So this is what the Lord says to
Jehoiakim son of Josiah king of Judah:
"The people of Judah will not cry
    loudly when Jehoiakim dies.
They will not say, 'Oh, my brother,
    I am so sad!
Oh, my sister, I am so sad!'
The people of Judah will not cry for
    him, saying:
'Oh, master, oh, my king.'
¹⁹The people of Jerusalem will bury
    him like a donkey.
They will just drag his body away.
Then they will throw it outside the
    gates of Jerusalem.
²⁰"Judah, go up to Lebanon and cry out.
    Let your voice be heard in Bashan.
Cry out from Abarim.
    All your friends are destroyed!
²¹Judah, when you were successful, I
    warned you.
But you refused to listen.
You have acted like this since you
    were young.
You have not obeyed me.
²²My punishment will come like a
    storm.

And it will blow all your shepherds
away.
Your friends will be taken away as
captives.
Then you will really be ashamed.
You will be disgraced because of
all the wicked things you did.
[23]King, you live in your palace.
You are cozy in your rooms of
cedar.
But you will groan when your
punishment comes.
You will hurt like a woman giving
birth to a baby!

Judgment upon Jehoiachin

[24]"As surely as I live," says the Lord,
"I will do this to you, Jehoiachin son of
Jehoiakim king of Judah: Even if you
were a signet[d] ring on my right hand,
I would still pull you off. [25]Jehoiachin,
I will give you to Nebuchadnezzar king
of Babylon. And I will hand you over to
the Babylonians. Those are the people
you are afraid of because they want to
kill you. [26]I will throw you and your
mother into another country. Neither of
you was born there. But both of you will
die there. [27]You will want to come back.
But you will never be able to return."

[28]Jehoiachin is like a broken pot
someone threw away.
He is like something no one wants.
Why will Jehoiachin and his
children be thrown out?
Why will they be thrown into a
foreign land?
[29]Land, land, land of Judah,
hear the word of the Lord!
[30]This is what the Lord says:
"Write this down about
Jehoiachin:
He is a man who is to have no
children.
He will not be successful in his
lifetime.
And none of his children will be
successful.
None of his children will sit on the
throne of David.
They will not rule in Judah."

The Evil Leaders

23 "How terrible it will be for the
leaders of Judah. They are destroying my people. They are making
them run in all directions," says the
Lord.
[2]They are responsible for the people.
And the Lord, the God of Israel, says to
them: "You have made my people run
away in all directions. You have forced
them away. And you have not taken
care of them. So I will punish you for
the evil things you have done," says
the Lord. [3]"I sent my people to other
countries. But I will gather my people
who are left alive. And I will bring them
back to their own country. When they
are back in their own land, they will
have many children. And they will grow
in number. [4]I will place new leaders
over my people. They will take care of
my people. And my people will not be
afraid or terrified. None of them will
be lost," says the Lord.

The Good Descendant

[5]"The days are coming," says the
Lord,
"when I will raise up a good
descendant[d] in David's family.
This descendant will be a king who
will rule in a wise way.
And he will do what is fair and
right in the land.
[6]In his time Judah will be saved.
Israel will live in safety.
This will be his name:
The Lord Does What Is Right.
[7]"So the days are coming," says the
Lord, "when people will not say: 'As
surely as the Lord lives, who brought
Israel out of Egypt . . .' [8]But people will
say something new: 'As surely as the
Lord lives, who brought Israel from the
land of the north and from all the countries where he had sent them away . . .'
Then the people of Israel will live in
their own land."

False Prophets

[9]A message to the prophets:[d]
My heart is broken.

All my bones shake.
I'm like a man who is drunk.
I'm like a man who has been
  overcome with wine.
This is because of the Lord
and his holy words.
¹⁰The land of Judah is full of people
  who are guilty of adultery.ᵈ
Because of this, the Lord cursed
  the land.
And it has become very dry.
The pastures have dried up.
The people are evil.
They use their power in the wrong
  way.

¹¹"Both the prophets and the priests
  are evil.
I have seen them doing evil things
  even in my own Temple,"ᵈ
  says the Lord.
¹²"So they will be in danger.
They will be forced into darkness.
There they will be defeated.
I will bring disaster on them.
At that time I will punish those
  prophets and priests," says the
  Lord.

¹³"I saw the prophets of Samaria
  do something wrong.
I saw those prophets prophesy by
  the false god Baal.ᵈ
And they led my people, the
  Israelites, away.
¹⁴And I have seen the prophets of
  Jerusalem
  do some terrible things.
These prophets are guilty of adultery
  and live by lies.
They encourage evil people to keep
  on doing evil.
So the people don't stop sinning.
All of those people are like the city
  of Sodom.
The people of Jerusalem are like
  the city of Gomorrah to me!"

¹⁵So this is what the Lord of heaven's armies says about the prophets:
"I will make those prophets eat
  bitter food.
I will make them drink poisoned
  water.

This is because the prophets of
  Jerusalem spread wickedness
  through the whole country."

¹⁶This is what the Lord of heaven's armies says:
"Don't pay attention to the things
  those prophets are saying to
  you.
They are trying to fool you.
Those prophets talk of visions from
  their own minds.
But they did not get their visions
  from me.
¹⁷They say to those who hate me:
  'The Lord says: You will have
  peace.'
They say to those who are stubborn
  and do as they please:
  'Nothing bad will happen to you!'
¹⁸But none of these prophets has
  stood in the meeting of angels.
None of them has seen or heard
  the message of the Lord.
None of them has paid close
  attention to the Lord's message.
¹⁹Look, the punishment from the
  Lord
will come like a storm.
His anger will be like a hurricane.
It will come crashing down on the
  heads of those wicked people.
²⁰The Lord's anger will not stop
until he finishes what he plans to do.
When that day is over,
  you will understand this clearly.
²¹I did not send those prophets.
But they ran to tell their message.
I did not speak to them.
But they prophesied anyway.
²²But if they had stood in the meeting
  of angels,
they would have told my message
  to my people.
They would have turned the people
  from their evil ways.
They would have turned them
  from doing evil.

²³"I am a God who is near," says the
  Lord.
"I am also a God who is far away."
²⁴"No one can hide

where I cannot see him," says the Lord.

"I fill all of heaven and earth," says the Lord.

25"I have heard the prophets who prophesy lies in my name. They say, 'I have had a dream! I have had a dream!' 26How long will this continue in the minds of these lying prophets? They prophesy from their own wishful thinking. 27They are trying to make the people of Judah forget me. They are doing this by telling each other these dreams. They are trying to make my people forget me in the same way that their ancestors forgot me. Their ancestors forgot me and worshiped Baal. 28Straw is not the same thing as wheat!" says the Lord. "If a prophet wants to tell about his dreams, let him! But let the person who hears my message speak it truthfully! 29My message is like a fire," says the Lord. "It is like a hammer that smashes a rock!

30"So I am against the false prophets," says the Lord. "These prophets keep stealing words from each other. They say these words are from me. 31I am against the false prophets," says the Lord. "They use their own words and pretend it is a message from me. 32I am against the prophets who prophesy false dreams," says the Lord. "They mislead my people with their lies and false teachings! I did not send those prophets to teach the people. I never commanded them to do anything for me. They can't help the people of Judah at all," says the Lord.

The Sad Message from the Lord

33"The people of Judah, a prophet*d* or a priest may ask you: 'Jeremiah, what is the message from the Lord?' You will answer them and say, 'You are a heavy load to the Lord. And I will throw down this heavy load, says the Lord!' 34A prophet or a priest or one of the people might say, 'This is a message from the Lord!' That person has lied. So I will punish him and his whole family. 35This is what you will say to each

other: 'What did the Lord answer?' or 'What did the Lord say?' 36But you will never again say, 'The message of the Lord.' This is because the only message you speak is your own words. You used to change the words of our God. He is the living God, the Lord of heaven's armies. 37This is how you speak to the prophets: 'What answer did the Lord give you?' or 'What did the Lord say?' 38But don't say, 'What was the message from the Lord?' If you use these words, the Lord will say this to you: You should not have called it a message from the Lord. I told you not to use those words. 39I will pick you up like a heavy load. And I'll throw you away from me. I gave the city of Jerusalem to your ancestors and to you. But I will throw you and that city away from me. 40And I will make a disgrace of you forever. You will never forget your shame."

The Good and Bad Figs

24 I saw a vision after Nebuchadnezzar king of Babylon took Jehoiachin son of Jehoiakim as a prisoner. Jehoiachin king of Judah and his officers were taken away from Jerusalem. They were taken to Babylon. Nebuchadnezzar also took away all the craftsmen and metalworkers of Judah. It was then that the Lord showed me these things: I saw two baskets of figs. They were arranged in front of the Temple*d* of the Lord. 2One of the baskets had very good figs in it. They were like figs that ripen early in the season. But the other basket had rotten figs. They were too rotten to eat.

3The Lord said to me, "What do you see, Jeremiah?"

I answered, "I see figs. The good figs are very good. But the rotten figs are too rotten to eat."

4Then the Lord spoke his word to me. 5This is what the Lord, the God of Israel, said: "I sent the people of Judah out of their country into Babylon. Those people will be like these good figs. I think of them as good. 6I will look after them. I will bring them back to the land of Judah. I will not tear them down. I will build them up. I will not pull them up. I will plant them so they can grow. [7]I will make them want to know me. They will know that I am the Lord. They will be my people, and I will be their God. This is because they will return to me with their whole hearts.

[8]"But the bad figs are too rotten to eat," says the Lord. "Zedekiah king of Judah and his officers will be like those rotten figs. All the people from Jerusalem who are left alive will be like that. This will be true even if those people now live in Egypt. [9]I will make those people hated as an evil people by all the kingdoms of the earth. People will make fun of the people from Judah and tell jokes about them. People will point fingers at them. They will curse them everywhere I scatter them. [10]I will send war, hunger and disease against them. I will attack them until they have all been killed. Then they will no longer be in the land I gave to them and their ancestors."

A Summary of Jeremiah's Preaching

25 This is the message that came to Jeremiah concerning all the people of Judah. It came in the fourth year that Jehoiakim son of Josiah was king of Judah. This was the first year Nebuchadnezzar was king of Babylon. [2]This is the message Jeremiah the prophet[d] spoke to all the people of Judah and Jerusalem:

[3]The Lord has spoken his word to me again and again for these past 23 years. I have been a prophet since the thirteenth year of Josiah. Josiah was the son of Amon king of Judah. I have spoken messages from the Lord to you from that time until today. But you have not listened.

[4]The Lord has sent his servants the prophets to you over and over again. But you have not listened to them. You have not paid any attention to them. [5]They have said, "Stop your evil ways.

Stop doing what is wrong. Do this so you can stay in the land. This is the land that the Lord gave to you and your ancestors long ago. He gave it to you to live in forever. [6]Don't follow other gods to serve them or to worship them. You must not worship idols that are the work of someone's hands. That makes the Lord angry, and he will punish you."

[7]"But you did not listen to me," says the Lord. "You worshiped idols that were the work of someone's hands. That made me angry. So I punished you.

[8]So this is what the Lord of heaven's armies says: "You have not listened to my messages. [9]So I will soon send for all the peoples of the north," says the Lord. "I will soon send for my servant Nebuchadnezzar king of Babylon. I will bring them all against Judah and all the nations around you, too. I will completely destroy all those countries. I will leave them in ruins forever. People will be shocked when they see how badly they will be destroyed. [10]I will bring an end to the sounds of joy and happiness. There will be no more happy sounds of brides and bridegrooms. I will take away the sound of people grinding meal. And I will take away the light of the lamp. [11]That whole area will be an empty desert. And these nations will be slaves of the king of Babylon for 70 years.

[12]"But when the 70 years have passed, I will punish the king of Babylon and his nation," says the Lord. "I will punish the Babylonians for their evil. I will make that land a desert forever. [13]I have said many terrible things will happen to Babylonia. All of them will happen. Jeremiah prophesied about those foreign nations. And the warnings are written in this book. [14]The Babylonians will have to serve many nations and many great kings. I will give them the punishment they deserve. They will be punished for all the things they do."

Judgment on the Nations

[15]The Lord, the God of Israel, said this to me: "My anger is like the wine

in a cup. Take it from my hand. I am sending you to all the nations. Make them drink all of my anger from this cup. [16]They will drink my anger like wine. Then they will not be able to walk straight. They will act like madmen. They will do this because of the war that I am going to send among them."

[17]So I took the cup from the Lord's hand. I went to those nations. And I made them drink from the cup. [18]I poured this wine for the people of Jerusalem and the towns of Judah. I made the kings and officers of Judah drink from the cup. I did it so that they would become a ruin. People would be shocked when they saw how badly they were destroyed. People would insult them and speak evil of them. And it happened. Judah is like that now. [19]I also made these people drink from that cup of my anger: the king of Egypt, his servants, his officers and all his people; [20]all the Arabs, and all the kings of the land of Uz; all the kings of the Philistines (the kings of the cities of Ashkelon, Gaza, Ekron and the people left at Ashdod); [21]the people of Edom, Moab and Ammon; [22]all the kings of Tyre and Sidon; all the kings of the faraway countries; [23]the people of Dedan and Tema and Buz; all who cut their hair short; [24]all the kings of Arabia; and the kings of the people who live in the desert; [25]all the kings of Zimri, Elam and Media; [26]and all the kings of the north, near and far, one after the other. I made all the kingdoms on earth drink from the cup of the Lord's anger. But the king of Babylon will drink from this cup after all the others.

[27]"Then say this to them: 'This is what the Lord of heaven's armies, the God of Israel, says: Drink this cup of my anger. Get drunk from it and vomit. Fall down and don't get up. Don't get up because I am sending a war to kill you!'

[28]"They will refuse to take the cup from your hand. They will refuse to drink it. Then say this to them: 'The Lord of heaven's armies says this: You must drink from this cup. [29]I am already bringing disaster on Jerusalem. And it is the city that is called by my name. And do you think you will not be punished? You will be punished! I am sending war on all the people of the earth, says the Lord of heaven's armies.'

[30]"You will prophesy[d] against them with these words. Say to them:
'The Lord roars from heaven.
   He shouts from his Holy Temple.[d]
He roars against his land.
He will shout like people who walk
      on grapes to make wine.
He will shout against all who live
      on the earth.
[31]The noise will spread all over the
      earth.
   This is because the Lord is
      punishing all the nations.
He judges and tells what is wrong
      with all people.
   And he is killing the evil people
      with a sword,'" says the Lord.

[32]This is what the Lord of heaven's armies says:
"Disasters will soon spread
      from nation to nation.
They will come like a powerful
      storm
   to all the faraway places on earth."

[33]At that time the dead bodies will reach from one end of the earth to the other. No one will cry for them. No one will gather up their bodies and bury them. They will be left lying on the ground like dung.

[34]Cry, you leaders! Cry out loud!
   Roll around in the dust, leaders of
      the people!
It is now time for you to be killed.
   You will fall and be scattered
      everywhere, like pieces of a
      broken jar.
[35]There will be no place for the
      leaders to hide.
   These leaders will not escape.
[36]I hear the leaders shouting.
   I hear the leaders of the people
      crying loudly.
This is because the Lord is
      destroying their land.

[37]Those peaceful pastures will be like
an empty desert.
This happened because the Lord is
very angry.
[38]The Lord, like a lion, has left his
den.
Their land has been destroyed.
It is because of his destroying anger.
It is because of his fierce anger.

Jeremiah's Lesson at the Temple

26 This message came from the Lord. It was during the first year Jehoiakim son of Josiah was king of Judah. [2]This is what the Lord said: "Jeremiah, stand in the courtyard of the Temple[d] of the Lord. Give this message to all the people of the towns of Judah. They are coming to worship at the Temple of the Lord. Tell them everything I tell you to say. Don't leave out any part of my message. [3]Maybe they will listen and stop their evil ways. I have plans to bring disaster on them because of the evil they have done. But if they change, I will change my mind about bringing disaster on them. [4]Say to them: 'This is what the Lord says: I gave my teachings to you. You must obey me and follow my teachings. [5]You must listen to what my servants the prophets[d] say to you. I have sent prophets to you again and again. But you did not listen to them. [6]If you don't obey me, I will destroy my Temple in Jerusalem. I will destroy it as I destroyed my Holy Tent[d] at Shiloh. People all over the world will curse Jerusalem.'"

[7]The priests, the prophets and all the people heard Jeremiah. He said all of these words in the Temple of the Lord. [8]Jeremiah finished speaking everything the Lord had commanded him to say. Then the priests, prophets and all the people grabbed Jeremiah. They said, "You must die! [9]How dare you prophesy such a thing in the name of the Lord! How dare you say that this Temple will be destroyed like the one at Shiloh! How dare you say that Jerusalem will become a desert without anyone to live in it!" All the people crowded around Jeremiah in the Temple of the Lord.

[10]Now the officers of Judah heard about what was happening. So they came out of the king's palace and went up to the Temple of the Lord. There they took their places at the entrance of the New Gate. [11]Then the priests and prophets spoke to the officers and all the other people. They said, "Jeremiah should be killed. He said bad things about Jerusalem! You heard him say it."

[12]Then Jeremiah spoke to all the officers of Judah and all the other people. He said, "The Lord sent me to say these things about this Temple and this city. Everything that you have heard is from the Lord. [13]Now change your lives! You must start doing good things. You must obey the Lord your God. If you do that, the Lord will change his mind. He will not bring on you the disaster he has told you about. [14]As for me, I am in your power. Do to me what you think is good and right. [15]But if you kill me, be sure of one thing. You will be guilty of killing an innocent person. You will make this city and everyone who lives in it guilty, too! The Lord sent me to you. The message you heard is from the Lord!"

[16]Then the officers and all the people spoke. They said to the priests and the prophets, "Jeremiah must not be killed. What he told us comes from the Lord our God."

[17]Then some of the older leaders stood up. They spoke to all the people. [18]They said, "Micah the prophet was from the city of Moresheth. He was a prophet during the time Hezekiah was king of Judah. Micah said these things to all the people of Judah: 'This is what the Lord of heaven's armies says:
Jerusalem will be plowed like a field.
Jerusalem will become a pile of
rocks.
The hill where the Temple stands
will be covered with bushes.'
[19]"Hezekiah was the king of Judah. And he did not kill Micah. No one else

in Judah killed him. You know that Hezekiah feared the Lord. He wanted to please the Lord. So the Lord changed his mind. He did not bring on Judah the disaster he had promised. If we hurt Jeremiah, we will bring a terrible disaster on ourselves!"

20 (Now there was another man who prophesied in the name of the Lord. His name was Uriah the son of Shemaiah. Uriah was from the city of Kiriath Jearim. He preached the same things against this city and land that Jeremiah did. 21King Jehoiakim, all his army officers and all the leaders of Judah heard Uriah preach. King Jehoiakim wanted to kill Uriah. But Uriah heard about it and was afraid. So he escaped to Egypt. 22But King Jehoiakim sent Elnathan son of Acbor and some other men to Egypt. 23They brought Uriah back from Egypt. Then they took him to King Jehoiakim. Jehoiakim ordered Uriah to be killed with a sword. His body was thrown into the burial place where poor people are buried.)

24There was an important man named Ahikam son of Shaphan. Ahikam supported Jeremiah. So Ahikam kept Jeremiah from being killed by the people.

Nebuchadnezzar Is Made Ruler

27 The Lord spoke his word to Jeremiah. This happened when Zedekiah son of Josiah was king of Judah. 2This is what the Lord said to me: "Make a yoke^d out of straps and poles. Put it on the back of your neck. 3Then send messages to the kings of Edom, Moab, Ammon, Tyre and Sidon. Send the messages through the messengers of these kings. Those messengers have come to Jerusalem to see Zedekiah king of Judah. 4Tell them to give this message to their masters. Tell them, 'The Lord of heaven's armies, the God of Israel, says: "Tell your masters: 5I made the earth and everyone on it. I made all the animals on the earth. I did this with my great power and my strong arm. I can give the earth to anyone I want. 6Now I have given

all these lands to Nebuchadnezzar king of Babylon. He is my servant. I will make even the wild animals obey him. 7All nations will serve Nebuchadnezzar and his son and grandson. Then the time will come for Babylon to be defeated. Many nations and great kings will make Babylon their servant.

8"'But now some nations or kingdoms might refuse to serve Nebuchadnezzar king of Babylon. They might refuse to be under his control. If that happens, I will punish that nation with war, hunger and terrible sickness, says the Lord. I will do it until I destroy that nation. I will use Nebuchadnezzar to destroy the nation that fights against him. 9So don't listen to your false prophets.^d Don't listen to people who use magic to tell what will happen in the future. Don't listen to those who say they can tell what dreams mean. Don't listen to mediums^d or magicians. They all tell you, 'You will not be slaves to the king of Babylon.' 10They are telling you lies! They will only cause you to be taken far from your homeland. I will force you to leave your homes. And you will die in another land. 11But some nations will put themselves under the control of the king of Babylon. They will serve him. I will let those nations stay in their own country, says the Lord. The people from those nations will live in their own land and farm it."'"

12I gave the same message to Zedekiah king of Judah. I said, "You must put yourself under the control of the king of Babylon and serve him. If you serve him and his people, you will live. 13Why should you and your people die like those who do not serve the king of Babylon? Why should you die because of war, hunger and sickness? The Lord said this will happen. 14But the false prophets are saying this: 'You will never be slaves to the king of Babylon.' Don't listen to them because they are prophesying lies to you! 15'I did not send them,' says the Lord. 'They are prophesying lies. And they are saying the message is from me. So I will send Judah away. You will die! And those prophets who prophesy to you will die also.'"

[16]Then I, Jeremiah, said to the priests and all the people, "This is what the Lord says: Those false prophets are saying that what the Babylonians took from the Temple[d] of the Lord will be brought back soon. Don't listen to them! They are prophesying lies to you. [17]Don't listen to those prophets. But serve the king of Babylon, and you will live. There is no reason for you to cause Jerusalem to become a ruin. [18]They might be prophets and have the message from the Lord. If so, let them pray to the Lord of heaven's armies. Let them pray about the things that are still in the Temple of the Lord. Let them pray about the things that are still in the king's palace and in Jerusalem. Let them pray that all this will not be taken away to Babylon.

[19]"This is what the Lord of heaven's armies says about those things left in Jerusalem. In the Temple there are the pillars, the large bronze bowl, which is called the Sea, the stands that can be moved and other things. Nebuchadnezzar king of Babylon left them in Jerusalem. [20]Nebuchadnezzar did not take these away when he took Jehoiachin king of Judah captive. Jehoiachin was the son of King Jehoiakim. Nebuchadnezzar also took other important people away from Judah and Jerusalem. [21]This is what the Lord of heaven's armies, the God of Israel, says about the things left in the Temple of the Lord and in the king's palace and in Jerusalem: 'All of this will also be taken to Babylon. [22]And they will stay there until the day I go to get them,' says the Lord. 'Then I will bring them back and return them to this place.'"

The False Prophet Hananiah

28 It was the fifth month of King Zedekiah's fourth year as king of Judah. This was at the beginning of the king's rule. At that time Hananiah the prophet[d] spoke to me. He was the son of Azzur. And he was from the town of Gibeon. He was in the Temple[d] of the Lord when he spoke to me. In front of the priests and all the people, Hananiah said: [2]"The Lord of heaven's armies, the God of Israel, says: 'I will break the yoke[d] the king of Babylon has put on Judah. [3]Before two years are over, I will bring back everything that Nebuchadnezzar king of Babylon took from the Lord's Temple. [4]I will also bring Jehoiachin son of Jehoiakim king of Judah back here. And I will bring back all the other people of Judah as captives to Babylon,' says the Lord. 'So I will break the yoke the king of Babylon put on Judah.'"

[5]Then the prophet Jeremiah answered the prophet Hananiah. They were standing in the Temple[d] of the Lord. The priests and all the people there could hear Jeremiah's answer. [6]He said, "Amen! Let the Lord really do that! May the Lord make the message you prophesy come true. May the Lord bring everything from the Lord's Temple back from Babylon. And may he bring back to their homes all the people who were taken as captives.

[7]"But listen to what I must say to you and all the people. [8]There were prophets long before we became prophets, Hananiah. They prophesied that war, hunger and terrible sicknesses would come. They would come to many countries and great kingdoms. [9]But a prophet might prophesy that we will have peace. The message of that prophet might come true. If it does, only then can he be recognized as one truly sent by the Lord!"

[10]Then the prophet Hananiah took the yoke off Jeremiah's neck and broke it. [11]Hananiah said in front of all the people, "This is what the Lord says: 'In the same way I will break the yoke of Nebuchadnezzar king of Babylon. He put that yoke on all the nations of the world. But I will break it before two years are over.'" After Hananiah had said that, Jeremiah left the Temple.

[12]Then the Lord spoke his word to Jeremiah. This was not long after the

prophet Hananiah had broken the yoke off of the prophet Jeremiah's neck. [13]The Lord said, "Go and tell Hananiah, 'This is what the Lord says: You have broken a wooden yoke. But I will make a yoke of iron in the place of the wooden one! [14]The Lord of heaven's armies, the God of Israel, says: I will put a yoke of iron on the necks of all these nations. I will do that to make them serve Nebuchadnezzar king of Babylon. And they will be slaves to him. I will even give Nebuchadnezzar control over the wild animals.'"

[15]Then the prophet Jeremiah said to the prophet Hananiah, "Listen, Hananiah! The Lord did not send you. And you have made the people of Judah trust in lies. [16]So this is what the Lord says: 'Soon I will remove you from the earth. You will die this year. This is because you taught the people to turn against the Lord.'"

[17]Hananiah died in the seventh month of that same year.

A Letter to the Jews in Babylon

29 Jeremiah the prophet[d] sent a letter to the people taken as captives to Babylon. He sent it to the older leaders who were among the captives, the priests and the prophets. And he sent it to all the other people Nebuchadnezzar had taken from Jerusalem to Babylon. [2](This letter was sent after all these people were taken away: Jehoiachin and the queen mother; the officers and leaders of Judah and Jerusalem; and the craftsmen and metalworkers.) [3]Zedekiah king of Judah had sent Elasah son of Shaphan and Gemariah son of Hilkiah to King Nebuchadnezzar. So Jeremiah gave the letter to them to take to Babylon. This is what the letter said:

[4]This is what the Lord of heaven's armies, the God of Israel, says to all those people he sent away from Jerusalem as captives to Babylon: [5]"Build houses and settle in the land. Plant gardens and eat the food you grow. [6]Get married and have sons and daughters. Find wives for your sons. Let your daughters be married so they may also have sons and daughters. Have many children and grow in number in Babylon. Don't become fewer in number. [7]Also do good things for the city where I sent you as captives. Pray to the Lord for the city where you are living. If there is peace in that city, you will have peace also." [8]The Lord of heaven's armies, the God of Israel, says: "Don't let your prophets and the people who do magic fool you. Don't listen to their dreams. [9]They are prophesying lies. And they are saying that their message is from me. But I did not send them," says the Lord.

"**K**ids, just wait 'til you read in Jeremiah 29:11-13 about the plans God has for you."

[10]This is what the Lord says: "Babylon will be powerful for 70 years. After that time I will come to you who are living in Babylon. I will keep my promise to bring you back to Jerusalem. [11]I say this because I know what I have planned for you," says the Lord. "I have good plans for you. I don't plan to hurt you. I plan to give you hope and a good future. [12]Then you will call my name. You will come to me and pray to me. And I will listen to you. [13]You will search for me. And when you search for me with all your heart, you will find me! [14]I will let you find me," says the Lord. "And I will bring you back from your captivity. I forced you to leave this place. But I will gather you from all the nations. I will gather you from the places I have sent you as captives," says the Lord. "And I will bring you back to this place."

¹⁵You might say, "The Lord has given us prophets here in Babylon."

¹⁶But the Lord says this about the king who is sitting on David's throne now. And I'm also talking about all the other people still in Jerusalem. These are your relatives who did not go to Babylon with you. ¹⁷The Lord of heaven's armies says: "I will soon send war, hunger and terrible diseases against those still in Jerusalem. I will make them like bad figs that are too rotten to eat. ¹⁸I will chase them with war, hunger and terrible diseases. I will make them a hated people by all the kingdoms of the earth. People will speak evil of them. They will be shocked when they hear what has happened. And people will use them as a shameful example wherever I make them go. ¹⁹This is because those in Jerusalem have not listened to my message," says the Lord. "I sent my message to them again and again. I used my servants, the prophets, to give my messages to them. But they did not listen," says the Lord.

²⁰You captives, I forced you to leave Jerusalem and go to Babylon. So listen to the message from the Lord. ²¹The Lord of heaven's armies says this about Ahab son of Kolaiah. And he says it about Zedekiah son of Maaseiah: "These two men have been prophesying lies to you. They have said that their message is from me. But I will hand over those two prophets to Nebuchadnezzar king of Babylon. And Nebuchadnezzar will kill them in front of you who are captives in Babylon. ²²Because of this, all the captives from Judah will use this curse: 'May the Lord treat you like Zedekiah and Ahab. The king of Babylon burned them with fire.' ²³They have done evil things among the people of Israel. They are guilty of adultery*d* with their neighbors' wives. They have also spoken lies. And they said those lies were a message from me, the

Lord. I did not tell them to do that. I know what they have done. I am a witness!" says the Lord.

²⁴Also give a message to Shemaiah. He is from the Nehelamite family. ²⁵The Lord of heaven's armies, the God of Israel, says: "Shemaiah, you sent letters to all the people in Jerusalem. And you sent letters to the priest Zephaniah son of Maaseiah. You also sent letters to all the priests. You sent those letters in your own name. ²⁶You said to Zephaniah, 'The Lord has made you priest in place of Jehoiada. You are to be in charge of the Temple*d* of the Lord. You should arrest any madman who acts like a prophet. You should lock the hands and feet of that person between wooden blocks. And put iron rings around his neck. ²⁷Now Jeremiah from Anathoth is acting like a prophet. So why haven't you arrested him? ²⁸Jeremiah has sent this message to us in Babylon: You will be there for a long time. So build houses and settle down. Plant gardens and eat what you grow.'"

²⁹Zephaniah the priest read the letter to Jeremiah the prophet. ³⁰Then the Lord spoke his word to Jeremiah: ³¹"Send this message to all the captives in Babylon: 'This is what the Lord says about Shemaiah the Nehelamite: Shemaiah has prophesied to you, but I did not send him. He has made you believe a lie. ³²Because Shemaiah has done that, this is what the Lord says: I will soon punish Shemaiah the Nehelamite. He will not see the good things I will do for my people, says the Lord. None of his family will be left alive among the people. This is because he has taught the people to turn against me.'"

Promises of Hope

30 These are the words that the Lord spoke to Jeremiah. ²The Lord, the God of Israel, said: "Jeremiah, write in a book all the words I have spoken to you. ³The days will come when I will make everything as good as it was before," says the Lord. "I will bring Israel and Judah back from captivity," says the Lord. "I will return them to the land I gave their ancestors. Then my people will own that land again!"

⁴The Lord spoke this message about the people of Israel and Judah: ⁵This is what the Lord said:

"We hear people crying from fear.
　They are afraid. There is no peace.
⁶Ask this question, and consider it:
　A man cannot have a baby.
So why do I see every strong man
　holding his stomach in pain like a
　woman having a baby?
Why is everyone's face turning
　white like a dead man's face?
⁷This will be a terrible day!
　There will never be another time
　like this.
This is a time of great trouble for
　the people of Jacob.
But they will be saved from it."

⁸The Lord of heaven's armies says,
　"At that time
I will break the yoke*ᵈ* from their
　necks.
And I will break the ropes holding
　them.
Foreign people will never again
　make my people slaves!
⁹They will serve the Lord their God.
　And they will serve David their king.
　I will send that king to them.

¹⁰"So people of Jacob, my servants,
　don't be afraid!
Israel, don't be frightened," says
　the Lord.
"I will save you from that faraway
　place where you are captives.
I will save your family from that
　land.
The people of Jacob will be safe and
　have peace again.
There will be no enemy to frighten
　them.
¹¹I am with you and will save you,"
　says the Lord.
"I scattered you among those
　nations.
Even if I completely destroy all
　those nations,

I will not destroy you.
You will be punished fairly.
　But I will punish you."

¹²This is what the Lord said:
"You people have a wound that
　cannot be cured.
　Your injury will not heal.
¹³There is no one to argue your case.
　There is no cure for your sores.
　So you will not be healed.
¹⁴All those nations who were your
　friends have forgotten you.
　They don't care about you.
I hurt you as an enemy would.
　I punished you very hard.
I did this because your guilt was so
　great.
I did this because your sins were
　so many.
¹⁵Why are you crying about your injury?
　There is no cure for your pain.
I, the Lord, did these things to you
　because of your great guilt.
I did these things because of your
　many sins.
¹⁶But those nations that destroyed
　you will now be destroyed.
　Your enemies will become captives.
Those who stole from you will have
　their own things stolen.
Those who took things from you
　in war will have their own
　things taken.
¹⁷I will bring back your health.
　And I will heal your injuries," says
　the Lord.
"This is because other people forced
　you out from among them.
Those people said about you, 'No
　one cares about Jerusalem!'"

¹⁸This is what the Lord said:
"I will make the tents of Jacob's
　people as they used to be.
And I will have pity on Israel's
　houses.
The city will be rebuilt on its hill of
　ruins.
And the king's palace will stand in
　its proper place.
¹⁹People in those places will sing
　songs of praise.

There will also be the sound of
laughter.
I will give them many children.
They will not be small.
I will bring honor to them.
No one will look down on them.
20 Their descendants[d] will be like they
were in the old days.
I will make their people strong
before me.
And I will punish the nations who
have hurt them.
21 One of their own people will lead
them.
Their ruler will come from among
them.
He will come near to me when I
invite him.
Who would dare to come
uninvited?" says the Lord.
22 "So you will be my people,
and I will be your God."

23 The Lord was very angry.
He punished the people.
And the punishment came like a
storm.
It came like a hurricane against
the evil people.
24 The Lord will stay angry
until he finishes punishing the
people.
He will stay angry
until he finishes the punishment
he planned.
When that day comes,
you will understand this.

The New Israel

31 The Lord says, "At that time I
will be God of all Israel's family
groups. And they will be my people."
2 This is what the Lord says:
"Some of the people were not killed
by the enemy's sword.
Those people will find help in the
desert.
I have come to give rest to Israel."

3 And from far away the Lord appeared to his people. He said,
"I love you people
with a love that will last forever.

I became your friend
because of my love and kindness.
4 People of Israel, I will build you up
again,
and you will be rebuilt.
You will pick up your tambourines[d]
again.
You will dance with those who are
joyful.
5 You will plant vineyards again
on the hills around Samaria.
The farmers will plant them
and enjoy their fruit.
6 There will be a time when
watchmen in the mountains of
Ephraim shout this message:
'Come, let's go up to Jerusalem to
worship the Lord our God!'"

7 This is what the Lord says:
"Be happy and sing for the people of
Jacob.
Shout for Israel, the greatest of the
nations.
Sing your praises and shout this:
'Lord, save your people!
Save those who are left alive from
the nation of Israel!'
8 Look, I will bring Israel from the
country in the north.
I will gather them from the
faraway places on earth.
Some of the people are blind and
crippled.
Some of the women will be pregnant
and ready to give birth.
A great many people will come
back.
9 Those people will be crying as they
come back.
But they will pray as I bring them
back.
I will lead those people by streams
of water.
I will lead them on an even road
where they will not stumble.
This is because I am Israel's father.
And Israel is my firstborn[d] son.

10 "Nations, listen to the message from
the Lord.
Tell this message in the faraway
lands by the sea:

'The one who scattered the people
of Israel will bring them back
together.
And he will watch over his people
like a shepherd.'
¹¹ The Lord will bring the people of
Jacob back.
The Lord will buy them back from
people stronger than they
were.
¹² The people of Israel will come to the
high points of Jerusalem.
There they will shout for joy.
Their faces will shine with
happiness about all the good
things from the Lord:
the grain, new wine, oil, young
sheep and cows.
They will be like a garden that has
plenty of water.
And the people of Israel will not be
troubled anymore.
¹³ Then young women of Israel will be
happy and dance.
The young men and old men will
also dance.
I will change their sadness into
happiness.
I will give them comfort and joy
instead of sadness.
¹⁴ The priests will have more than
enough sacrifices.
And my people will be filled with
the good things I give them!"
says the Lord.

¹⁵ This is what the Lord says:
"A sound was heard in Ramah.
It was painful crying and much
sadness.
Rachel cries for her children.
And she cannot be comforted,
because her children are dead!"

¹⁶ But this is what the Lord says:
"Stop crying.
Don't let your eyes fill with tears.
You will be rewarded for your
work!" says the Lord.
"The people will come back from
their enemy's land.
¹⁷ So there is hope for you!" says the
Lord.

"Your children will come back to
their own land.

¹⁸ "I have heard Israel moaning:
'Lord, you punished me, and I
have learned my lesson.
I was like a calf that had never
been trained.
Take me back, and I will come back.
You truly are the Lord my God.
¹⁹ Lord, I wandered away from you.
But I changed my heart and life.
Once I understood,
I beat my breast with sorrow.
I am ashamed and disgraced
because of the foolish things I did
when I was young.'

²⁰ "You know that Israel is my dear son.
I love that child.
Yes, I often speak against Israel,
but I still remember him.
I love him very much.
And I want to comfort him," says
the Lord.

²¹ "People of Israel, fix the road signs.
Put up the signs that show you the
way home.
Watch the road.
Pay attention to the road on which
you travel.
People of Israel, come home.
Come back to your towns.
²² You are an unfaithful daughter.
How long will you wander before
you come home?
The Lord will make something new
happen in the land:
A woman will go seeking a man."

²³ The Lord of heaven's armies, the
God of Israel, says: "I will again do good
things for the people of Judah. At that
time the people in the land of Judah and
its towns will again say: 'May the Lord
bless you. You are a righteous dwelling.
You are a holy mountain.' ²⁴ People in
all the towns of Judah will live together in peace. Farmers and those who
move around with their flocks will live
together in peace. ²⁵ I will give rest and
strength to those who are weak and
tired."

26After hearing that, I, Jeremiah, woke up and looked around. My sleep had been very pleasant.

27The Lord says, "The days are coming when I will help the families of Israel and Judah to grow. I will help their children and animals to grow, too. It will be like planting and caring for a plant. 28In the past I watched over Israel and Judah, but I watched for the time to pull them up. I tore them down. I destroyed them. I brought disaster to them. But now I will watch over them to build them up and make them strong," says the Lord. 29"At that time people will no longer say:

'The fathers have eaten sour grapes.
  And that caused the children to
    grind their teeth from the sour
    taste.'

30But each person will die for his own sin. The person who eats sour grapes will grind his own teeth.

The New Agreement

31"Look, the time is coming," says the Lord,
  "when I will make a new
    agreement.
  It will be with the people of Israel
    and the people of Judah.
32It will not be like the agreement
  I made with their ancestors.
  That was when I took them by the
    hand
    to bring them out of Egypt.
  I was a husband to them,
    but they broke that agreement,"
    says the Lord.
33"I will make this agreement
  with the people of Israel," says the
    Lord.
  "I will put my teachings in their
    minds.
  And I will write them on their
    hearts.
  I will be their God,
    and they will be my people.
34People will no longer have to teach
    their neighbors and relatives
    to know the Lord.

This is because all people will
    know me,
  from the least to the most
    important," says the Lord.
"I will forgive them for the wicked
    things they did.
  I will not remember their sins
    anymore."

The Lord Will Never Leave Israel

35This is what the Lord says:
  "The Lord makes the sun shine in
    the day.
  And he makes the moon and stars
    shine at night.
  He stirs up the sea so that its
    waves crash on the shore.
  The Lord of heaven's armies is his
    name.
36"Only if these laws should ever fail,"
    says the Lord,
  "will Israel's descendants*d* stop
    being a nation before me."

37This is what the Lord says:
  "There's only one way I will reject
    all the descendants of Israel.
  That is if people can measure the
    sky above.
  It is if they can learn the secrets of
    the earth below.
  Then I will reject them because of
    what they have done," says the
    Lord.

The New Jerusalem

38The Lord says, "The days are coming when Jerusalem will be rebuilt for me. Everything from the Tower of Hananel to the Corner Gate will be rebuilt. 39The measuring line will stretch from the Corner Gate straight to the hill of Gareb. Then it will turn to the place named Goah. 40There is the whole valley where dead bodies and ashes are thrown. It will be holy to the Lord. And all the terraces out to the Kidron Valley will be included. They are on the east as far as the corner of the Horse Gate. All that area will be holy to the Lord. The city of Jerusalem will never again be torn down or destroyed."

Jeremiah Buys a Field

32 This is the word the Lord spoke to Jeremiah. It was in the tenth year that Zedekiah was king of Judah. The tenth year of Zedekiah was the eighteenth year of Nebuchadnezzar. ²At that time the army of Babylon was surrounding Jerusalem. Jeremiah was under arrest in the courtyard of the guard. This courtyard was at the palace of the king of Judah.

³Zedekiah king of Judah had put Jeremiah in prison there. Zedekiah had asked, "Why have you prophesied*ᵈ* the things you have?" (Jeremiah had said, "This is what the Lord says: 'I will soon give the city of Jerusalem to the king of Babylon. Nebuchadnezzar will capture this city. ⁴Zedekiah king of Judah will not escape from the army of the Babylonians. But he will surely be given to the king of Babylon. And Zedekiah will speak to the king of Babylon face to face. Zedekiah will see him with his own eyes. ⁵The king of Babylon will take Zedekiah to Babylon. Zedekiah will stay there until I have punished him,' says the Lord. 'If you fight against the Babylonians, you will not succeed.'")

⁶While Jeremiah was prisoner, he said, "The Lord spoke his word to me. He said: ⁷Jeremiah, your cousin Hanamel will come to you soon. He is the son of your uncle Shallum. Hanamel will say to you, 'Jeremiah, you are my nearest relative. So buy my field near the town of Anathoth. It is your right and your responsibility to buy that field.'

⁸"Then it happened just as the Lord had said. My cousin Hanamel came to me in the courtyard of the guard. He said to me, 'Buy my field near Anathoth in the land of Benjamin. Buy that land for yourself. It is your right to buy it and own it.' So I knew this was a message from the Lord.

⁹"I bought the field at Anathoth from my cousin Hanamel. I weighed out seven ounces of silver for him. ¹⁰I signed the record that showed I now owned the field. And I had a copy of the record sealed up. Some men witnessed it and signed it also. And I weighed out the silver on the scales. ¹¹Then I took the sealed copy of the record of ownership. And I took the copy that was not sealed. ¹²And I gave them to Baruch son of Neriah. Neriah was the son of Mahseiah. The sealed copy of the record of ownership had all the demands and limits of my purchase. I gave this paper of ownership to Baruch. It was while my cousin Hanamel and the other witnesses were there. Those witnesses also signed the record of ownership. There were also many Jews sitting in the courtyard. And they saw me give the record of ownership to Baruch.

¹³"With all the people watching, I said to Baruch, ¹⁴'This is what the Lord of heaven's armies, the God of Israel, says: Take both copies of the record of ownership. Take both the sealed copy and the copy that was not sealed. And put them in a clay jar. Do this so that they will last a long time. ¹⁵This is what the Lord of heaven's armies, the God of Israel, says: In the future my people will once again buy houses. They will also buy fields for grain and vineyards in the land of Israel.'

¹⁶"I gave the record of ownership to Baruch son of Neriah. Then I prayed to the Lord. I said: ¹⁷Oh, Lord God, you made the skies and the earth. You made them with your very great power. There is nothing too wonderful for you to do. ¹⁸Lord, you show love and kindness to thousands of people. But you also bring punishment to children for their fathers' sins. Great and powerful God, your name is the Lord of heaven's armies. ¹⁹You plan and do great things, Lord. You see everything that people do. You reward people for the way they live and for what they do. ²⁰Lord, you did miracles*ᵈ* and wonderful things in the land of Egypt. You have kept on doing them even until today. You did miracles in Israel and among the other nations. You have become well known. ²¹Lord, you used signs and miracles and brought your people, the Israelites, out of Egypt. You used your great

power and strength to do those things. You brought great terror on everyone. [22]Lord, you gave this land to the people of Israel. This is the land you promised to their ancestors long ago. It's a land where much food grows. [23]The people of Israel came into this land and took it for their own. But those people did not obey you. They did not follow your teachings. They did not do the things you commanded. So you made all these terrible things happen to them.

[24]"And now, the enemy has surrounded the city. They are building roads to the top of the walls. There will be war, hunger and terrible diseases. These will cause the city to be handed over to the Babylonians. They are attacking the city now. Lord, you said this would happen. And now you see it is happening. [25]But now, Lord God, you are telling me, 'Buy the field with silver. Choose some men to watch while I purchase it.' You are telling me this while the Babylonian army is ready to capture the city."

[26]Then the Lord spoke his word to Jeremiah: [27]"I am the Lord. I am the God of every person on the earth. You know that nothing is impossible for me. [28]So this is what I say: I will soon give the city of Jerusalem to the Babylonian army. And I will give it to Nebuchadnezzar king of Babylon. That army will capture the city. [29]The Babylonian army is already attacking the city of Jerusalem. They will soon enter the city and start a fire to burn down the city. They will also burn down the houses. The people of Jerusalem made me angry. They offered sacrifices to Baal[d] on the roofs[n] of their houses. And the people poured out drink offerings to other idols. [30]The people of Israel and Judah have done only the things I said were wrong. They have done this since they were young. They have made me angry by worshiping idols made with their own hands," says the Lord. [31]"From the day Jerusalem was built

until now, they have made me very angry. Jerusalem has made me so angry I must remove it from my sight. [32]I will destroy it. This is because of the evil the people of Israel and Judah have done. The people, their kings and officers have made me angry. Their priests and prophets have made me angry. All the men of Judah and the people of Jerusalem have made me angry. [33]They turned their backs to me. I tried to teach them again and again. But they wouldn't listen to me. I tried to correct them, but they wouldn't listen. [34]They put their hated idols in the place where I have chosen to be worshiped. In this way they made it unclean.[d] [35]In the Valley of Ben Hinnom those people built places to worship Baal. They built them so they could burn their sons and daughters as sacrifices to Molech.[d] But I never commanded them to do such a hated thing. I never even thought of it! This would make Judah sin.

[36]"You are saying, 'There will be war, hunger and terrible diseases. So the city will be handed over to the king of Babylon.' But the Lord, the God of Israel, says: [37]I have forced the people of Israel and Judah to leave their land. I was very furious and angry with them. But I will gather them from the land where I forced them to go. I will bring them back to this place. I will let them live in peace and safety. [38]The people of Israel and Judah will be my people. And I will be their God. [39]I will make them want to be truly one people. They will have one goal. They will truly want to worship me all their lives. They will do this for their own good and for their children after them.

[40]"I will make an agreement with them. This agreement will last forever. And I will never turn away from them. I will always be good to them. I will make them want to respect me. Then they will never turn away from me. [41]I will enjoy doing good to them.

---

[n]**roofs** In Bible times houses were built with flat roofs. The roof was used for drying things such as flax and fruit. And it was used as an extra room, as a place for worship and as a place to sleep in the summer.

And I will surely plant them in this land and make them grow. I will do this with my whole being."

⁴²This is what the Lord says: "I have brought this great disaster to the people of Israel and Judah. In the same way I will bring good things to them. I promise to do good things for them. ⁴³You are saying, 'This land is an empty desert. There are no people or animals here. The Babylonian army defeated this country.' But in the future, people will once again buy fields in this land. ⁴⁴They will use their money and buy fields. They will sign and seal their agreements. People will witness their signing records of ownership. They will again buy fields in the land of Benjamin and in the area around Jerusalem. They will buy fields in the towns of Judah and in the mountains. They will buy them in the western mountain slopes and in southern Judah. This is because I will make everything as good as it once was," says the Lord.

The Promise of God

33 Now Jeremiah was still locked up in the courtyard of the guards. And the Lord spoke his word to him a second time: ²"The Lord made the earth. He made it, and he keeps it safe. The Lord is his name. This is what the Lord says: ³'Judah, pray to me, and I will answer you. I will tell you important secrets. You have never heard these things before.' ⁴The Lord is the God of Israel. He says these things about the houses in Jerusalem and the royal palaces of Judah. They have been torn down to be used against the attack by the Babylonian army. ⁵The Lord says, 'Some people will come to fight against the Babylonians. They will fill these houses with dead bodies. I killed those people in my hot anger. I have turned away from this city because of all the evil its people have done.

⁶"'But then I will bring health and heal the people there. I will let them enjoy peace and safety. ⁷I will make good things happen to Judah and Israel

again. I will make them strong as in the past. ⁸They sinned against me. But I will wash away that sin. They did evil and turned away from me, but I will forgive them. ⁹Then Jerusalem will be a wonderful place! People who live there will be happy. And people from all nations will praise it. This will happen because they will hear about the good things I am doing there. They will be surprised and shocked at the good things and peace I will bring to Jerusalem.'

¹⁰"You are saying, 'Our country is an empty desert. There are no people or animals living there.' It is now quiet in the streets of Jerusalem and in the towns of Judah. There are no people or animals there either. But it will be noisy there soon! ¹¹There will be sounds of joy and gladness. There will be the happy sounds of brides and bridegrooms. There will be the sounds of people bringing their offerings to the Temple[d] of the Lord. Their offerings will be to show thanks to the Lord. They will say,

'Praise the Lord of heaven's armies!
  The Lord is good!
  His love continues forever!'

They will say this because I will again do good things for Judah. It will be as in the beginning," says the Lord.

¹²This is what the Lord of heaven's armies says: "This place is empty now. There are no people or animals living here. But there will be shepherds in all the towns of Judah. And there will be pastures where they let their flocks of sheep rest. ¹³Shepherds will again count their sheep as the sheep walk in front of them. People will be counting their sheep all around the country. They will count them in the mountains and in the western mountain slopes. They will count them in southern Judah and the land of Benjamin. They will count them around Jerusalem and the other towns of Judah!"

The Good Branch

¹⁴The Lord says, "The time is coming

when I will do the things I promised. I made a special promise to the people of Israel and Judah. ¹⁵In those days and at that time,

I will make a righteous branch
     sprout from David's
     family.
He will do what is fair and right in
     the land.
¹⁶At this time Judah will be
     saved.
The people of Jerusalem will live
     in safety.
The branch will be named:
     The Lord Does What Is
     Right."

¹⁷This is what the Lord says: "Someone from David's family will always sit on the throne. And he will rule the family of Israel. ¹⁸And there will always be priests from the family of Levi. Those priests will always stand before me. And they will offer burnt offerings and grain offerings. And they will offer sacrifices to me."

¹⁹The Lord spoke his word to Jeremiah. ²⁰"This is what the Lord says: I have an agreement with day and night. I agreed that they will continue forever. Day and night will always come at the right times. If you could change that agreement, ²¹you could also change my agreement with David and Levi. Only then would descendants*d* from my servant David not be the kings on their thrones. And only then would the family of Levi not be priests serving me in the Temple.*d* ²²But I will give many descendants to my servant David. And I will give them to the family group of Levi who serve me in the Temple. They will be as many as the stars in the sky that no one can count. And they will be as many as the grains of sand on the seashore that no one can count."

²³The Lord spoke his word to Jeremiah: ²⁴"Jeremiah, have you heard what the people are saying? They are saying: 'The Lord turned away from the two families of Israel and Judah. He chose those people. But now he doesn't think of them as a nation anymore!'"

²⁵This is what the Lord says: "If I had not made my agreement with day and night, and if I had not made the laws for the sky and earth, ²⁶only then might I turn away from Jacob's descendants. And only then I might not let the descendants of David my servant rule over the descendants of Abraham, Isaac and Jacob. And I will be kind to those people. I will cause good things to happen to them again."

A Warning to Zedekiah

34 The Lord spoke his word to Jeremiah. It came when Nebuchadnezzar king of Babylon was fighting against Jerusalem and all the towns around it. Nebuchadnezzar had with him all his army. And he had the armies of all the kingdoms and peoples he ruled. ²This is what the Lord, the God of Israel, said: "Jeremiah, go to Zedekiah king of Judah and tell him: 'This is what the Lord says: I will hand the city of Jerusalem over to the king of Babylon very soon. And he will burn it down! ³You will not escape from the king of Babylon. You will surely be caught and given to him. You will see the king of Babylon with your own eyes. He will talk to you face to face. And you will go to Babylon. ⁴But, Zedekiah king of Judah, listen to the promise of the Lord. This is what the Lord says about you: You will not be killed with a sword. ⁵You will die in a peaceful way. People made funeral fires to honor your ancestors, who ruled before you. In the same way, people will make a funeral fire to honor you. They will cry for you. They will sadly say, "Ah, master!" I myself make this promise to you, says the Lord.'"

⁶So Jeremiah the prophet*d* gave the message from the Lord to Zedekiah in Jerusalem. ⁷This was while the army of the king of Babylon was fighting against Jerusalem. It was also fighting against the cities of Judah that had not been taken prisoners—Lachish and Azekah. These were the only strong, walled cities left in the land of Judah.

Slaves Are Free

⁸King Zedekiah had made an agreement with all the people in Jerusalem. He agreed to give freedom to all the Hebrew slaves. After Zedekiah made that agreement, the Lord spoke his word to Jeremiah. ⁹Everyone was supposed to free his Hebrew slaves. This included all male and female Hebrew slaves. No one was to keep a fellow Jew as a slave. ¹⁰So the officers and all the people accepted this agreement. Everyone would free their male and female slaves. They would no longer keep them as slaves. So all the slaves were set free. ¹¹But after that, the people who had slaves changed their minds. So they took back the people they had set free. And they made them slaves again.

¹²Then the Lord spoke his word to Jeremiah: ¹³"This is what the Lord, the God of Israel, says: I brought your ancestors out of Egypt where they were slaves. When I did that, I made an agreement with them. ¹⁴I said to your ancestors: 'At the end of every seven years, each one of you must set his Hebrew slaves free. You might have a fellow Hebrew who has sold himself to you. You must let him go free after he has served you for six years.' But your ancestors did not listen or pay attention to me. ¹⁵A short time ago you changed your hearts and did what is right. Each of you gave freedom to his fellow Hebrews who were slaves. And you even made an agreement before me. You made it in the place where I have chosen to be worshiped. ¹⁶But now you have changed your minds. You have shown you do not honor me. Each of you has taken back the male and female slaves you had set free. You have forced them to become slaves again.

¹⁷"So this is what the Lord says: You have not obeyed me. You have not given freedom to your fellow Hebrews. Because you have not kept the agreement, I will give freedom, says the Lord. I will give freedom to war. And I will give freedom to terrible diseases and to hunger to kill you. I will make you hated by all the kingdoms of the earth. ¹⁸I will hand over the men who broke my agreement. They have not kept the promises they made before me. These men cut a calf into two pieces before me. And they walked between the two pieces."ⁿ ¹⁹These people made the agreement before me: the leaders of Judah and Jerusalem; the officers of the court; the priests and all the people of the land. ²⁰So I will hand those people over to their enemies. I will hand them over to everyone who wants to kill them. Their bodies will become food for the birds of the air. And they will become food for the wild animals of the earth. ²¹I will hand Zedekiah king of Judah and his officers over to their enemies. I will hand them over to everyone who wants to kill them. I will hand Zedekiah and his people over to the army of the king of Babylon. I will do this even though that army has left Jerusalem. ²²I will give the order, says the Lord, to bring the Babylonian army back to Jerusalem. That army will fight against Jerusalem. They will capture it, set it on fire and burn it down. I will destroy the towns in the land of Judah. And they will become empty ruins. No one will live there!"

The Recabite Family

35 When Jehoiakim son of Josiah was king of Judah, the Lord spoke his word to Jeremiah. This was his message: ²"Jeremiah, go to the family of Recab. Invite them to come to one of the side rooms of the Temple*d* of the Lord. Offer them wine to drink."

³So I went to get Jaazaniah son of Jeremiah.ⁿ Jeremiah was the son of Habazziniah. And I gathered all of Jaazaniah's brothers and sons. I gathered the whole

---

ⁿ**they walked . . . pieces** This showed that the men were willing to be killed, like this animal, if they did not keep their agreement.
ⁿ**Jeremiah** Not the prophet Jeremiah, but a different man with the same name.

family of the Recabites together. ⁴Then I brought them into the Temple of the Lord. We went into the room of the sons of Hanan son of Igdaliah. Hanan was a man of God. The room was next to the one where the officers stay. It was over the room of Maaseiah son of Shallum. Maaseiah was the doorkeeper in the Temple. ⁵Then I put some bowls full of wine and some cups before the Recabite family. And I said to them, "Drink some wine."

⁶But the Recabite people answered, "We never drink wine. It is because of our ancestor Jonadab son of Recab. He gave us this command: 'You and your descendants^d must never drink wine. ⁷Also you must never build houses, plant seeds or plant vineyards. You must never do any of those things. You must live only in tents. Then you will live a long time in the land where you are a wanderer.' ⁸So we Recabites have obeyed everything Jonadab our ancestor commanded us. We never drink wine. And our wives, sons and daughters never drink wine. ⁹We never build houses in which to live. And we never own fields or vineyards. And we never plant crops. ¹⁰We have lived in tents. And we have obeyed everything our ancestor Jonadab commanded us. ¹¹But Nebuchadnezzar king of Babylon attacked the country of Judah. We said to each other, 'Come, we must enter Jerusalem. This is so we can escape the Babylonian army and the Aramean army.' So we have stayed in Jerusalem."

¹²Then the Lord spoke his word to Jeremiah: ¹³"This is what the Lord of heaven's armies, the God of Israel, says: Jeremiah, go and tell the men of Judah and the people of Jerusalem: 'You should learn a lesson and obey my message,' says the Lord. ¹⁴'Jonadab son of Recab ordered his sons not to drink wine. And that command has been obeyed. Until today the descendants of Jonadab obeyed their ancestor's command. They do not drink wine. But I am the Lord. I have given you messages again and again. But you did not

obey me. ¹⁵I sent my servants the prophets to you again and again. They said to you, "Each of you must stop doing evil. You must change and be good. Do not follow other gods to serve them. If you obey me, you will live in the land I have given to you and your ancestors." But you have not listened or paid attention to my message. ¹⁶The descendants of Jonadab obeyed the commands that their ancestor gave them. But the people of Judah have not obeyed me.'

¹⁷"So the Lord God of heaven's armies, the God of Israel, says: 'I said many disasters would come to Judah and on everyone living in Jerusalem. I will soon bring every one of those disasters on them. I spoke to those people, but they refused to listen. I called out to them, but they did not answer me.'"

¹⁸Then Jeremiah said to the Recabites, "This is what the Lord of heaven's armies, the God of Israel, says: 'You have obeyed the commands of your ancestor Jonadab. You have followed all of Jonadab's teachings. You have done everything he commanded.' ¹⁹So this is what the Lord of heaven's armies, the God of Israel, says: 'There will always be a descendant of Jonadab son of Recab to serve me.'"

Jehoiakim Burns Jeremiah's Scroll

36 The Lord spoke his word to Jeremiah. This was during the fourth year that Jehoiakim son of Josiah was king of Judah. This was his message: ²"Jeremiah, get a scroll. Write on it all the words I have spoken to you about Israel and Judah and all the nations. Write everything I have spoken to you since Josiah was king until now. ³Maybe the family of Judah will hear what disasters I am planning to bring on them. And maybe they will stop doing wicked things. Then I would forgive them for the sins and the evil things they have done."

⁴So Jeremiah called for Baruch son of Neriah. Jeremiah spoke the messages the Lord had given him. And

Baruch wrote those messages on the scroll. [5]Then Jeremiah said to Baruch, "I cannot go to the Temple[d] of the Lord. I must stay here. [6]So I want you to go to the Temple of the Lord. Go there on a day when the people are giving up eating. Read to all the people of Judah from the scroll. These people come into Jerusalem from the towns where they live. Read the messages from the Lord. Read the words that you wrote on the scroll as I spoke them to you. [7]Perhaps they will ask the Lord to help them. Perhaps each one will stop doing wicked things. The Lord has announced that he is very angry with them." [8]So Baruch son of Neriah did everything Jeremiah the prophet[d] told him to do. He read aloud the scroll that had the Lord's messages written on it. He read it in the Lord's Temple.

who had come into Jerusalem from the towns of Judah was supposed to give up eating. [10]At that time Baruch read the scroll that contained Jeremiah's words. Baruch read the scroll in the Temple of the Lord to all the people there. He was in the room of Gemariah son of Shaphan. Gemariah was a royal assistant. That room was in the upper courtyard at the entrance of the New Gate of the Temple.

[11]A man named Micaiah son of Gemariah, the son of Shaphan, heard all the messages from the Lord. Baruch read them from the scroll. [12]Micaiah went down to the royal assistant's room in the king's palace. All of the officers were sitting there: Elishama the royal assistant; Delaiah son of Shemaiah; Elnathan son of Acbor; Gemariah son of Shaphan; Zedekiah son of Hananiah; and all the other officers. [13]Micaiah told those officers everything he had heard Baruch read from the scroll.

Unsung Heroes

BARUCH • JEREMIAH 36

Baruch was a hero because he wrote a lot! The prophet Jeremiah was in prison for telling God's words to the people. Baruch was Jeremiah's helper. Jeremiah could not speak to the people from prison, so he told God's words to Baruch, who wrote all the words on a scroll. A scroll was a long piece of papyrus (like paper) that was rolled up from both ends. Then Baruch went to the temple and read Jeremiah's words from the scroll. But the king took the scroll and burned it because he didn't want to hear God's words. So then what happened? Baruch just got another scroll and wrote all the words again!

Like Baruch, we should keep doing what God wants us to, even if other people don't like it.

To read about a hero who rescued a prophet, fly to page 936.

[9]It was the ninth month of the fifth year that Jehoiakim son of Josiah was king. A special time to give up eating was announced. All the people of Jerusalem were supposed to give up eating to honor the Lord. And everyone

[14]Then the officers sent a man named Jehudi son of Nethaniah to Baruch. (Nethaniah was the son of Shelemiah, who was the son of Cushi.) Jehudi said to Baruch, "Bring the scroll that you read to the people and come with me."

So Baruch son of Neriah took the scroll and went with Jehudi to the officers. ¹⁵Then the officers said to Baruch, "Sit down and read the scroll to us."

So Baruch read the scroll to them. ¹⁶When the officers heard all the words, they became afraid. And they looked at one another. They said to Baruch, "We must certainly tell the king about these words." ¹⁷Then the officers asked Baruch, "Tell us, Baruch, where did you get these words you wrote on the scroll? Did you write down what Jeremiah said to you?"

¹⁸"Yes," Baruch answered. "Jeremiah spoke, and I wrote down all the words with ink on this scroll."

¹⁹Then the officers said to Baruch, "You and Jeremiah must go and hide. Don't tell anyone where you are hiding."

²⁰Then the officers put the scroll in the room of Elishama the royal assistant. Then they went to the king in the courtyard and told him all about the scroll. ²¹So King Jehoiakim sent Jehudi to get the scroll. Jehudi brought the scroll from the room of Elishama the royal assistant. Then Jehudi read the scroll to the king. And he read it to all the officers who stood around the king. ²²This happened in the ninth month of the year. So King Jehoiakim was sitting in the winter apartment. There was a fire burning in a small firepot in front of him. ²³Jehudi began to read from the scroll. But after he had read three or four columns, the king cut those columns off of the scroll with a pen knife. And he threw them into the firepot. Finally, the whole scroll was burned in the fire. ²⁴King Jehoiakim and his servants heard the message from the scroll. But they were not frightened! They did not tear their clothes to show their sorrow. ²⁵Elnathan, Delaiah and Gemariah tried to talk King Jehoiakim into not burning the scroll. But the king would not listen to them. ²⁶Instead, the king ordered some men to arrest Baruch the secretary and Jeremiah the prophet. Those men were Jerahmeel son of the king, Seraiah son of Azriel and Shelemiah son of Abdeel. But the Lord had hidden Baruch and Jeremiah.

²⁷The Lord spoke his word to Jeremiah. This happened after King Jehoiakim had burned the scroll. This was the scroll where Baruch had written all the words Jeremiah had spoken to him. The Lord said: ²⁸"Jeremiah, get another scroll. Write all the words on it that were on the first scroll. That was the scroll that Jehoiakim king of Judah burned up. ²⁹Also say this to Jehoiakim king of Judah: 'This is what the Lord says: You burned up that scroll. You said, "Why did Jeremiah write that the king of Babylon will come and destroy this land? Why did he say the king of Babylon will destroy both men and animals in it?" ³⁰So the Lord says this about Jehoiakim king of Judah: Jehoiakim's descendants*ᵈ* will not sit on David's throne. When Jehoiakim dies, his body will be thrown out on the ground. It will be left out in the heat of the day. And it will also be left in the cold frost of the night. ³¹I, the Lord, will punish Jehoiakim and his children. And I will punish his servants. I will do this because they have done evil things. I have promised to bring disasters upon them. And I will bring them upon all the people in Jerusalem and Judah, just as I promised. This is because they have not listened to me.'"

³²So Jeremiah took another scroll and gave it to Baruch. Baruch son of Neriah was his secretary. As Jeremiah spoke, Baruch wrote on the scroll. He wrote the same words that were on the scroll Jehoiakim king of Judah had burned in the fire. And many other words like those words were added to the second scroll.

Jeremiah in Prison

37 Nebuchadnezzar was king of Babylon. He appointed Zedekiah son of Josiah as king of Judah. Zedekiah took the place of Jehoiachin son of Jehoiakim. ²But Zedekiah, his servants and the people of Judah did not listen to the words of the Lord. The Lord had spoken his words through Jeremiah the prophet.*d*

³Now King Zedekiah sent Jehucal and Zephaniah with a message to Jeremiah the prophet. Jehucal was the son of Shelemiah. And Zephaniah the priest was the son of Maaseiah. This was the message: "Jeremiah, pray to the Lord our God for us."

⁴At that time Jeremiah had not yet been put into prison. So he was free to go anywhere he wanted. ⁵The army of the king of Egypt had marched from Egypt toward Judah. Now the Babylonian army had surrounded the city of Jerusalem so they could attack it. Then they had heard about the Egyptian army marching toward them. So the Babylonian army left Jerusalem to fight the Egyptian army.

⁶The Lord spoke his word to Jeremiah the prophet: ⁷"This is what the Lord, the God of Israel, says: Jehucal and Zephaniah, I know Zedekiah king of Judah sent you to ask me questions. Tell this to King Zedekiah: 'The army of the king of Egypt marched out of Egypt. They came here to help you against the Babylonian army. But that army will go back to Egypt. ⁸After that, the Babylonian army will come back here. And they will attack Jerusalem. Then the Babylonian army will take and burn Jerusalem.'

⁹"This is what the Lord says: People of Jerusalem, do not fool yourselves. Do not say to yourselves: 'The Babylonian army will surely leave us alone.' They will not! ¹⁰You might defeat all of the Babylonian army that is attacking you. But there would still be a few injured men left in their tents. Even those injured men would come from their tents and burn down Jerusalem!"

¹¹So the Babylonian army left Jerusalem. They left to fight the army of the king of Egypt. ¹²Now Jeremiah wanted to travel from Jerusalem to his home in the land of Benjamin. He was going there to get his share of the property that belonged to his family.

¹³Jeremiah got to the Benjamin Gate of Jerusalem. But then the captain in charge of the guards arrested him. The captain's name was Irijah son of Shelemiah son of Hananiah. So Irijah the captain arrested Jeremiah. Irijah said, "You are leaving us to join the Babylonian side!"

¹⁴Jeremiah said to Irijah, "That's not true! I am not leaving to join the Babylonians." But Irijah refused to listen to Jeremiah. So he arrested Jeremiah and took him to the officers of Jerusalem. ¹⁵Those rulers were very angry with Jeremiah. They gave an order for him to be beaten. Then they put him in prison in the house of Jonathan the royal assistant. Jonathan's house had been made into a prison. ¹⁶So those people put Jeremiah into a cell in a dungeon. And Jeremiah was there for a long time.

¹⁷Then King Zedekiah sent for Jeremiah and had him brought to the palace. Zedekiah talked to Jeremiah in private. He asked Jeremiah, "Is there any message from the Lord?"

Jeremiah answered, "Yes, there is a message from the Lord. Zedekiah, you will be handed over to the king of Babylon." ¹⁸Then Jeremiah said to King Zedekiah, "What crime have I done against you? What crime have I done to your officers or the people of Jerusalem? Why have you thrown me into prison? ¹⁹Where are your prophets now? Those prophets prophesied this message to you: 'The king of Babylon will not attack you or this land of Judah.' ²⁰But now, my master, king of Judah, please listen to me. And please do what I ask of you. Do not send me back to the house of Jonathan the royal assistant. If you do, I will die there!"

²¹So King Zedekiah gave orders for Jeremiah to be put under guard in the courtyard. And he ordered that Jeremiah be given bread from the street of the bakers. Jeremiah was to be given bread until there was no more bread in the city. So he stayed under guard in the courtyard.

Jeremiah Is Thrown into a Well

38 Some of the officers heard what Jeremiah was prophesying.[d] They were Shephatiah son of Mattan, Gedaliah son of Pashhur, Jehucal son of Shelemiah and Pashhur son of Malkijah. Jeremiah was telling all the people this message: [2]"This is what the Lord says: 'Everyone who stays in Jerusalem will die in war. Or he will die of hunger or terrible diseases. But everyone who surrenders to the Babylonian army will live. They will escape with their lives and live.' [3]And this is what the Lord says: 'This city of Jerusalem will surely be handed over to the army of the king of Babylon. He will capture this city!'"

[4]Then the officers said to the king, "Jeremiah must be put to death! He is making the soldiers who are still in the city become discouraged. He is discouraging everyone by the things he is saying. He does not want good to happen to us. He wants to ruin the people of Jerusalem."

[5]King Zedekiah said to them, "Jeremiah is in your control. I cannot do anything to stop you!"

[6]So the officers took Jeremiah and put him into the well of Malkijah, the king's son. That well was in the courtyard of the guards. The officers used ropes to lower Jeremiah into the well. It did not have any water in it, only mud. And Jeremiah sank down into the mud.

[7]But Ebed-Melech heard that the officers had put Jeremiah into the well. Ebed-Melech was a Cushite, and he was a eunuch[d] in the palace. King Zedekiah was sitting at the Benjamin Gate. [8]So Ebed-Melech left the palace and went to the king. Ebed-Melech said, [9]"My master and king, the rulers have acted in an evil way. They have treated Jeremiah the prophet badly! They have thrown him into a well! They have left him there to die! When there is no more bread in the city, he will starve."

[10]Then King Zedekiah commanded Ebed-Melech the Cushite: "Ebed-Melech, take 30 men from the palace with you. Go and lift Jeremiah the prophet out of the well before he dies."

[11]So Ebed-Melech took the men with him. And he went to a room under the

Unsung Heroes
EBED-MELECH • JEREMIAH 38:6-13

If it hadn't been for the kindness of a royal official named Ebed-Melech, Jeremiah would have been left to die in a deep well. Jeremiah had been telling the people what God said, but they didn't like it. The king wanted to keep him quiet, so he put him in a well. This was a large hole in the ground lined with rocks. It was a place to collect rainwater for drinking and washing. Sometimes a well would be full of water. The one Jeremiah was put into was full of mud. Ebed-Melech went to the king and asked him to release Jeremiah. Then he helped pull Jeremiah out of the well. Jeremiah was able to keep speaking for God to the people.

God wants us to stand up for people who are serving him. How can you help someone who is serving God?

To read about a hero who risked his reputation, fly to page 1214.

storeroom in the palace. He took some old rags and worn-out clothes from that room. Then he let those rags down with some ropes to Jeremiah in the well. ¹²Ebed-Melech the Cushite said to Jeremiah, "Put these old rags and worn-out clothes under your arms. They will be pads for the ropes." So Jeremiah did as Ebed-Melech said. ¹³The men pulled Jeremiah up with the ropes and lifted him out of the well. And Jeremiah stayed under guard in the courtyard.

Zedekiah Questions Jeremiah

¹⁴Then King Zedekiah sent someone to get Jeremiah the prophet.ᵈ He had Jeremiah brought to the third entrance to the Templeᵈ of the Lord. Then the king said to Jeremiah, "I am going to ask you something. Do not hide anything from me. But tell me everything honestly."

¹⁵Jeremiah said to Zedekiah, "If I give you an answer, you will probably kill me. And even if I give you advice, you will not listen to me."

¹⁶But King Zedekiah made a secret promise to Jeremiah. He said, "As surely as the Lord lives who has given us breath and life, I will not kill you. And I promise not to give you to the officers who want to kill you."

¹⁷Then Jeremiah said to Zedekiah, "This is what the Lord God of heaven's armies, the God of Israel, says: 'You must surrender to the officers of the king of Babylon. Then your life will be saved. And Jerusalem will not be burned down. And you and your family will live. ¹⁸You must not refuse to surrender to the officers of the king of Babylon. If you do, Jerusalem will be given to the Babylonian army. They will burn Jerusalem down. And you will not escape from them.'"

¹⁹Then King Zedekiah said to Jeremiah, "I'm afraid of some of the Jews. They have already gone over to the side of the Babylonian army. I'm afraid the Babylonians may hand me over to them. And they will treat me badly."

²⁰But Jeremiah answered, "The Babylonians will not hand you over to the Jews. Obey the Lord by doing what I tell you. Then things will go well for you. And your life will be saved. ²¹But if you refuse to surrender to the Babylonians, the Lord has shown me what will happen. ²²All the women left in the palace of the king of Judah will be brought out. They will be taken to the important officers of the king of Babylon. Your women will make fun of you with this song:

'Your good friends led you the
     wrong way and were stronger
     than you.
Those were friends that you trusted.
Your feet are stuck in the mud.
Your friends have left you.'

²³"All your wives and children will be brought out. They will be given to the Babylonian army. You yourself will not even escape from them. You will be taken prisoner by the king of Babylon. And Jerusalem will be burned down."

²⁴Then Zedekiah said to Jeremiah, "Do not tell anyone that I have been talking to you. If you do, you will die. ²⁵Those officers might find out that I talked to you. Then they will come to you and say, 'Tell us what you said to King Zedekiah. And tell us what King Zedekiah said to you. Don't keep any secrets from us. If you don't tell us everything, we will kill you.' ²⁶If they ask you, tell them this: 'I was begging the king not to send me back to Jonathan's house to die.'"

²⁷The officers did come to question Jeremiah. So he told them everything the king had ordered him to say. Then the officers said no more to Jeremiah. This was because no one had heard what Jeremiah and the king had discussed. ²⁸So Jeremiah stayed under guard in the courtyard until the day Jerusalem was captured.

The Fall of Jerusalem

39 This is how Jerusalem was captured: ¹Nebuchadnezzar king of Babylon marched against Jerusalem with his whole army. He surrounded the city to attack it. This was during the tenth month of the ninth year Zedekiah was king of Judah. ²This lasted until the ninth day of the fourth month in Zedekiah's eleventh year. Then the city wall was broken through. ³And all the officers of the king of Babylon came into Jerusalem. They sat down at the Middle Gate. They were Nergal-Sharezer of the district of Samgar; Nebo-Sarsekim, a chief officer; Nergal-Sharezer, an important leader; and all the other important officers.

⁴When Zedekiah king of Judah and all his soldiers saw them, they ran away. They left Jerusalem at night and went out from the king's garden. They went through the gate that was between the two walls. Then they headed toward the Jordan Valley. ⁵But the Babylonian army chased them. They caught up with Zedekiah in the plains of Jericho. They captured him and took him to Nebuchadnezzar king of Babylon. Nebuchadnezzar was at Riblah in the land of Hamath. There Nebuchadnezzar passed his sentence on Zedekiah. ⁶There at Riblah the king of Babylon killed Zedekiah's sons as he watched. And Nebuchadnezzar killed all the important officers of Judah as Zedekiah watched. ⁷Then he put out Zedekiah's eyes. He put bronze chains on Zedekiah and took him to Babylon.

⁸The Babylonians set fire to the palace. And they set fire to the houses of the people of Jerusalem. And they broke down the walls around Jerusalem. ⁹Nebuzaradan was commander of the king's special guards. He took the people left in Jerusalem as captives. He also took those captives who had surrendered to him earlier. And he took the rest of the people of Jerusalem. He carried them all away to Babylon. ¹⁰But Nebuzaradan, commander of the guard, left some of the poor people of Judah behind. They were the people who owned nothing. So on that day he gave them vineyards and fields.

¹¹Nebuchadnezzar had given these orders about Jeremiah through Nebuzaradan, commander of the guard: ¹²"Find Jeremiah and take care of him. Do not hurt him. Give him whatever he asks for." ¹³So these men sent for Jeremiah: Nebuzaradan, commander of the guards; Nebushazban, a chief officer; Nergal-Sharezer, an important leader; and all the other officers of the king of Babylon. ¹⁴They had Jeremiah taken out of the courtyard of the guard. They turned him over to Gedaliah son of Ahikam son of Shaphan. Gedaliah had orders to take Jeremiah back home. So they took him home, and he stayed among his own people.

¹⁵While Jeremiah was guarded in the courtyard, the Lord spoke his word to him: ¹⁶"Jeremiah, go and tell Ebed-Melech the Cushite this message: 'This is what the Lord of heaven's armies, the God of Israel, says: Very soon I will make my words about Jerusalem come true. They will come true through disaster, not through good times. You will see everything come true with your own eyes. ¹⁷But I will save you on that day, Ebed-Melech, says the Lord. You will not be handed over to the people you fear. ¹⁸I will surely save you, Ebed-Melech. You will not die from a sword. But you will escape and live. This will happen because you have trusted in me, says the Lord.'"

Jeremiah Is Set Free

40 The Lord spoke his word to Jeremiah. This was after Nebuzaradan, commander of the guards, had set Jeremiah free at the city of Ramah. He had found Jeremiah in Ramah bound in chains. He was with all the captives from Jerusalem and Judah. They were being taken away to Babylon. ²When commander Nebuzaradan found Jeremiah, Nebuzaradan said to him, "The Lord your God announced this disaster would come to this place. ³And now the Lord has done everything he said he would do. This disaster happened because the people of Judah sinned against the Lord. You people did not obey the Lord. ⁴But now I will set you free. I am taking the chains off your wrists. If you want to, come with me to Babylon. And I will take good care of you. But if you don't want to come, then don't. Look, the whole country is open to you." ⁵Before Jeremiah turned to leave, Nebuzaradan said, "Or go back to Gedaliah son of Ahikam, the son of Shaphan. The king of Babylon has chosen Gedaliah to be governor over the towns of Judah. Go and live with Gedaliah among the people. Or go anywhere you want."

Then Nebuzaradan gave Jeremiah some food and a present and let him go. ⁶So Jeremiah went to Gedaliah son of Ahikam at Mizpah. And Jeremiah stayed with him there. He lived among the people who were left behind in Judah.

The Short Rule of Gedaliah

⁷There were some officers and their men from the army of Judah. These men were still out in the open country. They heard that the king of Babylon had put Gedaliah son of Ahikam in charge. He was put in charge of the people who were left in the land: the men, women and children who were very poor. They were the ones who were not carried off to Babylon as captives. ⁸So these soldiers came to Gedaliah at Mizpah. They were Ishmael son of Nethaniah, and Johanan and Jonathan sons of Kareah. Also Seraiah son of Tanhumeth and the sons of Ephai the Netophathite came. And Jaazaniah son of the Maacathite and their men came. ⁹Gedaliah son of Ahikam, the son of Shaphan, made a promise to them. Gedaliah said, "Do not be afraid to serve the Babylonians. Live in the land and serve the king of Babylon. Then everything will go well for you. ¹⁰I myself will live in Mizpah. I will speak for you before the Babylonians who come here. You harvest the wine, the summer fruit and the oil. Put what you harvest in your storage jars. Live in the towns you control."

¹¹Some Jews were in Moab, Ammon, Edom and other countries. They heard that the king of Babylon had left a few Jews alive in the land. And they heard the king of Babylon had chosen Gedaliah as governor over them. (Gedaliah was the son of Ahikam, the son of Shaphan.) ¹²When the people of Judah heard this news, they came back to Judah. They came back to Gedaliah at Mizpah. They came from all the countries where they had been scattered. They gathered a large harvest of wine and summer fruit.

¹³Johanan son of Kareah came to Gedaliah at Mizpah. All the army officers of Judah still in the open country also came. ¹⁴Johanan and the officers with him said to Gedaliah, "Don't you know that Baalis king of the Ammonite people wants you dead? He has sent Ishmael son of Nethaniah to kill you." But Gedaliah son of Ahikam did not believe them.

¹⁵Then Johanan son of Kareah spoke to Gedaliah in private at Mizpah. He said to Gedaliah, "Let me go and kill Ishmael son of Nethaniah. No one will know anything about it. We should not let Ishmael kill you. All the Jews gathered around you would be scattered to different countries again. Then the few people of Judah who are left alive would be lost."

¹⁶But Gedaliah son of Ahikam said to Johanan son of Kareah, "Do not kill Ishmael! The things you are saying about Ishmael are not true!"

41 In the seventh month Ishmael son of Nethaniah came to Gedaliah son of Ahikam. (Nethaniah was the son of Elishama.) Ishmael came with ten of his men to Mizpah. Now Ishmael was a member of the king's family. He had been one of the officers of the king of Judah. Ishmael and his men ate a meal with Gedaliah at Mizpah. ²While they were eating together, Ishmael and his ten men got up. They killed Gedaliah son of Ahikam with a sword. Gedaliah was the man the king of Babylon had chosen as governor over Judah. ³Ishmael killed all the Jews with

Gedaliah at Mizpah, too. He also killed the Babylonian soldiers who were there with Gedaliah.

⁴⁵The day after Gedaliah was murdered, 80 men came to Mizpah. They were bringing grain offerings and incense*d* to the Temple*d* of the Lord. Those 80 men had shaved off their beards, torn their clothes and cut themselves.*n* They came from Shechem, Shiloh and Samaria. None of them knew that Gedaliah had been murdered. ⁶Ishmael son of Nethaniah went out from Mizpah to meet them. He cried as he walked. When he met them, he said, "Come with me to meet Gedaliah son of Ahikam." ⁷So they went into Mizpah. Then Ishmael son of Nethaniah and his men killed 70 of them! They threw the bodies into a deep well. ⁸But the 10 men who were left alive said to Ishmael, "Don't kill us! We have wheat and barley. And we have oil and honey. We have hidden these things in a field." So Ishmael let those 10 men alone. He did not kill them with the others. ⁹Now the well where he had thrown the bodies had been made by King Asa. Asa had made the well as a part of his defenses against Baasha king of Israel. But Ishmael son of Nethaniah put dead bodies in it until it was full.

¹⁰Ishmael captured all the other people in Mizpah. He captured the king's daughters and all the other people who were left there. They were the people whom Nebuzaradan commander of the guard had chosen Gedaliah son of Ahikam to take care of. So Ishmael son of Nethaniah captured those people. And he started to cross over to the country of the Ammonites.

¹¹Johanan son of Kareah heard about all the evil things Ishmael son of Nethaniah had done. All the army officers with him heard it, too. ¹²So Johanan and the army officers took their men and went to fight Ishmael son of Nethaniah. They caught him near the big pool of water at Gibeon. ¹³The captives Ishmael had taken saw Johanan and the army officers. And they became very happy. ¹⁴Then all the people Ishmael had taken captive turned around. They ran to Johanan son of Kareah. ¹⁵But Ishmael son of Nethaniah and eight of his men escaped from Johanan. And they ran away to the Ammonites.

¹⁶So Johanan son of Kareah and all his army officers saved the captives. Ishmael son of Nethaniah had murdered Gedaliah son of Ahikam. Then he had taken those people from Mizpah. Among those left alive were soldiers, women, children and court officers. Johanan brought them back from the town of Gibeon.

The Escape to Egypt

¹⁷⁻¹⁸Johanan and the other army officers were afraid of the Babylonians. The king of Babylon had chosen Gedaliah son of Ahikam to be governor of Judah. But Ishmael son of Nethaniah had murdered Gedaliah. So Johanan was afraid that the Babylonians would be angry. They decided to run away to Egypt. On the way they stayed at Geruth Kimham, near the town of Bethlehem.

42 While there, Johanan son of Kareah and Jezaniah son of Hoshaiah went to Jeremiah the prophet.*d* All the army officers went with Johanan and Jezaniah. All the people, from the least important to the greatest, all went along, too. ²They said to him, "Jeremiah, please listen to what we ask. Pray to the Lord your God. Pray for all the people left alive from the family of Judah. At one time there were many of us. You can see that there are few of us now. ³So pray that the Lord your God will tell us where we should go. And pray he will tell us what we should do."

⁴Then Jeremiah the prophet answered, "I understand what you want me to do. I will pray to the Lord your God as you have asked. I will tell you everything he says. I will not hide anything from you."

---

*n***shaved . . . themselves** The men did this to show they were sad about the Temple in Jerusalem being destroyed.

[5]Then the people said to Jeremiah, "We will do everything the Lord your God tells us. If we don't, may the Lord be a true and loyal witness against us. We know he will send you to tell us what to do. [6]It does not matter if we like the message or not. We will obey the Lord our God. We are sending you to the Lord for a message from him. We will obey what he says. Then good things will happen to us."

[7]Ten days later the Lord spoke his word to Jeremiah. [8]Then Jeremiah called for Johanan son of Kareah and the army officers who were with him. Jeremiah also called all the other people, from the least important to the greatest. [9]Then Jeremiah said to them, "You sent me to ask the Lord for what you wanted. This is what the Lord, the God of Israel, says: [10]'If you will stay in Judah, I will make you strong. I will not destroy you. I will plant you, and I will not pull you up. This is because I am sad about the disaster I brought on you. [11]Now you are afraid of the king of Babylon. But don't be afraid of him. Don't be afraid of the king of Babylon,' says the Lord. 'I am with you. I will save you. I will rescue you from his power. [12]I will be kind to you. And the king of Babylon will also treat you with mercy. He will bring you back to your land.'

[13]"But you might say, 'We will not stay in Judah.' If you say that, you will disobey the Lord your God. [14]Or you might say, 'No, we will go and live in Egypt. We will not be bothered with war there. We will not hear the trumpets of war. And in Egypt we will not be hungry.' [15]If you say that, listen to the message of the Lord. It is to you who are left alive from Judah. This is what the Lord of heaven's armies, the God of Israel, says: 'If you make up your mind to go and live in Egypt, these things will happen: [16]You are afraid of war. But it will defeat you in the land of Egypt. And you are worried about hunger. But you will be hungry in Egypt. You will die there. [17]Everyone who goes to live in Egypt will die in war. Or he

will die from hunger or terrible disease. No one who goes to Egypt will live. No one will escape the terrible things I will bring to them.'

[18]"This is what the Lord of heaven's armies, the God of Israel, says: 'I showed my anger against Jerusalem. I punished the people who lived in Jerusalem. In the same way I will show my anger against you when you go to Egypt. Other nations will speak evil of you. People will be shocked by what has happened to you. You will become a curse word. People will insult you. And you will never see Judah again.'

[19]"You who are left alive in Judah, the Lord has told you, 'Don't go to Egypt.' I warn you today. [20]You are making a mistake that will cause your deaths. You sent me to the Lord your God. You said to me, 'Pray to the Lord our God for us. Tell us everything the Lord says, and we will do it.' [21]So today I have told you the message from the Lord. But you have not obeyed the Lord your God. You have not done all that he sent me to tell you to do. [22]So now be sure you understand this: You want to go to live in Egypt. But you will die by war, hunger or terrible diseases."

43

So Jeremiah finished telling the people the message from the Lord their God. He told them everything the Lord their God had sent him to tell them.

[2]Azariah son of Hoshaiah, Johanan son of Kareah and some other men were too proud. They said to Jeremiah, "Jeremiah, you are lying! The Lord our God did not send you to say, 'You must not go to Egypt to live there.' [3]Baruch son of Neriah is causing you to be against us. He wants you to hand us over to the Babylonians. Then they will kill us. Or they will capture us and take us to Babylon."

[4]So Johanan, the army officers and all the people disobeyed the Lord's command. He had commanded them to stay in Judah. [5]But Johanan son of Kareah and the army officers took those who were left alive from Judah to Egypt.

These were the people who had run away from the Babylonians to other countries. But they had come back to Judah. ⁶Now Johanan and the army officers took the men, women and children. Among those people were the king's daughters. And they led them to Egypt. Nebuzaradan commander of the guard had put Gedaliah in charge of those people. (Gedaliah was the son of Ahikam son of Shaphan.) Johanan also took Jeremiah the prophet*d* and Baruch son of Neriah. ⁷These people did not listen to the Lord. So they all went to Egypt to the town of Tahpanhes.

⁸In Tahpanhes the Lord spoke his word to Jeremiah: ⁹"Take some large stones. Bury them in the clay in the brick pavement. This is in front of the king of Egypt's palace in Tahpanhes. Do this while the Jews are watching you. ¹⁰Then say to them, 'This is what the Lord of heaven's armies, the God of Israel, says: I will send for my servant, Nebuchadnezzar king of Babylon. And I will set his throne over these stones I have buried. He will spread his covering for shade above these stones. ¹¹He will come here and attack Egypt. He will bring death to those who are supposed to die. He will make prisoners of those who are to be taken captive. And he will bring war to those who are to be killed with a sword. ¹²Nebuchadnezzar will set fire to the temples of the gods of Egypt. He will burn those temples. And he will take the idols away. A shepherd wraps himself in his clothes. In the same way Nebuchadnezzar will wrap Egypt around him. Then he will safely leave Egypt. ¹³He will destroy the stone pillars in the temple of the sun god in Egypt. And he will burn down the temples of the gods of Egypt.'"

Disaster in Egypt

44 Jeremiah received a message from the Lord. It was for all the Jews living in Egypt. It was for the Jews in Migdol, Tahpanhes, Memphis and southern Egypt. This was the message:

²"The Lord of heaven's armies, the God of Israel, says: You saw the terrible things I brought on Jerusalem and the towns of Judah. Those towns are empty ruins today. ³And it is because the people who lived there did evil. Those people burned incense*d* to other gods. And that made me angry! Your people and your ancestors did not worship those gods before. ⁴I sent my prophets*d* to them again and again. Those prophets were my servants. They spoke my message and said to the people, 'Don't do this terrible thing. The Lord hates for you to worship other gods.' ⁵But they did not listen to the prophets. They did not pay attention. They did not stop doing evil things. They did not stop burning incense to other gods. ⁶So I showed my great anger against them. I punished the towns of Judah and the streets of Jerusalem. My anger made Jerusalem and the towns of Judah empty. They are only ruins and piles of stones today.

⁷"So the Lord of heaven's armies, the God of Israel, says: Why are you doing such great harm to yourselves by continuing to worship other gods? You are cutting off the men and women, children and babies from the family of Judah. So you leave yourselves without anyone from the family of Judah. ⁸Why do you want to make me angry by making idols? Why do you burn incense to the gods of Egypt, where you have come to live? You will destroy yourselves. Other nations will speak evil of you. And all the other nations on the earth will make fun of you. ⁹Have you forgotten about the evil things your ancestors did? And have you forgotten the evil the kings and queens of Judah did? Have you forgotten about the evil you and your wives did? They did these things in Judah and in the streets of Jerusalem. ¹⁰Even to this day the people of Judah are still too proud. They have not learned to respect me. And they have not followed my teachings. They have not obeyed the laws I gave you and your ancestors!

[11]"So this is what the Lord of heaven's armies, the God of Israel, says: I am determined to bring disasters on you. I will destroy the whole family of Judah. [12]There were a few left alive from Judah. They were determined to go to Egypt and settle there. But they will all die in Egypt. They will be killed in war or die from hunger. From the least important to the greatest, they will be killed in war or die from hunger. Other nations will speak evil about them. People will be shocked by what has happened to them. They will become a curse word. People will insult them. [13]I will punish those people who have gone to live in Egypt. I will use swords, hunger and terrible diseases to punish them. I will punish them just as I punished Jerusalem. [14]Of the people of Judah who were left alive and have gone to Egypt none will escape my punishment. They want to return to Judah and live there. But none of them will live to return to Judah. None of them will return to Judah, except a few people who escape."

[15]A large group of the people of Judah, who lived in southern Egypt, were meeting together. Among them were many women of Judah who lived in Egypt. They were burning incense to other gods, and their husbands knew it. All these people said to Jeremiah, [16]"We will not listen to the message from the Lord that you spoke to us. [17]We promised to make sacrifices to the Queen Goddess![d] And we will do everything we promised. We will burn incense and pour out drink offerings to worship her. We did that in the past. And our ancestors, kings and officers did that in the past. All of us did those things in the towns of Judah and in the streets of Jerusalem. At that time we had plenty of food. We were successful. Nothing bad happened to us. [18]But then we stopped making sacrifices to the Queen Goddess. And we stopped pouring out drink offerings to her. Since then we have had problems. Our people have been killed in war and by hunger."

[19]The women said, "Our husbands knew what we were doing. We had their permission to burn incense to the Queen Goddess! We had their permission to pour out drink offerings to her. Our husbands knew we were making cakes that looked like her and that we poured out drink offerings to her."

[20]Then Jeremiah spoke to all the people—men and women—who answered him. [21]He said to them, "The Lord remembered that you burned incense. You burned it in the towns of Judah and in the streets of Jerusalem. You and your ancestors, kings and officers did that. And the people of the land did that. The Lord remembered and thought about it. [22]Then he could not be patient with you any longer. He hated the terrible things you did. So he made your country an empty desert. No one lives there now. Other people curse that country. [23]All this happened because you burned incense to other gods. You sinned against the Lord. You did not obey him. You did not follow his teachings or the laws he gave you. You did not keep your part of the agreement. This disaster has happened. It is there for you to see."

[24]Then Jeremiah spoke to all those men and also to the women. He said, "People of Judah who are now in Egypt, hear the word of the Lord: [25]The Lord of heaven's armies, the God of Israel, says: You women did what you said you would do. You said, 'We will keep the promises we made. We promised to make sacrifices to the Queen Goddess. And we promised to pour out drink offerings to her.' So, go ahead. Do the things you promised you would do. Keep your promises. [26]But hear the word of the Lord. Listen, all you Jews living in Egypt. The Lord says, 'I use my great name and make this promise: The people of Judah now living in Egypt will never again use my name to make promises. They will never again say, "As surely as the Lord God lives . . ." [27]I am watching over them. I am not watching over them to take care of them, but to hurt them. The Jews who

live in Egypt will die from swords or hunger until they are all destroyed. [28]Some people will escape being killed by the sword. They will come back to Judah from Egypt. But there will only be a very few who escape. Then, of the people of Judah who came to live in Egypt, those who are left alive will know. They will know whether my word or their word came true. [29]I will give you a sign that I will punish you here in Egypt,' says the Lord. 'Then you will know my promises to hurt you will really happen.' [30]This is what the Lord says: 'Hophra king of Egypt has enemies who want to kill him. I will hand over King Hophra to his enemies. I will do this just as I handed Zedekiah king of Judah over to Nebuchadnezzar king of Babylon. Nebuchadnezzar wanted to kill Zedekiah.'"

A Message to Baruch

45 It was the fourth year that Jehoiakim son of Josiah was king of Judah. Jeremiah the prophet[d] told these things to Baruch son of Neriah. And Baruch wrote them on a scroll. This is what Jeremiah said to Baruch: [2]"This is what the Lord, the God of Israel, says to you: [3]Baruch, you have said, 'How terrible it is for me! The Lord has given me sorrow along with my pain. I am tired because of my suffering. I cannot rest.'"

[4]The Lord said, "Say this to Baruch: 'This is what the Lord says: I will tear down what I have built. And I will pull up what I have planted. I will do that everywhere in Judah. [5]Baruch, you are looking for great things for yourself. Don't do that! Don't look for them because I will bring disaster on all the people. The Lord says these things! You will have to go many places. But I will let you escape alive wherever you go.'"

Messages About the Nations

46 The Lord spoke this word to Jeremiah the prophet[d] about the nations:

[2]This message is about Egypt: This message is about the army of King Neco, king of Egypt. His army was defeated at the city of Carchemish on the Euphrates River. It was defeated by Nebuchadnezzar king of Babylon. This was in the fourth year that Jehoiakim son of Josiah was king of Judah. This is the Lord's message to Egypt:

[3]"Prepare your shields, large and
     small.
  March out for battle!
[4]Harness the horses.
  Soldiers, get on your horses!
  Go to your places for battle.
  Put on your helmets!
  Polish your spears.
  Put on your armor!
[5]What do I see?
  That army is terrified.
  The soldiers are running away.
  Their warriors are defeated.
  They run away quickly.
  They don't look back.
  There is terror on every side!"
     says the Lord.
[6]"The fast runners cannot run away.
  The strong soldiers cannot escape.
  They will stumble and fall
  in the north, by the Euphrates River.
[7]Who is this, rising up like the Nile
     River?
  Who comes like that strong, fast
     river?
[8]Egypt rises up like the Nile River.
  It is Egypt that comes like that
     strong, fast river.
  Egypt says, 'I will rise up and cover
     the earth.
  I will destroy cities and the people
     in them!'
[9]Horsemen, charge into battle!
  Chariot drivers, drive hard!
  March on, brave soldiers—
     soldiers from Cush and Put who
     carry shields.
  March on, soldiers from Lydia
     who use bows.

[10]"But that day belongs to the Master,
     the Lord of heaven's armies.
  At that time he will give those
     people the punishment they
     deserve.

The sword will kill until it is
    finished.
The sword will kill until it satisfies
    its thirst for blood.
This is because the Master, the
    Lord of heaven's armies, will
    offer a sacrifice.
That sacrifice is Egypt's army in
    the land of the north, by the
    Euphrates River.

[11] "Go to Gilead and get some balm.[d]
  Go up, people of Egypt!
You will make up many medicines,
  but you will not be healed.
[12] The nations will hear of your shame.
  Your cries will fill all the earth.
One warrior will run into another.
  And both of them will fall down
    together!"

[13] This is the message the Lord spoke to Jeremiah the prophet.[d] This message is about Nebuchadnezzar king of Babylon as he came to attack Egypt:
[14] "Announce this message in Egypt,
    and prophesy it in Migdol.
Preach this message also in
    Memphis and Tahpanhes:
'Get ready for war.
  The battle is all around you.'
[15] Egypt, why will your warriors be
    killed?
They cannot stand because the
    Lord will push them down.
[16] Those soldiers will stumble again
    and again.
They will fall over each other.
They will say, 'Get up. Let's go
    back
to our own people and our
    homeland.
We must get away from our
    enemy's sword!'
[17] In their homelands those soldiers
    will say,
'The king of Egypt is only a lot of
    noise.
His time of glory is over!'"

[18] The King's name is the Lord of
    heaven's armies.
He says, "As surely as I live,
a powerful leader will come.
He will be strong as great Mount
    Tabor is higher than other
    mountains.
He will be mighty as Mount
    Carmel is higher than the sea.
[19] People of Egypt, pack your things
  to be taken away as captives.
This is because Memphis will be
    destroyed.
The cities will be ruins, and no one
    will live there.

[20] "Egypt is like a beautiful young cow.
  But a horsefly is coming
from the north to attack her.
[21] The hired soldiers in Egypt's army
  are like fat calves.
They will all turn and run away
    together.
They will not stand strong against
    the attack.
Their time of destruction is coming.
  They will soon be punished.
[22] Egypt is like a hissing snake that is
    trying to escape.
The enemy comes closer and
    closer.
They will come against Egypt with
    axes.
They are like men who cut down
    trees.
[23] They will chop down Egypt's army
    as if it were a great forest," says
    the Lord.
"There are more enemy soldiers
    than locusts.[d]
There are too many soldiers to
    count.
[24] The people of Egypt will be
    ashamed.
They will be handed over to the
    enemy from the north."

[25] The Lord of heaven's armies, the God of Israel, says: "Very soon I will punish Amon, the god of Thebes. And I will punish Egypt, her king and her gods. And I will punish the people who depend on the king. [26] I will let all those people be defeated by their enemies. And those enemies want to kill them. I will give them to Nebuchadnezzar king of Babylon and his officers. But

in the future, Egypt will live in peace as it once did," says the Lord.

A Message to Israel

27"People of Jacob, my servants, don't
    be afraid.
  Don't be frightened, Israel.
  I will surely save you from those
      faraway places.
  I will save your children from the
      lands where they are captives.
  The people of Jacob will have peace
      and safety again.
  And no one will make them
      afraid.
28People of Jacob, my servants, do not
    be afraid.
  I am with you," says the Lord.
  "I scattered you to many different
      nations.
  And I will completely destroy all
      those nations.
  But I will not completely destroy
      you.
  I will punish you fairly.
  But I cannot let you escape your
      punishment."

A Message About the Philistines

47 The Lord spoke his word to Jeremiah the prophet.[d] This message is about the Philistine people. It came before the king of Egypt attacked the city of Gaza.

2This is what the Lord says:
"See, the enemy is gathering in the
    north like rising waters.
  They will become like an
      overflowing stream.
  They will cover the whole country
      like a flood.
  They will cover the towns and the
      people living in them.
  Everyone living in that country
    will cry for help.
  The people will cry painfully.
3 They will hear the sound of the
      running horses.
  They will hear the noisy chariots.
  They will hear the rumbling
      chariot wheels.

Fathers will not help their children
    to safety.
  Those fathers will be too weak to
      help.
4The time has come
  to destroy all the Philistines.
  It's time to destroy all who are left
      alive
  who could help Tyre and Sidon.
  The Lord will soon destroy the
      Philistines.
  He will destroy those left alive
      from the island of Crete.
5The people from Gaza will be sad
    and shave their heads.
  The people from Ashkelon will be
      made silent.
  Those left alive from the valley,
  how long will you cut
      yourselves?[n]

6"You cry, 'Sword of the Lord,
  how long will you keep fighting?
  Return to your holder.
    Stop! Be still.'
7But how can the sword of the Lord
    rest?
  The Lord gave it a command.
  The Lord has ordered it
    to attack the city of Ashkelon and
        the seacoast."

A Message About Moab

48 This message is about the country of Moab. This is what the Lord of heaven's armies, the God of Israel, says:
"How terrible it will be for Nebo.
  It will be ruined.
  The town of Kiriathaim will be
      disgraced and captured.
  The strong city will be disgraced
      and shattered.
2Moab will not be praised again.
  Men in the town of Heshbon plan
      Moab's defeat.
  They say, 'Come, let us put an end
      to that nation!'
  Town of Madmen, you will also be
      silenced.
  The sword will chase you.

---

[n]**sad and . . . yourselves?** The people did these things to show their sadness.

³Listen to the cries from the town of
  Horonaim.
  They are cries of much confusion
    and destruction.
⁴Moab will be broken up.
  Her little children will cry for help.
⁵Moab's people go up the path to
    Luhith.
  They cry loudly as they go.
On the road down to the town of
    Horonaim,
  cries of pain and suffering can be
    heard.
⁶Run! Run for your lives!
  Go like a bush being blown
    through the desert.
⁷You trust in the things you do and
    in your wealth.
  So you also will be captured.
The god Chemosh*d* will be taken
    into captivity.
  And his priests and officers will be
    taken with him.
⁸The destroyer will come against
    every town.
  Not one town will escape.
The valley will be ruined.
  The high plain will be destroyed.
  The Lord said this would happen.
⁹Spread salt*n* over the fields in Moab.
  The country will be an empty
    desert.
Moab's towns will become empty.
  No one will live in them.
¹⁰A curse will be on anyone who
    doesn't do what the Lord says.
  A curse will be on anyone who keeps
    back his sword from killing.

¹¹"The people of Moab have never
    known trouble.
  They are like wine left to settle.
They have never been poured like
    wine from one jar to another.
They have not been taken into
    captivity.
So they taste as they did before.
  And their smell has not changed.
¹²A time is coming," says the Lord.
  "And I will soon send men to pour
    you from your jars.

Those men will empty Moab's jars.
  And they will smash their jugs.
¹³The people of Israel trusted that
    god in Bethel.
  They were ashamed when there
    was no help.
In the same way Moab will be
    ashamed of their god
    Chemosh.

¹⁴"You cannot say, 'We are warriors!
  We are brave men in battle!'
¹⁵The enemy will attack Moab and
    destroy their towns.
  Their best young men will be
    killed!" says the King.
  The King's name is the Lord of
    heaven's armies.
¹⁶"The end of Moab is near.
  They will soon be destroyed.
¹⁷All you who live around Moab, cry
    for her.
  All you who know about her, cry
    for her.
Say, 'The ruler's power is broken.
  Moab's power and glory are gone.'

¹⁸"You people living in Dibon, come
    down from your place of honor.
  Sit on the dry ground.
This is because the destroyer of
    Moab is coming against you.
  And he will destroy your strong,
    walled cities.
¹⁹You people living in Aroer,
  stand next to the road and watch.
See the man running away and the
    woman escaping.
  Ask them what happened.
²⁰Moab will be ruined and filled with
    shame.
  Cry, Moab, cry out!
Announce at the Arnon River
  that Moab is destroyed.
²¹People on the high plain have been
    punished.
  Judgment has come to these towns:
    Holon, Jahzah and Mephaath;
²² Dibon, Nebo and Beth Diblathaim;
²³ Kiriathaim, Beth Gamul and Beth
    Meon;
²⁴ Kerioth and Bozrah.

---

*n*salt   The salt would keep crops from growing there.

Judgment has come to all the
towns of Moab, far and
near.
25 Moab's strength has been cut off.
Moab's arm is broken!" says the
Lord.

26 "The people of Moab thought they
were greater than the Lord.
So punish Moab until they act as if
they are drunk.
Moab will fall and roll around in
their own vomit.
People will make fun of them.
27 Moab, you made fun of Israel.
Israel was caught in the middle of
a gang of thieves.
You often spoke about Israel.
And you shook your head and
acted as if you were better
than Israel.
28 People in Moab, leave your towns
empty.
Go live among the rocks.
Be like a dove that makes its nest
at the entrance of a cave!

29 "We have heard that the people of
Moab are proud
and very conceited.
They are proud and think they are
important.
They were very proud in their
hearts."
30 The Lord says,
"I know Moab's quick anger, but it
is useless.
Moab's bragging accomplishes
nothing.
31 So I cry sadly for Moab.
I cry out for everyone in Moab.
I moan for the men from Kir
Hareseth.
32 I cry with the people of Jazer
for the grapevines of Sibmah.
In the past your vines spread all the
way to the sea.
They reached as far as the sea of
Jazer.
But the destroyer has taken
your fruit and grapes.
33 Joy and happiness are gone
from the large fields of Moab.

I have stopped the flow of wine from
the winepresses.[d]
No one walks on the grapes with
shouts of joy.
There are shouts,
but not shouts of joy.

34 "Their crying can be heard
from Heshbon to Elealeh and Jahaz.
It can be heard from Zoar as far
away as Horonaim and Eglath
Shelishiyah.
Even the waters of Nimrim are
dried up.
35 I will stop Moab
from making burnt offerings at the
places of worship.
I will stop them from burning
incense[d] to their gods," says
the Lord.
36 "My heart cries for Moab like a flute
playing a funeral song.
It cries for the people from Kir
Hareseth.
Their money and riches have all
been taken away.
37 Everyone has a shaved head.
Everyone's beard is cut off.
Everyone's hands are cut.
Everyone wears rough cloth
around his waist.[n]
38 People are crying on every roof[n] in
Moab
and in every public square.
There is nothing but sadness
because I have broken Moab
like a jar no one wants," says the
Lord.
39 "Moab is shattered! The people are
crying!
Moab turns away in shame!
People all around her make fun of
her.
The things that happened fill them
with fear."

40 This is what the Lord says:
"Look! An eagle is diving down
from the sky.
It spreads its wings over Moab.
41 The towns of Moab will be captured.
The strong, walled cities will be
defeated.

At that time Moab's warriors will be
    frightened.
They will feel pain like a woman
    who is having a baby.
42The nation of Moab will be destroyed.
This is because they thought they
    were greater than the Lord.
43Fear, deep pits and traps wait for you,
    people of Moab," says the Lord.
44"People will run from fear.
But they will fall into the pits.
Anyone who climbs out of the pits
    will be caught in the traps.
I will bring the year of punishment
    to Moab," says the Lord.

45"People have run from the powerful
    enemy.
They ran to Heshbon for safety.
But fire started in Heshbon.
A blaze broke out in Sihon's town.
And it burns the leaders of Moab.
It destroys those proud people.
46How terrible it will be for you, Moab!
Chemosh's people are being
    destroyed.
Your sons and daughters are being
    taken away as captives.

47"But in days to come,
I will make good things happen
    again to Moab," says the Lord.

This ends the judgment on Moab.

A Message About Ammon

49 This message is about the Am-
monite people. This is what the
Lord says:
"Do you think that Israel has no sons?
Do you think there is no one to take
    the land when the parents die?
Maybe that is why Molech[d] took
    Gad's land.
Maybe that is why Molech's
    people live in Gad's towns."
2The Lord says,
"The time will come when I will make
    the capital city of Rabbah Ammon
    hear the battle cry.

It will be a hill covered with ruins.
And the towns around it will be
    burned.
Those people forced Israel out of
    that land.
But now the people of Israel will
    force them out!" says the Lord.
3"People in Heshbon, cry because
    the town of Ai is destroyed!
Those who live in Rabbah Ammon,
    cry out!
Put on your rough cloth to show
    your sadness, and cry loudly.
Run here and there for safety
    inside the walls.
This is because the enemy will take
    Molech away as a captive.
They will also take away his
    priests and officers with him.
4You brag about your valleys.
You brag about the fruit in your
    valleys.
You are like an unfaithful child.
You believe your treasures will
    save you.
You think, 'Who would attack me?'
5I will bring terror on you
    from every side,"
says the Master, the Lord of
    heaven's armies.
"You will all be forced away.
No one will be able to gather you.

6"But the time will come
when I will make good things
    happen to the Ammonites
    again,"
says the Lord.

A Message About Edom

7This message is about Edom. This is
what the Lord of heaven's armies says:
"Is there no more wisdom in Teman?
Can the wise men of Edom no
    longer give good advice?
Have they lost their wisdom?
8You people living in Dedan,
    run away and hide in deep caves.
This is because I will punish

---

[n]**shaved head . . . waist** The people did these things to show their sadness for those who had died.
[n]**roof** In Bible times houses were built with flat roofs. The roof was used for drying things such as flax
and fruit. And it was used as an extra room, as a place for worship and as a place to sleep in the summer.

the people of Esau with disaster
for what they did.
⁹If workers came and picked the
grapes from your vines,
they would leave a few grapes
behind.
If robbers came at night,
they would steal only enough for
themselves.
¹⁰But I will strip Esau bare.
I will find all their hiding places.
They will not be able to hide
from me.
The children, relatives and
neighbors will die.
¹¹Leave the orphans, and I will take
care of them.
Your widows also can trust in me."

¹²This is what the Lord says: "Some
people did not deserve to be punished.
But they had to drink from the cup of
suffering anyway. People of Edom, you
deserve to be punished. So you will not
escape punishment. You must drink
from the cup of suffering." ¹³The Lord
says, "I make this promise in my own
name. The city of Bozrah will become
a pile of ruins! People will be shocked
by what happened there. People will
insult that city and speak evil of it. And
all the towns around Bozrah will become ruins forever."

¹⁴I have heard a message from the
Lord.
A messenger has been sent among
the nations, saying,
"Gather your armies to attack it!
Get ready for battle!"

¹⁵"Soon I will make you the smallest
of nations!
You will be greatly hated.
¹⁶Edom, you frightened other nations.
Your pride has fooled you.
You live in the hollow places of the
cliff.
You live on the high places of the
hills.
Even if you build your home as high
as an eagle's nest,
I will bring you down from there!"
says the Lord.

¹⁷"Edom will be destroyed.
People will be shocked to see the
destroyed cities.
They will be amazed at the injuries.
¹⁸Edom will be destroyed like the
cities of Sodom and Gomorrah
and the towns around them," says
the Lord.
"No one will live there!
No man will stay in Edom."

¹⁹"A lion will come from the thick
bushes near the Jordan River.
And it will go into the rich pastures
where people feed their flocks.
I am like that lion! I will suddenly
chase Edom from their land.
Who is the one I have chosen to
do this?
There is no one like me.
There is no one who can challenge
me.
None of their leaders can stand up
against me."

²⁰So listen to what the Lord has
planned to do against Edom.
Listen to what he has decided to
do to the people in Teman.
The Lord will surely drag away the
young ones of Edom.
Edom's pastures will surely be
destroyed because of them.
²¹At the sound of Edom's fall, the
earth will shake.
Their cry will be heard all the way
to the Gulf of Aqaba.
²²The Lord is like an eagle swooping
down.
He is like an eagle spreading its
wings over the city of Bozrah.
At that time Edom's soldiers will
become very frightened.
They will be crying from fear like a
woman having a baby.

A Message About Damascus

²³This message is about the city of
Damascus:
"The towns of Hamath and Arpad
are put to shame.
They are afraid because they have
heard bad news.

They are discouraged.
They are troubled like the tossing
sea.
24The city of Damascus has become
weak.
The people want to run away.
The people are ready to panic.
The people feel pain and suffering
like a woman having a baby.
25Damascus was a city of my joy.
Why have the people not left that
famous city yet?
26Surely the young men will die in the
public squares of that city.
All of her soldiers will be killed at
that time," says the Lord of
heaven's armies.
27"I will set fire to the walls of
Damascus.
The fire will completely burn the
strong cities of Ben-Hadad."

A Message About Kedar and Hazor

28This message is about the tribe[d] of
Kedar and the kingdoms of Hazor. Neb-
uchadnezzar king of Babylon defeated
them. This is what the Lord says:
"Go and attack the people of Kedar.
Destroy the people of the East.
29Their tents and flocks will be taken
away.
Their tents and all their things will
be carried off.
Their enemy will take away their
goods and camels.
Men will shout to them,
'Terror on every side!'
30"Run away quickly!
People in Hazor, find a good place
to hide!" says the Lord.
"Nebuchadnezzar king of Babylon
has made plans against you.
He has made plans to defeat you!
31"There is a nation that is comfortable.
It is sure that no one will defeat it,"
says the Lord.
"That nation does not have gates or
fences to protect it.
Its people live alone.
Attack that nation!
32The enemy will steal their camels

and their large herds of cattle.
I will scatter the Arabs to every part
of the earth.
And I will bring disaster on them
from everywhere," says the
Lord.
33"Hazor will become a place where
wild dogs live.
It will become an empty desert
forever.
No one will live there.
No man will stay in it."

A Message About Elam

34It was early in the time when Zedekiah was king of Judah. The Lord
spoke this word to Jeremiah the prophet.[d] This message is about the nation
of Elam.
35This is what the Lord of heaven's
armies says:
"I will break Elam's bow.
I will break its strength.
36I will bring the four winds against
Elam.
I will bring them from the four
corners of the skies.
I will scatter the people of Elam
everywhere the four winds
blow.
And its captives will go to every
nation.
37I will break Elam to pieces in front
of their enemies.
The enemies want to destroy
Elam.
I will bring disaster to Elam.
I will show them how angry I am!"
says the Lord.
"I will send a sword to chase Elam.
It will chase them until I have
killed them all.
38I will show Elam that I am king.
And I will destroy her king and her
officers!" says the Lord.
39"But I will make good things
happen to Elam again
in the future," says the Lord.

A Message About Babylon

50 This is the message the Lord
spoke about Babylon and the

Babylonian people. He spoke this message through Jeremiah the prophet.[d]

2"Announce this to the nations.
  Lift up a banner and tell them.
  Speak the whole message and say:
  'Babylon will be captured.
  The god Bel[d] will be put to shame.
  The god Marduk[d] will be very
      afraid.
  Babylon's idols will be put to shame.
  Her idols will be filled with terror!'
3A nation from the north will attack
      Babylon.
  That nation will make Babylon like
      an empty desert.
  No people will live there.
  Both men and animals will run
      away from there."

4The Lord says, "At that time
  the people of Israel and Judah will
      be together.
  They will cry and look for the Lord
      their God.
5Those people will ask how to go to
      Jerusalem.
  They will start to go in that
      direction.
  They will come and join themselves
      to the Lord.
  They will make an agreement that
      will last forever.
  It will be an agreement that will
      never be forgotten.

6"My people have been like lost sheep.
  Their leaders have led them in the
      wrong way.
  Their leaders made them wander
      around in the mountains and
      hills.
  They forgot where their resting
      place was.
7Whoever found my people hurt them.
  And those enemies said, 'We did
      nothing wrong.
  Those people sinned against the
      Lord, their true resting place.
  He was the God their fathers
      trusted.'

8"Run away from Babylon.
  Leave the land of the Babylonians.
  Be like the goats that lead the flock.

9I will bring against Babylon
  many nations from the north.
  This group of nations will take their
      places for war against Babylon.
  Babylon will be captured by people
      from the north.
  Their arrows are like trained soldiers
      who do not return from war with
      empty hands.
10The enemy will take all the wealth
      from the Babylonians.
  Those enemy soldiers will get all
      they want!" says the Lord.

11"Babylon, you are excited and happy.
  You took my land.
  You dance around like a young cow
      in the grain.
  Your laughter is like the neighing
      of male horses.
12Your mother will be very ashamed.
  The woman who gave you birth
      will be disgraced.
  Babylonia will be the least
      important of all the nations.
  She will be an empty, dry desert.
13The Lord will show his anger.
  No people will live there.
  Babylon will be completely empty.
  Everyone who passes by Babylon
      will be afraid.
  They will shake their heads when
      they see how it has been
      destroyed.

14"Take your positions for war against
      Babylon,
  all you soldiers with bows.
  Shoot your arrows at Babylon! Do
      not save any of them.
  This is because Babylon has
      sinned against the Lord.
15Soldiers around Babylon, shout the
      war cry!
  Babylon has surrendered. Her
      towers have fallen.
  Her walls have been torn down.
  The Lord is giving them the
      punishment they deserve.
  You nations should give Babylon
      what she deserves.
  Do to her what she has done to
      others.

[16]Don't let the people from Babylon
    plant their crops.
Don't let them gather the harvest.
The soldiers of Babylon treated
    their captives cruelly.
Now, let everyone go back home!
Let everyone run to his own
    country.

[17] "The people of Israel are like a flock
    of sheep that are scattered.
They are like sheep that have been
    chased away by lions.
The first lion to eat them up
    was the king of Assyria.
The last lion to crush their bones
    was Nebuchadnezzar king of
    Babylon."

[18]So this is what the Lord of heav-
en's armies, the God of Israel, says:
"I will punish the king of Babylon
    and his country.
I will punish him as I punished the
    king of Assyria.
[19]But I will bring the people of Israel
    back to their own pasture.
They will eat on Mount Carmel
    and in Bashan.
They will eat and be full.
They will eat on the hills of
    Ephraim and Gilead."
[20] The Lord says,
"At that time people will try to find
    Israel's guilt.
But there will be no guilt.
People will try to find Judah's sins.
But no sins will be found.
This is because I am saving the few
    people left alive from Israel
    and Judah.
And I am forgiving their sins.

[21]"Attack the land of Merathaim.
Attack the people who live in
    Pekod.
Chase them, kill them and
    completely destroy them.
Do everything I commanded you!"
    says the Lord.

[22] "The noise of battle can be heard all
    over the country.
It is the noise of much destruction.

[23]Babylon was the hammer of the
    whole earth.
But how broken and shattered that
    hammer is now!
Babylon is truly the most ruined
    of all the nations.
[24]Babylon, I set a trap for you.
And you were caught before you
    knew it.
You fought against the Lord.
So you were found and taken
    prisoner.
[25]The Lord has opened up his
    storeroom.
He has brought out the weapons
    of his anger.
This is because the Lord God of
    heaven's armies has work
    to do.
He has work to do in the land of
    the Babylonians.
[26]Come against Babylon from far
    away.
Break open her storehouses of
    grain.
Pile up her dead bodies like big
    piles of grain.
Completely destroy Babylon
    and do not leave anyone alive.
[27]Kill all the young men in Babylon.
Let them be killed.
The time has come for their defeat.
How terrible it will be for them!
It is time for them to be punished.
[28]Listen to the people running from
    the country of Babylon!
They are telling Jerusalem
how the Lord our God is punishing
    Babylon as it deserves.
This is because Babylon destroyed
    his Temple.[d]

[29]"Call for the men who shoot arrows
    to come against Babylon.
Tell them to surround the city.
Don't let anyone escape.
Pay her back for the bad things she
    has done.
Do to her what she has done to
    other nations.
Babylon acted with pride against
    the Lord,
the Holy One of Israel.

³⁰So Babylon's young men will be
killed in the streets.
All her soldiers will die on that
day," says the Lord.
³¹"Babylon, you are too proud. And I
am against you,"
says the Master, the Lord of
heaven's armies.
"This is because the time has come
for you to be punished.
³²Proud Babylon will stumble and fall.
And no one will help her get up.
I will start a fire in her towns.
It will completely burn up
everything around her."

³³This is what the Lord of heaven's
armies says:
"The people of Israel
and Judah both are slaves.
The enemy took them as prisoners.
And they won't let them go.
³⁴But God is strong and will buy them
back.
His name is the Lord of heaven's
armies.
He will defend them with power
so he can give rest to their land.
But he will not give rest to those
living in Babylon."

³⁵The Lord says,
"Let a sword kill the people living in
Babylon!
Let a sword kill its officers and
wise men!
³⁶Let a sword kill its false prophets!^d
They will become fools.
Let a sword kill Babylon's warriors!
They will be full of terror.
³⁷Let a sword kill its horses and
chariots.
Let a sword kill all the soldiers
hired from other countries!
They will be like frightened
women.
Let there be a sword against
Babylon's treasures!
They will be taken away.
³⁸Let there be a sword against its
waters!
They will be dried up.
It is a land of idols.

Those idols will go crazy with fear.
³⁹"Babylon will never be filled with
people again.
Desert animals and hyenas will
live there.
Owls will live there.
But no people will live there ever
again.
⁴⁰God completely destroyed the cities
of Sodom and Gomorrah
and the towns around them," says
the Lord.
"In the same way no people will live
in Babylon.
No man will stay there.

⁴¹"Look! An army is coming from the
north.
It comes from a powerful nation.
Many kings are coming together
from all around the world.
⁴²Their armies have bows and spears.
The soldiers are cruel and have no
mercy.
The soldiers come riding on their
horses.
And the sound is loud like the
roaring sea.
They stand in their places, ready for
battle.
They are ready to attack you, city
of Babylon.
⁴³The king of Babylon heard about
those armies.
And he became helpless because
of his fear.
His fear is like pain.
It is like the pain of a woman
having a baby.

⁴⁴"A lion will come from the thick
bushes near the Jordan River.
It will go into the rich pastures
where people feed their
flocks.
I am like that lion! I will suddenly
chase the people of Babylon
from their land.
Who is the one I have chosen to
do this?
There is no one like me.
There is no one who can
challenge me.

None of their leaders can stand up
against me."

⁴⁵So listen to what the Lord has
planned to do against Babylon.
Listen to what he has decided to
do to the people in Babylon.
He will surely drag away the young
ones of Babylon.
Babylon's pastures will be
destroyed because of them.
⁴⁶At the sound of Babylon's fall, the
earth will shake.
People in all nations will hear
about their destruction.

51 This is what the Lord says:
"I will cause a destroying wind
to blow.
It will blow against Babylon and
the Babylonian people.
²I will send foreign people to destroy
Babylon
like a wind that blows chaff ᵈ away.
Those people will make Babylon
empty.
Armies will surround the city
when disaster comes upon her.
³The Babylonian soldiers will not use
their bows and arrows.
Those soldiers will not even put on
their armor.
Don't feel sorry for the young men
of Babylon.
Completely destroy her army.
⁴Babylon's soldiers will be killed in
Babylon.
They will be badly injured in
Babylon's streets.
⁵The Lord God of heaven's armies
did not leave Israel and Judah
alone.
They are fully guilty of leaving the
Holy One of Israel.
But he has not left them.

⁶"Run away from Babylon!
Run to save your lives!
Don't stay and be killed because of
Babylon's sins.
It is time for the Lord to punish
Babylon.
Babylon will get the punishment it
deserves.

⁷Babylon was like a gold cup in the
Lord's hand.
It made the whole earth drunk.
The nations drank Babylon's wine.
So they went crazy.
⁸Babylon will suddenly fall and be
broken.
Cry for her!
Get balm ᵈ for her pain.
Maybe she can be healed.

⁹"Foreigners in Babylon say, 'We
tried to heal Babylon.
But she cannot be healed.
So let us leave her and each go to
his own country.
Babylon's guilt is as high as the
clouds.
Babylon's guilt reaches to
the sky.'

¹⁰"The people of Judah say, 'The
Lord has shown us to be right.
Come, let us tell about it in
Jerusalem.
Let us tell about what the Lord our
God has done.'

¹¹"Sharpen the arrows.
Pick up your shields!
The Lord has stirred up the kings of
the Medes.
He has stirred them up because he
wants to destroy Babylon.
The Lord will give the people of
Babylon the punishment they
deserve.
This is because Babylon destroyed
his Temple ᵈ in Jerusalem.
¹²Lift up a banner against the walls of
Babylon!
Bring more guards.
Put the watchmen in their places.
Get ready for a secret attack!
The Lord will do what he has
planned.
He will do what he said he would
do against the people of
Babylon.
¹³People of Babylon, you live near
much water.
You are rich with treasures.
But your end as a nation has come.
It is time for you to be destroyed.

¹⁴The Lord of heaven's armies has
  promised in his own name:
'Babylon, I will surely fill you with
  so many enemy soldiers they
  will be like a swarm of locusts.ᵈ
They will stand over you and shout
  their victory.'

¹⁵"The Lord made the earth by his
  power.
He used his wisdom to build the
  world.
He used his understanding to
  stretch out the skies.
¹⁶When he thunders, the waters in
  the skies roar.
He makes clouds rise in the sky all
  over the earth.
He sends lightning with the rain.
He brings out the wind from his
  storehouses.

¹⁷"People are so stupid and know so
  little.
Goldsmiths are made ashamed by
  their idols.
Those statues are only false gods.
They have no breath in them.
¹⁸They are worth nothing.
People make fun of them.
When they are judged, they will be
  destroyed.
¹⁹But God, who is Jacob's Portion,ᵈ is
  not like the idols.
God made everything.
And he made Israel to be his special
  people.
The Lord of heaven's armies is his
  name.

²⁰"You are my war club.
You are my battle weapon.
I use you to smash nations.
I use you to destroy kingdoms.
²¹I use you to smash horse and rider.
I use you to smash chariot and
  driver.
²²I use you to smash men and women.
I use you to smash old men and
  young men.
I use you to smash young men and
  young women.
²³I use you to smash shepherds and
  flocks.

I use you to smash farmers and
  oxen.
I use you to smash governors and
  officers.

²⁴"But I will pay Babylon back, and I
will pay back all the Babylonians for all
the evil things they did to Jerusalem,"
says the Lord.

²⁵The Lord says,
"Babylon, you are a destroying
  mountain.
And I am against you.
You have destroyed the whole land.
I will put my hand out against you.
I will roll you off the cliffs.
I will make you a burned-out
  mountain.
²⁶People will not find any rocks in
  Babylon big enough for
  cornerstones.ᵈ
People will not take any rocks
  from Babylon to use for the
  foundation of a building.
This is because your city will be
  just a pile of ruins forever,"
  says the Lord.

²⁷"Lift up the banner in the land!
Blow the trumpet among the
  nations!
Get the nations ready for battle
  against Babylon.
Call these kingdoms to come fight
  against Babylon:
Ararat, Minni and Ashkenaz.
Choose a commander to lead the
  army against Babylon.
Send so many horses that they are
  like a swarm of locusts.
²⁸Get the nations ready for battle
  against Babylon.
Get the kings of the Medes ready.
Get their governors and all their
  officers ready.
Get all the countries they rule ready
  for battle against Babylon.
²⁹The land shakes and moves like it is
  in pain.
It will shake when the Lord does
  what he planned to Babylon.
His plan is to make Babylon into an
  empty desert.

No one will live there.

30 Babylon's warriors have stopped
fighting.
They stay in their protected cities.
Their strength is gone.
They have become like frightened
women.
Babylon's houses are burning.
The bars of her gates are broken.

31 One messenger follows another.
Messenger follows messenger.
They announce to the king of
Babylon
that his whole city has been
captured.

32 The river crossings have been
captured.
The swamplands are burning.
All of Babylon's soldiers are
terribly afraid."

33 This is what the Lord of heaven's
armies, the God of Israel, says:
"The city of Babylon is like a
threshing^d floor,
where people crush the grain at
harvest time.
The time to harvest Babylon is
coming soon."

34 "Nebuchadnezzar king of Babylon
has destroyed us.
In the past he took our people away.
And we became like an empty jar.
He was like a giant snake that
swallowed us.
He ate everything until he was full
of our best things.
Then he spit us out.

35 Babylon did terrible things to
hurt us.
Now let those things happen to
Babylon,"
say the people of Jerusalem.
"The people of Babylon are guilty of
killing our people.
Now let them be punished for the
evil they did," says Jerusalem.

36 So this is what the Lord says:
"I will defend you, Judah.
I will make sure that Babylon is
punished.
I will dry up Babylon's sea.

And I will make her springs
become dry.

37 Babylon will become a pile of ruins.
Wild dogs will live there.
People will be shocked by what
happened there.
No one lives there anymore.

38 Babylon's people are like roaring
young lions.
They growl like baby lions.

39 While they are stirred up,
I will give a feast for them.
I will make them drunk.
They will shout and laugh.
And they will sleep forever and
never wake up!" says the Lord.

40 "I will take the people of Babylon to
be killed.
They will be like lambs,
like male sheep and goats waiting
to be killed.

41 "How Babylon will be defeated!
The pride of the whole earth will
be taken captive.
People from other nations will be
shocked at what happened to
Babylon.
And the things they see will make
them afraid.

42 The sea will rise over Babylon.
Its roaring waves will cover her.

43 Babylon's towns will be ruined and
empty.
Babylon will become a dry, desert
land.
It will become a land where no one
lives.
People will not even travel through
Babylon.

44 I will punish the god Bel^d in
Babylon.
I will make him spit out what he
has swallowed.
Nations will no longer come to
Babylon.
And the wall around the city will
fall.

45 "Come out of Babylon, my people!
Run for your lives!
Run from the Lord's great anger.

46 Don't lose courage.

Rumors will spread, but don't be
    afraid.
One rumor comes this year, and
    another comes the next year.
There will be rumors of terrible
    fighting in the country.
There will be rumors of rulers
    fighting against rulers.
⁴⁷The time will surely come
    when I will punish the idols of
    Babylon.
And the whole land will be
    disgraced.
There will be many dead people
    lying all around.
⁴⁸Then heaven and earth and all that
    is in them
will shout for joy about Babylon.
They will shout because the army
    came from the north
and fought against Babylon," says
    the Lord.

⁴⁹"Babylon killed people from Israel.
    Babylon killed people from
    everywhere on earth.
So Babylon must fall.
⁵⁰You people escaped being killed
    with swords.
    You must hurry and leave
    Babylon.
Don't wait!
Remember the Lord in the faraway
    land where you are.
And think about Jerusalem."

⁵¹"We people of Judah are disgraced.
    We have been insulted.
    We have been shamed.
This is because strangers have gone
    into
    the holy places of the Lord's
    Temple!"ᵈ

⁵²The Lord says, "The time is coming
    when I will punish the idols of
    Babylon.
Wounded people will cry with pain
    all over that land.
⁵³Babylon might grow until she
    touches the sky.
    She might make her cities strong.
But I will send people to destroy
    that city," says the Lord.

⁵⁴"We can hear people crying in
    Babylon.
We hear the sound of people
    destroying things
in the land of the Babylonians.
⁵⁵The Lord will destroy Babylon.
    He will make the loud sounds of
    the city become silent.
Enemies will come roaring in like
    ocean waves.
People all around will hear that
    roar.
⁵⁶The army will come and destroy
    Babylon.
    Babylon's soldiers will be taken
    captive.
    Their bows will be broken.
This is because the Lord is a God
    who punishes people for the
    evil they do.
He gives them the full punishment
    they deserve.
⁵⁷I will make Babylon's rulers and
    wise men drunk.
    I will make her governors, officers
    and soldiers drunk, too.
Then they will sleep forever and
    never wake up," says the King.
    His name is the Lord of heaven's
    armies.

⁵⁸This is what the Lord of heaven's
armies says:
"Babylon's thick wall will be pulled
    down.
    Her high gates will be burned.
The people will work hard, but it
    won't help.
    Their work will only become fuel
    for the flames!"

A Message to Babylon

⁵⁹This is the message that Jeremiah
the prophetᵈ gave to the officer Seraiah. Seraiah was the son of Neriah,
who was the son of Mahseiah. Seraiah
went to Babylon with Zedekiah king of
Judah. This happened in the fourth year
Zedekiah was king of Judah. ⁶⁰Jeremiah
had written on a scroll all the terrible
things that would happen to Babylon.
He had written all these words about
Babylon. ⁶¹Jeremiah said to Seraiah,

"Go to Babylon. Be sure to read this message so all the people can hear you. 62Then say, 'Lord, you have said that you will destroy this place. You will destroy it so that no people or animals will live in it. It will be an empty ruin forever.' 63After you finish reading this scroll, tie a stone to it. And throw it into the Euphrates River. 64Then say, 'In the same way Babylon will sink. It will not rise again. It will sink because of the terrible things I will make happen here. Her people will fall.'"

The words of Jeremiah end here.

The Fall of Jerusalem

52 Zedekiah was 21 years old when he became king. And he was king in Jerusalem for 11 years. His mother's name was Hamutal daughter of Jeremiah.*n* She was from Libnah. 2Zedekiah did what the Lord said was wrong, just as Jehoiakim had done. 3All this happened in Jerusalem and Judah because the Lord was angry with them. Finally, he threw them out of his presence.

Zedekiah turned against the king of Babylon.

4Then Nebuchadnezzar king of Babylon marched against Jerusalem with his whole army. They made a camp around the city. Then they built devices all around the city walls to attack it. This happened during Zedekiah's ninth year, tenth month and tenth day as king. 5The city was under attack until Zedekiah's eleventh year as king.

6By the ninth day of the fourth month, the hunger was terrible in the city. There was no food for the people to eat. 7Then the city wall was broken through. And the whole army ran away at night. They went through the gate between the two walls by the king's garden. The Babylonians were still surrounding the city. Zedekiah and his men ran toward the Jordan Valley.

8But the Babylonian army chased King Zedekiah. They caught up with him in the plains of Jericho. All of his army was scattered from him. 9So they captured Zedekiah and took him to the king of Babylon at Riblah. Riblah is in the land of Hamath. There he passed sentence on Zedekiah. 10There at Riblah the king of Babylon killed Zedekiah's sons as he watched. The king also killed all the officers of Judah. 11Then he put out Zedekiah's eyes. He put bronze chains on him and took him to Babylon. And the king kept Zedekiah in prison there until the day he died.

12Nebuzaradan was the commander of the king's special guards. This servant of the king of Babylon came to Jerusalem. This was on the tenth day of the fifth month. This was in Nebuchadnezzar's nineteenth year as king of Babylon. 13Nebuzaradan set fire to the Temple*d* of the Lord and the palace. He also set fire to all the houses of Jerusalem. Every important building was burned. 14The whole Babylonian army broke down the walls around Jerusalem. That army was led by the commander of the king's special guards. 15Nebuzaradan, the commander of the guards, took captive some of the poorest people. And he took those who were left in Jerusalem. He took captive those who had surrendered to the king of Babylon. And he took away the skilled craftsmen who were left in Jerusalem. 16But Nebuzaradan left behind the rest of the poorest people of the land. They were to take care of the vineyards and fields.

17The Babylonians broke up the bronze pillars, the bronze stands and the large bronze bowl, which was called the Sea. These were in the Temple of the Lord. Then they carried all the bronze to Babylon. 18They also took the pots, shovels, wick trimmers, bowls, dishes and all the bronze objects. They were used to serve in the Temple. 19The commander of the king's special guards took these things away: bowls, pans for carrying hot coals and large bowls; pots, lampstands, pans and bowls used for drink offerings. He took everything

---

*n***Jeremiah** This is not the prophet Jeremiah but a different man with the same name.

that was made of pure gold or silver.
20There was so much bronze that it could not be weighed. There were two pillars. There was the large bronze bowl with the 12 bronze bulls under it. And there were the movable stands, which King Solomon had made for the Temple of the Lord.

21Each of the pillars was about 27 feet high. Each pillar was 18 feet around and hollow. The wall of each pillar was 3 inches thick. 22The bronze capital*d* on top of the pillar was about 7½ feet high. It was decorated with a net design and bronze pomegranates*d* all around it. The other pillar also had pomegranates. It was like the first pillar. 23There were 96 pomegranates on the sides of the pillars. There was a total of 100 pomegranates above the net design.

24The commander of the guards took some prisoners. He took Seraiah the chief priest, Zephaniah the priest next in rank, and the three doorkeepers. 25The commander also took other people who were still in the city. He took the officer in charge of the fighting men. He also took seven people who advised the king. He also took the royal assistant who selected people for the army. And he took 60 other men who were in the city. 26Nebuzaradan, the commander, took all these people. And he brought them to the king of Babylon at Riblah. 27There at Riblah, in the land of Hamath, the king had them killed.

So the people of Judah were led away from their country as captives. 28This is how many people Nebuchadnezzar took away as captives: in the seventh year, 3,023 Jews; 29in Nebuchadnezzar's eighteenth year, 832 people from Jerusalem; 30in Nebuchadnezzar's twenty-third year, Nebuzaradan took 745 Jews as captives. Nebuzaradan was the commander of the king's special guards.

In all 4,600 people were taken captive.

Jehoiachin Is Set Free

31Jehoiachin king of Judah was in prison in Babylon for 37 years. That year Evil-Merodach became king of Babylon. He let Jehoiachin king of Judah out of prison that year. He set Jehoiachin free on the twenty-fifth day of the twelfth month. 32Evil-Merodach spoke kindly to Jehoiachin. He gave Jehoiachin a seat of honor. It was above the seats of the other kings who were with him in Babylon. 33So Jehoiachin put away his prison clothes. For the rest of his life, he ate at the king's table. 34Every day the king of Babylon gave Jehoiachin an allowance. This lasted as long as he lived, until Jehoiachin died.

LAMENTATIONS

*Sad Songs
About Jerusalem*

Jerusalem Cries over Her Destruction

1 Jerusalem once was full of people.
But now the city is empty.
Jerusalem once was a great city
among the nations.
But now she[n] has become like a
widow.
She was like a queen of all the other
cities.
But now she is a slave.

2 She cries loudly at night.
Tears are on her cheeks.
There is no one to comfort her.
All her lovers are gone.
All her friends have turned
against her.
They have become her enemies.

3 Judah has gone into captivity.
She has suffered and worked hard.
She lives among other nations.
But she has found no rest.
Those who chased her caught her.
They caught her when she was in
trouble.

4 The roads to Jerusalem are sad.
No one comes to Jerusalem for
the feasts.
No one passes through her gates.
And her priests groan.
Her young women are suffering.
And Jerusalem suffers terribly.

5 Her enemies have become her
masters.
Her enemies enjoy the wealth they
have won.
The Lord is punishing her
for her many sins.

Her children have gone away.
They are captives of the enemy in
a foreign land.

6 The beauty of Jerusalem
has gone away.
Her rulers are like deer
that cannot find food.
They are weak and have run away
from those who chased them.

7 Jerusalem is suffering and homeless.
She remembers all the precious
things
she had in the past.
She remembers when her people
were defeated by the enemy.
There was no one to help her.
When her enemies saw her,
they laughed to see her ruined.

8 Jerusalem sinned terribly.
So she has become unclean.[d]
Those who honored her hate her
now
because they have seen her
nakedness.
Jerusalem groans
and turns away.

9 Jerusalem made herself dirty by
her sins.
She did not think about what
would happen to her.
Her defeat was surprising.
There was no one to comfort her.
She says, "Lord, see how I suffer.
The enemy has won."

10 The enemy reached out and took
all her precious things.
She even saw foreigners
enter her Temple.[d]

---

[n]**she** In this poem the city of Jerusalem is described as a woman.

Lord, you had commanded
　that they should not enter the
　　meeting of your people.

11 All of Jerusalem's people are
　　groaning.
　They are looking for bread.
　They are giving away their precious
　　things for food
　so they can stay alive.
　The city says, "Look, Lord, and see.
　I am hated."

12 Jerusalem says, "You who pass by
　　on the road don't seem to care.
　Come, look at me and see.
　Is there any pain like mine?
　Is there any pain like that he has
　　caused me?
　The Lord has punished me
　on the day of his great anger.

13 "The Lord sent fire from above.
　It went down into my bones.
　He stretched out a net for my feet.
　He turned me back.
　He made me sad and lonely.
　I am weak all day.

14 "He has noticed my sins.
　They are tied together by his
　　hands.
　They hang around my neck.
　He has turned my strength into
　　weakness.
　The Lord has let me be defeated
　by those who are stronger than I
　　am.

15 "The Lord has rejected
　all my mighty men inside my
　　walls.
　He brought an army against me
　to destroy my young men.
　As if in a winepress,[d] the Lord has
　　crushed
　the capital city of Judah.

16 "I cry about these things.
　My eyes overflow with tears.
　There is no one near to comfort me.
　There is no one who can give me
　　strength again.
　My children are left sad and lonely
　because the enemy has won."

17 Jerusalem reaches out her hands,
　but there is no one to comfort her.
　The Lord has commanded for the
　　people of Jacob
　that their enemies surround them.
　Jerusalem has become unclean
　like those around her.

18 Jerusalem says, "The Lord is right.
　But I refused to obey him.
　Listen, all you people.
　Look at my pain.
　My young women and men
　have gone into captivity.

19 "I called out to my friends,
　but they turned against me.
　My priests and my older leaders
　have died in the city.
　They were looking for food
　so they could stay alive.

20 "Look at me, Lord. I am upset.
　I am troubled.
　My heart is troubled
　because I have been so stubborn.
　Out in the streets, the sword kills.
　Inside the houses, death destroys.

21 "People have heard my groaning.
　There is no one to comfort me.
　All my enemies have heard of my
　　trouble.
　They are happy that you have
　　done this to me.
　Now bring that day you have
　　announced.
　Let my enemies be like me.

22 "Look at all their evil.
　Do to them what you have done
　　to me
　because of all my sins.
　I groan over and over again,
　and I am afraid."

The Lord Destroyed Jerusalem

2 Look how the Lord in his anger
　has brought Jerusalem to shame.
　He has thrown down the greatness
　　of Israel
　from the sky to the earth.
　He did not remember the Temple,[d]
　　his footstool,
　on the day of his anger.

²The Lord swallowed up without
    mercy
  all the houses of the people of
    Jacob.
In his anger he pulled down
  the strong places of Judah.
He threw her kingdom and its
    rulers
  down to the ground in dishonor.

³In his anger the Lord has removed
  all the strength of Israel.
He took away his power from Israel
  when the enemy came.
He burned against the people of
    Jacob like a flaming fire
  that burns up everything around it.

⁴Like an enemy, the Lord prepared
    to shoot his bow.
  He took hold of his sword.
Like an enemy, he killed
  all the good-looking people.
He poured out his anger like fire
  on the tents of Jerusalem.

⁵The Lord has become like an enemy.
  He has swallowed up Israel.
He has swallowed up all her palaces.
  He has destroyed all her strong
    places.
He has caused more moaning and
    groaning
  for Judah.

⁶He has destroyed his Temple as if it
    were a garden tent.
He has destroyed the place where
  he met with his people.
The Lord has made Jerusalem forget
  the set feasts and Sabbath*ᵈ* days.
He has rejected the king and the
    priest
  in his great anger.

⁷The Lord has rejected his altar
  and abandoned his Temple.
He has given to the enemy
  the walls of Jerusalem's palaces.
The enemy shouted in the Lord's
    Temple
  as if it were a feast day.

⁸The Lord planned to destroy
  the wall around Jerusalem.

He marked the wall off with a
    measuring line.
He did not stop himself from
    destroying it.
He made the walls and defenses sad.
  Together they have fallen.

⁹Jerusalem's gates have fallen to the
    ground.
He destroyed and smashed the
    bars of the gates.
Her king and her princes are sent
  away among the nations.
The teaching of the Lord has
    stopped.
The prophets*ᵈ* have not had
  any visions from the Lord.

¹⁰The older leaders of Jerusalem
  sit on the ground and are silent.
They pour dust on their heads
  and put on rough cloth to show
    how sad they are.
The young women of Jerusalem
  bow their heads to the ground in
    sorrow.

¹¹My eyes are weak from crying.
  I am troubled.
I feel as if I have been poured out on
    the ground
  because my people have been
    destroyed.
Children and babies are fainting
  in the streets of the city.

¹²They say to their mothers,
  "Where is some bread and wine?"
They faint like wounded soldiers
  in the streets of the city.
  They die in their mothers' arms.

¹³What can I say about you,
    Jerusalem?
  What can I compare you to?
What can I say you are like?
  How can I comfort you, Jerusalem?
Your ruin is as big as the sea.
  No one can heal you.

¹⁴Your prophets saw visions about
    you.
  But they were false and worth
    nothing.
They did not expose your sins.

They did not keep you from being
captured.
The messages they preached to you
were false.
They fooled you.

He has carried out the order
that he commanded long ago.
He has destroyed without mercy.
He has made your enemies happy
because of what happened
to you.
He has strengthened your
enemies.

People Who Spoke God's Words
JEREMIAH • LAMENTATIONS 2:11

Jeremiah was also a great prophet, like Isaiah. He is called the "weeping prophet" because of this book, Lamentations. Jeremiah was very sad about what was going to happen to his country. Jeremiah spoke God's words to the people of Judah during the reigns of the last five kings, before the nation was conquered by Babylon and the people taken into captivity. He told about the coming destruction, and he was so sad that he cried. He cried for his people because they would not listen to God. He loved them and wanted them to do what was right. Jeremiah was very sad, but he also did what God wanted him to do by telling the people God's messages.

Do you love others so much that you want them to know about Jesus? People may not know that they can be saved from their sins unless you tell them.

To meet a prophet who spoke to his people in a faraway land, fly to page 972.

15All who pass by on the road
clap their hands at you.
They make fun and shake their
heads
at Jerusalem.
They ask, "Is this the city that
people called
the most beautiful city,
the happiest city on earth?"

16All your enemies open their mouths
to say things against you.
They make fun and grind their
teeth in anger.
They say, "We have swallowed
her up.
This is the day we were waiting for.
We have finally seen it happen."

17The Lord has done what he
planned.

18The people
cry out to the Lord.
Wall of Jerusalem,
let your tears flow
like a river day and night.
Do not stop.
Do not let your eyes rest.

19Get up, cry out in the night.
Cry all through the night.
Pour out your heart like water
in prayer to the Lord.
Lift up your hands in prayer to him.
Pray for the life of your children.
They are fainting with hunger
on every street corner.

20Jerusalem says: "Look, Lord, and
see.
You have never done this to
anyone else.

Women eat their own babies,
the children they have cared for.
Priests and prophets
are killed in the Temple of the Lord.

21 "Young men and old men
lie on the ground in the streets of
the city.
My young women and young men
have been killed by the sword.
You, Lord, killed them on the day of
your anger.
You killed them without mercy.

22 "You invited terrors to come against
me on every side.
It was as if you were inviting them
to a feast.
No one escaped or remained alive
on the day of the Lord's anger.
My enemy has killed
those whom I gave birth to and
brought up."

The Meaning of Suffering

3 I am a man who has seen the
suffering
that comes from the rod of the
Lord's anger.
2 He led me
into darkness, not light.
3 He turned his hand against me
again and again, all day long.
4 He caused my flesh and skin to
wear out.
He broke my bones.
5 He surrounded me and attacked me
with sadness and grief.
6 He made me sit in the dark,
like someone who has been dead a
long time.
7 He shut me in so I could not get out.
He put heavy chains on me.
8 I cry out and beg for help.
But he ignores my prayer.
9 He has blocked my way with stones.
He has made my life difficult.
10 The Lord is like a bear ready to
attack me.
He is like a lion in hiding.
11 He led me the wrong way and tore
me to pieces.

He left me without help.
12 He prepared to shoot his bow.
He made me the target for his
arrows.
13 He shot me in the kidneys
with the arrows from his arrow bag.
14 I have become a joke to all my
people.
All day long they make fun of me
with songs.
15 The Lord filled me with misery.
He filled me with suffering.
16 The Lord broke my teeth with
gravel.
He crushed me into the dirt.
17 I have no more peace.
I have forgotten what happiness is.
18 I said, "My strength is gone.
I have no more hope that the Lord
will help me."

19 Lord, remember my suffering and
how I have no home.
Remember the misery and
suffering.
20 I remember them well.
And I am very sad.

"I want to put Lamentations 3:22-23 where I can read it every morning after I get up. It's one of my favorite passages."

21 But I have hope
when I think of this:

22 The Lord's love never ends.
His mercies never stop.
23 They are new every morning.
Lord, your loyalty is great.
24 I say to myself, "The Lord is what I
have left.
So I have hope."

25 The Lord is good to those who put
their hope in him.
He is good to those who look to
him for help.

26It is good to wait quietly
for the Lord to save.
27It is good for a man to work hard
while he is young.

28He should sit alone and be quiet
because the Lord has given him
hard work to do.
29He should bow to the Lord with his
face to the ground.
Maybe there is still hope.
30He should offer his cheek if
someone wants to hit him.
He should be filled with shame.

31The Lord will not reject
his people forever.
32Although the Lord brings sorrow,
he also has mercy.
His love is great.
33The Lord does not like to punish
people
or make them sad.

34The Lord sees if any prisoner of
the earth
is crushed under his feet.
35He sees if someone is treated
unfairly
before the Most High God.
36The Lord sees
if someone is cheated in his case
in court.

37Nobody can speak and have it
happen
unless the Lord commands it.
38Both bad and good things
come by the command of the
Most High God.
39No man should complain
when he is punished for his sins.

40Let us examine and look at what
we have done.
Then let us return to the Lord.
41Let us lift up our hands and pray
from our hearts.
Let us say to God in heaven,
42"We have sinned and turned
against you.
And you have not forgiven us.

43"You wrapped yourself in anger and
chased us.

You killed us without mercy.
44You wrapped yourself in a cloud.
No prayer could get through.
45You made us like scum and trash
among the other nations.

46"All of our enemies
open their mouths and say things
against us.
47We have been frightened and
fearful.
We have been ruined and
destroyed."
48Streams of tears flow from my eyes
because my people are destroyed.

49My tears flow continually,
without stopping,
50until the Lord looks down
and sees from heaven.
51I am sad when I see
what has happened to all the
women of my city.

52Those who are my enemies for
no reason
hunted me like a bird.
53They threw me alive into a pit.
They threw stones at me.
54Water came up over my head.
I said to myself, "I am going to die."
55I called out to you, Lord,
from the bottom of the pit.
56You heard me calling, "Do not close
your ears.
Do not ignore my cry for help."
57You came close when I called out
to you.
You said, "Don't be afraid."

58Lord, you have taken my case.
You have given me back my life.
59Lord, you have seen how I have
been wronged.
Now judge my case for me.
60You have seen how my enemies
took revenge on me.
You have seen all their evil plans
against me.

61Lord, you have heard their insults
and all their evil plans against me.
62The words and thoughts of my
enemies
are against me all the time.

⁶³Look! In everything they do
   they make fun of me with songs.

⁶⁴Punish them as they should be
     punished, Lord.
   Pay them back for what they have
     done.
⁶⁵Make them stubborn.
   Put your curse on them.
⁶⁶Chase them in anger.
   Destroy them from the Lord's
     earth.

The Attack on Jerusalem

4 See how the gold has lost its shine!
   See how the good gold has
     changed!
The stones of the Temple*d* are
     scattered
   at every street corner.

²The precious people of Jerusalem
   were more valuable than gold.
But now they are thought of as clay
     jars
   made by the hands of a potter.

³Even wild dogs give their milk
   to feed their young.
But my people are cruel
   like ostriches in the desert.

⁴The baby is so thirsty
   that his tongue sticks to the roof of
     his mouth.
Children beg for bread.
   But no one breaks off a piece to
     share with them.

⁵Those who once ate fine foods
   are now starving in the streets.
The people who grew up wearing
     nice clothes
   now pick through trash piles.

⁶My people have been punished
   more than Sodom was.
Sodom was destroyed suddenly.
   No hands reached out to help her.

⁷Our princes were purer than snow.
   They were whiter than milk.
Their bodies were redder than
     rubies.
   Their faces shined like sapphires.
⁸But now they are blacker than coal.

No one even recognizes them in
     the streets.
Their skin is stretched over their
     bones.
   It is as dry as wood.

⁹Those people who were killed by
     the sword had it better
   than those killed by hunger.
They starved in pain and died
   because there was no food from
     the field.

¹⁰With their own hands kind women
   cooked their own children.
The children became food for their
     parents.
   This happened when my people
     were destroyed.

¹¹The Lord turned loose all of
     his anger.
He poured out his strong anger.
He set fire to Jerusalem.
   It burned down to the foundations.

¹²Kings of the earth and people of
     the world
   could not believe it.
They could not believe that enemies
   could come through the gates of
     Jerusalem.

¹³But it happened because her
     prophets*d* had sinned.
   And her priests had done evil.
They killed in the city
   the people who did what was right.

¹⁴They wandered in the streets
   like blind men.
They became dirty with blood.
   So no one could touch their
     clothes.

¹⁵"Go away! You are unclean,"*d* people
     shouted at them.
   "Get away! Get away! Do not touch
     us!"
So they left and wandered around.
   The other nations said, "Don't stay
     here."

¹⁶The Lord himself scattered them.
   He did not look after them
     anymore.

He did not respect the priests.
　　He showed no mercy to the older
　　　leaders.

17Also, our eyes grew tired
　　looking for help that never came.
　　We kept watch from our towers
　　　for a nation to save us.

18Our enemies hunted us
　　so we could not even walk in the
　　　streets.
　　Our end came near. Our time was up.
　　Our end came.

19The men who chased us
　　were faster than eagles in the sky.
　　They ran us into the mountains.
　　They ambushed us in the desert.

20The Lord's appointed king, who was
　　　our very breath,
　　was caught in their traps.
　　We had said about him, "We will be
　　　protected by him
　　among the nations."

21Be happy and glad, people of Edom,
　　you who live in the land of Uz.
　　But the Lord's anger is like a cup
　　　of wine that you also will have
　　　to drink.
　　Then you will get drunk on it and
　　　make yourselves naked.

22Your punishment is complete,
　　　Jerusalem.
　　He will not keep you in captivity
　　　any longer.
　　But the Lord will punish your
　　　wrongs, people of Edom.
　　He will uncover your sins.

A Prayer to the Lord

5 Remember, Lord, what happened
　　to us.
　　Look and see our disgrace.
2Our land has been turned over to
　　　strangers.
　　Our houses have been given to
　　　foreigners.
3We have become orphans with no
　　　father.
　　Our mothers have become like
　　　widows.

4We have to buy the water we drink.
　　We must pay for the wood for our
　　　fires.
5They work us hard as if we were
　　　animals with a yoke*d* on our
　　　necks.
　　We get tired and have no rest.
6We made an agreement with Egypt
　　and with Assyria to get enough
　　　food.
7Our ancestors sinned against you.
　　But they are gone.
　　Now we must suffer because of
　　　their sins.
8Slaves have become our rulers.
　　There is no one who can save us
　　　from them.
9We risk our lives to get our food
　　because there are men with
　　　swords in the desert.
10Our skin is hot like an oven.
　　We burn with fever because of the
　　　terrible hunger.
11The enemy attacked the women of
　　　Jerusalem
　　and the girls in the cities of Judah.
12The enemy hung our princes by the
　　　hands.
　　They do not honor our older
　　　leaders.
13The young men grind grain at the
　　　mill.
　　Boys stumble while carrying loads
　　　of wood.
14The older leaders no longer sit at
　　　the city gates.
　　The young men no longer make
　　　music.
15We have no more joy in our hearts.
　　Our dancing has turned into
　　　sadness.
16The glory has gone from Jerusalem.
　　How terrible it is for us because
　　　we have sinned.
17Because of this we are afraid.
　　Because of these things our eyes
　　　are dim.
18Mount Zion*d* is empty.
　　Now wild dogs wander around it.

19But you rule forever, Lord.
　　You will be King from now on.

²⁰Why have you forgotten us for so long?

Why have you left us for so long?

²¹Bring us back to you, Lord.

We will return.

Make our days as they were before.

²²Or have you completely rejected us?

Will your anger never end?

EZEKIEL

God's Message to the Captives

Ezekiel's Vision of Living Things

1 It was the thirtieth year, on the fifth day of the fourth month of our captivity. I, Ezekiel, was by the Kebar River in Babylon. I was among the people who had been carried away as captives from the land of Judah. The sky opened, and I saw visions of God. ²It was the fifth year that King Jehoiachin had been a prisoner. It was on the fifth day of the month. ³The Lord spoke his word to Ezekiel son of Buzi. This was in the land of the Babylonians by the Kebar River. There he felt the power of the Lord.

⁴When I looked, I saw a stormy wind coming from the north. There was a great cloud with a bright light around it. Fire was flashing out of it. And there was something that looked like glowing metal in the center of the fire. ⁵Inside the cloud were what looked like four living creatures. They were shaped like men. ⁶Each of them had four faces. And each of them had four wings. ⁷Their legs were straight. Their feet were like a calf's hoofs. And they sparkled like polished bronze. ⁸The living creatures had men's hands. They were under their wings on their four sides. All four of them had faces and wings. ⁹And their wings touched each other. The living creatures did not turn when they moved. Each went straight ahead.

¹⁰Their faces looked like this: In front each living creature had the face of a man. Each one had the face of a lion on the right side. Each one had the face of an ox on the left side. And in back each one had the face of an eagle. ¹¹This was what their faces looked like. Their wings were spread out above. Each had two wings that touched one of the other living creatures. Each living creature had two wings that covered its body. ¹²Each went straight ahead. Wherever the spirit would go, the living creatures would also go. When they went, they did not turn. ¹³The living creatures looked like burning coals of fire. They were like torches. Fire went back and forth among the living creatures. It was bright, and lightning flashed from it. ¹⁴The living creatures ran back and forth like bolts of lightning.

¹⁵Now I looked at the living creatures. And I saw a wheel on the ground by each of the living creatures with its four faces. ¹⁶The wheels and the way they were made were like this: They looked like sparkling chrysolite. All four of them looked the same. The wheels looked like one wheel crossways inside another wheel. ¹⁷When they moved, they went in any one of the four directions. They did not turn as they went. ¹⁸I saw the rims of the wheels. The rims were full of eyes all around.

¹⁹When the living creatures moved, the wheels moved beside them. When the living creatures were lifted up from the ground, the wheels also were lifted up. ²⁰Wherever the spirit would go, the living creatures would go. And the wheels were lifted up beside them. This is because the spirit of the living creatures was in the wheels. ²¹When the living creatures moved, the wheels moved. When the living creatures stopped, the wheels stopped. And when the living creatures were lifted

from the ground, the wheels were lifted beside them. This is because the spirit of the living creatures was in the wheels.

²²Now there was something like a dome over the heads of the living creatures. It sparkled like ice and was frightening. ²³And under the dome the wings of the living creatures were stretched out straight toward one another. Each living creature also had two wings covering its body. ²⁴I heard the sound of their wings as they moved. It was like the roaring sound of the sea. It was like the voice of God All-Powerful. It was a roaring sound like a noisy army. When the living creatures stood still, they lowered their wings.

²⁵And a voice came from above the dome over the heads of the living creatures. When the living creatures stood still, they lowered their wings. ²⁶Now above the dome there was something that looked like a throne. It looked like a sapphire gem. And on the throne was a shape like a man. ²⁷Then I noticed what he looked like from the waist up. He looked like glowing metal with fire inside it. And from his waist down he looked like fire. I saw a bright light all around him. ²⁸The glow around him looked like the rainbow in the clouds on a rainy day. It seemed to look like the glory of the Lord. So when I saw it, I bowed facedown on the ground. And I heard a voice speaking.

The Lord Speaks to Ezekiel

2 He said to me, "Human being, stand up on your feet. Then I will speak with you." ²While he spoke to me, the Spirit*ᵈ* entered me and put me on my feet. Then I heard the Lord speaking to me.

³He said, "Human being, I am sending you to the people of Israel. They are a nation of people who turned against me. They broke away from me. They and their ancestors have sinned against me until this very day. ⁴And I am sending you to people who are stubborn. They do not obey. You will

say this to them, 'This is what the Lord God says.' ⁵The people may listen, or they may not. They are a people who turn against me. But whatever they do, they will know that a prophet*ᵈ* has been among them. ⁶You, human being, don't be afraid of the people or their words. Thorny branches and thorns may be all around you. And you may live with insects that sting with poison. Don't be afraid of their words. Don't be afraid of their looks. They are a people who turn against me. ⁷But speak my words to them. They may listen, or they may not, because they turn against me. ⁸But you, human being, listen to what I say to you. Don't turn against me as those people do. Open your mouth and eat what I am giving you."

⁹I looked and saw a hand stretched out to me. A scroll was in the hand. ¹⁰The Lord opened the scroll in front of me. The scroll was written on the front and back. Funeral songs, sad writings and troubles were written on the scroll.

3 Then the Lord said to me, "Human being, eat what you find. Eat this scroll. Then go and speak to the people of Israel." ²So I opened my mouth, and the Lord gave me the scroll.

³The Lord said to me, "Human being, eat this scroll which I am giving you. Fill your stomach with it." Then I ate it. And it was sweet like honey in my mouth.

⁴Then the Lord said to me, "Human being, go to the people of Israel. Speak my words to them. ⁵You are not being sent to people whose speech you can't understand. Their language is not difficult. You are being sent to Israel. ⁶You are not being sent to many nations whose speech you can't understand. The language of Israel is not difficult. You are not being sent to people whose words you cannot understand. If I had sent you to them, they would have listened to you. ⁷But the people of Israel are not willing to listen to you. This is because they are not willing to listen to me. Yes, all the people of Israel are

stubborn and will not obey. ⁸See, I have made you as stubborn as they are. You will be as hard as they are. ⁹I have made you as hard as a diamond, harder than stone. Don't be afraid of them. Don't be frightened by them. They are a people who turn against me."

Israel's Warning

¹⁶After seven days the Lord spoke his word to me again. He said, ¹⁷"Human being, I have made you a watchman for Israel. Any time you hear a word from my mouth, warn them for me. ¹⁸When I say to an evil person, 'You will surely die,' you must warn him. If you don't speak out to warn the evil person to leave his evil way, he will die

People Who Spoke God's Words

EZEKIEL • EZEKIEL 3:10-11

Ezekiel was a great prophet who spoke God's words to his people after they had been taken away from their country to Babylon. Ezekiel had a special job to do among these people. They had seen their land and temple destroyed. God wanted them to learn from their mistakes and turn back to him. God told Ezekiel to do some very strange things, like eating bread made from barley and beans and shaving off all his hair, to get the people's attention. Also, he was to continue to speak to the people whether they listened or not.

It is difficult to tell people about God when they don't seem to be interested. But God wants you to serve him no matter what.

To meet a prophet who spoke to the kings of great empires, fly to page 1030.

¹⁰Also, the Lord said to me, "Human being, believe all the words that I will speak to you. And listen carefully. ¹¹Go to the captives, your people. And speak to them, whether they listen or not. Tell them, 'The Lord God says this.'"

¹²Then the Spirit lifted me up. And I heard a loud rumbling sound behind me. A voice said, "Praise God in heaven." ¹³I heard the wings of the living creatures touching each other. And I heard the sound of the wheels by them. It was a loud rumbling sound. ¹⁴So the Spirit lifted me up and took me away. I was unhappy and angry. I felt the great power of the Lord. ¹⁵I came to the captives from Judah. They lived by the Kebar River at Tel Abib. I sat there seven days where these people lived. I was shocked.

in his sin. But I will hold you responsible for his death. ¹⁹You must warn the evil person. Then if he does not turn from his wickedness or his evil ways, he will die because of his sin. But you will have saved yourself.

²⁰"Again, a person who does right may turn away from his goodness. He may do evil. If I caused him to sin, he will die. Because you have not warned him, he will die because of his sin. And the good he did will not be remembered. But I will hold you responsible for his death. ²¹But if you do warn that good person not to sin, he may not sin. Then he will surely live. This is because he was warned. And you will save yourself."

²²Then I felt the power of the Lord there. He said to me, "Get up and go

out to the plain. There I will speak to you." 23So I got up and went out to the plain. I saw the glory of the Lord standing there. It was like the glory I saw by the Kebar River. And I bowed face-down on the ground.

24Then the Spirit*d* entered me and made me stand on my feet. He spoke to me and said, "Go, shut yourself up in your house. 25As for you, human being, the people will tie you up with ropes. They will tie you up, and you will not be able to go out among them. 26Also, I will make your tongue stick to the roof of your mouth. Then you will be silent. And you will not be able to argue with the people, even though they turn against me. 27But when I speak to you, I will open your mouth. And you will say, 'The Lord God says this.' Whoever will listen, let him listen. Whoever refuses, let him refuse. They are a people who turn against me.

The Map of Jerusalem

4 "Now, human being, get yourself a brick. Put it in front of you and draw a map of Jerusalem on it. 2Then surround it with an army. Build battle works against the city. Build a road of earth to the top of the city walls. Set up camps around it. Put heavy logs in place to break down the walls. 3Then get yourself an iron plate. Put it up like an iron wall between you and the city. Turn your face toward the city as if to attack it. Then surround it and attack it. This is a sign to Israel.

4"Then lie down on your left side. Take the guilt of Israel on yourself. Their guilt will be on you for the number of days you lie on your left side. 5I have given you the same number of days as the years of the people's sin. So you will have the guilt of Israel's sin on you for 390 days.

6"When you have finished these 390 days, lie down a second time. This time lie on your right side. You will then have the guilt of Judah on you. I have given it to you for 40 days. This is a day for each year of their sin. 7Then you will

turn your face toward the army attacking Jerusalem. With your arm bare, you will prophesy*d* against Jerusalem. 8I will put ropes on you so you cannot turn from one side to the other. This will last until you have finished the days of your attack on Jerusalem.

9"Take wheat, barley, beans, small peas and millet seeds. And put them in one bowl. Make them into bread for yourself. You will eat it the 390 days you lie on your side. 10You will eat eight ounces of food every day. You will eat it at set times. 11You will drink about two-thirds of a quart of water every day. Drink it at set times. 12Eat your food as you would eat a barley cake. Bake it over human dung where the people can see." 13Then the Lord said, "In the same way Israel will eat unclean*d* food. They will eat it among the nations where I force them to go."

14But I said, "No, Lord God! I have never been made unclean. From the time I was young until now I've never eaten anything that died by itself. And I've never eaten anything torn by animals. Unclean meat has never entered my mouth."

15"Very well," he said. "Then I will give you cow's dung instead of human dung. You may use it for your fire to bake your bread."

16Then the Lord said to me, "Human being, look! I am going to cut off the supply of bread to Jerusalem. They will eat the bread that is measured out to them. And they will worry as they eat it. They will drink water that is measured out to them. And they will be in shock as they drink it. 17This is because bread and water will be hard to find. And the people will be shocked at the sight of each other. They will become weak because of their sin.

Ezekiel Cuts His Hair

5 "Now, human being, take a sharp sword. Use it like a barber's razor to shave your head and beard. Then take scales and weigh and divide the hair. 2Burn one-third with fire when

the days of the attack on Jerusalem are over. Burn it in the middle of the city. Then take one-third and cut it up with the knife all around the city. And scatter one-third to the wind. This is how I will chase them with a sword. ³Also take a few of these hairs and tie them in the folds of your clothes. ⁴Take a few more and throw them into the fire and burn them up. From there a fire will spread to all the people of Israel.

⁵"This is what the Lord says: This is Jerusalem. I have put her at the center of the nations with countries all around her. ⁶But she has refused to obey my laws. She has been more evil than the nations. She has refused to obey my rules even more than those around her. The people of Jerusalem have rejected my laws and have not lived by my rules.

⁷"So this is what the Lord God says: You caused more confusion than the nations around you. You did not follow my rules or obey my laws. You have not even obeyed the laws of the nations around you.

⁸"So this is what the Lord God says: I myself am against you. I will punish you and the nations will watch. ⁹I will do things among you that I have not done before. I will never do anything like them again. I will do them because you do the things I hate. ¹⁰So fathers among you will eat their children. And children will eat their fathers. I will punish you. I will scatter to the winds all who are left alive. ¹¹So the Lord God says: As surely as I live, you have made my Temple*d* unclean.*d* You have done it with all your evil idols and the hated things you do. Because of this I will cut you off. I will have no pity. I will show no mercy. ¹²A third of you will die by disease or be destroyed by hunger inside your walls. A third will fall dead by the sword outside your walls. And a third I will scatter in every direction. I will chase them with a sword. ¹³Then my anger will come to an end. I will use it up against them. Then I will be satisfied. Then they will

know that I, the Lord God, have spoken. After I have carried out my anger against them, they will know how strongly I felt.

¹⁴"I will make you a ruin. And I will make you a shame among the nations around you. All who pass by will see this. ¹⁵Then you will be shamed by the nations around you. They will make fun of you. You will be a warning to them. They will be terrified. This will happen when I punish you in my great anger. I, the Lord, have spoken. ¹⁶I will send a time of hunger to destroy you. Then I will make your hunger get even worse. I will cut off your supply of food. ¹⁷I will send a time of hunger and wild animals against you. They will kill your children. Disease and death will sweep through your people. I will bring the sword against you to kill you. I, the Lord, have spoken."

Prophecies Against the Mountains

6 Again the Lord spoke his word to me. The Lord said, ²"Human being, look toward the mountains of Israel. Prophesy*d* against them. ³Say, 'Mountains of Israel, listen to the word of the Lord God. The Lord God says this to the mountains, the hills, the ravines and the valleys: I will bring a sword against you. I will destroy your places of idol worship. ⁴Your altars will be destroyed. Your incense*d* altars will be broken down. Your people will be killed in front of your idols. ⁵I will lay the dead bodies of the Israelites before their idols. And I will scatter your bones around your altars. ⁶In all the places you live, cities will become empty. And the places of idol worship will be ruined. Your altars will become lonely ruins. Your idols will be broken and brought to an end. Your incense altars will be cut down. And the things you made will be wiped out. ⁷Your people will be killed and fall among you. Then you will know that I am the Lord God.

⁸"'But I will leave some people alive. Some will not be killed by the nations

when you are scattered among the foreign lands. ⁹Then those who have escaped will remember me. They will be living among the nations where they have been taken as captives. They will remember how I was hurt because they were unfaithful to me. They had turned away from me. They will remember how I was hurt because they desired to worship their idols. They will hate themselves because of the evil things they did that I hate. ¹⁰Then they will know that I am the Lord. I did not bring this terrible thing on them for no reason.

¹¹"'This is what the Lord God says: Clap your hands, stamp your feet. Say, "Oh!" because the people of Israel have done terrible things. So they will die by war, hunger and disease. ¹²The person who is far way will die by disease. The one who is nearby will die in war. The person who is still alive and has escaped these will die from hunger. So I will carry out my anger on them. ¹³Their people will lie dead among their idols around the altars. They will be on every high hill, on all the mountain tops and under every green tree and leafy oak. These are the places where they offered sweet-smelling incense to their idols. Then you will know that I am the Lord. ¹⁴I will use my power against them. I will make the land empty and wasted from the desert to Diblah, wherever they live. Then they will know that I am the Lord.'"

Ezekiel Tells of the End

7 Again the Lord spoke his word to me. He said: ²"Human being, the Lord says this to the land of Israel: An end! The end has come on the four corners of the land. ³Now the end has come for you. I will send my anger against you. I will judge you for the way you have lived. I will make you pay for your terrible actions. ⁴I will have no pity on you. I will not hold back punishment from you. I will make you pay for your ways and for your terrible actions. Then you will know that I am the Lord.

⁵"This is what the Lord God says: Disaster on top of disaster is coming. ⁶The end has come! The end has come! It has stirred itself up against you! Look! It has come! ⁷The end has come for you who live in the land! The time has come. The day of confusion is near. There will be no happy shouting on the mountains. ⁸Soon I will pour out my anger against you. I will carry out my anger against you. I will judge you for the way you have lived. I will make you pay for all the things you have done that I hate. ⁹I will show no pity. I will not hold back punishment. I will pay you back for the way you have lived and the terrible things you have done. Then you will know that I am the Lord who punishes.

¹⁰"Look, the day is here. It has come. Destruction has come. Violence has grown. There is more pride than ever. ¹¹Violence has grown into a weapon for punishing wickedness. None of the people will be left. None of that crowd, none of their wealth, and nothing of value will be left among them. ¹²The time has come. The day has arrived. Don't let the buyer be happy or the seller be sad. My burning anger is against the whole crowd. ¹³Sellers will not return to the land they have sold as long as they live. This is because the vision against all that crowd will not be changed. Because of their sins, no one will save his life. ¹⁴They have blown the trumpet, and everything is ready. But no one is going to the battle. My anger is against all that crowd.

¹⁵"The sword is outside. Disease and hunger are inside. The person who is in the field will die by the sword. Hunger and disease will destroy those in the city. ¹⁶Those who are left alive and who escape will be on the mountains. They will moan like doves of the valleys. Each person will groan about his own sin. ¹⁷All hands will hang weakly. All knees will become as weak as water. ¹⁸They will put on rough cloth to show how sad they are. They will tremble all over with fear. Their faces will

show their shame. And all their heads will be shaved. [19]The people will throw their silver into the streets. Their gold will be like trash. Their silver and gold will not save them from the Lord's anger. It will not satisfy their hunger or fill their stomachs. It was what caused them to fall into sin. [20]They were proud of their beautiful jewelry. They used it to make their idols, which I hate, and their evil statues. So I will turn their wealth into something they hate. [21]And I will give it to the foreigners as treasures from war. I will give it to the evil people of the earth as treasure. These foreigners and evil people will dishonor the people's jewelry. [22]I will also turn away from the people of Israel. They will dishonor my treasured place. Then robbers will enter and dishonor it.

[23]"Make chains for captives. The land is full of bloody crimes. And the city is full of violence. [24]So I will bring the worst of the nations to take over the people's houses. I will also end the pride of the rich. And their holy places will be dishonored. [25]When the people are suffering greatly, they will look for peace. But there will be none. [26]Disaster will come on top of disaster. Rumor will be added to rumor. Then they will try to get a vision from a prophet.[d] Even the teachings of God from the priest will be lost. And advice from the older leaders will also be lost. [27]The king will cry greatly. The prince will give up hope. The hands of the people who owned land will shake with fear. I will punish them for the way they have lived. The way they have judged others is the way I will judge them. Then they will know that I am the Lord."

Ezekiel's Vision of Jerusalem

8 It was the sixth year, on the fifth day of the sixth month of our captivity. I was sitting in my house with the older leaders of Judah before me. There I felt the power of the Lord God. [2]I looked and saw something that looked like a man. From his waist down he looked like fire. From his waist up he looked like bright glowing metal. [3]He stretched out the shape of a hand. And he caught me by the hair on my head. The Spirit[d] lifted me up between the earth and the sky. He took me in the visions of God to Jerusalem. He took me to the entrance to the north gate of the inner courtyard of the Temple.[d] The courtyard was where the idol was that caused God to be jealous. [4]The glory of the God of Israel was there. It was like what I had seen on the plain.

[5]Then God said to me, "Human being, now look toward the north." So I looked up toward the north. I saw an altar to the north of the gate. The idol that caused God to be jealous was in the entrance.

[6]The Lord said to me, "Human being, do you see what they are doing? Do you see how many hated things the people of Israel are doing here? This will drive me far away from my Temple. But you will see things more hated than these."

[7]Then the Lord brought me to the entry of the courtyard. When I looked, I saw a hole in the wall. [8]The Lord said to me, "Human being, dig through the wall." So I dug through the wall and saw an entrance.

[9]Then the Lord said to me, "Go in and see the terrible, evil things they are doing here." [10]So I entered and looked. And I saw pictures of every kind of crawling thing. I saw awful beasts and all the idols of the people of Israel. They were carved on the wall all around. [11]Seventy of the older leaders of Israel were standing there. They were in front of these carvings and idols. Jaazaniah son of Shaphan stood with them. Each man had his pan for burning incense[d] in his hand. A sweet-smelling cloud of incense was rising.

[12]Then the Lord said to me, "Human being, have you seen what the older leaders of Israel are doing in the dark? Have you seen each man in the room of his own idol? They say, 'The Lord doesn't see us. The Lord has left the

land.'" [13]And he said to me, "You will see even more terrible things that they are doing."

[14]Then the Lord brought me to the opening of the north gate of the Temple. And I saw women sitting there crying for Tammuz.[n] [15]The Lord said to me, "Do you see, human being? You will see things even more terrible than these."

[16]Then the Lord brought me into the inner courtyard of the Temple. And I saw about 25 men. They were at the entrance to the Temple, between the porch and the altar. Their backs were turned to the Temple of the Lord. They faced east. They were worshiping the sun in the east.

[17]The Lord said to me, "Do you see, human being? Is it unimportant that the people of Judah are doing the terrible things they have done here? They have filled the land with violence. They continually make me angry. Look, they are insulting me every way they can. [18]So I will act in anger. I will have no pity. I will not show mercy. Even if they shout in my ears, I won't listen to them."

Vision of the Angels

9 The Lord shouted with a loud voice in my ears. He said, "You who are chosen to punish this city, come near. Bring your weapon in your hand." [2]Then six men came from the direction of the upper gate, which faces north. Each had his powerful weapon in his hand. Among them was a man dressed in linen. At his side he had things to write with. The men went in and stood by the bronze altar.

[3]Then the glory of the God of Israel went up. It had been above the creatures with wings. It moved to the place in the Temple[d] where the door opened. Then the Lord called the man dressed in linen. He had the things to write with at his side. [4]The Lord said to him, "Go through Jerusalem. Put a mark on the

foreheads of the people who groan and cry about all the terrible things being done among them."

[5]As I listened, the Lord spoke to the other men. He said, "Go through the city behind the man dressed in linen and kill. Don't pity anyone. Don't show mercy. [6]Kill and destroy old men, young men and women, little children and older women. But don't touch anyone who has the mark on him. Start at my Temple." So they started with the older leaders who were in front of the Temple.

[7]And the Lord said to the men, "Make the Temple unclean.[d] Fill the courtyards with those who have been killed. Go out!" Then the men went out and killed the people in the city. [8]While the men were killing the people, I was left alone. I bowed facedown on the ground. I cried out, "Oh, Lord God! Will you destroy everyone left alive in Israel when you turn loose your anger on Jerusalem?"

[9]Then the Lord said to me, "The sin of the people of Israel and Judah is very great. The land is filled with people who murder. And the city is full of people who are not fair. The people say, 'The Lord has left the land. And the Lord does not see.' [10]But I will have no pity. I will show no mercy. But I will bring their evil acts back on their heads."

[11]Then the man dressed in linen reported to the Lord. He was the man who had things to write with at his side. He said, "I have done just as you have commanded me."

The Coals of Fire

10 Then I looked and saw the sky above the heads of the living creatures. I saw something like a sapphire gem. It looked like a throne. [2]The Lord said to the man dressed in linen, "Go in between the wheels under the living creatures. And fill your hands with coals of fire from between the living creatures. Scatter the coals over the city."

As I watched, the man with linen clothes went in. ³Now the living creatures were standing on the south side of the Temple*ᵈ* when the man went in. And the cloud from the Lord filled the inner courtyard. ⁴Then the glory of the Lord went up from the living creatures. And it stood over the door of the Temple. The Temple was filled with the cloud. And the courtyard was full of the brightness from the glory of the Lord. ⁵The sound of the wings of the living creatures was heard all the way to the outer courtyard. It was like the voice of God All-Powerful when he speaks.

⁶The Lord commanded the man dressed in linen, "Take fire from between the wheels, from between the living creatures." Then the man went in and stood by a wheel. ⁷One living creature put out his hand to the fire that was among them. The living creature took some of the fire. And he put it in the hands of the man dressed in linen. The man took the fire and went out.

The Wheels and the Creatures

⁸Something that looked like a man's hand appeared under the wings of the living creatures. ⁹I saw the four wheels by the living creatures. One wheel was by each living creature. The wheels looked like shining chrysolite. ¹⁰All four wheels looked alike. Each looked like a wheel crossways inside another wheel. ¹¹When the wheels moved, they went in any of the directions that the four living creatures faced. The wheels did not turn about. The living creatures did not turn their bodies as they went. But they followed wherever their faces pointed. ¹²All their bodies, their backs, hands, wings and the wheels were full of eyes all over. Now each of the four living creatures had a wheel. ¹³I heard the wheels being called "whirling wheels." ¹⁴Each living creature had four faces. The first face was the face of a creature with wings. The second face was the face of a

man. The third was the face of a lion. And the fourth was the face of an eagle.

¹⁵The living creatures flew up. They were the same living creatures I had seen by the Kebar River. ¹⁶And when the living creatures moved, the wheels moved by their sides. The living creatures lifted their wings to fly up from the ground. And the wheels did not leave their sides. ¹⁷When the living creatures stopped, the wheels stopped. When the creatures went up, the wheels went up also. This was because the spirit of the living creatures was in the wheels.

¹⁸Then the glory of the Lord left the door of the Temple*ᵈ* and stood over the living creatures. ¹⁹The living creatures spread their wings. And they flew up from the ground while I watched. As they went up, the wheels stayed by their sides. They stood where the east gate of the Temple of the Lord opened. The glory of the God of Israel was over them.

²⁰These are the living creatures I had seen under the God of Israel. This was by the Kebar River. I knew they were called cherubim. ²¹Each one had four faces. Each one had four wings. Things that looked like a man's hands were under their wings. ²²Their faces looked the same as the ones I had seen by the Kebar River. They each went straight ahead.

Prophecies Against Evil Leaders

11 The Spirit*ᵈ* lifted me up. And he brought me to the front gate of the Temple*ᵈ* of the Lord. This gate faces east. I saw 25 men where the gate opens. I saw Jaazaniah son of Azzur and Pelatiah son of Benaiah. They were leaders of the people. They were among these 25 men. ²Then the Lord said to me, "Human being, these are the men who plan evil. And they give wicked advice in this city of Jerusalem. ³They say, 'It is almost time for us to build houses. This city is like a cooking pot. And we are like the best meat.' ⁴So prophesy*d* against them. Prophesy, human being."

⁵Then the Spirit of the Lord entered me. He told me to say: "This is what the Lord says: You have said these things, people of Israel. But I know what is going through your mind. ⁶You have killed many people in this city. You have filled its streets with their bodies.

⁷"So this is what the Lord God says: Those people you have killed and left in the middle of the city are like the best meat. And this city is like the cooking pot. But I will force you out of the city. ⁸You have feared the sword. But I will bring a sword against you, says the Lord God. ⁹I will force you out of the city. I will hand you over to strangers. I will surely punish you. ¹⁰You will die by the sword. I will punish you at the border of Israel. Then you will know that I am the Lord. ¹¹This city will not be your cooking pot. You will not be the best meat in the middle of the city. I will punish you at the border of Israel. ¹²Then you will know that I am the Lord. You did not live by my rules. You did not obey my laws. You did the same things that the nations around you do."

¹³As I prophesied, Pelatiah son of Benaiah died. Then I bowed facedown on the ground. I shouted with a loud voice and said, "Oh no, Lord God! Will you completely destroy the Israelites who are left alive?"

Promise to Those Remaining

¹⁴The Lord spoke his word to me. He said, ¹⁵"Human being, the people still in Jerusalem have spoken about your relatives. And they have spoken about all the people of Israel who are captives with you. The people still in Jerusalem have said, 'They are far from the Lord. This land was given to us as our property.'

¹⁶"So say, 'This is what the Lord God says: I sent the people far away among the nations. I scattered them among the countries. But for a little while I

have become a Temple*d* to them in the countries where they have gone.'

¹⁷"So say: 'This is what the Lord God says: I will gather you from the nations. And I will bring you together from the countries where you have been scattered. Then I will give you back the land of Israel.'

¹⁸"They will come to this land. Then they will take away all the hated idols from the land. They will take all the terrible images from there. ¹⁹I will give them a desire to respect me completely. I will put a new way to think inside them. I will take out the stubborn heart like stone from their bodies. Then I will give them an obedient heart of flesh. ²⁰Then they will live by my rules. They will obey my laws and keep them. They will be my people, and I will be their God. ²¹But some people will want to serve their evil statues and hated idols. And I will pay them back for their evil ways, says the Lord God."

Ezekiel's Vision Ends

²²Then the living creatures lifted their wings. The wheels went beside them. And the glory of the God of Israel was above them. ²³The glory of the Lord went up from inside Jerusalem. And it stopped on the mountain on the east side of the city. ²⁴The Spirit*d* lifted me up. And he brought me to the captives who had been taken from Judah to Babylonia. He did this in a vision given by the Spirit of God. Then the vision I had seen ended. ²⁵And I told the things that the Lord had shown me. I told it to the captives from Judah.

Ezekiel Moves Out

12 Again the Lord spoke his word to me. He said: ²"Human being, you are living among a people who refuse to obey. They have eyes to see, but they do not see. They have ears to hear, but they do not hear. This is because they are a family that refuses to obey.

[3]"So, human being, pack your things as if you will be taken away captive. And walk away like a captive. Do this in the daytime with the people watching. Move from your place to another with the people watching. Maybe they will understand, even though they are a people who refuse to obey. [4]Bring out the things you would pack as a captive. Do it during the day when the people are watching. At evening go out with the people watching. Go like those who are taken away as captives from their country. [5]Dig a hole through the wall while they watch. Bring your things out through the hole. [6]Lift them onto your shoulders with the people watching. Carry them out in the dark. Cover your face so you cannot see the ground. I have made you a sign to the people of Israel."

[7]I did these things as I was commanded. In the daytime I brought out my things. I was packed, ready to go away as a captive. Then in the evening I dug through the wall with my hands. I brought my things out in the dark. I carried them on my shoulders. And the people saw all this.

[8]Then in the morning the Lord spoke his word to me. He said: [9]"Human being, Israel refuses to obey. Didn't those people ask you, 'What are you doing?'

[10]"Say to them, 'This is what the Lord God says: This message is about the king in Jerusalem. And it is about all the people of Israel who live there.' [11]Say, 'I am a sign to you.'

"The same things I have done will be done to the people in Jerusalem. They will be taken away from their country as captives. [12]The king among them will put his things on his shoulder in the dark. And he will leave. The people will dig a hole through the wall to bring him out. He will cover his face so he cannot see the ground. [13]But I will spread my net over him. He will be caught in my trap. Then I will bring him to Babylon in the land of the Babylonians. He will not see that land,

but he will die there. [14]All who are around the king I will scatter in every direction. I will scatter his helpers and all his army. I will chase them with a sword.

[15]"Then they will know that I am the Lord. I will scatter them among the nations. And I will spread them among the countries. [16]But I will save a few of them from the sword. I will save a few from hunger and disease. Then they can tell about their hated actions among the nations where they go. Then they will know that I am the Lord."

The Lesson of Ezekiel's Shaking

[17]The Lord spoke his word to me. He said: [18]"Human being, shake as you eat your food. Shake with fear as you drink your water. [19]Then say to the people of the land: 'This is what the Lord God says about the people who live in Jerusalem in the land of Israel: They will eat their food with fear. And they will drink their water in shock. This is because their land will be made empty. This is because of the violence of the people who live in it. [20]And the cities where people live will become ruins. The land will become empty. Then you will know that I am the Lord.'"

The Visions Will Come True

[21]The Lord spoke his word to me. He said: [22]"Human being, what is this saying you have in the land of Israel: 'The days go by and every vision comes to nothing'? [23]So say to them, 'This is what the Lord God says: I will make them stop saying this. Then nobody in Israel will use it anymore.' But tell them, 'The time is near when every vision will come true. [24]There will be no more false visions or pleasing prophecies[d] inside the nation of Israel. [25]This is because I, the Lord God, will speak. What I say will be done. It will not be delayed. You are a people who refuse to obey. And in your time I will say the word and do it, says the Lord God.'"

²⁶The Lord spoke his word to me. He said: ²⁷"Human being, look! The people of Israel are saying this: 'The vision that Ezekiel sees is for a time many years from now. He is prophesying about times far away.'

²⁸"So say to them: 'The Lord God says this: None of my words will be delayed anymore. What I have said will be done, says the Lord God.'"

Ezekiel Speaks Against False Prophets

13 The Lord spoke his word to me. He said: ²"Human being, prophesy^d against the prophets of Israel. Say to those who make up their own prophecies: 'Listen to the word of the Lord. ³This is what the Lord God says: How terrible it will be for the foolish prophets. They are the ones who follow their own ideas. And they have not seen a vision from me. ⁴People of Israel, your prophets have been like wild dogs hunting to kill and eat among ruins. ⁵Israel is like a house in ruins. But you have not gone up into the broken places. Your prophets have not repaired the wall. So how can Israel hold back the enemy in the battle on the Lord's day of judging? ⁶Your prophets see false visions. They prophesy lies. They say, "This is the message of the Lord." The Lord has not sent them. But they still hope their words will come true. ⁷You said, "This is the message of the Lord." But that is a false vision. Your prophecies are lies because I have not spoken.

⁸"So this is what the Lord God says: You prophets spoke things that are false. You saw visions that do not come true. That is why I am against you, says the Lord God. ⁹So I will punish the prophets who see false visions and prophesy lies. They will have no place among my people. Their names will not be written on the list of the people of Israel. They will not enter the land of Israel. Then you will know that I am the Lord God.

¹⁰"It is because they led my people away. They said, "Peace!" but there is no peace. When the people build a weak wall, the prophets cover it with whitewash to make it look strong. ¹¹So tell those who cover a weak wall with whitewash that it will fall down. Rain will pour down. Hailstones will fall. And a stormy wind will break the wall down. ¹²When the wall has fallen, people will ask you, "Where is the whitewash you used on the wall?"

¹³"So this is what the Lord God says: I will break the wall with a stormy wind. In my anger rain will pour down. And hailstones will destroy the wall. ¹⁴I will tear down the wall on which you put whitewash. I will level it to the ground. Then people will see the wall's foundation. And when the wall falls, you will be destroyed under it. Then you will know that I am the Lord. ¹⁵So I will carry out my anger on the wall and against those who covered it with whitewash. Then I will tell you, "The wall is gone. And those who covered it with whitewash are also gone. ¹⁶The prophets of Israel who prophesy to Jerusalem will be gone. And those who see visions of peace for Jerusalem will be gone also. There will be no peace, says the Lord God."'

False Women Prophets

¹⁷"Now, human being, reject the women among your people who make up their own prophecies.^d Prophesy against them. ¹⁸Say, 'This is what the Lord God says: How terrible it will be for women who sew magic charms on their wrists. How terrible it will be for those who make veils of every length. These women do this to trap people. You ruin the lives of my people but try to save your own lives! ¹⁹And you have dishonored me among my people. You have done it for handfuls of barley and pieces of bread. You have killed people who should not die. And you have kept alive those who should die. You have done this by lying to my people. And my people are willing to listen to lies.

²⁰"So this is what the Lord God says: I am against your magic charms.

You use them to trap people as if they were birds. I will tear these charms off your arms. I will free those people you have trapped like birds. ²¹I will also tear off your veils. I will save my people from your hands. They will no longer be in your power. You will not trap them. Then you will know that I am the Lord. ²²By your lies you caused the heart of the person who did right to be sad. I did not make him sad. You have encouraged the evil person not to stop being evil. And that would have saved his life. ²³So you will not see any more false visions. You will not prophesy anymore. And I will save my people from your power. Then you will know that I am the Lord.'"

Stop Worshiping Idols

14 Some of the older leaders of Israel came to me and sat down before me. ²Then the Lord spoke his word to me. He said: ³"Human being, these men love to worship idols. They put up evil things that cause people to sin. Should I allow them to ask me for help? ⁴So speak to them. Tell them, 'This is what the Lord God says: Any person in Israel might want to worship idols. He might even put up evil things that cause people to sin. Then he might come to the prophet.ᵈ When he does, I, the Lord, will answer him. I will put him to death because he worshiped idols. ⁵Then I will win back my people Israel. They have left me because of all their idols.'

⁶"So say this to the people of Israel: 'This is what the Lord God says: Change your hearts and lives. Stop worshiping idols. Stop doing all the things I hate. ⁷Any Israelite or any foreigner in Israel can separate himself from me. He can do this by wanting to worship idols. Or he can put up the things that cause people to sin. Then if he comes to the prophet to ask me questions, I, the Lord, will answer him myself. ⁸I will reject him. I will make him a sign and an example. I will sep-

arate him from my people. Then you will know that I am the Lord.

⁹"But the prophet may be tricked into giving a prophecy. Then it is because I, the Lord, have tricked that prophet to speak. Then I will use my power against him. I will destroy him from among my people Israel. ¹⁰The prophet will be as guilty as the one who asks him for help. They both will be responsible for their guilt. ¹¹Then the nation of Israel will not leave me anymore. And they will not make themselves uncleanᵈ anymore with all their sins. Then they will be my people. And I will be their God, says the Lord God.'"

Jerusalem Will Not Be Spared

¹²The Lord spoke his word to me. He said: ¹³"Human being, sometimes the people of a country will sin against me by not being loyal. When that happens, I will use my power against them. I will cut off their supply of food. I will send them a time of hunger. I will destroy both their people and animals. ¹⁴Three great men like Noah, Daniel and Job might be in that country. But their goodness could save only themselves, says the Lord God.

¹⁵"I might even send wild animals into that land. They would leave the land empty and without children. Then no one would pass through it because of the animals. ¹⁶As surely as I live, says the Lord God, not even Noah, Daniel and Job could help. Even if they were in the land, they could not save their own sons or daughters. They could only save themselves. And that country would remain empty.

¹⁷"Or, I might bring a war against that country. I might say, 'Let a war be fought in that land. Let it destroy its men and animals.' ¹⁸As surely as I live, says the Lord God, not even these three men could help. Even if they were in the land, they could not save their sons or daughters. They could only save themselves.

¹⁹"Or, I might cause a disease to spread in that country. I might pour

out my anger against that country, destroying and killing people and animals. ²⁰As surely as I live, says the Lord God, not even Noah, Daniel and Job could help. Even if they were in the land, they could not save their son or daughter. They could save only themselves because they did what was right.

²¹"This is what the Lord God says: I will send my four terrible punishments against Jerusalem. They are war, hunger, wild animals and disease. They will destroy people and animals from Jerusalem. ²²But some people will escape. Some sons and daughters will be led out. They will come out to you. You will see how they live. Then you will be comforted after the disasters I have brought against Jerusalem. You will be comforted after all the things I will bring against it. ²³You will be comforted when you see how they live. You will know there was a good reason for what I did to Jerusalem, says the Lord God."

Story of the Vine

15 The Lord spoke his word to me. He said: ²"Human being, what good is the wood of the vine? Is it better than the wood of a tree in the forest? ³Can wood be taken from the vine to make anything? Can you use it to make a peg on which to hang something? ⁴The vine is thrown into the fire for fuel. The fire burns up both ends and starts to burn the middle. Then is it useful for anything? ⁵When the vine was whole, it couldn't be made into anything. When the fire has burned it completely, it certainly cannot be made into anything."

⁶So this is what the Lord God says: "Out of all the trees in the forest, I gave the wood of the vine as fuel for fire. In the same way I have given up the people who live in Jerusalem. ⁷I will turn against them. They came through one fire. But fire will still destroy them. When I turn against them, you will

know that I am the Lord. ⁸So I will make the land empty. This is because the people have not been loyal, says the Lord God."

The Lord's Kindness to Jerusalem

16 The Lord spoke his word to me. He said: ²"Human being, tell Jerusalem about her hated actions. ³Say, 'This is what the Lord God says to Jerusalem: Your beginnings and your ancestors were in the land of the Canaanites. Your father was an Amorite. And your mother was a Hittite. ⁴On the day you were born, your cordⁿ was not cut. You were not washed with water for cleansing. You were not rubbed with salt. You were not wrapped in cloths. ⁵No one felt sorry for you. No one would do any of these things for you. No, you were thrown out into the open field. This is because you were hated on the day you were born.

⁶"'Then I passed by and saw you kicking about in your blood. I said to you, "Live!" ⁷I made you grow like a plant in the field. You grew up and became tall. You grew up and became like a beautiful jewel. Your breasts formed. Your hair grew. But you were naked and without clothes.

⁸"'Later I passed by you and looked at you. I saw that you were at the time for love. So I spread my robe over you and covered your nakedness. I also made a marriage promise to you. I entered into an agreement with you. Then you became mine, says the Lord God.

⁹"'Then I bathed you with water and washed all the blood off of you. I put oil on you. ¹⁰I put beautiful clothes made with needlework on you. I put sandals of fine leather on your feet. I wrapped you in fine linen and covered you with silk. ¹¹I put jewelry on you. I put bracelets on your arms and a necklace around your neck. ¹²I also put a ring in your nose and earrings in your ears. And I put a beautiful crown on your

ⁿ**cord** The umbilical cord that gives the unborn baby food and air from its mother.

head. [13]So you wore gold and silver. Your dress was made of fine linen, silk and beautiful needlework. You ate fine flour, honey and olive oil. You were very beautiful and became a queen. [14]Then you became famous among the nations because you were so beautiful. Your beauty was perfect, because of the glory I gave you, says the Lord God.

Jerusalem Becomes a Prostitute

[15]"But you trusted in your beauty. You became a prostitute[d] because you were so famous. You had sexual relations with anyone who passed by. [16]And you took some of your clothes and made your places of worship colorful. This is where you carried on your prostitution. These things should not have happened. They should never happen again. [17]You also took your beautiful jewelry. It was made from gold and silver I had given you. Then you made for yourselves male idols. And you were a prostitute with them. [18]Then you took your clothes with beautiful needlework and covered the idols. You gave my oil and incense[d] as an offering to them. [19]Also, you took the bread I gave you. You took the fine flour, oil and honey I gave you to eat. And you offered them before the false gods as a pleasing smell. This is what happened, says the Lord God.

[20]"Also, you took your sons and daughters who were my children. And you sacrificed them to idols as food. Your sexual sins were not enough for you. [21]You killed my children and offered them up in fire to idols. [22]You did all your hated acts and sexual sins. But you did not remember when you were young. At that time you were naked and had no clothes. You were left in your blood.

[23]"How terrible! How terrible it will be for you, says the Lord God. This is what you did after all these evil things. [24]You built yourself a place to worship false gods. You made for yourself a place of worship in every city square.

[25]You built a place of worship at the head of every street. You made your beauty hateful. You offered your body for sex to anyone who passed by. Your sexual sins became worse and worse. [26]You also had sexual relations with the Egyptians. They were your neighbors and partners in sexual sin. Your sexual sins became even worse. And they caused me to be angry. [27]So then, I used my power against you. I took away some of your land. I let those who hated you defeat you. They were the Philistine women. Even they were ashamed of your evil ways. [28]Also, you had sexual relations with the Assyrians because you could not be satisfied. You had sexual relations with them, but you still were not satisfied. [29]You did even more sexual sins in the land of Babylonia. The Babylonians were traders. But you were not satisfied even with this.

[30]"Truly your will is weak, says the Lord God. You do all the things a stubborn prostitute does. [31]You built your place to worship false gods at the beginning of every street. And you made places of worship in every city square. But you were not like a prostitute because you refused payment.

[32]"You are a wife who is guilty of adultery.[d] You desire strangers instead of your husband. [33]Men pay prostitutes, but you pay all your lovers. You pay them to come to you. And they come from all around for sexual relations. [34]So you are different from other prostitutes. No one acts like a prostitute the same way you do. You give money, and no money is given to you. Yes, you are different.

The Prostitute Is Judged

[35]"So, prostitute,[d] hear the word of the Lord. [36]This is what the Lord God says: You showed your riches to other countries. And you uncovered your body in your sexual sins with your lovers. And you even did it with all your hated idols. You killed your children and offered their blood to your idols.

³⁷So I will gather all your lovers with whom you found pleasure. Yes, I will gather all those you loved and those you hated. Yes, I will gather them against you from all around. I will strip you naked in front of them. Then they will be able to see your nakedness. ³⁸So I will punish you as judges punish women guilty of adultery.^d I will punish you as murderers are punished. I will put you to death because I am angry and jealous. ³⁹I will also hand you over to your lovers. They will tear down your places of worship. They will destroy the places where you worship false gods. They will tear off your clothes and take away your jewelry. They will leave you naked and bare. ⁴⁰They will bring a crowd against you. They will throw stones at you and cut you into pieces with their swords. ⁴¹They will burn your houses with fire. They will punish you in front of many women. Then I will put an end to your sexual sins. And you will no longer pay your lovers. ⁴²Then I will rest from my anger against you. I will stop being jealous. I will be quiet and not angry anymore.

⁴³"You didn't remember when you were young. So you have made me angry in all these ways. And I will repay you for what you have done, says the Lord God. Didn't you add sexual sins to all your other acts which I hate?

⁴⁴"Everyone who uses wise sayings will say this about you: "The daughter is like her mother." ⁴⁵You are like your mother. She hated her husband and children. You are also like your sisters. They hated their husbands and children. Your mother was a Hittite. And your father was an Amorite. ⁴⁶Now your older sister is Samaria. She lived north of you with her daughters. And your younger sister Sodom lived south of you with her daughters. ⁴⁷You followed their ways. And you did what they did. But you were even worse than they were in everything you did. ⁴⁸As surely as I live, says the Lord God, this is true. Your sister Sodom and her daughters never did what you and your daughters have done.

⁴⁹"This was the sin of your sister Sodom: She and her daughters were proud. They had plenty of food. They lived in great comfort. But she did not help the poor and needy. ⁵⁰So Sodom and her daughters were proud. And they did things I hate in front of me. So I got rid of them when I saw what they did. ⁵¹Also, Samaria did not do half the sins you do. You have done more hated things than they did. So you make your sisters look good because of all the hated things you have done. ⁵²You will suffer disgrace because you have provided an excuse for your sisters. They are more right than you are. Your sins were even more terrible than theirs. Be ashamed and suffer disgrace because you made your sisters seem right.

⁵³"But I will give Sodom and her daughters their riches back. I will give Samaria and her daughters their riches back. And with them I will also give you back your riches. ⁵⁴But you will have to suffer disgrace. You will feel ashamed for all the things you have done. You even gave comfort to your sisters in their sins. ⁵⁵Your sisters are Sodom with her daughters and Samaria with her daughters. They will return to what they were before. You and your daughters will also return to what you were before. ⁵⁶You would not even mention your sister Samaria when you were proud. ⁵⁷Nor would you mention her before your evil was uncovered. And now the Edomite women and their neighbors say bad things about you. Even the Philistine women say bad things about you. Those around you hate you. ⁵⁸You will be punished for your sexual sins and actions that I hate, says the Lord.

God Keeps His Promises

⁵⁹"This is what the Lord God says: I will give you what you should have. You hated and broke the marriage agreement. ⁶⁰But I will remember my agreement I made with you when you

were young. I will make an agreement that will continue forever with you. [61]Then you will remember what you have done. You will be ashamed when you receive your sisters—both your older and your younger sisters. I will give them to you like daughters. But it will not be because of my agreement with you. [62]I will set up my agreement with you. And you will know that I am the Lord. [63]You will remember and be ashamed. You will not open your mouth again because of your shame. This is because I will forgive you for all the things you have done, says the Lord God.'"

The Eagle and the Vine

17 The Lord spoke his word to me. He said: [2]"Human being, give a riddle. Tell a story to the people of Israel. [3]Say, 'This is what the Lord God says: A great eagle came to Lebanon. He had great wings with long feathers of many different colors. The eagle took hold of the top of a cedar tree. [4]He pulled off the top branch. And he brought it to a land of traders. The eagle planted it in a city of traders.

[5]"'The eagle took a young plant from the land. And he planted it in a good field near plenty of water. He planted it to grow like a willow tree. [6]The plant grew and became a low vine that spread over the ground. The vine's branches turned toward the eagle. The vine's roots were under the eagle. So the plant became a vine. And its branches grew, sending out leaves.

[7]"'But there was another eagle with great wings and many feathers. The vine then bent its roots toward this eagle. The vine also sent out its branches toward the eagle so he could water it. The vine turned away from the area where it was planted. [8]It was planted in a good field. It was by plenty of water so it could grow branches and give fruit. It could have become a fine vine.'

[9]"Say to them, 'This is what the Lord God says: The vine will not continue to grow. The first eagle will pull up the

vine's roots and strip off its fruit. Then the vine will dry up. All its new leaves will dry up and die. It will not take a strong arm or many people to pull the vine up by its roots. [10]It might be planted again. But it will not continue to grow. It will completely die when the east wind hits it. It will dry up in the area where it grew.'"

Zedekiah Against Nebuchadnezzar

[11]Then the Lord spoke his word to me. He said: [12]"Say now to the people who refuse to obey: 'Do you know what these things mean?' Say: 'The king of Babylon came to Jerusalem. He took the king and important men of Jerusalem and brought them to Babylon. [13]Then he took a member of the family of the king of Judah. He made an agreement with him. The king of Babylon made this person promise to support him. The king also took away the leaders of Judah. [14]He did this to make the kingdom of Judah weak so it would not be strong again. Then the kingdom of Judah could continue only by keeping its agreement with the king of Babylon. [15]But the king of Judah turned against the king of Babylon. The king of Judah sent his messengers to Egypt. He asked the Egyptians for horses and many soldiers. Will the king of Judah succeed? Will the one who does such things escape? He cannot break the agreement and escape.

[16]"'As surely as I live, says the Lord God, he will die in Babylon. He will die in the land of the king who made him king of Judah. The king of Judah hated his promise. He broke his agreement with the king of Babylon. [17]The king of Egypt will not help the king of Judah in the war. He will not help with his mighty army and many people. The Babylonians will build devices to attack the cities and to kill many people. [18]The king of Judah showed that he hated the promise by breaking the agreement. He promised to support

Babylon, but he did all these things. So he will not escape.

19 "So this is what the Lord God says: As surely as I live, this is true: I will pay back the king of Judah for hating my promise and breaking my agreement. 20 I will spread my net over him. He will be caught in my trap. Then I will bring him to Babylon. There I will judge him for the unfaithful acts he did against me. 21 And all the best of his soldiers who escape will die by the sword. Those who live will be scattered to every wind. Then you will know that I, the Lord, have spoken.

22 "This is what the Lord God says: I myself will also take a young branch from the top of a cedar tree. And I will plant it. I will cut off a small twig. It will be from the top of the tree's young branches. I will plant it on a high and great mountain. 23 I will plant it on the high mountain of Israel. Then it will grow branches and give fruit. And it will become a great cedar tree. Birds of every kind will build nests in it. They will live in the shelter of the tree's branches. 24 Then all the trees of the field will know that I am the Lord. I am the one who brings down the high tree. I make the low tree tall. I dry up the green tree. And I make the dry tree grow. I am the Lord. I have spoken, and I will do it.'"

God Is Fair

18 The Lord spoke his word to me. He said: 2 "What do you mean by using this saying about the land of Israel:

'The fathers have eaten sour grapes.
    And that caused the children to
        grind their teeth from the sour
        taste'?

3 "As surely as I live, says the Lord God, this is true: You will not use this saying in Israel anymore. 4 Every living thing belongs to me. The life of the father is mine. And the life of the son is mine. The person who sins will die.

5 "There may be a good person. This person does what is fair and right. 6 He does not eat at the mountain places of worship. He does not look to the idols of Israel for help. He does not have sexual relations with his neighbor's wife. He does not have sexual relations with a woman during her time of monthly bleeding. 7 He does not mistreat anyone. But he returns what was given as a promise for a loan. He does not rob other people. He gives bread to hungry people. He gives clothes to those who have no clothes. 8 He does not lend money to get too much interest or profit. He keeps his hand from doing wrong. He judges fairly between men. 9 He lives by my rules and obeys my laws faithfully. The person who does all these things is good. He will surely live, says the Lord God.

10 "But this person might have a wild son who murders people. This son may do any of these other bad things. 11 (But the father himself has not done any of these things.) This son eats at the mountain places of worship. He has sexual relations with his neighbor's wife. 12 He mistreats the poor and needy. He steals things. He refuses to return what was promised for a loan. He looks to idols for help. He does things which I hate. 13 He lends money for too much interest and profit. Will this son live? No, he will not live! He has done all these hated things. He will surely be put to death. He will be responsible for his own sins.

14 "But this son might have a son who has seen the sins his father did. But after seeing them, he does not do those things. 15 He does not eat at the mountain places of worship. He does not look to the idols of Israel for help. He does not have sexual relations with his neighbor's wife. 16 He does not mistreat anyone. He does not keep something promised for a loan. He does not steal. But he gives bread to the hungry people. He gives clothes to people without clothes. 17 He keeps his hand from doing wrong. He does not take too much interest or profit when he lends money. He obeys my laws and

lives by my rules. He will not die for his father's sin. He will surely live. [18]But his father took other people's money unfairly. He robbed his brother. He did what was wrong among his people. So he will die for his own sin.

[19]"But you ask, 'Why is the son not punished for the father's sin?' The son has done what is fair and right. He obeys all my rules. So he will surely live. [20]It is the person who sins that will die. The son will not be punished for the father's sin. The father will not be punished for the son's sin. The person who does right is responsible for his own goodness. The evil person is responsible for his own evil.

[21]"But the evil person might stop doing all the sins he has done. And he might obey all my rules and do what is fair and right. Then he will surely live. He will not die. [22]His sins will be forgotten. Now he does what is right. So he will live. [23]I do not really want the evil person to die, says the Lord God. I want him to stop his bad ways and live.

[24]"But a person who does right might stop doing good and do wrong. And he might do the same hated things an evil person does. Will he live? All his good acts will be forgotten. This is because he became unfaithful. He has sinned. So he will die because of his sins.

[25]"But you say, 'What the Lord does isn't fair.' Hear now, people of Israel. I am fair. It is what you do that is not fair! [26]A good person might stop doing good. He might do wrong and die because of it. He will die because he did wrong. [27]An evil person might stop doing the evil things he has done. And he might do what is fair and right. He will save his life. [28]He thought about it and stopped doing all the sins he had done. He will surely live. He will not die. [29]But the people of Israel still say, 'What the Lord does isn't fair.' People of Israel, I am fair. It is what you do that is not fair.

[30]"So I will judge you, people of Israel. I will judge each person by what he does, says the Lord God. Change your hearts. Stop all your sinning. Then sin will not bring your ruin. [31]Get rid of all the sins you have done. And get for yourselves a new heart and a new way to think. Why do you want to die, people of Israel? [32]I do not want anyone to die. So change your hearts and lives so you may live.

A Sad Song for Israel

19 "Sing a funeral song for the leaders of Israel. [2]Say:

'Your mother was like a female lion.
  She lay down among the young
    lions.
  She had many cubs.
[3]She brought up one of her cubs.
  And he became a strong lion.
  He learned to tear the animals he
    hunted.
  And he ate people.
[4]The nations heard about him.
  He was trapped in their pit.
  And they brought him with hooks
    to the land of Egypt.

[5]"'The mother lion waited and saw
    that there was no hope for her cub.
  So she took another one of her cubs
    and made him a strong lion.
[6]This cub roamed among the lions.
  He was now a strong lion.
  He learned to tear the animals he
    hunted.
  And he ate people.
[7]He destroyed their strong places.
  He destroyed their cities.
  The land and everything in it
    were terrified by the sound of his
      roar.
[8]Then the nations came against him
    from areas all around.
  And they spread their net over him.
  He was trapped in their pit.
[9]Then they put him into a cage with
    chains.
  And they brought him to the king
    of Babylon.
  They put him into prison.
  Then his roar could not be heard
    again
  on the mountains of Israel.

¹⁰"'Your mother was like a vine in
  your vineyard.
It was planted beside the water.
The vine had many branches and
  gave much fruit
because there was plenty of water.
¹¹The vine had strong branches.
They were good enough for a
  king's scepter.ᵈ
The vine became tall
among the thick branches.
And it was seen because it was tall
with many branches.
¹²But it was pulled up by its roots
  in anger.
It was thrown down to the ground.
The east wind dried it up.
Its fruit was torn off.
Its strong branches were broken off.
They were burned up.
¹³Now the vine is planted in the
  desert,
in a dry and thirsty land.
¹⁴And fire has spread from the vine's
  main branch.
It has destroyed its fruit.
There is not a strong branch left
  on it
that could become a scepter for
  a king.'

This is a funeral song. It is to be used
as a funeral song."

Israel Has Refused God

20 It was the seventh year, in the
fifth month of our captivity. It
was the tenth day of the month. Some
of the older leaders of Israel came to
ask about the Lord. They sat down
before me.

²The Lord spoke his word to me. He
said: ³"Human being, speak to the
older leaders of Israel. Say to them:
'This is what the Lord God says: Did
you come to ask me questions? As
surely as I live, I will not let you ask me
questions.'

⁴"Will you judge them? Will you
judge them, human being? Let them
know the hated things their fathers
did. ⁵Say to them: 'This is what the
Lord God says: I chose Israel and

made a promise to the descendantsᵈ
of Jacob. At that time I made myself
known to them in Egypt. I promised
them, "I am the Lord your God." ⁶At
that time I promised them I would
bring them out of Egypt. I promised to
bring them into a land I had chosen for
them. This is a land where much food
grows. It is the best of all lands. ⁷I said
to them, "Each one of you must throw
away the hateful idols you have set
your eyes on. Don't make yourselves
uncleanᵈ with the idols of Egypt. I am
the Lord your God."

⁸"'But they turned against me and
refused to listen to me. They did not
throw away the hated idols which they
saw and liked. They did not leave the
idols of Egypt. Then I decided to pour
out my anger against them in the land
of Egypt. ⁹But I acted to show who I
am. I did not allow myself to be dishonored before the nations where the
Israelites lived. I made myself known
to the Israelites. I did this by bringing
them out of Egypt while the nations
were watching. ¹⁰So I took them out of
Egypt and brought them into the
desert. ¹¹I gave them my rules. I told
them about my laws. If a person obeys
them, he will live. ¹²I also gave them
my Sabbaths.ᵈ They were to be a sign
between us. Then they would know
that I am the Lord. I make them holy.

¹³"'But in the desert Israel turned
against me. They did not follow my
rules. They rejected my laws. But if a
person obeys them, he will live. They
dishonored my Sabbaths. Then I
decided to pour out my anger against
them and destroy them in the desert.
¹⁴But I acted for the sake of my name.
I did not allow it to be dishonored
before the nations. As the nations
watched, I had brought the Israelites
out of Egypt. ¹⁵But in the desert I had
to make another promise to the
Israelites. I had to promise I would not
bring them into the land I had given
them. It is a land where much food
grows. It is the best of all the lands.
¹⁶This is because they rejected my

laws. They did not follow my rules. They dishonored my Sabbaths. They would rather worship their idols. ¹⁷But I had pity on them. I did not destroy them. I did not put an end to them in the desert. ¹⁸I said to their children in the desert, "Don't live by the rules of your fathers. Don't obey their laws. Don't make yourselves unclean with their idols. ¹⁹I am the Lord your God. Live by my rules. Obey my laws and do them. ²⁰Keep my Sabbaths holy. They will be a sign between me and you. Then you will know that I am the Lord your God."

²¹"But the people turned against me. If a person obeys my laws, he will live. But they did not live by my rules. They were not careful to obey my laws. They dishonored my Sabbaths. So I decided to pour out my anger against them. I decided to carry out my anger against them in the desert. ²²But I held back my anger. I acted for the sake of my name. Then my name would not be dishonored with the nations watching. As the nations watched, I had brought the Israelites out from Egypt. ²³Also in the desert I had to make a promise to the Israelites. I had to promise to scatter them among the nations and spread them among the countries. ²⁴This is because they did not obey my laws. They had rejected my rules and dishonored my Sabbaths. And they worshiped the idols of their ancestors. ²⁵I also allowed them to follow rules that were not good. And they followed laws by which they could not live. ²⁶I let the Israelites make themselves unclean by the gifts they brought to their false gods. They sacrificed their oldest children in the fire. This is how I shocked them so they would know that I am the Lord.'

²⁷"So, human being, speak to the people of Israel. Say to them, 'This is what the Lord God says: Your ancestors spoke against me by being unfaithful to me in this way: ²⁸I had brought them into the land I promised to give them. They saw every high hill and every leafy tree. There they offered their sacrifices to false gods. They brought offerings that made me angry. There, also, they burned their incense.ᵈ There they poured out their drink offerings. ²⁹Then I said to them: What is this place where you go to worship false gods?'" (It is still called High Place today.)

³⁰"So say to the people of Israel: 'This is what the Lord God says: Will you make yourselves unclean as your ancestors did? Will you be unfaithful and desire their hated idols? ³¹You offer your children as gifts to the false gods. You sacrifice them in the fire. You make yourselves unclean with all your idols even today. So, people of Israel, should I let you ask me questions? As surely as I live, says the Lord God, I will not accept questions from you.

³²"What you want will not come true. You say, "We want to be like the other nations and the people in other lands. We want to worship idols made of wood and stone." ³³As surely as I live, says the Lord God, I will rule you. I will rule you with my great power and strength and anger. ³⁴I will bring you out from the foreign nations. I will gather you from the lands where you are scattered. I will do this with my great power and strength and anger. ³⁵I will bring you among the nations as I brought your ancestors into the desert with Moses. There I will judge you face to face. ³⁶I will judge you the same way I judged your ancestors. That was in the desert of the land of Egypt. So I will judge you, says the Lord God. ³⁷I will take control of you. I will punish you by my agreement. ³⁸I will get rid of those who refuse to obey me and who turn against me. I will bring them out of the land where they are now living. But they will never enter the land of Israel. Then you will know that I am the Lord.

³⁹"This is what the Lord God says: People of Israel, go serve your idols for now. But later you will listen to me. You will not continue to dishonor my

holy name with your gifts and false gods. ⁴⁰My holy mountain is the high mountain of Israel. There all Israel will serve me in the land, says the Lord God. There I will accept you. There I will look for your offerings. I will look for the first harvest of your offerings and all your holy gifts. ⁴¹I will accept you like a pleasing smell. This will happen when I bring you out from the foreign nations. It will take place when I gather you from the lands where you are scattered. Then through you I will show how holy I am. The nations will see it. ⁴²When I bring you into the land of Israel, you will know that I am the Lord. I will bring you into the land I promised your ancestors. ⁴³There you will remember everything you did that made you unclean. Then you will hate yourselves for all the evil things you have done. ⁴⁴I will deal with you to show who I am. Then you will know I am the Lord, people of Israel. But it's not because of your evil ways or unclean actions, says the Lord God.'"

⁴⁵Now the Lord spoke his word to me. He said: ⁴⁶"Human being, look toward the south. Prophesy*d* against the south. Prophesy against the forest of the southern area. ⁴⁷Say to that forest: 'Hear the word of the Lord. This is what the Lord God says: I am ready to start a fire in you. The fire will destroy all your green trees and all your dry trees. The flame that burns will not be put out. All the land from south to north will be burned by the fire. ⁴⁸Then all the people will see that I, the Lord, have started the fire. It will not be put out.'"

⁴⁹Then I said, "Ah, Lord God! The people are saying about me, 'He is only telling stories.'"

Babylon, the Lord's Sword

21 Then the Lord spoke his word to me. He said: ²"Human being, look toward Jerusalem and speak against their holy place. Prophesy*d* against the land of Israel. ³Say to Israel: 'This is what the Lord says: I am against you.

I will pull my sword out of its holder. I will separate you from both wicked people and those who do right. ⁴I am going to separate the wicked and those who do right. So my sword will come out from its holder. And it will come against all people from south to north. ⁵Then all people will know that I, the Lord, have pulled my sword out from its holder. My sword will not go back in again.'

⁶"So, human being, groan with breaking heart and great sadness. Make these sad sounds in front of the people. ⁷They will ask you, 'Why do you make these sad sounds?' Then you will say, 'Because of the news that is coming. Every heart will melt with fear. All hands will become weak. Everyone will be afraid. All knees will become weak as water. Look, it is coming. It will happen, says the Lord God.'"

⁸The Lord spoke his word to me. He said, ⁹"Human being, prophesy and say, 'This is what the Lord says:

A sword, a sword,
    made sharp and polished.
¹⁰It is made sharp for the killing.
    It is polished to flash like
        lightning.

"'You are not happy about this horrible punishment by the sword. But my son, Judah, you did not change when you were only beaten with a rod. ¹¹The sword should be polished.
    The sword is meant to be held in
        the hand.
    It is made sharp and polished.
    It is made ready for the hand of
        the killer.
¹²Shout and yell, human being.
    This is because the sword is
        against my people.
    It is against all the rulers of Israel.
    They will be killed by the sword,
        along with my people.
    So beat your chest in sadness.
¹³"'The test will come. And Judah, who is hated by the armies of Babylon, will not last, says the Lord God.'

¹⁴"So, human being, prophesy.
    And clap your hands.

Let the sword hit
    two or three times.
It is the sword for killing.
    It is the sword for much killing.
    This sword surrounds the people.
¹⁵Their hearts will melt with fear.
    And many people will die.
I have placed the killing sword
    at all their gates.
Oh! The sword is made to flash like
        lightning.
    It is held, ready for killing.
¹⁶Sword, cut on the right side.
    Then cut on the left side.
    Cut anywhere your blade is
        turned.
¹⁷I will also clap my hands.
    Then my anger will rest.
    I, the Lord, have spoken."

Jerusalem to Be Destroyed

¹⁸The Lord spoke his word to me. He said: ¹⁹"Human being, mark two roads that the king of Babylon and his sword can follow. Both of these roads will start from the same country. And make signs where the road divides and one way goes toward the city. ²⁰One sign shows the road he can take with his sword to Rabbah. It is in the land of the Ammonites. And the other sign shows the road he can take to Judah and Jerusalem. Jerusalem is protected with strong walls. ²¹The king of Babylon will come to where the road divides into two. He will use magic. He will throw lots[d] with arrows. He will ask questions of his family idols. He will look at the liver of a sacrificed animal to learn where he should go. ²²The lots will tell him to go toward his right to Jerusalem. They will tell him these things: Use logs to break down the city gates. Shout the battle cry and give the order to kill. Build a dirt road to the top of the walls and devices to attack the walls. ²³The people of Jerusalem have made agreements with other nations to help them fight Babylon. So they will think this prediction is wrong. But the king of Babylon will remind them of their sin. And he will capture them.

²⁴"So this is what the Lord God says: 'You have shown how sinful you are by turning against the Lord. Your sins are seen in all the things you do. So you will be taken captive by the enemy.

²⁵"'You unclean[d] and evil leader of Israel, you will be killed! The time of your final punishment has come. ²⁶This is what the Lord God says: Take off the turban. Take off the crown. Things will change. Those who are important now will be made unimportant. And those who are unimportant now will be made important. ²⁷A ruin! A ruin! I will make it a ruin! This place will not be rebuilt until the one comes who has a right to be king. Then I will give it to him.'

The Punishment of Ammon

²⁸"And you, human being, prophesy[d] and say: 'This is what the Lord God says about the people of Ammon and their insults:
    A sword, a sword
        is pulled out of its holder.
    It is polished to kill and destroy.
        It will flash like lightning!
²⁹Prophets[d] see false visions about
            you
        and prophesy lies about you.
    The sword will be put on the necks
        of these evil people who are to
        be killed.
    Their day has come.
        The time of your final punishment
            has come.
³⁰Put the sword back in its holder.
    I will judge you in the place where
        you were created.
    I will judge you in the land where
        you were born.
³¹I will pour out my anger against
            you.
    I will breathe on you with the fire
        of my anger.
    I will hand you over to cruel men
        who are skilled in destruction.
³²You will be like fuel for the fire.
    You will die in the land.
    You will not be remembered.
    I, the Lord, have spoken.'"

The Sins of Jerusalem

22 The Lord spoke his word to me. He said: ²"And you, human being, will you judge? Will you judge the city of murderers? Then tell her about all her hated acts. ³You will say: 'This is what the Lord God says: You are a city that kills those who come to live there. You make yourself unclean*d* by making idols. ⁴You have become guilty of murder. And you have become unclean by your idols which you have made. So you have brought your time of punishment near. You have come to the end of your years. So I have made you a thing of shame to the nations. All lands will laugh at you. ⁵Those near and those far away will laugh at you. You will have a bad name. You will be full of confusion.

⁶"'Jerusalem, see how each ruler of Israel in you has been trying to kill people. ⁷The people in you hate their fathers and mothers. They mistreat the foreigners in you. They wrong the orphans and widows in you. ⁸You hate my holy things. You dishonor my Sabbaths.*d* ⁹The men in you tell lies to cause the death of others. The people in you eat food offered to idols at the mountain places of worship. They do sexual sins in you. ¹⁰The people in you have sexual relations with their fathers' wives. The men in you have sexual relations with women who are unclean, during their time of monthly bleeding. ¹¹One person in you does a hated act with his neighbor's wife. Another has shamefully made his daughter-in-law unclean sexually. And another forces his half sister to have sexual relations with him. ¹²The people in you take money to kill people. You take unfair interest and profits. You make profits by mistreating your neighbor. And you have forgotten me, says the Lord God.

¹³"'So with my fists I will hit you who have stolen money and you who have murdered people. ¹⁴Will you still be brave and strong when I punish you? I, the Lord, have spoken, and I will act. ¹⁵I will scatter you among the nations. I will spread you through the countries. I will get rid of your uncleanness. ¹⁶But you, yourself, will be dishonored in the sight of the nations. Then you will know that I am the Lord.'"

Israel Is Worthless

¹⁷The Lord spoke his word to me. He said: ¹⁸"Human being, the people of Israel have become useless like scum to me. They are like the copper, tin, iron and lead left in the furnace. These are left when silver is purified by melting. ¹⁹So this is what the Lord God says: 'You have become useless like scum. I am going to gather you into Jerusalem. ²⁰People gather silver, copper, iron, lead and tin into a furnace. Then they melt it in a blazing fire. In the same way I will gather you in my hot anger. I will put you in Jerusalem and melt you. ²¹I will gather you. And I will make you feel the heat of my anger. You will be melted in the fire. ²²Silver is melted in the furnace. In the same way you will be melted in the city. Then you will know that I, the Lord, have poured out my anger against you.'"

Sins of the People

²³The Lord spoke his word to me. He said: ²⁴"Human being, say to the land, 'You are a land that has not had rain or showers in a day of anger.' ²⁵Israel's rulers make evil plans. They are like a roaring lion that tears the animal it has caught. They have destroyed lives. They have taken treasure and valuable things. They have caused many women to become widows. ²⁶Israel's priests do cruel things to my teachings. They do not honor my holy things. They make no difference between holy and unholy things. They teach there is no difference between clean*d* and unclean things. They do not remember my Sabbaths.*d* So I am dishonored by them. ²⁷Jerusalem's leaders are like wolves tearing a dead animal. They have killed people for profit. ²⁸And the prophets*d* try to cover this up by false

visions and by lying. They say, 'This is what the Lord God says' when the Lord has not spoken. ²⁹The people cheat others. They steal. They hurt people who are poor and needy. They cheat foreigners and don't treat them fairly.

³⁰"I looked for someone to build up the walls. I looked for someone to stand before me where the walls are broken to defend these people. Then I would not have to destroy them. But I did not find anyone. ³¹So I will let them see my anger. I will destroy them with an anger that is like fire. This is because of all the things they have done, says the Lord God."

Samaria and Jerusalem

23 The Lord spoke his word to me. He said: ²"Human being, a woman had two daughters. ³While they were young, they went to Egypt and became prostitutes.ᵈ They let men touch and hold their breasts. ⁴The older girl was named Oholah, and her sister was named Oholibah. They were mine and had sons and daughters. Oholah is Samaria, and Oholibah is Jerusalem.

⁵"Samaria left me. She went to her lover, Assyria. The Assyrians were warriors. ⁶They wore blue uniforms. And all of them—governors, commanders and horsemen—were handsome. ⁷Samaria became a prostitute for all the important men in Assyria. And she made herself uncleanᵈ with all the idols of everyone she desired. ⁸She continued the prostitution she began in Egypt. When she was young, she slept with men. They touched her breasts and had sexual relations with her.

⁹"So I gave her to her lovers, the Assyrians, that she wanted so badly. ¹⁰They stripped her naked and took away her sons and daughters. Then they killed her with a sword. Women everywhere began talking about how she had been punished.

¹¹"Her sister Jerusalem saw what happened to Samaria. And so Jerusalem became worse than her sister in her sexual desire and prostitution. ¹²She also desired the Assyrians. All of them—governors, commanders, warriors dressed in uniform, and horsemen—were handsome. ¹³I saw that both girls were alike. Both of them were prostitutes.

¹⁴"But Jerusalem went even further. She saw carvings of Babylonian men on a wall. They wore red ¹⁵and had belts around their waists. They wore turbans on their heads. They all looked like chariot officers born in Babylonia. ¹⁶When she saw them, she wanted to have sexual relations with them. So she sent messengers to them in Babylonia. ¹⁷So these Babylonian men came and had sexual relations with her. They made her unclean. After that, she became sick of them. ¹⁸But she continued her prostitution so that everyone knew about it. And I finally became sick of her, as I had her sister. ¹⁹But she remembered how she was a young prostitute in Egypt. So she took part in even more prostitution. ²⁰She wanted men who behaved like animals in their sexual desire. ²¹In the same way you desired to do the sinful things you had done in Egypt. There men touched and held your young breasts.

God's Judgment on Jerusalem

²²"So, Jerusalem, this is what the Lord God says: You have tired of your lovers. So now I will make them angry with you. And they will surround you. ²³Men from Babylon and all Babylonia and men from Pekod, Shoa and Koa will come against you. All the Assyrians will come against you. They are governors, commanders, chariot drivers and important men, all riding horses. ²⁴Those men will come with great armies. They will come with their weapons, chariots and wagons. They will surround you with large and small shields and with helmets. And I will hand you over to them for punishment. And they will punish you with their own kind of punishment. ²⁵Then you will see how strong my anger can be.

They will punish you in their anger. They will cut off your noses and ears. They will take away your sons and daughters. Those who are left will be burned. 26They will take off your clothes and steal your jewelry. 27I will put a stop to the sinful life you began when you were in Egypt. You will not desire these things anymore. And you will not remember Egypt anymore.

28"This is what the Lord God says: You became sick of your lovers. But I am giving you to those men you now hate. 29They will treat you with hate and take away everything you worked for. They will leave you empty and naked. Everyone will know about the sinful things you did. Your sexual sins 30have brought this on you. You have made yourselves unclean*d* by worshiping their idols. 31You did the same things your sister did. So you will get the same punishment.

32"This is what the Lord God says:
You will drink the same cup your
    sister did.
And that cup is deep and wide.
Everyone will make fun of you,
    because the cup is full.
33It will make you miserable and
    drunk.
It is the cup of fear and ruin.
It is the cup of your sister Samaria.
34You will drink everything in it.
Then you will smash it
    and tear at your breasts.
I have spoken, says the Lord God.

35"So this is what the Lord God says: You have forgotten me and turned your back on me. So you will be punished for your sexual sins."

Judgment on Samaria and Jerusalem

36The Lord said to me: "Human being, will you judge Samaria and Jerusalem? Then show them their hated acts. 37They are guilty of adultery*d* and murder. They have taken part in adultery with their idols. They even offered their children as sacrifices in the fire. They were to be food for

these idols. 38They have also done this to me: They made my Temple*d* unclean*d* at the same time they dishonored my Sabbaths.*d* 39They offered their children to their idols. Then they entered my Temple at that very time to dishonor it. That is what they did inside my Temple.

40"They even sent for men from far away. A messenger was sent to them, and they came. The two sisters bathed themselves for them, painted their eyes and put on jewelry. 41They sat on a fine bed with a table set before it. They put my incense*d* and my oil on the table.

42"There was the noise of a reckless crowd in the city. Common people gathered, and drunkards were brought from the desert. They put bracelets on the hands of the two sisters. And they put beautiful crowns on their heads. 43Then I said about the one who was worn out by her acts of adultery, 'Let them continue their sexual sins with her. She is nothing but a prostitute.'*d* 44They kept going to her as they would go to a prostitute. So they continued to go to Oholah, which was Samaria, and Oholibah, which was Jerusalem. These were the shameful women. 45But men who do right will judge them as they judge women who take part in adultery. And they will judge them as they judge women who murder people. This is because Samaria and Jerusalem are guilty of adultery and murder.

46"This is what the Lord God says: Bring together a mob against Samaria and Jerusalem. And hand them over to be frightened and robbed. 47Let the mob kill them by throwing stones at them. Let the mob cut them down with their swords. Let them kill their sons and daughters and burn their houses with fire.

48"So I will put an end to sexual sins in the land. Then all women will be warned. And they will not do the sexual sins you have done. 49You will be punished for your sexual sins and the sin of worshiping idols. Then you will know that I am the Lord God."

The Pot and the Meat

24 The Lord spoke his word to me. It was in the ninth year, in the tenth month of our captivity. It was on the tenth day of the month. He said: [2]"Human being, write for yourself this date, this very date. The king of Babylon has surrounded Jerusalem this very day. [3]And tell a story to the people who refuse to obey me. Say to them: 'This is what the Lord God says:

Put on the pot. Put it on
  and pour water in it.
[4]Put in the pieces of meat.
  Put in the best pieces—the legs
    and the shoulders.
Fill it with the best bones.
[5] Take the best of the flock.
Pile wood under the pot.
  Boil the pieces of meat
  until even the bones are cooked.

[6]"'This is what the Lord God says:
How terrible it will be for the city of
  murderers!
  How terrible it will be for the rusty
    pot!
  Its rust will not go away!
Take the meat out of it, piece by
  piece.
  Don't choose any special piece.

[7]"'The blood from her killings is still
  in the city.
  She poured the blood on the bare
    rock.
  She did not pour it on the ground
  where dust would cover it.
[8]To stir up my anger and revenge,
  I put the blood she spilled on the
    bare rock.
  So it will not be covered.

[9]"'So this is what the Lord God says:
How terrible it will be for the city of
  murderers!
  I will also pile the wood high for
    burning.
[10]Pile up the wood
  and light the fire.
  Finish cooking the meat.
  Mix in the spices.
  And let the bones burn.

[11]Then set the empty pot on the coals.
  It will become hot, and its copper
    sides will glow.
  The dirty scum stuck inside it may
    then melt
  and its rust burn away.
[12]But efforts to clean the pot have
    failed.
  Its heavy rust cannot be removed,
  even in the fire.

[13]"'In your sinful action there is shame. I wanted to cleanse you, but you are still unclean.[d] You will never be cleansed from your sin until my anger against you is carried out. [14]"'I, the Lord, have spoken. The time has come for me to act. I will not hold back punishment. I will not feel pity. I will judge you by your ways and actions, says the Lord God.'"

The Death of Ezekiel's Wife

[15]Then the Lord spoke his word to me. He said: [16]"Human being, I am going to take your wife from you. She is the desire of your eyes. She will die suddenly. But you must not be sad or cry loudly for her. You must not shed any tears. [17]Groan silently. Do not cry loudly for the dead. Tie on your turban, and put your sandals on your feet. Do not cover your face. And do not eat the food people eat when they are sad about a death." [18]So I spoke to the people in the morning. Then my wife died in the evening. The next morning I did as I had been commanded. [19]Then the people asked me, "Tell us, what do the things you are doing mean for us?" [20]Then I said to them, "The Lord spoke his word to me. He said, [21]'Say to the people of Israel, This is what the Lord God says: I am going to dishonor my Temple.[d] You think it gives you strength. You are proud of it. You love to look at it. It makes you happy. But your sons and daughters that you left behind in Jerusalem will fall dead by the sword. [22]And you will do as I have done. You will not cover your face.

You will not eat the food people eat when they are sad about a death. ²³Your turbans will be on your heads. And your sandals will be on your feet. You will not cry loudly. But you will rot away in your sins. You will groan to each other. ²⁴So Ezekiel will be a sign for you. You will do all the same things he did. When it happens, you will know that I am the Lord God.'

²⁵"And as for you, human being, this is how it will be. I will take away the Temple that gives them strength. It makes them happy and proud. They love to look at it. It makes them happy. And I will take away their sons and daughters also. ²⁶At that time the person who escapes will come to you. He will have information for you to hear. ²⁷At that time your mouth will be opened. You will speak and be silent no more. So you will be a sign for them. Then they will know that I am the Lord."

Prophecy Against Ammon

25 The Lord spoke his word to me. He said: ²"Human being, look toward the people of Ammon and prophesy*d* against them. ³Say to them, 'Hear the word of the Lord God. This is what the Lord God says: You were glad when my Temple*d* was dishonored. You were glad when the land of Israel was ruined. And you were glad when the people of Judah were taken away as captives. ⁴So I am going to give you to the people of the East to be theirs. They will set up their camps among you. They will make their homes among you. They will eat your fruit and drink your milk. ⁵And I will make the city of Rabbah a pasture for camels. And the land of Ammon will become a resting place for sheep. Then you will know that I am the Lord. ⁶This is what the Lord God says: You clapped your hands and stamped your feet. You are happy about all the insults you have made against the land of Israel. ⁷So I will use my power against you. I will give you to the nations as if you were valuables taken in war. I will wipe you out of the lands so you will no longer be a nation. I will destroy you. And you will know that I am the Lord.'"

Prophecy Against Moab and Edom

⁸"This is what the Lord God says: 'Moab and Edom say, "The people of Judah are like all the other nations." ⁹So I am going to take away the cities that protect Moab's borders. They are the best cities in that land. They are Beth Jeshimoth, Baal Meon and Kiriathaim. ¹⁰Then I will give Moab, along with the Ammonites, to the people of the East. They will take over these people. Then along with the Ammonites, Moab will not be a nation anymore. ¹¹So I will punish the people of Moab. And they will know that I am the Lord.'"

Prophecy Against Edom

¹²"This is what the Lord God says: 'Edom took revenge on the people of Judah. And the Edomites became guilty because of it. ¹³So this is what the Lord God says: I will use my power against Edom. I will kill every man and animal in Edom. And I will destroy Edom all the way from Teman to Dedan. The Edomites will die in battle. ¹⁴I will take revenge on Edom through my people Israel. So the Israelites will do to Edom what my hot anger demands. Then the Edomites will know my revenge, says the Lord God.'"

Prophecy Against Philistia

¹⁵"This is what the Lord God says: 'The Philistines have taken revenge with hateful hearts. Because of their strong hatred, they have tried to destroy Judah. ¹⁶So this is what the Lord God says: I will use my power against the Philistines. I will remove the Kerethites. I will destroy those people still alive on the coast of the Mediterranean Sea. ¹⁷I will punish them in my anger until they have had enough. They will know that I am the Lord when I punish them.'"

Prophecy Against Tyre

26 It was the eleventh year, on the first day of the month of our captivity. The Lord spoke his word to me. He said: [2]"Human being, the city of Tyre has spoken against Jerusalem: 'The city that traded with the nations is destroyed. Now we can be the trading center. The city Jerusalem is ruined. Now we can make money.' [3]So this is what the Lord God says: I am against you, Tyre. I will bring many nations against you. They will come like the sea beating its waves on your island shores. [4]They will destroy the walls of Tyre and pull down her towers. I will also scrape away her ruins. I will make Tyre a bare rock. [5]Tyre will be an island where fishermen dry their nets. I have spoken, says the Lord God. The nations will steal valuable things from Tyre. [6]Also, her villages on the shore across from the island will be destroyed by war. Then they will know that I am the Lord.

Nebuchadnezzar to Attack Tyre

[7]"This is what the Lord God says: I will bring a king from the north against Tyre. He is Nebuchadnezzar king of Babylon, the greatest king. He will bring horses, chariots, horsemen and a great army. [8]He will fight a battle and destroy your villages on the shore across from the island. He will set up devices to attack you. He will build a road of earth to the top of the walls. He will raise his shields against you. [9]He will bring logs to pound through your city walls. And he will break down your towers with his iron bars. [10]His horses will be so many that they will cover you with their dust. Your walls will shake at the noise of horsemen, wagons and chariots. The king of Babylon will enter your city gates. He will enter as men enter a city where the walls are broken through. [11]The hoofs of his horses will run over your streets. He will kill your people with the sword. Your strong pillars will fall down to the ground. [12]Also, his men

will take away your riches. They will steal the things you sell. They will break down your walls and destroy your nice houses. They will throw your stones, wood and trash into the sea. [13]So I will stop your songs. The music of your harps will not be heard anymore. [14]I will make you a bare rock. You will be a place for drying fishing nets. You will not be built again. This is because I, the Lord, have spoken, says the Lord God.

[15]"This is what the Lord God says to Tyre: The people who live along the seacoast will shake with fear when they hear your defeat. Those of you who are injured and dying will groan. [16]Then all the leaders of the seacoast will go down from their thrones. They will take off their beautiful needlework clothes. They will clothe themselves with fear. They will sit on the ground. They will shake with fear all the time. They will be shocked when they see you. [17]They will begin singing a funeral song about you. They will say to you:

'Tyre, you famous city, you have
        been destroyed!
    Once seamen lived in you.
You and your people
    had great power on the seas.
All the people around you
    were afraid of you.
[18]Now the people who live by the
        coast
    will shake with fear on the day
        you fall.
The islands of the sea
    will be afraid because you have
        been defeated.'

[19]"This is what the Lord God says: I will make you an empty city. You will be like the cities that have no people living in them. I will bring the deep ocean waters over you. The Mediterranean Sea will cover you. [20]At that time I will send you down to the place of the dead. You will join the people who died long ago. I will make you live with the dead below the earth among old ruined places. You will not come back from there. People will never live

in you again. [21]Other people will be afraid of what happened to you. It will be the end of you. People will look for you. But they will never find you again, says the Lord God."

A Funeral Song for Tyre

27 The Lord spoke his word to me. He said: [2]"Human being, sing a funeral song for the city of Tyre. [3]Speak to Tyre that is at the entrance to the Mediterranean Sea. For the people of many lands along the seacoast, Tyre is a place for trade. 'This is what the Lord God says:

Tyre, you have said,
"I am like a beautiful ship."
[4]You were at home on the high seas.
Your builders have made your
beauty perfect.
[5]Your builders made all your boards
of fir trees from Mount Hermon.
They have taken a cedar tree from
Lebanon.
They took it to make a ship's mast
for you.
[6]They made your oars
from oak trees in Bashan.
They made your deck
from cypress trees from the coast
of Cyprus.
Your deck has ivory set into it.
[7]Your sail of linen with designs
sewed on it came from Egypt.
Your sail became like a flag for
you.
Your cloth shades over the deck
were blue and purple.
They came from the island of
Cyprus.
[8]Men from Sidon and Arvad used
oars to row you.
Tyre, your skilled men were the
sailors on your deck.
[9]Workers of Byblos were on board
ship with you.
They put caulk[n] in your ship's
seams.
All the ships of the sea and their
sailors
came alongside to trade with you.

[10]"'Men of Persia, Lydia and Put
were soldiers in your army.
They hung their shields and
helmets on your walls.
Their victories made you famous.
[11]Men of Arvad and Celicia
guarded your city walls all around.
Men of Gammad
were in your watchtowers.
They hung their shields around
your walls.
They made your beauty perfect.

[12]"'Tarshish traded with you for many kinds of things. They paid for them with silver, iron, tin and lead. [13]"'People of Greece, Tubal and Meshech traded with you. They traded slaves and bronze things for the things you sell. [14]"'People of Beth Togarmah traded work horses, war horses and mules for the things you sell. [15]"'People of Rhodes traded with you. You sold your things on many coastlands. They paid you with ivory tusks and valuable black wood. [16]"'Aram traded with you because you had so many good things to sell. They traded turquoise, purple cloth and cloth with designs sewed on. They also traded fine linen, coral and rubies for the things you sell. [17]"'Judah and Israel traded with you. They paid for the things you sell with wheat from Minnith. They also paid with honey, olive oil and balm.[d] [18]"'Damascus traded with you because you have many good things. They paid for them with wine from Helbon and wool from Zahar. [19]"'The Greeks from Uzal traded for the things you sold. They paid with wrought iron, cassia[d] and sugar cane for your good things. [20]"'Dedan traded saddle blankets to you. [21]"'Arabia and all the rulers of Kedar traded with you. They traded lambs, male sheep and goats to you. [22]"'The traders of Sheba and Raamah

[n]**caulk** Something like tar put between the boards of a ship to make it waterproof so it will not sink.

traded with you. They paid with all the best spices, valuable gems and gold.

23"'Haran, Canneh, Eden and the traders of Sheba, Asshur and Kilmad traded with you. 24They paid with the best clothes, blue cloth and cloth with designs sewed on. They traded carpets of many colors and tightly wound ropes.

25"'Trading ships
carried the things you sold.
You were like a ship full of heavy
cargo
in the middle of the sea.
26The men who rowed you
brought you out into the high seas.
But the east wind has broken you
to pieces
in the middle of the sea.
27Your wealth, your trade and the
things you sell will sink.
Your seamen, your sailors and
your workers will sink.
Your traders, your soldiers,
and everyone else on board
will sink into the sea.
This will happen on the day your
ship is wrecked.
28The people on the shore will shake
with fear
when your sailors cry out.
29All the men who row
will leave their ships.
The seamen and the sailors of
other ships
will stand on the shore.
30They will cry loudly about you.
They will cry very much.
They will throw dust on their heads.
They will roll in ashes to show
they are sad.
31They will shave their heads for you.
And they will put on rough cloth to
show they are upset.
They will cry very much for you.
They will cry loudly.
32And in their loud crying
they will sing a funeral song for
you.
"No one was ever destroyed
like Tyre,
surrounded by the sea."

33The things you traded went out over
the seas.
You met the needs of many
nations.
With your great wealth and things
you sold,
you made kings of the earth rich.
34But now you are broken by the sea.
You have sunk to the bottom.
The things you sell and all your
people
have gone down with you.
35All those who live along the shore
are shocked by what happened
to you.
Their kings are terribly afraid.
Their faces show their fear.
36The traders among the nations hiss
at you.
You have come to a terrible end.
And you are gone forever.'"

Prophecy Against the King of Tyre

28 The Lord spoke his word to me. He said: 2"Human being, say to the ruler of Tyre: 'This is what the Lord God says:
You are too proud.
And you say, "I am a god.
I sit on the throne of a god
in the middle of the seas."
You think you are as wise as a god.
But you are a man, not a god.
3You think you are wiser than Daniel.
You think you can find out all
secrets.
4Through your wisdom and
understanding
you have made yourself rich.
You have gained gold and silver.
And you have saved it in your
storerooms.
5Through your great skill in trading,
you have made your riches grow.
You are too proud
because of your riches.

6"'So this is what the Lord God says:
You think you are wise
like a god.
7But I will bring foreign people
against you.

They will be the cruelest nation.
They will pull out their swords
and destroy all that your wisdom
has built.
And they will dishonor your
greatness.
⁸They will kill you.
You will die a terrible death
like those who are killed at sea.
⁹While they are killing you,
you will not be able to say
anymore, "I am a god."
You will be only a man, not a god,
when your murderers kill you.
¹⁰You will die like an unclean*d* person.
Foreigners will kill you.

I have spoken, says the Lord God.'"

¹¹The Lord spoke his word to me. He
said: ¹²"Human being, sing a funeral
song for the king of Tyre. Say to him:
'This is what the Lord God says:
You were an example of what was
perfect.
You were full of wisdom and
perfect in beauty.
¹³You had a wonderful life,
like those in Eden, the garden
of God.
Every valuable gem was on you:
ruby, topaz and emerald,
yellow quartz, onyx and jasper,
sapphire, turquoise and chrysolite.
Your jewelry was made of gold.
It was prepared on the day you
were created.
¹⁴I appointed a living creature to
guard you.
I put you on the holy mountain
of God.
You walked among the gems
of fire.
¹⁵Your life was right and good.
This was from the day you were
created,
until evil was found in you.
¹⁶Because you traded with countries
far away,
you learned to be cruel, and you
sinned.
So I threw you down in disgrace
from the mountain of God.

And the living creature who
guarded you
forced you out from among the
gems of fire.
¹⁷You became too proud
because of your beauty.
You ruined your wisdom
because of your greatness.
I threw you down to the ground.
Your example taught a lesson to
other kings.
¹⁸You dishonored your places of
worship
through your many sins and
dishonest trade.
So I set your city on fire.
And it burned up.
I turned you into ashes on the
ground
for all those watching to see.
¹⁹All the nations who knew you
are shocked about you.
Your punishment was so terrible.
And you are gone forever.'"

Prophecy Against Sidon

²⁰The Lord spoke his word to me.
He said: ²¹"Human being, look toward
the city of Sidon and prophesy*d* against
her. ²²Say: 'This is what the Lord God
says:
I am against you, Sidon.
I will show my greatness among
you.
Then people will know that I am
the Lord
when I have punished Sidon.
I will show my holiness by
defeating her.
²³I will send diseases to Sidon,
and blood will flow in her streets.
Those who are wounded in Sidon
will fall dead.
She will be attacked from all sides.
Then they will know that I am
the Lord.

God Will Help Israel

²⁴"No more will neighboring nations
be like thorny branches or sharp stick-
ers to hurt Israel. Then they will know
that I am the Lord God.

²⁵"'This is what the Lord God says: I will gather the people of Israel from the nations where they are scattered. I will show my holiness when the nations see what I do to my people. Then they will live in their own land—the land I gave to my servant Jacob. ²⁶Then they will live safely in the land. They will build houses and plant vineyards. They will live in safety after I have punished all the nations around who hate them. Then they will know that I am the Lord their God.'"

Prophecy Against Egypt

29 It was the tenth year, in the tenth month of our captivity. It was on the twelfth day of the month. The Lord spoke his word to me. He said: ²"Human being, look toward the king of Egypt. And prophesy*ᵈ* against him and all Egypt. ³Say: 'This is what the Lord God says:

I am against you, king of Egypt.
You are like a great crocodile that
     lies in the Nile River.
You say, "The Nile is mine.
I made it for myself."
⁴But I will put hooks in your jaws.
I will make the fish of the Nile
     stick to your sides.
I will pull you up out of your rivers,
     with all the fish sticking to your
     sides.
⁵I will leave you in the desert.
I will leave you and all the fish
     from your rivers.
You will fall on the open field.
You will not be picked up or
     buried.
I have given you to the wild animals.
And I have given you to the birds
     of the sky for food.
⁶Then all the people who live in Egypt will know that I am the Lord.

"'Israel tried to lean on you for help. But you were like a crutch made out of a weak stalk of grass. ⁷When their hands grabbed you, you splintered and tore open their shoulders. When they leaned on you, you broke and made all their backs twist.

⁸"'So this is what the Lord God says: I will cause an enemy to attack you. He will kill your men and animals. ⁹Then Egypt will become an empty desert. They will know that I am the Lord.

"'This is because you said, "The Nile River is mine. And I have made it." ¹⁰So, I am against you. I am against your rivers. I will destroy the land of Egypt. It will be empty desert from Migdol in the north to Aswan in the south. It will be empty all the way to the southern border of Cush. ¹¹No man or animal will walk through it. No one will live in Egypt for 40 years. ¹²I will make the land of Egypt the emptiest country of all. And her cities will be the emptiest of all ruined cities for 40 years. And I will scatter the Egyptians among the nations. And I will spread them among the countries.

¹³"'This is what the Lord God says: After 40 years I will gather Egypt from the nations where they have been scattered. ¹⁴I will bring back the Egyptian captives. I will make the Egyptians return to southern Egypt. They will return to the land that they came from. They will become a weak kingdom there. ¹⁵It will be the weakest kingdom. It will never again rule other nations. I will make it so weak it will never again rule over the nations. ¹⁶The Israelites will never again depend on Egypt. Egypt's punishment will remind the Israelites of their sin. They turned to Egypt for help and not to God. Then they will know that I am the Lord God.'"

Egypt Is Given to Babylon

¹⁷It was the twenty-seventh year of our captivity, in the first month. It was on the first day of the month. The Lord spoke his word to me. He said: ¹⁸"Human being, Nebuchadnezzar king of Babylon made his army fight hard against Tyre. Every soldier's head was rubbed bare. Every shoulder was rubbed raw. But Nebuchadnezzar and his army gained nothing from fighting Tyre. ¹⁹So this is what the Lord God

says: I will give the land of Egypt to Nebuchadnezzar king of Babylon. And Nebuchadnezzar will take away Egypt's people. He will take Egypt's wealth and its valuable things as pay for his army. [20]I have given Nebuchadnezzar the land of Egypt. It is a reward for working hard to defeat Egypt for me. That is what the Lord God says.

[21]"On that day I will make Israel grow strong again. I will let you, Ezekiel, speak to them. Then they will know that I am the Lord God."

Egypt Will Be Punished

30 The Lord spoke his word to me. He said, [2]"Human being, prophesy[d] and say, 'This is what the Lord God says:
Cry and say,
  "The terrible day is coming."
[3]The day is near.
  The Lord's day of judging is near.
  It is a cloudy day.
  It is a time when the nations will
    be judged.
[4]An enemy will attack Egypt.
  And Cush will tremble with fear.
  When the killing begins in Egypt,
    her wealth will be taken away.
  Egypt's foundations will be torn
    down.

[5]Cush, Put, Lydia, Arabia, Libya and my people will die. All these who made an agreement with Egypt will fall dead in war.
  [6]'This is what the Lord God says:
  Those who fight on Egypt's side
    will fall.
  The power she is proud of will
    go down.
  The people in Egypt will fall dead
    in war
    from Migdol in the north to Aswan
      in the south,
    says the Lord God.
[7]They will be
  the emptiest land.
  Egypt's cities will be
    like other cities that lie in ruin.
[8]Then they will know that I am
  the Lord.

This will happen when I set fire
    to Egypt
  and when all those nations on her
    side are crushed.
[9]"At that time I will send messengers in ships. They will frighten Cush which now feels safe. The people of Cush will tremble with fear when Egypt is punished. And that time is sure to come.

[10]"This is what the Lord God says:
  I will destroy great numbers of
    people in Egypt.
  I will do it through Nebuchadnezzar
    king of Babylon.
[11]Nebuchadnezzar and his army
  are the cruelest army of any nation.
  They will be brought in to destroy
    the land.
  They will pull out their swords
    against Egypt.
  They will fill the land with those
    they kill.
[12]I will make the streams of the Nile
    River become dry land.
  Then I will sell the dry land to
    evil people.
  I will destroy the land and
    everything in it.
  I will do it through the power of
    strangers.

I, the Lord, have spoken.

Egypt's Idols Are Destroyed

[13]"This is what the Lord God says:
  I will destroy the idols.
  And I will take away the statues of
    false gods from the city of
    Memphis.
  There will no longer be a leader
    in Egypt.
  And I will spread fear through the
    land of Egypt.
[14]I will make southern Egypt empty.
  I will start a fire in Zoan.
  I will punish Thebes.
[15]And I will pour out my anger against
    Pelusium,
  the strong place of Egypt.
  I will destroy great numbers of
    people in Thebes.
[16]I will set fire to Egypt.

Pelusium will be in great pain.
The walls of Thebes will be broken
    open.
And Memphis will have troubles
    every day.
[17]The young men of Heliopolis and
    Bubastis
will fall dead in war.
And the people will be taken away
    as captives.
[18]In Tahpanhes the day will be dark
when I break Egypt's power.
A cloud will cover Egypt.
And her villages will be captured
    and taken away.
[19]So I will punish Egypt.
And they will know I am the Lord.'"

Egypt Becomes Weak

[20]It happened in the eleventh year of
our captivity, in the first month. It was
on the seventh day of the month. The
Lord spoke his word to me. He said:
[21]"Human being, I have broken the
powerful arm of the king of Egypt. It
has not been tied up so it will not get
well. It has not been wrapped with a
bandage. So his arm will not be strong
enough to hold a sword in war. [22]So
this is what the Lord God says: I am
against the king of Egypt. I will break
his arms. I will break both the strong
arm and the broken arm. I will make
the sword fall from his hand. [23]I will
scatter the Egyptians among the
nations. And I will spread them among
the countries. [24]I will make the arms of
the king of Babylon strong. I will put
my sword in his hand. But I will break
the arms of the king of Egypt. Then he
will cry out in pain as a wounded man
cries out. [25]So I will make the arms of
the king of Babylon strong. But the
arms of the king of Egypt will fall.
Then they will know that I am the
Lord. I will put my sword into the hand
of the king of Babylon. And he will use
the sword in war against Egypt. [26]Then
I will scatter the Egyptians among the
nations. And I will spread them among
the countries. And they will know that
I am the Lord."

A Cedar Tree

31 It happened in the eleventh year
of our captivity, in the third
month. It was on the first day of the
month. The Lord spoke his word to
me. He said: [2]"Human being, say to
the king of Egypt and his people:
'No one was like you in your
    greatness.
[3]Assyria was once like a cedar tree
    in Lebanon.
It had beautiful branches that
    shaded the forest.
It was very tall.
Its top was among the clouds.
[4]Much water made the tree grow.
The deep springs of water made
    the tree tall.
Rivers flowed
    around the bottom of the tree.
They sent their streams
    to all other trees of the field.
[5]So the tree was taller
    than all the other trees of the field.
Its branches became long and big
    because of so much water.
[6]All the birds of the sky
    made their nests in the tree's
        branches.
And all the wild animals
    gave birth under the tree's
        branches.
All great nations
    lived in the tree's shade.
[7]So the tree was great and beautiful,
    with its long branches.
Its roots reached down to many
        waters.
[8]The cedar trees in the garden of God
    were not as great as it was.
The pine trees
    did not have such great branches.
The plane trees
    did not have such branches.
No tree in the garden of God
    was as beautiful as this tree.
[9]I made it beautiful
    with many branches.
And all the trees of Eden in the
        garden of God
    wanted to be like it.

¹⁰"'So this is what the Lord God says: The tree has grown tall. Its top has reached the clouds. And it has become proud of its height. ¹¹So I have let a mighty ruler of the nations take care of the tree. The ruler will surely punish the tree. Because it is evil I will get rid of it. ¹²The cruelest foreign nation cut it down and left it. The tree's branches fell on the mountains and in all the valleys. Its broken branches were in all the ravines of the land. All the nations of the earth left the shade of that tree. ¹³The birds of the sky live on the fallen tree. The wild animals live among the tree's fallen branches. ¹⁴Then the trees that grow by the water will not be proud to be tall. They will not put their tops among the clouds. None of the trees that are watered well will grow that tall. They all are meant to die and go under the ground. They will be with those who have died and have gone down to where the dead are.

¹⁵"'This is what the Lord God says: On the day when the tree went down to where the dead are, I made people cry loudly. I covered the deep springs and held back their rivers. And the great waters stopped flowing. I made Lebanon cry loudly for the great tree. All the trees of the field dried up and died. ¹⁶I made the nations shake with fear at the sound of the tree falling. I brought the tree down to where the dead are. It went with those who go down to the grave. Then trees of Eden and the best trees of Lebanon were comforted. All the well-watered trees were comforted in the earth below. ¹⁷But these trees also went down with the great tree to the place where the dead are. They went to join those who were killed in war. They had lived under the great tree's shade. They were its friends among the nations.

¹⁸"'So no tree in Eden is equal to you in greatness and honor. But you will go down with the trees of Eden to the earth below. You will lie among unclean^d people who were killed in war.

"'This will happen to the king of Egypt and all his people, says the Lord God.'"

A Funeral Song

32 It happened in the twelfth year, in the twelfth month of our captivity. It was on the first day of the month. The Lord spoke his word to me. He said: ²"Human being, sing a funeral song about the king of Egypt. Say to him:

'You are like a young lion among
    the nations.
You are like a crocodile in the
    seas.
You splash around in your streams.
And you stir up the waters with
    your feet.
You make the rivers muddy.

³"'This is what the Lord God says:
I will spread my net over you.
And I will use a large group
    of people
    to pull you up in my net.
⁴Then I will throw you on the land.
I will toss you into the open field.
I will let the birds of the sky rest
    on you.
And I will let the animals of the
    earth eat you until they are
    full.
⁵I will scatter your flesh on the
    mountains.
And I will fill the valleys with what
    is left of you.
⁶I will drench the land with your
    flowing blood.
I will soak the mountains,
and the ravines will be full of
    your flesh.
⁷I will make you disappear.
And I will cover the sky and make
    the stars dark.
I will cover the sun with a cloud.
And the moon will not shine.
⁸I will make all the shining lights in
    the sky
become dark over you.
I will bring darkness over your
    land,
says the Lord God.

⁹I will cause many people to be afraid
    when I have another nation
        destroy you.
    Nations you have not known will
        be afraid because of you.
¹⁰I will cause people to be shocked
        about you.
    Their kings will tremble with fear
        because of you
    when I swing my sword before
        them.
    They will shake every moment
        on the day you fall.
    Each king will be afraid for his
        own life.

¹¹"'So this is what the Lord God says:
    The sword of the king of Babylon
        will come on you.
¹²I will cause your people to fall
    by the swords of mighty soldiers.
        They are the most terrible of all
            the nations.
    They will destroy the pride of Egypt.
    All Egypt's people will be destroyed.
¹³I will also destroy all Egypt's cattle
    which live alongside many waters.
    The foot of man will not stir the
        waters.
    And the hoofs of cattle will not
        muddy them anymore.
¹⁴So I will let the Egyptians' waters
        become quiet.
    I will cause their rivers to run as
        smoothly as olive oil,
    says the Lord God.
¹⁵I will make the land of Egypt empty.
    I will take everything that is in
        the land.
    I will destroy all those who live
        in Egypt.
    Then they will know that I am
        the Lord.'

¹⁶"This is the funeral song people
will sing for Egypt. The women of the
nations will sing it for Egypt. They will
sing a funeral song for Egypt and all
its people, says the Lord God."

Egypt to Be Destroyed

¹⁷It happened in the twelfth year of
our captivity. It was on the fifteenth
day of the month. The Lord spoke his
word to me. He said: ¹⁸"Human being,
cry for the people of Egypt. Bring
down Egypt, together with the women
of the powerful nations. Bring them
down to the earth below. Bring them
down with those who go to the place of
the dead. ¹⁹Say to them: 'Are you more
beautiful than others? Go lie down in
death with those who are unclean.'ᵈ
²⁰The Egyptians will fall among those
killed by war. Egypt is going to be
killed by the sword. The enemy will
drag her and all her people away.
²¹The leaders of the mighty ones will
speak from the place of death. They
will say about the king of Egypt and
the nations which help him: 'The king
and the nations which help him have
come down here. They lie killed by the
sword among those who are unclean.'
²²"Assyria and all its army lie dead
there. The graves of their soldiers are
all around. All were killed in war. ²³As-
syria's grave was put in the deep parts
of the place where the dead are. And
its army lies around its grave. When
they lived, they frightened people in
the land of the living. But now all of
them have been killed in war.
²⁴"The nation of Elam is there. And
all its army is around its grave. All of
them were killed in war. They had
frightened people on earth and were
unclean. So they went down to the
lowest parts of the place where the
dead are. And they must carry their
shame with those who go down to the
place where the dead are. ²⁵A bed is
made for Elam with all those killed in
war. They will be in the place where
the dead are. The graves of her soldiers are all around her. Elam's people
are unclean. So they have been killed
in war. They also scared people who
live on earth. But they must also carry
their shame with those who go down
to where the dead are. Their graves
are with the rest who were killed.
²⁶"Meshech and Tubal are there.
The graves of all their soldiers surround them. All of them are unclean.

So they have been killed in war. They also frightened people who live on earth. 27But they are not buried with the other unclean soldiers who have been killed in battle. They are not with those who went where the dead are with their weapons of war. These soldiers had their swords laid under their heads and their shields on their bodies. People who live on earth used to be afraid of these mighty soldiers.

28"You, king of Egypt, will be broken and lie among those who are unclean. You will be with those who were killed in war.

29"Edom is there also. Its kings and all its leaders are there. They were mighty. But now they lie in death with those killed in war. They will lie with those who are unclean. And they will be with those who go down to where the dead are.

30"All the rulers of the north are there. And all the Sidonians are there. Their strength frightened people. These rulers of the north and the Sidonians have gone down in shame with those who were killed. They are unclean, lying with those killed in war. They have carried their shame with those who go down to where the dead are.

31"The king of Egypt and his army will see these who have been killed in war. Then the king and all his army will be comforted for all his soldiers killed in war, says the Lord God. 32I made people who live on earth afraid of the king of Egypt. But he and his people will lie among those who are unclean. They will lie with those who were killed by the sword, says the Lord God."

Ezekiel Is Watchman for Israel

33 The Lord spoke his word to me. He said: 2"Human being, speak to your people. Say to them: 'I might bring a war against a land. The people of the land may choose one of their men. They may make him their watchman. 3This watchman might see the enemy coming to attack the land. And he blows the trumpet and warns the people. 4A person might hear the sound of the trumpet, but do nothing. Then the enemy will come and kill him. That person will be responsible for his own death. 5He heard the sound of the trumpet. But he did not do anything. So he is to blame for his own death. If he had done something, he would have saved his own life. 6But the watchman might see the enemy coming to attack and not blow the trumpet. So the people are not warned. Then the enemy comes and kills one of them. That person has died because of his own sin. But I will punish the watchman for the person's death.'

7"As for you, human being, I have made you a watchman for Israel. If you hear a message from me, you must warn them for me. 8I might say to the wicked person: 'Wicked man, you will surely die.' But you might not speak to warn the evil person to stop doing evil. Then he will die while still a sinner. But I will punish you for his death. 9But you might warn a wicked person to stop doing evil. If he does not stop, he will die while still a sinner. But you have saved your life.

10"So you, human being, say to Israel: 'You have said: Surely our law-breaking and sins are hurting us. They will kill us. What can we do so we will live?' 11Say to them: 'The Lord God says: As surely as I live, this is true. I do not want a wicked person to die. I want him to stop doing evil and live. Turn back! Turn back from your wicked ways! You don't want to die, people of Israel.'

12"And you, human being, say to your people: 'The goodness of a good person will not save him when he sins. The evil of the wicked person will not cause him to be punished if he turns from it. A good person will not be able to live by the good he did earlier if he sins.' 13I might tell the good person, "You will surely live." But he might think he has done enough good and then do evil. Then none of the good things he did will be remembered. He will die because of the evil he has done. ¹⁴Or, I might say to the wicked person, "You will surely die." But he might turn from his sin and do what is right and honest. ¹⁵He returns what somebody gave him as a promise to repay a loan. He pays back what he stole. He lives by the rules that give life. He does not sin. Then that one will surely live. He will not die. ¹⁶He will not be punished for any of his sins. He now does what is right and fair. He will surely live.

¹⁷"But your people say: 'The way of the Lord is not fair.' But it is their own way that is not fair. ¹⁸The good person might turn from his goodness and do evil. Then he will die for his evil. ¹⁹But the wicked person might stop doing evil and do what is right and fair. Then he will live. ²⁰You still say: 'The way of the Lord is not fair.' Israel, I will judge each of you by his own ways."

The Fall of Jerusalem Explained

²¹It happened in the twelfth year of our captivity. It was on the fifth day of the tenth month. A person who had escaped from Jerusalem came to me. He said, "Jerusalem has been defeated." ²²Now I had felt the power of the Lord on me the evening before. The Lord had made me able to talk again. He did this before the person came to me in the morning. I could speak. I was not without speech anymore.

²³Then the Lord spoke his word to me. He said: ²⁴"Human being, people who live in the ruins in the land of Israel are saying: 'Abraham was only one person. Yet he was given the land as his own. Surely the land has been given to us, who are many, as our very own.' ²⁵So say to them: 'This is what the Lord God says: You eat meat with the blood still in it. You ask your idols for help. You murder people. Should you then have the land as your very own? ²⁶You depend on your sword. You do terrible things which I hate.

Each of you has sexual relations with his neighbor's wife. So should you have the land?'

²⁷"Say to them: 'This is what the Lord God says: As surely as I live, this is true. Those who are among the city ruins in Israel will be killed in war. Those who live in the country will be eaten by wild animals. People hiding in the strong places and caves will die of disease. ²⁸I will make the land an empty desert. The people's pride in the land's power will end. The mountains of Israel will become empty. No one will pass through them. ²⁹They will know that I am the Lord when I make the land an empty desert. This is because of the things they have done that I hate.'

³⁰"But as for you, human being, your people talk against you. They talk by the walls and in the doorways of houses. They say to each other: 'Come now, and hear the message from the Lord.' ³¹So they come to you as if they are still my people. They sit before you. They hear your words. But they will not do them. With their mouths they tell me they love me. But their hearts desire their selfish profits. ³²To your people you are nothing more than a singer who sings love songs. You are like one who has a beautiful voice. You are like one who plays a musical instrument well. They hear your words, but they will not do them.

³³"This will come true. It will surely happen. Then the people will know that a prophet[d] has been among them."

The Leaders Are like Shepherds

34 The Lord spoke his word to me. He said: ²"Human being, prophesy[d] against the leaders of Israel, who are like shepherds. Prophesy and say to them: 'This is what the Lord God says: How terrible it will be for the shepherds of Israel who feed only themselves! Why don't the shepherds feed the flock? ³You eat the milk curds from the sheep. You clothe yourselves with the wool from the sheep. You kill the fat sheep. But you do not feed the flock. ⁴You have not made the weak strong. You have not healed the sick. You have not put bandages on those that were hurt. You have not brought back those who strayed away. You have not searched for the lost. You ruled the sheep with cruel force. ⁵The sheep were scattered because there was no shepherd. Then they became food for every wild animal. ⁶My flock wandered over all the mountains and on every high hill. They were scattered over all the face of the earth. And no one searched or looked for them.

⁷"So, you shepherds, hear the word of the Lord. This is what the Lord God says: ⁸As surely as I live, my flock has been caught. It has become food for all the wild animals. This is because the flock has no shepherd. The shepherds did not search for my flock. No, they fed themselves instead of my flock. ⁹So, you shepherds, hear the word of the Lord. ¹⁰This is what the Lord God says: I am against the shepherds. I will blame them for what has happened to my sheep. I will not let them tend the flock anymore. Then the shepherds will stop feeding themselves. And I will take my flock from their mouths. My sheep will no longer be their food.

¹¹"This is what the Lord God says: I, myself, will search for my sheep. I will take care of them. ¹²A shepherd will take care of his scattered flock when it is found. In the same way I will take care of my sheep. I will save them from all the places where they are scattered. I will do this on a cloudy and dark day. ¹³I will bring them out from the nations. I will gather them from the countries. I will bring them to their own land. I will pasture them on the mountains and in the ravines of Israel. And I will feed them in all the places where people live in the land. ¹⁴I will feed them in a good pasture. They will eat grass on the high mountains of Israel. They will lie down on good ground where they eat grass. They will eat in rich grassland on the

mountains of Israel. ¹⁵I will feed my flock and lead them to rest, says the Lord God. ¹⁶I will search for the lost. I will bring back those that were scattered. I will put bandages on those that were hurt. I will make the weak strong. I will destroy those sheep that are fat and strong. I will tend the sheep with fairness.

¹⁷"This is what the Lord God says: And as for you, my flock, I will judge between one sheep and another. I will judge between the male sheep and the male goats. ¹⁸Is it not enough for you to eat grass in the good land? Must you crush the rest of the grass with your feet? Is it not enough for you to drink clear water? Must you make the rest of the water muddy with your feet? ¹⁹Must my flock eat what you crush? And must they drink what you make muddy with your feet?

²⁰"So this is what the Lord God says to them: I, myself, will judge between the fat sheep and the thin sheep. ²¹You push with your side and with your shoulder. You knock down all the weak sheep with your horns. You do this until you have forced them away. ²²So I will save my flock. They will not be hurt anymore. I will judge between one sheep and another. ²³Then I will put one shepherd over them, my servant David. He will feed them. He will tend them and will be their shepherd. ²⁴Then I, the Lord, will be their God. And my servant David will be a ruler among them. I, the Lord, have spoken.

²⁵"And I will make an agreement of peace with my sheep. I will remove harmful animals from the land. Then the sheep will live safely in the desert. And they will sleep in the woods without danger. ²⁶I will bless them and let them live around my hill. I will cause the rains to come when it is time for them. There will be showers to bless them. ²⁷Also the trees of the field will give their fruit. The land will give its harvest. And the sheep will be safe on their land. Then they will know that I am the Lord. I will break the bars of

their captivity. And I will save them from the power of those who made them slaves. ²⁸They will not be led captive by the nations again. The wild animals will not eat them. But they will live safely. No one will make them afraid. ²⁹I will give them a place famous for its good crops. Then they will no longer suffer from hunger in the land. They will not suffer the insults of other nations anymore. ³⁰Then they will know that I, the Lord their God, am with them. The nation of Israel will know that they are my people, says the Lord God. ³¹And you, my sheep, are the sheep of my pasture. You are my people and I am your God, says the Lord God.'"

Prophecy Against Edom

35 The Lord spoke his word to me. He said: ²"Human being, look toward Mount Edom and prophesy[d] against it. ³Say to it: 'This is what the Lord God says: I am against you, Mount Edom. I will stretch out my hand against you. And I will make you an empty desert. ⁴I will destroy your cities. And you will become empty. Then you will know that I am the Lord.

⁵"'This is because you have always been an enemy of Israel. You let them be defeated in war when they were in trouble. It was the time of their final punishment. ⁶So the Lord God says, As surely as I live, I will let you be murdered. Murder will chase you. You did not hate murdering people, so murder will chase you. ⁷And I will make Mount Edom an empty ruin. And I will destroy everyone who goes in or comes out of it. ⁸I will fill its mountains with those who are killed. Those killed in war will fall on your hills. They will fall in your valleys and in all your ravines. ⁹I will make you a ruin forever. No one will live in your cities. Then you will know that I am the Lord.

¹⁰"'You said, "These two nations, Israel and Judah, and these two lands will be ours. We will take them for our own." But the Lord was there. ¹¹So this is what the Lord God says: As surely as I live, this is true. I will treat you just as you treated them. When you were angry and jealous, you acted hatefully against them. I will punish you. And that is how I will show the Israelites who I am. ¹²Then you will know that I, the Lord God, have heard all your insults. Those insults were against the mountains of Israel. You said, "They have been ruined. They have been given to us to eat." ¹³You have not stopped your proud talk against me. I have heard you. ¹⁴This is what the Lord God says: All the earth will be happy when I make you an empty ruin. ¹⁵You were happy when the land of Israel was ruined. But I will do the same thing to you. Mount Edom and all Edom, you will become an empty ruin. Then you will know that I am the Lord God.'"

Israel to Come Home

36 "Human being, prophesy[d] to the mountains of Israel and say: 'Mountains of Israel, hear the word of the Lord. ²This is what the Lord God says: The enemy has said this against you: "Now the old places to worship false gods have become ours."' ³So prophesy and say: 'This is what the Lord God says: They have made you an empty ruin. They have crushed you from all around. You belonged to the other nations. People talked and whispered against you. ⁴So, mountains of Israel, hear the word of the Lord God. The Lord God speaks to the mountains, hills, ravines and valleys. And he speaks to the empty ruins and abandoned cities that have been robbed and laughed at by the other nations. ⁵This is what the Lord God says: I have spoken in hot anger against the other nations. I have spoken against Edom. The Edomites took my land for themselves. They did this with joy and with hate in their hearts. They forced out the people and took their pastureland.' ⁶So prophesy about the land of Israel. Say to the mountains, hills, ravines and valleys: 'This is what the Lord God says: I speak in my jealous anger. This is because you have suffered the insults of the nations. [7]So this is what the Lord God says: I promise that the nations around you will also have to suffer insults.

[8]"But you, mountains of Israel, you will grow branches and fruit for my people. My people will soon come home. [9]I am concerned about you. I am for you. You will be plowed, and seed will be planted in you. [10]I will multiply the people who live on you. All the people of Israel will come. The cities will have people living in them. The ruins will be rebuilt. [11]I will make the people and animals living on you increase in number. They will grow and be fruitful. You will have people living on you as you did before. I will make you better off than at the beginning. Then you will know that I am the Lord. [12]I will cause my people Israel to walk on you. Then they will take you, and you will belong to them. You will never again take their children away from them.

[13]"This is what the Lord God says: People say about you: "You eat people and take children from your nation." [14]You will not destroy people anymore. You will not make your nation stumble anymore, says the Lord God. [15]I will not make you listen to insults from the nations anymore. You will not suffer shame from them anymore, says the Lord God.'"

The Lord Acts for Himself

[16]The Lord spoke his word to me again. He said: [17]"Human being, the nation of Israel was living in their own land. But they made it unclean[d] by their ways and the things they did. Their ways were like a woman's uncleanness in her time of monthly bleeding. [18]So I poured out my anger against them. I did it because of the murders they did in the land. And I did it because they made the land unclean with their idols. [19]I scattered them among the nations. And they were spread through all the countries. I punished them for how they lived and the things they did. [20]They dishonored my holy name in the nations where they went. The nations said about them: 'These are the people of the Lord. But they had to leave the land which he gave them.' [21]But I felt bad about my holy name. The nation of Israel had dishonored it among the nations where they went.

[22]"So say to the people of Israel, 'This is what the Lord God says: Israel, I am going to act, but not for your sake. Israel, I will do something to help my holy name. You have dishonored it among the nations where you went. [23]I will prove the holiness of my great name. It has been dishonored among the nations. You have dishonored it among these nations. But the nations will know that I am the Lord. I will prove myself holy before their eyes, says the Lord God.

[24]"I will take you from the nations. I will gather you out of all the lands. And I will bring you back into your own land. [25]Then I will sprinkle clean water on you, and you will be clean. I will cleanse you from all your uncleanness and your idols. [26]Also, I will teach you to respect me completely. I will put a new way to think inside you. I will take out the stubborn heart like stone from your bodies. And I will give you an obedient heart of flesh. [27]I will put my Spirit[d] inside you. And I will help you live by my rules. You will be careful to obey my laws. [28]Then you will live in the land I gave to your ancestors. So you will be my people, and I will be your God. [29]Also, I will save you from all your uncleanness. I will command the grain to come and grow. I will not allow a time of hunger to hurt you. [30]I will multiply the harvest of the field. You will never again suffer shame among the nations because of hunger. [31]And you will remember your evil ways and the things you did that were not good. Then you will hate yourselves because of your sins and terrible acts that I hate. [32]I want you to know

that I am not doing this for your sake, says the Lord God. Be ashamed and embarrassed about your ways, Israel.

33"'This is what the Lord God says: This is what will happen on the day I cleanse you from all your sins: I will cause the cities to have people living in them again. And the destroyed places will be rebuilt. 34The empty land will be plowed. It will no longer be a ruin for everyone who passes by to see. 35They will say: "This land was ruined. Now it has become like the garden of Eden. The cities were destroyed. They were empty and ruined. But now they are protected and have people living in them." 36Then those nations still around you will know. They will know that I, the Lord, have rebuilt what was destroyed. And I have planted what was empty. I, the Lord, have spoken. And I will do it.'

37"This is what the Lord God says: I will again be asked by the people of Israel to do this thing for them. I will make their people grow to be as many as a flock of sheep. 38They will be like the flocks brought to Jerusalem during her holy feasts. Her ruined cities will be filled with flocks of people. Then they will know that I am the Lord."

The Vision of Dry Bones

37 I felt the power of the Lord was on me. He brought me out by the Spirit*d* of the Lord. And he put me down in the middle of a valley. It was full of bones. 2The Lord led me around among the bones. There were many bones on the bottom of the valley. I saw the bones were very dry. 3Then he asked me, "Human being, can these bones live?"

I answered, "Lord God, only you know."

4The Lord said to me, "Prophesy*d* to these bones. Say to them, 'Dry bones, hear the word of the Lord. 5This is what the Lord God says to the bones: I will cause breath to enter you. Then you will live. 6I will put muscles on you.

I will put flesh on you. I will cover you with skin. Then I will put breath in you, and you will live. Then you will know that I am the Lord.'"

"**D**o you know what Ezekiel saw in the valley? Read Ezekiel 37:1-14 and find out."

7So I prophesied as I was commanded. While I prophesied, there was a noise and a rattling. The bones came together, bone to bone. 8I looked and saw muscles come on the bones. Flesh grew, and skin covered the bones. But there was no breath in them.

9Then the Lord said to me, "Prophesy to the wind.*n* Prophesy, human being, and say to the wind: 'This is what the Lord God says: Wind, come from the four winds. Breathe on these people who were killed so they can live again.'" 10So I prophesied as the Lord commanded me. And the breath came into them, and they came to life. They stood on their feet. They were a very large army.

11Then the Lord said to me: "Human being, these bones are like all the people of Israel. They say, 'Our bones are dried up, and our hope has gone. We are destroyed.' 12So, prophesy, and say to them: 'This is what the Lord God says: My people, I will open your graves. And I will cause you to come up out of your graves. Then I will bring you into the land of Israel. 13This is how you, my people, will know that I am the Lord. I will open your graves and cause you to come up from them. 14And I will put my Spirit inside you. You will come to life. Then I will put you in your own land. And you will know that I, the Lord, have spoken and done it, says the Lord.'"

*n*wind This Hebrew word could also mean "breath" or "spirit."

Judah and Israel Back Together

[15]The Lord spoke his word to me. He said, [16]"Human being, take a stick of wood. Write on it, 'For Judah and all the Israelites with him.' Then take another stick of wood. Write on it, 'The stick of Ephraim, for Joseph and all the Israelites with him.' [17]Then join them together into one stick. Then they will be one in your hand.

[18]"Your people will say to you, 'Explain to us what you mean by this.' [19]Tell them, 'This is what the Lord God says: I will take the stick which is for Joseph and the tribes[d] of Israel with him. This stick is in the hand of Ephraim. Then I will put it with the stick of Judah. And I will make them into one stick. And they will be one in my hand.' [20]Hold the sticks of wood on which you wrote these names. Hold them in your hands so the people can see them. [21]Say to the people: 'This is what the Lord God says: I will take the people of Israel from among the nations where they have gone. I will gather them from all around. I will bring them into their own land. [22]I will make them one nation in the land, on the mountains of Israel. One king will rule all of them. They will never again be two nations. They will not be divided into two kingdoms anymore. [23]They will not continue to make themselves unclean[d] by their idols, their statues of gods which I hate or their sins. But I will save them from all the ways they sin and turn against me. And I will make them clean. Then they will be my people. And I will be their God.

[24]"'And my servant David will be their king. They will all have one shepherd. They will live by my rules and obey my laws. [25]They will live on the land I gave to my servant Jacob. It is the land in which your ancestors lived. They will all live on the land forever: they, their children and their grandchildren. David my servant will be their king forever. [26]And I will make an agreement of peace with them. It will be an agreement that continues forever. I will

put them in their land. I will make them grow in number. Then I will put my Temple[d] among them forever. [27]The place where I live will be with them. I will be their God, and they will be my people. [28]When my Temple is among them forever, the nations will know that I, the Lord, make Israel holy.'"

Prophecy Against Gog

38 The Lord spoke his word to me. He said: [2]"Human being, turn toward Gog of the land of Magog. He is the chief ruler of the nations of Meshech and Tubal. Prophesy[d] against him. [3]Say, 'The Lord God says this: I am against you, Gog, chief ruler of Meshech and Tubal. [4]I will turn you around. I will put hooks in your jaws. And I will bring you out with all your army, horses and horsemen. All of them will be finely dressed. They will be a large army with large and small shields. All of them will have swords. [5]Persia, Cush and Put will be with them. All of them will have shields and helmets. [6]There will also be Gomer with all its troops. And there will be the nation of Togarmah from the far north. It will have all its troops. There will be many other nations with you.

[7]"'Be prepared. Be prepared, you and all the armies that have come together to make you their commander. [8]After many days you will be called for service. After many years you will come into a land that has been rebuilt from war. The people in the land will be gathered from many nations to the mountains of Israel. Those mountains were empty for a long time. These people were brought out from the nations. They will all be living in safety. [9]And you will go up like a storm. You will be like a cloud covering the land. It will be you, all your troops and many nations with you.

[10]"'This is what the Lord God says: At that time ideas will come into your mind. You will think up an evil plan. [11]You will say, "I will march against a land of towns without walls. I will

attack those who are at rest and live in safety. All of them live without city walls. They have no gate bars or gates. [12]I will capture valuable things and take good things. I will turn my power against the rebuilt ruins that now have people living in them. I will go against these people who have been gathered from the nations. They have become rich with farm animals and property. They live at the center of the world." [13]Sheba, Dedan and the traders of Tarshish, with all its villages, will say this to you: "Did you come to capture valuable things? Did you bring your troops together to take things? Did you bring them to carry away silver and gold? Did you bring them to take away farm animals and property?"'

[14]"So prophesy, human being, and say to Gog: 'This is what the Lord God says: Now that my people Israel are living in safety, you will know about it. [15]You will come from your place in the far north. And many people will be with you. All of them will ride on horses. You will be a large group with a mighty army. [16]You will come against my people Israel like a cloud that covers the land. This will happen in the days to come. I will bring you against my land. Gog, then the nations will know me. They will see me show my greatness by what I do through you.

[17]"'This is what the Lord God says: You are the one about whom I spoke in past days. I spoke through my servants the prophets of Israel. These prophets of Israel prophesied for many years. They said that I would bring you against them. [18]This is what will happen: On the day Gog comes against the land of Israel, my anger will become very great, says the Lord God. [19]With jealousy and great anger I tell you this. At that time there will surely be a great earthquake in Israel. [20]The fish of the sea and the birds of the sky will shake with fear before me. The wild animals and everything that crawls on the ground will shake with fear. And all the people on the earth

will shake with fear before me. Also the mountains will be thrown down. And the cliffs will fall. Every wall will fall to the ground. [21]And I will call for a war against Gog on all my mountains, says the Lord God. Every man's sword will be against his brother. [22]I will punish Gog with disease and death. I will send a heavy rain, with hailstones and burning sulfur on Gog. I will send it on his army and on the many nations with him. [23]Then I will show how great I am. I will show my holiness. And I will make myself known to the many nations that watch. Then they will know that I am the Lord.'

The Death of Gog and His Army

39 "Human being, prophesy[d] against Gog and say: 'This is what the Lord God says: I am against you, Gog, chief ruler of Meshech and Tubal. [2]I will turn you around and lead you. I will bring you from the far north. I will send you to attack the mountains of Israel. [3]I will knock your bow out of your left hand. I will throw down your arrows from your right hand. [4]You will fall dead on the mountains of Israel. You, all your troops and the nations with you will fall dead. I will let you be food for every bird that eats meat and every wild animal. [5]You will die in the country. I have spoken, says the Lord God. [6]I will send fire on Magog and those who live in safety on the coastlands. Then they will know that I am the Lord.

[7]"'And I will make myself known among my people Israel. I will not let myself be dishonored anymore. Then the nations will know that I am the Lord. They will know I am the Holy One in Israel. [8]It is coming! It will happen, says the Lord God. The day I talked about is coming.

[9]"'Then those who live in the cities of Israel will go out. They will make fires with the enemy's weapons and burn them. They will burn both large and small shields. They will burn bows and arrows, war clubs and spears. They

will use the weapons to burn in their fires for seven years. [10]They won't need to take wood from the field or chop firewood from the forests. This is because they will make fires with the weapons. They will take the valuable things of those who took their valuable things. They will grab the things of those who grabbed their things, says the Lord God.

[11]"On that day I will give Gog a place to be buried in Israel. It will be the Valley of the Travelers, east of the Dead Sea.[d] It will block the road for travelers. This is because Gog and all his army will be buried there. People will call it The Valley of Gog's Army.

[12]"The people of Israel will be burying them for seven months to make the land clean[d] again. [13]All the people of the land will bury them. The people of Israel will be honored on the day of my victory, says the Lord God.

[14]"They will choose men to work through the land to make it clean. With others they will bury Gog's soldiers still lying dead on the ground. After the seven months are finished, they will still search. [15]They will go through the land. If one person sees a human bone, he will put a marker by it. The sign will stay there until the gravediggers come. They will bury the bone in The Valley of Gog's Army. [16]A city will be there named Hamonah. So they will make the land clean again.'

[17]"Human being, this is what the Lord God says: Speak to every kind of bird and wild animal: 'Come together, come! Come together from all around to my sacrifice. I will prepare it for you. It is a great sacrifice on the mountains of Israel. Then you can eat flesh and drink blood. [18]You will eat the flesh of mighty men. You will drink the blood of the rulers of the earth. You will do it as people eat all the fat animals from Bashan: male sheep, lambs, goats and bulls. [19]You will eat and drink from my sacrifice which I have made ready for you. So you will eat fat until you are full. You will drink blood until you are

drunk. [20]At my table you will eat until you are full of horses and riders and all kinds of soldiers,' says the Lord God.

[21]"And I will show my greatness among the nations. All the nations will feel my power when I punish them. [22]From that day on the people of Israel will know that I am the Lord their God. [23]And the nations will know Israel was taken away captive because they turned against me. So I turned away from them. And I let their enemies defeat them. All of them died in war. [24]I punished them for their uncleanness[d] and their sins. I turned away from them.

[25]"So this is what the Lord God says: Now I will bring the people of Jacob back from captivity. I will have mercy on the whole nation of Israel. I will not let them dishonor me. [26]The people will forget their shame. And they will forget how they rejected me. They will live in safety on their own land. No one will make them afraid. [27]I will bring the people back from other lands. I will gather them from the lands of their enemies. That is how I will show that I am holy through my people. And many nations will see that I am holy. [28]Then my people will know that I am the Lord their God. This is because I sent them into captivity among the nations. But then I brought them back to their own land. And I didn't leave any behind. [29]I will not turn away from them anymore. I will put my Spirit[d] into the people of Israel, says the Lord God."

The New Temple

40 It was the twenty-fifth year of our captivity. It was at the beginning of the year, on the tenth day of the month. It was in the fourteenth year after Jerusalem was defeated. On that same day I felt the power of the Lord. He brought me to Jerusalem. [2]In the visions of God he brought me into the land of Israel. He put me on a very high mountain. On the south of the mountain there were some buildings that looked like a city. [3]The Lord took me closer to the buildings. I saw a man who looked as if he were made of bronze. He was standing in the gateway. He had a cord made of linen and a stick in his hand, both for measuring. [4]The man said to me, "Human being, look with your eyes and hear with your ears. And pay attention to all that I will show you. That's why you have been brought here. Tell the people of Israel all that you see."

The East Gate

[5]I saw a wall that surrounded the Temple.[d] The measuring stick in the man's hand was 10½ feet long. So the man measured the wall. It was 10½ feet thick and 10½ feet high.

[6]Then the man went to the east gate. He went up its steps and measured the opening of the gate. It was more than 10½ feet wide. [7]There were rooms for the guards. They were 10½ feet long and 10½ feet wide. The walls that came out between the guards' rooms were about 9 feet thick. And there was a gate next to the porch that faced the Temple. The opening of this gate was 10½ feet wide.

[8]Then the man measured the porch of the gate. [9]It was about 14 feet deep. And its doors were 3½ feet thick. The porch of the gate faced the Temple.

[10]There were three little rooms on each side of the last gate. These three rooms measured the same on each side. The walls between each room were the same thickness. [11]The man measured the width of the entrance to the gateway. It was 17½ feet wide. The length of the gate was about 23 feet. [12]And there was a low wall about 21 inches high in front of each room. The rooms were 10½ feet on each side. [13]The man measured the gateway from the roof of one room to the roof of the opposite room. It was about 44 feet from one door to the opposite door. [14]The man also measured the porch. It was about 35 feet wide. The courtyard was around the porch. [15]From the front of the outer side of the gate to the front of the porch of the inner side of the gate was 87½ feet. [16]The rooms and porch had small windows on all sides. The windows were narrower on the side facing the gateway. Carvings of palm trees were on each inner wall of the rooms.

The Outer Courtyard

[17]Then the man brought me into the outer courtyard. I saw rooms and a pavement of stones. Thirty rooms were along the edge of the paved walkway. [18]The pavement ran alongside the gates. It was as long as the gates were wide. This was the lower pavement. [19]Then the man measured from the outer wall to the inner wall. The outer court between these two walls was 175 feet on the east and on the north.

The North Gate

[20]The man measured the length and width of the gate leading to the outer courtyard. It faced north. [21]It had three rooms on each side. Its inner walls and its porch measured the same as the first gate. It was 87½ feet long. And it was 44 feet wide. [22]Its windows, porch and carvings of palm trees measured the same as the east gate. Seven steps went up to the gate. And the gate's porch was opposite them. [23]The inner courtyard had a gate across from the northern gate like the one on the east. The man measured it and found it was 175 feet from inner gate to outer gate.

The South Gate

[24]Then the man led me south. I saw a gate facing south. He measured its inner walls and its porch. They measured the same as the other gates. [25]The gate and its porch had windows all around like the other gates. It was 87½ feet long and 44 feet wide. [26]Seven steps went up to this gate. Its porch was in front of them. It had carvings of palm trees on its inner walls. [27]A gate was on the south side of the inner courtyard. The man measured from gate to gate on the south side. It was 175 feet.

The Inner Courtyard

²⁸Then the man brought me through the south gate to the inner courtyard. The inner south gate measured the same as the gates in the outer wall. ²⁹The inner southgate's rooms, inner walls and porch measured the same as the gates in the outer wall. There were windows all around the gate and its porch. The gate was 87½ feet long and 44 feet wide. ³⁰Each porch of each inner gate was about 44 feet long and about 9 feet wide. ³¹The inner south gate's porch faced the outer courtyard. Carvings of palm trees were on its inside walls. Its stairway had eight steps.

³²The man brought me into the inner courtyard on the east side. He measured the inner east gate. It measured the same as the other gates. ³³The inner east gate's rooms, inside walls and porch measured the same as the other gates. Windows were all around the gate and its porch. The inner east gate was 87½ feet long and 44 feet wide. ³⁴Its porch faced the outer courtyard. Carvings of palm trees were on its inner walls on each side. Its stairway had eight steps.

³⁵Then the man brought me to the inner north gate. He measured it. It measured the same as the other gates. ³⁶Its rooms, inner walls and porch measured the same as the other gates. Windows were all around the gate. It was 87½ feet long and 44 feet wide. ³⁷Its porch faced the outer courtyard. Carvings of palm trees were on its inner walls on each side. And its stairway had eight steps.

Rooms for Preparing Sacrifices

³⁸There was a room with a door that opened onto the porch of the inner north gate. In this room the priests washed animals for the burnt offerings. ³⁹There were two tables on each side of the room. Animals for burnt offerings, sin offerings and penalty offerings were killed on these tables. ⁴⁰On each side of the porch, outside the door to the room, were two tables. ⁴¹So four tables were on one side of the gate. And four tables were on the other side of the gate. In all there were eight tables on which the priests killed animals for sacrifices. ⁴²There were four tables of cut stone for the burnt offering. These tables were about 3 feet long and 3 feet wide. And they were about 2 feet high. On these tables the priests put their tools. They used the tools to kill animals for burnt offerings and the other sacrifices. ⁴³Double hooks 3 inches long were put up on all the walls. The flesh for the offering was put on the tables.

The Priests' Rooms

⁴⁴There were two rooms in the inner courtyard. One was beside the north gate. It faced south. The other room was beside the south gate. It faced north. ⁴⁵The man said to me, "The room which faces the south is for the priests. They serve in the Temple.ᵈ ⁴⁶And the room that faces north is for the priests who serve at the altar. These priests are descendantsᵈ of Zadok. They are the only descendants of Levi who can come near the Lord to serve him."

⁴⁷The man measured the Temple courtyard. It was a perfect square. It was 175 feet long and 175 feet wide. The altar was in front of the Temple.

The Temple Porch

⁴⁸The man brought me to the porch of the Temple.ᵈ And he measured each wall of the porch. It was about 9 feet on each side. The gate was 24½ feet wide. The walls of the gate were about 5 feet on each side. ⁴⁹The porch was 35 feet long and 21 feet wide. Ten steps went up to the porch. Pillars were by the walls, one on each side of the entrance.

The Holy Place of the Temple

41 The man brought me to the Holy Place. He measured its walls. They were 10½ feet wide on each side.

²The entrance was 17½ feet wide. The walls alongside the entrance were about 9 feet wide on each side. The man measured the Holy Place. It was 70 feet long and 35 feet wide.

³Then the man went inside. And he measured the walls of the doorway. Each was 3½ feet wide. The doorway was 10½ feet wide. The walls next to it were more than 12 feet thick. ⁴Then the man measured the room at the end of the Holy Place. It was 35 feet long and 35 feet wide. The man said to me, "This is the Most Holy Place."

⁵Then the man measured the wall of the Temple.ᵈ It was 10½ feet wide. The side rooms were 7 feet wide all around the Temple. ⁶The side rooms were on three different stories, each above the other. There were 30 rooms on each story. The side rooms had ledges on the wall all around. The rooms rested on the ledges but were not attached to the walls. ⁷The side rooms around the Temple were wider on each higher story. So rooms were wider on the top story. A stairway went up from the lowest story to the highest through the middle story.

⁸I also saw that the Temple had a raised base all around. It was the foundation for the side rooms and was 10½ feet thick. ⁹The outer wall of the side rooms was about 9 feet thick. There was an open area between the side rooms of the Temple ¹⁰and the priests' rooms. It was 35 feet wide and went all around the Temple. ¹¹The doors of the side rooms led to a paved base around the outside of the Temple. One door faced north. And the other door faced south. The paved base was about 9 feet wide all around.

¹²There was a building facing the Temple courtyard at the west side. It was 122½ feet wide. The wall of the building was about 9 feet thick all around. It was 157½ feet long.

¹³Then the man measured the Temple. The Temple was 175 feet long. This included the courtyard with the building and its walls. It was all 175 feet long. ¹⁴Also the eastern front of the Temple and its courtyard was 175 feet wide.

¹⁵The man measured the length of the building facing the courtyard on the west side, including its side rooms. Its walls from one side to the other were 175 feet.

The Holy Place, the Most Holy Place and the porch of the courtyard ¹⁶had wood panels on the walls. By the doorway, the Temple had wood panels on the walls. The wood covered all the walls from the floor up to the windows. The windows were covered with crossed strips of wood.

¹⁷In the space above the entrance to the Most Holy Place there were carvings. And on the outside and all the walls around the Most Holy Place and the Holy Place were carvings. ¹⁸The carvings were of creatures with wings and palm trees. A palm tree was between each carved creature. Every creature had two faces. ¹⁹One was a man's face looking toward the palm tree on one side. The other was a lion's face looking toward the palm tree on the other side. They were carved all around the Temple wall. ²⁰This was from the floor to above the door. Palm trees and creatures with wings were carved on all the walls of the Holy Place. ²¹The walls of the Holy Place were square. In front of the Most Holy Place was something that looked like ²²an altar of wood. It was more than 5 feet high and 3 feet wide. Its corners, base and sides were wood. The man said to me, "This is the table that is in the presence of the Lord." ²³Both the Holy Place and the Most Holy Place had double doors. ²⁴Each of the doors had two pieces that would swing open. ²⁵Palm trees and creatures with wings were also carved on the doors of the Holy Place. They were like those carved on the walls. And there was a wood roof on the front Temple porch. ²⁶There were windows and palm trees on both side walls of the porch. The side rooms of the Temple were also covered by a roof.

The Priests' Room

42 Then the man led me north out into the outer courtyard. He led me to the rooms across from the Temple*ᵈ* courtyard. The outer wall was north of these rooms. ²The building on the north side was 175 feet long and 87½ feet wide. ³There was 35 feet of the Temple courtyard between this building and the Temple. On the other side, this building faced the stone pavement of the outer courtyard. The building had rooms and balconies on three stories. ⁴There was a hallway on the north side of the rooms. It was 17½ feet wide and 175 feet long. Doors led into the rooms from this hallway. ⁵The top rooms were narrower. This was because the balconies took more space from them. The rooms on the first and second stories of the building were wider. ⁶The rooms were on three stories. They did not have pillars like the pillars of the courtyards. So the top rooms were farther back than those on the first and second stories. ⁷There was a wall outside parallel to the rooms and to the outer courtyard. It ran in front of the rooms for 87½ feet. ⁸The row of rooms along the outer courtyard was 87½ feet long. The rooms that faced the Temple were about 175 feet long. ⁹The lower rooms had an entrance on the east end of the building. This was so a person could enter them from the courtyard.

¹⁰There were rooms on the south side, parallel to the wall of the outer courtyard. They faced the Temple courtyard. ¹¹These rooms had a hallway in front of them. They were like the rooms on the north. They had the same length and width. And the doors were the same. ¹²The doors of the south rooms were like the doors of the north rooms. There was a door at the east end of a hall. This hall went to all the rooms.

¹³The man said to me, "The north and south rooms across from the Temple courtyard are holy rooms. There the priests who go near the Lord will eat the most holy offerings. There they will put the most holy offerings: the grain offerings, sin offerings and the penalty offerings. ¹⁴The priests who enter the Holy Place must leave their serving clothes there. Then they may go into the outer courtyard. This is because these clothes are holy. The priests must put on other clothes. Then they may go to the part of the Temple which is for the people."

The Outside of the Temple

¹⁵The man finished measuring inside the Temple.*ᵈ* Then he brought me out through the east gate. He measured the area all around. ¹⁶The man measured the east side with the measuring stick. It was 875 feet by the measuring stick. ¹⁷He measured the north side. It was 875 feet by the measuring stick. ¹⁸He measured the south side. It was 875 feet by the measuring stick. ¹⁹He went around to the west side. And it measured 875 feet by the measuring stick. ²⁰So he measured the Temple on all four sides. The Temple had a wall all around it. It was 875 feet long and 875 feet wide. It separated the holy from that which is not holy.

The Lord Among His People

43 The man led me to the outer east gate. ²And I saw the greatness of the God of Israel coming from the east. God's voice was like the roar of rushing water. His greatness made the earth shine. ³I saw a vision. It was like the vision I had seen when the Lord came to destroy the city. It was also like the vision I had seen by the Kebar River. I bowed facedown on the ground. ⁴The greatness of the Lord came into the Temple*ᵈ* through the east gate.

⁵Then the Spirit*ᵈ* picked me up. And he brought me into the inner courtyard. There the Lord's greatness filled the Temple. ⁶The man stood at my side. I heard someone speaking to me from inside the Temple. ⁷The voice

from the Temple said to me, "Human being, this is my throne. And this is the place my feet rest. I will live here among the Israelites forever. The people of Israel will not make my holy name unclean[d] again. Neither the people nor their kings will make it unclean by their sexual sins. Nor will they make it unclean with the dead bodies of their kings. 8They made my name unclean by putting their doorway next to my doorway. And they put their doorpost next to my doorpost. Only a wall separated me from them. When they did their acts that I hate, they made my holy name unclean. So I destroyed them in my anger. 9Now let them stop their sexual sins. And let them take the dead bodies of their kings far away from me. Then I will live among them forever.

10"Human being, tell the people of Israel about the Temple. Then they will be ashamed of their sins. Let them think about the plan of the Temple. 11Then they will be ashamed of all they have done. Let them know the design of the Temple. Let them know how it is built. Show them its exits and entrances. Show them all its designs, all its rules and all its teachings. And write the rules as they watch. Do this so they can obey all the Temple's teachings and rules. 12This is the teaching of the Temple: All the area around the top of the mountain is most holy. This is the teaching of the Temple.

The Altar

13"And these are the measurements of the altar, using the measuring stick. It is 21 inches long. The altar's base is 21 inches high and 21 inches long. Its rim is about 9 inches around its edge. And the altar is this tall: 14From the ground up to the lower ledge, it measures 3½ feet. It is 21 inches wide. It measures 7 feet from the smaller ledge to the larger ledge and is 21 inches wide. 15The place where the sacrifice is burned on the altar is 7 feet high. The four corners are shaped like horns and reach up above it. 16It is square. It is 21 feet long and 21 feet wide. 17The upper ledge is also square, 24½ feet long and 24½ feet wide. The border around it is 10½ inches wide. Its base is 21 inches around. Its steps are on the east."

18Then the man said to me, "Human being, this is what the Lord God says: These are the rules for the altar. When it is built, use these rules to offer burnt offerings and sprinkle blood on it. 19You must give a young bull as a sin offering to the priests. These priests are the Levites from the family of Zadok. They come near me to serve me, says the Lord God. 20Take some of the bull's blood and put it on the altar's four corners. Put it also on the four corners of the ledge. And put it on the border all around. This is how you will make the altar pure and ready for God's service. 21Then take the bull for the sin offering and burn it in the proper place in the Temple[d] area. It will be outside the Holy Place.

22"On the second day offer a male goat. It must have nothing wrong with it. It will be for a sin offering. The priests will make the altar pure and ready for God's service. They will do it the same way they did with the young bull. 23When you finish making the altar pure and ready, offer a young bull and a male sheep from the flock. They must also have nothing wrong with them. 24You must offer them before the Lord. The priests will throw salt on them. Then they will offer them as a burnt offering to the Lord.

25"You must prepare a goat every day for seven days as a sin offering. Also, you must prepare a young bull and male sheep from the flock. They must have nothing wrong with them. 26For seven days the priests will make the altar pure and ready for God's service. Then the priests will give the altar to God. 27After these seven days, on the eighth day, the priests must present your offerings. They must offer your burnt offerings and your fellowship offerings on the altar. Then I will accept you, says the Lord God."

The Outer East Gate

44 Then the man brought me back to the outer east gate of the Temple[d] area. The gate was shut. [2]The Lord said to me, "This gate will stay shut. It will not be opened. No one may enter through it. This is because the Lord God of Israel has entered through it. So it must stay shut. [3]Only the ruler himself may sit in the gateway to eat bread before the Lord. He must enter through the porch of the gateway and go out the same way."

[4]Then the man brought me through the outer north gate. He brought me to the front of the Temple. I looked and saw the greatness of the Lord. It was filling the Temple of the Lord. I bowed facedown on the ground.

[5]The Lord said to me, "Human being, pay attention. See this with your eyes. And hear this with your ears. See and hear everything I tell you about all the rules and teachings of the Temple of the Lord. Pay attention to the entrance to the Temple and to all the exits from the Temple area. [6]Then speak to those who refuse to obey. Say to the people of Israel, 'This is what the Lord God says: Stop doing all your acts that I hate, Israel! [7]You brought foreigners into my Holy Place. They were not circumcised[d] in the flesh. They had not given themselves to serving me. You dishonored my Temple when you offered me food, fat and blood. You broke my agreement by all your ways that I hate. [8]And you have not taken care of my holy things. You put foreigners in charge of my Temple. [9]This is what the Lord God says: Foreigners who are not circumcised in flesh and who do not give themselves to serving me may not enter my Temple. Even a foreigner living among the people of Israel may not enter.

[10]"Some Levites stopped obeying me when Israel left me and followed their idols. These Levites must be punished for their sin. [11]These Levites are to be servants in my Holy Place. They may guard the gates of the Temple. They may serve in the Temple. They may kill the animals for the burnt offering and the sacrifices for the people. They may stand before the people to serve them. [12]But these Levites helped the people worship their idols and caused the people of Israel to fall. So I have made this promise: They will be punished for their sin, says the Lord God. [13]They will not come near me to serve as priests. They will not come near any of my holy things or the most holy offerings. But they will be ashamed of the things they did that I hate. [14]But I will make them take care of the Temple. They will take care of everything that must be done in it.

[15]"But this is not true for priests who are Levites and descendants[d] of Zadok. They took care of my Holy Place when Israel left me. They may come near to serve me. They may stand in my presence. They will offer me the fat and blood of the animals they sacrifice, says the Lord God. [16]They are the only ones who may enter my Holy Place. They may come near my table to serve me. They may take care of the things I gave them.

[17]"When they enter the gates of the inner courtyard, they must wear linen robes. They must not wear wool to serve at the gates of the inner courtyard or in the Temple. [18]They will wear linen turbans on their heads and linen underclothes. They will not wear anything that makes them perspire. [19]At times they will go out into the outer courtyard to the people. But before they go, they must take off their serving clothes. They must put these clothes away in the holy rooms. And they must put on other clothes. Then they will not let their holy clothes hurt the people. [20]"They must not shave their heads or let their hair grow long. They must keep the hair of their heads trimmed.

21None of the priests may drink wine when they enter the inner courtyard. 22The priests must not marry a widow or a divorced woman. They may marry only virgins*d* from the people of Israel. Or they may marry a widow of a priest. 23They must teach my people the difference between what is holy and what is not holy. They must help my people know what is unclean*d* and what is clean.

24"In court they will act as judges. When they judge, they will follow my teachings. They must obey my laws and my rules at all my special feasts. They must keep my Sabbaths*d* holy.

25"They must not go near a dead person, making themselves unclean.*d* But they are allowed to make themselves unclean if the dead person is a relative. It might be his father, mother, son, daughter, brother or a sister who has not married. 26After the priest has been made clean again, he must wait seven days. 27Then he may go into the inner courtyard to serve in the Temple. But he must offer a sin offering for himself, says the Lord God.

28"These are the rules about the priests and their property: They will have me instead of property. You will not give them any land to own in Israel. I am what they will own. 29They will eat the grain offerings, sin offerings and penalty offerings. Everything Israel offers will be theirs. 30And the best fruits of all the first harvests will be for the priests. And they will have all the special gifts offered to me. You will also give to the priests the first part of your grain that you grind. This will cause a blessing to come on your house. 31The priests must not eat any bird or animal that died a natural death. And they must not eat one that has been torn by wild animals.

The Land Is Divided

45 "Divide the land for the Israelite tribes*d* by throwing lots.*d* At that time you will give a part of the land to belong to the Lord. It will be about 7 miles long and about 6 miles wide. All of this land will be holy. 2An area of 875 feet square will be for the Temple.*d* There will be an open space around the Temple that is 87½ feet wide. 3In the holy area you will measure a part about 7 miles long and 3 miles wide. The Most Holy Place will be in this holy area. 4This holy part of the land will be for the priests who serve in the Temple. This is where they come near to serve the Lord. It will be a place for the priests' houses. And it will be the place for the Temple. 5Another area will be about 7 miles long and more than 3 miles wide. It will be for the Levites, who serve in the Temple. It will belong to them so they will have cities in which to live.

6"And you will give the city an area that is about 1½ miles wide and about 7 miles long. It will be along the side of the holy area. It will belong to all the people of Israel.

7"The ruler will have land on both sides of the holy area and the city. On the west of the holy area, his land will reach to the Mediterranean Sea. On the east of the holy area, his land will reach to the eastern border. It will be as long as the land given to each tribe. 8This land will be the ruler's property in Israel. So my rulers will not be cruel to my people anymore. But they will give land to each tribe in the nation of Israel.

9"This is what the Lord God says: You have gone far enough, you rulers of Israel! Stop being cruel and hurting people. Do what is right and fair. Stop forcing my people out of their homes, says the Lord God. 10You must have honest scales, an honest dry measurement and an honest liquid measurement. 11The dry measure and the liquid measure will be the same: The liquid measure will always be a tenth of a homer.*n* The ephah will always be a tenth of a homer. The measurement they follow will be the homer. 12The

---

*n***homer**   The Hebrew word means "donkey-load." It measured about 5 dry bushels or 175 liquid quarts. So an ephah was about one-half bushel. And a bath was about 18 quarts.

shekel[n] will be worth 20 gerahs. A mina will be worth 60 shekels.

Offerings and Holy Days

13 "'This is the gift you will offer: a sixth of an ephah from a homer of wheat; a sixth of an ephah from a homer of barley. 14 The amount of oil you are to offer is a tenth of a bath from each cor. (Ten baths make a homer and also make a cor.) 15 You should give 1 sheep from each flock of 200 from the watering places of Israel. They are to be offered with the grain offerings, burnt offerings and fellowship offerings. These offerings are to remove sins so you will belong to God, says the Lord God. 16 All people in the land will give this special offering for the ruler of Israel. 17 It will be the ruler's responsibility to supply the burnt offerings, grain offerings and drink offerings. These offerings will be given at the feasts and at the New Moons.[d] They will also be given on the Sabbaths[d] and at all the other feasts of Israel. The ruler will supply the sin offerings, grain offerings and fellowship offerings. These offerings are to pay for the sins of Israel.

18 "'This is what the Lord God says: On the first day of the first month take a young bull that has nothing wrong with it. Use it to make the Temple[d] pure and ready for God's service. 19 The priest will take some of the blood from the sin offering. And he will put it on the doorposts of the Temple. He will put it on the four corners of the ledge of the altar. And he will put it on the posts of the gate of the inner courtyard. 20 You will do the same thing on the seventh day of the month. You will do it for anyone who has sinned by accident or without knowing it. This is how you make the Temple pure and ready for God's service.

Passover Feast Offerings

21 "'On the fourteenth day of the first month you will celebrate the Feast[d] of Passover. It will be a feast of seven days when you eat bread made without yeast. 22 On that day the ruler must offer a bull for himself and for all the people of the land. The bull will be a sin offering. 23 During the seven days of the feast the ruler must offer seven bulls. And he must offer seven male sheep. The bulls and sheep must have nothing wrong with them. They will be burnt offerings to the Lord. The ruler will offer them every day of the seven days of the feast. He must also offer a male goat every day as a sin offering. 24 The ruler must give as a grain offering a half bushel for each bull and a half bushel for each sheep. He must give a gallon of olive oil for each half bushel.

25 "'Beginning on the fifteenth day of the seventh month, you will celebrate the Feast[d] of Shelters. During the feast, the ruler will do the same things for seven days. He will supply the sin offering, burnt offering, grain offering and the olive oil.

Rules for Worship

46 "'This is what the Lord God says: The east gate of the inner courtyard will be shut on the six working days. But it will be opened on the Sabbath[d] day. And it will be open on the day of the New Moon.[d] 2 The ruler will enter through the porch of the gateway. He will enter from outside and stand by the gatepost. Then the priests will offer the ruler's burnt offering and fellowship offerings. The ruler will worship at the entrance of the gate. Then he will go out. But the gate will not be shut until evening. 3 The people of the land will worship at the entrance of that gateway. They will worship there in the presence of the Lord on the Sabbaths and New Moons. 4 This is the burnt offering the ruler will offer to the Lord on the Sabbath day. It will be six male lambs

---

[n]**shekel**　In Ezekiel's time a shekel weighed about two-fifths of an ounce.

that have nothing wrong with them. And it will be a male sheep that has nothing wrong with it. [5]He must give a half bushel grain offering with the male sheep. But he can give as much grain offering with the lambs as he pleases. He must also give a gallon of olive oil for each half bushel of grain. [6]On the day of the New Moon he must offer a young bull. It must have nothing wrong with it. He must also offer six lambs and a male sheep. They also must have nothing wrong with them. [7]The ruler must give a half bushel grain offering with the bull. And he must give the same with the male sheep. With the lambs, he can give as much grain as he pleases. But he must give a gallon of olive oil for each half bushel of grain. [8]And when the ruler enters, he must go in through the porch of the gateway. He must go out the same way.

[9]"'The people of the land must come before the Lord at the special feasts. Anyone who enters through the north gate to worship must go out through the south gate. Anyone who enters through the south gate must go out through the north gate. No one will return the same way he entered. Each person will go out straight ahead. [10]When the people go in, the ruler will go in with them. When they go out, the ruler will go out.

[11]"'At the feasts and regular times of worship a half bushel of grain must be offered. It will be offered with a young bull. And a half bushel of grain must be offered with a male sheep. But with an offering of lambs, the ruler may give as much grain as he pleases. He should give a gallon of olive oil for each half bushel of grain. [12]The ruler may give an offering as a special gift to the Lord. It may be a burnt offering or fellowship offering. When he gives it to the Lord, the inner east gate will be opened for him. He must offer his burnt offering and his fellowship offerings as he does on the Sabbath[d] day. Then he will go out. After he has gone out, the gate will be shut.

[13]"'Every morning you will give a year-old lamb that has nothing wrong with it. It will be for a burnt offering to the Lord every day. [14]Also, you must offer a grain offering with the lamb every morning. With it you will give three and a third quarts of grain and one and a third quarts of olive oil. This is to make the fine flour moist. It will be a grain offering to the Lord. This is a rule that must be kept from now on. [15]So they must always give the lamb, the grain offering and the olive oil every morning as a burnt offering.

Rules for the Ruler

[16]"'This is what the Lord God says: The ruler might give a gift from his land to one of his sons. Then that land will belong to that son's children. It is their property from their family. [17]But the ruler might give a gift from his land to one of his slaves. That land will belong to the slave only until the year of freedom. Then the land will go back to the ruler. Only the ruler's sons may keep a gift of land from the ruler. [18]The ruler must not take any of the people's land. He must not force them out of their land. He must give his sons land from his own land. Then my people will not be scattered out of their own land.'"

The Special Kitchens

[19]The man led me through the entrance at the side of the gateway. He led me to the priests' holy rooms that face north. There I saw a place at the west end. [20]The man said to me, "This is where the priests will boil the meat of the penalty offering and sin offering. There the priests will bake the grain offering. Then they will not need to bring these offerings into the outer courtyard. That would hurt the people."

[21]Then the man brought me out to the outer courtyard. He led me to its four corners. In each corner of the courtyard was a smaller courtyard. [22]Small courtyards were in the four

corners of the courtyard. Each small courtyard was 70 feet long and 52½ feet wide. All four corners measured the same. ²³A stone wall was around each of the four small courtyards. Places for cooking were built in each of the stone walls. ²⁴The man said to me, "These are the kitchens. The Temple*d* priests will boil the sacrifices for the people here."

The River from the Temple

47 The man led me back to the door of the Temple.*d* I saw water coming out from under the doorway that faces east. (The Temple faced east.) The water flowed down from the south end of the Temple. It was south of the altar. ²The man brought me out through the outer north gate. And he led me around outside to the outer east gate. The water was coming out on the south side of the gate.

³The man went toward the east with a line in his hand. He measured about a third of a mile. Then he led me through water that came up to my ankles. ⁴The man measured about a third of a mile again. Then he led me through water that came up to my knees. Then he measured about a third of a mile again. And he led me through water up to my waist. ⁵The man measured about a third of a mile again. But it was now a river that I could not cross. The water had risen too high. It was deep enough for swimming. It was a river that no one could cross. ⁶The man asked me, "Human being, do you see this?"

Then the man led me back along the bank of the river. ⁷As I went back, I saw many trees on both sides of the water. ⁸The man said to me, "This water will flow toward the eastern areas. It will go down into the Jordan Valley. When the water enters the Dead Sea,*d* it will become fresh. ⁹And everywhere the river goes, there will be many animals and fish. Wherever this water goes the Dead Sea will become fresh. So where the river goes there will be many living

things. ¹⁰Fishermen will stand by the sea. From En Gedi all the way to En Eglaim will become a place to spread fishing nets. There will be many kinds of fish in the Dead Sea. There will be as many kinds of fish as there are in the Mediterranean Sea. ¹¹But the swamps and marshes will not become fresh. They will be left for salt. ¹²All kinds of fruit trees will grow on both banks of the river. Their leaves will not dry and die. The trees will have fruit every month because the water for them comes from the Temple. The fruit from the trees will be for food. And their leaves will be for medicine."

Borders of the Land

¹³This is what the Lord God says: "These are the borders to divide the land among the 12 tribes*d* of Israel. Joseph will have two parts of land. ¹⁴You will divide the land equally. I promised to give it to your ancestors. So this land will belong to you from your family.

¹⁵"This will be the border line of the land.

"On the north side it will start at the Mediterranean Sea. It will go by the Hethlon Road. This is where the road turns toward Lebo Hamath. And it will go to the cities of Zedad, ¹⁶Berothah and Sibraim. Sibraim is on the border between Damascus and Hamath. And it will go on to the city of Hazer Hatticon on the border of the country of Hauran. ¹⁷So the border line will go from the Mediterranean Sea east to the city of Hazar Enan. This is on the northern border of Damascus. And the country of Hamath will be on the north side of the border.

¹⁸"On the east side the border runs south from a point between Hauran and Damascus. It will go along the Jordan between Gilead and the land of Israel. It will continue to the city of Tamar on the Dead Sea.*d* This will be the east side of the land.

¹⁹"On the south side the border line will go east from Tamar. It will go all

the way to the waters of Meribah Hadesh. Then it will run along the brook of Egypt to the Mediterranean Sea. This will be the south side of the land.

²⁰"On the west side the Mediterranean Sea will be the border line. It will go to a place across from Lebo Hamath. This will be the west side of your land.

²¹"So you will divide this land among the tribes of Israel. ²²You will divide it as a property for yourselves. And it will be for you and for the foreigners who live and have children among you. These foreigners will be like people born in Israel. You will divide some land for them among the tribes of Israel. ²³In whatever tribe the foreigner lives, you will give him some land," says the Lord God.

Dividing the Land

48 "These are the names of the tribes.ᵈ Dan will have one share. It will begin at the northern border. It will go from the sea and over the Hethlon Road. It will follow the road to Lebo Hamath. It will go all the way to Hazar Enan. This is on the northern border of Damascus. It will stop there next to Hamath. This will be Dan's northern border from the east side to the Mediterranean Sea on the west side.

²"South of Dan's border, Asher will have one share. It will go from the east side to the west side.

³"South of Asher's border, Naphtali will have one share. It will go from the east side to the west side.

⁴"South of Naphtali's border, Manasseh will have one share. It will go from the east side to the west side.

⁵"South of Manasseh's border, Ephraim will have one share. It will go from the east side to the west side.

⁶"South of Ephraim's border, Reuben will have one share. It will go from the east side to the west side.

⁷"South of Reuben's border, Judah will have one share. It will go from the east side to the west side.

⁸"South of Judah's border will be the holy area which you are to give. It will be about 7 miles wide. It will be as long and wide as one of the tribes' shares. It will run from the east side to the west side. The Templeᵈ will be in the middle of this area.

⁹"The share which you will give the Lord will be about 7 miles long and 3 miles wide. ¹⁰The holy area will be divided among these people. For the priests on the north side, the land will measure about 7 miles. It will be 3 miles wide on the west side and 3 miles wide on the east side. It will be about 7 miles on the south side. The Temple of the Lord will be in the middle of it. ¹¹This land is for the priests who are given to serve the Lord. They are the descendantsᵈ of Zadok who did my work. They did not leave me. The other Levites left me when Israel did. ¹²This share from the holy portion of the land will be a gift for these priests. It will be next to the land of the Levites.

¹³"Alongside the land for the priests, the Levites will have a share. It will be about 7 miles long and 3 miles wide. Its full length will be about 7 miles. And its full width will be about 3 miles. ¹⁴The Levites are not to sell or trade any of this land. They will not sell any of this best part of the land. It belongs to the Lord.

City Property

¹⁵"The rest of the land will be an area about 1½ miles wide and 7 miles long. It will be for the other people's use. It will be for the city, for homes and for pastures. The city will be in the middle of it. ¹⁶These are the city's measurements: the north side will be about a mile. The south side will be about a mile. The east side will be about a mile. And the west side will be about a mile. ¹⁷The city's land for pastures will be about 437 feet on the north, 437 feet on the south, 437 feet on the east and 437 feet on the west. ¹⁸Alongside the length of the holy area there will be left 3 miles on the east and 3 miles on the west. It will be used to grow food

for the city workers. [19]The city workers will plow this land. The workers will be from all the tribes[d] of Israel. [20]This whole area will be square, 7 miles by 7 miles. You shall give to the Lord the holy share along with the city property.

[21]"Land that is left over on both sides of the holy area and city property will belong to the ruler. That land will extend east of the holy area to the eastern border. And it will extend west of it to the Mediterranean Sea. Both of these areas run the length of the lands of the tribes. They belong to the ruler. The holy area with the Holy Place of the Temple[d] will be in the middle. [22]The Levites' land and the city property will be between the lands belonging to the ruler. The ruler's land will be between Judah's border and Benjamin's border.

The Other Tribes' Land

[23]"Here is what the rest of the tribes will receive: Benjamin will have one share. It will go from the east side to the Mediterranean Sea on the west side. [24]"South of Benjamin's land, Simeon will have one share. It will go from the east side to the west side. [25]"South of Simeon's land, Issachar will have one share. It will go from the east side to the west side. [26]"South of Issachar's land, Zebulun will have one share. It will go from the

east side to the west side. [27]"South of Zebulun's land, Gad will have one share. It will go from the east side to the west side. [28]"The southern border of Gad's land will go east from Tamar on the Dead Sea[d] to the waters of Meribah Kadesh. Then it will run along the brook of Egypt to the Mediterranean Sea. [29]"This is the land you will divide among the tribes of Israel. These are to be their shares," says the Lord God.

The Gates of the City

[30]"These will be the outside borders of the city: The north side will measure more than a mile. [31]There will be three gates facing north. They are Reuben's Gate, Judah's Gate and Levi's Gate. The city's gates will be named for the tribes[d] of Israel. [32]"The east side will measure more than a mile. There will be three gates facing east. They are Joseph's Gate, Benjamin's Gate and Dan's Gate. [33]"The south side will measure more than a mile. There will be three gates facing south. They are Simeon's Gate, Issachar's Gate and Zebulun's Gate. [34]"The west side will measure more than a mile. There will be three gates facing west. They are Gad's Gate, Asher's Gate and Naphtali's Gate. [35]"The city will measure about six miles around. From then on the name of the city will be The Lord God Is There."

DANIEL

The Life and Visions of Daniel

Daniel Taken to Babylon

1 Nebuchadnezzar king of Babylon came to Jerusalem and surrounded it with his army. This happened during the third year that Jehoiakim was king of Judah. ²The Lord allowed Nebuchadnezzar to capture Jehoiakim king of Judah. Nebuchadnezzar also took some of the things from the Temple *d* of God. He carried them to Babylonia and put them in the temple of his gods.

³Then King Nebuchadnezzar gave an order to Ashpenaz, his chief officer. He told Ashpenaz to bring some of the Israelite men into his house. He wanted them to be from important families. And he wanted those who were from the family of the king of Judah. ⁴King Nebuchadnezzar wanted only healthy, young, Israelite men. These men were not to have anything wrong with their bodies. They were to be handsome and well educated. They were to be able to learn and understand things. He wanted those who were able to serve in his palace. Ashpenaz was to teach them the language and writings of the Babylonians. ⁵The king gave the young men a certain amount of food and wine every day. That was the same kind of food that the king ate. They were to be trained for three years. Then the young men would become servants of the king of Babylon. ⁶Among those young men were some from the people of Judah. These were Daniel, Hananiah, Mishael and Azariah.

⁷Then Ashpenaz, the chief officer, gave them Babylonian names. Daniel's new name was Belteshazzar. Hananiah's was Shadrach. Mishael's was Meshach. And Azariah's new name was Abednego.

⁸Daniel decided not to eat the king's food and wine because that would make him unclean.*d* So he asked Ashpenaz for permission not to make himself unclean in this way.

⁹God made Ashpenaz want to be kind and merciful to Daniel. ¹⁰But Ashpenaz said to Daniel, "I am afraid of my master, the king. He ordered me to give you this food and drink. If you don't eat this food, you will begin to look worse than other young men your age. The king will see this. And he will cut off my head because of you."

¹¹Ashpenaz had ordered a guard to watch Daniel, Hananiah, Mishael and Azariah. ¹²Daniel said to the guard, "Please give us this test for ten days: Don't give us anything but vegetables to eat and water to drink. ¹³Then after ten days compare us with the other young men who eat the king's food. See for yourself who looks healthier. Then you judge for yourself how you want to treat us, your servants."

¹⁴So the guard agreed to test them for ten days. ¹⁵After ten days they looked very healthy. They looked better than all of the young men who ate the king's food. ¹⁶So the guard took away the king's special food and wine. He gave Daniel, Hananiah, Mishael and Azariah vegetables instead.

¹⁷God gave these four men wisdom and the ability to learn. They learned many kinds of things people had written and studied. Daniel could also understand all kinds of visions and dreams.

¹⁸The end of the three years came. And Ashpenaz brought all of the young men to King Nebuchadnezzar.

¹⁹The king talked to them. He found that none of the young men were as good as Daniel, Hananiah, Mishael and Azariah. So those four young men became the king's servants. ²⁰Every time the king asked them about something important, they showed much wisdom and understanding. He found they were ten times better than all the fortune-tellers and magicians in his kingdom. ²¹So Daniel continued to be the king's servant until the first year Cyrus was king.

Nebuchadnezzar's Dream

2 During Nebuchadnezzar's second year as king, he had some dreams. Those dreams bothered him, and he could not sleep. ²So the king called for his fortune-tellers, magicians, wizards and wise men. The king wanted those men to tell him what he had dreamed. So they came in and stood in front of the king.

³Then the king said to them, "I had a dream that bothers me. I want to know what the dream means."

⁴Then the wise men answered the king in the Aramaic language. They said, "Our king, live forever! We are your servants. Please tell us your dream. Then we will tell you what it means."

⁵Then King Nebuchadnezzar said to them, "No! You must tell me the dream. And then you must tell me what it means. If you don't do these things, I will have you torn apart. And I will turn your houses into piles of stones. ⁶But if you tell me my dream and its meaning, I will reward you. I will give you gifts and great honor. So tell me the dream, and tell me what it means."

⁷Again the wise men said to the king, "Please, tell us the dream. And we will tell you what it means."

⁸King Nebuchadnezzar answered, "Now I know that you are trying to get more time. You know that I meant what I said. ⁹If you don't tell me my dream, you will be punished. You have all agreed to tell me lies and wicked things. You are hoping things will change. Now, tell me the dream. Then I will know you can tell me what it really means!"

¹⁰The wise men answered the king. They said, "No one on earth can do what the king asks! Not even a great and powerful king has ever asked the fortune-tellers, magicians or wise men to do this. ¹¹The king is asking something that is too hard. Only the gods could tell the king this. But the gods do not live among people."

¹²When the king heard that, he became very angry. He gave an order for all the wise men of Babylon to be killed. ¹³So King Nebuchadnezzar's order was announced. All the wise men were to be put to death. Men were sent to look for Daniel and his friends to kill them.

¹⁴Arioch was the commander of the king's guards. He was going to put to death the wise men of Babylon. But Daniel spoke to him with wisdom and skill. ¹⁵Daniel asked, "Why did the king order such a terrible punishment?" Then Arioch explained everything to Daniel. ¹⁶When Daniel heard the story, he went to King Nebuchadnezzar. Daniel asked him to give him some more time. Then he would tell the king what he had dreamed and what it meant.

¹⁷So Daniel went to his house. He explained the whole story to his friends Hananiah, Mishael and Azariah. ¹⁸Daniel asked his friends to pray to the God of heaven. Daniel asked them to pray that God would show them mercy and help them understand this secret. Then Daniel and his friends would not be put to death with the other wise men of Babylon.

¹⁹During the night God explained the secret to Daniel in a vision. Then Daniel praised the God of heaven. ²⁰Daniel said:

"Praise God forever and ever.
    He has wisdom and power.
²¹He changes the times and seasons
    of the year.

He takes away the power of kings.
And he gives their power to new
    kings.
He gives wisdom to people so they
    become wise.
And he helps people learn and
    know things.
22He makes known secrets that are
    deep and hidden.
He knows what is hidden in
    darkness,
and light lives with him.
23I thank you and praise you, God of
    my ancestors.
You have given me wisdom and
    power.
You told me what we asked of you.
You told us about the king's
    dream."

25So very quickly Arioch took Daniel
to the king. Arioch said to the king, "I
have found a man among the captives
from Judah. He can tell the king what
his dream means."

26The king asked Daniel (also called
Belteshazzar) a question. He asked,
"Are you able to tell me what I dreamed
and what it means?"

27Daniel answered, "No person can
explain to the king the secret he has
asked about. No wise man, magician
or fortune-teller can do this. 28But
there is a God in heaven who explains
secret things. God has shown King
Nebuchadnezzar what will happen at a
later time. This is your dream. This is
the vision you saw while lying on your
bed: 29My king, as you were lying
there, you thought about things to
come. God, who can tell people about
secret things, showed you what is
going to happen. 30God also told this

People Who Spoke God's Words

DANIEL · DANIEL 2:17-28

Daniel spoke God's truth in a country where the people didn't even
know about God. He spoke to the most powerful leaders of two great
kingdoms. Even though Daniel had been taken away from his home, he
served God by working for the rulers and telling them God's messages.
When King Nebuchadnezzar had a dream and wanted to know the interpretation, Daniel asked his friends to pray. God told Daniel what the dream
meant, and then Daniel told the king. The king wanted to praise Daniel,
but Daniel told him to praise God instead.

Like Daniel, we should always point people to God. He is the one who
deserves all the praise!

To meet a prophet who was tired of excuses, fly to page 1103.

The Meaning of the Dream

24Then Daniel went to Arioch. King
Nebuchadnezzar had chosen Arioch to
put to death the wise men of Babylon.
Daniel said to Arioch, "Don't put the
wise men of Babylon to death. Take
me to the king. I will tell him what his
dream means."

secret to me. It is not because I have
greater wisdom than other men. It is
so that you, my king, may know what
it means. In that way you will understand what went through your mind.

31"My king, in your dream you saw a
large statue in front of you. It was huge,
shiny and frightening. 32The head of
the statue was made of pure gold. Its

chest and arms were made of silver. Its middle and the upper part of its legs were made of bronze. ³³The lower part of the legs were made of iron. Its feet were made partly of iron and partly of baked clay. ³⁴While you were looking at the statue, you saw a rock cut free. But no human being touched the rock. It hit the statue on its feet of iron and clay and smashed them. ³⁵Then the iron, clay, bronze, silver and gold broke to pieces at the same time. They became like chaff*d* on a threshing*d* floor in the summertime. The wind blew them away, and there was nothing left. Then the rock that hit the statue became a very large mountain. It filled the whole earth.

³⁶"That was your dream. Now we will tell the king what it means. ³⁷My king, you are the greatest king. God of heaven has given you a kingdom. He has given you power, strength and glory. ³⁸God has given you power over people, wild animals and birds. Wherever they live, God has made you ruler over them all. King Nebuchadnezzar, you are the head of gold on that statue.

³⁹"Another kingdom will come after you. But that kingdom will not be as great as yours. Next a third kingdom will rule over the earth. That is the bronze part. ⁴⁰Then there will be a fourth kingdom, strong as iron. Iron crushes and smashes things to pieces. In the same way the fourth kingdom will smash and crush all the other kingdoms.

⁴¹"You saw that the statue's feet and toes were partly baked clay and partly iron. That means the fourth kingdom will be a divided kingdom. It will have some of the strength of iron in it. As you saw, iron was mixed with clay. ⁴²The toes of the statue were partly iron and partly clay. So the fourth kingdom will be partly strong like iron and partly breakable like clay. ⁴³You saw the iron mixed with clay. But iron and clay don't mix completely together. In the same way the people of the fourth kingdom will be a mixture. Those peo-

ple will not be united as one people.

⁴⁴"During the time of those kings, the God of heaven will set up another kingdom. It will never be destroyed. And it will not be given to another group of people. This kingdom will crush all the other kingdoms. It will bring them to an end. But that kingdom itself will continue forever.

⁴⁵"King Nebuchadnezzar, you saw a rock cut from a mountain. But no human being touched it. The rock broke the iron, bronze, clay, silver and gold to pieces. In this way the great God showed you what will happen. The dream is true, and you can trust this explanation."

⁴⁶Then King Nebuchadnezzar fell facedown on the ground in front of Daniel. The king honored him. He ordered that an offering and incense*d* be presented to Daniel. ⁴⁷Then the king said to Daniel, "Truly I know your God is the greatest of all gods. And he is the Lord of all the kings. He tells people about things they cannot know. I know this is true. You were able to tell these secret things to me."

⁴⁸Then the king gave Daniel an important position in his kingdom. And he gave many gifts to Daniel. Nebuchadnezzar made him ruler over the whole area of Babylon. And he put Daniel in charge of all the wise men of Babylon. ⁴⁹Daniel asked the king to make Shadrach, Meshach and Abednego important leaders over the area of Babylon. And the king did as Daniel asked. Daniel himself became one of the important people who stayed at the royal court.

The Gold Idol and Blazing Furnace

3 Now King Nebuchadnezzar had a gold statue made. That statue was 90 feet high and 9 feet wide. He set up the statue on the plain of Dura in the area of Babylon. ²Then the king called the important leaders: the governors, assistant governors, captains of the soldiers, people who advised the king, keepers of the treasury, judges, rulers and all other officers in his kingdom. He wanted these men to come to the special service for the statue he had set up. ³So they all came for the special service. And they stood in front of the statue that King Nebuchadnezzar had set up. ⁴Then the man who made announcements for the king spoke in a loud voice. He said, "People, nations and men of every language, this is what you are commanded to do: ⁵You will hear the sound of the horns, flutes, lyres,^{d} zithers,^{n} harps, pipes and all the other musical instruments. When this happens, you must bow down and worship the gold statue. This is the one King Nebuchadnezzar has set up. ⁶Everyone must bow down and worship this gold statue. Anyone who doesn't will be quickly thrown into a blazing furnace."

they heard the sound of the horns, flutes, lyres, zithers, pipes and all the other musical instruments. So they bowed down and worshiped the gold statue that King Nebuchadnezzar had set up.

⁸Then some Babylonians came up to the king. They began speaking against the men of Judah. ⁹They said to King Nebuchadnezzar, "Our king, live forever! ¹⁰Our king, you gave a command. You said that everyone would hear the horns, lyres, zithers, harps, pipes and all the other musical instruments. Then they would have to bow down and worship the gold statue. ¹¹Anyone who wouldn't do this was to be thrown into a blazing furnace. ¹²Our king, there are some men of Judah who did not pay attention to your order. You made them important officers in the area of Babylon. Their names are Shadrach, Meshach and Abednego. They do not serve your gods. And they do not worship the gold statue you have set up."

People Who Depended on God
SHADRACH, MESHACH, AND ABEDNEGO • DANIEL 3:16-27

Shadrach, Meshach, and Abednego trusted God and did what was right—even though it was difficult. These three men had been taken from their home in Judah when King Nebuchadnezzar of Babylon conquered their country. They served King Nebuchadnezzar, but they served God first. Shadrach, Meshach, and Abednego would not obey the king's law because God had said that no one should worship idols. It was very dangerous to disobey the king, and Shadrach, Meshach, and Abednego were sentenced to die in a fiery furnace. This was a room made of stone where fire was always burning.

But they didn't die, because God was glad that they had obeyed him and not the king. He kept them safe. Remember that you must always serve God first and do what is right, even if it is difficult.

To read about a man who amazed Jesus by what he said,
fly to page 1138.

⁷Now people, nations and men who spoke every language were there. And

¹³Nebuchadnezzar became very angry. He called for Shadrach, Meshach

---

^{n}**zithers** Musical instruments with 30 to 40 strings.

and Abednego. So those men were brought to the king. ¹⁴And Nebuchadnezzar said, "Shadrach, Meshach and Abednego, is it true that you do not serve my gods? And is it true that you did not worship the gold statue I have set up? ¹⁵Now, you will hear the sound of the horns, flutes, lyres, zithers, harps, pipes and all the other musical instruments. And you must be ready to bow down and worship the statue I made. That will be good. But if you do not worship it, you will be thrown quickly into the blazing furnace. Then no god will be able to save you from my power!"

¹⁶Shadrach, Meshach and Abednego answered the king. They said, "Nebuchadnezzar, we do not need to defend ourselves to you. ¹⁷You can throw us into the blazing furnace. The God we serve is able to save us from the furnace and your power. If he does this, it is good. ¹⁸But even if God does not save us, we want you, our king, to know this: We will not serve your gods. We will not worship the gold statue you have set up."

¹⁹Then Nebuchadnezzar was furious with Shadrach, Meshach and Abednego. He ordered the furnace to be heated seven times hotter than usual. ²⁰Then he commanded some of the strongest soldiers in his army to tie up Shadrach, Meshach and Abednego. The king told the soldiers to throw them into the blazing furnace.

²¹So Shadrach, Meshach and Abednego were tied up and thrown into the blazing furnace. They were still wearing their robes, trousers, turbans and other clothes. ²²The king was very angry when he gave the command. And the furnace was made very hot. The fire was so hot that the flames killed the strong soldiers who took Shadrach, Meshach and Abednego there. ²³Firmly tied, Shadrach, Meshach and Abednego fell into the blazing furnace.

²⁴Then King Nebuchadnezzar was very surprised and jumped to his feet.

He asked the men who advised him, "Didn't we tie up only three men? Didn't we throw them into the fire?"

They answered, "Yes, our king."

"**D**aniel's friends were thrown into a blazing furnace and didn't even get their hair singed!" Read all about it in Daniel 3:1-30.

²⁵The king said, "Look! I see four men. They are walking around in the fire. They are not tied up, and they are not burned. The fourth man looks like a son of the gods."

²⁶Then Nebuchadnezzar went to the opening of the blazing furnace. He shouted, "Shadrach, Meshach and Abednego, come out! Servants of the Most High God, come here!"

So Shadrach, Meshach and Abednego came out of the fire. ²⁷When they came out, the princes, assistant governors, governors and royal advisers crowded around them. They saw that the fire had not harmed their bodies. Their hair was not burned. Their robes were not burned. And they didn't even smell like smoke.

²⁸Then Nebuchadnezzar said, "Praise the God of Shadrach, Meshach and Abednego. Their God has sent his angel and saved his servants from the fire! These three men trusted their God. They refused to obey my command. And they were willing to die rather than serve or worship any god other than their own. ²⁹So I now make this law: The people of any nation or language must not say anything against the God of Shadrach, Meshach and Abednego. Anyone who does will be torn apart. And his house will be turned into a pile of stones. No other god can save his people like this." ³⁰Then the king promoted Shadrach, Meshach and Abednego in the area of Babylon.

Nebuchadnezzar's Dream of a Tree

4 King Nebuchadnezzar sent a letter. It went to the people, nations and those who speak every language in all the world. The letter said:

I wish you great wealth!

²The Most High God has done miracles^d and wonderful things for me. I am happy to tell you about these things.

³The things he has done are great.
His miracles are mighty.
His kingdom continues forever.
His rule will continue for all time.

⁴I, Nebuchadnezzar, was at my palace. I was happy and successful. ⁵I had a dream that made me afraid. As I was lying on my bed, I saw pictures and visions in my mind. Those things made me very afraid. ⁶So I gave an order. All the wise men of Babylon were to be brought to me. I wanted them to tell me what my dream meant. ⁷The fortune-tellers, magicians and wise men came. I told them about the dream. But those men could not tell me what it meant.

⁸Finally, Daniel came to me. (I called him Belteshazzar to honor my god. The spirit of the holy gods is in him.) I told my dream to Daniel. ⁹I said, "Belteshazzar, you are the most important of all the fortune-tellers. I know that the spirit of the holy gods is in you. I know there is no secret that is too hard for you to understand. This was what I dreamed. Tell me what it means.

¹⁰These are the visions I saw while I was lying in my bed: I looked, and there in front of me was a tree. It was standing in the middle of the earth. The tree was very tall. ¹¹The tree grew large and strong. The top of the tree touched the sky. It could be seen from anywhere on earth. ¹²The leaves of the tree were beautiful. It had plenty of good fruit on it. On the tree was food for everyone.

The wild animals found shelter under the tree. And the birds lived in its branches. Every animal ate from it.

¹³"I was looking at those things in the vision while lying on my bed. And then I saw a holy angel coming down from heaven. ¹⁴He spoke very loudly. He said, 'Cut down the tree, and cut off its branches. Strip off its leaves. Scatter its fruit around. Let the animals that are under the tree run away. Let the birds that were in its branches fly away. ¹⁵But let the stump and its roots stay in the ground. Put a band of iron and bronze around it. Let it stay in the field with the grass around it.

"'Let the man become wet with dew. Let him live among the animals and plants of the earth. ¹⁶Let him not think like a man any longer. Let him have the mind of an animal for seven years.

¹⁷"'Messengers gave this command. The holy ones declared the sentence. This is so all the people may know that the Most High God rules over the kingdoms of men. God gives those kingdoms to anyone he wants. And he chooses people to rule them who are not proud.'

¹⁸"That is what I, King Nebuchadnezzar, dreamed. Now Daniel, called Belteshazzar, tell me what the dream means. None of the wise men in my kingdom can explain it to me. But you can, because the spirit of the holy gods is in you."

Daniel Explains the Dream

¹⁹Then Daniel (also called Belteshazzar) was very quiet for a while. His thoughts made him afraid. So the king said, "Belteshazzar, do not let the dream or its meaning make you afraid."

Then Daniel, called Belteshazzar, answered the king. He said, "My master, I wish the dream were about your enemies. And I wish its meaning were for those who are against you! ²⁰You saw a tree in your dream. The tree grew large and strong. Its top touched the sky. It could be seen from all over the earth. ²¹Its leaves were beautiful, and it had plenty of fruit. The fruit gave food for everyone. It was a home for the wild animals. And its branches were nesting places for the birds. That is the tree you saw. ²²My king, you are that tree! You have become great and powerful. You are like the tall tree that touched the sky. And your power reaches to the far parts of the earth.

to happen to my master the king: ²⁵You will be forced away from people. You will live among the wild animals. People will feed you grass like an ox. And dew from the sky will make you wet. Seven years will pass, and then you will learn this lesson: The Most High God is ruler over the kingdoms of men. And the Most High God gives those kingdoms to anyone he wants.

²⁶"The stump of the tree and its roots were to be left in the ground. This means your kingdom will be given back to you. This will happen when you learn that heaven rules your kingdom. ²⁷So, my king, please

Good Kings and Bad Kings
NEBUCHADNEZZAR • DANIEL 4:28-33

Nebuchadnezzar was a powerful king. He ruled—not a city or a country—but an entire empire! He ruled over many countries. Nebuchadnezzar became proud. He thought that he had built the empire all by himself. He did not realize that God had given him his power and that God could take it away. So God taught Nebuchadnezzar a lesson. God is in charge of everything that happens in the world. The people who become leaders of countries are only there because God wants them there. He puts people in power and takes them out of power. Everything happens according to his plan. God is also in charge of your life. When good things happen, don't become proud—instead, thank God.

To meet a whole family of bad kings, fly to page 1267.

²³"My king, you saw a holy angel coming down from heaven. He said, 'Cut down the tree and destroy it. But leave the stump and its roots in the ground. Put a band of iron and bronze around it. Leave it in the field with the grass. Let him become wet with dew. He will live like a wild animal for seven years.' ²⁴"This is the meaning of the dream, my king. The Most High God has commanded these things

accept my advice. I advise you to stop sinning and do what is right. Stop doing wicked things and be kind to poor people. Then you might continue to be successful."

The King's Dream Comes True

²⁸All these things happened to King Nebuchadnezzar. ²⁹Twelve months after the dream, King Nebuchadnezzar was walking on the roof[n] of his palace in Babylon. ³⁰And

---

*ⁿ***roof** In Bible times houses were built with flat roofs. The roof was used for drying things such as flax and fruit. And it was used as an extra room, as a place for worship and as a place to sleep in the summer.

he said, "Look at Babylon. I built this great city. It is my palace. I built this great place by my power to show how great I am."

[31]The words were still in his mouth when a voice came from heaven. The voice said, "King Nebuchadnezzar, these things will happen to you: Your royal power has been taken away from you. [32]You will be forced away from people. You will live with the wild animals. You will be fed grass like an ox. Seven years will pass before you learn this lesson: The Most High God rules over the kingdoms of men. And the Most High God gives those kingdoms to anyone he wants."

[33]Those things happened quickly. Nebuchadnezzar was forced to go away from people. He began eating grass like an ox. He became wet from dew. His hair grew long like the feathers of an eagle. And his nails grew long like the claws of a bird.

[34]Then at the end of that time, I, Nebuchadnezzar, looked up toward heaven. And I could think correctly again. Then I gave praise to the Most High God. I gave honor and glory to him who lives forever.

God's rule is forever.
His kingdom continues for
    all time.
[35]People on earth
are not truly important.
God does what he wants
    with the powers of heaven
    and the people on earth.
No one can stop his powerful hand.
No one can question the things
    he does.

[36]So, at that time I could think correctly again. And God gave back my great honor and power as king. The people who advise me and the royal family came to me for help again. I became king again. And I became even greater and more powerful than before. [37]Now I, Nebuchadnezzar, give praise and honor and glory to the King of heaven. Everything he does is right. He is always fair. And he is able to make proud people humble.

The Writing on the Wall

5 King Belshazzar gave a big banquet for 1,000 royal guests. And he drank wine with them. [2]As Belshazzar was drinking his wine, he gave an order to his servants. He told them to bring the gold and silver cups that his ancestor Nebuchadnezzar had taken from the Temple[d] in Jerusalem. King Belshazzar wanted his royal guests to drink from those cups. He also wanted his wives and his slave women[d] to drink from them. [3]So they brought the gold cups. They had been taken from the Temple of God in Jerusalem. And the king and his royal guests, his wives and his slave women drank from them. [4]As they were drinking, they praised their gods. Those gods were made from gold, silver, bronze, iron, wood and stone.

[5]Then suddenly a person's hand appeared. The fingers wrote words on the plaster on the wall. This was near the lampstand in the royal palace. The king watched the hand as it wrote. [6]King Belshazzar was very frightened. His face turned white, and his knees knocked together. He could not stand up because his legs were too weak. [7]The king called for the magicians and wise men to be brought to him. He said to the wise men of Babylon, "I will give a reward to anyone who can read this writing and explain it. I will give him purple clothes fit for a king. I will put a gold chain around his neck. And I will make him the third highest ruler in the kingdom."

[8]So all the king's wise men came in. But they could not read the writing. And they could not tell the king what it meant. [9]King Belshazzar became even more afraid. His face became

even whiter. His royal guests were confused.

¹⁰ Then the king's mother came into the banquet room. She had heard the voices of the king and his royal guests. She said, "My king, live forever! Don't be afraid! Don't let your face be white with fear! ¹¹There is a man in your kingdom who has the spirit of the holy gods in him. In the days of your father, this man showed understanding, knowledge and wisdom. He was like the gods in these things. Your father, King Nebuchadnezzar, put this man in charge of all the wise men. He ruled over all the fortune-tellers, magicians and wise men. ¹²The man I am talking about is named Daniel. The king gave him the name Belteshazzar. He was very smart, and he had knowledge and understanding. He could explain dreams and secrets. He could answer very hard problems. Call for Daniel. He will tell you what the writing on the wall means."

¹³ So they brought Daniel to the king. The king said to him, "Is your name Daniel? Are you one of the captives my father the king brought from Judah? ¹⁴I have heard that the spirit of the gods is in you. And I have heard that you are very smart and have knowledge and understanding. ¹⁵The wise men and magicians were brought to me to read this writing on the wall. I wanted those men to explain to me what it means. But they could not explain it. ¹⁶I have heard that you are able to explain what things mean. And you can find the answers to hard problems. Read this writing on the wall and explain it to me. If you can, I will give you purple clothes fit for a king. And I will put a gold chain around your neck. And you will become the third highest ruler in the kingdom."

¹⁷ Then Daniel answered the king, "You may keep your gifts for yourself. Or you may give those rewards to someone else. I will read the writing on the wall for you. And I will explain to you what it means.

¹⁸ "My king, the Most High God made your father Nebuchadnezzar a great, important and powerful king. ¹⁹God made him very important. So all the people, nations and those who spoke every language were very afraid of Nebuchadnezzar. If he wanted a person to die, he put that person to death. And if he wanted a person to live, he let that person live. If he wanted to promote a person, he promoted him. And if he wanted a person to be unimportant, he made him unimportant.

²⁰ "But Nebuchadnezzar became too proud and stubborn. So he was taken off his royal throne. His glory was taken away. ²¹Then Nebuchadnezzar was forced away from people. His mind became like the mind of an animal. He lived with the wild donkeys and was fed grass like an ox. He became wet with dew. These things happened to him until he learned his lesson: The Most High God rules over the kingdoms of men. And the Most High God sets anyone he wants over those kingdoms.

²² "But, Belshazzar, you already knew these things. You are a descendant[d] of Nebuchadnezzar. But still you have not been sorry for what you have done. ²³Instead, you have turned against the Lord of heaven. You ordered the drinking cups from the Temple of the Lord to be brought to you. Then you and your royal guests drank wine from them. Your wives and your slave women also drank wine from them. You praised the gods of silver, gold, bronze, iron, wood and stone. They are not really gods. They cannot see or hear or understand anything. But you did not honor God. He is the One who has power over your life and everything you do. ²⁴So God sent the hand that wrote on the wall.

²⁵ "These are the words that were written on the wall: 'Mene, mene, tekel, parsin.'

²⁶ "This is what these words mean: Mene: God has counted the days until your kingdom will end. ²⁷Tekel: You

have been weighed on the scales and found not good enough. ²⁸Parsin: Your kingdom is being divided. It will be given to the Medes and the Persians."

²⁹Then Belshazzar gave an order for Daniel to be dressed in purple clothes. A gold chain was put around his neck. And he was announced to be the third highest ruler in the kingdom. ³⁰That

visors and the governors tried to find reasons to accuse Daniel. But he went on doing the business of the government. And they could not find anything wrong with him. So they could not accuse him of doing anything wrong.

Thankfulness
DANIEL 6:10

What is something you do every single day that you never forget to do? (Breathing doesn't count!) Most people have more than one thing they do every day. No matter what happens, they always do it—like eating or brushing their teeth.

Daniel's schedule looked like this every day: "First, I've got to thank God. Later on, I'll spend some more time thanking him. The third thing I'll do today is . . . oh, yeah, thank God!" Every day. Just like we wouldn't dare go for a whole day without eating, Daniel decided not to go a single day without giving God thanks.

You don't have to be like Daniel and go to your window each time you want to thank God. And you don't have to thank God three times a day. But at least thank him once every day. God would love for you to thank him as often as you think of him. What can you thank him for today?

To learn more about thankfulness, zoom to page 1256.

very same night Belshazzar, king of the Babylonian people, was killed. ³¹A man named Darius the Mede became the new king. Darius was 62 years old.

Daniel and the Lions

6 Darius thought it would be a good idea to choose 120 governors. They would rule through all of his kingdom. ²And he chose three men as supervisors over those 120 governors. Daniel was one of these three supervisors. The king set up these men so that he would not be cheated. ³Daniel showed that he could do the work better than the other supervisors and the governors. Because of this, the king planned to put Daniel in charge of the whole kingdom. ⁴So the other super-

Daniel was trustworthy. He was not lazy and did not cheat the king. ⁵Finally these men said, "We will never find any reason to accuse Daniel. But we must find something to complain about. It will have to be about the law of his God."

⁶So the supervisors and the governors went as a group to the king. They said: "King Darius, live forever! ⁷The supervisors, assistant governors, governors, the people who advise you and the captains of the soldiers have all agreed on something. We think the king should make this law that everyone would have to obey: No one should pray to any god or man except to you, our king. This should be done for the next 30 days. Anyone who doesn't obey

will be thrown into the lions' den. ⁸Now, our king, make the law. Write it down so it cannot be changed. The laws of the Medes and Persians cannot be canceled." ⁹So King Darius made the law and had it written.

¹⁰When Daniel heard that the new law had been written, he went to his house. He went to his upstairs room. The windows of that room opened toward Jerusalem. Three times each day Daniel got down on his knees and prayed. He prayed and thanked God, just as he always had done.

¹¹Then those men went as a group and found Daniel. They saw him praying and asking God for help. ¹²So they went to the king. They talked to him about the law he had made. They said, "Didn't you write a law that says no one may pray to any god or man except you, our king? Doesn't it say that anyone who disobeys during the next 30 days

will be thrown into the lions' den?" The king answered, "Yes, I wrote that law. And the laws of the Medes and Persians cannot be canceled."

¹³Then those men spoke to the king. They said, "Daniel is one of the captives from Judah. And he is not paying attention to the law you wrote. Daniel still prays to his God three times every day." ¹⁴The king became very upset when he heard this. He decided he had to save Daniel. He worked until sunset trying to think of a way to save him.

¹⁵Then those men went as a group to the king. They said, "Remember, our king, the law of the Medes and Persians. It says that no law or command given by the king can be changed."

¹⁶So King Darius gave the order. They brought Daniel and threw him into the lions' den. The king said to Daniel, "May the God you serve all the time save you!" ¹⁷A big stone was brought. It was put over the opening of the lions' den. Then the king used his signet*d* ring to put his special seal*d* on

Visiting Angels
DANIEL 6:22

Sometimes God sent angels to protect people. Daniel had been taken from his homeland when the king of Babylon conquered Judah. Daniel was chosen to serve the king. Over his lifetime he served three kings in Babylon. Daniel served the kings well, but he never forgot about serving God first.

Some of the king's other helpers were jealous of Daniel, so they tricked the king into making a law against prayer. Of course, Daniel didn't obey the law because he knew he was supposed to pray to God. The punishment for disobeying the law was to be thrown into a den of hungry lions. Daniel was thrown into the den, but the lions didn't hurt him because God sent an angel to protect him.

Angels still protect God's people at times, even though we cannot see them and may not know it.

We can thank God for his love and protection.

To read about an angel God sent as an answer to someone's prayer, fly to page 1045.

the rock. And he used the rings of his royal officers to put their seals on the rock also. This showed that no one could move that rock and bring Daniel out. [18]Then King Darius went back to his palace. He did not eat that night. He did not have any entertainment brought to entertain him. And he could not sleep.

[19]The next morning King Darius got up at dawn. He hurried to the lions' den. [20]As he came near the den, he was worried. He called out to Daniel. He said, "Daniel, servant of the living God! Has your God that you always worship been able to save you from the lions?"

[21]Daniel answered, "My king, live forever! [22]My God sent his angel to close the lions' mouths. They have not hurt me, because my God knows I am innocent. I never did anything wrong to you, my king."

[23]King Darius was very happy. He told his servants to lift Daniel out of the lions' den. So they lifted him out and did not find any injury on him. This was because Daniel had trusted in his God.

[24]Then the king gave a command. The men who had accused Daniel were brought to the lions' den and thrown into it. Their wives and children were also thrown into it. The lions grabbed them before they hit the floor of the den. And the lions crushed their bones.

[25]Then King Darius wrote a letter. It was to all people and all nations, to those who spoke every language in the world:

I wish you great wealth.

[26]I am making a new law. This law is for people in every part of my kingdom. All of you must fear and respect the God of Daniel.

Daniel's God is the living God.
He lives forever.
His kingdom will never be destroyed.
His rule will never end.
[27]God rescues and saves people.
God does mighty miracles[d]
in heaven and on earth.

God saved Daniel
from the power of the lions.

[28]So Daniel was successful during the time that Darius was king. This was also the time that Cyrus the Persian was king.

Daniel's Dream about Four Animals

7 In Belshazzar's first year as king of Babylon, Daniel had a dream. He saw visions as he was lying on his bed. Daniel wrote down what he had dreamed.

[2]Daniel said: "I saw my vision at night. In the vision the wind was blowing from all four directions. These winds made the sea very rough. [3]I saw four huge animals come up from the sea. Each animal was different from the others.

[4]"The first animal looked like a lion. But it had wings like an eagle. I watched this animal until its wings were torn off. It was lifted from the ground so that it stood up on two feet like a man. And it was given the mind of a man.

[5]"And then I saw a second animal before me. It looked like a bear. It was raised up on one of its sides. And it had three ribs in its mouth between its teeth. It was told, 'Get up and eat all the meat you want!'

[6]"After that, I looked, and there before me was another animal. This animal looked like a leopard. And the leopard had four wings on its back. The wings looked like a bird's wings. This animal had four heads. It was given power to rule.

[7]"After that, in my vision at night I continued looking. There in front of me was a fourth animal. This animal looked cruel and terrible and very strong. It had large iron teeth. It crushed and ate what it killed. Then it walked on whatever was left. This fourth animal was different from all the animals I had seen before it. It had ten horns.

[8]"While I was thinking about the horns, another horn grew up among

them. It was a little horn. It had eyes like a person's eyes. It also had a mouth. And the mouth was bragging. The little horn pulled out three of the other horns.

9"As I looked,

thrones were put in their places.
And God, who has been alive
   forever, sat on his throne.
His clothes were white like snow.
   And the hair on his head was white
   like wool.
His throne was made from fire.
   And the wheels of his throne were
   blazing with fire.
10A river of fire was flowing
   from in front of him.
Many thousands of angels were
   serving him.
   Millions of angels stood before
   him.
Court was ready to begin.
   And the books were opened.

11"I kept on looking because the little horn was bragging. I kept watching until finally the fourth animal was killed. Its body was destroyed, and it was thrown into the burning fire. 12(The power and rule of the other animals had been taken from them. But they were permitted to live for a certain period of time.)

13"In my vision at night I looked. There in front of me was someone who looked like a human being. He was coming with clouds in the sky. He came near God, who has been alive forever. And he was led to God. 14The one who looked like a human being was given the power to rule. He was also given glory and royal power. All peoples, nations and men who spoke every language will serve him. His rule will last forever. His kingdom will never be destroyed.

The Meaning of the Dream

15"I, Daniel, was worried. The visions that went through my mind frightened me. 16I came near one of those standing there. I asked him what all this meant.

"So he told me. He explained to me

what these things meant. 17He said, 'The four great animals are four kingdoms. Those four kingdoms will come from the earth. 18But the people who belong to the Most High God will receive the power to rule. And they will have the power to rule forever. They will have it from now on.'

19"Then I wanted to know what the fourth animal meant. It was different from all the other animals. It was very terrible. It had iron teeth and bronze claws. It was the animal that crushed and ate what it killed. And it walked on whatever was left. 20I also wanted to know about the ten horns on its head. And I wanted to know about the little horn that grew there. It had pulled out three of the other ten horns. It looked greater than the others. And it had eyes and a mouth that kept bragging. 21As I watched, the little horn began making war against God's people. And the horn kept killing them 22until God, who has been alive forever, came. He judged in favor of the people who belong to the Most High God. And the time came for them to receive the power to rule.

23"And he explained this to me: 'The fourth animal is a fourth kingdom that will come on the earth. It will be different from all the other kingdoms. It will destroy people all over the world. It will walk on and crush the whole earth. 24The ten horns are ten kings who will come from this fourth kingdom. After those ten kings are gone, another king will come. He will be different from the kings who ruled before him. He will defeat three of the other kings. 25This king will say things against the Most High God. And he will hurt and kill God's people. He will try to change times and laws that have already been set. The people that belong to God will be in that king's power for three and one-half years.

26" 'But the court will decide what should happen. And the power of the king will be taken away. His kingdom will be completely destroyed. 27Then the people who belong to the Most

High God will have the power to rule. They will rule over all the kingdoms under heaven with power and greatness. Their power to rule will last forever. And people from all the other kingdoms will respect and serve them.'

28"And that was the end of the dream. I, Daniel, was very afraid. My face became very white from fear. But I kept everything to myself."

Daniel's Vision

8 During the third year Belshazzar was king, I saw this vision. This was after the other one. ²In this vision I saw myself in the capital city of Susa. Susa is in the area of Elam. I was standing by the Ulai River. ³I looked up, and I saw a male sheep standing beside the river. It had two long horns. But one horn was longer than the other. The long horn was newer than the other horn. ⁴I watched the male sheep charge to the west. He also charged to the north and the south. No animal could stand before him. And none could save another animal from his power. He did whatever he wanted. And he became very powerful.

⁵While I was thinking about this, I saw a male goat come from the west. This goat had one large horn that was easy to see. It was between his eyes. He crossed over the whole earth. But his feet did not touch the ground.

⁶That goat charged the male sheep with the two horns. This was the male sheep I had seen standing by the river. The goat was very angry. ⁷I watched the goat attack the male sheep. It broke the sheep's two horns. The sheep could not stop it. The goat knocked the sheep to the ground. Then the goat walked all over him. No one was able to save the sheep from the goat. ⁸So the male goat became very great. But when he was strong, his big horn broke off. Then four horns grew in place of the one big horn. Those four horns were easy to see. They pointed in four different directions.

⁹Then a little horn grew from one of those four horns. It became very big. It grew to the south and the east and toward the beautiful land of Judah. ¹⁰That little horn grew until it reached to the sky. It even threw some of the army of heaven to the ground. And it walked on them. ¹¹That little horn became very strong against God, the commander of heaven's armies. It stopped the daily sacrifices that were offered to the commander. The place where people worshiped the commander was pulled down. ¹²There was a turning away from God. Because of this the people stopped the daily sacrifices. It was like throwing truth down to the ground. The horn was successful in everything it did.

¹³Then I heard one angel speaking. Another angel asked the first one, "How long will the things in this vision last? The vision is about the daily sacrifices. It is about the turning away from God that brings destruction. It is about the Temple*d* being pulled down. It is about the army of heaven being walked on."

¹⁴He said to me, "This will happen for 2,300 evenings and mornings.*n* Then the holy place will be repaired."

¹⁵I, Daniel, saw this vision. And I tried to understand what it meant. Then someone who looked like a man suddenly stood before me. ¹⁶And I heard a man's voice calling from the Ulai River: "Gabriel, explain the vision to this man."

¹⁷Gabriel came to where I was standing. When he came close to me, I was very afraid. I bowed facedown on the ground. But Gabriel said to me, "Human being, understand that this vision is about the time of the end."

¹⁸While Gabriel was speaking, I fell into a deep sleep. My face was on the ground. Then he touched me and lifted me to my feet. ¹⁹He said, "Now, I will explain the vision to you. I will tell you what will happen later, in the time of God's anger. Your vision was about the set time of the end.

*n*2,300 evenings and mornings   This could mean 1,150 days or 2,300 days.

²⁰"You saw a male sheep with two horns. Those horns are the kings of Media and Persia. ²¹The male goat is the king of Greece. The big horn between its eyes is the first king. ²²After that horn broke, four horns grew in its place. Those four horns are four kingdoms. Those four kingdoms will come from the nation of the first king. But they will not be as strong as the first king.

²³"When the end comes near for those kingdoms, a bold and cruel king will come. This king will tell lies. This will happen when many people have turned against God. ²⁴This king will be very powerful. But his power will not come from himself. He will cause terrible destruction. He will be successful in everything he does. He will destroy powerful people and even God's people. ²⁵This king will use his wisdom to make lies successful. He will think that he is very important. He will destroy many people without warning. He will try to fight even God, the Prince of princes! But that cruel king will be destroyed. And it will not be human power that destroys him.

²⁶"The vision that has been shown to you about those times is true. But seal up the vision. Those things won't happen for a long time."

²⁷I, Daniel, became very weak. I was sick for several days after that vision. Then I got up and went back to work for the king. But I was very upset about the vision. I didn't understand what it meant.

Daniel's Prayer

9 These things happened during the first year Darius son of Xerxes was king. He was a descendant*d* of the Medes. ²During Darius' first year as king, I, Daniel, was reading the Scriptures.*d* In them I saw what the Lord told Jeremiah. He said Jerusalem would be an empty desert for 70 years.

³Then I turned to the Lord God. I prayed to him and asked him for help. I did not eat any food. To show how sad I was I put on rough cloth and sat in ashes. ⁴I prayed to the Lord my God. I told him about all of my sins. I said, "Lord, you are a great God. You cause fear and wonder. You keep your agreement of love with all who love you and obey your commands.

⁵"But we have sinned and done wrong. We have been wicked and turned against you. We have not obeyed your commands and laws. ⁶We did not listen to your servants, the prophets. They spoke for you to our kings, our leaders and our ancestors. They spoke to all the people of the land.

⁷"Lord, you are good and right. But we are full of shame today. The people of Judah and Jerusalem and all the people of Israel are ashamed. People near and far whom you scattered among many nations are ashamed. We were not loyal to you. ⁸Lord, we are all ashamed. Our kings and leaders and our fathers are ashamed. This is because we have sinned against you.

⁹"But, Lord our God, you show us mercy. You forgive us even though we have turned against you. ¹⁰We have not obeyed the Lord our God. We have not obeyed the teachings he gave us through his servants, the prophets. ¹¹All the people of Israel have disobeyed your teachings. They all have turned away and refused to obey you. So you brought on us the curses and promises of punishment written in the Teachings of Moses, the servant of God. These things have happened to us because we sinned against you.

¹²"God said these things would happen to us and our leaders. And he made them happen. You brought on us a great disaster. Nothing has ever been done here on earth like what was done to Jerusalem. ¹³All this disaster came to us just as it is written in the Teachings of Moses. But we still have not stopped sinning. We still do not pay attention to your truth. ¹⁴The Lord was ready to bring the disaster on us. This is because he is right in every-

thing he does. But we still have not obeyed him.

15"Lord our God, you used your power and brought us out of Egypt. Because of that, your name is known even today. Lord, we have sinned. We have done wrong. 16Lord, you do the right things. So do not be angry with Jerusalem. Jerusalem is your city on your holy hill. All this has happened because of our sins and the evil things done by our ancestors. So now people all around insult and make fun of Jerusalem and your people.

17"Now, our God, hear my prayers. I am your servant. Listen to my prayer for help. Do good things for your holy place that is in ruins. Do this for your sake. 18My God, pay attention and hear me. Open your eyes and see all the terrible things that have happened to us. See what has happened to the city that is called by your name. We do not ask these things because we are good. We ask because of your mercy. 19Lord, listen! Lord, forgive! Lord, hear us and do something! For your sake, don't wait! Your city and your people are called by your name."

Gabriel's Explanation

20I was saying those things in my prayer to the Lord, my God. I was confessing my sins and the sins of the people of Israel. I was praying for God's holy hill. 21While I was still praying, Gabriel came to me. Gabriel was the person I had seen in my last vision. He came flying quickly to me about the time of the evening sacrifice. 22Gabriel said to me, "Daniel, I have come to give you wisdom and to help you understand. 23When you first started praying, an answer was given. And I came to tell you, because God loves you very much. So think about the message and understand the vision.

24"God has ordered 490 years for your people and your holy city. These years are ordered for these reasons: to stop people from turning against God; to put an end to sin; to take away evil; to bring in goodness that continues forever; to make the vision and prophecy[d] come true; and to appoint a most holy place.

25"Learn and understand these things. A command will come to rebuild Jerusalem. The time from this command until the appointed leader comes will be 49 years and 434 years. Jerusalem will be rebuilt with streets and a trench around it. But it will be built in times of trouble. 26After the 434 years the appointed leader will be killed. He will have nothing. The people of the leader who is to come will destroy the city. They will also destroy the holy place. That end will come like a flood. War will continue until the end. God has ordered that place to be completely destroyed. 27That leader will make an agreement with many people for 7 years. He will put a stop to offerings and sacrifices after 3½ years. And the horrible thing that destroys will be placed on the highest point of the Temple.[d] But God has ordered him to be destroyed!"

Daniel's Vision of a Man

10 During Cyrus' third year as king of Persia, Daniel learned about these things. (Daniel's other name is Belteshazzar.) The message was true. It was about a great war. But Daniel understood it, because it was explained to him in a vision.

2At that time I, Daniel, was very sad for three weeks. 3I did not eat any fancy food. I did not eat any meat or drink any wine. I did not use any perfumed oil. I did not do any of these things for three weeks.

4On the twenty-fourth day of the first month, I was standing beside the great Tigris River. 5While standing there, I looked up. And I saw a man dressed in linen clothes. A belt made of fine gold was wrapped around his waist. 6His body was like shiny yellow quartz. His face was bright like lightning, and his eyes were like fire. His arms and legs were shiny like polished bronze. His voice sounded like the roar of a crowd. [7]I, Daniel, was the only person who saw the vision. The men with me did not see it. But they were badly frightened. They were so afraid they ran away and hid. [8]So I was left alone, watching this great vision. I lost my strength. My face turned white like a dead person, and I was helpless. [9]Then I heard the man in the vision speaking. As I listened, I fell into a deep sleep. My face was on the ground.

[10]Then a hand touched me and set me on my hands and knees. I was so afraid that I was shaking. [11]The man in the vision said to me, "Daniel, God loves you very much. Think very carefully about the words I will speak to you. Stand up because I have been sent to you." And when he said this, I stood up. I was still shaking.

you. And I came to you because you have been praying. [13]But the prince of Persia has been fighting against me for 21 days. Then Michael, one of the most important angels, came to help me. He came because I had been left there with the king of Persia. [14]Now I have come to you, Daniel. I will explain to you what will happen to your people. The vision is about a time in the future."

[15]While he was speaking to me, I bowed facedown. I could not speak. [16]Then one who looked like a man touched my lips. I opened my mouth and started to speak. I said to the one standing in front of me, "Master, I am upset and afraid. It is because of what I saw in the vision. I feel helpless. [17]Master, I am Daniel your servant. How can I talk with you! My strength is gone, and it is hard for me to breathe."

[18]The one who looked like a man touched me again. And he gave me

Visiting Angels

DANIEL 10:4-12

Sometimes God uses an angel to help answer a person's prayers. Daniel was praying, because God had told him about a terrible war that was going to happen in the future. This made Daniel very sad. He prayed to God to try and understand more about the war. He prayed all the time for three weeks. Finally, God sent an angel to Daniel. The angel told him he would help Daniel understand what God had told him about the war. Daniel was encouraged because of the angel's visit. God sent the angel to let David know he had heard David's prayers.

God hears every word we say when we pray. Remember that whenever it seems like it takes a long time for him to answer. God will always answer our prayers—even if he does not send an angel to do it!

To read about an angel who told a man to get married, *fly to page 1122.*

[12]Then the man said to me, "Daniel, do not be afraid. Some time ago you decided to try to get understanding. You wanted to be humble before God. Since that time God has listened to

strength. [19]He said, "Daniel, don't be afraid. God loves you very much. Peace be with you. Be strong now, be strong."

When he spoke to me, I became

stronger. Then I said, "Master, speak, since you have given me strength."

20So then he said, "Daniel, do you know why I have come to you? Soon I must go back to fight against the prince of Persia. When I go, the prince of Greece will come. 21But before I go, I must first tell you what is written in the Book of Truth. No one stands with me against them except Michael. He is the angel ruling over your people.

11 In the first year Darius the Mede was king, I stood up to support Michael. I supported him in his fight against the prince of Persia.

Kingdoms of the South and North

2"Now then, Daniel, I tell you the truth: Three more kings will rule in Persia. Then a fourth king will come. He will be much richer than all the kings of Persia before him. He will use his riches to get power. And he will stir up everyone against the kingdom of Greece. 3Then a mighty king will come. He will rule with great power. He will do anything he wants. 4After that king has come, his kingdom will be broken up. It will be divided out toward the four parts of the world. His kingdom will not go to his descendants.d And it will not have the power that he had. This is because his kingdom will be pulled up and given to other people.

5"The king of the South will become strong. But one of his commanders will become even stronger. He will begin to rule his own kingdom with great power. 6Then after a few years, the king of the South and the commander will become friends. The daughter of the king of the South will marry the king of the North. She will do this to bring peace. But she will not keep her power. And his family will not last. She, her husband, her child and those who brought her to that country will be killed.

7"But a person from her family will become king of the South. He will attack the armies of the king of the North. He will go into that king's strong, walled city. He will fight and win. 8He will take their gods and their metal idols. He will also take their valuable things made of silver and gold. He will take those things to Egypt. Then he will not bother the king of the North for a few years. 9Next, the king of the North will attack the king of the South. But he will be beaten back to his own country.

10"The sons of the king of the North will prepare for war. They will get a large army together. That army will move through the land very quickly, like a powerful flood. Later, that army will come back and fight. They will fight all the way to the strong, walled city of the king of the South. 11Then the king of the South will become very angry. He will march out to fight against the king of the North. The king of the North will have a large army. But he will lose the battle. 12The soldiers will be carried away. So the king of the South will be very proud. And he will kill thousands of soldiers from the northern army. But he will not continue to be successful. 13The king of the North will gather another army. That army will be larger than the first one. After several years he will attack. That army will be very large, and it will have plenty of weapons.

14"In those times many people will be against the king of the South. Some of your own people who love to fight will turn against the king of the South. They will think it is time for God's promises to come true. But it will not be the time yet. And they will fail. 15Then the king of the North will come. He will build dirt roads to the tops of the city walls. And he will capture a strong, walled city. The southern army will not have the power to fight back. Even their best soldiers will not be strong enough to stop the northern army. 16The king of the North will do whatever he wants. No one will be able to stand against him. He will gain power and control in the beautiful land of Israel. And he will have the power to destroy it. ¹⁷The king of the North will decide to use all his power to fight against the king of the South. He will make an agreement with the king of the South. The king of the North will give one of his daughters as a wife to the king of the South. He will do that so he can defeat the king of the South. But those plans will not succeed or help him. ¹⁸Then the king of the North will turn his attention to other places. He will take many cities along the coast of the Mediterranean Sea. But a commander will put an end to the pride of the king of the North. The commander will turn that pride back on him. ¹⁹After that happens the king of the North will go back to the strong, walled cities of his own country. But he will lose his power. That will be the end of him.

²⁰"The next king of the North will send out a tax collector. He will then have plenty of money. In a few years that ruler will be killed. But he will not die in anger or in a battle.

²¹"That ruler will be followed by a very cruel and hated man. He will not have the honor of being from a king's family. He will attack the kingdom when the people feel safe. He will take power by lying to the people. ²²He will sweep away in defeat large and powerful armies. He will even defeat a prince who made an agreement. ²³Many nations will make agreements with that cruel and hated ruler. But he will lie to them. He will gain much power. But only a few people will support him. ²⁴The richest areas will feel safe. But that cruel and hated ruler will attack them. And he will succeed where his ancestors did not. He will take things from the countries he defeated. And he will give those things to his followers. He will plan to defeat and destroy strong cities. He will be successful, but only for a short time.

²⁵"That very cruel and hated ruler will have a large army. He will use it to stir up his strength and courage. He will attack the king of the South. The king of the South will get a large and very powerful army and get ready for war. But the people who are against him will make secret plans. And the king of the South will be defeated. ²⁶There were people who were supposed to be good friends of the king of the South. But they will try to destroy him. His army will be swept away in defeat. Many of his soldiers will be killed in battle. ²⁷Those two kings will want to hurt each other. They will sit at the same table and lie to each other. But it will not do either one any good. This is because God has set a time for their end to come. ²⁸The king of the North will go back to his own country with much wealth. Then he will decide to go against the holy agreement. He will do what he planned. Then he will go back to his own country.

²⁹"At the right time the king of the North will attack the king of the South again. But this time he will not be successful as he was before. ³⁰Ships from the west will come and fight against the king of the North. He will see those ships coming and be afraid. Then he will return and show his anger against God's people who obey the holy agreement. He will be good to those who have stopped obeying the holy agreement.

³¹"The king of the North will send his army. They will make the Temple*ᵈ* in Jerusalem unclean.*ᵈ* They will stop the people from offering the daily sacrifice. Then they will set up the horrible thing that destroys. ³²The king of the North will tell lies to God's people. Those who have not obeyed God will be ruined. But there will be some who know God and obey him. They will be strong and fight back.

³³"Those who are wise will help the others understand what is happening. But some of them will be killed with swords. Some will be burned or taken captive. Some of them will have their homes and things taken away. These things will continue for many days.

³⁴When the wise ones are suffering, they will get a little help. Many who join the wise ones will not love God. ³⁵Some of the wise ones will be killed. But the hard times must come. This is so they can be made stronger and purer. They will be without faults until the time of the end comes. Then, at the right time the end will come.

The King Who Praises Himself

³⁶"The king of the North will do whatever he wants. He will brag about himself. He will praise himself and think he is even better than a god. He will say things against the God of gods that no one has ever heard. He will be successful until all the bad things have happened. What God has planned to happen will happen. ³⁷That king of the North will not care about the gods his ancestors worshiped. He won't care about the god that women worship. He won't care about any god. Instead, he will make himself more important than any god. ³⁸The king of the North will worship power and strength. His ancestors did not love power as he will. He will honor the god of power with gold and silver, expensive jewels and gifts. ³⁹That king will attack strong, walled cities. He will do it with the help of a foreign god. He will give much honor to the people who join him. He will make them rulers in charge of many other people. He will make those rulers pay him for the land they rule.

⁴⁰"At the time of the end, the king of the South will fight a battle against the king of the North. The king of the North will attack him. He will attack with chariots and soldiers on horses and many large ships. He will invade many countries and sweep through their lands like a flood. ⁴¹The king of the North will attack the beautiful land of Judah. He will defeat many countries. But Edom, Moab and the leaders of Ammon will be saved from him. ⁴²The king of the North will show his power in many countries. Egypt will not escape. ⁴³The king will get trea-sures of gold and silver. And he will get all the riches of Egypt. The Libyan and Nubian people will obey him. ⁴⁴But the king of the North will hear news from the east and the north. And it will make him afraid and angry. He will go to destroy completely many nations. ⁴⁵He will set up his royal tents. They will be between the sea and the beautiful mountain where the Temple*d* is built. But, finally, his end will come. There will not be anyone to help him when he dies.

The Time of the End

12 "Daniel, at that time Michael, the great prince, will stand up. (He is the one who protects your people.) There will be a time of much trouble. It will be the worst time since nations have been on earth. But your people will be saved. Everyone whose name is written in God's book will be saved. ²Many people who have already died will live again. Some of them will wake up to have life forever. But some will wake up to find shame and disgrace forever. ³The wise people will shine like the brightness of the sky. Those who teach others to live right will shine like stars forever and ever.

⁴"But you, Daniel, close up the book and seal it. These things will happen at the time of the end. Many people will go here and there to find true knowledge."

⁵Then I, Daniel, looked, and I saw two other men. One was standing on my side of the river. And the other was standing on the far side. ⁶The man who was dressed in linen was standing over the water in the river. One of the two men spoke to him. He asked, "How long will it be before these amazing things come true?"

⁷The man dressed in linen who stood over the water raised his hands toward heaven. And I heard him make a promise. He used the name of God who lives forever. He said, "It will be for three and one-half years. The power of the holy people will finally be

broken. Then all these things will come true."

⁸I heard the answer, but I did not really understand. So I asked, "Master, what will happen after all these things come true?"

⁹He answered, "Go your way, Daniel. The message is closed up and sealed until the time of the end. ¹⁰Many people will be made clean,ᵈ pure and spotless. But the wicked will continue to be wicked. And those wicked people will not understand these things. But the wise people will understand them. ¹¹"The daily sacrifice will be stopped. There will be 1,290 days from that time. Then the horrible thing that destroys will be set up. ¹²Those who wait for the end of the 1,335 days will be happy.

¹³"As for you, Daniel, go your way till the end. You will get your rest when you die. And at the end you will rise from the dead to get your reward."

HOSEA

Israel Acts Like an Unfaithful Wife

1 The Lord spoke his word to Hosea son of Beeri. This was during the time that Uzziah, Jotham, Ahaz and Hezekiah were kings of Judah. During part of this time Jeroboam son of Jehoash was king of Israel.

Hosea's Wife and Children

²The Lord said to him, "Go, and marry a woman who will be unfaithful to you. She will give you children whose fathers are other men. Do this because people in this country have acted like an unfaithful wife toward the Lord." ³So Hosea married Gomer daughter of Diblaim. Gomer became pregnant and gave birth to Hosea's son.

⁴The Lord said to Hosea, "Name him Jezreel. This is because soon I will punish the family of Jehu for the people they killed at Jezreel. Then I will put an end to the kingdom of Israel. ⁵And I will also break the power of Israel's army in the Valley of Jezreel."

⁶Gomer became pregnant again and gave birth to a daughter. The Lord said to Hosea, "Name her Lo-Ruhamah." This is because I will not pity Israel anymore. I will no longer forgive them. ⁷But I will show pity to the people of Judah. I will save them. I will not use bows or swords, horses or horsemen, or weapons of war to save them. I, the Lord their God, will save them."

⁸After Gomer had finished nursing Lo-Ruhamah, she became pregnant again. And she gave birth to another son. ⁹The Lord said, "Name him Lo-Ammi" because you are not my people. And I am not your God.

God's Promise to Israel

¹⁰"But the people of Israel will become like the grains of sand of the sea. You cannot measure or count them. Now it is said to Israel, 'You are not my people.' But later they will be called 'children of the living God.' ¹¹Then the people of Judah and Israel will be joined together again. They will choose one leader for themselves. And again they will grow in their land. The day of Jezreel, when God plants, will be truly great.

2 "Your brothers and your sisters will be called 'my people' and 'you have been shown love.'

God Speaks About Israel

²"Plead with your mother."
   Plead with her because she no
      longer acts like a wife to me.
   And I am not treated like her
      husband.
Tell her to stop acting like a
      prostitute.ᵈ
Tell her to stop behaving like an
      unfaithful wife.
³If she refuses, I will strip her naked.
   I will leave her bare like the day
      she was born.
   I will make her dry like a desert.
   I will make her like a land
      without water.
   I will kill her with thirst.
⁴I will not take pity on her children.
   They are the children of an
      unfaithful wife.

"**Lo-Ruhamah** This name in Hebrew means "not pitied."
"**Lo-Ammi** This name in Hebrew means "not my people."
"**mother** This refers to the nation of Israel here.

⁵Their mother has acted like a
   prostitute.
The one who became pregnant
   with them has acted
   disgracefully.
She said, 'I will chase after my
   lovers.ⁿ
They give me food and water.
They give me wool and linen.
They give me wine and olive oil.'
⁶So I will block her road with
   thornbushes.
I will build a wall around her
so she cannot find her way.
⁷She will run after her lovers.
But she won't catch up to them.
She will look for them.
But she won't find them.
Then she will say, 'I will go back to
   my first husband.ⁿ
Life was better for me then than
   it is now.'
⁸But she has not accepted that I
   was the one
who gave her grain, wine and oil.
I gave her much silver and gold.
But she used it to make statues of
   Baal.ᵈ

⁹"So I will take away my grain at
   harvest time.
And I will take away my wine
   when it is ready.
I will take back my wool and linen.
I gave her those things to cover
   her nakedness.
¹⁰So I will show her nakedness to her
   lovers.
No one will save her from my
   punishment.
¹¹I will put an end to all her
   celebrations:
her yearly festivals, her New
   Moonᵈ festivals and her
   Sabbaths.ᵈ
I will stop all of her special feasts.
¹²I will destroy her vines and fig trees.
She said they were her pay from
   her lovers.

I will turn them into a forest.
Wild animals will eat those plants.
¹³I will punish her for all the times
   she burned incenseᵈ to the Baals.
She put on her rings and jewelry.
Then she went chasing after her
   lovers.
But she has forgotten me!"
   says the Lord.

¹⁴"So I am going to attract her.
I will lead her into the desert
and speak tenderly to her.
¹⁵Then I will give her back her
   vineyards.
And I will make the Valley of
   Achorⁿ a door of hope.
Then she will respond as when she
   was young,
as when she came out of Egypt."

¹⁶The Lord says, "Then she will call
   me 'my husband.'
She will no longer call me 'my
   baal.'ⁿ
¹⁷I will never let her say the names of
   Baal again.
Then people won't use their names
   anymore.
¹⁸At that time I will make an
   agreement for them.
It will be with the wild animals, the
   birds and the crawling things.
I will remove from the land
the bow and the sword and the
   weapons of war.
Then my people will live in safety.
¹⁹And I will make you my promised
   bride forever.
I will be good and fair.
I will show you my love and
   mercy.
²⁰I will be true to you as my
   promised bride.
Then you will accept that I
   am the Lord.

²¹"And at that time I will answer you,"
   says the Lord.
"I will speak to the skies.

ⁿ**lovers**   This refers to the nations surrounding Israel, who led Israel to worship false gods.
ⁿ**husband**   This refers to God here.
ⁿ**Achor**   This name in Hebrew means "trouble." It refers here to punishment as the way to blessing.
ⁿ**baal**   Another Hebrew word for husband. But it was the same word as the false god Baal.

And they will give rain to the
earth.
22The earth will produce grain, wine
and oil.
Much will grow because my
people are called Jezreel—
God plants.
23I will plant my people in the land.
I will show pity to the one I had
called 'not shown pity.'
I will say, 'You are my people'
to those I had called 'not my
people.'
And they will say to me, 'You are
our God.'"

Hosea Buys Gomer Back

3 The Lord said to me, "Go, show
your love to your wife again. She
has had other lovers and has been
unfaithful to you. But you must keep
on loving her the way the Lord loves
the people of Israel. This is true even
though the Israelites worship other
gods. They love to eat the raisin
cakes."*n*

2So I bought Gomer for six ounces of
silver and about ten bushels of barley.
3Then I told her, "You must wait for me
for many days. You must not be a
prostitute.*d* You must not be any other
man's lover. I, in turn, will wait for you."

4In the same way Israel will live
many days without a king or leader.
They will not have sacrifices or holy
stone pillars. They will be without the
holy vest*d* or an idol. 5After this, the
people of Israel will return to the Lord
their God. They will follow the Lord
and the king from David's family. In
the last days they will come to the
Lord. And he will bless them.

The Lord's Word Against Israel

4 People of Israel, listen to the Lord's
message.
The Lord says he has this
against you who live in this
country:
"The people are not true, not loyal
to God.

They do not even know him.
2They curse. They lie. They kill.
They steal.
They are guilty of adultery.*d*
They break all my laws.
One murder follows another.
3Because of this the land dries up,
and all its people are dying off.
Even the wild animals are dying.
Even the birds of the air and the
fish of the sea are dying.

God's Case Against the Priests

4"No one should accuse
or blame another person.
Don't blame the people, you priests,
when they quarrel with you.
5You will be ruined one of these days.
And your prophets*d* will be ruined
with you one of these nights.
I will also destroy your mother, the
nation of Israel.
6My people will be destroyed
because they have no knowledge.
You priests have refused to learn.
So I will refuse to let you be priests
to me.
You have forgotten the teachings of
your God.
So I will reject your children.
7The more priests there are,
the more they sin against me.
I will take away their honor
and give them nothing but shame.
8The priests live off the sin offerings
of the people.
So they want the people to sin
more and more.
9The priests are as wrong as the
people.
I will punish them both for what
they have done.
I will repay them for the wrong
they have done.

10"They will eat
but not have enough.
They will have sexual relations with
the prostitutes.*d*
But they will not have children.
This is because they left the Lord.

*n*raisin cakes   This food may have been used in the feasts that honored false gods.

God's Case Against the People

[11]"Sexual sins, old wine and new wine
take away my people's ability to
understand.
[12]My people ask wooden idols for
advice.
They ask those sticks of wood to
advise them!
Like prostitutes, they have chased
after other gods.
They have left their own God.
[13]They make sacrifices on the tops of
the mountains.
They burn offerings on the hills,
under oaks, poplars and other trees.
They think the shade under those
trees is nice.
So your daughters become
prostitutes.
And your daughters-in-law are
guilty of adultery.[d]

[14]"But I will not punish your daughters
when they become prostitutes.
I will not punish your daughters-
in-law
for their sins of adultery.
I will not punish them
because you yourselves have
sexual relations with
prostitutes.
You offer sacrifices with the temple
prostitutes.
You foolish people are destroying
yourselves.

[15]"Israel, you act like a prostitute.
But don't let Judah be guilty.
Don't go to sacrifice at Gilgal.
Don't go up to give offerings at
Beth Aven.[n]
Don't use the Lord's name to make
promises.
Don't say, 'As surely as the Lord
lives...'
[16]The people of Israel are stubborn
like a stubborn young cow.
How then can the Lord feed them
like lambs in a meadow?
[17]Israel has chosen to worship idols.
So, let them.

[18]Her rulers get drunk.
Then they give themselves to
being prostitutes.
They love these disgraceful things.
[19]They will be swept away as by a
whirlwind.
Their sacrifices will bring them
only shame.

The Lord's Word Against the Leaders

5 "Listen, you priests.
Pay attention, people of Israel.
Listen, royal family.
You will all be judged.
You have been like a trap at Mizpah.
You have been like a net spread
out at Mount Tabor.
[2]You have done many bad things.
So I will punish you all.
[3]I know all about Israel.
What they have done is not hidden
from me.
They all act like prostitutes.[d]
Israel has made itself unclean.[d]

[4]"And those bad things they
have done
keep them from returning to
their God.
They are determined to be
unfaithful to me.
They do not know the Lord.
[5]Israel's pride testifies against them.
The people of Israel will stumble
because of their sin.
The people of Judah will also
stumble with them.
[6]The people will come to worship
the Lord.
They will come with their sheep
and cattle.
But they will not be able to find him,
because he has left them.
[7]They have not been true to the Lord.
Their children do not belong
to him.
So their false worship
will destroy them and their land.

[8]"Blow the horn in Gibeah.
Blow the trumpet in Ramah.

[n]**Gilgal and Beth Aven** Cities in Israel where people worshiped false gods.

Give the warning at Beth Aven.
  Be first into battle, people of
      Benjamin.
9A time of punishment is coming.
  Israel will be destroyed.
I warn the tribes[d] of Israel
  that this will surely happen.
10The leaders of Judah are like
      thieves.
  They try to steal the property of
      others.
My punishment will overwhelm
      them
  like a flood of water.
11Israel will be crushed by the
      punishments,
  because they decided to follow
      idols.
12I will destroy Israel
  as a moth destroys clothing.
I will destroy Judah
  as rot destroys wood.

13"Israel saw how weak she was.
  Judah saw the wounds she
      suffered.
So Israel turned to Assyria for help.
  She sent to the great king of
      Assyria for help.
But he cannot heal you.
  He cannot cure your wound.
14I will be like a lion to Israel.
  I will be like a young lion to Judah.
I will attack them
  and tear them to pieces.
I will drag them off,
  and no one will be able to save
      them.
15Then I will go back to my place
  until the people admit they are
      guilty.
At that time they must look for me.
  In their trouble they must turn
      to me."

The People Are Not Faithful

6 You people say,
  "Come, let's go back to the Lord.
He has hurt us, but he will heal us.
  He has wounded us, but he will
      bandage our wounds.

2In a short while he will put new life
      in us.
  We will not have to wait long for
      him to raise us up.
  Then we may live in his presence.
3Let's learn about the Lord.
  Let's try hard to know who he is.
He will come to us
  as surely as the dawn comes.
The Lord will come to us like
      the rain,
  like the spring rain that waters
      the ground."

4The Lord says, "Israel, what should
      I do with you?
  Judah, what should I do with you?
Your faithfulness is like a morning
      mist.
  It lasts only as long as the dew in
      the morning.
5I have warned you by my prophets[d]
  that I will kill you and destroy you.
My judgments will flash forth like
      lightning against you.
6I want faithful love
  more than I want animal sacrifices.
I want people to know me
  more than I want burnt offerings.
7But you have broken the agreement
      as Adam did.
  You have been unfaithful to me.
8Gilead is full of people who do evil.
  It is covered with bloody
      footprints.
9Some of the priests are like
      robbers waiting in ambush.
  They murder people on the way to
      Shechem.[n]
  They do wicked crimes.
10I have seen horrible things in Israel.
  The people are unfaithful to God,
  and Israel has become unclean.[d]

11"Judah, I have set a time to punish
      you also.

"I would like to give my people back
      their riches.
7 I would like to heal Israel.
  But their sin can be seen by
      everyone.

---

[n]Shechem A city of safety where men could go for protection.

The wickedness of Israel is too
    well-known.
They cheat one another.
    They break into other peoples'
        houses.
    There are robberies in the streets.
²It never enters their minds
    that I remember all their wicked
        deeds.
The bad things they do are all
    around,
    and I can see their sins clearly.

Israel Destroys Her Rulers

³"They make the king happy with
    their wickedness.
    They make their rulers glad with
        their lies.
⁴But all of them are traitors.
    They are like an oven heated by
        a baker.
While he mixes the dough,
    he does not stir up the flame.
⁵They hold a festival day for the king.
    On that day the rulers become
        drunk with wine.
    The king joins in with those who
        had made evil plans.
⁶They approach him with murder
    in mind.
    Their hearts are like a hot oven.
All night long its fire is low.
    When morning comes, it is fanned
        into flame.
⁷So all these people are as hot as
    an oven.
    Like a fire they destroy their
        rulers.
Their kings fall one after another.
    And no one calls on me.

Israel and the Other Nations

⁸"Israel mixes with other nations.
    Israel is useless like a pancake
        cooked only on one side.
⁹Foreign nations are using up
    Israel's strength.
    And Israel doesn't even know it.
Israel is weak and feeble, like an
    old man.
    And they don't even know it.

¹⁰Israel's pride will cause their defeat.
    They have had many troubles.
But they still do not turn to the Lord
    their God.
    They do not look to him for help.
¹¹Israel has become like a silly
    pigeon.
    The people have no
        understanding.
First they call to Egypt for help.
    Then they run for help to Assyria.
¹²When they go, I will catch them
    as men catch birds in a net.
Then I will punish them
    as I have warned them.
¹³How terrible for them because
    they left me!
    They will be destroyed because
        they turned against me.
I want to save them.
    But they have spoken lies
        against me.
¹⁴They do not call to me from
    their hearts.
    They just lie on their beds and cry.
They come together to ask for grain
    and new wine.
    But they really turn away from me.
¹⁵I trained them and gave them
    strength.
    But they have made evil plans
        against me.
¹⁶They did not turn to the Most
    High God.
    They are like a crooked bow that
        does not shoot straight.
Their leaders brag about their
    strength.
    But they will be killed with
        swords.
Then the people in Egypt
    will laugh at them.

Israel Has Trusted Wrong Things

8 "Put the trumpet to your lips and
    give the warning!
The enemy swoops down on my
    people like an eagle.
The Israelites have broken my
    agreement.
    They have turned against my
        teachings.

²They cry out to me,
  'Our God, we in Israel know you!'
³But Israel has rejected what is good.
  So the enemy chases them.
⁴They chose their own kings
  without asking my permission.
They chose their own leaders,
  men I did not know.
They made their silver and gold into
  idols.
For all this they will be destroyed.
⁵I hate that calf-shaped idol.
  I am very angry with the people.
How long will they remain
  unclean?ᵈ
⁶The idol is something a craftsman
  made.
  It is not God.
Israel's calf-shaped idol
  will surely be smashed to pieces.

⁷"Israel's foolish plans are like
  planting the wind.
But they will harvest a whirlwind.
Her plans are like a stalk with no
  head of grain.
  It produces nothing.
Even if it produces something,
  other nations would eat it.
⁸Israel is destroyed.
  The people are mixed among the
    other nations.
  They have become useless to me.
⁹Like a wild donkey,
  Israel has run to Assyria.
Israel has hired other nations to
  protect her.
¹⁰Although Israel is mixed among
  the nations,
  I will gather them together.
They will become weaker and
  weaker
  as they suffer under the great king
    of Assyria.

¹¹"The more altars Israel built to
  remove sin,
  the more they have become
    altars for sinning.
¹²They reject the many teachings I
  have written for them.
  They act as if the teachings were
    strange and foreign to them.

¹³The Israelites offer sacrifices to me
  and eat the meat.
But the Lord is not pleased
  with them.
He remembers the evil they
  have done.
And he will punish them for
  their sins.
They will be slaves again as they
  were in Egypt.
¹⁴The people of Israel have forgotten
  their Maker.
They trust in the palaces they
  have built.
And Judah trusts in her many
  strong, walled cities.
But I will send fire on their cities
  and destroy their strong towers."

Israel's Punishment

9 Israel, do not rejoice.
  Don't celebrate as the other
    nations do.
You have been unfaithful to your
  God.
  You love the grain on your
    threshingᵈ floors.
  So you worship the gods who
    supposedly gave it.
²But there won't be enough grain to
  feed the people.
  And there won't be enough wine
    to go around.
³The Israelites will not stay in the
  Lord's land.
Israel will return to being captives
  as they were in Egypt.
In Assyria they will eat food that
  they are not allowed to eat.
⁴The Israelites will not give offerings
  of wine to the Lord.
Their sacrifices will not please him.
Their sacrifices will be like food that
  is eaten at a funeral.
It is unclean,ᵈ and everyone who
  eats it becomes unclean.
Their food will only satisfy their
  hunger.
They cannot sacrifice it in the
  Temple.ᵈ
⁵What will you do then on the day
  of feasts

and on the festival days of the Lord?

[6] Even if the people are not destroyed,
Egypt will take them as captives.
They will be buried in Memphis.[n]
Weeds will grow over their silver
treasures.
Thorns will grow over their
houses.

[7] Let Israel know this.
The time of punishment has come.
The time to pay for your sins
has come.
You have sinned very much,
and your hatred is great.
You think the prophet[d] is a fool.
You say the spiritual man is crazy.

[8] The prophet is God's watchman
to warn Israel of danger.
But everywhere he goes you set
traps for him.
You treat him as an enemy in
God's own land.

[9] The men of Israel have become
as sinful
as the men of Gibeah[n] were.
The Lord will remember the evil
things they have done.
He will punish them for their sins.

[10] "When I found Israel,
it was like finding grapes in
the desert.
Your ancestors were like
finding the first figs on the tree.
But when they came to Baal Peor,
they began worshiping an idol.
They became as disgusting as the
thing they worshiped.

[11] Israel's glory will fly away like
a bird.
There will be no more
pregnancies, no more births,
no more babies.

[12] But even if the Israelites bring up
children,
I will take them all away.
How terrible it will be for them
when I turn away from them!

[13] I have seen Israel, like Tyre,
given a pleasant place.
But the people of Israel will soon
bring out
their children to be killed."

[14] Lord, give them what they should
have.
What will you give them?
Make their women unable to have
children.
Give them breasts that cannot feed
their babies.

[15] "The Israelites were wicked in
Gilgal,
so I began to hate them there.
Because of the sinful things they
have done,
I will force them to leave my land.
I will no longer love them.
Their leaders have turned
against me.

[16] Israel is like a sick plant.
Its root is dying, and it has no fruit.
So the people will have no more
children.
And if they did, I would kill the
children they love."

[17] God will reject them,
because they have not obeyed
him.
They will wander among the
nations.

Israel Will Pay for Sin

10 Israel is like a vine
that produced plenty of fruit.
As the people became richer,
they built more altars for idols.
As their land became better,
they put up better stone pillars to
honor false gods.

[2] Their heart was false.
Now they must pay for their guilt.
The Lord will break down their
altars.
He will destroy their holy stone
pillars.

[3] Then the Israelites will say, "We
have no king,
because we didn't honor the Lord.

---

[n] **Memphis** A city in Egypt famous for its tombs.
[n] **Gibeah** The sins of the men of Gibeah caused a civil war. See Judges 19-21.

But even if we had one,
  he couldn't do anything for us."
⁴They make many false promises.
  They make agreements they don't
    keep.
So people sue each other in court.
  They are like poisonous weeds
    growing in a plowed field.
⁵The people from Israel are worried
    about
  the calf-shaped idol at Beth Aven.
The people and the priests will cry
  because their glorious idol is gone.
⁶It will be carried off as a payment
    that was demanded
  to the great king of Assyria.
Israel will be disgraced.
  The people will be ashamed of
    trusting that idol.
⁷The king of Israel will be carried off
  like a chip of wood floating on
    the water.
⁸The places of worship at Beth Aven
    will be destroyed.
  They are where Israel sins.
Thorns and weeds will grow up
  and cover their altars.
Then they will say to the mountains,
    "Cover us!"
  And they will say to the hills, "Fall
    on us!"

⁹"Israel, you have sinned since the
    time of Gibeah.ⁿ
  The people there have continued
    sinning.
But war will surely overwhelm
    them,
  because of the evil they have done
    there.
¹⁰When I am ready,
  I will come to punish them.
Armies will come together against
    them.
  They will be punished for their
    many sins.
¹¹Israel is like a well-trained young cow
  that likes to threshᵈ grain.
But I will put a yokeᵈ on her neck.
  I will make Israel work hard in the
    field.

Judah will plow.
  Israel will break up the ground.
¹²I said, 'Break new ground.
  Plant what is right.
Then you will harvest good things
  from your loyalty to me.
It is time for you to turn back to me,
    the Lord.
  Do it until I come and pour out my
    goodness on you.'
¹³But you have planted evil.
  So you have harvested trouble.
You have trusted in your own power
  and your many soldiers.
Now you must live with the result
    of your lies.
¹⁴So your armies will hear the noise
    of battle.
  And all your strong, walled cities
    will be destroyed.
It will be like the time King Shalman
  destroyed Beth Arbel in battle.
Mothers and children were
  crushed to the ground together.
¹⁵The same will happen to you,
    people of Bethel,
  because you did so much evil.
When that time comes,
  the king of Israel will die.

God's Love for Israel

11 "When Israel was a child, I
  loved him.
  And I called my son out of Egypt.
²But the more I called to the people
    of Israel,
  the further they went from me.
They offered sacrifices to the
    Baals.ᵈ
  They burned incenseᵈ to the idols.
³But it was I who taught Israel
    to walk.
  I took them by the arms.
But they did not understand
  that I had healed them.
⁴I led them with cords of human
    kindness,
  with ties of love.
I lifted the yokeᵈ from their neck.
  I bent down and fed them.

ⁿ**Gibeah** The sins of the men of Gibeah caused a civil war. See Judges 19-21.

5"The Israelites will become captives
again, as they were in Egypt.
The king of Assyria will become
their king.
This is because they refuse to
turn to God.
6War will sweep through their cities.
It will destroy them,
because of their wicked plans.
7My people have made up their minds
to turn away from me.
The prophets[d] call them to turn to me.
But none of them honors me at all.

8"Israel, I don't want to give you up.
I don't want to go away and leave
you.
I don't want to make you like Admah.
I don't want to treat you like
Zeboiim.[n]
My heart beats for you.
My love for you stirs up my pity.
9I won't punish you in my anger.
I won't destroy Israel again.
I am God and not man.
I am the Holy One, and I am
among you.
I will not come against you in anger.
10I will call for my people like
a lion calling for its young.
My children will come and follow me.
They will hurry to me from the
west.
11They will come swiftly
like birds from a captivity like
Egypt was,
and like doves from Assyria.
I will settle them again in their
homes,"
says the Lord.

The Lord Is Against Israel

12Israel has surrounded me with lies.
The people of Israel have made
their secret plans.
And Judah turns against God,
the faithful Holy One.

12 What Israel does is as useless as
chasing the wind,
as dangerous as being in a
windstorm.

They tell more and more lies
and do more and more violence.
They make agreements with Assyria,
and they send a gift of olive oil
to Egypt.
2The Lord also has some things
against Judah.
He will punish Israel for what they
have done.
He will give them what they
deserve.
3Their ancestor Jacob held on to his
brother's heel
while the two of them were being
born.
When Jacob grew to be a man,
he wrestled with God.
4He wrestled with the angel and won.
Jacob cried and asked for his
blessing.
Later, God met with him at Bethel
and spoke with him there.
5He is the Lord God of heaven's
armies.
He wants to be remembered as
the Lord.
6Like Jacob you must return to him.
You must be loyal and true to him.
You must do what is honest and
just.
You must always trust in him as
your God.

7The merchants use dishonest scales.
They like to cheat people.
8The people of Israel brag that they
are rich.
They think that because they
are rich
no one will learn about their sins.

9"But I am the Lord your God.
I brought you out of Egypt.
I will make you live in tents again
as you used to do in the desert.
10I spoke to the prophets[d]
and gave them many visions.
Through them, I taught my
lessons to you."

11The people of Gilead are evil.
They are worth nothing.

[n]**Admah and Zeboiim** Two other cities destroyed when God destroyed Sodom and Gomorrah.

People sacrifice bulls at Gilgal.
But their altars will become like
piles of stone in a plowed field.

¹²Your ancestor Jacob fled to
Northwest Mesopotamia.
There he worked to get a wife.
He tended sheep to pay for her.

¹³Later the Lord used a prophet
to bring Jacob's descendants*d*
out of Egypt.
The Lord used a prophet
to take care of the Israelites.

¹⁴But the Israelites made the Lord
angry.
They killed other people.
They deserve to die for their
crimes.
The Lord will make them pay
for the disgraceful things they
have done.

The Final Word Against Israel

13 People used to fear the tribe*d* of
Ephraim.
They were important people
in Israel.
But they sinned by worshiping Baal.*d*
So they must die.

²But they keep on sinning more
and more.
They make idols of their silver.
Those idols are cleverly made.
They are the work of a craftsman.
Yet the people of Israel say to each
other,
"Kiss those calf idols and sacrifice
to them."

³So those people will be like the
morning dew.
They will disappear like the
morning mist.
They will be like chaff*d* blown from
the threshing*d* floor.
They will vanish away like smoke
rising from a chimney.

⁴"I have been the Lord their God
since they were in the land of Egypt.
They have really known no other
God except me.
I am the one who has saved them.

⁵I cared for them in the desert
where it was hot and dry.

⁶I gave them food, and they became
full and satisfied.
But then they became proud and
forgot me.

⁷That is why I will be like a lion
to them.
I will be like a leopard waiting by
the road.

⁸I will attack like a bear robbed of
her cubs.
I will rip their bodies open.
I will devour them like a lion.
I will tear them apart like a wild
animal.

⁹"Israel, I will destroy you
for turning against me, your helper.

¹⁰What good are your kings and your
leaders now?
Can they save you in any of your
towns?
You asked for them, saying,
'Give us a king and leaders.'

¹¹So I gave you kings, but only in anger.
And I took them away in my
great anger.

¹²The sins of Israel are on record.
They are filed away, waiting for
punishment.

¹³Israel has a chance to live again,
but the people are too foolish to
take it.
They are like an unborn baby
who won't come out of its
mother's womb.

¹⁴So I will not save them from the
place where the dead are.
I will not rescue them from death.
I will call on death to hurt them.
I will call on the place where the
dead are to destroy them.
I will show them no mercy.

¹⁵Israel has become important among
the nations.
But the Lord will send a destroyer
from the east.
He will come like a wind from
the desert
that dries up all the springs and
wells of water.
He will destroy all their treasures,
everything of value.

¹⁶The nation of Israel will be punished,

because it fought against God.
The people of Israel will die by
    the sword.
Their children will be torn to pieces.
And their pregnant women will be
    ripped open."

Israel Returns to God

14 Israel, return to the Lord your
    God.
Your sins have caused your ruin.
2Come back to the Lord
   and say these words to him:
"Take away all our sin
   and kindly receive us.
Then we will give you the praise we
   promised you.
3Assyria cannot save us.
   We will not trust in our horses.
We will not say again, 'Our gods,'
   to the things our hands have made.
You show mercy to us, who are
    like orphans."

4The Lord says,
"I will forgive them for leaving me.
I will love them freely.
I am not angry with them
   anymore.
5I will be like the dew to Israel.
   It will blossom like a lily.

Like the cedar trees in Lebanon,
   its roots will be firm.
6The people will be like spreading
    branches.
They will be like the beautiful olive
    trees.
They will be like the sweet-
    smelling cedars in Lebanon.
7The people of Israel will again live
    under my protection.
They will grow like the grain.
They will bloom like a vine.
They will be as famous as the wine
    of Lebanon.
8Israel, have nothing to do with idols.
I, the Lord, am the one who
   answers your prayers.
I am the one who watches over you.
I am like a green pine tree.
   Your blessings come from me."

9A wise person will know these things.
   An understanding person will take
    them to heart.
The Lord's ways are right.
   Good people live by following them,
   but those who turn against God
    die because of them.

Get Ready, Get Set, Grow!
HOSEA 14:9

When you think about growing up, you think about getting taller and stronger. The cells in your body are working and changing to help you get bigger. You don't even notice it, but suddenly your pants are too short, and your shoes are too small.

Growing in your faith is like that too. You hardly even notice it. You grow as you live each day by following God's ways. The more you learn about God, the more you know about what he wants you to do. Then you can take what you know and use it when you have to make a decision, talk to a friend, or solve a problem. That's what it means to live by following the Lord's ways. That's what it means to grow in your faith.

How much "taller" is your faith today than it was when you first trusted in Jesus?

To find out more about growing in your faith, zoom to page 1223.

JOEL

God Will Punish Judah

Locusts Destroy the Crops

1 The Lord spoke his word to Joel son of Pethuel:

²Older leaders, listen to this message.
Listen to me, all you people who live
in the land.
Nothing like this has ever happened
during your lifetime.
Nothing like this has ever happened
during your fathers' lifetimes.
³Tell your children about these things.
And let your children tell their
children.
And let your grandchildren tell their
children.
⁴What the cutting locusts have
not eaten,
the swarming locusts have eaten.
And what the swarming locusts
have left,
the hopping locusts have eaten.
And what the hopping locusts
have left,
the destroying locusts*ⁿ* have eaten.

⁵Drunks, wake up and cry!
All of you people who drink wine,
cry!
Cry because your sweet wine
has been taken away from you.
⁶A powerful nation has come into
my land.
It has too many soldiers to count.
It has teeth like a lion.
And it has fangs like a female lion.
⁷That army has eaten my grapevines.
It has destroyed my fig trees.
It has eaten the bark off my trees
and left the branches white.

⁸Cry as a young woman cries
when the man she was going to
marry is killed.
⁹There will be no more grain or
drink offerings
to offer in the Temple*ᵈ* of the Lord
Because of this, the priests,
the servants of the Lord, cry.
¹⁰The fields are ruined.
Even the ground is dried up.
The grain is destroyed.
The new wine is dried up.
And the olive oil runs out.
¹¹Be sad, farmers.
Cry loudly, you who grow grapes.
Cry for the wheat and the barley.
Cry because the harvest in the field
is lost.
¹²The vines have become dry.
And the fig trees are dying.
The pomegranate*ᵈ* trees, the date
palm trees and the apple trees
have dried up.
All the trees in the field have died.
And the happiness of the people has
died, too.
¹³Priests, put on your rough cloth and
cry to show your sadness.
Servants of the altar, cry out loud.
Servants of my God,
sleep in your rough cloth to show
your sadness.
Cry because there will be no more
grain or drink offerings
to offer in the Temple of your God
¹⁴Call the people together.
Tell them there will be a time to
give up food.
Bring together the older leaders

ⁿcutting . . . locusts These are different names for an insect like a large grasshopper. The locust
can quickly destroy trees, plants and crops. In this destruction by locusts, Joel sees a warning. God
will cause this type of destruction when he punishes his people.

and everyone who lives in the land.
Bring them to the Temple of the
    Lord your God.
And cry out to the Lord.
¹⁵This will be a terrible day!
The Lord's day of judging is near.
At that time punishment will come
    like an attack from God All-Powerful.

¹⁶Our food is taken away
    while we watch.
Joy and happiness are gone
    from the Temple of our God.
¹⁷We planted seeds,
    but they lie dry and dead in the dirt.
Our barns are empty and falling down.
    The storerooms for grain have been
      broken down.
This is because the grain has
    dried up.
¹⁸The animals are hungry and groaning!
    The herds of cattle wander around
      confused.
They have no grass to eat.
    Even the flocks of sheep suffer.
¹⁹Lord, I am calling to you for help.
    Fire has burned up the open
      pastures.
Flames have burned all the trees in
    the field.
²⁰Wild animals also need your help.
    The water in the streams has
      dried up.
Fire has burned up the open
    pastures.

The Coming Day of Judgment

2 Blow the trumpet in Jerusalem.
Shout a warning on my holy
    mountain.
Let all the people who live in the land
    shake with fear.
The Lord's day of judging is coming.
    The Lord's day of judging is near.
²It will be a dark, gloomy day.
    It will be a cloudy and black day.
Like the light at sunrise,
    the great and powerful army will
      spread over the mountains.
There has never been anything like
    it before.
And there will never be anything
    like it again.

³The army destroys the land
    like a burning fire.
The land in front of them is like the
    garden of Eden.
The land behind them is like an
    empty desert.
Nothing will escape them.
⁴They look like horses.
    They run like war horses.
⁵Listen to them!
It is like the noise of chariots
    rumbling over the mountains.
It is like the noise of crackling flames
    burning dry stalks.
They are like a powerful army lined
    up for battle.
⁶Before this army, nations shake
    with fear.
Their faces become pale.

⁷The army charges ahead like soldiers.
    They climb over the walls like
      warriors.
They all march straight ahead.
    They do not move off their path.
⁸They do not run into each other.
    Each one walks in line.
They charge through all efforts to
    stop them
    and stay in line.
⁹They run into the city.
    They run along the tops of the walls.
They climb into the houses.
    They enter through windows like
      a thief.

¹⁰Before them, earth and sky shake.
    The sun and the moon become dark,
    and the stars stop shining.
¹¹The Lord calls out orders loudly
    as he leads his army.
That army obeys his commands.
    It is very large and powerful.
The Lord's day of judging
    is an overwhelming and terrible day.
No one can stand up against it.

Change Your Hearts

¹²The Lord says, "Now, come back to
    me with all your heart.
Go without food, and cry and be sad."

¹³Tearing your clothes is not enough
    to show you are sad.

Let your heart be broken.
Come back to the Lord your God.
He is kind and shows mercy.
He doesn't become angry quickly.
He has great love.
He would rather forgive than punish.
14Who knows? Maybe the Lord will
    change his mind
and leave behind a blessing for you.
Then you may give grain and drink
    offerings
    to the Lord your God.

15Blow the trumpet in Jerusalem.
    Call for a special time of going
        without food.
    Call for a special meeting.
16Bring the people together.
    Make the meeting holy for the Lord.
    Bring together the older leaders.
    Bring together the children,
    even babies that still feed at their
        mothers' breasts.
    The bridegroom should come from
        his room.
    The bride should come from her
        bedroom.
17The priests, the Lord's servants,
        should cry.
    They should cry between the altar
        and entrance to the Temple.*d*
    They should say, "Lord, have mercy
        on your people.
    Don't let them be put to shame.
    Don't let other nations make fun of
        them.
    Don't let people in other nations ask,
    'Where is their God?'"

The Lord Restores the Land

18Then the Lord became concerned
        about his land.
    He felt sorry for his people.
19The Lord said to them:
    "I will send you grain, wine and
        olive oil.
    You will have plenty.
    No more will I shame you
        among the nations.

20I will force the army from the north
        to leave your land.
    I will force them into a dry, empty
        land.
    Their soldiers in front will be forced
        into the Dead Sea.*d*
    And those in the rear will be forced
        into the Mediterranean Sea.
    Their bodies will rot and stink
    because they did horrible things."

21But, land, don't be afraid.
    Be happy and full of joy
    because the Lord has begun to do
        wonderful things.
22Wild animals, don't be afraid.
    The open pastures will grow grass.
    The trees will grow fruit.
    The fig trees and the vines will
        grow much fruit.
23So be happy, people of Jerusalem.
    Be joyful in the Lord your God.
    He will do what is right
    and will give you rain.
    He will send the early rain
    and the late rain for you, as before.
24And the threshing*d* floors will be
        full of wheat.
    And the barrels will overflow with
        wine and olive oil.

The Lord Speaks

25"I sent my great army against you.
    Those swarming locusts and the
        hopping locusts,
    the destroying locusts and the
        cutting locusts*n* ate your crops.
    But I will pay you back
    for those years of trouble.
26Then you will have plenty to eat.
    You will be full.
    You will praise the name of the Lord
        your God.
    He has done miracles*d* for you.
    My people will never again be shamed.
27Then you will know that I am among
        the people of Israel.
    You will know that I am the Lord
        your God.

---

*n*swarming . . . locust These are different names for an insect like a large grasshopper. The locust
can quickly destroy trees, plants and crops. In this destruction by locusts, Joel sees a warning. God
will cause this type of destruction when he punishes his people.

There is no other God.
My people will never be shamed
again.

28"After this,
I will give my Spirit*d* freely to all
kinds of people.
Your sons and daughters will
prophesy.*d*
Your old men will dream dreams.
Your young men will see visions.
29At that time I will give my Spirit
even to servants, both men and
women.
30I will show miracles
in the sky and on the earth:
blood, fire and thick smoke.
31The sun will become dark.
The moon will become red as blood.
And then the Lord's overwhelming
and terrible day of judging
will come.
32Then anyone who asks the Lord
for help
will be saved.
Even on Mount Zion*d* and in Jerusalem
there will be people who will be
saved.
This will happen just as the Lord
has said.
Those left alive after the day of
punishment
are the people whom the Lord
called.

Punishment for Judah's Enemies

3 "In those days and at that time,
I will give Judah and Jerusalem
back their riches.
2I will also gather all the nations
together.
I will bring them down into the
Valley Where the Lord Judges.
And there I will judge them.
Those nations scattered my own
people, Israel.
They forced my people to live in
other nations.
They divided up my land.
3They threw lots*d* for my people.
They traded boys for prostitutes.*d*
And they sold girls to buy wine
to drink.

4"Tyre and Sidon and all of you
regions of Philistia! What do you have
against me? Are you punishing me for
something I did? Or are you doing
something to hurt me? Then I will
quickly do to you what you have done
to me. 5You took my silver and gold.
You took my precious treasures and
put them in your temples. 6You sold
the people of Judah and Jerusalem to
the Greeks. That way you could send
them far from their land.

7"You sent my people to that faraway place. But I will bring them
back. And I will do to you what you
have done to them. 8I will sell your
sons and daughters to the people of
Judah. Then they will sell them to the
Sabean people far away." The Lord
said this.

God Judges the Nations

9Announce this among the nations:
Prepare for war!
Wake up the soldiers!
Let all the men of war come near
and attack.
10Make your plows into swords.
Make spears from your hooks for
trimming trees.
Let the weak say,
"I am strong."
11All of you nations, hurry.
Come together in that place.
Lord, send your strong soldiers
to gather the nations.

12"Wake up, nations.
Come to the Valley Where the
Lord Judges.
There I will sit to judge
all the nations on every side.
13Cut them down like grain
because the harvest is ripe
with sin.
Come, walk on them as you would
walk on grapes,
because the winepress*d* is full.
The barrels are full of their sins
and spilling over.
These people are so evil!"

14There are many people

in the Valley of Decision.[n]
The Lord's day of judging is near
in the Valley of Decision.
15 The sun and the moon will become
dark.
The stars will stop shining.
16 The Lord will roar like a lion from
Jerusalem.
His loud voice will sound like a
growl from Jerusalem.
And the sky and the earth will shake.
But the Lord will be a safe place for
his people.
He will be a strong place of safety
for the people of Israel.

17 "Then you will know that I am the
Lord your God.
I stay in my holy Mount Zion.[d]
Jerusalem will become holy.
Strangers will never take over that
city again.

A New Life Promised for Judah

18 "On that day the mountains will be
covered with grapes for
sweet wine.
The hills will be covered with cows
to give milk.
And water will flow through all the
ravines of Judah.
A fountain will flow from the
Temple [d] of the Lord.
It will give water to the valley of
acacia trees.
19 But Egypt will become empty.
And Edom will become an empty
desert.
This is because they were cruel to
the people of Judah.
They killed innocent people in the
land of Judah.
20 But there will always be people
living in Judah.
And people will live in Jerusalem
from now on.
21 Egypt and Edom killed my people.
So I will definitely punish them."

The Lord lives in Jerusalem!

[n]**Valley of Decision** This is like the name "The Valley Where the Lord Judges" in 3:2 and 3:12.

AMOS

God Warns
Israel to Stop Sinning

1 Amos was one of the shepherds from the town of Tekoa. God showed him this vision about Israel. It was at the time Uzziah was king of Judah and Jeroboam son of Jehoash was king of Israel. This happened two years before the earthquake.

²Amos said,
"The Lord will roar like a lion from Jerusalem.
His loud voice will sound like a growl from Jerusalem.
The green pastures of the shepherds will become dry.
Even Mount Carmel will dry up."

Israel's Neighbors Are Punished

The People of Aram

³This is what the Lord says:
"For the many crimes Damascus is doing,
I will punish them.
They beat the people of Gilead with threshing[d] boards that had iron teeth.
⁴So I will send fire upon the house of Hazael.
That fire will destroy the strong towers of Ben-Hadad.
⁵I will break down the gate of Damascus.
I will destroy the king who is in the Valley of Aven.
I will also destroy the king of Beth Eden.
The people of Aram will be taken captive to the country of Kir," says the Lord.

The People of Philistia

⁶This is what the Lord says:

"For the many crimes Gaza is doing,
I will punish them.
They sold all the people of one area as slaves to Edom.
⁷So I will send a fire on the walls of Gaza.
That fire will destroy the city's strong towers.
⁸I will destroy the king of the city of Ashdod.
I will destroy the king of the city of Ashkelon.
Then I will turn against the people of the city of Ekron.
I will punish the Philistines until they are all dead," says the Lord God.

The People of Phoenicia

⁹This is what the Lord says:
"For the many crimes Tyre is doing,
I will punish them.
They sold all the people of one area as slaves to Edom.
They forgot the brotherly agreement they had made with Israel.
¹⁰So I will send fire on the walls of Tyre.
That fire will destroy the city's strong towers."

The People of Edom

¹¹This is what the Lord says:
"For the many crimes Edom is doing,
I will punish them.
They hunted down their brothers, the Israelites, with the sword.
They showed them no mercy.
The people of Edom were continually angry.

And they did not hold back their
    great anger.
[12]So I will send fire on the city of
    Teman.
That fire will even destroy the
    strong towers of Bozrah.”[n]

The People of Ammon

[13]This is what the Lord says:
“For the many crimes Ammon is
    doing,
I will punish them.
They ripped open the pregnant
    women in Gilead.
They did this so they could take
    over that land
and make their own country larger.
[14]So I will send fire on the walls of
    Rabbah.
That fire will destroy the city's
    strong towers.
It will come during a day of battle.
There will be strong winds on a
    stormy day.
[15]Then their king and leaders will be
    captured.
They will all be taken away
    together,” says the Lord.

The People of Moab

2 This is what the Lord says:
“For the many crimes Moab is
    doing,
I will punish them.
They burned the bones of the king
    of Edom into lime.
[2]So I will send fire on Moab.
And it will destroy the strong
    towers of the city of Kerioth.
The people of Moab will die in a
    great noise.
They will die in the middle of
    sounds of war and trumpets.
[3]So I will bring an end to the king
    of Moab.
And I will kill all its leaders with
    him,” says the Lord.

The People of Judah

[4]This is what the Lord says:

“For the many crimes Judah is
    doing,
I will punish them.
They rejected the teachings of
    the Lord.
They did not keep his commands.
Their ancestors followed false gods.
And Judah followed those same
    gods.
[5]So I will send fire on Judah.
It will destroy the strong towers of
    Jerusalem.”

Israel Is Punished

[6]This is what the Lord says:
“For the many crimes Israel is
    doing,
I will punish them.
For silver they sell people who have
    done nothing wrong.
They sell poor people for the price
    of a pair of sandals.
[7]They walk on poor people
as if they were dirt.
They refuse to be fair to those who
    are suffering.
Fathers and sons have sexual
    relations with the same
    woman.
By doing this they ruin my holy
    name.
[8]As they worship at their altars,
they lie down on clothes taken
    from poor people.
They make people pay money as
    punishment.
With that money they buy wine to
    drink in the house of
    their god.

[9]“But it was I who destroyed the
    Amorites before them.
The Amorites were tall like cedar
    trees and as strong as oaks.
But I destroyed them completely.
[10]It was I who brought you from the
    land of Egypt.
For 40 years I led you through the
    desert.
I led you so I could give you the
    land of the Amorites.

---

[n] **Teman and Bozrah** Teman was in northern Edom, and Bozrah was in southern Edom. So this
means the whole country will be destroyed.

[11]I made some of your sons to be
    prophets.[d]
  I made some of your young men to
    be Nazirites.[d]
  People of Israel, isn't this true?"
    says the Lord.
[12]"But you made the Nazirites drink
    wine.
  You told the prophets not to
    prophesy my message.
[13]Now I will crush you
  as a wagon loaded with grain
    crushes anything beneath it.
[14]No one will escape, not even the
    fastest runner.
  Strong men will not be strong
    enough.
  Warriors will not be able to save
    themselves.
[15]Soldiers with bows and arrows will
    not stand and fight.
  Even soldiers who run quickly will
    not get away.
  Soldiers on horses will not escape
    alive.
[16]At that time even the bravest
    warriors
  will run away without their armor,"
    says the Lord.

Warning to Israel

3 Listen to this message that the Lord
  has spoken against you, people of
Israel. The message is against the
whole nation the Lord brought out of
Egypt.
[2]"I have chosen only you
  out of all the families of the earth.
  So I will punish you
    for all your sins."

[3]Two people will not walk together
    unless they have agreed to do this.
[4]A lion in the forest will roar
    when he has caught an animal.
  He does not growl in his den
    when he has caught nothing.
[5]A bird will not fall into a trap
    where there is no bait.
  The trap will not spring shut
    if there is nothing to catch.
[6]When a trumpet blows a warning,
    the people tremble.

  When trouble comes to a city,
    the Lord has caused it.
[7]Before the Lord God does anything,
  he tells his servants the prophets.[d]
[8]The lion has roared!
  Who wouldn't be afraid?
  The Lord God has spoken,
    and I must prophesy his message.

[9]Announce this to the strong towers
    of Ashdod.
  Announce it to the strong cities of
    Egypt:
  "Come to the mountains of Samaria.
  There you will see great confusion.
  You will see people hurting others."

[10]"The people don't know how to do
    what is right," says the Lord.
  "Their strong cities are filled with
    treasures they took by force
    from others."

[11]So this is what the Lord God says:
"An enemy will take over the land.
  He will pull down your strong
    towers.
  He will take the treasures you hid
    in your strong cities."

[12]This is what the Lord says:
"A shepherd might save from a
    lion's mouth
  only two leg bones or a scrap of an
    ear of his sheep.
In the same way only a few
    Israelites will be saved.
  These people now sit on their beds
    in Samaria.
  They sit on their couches."

[13]"You nations, listen to what I say
against the family of Israel. You are
my witnesses against them," says the
Lord God, the God of heaven's armies.

[14]"The people of Israel sinned, and I
    will punish them.
  I will also destroy the altars at
    Bethel.
The corners of the altar will be
    cut off,
  and they will fall to the ground.
[15]I will tear down the winter house,
  together with the summer house.

The houses decorated with ivory
    will be destroyed.
And the great houses will come to
    an end," says the Lord.

Israel Will Not Return

4 Listen to this message, you rich
women on the Mountain of Samaria.
You take things from the poor
    and crush people who are in need.
You tell your husbands,
    "Bring us money so we can drink!"
²The Lord God has promised this:
    "It is certain that I am a holy God.
So it is certain that the time will come
    when some of you will be taken
    away by hooks.
The rest of you will be taken away
    with fishhooks.
³You will go straight out of the city
    through holes in the walls.
And you will be thrown on the
    garbage dump," says the Lord.

⁴"Go to the city of Bethel and sin.
    Go to Gilgal and sin even more.
Offer your sacrifices every
    morning.
Bring one-tenth of your crops on
    the third day.
⁵Offer bread made with yeast as a
    sacrifice to show your thanks.
And brag about the offerings you
    bring to show thanks to
    the Lord.
Brag about these things, Israelites.
    This is what you love to do," says
    the Lord God.

⁶"I did not give you any food to eat.
    There was not enough food in any
    of your towns.
But you did not come back to me,"
    says the Lord.
⁷"I held back the rain from you
    three months before harvest time.
Then I let it rain on one city
    but not on another.
Rain fell on one field,
    but another field got none and
    dried up.
⁸People weak from thirst went from
    town to town for water.

But they could not get enough
    water to drink.
But you still did not come back to
    me," says the Lord.
⁹"I made your crops die from disease
    and mildew.ᵈ
I destroyed your gardens and your
    vineyards.
Locustsᵈ ate your fig trees and olive
    trees.
But you still did not come back to
    me," says the Lord.
¹⁰"I sent disasters against you,
    as I did to Egypt.
I killed your young men with swords.
    I also killed your horses.
I made you smell the stink from all
    the dead bodies.
But you still did not come back to
    me," says the Lord.
¹¹"I destroyed some of you
    as I destroyed Sodom and
    Gomorrah.
You were like a burning stick pulled
    from a fire.
But you still have not come back
    to me," says the Lord.

¹²"So this is what I will do to you, Israel.
    And because I will do this to you,
    get ready to meet your God, Israel."

¹³He is the one who makes the
    mountains.
He creates the wind.
He makes his thoughts known
    to man.
He changes the dawn into darkness.
He walks over the mountains of
    the earth.
His name is the Lord God of
    heaven's armies.

Israel Needs to Repent

5 Listen to this funeral song that I
sing about you, people of Israel.
²"Israel has fallen.
    It will not rise up again.
It was left alone in the land.
    There is no one to lift it up."

³This is what the Lord God says:
    "If 1,000 soldiers leave a city,
    only 100 will return.

If 100 soldiers leave a city,
    only 10 will return."

⁴This is what the Lord says to the
nation of Israel:
    "Come to me and live.
⁵ But do not look in Bethel.
Do not go to Gilgal,
    and do not go down to Beersheba.
The people of Gilgal will be taken
    away as captives.
And Bethel will become nothing."
⁶Come to the Lord and live.
    If you don't, he will destroy the
      descendants^d of Joseph as a
      fire would.
The fire will burn.
    But there will be no one to put it
      out for Bethel.
⁷You change the justice of the courts
    into something unfair.
    You reject what is right.

⁸God is the one who made the star
    groups Pleiades and Orion.
He changes darkness into the
    morning light.
And he changes the day into the
    dark night.
He calls for the waters of the sea
    to pour out on the earth.
The Lord is his name.
⁹He destroys the protected city.
    And he ruins the strong, walled city.

¹⁰You hate those who speak in court
    against evil.
    And you hate those who tell
      the truth.
¹¹You walk on poor people.
    You force them to give you grain.
You have built fancy houses of
    cut stone.
    But you will not live in them.
You have planted beautiful vineyards.
    But you will not drink the wine
      from them.
¹²It is because I know your many
    crimes.
    I know your terrible sins.
You hurt people who do right.
    You accept money to do wrong.
You keep the poor from getting
    justice in court.

¹³In such times the wise man will
    keep quiet,
    because it is a bad time.

¹⁴Try to do good, not evil.
    Then you will live.
And the Lord God of heaven's
    armies will be with you
    just as you say he is.
¹⁵Hate evil and love good.
    Be fair in the courts.
Maybe the Lord God of heaven's
    armies will be kind
    to the people of Joseph who are
      left alive.

¹⁶This is what the Lord, the Lord
God of heaven's armies, says:
    "People will be crying in all the
      public places.
    They will be saying, 'Oh, no!' in
      the streets.
    They will call the farmers to come
      and weep.
    They will pay people to cry out
      loud for them.
¹⁷People will be crying in all the
    vineyards.
    This is because I will pass among
      you to punish you," says
      the Lord.

The Lord's Day of Judging

¹⁸How terrible it will be for you who
    want
    the Lord's day of judging to come.
Why do you want that day to come?
    It will bring darkness for you,
      not light.
¹⁹It will be like a man who runs
    from a lion
    and meets a bear.
It will be like him going into his house
    and putting his hand on the wall.
    And then a snake bites him.
²⁰So the Lord's day of judging will
    bring darkness, not light.
    It will be a time of sadness, not joy.

²¹The Lord says, "I hate your feasts.
    I cannot stand your religious
      meetings.
²²You offer me burnt offerings and
    grain offerings.

But I won't accept them.
You bring the best fellowship
　　offerings.
But I will ignore them.
23Take the noise of your songs away
　　from here!
I won't listen to the music of your
　　harps.
24But let justice flow like a river.
Let goodness flow like a stream
　　that never stops.

25"People of Israel, you did not bring
　　me sacrifices and offerings
while you traveled in the desert for
　　40 years.
26But now you will have to carry
　　with you
your king, the false god Sakkuth,
　　and Kaiwan your idol
and the idols of your other star
　　gods you have made.
27This is because I will send you away
　　as captives beyond
　　Damascus,"
　　says the Lord. His name is God of
　　heaven's armies.

Israel Will Be Destroyed

6 How terrible it will be for you who
have it easy in Jerusalem.
　　How terrible for you who live on
　　　　Mount Samaria and feel safe.
You think you are important people
　　of the best nation in the world.
The Israelites come to you for help.
2Go look at the city of Calneh.
　　From there go to the great city
　　　　Hamath.
Go down to Gath of the Philistines.
Are you better than these kingdoms?
Are their lands larger than yours?
3You put off the day of punishment.
　　But you bring near the day when
　　　　you can do evil to others.
4You lie on beds decorated with ivory.
　　You stretch out on your couches.
You eat tender lambs
　　and fattened calves.
5You play your harps.

Like David, you compose songs on
　　musical instruments.
6You drink wine by the bowlful.
　　You use the best perfumed lotions.
But you are not sad over the ruin
　　of Israel, Joseph's
　　descendants.[d]
7So you will be some of the first ones
　　taken as slaves.
　　Your feasting and lying around will
　　　　come to an end.

8The Lord God made this promise.
The Lord God of heaven's armies says:
"I hate the pride of the people of
　　Israel.
I hate their strong towers.
So I will let the enemy take
　　the city
and everything in it."

9At that time there might be ten
people left alive in a house. But they
will also die. 10A relative and one who
is to prepare bodies for burial may
come to get the bodies. One of them
will take the bodies out to burn them.
He will call to the other and ask, "Are
there any other dead bodies with you?"
　　That person will answer, "No."
　　Then the one who asked will say,
"Hush! We must not speak the name
of the Lord."

11The Lord has given the command.
　　The large house will be broken
　　　　into pieces.
And the small house will be
　　broken into bits.
12Horses do not run on rocks.
　　People do not plow rocks with oxen.
But you have changed fairness
　　into poison.
You have changed what is right
　　into something wrong.
13You are happy that the town of Lo
　　Debar[n] was taken.
You say, "We have taken Karnaim[n]
　　by our own strength."

14The Lord God of heaven's armies
　　says,

---

[n]**Lo Debar** This name means "nothing at all."
[n]**Karnaim** This name means "horns," a symbol of strength.

"Israel, I will bring a nation
    against you.
It will bring trouble for you from
    Lebo Hamath in the north
to the valley south of the Dead
    Sea."[d]

The Vision of Locusts

7 This is what the Lord God showed
me: He was forming a swarm of
locusts.[d] This was after the king had
taken his share of the first crop. The
second crop had just begun growing.
[2]The locusts ate all the crops in the
country. After that I said, "Lord God,
forgive us, I beg you! No one in Israel
could live through this. Israel is too
small already!"

[3]So the Lord felt sorry about this.
"This will not happen," said the Lord.

The Vision of Fire

[4]This is what the Lord God showed
me: The Lord God was calling for fire
to come to punish. The fire dried up
the deep water and destroyed the land.
[5]Then I cried out, "Lord God, stop, I beg
you! No one in Israel could live through
this. Israel is too small already."

[6]So the Lord felt sorry about this.
"This will not happen either," said the
Lord God.

The Vision of the Plumb Line

[7]This is what the Lord showed me:
The Lord stood by a straight wall. He
had a plumb line[d] in his hand. [8]The
Lord said to me, "Amos, what do you
see?"

I said, "A plumb line."

Then the Lord said, "See, I will put a
plumb line among my people Israel to
show how crooked they are. I will not
feel sorry for them any longer.

[9]"The places where Isaac's
    descendants[d] worship will be
    destroyed.
Israel's holy places will be turned
    into ruins.
And I will attack King Jeroboam's
    family with the sword."

Amaziah and Amos

[10]So Amaziah, a priest at Bethel,
sent this message to Jeroboam king of
Israel: "Amos is making evil plans
against you with the people of Israel.
He has been speaking so much that
this land can't hold all his words.
[11]Amos has said this:
    'Jeroboam will die by the sword,
    and the people of Israel will be
        taken as captives
    out of their own country.'"

[12]Then Amaziah said to Amos,
"Seer,[d] go, run away to Judah. Do your
prophesying[d] and earn your living
there. [13]But don't prophesy anymore
here at Bethel. This is King Jeroboam's
holy place. This is Israel's temple."

[14]Then Amos answered Amaziah, "I
do not make my living as a prophet.
And I am not a member of a group of
prophets. I make my living as a shepherd. And I take care of sycamore
trees. [15]But the Lord took me away
from tending the sheep. He said to me,
'Go, prophesy to my people, the Israelites.' [16]So listen to the Lord's message.
You tell me,
    'Don't prophesy against Israel.
    And stop prophesying against the
        descendants of Isaac.'

[17]"Because you have said this, the
Lord says:
    'Your wife will become a prostitute[d]
        in the city.
    Your sons and daughters will be
        killed with swords.
    Other people will take your land and
        divide it among themselves.
    And you will die in a foreign
        country.
    The people of Israel will definitely
        be taken
    from their own land as captives.'"

The Vision of Ripe Fruit

8 This is what the Lord showed me:
a basket of ripe fruit. [2]The Lord
said to me, "Amos, what do you see?"

I said, "A basket of fruit from the
end of the harvest."

Then the Lord said to me, "An end has come for my people, the Israelites. I will not overlook their sins anymore.
³"On that day the palace songs will become funeral songs," says the Lord God. "There will be dead bodies thrown everywhere! Silence!"

⁴Listen to me you who walk on
  helpless people.
  You are trying to destroy the poor
    people of this country.
⁵Your businessmen say,
"When will the New Moonᵈ Festival
    be over
  so we can sell grain?
When will the Sabbathᵈ be over
  so we can bring out wheat to sell?
We can charge them more
  and give them less.
We can change the scales to cheat
    the people.
⁶We will buy poor people for silver.
  And we will buy needy people for
    the price of a pair of sandals.
  We will even sell the wheat that
    was swept up from the floor."

⁷The Lord used his name, the Pride of Jacob, to make a promise. He said, "I will never forget what these people did.
⁸The whole land will shake because
    of it.
  Everyone who lives in the land will
    cry for those who died.
  The whole land will rise like the Nile.
  It will be shaken, and then it will fall
    like the Nile River in Egypt."

⁹The Lord God says:
"At that time I will cause the sun to
    go down at noon.
  I will make the earth dark on a
    clear day.
¹⁰I will change your festivals into days
    of crying for the dead.
  All your songs will become songs
    of sadness for the dead.
  I will make all of you wear rough
    cloth to show your sadness.
  You will shave your heads to show
    sadness.

I will make that day like the crying
    for the death of an only son.
  Its end will be very painful."

¹¹The Lord God says: "The days are
    coming
  when I will cause a time of hunger
    in the land.
  The people will not be hungry for
    bread or thirsty for water.
  But they will be hungry for words
    from the Lord.
¹²People will wander from the
    Mediterranean Sea to the
    Dead Sea.ᵈ
  They will wander from the north to
    the east.
  They will search for the word of
    the Lord.
  But they won't find it.
¹³At that time the beautiful young
    women and the young men
  will become weak from thirst.
¹⁴They made promises by the idol in
    Samaria.
  They said, 'As surely as the god of
    Dan lives . . . .'
  And they said, 'As surely as the
    god of Beershebaⁿ lives, we
    promise . . . .'
So they will fall
  and never get up again."

Israel Will Be Destroyed

9 I saw the Lord standing by the altar. He said:
"Smash the top of the pillars
  so that even the bottom of the
    doors will shake.
  Make the pillars fall on the people's
    heads.
  Anyone left alive I will kill with a
    sword.
  Not one person will get away.
  No one will escape.
²If they dig down as deep as where
    the dead are,
  I will pull them up from there.
  If they climb up into the skies,
  I will bring them down from
    there.

ⁿDan . . . Beersheba Dan was the city farthest north in Israel, and Beersheba was the city farthest

"STILTED BEHAVIOR"

Dylan and Jessie learn about obedience

A story based on Ephesians 6:1-3

WOOO! THIS IS A *BLAST!* THESE STILTS ARE EXCELLENT!

HEY, DYLAN, LOOK AT ME! I CAN ALMOST CROSS THE WHOLE DRIVEWAY!

SOON, AT WHIT'S END...

MISTER WHITTAKER, DO YOU HAVE SOME BOARDS I CAN USE?

WHAT FOR, DYLAN?

I'M GOING TO MAKE SOME STILTS!

WELL, THERE IS SOME LUMBER OUT BACK. DO YOUR FOLKS KNOW ABOUT THIS, DYLAN?

WELL, I HAVEN'T TOLD THEM YET, BUT I WILL.

BE SURE YOU DO. STILTS CAN BE FUN, BUT THEY CAN BE *DANGEROUS* IF YOU DON'T KNOW WHAT YOU'RE DOING.

THANKS, MR. WHITTAKER!

THESE STILTS WILL BE TALLER THAN ANYBODY'S!

[3]If they hide at the top of Mount
　　Carmel,
　I will find them and take them away.
If they try to hide from me at the
　　bottom of the sea,
　I will command a snake to bite
　　them.
[4]If they are captured and taken away
　　by their enemies,
　I will command the sword to kill
　　them.
I will keep watch over them.
But I will keep watch to give them
　　trouble, not to do them good."

[5]The Master, the Lord of heaven's
　　armies, will touch the land.
　And the land will shake.
Then everyone who lives in the
　　land will cry for the dead.
The whole land will rise like the
　　Nile River.
　It will fall like the river of
　　Egypt.
[6]The Lord built his upper rooms
　　above the skies.
　He sets their foundations on
　　the earth.
He calls for the waters of the sea.
　He pours them out on the land.
　The Lord is his name.

[7]The Lord says this:
"Israel, you are no different to me
　　than the people of Cush.
I brought Israel out of the land of
　　Egypt.
　I also brought the Philistines from
　　Crete
　and the Arameans from Kir.
[8]I, the Lord God, am watching the
　　sinful kingdom Israel.
I will destroy Israel
　from the earth's surface.
But I will not completely destroy
　Jacob's descendants,"[d] says the
　　Lord.
[9]"I am giving the command
　to scatter the nation of Israel
　　among all nations.
It will be like someone sifting flour.

A person shakes flour through
　　a sifter.
　The good flour falls through, but
　　not the bad clumps.
[10]Sinners among my people
　will die by the sword.
All of them say,
　'Nothing bad will happen to us.'

The Lord Promises to Restore Israel

[11]"The kingdom of David is like a
　　fallen tent.
　But in that day I will set it up again
　and mend its broken places.
I will rebuild its ruins.
　I will rebuild it as it was before.
[12]Then Israel will take over what is
　　left of Edom
　and the other nations that belong
　　to me,"
says the Lord.
　And he will make it happen.

[13]The Lord says, "The time is coming
　　when there will be plenty
　　of food.
A person will still be harvesting his
　　crops
　when it's time to plow again.
A person will still be taking the juice
　　from his grapes
　when it's time to plant again.
Sweet wine will drip from the
　　mountains.
　And it will pour from the hills.
[14]I will bring my people Israel back
　　from captivity.
　They will build the ruined cities
　　again.
　And they will live in them.
They will plant vineyards and drink
　　the wine from them.
　They will plant gardens and eat
　　their fruit.
[15]I will plant my people on their land.
　And they will not be pulled out again
　from the land which I have given
　　them,"
says the Lord your God.

OBADIAH

God Will Punish Edom

The Lord Will Punish the Edomites

¹This is the vision of Obadiah.

This is what the Lord God says about Edom:[n]
We have heard a message from the Lord.
A messenger has been sent among the nations, saying
"Let's go attack Edom!"

The Lord Speaks to the Edomites

²"Look, I have made you only a small nation.
Others do not respect you.
³But your pride has fooled you.
You live in the hollow places of the cliff.
Your home is up high.
And you say to yourself,
'No one can bring me down to the ground.'
⁴You fly high like the eagle.
You make your nest among the stars.
But I will bring you down from there," says the Lord.
⁵"You will really be ruined!
It would be better if thieves come to you,
if robbers come by night.
They would steal only enough for themselves.
Workers come and pick the grapes from your vines.
But they would leave a few grapes behind.
⁶But you, Edom, will really lose everything!

People will find even your hidden treasures!
⁷All the people who are your friends will force you out of the land.
The people who are at peace with you
will trick you and defeat you.
They eat your bread with you now.
But they are planning a trap for you.
And you will not notice it."

⁸The Lord says, "On that day
I will surely destroy the wise men from Edom.
I will destroy these men of understanding from the mountains of Edom.
⁹Then, city of Teman, your mighty men will be afraid.
And everyone from the mountains of Edom will be killed.
¹⁰You did violence against your relatives, the people of Israel.
So you will be covered with shame.
You will be destroyed forever.
¹¹You stood aside without helping while strangers carried Israel's treasures away.
Foreigners entered Israel's city gate.
They threw lots[d] to decide what part of Jerusalem they would take.
At that time you were like one of those foreigners.

Commands That Edom Broke

¹²"Do not laugh at your brothers' trouble.

---

[n]**Edom** The Edomites were the people who came from Esau, Jacob's twin brother. They were enemies of the Israelites.

Do not be happy when people
destroy Judah.
Do not brag about the cruel things
done to them.
¹³Do not enter the city gate of my
people
in their time of trouble.
Do not laugh at their problems
in their time of trouble.
Do not take their treasures
in their time of trouble.
¹⁴Do not stand at the crossroads
to destroy those who are trying
to escape.
Do not capture those who escape
alive
in a time of trouble.

The Nations Will Be Judged

¹⁵"The Lord's day of judging is
coming soon
to all the nations.
You did evil things to other people.
Those same things will happen to
you.
They will come back upon your
own head.
¹⁶Because you joined the nations in
robbing my Temple,[d]
you drank my anger.
So all the nations will drink my anger.
They will be punished so much
that they will disappear.
¹⁷But on Mount Zion[d] some will be
left alive.
The mountain will be a holy place.
The people of Jacob will take back
their land.
They will take it from those who
took it from them.

¹⁸The people of Jacob, the Israelites,
will be like a fire.
And the people of Joseph will be
like a flame.
But the people of Esau, the
Edomites, will be like dry
stalks.
The people of Jacob will set these
stalks on fire.
They will burn up the Edomites.
Then there will be no one left of
the people of Esau."
This will happen because the Lord
has said it.

¹⁹Then God's people will regain
southern Judah from Edom,
the mountain of Esau.
They will take back the western
mountain slopes
from the Philistines.
They will regain the lands of
Ephraim and Samaria.
And Benjamin will take over Gilead.
²⁰People from Israel once were forced
to leave their homes.
But at that time they will take the
land of the Canaanites.
They will take it all the way to
Zarephath.
People from Judah were once
forced to leave Jerusalem
and live in Sepharad.
But at that time they will take back
the cities of southern Judah.
²¹Powerful warriors will go up on
Mount Zion.
There they will rule the people
living on Edom's mountain.
And the kingdom will belong to
the Lord.

JONAH

A Prophet
Runs from God

God Calls and Jonah Runs

1 The Lord spoke his word to Jonah son of Amittai: [2]"Get up, go to the great city of Nineveh and preach against it. I see the evil things they do."

[3]But Jonah got up to run away from the Lord. He went to the city of Joppa. There he found a ship that was going to the city of Tarshish. Jonah paid for the trip and went aboard. He wanted to go to Tarshish to run away from the Lord.

[4]But the Lord sent a great wind on the sea. This wind made the sea very rough. So the ship was in danger of breaking apart. [5]The sailors were afraid. Each man cried to his own god.

The men began throwing the cargo into the sea. This would make the ship lighter so it would not sink.

But Jonah had gone down into the ship to lie down. He fell fast asleep. [6]The captain of the ship came and said, "Why are you sleeping? Get up! Pray to your god! Maybe your god will pay attention to us. Maybe he will save us!"

[7]Then the men said to each other, "Let's throw lots[d] to see who caused these troubles to happen to us."

So the men threw lots. The lot showed that the trouble had happened because of Jonah. [8]Then the men said to Jonah, "Tell us what you have done. Why has this terrible thing happened to us? What is your job? Where do you come from? What is your country? Who are your people?"

Boats with Precious Cargo

JONAH 1

Do you know there was a boat with a passenger who wanted to be thrown overboard? God wanted Jonah to go east across the desert to Nineveh, a big, evil city where the people needed to hear about God. But Jonah went west instead, across the sea on a big trading ship headed for another country. Jonah went below the deck to hide from God (of course, that's impossible).

But God still wanted Jonah to go to Nineveh, so he sent a bad storm. Jonah told the sailors to throw him overboard, and when they did the sea grew calm. The boat sailed on to Tarshish with a crew that had learned about God's power. Jonah ended up on a very different kind of boat–a huge fish that took him back where he started.

Jonah finally went to Nineveh as God had said. It is always better to obey God first.

To read about a boat in a big storm, fly to page 1139.

⁹Then Jonah said to them, "I am a Hebrew. I fear the Lord, the God of heaven. He is the God who made the sea and the land."

"**I** guess Jonah had to learn not to rock the boat! Read about his lesson in Jonah 1:1-16."

¹⁰Then the men were very afraid. They asked Jonah, "What terrible thing did you do?" They knew Jonah was running away from the Lord because Jonah had told them.

¹¹The wind and the waves of the sea were becoming much stronger. So the men said to Jonah, "What should we do to you to make the sea calm down?"

¹²Jonah said to them, "Pick me up, and throw me into the sea. Then it will calm down. I know it is my fault that this great storm has come on you."

¹³Instead, the men tried to row the ship back to the land. But they could not. The wind and the waves of the sea were becoming much stronger.

Jonah's Punishment

¹⁴So the men cried to the Lord, "Lord, please don't let us die because of taking this man's life. Please don't think we are guilty of killing an innocent man. Lord, you have caused all this to happen. You wanted it this way." ¹⁵Then the men picked up Jonah and threw him into the sea. So the sea became calm. ¹⁶Then they began to fear the Lord very much. They offered a sacrifice to the Lord. They also made promises to him.

¹⁷And the Lord caused a very big fish to swallow Jonah. Jonah was in the stomach of the fish three days and three nights.

2 While Jonah was in the stomach of the fish, he prayed to the Lord his God. Jonah said,

²"I was in danger.
So I called to the Lord,
and he answered me.
I was about to die.
So I cried to you,
and you heard my voice.
³You threw me into the sea.
I went down, down into the deep sea.
The water was all around me.
Your powerful waves flowed over me.
⁴I said, 'I was driven out of your presence.
But I hope to see your Holy Temple*ᵈ* again.'
⁵The waters of the sea closed over me.
I was about to die.
The deep sea was all around me.
Seaweed wrapped around my head.
⁶I went down to where the mountains of the sea start to rise.
I thought I was locked in this prison forever.
But you saved me from death,
Lord my God.

⁷"When my life had almost gone,
I remembered the Lord.
Lord, I prayed to you.
And you heard my prayers in your Holy Temple.

⁸"People who worship useless idols give up their loyalty to you.
⁹Lord, I will praise and thank you while I give sacrifices to you.
I will make promises to you.
And I will do what I promise.
Salvation comes from the Lord!"

¹⁰Then the Lord spoke to the fish. And the fish spit Jonah out of its stomach onto the dry land.

God Calls and Jonah Obeys

3 Then the Lord spoke his word to Jonah again. The Lord said, ²"Get up. Go to the great city Nineveh. Preach against it what I tell you."

³So Jonah obeyed the Lord. He got up and went to Nineveh. It was a very

large city. It took a person three days just to walk across it. ⁴Jonah entered the city. When he had walked for one day, he preached to the people. He said, "After 40 days, Nineveh will be destroyed!"

rough cloth. People should cry loudly to God. Everyone must turn away from his evil life. Everyone must stop doing harm. ⁹Maybe

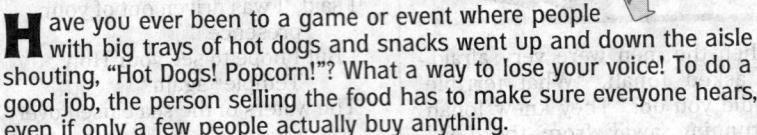

Witnessing
JONAH 3:1-5

Have you ever been to a game or event where people with big trays of hot dogs and snacks went up and down the aisle shouting, "Hot Dogs! Popcorn!"? What a way to lose your voice! To do a good job, the person selling the food has to make sure everyone hears, even if only a few people actually buy anything.

Jonah didn't carry a tray of food, but he had a message from God. For one whole day he walked through the big city of Nineveh and made sure that everyone heard his message. He had no way of knowing how the people would respond to what he said.

The same thing can happen to us when we tell people about God. We never know how they will act. Maybe they'll be like the Ninevites and decide to believe in God. Maybe they won't. Our job is to make sure our friends hear about God, even if only a few of them decide to believe in him.

To learn more about witnessing, zoom to page 1129.

⁵The people of Nineveh believed in God. They announced they would stop eating for a while. They put on rough cloth to show how sad they were. All the people in the city wore the cloth. People from the most important to the least important did this.

⁶When the king of Nineveh heard this news, he got up from his throne. He took off his robe. He covered himself with rough cloth and sat in ashes to show how upset he was.

⁷He made an announcement and sent it through the city. The announcement said:

By command of the king and his important men: No person or animal should eat anything. No herd or flock will be allowed to taste anything. Do not let them eat food or drink water. ⁸But every person and animal should be covered with

God will change his mind. Maybe he will stop being angry. Then we will not die.

¹⁰God saw what the people did. He saw that they stopped doing evil things. So God changed his mind and did not do what he had warned. He did not punish them.

God's Mercy Makes Jonah Angry

4 But Jonah was very unhappy that God did not destroy the city. He was angry. ²He complained to the Lord and said, "I knew this would happen. I knew it when I was still in my own country. It is why I quickly ran away to Tarshish. I knew that you are a God who is kind and shows mercy. You don't become angry quickly. You have great love. I knew you would rather forgive than punish them. ³So now I ask you, Lord, please kill me. It is better for me to die than to live."

[4] Then the Lord said, "Do you think it is right for you to be angry?"

[5] Jonah went out and sat down east of the city. There he made a shelter for himself. And he sat there in the shade. He was waiting to see what would happen to the city. [6] The Lord made a plant grow quickly up over Jonah. This made a cool place for him to sit. And it helped him to be more comfortable. Jonah was very pleased to have the plant for shade. [7] The next day the sun rose. And God sent a worm to attack the plant. Then the plant died.

[8] When the sun was high in the sky, God sent a hot east wind to blow. The sun became very hot on Jonah's head. And he became very weak. He wished he were dead. Jonah said, "It is better for me to die than to live."

[9] But God said this to Jonah: "Do you think it is right for you to be angry because of the plant?"

Jonah answered, "It is right for me to be angry! I will stay angry until I die!"

[10] And the Lord said, "You showed concern for that plant. But you did not plant it or make it grow. It appeared in the night, and the next day it died. [11] Then surely I can show concern for the great city Nineveh. There are many animals in that city. And there are more than 120,000 people living there. Those people simply do not know right from wrong!"

MICAH

*Assyria Will
Punish Israel and Judah*

Samaria and Israel to Be Punished

1 Jotham, Ahaz and Hezekiah were kings of Judah. During the time they were kings, the word of the Lord came to Micah, who was from Moresheth. He saw these visions about Samaria and Jerusalem.

2Hear this, all you nations.
  Listen, all you who live on
    the earth.
  The Lord God will come from his
    Holy Temple.*d*
  He will come as a witness against
    you.
3See, the Lord is coming out of his
    place in heaven.
  He is coming down to walk on the
    tops of the mountains.
4The mountains will melt under him
    like wax in a fire.
  The valleys will crack open
    as if split by water raging down a
      mountain.
5This is because of Jacob's sin.
  It is because of the sins of the
    nation of Israel.
  Who is responsible for Jacob's sin?
  Samaria!
  Who is responsible for Judah's
    worshiping idols?
  Jerusalem!

The Lord Speaks

6"So I will make Samaria a pile of
    ruins in the open country.
  It will be like a place for planting
    vineyards.
  I will pour Samaria's stones down
    into the valley.
  And I will destroy her down to her
    foundations.
7All her idols will be broken into
    pieces.
  All the gifts to her idols will be
    burned with fire.
  I will destroy all her idols.
  This is because Samaria earned her
    money by being unfaithful
      to me.
  So this money will be carried off
    by other people who are not
      faithful to me."

Micah's Great Sadness

8I will moan and cry because of
    this evil.
  I will go around barefoot and
    without clothes.
  I will cry loudly like the wild dogs.
  I will cry like the ostriches.
9I will do this because Samaria's
    wound cannot be healed.
  Her destruction will spread to
    Judah.
  It will reach the city gate of my
    people.
  It will come all the way to
    Jerusalem.
10Don't tell it in Gath.*n*
  Don't cry in Acco.*n*
  Cry and roll in the dust
    at Beth Ophrah.*n*
11Pass on your way, naked and
    ashamed,
  you who live in Shaphir.*n*

*n***Gath**   This name sounds like the Hebrew word for "tell."
*n***Acco**   This name sounds like the Hebrew word for "cry."
*n***Beth Ophrah**   This name means "house of dust."
*n***Shaphir**   This name means "beautiful."

Those who live in Zaanan[n]
  won't come out to help you.
The people in Beth Ezel[n] will cry.
  But they will not give you any
  support.
¹²Those who live in Maroth[n]
  will be anxious for good news to
  come.
This is because trouble will come
  from the Lord.
It will come all the way to the gate
  of Jerusalem.
¹³You people living in Lachish,[n]
  harness the fastest horse to the
  chariot.
Jerusalem's sins started in you.
  This is because you followed in
  Israel's sins.
¹⁴So you must give farewell gifts
  to Moresheth[n] in Gath.
The houses in Aczib[n] will be
  false help
  to the kings of Israel.
¹⁵I will bring an enemy against you
  who live in Mareshah.[n]
He will take what you own.
The leaders Israel brags about
  will hide in the cave at Adullam.
¹⁶Cut off your hair to show you
  are sad.
  Cry for the children you love.
Make yourself bald like the eagle,
  because your children will be
  forced to live in a foreign land.

The Evil Plans of People

2 How terrible it will be for people
  who plan wickedness.
  They lie on their beds and make
  evil plans.
When the morning light comes,
  they do the things they
  planned.
They do them just because they
  have the power to do so.
²They want fields; so they take them.

They want houses; so they take
  them.
They cheat a man and take his house.
They cheat a man and take his
  property.

³That is why the Lord says:
"Look, I am planning trouble
  against such people.
You won't be able to save
  yourselves.
You will no longer walk proudly,
  because it will be a terrible time.
⁴At that time people will make fun
  of you.
They will sing this sad song
  about you:
'We are completely ruined.
  The Lord has taken away our land.
Yes, he has taken our land away
  from us.
He has divided our fields among
  our enemies!'"
⁵So you will have no land for people
  to measure.
  They will not throw lots[d] to divide
  the land among the Lord's
  people.

Micah Is Asked Not to Prophesy

⁶People say, "Don't prophesy[d] to us!
  Don't say those bad things about us!
Nothing like that will happen to
  us!"
⁷But I must say this, people of Jacob.
  The Lord is becoming angry about
  what you have done.
If you lived right,
  I could say nice words to you.
⁸But recently, my people have
  become my enemy.
You take the coats from people
  who pass by.
They think they are safe.
  But you rob them
as if they were prisoners of war.

---

[n]**Zanaan**   This name sounds like the Hebrew word for "come out."
[n]**Beth Ezel**   This name means "house by the side of another," suggesting help or support.
[n]**Maroth**   This name sounds like the Hebrew word for "sad" or "miserable."
[n]**Lachish**   This name sounds like the Hebrew word for "horses."
[n]**Moresheth**   This may be a wordplay on the word "engaged," referring to a farewell gift to a bride.
[n]**Aczib**   This name means "lie" or "trick."
[n]**Mareshah**   This name sounds like the Hebrew word for a person who captures other cities and lands.

⁹You've forced the women of my
    people
  from their nice houses.
You've taken my glory
  from their children forever.
¹⁰Get up and leave.
  This is not your promised place of
    rest anymore.
  You have made this place unclean.*d*
  It is doomed to destruction.
¹¹But you people want a false prophet
  who will tell you nothing but lies.
You want one who promises to
    prophesy good things for you
  if you give him wine and beer.
  He's just the prophet for you.

The Lord Promises to Rescue His People

¹²"Yes, people of Jacob, I will bring all
    of you together.
  I will bring together all those left
    alive in Israel.
I'll put them together like sheep
    in a pen,
  like a flock in its pasture.
  Then the place will be filled with
    many people.
¹³Someone will open the way and lead
    the people out.
  The people will break through the
    gate and leave the city where
    they were held captive.
Their king will go out in front
    of them.
  The Lord will lead his people."

The Leaders of Israel Are Guilty of Evil

3 Then I said,
    "Listen, leaders of the people
      of Jacob.
  Listen, you rulers of the nation
    of Israel.
  You should know how to decide
    cases fairly.
² But you hate good and love evil.
  You skin my people alive.
    You tear the flesh off their bones.
³You are destroying my people.
  You skin them and break their
    bones.

You chop them up in pieces
  like meat to put in the pot.
⁴Then you will pray to the Lord.
  But he won't answer you.
He will hide his face from you,
  because you have done evil."

⁵The Lord says this about the proph-
ets*d* who teach his people the wrong
way of living:
"If someone gives these prophets
    food to eat,
  they shout, 'Peace!'
But if he doesn't give them food,
  they prepare for war against him.
⁶So it will become like night to the
    prophets.
  They won't have any visions from
    the Lord.
It will become dark for them.
  They won't be able to tell what will
    happen in the future.
The sun is about to set for
    the prophets.
  Their days will become dark.
⁷The seers*d* will be ashamed.
  The people who see the future will
    be embarrassed.
Yes, all of them will cover their
    mouths.
  This is because there will be no
    answer from God."

Micah Is an Honest Prophet of God

⁸But the Lord's Spirit*d* has filled me
  with power and strength to preach
    fairness.
I will tell the people of Jacob how
    they have turned against God.
  I will tell the people of Israel how
    they have done wrong.
⁹Leaders of Jacob and rulers of Israel,
    listen to me.
  You hate fairness.
    You destroy what is right.
¹⁰You build Jerusalem by murdering
    people.
  You build it with the sins you do.
¹¹The judges in Jerusalem take money
    to decide who wins in court.
  The priests in Jerusalem only teach
    for pay.

The prophets[d] only look into the
future when they get paid.
But yet those leaders say,
"The Lord is with us.
Nothing bad will happen to us."
[12]Because of you,
Jerusalem will be plowed like
a field.
Jerusalem will become a pile of rocks.
The hill on which the Temple[d]
stands will be covered with
bushes.

The Mountain of the Lord

4 In the last days
the mountain on which the Lord's
Temple[d] stands
will become the most important of
all mountains.
It will be raised above the hills.
People from other nations will
come streaming to it.
[2]Many nations will come and say,
"Come, let us go up to the
mountain of the Lord.
Let us go to the Temple of the God
of Jacob!
Then God will teach us his ways.
And we will obey his teachings."
The Lord's teachings will go out
from Jerusalem.
The word of the Lord will go out
from Jerusalem.
[3]The Lord will settle arguments
among many nations.
He will decide between strong
nations that are far away.
Then the nations will make their
swords into plows.
They will make their spears into
hooks for trimming trees.
Nations will no longer fight other
nations.
They will not even train for war
anymore.
[4]Everyone will sit under his own vine
and fig tree.
No one will make them afraid.
This is because the Lord of
heaven's armies has said it.

[5]All other nations follow their
own gods.
But we will follow the Lord our
God forever and ever.

[6]The Lord says, "At that time,
I will bring back to me the crippled.
I will bring back to Jerusalem
those who were sent away.
I will bring back to me those who
were hurt.
[7]I will keep alive those who were
crippled.
I will make a strong nation of
those who were sent away.
The Lord will be their king in
Mount Zion[d] forever.
[8]And you, watchtower of the flocks,[n]
strong city of Jerusalem,
you will be a kingdom as in
the past.
Jerusalem, the right to rule will
come again to you."

Why the Israelites Must Go to Babylon

[9]Now, why do you cry so loudly?
Is your king gone?
Have you lost your leader?
You are in pain like a woman
trying to give birth.
[10]People of Jerusalem, be in pain.
Be like a woman trying to give
birth.
Now you must leave the city
and live in the field.
You will go to Babylon.
But you will be saved from
that place.
The Lord will go there
and take you back from your
enemies.
[11]But now many nations
have come to fight against you.
They say, "Let's destroy Jerusalem
and be proud we have defeated her."
[12]But they don't know
what the Lord is thinking.
They don't understand his plan
for them.

---

[n]**watchtower . . . flocks** This probably means a part of Jerusalem. The leaders would be like shepherds in a tower watching their sheep.

He will crush them like a bundle of grain on the threshing*d* floor.

13"Get up and crush them, people of Jerusalem.
I will make you strong as if you had horns of iron.
I will make you strong as if you had hoofs of bronze.
You will beat many nations into small pieces.
You will give their wealth to the Lord.
You will give their treasure to the Lord of all the earth."

5 So, strong city, gather your soldiers together.
We are surrounded and attacked.
The enemy will swing his club.
He will hit the leader of Israel in the face.

The Ruler to Be Born in Bethlehem

2"But you, Bethlehem Ephrathah, are one of the smallest towns in Judah.
But from you will come one who will rule Israel for me.

He comes from very old times, from days long ago."

3The Lord will leave his people in Babylon
until Jerusalem, who is in labor, gives birth to her children.
Then his brothers who are in captivity will return.
They will come back to the people of Israel living in Judah.
4Then the ruler of Israel will stand and take care of his people.
He will lead them with the Lord's power.
He will lead them in the wonderful name of the Lord his God.
They will live in safety.
And his greatness will be known all over the earth.
5 He will bring peace.

Rescue and Punishment

The Assyrian army will come into our country.
They will destroy our large houses.
But we will choose seven or eight leaders.
They will shepherd our people.
6They will destroy the Assyrians with their swords.

Touring Bible Lands
BETHLEHEM • MICAH 5:2

Bethlehem was a small town built on the hills where King David once took care of his father's sheep. It was located on a major road between Jerusalem and Egypt. Trading caravans often stopped there to rest at the inns.

Are you surprised to find the city of Bethlehem, where Jesus was born, in this little book in the Old Testament? God told the prophet Micah where Jesus would be born hundreds of years before it happened! He wrote down what God told him. Many years later, when the wise men came looking for Jesus, some of the Jewish teachers told the wise men that Jesus would be born in Bethlehem, because they had read about it in Micah's prophecy. So the wise men went to Bethlehem where they found Jesus just as Micah had said. (You can read about that in Matthew 2:4-6).

Fly north along the Jordan River to find the lake of sudden storms 1195.

They will conquer the land of
Assyria with their swords
drawn.
The Assyrians will come into our
land.
They will come within our borders.
But the leaders of Israel
will save us from them.

⁷Then the people of Jacob who are
left alive
will be like dew from the Lord to
many people.
They will be like rain which does
not wait for man.
They will be like showers which
do not wait for human beings.
⁸Those left alive of Jacob's people
will be scattered among the
nations.
They will be among many peoples.
They will be like a lion among the
animals of the forest.
They will be like a young lion
going through the flock.
He steps on what is in his way.
No one can save the nations from
God's people.
⁹So you will raise your fist in victory
over your enemies,
and you will destroy them.

¹⁰The Lord says, "At that time,
I will take your horses from you.
I will destroy your chariots.
¹¹I will destroy the walled cities in
your country.
I will tear down all your defenses.
¹²You will no longer be able to do
witchcraft.ᵈ
You will not have anyone who can
tell the future.
¹³I will destroy your statues of false
gods.
I will tear down the stone pillars
you worship.
You will no longer worship
what your hands have made.
¹⁴I will destroy the Asherahᵈ idols.
I will destroy your cities.
¹⁵Some people won't obey me.
I will show my anger and punish
them."

The Lord's Complaint

6 Now hear what the Lord says:
"Get up; plead your case in front
of the mountains.
Let the hills hear your story.
²Mountains, listen to the Lord's
complaint.
Foundations of the earth, listen to
the Lord.
The Lord has a complaint against
his people.
He will prove that Israel is wrong."

³The Lord says, "My people, did I do
something wrong to you?
How did I make you tired of me?
Tell me.
⁴I brought you from the land of Egypt.
I freed you from slavery.
I sent Moses, Aaron and Miriam
to you.
⁵My people, remember
the evil plans of Balak king of Moab.
Remember what Balaam son of
Beor told Balak.
Remember what happened from
Acacia to Gilgal.
Then you will know the Lord does
what is right!"

⁶You say, "What can I bring with me
when I come before the Lord?
What can I bring
when I bow before God on high?
Should I come before the Lord with
burnt offerings,
with year-old calves?
⁷Will the Lord be pleased with 1,000
male sheep?
Will he be pleased with 10,000
rivers of oil?
Should I give my first child for the
evil I have done?
Should I give my very own child
for my sin?"
⁸The Lord has told you what is good.
He has told you what he wants
from you:
Do what is right to other people.
Love being kind to others.
And live humbly, trusting
your God.

The Lord has told you what is good.
He has told you what he wants from you:
Do what is right to other people. Love being kind to others. And live humbly, trusting your God.
• Micah 6:8

⁹The voice of the Lord shouts to the city.
The wise person honors the Lord.
So pay attention to the rod of punishment.
Pay attention to the One who threatens to punish.
¹⁰Can the Lord forget that the wicked still hide
treasures they have stolen?
Do they still cheat others?
I curse their false measure!
¹¹Can I forgive people who cheat others with wrong weights and scales?
¹²The rich men in the city still do cruel things.
The people still tell lies.

They do not tell the truth.
¹³So I have started to punish you.
I will destroy you because of your sins.
¹⁴You will eat, but you won't become full.
You will still be hungry and empty.
You will store up but save nothing.
What you store up the sword will destroy.
¹⁵You will plant,
but you won't harvest.
You will squeeze your olives.
But you won't get any oil from them to put on your skin.
You will crush the grapes.
But you will not drink the wine.
¹⁶This is because you obey the wicked laws of King Omri.
You do all the evil that Ahab's family does.
You follow their teachings.
So I will let you be destroyed.
The people in your city will be laughed at.
Other nations will make fun of you.

Humility
MICAH 6:8

Sometimes being a Christian seems pretty complicated.
You have to go to church and Sunday school, honor your father and mother, read your Bible, try to get along with your little sister, say your prayers . . . whew! There's a lot to remember and keep up with . . . isn't there?

Not so, said the prophet Micah. What God wants from us is very simple. We are *"to do what is right to other people, love being kind to others, and live humbly, obeying your God."* That's all. We are to treat others right, be kind, and live humbly before God. These three things are very important to God.

Being humble means not thinking of yourself as more important than you really are. It also means treating others with respect. If you do this, God will be pleased with you!

To learn more about humility, zoom to page 1157.

Micah Is Upset at the Evil That People Do

7 Poor me! I am like a hungry man.
And all the summer fruit has been
picked.

There are no grapes left to eat.
There are none of the early figs
I love.
[2] All of the faithful people are gone.
There is not one good person left
in this country.

Everyone is waiting to kill someone.
Everyone is trying to trap his
brother.
[3] People are good at doing evil with
both hands.

Rulers ask for money.
And judges' decisions are bought
for a price.

Rich people make their wishes
known.
They all join in their evil plans.
[4] Even the best of them is like a
thornbush.

Even the nicest of them is worse
than a thornbush.
Your watchmen[n] warned you about
this day.

Now it has come.
Now you will be punished.
Your punishment will amaze you.
[5] Don't trust your neighbor.
Don't even trust a friend.
Be careful what you say,
even to your wife.
[6] A son will not honor his father.
A daughter will turn against
her mother.
A daughter-in-law will fight with her
mother-in-law.
A person's enemies will be
members of his own family.

The Lord's Kindness

[7] Israel says, "I will look to the Lord
for help.
I will wait for God to save me.
My God will hear me.
[8] Enemy, don't laugh at me.

I have fallen, but I will get up
again.
I sit in the shadow of trouble now.
But the Lord will be a light for me.
[9] I sinned against the Lord.
So he was angry with me.
But he will defend my case in court.
He will do what is right for me.
Then he will bring me out into
the light.
I will see him set things right.
[10] Then my enemies will see this,
and they will be ashamed.
My enemies said to me,
'Where is the Lord your God?'
Now I will laugh at them.
They will fall down defeated, like
the mud people walk on."

The Jews to Return

[11] The time will come when your walls
will be built again.
At that time your country will
grow.
[12] Your people will come back to
your land.
They will come from Assyria and
the cities of Egypt.
They will come from the countries
between the river of Egypt and the
Euphrates River.
They will come from the countries
between the Mediterranean Sea in
the west and the mountains in
the east.
[13] The rest of the earth will be ruined.
This is because of what the people
who lived in it did.

A Prayer to God

[14] So shepherd your people with
your stick.
Tend the flock of people who
belong to you.
That flock now lives alone in
the desert.
But there is fertile pasture nearby.
Let them feed in Bashan and Gilead
as they did long ago.

[n] **watchmen** Another name for a prophet. The prophets were like guards who stood on a city's wall.
They watched for trouble coming from far away.

¹⁵The Lord says, "I did many
miracles^d when I brought you
out of Egypt.
I will show you more miracles
like that."

¹⁶The nations will see those miracles.
Then they will no longer brag
about their power.
They will be amazed and put their
hands over their mouths.
They will refuse to listen.
¹⁷They will crawl in the dust like
a snake.
They will shake with fear.
They will crawl on the ground
like insects crawling from their
holes.
They will come trembling to you,
Lord our God.
They will tremble in fear before
you.

¹⁸There is no God like you.
You forgive people who are guilty
of sin.
You don't look at the sins of
your people
who are left alive.
You, Lord, will not stay angry forever.
You enjoy being kind.
¹⁹Lord, you will have mercy on
us again.
You will conquer our sins.
You will throw away all our sins
into the deepest sea.
²⁰You will be true to the people
of Jacob!
You will be kind to the people of
Abraham.
You will do what you promised
to our ancestors long ago.

God's Love for Us
MICAH 7:18-19

Have you ever made your mom (or dad) so
mad you thought she (or he) would never get over it? "Uh-oh! This
time I've *really* done it. Mom is so mad she'll never forgive me. I wonder if
I can live with the Johnsons for a while. . . ." But sooner or later Mom (or
Dad) cooled off and let you back into the house *and* the family.

God is like that. He gets angry with us—all parents who truly love their
children get angry, because they care so much. If God didn't care, there
would be no reason for him to be angry. But he does care about us—
deeply—and so he sometimes gets very upset with us. But the good
news is, he doesn't *stay* angry. He loves you too much to want you to
stay away from him out of fear. Just as your parents eventually let you
back into the house (or out of your room), God gets over his anger. Don't
let fear keep you from being close to him.

For more about God's love for us, zoom to page 1140.

NAHUM

*God Will
Punish Assyria*

1 This is the message for the city of Nineveh.ⁿ This is the vision of Nahum, who was from the town of Elkosh.

The Lord Is Angry with Nineveh

²The Lord is a jealous God who gives punishment.
The Lord punishes wicked people and is filled with anger.
The Lord punishes those who are against him.
He stays angry with his enemies.
³The Lord does not become angry quickly.
His power is great.
The Lord will not let the guilty go unpunished.
Where the Lord goes, whirlwinds and storms show his power.
The clouds are the dust that his feet kick up.
⁴The Lord speaks to the sea and makes it dry.
He dries up all the rivers.
The areas of Bashan and Carmel dry up.
And the flowers of Lebanon die.
⁵He shakes the mountains
and makes the hills melt away.
The earth trembles when he comes.
The world and all who live in it shake with fear.
⁶No one can stay alive when the Lord is angry with him.
No one can survive his strong anger.
His anger is poured out like fire.
He smashes rocks that are in his path.

> **The Lord is good.
> He gives protection
> in times of trouble.
> He knows who trusts
> in him.**
> • **Nahum 1:7**

⁷The Lord is good.
He gives protection in times of trouble.
He knows who trusts in him.
⁸But he will completely destroy the city of Nineveh.
An army will come like a rushing flood.
The Lord will chase his enemies until he kills them.

⁹The Lord will completely destroy the plans that are made against him.
Trouble will not come a second time.
¹⁰Those people will be like tangled thorns
or like people drunk from their wine.
They will be destroyed quickly like dry weeds.
¹¹Someone has come from Nineveh.
He makes evil plans against the Lord.
And he gives wicked advice.

¹²This is what the Lord says:
"Assyria is strong and has many people.
But it will be defeated and brought to an end.

ⁿ**Nineveh** The capital city of the country of Assyria. Nahum uses Nineveh to stand for all of Assyria.

Judah, I have punished you, my
  people.
But I will punish you no more.
[13] Now I will free you from their
  control.
And I will tear away the chains
  with which they hold you."

[14] The Lord has given you this
  command, Nineveh:
"You will not have descendants[d] to
  carry on your name.
I will destroy the idols and metal
  images
that are in the temple of your gods.
I will dig your grave
  because you are wicked."

[15] Look, there on the hills,
  someone is bringing good news!
He is announcing peace!
Celebrate your feasts, people of
  Judah.
And do what you promised to God.
The wicked will not attack you again.
They have been completely
  destroyed.

Nineveh Will Be Defeated

2 The destroyer[n] is coming to attack
  you, Nineveh.
Guard the defenses.
Watch the road.
Get ready.
Gather all your strength!
[2] Destroyers have destroyed God's
  people
and ruined their vines.
But the Lord will make the people
  of Jacob
and the people of Israel great
  again.

[3] The shields of the soldiers are red.
The army is dressed in red.
The metal on the chariots flashes
  when they are ready to attack.
Their horses are excited.
[4] The chariots race through the
  streets.

They rush back and forth through
  the city squares.
They look like torches.
They run like lightning.

[5] He[n] calls his officers.
But they fall down on the way.
They hurry to the city wall.
The shield is put into place.
[6] The river gates are thrown open.
And the palace is destroyed.
[7] It has been announced that the
  people of Nineveh
will be captured and carried away.
The slave girls moan like doves.
They beat their breasts because
  they are sad.
[8] Nineveh is like a pool.
And its water is draining away.
"Stop! Stop!" the people yell.
But no one turns back.
[9] Take the silver!
Take the gold!
There is no end to the treasure.
There is wealth of every kind.
[10] Nineveh is robbed, ruined and
  destroyed.
The people lose their courage.
  Their knees knock with fear.
Stomachs ache. And everyone's
  face grows pale from fright.

[11] Where is the lions'[n] den?
Where do they feed their young?
Where did the lion, lioness and
  cubs go?
Where were they not afraid?
[12] The lion killed enough for his cubs.
He killed it for his mate.
He filled his cave with the animals
  he caught.
He filled his den with what he had
  killed.

[13] "I am against you, Nineveh,"
  says the Lord of heaven's armies.
"I will burn up your chariots in
  smoke.
And I will kill your young lions
  with a sword.

[n] **destroyer**   The Babylonians, the Scythians and the Medes destroyed Nineveh.
[n] **He**   This probably means the king of Assyria.
[n] **lions'**   The symbol of Assyria was the lion.

I will stop you from hunting down
others on the earth.
Your messengers' voices
will no longer be heard."

It Will Be Terrible for Nineveh

3 How terrible it will be for the city
which has killed so many.
It is full of lies.
It is full of stolen things from other
countries.
It is always hurting or killing
somebody.
[2]Hear the sound of whips.
Listen to the wheels.
Hear horses galloping
and chariots bouncing along!
[3]Soldiers on horses are charging.
Their swords are shining.
Their spears are gleaming!
There are many bodies.
Dead people are piled up.
There are too many to count.
People fall over the dead bodies.
[4]The city was like a prostitute.[d]
She was charming and a lover
of magic.
She made nations slaves with her
evil ways
and her witchcraft.[d]

[5]"I am against you, Nineveh," says
the Lord of heaven's armies.
"I will pull your dress up over
your face.
I will show the nations your
nakedness.
And I will show the kingdoms
your shame.
[6]I will throw dirt on you.
I will make a fool of you.
People will see you and make fun
of you.
[7]Everyone who sees you will run
away and say,
'Nineveh is in ruins. Who will cry
for her?'
Nineveh, I cannot find anyone to
comfort you."

[8]Nineveh, you are no better than
Thebes.[n]

She sits by the Nile River
with water all around her.
The river was her defense.
The waters were like a wall
around her.
[9]Cush and Egypt gave her endless
strength.
Put and Libya supported her.
[10]But Thebes was captured.
And she went into captivity.
Her small children were beaten to
death
at every street corner.
Lots[d] were thrown for her important
men.
And all of her leaders were put in
chains.

[11]Nineveh, you will be drunk, too.
You will hide.
You will look for a place safe from
the enemy.
[12]All your defenses are like fig trees
with ripe fruit.
When the tree is shaken, the figs
fall into the mouth of the eater.
[13]Look at your soldiers.
They are all women!
The gates of your land
are wide open for your enemies.
Fire has burned the bars of those
gates.

[14]Get enough water before the attack
begins.
Make your defenses strong!
Make the bricks.
Mix the mortar.
Repair the wall!
[15]There the fire will burn you up.
The sword will kill you.
Like grasshoppers eating crops,
the battle will completely
destroy you.
Grow in number like hopping
locusts.[d]
Grow in number like swarming
locusts!
[16]Your traders are more than the
stars in the sky.
But like locusts, they strip the land
and then fly away.

[n]**Thebes**   A great city in Egypt.

17Your guards are like locusts.
Your officers are like swarms
of locusts
that settle in the walls on a
cold day.
But when the sun comes up they
fly away.
And no one knows where they
have gone.
18King of Assyria, your rulers are
asleep.

Your important men lie down
to rest.
Your people have been scattered on
the mountains.
And there is no one to bring
them back.
19Nothing can heal your wound.
Your injury will not heal.
Everyone who hears about you
applauds
because everyone has felt your
endless cruelty.

HABAKKUK

*Learning How
to Trust God*

1 This is the message that was given to Habakkuk the prophet.*ᵈ*

Habakkuk Complains

²Lord, I continue to ask for help.
 How long will you ignore me?
I cry out to you about violence,
 but you do not save us!
³Why do you let me see wrong things?
 Why do you put up with evil?
People are destroying things and
 hurting others while I am
 looking.
 They are arguing and fighting.
⁴People are not forced to obey the
 teachings.
 No one receives a fair trial.
Evil people gain while good people
 lose.
 The judges no longer make fair
 decisions.

The Lord Answers

⁵"You and your people, look at the
 nations!
 Watch them and be amazed.
I will do something in your lifetime
 that will amaze you.
 You won't believe it even when
 you are told about it.
⁶I will use the Babylonian people to
 punish the evil people.
The Babylonians are cruel and
 powerful fighters.
They march across the earth.
 They take lands that don't belong
 to them.
⁷The Babylonians frighten other
 people.
They do what they want to do.
 They are good only to themselves.
⁸Their horses are faster than leopards

and more cruel than wolves at
 sunset.
Their horse soldiers attack quickly.
 They come from places that are
 far away.
They attack quickly, like an eagle
 swooping down for food.
⁹ They all come to fight.
Their armies march quickly like a
 whirlwind in the desert.
 Their prisoners are as many as the
 grains of sand.
¹⁰The Babylonian soldiers laugh at
 kings.
 They make fun of rulers.
They laugh at all the strong, walled
 cities.
They build dirt roads up to the top
 of the walls.
 They capture the cities.
¹¹Then they leave like the wind and
 move on.
 They are guilty of worshiping their
 own strength."

Habakkuk Complains Again

¹²Lord, you are the Lord who lives
 forever.
 You are my God, my holy God.
 You will not let those who trust
 you die.
Lord, you have chosen the
 Babylonians to punish people.
Our Rock,*ᵈ* you created them to
 punish the people.
¹³Your eyes are too good to look at evil.
 You cannot stand to see people
 do wrong.
So how can you put up with those
 evil people?
 How can you be quiet when
 wicked people defeat people

who are better than they are?
¹⁴You treat people like fish in the sea.
You treat them like sea animals
without a leader.
¹⁵The enemy catches all of them
with hooks.
He catches them in his net.
He drags them in.
He is glad that he has caught them.
¹⁶The enemy offers sacrifices to his net.
He burns incense*d* to worship it.
This is because his net lets him live
like a rich man.
His net lets him enjoy the best food.
¹⁷Will he keep on taking riches with
his net?
Will he go on destroying people
without showing mercy?

2 I will stand like a guard to watch.
I will stand on the tower.
I will wait to see what the Lord will
say to me.
I will wait to learn how to answer
his complaint.

The Lord Answers

²The Lord answered me:
"Write down what I show you.
Write it clearly on stone tablets
so whoever reads it can run to tell
others.

³It is not yet time for the message to
come true.
But that time is coming soon.
The message will come true.
It may seem like a long time before
it happens.
But be patient and wait for it.
These things will happen.
They will not be delayed.
⁴See, the nation that is evil and trusts
in itself will fail.
But those who do right because
they trust in God will live.

⁵"Wine can trick a person.
In the same way the Babylonians
are fooled by their pride.
Their desire for wealth is like a
grave's desire for death.
They always want more and more.
And, like death, they collect other
nations for themselves.
They make them their own people.
⁶But all the nations the Babylonians
have hurt will laugh at them.
They will make fun of the
Babylonians.

Faith and How It Works
HABAKKUK 2:4

If you wanted to learn how to swim or how to ride a bike, what would you do? The answer is easy: you would ask someone to teach you. That person would show you how and then would help you practice.

If you want to know how to live as a Christian, what should you do? The answer is also easy: ask God to show you how. God says that Christians are to live by trusting in him. Trusting in God is called *faith*. As you trust in God, he shows you how to live the way he wants. During your whole life, you will keep learning more about God, your faith will keep getting stronger, and you will learn how to please God every day.

Ask God to help you live today "by trusting in him."

To find out more about faith and how it works, fly to page 1253.

They will say, 'How terrible it will
    be for the nation that steals
    many things.
How long will that nation get rich
    by forcing others to pay them?'

[7]"One day the people you have taken
    money from will turn against
    you.
They will realize what is happening
    and make you shake with fear.
Then they will hurt you.
[8]You have stolen from many nations.
So the people who are left will take
    much from you.
This is because you have killed
    many people.
You have destroyed countries and
    cities and everyone in them.

[9]"How terrible it will be for the
    nation that becomes rich by
    doing wrong.
They do those things to live in a
    safe place.
They think they will be safe from
    harm.
[10]You have made plans to destroy
    many people.
This has made your own houses
    ashamed of you.
Because of it, you will lose your
    lives.
[11]The stones of the walls will cry out
    against you.
Even the wooden boards that
    support the roof will agree that
    you are wrong.

[12]"How terrible it will be for the nation
    that kills people to build a city.
How terrible for that nation that
    wrongs others to start a town.
[13]The Lord of heaven's armies will
    send fire
to destroy what those people
    have built.
All the nations' work will be
    for nothing.
[14]Then people everywhere will know
    the Lord's greatness.
This news will spread like water
    covering the sea.

[15]"How terrible for the nation that
    becomes angry and makes
    others suffer.
In anger they knock other people
    to the ground.
And they treat them as if they are
    naked and drunk.
[16]You Babylonians will receive the
    Lord's anger, not respect.
This anger will be like a cup of
    poison in the Lord's right hand.
You will taste this anger and fall to
    the ground like a drunk person.
You will drink from this cup.
You will receive disgrace, not
    respect.
[17]You hurt many people in Lebanon.
Now you will be hurt.
You killed many animals there.
And now you must be afraid.
You will be afraid because of what
    you did
to those cities and the people who
    lived in them.

The Message About Idols

[18]"An idol does no good, because a
    man made it.
It is only a statue that teaches lies.
The person who made it expects his
    own work to help him.
But it can't even speak!
[19]How terrible it will be for the nation
    that says to a wooden statue,
    'Come to life!'
How terrible it will be when this
    nation says to a stone that
    cannot speak, 'Get up!'
These things cannot tell them what
    to do.
That idol is only a statue covered
    with gold and silver.
There is no life in it.
[20]The Lord is in his Holy Temple.[d]
So all the earth should be silent in
    his presence."

Habakkuk's Prayer

3 This is the prayer of Habakkuk the
prophet,[d] on shigionoth.[d]

[2]Lord, I have heard the news about
you.

Lord, I am amazed at the powerful
    things you have done.
Do great things once again in our time.
Make those things happen again
    in our own days.
Even when you are angry,
    remember to be gentle with us.

3God is coming from Teman in the
    south.
The Holy One comes from Mount
    Paran.ⁿ   Selahᵈ
The Lord's greatness covers the
    heavens.
His praise fills the earth.
4He is like a bright light.
Rays of light shine from his hand.
And there he hides his power.
5Sickness goes before him,
    and fever follows behind him.
6The Lord stands and shakes the earth.
He looks, and the nations shake
    with fear.
The mountains, which stood for
    ages, break into pieces.
The old hills fall down.
God has always done this.

7I saw that the tents of Cushan were
    in trouble.
The tents of Midian trembled.
8Lord, were you angry at the rivers?
Were you angry at the streams?
Were you angry with the sea
    when you rode your horses and
    chariots to victory?ⁿ
9You uncovered your bow.
You commanded many arrows to
    be brought to you.   Selah
You split the earth with rivers.
10   The mountains saw you and
    shook with fear.
The rushing water flowed by.
The sea made a loud noise,
    and its waves rose high.
11The sun and moon stood still in
    the sky.
They stopped when they saw the
    flash of your flying arrows.
They stopped when they saw the

gleam of your shining spear.
12In anger you marched on the earth.
In anger you punished the nations.
13You came to save your people.
You came to save your chosen one.
You crushed the leader of the
    wicked ones.
You took everything away from
    them.   Selah
14With the enemy's own spear you
    stabbed the leader of his army.
His soldiers rushed out like a
    storm to scatter us.
They were happy as if
    they were robbing the poor people
    in secret.
15But you marched through the sea
    with your horses,
    stirring the great waters.

16I hear these things, and my body
    trembles.
My lips tremble when I hear the
    sound.
My bones feel weak.
My legs shake.

But I will wait patiently for the day
    of disaster.
That day is coming to the people
    who attack us.
17Fig trees may not grow figs.
There may be no grapes on
    the vines.
There may be no olives growing on
    the trees.
There may be no food growing in
    the fields.
There may be no sheep in the pens.
There may be no cattle in the barns.
18But I will still be glad in the Lord.
I will rejoice in God my Savior.
19The Lord God gives me my strength.
He makes me like a deer, which
    does not stumble.
He leads me safely on the steep
    mountains.

For the director of music. On my
stringed instruments.

ⁿ**Teman . . . Paran**   God is seen as again coming from the direction of Mount Sinai. He came from
Sinai when he rescued his people from Egypt.
ⁿ**sea . . . victory**   This is probably talking about the Israelites crossing the Red Sea.

ZEPHANIAH

God Will
Judge the World

1 This is the message of the Lord that came through Zephaniah. It came while Josiah son of Amon was king of Judah. Zephaniah was the son of Cushi, who was the son of Gedaliah. Gedaliah was the son of Amariah, who was the son of Hezekiah.

The Lord's Judgment

2 "I will destroy everything
  on earth," says the Lord.
3 "I will destroy the people and
    animals.
  I will destroy the birds in the air
    and the fish of the sea.
  I will ruin the evil people.
  I will remove all the people from
    the earth," says the Lord.

The Future of Judah

4 "I will punish Judah
  and all the people living in
    Jerusalem.
  I will remove from this place
    all signs of Baal[d] and his priests.
5 I will destroy those who worship
    the stars from the roofs.[n]
  I will destroy those who worship
    and make promises
  by both the Lord and the god
    Molech.[d]
6 I will destroy those who turned
    away from the Lord.
  They quit following the Lord and
    consulting him.
7 Be silent before the Lord God.
  His day for judging people is
    coming soon.
  The Lord has prepared to sacrifice
    Judah.

He has appointed the invited
  guests to feast on Judah.
8 On that day the Lord will sacrifice
    Judah.
  I, the Lord, will punish the princes
    and the king's sons.
  And I will punish all
    those who wear foreign clothes.
9 On that day I will punish those who
    worship Dagon.[d]
  I will punish those who hurt others
  and tell lies in the temples of their
    gods.

10 "On that day this will happen," says
    the Lord.
  "A cry will be heard at the Fish Gate.
  A wail will come from the new area
    of the city.
  A loud crash will echo from
    the hills.
11 The people living in the market area
    will wail.
  All the merchants will be dead.
  All the silver traders will be gone.
12 At that time I, the Lord, will search
    Jerusalem with lamps.
  I will punish those who are settled
    and satisfied with themselves.
  They are like wine left to settle.
  They think, 'The Lord never does
    anything.
  He won't help us or punish us.'
13 Their wealth will be stolen.
  Their houses will be destroyed.
  They may build houses,
    but they will never live in them.
  They may plant vineyards,
    but they will never drink any wine
      from them.

---

roofs In Bible times houses were built with flat roofs. The roof was used for drying things such as flax and fruit. And it was used as an extra room, as a place for worship and as a place to sleep in the summer.

The Lord's Day of Judging

[14] "The Lord's day of judging is
    coming soon.
That great day is near and
    coming fast.
The cry will be very sad on that day.
Even soldiers will cry.
[15] That day will be a day of anger.
It will be a day of terror and trouble.
It will be a day of destruction and
    ruin.
It will be a day of darkness and
    gloom.
It will be a day of clouds and
    blackness.
[16] It will be a day of alarms and
    battle cries.
'Attack the strong, walled cities!
Attack the corner towers!'
[17] I will make life hard on the people.
They will walk around like
    blind men.
This is because they have sinned
    against the Lord.
Their blood will be poured out
    like dust.
And their bodies will be dumped
    like trash.
[18] On that day God will show
    his anger.
Then neither their silver nor gold
    will save them.
The Lord's anger will be like fire.
And the whole world will be
    burned up.
Suddenly he will bring an end
    to everyone on earth."

God Asks People to Change

2 Gather together,
    you unwanted people.
[2] Do it before it's too late.
Do it before you are blown away
    like chaff.[d]
Do it before the Lord's terrible
    anger reaches you.
Do it before the day of the Lord's
    anger comes to you.
[3] All you who are not proud, come to
    the Lord.

You who obey his laws, come to him.
Do what is right. Learn to be
    humble.
Maybe you will escape
on the day the Lord shows his anger.

Philistia Will Be Punished

[4] No one will be left in the city of Gaza.
The city of Ashkelon will be
    destroyed.
Ashdod will be empty by noon.
And the people of Ekron will be
    chased away.
[5] How terrible it will be for you who
    live by the Mediterranean Sea,
you Philistines!
This message from the Lord is
    for you,
people of Canaan, land of the
    Philistines.

"I will destroy you.
No one will be left."
[6] You live in the land by the
    Mediterranean Sea.
It will be a place for shepherds and
    sheep.
[7] Your land will belong to the
    descendants[d] of Judah who are
    left alive.
There they will let their sheep
    eat grass.
At night they will sleep
    in the houses of Ashkelon.
The Lord their God will come to be
    with them.
He will give them back their
    riches.

Moab and Ammon Will Be Punished

[8] "I heard the country of Moab insult
    my people.
The country of Ammon threatened
    to take their land."
[9] So the Lord of heaven's armies, the
    God of Israel, says,
"As surely as I live,
Moab will be destroyed like Sodom.
Ammon will be destroyed like
    Gomorrah."[n]

[n] **Sodom and Gomorrah**   Two cities God destroyed because the people were so evil.

Their land will be covered with
weeds and salt.
It will be destroyed forever.
Those of my people who are left
alive will take whatever they
want from them.
Those who are left from my nation
will take their land."

¹⁰ This is what Moab and Ammon get
for being proud.
This will happen because they
insulted and made fun of the
people of the Lord of heaven's
armies.
¹¹Those people will be afraid of
the Lord.
He will destroy all the gods of
the earth.
Then those people in faraway places
will worship the Lord in their own
countries.

Cush and Assyria Will Be Destroyed

¹²"You Cushites also
will be killed by my sword."
¹³Then the Lord will turn against
the north
and punish Assyria.
He will destroy Nineveh.
It will be dry like a desert.
¹⁴Sheep and goats will lie down there.
Wild animals will live there.
The owls and crows will sit
on the stone pillars that are left
standing.
Their calls will be heard through
the windows.
Trash will be in the doorways.
The wooden boards of the
buildings will be gone.
¹⁵This is the happy and safe city.
It thinks there is no one else as
strong as it is.
But that city will be destroyed.
Only animals will stay there.
Those who pass by will make fun
and shake their fists.

Jerusalem Will Be Punished

3 How terrible it will be for Jerusalem
that hurts its own people.

It's a wicked, stubborn city.
²Her people don't listen.
They can't be taught to do right.
They don't trust the Lord.
They don't worship their God.
³Their officers are like roaring lions.
Their rulers are like hungry
wolves that attack in the
evening.
In the morning nothing is left of
those they attacked.
⁴Their prophets*ᵈ* are proud.
They cannot be trusted.
Their priests don't respect holy
things.
They break God's teachings.
⁵But the Lord is good, and he is
there in that city.
He does no wrong.
Every morning he governs the
people fairly.
Every day he can be trusted by
his people.
But evil people are not ashamed of
the bad things they do.

⁶"I have destroyed other nations.
Their towers have fallen.
I made their streets empty.
No one goes there anymore.
Their cities are ruined.
No one lives there anymore.
⁷I said, 'Maybe now Jerusalem will
respect me.
Maybe now my people will let me
teach them to do right.'
Then the place where they lived
would not be destroyed.
Then I would not have punished
them.
They got up early in order to
do evil.
Everything they did was bad.
⁸Just wait," says the Lord.
"Some day I will hold court and be
the judge.
I will gather nations.
I will assemble kingdoms.
I will pour out my anger on them.
My anger will be very strong.
My anger will be like fire.
And the whole world will be
burned up.

A New Day for God's People

9 "Then I will make the people of all
        nations speak a pure language.
    All of them will speak the name of
        the Lord.
    And they will worship me
        together.
10 People will come from where the
        Nile River begins.
    My scattered people will come
        with gifts for me.
11 Then Jerusalem will not be
        ashamed
    of the wrongs done against me.
    I will remove from this city
        those who like to brag.
    There will never be any more proud
        people
    on my holy mountain in Jerusalem.
12 Only the meek and humble will
        stay in my city.
    And they will trust in the Lord.
13 Those who are left alive of Israel
        won't do wrong.
    They won't tell lies.
    They won't trick people with
        their words.
    They will be like sheep that eat and
        lie down.
    No one will bother them."

A Happy Song

14 Sing, Jerusalem.
    Israel, shout for joy!
    Jerusalem, be happy.
    Rejoice with all your heart.
15 The Lord has stopped punishing you.

He has sent your enemies away.
    The King of Israel, the Lord, is
        with you.
    You will never again be afraid of
        being harmed.
16 On that day Jerusalem will be told,
    "Don't be afraid, city of Jerusalem.
    Don't be so discouraged that you
        can't do anything.
17 The Lord your God is with you.
    The mighty One will save you.
    The Lord will be happy with you.
    You will rest in his love.
    He will sing and be joyful about
        you."

18 "I will take away the sadness
        planned for you.
    It would have made you very
        ashamed.
19 At that time I will punish
        all those who harmed you.
    I will save my people who are hurt.
    I will gather my people who are
        scattered.
    I will give them praise and honor
        in every place where they were
        disgraced.
20 At that time I will gather you.
    At that time I will bring you back
        home.
    I will give you honor and praise
        from people everywhere.
    That will happen when I give you
        back your riches.
    You will see this with your own
        eyes," says the Lord.

HAGGAI

The Temple Is Rebuilt

It Is Time to Build the Temple

1 The prophet[d] Haggai spoke the word of the Lord to Zerubbabel and to Joshua. Zerubbabel son of Shealtiel was governor of Judah. Joshua son of Jehozadak was high priest. This message came in the second year that Darius was king of Persia. It came on the first day of the sixth month of that year. This was the message:

[2]"This is what the Lord of heaven's armies says: 'The people say the right time has not come to rebuild the Temple[d] of the Lord.'"

[3]Then Haggai the prophet spoke the word of the Lord: [4]"The Temple is still in ruins. Is it right for you to be living in fancy houses?"

[5]This is why the Lord of heaven's armies says: "Think about what you have done. [6]You have planted much, but you harvest little. You eat, but you do not become full. You drink, but you are still thirsty. You put on clothes,

People Who Spoke God's Words
HAGGAI • HAGGAI 1:5

What would you think of a girl who always found an excuse for not doing her homework? One day she tells the teacher she wants to go swimming before the weather turns cold. The next day she says that she wants to watch a new television program with her family. The day after that, she claims that she has to go to a youth-group soccer game. Even though her excuses might be good, from time to time, they are keeping her from doing what's more important—her schoolwork.

The prophet Haggai reminded the people of Israel that they were making excuses and forgetting about God. Instead of rebuilding the temple—a job they had started fifteen years earlier but hadn't finished—they spent time on their own plans. Haggai told the people that their plans would never be successful unless they made God first. If they decided to honor God, they would receive great blessings. But if they didn't, they would never find happiness or peace.

Many times your life will be full of plans and activities. But God wants you to remember that getting to know him should be the most important activity in your life.

To meet a prophet who led people to his cousin, fly to page 1180.

but you are not warm enough. You earn money, but then you lose it all. It is as if you put it into a purse full of holes."

[7]This is what the Lord of heaven's armies says: "Think about what you have done. [8]Go up to the mountains. Bring back wood and build the Temple. Then I will be pleased with it and be honored," says the Lord. [9]The Lord of heaven's armies says: "You look for much, but you find little. When you bring it home, I destroy it. Why? Because you are busy working on your own houses. But my house is still in ruins! [10]Because of what you have done, the sky holds back its rain. And the ground holds back its crops.[d] [11]I have called for a dry time in the land. There will be no rain in the mountains for the grain, new wine and olive oil. It will be a dry time for the plants which the earth produces. It will be a dry time for men and farm animals. The dry time will make your hard work useless."

[12]Zerubbabel was the son of Shealtiel. And Joshua, the high priest, was the son of Jehozadak. Zerubbabel and Joshua obeyed the Lord their God. And they obeyed the message from Haggai the prophet. All the rest of the people who were left alive also obeyed. This was because they realized that the Lord their God had sent Haggai. And they feared the Lord.

[13]The Lord sent a message to Haggai, the Lord's messenger. Haggai gave this message to the people. He said: "The Lord says, 'I am with you.'"
[14]The Lord made Zerubbabel and Joshua excited about building the Temple. Zerubbabel son of Shealtiel was the governor of Judah. Joshua son of Jehozadak was the high priest. The Lord made all the rest of the people who were left alive excited, too. They came and worked on the Temple of their God, the Lord of heaven's armies.
[15]They began on the twenty-fourth day of the sixth month. This was in the second year that Darius was king of Persia.

The Beauty of the Temple

2 The Lord spoke his word through Haggai the prophet[d] on the twenty-first day of the seventh month. This is what the Lord said: [2]"Speak to Zerubbabel son of Shealtiel, governor of Judah. Speak also to Joshua son of Jehozadak, the high priest. And speak to the rest of the people who were left alive. Say: [3]'Do any of you who are still alive remember how beautiful the Temple[d] was before it was destroyed? What does it look like now? The truth is it means nothing to you!' [4]But the Lord says: 'Zerubbabel, be brave. Joshua son of Jehozadak, the high priest, be brave. And all you people who live in the land, be brave,' says the Lord. 'Work, because I am with you,' says the Lord of heaven's armies. [5]I made a promise to you when you came out of Egypt. My Spirit[d] is still with you. So don't be afraid.'

[6]"This is what the Lord of heaven's armies says: 'In a short time I will shake the heavens and earth once again. And I will shake the sea and the dry land. [7]I will shake all the nations. All the nations will bring their wealth. Then I will fill this Temple with glory,' says the Lord of heaven's armies. [8]'The silver is mine, and the gold is mine,' says the Lord of heaven's armies. [9]'The new Temple will be more beautiful than the one that was destroyed,' says the Lord of heaven's armies. 'And in this place I will give peace to the people,' says the Lord of heaven's armies."

[10]The Lord spoke his word to Haggai the prophet. This was on the twenty-fourth day of the ninth month. It was in the second year that Darius was king of Persia. This is what the Lord said: [11]"This is what the Lord of heaven's armies says: 'Ask the priests what the teachings say. [12]A person might carry meat made holy for the Lord in the fold of his clothes. And that fold might touch bread, cooked food, wine, olive oil or some other food. Will the thing the fold touches be made holy for the Lord, too?'"

The priests answered, "No."

[13]Then Haggai said, "A person who touches a dead body will become unclean.[d] If he touches any of these foods, will it become unclean, too?"

The priests answered, "Yes. It would become unclean."

[14]Then Haggai answered, "The Lord says this: 'This is also true for the people of this nation. They are unclean, and everything they do with their hands is unclean to me. If these people offer something at the altar to me, it is also unclean.

[15]"'Think about this from now on! Think about how it was before you started piling stones on top of stones. Think about how it was before you started building the Temple of the Lord. [16]A person used to come to a pile of grain expecting to find 20 basketfuls. But there were only 10. And a person used to come to the wine vat to take out 50 jarfuls. But only 20 were there. [17]I destroyed your work with diseases, mildew[d] and hail. But you still did not come to me.' The Lord says this. [18]It is the twenty-fourth day of the ninth month. On this day the people finished working on the foundation of the Temple of the Lord. From now on, think about these things: [19]Do you have seeds for your crops already in the barn? No! Your vines and trees are not giving fruit yet, either. You don't have any figs, pomegranates[d] or olives yet. But from now on I will bless you!'"

The Lord Makes a Promise to Zerubbabel

[20]Then the Lord spoke his word a second time to Haggai. It was on the twenty-fourth day of the month. This is what the Lord said: [21]"Tell Zerubbabel, the governor of Judah: 'I am going to shake the heavens and the earth. [22]I will destroy the foreign kingdoms. I will take away the power of the kingdoms of the nations. I will destroy the chariots and their riders. The horses will fall with their riders. People will kill each other with swords.' [23]The Lord of heaven's armies says this: 'On that day I will take you, Zerubbabel son of Shealtiel, my servant.' The Lord says this: 'I will make you important like my signet[d] ring. This is because I have chosen you!' says the Lord of heaven's armies."

ZECHARIAH

Encouraging the People

The Lord Calls His People Back

1 It was the eighth month of the second year Darius was king of Persia. The Lord spoke his word to the prophet[d] Zechariah son of Berekiah. Berekiah was the son of Iddo. The Lord said:

²"The Lord was very angry with your ancestors. ³So tell the people: This is what the Lord of heaven's armies says: Return to me, and I will return to you. ⁴Don't be like your ancestors. In the past the prophets spoke to them. They said: This is what the Lord of heaven's armies says: 'Stop your evil ways and evil actions.' But they wouldn't listen or pay attention to me, says the Lord. ⁵Your ancestors are dead. And those prophets didn't live forever. ⁶I commanded my words and laws to my servants the prophets. They preached to your ancestors, who returned to me. They said, 'The Lord of heaven's armies did as he said he would. He punished us for the way we lived and for what we did.'"

The Vision of the Horses

⁷It was on the twenty-fourth day of the eleventh month, which is called Shebat. It was Darius's second year as king. The Lord spoke his word to the prophet[d] Zechariah son of Berekiah. Berekiah was the son of Iddo.

⁸During the night I had a vision. I saw a man riding a red horse. He was standing among some myrtle trees in the ravine. Behind him were red, brown and white horses.

⁹I asked, "What are these, sir?"

The angel who was talking with me answered. He said, "I'll show you what they are."

¹⁰Then the man standing among the myrtle trees explained. He said, "They are the ones the Lord sent through all the earth."

¹¹Then they spoke to the Lord's angel. He was standing among the myrtle trees. They said, "We have gone through all the earth. Everything is calm and quiet."

¹²Then the Lord's angel asked, "Lord of heaven's armies, how long before you show mercy to Jerusalem and the cities of Judah? You have been angry with them for 70 years now." ¹³Then the Lord answered the angel who was talking with me. His words were comforting and good.

¹⁴Then the angel told me, "Announce this: This is what the Lord of heaven's armies says: 'I have a strong love for Jerusalem. ¹⁵And I am very angry with the nations that feel so safe. I was only a little angry, but they made things worse for my people.'

¹⁶"So this is what the Lord says: 'I will return to Jerusalem with mercy. My Temple[d] will be rebuilt,' says the Lord of heaven's armies. 'And the measuring line will be used to rebuild Jerusalem.'

¹⁷"Also announce: This is what the Lord of heaven's armies says: 'My towns will be rich again. I will comfort Jerusalem again. I will still choose Jerusalem.'"

The Vision of the Horns

¹⁸Then I looked up and saw four animal horns. ¹⁹I asked the angel who was talking with me, "What are these?"

He said, "These are the strong nations that scattered the people of Judah, Israel and Jerusalem."

[20]Then the Lord showed me four craftsmen. [21]I asked, "What are they coming to do?"

He answered, "They have come to scare and throw down the horns. Those horns scattered the people of Judah. No one could even lift up his head. The horns stand for the strong nations that attacked the people of Judah and scattered them."

The Vision of the Measuring Line

2 Then I looked up. And I saw a man holding a line for measuring things. [2]I asked him, "Where are you going?"

He said to me, "I am going to measure Jerusalem. I will see how wide and how long it is."

[3]Then the angel who was talking with me left. And another angel came out to meet him. [4]The second angel said to him, "Run and tell that young man this: 'Jerusalem will become a city without walls because there will be so many people and cattle in it. [5]I will be a wall of fire around it,' says the Lord. 'And I will be the glory within it.'

[6]"Hurry! Run away from Babylon. I have scattered you in all directions," says the Lord.

[7]"Hurry, people of Jerusalem! Escape from Babylon." [8]This is what the Lord of heaven's armies says: "Whoever hurts you hurts what is precious to me."

So the Lord will honor me. And he will send me to speak against those nations who scattered you. [9]"I will raise my hand against them. Their slaves will rob them."

Then you will know that the Lord of heaven's armies sent me.

[10]"Shout and be glad, Jerusalem. I am coming, and I will live among you," says the Lord. [11]"At that time people from many nations will come to the Lord. And they will become my people. I will live among you. And you will know that the Lord of heaven's armies has sent me to you. [12]Judah will be the Lord's special part of the holy land. And Jerusalem will be his chosen city again. [13]Be silent, everyone. The Lord is coming out of the holy place where he lives."

The Vision of the High Priest

3 Then he showed me Joshua the high priest. He was standing in front of the Lord's angel. And Satan was standing by Joshua's right side to accuse him. [2]The Lord said to Satan, "The Lord says you are guilty, Satan. The Lord who has chosen Jerusalem says you are guilty. This man was like a burning stick pulled from the fire."

[3]Joshua was standing in front of the angel. And Joshua was wearing dirty clothes. [4]Then the angel spoke to those standing near him. He said, "Take those dirty clothes off Joshua."

Then the angel said to Joshua, "Look, I have taken away your sin. And I am giving you new clothes."

[5]Then I said, "Put a clean turban on his head." So they put a clean turban on his head. They also dressed him while the Lord's angel stood there.

[6]Then the Lord's angel said to Joshua, "This is what the Lord of heaven's armies says: [7]'Do as I tell you and serve me. Then you will be in charge of my Temple.[d] You will take care of my courtyards. And I will let you be with these angels who are standing here.

[8]"'Listen, high priest Joshua and the people with you. You stand for things that will happen. I am going to bring my servant called the Branch. [9]Look, I put this stone in front of Joshua. The stone has seven sides. I will carve a message on it,' says the Lord of heaven's armies. 'And in one day I will take away the sin of this land.'

[10]"The Lord of heaven's armies says, 'In that day, each of you will invite your neighbor to join you. And you will sit together under your own grapevine and under your own fig tree.'"

The Vision of the Lampstand

4 Then the angel who was talking with me came back. He woke me up as if I had been asleep. [2]He asked me, "What do you see?"

I said, "I see a solid gold lampstand. There is a bowl at the top. And there are seven lamps. There are also seven places for wicks. ³There are two olive trees by it. One is on the right of the bowl. And one is on the left."

⁴I asked the angel who talked with me, "Sir, what are these?"

⁵The angel said, "Don't you know what they are?"

"No, sir," I said.

⁶Then he told me, "This is the message from the Lord to Zerubbabel: 'You will not succeed by your own strength or power. The power will come from my Spirit,'ᵈ says the Lord of heaven's armies.

⁷"No mountain can stand in Zerubbabel's way. It will be flattened. Then he will bring out the topmost stone. There will be shouts of 'It's beautiful! It's beautiful!'"

⁸Then the Lord spoke his word to me again. He said: ⁹"Zerubbabel has laid the foundation of this Temple.ᵈ He will also complete it. Then you will know that the Lord of heaven's armies has sent me to you.

¹⁰"The people should not think that small beginnings are unimportant. They will be happy when they see Zerubbabel with tools, building the Temple.

"(These seven lamps stand for the eyes of the Lord. They look back and forth across the earth.)"

¹¹Then I asked the angel, "What are the two olive trees on the right and left of the lampstand?"

¹²I also asked him, "What are the two branches full of olives? The olive oil flows through the two gold pipes to the lamps."

¹³He answered, "Don't you know what they are?"

"No, sir," I said.

¹⁴So he said, "They stand for two men. They have been appointed to serve the Lord of all the earth."

The Vision of the Flying Scroll

5 I looked up again. And I saw a flying scroll.

²The angel asked me, "What do you see?"

I answered, "I see a flying scroll. It is 30 feet long and 15 feet wide."

³And he said to me, "This is the curse that will go all over the land. One side says every thief will be sent away. The other side says everyone who makes false promises will be sent away. ⁴The Lord of heaven's armies says, 'I will send it to the houses of thieves. I will also send it to those who use my name to make false promises. The scroll will stay in that person's house. And it will destroy the house with its wood and stones.'"

The Vision of the Woman

⁵Then the angel who was talking with me came forward. He said to me, "Look up and see what is coming."

⁶I asked, "What is it?"

He answered, "It is a measuring basket." He also said, "It stands for the people's sins in all the land."

⁷Then the lid made of lead was raised. There was a woman sitting in the basket. ⁸The angel said, "The woman stands for wickedness." Then he pushed her back into the basket. And he put the lid back down.

⁹Then I looked up. I saw two women. They had wind in their wings. Their wings were like those of a stork. They lifted up the basket into the sky.

¹⁰I spoke to the angel who was talking with me. I asked, "Where are they taking the basket?"

¹¹He answered, "They are going to Babylonia. They will build a temple for it. When the temple is ready, they will set the basket there in its place."

The Vision of the Four Chariots

6 I looked up again. I saw four chariots coming from between two mountains. They were mountains of bronze. ²Red horses pulled the first chariot. Black horses pulled the second chariot. ³White horses pulled the third chariot. And strong, spotted horses pulled the fourth chariot. ⁴I spoke to the angel who was talking with me.

I asked, "What are these, sir?"

5He said, "These are going to the four directions on earth. They have just come from the presence of the Lord of the whole world. 6The chariot pulled by the black horses will go north. The white horses will go west. And the spotted horses will go south."

7The powerful horses were trying to go through all the earth. So he said, "Go through all the earth." And they did.

8Then he called to me, "Look. The horses that went north have calmed the Lord's anger that came from there to punish."

A Crown for Joshua

9The Lord spoke his word to me. He said: 10"Heldai, Tobijah and Jedaiah were captives in Babylon. Get silver and gold from them. Go that same day to the house of Josiah son of Zephaniah. 11Make the silver and gold into a crown. And put it on the head of Joshua son of Jehozadak. Joshua is the high priest. 12Tell him this is what the Lord of heaven's armies says: 'There is a man whose name is the Branch. He will branch out from where he is. He will build the Temple[d] of the Lord. 13One man[n] will build the Temple of the Lord. And the other[n] will receive the honor of a king. One man will sit on his throne and rule. And the other will be a priest on his throne. And these two men will work together in peace.' 14The crown will be kept in the Temple of the Lord. It will remind Heldai, Tobijah, Jedaiah and Josiah son of Zephaniah of God's king. 15People living far away will come and build the Temple of the Lord. Then you will know the Lord of heaven's armies has sent me to you. This will happen if you completely obey the Lord your God."

The People Should Show Mercy

7 It was the fourth year of King Darius's rule. It was on the fourth day of the ninth month, which is called Kislev. The Lord spoke his word to Zechariah. 2The city of Bethel sent Sharezer, Regem-Melech and their men to ask the Lord a question. 3They went to the prophets[d] and priests. They were at the Temple[d] of the Lord of heaven's armies. The men said, "For years the fifth month of each year has been a special time for us. We have shown our sadness and gone without food in this month. Should we continue to do this?"

4The Lord of heaven's armies spoke his word to me. He said, 5"Tell the priests and the people in the country this: 'For 70 years you went without food and cried in the fifth and seventh months. But that was not really for me. 6And when you ate and drank, it was really for yourselves. 7The Lord used the earlier prophets to say the same thing. Jerusalem and the surrounding towns were at peace and wealthy then. People lived in the southern area and the western mountain slopes.'"

8And the Lord spoke his word to Zechariah again: 9"This is what the Lord of heaven's armies says: 'Do what is right and fair. Be kind and merciful to each other. 10Don't hurt widows and orphans, foreigners or the poor. Don't even think of doing evil to somebody else.'

11"But they refused to pay attention. They were stubborn and would not listen. 12They made their hearts as hard as rock. They would not listen to the teachings of the Lord of heaven's armies. And they would not hear his words through the earlier prophets. So the Lord of heaven's armies became very angry.

13"The Lord of heaven's armies says, 'When I called to them, they would not listen. So when they called to me, I would not listen. 14I scattered them like a hurricane to other countries. These were countries they did not know. This good land was left so ruined that no one could live there.'"

---

[n]**One man** This probably refers to Zerubbabel.
[n]**other** This probably refers to Joshua.

The Lord Will Bless Jerusalem

8 The Lord of heaven's armies spoke his word to me again. ²This is what the Lord of heaven's armies says: "I have a very strong love for Jerusalem. My strong love for her is like a fire burning in me."

³This is what the Lord says: "I will return to Jerusalem. I will live in Jerusalem. Then it will be called the City of Truth. And the mountain of the Lord of heaven's armies will be called the Holy Mountain."

⁴This is what the Lord of heaven's armies says: "Old men and old women will again sit along Jerusalem's streets. Each will carry a cane because of his age. ⁵And the streets will be filled with boys and girls playing."

⁶This is what the Lord of heaven's armies says: "Those who are left alive then may think it is too difficult to happen. But it is not too difficult for me," says the Lord of heaven's armies. ⁷This is what the Lord of heaven's armies says: "I will save my people from countries in the east and west. ⁸I will bring them back. And they will live in Jerusalem. They will be my people. And I will be their good and loyal God."

⁹This is what the Lord of heaven's armies says: "Be strong, you who are hearing these words today. The prophets spoke these words when the foundation was laid for the building of the Temple.ᵈ ¹⁰Before that time there was no money to hire men or animals. People could not safely come and go because of the enemies. I had turned everyone against his neighbor. ¹¹But I will not do to these people who are left alive what I did in the past," says the Lord of heaven's armies.

¹²"Their seeds will come up. Their grapevines will have fruit. The ground will give good crops. And the sky will send rain. I will give all this to those who are left alive. ¹³Judah and Israel, your names have been used as curses. But I will save you. And you will be a blessing. So don't be afraid. Be strong."

¹⁴This is what the Lord of heaven's armies says: "Your ancestors made me angry. So I planned to punish you. I had no mercy," says the Lord of heaven's armies. ¹⁵"But now I am planning to do good to Jerusalem and Judah. So don't be afraid. ¹⁶But do these things: Tell each other the truth. In the courts judge with truth and complete fairness. ¹⁷Do not make plans to hurt your neighbors. And don't make false promises. I hate all these things," says the Lord.

¹⁸The Lord of heaven's armies spoke his word to me again. ¹⁹This is what the Lord of heaven's armies says: "You have special days when you give up eating. These days are in the fourth, fifth, seventh and tenth months. Those days will become good, joyful, happy feasts in Judah. But you must love truth and peace."

²⁰This is what the Lord of heaven's armies says: "Many people from many cities will still come to Jerusalem. ²¹People from one city will say to those from another city, 'We are going to pray to the Lord. We want to ask the Lord of heaven's armies for help. Come and go with us.' ²²Many people and powerful nations will come to Jerusalem. They will worship the Lord of heaven's armies. They will pray to the Lord."

²³This is what the Lord of heaven's armies says: "At that time, ten men from different countries with different languages will come. They will take hold of one Jew by his coat. They will say to him, 'Let us go with you. We have heard that God is with you.'"

Punishment on Israel's Enemies

9 This message is the word of the Lord.

The message is against the land of Hadrach.
  And it is against the city of Damascus.
The tribesᵈ of Israel and all people belong to the Lord.
  ²The Lord's message is also against the city of Hamath, which is on the border of the land of Hadrach.

The Lord's message is against
Tyre and Sidon, with their
skill.
3Tyre has built a strong, walled city.
The people have piled up silver
like dust.
They have as much gold as mud in
the streets.
4But the Lord will take away all
she has.
He will destroy her power on
the sea.
That city will be destroyed by fire.
5The city of Ashkelon will see it and
be afraid.
The people of Gaza will shake
with fear.
And the people of Ekron will
lose hope.
No king will be left in Gaza.
And no one will live in Ashkelon
anymore.
6Foreigners will live in Ashdod.
And I will destroy the pride of
the Philistines.
7I will stop them from drinking
blood.
They will not eat any other
forbidden food.
Those left alive will belong to God.
They will be leaders in Judah.
And Ekron will become part of my
people like the Jebusites.
8I will protect my Temple*d*
from armies who come and go.
No one will hurt my people again
because now I am guarding it.

The King Is Coming

9Rejoice, people of Jerusalem.
Shout for joy, people of Jerusalem.
Your king is coming to you.
He does what is right, and he
saves.
He is gentle and riding on a
donkey.
He is on the colt of a donkey.
10I will take away the chariots from
Ephraim
and the horses from Jerusalem.
The bows used in war will be
broken.

The king will talk to the nations
about peace.
His kingdom will go from sea to
sea,
and from the Euphrates River to
the ends of the earth.
11My people, I made an agreement
with you
and sealed it with the blood of
sacrifices.
Because of this, I will set your
prisoners free from captivity,
which is like a dry pit.
12You prisoners who have hope,
return to your place of safety.
Today I am telling you
that I will give you back twice as
much as before.
13I will use Judah like a bow.
And Ephraim will be like the
arrows.
Jerusalem, I will use your men
to fight the men of Greece.
I will make you like the sword
of a warrior.
14Then the Lord will appear to them.
He will shoot his arrows like
lightning.
The Lord God will blow the
trumpet.
And he will march in the storms
of the south.
15The Lord of heaven's armies will
protect them.
They will destroy the enemy with
slingshots.
They will drink and shout like
drunk men.
They will be filled like a bowl
used for sprinkling blood at the
corners of the altar.
16On that day the Lord their God will
save them
as if his people were sheep.
They will shine in his land
like jewels in a crown.
17They will be so pretty and beautiful.
The young men will grow strong
on the grain.
And the young women will grow
strong on new wine.

The Lord's Promises

10 Ask the Lord for rain in the springtime.
The Lord makes the clouds.
He sends the showers.
And he gives everyone green fields.
²Idols tell lies.
Fortune-tellers see false visions.
They tell about false dreams.
The comfort they give is worth nothing.
So the people are like lost sheep.
They are abused because there is no shepherd.

³The Lord says, "I am angry at my shepherds.
I will punish the leaders.
I, the Lord of heaven's armies, will care
for my flock, which is the people of Judah.
I will make them like my proud war horses.
⁴From Judah will come the cornerstone[d]
and the tent peg.
From him will come the battle bow.
From him will come every ruler.
⁵They will be like soldiers marching to battle through muddy streets.
The Lord is with them.
So they will fight and defeat the horsemen.

⁶"I will strengthen the people of Judah.
And I will save the people of Joseph.
I will bring them back because I care for them.
It will be as though I had never left them.
I am the Lord their God,
and I will answer their calls for help.
⁷The people of Ephraim will be strong like soldiers.

They will be glad as when they have drunk wine.
Their children will see it and rejoice.
They will be happy in the Lord.
⁸I will call my people
and gather them together.
I will save them.
And there will be as many of them as there used to be.
⁹I have scattered them among the nations.
But in those faraway places, they will remember me.
They and their children will live and return.
¹⁰I will bring them back from Egypt.
I will gather them from Assyria.
I will bring them to Gilead and Lebanon.
There won't be enough room in the land for them all.
¹¹They will come through their sea of trouble.
The waves of the sea will be calm.
And the Nile River will dry up.
I will defeat Assyria's pride.
I will destroy Egypt's power over other countries.
¹²I will make my people strong.
And they will live as I say," says the Lord.

11 Lebanon, open your gates
so fire may burn your cedar trees."[n]
²Cry, pine trees, because the cedar has fallen.
The tall trees are ruined.
Cry, oaks in Bashan,
because the mighty forest has been cut down.
³Listen to the shepherds crying.
Their rich pastures are destroyed.
Listen to the lions roaring.
The thick bushes near the Jordan River are ruined.

⁴This is what the Lord my God says: "Feed the sheep that are about to be killed. ⁵Their buyers kill them and are not punished. Those who sell them say,

---

[n]**trees** In this poem, trees, bushes and animals stand for leaders of countries around Judah.

'Praise the Lord. I am rich.' Even the shepherds don't feel sorry for their sheep. ⁶Even I don't feel sorry anymore for the people of this country," says the Lord. "I will let everyone be under the power of his neighbor and king. They will bring trouble to the country. And I will not stop them."

⁷So I fed the sheep about to be killed, particularly the weakest ones. Then I took two sticks. I called one Favor. I called the other Union. And I fed the sheep. ⁸In one month I got rid of three shepherds. The flock hated me, and I got impatient with them. ⁹I said, "I will no longer take care of you like a shepherd. Let those that are dying die. Let those that are to be destroyed be destroyed. Let those that are left eat each other."

¹⁰Then I broke the stick named Favor. This broke the agreement God made with his people. ¹¹That day it was broken. Those weak sheep were watching me. They knew this message was from the Lord.

¹²Then I said, "If you want to pay me, then pay me. If not, then don't." So they paid me 30 pieces of silver.

¹³The Lord said to me, "Throw the money to the potter." That is how little they thought I was worth.ⁿ So I threw the money to the potter in the Templeᵈ of the Lord.

¹⁴Then I broke the second stick named Union. This broke the tie between Judah and Israel.

¹⁵Then the Lord said to me, "Become a foolish shepherd again. ¹⁶I am going to get a new shepherd for the country. He will not care for the dying sheep. He will not look for the young ones. He will not heal the injured ones. He will not feed the healthy. But he will eat the best sheep and tear off their hoofs.

¹⁷"How terrible it will be for the
    useless shepherd.
He abandoned the flock.
May war destroy his power and
    wisdom.

May his power become useless.
May his wisdom be taken away."

Jerusalem Will Be Saved

12 This message is the word of the Lord to Israel. The Lord stretched out the skies. He laid the foundations of the earth. He put man's spirit in him. And the Lord says this: ²"I will make Jerusalem like a cup of poison to the nations around her. They will come and attack Jerusalem and Judah. ³One day all the nations on earth will come together to attack Jerusalem. But I will make Jerusalem like a heavy rock. Anyone who tries to move it will get hurt. ⁴At that time I will scare every horse. And its rider will panic," says the Lord. "I will watch over Judah. But I will blind all the horses of the enemies. ⁵Then the leaders of Judah will say to themselves, 'The people of Jerusalem are strong. This is because the Lord of heaven's armies is their God.'

⁶"At that time I will make the leaders of Judah like a fire burning a stack of wood. They will be like a fire burning straw. They will destroy all the people around them left and right. But Jerusalem will remain safe.

⁷"The Lord will save the people of Judah first. Then the people in Jerusalem, David's city, won't have more honor than Judah. ⁸At that time the Lord will protect the people in Jerusalem. Then even the weakest of them will be strong like David. And the family of David will be like God. They will be like an angel of the Lord leading the people. ⁹At that time I will go to destroy all the nations that attack Jerusalem.

Crying for the One They Stabbed

¹⁰"I will give David's family and people in Jerusalem a spirit of kindness and mercy. They will look at me, the one they have stabbed. And they will cry like someone crying over the death of an only child. They will be as sad as someone who has lost a firstbornᵈ son. ¹¹At that time there will be much crying

in Jerusalem. It will be like the crying for Hadad Rimmon in the plain of Megiddo. ¹²The land will cry. Each family will cry alone. The family of David and their wives will cry. The family of Nathan and their wives will cry. ¹³The family of Levi and their wives will cry. The family of Shimei and their wives will cry. ¹⁴And all the rest of the families and their wives will cry.

13 "At that time a fountain will be opened. It will be for David's descendants[d] and for the people of Jerusalem. It will cleanse them of their sins and wrongs."

²The Lord of heaven's armies says, "At that time I will get rid of the names of the idols from the land. No one will remember them anymore. I will also remove the prophets[d] and unclean[d] spirits. ³A person might continue to prophesy. If he does, his own father and mother will tell him, 'You have told lies using the Lord's name. So you must die.' When he prophesies, his own parents should stab him.

⁴"At that time the prophets will be ashamed of their visions and prophecies. They won't wear the prophet's clothes made of hair to trick people. ⁵They will say, 'I am not a prophet. I am a farmer. I have been a farmer since I was young.' ⁶But someone will ask, 'What are the deep cuts on your body?' And he will answer, 'I was hurt at my friend's house.'

The Shepherd Is Killed

⁷"Sword, hit the shepherd.
  Attack the man who is my friend,"
  says the Lord of heaven's armies.
"Kill the shepherd,
  and the sheep will scatter.
  I will punish the little ones."
⁸The Lord says, "Two-thirds of the people
  through all the land will die.
  And one-third will be left.
⁹I will test the ones left with fire.
  I will purify them like silver.
  I will test them like gold.
  Then they will call on me.

And I will answer them.
I will say, 'You are my people.'
  And they will say, 'The Lord is our
    God.'"

The Day of Punishment

14 The Lord's day of judging is coming. The wealth you have taken will be divided among you.

²I will bring all the nations together to fight Jerusalem. They will capture the city and rob the houses. The women will be attacked. Half the people will be taken away as captives. But the rest won't be taken from the city.

³Then the Lord will go to war against those nations. He will fight as in a day of battle. ⁴On that day he will stand on the Mount of Olives,[d] east of Jerusalem. The Mount of Olives will split in two. A deep valley will run east and west. Half the mountain will move north. And half will move south. ⁵You will run through this mountain valley to the other side. You will run as you ran from the earthquake. That was when Uzziah was king of Judah. Then the Lord my God will come. And all the holy ones will be with him.

⁶On that day there will be no light, cold or frost. ⁷There will be no other day like it. The Lord knows when it will come. There will be no day or night. Even at evening it will still be light.

⁸At that time fresh water will flow from Jerusalem. Half of it will flow east to the Dead Sea.[d] And half of it will flow west to the Mediterranean Sea. It will flow summer and winter.

⁹Then the Lord will be king over the whole world. At that time there will be only one Lord. And his name will be the only name.

¹⁰All the land south of Jerusalem from Geba to Rimmon will be turned into a plain. Jerusalem will be raised up. But it will stay in the same place. The city will reach from the Benjamin Gate to the First Gate to the Corner Gate. It will go from the Tower of Hananel to the king's winepresses.[d] ¹¹People will live there. It will never be

destroyed again. Jerusalem will be safe. [12]But the Lord will punish the nations that fought against Jerusalem. He will bring a terrible disease on them. Their flesh will rot away while they are still standing up. Their eyes will rot in their sockets. And their tongues will rot in their mouths. [13]At that time the Lord will cause panic. Everybody will grab his neighbor. They will attack each other. [14]The people of Judah will fight in Jerusalem. And the wealth of the nations around them will be collected. There will be much gold, silver and clothes. [15]A similar disease will strike the horses, mules, camels and donkeys. All the animals in the camps will have the disease.

[16]Some of the people who came to fight Jerusalem will be left alive. They will come back to Jerusalem year after year. They will come to worship the King, the Lord of heaven's armies. They will celebrate the Feast[d] of Shelters. [17]Some people from the nations might not go to Jerusalem. They might not worship the King, the Lord of heaven's armies. Then rain will not fall on their land. [18]The Egyptians might not go to Jerusalem. They might not celebrate the Feast of Shelters. Then the Lord will send them the same terrible disease the other nations got. [19]This will be the punishment. It will be for Egypt and any nation which does not go to celebrate the Feast of Shelters.

[20]At that time the horses' bells will have written on them: Holy to the Lord. The cooking pots in the Temple[d] of the Lord will be like the holy altar bowls. [21]Every pot in Jerusalem and Judah will be holy to the Lord of heaven's armies. And everyone who offers sacrifices will be able to cook in them. At that time there will not be any traders in the Temple of the Lord of heaven's armies.

Animals in the Bible
CAMELS · ZECHARIAH 14:15

Have you ever been in a hot desert? Did you get thirsty? People cannot go very long without water, but a camel can. Camels can live up to four days without drinking. They have their own built-in water tank. Their three stomachs can hold many gallons of water each. When camels are thirsty, they can drink up to twenty-five gallons of water in ten minutes. The people in the Bible times did not have cars or trucks. They used camels for transportation and to carry things. Camels are very dependable helpers. God wants us to be dependable helpers too.

To find out about the animal who teaches us not to worry, fly to page 1135.

MALACHI

God Tells Israel to Be Loyal

1 This message is the word of the Lord. It is given to Israel through Malachi.

God Loves Israel

²The Lord said, "I love you."

But you ask, "How have you loved us?"

The Lord said, "Esau and Jacob were brothers. I loved Jacob, ³but I hated Esau. I destroyed his mountain country. I left his land to the wild dogs of the desert."

⁴The people of Edom might say, "We were destroyed. But we will go back and rebuild the ruins."

But the Lord of heaven's armies says, "If they rebuild them, I will destroy them. People will say, 'Edom is the Wicked Country. The Lord is always angry with the Edomites.' ⁵You will see these things with your own eyes. You will say, 'The Lord is great, even outside the borders of Israel!'"

The Priests Don't Respect God

⁶The Lord of heaven's armies says, "A child honors his father. A servant honors his master. I am a father. So why don't you honor me? I am a master. So why don't you respect me? You priests do not respect me.

"But you ask, 'How have we shown you disrespect?'

⁷"You have shown it by bringing unclean_d_ sacrifices to my altar.

"But you ask, 'What makes them unclean?'

"They are unclean because you don't show respect for my altar. ⁸You bring blind animals as sacrifices, and that is wrong. You bring crippled and sick animals. That is wrong. Try giving them to your governor. Would he be pleased with you? He wouldn't accept you," says the Lord of heaven's armies.

⁹"Now ask God to be kind to you. But he won't accept you with such offerings," says the Lord of heaven's armies. ¹⁰"I wish one of you would close the Temple_d_ doors. Then you would not light useless fires on my altar! I am not pleased with you. I will not accept your gifts," says the Lord of heaven's armies. ¹¹"From the east to the west I will be honored among the nations. Everywhere they will bring incense_d_ and clean offerings to me. I will be honored among the nations," says the Lord of heaven's armies. ¹²"But you don't honor me. You say about the Lord's altar, 'It is unclean. The food has no worth.' ¹³You say, 'We are tired of doing this.' And you sniff at it in disgust," says the Lord of heaven's armies.

"And you bring hurt, crippled and sick animals. You bring them as gifts. But I won't accept them from you," says the Lord. ¹⁴"The cheat will be cursed. He has an animal in his flock. He promises to offer it. But then he offers me an animal that has something wrong with it. I am a great king," says the Lord of heaven's armies. "I am feared by all the nations.

Rules for Priests

2 "Priests, this command is for you. ²Listen to me. Pay attention to what I say. Honor my name," says the Lord of heaven's armies. "If you don't, I will send a curse on you. I will curse your blessings. I have already cursed them because you don't pay attention to what I say.

³"I will punish your descendants.ᵈ I will smear your faces with the garbage from your feasts. And you will be thrown away with it. ⁴Then you will know why I am giving you this command. It is so that my agreement with Levi will continue," says the Lord of heaven's armies. ⁵"My agreement for priests was with the tribeᵈ of Levi. I promised them life and peace. And I gave these to them so they would honor me. They did honor me and fear me. ⁶They taught the true teachings. They spoke no lies. With peace and honesty they did what I said they should do. They kept many people from sinning.

⁷"A priest should teach what he knows. People should learn the teachings from him because he is the messenger of the Lord of heaven's armies. ⁸But you priests have stopped obeying me. With your teachings you have caused many people to do wrong. You have broken the agreement with the tribeᵈ of Levi!" says the Lord of heaven's armies. ⁹"You have not been careful to do what I say. You take sides in court cases. So I have caused you to be hated and disgraced in front of everybody."

Judah Was Not Loyal to God

¹⁰We all have the same father. The same God made us. So why do people break their promises to each other? They don't respect the agreement that our ancestors made with God. ¹¹The people of Judah have broken their promises. They have done something God hates in Israel and Jerusalem. The people of Judah did not respect the Templeᵈ that the Lord loves. The men of Judah married the women who worship foreign gods. ¹²The man who does this might bring offerings to the Lord of heaven's armies. But the Lord will still separate him from the community of Israel.

¹³This is another thing you do. You cover the Lord's altar with your tears. You cry and moan because the Lord does not accept your offerings. He is not pleased with what you bring. ¹⁴You ask, "Why?" It is because the Lord sees how you treated the wife you married when you were young. You broke your promise with her. She was your partner. You promised yourself to her. ¹⁵God made husbands and wives to become one body and one spirit for his purpose. This is so they would have children who are true to God. So be careful. Do not break your promise with the wife you married when you were young.

¹⁶The Lord God of Israel says, "I hate divorce. And I hate people who do cruel things as easily as they put on clothes," says the Lord of heaven's armies. So be careful. And do not break your trust.

The Special Day of Judging

¹⁷You have tired the Lord with what you say.

You ask, "How have we tired him?"

You did it by saying, "God thinks anyone who does evil is good. And he is pleased with them." Or you asked, "Where is the God who is fair?"

3 The Lord of heaven's armies says, "I will send my messenger. He will prepare the way for me to come. Suddenly, the Lord you are looking for will come to his Temple.ᵈ The messenger of the agreement, whom you want, will come." ²No one can live through that time. No one can survive when he comes. He will be like a purifying fire. He will be like laundry soap. ³He will be like someone who heats and purifies silver. He will purify the Levites. He will make them pure like gold and silver. Then they will bring offerings to the Lord in the right way. ⁴And he will accept the offerings from Judah and Jerusalem. It will be as it was in the past. ⁵The Lord of heaven's armies says, "Then I will come to you and judge you. I will testify against those who take part in evil magic, adulteryᵈ and lying. I will testify against those who cheat workers of their pay and who cheat widows and orphans. And I will testify against those who are unfair to foreigners. These people do not respect me.

Stealing from God

6"I am the Lord. I do not change. So you descendants*d* of Jacob have not been destroyed. 7Like your ancestors before you, you have disobeyed my rules. You have not kept them. Return to me. Then I will return to you," says the Lord of heaven's armies.

"But you ask, 'How can we return?'

8"Should a man rob God? But you rob me.

"You ask, 'How have we robbed you?'

"You have robbed me in your offerings and the tenth of your crops. 9So a curse is on you because the whole nation has robbed me. 10Bring to the storehouse a tenth of what you gain. Then there will be food in my house. Test me in this," says the Lord of heaven's armies. "I will open the windows of heaven for you. I will pour out more blessings than you have room for. 11I will stop the insects so they won't eat your crops. The grapes won't fall from your vines before they are ready to pick," says the Lord of heaven's armies. 12"All the nations will call you blessed. You will have a pleasant country," says the Lord of heaven's armies.

The Lord's Promise of Mercy

13The Lord says, "You have said terrible things about me.

"But you ask, 'What have we said about you?'

14"You have said, 'It is useless to serve God. It did no good to obey his laws. And it did no good to show the Lord of heaven's armies that we are sorry for what we did. 15So we say that proud people are happy. Evil people succeed. They challenge God and get away with it.'"

16Then those who honored the Lord spoke with each other. The Lord listened and heard them. The names of those who honored the Lord and respected him were written in a book. The Lord will remember them.

17The Lord of heaven's armies says, "They belong to me. On that day they will be my very own. A father shows mercy to his son who serves him. In the same way I will show mercy to my people. 18You will again see the difference between good and evil people. You will see the difference between those who serve God and those who don't.

The Day of the Lord's Judging

4 "There is a day coming that will be like a hot furnace. All the proud and evil people will be like straw. On that day they will be completely burned up. Not a root or branch will be left," says the Lord of heaven's armies. 2"But for you who honor me, goodness will shine on you like the sun. There will be healing in its rays. You will jump around, like calves freed from their stalls. 3Then you will crush the wicked. They will be like ashes under your feet. I will do this on that day," says the Lord of heaven's armies.

4"Remember the teaching of Moses my servant. I gave those laws and rules to him at Mount Sinai. They are for all the Israelites.

5"But I will send Elijah the prophet*d* to you. He will come before that great and terrible day of the Lord's judging. 6Elijah will help fathers love their children. And he will help the children love their fathers. Otherwise, I will come and put a curse on the land."

NEW TESTAMENT

MATTHEW

Matthew Tells the Jews About Jesus

"Just for the fun of it, how many names do you recognize among the ancestors of Jesus? Read over Matthew 1:1-17."

The Family History of Jesus

1 This is the family history of Jesus Christ. He came from the family of David. David came from the family of Abraham.

[2] Abraham was the father[n] of Isaac. Isaac was the father of Jacob. Jacob was the father of Judah and his brothers.

[3] Judah was the father of Perez and Zerah.

(Their mother was Tamar.)

Perez was the father of Hezron. Hezron was the father of Ram.

[4] Ram was the father of Amminadab. Amminadab was the father of Nahshon.

Nahshon was the father of Salmon.

[5] Salmon was the father of Boaz.

(Boaz's mother was Rahab.)

Boaz was the father of Obed.

(Obed's mother was Ruth.)

Salvation
MATTHEW 1:18-25

Did you know that Jesus' name tells us about what he did for us? We read earlier that Isaiah predicted the birth of a child named *Immanuel*, which means "God with us." Over 700 years later, at a stable in Bethlehem, Joseph named God's son *Jesus*, which means "salvation." Matthew put these two events together because God told him to and because our *salvation* depends on *God* being *with us.*

Many people will tell you that education, money, hard work, or something else is the most important thing in life. These things are good, but they cannot save a person from sin. Only God can do that. The good news is that God has come to us. He is Jesus of Nazareth, who was born to Joseph and Mary. *God is with us*—he was born in a manger in Bethlehem.

Aren't you glad Jesus came as our savior?

To learn more about salvation, zoom to page 1277.

---

[n]**father** "Father" in Jewish lists of ancestors can sometimes mean grandfather or more distant relative.

Obed was the father of Jesse.
⁶Jesse was the father of King David.
David was the father of Solomon.
  (Solomon's mother had been
    Uriah's wife.)
⁷Solomon was the father of
  Rehoboam.
Rehoboam was the father of Abijah.
Abijah was the father of Asa.

Abiud was the father of Eliakim.
Eliakim was the father of Azor.
¹⁴Azor was the father of Zadok.
Zadok was the father of Akim.
Akim was the father of Eliud.
¹⁵Eliud was the father of Eleazar.
Eleazar was the father of Matthan.
Matthan was the father of Jacob.
¹⁶Jacob was the father of Joseph.
Joseph was the husband of Mary,
and Mary was the mother of Jesus.
Jesus is called the Christ.ᵈ

Visiting Angels

MATTHEW 1:20-21

Sometimes angels give guidance from God. Joseph didn't know what to do. He was supposed to get married to Mary, but she had just told him that she was going to have a baby. It was difficult for Joseph to believe Mary's story about an angel visiting her and telling her that she would have a special baby, God's Son. So Joseph decided not to marry her. But then an angel came while Joseph was sleeping. The angel told Joseph in a dream that Mary was telling the truth and that he should marry her. So Joseph obeyed. He took care of Mary when Jesus was born, and he was Jesus' father on earth while Jesus was growing up.

To read about an angel who told about a baby's birth,
fly to page 1217.

⁸Asa was the father of Jehoshaphat.
Jehoshaphat was the father of
  Jehoram.
Jehoram was the ancestor of Uzziah.
⁹Uzziah was the father of Jotham.
Jotham was the father of Ahaz.
Ahaz was the father of Hezekiah.
¹⁰Hezekiah was the father of
  Manasseh.
Manasseh was the father of Amon.
Amon was the father of Josiah.
¹¹Josiah was the grandfather of
  Jehoiachin and his brothers.
  (This was at the time that the
    people were taken to Babylon.)
¹²After they were taken to Babylon:
Jehoiachin was the father of Shealtiel.
Shealtiel was the grandfather of
  Zerubbabel.
¹³Zerubbabel was the father of Abiud.

¹⁷So there were 14 generations from Abraham to David. And there were 14 generations from David until the time when the people were taken to Babylon. And there were 14 generations from the time when the people were taken to Babylon until Christ was born.

The Birth of Jesus Christ

¹⁸The mother of Jesus Christ was Mary. And this is how the birth of Jesus came about. Mary was engaged to marry Joseph. But before they married, she learned that she was going to have a baby. She was pregnant by the power of the Holy Spirit.ᵈ ¹⁹Mary's husband, Joseph, was a good man. He did not want to disgrace her in public, so he planned to divorce her secretly. ²⁰While Joseph thought about this,

an angel of the Lord came to him in a dream. The angel said, "Joseph, descendant[d] of David, don't be afraid to take Mary as your wife. The baby in her is from the Holy Spirit. [21]She will give birth to a son. You will name the son Jesus.[n] Give him that name because he will save his people from their sins."

[22]All this happened to make clear the full meaning of what the Lord had said through the prophet:[d] [23]"The virgin[d] will be pregnant. She will have a son, and they will name him Immanuel."[n] This name means "God is with us."

[24]When Joseph woke up, he did what the Lord's angel had told him to do. Joseph married Mary. [25]But he did not have sexual relations with her until she gave birth to the son. And Joseph named the son Jesus.

Wise Men Come to Visit Jesus

2 Jesus was born in the town of Bethlehem in Judea during the time when Herod was king. After Jesus was born, some wise men from the

"**W**hat would *you* have brought as a gift to honor Jesus' birth? Why were the first Christmas gifts given? Read Matthew 2:1-12."

east came to Jerusalem. [2]They asked, "Where is the baby who was born to be the king of the Jews? We saw his star in the east. We came to worship him."

[3]When King Herod heard about this new king of the Jews, he was troubled. And all the people in Jerusalem were worried too. [4]Herod called a meeting of all the leading priests and teachers of the law. He asked them where the Christ[d] would be born. [5]They answered, "In the town of Bethlehem in Judea. The prophet[d] wrote about this in the Scriptures:[d]

[6]'But you, Bethlehem, in the land of Judah,
    you are important among the rulers of Judah.

Amazing Events That Showed God's Power

MATTHEW 2:1-2

Did you ever try to count the stars? God made so many stars that we can't count them all.

Once there was a very important star. Some men who lived thousands of miles east of the country where Jesus was born saw a super bright star in the sky. These men were called wise men. They were sort of like astronomers (people who study stars). When they saw the star, they knew it meant something important. So they loaded food and supplies on their donkeys and set out on a long journey to follow the star. The star led them to the baby Jesus.

Even these men from thousands of miles away came to worship baby Jesus! God wants everyone to worship him.

To find how God showed his power over a plant, fly to page 1204.

[n]**Jesus** The name Jesus means "salvation."
[n]**"The virgin . . . Immanuel."** Quotation from Isaiah 7:14.

A ruler will come from you.
He will be like a shepherd for my
    people, the Israelites.'"

Micah 5:2

⁷Then Herod had a secret meeting with the wise men from the east. He learned from them the exact time they first saw the star. ⁸Then Herod sent the wise men to Bethlehem. He said to them, "Go and look carefully to find the child. When you find him, come tell me. Then I can go worship him too."

⁹The wise men heard the king and then left. They saw the same star they had seen in the east. It went before them until it stopped above the place where the child was. ¹⁰When the wise men saw the star, they were filled with joy. ¹¹They went to the house where the child was and saw him with his mother, Mary. They bowed down and worshiped the child. They opened the gifts they brought for him. They gave him treasures of gold, frankincense,[d] and myrrh.[d] ¹²But God warned the wise men in a dream not to go back to Herod. So they went home to their own country by a different way.

Jesus' Parents Take Him to Egypt

¹³After they left, an angel of the Lord came to Joseph in a dream. The angel said, "Get up! Take the child and his mother and escape to Egypt. Herod will start looking for the child to kill him. Stay in Egypt until I tell you to return."

¹⁴So Joseph got up and left for Egypt during the night with the child and his mother. ¹⁵Joseph stayed in Egypt until Herod died. This was to make clear the full meaning of what the Lord had said through the prophet.[d] The Lord said, "I called my son out of Egypt."[n]

Herod Kills the Baby Boys

¹⁶When Herod saw that the wise men had tricked him, he was very angry. So he gave an order to kill all the baby boys in Bethlehem and in all the area around Bethlehem who were two years old or younger. This was in keeping with the time he learned from the wise men. ¹⁷So what God had said through the prophet[d] Jeremiah came true:

¹⁸"A sound was heard in Ramah.
  It was painful crying and much
    sadness.
Rachel cries for her children,
  and she cannot be comforted,
  because her children are dead."

Jeremiah 31:15

Joseph and Mary Return

¹⁹After Herod died, an angel of the Lord came to Joseph in a dream. This happened while Joseph was in Egypt. ²⁰The angel said, "Get up! Take the child and his mother and go to Israel. The people who were trying to kill the child are now dead."

²¹So Joseph took the child and his mother and went to Israel. ²²But he heard that Archelaus was now king in Judea. Archelaus became king when his father Herod died. So Joseph was afraid to go there. After being warned in a dream, he went to the area of Galilee. ²³He went to a town called Nazareth and lived there. And so what God had said through the prophets[d] came true: "He will be called a Nazarene."[n]

The Work of John the Baptist

3 About that time John the Baptist[d] came and began preaching in the desert area of Judea. ²John said, "Change your hearts and lives because the kingdom of heaven is coming soon." ³John the Baptist is the one Isaiah the prophet[d] was talking about. Isaiah said:

"This is a voice of a man
  who calls out in the desert:
'Prepare the way for the Lord.
  Make the road straight for him.'"

Isaiah 40:3

⁴John's clothes were made from camel's hair. He wore a leather belt around his waist. For food, he ate locusts[d] and wild honey. ⁵Many people

---

[n]**"I called . . . Egypt."** Quotation from Hosea 11:1.
[n]**Nazarene** A person from the city of Nazareth, a name probably meaning "branch" (see Isaiah 11:1).

went to hear John preach. They came from Jerusalem and all Judea and all the area around the Jordan River. [6]They told of the sins they had done, and John baptized them in the Jordan River.

[7]Many of the Pharisees[d] and Sadducees[d] came to the place where John was baptizing people. When John saw

Every tree that does not produce good fruit will be cut down and thrown into the fire.[n]

[11]"I baptize you with water to show that your hearts and lives have changed. But there is one coming later who is greater than I am. I am not good enough to carry his sandals. He will baptize you with the Holy Spirit[d] and with fire. [12]He will come ready to clean the grain. He will separate the good grain from the chaff.[d] He will put the good part of the grain into his barn. And he will burn

Plans That Backfired
HEROD THE GREAT • MATTHEW 3

Even though Herod was the king, he was afraid someone might come along and try to steal his power. He did anything he could to keep that from happening. He even had some of his own children and one of his wives killed.

When Herod heard there was a new king born in Bethlehem, he wanted to get rid of him, too. This new king was Jesus. First, Herod pretended to want to find the baby king so he could worship him. But Herod really planned to kill him. Two years or so passed and Herod had not yet found the baby, so he ordered all the baby boys in the area two years old and younger to be killed.

However, God made sure Jesus and his family escaped the awful plans of Herod. Sometimes evil people seem to be very powerful. We should be encouraged to know that God is always more powerful.

To meet one of Jesus' friends that turned out to be a bad friend,
fly to page 1209.

them, he said: "You are all snakes! Who warned you to run away from God's anger that is coming? [8]You must do the things that show that you have really changed your hearts and lives. [9]And don't think that you can say to yourselves, 'Abraham is our father.' I tell you that God could make children for Abraham from these rocks. [10]The ax is now ready to cut down the trees.

the chaff with a fire that cannot be put out."[n]

Jesus Is Baptized by John

[13]At that time Jesus came from Galilee to the Jordan River. He came to John and wanted John to baptize him. [14]But John tried to stop him. John said, "Why do you come to me to be baptized? I should be baptized by you!"

---

[n]**The ax . . . fire.**   This means that God is ready to punish his people who do not obey him.
[n]**He will . . . out.**   This means that Jesus will come to separate the good people from the bad people, saving the good and punishing the bad.

¹⁵Jesus answered, "Let it be this way for now. We should do all things that are right." So John agreed to baptize Jesus.

¹⁶Jesus was baptized and came up out of the water. Heaven opened, and he saw God's Spirit[d] coming down on him like a dove. ¹⁷And a voice spoke from heaven. The voice said, "This is my Son and I love him. I am very pleased with him."

The Temptation of Jesus

4 Then the Spirit[d] led Jesus into the desert to be tempted by the devil. ²Jesus ate nothing for 40 days and nights. After this, he was very hungry. ³The devil came to Jesus to tempt him. The devil said, "If you are the Son of God, tell these rocks to become bread."

⁴Jesus answered, "It is written in the Scriptures,[d] 'A person does not live only by eating bread. But a person lives by everything the Lord says.'"[n]

⁵Then the devil led Jesus to the holy city of Jerusalem. He put Jesus on a very high place of the Temple.[d] ⁶The devil said, "If you are the Son of God, jump off. It is written in the Scriptures,

'He has put his angels in charge of
    you.
They will catch you with their hands.
And you will not hit your foot on a
    rock.'"   *Psalm 91:11-12*

⁷Jesus answered him, "It also says in the Scriptures, 'Do not test the Lord your God.'"[n]

⁸Then the devil led Jesus to the top of a very high mountain. He showed Jesus all the kingdoms of the world and all the great things that are in those kingdoms. ⁹The devil said, "If you will bow down and worship me, I will give you all these things."

¹⁰Jesus said to the devil, "Go away from me, Satan! It is written in the Scriptures, 'You must worship the Lord your God. Serve only him!'"[n]

¹¹So the devil left Jesus. And then some angels came to Jesus and helped him.

Jesus Begins Work in Galilee

¹²Jesus heard that John had been put in prison. So Jesus went back to Galilee. ¹³He left Nazareth and went and lived in Capernaum, a town near Lake Galilee. Capernaum is in the area near Zebulun and Naphtali. ¹⁴Jesus did this to make true what the prophet[d] Isaiah said:

Jobs in the Bible

FISHERMAN • MATTHEW 4:18

Fishing was an important business in Bible times because many people ate fish. In northern Israel, around the Sea of Galilee, there were about thirty fishing villages that supplied fish for markets all over the country. Fishing was usually done with nets from boats that were sailed out onto the lake. Peter and Andrew were brothers who were fishermen. They were in business with James and John, brothers who were also fishermen. Although their business was going very well, they willingly left it when Jesus called them to "fish for people," to tell people the good news of Jesus Christ.

To read about people most disliked because of their job,
fly to page 1184.

---

[n]'A person . . . says.'   Quotation from Deuteronomy 8:3.
[n]'Do . . . God.'   Quotation from Deuteronomy 6:16.
[n]'You . . . him!'   Quotation from Deuteronomy 6:13.

15"Land of Zebulun and land of Naphtali
are on the way to the sea.
They are along the Jordan River.
This is Galilee where the non-
Jewish people live.
16These people who live in darkness
will see a great light.
They live in a place that is very dark.
But a light will shine on them."

Isaiah 9:1-2

Jesus Chooses Some Followers

17From that time Jesus began to preach, saying, "Change your hearts and lives, because the kingdom of heaven is coming soon."

18Jesus was walking by Lake Galilee. He saw two brothers, Simon (called Peter) and Simon's brother Andrew. The brothers were fishermen, and they were fishing in the lake with a net. 19Jesus said, "Come follow me. I will make you fishermen for men." 20At once Simon and Andrew left their nets and followed him.

21Jesus continued walking by Lake Galilee. He saw two other brothers, James and John, the sons of Zebedee. They were in a boat with their father Zebedee, preparing their nets to catch fish. Jesus told them to come with him. 22At once they left the boat and their father, and they followed Jesus.

Jesus Teaches and Heals People

23Jesus went everywhere in Galilee. He taught in the synagogues*d* and preached the Good News*d* about the kingdom of heaven. And he healed all the people's diseases and sicknesses. 24The news about Jesus spread all over Syria, and people brought all the sick to him. These sick people were suffering from different kinds of diseases and pain. Some were suffering very great pain, some had demons,*d* some were epileptics,*n* and some were paralyzed. Jesus healed all of them. 25Many people

followed him. They came from Galilee, the Ten Towns,*n* Jerusalem, Judea, and the land across the Jordan River.

Jesus Teaches the People

5 Jesus saw the crowds who were there. He went up on a hill and sat down. His followers came to him. 2Jesus taught the people and said:
3"Those people who know they have
great spiritual needs are
happy.
The kingdom of heaven belongs to
them.
4Those who are sad now are happy.
God will comfort them.
5Those who are humble are happy.
The earth will belong to them.
6Those who want to do right more
than anything else are happy.
God will fully satisfy them.
7Those who give mercy to others are
happy.
Mercy will be given to them.
8Those who are pure in their thinking
are happy.
They will be with God.
9Those who work to bring peace are
happy.
God will call them his sons.
10Those who are treated badly for
doing good are happy.
The kingdom of heaven belongs to
them.
11"People will say bad things about you and hurt you. They will lie and say all kinds of evil things about you because you follow me. But when they do these things to you, you are happy. 12Rejoice and be glad. You have a great reward waiting for you in heaven. People did the same evil things to the prophets*d* who lived before you.

You Are like Salt and Light

13"You are the salt of the earth. But if the salt loses its salty taste, it cannot be made salty again. It is good for nothing.

---

*n***epileptics**   People with a disease that causes them sometimes to lose control of their bodies, and maybe faint, shake strongly, or not be able to move.
*n***Ten Towns**   In Greek, called "Decapolis." It was an area east of Lake Galilee that once had ten main towns.

Whit's Wisdom: The Beatitudes • Matthew 5

Maybe you've heard someone talk about the Beatitudes and wondered what they meant. The word sounds a little like "bad attitudes" but there's a big difference between beatitudes and bad attitudes. We saw a very clear example last week in my ice cream parlor, Whit's End.

Dylan and his friends were there having a soft drink after school. Dylan's younger sister, Jessie, walked in and spotted her brother. I could tell from behind the counter that Dylan wasn't pleased to see Jessie. But he ignored her until she tapped him on the shoulder.

"**D**ylan, could I borrow some money?" she asked. "I'm too thirsty to walk to the house for mine. I'll pay you back as soon as we get home."

Dylan turned to her with a smile and said, "Jessie, can't you see I'm busy? If I had a million dollars in my pocket I wouldn't lend you a dime."

Jessie's feelings were hurt. She also got mad. She started to walk away from her brother but turned around and took a deep breath, almost like she was going to blow fire at Dylan. Before I could do anything she almost yelled, "Dylan Taylor, you've really got a–a–beatitude!"

I caught up with her before she left and tried to calm her down. I told her she had certainly gotten her point across even if she hadn't used the right word to say it. I suggested we go back and talk to Dylan. You see, I know Dylan pretty well. Sometimes he's a mean big brother before he thinks about how much he's going to hurt his little sister.

When we walked up to the table again, Dylan was pulling some money out of his pocket. He said, "Sorry I was mean to you, Jess. Here's some money for a drink. And you don't have to pay me back, either. But what's a beatitude?"

Jessie looked at me, so I explained quickly that she had meant to say "bad attitude." Acutally, a beatitude is just the opposite of a bad attitude. I showed them Matthew 5:2-10 and explained that Jesus was telling us about the good attitudes (beatitudes) he wants us to have. Then I read each beatitude and asked them to tell me what kind of attitude Jesus was describing. We talked about things like being humble, wanting to do what is right, and being kind to others. I also asked them to tell me what the opposite, bad attitude would be like. You could learn a lot by doing the same thing right now.

Related Passages: Luke 6:20-36; James 1:19-27

Teacher/Parent Hint: Help the children with the suggested study. Guide them in discovering a description of each beatitude and its opposite bad attitude. Then encourage them to suggest ways they could put each beatitude into practice. Have children think in different settings: for instance, how would someone who "works to bring peace" (verse 9) act in school? How would someone who wants to be "pure in their thinking" (verse 8) watch television? etc.

Witnessing
MATTHEW 5:14-15

"Lights out!" Do you get frustrated when your parents say that? And they always seem to say it when you've reached the good part in a book. Did you ever try to finish the chapter with a flashlight under the covers?

You thought no one could see you, right?

Bad news. They can. It must be a funny sight for a parent to see a glowing mound of bed covers! You just can't hide light. It seeps through your fingers. It shows through the cracks. It even shines through you, when it's a heavenly sort of light.

Jesus said he is the Light of the World. He lives inside those who believe in him, and he shines out for all to see.

When people see that you are different, you can tell them that is because Jesus lives inside of you. Let your light shine onto everyone you meet.

To learn more about witnessing, zoom to page 1179.

It must be thrown out for people to walk on.

¹⁴"You are the light that gives light to the world. A city that is built on a hill cannot be hidden. ¹⁵And people don't hide a light under a bowl. They put the light on a lampstand. Then the light shines for all the people in the house. ¹⁶In the same way, you should be a light for other people. Live so that they will see the good things you do. Live so that they will praise your Father in heaven.

The Importance of the Law

¹⁷"Don't think that I have come to destroy the law of Moses or the teaching of the prophets.[d] I have not come to destroy their teachings but to do what they said. ¹⁸I tell you the truth. Nothing will disappear from the law until heaven and earth are gone. The law will not lose even the smallest letter or the smallest part of a letter until all has happened. ¹⁹Whoever refuses to obey any command and teaches other people not to

obey that command will be the least important in the kingdom of heaven. But whoever obeys the law and teaches other people to obey the law will be great in the kingdom of heaven. ²⁰I tell you that you must do better than the teachers of the law and the Pharisees.[d] If you are not better than they are, you will not enter the kingdom of heaven.

Jesus Teaches About Anger

²¹"You have heard that it was said to our people long ago, 'You must not murder anyone.[n] Anyone who murders another will be judged.' ²²But I tell you, if you are angry with your brother, you will be judged. And if you say bad things to your brother, you will be judged by the Jewish council. And if you call your brother a fool, then you will be in danger of the fire of hell.

²³"So when you offer your gift to God at the altar, and you remember that your brother has something against you, ²⁴leave your gift there at the altar. Go

[n]**You . . . anyone.** Quotation from Exodus 20:13; Deuteronomy 5:17.

The Bible
MATTHEW 5:18

Think of a special event that seems a long time away. It could be your birthday, Christmas, or summer vacation. When you're waiting, it seems to take forever to arrive. Now think of something even further away: college, marriage, having children, growing old and having grandchildren. For someone your age, it's almost impossible to think of events so far in the future.

Now, try to imagine this: long after you have lived and died, after your children and grandchildren have come and gone, after even heaven and earth have disappeared, the Bible—the word of God—will still be here. That's right—the words you read in the Bible will outlast everything else in the universe. These words of Jesus guarantee it.

When you read the Bible, you are looking at God's forever truths for his people. You can count on them for always.

To learn more about the Bible, zoom to page 1234.

and make peace with him. Then come and offer your gift.

25"If your enemy is taking you to court, become friends with him quickly. You should do that before you go to court. If you don't become his friend, he might turn you over to the judge. And the judge might give you to a guard to put you in jail. 26I tell you that you will not leave that jail until you have paid everything you owe.

Jesus Teaches About Sexual Sin

27"You have heard that it was said, 'You must not be guilty of adultery.'[n] 28But I tell you that if anyone looks at a woman and wants to sin sexually with her, then he has already done that sin with the woman in his mind. 29If your right eye causes you to sin, then take it out and throw it away. It is better to lose one part of your body than to have your whole body thrown into hell. 30If

your right hand causes you to sin, then cut it off and throw it away. It is better to lose one part of your body than for your whole body to go into hell.

Jesus Teaches About Divorce

31"It was also said, 'Anyone who divorces his wife must give her a written divorce paper.'[n] 32But I tell you that anyone who divorces his wife is causing his wife to be guilty of adultery.[d] The only reason for a man to divorce his wife is if she has sexual relations with another man. And anyone who marries that divorced woman is guilty of adultery.

Make Promises Carefully

33"You have heard that it was said to our people long ago, 'When you make a promise, don't break your promise. Keep the promises that you make to the Lord.'[n] 34But I tell you, never make an oath. Don't make an oath using the

[n]'You . . . adultery.' Quotation from Exodus 20:14; Deuteronomy 5:18.
[n]'Anyone . . . divorce paper.' Quotation from Deuteronomy 24:1.
[n]'When . . . Lord.' Quotation from Leviticus 19:12; Numbers 30:2; Deuteronomy 23:21.

name of heaven, because heaven is God's throne. [35]Don't make an oath using the name of the earth, because the earth belongs to God. Don't make an oath using the name of Jerusalem, because that is the city of the great King. [36]And don't even say that your own head is proof that you will keep your oath. You cannot make one hair on your head become white or black. [37]Say only 'yes' if you mean 'yes,' and say only 'no' if you mean 'no.' If you must say more than 'yes' or 'no,' it is from the Evil One.

miles. [42]If a person asks you for something, then give it to him. Don't refuse to give to a person who wants to borrow from you.

Love All People

[43]"You have heard that it was said, 'Love your neighbor[n] and hate your enemies.' [44]But I tell you, love your enemies. Pray for those who hurt you. [45]If you do this, then you will be true sons of your Father in heaven. Your Father causes

Sin
MATTHEW 5:21-22, 27-28

One time a little girl was taking her first airplane trip with her parents. She was very excited, and she climbed in and out of her seat and ran up and down the aisles of the plane. Her father got upset with her. He put her in her seat, fastened the seat belt, and told her she had better stay there. After a few minutes he noticed that she was sitting still as he had told her, but with a funny smile on her face.

"*Now* what are you smiling about?" he asked.

"I may be sitting still on the outside, but inside I'm moving all over the place," she answered.

It's possible to be good and obedient in our outward actions, and still disobey God in our minds. Matthew 5:21-22 says that sin happens in our hearts as well as our actions. We need to obey God inwardly *and* outwardly.

To learn more about sin, zoom to page 1181.

Don't Fight Back

[38]"You have heard that it was said, 'An eye for an eye, and a tooth for a tooth.'[n] [39]But I tell you, don't stand up against an evil person. If someone slaps you on the right cheek, then turn and let him slap the other cheek too. [40]If someone wants to sue you in court and take your shirt, then let him have your coat too. [41]If a soldier forces you to go with him one mile, then go with him two

the sun to rise on good people and on bad people. Your Father sends rain to those who do good and to those who do wrong. [46]If you love only the people who love you, then you will get no reward. Even the tax collectors do that. [47]And if you are nice only to your friends, then you are no better than other people. Even people without God are nice to their friends. [48]So you must be perfect, just as your Father in heaven is perfect.

[n]'An eye . . . tooth.'   Quotation from Exodus 21:24; Leviticus 24:20; Deuteronomy 19:21.
[n]Love your neighbor   Quotation from Leviticus 19:18.

Friendships
MATTHEW 5:43-48

Do you have a friend or classmate that gets on your nerves? Maybe you have a brother or sister who makes life hard for you!

Jesus told us that we should be nice, not only to our friends but to the people who are mean to us. If we were kind only to our friends, then we really wouldn't be any different than everybody else. One good way to show that we love God is to love others, even the ones who are hard to get along with.

Nobody is perfect. So, unfortunately, there will always be someone around who bugs you or makes you mad! Instead of giving that person a dirty look or a mean insult, surprise that person with kindness!

To find out what it means to love others, zoom to page 1300.

Jesus Teaches About Giving

6 "Be careful! When you do good things, don't do them in front of people to be seen by them. If you do that, then you will have no reward from your Father in heaven.

²"When you give to the poor, don't be like the hypocrites.*ᵈ* They blow trumpets before they give so that people will see them. They do that in the synagogues*ᵈ* and on the streets. They want other people to honor them. I tell you the truth. Those hypocrites already have their full reward. ³So when you give to the poor, give very secretly. Don't let anyone know what you are doing. ⁴Your giving should be done in secret. Your Father can see what is done in secret, and he will reward you.

Jesus Teaches About Prayer

⁵"When you pray, don't be like the hypocrites.*ᵈ* They love to stand in the synagogues*ᵈ* and on the street corners and pray loudly. They want people to see them pray. I tell you the truth. They already have their full reward. ⁶When you pray, you should go into your room and close the door. Then pray to your Father who cannot be seen. Your Father can see what is done in secret, and he will reward you.

"**A**nd God, I want to learn to talk to you the way you want me to talk. I want to pray like Jesus prayed in Matthew 6:9-13."

⁷"And when you pray, don't be like those people who don't know God. They continue saying things that mean nothing. They think that God will hear them because of the many things they say. ⁸Don't be like them. Your Father knows the things you need before you ask him. ⁹So when you pray, you should pray like this:

'Our Father in heaven,
  we pray that your name will always
      be kept holy.
¹⁰We pray that your kingdom will
      come.
  We pray that what you want will be
      done,

here on earth as it is in heaven.
[11] Give us the food we need for each day.
[12] Forgive the sins we have done,
  just as we have forgiven those who
    did wrong to us.
[13] Do not cause us to be tested;
  but save us from the Evil One.'
[14] Yes, if you forgive others for the things they do wrong, then your Father in heaven will also forgive you for the things you do wrong. [15] But if you don't forgive the wrongs of others, then your Father in heaven will not forgive the wrong things you do.

God Is More Important than Money

[19] "Don't store treasures for yourselves here on earth. Moths and rust will destroy treasures here on earth. And thieves can break into your house and steal the things you have. [20] So store your treasure in heaven. The treasures in heaven cannot be destroyed by moths or rust. And thieves cannot break in and steal that treasure. [21] Your heart will be where your treasure is.

Character
MATTHEW 5:48

Have you ever noticed that when two people hang around together a lot, they start to talk like each other? They may even start to dress like one another, play the same games, read the same books, and so on. It is natural for them to become like each other.

God isn't just somebody we hang out with. He's more important than that. He lets us spend time with him by reading the Bible and praying to him. That is how we become like him. When Jesus said that we are to be perfect, just like God, he didn't mean that we will become perfect right away. It doesn't happen the minute we become a Christian. But as we spend time getting to know God, he will mold our character until it becomes more and more like his own.

Spend time getting to know God better and better.

To learn more about character, zoom to page 1171.

Jesus Teaches About Worship

[16] "When you give up eating,"[n] don't put on a sad face like the hypocrites.[d] They make their faces look strange to show people that they are giving up eating. I tell you the truth, those hypocrites already have their full reward. [17] So when you give up eating, comb your hair and wash your face. [18] Then people will not know that you are giving up eating. But your Father, whom you cannot see, will see you. Your Father sees what is done in secret, and he will reward you.

[22] "The eye is a light for the body. If your eyes are good, then your whole body will be full of light. [23] But if your eyes are evil, then your whole body will be full of darkness. And if the only light you have is really darkness, then you have the worst darkness.

[24] "No one can be a slave to two masters. He will hate one master and love the other. Or he will follow one master and refuse to follow the other. So you cannot serve God and money at the same time.

[n] **give up eating** This is called "fasting." The people would give up eating for a special time of prayer and worship to God. It was also done to show sadness.

No one can be a slave to two masters. He will hate one master and love the other. Or he will follow one master and refuse to follow the other. So you cannot serve God and money at the same time.
• Matthew 6:24

28"And why do you worry about clothes? Look at the flowers in the field. See how they grow. They don't work or make clothes for themselves. 29But I tell you that even Solomon with his riches was not dressed as beautifully as one of these flowers. 30God clothes the grass in the field like that. The grass is living today, but tomorrow it is thrown into the fire to be burned. So you can

Prayer
MATTHEW 6:7

"**N**ow I lay me down to sleep . . ."

"**A**nd bless Mommy and Daddy and all the missionaries in Africa and . . ."

Do your prayers often sound like that? Do you say the same words, in the same way, in every prayer? It can be difficult to know what to say to God.

In this verse, Jesus doesn't tell us what to pray. Instead, he tells us what not to pray—the same old thing in the same old way, over and over. It's not that we can't bring the same problems to God in prayer many times. The problem is that our prayers can lose their meaning when we repeat them too much. If we do it often enough, we can mumble through our prayers by memory, never thinking about what we are saying. That's what this verse warns us not to do.

So when you pray, think of some new things to say. And remember that you are talking to your heavenly father. You are not just repeating a list of religious words.

To learn more about prayer, zoom to page 1174.

Don't Worry

25"So I tell you, don't worry about the food you need to live. And don't worry about the clothes you need for your body. Life is more important than food. And the body is more important than clothes. 26Look at the birds in the air. They don't plant or harvest or store food in barns. But your heavenly Father feeds the birds. And you know that you are worth much more than the birds. 27You cannot add any time to your life by worrying about it.

be even more sure that God will clothe you. Don't have so little faith! 31Don't worry and say, 'What will we eat?' or 'What will we drink?' or 'What will we wear?' 32All the people who don't know God keep trying to get these things. And your Father in heaven knows that you need them. 33The thing you should want most is God's kingdom and doing what God wants. Then all these other things you need will be given to you. 34So don't worry about tomorrow. Each day has enough trouble of its own. Tomorrow will have its own worries.

> The thing you should want most is God's kingdom and doing what God wants. Then all these other things you need will be given to you.
> • Matthew 6:33

only trample on them. And the dogs will only turn to attack you.

Ask God for What You Need

[7]"Continue to ask, and God will give to you. Continue to search, and you will find. Continue to knock, and the door will open for you. [8]Yes, everyone who continues asking will receive. He who continues searching will find. And he who continues knocking will have the door opened for him.

[9]"What would you do if your son asks

Animals in the Bible
BIRDS • MATTHEW 6:26-27

Do you ever watch birds fly? It is wonderful to see them soar and swoop from the sky to land on top of a branch on a high tree. Wouldn't it be fun to fly? If you had wings, where would you go?

Jesus said that birds can remind us not to worry. Because God takes care of the birds and feeds them, so we know he will take care of us. Many people waste time worrying that bad things will happen to them. But that is silly. We should trust God to take care of us, because we are more valuable to him than birds.

To discover the animal that stands for peace, fly to page 1142.

Be Careful About Judging Others

7 "Don't judge other people, and you will not be judged. [2]You will be judged in the same way that you judge others. And the forgiveness you give to others will be given to you.

[3]"Why do you notice the little piece of dust that is in your brother's eye, but you don't notice the big piece of wood that is in your own eye? [4]Why do you say to your brother, 'Let me take that little piece of dust out of your eye'? Look at yourself first! You still have that big piece of wood in your own eye. [5]You are a hypocrite![d] First, take the wood out of your own eye. Then you will see clearly enough to take the dust out of your brother's eye.

[6]"Don't give holy things to dogs. Don't throw your pearls before pigs. Pigs will

> Continue to ask, and God will give to you. Continue to search, and you will find. Continue to knock, and the door will open for you. Yes, everyone who continues asking will receive. He who continues searching will find. And he who continues knocking will have the door opened for him.
> • Matthew 7:7-8

for bread? Which of you would give him a stone? [10]Or if your son asks for a fish, would you give him a snake? [11]Even though you are bad, you know how to give good gifts to your children. So surely your heavenly Father will give good things to those who ask him.

The Most Important Rule

¹²"Do for other people the same things you want them to do for you. This is the meaning of the law of Moses and the teaching of the prophets.ᵈ

"**W**hen you hear people talking about the Golden Rule, they're not talking about a ruler made out of shiny metal. They're talking about what Jesus said in Matthew 7:12."

The Way to Heaven Is Hard

¹³"Enter through the narrow gate. The road that leads to hell is a very easy road. And the gate to hell is very wide. Many people enter through that gate. ¹⁴But the gate that opens the way to true life is very small. And the road to true life is very hard. Only a few people find that road.

People Know You by Your Actions

¹⁵"Be careful of false prophets.ᵈ They come to you and look gentle like sheep. But they are really dangerous like wolves. ¹⁶You will know these people because of the things they do. Good things don't come from bad people, just as grapes don't come from thornbushes. And figs don't come from thorny weeds. ¹⁷In the same way, every good tree produces good fruit. And bad trees produce bad fruit. ¹⁸A good tree cannot produce bad fruit. And a bad tree cannot produce good fruit. ¹⁹Every tree that does not produce good fruit is cut down and thrown into the fire. ²⁰You will know these false prophets by what they produce.

²¹"Not everyone who says that I am

his Lord will enter the kingdom of heaven. The only people who will enter the kingdom of heaven are those who do the things that my Father in heaven wants. ²²On the last day many people will say to me, 'You are our Lord! We spoke for you. And through you we forced out demonsᵈ and did many miracles.'ᵈ ²³Then I will tell them clearly, 'Get away from me, you who do evil. I never knew you.'

Two Kinds of People

²⁴"Everyone who hears these things I say and obeys them is like a wise man. The wise man built his house on rock. ²⁵It rained hard and the water rose. The winds blew and hit that house. But the house did not fall, because the house was built on rock. ²⁶But the person who hears the things I teach and does not obey them is like a foolish man. The foolish man built his house on sand. ²⁷It rained hard, the water rose, and the winds blew and hit that house. And the house fell with a big crash."

> Everyone who hears these things I say and obeys them is like a wise man. The wise man built his house on rock.
> • Matthew 7:24

²⁸When Jesus finished saying these things, the people were amazed at his teaching. ²⁹Jesus did not teach like their teachers of the law. He taught like a person who had authority.

Jesus Heals a Sick Man

8 When Jesus came down from the hill, great crowds followed him. ²Then a man sick with a harmful skin disease came to Jesus. The man bowed down before him and said, "Lord, you have the power to heal me if you want." ³Jesus touched the man and said, "I want to heal you. Be healed!" And immediately the man was healed from his skin disease. ⁴Then Jesus said to him,

Whit's Wisdom: A Solid Foundation • Matthew 7:24-29

My place has a name, kids. I call it Whit's End. I sure do enjoy Whit's End, and I enjoy having all the visitors who come. You can even visit in your imagination.

Say, it might be fun to talk with your family about having a name for your house. What would you call the place where you live?

Whit's End is an old house, but it was built very carefully. The other day, Sal, one of the kids here in Odyssey, asked me, "Mr. Whittaker, how come Whit's End is still standing so straight when a lot of the other houses here in Odyssey are crooked and look like they might fall down?"

"**W**ell, Sal," I said, "this might surprise you, but Jesus said something that answers your question."

"**J**esus talked about your house?" Sal asked.

"**W**ell, not exactly Sal," I answered, "but he did give the reason why Whit's End has stood through all the years."

"**I** gotta see this," said Sal. He grabbed a Bible and asked me where to look. He turned right to this page, Matthew 7. I had him start reading at verse 24. His lips moved as he read the words silently. Take a moment and read what he found in verses 24 until 27. "I see it!" he said when he was done reading. Can you find what he found? Why has Whit's End lasted so long?

"**L**ook again at those verses," I asked him, "and tell me what Jesus was talking about."

After he read and thought for a minute he said, "Well, Jesus says that people are like houses. Those built on sand fall, and those built on rock stand."

"**H**ow did Jesus explain what it means to be built on rock, Sal?" I asked.

"**W**hen people hear and obey Jesus' words," he said. Then he quickly added, "And when they hear but don't obey Jesus' words, they are built on sand—they crash!"

I was going to ask one more question, but Sal surprised me.

"**I** already know what you're going to ask, Mr. Whittaker. Yes, I want to be a person whose life is built on rock, so I need to listen to Jesus words and obey them, right?"

I laughed and said, "Right, Sal! That's exactly what we all need to do. Now, let me show you down in the basement where you can still see the solid rock they blasted out to build Whit's End."

Related Passages: Matthew 7:24-29; 1 Corinthians 3:9-16.

Teacher/Parent Hint: Discuss how we can listen to Christ and obey his words. Ask the children how many of Christ's words they know by heart. Use the experience to challenge them to learn more about the Bible.

People Who Depended on God
ROMAN OFFICER • MATTHEW 8:8-12

Have you ever heard someone say, "Seeing is believing"? It means that it is hard to believe something is true unless you see it yourself.

The officer in this story did not have to see Jesus heal his servant in order to believe Jesus could do it. Jesus was on his way to the officer's house to heal the officer's sick servant. But before Jesus could get to the house, some people came to him with a message from the Roman officer. The officer said Jesus did not have to come to the house. He believed Jesus could just say the word and his servant would be healed. The officer had great faith in Jesus.

It pleases God when you depend on him to help you. He will never let you down when you trust in him.

To read about a woman who knew God could help her get well,
fly to page 1190.

"Don't tell anyone about what happened. But go and show yourself to the priest.[n] And offer the gift that Moses commanded[n] for people who are made well. This will show people that you are healed."

Jesus Heals a Soldier's Servant

[5]Jesus went to the city of Capernaum. When he entered the city, an army officer came to Jesus and begged for help. [6]The officer said, "Lord, my servant is at home in bed. He can't move his body and is in much pain."

[7]Jesus said to the officer, "I will go and heal him."

[8]The officer answered, "Lord, I am not good enough for you to come into my house. All you need to do is command that my servant be healed, and he will be healed. [9]I myself am a man under the authority of other men. And I have soldiers under my command. I tell one soldier, 'Go,' and he goes. I tell another soldier, 'Come,' and he comes. I say to my servant, 'Do this,' and my servant obeys me.

[10]When Jesus heard this, he was amazed. He said to those who were with him, "I tell you the truth. This man has more faith than any other person I have found, even in Israel. [11]Many people will come from the east and from the west. They will sit and eat with Abraham, Isaac, and Jacob in the kingdom of heaven. [12]And those people who should have the kingdom will be thrown outside into the darkness. In that place people will cry and grind their teeth with pain."

[13]Then Jesus said to the officer, "Go home. Your servant will be healed just as you believed he would." And at that same time his servant was healed.

Jesus Heals Many People

[14]Jesus went to Peter's house. There

---

[n]**show . . . priest** The law of Moses said a priest must say when a Jew who had a harmful skin disease was well.
[n]**Moses commanded** Read about this in Leviticus 14:1-32.

Jesus saw that Peter's mother-in-law was in bed with a high fever. ¹⁵Jesus touched her hand, and the fever left her. Then she stood up and began to serve Jesus.

¹⁶That evening people brought to Jesus many who had demons.ᵈ Jesus spoke and the demons left them. Jesus healed all the sick. ¹⁷He did these things to make come true what Isaiah the prophetᵈ said:

"He took our suffering on him.
And he felt our pain for us."

Isaiah 53:4

People Want to Follow Jesus

¹⁸When Jesus saw the crowd around him, he told his followers to go to the other side of the lake. ¹⁹Then a teacher of the law came to Jesus and said, "Teacher, I will follow you any place you go."

²⁰Jesus said to him, "The foxes have holes to live in. The birds have nests to live in. But the Son of Manᵈ has no place where he can rest his head."

²¹Another man, one of Jesus' followers, said to Jesus, "Lord, let me go and bury my father first."

²²But Jesus said to him, "Follow me, and let the people who are dead bury their own dead."

Jesus Stops a Storm

²³Jesus got into a boat, and his followers went with him. ²⁴A very bad storm arose on the lake. The waves covered the boat. But Jesus was sleeping. ²⁵The followers went to Jesus and woke him. They said, "Lord, save us! We will drown!"

²⁶Jesus answered, "Why are you afraid? You don't have enough faith." Then Jesus got up and gave a command to the wind and the sea. The wind stopped, and the sea became very calm.

²⁷The men were amazed. They said, "What kind of man is this? Even the wind and the sea obey him!"

Jesus Heals Two Men with Demons

²⁸Jesus arrived at the other side of the lake in the country of the Gadareneⁿ people. There, two men came to Jesus.

Boats with Precious Cargo
MATTHEW 8:23-27

Do you know which boat in the Bible carried a very sleepy passenger? Jesus was tired after teaching and healing people all day. As the disciples set sail, Jesus fell asleep on a cushion in the back of the boat. The Sea of Galilee (a large lake) often had powerful storms with high waves and strong winds. As Jesus and the disciples crossed the lake, suddenly a bad storm began to splash waves into the boat. But Jesus didn't even wake up! He must have been very tired.

The disciples were scared, so they woke Jesus up. They thought that somehow he could help them. But they didn't expect him to stop the storm!

The boat landed safely right on course. The disciples had learned that Jesus' power is greater than even big storms.

To read about a boat with passengers who walked on the water,
fly to page 1152.

ⁿ**Gadarene**   From Gadara, an area southeast of Lake Galilee.

They had demons*d* in them. These men lived in the burial caves. They were so dangerous that people could not use the road by those caves. [29]The two men came to Jesus and shouted, "What do you want with us, Son of God? Did you come here to punish us before the right time?"

[30]Near that place there was a large herd of pigs feeding. [31]The demons begged Jesus, "If you make us leave these men, please send us into that herd of pigs."

town. [2]Some people brought to Jesus a man who was paralyzed. The man was lying on his mat. Jesus saw that these people had great faith, so he said to the paralyzed man, "Be happy, young man. Your sins are forgiven."

[3]Some of the teachers of the law heard this. They said to themselves, "This man speaks as if he were God—that is blasphemy!"*n*

[4]Jesus knew what they were thinking.

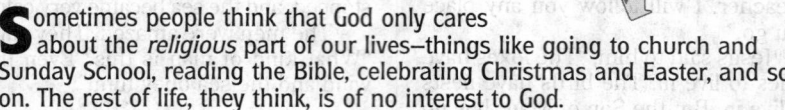

God's Love for Us
MATTHEW 9:1-8

Sometimes people think that God only cares about the *religious* part of our lives—things like going to church and Sunday School, reading the Bible, celebrating Christmas and Easter, and so on. The rest of life, they think, is of no interest to God.

But God is interested in every part of our lives. He cares about what goes on in our families, our schools, our parents' marriages and jobs, our hobbies, how we spend our money, and every other area. He isn't just a God for Sundays.

Jesus showed the paralyzed man that God cares about all of our problems. Some people probably told the man not to bother Jesus. After all, Jesus was a religious teacher, not a doctor. But Jesus cared about the man's physical needs, not just his spiritual needs, and healed him. God cares about your *whole* life, not just the religious part.

To learn more about God's love for us, turn to page 1233.

[32]Jesus said to them, "Go!" So the demons left the men and went into the pigs. Then the whole herd of pigs ran down the hill into the lake and were drowned. [33]The men who were caring for the pigs ran away and went into town. They told about all of this and what had happened to the men who had demons. [34]Then the whole town went out to see Jesus. When they saw him, they begged him to leave their area.

Jesus Heals a Paralyzed Man

9 Jesus got into a boat and went back across the lake to his own

So he said, "Why are you thinking evil thoughts? [5]Which is easier: to tell this paralyzed man, 'Your sins are forgiven,' or to tell him, 'Stand up and walk'? [6]But I will prove to you that the Son of Man*d* has power on earth to forgive sins." Then Jesus said to the paralyzed man, "Stand up. Take your mat and go home." [7]And the man stood up and went home. [8]The people saw this and were amazed. They praised God for giving power like this to men.

Jesus Chooses Matthew

[9]When Jesus was leaving, he saw a

---

*n***blasphemy** Saying things against God.

man named Matthew. Matthew was sitting in the tax office. Jesus said to him, "Follow me." And Matthew stood up and followed Jesus.

[10]Jesus had dinner at Matthew's house. Many tax collectors and "sinners" came and ate with Jesus and his followers. [11]The Pharisees[d] saw this and asked Jesus' followers, "Why does your teacher eat with tax collectors and 'sinners'?"

[12]Jesus heard the Pharisees ask this. So he said, "Healthy people don't need a doctor. Only the sick need a doctor. [13]Go and learn what this means: 'I want faithful love more than I want animal sacrifices.'[n] I did not come to invite good people. I came to invite sinners."

Jesus Is Not like Other Jews

[14]Then the followers of John[n] came to Jesus. They said to Jesus, "We and the Pharisees[d] often give up eating.[n] But your followers don't. Why?"

[15]Jesus answered, "The friends of the bridegroom are not sad while he is with them. But the time will come when the bridegroom will leave them. Then his friends are sad, and they will give up eating.

[16]"When someone sews a patch over a hole in an old coat, he never uses a piece of cloth that is not yet shrunk. If he does, the patch will shrink and pull away from the coat. Then the hole will be worse. [17]Also, people never pour new wine into old leather bags for holding wine. If they do, the old bags will break. The wine will spill, and the wine bags will be ruined. But people always pour new wine into new wine bags. Then the wine and the wine bags will continue to be good."

Jesus Gives Life to a Dead Girl and Heals a Sick Woman

[18]While Jesus was saying these things, a ruler of the synagogue[d] came to him.

The ruler bowed down before Jesus and said, "My daughter has just died. But come and touch her with your hand, and she will live again."

[19]So Jesus stood up and went with the ruler. Jesus' followers went too.

[20]Then a woman who had been bleeding for 12 years came behind Jesus and touched the edge of his coat. [21]She was thinking, "If I can touch his coat, then I will be healed."

[22]Jesus turned and saw the woman. He said, "Be happy, dear woman. You are made well because you believed." And the woman was healed at once.

[23]Jesus continued along with the ruler and went into the ruler's house. Jesus saw people there who play music for funerals. And he saw many people there crying. [24]Jesus said, "Go away. The girl is not dead. She is only asleep." But the people laughed at Jesus. [25]After the crowd had been put outside, Jesus went into the girl's room. He took her hand, and she stood up. [26]The news about this spread all around the area.

Jesus Heals More People

[27]When Jesus was leaving there, two blind men followed him. They cried out, "Show kindness to us, Son of David!"[d]

[28]Jesus went inside, and the blind men went with him. He asked the men, "Do you believe that I can make you see again?"

They answered, "Yes, Lord."

[29]Then Jesus touched their eyes and said, "You believe that I can make you see again. So this will happen." [30]Then the men were able to see. But Jesus warned them very strongly, saying, "Don't tell anyone about this." [31]But the blind men left and spread the news about Jesus all around that area.

[32]When the two men were leaving, some people brought another man to Jesus. This man could not talk because he had a demon[d] in him. [33]Jesus forced

---

[n]**'I want . . . sacrifices.'**　Quotation from Hosea 6:6.

[n]**John**　John the Baptist, who preached to people about Christ's coming (Matthew 3, Luke 3).

[n]**give up eating**　This is called "fasting." The people would give up eating for a special time of prayer and worship to God. It was also done to show sadness.

the demon to leave the man. Then the man who couldn't talk was able to speak. The crowd was amazed and said, "We have never seen anything like this in Israel."

34But the Pharisees*d* said, "The leader of demons is the one that gives him power to force demons out."

35Jesus traveled through all the towns and villages. He taught in their synagogues*d* and told people the Good News*d* about the kingdom. And he healed all kinds of diseases and sicknesses. 36He saw the crowds of people and felt sorry for them because they were worried and helpless. They were like sheep without a shepherd. 37Jesus said to his followers, "There are many people to harvest, but there are only a few workers to help harvest them. 38God owns the harvest. Pray to him that he will send more workers to help gather his harvest."*n*

Jesus Sends Out His Apostles

10 Jesus called his 12 followers together. He gave them power to drive out evil spirits and to heal every kind of disease and sickness. 2These are the names of the 12 apostles:*d* Simon (also called Peter) and his brother Andrew; James son of Zebedee, and his brother John; 3Philip and Bartholomew; Thomas and Matthew, the tax collector; James son of Alphaeus, and Thaddaeus; 4Simon the Zealot*d* and Judas Iscariot. Judas is the one who turned against Jesus.

5These 12 men he sent out with the following order: "Don't go to the non-Jewish people. And don't go into any town where the Samaritans*d* live. 6But go to the people of Israel. They are like sheep that are lost. 7When you go, preach this: 'The kingdom of heaven is coming soon.' 8Heal the sick. Give dead people life again. Heal those who have harmful skin diseases. Force demons*d* to leave people. I give you these powers freely. So help other people freely. 9Don't carry any money with you—gold or silver or copper. 10Don't carry a bag. Take for your trip only the clothes and sandals you are wearing. Don't take a walking stick. A worker should be given the things he needs. 11"When you enter a city or town, find some worthy person there and stay in

Animals in the Bible

DOVES • MATTHEW 10:16

The Bible talks about doves more than any other bird. The Hebrews offered doves as sacrifices to God. Doves reminded God's people of peace. Noah sent a dove out of the ark to see if all the floodwaters had left so the people could get out on dry land. You can read about that in Genesis 8.

Jesus told his disciples that they should act like doves. He meant that they should be peaceful and not hurt anyone. It is not always easy to be peaceful, but we need to try. We should not pick fights and be mean to people. Instead, we should be peaceful and try to get along with our family, friends, and neighbors.

To learn about an animal that slithers with excitement, fly to page 1369.

n"**There are . . . harvest."** As a farmer sends workers to harvest the grain, Jesus sends his followers to bring people to God.

his home until you leave. [12]When you enter that home, say, 'Peace be with you.' [13]If the people there welcome you, let your peace stay there. But if they don't welcome you, take back the peace you wished for them. [14]And if a home or town refuses to welcome you or listen to you, then leave that place. Shake its dust off your feet.[n] [15]I tell you the truth. On the Judgment Day it will be worse for that town than for the towns of Sodom and Gomorrah.[n]

Jesus Warns His Apostles

[16]"Listen! I am sending you out, and you will be like sheep among wolves. So be as smart as snakes. But also be like doves and do nothing wrong. [17]Be careful of people. They will arrest you and take you to court. They will whip you in their synagogues.[d] [18]Because of me you will be taken to stand before governors and kings. You will tell them and the non-Jewish people about me. [19]When you are arrested, don't worry about what to say or how you should say it. At that time you will be given the things to say. [20]It will not really be you speaking. The Spirit of your Father will be speaking through you.

[21]"Brothers will turn against their own brothers and give them over to be killed. Fathers will turn against their own children and give them to be killed. Children will fight against their own parents and have them killed. [22]All people will hate you because you follow me. But the person who continues strong until the end will be saved. [23]When you are treated badly in one city, go to another city. I tell you the truth. You will not finish going through all the cities of Israel before the Son of Man[d] comes.

[24]"A student is not better than his teacher. A servant is not better than his master. [25]A student should be satisfied to become like his teacher. A servant should be satisfied to become like his master. If the head of the family is called Beelzebul,[d] then the other members

of the family will be called worse names!

Fear God, Not People

[26]"So don't be afraid of those people. Everything that is hidden will be shown. Everything that is secret will be made known. [27]I tell you these things in the dark, but I want you to tell them in the light. I speak these things only to you, but you should tell them to everyone. [28]Don't be afraid of people. They can only kill the body. They cannot kill the soul. The only one you should fear is the One who can destroy the body and the soul in hell. [29]When birds are sold, two small birds cost only a penny. But not even one of the little birds can die without your Father's knowing it. [30]God even knows how many hairs are on your head. [31]So don't be afraid. You are worth much more than many birds.

Tell People About Your Faith

[32]"If anyone stands before other people and says he believes in me, then I will say that he belongs to me. I will say this before my Father in heaven. [33]But if anyone stands before people and says he does not believe in me, then I will say that he does not belong to me. I will say this before my Father in heaven.

[34]"Don't think that I have come to bring peace to the earth. I did not come to bring peace, but a sword. [35]I have come to make this happen:

'A son will be against his father,
  a daughter will be against her
    mother,
  a daughter-in-law will be against her
    mother-in-law.
[36] A person's enemies will be
    members of his own family.'

Micah 7:6

[37]"Whoever loves his father or mother more than he loves me is not worthy to be my follower. Whoever loves his son or daughter more than he loves me is not worthy to be my follower. [38]Whoever is not willing to die on a cross and follow me is not worthy of me.

---

[n]**Shake . . . feet.** A warning. It showed that they were finished talking to these people.
[n]**Sodom and Gomorrah** Two cities that God destroyed because the people were so evil.

³⁹Whoever tries to hold on to his life will give up true life. Whoever gives up his life for me will hold on to true life. ⁴⁰Whoever accepts you also accepts me. And whoever accepts me also accepts the One who sent me. ⁴¹Whoever meets a prophet*d* and accepts him will receive the reward of a prophet. And whoever accepts a good man because that man is good will receive the reward of a good man. ⁴²Whoever helps one of these little ones because they are my followers will truly get his reward. He will get his reward even if he only gave my follower a cup of cold water."

and tell him about the things you hear and see: ⁵The blind can see. The crippled can walk. People with harmful skin diseases are healed. The deaf can hear. The dead are raised to life. And the Good News*d* is told to the poor. ⁶The person who does not lose faith because of me is blessed."

⁷As John's followers were leaving, Jesus began talking to the people about John. Jesus said, "What did you go out to the desert to see? A reed*n* blown by the wind? No. ⁸Really, what did you go

Helping Others
MATTHEW 10:40-42

We've all heard stories about a wise, beautiful, and powerful princess who disguises herself as someone poor and weak, like a beggar. Because she seems to be poor and old, no one wants to help her or be kind. But finally someone does show kindness. Then the princess reveals her true identity and grants the kind person a special favor.

These verses teach that something like that happens whenever we help someone, no matter how small or unimportant that person seems to be. God, who created each person in his own image, notices each act of kindness. He even sees something as small as giving someone a cup of cold water. And he treats it as though we had given it to the Lord himself!

Remember that each time you help another person God says you have helped him. If you would like to do something to help the Lord today, be kind to someone.

To learn more about helping others, zoom to page 1167.

Jesus and John the Baptist

11 Jesus finished telling these things to his 12 followers. Then he left there and went to the towns in Galilee to teach and preach.

²John the Baptist*d* was in prison, but he heard about the things Christ was doing. So John sent some of his followers to Jesus. ³They asked Jesus, "Are you the man who John said was coming, or should we wait for another one?"

⁴Jesus answered, "Go back to John

out to see? A man dressed in fine clothes? No. Those people who wear fine clothes live in kings' palaces. ⁹So what did you go out to see? A prophet?*d* Yes, and I tell you, John is more than a prophet. ¹⁰This was written about John in the Scriptures:*d*

'I will send my messenger ahead of you.

He will prepare the way for you.'

Malachi 3:1

¹¹I tell you the truth: John the Baptist

---

*n***reed** It means that John was not weak like grass blown by the wind.

is greater than any other man who has ever lived. But even the least important person in the kingdom of heaven is greater than John. ¹²Since the time John the Baptist came until now, the kingdom of heaven has been going forward in strength. People using force have been trying to take the kingdom. ¹³All the prophets and the law of Moses spoke until the time John came. They told about the things that would happen. ¹⁴And if you will believe the things the law and the prophets said, then you will believe that John is Elijah. The law and the prophets said he would come. ¹⁵You people who hear me, listen!

¹⁶"What can I say about the people who live today? What are they like? They are like children sitting in the marketplace. One group calls to the other,
¹⁷'We played music for you, but you
    did not dance;
we sang a sad song, but you did
    not cry.'
¹⁸John came, and he did not eat like other people or drink wine. And people say, 'He has a demon.'ᵈ ¹⁹The Son of Manᵈ came, eating and drinking wine, and people say, 'Look at him! He eats too much and drinks too much. He is a friend of tax collectors and "sinners."' But wisdom is proved to be right by the things it does."

Jesus Warns Unbelievers

²⁰Then Jesus criticized the cities where he did most of his miracles.ᵈ He criticized them because the people there did not change their lives and stop sinning. ²¹Jesus said, "How terrible for you, Korazin! How terrible for you, Bethsaida! I did many miracles in you. If those same miracles had happened in Tyre and Sidon,ⁿ then the people there would have changed their lives a long time ago. They would have worn rough cloth and put ashes on themselves to show that they had changed. ²²But I tell you, on the Judgment Day it will be worse

for you than for Tyre and Sidon. ²³And you, Capernaum,ⁿ will you be lifted up to heaven? No. You will be thrown down to the depths. I did many miracles in you. If those same miracles had happened in Sodom,ⁿ its people would have stopped sinning, and it would still be a city today. ²⁴But I tell you it will be worse for you on the Judgment Day than for Sodom."

Jesus Offers Rest to People

²⁵Then Jesus said, "I thank you, Father, Lord of heaven and earth. I praise you because you have hidden these things from the people who are wise and smart. But you have shown them to those who are like little children. ²⁶Yes, Father, this is what you really wanted.

²⁷"My Father has given me all things. No one knows the Son—only the Father knows the Son. And no one knows the Father—only the Son knows the Father. And the only people who will know about the Father are those whom the Son chooses to tell.

²⁸"Come to me, all of you who are tired and have heavy loads. I will give you rest. ²⁹Accept my work and learn from me. I am gentle and humble in spirit. And you will find rest for your souls. ³⁰The work that I ask you to accept is easy. The load I give you to carry is not heavy."

Jesus Is Lord of the Sabbath

12 About that same time, Jesus was walking through some fields of grain on a Sabbathᵈ day. His followers were with him, and they were hungry. So they began to pick the grain and eat it. ²The Phariseesᵈ saw this, and they said to Jesus, "Look! Your followers are doing something that is against the Jewish law to do on the Sabbath day." ³Jesus answered, "Have you not read what David did when he and the people with him were hungry? ⁴David went

---

ⁿ**Tyre and Sidon** Towns where wicked people lived.
ⁿ**Korazin, Bethsaida, Capernaum** Towns by Lake Galilee where Jesus preached to the people.
ⁿ**Sodom** City that God destroyed because the people were so evil.

into God's house. He and those with him ate the bread that was made holy for God. It was against the law for them to eat that bread. Only the priests were allowed to eat it. ⁵And have you not read in the law of Moses that on every Sabbath day the priests in the Temple*d* break this law about the Sabbath day? But the priests are not wrong for doing that. ⁶I tell you that there is something here that is greater than the Temple. ⁷The Scripture*d* says, 'I want faithful love more than I want animal sacrifices.'*n* You don't really know what those words mean. If you understood them, you would not judge those who have done nothing wrong.

was a man with a crippled hand. Some Jews there were looking for a reason to accuse Jesus of doing wrong. So they asked him, "Is it right to heal on the Sabbath*d* day?"*n*

¹¹Jesus answered, "If any of you has a sheep, and it falls into a ditch on the Sabbath day, then you will take the sheep and help it out of the ditch. ¹²Surely a man is more important than a sheep. So the law of Moses allows people to do good things on the Sabbath day."

¹³Then Jesus said to the man with the crippled hand, "Let me see your hand." The man put his hand out, and the hand became well again, the same as the other hand. ¹⁴But the Pharisees*d* left and made plans to kill Jesus.

Words to Know: New Testament

SABBATH • MATTHEW 12:1-14

The **Sabbath** was (and still is) an important day of every week for the Jewish people. Celebrated every Saturday, Sabbath was a time to rest from work and to worship God. But in Jesus' time, a lot of laws had been added that told people exactly what they could and could not do on that day. Some people got angry at Jesus because he was healing people on the Sabbath. They thought he was doing work, and that was against the law. Jesus showed the people that the purpose of the Sabbath was not only to rest but also to worship God.

Your day of worship is probably Sunday. God wants you to think about him and worship him on that day. Ask God to show you what you can do to honor him on Sundays.

To read about some men who did not believe that people can be raised from the dead, fly to page 1165.

⁸"The Son of Man*d* is Lord of the Sabbath day."

Jesus Heals a Man's Crippled Hand

⁹Jesus left there and went into their synagogue.*d* ¹⁰In the synagogue, there

Jesus Is God's Chosen Servant

¹⁵Jesus knew what the Pharisees*d* were doing, so he left that place. Many people followed him, and he healed all who were sick. ¹⁶But Jesus warned the people not to tell who he

n"**I . . . sacrifices.'** Quotation from Hosea 6:6.
n"**Is it right . . . day?** It was against Jewish law to work on the Sabbath day.

was. [17]He did these things to make come true what Isaiah the prophet[d] had said:

[18]"Here is my servant whom I have
  chosen.
  I love him, and I am pleased with
    him.
  I will put my Spirit[d] in him.
  Then he will tell how I will judge
    all people fairly.
[19]He will not argue or shout.
  No one will hear his voice in the
    streets.
[20]He will not break a crushed blade of
    grass.
  He will not put out even a weak
    flame.
  He will continue until he makes fair
    judgment win the victory.
[21] In him will the nations find hope."

Isaiah 42:1-4

Jesus' Power Is from God

[22]Then some people brought a man to Jesus. This man was blind and could not talk, because he had a demon.[d] Jesus healed the man, and the man could talk and see. [23]All the people were amazed. They said, "Perhaps this man is the Son of David!"[d]

[24]The Pharisees[d] heard the people saying this. The Pharisees said, "Jesus uses the power of Beelzebul[d] to force demons out of people. Beelzebul is the ruler of demons."

[25]Jesus knew what the Pharisees were thinking. So he said to them, "Every kingdom that is fighting against itself will be destroyed. And every city that is divided will fall. And every family that is divided cannot succeed. [26]So if Satan forces out his own demons, then Satan is divided, and his kingdom will not continue. [27]You say that I use the power of Satan when I force out demons. If that is true, then what power do your people use when they force out demons? So your own people prove that you are wrong. [28]But if I use the power of God's Spirit[d] to force out demons, this shows that the kingdom of God has come to you.

[29]"If anyone wants to enter a strong man's house and steal his things, first he must tie up the strong man. Then he can steal the things from the strong man's house.

[30]"If anyone is not with me, then he is against me. He who does not work with me is working against me. [31]So I tell you, people can be forgiven for every sin they do. And people can be forgiven for every bad thing they say. But if anyone speaks against the Holy Spirit, then he will not be forgiven. [32]Anyone who says things against the Son of Man[d] can be forgiven. But anyone who says things against the Holy Spirit will not be forgiven. He will not be forgiven now or in the future.

People Know You by Your Words

[33]"If you want good fruit, you must make the tree good. If your tree is not good, then it will have bad fruit. A tree is known by the kind of fruit it produces. [34]You snakes! You are evil people! How can you say anything good? The mouth speaks the things that are in the heart. [35]A good person has good things in his heart. And so he speaks the good things that come from his heart. But an evil person has evil in his heart. So he speaks the evil things that come from his heart. [36]And I tell you that people will have to explain about every careless thing they have said. This will happen on the Judgment Day. [37]The words you have said will be used to judge you. Some of your words will prove you right, but some of your words will prove you guilty."

The Leaders Ask for a Miracle

[38]Then some of the Pharisees[d] and teachers of the law answered Jesus. They said, "Teacher, we want to see you work a miracle[d] as a sign."

[39]Jesus answered, "Evil and sinful people are the ones who want to see a miracle for a sign. But no sign will be given to them. The only sign will be what happened to the prophet[d] Jonah. [40]Jonah was in the stomach of the big fish for three days and three nights. In

the same way, the Son of Man[d] will be in the grave three days and three nights. [41]And on the Judgment Day the men from Nineveh[n] will stand up with you people who live today. They will show that you are guilty because when Jonah preached to them, they were sorry and changed their lives. And I tell you that someone greater than Jonah is here! [42]On the Judgment Day, the Queen of the South[n] will stand up with you people who live today. She will show that you are guilty because she came from far away to listen to Solomon's wise teaching. And I tell you that someone greater than Solomon is here!

People Today Are Full of Evil

[43]"When an evil spirit comes out of a man, it travels through dry places looking for a place to rest. But it finds no place to rest. [44]So the spirit says, 'I will go back to the home I left.' When the spirit comes back to the man, the spirit finds the home still empty. The home is swept clean and made neat. [45]Then the evil spirit goes out and brings seven other spirits even more evil than it is. Then all the spirits go into the man and live there. And that man has even more trouble than he had before. It is the same way with the evil people who live today."

Jesus' True Family

[46]While Jesus was talking to the people, his mother and brothers stood outside. They wanted to talk to him. [47]Someone told Jesus, "Your mother and brothers are waiting for you outside. They want to talk to you."

[48]He answered, "Who is my mother? Who are my brothers?" [49]Then he pointed to his followers and said, "See! These people are my mother and my brothers. [50]My true brothers and sisters and mother are those who do the things that my Father in heaven wants."

God's Children
MATTHEW 12:50

Here is a riddle: In what kind of family can you have brothers and sisters who are not related by birth? In other words, they do not have to have the same mother, and they can even grow up at the same time without even knowing each others' names! As strange as it sounds, there is such a family. In this verse, Jesus explains his idea of a family—his spiritual family.

God's spiritual family has people in it from all over the world: men, women, boys, and girls who have obeyed God and have trusted in Christ as their Savior. Although Jesus was raised in a family with parents, brothers, and sisters, his spiritual family includes those who obey God.

No matter how big or small your earthly family is, if you are a Christian, you also have a spiritual family with so many members that you could never count them.

To learn more about God's children, zoom to page 1262.

---

[n]**Nineveh**   The city where Jonah preached to warn the people. Read Jonah 3.
[n]**Queen of the South**   The Queen of Sheba. She traveled 1,000 miles to learn God's wisdom from Solomon. Read 1 Kings 10:1-13.

A Story About Planting Seed

13 That same day Jesus went out of the house and sat by the lake. [2]Large crowds gathered around him. So Jesus got into a boat and sat, while the people stayed on the shore. [3]Then Jesus used stories to teach them many things. He said: "A farmer went out to plant his seed. [4]While he was planting, some seed fell by the road. The birds came and ate all that seed. [5]Some seed fell on rocky ground, where there wasn't enough dirt. That seed grew very fast, because the ground was not deep. [6]But when the sun rose, the plants dried up because they did not have deep roots. [7]Some other seed fell among thorny weeds. The weeds grew and choked the good plants. [8]Some other seed fell on good ground where it grew and became grain. Some plants made 100 times more grain. Other plants made 60 times more grain, and some made 30 times more grain. [9]You people who hear me, listen!"

Why Jesus Used Stories to Teach

[10]The followers came to Jesus and asked, "Why do you use stories to teach the people?"

[11]Jesus answered, "Only you can know the secret truths about the kingdom of heaven. Other people cannot know these secret truths. [12]The person who has something will be given more. And he will have all he needs. But the person who does not have much, even what he has will be taken from him. [13]This is why I use stories to teach the people: They see, but they don't really see. They hear, but they don't really understand. [14]So they show that the things Isaiah said about them are true:

'You will listen and listen, but you will not understand.

You will look and look, but you will not learn.

[15]For these people have become stubborn.

They do not hear with their ears.

And they have closed their eyes.

Otherwise they might really understand

what they see with their eyes and hear with their ears.

They might really understand in their minds.

If they did this, they would come back to me and be forgiven.'

Isaiah 6:9-10

[16]But you are blessed. You understand the things you see with your eyes. And you understand the things you hear with your ears. [17]I tell you the truth. Many prophets[d] and good people wanted to see the things that you now see. But they did not see them. And many prophets and good people wanted to hear the things that you now hear. But they did not hear them.

Jesus Explains the Seed Story

[18]"So listen to the meaning of that story about the farmer. [19]What is the seed that fell by the road? That seed is like the person who hears the teaching about the kingdom but does not understand it. The Evil One comes and takes away the things that were planted in that person's heart. [20]And what is the seed that fell on rocky ground? That seed is like the person who hears the teaching and quickly accepts it with joy. [21]But he does not let the teaching go deep into his life. He keeps it only a short time. When trouble or persecution comes because of the teaching he accepted, then he quickly gives up. [22]And what is the seed that fell among the thorny weeds? That seed is like the person who hears the teaching but lets worries about this life and love of money stop that teaching from growing. So the teaching does not produce fruit[n] in that person's life. [23]But what is the seed that fell on the good ground? That seed is like the person who hears the teaching and understands it. That person grows and produces fruit, sometimes

---

[n]**produce fruit** To produce fruit means to have in your life the good things God wants.

100 times more, sometimes 60 times more, and sometimes 30 times more."

A Story About Wheat and Weeds

24Then Jesus told them another story. He said, "The kingdom of heaven is like a man who planted good seed in his field. 25That night, when everyone was asleep, his enemy came and planted weeds among the wheat. Then the enemy went away. 26Later, the wheat grew and heads of grain grew on the wheat plants. But at the same time the weeds also grew. 27Then the man's servants came to him and said, 'You planted good seed in your field. Where did the weeds come from?' 28The man answered, 'An enemy planted weeds.' The servants asked, 'Do you want us to pull up the weeds?' 29The man answered, 'No, because when you pull up the weeds, you might also pull up the wheat. 30Let the weeds and the wheat grow together until the harvest time. At harvest time I will tell the workers this: First gather the weeds and tie them together to be burned. Then gather the wheat and bring it to my barn.'"

Stories of Mustard Seed and Yeast

31Then Jesus told another story: "The kingdom of heaven is like a mustard seed. A man plants the seed in his field. 32That seed is the smallest of all seeds. But when it grows, it is one of the largest garden plants. It becomes a tree, big enough for the wild birds to come and make nests in its branches."

"**W**eeds make me think of a story Jesus told about weeds in Matthew 13:24-30. He also explained his story in Matthew 13:36-43."

33Then Jesus told another story: "The kingdom of heaven is like yeast that a woman mixes into a big bowl of flour. The yeast makes all the dough rise."

34Jesus used stories to tell all these things to the people. He always used stories to teach people. 35This is as the prophet[d] said:

"I will speak using stories;
　I will tell things that have been
　　secret since the world was
　　made."
　　　　　　　　　Psalm 78:2

Jesus Explains About the Wheat and Weeds

36Then Jesus left the crowd and went into the house. His followers came to him and said, "Explain to us the meaning of the story about the weeds in the field." 37Jesus answered, "The man who planted the good seed in the field is the Son of Man.[d] 38The field is the world. And the good seed are all of God's children in the kingdom. The weeds are those people who belong to the Evil One. 39And the enemy who planted the bad seed is the devil. The harvest time is the end of the world. And the workers who gather are God's angels.

40"The weeds are pulled up and burned in the fire. It will be this way at the end of the world. 41The Son of Man will send out his angels. They will gather out of his kingdom all who cause sin and all who do evil. 42The angels will throw them into the blazing furnace. There the people will cry and grind their teeth with pain. 43Then the good people will shine like the sun in the kingdom of their Father. You people who hear me, listen!

Stories of a Treasure and a Pearl

44"The kingdom of heaven is like a treasure hidden in a field. One day a man found the treasure, and then he hid it in the field again. The man was very happy to find the treasure. He went and sold everything that he owned to buy that field.

45"Also, the kingdom of heaven is like a man looking for fine pearls. 46One day he found a very valuable pearl. The man went and sold everything he had to buy that pearl.

A Story of a Fishing Net

47"Also, the kingdom of heaven is like a net that was put into the lake. The net caught many different kinds of fish. 48When it was full, the fishermen pulled the net to the shore. They sat down and put all the good fish in baskets. Then they threw away the bad fish. 49It will be this way at the end of the world. The angels will come and separate the evil people from the good people. 50The angels will throw the evil people into the blazing furnace. In that place the people will cry and grind their teeth with pain."

51Jesus asked his followers, "Do you understand all these things?"

They answered, "Yes, we understand."

52Then Jesus said to them, "So every teacher of the law who has been taught about the kingdom of heaven is like the owner of a house. He has both new things and old things saved in his house. And he brings out both those new things and old things."

Jesus Goes to His Hometown

53When Jesus finished teaching with these stories, he left there. 54He went to the town where he grew up. He taught the people in the synagogue,[d] and they were amazed. They said, "Where did this man get this wisdom and this power to do miracles?[d] 55He is only the son of the carpenter. And his mother is Mary. His brothers are James, Joseph, Simon and Judas. 56And all his sisters are here with us. So where does this man get all these things?" 57And the people refused to accept Jesus.

But Jesus said to them, "A prophet[d] is honored everywhere except in his own town or in his own home."

58The people there did not believe in Jesus. So Jesus did not do many miracles there.

How John the Baptist Was Killed

14 At that time Herod, the ruler of Galilee, heard the reports about Jesus. 2So Herod said to his servants, "Jesus is really John the Baptist.[d] He has risen from death. That is why he is able to do these miracles."[d]

3Sometime before this, Herod had arrested John, tied him up, and put him into prison. Herod did this because of Herodias. Herodias was the wife of Philip, Herod's brother. 4Herod arrested John because he told Herod: "It is not right for you to have Herodias." 5Herod wanted to kill John, but he was afraid of the people. They believed that John was a prophet.[d]

6On Herod's birthday, the daughter of Herodias danced for Herod and his guests. Herod was very pleased with her, 7so he promised he would give her anything she wanted. 8Herodias told her daughter what to ask for. So she said to Herod, "Give me the head of John the Baptist here on a platter." 9King Herod was very sad. But he had promised to give her anything she wanted, and the people eating with him had heard his promise. So Herod ordered that what she asked for be done. 10He sent men to the prison to cut off John's head. 11And the men brought John's head on a platter and gave it to the girl. She took it to her mother, Herodias. 12John's followers came and got his body and buried it. Then they went and told Jesus what happened.

More than 5,000 People Fed

13When Jesus heard what happened to John, Jesus left in a boat. He went to a lonely place by himself. But when the crowds heard about it, they followed him on foot from the towns. 14When Jesus arrived, he saw a large crowd. He felt sorry for them and healed those who were sick.

15Late that afternoon, his followers came to Jesus and said, "No one lives in this place. And it is already late. Send the people away so they can go to the towns and buy food for themselves."

16Jesus answered, "They don't need to go away. You give them some food to eat."

17The followers answered, "But we

have only five loaves of bread and two fish."

¹⁸Jesus said, "Bring the bread and the fish to me." ¹⁹Then he told the people to sit down on the grass. He took the five loaves of bread and the two fish. Then he looked to heaven and thanked God for the food. Jesus divided the loaves of bread. He gave them to his followers, and they gave the bread to

of him to the other side of the lake. Jesus stayed there to tell the people they could go home. ²³After he said good-bye to them, he went alone up into the hills to pray. It was late, and Jesus was there alone. ²⁴By this time, the boat was already far away on the lake. The boat was having trouble because of the waves, and the wind was blowing against it.

²⁵Between three and six o'clock in the morning, Jesus' followers were still in the boat. Jesus came to them.

Boats with Precious Cargo
MATTHEW 14:22-33

Do you know that one boat in the Bible picked up a passenger in the middle of the lake? The disciples left Jesus on land and set sail across the lake in a fishing boat. The boat wasn't very big. It was just large enough to carry all twelve men. They ran into a big storm and were terribly frightened.

Jesus walked out to them on the water, and they were even more scared because they thought he was a ghost. No one can walk on water, they thought. But they should have known that Jesus could do such a miracle because he was God's Son.

Jesus wants us to have faith and always believe in him.

To read about a boat that had a big audience, fly to page 1186.

the people. ²⁰All the people ate and were satisfied. After they finished eating, the followers filled 12 baskets with the pieces of food that were not eaten. ²¹There were about 5,000 men there who ate, as well as women and children.

"**I**'m going to try to walk on water too, but I'll wear my swimsuit, just in case. Jesus really did it in Matthew 14:22-33."

Jesus Walks on the Water

²²Then Jesus made his followers get into the boat. He told them to go ahead

He was walking on the water. ²⁶When the followers saw him walking on the water, they were afraid. They said, "It's a ghost!" and cried out in fear.

²⁷But Jesus quickly spoke to them. He said, "Have courage! It is I! Don't be afraid."

²⁸Peter said, "Lord, if that is really you, then tell me to come to you on the water."

²⁹Jesus said, "Come."

And Peter left the boat and walked on the water to Jesus. ³⁰But when Peter saw the wind and the waves, he became afraid and began to sink. He shouted, "Lord, save me!"

³¹Then Jesus reached out his hand and caught Peter. Jesus said, "Your faith is small. Why did you doubt?"

³²After Peter and Jesus were in the

boat, the wind became calm. ³³Then those who were in the boat worshiped Jesus and said, "Truly you are the Son of God!"

³⁴After they crossed the lake, they came to the shore at Gennesaret. ³⁵The people there saw Jesus and knew who he was. So they told people all around there that Jesus had come. They brought all their sick to him. ³⁶They begged Jesus to let them just touch the edge of his coat to be healed. And all the sick people who touched it were healed.

says cruel things to his father or mother must be put to death.'ⁿ ⁵But you say that a person can tell his father or mother, 'I have something I could use to help you. But I will not use it for you. I will give it to God.' ⁶You teach that person not to honor his father. You teach that it is not important to do what God said. You think that it is more important to follow the rules you have. ⁷You are hypocrites!ᵈ Isaiah was right when he spoke about you:

⁸'These people show honor to me
   with words.
But their hearts are far from me.
⁹Their worship of me is worthless.

Miracles from God
MATTHEW 15:29-39

Can you imagine packing a picnic for four thousand people? Thousands of people followed Jesus, listening to what he said. One time over four thousand people were listening to him speak. When the day got late, Jesus did not want to send them home hungry. So he did a great miracle on the mountainside. He made food for everyone to eat from seven loaves of bread and a few small fish.

As humans, there are many things we cannot do. But God can do anything! Jesus could have fed five people or five million people. There is no limit to what he can do!

To find out what happened to some men who tore up a roof, fly to page 1183.

Obey God's Law Not Men's

15 Then some Phariseesᵈ and teachers of the law came to Jesus from Jerusalem. They asked him, ²"Why do your followers not obey the rules given to us by the great people who lived before us? Your followers don't wash their hands before they eat!"

³Jesus answered, "And why do you refuse to obey God's command so that you can follow those rules you have? ⁴God said, 'Honor your father and mother.'ⁿ And God also said, 'Anyone who

The things they teach are nothing
   but human rules they have
   memorized.'"   *Isaiah 29:13*

¹⁰Jesus called the crowd to him. He said, "Listen and understand what I am saying. ¹¹It is not what a person puts into his mouth that makes him unclean.ᵈ It is what comes out of his mouth that makes him unclean."

¹²Then his followers came to Jesus and asked, "Do you know that the Pharisees are angry because of what you said?"

ⁿ"**Honor . . . mother.**" Quotation from Exodus 20:12; Deuteronomy 5:16.
ⁿ"**Anyone . . . death.**" Quotation from Exodus 21:17.

[13] Jesus answered, "Every plant that my Father in heaven has not planted himself will be pulled up by the roots. [14] Stay away from the Pharisees. They are blind leaders. And if a blind man leads another blind man, then both men will fall into a ditch."

[15] Peter said, "Explain the story to us."

[16] Jesus said, "You still have trouble understanding? [17] Surely you know that all the food that enters the mouth goes into the stomach. Then that food goes out of the body. [18] But what a person says with his mouth comes from the way he thinks. And these are the things that make him unclean. [19] Out of his mind come evil thoughts, murder, adultery,[d] sexual sins, stealing, lying, and saying bad things against other people. [20] These things make a person unclean. But eating with unwashed hands does not make him unclean."

Jesus Helps a Non-Jewish Woman

[21] Jesus left that place and went to the area of Tyre and Sidon. [22] A Canaanite woman from that area came to Jesus. The woman cried out, "Lord, Son of David,[d] please help me! My daughter has a demon,[d] and she is suffering very much."

[23] But Jesus did not answer the woman. So the followers came to Jesus and begged him, "Tell the woman to go away. She is following us and shouting."

[24] Jesus answered, "God sent me only to the lost sheep, the people of Israel."

[25] Then the woman came to Jesus again. She bowed before him and said, "Lord, help me!"

[26] Jesus answered, "It is not right to take the children's bread and give it to the dogs."

[27] The woman said, "Yes, Lord, but even the dogs eat the pieces of food that fall from their masters' table."

[28] Then Jesus answered, "Woman, you have great faith! I will do what you asked me to do." And at that moment the woman's daughter was healed.

Jesus Heals Many People

[29] Then Jesus left that place and went to the shore of Lake Galilee. He went up on a hill and sat there.

[30] Great crowds came to Jesus. They brought their sick with them: the lame, the blind, the crippled, the dumb and many others. They put them at Jesus' feet, and he healed them. [31] The crowd was amazed when they saw that people who could not speak were able to speak again. The crippled were made strong again. Those who could not walk were able to walk again. The blind were able to see again. And they praised the God of Israel for this.

More than 4,000 People Fed

[32] Jesus called his followers to him and said, "I feel sorry for these people. They have been with me three days, and now they have nothing to eat. I don't want to send them away hungry. They might faint while going home."

[33] His followers asked him, "Where can we get enough bread to feed all these people? We are far away from any town."

[34] Jesus asked, "How many loaves of bread do you have?"

They answered, "We have seven loaves and a few small fish."

[35] Jesus told the people to sit on the ground. [36] He took the seven loaves of bread and the fish and gave thanks to God for the food. Then Jesus divided the food and gave it to his followers. They gave the food to the people. [37] All the people ate and were satisfied. After this, the followers filled seven baskets with the pieces of food that were not eaten. [38] There were about 4,000 men there who ate, besides women and children. [39] After they ate, Jesus told the people to go home. He got into the boat and went to the area of Magadan.

The Leaders Ask for a Miracle

16 The Pharisees[d] and Sadducees[d] came to Jesus. They wanted to trap him. So they asked him to show them a miracle[d] to prove that he was from God.

[2]Jesus answered, "When you see the sunset, you know what the weather will be. If the sky is red, then you say we will have good weather. [3]And in the morning if the sky is dark and red, then you say that it will be a rainy day. You see these signs in the sky, and you know what they mean. In the same way, you see the things that are happening now. But you don't know their meaning. [4]Evil and sinful people ask for a miracle as a sign. But they will have no sign—only the sign of Jonah."[n] Then Jesus left them and went away.

Guard Against Wrong Teachings

[5]Jesus and his followers went across the lake. But the followers forgot to bring bread. [6]Jesus said to them, "Be careful! Guard against the yeast of the Pharisees[d] and the Sadducees."[d]

[7]The followers discussed the meaning of this. They said, "Did Jesus say this because we forgot to bring bread?"

[8]Jesus knew that they were talking about this. So he asked them, "Why are you talking about not having bread? Your faith is small. [9]You still don't understand? Remember the five loaves of bread that fed the 5,000 people? And remember that you filled many baskets with bread after the people finished eating? [10]And remember the seven loaves of bread that fed the 4,000 people? Remember that you filled many baskets then also? [11]So I was not talking to you about bread. Why don't you understand that? I am telling you to be careful and guard against the yeast of the Pharisees and the Sadducees." [12]Then the followers understood what Jesus meant. He was not telling them to guard against the yeast used in bread. He was telling them to guard against the teaching of the Pharisees and the Sadducees.

Peter Says Jesus Is the Christ

[13]Jesus went to the area of Caesarea Philippi. He said to his followers, "I am the Son of Man.[d] Who do the people say I am?"

[14]They answered, "Some people say you are John the Baptist.[d] Others say you are Elijah. And others say that you are Jeremiah or one of the prophets."[d]

[15]Then Jesus asked them, "And who do you say I am?"

[16]Simon Peter answered, "You are the Christ,[d] the Son of the living God."

[17]Jesus answered, "You are blessed, Simon son of Jonah. No person taught you that. My Father in heaven showed you who I am. [18]So I tell you, you are Peter.[n] And I will build my church on this rock. The power of death will not be able to defeat my church. [19]I will give you the keys of the kingdom of heaven. The things you don't allow on earth will be the things that God does not allow. The things you allow on earth will be the things that God allows." [20]Then Jesus warned his followers not to tell anyone that he was the Christ.

Jesus Says that He Must Die

[21]From that time on Jesus began telling his followers that he must go to Jerusalem. He explained that the older Jewish leaders, the leading priests, and the teachers of the law would make him suffer many things. And he told them that he must be killed. Then, on the third day, he would be raised from death.

[22]Peter took Jesus aside and began to criticize him. Peter said, "God save you from those things, Lord! Those things will never happen to you!"

[23]Then Jesus said to Peter, "Go away from me, Satan![n] You are not helping me! You don't care about the things of God. You care only about things that men think are important."

[24]Then Jesus said to his followers, "If anyone wants to follow me, he must say 'no' to the things he wants. He must be willing even to die on a cross, and he

---

[n]**sign of Jonah**   Jonah's three days in the big fish are like Jesus' three days in the tomb. The story about Jonah is in the book of Jonah.
[n]**Peter**   The Greek name "Peter," like the Aramaic name "Cephas," means "rock."
[n]**Satan**   Name for the devil, meaning "the enemy." Jesus means that Peter was talking like Satan.

must follow me. [25]Whoever wants to save his life will give up true life. And whoever gives up his life for me will have true life. [26]It is worth nothing for a man to have the whole world if he loses his soul. He could never pay enough to buy back his soul. [27]The Son of Man[d] will come again with his Father's glory and with his angels. At that time, he will reward everyone for what he has done. [28]I tell you the truth. There are some people standing here who, before they die, will see the Son of Man coming with his kingdom."

Jesus with Moses and Elijah

17 Six days later, Jesus took Peter, James, and John the brother of James up on a high mountain. They were all alone there. [2]While they watched, Jesus was changed. His face became bright like the sun. And his clothes became white as light. [3]Then two men were there, talking with him. The men were Moses and Elijah.[n]

[4]Peter said to Jesus, "Lord, it is good that we are here. If you want, I will put three tents here—one for you, one for Moses, and one for Elijah."

[5]While Peter was talking, a bright cloud covered them. A voice came from the cloud. The voice said, "This is my Son and I love him. I am very pleased with him. Obey him!"

[6]The followers with Jesus heard the voice. They were so frightened that they fell to the ground. [7]But Jesus went to them and touched them. He said, "Stand up. Don't be afraid." [8]When the followers looked up, they saw Jesus was now alone.

[9]When Jesus and the followers were coming down the mountain, Jesus commanded them, "Don't tell anyone about the things you saw on the mountain. Wait until the Son of Man[d] has been raised from death. Then you may tell."

[10]The followers asked Jesus, "Why do the teachers of the law say that Elijah must come first, before the Christ[d] comes?"

[11]Jesus answered, "They are right to say that Elijah is coming. And it is true that Elijah will make everything the way it should be. [12]But I tell you, Elijah has already come. People did not know who he was. They did to him everything they wanted to do. It will be the same with the Son of Man. Those same people will make the Son of Man suffer." [13]Then the followers understood that Jesus was talking about John the Baptist.[d]

Jesus Heals a Sick Boy

[14]Jesus and his followers went back to the crowd. A man came to Jesus and bowed before him. [15]The man said, "Lord, please help my son. He has epilepsy[n] and is suffering very much. He often falls into the fire or into the water. [16]I brought him to your followers, but they could not cure him."

[17]Jesus answered, "You people have no faith. Your lives are all wrong. How long must I stay with you? How long must I continue to be patient with you? Bring the boy here." [18]Jesus gave a strong command to the demon[d] inside the boy. Then the demon came out, and the boy was healed.

[19]The followers came to Jesus when he was alone. They said, "Why couldn't we force the demon out?"

[20]Jesus answered, "You were not able to drive out the demon because your faith is too small. I tell you the truth. If your faith is as big as a mustard seed,[n] you can say to this mountain, 'Move from here to there.' And the mountain will move. All things will be possible for you." [21][n]

Jesus Talks About His Death

[22]Later, the followers met together

---

[n]**Moses and Elijah** Two of the most important Jewish leaders in the past.

[n]**epilepsy** A disease that causes a person sometimes to lose control of his body, and maybe faint, shake strongly, or not be able to move.

[n]**mustard seed** This seed is very small, but the plant grows taller than a man.

[n]**Verse 21** Some Greek copies add verse 21: "That kind of spirit comes out only if you use prayer and give up eating."

in Galilee. Jesus said to them, "The Son of Man[d] will be given into the control of some men. 23They will kill him, but on the third day he will be raised from death." And the followers were filled with sadness.

"**W**ho did Jesus say was really the greatest? If you don't know, check it out in Matthew 18:1-4."

Jesus Talks About Paying Taxes

24Jesus and his followers went to Capernaum. There some men came to Peter. They were the men who collected the Temple[d] tax. They asked, "Does your teacher pay the Temple tax?"

25Peter answered, "Yes, Jesus pays the tax."

Peter went into the house where Jesus was. Before Peter could speak, Jesus said to him, "The kings on the earth collect different kinds of taxes. But who are the people who pay the taxes? Are they the king's children? Or do others pay the taxes? What do you think?"

26Peter answered, "Other people pay the taxes."

Jesus said to Peter, "Then the children of the king don't have to pay taxes. 27But we don't want to make these tax collectors angry. So go to the lake and fish. After you catch the first fish, open its mouth. Inside its mouth you will find a coin. Take that coin and give it to the tax collectors. That will pay the tax for you and me."

Who Is the Greatest?

18 At that time the followers came to Jesus and asked, "Who is greatest in the kingdom of heaven?" 2Jesus called a little child to him. He

Humility
MATTHEW 18:1-4

"**Y**ou're just a kid."

"**S**orry—you're not old enough."

"**G**row up, will you?"

Children often hear things like that, reminding them that they're just kids. But Jesus sees things differently. Instead of pointing out what's *wrong* with being a child, Jesus talks about what's *right*. Jesus says that everyone should be humble, like a small child. In fact, that's the only way to become great and important in his kingdom.

A lot of people don't think that way. They say that being rich, or smart, or athletic, or good looking makes a person important. But that's backward. What really makes a person great is being humble. (If that sounds strange to you, just wait! The more you get to know Jesus, the more surprises he has for you.) Don't be confused by what you see and hear in the world. Listen to Jesus.

To learn more about humility, zoom to page 1299.

stood the child before the followers. [3]Then he said, "I tell you the truth. You must change and become like little children. If you don't do this, you will never enter the kingdom of heaven. [4]The greatest person in the kingdom of heaven is the one who makes himself humble like this child.

[5]"Whoever accepts a little child in my name accepts me. [6]If one of these little children believes in me, and someone causes that child to sin, then it will be very bad for that person. It would be better for him to have a large stone tied around his neck and be drowned in the sea. [7]How terrible for the people of the world because of the things that cause them to sin. Such things will happen. But how terrible for the one who causes them to happen. [8]If your hand or your foot causes you to sin, cut it off and throw it away. It is better for you to have only part of your body but have life forever. That is much better than to have two hands and two feet but be thrown into the fire that burns forever. [9]If your eye causes you to sin, take it out and throw it away. It is better for you to have only one eye but have life forever. That is much better than to have two eyes but be thrown into the fire of hell.

A Lost Sheep

[10]"Be careful. Don't think these little children are worth nothing. I tell you that they have angels in heaven who are always with my Father in heaven. [11]*

[12]"If a man has 100 sheep, but 1 of the sheep gets lost, he will leave the other 99 sheep on the hill. He will go to look for the lost sheep. [13]And if he finds it, he is happier about that 1 sheep than about the 99 that were never lost. I tell you the truth. [14]In the same way, your Father in heaven does not want any of these little children to be lost.

When a Person Sins Against You

[15]"If your brother sins against you, go and tell him what he did wrong. Do this in private. If he listens to you, then you have helped him to be your brother again. [16]But if he refuses to listen, then go to him again and take one or two other people with you. 'Every case may be proved by two or three witnesses.'" [17]If he refuses to listen to them, then tell it to the church. If he refuses to listen to the church, then treat him as you would one who does not believe in God. Treat him as if he were a tax collector.

[18]"I tell you the truth. The things you don't allow on earth will be the things God does not allow. The things you allow on earth will be the things that God allows.

[19]"Also, I tell you that if two of you on earth agree about something, then you can pray for it. And the thing you ask for will be done for you by my Father in heaven. [20]This is true because if two or three people come together in my name, I am there with them."

An Unforgiving Servant

[21]Then Peter came to Jesus and asked, "Lord, when my brother sins against me, how many times must I forgive him? Should I forgive him as many as 7 times?"

[22]Jesus answered, "I tell you, you must forgive him more than 7 times. You must forgive him even if he does wrong to you 77 times.

[23]"The kingdom of heaven is like a king who decided to collect the money his servants owed him. [24]So the king began to collect his money. One servant owed him several million dollars. [25]But the servant did not have enough money to pay his master, the king. So the master ordered that everything the servant owned should be sold, even the servant's wife and children. The money would be used to pay the king what the servant owed.

[26]"But the servant fell on his knees and begged, 'Be patient with me. I will pay you everything I owe.' [27]The master felt sorry for his servant. So the master

---

*Verse 11   Some Greek copies add verse 11: "The Son of Man came to save lost people."
*'Every . . . witnesses.'   Quotation from Deuteronomy 19:15.

told the servant he did not have to pay. He let the servant go free.

28"Later, that same servant found another servant who owed him a few dollars. The servant grabbed the other servant around the neck and said, 'Pay me the money you owe me!'

29"The other servant fell on his knees and begged him, 'Be patient with me. I will pay you everything I owe.'

30"But the first servant refused to be patient. He threw the other servant into prison until he could pay everything he owed. 31All the other servants saw what happened. They were very sorry. So they went and told their master all that had happened.

32"Then the master called his servant in and said, 'You evil servant! You begged me to forget what you owed. So I told you that you did not have to pay anything. 33I had mercy on you. You should have had the same mercy on that other servant.' 34The master was very angry, and he put the servant in prison to be punished. The servant had to stay in prison until he could pay everything he owed.

35"This king did what my heavenly Father will do to you if you do not forgive your brother from your heart."

Jesus Teaches About Divorce

19 After Jesus said all these things, he left Galilee. He went into the area of Judea on the other side of the Jordan River. 2Large crowds followed Jesus, and he healed them there.

3Some Pharisees*d* came to Jesus and tried to trick him. They asked, "Is it right for a man to divorce his wife for any reason he chooses?"

4Jesus answered, "Surely you have read in the Scriptures:*d* When God made the world, 'he made them male and female.'*n* 5And God said, 'So a man will leave his father and mother and be unit-

ed with his wife. And the two people will become one body.'*n* 6So the two are not two, but one. God joined the two people together. No person should separate them."

7The Pharisees asked, "Why then did Moses give a command for a man to divorce his wife by giving her divorce papers?"

8Jesus answered, "Moses allowed you to divorce your wives because you refused to accept God's teaching. But divorce was not allowed in the beginning. 9I tell you that anyone who divorces his wife and marries another woman is guilty of adultery.*d* The only reason for a man to divorce and marry again is if his first wife has sexual relations with another man."

10The followers said to him, "If that is the only reason a man can divorce his wife, then it is better not to marry."

11Jesus answered, "Not everyone can accept this truth about marriage. But God has made some able to accept it. 12There are different reasons why some men cannot marry. Some men were born without the ability to become fathers. Others were made that way later in life by other people. And other men have given up marriage because of the kingdom of heaven. But the person who can marry should accept this teaching about marriage."*n*

Jesus Welcomes Children

13Then the people brought their little children to Jesus so that he could put his hands on them*n* and pray for them. When his followers saw this, they told the people to stop bringing their children to Jesus. 14But Jesus said, "Let the little children come to me. Don't stop them, because the kingdom of heaven belongs to people who are like these children." 15After Jesus put his hands on the children, he left there.

*n***he made . . . female.'** Quotation from Genesis 1:27 or 5:2.
*n***'So . . . body.'** Quotation from Genesis 2:24.
*n***But . . . marriage.** This may also mean, "The person who can accept this teaching about not marrying should accept it."
*n***put his hands on them** Showing that Jesus gave special blessings to these children.

A Rich Young Man's Question

[16] A man came to Jesus and asked, "Teacher, what good thing must I do to have life forever?"

[17] Jesus answered, "Why do you ask me about what is good? Only God is good. But if you want to have life forever, obey the commands."

[18] The man asked, "Which commands?"

Jesus answered, "'You must not murder anyone. You must not be guilty of adultery.[d] You must not steal. You must not tell lies about your neighbor in court. [19] Honor your father and mother.[n] Love your neighbor as you love yourself.'"[n]

[20] The young man said, "I have obeyed all these things. What else do I need to do?"

[21] Jesus answered, "If you want to be perfect, then go and sell all the things you own. Give the money to the poor. If you do this, you will have a treasure in heaven. Then come and follow me!"

[22] But when the young man heard this, he became very sad because he was very rich. So he left Jesus.

[23] Then Jesus said to his followers, "I tell you the truth. It will be very hard for a rich person to enter the kingdom of heaven. [24] Yes, I tell you that it is easier for a camel to go through the eye of a needle than for a rich person to enter the kingdom of God."

[25] When the followers heard this, they were very surprised. They asked, "Then who can be saved?"

[26] Jesus looked at them and said, "This is something that men cannot do. But God can do all things."

[27] Peter said to Jesus, "We left everything we had and followed you. So what will we have?"

[28] Jesus said to them, "I tell you the truth. When the new age comes, the Son of Man[d] will sit on his great throne. And all of you who followed me will also sit on 12 thrones. And you will judge the 12 tribes[d] of Israel. [29] And everyone who has left houses, brothers, sisters, father, mother, children, or farms to follow me will get much more than he left. And he will have life forever. [30] Many who have the highest place in life now will have the lowest place in the future. And many who have the lowest place now will have the highest place in the future.

A Story About Vineyard Workers

20 "The kingdom of heaven is like a man who owned some land. One morning, he went out very early to hire some people to work in his vineyard. [2] The man agreed to pay the workers one silver coin[n] for working that day. Then he sent them into the vineyard to work. [3] About nine o'clock the man went to the marketplace and saw some other people standing there, doing nothing. [4] So he said to them, 'If you go and work in my vineyard, I will pay you what your work is worth.' [5] So they went to work in the vineyard. The man went out again about twelve o'clock and again at three o'clock. Both times he hired people to work in his vineyard. [6] About five o'clock the man went to the marketplace again. He saw others standing there. He asked them, 'Why did you stand here all day doing nothing?' [7] They answered, 'No one gave us a job.' The man said to them, 'Then you can go and work in my vineyard.'

[8] "At the end of the day, the owner of the vineyard said to the boss of all the workers, 'Call the workers and pay them. Start by paying the last people I hired. Then pay all of them, ending with the workers I hired first.'

[9] "The workers who were hired at five o'clock came to get their pay. Each worker received one silver coin. [10] Then the workers who were hired first came to get their pay. They thought they would be paid more than the others. But each one of them also received one

[n] **'You . . . mother.'**   Quotation from Exodus 20:12-16; Deuteronomy 5:16-20.
[n] **'Love . . . yourself.'**   Quotation from Leviticus 19:18.
[n] **silver coin**   A Roman denarius. One coin was the average pay for one day's work.

Staying Away from Selfishness
MATTHEW 20:20-23

If you've ever been in a spelling contest, you know that if you get even one letter mixed up and misspell the word, you are out. Knowing the order of the letters in a word is the key to winning the contest. The key to winning in the Christian life is to remember the order of the letters in the word, joy: **J**esus, **O**thers, **Y**ou. As long as you put love for Jesus and others in front of love for yourself, you will have joy.

The mother in this story had one wish. She thought it would bring the greatest joy. The only problem was she got her letters mixed up. She was more concerned with what she wanted. Thinking about how you can please Jesus instead of pleasing yourself is a good way to say "so long" to selfishness. Remember to get the letters right: **J**esus, **O**thers, **Y**ou.

To learn more ways to stay away from selfishness,
zoom to page 1198.

silver coin. ¹¹When they got their silver coin, they complained to the man who owned the land. ¹²They said, 'Those people were hired last and worked only one hour. But you paid them the same as you paid us. And we worked hard all day in the hot sun.' ¹³But the man who owned the vineyard said to one of those workers, 'Friend, I am being fair to you. You agreed to work for one silver coin. ¹⁴So take your pay and go. I want to give the man who was hired last the same pay that I gave you. ¹⁵I can do what I want with my own money. Are you jealous because I am good to those people?'

¹⁶"So those who have the last place now will have the first place in the future. And those who have the first place now will have the last place in the future."

Jesus Talks About His Own Death

¹⁷Jesus was going to Jerusalem. His 12 followers were with him. While they were on the way, Jesus gathered the followers together and spoke to them privately. He said to them, ¹⁸"We are going to Jerusalem. The Son of Man*d* will be turned over to the leading priests and the teachers of the law. They will say that he must die. ¹⁹They will give the Son of Man to the non-Jewish people. They will laugh at him and beat him with whips, and then they will kill him on a cross. But on the third day after his death, he will be raised to life again."

A Mother Asks Jesus a Favor

²⁰Then the wife of Zebedee came to Jesus. Her sons were with her. The mother bowed before Jesus and asked him to do something for her.

²¹Jesus asked, "What do you want?"

She said, "Promise that one of my sons will sit at your right side in your kingdom. And promise that the other son will sit at your left side."

²²But Jesus said, "You don't understand what you are asking. Can you

accept the kind of suffering that I must suffer?"[n]

The sons answered, "Yes, we can!"

[23]Jesus said to them, "Truly you will suffer the same things that I will suffer. But I cannot choose who will sit at my right side or my left side. Those places belong to those for whom my Father has prepared them."

[24]The other ten followers heard this and were angry with the two brothers.

[25]Jesus called all the followers together. He said, "You know that the rulers of the non-Jewish people love to show their power over the people. And their important leaders love to use all their authority. [26]But it should not be that way among you. If one of you wants to become great, then he must serve the rest of you like a servant. [27]If one of you wants to become first, then he must serve the rest of you like a slave. [28]So it is with the Son of Man.[d] The Son of Man did not come for other people to serve him. He came to serve others. The Son of Man came to give his life to save many people."

Jesus Heals Two Blind Men

[29]When Jesus and his followers were leaving Jericho, a great many people followed Jesus. [30]There were two blind men sitting by the road. The blind men heard that Jesus was going by, so they shouted, "Lord, Son of David,[d] please help us!"

[31]All the people criticized the blind men. They told them to be quiet. But the blind men shouted more and more, "Lord, Son of David, please help us!"

[32]Jesus stopped and said to the blind men, "What do you want me to do for you?"

[33]They answered, "Lord, we want to be able to see."

[34]Jesus felt sorry for the blind men. He touched their eyes, and at once they

were able to see. Then the men followed Jesus.

Jesus Enters Jerusalem as a King

21 Jesus and his followers were coming closer to Jerusalem. But first they stopped at Bethphage at the hill called the Mount of Olives.[d] From there Jesus sent two of his followers into the town. [2]He said to them, "Go to the town you can see there. When you enter it, you will find a donkey tied there with its colt. Untie them and bring them to me. [3]If anyone asks you why you are taking the donkeys, tell him, 'The Master needs them. He will send them back soon.'"

[4]This was to make clear the full meaning of what the prophet[d] said:

[5]"Tell the people of Jerusalem,
  'Your king is coming to you.
He is gentle and riding on a
  donkey.
He is on the colt of a donkey.'"
        Isaiah 62:11; Zechariah 9:9

"**D**id you know that a one-person parade was held in Jesus' honor? Read about it in Matthew 21:1-11."

[6]The followers went and did what Jesus told them to do. [7]They brought the donkey and the colt to Jesus. They laid their coats on the donkeys, and Jesus sat on them. [8]Many people spread their coats on the road before Jesus. Others cut branches from the trees and spread them on the road. [9]Some of the people were walking ahead of Jesus. Others were walking behind him. All the people were shouting,

"Praise[n] to the Son of David![d]

---

[n]**accept . . . suffer** Literally, "drink the cup that I must drink." Jesus used the idea of drinking from a cup to mean accepting the terrible things that would happen to him.

[n]**Praise** Literally, "Hosanna," a Hebrew word used at first in praying to God for help. At this time it was probably a shout of joy used in praising God or his Messiah.

God bless the One who comes in the name of the Lord!

Psalm 118:26

Praise to God in heaven!"

[10]Then Jesus went into Jerusalem. The city was filled with excitement. The people asked, "Who is this man?"

[11]The crowd answered, "This man is Jesus. He is the prophet from the town of Nazareth in Galilee."

Jesus Goes to the Temple

[12]Jesus went into the Temple.[d] He threw out all the people who were buying and selling there. He turned over the tables that belonged to the men who were exchanging different kinds of money. And he upset the benches of those who were selling doves. [13]Jesus said to all the people there, "It is written in the Scriptures,[d] 'My Temple will be a house where people will pray.'[n] But you are changing God's house into a 'hideout for robbers.'"[n]

[14]The blind and crippled people came to Jesus in the Temple, and Jesus healed them. [15]The leading priests and the teachers of the law saw that Jesus was doing wonderful things. They saw the children praising him in the Temple. The children were saying, "Praise[n] to the Son of David."[d] All these things made the priests and the teachers of the law very angry.

[16]They asked Jesus, "Do you hear the things these children are saying?"

Jesus answered, "Yes. Haven't you read in the Scriptures, 'You have taught children and babies to sing praises'?"[n]

[17]Then Jesus left and went out of the city to Bethany, where he spent the night.

The Power of Faith

[18]Early the next morning, Jesus was going back to the city. He was very hungry. [19]He saw a fig tree beside the road. Jesus went to it, but there were no figs on the tree. There were only leaves. So Jesus said to the tree, "You will never again have fruit!" The tree immediately dried up.

[20]His followers saw this and were amazed. They asked, "How did the fig tree dry up so quickly?"

[21]Jesus answered, "I tell you the truth. If you have faith and do not doubt, you will be able to do what I did to this tree. And you will be able to do more. You will be able to say to this mountain, 'Go, mountain, fall into the sea.' And if you have faith, it will happen. [22]If you believe, you will get anything you ask for in prayer."

Leaders Doubt Jesus' Authority

[23]Jesus went to the Temple.[d] While he was teaching there, the leading priests and the older leaders of the people came to Jesus. They said to him, "Tell us! What authority do you have to do these things? Who gave you this authority?"

[24]Jesus answered, "I will ask you a question, too. If you answer me, then I will tell you what authority I have to do these things. [25]Tell me: When John baptized people, did that come from God or from man?"

The priests and the leaders argued about Jesus' question. They said to each other, "If we answer, 'John's baptism was from God,' then Jesus will say, 'Then why didn't you believe John?' [26]But if we say, 'It was from man,' we are afraid of what the people will do because they all believe that John was a prophet."[d]

[27]So they answered Jesus, "We don't know."

Then Jesus said, "Then I won't tell you what authority I have to do these things!

A Story About Two Sons

[28]"Tell me what you think about this:

---

[n]**'My Temple . . . pray.'**   Quotation from Isaiah 56:7.

[n]**'hideout for robbers.'**   Quotation from Jeremiah 7:11.

[n]**Praise**   Literally, "Hosanna," a Hebrew word used at first in praying to God for help. At this time it was probably a shout of joy used in praising God or his Messiah.

[n]**'You . . . praises'**   Quotation from the Septuagint (Greek) version of Psalm 8:3.

There was a man who had two sons. He went to the first son and said, 'Son, go and work today in my vineyard.' [29]The son answered, 'I will not go.' But later the son decided he should go, and he went. [30]Then the father went to the other son and said, 'Son, go and work today in my vineyard.' The son answered, 'Yes, sir, I will go and work.' But he did not go. [31]Which of the two sons obeyed his father?"

The priests and leaders answered, "The first son."

Jesus said to them, "I tell you the truth. The tax collectors and the prostitutes[d] will enter the kingdom of God before you do. [32]John came to show you the right way to live. And you did not believe him. But the tax collectors and prostitutes believed John. You saw this, but you still refused to change and believe him.

God Sends His Son

[33]"Listen to this story: There was a man who owned a vineyard. He put a wall around the vineyard and dug a hole for a winepress.[d] Then he built a tower. He leased the land to some farmers and left for a trip. [34]Later, it was time for the grapes to be picked. So the man sent his servants to the farmers to get his share of the grapes. [35]But the farmers grabbed the servants, beat one, killed another, and then killed a third servant with stones. [36]So the man sent some other servants to the farmers. He sent more servants than he sent the first time. But the farmers did the same thing to the servants that they had done before. [37]So the man decided to send his son to the farmers. He said, 'The farmers will respect my son.' [38]But when the farmers saw the son, they said to each other, 'This is the owner's son. This vineyard will be his. If we kill him, then his vineyard will be ours!' [39]So the farmers grabbed the son, threw him out of the vineyard, and killed him. [40]So what will the owner of the vineyard do to these farmers when he comes?"

[41]The priests and leaders said, "He will surely kill those evil men. Then he will lease the vineyard to some other farmers. They will give him his share of the crop at harvest time."

[42]Jesus said to them, "Surely you have read this in the Scriptures:[d]

'The stone that the builders did not want
became the cornerstone.[d]
The Lord did this,
and it is wonderful to us.'

Psalm 118:22-23

[43]"So I tell you that the kingdom of God will be taken away from you. It will be given to people who do the things God wants in his kingdom. [44]The person who falls on this stone will be broken. But if the stone falls on him, he will be crushed."

[45]The leading priests and the Pharisees[d] heard these stories that Jesus told. They knew he was talking about them. [46]They wanted to arrest him. But they were afraid of the people, because the people believed that Jesus was a prophet.[d]

A Story About a Wedding Feast

22 Jesus used stories to tell other things to the people. He said, [2]"The kingdom of heaven is like a king who prepared a wedding feast for his son. [3]The king invited some people to the feast. When the feast was ready, the king sent his servants to tell the people to come. But they refused to come to the feast.

[4]"Then the king sent other servants. He said to them, 'Tell those who have been invited that my feast is ready. I have killed my best bulls and calves for the dinner. Everything is ready. Come to the wedding feast.'

[5]"But the people refused to listen to the servants. They went to do other things. One went to work in his field, and another went to his business. [6]Some of the other people grabbed the servants, beat them, and killed them. [7]The king was very angry. He sent his army to kill the people who had killed his servants. And the army burned their city.

[8]"After that, the king said to his servants, 'The wedding feast is ready. I invited those people, but they were not worthy to come. [9]So go to the street corners and invite everyone you see. Tell them to come to my feast.' [10]So the servants went into the streets. They gathered all the people they could find, both good and bad. And the wedding hall was filled with guests.

[11]"Then the king came in to see all the guests. He saw a man there who was not dressed in the right clothes for a wedding. [12]The king said, 'Friend, how were you allowed to come in here? You are not wearing the right clothes for a wedding.' But the man said nothing. [13]So the king told some servants, 'Tie this man's hands and feet. Throw him out into the darkness. In that place, people will cry and grind their teeth with pain.'

[14]"Yes, many people are invited. But only a few are chosen."

The Pharisees Try to Trap Jesus

[15]Then the Pharisees[d] left the place where Jesus was teaching. They made plans to trap Jesus with a question. [16]They sent some of their own followers and some men from the group called Herodians.[n] These men said, "Teacher, we know that you are an honest man. We know that you teach the truth about God's way. You are not afraid of what other people think about you. All men are the same to you. [17]So tell us what you think. Is it right to pay taxes to Caesar[d] or not?"

[18]But Jesus knew that these men were trying to trick him. So he said, "You hypocrites![d] Why are you trying to trap me? [19]Show me a coin used for paying the tax." The men showed him a silver coin.[n] [20]Then Jesus asked, "Whose picture is on the coin? And whose name is written on the coin?"

[21]The men answered, "Caesar's."

Then Jesus said to them, "Give to Caesar the things that are Caesar's. And give to God the things that are God's."

[22]The men heard what Jesus said, and they were amazed. They left him and went away.

Sadducees Try to Trick Jesus

[23]That same day some Sadducees[d]

Words to Know: New Testament
SADDUCEES • MATTHEW 22:23

One of the groups of men who often spoke to Jesus was the **Sadducees**. These men were religious leaders in Israel. But they were different from other leaders because they did not believe that anyone would be resurrected from the dead. Also, they did not believe in the whole Old Testament. They only read and followed Genesis, Exodus, Leviticus, Numbers, and Deuteronomy. Jesus tried to show the Sadducees that all of the Bible (our Old Testament) is important to study and that people will one day be raised from the dead.

How sad it would be to not be able to look forward to living with Jesus forever!

To read about some other leaders who did not believe in Jesus, fly to page 1194.

[n]**Herodians**   A political group that followed Herod and his family.
[n]**silver coin**   A Roman denarius. One coin was the average pay for one day's work.

came to Jesus. (Sadducees believe that no person will rise from death.) The Sadducees asked Jesus a question. [24]They said, "Teacher, Moses told us that a married man might die without having children. Then his brother must marry the widow and have children for him. [25]There were seven brothers among us. The first one married but died. He had no children. So his brother married the widow. [26]Then the second brother also died. The same thing happened to the third brother and all the other brothers. [27]The woman was last to die. [28]But all seven men had married her. So when people rise from death, whose wife will she be?"

[29]Jesus answered, "You don't understand because you don't know what the Scriptures[d] say. And you don't know about the power of God. [30]When people rise from death, there will be no marriage. People will not be married to each other. They will be like the angels in heaven. [31]Surely you have read what God said to you about the rising from death? [32]God said, 'I am the God of Abraham, the God of Isaac, and the God of Jacob.'[n] God is the God of living people, not dead people."

[33]All the people heard this. They were amazed at Jesus' teaching.

The Most Important Command

[34]The Pharisees[d] learned that the Sadducees[d] could not argue with Jesus' answers to them. So the Pharisees met together. [35]One Pharisee was an expert in the law of Moses. That Pharisee asked Jesus a question to test him. [36]The Pharisee asked, "Teacher, which command in the law is the most important?"

[37]Jesus answered, "'Love the Lord your God with all your heart, soul and mind.'[n] [38]This is the first and most important command. [39]And the second command is like the first: 'Love your neighbor as you love yourself.'[n] [40]All the law and the writings of the prophets[d] depend on these two commands."

Jesus Questions the Pharisees

[41]While the Pharisees[d] were together, Jesus asked them a question. [42]He asked, "What do you think about the Christ?[d] Whose son is he?"

The Pharisees answered, "The Christ is the Son of David."[d]

[43]Then Jesus said to them, "Then why did David call him 'Lord'? David was speaking by the power of the Holy Spirit.[d] David said,
[44]'The Lord said to my Lord:
    Sit by me at my right side,
    until I put your enemies under
        your control.'   *Psalm 110:1*
[45]David calls the Christ 'Lord.' So how can he be David's son?"

[46]None of the Pharisees could answer Jesus' question. And after that day no one was brave enough to ask Jesus any more questions.

Jesus Accuses the Leaders

23 Then Jesus spoke to the crowds and to his followers. Jesus said, [2]"The teachers of the law and the Pharisees[d] have the authority to tell you what the law of Moses says. [3]So you should obey and follow whatever they tell you. But their lives are not good examples for you to follow. They tell you to do things, but they don't do the things themselves. [4]They make strict rules and try to force people to obey them. But they themselves will not try to follow any of those rules.

[5]"The reason they do good things is so other people will see them. They make the boxes[n] of Scriptures[d] that they wear bigger and bigger. And they make their special prayer clothes very long so that people will notice them. [6]Those Pharisees and teachers of the law love

---

[n]'**I am . . . Jacob.'** Quotation from Exodus 3:6.
[n]'**Love . . . mind.'** Quotation from Deuteronomy 6:5.
[n]'**Love . . . yourself.'** Quotation from Leviticus 19:18.
[n]**boxes** Small leather boxes containing four important Scriptures. Some Jews tied these to the forehead and left arm, probably to show they were very religious.

to have the most important seats at the feasts. And they love to have the most important seats in the synagogues.[d] [7]They love people to show respect to them in the marketplaces. And they love to have people call them 'Teacher.'

[8]"But you must not be called 'Teacher.' You are all brothers and sisters together. You have only one Teacher. [9]And don't call any person on earth 'Father.' You have one Father. He is in heaven. [10]And you should not be called 'Master.' You have only one Master, the Christ.[d] [11]He who serves you as a servant is the greatest among you. [12]Whoever makes himself great will be made humble. Whoever makes himself humble will be made great.

the law and Pharisees! You are hypocrites! You travel across land and sea to find one person who will follow your ways. When you find that person, you make him more fit for hell than you are.

[16]"How terrible for you, teachers of the law and Pharisees! You guide the people, but you are blind. You say, 'If anyone swears by the Temple[d] when he makes a promise, that means nothing. But if anyone swears by the gold that is in the Temple, then he must keep that promise.' [17]You are blind fools! Which is greater: the gold or the Temple? The Temple makes that gold holy.

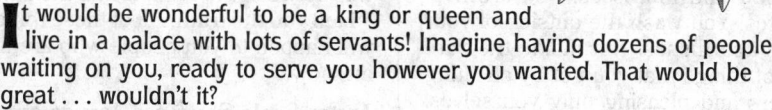

Helping Others
MATTHEW 23:11-12

It would be wonderful to be a king or queen and live in a palace with lots of servants! Imagine having dozens of people waiting on you, ready to serve you however you wanted. That would be great . . . wouldn't it?

Not according to Jesus. Not that there is anything wrong with being a king or queen, but Jesus said that it is *not* what makes someone great. In fact, he said it's the other way around: the person on the throne isn't great, the one who *serves* is great. According to these verses, that is the true definition of greatness—*helping others*.

Next time you and your friends are playing make-believe, let the others fight over who gets to be king, queen, president, or captain of the ship. After they have finished arguing over that, stand up and say, "Now that you've chosen your roles, could I be a *servant*?" They may not understand, but God will.

To learn more about helping others, zoom to page 1203.

[13]"How terrible for you, teachers of the law and Pharisees! You are hypocrites![d] You close the door for people to enter the kingdom of heaven. You yourselves don't enter, and you stop others who are trying to enter. [14][n]

[15]"How terrible for you, teachers of

[18]And you say, 'If anyone swears by the altar when he makes a promise, that means nothing. But if he swears by the gift on the altar, then he must keep his promise.' [19]You are blind! Which is greater: the gift or the altar? The altar makes the gift holy. [20]The person who

[n]**Verse 14** Some Greek copies add verse 14: "How terrible for you, teachers of the law and Pharisees. You are hypocrites. You take away widows' houses, and you make long prayers so that people can see you. So you will have a worse punishment."

swears by the altar is really using the altar and also everything on the altar. ²¹And the person who uses the Temple to make a promise is really using the Temple and also everything in the Temple. ²²The person who uses heaven to make a promise is also using God's throne and the One who sits on that throne.

²³"How terrible for you, teachers of the law and Pharisees! You are hypocrites! You give to God one-tenth of everything you earn—even your mint, dill, and cummin.[n] But you don't obey the really important teachings of the law—being fair, showing mercy, and being loyal. These are the things you should do, as well as those other things. ²⁴You guide the people, but you are blind! You are like a person who picks a fly out of his drink and then swallows a camel![n]

²⁵"How terrible for you, teachers of the law and Pharisees! You are hypocrites! You wash the outside of your cups and dishes. But inside they are full of things that you got by cheating others and pleasing only yourselves. ²⁶Pharisees, you are blind! First make the inside of the cup clean and good. Then the outside of the cup can be truly clean.

²⁷"How terrible for you, teachers of the law and Pharisees. You are hypocrites! You are like tombs that are painted white. Outside, those tombs look fine. But inside, they are full of the bones of dead people, and all kinds of unclean things are there. ²⁸It is the same with you. People look at you and think you are good. But on the inside you are full of hypocrisy and evil.

²⁹"How terrible for you, teachers of the law and Pharisees! You are hypocrites! You build tombs for the prophets.[d] You show honor to the graves of people who lived good lives. ³⁰And you

say, 'If we had lived during the time of our fathers, we would not have helped them kill the prophets.' ³¹But you give proof that you are children of those people who murdered the prophets. ³²And you will complete the sin that your fathers started!

³³"You are snakes! A family of poisonous snakes! You will not escape God. You will all be judged guilty and be sent to hell! ³⁴So I tell you this: I am sending to you prophets and wise men and teachers. You will kill some of these people. You will nail some of them to crosses. You will beat some of them in your synagogues. You will chase them from town to town. ³⁵So you will be guilty for the death of all the good people who have been killed on earth. You will be guilty for the murder of that good man Abel. And you will be guilty for the murder of Zechariah[n] son of Berakiah. He was murdered when he was between the Temple and the altar. ³⁶I tell you the truth. All of these things will happen to you people who are living now.

Jesus Feels Sorry for Jerusalem

³⁷"Jerusalem, Jerusalem! You kill the prophets[d] and kill with stones those men God sent to you. Many times I wanted to help your people! I wanted to gather them together as a hen gathers her chicks under her wings. But you did not let me. ³⁸Now your home will be left completely empty. ³⁹I tell you, you will not see me again until that time when you will say, 'God bless the One who comes in the name of the Lord.'"[n]

The Temple Will Be Destroyed

24 Jesus left the Temple[d] and was walking away. But his followers came to show him the Temple's buildings. ²Jesus asked, "Do you see all these buildings? I tell you the truth. Every

---

[n]**mint, dill, and cummin** Small plants grown in gardens and used for spices. Only very religious people would be careful enough to give a tenth of these plants.
[n]**You . . . camel!** Meaning, "You worry about the smallest mistakes but commit the biggest sin."
[n]**Abel . . . Zechariah** In the Hebrew Old Testament, the first and last men to be murdered.
[n]**God . . . Lord** Quotation from Psalm 118:26.

stone will be thrown down to the ground. Not one stone will be left on another."

[3]Later, Jesus was sitting on the Mount of Olives.[d] His followers came to be alone with him. They said, "Tell us when these things will happen. And what will happen to show us that it is time for you to come again and for the world to end?"

[4]Jesus answered: "Be careful that no one fools you. [5]Many people will come in my name. They will say, 'I am the Christ.'[d] And they will fool many people. [6]You will hear about wars and stories of wars that are coming. But don't be afraid. These things must happen before the end comes. [7]Nations will fight against other nations. Kingdoms will fight against other kingdoms. There will be times when there is no food for people to eat. And there will be earthquakes in different places. [8]These things are like the first pains when something new is about to be born.

[9]"Then men will arrest you and hand you over to be hurt and kill you. They will hate you because you believe in me. [10]At that time, many who believe will lose their faith. They will turn against each other and hate each other. [11]Many false prophets[d] will come and cause many people to believe false things. [12]There will be more and more evil in the world. So most people will stop showing their love for each other. [13]But the person who continues to be strong until the end will be saved. [14]The Good News[d] about God's kingdom will be preached in all the world, to every nation. Then the end will come.

[15]"Daniel the prophet spoke about 'The horrible thing that destroys.'[n] You will see this terrible thing standing in the holy place." (You who read this should understand what it means.) [16]"At that time, the people in Judea should run away to the mountains. [17]If a person is on the roof[n] of his house, he must not go down to get anything out of his house. [18]If a person is in the field, he must not go back to get his coat. [19]At that time, it will be hard for women who are pregnant or have nursing babies! [20]Pray that it will not be winter or a Sabbath[d] day when these things happen and you have to run away. [21]This is because that at that time there will be much trouble. There will be more trouble than has ever happened since the beginning of the world. And nothing as bad as that will ever happen again. [22]God has decided to make that terrible time short. If that time were not made short, then no one would go on living. But God will make that time short to help the people he has chosen. [23]At that time, someone might say to you, 'Look, there is the Christ!' Or another person might say, 'There he is!' But don't believe them. [24]False Christs and false prophets will come and perform great things and miracles.[d] They will do these things to the people God has chosen. They will fool them, if that is possible. [25]Now I have warned you about this before it happens.

[26]"If people tell you, 'The Christ is in the desert'—don't go there. If they say, 'The Christ is in the inner room'—don't believe it. [27]When the Son of Man[d] comes, he will be seen by everyone. It will be like lightning flashing in the sky that can be seen everywhere. [28]Wherever there is a dead body, there the vultures will gather.

[29]"Soon after the trouble of those days, this will happen:

'The sun will grow dark.
And the moon will not give its light.
The stars will fall from the sky.
And everything in the sky will be changed.'   *Isaiah 13:10; 34:4*

[30]"At that time, there will be something in the sky that shows the Son of Man is coming. All the peoples of the world will cry. They will see the Son of Man coming on clouds in the sky. He will come with great power and glory.

---

[n]**'horrible . . . destroys.'**   Mentioned in Daniel 9:27; 12:11 (cf. Daniel 11:31).
[n]**roof**   In Bible times houses were built with flat roofs. The roof was used for drying things such as flax and fruit. And it was used as an extra room, as a place for worship and as a place to sleep in the summer.

31He will use a loud trumpet to send his angels all around the earth. They will gather his chosen people from every part of the world.

32"The fig tree teaches us a lesson: When its branches become green and soft, and new leaves begin to grow, then you know that summer is near. 33So also, when you see all these things happening, you will know that the time is near, ready to come. 34I tell you the truth. All these things will happen while the people of this time are still living! 35The whole world, earth and sky, will be destroyed, but the words I have said will never be destroyed!

When Will Jesus Come Again?

36"No one knows when that day or time will be. Even the Son and the angels in heaven don't know. Only the Father knows. 37When the Son of Man[d] comes, it will be the same as what happened during Noah's time. 38In those days before the flood, people were eating and drinking. They were marrying and giving their children to be married. They were still doing those things until the day Noah entered the boat. 39They knew nothing about what was happening. But then the flood came, and all those people were destroyed. It will be the same when the Son of Man comes. 40Two men will be working together in the field. One man will be taken and the other left. 41Two women will be grinding grain with a hand mill.[n] One woman will be taken and the other will be left.

42"So always be ready. You don't know the day your Lord will come. 43Remember this: If the owner of the house knew what time a thief was coming, then the owner would be ready for him. The owner would watch and not let the thief enter his house. 44So you also must be ready. The Son of Man will come at a time you don't expect him.

45"Who is the wise and trusted servant? The master trusts one servant to give the other servants their food at the right time. 46When the master comes and finds the servant doing his work, the servant will be very happy. 47I tell you the truth. The master will choose that servant to take care of everything the master owns. 48But what will happen if the servant is evil and thinks his master will not come back soon? 49Then that servant will begin to beat the other servants. He will feast and get drunk with others like him. 50And the master will come when the servant is not ready and is not expecting him. 51Then the master will punish that servant. He will send him away to be among the hypocrites.[d] There people will cry and grind their teeth with pain.

A Story About Ten Girls

25 "At that time the kingdom of heaven will be like ten girls who went to wait for the bridegroom. They took their lamps with them. 2Five of the girls were foolish and five were wise. 3The five foolish girls took their lamps, but they did not take more oil for the lamps to burn. 4The wise girls took their lamps and more oil in jars. 5The bridegroom was very late. All the girls became sleepy and went to sleep.

6"At midnight someone cried out, 'The bridegroom is coming! Come and meet him!' 7Then all the girls woke up and got their lamps ready. 8But the foolish girls said to the wise, 'Give us some of your oil. Our lamps are going out.' 9The wise girls answered, 'No! The oil we have might not be enough for all of us. Go to the people who sell oil and buy some for yourselves.'

10"So the five foolish girls went to buy oil. While they were gone, the bridegroom came. The girls who were ready went in with the bridegroom to the wedding feast. Then the door was closed and locked.

11"Later the others came back. They called, 'Sir, sir, open the door to let us in.' 12But the bridegroom answered, 'I tell you the truth, I don't know you.'

13"So always be ready. You don't

---

*n***mill** Two large, round, flat rocks used for grinding grain to make flour.

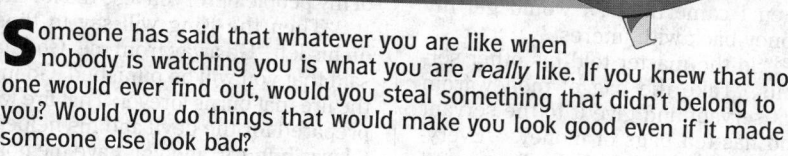

Character
MATTHEW 25:14-46

Someone has said that whatever you are like when nobody is watching you is what you are *really* like. If you knew that no one would ever find out, would you steal something that didn't belong to you? Would you do things that would make you look good even if it made someone else look bad?

These stories tell us the things people did when they thought no one was looking. But later everyone knew their actions and their thoughts, and they were either rewarded or punished accordingly. That doesn't always happen in real life. But we should always remember that wherever we are and whatever we do, our loving heavenly father *is* watching. He knows what we are really like . . . and he loves us anyway. We want him to be proud of us, so we do the things that please him.

Be someone he can be proud of—even when no one is watching!

To learn more about character, zoom to page 1378.

know the day or the time the Son of Man[d] will come.

A Story About Three Servants

[14]"The kingdom of heaven is like a man who was going to another place for a visit. Before he left, he talked with his servants. The man told them to take care of his things while he was gone. [15]He decided how much each servant would be able to care for. He gave one servant five bags of money. He gave another servant two bags of money. And he gave a third servant one bag of money. Then the man left. [16]The servant who got five bags went quickly to invest the money. The five bags of money earned five more. [17]It was the same with the servant who had two bags of money. He invested the money and earned two more. [18]But the servant who got one bag of money went out and dug a hole in the ground. Then he hid his master's money in the hole.

[19]"After a long time the master came home. He asked the servants what they did with his money. [20]The servant who

got five bags of money brought five more bags to the master. The servant said, 'Master, you trusted me to care for five bags of money. So I used your five bags to earn five more.' [21]The master answered, 'You did well. You are a good servant who can be trusted. You did well with small things. So I will let you care for much greater things. Come and share my happiness with me.'

[22]"Then the servant who got two bags of money came to the master. The servant said, 'Master, you gave me two bags of money to care for. So I used your two bags to earn two more.' [23]The master answered, 'You did well. You are a good servant who can be trusted. You did well with small things. So I will let you care for much greater things. Come and share my happiness with me.'

[24]"Then the servant who got one bag of money came to the master. The servant said, 'Master, I knew that you were a hard man. You harvest things you did not plant. You gather crops where you did not sow any seed. [25]So I was afraid. I went and hid your money in the

ground. Here is the bag of money you gave me.' ²⁶The master answered, 'You are a bad and lazy servant! You say you knew that I harvest things I did not plant, and that I gather crops where I did not sow any seed? ²⁷So you should have put my money in the bank. Then, when I came home, I would get my money back with interest.'

²⁸"So the master told his other servants, 'Take the bag of money from that servant and give it to the servant who has ten bags of money. ²⁹Everyone who uses what he has will get more. He will have much more than he needs. But the one who does not use what he has will have everything taken away from him.' ³⁰Then the master said, 'Throw that useless servant outside, into the darkness! There people will cry and grind their teeth with pain.'

The King Will Judge All People

³¹"The Son of Man^d will come again in his great glory. All his angels will come with him. He will be King and sit on his great throne. ³²All the people of the world will be gathered before him. Then he will separate them into two groups as a shepherd separates the sheep from the goats. ³³The Son of Man will put the sheep, the good people, on his right and the goats, the bad people, on his left.

³⁴"Then the King will say to the good people on his right, 'Come. My Father has given you his blessing. Come and receive the kingdom God has prepared for you since the world was made. ³⁵I was hungry, and you gave me food. I was thirsty, and you gave me something to drink. I was alone and away from home, and you invited me into your house. ³⁶I was without clothes, and you gave me something to wear. I was sick, and you cared for me. I was in prison, and you visited me.'

³⁷"Then the good people will answer, 'Lord, when did we see you hungry and give you food? When did we see you thirsty and give you something to drink? ³⁸When did we see you alone and away

from home and invite you into our house? When did we see you without clothes and give you something to wear? ³⁹When did we see you sick or in prison and care for you?'

⁴⁰"Then the King will answer, 'I tell you the truth. Anything you did for any of my people here, you also did for me.'

⁴¹"Then the King will say to those on his left, 'Go away from me. God has said that you will be punished. Go into the fire that burns forever. That fire was prepared for the devil and his helpers. ⁴²I was hungry, and you gave me nothing to eat. I was thirsty, and you gave me nothing to drink. ⁴³I was alone and away from home, and you did not invite me into your house. I was without clothes, and you gave me nothing to wear. I was sick and in prison, and you did not care for me.'

⁴⁴"Then those people will answer, 'Lord, when did we see you hungry or thirsty? When did we see you alone and away from home? Or when did we see you without clothes or sick or in prison? When did we see these things and not help you?'

⁴⁵"Then the King will answer, 'I tell you the truth. Anything you refused to do for any of my people here, you refused to do for me.'

⁴⁶"These people will go off to be punished forever. But the good people will go to live forever."

The Plan to Kill Jesus

26 After Jesus finished saying all these things, he told his followers, ²"You know that the day after tomorrow is the day of the Passover^d Feast. On that day the Son of Man^d will be given to his enemies to be killed on a cross."

³Then the leading priests and the older Jewish leaders had a meeting at the palace of the high priest. The high priest's name was Caiaphas. ⁴At the meeting, they planned to set a trap to arrest Jesus and kill him. ⁵But they said, "We must not do it during the feast. The people might cause a riot."

A Woman with Perfume for Jesus

[6]Jesus was in Bethany. He was at the house of Simon, who had a harmful skin disease. [7]While Jesus was there, a woman came to him. She had an alabaster[d] jar filled with expensive perfume. She poured this perfume on Jesus' head while he was eating.

[8]His followers saw the woman do this and were upset. They asked, "Why waste that perfume? [9]It could be sold for a great deal of money, and the money could be given to the poor."

[10]But Jesus knew what happened. He said, "Why are you troubling this woman? She did a very beautiful thing for me. [11]You will always have the poor with you. But you will not always have me. [12]This woman poured perfume on my body to prepare me for burial. [13]I tell you the truth. The Good News[d] will be told to people in all the world. And in every place where it is preached, what this woman has done will be told. And people will remember her."

Judas Becomes an Enemy of Jesus

[14]Then 1 of the 12 followers went to talk to the leading priests. This was the follower named Judas Iscariot. [15]He said, "I will give Jesus to you. What will you pay me for doing this?" The priests gave Judas 30 silver coins. [16]After that, Judas waited for the best time to give Jesus to the priests.

Jesus Eats the Passover Feast

[17]On the first day of the Feast[d] of Unleavened Bread, the followers came to Jesus. They said, "We will prepare everything for you to eat the Passover[d] Feast. Where do you want to have the feast?"

[18]Jesus answered, "Go into the city to a certain man. Tell him that the Teacher says, 'The chosen time is near. I will have the Passover Feast with my followers at your house.'" [19]The followers did what Jesus told them to do, and they prepared the Passover Feast.

[20]In the evening Jesus was sitting at the table with his 12 followers. [21]They were all eating. Then Jesus said, "I tell you the truth. One of you 12 will turn against me."

[22]This made the followers very sad. Each one said to Jesus, "Surely, Lord, I am not the one who will turn against you. Am I?"

[23]Jesus answered, "The man who has dipped his hand with me into the bowl is the one who will turn against me. [24]The Son of Man[d] will die. The Scriptures[d] say this will happen. But how terrible it will be for the person who gives the Son of Man to be killed. It would be better for him if he had never been born."

[25]Then Judas said to Jesus, "Teacher, surely I am not the one. Am I?" (Judas is the one who would give Jesus to his enemies.)

Jesus answered, "Yes, it is you."

The Lord's Supper

[26]While they were eating, Jesus took some bread. He thanked God for it and broke it. Then he gave it to his followers and said, "Take this bread and eat it. This bread is my body."

[27]Then Jesus took a cup. He thanked God for it and gave it to the followers. He said, "Every one of you drink this. [28]This is my blood which begins the new agreement that God makes with his people. This blood is poured out for many to forgive their sins. [29]I tell you this: I will not drink of this fruit of the vine[n] again until that day when I drink it new with you in my Father's kingdom."

[30]They sang a hymn. Then they went out to the Mount of Olives.[d]

Jesus' Followers Will All Leave Him

[31]Jesus told the followers, "Tonight you will lose your faith because of me. It is written in the Scriptures:[d]
'I will kill the shepherd,
   and the sheep will scatter.'
Zechariah 13:7

---

[n]**fruit of the vine**   Product of the grapevine; this may also be translated "wine."

³²But after I rise from death, I will go ahead of you into Galilee."

³³Peter said, "All the other followers may lose their faith because of you. But I will never lose my faith."

³⁴Jesus said, "I tell you the truth. Tonight you will say you don't know me. You will say this three times before the rooster crows."

³⁵But Peter said, "I will never say that I don't know you! I will even die with you!" And all the other followers said the same thing.

ble, do not give me this cup[n] of suffering. But do what you want, not what I want." ⁴⁰Then Jesus went back to his followers and found them asleep. Jesus said to Peter, "You men could not stay awake with me for one hour? ⁴¹Stay awake and pray for strength against temptation. Your spirit wants to do what is right. But your body is weak."

⁴²Then Jesus went away a second time. He prayed, "My Father, if it is

Prayer
MATTHEW 26:36-41

On some Sundays, you know you should get up and get ready for church, but you feel like you would rather sleep a little longer. Some days, you know you should spend time reading your Bible or praying, but you'd rather go outside and play.

The men who went with Jesus to pray in the garden (Peter, James, and John) felt the same way. They fought to stay awake so they could pray. Three times Jesus asked them to pray while he went off by himself to pray, but each time they fell asleep. They must have felt like total losers.

Jesus understood their weakness. He told them to ask God to help them win the struggle. That's what you should do, too, when you're caught in the struggle between what you know you should do and what you feel like doing.

To learn more about prayer, zoom to page 1182.

Jesus Prays Alone

³⁶Then Jesus went with his followers to a place called Gethsemane. He said to them, "Sit here while I go over there and pray." ³⁷He told Peter and the two sons of Zebedee to come with him. Then Jesus began to be very sad and troubled. ³⁸He said to Peter and the two sons of Zebedee, "My heart is full of sorrow and breaking with sadness. Stay here with me and watch."

³⁹Then Jesus walked a little farther away from them. He fell to the ground and prayed, "My Father, if it is possi-

not possible for this painful thing to be taken from me, and if I must do it, then I pray that what you want will be done."

⁴³Then Jesus went back to the followers. Again he found them asleep, because their eyes were heavy. ⁴⁴So Jesus left them and went away one more time and prayed. This third time he prayed, he said the same thing.

⁴⁵Then Jesus went back to the followers and said, "You are still sleeping and resting? The time has come for the Son of Man[d] to be given to sinful people. ⁴⁶Get up. We must go. Here comes the man who has turned against me."

---

[n]**cup** Jesus is talking about the bad things that will happen to him. Accepting these things will be very hard, like drinking a cup of something that tastes very bitter.

Jesus Is Arrested

⁴⁷While Jesus was still speaking, Judas came up. Judas was 1 of the 12 followers. He had many people with him. They had been sent from the leading priests and the older leaders of the people. They carried swords and clubs. ⁴⁸Judas had planned to give them a signal. He had said, "The man I kiss is Jesus. Arrest him." ⁴⁹At once Judas went to Jesus and said, "Greetings, Teacher!" Then Judas kissed him.

⁵⁰Jesus answered, "Friend, do the thing you came to do."

Then the men came and grabbed Jesus and arrested him. ⁵¹When that happened, one of Jesus' followers reached for his sword and pulled it out. The follower struck the servant of the high priest with the sword and cut off his ear.

⁵²Jesus said to the man, "Put your sword back in its place. All who use swords will be killed with swords. ⁵³Surely you know I could ask my Father, and he would give me more than 12 armies of angels. ⁵⁴But this thing must happen this way so that it will be as the Scriptures^d say."

⁵⁵Then Jesus said to the crowd, "You came to get me with swords and clubs as if I were a criminal. Every day I sat in the Temple^d teaching. You did not arrest me there. ⁵⁶But all these things have happened so that it will be as the prophets^d wrote." Then all of Jesus' followers left him and ran away.

Jesus Before the Jewish Leaders

⁵⁷Those men who arrested Jesus led him to the house of Caiaphas, the high priest. The teachers of the law and the older Jewish leaders were gathered there. ⁵⁸Peter followed Jesus but did not go near him. He followed Jesus to the courtyard of the high priest's house. He sat down with the guards to see what would happen to Jesus.

⁵⁹The leading priests and the Jewish council tried to find something false against Jesus so that they could kill him. ⁶⁰Many people came and told lies about him. But the council could find no real reason to kill Jesus. Then two people came and said, ⁶¹"This man said, 'I can destroy the Temple^d of God and build it again in three days.'"

⁶²Then the high priest stood up and said to Jesus, "Aren't you going to answer? Don't you have something to say about their charges against you?" ⁶³But Jesus said nothing.

Again the high priest said to Jesus, "You must swear to this. I command you by the power of the living God to tell us the truth. Tell us, are you the Christ,^d the Son of God?"

⁶⁴Jesus answered, "Yes, I am. But I tell you, in the future you will see the Son of Man^d sitting at the right hand of God, the Powerful One. And you will see him coming in clouds in the sky."

⁶⁵When the high priest heard this, he was very angry. He tore his clothes and said, "This man has said things that are against God! We don't need any more witnesses. You all heard him say these things against God. ⁶⁶What do you think?"

The people answered, "He is guilty, and he must die."

⁶⁷Then the people there spit in Jesus' face and beat him with their fists. Others slapped Jesus. ⁶⁸They said, "Prove to us that you are a prophet,^d you Christ! Tell us who hit you!"

Peter Says He Doesn't Know Jesus

⁶⁹At that time, Peter was sitting in the courtyard. A servant girl came to him and said, "You were with Jesus, that man from Galilee."

⁷⁰But Peter said that he was never with Jesus. He said this to all the people there. Peter said, "I don't know what you are talking about."

⁷¹Then he left the courtyard. At the gate, another girl saw him. She said to the people there, "This man was with Jesus of Nazareth."

⁷²Again, Peter said that he was never with Jesus. Peter said, "I swear that I don't know this man Jesus!"

⁷³A short time later, some people

standing there went to Peter. They said, "We know you are one of those men who followed Jesus. We know this because of the way you talk."

[74] Then Peter began to curse. He said, "May a curse fall on me if I'm not telling the truth. I don't know the man." After Peter said this, a rooster crowed. [75] Then he remembered what Jesus had told him: "Before the rooster crows, you will say three times that you don't know me." Then Peter went outside and cried painfully.

Jesus Is Taken to Pilate

27 Early the next morning, all the leading priests and older leaders of the people decided to kill Jesus. [2] They tied him, led him away, and turned him over to Pilate, the governor.

Judas Kills Himself

[3] Judas saw that they had decided to kill Jesus. Judas was the one who gave Jesus to his enemies. When Judas saw what happened, he was very sorry for what he had done. So he took the 30 silver coins back to the priests and the leaders. [4] Judas said, "I sinned. I gave you an innocent man to be killed."

The leaders answered, "What is that to us? That's your problem, not ours."

[5] So Judas threw the money into the Temple.[d] Then he went off and hanged himself.

[6] The leading priests picked up the silver coins in the Temple. They said, "Our law does not allow us to keep this money with the Temple money. This money has paid for a man's death." [7] So they decided to use the coins to buy a field called Potter's Field. This field would be a place to bury strangers who died while visiting Jerusalem. [8] That is why that field is still called the Field of Blood. [9] So the thing came true that Jeremiah the prophet[d] had said: "They took 30 silver coins. That is how little the Israelites thought he was worth. [10] They used those 30 silver coins to buy the potter's field, as the Lord commanded me."[n]

Pilate Questions Jesus

[11] Jesus stood before Pilate the governor. Pilate asked him, "Are you the King of the Jews?"

Jesus answered, "Yes, I am."

[12] When the leading priests and the older leaders accused Jesus, he said nothing.

[13] So Pilate said to Jesus, "Don't you hear these people accusing you of all these things?"

[14] But Jesus said nothing in answer to Pilate. Pilate was very surprised at this.

Pilate Tries to Free Jesus

[15] Every year at the time of Passover[d] the governor would free one person from prison. This was always a person the people wanted to be set free. [16] At that time there was a man in prison who was known to be very bad. His name was Barabbas. [17] All the people gathered at Pilate's house. Pilate said, "Which man do you want me to free: Barabbas, or Jesus who is called the Christ?"[d] [18] Pilate knew that the people gave Jesus to him because they were jealous.

[19] Pilate said these things while he was sitting on the judge's seat. While he was sitting there, his wife sent a message to him. The message said, "Don't do anything to that man. He is not guilty. Today I had a dream about him, and it troubled me very much."

[20] But the leading priests and older leaders told the crowd to ask for Barabbas to be freed and for Jesus to be killed.

[21] Pilate said, "I have Barabbas and Jesus. Which do you want me to set free for you?"

The people answered, "Barabbas!"

[22] Pilate asked, "What should I do with Jesus, the one called the Christ?"

They all answered, "Kill him on a cross!"

[23] Pilate asked, "Why do you want me

---

n**"They . . . commanded me."** See Zechariah 11:12-13 and Jeremiah 32:6-9.

to kill him? What wrong has he done?"

But they shouted louder, "Kill him on a cross!"

[24]Pilate saw that he could do nothing about this, and a riot was starting. So he took some water and washed his hands[n] in front of the crowd. Then he said, "I am not guilty of this man's death. You are the ones who are causing it!"

[25]All the people answered, "We will be responsible. We accept for ourselves and for our children any punishment for his death."

[26]Then Pilate freed Barabbas. Pilate told some of the soldiers to beat Jesus with whips. Then he gave Jesus to the soldiers to be killed on a cross.

[27]Pilate's soldiers took Jesus into the governor's palace. All the soldiers gathered around Jesus. [28]They took off his clothes and put a red robe on him. [29]Then the soldiers used thorny branches to make a crown. They put this crown of thorns on Jesus' head. They put a stick in his right hand. Then the soldiers bowed before Jesus and made fun of him. They said, "Hail, King of the Jews!" [30]They spit on Jesus. Then they took his stick and hit him on the head many times. [31]After they finished making fun of Jesus, the soldiers took off the robe and put his own clothes on him again. Then they led Jesus away to be killed on a cross.

Jesus Is Killed on a Cross

[32]The soldiers were going out of the city with Jesus. They forced another man to carry the cross to be used for Jesus. This man was Simon, from Cyrene. [33]They all came to the place called Golgotha. (Golgotha means the Place of the Skull.) [34]At Golgotha, the soldiers gave Jesus wine to drink. This wine was mixed with gall.[n] He tasted the wine but refused to drink it. [35]The soldiers nailed Jesus to a cross. They threw lots[d] to decide who would get his

clothes. [36]The soldiers sat there and continued watching him. [37]They put a sign above Jesus' head with the charge against him written on it. The sign read: "THIS IS JESUS, THE KING OF THE JEWS." [38]Two robbers were nailed to crosses beside Jesus, one on the right and the other on the left. [39]People walked by and insulted Jesus. They shook their heads, [40]saying, "You said you could destroy the Temple[d] and build it again in three days. So save yourself! Come down from that cross, if you are really the Son of God!"

[41]The leading priests, the teachers of the law, and the older Jewish leaders were also there. These men made fun of Jesus [42]and said, "He saved other people, but he can't save himself! People say he is the King of Israel! If he is the King, then let him come down now from the cross. Then we will believe in him. [43]He trusts in God. So let God save him now, if God really wants him. He himself said, 'I am the Son of God.'" [44]And in the same way, the robbers who were being killed on crosses beside Jesus also insulted him.

Jesus Dies

[45]At noon the whole country became dark. This darkness lasted for three hours. [46]About three o'clock Jesus cried out in a loud voice, "Eli, Eli, lema sabachthani?" This means, "My God, my God, why have you left me alone?"

[47]Some of the people standing there heard this. They said, "He is calling Elijah."

[48]Quickly one of them ran and got a sponge. He filled the sponge with vinegar and tied it to a stick. Then he used the stick to give the sponge to Jesus to drink from it. [49]But the others said, "Don't bother him. We want to see if Elijah will come to save him."

[50]Again Jesus cried out in a loud voice. Then he died.

---

[n]**washed his hands** He did this as a sign to show that he wanted no part in what the people d[...]
[n]**gall** Probably a drink of wine mixed with drugs to help a person feel less pain.
[n]**curtain in the Temple** A curtain divided the Most Holy Place from the other part of the Te[...]
    That was the special building in Jerusalem where God commanded the Jews to worship him.

51Then the curtain in the Templeⁿ split into two pieces. The tear started at the top and tore all the way down to the bottom. Also, the earth shook and rocks broke apart. 52The graves opened, and many of God's people who had died were raised from death. 53They came out of the graves after Jesus was raised from death. They went into the holy city, and many people saw them.

54The army officer and the soldiers guarding Jesus saw this earthquake and everything else that happened. They were very frightened and said, "He really was the Son of God!"

55Many women were standing at a distance from the cross, watching. These were women who had followed Jesus from Galilee to care for him. 56Mary Magdalene, and Mary the mother of James and Joseph, and the mother of James and John were there.

Jesus Is Buried

57That evening a rich man named Joseph came to Jerusalem. He was a follower of Jesus from the town of Arimathea. 58Joseph went to Pilate and asked to have Jesus' body. Pilate gave orders for the soldiers to give it to Joseph. 59Then Joseph took the body and wrapped it in a clean linen cloth. 60He put Jesus' body in a new tomb that he had cut in a wall of rock. He rolled a very large stone to block the entrance of the tomb. Then Joseph went away. 61Mary Magdalene and the other woman named Mary were sitting near the tomb.

The Tomb of Jesus Is Guarded

62That day was the day called Preparation^d Day. The next day, the leading priests and the Pharisees^d went to Pilate. 63They said, "Sir, we remember that while that liar was still alive he said, 'After three days I will rise from death.' 64So give the order for the tomb to be guarded closely till the third day. His followers might come and steal the body. Then they could tell the people that he has risen from death. That lie would be even worse than the first one."

65Pilate said, "Take some soldiers and go guard the tomb the best way you know." 66So they all went to the tomb and made it safe from thieves. They did this by sealing the stone in the entrance and then putting soldiers there to guard it.

"My pastor says that putting a rock and seal on Jesus' tomb was like putting a band-aid on a volcano! Read in Matthew 27:57-66 how they tried to keep Jesus dead."

Jesus Rises from Death

28 The day after the Sabbath^d day was the first day of the week. At dawn on the first day, Mary Magdalene and another woman named Mary went to look at the tomb.

2At that time there was a strong earthquake. An angel of the Lord came down from heaven. The angel went to the tomb and rolled the stone away from the entrance. Then he sat on the stone. 3He was shining as bright as lightning. His clothes were white as snow. 4The soldiers guarding the tomb were very frightened of the angel. They shook with fear and then became like dead men.

5The angel said to the women, "Don't be afraid. I know that you are looking for Jesus, the one who was killed on the cross. 6But he is not here. He has risen from death as he said he would. Come and see the place where his body was. 7And go quickly and tell his followers. Say to them: 'Jesus has risen from death. He is going into Galilee. He will be there before you. You will see him there.'" Then the angel said, "Now I have told you."

8The women left the tomb quickly. They were afraid, but they were also very happy. They ran to tell Jesus'

Witnessing
MATTHEW 28:18-20

What would be the last thing you would want to say to your family if you were going on a long trip and knew you would not see them for a long time? I love you? I'll miss you? Take care of the cat? Whatever you would choose to say, it would probably be something very important to you. It would be something that you would want to make sure they knew before you left.

Some of the last words that Jesus spoke to his disciples are written right here in this passage. Out of all the things he could have said, he wanted them to remember to be his witnesses. "Talk about me," he was saying, "everywhere and to everyone."

So it was Jesus' idea to be witnesses. And he says in the Bible that he wants every Christian to do it. Remember these last words of Jesus and start telling others about his love.

To learn more about witnessing, zoom to page 1189.

followers what had happened. ⁹Suddenly, Jesus met them and said, "Greetings." The women came up to Jesus, took hold of his feet, and worshiped him. ¹⁰Then Jesus said to them, "Don't be afraid. Go and tell my brothers to go on to Galilee. They will see me there."

The Soldiers Report to the Jewish Leaders

¹¹The women went to tell Jesus' followers. At the same time, some of the soldiers who had been guarding the tomb went into the city. They went to tell the leading priests everything that had happened. ¹²Then the priests met with the older Jewish leaders and made

a plan. They paid the soldiers a large amount of money. ¹³They said to the soldiers, "Tell the people that Jesus' followers came during the night and stole the body while you were asleep. ¹⁴If the governor hears about this, we will satisfy him and save you from trouble." ¹⁵So the soldiers kept the money and obeyed the priests. And that story is still spread among the Jews even today.

Jesus Talks to His Followers

¹⁶The 11 followers went to Galilee. They went to the mountain where Jesus told them to go. ¹⁷On the mountain they saw Jesus and worshiped him. But some of them did not believe that it was really Jesus. ¹⁸Then Jesus came to them and said, "All power in heaven and on earth is given to me. ¹⁹So go and make followers of all people in the world. Baptize them in the name of the Father and the Son and the Holy Spirit.ᵈ ²⁰Teach them to obey everything that I have told you. You can be sure that I will be with you always. I will continue with you until the end of the world."

"**D**o you know what job Jesus gave us to do? He told us he would always be with us, too! Read about it in Matthew 28:16-20."

MARK

*Mark Tells About
the Power of Jesus*

John Prepares for Jesus

1 This is the beginning of the Good News[d] about Jesus Christ, the Son of God,[n] ²as the prophet[d] Isaiah wrote:
"I will send my messenger ahead of you.
   He will prepare your way."

Malachi 3:1

³"There is a voice of a man who calls out in the desert:
'Prepare the way for the Lord.
   Make the road straight for him.'"

Isaiah 40:3

⁴John was baptizing people in the desert. He preached a baptism of changed hearts and lives for the forgiveness of sins. ⁵All the people from Judea and Jerusalem were going out to John. They told about the sins they had done. Then they were baptized by him in the Jordan River. ⁶John wore clothes made from camel's hair and had a leather belt around his waist. He ate locusts[d] and wild honey. ⁷This is what John preached to the people: "There is one coming later who is greater than I. I am not good enough even to kneel down and untie his sandals. ⁸I baptize you with water. But the one who is coming will baptize you with the Holy Spirit."[d]

Jesus Is Baptized

⁹At that time Jesus came from the town of Nazareth in Galilee to the place where John was. John baptized Jesus in the Jordan River. ¹⁰When Jesus was coming up out of the water, he saw

People Who Spoke God's Words

JOHN THE BAPTIST • MARK 1:4-8

John the Baptist spoke God's words to prepare the people for the coming of God's Son, Jesus. God's message was that the people should admit their sins. Then they would be ready to hear the good news about Jesus. John pointed people to Jesus, not to himself. He knew that Jesus (who was his cousin) was far greater. Jesus was God's Son who would die for the sins of the world. John never tried to make himself more important than Jesus. He always told people to follow Jesus.

We need to remember that we are to serve God first, not try to make ourselves important or noticed. What will matter most in our lives is what we do for God.

To meet a prophet who saw the end of the world, fly to page 1536.

ⁿ**the Son of God** Some Greek copies omit these words.

heaven open. The Holy Spirit[d] came down on him like a dove. [11]A voice came from heaven and said: "You are my Son and I love you. I am very pleased with you."

[12]Then the Spirit sent Jesus into the desert alone. [13]He was in the desert 40 days and was there with the wild animals. While he was in the desert, he was tempted by Satan. Then angels came and took care of Jesus.

Andrew immediately left their nets and followed him.

[19]Jesus continued walking by Lake Galilee. He saw two more brothers, James and John, the sons of Zebedee. They were in their boat, preparing their nets to catch fish. [20]Their father Zebedee and the men who worked for him were in the boat with the brothers.

Sin
MARK 1:14-15

Have you ever had to admit you were wrong about something—*really, really* wrong?

For most people, that's pretty hard to do. But when Jesus first began preaching to people, he told them they needed to admit how wrong they had been! Jesus said: "Change your hearts and lives and believe the Good News!" That caused people to think about their lives and beliefs in a new way. Some agreed with Jesus and many disagreed.

The Bible often uses the word *repent*. This means to admit that you are wrong and to change the way you are living. When Jesus told people to change their hearts and lives, he was saying they needed to turn *away* from their sins and turn *to* God.

Do you need to repent, to turn from your sins and turn to God? Do it today.

To learn more about sin, zoom to page 1376.

Jesus Chooses Some Followers

[14]After John was put in prison, Jesus went into Galilee and preached the Good News[d] from God. [15]Jesus said, "The right time has come. The kingdom of God is near. Change your hearts and lives and believe the Good News!"

[16]When Jesus was walking by Lake Galilee, he saw Simon[n] and Simon's brother, Andrew. They were fishermen and were throwing a net into the lake to catch fish. [17]Jesus said to them, "Come and follow me. I will make you fishermen for men." [18]So Simon and

When Jesus saw the brothers, he called them to come with him. They left their father and followed Jesus.

Jesus Removes an Evil Spirit

[21]Jesus and his followers went to Capernaum. On the Sabbath[d] day Jesus went to the synagogue[d] and began to teach. [22]The people there were amazed at his teaching. He did not teach like their teachers of the law. He taught like a person who had authority. [23]While he was in the synagogue, a man was there who had an evil spirit in him. The man shouted, [24]"Jesus of Nazareth! What do you want with us?

[n]**Simon** Simon's other name was Peter.

Did you come to destroy us? I know who you are—God's Holy One!"

²⁵Jesus said strongly, "Be quiet! Come out of the man!" ²⁶The evil spirit made the man shake violently. Then the spirit gave a loud cry and came out of him.

²⁷The people were amazed. They asked each other, "What is happening here? This man is teaching something new. And he teaches with authority. He even gives commands to evil spirits, and they obey him." ²⁸And the news about Jesus spread quickly everywhere in the area of Galilee.

³²That night, after the sun went down, the people brought to Jesus all who were sick. They also brought those who had demons*d* in them. ³³The whole town gathered at the door of the house. ³⁴Jesus healed many who had different kinds of sicknesses. He also forced many demons to leave people. But he would not allow the demons to speak, because they knew who he was.

³⁵Early the next morning, Jesus woke and left the house while it was still dark. He went to a place to be

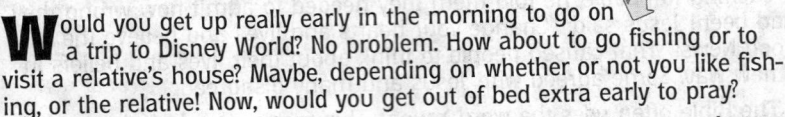

Prayer
MARK 1:35

Would you get up really early in the morning to go on a trip to Disney World? No problem. How about to go fishing or to visit a relative's house? Maybe, depending on whether or not you like fishing, or the relative! Now, would you get out of bed extra early to pray?

Hmmm. That's a tough question. You know you should say yes, but let's get real. Nobody gets up early just to pray, do they?

Jesus did. This verse tells about one time (and there were many others) when Jesus got up before sunrise to pray. We don't know what he prayed about, but we do know this. If prayer was that important for Jesus, it's important for us, too.

You may not have to get up before dawn to find time to pray. Whenever you choose to do it, make time to pray. It's that important. God will be waiting for you, no matter what time it is.

To learn more about prayer, zoom to page 1230.

Jesus Heals Many People

²⁹Jesus and his followers left the synagogue.*d* They all went at once with James and John to the home of Simon*n* and Andrew. ³⁰Simon's mother-in-law was sick in bed with a fever. The people there told Jesus about her. ³¹So Jesus went to her bed, took her hand, and helped her up. Immediately the fever left her, and she was healed. Then she began serving them.

alone and pray. ³⁶Later, Simon and his friends went to look for Jesus. ³⁷They found him and said, "Everyone is looking for you!"

³⁸Jesus answered, "We should go somewhere else, to other towns around here. Then I can preach there too. That is the reason I came." ³⁹So he traveled everywhere in Galilee. He preached in the synagogues and forced demons to leave people.

ⁿSimon Simon's other name was Peter.

Jesus Heals a Sick Man

[40]A man who had a harmful skin disease came to Jesus. The man fell to his knees and begged Jesus, "I know that you can heal me if you will."

[41]Jesus felt sorry for the man. So he touched him and said, "I want to heal you. Be healed!" [42]At once the disease left the man, and he was healed.

Jesus Heals a Paralyzed Man

2 A few days later, Jesus came back to Capernaum. The news spread that he was home. [2]So many people gathered to hear him preach that the house was full. There was no place to stand, not even outside the door. Jesus was teaching them. [3]Some people came, bringing a paralyzed man to Jesus. Four of them were carrying the paralyzed man. [4]But they could not get to Jesus because of the crowd. So

Miracles from God

MARK 2:1-12

Has your best friend ever been sick? In the Bible, some men had a sick friend they wanted to bring to Jesus. But there were so many crowds around the house that they couldn't get near to Jesus. Finally, they decided to rip a hole in the roof of the house. In those days the roofs were flat and made of mud, straw, and stone. So the men climbed up to the roof, tore open a hole, and lowered their friend down to Christ.

What strong faith they had! These men were not going to let anything keep them from taking their friend to Jesus. Their faith was rewarded when their friend was healed. Would you go to this much effort to take your friend to Jesus?

To find out what to do when a storm has you frightened, fly to page 1188.

To find out what to do when a storm has you frightened, fly to page 1188.

[43]Jesus told the man to go at once. But Jesus warned him strongly, [44]"Don't tell anyone about what I did for you. But go and show yourself to the priest. And offer a gift to God because you have been healed. Offer the gift that Moses commanded.[n] This will show the people that you are healed." [45]The man left there, but he told everyone he saw that Jesus had healed him. So the news about Jesus spread. That is the reason Jesus could not enter a town if people saw him. He stayed in places where nobody lived. But people came from all the towns to wherever he was.

they went to the roof above Jesus and made a hole in the roof. Then they lowered the mat with the paralyzed man on it. [5]Jesus saw that these men had great faith. So he said to the paralyzed man, "Young man, your sins are forgiven."

[6]Some of the teachers of the law were sitting there. They saw what Jesus did, and they said to themselves, [7]"Why does this man say things like that? He is saying things that are against God. Only God can forgive sins."

[8]At once Jesus knew what these teachers of the law were thinking. So he said to them, "Why are you thinking

[n]**Moses commanded** Read about this in Leviticus 14:1-32.

these things? [9]Which is easier: to tell this paralyzed man, 'Your sins are forgiven,' or to tell him, 'Stand up. Take your mat and walk'? [10]But I will prove to you that the Son of Man[d] has authority on earth to forgive sins." So Jesus said to the paralyzed man, [11]"I tell you, stand up. Take your mat and go home." [12]Immediately the paralyzed man stood up. He took his mat and walked out while everyone was watching him.

The people were amazed and praised God. They said, "We have never seen anything like this!"

this followed Jesus. [16]The teachers of the law who were Pharisees[d] saw Jesus eating with the tax collectors and "sinners." They asked his followers, "Why does he eat with tax collectors and sinners?"

[17]Jesus heard this and said to them, "Healthy people don't need a doctor. It is the sick who need a doctor. I did not come to invite good people. I came to invite sinners."

Jesus' Followers Are Criticized

[18]One day the followers of John[n] and the Pharisees[d] were giving up eating.[n] Some people came to Jesus and said, "John's followers and the followers of the Pharisees give up eating. But your followers don't. Why?"

Jobs in the Bible
TAX COLLECTOR • MARK 2:13-17

In Bible times, the tax collectors were the richest and most disliked people in any town. The tax collectors worked for the Roman Empire. Matthew (his name was also Levi) was a Jew who worked for Rome by collecting taxes from the people who lived in his city and from people who passed through. Sometimes the tax collectors made themselves rich by asking for more money than they had to. They sent to Rome what was expected and then kept the rest. The Jewish people did not like paying taxes because their money was supporting the evil leaders and religions in Rome. Matthew was probably very wealthy, but he gave up his job in order to follow Jesus.

To read about a person who made leather, fly to page 1333.

[13]Jesus went to the lake again. A crowd followed him there, and he taught them. [14]While he was walking beside the lake, he saw a tax collector named Levi son of Alphaeus. Levi was sitting in the tax office. Jesus said to him, "Follow me." And Levi stood up and followed Jesus.

[15]Later that day, Jesus ate at Levi's house. There were many tax collectors and "sinners" eating there with Jesus and his followers. Many people like

[19]Jesus answered, "When there is a wedding, the friends of the bridegroom are not sad while he is with them. They do not give up eating while the bridegroom is still there. [20]But the time will come when the bridegroom will leave them. Then the friends will be sad and will give up eating.

[21]"When a person sews a patch over a hole on an old coat, he never uses a piece of cloth that is not yet shrunk. If he does, the patch will shrink and pull

---

[n]**John** John the Baptist who preached to the Jews about Christ's coming (Mark 1:4-8).
[n]**giving up eating** This is called "fasting." The people would give up eating for a special time of prayer and worship to God. It was also done to show sadness.

away from the coat. Then the hole will be worse. [22]Also, no one ever pours new wine into old leather bags for holding wine. If he does, the new wine will break the bags, and the wine will be ruined along with the bags for the wine. People always put new wine into new leather bags."

Jesus Is Lord of the Sabbath

[23]On the Sabbath[d] day, Jesus was walking through some grainfields. His followers were with him and picked some grain to eat. [24]The Pharisees[d] saw this and said to Jesus, "Why are your followers doing what is not lawful on the Sabbath?"

[25]Jesus answered, "You have read what David did when he and those with him were hungry and needed food. [26]It was during the time of Abiathar the high priest. David went into God's house and ate the bread that was made holy for God. The law of Moses says that only priests may eat that bread. But David also gave some of the bread to those who were with him."

[27]Then Jesus said to the Pharisees, "The Sabbath day was made to help people. They were not made to be ruled by the Sabbath day. [28]The Son of Man[d] is Lord even of the Sabbath."

Jesus Heals a Man's Crippled Hand

3 Another time when Jesus went into a synagogue,[d] a man with a crippled hand was there. [2]Some people there wanted to see Jesus do something wrong so they could accuse him. They watched him closely to see if he would heal the man on the Sabbath[d] day.

[3]Jesus said to the man with the crippled hand, "Stand up here in front of everyone."

[4]Then Jesus asked the people, "Which is right on the Sabbath day: to do good, or to do evil? Is it right to save a life or to destroy one?" But they said nothing to answer him.

[5]Jesus was angry as he looked at the people. But he felt very sad because they were stubborn. Then he said to the man, "Let me see your hand." The man put his hand out for Jesus, and it was healed. [6]Then the Pharisees[d] left and began making plans with the Herodians[n] about a way to kill Jesus.

Many People Follow Jesus

[7]Jesus left with his followers for the lake. A large crowd from Galilee followed him. [8]Also many people came from Judea, from Jerusalem, from Idumea, from the lands across the Jordan River, and from the area of Tyre and Sidon. They came because they had heard about all the things Jesus was doing. [9]Jesus saw the crowds. So he told his followers to get a boat ready for him. He wanted the boat so that the many people would not crowd themselves against him. [10]He had healed many people. So all the sick were pushing toward him to touch him. [11]Some had evil spirits in them. When the evil spirits saw Jesus, they fell down before him and shouted, "You are the Son of God!" [12]But Jesus strongly commanded the spirits not to tell who he was.

Jesus Chooses His 12 Apostles

[13]Then Jesus went up on a hill and called some men to come to him. These were the men Jesus wanted, and they went up to him. [14]Jesus chose 12 men and called them apostles.[d] He wanted these 12 to be with him, and he wanted to send them to other places to preach. [15]He also wanted them to have the power to force demons[d] out of people. [16]These are the 12 men he chose: Simon (Jesus gave him the name Peter); [17]James and John, the sons of Zebedee (Jesus gave them the name Boanerges, which means "Sons of Thunder"); [18]Andrew, Philip, Bartholomew, Matthew, Thomas, James the son of Alphaeus, Thaddaeus, Simon the Zealot,[d]

[n]**Herodians** A political group that followed Herod and his family.

¹⁹and Judas Iscariot. Judas is the one who gave Jesus to his enemies.

People Say Jesus Has a Devil

²⁰Then Jesus went back home. But again a crowd gathered. There were so many people that Jesus and his followers could not eat. ²¹His family heard about all these things. They went to get him because people were saying that Jesus was out of his mind.

²²And the teachers of the law from Jerusalem were saying, "Beelzebul[d] is living inside him! He uses power from the ruler of demons[d] to force demons out."

things from the strong man's house. ²⁸I tell you the truth. All sins that people do can be forgiven. And all the bad things people say against God can be forgiven. ²⁹But any person who says bad things against the Holy Spirit[d] will never be forgiven. He is guilty of a sin that continues forever."

³⁰Jesus said this because the teachers of the law said that Jesus had an evil spirit inside him.

Jesus' True Family

³¹Then Jesus' mother and brothers arrived. They stood outside and sent someone in to tell him to come out. ³²Many people were sitting around Jesus. They said to him, "Your mother and brothers are waiting for you outside."

Boats with Precious Cargo

MARK 4:1

Do you know that once in the Bible a boat was used as a stage? While Jesus was on earth he was always teaching people. He taught them as he walked along the road, in synagogues (Jewish churches), on mountainsides, in houses, on the street, and on the beach next to the Sea of Galilee.

One time there were so many people crowded on the beach to listen that Jesus no longer had room to stand. He decided to get in a boat near the shore and teach from there. Jesus always wanted to talk to people and teach them about God.

Today we can learn from Jesus because we can read his teachings in the Bible. The Bible can always teach us more about God.

To read about a boat overflowing with fish, fly to page 1228.

²³So Jesus called the people together and used stories to teach them. He said, "Satan will not force his own demons out of people. ²⁴A kingdom that fights against itself cannot continue. ²⁵And a family that is divided cannot continue. ²⁶And if Satan is against himself and fights against his own people, then he cannot continue. And that is the end of Satan. ²⁷If a person wants to enter a strong man's house and steal his things, first he must tie up the strong man. Then the thief can steal the

³³Jesus asked, "Who is my mother? Who are my brothers?" ³⁴Then Jesus looked at those sitting around him. He said, "Here are my mother and my brothers! ³⁵My true brother and sister and mother are those who do the things God wants."

A Story About Planting Seed

4 Another time Jesus began teaching by the lake. A great crowd gathered around him. So he got into a boat and went out on the lake. All the people stayed on the shore close to the water. ²Jesus used many stories to teach them. He said, ³"Listen! A farmer went out to plant his seed. ⁴While the farmer was planting, some seed fell by the road. The birds came and ate all that seed. ⁵Some seed fell on rocky ground where there wasn't much dirt. The seed grew very fast there because the ground was not deep. ⁶But when the sun rose, the plants withered. The plants died because they did not have deep roots. ⁷Some other seed fell among thorny weeds. The weeds grew and choked the good plants. So those plants did not make grain. ⁸Some other seed fell on good ground. In the good ground, the seed began to grow. It grew and made a crop of grain. Some plants made 30 times more grain, some 60 times more grain, and some 100 times more grain."

"**S**ometimes I play in the mud and get dirty. In Mark 4:3-9, Jesus said we're all like dirt."

⁹Then Jesus said, "You people who hear me, listen!"

Jesus Tells Why He Used Stories

¹⁰Later, when Jesus was alone, the 12 apostles[d] and others around him asked him about the stories.

¹¹Jesus said, "Only you can know the secret truth about the kingdom of God. But to other people I tell everything by using stories. ¹²I do this so that:

'They will look and look, but they
    will not learn.
They will listen and listen, but they
    will not understand.
If they did learn and understand,
    they would come back to me and
    be forgiven.'"   *Isaiah 6:9-10*

Jesus Explains the Seed Story

¹³Then Jesus said to the followers, "Do you understand this story? If you don't, then how will you understand any story? ¹⁴The farmer is like a person who plants God's teaching in people. ¹⁵Sometimes the teaching falls on the road. This is like some people. They hear the teaching of God. But Satan quickly comes and takes away the teaching that was planted in them. ¹⁶Others are like the seed planted on rocky ground. They hear the teaching and quickly accept it with joy. ¹⁷But they don't allow the teaching to go deep into their lives. They keep it only a short time. When trouble or persecution comes because of the teaching, they quickly give up. ¹⁸Others are like the seed planted among the thorny weeds. They hear the teaching. ¹⁹But then other things come into their lives: worries, the love of money, and wanting all kinds of other things. These things stop the teaching from growing. So that teaching does not produce fruit[n] in their lives. ²⁰Others are like the seed planted in the good ground. They hear the teaching and accept it. Then they grow and produce fruit—sometimes 30 times more, sometimes 60 times more, and sometimes 100 times more."

Use What You Have

²¹Then Jesus said to them, "Do you hide a lamp under a bowl or under a bed? No! You put the lamp on a lampstand. ²²Everything that is hidden will be made clear. Every secret thing will be made known. ²³You people who hear me, listen!

²⁴"Think carefully about the things you hear. The way you give to others is the way God will give to you. But God will give you more than you give. ²⁵The person who has something will be given more. But the person who does not have much, even what he has will be taken from him."

[n]**produce fruit** To produce fruit means to have in your life the good things God wants.

Jesus Uses a Story About Seed

26Then Jesus said, "The kingdom of God is like a man who plants seed in the ground. 27The seed comes up and grows night and day. It doesn't matter whether the man is asleep or awake; the seed still grows. The man does not know how it grows. 28Without any help, the earth produces grain. First the plant grows, then the head, and then all the grain in the head. 29When the grain is ready, the man cuts it. This is the harvest time."

A Story About Mustard Seed

30Then Jesus said, "How can I show you what the kingdom of God is like? What story can I use to explain it? 31The kingdom of God is like a mustard seed. The mustard seed is the smallest seed you plant in the ground. 32But when you plant this seed, it grows and becomes the largest of all garden plants. It produces large branches. Even the wild birds can make nests in it and be protected from the sun."

33Jesus used many stories like these to teach them. He taught them all that they could understand. 34He always used stories to teach them. But when he and his followers were alone together, Jesus explained everything to them.

Jesus Stops a Storm

35That evening, Jesus said to his followers, "Come with me across the lake." 36He and the followers left the people there. They went in the boat that Jesus was already sitting in. There were also other boats with them. 37A very strong wind came up on the lake. The waves began coming over the sides and into the boat. It was almost full of water. 38Jesus was at the back of the boat, sleeping with his head on a pillow. The followers went to him and woke him. They said, "Teacher, do you care about us? We will drown!"

39Jesus stood up and commanded the wind and the waves to stop. He said, "Quiet! Be still!" Then the wind stopped, and the lake became calm.

40Jesus said to his followers, "Why are you afraid? Do you still have no faith?"

41The followers were very afraid and asked each other, "What kind of

Miracles from God

MARK 4:33-41

Storms can be pretty scary. Sometimes the thunder can be so loud that it seems to shake the house! One time the disciples were in a boat on the sea of Galilee and got caught in a big storm. The rough waves crashed all around them. Lightning flashed in the sky and the thunder boomed. The disciples were afraid the boat might sink at any moment.

But Jesus was asleep in the middle of the storm. When the disciples woke Jesus up to ask for his help, he wondered why they were so afraid. The disciples should have known that Jesus was more powerful than nature and could stop the storm.

In the same way, we do not need to be afraid when storms come along. Jesus will protect us and keep us safe.

To learn about a leper who said "thank you," fly to page 1255.

man is this? Even the wind and the waves obey him!"

A Man with Demons Inside Him

5 Jesus and his followers went across the lake to the region of the Gerasene people. [2]When Jesus got out of the boat, a man came to him from the caves where dead people were buried. This man, who lived in the caves, had an evil spirit living in him. [3]No one could tie him up, not even with a chain. [4]Many times people had used chains to tie the man's hands and feet. But he always broke the chains off. No one was strong enough to control him. [5]Day and night he would wander around the burial caves and on the hills, screaming and cutting himself with stones. [6]While Jesus was still far away, the man saw him. He ran to Jesus and knelt down before him. [7-8]Jesus said to the man, "You evil spirit, come out of that man."

But the man shouted in a loud voice, "What do you want with me, Jesus, Son of the Most High God? I beg you, promise God that you will not punish me!"

[9]Then Jesus asked the man, "What is your name?"

The man answered, "My name is Legion,[n] because I have many spirits in me." [10]The man begged Jesus again and again not to send the spirits out of that area.

[11]A large herd of pigs was eating on a hill near there. [12]The evil spirits begged Jesus, "Send us to the pigs. Let us go into them." [13]So Jesus allowed them to do this. The evil spirits left the man and went into the pigs. Then the herd of pigs rushed down the hill into the lake and were drowned. There were about 2,000 pigs in that herd.

[14]The men who took care of the pigs ran away. They went to the town and to the countryside, telling everyone about this. So people went out to see what had happened. [15]They came to Jesus and saw the man who had had the many evil spirits. The man was sitting there, clothed and in his right mind. The people were frightened. [16]Some

Witnessing
MARK 5:18-20

If you won a million dollars, who would you tell first? Who would you tell next? Before long, you would tell everyone about this amazing prize. Most likely, the first two people you thought of to tell are either really close friends or members of your family. We usually share good news with people we love.

Sure, winning a million dollars would be pretty awesome news. But think about this: what Jesus has done in our lives is the best news we'll ever have to tell anyone!

The man in this story would agree! Jesus did a miracle in his life—something he wouldn't trade for a million dollars. So he went home and told the people he knew all about it. Read the whole story in Mark 5:1-20 to find out what Jesus did for the man. And remember, you can be a witness by telling all your friends and family the best news ever.

To learn more about witnessing, zoom to page 1315.

---

[n]**Legion**   Means very many. A legion was about 5,000 men in the Roman army.

people were there who saw what Jesus had done. They told the others what had happened to the man who had the demons[d] living in him. And they also told about the pigs. [17]Then the people began to beg Jesus to leave their area.

[18]Jesus was getting ready to leave in the boat. The man who was freed from the demons begged to go with him.

[19]But Jesus would not allow the man to go. Jesus said, "Go home to your family and friends. Tell them how much the Lord has done for you and how he has had mercy on you." [20]So the man left and told the people in the Ten Towns[n] about the great things Jesus had done for him. All the people were amazed.

and bowed before him. [23]The ruler begged Jesus again and again. He said, "My little daughter is dying. Please come and put your hands on her. Then she will be healed and will live." [24]So Jesus went with the ruler, and many people followed Jesus. They were pushing very close around him.

[25]A woman was there who had been bleeding for the past 12 years. [26]She had suffered very much. Many doctors had tried to help her. She had spent all the money she had, but she was not improving. She was getting worse. [27]When the woman heard about Jesus, she followed him with the people and touched his coat. [28]The woman thought, "If I can even touch his coat, that will be enough to heal me." [29]When she touched his coat, her bleeding stopped. She could feel in her body that she was healed.

People Who Depended on God

A SICK WOMAN • MARK 5:25-34

This woman trusted Jesus to help her get well. We don't know her name. We just know that she had been sick for many years. When the woman heard that Jesus was in her town, she went to find him. She was so tired of being sick. She knew that if she could just touch Jesus' cloak, she would be healed.

It took a lot of courage and faith for this woman to push through the crowd. But the moment she touched Jesus' cloak, she was healed. Jesus wanted her to be well, but he also wanted her to believe in him.

God can take care of all your needs. You can pray to him about anything. Jesus promises to answer your prayers. Most important of all, he wants you to believe in him and obey him.

To read about someone who wanted to be saved, fly to page 1334.

Jesus Gives Life to a Dead Girl and Heals a Sick Woman

[21]Jesus went in the boat back to the other side of the lake. There, a large crowd gathered around him. [22]A ruler from the synagogue,[d] named Jairus, came to that place. Jairus saw Jesus

[30]At once Jesus felt power go out from him. So he stopped and turned around. Then he asked, "Who touched my clothes?"

[31]The followers said, "There are so many people pushing against you! And you ask, 'Who touched me?'"

---

[n]**Ten Towns**   In Greek, called "Decapolis." It was an area east of Lake Galilee that once had ten main towns.

³²But Jesus continued looking around to see who had touched him. ³³The woman knew that she was healed. So she came and bowed at Jesus' feet. Shaking with fear, she told him the whole story. ³⁴Jesus said to the woman, "Dear woman, you are made well because you believed. Go in peace. You will have no more suffering."

the people to leave. Then he went into the room where the child was. He took the child's father and mother and his three followers into the room with him. ⁴¹Then he took hold of the girl's hand and said to her, "Talitha, koum!" (This means, "Little girl, I tell you to stand up!") ⁴²The girl stood right up and began walking. (She was 12 years old.) The father and mother and the followers were amazed. ⁴³Jesus gave the

Children Who Saw God at Work

JAIRUS'S DAUGHTER • MARK 5:35-43

When people got really sick in Bible times, they would often die. There were doctors, but they didn't have lots of medicines like we do today. There were no big hospitals, or ambulances. Jairus' little girl was so sick that the doctors couldn't help her. Jairus loved his little girl, and when he heard Jesus was in his town he went to find Jesus to heal her. But before Jesus could get to Jairus' house, the little girl died. Then Jesus surprised everyone—he brought her back to life.

Usually, when you get sick, you can go to a doctor and get medicine to make you better. But someday everyone will die. However, if you believe in Jesus as your Savior, he promises you a new life in heaven!

To meet a boy who learned multiplication outside of math class, fly to page 1283.

³⁵Jesus was still speaking to her when some men came from the house of Jairus, the synagogue ruler. The men said, "Your daughter is dead. There is now no need to bother the teacher."

³⁶But Jesus paid no attention to what the men said. He said to the synagogue ruler, "Don't be afraid; only believe."

³⁷Jesus let only Peter, James, and John the brother of James go with him to Jairus's house. ³⁸They came to the house of the synagogue ruler, and Jesus found many people there crying loudly. There was much confusion. ³⁹Jesus entered the house and said to the people, "Why are you crying and making so much noise? This child is not dead. She is only asleep." ⁴⁰But they only laughed at Jesus. He told all

father and mother strict orders not to tell people about this. Then he told them to give the girl some food.

Jesus Goes to His Hometown

6 Jesus left there and went back to his hometown. His followers went with him. ²On the Sabbath[d] day he taught in the synagogue.[d] Many people heard him and were amazed. They said, "Where did this man get these teachings? What is this wisdom that has been given to him? And where did he get the power to work miracles?[d] ³He is only the carpenter. His mother is Mary. He is the brother of James, Joseph, Judas, and Simon. And his sisters are here with us." The people did not accept Jesus.

[4]Jesus said to them, "Other people give honor to a prophet.[d] But in his own town with his own people and in his own home, a prophet does not receive honor." [5]Jesus was not able to work many miracles there. The only miracles he did were to heal some sick people by putting his hands on them. [6]Jesus was amazed that they had no faith.

Then Jesus went to other villages in that area and taught. [7]He called the 12 followers together and sent them out in groups of 2. He gave them authority over evil spirits. [8]This is what Jesus told them: "Take nothing for your trip except a walking stick. Take no bread, no bag, and no money in your pockets. [9]Wear sandals, and take only the clothes you are wearing. [10]When you enter a house, stay there until you leave that place. [11]If any town refuses to accept you or its people refuse to listen to you, then leave that town. Shake its dust off your feet.[n] This will be a warning to them."

[12]The followers went out and preached to the people to change their hearts and lives. [13]The followers forced many demons[d] out and poured olive oil on many sick people and healed them.

How John the Baptist Was Killed

[14]King Herod heard about Jesus, because Jesus was now well-known. Some people said, "He is John the Baptist.[d] He is risen from death. That is the reason he can work these miracles."[d]

[15]Others said, "He is Elijah."[n]

Other people said, "Jesus is a prophet.[d] He is like the prophets who lived long ago."

[16]Herod heard all these things about Jesus. He said, "I killed John by cutting off his head. Now he has been raised from death!"

[17]Herod himself had ordered his soldiers to arrest John, and John was put in prison. Herod did this to please his wife, Herodias. Herodias was the wife of Philip, Herod's brother. But then Herod married her. [18]John told Herod that it was not lawful for him to be married to his brother's wife. [19]So Herodias hated John and wanted to kill him. But she could not because of Herod. [20]Herod was afraid to kill John because he knew John was a good and holy man. So Herod protected John. Also, Herod enjoyed listening to John preach. But John's preaching always bothered him.

[21]Then the perfect time came for Herodias to cause John's death. It happened on Herod's birthday. Herod gave a dinner party for the most important government leaders, the commanders of his army, and the most important people in Galilee. [22]The daughter of Herodias came to the party and danced. When she danced, Herod and the people eating with him were very pleased.

So King Herod said to the girl, "I will give you anything you want." [23]He promised her, "Anything you ask for I will give to you. I will even give you half of my kingdom."

[24]The girl went to her mother and asked, "What should I ask the king to give me?"

Her mother answered, "Ask for the head of John the Baptist."[d]

[25]Quickly the girl went back to the king. She said to him, "Please give me the head of John the Baptist. Bring it to me now on a platter."

[26]The king was very sad. But he had promised to give the girl anything she wanted. And the people eating there with him had heard his promise. So Herod could not refuse what she asked. [27]Immediately the king sent a soldier to bring John's head. The soldier went and cut off John's head in the prison [28]and brought it back on a platter. He gave it to the girl, and the girl gave it to her mother. [29]John's followers heard about what happened. So they came and got John's body and put it in a tomb.

[n]**Shake . . . feet** A warning. It showed that they were finished talking to these people.
[n]**Elijah** A man who spoke for God. He lived hundreds of years before Christ.

More than 5,000 People Fed

[30]The apostles[d] that Jesus had sent out to preach returned. They gathered around him and told him about all the things they had done and taught. [31]Crowds of people were coming and going. Jesus and his followers did not even have time to eat. He said to them, "Come with me. We will go to a quiet place to be alone. There we will get some rest."

[32]So they went in a boat alone to a place where there were no people. [33]But many people saw them leave and recognized them. So people from all the towns ran to the place where Jesus was going. They got there before Jesus arrived. [34]When he landed, he saw a great crowd waiting. Jesus felt sorry for them, because they were like sheep without a shepherd. So he taught them many things.

[35]It was now late in the day. Jesus' followers came to him and said, "No one lives in this place. And it is already very late. [36]Send the people away. They need to go to the farms and towns around here to buy some food to eat."

[37]But Jesus answered, "You give them food to eat."

They said to him, "We can't buy enough bread to feed all these people! We would all have to work a month to earn enough money to buy that much bread!"

[38]Jesus asked them, "How many loaves of bread do you have now? Go and see."

When they found out, they came to him and said, "We have five loaves and two fish."

[39]Then Jesus said to the followers, "Tell all the people to sit in groups on the green grass." [40]So all the people sat in groups. They sat in groups of 50 or groups of 100. [41]Jesus took the five loaves and two fish. He looked up to heaven and thanked God for the bread. He divided the bread and gave it to his followers for them to give to the people. Then he divided the two fish among them all. [42]All the people ate and were satisfied. [43]The followers filled 12 baskets with the pieces of bread and fish that were not eaten. [44]There were about 5,000 men there who ate.

Jesus Walks on the Water

[45]Then Jesus told his followers to get into the boat and go to Bethsaida on the other side of the lake. Jesus said that he would come later. He stayed there to tell the people they could go home. [46]After sending them away, he went into the hills to pray.

[47]That night, the boat was in the middle of the lake. Jesus was alone on the land. [48]He saw the followers working hard to row the boat because the wind was blowing against them. At some time between three and six o'clock in the morning, Jesus came to them, walking on the water. He continued walking until he was almost past the boat. [49]But when his followers saw him walking on the water, they thought he was a ghost and cried out. [50]They all saw him and were terrified. But Jesus spoke to them and said, "Have courage! It is I! Do not be afraid." [51]Then he got into the boat with them. And the wind became calm. The followers were greatly amazed. [52]They had seen Jesus make more bread from the five loaves. But they did not understand what it meant. Their minds were closed.

[53]When they had crossed the lake, they came to shore at Gennesaret. They tied the boat there. [54]When they got out of the boat, the people saw Jesus and immediately recognized him. [55]They ran to tell others everywhere in that area that Jesus was there. They brought sick people on mats to every place Jesus went. [56]Jesus went into towns and cities and farms around that area. And everywhere he went, the people brought the sick to the marketplaces. They begged him to let them just touch the edge of his coat. And all who touched him were healed.

Obey God's Law Not Men's

7 Some Pharisees[d] and some teachers of the law came from Jerusalem. They gathered around Jesus. [2]They saw that some of Jesus' followers ate food with hands that were not clean.[d] ("Not clean" means that they did not wash their hands in the way the Pharisees said people must. [3]The Pharisees and all the Jews never eat before washing their hands in this special way. They do this to follow the teaching given to them by their great people who lived before them. [4]And when the Jews buy something in the market, they never eat it until they wash it in a special way. They also follow other rules of their great people who lived before them. They follow rules about the washing of cups, pitchers, and pots.)

great people who lived before us. Your followers eat their food with hands that are not clean. Why do they do this?"

[6]Jesus answered, "You are all hypocrites![d] Isaiah was right when he spoke about you. Isaiah wrote,

'These people show honor to me
   with words.
But their hearts are far from me.
[7]Their worship of me is worthless.
   The things they teach are nothing
   but human rules they have
   memorized.'   *Isaiah 29:13*
[8]You have stopped following the commands of God. Now you only follow the teachings of men."

[9]Then Jesus said to them: "You think you are clever! You ignore the commands of God so that you can follow your own teachings! [10]Moses said, 'Honor your father and mother.'[n] Then Moses also said, 'Anyone who says cruel things to his father or mother

---

Words to Know: New Testament
PHARISEES • MARK 7:1

You'll read about **Pharisees** and Scribes (teachers of the law) in a lot of the stories about Jesus. The Pharisees and teachers of the law were religious leaders. They were supposed to teach the people about God and serve in God's temple. But they were not doing a very good job. The Pharisees had written a lot of extra laws for everyone to follow. They did their best to obey all the laws. They thought that would make them good enough for God. The teachers of the law studied God's law. They thought that would make them good enough for God. The Pharisees and Scribes got angry at Jesus for teaching that everyone can be saved by believing in him.

We don't have to obey laws to be good enough for God to love us. He loves us just as we are. And he forgives us and saves us if we ask him. Have you asked Jesus to be your Savior?

To read about why the cross is important to Christians, fly to page 1213.

---

[5]The Pharisees and the teachers of the law said to Jesus, "Your followers don't follow the rules given to us by our

must be put to death.'[n] [11]But you teach that a person can say to his father or mother, 'I have something I could use

---

[n]*'Honor your father and mother.'*   Quotation from Exodus 20:12; Deuteronomy 5:16.
[n]*'Anyone . . . death.'*   Quotation from Exodus 21:17.

to help you. But I will not use it for you. I will give it to God.' [12]You are telling that person that he does not have to do anything for his father or mother. [13]So you are teaching that it is not important to do what God said. You think that it is more important to follow your own rules, which you teach people. And you do many things like that."

[14]Jesus called the people to him again. He said, "Every person should listen to me and understand what I am saying. [15]There is nothing a person puts into his body that makes him unclean. A person is made unclean by the things that come out of him." [16]*n*

[17]When Jesus left the people and went inside, his followers asked him about this story. [18]Jesus said, "Do you still have trouble understanding? Surely you know that nothing that enters a man from the outside can make him unclean. [19]Food does not go into a person's mind. Food goes into his stomach. Then that food goes out of his body." (When Jesus said this, he meant that there is no food that is unclean for people to eat.)

[20]And Jesus said, "The things that come out of a man are the things that make him unclean. [21]All these evil things begin inside a person, in his mind: evil thoughts, sexual sins, stealing, murder, adultery,*d* [22]selfishness, doing bad things to other people, lying, doing sinful things, jealousy, saying bad things about people, pride, and foolish living. [23]All these evil things come from within a person. These things make a person unclean."

Jesus Helps a Non-Jewish Woman

[24]Jesus left that place and went to the area around Tyre. He went into a house and did not want anyone to know he was there. But Jesus could not stay hidden. [25]A woman heard that he was there. Her little daughter had

Touring Bible Lands
LAKE GALILEE • MARK 7:31

This harp-shaped body of water has several names in the Bible. Sometimes it is called the Sea of Galilee and other times it is called Lake Galilee. It is also simply known as the lake! It is bigger than many lakes because it stretches nearly eight miles across from shore to shore.

Jesus spent a lot of time around Lake Galilee. He often visited the towns near the lake to preach and to heal people. The lake was a favorite fishing spot for many fishermen. Jesus met some of these fishermen on the shore of this lake and they later became his disciples. There are also stories in the Bible about dangerous, sudden storms that still form on the lake today. Jesus walked across the rough waves of the Lake of Galilee during the middle of one of these storms. He also showed his power by calming the wind and the waves.

Look for all the stories about Jesus and the Sea of Galilee!

Fly north from Lake Galilee to a city where the name "Christian" was first used on page 1336.

---

*n***Verse 16**   Some Greek copies add verse 16: "You people who hear me, listen!"

an evil spirit in her. So the woman quickly came to Jesus and fell at his feet. 26She was not Jewish. She was Greek, born in Phoenicia, in Syria. She begged Jesus to force the demon*d* out of her daughter.

27Jesus told the woman: "It is not right to take the children's bread and give it to the dogs. First let the children eat all they want."

28She answered, "That is true, Lord. But the dogs under the table can eat the pieces of food that the children don't eat."

29Then Jesus said, "That is a very good answer. You may go. The demon has left your daughter."

30The woman went home and found her daughter lying in bed. The demon was gone.

Jesus Heals a Deaf Man

31Then Jesus left the area around Tyre. He went through Sidon to Lake Galilee, to the area of the Ten Towns.*n* 32While he was there, some people brought a man to him. This man was deaf and could not talk. The people begged Jesus to put his hand on the man to heal him.

33Jesus led the man away from the crowd, to be alone with him. Jesus put his fingers in the man's ears. Then Jesus spit and touched the man's tongue. 34Jesus looked up to heaven and took a deep breath. He said to the man, "Ephphatha!" (This means, "Be opened.") 35When Jesus did this, the man was able to hear. He was also able to use his tongue, and he spoke clearly.

36Jesus commanded the people not to tell anyone about what happened. But the more he commanded them, the more they told about it. 37They were really amazed. They said, "Jesus does everything well. He makes the deaf hear! And those who can't talk— Jesus makes them able to speak."

More than 4,000 People Fed

8 Another time there was a great crowd with Jesus. They had nothing to eat. So Jesus called his followers to him. He said, 2"I feel sorry for these people. They have been with me for three days, and now they have nothing to eat. 3I cannot send them home hungry. If they leave without eating, they will faint on the way home. Some of them live a long way from here."

4Jesus' followers answered, "But we are far away from any towns. Where can we get enough bread to feed all these people?"

5Jesus asked, "How many loaves of bread do you have?"

They answered, "We have seven loaves."

6Jesus told the people to sit on the ground. Then he took the seven loaves and gave thanks to God. Jesus divided the bread and gave the pieces to his followers. He told them to pass out the bread to the people, and they did so. 7The followers also had a few small fish. Jesus gave thanks for the fish and told his followers to give the fish to the people. 8All the people ate and were satisfied. Then the followers filled seven baskets with the pieces of food that were not eaten. 9There were about 4,000 men who ate. After they had eaten, Jesus told them to go home. 10Then he went in a boat with his followers to the area of Dalmanutha.

The Leaders Ask for a Miracle

11The Pharisees*d* came to Jesus and asked him questions. They wanted to trap him. So they asked Jesus to do a miracle*d* to show that he was from God. 12Jesus sighed deeply. He said, "Why do you people ask for a miracle as proof? I tell you the truth. No miracle will be given to you." 13Then Jesus left the Pharisees. He went in the boat to the other side of the lake.

*n***Ten Towns** In Greek, called "Decapolis." It was an area east of Lake Galilee that once had ten main towns.

Guard Against Wrong Teachings

¹⁴The followers had only one loaf of bread with them in the boat. They had forgotten to bring more bread. ¹⁵Jesus warned them, "Be careful! Guard against the yeast of the Pharisees*d* and the yeast of Herod."

¹⁶Among themselves, his disciples discussed the meaning of this. They said, "He said this because we have no bread."

¹⁷Jesus knew what his followers were talking about. So he asked them, "Why are you talking about having no bread? You still don't see or understand? Are your minds closed? ¹⁸You have eyes, but you don't really see. You have ears, but you don't really listen. Remember what I did before, when we did not have enough bread? ¹⁹I divided five loaves of bread for 5,000 people. Remember how many baskets you filled with pieces of food that were not eaten?"

They answered, "We filled 12 baskets."

²⁰"And remember that I divided seven loaves of bread for 4,000 people. Remember how many baskets you filled with pieces of food that were not eaten?"

They answered, "We filled 7 baskets."

²¹Then Jesus said to them, "You remember these things I did, but you still don't understand?"

Jesus Heals a Blind Man

²²Jesus and his followers came to Bethsaida. Some people brought a blind man to Jesus and begged him to touch the man. ²³So Jesus took the blind man's hand and led him out of the village. Then he spit on the man's eyes. He put his hands on the blind man and asked, "Can you see now?"

²⁴The man looked up and said, "Yes, I see people, but they look like trees walking around."

²⁵Again Jesus put his hands on the man's eyes. Then the man opened his eyes wide. His eyes were healed, and he was able to see everything clearly. ²⁶Jesus told him to go home, saying, "Don't go into the town."

Peter Says Jesus Is the Christ

²⁷Jesus and his followers went to the towns around Caesarea Philippi. While they were traveling, Jesus asked them, "Who do people say I am?"

²⁸They answered, "Some people say you are John the Baptist.*d* Others say you are Elijah.*n* And others say that you are one of the prophets."*d*

"**H**ow would you answer the question Jesus asked his disciples in Mark 8:27–9:1?"

²⁹Then Jesus asked, "Who do you say I am?"

Peter answered, "You are the Christ."*d*

³⁰Jesus ordered his followers, "Don't tell anyone who I am."

³¹Then Jesus began to teach them that the Son of Man*d* must suffer many things. He taught that the Son of Man would not be accepted by the older Jewish leaders, the leading priests, and the teachers of the law. He taught that the Son of Man must be killed and then rise from death after three days. ³²Jesus told them plainly what would happen. Then Peter took Jesus aside and began to criticize him. ³³But Jesus turned and looked at his followers. Then he criticized Peter and said, "Go away from me, Satan!*n* You don't care about the things of God. You care only about things men think are important."

*n*Elijah   A man who spoke for God. He lived hundreds of years before Christ.

*n*Satan   Name for the devil meaning "the enemy." Jesus means that Peter was talking like Satan.

³⁴Then Jesus called the crowd to him, along with his followers. He said, "If anyone wants to follow me, he must say 'no' to the things he wants. He must be willing to die on a cross, and he must follow me. ³⁵Whoever wants to save his life will give up true life. But whoever gives up his life for me and for the Good News[d] will have true life forever. ³⁶It is worth nothing for a person to have the whole world, if he loses his soul. ³⁷A person could never pay enough to buy back his soul. ³⁸The people who live now are living in a sinful and evil time. If anyone is ashamed

Jesus with Moses and Elijah

²Six days later Jesus took Peter, James, and John and went up on a high mountain. They were all alone there. While these followers watched, Jesus was changed. ³His clothes became shining white, whiter than any person could make them. ⁴Then two men appeared, talking with Jesus. The men were Moses and Elijah.[n]

⁵Peter said to Jesus, "Teacher, it is good that we are here. We will put

Staying Away from Selfishness
MARK 8:34-35

Here is a riddle: What is it that the more you lose, the more you have?

Answer: Your life!

That's what Jesus says in these verses. How can that be? It works like this. If you are a Christian, your life belongs to God. He tells Christians throughout the Bible to give their lives away to others by helping them. That's how you *lose* your life—you give it away freely. As we do that, God promises to give us more and more of *his* new life. That's how you can *have* more life—God gives you more from his never-ending supply. You lose your life for him by giving it to others, and you get more in return as he gives it to you.

What could you do today to "lose your life" by helping others? How about helping your mom, dad, brother, sister, classmate, or neighbor? *Remember: the more you lose, the more you gain.*

To learn more ways to stay away from selfishness, zoom to page 1278.

of me and my teaching, then I will be ashamed of him. I will be ashamed of him when I come with the glory of my Father and the holy angels."

9 Then Jesus said to the people, "I tell you the truth. Some of you standing here will see the kingdom of God come with power before you die."

three tents here—one for you, one for Moses, and one for Elijah." ⁶Peter did not know what to say, because he and the others were so frightened.

⁷Then a cloud came and covered them. A voice came from the cloud. The voice said, "This is my Son, and I love him. Obey him!"

---

[n]**Moses and Elijah** Two of the most important Jewish leaders in the past.

[8]Then Peter, James, and John looked around, but they saw only Jesus there alone with them.

[9]As Jesus and his followers were walking back down the mountain, he commanded them, "Don't tell anyone about the things you saw on the mountain. Wait till the Son of Man[d] rises from death. Then you may tell."

[10]So the followers obeyed Jesus and said nothing about what they had seen. But they discussed what Jesus meant about rising from death.

[11]They asked Jesus, "Why do the teachers of the law say that Elijah must come first?"

[12]Jesus answered, "They are right to say that Elijah must come first. Elijah makes all things the way they should be. But why does the Scripture[d] say that the Son of Man will suffer much and that people will treat him as if he were nothing? [13]I tell you that Elijah has already come. And people did to him whatever they wanted to do. The Scriptures said this would happen to him."

Jesus Heals a Sick Boy

[14]Then Jesus, Peter, James, and John went to the other followers. They saw a great crowd around them. The teachers of the law were arguing with them. [15]But when the crowd saw Jesus, they were surprised and ran to welcome him.

[16]Jesus asked, "What are you arguing about with the teachers of the law?"

[17]A man answered, "Teacher, I brought my son to you. He has a spirit from the devil in him. This spirit stops him from talking. [18]The spirit attacks him and throws him on the ground. My son foams at the mouth, grinds his teeth, and becomes very stiff. I asked your followers to force the evil spirit out, but they couldn't."

[19]Jesus answered, "You people don't believe! How long must I stay with you? How long must I go on being patient with you? Bring the boy to me!"

[20]So the followers brought him to Jesus. As soon as the evil spirit saw Jesus, it attacked the boy. He fell down and rolled on the ground, foaming from his mouth.

[21]Jesus asked the boy's father, "How long has this been happening?"

The father answered, "Since he was very young. [22]The spirit often throws him into a fire or into water to kill him. If you can do anything for him, please have pity on us and help us."

[23]Jesus said to the father, "You said, 'If you can!' All things are possible for him who believes."

[24]Immediately the father cried out, "I do believe! Help me to believe more!"

[25]Jesus saw that a crowd was running there to see what was happening. So he spoke to the evil spirit, saying, "You deaf and dumb spirit—I command you to come out of this boy and never enter him again!"

[26]The evil spirit screamed and caused the boy to fall on the ground again. Then the spirit came out. The boy looked as if he were dead. And many people said, "He is dead!" [27]But Jesus took hold of the boy's hand and helped him to stand up.

[28]Jesus went into the house. His followers were alone with him there. They said, "Why couldn't we force that evil spirit out?"

[29]Jesus answered, "That kind of spirit can only be forced out by prayer."

Jesus Talks About His Death

[30]Then Jesus and his followers left that place and went through Galilee. Jesus did not want anyone to know where he was [31]because he wanted to teach his followers alone. He said to them, "The Son of Man[d] will be given to men who will kill him. After three days, he will rise from death." [32]But the followers did not understand what Jesus meant. And they were afraid to ask.

Who Is the Greatest?

[33]Jesus and his followers went to Capernaum and went into a house

there. Then Jesus said to them, "What were you arguing about on the road?" [34]But the followers did not answer, because their argument on the road was about which one of them was the greatest.

[35]Jesus sat down and called the 12 apostles[d] to him. He said, "If anyone wants to be the most important, then he must be last of all and servant of all."

[36]Then Jesus took a small child and had him stand among them. He took the child in his arms and said, [37]"If anyone accepts children like these in my name, then he is also accepting me. And if he accepts me, then he is also accepting the One who sent me."

Anyone Not Against Us Is for Us

[38]Then John said, "Teacher, we saw a man using your name to force demons[d] out of a person. We told him to stop, because he does not belong to our group."

[39]Jesus said, "Don't stop him. Anyone who uses my name to do powerful things will not say evil things about me. [40]He who is not against us is with us. [41]I tell you the truth. If anyone helps you by giving you a drink of water because you belong to the Christ,[d] then he will truly get his reward.

[42]"If one of these little children believes in me, and someone causes that child to sin, then it will be very bad for him. It would be better for him to have a large stone tied around his neck and be drowned in the sea. [43]If your hand causes you to sin, cut it off. It is better for you to lose part of your body but have life forever. That is much better than to have two hands and go to hell. In that place the fire never goes out. [44 n] [45]If your foot causes you to sin, cut it off. It is better for you to lose part of your body but have life forever. That is much better than to have two feet

and be thrown into hell. [46 n] [47]If your eye causes you to sin, take it out. It is better for you to have only one eye but have life forever. That is much better than to have two eyes and be thrown into hell. [48]In hell the worm does not die; the fire is never stopped. [49]Every person will be salted with fire.

[50]"Salt is good. But if the salt loses its salty taste, then you cannot make it salty again. So, be full of goodness. And have peace with each other."

Jesus Teaches About Divorce

10 Then Jesus left that place. He went into the area of Judea and across the Jordan River. Again, crowds came to him. And Jesus taught them as he always did.

[2]Some Pharisees[d] came to Jesus and tried to trick him. They asked, "Is it right for a man to divorce his wife?"

[3]Jesus answered, "What did Moses command you to do?"

[4]They said, "Moses allowed a man to write out divorce papers and send her away."[n]

[5]Jesus said, "Moses wrote that command for you because you refused to accept God's teaching. [6]But when God made the world, 'he made them male and female.'[n] [7]So a man will leave his father and mother and be united with his wife. [8]And the two people will become one body.'[n] So the people are not two, but one. [9]God has joined the two people together. So no one should separate them."

[10]Later, the followers and Jesus were in the house. They asked Jesus again about the question of divorce. [11]He answered, "Anyone who divorces his wife and marries another woman is guilty of adultery[d] against her. [12]And the woman who divorces her husband and marries another man is also guilty of adultery."

---

[n]**Verse 44**　Some Greek copies of Mark add verse 44, which is the same as verse 48.
[n]**Verse 46**　Some Greek copies of Mark add verse 46, which is the same as verse 48.
[n]**"Moses . . . away."**　Quotation from Deuteronomy 24:1.
[n]**'he made . . . female.'**　Quotation from Genesis 1:27.
[n]**'So . . . body.'**　Quotation from Genesis 2:24.

Jesus Accepts Children

¹³Some people brought their small children to Jesus so he could touch them. But his followers told the people to stop bringing their children to him. ¹⁴When Jesus saw this, he was displeased. He said to them, "Let the little children come to me. Don't stop them. The kingdom of God belongs to people who are like these little children. ¹⁵I tell you the truth. You must accept the kingdom of God as a little child accepts things, or you will never enter it." ¹⁶Then Jesus took the children in his arms. He put his hands on them and blessed them.

"**W**hat was that young man thinking about when he asked Jesus his question? Read Mark 10:17-22."

A Rich Young Man's Question

¹⁷Jesus started to leave, but a man ran to him and fell on his knees before Jesus. The man asked, "Good teacher, what must I do to get the life that never ends?"

¹⁸Jesus answered, "Why do you call me good? No one is good except God alone. ¹⁹You know the commands: 'You must not murder anyone. You must not be guilty of adultery.ᵈ You must not steal. You must not tell lies about your neighbor in court. You must not cheat. Honor your father and mother.'"ⁿ

²⁰The man said, "Teacher, I have obeyed all these commands since I was a boy."

²¹Jesus looked straight at the man and loved him. Jesus said, "There is still one more thing you need to do. Go and sell everything you have, and give the money to the poor. You will

have a reward in heaven. Then come and follow me."

²²He was very sad to hear Jesus say this, and he left. The man was sad because he was very rich.

²³Then Jesus looked at his followers and said, "How hard it will be for those who are rich to enter the kingdom of God!"

²⁴The followers were amazed at what Jesus said. But he said again, "My children, it is very hard to enter the kingdom of God! ²⁵And it will be very hard for a rich person to enter the kingdom of God. It would be easier for a camel to go through the eye of a needle!"

²⁶The followers were even more amazed and said to each other, "Then who can be saved?"

²⁷Jesus looked straight at them and said, "This is something that men cannot do. But God can do it. God can do all things."

²⁸Peter said to Jesus, "We left everything to follow you!"

²⁹Jesus said, "I tell you the truth. Everyone who has left his home, brothers, sisters, mother, father, children, or fields for me and for the Good Newsᵈ ³⁰will get a hundred times more than he left. Here in this world he will have more homes, brothers, sisters, mothers, children, and fields. And with those things, he will also suffer for his belief. But in the age that is coming he will have life forever. ³¹Many who have the highest place now will have the lowest place in the future. And those who have the lowest place now will have the highest place in the future."

Jesus Talks About His Own Death

³²Jesus and the people with him were on the road to Jerusalem. Jesus was leading the way. The followers were amazed, but those who followed behind them were afraid. Jesus took the 12 apostlesᵈ aside and talked with them alone. He told them what would

---

ⁿ**'You . . . mother.'** Quotation from Exodus 20:12-16; Deuteronomy 5:16-20.

happen in Jerusalem. ³³He said, "We are going to Jerusalem. The Son of Man*ᵈ* will be given to the leading priests and teachers of the law. They will say that he must die. They will give him to the non-Jewish people, ³⁴who will laugh at him and spit on him. They will beat him with whips and kill him. But on the third day after his death, he will rise to life again."

be baptized with the same kind of baptism that I must have?"*ⁿ*

³⁹They answered, "Yes, we can!"

Jesus said to them, "You will drink the same cup that I will drink. And you will be baptized with the same baptism that I must have. ⁴⁰But I cannot choose who will sit at my right or my left. These places are for those for whom they are prepared."

⁴¹The ten followers heard this. They began to be angry with James and John.

⁴²Jesus called all the followers together. He said, "The non-Jewish

Brothers and Sisters

JAMES AND JOHN • MARK 10:35-40

James and John were brothers, and both were Jesus' disciples. They loved Jesus very much. They believed that Jesus would become a great king who would one day rule their land. One day they asked Jesus to do something special for them. They wanted Jesus to let them sit, one on each side of his throne. The people who sat on each side of the king were the most powerful people in the kingdom besides the king. James and John wanted to be the most important and powerful people in Jesus' kingdom.

Jesus told them that the people who would be important in his kingdom were the people who served others. Do you want to sit on a throne, or will you serve others?

To meet a brother who told about Jesus, fly to page 1273.

Two Followers Ask Jesus a Favor

³⁵Then James and John, sons of Zebedee, came to Jesus. They said, "Teacher, we want to ask you to do something for us."

³⁶Jesus asked, "What do you want me to do for you?"

³⁷They answered, "You will have glory in your kingdom. Let one of us sit at your right, and let one of us sit at your left."

³⁸Jesus said, "You don't understand what you are asking. Can you drink the cup that I must drink? And can you

people have men they call rulers. You know that those rulers love to show their power over the people. And their important leaders love to use all their authority. ⁴³But it should not be that way among you. If one of you wants to become great, then he must serve you like a servant. ⁴⁴If one of you wants to become the most important, then he must serve all of you like a slave. ⁴⁵In the same way, the Son of Man*ᵈ* did not come to be served. He came to serve. The Son of Man came to give his life to save many people."

*ⁿ**Can you . . . have?** Jesus was asking if they could suffer the same terrible things that would happen to him.*

Jesus Heals a Blind Man

⁴⁶Then they came to the town of Jericho. As Jesus was leaving there with his followers and a large crowd, a blind beggar named Bartimaeus (son of Timaeus) was sitting by the road. ⁴⁷He heard that Jesus from Nazareth was walking by. The blind man cried out, "Jesus, Son of David,ᵈ please help me!"

⁴⁸Many people scolded the blind man and told him to be quiet. But he shouted more and more, "Son of David, please help me!"

⁴⁹Jesus stopped and said, "Tell the man to come here."

So they called the blind man. They said, "Cheer up! Get to your feet. Jesus is calling you." ⁵⁰The blind man stood up quickly. He left his coat there and went to Jesus.

⁵¹Jesus asked him, "What do you want me to do for you?"

The blind man answered, "Teacher, I want to see again."

⁵²Jesus said, "Go. You are healed because you believed." At once the man was able to see again, and he followed Jesus on the road.

Jesus Enters Jerusalem as a King

11 Jesus and his followers were coming closer to Jerusalem. They came to the towns of Bethphage and Bethany near the Mount of Olives.ᵈ There Jesus sent two of his followers. ²He said to them, "Go to the town you see there. When you enter it, you will find a colt tied which no one has ever ridden. Untie it and bring it here to me. ³If anyone asks you why you are doing this, tell him, 'The Master needs the colt. He will send it back soon.'"

⁴The followers went into the town. They found a colt tied in the street near the door of a house, and they untied it. ⁵Some people were standing there and asked, "What are you doing? Why are you untying that colt?" ⁶The followers answered the way Jesus told them to answer. And the people let them take the colt.

⁷The followers brought the colt to

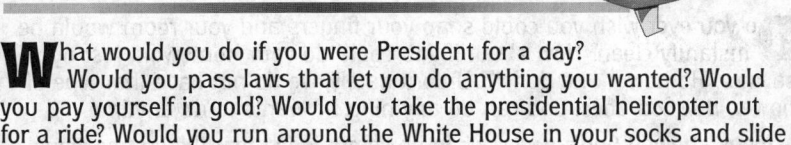

Helping Others
MARK 10:42-45

What would you do if you were President for a day? Would you pass laws that let you do anything you wanted? Would you pay yourself in gold? Would you take the presidential helicopter out for a ride? Would you run around the White House in your socks and slide across the polished floors?

You're *not* going to be President for a day, of course. Even if you were, maybe you wouldn't do any of those things. The real question is, if you had that kind of power, would you use it for yourself or to help others?

This passage makes it very clear that people in charge are not to use their authority just for their own advantage. They are to use it for the good of others.

You may not ever be President. But someday you may have some amount of authority over others. If so, use that power to help other people, not just yourself. That's what Jesus would do.

To learn more about helping others, zoom to page 1321.

Jesus. They put their coats on the colt, and Jesus sat on it. [8]Many people spread their coats on the road. Others cut branches in the fields and spread the branches on the road. [9]Some of the people were walking ahead of Jesus. Others were following him. All of them were shouting,

"Praise[n] God!
God bless the One who comes in
       the name of the Lord!
Psalm 118:26

[10]God bless the kingdom of our
       father David!
   That kingdom is coming!
   Praise to God in heaven!"

[11]Jesus entered Jerusalem and went into the Temple.[d] When he had looked at everything, and since it was already late, he went out to Bethany with the 12 apostles.[d]

[12]The next day as Jesus was leaving Bethany, he was hungry. [13]He saw a fig tree in leaf. So he went to the tree to see if it had any figs on it. But he found no figs, only leaves. It was not the right season for figs to grow. [14]So Jesus said to the tree, "May no one ever eat fruit from you again." Jesus' followers heard him say this.

Jesus Goes to the Temple

[15]Jesus returned to Jerusalem and went into the Temple.[d] He began to throw out those who were buying and selling things there. He overturned the tables that belonged to the men who were exchanging different kinds of money. And he turned over the benches of the men who were selling doves. [16]Jesus refused to allow anyone to carry goods through the Temple courts. [17]Then Jesus taught the people. He said, "It is written in the Scriptures,[d] 'My Temple will be a house where people from all nations will pray.'[n] But

Amazing Events that Showed God's Power

MARK 11:12-21

Do you ever wish you could snap your fingers and your room would be instantly clean? How about if you could do your homework just by saying, "Homework be done!"? Unfortunately, we do not have that type of power. But God does. God can do anything he wants to do anytime.

Jesus showed God's power when he commanded that the fig tree would never bear fruit again. When Jesus passed by with his disciples the next day they saw that the plant had died. It would never bear fruit again. Jesus did not kill the plant because he was angry at the plant. He used the plant to teach a lesson about the great power of God.

God wants us to know he is powerful. Aren't you glad God will use his power for good in our lives?

To find out what happened to Jesus after his time on earth, fly to page 1316.

---

[n]**Praise**   Literally, "Hosanna," a Hebrew word used at first in praying to God for help, but at this time it was probably a shout of joy used in praising God or his Messiah.
[n]**'My Temple . . . pray.'**   Quotation from Isaiah 56:7.

you are changing God's house into a 'hideout for robbers.'"[n]

[18]The leading priests and the teachers of the law heard all this. They began trying to find a way to kill Jesus. They were afraid of him because all the people were amazed at his teaching. [19]That night, Jesus and his followers left the city.

The Power of Faith

[20]The next morning, Jesus was passing by with his followers. They saw the fig tree, and it was dry and dead, even to the roots. [21]Peter remembered the tree and said to Jesus, "Teacher, look! Yesterday, you cursed the fig tree. Now it is dry and dead!"

[22]Jesus answered, "Have faith in God. [23]I tell you the truth. You can say to this mountain, 'Go, mountain, fall into the sea.' And if you have no doubts in your mind and believe that the thing you say will happen, then God will do it for you. [24]So I tell you to ask for things in prayer. And if you believe that you have received those things, then they will be yours. [25]When you are praying, and you remember that you are angry with another person about something, then forgive him. If you do this, then your Father in heaven will also forgive your sins." [26][n]

Leaders Doubt Jesus' Authority

[27]Jesus and his followers went again to Jerusalem. Jesus was walking in the Temple.[d] The leading priests, the teachers of the law, and the older Jewish leaders came to him. [28]They said to him, "Tell us! What authority do you have to do these things? Who gave you this authority?"

[29]Jesus answered, "I will ask you one question. You answer it. Then I will tell you whose authority I use to do these things. [30]Tell me: When John baptized people, was that from God or from man? Answer me!"

[31]They argued about Jesus' question. They said to each other, "If we answer, 'John's baptism was from God,' then Jesus will say, 'Then why didn't you believe John?' [32]But if we say, 'From man,' then the people will be against us." (These leaders were afraid of the people. All the people believed that John was a prophet.[d])

[33]So the leaders answered Jesus, "We don't know."

Jesus said, "Then I will not tell you what authority I use to do these things."

God Sends His Son

12 Jesus used stories to teach the people. He said, "A man planted a vineyard. He put a wall around it and dug a hole for a winepress.[d] Then he built a tower. He leased the vineyard to some farmers and left for a trip. [2]Later, it was time for the grapes to be picked. So the man sent a servant to the farmers to get his share of the grapes. [3]But the farmers grabbed the servant and beat him. They sent him away with nothing. [4]Then the man sent another servant. They hit him on the head and showed no respect for him. [5]So the man sent another servant. They killed this servant. The man sent many other servants. The farmers beat some of them and killed others.

[6]"The man had one person left to send, his son whom he loved. He sent him last of all, saying, 'The farmers will respect my son.'

[7]"But they said to each other, 'This is the owner's son. This vineyard will be his. If we kill him, then it will be ours.' [8]So they took the son, killed him, and threw him out of the vineyard.

[9]"So what will the man who owns the vineyard do? He will go to the vineyard and kill those farmers. Then he will give the vineyard to other farmers. [10]Surely you have read this Scripture:[d]

---

[n]**'hideout for robbers.'** Quotation from Jeremiah 7:11.
[n]**Verse 26** Some early Greek copies add verse 26: "But if you don't forgive other people, then your Father in heaven will not forgive your sins."

'The stone that the builders did not
    want
    became the cornerstone.[d]
[11]The Lord did this,
    and it is wonderful to us.'"

Psalm 118:22-23

[12]The Jewish leaders knew that the
story was about them. So they wanted
to find a way to arrest Jesus, but they
were afraid of the people. So the leaders left him and went away.

The Leaders Try to Trap Jesus

[13]Later, the Jewish leaders sent
some Pharisees[d] and some men from
the group called Herodians[n] to Jesus.
They wanted to catch Jesus saying
something wrong. [14]They came to him
and said, "Teacher, we know that you
are an honest man. You are not afraid
of what other people think about you.
All men are the same to you. And you
teach the truth about God's way. Tell
us: Is it right to pay taxes to Caesar?[d]
Should we pay them, or not?"

[15]But Jesus knew what these men
were really trying to do. He said, "Why
are you trying to trap me? Bring me a
silver coin. Let me see it." [16]They gave
Jesus a coin, and he asked, "Whose
picture is on the coin? And whose
name is written on it?"

They answered, "Caesar's."

[17]Then Jesus said to them, "Give to
Caesar the things that are Caesar's.
And give to God the things that are
God's." The men were amazed at what
Jesus said.

Sadducees Try to Trick Jesus

[18]Then some Sadducees[d] came to
Jesus. (Sadducees believe that no person will rise from death.) The Sadducees asked Jesus a question. [19]They
said, "Teacher, Moses wrote that a
man's brother might die. He leaves a
wife but no children. Then that man
must marry the widow and have children for the dead brother. [20]There

were seven brothers. The first brother
married but died. He had no children.
[21]So the second brother married the
widow. But he also died and had no
children. The same thing happened
with the third brother. [22]All seven
brothers married her and died. None
of the brothers had any children. The
woman was last to die. [23]But all seven
brothers had married her. So at the
time people rise from death, whose
wife will the woman be?"

[24]Jesus answered, "Why did you
make this mistake? Is it because you
don't know what the Scriptures[d] say?
Or is it because you don't know about
the power of God? [25]When people rise
from death, there will be no marriage.
People will not be married to each
other but will be like angels in heaven.
[26]Surely you have read what God said
about people rising from death. In the
book in which Moses wrote about the
burning bush,[n] it says that God told
Moses this: 'I am the God of Abraham,
the God of Isaac, and the God of
Jacob.'[n] [27]God is the God of living people, not dead people. You Sadducees
are wrong!"

"**S**o what do
you think?
Which is
the greatest
commandment?
Find out Jesus'
answer in
Mark 12:28-34."

The Most Important Command

[28]One of the teachers of the law
came to Jesus. He heard Jesus arguing
with the Sadducees[d] and the Pharisees.[d] He saw that Jesus gave good
answers to their questions. So he
asked Jesus, "Which of the commands
is most important?"

---

[n]**Herodians**   A political group that followed Herod and his family.
[n]**burning bush**   Read Exodus 3:1-12 in the Old Testament.
[n]**'I am . . . Jacob.'**   Quotation from Exodus 3:6.

[29]Jesus answered, "The most important command is this: 'Listen, people of Israel! The Lord our God, he is the only Lord. [30]Love the Lord your God. Love him with all your heart, all your soul, all your mind, and all your strength.'[n] [31]The second most important command is this: 'Love your neighbor as you love yourself.'[n] These two commands are the most important commands."

[32]The man answered, "That was a good answer, Teacher. You were right when you said these things. God is the only Lord, and there is no other God besides him. [33]One must love God with all his heart, all his mind, and all his strength. And one must love his neighbor as he loves himself. These commands are more important than all the animals and sacrifices we offer to God."

[34]Jesus saw that the man answered him wisely. So Jesus said to him, "You are close to the kingdom of God." And after that, no one was brave enough to ask Jesus any more questions.

[35]Jesus was teaching in the Temple.[d] He asked, "Why do the teachers of the law say that the Christ[d] is the son of David? [36]David himself, speaking by the Holy Spirit,[d] said:

'The Lord said to my Lord:
 Sit by me at my right side,
 until I put your enemies under
         your control.'   *Psalm 110:1*

[37]David himself calls the Christ 'Lord.' So how can the Christ be David's son?" The large crowd listened to Jesus with pleasure.

[38]Jesus continued teaching. He said, "Beware of the teachers of the law. They like to walk around wearing clothes that look important. And they love for people to show respect to them in the marketplaces. [39]They love to have the most important seats in the synagogues.[d] And they love to have the most important seats at the feasts. [40]They cheat widows and steal their homes. Then they try to make

themselves look good by saying long prayers. God will punish these people terribly."

True Giving

[41]Jesus sat near the Temple[d] money box where people put their gifts. He watched the people put in their money. Many rich people gave large sums of money. [42]Then a poor widow came and gave two very small copper coins. These coins were not worth even a penny.

[43]Jesus called his followers to him. He said, "I tell you the truth. This poor widow gave only two small coins. But she really gave more than all those rich people. [44]The rich have plenty; they gave only what they did not need. This woman is very poor. But she gave all she had. And she needed that money to help her live."

The Temple Will Be Destroyed

13 Jesus was leaving the Temple.[d] One of his followers said to him, "Look, Teacher! This Temple has beautiful buildings with very big stones."

[2]Jesus said, "Do you see all these great buildings? Every stone will be thrown to the ground. Not one stone will be left on another."

[3]Later, Jesus was sitting on the Mount of Olives.[d] He was alone with Peter, James, John, and Andrew. They could all see the Temple. They asked Jesus, [4]"Tell us, when will all these things happen? And what will show us that the time has come for them to happen?"

[5]Jesus said to them: "Be careful that no one fools you. [6]Many people will come and use my name. They will say, 'I am the One.' And they will fool many. [7]You will hear about wars and stories of wars that are coming. But don't be afraid. These things must happen before the end comes. [8]Nations will fight against other nations. Kingdoms

---

[n]**Listen . . . strength.'**   Quotation from Deuteronomy 6:4-5.
[n]**'Love . . . yourself.'**   Quotation from Leviticus 19:18.

will fight against other kingdoms. There will be times when there is no food for people to eat. And there will be earthquakes in different places. These things are like the first pains when something new is about to be born.

[9]"You must be careful. People will arrest you and take you to court. They will beat you in their synagogues.[d] You will be forced to stand before kings and governors, to tell them about me. This will happen to you because you follow me. [10]But before these things happen, the Good News[d] must be told to all people. [11]When you are arrested and judged, don't worry about what you should say. Say the things God gives you to say at that time. It will not really be you speaking. It will be the Holy Spirit.[d]

[12]"Brothers will turn against their own brothers and give them over to be killed. Fathers will turn against their own children and give them over to be killed. Children will fight against their own parents and cause their parents to be killed. [13]All people will hate you because you follow me. But the person who continues to be strong until the end will be saved.

[14]"You will see 'The horrible thing that destroys.'[n] You will see this thing standing in the place where it should not be." (You who read this should understand what it means.) "At that time, the people in Judea should run away to the mountains. [15]If a person is on the roof[n] of his house, he must not go down to take anything out of his house. [16]If a person is in the field, he must not go back to get his coat. [17]At that time, it will be hard for women who are pregnant or have nursing babies. [18]Pray that these things will not happen in winter. [19]This is because those days will be full of trouble. There will be more trouble than there has ever been since the beginning, when God made the world. And nothing as

bad will ever happen again. [20]God has decided to make that terrible time short. If that time were not made short, then no one would go on living. But God will make that time short to help his special people whom he has chosen. [21]At that time, someone might say to you, 'Look, there is the Christ!'[d] Or another person might say, 'There he is!' But don't believe them. [22]False Christs and false prophets[d] will come and perform great wonders and miracles.[d] They will do these things to the people God has chosen. They will do these things to try to fool them, if that is possible. [23]So be careful. For I have warned you about all this before it happens.

[24]"During the days after this trouble comes,

'The sun will grow dark.
　And the moon will not give its
　　light.
[25]The stars will fall from the sky.
　And everything in the sky will be
　　changed.'　　　*Isaiah 13:10; 34:4*

[26]"Then people will see the Son of Man[d] coming in clouds with great power and glory. [27]The Son of Man will send his angels all around the earth. They will gather his chosen people from every part of the earth.

[28]"The fig tree teaches us a lesson: When its branches become green and soft, and new leaves begin to grow, then you know that summer is near. [29]So also when you see all these things happening, then you will know that the time is near, ready to come. [30]I tell you the truth. All these things will happen while the people of this time are still living. [31]The whole world, earth and sky, will be destroyed, but the words I have said will never be destroyed.

[32]"No one knows when that day or time will be. The Son and the angels in heaven don't know. Only the Father knows. [33]Be careful! Always be ready! You don't know when that time will be.

---

[n]"**horrible . . . destroys.'** Mentioned in Daniel 9:27; 12:11 (cf. Daniel 11:31).
[n]**roof** In Bible times houses were built with flat roofs. The roof was used for drying things such as flax and fruit. And it was used as an extra room, as a place for worship and as a place to sleep in the summer.

34It is like a man who goes on a trip. He leaves his house and lets his servants take care of it. He gives each servant a special job to do. One servant has the work of guarding the door. The man tells this servant always to be watchful. This is what I am now telling you. 35You must always be ready. You don't know when the owner of the house will come back. He might come in the evening, or at midnight, or in the early morning, or when the sun rises. 36He might come back quickly. If you are always ready, then he will not find you sleeping. 37I tell you this, and I say this to everyone: 'Be ready!'"

The Plan to Kill Jesus

14 It was now only two days before the Passover[d] and the Feast[d] of Unleavened Bread. The leading priests and teachers of the law were trying to find a way to use some trick to arrest Jesus and kill him. 2But they said, "We must not do it during the feast. The people might cause a riot."

A Woman with Perfume for Jesus

3Jesus was in Bethany. He was at dinner in the house of Simon, who had a harmful skin disease. While Jesus was there, a woman came to him. She had an alabaster[d] jar filled with very expensive perfume, made of pure nard.[d] The woman opened the jar and poured the perfume on Jesus' head.

4Some of those who were there saw this and became angry. They complained to each other, saying, "Why waste that perfume? 5It was worth a full year's work. It could be sold, and the money could be given to the poor." They spoke to the woman sharply.

6Jesus said, "Don't bother the woman. Why are you troubling her? She did a beautiful thing for me. 7You will always have the poor with you. You can help them anytime you want. But you will not always have me. 8This woman did the only thing she could do for me. She poured perfume on my body. She did this before I die to prepare me for burial. 9I tell you the truth. The Good News[d] will be told to people in all the world. And in every place it is preached, what this woman has done

Plans That Backfired
JUDAS • MARK 14

Judas was one of Jesus' most trusted disciples. He was in charge of keeping the money people gave to help Jesus and his disciples. But sometimes Judas would take the money that was supposed to help Jesus and the disciples and spend it on himself. Eventually he planned to have Jesus arrested. That was a terrible thing to do. He was not a true friend of Jesus or the disciples.

A group of people promised to give Judas some money if he helped them arrest Jesus. Judas thought he had a plan for getting some extra money. But when Jesus was arrested, Judas realized that what he had done was wrong. He went to the people who gave him the money and threw the money on the ground in front of them. Then he killed himself. Judas' plan did not work out the way he wanted.

It is never good to plan to do something wrong. God wants us to do what is right.

To meet a leader who was very proud, fly to page 1337.

will be told. And people will remember her."

Judas Becomes an Enemy of Jesus

[10]One of the 12 followers, Judas Iscariot, went to talk to the leading priests. Judas offered to give Jesus to them. [11]The leading priests were pleased about this. They promised to pay Judas money. So he waited for the best time to give Jesus to them.

Jesus Eats the Passover Feast

[12]It was now the first day of the Feast[d] of Unleavened Bread. This was a time when the Jews always sacrificed the Passover[d] lambs. Jesus' followers came to him. They said, "We will go and prepare everything for the Passover Feast. Where do you want to eat the feast?"

[13]Jesus sent two of his followers and said to them, "Go into the city. A man carrying a jar of water will meet you. Follow him. [14]He will go into a house. Tell the owner of the house, 'The Teacher asks that you show us the room where he and his followers can eat the Passover Feast.' [15]The owner will show you a large room upstairs. This room is ready. Prepare the food for us there."

[16]So the followers left and went into the city. Everything happened as Jesus had said. So they prepared the Passover Feast.

[17]In the evening, Jesus went to that house with the 12. [18]While they were all eating, Jesus said, "I tell you the truth. One of you will give me to my enemies—one of you eating with me now."

[19]The followers were very sad to hear this. Each one said to Jesus, "I am not the one, am I?"

[20]Jesus answered, "The man who is against me is 1 of the 12. He is the 1 who dips his bread into the bowl with me. [21]The Son of Man[d] must go and die. The Scriptures[d] say this will happen.

But how terrible it will be for the person who gives the Son of Man to be killed. It would be better for that person if he had never been born."

The Lord's Supper

[22]While they were eating, Jesus took some bread. He thanked God for it and broke it. Then he gave it to his followers and said, "Take it. This bread is my body."

[23]Then Jesus took a cup. He thanked God for it and gave it to the followers. All the followers drank from the cup.

[24]Then Jesus said, "This is my blood which begins the new agreement that God makes with his people. This blood is poured out for many. [25]I tell you the truth. I will not drink of this fruit of the vine[n] again until that day when I drink it new in the kingdom of God."

[26]They sang a hymn and went out to the Mount of Olives.[d]

Jesus' Followers Will All Leave Him

[27]Then Jesus told the followers, "You will all lose your faith in me. It is written in the Scriptures:[d]

'I will kill the shepherd,
    and the sheep will scatter.'
                         Zechariah 13:7
[28]But after I rise from death, I will go ahead of you into Galilee."

[29]Peter said, "All the other followers may lose their faith. But I will not."

[30]Jesus answered, "I tell you the truth. Tonight you will say you don't know me. You will say this three times before the rooster crows twice."

[31]But Peter answered strongly, "I will never say that I don't know you! I will even die with you!" And all the other followers said the same thing.

Jesus Prays Alone

[32]Jesus and his followers went to a place called Gethsemane. He said to his followers, "Sit here while I pray." [33]Jesus told Peter, James, and John to

---

[n]**fruit of the vine** Product of the grapevine; this may also be translated "wine."

come with him. Then Jesus began to be very sad and troubled. [34]He said to them, "I am full of sorrow. My heart is breaking with sadness. Stay here and watch."

[35]Jesus walked a little farther away from them. Then he fell on the ground and prayed. He prayed that, if possible, he would not have this time of suffering. [36]He prayed, "Abba,[n] Father! You can do all things. Let me not have this cup[n] of suffering. But do what you want, not what I want."

[37]Then Jesus went back to his followers. He found them asleep. He said to Peter, "Simon, why are you sleeping? You could not stay awake with me for one hour? [38]Stay awake and pray that you will not be tempted. Your spirit wants to do what is right, but your body is weak."

[39]Again Jesus went away and prayed the same thing. [40]Then he went back to the followers. Again he found them asleep because their eyes were very heavy. And they did not know what to say to Jesus.

[41]After Jesus prayed a third time, he went back to his followers. He said to them, "You are still sleeping and resting? That's enough! The time has come for the Son of Man[d] to be given to sinful people. [42]Get up! We must go. Here comes the man who has turned against me."

Jesus Is Arrested

[43]While Jesus was still speaking, Judas came up. Judas was 1 of the 12 followers. He had many people with him. They were sent from the leading priests, the teachers of the law, and the older Jewish leaders. Those with Judas had swords and clubs.

[44]Judas had planned a signal for them. He had said, "The man I kiss is Jesus. Arrest him and guard him while you lead him away." [45]So Judas went to Jesus and said, "Teacher!" and kissed

him. [46]Then the men grabbed Jesus and arrested him. [47]One of the followers standing near drew his sword. He struck the servant of the high priest with the sword and cut off his ear.

[48]Then Jesus said, "You came to get me with swords and clubs as if I were a criminal. [49]Every day I was with you teaching in the Temple.[d] You did not arrest me there. But all these things have happened to make the Scriptures[d] come true." [50]Then all of Jesus' followers left him and ran away.

[51]A young man, wearing only a linen cloth, was following Jesus. The people also grabbed him. [52]But the cloth he was wearing came off, and he ran away naked.

Jesus Before the Leaders

[53]The people who arrested Jesus led him to the house of the high priest. All the leading priests, the older Jewish leaders, and the teachers of the law were gathered there. [54]Peter followed far behind and entered the courtyard of the high priest's house. There he sat with the guards, warming himself by the fire.

[55]The leading priests and all the Jewish council tried to find something that Jesus had done wrong so they could kill him. But the council could find no proof against him. [56]Many people came and told false things about him. But all said different things— none of them agreed.

[57]Then some men stood up and lied about Jesus. They said, [58]"We heard this man say, 'I will destroy this Temple[d] that men made. And three days later, I will build another Temple—a Temple not made by men.'" [59]But even the things these men said did not agree.

[60]Then the high priest stood before them and said to Jesus, "Aren't you going to answer the charges these men bring against you?" [61]But Jesus said nothing. He did not answer.

---

[n]**Abba**   Name that a child called his father.

[n]**cup**   Jesus is talking about the bad things that will happen to him. Accepting these things will be very hard, like drinking a cup of something that tastes very bitter.

The high priest asked Jesus another question: "Are you the Christ,[d] the Son of the blessed God?"

[62] Jesus answered, "I am. And in the future you will see the Son of Man[d] sitting at the right side of the Powerful One. And you will see the Son of Man coming on clouds in the sky."

[63] When the high priest heard this, he was very angry. He tore his clothes and said, "We don't need any more witnesses! [64] You all heard him say these things against God. What do you think?"

They all said that Jesus was guilty and should be killed. [65] Some of the people there spit at Jesus. They covered his eyes and hit him with their fists. They said, "Prove that you are a prophet!"[d] Then the guards led Jesus away and beat him.

Peter Says He Doesn't Know Jesus

[66] Peter was still in the courtyard when a servant girl of the high priest came there. [67] She saw Peter warming himself at the fire. She looked closely at him.

Then the girl said, "You were with Jesus, that man from Nazareth."

[68] But Peter said that he was never with Jesus. He said, "I don't know or understand what you are talking about." Then Peter left and went toward the entrance of the courtyard.[n]

[69] The servant girl saw Peter there. Again she said to the people who were standing there, "This man is one of those who followed Jesus." [70] Again Peter said that it was not true.

A short time later, some people were standing near Peter. They said, "We know you are one of those who followed Jesus. You are from Galilee, too."

[71] Then Peter began to curse. He said, "I swear that I don't know this man you're talking about!"

[72] As soon as Peter said this, the rooster crowed the second time. Then Peter remembered what Jesus had told him: "Before the rooster crows twice, you will say three times that you don't know me." Then Peter was very sad and began to cry.

Pilate Questions Jesus

15 Very early in the morning, the leading priests, the older Jewish leaders, the teachers of the law, and all the Jewish council decided what to do with Jesus. They tied him, led him away, and turned him over to Pilate, the governor.

[2] Pilate asked Jesus, "Are you the king of the Jews?"

Jesus answered, "Yes, I am."

[3] The leading priests accused Jesus of many things. [4] So Pilate asked Jesus another question. He said, "You can see that these people are accusing you of many things. Why don't you answer?"

[5] But Jesus still said nothing. Pilate was very surprised at this.

Pilate Tries to Free Jesus

[6] Every year at the Passover[d] time the governor would free one person from prison. He would free any person the people wanted him to free. [7] At that time, there was a man named Barabbas in prison. He was a rebel and had committed murder during a riot. [8] The crowd came to Pilate and asked him to free a prisoner as he always did.

[9] Pilate asked them, "Do you want me to free the king of the Jews?" [10] Pilate knew that the leading priests had given Jesus to him because they were jealous of Jesus. [11] And the leading priests had persuaded the people to ask Pilate to free Barabbas, not Jesus.

[12] Pilate asked the crowd again, "So what should I do with this man you call the king of the Jews?"

[13] They shouted, "Kill him on a cross!"

[14] Pilate asked, "Why? What wrong has he done?"

But they shouted louder and louder, "Kill him on a cross!"

[n] Verse 68 Many Greek copies add: "And the rooster crowed."

¹⁵Pilate wanted to please the crowd. So he freed Barabbas for them. And Pilate told the soldiers to beat Jesus with whips. Then he gave Jesus to the soldiers to be killed on a cross.

¹⁶Pilate's soldiers took Jesus into the governor's palace (called the Praetorium). They called all the other soldiers together. ¹⁷They put a purple robe on Jesus. Then they used thorny branches to make a crown. They put it on his head. ¹⁸Then they called out to him, "Hail, King of the Jews!" ¹⁹The man was Simon, the father of Alexander and Rufus. The soldiers forced Simon to carry the cross for Jesus. ²²They led Jesus to the place called Golgotha. (Golgotha means the Place of the Skull.) ²³At Golgotha the soldiers tried to give Jesus wine to drink. This wine was mixed with myrrh.^d But he refused to drink it. ²⁴The soldiers nailed Jesus to a cross. Then they divided his clothes among themselves. They threw lots^d to decide which clothes each soldier would get.

²⁵It was nine o'clock in the morning when they nailed Jesus to the cross.

Words to Know: New Testament

CROSS • MARK 15:21-24

You already know that Jesus died on a **cross**. Maybe there is a cross in your church. Perhaps you have seen pieces of jewelry with crosses on them. Why is the cross so important for Christians?

Dying on a cross (being crucified) was a terrible way to die. Jesus suffered very much when he was crucified. Christians remember the cross because when Jesus suffered there, he was taking the punishment that we deserved for our sins. Because Jesus died on the cross, we can come to God and ask forgiveness for our sins. That is why the cross is important to Christians.

What does the cross mean to you? Are you thankful Jesus died there for you?

To read about where Jesus was buried, fly to page 1215.

soldiers beat Jesus on the head many times with a stick. They also spit on him. Then they made fun of him by bowing on their knees and worshiping him. ²⁰After they finished making fun of him, the soldiers took off the purple robe and put his own clothes on him again. Then they led Jesus out of the palace to be killed on a cross.

Jesus Is Killed on a Cross

²¹There was a man from Cyrene coming from the fields to the city. The ²⁶There was a sign with the charge against Jesus written on it. The sign read: "THE KING OF THE JEWS." ²⁷They also put two robbers on crosses beside Jesus, one on the right, and the other on the left. ^{28 n 29}People walked by and insulted Jesus. They shook their heads, saying, "You said you could destroy the Temple^d and build it again in three days. ³⁰So save yourself! Come down from that cross!"

³¹The leading priests and the teachers of the law were also there. They

---

ⁿVerse 28 Some Greek copies add verse 28: "And the Scripture came true that says, 'They put him with criminals.'"

made fun of Jesus just as the other people did. They said among themselves, "He saved other people, but he can't save himself. ³²If he is really the Christ,ᵈ the king of Israel, then let him come down from the cross now. We will see this, and then we will believe in him." The robbers who were being killed on the crosses beside Jesus also insulted him.

Jesus Dies

³³At noon the whole country became dark. This darkness lasted for three hours. ³⁴At three o'clock Jesus cried in a loud voice, "Eloi, Eloi, lama sabachthani." This means, "My God, my God, why have you left me alone?"

³⁵Some of the people standing there heard this. They said, "Listen! He is calling Elijah."

³⁶One man there ran and got a sponge. He filled the sponge with vinegar and tied it to a stick. Then he used the stick to give the sponge to Jesus to drink from it. The man said, "We should wait now and see if Elijah will come to take him down from the cross."

³⁷Then Jesus cried in a loud voice and died.

³⁸When Jesus died, the curtain in the Templeⁿ split into two pieces. The tear started at the top and tore all the way to the bottom. ³⁹The army officer that was standing there before the cross saw what happened when Jesus died. The officer said, "This man really was the Son of God!"

⁴⁰Some women were standing at a distance from the cross, watching. Some of these women were Mary Magdalene, Salome, and Mary the mother of James and Joseph. (James was her youngest son.) ⁴¹These were the women who followed Jesus in Galilee and cared for him. Many other women were also there who had come with Jesus to Jerusalem.

Jesus Is Buried

⁴²This was Preparationᵈ Day. (That means the day before the Sabbathᵈ day.) It was becoming dark. ⁴³A man

Unsung Heroes

JOSEPH OF ARIMATHEA • MARK 15:42-46

Joseph of Arimathea was a Pharisee, a Jewish leader who strictly followed Jewish laws and traditions. Most of the Pharisees did not believe in Jesus. In fact, they had wanted Jesus to die. But Joseph loved Jesus. After Jesus was crucified, Joseph went to Pilate, the Roman leader, and asked to take Jesus' body from the cross and bury it in his own tomb.

Joseph might have worried that other Pharisees would not like him, or he might have been afraid of Pilate who had sentenced Jesus to die. But he went to Pilate anyway and took care of Jesus' body so it was buried properly.

Joseph of Arimathea was courageous and kind. That is why he is a hero!

To read about a hero who answered the door, fly to page 1339.

To read about a hero who answered the door, fly to page 1339.

ⁿcurtain in the Temple A curtain divided the Most Holy Place from the other part of the Temple. That was the special building in Jerusalem where God commanded the Jews to worship him.

named Joseph from Arimathea was brave enough to go to Pilate and ask for Jesus' body. Joseph was an important member of the Jewish council. He was one of the people who wanted the kingdom of God to come. 44Pilate wondered if Jesus was already dead. Pilate called the army officer who guarded Jesus and asked him if Jesus had already died. 45The officer told Pilate that he was dead. So Pilate told Joseph he could have the body. 46Joseph bought some linen cloth, took the body down from the cross and wrapped it in the linen. He put the body in a tomb that was cut in a wall of rock. Then he closed the tomb by rolling a very large stone to cover the entrance. 47And Mary Magdalene and Mary the mother of Joseph saw the place where Jesus was laid.

Jesus' body. 2Very early on that day, the first day of the week, the women were on their way to the tomb. It was soon after sunrise. 3They said to each other, "There is a large stone covering the entrance of the tomb. Who will move the stone for us?"

4Then the women looked and saw that the stone was already moved. The stone was very large, but it was moved away from the entrance. 5The women entered the tomb and saw a young man wearing a white robe. He was sitting on the right side, and the women were afraid.

6But the man said, "Don't be afraid. You are looking for Jesus from Nazareth, the one who was killed on a cross. He has risen from death. He is not here. Look, here is the place they laid him. 7Now go and tell his followers and Peter, 'Jesus is going into Galilee. He will be there before you. You will see him there as he told you before.'"

Words to Know: New Testament
TOMB • MARK 16:1-5

A **tomb** is a place where a dead person is buried. What did Jesus' tomb look like? Jesus was not put in a coffin and buried in a grave the way people are buried today. In Jesus' day, a person who died was wrapped up in long strips of cloth, and spices and perfumes were put in between the layers. Then the body was put in a tomb, a cave that had been dug in the side of a hill. The cave was big enough for people to walk in. They would lay the body on a shelf cut out of the rock in the cave. Then a big, heavy stone would be rolled in front of the opening.

Jesus died on the cross and was buried in a tomb, but he did not stay there! He rose again, and we know that one day we will be with him forever.

To read about how Jesus taught people, fly to page 1249.

Jesus Rises from Death

16 The day after the Sabbath[d] day, Mary Magdalene, Mary the mother of James, and Salome bought some sweet-smelling spices to put on

8The women were confused and shaking with fear. They left the tomb and ran away. They did not tell anyone about what happened, because they were afraid.[n]

[n]Verse 8 Some early Greek copies end the book with verse 8.

Some Followers See Jesus

[9]Jesus rose from death early on the first day of the week. He showed himself first to Mary Magdalene. One time in the past, he had forced seven demons[d] to leave Mary. [10]After Mary saw Jesus, she went and told his followers. They were very sad and were crying. [11]But Mary told them that Jesus was alive. She said that she had seen him, but the followers did not believe her.

[12]Later, Jesus showed himself to two of his followers while they were walking in the country. But Jesus did not look the same as before. [13]These followers went back to the others and told them what had happened. Again, the followers did not believe them.

Jesus Talks to the Apostles

[14]Later Jesus showed himself to the 11 followers while they were eating. He criticized them because they had little faith. They were stubborn and refused to believe those who had seen him after he had risen from death.

[15]Jesus said to the followers, "Go everywhere in the world. Tell the Good News[d] to everyone. [16]Anyone who believes and is baptized will be saved. But he who does not believe will be judged guilty. [17]And those who believe will be able to do these things as proof: They will use my name to force demons[d] out of people. They will speak in languages[n] they never learned. [18]They will pick up snakes without being hurt. And they will drink poison without being hurt. They will touch the sick, and the sick will be healed."

[19]After the Lord Jesus said these things to the followers, he was carried up into heaven. There, Jesus sat at the right side of God. [20]The followers went everywhere in the world and told the Good News to people. And the Lord helped them. The Lord proved that the Good News they told was true by giving them power to work miracles.[d]

---

[n]**languages**   This can also be translated "tongues."

LUKE

Luke Tells the
Non-Jews About Jesus

Luke Writes About Jesus' Life

1 To Theophilus:
Many have tried to give a history of the things that happened among us. [2]They have written the same things that we learned from others—the people who saw those things from the beginning and served God by telling people his message. [3]I myself studied everything carefully from the beginning, your Excellency." I thought I should write it out for you. So I put it in order in a book. [4]I write these things so that you can know that what you have been taught is true.

Zechariah and Elizabeth

[5]During the time Herod ruled Judea, there was a priest named Zechariah. He belonged to Abijah's group." Zechariah's wife came from the family of Aaron. Her name was Elizabeth. [6]Zechariah and Elizabeth truly did what God said was good. They did everything the Lord commanded and told people to do. They were without fault in keeping his law. [7]But Zechariah and Elizabeth had no children. Elizabeth could not have a baby; and both of them were very old.

[8]Zechariah was serving as a priest before God for his group. It was his

---

Visiting Angels
LUKE 1:5-19

Sometimes angels bring messages from God. In this story the angel was Gabriel, sent by God to bring a message to Zechariah, a priest. Zechariah was serving in the temple when the angel appeared and told him that he and his wife, Elizabeth, would have a son. At first, Zechariah didn't believe the angel because he thought that he and Elizabeth were too old to have a baby. Because he didn't believe, the angel told Zechariah that he would not be able to speak until after the baby was born. Sure enough, the angel's message came true. Zechariah and Elizabeth had a baby boy. They named him John. After he was born Zechariah could talk again.

This little baby grew up to be a special man, John the Baptist. He told everyone that Jesus, the Messiah, was coming soon. We can be like John the Baptist. We can tell people about Jesus too.

To read about a group of angels who sang, fly to page 1221.

"**Excellency** This word was used to show respect to an important person like a king or ruler.
"**Abijah's group** The Jewish priests were divided into 24 groups. See 1 Chronicles 24.

group's time to serve. ⁹According to the custom of the priests, he was chosen to go into the Temple[d] of the Lord and burn incense.[d] ¹⁰There were a great many people outside praying at the time the incense was offered. ¹¹Then, on the right side of the incense table, an angel of the Lord came and stood before Zechariah. ¹²When he saw the angel, Zechariah was confused and frightened. ¹³But the angel said to him, "Zechariah, don't be afraid. Your prayer has been heard by God. Your wife, Elizabeth, will give birth to a son. You will name him John. ¹⁴You will be very happy. Many people will be happy because of his birth. ¹⁵John will be a great man for the Lord. He will never drink wine or beer. Even at the time John is born, he will be filled with the Holy Spirit.[d] ¹⁶He will help many people of Israel return to the Lord their God. ¹⁷He himself will go first before the Lord. John will be powerful in spirit like Elijah. He will make peace between fathers and their children. He will bring those who are not obeying God back to the right way of thinking. He will make people ready for the coming of the Lord."

"Looks like Mr. Zechariah was speechless! Read Luke 1:5-25 to find out how it happened."

¹⁸Zechariah said to the angel, "How can I know that what you say is true? I am an old man, and my wife is old, too."

¹⁹The angel answered him, "I am Gabriel. I stand before God. God sent me to talk to you and to tell you this good news. ²⁰Now, listen! You will not be able to talk until the day these things happen. You will lose your speech because you did not believe what I told you. But these things will really happen."

²¹Outside, the people were still waiting for Zechariah. They were surprised that he was staying so long in the Temple. ²²Then Zechariah came outside, but he could not speak to them. So they knew that he had seen a vision in the Temple. Zechariah could not speak. He could only make signs to them. ²³When his time of service as a priest was finished, he went home.

²⁴Later, Zechariah's wife, Elizabeth, became pregnant. She did not go out of her house for five months. Elizabeth said, ²⁵"Look what the Lord has done for me! My people were ashamed[n] of me, but now the Lord has taken away that shame."

The Virgin Mary

²⁶⁻²⁷During Elizabeth's sixth month of pregnancy, God sent the angel Gabriel to a virgin[d] who lived in Nazareth, a town in Galilee. She was engaged to marry a man named Joseph from the family of David. Her name was Mary. ²⁸The angel came to her and said, "Greetings! The Lord has blessed you and is with you."

²⁹But Mary was very confused by what the angel said. Mary wondered, "What does this mean?"

³⁰The angel said to her, "Don't be afraid, Mary, because God is pleased with you. ³¹Listen! You will become pregnant. You will give birth to a son, and you will name him Jesus. ³²He will be great, and people will call him the Son of the Most High. The Lord God will give him the throne of King David, his ancestor. ³³He will rule over the people of Jacob forever. His kingdom will never end."

³⁴Mary said to the angel, "How will this happen? I am a virgin!"

³⁵The angel said to Mary, "The Holy Spirit[d] will come upon you, and the power of the Most High will cover you. The baby will be holy and will be called the Son of God. ³⁶Now listen! Elizabeth, your relative, is very old. But she is also pregnant with a son. Everyone thought

---

[n]ashamed   The Jews thought it was a disgrace for women not to have children.

Heroes Who Trusted God
MARY • LUKE 1:26-38

Just because we trust in God does not mean we won't have hard times.

Mary was only a young teenager when an angel told her that she would have a special baby, Jesus. But Mary wasn't married yet. She was supposed to marry Joseph. What would he think about her when he found out she was going to have a baby? And what would her parents think? And her friends and neighbors?

But Mary trusted God. She did what he wanted her to do. She took good care of baby Jesus.

When we believe in God, we must do what he says, even if it is not easy. God wants us to obey him, no matter how hard it might be.

she could not have a baby, but she has been pregnant for six months. ³⁷God can do everything!"

³⁸Mary said, "I am the servant girl of the Lord. Let this happen to me as you say!" Then the angel went away.

God can do everything!
• Luke 1:37

Mary's Visit

³⁹Mary got up and went quickly to a town in the mountains of Judea. ⁴⁰She went to Zechariah's house and greeted Elizabeth. ⁴¹When Elizabeth heard Mary's greeting, the unborn baby inside Elizabeth jumped. Then Elizabeth was filled with the Holy Spirit.ᵈ ⁴²She cried out in a loud voice, "God has blessed you more than any other woman. And God has blessed the baby which you will give birth to. ⁴³You are the mother of my Lord, and you have come to me! Why has something so good happened to

me? ⁴⁴When I heard your voice, the baby inside me jumped with joy. ⁴⁵You are blessed because you believed what the Lord said to you would really happen."

Mary Praises God

⁴⁶Then Mary said,
"My soul praises the Lord;
⁴⁷   my heart is happy because God is
        my Savior.
⁴⁸I am not important, but God has
        shown his care for me, his
        servant girl.
   From now on, all people will say
        that I am blessed,
⁴⁹   because the Powerful One has
        done great things for me.
   His name is holy.
⁵⁰God will always give mercy
   to those who worship him.
⁵¹God's arm is strong.
   He scatters the people who are
        proud
   and think great things about
        themselves.
⁵²God brings down rulers from their
        thrones,
   and he raises up the humble.

53 God fills the hungry with good things,
  but he sends the rich away with
    nothing.
54 God has helped his people Israel
    who serve him.
  He gave them his mercy.
55 God has done what he promised to
    our ancestors,
  to Abraham and to his children
    forever."

56 Mary stayed with Elizabeth for about three months and then returned home.

The Birth of John

57 When it was time for Elizabeth to give birth, she had a boy. 58 Her neighbors and relatives heard how good the Lord was to her, and they rejoiced.

59 When the baby was eight days old, they came to circumcise[d] him. They wanted to name him Zechariah because this was his father's name. 60 But his mother said, "No! He will be named John."

61 The people said to Elizabeth, "But no one in your family has this name!" 62 Then they made signs to his father, "What would you like to name him?"

63 Zechariah asked for something to write on. Then he wrote, "His name is John." Everyone was surprised. 64 Then Zechariah could talk again. He began to praise God. 65 And all their neighbors became alarmed. In all the mountains of Judea people continued talking about all these things. 66 The people who heard about these things wondered about them. They thought, "What will this child be?" They said this because the Lord was with him.

Zechariah Praises God

67 Then Zechariah, John's father, was filled with the Holy Spirit.[d] He told the people what would happen:
68 "Let us thank the Lord, the God of
    Israel.
  God has come to help his people
    and has given them freedom.
69 God has given us a powerful
    Savior

from the family of God's servant
    David.
70 God said that he would do this.
  He said it through his holy
    prophets[d] who lived long ago.
71 God will save us from our enemies
  and from the power of all those
    who hate us.
72 God said he would give mercy to
    our fathers.
  And he remembered his holy
    promise.
73 God promised Abraham, our father,
74   that he would free us from the
    power of our enemies,
  so that we could serve him
    without fear.
75 We will be righteous and holy
  before God as long as we live.

76 "Now you, child, will be called a
    prophet of the Most High God.
  You will go first before the Lord
  to prepare the people for
    his coming.
77 You will make his people know that
    they will be saved.
  They will be saved by having their
    sins forgiven.
78 With the loving mercy of our God,
  a new day from heaven will shine
    upon us.
79 God will help those who live
    in darkness,
  in the fear of death.
  He will guide us into the path that
    goes toward peace."

80 And so the child grew up and became strong in spirit. John lived away from other people until the time when he came out to preach to Israel.

The Birth of Jesus

2 At that time, Augustus Caesar[d] sent an order to all people in the countries that were under Roman rule. The order said that they must list their names in a register. 2 This was the first registration[n] taken while Quirinius was governor of Syria. 3 And everyone went to their own towns to be registered.

---

[n]registration   Census. A counting of all the people and the things they own.

⁴So Joseph left Nazareth, a town in Galilee. He went to the town of Bethlehem in Judea. This town was known as the town of David. Joseph went there because he was from the family of David. ⁵Joseph registered with Mary because she was engaged to marry him. (Mary was now pregnant.) ⁶While Joseph and Mary were in Bethlehem, the time came for her to have the baby. ⁷She gave birth to her first son. There were no rooms left in the inn. So she wrapped the baby with cloths and laid him in a box where animals are fed.

Some Shepherds Hear About Jesus

⁸That night, some shepherds were in the fields nearby watching their sheep. ⁹An angel of the Lord stood before them. The glory of the Lord was shining around them, and suddenly they became very frightened. ¹⁰The angel said to them, "Don't be afraid, because I am bringing you some good news. It will be a joy to all the people. ¹¹Today your Savior was born in David's town. He is Christ,ᵈ the Lord. ¹²This is how you will know him: You will find a baby wrapped in cloths and lying in a feeding box."

¹³Then a very large group of angels from heaven joined the first angel. All the angels were praising God, saying:
¹⁴"Give glory to God in heaven,
 and on earth let there be peace to
  the people who please God."

"**H**ear ye! Hear ye! Child born turns out to be Son of God. Angels give exclusive interview. Read Luke 2:1-20."

¹⁵Then the angels left the shepherds and went back to heaven. The shepherds said to each other, "Let us go to Bethlehem and see this thing that has happened. We will see this thing the Lord told us about."

¹⁶So the shepherds went quickly and found Mary and Joseph. ¹⁷And the shepherds saw the baby lying in a feeding box. Then they told what the angels had said about this child. ¹⁸Everyone was amazed when they heard what the shepherds said to them. ¹⁹Mary hid these things in her heart; she continued to think about them. ²⁰Then the shepherds went back to their sheep, praising God and thanking him for everything that

Visiting Angels
LUKE 2:9-14

Many angels live in heaven. God created the angels to deliver messages, to protect people, and to encourage people. One of the most important things the angels do is praise God. When Jesus was born, the angels were so happy that they sang songs praising God. An angel told the good news to shepherds in the fields outside Bethlehem. Then a large group of angels appeared and sang songs of praise to God. Can you imagine what beautiful music that must have been? No wonder the shepherds ran to see the newborn baby!

To read about some angels who looked like people, fly to page 1270.

they had seen and heard. It was just as the angel had told them.

²¹When the baby was eight days old, he was circumcised,[d] and he was named Jesus. This name had been given by the angel before the baby began to grow inside Mary.

Jesus Is Presented in the Temple

²²The time came for Mary and Joseph to do what the law of Moses taught about being made pure.[n] They took Jesus to Jerusalem to present him to the Lord. ²³It is written in the law of the Lord: "Give every firstborn[d] male to the Lord."[n] ²⁴Mary and Joseph also went to offer a sacrifice, as the law of the Lord says: "You must sacrifice two doves or two young pigeons."[n]

Simeon Sees Jesus

²⁵A man named Simeon lived in Jerusalem. He was a good man and very religious. He was waiting for the time when God would help Israel. The Holy Spirit[d] was in him. ²⁶The Holy Spirit told Simeon that he would not die before he saw the Christ[d] promised by the Lord. ²⁷The Spirit led Simeon to the Temple.[d] Mary and Joseph brought the baby Jesus to the Temple to do what the law said they must do. ²⁸Then Simeon took the baby in his arms and thanked God:

²⁹"Now, Lord, you can let me, your servant,
    die in peace as you said.
³⁰I have seen your Salvation[n] with my own eyes.
³¹ You prepared him before all people.
³²He is a light for the non-Jewish people to see.
    He will bring honor to your people, the Israelites."

Women Who Trusted God
ANNA • LUKE 2:36

We don't know much about the woman named Anna who was present when Jesus was brought to the temple. She was from the tribe of Asher. She was married for seven years, but she had been a widow for most of her long life. When she saw Jesus, she was a very old woman.

We do know, however, that Anna loved God. Luke tells us that she never left the temple and that she worshiped there day and night. She prayed and fasted all the time. When Ann saw Mary and Joseph with Jesus, she was thankful. God had told her that this child would save the people from their sins. Anna told everyone she knew that the Messiah had at last arrived.

Anna is remembered because she loved God. Make it your goal to be remembered that way, too.

To meet a woman who showed her love for Jesus in a special way, fly to page 1297.

To meet a woman who showed her love for Jesus in a special way, fly to page 1297.

[n]**pure**   The law of Moses said that 40 days after a Jewish woman gave birth to a baby, she must be cleansed by a ceremony at the Temple. Read Leviticus 12:2-8.
[n]**"Give . . . Lord"**   Quotation from Exodus 13:2.
[n]**"You . . . pigeons."**   Quotation from Leviticus 12:8.
[n]**Salvation**   Simeon was talking about Jesus. The name Jesus means "salvation."

[33]Jesus' father and mother were amazed at what Simeon had said about him. [34]Then Simeon blessed them and said to Mary, "Many in Israel will fall and many will rise because of this child. He will be a sign from God that many people will not accept. [35]The things they think in secret will be made known. And the things that will happen will make your heart sad, too."

Anna Sees Jesus

[36]Anna, a prophetess,[d] was there at the Temple.[d] She was from the family of Phanuel in the tribe[d] of Asher. Anna was very old. She had once been married for seven years. [37]Then her husband died and she lived alone. She was now 84 years old. Anna never left the Temple. She worshiped God by going without food and praying day and night. [38]She was standing there at that time, thanking God. She talked about Jesus to all who were waiting for God to free Jerusalem.

Joseph and Mary Return Home

[39]Joseph and Mary finished doing everything that the law of the Lord commanded. Then they went home to Nazareth, their own town in Galilee. [40]The little child began to grow up. He became stronger and wiser, and God's blessings were with him.

Jesus As a Boy

[41]Every year Jesus' parents went to Jerusalem for the Passover[d] Feast. [42]When Jesus was 12 years old, they went to the feast as they always did. [43]When the feast days were over, they went home. The boy Jesus stayed behind in Jerusalem, but his parents did not know it. [44]Joseph and Mary traveled for a whole day. They thought that Jesus was with them in the group. Then they began to look for him among their family and friends, [45]but they did not find him. So they went back to Jerusalem to look for him there. [46]After three days they found him. Jesus was sitting in the Temple[d] with the religious teachers, listening to them and asking them questions. [47]All who heard him were amazed at his understanding and wise answers. [48]When Jesus' parents saw him, they were amazed. His mother said to him, "Son, why did you do this to us? Your father and I were very worried about you. We have been looking for you."

Get Ready, Get Set, Grow!
LUKE 2:51-52

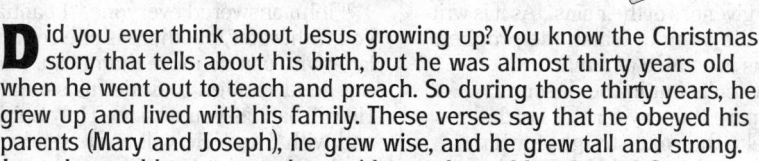

Did you ever think about Jesus growing up? You know the Christmas story that tells about his birth, but he was almost thirty years old when he went out to teach and preach. So during those thirty years, he grew up and lived with his family. These verses say that he obeyed his parents (Mary and Joseph), he grew wise, and he grew tall and strong. Jesus learned how to get along with people, and he pleased God.

No one else is perfect, as Jesus was, but God wants you to obey your parents, to make wise decisions, to get along with people, and to learn how to please God. The best part is that God will help you every step of the way! Trust him to help you grow!

To find out more about growing in your faith, zoom to page 1443.

⁴⁹Jesus asked, "Why did you have to look for me? You should have known that I must be where my Father's work is!" ⁵⁰But they did not understand the meaning of what he said.

⁵¹Jesus went with them to Nazareth and obeyed them. His mother was still thinking about all that had happened. ⁵²Jesus continued to learn more and more and to grow physically. People liked him, and he pleased God.

"I wonder if I can grow up the way Jesus grew up? How about you? Read about it in Luke 2:41-52."

The Preaching of John

3 It was the fifteenth year of the rule of Tiberius Caesar.*ᵈ* These men were under Caesar: Pontius Pilate was the ruler of Judea. Herod was the ruler of Galilee. Philip, Herod's brother, was the ruler of Iturea and Trachonitis. And Lysanias was the ruler of Abilene. ²Annas and Caiaphas were the high priests. At this time, a command from God came to John son of Zechariah. John was living in the desert. ³He went all over the area around the Jordan River and preached to the people. He preached a baptism of changed hearts and lives for the forgiveness of their sins. ⁴As it is written in the book of Isaiah the prophet:*ᵈ*

"This is a voice of a man
    who calls out in the desert:
'Prepare the way for the Lord.
    Make the road straight for him.
⁵Every valley should be filled in.
    Every mountain and hill should be
        made flat.
Roads with turns should be made
    straight,

and rough roads should be made
    smooth.
⁶And all people will know about the
    salvation of God!'" *Isaiah 40:3-5*

⁷Crowds of people came to be baptized by John. He said to them, "You poisonous snakes! Who warned you to run away from God's anger that is coming? ⁸You must do the things that will show that you really have changed your hearts. Don't say, 'Abraham is our father.' I tell you that God can make children for Abraham from these rocks here. ⁹The ax is now ready to cut down the trees. Every tree that does not produce good fruit will be cut down and thrown into the fire."*ⁿ*

¹⁰The people asked John, "What should we do?"

¹¹John answered, "If you have two shirts, share with the person who does not have one. If you have food, share that too."

¹²Even tax collectors came to John to be baptized. They said to John, "Teacher, what should we do?"

¹³John said to them, "Don't take more taxes from people than you have been ordered to take."

¹⁴The soldiers asked John, "What about us? What should we do?"

John said to them, "Don't force people to give you money. Don't lie about them. Be satisfied with the pay you get."

¹⁵All the people were hoping for the Christ*ᵈ* to come, and they wondered about John. They thought, "Maybe he is the Christ."

¹⁶John answered everyone, "I baptize you with water, but there is one coming later who can do more than I can. I am not good enough to untie his sandals. He will baptize you with the Holy Spirit*ᵈ* and with fire. ¹⁷He will come ready to clean the grain. He will separate the good grain from the chaff.*ᵈ* He will put the good part of the grain into his barn. Then he will burn the chaff with a fire that cannot be put out."*ⁿ* ¹⁸And John

*ⁿ***The ax . . . fire.**   This means that God is ready to punish his people who do not obey him.
*ⁿ***He will . . . out.**   This means that Jesus will come to separate the good people from the bad people, saving the good and punishing the bad.

continued to preach the Good News,[d] saying many other things to encourage the people.

[19]But John spoke against Herod, the governor, because of his sin with Herodias, the wife of Herod's brother. John also criticized Herod for the many other evil things Herod did. [20]So Herod did another evil thing: He put John in prison.

Jesus Is Baptized by John

[21]When all the people were being baptized by John, Jesus also was baptized. While Jesus was praying, heaven opened and [22]the Holy Spirit[d] came down on him. The Spirit was in the form of a dove. Then a voice came from heaven and said, "You are my Son and I love you. I am very pleased with you."

The Family History of Jesus

[23]When Jesus began to teach, he was about 30 years old. People thought that Jesus was Joseph's son.

Joseph was the son[n] of Heli.
[24]Heli was the son of Matthat.
Matthat was the son of Levi.
Levi was the son of Melki.
Melki was the son of Jannai.
Jannai was the son of Joseph.
[25]Joseph was the son of Mattathias.
Mattathias was the son of Amos.
Amos was the son of Nahum.
Nahum was the son of Esli.
Esli was the son of Naggai.
[26]Naggai was the son of Maath.
Maath was the son of Mattathias.
Mattathias was the son of Semein.
Semein was the son of Josech.
Josech was the son of Joda.
[27]Joda was the son of Joanan.
Joanan was the son of Rhesa.
Rhesa was the son of Zerubbabel.
Zerubbabel was the grandson of
   Shealtiel.
Shealtiel was the son of Neri.
[28]Neri was the son of Melchi.
Melchi was the son of Addi.
Addi was the son of Cosam.
Cosam was the son of Elmadam.

Elmadam was the son of Er.
[29]Er was the son of Joshua.
Joshua was the son of Eliezer.
Eliezer was the son of Jorim.
Jorim was the son of Matthat.
Matthat was the son of Levi.
[30]Levi was the son of Simeon.
Simeon was the son of Judah.
Judah was the son of Joseph.
Joseph was the son of Jonam.
Jonam was the son of Eliakim.
[31]Eliakim was the son of Melea.
Melea was the son of Menna.
Menna was the son of Mattatha.
Mattatha was the son of Nathan.
Nathan was the son of David.
[32]David was the son of Jesse.
Jesse was the son of Obed.
Obed was the son of Boaz.
Boaz was the son of Salmon.
Salmon was the son of Nahshon.
[33]Nahshon was the son of Amminadab.
Amminadab was the son of Admin.
Admin was the son of Arni.
Arni was the son of Hezron.
Hezron was the son of Perez.
Perez was the son of Judah.
[34]Judah was the son of Jacob.
Jacob was the son of Isaac.
Isaac was the son of Abraham.
Abraham was the son of Terah.
Terah was the son of Nahor.
[35]Nahor was the son of Serug.
Serug was the son of Reu.
Reu was the son of Peleg.
Peleg was the son of Eber.
Eber was the son of Shelah.
[36]Shelah was the son of Cainan.
Cainan was the son of Arphaxad.
Arphaxad was the son of Shem.
Shem was the son of Noah.
Noah was the son of Lamech.
[37]Lamech was the son of Methuselah.
Methuselah was the son of Enoch.
Enoch was the son of Jared.
Jared was the son of Mahalalel.
Mahalalel was the son of Kenan.
[38]Kenan was the son of Enosh.
Enosh was the son of Seth.
Seth was the son of Adam.
Adam was the son of God.

[n]**son**   "Son" in Jewish lists of ancestors can sometimes mean grandson or more distant relative.

Jesus Is Tempted by the Devil

4 Jesus, filled with the Holy Spirit,[d] returned from the Jordan River. The Spirit led Jesus into the desert [2]where the devil tempted Jesus for 40 days. Jesus ate nothing during that time. When those days were ended, he was very hungry.

[3]The devil said to Jesus, "If you are the Son of God, tell this rock to become bread."

[4]Jesus answered, "It is written in the Scriptures:[d] 'A person does not live only by eating bread.'"[n]

[5]Then the devil took Jesus and showed him all the kingdoms of the world in a moment of time. [6]The devil said to Jesus, "I will give you all these kingdoms and all their power and glory. It has all been given to me, and I can give it to anyone I wish. [7]If you worship me, all will be yours."

[8]Jesus answered, "It is written in the Scriptures: 'You must worship the Lord your God. Serve only him!'"[n]

[9]Then the devil led Jesus to Jerusalem and put him on a high place of the Temple.[d] He said to Jesus, "If you are the Son of God, jump off! [10]It is written in the Scriptures:

'He has put his angels in charge of you.
They will watch over you.'
Psalm 91:11

[11]'They will catch you with their hands.
And you will not hit your foot on a rock.'"
Psalm 91:12

[12]Jesus answered, "But it also says in the Scriptures: 'Do not test the Lord your God.'"[n]

[13]After the devil had tempted Jesus in every way, he went away to wait until a better time.

Jesus Teaches the People

[14]Jesus went back to Galilee with the power of the Holy Spirit.[d] Stories about Jesus spread all through the area. [15]He began to teach in the synagogues,[d] and all the people praised him.

[16]Jesus traveled to Nazareth, where he had grown up. On the Sabbath[d] day he went to the synagogue as he always did. Jesus stood up to read. [17]The book of Isaiah the prophet[d] was given to him. He opened the book and found the place where this is written:

[18]"The Spirit of the Lord is in me.
This is because God chose me to tell the Good News[d] to the poor.
God sent me to tell the prisoners of sin that they are free,
and to tell the blind that they can see again.
Isaiah 61:1
God sent me to free those who have been treated unfairly, *Isaiah 58:6*
[19] and to announce the time when the Lord will show kindness to his people."
Isaiah 61:2

[20]Jesus closed the book, gave it back, and sat down. Everyone in the synagogue was watching Jesus closely. [21]He began to speak to them. He said, "While you heard these words just now, they were coming true!"

[22]All the people praised Jesus. They were amazed at the beautiful words he spoke. They asked, "Isn't this Joseph's son?"

[23]Jesus said to them, "I know that you will tell me the old saying: 'Doctor, heal yourself.' You want to say, 'We heard about the things you did in Capernaum. Do those things here in your own town!'" [24]Then Jesus said, "I tell you the truth. A prophet is not accepted in his own town. [25]What I say is true. During the time of Elijah it did not rain in Israel for three and a half years. There was no food anywhere in the whole country. And there were many widows in Israel during that time. [26]But Elijah was sent to none of those widows. He was sent only to a widow in Zarephath, a town in Sidon. [27]And there were many with a harmful skin disease living in Israel during the time of the prophet

---

[n]**'A person . . . bread.'** Quotation from Deuteronomy 8:3.
[n]**'You . . . him!'** Quotation from Deuteronomy 6:13.
[n]**'Do . . . God.'** Quotation from Deuteronomy 6:16.

Elisha. But none of them were healed except Naaman, who was from the country of Syria."

²⁸When all the people in the synagogue heard these things, they became very angry. ²⁹They got up and forced Jesus out of town. The town was built on a hill. They took Jesus to the edge of the hill and wanted to throw him off. ³⁰But Jesus walked through the crowd and went on his way.

Jesus Removes an Evil Spirit

³¹Jesus went to Capernaum, a city in Galilee. On the Sabbath[d] day, Jesus taught the people. ³²They were amazed at his teaching, because he spoke with authority. ³³In the synagogue[d] there was a man who had an evil spirit from the devil inside him. The man shouted in a loud voice, ³⁴"Jesus of Nazareth! What do you want with us? Did you come here to destroy us? I know who you are—God's Holy One!"

³⁵But Jesus warned the evil spirit to stop. He said, "Be quiet! Come out of the man!" The evil spirit threw the man down to the ground before all the people. Then the evil spirit left the man and did not hurt him.

³⁶The people were amazed. They said to each other, "What does this mean? With authority and power he commands evil spirits, and they come out." ³⁷And so the news about Jesus spread to every place in the whole area.

Jesus Heals Many People

³⁸Jesus left the synagogue[d] and went to Simon's[n] house. Simon's mother-in-law was very sick with a high fever. They asked Jesus to do something to help her. ³⁹He stood very close to her and commanded the fever to leave. It left her immediately, and she got up and began serving them.

⁴⁰When the sun went down, the people brought their sick to Jesus. They had many different diseases. Jesus put his hands on each sick person and healed every one of them. ⁴¹Demons[d]

came out of many people. The demons would shout, "You are the Son of God." But Jesus gave a strong command for the demons not to speak. They knew Jesus was the Christ.[d]

⁴²At daybreak, Jesus went to a place to be alone, but the people looked for him. When they found him, they tried to keep him from leaving. ⁴³But Jesus said to them, "I must tell the Good News[d] about God's kingdom to other towns, too. This is why I was sent."

⁴⁴Then Jesus kept on preaching in the synagogues[d] of Judea.

Jesus' First Followers

5 One day Jesus was standing beside Lake Galilee. Many people were pressing all around him. They wanted to hear the word of God. ²Jesus saw two boats at the shore of the lake. The fishermen had left them and were washing their nets. ³Jesus got into one of the boats, the one which belonged to Simon.[n] Jesus asked Simon to push off a little from the land. Then Jesus sat down in the boat and continued to teach the people on the shore.

⁴When Jesus had finished speaking, he said to Simon, "Take the boat into deep water. If you will put your nets in the water, you will catch some fish."

⁵Simon answered, "Master, we worked hard all night trying to catch fish, but we caught nothing. But you say to put the nets in the water; so I will." ⁶The fishermen did as Jesus told them. And they caught so many fish that the nets began to break. ⁷They called to their friends in the other boat to come and help them. The friends came, and both boats were filled so full that they were almost sinking.

⁸⁻⁹The fishermen were all amazed at the many fish they caught. When Simon Peter saw what had happened, he bowed down before Jesus and said, "Go away from me, Lord. I am a sinful man!" ¹⁰James and John, the sons of Zebedee, were amazed too. (James and John were Simon's partners.)

[n]**Simon**   Simon's other name was Peter.

Boats with Precious Cargo
LUKE 5:1-11

Which boat had so many fish in it that it began to sink? Peter (who was also called Simon) and his brother Andrew worked with James and his brother John as fishermen. They often fished at night because the fish were closer to the surface of the lake. These fishermen used large nets with lead weights around the edges. They would throw a net out over the water and the weights would make it sink over the fish. Then they would pull a cord, draw the net tight, and haul the fish into the boat.

Even though Peter and his friends had fished all night, they had not caught anything. The next day Jesus told them to throw out their net again. This time the nets began to tear and the boats were filled so full of fish that they began to sink! Peter, Andrew, James, and John were so amazed that they decided to follow Jesus and be his disciples.

To read about a shipwreck, fly to page 1367.

Jesus said to Simon, "Don't be afraid. From now on you will be fishermen for men." [11] When the men brought their boats to the shore, they left everything and followed Jesus.

Jesus Heals a Sick Man

[12] One time Jesus was in a town where a very sick man lived. The man was covered with a harmful skin disease. When he saw Jesus, he bowed before Jesus and begged him, "Lord, heal me. I know you can if you want to."
[13] Jesus said, "I want to. Be healed!" And Jesus touched the man. Immediately the disease disappeared. [14] Then Jesus said, "Don't tell anyone about what happened. But go show yourself to the priest.[n] And offer a gift to God for your healing as Moses commanded.[n] This will prove to everyone that you are healed."
[15] But the news about Jesus was spreading more and more. Many people came to hear Jesus and to be healed of their sicknesses. [16] But Jesus often slipped away to other places to be alone so that he could pray.

Jesus Heals a Paralyzed Man

[17] One day Jesus was teaching the people. The Pharisees[d] and teachers of the law were there, too. They had come from every town in Galilee and from Judea and Jerusalem. The Lord was giving Jesus the power to heal people. [18] There was a man who was paralyzed. Some men were carrying him on a mat. They tried to bring him in and put him down before Jesus. [19] But because there were so many people there, they could not find a way to Jesus. So the men went up on the roof and made a hole in the ceiling. They lowered the mat so that the paralyzed man was lying right before Jesus. [20] Jesus saw that these men believed. So he said to the sick man, "Friend, your sins are forgiven."
[21] The Jewish teachers of the law and the Pharisees thought to themselves, "Who is this man? He is saying things

---

[n] **show . . . priest** The law of Moses said a priest must say when a Jew with a harmful skin disease was well.
[n] **Moses commanded** Read about this in Leviticus 14:1-32.

that are against God! Only God can forgive sins."

²²But Jesus knew what they were thinking. He said, "Why do you have thoughts like that in your hearts? ²³Which is easier: to tell this paralyzed man, 'Your sins are forgiven,' or to tell him, 'Stand up and walk'? ²⁴But I will prove to you that the Son of Man*ᵈ* has authority on earth to forgive sins." So Jesus said to the paralyzed man, "I tell you, stand up! Take your mat and go home."

²⁵Then the man stood up before the people there. He picked up his mat and went home, praising God. ²⁶All the people were fully amazed and began to praise God. They were filled with much respect and said, "Today we have seen amazing things!"

Levi Follows Jesus

²⁷After this, Jesus went out and saw a tax collector named Levi sitting in the tax office. Jesus said to him, "Follow me!" ²⁸Levi got up, left everything, and followed Jesus.

²⁹Then Levi gave a big dinner for Jesus. The dinner was at Levi's house. At the table there were many tax collectors and other people, too. ³⁰But the Pharisees*ᵈ* and the men who taught the law for the Pharisees began to complain to the followers of Jesus. They said, "Why do you eat and drink with tax collectors and 'sinners'?"

³¹Jesus answered them, "Healthy people don't need a doctor. It is the sick who need a doctor. ³²I have not come to invite good people. I have come to invite sinners to change their hearts and lives!"

Jesus Answers a Question

³³They said to Jesus, "John's followers often give up eating*ⁿ* and pray, just as the Pharisees*ᵈ* do. But your followers eat and drink all the time."

³⁴Jesus said to them, "When there is a wedding, you cannot make the friends of the bridegroom give up eating while he is still with them. ³⁵But the time will come when he will be taken away from them. Then his friends will give up eating."

³⁶Jesus told them this story: "No one takes cloth off a new coat to cover a hole in an old coat. If he does, he ruins the new coat, and the cloth from the new coat will not be the same as the old cloth. ³⁷People never pour new wine into old leather bags for holding wine. If they do, the new wine will break the bags, and the wine will spill out. Then the leather bags for holding wine will be ruined. ³⁸People always put new wine into new leather bags. ³⁹No one after drinking old wine wants new wine because he says, 'The old wine is better.'"

Jesus Is Lord over the Sabbath

6 One Sabbath*ᵈ* day Jesus was walking through some grainfields. His followers picked the heads of grain, rubbed them in their hands, and ate them. ²Some Pharisees*ᵈ* said, "Why are you doing that? It is against the law of Moses to do that on the Sabbath day."

³Jesus answered, "Haven't you read about what David did when he and those with him were hungry? ⁴David went into God's house. He took the bread that was made holy for God and ate it. And he gave some of the bread to the people with him. This was against the law of Moses. It says that only priests can eat that bread." ⁵Then Jesus said to the Pharisees, "The Son of Man*ᵈ* is Lord of the Sabbath day."

Jesus Heals a Man's Crippled Hand

⁶On another Sabbath*ᵈ* day Jesus went into the synagogue*ᵈ* and was teaching. A man with a crippled right hand was there. ⁷The teachers of the law and the Pharisees*ᵈ* were watching to see if Jesus would heal on the Sabbath day. They wanted to see Jesus do something wrong so that they could accuse him. ⁸But he knew what they were thinking. He said to the man with the crippled hand, "Get

---

*ⁿ***give up eating** This is called "fasting." The people would give up eating for a special time of prayer and worship to God. It was also done to show sadness.

up and stand before these people." The man got up and stood there. ⁹Then Jesus said to them, "I ask you, which is it right to do on the Sabbath day: to do good, or to do evil? Is it right to save a life or to destroy one?" ¹⁰Jesus looked around at all of them. He said to the man, "Let me see your hand." The man stretched out his hand, and it was completely healed.

¹¹The Pharisees and the teachers of the law became very angry. They said to each other, "What can we do to Jesus?"

Jesus Chooses His Apostles

¹²At that time Jesus went off to a mountain to pray. He stayed there all night, praying to God. ¹³The next morning, Jesus called his followers to him. He chose 12 of them, whom he named "apostles."*d* They were ¹⁴Simon (Jesus named him Peter) and Andrew, Peter's brother; James and John, Philip and Bartholomew; ¹⁵Matthew, Thomas, James son of Alphaeus, and Simon (called the Zealot*d*), ¹⁶Judas son of James and Judas Iscariot. This Judas was the one who gave Jesus to his enemies.

Jesus Teaches and Heals

¹⁷Jesus and the apostles*d* came down from the mountain. Jesus stood on level ground where there was a large group of his followers. Also, there were many people from all around Judea, Jerusalem, and the seacoast cities of Tyre and Sidon. ¹⁸They all came to hear Jesus teach and to be healed of their sicknesses. He healed those who were troubled by evil spirits. ¹⁹All the people were trying to touch Jesus, because power was coming from him and healing them all!

²⁰Jesus looked at his followers and said,

"Poor people, you are happy,
   because God's kingdom belongs to you.
²¹You people who are now hungry are happy,
   because you will be satisfied.
You people who are now crying are happy,
   because you will laugh with joy.

²²"You are happy when people hate you and are cruel to you. You are happy when they say that you are evil because you belong to the Son of Man.*d* ²³At that time be full of joy, because you have a great reward in heaven. Their fathers were cruel to the prophets*d* in the same way these people are cruel to you.

Prayer
LUKE 6:27-28

When you pray, you probably remember to pray for people who are close to you—your mother, father, brothers and sisters, grandparents, friends. But do you ever pray for those who aren't your friends or who have even been unkind to you?

Why would anybody do that? Because Jesus said we should. He said we are to love not just those who are easy to love, but even our enemies, and that we should do good to those who have not done good to us. That's hard to do! In fact, it's impossible to love our enemies and be kind to those who have been unkind to us . . . unless we let Jesus do it through us. And one way to do that is by praying for them.

To learn more about prayer, zoom to page 1242.

[24]"But how terrible it will be for you
who are rich,
because you have had your easy life.
[25]How terrible it will be for you who
are full now,
because you will be hungry.
How terrible it will be for you who
are laughing now,
because you will be sad and cry.
[26]"How terrible when all people say
only good things about you. Their
fathers always said good things about
the false prophets.

Love Your Enemies

[27]"I say to you who are listening to
me, love your enemies. Do good to
those who hate you. [28]Ask God to
bless those who say bad things to you.
Pray for those who are cruel to you. [29]If
anyone slaps you on one cheek, let
him slap the other cheek too. If someone takes your coat, do not stop him
from taking your shirt. [30]Give to everyone who asks you. When a person takes
something that is yours, don't ask for
it back. [31]Do for other people what you
want them to do for you. [32]If you love
only those who love you, should you get
some special praise for doing that? No!
Even sinners love the people who love
them! [33]If you do good only to those who
do good to you, should you get some
special praise for doing that? No! Even
sinners do that! [34]If you lend things to
people, always hoping to get something
back, should you get some special
praise for that? No! Even sinners lend
to other sinners so that they can get
back the same amount! [35]So love your
enemies. Do good to them, and lend
to them without hoping to get anything back. If you do these things, you
will have a great reward. You will be
sons of the Most High God. Yes, because God is kind even to people who
are ungrateful and full of sin. [36]Show
mercy just as your father shows mercy.

Look at Yourselves

[37]"Don't judge other people, and you
will not be judged. Don't accuse others

of being guilty, and you will not be accused of being guilty. Forgive other
people, and you will be forgiven. [38]Give,
and you will receive. You will be given
much. It will be poured into your
hands—more than you can hold. You
will be given so much that it will spill
into your lap. The way you give to others is the way God will give to you."

[39]Jesus told them this story: "Can a
blind man lead another blind man? No!
Both of them will fall into a ditch. [40]A
student is not better than his teacher.
But when the student has fully learned
all that he has been taught, then he will
be like his teacher.

[41]"Why do you notice the little piece
of dust that is in your brother's eye,
but you don't see the big piece of wood
that is in your own eye? [42]You say to
your brother, 'Brother, let me take that
little piece of dust out of your eye.' Why
do you say this? You cannot see that
big piece of wood in your own eye! You
are a hypocrite![d] First, take the piece
of wood out of your own eye. Then you
will see clearly to take the dust out of
your brother's eye.

Two Kinds of Fruit

[43]"A good tree does not produce bad
fruit. Also, a bad tree does not produce
good fruit. [44]Each tree is known by its
fruit. People don't gather figs from
thornbushes. And they don't get grapes
from bushes. [45]A good person has good
things saved up in his heart. And so
he brings good things out of his heart.
But an evil person has evil things saved
up in his heart. So he brings out bad
things. A person speaks the things that
are in his heart.

Two Kinds of People

[46]"Why do you call me, 'Lord, Lord,'
but do not do what I say? [47]Everyone
who comes to me and listens to my
words and obeys [48]is like a man building a house. He digs deep and lays his
foundation on rock. The floods come,
and the water tries to wash the house
away. But the flood cannot move the

house, because the house was built well. ⁴⁹But the one who hears my words and does not obey is like a man who builds his house on the ground without a foundation. When the floods come, the house quickly falls down. And that house is completely destroyed."

Jesus Heals a Soldier's Servant

7 When Jesus finished saying all these things to the people, he went to Capernaum. ²In Capernaum there was an army officer. He had a servant who was so sick he was nearly dead. The officer loved the servant very much. ³When the officer heard about Jesus, he sent some older Jewish leaders to him. The officer wanted the leaders to ask Jesus to come and heal his servant. ⁴The men went to Jesus and begged him saying, "This officer is worthy of your help. ⁵He loves our people, and he built us a synagogue."ᵈ

⁶So Jesus went with the men. He was getting near the officer's house when the officer sent friends to say, "Lord, you don't need to come into my house. I am not good enough for you to be under my roof. ⁷That is why I did not come to you myself. You only need to say the word, and my servant will be healed. ⁸I, too, am a man under the authority of other men. And I have soldiers under my command. I tell one soldier, 'Go,' and he goes. And I tell another soldier, 'Come,' and he comes. And I say to my servant, 'Do this,' and my servant obeys me."

⁹When Jesus heard this, he was amazed. He turned to the crowd following him and said, "I tell you, this is the greatest faith I have seen anywhere, even in Israel."

¹⁰The men who had been sent to Jesus went back to the house. There they found that the servant was healed.

Jesus Brings a Man Back to Life

¹¹The next day Jesus went to a town called Nain. His followers and a large crowd were traveling with him. ¹²When he came near the town gate, he saw a funeral. A mother, who was a widow, had lost her only son. A large crowd from the town was with the mother while her son was being carried out. ¹³When the Lord saw her, he felt very sorry for her. Jesus said to her, "Don't cry." ¹⁴He went up to the coffin and touched it. The men who were carrying it stopped. Jesus said, "Young man, I tell you, get up!" ¹⁵And the son sat up and began to talk. Then Jesus gave him back to his mother.

¹⁶All the people were amazed. They began praising God. They said, "A great prophetᵈ has come to us! God is taking care of his people."

¹⁷This news about Jesus spread through all Judea and into all the places around there.

John Asks a Question

¹⁸John's followers told him about all these things. He called for two of his followers. ¹⁹He sent them to the Lord to ask, "Are you the One who is coming, or should we wait for another?"

²⁰So the men came to Jesus. They said, "John the Baptistᵈ sent us to you with this question: 'Are you the One who is coming, or should we wait for another?'"

²¹At that time, Jesus healed many people of their sicknesses, diseases, and evil spirits. He healed many blind people so that they could see again. ²²Then Jesus said to John's followers, "Go tell John the things that you saw and heard here. The blind can see. The crippled can walk. People with a harmful skin disease are healed. The deaf can hear, and the dead are given life. And the Good Newsᵈ is told to the poor. ²³The person who does not lose faith is blessed!"

²⁴When John's followers left, Jesus began to tell the people about John: "What did you go out into the desert to see? A reedⁿ blown by the wind? ²⁵What did you go out to see? A man dressed in fine clothes? No. People who have fine clothes live in kings' palaces. ²⁶But what did you go out to see? A

ⁿ**reed** It means that John was not weak like grass blown by the wind.

prophet?[d] Yes, and I tell you, John is more than a prophet. [27]This was written about John:

'I will send my messenger ahead of you.
He will prepare the way for you.'

Malachi 3:1

[28]I tell you, John is greater than any other man ever born. But even the least important person in the kingdom of God is greater than John."

[29](When the people heard this, they all agreed that God's teaching was good. Even the tax collectors agreed. These were people who were already baptized by John. [30]But the Pharisees[d] and teachers of the law refused to accept God's plan for themselves; they did not let John baptize them.)

[31]Then Jesus said, "What shall I say about the people of this time? What are they like? [32]They are like children sitting in the marketplace. One group of children calls to the other group and says,

'We played music for you, but you did not dance.
We sang a sad song, but you did not cry.'

[33]John the Baptist came and did not eat like other people or drink wine. And you say, 'He has a demon[d] in him.' [34]The Son of Man[d] came eating like other people and drinking wine. And you say, 'Look at him! He eats too much and drinks too much wine! He is a friend of the tax collectors and "sinners"!' [35]But wisdom is shown to be right by the things it does."

Simon the Pharisee

[36]One of the Pharisees[d] asked Jesus to eat with him. Jesus went into the Pharisee's house and sat at the table. [37]A sinful woman in the town learned that Jesus was eating at the Pharisee's house. So she brought an alabaster[d] jar of perfume. [38]She stood at Jesus' feet, crying, and began to wash his feet with her tears. She dried his feet with her hair, kissed them many times and rubbed them with the perfume. [39]The Pharisee who asked Jesus to come to his house saw this. He thought to himself, "If Jesus were a prophet,[d] he would

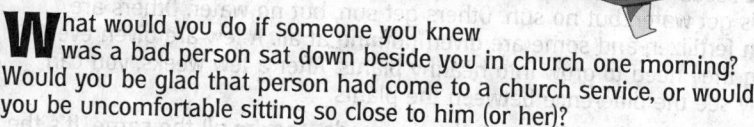

God's Love for Us
LUKE 7:36-50

What would you do if someone you knew was a bad person sat down beside you in church one morning? Would you be glad that person had come to a church service, or would you be uncomfortable sitting so close to him (or her)?

Most of us, if we are honest, would probably be pretty uncomfortable in that situation. Jesus found himself in a situation like that, but he wasn't at all embarrassed or uneasy about it. A woman known for her bad lifestyle made a real scene by pouring perfume on Jesus' feet and then drying them with her hair. The others who watched her do this were unhappy with her actions. But Jesus accepted her, sinful as she was, and made her feel loved.

The next time you are around someone that other people look down on, try to see past the outer appearance and accept that person. That's what Jesus did.

To learn more about God's love, zoom to page 1295.

know that the woman who is touching him is a sinner!"

40 Jesus said to the Pharisee, "Simon, I have something to say to you."

Simon said, "Teacher, tell me."

41 Jesus said, "There were two men. Both men owed money to the same banker. One man owed the banker 500 silver coins.*n* The other man owed the banker 50 silver coins. 42 The men had no money; so they could not pay what they owed. But the banker told the men that they did not have to pay him. Which one of the two men will love the banker more?"

43 Simon, the Pharisee, answered, "I think it would be the one who owed him the most money."

Jesus said to Simon, "You are right." 44 Then Jesus turned toward the woman and said to Simon, "Do you see this woman? When I came into your house, you gave me no water for my feet. But she washed my feet with her tears and dried my feet with her hair. 45 You did not kiss me, but she has been kissing my feet since I came in! 46 You did not rub my head with oil, but she rubbed my feet with perfume. 47 I tell you that her many sins are forgiven. This is clear because she showed great love. But the person who has only a little to be forgiven will feel only a little love."

48 Then Jesus said to her, "Your sins are forgiven."

49 The people sitting at the table began to think to themselves, "Who is this man? How can he forgive sins?"

50 Jesus said to the woman, "Because you believed, you are saved from your sins. Go in peace."

The Group with Jesus

8 The next day, while Jesus was traveling through some cities and small towns, he preached and told the Good News*d* about God's kingdom. The 12 apostles*d* were with him. 2 There were also some women with him who had

The Bible
LUKE 8:4-15

Maybe you've done this in science class. You plant seeds in paper cups full of dirt and set them out to grow. Some seeds get water, but no sun. Others get sun, but no water. Others are given fertilizer, and some are given nothing at all. A few are given everything they need to grow into healthy plants. After a few weeks, you can easily see the difference between the plants.

What makes the difference? Not the seeds—they're all the same. It's the other parts of the process, like soil, water, and fertilizer, that determine whether the seeds grow. This story that Jesus told uses the example of planting seeds to describe how we grow as Christians. In his story, the seed is the Word of God. That seed gets planted in all kinds of soil under all kinds of conditions. The soil is the hearts of people. Some hearts, like some soils, allow the seed to grow. Others don't.

What kind of soil does God's word find in your heart? Does his word find good soil?

To learn more about the Bible, zoom to page 1289.

n **silver coins** A Roman denarius. One coin was the average pay for one day's work.

been healed of sicknesses and evil spir-its. One of the women was Mary, called Magdalene, from whom seven demons[d] had gone out. [3]Also among the women were Joanna, the wife of Chuza (Her-od's helper), Susanna, and many other women. These women used their own money to help Jesus and his apostles.

A Story About Planting Seed

[4]A great crowd gathered. People were coming to Jesus from every town. He told them this story:

[5]"A farmer went out to plant his seed. While he was planting, some seed fell beside the road. People walked on the seed, and the birds ate all this seed. [6]Some seed fell on rock. It began to grow but then died because it had no water. [7]Some seed fell among thorny weeds. This seed grew, but later the weeds choked the good plants. [8]And some seed fell on good ground. This seed grew and made 100 times more grain."

Jesus finished the story. Then he called out, "You people who hear me, listen!"

[9]Jesus' followers asked him, "What does this story mean?"

[10]Jesus said, "You have been chosen to know the secret truths of the king-dom of God. But I use stories to speak to other people. I do this so that:

'They will look, but they may not see.
They will listen, but they may not
understand.'   *Isaiah 6:9*

[11]"This is what the story means: The seed is God's teaching. [12]What is the seed that fell beside the road? It is like the people who hear God's teaching, but then the devil comes and takes it away from their hearts. So they can-not believe the teaching and be saved. [13]What is the seed that fell on rock? It is like those who hear God's teaching and accept it gladly. But they don't have deep roots. They believe for a while, but then trouble comes. They stop believing and turn away from God. [14]What is the seed that fell among the thorny weeds? It is like those who hear God's teaching, but they let the worries, riches, and plea-sures of this life keep them from grow-ing. So they never produce good fruit. [15]And what is the seed that fell on the good ground? That is like those who hear God's teaching with a good, honest heart. They obey God's teaching and patiently produce good fruit.

Use What You Have

[16]"No one lights a lamp and then cov-ers it with a bowl or hides it under a bed. Instead, he puts the lamp on a lamp-stand so that those who come in will have enough light to see. [17]Everything that is hidden will become clear. Every secret thing will be made known. [18]So be careful how you listen. The person who has something will be given more. But to the person who has nothing, this will happen: Even what he thinks he has will be taken away from him."

Jesus' True Family

[19]Jesus' mother and brothers came to see him. There was such a crowd that they could not get to him. [20]Someone said to Jesus, "Your mother and your brothers are standing outside. They want to see you."

[21]Jesus answered them, "My mother and my brothers are those who listen to God's teaching and obey it!"

"**D**o you know what happened when Jesus spoke to the wind and the waves? To find out, read Luke 8:22-25."

Jesus Stops a Storm

[22]One day Jesus and his followers got into a boat. He said to them, "Come with me across the lake." And so they started across. [23]While they were sailing, Jesus fell asleep. A big storm blew up on the lake. The boat began to fill with water, and they were in danger.

24The followers went to Jesus and woke him. They said, "Master! Master! We will drown!"

Jesus got up and gave a command to the wind and the waves. The wind stopped, and the lake became calm. 25Jesus said to his followers, "Where is your faith?"

The followers were afraid and amazed. They said to each other, "What kind of man is this? He commands the wind and the water, and they obey him!"

A Man with Demons Inside Him

26Jesus and his followers sailed across the lake from Galilee to the area where the Gerasene people live. 27When Jesus got out of the boat, a man from the town came to Jesus. This man had demons[d] inside him. For a long time he had worn no clothes. He lived in the burial caves, not in a house. 28When he saw Jesus, he cried out and fell down before him. The man said with a loud voice, "What do you want with me, Jesus, Son of the Most High God? Please don't punish me!" 29He said this because Jesus had commanded the evil spirit to come out of him. Many times it had taken hold of him. He had been kept under guard and chained hand and foot. But he had broken his chains and had been driven by the demon out into the desert.

30Jesus asked him, "What is your name?"

The man answered, "Legion."[n] (He said his name was "Legion" because many demons were in him.) 31The demons begged Jesus not to send them into eternal darkness.[n] 32On the hill there was a large herd of pigs eating. The demons begged Jesus to allow them to go into the pigs. So Jesus allowed them to do this. 33Then the demons came out of the man and went into the pigs. The herd of pigs ran down the hill and into the lake. All the pigs drowned.

34The men who took care of the pigs ran away. They told about this in the town and the countryside. 35And people went to see what had happened. They came to Jesus and found the man sitting there at Jesus' feet. The man was clothed and in his right mind because the demons were gone. But the people were frightened. 36The men who saw these things happen told the others all about how Jesus had made the man well. 37All the people of the Gerasene country asked Jesus to go away. They were all very afraid. So Jesus got into the boat and went back to Galilee.

38The man that Jesus had healed begged to go with him. But Jesus sent him away, saying, 39"Go back home and tell people what God did for you." So the man went all over town telling how much Jesus had done for him.

Jesus Gives Life to a Dead Girl and Heals a Sick Woman

40When Jesus got back to Galilee, a crowd welcomed him. Everyone was waiting for him. 41A man named Jairus came to Jesus. Jairus was a ruler of the synagogue.[d] He bowed down at Jesus' feet and begged him to come to his house. 42Jairus had only one daughter. She was 12 years old, and she was dying.

While Jesus was on his way to Jairus' house, the people were crowding all around him. 43A woman was there who had been bleeding for 12 years. She had spent all her money on doctors, but no doctor was able to heal her. 44The woman came up behind Jesus and touched the edge of his coat. At that moment, her bleeding stopped. 45Then Jesus said, "Who touched me?"

All the people said they had not touched Jesus. Peter said, "Master, the people are all around you and are pushing against you."

46But Jesus said, "Someone did touch me! I felt power go out from me." 47When the woman saw that she could not hide, she came forward, shaking. She bowed down before Jesus. While all the people listened, she told why she had touched him. Then, she said, she

[n]**"Legion"** Means very many. A legion was about 5,000 men in the Roman army.
[n]**eternal darkness** Literally, "the abyss," something like a pit or a hole that has no end.

was healed immediately. [48]Jesus said to her, "Dear woman, you are healed because you believed. Go in peace."

[49]While Jesus was still speaking, someone came from the house of the synagogue ruler and said to the ruler, "Your daughter has died! Don't bother the teacher now."

[50]When Jesus heard this, he said to Jairus, "Don't be afraid. Just believe, and your daughter will be well."

[51]Jesus went to the house. He let only Peter, John, James, and the girl's father and mother go inside with him. [52]All the people were crying and feeling sad because the girl was dead. But Jesus said, "Don't cry. She is not dead; she is only sleeping."

[53]The people laughed at Jesus because they knew that the girl was dead. [54]But Jesus took her by the hand and called to her, "My child, stand up!" [55]Her spirit came back into her, and she stood up immediately. Jesus said, "Give her something to eat." [56]The girl's parents were amazed. Jesus told them not to tell anyone about what happened.

Jesus Sends Out the Apostles

9 Jesus called the 12 apostles[d] together. He gave them power to heal sicknesses and power over all demons.[d] [2]Jesus sent the apostles out to tell about God's kingdom and to heal the sick. [3]He said to them, "When you travel, don't take a walking stick. Also, don't carry a bag, or food, or money. Take for your trip only the clothes you are wearing. [4]When you go into a house, stay there until it is time to leave. [5]If the people in the town will not welcome you, go outside the town and shake the dust off of your feet.[n] This will be a warning to them."

[6]So the apostles went out. They traveled through all the towns. They told the Good News[d] and healed people everywhere.

Herod Is Confused About Jesus

[7]Herod, the governor, heard about all these things that were happening. He was confused because some people said, "John the Baptist[d] is risen from death." [8]Others said, "Elijah has come to us." And still others said, "One of the prophets[d] from long ago has risen from death." [9]Herod said, "I cut off John's head. So who is this man I hear these things about?" And Herod kept trying to see Jesus.

More than 5,000 People Fed

[10]When the apostles[d] returned, they told Jesus all the things they had done on their trip. Then Jesus took them away to a town called Bethsaida. There, Jesus and his apostles could be alone together. [11]But the people learned where Jesus went and followed him. Jesus welcomed them and talked with them about God's kingdom. He healed those who needed to be healed.

[12]Late in the afternoon, the 12 apostles came to Jesus and said, "No one lives in this place. Send the people away. They need to find food and places to sleep in the towns and countryside around here."

[13]But Jesus said to them, "You give them something to eat."

They said, "We have only five loaves of bread and two fish. Do you want us to go buy food for all these people?" [14](There were about 5,000 men there.)

Jesus said to his followers, "Tell the people to sit in groups of about 50 people."

[15]So the followers did this, and all the people sat down. [16]Then Jesus took the five loaves of bread and two fish. He looked up to heaven and thanked God for the food. Then Jesus divided the food and gave it to the followers to give to the people. [17]All the people ate and were satisfied. And there was much food left. Twelve baskets were filled with pieces of food that were not eaten.

Jesus Is the Christ

[18]One time when Jesus was praying alone, his followers came together there.

[n]**shake . . . feet** A warning. It showed that they were finished talking to these people.

Jesus asked them, "Who do the people say I am?"

[19]They answered, "Some say you are John the Baptist.[d] Others say you are Elijah.[n] And others say you are one of the prophets[d] from long ago who has come back to life."

[20] Then Jesus asked, "And who do you say I am?"

Peter answered, "You are the Christ[d] from God."

[21] Jesus warned them not to tell anyone. Then he said, [22]"The Son of Man[d] must suffer many things. He will be rejected by the older Jewish leaders, the leading priests, and the teachers of the law. The Son of Man will be killed. But after three days he will be raised from death."

[23] Jesus went on to say to all of them, "If anyone wants to follow me, he must say 'no' to the things he wants. Every day he must be willing even to die on a cross, and he must follow me. [24]Whoever wants to save his life will lose it. And whoever gives his life for me will save it. [25]It is worth nothing for a man to have the whole world, if he himself is destroyed or lost. [26]If anyone is ashamed of me and my teaching, then I[n] will be ashamed of him. I will be ashamed of him at the time I come with my glory and with the glory of the Father and the holy angels. [27]I tell you the truth. Some of you people standing here will see the kingdom of God before you die."

Jesus with Moses and Elijah

[28]About eight days after Jesus said these things, he took Peter, James, and John and went up on a mountain to pray. [29]While Jesus was praying, his face was changed, and his clothes became shining white. [30]Then two men were talking with Jesus. The men were Moses and Elijah.[n] [31]They appeared in heavenly glory, talking with Jesus about his death which would happen in Jerusalem. [32]Peter and the others were asleep.

But they woke up and saw the glory of Jesus. They also saw the two men who were standing with him. [33]When Moses and Elijah were about to leave, Peter said, "Master, it is good that we are here. We will put three tents here—one for you, one for Moses, and one for Elijah." (Peter did not know what he was saying.)

"**O**f all the conversations Jesus had with people, this was one of the most unusual ones. You can read it in Luke 9:28-36."

[34]While Peter was saying these things, a cloud came down all around them. Peter, James, and John became afraid when the cloud covered them. [35]A voice came from the cloud. The voice said, "This is my Son. He is the One I have chosen. Obey him."

[36]When the voice finished speaking, only Jesus was there. Peter, James, and John said nothing. At that time they told no one about what they had seen.

Jesus Heals a Sick Boy

[37]The next day, Jesus, Peter, James, and John came down from the mountain. A large crowd met Jesus. [38]A man in the crowd shouted to Jesus, "Teacher, please come and look at my son. He is the only child I have. [39]An evil spirit comes into my son, and then he shouts. He loses control of himself, and he foams at the mouth. The evil spirit keeps on hurting him and almost never leaves him. [40]I begged your followers to make the evil spirit leave my son, but they could not do it."

[41]Jesus answered, "You people who live now have no faith. Your lives are all wrong. How long must I be with you

---

[n]**Elijah**   A man who spoke for God. He lived hundreds of years before Christ.
[n]**I**   Literally, "the Son of Man."
[n]**Moses and Elijah**   Two of the most important Jewish leaders in the past.

and be patient with you?" Then Jesus said to the man, "Bring your son here."

[42]While the boy was coming, the demon[d] threw him on the ground. The boy lost control of himself. But Jesus gave a strong command to the evil spirit. Then the boy was healed, and Jesus gave him back to his father. [43]All the people were amazed at the great power of God.

Jesus Talks About His Death

The people were all wondering about the things Jesus did. But he said to his followers, [44]"Don't forget the things I tell you now: The Son of Man[d] will be handed over into the control of men." [45]But the followers did not understand what Jesus meant. The meaning was hidden from them so that they could not understand it. But they were afraid to ask Jesus about what he said.

The Most Important Person

[46]Jesus' followers began to have an argument about which one of them was the greatest. [47]Jesus knew what they were thinking. So he took a little child and stood the child beside him. [48]Then Jesus said, "If anyone accepts a little child like this in my name, then he accepts me. And when he accepts me, he accepts the One who sent me. He who is least among you all—he is the greatest."

Anyone Not Against Us Is for Us

[49]John answered, "Master, we saw someone using your name to force demons[d] out of people. We told him to stop because he does not belong to our group."

[50]Jesus said to him, "Don't stop him. If a person is not against you, then he is for you."

A Samaritan Town

[51]The time was coming near when Jesus would leave and be taken to heaven. He was determined to go to Jerusalem [52]and sent some men ahead of him. The men went into a town in Samaria to make everything ready for Jesus. [53]But the people there would not welcome him because he was going toward Jerusalem. [54]James and John, the followers of Jesus, saw this. They said, "Lord, do you want us to call fire down from heaven and destroy those people?"[n] [55]But Jesus turned and scolded them.[n] [56]Then he and his followers went to another town.

Following Jesus

[57]They were all going along the road. Someone said to Jesus, "I will follow you any place you go."

[58]Jesus answered, "The foxes have holes to live in. The birds have nests to live in. But the Son of Man[d] has no place to rest his head."

[59]Jesus said to another man, "Follow me!"

But the man said, "Lord, first let me go and bury my father."

[60]But Jesus said to him, "Let the people who are dead bury their own dead! You must go and tell about the kingdom of God."

[61]Another man said, "I will follow you, Lord, but first let me go and say goodbye to my family."

[62]Jesus said, "Anyone who begins to plow a field but keeps looking back is of no use in the kingdom of God."

Jesus Sends the 72 Men

10 After this, the Lord chose 72[n] others. He sent them out in pairs. He sent them ahead of him into every town and place where he planned to go. [2]He said to them, "There are a great many people to harvest. But there are only a few workers to harvest them. God owns the harvest. Pray to God that he will send more workers to help gather his harvest.

[n]**Verse 54** Here, some Greek copies add: ". . . as Elijah did."
[n]**Verse 55** Here, some copies add: "And Jesus said, 'You don't know what kind of spirit you belong to. [56]The Son of Man did not come to destroy the souls of men but to save them.'"
[n]**72** Many Greek copies read 70.

³You can go now. But listen! I am sending you, and you will be like sheep among wolves. ⁴Don't carry a purse, a bag, or sandals. Don't stop to talk with people on the road. ⁵Before you go into a house, say, 'Peace be with this house.' ⁶If a peaceful man lives there, your blessing of peace will stay with him. If the man is not peaceful, then your blessing of peace will come back to you. ⁷Stay in the peaceful house. Eat and drink what the people there give you. A worker should be given his pay. Don't move from house to house. ⁸If you go into a town and the people welcome you, eat what they give you. ⁹Heal the sick who live there. Tell them, 'The kingdom of God is soon coming to you!' ¹⁰But if you go into a town, and the people don't welcome you, then go out into the streets of that town. Say to them, ¹¹'Even the dirt from your town that sticks to our feet we wipe off against you.ⁿ But remember that the kingdom of God is coming soon.' ¹²I tell you, on the Judgment Day it will be worse for the people of that town than for the people of Sodom.ⁿ

Jesus Warns Unbelievers

¹³"How terrible for you, Korazin! How terrible for you, Bethsaida! I did many miraclesᵈ in you. If those same miracles had happened in Tyre and Sidon,ⁿ those people would have changed their lives and stopped sinning long ago. They would have worn rough cloth and put ashes on themselves to show that they had changed. ¹⁴But on the Judgment Day it will be worse for you than for Tyre and Sidon. ¹⁵And you, Capernaum,ⁿ will you be lifted up to heaven? No! You will be thrown down to the depths!

¹⁶"He who listens to you is really listening to me. He who refuses to accept you is really refusing to accept me. And he who refuses to accept me is refusing to accept the One who sent me."

Satan Falls

¹⁷When the 72ⁿ men came back from their trip, they were very happy. They said, "Lord, even the demonsᵈ obeyed us when we used your name!"

¹⁸Jesus said to the men, "I saw Satan falling like lightning from the sky. ¹⁹Listen! I gave you power to walk on snakes and scorpions. I gave you more power than the Enemy has. Nothing will hurt you. ²⁰You should be happy, but not because the spirits obey you. You should be happy because your names are written in heaven."

Jesus Prays to the Father

²¹Then the Holy Spiritᵈ made Jesus rejoice. He said, "I thank you, Father, Lord of heaven and earth, because you have hidden these things from the people who are wise and smart. But you have shown them to those who are like little children. Yes, Father, you did this because this is what you really wanted.

²²"My Father has given me all things. No one knows the Son—only the Father knows. And only the Son knows the Father. The only people who will know about the Father are those whom the Son chooses to tell."

²³Then Jesus turned to his followers and said privately, "You are blessed to see what you now see! ²⁴I tell you, many prophetsᵈ and kings wanted to see what you now see. But they did not see these things. And many prophets and kings wanted to hear what you now hear. But they did not hear these things."

The Good Samaritan

²⁵Then a teacher of the law stood up. He was trying to test Jesus. He said, "Teacher, what must I do to get life forever?"

²⁶Jesus said to him, "What is written in the law? What do you read there?"

²⁷The man answered, "Love the Lord

ⁿ**dirt . . . you** A warning. It showed that they were finished talking to these people.
ⁿ**Sodom** City that God destroyed because the people were so evil.
ⁿ**Tyre and Sidon** Towns where wicked people lived.
ⁿ**Korazin, Bethsaida, Capernaum** Towns by Lake Galilee where Jesus preached to the people.
ⁿ**72** Many Greek copies read 70.

your God. Love him with all your heart, all your soul, all your strength, and all your mind."[n] Also, "You must love your neighbor as you love yourself."[n]

[28] Jesus said to him, "Your answer is right. Do this and you will have life forever."

[29] But the man wanted to show that the way he was living was right. So he said to Jesus, "And who is my neighbor?"

[30] To answer this question, Jesus said, "A man was going down the road from Jerusalem to Jericho. Some robbers attacked him. They tore off his clothes and beat him. Then they left him lying there, almost dead. [31] It happened that a Jewish priest was going down that road. When the priest saw the man, he walked by on the other side of the road. [32] Next, a Levite[n] came there. He went over and looked at the man. Then he walked by on the other side of the road. [33] Then a Samaritan[n] traveling down the road came to where the hurt man was lying. He saw the man and felt very sorry for him. [34] The Samaritan went to him and poured olive oil and wine[n] on his wounds and bandaged them. He put the hurt man on his own donkey and took him to an inn. At the inn, the Samaritan took care of him. [35] The next day, the Samaritan brought out two silver coins[n] and gave them to the innkeeper. The Samaritan said, 'Take care of this man. If you spend more money on him, I will pay it back to you when I come again.'"

[36] Then Jesus said, "Which one of these three men do you think was a neighbor to the man who was attacked by the robbers?"

[37] The teacher of the law answered, "The one who helped him."

Jesus said to him, "Then go and do the same thing he did!"

Mary and Martha

[38] While Jesus and his followers were traveling, Jesus went into a town. A woman named Martha let Jesus stay at her house. [39] Martha had a sister named Mary. Mary was sitting at Jesus' feet and listening to him teach. [40] Martha became angry because she had so much work to do. She went in and said, "Lord, don't you care that my sister has left me alone to do all the work? Tell her to help me!"

[41] But the Lord answered her, "Martha, Martha, you are getting worried and upset about too many things. [42] Only one thing is important. Mary has chosen the right thing, and it will never be taken away from her."

Jesus Teaches About Prayer

11 One time Jesus was praying in a place. When he finished, one of his followers said to him, "John taught his followers how to pray. Lord, please teach us how to pray, too."

[2] Jesus said to them, "When you pray, say:

'Father, we pray that your name will
always be kept holy.
We pray that your kingdom will
come.
[3] Give us the food we need for each
day.
[4] Forgive us the sins we have done,
because we forgive every person
who has done wrong to us.
And do not cause us to be tested.'"

Continue to Ask

[5-6] Then Jesus said to them, "Suppose one of you went to your friend's house at midnight and said to him, 'A friend of mine has come into town to visit me. But I have nothing for him to eat. Please

---

[n] **"Love . . . mind."** Quotation from Deuteronomy 6:5.
[n] **"You . . . yourself."** Quotation from Leviticus 19:18.
[n] **Levite** Levites were men from the tribe of Levi who helped the Jewish priests with their work in the Temple. Read 1 Chronicles 23:24-32.
[n] **Samaritan** Samaritans were people from Samaria. These people were part Jewish, but the Jews did not accept them as true Jews. Samaritans and Jews hated each other.
[n] **olive oil and wine** Oil and wine were used like medicine to soften and clean wounds.
[n] **silver coins** A Roman denarius. One coin was the average pay for one day's work.

Prayer
LUKE 11:5-13

Let's say you really want something, like a new pair of roller blades or maybe a new video game. You ask your dad or mom for it, and the answer is, "No way." Do you give up?

No way!

If you really want it (whatever it is), you will keep asking. You'll look for ways to convince your parents that they should give you what you want.

According to these verses, prayer is sort of like that. If you ask God for something that you know is right and good, and he doesn't grant your request, keep asking. Does this mean that God doesn't want to give you good things, or that he can't make up his mind? No, he just wants to teach you to keep on praying.

If you want it, keep asking. God may surprise you by saying, "Yes!"

To learn more about prayer, zoom to page 1447.

loan me three loaves of bread.' ⁷Your friend inside the house answers, 'Don't bother me! The door is already locked. My children and I are in bed. I cannot get up and give you the bread now.' ⁸I tell you, maybe friendship is not enough to make him get up to give you the bread. But he will surely get up to give you what you need if you continue to ask. ⁹So I tell you, continue to ask, and God will give to you. Continue to search, and you will find. Continue to knock, and the door will open for you. ¹⁰Yes, if a person continues asking, he will receive. If he continues searching, he will find. And if he continues knocking, the door will open for him. ¹¹What would you fathers do if your son asks you for a fish? Would any of you give him a snake? ¹²Or, if your son asks for an egg, would you give him a scorpion? ¹³Even though you are bad, you know how to give good things to your children. So surely your heavenly Father knows how to give the Holy Spirit*ᵈ* to those who ask him."

Jesus' Power Is from God

¹⁴One time Jesus was sending a demon*ᵈ* out of a man who could not talk. When the demon came out, the man was able to speak. The people were amazed. ¹⁵But some of them said, "Jesus uses the power of Beelzebul*ᵈ* to force demons out of people. Beelzebul is the ruler of demons."

¹⁶Other people wanted to test Jesus. They asked him to give them a sign from heaven. ¹⁷But Jesus knew what they were thinking. So he said to them, "Every kingdom that is divided and fights against itself will be destroyed. And a family that fights against itself will break apart. ¹⁸So if Satan is fighting against himself, then how will his kingdom last? You say that I use the power of Beelzebul to force out demons. ¹⁹But if I use the power of Beelzebul to force out demons, then by what power do your people force out demons? So your own people prove that you are wrong. ²⁰But if I use the power of God

to force out demons, the kingdom of God has come to you!

²¹"When a strong man with many weapons guards his own house, then the things in his house are safe. ²²But suppose a stronger man comes and defeats him. The stronger man will take away the weapons that the first man trusted to keep his house safe. Then the stronger man will do what he wants with the first man's things.

²³"If anyone is not with me, he is against me. He who does not work with me is working against me.

The Empty Man

²⁴"When an evil spirit comes out of a person, it travels through dry places, looking for a place to rest. But that spirit finds no place to rest. So it says, 'I will go back to the home I left.' ²⁵When the spirit comes back to that person, it finds that home swept clean and made neat. ²⁶Then the evil spirit goes out and brings seven other spirits more evil than itself. Then all the evil spirits go into that person and live there. And he has even more trouble than he had before."

People Who Are Truly Blessed

²⁷When Jesus was saying these things, a woman in the crowd spoke out. She said to Jesus, "Your mother is blessed because she gave birth to you and nursed you."

²⁸But Jesus said, "Those who hear the teaching of God and obey it—they are the ones who are truly blessed."

Give Us Proof!

²⁹The crowd grew larger. Jesus said, "The people who live today are evil. They ask for a miracle[d] as a sign from God. But they will have no sign—only the sign of Jonah.[n] ³⁰Jonah was a sign for those people who lived in Nineveh. In the same way the Son of Man[d] will be a sign for the people of this time.

³¹On the Judgment Day the Queen of the South[n] will stand up with the men who live now. She will show that they are guilty because she came from far away to listen to Solomon's wise teaching. And I tell you that someone greater than Solomon is here! ³²On the Judgment Day the men of Nineveh will stand up with the people who live now. And they will show that you are guilty, because when Jonah preached to those people, they changed their hearts and lives. And I tell you that someone greater than Jonah is here!

Be a Light for the World

³³"No one takes a light and puts it under a bowl or hides it. Instead, he puts the light on a lampstand so that the people who come in can see. ³⁴Your eye is a light for the body. If your eyes are good, then your whole body will be full of light. But if your eyes are evil, then your whole body will be full of darkness. ³⁵So be careful! Don't let the light in you become darkness. ³⁶If your whole body is full of light, and none of it is dark, then you will shine bright, as when a lamp shines on you."

Jesus Accuses the Pharisees

³⁷After Jesus had finished speaking, a Pharisee[d] asked Jesus to eat with him. So Jesus went in and sat at the table. ³⁸But the Pharisee was surprised when he saw that Jesus did not wash his hands[n] before the meal. ³⁹The Lord said to him, "You Pharisees clean the outside of the cup and the dish. But inside you are full of greed and evil. ⁴⁰You are foolish. The same One who made what is outside also made what is inside. ⁴¹So give what is in your cups and dishes to the poor. Then you will be fully clean. ⁴²But how terrible for you Pharisees! You give God one-tenth of even your mint, your rue, and every other plant in your garden. But you

---

[n]**sign of Jonah** Jonah's three days in the big fish are like Jesus' three days in the tomb.
[n]**Queen of the South** The Queen of Sheba. She traveled 1,000 miles to learn God's wisdom from Solomon. Read 1 Kings 10:1-3.
[n]**wash his hands** This was a Jewish religious custom that the Pharisees thought was very important.

forget to be fair to other people and to love God. These are the things you should do. And you should also continue to do those other things—like giving one-tenth. [43]How terrible for you Pharisees, because you love to get the most important seats in the synagogues.[d] And you love people to show respect to you in the marketplaces. [44]How terrible for you, because you are like hidden graves. People walk on them without knowing it."

Jesus Talks to Teachers of the Law

[45]One of the teachers of the law said to Jesus, "Teacher, when you say these things, you are insulting us, too."

[46]Jesus answered, "How terrible for you, you teachers of the law! You make strict rules that are very hard for people to obey. But you yourselves don't even try to follow those rules. [47]How terrible for you, because you build tombs for the prophets.[d] But these are the prophets that your fathers killed! [48]And now you show that you approve of what your fathers did. They killed the prophets, and you build tombs for the prophets! [49]This is why in his wisdom God said, 'I will send prophets and apostles[d] to them. Some of my prophets and apostles will be killed, and others will be treated cruelly.' [50]So you who live now will be punished for the deaths of all the prophets who were killed since the beginning of the world. [51]You will be punished for the killing of Abel and for the killing of Zechariah.[n] Zechariah was killed between the altar and the Temple.[d] Yes, I tell you that you people who live now will be punished for them all.

[52]"How terrible for you, you teachers of the law. You have hidden the key to learning about God. You yourselves would not learn, and you stopped others from learning, too."

[53]When Jesus was leaving, the teachers of the law and the Pharisees[d] began to give him trouble, asking him questions about many things. [54]They were trying to catch Jesus saying something wrong.

Don't Be Like the Pharisees

12 Many thousands of people had gathered. There were so many people that they were stepping on each other. Before Jesus spoke to them, he said to his followers, "Be careful of the yeast of the Pharisees.[d] They are hypocrites.[d] [2]Everything that is hidden will be shown. Everything that is secret will be made known. [3]The things you say in the dark will be told in the light. The things you have whispered in an inner room will be shouted from the top of the house."

Fear Only God

[4]Then Jesus said to the people, "I tell you, my friends, don't be afraid of people. People can kill the body, but after that they can do nothing more to hurt you. [5]I will show you the One to fear. You should fear him who has the power to kill you and also to throw you into hell. Yes, he is the One you should fear. [6]"When five sparrows are sold, they cost only two pennies. But God does not forget any of them. [7]Yes, God even knows how many hairs you have on your head. Don't be afraid. You are worth much more than many sparrows.

Don't Be Ashamed of Jesus

[8]"I tell you, if anyone stands before others and says that he believes in me, then I will say that he belongs to me. I will say this before the angels of God. [9]But if anyone stands before others and says he does not believe in me, then I will say that he does not belong to me. I will say this before the angels of God.

[10]"If a person says something against the Son of Man,[d] he can be forgiven. But a person who says bad things against the Holy Spirit[d] will not be forgiven.

[11]"When men bring you into the synagogues[d] before the leaders and other important men, don't worry about how to defend yourself or what

---

[n]**Abel . . . Zechariah** In the Hebrew Old Testament, the first and last men to be murdered.

to say. [12]At that time the Holy Spirit will teach you what you must say."

Jesus Warns Against Selfishness

[13]One of the men in the crowd said to Jesus, "Teacher, tell my brother to divide with me the property our father left us."

[14]But Jesus said to him, "Who said that I should be your judge or decide how to divide the property between you two?" [15]Then Jesus said to them, "Be careful and guard against all kinds of greed. A man's life is not measured by the many things he owns."

[16]Then Jesus used this story: "There was a rich man who had some land, which grew a good crop of food. [17]The rich man thought to himself, 'What will I do? I have no place to keep all my crops.' [18]Then he said, 'I know what I will do. I will tear down my barns and build bigger ones! I will put all my grain and other goods together in my new barns. [19]Then I can say to myself, I have enough good things stored to last for many years. Rest, eat, drink, and enjoy life!'

[20]"But God said to that man, 'Foolish man! Tonight you will die. So who will get those things you have prepared for yourself?'

[21]"This is how it will be for anyone who stores things up only for himself and is not rich toward God."

"**W**hat do you mean that I'm not supposed to worry? Is that what Luke 12:22-31 means?"

Don't Worry

[22]Jesus said to his followers, "So I tell you, don't worry about the food you need to live. Don't worry about the clothes you need for your body. [23]Life is more important than food. And the body is more important than clothes.

[24]Look at the birds. They don't plant or harvest. They don't save food in houses or barns. But God takes care of them. And you are worth much more than birds. [25]None of you can add any time to your life by worrying about it. [26]If you cannot do even the little things, then why worry about the big things? [27]Look at the wild flowers. See how they grow. They don't work or make clothes for themselves. But I tell you that even Solomon, the great and rich king, was not dressed as beautifully as one of these flowers. [28]God clothes the grass in the field like that. That grass is living today, but tomorrow it will be thrown into the fire. So you know how much more God will clothe you. Don't have so little faith! [29]Don't always think about what you will eat or what you will drink. Don't worry about it. [30]All the people in the world are trying to get those things. Your Father knows that you need them. [31]The thing you should seek is God's kingdom. Then all the other things you need will be given to you.

Don't Trust in Money

[32]"Don't fear, little flock. Your Father wants to give you the kingdom. [33]Sell the things you have and give to the poor. Get for yourselves purses that don't wear out. Get the treasure in heaven that never runs out. Thieves can't steal it in heaven, and moths can't destroy it. [34]Your heart will be where your treasure is.

Always Be Ready

[35]"Be ready! Be dressed for service and have your lamps shining. [36]Be like servants who are waiting for their master to come home from a wedding party. The master comes and knocks. The servants immediately open the door for him. [37]Those servants will be blessed when their master comes home, because he sees that his servants are ready and waiting for him. I tell you the truth. The master will dress himself to serve and tell the servants to sit at the table. Then the master will serve them.

38Those servants might have to wait until midnight or later for their master. But they will be happy when he comes in and finds them still waiting.

39"Remember this: If the owner of the house knew what time a thief was coming, then the owner would not allow the thief to enter his house. 40So you also must be ready! The Son of Man[d] will come at a time when you don't expect him!"

Who Is the Trusted Servant?

41Peter said, "Lord, did you tell this story for us or for all people?"

42The Lord said, "Who is the wise and trusted servant? Who is the servant the master trusts to give the other servants their food at the right time? 43When the master comes and finds his servant doing the work he gave him, that servant will be very happy. 44I tell you the truth. The master will choose that servant to take care of everything the master owns. 45But what will happen if the servant is evil and thinks that his master will not come back soon? That servant will begin to beat the other servants, men and women. He will eat and drink and get drunk. 46Then the master will come when that servant is not ready. It will be a time when the servant is not expecting him. Then the master will cut him in pieces and send him away to be with the others who don't obey.

47"The servant who knows what his master wants but is not ready or does not do what the master wants will be beaten with many blows! 48But the servant who does not know what his master wants and does things that should be punished will be beaten with few blows. Everyone who has been given much will be responsible for much. Much more will be expected from the one who has been given more."

Jesus Causes Division

49Jesus continued speaking, "I came to set fire to the world. I wish it were already burning! 50I must be baptized with a different kind of baptism.[n] I feel very troubled until it is over. 51Do you think that I came to give peace to the world? No! I came to divide the world! 52From now on, a family with five people will be divided, three against two, and two against three. 53A father and son will be divided: The son will be against his father. The father will be against his son. A mother and her daughter will be divided: The daughter will be against her mother. The mother will be against her daughter. A mother-in-law and her daughter-in-law will be divided: The daughter-in-law will be against her mother-in-law. The mother-in-law will be against her daughter-in-law."

Understanding the Times

54Then Jesus said to the people, "When you see clouds coming up in the west, you say, 'It's going to rain.' And soon it begins to rain. 55When you feel the wind begin to blow from the south, you say, 'It will be a hot day.' And you are right. 56Hypocrites![d] You can understand the weather. Why don't you understand what is happening now?

Settle Your Problems

57"Why can't you decide for yourselves what is right? 58When someone is suing you, and you are going with him to court, try hard to settle it on the way. If you don't settle it, he may take you to the judge. The judge might turn you over to the officer. And the officer might throw you into jail. 59You will not get out of there until they have taken everything you have."

Change Your Hearts

13 At that time some people were there with Jesus. They told him about what had happened to some people from Galilee. Pilate[n] killed those people while they were worshiping. He mixed their blood with the blood of the animals they were sacrificing to God. [2]Jesus answered, "Do you think this happened to them because they were more sinful than all others from Galilee? [3]No, they were not! But if all of you don't change your hearts and lives, then you will be destroyed as they were! [4]What about those 18 people who died when the tower of Siloam fell on them? Do you think they were more sinful than all the others who live in Jerusalem? [5]They were not! But I tell you, if you don't change your hearts and lives, then you will all be destroyed too!"

The Useless Tree

[6]Jesus told this story: "A man had a fig tree planted in his vineyard. He came looking for some fruit on the tree, but he found none. [7]So the man said to his servant who took care of his vineyard, 'I have been looking for fruit on this tree for three years, but I never find any. Cut it down! Why should it waste the ground?' [8]But the servant answered, 'Master, let the tree have one more year to produce fruit. Let me dig up the dirt around it and put on some fertilizer. [9]Maybe the tree will produce fruit next year. If the tree still doesn't produce fruit, then you can cut it down.'"

Jesus Heals on the Sabbath

[10]Jesus was teaching in one of the synagogues[d] on the Sabbath[d] day. [11]In the synagogue there was a woman who had an evil spirit in her. This spirit had made the woman a cripple for 18 years. Her back was always bent; she could not stand up straight. [12]When Jesus saw her, he called her over and said, "Woman, your sickness has left you!" [13]Jesus put his hands on her. Immediately she was able to stand up straight and began praising God.

[14]The synagogue leader was angry because Jesus healed on the Sabbath day. He said to the people, "There are six days for work. So come to be healed on one of those days. Don't come for healing on the Sabbath day."

[15]The Lord answered, "You people are hypocrites![d] All of you untie your work animals and lead them to drink water every day—even on the Sabbath day! [16]This woman that I healed is our Jewish sister. But Satan has held her for 18 years. Surely it is not wrong for her to be freed from her sickness on a Sabbath day!" [17]When Jesus said this, all the men who were criticizing him were ashamed. And all the people were happy for the wonderful things Jesus was doing.

Stories of Mustard Seed and Yeast

[18]Then Jesus said, "What is God's kingdom like? What can I compare it with? [19]God's kingdom is like the seed of the mustard plant.[n] A man plants this seed in his garden. The seed grows and becomes a tree. The wild birds build nests on its branches."

[20]Jesus said again, "What can I compare God's kingdom with? [21]It is like yeast that a woman mixes into a big bowl of flour. The yeast makes all the dough rise."

The Narrow Door

[22]Jesus was teaching in every town and village. He continued to travel toward Jerusalem. [23]Someone said to Jesus, "Lord, how many people will be saved? Only a few?"

Jesus said, [24]"Try hard to enter through the narrow door that opens the way to heaven! Many people will try to enter there, but they will not be able. [25]A man gets up and closes the door of his house. You can stand outside and knock on the door. You can say, 'Sir, open the door for us!' But he will answer, 'I don't know you! Where did you come from?' [26]Then you will say, 'We ate and drank with you. You taught in the streets of our town.' [27]But he will say to you, 'I don't know you! Where did you come from? Go away from me! All of you do evil!' [28]You will see Abraham, Isaac, Jacob, and all the prophets[d] in God's kingdom. But you will be thrown

---

[n]**mustard plant** The seed is very small, but the plant grows taller than a man.

outside. Then you will cry and grind your teeth with pain. [29]People will come from the east, west, north, and south. They will sit down at the table in the kingdom of God. [30] Those who have the lowest place in life now will have the highest place in the future. And those who have the highest place now will have the lowest place in the future."

Jesus Will Die in Jerusalem

[31]At that time some Pharisees[d] came to Jesus and said, "Go away from here! Herod wants to kill you!"

[32]Jesus said to them, "Go tell that fox Herod, 'Today and tomorrow I am forcing demons[d] out of people and finishing my work of healing. Then, on the third day, I will reach my goal.' [33]Yet I must be on my way today and tomorrow and the next day. Surely it cannot be right for a prophet[d] to be killed anywhere except in Jerusalem.

[34]"Jerusalem, Jerusalem! You kill the prophets. You kill with stones those men that God has sent you. Many times I wanted to help your people. I wanted to gather them together as a hen gathers her chicks under her wings. But you did not let me. [35]Now your home will be left completely empty. I tell you, you will not see me again until that time when you will say, 'God bless the One who comes in the name of the Lord.'"[n]

Is It Right to Heal on the Sabbath?

14 On a Sabbath[d] day, Jesus went to the home of a leading Pharisee[d] to eat with him. The people there were all watching Jesus very closely. [2]A man with dropsy[n] was brought before Jesus. [3]Jesus said to the Pharisees and teachers of the law, "Is it right or wrong to heal on the Sabbath day?" [4]But they would not answer his question. So Jesus took the man, healed him, and sent him away. [5]Jesus said to the Pharisees and teachers of the law, "If your son or ox falls into a well on the Sabbath day, will

you not pull him out quickly?" [6]And they could not answer him.

Don't Make Yourself Important

[7]Then Jesus noticed that some of the guests were choosing the best places to sit. So Jesus told this story: [8]"When someone invites you to a wedding feast, don't take the most important seat. The host may have invited someone more important than you. [9]And if you are sitting in the most important seat, the host will come to you and say, 'Give this man your seat.' Then you will begin to move down to the last place. And you will be very embarrassed. [10]So when you are invited, go sit in a seat that is not important. Then the host will come to you and say, 'Friend, move up here to a more important place!' Then all the other guests will respect you. [11]Everyone who makes himself great will be made humble. But the person who makes himself humble will be made great."

You Will Be Rewarded

[12]Then Jesus said to the man who had invited him, "When you give a lunch or a dinner, don't invite only your friends, brothers, relatives, and rich neighbors. At another time they will invite you to eat with them. Then you will have your reward. [13]Instead, when you give a feast, invite the poor, the crippled, the lame and the blind. [14]Then you will be blessed, because they cannot pay you back. They have nothing. But you will be rewarded when the good people rise from death."

A Story About a Big Banquet

[15]One of the men sitting at the table with Jesus heard these things. The man said to Jesus, "The people who will eat a meal in God's kingdom are blessed."

[16]Jesus said to him, "A man gave a big banquet and invited many people. [17]When it was time to eat, the man sent his servant to tell the guests, 'Come! Everything is ready!'

---

[n]**'God . . . Lord.'** Quotation from Psalm 118:26.
[n]**dropsy** A sickness that causes the body to swell larger and larger.

18"But all the guests said they could not come. Each man made an excuse. The first one said, 'I have just bought a field, and I must go look at it. Please excuse me.' 19Another man said, 'I have just bought five pairs of oxen; I must go and try them. Please excuse me.' 20A third man said, 'I just got married; I can't come.' 21So the servant returned. He told his master what had happened. Then the master became angry and said, 'Go at once into the streets and alleys of the town. Bring in the poor, the crippled, the blind, and the lame.' 22Later the servant said to him, 'Master, I did what you told me to do, but we still have places for more people.' 23The master said to the servant, 'Go out to the roads and country lanes. Tell the people there to come. I want my house to be full! 24None of those men that I invited first will ever eat with me!'"

You Must First Plan

25Large crowds were traveling with Jesus. He turned and said to them, 26"If anyone comes to me but loves his father, mother, wife, children, brothers, or sisters more than he loves me, then he cannot be my follower. A person must love me more than he loves himself! 27If anyone is not willing to die on a cross when he follows me, then he cannot be my follower. 28If you wanted to build a tower, you would first sit down and decide how much it would cost. You must see if you have enough money to finish the job. 29If you don't do that, you might begin the work, but you would not be able to finish. And if you could not finish it, then all who would see it would laugh at you. 30They would say, 'This man began to build but was not able to finish!'

31"If a king is going to fight against another king, first he will sit down and plan. If the king has only 10,000 men, he will plan to see if he is able to defeat the other king who has 20,000 men. 32If he cannot defeat the other king, then he will send some men to speak to the other king and ask for peace. 33In the same way, you must give up everything you have to follow me. If you don't, you cannot be my follower!

Don't Lose Your Influence

34"Salt is a good thing. But if the salt loses its salty taste, then it is worth nothing. You cannot make it salty again. 35It is no good for the soil or for manure. People throw it away.

"You people who hear me, listen!"

Words to Know: New Testament
PARABLE • LUKE 15:3-7

When Jesus spoke to crowds of people, the Bible says he used **parables**. A parable is a story that uses everyday objects or people to explain something that is difficult to understand. For example, Jesus told about how much God loves us by comparing God to a shepherd who goes out and looks for one lost sheep, not stopping until he finds it. People who truly wanted to know more about God understood the parables and the meaning behind these stories. But Jesus' enemies could not understand them.

Ask God to help you understand his words in the Bible so you can know how you should live.

To read about a dangerous disease, fly to page 1254.

A Lost Sheep and a Lost Coin

15 Many tax collectors and "sinners" came to listen to Jesus. [2]The Pharisees[d] and the teachers of the law began to complain: "Look! This man welcomes sinners and even eats with them!"

[3]Then Jesus told them this story: [4]"Suppose one of you has 100 sheep, but he loses 1 of them. Then he will leave the other 99 sheep alone and go out and look for the lost sheep. The man will keep on searching for the lost sheep until he finds it. [5]And when he finds it, the man is very happy. He puts it on his shoulders [6]and goes home. He calls to his friends and neighbors and says, 'Be happy with me because I found my lost sheep!' [7]In the same way, I tell you there is much joy in heaven when 1 sinner changes his heart. There is more joy for that 1 sinner than there is for 99 good people who don't need to change.

[8]"Suppose a woman has ten silver coins,[n] but she loses one of them. She will light a lamp and clean the house. She will look carefully for the coin until she finds it. [9]And when she finds it, she will call her friends and neighbors and say, 'Be happy with me because I have found the coin that I lost!' [10]In the same way, there is joy before the angels of God when 1 sinner changes his heart."

"**I** know I'm an older brother, but I sure wouldn't want to act like the one in Jesus' story here in Luke 15:11-32."

The Son Who Left Home

[11]Then Jesus said, "A man had two sons. [12]The younger son said to his father, 'Give me my share of the prop- erty.' So the father divided the property between his two sons. [13]Then the younger son gathered up all that was his and left. He traveled far away to another country. There he wasted his money in foolish living. [14]He spent everything that he had. Soon after that, the land became very dry, and there was no rain. There was not enough food to eat anywhere in the country. The son was hungry and needed money. [15]So he got a job with one of the citizens there. The man sent the son into the fields to feed pigs. [16]The son was so hungry that he was willing to eat the food the pigs were eating. But no one gave him anything. [17]The son realized that he had been very foolish. He thought, 'All of my father's servants have plenty of food. But I am here, almost dying with hunger. [18]I will leave and return to my father. I'll say to him: Father, I have sinned against God and have done wrong to you. [19]I am not good enough to be called your son. But let me be like one of your servants.' [20]So the son left and went to his father.

"While the son was still a long way off, his father saw him coming. He felt sorry for his son. So the father ran to him, and hugged and kissed him. [21]The son said, 'Father, I have sinned against God and have done wrong to you. I am not good enough to be called your son.' [22]But the father said to his servants, 'Hurry! Bring the best clothes and put them on him. Also, put a ring on his fin- ger and sandals on his feet. [23]And get our fat calf and kill it. Then we can have a feast and celebrate! [24]My son was dead, but now he is alive again! He was lost, but now he is found!' So they began to celebrate.

[25]"The older son was in the field. As he came closer to the house, he heard the sound of music and dancing. [26]So he called to one of the servants and asked, 'What does all this mean?' [27]The servant said, 'Your brother has come back. Your father killed the fat calf to eat because your brother came home safely!' [28]The

---

[n]**silver coins** A Roman denarius. One coin was the average pay for one day's work.

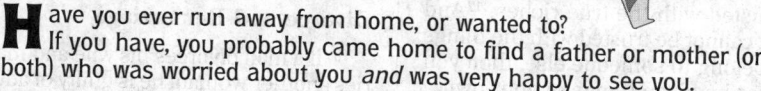

What God Is Like
LUKE 15:11-32

Have you ever run away from home, or wanted to? If you have, you probably came home to find a father or mother (or both) who was worried about you *and* was very happy to see you.

Luke 15:11-32 tells the story of a young man who didn't exactly run away from home—he was too old for that—but he left his home and his family to travel far away. After spending a lot of time on his own, he was poor, hungry, miserable, and homesick. He decided to go home and ask his father to take him back. The story has a happy ending: his father was thrilled to have him home and took him back eagerly.

That's a great story and a picture of God's love for us. Even though we often "run away" from him, our heavenly Father is eager to take us back. Remember that when you feel far away from him and don't know where to turn. Turn back to him. He is waiting for you.

To learn more about what God is like, zoom to page 1389.

older son was angry and would not go in to the feast. So his father went out and begged him to come in. 29The son said to his father, 'I have served you like a slave for many years! I have always obeyed your commands. But you never even killed a young goat for me to have a feast with my friends. 30But your other son has wasted all your money on prostitutes.*d* Then he comes home, and you kill the fat calf for him!' 31The father said to him, 'Son, you are always with me. All that I have is yours. 32We had to celebrate and be happy because your brother was dead, but now he is alive. He was lost, but now he is found.'"

True Wealth

16 Jesus also said to his followers, "Once there was a rich man. He had a manager to take care of his business. Later, the rich man learned that his manager was cheating him. 2So he called the manager in and said to him, 'I have heard bad things about you. Give me a report of what you have done with my money. You can't be my manager any longer!' 3Later, the manager thought to himself, 'What will I do? My master is taking my job away from me! I am not strong enough to dig ditches. I am too proud to beg. 4I know! I'll do something so that when I lose my job, people will welcome me into their homes.'

5"So the manager called in everyone who owed the master any money. He said to the first man, 'How much do you owe my master?' 6The man answered, 'I owe him 800 gallons of olive oil.' The manager said to him, 'Here is your bill; sit down quickly and make the bill less. Write 400 gallons.' 7Then the manager said to another man, 'How much do you owe my master?' The man answered, 'I owe him 1,000 bushels of wheat.' Then the manager said to him, 'Here is your bill; you can make it less. Write 800 bushels.' 8Later, the master praised the dishonest manager for being smart. Yes, worldly people are smarter with their own kind than spiritual people are.

9"I tell you, make friends for yourselves using worldly riches. Then, when those things are gone, you will be welcomed in that home that continues forever. [10]Whoever can be trusted with small things can also be trusted with large things. Whoever is dishonest in little things will be dishonest in large things too. [11]If you cannot be trusted with worldly riches, then you will not be trusted with the true riches. [12]And if you cannot be trusted with the things that belong to someone else, then you will not be given things of your own.

[13]"No servant can serve two masters. He will hate one master and love the other. Or he will follow one master and refuse to follow the other. You cannot serve both God and money."

God's Law Cannot Be Changed

[14]The Pharisees[d] were listening to all these things. They made fun of Jesus because they all loved money. [15]Jesus said to them, "You make yourselves look good in front of people. But God knows what is really in your hearts. The things that are important to people are worth nothing to God.

[16]"God wanted the people to live by the law of Moses and the writings of the prophets.[d] But ever since John[n] came, the Good News[d] about the kingdom of God is being told. Now everyone is trying hard to get into the kingdom. [17]Even the smallest part of a letter in the law cannot be changed. It would be easier for heaven and earth to pass away.

Divorce and Remarriage

[18]"If a man divorces his wife and marries another woman, he is guilty of adultery.[d] And the man who marries a divorced woman is also guilty of adultery."

The Rich Man and Lazarus

[19]Jesus said, "There was a rich man who always dressed in the finest clothes. He lived in luxury every day. [20]There was also a very poor man named Lazarus, whose body was covered with sores. Lazarus was often placed at the rich man's gate. [21]He wanted to eat only the small pieces of food that fell from the rich man's table. And the dogs would

Honesty
LUKE 16:10

Would you let a baby drive a race car? Of course not. First, a child learns to ride a tricycle, then a bicycle, then much later a car. Some day the person might even go on to drive race cars. The point is, you give a child a little bit of responsibility at first. Then if the child handles that well, you give a little more and so on.

This verse says it's the same way with trust. First you trust a person with a little to see if the person is honest with that responsibility. An honest person can be trusted to do what is right. If so, you give the person some bigger responsibility. If not, you cannot trust that person with anything else. And that is a very sad.

When it comes to truth, how trustworthy are you? Are you ready for a race car, or are you still riding around on a tricycle?

To learn more about honesty, zoom to page 1322.

[n]John   John the Baptist, who preached to people about Christ's coming (Matthew 3, Luke 3).

come and lick his sores! [22]Later, Lazarus died. The angels took Lazarus and placed him in the arms of Abraham.[d] The rich man died, too, and was buried. [23]But he was sent to where the dead are and had much pain. The rich man saw Abraham far away with Lazarus in his arms. [24]He called, 'Father Abraham, have mercy on me! Send Lazarus to me so that he can dip his finger in water and cool my tongue. I am suffering in this fire!' [25]But Abraham said, 'My child, remember when you lived? You had all the good things in life, but all the bad things happened to Lazarus. Now Lazarus is comforted here, and you are suffering. [26]Also, there is a big pit between you and us. No one can cross over to help you. And no one can leave there and come here.' [27]The rich man said, 'Then please send Lazarus to my father's house on earth! [28]I have five brothers. Lazarus could warn my brothers so that they will not come to this place of pain.' [29]But Abraham said, 'They have the law of Moses and the writings of the prophets[d] to read; let them learn from them!' [30]The rich man said, 'No, father Abraham! If someone came to them from the dead, they would believe and change their hearts and lives.' [31]But Abraham said to him, 'No! If your brothers won't listen to Moses and the prophets, then they won't listen to someone who comes back from death.'"

Sin and Forgiveness

17 Jesus said to his followers, "Things will surely happen that cause people to sin. But how terrible for the one who causes them to happen. [2]It would be better for him to be thrown into the sea with a large stone around his neck than to cause one of these weak people to sin. [3]So be careful!

"If your brother sins, tell him he is wrong. But if he is sorry and stops sinning, forgive him. [4]If your brother sins against you seven times in one day, but he says that he is sorry each time, then forgive him."

How Big Is Your Faith?

[5]The apostles[d] said to the Lord, "Give us more faith!"

[6]The Lord said, "If your faith is as big as a mustard seed,[n] then you can say to this mulberry tree, 'Dig yourself up and plant yourself in the sea!' And the tree will obey you.

Be Good Servants

[7]"Suppose one of you has a servant who has been plowing the ground or

Faith and How It Works
LUKE 17:5-6

Have you ever planted a garden? Some flower and vegetable seeds are very tiny. It's hard to believe that such a tiny seed can grow into a flower or a tomato plant. The mustard seed that Jesus spoke about was so tiny you could hardly see it! Jesus explained that if you truly have faith in him—even if it's not very big or strong, even if it's still tiny like a mustard seed—it's enough to serve Jesus. The tiny mustard seed grows into a plant big enough for birds to sit in.

Your faith will grow too as you learn more about Jesus and live for him every day.

To find out more about faith and how it works, fly to page 1272.

[n]**mustard seed** This seed is very small, but the plant grows taller than a man.

Words to Know: New Testament

LEPROSY • LUKE 17:11-14

These ten men who were healed of **leprosy** were certainly very happy. Leprosy was a serious disease because it could not be cured. Some types of leprosy were contagious (could be passed from one person to another), so a person who had leprosy (called a leper) had to leave family and friends and go live with others who had the same disease.

Although the doctors couldn't cure leprosy, God can cure any disease. Jesus only spoke a word and the ten men were healed. That meant they could return to their families and friends! But only one man came back and thanked Jesus for healing him.

Jesus has done wonderful things for you too. Have you remembered to thank him?

To read about people who are sent out with a message, fly to page 1314.

caring for the sheep. When the servant comes in from working in the field, would you say, 'Come in and sit down to eat'? [8]No, you would say to your servant, 'Prepare something for me to eat. Then get yourself ready and serve me. When I finish eating and drinking, then you can eat.' [9]The servant does not get any special thanks for doing what his master told him to do. [10]It is the same with you. When you do everything you are told to do, you should say, 'We don't deserve any special thanks. We have only done the work we should do.'"

Be Thankful

[11]Jesus was on his way to Jerusalem. Traveling from Galilee to Samaria, [12]he came into a small town. Ten men met him there. These men did not come close to Jesus, because they all had a harmful skin disease. [13]But they called to him, "Jesus! Master! Please help us!" [14]When Jesus saw the men, he said, "Go and show yourselves to the priests."[n]

While the ten men were going, they were healed. [15]When one of them saw that he was healed, he went back to Jesus. He praised God in a loud voice. [16]Then he bowed down at Jesus' feet and thanked him. (This man was a Samaritan.[d]) [17]Jesus asked, "Ten men were healed; where are the other nine? [18]Is this Samaritan the only one who came back to thank God?" [19]Then Jesus said to him, "Stand up and go on your way. You were healed because you believed."

God's Kingdom Is Within You

[20]Some of the Pharisees[d] asked Jesus, "When will the kingdom of God come?"

Jesus answered, "God's kingdom is coming, but not in a way that you will be able to see with your eyes. [21]People will not say, 'Look, God's kingdom is here!' or, 'There it is!' No, God's kingdom is within you."

[n]**show . . . priests** The law of Moses said a priest must say when a Jew with a harmful skin disease became well.

Miracles from God
LUKE 17:11-19

In Bible days, leprosy was a terrible sickness. It was an infection that caused a person to have sores all over his or her body. In worse cases, fingers and toes would become infected and eventually fall off. When Christ healed the ten lepers, only one returned to say "thank you." The other nine quickly forgot about the miracle the Lord did for them. You would think that after being healed from this terrible sickness, a person would say thank you, but nine of the lepers forgot about the Lord's kindness.

Have you ever stopped to think of all the wonderful things that people have done for you? Whether it be your parents, teachers, friends or neighbors, a lot of people have been there to help and guide you. When was the last time you thanked these people and let them know how much they mean to you?

To discover a miracle on the water, fly to page 1284.

22Then Jesus said to his followers, "The time will come when you will want very much to see one of the days of the Son of Man.[d] But you will not be able to see it. 23People will say to you, 'Look, there he is!' or, 'Look, here he is!' Stay where you are; don't go away and search.

When Jesus Comes Again

24"The Son of Man[d] will come again. On the day he comes he will shine like lightning, which flashes across the sky and lights it up from one side to the other. 25But first, the Son of Man must suffer many things and be rejected by the people of this time. 26When the Son of Man comes again, it will be as it was when Noah lived. 27In the time of Noah, people were eating, drinking, and getting married even on the day when Noah entered the boat. Then the flood came and killed all the people. 28It will be the same as during the time of Lot. Those people were eating, drinking, buying, selling, planting, and building. 29They were doing these things even on the day Lot left Sodom.[n] Then fire and sulfur rained down from the sky and killed them all. 30This is exactly how it will be when the Son of Man comes again.

31"On that day, if a man is on his roof, he will not have time to go inside and get his things. If a man is in the field, he cannot go back home. 32Remember what happened to Lot's wife?[n] 33Whoever tries to keep his life will give up true life. But whoever gives up his life will have true life. 34At the time when I come again, there may be two people sleeping in one bed. One will be taken and the other will be left. 35There may be two women grinding grain together. One will be taken and the other will be left." 36[n]

[n]**Sodom** City that God destroyed because the people were so evil.
[n]**Lot's wife** A story about what happened to Lot's wife is found in Genesis 19:15-17,26.
[n]**Verse 36** A few Greek copies add verse 36: "Two men will be in the same field. One man will be taken, but the other man will be left behind."

37The followers asked Jesus, "Where will this be, Lord?"

Jesus answered, "People can always find a dead body by looking for the vultures."

God Will Answer His People

18 Then Jesus used this story to teach his followers that they should always pray and never lose hope. 2"Once there was a judge in a town. He did not care about God. He also did not care what people thought about him. 3In that same town there was a widow who kept coming to this judge. She said, 'There is a man who is not being fair to me. Give me my rights!' 4But the judge did not want to help the widow. After a long time, he thought to himself, 'I don't care about God. And I don't care about what people think. 5But this widow is bothering me. I will see that she gets her rights, or she will bother me until I am worn out!'"

6The Lord said, "Listen to what the bad judge said. 7God's people cry to him night and day. God will always give them what is right, and he will not be slow to answer them. 8I tell you, God will help his people quickly! But when the Son of Man[d] comes again, will he find those on earth who believe in him?"

Being Right with God

9There were some people who thought that they were very good and looked down on everyone else. Jesus used this story to teach them: 10"One day there was a Pharisee[d] and a tax collector. Both went to the Temple[d] to pray. 11The Pharisee stood alone, away from the tax collector. When the Pharisee prayed, he said, 'God, I thank you that I am not as bad as other people. I am not like men who steal, cheat, or take part in adultery.[d] I thank you that I am better than this tax collector. 12I give up eating[n]

Thankfulness
LUKE 17:11-19

Think about a time when you received a present from a friend or one of your relatives at a birthday party or at Christmas. One of the first things your parents probably said to you after you opened it was, "What do you say?" or something like that. They were reminding you to thank the person who gave you the gift.

Sometimes we can get so caught up in the excitement of receiving a special gift that we forget to express our thanks.

Sometimes we pray and ask God to do something. Then when he does it, we are so glad, but we forget to thank him right away. In this story, nine of the ten men whom Jesus healed forgot to thank Jesus for what he had done for them. They were so excited and thrilled to see that they were healed, they ran off and forgot to say thanks! Only one returned to tell Jesus thank you.

Others may forget to tell God thank you. You be the one who remembers.

To learn more about thankfulness, zoom to page 1415.

---

ngive up eating This is called "fasting." The people would give up eating for a special time of prayer and worship to God. It was also done to show sadness.

Whit's Wisdom: Money and Possessions • Luke 18:18-27

One sunny summer afternoon, a few of my young friends were having ice cream cones on the front steps of my shop. I couldn't help overhear them. In fact, there were getting excited and talking louder and louder. The topic was money, how great it would be to be rich, and what they would do with a million dollars. I stepped outside and interrupted by asking: "Kids, what would it take to get Sherman to fit through the keyhole in my front door?" They laughed and told me it would be impossible–Sherman may not be a large dog, but that keyhole is mighty small!

Then I added, "If you think that sounds impossible, try it with a camel! Believe it or not, that's how hard it is for a rich person to get into heaven."

Suddenly I had their attention. Then I got out my Bible and told them this story about a rich young man.

I explained that one day this man came up to Jesus and asked what he could do to get eternal life. Jesus answered that he had to sell everything he had, give the money to the poor, and then follow him. Jesus' answer was just too tough for the young man, so he sadly turned and walked away. That's when Jesus said, "It is easier for a camel to go through the eye of a needle than for a rich person to enter the kingdom of God." Just like the kids on my front steps, the people who heard Jesus wondered what he meant and if anyone could be saved.

Well, we talked about the story for a while. Eventually we saw that Jesus was teaching several important lessons. Dylan pointed out that Jesus was saying that in order to truly follow him, a person must be willing to give up what is most important in his or her life. For the young man, it was his money. For others it might be a friendship, a talent, a possession, or something else. I sure like Whit's End, but I have to realize that Jesus must be more important to me than my workshop.

Mark, a boy who just moved to Odyssey, said that Jesus was teaching that money can take over a person's life. The young man sure couldn't give it up.

Mark was right–some people spend their whole lives trying to get more and more money and buying more and more things. But money can't buy happiness or eternal life, as the young man found out.

Holly looked at the verses at the end of the story and explained that Jesus was saying that God can do anything, even save people who we think are impossible.

In those few minutes of looking into God's Word, we all learned some important lessons. And we decided that having money is all right, but it's not nearly as important as doing what God wants.

Related Passages: Matthew 6:19-21, 24, 33-34; Philippians 3:7-11.

Teacher/Parent Hint: Discuss the kinds of things that can take over a person's life. Also, this would be a good time to explain how to become a Christian.

twice a week, and I give one-tenth of everything I earn!'

[13] "The tax collector stood at a distance. When he prayed, he would not even look up to heaven. He beat on his chest because he was so sad. He said, 'God, have mercy on me. I am a sinner!' [14] I tell you, when this man went home, he was right with God. But the Pharisee was not right with God. Everyone who makes himself great will be made humble. But everyone who makes himself humble will be made great."

Who Will Enter God's Kingdom?

[15] Some people brought their small children to Jesus so that he could touch them. When the followers saw this, they told the people not to do this. [16] But Jesus called the little children to him and said to his followers, "Let the little children come to me. Don't stop them, because the kingdom of God belongs to people who are like these little children. [17] I tell you the truth. You must accept God's kingdom like a little child, or you will never enter it!"

A Rich Man's Question

[18] A Jewish leader asked Jesus, "Good Teacher, what must I do to get the life that continues forever?"

[19] Jesus said to him, "Why do you call me good? Only God is good. [20] You know the commands: 'You must not be guilty of adultery.[d] You must not murder anyone. You must not steal. You must not tell lies about your neighbor in court. Honor your father and mother.'"[n]

[21] But the leader said, "I have obeyed all these commands since I was a boy!"

[22] When Jesus heard this, he said to him, "But there is still one more thing you need to do. Sell everything you have and give the money to the poor. You will have a reward in heaven. Then come and follow me!" [23] But when the man heard this, he became very sad because he was very rich.

[24] When Jesus saw that the man was sad, he said, "It will be very hard for rich people to enter the kingdom of God! [25] It would be easier for a camel to go through the eye of a needle than for a rich person to enter the kingdom of God!"

Who Can Be Saved?

[26] When the people heard this, they asked, "Then who can be saved?"

[27] Jesus answered, "God can do things that are not possible for men to do!"

[28] Peter said, "Look, we left everything we had and followed you!"

[29] Jesus said, "I tell you the truth. Everyone who has left his house, wife, brothers, parents, or children for God's kingdom [30] will get much more than he left. He will receive many times more in this life. And after he dies, he will live with God forever."

Jesus Will Rise from Death

[31] Then Jesus talked to the 12 apostles[d] alone. He said to them, "Listen! We are going to Jerusalem. Everything that God told the prophets[d] to write about the Son of Man[d] will happen! [32] He will be turned over to the non-Jewish people. They will laugh at him, insult him, and spit on him. [33] They will beat him with whips and then kill him. But on the third day after his death, he will rise to life again." [34] The apostles tried to understand this, but they could not; the meaning was hidden from them.

Jesus Heals a Blind Man

[35] Jesus was coming near the city of Jericho. There was a blind man sitting beside the road, begging for money. [36] When he heard the people coming down the road, he asked, "What is happening?"

[37] They told him, "Jesus, the one from Nazareth, is coming here."

[38] The blind man cried out, "Jesus, Son of David![d] Please help me!"

[39] The people who were in front, leading the group, told the blind man

[n] "You . . . mother.' Quotation from Exodus 20:12-16; Deuteronomy 5:16-20.

to be quiet. But the blind man shouted more and more, "Son of David, please help me!"

[40]Jesus stopped and said, "Bring the blind man to me!" When he came near, Jesus asked him, [41]"What do you want me to do for you?"

He said, "Lord, I want to see again."

[42]Jesus said to him, "Then see! You are healed because you believed."

[43]At once the man was able to see, and he followed Jesus, thanking God. All the people who saw this praised God.

Zacchaeus

19 Jesus was going through the city of Jericho. [2]In Jericho there was a man named Zacchaeus. He was a wealthy, very important tax collector. [3]He wanted to see who Jesus was, but he was too short to see above the crowd. [4]He ran ahead to a place where he knew Jesus would come. He climbed a sycamore tree so he could see Jesus. [5]When Jesus came to that place, he looked up and saw Zacchaeus in the tree. He said to him, "Zacchaeus, hurry and come down! I must stay at your house today."

[6]Zacchaeus came down quickly. He was pleased to have Jesus in his house. [7]All the people saw this and began to complain, "Look at the kind of man Jesus stays with. Zacchaeus is a sinner!"

[8]But Zacchaeus said to the Lord, "I will give half of my money to the poor. If I have cheated anyone, I will pay that person back four times more!"

[9]Jesus said, "Salvation has come to this house today. This man truly belongs to the family of Abraham. [10]The Son of Man[d] came to find lost people and save them."

A Story About Three Servants

[11]Jesus traveled closer to Jerusalem. Some of the people thought that God's kingdom would appear soon. [12]Jesus knew that the people thought this, so he told them this story: "A very important man was preparing to go to a country far away to be made a king. Then he planned to return home and rule his people. [13]So the man called ten of his servants together. He gave a bag of money[n] to each servant. He said, 'Do business with this money till I get back.' [14]But the people in the kingdom hated the man. So they sent a group to follow him and say, 'We don't want this man to be our king!'

[15]"But the man became king. When he came home, he said, 'Call those servants who have my money. I want to know how much they earned with it.'

[16]"The first servant came and said, 'Sir, I earned ten bags of money with the one bag you gave me!' [17]The king said to the servant, 'Fine! You are a good servant. I see that I can trust you with small things. So now I will let you rule over ten of my cities.'

[18]"The second servant said, 'Sir, with your one bag of money I earned five bags!' [19]The king said to this servant, 'You can rule over five cities.'

[20]"Then another servant came in. The servant said to the king, 'Sir, here is your bag of money. I wrapped it in a piece of cloth and hid it. [21]I was afraid of you because you are a hard man. You even take money that you didn't earn and gather food that you didn't plant.' [22]Then the king said to the servant, 'You evil servant! I will use your own words to condemn you. You said that I am a hard man. You said that I even take money that I didn't earn and gather food that I didn't plant. [23]If that is true, then you should have put my money in the bank. Then, when I came back, my money would have earned some interest.'

[24]"Then the king said to the men who were watching, 'Take the bag of money away from this servant and give it to the servant who earned ten bags of money.' [25]They said to the king, 'But sir, that servant already has ten bags of money!' [26]The king said, 'The one who uses what he has will get more. But the one who does not use what he has will have

---

[n]**bag of money** One bag of money was a Greek "mina." One mina was enough money to pay a person for working three months.

everything taken away from him. [27] Now where are my enemies who didn't want me to be king? Bring them here and kill them before me.'"

Jesus Enters Jerusalem as a King

[28] After Jesus said this, he went on toward Jerusalem. [29] Jesus came near Bethphage and Bethany, towns near the hill called the Mount of Olives.[d] Then he sent out two of his followers. [30] He said, "Go into the town you can see there. When you enter it, you will find a colt tied there. No one has ever ridden this colt. Untie it, and bring it here to me. [31] If anyone asks you why you are taking it, say, 'The Master needs it.'"

[32] The two followers went into town. They found the colt just as Jesus told them. [33] The followers untied it, but the owners of the colt came out. They asked the followers, "Why are you untying our colt?"

[34] The followers answered, "The Master needs it." [35] So they brought it to Jesus. They threw their coats on the colt's back and put Jesus on it. [36] As Jesus rode toward Jerusalem, the followers spread their coats on the road before him.

[37] Jesus was coming close to Jerusalem. He was already near the bottom of the Mount of Olives. The whole crowd of followers was very happy. They began shouting praise to God for all the powerful works they had seen. They said, [38] "God bless the king who comes in the name of the Lord!

There is peace in heaven and glory to God!"   *Psalm 118:26*

[39] Some of the Pharisees[d] said to Jesus, "Teacher, tell your followers not to say these things!"

[40] But Jesus answered, "I tell you, if my followers don't say these things, then the stones will cry out."

Jesus Cries for Jerusalem

[41] Jesus came near Jerusalem. He saw the city and began to cry for it. [42] Jesus said to Jerusalem, "I wish you knew today what would bring you peace! But you can't know it, because it is hidden from you. [43] A time is coming when your enemies will build a wall around you and will hold you in on all sides. [44] They will destroy you and all your people. Not one stone of your buildings will be left on another. All this will happen because you did not know the time when God came to save you."

Jesus Goes to the Temple

[45] Jesus went into the Temple.[d] He began to throw out the people who were selling things there. [46] He said, "It is written in the Scriptures,[d] 'My Temple will be a house where people will pray.'[n] But you have changed it into a 'hideout for robbers'!"[n]

[47] Jesus taught in the Temple every day. The leading priests, the teachers of the law, and some of the leaders of the people wanted to kill Jesus. [48] But all the people were listening closely to him and were interested in all the things he said. So the leading priests, the teachers of the law, and the leaders did not know how they could kill him.

Jewish Leaders Question Jesus

20 One day Jesus was in the Temple,[d] teaching the people and telling them the Good News.[d] The leading priests, teachers of the law, and older Jewish leaders came up to talk with him. [2] They said, "Tell us! What authority do you have to do these things? Who gave you this authority?"

[3] Jesus answered, "I will ask you a question too. Tell me: [4] When John baptized people, did that come from God or from man?"

[5] The priests, the teachers of the law, and the Jewish leaders all talked about this. They said to each other, "If we answer, 'John's baptism was from God,' then Jesus will say, 'Then why did you

---

[n]'My Temple . . . pray.'   Quotation from Isaiah 56:7.
[n]'hideout for robbers'   Quotation from Jeremiah 7:11.

not believe John?' ⁶But if we say, 'John's baptism was from man,' then all the people will kill us with stones because they believe that John was a prophet."ᵈ ⁷So they answered, "We don't know the answer."

⁸So Jesus said to them, "Then I will not tell you by what authority I do these things!"

God Sends His Son

⁹Then Jesus told the people this story: "A man planted a vineyard. The man leased the land to some farmers. Then he went away for a long time. ¹⁰Later, it was time for the grapes to be picked. So the man sent a servant to those farmers to get his share of the grapes. But they beat the servant and sent him away with nothing. ¹¹Then he sent another servant. They beat this servant too. They showed no respect for him and sent him away with nothing. ¹²So the man sent a third servant. The farmers hurt this servant badly and threw him out. ¹³The owner of the vineyard said, 'What will I do now? I will send my son whom I love very much. Maybe they will respect him!' ¹⁴When they saw the son, they said to each other, 'This is the owner's son. This vineyard will be his. If we kill him, then it will be ours!' ¹⁵So the farmers threw the son out of the vineyard and killed him.

"What will the owner of this vineyard do? ¹⁶He will come and kill those farmers! Then he will give the vineyard to other farmers."

The people heard this story. They said, "No! Let this never happen!"

¹⁷But Jesus looked at them and said, "Then what does this verse mean:

'The stone that the builders did not want
became the cornerstone'?ᵈ

Psalm 118:22

¹⁸Everyone who falls on that stone will be broken. If that stone falls on you, it will crush you!"

¹⁹The teachers of the law and the priests heard this story that Jesus told. They knew the story was about them.

So they wanted to arrest Jesus at once. But they were afraid of what the people would do.

The Leaders Try to Trap Jesus

²⁰So they waited for the right time to get Jesus. They sent some spies who acted as if they were good men. They wanted to trap Jesus in what he said so they could hand him over to the authority and power of the governor. ²¹So the spies asked Jesus, "Teacher, we know that what you say and teach is true. You teach the same to all people. You always teach the truth about God's way. ²²Tell us, is it right that we pay taxes to Caesarᵈ or not?"

²³But Jesus knew that these men were trying to trick him. He said, ²⁴"Show me a coin. Whose name is on the coin? And whose picture is on it?"

They said, "Caesar's."

²⁵Jesus said to them, "Then give to Caesar the things that are Caesar's. And give to God the things that are God's."

²⁶The men were amazed at his answer. They could say nothing. They were not able to trap Jesus in anything he said before the people.

Sadducees Try to Trick Jesus

²⁷Some Sadduceesᵈ came to Jesus. (Sadducees believe that people will not rise from death.) They asked, ²⁸"Teacher, Moses wrote that a man's brother might die. He leaves a wife but no children. Then that man must marry the widow and have children for his dead brother. ²⁹One time there were seven brothers. The first brother married, but died. He had no children. ³⁰Then the second brother married the widow, and he died. ³¹And the third brother married the widow, and he died. The same thing happened with all the other brothers. They all died and had no children. ³²The woman was the last to die. ³³But all seven brothers married her. So when people rise from death, whose wife will the woman be?"

³⁴Jesus said to the Sadducees, "On earth, people marry each other. ³⁵But

those who will be worthy to be raised from death and live again will not marry. ³⁶In that life they are like angels and cannot die. They are children of God, because they have been raised from death. ³⁷Moses clearly showed that the dead are raised to life. When Moses wrote about the burning bush,ⁿ he said that the Lord is 'The God of Abraham, the God of Isaac, and the God of Jacob.'ⁿ ³⁸God is the God of living people, not dead people. All people are alive to God."

³⁹Some of the teachers of the law said, "Teacher, your answer was good." ⁴⁰No one was brave enough to ask him another question.

Is the Christ the Son of David?

⁴¹Then Jesus said, "Why do people say that the Christᵈ is the Son of David?ᵈ ⁴²In the book of Psalms, David himself says:

'The Lord said to my Lord:
   Sit by me at my right side,
⁴³until I put your enemies under your
         control.'ⁿ   *Psalm 110:1*
⁴⁴David calls the Christ 'Lord.' But the

Christ is also the son of David. How can both these things be true?"

Jesus Accuses the Leaders

⁴⁵While all the people were listening, Jesus said to his followers, ⁴⁶"Be careful of the teachers of the law. They like to walk around wearing clothes that look important. And they love for people to show respect to them in the marketplaces. They love to have the most important seats in the synagoguesᵈ and at the feasts. ⁴⁷But they cheat widows and steal their houses. Then they try to make themselves look good by saying long prayers. God will punish these men very much."

True Giving

21 Jesus saw some rich people putting their gifts into the Templeᵈ money box.ⁿ ²Then Jesus saw a poor widow. She put two small copper coins into the box. ³He said, "I tell you the truth. This poor widow gave only two

---

God's Children
LUKE 20:36

If you've ever joined a club, you know that certain privileges go along with being a member. These privileges make you different from other people. Only members can use the clubhouse, wear the uniform, and do the club activities.

There are also special privileges that come to members of God's family. They set God's children apart from others. One of these is that a child of God will go to heaven after death. That is why Jesus says a child of God is like an angel because angels never die. Only God's children are like this.

When Christians die God makes sure they are with him in heaven.

To learn more about God's children, zoom to page 1445.

ⁿ**burning bush**   Read Exodus 3:1-12 in the Old Testament.
ⁿ**'The God of . . . Jacob'**   These words are taken from Exodus 3:6.
ⁿ**until . . . control**   Literally, "until I make your enemies a footstool for your feet."
ⁿ**money box**   A special box in the Jewish place for worship where people put their gifts to God.

small coins. But she really gave more than all those rich people. ⁴The rich have plenty; they gave only what they did not need. This woman is very poor, but she gave all she had. And she needed that money to live on."

The Temple Will Be Destroyed

⁵Some of the followers were talking about the Temple[d] and how it was decorated with beautiful stones and gifts offered to God.

⁶But Jesus said, "The time will come when all that you see here will be destroyed. Every stone will be thrown down to the ground. Not one stone will be left on another!"

⁷Some followers asked Jesus, "Teacher, when will these things happen? What will show us that it is time for them to take place?"

⁸Jesus said, "Be careful! Don't be fooled. Many people will come using my name. They will say, 'I am the Christ'[d] and, 'The right time has come!' But don't follow them. ⁹When you hear about wars and riots, don't be afraid. These things must happen first. Then the end will come later."

¹⁰Then he said to them, "Nations will fight against other nations. Kingdoms will fight against other kingdoms. ¹¹There will be great earthquakes, sicknesses, and other terrible things in many places. In some places there will be no food for the people to eat. Fearful events and great signs will come from heaven.

¹²"But before all these things happen, people will arrest you and treat you cruelly. They will judge you in their synagogues[d] and put you in jail. You will be forced to stand before kings and governors. They will do all these things to you because you follow me. ¹³But this will give you an opportunity to tell about me. ¹⁴Don't worry about what you will say. ¹⁵I will give you the wisdom to say things so that none of your enemies will be able to show that you are wrong. ¹⁶Even your parents, brothers, relatives and friends will turn against

you. They will kill some of you. ¹⁷All people will hate you because you follow me. ¹⁸But none of these things can really harm you. ¹⁹You will save yourselves by continuing strong in your faith through all these things.

Jerusalem Will Be Destroyed

²⁰"When you see armies all around Jerusalem, then you will know that it will soon be destroyed. ²¹At that time, the people in Judea should run away to the mountains. The people in Jerusalem must get out. If you are near the city, don't go in! ²²These are the days of punishment to make come true all that is written in the Scriptures.[d] ²³At that time, it will be hard for women who are pregnant or have nursing babies! Great trouble will come upon this land, and God will be angry with these people. ²⁴Some will be killed by the sword and taken as prisoners to all nations. Jerusalem will be crushed by non-Jewish people until their time is over.

Don't Fear

²⁵"Amazing things will happen to the sun, moon, and stars. On earth, nations will be afraid because of the roar and fury of the sea. They will not know what to do. ²⁶People will be so afraid they will faint. They will wonder what is happening to the whole world. Everything in the sky will be changed. ²⁷Then people will see the Son of Man[d] coming in a cloud with power and great glory. ²⁸When these things begin to happen, don't fear. Look up and hold your heads high because the time when God will free you is near!"

My Words Will Live Forever

²⁹Then Jesus told this story: "Look at the fig tree and all the other trees. ³⁰When their leaves appear, you know that summer is near. ³¹In the same way, when you see all these things happening, then you will know that God's kingdom is coming very soon.

³²"I tell you the truth. All these things will happen while the people of this

time are still living! [33]The whole world, earth and sky, will be destroyed; but the words I have said will never be destroyed!

Be Ready All the Time

[34]"Be careful! Don't spend your time feasting and drinking. Or don't be too busy with worldly things. If you do that, you will not be able to think straight. And then that day might come when you are not ready. [35]It will close like a trap on all people on earth. [36]So be ready all the time. Pray that you will be strong enough to escape all these things that will happen. And pray that you will be able to stand before the Son of Man."[d]

[37]During the day, Jesus taught the people in the Temple.[d] At night he went out of the city and stayed on the Mount of Olives.[d] [38]Every morning all the people got up early to go to the Temple to listen to him.

Plans to Kill Jesus

22 It was almost time for the Jewish Feast[d] of Unleavened Bread, called the Passover[d] Feast. [2]The leading priests and teachers of the law were trying to find a way to kill Jesus. But they were afraid of the people.

[3]One of Jesus' 12 apostles[d] was named Judas Iscariot. Satan entered Judas, and he went to [4]the leading priests and some of the soldiers who guarded the Temple.[d] He talked to them about a way to give Jesus to them. [5]They were pleased and promised to give Judas money. [6]Judas agreed. Then he waited for the best time to turn Jesus over to them without the crowd knowing it.

Preparation of the Passover Meal

[7]The Day of Unleavened[d] Bread came. This was the day the Passover[d] lambs had to be sacrificed. [8]Jesus said to Peter and John, "Go and prepare the Passover meal for us to eat."

[9]They asked, "Where do you want us to prepare it?"

Jesus said to them, [10]"Listen! After you go into the city, you will see a man carrying a jar of water. Follow him into the house that he enters. [11]Tell the person who owns that house, 'The Teacher asks that you please show us the room where he and his followers may eat the Passover meal.' [12]Then he will show you a large room upstairs. This room is ready for you. Prepare the Passover meal there."

[13]So Peter and John left. Everything happened as Jesus had said. So they prepared the Passover meal.

The Lord's Supper

[14]When the time came, Jesus and the apostles[d] were sitting at the table. [15]He said to them, "I wanted very much to eat this Passover[d] meal with you before I die. [16]I will never eat another Passover meal until it is given its true meaning in the kingdom of God."

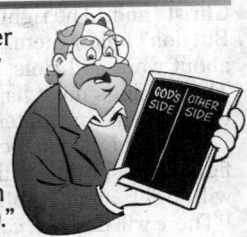

"**H**ave you ever wondered how *Communion* or the *Lord's Supper* got started? You can find out in Luke 22:14-20."

[17]Then Jesus took a cup. He gave thanks to God for it and said, "Take this cup and give it to everyone here. [18]I will not drink again from the fruit of the vine[n] until God's kingdom comes."

[19]Then Jesus took some bread. He thanked God for it, broke it, and gave it to the apostles. Then Jesus said, "This bread is my body that I am giving for you. Do this to remember me." [20]In the same way, after supper, Jesus took the cup and said, "This cup shows the new agreement that God makes with his people. This new agreement begins with my blood which is poured out for you."[n]

---

[n]**fruit of the vine**   Product of the grapevine; this may also be translated "wine."
[n]**Verse 20**   A few Greek copies do not have the last part of verse 19 and all of verse 20.

Who Will Turn Against Jesus?

[21]Jesus said, "One of you will turn against me. His hand is by my hand on the table. [22]The Son of Man[d] will do what God has planned. But how terrible it will be for that man who gives the Son of Man to be killed."

[23]Then the apostles[d] asked each other, "Which one of us would do that to Jesus?"

Be Like a Servant

[24]Then the apostles[d] began to argue about which one of them was the most important. [25]But Jesus said to them, "The kings of the world rule over their people. Men who have authority over others are called 'very important.' [26]But you must not be like that. The greatest among you should be like the youngest, and the leader should be like the servant. [27]Who is more important: the one sitting at the table or the one serving him? You think the one at the table is more important. But I am like a servant among you!

[28]"You men have stayed with me through many struggles. [29]My Father has given me the power to rule. I also give you authority to rule with me. [30]You will eat and drink at my table in my kingdom. You will sit on thrones and judge the 12 tribes[d] of Israel.

Don't Lose Your Faith!

[31]"Satan has asked to test all of you as a farmer tests his wheat. Simon, Simon, [32]I have prayed that you will not lose your faith! Help your brothers be stronger when you come back to me."

[33]But Peter said to Jesus, "Lord, I am ready to go to prison with you. I will even die with you!"

[34]But Jesus said, "Peter, before the rooster crows tonight, you will say you don't know me. You will say this three times!"

Be Ready for Trouble

[35]Then Jesus said to the apostles,[d] "When I sent you out without money, a bag, or sandals, did you need anything?"

They said, "No."

[36]He said to them, "But now if you have money or a bag, carry that with you. If you don't have a sword, sell your coat and buy one. [37]The Scripture[d] says, 'He was treated like a criminal.'[n] This scripture must have its full meaning. It was written about me, and it is happening now."

[38]The followers said, "Look, Lord, here are two swords!"

He said to them, "That's enough."

Jesus Prays Alone

[39-40]Jesus left the city and went to the Mount of Olives.[d] His followers went with him. (Jesus went there often.) He said to his followers, "Pray for strength against temptation."

[41]Then Jesus went about a stone's throw away from them. He kneeled down and prayed, [42]"Father, if it is what you want, then let me not have this cup[n] of suffering. But do what you want, not what I want." [43]Then an angel from heaven appeared to him to help him. [44]Jesus was full of pain; he prayed even more. Sweat dripped from his face as if he were bleeding. [45]When he finished praying, he went to his followers. They were asleep. (Their sadness had made them very tired.) [46]Jesus said to them, "Why are you sleeping? Get up and pray for strength against temptation."

Jesus Is Arrested

[47]While Jesus was speaking, a crowd came up. One of the 12 apostles[d] was leading them. He was Judas. He came close to Jesus so that he could kiss him.

[48]But Jesus said to him, "Judas, are you using the kiss to give the Son of Man[d] to his enemies?"

---

[n]'He . . . criminal.' Quotation from Isaiah 53:12.
[n]cup Jesus is talking about the bad things that will happen to him. Accepting these things will be hard, like drinking a cup of something that tastes very bitter.

Temptation
LUKE 22:40

There is an old story about a little boy who was trying to move a large stone. A short distance away his father was working. Every now and then, the father would stop to watch his son's struggle. Try as he might, the boy could not budge the stone.

Finally, his father asked him, "Son, are you using all the strength you have?"

"Of course I am!" the boy replied. "Can't you see that?"

"No, son, you're not," his father said. "You haven't asked *me* to help you."

Sometimes you will be faced with temptations that seem almost impossible to resist. And time after time, you may give in to them and sin. When you realize that you do not have the strength to say no to those temptations, do what the boy in the story should have done to start with: ask your heavenly father to give you *his* strength.

To learn more about temptation, zoom to page 1381.

⁴⁹The followers of Jesus were standing there too. They saw what was happening. They said to Jesus, "Lord, should we use our swords?" ⁵⁰And one of them did use his sword. He cut off the right ear of the servant of the high priest.

⁵¹Jesus said, "Stop!" Then he touched the servant's ear and healed him.

⁵²Those who came to arrest Jesus were the leading priests, the soldiers who guarded the Temple,*ᵈ* and the older Jewish leaders. Jesus said to them, "Why did you come out here with swords and sticks? Do you think I am a criminal? ⁵³I was with you every day in the Temple. Why didn't you try to arrest me there? But this is your time—the time when darkness rules."

Peter Says He Doesn't Know Jesus

⁵⁴They arrested Jesus and took him away. They brought him into the house of the high priest. Peter followed them, but he did not go near Jesus. ⁵⁵The soldiers started a fire in the middle of the courtyard and sat together. Peter sat with them. ⁵⁶A servant girl saw Peter sitting there near the light. She looked closely at Peter's face and said, "This man was also with him!"

⁵⁷But Peter said this was not true. He said, "Girl, I don't know him."

⁵⁸A short time later, another person saw Peter and said, "You are also one of them."

But Peter said, "Man, I am not!"

⁵⁹About an hour later, another man insisted, "It is true! This man was with him. He is from Galilee!"

⁶⁰But Peter said, "Man, I don't know what you are talking about!"

Immediately, while Peter was still speaking, a rooster crowed. ⁶¹Then the Lord turned and looked straight at Peter. And Peter remembered what the Lord had said: "Before the rooster crows tonight, you will say three times that you don't know me." ⁶²Then Peter went outside and cried with much pain in his heart.

"THE BIG SPLASH!"

Dylan learns about responsibility
A story based on **Proverbs 3:7**

ONE SUNNY DAY IN ODYSSEY, DYLAN STROLLS MERRILY ALONG...

♪

♪ ♪ ♪

SPLOOSH!

HEY, WATCH IT! YOU JUST *MISSED* ME!

HA-HA! ALMOST GOTCHA, DYLAN!

NEARLY A BULLSEYE! HA-HA-HA!

COME ON UP, THIS IS A LOT OF *FUN!*

STAY OUT!

OKAY! HOLD ON, I'M ON MY WAY!

What should Dylan do? While the other boys don't intend to harm anyone, they aren't thinking about what might happen if something goes a little bit wrong.

Dylan senses they're doing something they probably shouldn't be doing, but he's not sure why, exactly. These verses would help him decide. You can read them and decide what you think:

Leviticus 5:5   Psalm 32:5
Proverbs 1:11   Proverbs 3:7
Proverbs 14:16   1 John 1:9
Jeremiah 5:26

The People Laugh at Jesus

63-64Some men were guarding Jesus. They made fun of him like this: They covered his eyes so that he could not see them. Then they hit him and said, "Prove that you are a prophet,[d] and tell us who hit you!" 65The men said many cruel things to Jesus.

Jesus Before the Leaders

66When day came, the older leaders of the people, the leading priests, and the teachers of the law came together. They led Jesus away to their highest court. 67They said, "If you are the Christ,[d] then tell us that you are!"

Jesus said to them, "If I tell you I am the Christ, you will not believe me. 68And if I ask you, you will not answer. 69But beginning now, the Son of Man[d] will sit at the right hand of the powerful God."

70They all said, "Then are you the Son of God?"

Jesus said to them, "Yes, you are right when you say that I am."

71They said, "Why do we need witnesses now? We ourselves heard him say this!"

Governor Pilate Questions Jesus

23 Then the whole group stood up and led Jesus to Pilate.[n] 2They began to accuse Jesus. They told Pilate, "We caught this man telling things that were confusing our people. He says that we should not pay taxes to Caesar.[d] He calls himself the Christ,[d] a king."

3Pilate asked Jesus, "Are you the king of the Jews?"

Jesus answered, "Yes, that is right."

4Pilate said to the leading priests and the people, "I find nothing wrong with this man."

5They said again and again, "But Jesus is making trouble with the people! He teaches all around Judea. He began in Galilee, and now he is here!"

Pilate Sends Jesus to Herod

6Pilate heard this and asked if Jesus was from Galilee. 7If so, Jesus was under

Good Kings and Bad Kings

THE HEROD FAMILY • LUKE 23:6-12

You will read about several kings named Herod in the Bible. There was Herod the Great, who was ruling when Jesus was born (you can read about him in Matthew 2:1-8). The leader described here is Herod Philip I, a son of Herod the Great. Herod Philip listened to John the Baptist's teaching, but he eventually had John killed (see Mark 6:14-29). Herod also could have listened to Jesus himself, but all Herod was interested in was seeing Jesus do a miracle. Herod could have heard the gospel and chosen to believe in Jesus, but he missed out because he was too concerned about being important, having power, and doing what he wanted. He did not take time to listen to God.

What are you concerned about? What do you want in life? Seek God first and trust him, then you will become all that God wants you to be.

To meet a king who was also a priest, fly to page 1492.

To meet a king who was also a priest, fly to page 1492.

---

[n]**Pilate** Pontius Pilate was the Roman governor of Judea from A.D. 26 to A.D. 36.

Herod's authority. Herod was in Jerusalem at that time; so Pilate sent Jesus to him. 8When Herod saw Jesus, he was very glad. He had heard about Jesus and had wanted to meet him for a long time. Herod was hoping to see Jesus work a miracle.*d* 9Herod asked Jesus many questions, but Jesus said nothing. 10The leading priests and teachers of the law were standing there. They were shouting things against Jesus. 11Then Herod and his soldiers made fun of Jesus. They dressed him in a kingly robe and then sent him back to Pilate. 12In the past, Pilate and Herod had always been enemies. But on that day they became friends.

Jesus Must Die

13Pilate called all the people together with the leading priests and the Jewish leaders. 14He said to them, "You brought this man to me. You said that he was making trouble among the people. But I have questioned him before you all, and I have not found him guilty of the things you say. 15Also, Herod found nothing wrong with him; he sent him back to us. Look, he has done nothing for which he should die. 16So, after I punish him, I will let him go free." 17 *n*

18But all the people shouted, "Kill him! Let Barabbas go free!" 19(Barabbas was a man who was in prison because he started a riot in the city. He was guilty of murder.)

20Pilate wanted to let Jesus go free. So he told this to the crowd. 21But they shouted again, "Kill him! Kill him on a cross!"

22A third time Pilate said to them, "Why? What wrong has he done? I can find no reason to kill him. So I will have him punished and set him free."

23But they continued to shout. They demanded that Jesus be killed on the cross. Their yelling became so loud that 24Pilate decided to give them what they wanted. 25They wanted Barabbas to go free, the man who was in jail for starting a riot and for murder. Pilate let Barabbas go free and gave Jesus to them to be killed.

Jesus Is Killed on a Cross

26The soldiers led Jesus away. At that time, there was a man coming into the city from the fields. His name was Simon, and he was from the city of Cyrene. The soldiers forced Simon to carry Jesus' cross and walk behind him.

27A large crowd of people was following Jesus. Some of the women were sad and crying. 28But Jesus turned and said to them, "Women of Jerusalem, don't cry for me. Cry for yourselves and for your children too! 29The time is coming when people will say, 'Happy are the women who cannot have children! Happy are the women who have no babies to nurse.' 30Then people will say to the mountains, 'Fall on us!' And they will say to the hills, 'Cover us!' 31If they act like this now when life is good, what will happen when bad times come?"*n*

"Every time I read about how Jesus died I get sad because I know he died for me. Read the story in Luke 23:32-49."

32There were two criminals led out with Jesus to be killed. 33Jesus and the two criminals were taken to a place called the Skull. There the soldiers nailed Jesus to his cross. They also nailed the criminals to their crosses, one beside Jesus on the right and the other beside Jesus on the left. 34Jesus said, "Father, forgive them. They don't know what they are doing."*n*

---

*nVerse 17   A few Greek copies add verse 17: "Every year at the Passover Feast, Pilate had to release one prisoner to the people."

*nIf . . . come?   Literally, "If they do these things in the green tree, what will happen in the dry?"

*nVerse 34   Some early Greek copies do not have this part of the verse.

The soldiers threw lots[d] to decide who would get his clothes. 35The people stood there watching. The leaders made fun of Jesus. They said, "If he is God's Chosen One, the Christ,[d] then let him save himself. He saved other people, didn't he?"

36Even the soldiers made fun of him. They came to Jesus and offered him some vinegar. 37They said, "If you are the king of the Jews, save yourself!" 38(At the top of the cross these words were written: "THIS IS THE KING OF THE JEWS.")

39One of the criminals began to shout insults at Jesus: "Aren't you the Christ? Then save yourself! And save us too!"

40But the other criminal stopped him. He said, "You should fear God! You are getting the same punishment as he is. 41We are punished justly; we should die. But this man has done nothing wrong!" 42Then this criminal said to Jesus, "Jesus, remember me when you come into your kingdom!"

43Then Jesus said to him, "Listen! What I say is true: Today you will be with me in paradise!"[n]

Jesus Dies

44It was about noon, and the whole land became dark until three o'clock in the afternoon. 45There was no sun! The curtain in the Temple[n] was torn into two pieces. 46Jesus cried out in a loud voice, "Father, I give you my life." After Jesus said this, he died.

47The army officer there saw what happened. He praised God, saying, "I know this was a good man!"

48Many people had gathered there to watch this thing. When they saw what happened, they returned home. They beat their chests because they were so sad. 49Those who were close friends of Jesus were there. Some were women who had followed Jesus from Galilee. They all stood far away from the cross and watched.

Joseph of Arimathea

50-51A man from the Jewish town of Arimathea was there, too. His name was Joseph. He was a good, religious man. He wanted the kingdom of God to come. Joseph was a member of the Jewish council, but he had not agreed when the other leaders decided to kill Jesus. 52Joseph went to Pilate to ask for the body of Jesus. 53So Joseph took the body down from the cross and wrapped it in cloth. Then he put Jesus' body in a tomb that was cut in a wall of rock. This tomb had never been used before. 54This was late on Preparation[d] Day. When the sun went down, the Sabbath[d] day would begin.

55The women who had come from Galilee with Jesus followed Joseph. They saw the tomb and saw inside where the body of Jesus was laid. 56Then the women left to prepare perfumes and spices.

On the Sabbath day they rested, as the law of Moses commanded.

Jesus Rises from Death

24 Very early on the first day of the week, the women came to the tomb where Jesus' body was laid. They brought the spices they had prepared. 2They found that the stone had been rolled away from the entrance of the tomb. 3They went in, but they did not find the body of the Lord Jesus. 4While they were wondering about this, two men in shining clothes suddenly stood beside them. 5The women were very afraid; they bowed their heads to the ground. The men said to the women, "Why are you looking for a living person here? This is a place for the dead. 6Jesus is not here. He has risen from death! Do you remember what he said in Galilee? 7He said that the Son of Man[d] must be given to evil men, be killed on a cross, and rise from death on the third day." 8Then the women remembered what Jesus had said.

---

[n]**paradise** A place where people who obey God go when they die.
[n]**curtain in the Temple** A curtain divided the Most Holy Place from the other part of the Temple. This was the special building in Jerusalem where God commanded the Jews to worship him.

Visiting Angels
LUKE 24:4-8

Sometimes angels look like humans. After Jesus died on the cross and was buried, some of the women who loved Jesus went to his tomb to put spices on his body. When they got to the tomb, Jesus' body was gone. They saw only two angels who looked like men dressed in shining white clothes. These angels told them the news that Jesus had risen from the dead, just as he said he was going to do. The angels told the women to tell the disciples. The women obeyed and ran to tell the disciples the amazing news that Jesus was alive!

This is amazing, good news for us too!

To read about an angel who freed a man from prison, fly to page 1338.

⁹The women left the tomb and told all these things to the 11 apostles[d] and the other followers. ¹⁰These women were Mary Magdalene, Joanna, Mary the mother of James, and some other women. The women told the apostles everything that had happened at the tomb. ¹¹But they did not believe the women. It sounded like nonsense. ¹²But Peter got up and ran to the tomb. He looked in, but he saw only the cloth that Jesus' body had been wrapped in. Peter went away to be alone, wondering about what had happened.

On the Road to Emmaus

¹³That same day two of Jesus' followers were going to a town named Emmaus. It is about seven miles from Jerusalem. ¹⁴They were talking about everything that had happened. ¹⁵While they were discussing these things, Jesus himself came near and began walking with them. ¹⁶(They were not allowed to recognize Jesus.) ¹⁷Then he said, "What are these things you are talking about while you walk?"

The two followers stopped. Their faces were very sad. ¹⁸The one named Cleopas answered, "You must be the only one in Jerusalem who does not know what just happened there."

¹⁹Jesus said to them, "What are you talking about?"

The followers said, "It is about Jesus of Nazareth. He was a prophet[d] from God to all the people. He said and did many powerful things. ²⁰Our leaders and the leading priests gave him up to be judged and killed. They nailed him to a cross. ²¹But we were hoping that he would free the Jews. It is now the third day since this happened. ²²And today some women among us told us some amazing things. Early this morning they went to the tomb, ²³but they did not find his body there. They came and told us that they had seen a vision of angels. The angels said that Jesus was alive! ²⁴So some of our group went to the tomb, too. They found it just as the women said, but they did not see Jesus."

²⁵Then Jesus said to them, "You are foolish and slow to realize what is true. You should believe everything the prophets said. ²⁶They said that the Christ[d] must suffer these things before

he enters his glory." [27]Then Jesus began to explain everything that had been written about himself in the Scriptures.[d] He started with Moses, and then he talked about what all the prophets had said about him.

[28]They came near the town of Emmaus, and Jesus acted as if he did not plan to stop there. [29]But they begged him, "Stay with us. It is late; it is almost night." So he went in to stay with them.

[30]Jesus sat down with them and took some bread. He gave thanks for the food and divided it. Then he gave it to them. [31]And then, they were allowed to recognize Jesus. But when they saw who he was, he disappeared. [32]They said to each other, "When Jesus talked to us on the road, it felt like a fire burning in us. It was exciting when he explained the true meaning of the Scriptures."

[33]So the two followers got up at once and went back to Jerusalem. There they found the 11 apostles[d] and others gathered. [34]They were saying, "The Lord really has risen from death! He showed himself to Simon."

[35]Then the two followers told what had happened on the road. They talked about how they recognized Jesus when he divided the bread.

Jesus Appears to His Followers

[36]While the two followers were telling this, Jesus himself stood among those gathered. He said to them, "Peace be with you."

[37]They were fearful and terrified. They thought they were seeing a ghost. [38]But Jesus said, "Why are you troubled? Why do you doubt what you see? [39]Look at my hands and my feet. It is I myself! Touch me. You can see that I have a living body; a ghost does not have a body like this."

[40]After Jesus said this, he showed them his hands and feet. [41]The followers were amazed and very happy. They still could not believe it. Jesus said to them, "Do you have any food here?" [42]They gave him a piece of cooked fish. [43]While the followers watched, Jesus took the fish and ate it.

[44]He said to them, "Remember when I was with you before? I said that everything written about me must happen—everything in the law of Moses, the books of the prophets,[d] and the Psalms."

[45]Then Jesus opened their minds so they could understand the Scriptures.[d] [46]He said to them, "It is written that the Christ[d] would be killed and rise from death on the third day. [47-48]You saw these things happen—you are witnesses. You must tell people to change their hearts and lives. If they do this, their sins will be forgiven. You must start at Jerusalem and preach these things in my name to all nations. [49]Listen! My Father has promised you something; I will send it to you. But you must stay in Jerusalem until you have received that power from heaven."

Jesus Goes Back to Heaven

[50]Jesus led his followers out of Jerusalem almost to Bethany. He raised his hands and blessed them. [51]While he was blessing them, he was separated from them and carried into heaven. [52]They worshiped him and then went back to the city very happy. [53]They stayed in the Temple[d] all the time, praising God.

JOHN

*John Tells
About Jesus, the Son of God*

Christ Comes to the World

1 Before the world began, there was the Word." The Word was with God, and the Word was God. ²He was with

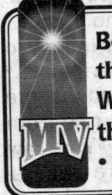

> **Before the world began, there was the Word. The Word was with God, and the Word was God.**
> • John 1:1

God in the beginning. ³All things were made through him. Nothing was made without him. ⁴In him there was life. That life was light for the people of the world. ⁵The Light shines in the darkness. And the darkness has not overpowered the Light.

⁶There was a man named John" who was sent by God. ⁷He came to tell people about the Light. Through him all people could hear about the Light and believe. ⁸John was not the Light, but he came to tell people about the Light. ⁹The true Light was coming into the world. The true Light gives light to all.

¹⁰The Word was in the world. The world was made through him, but the world did not know him. ¹¹He came to the world that was his own. But his own people did not accept him. ¹²But some people did accept him. They believed in him. To them he gave the right to become children of God. ¹³They did not become his children in the human

Faith and How It Works
JOHN 1:12

Being God's child is a special privilege. God says that anyone who accepts and believes in Jesus can become one of his children. What does God want you to believe? First, you should believe that Jesus is the Son of God. Second, you should believe in what Jesus did—that he died on the cross in your place and then rose again from the dead.

Your faith in Christ is faith in a real person who lived on earth, who died for you, and who rose again. Hebrews 11:6 says, "Without faith no one can please God. Anyone who comes to God must believe that he is real and that he rewards those who truly want to find him." Do you have faith in who Jesus is and what he has done for you?

To find out more about faith and how it works, fly to page 1388.

"**Word** The Greek word is "logos," meaning any kind of communication. It could be translated "message." Here, it means Christ. Christ was the way God told people about himself.
"**John** John the Baptist, who preached to people about Christ's coming (Matthew 3, Luke 3).

way. They were not born because of the desire or wish of some man. They were born of God.

¹⁴The Word became a man and lived among us. We saw his glory—the glory that belongs to the only Son of the Father. The Word was full of grace and truth. ¹⁵John told about him. He said, "This is the One I was talking about. I said, 'The One who comes after me is greater than I am. He was living before me.'"

²⁰John spoke freely and did not refuse to answer. He said clearly, "I am not the Christ."[d]

²¹So they asked him, "Then who are you? Are you Elijah?"[n]

He answered, "No, I am not Elijah."

Then they asked, "Are you the Prophet?"[n]

He answered, "No, I am not the Prophet."

²²Then they said, "Who are you? Give us an answer to tell those who sent us. What do you say about yourself?"

Brothers and Sisters

PETER AND ANDREW • JOHN 1:41

You have probably heard a lot about the apostle Peter. He became a great leader among the apostles in teaching the gospel. But did you know that it was his brother, Andrew, who first brought Peter to Jesus? Andrew had been following John the Baptist. When Jesus began to teach, John the Baptist said that people should follow Jesus. So Andrew decided to follow Jesus and brought his brother Peter to follow him too.

You can tell your brothers and sisters about Jesus if they don't know him, and you can be a good example of Jesus by your kindness and love. Your brothers and sisters might accept Jesus as their Savior because of you!

To find out what Jesus' brothers thought about him, fly to page 1286.

¹⁶The Word was full of grace and truth. From him we all received more and more blessings. ¹⁷The law was given through Moses, but grace and truth came through Jesus Christ. ¹⁸No man has ever seen God. But God the only Son is very close to the Father.[n] And the Son has shown us what God is like.

John Tells People About Jesus

¹⁹The Jews in Jerusalem sent some priests and Levites to John.[n] The Jews sent them to ask, "Who are you?"

²³John told them in the words of the prophet Isaiah:

"I am the voice of a man
 calling out in the desert:
'Make the road straight for the
 Lord.'"   *Isaiah 40:3*

²⁴In the group of Jews who were sent, there were some Pharisees.[d] ²⁵They said to John: "You say you are not the Christ. You say you are not Elijah or the Prophet. Then why do you baptize people?"

²⁶John answered, "I baptize people

---

[n]**But . . . Father** This could be translated, "But the only God is very close to the Father." Also, some Greek copies say, "But the only Son is very close to the Father."

[n]**John** John the Baptist, who preached to people about Christ's coming (Matthew 3, Luke 3).

[n]**Elijah** A man who spoke for God. He lived hundreds of years before Christ.

[n]**Prophet** They probably meant the prophet that God told Moses he would send (Deuteronomy 18:15-19).

with water. But there is one here with you that you don't know. 27He is the One who comes after me. I am not good enough to untie the strings of his sandals."

28This all happened at Bethany on the other side of the Jordan River. This is where John was baptizing people.

29The next day John saw Jesus coming toward him. John said, "Look, the Lamb of God.n He takes away the sins of the world! 30This is the One I was talking about. I said, 'A man will come after me, but he is greater than I am, because he was living before me.' 31Even I did not know who he was. But I came baptizing with water so that the people of Israel could know who he is."

32-33Then John said, "I did not know who the Christ was. But God sent me to baptize with water. And God told me, 'You will see the Spiritd come down and rest on a man. That man is the One who will baptize with the Holy Spirit.'" John said, "I saw the Spirit come down from heaven. The Spirit looked like a dove and rested on him. 34I have seen this happen. So I tell people: 'He is the Son of God.'"

"Do you think Jesus found his disciples by placing an ad in the newspaper? I don't think so. Check out John 1:35-51."

The First Followers of Jesus

35The next day Johnn was there again with two of his followers. 36He saw Jesus walking by and said, "Look, the Lamb of God!"n

37The two followers heard John say this. So they followed Jesus. 38Jesus turned and saw them following him. He asked, "What do you want?"

They said, "Rabbi, where are you staying?" ("Rabbi" means "Teacher.")

39Jesus answered, "Come with me and you will see." So the two men went with Jesus. They saw the place where Jesus was staying and stayed there with him that day. It was then about four o'clock.

40These two men followed Jesus after they heard about him from John. One of the men was Andrew. He was Simon Peter's brother. 41The first thing Andrew did was to find his brother, Simon. He said to Simon, "We have found the Messiah." ("Messiah" means "Christ."d)

42Then Andrew took Simon to Jesus. Jesus looked at Simon and said, "You are Simon son of John. You will be called Cephas." ("Cephas" means "Peter."n)

43The next day Jesus decided to go to Galilee. He found Philip and said to him, "Follow me." 44Philip was from the town of Bethsaida, where Andrew and Peter lived. 45Philip found Nathanael and told him, "Remember that Moses wrote in the law about a man who was coming, and the prophetsd also wrote about him. We have found him. He is Jesus, the son of Joseph. He is from Nazareth."

46But Nathanael said to Philip, "Nazareth! Can anything good come from Nazareth?"

Philip answered, "Come and see."

47Jesus saw Nathanael coming toward him. He said, "Here is truly a person of Israel. There is nothing false in him."

48Nathanael asked, "How do you know me?"

Jesus answered, "I saw you when you were under the fig tree. That was before Philip told you about me."

49Then Nathanael said to Jesus, "Teacher, you are the Son of God. You are the King of Israel."

50Jesus said to Nathanael, "You believe in me because I told you I saw you under the fig tree. But you will see

nLamb of God   Name for Jesus. Jesus is like the lambs that were offered for a sacrifice to God.
nJohn   John the Baptist, who preached to people about Christ's coming (Matthew 3, Luke 3).
nPeter   The Greek name "Peter," like the Aramaic name "Cephas," means "rock."

greater things than that!" [51]And Jesus' said to them, "I tell you the truth. You will all see heaven open. You will see 'angels of God going up and coming down'[n] on the Son of Man."[d]

The Wedding at Cana

2 Two days later there was a wedding in the town of Cana in Galilee. Jesus' mother was there. [2]Jesus and his followers were also invited to the wedding. [3]When all the wine was gone, Jesus' mother said to him, "They have no more wine."

[4]Jesus answered, "Dear woman, why come to me? My time has not yet come."

[5]His mother said to the servants, "Do whatever he tells you to do."

[6]In that place there were six stone water jars. The Jews used jars like these in their washing ceremony.[n] Each jar held about 20 or 30 gallons.

[7]Jesus said to the servants, "Fill the jars with water." So they filled the jars to the top.

[8]Then he said to them, "Now take some out and give it to the master of the feast."

So the servants took the water to the master. [9]When he tasted it, the water had become wine. He did not know where the wine came from. But the servants who brought the water knew. The master of the wedding called the bridegroom [10]and said to him, "People always serve the best wine first. Later, after the guests have been drinking a lot, they serve the cheaper wine. But you have saved the best wine till now."

[11]So in Cana of Galilee, Jesus did his first miracle.[d] There he showed his glory, and his followers believed in him.

Jesus in the Temple

[12]Then Jesus went to the town of Capernaum with his mother, brothers and his followers. They all stayed in Capernaum for a few days. [13]But it was almost time for the Jewish Passover[d] Feast. So Jesus went to Jerusalem. [14]In the Temple[d] he found men selling cattle, sheep, and doves. He saw others sitting at tables, exchanging money. [15]Jesus made a whip out of cords. Then he forced all these men, with the sheep and cattle, to leave the Temple. He turned over the tables and scattered the money of the men who were exchanging it. [16]Then he said to those who were selling pigeons, "Take these things out of here! Don't make my Father's house a place for buying and selling!"

[17]When this happened the followers remembered what was written in the Scriptures:[d] "My strong love for your Temple completely controls me."[n]

[18]The Jews said to Jesus, "Show us a miracle[d] for a sign. Prove that you have the right to do these things."

[19]Jesus answered, "Destroy this temple, and I will build it again in three days."

[20]The Jews answered, "Men worked 46 years to build this Temple! Do you really believe you can build it again in three days?"

[21](But the temple Jesus meant was his own body. [22]After Jesus was raised from death, his followers remembered that Jesus had said this. Then they believed the Scripture[d] and the words Jesus said.)

[23]Jesus was in Jerusalem for the Passover Feast. Many people believed in him because they saw the miracles he did. [24]But Jesus did not trust himself to them because he knew them all. [25]He did not need anyone to tell him about people. Jesus knew what was in a person's mind.

Jesus and Nicodemus

3 There was a man named Nicodemus who was one of the Pharisees.[d] He was an important Jewish leader. [2]One night Nicodemus came to Jesus.

---

[n]**'angels . . . down'**   These words are from Genesis 28:12.
[n]**washing ceremony**   The Jews washed themselves in special ways before eating, before worshiping in the Temple, and at other special times.
[n]**"My . . . me."**   Quotation from Psalm 69:9.

Whit's Wisdom: Eternal Life • John 3

The best part of living in Odyssey is the kids who have become my friends. I'm sure you're just like them. We have fun together, and they always ask such great questions! If you don't ask questions, you won't find answers.

Sal came up with a good question just the other day. "Hey, Mr. Whittaker, what do people mean when they say 'born again'?"

"**W**hat do *you* think they mean, Sal," I answered.

"**I**'m not sure. I think the Bible talks about it, though, doesn't it?"

"**T**hat's right, Sal. Jesus himself told a man named Nicodemus that he needed to be born again. And do you know what Nicodemus said? The exact same thing you did, Sal. He asked Jesus, 'What does it mean to be born again?'"

I had Sal look up John 3, the page you're on right now. Why don't you take a minute and read what happened yourself. Start at verse 1 and go to verse 21. Read it slowly. You probably won't understand everything, but that's OK. I learn something new from John 3 almost every time I read it!

First, find each time the word *born* is used (there are six). Notice that Nicodemus says "born again" or "born a second time" but he doesn't understand at all. What does he think Jesus is saying? (See verse 4). Nicodemus was a smart adult, but he couldn't understand. So don't worry if it's hard for you.

Now, notice that Jesus said we can't be "in God's kingdom" unless we are born again (see verses 3 and 5). But he doesn't just say "born again" over and over, does he? In verses 5 and 8 he changes it to "born of the Spirit." So, we can say that being born again is being born of the Spirit, right? We know Jesus was talking about God's Spirit. That means that God gives us our second birth.

Nicodemus asked "How can this happen?" Jesus tried to make him think. Then he told Nicodemus the way. You probably know verse 16 by heart. Read it again, but try saying "born again" when you read "have eternal life." Does it make sense to you? So, then, back to Sal's and Nicodemus's question: How can somebody be born again? By believing in Jesus!

Related Passages: Romans 10:8-10; 2 Corinthians 5:17

Teacher/Parent Hint: The message is simple, but the language may seem unusual to your children. Encourage them to ask questions. It may help to draw the parallel between God's kingdom, an eternal place, and Jesus' promise of eternal life. The children might enjoy trying to dramatize this conversation in their own words.

He said, "Teacher, we know that you are a teacher sent from God. No one can do the miracles[d] you do, unless God is with him."

[3]Jesus answered, "I tell you the truth. Unless one is born again, he cannot be in God's kingdom."

[4]Nicodemus said, "But if a man is already old, how can he be born again? He cannot enter his mother's body again. So how can he be born a second time?"

teacher in Israel. But you still don't understand these things? [11]I tell you the truth. We talk about what we know. We tell about what we have seen. But you don't accept what we tell you. [12]I have told you about things here on earth, but you do not believe me. So surely you will not believe me if I tell you about the things of heaven! [13]The only one

Salvation
JOHN 3:1-17

Is a Christian someone who goes to church, doesn't use bad language, reads the Bible, doesn't get into trouble, prays every day, and tries to be good? All these things are good, and hopefully all of them are true of you. But *they don't make you a Christian.*

What does?

These verses tell us that a Christian is *someone who believes in Jesus.* That's right—it does not say someone who goes to church, reads the Bible, or does good things. These are important, but *they don't make a person a Christian.* Believing in Jesus does.

This would be a good place to stop and ask yourself, "Do I believe in Jesus? Have I put my trust in him for my salvation? Have I been born again?" If so, *great!* If not—why not do it now?

To learn more about salvation, zoom to page 1347.

[5]But Jesus answered, "I tell you the truth. Unless one is born from water and the Spirit,[d] he cannot enter God's kingdom. [6]A person's body is born from his human parents. But a person's spiritual life is born from the Spirit. [7]Don't be surprised when I tell you, 'You must all be born again.' [8]The wind blows where it wants to go. You hear the wind blow. But you don't know where the wind comes from or where it is going. It is the same with every person who is born from the Spirit."

[9]Nicodemus asked, "How can all this be possible?"

[10]Jesus said, "You are an important

who has ever gone up to heaven is the One who came down from heaven—the Son of Man.[d]

[14]"Moses lifted up the snake in the desert.[n] It is the same with the Son of Man. The Son of Man must be lifted up too. [15]Then everyone who believes in him can have eternal life.

[16]"For God loved the world so much that he gave his only Son. God gave his Son so that whoever believes in him may not be lost, but have eternal life. [17]God did not send his Son into the world to judge the world guilty, but to save the world through him. [18]He who believes in God's Son is not judged

[n]**Moses . . . desert** The people of Israel were dying from snake bites. God told Moses to put a brass snake on a pole. The people who looked at the snake were healed (Numbers 21:4-9).

For God loved the world so much that he gave his only Son. God gave his Son so that whoever believes in him may not be lost, but have eternal life.
• **John 3:16**

guilty. He who does not believe has already been judged guilty, because he has not believed in God's only Son. ¹⁹People are judged by this fact: I am the Light from God that has come into the world. But men did not want light. They wanted darkness because they were doing evil things. ²⁰Everyone who does evil hates the light. He will not come to the light because it will show all the evil things he has done. ²¹But he who follows the true way comes to the light. Then the light will show that the things he has done were done through God."

Jesus and John the Baptist

²²After this, Jesus and his followers went into the area of Judea. There Jesus stayed with his followers and baptized people. ²³John was also baptizing in Aenon, near Salim, because there was plenty of water there. People were going there to be baptized. ²⁴(This was before John was put into prison.)

²⁵Some of John's followers had an argument with a Jew about religious washing.ⁿ ²⁶So they came to John and said, "Teacher, remember the man who was with you on the other side of the Jordan River, the one you spoke about? He is baptizing, and everyone is going to him."

²⁷John answered, "A man can get only what God gives him. ²⁸You yourselves heard me say, 'I am not the Christ.ᵈ I am only the one God sent to prepare the way for him.' ²⁹The bride belongs only to the bridegroom. The friend who

Staying Away from Selfishness
JOHN 3:30

John the Baptist was enjoying great success with his preaching. Hundreds of people were coming to hear him. They were listening carefully to his message and turning away from their sins. Suddenly, when Jesus came the big crowds stopped listening to John and started following Jesus. Even many of John's closest followers and friends became Jesus' disciples.

Instead of being upset and jealous, John explained that Jesus "must become greater, and I must become less important." John knew that Jesus was the Lord and that people should become his followers. John felt alright about Jesus being in the spotlight instead of him.

How do you feel when others become popular and win awards instead of you? Instead of being jealous, be happy for them and thank God for what he has given you. Be like John the Baptist.

To learn more ways to stay away from selfishness, zoom to page 1318.

ⁿ**religious washing** The Jews washed themselves in special ways before eating, before worshiping in the Temple, and at other special times.

helps the bridegroom waits and listens for him. He is glad when he hears the bridegroom's voice. That is the same pleasure I have. And my time of joy is now here. ³⁰He must become greater. And I must become less important.

The One Who Comes from Heaven

³¹"The One who comes from above is greater than all. He who is from the earth belongs to the earth and talks about things on the earth. But the One who comes from heaven is greater than all. ³²He tells what he has seen and heard, but no one accepts what he says. ³³The person who accepts what he says has proven that God is true. ³⁴God sent him, and he tells the things that God says. God gives him the Spirit^d fully. ³⁵The Father loves the Son and has given him power over everything. ³⁶He who believes in the Son has eternal life. But he who does not obey the Son will never have that life. God's anger stays with him."

"I heard that Jesus changed a whole town when he stopped to get a drink of water! Read about it in John 4:1-42."

Jesus and a Samaritan Woman

4 The Pharisees^d heard that Jesus was making and baptizing more followers than John. ²(But really Jesus himself did not baptize people. His followers did the baptizing.) Jesus knew that the Pharisees had heard about him. ³So he left Judea and went back to Galilee. ⁴On the way he had to go through the country of Samaria.

⁵In Samaria Jesus came to the town called Sychar. This town is near the field that Jacob gave to his son Joseph.

Worship
JOHN 4:19-24

"**W**here do you go to church?"

Have you ever been asked that question? Most people think of worship in terms of the church building where people meet. But Jesus says that it is not important *where* we worship, but *how*. We can worship God anywhere, as long as our attitude is right. Throughout the Bible, we read about people praising the Lord in all kinds of places—mountaintops, prisons, palaces, homes, and even in the stomach of a huge fish.

The important ingredient in worship isn't where we do it, but *how*. When you attend worship services at your church, check your attitude: are you glad to be there, or did your parents drag you? Do you listen and participate, or look for ways to distract yourself (and others)? Do you understand that worship brings you into the presence of God himself, or is it just something you have to get through on Sundays?

How do *you* worship him?

To learn more about worship, zoom to page 1317.

⁶Jacob's well was there. Jesus was tired from his long trip. So he sat down beside the well. It was about six o'clock in the evening. ⁷A Samaritan*d* woman came to the well to get some water. Jesus said to her, "Please give me a drink." ⁸(This happened while Jesus' followers were in town buying some food.)

⁹The woman said, "I am surprised that you ask me for a drink. You are a Jew and I am a Samaritan." (Jews are not friends with Samaritans.*n*)

¹⁰Jesus said, "You don't know what God gives. And you don't know who asked you for a drink. If you knew, you would have asked me, and I would have given you living water."

¹¹The woman said, "Sir, where will you get that living water? The well is very deep, and you have nothing to get water with. ¹²Are you greater than Jacob, our father? Jacob is the one who gave us this well. He drank from it himself. Also, his sons and flocks drank from this well."

¹³Jesus answered, "Every person who drinks this water will be thirsty again. ¹⁴But whoever drinks the water I give will never be thirsty again. The water I give will become a spring of water flowing inside him. It will give him eternal life."

¹⁵The woman said to him, "Sir, give me this water. Then I will never be thirsty again. And I will not have to come back here to get more water."

¹⁶Jesus told her, "Go get your husband and come back here."

¹⁷The woman answered, "But I have no husband."

Jesus said to her, "You are right to say you have no husband. ¹⁸Really you have had five husbands. But the man you live with now is not your husband. You told the truth."

¹⁹The woman said, "Sir, I can see that you are a prophet.*d* ²⁰Our fathers worshiped on this mountain. But you Jews say that Jerusalem is the place where people must worship."

²¹Jesus said, "Believe me, woman.

The time is coming when you will not have to be in Jerusalem or on this mountain to worship the Father. ²²You Samaritans worship what you don't understand. We Jews understand what we worship. Salvation comes from the Jews. ²³The time is coming when the true worshipers will worship the Father in spirit and truth. That time is now here. And these are the kinds of worshipers the Father wants. ²⁴God is spirit. Those who worship God must worship in spirit and truth."

²⁵The woman said, "I know that the Messiah is coming." (Messiah is the One called Christ.*d*) "When the Messiah comes, he will explain everything to us."

²⁶Then Jesus said, "He is talking to you now. I am he."

²⁷Just then his followers came back from town. They were surprised because they saw Jesus talking with a woman. But none of them asked, "What do you want?" or "Why are you talking with her?"

²⁸Then the woman left her water jar and went back to town. She said to the people, ²⁹"A man told me everything I have ever done. Come see him. Maybe he is the Christ!" ³⁰So the people left the town and went to see Jesus.

³¹While the woman was away, the followers were begging him, "Teacher, eat something!"

³²But Jesus answered, "I have food to eat that you know nothing about."

³³So the followers asked themselves, "Did somebody already bring Jesus some food?"

³⁴Jesus said, "My food is to do what the One who sent me wants me to do. My food is to finish the work that he gave me to do. ³⁵You say, 'Four more months to wait before we gather the grain.' But I tell you, open your eyes. Look at the fields that are ready for harvesting now. ³⁶Even now, the one who harvests the crop is being paid. He is gathering crops for eternal life. So now the one who plants can be happy along with the one who harvests. ³⁷It

---

*n***Jews . . . Samaritans** This can also be translated "Jews don't use things that Samaritans have used."

is true when we say, 'One person plants, but another harvests the crop.' [38]I sent you to harvest a crop that you did not work for. Others did the work, and you get the profit from their work."[n]

[39]Many of the Samaritans in that town believed in Jesus. They believed because of what the woman said: "He told me everything I have ever done." [40]The Samaritans came to Jesus and begged him to stay with them. So he stayed there two days. [41]Many more believed because of the things he said.

[42]They said to the woman, "First we believed in Jesus because of what you told us. But now we believe because we heard him ourselves. We know that this man really is the Savior of the world."

Jesus Heals an Officer's Son

[43]Two days later, Jesus left and went to Galilee. [44](Jesus had said before that a prophet[d] is not respected in his own country.) [45]When Jesus arrived in Galilee, the people there welcomed him. They had seen all the things he did at the Passover[d] Feast in Jerusalem. They had been at the Passover Feast, too.

[46]Jesus went to visit Cana in Galilee again. This is where Jesus had changed the water into wine. One of the king's important officers lived in the city of Capernaum. This man's son was sick. [47]The man heard that Jesus had come from Judea and was now in Galilee. He went to Jesus and begged him to come to Capernaum and heal his son. His son was almost dead. [48]Jesus said to him, "You people must see signs and miracles[d] before you will believe in me."

[49]The officer said, "Sir, come before my child dies."

[50]Jesus answered, "Go. Your son will live."

The man believed what Jesus told him and went home. [51]On the way the man's servants came and met him. They told him, "Your son is well."

[52]The man asked, "What time did my son begin to get well?"

They answered, "It was about one o'clock yesterday when the fever left him."

[53]The father knew that one o'clock was the exact time that Jesus had said, "Your son will live." So the man and all the people of his house believed in Jesus.

[54]That was the second miracle that Jesus did after coming from Judea to Galilee.

Jesus Heals a Man at a Pool

5 Later Jesus went to Jerusalem for a special Jewish feast. [2]In Jerusalem there is a pool with five covered porches. In the Jewish language[n] it is called Bethzatha.[n] This pool is near the Sheep Gate. [3]Many sick people were lying on the porches beside the pool. Some were blind, some were crippled, and some were paralyzed.[n] [5]There was a man lying there who had been sick for 38 years. [6]Jesus saw the man and knew that he had been sick for a very long time. So Jesus asked him, "Do you want to be well?"

[7]The sick man answered, "Sir, there is no one to help me get into the pool

"I've heard of people having to wait a long time in the doctor's office, but the guy in this story had to wait thirty-eight years!" Read about it in John 5:1-18.

[n]**Look at . . . their work.** As a farmer sends workers to harvest grain, Jesus sends his followers out to bring people to God.
[n]**Jewish language** Aramaic, the language of the Jews in the first century.
[n]**Bethzatha** Also called Bethsaida or Bethesda, a pool of water north of the Temple in Jerusalem.
[n]**Verse 3** Some Greek copies add "and they waited for the water to move." A few later copies add verse 4: "Sometimes an angel of the Lord came down to the pool and stirred up the water. After the angel did this, the first person to go into the pool was healed from any sickness he had."

when the water starts moving. I try to be the first one into the water. But when I try, someone else always goes in before I can."

[8]Then Jesus said, "Stand up. Pick up your mat and walk." [9]And immediately the man was well. He picked up his mat and began to walk.

The day all this happened was a Sabbath[d] day. [10]So the Jews said to the man who had been healed, "Today is the Sabbath. It is against our law for you to carry your mat on the Sabbath day."

[11]But he answered, "The man who made me well told me, 'Pick up your mat and walk.'"

[12]Then they asked him, "Who is the man who told you to pick up your mat and walk?"

[13]But the man who had been healed did not know who it was. There were many people in that place, and Jesus had left.

[14]Later, Jesus found the man at the Temple.[d] Jesus said to him, "See, you are well now. But stop sinning or something worse may happen to you!"

[15]Then the man left and went back to the Jews. He told them that Jesus was the one who had made him well.

[16]Jesus was doing this on the Sabbath day. So the Jews began to do bad things to him. [17]But Jesus said to them, "My Father never stops working. And so I work, too."

[18]This made the Jews try harder to kill him. They said, "First Jesus was breaking the law about the Sabbath day. Then he said that God is his own Father! He is making himself equal with God!"

Jesus Has God's Authority

[19]But Jesus said, "I tell you the truth. The Son can do nothing alone. The Son does only what he sees his Father doing. The Son does whatever the Father does. [20]The Father loves the Son, and the Father shows the Son all the things he himself does. But the Father will show the Son greater things than this to do. Then you will all be amazed. [21]The Father raises the dead and gives them life. In the same way, the Son gives life to those he wants to. [22]Also, the Father judges no one. But the Father has given the Son power to do all the judging. [23]God did this so that all people will respect the Son the same way they respect the Father. He who does not respect the Son does not respect the Father. The Father is the One who sent the Son.

[24]"I tell you the truth. Whoever hears what I say and believes in the One who sent me has eternal life. He will not be judged guilty. He has already left death and has entered into life. [25]I tell you the truth. The time is coming and is already here when the dead will hear the voice of the Son of God. And those who hear will have life. [26]Life comes from the Father himself. So the Father has allowed the Son to give life. [27]And the Father has given the Son the power to judge because he is the Son of Man.[d] [28]Don't be surprised at this. A time is coming when all who are dead and in their graves will hear his voice. [29]Then they will come out of their graves. Those who did good will rise and have life forever. But those who did evil will rise to be judged guilty.

Jesus Is God's Son

[30]"I can do nothing alone. I judge only the way I am told, so my judgment is right. I don't try to please myself. I try to please the One who sent me.

[31]"If I tell people about myself, then they will not accept what I say about myself. [32]But there is another who tells about me. And I know that the things he says about me are true.

[33]"You have sent men to John. And he has told you about the truth. [34]But I don't need a man to tell about me. I tell you this so that you can be saved. [35]John was like a burning and shining lamp. And you were happy to enjoy his light for a while.

[36]"But I have a proof about myself that is greater than that of John. The things I do are my proof. These are the things my Father gave me to do. They

show that the Father sent me. ³⁷And the Father who sent me has given proof about me himself. You have never heard his voice. You have never seen what he looks like. ³⁸His teaching does not live in you because you don't believe in the One that the Father sent. ³⁹You carefully study the Scriptures*ᵈ* because you think that they give you eternal life. Those are the same Scriptures that tell about me! ⁴⁰But you refuse to come to me to have that life.

More than 5,000 People Fed

6 After this, Jesus went across Lake Galilee (or, Lake Tiberias). ²Many people followed him because they saw the miracles*ᵈ* he did to heal the sick. ³Jesus went up on a hill and there sat down with his followers. ⁴It was almost the time for the Jewish Passover*ᵈ* Feast.

⁵Jesus looked up and saw a large crowd coming toward him. He said to Philip, "Where can we buy bread for all these people to eat?" ⁶(Jesus asked

Children Who Saw God at Work
THE BOY IN THE CROWD • JOHN 6:2-13

What is your favorite food? Hot dogs? Pizza? Bread and fish? Not bread and fish? That is what a little boy who went to hear Jesus speak brought in his lunch basket. People made their own bread in Bible times that was hard and flat. And everyone liked fish. There were lots of fishermen on the Sea of Galilee who caught fish to sell at the markets.

When Jesus' disciples were trying to find food to feed all the people who had come to hear Jesus, this little boy gave them his lunch. You can read what happened when Jesus took it. It all happened when the little boy gave Jesus everything he had. What can you give to Jesus?

To meet a boy who stayed up too late, fly to page 1355.

⁴¹"I don't want praise from men. ⁴²But I know you—I know that you don't have God's love in you. ⁴³I have come from my Father—I speak for him. But you don't accept me. But when another person comes, speaking only for himself, you will accept him. ⁴⁴You like to have praise from each other. But you never try to get the praise that comes from the only God. So how can you believe? ⁴⁵Don't think that I will stand before the Father and say that you are wrong. Moses is the one who says that you are wrong. And he is the one that you hoped would save you. ⁴⁶If you really believed Moses, you would believe me because Moses wrote about me. ⁴⁷But you don't believe what Moses

wrote. So how can you believe what I say?"

⁷Philip answered, "We would all have to work a month to buy enough bread for each person here to have only a little piece."

⁸Another follower there was Andrew. He was Simon Peter's brother. Andrew said, ⁹"Here is a boy with five loaves of barley bread and two little fish. But that is not enough for so many people."

¹⁰Jesus said, "Tell the people to sit down." This was a very grassy place. There were about 5,000 men who sat down there. ¹¹Then Jesus took the loaves of bread. He thanked God for the bread and gave it to the people who were sitting there. He did the same with

the fish. He gave them as much as they wanted.

¹²They all had enough to eat. When they had finished, Jesus said to his followers, "Gather the pieces of fish and bread that were not eaten. Don't waste anything." ¹³So they gathered up the pieces that were left. They filled 12 large baskets with the pieces that were left of the five barley loaves.

¹⁴The people saw this miracle that Jesus did. They said, "He must truly be the Prophet[n] who is coming into the world."

¹⁹They rowed the boat about three or four miles. Then they saw Jesus walking on the water, coming toward the boat. The followers were afraid. ²⁰But Jesus said to them, "Don't be afraid. It is I." ²¹Then they were glad to take him into the boat. At once the boat came to land at the place where they wanted to go.

The People Seek Jesus

²²The next day came. Some people had stayed on the other side of the lake. They knew that Jesus had not gone in the boat with his followers but that they had left without him. And they knew that only one boat had been

Miracles from God

JOHN 6:16-21

Wouldn't it be fun to be able to walk on water? If your friends were in a boat, you could walk across the water and see them. You wouldn't need to water ski if you could walk on the water! Unfortunately, we cannot walk on water, but Jesus could.

Jesus walked across the top of the water to see his disciples who were in a boat on the sea of Galilee. Jesus proved he had power to do things that ordinary people could never do. He showed that nothing in the world has any power over him. Since Jesus made everything and everyone in the universe, he can do anything he wants.

We do not need to be afraid when we have problems. God has the power to help us.

To learn about a spot where the fishing is great, fly to page 1312.

¹⁵Jesus knew that the people planned to come and take him by force and make him their king. So he left and went into the hills alone.

Jesus Walks on the Water

¹⁶That evening Jesus' followers went down to Lake Galilee. ¹⁷It was dark now and Jesus had not yet come to them. The followers got into a boat and started across the lake to Capernaum. ¹⁸By now a strong wind was blowing, and the waves on the lake were getting bigger.

there. ²³But then some boats came from Tiberias. They landed near the place where the people had eaten the bread after the Lord had given thanks. ²⁴The people saw that Jesus and his followers were not there now. So they got into boats and went to Capernaum. They wanted to find Jesus.

Jesus, the Bread of Life

²⁵The people found Jesus on the other side of the lake. They asked him, "Teacher, when did you come here?"

ⁿ**Prophet** They probably meant the prophet God told Moses he would send (Deuteronomy 18:15-19).

26Jesus answered, "Are you looking for me because you saw me do miracles?[d] No! I tell you the truth. You are looking for me because you ate the bread and were satisfied. 27Earthly food spoils and ruins. So don't work to get that kind of food. But work to get the food that stays good always and gives you eternal life. The Son of Man[d] will give you that food. God the Father has shown that he is with the Son of Man."

28The people asked Jesus, "What are the things God wants us to do?"

29Jesus answered, "The work God wants you to do is this: to believe in the One that God sent."

30So the people asked, "What miracle will you do? If we can see a miracle, then we will believe you. What will you do? 31Our fathers ate the manna[d] in the desert. This is written in the Scriptures:[d] 'God gave them bread from heaven to eat.'"[n]

"**D**id you ever wonder why Jesus called himself 'the bread from heaven'? He explained what he meant in John 6:32-59."

32Jesus said, "I tell you the truth. Moses was not the one who gave you bread from heaven. But my Father gives you the true bread from heaven. 33God's bread is the One who comes down from heaven and gives life to the world."

34The people said, "Sir, give us this bread always."

35Then Jesus said, "I am the bread that gives life. He who comes to me will never be hungry. He who believes in me will never be thirsty. 36But as I told you before, you have seen me, and still you don't believe. 37The Father gives me my people. Every one of them will come to me, and I will always accept

them. 38I came down from heaven to do what God wants me to do. I did not come to do what I want to do. 39I must not lose even one of those that God has given me, but I must raise them up on the last day. This is what the One who sent me wants me to do. 40Everyone who sees the Son and believes in him has eternal life. I will raise him up on the last day. This is what my Father wants."

41The Jews began to complain about Jesus. They complained because he said, "I am the bread that comes down from heaven." 42The Jews said, "This is Jesus. We know his father and mother. He is only Joseph's son. How can he say, 'I came down from heaven'?"

43But Jesus answered, "Stop complaining to each other. 44The Father is the One who sent me. No one can come to me unless the Father draws him to me. And I will raise him up on the last day. 45It is written in the prophets,[d] 'God will teach all the people.'[n] Everyone who listens to the Father and learns from him comes to me. 46No one has seen the Father except the One who is from God. Only he has seen the Father. 47I tell you the truth. He who believes has eternal life. 48I am the bread that gives life. 49Your ancestors ate the manna in the desert. But still they died. 50Here is the bread that comes down from heaven. If anyone eats this bread, he will never die. 51I am the living bread that came down from heaven. If anyone eats this bread, he will live forever. This bread is my flesh. I will give my flesh so that the people in the world may have life."

52Then the Jews began to argue among themselves. They said, "How can this man give us his flesh to eat?"

53Jesus said, "I tell you the truth. You must eat the flesh of the Son of Man. And you must drink his blood. If you don't do this, then you won't have real life in you. 54He who eats my flesh and

---

n"**God gave . . . eat.'**   Quotation from Psalm 78:24.
n"**God . . . people.'**   Quotation from Isaiah 54:13.

drinks my blood has eternal life. I will raise him up on the last day. ⁵⁵My flesh is true food. My blood is true drink. ⁵⁶Whoever eats my flesh and drinks my blood lives in me, and I live in him. ⁵⁷The Father sent me. The Father lives, and I live because of the Father. So he who eats me will live because of me. ⁵⁸I am not like the bread our ancestors ate. They ate that bread, but still they died. I am the bread that came down from heaven. He who eats this bread will live forever." ⁵⁹Jesus said all these things while he was teaching in the synagogue*d* in Capernaum.

The Words of Eternal Life

⁶⁰The followers of Jesus heard this. Many of them said, "This teaching is hard. Who can accept it?"

⁶¹Jesus knew that his followers were complaining about this. So he said, "Does this teaching bother you? ⁶²Then will it also bother you to see the Son of Man*d* going back to the place where he came from? ⁶³It is not the flesh that gives a person life. It is the spirit that gives life. The words I told you are spirit, and so they give life. ⁶⁴But some of you don't believe." (Jesus knew who

did not believe. He knew this from the beginning. And he knew who would turn against him.) ⁶⁵Jesus said, "That is the reason I said, 'If the Father does not let a person come to me, then he cannot come.'"

⁶⁶After Jesus said this, many of his followers left him. They stopped following him.

⁶⁷Jesus asked the 12 followers, "Do you want to leave, too?"

⁶⁸Simon Peter answered Jesus, "Lord, where would we go? You have the words that give eternal life. ⁶⁹We believe in you. We know that you are the Holy One from God."

⁷⁰Then Jesus answered, "I chose all 12 of you. But 1 of you is a devil."

⁷¹Jesus was talking about Judas, the son of Simon Iscariot. Judas was 1 of the 12. But later he was going to turn against Jesus.

Jesus and His Brothers

7 After this, Jesus traveled around Galilee. He did not want to travel in Judea, because the Jews there wanted to kill him. ²It was time for the Jewish Feast*d* of Shelters. ³So Jesus' brothers said to him, "You should leave here and go to Judea. Then your followers there can see the miracles*d* you do. ⁴Anyone who wants to be well known does not hide what he does. If

Brothers and Sisters
JESUS' BROTHERS • JOHN 7:1-5

Jesus grew up in a family. Jesus' mother was Mary and his father was God. Jesus also had half-brothers and half-sisters. Their mother was Mary and their father was Joseph. Jesus lived with his family until he was thirty years old, working as a carpenter. Then he left his family to begin teaching about the kingdom of God. When he began to teach, his brothers and sisters did not believe in him. They thought he was crazy! We only know of one of Jesus' brothers who changed his mind about Jesus and finally believed in him.

We should pray for our brothers and sisters if they do not believe in Jesus.

To meet some brothers and a sister who invited people to their home, fly to page 1294.

you are doing these things, show yourself to the world." [5](Even Jesus' brothers did not believe in him.)

[6]Jesus said to his brothers, "The right time for me has not yet come. But any time is right for you. [7]The world cannot hate you. But it hates me, because I tell about the evil things it does. [8]So you go to the feast. I will not go now. The right time for me has not yet come." [9]After saying this, Jesus stayed in Galilee.

[10]So Jesus' brothers left to go to the feast. When they had gone, Jesus went, too. But he did not let people see him. [11]At the feast the Jews were looking for him. They said, "Where is that man?"

[12]There was a large crowd of people there. Many of them were whispering to each other about Jesus. Some said, "He is a good man."

Others said, "No, he fools the people." [13]But no one was brave enough to talk about Jesus openly. They were afraid of the Jews.

Jesus Teaches at the Feast

[14]The feast was about half over. Then Jesus went to the Temple[d] and began to teach. [15]The Jews were amazed. They said, "This man has never studied in school. How did he learn so much?"

[16]Jesus answered, "The things I teach are not my own. My teaching comes from him who sent me. [17]If anyone chooses to do what God wants, then he will know that my teaching comes from God. He will know that this teaching is not my own. [18]He who teaches his own ideas is trying to get honor for himself. But he who tries to bring honor to the one who sent him—that person speaks the truth. There is nothing false in him. [19]Moses gave you the law,[n] but none of you obey that law. Why are you trying to kill me?"

[20]The people answered, "A demon[d] has come into you. We are not trying to kill you."

[21]Jesus said to them, "I did one miracle,[d] and you are all amazed. [22]Moses gave you the law about circumcision.[d] (But really Moses did not give you circumcision. Circumcision came from our ancestors.) And yet you circumcise a baby on a Sabbath[d] day. [23]This shows that a baby can be circumcised on a Sabbath day to obey the law of Moses. So why are you angry at me for healing a person's whole body on the Sabbath day? [24]Stop judging by the way things look! Be fair, and judge by what is really right."

Is Jesus the Christ?

[25]Then some of the people who lived in Jerusalem said, "This is the man they are trying to kill. [26]But he is teaching where everyone can see and hear him. And no one is trying to stop him. Maybe the leaders have decided that he really is the Christ.[d] [27]But we know where this man is from. And when the real Christ comes, no one will know where he comes from."

[28]Jesus was still teaching in the Temple.[d] He cried out, "Yes, you know me, and you know where I am from. But I have not come by my own authority. I was sent by the One who is true. You don't know him. [29]But I know him. I am from him, and he sent me."

[30]When Jesus said this, the people tried to take him. But no one was able to touch him. It was not yet the right time. [31]But many of the people believed in Jesus. They said, "When the Christ comes, will he do more miracles[d] than this man has done?"

Some Leaders Try to Arrest Jesus

[32]The Pharisees[d] heard the crowd whispering these things about Jesus. So the leading priests and the Pharisees sent some Temple[d] guards to arrest him. [33]Then Jesus said, "I will be with you a little while longer. Then I will go back to the One who sent me. [34]You will look for me, but you will not find me. And you cannot come where I am."

[35]The Jews said to each other, "Where will this man go so we cannot

---

[n]**law**   Moses gave God's people the law that God gave him on Mount Sinai (Exodus 34:29-32).

find him? Will he go to the Greek cities where our people live? Will he teach the Greek people there? ³⁶This man says, 'You will look for me but you will not find me.' He also says, 'You cannot come where I am.' What does this mean?"

Jesus Talks About the Spirit

³⁷The last day of the feast came. It was the most important day. On that day Jesus stood up and said in a loud voice, "If anyone is thirsty, let him come to me and drink. ³⁸If a person believes in me, rivers of living water will flow out from his heart. This is what the Scripture*d* says." ³⁹Jesus was talking about the Holy Spirit.*d* The Spirit had not yet been given because Jesus had not yet been raised to glory. But later, those who believed in Jesus would receive the Spirit.

The People Argue About Jesus

⁴⁰The people heard these things that Jesus said. Some of them said, "This man really is the Prophet."*n*

⁴¹Others said, "He is the Christ."*d*

Still others said, "The Christ will not come from Galilee. ⁴²The Scripture*d* says that the Christ will come from David's family. And the Scripture says that the Christ will come from Bethlehem, the town where David lived." ⁴³So the people did not agree with each other about Jesus. ⁴⁴Some of them wanted to arrest him, but no one was able to touch him.

The Leaders Won't Believe

⁴⁵The Temple*d* guards went back to the leading priests and the Pharisees.*d* The priests and the Pharisees asked, "Why didn't you bring Jesus?"

⁴⁶The Temple guards answered, "The things he says are greater than the words of any man!"

⁴⁷The Pharisees answered, "So Jesus has fooled you too! ⁴⁸Have any of the

leaders or the Pharisees believed in him? No! ⁴⁹But those people, who know nothing about the law, are under God's curse!"

⁵⁰But Nicodemus was there in that group. He was the one who had gone to see Jesus before.*n* Nicodemus said, ⁵¹"Our law does not judge a man without hearing him. We cannot judge him until we know what he has done."

⁵²They answered, "Are you from Galilee too? Study the Scriptures.*d* You will learn that no prophet*d* comes from Galilee."

⁵³And everyone left and went home.*n*

The Woman Caught in Adultery

8 Jesus went to the Mount of Olives.*d* ²But early in the morning he went back to the Temple.*d* All the people came to Jesus, and he sat and taught them. ³The teachers of the law and the Pharisees*d* brought a woman there. She had been caught in adultery.*d* They forced the woman to stand before the people. ⁴They said to Jesus, "Teacher, this woman was caught having sexual relations with a man who is not her husband. ⁵The law of Moses commands that we kill with stones every woman who does this. What do you say we should do?" ⁶They were asking this to trick Jesus so that they could have some charge against him.

But Jesus knelt down and started writing on the ground with his finger. ⁷They continued to ask Jesus their question. So he stood up and said, "Is there anyone here who has never sinned? The person without sin can throw the first stone at this woman." ⁸Then Jesus knelt down again and wrote on the ground.

⁹Those who heard Jesus began to leave one by one. The older men left first, and then the others. Jesus was left there alone with the woman. She was standing before him. ¹⁰Jesus stood up again and asked her, "Woman, all of

---

*n***Prophet**   They probably meant the prophet God told Moses he would send (Deuteronomy 18:15-19).
*n***But Nicodemus . . . before**   The story about Nicodemus going and talking to Jesus is in John 3:1-21.
*n***Verse 53**   Some early Greek manuscripts do not contain 7:53—8:11.

those people have gone. Has no one judged you guilty?"

[11]She answered, "No one has judged me, sir."

Then Jesus said, "So I also don't judge you. You may go now, but don't sin again."

Jesus Is the Light of the World

[12]Later, Jesus talked to the people again. He said, "I am the light of the world. The person who follows me will never live in darkness. He will have the light that gives life."

say the same thing, then you must accept what they say. [18]I am one of the witnesses who speaks about myself. And the Father who sent me is my other witness."

[19]They asked, "Where is your father?"

Jesus answered, "You don't know me or my Father. But if you knew me, then you would know my Father, too." [20]Jesus said these things while he was

The Bible
JOHN 8:31-32

If you like to play football, you know how exciting it is when your team moves down the field toward the goal line. But what if one day you played with no rules? "Great!" you say. "We could do whatever we want!" But think about it. Would it really be fun with no rules?

With no rules, you wouldn't know which way to move the ball, where the out of bounds line was, or how many downs the other team got before they had to turn the ball over. With no rules, you wouldn't know when time was up or when somebody had won. When you think about it that way, playing without rules wouldn't be so great after all.

We need rules and guidelines in our games and in every other part of life. When Jesus said his word is truth, and the truth shall make you free, he wasn't thinking about football, but he was thinking about the rules and guidelines in the Bible that help us to live a good life.

To learn more about the Bible, zoom to page 1350.

[13]But the Pharisees[d] said to Jesus, "When you talk about yourself, you are the only one to say these things are true. We cannot accept these things you say."

[14]Jesus answered, "Yes, I am saying these things about myself, but they are true. I know where I came from. And I know where I am going. You don't know where I came from or where I am going. [15]You judge me the way you would judge any man. I don't judge anyone. [16]But if I judge, my judging is true. When I judge, I am not alone. The Father who sent me is with me. [17]Your own law says that when two witnesses

teaching in the Temple.[d] He was near the place where the money that the people give is kept. But no one arrested him. The right time for Jesus had not yet come.

The People Misunderstand Jesus

[21]Again, Jesus said to the people, "I will leave you. You will look for me, but you will die in your sins. You cannot come where I am going."

[22]So the Jews asked, "Will Jesus kill himself? Is that why he said, 'You cannot come where I am going'?"

[23]But Jesus said, "You people are

from here below. But I am from above. You belong to this world, but I don't belong to this world. ²⁴So I told you that you would die in your sins. Yes, you will die in your sins if you don't believe that I am he."

²⁵They asked, "Then who are you?"

Jesus answered, "I am what I have told you from the beginning. ²⁶I have many things to say about you and to judge you for. But I tell people only the things I have heard from the One who sent me. And he speaks the truth."

²⁷The people did not understand that Jesus was talking to them about the Father. ²⁸So Jesus said to them, "You will lift up the Son of Man.ᵈ Then you will know that I am he. You will know that these things I do are not by my own authority. You will know that I say only what the Father has taught me. ²⁹The One who sent me is with me. I always do what is pleasing to him. So he has not left me alone." ³⁰While Jesus was saying these things, many people believed in him.

"**W**hat did Jesus mean when he said the truth would make us free? Find out in John 8:31-47."

Freedom from Sin

³¹So Jesus said to the Jews who believed in him, "If you continue to obey my teaching, you are truly my followers. ³²Then you will know the truth. And the truth will make you free."

³³They answered, "We are Abraham's children. And we have never been slaves. So why do you say that we will be free?"

³⁴Jesus answered, "I tell you the truth. Everyone who lives in sin is a slave to sin. ³⁵A slave does not stay with a family forever, but a son belongs to the family forever. ³⁶So if the Son makes you free, then you will be truly free. ³⁷I

know you are Abraham's children. But you want to kill me because you don't accept my teaching. ³⁸I am telling you what my Father has shown me. But you do what your father has told you."

³⁹They answered, "Our father is Abraham."

Jesus said, "If you were really Abraham's children, you would do the things that Abraham did. ⁴⁰I am a man who has told you the truth which I heard from God. But you are trying to kill me. Abraham did nothing like that. ⁴¹So you are doing the things that your own father did."

But they said, "We are not like children who never knew who their father was. God is our Father. He is the only Father we have."

⁴²Jesus said to them, "If God were really your Father, you would love me. I came from God and now I am here. I did not come by my own authority. God sent me. ⁴³You don't understand what I say because you cannot accept my teaching. ⁴⁴Your father is the devil. You belong to him and want to do what he wants. He was a murderer from the beginning. He was against the truth, for there is no truth in him. He is a liar, and he is like the lies he tells. He is the father of lies. ⁴⁵But I speak the truth. That is why you don't believe me. ⁴⁶Can any of you prove that I am guilty of sin? If I am telling the truth, why don't you believe me? ⁴⁷He who belongs to God accepts what God says. But you don't accept what God says, because you don't belong to God."

Jesus and Abraham

⁴⁸The Jews answered, "We say you are a Samaritan!ᵈ We say a demonᵈ has come into you. Are we not right?"

⁴⁹Jesus answered, "I have no demon in me. I give honor to my Father, but you dishonor me. ⁵⁰I am not trying to get honor for myself. There is One who wants this honor for me, and he is the judge. ⁵¹I tell you the truth. If anyone obeys my teaching, he will never die."

⁵²The Jews said to Jesus, "Now we

know that you have a demon in you! Even Abraham and the prophets[d] died. But you say, 'Whoever obeys my teaching will never die.' [53]Do you think that you are greater than our father Abraham? Abraham died. And the prophets died, too. Who do you think you are?"

[54]Jesus answered, "If I give honor to myself, that honor is worth nothing. The One who gives me honor is my Father. And you say that he is your God. [55]But you don't really know him. I know him. If I said I did not know him, then I would be a liar as you are liars. But I do know him, and I obey what he says. [56]Your father Abraham was very happy that he would see my day. He saw that day and was glad."

[57]The Jews said to him, "What? You have never seen Abraham! You are not even 50 years old!"

[58]Jesus answered, "I tell you the truth. Before Abraham was born, I am!" [59]When Jesus said this, the people picked up stones to throw at him. But Jesus hid himself, and then he left the Temple.[d]

Jesus Heals a Man Born Blind

9 As Jesus was walking along, he saw a man who had been born blind. [2]His followers asked him, "Teacher, whose sin caused this man to be born blind—his own sin or his parents' sin?"

[3]Jesus answered, "It is not this man's sin or his parents' sin that made him be blind. This man was born blind so that God's power could be shown in him. [4]While it is daytime, we must continue doing the work of the One who sent me. The night is coming. And no one can work at night. [5]While I am in the world, I am the light of the world."

[6]After Jesus said this, he spit on the ground and made some mud with it. He put the mud on the man's eyes. [7]Then he told the man, "Go and wash in the Pool of Siloam." (Siloam means Sent.) So the man went to the pool. He washed and came back. And he was able to see.

[8]Some people had seen this man begging before. They and the man's neighbors said, "Look! Is this the same man who always sits and begs?"

[9]Some said, "Yes! He is the one." But others said, "No, he's not the same man. He only looks like him."

So the man himself said, "I am the man."

[10]They asked, "What happened? How did you get your sight?"

[11]He answered, "The man named Jesus made some mud and put it on my eyes. Then he told me to go to Siloam and wash. So I went and washed and came back seeing."

[12]They asked him, "Where is this man?"

The man answered, "I don't know."

Pharisees Question the Healing

[13]Then the people took to the Pharisees[d] the man who had been blind. [14]The day Jesus had made mud and healed his eyes was a Sabbath[d] day. [15]So now the Pharisees asked the man, "How did you get your sight?"

He answered, "He put mud on my eyes. I washed, and now I can see."

[16]Some of the Pharisees were saying, "This man does not keep the Sabbath day. He is not from God!"

Others said, "But a man who is a sinner can't do miracles[d] like these." So they could not agree with each other.

[17]They asked the man again, "What do you say about him? It was your eyes he opened."

The man answered, "He is a prophet."[d]

[18]The Jews did not believe that he had been blind and could now see again. So they sent for the man's parents [19]and asked them, "Is this your son? You say that he was born blind. Then how does he see now?"

[20]His parents answered, "We know that this is our son, and we know that he was born blind. [21]But we don't know how he can see now. We don't know who opened his eyes. Ask him. He is old enough to answer for himself." [22]His parents said this because they were afraid of the Jews. The Jews had already

decided that anyone who said that Jesus was the Christ[d] would be put out of the synagogue.[d] 23That is why his parents said, "He is old enough. Ask him."

24So for the second time, they called the man who had been blind. They said, "You should give God the glory by telling the truth. We know that this man is a sinner."

25He answered, "I don't know if he is a sinner. But one thing I do know. I was blind, and now I can see."

26They asked, "What did he do to you? How did he make you see again?"

27He answered, "I have already told you that. But you would not listen to me. Why do you want to hear it again? Do you want to become his followers, too?"

28Then they insulted him and said, "You are his follower. We are followers of Moses. 29We know that God spoke to Moses. But we don't even know where this man comes from!"

30The man answered, "This is a very strange thing. You don't know where he comes from, and yet he opened my eyes. 31We all know that God does not listen to sinners. But God listens to anyone who worships and obeys him. 32Nobody has ever heard of anyone giving sight to a man born blind. 33If this man were not from God, he could do nothing."

34They answered, "You were born full of sin! Are you trying to teach us?" And they threw the man out.

Spiritual Blindness

35Jesus heard that they had thrown him out. So Jesus found him and said, "Do you believe in the Son of Man?"[d]

36He asked, "Who is the Son of Man, sir? Tell me, so I can believe in him!"

37Jesus said to him, "You have already seen him. The Son of Man is the one talking with you now."

38He said, "Yes, Lord, I believe!" Then the man bowed and worshiped Jesus.

39Jesus said, "I came into this world so that the world could be judged. I came so that the blind[n] could see and so that those who see will become blind."

40Some of the Pharisees[d] were near Jesus. When they heard him say this, they asked, "What? Are you saying that we are blind, too?"

41Jesus said, "If you were really blind, you would not be guilty of sin. But now that you say you can see, your guilt remains."

The Shepherd and His Sheep

10 Jesus said, "I tell you the truth. The man who does not enter the sheepfold by the door, but climbs in some other way, is a thief and a robber. 2The one who enters by the door is the shepherd of the sheep. 3The man who guards the door opens it for him. And the sheep listen to the voice of the shepherd. He calls his own sheep, using their names, and he leads them out. 4He brings all of his sheep out. Then he goes ahead of them and leads them. They follow him because they know his voice. 5But they will never follow a stranger. They will run away from him because they don't know his voice." 6Jesus told the people this story, but they did not understand what it meant.

"I guess if Jesus is my shepherd, I don't mind being his lamb. Check out John 10:7-18."

Jesus Is the Good Shepherd

7So Jesus said again, "I tell you the truth. I am the door for the sheep. 8All the people who came before me were thieves and robbers. The sheep did not listen to them. 9I am the door. The person who enters through me will be saved. He will be able to come in and go out and find pasture. 10A thief comes to steal and kill and destroy. But I came to give life—life in all its fullness.

---

[n]**blind** Jesus is talking about people who are spiritually blind, not physically blind.

[11]"I am the good shepherd. The good shepherd gives his life for the sheep. [12]The worker who is paid to keep the sheep is different from the shepherd who owns them. So when the worker sees a wolf coming, he runs away and leaves the sheep alone. Then the wolf attacks the sheep and scatters them. [13]The man runs away because he is only a paid worker. He does not really care for the sheep.

[14-15]"I am the good shepherd. I know my sheep, as the Father knows me. And my sheep know me, as I know the Father. I give my life for the sheep. [16]I have other sheep that are not in this flock here. I must bring them also. They will listen to my voice, and there will be one flock and one shepherd. [17]The Father loves me because I give my life. I give my life so that I can take it back again. [18]No one takes it away from me. I give my own life freely. I have the right to give my life, and I have the right to take it back. This is what my Father commanded me to do."

[19]Again the Jews did not agree with each other because of these words Jesus said. [20]Many of them said, "A demon[d] has come into him and made him crazy. Why listen to him?"

[21]But others said, "A man who is crazy with a demon does not say things like this. Can a demon open the eyes of the blind?"

[22]The time came for the Feast[d] of Dedication at Jerusalem. This was during the winter. [23]Jesus was walking in the Temple[d] in Solomon's Porch.[d] [24]The Jews gathered around him and said, "How long will you make us wonder about you? If you are the Christ,[d] then tell us plainly."

Jesus Is the Son of God

[25]Jesus answered, "I told you already, but you did not believe. I do miracles[d] in my Father's name. Those miracles show who I am. [26]But you don't believe because you are not my sheep. [27]My sheep listen to my voice. I know them,

and they follow me. [28]I give them eternal life, and they will never die. And no person can steal them out of my hand. [29]My Father gave my sheep to me. He is greater than all, and no person can steal my sheep out of my Father's hand. [30]The Father and I are one."

[31]Again the Jews picked up stones to kill Jesus. [32]But Jesus said to them, "I have done many good works from the Father. Which of these good works are you killing me for?"

[33]The Jews answered, "We are not killing you for any good work you did. But you say things that are against God. You are only a man, but you say you are the same as God!"

[34]Jesus answered, "It is written in your law that God said, 'I have said you are gods!'[n] [35]This Scripture[d] called those people gods, the people who received God's message. And Scripture is always true. [36]So why do you say that I speak against God because I said, 'I am God's Son'? I am the one God chose and sent into the world. [37]If I don't do what my Father does, then don't believe me. [38]But if I do what my Father does, even though you don't believe in me, believe what I do. Then you will know and understand that the Father is in me and I am in the Father."

[39]They tried to take Jesus again, but he escaped from them.

[40]Then Jesus went back across the Jordan River to the place where John had first baptized. Jesus stayed there, [41]and many people came to him. They said, "John never did a miracle. But

"**A** lot of kids know that this verse is one of the shortest in the Bible. But not many know why Jesus cried. Do you? Read what happened in John 11:1-44."

[n]"I . . . gods.' Quotation from Psalm 82:6.

everything John said about this man is true." [42]And in that place many believed in Jesus.

The Death of Lazarus

11 There was a man named Lazarus who was sick. He lived in the town of Bethany, where Mary and her sister Martha lived. [2]Mary is the woman who later put perfume on the Lord and wiped his feet with her hair. Mary's brother was Lazarus, the man who was now sick. [3]So Mary and Martha sent someone to tell Jesus, "Lord, the one you love is sick."

he can see by this world's light. [10]But if anyone walks at night he stumbles because there is no light to help him see."

[11]After Jesus said this, he added, "Our friend Lazarus has fallen asleep. But I am going there to wake him."

[12]The followers said, "But Lord, if he can sleep, he will get well."

[13]Jesus meant that Lazarus was dead. But Jesus' followers thought that he meant Lazarus was really sleeping. [14]So then Jesus said plainly, "Lazarus is dead. [15]And I am glad for your sakes that I was not there so that you may believe. But let us go to him now."

[16]Then Thomas (the one called Didymus) said to the other followers, "Let us go, too. We will die with him."

Brothers and Sisters

MARY, MARTHA, AND LAZARUS • JOHN 11:1-6

Mary, Martha, and Lazarus were sisters and a brother who loved Jesus very much. They lived together in the little village of Bethany, not far from Jerusalem. Often when Jesus and the disciples traveled near Jerusalem, they would stay at Mary and Martha's home. They gave Jesus and the disciples a place to stay and food to eat. Jesus and the disciples must have enjoyed staying with these sisters and their brother who were so kind and friendly.

Do you and your brothers and sisters enjoy having company at your house? Do you help your parents so the company will enjoy visiting with you?

[4]When Jesus heard this he said, "This sickness will not end in death. It is for the glory of God. This has happened to bring glory to the Son of God." [5]Jesus loved Martha and her sister and Lazarus. [6]But when he heard that Lazarus was sick, he stayed where he was for two more days. [7]Then Jesus said to his followers, "Let us go back to Judea."

[8]The followers said, "But Teacher, the Jews there tried to kill you with stones. That was only a short time ago. Now you want to go back there?"

[9]Jesus answered, "Are there not 12 hours in the day? If anyone walks in the daylight, he will not stumble because

Jesus in Bethany

[17]Jesus arrived in Bethany. There he learned that Lazarus had already been dead and in the tomb for four days. [18]Bethany was about two miles from Jerusalem. [19]Many Jews had come there to comfort Martha and Mary about their brother.

[20]Martha heard that Jesus was coming, and she went out to meet him. But Mary stayed at home. [21]Martha said to Jesus, "Lord, if you had been here, my brother would not have died. [22]But I know that even now God will give you anything you ask."

²³Jesus said, "Your brother will rise and live again."

²⁴Martha answered, "I know that he will rise and live again in the resurrection[n] on the last day."

²⁵Jesus said to her, "I am the resurrection and the life. He who believes in me will have life even if he dies. ²⁶And he who lives and believes in me will never die. Martha, do you believe this?"

²⁷Martha answered, "Yes, Lord. I believe that you are the Christ,[d] the Son of God. You are the One who was coming to the world."

Jesus Cries

²⁸After Martha said this, she went back to her sister Mary. She talked to Mary alone. Martha said, "The Teacher is here and he is asking for you." ²⁹When Mary heard this, she got up quickly and went to Jesus. ³⁰Jesus had not yet come into the town. He was still at the place where Martha had met him. ³¹The Jews were with Mary in the house, comforting her. They saw Mary stand and leave quickly. They followed her, thinking that she was going to the tomb to cry there. ³²But Mary went to the place where Jesus was. When she saw him, she fell at his feet and said, "Lord, if you had been here, my brother would not have died."

³³Jesus saw that Mary was crying and that the Jews who came with her were crying, too. Jesus felt very sad in his heart and was deeply troubled. ³⁴He asked, "Where did you bury him?"

"Come and see, Lord," they said.

³⁵Jesus cried.

³⁶So the Jews said, "See how much he loved him."

³⁷But some of them said, "If Jesus healed the eyes of the blind man, why didn't he keep Lazarus from dying?"

Jesus Raises Lazarus

³⁸Again Jesus felt very sad in his heart. He came to the tomb. The tomb was a cave with a large stone covering the entrance. ³⁹Jesus said, "Move the stone away."

Martha said, "But, Lord, it has been four days since he died. There will be a bad smell." Martha was the sister of the dead man.

God's Love for Us
JOHN 11:28-45

Having someone you love die is one of the most painful things that can happen. The sense of hurt and loss are overwhelming. If someone you love dies, you may feel like asking God, "Why? Why did it have to be *my* friend (or mother, or father, or whoever)? Why did *that* person have to die?" You may even wonder if God understands how sad you feel.

He does. John 11 tells the story of the death of Lazarus, a close friend of Jesus. Even though Jesus knew he was going to raise Lazarus from the dead, he still felt the pain and loss of his friend. Jesus loved us so much that he was willing to experience the same pain and sorrow we do.

The next time you wonder if God understands your sadness and loneliness, read John 11, and you'll know: *he does.*

To learn more about God's love for us, zoom to page 1379.

[n]**resurrection** Being raised from death to live again.

⁴⁰Then Jesus said to her, "Didn't I tell you that if you believed, you would see the glory of God?"

⁴¹So they moved the stone away from the entrance. Then Jesus looked up and said, "Father, I thank you that you heard me. ⁴²I know that you always hear me. But I said these things because of the people here around me. I want them to believe that you sent me." ⁴³After Jesus said this, he cried out in a loud

come and take away our Temple*d* and our nation."

⁴⁹One of the men there was Caiaphas. He was the high priest that year. Caiaphas said, "You people know nothing! ⁵⁰It is better for one man to die for the people than for the whole nation to be destroyed. But you don't realize this."

Feelings
JOHN 11:35

The shortest verse in the bible is "Jesus cried." Believe it or not, these two little words can actually teach us a lot!

Jesus wants us to follow his example. One important part of his character was his willingness to show his feelings. He was perfect, yet he didn't try to hide his feelings from others. There are many stories in the Bible that describe Jesus showing sadness, compassion, love, frustration, sorrow, and even anger.

Don't try to hide your feelings from Jesus. Be honest with him. He understands how you feel because he's had many of the same problems that you have! He is waiting to hear from you and to help you.

To find out why you sometimes have different feelings than others, zoom to page 1305.

voice, "Lazarus, come out!" ⁴⁴The dead man came out. His hands and feet were wrapped with pieces of cloth, and he had a cloth around his face.

Jesus said to them, "Take the cloth off of him and let him go."

The Leaders Plan to Kill Jesus

⁴⁵There were many Jews who had come to visit Mary. They saw what Jesus did. And many of them believed in him. ⁴⁶But some of them went to the Pharisees.*d* They told the Pharisees what Jesus had done. ⁴⁷Then the leading priests and Pharisees called a meeting of the Jewish council. They asked, "What should we do? This man is doing many miracles.*d* ⁴⁸If we let him continue doing these things, everyone will believe in him. Then the Romans will

⁵¹Caiaphas did not think of this himself. He was high priest that year. So he was really prophesying*d* that Jesus would die for the Jewish nation ⁵²and for God's scattered children. This would bring them all together and make them one.

⁵³That day they started planning to kill Jesus. ⁵⁴So Jesus no longer traveled openly among the Jews. He left there and went to a place near the desert. He went to a town called Ephraim and stayed there with his followers.

⁵⁵It was almost time for the Jewish Passover*d* Feast. Many from the country went up to Jerusalem before the Passover. They went to do the special things to make themselves pure. ⁵⁶The people looked for Jesus. They stood in the Temple and were asking each other,

"Is he coming to the Feast? What do you think?" [57]But the leading priests and the Pharisees had given orders about Jesus. They said that if anyone knew where Jesus was, he must tell them. Then they could arrest Jesus.

Jesus with Friends in Bethany

12 Six days before the Passover[d] Feast, Jesus went to Bethany, where Lazarus lived. (Lazarus is the man Jesus raised from death.) [2]There they had a dinner for Jesus. Martha served the food. Lazarus was one of the people eating with Jesus. [3]Mary brought in a pint of very expensive perfume made from pure nard.[d] She poured the perfume on Jesus' feet, and then she wiped his feet with her hair. And the sweet smell from the perfume filled the whole house.

[4]Judas Iscariot, one of Jesus' followers, was there. (He was the one who would later turn against Jesus.) Judas said, [5]"This perfume was worth 300 silver coins.[n] It should have been sold and the money given to the poor." [6]But Judas did not really care about the poor. He said this because he was a thief. He was the one who kept the money box, and he often stole money from it.

[7]Jesus answered, "Let her alone. It was right for her to save this perfume for today—the day for me to be prepared for burial. [8]The poor will always be with you, but you will not always have me."

The Plot Against Lazarus

[9]A large crowd of Jews heard that Jesus was in Bethany. So they went there to see not only Jesus but also Lazarus. Lazarus was the one Jesus raised from death. [10]So the leading priests made plans to kill Lazarus, too. [11]Because of Lazarus many Jews were leaving them and believing in Jesus.

Jesus Enters Jerusalem

[12]The next day a great crowd in Jerusalem heard that Jesus was coming

Women Who Trusted God
MARY • JOHN 12:1-3

Mary loved Jesus very much. Mary, her sister Martha, and her brother Lazarus always welcomed Jesus and the disciples into their home. As Jesus was on his way to Jerusalem where he would die, he stopped at Mary's house to eat. Mary had an expensive bottle filled with a special perfume called nard. The bottle and perfume were worth as much money as a working person could make in a whole year!

While Jesus was sitting at the table, Mary took the bottle, broke it, and poured the perfume on Jesus' head and feet. This was called *anointing*. It was a way of honoring a special guest. In Old Testament times, kings were anointed with nard.

Mary loved Jesus and she knew he was someone very special. How special is Jesus to you? Is he worth more to you than your most valuable possession?

To meet a woman who became the first believer in a city, fly to page 1345.

[n]**silver coin** One coin, a denarius, was the average pay for one day's work.

there. These were the people who had come to the Passover[d] Feast. [13]They took branches of palm trees and went out to meet Jesus. They shouted,

"Praise[n] God!
God bless the One who comes in the name of the Lord!
God bless the King of Israel!"
    Psalm 118:25-26

[14]Jesus found a colt and sat on it. This was as the Scripture[d] says,

[15]"Don't be afraid, people of Jerusalem!
Your king is coming.
He is sitting on the colt of a donkey."   *Zechariah 9:9*

[16]The followers of Jesus did not understand this at first. But after Jesus was raised to glory, they remembered that this had been written about him. And they remembered that they had done these things to him.

People Tell About Jesus

[17]There had been many people with Jesus when he raised Lazarus from death and told him to come out of the tomb. Now they were telling others about what Jesus did. [18]Many people went out to meet Jesus, because they had heard about this miracle.[d] [19]So the Pharisees[d] said to each other, "You can see that nothing is going right for us. Look! The whole world is following him."

Jesus Talks About His Death

[20]There were some Greek people, too, who came to Jerusalem to worship at the Passover[d] Feast. [21]They went to Philip. (Philip was from Bethsaida, in Galilee.) They said, "Sir, we would like to see Jesus." [22]Philip told Andrew. Then Andrew and Philip told Jesus.

[23]Jesus said to them, "The time has come for the Son of Man[d] to receive his glory. [24]I tell you the truth. A grain of wheat must fall to the ground and die. Then it makes many seeds. But if it never dies, it remains only a single seed. [25]The person who loves his life will give up true life. But the person who hates his life in this world will keep true life forever. [26]Whoever serves me must follow me. Then my servant will be with me everywhere I am. My Father will honor anyone who serves me.

[27]"Now I am very troubled. What should I say? Should I say, 'Father, save me from this time'? No, I came to this time so that I could suffer. [28]Father, bring glory to your name!"

Then a voice came from heaven, "I have brought glory to it, and I will do it again."

[29]The crowd standing there heard the voice. They said it was thunder.

But others said, "An angel has spoken to him."

[30]Jesus said, "That voice was for you, not for me. [31]Now is the time for the world to be judged. Now the ruler of this world will be thrown down. [32]I will be lifted up from the earth. And when this happens, I will draw all people toward me." [33]Jesus said this to show how he would die.

[34]The crowd said, "We have heard from the law that the Christ[d] will live forever. So why do you say, 'The Son of Man must be lifted up'? Who is this 'Son of Man'?"

[35]Then Jesus said, "The light will be with you for a little longer. So walk while you have the light. Then the darkness will not catch you. He who walks in the darkness does not know where he is going. [36]So believe in the light while you still have it. Then you will become sons of light." When Jesus had said this, he left and hid himself from them.

Some Don't Believe in Jesus

[37]Though Jesus had done many miracles[d] before the people, they still did not believe in him. [38]This was to make clear the full meaning of what Isaiah the prophet[d] said:

"Lord, who believed the things we told them?

---

[n]**Praise** Literally, "Hosanna," a Hebrew word used at first in praying to God for help, but at this time it was probably a shout of joy used in praising God or his Messiah.

Who has seen the Lord's power?"

Isaiah 53:1

[39]This is why the people could not believe: Isaiah also said,

[40]"He has blinded their eyes.

He has closed their minds.

This is so that they will not see with their eyes

nor understand in their minds.

This is so they will not

come back to me and be forgiven."

Isaiah 6:10

[41]Isaiah said this because he saw Jesus' glory and spoke about him.

come as light into the world. I came so that whoever believes in me would not stay in darkness.

[47]"If anyone hears my words and does not obey them, I do not judge him. For I did not come to judge the world, but to save the world. [48]There is a judge for the one who refuses to believe in me and does not accept my words. The word I have taught will be his judge on the last day. [49]The things

Humility
JOHN 13:1-17

Imagine that it is summer. You and your friends are enjoying the warm weather and being out of school. You play baseball for a couple of hours. After the game, you're sitting around on the ground, hot, dirty, and sweaty. One of your friends looks at you and says, "Hey—how about getting some nice, cool water in a bucket and washing all of our feet?" *What would you say?*

Most of us would say something like "gross!" Who would want to wash a bunch of dirty, sweaty feet?

Jesus would.

In fact, that is just what he did. And he did it not just because it needed to be done (which it did), and not just because no one else offered (which they did not). Jesus washed the disciples' feet to show what it means to serve others and to be humble. That is how important humility is to Jesus. It means being willing to do the dirty work around the house and to look for ways to help others.

What do you say-are you ready to wash some feet?

To learn more about humility, zoom to page 1450.

[42]But many people believed in Jesus, even many of the leaders. But because of the Pharisees,[d] they did not say that they believed in him. They were afraid that they would be put out of the synagogue.[d] [43]They loved praise from men more than praise from God.

[44]Then Jesus cried out, "He who believes in me is really believing in the One who sent me. [45]He who sees me sees the One who sent me. [46]I have

I taught were not from myself. The Father who sent me told me what to say and what to teach. [50]And I know that eternal life comes from what the Father commands. So whatever I say is what the Father told me to say."

Jesus Washes His Followers' Feet

13 It was almost time for the Jewish Passover[d] Feast. Jesus knew that it was time for him to leave this world and go back to the Father. He had always loved those who were his own in the world, and he loved them all the way to the end.

"**D**id you know that Jesus washed someone's feet? Look at John 13:1-17 to find out whose."

²Jesus and his followers were at the evening meal. The devil had already persuaded Judas Iscariot to turn against Jesus. (Judas was the son of Simon.) ³Jesus knew that the Father had given him power over everything. He also knew that he had come from God and was going back to God. ⁴So during the meal Jesus stood up and took off his outer clothing. Taking a towel, he wrapped it around his waist. ⁵Then he poured water into a bowl and began to wash the followers' feet. He dried them with the towel that was wrapped around him.

⁶Jesus came to Simon Peter. But Peter said to Jesus, "Lord, are you going to wash my feet?"

⁷Jesus answered, "You don't understand what I am doing now. But you will understand later."

⁸Peter said, "No! You will never wash my feet."

Jesus answered, "If I don't wash your feet, then you are not one of my people."

⁹Simon Peter answered, "Lord, after you wash my feet, wash my hands and my head, too!"

¹⁰Jesus said, "After a person has had a bath, his whole body is clean. He needs only to wash his feet. And you men are clean,ᵈ but not all of you." ¹¹Jesus knew who would turn against him. That is why Jesus said, "Not all of you are clean."

¹²When he had finished washing their feet, he put on his clothes and sat down again. Jesus asked, "Do you understand what I have just done for you? ¹³You call me 'Teacher' and 'Lord.' And this is right, because that is what

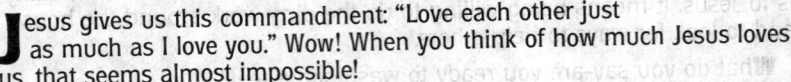

Friendships
JOHN 13:34-35

Jesus gives us this commandment: "Love each other just as much as I love you." Wow! When you think of how much Jesus loves us, that seems almost impossible!

Thankfully, Jesus never gives us rules that are impossible to obey. In this instance, we just have to understand what Jesus meant by the word *love*.

Some people think that love is a warm, fuzzy feeling that just comes naturally! But loving others isn't that easy. Most of the time we have to make the decision to act kindly toward others. If we hang around waiting for warm, fuzzy feelings to appear, we may be waiting for a long time!

Make the choice to be kind to others, even when you don't feel like it. You may surprise yourself—after you do nice things for others, those loving feelings might show up after all!

To discover what it means to be God's friend, zoom to page 1302.

I am. 14I, your Lord and Teacher, have washed your feet. So you also should wash each other's feet. 15I did this as an example for you. So you should do as I have done for you. 16I tell you the truth. A servant is not greater than his master. A messenger is not greater than the one who sent him. 17If you know these things, you will be happy if you do them.

18"I am not talking about all of you. I know those I have chosen. But what the Scripture*d* said must happen: 'The man who ate at my table has now turned against me.'*n* 19I am telling you this now before it happens. Then when it happens you will believe that I am he. 20I tell you the truth. Whoever accepts anyone I send also accepts me. And whoever accepts me also accepts the One who sent me."

Jesus Talks About His Death

21After Jesus said this, he was very troubled. He said openly, "I tell you the truth. One of you will turn against me."

22The followers all looked at each other. They did not know whom Jesus was talking about. 23One of the followers was sitting*n* next to Jesus. This was the follower Jesus loved. 24Simon Peter made signs to him to ask Jesus who it was that he was talking about.

25That follower leaned closer to Jesus and asked, "Lord, who is it that will turn against you?"

26Jesus answered, "I will dip this bread into the dish. The man I give it to is the man who will turn against me." So Jesus took a piece of bread. He dipped it and gave it to Judas Iscariot, the son of Simon. 27As soon as Judas took the bread, Satan entered him. Jesus said to Judas, "The thing that you will do—do it quickly!" 28None of the men at the table understood why Jesus said this to Judas. 29He was the one who kept the money box. So some of the followers thought that Jesus was telling Judas to buy what was needed for the feast. Or they thought that Jesus wanted Judas to give something to the poor.

30Judas accepted the bread Jesus gave him and immediately went out. It was night.

31When Judas was gone, Jesus said, "Now the Son of Man*d* receives his glory. And God receives glory through him. 32If God receives glory through him, then God will give glory to the Son through himself. And God will give him glory quickly."

33Jesus said, "My children, I will be with you only a little longer. You will look for me. And what I told the Jews, I tell you now: Where I am going you cannot come.

34"I give you a new command: Love each other. You must love each other as I have loved you. 35All people will know that you are my followers if you love each other."

Peter Will Say He Doesn't Know Jesus

36Simon Peter asked Jesus, "Lord, where are you going?"

Jesus answered, "Where I am going you cannot follow now. But you will follow later."

37Peter asked, "Lord, why can't I follow you now? I am ready to die for you!"

38Jesus answered, "Will you really die for me? I tell you the truth. Before the rooster crows, you will say three times that you don't know me."

The 'one way' road sign reminds me of something important that Jesus said in John 14:1-6.

Jesus Comforts His Followers

14 Jesus said, "Don't let your hearts be troubled. Trust in God. And trust in me. 2There are many rooms in my Father's house. I would not tell

---

n'**The man . . . me.**' Quotation from Psalm 41:9.
*n***sitting** Literally, "lying." The people of that time ate lying down and leaning on one arm.

you this if it were not true. I am going there to prepare a place for you. ³After I go and prepare a place for you, I will come back. Then I will take you to be with me so that you may be where I am. ⁴You know the way to the place where I am going."

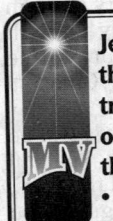

> Jesus answered, "I am the way. And I am the truth and the life. The only way to the Father is through me."
> • John 14:6

⁵Thomas said to Jesus, "Lord, we don't know where you are going. So how can we know the way?"

⁶Jesus answered, "I am the way. And I am the truth and the life. The only way to the Father is through me. ⁷If you really knew me, then you would know my Father, too. But now you do know him, and you have seen him."

⁸Philip said to him, "Lord, show us the Father. That is all we need."

⁹Jesus answered, "I have been with you a long time now. Do you still not know me, Philip? He who has seen me has seen the Father. So why do you say, 'Show us the Father'? ¹⁰Don't you believe that I am in the Father and the Father is in me? The words I say to you don't come from me. The Father lives in me, and he is doing his own work. ¹¹Believe me when I say that I am in the Father and the Father is in me. Or believe because of the miracles[d] I have done. ¹²I tell you the truth. He who believes in me will do the same things that I do. He will do even greater things than these because I am going to the Father. ¹³And if you ask for anything in my name, I will do it for you. Then the Father's glory will be shown through the Son. ¹⁴If you ask me for anything in my name, I will do it.

The Promise of the Holy Spirit

¹⁵"If you love me, you will do the things I command. ¹⁶I will ask the Father, and he will give you another Helper.[n] He will give you this Helper to be with you forever. ¹⁷The Helper is the Spirit[d] of truth. The world cannot accept him because it does not see him or know him. But you know him. He lives with you and he will be in you.

Friendships
JOHN 14:15

Friendship is a two-way street. You can't expect someone to be your friend if you are never willing to spend time together or if you treat that person badly when you are together. Friends expect certain things from each other, like kindness and loyalty.

Your relationship with God is also two-sided. You can depend on him to always be there for you. But he also expects something from you: obedience. He says, "If you love me, you will obey my commands."

If we turn to God only when we're in trouble and need his help, we aren't being very good friends. If we love him, we will want to obey him.

To find out how to treat people who don't believe in God, zoom to page 1422.

ⁿHelper   "Counselor," or "Comforter." Jesus is talking about the Holy Spirit.

¹⁸"I will not leave you all alone like orphans. I will come back to you. ¹⁹In a little while the world will not see me anymore, but you will see me. Because I live, you will live, too. ²⁰On that day you will know that I am in my Father. You will know that you are in me and I am in you. ²¹He who knows my commands and obeys them is the one who loves me. And my Father will love him who loves me. I will love him and will show myself to him."

²²Then Judas (not Judas Iscariot) said, "But, Lord, why do you plan to show yourself to us, but not to the world?"

²³Jesus answered, "If anyone loves me, then he will obey my teaching. My Father will love him, and we will come to him and make our home with him. ²⁴He who does not love me does not obey my teaching. This teaching that you hear is not really mine. It is from my Father, who sent me.

²⁵"I have told you all these things while I am with you. ²⁶But the Helper will teach you everything. He will cause you to remember all the things I told you. This Helper is the Holy Spirit whom the Father will send in my name.

²⁷"I leave you peace. My peace I give you. I do not give it to you as the world does. So don't let your hearts be troubled. Don't be afraid. ²⁸You heard me say to you, 'I am going, but I am coming back to you.' If you loved me, you should be happy that I am going back to the Father because he is greater than I am. ²⁹I have told you this now, before it happens. Then when it happens, you will believe. ³⁰I will not talk with you much longer. The ruler of this world is coming. He has no power over me. ³¹But the world must know that I love the Father. So I do exactly what the Father told me to do.

"Come now, let us go.

Jesus Is Like a Vine

15 "I am the true vine; my Father is the gardener. ²He cuts off every branch of mine that does not produce fruit. And he trims and cleans every branch that produces fruit so that it will produce even more fruit. ³You are already clean*ᵈ* because of the words I have spoken to you. ⁴Remain in me, and I will remain in you. No branch can produce fruit alone. It must remain in the vine. It is the same with you. You cannot produce fruit alone. You must remain in me.

⁵"I am the vine, and you are the branches. If a person remains in me and I remain in him, then he produces much fruit. But without me he can do nothing. ⁶If anyone does not remain in me, then he is like a branch that is thrown away. That branch dies. People pick up dead branches, throw them into the fire, and burn them. ⁷Remain in me and follow my teachings. If you do this, then you can ask for anything you want, and it will be given to you. ⁸You should produce much fruit and show that you are my followers. This brings glory to my Father. ⁹I loved you as the Father loved me. Now remain in my love. ¹⁰I have obeyed my Father's commands, and I remain in his love. In the same way, if you obey my commands, you will remain in my love. ¹¹I have told you these things so that you can have the same joy I have. I want your joy to be the fullest joy.

¹²"This is my command: Love each other as I have loved you. ¹³The greatest love a person can show is to die for his friends. ¹⁴You are my friends if you do what I command you. ¹⁵I don't call you servants now. A servant does not know what his master is doing. But now I call you friends because I have made known to you everything I heard from my Father. ¹⁶You did not choose me; I chose you. And I gave you this work, to go and produce fruit. I want you to produce fruit that will last. Then the Father will give you anything you ask for in my name. ¹⁷This is my command: Love each other.

Jesus Warns His Followers

¹⁸"If the world hates you, remember that it hated me first. ¹⁹If you belonged

to the world, then it would love you as it loves its own. But I have chosen you out of the world. So you don't belong to it. That is why the world hates you. [20]Remember what I told you: A servant is not greater than his master. If people did wrong to me, they will do wrong to you, too. And if they obeyed my teaching, they will obey yours, too. [21]They will do all this to you because of me. They don't know the One who sent me. [22]If I had not come and spoken to them, they would not be guilty of sin. But now they have no excuse for their sin. [23]He who hates me also hates my Father. [24]I did works among them that no one else has ever done. If I had not done those works, they would not be guilty of sin. But now they have seen what I did, and yet they have hated both me and my Father. [25]But this happened so that what is written in their law would be true: 'They hated me for no reason.'[n]

[26]"I will send you the Helper[n] from the Father. He is the Spirit of truth who comes from the Father. When he comes, he will tell about me. [27]And you also must tell people about me because you have been with me from the beginning.

16 "I have told you these things to keep you from giving up. [2]People will put you out of their synagogues.[d] Yes, the time is coming when whoever kills you will think that he is offering service to God. [3]They will do this because they have not known the Father and they have not known me. [4]I have told you these things now. So when the time comes, you will remember that I warned you.

The Work of the Holy Spirit

"I did not tell you these things at the beginning, because I was with you then. [5]Now I am going back to the One who sent me. But none of you asks me, 'Where are you going?' [6]Your hearts are filled with sadness because I have told you these things. [7]But I tell you the truth. It is better for you that I go away. When I go away I will send the Helper[n] to you. If I do not go away, then the Helper will not come. [8]When the Helper comes, he will prove to the people of the world the truth about sin, about being right with God, and about judgment. [9]He will prove to them about sin, because they don't believe in me. [10]He will prove to them that I am right with God, because I am going to the Father. You will not see me anymore. [11]And the Helper will prove to them the truth about judgment, because the ruler of this world is already judged.

[12]"I have many more things to say to you, but they are too much for you now. [13]But when the Spirit[d] of truth comes he will lead you into all truth. He will not speak his own words. He will speak only what he hears and will tell you what is to come. [14]The Spirit of truth will bring glory to me. He will take what I have to say and tell it to you. [15]All that the Father has is mine. That is why I said that the Spirit will take what I have to say and tell it to you.

Sadness Will Become Happiness

[16]"After a little while you will not see me. And then after a little while you will see me again."

[17]Some of the followers said to each other, "What does Jesus mean when he says, 'After a little while you will not see me, and then after a little while you will see me again'? And what does he mean when he says, 'Because I am going to the Father'?" [18]They also asked, "What does he mean by 'a little while'? We don't understand what he is saying."

[19]Jesus saw that the followers wanted to ask him about this. So Jesus said to the followers, "Are you asking each other what I meant when I said, 'After a little while you will not see me. And then after a little while you will see me again'? [20]I tell you the truth. You will cry and be sad, but the world will be happy. You will be sad, but your sadness will

---

[n]**'They . . . reason.'**   These words could be from Psalm 35:19 or Psalm 69:4.
[n]**Helper**   "Counselor," or "Comforter." Jesus is talking about the Holy Spirit.

become joy. ²¹When a woman gives birth to a baby, she has pain, because her time has come. But when her baby is born, she forgets the pain. She forgets because she is so happy that a child has been born into the world. ²²It is the same with you. Now you are sad. But I will see you again and you will be happy. And no one will take away your joy. ²³In

loved me. And he loves you because you have believed that I came from God. ²⁸I came from the Father into the world. Now I am leaving the world and going back to the Father."

Feelings
JOHN 16:20

Jesus warned his friends that they would have different feelings from most people around them. They would be sad when others were happy, but that after a while their sadness would be turned to joy. Actually, Jesus was talking about his own death and the future they could expect after he was killed. He didn't want his friends to worry when he died, because three days later he would rise from the dead. Jesus warned them in advance so that in the middle of their sorrow they could look forward to seeing him again.

Because we are Christians, our feelings will often be different from the people around us. When our problems seem too big for us to handle, we don't have to give up hope. God has told us that life will be hard, but obeying him will be worth it in the long run. We will live with God forever in heaven.

To discover what God wants you to do when you are upset, zoom to page 1444.

that day you will not ask me for anything. I tell you the truth. My Father will give you anything you ask for in my name. ²⁴You have never asked for anything in my name. Ask and you will receive. And your joy will be the fullest joy.

Victory over the World

²⁵"I have told you these things, using words that hide the meaning. But the time will come when I will not use words like that to tell you things. I will speak to you in plain words about the Father. ²⁶In that day you will ask the Father for things in my name. I am saying that I will not need to ask the Father for you. ²⁷No! The Father himself loves you. He loves you because you have

²⁹Then the followers of Jesus said, "You are speaking clearly to us now. You are not using words that are hard to understand. ³⁰We can see now that you know all things. You can answer a person's question even before he asks it. This makes us believe that you came from God."

³¹Jesus answered, "So now you believe? ³²Listen to me. A time is coming when you will be scattered. Each of you will be scattered to his own home. That time is now here. You will leave me. I will be alone. But I am never really alone. Why? Because the Father is with me.

³³"I told you these things so that you can have peace in me. In this world you will have trouble. But be brave! I have defeated the world!"

Jesus Prays for His Followers

17 After Jesus said these things he looked toward heaven. Jesus prayed, "Father, the time has come. Give glory to your Son so that the Son can give glory to you. [2]You gave the Son power over all people so that the Son could give eternal life to all those people you have given to him. [3]And this is eternal life: that men can know you, the only true God, and that men can know Jesus Christ, the One you sent. [4]I finished the work you gave me to do. I brought you glory on earth. [5]And now, Father, give me glory with you. Give me the glory I had with you before the world was made.

[6]"You gave me some men from the world. I have shown them what you are like. Those men belonged to you, and you gave them to me. They have obeyed your teaching. [7]Now they know that everything you gave me comes from you. [8]I gave these men the teachings that you gave me. They accepted those teachings. They know that I truly came from you. [9]I pray for them now. I am not praying for the people in the world. But I am praying for those men you gave me, because they are yours. [10]All I have is yours, and all you have is mine. And my glory is shown through these men. [11]Now I am coming to you. I will not stay in the world now. But these men are still in the world. Holy Father, keep them safe. Keep them safe by the power of your name (the name you gave me), so that they will be one, the same as you and I are one. [12]While I was with them, I kept them safe. I kept them safe by the power of your name—the name you gave me. I protected them. And only one of them, the one who is going to hell, was lost. He was lost so that what was said in the Scripture[d] would happen.

[13]"I am coming to you now. But I pray these things while I am still in the world. I say these things so that these men can have my joy. I want them to have all of my joy. [14]I have given them your teaching. And the world has hated

them. The world hated these men, because they don't belong to the world, the same as I don't belong to the world. [15]I am not asking you to take them out of the world. But I am asking that you keep them safe from the Evil One. [16]They don't belong to the world, the same as I don't belong to the world. [17]Make them ready for your service through your truth. Your teaching is truth. [18]I have sent them into the world, the same as you sent me into the world. [19]I am making myself ready to serve. I do this for them so that they can truly be ready for your service.

[20]"I pray for these men. But I am also praying for all people who will believe in me because of the teaching of these men. [21]Father, I pray that all people who believe in me can be one. You are in me and I am in you. I pray that these people can also be one in us, so that the world will believe that you sent me. [22]I have given these people the glory that you gave me. I gave them this glory so that they can be one, the same as you and I are one. [23]I will be in them and you will be in me. So they will be completely one. Then the world will know that you sent me. And the world will know that you loved these people the same as you loved me.

[24]"Father, I want these people that you have given me to be with me in every place I am. I want them to see my glory. This is the glory you gave me because you loved me before the world was made. [25]Father, you are the One who is good. The world does not know you, but I know you. And these people know that you sent me. [26]I showed them what you are like. And again I will show them what you are like. Then they will have the same love that you have for me. And I will live in them."

Jesus Is Arrested

18 When Jesus finished praying, he left with his followers. They went across the Kidron Valley. On the other side there was a garden of olive trees.

Jesus and his followers went there.

[2]Judas knew where this place was, because Jesus met there often with his followers. Judas was the one who turned against Jesus. [3]So Judas led a group of soldiers to the garden. Judas also brought some guards from the leading priests and the Pharisees.[d] They were carrying torches, lanterns, and weapons.

[4]Jesus knew everything that would happen to him. Jesus went out and asked, "Who is it you are looking for?"

[5]The men answered, "Jesus from Nazareth."

Jesus said, "I am Jesus." (Judas, the one who turned against Jesus, was standing there with them.) [6]When Jesus said, "I am Jesus," the men moved back and fell to the ground.

[7]Jesus asked them again, "Who is it you are looking for?"

They said, "Jesus of Nazareth."

[8]Jesus said, "I told you that I am he. So if you are looking for me, then let these other men go." [9]This happened so that the words Jesus said before might come true: "I have not lost any of the men you gave me."

[10]Simon Peter had a sword. He took out the sword and struck the servant of the high priest, cutting off his right ear. (The servant's name was Malchus.) [11]Jesus said to Peter, "Put your sword back. Shall I not drink of the cup[n] the Father has given me?"

Jesus Is Brought Before Annas

[12]Then the soldiers with their commander and the Jewish guards arrested Jesus. They tied him [13]and led him first to Annas. Annas was the father-in-law of Caiaphas, the high priest that year. [14]Caiaphas was the one who had told the Jews that it would be better if one man died for all the people.

Peter Says He Doesn't Know Jesus

[15]Simon Peter and another one of Jesus' followers went along after Jesus.

This follower knew the high priest. So he went with Jesus into the high priest's courtyard. [16]But Peter waited outside near the door. The follower who knew the high priest came back outside. He spoke to the girl at the door and brought Peter inside. [17]The girl at the door said to Peter, "Aren't you also one of that man's followers?"

Peter answered, "No, I am not!"

[18]It was cold, so the servants and guards had built a fire. They were standing around it and warming themselves. Peter was standing with them, warming himself.

The High Priest Questions Jesus

[19]The high priest asked Jesus questions about his followers and his teaching. [20]Jesus answered, "I have spoken openly to everyone. I have always taught in synagogues[d] and in the Temple,[d] where all the Jews come together. I never said anything in secret. [21]So why do you question me? Ask the people who heard my teaching. They know what I said."

[22]When Jesus said this, one of the guards standing there hit him. The guard said, "Is that the way you answer the high priest?"

[23]Jesus answered him, "If I said something wrong, then say what was wrong. But if what I said is true, why do you hit me?"

[24]Then Annas sent Jesus to Caiaphas, the high priest. Jesus was still tied.

Peter Says Again He Doesn't Know Jesus

[25]Simon Peter was standing and warming himself. They said to him, "Aren't you one of that man's followers?"

Peter denied it and said, "No, I am not."

[26]One of the servants of the high priest was there. This servant was a relative of the man whose ear Peter had cut off. The servant said, "Didn't I see you with him in the garden?"

[n]**cup** Jesus is talking about the bad things that will happen to him. Accepting these things will be very hard, like drinking a cup of something that tastes very bitter.

[27]Again Peter said it wasn't true. Just then a rooster crowed.

Jesus Is Brought Before Pilate

[28]Then they led Jesus from Caiaphas' house to the Roman governor's palace. It was early in the morning. The Jews would not go inside the palace. They did not want to make themselves unclean,[n] because they wanted to eat the Passover[d] meal. [29]So Pilate went outside to them. He asked, "What charges do you bring against this man?"

[35]Pilate answered, "I am not a Jew. It was your own people and their leading priests who brought you before me. What have you done wrong?"

[36]Jesus said, "My kingdom does not belong to this world. If it belonged to this world, my servants would fight so that I would not be given over to the Jews. But my kingdom is from another place."

[37]Pilate said, "So you are a king!"

Jesus answered, "You say that I am a king. That is true. I was born for this: to tell people about the truth. That is why I came into the world. And everyone who belongs to the truth listens to me."

People Who Made Mistakes
PETER • JOHN 18:25-27

Sometimes it is difficult to stand up for what we believe. It was difficult for Peter. He was one of Jesus' closest disciples. Yet when Jesus needed him the most, Peter said he did not even know who Jesus was. Jesus had warned Peter that before the rooster crowed in the morning, Peter would deny him three times. Peter did not believe it would happen. But when Christ was on trial to be crucified, Peter did just what the Lord had said he would do. Three times he told the people that he did not know who Jesus was.

Later, Peter was sorry for what he had done. He was so sad that he had denied Jesus. We don't want to make the mistake Peter made. Let's tell others that Jesus is our friend.

To discover a couple who tried to lie to God, fly to page 1323.

[30]They answered, "He is a criminal. That is why we brought him to you."

[31]Pilate said to them, "Take him yourselves and judge him by your own law."

They answered, "But we are not allowed to put anyone to death." [32](This happened so that what Jesus had said about how he would die would come true.)

[33]Then Pilate went back inside the palace. He called Jesus to him and asked, "Are you the king of the Jews?"

[34]Jesus said, "Is that your own question, or did others tell you about me?"

[38]Pilate said, "What is truth?" After he said this, he went out to the Jews again. He said to them, "I can find nothing to charge against this man. [39]But it is your custom that I free one prisoner to you at the time of the Passover. Do you want me to free this 'king of the Jews'?"

[40]They shouted back, "No, not him! Let Barabbas go free!" (Barabbas was a robber.)

19 Then Pilate ordered that Jesus be taken away and whipped. [2]The soldiers used some thorny branches

[n]**unclean** Going into a non-Jewish place would make them unfit to eat the Passover Feast, according to Jewish law.

to make a crown. They put this crown on Jesus' head and put a purple robe around him. [3]Then they came to Jesus many times and said, "Hail, King of the Jews!" They hit Jesus in the face.

[4]Again Pilate came out and said to them, "Look! I am bringing Jesus out to you. I want you to know that I find nothing I can charge against him." [5]Then Jesus came out, wearing the crown of thorns and the purple robe. Pilate said to the Jews, "Here is the man!"

[6]When the leading priests and the guards saw Jesus they shouted, "Kill him on a cross! Kill him on a cross!"

But Pilate answered, "Take him and nail him to a cross yourselves. I find nothing I can charge against him."

[7]The Jews answered, "We have a law that says he should die, because he said he is the Son of God."

[8]When Pilate heard this, he was even more afraid. [9]He went back inside the palace and asked Jesus, "Where are you from?" But Jesus did not answer him. [10]Pilate said, "You refuse to speak to me? Don't you know that I have power to set you free and power to have you killed on a cross?"

[11]Jesus answered, "The only power you have over me is the power given to you by God. The man who gave me to you is guilty of a greater sin."

[12]After this, Pilate tried to let Jesus go free. But the Jews cried out, "Anyone who makes himself king is against Caesar. If you let this man go free, you are not Caesar's friend."

[13]Pilate heard what the Jews were saying. So he brought Jesus out to the place called The Stone Pavement. (In the Jewish language[n] the name is Gabbatha.) Pilate sat down on the judge's seat there. [14]It was about six o'clock in the morning on Preparation[d] Day of Passover[d] week. Pilate said to the Jews, "Here is your king!"

[15]They shouted, "Take him away! Take him away! Kill him on a cross!"

Pilate asked them, "Do you want me to kill your king on a cross?"

The leading priests answered, "The only king we have is Caesar!"

[16]So Pilate gave Jesus to them to be killed on a cross.

Jesus Is Killed on a Cross

The soldiers took charge of Jesus. [17]Carrying his own cross, Jesus went out to a place called The Place of the Skull. (In the Jewish language[n] this place is called Golgotha.) [18]There they nailed Jesus to the cross. They also put two other men on crosses, one on each side of Jesus with Jesus in the middle. [19]Pilate wrote a sign and put it on the cross. It read: JESUS OF NAZARETH, THE KING OF THE JEWS. [20]The sign was written in the Jewish language, in Latin, and in Greek. Many of the Jews read the sign, because this place where Jesus was killed was near the city. [21]The leading Jewish priests said to Pilate, "Don't write, 'The King of the Jews.' But write, 'This man said, I am the King of the Jews.'"

[22]Pilate answered, "What I have written, I have written!"

[23]After the soldiers nailed Jesus to the cross, they took his clothes. They divided them into four parts. Each soldier got one part. They also took his long shirt. It was all one piece of cloth, woven from top to bottom. [24]So the soldiers said to each other, "We should not tear this into parts. We should throw lots[d] to see who will get it." This happened to give full meaning to the Scripture:[d]

"They divided my clothes among
     them.
And they threw lots[d] for my
     clothing."   *Psalm 22:18*

So the soldiers did this.

[25]Jesus' mother stood near his cross. His mother's sister was also standing there, with Mary the wife of Clopas, and Mary Magdalene. [26]Jesus saw his mother. He also saw the follower he loved standing there. He said to his mother, "Dear woman, here is your son." [27]Then he said to the follower, "Here is your mother." From that time on, this follower took her to live in his home.

---

[n]**Jewish language**   Aramaic, the language of the Jews in the first century.

Jesus Dies

28After this, Jesus knew that everything had been done. To make the Scripture*d* come true, he said, "I am thirsty."*n* 29There was a jar full of vinegar there, so the soldiers soaked a sponge in it. Then they put the sponge on a branch of a hyssop plant and lifted it to Jesus' mouth. 30Jesus tasted the vinegar. Then he said, "It is finished." He bowed his head and died.

31This day was Preparation*d* Day. The next day was a special Sabbath*d* day. The Jews did not want the bodies to stay on the cross on the Sabbath day. So they asked Pilate to order that the legs of the men be broken*n* and the bodies be taken away. 32So the soldiers came and broke the legs of the first man on the cross beside Jesus. Then they broke the legs of the man on the other cross beside Jesus. 33But when the soldiers came to Jesus, they saw that he was already dead. So they did not break his legs. 34But one of the soldiers stuck his spear into Jesus' side. At once blood and water came out. 35(The one who saw this happen has told about it. The things he says are true. He knows that he tells the truth. He told about it so that you also can believe.) 36These things happened to make the Scripture come true: "Not one of his bones will be broken."*n* 37And another Scripture said, "They will look at the one they have stabbed."*n*

Jesus Is Buried

38Later, a man named Joseph from Arimathea asked Pilate if he could take the body of Jesus. (Joseph was a secret follower of Jesus, because he was afraid of the Jews.) Pilate gave his permission. So Joseph came and took Jesus' body away. 39Nicodemus went with Joseph. Nicodemus was the man who earlier had come to Jesus at night. He brought about 75 pounds of spices. This was a mixture of myrrh*d* and aloes.*d* 40These two men took Jesus' body and wrapped it with the spices in pieces of linen cloth. (This is how the Jews bury people.) 41In the place where Jesus was killed, there was a garden. In the garden was a new tomb where no one had ever been buried. 42The men laid Jesus in that tomb because it was near, and the Jews were preparing to start their Sabbath*d* day.

"**S**omething pretty exciting happened on the first Easter Sunday. Do you know what it was? Read John 20:1-29 to find out."

Jesus' Tomb Is Empty

20 Early on the first day of the week, Mary Magdalene went to the tomb. It was still dark. Mary saw that the large stone had been moved away from the tomb. 2So Mary ran to Simon Peter and the other follower (the one Jesus loved). Mary said, "They have taken the Lord out of the tomb. We don't know where they have put him."

3So Peter and the other follower started for the tomb. 4They were both running, but the other follower ran faster than Peter. So the other follower reached the tomb first. 5He bent down and looked in. He saw the strips of linen cloth lying there, but he did not go in. 6Then following him came Simon Peter. He went into the tomb and saw the strips of linen lying there. 7He also saw the cloth that had been around Jesus' head. The cloth was folded up and laid in a different place from the strips of linen. 8Then the other follower, who had reached the tomb first, also went in. He saw and believed. 9(These

---

*n***"I am thirsty."**   Read Psalms 22:15; 69:21.
*n***broken**   The breaking of the men's bones would make them die sooner.
*n***"Not one . . . broken."**   Quotation from Psalm 34:20. The idea is from Exodus 12:46; Numbers 9:12.
*n***"They . . . stabbed."**   Quotation from Zechariah 12:10.

followers did not yet understand from the Scriptures[d] that Jesus must rise from death.)

Jesus Appears to Mary Magdalene

[10]Then the followers went back home. [11]But Mary stood outside the tomb, crying. While she was still crying, she bent down and looked inside the tomb. [12]She saw two angels dressed in white. They were sitting where Jesus' body had been, one at the head and one at the feet.

[13]They asked her, "Woman, why are you crying?"

She answered, "They have taken away my Lord. I don't know where they have put him." [14]When Mary said this, she turned around and saw Jesus standing there. But she did not know that it was Jesus.

[15]Jesus asked her, "Woman, why are you crying? Whom are you looking for?"

Mary thought he was the gardener. So she said to him, "Did you take him away, sir? Tell me where you put him, and I will get him."

[16]Jesus said to her, "Mary."

Mary turned toward Jesus and said in the Jewish language,[n] "Rabboni." (This means Teacher.)

[17]Jesus said to her, "Don't hold me. I have not yet gone up to the Father. But go to my brothers and tell them this: 'I am going back to my Father and your Father. I am going back to my God and your God.'"

[18]Mary Magdalene went and said to the followers, "I saw the Lord!" And she told them what Jesus had said to her.

Jesus Appears to His Followers

[19]It was the first day of the week. That evening the followers were together. The doors were locked, because they were afraid of the Jews. Then Jesus came and stood among them. He said, "Peace be with you!" [20]After he said this, he showed them his hands and his side. The followers were very happy when they saw the Lord.

[21]Then Jesus said again, "Peace be with you! As the Father sent me, I now send you." [22]After he said this, he breathed on them and said, "Receive the Holy Spirit.[d] [23]If you forgive anyone his sins, they are forgiven. If you don't forgive them, they are not forgiven."

Jesus Appears to Thomas

[24]Thomas (called Didymus) was not with the followers when Jesus came. Thomas was 1 of the 12. [25]The other followers told Thomas, "We saw the Lord."

But Thomas said, "I will not believe it until I see the nail marks in his hands. And I will not believe until I put my finger where the nails were and put my hand into his side."

[26]A week later the followers were in the house again. Thomas was with them. The doors were locked, but Jesus came in and stood among them. He said, "Peace be with you!" [27]Then he said to Thomas, "Put your finger here. Look at my hands. Put your hand here in my side. Stop doubting and believe."

[28]Thomas said to him, "My Lord and my God!"

[29]Then Jesus told him, "You believe because you see me. Those who believe without seeing me will be truly happy."

Why John Wrote This Book

[30]Jesus did many other miracles[d] before his followers that are not written in this book. [31]But these are written so that you can believe that Jesus is the Christ,[d] the Son of God. Then, by believing, you can have life through his name.

Jesus Appears to Seven Followers

21 Later, Jesus showed himself to his followers by Lake Galilee.[n] This is how it happened: [2]Some of the followers were together. They were Simon Peter, Thomas (called Didymus), Nathanael from Cana in Galilee,

[n]**Jewish language** Aramaic, the language of the Jews in the first century.
[n]**Lake Galilee** Literally, "Sea of Tiberias."

the two sons of Zebedee, and two other followers. [3]Simon Peter said, "I am going out to fish."

The other followers said, "We will go with you." So they went out and got into the boat. They fished that night but caught nothing.

[4]Early the next morning Jesus stood on the shore. But the followers did not know that it was Jesus. [5]Then he said to them, "Friends, have you caught any fish?"

They answered, "No."

[6]He said, "Throw your net into the water on the right side of the boat, and you will find some." So they did this. They caught so many fish that they could not pull the net back into the boat.

[7]The follower whom Jesus loved said to Peter, "It is the Lord!" When Peter heard him say this, he wrapped his coat around himself. (Peter had taken his clothes off.) Then he jumped into the water. [8]The other followers went to shore in the boat, dragging the net full of fish. They were not very far from shore, only about 100 yards. [9]When the followers stepped out of the boat and onto the shore, they saw a fire of hot coals. There were fish on the fire, and there was bread.

[10]Then Jesus said, "Bring some of the fish that you caught."

"Peter sure loved Jesus a lot! Read their special conversation in John 21:15-22."

[11]Simon Peter went into the boat and pulled the net to the shore. It was full of big fish. There were 153. Even though there were so many, the net did not tear. [12]Jesus said to them, "Come and eat." None of the followers dared ask him, "Who are you?" They knew it was the Lord. [13]Jesus came and took the bread and gave it to them. He also gave them the fish.

[14]This was now the third time Jesus showed himself to his followers after he was raised from death.

Miracles from God

JOHN 21:1-14

Have you ever been fishing? It is fun to catch a lot of fish, and the fish always seem to taste better when you catch them yourself.

Many of Christ's disciples were fisherman, so they knew how to catch fish. But one night they did not catch a thing. They were about ready to go home when a man yelled from the shore. He told them to throw their nets on the other side of the boat. That seemed a little silly to the fishermen. But they did what the man said. Sure enough, they caught so many fish that their nets almost broke. Immediately, the fishermen knew that the man who had spoken to them was Jesus and that their catch of fish was a miracle.

When God tells us to do something, we should do it and not doubt his word.

To discover a woman who came back to life, fly to page 1332.

Jesus Talks to Peter

[15]When they finished eating, Jesus said to Simon Peter, "Simon son of John do you love me more than these?"

He answered, "Yes, Lord, you know that I love you."

Jesus said, "Take care of my lambs."

[16]Again Jesus said, "Simon son of John do you love me?"

He answered, "Yes, Lord, you know that I love you."

Jesus said, "Take care of my sheep."

[17]A third time he said, "Simon son of John do you love me?"

Peter was hurt because Jesus asked him the third time, "Do you love me?" Peter said, "Lord, you know everything. You know that I love you!"

He said to him, "Take care of my sheep. [18]I tell you the truth. When you were younger, you tied your own belt and went where you wanted. But when you are old, you will put out your hands and someone else will tie them. They will take you where you don't want to go." [19](Jesus said this to show how Peter would die to give glory to God.)

Then Jesus said to Peter, "Follow me!"

[20]Peter turned and saw that the follower Jesus loved was walking behind them. (This was the follower who had leaned against Jesus at the supper and had said, "Lord, who will turn against you?") [21]When Peter saw him behind them he asked Jesus, "Lord, what about him?"

[22]Jesus answered, "Perhaps I want him to live until I come back. That should not be important to you. You follow me!"

[23]So a story spread among the brothers that this follower would not die. But Jesus did not say that he would not die. He only said, "Perhaps I want him to live until I come back. That should not be important to you."

[24]That follower is the one who is telling these things. He is the one who has now written them down. We know that what he says is true.

[25]There are many other things that Jesus did. If every one of them were written down, I think the whole world would not be big enough for all the books that would be written.

ACTS

The Good News of Jesus Spreads

Luke Writes Another Book

1 To Theophilus,
The first book I wrote was about everything that Jesus did and taught. [2]I wrote about the whole life of Jesus, from the beginning until the day he was taken up into heaven. Before this, Jesus talked to the apostles[d] he had chosen. With the help of the Holy Spirit,[d] Jesus told them what they should do. [3]After his death, he showed

himself to them and proved in many ways that he was alive. The apostles saw Jesus during the 40 days after he was raised from death. He spoke to them about the kingdom of God. [4]Once when he was eating with them, he told them not to leave Jerusalem. He said, "The Father has made you a promise

which I told you about before. Wait here to receive this promise. [5]John baptized people with water, but in a few days you will be baptized with the Holy Spirit."

Jesus Is Taken Up into Heaven

[6]The apostles[d] were all together. They asked Jesus, "Lord, are you at this time going to give the kingdom back to Israel?"

[7]Jesus said to them, "The Father is the only One who has the authority to decide dates and times. These things are not for you to know. [8]But the Holy Spirit[d] will come to you. Then you will receive power. You will be my witnesses—in Jerusalem, in all of Judea, in Samaria, and in every part of the world."

[9]After he said this, as they were watching, he was lifted up. A cloud hid him from their sight. [10]As he was going, they were looking into the sky.

Words to Know: New Testament

DISCIPLE/APOSTLE • ACTS 1:2

The twelve men whom Jesus chose to follow him during his time on earth were called **disciples**. Jesus knew that he would return to heaven, so he spent time training the disciples so they could tell people how to be saved. In this verse in Acts, the men were called **apostles**. These were the same men (except there were only eleven because Judas had died), but the new name explains their new job. The word apostle means "a person who is sent." The apostles had been sent out into the world to spread the good news that people can be saved if they believe in Jesus Christ. God also wants you to tell people about him.

To read about the place where Jewish people worship, fly to page 1349.

Suddenly, two men wearing white clothes stood beside them. ¹¹They said, "Men of Galilee, why are you standing here looking into the sky? You saw Jesus taken away from you into heaven. He will come back in the same way you saw him go."

"**C**an you think of any place where Jesus *doesn't* want us to be his witnesses? Notice all the places he mentioned in Acts 1:8."

But the Holy Spirit*ᵈ* will come to you. Then you will receive power. You will be my witnesses— in Jerusalem, in all of Judea, in Samaria, and in every part of the world."
• Acts 1:8

A New Apostle Is Chosen

¹²Then they went back to Jerusalem from the Mount of Olives.*ᵈ* (This mountain is about half a mile from Jerusalem.) ¹³When they entered the city, they went to the upstairs room where they were staying. Peter, John, James, Andrew, Philip, Thomas, Bartholomew, Matthew, James son of Alphaeus, Simon (known as the Zealot*ᵈ*), and Judas son of James were there. ¹⁴They all continued praying together. Some women, including Mary the mother of Jesus, and Jesus' brothers were also there with the apostles.

¹⁵During this time there was a meeting of the believers. (There were about 120 of them.) Peter stood up and said, ¹⁶⁻¹⁷"Brothers, in the Scriptures*ᵈ* the Holy Spirit*ᵈ* said through David that something must happen. The Spirit was talking about Judas, one of our own group, who served together with us. The Spirit said that Judas would lead men to arrest Jesus. ¹⁸Judas bought a field with the money he got for his evil act. (But Judas fell to his death, his body burst open, and all his intestines poured out.) ¹⁹Everyone in Jerusalem

Witnessing
ACTS 1:8

Can you imagine what a car would be like without a motor? Or what a television would sound like without electricity? Neither would work because they would be missing their power. The motor provides the power for a car. And electricity is the power to make sound come out of a television. In this verse, Jesus explains that the Holy Spirit gives the power in a Christian's life.

We need power to witness for God. We may need courage and just the right words to tell a friend who Jesus is. The Holy Spirit can give us power, courage, and the right words.

What do you need the Holy Spirit to give you so you can be a better witness for Jesus Christ? Just ask him!

To learn more about witnessing, zoom to page 1351.

learned about this. This is why they named the field Akeldama. (In their language Akeldama means "field of blood.") [20]In the book of Psalms, this is written:

'May his place be empty.
Leave no one to live in it.'

Psalm 69:25

And it is also written:

'Let another man replace him as leader.'

Psalm 109:8

prayed, "Lord, you know the minds of everyone. Show us which one of these two you have chosen to do this work. Judas turned away from it and went where he belongs. Lord, show us which one should take his place as an apostle!"[d] [26]Then they used lots[d] to choose between them, and the lots showed that Matthias was the one. So he became an apostle with the other 11.

The Coming of the Holy Spirit

2 When the day of Pentecost[d] came, they were all together in one place. [2]Suddenly a noise came from heaven.

Amazing Events That Showed God's Power

ACTS 1:10-11

Did you know that Jesus is alive up in heaven right now?

After Jesus died on the cross and then came back to life, he spent about fifty days on earth talking to his disciples and other people about the work he wanted them to do. He wanted them to tell people how to believe in him. Then one day, Jesus was with his followers on a mountain near the city of Jerusalem. He gave them some more instructions, and then he floated right up into the clouds!

The Bible tells us that Jesus is in heaven with God. But if we believe in him, he is also living in our hearts by his Holy Spirit. Jesus loves us and promises to be with us always.

[21-22]"So now a man must join us and become a witness of Jesus' being raised from death. He must be one of the men who were part of our group during all the time the Lord Jesus was with us. He must have been with us from the time John began to baptize people until the day when Jesus was taken up from us to heaven."

[23]They put the names of two men before the group. One was Joseph Barsabbas, who was also called Justus. The other was Matthias. [24-25]The apostles

It sounded like a strong wind blowing. This noise filled the whole house where they were sitting. [3]They saw something that looked like flames of fire. The flames were separated and stood over each person there. [4]They were all filled with the Holy Spirit,[d] and they began to speak different languages.[n] The Holy Spirit was giving them the power to speak these languages.

[5]There were some religious Jews staying in Jerusalem who were from

[n]**languages** This can also be translated "tongues."

every country in the world. [6]When they heard this noise, a crowd came together. They were all surprised, because each one heard them speaking in his own language. [7]They were completely amazed at this. They said, "Look! Aren't all these men that we hear speaking from Galilee?[n] [8]But each of us hears them in his own language. How is this possible? We are from different places: [9]Parthia, Media, Elam, Mesopotamia, Judea, Cappadocia, Pontus, Asia, [10]Phrygia, Pamphylia, Egypt, the areas of Libya near Cyrene, Rome [11](both Jews and those who had become Jews), Crete and Arabia. But we hear these men telling in our own languages about the great things God has done!" [12]They were all amazed and confused. They asked each other, "What does this mean?"

[13]But others were making fun of them, saying, "They have had too much wine."

Peter Speaks to the People

[14]But Peter stood up with the 11 apostles.[d] In a loud voice he spoke to the crowd: "My fellow Jews, and all of you who are in Jerusalem, listen to me. Pay attention to what I have to say. [15]These men are not drunk, as you think; it is only nine o'clock in the morning! [16]But Joel the prophet[d] wrote about what is happening here today: [17]'God says: In the last days

I will give my Spirit[d] freely to all kinds of people.
Your sons and daughters will prophesy.[d]
Your old men will dream dreams.
Your young men will see visions.
[18]At that time I will give my Spirit even to my servants, both men and women.
And they will prophesy.
[19]I will show miracles[d]
in the sky and on the earth:
blood, fire and thick smoke.
[20]The sun will become dark.
The moon will become red as blood.
And then the great and glorious day of the Lord will come.

Worship
ACTS 2:42

If your house burned down with all your toys and clothes in it, where would you go for help? Grandma and grandpa? Neighbors? Friends from school? Those groups would be good. But if you lived in Jerusalem at the time Peter spoke these words, you probably would have said, "The church!"

The Christians did more than just meet once or twice a week. They shared their lives, their homes, their meals, and just about everything else with each other. The Bible doesn't say that churches everywhere must always do this, but it does make us stop and think. Would the people in my church be there to help me if I needed them? More importantly: would I be there to help someone in my church if he or she needed me?

As you praise God this Sunday, ask him to help you be the kind of Christian who stands by other people no matter what.

To learn more about worship, zoom to page 1442.

[n]**from Galilee** The people thought men from Galilee could speak only their own language.

²¹Then anyone who asks the Lord
for help
will be saved.'   *Joel 2:28-32*

²²"Men of Israel, listen to these words: Jesus from Nazareth was a very special man. God clearly showed this to you by the miracles,ᵈ wonders, and

"**H**ow was the very first church like the church you attend? How did the first Christians treat each other? Find out it in Acts 2:43-47."

signs God did through him. You all know this, because it happened right here among you. ²³Jesus was given to you, and you killed him. With the help of evil men you nailed him to a cross. But God knew all this would happen. This was God's plan which he had made long ago. ²⁴God raised Jesus from death. God set him free from the pain

of death. Death could not hold him. ²⁵For David said this about him:
'I keep the Lord before me always.
Because he is close by my side,
I will not be hurt.
²⁶So I am glad, and I rejoice.
Even my body has hope.
²⁷This is because you will not leave me
in the grave.
You will not let your Holy One rot.
²⁸You will teach me God's way to live.
Being with you will fill me with joy.'
     Psalm 16:8-11

²⁹"Brothers, I can tell you truly about David, our ancestor. He died and was buried. His grave is still here with us today. ³⁰David was a prophetᵈ and knew what God had said. God had promised David that he would make a person from David's family a king just as he was.ⁿ ³¹David knew this before it happened. That is why he said:
'He was not left in the grave.
His body did not rot.'

Staying Away from Selfishness
ACTS 2:44-45

Imagine this: Your parents come into your room one night and tell you they've decided to move out of the house and give it away to a homeless man and his family. Not only that, they are going to sell everything they own and give that money away, too. WHAT?! You must be dreaming, or *they* must be kidding—right?

That may sound a little crazy, but that is what many Christians in the early church did with the things they owned. God may not ask you to do what those early believers did, but he wants you to have the same attitude toward the things you own. What can you do to share your possessions with others?

Be willing to share all you have with your friends and family. Then you will be on your way to winning over selfishness.

To learn more ways to stay away from selfishness, zoom to page 1514.

ⁿ**God . . . was** See 2 Samuel 7:13; Psalm 132:11.

David was talking about the Christ[d] rising from death. [32]So Jesus is the One who God raised from death! And we are all witnesses to this. [33]Jesus was lifted up to heaven and is now at God's right side. The Father has given the Holy Spirit[d] to Jesus as he promised. So now Jesus has poured out that Spirit. This is what you see and hear. [34]David was not the one who was lifted up to heaven. But he said:

'The Lord said to my Lord:
　Sit by me at my right side,
[35]until I put your enemies under your
　control.'[n]　　　　　　*Psalm 110:1*

[36]"So, all the people of Israel should know this truly: God has made Jesus both Lord and Christ. He is the man you nailed to the cross!"

[37]When the people heard this, they were sick at heart. They asked Peter and the other apostles, "What shall we do?"

[38]Peter said to them, "Change your hearts and lives and be baptized, each one of you, in the name of Jesus Christ for the forgiveness of your sins. And you will receive the gift of the Holy Spirit. [39]This promise is for you. It is also for your children and for all who are far away. It is for everyone the Lord our God calls to himself."

[40]Peter warned them with many other words. He begged them, "Save yourselves from the evil of today's people!" [41]Then those people who accepted what Peter said were baptized. About 3,000 people were added to the number of believers that day. [42]They spent their time learning the apostles' teaching. And they continued to share, to break bread,[n] and to pray together.

The Believers Share

[43]The apostles[d] were doing many miracles[d] and signs. And everyone felt great respect for God. [44]All the believers stayed together. They shared everything. [45]They sold their land and the things they owned. Then they divided the money and gave it to those people who needed it. [46]The believers met together in the Temple[d] every day. They all had the same purpose. They broke bread in their homes, happy to share their food with joyful hearts. [47]They praised God, and all the people liked them. More and more people were being saved every day; the Lord was adding those people to the group of believers.

Peter Heals a Crippled Man

3 One day Peter and John went to the Temple.[d] It was three o'clock in the afternoon. This was the time for the daily prayer service. [2]There, at the Temple gate called Beautiful Gate, was a man who had been crippled all his life. Every day he was carried to this gate to beg. He would ask for money from the people going into the Temple. [3]The man saw Peter and John going into the Temple and asked them for money. [4]Peter and John looked straight at him and said, "Look at us!" [5]The man looked at them; he thought they were going to give him some money. [6]But Peter said, "I don't have any silver or gold, but I do have something else I can give you: By the power of Jesus Christ from Nazareth—stand up and walk!" [7]Then Peter took the man's right hand and lifted him up. Immediately the man's feet and ankles became strong. [8]He jumped up, stood on his feet, and began to walk. He went into the Temple with them, walking and jumping, and praising God. [9-10]All the people recognized him. They knew he was the crippled man who always sat by the Beautiful Gate begging for money. Now they saw this same man walking and praising God. The people were amazed. They could not understand how this could happen.

---

[n]**until . . . control**　Literally, "until I make your enemies a footstool for your feet."
[n]**break bread**　This may mean a meal as in verse 46, or the Lord's Supper, the special meal Jesus told his followers to eat to remember him (Luke 22:14-20).

Peter Speaks to the People

[11]The man was holding on to Peter and John. All the people were amazed and ran to Peter and John at Solomon's Porch.[d] [12]When Peter saw this, he said to them, "Men of Israel, why are you surprised? You are looking at us as if it were our own power that made this man walk. Do you think this happened because we are good? No! [13]The God of Abraham, Isaac and Jacob, the God of our ancestors, gave glory to Jesus, his servant. But you gave him up to be killed. Pilate decided to let him go free. But you told Pilate you did not want Jesus. [14]He was pure and good, but you said you did not want him. You told Pilate to give you a murderer[n] instead of Jesus. [15]And so you killed the One who gives life! But God raised him from death. We are witnesses to this. [16]It was the power of Jesus that made this crippled man well. This happened because we trusted in the power of Jesus. You can see this man, and you know him. He was made completely well because of trust in Jesus. You all saw it happen!

[17]"Brothers, I know you did those things to Jesus because you did not understand what you were doing. Your leaders did not understand either. [18]God said this would happen. He said through the prophets[d] that his Christ[d] would suffer and die. And now God has made these things come true in this way. [19]So you must change your hearts and lives! Come back to God, and he will forgive your sins. [20]Then the Lord will give you times of spiritual rest. He will give you Jesus, the One he chose to be the Christ. [21]But Jesus must stay in heaven until the time comes when all things will be made right again. God told about this time long ago when he spoke through his holy prophets. [22]Moses said, 'The Lord your God will give you a prophet like me. He will be one of your own people. You must obey everything he tells you. [23]Anyone who does not obey him will die, separated from God's people.'[n] [24]Samuel, and all the other prophets who spoke for God after Samuel, told about this time now. [25]You have received what the prophets talked about. You have received the agreement God made with your ancestors. He said to your father Abraham, 'Through your descendants[d] all the nations on the earth will be blessed.'[n] [26]God has raised up his servant and sent him to you first. He sent Jesus to bless you by turning each of you away from doing evil things."

Peter and John at the Council

4 While Peter and John were speaking to the people, a group of men came up to them. There were Jewish priests, the captain of the soldiers that guarded the Temple,[d] and some Sadducees.[d] [2]They were upset because the two apostles[d] were teaching the people. Peter and John were preaching that people will rise from death through the power of Jesus. [3]The Jewish leaders grabbed Peter and John and put them in jail. It was already night, so they kept them in jail until the next day. [4]But many of those who heard Peter and John preach believed the things they said. There were now about 5,000 men in the group of believers.

[5]The next day the Jewish leaders, the older Jewish leaders, and the teachers of the law met in Jerusalem. [6]Annas the high priest, Caiaphas, John, and Alexander were there. Everyone from the high priest's family was there. [7]They made Peter and John stand before them. The Jewish leaders asked them: "By what power or authority did you do this?"

[8]Then Peter was filled with the Holy Spirit.[d] He said to them, "Rulers of the people and you older leaders, [9]are you

---

[n]**murderer** Barabbas, the man the Jews asked Pilate to let go free instead of Jesus (Luke 23:18).
[n]**'The Lord . . . people.'** Quotation from Deuteronomy 18:15,19 and Leviticus 23:39.
[n]**'Through . . . blessed.'** Quotation from Genesis 22:18; 26:24.

questioning us about a good thing that was done to a crippled man? Are you asking us who made him well? [10]We want all of you and all the Jewish people to know that this man was made well by the power of Jesus Christ from Nazareth! You nailed him to a cross, but God raised him from death. This man was crippled, but he is now well and able to stand here before you because of the power of Jesus! [11]Jesus is

'The stone[n] that you builders did
    not want.
It has become the cornerstone.'[d]
                Psalm 118:22

[12]Jesus is the only One who can save people. His name is the only power in the world that has been given to save people. And we must be saved through him!"

[13]The Jewish leaders saw that Peter and John were not afraid to speak. They understood that these men had no special training or education. So they were amazed. Then they realized that Peter and John had been with Jesus. [14]They saw the crippled man standing there beside the two apostles. They saw that the man was healed. So they could say nothing against them. [15]The Jewish leaders told them to leave the meeting. Then the leaders talked to each other about what they should do. [16]They said, "What shall we do with these men? Everyone in Jerusalem knows that they have done a great miracle![d] We cannot say it is not true. [17]But we must warn them not to talk to people anymore using that name. Then this thing will not spread among the people."

[18]So they called Peter and John in again. They told them not to speak or to teach at all in the name of Jesus. [19]But Peter and John answered them, "What do you think is right? What would God want? Should we obey you or God? [20]We cannot keep quiet. We must speak about what we have seen

Helping Others
ACTS 4:32

Imagine that you and several friends decide to play baseball one afternoon. As you arrive at the field, some kids have gloves, three or four have their own bats, and you have the only ball. Everyone is ready to play. Then the kids with gloves say, "No one else is using *my* glove." Those with bats say, "I'm the only one who can hit with *my* bat." And you say, "I'm not letting anyone else throw, hit, or catch *my* ball." What kind of fun would that be?

No fun at all. It always works better when you share. This verse says that the Christians in the church in Jerusalem shared everything they had with each other. Their love for one another was so strong that they gave everything they had to whoever needed it. Those Christians show us how to help other people.

Think about what you can share with others today.

To learn more about helping others, zoom to page 1356.

[n]**stone**   A symbol meaning Jesus.

and heard." ²¹⁻²²The Jewish leaders could not find a way to punish them because all the people were praising God for what had been done. (This miracle was a proof from God. The man who was healed was more than 40 years old!) So the Jewish leaders warned the apostles again and let them go free.

The Believers' Prayer

²³Peter and John left the meeting of Jewish leaders and went to their own group. They told them everything that the leading priests and the older Jewish leaders had said to them. ²⁴When the believers heard this, they prayed to God with one purpose. They prayed, "Lord, you are the One who made the sky, the earth, the sea, and everything in the world. ²⁵Our father David was your servant. With the help of the Holy Spirit*d* he said:

'Why are the nations so angry?
Why are the people making
     useless plans?
²⁶The kings of the earth prepare to
     fight.
  Their leaders make plans together
     against the Lord
  and against his Christ.'*d*   Psalm 2:1-2

²⁷These things really happened when Herod, Pontius Pilate, the non-Jewish people, and the Jewish people all came together against Jesus here in Jerusalem. Jesus is your holy Servant. He is the One you made to be the Christ. ²⁸These people made your plan happen; it happened because of your power and your will. ²⁹And now, Lord, listen to what they are saying. They are trying to make us afraid! Lord, we are your servants. Help us to speak your word without fear. ³⁰Help us to be brave by showing us your power; make sick people well, give proofs, and make miracles*d* happen by the power of Jesus, your holy servant."

³¹After they had prayed, the place where they were meeting was shaken. They were all filled with the Holy Spirit,*d* and they spoke God's word without fear.

The Believers Share

³²The group of believers were joined in their hearts, and they had the same spirit. No person in the group said that the things he had were his own. Instead, they shared everything. ³³With great power the apostles*d* were telling people that the Lord Jesus was truly raised from death. And God blessed all the believers very much. ³⁴They all received the things they needed.

Honesty
ACTS 5:1-11

Have you ever heard, "Honesty is the best policy"? These verses tell the story of a man and woman who found that to be very true.

Ananias and Sapphira sold a piece of land and decide to give part of the money to the church. That was fine. The problem was that they lied and said that they were giving *all* the money they had made by selling the property. God was so angry with them that he killed them.

Even though God doesn't usually deal with liars that way, he always hates lies. Be honest with God and with others.

To learn more about honesty, zoom to page 1421.

Everyone that owned fields or houses sold them. They brought the money [35]and gave it to the apostles. Then each person was given the things he needed.

[36]One of the believers was named Joseph. The apostles called him Barnabas. (This name means "one who encourages.") He was a Levite, born in Cyprus. [37]Joseph owned a field. He sold it, brought the money, and gave it to the apostles.

Ananias and Sapphira

5 A man named Ananias and his wife Sapphira sold some land. [2]But he gave only part of the money to the apostles.[d] He secretly kept some of it for himself. His wife knew about this, and she agreed to it. [3]Peter said, "Ananias, why did you let Satan rule your heart? You lied to the Holy Spirit.[d] Why did you keep part of the money you received for the land for yourself? [4]Before you sold the land, it belonged to you. And even after you sold it, you could have used the money any way you wanted. Why did you think of

doing this? You lied to God, not to men!" [5-6]When Ananias heard this, he fell down and died. Some young men came in, wrapped up his body, carried it out, and buried it. And everyone who heard about this was filled with fear.

[7]About three hours later his wife came in. She did not know what had happened. [8]Peter said to her, "Tell me how much money you got for your field. Was it this much?"

Sapphira answered, "Yes, that was the price."

[9]Peter said to her, "Why did you and your husband agree to test the Spirit of the Lord? Look! The men who buried your husband are at the door! They will carry you out." [10]At that moment Sapphira fell down by his feet and died. The young men came in and saw that she was dead. They carried her out and buried her beside her husband. [11]The whole church and all the others who heard about these things were filled with fear.

Proofs from God

[12]The apostles[d] did many signs and miracles[d] among the people. And they would all meet together on Solomon's Porch.[d] [13]None of the others dared to

---

People Who Made Mistakes
ANANIAS AND SAPPHIRA • ACTS 5:1-11

We all know that it is wrong to lie, right? Well, if Ananias and Sapphira knew it, they sure forgot. When the Christians started the first church, they often sold some of their belongings and gave the money to the disciples. The disciples would use the money to help poor people and to pay for the work of the church.

When Ananias and Sapphira sold some land and gave the money to Peter, they lied about the money. They said that they were giving all the money to the church, but they were secretly keeping part of it for themselves. Because Ananias and Sapphira lied, they were punished by God.

This is an important lesson for us to learn: God wants us to be honest— all the time.

To discover the person who thought he could buy God, fly to page 1329.

stand with them. All the people were saying good things about them. ¹⁴More and more men and women believed in the Lord and were added to the group of believers. ¹⁵As Peter was passing by, the people brought their sick into the streets. They put their sick on beds and mats so at least Peter's shadow might fall on them. ¹⁶Crowds came from all the towns around Jerusalem. They brought their sick and those who were bothered by evil spirits. All of them were healed.

The Apostles Obey God

¹⁷The high priest and all his friends (a group called the Sadducees[d]) became very jealous. ¹⁸They took the apostles[d] and put them in jail. ¹⁹But during the night, an angel of the Lord opened the doors of the jail. He led the apostles outside and said, ²⁰"Go and stand in the Temple.[d] Tell the people everything about this new life." ²¹When the apostles heard this, they obeyed and went into the Temple. It was early in the morning, and they began to teach.

The high priest and his friends arrived. They called a meeting of the Jewish leaders and all the important older men of the Jews. They sent some men to the jail to bring the apostles to them. ²²When the men went to the jail, they could not find the apostles. So they went back and told the Jewish leaders about this. ²³They said, "The jail was closed and locked. The guards were standing at the doors. But when we opened the doors, the jail was empty!" ²⁴Hearing this, the captain of the Temple guards and the leading priests were confused. They wondered, "What will happen because of this?"

²⁵Then someone came and told them, "Listen! The men you put in jail are standing in the Temple. They are teaching the people!" ²⁶Then the captain and his men went out and brought the apostles back. But the soldiers did not use force, because they were afraid that the people would kill them with stones.

²⁷The soldiers brought the apostles to the meeting and made them stand before the Jewish leaders. The high priest questioned them. ²⁸He said, "We gave you strict orders not to go on teaching in that name. But look what you have done! You have filled Jerusalem with your teaching. You are trying to make us responsible for this man's death."

²⁹Peter and the other apostles answered, "We must obey God, not men! ³⁰You killed Jesus. You hung him

Peter and the other apostles answered, "We must obey God, not men!"
• Acts 5:29

on a cross. But God, the same God our ancestors had, raised Jesus up from death! ³¹Jesus is the One whom God raised to be on his right side. God made Jesus our Leader and Savior. God did this so that all Jews could change their hearts and lives and have their sins forgiven. ³²We saw all these things happen. The Holy Spirit[d] also proves that these things are true. God has given the Spirit to all who obey him."

³³When the Jewish leaders heard this, they became very angry and wanted to kill them. ³⁴A Pharisee[d] named Gamaliel stood up in the meeting. He was a teacher of the law, and all the people respected him. He ordered the apostles to leave the meeting for a little while. ³⁵Then he said to them, "Men of Israel, be careful of what you are planning to do to these men! ³⁶Remember when Theudas appeared? He said that he was a great man, and about 400 men joined him. But he was killed. And all his followers were scattered. They were able to do nothing. ³⁷Later, a man named Judas came from Galilee at the time of the

registration.[n] He led a group of followers, too. He was also killed, and all his followers were scattered. [38]And so now I tell you: Stay away from these men. Leave them alone. If their plan comes from men, it will fail. [39]But if it is from God, you will not be able to stop them. You might even be fighting against God himself!"

The Jewish leaders agreed with what Gamaliel said. [40]They called the apostles in again. They beat the apostles and told them not to speak in the name of Jesus again. Then they let them go free. [41]The apostles left the meeting full of joy because they were given the honor of suffering disgrace for Jesus. [42]The apostles did not stop teaching people. Every day in the Temple and in people's homes they continued to tell the Good News—that Jesus is the Christ.[d]

Seven Men Are Chosen

6 More and more people were becoming followers of Jesus. But during this same time, the Greek-speaking followers had an argument with the other Jewish followers. The Greek-speaking Jews said that their widows were not getting their share of the food that was given out every day. [2]The 12 apostles[d] called the whole group of followers together. They said, "It is not right for us to stop our work of teaching God's word in order to serve tables. [3]So, brothers, choose seven of your own men. They must be men who are good. They must be full of wisdom and full of the Spirit.[d] We will put them in charge of this work. [4]Then we can use all our time to pray and to teach the word of God."

[5]The whole group liked the idea. So they chose these seven men: Stephen (a man with great faith and full of the Holy Spirit), Philip,[n] Procorus, Nicanor, Timon, Parmenas, and Nicolas (a man from Antioch who had become a Jew).

[6]Then they put these men before the apostles. The apostles prayed and laid their hands on[n] the men.

[7]The word of God was reaching more and more people. The group of followers in Jerusalem became larger and larger. A great number of the Jewish priests believed and obeyed.

Stephen Is Arrested

[8]Stephen was richly blessed by God. God gave him the power to do great miracles[d] and signs among the people. [9]But some Jews were against him. They belonged to a synagogue[d] of Free Men[n] (as it was called). (This synagogue was also for Jews from Cyrene and from Alexandria.) Jews from Cilicia and Asia were also with them. They all came and argued with Stephen. [10]But the Spirit[d] was helping him to speak with wisdom. His words were so strong that they could not argue with him. [11]So they paid some men to say, "We heard him say things against Moses and against God!"

[12]This upset the people, the older Jewish leaders, and the teachers of the law. They came to Stephen, grabbed him and brought him to a meeting of the Jewish leaders. [13]They brought in some men to tell lies about Stephen. They said, "This man is always saying things against this holy place and the law of Moses. [14]We heard him say that Jesus from Nazareth will destroy this place. He also said that Jesus will change the things that Moses told us to do." [15]All the people in the meeting were watching Stephen closely. His face looked like the face of an angel.

Stephen's Speech

7 The high priest said to Stephen, "Are these things true?"

[2]Stephen answered, "Brothers and fathers, listen to me. Our glorious God appeared to Abraham, our ancestor.

---

[n]**registration** Census. A counting of all the people and the things they own.
[n]**Philip** Not the apostle named Philip.
[n]**laid their hands on** Here, doing this showed that these men were given a special work of God.
[n]**Free Men** Jews who had been slaves or whose fathers had been slaves, but were now free.

Abraham was in Mesopotamia before he lived in Haran. ³God said to Abraham, 'Leave your country and your relatives. Go to the land I will show you.'[n] ⁴So Abraham left the country of Chaldea and went to live in Haran. After Abraham's father died, God sent him to this place where you now live. ⁵God did not give Abraham any of this land, not even a foot of it. But God promised that he would give him and his descendants[d] this land. (This was before Abraham had any descendants.) ⁶This is what God said to him: 'Your descendants will be strangers in a land they don't own. The people there will make them slaves. And they will do cruel things to them for 400 years. ⁷But I will punish the nation where they are slaves. Then your descendants will leave that land. Then they will worship me in this place.'[n] ⁸God made an agreement with Abraham; the sign for this agreement was circumcision.[d] And so when Abraham had his son Isaac, Abraham circumcised him when he was eight days old. Isaac also circumcised his son Jacob. And Jacob did the same for his sons, the 12 ancestors[n] of our people.

⁹"These sons became jealous of Joseph. They sold him to be a slave in Egypt. But God was with him. ¹⁰Joseph had many troubles there, but God saved him from all those troubles. The king of Egypt liked Joseph and respected him because of the wisdom that God gave him. The king made him governor of Egypt. He put Joseph in charge of all the people in his palace.

¹¹"Then all the land of Egypt and of Canaan became so dry that nothing would grow there. This made the people suffer very much. The sons could not find anything to eat. ¹²But when Jacob heard that there was grain in Egypt, he sent his sons, our ancestors, there. This was their first trip to Egypt. ¹³Then they went there a second time.

This time, Joseph told his brothers who he was. And the king learned about Joseph's family. ¹⁴Then Joseph sent some men to invite Jacob, his father, to come to Egypt. He also invited all his relatives (75 persons altogether). ¹⁵So Jacob went down to Egypt, where he and his sons died. ¹⁶Later their bodies were moved to Shechem and put in a grave there. (It was the same grave that Abraham had bought in Shechem from the sons of Hamor for a sum of money.)

¹⁷"The number of people in Egypt grew large. There were more and more of our people there. (The promise that God made to Abraham was soon to come true.) ¹⁸Then a new king began to rule Egypt. He did not know who Joseph was. ¹⁹This king tricked our people and was cruel to our ancestors. He forced them to put their babies outside to die. ²⁰This was the time when Moses was born. He was a fine child. For three months Moses was cared for in his father's house. ²¹When they put Moses outside, the king's daughter took him. She raised him as if he were her own son. ²²The Egyptians taught Moses all the things they knew. He was a powerful man in the things he said and did.

²³"When Moses was about 40 years old, he thought it would be good to visit his brothers, the people of Israel. ²⁴Moses saw an Egyptian doing wrong to a Jew. So he defended the Jew and punished the Egyptian for hurting him. Moses killed the Egyptian. ²⁵Moses thought that his fellow Jews would understand that God was using him to save them. But they did not understand. ²⁶The next day, Moses saw two Jewish men fighting. He tried to make peace between them. He said, 'Men, you are brothers! Why are you hurting each other?' ²⁷The man who was hurting the other man pushed Moses away. He said, 'Who made you our ruler and judge? ²⁸Are you going to kill me as you killed

---

[n]'**Leave . . . you'** Quotation from Genesis 12:1.
[n]'**Your descendants . . . place.'** Quotation from Genesis 15:13-14 and Exodus 12.
[n]**12 ancestors** Important ancestors of the Jews; the leaders of the 12 Jewish tribes.

the Egyptian yesterday?'[n] [29]When Moses heard him say this, he left Egypt. He went to live in the land of Midian where he was a stranger. While Moses lived in Midian, he had two sons.

[30]"After 40 years Moses was in the desert near Mount Sinai. An angel appeared to him in the flames of a burning bush. [31]When Moses saw this, he was amazed. He went near to look closer at it. Moses heard the Lord's voice. [32]The Lord said, 'I am the God of your ancestors. I am the God of Abraham, Isaac and Jacob.'[n] Moses began to shake with fear and was afraid to look. [33]The Lord said to him, 'Take off your sandals. You are standing on holy ground. [34]I have seen the troubles my people have suffered in Egypt. I have heard their cries. I have come down to save them. And now, Moses, I am sending you back to Egypt.'[n]

[35]"This Moses was the same man the Jews said they did not want. They had said to him, 'Who made you our ruler and judge?'[n] Moses is the same man God sent to be a ruler and savior, with the help of an angel. This was the angel Moses saw in the burning bush. [36]So Moses led the people out of Egypt. He worked miracles[d] and signs in Egypt, at the Red Sea,[d] and then in the desert for 40 years. [37]This is the same Moses that said to the Jewish people: 'God will give you a prophet[d] like me. He will be one of your own people.'[n] [38]This is the same Moses who was with the gathering of the Jews in the desert. He was with the angel that spoke to him at Mount Sinai, and he was with our ancestors. He received commands from God that give life, and he gave those commands to us.

[39]"But our fathers did not want to obey Moses. They rejected him. They wanted to go back to Egypt again.

[40]They said to Aaron, 'Moses led us out of Egypt. But we don't know what has happened to him. So make us gods who will lead us.'[n] [41]So the people made an idol that looked like a calf. Then they brought sacrifices to it. The people were proud of what they had made with their own hands! [42]But God turned against them. He did not try to stop them from worshiping the sun, moon and stars. This is what is written in the book of the prophets: God says,

'People of Israel, you did not bring
    me sacrifices and offerings
  while you traveled in the desert for
    40 years.
[43]But now you will have to carry
    with you
  the tent to worship the false
    god Molech[d]
  and the idols of the star god Rephan
    that you made to worship.
This is because I will send you away
    beyond Babylon.' *Amos 5:25-27*

[44]"The Holy Tent[d] where God spoke to our fathers was with the Jews in the desert. God told Moses how to make this Tent. He made it like the plan God showed him. [45]Later, Joshua led our fathers to capture the lands of the other nations. Our people went in, and God drove the other people out. When our people went into this new land, they took with them this same Tent. They received this Tent from their fathers and kept it until the time of David. [46]God was very pleased with David. He asked God to let him build a house for him, the God of Jacob. [47]But Solomon was the one who built the Temple.[d]

[48]"But the Most High does not live in houses that men build with their hands. This is what the prophet says:
[49]'Heaven is my throne.
  The earth is my footstool.
So do you think you can build a house
    for me? says the Lord.

---

[n]'**Who . . . yesterday?'**   Quotation from Exodus 2:14.
[n]'**I am . . . Jacob.'**   Quotation from Exodus 3:6.
[n]'**Take . . . Egypt.'**   Quotation from Exodus 3:5-10.
[n]'**Who . . . judge?'**   Quotation from Exodus 2:14.
[n]'**God . . . people.'**   Quotation from Deuteronomy 18:15.
[n]'**Moses . . . us.'**   Quotation from Exodus 32:1.

There is no place where I need to
rest.
⁵⁰Remember, I made all these things!"

Isaiah 66:1-2

⁵¹Stephen continued speaking: "You
stubborn Jewish leaders! You have not
given your hearts to God! You won't
listen to him! You are always against
what the Holy Spirit[d] is trying to tell
you. Your ancestors were like this, and
you are just like them! ⁵²Your fathers
tried to hurt every prophet who ever
lived. Those prophets said long ago
that the Righteous One would come.
But your fathers killed them. And now
you have turned against the Righteous
One and killed him. ⁵³You received the
law of Moses, which God gave you
through his angels. But you don't
obey it!"

"I've heard of peo-
ple not wanting to
listen, but this was
ridiculous! Look at
what happened to
Stephen and also
what he did. Read
Acts 7:54-60."

Stephen Is Killed

⁵⁴When the leaders heard Stephen
saying all these things, they became
very angry. They were so mad that they
were grinding their teeth at Stephen.
⁵⁵But Stephen was full of the Holy
Spirit.[d] He looked up to heaven and saw
the glory of God. He saw Jesus standing
at God's right side. ⁵⁶He said, "Look! I
see heaven open. And I see the Son of
Man[d] standing at God's right side!"

⁵⁷Then they all shouted loudly. They
covered their ears with their hands
and all ran at Stephen. ⁵⁸They took him
out of the city and threw stones at him
until he was dead. The men who told
lies against Stephen left their coats
with a young man named Saul. ⁵⁹While
they were throwing stones, Stephen

prayed, "Lord Jesus, receive my spirit!" ⁶⁰He fell on his knees and cried in
a loud voice, "Lord, do not hold this
sin against them!" After Stephen said
this, he died.

8 Saul agreed that the killing of
Stephen was a good thing.

Trouble for the Believers

²⁻³Some religious men buried
Stephen. They cried very loudly for
him. On that day people began trying
to hurt the church in Jerusalem and
make it suffer. Saul was also trying to
destroy the church. He went from
house to house. He dragged out men
and women and put them in jail. All the
believers, except the apostles,[d] went to
different places in Judea and Samaria.
⁴And everywhere they were scattered,
they told people the Good News.[d]

Philip Preaches in Samaria

⁵Philip[n] went to the city of Samaria
and preached about the Christ.[d] ⁶The
people there heard Philip and saw the
miracles[d] he was doing. They all listened carefully to the things he said.
⁷Many of these people had evil spirits
in them. But Philip made the evil spirits leave them. The spirits made a loud
noise when they came out. There were
also many weak and crippled people
there. Philip healed them, too. ⁸So the
people in that city were very happy.

⁹But there was a man named Simon
in that city. Before Philip came there,
Simon had practiced magic. He amazed
all the people of Samaria with his
magic. He bragged and called himself a
great man. ¹⁰All the people—the least
important and the most important—
paid attention to what Simon said. They
said, "This man has the power of God,
called 'The Great Power'!" ¹¹Simon
had amazed them with his magic
tricks so long that the people became
his followers. ¹²But Philip told them
the Good News[d] about the kingdom of
God and the power of Jesus Christ.
Men and women believed Philip and

ⁿ**Philip** Not the apostle named Philip.

were baptized. [13]Simon himself believed and was baptized. He stayed very close to Philip. When he saw the miracles and the very powerful things that Philip did, Simon was amazed.

[14]The apostles[d] were still in Jerusalem. They heard that the people of Samaria had accepted the word of God. So they sent Peter and John to them. [15]When Peter and John arrived, they prayed that the Samaritan believers might receive the Holy Spirit.[d] [16]These people had been baptized in the name of the Lord Jesus. But the Holy Spirit had not yet entered any of them. [17]Then, when the two apostles began laying their hands on[n] the people, they received the Holy Spirit.

[18]Simon saw that the Spirit was given to people when the apostles laid their hands on them. So he offered the apostles money. [19]He said, "Give me also this power so that when I lay my hands on a person, he will receive the Holy Spirit."

[20]Peter said to him, "You and your money should both be destroyed! You thought you could buy God's gift with money. [21]You cannot share with us in this work. Your heart is not right before God. [22]Change your heart! Turn away from this evil thing you have done. Pray to the Lord. Maybe he will forgive you for thinking this. [23]I see that you are full of bitter jealousy and ruled by sin."

"**P**hilip followed the road God told him to take and got to tell someone about Jesus. Read Acts 8:26-39 to learn how it happened."

[24]Simon answered, "Both of you pray for me to the Lord. Pray that the things you have said will not happen to me!"

[25]Then the two apostles told the people the things they had seen Jesus do. And after the apostles had given the message of the Lord, they went back to Jerusalem. On the way, they went through many Samaritan towns and preached the Good News to the people.

Philip Teaches an Ethiopian

[26]An angel of the Lord spoke to Philip.[n] The angel said, "Get ready

People Who Made Mistakes
SIMON THE SORCERER • ACTS 8:9-25

Some people think that money can buy everything—happiness, love, friends, or power. Simon felt this way. In Samaria, Peter and John were laying their hands on the believers so they could receive the Holy Spirit. When Simon saw the great things Peter and John were doing, he wanted to buy this amazing power.

But Peter scolded Simon for thinking this way. No one can buy God's power. And no one needs to! He gives it freely to everyone who believes in him.

To learn about a man who loved the world more than God, fly to page 1479.

[n]**laying their hands on** Here, doing this showed that these men were given a special work of God.
[n]**Philip** Not the apostle named Philip.

and go south. Go to the road that leads down to Gaza from Jerusalem—the desert road." [27]So Philip got ready and went. On the road he saw a man from Ethiopia, a eunuch.[d] He was an important officer in the service of Candace, the queen of the Ethiopians. He was responsible for taking care of all her money. He had gone to Jerusalem to worship, and [28]now he was on his way home. He was sitting in his chariot and reading from the book of Isaiah, the prophet.[d] [29]The Spirit[d] said to Philip, "Go to that chariot and stay near it."

[30]So Philip ran toward the chariot. He heard the man reading from Isaiah, the prophet. Philip asked, "Do you understand what you are reading?"

[31]He answered, "How can I understand? I need someone to explain it to me!" Then he invited Philip to climb in and sit with him. [32]The verse of Scripture[d] that he was reading was this:

"He was like a sheep being led to be killed.

He was quiet, as a sheep is quiet while its wool is being cut.

He said nothing.

[33] He was shamed and was treated unfairly.

He died without children to continue his family.

His life on earth has ended."

Isaiah 53:7-8

[34]The officer said to Philip, "Please tell me, who is the prophet talking about? Is he talking about himself or about someone else?" [35]Philip began to speak. He started with this same Scripture and told the man the Good News[d] about Jesus.

[36]While they were traveling down the road, they came to some water. The officer said, "Look! Here is water! What is stopping me from being baptized?" [37] [n] [38]Then the officer commanded the chariot to stop. Both Philip and the officer went down into the water, and Philip baptized him. [39]When they came up out of the water, the Spirit of the Lord took Philip away; the officer never saw him again. The officer continued on his way home, full of joy. [40]But Philip appeared in a city called Azotus and preached the Good News in all the towns on the way from Azotus to Caesarea.

Saul Is Converted

9 In Jerusalem Saul was still trying to frighten the followers of the Lord by saying he would kill them. So he went to the high priest [2]and asked him to write letters to the synagogues[d] in the city of Damascus. Saul wanted the high priest to give him the authority to find people in Damascus who were followers of Christ's Way. If he found any there, men or women, he would arrest them and bring them back to Jerusalem.

[3]So Saul went to Damascus. As he came near the city, a bright light from heaven suddenly flashed around him. [4]Saul fell to the ground. He heard a voice saying to him, "Saul, Saul! Why are you doing things against me?"

[5]Saul said, "Who are you, Lord?"

The voice answered, "I am Jesus. I am the One you are trying to hurt. [6]Get up now and go into the city. Someone there will tell you what you must do."

[7]The men traveling with Saul stood there, but they said nothing. They heard the voice, but they saw no one. [8]Saul got up from the ground. He opened his eyes, but he could not see. So the men with Saul took his hand and led him into Damascus. [9]For three days Saul could not see, and he did not eat or drink.

[10]There was a follower of Jesus in Damascus named Ananias. The Lord spoke to Ananias in a vision, "Ananias!"

Ananias answered, "Here I am, Lord."

[11]The Lord said to him, "Get up and go to the street called Straight Street. Find the house of Judas.[n] Ask for a man

[n]**Verse 37** Some late copies of Acts add verse 37: "Philip answered, 'If you believe with all your heart, you can.' The officer said, 'I believe that Jesus Christ is the Son of God.'"
[n]**Judas** This is not either of the apostles named Judas.

named Saul from the city of Tarsus. He is there now, praying. [12]Saul has seen a vision. In it a man named Ananias comes to him and lays his hands on him. Then he sees again."

[13]But Ananias answered, "Lord, many people have told me about this man and the terrible things he did to your people in Jerusalem. [14]Now he has come here to Damascus. The leading priests have given him the power to arrest everyone who worships you."

[15]But the Lord said to Ananias, "Go! I have chosen Saul for an important work. He must tell about me to non-Jews, to kings, and to the people of Israel. [16]I will show him how much he must suffer for my name."

[17]So Ananias went to the house of Judas. He laid his hands on Saul and said, "Brother Saul, the Lord Jesus sent me. He is the one you saw on the road on your way here. He sent me so that you can see again and be filled with the Holy Spirit."[d] [18]Immediately, something that looked like fish scales fell from Saul's eyes. He was able to see again! Then Saul got up and was baptized. [19]After eating some food, his strength returned.

Saul Preaches in Damascus

Saul stayed with the followers of Jesus in Damascus for a few days. [20]Soon he began to preach about Jesus in the synagogues,[d] saying, "Jesus is the Son of God!"

[21]All the people who heard him were amazed. They said, "This is the man who was in Jerusalem. He was trying to destroy those who trust in this name! He came here to do the same thing. He came here to arrest the followers of Jesus and take them back to the leading priests."

[22]But Saul became more and more powerful. His proofs that Jesus is the Christ[d] were so strong that the Jews in Damascus could not argue with him.

Saul Escapes from Damascus

[23]After many days, the Jews made plans to kill Saul. [24]They were watching

People Who Got Away

SAUL • ACTS 9:20-25

Saul (also called Paul) was a Jew who believed in God and tried to serve God with his whole heart. When he learned about Jews who believed in Jesus, he hated them because he thought they were wrecking his religion. One day, Saul traveled to the city of Damascus to try to capture some followers of Christ and bring them back to Jerusalem to be punished. But on the way, a miracle happened, and Saul became a believer himself! In fact, he began talking about Jesus right there in Damascus. This made the Jewish leaders angry. They made plans to kill Saul when he left Damascus. But some of Saul's friends helped him escape by lowering him in a basket tied with some ropes down through an opening in the city wall. Then Saul ran away in the darkness.

God had great work for Saul to do. God also has a plan for your life, and he will help you to do it.

To find out how many times Paul was able to escape from harm, fly to page 1426.

the city gates day and night. They wanted to kill him, but Saul learned about their plan. ²⁵One night some followers of Saul helped him leave the city. They lowered him in a basket through an opening in the city wall.

Saul in Jerusalem

²⁶Then Saul went to Jerusalem. He tried to join the group of followers, but they were all afraid of him. They did not believe that he was really a follower. ²⁷But Barnabas accepted Saul and took him to the apostles.*ᵈ* Barnabas told them that Saul had seen the Lord on the road. He explained how the Lord had spoken to Saul. Then he told them how boldly Saul had preached in the name of Jesus in Damascus.

²⁸And so Saul stayed with the followers. He went everywhere in Jerusalem, preaching boldly in the name of Jesus. ²⁹He would often talk and argue with the Jews who spoke Greek. But they were trying to kill him. ³⁰When the brothers learned about this, they took Saul to Caesarea. From there they sent him to Tarsus.

³¹The church everywhere in Judea, Galilee, and Samaria had a time of peace. With the help of the Holy Spirit,*ᵈ*

the group became stronger. The believers showed that they respected the Lord by the way they lived. Because of this, the group of believers grew larger and larger.

Peter Heals Aeneas

³²As Peter was traveling through all the area, he visited God's people who lived in Lydda. ³³There he met a paralyzed man named Aeneas. Aeneas had not been able to leave his bed for the past eight years. ³⁴Peter said to him, "Aeneas, Jesus Christ heals you. Stand up and make your bed!" Aeneas stood up immediately. ³⁵All the people living in Lydda and on the Plain of Sharon saw him. These people turned to the Lord.

Peter in Joppa

³⁶In the city of Joppa there was a follower named Tabitha. (Her Greek name, Dorcas, means "a deer.") She was always doing good and helping the poor. ³⁷While Peter was in Lydda, Tabitha became sick and died. Her body was washed and put in a room upstairs. ³⁸The followers in Joppa heard that Peter was in Lydda. (Lydda is near Joppa.) So they sent two men to Peter. They begged him, "Hurry, please come to us!" ³⁹Peter got ready and went with them. When he arrived, they took

Miracles from God

ACTS 9:36-42

It is sad when someone dies, especially if that person is a friend or someone we love. We miss that person.

When Dorcas died, the people in her town were sad because she was a kind person. They loved her dearly and would miss her and all the good things she did. But Peter prayed for her and God raised her from the dead. This miracle made the people very happy. It showed them that God has power over life and death.

As God's children we do not need to be afraid to die. Jesus has promised that we will go to heaven to live with him.

him to the upstairs room. All the widows stood around Peter, crying. They showed him the shirts and coats that Tabitha had made when she was still alive. ⁴⁰Peter sent everyone out of the room. He kneeled and prayed. Then he turned to the body and said, "Tabitha, stand up!" She opened her eyes, and when she saw Peter, she sat up. ⁴¹He gave her his hand and helped her up. Then he called the saints*ᵈ* and the widows into the room. He showed them Tabitha; she was alive! ⁴²People everywhere in Joppa learned about this, and many believed in the Lord. ⁴³Peter stayed in Joppa for many days with a man named Simon who was a leatherworker.

prayed to God often. ³One afternoon about three o'clock, Cornelius saw a vision clearly. In the vision an angel of God came to him and said, "Cornelius!"

⁴Cornelius stared at the angel. He became afraid and said, "What do you want, Lord?"

The angel said, "God has heard your prayers. He has seen what you give to the poor. And God remembers you. ⁵Send some men now to Joppa to bring back a man named Simon. Simon is also called Peter. ⁶Simon is staying with a man, also named Simon, who is a leatherworker. He has a house beside the sea." ⁷Then the angel who spoke to Cornelius left. Cornelius called two of his servants and a soldier. The soldier was a religious man who worked for Cornelius. ⁸Cornelius explained everything to these three men and sent them to Joppa.

Jobs in the Bible

TANNER • ACTS 9:43

Simon was a tanner. This meant that he made animal hides into leather. His job involved skinning dead animals and soaking the hides in a hot water bath prepared with bark from oak or hemlock trees. This gave the hides their rich color. Because Simon worked with dead animals, he was considered "unclean" by the Jews. That meant they should not have any contact with him because of his job. But Peter knew that God loves all people and that a job does not mean a person should not hear the gospel. So although Peter was a Jew, he stayed at Simon the tanner's home and shared the good news of Jesus with him.

To read about Paul's job, fly to page 1352.

Peter and Cornelius

10 At Caesarea there was a man named Cornelius. He was an officer in the Italian group of the Roman army. ²Cornelius was a religious man. He and all the other people who lived in his house worshiped the true God. He gave much of his money to the poor and

⁹The next day as they came near Joppa, Peter was going up to the roof*ⁿ* to pray. It was about noon. ¹⁰Peter was hungry and wanted to eat. But while the food was being prepared, he had a vision. ¹¹He saw heaven opened and something coming down. It looked like a big sheet being lowered to earth by its four corners. ¹²In it were all kinds of

*ⁿ***roof** In Bible times houses were built with flat roofs. The roof was used for drying things such as flax and fruit. And it was used as an extra room, as a place for worship and as a place to sleep in the animals, reptiles, and birds. [13]Then a voice said to Peter, "Get up, Peter; kill and eat."

man; he worships God. All the Jewish people respect him. The angel told Cornelius to ask you to his house so that he can hear what you have to say." [23]Peter asked the men to come in and spend the night.

People Who Depended on God
CORNELIUS • ACTS 10:1-8

Cornelius was an important man in the army of the Roman Empire. He was not like most Romans who worshiped idols. He loved and worshiped God. But Cornelius didn't know about Jesus, so God sent an angel who told Cornelius to send for Peter. Peter came and told Cornelius and his family how they could be saved from their sins by trusting in Jesus. They all believed and were saved!

When the church first began, most of the believers were Jewish. They didn't know that God also wanted to save people who were not Jewish (such as the Romans). So when God saved Cornelius and his family, who were Romans, the believers knew they should tell everyone about Jesus. God wants everyone to believe in Jesus. Have you trusted Jesus as your Savior?

[14]But Peter said, "No, Lord! I have never eaten food that is unholy or unclean."[d]

[15]But the voice said to him again, "God has made these things clean. Don't call them 'unholy'!" [16]This happened three times. Then the sheet was taken back to heaven.

[17]While Peter was wondering what this vision meant, the men Cornelius sent had found Simon's house. They were standing at the gate. [18]They asked, "Is Simon Peter staying here?"

[19]Peter was still thinking about the vision. But the Spirit[d] said to him, "Listen! Three men are looking for you. [20]Get up and go downstairs. Go with them and don't ask questions. I have sent them to you."

[21]So Peter went down to the men. He said, "I am the man you are looking for. Why did you come here?"

[22]They said, "A holy angel spoke to Cornelius, an army officer. He is a good

The next day Peter got ready and went with them. Some of the brothers from Joppa joined him. [24]On the following day they came to Caesarea. Cornelius was waiting for them. He had called together his relatives and close friends. [25]When Peter entered, Cornelius met him. He fell at Peter's feet and worshiped him. [26]But Peter helped him up, saying, "Stand up! I too am only a man." [27]Peter went on talking with Cornelius as they went inside. There Peter saw many people together. [28]He said, "You people understand that it is against our Jewish law for a Jew to associate with or visit anyone who is not a Jew. But God has shown me that I should not call any person 'unholy' or 'unclean.' [29]That is why I did not argue when I was asked to come here. Now, please tell me why you sent for me."

[30]Cornelius said, "Four days ago, I was praying in my house. It was at this same time—three o'clock in the

afternoon. Suddenly, there was a man standing before me wearing shining clothes. [31]He said, 'Cornelius! God has heard your prayer. He has seen what you give to the poor. And God remembers you. [32]So send some men to Joppa and ask Simon Peter to come. Peter is staying in the house of a man, also named Simon, who is a leatherworker. His house is beside the sea.' [33]So I sent for you immediately, and it was very good of you to come. Now we are all here before God to hear everything the Lord has commanded you to tell us."

Peter's Speech

[34]Peter began to speak: "I really understand now that to God every person is the same. [35]God accepts anyone who worships him and does what is right. It is not important what country a person comes from. [36]You know that God has sent his message to the people of Israel. That message is the Good News[d] that peace has come through Jesus Christ. Jesus is the Lord of all people! [37]You know what has happened all over Judea. It began in Galilee after John[n] preached to the people about baptism. [38]You know about Jesus from Nazareth. God made him the Christ[d] by giving him the Holy Spirit[d] and power. You know how Jesus went everywhere doing good. He healed those who were ruled by the devil, for God was with Jesus. [39]We saw all the things that Jesus did in Judea and in Jerusalem. But they killed him by nailing him to a cross. [40]Yet, on the third day, God raised Jesus to life and caused him to be seen. [41]But he was not seen by all the people. Only the witnesses that God had already chosen saw him, and we are those witnesses. We ate and drank with him after he was raised from death. [42]He told us to preach to the people and to tell them that he is the one whom God chose to be the judge of the living and the dead. [43]Everyone who

believes in Jesus will be forgiven. God will forgive his sins through Jesus. All the prophets[d] say this is true."

Non-Jews Receive the Holy Spirit

[44]While Peter was still saying this, the Holy Spirit[d] came down on all those who were listening. [45]The Jewish believers who came with Peter were amazed that the gift of the Holy Spirit had been given even to the non-Jewish people. [46]These Jewish believers heard them speaking in different languages[n] and praising God. Then Peter said, [47]"Can anyone keep these people from being baptized with water? They have received the Holy Spirit just as we did!" [48]So Peter ordered that they be baptized in the name of Jesus Christ. Then they asked Peter to stay with them for a few days.

Peter Returns to Jerusalem

11 The apostles[d] and the believers in Judea heard that non-Jewish people had accepted God's teaching too. [2]But when Peter came to Jerusalem, some Jewish believers argued with him. [3]They said, "You went into the homes of people who are not Jews and are not circumcised![d] You even ate with them!"

[4]So Peter explained the whole story to them. [5]He said, "I was in the city of Joppa. While I was praying, I had a vision. In the vision, I saw something which looked like a big sheet coming down from heaven. It was being lowered to earth by its four corners. It came down very close to me, and [6]I looked inside it. I saw animals, wild beasts, reptiles, and birds. [7]I heard a voice say to me, 'Get up, Peter. Kill and eat.' [8]But I said, 'No, Lord! I have never eaten anything that is unholy or unclean.'[d] [9]But the voice from heaven answered again, 'God has made these things clean. Don't call them unholy!' [10]This happened three times. Then the whole thing was taken back to heaven.

---

[n]**John**   John the Baptist, who preached to people about Christ's coming (Matthew 3, Luke 3).
[n]**languages**   This can also be translated "tongues."

¹¹Right then three men came to the house where I was staying. They were sent to me from Caesarea. ¹²The Spirit*d* told me to go with them without doubting. These six believers here also went with me. We went to the house of Cornelius. ¹³He told us about the angel he saw standing in his house. The angel said to him, 'Send some men to Joppa and invite Simon Peter to come. ¹⁴He will speak to you. The things he will say will save you and all your family.' ¹⁵When I began my speech, the Holy Spirit came on them just as he came on us at the beginning. ¹⁶Then I remembered the words of the Lord. He said, 'John baptized in water, but you will be baptized in the Holy Spirit!' ¹⁷God gave to them the same gift that he gave to us who believed in the Lord Jesus Christ. So could I stop the work of God? No!"

¹⁸When the Jewish believers heard this, they stopped arguing. They praised God and said, "So God is allowing the non-Jewish people also to turn to him and live."

The Good News Comes to Antioch

¹⁹Many of the believers were scattered by the terrible things that happened after Stephen was killed. Some of them went to places as far away as Phoenicia, Cyprus, and Antioch. They were telling the message to others, but only to Jews. ²⁰Some of these believers were men from Cyprus and Cyrene. When they came to Antioch, they spoke also to Greeks, telling them the Good News*d* about the Lord Jesus. ²¹The Lord was helping the believers. And a large group of people believed and turned to the Lord.

²²The church in Jerusalem heard about all of this, so they sent Barnabas to Antioch. ²³⁻²⁴Barnabas was a good man, full of the Holy Spirit*d* and full of faith. When he reached Antioch and saw how God had blessed the people, he was glad. He encouraged all the believers in Antioch. He told them, "Never lose your faith. Always obey the Lord with all your hearts." Many people became followers of the Lord.

²⁵Then Barnabas went to the city of Tarsus to look for Saul. ²⁶When he found Saul, he brought him to Antioch. And for a whole year Saul and

Touring Bible Lands
ANTIOCH • ACTS 11:26

Antioch was called the Beautiful and Golden City. It was built on a river just a few miles from the Mediterranean Sea in a broad and fertile valley. It was surrounded by tall, snow-capped mountains.

This was the first place that people who believed in Jesus were called Christians or people who belong to Christ. They were not always called Christians because at first most of the people who believed were Jewish. But these Jewish people traveled to other places like Antioch to tell people who were not Jewish about Jesus. The people in these other cities believed too.

Many different kinds of people believe in Jesus today. They are all Christians!

Fly west from Antioch over a large sea on page 1340.

Barnabas met with the church. They taught many people there. In Antioch the followers were called Christians for the first time.

²⁷About that time some prophets^d came from Jerusalem to Antioch. ²⁸One of them was named Agabus. He stood up and spoke with the help of the Holy Spirit. He said, "A very hard time is coming to the whole world. There will be no food for people to eat." (This happened when Claudius ruled.) ²⁹The followers all decided to help their brothers who lived in Judea. Each one planned to send them as much as he could. ³⁰They gathered the money and gave it to Barnabas and Saul, who brought it to the elders^d in Judea.

Herod Agrippa Hurts the Church

12 During that same time King Herod began to do terrible things to some who belonged to the church. ²He ordered James, the brother of John, to be killed by the sword. ³Herod saw that the Jews liked this, so he decided to arrest Peter, too. (This happened during the time of the Feast^d of Unleavened Bread.)

⁴After Herod arrested Peter, he put him in jail and handed him over to be guarded by 16 soldiers. Herod planned to bring Peter before the people for trial after the Passover^d Feast. ⁵So Peter was kept in jail. But the church kept on praying to God for him.

Peter Leaves the Jail

⁶The night before Herod was to bring him to trial, Peter was sleeping. He was between two soldiers, bound with two chains. Other soldiers were guarding the door of the jail. ⁷Suddenly, an angel of the Lord stood there. A light shined in the room. The angel touched Peter on the side and woke him up. The angel said, "Hurry! Get up!" And the chains fell off Peter's hands. ⁸The angel said to him, "Get dressed and put on your sandals." And so Peter did this. Then the angel said, "Put on your coat and follow me." ⁹So the angel went out, and Peter followed him. Peter did not know if what the angel was doing was real. He thought he might be seeing a vision. ¹⁰They went past the first and the second guard. They came to the iron gate that separated them from the city. The

Plans That Backfired

HEROD AGRIPPA • ACTS 12

What would you do if you were expecting a visit from the President of the United States? Hopefully you would at least clean your room! The people in this city were excited to have King Herod Agrippa visit their city. The king put on his royal robes, sat on his throne, and gave them a speech. The people were really impressed by the king. They thought he was a god.

Being called a god was just what the king liked to hear. But God knew that Herod was really evil. In fact, Herod had killed one of Jesus' followers and put another one in prison. Just when Herod planned on living like a god, God punished him. Immediately after his speech, the king was struck with a terrible disease. He died within one week.

Sometimes pride can make us think more highly of ourselves than we should. Remember God's plan for us is to be humble.

gate opened itself for them. They went through the gate and walked down a street. And the angel suddenly left him.

[11] Then Peter realized what had happened. He thought, "Now I know that the Lord really sent his angel to me. He rescued me from Herod and from all the things the Jewish people thought would happen."

[12] When he realized this, he went to the home of Mary. She was the mother of John. (John was also called Mark.) Many people were gathered there, praying. [13] Peter knocked on the outside door. A servant girl named Rhoda came to answer it. [14] She recognized Peter's voice, and she was very happy. She even forgot to open the door. She ran inside and told the group, "Peter is at the door!"

[15] They said to her, "You are crazy!" But she kept on saying that it was true. So they said, "It must be Peter's angel."

[16] Peter continued to knock. When they opened the door, they saw him and were amazed. [17] Peter made a sign with his hand to tell them to be quiet. He explained how the Lord led him out of the jail. And he said, "Tell James and the other believers what happened."

Then he left to go to another place.

[18] The next day the soldiers were very upset. They wondered what had happened to Peter. [19] Herod looked everywhere for Peter but could not find him. So he questioned the guards and ordered that they be killed.

The Death of Herod Agrippa

Later Herod moved from Judea and went to the city of Caesarea, where he stayed for a while. [20] Herod was very angry with the people of Tyre and Sidon. But the people of those cities all came in a group to Herod. They were able to get Blastus, the king's personal servant, on their side. They asked Herod for peace because their country got its food from his country.

[21] On a chosen day Herod put on his royal robes. He sat on his throne and made a speech to the people. [22] They shouted, "This is the voice of a god, not a man!" [23] Herod did not give the glory to God. So an angel of the Lord caused him to become sick. He was eaten by worms and died.

[24] God's message continued to spread and reach more and more people.

[25] After Barnabas and Saul finished their task in Jerusalem, they returned to Antioch. John, also called Mark, was with them.

Visiting Angels
ACTS 12:7-10

One time an angel freed Peter from prison. Peter had been arrested for teaching about Jesus. He was put in prison, chained by his wrists and his feet between two soldiers. King Herod wanted to make sure that Peter could not escape. But no king or soldier is more powerful than God.

During the night, while everyone was asleep, an angel woke Peter up. The angel told Peter what to do, and then walked him out of the prison! Peter must have thought he was dreaming. But then the angel left and he realized he was standing in the street outside the prison! God had more work for Peter to do, and no prison was going to stop him.

To read about angels singing in heaven, fly to page 1542.

Barnabas and Saul Are Chosen

13 In the church at Antioch there were these prophets[d] and teachers: Barnabas, Simeon (also called Niger), Lucius (from the city of Cyrene), Manaen (who had grown up with Herod, the ruler) and Saul. [2]They were all worshiping the Lord and giving up eating.[n] The Holy Spirit[d] said to them, "Give Barnabas and Saul to me

of God in the Jewish synagogues.[d] John Mark was with them to help.
[6]They went across the whole island to Paphos. In Paphos they met a Jew who was a magician. His name was Bar-Jesus. He was a false prophet,[d] [7]who always stayed close to Sergius Paulus, the governor. Sergius Paulus was a smart man. He asked Barnabas and Saul to come to him, because he wanted to hear the message of God. [8]But Elymas, the magician, was against them. (Elymas is the name for Bar-Jesus in the Greek language.) He tried

Unsung Heroes
RHODA • ACTS 12:13-14

If it hadn't been for Rhoda, Peter might have been standing outside Mary's house for a long time! Peter had been in prison because he was preaching about Jesus. All the Christians were worried about Peter and were afraid that they might be put in prison too. So they were together in Mary's house, praying that God would take care of Peter. While they prayed, Peter arrived at the door. Rhoda was a servant in Mary's house, so she answered the door. When she told the others that Peter was at the door, no one believed her! Fortunately, they went to check for themselves and let Peter in. Their prayers had been answered!

Rhoda helped Peter and she helped the other Christians. Can you think of ways to help others?

To read about a jailer who learned from his prisoners, fly to page 1348.

to do a special work. I have chosen them for it."
[3]So they gave up eating and prayed. They laid their hands on[n] Barnabas and Saul and sent them out.

Barnabas and Saul in Cyprus

[4]Barnabas and Saul were sent out by the Holy Spirit.[d] They went to the city of Seleucia. From there they sailed to the island of Cyprus. [5]When they came to Salamis, they preached the Good News[d]

to stop the governor from believing in Jesus. [9]But Saul was filled with the Holy Spirit. (Saul's other name was Paul.) He looked straight at Elymas [10]and said, "You son of the devil! You are an enemy of everything that is right! You are full of evil tricks and lies. You are always trying to change the Lord's truths into lies! [11]Now the Lord will touch you, and you will be blind. For a time you will not be able to see anything—not even the light from the sun."

[n]**giving up eating** This is called "fasting." The people would give up eating for a special time of prayer and worship to God. It was also done to show sadness.
[n]**laid their hands on** Here, this was a sign to show that these men were given a special work of God.

Then everything became dark for Elymas. He walked around, trying to find someone to lead him by the hand. [12]When the governor saw this, he believed. He was amazed at the teaching about the Lord.

"**O**ur church has missionaries in other countries. We help them as they tell others about Jesus. Do you know who the first missionaries were? Find out in Acts 13:1-12."

Paul and Barnabas Leave Cyprus

[13]Paul and those with him sailed away from Paphos. They came to Perga, in Pamphylia. But John Mark left them and returned to Jerusalem. [14]They continued their trip from Perga and went to Antioch, a city in Pisidia. On the Sabbath[d] day they went into the synagogue[d] and sat down. [15]The law of Moses and the writings of the prophets[d] were read. Then the leaders of the synagogue sent a message to Paul and Barnabas: "Brothers, if you have any message that will encourage the people, please speak!"

[16]Paul stood up. He raised his hand and said, "Men of Israel and you other people who worship God, please listen! [17]The God of the people of Israel chose our ancestors. He made the people great during the time they lived in Egypt. He brought them out of that country with great power. [18]And he was patient with them for 40 years in the desert. [19]God destroyed seven nations in the land of Canaan and gave the land to his people. [20]All this happened in about 450 years.

"After this, God gave them judges until the time of Samuel the prophet. [21]Then the people asked for a king. God gave them Saul son of Kish. Saul was from the tribe[d] of Benjamin. He was king for 40 years. [22]After God took him away, God made David their king. This is what God said about him: 'I have found David son of Jesse. He is the kind of man I want. He will do all that I want him to do.' [23]So God has brought one of David's descendants[d] to Israel to be

Touring Bible Lands

THE MEDITERRANEAN SEA • ACTS 13:4

People in Bible times called the Mediterranean Sea the Great Sea. This sea formed one of the borders of Canaan. And Jonah was swallowed by a whale in this sea. The Mediterranean Sea was an important trade route for ships that carried products like cedar logs to sell between cities.

Paul traveled across the Mediterranean Sea on his missionary journeys. In fact, he probably swam in the sea when his ship was wrecked near the Island of Crete. Many people who lived around the sea heard about Jesus and believed in him.

Would you like to be a missionary and travel on a boat?

Fly north from the Mediterranean Sea to an important city in Italy on page 1370.

their Savior.*d* That descendant is Jesus. And God promised to do this. [24]Before Jesus came, John[n] preached to all the people of Israel. He told them about a baptism of changed hearts and lives. [25]When he was finishing his work, he said, 'Who do you think I am? I am not the Christ.*d* He is coming later. I am not worthy to untie his sandals.'

[26]"Brothers, sons in the family of Abraham, and you non-Jews who worship God, listen! The news about this salvation has been sent to us. [27]Those who live in Jerusalem and their leaders did not realize that Jesus was the Savior. They did not understand the words that the prophets wrote, which are read every Sabbath*d* day. But they made them come true when they said Jesus was guilty. [28]They could not find any real reason for Jesus to die, but they asked Pilate to have him killed. [29]They did to him all that the Scriptures*d* had said. Then they took him down from the cross and laid him in a tomb. [30]But God raised him up from death! [31]After this, for many days, the people who had gone with Jesus from Galilee to Jerusalem saw him. They are now his witnesses to the people. [32]We tell you the Good News*d* about the promise God made to our ancestors. [33]We are their children, and God has made this promise come true for us. God did this by raising Jesus from death. We read about this also in Psalm 2:

'You are my Son.

Today I have become your Father.'
Psalm 2:7

[34]God raised Jesus from death. He will never go back to the grave and become dust. So God said:

'I will give you the holy and sure
      blessings

   that I promised to David.' *Isaiah 55:3*

[35]But in another place God says:

'You will not let your Holy One
   rot in the grave.'   *Psalm 16:10*

[36]David did God's will during his lifetime. Then he died and was buried with his fathers. And his body did rot in the grave! [37]But the One God raised from death did not rot in the grave. [38-39]Brothers, you must understand what we are telling you: You can have forgiveness of your sins through Jesus. The law of Moses could not free you from your sins. But everyone who believes is free from all sins through him. [40]Be careful! Don't let what the prophets said happen to you:

[41]'Listen, you people who doubt!

   You can wonder, and then die.

I will do something in your lifetime
      that will amaze you.

   You won't believe it even when you
      are told about it!'" *Habakkuk 1:5*

[42]While Paul and Barnabas were leaving the synagogue, the people asked them to tell them more about these things on the next Sabbath. [43]After the meeting, many Jews followed Paul and Barnabas from that place. With the Jews there were many who had changed to the Jewish religion and worshiped God. Paul and Barnabas were persuading them to continue trusting in God's kindness.

[44]On the next Sabbath day, almost all the people in the city came to hear the word of the Lord. [45]Seeing the crowd, the Jews became very jealous. They said insulting things and argued against what Paul said. [46]But Paul and Barnabas spoke very boldly. They said, "We must speak the message of God to you first. But you refuse to listen. You are judging yourselves not worthy of having eternal life! So we will now go to the people of other nations! [47]This is what the Lord told us to do. The Lord said:

'I have made you a light for the non-Jewish nations.

   You will show people all over the
      world the way to be saved.'"
Isaiah 49:6

[48]When the non-Jewish people heard Paul say this, they were happy. They gave honor to the message of the Lord. And many of the people believed the

---

[n]**John**   John the Baptist, who preached to people about Christ's coming (Matthew 3, Luke 3).

message. They were the ones chosen to have life forever.

⁴⁹And so the message of the Lord was spreading through the whole country. ⁵⁰But the Jews stirred up some of the important religious women and the leaders of the city against Paul and Barnabas. They started trouble against Paul and Barnabas and drove them out of their area. ⁵¹So Paul and Barnabas shook the dust off their feet[n] and went to Iconium. ⁵²But the followers were filled with joy and the Holy Spirit.[d]

Paul and Barnabas in Iconium

14 In Iconium, Paul and Barnabas went as usual to the Jewish synagogue.[d] They spoke so well that a great many Jews and Greeks believed. ²But some of the Jews who did not believe excited the non-Jewish people and turned them against the believers. ³But Paul and Barnabas stayed in Iconium a long time and spoke bravely for the Lord. The Lord showed that their message about his grace was true by giving them the power to work miracles[d] and signs. ⁴But some of the people in the city agreed with the Jews. Others believed the apostles.[d] So the city was divided.

⁵Some non-Jewish people, some Jews, and some of their rulers wanted to harm Paul and Barnabas by killing them with stones. ⁶When Paul and Barnabas learned about this, they went to Lystra and Derbe, cities in Lycaonia, and to the areas around those cities. ⁷They announced the Good News[d] there, too.

Paul in Lystra and Derbe

⁸In Lystra there sat a man who had been born crippled; he had never walked. ⁹This man was listening to Paul speak. Paul looked straight at him and saw that the man believed God could heal him. ¹⁰So he cried out, "Stand up on your feet!" The man jumped up

and began walking around. ¹¹When the crowds saw what Paul did, they shouted in their own Lycaonian language. They said, "The gods have become like men! They have come down to us!" ¹²And the people began to call Barnabas "Zeus."[n] They called Paul "Hermes,"[n] because he was the main speaker. ¹³The temple of Zeus was near the city. The priest of this temple brought some bulls and flowers to the city gates. The priest and the people wanted to offer a sacrifice to Paul and Barnabas. ¹⁴But when the apostles,[d] Barnabas and Paul, understood what they were about to do, they tore their clothes in anger. Then they ran in among the people and shouted, ¹⁵"Men, why are you doing these things? We are only men, human beings like you! We are bringing you the Good News.[d] We are telling you to turn away from these worthless things and turn to the true living God. He is the One who made the sky, the earth, the sea, and everything that is in them. ¹⁶In the past, God let all the nations do what they wanted. ¹⁷Yet he did things to prove he is real: He shows kindness to you. He gives you rain from heaven and crops at the right times. He gives you food and fills your hearts with joy." ¹⁸Even with these words, they were barely able to keep the crowd from offering sacrifices to them.

¹⁹Then some Jews came from Antioch and Iconium. They persuaded the people to turn against Paul. And so they threw stones at Paul and dragged him out of town. They thought that they had killed him. ²⁰But the followers gathered around him, and he got up and went back into the town. The next day, he and Barnabas left and went to the city of Derbe.

The Return to Antioch in Syria

²¹Paul and Barnabas told the Good News[d] in Derbe and many became followers. Paul and Barnabas returned to

---

*n***shook . . . feet** A warning. It showed that they were finished talking to these people.
*n***"Zeus"** The Greeks believed in many gods. Zeus was their most important god.
*n***"Hermes"** The Greeks believed he was a messenger for the other gods.

Lystra, Iconium, and Antioch. 22In those cities they made the followers of Jesus stronger. They helped them to stay in the faith. They said, "We must suffer many things to enter God's kingdom." 23They chose elders[d] for each church, by praying and giving up eating.[n] These elders were men who had trusted the Lord. So Paul and Barnabas put them in the Lord's care.

24Then they went through Pisidia and came to Pamphylia. 25They preached the message in Perga, and then they went down to Attalia. 26And from there they sailed away to Antioch. This is where the believers had put them into God's care and had sent them out to do this work. And now they had finished the work.

27When they arrived in Antioch, they gathered the church together. Paul and Barnabas told them all about what God had done with them. They told how God had made it possible for the non-Jews to believe! 28And they stayed there a long time with the followers.

The Meeting at Jerusalem

15 Then some men came to Antioch from Judea. They began teaching the non-Jewish brothers: "You cannot be saved if you are not circumcised.[d] Moses taught us to do this."

"**E**ven the first Christians had to get together and talk about their problems. What problem does Acts 15:1-21 tell about?"

2Paul and Barnabas were against this teaching and argued with the men about it. So the group decided to send Paul, Barnabas, and some other men to Jerusalem. There they could talk more about this with the apostles[d] and elders.[d]

3The church helped the men leave on the trip. They went through the countries of Phoenicia and Samaria, telling all about how the non-Jewish people had turned to God. This made all the believers very happy. 4When they arrived in Jerusalem, the apostles, the elders, and the church welcomed them. Paul, Barnabas, and the others told about all the things that God had done with them. 5But some of the believers who had belonged to the Pharisee[d] group came forward. They said, "The non-Jewish believers must be circumcised. We must tell them to obey the law of Moses!"

6The apostles and the elders gathered to study this problem. 7There was a long debate. Then Peter stood up and said to them, "Brothers, you know what happened in the early days. God chose me from among you to preach the Good News[d] to the non-Jewish people. They heard the Good News from me, and they believed. 8God, who knows the thoughts of all men, accepted them. He showed this to us by giving them the Holy Spirit,[d] just as he did to us. 9To God, those people are not different from us. When they believed, he made their hearts pure. 10So now why are you testing God? You are putting a heavy load around the necks of the non-Jewish brothers. It is a load that neither we nor our fathers were able to carry. 11But we believe that we and they too will be saved by the grace of the Lord Jesus!"

12Then the whole group became quiet. They listened to Paul and Barnabas speak. Paul and Barnabas told about all the miracles[d] and signs that God did through them among the non-Jewish people. 13After they finished speaking, James spoke. He said, "Brothers, listen to me. 14Simon has told us how God showed his love for the non-Jewish people. For the first time he has accepted them and made them his people. 15The words of the

---

[n]**giving up eating** This is called "fasting." The people would give up eating for a special time of prayer and worship to God. It was also done to show sadness.

prophets[d] agree with this too:

[16]'After these things I will return.
   The kingdom of David is like a
      fallen tent.
   But I will rebuild it.
   And I will again build its ruins.
   And I will set it up.
[17]Then those people who are left alive
      may ask the Lord for help.
   And all people from other nations
      may worship me,
   says the Lord.
   And he will make it happen.
[18] And these things have been
      known for a long time.'
                              Amos 9:11-12

[19]"So I think we should not bother the non-Jewish brothers who have turned to God. [20]Instead, we should write a letter to them. We should tell them these things: Do not eat food that has been offered to idols. (This makes the food unclean.[d]) Do not take part in any kind of sexual sin. Do not taste blood. Do not eat animals that have been strangled. [21]They should not do these things, because there are still men in every city who teach the law of Moses. For a long time the words of Moses have been read in the synagogue[d] every Sabbath[d] day."

Letter to Non-Jewish Believers

[22]The apostles,[d] the elders,[d] and the whole church decided to send some of their men with Paul and Barnabas to Antioch. They chose Judas Barsabbas and Silas, who were respected by the believers. [23]They sent the following letter with them:

From the apostles and elders, your brothers.

To all the non-Jewish brothers in Antioch, Syria and Cilicia:

Dear Brothers,

[24]We have heard that some of our men have come to you and said things that trouble and upset you. But we did not tell them to do this! [25]We have all agreed to choose some men and send

them to you. They will be with our dear friends Barnabas and Paul— [26]men who have given their lives to serve our Lord Jesus Christ. [27]So we have sent Judas and Silas with them. They will tell you the same things. [28]It has pleased the Holy Spirit[d] that you should not have a heavy load to carry, and we agree. You need to do only these things: [29]Do not eat any food that has been offered to idols. Do not taste blood. Do not eat any animals that have been strangled. Do not take part in any kind of sexual sin. If you stay away from these things, you will do well.

Good-bye.

[30]So the men left Jerusalem and went to Antioch. There they gathered the church and gave them the letter. [31]When they read it, they were very happy because of the encouraging letter. [32]Judas and Silas were also prophets,[d] who said many things to encourage the believers and make them stronger. [33]After some time Judas and Silas were sent off in peace by the believers. They went back to those who had sent them. [34] [n]

[35]But Paul and Barnabas stayed in Antioch. They and many others preached the Good News[d] and taught the people the message of the Lord.

Paul and Barnabas Separate

[36]After some time, Paul said to Barnabas, "We preached the message of the Lord in many towns. We should go back to all those towns to visit the believers and see how they are doing." [37]Barnabas wanted to take John Mark with them too. [38]But John Mark had left them at Pamphylia; he did not continue with them in the work. So Paul did not think it was a good idea to take him. [39]Paul and Barnabas had a serious argument about this. They separated and went different ways. Barnabas sailed to Cyprus and took Mark with him. [40]But Paul chose Silas and left. The believers in Antioch put Paul into

[n]**Verse 34** Some Greek copies add verse 34: ". . .but Silas decided to remain there."

the Lord's care. ⁴¹And he went through Syria and Cilicia, giving strength to the churches.

Timothy Goes with Paul and Silas

16 Paul came to Derbe and Lystra. A follower named Timothy was there. Timothy's mother was Jewish and a believer. His father was a Greek. ²The brothers in Lystra and Iconium respected Timothy and said good things about him. ³Paul wanted Timothy to travel with him. But all the Jews living in that area knew that Timothy's father was Greek. So Paul circumcised*d* Timothy to please the Jews. ⁴Paul and the men with him traveled from town to town. They gave the decisions made by the apostles*d* and elders*d* in Jerusalem for the people to obey. ⁵So the churches became stronger in the faith and grew larger every day.

Paul Is Called Out of Asia

⁶Paul and the men with him went through the areas of Phrygia and Galatia. The Holy Spirit*d* did not let them preach the Good News*d* in the country of Asia. ⁷When they came near the country of Mysia, they tried to go into Bithynia. But the Spirit of Jesus did not let them. ⁸So they passed by Mysia and went to Troas. ⁹That night Paul had a vision. In the vision, a man from Macedonia came to him. The man stood there and begged, "Come over to Macedonia. Help us!" ¹⁰After Paul had seen the vision, we immediately prepared to leave for Macedonia. We understood that God had called us to tell the Good News to those people.

Lydia Becomes a Christian

¹¹We left Troas in a ship, and we sailed straight to the island of Samothrace. The next day we sailed to Neapolis.*n* ¹²Then we went by land to Philippi, the leading city in that part of Macedonia. It is also a Roman colony.*n* We stayed there for several days.

¹³On the Sabbath*d* day we went outside the city gate to the river. There we thought we would find a special place for prayer. Some women had gathered there, so we sat down and talked with them. ¹⁴There was a woman named Lydia from the city of Thyatira. Her job was selling purple cloth. She worshiped the true God. The Lord

Women Who Trusted God
LYDIA • ACTS 16:14

Lydia was a businesswoman who sold purple cloth. The purple cloth was made by dyeing cloth with a rare and expensive dye. Usually only kings or wealthy people wore purple clothing. One day Lydia and some other women were worshiping God beside the river in Philippi. Paul and Silas went down to the river and told the women about Jesus. Lydia listened to what they said and wanted to believe in Jesus.

Like Lydia, you can open your heart and accept salvation. All you have to do is ask Jesus to forgive you for your sins and believe in him. Have you believed in Jesus?

To meet a woman who helped Paul, fly to page 1395.

To meet a woman who helped Paul, fly to page 1395.

---

*ⁿ***Neapolis** City in Macedonia. It was the first city Paul visited on the continent of Europe.
*ⁿ***Roman colony** A town begun by Romans with Roman laws, customs and privileges.

Whit's Wisdom: Singing to God • Acts 16:16-34

One day after school I noticed that Jessie was sitting by herself. She looked sad. I wandered over and asked if she was all right.

"Mr. Whittaker," she began, almost crying, "Dylan heard me singing in the shower this morning and teased me all day. He said Mom and Dad almost called an ambulance because they thought I had fallen in the bathroom and was hurt! At first we all laughed, but later I started feeling sad. Maybe I can't sing."

"Let me show you something," I said. I called Sherman the dog over and then began to sing "My Bonnie Lies Over the Ocean." When I got to "ocean," Sherman began to howl loudly. Jessie smiled and then laughed. That got me laughing, too. "Sherman always lets me know what he thinks of my singing," I said. "Now Jessie, I can carry a tune, but I'm not a great singer. In fact, most of us are really not great singers, but all of us can sing well! We can have fun doing it. Remember, the Bible doesn't say, "Sing to the Lord if you're a good singer." It says "Sing to him" (Psalm 105:2).

"But what's the use of singing if you're not a good singer?" said Jessie, still looking a little sad.

"Well, what were you singing and how were you feeling before Dylan teased you?" I asked.

"I was singing a song we learned in church last week, and I was feeling really happy!"

"Then I guess I would have to say that Dylan had fun teasing you, but he would have had more fun singing along with you. Songs are one of the best ways we have to tell God how we feel. Songs can even be a special way to talk to God. There are lots of examples in the Bible. Let me show you one."

We opened a Bible to this page (Acts 16:16-34) and read the story about Paul and Silas stuck in a dark, dank, dingy dungeon. Something pretty exciting happened while they were singing in the middle of the night! Read it yourself.

Afterwards, we talked about the way God can help us when we sing to him. Jessie said, "Well, if those guys could sing in a yucky place like that, then I can sing in the shower! Even if Dylan doesn't think I sound so good."

Related passages: Psalm 98, Colossians 3:16-17.

Teacher/Parent Hint: Whether or not your group are singers, encourage them to sing several simple songs together.

opened her mind to pay attention to what Paul was saying. [15]She and all the people in her house were baptized. Then Lydia invited us to her home. She said, "If you think I am truly a believer in the Lord, then come stay in my house." And she persuaded us to stay with her.

Paul and Silas in Jail

[16]Once, while we were going to the place for prayer, a servant girl met us. She had a special spirit[n] in her. She earned a lot of money for her owners by telling fortunes. [17]This girl followed Paul and us. She said loudly, "These men are servants of the Most High God! They are telling you how you can be saved!"

[18]She kept this up for many days. This bothered Paul, so he turned and said to the spirit, "By the power of Jesus Christ, I command you to come out of her!" Immediately, the spirit came out.

[19]The owners of the servant girl saw this. These men knew that now they could not use her to make money. So they grabbed Paul and Silas and dragged them before the city rulers in the marketplace. [20]Here they brought Paul and Silas to the Roman rulers and said, "These men are Jews and are making trouble in our city. [21]They are teaching things that are not right for us as Romans to do."

[22]The crowd joined the attack against them. The Roman officers tore the clothes of Paul and Silas and had them beaten with rods again and again. [23]Then Paul and Silas were thrown into

Salvation
ACTS 16:25-31

Suppose you are very sick, and someone comes to you and says, "I have the cure for your sickness right here. Do you want it?" What would you say?

"**O**f course I want it! What do I have to do to get it?" You would do anything or pay any amount of money for the medicine, because without it, you would die.

Then the person says, "You don't have to *do* anything. You cannot buy it, either. All I ask is that you *believe* that I have the cure."

"**T**hat's it? Just *believe*?" you ask.

"**T**hat's it," the person answers. "What do you say?"

The jailer who felt the earthquake and saw Paul and Silas released from their chains realized that he too was sick. His problem was sin. Sin is the fatal disease that infects every person who has ever lived. These verses in Acts tell us that the only cure is to believe in the Lord Jesus Christ. We cannot heal ourselves or find another treatment. All we have to do is believe in Jesus, and we can be saved.

What do you say?

To learn more about salvation, zoom to page 1375.

---

[n]**spirit** This was a spirit from the devil. It caused her to say she had special knowledge.

jail. The jailer was ordered to guard them carefully. ²⁴When he heard this order, he put them far inside the jail. He pinned down their feet between large blocks of wood.

²⁵About midnight Paul and Silas were praying and singing songs to God. The other prisoners were listening to them. ²⁶Suddenly, there was a big earthquake. It was so strong that it shook the foundation of the jail. Then all the doors of the jail broke open. All the prisoners were freed from their chains. ²⁷The jailer woke up and saw that the jail doors were open. He thought that the prisoners had already escaped. So he got his sword and was about to kill himself." ²⁸But Paul shouted, "Don't hurt yourself! We are all here!"

²⁹The jailer told someone to bring a light. Then he ran inside. Shaking with fear, he fell down before Paul and Silas. ³⁰Then he brought them outside and said, "Men, what must I do to be saved?"

³¹They said to him, "Believe in the Lord Jesus and you will be saved—you and all the people in your house." ³²So Paul and Silas told the message of the Lord to the jailer and all the people in his house. ³³At that hour of the night the jailer took Paul and Silas and washed their wounds. Then he and all his people were baptized immediately. ³⁴After this the jailer took Paul and Silas home and gave them food. He and his family were very happy because they now believed in God.

³⁵The next morning, the Roman officers sent the police to tell the jailer, "Let these men go free!"

³⁶The jailer said to Paul, "The officers have sent an order to let you go free. You can leave now. Go in peace."

³⁷But Paul said to the police, "They beat us in public without a trial, even though we are Roman citizens." And they threw us in jail. Now they want to make us go away quietly. No! Let them come themselves and bring us out!"

³⁸The police told the Roman officers what Paul said. When the officers heard

Unsung Heroes
PHILIPPIAN JAILER • ACTS 16:25-34

The Philippian jailer acted courageously. Paul and Silas were beaten and thrown in prison in the city of Philippi because they taught about Jesus. The jailer was supposed to make sure that prisoners didn't escape. If a prisoner got away, the jailer could be killed for it.

God wanted to free Paul and Silas. He caused an earthquake to shake the prison, but none of the prisoners ran away. Instead, Paul and Silas told the jailer about Jesus. The jailer believed in Jesus. Then he washed the scratches and cuts on the prisoners' backs.

The jailer was glad that he had learned about Jesus from two of his prisoners. Like Paul and Silas, we should always be ready to tell people about Jesus.

To read about a young boy who saved his uncle's life, fly to page 1361.

"**kill himself** He thought the leaders would kill him for letting the prisoners escape.
"**Roman citizens** Roman law said that Roman citizens must not be beaten before they had a trial.

that Paul and Silas were Roman citizens, they were afraid. ³⁹So they came and told Paul and Silas they were sorry. They took Paul and Silas out of jail and asked them to leave the city. ⁴⁰So when they came out of the jail, they went to Lydia's house. There they saw some of the believers and encouraged them. Then they left.

Paul and Silas in Thessalonica

17 Paul and Silas traveled through Amphipolis and Apollonia and came to Thessalonica. In that city there was a Jewish synagogue.ᵈ ²Paul went into the synagogue as he always did. On each Sabbathᵈ day for three weeks, Paul talked with the Jews about the Scriptures.ᵈ ³He explained and proved that the Christᵈ must die and then rise from death. He said, "This Jesus I am telling you about is the Christ." ⁴Some of the Jews were convinced and joined Paul and Silas. Many of the Greeks who worshiped the true God and many of the important women joined them.

⁵But the Jews became jealous. They got some evil men from the marketplace, formed a mob and started a riot.

They ran to Jason's house, looking for Paul and Silas. The men wanted to bring Paul and Silas out to the people. ⁶But they did not find them. So they dragged Jason and some other believers to the leaders of the city. The people were yelling, "These men have made trouble everywhere in the world. And now they have come here too! ⁷Jason is keeping them in his house. All of them do things against the laws of Caesar.ᵈ They say that there is another king called Jesus."

⁸When the people and the leaders of the city heard these things, they became very upset. ⁹They made Jason and the others put up a sum of money. Then they let the believers go free.

Paul and Silas Go to Berea

¹⁰That same night the believers sent Paul and Silas to Berea. There Paul and Silas went to the Jewish synagogue.ᵈ ¹¹These Jews were better than the Jews in Thessalonica. They were eager to hear the things Paul and Silas said. These Jews in Berea studied the Scripturesᵈ every day to find out if these things were true. ¹²So, many of them believed. Many important Greek men and women also believed. ¹³But when the Jews in Thessalonica learned that Paul was preaching the word of God in Berea, they came there, too. They

Words to Know: New Testament
SYNAGOGUE • ACTS 17:1-2

When Jesus traveled around Israel, he would often speak in **synagogues** (see Mark 1:21). A synagogue was a place of worship where Jewish men gathered to read from God's word and to pray. Wherever there were ten Jewish men who wanted to worship together, they could start a synagogue. Often, traveling preachers were invited to speak there. That's why Jesus had a lot of opportunities to speak in synagogues. As the apostles traveled, they spoke in synagogues too. Usually, Paul went first to the synagogue in a town to speak to the people about Jesus.

Where do you worship? Is your church important to you?

To read about some soldiers, fly to page 1360.

upset the people and made trouble. [14]So the believers quickly sent Paul away to the coast. But Silas and Timothy stayed in Berea. [15]The men who took Paul went with him to Athens. Then they carried a message from Paul back to Silas and Timothy. It said, "Come to me as soon as you can."

Paul in Athens

[16]Paul was waiting for Silas and Timothy in Athens. He was troubled because he saw that the city was full of idols. [17]In the synagogue,[d] he talked with the Jews and the Greeks who worshiped the true God. He also talked every day with people in the marketplace.

[18]Some of the Epicurean and Stoic philosophers[n] argued with him. Some of them said, "This man doesn't know what he is talking about. What is he trying to say?" Paul was telling them the Good News[d] of Jesus' rising from death. They said, "He seems to be telling us about some other gods." [19]They got Paul and took him to a meeting of the Areopagus.[n] They said, "Please explain to us this new idea that you have been teaching. [20]The things you are saying are new to us. We want to know what this teaching means." [21](All the people of Athens and those from other countries always used their time talking about all the newest ideas.)

"If Paul came to your city, what would he see that might make him speak like he did in Athens? Read Acts 17:16-34."

[22]Then Paul stood before the meeting of the Areopagus. He said, "Men of Athens, I can see that you are very

The Bible
ACTS 17:10-12

How do you know that what you believe about God is true? That's a hard question, but one that someone will probably ask you sooner or later. How can we know that Christianity is true, instead of other religions?

One key to the answer is right in your hands: *the Bible*. The Bible is our most powerful tool in telling others why we believe Christianity is true. The Bible, unlike the important books of other religions, claims to be the word of God himself. And it supports that claim by giving an accurate story of people and events that actually happened. You can count on the Bible to be right about God because it is right about everything else in it.

When you have doubts about your beliefs, or when you need to help answer other people's questions, do what Paul and Silas did. Study the Bible.

To learn more about the Bible, zoom to page 1478.

[n]**Epicurean and Stoic philosophers** Philosophers were those who searched for truth. Epicureans believed that pleasure, especially pleasures of the mind, were the goal of life. Stoics believed that life should be without feelings of joy or grief.
[n]**Areopagus** A council or group of important leaders in Athens. They were like judges.

religious in all things. ²³I was going through your city, and I saw the things you worship. I found an altar that had these words written on it: "TO A GOD WHO IS NOT KNOWN." You worship a god that you don't know. This is the God I am telling you about! ²⁴He is the God who made the whole world and everything in it. He is the Lord of the land and the sky. He does not live in temples that men build! ²⁵This God is the One who gives life, breath, and everything else to people. He does not need any help from them. He has everything he needs. ²⁶God began by making one man. From him came all the different people who live everywhere in the world. He decided exactly when and where they must live. ²⁷God wanted them to look for him and perhaps search all around for him and find him. But he is not far from any of us: ²⁸'We live in him. We walk in him. We are in him.' Some of your own poets have said: 'For we are his children.' ²⁹We are God's children. So, you must not think that God is like something that people imagine or make. He is not like gold, silver, or rock. ³⁰In the past, people did not understand God, but God ignored this. But now, God tells everyone in the world to change his heart and life. ³¹God has decided on a day that he will judge all the world. He will be fair. He will use a man to do this. God chose that man long ago. And God has proved this to everyone by raising that man from death!"

³²When the people heard about Jesus being raised from death, some of them laughed. They said, "We will hear more about this from you later." ³³So Paul went away from them. ³⁴But some of the people believed Paul and joined him. One of those who believed was Dionysius, a member of the Areopagus. Also a woman named Damaris and some others believed.

Paul in Corinth

18 Later, Paul left Athens and went to Corinth. ²Here he met a Jew named Aquila. Aquila was born in the country of Pontus. But Aquila and his

Witnessing
ACTS 17:32-34

Have you ever had someone laugh at you for doing something that was not supposed to be funny? When they laughed, you probably wanted to tackle them and make them stop. Or maybe you felt like running away to hide. Nobody likes to be made fun of.

You can bet Paul was not trying to be funny when he told the crowd in Athens that Jesus Christ had risen from the dead. He was being a witness. But then some of the people laughed at him. But instead of getting angry or insulting them, Paul just walked away. He probably didn't like what they said, but he didn't worry about it. We should do the same thing if someone laughs at us for our beliefs or for being a witness.

By the way, not everyone listening that day laughed. Some of the people believed in God because of what Paul had told them. So don't worry if someone laughs when you are a witness.

wife, Priscilla, had recently moved to Corinth from Italy. They left Italy because Claudius[n] commanded that all Jews must leave Rome. Paul went to visit Aquila and Priscilla. [3]They were tentmakers, just as he was. He stayed with them and worked with them. [4]Every Sabbath[d] day he talked with the Jews and Greeks in the synagogue.[d] Paul tried to persuade these people to believe in Jesus.

[5]Silas and Timothy came from Macedonia and joined Paul in Corinth. After this, Paul used all his time telling people the Good News.[d] He showed the Jews that Jesus is the Christ.[d] [6]But they would not accept Paul's teaching and said some evil things. So he shook off the dust from his clothes.[n] He said to them, "If you are not saved, it will be your own fault! I have done all I can do! After this, I will go only to non-Jewish people!" [7]Paul left the synagogue and moved into the home of Titius Justus. It was next to the synagogue. This man worshiped the true God. [8]Crispus was the leader of that synagogue. He and all the people living in his house believed in the Lord. Many others in Corinth also listened to Paul. They too believed and were baptized.

[9]During the night, Paul had a vision. The Lord said to him, "Don't be afraid! Continue talking to people and don't be quiet! [10]I am with you. No one will hurt you because many of my people are in this city." [11]Paul stayed there for a year and a half, teaching God's word to the people.

Paul Is Brought Before Gallio

[12]Gallio became the governor of the country of Southern Greece. At that time, some of the Jews came together against Paul and took him to the court. [13]They said to Gallio, "This man is teaching people to worship God in a way that is against our law!"

[14]Paul was about to say something, but Gallio spoke to the Jews. Gallio said, "I would listen to you Jews if you were complaining about a crime or some wrong. [15]But the things you are saying are only questions about words and names—arguments about your own law. So you must solve this problem yourselves. I don't want to be a judge of these things!" [16]Then Gallio made them leave the court.

Jobs in the Bible
TENTMAKER • ACTS 18:3

As Paul traveled around the Roman Empire telling people about Jesus, he sometimes earned money to support himself. He did this by making tents. Paul had grown up in an area noted for the goat's-hair cloth it produced, the cloth most often used in tents. Jewish boys learned trades. So, as a young man, Paul learned how to cut and sew the cloth to make tents. Most of the tents that Paul and his friends Priscilla and Aquila made were probably sold to the Roman army for the soldiers.

Paul was a hard worker, whether he was making tents or telling people about Jesus. We should be hard workers too.

[n]**Claudius**   The emperor (ruler) of Rome, A.D. 41–54.
[n]**shook . . . clothes**   This was a warning. It showed that Paul was finished talking to the Jews.

[17]Then they all grabbed Sosthenes. (Sosthenes was now the leader of the synagogue.[d]) They beat him there before the court. But this did not bother Gallio.

Paul Returns to Antioch

[18]Paul stayed with the believers for many more days. Then he left and sailed for Syria. Priscilla and Aquila went with him. At Cenchrea, Paul cut off his hair.[n] This showed that he had made a promise to God. [19]Then they went to Ephesus, where Paul left Priscilla and Aquila. While Paul was there, he went into the synagogue[d] and talked with the Jews. [20]When they asked him to stay with them longer, he refused. [21]He left them, but he said, "I will come back to you again if God wants me to." And so he sailed away from Ephesus.

[22]Paul landed at Caesarea. Then he went and gave greetings to the church in Jerusalem. After that, Paul went to Antioch. [23]He stayed there for a while and then left and went through the countries of Galatia and Phrygia. He traveled from town to town in these countries, giving strength to all the followers.

Apollos in Ephesus and Corinth

[24]A Jew named Apollos came to Ephesus. He was born in the city of Alexandria. He was an educated man who knew the Scriptures[d] well. [25]He had been taught about the Lord. He was always very excited when he spoke and taught the truth about Jesus. But the only baptism that Apollos knew about was the baptism that John[n] taught. [26]Apollos began to speak very boldly in the synagogue,[d] and Priscilla and Aquila heard him. So they took him to their home and helped him better understand the way of God. [27]Now Apollos wanted to go to the country of Southern Greece, so the believers helped him. They wrote a letter to the followers there, asking them to accept him. These followers had believed in Jesus because of God's grace. When Apollos went there, he helped them very much. [28]He argued very strongly with the Jews before all the people. Apollos clearly proved that the Jews were wrong. Using the Scriptures, he proved that Jesus is the Christ.[d]

Paul in Ephesus

19 While Apollos was in Corinth, Paul was visiting some places on the way to Ephesus. There he found some followers. [2]Paul asked them, "Did you receive the Holy Spirit[d] when you believed?"

They said, "We have never even heard of a Holy Spirit!"

[3]So he asked, "What kind of baptism did you have?"

They said, "It was the baptism that John[n] taught."

[4]Paul said, "John's baptism was a baptism of changed hearts and lives. He told people to believe in the One who would come after him. That One is Jesus."

[5]When they heard this, they were baptized in the name of the Lord Jesus. [6]Then Paul laid his hands on them,[n] and the Holy Spirit came upon them. They began speaking different languages[n] and prophesying.[d] [7]There were about 12 men in this group.

[8]Paul went into the synagogue[d] and spoke out boldly for three months. He talked with the Jews and persuaded them to accept the things he said about the kingdom of God. [9]But some of the Jews became stubborn and refused to believe. These Jews said evil things about the Way of Jesus. All the people heard these things. So Paul left them

---

[n]**cut . . . hair** Jews did this to show that the time of a special promise to God was finished.
[n]**John** John the Baptist, who preached to people about Christ's coming (Matthew 3, Luke 3).
[n]**John** John the Baptist, who preached to people about Christ's coming (Matthew 3, Luke 3).
[n]**laid his hands on them** Here, doing this was a sign to show that Paul had God's authority or power to give these people special powers of the Holy Spirit.
[n]**languages** This can also be translated "tongues."

and took the followers with him. He went to a place where a man named Tyrannus had a school. There Paul talked with people every day [10]for two years. Because of his work, every Jew and Greek in the country of Asia heard the word of the Lord.

The Sons of Sceva

[11]God used Paul to do some very special miracles.[d] [12]Some people took handkerchiefs and clothes that Paul had used and put them on the sick. When they did this, the sick were healed and evil spirits left them.

[13-14]But some Jews also were traveling around and making evil spirits go out of people. The seven sons of Sceva were doing this. (Sceva was a leading Jewish priest.) These Jews tried to use the name of the Lord Jesus to force the evil spirits out. They would say, "By the same Jesus that Paul talks about, I order you to come out!"

[15]But one time an evil spirit said to these Jews, "I know Jesus, and I know about Paul, but who are you?"

[16]Then the man, who had the evil spirit in him, jumped on these Jews. He was much stronger than all of them. He beat them and tore their clothes off, so they ran away from the house. [17]All the people in Ephesus, Jews and Greeks, learned about this. They were filled with fear. And the people gave great honor to the Lord Jesus. [18]Many of the believers began to confess openly and tell all the evil things they had done. [19]Some of them had used magic. These believers brought their magic books and burned them before everyone. Those books were worth about 50,000 silver coins.[n]

[20]So in a powerful way the word of the Lord kept spreading and growing.

Paul Plans a Trip

[21]After these things, Paul made plans to go to Jerusalem. He planned to go through the countries of Macedonia and Southern Greece, and then on to Jerusalem. He said, "After I have been to Jerusalem, I must also visit Rome." [22]Paul sent Timothy and Erastus, two of his helpers, ahead to Macedonia. He himself stayed in Asia for a while.

Trouble in Ephesus

[23]But during that time, there was some serious trouble in Ephesus about the Way of Jesus. [24]There was a man named Demetrius, who worked with silver. He made little silver models that looked like the temple of the goddess Artemis.[n] The men who did this work made much money. [25]Demetrius had a meeting with these men and some others who did the same kind of work. He told them, "Men, you know that we make a lot of money from our business. [26]But look at what this man Paul is doing! He has convinced and turned away many people in Ephesus and in almost all of Asia! He says the gods that men make are not real. [27]There is a danger that our business will lose its good name. But there is also another danger: People will begin to think that the temple of the great goddess Artemis is not important! Her greatness will be destroyed. And Artemis is the goddess that everyone in Asia and the whole world worships."

[28]When the men heard this, they became very angry. They shouted, "Artemis, the goddess of Ephesus, is great!" [29]The whole city became confused. The people grabbed Gaius and Aristarchus. (These two men were from Macedonia and were traveling with Paul.) Then all the people ran to the theater. [30]Paul wanted to go in and talk to the crowd, but the followers did not let him. [31]Also, some leaders of Asia were friends of Paul. They sent him a message, begging him not to go into the theater. [32]Some people were shouting one thing, and some were shouting another. The meeting was completely confused. Most of the people did not

---

[n]**50,000 silver coins** Probably drachmas. One coin was enough to pay a man for working one day.
[n]**Artemis** A Greek goddess that the people of Asia Minor worshiped.

know why they had come together.
³³The Jews put a man named
Alexander in front of the people. Some
of them had told him what to do.
Alexander waved his hand because he
wanted to explain things to the people.
³⁴But when they saw that Alexander
was a Jew, they all began shouting the
same thing. They continued shouting
for two hours: "Great is Artemis of
Ephesus!"

³⁵Then the city clerk made the crowd
be quiet. He said, "Men of Ephesus,
everyone knows that Ephesus is the
city that keeps the temple of the great
goddess Artemis. All people know that
we also keep her holy stone" that fell
from heaven. ³⁶No one can say that this
is not true. So you should be quiet.
You must stop and think before you do
anything. ³⁷You brought these men
here, but they have not said anything
evil against our goddess. They have not
stolen anything from her temple. ³⁸We
have courts of law, and there are judges.
Do Demetrius and the men who work

with him have a charge against anyone? They should go to the courts!
That is where they can argue with each
other! ³⁹Is there something else you
want to talk about? It can be decided at
the regular town meeting of the peo-
ple. ⁴⁰I say this because some people
might see this trouble today and say
that we are rioting. We could not explain this because there is no real reason for this meeting." ⁴¹After the city
clerk said these things, he told the
people to go home.

Paul In Macedonia and Greece

20 When the trouble stopped, Paul
sent for the followers to come to
him. He encouraged them and then
told them good-bye. Paul left and went
to the country of Macedonia. ²He said
many things to strengthen the followers
in the different places on his way
through Macedonia. Then he went to
Southern Greece. ³He stayed there
three months. He was ready to sail for
Syria, but some Jews were planning
something against him. So Paul decided to go back through Macedonia to
Syria. ⁴Some men went with him. They
were Sopater son of Pyrrhus, from the

Children Who Saw God at Work
EUTYCHUS • ACTS 20:7-12

I t's fun to stay up late sometimes isn't it? Have you ever stayed up so
late that you fell asleep before you could get to bed? That's what happened to Eutychus. He was sitting in an upstairs window seat listening to
Paul preach. Houses in Bible times didn't have glass windows. They were
just big holes in the wall that were covered with heavy blankets for curtains. The curtains were pulled back while Paul was preaching because it
was probably hot in the crowded room lit by lanterns and candles.
Eutychus went to sleep in the window and fell down to the ground! He
got hurt, but Paul prayed for him and he was healed.

It's fun to stay up late, but God knows your body needs lots of sleep.
Take good care of your body and get the sleep you need!

ⁿ**holy stone**   Probably a meteorite or stone that the people thought looked like Artemis.

city of Berea; Aristarchus and Secundus, from the city of Thessalonica; Gaius, from Derbe; and Timothy; and Tychicus and Trophimus, two men from the country of Asia. [5]These men went first, ahead of Paul, and waited for us at Troas. [6]We sailed from Philippi after the Feast[d] of Unleavened Bread and we met them in Troas five days later. We stayed there seven days.

Paul's Last Visit to Troas

[7]On the first day of the week,[n] we all met together to break bread.[n] Paul spoke to the group. Because he was planning to leave the next day, he kept on talking till midnight. [8]We were all together in a room upstairs, and there were many lamps in the room. [9]A young man named Eutychus was sitting in the window. As Paul continued talking, Eutychus was falling into a deep sleep. Finally, he went sound asleep and fell to the ground from the third floor. When they picked him up, he was dead. [10]Paul went down to Eutychus. He knelt down and put his arms around him. He said, "Don't worry. He is alive now." [11]Then Paul went upstairs again, broke bread, and ate. He spoke to them a long time, until it was early morning. Then he left. [12]They took the young man home alive and were greatly comforted.

The Trip from Troas to Miletus

[13]We sailed for the city of Assos. We went first, ahead of Paul. He wanted to join us on the ship there. Paul planned it this way because he wanted to go to Assos by land. [14]When he met us at Assos, we took him aboard and went to Mitylene. [15]The next day, we sailed from Mitylene and came to a place near Chios. The next day, we sailed to Samos. A day later, we reached Miletus. [16]Paul had already decided not to stop at Ephesus. He did not want to stay too

Helping Others
ACTS 20:35

Imagine that you and your sister are watching TV. You each want to watch a different program at the same time. You could both grab the remote control; then, whoever was faster would get to choose. Or you could flip a coin. Or you could turn the TV off, and neither of you would get to watch your program.

Or you could say, "You watch your program. I'll see mine another time."

What would be the best thing to do? According to this verse, the fourth choice is definitely the right way to solve the problem. "It is more blessed to give than to receive." That means it is better to let the other person have his or her way.

When you have to give up something, you don't get what you want. But in the long run, God will get what he wants: a more mature Christian boy or girl. That's a lot more important than any TV show.

To learn more about helping others, zoom to page 1392.

To learn more about helping others, zoom to page 1392.

[n]**first day of the week**   Sunday, which for the Jews began at sunset on our Saturday. But if in this part of Asia a different system of time was used, then the meeting was on our Sunday night.
[n]**break bread**   Probably the Lord's Supper, the special meal that Jesus told his followers to eat to remember him (Luke 22:14-20).

long in the country of Asia. He was hurrying to be in Jerusalem on the day of Pentecost,[d] if that was possible.

The Elders from Ephesus

[17]Now from Miletus Paul sent to Ephesus and called for the elders[d] of the church. [18]When they came to him, he said, "You know about my life from the first day I came to Asia. You know the way I lived all the time I was with you. [19]The Jews plotted against me. This troubled me very much. But you know that I always served the Lord. I never thought of myself first, and I often cried. [20]You know I preached to you, and I did not hold back anything that would help you. You know that I taught you in public and in your homes. [21]I warned both Jews and Greeks to change their lives and turn to God. And I told them all to believe in our Lord Jesus. [22]But now I must obey the Holy Spirit[d] and go to Jerusalem. I don't know what will happen to me there. [23]I know only that in every city the Holy Spirit tells me that troubles and even jail wait for me. [24]I don't care about my own life. The most important thing is that I complete my mission. I want to finish the work that the Lord Jesus gave me—to tell people the Good News[d] about God's grace.

[25]"And now, I know that none of you will ever see me again. All the time I was with you, I was preaching the kingdom of God. [26]So today I can tell you one thing that I am sure of: If any of you should be lost, I am not responsible. [27]This is because I have told you everything God wants you to know. [28]Be careful for yourselves and for all the people God has given you. The Holy Spirit gave you the work of caring for this flock. You must be like shepherds to the church of God.[n] This is the church that God bought with his own death. [29]I know that after I leave, some men will come like wild wolves and try to destroy the flock. [30]Also, men from your own group will rise up and twist the truth. They will lead away followers after them. [31]So be careful! Always remember this: For three years I never stopped warning each of you. I taught you night and day. I often cried over you.

[32]"Now I am putting you in the care of God and the message about his grace. That message is able to give you strength, and it will give you the blessings that God has for all his holy people. [33]When I was with you, I never wanted anyone's money or fine clothes. [34]You know that I always worked to take care of my own needs and the needs of those who were with me. [35]I showed you in all things that you should work as I did and help the weak. I taught you to remember the words of Jesus. He said, 'It is more blessed to give than to receive.'"

[36]When Paul had said this, he knelt down with all of them and prayed. [37-38]And they all cried because Paul had said that they would never see him again. They put their arms around him and kissed him. Then they went with him to the ship.

Paul Goes to Jerusalem

21 We all said good-bye to them and left. We sailed straight to Cos island. The next day, we reached Rhodes, and from Rhodes we went to Patara. [2]There we found a ship that was going to Phoenicia. We went aboard and sailed away. [3]We sailed near the island of Cyprus. We could see it to the north, but we sailed on to Syria. We stopped at Tyre because the ship needed to unload its cargo there. [4]We found some followers in Tyre, and we stayed with them for seven days. Through the Holy Spirit[d] they warned Paul not to go to Jerusalem. [5]When we finished our visit, we left and continued our trip. All the followers, even the women and children, came outside the city with us. We all knelt down on the beach and prayed. [6]Then we said good-bye and got on the ship. The followers went back home.

---

[n]**of God** Some Greek copies say, "of the Lord."

[7]We continued our trip from Tyre and arrived at Ptolemais. We greeted the believers there and stayed with them for a day. [8]We left Ptolemais and went to the city of Caesarea. There we went into the home of Philip and stayed with him. Philip had the work of telling the Good News.[d] He was one of the seven helpers.[n] [9]He had four unmarried daughters who had the gift of prophesying.[d] [10]After we had been there for some time, a prophet named Agabus arrived from Judea. [11]He came to us and borrowed Paul's belt. Then he used the belt to tie his own hands and feet. He said, "The Holy Spirit says, 'This is how the Jews in Jerusalem will tie up the man who wears this belt. Then they will give him to the non-Jewish people.'"

[12]We all heard these words. So we and the people there begged Paul not to go to Jerusalem. [13]But he said, "Why are you crying and making me so sad? I am ready to be tied up in Jerusalem. And I am ready to die for the Lord Jesus!"

[14]We could not persuade him to stay away from Jerusalem. So we stopped begging him and said, "We pray that what the Lord wants will be done."

[15]After this, we got ready and started on our way to Jerusalem. [16]Some of the followers from Caesarea went with us. They took us to the home of Mnason, a man from Cyprus. Mnason was one of the first followers. They took us to his home so that we could stay with him.

Paul Visits James

[17]In Jerusalem the believers were glad to see us. [18]The next day, Paul went with us to visit James. All the elders[d] were there, too. [19]Paul greeted them and told them everything that God had done among the non-Jewish people through him. [20]When they heard this, they praised God. Then they said to Paul, "Brother, you can see that many thousands of Jews have become believers. But they think it is very important to obey the law of Moses. [21]These Jews have heard about your teaching. They heard that you tell the Jews who live among non-Jews to leave the law of Moses. They heard that you tell them not to circumcise[d] their children and not to obey Jewish customs. [22]What should we do? The Jewish believers here will learn that you have come. [23]So we will tell you what to do: Four of our men have made a promise to God. [24]Take these men with you and share in their cleansing ceremony.[n] Pay their expenses. Then they can shave their heads.[n] Do this and it will prove to everyone that what they have heard about you is not true. They will see that you follow the law of Moses in your own life. [25]We have already sent a letter to the non-Jewish believers. The letter said: 'Do not eat food that has been offered to idols. Do not taste blood. Do not eat animals that have been strangled. Do not take part in any kind of sexual sin.'"

[26]Then Paul took the four men with him. The next day, he shared in the cleansing ceremony. Then he went to the Temple.[d] Paul announced the time when the days of the cleansing ceremony would be finished. On the last day an offering would be given for each of the men.

[27]The seven days were almost over. But some Jews from Asia saw Paul at the Temple. They caused all the people to be upset, and they grabbed Paul. [28]They shouted, "Men of Israel, help us! This is the man who goes everywhere teaching things that are against the law of Moses, against our people, and against this Temple. And now he has brought some Greek men into the Temple. He has made this holy place unclean!"[d] [29](The Jews said this because they had seen Trophimus with Paul in Jerusalem. Trophimus was a man from Ephesus. The Jews

---

[n]**helpers** The seven men chosen for a special work described in Acts 6:1-6.
[n]**cleansing ceremony** The special things Jews did to end the Nazirite promise.
[n]**shave their heads** The Jews did this to show that their promise was finished.

thought that Paul had brought him into the Temple.)

³⁰All the people in Jerusalem became very upset. They ran and took Paul and dragged him out of the Temple. The Temple doors were closed immediately. ³¹The people were about to kill Paul. Now the commander of the Roman army in Jerusalem learned that there was trouble in the whole city. ³²Immediately he ran to the place where the crowd was gathered. He brought officers and soldiers with him, and the people saw them. So they stopped beating Paul. ³³The commander went to Paul and arrested him. He told his soldiers to tie Paul with two chains. Then he asked, "Who is this man? What has he done wrong?" ³⁴Some in the crowd were yelling one thing, and some were yelling another. Because of all this confusion and shouting, the commander could not learn what had happened. So he ordered the soldiers to take Paul to the army building. ³⁵⁻³⁶The whole mob was following them. When the soldiers came to the steps, they had to carry Paul. They did this because the people were ready to hurt him. They were shouting, "Kill him!"

³⁷The soldiers were about to take Paul into the army building. But he spoke to the commander, "May I say something to you?"

The commander said, "Do you speak Greek? ³⁸I thought you were the Egyptian who started some trouble against the government not long ago. He led 4,000 killers out to the desert."

³⁹Paul said, "No, I am a Jew from Tarsus in the country of Cilicia. I am a citizen of that important city. Please, let me speak to the people."

⁴⁰The commander gave permission, so Paul stood on the steps. He waved with his hand so that the people would be quiet. When there was silence, Paul spoke to them in the Jewish language.ⁿ

Paul Speaks to the People

22 Paul said, "Brothers and fathers, listen to me! I will make my defense to you." ²When the Jews heard him speaking the Jewish language,ⁿ they became very quiet. Paul said, ³"I am a Jew. I was born in Tarsus in the country of Cilicia. I grew up in this city. I was a student of Gamaliel.ⁿ He carefully taught me everything about the law of our ancestors. I was very serious about serving God, just as are all of you here today. ⁴I hurt the people who followed the Way of Jesus. Some of them were even killed. I arrested men and women and put them in jail. ⁵The high priest and the whole council of older Jewish leaders can tell you that this is true. These leaders gave me letters to the Jewish brothers in Damascus. So I was going there to arrest these people and bring them back to Jerusalem to be punished.

⁶"But something happened to me on my way to Damascus. It was about noon when I came near Damascus. Suddenly a bright light from heaven flashed all around me. ⁷I fell to the ground and heard a voice saying, 'Saul, Saul, why are you doing things against me?' ⁸I asked, 'Who are you, Lord?' The voice said, 'I am Jesus from Nazareth. I am the One you are trying to hurt.' ⁹The men who were with me did not understand the voice. But they saw the light. ¹⁰I said, 'What shall I do, Lord?' The Lord answered, 'Get up and go to Damascus. There you will be told about all the things I have planned for you to do.' ¹¹I could not see, because the bright light had made me blind. So the men led me into Damascus.

¹²"There a man named Ananias came to me. He was a religious man; he obeyed the law of Moses. All the Jews who lived there respected him. ¹³Ananias came to me, stood by me, and said, 'Brother Saul, see again!'

ⁿ**Jewish language**   Aramaic, the language of the Jews in the first century.
ⁿ**Jewish language**   Aramaic, the language of the Jews in the first century.
ⁿ**Gamaliel**   A very important teacher of the Pharisees, a Jewish religious group (Acts 5:34).

Immediately I was able to see him. [14]Ananias told me, 'The God of our fathers chose you long ago. He chose you to know his plan. He chose you to see the Righteous One and to hear words from him. [15]You will be his witness to all people. You will tell them about the things you have seen and heard. [16]Now, why wait any longer? Get up, be baptized, and wash your sins away. Do this, trusting in him to save you.'

[17]"Later, I returned to Jerusalem. I was praying in the Temple,[d] and I saw a vision. [18]I saw the Lord saying to me, 'Hurry! Leave Jerusalem now! The people here will not accept the truth about me.' [19]But I said, 'Lord, they know that in every synagogue[d] I put the believers in jail and beat them. [20]They also know that I was there when Stephen, your witness, was killed. I stood there and agreed that they should kill him. I even held the coats of the men who were killing him!' [21]But the Lord said to me,

'Leave now. I will send you far away to the non-Jewish people.'"

[22]The crowd listened to Paul until he said this. Then they began shouting, "Kill him! Get him out of the world! A man like this should not be allowed to live!" [23]They shouted and threw off their coats.[n] They threw dust into the air.[n]

[24]Then the commander ordered the soldiers to take Paul into the army building and beat him. The commander wanted to make Paul tell why the people were shouting against him like this. [25]So the soldiers were tying him up, preparing to beat him. But Paul said to an officer there, "Do you have the right to beat a Roman citizen[n] who has not been proven guilty?"

[26]When the officer heard this, he went to the commander and told him about it. The officer said, "Do you know what you are doing? This man is a Roman citizen!"

[27]The commander came to Paul and said, "Tell me, are you really a Roman citizen?"

He answered, "Yes."

[28]The commander said, "I paid a lot of money to become a Roman citizen."

Words to Know: New Testament
ROMAN SOLDIERS • ACTS 22:22-29

Roman soldiers appear in many of the Bible stories about Jesus and the apostles. A Roman centurion (a commanding officer) asked Jesus to heal his servant. Later, some Roman soldiers crucified Jesus. Where did the Roman soldiers come from and why were they in Palestine? At that time, the land where Jesus lived and most of the area where Paul traveled was under the control of Rome. Many different countries were part of the Roman Empire. All the people in the empire had to pay taxes (you can read about tax collectors on another journey). Rome put soldiers in all the cities to keep peace and to make sure the people obeyed the laws. Some Roman soldiers became followers of Jesus.

Have you decided to follow Jesus?

---

[n]**threw off their coats** This showed that the Jews were very angry at Paul.
[n]**threw dust into the air** This showed even greater anger.
[n]**Roman citizen** Roman law said that Roman citizens must not be beaten before they had a trial.

But Paul said, "I was born a citizen."

²⁹The men who were preparing to question Paul moved away from him immediately. The commander was frightened because he had already tied Paul, and Paul was a Roman citizen.

Paul Speaks to Jewish Leaders

³⁰The next day the commander decided to learn why the Jews were accusing Paul. So he ordered the leading priests and the Jewish council to meet. The commander took Paul's chains off. Then he brought Paul out and stood him before their meeting.

23 Paul looked at the Jewish council and said, "Brothers, I have lived my life in a good way before God up to this day." ²Ananias,ⁿ the high priest, heard this and told the men who were standing near Paul to hit him on his mouth. ³Paul said to Ananias, "God will hit you too! You are like a wall that has been painted white! You sit there and judge me, using the law of Moses. But you are telling them to hit me, and that is against the law."

⁴The men standing near Paul said to him, "You cannot talk like that to God's high priest! You are insulting him!"

⁵Paul said, "Brothers, I did not know this man was the high priest. It is written in the Scriptures,ᵈ 'You must not curse a leader of your people.'"ⁿ

⁶Some of the men in the meeting were Sadducees,ᵈ and others were Pharisees.ᵈ So Paul shouted to them, "My brothers, I am a Pharisee and my father was a Pharisee! I am on trial here because I hope that people will rise from death!"

⁷When Paul said this, there was an argument between the Pharisees and the Sadducees. The group was divided. ⁸(The Sadducees believe that after people die, they cannot live again. The Sadducees also teach that there are no angels or spirits. But the Pharisees believe in them all.) ⁹So there was a great uproar. Some of the teachers of the law, who were Pharisees, stood up and argued, "We find nothing wrong with this man! Maybe an angel or a spirit did speak to him."

¹⁰The argument was beginning to turn into a fight. The commander was afraid that the Jews would tear Paul to

Unsung Heroes

PAUL'S NEPHEW • ACTS 23:12-22

The apostle Paul had a nephew who saved his life. Paul had been a Pharisee. That meant he obeyed all the Jewish laws and traditions. Most of the Pharisees did not believe in Jesus. In fact, they had wanted Jesus to die. Paul did not believe in Jesus either. He even captured Christians and put them in prison. But then Paul became a Christian and began preaching about Jesus. This made his former friends, the Pharisees, very angry. When Paul was in Jerusalem, the Pharisees plotted to kill him. But Paul's nephew found out about the plot and warned Paul. Paul's life was saved and he continued to teach about Jesus.

This young man was brave. He was a true hero!

To read about a soldier who saved his prisoner's life, fly to page 1368.

ⁿ**Ananias** This is not the same man named Ananias in Acts 22:12.
ⁿ**'You . . . people.'** Quotation from Exodus 22:28.

pieces. So the commander told the soldiers to go down and take Paul away and put him in the army building.

[11]The next night the Lord came and stood by Paul. He said, "Be brave! You have told people in Jerusalem about me. You must do the same in Rome also."

[12]In the morning some of the Jews made a plan to kill Paul. They made a promise that they would not eat or drink anything until they had killed him. [13]There were more than 40 Jews who made this plan. [14]They went and talked to the leading priests and the older Jewish leaders. They said, "We have made a promise to ourselves that we will not eat or drink until we have killed Paul! [15]So this is what we want you to do: Send a message to the commander to bring Paul out to you. Tell him you want to ask Paul more questions. We will be waiting to kill him while he is on the way here."

[16]But Paul's nephew heard about this plan. He went to the army building and told Paul about it. [17]Then Paul called one of the officers and said, "Take this young man to the commander. He has a message for him."

[18]So the officer brought Paul's nephew to the commander. The officer said, "The prisoner, Paul, asked me to bring this young man to you. He wants to tell you something."

[19]The commander led the young man to a place where they could be alone. The commander asked, "What do you want to tell me?"

[20]The young man said, "The Jews have decided to ask you to bring Paul down to their council meeting tomorrow. They want you to think that they are going to ask him more questions. [21]But don't believe them! There are more than 40 men who are hiding and waiting to kill Paul. They have all made a promise not to eat or drink until they have killed him! Now they are waiting for you to agree."

[22]The commander sent the young man away. He said to him, "Don't tell anyone that you have told me about their plan."

Paul Is Sent to Caesarea

[23]Then the commander called two officers. He said to them, "I need some men to go to Caesarea. Get 200 soldiers ready. Also, get 70 horsemen and 200 men with spears. Be ready to leave at nine o'clock tonight. [24]Get some horses for Paul to ride. He must be taken to Governor Felix safely." [25]And he wrote a letter that said:

[26]From Claudius Lysias.

To the Most Excellent Governor Felix:

Greetings.

[27]The Jews had taken this man, and they planned to kill him. But I learned that he is a Roman citizen, so I went with my soldiers and saved him. [28]I wanted to know why they were accusing him. So I brought him before their council meeting. [29]I learned that the Jews said Paul did some things that were wrong. But these charges were about their own laws. And no charge was worthy of jail or death. [30]I was told that some of the Jews were planning to kill Paul. So I sent him to you at once. I also told those Jews to tell you what they have against him.

[31]So the soldiers did what they were told. They took Paul and brought him to the city of Antipatris that night. [32]The next day the horsemen went with Paul to Caesarea. But the other soldiers went back to the army building in Jerusalem. [33]The horsemen came to Caesarea and gave the letter to the governor. Then they turned Paul over to him. [34]The governor read the letter. Then he asked Paul, "What area are you from?" He learned that Paul was from Cilicia. [35]He said, "I will hear your case when those who are against you come here too." Then the governor gave orders for Paul to be kept under guard in the palace. (This building had been built by Herod.)

The Jews Accuse Paul

24 Five days later Ananias, the high priest, went to the city of Caesarea. With him were some of the older Jewish leaders and a lawyer named Tertullus. They had come to make charges against Paul before the governor. [2]Paul was called into the meeting, and Tertullus began to accuse him, saying: "Most Excellent Felix! Our people enjoy much peace because of you, and many wrong things in our country are being made right through your wise help. [3]We accept these things always and in every place. And we are thankful for them. [4]But I do not want to take any more of your time. I beg you to be kind and listen to our few words. [5]This man is a troublemaker. He makes trouble among the Jews everywhere in the world. He is a leader of the Nazarene[d] group. [6]Also, he was trying to make the Temple[d] unclean,[d] but we stopped him.[n] [8]You can decide if all these things are true. Ask him some questions yourself." [9]The other Jews agreed and said that all of this was true.

[10]The governor made a sign for Paul to speak. So Paul said, "Governor Felix, I know that you have been a judge over this nation for a long time. So I am happy to defend myself before you. [11]I went to worship in Jerusalem only 12 days ago. You can learn for yourself that this is true. [12]Those who are accusing me did not find me arguing with anyone in the Temple. I was not stirring up the people. And I was not making trouble in the Temple or in the synagogues[d] or in the city. [13]They cannot prove the things they are saying against me now. [14]But I will tell you this: I worship the God of our ancestors as a follower of the Way of Jesus. The Jews say that the Way of Jesus is not the right way. But I believe everything that is taught in the law of Moses and that is written in the books of the Prophets.[d]

[15]I have the same hope in God that they have—the hope that all people, good and bad, will be raised from death. [16]This is why I always try to do what I believe is right before God and men.

[17]"I was away from Jerusalem for several years. I went back there to bring money to my people and to offer sacrifices. [18]I was doing this when they found me in the Temple. I had finished the cleansing ceremony. I had not made any trouble; no people were gathering around me. [19]But some Jews from the country of Asia were there. They should be here, standing before you. If I have really done anything wrong, they are the ones who should accuse me. [20]Or ask these Jews here if they found any wrong in me when I stood before the Jewish council in Jerusalem. [21]But I did say one thing when I stood before them: 'You are judging me today because I believe that people will rise from death!'"

[22]Felix already understood much about the Way of Jesus. He stopped the trial and said, "When commander Lysias comes here, I will decide about your case." [23]Felix told the officer to keep Paul guarded. But he told the officer to give Paul some freedom and to let his friends bring what he needed.

Paul Speaks to Felix and His Wife

[24]After some days Felix came with his wife, Drusilla, who was a Jew. He asked for Paul to be brought to him. He listened to Paul talk about believing in Christ Jesus. [25]But Felix became afraid when Paul spoke about things like right living, self-control, and the time when God will judge the world. He said, "Go away now. When I have more time, I will call for you." [26]At the same time Felix hoped that Paul would give him some money. So he sent for Paul often and talked with him.

[27]But after two years, Porcius Festus became governor. Felix was no longer

---

[n]**Verse 6** Some Greek copies add 6b-8a: "And we wanted to judge him by our own law. [7]But the officer Lysias came and used much force to take him from us. [8]And Lysias commanded his people to come to you to accuse us."

governor, but he had left Paul in prison to please the Jews.

Paul Asks to See Caesar

25 Three days after Festus became governor, he went from Caesarea to Jerusalem. ²There the leading priests and the important Jewish leaders made charges against Paul before Festus. ³They asked Festus to do something for them; they wanted him to send Paul back to Jerusalem. (They had a plan to kill Paul on the way.) ⁴But Festus answered, "No! Paul will be kept in Caesarea. I will return there soon myself. ⁵Some of your leaders should go with me. They can accuse the man there in Caesarea, if he has really done something wrong."

⁶Festus stayed in Jerusalem another eight or ten days. Then he went back to Caesarea. The next day he told the soldiers to bring Paul before him. Festus was seated on the judge's seat ⁷when Paul came into the room. The Jews who had come from Jerusalem stood around him. They started making serious charges against Paul. But they could not prove any of them. ⁸This is what Paul said to defend himself: "I have done nothing wrong against the Jewish law, against the Temple,*ᵈ* or against Caesar!"*ᵈ*

⁹But Festus wanted to please the Jews. So he asked Paul, "Do you want to go to Jerusalem? Do you want me to judge you there on these charges?"

¹⁰Paul said, "I am standing at Caesar's judgment seat now. This is where I should be judged! I have done nothing wrong to the Jews; you know this is true. ¹¹If I have done something wrong and the law says I must die, I do not ask to be saved from death. But if these charges are not true, then no one can give me to them. No! I want Caesar to hear my case!"

¹²Festus talked about this with the people who advised him. Then he said, "You have asked to see Caesar; so you will go to Caesar!"

Paul Before King Agrippa

¹³A few days later King Agrippa and Bernice came to Caesarea to visit Festus. ¹⁴They stayed there for some time, and Festus told the king about Paul's case. Festus said, "There is a man that Felix left in prison. ¹⁵When I went to Jerusalem, the leading priests and the older Jewish leaders there made charges against him. They wanted me to sentence him to death. ¹⁶But I answered, 'When a man is accused of a crime, Romans do not hand him over just to please someone. The man must be allowed to face his accusers and defend himself against their charges.' ¹⁷So these Jews came here to Caesarea for the trial. And I did not waste time. The next day I sat on the judge's seat and commanded that the man be brought in. ¹⁸The Jews stood up and accused him. But they did not accuse him of any serious crime as I thought they would. ¹⁹The things they said were about their own religion and about a man named Jesus. Jesus died, but Paul said that he is still alive. ²⁰I did not know much about these things; so I did not ask questions. But I asked Paul, 'Do you want to go to Jerusalem and be judged there?' ²¹But he asked to be kept in Caesarea. He wants a decision from the Emperor.*ⁿ* So I ordered that Paul be held until I could send him to Caesar*ᵈ* in Rome."

²²Agrippa said to Festus, "I would like to hear this man, too."

Festus said, "Tomorrow you will hear him!"

²³The next day Agrippa and Bernice appeared. They dressed and acted like very important people. Agrippa and Bernice, the army leaders, and the important men of Caesarea went into the judgment room. Then Festus ordered the soldiers to bring Paul in. ²⁴Festus said, "King Agrippa and all who are gathered here with us, you see this man. All the Jewish people, here and in Jerusalem, have complained to

---

*ⁿ***Emperor** The ruler of the Roman Empire, which was almost all the world.

me about him. They shout that he should not live any longer. ²⁵When I judged him, I could find nothing wrong. I found no reason to order his death. But he asked to be judged by Caesar. So I decided to send him. ²⁶But I have nothing definite to write the Emperor about him. So I have brought him before all of you—especially you, King Agrippa. I hope that you can question him and give me something to write. ²⁷I think it is foolish to send a prisoner to Caesar without telling what the charges are against him."

Paul Defends Himself

26 Agrippa said to Paul, "You may now speak to defend yourself." Then Paul raised his hand and began to speak. ²He said, "King Agrippa, I will answer all the charges that the Jews make against me. I think it is a blessing that I can stand here before you today. ³I am very happy to talk to you, because you know so much about all the Jewish customs and the things that the Jews argue about. Please listen to me patiently.

⁴"All the Jews know about my whole life. They know the way I lived from the beginning in my own country and later in Jerusalem. ⁵They have known me for a long time. If they want to, they can tell you that I was a good Pharisee.ᵈ And the Pharisees obey the laws of the Jewish religion more carefully than any other group of Jewish people. ⁶Now I am on trial because I hope for the promise that God made to our ancestors. ⁷This is the promise that the 12 tribesᵈ of our people hope to receive. For this hope the Jews serve God day and night. My king, the Jews have accused me because I hope for this same promise! ⁸Why do any of you people think it is impossible for God to raise people from death?

⁹"I too thought I ought to do many things against Jesus from Nazareth. ¹⁰And in Jerusalem I did many things against God's people. The leading

priests gave me the power to put many of them in jail. When they were being killed, I agreed that it was a good thing. ¹¹In every synagogue,ᵈ I often punished them. I tried to make them say evil things against Jesus. I was so angry against them that I even went to other cities to find them and punish them.

¹²"One time the leading priests gave me permission and the power to go to Damascus. ¹³On the way there, at noon, I saw a light from heaven. The light was brighter than the sun. It flashed all around me and the men who were traveling with me. ¹⁴We all fell to the ground. Then I heard a voice speaking to me in the Jewish language.ⁿ The voice said, 'Saul, Saul, why are you doing things against me? You are only hurting yourself by fighting me.' ¹⁵I said, 'Who are you, Lord?' The Lord said, 'I am Jesus. I am the One you are trying to hurt. ¹⁶Stand up! I have chosen you to be my servant. You will be my witness—you will tell people the things that you have seen and the things that I will show you. This is why I have come to you today. ¹⁷I will not let your own people hurt you. And I will keep you safe from the non-Jewish people too. These are the people I am sending you to. ¹⁸I send you to open their eyes that they may turn away from darkness to the light. I send you that they may turn away from the power of Satan and turn to God. Then their sins can be forgiven and they can have a place with those people who have been made holy by believing in me.'

¹⁹"King Agrippa, after I had this vision from heaven, I obeyed it. ²⁰I began telling people that they should change their hearts and lives and turn to God. I told them to do things to show that they really had changed. I told this first to those in Damascus, then in Jerusalem and in every part of Judea, and also to the non-Jewish people. ²¹This is why the Jews took me and were trying to kill me in the Temple.ᵈ ²²But God helped me and is still helping me today.

ⁿ**Jewish language** Aramaic, the language of the Jews in the first century.

With God's help I am standing here today and telling all people what I have seen. But I am saying nothing new. I am saying what Moses and the prophets[d] said would happen. [23]They said that the Christ[d] would die and be the first to rise from death. They said that the Christ would bring light to the Jewish and non-Jewish people."

Paul Tries to Persuade Agrippa

[24]While Paul was saying these things to defend himself, Festus said loudly, "Paul, you are out of your mind! Too much study has driven you crazy!"

[25]Paul said, "Most Excellent Festus, I am not crazy. My words are true. They are not the words of a foolish man. [26]King Agrippa knows about these things. I can speak freely to him. I know that he has heard about all of these things. They did not happen off in a corner. [27]King Agrippa, do you believe what the prophets[d] wrote? I know you believe!"

[28]King Agrippa said to Paul, "Do you think you can persuade me to become a Christian in such a short time?"

[29]Paul said, "Whether it is a short or a long time, I pray to God that not only you but every person listening to me today would be saved and be like me— except for these chains I have!"

[30]Then King Agrippa, Governor Festus, Bernice, and all the people sitting with them stood up [31]and left the room. They were talking to each other. They said, "There is no reason why this man should die or be put in jail." [32]And Agrippa said to Festus, "We could let this man go free, but he has asked Caesar[d] to hear his case."

Paul Sails for Rome

27 It was decided that we would sail for Italy. An officer named Julius, who served in the Emperor's[n] army, guarded Paul and some other prisoners. [2]We got on a ship and left.

"I'm feeling a little seasick after hearing what Paul had to go through to get to Rome." Read all about it in Acts 27:1-44.

The ship was from the city of Adramyttium and was about to sail to different ports in the country of Asia. Aristarchus, a man from the city of Thessalonica in Macedonia, went with us. [3]The next day we came to Sidon. Julius was very good to Paul. He gave Paul freedom to go visit his friends, who took care of his needs. [4]We left Sidon and sailed close to the island of Cyprus because the wind was blowing against us. [5]We went across the sea by Cilicia and Pamphylia. Then we came to the city of Myra, in Lycia. [6]There the officer found a ship from Alexandria that was going to Italy. So he put us on it.

[7]We sailed slowly for many days. We had a hard time reaching Cnidus because the wind was blowing against us. We could not go any farther that way. So we sailed by the south side of the island of Crete near Salmone. [8]We sailed along the coast, but the sailing was hard. Then we came to a place called Safe Harbors, near the city of Lasea.

[9]But we had lost much time. It was now dangerous to sail, because it was already after the Day of Cleansing.[n] So Paul warned them, [10]"Men, I can see there will be a lot of trouble on this trip. The ship and the things in the ship will be lost. Even our lives may be lost!" [11]But the captain and the owner of the ship did not agree with Paul. So the officer did not believe Paul. Instead, the officer believed what the captain and owner of the ship said. [12]And that harbor was not a good place for the ship to

---

[n]**Emperor** The ruler of the Roman Empire, which was almost all the world.
[n]**Day of Cleansing** An important Jewish holy day in the fall of the year. This was the time of year that bad storms happened on the sea.

stay for the winter. So most of the men decided that the ship should leave. The men hoped we could go to Phoenix. The ship could stay there for the winter. (Phoenix was a city on the island of Crete. It had a harbor which faced southwest and northwest.)

The Storm

[13]Then a good wind began to blow from the south. The men on the ship thought, "This is the wind we wanted, and now we have it!" So they pulled up the anchor. We sailed very close to the island of Crete. [14]But then a very strong wind named the "Northeaster" came from the island. [15]This wind took the ship and carried it away. The ship could not sail against it. So we stopped trying and let the wind blow us. [16]We went below a small island named Cauda. Then we were able to bring in the lifeboat, but it was very hard to do.

[17]After the men took the lifeboat in, they tied ropes around the ship to hold it together. The men were afraid that the ship would hit the sandbanks of Syrtis.[n] So they lowered the sail and let the wind carry the ship. [18]The next day the storm was blowing us so hard that the men threw out some of the cargo. [19]A day later they threw out the ship's equipment. [20]For many days we could not see the sun or the stars. The storm was very bad. We lost all hope of staying alive—we thought we would die.

[21]The men had gone without food for a long time. Then one day Paul stood up before them and said, "Men, I told you not to leave Crete. You should have listened to me. Then you would not have all this trouble and loss. [22]But now I tell you to cheer up. None of you will die! But the ship will be lost. [23]Last night an angel from God came to me. This is the God I worship. I am his. [24]God's angel said, 'Paul, do not be afraid! You must stand before Caesar.[d] And God has given you this promise: He will save the lives of all

Boats with Precious Cargo
ACTS 27:27-41

What would you do if your ship got stuck on a sandbank and was wrecked? Paul was on his way to Rome in a big ship. Usually ships did not sail during the winter because the Mediterranean Sea could be very rough. The pilot of this ship took a chance and sailed right into a terrible storm. The sailors passed ropes around the ship to try to hold it together in the rough waves. They didn't want the boat to crash into rocks at night when they couldn't see land.

When daylight came and they could see land, the sailors tried to steer the ship into a harbor. But it got stuck on a sandbank and was wrecked by the waves. During the storm God had told Paul that everyone on the ship would be safe and that Paul would get to Rome. Sure enough, everyone got ashore safely, and later Paul did get to Rome.

Even when things are rough and we have problems, we can trust God to take care of us.

[n]**Syrtis** Shallow area in the sea near the Libyan coast.

those men sailing with you.' ²⁵So men, be cheerful! I trust in God. Everything will happen as his angel told me. ²⁶But we will crash on an island."

²⁷On the fourteenth night we were floating around in the Adriatic Sea." The sailors thought that we were close to land. ²⁸They threw a rope into the water with a weight on the end of it. They found that the water was 120 feet deep. They went a little farther and threw the rope in again. It was 90 feet deep. ²⁹The sailors were afraid that we would hit the rocks, so they threw four anchors into the water. Then they prayed for daylight to come. ³⁰Some of the sailors wanted to leave the ship, and they lowered the lifeboat. These sailors wanted the other men to think that they were throwing more anchors from the front of the ship. ³¹But Paul told the officer and the other soldiers, "If these men do not stay in the ship, your lives cannot be saved!" ³²So the soldiers cut the ropes and let the lifeboat fall into the water.

³³Just before dawn Paul began persuading all the people to eat something. He said, "For the past 14 days you have been waiting and watching. You have not eaten. ³⁴Now I beg you to eat something. You need it to stay alive. None of you will lose even one hair off your heads." ³⁵After he said this, Paul took some bread and thanked God for it before all of them. He broke off a piece and began eating. ³⁶All the men felt better. They all started eating too. ³⁷(There were 276 people on the ship.) ³⁸We ate all we wanted. Then we began making the ship lighter by throwing the grain into the sea.

The Ship Is Destroyed

³⁹When daylight came, the sailors saw land. They did not know what land it was, but they saw a bay with a beach. They wanted to sail the ship to the beach, if they could. ⁴⁰So they cut the ropes to the anchors and left the anchors in the sea. At the same time, they untied the ropes that were holding the rudders. Then they raised the front sail into the wind and sailed

Unsung Heroes

JULIUS • ACTS 27:42-44

Paul was a prisoner on his way to Rome with lots of other prisoners. They were guarded by some Roman soldiers. The leader of the soldiers was a centurion named Julius. The ship they were sailing on crashed in a storm. The soldiers knew that if the prisoners escaped they might have to die for it. So the soldiers were going to kill the prisoners rather than let them escape. But Julius liked Paul and didn't want him killed, so he commanded the soldiers not to kill the prisoners. Because Julius protected him, Paul made it safely to Rome.

In Rome Paul was in prison, but he still preached about Jesus and wrote many of the letters that are in the New Testament. Aren't you glad Julius helped to save Paul's life?

To read about a hero who kept the church from arguing,
fly to page 1504.

"**Adriatic Sea**   The sea between Greece and Italy, including the central Mediterranean.

toward the beach. [41]But the ship hit a sandbank. The front of the ship stuck there and could not move. Then the big waves began to break the back of the ship to pieces.

[42]The soldiers decided to kill the prisoners so that none of them could swim away and escape. [43]But Julius, the officer, wanted to let Paul live. He did not allow the soldiers to kill the prisoners. Instead he ordered everyone who could swim to jump into the water and swim to land. [44]The rest used wooden boards or pieces of the ship. And this is how all the people made it safely to land.

Paul on the Island of Malta

28 When we were safe on land, we learned that the island was called Malta. [2]It was raining and very cold. But the people who lived there were very good to us. They made us a fire and welcomed all of us. [3]Paul gathered a pile of sticks for the fire. He was putting them on the fire when a poisonous snake came out because of the heat and bit him on the hand. [4]The people living on the island saw the snake hanging from Paul's hand. They said to each other, "This man must be a murderer! He did not die in the sea, but Justice[n] does not want him to live." [5]But Paul shook the snake off into the fire. He was not hurt. [6]The people thought that Paul would swell up or fall down dead. The people waited and watched him for a long time, but nothing bad happened to him. So they changed their minds about Paul. Now they said, "He is a god!"

[7]There were some fields around there owned by a very important man on the island. His name was Publius. He welcomed us into his home and was very good to us. We stayed in his house for three days. [8]Publius' father was very sick with a fever and dysentery.[n] But Paul went to him and prayed. Then he put his hands on the man and healed him. [9]After this, all the other sick people on the island came to Paul, and he healed

Animals in the Bible
SNAKES • ACTS 28:1-6

Snakes like to be left alone. That is why they hide inside of tall grass, gardens or old piles of wood. They usually will not bother you unless you bother them first.

Paul accidentally disturbed a poisonous snake when he was shipwrecked on the island of Malta. He had gathered some wood to put on a fire that others had built to keep warm. Suddenly a snake crawled out because of the heat and bit Paul on the hand. Paul quickly shook the snake off his hand, and it landed in the fire. Because the snake was poisonous, the other men thought Paul would die instantly.

But God protected Paul. He did not even get sick from the poison. God used this snake to show the others on the island his great power.

To learn about the king of the beasts, fly to page 1539.

[n]**Justice**   The people thought there was a god named Justice who would punish bad people.
[n]**dysentery**   A sickness like diarrhea.

them, too. 10-11 The people on the island gave us many honors. We stayed there three months. When we were ready to leave, they gave us the things we needed.

Paul Goes to Rome

We got on a ship from Alexandria. The ship had stayed on the island during the winter. On the front of the ship was the sign of the twin gods." 12We stopped at Syracuse for three days and

Three Inns" to meet us. When Paul saw them, he was encouraged and thanked God.

Paul in Rome

16Then we arrived at Rome. There, Paul was allowed to live alone. But a soldier stayed with him to guard him.

17Three days later Paul sent for the Jewish leaders there. When they came together, he said, "Brothers, I have done nothing against our people. I have done nothing against the customs of our fathers. But I was arrested in Jerusalem and given to the Romans. 18The Romans asked me many questions. But

Touring Bible Lands
ROME • ACTS 28:14

In the Old Testament there were many different empires. But in the New Testament there was only one empire—the Roman Empire. The capital city was Rome. This city still exists today in the country of Italy.

At the time when Jesus and the apostles lived, the Roman Empire covered more land than all the other empires we read about in the Old Testament. It was very powerful. The apostle Paul traveled and preached in many places, but most of all he wanted to go to Rome. He knew that from the capital city, the story of Jesus would spread all across the world.

Paul finally did travel to Rome. He was a prisoner, but he still told people about Jesus. He also wrote letters to many new churches telling them how to follow Jesus. We can read some of these letters in the New Testament.

Paul was right! The good news about salvation in Jesus spread out from Rome all over the world.

then left. 13From there we sailed to Rhegium. The next day a wind began to blow from the southwest, so we were able to leave. A day later we came to Puteoli. 14We found some believers there, and they asked us to stay with them for a week. Finally, we came to Rome. 15The believers in Rome heard that we were there. They came out as far as the Market of Appius" and the

they could find no reason why I should be killed. They wanted to let me go free, 19but the Jews there did not want that. So I had to ask to come to Rome to have my trial before Caesar.d But I have no charge to bring against my own people. 20That is why I wanted to see you and talk with you. I am bound with this chain because I believe in the hope of Israel."

21The Jews answered Paul, "We have

"twin gods   Statues of Castor and Pollux, gods in old Greek tales.
"Market of Appius   A town about 27 miles from Rome.
"Three Inns   A town about 30 miles from Rome.

received no letters from Judea about you. None of our Jewish brothers who have come from there brought news about you or told us anything bad about you. [22] We want to hear your ideas. We know that people everywhere are speaking against this religious group."

[23] Paul and the Jews chose a day for a meeting. On that day many more of the Jews met with Paul at the place he was staying. Paul spoke to them all day long, explaining the kingdom of God to them. He tried to persuade them to believe these things about Jesus. He used the law of Moses and the writings of the prophets[d] to do this. [24] Some of the Jews believed what Paul said, but others did not. [25] So they argued, and the Jews were ready to leave. But Paul said one more thing to them: "The Holy Spirit[d] spoke the truth to your fathers through Isaiah the prophet. He said,

[26] 'Go to this people and say:

You will listen and listen, but you will not understand.

You will look and look, but you will not learn.

[27] For these people have become stubborn.

They don't hear with their ears.

And they have closed their eyes.

Otherwise, they might really understand

what they see with their eyes

and hear with their ears.

They might really understand in their minds.

If they did this, they would come back to me and be forgiven.'

Isaiah 6:9-10

[28] "I want you Jews to know that God has also sent his salvation to the non-Jewish people. They will listen!" [29][n]

[30] Paul stayed two full years in his own rented house. He welcomed all people who came and visited him. [31] He preached about the kingdom of God and taught about the Lord Jesus Christ. He was very bold, and no one tried to stop him from speaking.

---

[n]**Verse 29** Some late Greek copies add verse 29: "After Paul said this, the Jews left. They were arguing very much with each other."

ROMANS

God's Plan to Save Us

1 From Paul, a servant of Christ Jesus. God called me to be an apostle[d] and chose me to tell the Good News.[d]

[2]God promised this Good News long ago through his prophets.[d] That promise is written in the Holy Scriptures.[d] [3-4]The Good News is about God's Son, Jesus Christ our Lord. As a man, he was born from the family of David. But through the Spirit[d] of holiness he was appointed to be God's Son with great power by rising from death. [5]Through Christ, God gave me the special work of an apostle. This was to lead people of all nations to believe and obey. I do this work for Christ. [6]And you who are in Rome are also called to belong to Jesus Christ.

[7]This letter is to all of you in Rome whom God loves and has called to be his holy people.

May God our Father and the Lord Jesus Christ show you kindness and give you peace.

A Prayer of Thanks

[8]First I want to say that I thank my God through Jesus Christ for all of you. I thank God because people everywhere in the world are talking about your great faith. [9-10]God knows that every time I pray I always mention you. God is the One I serve with my whole heart by telling the Good News[d] about his Son. I pray that I will be allowed to come to you, and this will happen if God wants it. [11]I want very much to see you, to give you some spiritual gift to make you strong. [12]I mean that I want us to help each other with the faith that we have. Your faith will help me, and my faith will help you. [13]Brothers, I want you to know that I planned many times to come to you. But this has not been possible. I wanted to come so that I could help you grow spiritually. I wanted to help you as I have helped the other non-Jewish people.

[14]I must serve all people—Greeks and non-Greeks, the wise and the foolish. [15]That is why I want so much to preach the Good News to you in Rome.

[16]I am proud of the Good News. It is the power God uses to save everyone who believes—to save the Jews first, and also to save the non-Jews. [17]The Good News shows how God makes people right with himself. God's way of making people right with him begins and ends with faith. As the Scripture[d] says, "The person who is made right with God by faith will live forever."[n]

All People Have Done Wrong

[18]God's anger is shown from heaven against all the evil and wrong things that people do. By their own evil lives they hide the truth. [19]God shows his anger because everything that may be known about God has been made clear. Yes, God has clearly shown them everything that may be known about him. [20]There are things about God that people cannot see—his eternal power and all the things that make him God. But since the beginning of the world those things have been easy to understand. They are made clear by what God has made. So people have no excuse for the bad things they do. [21]They knew God. But they did not give glory to

---

[n]"The person . . . forever." Quotation from Habakkuk 2:4.

God, and they did not thank him. Their thinking became useless. Their foolish minds were filled with darkness. ²²They said they were wise, but they became fools. ²³They gave up the glory of God who lives forever. They traded that glory for the worship of idols made to look like earthly people. They traded God's glory for things that look like birds, animals, and snakes.

²⁴People were full of sin, wanting only to do evil. So God let them go their sinful way. They became full of sexual sin, using their bodies wrongly with each other. ²⁵They traded the truth of God for a lie and worshiped and served things that were made by man. But they did not worship and serve the God who made those things. God should be praised forever. Amen.

²⁶Because people did those things, God left them and let them do the shameful things they wanted to do. Women stopped having natural sex and started having sex with other women. ²⁷In the same way, men stopped having natural sex and began wanting each other. Men did shameful things with other men. And in their bodies they received the punishment for those wrongs.

²⁸People did not think it was important to have a true knowledge of God. So God left them and allowed them to have their own worthless thinking. And so those people do the things that they should not do. ²⁹They are filled with every kind of sin, evil, selfishness, and hatred. They are full of jealousy, murder, fighting, lying, and thinking the worst about each other. They gossip ³⁰and say evil things about each other. They hate God. They are rude and conceited and brag about themselves. They invent ways of doing evil. They do not obey their parents. ³¹They are foolish, they do not keep their promises, and they show no kindness or mercy to other people. ³²They know God's law says that those who live like this should die. But they continue to do these evil things. And they also feel that those who do these things are doing right.

You People Also Are Sinful

2 If you think that you can judge others, then you are wrong. You too are guilty of sin. You judge people, but you do the same bad things they do. So when you judge them, you are really judging yourself guilty. ²God judges those who do wrong things. And we know that God's judging is right. ³You judge those who do wrong, but you do wrong yourselves. Do you think you will be able to escape the judgment of God? ⁴God has been very kind to you, and he has been patient with you. God has been waiting for you to change. But you think nothing of his kindness. Perhaps you do not understand that God is kind to you so that you will change your hearts and lives. ⁵But you are hard and stubborn and refuse to change. So you are making your own punishment greater and greater on the day God shows his anger. On that day all people will see God's right judgments. ⁶God will reward or punish every person for what he has done. ⁷Some people live for God's glory, for honor, and for life that has no end. They live for those things by always continuing to do good. God will give life forever to them. ⁸But other people are selfish and refuse to follow truth. They follow evil. God will give them his punishment and anger. ⁹He will give trouble and suffering to everyone who does evil—to the Jews first and also to the non-Jews. ¹⁰But God will give glory, honor, and peace to everyone who does good—to the Jews first and also to the non-Jews. ¹¹For God judges all people in the same way.

¹²People who have God's law and those who have never heard of the law are all the same when they sin. Those who do not have the law and are sinners will be lost. And, in the same way, people who have the law and are sinners will be judged by the law. ¹³Hearing the law does not make people right with God. The law makes people right with God only if they obey what the law says. ¹⁴(The non-Jews do not have

the law. But when they freely do things that the law commands, then they are the law for themselves. This is true even though they do not have the law. [15]They show that in their hearts they know what is right and wrong, just as the law commands. And they also show this by the way they feel about right and wrong. Sometimes their thoughts tell them they did wrong. And sometimes their thoughts tell them they did right.) [16]All these things will happen on the day when God will judge the secret thoughts of people's hearts. The Good News[d] that I preach says that God will judge everyone through Christ Jesus.

The Jews and the Law

[17]What about you? You call yourself a Jew. You trust in the law of Moses and brag that you are close to God. [18]You know what God wants you to do. And you know the things that are important because you have learned the law. [19]You think you are a guide for the blind and a light for those who are in darkness. [20]You think you can show foolish people what is right and teach those who know nothing. You have the law; so you think you know everything and have all truth. [21]You teach other people. So why don't you teach yourself? You tell others not to steal. But you yourselves steal. [22]You say that others must not take part in adultery.[d] But you yourselves are guilty of that sin. You hate idols. But you steal from temples. [23]You brag about having God's law. But you bring shame to God by breaking his law. [24]It is written in the Scriptures:[d] "The non-Jews speak against God's name because of you Jews."[n]

[25]If you follow the law, then your circumcision[d] has meaning. But if you break the law, then it is as if you were never circumcised. [26]The non-Jews are not circumcised. But if they do what the law says, then it is as if they were circumcised. [27]You Jews have the written law and circumcision, but you break the law. So those who are not circum-

cised in their bodies, but still obey the law, will show that you are guilty. [28]A person is not a true Jew if he is only a Jew in his physical body. True circumcision is not only on the outside of the body. [29]A person is a true Jew only if he is a Jew inside. True circumcision is done in the heart by the Spirit,[d] not by the written law. Such a person gets praise from God, not from other people.

3 So, do Jews have anything that other people do not have? Is there anything special about being circumcised? [2]Yes, of course, there is in every way. The most important thing is this: God trusted the Jews with his teachings. [3]It is true that some Jews were not faithful to God. But will that stop God from doing what he promised? [4]No! God will continue to be true even when every person is false. As the Scriptures[d] say:

"So your words may be shown to be right.
    You are fair when you judge me."
                                Psalm 51:4

[5]When we do wrong, that shows more clearly that God is right. So can we say that God is wrong to punish us? (I am talking as men might talk.) [6]No! If God could not punish us, then God could not judge the world.

[7]A person might say, "When I lie, it really gives God glory, because my lie shows God's truth. So why am I judged a sinner?" [8]It would be the same to say, "We should do evil so that good will come." Some people find fault with us and say that we teach this. Those who say such things about us are wrong, and they should be punished.

All People Are Guilty

[9]So are we Jews better than others? No! We have already said that Jews and non-Jews are the same. They are all guilty of sin. [10]As the Scriptures[d] say:

"There is no one without sin. None!
[11] There is no one who understands.
    There is no one who looks to God for help.
[12]All have turned away.

---

[n]**"The non-Jews . . . Jews."** Quotation from Isaiah 52:5; Ezekiel 36:20.

Together, everyone has become evil.
None of them does anything good."

Psalm 14:1-3

[13]"Their throats are like open
graves.
They use their tongues for
telling lies." *Psalm 5:9*
"Their words are like snake's
poison." *Psalm 140:3*
[14] "Their mouths are full of cursing
and hate." *Psalm 10:7*

right with him without the law. And God
has now shown us that way which the
law and the prophets[d] told us about.
[22]God makes people right with himself through their faith in Jesus Christ.
This is true for all who believe in Christ,
because all are the same. [23]All people
have sinned and are not good enough
for God's glory. [24]People are made right

Salvation
ROMANS 3:21-26

How does God decide who belongs to him and who
doesn't?

Some people might answer, "He takes the good people, and he doesn't
take the bad people."

But in these verses, Paul gives a different answer. If God only took
good people as his, he wouldn't take anyone, because: *"All have sinned
and are not good enough for God's glory"* (verse 23). That's right—no one
is good enough for God!

So does God reject everyone? No. He accepts us, not because of how
good we are but because of our *faith in Christ.*

Salvation is for those who put their faith in Christ, period. Salvation is a
gift from God for all who believe. Are you enjoying God's gift?

To learn more about salvation, zoom to page 1387.

[15]"They are always ready to kill people.
[16] Everywhere they go they cause
ruin and misery.
[17]They don't know how to live in
peace." *Isaiah 59:7-8*
[18] "They have no fear of or respect
for God." *Psalm 36:1*
[19]The law commands many things.
We know that those commands are for
those who are under the law. This stops
all excuses and brings the whole world
under God's judgment, [20]because no
one can be made right with God by
following the law. The law only shows
us our sin.

How God Makes People Right

[21]But God has a way to make people

with God by his grace, which is a free
gift. They are made right with God by
being made free from sin through Jesus
Christ. [25]God gave Jesus as a way to forgive sin through faith. And all of this is
because of the blood of Jesus' death.
This showed that God always does what
is right and fair. God was right in the
past when he was patient and did not
punish people for their sins. [26]And God

All people have sinned
and are not good
enough for God's glory.
• Romans 3:23

gave Jesus to show today that God does what is right. God did this so that he could judge rightly and also make right any person who has faith in Jesus.

27So do we have a reason to brag about ourselves? No! And why not? It is the way of faith that stops all bragging, not the way of following the law. 28A person is made right with God through faith, not through what he does to follow the law. 29Is God only the God of the Jews? Is he not also the God of the non-Jews? 30Of course he is, for there is only one God. He will make Jews right with him by their faith. And he will also make non-Jews right with him through their faith. 31So do we destroy the law by following the way of faith? No! Faith causes us to be what the law truly wants.

The Example of Abraham

4 So what can we say about Abraham,[n] the father of our people? What did he learn about faith? 2If Abraham was made right by the things he did, then he had a reason to brag. But he could not brag before God. 3The Scrip-

ture[d] says, "Abraham believed God. And that faith made him right with God."[n]

4When a person works, his pay is not given to him as a gift. He earns the pay he gets. 5But a person cannot do any work that will make him right with God. So he must trust in God. Then God accepts his faith, and that makes him right with God. God is the One who can make even those who are evil right in his sight. 6David said the same thing. He said that a person is truly blessed when God does not look at what he has done but accepts him as good:

7"Happy are they
   whose sins are forgiven,
   whose wrongs are pardoned.
8Happy is the person
   whom the Lord does not consider
    guilty."   *Psalm 32:1-2*

9Is this blessing only for those who are circumcised?[d] Or is it also for those who are not circumcised? We have already said that God accepted Abraham's faith, and that faith made him right with God. 10So how did this happen? Did God

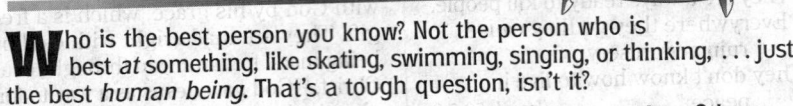

Sin
ROMANS 3:23

Who is the best person you know? Not the person who is best *at* something, like skating, swimming, singing, or thinking, . . . just the best *human being*. That's a tough question, isn't it?

The best person many people know is their father or mother. Others may think of a teacher or a pastor. Still others might name someone famous. But even people who are good have one thing in common: no matter how *good* they are, they are all still *sinners*.

This does not mean we should put people down or criticize them. It is simply the truth as stated in this verse. It says that *all* people are sinners, no matter how good they are. All of us need God's love, forgiveness, and mercy.

To learn more about sin, zoom to page 1380.

---

[n]**Abraham** Most respected ancestor of the Jews. Every Jew hoped to see Abraham.
[n]**"Abraham . . . God."** Quotation from Genesis 15:6.

accept Abraham before or after he was circumcised? God accepted him before his circumcision. [11]Abraham was circumcised later to show that God accepted him. His circumcision was proof that he was right with God through faith before he was circumcised. So Abraham is the father of all those who believe but are not circumcised. He is the father of all believers who are accepted as being right with God. [12]And Abraham is also the father of those who have been circumcised. But it is not their circumcision that makes him their father. He is their father only if they live following the faith that our father Abraham had before he was circumcised.

God Keeps His Promise

[13]Abraham[n] and his descendants[d] received the promise that they would get the whole world. But Abraham did not receive that promise through the law. He received it because he was right with God through his faith. [14]If people could receive what God promised by following the law, then faith is worthless. And God's promise to Abraham is worthless, [15]because the law can only bring God's anger. But if there is no law, then there is nothing to disobey.

[16]So people receive God's promise by having faith. This happens so that the promise can be a free gift. And if the promise is a free gift, then all of Abraham's children can have that promise. The promise is not only for those people that live under the law of Moses. It is for anyone who lives with faith like Abraham. He is the father of us all. [17]As it is written in the Scriptures:[d] "I am making you a father of many nations."[n] This is true before God. Abraham believed in God—the God who gives life to the dead and decides that things will happen that have not yet happened.

[18]There was no hope that Abraham would have children. But Abraham believed God and continued hoping. And that is why he became the father of many nations. As God told him, "Your descendants will also be too many to count."[n] [19]Abraham was almost 100 years old, much past the age for having children. Also, Sarah could not have children. Abraham thought about all this. But his faith in God did not become weak. [20]He never doubted that God would keep his promise. Abraham never stopped believing. He grew stronger in his faith and gave praise to God. [21]Abraham felt sure that God was able to do the thing that God promised. [22]So, "God accepted Abraham's faith, and that made him right with God."[n] [23]Those words ("God accepted Abraham's faith") were written not only for Abraham. [24]They were written also for us. God will accept us also because we believe. We believe in the One who raised Jesus our Lord from death. [25]Jesus was given to die for our sins. And he was raised from death to make us right with God.

"This is one of my favorite parts of the Bible. Do you know how to have peace with God? These verses will help you—Romans 5:1-11."

Right with God

5 We have been made right with God because of our faith. So we have peace with God through our Lord Jesus Christ. [2]Through our faith, Christ has brought us into that blessing of God's grace that we now enjoy. And we are happy because of the hope we have of sharing God's glory. [3]And we also have joy with our troubles because we know that these troubles produce patience. [4]And patience produces character, and

---

[n]**Abraham** Most respected ancestor of the Jews. Every Jew hoped to see Abraham.
[n]**"I . . . nations."** Quotation from Genesis 17:5.
[n]**"Your . . . count."** Quotation from Genesis 15:5.
[n]**"God . . . God."** Quotation from Genesis 15:6.

character produces hope. ⁵And this hope will never disappoint us, because God has poured out his love to fill our hearts. God gave us his love through the Holy Spirit,ᵈ whom God has given to us.

> But Christ died for us while we were still sinners. In this way God shows his great love for us.
> • Romans 5:8

⁶Christ died for us while we were still weak. We were living against God, but at the right time, Christ died for us. ⁷Very few people will die to save the life of someone else. Although perhaps for a good man someone might possibly die. ⁸But Christ died for us while we were still sinners. In this way God shows his great love for us.

⁹We have been made right with God by the blood of Christ's death. So through Christ we will surely be saved from God's anger. ¹⁰I mean that while we were God's enemies, God made friends with us through the death of his Son. Surely, now that we are God's friends, God will save us through his Son's life. ¹¹And not only that, but now we are also very happy in God through our Lord Jesus Christ. Through Jesus we are now God's friends again.

Adam and Christ

¹²Sin came into the world because of what one man did. And with sin came death. And this is why all men must die—because all men sinned. ¹³Sin was in the world before the law of Moses. But God does not judge people guilty of sin if there is no law. ¹⁴But from the time of Adam to the time of Moses, everyone had to die. Adam died because he sinned by not obeying God's command. But even those who did not sin in the same way had to die.

Adam was like the One who was coming in the future. ¹⁵But God's free gift is not like Adam's sin. Many people died because of the sin of that one man. But the grace that they received from God was much greater. Many people received God's gift of life by the grace of the one man, Jesus Christ. ¹⁶After Adam sinned once, he was judged guilty. But the gift of God is different.

Character
ROMANS 5:3-4

Have you ever run a race or gone roller-blading until you felt your muscles burn? As you exercise, your muscles strain, trying to move faster and faster. Eventually you have to stop and rest. But if you keep running and roller-blading, your muscles will get stronger. You will be able to run farther and faster—all because you have struggled against the resistance.

These verses say something like that happens to help us develop good qualities in our lives. We encounter troubles of various kinds, and these troubles cause us to develop patience. This patience, in turn, improves our character, which, in turn, leads to hope. This process can be very difficult—like running when you want to rest. But that is how God makes us more like himself. Try to see your struggles as God's exercise program for your character.

To learn more about character, zoom to page 1411.

God's free gift came after many sins. And the gift makes people right with God. [17]One man sinned, and so death ruled all people because of that one man. But now some people accept God's full grace and the great gift of being made right with him. They will surely have true life and rule through the one man, Jesus Christ.

[18]So one sin of Adam brought the punishment of death to all people. But in the same way, one good act that Christ did makes all people right with God. And that brings true life for all. [19]One man disobeyed God, and many

died to our old sinful lives. So how can we continue living with sin? [3]Did you forget that all of us became part of Christ when we were baptized? We shared his death in our baptism. [4]So when we were baptized, we were buried with Christ and shared his death. We were buried with him so that we could live a new life, just as Christ was raised from death by the wonderful power of the Father.

[5]Christ died, and we have been joined with Christ by dying too. So we will also

God's Love for Us
ROMANS 5:6-8

Imagine that you have a rare blood type. Unbelievably, your best friend has the same, rare type. Even harder to imagine, your worst enemy in the world also has this unusual blood type. If somehow your friend and your enemy were in an accident together and both needed your blood, would you give it? Before you answer, you should know that if you give such a large amount of your blood, there is a good possibility you could die. *Now* what would you say?

You might be willing to risk your life for your good friend. Very few of us, however, would do the same for an enemy. Yet that is exactly what God did for us—he gave his life for us when we were his enemies. Our sins made us God's enemies, and Jesus died so that we could be God's friends. That is an amazing kind of love.

To learn more about God's love for us, zoom to page 1385.

became sinners. But in the same way, one man obeyed God, and many will be made right. [20]The law came to make people have more sin. But when people had more sin, God gave them more of his grace. [21]Sin once used death to rule us. But God gave people more of his grace so that grace could rule by making people right with him. And this brings life forever through Jesus Christ our Lord.

Dead to Sin but Alive in Christ

6 So do you think that we should continue sinning so that God will give us more and more grace? [2]No! We

be joined with him by rising from death as he did. [6]We know that our old life died with Christ on the cross. This was so that our sinful selves would have no power over us, and we would not be slaves to sin. [7]Anyone who has died is made free from sin's control.

[8]If we died with Christ, we know that we will also live with him. [9]Christ was raised from death. And we know that he cannot die again. Death has no power over him now. [10]Yes, when Christ died, he died to defeat the power of sin one time—enough for all time. He now has a new life, and his new life is with God. [11]In the same way, you

should see yourselves as being dead to the power of sin and alive with God through Christ Jesus.

¹²So, do not let sin control you in your life here on earth. You must not be ruled by the things your sinful self makes you want to do. ¹³Do not offer the parts of your body to serve sin. Do not use your

him. ¹⁷In the past you were slaves to sin—sin controlled you. But thank God, you fully obeyed the things that were taught to you. ¹⁸You were made free from sin, and now you are slaves to goodness. ¹⁹I use this example because

Sin
ROMANS 6:23

What would you do if you owed someone a *billion* dollars? No matter how hard you tried, you could never pay off that kind of debt. But if you could not pay it back, you would have to die.

Now, imagine that someone comes along and says, "I can pay your debt. I have more money than you can imagine. Will you let me?"

You would probably answer, "Yes! Thank you!"

But you don't have to say yes. You could say, "No, thank you. It's *my* debt, and *I'll* pay it off somehow." That would be foolish, and you would die trying, but you could answer that way.

The Bible says we are indebted to God because of our sins. It is a debt we can never repay, no matter how hard we work. And the penalty is death. Jesus says, "May I pay off your debt?" We have a choice. We can say yes to Jesus. We can try to do it ourselves. Or we can just give up.

Jesus offers to pay your debt. Will you accept his free gift?

To learn more about sin, zoom to page 1383.

bodies as things to do evil with, but offer yourselves to God. Be like people who have died and now live. Offer the parts of your body to God to be used for doing good. ¹⁴Sin will not be your master, because you are not under law but under God's grace.

Slaves of Righteousness

¹⁵So what should we do? Should we sin because we are under grace and not under law? No! ¹⁶Surely you know that when you give yourselves like slaves to obey someone, then you are really slaves of that person. The person you obey is your master. You can follow sin, or obey God. Sin brings spiritual death. But obeying God makes you right with

this is hard for you to understand. In the past you offered the parts of your body to be slaves to sin and evil. You lived only for evil. In the same way now you must give yourselves to be slaves of goodness. Then you will live only for God.

²⁰In the past you were slaves to sin, and goodness did not control you. ²¹You did evil things, and now you are ashamed of them. Those things only bring death. ²²But now you are free from sin and have become slaves of God. This brings you a life that is only for God. And this gives you life forever. ²³When someone sins, he earns what sin pays—death. But God gives us a free gift—life forever in Christ Jesus our Lord.

When someone sins, he
earns what sin pays—
death. But God gives us
a free gift—life forever
in Christ Jesus our Lord.
• Romans 6:23

An Example from Marriage

7 Brothers, all of you understand the law of Moses. So surely you know that the law rules over a person only while he is alive. ²For example, a woman must stay married to her husband as long as he is alive. But if her husband dies, then she is free from the law of marriage. ³But if she marries another man while her husband is still alive, the law says she is guilty of adultery.*d* But if her husband dies, then the woman is free from the law of marriage. So if she marries another man after her husband dies, she is not guilty of adultery.

⁴In the same way, my brothers, your old selves died, and you became free from the law through the body of Christ. Now you belong to someone else. You belong to the One who was raised from death. We belong to Christ so that we can be used in service to God. ⁵In the past, we were ruled by our sinful selves. The law made us want to do sinful things. And those sinful things we wanted to do controlled our bodies, so that the things we did were only bringing us death. ⁶In the past, the law held us like prisoners. But our old selves died, and we were made free from the law. So now we serve God in

Temptation
ROMANS 7:18-25

"**Y**es I will!"

"No you won't!"

"Yes I will!"

"No you won't!"

If you've ever argued with a brother, sister, or friend over something silly, it may have sounded like that. Arguments are often just two people playing tug-of-war with words over who is going to get his or her way. As unpleasant as such arguments can be, the ones we have with *ourselves* are even worse.

"Yes I will! . . . No I won't!"

"Yes I will! . . . No I won't!"

The apostle Paul describes this kind of an argument with himself in these verses. Paul wanted to do what was right, but he continually ended up doing what was wrong. Do you ever feel that way—torn between doing what would please God and what would please yourself? If so, you and Paul have something in common. His answer will help you, too, when you feel the pressure to sin. Look to Jesus to help you and end the argument.

To learn more about temptation, zoom to page 1406.

a new way, not in the old way with written rules. Now we serve God in the new way, with the Spirit.[d]

Our Fight Against Sin

[7]You might think that I am saying that sin and the law are the same thing. That is not true. But the law was the only way I could learn what sin meant. I would never have known what it means to want something wrong if the law had not said, "You must not want to take your neighbor's things."[n] [8]And sin found a way to use that command and cause me to want every kind of wrong thing. So sin came to me because of that command. But without the law, sin has no power. [9]I was alive without the law before I knew the law. But when the law's command came to me, then sin began to live. [10]And I died because of sin. The command was meant to bring life, but for me that command brought death. [11]Sin found a way to fool me by using the command. Sin used the command to make me die.

[12]So the law is holy, and the command is holy and right and good. [13]Does this mean that something that is good brought death to me? No! Sin used something that is good to bring death to me. This happened so that I could see what sin is really like. The command was used to show that sin is something very evil.

The War Within Man

[14]We know that the law is spiritual. But I am not spiritual. Sin rules me as if I were its slave. [15]I do not understand the things I do. I do not do the good things I want to do. And I do the bad things I hate to do. [16]And if I do not want to do the bad things I do, then that means that I agree that the law is good. [17]But I am not really the one who is doing these bad things. It is sin living in me that does these things. [18]Yes, I know that nothing good lives in me—I mean nothing good lives in the part of me that is earthly and sinful. I want to

do the things that are good. But I do not do them. [19]I do not do the good things that I want to do. I do the bad things that I do not want to do. [20]So if I do things I do not want to do, then I am not the one doing those things. It is sin living in me that does those bad things.

[21]So I have learned this rule: When I want to do good, evil is there with me. [22]In my mind, I am happy with God's law. [23]But I see another law working in my body. That law makes war against the law that my mind accepts. That other law working in my body is the law of sin, and that law makes me its prisoner. [24]What a miserable man I am! Who will save me from this body that brings me death? [25]God will. I thank him for saving me through Jesus Christ our Lord!

So in my mind I am a slave to God's law. But in my sinful self I am a slave to the law of sin.

Life in the Spirit

8 So now, those who are in Christ Jesus are not judged guilty. [2]I am not judged guilty because in Christ Jesus the law of the Spirit[d] that brings life made me free. It made me free from the law that brings sin and death. [3]The law was without power, because the law was made weak by our sinful selves. But God did what the law could not do. He sent his own Son to earth with the same human life that others use for sin. He sent his Son to be an offering to pay for sin. So God used a human life to destroy sin. [4]He did this so that we could be right as the law said we must be. Now we do not live following our sinful selves, but we live following the Spirit.

[5]Those who live following their sinful selves think only about things that their sinful selves want. But those who live following the Spirit are thinking about the things that the Spirit wants them to do. [6]If a person's thinking is controlled by his sinful self, then there is death. But if his thinking is controlled by the Spirit, then there is life

---

[n]**"You . . . things."**   Quotation from Exodus 20:13,15-17.

and peace. [7]This is true because if a person's thinking is controlled by his sinful self, then he is against God. He refuses to obey God's law. And really he is not able to obey God's law. [8]Those people who are ruled by their sinful selves cannot please God.

[9]But you are not ruled by your sinful selves. You are ruled by the Spirit, if that Spirit of God really lives in you. But if anyone does not have the Spirit of Christ, then he does not belong to Christ. [10]Your body will always be dead

things your sinful selves want, then you will die spiritually. But if you use the Spirit's help to stop doing the wrong things you do with your body, then you will have true life.

[14]The true children of God are those who let God's Spirit lead them. [15]The Spirit that we received is not a spirit that makes us slaves again to fear. The Spirit that we have makes us children of God. And with that Spirit we

---

Sin
ROMANS 8:1-2

Does this sound familiar? You did something that hurt someone else. Maybe you said something bad about someone, broke something that belonged to another person, or told a lie. Then you apologized and asked the person to forgive you, and everything seemed to be OK ... but you still felt like something was wrong. That feeling is called *guilt*.

Everyone feels guilty from time to time. Often it is because we have done something wrong, and we really are guilty. But there are other times when we have admitted our wrong, said that we are sorry, and done whatever we could to make things right, yet we still feel guilty!

That's when it's good for us to know that we are truly forgiven. God has taken away our guilt through Jesus' death on the cross. We are not guilty any more! We are forgiven! We are free!

The next time you struggle with guilt, read Romans 8:1-2. Then relax. God has set you free!

To learn more about sin, zoom to page 1523.

---

because of sin. But if Christ is in you, then the Spirit gives you life, because Christ made you right with God. [11]God raised Jesus from death. And if God's Spirit is living in you, then he will also give life to your bodies that die. God is the One who raised Christ from death. And he will give life through his Spirit that lives in you.

[12]So, my brothers, we must not be ruled by our sinful selves. We must not live the way our sinful selves want. [13]If you use your lives to do the wrong

say, "Father, dear Father."[n] [16]And the Spirit himself joins with our spirits to say that we are God's children. [17]If we are God's children, then we will receive the blessings God has for us. We will receive these things from God together with Christ. But we must suffer as Christ suffered, and then we will have glory as Christ has glory.

Our Future Glory

[18]We have sufferings now. But the sufferings we have now are nothing

---

[n]**"Father, dear Father."**   Literally, "Abba, Father." Jewish children called their fathers "Abba."

compared to the great glory that will be given to us. [19]Everything that God made is waiting with excitement for the time when God will show the world who his children are. The whole world wants very much for that to happen. [20]Everything that God made was changed to become useless. This was not by its own wish. It happened because God wanted it. But there was this hope: [21]that everything God made would be set free from ruin. There was hope that everything God made would have the freedom and glory that belong to God's children.

[22]We know that everything God made has been waiting until now in pain, like a woman ready to give birth. [23]Not only the world, but we also have been waiting with pain inside us. We have the Spirit[d] as the first part of God's promise. So we are waiting for God to finish making us his own children. I mean we are waiting for our bodies to be made free. [24]We were saved, and we have this hope. If we see what we are waiting for, then that is not really hope. People do not hope for something they already have. [25]But we are hoping for something that we do not have yet. We are waiting for it patiently.

[26]Also, the Spirit helps us. We are very weak, but the Spirit helps us with our weakness. We do not know how to pray as we should. But the Spirit himself speaks to God for us, even begs God for

> We know that in everything God works for the good of those who love him. They are the people God called, because that was his plan.
> • Romans 8:28

us. The Spirit speaks to God with deep feelings that words cannot explain. [27]God can see what is in people's hearts. And he knows what is in the mind of the Spirit, because the Spirit speaks to

God for his people in the way that God wants.

[28]We know that in everything God works for the good of those who love him. They are the people God called, because that was his plan. [29]God knew them before he made the world. And God decided that they would be like his Son. Then Jesus would be the firstborn[n] of many brothers. [30]God planned for them to be like his Son. And those he planned to be like his Son, he also called. And those he called, he also made right with him. And those he made right, he also glorified.

> "**B**ig things help me understand just how much bigger God's love is. Check out God's special love in Romans 8:31-39."

God's Love in Christ Jesus

[31]So what should we say about this? If God is with us, then no one can defeat us. [32]God let even his own Son suffer for us. God gave his Son for us all. So with Jesus, God will surely give us all things. [33]Who can accuse the people that God has chosen? No one! God is the One who makes them right. [34]Who can say that God's people are guilty? No one! Christ Jesus died, but that is not all. He was also raised from death. And now he is on God's right side and is begging God for us. [35]Can anything separate us from the love Christ has for us? Can troubles or problems or sufferings? If we have no food or clothes, if we are in danger, or even if death comes—can any of these things separate us from Christ's love? [36]As it is written in the Scriptures:[d]

> "For you we are in danger of death
> all the time.
> People think we are worth no
> more than sheep to be killed."
> *Psalm 44:22*

---

[n]firstborn　Here this probably means that Christ was the first in God's family to share God's glory.

[37]But in all these things we have full victory through God who showed his love for us. [38-39]Yes, I am sure that nothing can separate us from the love God has for us. Not death, not life, not angels, not ruling spirits, nothing now, nothing in the future, no powers, nothing above us, nothing below us, or anything else in the whole world will ever

And God gave his promises to them. [5]They are the descendants[d] of our great ancestors, and they are the earthly family of Christ. Christ is God over all. Praise him forever![n] Amen.

[6]I do not mean that God failed to keep his promise to them. But only

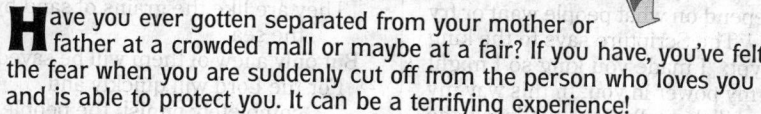

God's Love for Us
ROMANS 8:35-39

Have you ever gotten separated from your mother or father at a crowded mall or maybe at a fair? If you have, you've felt the fear when you are suddenly cut off from the person who loves you and is able to protect you. It can be a terrifying experience!

The Christian doesn't have to worry about being separated from Jesus. Romans 8 tells us that *nothing* can separate us from the love of God. Hopefully, you will never experience the panic of being separated from your parents. But even if you do, remember: *nothing can take you away from the love of God.* His love will always be with you, no matter what.

To learn more about the love of God, zoom to page 1528.

be able to separate us from the love of God that is in Christ Jesus our Lord.

God and the Jewish People

9 I am in Christ, and I am telling you the truth. I do not lie. My feelings are ruled by the Holy Spirit,[d] and they tell me that I am not lying. [2]I have great sorrow and always feel much sadness for the Jewish people. [3]I wish I could help my Jewish brothers, my people. I would even wish that I were cursed and cut off from Christ if that would help them. [4]They are the people of Israel. They were God's chosen children. They have the glory of God and the agreements that God made between himself and his people. God gave them the law of Moses and the right way of worship.

some of the people of Israel are truly God's people.[n] [7]And only some of Abraham's[n] descendants are true children of Abraham. But God said to Abraham: "The descendants I promised you will be from Isaac."[n] [8]This means that not all of Abraham's descendants are God's true children. Abraham's true children are those who become God's children because of the promise God made to Abraham. [9]God's promise to Abraham was this: "At the right time I will return, and Sarah will have a son."[n] [10]And that is not all. Rebekah also had sons. And those sons had the same father, our father Isaac. [11-12]But before the two boys were born, God told Rebekah, "The older will serve the younger."[n]

[n]**Christ . . . forever!** This can also mean, "May God, who rules over all things, be praised forever!"
[n]**God's people** Literally, "Israel," the people God chose to bring his blessings to the world.
[n]**Abraham** Most respected ancestor of the Jews. Every Jew hoped to see Abraham.
[n]**"The descendants . . . Isaac."** Quotation from Genesis 21:12.
[n]**"At . . . son."** Quotation from Genesis 18:10,14.
[n]**"The older . . . younger."** Quotation from Genesis 25:23.

This was before the boys had done anything good or bad. God said this before they were born so that the one chosen would be chosen because of God's own plan. He was chosen because he was the one God wanted to call, not because of anything he did. [13]As the Scripture[d] says, "I loved Jacob, but I hated Esau."[n]

[14]So what should we say about this? Is God unfair? In no way. [15]God said to Moses, "I will show kindness to anyone I want to show kindness. I will show mercy to anyone I want to show mercy."[n] [16]So God will choose the one he decides to show mercy to. And his choice does not depend on what people want or try to do. [17]The Scripture says to the king of Egypt: "I made you king so I might show my power in you. In this way my name will be talked about in all the earth."[n] [18]So God shows mercy where he wants to show mercy. And he makes stubborn the people he wants to make stubborn.

[19]So one of you will ask me: "If God controls the things we do, then why does he blame us for our sins? Who can fight his will?" [20]Do not ask that. You are only human. And human beings have no right to question God. An object cannot tell the person who made it, "Why did you make me like this?" [21]The man who makes a jar can make anything he wants to make. He can use the same clay to make different things. He can make one thing for special use and another thing for daily use.

[22]It is the same way with what God has done. God wanted to show his anger and to let people see his power. But God patiently stayed with those people he was angry with—people who were ready to be destroyed. [23]God waited with patience so that he could make known his rich glory. He wanted to give that glory to the people who receive his mercy. He has prepared these people to have his glory, and [24]we are those people whom God called. He called us from the Jews and from the non-Jews. [25]As the Scripture says in Hosea:

"I will say, 'You are my people'
  to those I had called 'not my people.'
And I will show my love
  to those people I did not love."
Hosea 2:1,23

[26]"Now it is said to Israel,
  'You are not my people.'
But later they will be called
  'children of the living God.'"
Hosea 1:10

[27]And Isaiah cries out about Israel:

"There are so many people of Israel.
  They are like the grains of sand by
    the sea.
But only a few of them will be saved.
[28] For the Lord will quickly and
    completely punish the people
    on the earth."   Isaiah 10:22-23

[29]It is as Isaiah said:

"The Lord of heaven's armies
  allowed a few of our descendants
    to live.
Otherwise we would have been
    completely destroyed
like the cities of Sodom and
    Gomorrah."[n]   Isaiah 1:9

[30]So what does all this mean? It means this: the non-Jews were not trying to make themselves right with God. But they were made right with God because of their faith. [31]And the people of Israel tried to follow a law to make themselves right with God. But they did not succeed, [32]because they tried to make themselves right by the things they did. They did not trust in God to make them right. They fell over the stone that causes people to fall. [33]As it is written in the Scripture:

"I will put in Jerusalem a stone that
  causes people to stumble.
It is a rock that makes them fall.
Anyone who trusts in him will not
  be disappointed."
Isaiah 8:14; 28:16

---

[n]**"I . . . Esau."** Quotation from Malachi 1:2-3.
[n]**"I . . . mercy."** Quotation from Exodus 33:19.
[n]**"I . . . earth."** Quotation from Exodus 9:16.
[n]**Sodom, Gomorrah** Two cities that God destroyed because the people were so evil.

10 Brothers, the thing I want most is for all the Jews to be saved. That is my prayer to God. [2]I can say this about them: They really try to follow God. But they do not know the right way. [3]They did not know the way that God makes people right with him. And they tried to make themselves right in their own way. So they did not accept God's way of making people right. [4]Christ ended the law, so that everyone who believes in him may be right with God.

[5]Moses writes about being made right by following the law. He says, "A person who does these things will have life forever because of them."[n] [6]But this is what the Scripture says about being made right through faith: "Don't say to yourself, 'Who will go up into heaven?'" (That means, "Who will go up to heaven to get Christ and bring him down to earth?") [7]"And do not say, 'Who will go down into the world below?'" (That means, "Who will go down to get Christ and bring him up from death?") [8]This is what the Scripture says: "God's teaching is near you; it is in your mouth and in your heart."[n] That is the teaching of faith that we tell. [9]If you use your mouth to say, "Jesus is Lord," and if you believe in your heart that God raised Jesus from death, then you will be saved. [10]We believe with our hearts, and so we are made right with God. And we use our mouths to say that we believe, and so we are saved. [11]As the Scripture says, "Anyone who trusts in him will never be disappointed."[n] [12]That Scripture says "anyone" because there is no difference between Jew and non-Jew. The same Lord is the Lord of all and gives many blessings to all who trust in him. [13]The Scripture says, "Anyone who asks the Lord for help will be saved."[n]

[14]But before people can trust in the Lord for help, they must believe in him. And before they can believe in the Lord, they must hear about him. And for them to hear about the Lord, someone must tell them. [15]And before someone can go and tell them, he must be sent. It is written, "How beautiful is the person who comes to bring good news."[n]

[16]But not all the Jews accepted the

Salvation
ROMANS 10:8-10

Faith is important for salvation. Faith means more than just believing; it also means putting your trust in someone or something. When the Bible talks about faith in God, it means more than just believing that God exists. It means counting on him to forgive you of your sins, to give you the strength to live for him, and to give you eternal life.

We cannot have salvation by believing in just anything, even if we believe sincerely. We must believe that Jesus is Lord, and that God raised him from the dead. If you can say that and really mean it, then you are saved. You belong to Jesus. You are a Christian.

If you are not sure you can say that, or you don't understand exactly what that means, why don't you ask your parents or your Sunday school teacher?

To learn more about salvation, zoom to page 1439.

---

[n]**"A person . . . them."** Quotation from Leviticus 18:5.
[n]**Verses 6-8** Quotations from Deuteronomy 9:4; 30:12-14; Psalm 107:26.
[n]**"Anyone . . . disappointed."** Quotation from Isaiah 28:16.
[n]**"Anyone . . . saved."** Quotation from Joel 2:32.
[n]**"How . . . news."** Quotation from Isaiah 52:7.

good news. Isaiah said, "Lord, who believed what we told them?"[n] [17]So faith comes from hearing the Good News.[d] And people hear the Good News when someone tells them about Christ.

[18]But I ask: Didn't people hear the Good News? Yes, they heard—as the Scripture says:

"Their message went out through
    all the world.
It goes everywhere on earth."

Psalm 19:4

God Shows Mercy to All People

11 So I ask: Did God throw out his people? No! I myself am an Israelite. I am from the family of Abraham, from the tribe[d] of Benjamin. [2]God chose the Israelites to be his people before they were born. And God did not leave his people. Surely you know what the

Faith and How It Works
ROMANS 10:17

Do you remember when you became a Christian? Probably someone told you about Jesus and what he did for you. Then you believed and prayed to accept him as your Savior. That person could tell you about Jesus because he or she had heard about Jesus from someone else.

People have been telling other people about Christ since the days when he was here on earth. People can have faith because they hear the message. The message is always the same—faith in Jesus is based on who Jesus is and what he did for us. If you want other people to have faith in Jesus, you need to let them hear the message. Who can you tell about Jesus?

To find out more about faith and how it works, fly to page 1431.

[19]Again I ask: Didn't the people of Israel understand? Yes, they did understand. First, Moses says:

"I will use those who are not a
    nation to make you jealous.
I will use a nation that does not
    understand to make
    you angry."   *Deuteronomy 32:21*

[20]Then Isaiah is bold enough to say:

"I was found by those who were not
    asking me for help.
I made myself known to people
    who were not looking for me."

Isaiah 65:1

[21]But about Israel God says,

"All day long I stood ready to accept
    people who disobey and
    are stubborn."   *Isaiah 65:2*

Scripture[d] says about Elijah, how he prayed to God against the people of Israel. Elijah said, [3]"They have killed your prophets,[d] and they have destroyed your altars. I am the only prophet left. And now they are trying to kill me, too."[n] [4]But what answer did God give Elijah? He said, "But I have left 7,000 people in Israel. Those 7,000 have never bowed down before Baal."[n] [5]It is the same now. There are a few people that God has chosen by his grace. [6]And if God chose them by grace, then it is not for the things they have done. If they could be made God's people by what they did, then God's gift of grace would not really be a gift.

[7]So this is what has happened: The

---

[n]**"Lord, . . . them?"** Quotation from Isaiah 53:1.
[n]**"They . . . too."** Quotation from 1 Kings 19:10,14.
[n]**"But . . . Baal."** Quotation from 1 Kings 19:18.

people of Israel tried to be right with God. But they did not succeed. But the ones God chose did become right with him. The others became hard and refused to listen to God. [8]As it is written in the Scriptures:[d]

"God gave the people a dull mind so they could not understand."

Isaiah 29:10

"God closed their eyes so they could not see,
and God closed their ears so they could not hear.
This continues until today."

Deuteronomy 29:4

blessings for the non-Jewish people. So surely the world will get much richer blessings when enough Jews become the kind of people God wants.

[13]Now I am speaking to you who are not Jews. I am an apostle[d] to the non-Jews. So while I have that work, I will do the best I can. [14]I hope I can make my own people jealous. That way, maybe I can help some of them to be saved. [15]God turned away from the Jews. When that happened, God became friends with the other people in

What God Is Like
ROMANS 11:33

Sometimes grown-ups make decisions that you don't understand. Your parents decide you have to move to another city, or your teacher gives you a homework assignment that seems way over your head. At the time, you don't understand it, and you certainly don't like it. But later . . . later you look back and think, *Oh—now I understand why they did that.*

God is like that. Sometimes he does things in our lives that we don't enjoy or can't understand. But he is bigger and smarter than we are, and he sees things we can't. When God causes or allows something in your life that doesn't make sense, it is because he knows better than you do what you need—and what you don't need. Trust God. He loves you and knows what is best for you.

To learn more about what God is like, zoom to page 1529.

[9]And David says:
"Let their own feasts trap them and cause their ruin.
Let their feasts cause them to sin and be paid back.
[10]Let their eyes be closed so they cannot see.
Let their backs be forever weak from troubles."   *Psalm 69:22-23*

[11]So I ask: When the Jews fell, did that fall destroy them? No! But their mistake brought salvation to the non-Jews. This took place to cause the Jews to be jealous. [12]The Jews' mistake brought rich blessings for the world. And what the Jews lost brought rich

the world. So when God accepts the Jews, then surely that will bring to them life after death.

[16]If the first piece of bread is offered to God, then the whole loaf is made holy. If the roots of a tree are holy, then the tree's branches are holy too.

[17]Some of the branches from an olive tree have been broken off, and the branch of a wild olive tree has been joined to that first tree. You non-Jews are the same as that wild branch, and you now share the strength and life of the first tree, the Jews. [18]So do not brag about those branches that were broken off. You have no reason

to brag. Why? You do not give life to the root. The root gives life to you. ¹⁹You will say, "Branches were broken off so that I could be joined to their tree." ²⁰That is true. But those branches were broken off because they did not believe. And you continue to be part of the tree only because you believe. Do not be proud, but be afraid. ²¹If God did not let the natural branches of that tree stay, then he will not let you stay if you don't believe.

²²So you see that God is kind, but he can also be very strict. God punishes those who stop following him. But God is kind to you, if you continue following in his kindness. If you do not continue following him, you will be cut off from the tree. ²³And if the Jews will believe in God again, then God will accept the Jews back again. God is able to put them back where they were. ²⁴It is not natural for a wild branch to be part of a good tree. But you non-Jews are like a branch cut from a wild olive tree. And you were joined to a good olive tree. But those Jews are like a branch that grew from the good tree. So surely they can be joined to their own tree again.

²⁵I want you to understand this secret truth, brothers. This truth will help you understand that you do not know everything. The truth is this: Part of Israel has been made stubborn. But that will change when many non-Jews have come to God. ²⁶And that is how all Israel will be saved. It is written in the Scriptures:

"The Savior will come from
    Jerusalem;
he will take away all evil from the
    family of Jacob."ⁿ
²⁷And I will make this agreement with
    those people
when I take away their sins."

Isaiah 59:20-21; 27:9

²⁸The Jews refuse to accept the Good News,ᵈ so they are God's enemies. This has happened to help you non-Jews. But the Jews are still God's chosen people, and God loves them very much.

He loves them because of the promises he made to their ancestors. ²⁹God never changes his mind about the people he calls and the things he gives them. ³⁰At one time you refused to obey God. But now you have received mercy, because those people refused to obey. ³¹And now the Jews refuse to obey, because God showed mercy to you. But this happened so that they also can receive mercy from God. ³²All people have refused to obey God. God has given them all over to their stubborn ways, so that God can show mercy to all.

Praise to God

³³Yes, God's riches are very great! God's wisdom and knowledge have no end! No one can explain the things God decides. No one can understand God's ways. ³⁴As the Scriptureᵈ says,

"Who has known the mind of the
    Lord?
Who has been able to give the
    Lord advice?"   *Isaiah 40:13*
³⁵"No one has ever given God anything
    that he must pay back."   *Job 41:11*
³⁶Yes, God made all things. And everything continues through God and for God. To God be the glory forever! Amen.

"**H**ow can you be a sacrifice and be alive at the same time? That's a great question. Look at how the Bible answers it in Romans 12:1-21."

Give Your Lives to God

12 So brothers, since God has shown us great mercy, I beg you to offer your lives as a living sacrifice to him. Your offering must be only for God and pleasing to him. This is the spiritual way for you to worship. ²Do not change yourselves to be like the people of this world. But be changed with-

---

ⁿ**Jacob** Father of the 12 family groups of Israel, the people God chose to be his people.

in by a new way of thinking. Then you will be able to decide what God wants for you. And you will be able to know what is good and pleasing to God and what is perfect. [3]God has given me a special gift. That is why I have something to say to everyone among you.

others, that person should do so with joy. [9]Your love must be real. Hate what is evil. Hold on to what is good. [10]Love each other like brothers and sisters. Give your brothers and sisters more honor than you want for yourselves. [11]Do not be lazy but work hard. Serve

So brothers, since God has shown us great mercy, I beg you to offer your lives as a living sacrifice to him. Your offering must be only for God and pleasing to him. This is the spiritual way for you to worship. Do not change yourselves to be like the people of this world. But be changed within by a new way of thinking. Then you will be able to decide what God wants for you. And you will be able to know what is good and pleasing to God and what is perfect.
• Romans 12:1-2

Do not think that you are better than you are. You must see yourself as you really are. Decide what you are by the amount of faith God has given you. [4]Each one of us has a body, and that body has many parts. These parts all have different uses. [5]In the same way, we are many, but in Christ we are all one body. Each one is a part of that body. And each part belongs to all the other parts. [6]We all have different gifts. Each gift came because of the grace that God gave us. If one has the gift of prophecy,[d] he should use that gift with the faith he has. [7]If one has the gift of serving, he should serve. If one has the gift of teaching, he should teach.

Love each other like brothers and sisters. Give your brothers and sisters more honor than you want for yourselves.
• Romans 12:10

[8]If one has the gift of encouraging others, he should encourage. If one has the gift of giving to others, he should give freely. If one has the gift of being a leader, he should try hard when he leads. If one has the gift of showing kindness to

the Lord with all your heart. [12]Be joyful because you have hope. Be patient when trouble comes. Pray at all times. [13]Share with God's people who need help. Bring strangers in need into your homes.

[14]Wish good for those who do bad things to you. Wish them well and do not curse them. [15]Be happy with those who are happy. Be sad with those who are sad. [16]Live together in peace with each other. Do not be proud, but make friends with those who seem unimportant. Do not think how smart you are.

[17]If someone does wrong to you, do not pay him back by doing wrong to him. Try to do what everyone thinks is right. [18]Do your best to live in peace with everyone. [19]My friends, do not try to punish others when they wrong you. Wait for God to punish them with his anger. It is written: "I am the One who punishes; I will pay people back,"[n] says the Lord. [20]But you should do this:
"If your enemy is hungry, feed him;
    if your enemy is thirsty, give him
        a drink.
Doing this will be like pouring
    burning coals on his head."
Proverbs 25:21-22
[21]Do not let evil defeat you. Defeat evil by doing good.

[n]**"I . . . back"** Quotation from Deuteronomy 32:35.

Christians Should Obey the Law

13 All of you must obey the government rulers. No one rules unless God has given him the power to rule. And no one rules now without that power from God. [2] So if anyone is against the government, he is really against what God has commanded. And so he

their time to their work. [7] Pay everyone, then, what you owe him. If you owe any kind of tax, pay it. Show respect and honor to them all.

Loving Others

[8] Do not owe people anything. But you

Helping Others
ROMANS 12:10

"**L**ove each other like brothers and sisters."

That's what this verse says to do. But if you have brothers or sisters, you know how difficult it can be to love them sometimes. You fight, argue, compete, and generally make each other unhappy at times. In fact, it's often easier to love almost anyone *but* your family members.

Yet your family is where you turn when you need help. At times like that, you forget about the little arguments and the irritations that are part of family life, and just hang together. You know that even if everybody else leaves you, your family (including your brothers and sisters) will be there for you. After all, you're *family*.

Christians are brothers and sisters in God's family. Sometimes we fight and hurt each other, just like normal brothers and sisters. But we always need to be there to help one another. After all, we're *family*.

To learn more about helping others, zoom to page 1405.

brings punishment on himself. [3] Those who do right do not have to fear the rulers. But people who do wrong must fear them. Do you want to be unafraid of the rulers? Then do what is right, and the ruler will praise you. [4] He is God's servant to help you. But if you do wrong, then be afraid. The ruler has the power to punish; he is God's servant to punish those who do wrong. [5] So you must obey the government. You must obey not only because you might be punished, but because you know it is the right thing to do. [6] And this is also why you pay taxes. Rulers are working for God and give

will always owe love to each other. The person who loves others has obeyed all the law. [9] The law says, "You must not be guilty of adultery.[d] You must not murder anyone. You must not steal. You must not want to take your neighbor's things."[n] All these commands and all others are really only one rule: "Love your neighbor as you love yourself."[n] [10] Love never hurts a neighbor. So loving is obeying all the law.

[11] I say this because we live in an important time. Yes, it is now time for you to wake up from your sleep. Our salvation is nearer now than when we first believed. [12] The "night"[n] is almost

---

[n]**"You . . . things."** Quotation from Exodus 20:13-15,17.
[n]**"Love . . . yourself."** Quotation from Leviticus 19:18.
[n]**"night"** This is used as a symbol of the sinful world we live in. This world will soon end.

finished. The "day"[n] is almost here. So we should stop doing things that belong to darkness and take up the weapons used for fighting in the light. [13]Let us live in a right way, like people who belong to the day. We should not have wild parties or get drunk. There should be no sexual sins of any kind, no fighting or jealousy. [14]But clothe yourselves with the Lord Jesus Christ. Forget about satisfying your sinful self.

Do Not Criticize Other People

14 Do not refuse to accept into your group someone who is weak in faith. And do not argue with him about opinions. [2]One person believes that he can eat all kinds of food.[n] But if another man's faith is weak, then he believes he can eat only vegetables. [3]The one who knows that he can eat any kind of food must not feel that he is better than the one who eats only vegetables. And the person who eats only vegetables must not think that the one who eats all foods is wrong. God has accepted him. [4]You cannot judge another man's servant. His own master decides if he is doing well or not. And the Lord's servant will do well because the Lord helps him do well.

[5]One person thinks that one day is more important than another. And someone else thinks that every day is the same. Each one should be sure in his own mind. [6]The person who thinks one day is more important than other days is doing that for the Lord. And the one who eats all kinds of food is doing that for the Lord. Yes, he gives thanks to God for that food. And the man who refuses to eat some foods does that for the Lord, and he gives thanks to God. [7]For we do not live or die for ourselves. [8]If we live, we are living for the Lord. And if we die, we are dying for the Lord. So living or dying, we belong to the Lord.

[9]That is why Christ died and rose from death to live again. He did this so that he would be Lord over both the dead and the living. [10]So why do you judge your brother in Christ? And why do you think that you are better than he is? We will all stand before God, and he will judge us all. [11]Yes, it is written in the Scriptures:[d]

"Everyone will bow before me;
    everyone will say that I am God.
As surely as I live, these things will
        happen, says the Lord."

Isaiah 45:23

[12]So each of us will have to answer to God for what he has done.

Do Not Cause Others to Sin

[13]So we should stop judging each other. We must make up our minds not to do anything that will make a Christian brother sin. [14]I am in the Lord Jesus, and I know that there is no food that is wrong to eat. But if a person believes that something is wrong, then that thing is wrong for him. [15]If you hurt your brother's faith because of something you eat, then you are not really following the way of love. Do not destroy his faith by eating food that he thinks is wrong. Christ died for him. [16]Do not allow what you think is good to become what others say is evil. [17]In the kingdom of God, eating and drinking are not important. The important things are living right with God, peace, and joy in the Holy Spirit.[d] [18]Anyone who serves Christ by living this way is pleasing God and will be accepted by other people.

[19]So let us try to do what makes peace and helps one another. [20]Do not let the eating of food destroy the work of God. All foods are all right to eat, but it is wrong to eat food that causes someone else to sin. [21]It is better not to eat meat or drink wine or do anything that will cause your brother to sin.

[22]Your beliefs about these things should be kept secret between you and God. A person is blessed if he can

---

[n]**"day"** This is used as a symbol of the good time that is coming, when we will be with God.

[n]**all . . . food** The Jewish law said there were some foods Jews should not eat. When Jews became Christians, some of them did not understand they could now eat all foods.

do what he thinks is right without feeling guilty. [23]But if he eats something without being sure that it is right, then he is wrong because he did not believe that it was right. And if he does anything without believing that it is right, then it is a sin.

15 We who are strong in faith should help those who are weak. We should help them with their weaknesses, and not please only ourselves. [2]Let each of us please his neighbor for his good, to help him be stronger in faith. [3]Even Christ did not live to please himself. It was as the Scriptures[d] said: "When people insult you, it hurts me."[n] [4]Everything that was written in the past was written to teach us, so that we could have hope. That hope comes from the patience and encouragement that the Scriptures give us. [5]Patience and encouragement come from God. And I pray that God will help you all agree with each other the way Christ Jesus wants. [6]Then you will all be joined together, and you will give glory to God the Father of our Lord Jesus Christ. [7]Christ accepted you, so you should accept each other. This will bring glory to God. [8]I tell you that Christ became a servant of the Jews. This was to show that God's promises to the Jewish ancestors are true. [9]And he also did this so that the non-Jews could give glory to God for the mercy he gives to them. It is written in the Scriptures:

"So I will praise you among the non-Jewish people.
I will sing praises to your name."
Psalm 18:49

[10]The Scripture also says,

"Be happy, you non-Jews, together with God's people."
Deuteronomy 32:43

[11]Again the Scripture says,

"All you non-Jews, praise the Lord.
All you people, sing praises to him."
Psalm 117:1

[12]And Isaiah says,

"A new king will come from Jesse's family.[n]
He will come to rule over the non-Jews;
and the non-Jews will have hope because of him."
Isaiah 11:10

[13]I pray that the God who gives hope will fill you with much joy and peace while you trust in him. Then your hope will overflow by the power of the Holy Spirit.[d]

Paul Talks About His Work

[14]My brothers, I am sure that you are full of goodness. I know that you have all the knowledge you need and that you are able to teach each other. [15]But I have written to you very openly about some things that I wanted you to remember. I did this because God gave me this special gift: [16]to be a minister of Christ Jesus to the non-Jewish people. I served God by teaching his Good News,[d] so that the non-Jewish people could be an offering that God would accept—an offering made holy by the Holy Spirit.[d]

[17]So I am proud of what I have done for God in Christ Jesus. [18]I will not talk about anything I did myself. I will talk only about what Christ has done through me in leading the non-Jewish people to obey God. They have obeyed God because of what I have said and done. [19]And they have obeyed God because of the power of miracles[d] and the great things they saw, and the power of the Holy Spirit. I preached the Good News from Jerusalem all the way around to Illyricum. And so I have finished that part of my work. [20]I always want to preach the Good News in places where people have never heard of Christ. I do this because I do not want to build on the work that someone else has already started. [21]But it is written in the Scriptures:[d]

"Those who were not told about him will see,

---

[n]**"When . . . me."** Quotation from Psalm 69:9.
[n]**Jesse's family** Jesse was the father of David, king of Israel. Jesus was from their family.

and those who have not heard about him will understand."

Isaiah 52:15

Paul's Plan to Visit Rome

²²That is why many times I was stopped from coming to you. ²³Now I have finished my work here. Since for many years I have wanted to come to you, ²⁴I hope to visit you on my way to Spain. I will enjoy being with you, and you can help me on my trip. ²⁵Now I am going to Jerusalem to help God's people. ²⁶The believers in Macedonia and Southern Greece were happy to give their money to help the poor among God's people at Jerusalem. ²⁷They were

that has been given for them. After I do this, I will leave for Spain and stop and visit you. ²⁹I know that when I come to you, I will bring Christ's full blessing.

³⁰Brothers, I beg you to help me in my work by praying for me to God. Do this because of our Lord Jesus and the love that the Holy Spirit*d* gives us. ³¹Pray that I will be saved from the non-believers in Judea. And pray that this help I bring to Jerusalem will please God's people there. ³²Then, if God wants me to, I will come to you. I will come with joy, and together you and I will have a time of rest. ³³The God who gives peace be with you all. Amen.

Greetings to the Christians

16 I recommend to you our sister Phoebe. She is a helper*ⁿ* in the church in Cenchrea. ²I ask you to accept

Women Who Trusted God

PHOEBE • ROMANS 16:1

Phoebe was a Christian woman who helped Paul. She served in her church in Cenchrea. This town was about six miles from Corinth where Paul was living when he wrote a letter to the believers in Rome. She was traveling from Corinth to Rome, perhaps on business, so Paul asked her to deliver his letter to the church in Rome

Many people helped Paul in his ministry. Sometimes we read only their names, and we don't know much more about them. But Phoebe helped Paul by carrying an important letter to Rome. That letter is this Bible book—Romans.

You may not feel like you are doing important things for God. But if you are serving him and doing your best, you are important to him and to his work in the world.

To meet two women who taught a young boy about Jesus, fly to page 1475.

happy to do this, and really they owe it to them. These non-Jews have shared in the Jews' spiritual blessings. So they should use their material possessions to help the Jews. ²⁸I must be sure that the poor in Jerusalem get the money

her in the Lord in the way God's people should. Help her with anything she needs because she has helped me and many other people too.

³Give my greetings to Priscilla and Aquila, who work together with me in

*ⁿ***helper** Literally, "deaconess." This might mean the same as one of the special women helpers in 1 Timothy 3:11.

Christ Jesus. [4]They risked their own lives to save my life. I am thankful to them, and all the non-Jewish churches are thankful to them as well. [5]Also, greet for me the church that meets at their house.

Greetings to my dear friend Epenetus. He was the first person in the country of Asia to follow Christ. [6]Greetings to Mary, who worked very hard for you. [7]Greetings to Andronicus and Junias, my relatives, who were in prison with me. The apostles feel they are very important. They were believers in Christ before I was. [8]Greetings to Ampliatus, my dear friend in the Lord. [9]Greetings to Urbanus. He is a worker together with me for Christ. And greetings to my dear friend Stachys. [10]Greetings to Apelles. He was tested and proved that he truly loves Christ. Greetings to all those who are in the family of Aristobulus. [11]Greetings to Herodion, my relative. Greetings to all those in the family of Narcissus who belong to the Lord. [12]Greetings to Tryphena and Tryphosa. Those women work very hard for the Lord. Greetings to my dear friend Persis. She also has worked very hard for the Lord. [13]Greetings to Rufus who is a special person in the Lord. Greetings to his mother, who has been a mother to me also. [14]Greetings to Asyncritus, Phlegon, Hermes, Patrobas, Hermas, and all the brothers who are with them. [15]Greetings to Philologus and Julia, Nereus and his sister, and Olympas. And greetings to all God's people with them. [16]Greet each other with a holy kiss. All of Christ's churches send greetings to you.

[17]Brothers, I ask you to look out for those who cause people to be against each other and who upset other people's faith. They are against the true teaching you learned. Stay away from them. [18]For such people are not serving our Lord Christ. They are only doing what pleases themselves. They use fancy talk and fine words to fool the minds of those who do not know about evil. [19]All the believers have heard that you obey. So I am very happy because of you. But I want you to be wise in what is good and innocent in what is evil.

[20]The God who brings peace will soon defeat Satan and give you power over him.

The grace of our Lord Jesus be with you.

[21]Timothy, a worker together with me, sends greetings, as well as Lucius, Jason, and Sosipater, my relatives.

[22]I am Tertius, and I am writing this letter from Paul. I send greetings to you in the Lord.

[23]Gaius is letting me and the whole church here use his home. He also sends greetings to you, as do Erastus and our brother Quartus. Erastus is the city treasurer here. [24][n]

[25]Glory to God! God is the One who can make you strong in faith by the Good News[d] that I tell people and by the message about Jesus Christ. The message about Christ is the secret truth that was hidden for long ages past, but is now made known. [26]It has been made clear through the writings of the prophets.[d] And by the command of the eternal God it is made known to all nations, that they might believe and obey.

[27]To the only wise God be glory forever through Jesus Christ! Amen.

---

[n]**Verse 24** Some Greek copies add verse 24: "The grace of our Lord Jesus Christ be with all of you. Amen."

1 CORINTHIANS

Help for a Church with Problems

1 From Paul. I was called to be an apostle[d] of Christ Jesus because that is what God wanted. Also from Sosthenes, our brother in Christ.

[2] To the church of God in Corinth, to those people who have been made holy in Christ Jesus. You were called to be God's holy people with all people everywhere who trust in the name of the Lord Jesus Christ—their Lord and ours:

[3] Grace and peace to you from God our Father and the Lord Jesus Christ.

Paul Gives Thanks to God

[4] I always thank my God for you because of the grace that God has given you in Christ Jesus. [5] In Jesus you have been blessed in every way, in all your speaking and in all your knowledge. [6] The truth about Christ has been proved in you. [7] So you have every gift from God while you wait for our Lord Jesus Christ to come again. [8] Jesus will keep you strong until the end. He will keep you strong, so that there will be no wrong in you on the day our Lord Jesus Christ comes again. [9] God is faithful. He is the One who has called you to share life with his Son, Jesus Christ our Lord.

Problems in the Church

[10] I beg you, brothers, in the name of our Lord Jesus Christ. I beg that all of you agree with each other, so that you will not be divided into groups. I beg that you be completely joined together by having the same kind of thinking and the same purpose. [11] My brothers, some people from Chloe's family have told me that there are arguments among you. [12] This is what I mean: One of you says, "I follow Paul"; another says, "I follow Apollos"; another says, "I follow Peter"; and another says, "I follow Christ." [13] Christ cannot be divided into different groups! Did Paul die on the cross for you? No! Were you baptized in the name of Paul? No! [14] I am thankful that I did not baptize any of you except Crispus and Gaius. [15] I am thankful, because now no one can say that you were baptized in my name. [16] (I also baptized the family of Stephanas. But I do not remember that I myself baptized any others.) [17] Christ did not give me the work of baptizing people. He gave me the work of preaching the Good News,[d] and he sent me to preach the Good News without using words of worldly wisdom. If I used worldly wisdom to tell the Good News, the cross[n] of Christ would lose its power.

Christ Is God's Power and Wisdom

[18] The teaching about the cross seems foolish to those who are lost. But to us who are being saved it is the power of God. [19] It is written in the Scriptures:[d]

"I will cause the wise men to lose
　　their wisdom.
I will make the wise men unable to
　　understand."　　*Isaiah 29:14*

[20] Where is the wise person? Where is the educated person? Where is the philosopher[n] of our times? God has made the wisdom of the world foolish.

---

[n]**cross** Paul uses the cross as a picture of the gospel, the story of Christ's death and rising from death to pay for men's sins. The cross, or Christ's death, was God's way to save men.

[n]**philosopher** Philosophers were those who searched for truth.

21The world did not know God through its own wisdom. So God chose to use the message that sounds foolish to save those who believe it. 22The Jews ask for miracles[d] as proofs. The Greeks want wisdom. 23But we preach Christ on the cross. This is a big problem to the Jews. And it seems foolish to the non-Jews. 24But Christ is the power of God and the wisdom of God to those people God has called—Jews and Greeks. 25Even the foolishness of God is wiser than men. Even the weakness of God is stronger than men.

26Brothers, look at what you were when God called you. Not many of you were wise in the way the world judges wisdom. Not many of you had great influence. Not many of you came from important families. 27But God chose the foolish things of the world to shame the wise. He chose the weak things of the world to shame the strong. 28And he chose what the world thinks is not important. He chose what the world hates and thinks is nothing. He chose these to destroy what the world thinks is important. 29God did this so that no man can brag before him. 30It is God who has made you part of Christ Jesus. Christ has become wisdom for us from God. Christ is the reason we are right with God and have freedom from sin; Christ is the reason we are holy. 31So, as the Scripture[d] says, "If a person brags, he should brag only about the Lord."[n]

The Message of Christ's Death

2 Dear brothers, when I came to you, I did not come as a proud man. I preached God's truth, but not with fancy words or a show of great learning. 2I decided that while I was with you I would forget about everything except Jesus Christ and his death on the cross. 3When I came to you, I was weak and shook with fear. 4My teaching and my speaking were not with wise words that persuade people. But the proof of my teaching was the power that the Spirit[d] gives. 5I did this so that your faith would be in God's power, not in the wisdom of a man.

God's Wisdom

6Yet I speak wisdom to those who are mature. But this wisdom is not from this world or of the rulers of this world. (These rulers are losing their power.) 7But I speak God's secret wisdom, which he has kept hidden. God planned this wisdom for our glory, before the world began. 8None of the rulers of this world understood it. If they had, they would not have killed the Lord of glory on a cross. 9But as it is written in the Scriptures:[d]

"No one has ever seen this.
No one has ever heard about it.
No one has ever imagined
what God has prepared for those
who love him."   *Isaiah 64:4*

10But God has shown us these things through the Spirit.[d]

The Spirit knows all things, even the deep secrets of God. 11It is like this: No one knows the thoughts that another person has. Only a person's spirit that lives in him knows his thoughts. It is the same with God. No one knows the thoughts of God. Only the Spirit of God knows God's thoughts. 12We did not receive the spirit of the world, but we received the Spirit that is from God. We received this Spirit so that we can know all that God has given us. 13When we speak, we do not use words taught to us by the wisdom that men have. We use words taught to us by the Spirit. We use spiritual words to explain spiritual things. 14A person who is not spiritual does not accept the gifts that come from the Spirit of God. That person thinks they are foolish. He cannot understand the Spirit's gifts, because they can only be judged spiritually. 15But the spiritual person is able to judge all things. Yet no one can judge him. The Scripture says:
16"Who has known the mind of the
Lord?

---

[n]"If . . . Lord."   Quotation from Jeremiah 9:24.

Who has been able to teach him?"

Isaiah 40:13

But we have the mind of Christ.

Following Men Is Wrong

3 Brothers, in the past I could not talk to you as I talk to spiritual people. I had to talk to you as I would to people of the world—babies in Christ. [2] The teaching I gave you was like milk, not solid food. I did this because you were not ready for solid food. And even now you are not ready. [3] You are still not spiritual. You have jealousy and arguing among you. This shows that you are not spiritual. You are acting like people of the world. [4] One of you says, "I follow Paul," and another says, "I follow Apollos." When you say things like this, you are acting like worldly people.

[5] Is Apollos important? No! Is Paul important? No! We are only servants of God who helped you believe. Each one of us did the work God gave us to do. [6] I planted the seed of the teaching in you, and Apollos watered it. But God is the One who made the seed grow. [7] So the one who plants is not important, and the one who waters is not important. Only God is important, because he is the One who makes things grow. [8] The one who plants and the one who waters have the same purpose. And each will be rewarded for his own work. [9] We are workers together for God. And you are like a farm that belongs to God.

And you are a house that belongs to God. [10] Like an expert builder I built the foundation of that house. I used the gift that God gave me to do this. Others are building on that foundation. But everyone should be careful how he builds. [11] The foundation has already been built. No one can build any other foundation. The foundation that has already been laid is Jesus Christ. [12] Anyone can build on that foundation, using gold, silver, jewels, wood, grass, or straw.

[13] But the work that each person does will be clearly seen, because the Day[n] will make it plain. That Day will appear with fire, and the fire will test every man's work. [14] If the building that a man puts on the foundation still stands, he will get his reward. [15] But if his building is burned up, he will suffer loss. The man will be saved, but it will be as if he escaped from a fire.

[16] You should know that you yourselves are God's temple. God's Spirit[d] lives in you. [17] If anyone destroys God's temple, God will destroy him, because God's temple is holy. You yourselves are God's temple.

[18] Do not fool yourselves. If anyone among you thinks he is wise in this world, he should become a fool. Then he can become truly wise, [19] because the wisdom of this world is foolishness to God. It is written in the Scriptures,[d] "He catches wise men in their own clever traps."[n] [20] It is also written in the Scriptures, "The Lord knows what people think. He knows they are just a puff of wind."[n] [21] So you should not brag about men. All things are yours: [22] Paul, Apollos and Peter; the world, life, death, the present, and the future—all these things are yours. [23] And you belong to Christ, and Christ belongs to God.

Apostles of Christ

4 This is what people should think about us: We are servants of Christ. We are the ones God has trusted with his secret truths. [2] A person who is trusted with something must show that he is worthy of that trust. [3] I do not care if I am judged by you or if I am judged by any human court. I do not even judge myself. [4] I know of no wrong that I have done. But this does not make me innocent. The Lord is the One who judges me. [5] So do not judge before the right time; wait until the Lord comes. He will bring to light things that are now hidden in darkness. He will make

---

[n]**Day** The day Christ will come to judge all people and take his people home to live with him.
[n]**"He . . . traps."** Quotation from Job 5:13.
[n]**"The Lord . . . wind."** Quotation from Psalm 94:11.

known the secret purposes of people's hearts. Then God will give everyone the praise he should get.

[6]Brothers, I have used Apollos and myself as examples. I did this so that you could learn from us the meaning of the words, "Follow only what is written in the Scriptures."[d] Then you will not be proud of one man and hate another. [7]Who says that you are better than others? Everything you have was given to you. And if this is so, why do you brag as if you got these things by your own power?

[8]You think you have everything you need. You think you are rich. You think you have become kings without us. I wish you really were kings! Then we could be kings together with you. [9]But it seems to me that God has given me and the other apostles[d] the last place. We are like men sentenced to die. We are like a show for the whole world to see—angels and people. [10]We are fools for Christ's sake. But you think you are very wise in Christ. We are weak, but you think you are strong. You receive honor, but we are hated. [11]Even now we still do not have enough to eat or drink or enough clothes. We are often beaten. We have no homes. [12]We work hard with our own hands for our food. People curse us, but we bless them. They hurt us, and we accept it. [13]They say evil things against us, but we say only kind things to them. Even today, we are treated as though we are the garbage of the world—the dirt of the earth.

[14]I am not trying to make you feel ashamed. I am writing this to give you a warning as if you were my own dear children. [15]For though you may have 10,000 teachers in Christ, you do not have many fathers. Through the Good News[d] I became your father in Christ Jesus. [16]So I beg you, please be like me. [17]That is why I am sending Timothy to you. He is my son in the Lord. I love Timothy, and he is faithful. He will help you remember the way I live in Christ

Jesus. This way of life is what I teach in all the churches everywhere.

[18]Some of you have become proud, thinking that I will not come to you again. [19]But I will come very soon if the Lord wants me to. Then I will see what those who are proud can do, not what they say. [20]I want to see this because the kingdom of God is not talk but power. [21]Which do you want: that I come to you with punishment, or that I come with love and gentleness?

Wickedness in the Church

5 Now, it is actually being said that there is sexual sin among you. And it is of such a bad kind that it does not happen even among those who do not know God. A man there has his father's wife. [2]And still you are proud of yourselves! You should have been filled with sadness. And the man who did that sin should be put out of your group. [3]My body is not there with you, but I am with you in spirit. And I have already judged the man who did that sin. I judged him just as I would if I were really there. [4]Meet together as the people of our Lord Jesus. I will be with you in spirit, and you will have the power of our Lord Jesus with you. [5]Then give this man to Satan, so that his sinful self[n] will be destroyed. And then his spirit can be saved on the day of the Lord.

[6]Your bragging is not good. You know the saying, "Just a little yeast makes the whole batch of dough rise." [7]Take out all the old yeast so that you will be a new batch of dough. And you really are new dough without yeast. For Christ, our Passover[d] lamb, was killed to cleanse us. [8]So let us continue our feast, but not with the bread that has the old yeast. That old yeast is the yeast of sin and wickedness. But let us eat the bread that has no yeast. This is the bread of goodness and truth.

[9]I wrote to you in my letter that you should not associate with those who take part in sexual sin. [10]But I did not mean that you should not associate

---

[n]**sinful self** Literally, "flesh." This could also mean his body.

with the sinful people of this world. People of the world do take part in sexual sin, or they are selfish and they cheat each other, or they worship idols. But to get away from them you would have to leave this world. [11]I am writing to tell you that the person you must not associate with is this: anyone who calls himself a brother in Christ but who takes part in sexual sin, or is selfish, or worships idols, or lies about others, or gets drunk, or cheats people. Do not even eat with someone like that.

[12-13]It is not my business to judge those who are not part of the church. God will judge them. But you must judge the people who are part of the church. The Scripture[d] says, "You must get rid of the evil person among you."[n]

Judging Problems Among Christians

6 When one of you has something against a brother in Christ, why do you go to the judges in the law courts? Those people are not right with God. So why do you let them decide who is right? You should be ashamed! Why do you not let God's people decide who is right? [2]Surely you know that God's people will judge the world. So if you are to judge the world, then surely you are able to judge small things as well. [3]You know that in the future we will judge angels. So surely we can judge things in this life. [4]So if you have disagreements that must be judged, why do you take them to those who are not part of the church? They mean nothing to the church. [5]I say this to shame you. Surely there is someone among you wise enough to judge a complaint between two brothers in Christ. [6]But now one brother goes to court against another brother. And you let men who are not believers judge their case!

[7]The lawsuits that you have against each other show that you are already defeated. It would be better for you to

let someone wrong you! It would be better for you to let someone cheat you! [8]But you yourselves do wrong and cheat! And you do this to your own brothers in Christ!

[9-10]Surely you know that the people who do wrong will not receive God's kingdom. Do not be fooled. These people will not receive God's kingdom: those who sin sexually, or worship idols, or take part in adultery,[d] or men who have sexual relations with other men, or steal, or are selfish, or get drunk, or lie about others, or cheat. [11]In the past, some of you were like that. But you were washed clean. You were made holy. And you were made right with God in the name of the Lord Jesus Christ and by the Spirit of our God.

Use Your Bodies for God's Glory

[12]"I am allowed to do all things." But all things are not good for me to do. "I am allowed to do all things." But I must not do those things that will make me their slave. [13]"Food is for the stomach, and the stomach for food." Yes. But God will destroy them both. The body is not for sexual sin. The body is for the Lord, and the Lord is for the body. [14]By God's power God raised the Lord Jesus from death. And God will also raise us from death. [15]Surely you know that your bodies are parts of Christ himself. So I must never take parts of Christ and join them to a prostitute![d] [16]It is written in the Scriptures,[d] "The two people will become one body."[n] So you should know that a man who joins himself with a prostitute becomes one with her in body. [17]But the one who joins himself with the Lord is one with the Lord in spirit.

[18]So run away from sexual sin. Every other sin that a man does is outside his body. But the one who sins sexually sins against his own body. [19]You should know that your body is a temple for the Holy Spirit.[d] The Holy Spirit is in you. You have received the Holy Spirit from

[n]**"You . . . you."**   Quotation from Deuteronomy 17:7; 19:19; 22:21,24; 24:7.
[n]**"The two . . . body."**   Quotation from Genesis 2:24.

t

God. You do not own yourselves. 20You were bought by God for a price. So honor God with your bodies.

You should know that your body is a temple for the Holy Spirit. The Holy Spirit is in you. You have received the Holy Spirit from God. You do not own yourselves. You were bought by God for a price. So honor God with your bodies.
• 1 Corinthians 6:19–20

About Marriage

7 Now I will discuss the things you wrote to me about. It is good for a man not to marry. 2But sexual sin is a danger. So each man should have his own wife. And each woman should have her own husband. 3The husband should give his wife all that she should have as his wife. And the wife should give her husband all that he should have as her husband. 4The wife does not have power over her own body. Her husband has the power over her body. And the husband does not have power over his own body. His wife has the power over his body. 5Do not refuse to give your bodies to each other. But you might both agree to stay away from sexual relations for a time. You might do this so that you can give your time to prayer. Then come together again. This is so that Satan cannot tempt you in your weakness. 6I say this to give you permission. It is not a command. 7I wish everyone were like me. But each person has his own gift from God. One has one gift, another has another gift.

8Now for those who are not married and for the widows I say this: It is good for them to stay single as I am. 9But if they cannot control their bodies, then they should marry. It is better to marry than to burn with sexual desire.

10Now I give this command for the married people. (The command is not from me; it is from the Lord.) A wife should not leave her husband. 11But if she does leave, she must not marry again. Or she should go back to her husband. Also the husband should not divorce his wife.

12For all the others I say this (I am saying this, not the Lord): A brother in Christ might have a wife who is not a believer. If she will live with him, he must not divorce her. 13And a woman might have a husband who is not a believer. If he will live with her, she must not divorce him. 14The husband who is not a believer is made holy through his believing wife. And the wife who is not a believer is made holy through her believing husband. If this were not true, then your children would not be clean.*d* But now your children are holy.

15But if the person who is not a believer decides to leave, let him leave. When this happens, the brother or sister in Christ is free. God called us to a life of peace. 16Wives, maybe you will save your husband; and husbands, maybe you will save your wife. You do not know now what will happen later.

Live as God Called You

17But each one should continue to live the way God has given him to live— the way he was when God called him. This is a rule I make in all the churches. 18If a man was already circumcised*d* when he was called, he should not change his circumcision. If a man was without circumcision when he was called, he should not be circumcised. 19It is not important if a man is circumcised or not circumcised. The important thing is obeying God's commands. 20Each one should stay the way he was when God called him. 21If you were a slave when God called you, do not let that bother you. But if you can be free, then become free. 22The person who was a slave when the Lord called him is free in the Lord. He belongs to the Lord. In the same way, the one who was free when he was called is now Christ's slave. ²³You all were bought for a price. So do not become slaves of men. ²⁴Brothers, in your new life with God each one of you should continue the way you were when you were called.

Questions About Getting Married

²⁵Now I write about people who are not married. I have no command from the Lord about this, but I give my opinion. And I can be trusted, because the Lord has given me mercy. ²⁶This is a time of trouble. So I think that it is good for you to stay the way you are. ²⁷If you have a wife, then do not try to become free from her. If you are not married, then do not try to find a wife. ²⁸But if you decide to marry, this is not a sin. And it is not a sin for a girl who has never married to get married. But those who marry will have trouble in this life. And I want you to be free from this trouble.

²⁹Brothers, this is what I mean: We do not have much time left. So starting now, those who have wives should use their time to serve the Lord as if they had no wives. ³⁰Those who are sad should live as if they are not sad. Those who are happy should live as if they are not happy. Those who buy things should live as if they own nothing. ³¹Those who use the things of the world should live as if those things are not important to them. You should live like this, because this world, the way it is now, will soon be gone.

³²I want you to be free from worry. A man who is not married is busy with the Lord's work. He is trying to please the Lord. ³³But a man who is married is busy with things of the world. He is trying to please his wife. ³⁴He must think about two things—pleasing his wife and pleasing the Lord. A woman who is not married or a girl who has never married is busy with the Lord's work. She wants to give herself fully—body and soul—to the Lord. But a married woman is busy with things of the world. She is trying to please her hus-

band. ³⁵I am saying this to help you. I am not trying to limit you. But I want you to live in the right way. And I want you to give yourselves fully to the Lord without giving your time to other things.

³⁶A man might think that he is not doing the right thing with the girl he is engaged to. The girl might be almost past the best age to marry. So he might feel that he should marry her. He should do what he wants. They should get married. It is no sin. ³⁷But another man might be more sure in his mind. There may be no need for marriage, so he is free to do what he wants. If he has decided in his own heart not to marry, he is doing the right thing. ³⁸So the man who marries his girl does right. And the man who does not marry does even better.

³⁹A woman must stay with her husband as long as he lives. If the husband dies, she is free to marry any man she wants. But she must marry in the Lord. ⁴⁰The woman is happier if she does not marry again. This is my opinion, and I believe that I have God's Spirit.

About Food Offered to Idols

8 Now I will write about meat that is sacrificed to idols. We know that "we all have knowledge." Knowledge puffs you up with pride, but love builds up. ²Whoever thinks he knows something does not yet know anything as he should. ³But he who loves God is known by God.

⁴So this is what I say about eating meat sacrificed to idols: We know that an idol is really nothing in the world. And we know that there is only one God. ⁵It is really not important if there are things called gods, in heaven or on earth. (And there are many things that people call "gods" and "lords.") ⁶But for us there is only one God. He is our Father. All things came from him, and we live for him. And there is only one Lord—Jesus Christ. All things were made through Jesus, and we also have life through him.

⁷But not all people know this. Until

now, some people have had the habit of worshiping idols. So now when they eat meat, they still feel as if it belongs to an idol. They are not sure that it is right to eat this meat. When they eat it, they feel guilty. [8]But food will not make us closer to God. Refusing to eat does not make us less pleasing to God. And eating does not make us better in God's sight.

[9]But be careful with your freedom. Your freedom may cause those who are weak in faith to fall into sin. [10]You have "knowledge," so you might eat in an idol's temple.[n] Someone who is weak in faith might see you eating there. This would encourage him to eat meat sacrificed to idols. But he really thinks it is wrong. [11]So this weak brother is ruined because of your "knowledge." And Christ died for this brother. [12]When you sin against your brothers in Christ like this and cause them to do what they feel is wrong, you are also sinning against Christ. [13]So if the food I eat makes my brother fall into sin, I will never eat meat again. I will stop eating meat, so that I will not cause my brother to sin.

Paul Is like the Other Apostles

9 I am a free man. I am an apostle.[d] I have seen Jesus our Lord. You people are all an example of my work in the Lord. [2]Others may not accept me as an apostle, but surely you accept me. You are proof that I am an apostle in the Lord.

[3]Some people want to judge me. So this is the answer I give them: [4]Do we not have the right to eat and drink? [5]Do we not have the right to bring a believing wife with us when we travel? The other apostles, the Lord's brothers, and Peter all do this. [6]And are Barnabas and I the only ones who must work to earn our living? [7]No soldier ever serves in the army and pays his own salary. No one ever plants a vineyard without eating some of the grapes himself. No person

takes care of a flock of sheep without drinking some of the milk himself.

[8]This is not only what men think. God's law says the same thing. [9]Yes, it is written in the law of Moses: "When an ox is working in the grain, do not cover its mouth and keep it from eating."[n] When God said this, was he thinking only about oxen? No. [10]He was really talking about us. Yes, that Scripture[d] was written for us. The one who plows and the one who works in the grain should hope to get some of the grain for their work. [11]We planted spiritual seed among you. So we should be able to harvest from you some things for this life. Surely this is not asking too much. [12]Other men have the right to get something from you. So surely we have this right, too. But we do not use this right. No, we put up with everything ourselves so that we will not stop anyone from obeying the Good News[d] of Christ. [13]Surely you know that those who work at the Temple[d] get their food from the Temple. And those who serve at the altar get part of what is offered at the altar. [14]It is the same with those who tell the Good News. The Lord has commanded that those who tell the Good News should get their living from this work.

[15]But I have not used any of these rights. And I am not writing this now to get anything from you. I would rather die than to have my reason for bragging taken away. [16]Telling the Good News is not my reason for bragging. Telling the Good News is my duty—something I must do. And how bad it will be for me if I do not tell the Good News. [17]If I preach because it is my own choice, I should get a reward. But I have no choice. I must tell the Good News. I am only doing the duty that was given to me. [18]So what reward do I get? This is my reward: that when I tell the Good News I can offer it freely. In this way I do not use my right to be paid in my work for the Good News.

---

[n]**idol's temple**   Building where a false god is worshiped.
[n]**"When an ox . . . eating."**   Quotation from Deuteronomy 25:4.

¹⁹I am free. I belong to no man. But I make myself a slave to all people. I do this to help save as many people as I can. ²⁰To the Jews I became like a Jew. I did this to help save the Jews. I myself am not ruled by the law. But to those who are ruled by the law I became like a person who is ruled by the law. I did this to help save those who are ruled by the law. ²¹To those who are without the law I became like a person who is without the law. I did this to help save those people who are without the law. (But really, I am not without God's law—I am ruled by Christ's law.) ²²To those who are weak, I became weak so that I could help save them. I have become all things to all people. I did this so that I could save some of them in any way possible. ²³I do all this because of the Good News. I do it so that I can share in the blessings of the Good News.

²⁴You know that in a race all the runners run. But only one gets the prize. So run like that. Run to win! ²⁵All those who compete in the games use strict training. They do this so that they can win a crown. That crown is an earthly thing that lasts only a short time. But our crown will continue forever. ²⁶So I do not run without a goal. I fight like a boxer who is hitting something—not just the air. ²⁷It is my own body that I hit. I make it my slave. I do this so that I myself will not be rejected after I have preached to others.

Don't Be like the Jews

10 Brothers, I want you to know what happened to our ancestors who followed Moses. They were all under the cloud, and they all went through the sea. ²They were all baptized as followers of Moses in the cloud and in the sea. ³They all ate the same spiritual food. ⁴And they all drank the same spiritual drink. They drank from that spiritual rock that was

Helping Others
1 CORINTHIANS 9:19-23

Imagine that a creature from the planet Ziptang beamed down to your house one day. "Greetings, earth creatures," he says in Ziptangese. "I'm here to help you solve all your problems." "Great," you say. "Want to have dinner with us first?"

Your family and the creature settle down for dinner, but there are problems. He can't eat meat, vegetables, or grains, and he is shocked that you do. He tries to drink some water, but it keeps getting in what look like his ears. And when your mom brings out a cake with candles on it in his honor, he screams and flies away.

"You earthlings are so gross! How will I ever help you?" he says, horrified.

By this time, you probably would wish that he would beam back to Ziptang. No one appreciates that kind of "help."

Sometimes it is difficult to know how to help other people, especially if they are very different from us. But Jesus wants us to help others, and he will show us how to be their friend.

To learn more about helping others, zoom to page 1491.

The only temptations that you have are the temptations that all people have. But you can trust God. He will not let you be tempted more than you can stand. But when you are tempted, God will also give you a way to escape that temptation. Then you will be able to stand it.
• 1 Corinthians 10:13

with them. That rock was Christ. [5]But God was not pleased with most of them. They died in the desert.

[6]And these things that happened are examples for us. They should stop us from wanting evil things as those people did. [7]Do not worship idols, as some of them did. It is written in the Scriptures:[d] "The people sat down to eat and drink. Then they got up and sinned sexually."[n] [8]We should not take part in sexual sins, as some of them did. In one day 23,000

of them died because of their sins. [9]We should not test the Lord as some of them did. They were killed by snakes. [10]And do not complain as some of them did. They were killed by the angel that destroys.

[11]The things that happened to those people are examples. And they were written down to be warnings for us. For we live in a time when all these things of the past have reached their goal. [12]So anyone who thinks he is standing strong should be careful not to fall. [13]The only temptations that you have are the temptations that all people have. But you can trust God. He will not let you be tempted more than you can stand. But when you are tempted, God will also give you a way to escape that temptation. Then you will be able to stand it.

[14]So, my dear friends, stay away from worshiping idols. [15]I am speaking to you, as to intelligent people; judge for yourselves what I say. [16]We give thanks

Temptation
1 CORINTHIANS 10:13

"I couldn't help it! The desire to do wrong was too strong. Anybody else in my position would have done the same thing."

People often talk that way when they get caught doing something wrong. It's natural to try to blame the situation or someone else rather than admit that we chose to commit a sin. But in this verse, God says that we *are* responsible for what we do. Paul says that the temptations we run into are the same ones that people everywhere have. He also says that God won't allow us to be tempted more than we can handle. And further, Paul says that God will always make a way out of the temptation. The question is, do we want to take God's way? Sometimes the best way out of a tempting situation is not to put ourselves in it in the first place.

When you are struggling with the desire to do something wrong, try memorizing 1 Corinthians 10:13. It may be just the escape you need.

To learn more about temptation, zoom to page 1473.

[n]"The people . . . sexually." Quotation from Exodus 32:6.

for the cup of blessing.[n] It is a sharing in the blood of Christ's death. And the bread that we break is a sharing in the body of Christ. [17]There is one loaf of bread. And we are many people. But we all share from that one loaf. So we are really one body.

[18]Think about the people of Israel: Do not those who eat the sacrifices share in the altar? [19]I do not mean that the food sacrificed to an idol is something important. And I do not mean that an idol is anything at all. [20]But I say that what is sacrificed to idols is offered to demons,[d] not to God. And I do not want you to share anything with demons. [21]You cannot drink the cup of the Lord and the cup of demons, too. You cannot share in the Lord's table and the table of demons, too. [22]Do we want to make the Lord jealous? We are not stronger than he is, are we?

How to Use Christian Freedom

[23]"We are allowed to do all things." Yes. But all things are not good for us to do. "We are allowed to do all things." Yes. But not all things help others grow stronger. [24]No one should try to do what will help only himself. He should try to do what is good for others.

[25]Eat any meat that is sold in the meat market. Do not ask questions about the meat to see if it is something you think is wrong to eat. [26]You can eat it, "because the earth and everything on it belong to the Lord."[n]

[27]Someone who is not a believer may invite you to eat with him. If you want to go, eat anything that is put before you. Do not ask questions to see if it is something you think might be wrong to eat. [28]But if anyone says to you, "That food was offered to idols," then do not eat it. Do not eat it because of that person who told you and because eating it would be something that might be thought wrong. [29]I don't mean that

you think it is wrong. But the other person might think it is wrong. My own freedom should not be judged by what someone else thinks. [30]I eat the meal with thankfulness. And I do not want to be criticized because of something I thank God for.

[31]So if you eat, or if you drink, or if you do anything, do everything for the glory of God. [32]Never do anything that might make others do wrong—Jews, Greeks, or God's church. [33]I do the same thing. I try to please everybody in every way. I am not trying to do what is good for me. I try to do what is good for the most people. I do this so that they can be saved.

11 Follow my example, as I follow the example of Christ.

Being Under Authority

[2]I praise you because you remember me in everything. You follow closely the teachings that I gave you. [3]But I want you to understand this: The head of every man is Christ. And the head of a woman is the man.[n] And the head of Christ is God. [4]Every man who prophesies[d] or prays with his head covered brings shame to his head. [5]But every woman who prays or prophesies should have her head covered. If her head is not covered, she brings shame to her head. She is the same as a woman who has her head shaved. [6]If a woman does not cover her head, it is the same as cutting off all her hair. But it is shameful for a woman to cut off her hair or to shave her head. So she should cover her head. [7]But a man should not cover his head, because he is made like God and is God's glory. But woman is man's glory. [8]Man did not come from woman, but woman came from man. [9]And man was not made for woman. Woman was made for man. [10]So that is why a woman should have her head covered with something to show that she is under

---

[n]**cup of blessing**   The cup of the fruit of the vine that Christians thank God for and drink at the Lord's Supper.
[n]**"because . . . Lord"**   Quotation from Psalms 24:1; 50:12; 89:11.
[n]**the man**   This could also mean "her husband."

authority. And also she should do this because of the angels.

¹¹But in the Lord the woman is important to the man, and the man is important to the woman. ¹²This is true because woman came from man, but also man is born from woman. Really, everything comes from God. ¹³Decide this for yourselves: Is it right for a woman to pray to God without something on her head? ¹⁴Even nature itself teaches you that wearing long hair is shameful for a man. ¹⁵But wearing long hair is a woman's honor. Long hair is given to the woman to cover her head. ¹⁶Some people may still want to argue about this. But I would add that neither we nor the churches of God accept any other practice.

"I guess taking communion with other Christians is a serious and special part of obeying Jesus. Read about it in 1 Corinthians 11:17-34."

The Lord's Supper

¹⁷In the things I tell you now I do not praise you. Your meetings hurt you more than they help you. ¹⁸First, I hear that when you meet together as a church you are divided. And I believe some of this. ¹⁹(It is necessary for there to be differences among you. That is the way to make it clear which of you are really doing right.) ²⁰When you all come together, you are not really eating the Lord's Supper.ⁿ ²¹This is because when you eat, each person eats without waiting for the others. Some people do not get enough to eat, while others have too much to drink. ²²You can eat and drink in your own homes! It seems that you think God's church is not important. You embarrass those who are poor. What should I tell you? Should I praise you for doing this? I do not praise you.

²³The teaching that I gave you is the same teaching that I received from the Lord: On the night when Jesus was handed over to be killed, he took bread ²⁴and gave thanks for it. Then he broke the bread and said, "This is my body; it is for you. Do this to remember me." ²⁵In the same way, after they ate, Jesus took the cup. He said, "This cup shows the new agreement from God to his people. This new agreement begins with the blood of my death. When you drink this, do it to remember me." ²⁶Every time you eat this bread and drink this cup, you show others about the Lord's death until he comes.

²⁷So a person should not eat the bread or drink the cup of the Lord in a way that is not worthy of it. If he does he is sinning against the body and the blood of the Lord. ²⁸Everyone should look into his own heart before he eats the bread and drinks the cup. ²⁹If someone eats the bread and drinks the cup without recognizing the body, then he is judged guilty by eating and drinking. ³⁰That is why many in your group are sick and weak. And many have died. ³¹But if we judged ourselves in the right way, then God would not judge us. ³²But when the Lord judges us, he punishes us to show us the right way. He does this so that we will not be destroyed along with the world.

³³So my brothers, when you come together to eat, wait for each other. ³⁴If anyone is too hungry, he should eat at home. Do this so that your meeting together will not bring God's judgment on you. I will tell you what to do about the other things when I come.

Gifts from the Holy Spirit

12 Now, brothers, I want you to understand about spiritual gifts. ²You remember the lives you lived before you were believers. You let yourselves be influenced and led away to worship idols—things that have no life. ³So I tell you that no one who is speaking with the help of God's Spirit

---

ⁿ**Lord's Supper** The meal Jesus told his followers to eat to remember him (Luke 22:14-20).

Whit's Wisdom: The Body of Christ
1 Corinthians 12:12-27

You can never tell what someone's going to ask when the kids show up at Whit's End, my ice cream parlor in Odyssey. Last week, Calvin was wondering why God made all of us so different. He thought that things might be better if we were all the same. I asked the others what they thought. Some agreed with Calvin. Others wondered what we would be like if we were all the same. Then someone said if we were all the same we wouldn't need each other. Somebody else asked what I thought.

"**K**ids," I answered, "I'd be happy to tell you what I think. But before I do that, maybe we should take a look at what God thinks." I opened a Bible to 1 Corinthians 12:12-27 and handed it to one of the kids. If you were there, I might have handed it to you. Why don't you read those verses out loud?

The kids laughed several times during the reading. They thought it was funny that an eye or an ear or a hand might think it could get along without the rest of the body. Or that the rest of the body wouldn't miss the ear or hand. "Yeah," added Jessie, "without a brain how would we even think!"

After the jokes quieted down, Calvin said, "So, Mr. Whittaker, what the Bible is saying is that we are like the different parts of a body?"

"**R**ight, Calvin," I answered. "Each of us has an important function, or job, but none of us can really get along without the rest of us. We need each other."

Calvin nodded his head like he understood, so I asked the rest of the kids, "Who was Paul writing about here? Was it a certain group of people, or everybody?" Some thought it was everybody; others thought he must have had a group in mind. "Well," I said, "the best way to settle this is to find out what the Bible says, right?" They agreed so I had one of them look at 1 Corinthians 1:2. That's where we found our answer. There is a group of people God calls a body. Can you find who that group is? Are you part of it?

Related Passages: Romans 12:1-13; Ephesians 4:1-16.

Teacher/Parent Hint: Use this little study to teach your children about the church and their participation in it. The study may challenge your own family's level of participation in the local church.

---

says, "Jesus be cursed." And no one can say, "Jesus is Lord," without the help of the Holy Spirit.[d]

[4]There are different kinds of gifts; but they are all from the same Spirit. [5]There are different ways to serve; but all these ways are from the same Lord. [6]And there are different ways that God

works in people; but all these ways are from the same God. God works in us all in everything we do. [7]Something from the Spirit can be seen in each person, to help everyone. [8]The Spirit gives one person the ability to speak with wisdom. And the same Spirit gives another the ability to speak with knowlanother gifts of healing. [10]The Spirit gives to another person the power to do miracles,[d] to another the ability to prophesy.[d] And he gives to another the ability to know the difference between good and evil spirits. The Spirit gives one person the ability to speak in different kinds of languages[n] and to another the ability to interpret those languages. [11]One Spirit, the same Spirit, does all these things. The Spirit decides what to give each person.

The Body of Christ

[12]A person's body is only one thing, but it has many parts. Yes, there are many parts to a body, but all those parts make only one body. Christ is like that too. [13]Some of us are Jews, and some of us are Greeks. Some of us are slaves, and some of us are free. But we were all baptized into one body through one Spirit.[d] And we were all made to share in the one Spirit.

[14]And a person's body has more than one part. It has many parts. [15]The foot might say, "I am not a hand. So I am not part of the body." But saying this would not stop the foot from being a part of the body. [16]The ear might say, "I am not an eye. So I am not part of the body." But saying this would not make the ear stop being a part of the body. [17]If the whole body were an eye, the body would not be able to hear. If the whole body were an ear, the body would not be able to smell anything. [18-19]If each part of the body were the same part, there would be no body. But truly God put the parts in the body as he wanted them. He made a place for each one of them. [20]And so there are many parts, but only one body.

[21]The eye cannot say to the hand, "I don't need you!" And the head cannot say to the foot, "I don't need you!" [22]No! Those parts of the body that seem to be weaker are really very important. [23]And the parts of the body that we think are not worth much are the parts that we give the most care to. And we give special care to the parts of the body that we want to hide. [24]The more beautiful parts of our body need no special care. But God put the body together and gave more honor to the parts that need it. [25]God did this so that our body would not be divided. God wanted the different parts to care the same for each other. [26]If one part of the body suffers, then all the other parts suffer with it. Or if one part of our body is honored, then all the other parts share its honor.

[27]All of you together are the body of Christ. Each one of you is a part of that body. [28]And in the church God has given a place first to apostles,[d] second to prophets,[d] and third to teachers. Then God has given a place to those who do miracles,[d] those who have gifts of healing, those who can help others, those who are able to lead, and those who can speak in different languages.[n] [29]Not all are apostles. Not all are prophets. Not all are teachers. Not all do miracles. [30]Not all have gifts of healing. Not all speak in different languages. Not all interpret those languages. [31]But you should truly want to have the greater gifts.

Love

And now I will show you the best way of all.

> "This chapter, 1 Corinthians 13, is like God's valentine card to the world. It tells us what real love is like. Read it."

13 I may speak in different languages[n] of men or even angels. But if I do not have love, then I am only a noisy bell or a ringing cymbal. [2]I may have the gift of prophecy;[d] I may

---

[n]**languages** This can also be translated "tongues."

understand all the secret things of God and all knowledge; and I may have faith so great that I can move mountains. But even with all these things, if I do not have love, then I am nothing. ³I may give everything I have to feed the poor. And I may even give my body as an offering to be burned. But I gain nothing by doing these things if I do not have love.

⁴Love is patient and kind. Love is not jealous, it does not brag, and it is not proud. ⁵Love is not rude, is not selfish, and does not become angry easily. Love does not remember wrongs done against it. ⁶Love is not happy with evil, but is happy with the truth. ⁷Love patiently accepts all things. It always trusts, always hopes, and always continues strong.

⁸Love never ends. There are gifts of prophecy,ᵈ but they will be ended. There are gifts of speaking in different languages, but those gifts will end. There is the gift of knowledge, but it will be ended. ⁹These things will end, because this knowledge and these prophecies we have are not complete. ¹⁰But when perfection comes, the things that are not complete will end. ¹¹When I was a child, I talked like a child; I thought like a child; I made plans like a child. When I became a man, I stopped those childish ways. ¹²It is the same with us. Now we see as if we are looking into a dark mirror. But at that time, in the future, we shall see clearly. Now I know only a part. But at that time I will know fully, as God has known me. ¹³So these three things continue forever: faith, hope and love. And the greatest of these is love.

Spiritual Gifts

14 Love, then, is what you should try for. And you should truly want to have the spiritual gifts. And the gift you should want most is to be able to prophesy.ᵈ ²I will explain why. One who has the gift of speaking in a different languageⁿ is not speaking to people. He is speaking to God. No one understands him—he is speaking secret things through the Spirit.ᵈ ³But one who prophesies is speaking to people. He

Character
1 CORINTHIANS 13:2-7

We have been talking about how to develop good qualities in our lives: qualities like honesty, loyalty, patience, and others. All of these are good, and we should try to have them in our lives. But of all the qualities the Bible teaches us to develop, these verses say that the most important is *love.*

Love is really all the good character traits joined together. In fact, the Bible says that without love, all the others aren't worth anything at all.

So be honest, but make sure you do it lovingly. Be loyal, but make sure your loyalty is powered by love. Be patient, but not just because you know you have to be. Show patience to others because you love them.

Let love be the mark on all that you do and all that you are.

To learn more about character, zoom to page 1435.

ⁿ**language**   This can also be translated "tongue."

gives people strength, encouragement, and comfort. [4]The one who speaks in a different language is helping only himself. But the one who prophesies is helping the whole church. [5]I would like all of you to have the gift of speaking in different kinds of languages. But more, I want you to prophesy. The person who prophesies is greater than the one who can only speak in different languages—unless someone is there who can explain what he says. Then the whole church can be helped.

[6]Brothers, will it help you if I come to you speaking in different languages? No! It will help you only if I bring you a new truth or some knowledge, or some prophecy, or some teaching. [7]It is the same as with non-living things that make sounds—like a flute or a harp. If different musical notes are not made clear, you will not know what song is being played. Each note must be played clearly for you to be able to understand the tune. [8]And in a war, if the trumpet does not sound clearly, the soldiers will not know it is time to prepare for fighting. [9]It is the same with you. The words you speak with your tongue must be clear. Unless you speak clearly, no one can understand what you are saying. You will be talking in the air! [10]It is true that there are many kinds of speech in the world. And they all have meaning. [11]So unless I understand the meaning of what someone says to me, I am a stranger to him, and he is a stranger to me. [12]It is the same with you. You want spiritual gifts very much. So try most to have the gifts that help the church grow stronger.

[13]The one who has the gift of speaking in a different language should pray that he can also interpret what he says. [14]If I pray in a different language, my spirit is praying, but my mind does nothing. [15]So what should I do? I will pray with my spirit, but I will also pray with my mind. I will sing with my spirit, but I will also sing with my mind. [16]You might be praising God with your spirit.

But a person there without understanding cannot say "Amen"[n] to your prayer of thanks. He does not know what you are saying. [17]You may be thanking God in a good way, but the other person is not helped.

[18]I thank God that my gift of speaking in different kinds of languages is greater than any of yours. [19]But in the church meetings I would rather speak five words that I understand than thousands of words in a different language. I would rather speak with my understanding, so that I can teach others.

[20]Brothers, do not think like children. In evil things be like babies. But in your thinking you should be like full-grown men. [21]It is written in the Scriptures:[d]

"I will use strange words and
    foreign languages
  to speak to these people.
But even then they will not listen."

Isaiah 28:11-12

That is what the Lord says.

[22]So the gift of speaking in different kinds of languages is a proof for those who do not believe, not for those who believe. And prophecy is for people who believe, not for those who do not believe. [23]Suppose the whole church meets together and everyone speaks in different languages. If some people come in who are without understanding or do not believe, they will say you are crazy. [24]But suppose everyone is prophesying and someone comes in who does not believe or is without understanding. If everyone is prophesying, his sin will be shown to him, and he will be judged by all that he hears. [25]The secret things in his heart will be made known. So he will bow down and worship God. He will say, "Truly, God is with you."

Meetings Should Help the Church

[26]So, brothers, what should you do? When you meet together, one person has a song. Another has a teaching. Another has a new truth from God.

---

[n]"Amen" When a person says "Amen," it means he agrees with the things that were said.

Another speaks in a different language,[n] and another person interprets that language. The purpose of all these things should be to help the church grow strong. [27]When you meet together, if anyone speaks in a different language, then it should be only two, or not more than three, who speak. They should speak one after the other. And someone else should interpret what they say. [28]But if there is no interpreter, then anyone who speaks in a different language should be quiet in the church meeting. He should speak only to himself and to God.

[29]And only two or three prophets[d] should speak. The others should judge what they say. [30]And if a message from God comes to another person who is sitting, then the first speaker should stop. [31]You can all prophesy one after the other. In this way all the people can be taught and encouraged. [32]The spirits of prophets are under the control of the prophets themselves. [33]God is not a God of confusion but a God of peace.

This is true in all the churches of God's people. [34]Women should keep quiet in the church meetings. They are not allowed to speak. They must be under control. This is also what the law of Moses says. [35]If there is something the women want to know, they should ask their own husbands at home. It is shameful for a woman to speak in the church meeting. [36]Did God's teaching come from you? Or are you the only ones who have received that teaching?

[37]If anyone thinks that he is a prophet or that he has a spiritual gift, then he should understand that what I am writing to you is the Lord's command. [38]If that person does not know this, then he is not known by God.

[39]So my brothers, you should truly want to prophesy. And do not stop people from using the gift of speaking in different kinds of languages. [40]But let everything be done in a way that is right and orderly.

The Good News About Christ

15 Now, brothers, I want you to remember the Good News[d] I brought to you. You received this Good News, and you continue strong in it. [2]And you are saved by this Good News. But you must continue believing what I told you. If you do not, then you believed for nothing.

[3]I passed on to you what I received. And this was the most important: that

> "**W**ould it make a big difference if Jesus hadn't risen from the dead? What if Easter was just a nice story? The Bible answers that question in 1 Corinthians 15:1-34."

Christ died for our sins, as the Scriptures[d] say; [4]that he was buried and was raised to life on the third day as the Scriptures say; [5]and that he showed himself to Peter and then to the twelve apostles.[d] [6]After that, Jesus showed himself to more than 500 of the believers at the same time. Most of them are still living today. But some have died. [7]Then Jesus showed himself to James and later to all the apostles. [8]Last of all he showed himself to me—as to a person not born at the normal time. [9]All the other apostles are greater than I am. This is because I persecuted the church of God. And this is why I am not even good enough to be called an apostle. [10]But God's grace has made me what I am. And his grace to me was not wasted. I worked harder than all the other apostles. (But I was not really the one working. It was God's grace that was with me.) [11]So then it is not important if I preached to you or if the other apostles preached to you. We all preach the same thing, and this is what you believed.

[n]**language** This can also be translated "tongue."

We Will Be Raised from Death

[12]It is preached that Christ was raised from death. So why do some of you say that people will not be raised from death? [13]If no one will ever be raised from death, then Christ was not raised from death. [14]And if Christ was not raised, then our preaching is worth nothing. And your faith is worth nothing. [15]And also, we will be guilty of lying about God. Because we have preached about him by saying that he raised Christ from death. And if people are not raised from death, then God never raised Christ from death. [16]If the dead are not raised, Christ has not been raised either. [17]And if Christ has not been raised, then your faith is for nothing; you are still guilty of your sins. [18]And also, those in Christ who have already died are lost. [19]If our hope in Christ is for this life only, we should be pitied more than anyone else in the world.

[20]But Christ has truly been raised from death—the first one and proof that those who are asleep in death will also be raised. [21]Death comes to everyone because of what one man did. But the rising from death also happens because of one man. [22]In Adam all of us die. In the same way, in Christ all of us will be made alive again. [23]But everyone will be raised to life in the right order. Christ was first to be raised. When Christ comes again, those who belong to him will be raised to life. [24]Then the end will come. Christ will destroy all rulers, authorities, and powers. And he will give the kingdom to God the Father. [25]Christ must rule until God puts all enemies under Christ's control. [26]The last enemy to be destroyed will be death. [27]The Scripture[d] says, "God put all things under his control."[n] When it says that "all things" are put under him, it is clear that this does not include God himself. God is the one putting every-thing under Christ's control. [28]After everything has been put under Christ, then the Son himself will be put under God. God is the One who put all things under Christ. And Christ will be put under God, so that God will be the complete ruler over everything.

[29]If the dead are never raised, then what will people do who are baptized for those who have died? If the dead are not raised at all, why are people baptized for them?

[30]And what about us? Why do we put ourselves in danger every hour? [31]I die every day. That is true, brothers, just as it is true that I brag about you in Christ Jesus our Lord. [32]If I fought wild animals in Ephesus only for human reasons, I have gained nothing. If the dead are not raised, then, "Let us eat and drink, because tomorrow we will die."[n]

[33]Do not be fooled: "Bad friends will ruin good habits." [34]Come back to your right way of thinking and stop sinning. I say this to shame you—some of you do not know God.

What Kind of Body Will We Have?

[35]But someone may ask, "How are the dead raised? What kind of body will they have?" [36]Those are stupid questions. When you plant something, it must die in the ground before it can live and grow. [37]And when you plant it, what you plant does not have the same "body" that it will have later. What you plant is only a seed, maybe wheat or something else. [38]But God gives it a body that he has planned for it. And God gives each kind of seed its own body. [39]All things made of flesh are not the same kinds of flesh: People have one kind of flesh, animals have another kind, birds have another, and fish have another. [40]Also there are heavenly bodies and earthly bodies. But the beauty of the heavenly bodies is one kind. The beauty of the earthly bodies is another kind. [41]The sun has one kind of beauty. The moon has another

[n]"God put . . . control."   Quotation from Psalm 8:6.
[n]"Let us . . . die."   Quotation from Isaiah 22:13; 56:12.

beauty, and the stars have another. And each star is different in its beauty.

⁴²It is the same with the dead who are raised to life. The body that is "planted" will ruin and decay. But the body that is raised to a life that cannot be destroyed. ⁴³When the body is "planted," it is without honor. But it is raised in glory. When the body is "planted," it is weak. But when it is raised, it has power. ⁴⁴The body that is "planted" is a physical body. When it is raised, it is a spiritual body.

There is a physical body. And there is also a spiritual body. ⁴⁵It is written in the Scriptures:ᵈ "The first man became a living person."ⁿ But the last Adam became a spirit that gives life. ⁴⁶The spiritual man did not come first. It was the physical man who came first; then came the spiritual. ⁴⁷The first man came from the dust of the earth. The second man came from heaven. ⁴⁸People belong to the earth. They are like the first man of earth. But those people who belong to heaven are like the man of heaven. ⁴⁹We were made like the man of earth. So we will also be made like the man of heaven.

⁵⁰I tell you this, brothers: Flesh and blood cannot have a part in the kingdom of God. A thing that will ruin cannot have a part in something that never ruins. ⁵¹But listen, I tell you this secret: We will not all die, but we will all be changed. ⁵²It will only take a second. We will be changed as quickly as an eye blinks. This will happen when the last trumpet sounds. The trumpet will sound and those who have died will be raised to live forever. And we will all be changed. ⁵³This body that will ruin must clothe itself with something that will never ruin. And this body that dies must clothe itself with something that will never die. ⁵⁴So this body that ruins will clothe itself with that which never ruins. And this body that dies will clothe itself with that which never dies. When this happens, then this Scripture will be made true:

"Death is destroyed forever in
    victory."   *Isaiah 25:8*
⁵⁵"Death, where is your victory?
  Death, where is your power to
    hurt?"   *Hosea 13:14*
⁵⁶Death's power to hurt is sin. The power of sin is the law. ⁵⁷But we thank

Thankfulness
1 CORINTHIANS 15:57

Imagine that you have just watched a runner streak by the finish line in a big race. Then you see the judge give the hot, sweaty runner one of the biggest trophies you've ever seen. Suddenly the runner walks over to you, gives you the trophy, and says that you are the winner! He did all the work, but thanks to him, you receive the prize.

That's a picture of what Jesus did for us. Jesus won eternal life for us because he died on the cross for our sins, the things we do wrong. We didn't die on the cross, but he gives us his prize—eternal life with him. Thanks to Jesus, we get the trophy.

What a gift! That's why Paul says, "Thank God for Jesus!" Thanking God for Jesus is one of the most important things we can do.

For more on thankfulness, zoom to page 1424.

ⁿ**"The first . . . person."** Quotation from Genesis 2:7.

God! He gives us the victory through our Lord Jesus Christ.

58 So my dear brothers, stand strong. Do not let anything change you. Always give yourselves fully to the work of the Lord. You know that your work in the Lord is never wasted.

The Gift for Other Believers

16 Now I will write about the collection of money for God's people. Do the same thing that I told the Galatian churches to do: 2 On the first day of every week, each one of you should put aside as much money as you can from what you are blessed with. You should save it up, so that you will not have to collect money after I come. 3 When I arrive, I will send some men to take your gift to Jerusalem. These will be men who you all agree should go. I will send them with letters of introduction. 4 If it seems good for me to go also, these men will go along with me.

Paul's Plans

5 I plan to go through Macedonia. So I will come to you after I go through there. 6 Maybe I will stay with you for a time. I might even stay all winter. Then you can help me on my trip, wherever I go. 7 I do not want to come to see you now, because I would have to leave to go other places. I hope to stay a longer time with you if the Lord allows it. 8 But I will stay at Ephesus until Pentecost.*d* 9 I will stay, because a good opportunity for a great and growing work has been given to me now. And there are many people working against me.

10 Timothy might come to you. Try to make him feel comfortable with you. He is working for the Lord just as I am. 11 So none of you should refuse to accept Timothy. Help him on his trip in peace, so that he can come back to me. I am expecting him to come back with the brothers.

12 Now about our brother Apollos: I strongly encouraged him to visit you with the other brothers. But he was sure that he did not want to go now. But when he has the opportunity, he will go to you.

Paul Ends His Letter

13 Be careful. Continue strong in the faith. Have courage, and be strong. 14 Do everything in love.

15 You know that the family of Stephanas were the first believers in Southern Greece. They have given themselves to the service of God's people. I ask you, brothers, 16 to follow the leading of people like these and anyone else who works and serves with them.

17 I am happy that Stephanas, Fortunatus, and Achaicus have come. You are not here, but they have filled your place. 18 They have given rest to my spirit and to yours. You should recognize the value of men like these.

19 The churches in the country of Asia send greetings to you. Aquila and Priscilla greet you in the Lord. Also the church that meets in their house greets you. 20 All the brothers here send greetings. Give each other a holy kiss when you meet.

21 I am Paul, and I am writing this greeting with my own hand.

22 If anyone does not love the Lord, then let him be separated from God— lost forever!

Come, O Lord!

23 The grace of the Lord Jesus be with you.

24 My love be with all of you in Christ Jesus.

2 CORINTHIANS

Paul Answers Those
Who Accuse Him

1 From Paul, an apostle[d] of Christ Jesus. I am an apostle because that is what God wanted.

Also from Timothy our brother in Christ.

To the church of God in Corinth, and to all of God's people in the whole country of Southern Greece:

[2] Grace and peace to you from God our Father and the Lord Jesus Christ.

Paul Gives Thanks to God

[3] Praise be to the God and Father of our Lord Jesus Christ. God is the Father who is full of mercy. And he is the God of all comfort. [4] He comforts us every time we have trouble, so that we can comfort others when they have trouble. We can comfort them with the same comfort that God gives us. [5] We share in the many sufferings of Christ. In the same way, much comfort comes to us through Christ. [6] If we have troubles, it is for your comfort and salvation. If we have comfort, then you also have comfort. This helps you to accept patiently the same sufferings that we have. [7] Our hope for you is strong. We know that you share in our sufferings. So we know that you also share in the comfort we receive.

[8] Brothers, we want you to know about the trouble we suffered in the country of Asia. We had great burdens there that were greater than our own strength. We even gave up hope for life. [9] Truly, in our own hearts we believed that we would die. But this happened so that we would not trust in ourselves. It happened so that we would trust in God, who raises people from death. [10] God saved us from these great dangers of death. And he will continue to save us. We have put our hope in him, and he will save us again. [11] And you can help us with your prayers. Then many people will give thanks for us—that God blessed us because of their many prayers.

The Change in Paul's Plans

[12] This is what we are proud of, and I can say with all my heart that it is true: In all the things we have done in the world, we have done everything with an honest and pure heart from God. And this is even more true in what we have done with you. We did this by God's grace, not by the kind of wisdom the world has. [13] For we write to you only what you can read and understand. And I hope that [14] as you have understood some things about us, you may come to know everything about us. Then you can be proud of us, as we will be proud of you on the day our Lord Jesus Christ comes again.

[15] I was very sure of all this. That is why I made plans to visit you first. Then you could be blessed twice. [16] I planned to visit you on my way to Macedonia. Then I planned to visit you again on my way back. I wanted to get help from you for my trip to Judea. [17] Do you think that I made these plans without really thinking? Or maybe you think I make plans as the world does, so that I say "Yes, yes," and at the same time "No, no."

[18] But if you can believe God, then you can believe that what we tell you is never both "Yes" and "No." [19] The Son of God, Jesus Christ, that Silas and Timothy and I preached to you, was not

"Yes" and "No." In Christ it has always been "Yes." [20]The "Yes" to all of God's promises is in Christ. And that is why we say "Amen"[n] through Christ to the glory of God. [21]And God is the One who makes you and us strong in Christ. God made us his chosen people. [22]He put his mark on us to show that we are his. And he put his Spirit[d] in our hearts to be a guarantee for all he has promised.

[23]I tell you this, and I ask God to be my witness that this is true: The reason I did not come back to Corinth was that I did not want to punish or hurt you. [24]I do not mean that we are trying to control your faith. You are strong in faith. But we are workers with you for your own happiness.

2 So I decided that my next visit to you would not be another visit to make you sad. [2]If I make you sad, who will make me happy? Only you can make me happy—you whom I made sad. [3]I wrote you a letter for this reason: that when I came to you I would not be made sad by the people who should make me happy. I felt sure of all of you. I felt sure that you would share my joy. [4]When I wrote to you before, I was very troubled and unhappy in my heart. I wrote with many tears. I did not write to make you sad, but to let you know how much I love you.

Forgive the Sinner

[5]Someone there among you has caused sadness. He caused this not to me, but to all of you—I mean he caused sadness to all in some way. (I do not want to make it sound worse than it really is.) [6]The punishment that most of you gave him is enough for him. [7]But now you should forgive him and comfort him. This will keep him from having too much sadness and giving up completely. [8]So I beg you to show him that you love him. [9]This is why I wrote to you. I wanted to test you and see if you obey in everything. [10]If you forgive someone, I also forgive him. And what

I have forgiven—if I had anything to forgive—I forgave it for you, and Christ was with me. [11]I did this so that Satan would not win anything from us. We know very well what Satan's plans are.

Paul's Concern in Troas

[12]I went to Troas to preach the Good News[d] of Christ. The Lord gave me a good opportunity there. [13]But I had no peace because I did not find my brother Titus there. So I said good-bye and went to Macedonia.

Victory Through Christ

[14]But thanks be to God, who always leads us in victory through Christ. God uses us to spread his knowledge everywhere like a sweet-smelling perfume. [15]Our offering to God is this: We are the sweet smell of Christ among those who are being saved and among those who are being lost. [16]To those who are lost, we are the smell of death that brings death. But to those who are being saved, we are the smell of life that brings life. So who is able to do this work? [17]We do not sell the word of God for a profit as many other people do. But in Christ we speak the truth before God. We speak as men sent from God.

Servants of the New Agreement

3 Are we starting to brag about ourselves again? Do we need letters of introduction to you or from you, like some other people? [2]You yourselves are our letter, written on our hearts. It is known and read by everyone. [3]You show that you are a letter from Christ that he sent through us. This letter is not written with ink, but with the Spirit[d] of the living God. It is not written on stone tablets.[n] It is written on human hearts.

[4]We can say this, because through Christ we feel sure before God. [5]I do not mean that we are able to say that we can do this work ourselves. It is God who makes us able to do all that we

---

[n]**"Amen"** When a person says "Amen," it means he agrees with the things that were said.
[n]**stone tablets** Meaning the law of Moses that was written on stone tablets (Exodus 24:12; 25:16).

do. ⁶God made us able to be servants of a new agreement from himself to his people. This new agreement is not a written law. It is of the Spirit. The written law brings death, but the Spirit gives life.

⁷The law that brought death was written in words on stone. It came with God's glory. Moses' face was so bright with glory that the people of Israel could not continue to look at his face. And that glory later disappeared. ⁸So surely the new way that brings the Spirit has even more glory. ⁹That law judged people guilty of sin, but it had glory. So surely the new way that makes people right with God has much greater glory. ¹⁰That old law had glory. But it really loses its glory when it is compared to the much greater glory of this new way. ¹¹If that law which disappeared came with glory, then this new way which continues forever has much greater glory.

¹²We have this hope, so we are very brave. ¹³We are not like Moses. He put a covering over his face so that the people of Israel would not see it. The glory was disappearing, and Moses did not want them to see it end. ¹⁴But their minds were closed. Even today that same covering hides the meaning when they read the old agreement. That covering is taken away only through Christ. ¹⁵But even today, when they read the law of Moses, there is a covering over their minds. ¹⁶But when a person changes and follows the Lord, that covering is taken away. ¹⁷The Lord is the Spirit. And where the Spirit of the Lord is, there is freedom. ¹⁸Our faces, then, are not covered. We all show the Lord's glory, and we are being changed to be like him. This change in us brings more and more glory. And it comes from the Lord, who is the Spirit.

Preaching the Good News

4 God, with his mercy, gave us this work to do. So we don't give up. ²But we have turned away from secret and shameful ways. We use no trickery, and we do not change the teaching of God. We teach the truth plainly. This is how we show everyone who we are. And this is how they can know in their hearts what kind of people we are before God. ³The Good News*ᵈ* that we preach may be hidden. But it is hidden only to those who are lost. ⁴The devil who rules this world has blinded the minds of those who do not believe. They cannot see the light of the Good News—the Good News about the glory of Christ, who is exactly like God. ⁵We do not preach about ourselves. But we preach that Jesus Christ is Lord; and we preach that we are your servants for Jesus. ⁶God once said, "Let the light shine out of the darkness!" And this is the same God who made his light shine in our hearts. He gave us light by letting us know the glory of God that is in the face of Christ.

"**T**he older I get, the more I realize how true God's word is. These verses tell us that we are like a pottery jar. But look at what's inside when you read 2 Corinthians 4:7-15."

Spiritual Treasure in Clay Jars

⁷We have this treasure from God. But we are only like clay jars that hold the treasure. This shows that this great power is from God, not from us. ⁸We have troubles all around us, but we are not defeated. We do not know what to do, but we do not give up. ⁹We are persecuted, but God does not leave us. We are hurt sometimes, but we are not destroyed. ¹⁰We carry the death of Jesus in our own bodies, so that the life of Jesus can also be seen in our bodies. ¹¹We are alive, but for Jesus we are always in danger of death. This is so that the life of Jesus can be seen in our bodies that die.

¹²So death is working in us, but life is working in you.

¹³It is written in the Scriptures,ᵈ "I believed, so I spoke."ⁿ Our faith is like this, too. We believe, and so we speak. ¹⁴God raised the Lord Jesus from death. And we know that God will also raise us with Jesus. God will bring us together with you, and we will stand before him. ¹⁵All these things are for you. And so the grace of God is being given to more and more people. This will bring more and more thanks to God for his glory.

Living by Faith

¹⁶So we do not give up. Our physical body is becoming older and weaker, but our spirit inside us is made new every day. ¹⁷We have small troubles for a while now, but they are helping us gain an eternal glory. That glory is much greater than the troubles. ¹⁸So we set our eyes not on what we see but on what we cannot see. What we see will last only a short time. But what we cannot see will last forever.

5 We know that our body—the tent we live in here on earth—will be destroyed. But when that happens, God will have a house for us to live in. It will not be a house made by men. It will be a home in heaven that will last forever. ²But now we are tired of this body. We want God to give us our heavenly home. ³It will clothe us, and we will not be naked. ⁴While we live in this body, we have burdens, and we complain. We do not want to be naked. We want to be clothed with our heavenly home. Then this body that dies will be fully covered with life. ⁵This is what God made us for. And he has given us the Spiritᵈ to be a guarantee for this new life.

⁶So we always have courage. We know that while we live in this body, we are away from the Lord. ⁷We live by what we believe, not by what we can see. ⁸So I say that we have courage. And we really want to be away from this body and be at home with the Lord.

⁹Our only goal is to please God. We want to please him whether we live here or there. ¹⁰For we must all stand before Christ to be judged. Each one will receive what he should get—good or bad—for the things he did when he lived in the earthly body.

Becoming Friends with God

¹¹We know what it means to fear the Lord. So we try to help people accept the truth. God knows what we really are. And I hope that in your hearts you know, too. ¹²We are not trying to prove ourselves to you again. But we are telling you about ourselves, so you will be proud of us. Then you will have an answer for those who are proud about things that can be seen. They do not care about what is in the heart. ¹³If we are out of our minds, it is for God. If we have our right mind, then it is for you. ¹⁴The love of Christ controls us. Because we know that One died for all. So all have died. ¹⁵Christ died for all so that those who live would not continue to live for themselves. He died for them and was raised from death so that they would live for him.

¹⁶From this time on we do not think of anyone as the world does. It is true that in the past we thought of Christ as the world thinks. But we no longer think of him in that way. ¹⁷If anyone belongs to Christ, then he is made new. The old things have gone; everything is made new! ¹⁸All this is from God. Through Christ, God made peace between us and himself. And God gave us the work of bringing everyone into peace with him. ¹⁹I mean that God was in Christ, making peace between the world and himself. In Christ, God did not hold the world guilty of its sins. And he gave us this message of peace. ²⁰So we have been sent to speak for Christ. It is as if God is calling to you through us. We speak for Christ when we beg you to be at peace with God. ²¹Christ had no sin. But God made him become sin. God did this for us so that

---

ⁿ**"I ... spoke."** Quotation from Psalm 116:10.

in Christ we could become right with God.

6 We are workers together with God. So we beg you: Do not let the grace that you received from God be for nothing. ²God says,

"I heard your prayers at the right time,
and I gave you help on the day of salvation."　　*Isaiah 49:8*

I tell you that the "right time" is now. The "day of salvation" is now.

³We do not want anyone to find anything wrong with our work. So we do nothing that will be a problem for anyone. ⁴But in every way we show that we are servants of God: in accepting many hard things, in troubles, in difficulties, and in great problems. ⁵We are beaten and thrown into prison. Men become upset and fight us. We work hard, and sometimes we get no sleep or food. ⁶We show that we are servants of God by living a pure life, by our understanding, by our patience, and by our kindness. We show this by the Holy Spirit,ᵈ by true love, ⁷by speaking the truth, and by God's power. We use our right living to defend ourselves against everything. ⁸Some people honor us, but other people shame us. Some people say good things about us, but other people say bad things. Some people say we are liars, but we speak the truth. ⁹We are not known, but we are well-known. We seem to be dying, but look—we continue to live. We are punished, but we are not killed. ¹⁰We have much sadness, but we are always rejoicing. We are poor, but we are making many people rich in faith. We have nothing, but really we have everything.

¹¹We have spoken freely to you in Corinth. We have opened our hearts to you. ¹²Our feelings of love for you have not stopped. It is you that have stopped your feelings of love for us. ¹³I speak to you as if you were my children. Do to us as we have done—open your hearts to us.

Warning About Non-Christians

¹⁴You are not the same as those who do not believe. So do not join yourselves to them. Good and bad do not belong together. Light and darkness cannot share together. ¹⁵How can Christ and Belial, the devil, have any agreement?

Honesty
2 CORINTHIANS 6:6-7

Do people ever say to you, "You look just like your mother (or father)?" They probably think that your nose or eyes or the shape of your face reminds them of your mom or dad. Who do you think you look like?

These verses list many ways that Christians are like their heavenly father. One of those ways is "speaking the truth." Because God is always truthful, we are like him when we are truthful. (Read John 8:42-47 for some strong words from Jesus about liars and who *their* real father is.)

These verses tell other ways that we are to be like God.

Remember, when you speak the truth, you look just like your heavenly father.

To learn more about honesty, zoom to page 1481.

What can a believer have together with a non-believer? [16]The temple of God cannot have any agreement with idols. And we are the temple of the living God. As God said: "I will live with them and walk with them. And I will be their God. And they will be my people."[n]

[17]"Leave those people,
    and make yourselves pure, says the Lord.
Touch nothing that is unclean,[d]
    and I will accept you."
                    Isaiah 52:11; Ezekiel 20:34,41

[18]"I will be your father,
    and you will be my sons and daughters,
    says the Lord All-Powerful."
                    2 Samuel 7:14; 7:8

7 Dear friends, we have these promises from God. So we should make ourselves pure—free from anything that makes body or soul unclean. We should try to become perfect in the way we live, because we respect God.

Paul's Joy

[2]Open your hearts to us. We have not done wrong to anyone. We have not ruined the faith of any person, and we have cheated no one. [3]I do not say this to blame you. I told you before that we love you so much that we would live or die with you. [4]I feel very sure of you. I am very proud of you. You give me much comfort. And in all of our troubles I have great joy.

[5]When we came into Macedonia, we had no rest. We found trouble all around us. We had fighting on the outside and fear on the inside. [6]But God comforts those who are troubled. And God comforted us when Titus came. [7]We were comforted by his coming and also by the comfort that you gave him. Titus told us about your wish to see me. He told us that you are very sorry for what you did. And he told me about your great care for me. When I heard this, I was much happier.

[8]Even if the letter I wrote you made you sad, I am not sorry I wrote it. I know it made you sad, and I was sorry for that. But it made you sad only for a short time. [9]Now I am happy, but not

Friendships
2 CORINTHIANS 6:14-16

Think about your friends. How have they rubbed off on you? You probably use the same words, laugh at the same jokes, and want to do the same things. It is natural for friends who spend a lot of time together to become more like each other.

Hanging around with people who don't believe in God will probably not help us become better Christians. God doesn't want us to ignore people who don't know him. We should try to help them understand the importance of obeying him. But we need to be careful. We want them to get closer to God. We don't want them to pull us further away from him!

Spending time with friends who believe in God will help you grow closer to him.

To find out why you should obey your parents, zoom to page 1446.

[n]**"I . . . people."** Quotation from Leviticus 26:11-12; Jeremiah 32:38; Ezekiel 37:27.

because you were made sad. I am happy because your sorrow made you change your hearts. You became sad in the way God wanted you to. So you were not hurt by us in any way. [10]Being sorry in the way God wants makes a person change his heart and life. This leads to salvation, and we cannot be sorry for that. But the kind of sorrow the world has will bring death. [11]You had the kind of sorrow God wanted you to have. Now see what this sorrow has brought you: It has made you very serious. It made you want to prove that you were not wrong. It made you angry and afraid. It made you want to see me. It made you care. It made you want the right thing to be done. You proved that you were not guilty in any part of the problem. [12]I wrote that letter, but not because of the one who did the wrong. And it was not written because of the person who was hurt. But I wrote the letter so that you could see, before God, the great care that you have for us. [13]That is why we were comforted.

We were very comforted. And we were even happier to see that Titus was so happy. All of you made him feel much better. [14]I bragged to Titus about you. And you showed that I was right. Everything that we said to you was true. And you have proved that what we bragged about to Titus is true. [15]And his love for you is stronger when he remembers that you were all ready to obey. You welcomed him with respect and fear. [16]I am very happy that I can trust you fully.

Christian Giving

8 And now, brothers, we want you to know about the grace that God gave the churches in Macedonia. [2]They have been tested by great troubles. And they are very poor. But they gave much because of their great joy. [3]I can tell you that they gave as much as they were able. They gave even more than they could afford. No one told them to do it. [4]But they asked us again and again— they begged us to let them share in

this service for God's people. [5]And they gave in a way that we did not expect: They first gave themselves to the Lord and to us. This is what God wants. [6]So we asked Titus to help you finish this special work of grace. He is the one who started this work. [7]You are rich in everything—in faith, in speaking, in knowledge, in truly wanting to help, and in the love you learned from us. And so we want you to be rich also in this gift of giving.

[8]I am not commanding you to give. But I want to see if your love is true love. I do this by showing you that others really want to help. [9]You know the grace of our Lord Jesus Christ. You know that Christ was rich, but for you he became poor. Christ did this so that by his being poor you might become rich.

[10]This is what I think you should do: Last year you were the first to want to give. And you were the first who gave. [11]So now finish the work that you started. Then your "doing" will be equal to your "wanting to do." Give from what you have. [12]If you want to give, your gift will be accepted. Your gift will be judged by what you have, not by what you do not have. [13]We do not want you to have troubles while other people are at ease. We want everything to be equal. [14]At this time you have plenty. What you have can help others who are in need. Then later, when they have plenty, they can help you when you are in need. Then all will be equal. [15]As it is written in the Scriptures,[d] "The person who gathered more did not have too much. The person who gathered less did not have too little."[n]

Titus and His Companions

[16]I thank God because he gave Titus the same love for you that I have. [17]Titus accepted what we asked him to do. He wanted very much to go to you. This was his own idea. [18]We are sending with him the brother who is praised

by all the churches. This brother is praised because of his service in preaching the Good News.[d] 19Also, this brother was chosen by the churches to go with us when we deliver this gift of money. We are doing this service to bring glory to the Lord and to show that we really want to help.

20We are being careful so that no one will criticize us about the way we are handling this large gift. 21We are trying to do what is right. We want to do what the Lord accepts as right and also what people think is right.

Help for Fellow Christians

9 I really do not need to write to you about this help for God's people. 2I know that you want to help. I have been bragging about this to the people in Macedonia. I have told them that you in Southern Greece have been ready to give since last year. And your wanting to give has made most of them here ready to give also. 3But I am sending the brothers to you. I do not want our bragging about you in this to be for

---

Thankfulness
2 CORINTHIANS 9:11-12

Why do people say yawns are contagious? If you have ever been around someone sleepy who gives a really big yawn, then you know why. It makes you yawn right back! You can even try it to see if you can make someone else yawn!

You can do the same thing with thankfulness. You can actually cause others to give thanks to God. For example, when you give money to your church on Sundays, the money may go to help other Christians somewhere, and they will thank God for meeting their needs. Also, if we pray for a person who is sick and the person gets better, that person will thank God for answering our prayers.

When you serve God, others have a chance to thank him. What can you do to make thanking God contagious to others?

To learn more about thankfulness, zoom to page 1438.

22Also, we are sending with them our brother who is always ready to help. He has proved this to us in many ways. And he wants to help even more now because he has much faith in you.

23Now about Titus—he is my partner who is working with me to help you. And about the other brothers—they are sent from the churches, and they bring glory to Christ. 24So show these men that you really have love. Show them why we are proud of you. Then all the churches can see it.

nothing. I want you to be ready, as I said you would be. 4If any of the people from Macedonia come with me and find that you are not ready, we will be ashamed. We will be ashamed that we were so sure of you. (And you will be ashamed, too!) 5So I thought that I should ask these brothers to go to you before we come. They will finish getting in order the gift you promised. Then the gift will be ready when we come, and it will be a gift you wanted to give—not a gift that you hated to give.

⁶Remember this: The person who plants a little will have a small harvest. But the person who plants a lot will have a big harvest. ⁷Each one should give, then, what he has decided in his heart to give. He should not give if it makes him sad. And he should not give if he thinks he is forced to give. God loves the person who gives happily. ⁸And God can give you more blessings than you need. Then you will always have plenty of everything. You will have enough to give to every good work. ⁹It is written in the Scriptures:*d*

"He gives freely to the poor.
The things he does are right and
will continue forever."

Psalm 112:9

¹⁰God is the One who gives seed to the farmer. And he gives bread for food. And God will give you all the seed you need and make it grow. He will make a great harvest from your goodness. ¹¹God will make you rich in every way so that you can always give freely. And your giving through us will cause many to give thanks to God. ¹²This service that you do helps the needs of God's people. It is also bringing more and more thanks to God. ¹³This service you do is a proof of your faith. Many people will praise God because of it. They will praise God because you follow the Good News*d* of Christ—the gospel you say you believe. They will praise God because you freely share with them and with all others. ¹⁴And when they pray, they will wish they could be with you. They will feel this because of the great grace that God has given you. ¹⁵Thanks be to God for his gift that is too wonderful to explain.

Paul Defends His Ministry

10 I, Paul, am begging you with the gentleness and the kindness of Christ. Some people say that I am easy on you when I am with you and strict when I am away. ²They think that we live in a worldly way. I plan to be very strict against them when I come. I beg you that when I come I will not need to use that same strictness with you. ³We do live in the world. But we do not fight in the same way that the world fights. ⁴We fight with weapons that are different from those the world uses. Our weapons have power from God. These weapons can destroy the enemy's strong places. We destroy men's arguments. ⁵And we destroy every proud thing that raises itself against the knowledge of God. We capture every thought and make it give up and obey Christ. ⁶We are ready to punish anyone there who does not obey. But first we want you to obey fully.

⁷You must look at the facts before you. If anyone feels sure that he belongs to Christ, then he must remember that we belong to Christ just as he does. ⁸It is true that we brag freely about the authority the Lord gave us. But he gave us this authority to strengthen you, not to hurt you. So I will not be ashamed of the bragging we do. ⁹I don't want you to think that I am trying to scare you with my letters. ¹⁰Some people say, "Paul's letters are powerful and sound important. But when he is with us, he is weak. And his speaking is nothing." ¹¹They should know this: We are not there with you now, so we say these things in letters. But when we are there with you, we will show the same authority that we show in our letters.

¹²We do not dare to put ourselves in the same group with those who think that they are very important. We do not compare ourselves to them. They use themselves to measure themselves, and they judge themselves by what they themselves are. This shows that they know nothing. ¹³But we will not brag about things outside the work that was given us to do. We will limit our bragging to the work that God gave us. And this work includes our work with you. ¹⁴We are not bragging too much. We would be bragging too much if we had not already come to you. But we have come to you with the Good News*d* of Christ. ¹⁵We limit our bragging to the work that is ours. We do not brag

in the work other men have done. We hope that your faith will continue to grow. And we hope that you will help our work to grow much larger. [16] We want to tell the Good News in the areas beyond your city. We do not want to brag about work that has already been done in another man's area. [17] But, "If a person brags, he should brag only about the Lord."[n] [18] It is not the one who says he is good who is accepted but the one that the Lord thinks is good.

Paul and the False Apostles

11 I wish you would be patient with me even when I am a little foolish. But you are already doing that. [2] I am jealous over you. And this jealousy comes from God. I promised to give you to Christ. He must be your only husband. I want to give you to Christ to be his pure bride. [3] But I am afraid that your minds will be led away from your true and pure following of Christ. This might happen just as Eve was tricked by the snake with his evil ways. [4] You are very patient with anyone who comes to you and preaches a different Jesus than the one we preached. You are very willing to accept a spirit or Good News that is different from the Spirit[d] and Good News[d] that you received from us.

[5] I do not think that those "great apostles" are any better than I am. [6] I may not be a trained speaker, but I do have knowledge. We have shown this to you clearly in every way.

[7] I preached God's Good News to you without pay. I made myself unimportant to make you important. Do you think that was wrong? [8] I accepted pay from other churches. I took their money so that I could serve you. [9] If I needed something when I was with you, I did not trouble any of you. The brothers who came from Macedonia gave me all that I needed. I did not allow myself to depend on you in any way. And I will never depend on you. [10] No one in Southern Greece will stop me from bragging about that. I say this

People Who Got Away
PAUL • 2 CORINTHIANS 11

You hold your breath as the magician climbs into the trunk. After he waves to the crowd, his assistant chains his hands and feet together. He stoops down, and the lid is pulled shut and locked. Another assistant takes ten razor-sharp swords and plunges each one into the trunk. Then the swords are pulled out. The lock is taken off, the lid is opened—and the magician steps out unharmed!

The apostle Paul had many close escapes. He was roughed up by crowds, beaten with whips, thrown into prison, stoned, shipwrecked, and robbed—not just once but many times. He often went without food, water, and warm clothes. But that didn't stop Paul from sharing the good news of Jesus. He trusted God to protect him from anything his enemies did to him.

Paul knew what we should always remember—those who love and obey God can count on him to take care of any situation.

To meet someone who ran away and became a Christian, fly to page 1484.

---

[n]"If a person . . . Lord."   Quotation from Jeremiah 9:24.

with the truth of Christ in me. [11]And why do I not depend on you? Do you think it is because I do not love you? No. God knows that I love you.

[12]And I will keep on doing what I am doing now. I will continue because I want to stop those people from having a reason to brag. They would like to say that the work they brag about is the same as ours. [13]Such men are not true apostles.[d] They are workers who lie. And they change themselves to look like apostles of Christ. [14]This does not surprise us. Even Satan changes himself to look like an angel of light.[n] [15]So it does not surprise us if Satan's servants also make themselves look like servants who work for what is right. But in the end they will be punished for the things they do.

Paul Tells About His Sufferings

[16]I tell you again: No one should think that I am a fool. But if you think that I am a fool, then accept me as you would accept a fool. Then I can brag a little, too. [17]I brag because I feel sure of myself. But I am not talking as the Lord would talk. I am bragging like a fool. [18]Many people are bragging about their lives in the world. So I will brag, too. [19]You are wise, so you will gladly be patient with fools! [20]You are even patient with someone who orders you around and uses you! You are patient with those who trick you, or think they are better than you, or hit you in the face! [21]It is shameful to me to say this, but we were too "weak" to do those things to you!

But if anyone else is brave enough to brag, then I also will be brave and brag. (I am talking like a fool.) [22]Are they Hebrews?[n] So am I. Are they Israelites? So am I. Are they from Abraham's family? So am I. [23]Are they serving Christ? I am serving him more. (I am crazy to talk like this.) I have worked much harder than they. I have been in prison more often. I

have been hurt more in beatings. I have been near death many times. [24]Five times the Jews have given me their punishment of 39 lashes with a whip. [25]Three different times I was beaten with rods. One time they tried to kill me with stones. Three times I was in ships that were wrecked, and one of those times I spent the night and the next day in the sea. [26]I have gone on many travels. And I have been in danger from rivers, from thieves, from my own people, the Jews, and from those who are not Jews. I have been in danger in cities, in places where no one lives, and on the sea. And I have been in danger with false brothers. [27]I have done hard and tiring work, and many times I did not sleep. I have been hungry and thirsty. Many times I have been without food. I have been cold and without clothes. [28]Besides all this, there is on me every day the load of my concern for all the churches. [29]I feel weak every time someone is weak. I feel upset every time someone is led into sin.

[30]If I must brag, I will brag about the things that show I am weak. [31]God knows that I am not lying. He is the God and Father of the Lord Jesus Christ, and he is to be praised forever. [32]When I was in Damascus, the governor under King Aretas wanted to arrest me. So he put guards around the city. [33]But my friends put me in a basket. Then they put the basket through a hole in the wall and lowered me down. So I escaped from the governor.

A Special Blessing in Paul's Life

12 I must continue to brag. It will do no good, but I will talk now about visions and revelations[n] from the Lord. [2]I know a man in Christ who was taken up to the third heaven. This happened 14 years ago. I do not know whether the man was in his body or out of his body. But God knows. [3-4]And I know

---

"angel of light Messenger from God. The devil fools people so that they think he is from God.
"Hebrews A name for the Jews that some Jews were very proud of.
"revelations Revelation is making known a truth that was hidden.

that this man was taken up to paradise.[n] I don't know if he was in his body or away from his body. But he heard things he is not able to explain. He heard things that no man is allowed to tell. [5]I will brag about a man like that. But I will not brag about myself, except about my weaknesses. [6]But if I wanted to brag about myself, I would not be a fool. I would not be a fool, because I would be telling the truth. But I will not brag about myself. I do not want people to think more of me than what they see me do or hear me say.

[7]But I must not become too proud of the wonderful things that were shown to me. So a painful problem[n] was given to me. This problem is a messenger from Satan. It is sent to beat me and keep me from being too proud. [8]I begged the Lord three times to take this problem away from me. [9]But the Lord said to me, "My grace is enough for you. When you are weak, then my power is made perfect in you." So I am very happy to brag about my weaknesses. Then Christ's power can live in me. [10]So I am happy when I have weaknesses, insults, hard times, sufferings, and all kinds of troubles. All these things are for Christ. And I am happy, because when I am weak, then I am truly strong.

Paul's Love for the Christians

[11]I have been talking like a fool. But you made me do it. You are the ones who should say good things about me. I am worth nothing, but those "great apostles" are not worth any more than I am! [12]When I was with you, I did what proves that I am an apostle[d]—signs, wonders, and miracles.[d] And I did these things with much patience. [13]So you received everything that the other churches have received. Only one thing was different: I was not a burden to you. Forgive me for this!

[14]I am now ready to visit you the third time. And I will not be a burden to you. I want nothing from you, I only want you. Children should not have to save up to give to their parents. Parents should save to give to their children. [15]So I am happy to give everything I have for you. I will even give myself for you. If I love you more, will you love me less? [16]It is clear that I was not a burden to you. But you think that I was tricky and used lies to catch you. [17]Did I cheat you by using any of the men I sent to you? No, you know I did not. [18]I asked Titus to go to you. And I sent our brother with him. Titus did not cheat you, did he? No, you know that Titus and I did the same thing and with the same spirit.

[19]Do you think that we have been defending ourselves to you all this time? We have been speaking in Christ and before God. You are our dear friends. And everything that we do is to make you stronger. [20]I do this because I am afraid that when I come, you will not be what I want you to be. And I am afraid that I will not be what you want me to be. I am afraid that among you there may be arguing, jealousy, anger, selfish fighting, evil talk, gossip, pride, and confusion. [21]I am afraid that when I come to you again, my God will make me ashamed before you. I may be saddened by many of those who have sinned. I may be saddened because they have not changed their hearts and have not turned away from their sexual sins and from the shameful things they have done.

Final Warnings and Greetings

13 I will come to you for the third time. And remember, "Every case must be proved by two or three witnesses."[n] [2]When I was with you the second time, I gave a warning to those who had sinned. Now I am away from you, and I give a warning to all the others. When I come to you again, I will not be easy with them. [3]You want proof that

---

[n]**paradise**   A place where people who obey God go when they die.
[n]**painful problem**   Literally, "thorn in the flesh."
[n]**"Every . . . witnesses."**   Quotation from Deuteronomy 19:15.

Christ is speaking through me. My proof is that he is not weak among you, but he is powerful. [4]It is true that he was weak when he was killed on the cross. But he lives now by God's power. It is true that we are weak in Christ. But for you we will be alive in Christ by God's power.

[5]Look closely at yourselves. Test yourselves to see if you are living in the faith. You know that Christ Jesus is in you—unless you fail the test. [6]But I hope you will see that we ourselves have not failed the test. [7]We pray to God that you will not do anything wrong. It is not important to see that we have passed the test. But it is important that you do what is right, even if it seems that we have failed. [8]We cannot do anything against the truth, but only for the truth. [9]We are happy to be weak, if you are strong. And we pray that you will grow stronger and stronger. [10]I am writing this while I am away from you. I am writing so that when I come I will not have to be harsh in my use of authority. The Lord gave me this authority to use to make you stronger, not to destroy you.

[11]Now, brothers, I say good-bye. Try to be perfect. Do what I have asked you to do. Agree with each other, and live in peace. Then the God of love and peace will be with you.

[12]Give each other a holy kiss when you greet each other. [13]All of God's holy people send greetings to you.

[14]The grace of the Lord Jesus Christ, the love of God, and the fellowship of the Holy Spirit[d] be with you all.

GALATIANS

Christians Are
Saved by Grace

1 From Paul, an apostle.[d]
I was not chosen to be an apostle by men. I was not sent from men. It was Jesus Christ and God the Father who made me an apostle. God is the One who raised Jesus from death.

²This letter is also from all the brothers who are with me.

To the churches in Galatia.[n]

³I pray that God our Father and the Lord Jesus Christ will be good to you and give you peace. ⁴Jesus gave himself for our sins to free us from this evil world we live in. This is what God the Father wanted. ⁵The glory belongs to God forever and ever. Amen.

The Only Good News

⁶A short time ago God called you to follow him. He called you by his grace that came through Christ. But now I am amazed at you! You are already turning away and believing something

> Do you think I am trying to make people accept me? No! God is the One I am trying to please. Am I trying to please men? If I wanted to please men, I would not be a servant of Christ.
> • Galatians 1:10

different than the Good News.[d] ⁷Really, there is no other Good News. But some people are confusing you and want to change the Good News of Christ. ⁸We

preached to you the Good News. So if we ourselves, or even an angel from heaven, preach to you something different than the Good News, he should be condemned! ⁹I said this before. Now I say it again: You have already accepted the Good News. If anyone tells you another way to be saved, he should be condemned!

¹⁰Do you think I am trying to make people accept me? No! God is the One I am trying to please. Am I trying to please men? If I wanted to please men, I would not be a servant of Christ.

Paul's Authority Is from God

¹¹Brothers, I want you to know that the Good News[d] I preached to you was not made by men. ¹²I did not get it from men, nor did any man teach it to me. Jesus Christ showed it to me.

¹³You have heard about my past life. I belonged to the Jewish religion. I hurt the church of God very much and tried to destroy it. ¹⁴I was becoming a leader in the Jewish religion. I did better than most other Jews of my age. I tried harder than anyone else to follow the old rules. These rules were the customs handed down by our ancestors.

¹⁵But God had special plans for me even before I was born. So he called me through his grace that I might ¹⁶tell the Good News about his Son to the non-Jewish people. So God showed me about his Son. When God called me, I did not get advice or help from any man. ¹⁷I did not go to Jerusalem to see those who were apostles[d] before I was. But, without waiting, I went away

---

Galatia Probably the same country where Paul preached and began churches on his first missionary trip. Read the book of Acts, chapters 13 and 14.

to Arabia and later went back to Damascus.

[18] After three years I went to Jerusalem to meet Peter and stayed with him for 15 days. [19] I met no other apostles, except James, the brother of the Lord. [20] God knows that these things I write are not lies. [21] Later, I went to the areas of Syria and Cilicia.

[22] In Judea the churches in Christ had never met me. [23] They had only heard this about me: "This man was trying to hurt us. But now he is preaching the same faith that he once tried to destroy." [24] And these believers praised God because of me.

Other Apostles Accepted Paul

2 After 14 years, I went to Jerusalem again, this time with Barnabas. I also took Titus with me. [2] I went because God showed me that I should go. I met

because some false brothers had come into our group secretly. They came in like spies to find out about the freedom we have in Christ Jesus. They wanted to make us slaves. [5] But we did not agree with anything those false brothers wanted! We wanted the truth of the Good News to continue for you.

[6] Those men who seemed to be important did not change the Good News that I preach. (It doesn't matter to me if they were "important" or not. To God all men are the same.) [7] But these leaders saw that God had given me special work, just as he had to Peter. God gave Peter the work of telling the Good News to the Jews. But God gave me the work of telling the Good News to the non-Jewish people. [8] God gave Peter the power to work as an apostle[d]

Faith and How It Works
GALATIANS 2:16

You didn't have to do anything in order to be born, did you? You couldn't tell your mom and dad what you would be like so they could decide whether or not to have you. Instead, you were born, and here you are. The same is true when you become a Christian—when you are *reborn*. You don't have to *do* anything—except believe in Jesus.

In this verse, Paul wanted to teach the Galatian people that they didn't have to keep a lot of laws in order to be saved. They couldn't send a list of good things they had done to God so he could decide whether to save them or not. God wants to save everyone who comes to him.

Thank Jesus that you didn't have to be good enough for him to save you; instead, you are saved because you believe in Jesus.

To find out more about faith and how it works, fly to page 1490.

with those men who were the leaders of the believers. When we were alone, I told them the Good News[d] that I preach to the non-Jewish people. I did not want my past work and the work I am now doing to be wasted. [3] Titus was with me. But Titus was not forced to be circumcised,[d] even though he was a Greek. [4] We talked about this problem

for the Jewish people. But he also gave me the power to work as an apostle for those who are not Jews. [9] James, Peter, and John, who seemed to be the leaders, saw that God had given me this special grace. So they accepted Barnabas and me. They said, "Paul and Barnabas, we agree that you should go to the people who are not Jews. We will go to the

Jews." [10]They asked us to do only one thing—to remember to help the poor. And this was something that I really wanted to do.

Paul Shows that Peter Was Wrong

[11]When Peter came to Antioch, I was against him because he was wrong. [12]This is what happened: When Peter first came to Antioch, he ate with the non-Jewish people. But then some Jewish men were sent from James. When they arrived, Peter stopped eating with the non-Jewish people and separated himself from them. He was afraid of the Jews who believe that all non-Jewish people must be circumcised.[d] [13]So Peter was a hypocrite.[d] The other Jewish believers joined with him and were hypocrites, too. Even Barnabas was influenced by what these Jewish believers did. [14]I saw what they did. They were not following the truth of the Good News.[d] So I spoke to Peter in front of them all. I said: "Peter, you are a Jew, but you are not living like a Jew. You are living like the non-Jewish people. So why do you now try to force the non-Jewish people to live like Jews?"

[15]We were not born as non-Jewish "sinners," but we were born as Jews. [16]Yet we know that a person is not made right with God by following the law. No! It is trusting in Jesus Christ that makes a person right with God. So we, too, have put our faith in Christ Jesus, that we might be made right with God. And we are right with God because we trusted in Christ—not because we followed the law. For no one can be made right with God by following the law.

[17]We Jews came to Christ to be made right with God. So it is clear that we were sinners too. Does this mean that Christ makes us sinners? No! [18]But I would really be wrong to begin teaching again those things of the Law of Moses that I gave up. [19]I stopped living for the law. It was the law that put me to death. I died to the law so that I can now live for God. I was put to death on the cross with Christ. [20]I do not live anymore—it is Christ living in me. I still live in my body, but I live by faith in the Son of God. He loved me and gave himself to save me. [21]This gift is from God, and it is very important to me. If the law could make us right with God, then Christ did not have to die.

Blessing Comes Through Faith

3 You people in Galatia were told very clearly about the death of Jesus Christ on the cross. But you were very foolish. You let someone trick you. [2]Tell me this one thing: How did you receive the Holy Spirit?[d] Did you receive the Spirit by following the law? No! You received the Spirit because you heard the Good News[d] and believed it. [3]You began your life in Christ by the Spirit. Now do you try to continue it by your own power? That is foolish. [4]You have experienced many things. Were all those experiences wasted? I hope not! [5]Does God give you the Spirit because you follow the law? No! Does God work miracles[d] among you because you follow the law? No! God gives you his Spirit and works miracles among you because you heard the Good News and believed it.

[6]The Scriptures[d] say the same thing about Abraham: "Abraham believed God, and God accepted Abraham's faith, and that faith made him right with God."[n] [7]So you should know that the true children of Abraham are those who have faith. [8]The Scriptures told what would happen in the future. They said that God would make the non-Jewish people right through their faith. This Good News was told to Abraham beforehand, as the Scripture says: "All nations will be blessed through you."[n] [9]Abraham believed this, and because he believed, he was blessed. It is the same today. All who believe today are blessed just as Abraham was blessed. [10]But those who depend on following the law

[n]"Abraham . . . God." Quotation from Genesis 15:6.
[n]"All . . . you." Quotation from Genesis 12:3.

to make them right are under a curse because the Scriptures say, "Anyone will be cursed who does not always obey what is written in the Book of the Law!"[n] [11]So it is clear that no one can be made right with God by the law. The Scriptures say, "He who is right with God by faith will live." [12]The law does not use faith. It says, "A person who does these things will live forever because of them."[n] [13]So the law put a curse on us, but Christ took away that curse. He changed places with us and put himself under that curse. It is written in the Scriptures, "Everyone whose body is displayed on a tree[n] is cursed." [14]Christ did this so that God's blessing promised to Abraham might come to the non-Jews. This blessing comes through Jesus Christ. Jesus died so that we could have the Spirit that God promised and receive this promise by believing.

The Law and the Promise

[15]Brothers, let me give you an example: Think about an agreement that a person makes with another person. After that agreement is accepted by both people, no one can stop that agreement or add anything to it. [16]God made promises to Abraham and his descendant.[d] God did not say, "and to your descendants." That would mean many people. But God said, "and to your descendant." That means only one person; that person is Christ. [17]This is what I mean: God had an agreement with Abraham and promised to keep it. The law, which came 430 years later, cannot change God's promise to Abraham. [18]Can following the law give us what God promised? No! If this is so, it is not God's promise that brings us the blessings. Instead God freely gave his blessings to Abraham through the promise he had made.

[19]So what was the law for? The law was given to show the wrong things people do. It continued until the special descendant of Abraham came. God's promise was about this descendant. The law was given through angels who used Moses for a mediator[n] to give the law to men. [20]But a mediator is not needed when there is only one side. And God is only one.

The Purpose of the Law of Moses

[21]Does this mean that the law is against God's promises? Never! If there were a law that could give men life, then we could be made right by following that law. [22]But this is not true, because the Scriptures[d] showed that the whole world is bound by sin. This was so that the promise would be given through faith. And it is given to people who believe in Jesus Christ.

[23]Before this faith came, we were all held prisoners by the law. We had no freedom until God showed us the way of faith that was coming. [24]So the law was our master until Christ came. After Christ came, we could be made right with God through faith. [25]Now the way of faith has come, and we no longer live under the law.

[26-27]You were all baptized into Christ, and so you were all clothed with Christ. This shows that you are all children of God through faith in Christ Jesus. [28]Now, in Christ, there is no difference between Jew and Greek. There is no difference between slaves and free men. There is no difference between male and female. You are all the same in Christ Jesus. [29]You belong to Christ. So you are Abraham's descendants.[d] You get all of God's blessings because of the promise that God made to Abraham.

4 I want to tell you this: While the one who will inherit his father's property is still a child, he is no different from a slave. It does not matter that the

---

[n]**"Anyone . . . Law!"**   Quotation from Deuteronomy 27:26.
[n]**"A person . . . them."**   Quotation from Leviticus 18:5.
[n]**displayed on a tree**   Deuteronomy 21:22-23 says that when a person was killed for doing wrong, his body was hung on a tree to show shame. Paul means that the cross of Jesus was like that.
[n]**mediator**   A person who helps one person talk to or give something to another person.

child owns everything. ²While he is a child, he must obey those who are chosen to care for him. But when the child reaches the age set by his father, he is free. ³It is the same for us. We were once like children. We were slaves to the useless rules of this world. ⁴But when the right time came, God sent his Son. His Son was born of a woman and lived under the law. ⁵God did this so that he could buy freedom for those who were under the law. His purpose was to make us his children.

⁶And you are God's children. That is why God sent the Spirit of his Son into your hearts. The Spirit*d* cries out, "Father, dear Father."*n* ⁷So now you are not a slave; you are God's child, and God will give you what he promised, because you are his child.

Paul's Love for the Christians

⁸In the past you did not know God. You were slaves to gods that were not real. ⁹But now you know the true God. Really, it is God who knows you. So why do you turn back to those weak and useless rules you followed before? Do you want to be slaves to those things again? ¹⁰You still follow teachings about special days, months, seasons, and years. ¹¹I am afraid for you. I fear that my work for you has been wasted.

¹²Brothers, I was like you; so I beg you to become like me. You were very good to me before. ¹³You remember that I came to you the first time because I was sick. That was when I preached the Good News*d* to you. ¹⁴Though my sickness was a trouble for you, you did not hate me or make me leave. But you welcomed me as an angel from God, as if I were Jesus Christ himself! ¹⁵You were very happy then. Where is that joy now? I remember that you would have taken out your eyes and given them to me if that were possible. ¹⁶Now am I your enemy because I tell you the truth?

¹⁷Those people*n* are working hard to persuade you. But this is not good for you. They want to persuade you to turn against us. They want you to follow only them. ¹⁸It is good for people to show interest in you, but only if their purpose is good. This is always true. It is true when I am with you and when I am away. ¹⁹My little children, again I feel pain for you as a mother feels when she gives birth. I will feel this until you truly become like Christ. ²⁰I wish I could be with you now. Then maybe I could change the way I am talking to you. Now I do not know what to do about you.

The Example of Hagar and Sarah

²¹Some of you people still want to be under the law of Moses. Tell me, do you know what the law says? ²²The Scriptures*d* say that Abraham had two sons. The mother of one son was a slave woman. The mother of the other son was a free woman. ²³Abraham's son from the slave woman was born in the normal human way. But the son from the free woman was born because of the promise God made to Abraham.

²⁴This makes a picture for us. The two women are like the two agreements between God and men. One agreement is the law that God made on Mount Sinai.*n* The people who are under this agreement are like slaves. The mother named Hagar is like that agreement. ²⁵She is like Mount Sinai in Arabia and is a picture of the earthly Jewish city of Jerusalem. This city is a slave, and all its people, the Jews, are slaves to the law. ²⁶But the heavenly Jerusalem which is above is like the free woman. She is our mother. ²⁷It is written in the Scriptures:

"Be happy, Jerusalem.
You are like a woman who never gave birth to children.
Start singing and shout for joy.
You never felt the pain of giving birth to children.

---

*n***"Father, dear Father"** Literally, "Abba, Father." Jewish children called their fathers "Abba."
*n***Those people** They are the false teachers who were bothering the believers in Galatia (Galatians 1:7).
*n***Mount Sinai** Mountain in Arabia where God gave his laws to Moses (Exodus 19 and 20).

But you will have more children
than the woman who has a
husband."   *Isaiah 54:1*

[28] My brothers, you are God's children because of his promise, as Isaac was then. [29] The son who was born in the normal way treated the other son badly. It is the same today. [30] But what does the Scripture say? "Throw out the slave woman and her son! The son of the free woman will receive everything his father has. But the son of the slave woman will receive nothing."[n] [31] So, my brothers, we are not children of the slave woman. We are children of the free woman.

Keep Your Freedom

5 We have freedom now because Christ made us free. So stand strong. Do not change and go back into the slavery of the law. [2] Listen! I am Paul. I tell you that if you go back to the law by being circumcised,[d] then Christ is no good for you. [3] Again, I warn every man: If you allow yourselves to be circumcised, then you must follow all the law. [4] If you try to be made right with God through the law, then your life with Christ is over—you have left God's grace. [5] But we hope to be made right with God through faith, and we wait for this hope anxiously with the Spirit's[d] help. [6] When we are in Christ Jesus, it is not important if we are circumcised or not. The important thing is faith—the kind of faith that works through love.

[7] You were running a good race. You were obeying the truth. Who stopped you from following the true way? [8] Whatever way he used did not come from the One who chose you. [9] Be careful! "Just a little yeast makes the whole batch of dough rise." [10] But I trust in the Lord that you will not believe those different ideas. Someone is confusing you with such ideas. And he will be punished, whoever he is.

[11] My brothers, I do not teach that a man must be circumcised. If I teach circumcision, then why am I still being treated badly? If I still taught circumcision, my preaching about the cross would not be a problem. [12] I wish the people who are bothering you would castrate[n] themselves!

[13] My brothers, God called you to be free. But do not use your freedom as an excuse to do the things that please your sinful self. Serve each other with love.

Character
GALATIANS 5:22-23

Look at this list of character qualities! The Bible calls them *fruit*. The secret to having these fruits in our lives is to let God produce them in us. An apple doesn't pop out on the tree because the tree tries hard or wishes for it to happen. The apple comes out because that's what apple trees produce.

So if you want to produce these good fruits in your life, you need to become the right kind of "tree" or person—a person who loves God and stays close to him.

Let God produce these good qualities inside of you!

---

[n] **"Throw . . . nothing."**   Quotation from Genesis 21:10.
[n] **castrate**   To cut off part of the male sex organ. Paul uses this word because it is similar to "circumcision." Paul wanted to show that he is very upset with the false teachers.

[14]The whole law is made complete in this one command: "Love your neighbor as you love yourself."[n] [15]If you go on hurting each other and tearing each other apart, be careful! You will completely destroy each other.

The Spirit and Human Nature

[16]So I tell you: Live by following the Spirit.[d] Then you will not do what your sinful selves want. [17]Our sinful selves want what is against the Spirit. The Spirit wants what is against our sinful selves. The two are against each other. So you must not do just what you please. [18]But if you let the Spirit lead you, you are not under the law.

[19]The wrong things the sinful self does are clear: being sexually unfaithful, not being pure, taking part in sexual sins, [20]worshiping false gods, doing witchcraft,[d] hating, making trouble, being jealous, being angry, being selfish, making people angry with each other, causing divisions among people, [21]having envy, being drunk, having wild and wasteful parties, and doing other things like this. I warn you now as I warned you before: Those who do these things will not be in God's kingdom. [22]But the Spirit gives love, joy, peace, patience, kindness, goodness,

But the Spirit gives love, joy, peace, patience, kindness, goodness, faithfulness, gentleness, self-control. There is no law that says these things are wrong.
• Galatians 5:22-23

faithfulness, [23]gentleness, self-control. There is no law that says these things are wrong. [24]Those who belong to Christ Jesus have crucified their own sinful selves. They have given up their old selfish feelings and the evil things they wanted to do. [25]We get our new life from the Spirit. So we should follow the Spirit. [26]We must not be proud. We must not make trouble with each other. And we must not be jealous of each other.

Help Each Other

6 Brothers, someone in your group might do something wrong. You who are spiritual should go to him and help make him right again. You should do this in a gentle way. But be careful! You might be tempted to sin, too. [2]Help each other with your troubles. When you do this, you truly obey the law of Christ. [3]If anyone thinks that he is important when he is really not important, he is only fooling himself. [4]He should not compare himself with others. Each person should judge his own actions. Then he can be proud for what he himself has done. [5]Each person must be responsible for himself.

[6]Anyone who is learning the teaching of God should share all the good things he has with his teacher.

Life Is like Planting a Field

[7]Do not be fooled: You cannot cheat God. A person harvests only what he plants. [8]If he plants to satisfy his sinful self, his sinful self will bring him eternal death. But if he plants to please the Spirit,[d] he will receive eternal life from the Spirit. [9]We must not become tired of doing good. We will receive our harvest of eternal life at the right time. We must not give up! [10]When we have the opportunity to help anyone, we should do it. But we should give special attention to those who are in the family of believers.

Paul Ends His Letter

[11]I am writing this myself. See what large letters I use. [12]Some men are trying to force you to be circumcised.[d] They do these things so that the Jews will accept them. They are afraid that

---

[n]"Love . . . yourself." Quotation from Leviticus 19:18.

they will be treated badly if they follow only the cross of Christ." [13]Those who are circumcised do not obey the law themselves, but they want you to be circumcised. Then they can brag about what they forced you to do. [14]I hope I will never brag about things like that. The cross of our Lord Jesus Christ is my only reason for bragging. Through the cross of Jesus my world was crucified and I died to the world. [15]It is not important if a man is circumcised or not circumcised. The important thing is being the new people God has made. [16]Peace and mercy to those who follow this rule—to all of God's people.

[17]So do not give me any more trouble. I have scars on my body. These show" I belong to Christ Jesus.

[18]My brothers, I pray that the grace of our Lord Jesus Christ will be with your spirit. Amen.

"**cross of Christ**   Paul uses the cross as a picture of the gospel, the story of Christ's death and rising from death to pay for men's sins. The cross, or Christ's death, was God's way to save men.

"**These show**   Many times Paul was beaten and whipped by people who were against him because he was teaching about Christ. The scars were from these beatings.

EPHESIANS

*God Unites
His People*

1 From Paul, an apostle[d] of Christ Jesus. I am an apostle because that is what God wanted.

To God's holy people living in Ephesus, believers in Christ Jesus.

[2] Grace and peace to you from God our Father and the Lord Jesus Christ.

Spiritual Blessings in Christ

[3] Praise be to the God and Father of our Lord Jesus Christ. In Christ, God has given us every spiritual blessing in heaven. [4] In Christ, he chose us before the world was made. In his love he chose us to be his holy people—people without blame before him. [5] And before the world was made, God decided to make us his own children through Jesus Christ. That was what he wanted and what pleased him. [6] This brings praise to God because of his wonderful grace. God gave that grace to us freely, in Christ, the One he loves. [7] In Christ we are set free by the blood of his death. And so we have forgiveness of sins because of God's rich grace. [8] God gave us that grace fully and freely. God, with full wisdom and understanding, [9] let us know his secret purpose. This was what God wanted, and he planned to do it through Christ. [10] His goal was to carry out his plan when the right time came. He planned that all things in heaven and on earth would be joined together in Christ as the head.

[11] In Christ we were chosen to be God's people. God had already chosen

Thankfulness
EPHESIANS 1:16

Whenever you think of your close friends, do you smile because you remember all the fun things you've done together? Do you suddenly remember something you need to tell them? Or maybe you're sad when you think of a close friend because you or your friend has moved away. Whatever you do, remember to thank God for your friends.

That's what Paul says he did with his special friends at the church in the city of Ephesus. He knew that God had given him those dear friends, and he wanted to show God he was grateful. Paul didn't thank God just once or even twice for these friends. He thanked God all the time!

God has given you some very good friends. When you think of them, thank God.

To learn more about thankfulness, zoom to page 1464.

Salvation
EPHESIANS 2:1-10

Suppose you have a friend whose father is a famous inventor. One day your friend comes over to your house on an amazing skateboard that his father built. This skateboard glides over pavement, sand, water, and even air—all you have to do is ride it.

As you stand there, your friend starts bragging: "Look at this great skateboard I made! Watch how fast I can make it go! Check out all the places I can take it!"

Wouldn't that be silly? You know your friend can't take credit for that skateboard. His father, the inventor, designed it, built it, and made it do all those wonderful things. Your buddy was just fortunate to have a great inventor for a father.

In these verses, Paul says that our salvation is like that. We didn't do anything to earn it or to make it happen. It is God's kind gift to us—even though we don't deserve it.

Always remember that salvation is a gift from God, not something that you can brag about.

us to be his people, because that is what he wanted. And God is the One who makes everything agree with what he decides and wants. ¹²We are the first people who hoped in Christ. And we were chosen so that we would bring praise to God's glory. ¹³So it is with you. You heard the true teaching—the Good News*d* about your salvation. When you heard it, you believed in Christ. And in Christ, God put his special mark on you by giving you the Holy Spirit*d* that he had promised. ¹⁴That Holy Spirit is the guarantee that we will get what God promised for his people. This will bring full freedom to the people who belong to God, to bring praise to God's glory.

Paul's Prayer

¹⁵⁻¹⁶That is why I always remember you in my prayers and always thank God for you. I have always done this since the time I heard about your faith in the Lord Jesus and your love for all God's people. ¹⁷I always pray to the God of our Lord Jesus Christ—to the glorious Father. I pray that he will give you a spirit that will make you wise in the knowledge of God—the knowledge that he has shown you. ¹⁸I pray that you will have greater understanding in your heart. Then you will know the hope that God has chosen to give us. I pray that you will know that the blessings God has promised his holy people are rich and glorious. ¹⁹And you will know that God's power is very great for us who believe. That power is the same as the great strength ²⁰God used to raise Christ from death and put him at his right side in heaven. ²¹God made Christ more important than all rulers, authorities, powers, and kings. Christ is more important than anything in this world or in the next world. ²²God put everything under his power. And God made him the head over everything for the church. ²³The church is Christ's body. The church is

filled with Christ, and Christ fills everything in every way.

From Death to Life

2 In the past your spiritual lives were dead because of your sins and the things you did wrong against God. [2]Yes, in the past you lived the way the world lives. You followed the ruler of the evil powers that are above the earth. That same spirit is now working in those who refuse to obey God. [3]In the past all of us lived like them. We lived trying to please our sinful selves. We did all the things our bodies and minds wanted. We should have suffered God's anger because of the way we were. We were the same as all other people.

"**Do** you know how good God is to us? Do you want to find out? Read Ephesians 2:4-10."

[4]But God's mercy is great, and he loved us very much. [5]We were spiritually dead because of the things we did wrong against God. But God gave us new life with Christ. You have been saved by God's grace. [6]And he raised us up with Christ and gave us a seat with him in the heavens. He did this for those of us who are in Christ Jesus. [7]He did this so that for all future time he could show the very great riches of his grace. He shows that grace by being kind to us in Christ Jesus. [8]I mean that you have been saved by grace because you believe. You did not save yourselves. It was a gift from God. [9]You cannot brag that you are saved by the work you have done. [10]God has made us what we are. In Christ Jesus, God made us new people so that we would do good works. God had planned in advance those good works for us. He had planned for us to live our lives doing them.

One in Christ

[11]You were born non-Jews. You are the people the Jews call "uncircumcised."[n] Those who call you "uncircumcised" call themselves "circumcised."[d] (Their circumcision is only something they themselves do on their bodies.) [12]Remember that in the past you were without Christ. You were not citizens of Israel. And you had no part in the agreements[n] with the promise that God made to his people. You had no hope, and you did not know God. [13]Yes, at one time you were far away from God. But now in Christ Jesus you are brought near to God through the blood of Christ's death. [14]Because of Christ we now have peace. Christ made both Jews and non-Jews one people. They were separated as if there were a wall between them. But Christ broke down that wall of hate by giving his own body. [15]The Jewish law had many commands and rules. But Christ ended that law. Christ's purpose was to make the two groups of people become one new people in him. By doing this Christ would make peace. [16]Through the cross Christ ended the hatred between the two groups. And after Christ made the two groups to be one body, he wanted to bring them back to God. Christ did this with his death on the cross. [17]Christ came and preached peace to you non-Jews who were far away from God. And he preached peace to those Jews who

I mean that you have been saved by grace because you believe. You did not save your selves. It was a gift from God. You cannot brag that you are saved by the work you have done.
• Ephesians 2:8-9

---

[n]**uncircumcised** People not having the mark of circumcision as the Jews have.
[n]**agreements** The agreements that God gave to his people in the Old Testament.

were near to God. [18]Yes, through Christ we all have the right to come to the Father in one Spirit.[d]

[19]So now you non-Jews are not visitors or strangers. Now you are citizens together with God's holy people. You belong to God's family. [20]You believers are like a building that God owns. That building was built on the foundation of the apostles[d] and prophets.[d] Christ Jesus himself is the most important stone[n] in that building. [21]That whole building is joined together in Christ. And Christ makes it grow and become a holy temple in the Lord. [22]And in Christ you, too, are being built together with the Jews. You are being built into a place where God lives through the Spirit.

Paul's Work for the Non-Jews

3 So I, Paul, am a prisoner of Christ Jesus. I am a prisoner for you who are not Jews. [2]Surely you know that God gave me this work through his grace to help you. [3]God let me know his secret plan. He showed it to me. I have already written a little about this. [4]And if you read what I wrote, then you can see that I truly understand the secret truth about the Christ.[d] [5]People who lived in other times were not told that secret truth. But now, through the Spirit,[d] God has shown that secret truth to his holy apostles[d] and prophets.[d] [6]This is that secret truth: that the non-Jews will receive what God has for his people, just as the Jews will. The non-Jews are together with the Jews as part of the same body. And they share together in the promise that God made in Christ Jesus. The non-Jews have all of this because of the Good News.[d]

[7]By God's special gift of grace, I became a servant to tell that Good News. God gave me that grace through his power. [8]I am the least important of all God's people. But God gave me this gift—to tell the non-Jewish people the Good News about the riches of Christ. Those riches are too great to understand fully. [9]And God gave me the work

of telling all people about the plan for God's secret truth. That secret truth has been hidden in God since the beginning of time. God is the One who created everything. [10]His purpose was that through the church all the rulers and powers in the heavenly world will now know God's wisdom, which has so many forms. [11]This agrees with the purpose God had since the beginning of time. And God carried out his plan through Christ Jesus our Lord. [12]In Christ we can come before God with freedom and without fear. We can do this through faith in Christ. [13]So I ask you not to become discouraged because of the sufferings I am having for you. My sufferings bring honor to you.

The Love of Christ

[14]So I bow in prayer before the Father. [15]Every family in heaven and on earth gets its true name from him. [16]I ask the Father in his great glory to give you the power to be strong in spirit. He will give you that strength through his Spirit.[d] [17]I pray that Christ will live in your hearts because of your faith. I pray that your life will be strong in love and be built on love. [18]And I pray that you and all God's holy people will have the power to understand the greatness of Christ's love. I pray that you can understand how wide and how long and how high and how deep that love is. [19]Christ's love is greater than any person can ever know. But I pray that you will be able to know that love. Then you can be filled with the fullness of God.

[20]With God's power working in us, God can do much, much more than anything we can ask or think of. [21]To him be glory in the church and in Christ Jesus for all time, forever and ever. Amen.

The Unity of the Body

4 I am in prison because I belong to the Lord. God chose you to be his people. I tell you now to live the way God's people should live. [2]Always be

---

[n]**most important stone** Literally, "cornerstone." The first and most important stone in a building.

Worship
EPHESIANS 4:11-13

A lot of people think worship is like watching a sport, like football or baseball. They go to church, put a few dollars in the offering plate, and then sit back and watch the choir, the musicians, and the preacher.

Wrong!

That kind of thinking is not what the Bible teaches. The Bible says that all Christians should serve God, even in worship. We can't all sing, or preach, or play the piano, but we all have something to contribute: our time, voices, helpful hearts, servant attitudes, money, and so on. God is watching and listening as we bring our worship before him.

humble and gentle. Be patient and accept each other with love. ³You are joined together with peace through the Spirit.*ᵈ* Do all you can to continue together in this way. Let peace hold you together. ⁴There is one body and one Spirit. And God called you to have one hope. ⁵There is one Lord, one faith, and one baptism. ⁶There is one God and Father of everything. He rules everything. He is everywhere and in everything.

⁷Christ gave each one of us a special gift. Each one received what Christ wanted to give him. ⁸That is why it says in the Scriptures,*ᵈ*

"When he went up to the heights,
  he led a parade of captives.
And he gave gifts to people."
Psalm 68:18

⁹When it says, "He went up," what does it mean? It means that he first came down to the earth. ¹⁰So Jesus came down, and he is the same One who went up. He went up above all the heavens. Christ did that to fill everything with himself. ¹¹And Christ gave gifts to men—he made some to be apostles,*ᵈ* some to be prophets,*ᵈ* some to go and tell the Good News,*ᵈ* and some to have the work of caring for and teaching

God's people. ¹²Christ gave those gifts to prepare God's holy people for the work of serving. He gave those gifts to make the body of Christ stronger. ¹³This work must continue until we are all joined together in the same faith and in the same knowledge about the Son of God. We must become like a mature person—we must grow until we become like Christ and have all his perfection.

¹⁴Then we will no longer be babies. We will not be tossed about like a ship that the waves carry one way and then another. We will not be influenced by every new teaching we hear from men who are trying to fool us. Those men make plans and try any kind of trick to fool people into following the wrong path. ¹⁵No! We will speak the truth with love. We will grow up in every way to be like Christ, who is the head. ¹⁶The whole body depends on Christ. And all the parts of the body are joined and held together. Each part of the body does its own work. And this makes the whole body grow and be strong with love.

The Way You Should Live

¹⁷In the Lord's name, I tell you this. I warn you: Do not continue living like those who do not believe. Their

thoughts are worth nothing. [18]They do not understand. They know nothing, because they refuse to listen. So they cannot have the life that God gives. [19]They have lost their feeling of shame. And they use their lives for doing evil. More and more they want to do all kinds of evil things. [20]But the things you learned in Christ were not like this. [21]I know that you heard about him, and you are in him; so you were taught the truth. Yes, the truth is in Jesus. [22]You were taught to leave your old self—to stop living the evil way you lived before. That old self becomes worse and worse because people are fooled by the evil things they want to do. [23]But you were taught to be made new in your hearts. [24]You were taught to become a new person. That new person is made to be like God—made to be truly good and holy.

[25]So you must stop telling lies. Tell each other the truth because we all belong to each other in the same body.[*n*] [26]When you are angry, do not sin. And do not go on being angry all day. [27]Do not give the devil a way to defeat you. [28]If a person is stealing, he must stop stealing and start working. He must use his hands for doing something good.

Then he will have something to share with those who are poor.

Be kind and loving to each other. Forgive each other just as God forgave you in Christ.
• **Ephesians 4:32**

[29]When you talk, do not say harmful things. But say what people need—words that will help others become stronger. Then what you say will help those who listen to you. [30]And do not make the Holy Spirit[*d*] sad. The Spirit is God's proof that you belong to him. God gave you the Spirit to show that God will make you free when the time comes. [31]Do not be bitter or angry or mad. Never shout angrily or say things to hurt others. Never do anything evil. [32]Be kind and loving to each other. Forgive each other just as God forgave you in Christ.

Get Ready, Get Set, Grow!
EPHESIANS 4:15-16

As you are getting taller, you probably notice that your friends are getting taller too. Some of them are getting tall very quickly. Others aren't growing as fast. But if you all had to play together on a team, everyone would do his or her part to run or jump or catch in order to win the game.

In the same way, your Christian friends are growing in their faith just as you are. Some may grow more quickly than others, but God is working in each person's life to help that person grow. Then, as you serve God together, God uses all of you. All of you work together in various ways to tell others about God. As you grow, God wants you to be a part of his growing family by joining with others to serve him.

To find out more about growing in your faith, zoom to page 1448.

---

*[n]***Tell . . . body.**　Quotation from Zechariah 8:16.

Feelings
EPHESIANS 4:31

We have learned that God gave us our feelings and wants us to tell him about them. In this verse, however, it is very clear that it is wrong for us to use our feelings as an excuse to be mean or selfish.

While it is natural to feel angry or upset sometimes, God doesn't want us to say and do mean things to others! There is a big difference between feeling angry and letting anger control the way we treat our friends and family.

When you are tempted to argue with your brother or say a dirty word or do something mean to your friend, stop in your tracks. Ask God to help you handle your feelings in the right way, in a way that won't hurt others!

Living in the Light

5 You are God's children whom he loves. So try to be like God. ²Live a life of love. Love other people just as Christ loved us. Christ gave himself for us—he was a sweet-smelling offering and sacrifice to God.

³But there must be no sexual sin among you. There must not be any kind of evil or greed. Those things are not right for God's holy people. ⁴Also, there must be no evil talk among you. You must not speak foolishly or tell evil jokes. These things are not right for you. But you should be giving thanks to God. ⁵You can be sure of this: No one will have a place in the kingdom of Christ and of God if he does sexual sins, or does evil things, or is greedy. Anyone who is greedy is serving a false god.

⁶Do not let anyone fool you by telling you things that are not true. These things will bring God's anger on those who do not obey him. ⁷So have no part with them. ⁸In the past you were full of darkness, but now you are full of light in the Lord. So live like children who belong to the light. ⁹Light brings every kind of goodness, right living, and truth. ¹⁰Try to learn what pleases the Lord. ¹¹Do not do the things that people in darkness do. That brings nothing good. But do good things to show that the things done in darkness are wrong. ¹²It is shameful even to talk about what those people do in secret. ¹³But the light makes all things easy to see. ¹⁴And everything that is made easy to see can become light. This is why it is said:

"Wake up, sleeper!
   Rise from death,
   and Christ will shine on you."

¹⁵So be very careful how you live. Do not live like those who are not wise. Live wisely. ¹⁶I mean that you should use every chance you have for doing good, because these are evil times. ¹⁷So do not be foolish with your lives. But learn what the Lord wants you to do. ¹⁸Do not be drunk with wine. That will ruin you spiritually. But be filled with the Spirit.ᵈ ¹⁹Speak to each other with psalms, hymns, and spiritual songs. Sing and make music in your hearts to the Lord. ²⁰Always give thanks to God the Father for everything, in the name of our Lord Jesus Christ.

Wives and Husbands

21 Be willing to obey each other. Do this because you respect Christ.

22 Wives, be under the authority of your husbands, as of the Lord. 23 The husband is the head of the wife, as Christ is the head of the church. The church is Christ's body—Christ is the Savior of the body. 24 The church is under the authority of Christ. So it is the same with you wives. You should be under the authority of your husbands in everything.

25 Husbands, love your wives as Christ loved the church. Christ died for the church 26 to make it belong to God. Christ used the word to make the church clean by washing it with water. 27 Christ died so that he could give the church to himself like a bride in all her beauty. He died so that the church could be pure and without fault, with no evil or sin or any other wrong thing in it. 28 And husbands should love their wives in the same way. They should love their wives as they love their own bodies. The man who loves his wife loves himself. 29 No person ever hates his own body, but feeds and takes care of it. And that is what Christ does for the church, 30 because we are parts of his body. 31 The Scripture says, "So a man will leave his father and mother and be united with his wife. And the two people will become one body."[n]
32 That secret truth is very important— I am talking about Christ and the church. 33 But each one of you must love his wife as he loves himself. And a wife must respect her husband.

Children and Parents

6 Children, obey your parents the way the Lord wants. This is the right thing to do. 2 The command says, "Honor your father and mother."[n] This is the first command that has a promise with it. 3 The promise is: "Then everything will be well with you, and you will have a long life on the earth."[n]

4 Fathers, do not make your children angry, but raise them with the training and teaching of the Lord.

God's Children
EPHESIANS 5:1

People love to try to figure out which parent a newborn baby looks like. They may think the baby has the daddy's nose or the mother's eyes. When the baby gets older, people still like to say things like, "You walk just like your father" or "You talk just like your mother." Maybe that has happened to you. Children grow up to be like their parents—they can't help it because of heredity and because they have lived so close with their mom and dad.

God is our heavenly Father, and he wants us to grow up to be like him. That happens by spending time with him. And we can spend time with our heavenly Father by praying, reading the Bible, and worshiping. We will become more like God naturally, and that's the way God wants it.

To learn more about God's children, zoom to page 1451.

[n]"So . . . body." Quotation from Genesis 2:24.
[n]"Honor . . . mother." Quotation from Exodus 20:12; Deuteronomy 5:16.
[n]"Then . . . earth." Quotation from Exodus 20:12; Deuteronomy 5:16.

Friendships
EPHESIANS 6:1-3

Sometimes it is hard to believe that our parents are really doing what is best for us. But the Bible tells us to obey and honor our parents. Not just once in a while, or when they ask us to do things we already want to do. We need to listen to them and obey them every day.

God placed our parents over us to love us and make our lives safe and happy. They protect us, help us, and teach us. They also tell us to do things we don't always want to do. And sometimes they have to punish us for messing up.

When is it hard for you to do what your parents say? When you don't understand what your parents are thinking or why they make you do certain things, remind yourself of what the Bible promises. If you obey them, "everything will be well with you."

To find out why we should love others, zoom to page 1527.

Slaves and Masters

⁵Slaves, obey your masters here on earth with fear and respect. And do that with a heart that is true, just as you obey Christ. ⁶You must do more than obey your masters to please them only while they are watching you. You must obey them as you are obeying Christ. With all your heart you must do what God wants. ⁷Do your work, and be happy to do it. Work as if you were serving the Lord, not as if you were serving only men. ⁸Remember that the Lord will give a reward to everyone, slave or free, for doing good.

⁹Masters, in the same way, be good to your slaves. Do not say things to scare them. You know that the One who is your Master and their Master is in heaven. And that Master treats everyone alike.

Wear the Full Armor of God

¹⁰Finally, be strong in the Lord and in his great power. ¹¹Wear the full armor of God. Wear God's armor so that you can fight against the devil's evil tricks.

¹²Our fight is not against people on earth. We are fighting against the rulers and authorities and the powers of this world's darkness. We are fighting against the spiritual powers of evil in the heavenly world. ¹³That is why you need to get God's full armor. Then on the day of evil you will be able to stand strong. And when you have finished the whole fight, you will still be standing. ¹⁴So stand strong, with the belt of truth tied around your waist. And on your chest wear the protection of right living. ¹⁵And on your feet wear the Good News*d* of peace to help you stand strong. ¹⁶And also use the shield of faith. With that you can stop all the burning arrows of the Evil One. ¹⁷Accept God's salvation to be your helmet. And take the sword of the Spirit*d*—that sword is the teaching of God. ¹⁸Pray in the Spirit at all times. Pray with all kinds of prayers, and ask for everything you need. To do this you must always be ready. Never give up. Always pray for all God's people.

¹⁹Also pray for me. Pray that when I speak, God will give me words so that I can tell the secret truth of the Good

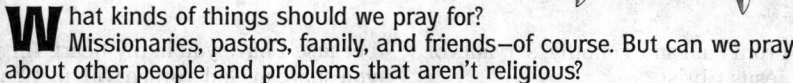

Prayer
EPHESIANS 6:18

What kinds of things should we pray for?
Missionaries, pastors, family, and friends—of course. But can we pray about other people and problems that aren't religious?

According to this verse, the answer is yes. Paul says that we can pray "all kinds of prayers," and that we can ask for *everything* we need. God is interested in every area of your life, not just those parts that are connected to church. He is concerned about you all the time, not just on Sundays. He wants to hear about *all* your problems. And he will help you.

So with this verse as your guideline and the Holy Spirit as your helper, go to God with all your needs and problems.

To learn more about prayer, zoom to page 1453.

News without fear. [20]I have the work of speaking that Good News. I am doing that now, here in prison. Pray that when I preach the Good News I will speak without fear, as I should.

Final Greetings

[21]I am sending to you Tychicus, our brother whom we love. He is a faithful servant of the Lord's work. He will tell you everything that is happening with me. Then you will know how I am and what I am doing. [22]That is why I am sending him. I want you to know how we are. I am sending him to encourage you.

[23]Peace and love with faith to you from God the Father and the Lord Jesus Christ. [24]God's grace to all of you who love our Lord Jesus Christ with love that never ends.

PHILIPPIANS

Serve
Others with Joy

1 From Paul and Timothy, servants of Jesus Christ.

To all of God's holy people in Christ Jesus who live in Philippi. And to your elders[d] and deacons.[d]

[2]Grace and peace to you from God our Father and the Lord Jesus Christ.

Paul's Prayer

[3]I thank God every time I remember you. [4]And I always pray for all of you with joy. [5]I thank God for the help you gave me while I preached the Good News.[d] You helped from the first day you believed until now. [6]God began doing a good work in you. And he will continue it until it is finished when Jesus Christ comes again. I am sure of that.

[7]And I know that I am right to think like this about all of you. I am sure because I have you in my heart. All of you share in God's grace with me. You share in God's grace with me while I am in prison, while I am defending the Good News, and while I am proving the truth of the Good News. [8]God knows that I want to see you very much. I love all of you with the love of Christ Jesus.

[9]This is my prayer for you: that your love will grow more and more; that you will have knowledge and understanding with your love; [10]that you will see the difference between good and bad and choose the good; that you will be pure and without wrong for the coming of Christ; [11]that you will do many good things with the help of Christ to bring glory and praise to God.

Get Ready, Get Set, Grow!
PHILIPPIANS 1:6

When you were born, you weren't left alone to get your own food. Someone fed you and took care of you. In the same way, when we first trust in Jesus, we are not left alone to figure out how to be a Christian.

In this verse, Paul explains that God, who gave us a new life when we became a Christian, will help us grow. He will keep on working in our lives until his work is finished.

That will happen when Jesus returns and we go to heaven to be with God. Then we will be exactly the way God wants us to be. It is important for you to study God's Word and live as he wants you to live. And remember, God is helping you grow. He is always there to teach and to help you.

To find out more about growing in your faith, zoom to page 1456.

Paul's Troubles Help the Work

[12]Brothers, I want you to know that what has happened to me has helped to spread the Good News.[d] [13]I am in prison because I am a believer in Christ. All the palace guards and everyone else knows this. [14]I am still in prison, but most of the believers feel better about it now. And so they are much braver about telling the Good News about Christ.

[15]It is true that some preach about Christ because they are jealous and bitter. But others preach about Christ because they want to help. [16]They preach because they have love, and they know that God gave me the work of defending the Good News. [17]But others preach about Christ because they are selfish. Their reason for preaching is wrong. They want to make trouble for me in prison.

[18]But I do not care if they make trouble for me. The important thing is that they are preaching about Christ. They should do it for the right reasons. But I am happy even if they do it for wrong reasons. And I will continue to be happy. [19]You are praying for me, and the Spirit of Jesus Christ helps me. So I know that this trouble will bring my freedom. [20]The thing I want and hope for is that I will not fail Christ in anything. I hope that I will have the courage now, as always, to show the greatness of Christ in my life here on earth. I want to do that if I die or if I live. [21]To me the only important thing about living is Christ. And even death would be profit for me. [22]If I continue living in the body, I will be able to work for the Lord. But what should I choose—living or dying? I do not know. [23]It is hard to choose between the two. I want to leave this life and be with Christ. That is much better. [24]But you need me here in my body. [25]I know that you need me, and so I know that I will stay with you. I will help you grow and have joy in your faith. [26]You will be very happy in Christ Jesus when I am with you again.

[27]Be sure that you live in a way that brings honor to the Good News of Christ. Then whether I come and visit you or am away from you, I will hear good things about you. I will hear that you continue strong with one purpose and that you work together as a team for the faith of the Good News. [28]And you will not be afraid of those who are against you. All of these things are proof from God that you will be saved and that your enemies will be lost. [29]God gave you the honor both of believing in Christ and suffering for Christ. Both these things bring glory to Christ. [30]When I was with you, you saw the struggles I had. And you hear about the struggles I am having now. You yourselves are having the same kind of struggles.

2 Does your life in Christ give you strength? Does his love comfort you? Do we share together in the Spirit?[d] Do you have mercy and kindness? [2]If so, make me very happy by having the same thoughts, sharing the same love, and having one mind and purpose. [3]When you do things, do not let selfishness or pride be your guide. Be humble and give more honor to others than to yourselves. [4]Do not be interested only in your own life, but be interested in the lives of others.

When you do things, do not let selfishness or pride be your guide. Be humble and give more honor to others than to yourselves. Do not be interested only in your own life, but be interested in the lives of others.
• Philippians 2:3-4

Be Unselfish like Christ

[5]In your lives you must think and act like Christ Jesus.
[6]Christ himself was like God in everything.
He was equal with God.
But he did not think that being

Humility
PHILIPPIANS 2:1-11

If you were a member of a royal family, living in a palace and surrounded by beautiful treasures, delicious food, and servants, would you give all that up to live in a pigpen? Probably not. But here we read that Jesus did something like that when he willingly left his place beside his Father in heaven and became a human being. Jesus, who is God, had all the glory and privileges you can imagine. Yet he gave all that up to come to earth and live with us. It was like moving from a palace to a pigpen.

And that is as good a picture of humility as we will ever see. Someone with everything gave it all up and became nothing in order to help others. We should thank God that Jesus did this for us! Otherwise we would be lost and without hope. Jesus loved us so much he gave *his* life so that we could live.

What could you give up to help someone else?

To learn more about humility, zoom to page 1509.

equal with God was something to be held on to.
⁷He gave up his place with God and made himself nothing.
He was born to be a man and became like a servant.
⁸And when he was living as a man, he humbled himself and was fully obedient to God.
He obeyed even when that caused his death—death on a cross.
⁹So God raised Christ to the highest place.
God made the name of Christ greater than every other name.
¹⁰God wants every knee to bow to Jesus—
everyone in heaven, on earth, and under the earth.
¹¹Everyone will say, "Jesus Christ is Lord"
and bring glory to God the Father.

Be the People God Wants You to Be

¹²My dear friends, you have always obeyed. You obeyed God when I was with you. It is even more important that you obey now while I am not with you. Keep on working to complete your salvation, and do it with fear and trembling. ¹³Yes, God is working in you to help you want to do what pleases him. Then he gives you the power to do it.

"**J**ust look at how much Jesus gave up for us! How does the Bible say *we're* supposed to act? Check out Philippians 2:5-11 to find out."

¹⁴Do everything without complaining or arguing. ¹⁵Then you will be innocent and without anything wrong in you. You will be God's children without fault. But you are living with crooked and mean people all around you. Among them you shine like stars in the dark world.

God's Children
PHILIPPIANS 2:15

We can see stars only at night, when the sky is dark. The darker the sky, the more stars we can see and the brighter they shine in the night sky.

If you ever feel a little different from most other people, it is because you *are* different. God's children shine like stars of kindness, joy, and hope. They stand out in a huge, dark world of unkind people. When others around you are being mean and hateful, remember that is when your deeds of kindness *really* stand out—just like stars at night.

One night, just before you go to sleep, spend some time looking at the stars. And think of how you are like a star. You may be different from many other people, but you are not alone. Think of how you can shine for Christ.

To learn more about God's children, zoom to page 1500.

To learn more about God's children, zoom to page 1500.

¹⁶You offer to them the teaching that gives life. So when Christ comes again, I can be happy because my work was not wasted. I ran in the race and won.

¹⁷Your faith makes you offer your lives as a sacrifice in serving God. Perhaps I will have to offer my own blood with your sacrifice. But if that happens, I will be happy and full of joy with all of you. ¹⁸You also should be happy and full of joy with me.

Timothy and Epaphroditus

¹⁹I hope in the Lord Jesus to send Timothy to you soon. I will be happy to learn how you are. ²⁰I have no other person like Timothy. He truly cares for you. ²¹Other people are interested only in their own lives. They are not interested in the work of Christ Jesus. ²²You know the kind of person Timothy is. You know that he has served with me in telling the Good News,ᵈ as a son serves his father. ²³I plan to send him to you quickly when I know what will happen to me. ²⁴I am sure that the Lord will help me to come to you soon.

²⁵Epaphroditus is my brother in Christ. He works and serves with me in the army of Christ. When I needed help, you sent him to me. I think now that I must send him back to you ²⁶because he wants very much to see all of you. He is worried because you heard that he was sick. ²⁷Yes, he was sick, and nearly died. But God helped him and me too, so that I would not have more sadness. ²⁸So I want very much to send him to you. When you see him, you can be happy. And I can stop worrying about you. ²⁹Welcome him in the Lord with much joy. Give honor to people like Epaphroditus. ³⁰He should be honored because he almost died for the work of Christ. He put his life in danger so that he could help me. This was help that you could not give me.

The Importance of Christ

3 My brothers, be full of joy in the Lord. It is no trouble for me to write the same things to you again, and it will help you to be more ready. ²Be careful of those who do evil. They are like dogs.

They demand to cut[n] the body. [3]But we are the ones who are truly circumcised.[d] We worship God through his Spirit.[d] We are proud to be in Christ Jesus. And we do not trust in ourselves or anything we can do. [4]Even if I am able to trust in myself, still I do not. If anyone thinks that he has a reason to trust in himself, he should know that I have greater reason for trusting in myself. [5]I was circumcised eight days after my birth. I am from the people of Israel and the tribe[d] of Benjamin. I am a Hebrew, and my parents were Hebrews. The law of Moses was very important to me. That is why I became a Pharisee.[d] [6]I was so enthusiastic that I tried to hurt the church. No one could find fault with the way I obeyed the law of Moses. [7]At one time all these things were important to me. But now I think those things are worth nothing because of Christ. [8]Not only those things, but I think that all things are worth nothing compared with the greatness of knowing Christ Jesus my Lord. Because of Christ, I have lost all those things. And now I know that all those things are worthless trash. This allows me to have Christ [9]and to belong to him. Now that I belong to Christ, I am right with God and this being right does not come from my following the law. It comes from God through faith. God uses my faith in Christ to make me right with him. [10]All I want is to know Christ and the power of his rising from death. I want to share in Christ's sufferings and become like him in his death. [11]If I have those things, then I have hope that I myself will be raised from death.

Continuing Toward Our Goal

[12]I do not mean that I am already as God wants me to be. I have not yet reached that goal. But I continue trying to reach it and to make it mine. Christ wants me to do that. That is the reason Christ made me his. [13]Brothers, I know that I have not yet reached that goal. But there is one thing I always do: I forget the things that are past. I try as hard as I can to reach the goal that is before me. [14]I keep trying to reach the goal and get the prize. That prize is mine because God called me through Christ to the life above.

[15]All of us who have grown spiritually to be mature should think this way, too. And if there are things you do not agree with, God will make them clear to you. [16]But we should continue following the truth we already have.

[17]Brothers, all of you should try to follow my example and to copy those who live the way we showed you. [18]Many people live like enemies of the cross of Christ. I have often told you about them, and it makes me cry to tell you about them now. [19]The way they live is leading them to destruction. Instead of serving God, they do whatever their bodies want. They do shameful things, and they are proud of it. They think only about earthly things. [20]But our homeland is in heaven, and we are waiting for our Savior, the Lord Jesus Christ, to come from heaven. [21]He will change our simple bodies and make them like his own glorious body. Christ can do this by his power. With that power he is able to rule all things.

What the Christians Are to Do

4 My dear brothers, I love you and want to see you. You bring me joy and make me proud of you. Continue following the Lord as I have told you.

[2]I ask Euodia and Syntyche to agree in the Lord. [3]And because you serve faithfully with me, my friend, I ask you to help these women to do this. They served with me in telling people the Good News.[d] They served together with Clement and others who worked with me. Their names are written in the book of life.[n]

[4]Be full of joy in the Lord always. I will say again, be full of joy.

[5]Let all men see that you are gentle

Prayer
PHILIPPIANS 4:6

Choose the correct answer:

Worry . . .

a. keeps bad things from happening

b. makes it better when something bad does happen

c. keeps people from getting sick

d. helps you recover faster from illness or tragedy

e. none of the above

The correct answer, in case you're not sure, is "none of the above." Worry doesn't prevent anything bad from happening, it doesn't make it any less painful when it does happen, and it won't help you recover any faster. In other words, worry is no help at all in dealing with the rough times that everyone goes through. So what should you do instead? According to this verse, the answer, is "pray." Ask God to protect you and your loved ones. If that's not what God wants, ask him to to help you accept his will with a good attitude.

Prayer won't keep you free from all of life's problems, but it will help you to face them in a way that pleases God and makes you more like him.

To learn more about prayer, zoom to page 1540.

and kind. The Lord is coming soon. ⁶Do not worry about anything. But pray and ask God for everything you need. And when you pray, always give thanks. ⁷And God's peace will keep your hearts and minds in Christ Jesus. The peace that God gives is so great that we cannot understand it.

⁸Brothers, continue to think about the things that are good and worthy of praise. Think about the things that are true and honorable and right and pure and beautiful and respected. ⁹And do what you learned and received from me. Do what I told you and what you saw me do. And the God who gives peace will be with you.

Paul Thanks the Christians

¹⁰I am very happy in the Lord that you have shown your care for me again. You continued to care about me, but there was no way for you to show it. ¹¹I am telling you this, but it is not because I need anything. I have learned to be satisfied with the things I have and with everything that happens. ¹²I know how to live when I am poor. And I know how to live when I have plenty. I have learned the secret of being happy at any time in everything that happens. I have learned to be happy when I have enough to eat and when I do not have enough to eat. I have learned to be happy when I have all that I need

and when I do not have the things I need. ¹³I can do all things through Christ because he gives me strength.

I can do all things through Christ because he gives me strength.
• Philippians 4:13

¹⁴But it was good that you helped me when I needed help. ¹⁵You people in Philippi remember when I first preached the Good News*ᵈ* there. When I left Macedonia, you were the only church that gave me help. ¹⁶Several times you sent me things I needed when I was in Thessalonica. ¹⁷Really, it is not that I want to receive gifts from you. But I want you to have the good that comes from giving. ¹⁸And now I have everything, and more. I have all I need because Epaphroditus brought your gift to me. Your gift is like a sweet-smelling sacrifice offered to God. God accepts that sacrifice, and it pleases him. ¹⁹My God will use his wonderful riches in Christ Jesus to give you everything you need. ²⁰Glory to our God and Father forever and ever! Amen.

²¹Greet each of God's people in Christ. God's people who are with me send greetings to you. ²²All of God's people greet you. And those believers from the palace of Caesar*ᵈ* greet you, too.

²³The grace of the Lord Jesus Christ be with you all.

COLOSSIANS

Only Christ Can Save People

1 From Paul, an apostle[d] of Christ Jesus. I am an apostle because that is what God wanted.

Also from Timothy, our brother.

[2] To the holy and faithful brothers in Christ that live in Colosse. Grace and peace from God our Father.

[3] In our prayers for you we always thank God, the Father of our Lord Jesus Christ. [4] We thank God because we have heard about the faith you have in Christ Jesus and the love you have for all of God's people. [5] You have this faith and love because of your hope, and what you hope for is saved for you in heaven. You learned about this hope when you heard the true teaching, the Good News[d] [6] that was told to you. Everywhere in the world that Good News is bringing blessings and is growing. This has happened with you, too, since you heard the Good News and understood the truth about the grace of God. [7] You learned about God's grace from Epaphras, whom we love. Epaphras works together with us and is a faithful servant of Christ for us. [8] He also told us about the love you have from the Holy Spirit.[d]

[9] Since the day we heard this about you, we have continued praying for you. We ask God that you will know fully what God wants. We pray that you will also have great wisdom and understanding in spiritual things. [10] Then you will live the kind of life that honors and pleases the Lord in every way. You will produce fruit in every good work and grow in the knowledge of God. [11] Then God will strengthen you with his own great power. And you will not give up when troubles come, but you will be patient. [12] Then you will joyfully give thanks to the Father. He has made you able to have all that he has prepared for his people who live in the light. [13] God made us free from the power of darkness, and he brought us into the kingdom of his dear Son. [14] The Son paid for our sins, and in him we have forgiveness.

The Importance of Christ

[15] No one has seen God, but Jesus is exactly like him. Christ ranks higher than all the things that have been made. [16] Through his power all things were made—things in heaven and on earth, things seen and unseen, all powers, authorities, lords, and rulers. All things were made through Christ and for Christ. [17] Christ was there before anything was made. And all things continue because of him. [18] He is the head of the body. (The body is the church.) Everything comes from him. And he is the first one who was raised from death. So in all things Jesus is most important. [19] God was pleased for all of himself to live in Christ. [20] And through Christ, God decided to bring all things back to himself again—things on earth and things in heaven. God made peace by using the blood of Christ's death on the cross.

[21] At one time you were separated from God. You were God's enemies in your minds because the evil deeds you did were against God. [22] But now Christ has made you God's friends again. He did this by his death while he was in the body, that he might bring you into God's presence. He brings you before God as people who are holy, with no wrong in you, and with nothing that God can judge you guilty of. [23] And Christ will do this if you continue to believe

in the Good News[d] you heard. You must continue strong and sure in your faith. You must not be moved away from the hope that Good News gave you. That same Good News has been told to everyone in the world. I, Paul, help in preaching that Good News.

Paul's Work for the Church

24I am happy in my sufferings for you. There are many things that Christ must still suffer through his body, the church. I am accepting my part of these things that must be suffered. I accept these sufferings in my body. I suffer for his body, the church. 25I became a servant of the church because God gave me a special work to do that helps you. My work is to tell fully the teaching of God. 26This teaching is the secret truth that was hidden since the beginning of time. It was hidden from everyone, but now it is made known to God's holy people. 27God decided to let his people know this rich and glorious truth which he has for all people. This truth is Christ himself, who is in you. He is our only hope for glory. 28So we continue to preach Christ to all men. We use all wisdom to warn and to teach everyone. We are trying to bring each one into God's presence as a mature per-

son in Christ. 29To do this, I work and struggle, using Christ's great strength that works so powerfully in me.

2 I want you to know that I am trying very hard to help you. And I am trying to help those in Laodicea and others who have never seen me. 2I want them to be strengthened and joined together with love. I want them to be rich in the strong belief that comes from understanding. I mean I want you to know fully God's secret truth. That truth is Christ himself. 3And in him all the treasures of wisdom and knowledge are safely kept.

4I say this so that no one can fool you by arguments that seem good, but are false. 5I am not there with you, but my heart is with you. I am happy to see your good lives and your strong faith in Christ.

Continue to Live in Christ

6As you received Christ Jesus the Lord, so continue to live in him. 7Keep your roots deep in him and have your lives built on him. Be strong in the faith, just as you were taught. And always be thankful.

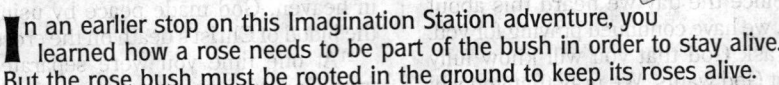

Get Ready, Get Set, Grow!
COLOSSIANS 2:6-7

In an earlier stop on this Imagination Station adventure, you learned how a rose needs to be part of the bush in order to stay alive. But the rose bush must be rooted in the ground to keep its roses alive.

Paul wrote to the Christians in Colosse that they should keep their roots deep in Christ. Christians who are rooted in Christ know that he is the center of their lives. He is the one who will help them live to please God. Just as the rose bush grows and blossoms, so Christians grow in their faith if they stay rooted in Christ.

Have you put your "roots" down into Christ? If he is the center of your life, you will be a strong Christian.

To find out more about growing in your faith, zoom to page 1470.

Whit's Wisdom: The Source of Faith • Colossians 2:6-7

In Odyssey, everyone likes the large oak and maple trees that shade our homes and streets. During the fall season, the colors look as if someone had dumped huge buckets of bright paint all over the town! In spring, the trees tell us with their new leaves that winter is over. On windy days, those trees seem to hum tunes. During summer, our tall green friends keep the town cool.

The other day, I was admiring a huge oak tree near Whit's End. The trunk was bigger around than three or four people holding hands. That tree has seen a lot of history. It was here before the town was ever built. I had to lean my head way back to see the whole tree. Great, green, and grand, it towered over me.

Then I remembered something I once heard: that a healthy tree has a root system *under* the ground that is just as large as the tree is *above* the ground. For something that large to stand, it has to be firmly rooted. Without roots, it will never grow very large.

That reminded me of two verses I often read in my Bible. Take a look at Colossians 2:6, 7. The apostle Paul compares us to trees. He says that we need Jesus Christ just as much as a tree needs to have its roots in the ground. Notice how verse 6 talks about receiving and living in Christ Jesus? That's like being planted in him. We depend on Jesus for our life! But then verse 7 mentions our roots going deep, our lives being built, our faith growing strong. Those are all pictures of learning what Jesus wants us to know and obeying him every day. Paul also says that we should always be thankful.

When you look at a beautiful tree, notice how the branches almost always curve or point up. When the wind blows it looks like they are waving. Doesn't it almost look like they are waving "thanks" to their Creator?

Related passages: Psalm 1

Parent/Teacher Hint: If the weather allows, this lesson can be illustrated with a walk outside. Ask the kids to choose a tree that shows them how we should depend on Christ.

[8] Be sure that no one leads you away with false ideas and words that mean nothing. Those ideas come from men. They are the worthless ideas of this world. They are not from Christ. [9] All of God lives in Christ fully (even when Christ was on earth). [10] And in him you have a full and true life. He is ruler over all rulers and powers.

[11] In Christ you had a different kind of circumcision.[d] That circumcision was not done by hands. I mean, you were made free from the power of your sinful self. That is the kind of circumcision Christ does. [12] When you were baptized, you were buried with Christ and you were raised up with Christ because of your faith in God's power. That power was shown when he raised Christ from death. [13] You were spiritually dead because of your sins and because you were not free from the power of your

sinful self. But God made you alive with Christ. And God forgave all our sins. ¹⁴We owed a debt because we broke God's laws. That debt listed all the rules we failed to follow. But God forgave us that debt. He took away that debt and nailed it to the cross. ¹⁵God defeated the spiritual rulers and powers. With the cross God won the victory and defeated them. He showed the world that they were powerless.

Don't Follow People's Rules

¹⁶So do not let anyone make rules for you about eating and drinking or about a religious feast, a New Moon^d Festival, or a Sabbath^d day. ¹⁷In the past, these things were like a shadow of what was to come. But the new things that were coming are found in Christ. ¹⁸Some enjoy acting as if they were humble and love to worship angels. They are always talking about the visions they have seen. Do not let them tell you that you are wrong. They are full of foolish pride because of their human way of thinking. ¹⁹They do not keep themselves under the control of Christ, the head. The whole body depends on Christ. Because of him all the parts of the body care for each other and help each other. This strengthens the body and holds it together. And so the body grows in the way God wants.

²⁰You died with Christ and were made free from the worthless rules of the world. So why do you act as if you still belong to this world? I mean, why do you follow rules like these: ²¹"Don't eat this," "Don't taste that," "Don't touch that thing"? ²²These rules are talking about earthly things that are gone as soon as they are used. They are only man-made commands and teachings. ²³These rules seem to be wise. But they are only part of a man-made religion. They make people pretend not to be proud and make them punish their bodies. But they do not really control the evil desires of the sinful self.

Your New Life in Christ

3 You were raised from death with Christ. So aim at what is in heaven, where Christ is sitting at the right hand of God. ²Think only about the things in heaven, not the things on earth. ³Your old sinful self has died, and your new life is kept with Christ in God. ⁴Christ is your life. When he comes again, you will share in his glory.

"**A**fter my bath, I'll have to change my clothes, too. Now that reminds me of the way the Bible talks in Colossians 3:1-17 about living as a Christian."

⁵So put all evil things out of your life: sexual sinning, doing evil, letting evil thoughts control you, wanting things that are evil, and always selfishly wanting more and more. This really means living to serve a false god. ⁶These things make God angry.^{n} ⁷In your evil life in the past, you also did these things.

⁸But now put these things out of your life: anger, bad temper, doing or saying things to hurt others, and using evil words when you talk. ⁹Do not lie to each other. You have left your old sinful life and the things you did before. ¹⁰You have begun to live the new life. In your new life you are being made new. You are becoming like the One who made you. This new life brings you the true knowledge of God. ¹¹In the new life there is no difference between Greeks and Jews. There is no difference between those who are circumcised^d and those who are not circumcised, or people that are foreigners, or Scythians.^{n} There is no difference between slaves and free people. But Christ is in all believers. And Christ is all that is important.

¹²God has chosen you and made you

---

^{n}**These . . . angry** Some Greek copies add: "against the people who do not obey God."
^{n}**Scythians** The Scythians were known as very wild and cruel people.

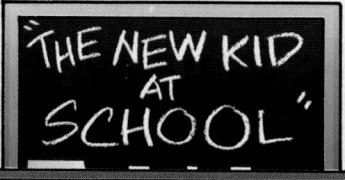

"THE NEW KID AT SCHOOL"

Dylan learns the importance of kindness
A story based on Mark 12:31

CLASS, I'D LIKE TO INTRODUCE OUR NEW CLASSMATE...

...*GRANT MORLEY.* GRANT IS FROM JAMAICA AND HIS FAMILY HAS JUST MOVED HERE TO ODYSSEY.

GRANT, YOU CAN SIT RIGHT BACK THERE AT THE EMPTY DESK.

LOOKS KIND OF *SMALL* FOR THE SIXTH GRADE!

HI, GRANT. WELCOME TO ODYSSEY SCHOOL! MY NAME'S DYLAN.

THANKS, DYLAN!

A*s THE SCHOOL DAY PASSES, GRANT PROVES TO BE QUITE THE STUDENT...*

YES, GRANT, YOU HAVE THE ANSWER?

225.

WOW, GRANT! HOW DO YOU *KNOW* ALL THIS STUFF?!

MY *DAD* HELPS ME WITH MY HOMEWORK.

HEY, WHO DOES THIS KID THINK HE IS, *MR. WIZARD?!*

TOO BAD HIS *BODY* ISN'T AS BIG AS HIS *BRAIN!*

his holy people. He loves you. So always do these things: Show mercy to others; be kind, humble, gentle, and patient. [13]Do not be angry with each other, but forgive each other. If someone does wrong to you, then forgive him. Forgive each other because the Lord forgave you. [14]Do all these things; but most important, love each other. Love is what holds you all together in perfect unity. [15]Let the peace that Christ gives control your thinking. You were all called together in one body[n] to have peace. Always be thankful. [16]Let the teaching of Christ live in you richly. Use all wisdom to teach and strengthen each other. Sing psalms, hymns, and spiritual songs with thankfulness in your hearts to God. [17]Everything you say and everything you do should all be done for Jesus your Lord. And in all you do, give thanks to God the Father through Jesus.

Your New Life with Other People

[18]Wives, be under the authority of your husbands. This is the right thing to do in the Lord.

[19]Husbands, love your wives, and be gentle to them.

[20]Children, obey your parents in all things. This pleases the Lord.

Children, obey your parents in all things. This pleases the Lord.
• Colossians 3:20

[21]Fathers, do not nag your children. If you are too hard to please, they may want to stop trying.

[22]Slaves, obey your masters in all things. Do not obey just when they are watching you, to gain their favor. But serve them honestly, because you respect the Lord. [23]In all the work you are doing, work the best you can. Work as if you were working for the Lord, not for men. [24]Remember that you will receive your reward from the Lord, which he promised to his people. You are serving the Lord Christ. [25]But remember that anyone who does wrong will be punished for that wrong. And the Lord treats everyone the same.

4 Masters, give the things that are good and fair to your slaves. Remember that you have a Master in heaven.

What the Christians Are to Do

[2]Continue praying and keep alert. And when you pray, always thank God. [3]Also pray for us. Pray that God will give us an opportunity to tell people his message. Pray that we can preach the secret truth that God has made known about Christ. I am in prison because I preach this truth. [4]Pray that I can speak in a way that will make it clear as I should.

[5]Be wise in the way you act with people who are not believers. Use your time in the best way you can. [6]When you talk, you should always be kind and wise. Then you will be able to answer everyone in the way you should.

News About the People with Paul

[7]Tychicus is my dear brother in Christ. He is a faithful minister and servant with me in the Lord. He will tell you all the things that are happening to me. [8]That is why I am sending him. I want you to know how we are. I am sending him to encourage you. [9]I send him with Onesimus. Onesimus is a faithful and dear brother in Christ. He is one of your group. They will tell you all that has happened here.

[10]Aristarchus greets you. He is a prisoner with me. And Mark, the cousin of Barnabas, also greets you. (I have already told you what to do about Mark. If he comes, welcome him.) [11]Jesus, who is called Justus, also greets you. These are the only Jewish believers who work with me for the kingdom of God. They have been a comfort to me. [12]Epaphras also greets you. He is a

[n]**body** The spiritual body of Christ, meaning the church or his people.

servant of Jesus Christ. And he is from your group. He always prays for you. He prays that you will grow to be spiritually mature and have everything that God wants for you. [13]I know that he has worked hard for you and the people in Laodicea and in Hierapolis. [14]Demas and our dear friend Luke, the doctor, greet you.

[15]Greet the brothers in Laodicea. And greet Nympha and the church that meets in her house. [16]After this letter is read to you, be sure that it is also read to the church in Laodicea. And you read the letter that I wrote to Laodicea. [17]Tell Archippus, "Be sure to do the work the Lord gave you."

[18]I, Paul, greet you and write this with my own hand. Remember me in prison. God's grace be with you.

1 THESSALONIANS

Paul Encourages
New Christians

1 From Paul, Silas, and Timothy.
To the church in Thessalonica, the church in God the Father and the Lord Jesus Christ. May God's grace and peace be yours.

The Faith of the Thessalonians

[2]We always remember you when we pray and thank God for all of you. [3]When we pray to God our Father, we always thank him for the things you have done because of your faith. And we thank him for the work you have done because of your love. And we thank him that you continue to be strong because of your hope in our Lord Jesus Christ.

[4]Brothers, God loves you. And we know that he has chosen you to be his. [5]We brought the Good News[d] to you. But we did not use only words. We brought the Good News with power, with the Holy Spirit,[d] and with sure knowledge that it is true. Also you know how we lived when we were with you. We lived that way to help you. [6]And you became like us and like the Lord. You suffered much, but still you accepted the teaching with the joy that comes from the Holy Spirit. [7]So you became an example to all the believers in Macedonia and Southern Greece. [8]The Lord's teaching spread from you in Macedonia and Southern Greece. And your faith in God has become known everywhere. So we do not need to say anything about your faith. [9]People everywhere are telling about the good way you accepted us when we were there with you. They tell about how you stopped worshiping idols and changed to serving the living and true God. [10]And you changed to wait for God's

Son to come from heaven. God raised that Son from death. He is Jesus, who saves us from God's angry judgment that is sure to come.

Paul's Work in Thessalonica

2 Brothers, you know that our visit to you was not a failure. [2]Before we came to you, we suffered in Philippi. People there insulted us. You know about that. And when we came to you, many people were against us. But our God helped us to be brave and to tell you his Good News.[d] [3]Our message was a message to encourage you. We were not trying to lie. We had no evil plan. We were not trying to trick you. [4]But we speak the Good News because God tested us and trusted us to do it. When we speak, we are not trying to please men. But we are trying to please God, who tests our hearts. [5]You know that we never tried to influence you by saying nice things about you. We were not trying to get your money. We had no selfishness to hide from you. God knows that this is true. [6]We were not looking for praise from you or anyone else. We are apostles[d] of Christ. When we were with you, we could have used our authority to make you do things.

[7]But we were very gentle with you. We were like a mother caring for her little children. [8]Because we loved you, we were happy to share God's Good News with you. But not only that, we were also happy to share even our own lives with you. [9]Brothers, I know that you remember how hard we worked. We worked night and day so that we would not burden any of you while we preached God's Good News to you.

[10]When we were with you, we lived in a holy and right way, without fault. You know that this is true, and God knows that this is true. [11]You know that we treated each of you as a father treats his own children. [12]We strengthened you, we comforted you, and we told you to live good lives for God. It is God who calls you to his glorious kingdom.

[13]Also, we always thank God because of the way you accepted his message. You heard his message from us, and you accepted it as the word of God, not the words of men. And it really is God's message. And that message works in you who believe. [14]Brothers, you have been like God's churches in Christ that are in Judea.[n] God's people suffered bad things from the other Jews there. And you suffered the same bad things from the people of your own country. [15]Those Jews killed both the Lord Jesus and the prophets.[d] And they forced us to leave that country. They do not please God. They are against all people. [16]They try to stop us from teaching the non-Jews so that they may be saved. But those Jews are adding more and more sins to the sins they already have. The anger of God has come to them at last.

Paul Wants to Visit Them Again

[17]Brothers, we were separated from you for a short time, but our thoughts were still with you. We wanted very much to see you, and tried very hard to do so. [18]I, Paul, tried to come many times, but Satan stopped us. [19]For you are our hope, our joy, and the crown we will be proud of when our Lord Jesus Christ comes. [20]Truly you are our glory and our joy.

3 We could not come to you, but it was very hard to wait any longer. So we decided to stay in Athens alone [2]and send Timothy to you. Timothy is our brother, who works with us for God. He helps us tell people the Good News[d] about Christ. We sent Timothy to strengthen and comfort you in your faith. [3]We sent him so that none of

you would be upset by these troubles we have now. You yourselves know that we must have these troubles. [4]Even when we were with you, we told you that we all would have to suffer. And you know that it has happened the way we said. [5]This is why I sent Timothy to you, so that I could know about your faith. I sent him when I could not wait any longer. I was afraid that the devil had tempted you, and then our hard work would have been wasted.

[6]But Timothy now has come back to us from you and has brought us good news about your faith and love. He told us that you always remember us in a good way. He told us that you want to see us just as much as we want to see you. [7]So, brothers, we are comforted about you, because of your faith. We have much trouble and suffering, but still we are comforted. [8]For our life is really full if you stand strong in the Lord. [9]We have so much joy before our God because of you, and we thank him for you. But we cannot thank him enough for all the joy we feel. [10]And we continue praying with all our heart for you night and day. We pray that we can see you again and give you all the things you need to make your faith strong.

[11]We pray that our God and Father and our Lord Jesus will prepare the way for us to come to you. [12]We pray that the Lord will make your love grow more and more for each other and for all people. We pray that you will love others as we love you and [13]that your hearts will be made strong. Then you will be holy and without fault before our God and Father when our Lord Jesus comes with all his holy people.

A Life that Pleases God

4 Brothers, now I have some other things to tell you. We taught you how to live in a way that will please God. And you are living that way. Now we ask you and encourage you in the Lord Jesus to live that way more and more. [2]You know what we told you to do by

---

[n]**Judea** The Jewish land where Jesus lived and taught and where the church first began.

the authority of the Lord Jesus. ³God wants you to be holy and to stay away from sexual sins. ⁴He wants each one of you to learn how to take a wife[n] in a way that is holy and honorable. ⁵Don't use your body for sexual sin. The people who do not know God use their bodies for that. ⁶So do not wrong your brother or cheat him in this way. The Lord will punish people who do those things. We have already told you and warned you about that. ⁷God called us to be holy and does not want us to live in sin. ⁸So the person who refuses to obey this teaching is refusing to obey God, not man. And God is the One who gives us his Holy Spirit.[d]

⁹We do not need to write to you about having love for your brothers and sisters in Christ. God has already taught you to love each other. ¹⁰And truly you do love the brothers in all of Macedonia. Brothers, now we encourage you to love them more and more.

¹¹Do all you can to live a peaceful life. Take care of your own business. Do your own work. We have already told you to do these things. ¹²If you do, then people who are not believers will respect you. And you will not have to depend on others for what you need.

The Lord's Coming

¹³Brothers, we want you to know about those who have died. We do not want you to be sad as others who have no hope. ¹⁴We believe that Jesus died and that he rose again. So, because of Jesus, God will bring together with Jesus those who have died. ¹⁵What we tell you now is the Lord's own message. We who are living now may still be living when the Lord comes again. We who are living at that time will be with the Lord, but not before those who have already died. ¹⁶The Lord himself will come down from heaven. There will be a loud command with the voice of the archangel[n] and with the trumpet call of God. And those who have died and

were in Christ will rise first. ¹⁷After that, those who are still alive at that time will be gathered up with them. We will be taken up in the clouds to meet the Lord in the air. And we will be with the Lord forever. ¹⁸So comfort each other with these words.

"Yes, I know that every day isn't a party. But that shouldn't stop us from being happy. Look at what the Bible says in 1 Thessalonians 4:16-18 about what we can look forward to."

Be Ready for the Lord's Coming

5 Now, brothers, we do not need to write to you about times and dates. ²You know very well that the day the Lord comes again will be a surprise like a thief that comes in the night. ³People will say, "We have peace and we are safe." At that time they will be destroyed quickly, as pains come quickly to a woman having a baby. And those people will not escape. ⁴But you, brothers, are not living in darkness. And so that day will not surprise you like a thief. ⁵You are all people who belong to the light. You belong to the day. We do not belong to the night or to darkness. ⁶So we should not be like other people. We should not be sleeping, but we should be awake and have self-control. ⁷Those who sleep, sleep at night. Those who get drunk, get drunk at night. ⁸But we belong to the day; so we should control ourselves. We should wear faith and love to protect us. And the hope of salvation should be our helmet. ⁹God did not choose us to suffer his anger, but to have salvation through our Lord Jesus Christ. ¹⁰Jesus died for us so that we can live together with him. It is not important if we are alive or dead when Jesus

[n]**learn . . . wife** This might also mean "learn to control your own body."
[n]**archangel** The leader among God's angels or messengers.

comes. ¹¹So comfort each other and give each other strength, just as you are doing now.

Final Instructions and Greetings

¹²Now, brothers, we ask you to respect those people who work hard with you, who lead you in the Lord and teach you. ¹³Respect them with a very special love because of the work they do with you.

Live in peace with each other. ¹⁴We ask you, brothers, to warn those who do not work. Encourage the people who are afraid. Help those who are weak. Be patient with every person. ¹⁵Be sure that no one pays back wrong for wrong. But always try to do what is good for each other and for all people.

¹⁶Always be happy. ¹⁷Never stop praying. ¹⁸Give thanks whatever happens. That is what God wants for you in Christ Jesus.

¹⁹Do not stop the work of the Holy Spirit.ᵈ ²⁰Do not treat prophecyᵈ as if it were not important. ²¹But test everything. Keep what is good. ²²And stay away from everything that is evil.

²³We pray that God himself, the God of peace, will make you pure, belonging only to him. We pray that your whole self—spirit, soul, and body—will be kept safe and be without wrong when our Lord Jesus Christ comes. ²⁴The One who calls you will do that for you. You can trust him.

²⁵Brothers, please pray for us.

²⁶Give all the brothers a holy kiss when you meet. ²⁷I tell you by the authority of the Lord to read this letter to all the brothers.

²⁸The grace of our Lord Jesus Christ be with you.

Thankfulness
1 THESSALONIANS 5:18

Bad guys, good guys, a princess in danger, and adventure are all good parts of a story about heroes. The best part is that we know whatever may happen, everything will turn out all right for the hero and the princess.

This is an important lesson about thankfulness. This verse says to be thankful no matter what happens. Why should we do that? Because God will make everything that happens to us, from losing our homework to losing our best friend, turn out all right.

"So, am I supposed to feel thankful for losing my friend?" No, it just means that you can thank God that he is with you and that he will work out even something sad for your good. Do you see the difference? It's not always easy to be thankful, but it will be easier if you remember that God makes everything turn out right.

2 THESSALONIANS

The Problems of New Christians

1 From Paul, Silas, and Timothy.
To the church in Thessalonica in God our Father and the Lord Jesus Christ.

²Grace and peace to you from God the Father and the Lord Jesus Christ.

Paul Talks About God's Judgment

³We must always thank God for you. And we should do this because it is right. It is right because your faith is growing more and more. And the love that every one of you has for each other is also growing. ⁴So we brag about you to the other churches of God. We tell them about the way you continue to be strong and have faith. You are being treated badly and are suffering many troubles, but you continue with strength and faith.

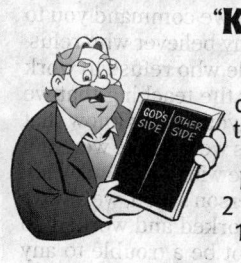

"Kids, one of the greatest gifts someone can give you is to pray for you. Notice how Paul prayed in 2 Thessalonians 1:3-12. We can do that too."

⁵This is proof that God is right in his judgment. God wants you to be worthy of his kingdom. Your suffering is for that kingdom. ⁶And God will do what is right. He will give trouble to those who trouble you. ⁷And he will give peace to you people who are troubled and to us also. God will give us this help when the Lord Jesus is shown to us from heaven

with his powerful angels. ⁸He will come from heaven with burning fire to punish those who do not know God. He will punish those who do not obey the Good News^d of our Lord Jesus Christ. ⁹Those people will be punished with a destruction that continues forever. They will not be allowed to be with the Lord, and they will be kept away from his great power. ¹⁰This will happen on the day when the Lord Jesus comes to receive glory with his holy people. And all the people who have believed will be amazed at Jesus. You will be in that group of believers because you believed what we told you.

¹¹That is why we always pray for you. We ask our God to help you live the good way that he called you to live. The goodness you have makes you want to do good, and the faith you have makes you work. We pray that with his power God will help you do these things more and more. ¹²We pray all this so that the name of our Lord Jesus Christ can have glory in you. And you can have glory in him. That glory comes from the grace of our God and the Lord Jesus Christ.

Evil Things Will Happen

2 Brothers, we have something to say about the coming of our Lord Jesus Christ. We want to talk to you about that time when we will meet together with him. ²Do not become easily upset in your thinking or afraid if you hear that the day of the Lord has already come. Someone may say this in a prophecy^d or in a message. Or you may read it in a letter that someone tells you came from us. ³Do not let any person fool you in any way. That day of the Lord will not come until the turning away from God happens. And that day will not come until the Man of Evil appears. He belongs to hell. [4]He is against anything called God or anything that people worship. And the Man of Evil puts himself above anything called God or anything that people worship. And that Man of Evil even goes into God's Temple[d] and sits there. Then he says that he is God.

[5]I told you when I was with you that all this would happen. Do you not remember? [6]And you know what is stopping that Man of Evil now. He is being stopped now so that he will appear at the right time. [7]The secret power of evil is already working in the world now. But there is one who is stopping that power. And he will continue to stop it until he is taken out of the way. [8]Then that Man of Evil will appear. And the Lord Jesus will kill him with the breath that comes from his mouth and will destroy him with the glory of his coming. [9]The Man of Evil will come by the power of Satan. He will have great power, and he will do many different false miracles,[d] signs, and wonders. [10]He will use every kind of evil to trick those who are lost. They are lost because they refused to love the truth. (If they loved the truth, they would be saved.) [11]But they refused to love the truth; so God sends them something powerful that leads them away from the truth. He sends them that power so they will believe something that is not true. [12]So all those who do not believe the truth will be judged guilty. They did not believe the truth, and they enjoyed doing evil.

You Are Chosen for Salvation

[13]Brothers, the Lord loves you. God chose you from the beginning to be saved. So we must always thank God for you. You are saved by the Spirit[d] that makes you holy and by your faith in the truth. [14]God used the Good News[d] that we preached to call you to be saved. He called you so that you can share in the glory of our Lord Jesus Christ. [15]So,

brothers, stand strong and continue to believe the teachings we gave you. We taught you those things in our speaking and in our letter to you.

[16-17]We pray that the Lord Jesus Christ himself and God our Father will comfort you and strengthen you in every good thing you do and say. God loved us. Through his grace he gave us a good hope and comfort that continues forever.

Pray for Us

3 And now, brothers, pray for us. Pray that the Lord's teaching will continue to spread quickly. And pray that people will give honor to that teaching, just as happened with you. [2]And pray that we will be protected from bad and evil people. (Not all people believe in the Lord.)

[3]But the Lord is faithful. He will give you strength and protect you from the Evil One. [4]The Lord makes us feel sure that you are doing the things we told you. And we know that you will continue to do those things. [5]We pray that the Lord will lead your hearts into God's love and Christ's patience.

The Duty to Work

[6]Brothers, by the authority of our Lord Jesus Christ we command you to stay away from any believer who refuses to work. People who refuse to work are not following the teaching that we gave them. [7]You yourselves know that you should live as we live. We were not lazy when we were with you. [8]And when we ate another person's food, we always paid for it. We worked and worked so that we would not be a trouble to any of you. We worked night and day. [9]We had the right to ask you to help us. But we worked to take care of ourselves so that we would be an example for you to follow. [10]When we were with you, we gave you this rule: "If anyone will not work, he will not eat."

[11]We hear that some people in your group refuse to work. They do nothing. And they busy themselves in other people's lives. [12]We command those people

to work quietly and earn their own food. In the Lord Jesus Christ we beg them to do this. [13]Brothers, never become tired of doing good.

[14]If anyone does not obey what we tell you in this letter, then remember who he is. Do not associate with him. Then maybe he will feel ashamed. [15]But do not treat him as an enemy. Warn him as a brother.

Final Words

[16]We pray that the Lord of peace will give you peace at all times and in every way. May the Lord be with all of you.

[17]I am Paul, and I end this letter now in my own handwriting. All my letters have this to show they are from me. This is the way I write.

[18]May our Lord Jesus Christ show all of you his grace.

1 TIMOTHY

Advice to a
Young Preacher

1 From Paul, an apostle*d* of Christ Jesus, by the command of God our Savior and Christ Jesus our hope.

²To Timothy, a true son to me because you believe.

Grace, mercy, and peace from God the Father and Christ Jesus our Lord.

Warning Against False Teaching

³I want you to stay in Ephesus. I asked you to do that when I went into Macedonia. Some people there in Ephesus are teaching false things. Stay there so that you can command them to stop. ⁴Tell them not to spend their time on stories that are not true and on long lists of names in family histories. These things only bring arguments; they do not help God's work. God's work is done by faith. ⁵The purpose of this command is for people to have love. To have this love they must have a pure heart, they must do what they know is right, and they must have true faith. ⁶Some people have wandered away from these things. They talk about things that are worth nothing. ⁷They want to be teachers of the law, but they do not know what they are talking about. They do not even understand what they say they are sure about.

⁸We know that the law is good if a man uses it right. ⁹We also know that the law is not made for good men. The law is made for people who are against the law and for those who refuse to follow the law. It is for people who are against God and are sinful, who are not holy and have no religion, who kill their fathers and mothers, who murder, ¹⁰who take part in sexual sins, men who have sexual relations with other men, those who sell slaves, who tell lies, who speak falsely, and who do anything against the true teaching of God. ¹¹That teaching is part of the Good News*d* that God gave me to tell. That glorious Good News is from the blessed God.

Thanks for God's Mercy

¹²I thank Christ Jesus our Lord because he trusted me and gave me this work of serving him. And he gives me strength. ¹³In the past I spoke against Christ and persecuted him and did all kinds of things to hurt him. But God showed mercy to me because I did not know what I was doing. I did those things when I did not believe. ¹⁴But the grace of our Lord was fully given to me. And with that grace came the faith and love that are in Christ Jesus.

¹⁵What I say is true, and you should fully accept it: Christ Jesus came into the world to save sinners. And I am the worst of those sinners. ¹⁶But I was given mercy. I was given mercy so that in me Christ Jesus could show that he has patience without limit. And he showed his patience with me, the worst of all sinners. Christ wanted me to be an example for those who would believe in him and have life forever. ¹⁷Honor and glory to the King that rules forever! He cannot be destroyed and cannot be seen. Honor and glory forever and ever to the only God. Amen.

¹⁸Timothy, you are like a son to me. I am giving you a command that agrees with the prophecies*d* that were given about you in the past. I tell you this so that you can follow those prophecies and fight the good fight of faith. ¹⁹Continue to have faith and do what you know is right. Some people have

not done this. Their faith has been destroyed. [20]Hymenaeus and Alexander are men who have done that. I have given them to Satan so that they will learn not to speak against God.

Some Rules for Men and Women

2 First, I tell you to pray for all people. Ask God for the things people need, and be thankful to him. [2]You should pray for kings and for all who have authority. Pray for the leaders so that we can have quiet and peaceful lives—lives full of worship and respect for God. [3]This is good, and it pleases God our Savior. [4]God wants all people to be saved. And he wants everyone to know the truth. [5]There is only one God. And there is only one way that people can reach God. That way is through Jesus Christ, who is also a man. [6]Jesus gave himself to pay for the sins of all people. Jesus is proof that God wants all people to be saved. And that proof came at the right time. [7]That is why I was chosen to tell the Good News[d] and was chosen to be an apostle.[d] (I am telling the truth. I am not lying.) I was chosen to teach the non-Jewish people to believe and to know the truth.

[8]I want men everywhere to pray. These men who lift up their hands in prayer must be holy. They must not be men who become angry and have arguments.

[9]I also want women to wear clothes that are right for them. They should dress with respect and right thinking. They should not use fancy braided hair or gold or pearls or expensive clothes to make themselves beautiful. [10]But they should make themselves beautiful by doing good deeds. Women who say they worship God should make themselves beautiful in that way.

[11]A woman should learn by listening quietly and being fully ready to obey. [12]I do not allow a woman to teach a man or to have authority over a man. She must remain silent. [13]For Adam was made

first; Eve was made later. [14]Also, Adam was not the one who was tricked by the devil. It was the woman who was tricked and became a sinner. [15]But women will be saved through having children. They will be saved if they continue in faith, love, holiness, and self-control.

Leaders in the Church

3 What I say is true: If anyone wants to become an elder,[d] he is wanting a good work. [2]An elder must be so good that people cannot rightly criticize him. He must have only one wife. He must have self-control and be wise. He must be respected by other people and must be ready to help people by accepting them into his home. He must be a good teacher. [3]He must not drink too much wine, and he must not be a man who likes to fight. He must be gentle and peaceful. He must not love money. [4]He must be a good leader of his own family so that his children obey him with full respect. [5](If a man does not know how to be a leader over his own family, he will not be able to take care of God's church.) [6]But an elder must not be a new believer. A new believer might be too proud of himself. Then he would be judged guilty for his pride just as the devil was. [7]An elder must also have the respect of people who are not in the church. Then he will not be criticized by others and caught in the devil's trap.

Helpers in the Church

[8]In the same way, deacons[d] must be men that people can respect. They must not say things they do not mean. They must not use their time drinking too much wine, and they must not be men who are always trying to get rich by cheating others. [9]They must follow the faith that God made known to us and always do what they know is right. [10]You should test those men first. If you find nothing wrong in them, then they can serve as deacons. [11]In the same way, the women[n] must have the respect of other

---

[n]**women** This might mean the wives of the deacons, or it might mean women who serve in the same way as deacons.

people. They must not be women who repeat evil gossip about other people. They must have self-control and be women who can be trusted in everything. [12]Deacons must have only one wife. They must be good leaders of their children and their own families. [13]Those who serve well as deacons are making an honorable place for themselves. And they will feel very sure of their faith in Christ Jesus.

The Secret of Our Life

[14]I hope I can come to you soon. But I am writing these things to you now. [15]Then, even if I cannot come soon, you will know about the things that people must do in the family of God. That family is the church of the living God, the support and foundation of the truth. [16]Without doubt, the secret of our life of worship is great:

He was shown to us in a human
      body,
   proved right by the Spirit,[d]
and seen by angels.

He was preached to the nations,
   believed in by the world,
   and taken to heaven in glory.

A Warning About False Teachers

4 The Holy Spirit[d] clearly says that in the later times some people will stop believing the true faith. They will obey spirits that lie and will follow the teachings of demons.[d] [2]Such teachings come from hypocrites,[d] men who cannot see what is right and what is wrong. It is as if their understanding were destroyed by a hot iron. [3]They tell people that it is wrong to marry. And they tell people that there are some foods that must not be eaten. But God made those foods, and the people who believe and who know the truth can eat those foods with thanks. [4]Everything that God made is good. Nothing that God made should be refused if it is accepted with thanks to God. [5]Everything God made is made holy by what God has said and by prayer.

Be a Good Servant of Christ

[6]Tell these things to the brothers. This will show that you are a good servant of Christ Jesus. You will show that you are made strong by the words of faith and good teaching that you have been following. [7]People tell silly stories

Get Ready, Get Set, Grow!
1 TIMOTHY 4:6

You hardly ever think about growing, do you? As your body grows, you don't decide that today you're going to get bigger feet or longer hair. Your body just grows on its own. But it helps to eat healthy foods and get lots of exercise.

We probably don't realize it when our Christian faith is growing either. But it helps to get "healthy foods" (teaching about God's Word) and lots of "exercise" (practice in obeying God's Word). Paul told Timothy that he would be made strong by following "the words of faith and the good teaching."

If you want your faith to grow, give yourself the spiritual food of the Bible, and then follow what it says. Eat and exercise well so that your faith can grow.

To find out more about growing in your faith, zoom to page 1477.

Whit's Wisdom: Growing in Faith • 1 Timothy 4:12

"**I** can't *wait* 'til I grow up!" said Jessie as I served her a kid's size cone at Whit's End, my ice cream shop.

"**Y**ou don't have to wait, you know," I said.

"**W**hat do you mean, Mr. Whittaker? Have you invented a machine that will make me bigger or give me some extra birthdays?" she said.

"**N**ow hold on," I said. "There are more important ways to grow up than getting bigger and adding birthdays."

"**I** know, I know," she answered. "I have to eat my beans and peas, drink my milk, get enough sleep and stay out of my brother Dylan's way. Then maybe someday I'll get so big that Dylan will have to stay out of *my* way."

She had me laughing. "I'll warn Dylan," I said. "But in the meantime, let me tell you at least five important ways you can grow to be a better person."

Well, I had her attention. Have I got yours? Here are the five ways I showed Jessie.

Find 1 Timothy 4:12 and read it out loud. This would be a good verse for you to memorize while you are young. Can you tell why?

First, isn't it nice to know that God doesn't think you're unimportant just because you're young. Remember that. If you're old enough to believe in Jesus, you are already old enough to help other people believe in him.

OK, now find the five ways to grow that I talked about. See them? They are (1) words, (2) actions, (3) love, (4) faith, and (5) a pure life. How do you grow in your words? By watching what you say; by asking yourself if God would want you to use certain words. How can you grow in your actions? By learning to live like Jesus. By getting in the habit of asking, "What would Jesus do?" Now, think about the other three. Can you come up with some ways to grow in those areas? You might have to ask an older Christian for help.

You can use all five of these ways to grow today. That's what I told Jessie that day. She got down from her stool at the counter and skipped to the door. She stopped there and said, "See you later, Mr. Whittaker. I'm going to go grow up!"

I'm sure you are, too.

Related passages: Psalm 1; Psalm 119:9-11

Teacher/Parent Hint: Work with your child on memorization. Children memorize Scripture easily, but it can be more difficult for them to understand how to apply the Scriptures to daily living. Discuss with children what they can *do* to be obedient to Scripture.

that do not agree with God's truth. Do not follow what those stories teach. But teach yourself only to serve God. [8]Training your body helps you in some ways, but serving God helps you in every way. Serving God brings you blessings in this life and in the future life, too. [9]What I say is true, and you should fully accept it. [10]For this is why we work and struggle: We hope in the living God. He is the Savior of all people. And in a very special way, he is the Savior of all who believe in him.

[11]Command and teach these things. [12]You are young, but do not let anyone treat you as if you were not important. Be an example to show the believers how they should live. Show them with your words, with the way you live, with your love, with your faith, and with your pure life. [13]Continue to read the Scriptures[d] to the people, strengthen them, and teach them. Do these things until I come. [14]Remember to use the gift that you have. That gift was given to you through a prophecy[d] when the group of elders[d] laid their hands on[n] you. [15]Continue to do those things. Give your life to doing them. Then everyone can see that your work is progressing. [16]Be careful in your life and in your teaching. Continue to live and teach rightly. Then you will save yourself and those people who listen to you.

Rules for Living with Others

5 Do not speak angrily to an older man, but talk to him as if he were your father. Treat younger men like brothers. [2]Treat older women like mothers, and younger women like sisters. Always treat them in a pure way.

[3]Take care of widows who are all alone. [4]But if a widow has children or grandchildren, the first thing they need to learn is to do their duty to their own family. When they do this, they will be repaying their parents or grandparents. That pleases God. [5]If a widow is all alone and without help, then she puts

her hope in God and prays night and day for God's help. [6]But the widow who uses her life to please herself is really dead while she is still living. [7]Tell the believers there to do these things so that no one can say they are doing wrong. [8]A believer should take care of his own relatives, especially his own family. If he does not do that, he has turned against the faith. He is worse than a person who does not believe in God.

[9]To be on your list of widows, a woman must be 60 years old or older. She must have been faithful to her husband. [10]She must be known as a woman who has done good works. By this, I mean good works such as raising her children, accepting visitors in her home, washing the feet of God's people, helping those in trouble, and using her life to do all kinds of good deeds.

[11]But do not put younger widows on that list. After they give themselves to Christ, they are often pulled away from him by their physical needs. And then they want to marry again. [12]And they will be judged for not doing what they first promised to do. [13]Also, those younger widows begin to waste their time going from house to house. They begin to gossip and busy themselves with other people's lives. They say things that they should not say. [14]So I want the younger widows to marry, have children, and take care of their homes. If they do this, then no enemy will have any reason to criticize them. [15]But some of the younger widows have already turned away to follow Satan.

[16]If any woman who is a believer has widows in her family, then she should care for them herself. The church should not have to care for them. Then the church will be able to care for the widows who have no living family.

[17]The elders[d] who lead the church well should receive great honor. Those who work hard by speaking and teaching especially should receive great honor. [18]For the Scripture[d] says, "When

---

[n]**laid their hands on** A sign to show that Timothy was being given a special work of God.

an ox is working in the grain, do not cover its mouth to keep it from eating."[n] And the Scripture also says, "A worker should be given his pay."[n]

[19]Do not listen to someone who accuses an elder, unless there are two or three other persons who say he did wrong. [20]Tell those who keep on sinning that they are wrong. Do this in front of the whole church so that the others will have a warning.

[21]Before God and Jesus Christ and the chosen angels, I command you to do these things. Be careful to do them without showing favor to anyone.

[22]Think carefully before you lay your hands on[n] anyone for the Lord's service. Do not share in the sins of others. Keep yourself pure.

[23]Timothy, you stop drinking only water and drink a little wine. This will help your stomach, and you will not be sick so often.

[24]The sins of some people are easy to see even before they are judged. But the sins of others are seen only later.

[25]So also good deeds are easy to see. But even when they are not easy to see, they cannot stay hidden.

6 All who are slaves should show full respect to their masters. Then no one will speak against God's name and our teaching. [2]Some slaves have masters who are believers. This means they are all brothers. But the slaves should not show their masters any less respect. They should serve their masters even better, because they are helping believers they love.

False Teaching and True Riches

You must teach and preach these things. [3]If anyone has a different teaching, he does not accept the true teaching of our Lord Jesus Christ. And that teaching shows him the true way to serve God. [4]The person who teaches falsely is full of pride and understands nothing. He is sick with a love for arguing and fighting about words. And that brings

Temptation
1 TIMOTHY 6:6-10

One of the richest men in the world was once asked, "How much money is enough?" He answered, "Just a little bit more."

He had billions of dollars, but he still wanted more! Money is like that. It presents a special kind of temptation. No matter how much or how little we have, we always seem to want a little bit more.

Of course this is nothing new. Almost 2000 years ago, Paul wrote to Timothy that people who only think about money "bring temptation to themselves and are caught in a trap.... The love of money causes all kinds of evil" (verses 9-10). Money is good to use, but we shouldn't live for it. Watch your own attitude toward money and the things it can buy. If necessary, take that attitude to God and ask him to replace it with one that is more pleasing to him.

To learn more about temptation, zoom to page 1489.

[n]**"When . . . eating."** Quotation from Deuteronomy 25:4.
[n]**"A worker . . . pay."** Quotation from Luke 10:7.
[n]**lay your hands on** A sign of giving authority or power to another person.

jealousy, making trouble, insults, and evil mistrust. [5]And that also brings arguments from men who have evil minds. They have lost the truth. They think that serving God is a way to get rich.

[6]It is true that serving God makes a person very rich, if he is satisfied with what he has. [7]When we came into the world, we brought nothing. And when we die, we can take nothing out. [8]So, if we have food and clothes, we will be satisfied with that. [9]Those who want to become rich bring temptation to themselves. They are caught in a trap. They begin to want many foolish things that will hurt them, things that ruin and destroy people. [10]The love of money causes all kinds of evil. Some people have left the true faith because they want to get more and more money. But they have caused themselves much sorrow.

Some Things to Remember

[11]But you are a man of God. So you should stay away from all those things. Try to live in the right way, serve God, have faith, love, patience, and gentleness. [12]Keeping your faith is like running a race. Try as hard as you can to win. Be sure you receive the life that continues forever. You were called to have that life. And you confessed the great truth about Christ in a way that many people heard. [13]Before God and Christ Jesus I give you a command. Christ Jesus confessed that same great truth when he stood before Pontius Pilate. And God gives life to everything.

Now I tell you: [14]Do the things you were commanded to do. Do them without wrong or blame until the time when our Lord Jesus Christ comes again. [15]God will make that happen at the right time. He is the blessed and only Ruler. He is the King of all kings and the Lord of all lords. [16]God is the only One who never dies. He lives in light so bright that men cannot go near it. No one has ever seen God, or can see him. May honor and power belong to God forever. Amen.

[17]Give this command to those who are rich with things of this world. Tell them not to be proud. Tell them to hope in God, not their money. Money cannot be trusted, but God takes care of us richly. He gives us everything to enjoy. [18]Tell the rich people to do good and to be rich in doing good deeds. Tell them to be happy to give and ready to share. [19]By doing that, they will be saving a treasure for themselves in heaven. That treasure will be a strong foundation. Their future life can be built on that treasure. Then they will be able to have the life that is true life.

[20]Timothy, God has trusted you with many things. Keep those things safe. Stay away from people who say foolish things that are not from God. Stay away from those who argue against the truth. They use something they call "knowledge," but it is really not knowledge. [21]They say that they have that "knowledge," but they have left the true faith.

God's grace be with you.

2 TIMOTHY

Paul
Encourages Timothy

1 From Paul, an apostle[d] of Christ Jesus by the will of God. God sent me to tell about the promise of life that is in Christ Jesus.

[2] To Timothy, a dear son to me. Grace, mercy, and peace to you from God the Father and Christ Jesus our Lord.

Encouragement for Timothy

[3] I always remember you in my prayers, day and night. And I thank God for you in these prayers. He is the God my ancestors served. And I serve him, doing what I know is right. [4] I remember that you cried for me. And I want very much to see you so that I can be filled with joy. [5] I remember your true faith. That kind of faith first belonged to your grandmother Lois and to your mother Eunice. And I know that you now have that same faith. [6] That is why I remind you to use the gift God gave you. God gave you that gift when I laid my hands on[n] you. Now let it grow, as a small flame grows into a fire. [7] God did not give us a spirit that makes us afraid. He gave us a spirit of power and love and self-control.

[8] So do not be ashamed to tell people about our Lord Jesus. And do not be ashamed of me. I am in prison for the Lord. But suffer with me for the Good News.[d] God gives us the strength to do that. [9] God saved us and made us his holy people. That was not because of anything we did ourselves but because of what he wanted and because of his grace. That grace was given to us through Christ Jesus before time began. [10] It was not shown to us until our

Women Who Trusted God

LOIS AND EUNICE • 2 TIMOTHY 1:5

Lois was Timothy's mother, and Eunice was his grandmother. Lois and Eunice came to believe in Jesus, probably when Paul visited their hometown of Lystra. They taught Timothy about Jesus so he could believe and accept Jesus as his Savior. Timothy's father probably was not a Christian. Because Eunice and Lois taught Timothy, he believed in Jesus and later traveled with Paul to tell others about Jesus.

Your parents and grandparents love you very much. If they believe in Jesus, you should learn as much as you can from them about how to serve Jesus. If they don't believe in Jesus, you should try to be a good example to them by being obedient and kind.

[n]**laid . . . on** A sign to show that Paul had power from God to give Timothy a special blessing.

Savior Christ Jesus came. Jesus destroyed death. And through the Good News, he showed us the way to have life that cannot be destroyed. [11]I was chosen to tell that Good News and to be an apostle[d] and a teacher. [12]And I suffer now because I tell the Good News. But I am not ashamed. I know Jesus, the One I have believed in. And I am sure that he is able to protect what he has trusted me with until that Day.[n] [13]Follow the true teachings you heard from me. Follow them as an example of the faith and love we have in Christ Jesus. [14]Protect the truth that you were given. Protect it with the help of the Holy Spirit[d] who lives in us.

[15]You know that everyone in the country of Asia has left me, even Phygelus and Hermogenes. [16]I pray that the Lord will show mercy to the family of Onesiphorus. He has often helped me and was not ashamed that I was in prison. [17]When he came to Rome, he looked for me until he found me. [18]I pray that the Lord will allow Onesiphorus to have mercy from the Lord on that Day. You know how many ways Onesiphorus helped me in Ephesus.

A Loyal Soldier of Christ Jesus

2 Timothy, you are like a son to me. Be strong in the grace that we have in Christ Jesus. [2]You and many others have heard what I taught. You should teach the same thing to some people you can trust. Then they will be able to teach it to others. [3]Share in the troubles that we have. Accept them like a true soldier of Christ Jesus. [4]A soldier wants to please his commanding officer, so he does not waste his time doing the things that most people do. [5]If an athlete is running a race, he must obey all the rules in order to win. [6]The farmer who works hard should be the first person to get some of the food that he grew. [7]Think about these things that I am saying. The Lord will give you the ability to understand all these things.

[8]Remember Jesus Christ. He is from the family of David. After Jesus died, he was raised from death. This is the Good News[d] that I preach, [9]and I am suffering because of that Good News. I am even bound with chains like a criminal. But God's teaching is not in chains. [10]So I patiently accept all these troubles. I do this so that those whom God has chosen can have the salvation that is in Christ Jesus. With that salvation comes glory that never ends.

[11]This teaching is true:
If we died with him,
   then we will also live with him.
[12]If we accept suffering,
   then we will also rule with him.
If we refuse to accept him,
   then he will refuse to accept us.
[13]If we are not faithful,
   he will still be faithful,
   because he cannot be false to
      himself.

A Worker Pleasing to God

[14]Continue teaching these things. And warn people before God not to argue about words. Arguing about words does not help anyone, and it ruins those who listen. [15]Do the best you can to be the kind of person that God will accept, and give yourself to him. Be a worker who is not ashamed of his work—a worker who uses the true teaching in the right way. [16]Stay away from those who talk about useless worldly things. That kind of talk will lead a person more and more away from God. [17]Their evil teaching will spread like a sickness inside the body. Hymenaeus and Philetus are men like that. [18]They have left the true teaching. They say that the rising from death of all men has already taken place. And those two men are destroying the faith of some people. [19]But God's strong foundation continues to stand. These words are written on that foundation: "The Lord knows those who belong to him."[n] And also these words are written on that foundation, "Everyone who

---

[n]**Day**   The day Christ will come to judge all people and take his people to live with him.
[n]**"The Lord . . . him."**   Quotation from Numbers 16:5.

says that he believes in the Lord must stop doing wrong."

²⁰In a large house there are things made of gold and silver. But also there are things made of wood and clay. Some things are used for special purposes, and others are made for ordinary jobs. ²¹If anyone makes himself clean*d* from evil things, he will be used for special purposes. He will be made holy, and the Master can use him. He will be ready to do any good work.

²²Stay away from the evil things young people love to do. Try hard to live right and to have faith, love, and peace. Work for these things together with those who have pure hearts and who trust in the Lord. ²³Stay away from foolish and stupid arguments. You know that such arguments grow into bigger arguments. ²⁴And a servant of the Lord must not quarrel! He must be kind to everyone. He must be a good teacher. He must be patient. ²⁵The Lord's servant must gently teach those who do not agree with him. Maybe God will let them change their hearts so that they can accept the truth. ²⁶The devil has trapped them and causes them to do what he wants. But maybe they can wake up and free themselves from the devil's trap.

The Last Days

3 Remember this! There will be many troubles in the last days. ²In those times people will love only themselves and money. They will brag and be proud. They will say evil things against others. They will not obey their parents. People will not be thankful or be the kind of people God wants. ³They will not have love for others. They will refuse to forgive others and will speak bad things. They will not control themselves. They will be cruel and will hate what is good. ⁴In the last days, people will turn against their friends. They will do foolish things without thinking. They will be conceited and proud. They will love pleasure. They will not love God. ⁵They will continue to act as if they serve God, but they will not really serve God. Stay away from those people. ⁶Some of them go into homes and get control of weak women who are full of sin. They are led to sin by the many evil desires they have. ⁷Those women always try to learn new teachings, but they are never able to understand the truth fully. ⁸Just as Jannes and Jambres were against Moses, these people are against the truth.

Get Ready, Get Set, Grow!
2 TIMOTHY 2:15

Even though you are still young, God can use you. When you became a Christian, you began a new life. Now you are serving God, the King. You know how much he loves you, and you know he wants to help you grow to know him better. Every day of your life is a chance to "give yourself to God as the kind of person he will accept" and to "be a worker who is not ashamed" to serve Jesus.

Your work is to follow Jesus and do what he wants you to do. Sometimes that will be difficult—if your friends want to do bad things, or if you're tempted to do something you know is wrong. But remember that you are God's servant. Ask God to help you be a good worker for him.

To find out more about growing in your faith, zoom to page 1515.

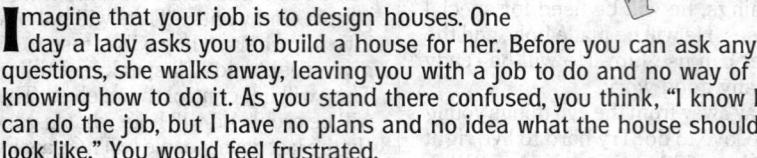

The Bible
2 TIMOTHY 3:16-17

Imagine that your job is to design houses. One day a lady asks you to build a house for her. Before you can ask any questions, she walks away, leaving you with a job to do and no way of knowing how to do it. As you stand there confused, you think, "I know I can do the job, but I have no plans and no idea what the house should look like." You would feel frustrated.

Just as you are ready to give up, another lady comes along. She says, "I just spoke with the woman who wants this house built. Here are the plans and the schedule. Get to work!" *Now* you can do the job.

Christians don't have to feel like a frustrated builder without any plans. Because these verses explain that the Bible provides the plans, as well as the tools and directions. We can use these plans to build our lives.

To learn more about the Bible, zoom to page 1488.

They are people whose thinking has been confused. They have failed in trying to follow the faith. ⁹But they will not be successful in what they do. Everyone will see that they are foolish. That is what happened to Jannes and Jambres.

Obey the Teachings

¹⁰But you know all about me. You know what I teach and the way I live. You know my goal in life. You know my faith, my patience, and my love. You know that I never stop trying. ¹¹You know how I have been hurt and have suffered. You know all that happened to me in Antioch, Iconium, and Lystra. You know the hurts I suffered in those places. But the Lord saved me from all those troubles. ¹²Everyone who wants to live the way God wants, in Christ Jesus, will be hurt. ¹³People who are evil and cheat other people will go from bad to worse. They will fool others, but they will also be fooling themselves.

¹⁴But you should continue following the teachings that you learned. You know that these teachings are true. And you know you can trust those who taught you. ¹⁵You have known the Holy Scriptures*ᵈ* since you were a child. The Scriptures are able to make you wise. And that wisdom leads to salvation through faith in Christ Jesus. ¹⁶All Scripture is given by God and is useful for teaching and for showing people what is wrong in their lives. It is useful for correcting faults and teaching how to live right. ¹⁷Using the Scriptures, the person who serves God will be ready and will have everything he needs to do every good work.

4 Before God and Jesus Christ I give you a command. Christ Jesus is the One who will judge all who are living and all who have died. Jesus has a kingdom, and he is coming again. So I give you this command: ²Preach the Good News.*ᵈ* Be ready at all times. Tell people what they need to do, tell them when they are wrong, and encourage them. Do these things with great patience and careful teaching. ³The time will come when people will not listen to the true teaching. They will find more and more teachers who are pleasing to them, teachers who say the things they want to hear. [4]They will stop listening to the truth. They will begin to follow the teaching in false stories. [5]But you should control yourself at all times. When troubles come, accept them. Do the work of telling the Good News. Do all the duties of a servant of God.

[6]My life is being given as an offering to God. The time has come for me to leave this life. [7]I have fought the good fight. I have finished the race. I have kept the faith. [8]Now, a crown is waiting for me. I will get that crown for being right with God. The Lord is the judge who judges rightly, and he will give me the crown on that Day.[n] He will give that crown not only to me but to all those who have waited with love for him to come again.

Personal Words

[9]Do your best to come to me as soon as you can. [10]Demas loved this world too much. He left me and went to Thessalonica. Crescens went to Galatia. And Titus went to Dalmatia. [11]Luke is the only one still with me. Get Mark and bring him with you when you come. He can help me in my work here. [12]I sent Tychicus to Ephesus.

[13]When I was in Troas, I left my coat there with Carpus. So when you come, bring it to me. Also, bring my books, particularly the ones written on parchment.[n]

[14]Alexander the metalworker did many harmful things against me. The Lord will punish him for the things he did. [15]You should be careful that he does not hurt you too. He fought strongly against our teaching.

[16]The first time I defended myself, no one helped me. Everyone left me. I pray that God will forgive them. [17]But the Lord stayed with me. He gave me strength so that I could fully tell the Good News[d] to the non-Jews. The Lord wanted all the non-Jews to hear it. So I was saved from the lion's mouth. [18]The Lord will save me when anyone tries to hurt me. The Lord will bring me safely to his heavenly kingdom. Glory forever and ever be the Lord's. Amen.

People Who Made Mistakes
DEMAS • 2 TIMOTHY 4:10

Has a friend ever hurt you and decided not to be your friend any more? The apostle Paul had a friend like that. His name was Demas. Demas started out to be a good friend (Colossians 4:14; Philemon 1:24), but later he left Paul because he loved the world too much. Unfortunately, Demas stopped obeying God and sought after sin and wickedness.

We need to be careful not to make the same mistake. We can't make the things of the world so important that we stop following God. God must be more important to us than our friends, sports, toys, money-or anything!

To learn about a man who got upset and murdered his brother, fly to page 1526.

To learn about a man who got upset and murdered his brother, fly to page 1526.

[n]**Day** The day Christ will come to judge all people and take his people to live with him.
[n]**parchment** Something like paper made from the skins of sheep and used for writing on.

Final Greetings

[19] Greet Priscilla and Aquila and the family of Onesiphorus. [20] Erastus stayed in Corinth. And I left Trophimus sick in Miletus. [21] Try as hard as you can to come to me before winter.

Eubulus sends greetings to you. Also Pudens, Linus, Claudia, and all the brothers in Christ greet you.

[22] The Lord be with your spirit. Grace be with you.

TITUS

*Paul
Instructs Titus*

1 From Paul, a servant of God and an apostle[d] of Jesus Christ. I was sent to help the faith of God's chosen people. I was sent to help them to know the truth. And that truth shows people how to serve God. [2]That faith and that knowledge come from our hope for life forever. God promised that life to us before time began, and God does not lie. [3]At the right time God let the world know about that life through preaching. He trusted me with that work, and I preached because God our Savior commanded me to.

[4]To Titus. You are like a true son to me in the faith we share.

Grace and peace to you from God the Father and Christ Jesus our Savior.

Titus' Work in Crete

[5]I left you in Crete so that you could finish doing the things that still needed to be done. I left you there also so that you could choose men to be elders[d] in every town. [6]To be an elder, a man must not be guilty of doing wrong. He must have only one wife. His children must be believers. They must not be known as children who are wild and who do not obey. [7]An elder has the job of taking care of God's work. So he must not be guilty of doing wrong. He must not be a man who is proud and selfish or who becomes angry quickly. He must not drink too much wine. He must not

Honesty
TITUS 1:7

How many ways are there to tell a lie? Think carefully before you answer. Someone might say, "Just one. You lie when you say something you know is not true." That certainly is a lie, but there are other ways of being dishonest.

You can be dishonest by *not* saying something. For example, suppose you broke something at school, but the teacher blamed one of your classmates. If you remained silent and did not confess, that would be the same as lying. This verse says that elders in the church are not to "try to get rich by cheating others." Hurting someone that way is also dishonest.

There is more to being honest than simply not telling lies. Why not ask your mother or father to talk with you about other ways of being honest and how not to be dishonest?

To learn more about honesty, zoom to page 1524.

be a person who likes to fight. And he must not be a person who always tries to get rich by cheating people. [8]An elder must be ready to help others by accepting them into his home. He must love what is good. He must be wise. He must live right. He must be holy. And he must be able to control himself. [9]An elder must faithfully follow the truth just as we teach it. He must be able to help people by using true and right teaching. And he must be able to show those who are against the true teaching that they are wrong.

[10]There are many people who refuse to obey—people who talk about worthless things and lead others into the wrong way. I am talking mostly about those who say that all non-Jews must be circumcised.[d] [11]These people must be stopped from talking. They are destroying whole families by teaching things that they should not teach. They teach them only to cheat people and make money. [12]Even one of their own prophets from Crete said, "Cretan people are always liars. They are evil animals and lazy people who do nothing but eat." [13]The words that prophet said are true. So tell those people that they are wrong. You must be strict with them. Then they will become strong in the faith [14]and stop accepting Jewish stories. And they will stop following the commands of others who do not accept the truth. [15]To those who are pure, all things are pure. But to those who are full of sin and do not believe, nothing is pure. The thinking of those people has become evil and their knowledge of what is right has been ruined. [16]They say they know God, but the evil things they do show that they do not accept God. They are terrible people, they refuse to obey, and they are useless for doing anything good.

Following the True Teaching

2 You must speak things that make the true teaching attractive. [2]Teach older men to have self-control, to be serious, and to be wise. They should be strong in faith, strong in love, and strong in patience.

[3]Also, teach older women to be holy in the way they live. Teach them not to speak against others or have the habit of drinking too much wine. They should teach what is good. [4]In that way they can teach younger women to love their husbands and children. [5]They can teach younger women to be wise and pure, to take care of their homes, to be kind, and to obey their husbands. Then no one will be able to criticize the teaching God gave us.

[6]In the same way, tell young men to be wise. [7]You should do good deeds to be an example in every way for young men. When you teach, be honest and serious. [8]And when you speak, speak the truth so that you cannot be criticized. Then anyone who is against you will be ashamed because there is nothing bad that he can say against us.

[9]And tell slaves to obey their masters at all times. They should try to please them and not argue with them. [10]They should not steal from them. And they should show their masters that they can be fully trusted. Then, in everything they do they will make the teaching of God our Savior attractive.

[11]That is the way we should live, because God's grace has come. That grace can save every person. [12]It teaches us not to live against God and not to do the evil things the world wants to do. That grace teaches us to live on earth now in a wise and right way—a way that shows that we serve God. [13]We should live like that while we are waiting for the coming of our great God and Savior Jesus Christ. He is our great hope, and he will come with glory. [14]He gave himself for us; he died to free us from all evil. He died to make us pure people who belong only to him—people who are always wanting to do good things.

[15]Tell everyone these things. You have full authority. So use that authority to strengthen the people and tell them what they should do. And do not let anyone treat you as if you were not important.

The Right Way to Live

3 Remind the believers to do these things: to be under the authority of rulers and government leaders, to obey them and be ready to do good, [2]to speak no evil about anyone, to live in peace with all, to be gentle and polite to all people.

[3]In the past we were foolish people, too. We did not obey, we were wrong, and we were slaves to many things our bodies wanted and enjoyed. We lived doing evil and being jealous. People hated us and we hated each other. [4]But then the kindness and love of God our Savior was shown. [5]He saved us because of his mercy, not because of good deeds we did to be right with God. He saved us through the washing that made us new people. He saved us by making us new through the Holy Spirit.[d] [6]God poured out to us that Holy Spirit fully through Jesus Christ our Savior. [7]We were made right with God by His grace. And God gave us the Spirit so that we could receive the life that never ends. That is what we hope for.

[8]This teaching is true. And I want you to be sure that the people understand these things. Then those who believe in God will be careful to use their lives for doing good. These things are good and will help all people.

[9]Stay away from those who have foolish arguments, who talk about useless family histories, who make trouble and fight about what the law of Moses teaches. Those things are worth nothing and will not help anyone. [10]If someone causes arguments, then give him a warning. If he continues to cause arguments, warn him again. If he still continues causing arguments, then do not be around him. [11]You know that such a person is evil and sinful. His sins prove that he is wrong.

Some Things to Remember

[12]I will send Artemas and Tychicus to you. When I send them, try hard to come to me at Nicopolis. I have decided to stay there this winter. [13]Zenas the lawyer and Apollos will be traveling from there. Do all that you can to help them on their way. Be sure that they have everything they need. [14]Our people must learn to use their lives for doing good deeds. They should do good to those in need. Then our people will not have useless lives.

[15]All who are with me greet you. Greet those who love us in the faith.

Grace be with you all.

PHILEMON

A Slave Becomes a Christian

¹From Paul, a prisoner of Jesus Christ, and from Timothy, our brother.

To Philemon, our dear friend and worker with us; ²to Apphia, our sister; to Archippus, a worker with us; and to the church that meets in your home.

³Grace and peace to you from God our Father and the Lord Jesus Christ.

Philemon's Love and Faith

⁴I remember you in my prayers. And I always thank my God for you. ⁵I hear about the love you have for all God's holy people and the faith you have in the Lord Jesus. ⁶I pray that the faith you share will make you understand every blessing that we have in Christ. ⁷My brother, you have shown love to God's people. You have made them feel happy. This has given me great joy and comfort.

Accept Onesimus as a Brother

⁸There is something that you should do. And because of your love in Christ, I feel free to order you to do it. ⁹But because I love you, I am asking you instead. I, Paul, am an old man now, and a prisoner for Christ Jesus. ¹⁰I am asking you a favor for my son Onesimus. He became my son while I was in prison. ¹¹In the past he was useless to

People Who Got Away

ONESIMUS • PHILEMON 12

How would you feel if a classmate stole your bike and then ran away? Now imagine that he comes to your house a few weeks later with the bike and a note from your pastor. The notes says, "Jason is sorry he stole your bike. He is a Christian now. He would like to go with you to Sunday school next week." Would you be able to forgive your classmate?

Philemon faced a situation like that. He was a master who owned a slave named Onesimus. One day Onesimus escaped and met a group of Christians, including Paul. Paul loved Onesimus, but he didn't want Philemon to think he had been cheated out of a valuable slave. So he sent Onesimus back with a letter. He asked Philemon, who was a Christian, to forgive Onesimus for running away and to treat him well.

Paul's letter to Philemon reminds us that it's important to forgive others, no matter how much they have cheated or hurt us. We shouldn't hold a grudge or say bad things about a person who has wronged us. We should go to that person and get things right.

you. But now he has become useful for both you and me.

[12]I am sending him back to you, and with him I am sending my own heart. [13]I wanted to keep him with me to help me while I am in prison for the Good News.[d] By helping me he would be serving you. [14]But I did not want to do anything without asking you first. Then any favor you do for me will be because you want to do it, not because I forced you to do it.

[15]Onesimus was separated from you for a short time. Maybe that happened so that you could have him back forever— [16]not to be a slave, but better than a slave, to be a loved brother. I love him very much. But you will love him even more. You will love him as a man and as a brother in the Lord.

[17]If you think of me as your friend, then accept Onesimus back. Welcome him as you would welcome me. [18]If Onesimus has done anything wrong to you, charge that to me. If he owes you anything, charge that to me. [19]I, Paul, am writing this with my own hand. I will pay back anything Onesimus owes. And I will say nothing about what you owe me for your own life. [20]So, my brother, I ask that you do this for me in the Lord. Comfort my heart in Christ. [21]I write this letter, knowing that you will do what I ask you and even more.

[22]Also, please prepare a room for me to stay in. I hope that God will answer your prayers and I will be able to come to you.

Final Greetings

[23]Epaphras is a prisoner with me for Christ Jesus. He sends greetings to you. [24]And also Mark, Aristarchus, Demas, and Luke send greetings. They are workers together with me.

[25]The grace of our Lord Jesus Christ be with your spirit.

HEBREWS

A Better Life
Through Christ

God Spoke Through His Son

1 In the past God spoke to our ancestors through the prophets.*d* He spoke to them many times and in many different ways. ²And now in these last days God has spoken to us through his Son. God has chosen his Son to own all things. And he made the world through the Son. ³The Son reflects the glory of God. He is an exact copy of God's nature. He holds everything together with his powerful word. The Son made people clean from their sins. Then he sat down at the right side of God, the Great One in heaven. ⁴The Son became much greater than the angels. And God gave him a name that is much greater than theirs.

⁵This is because God never said to any of the angels,

"You are my Son.
  Today I have become your
    Father." *Psalm 2:7*

Nor did God say of any angel,

"I will be his Father,
  and he will be my Son."

2 Samuel 7:14

⁶And when God brings his firstborn Son into the world, he says,

"Let all God's angels worship him."*n*

Psalm 97:7

⁷This is what God said about the angels:

"God makes his angels become like
    winds.
  He makes his servants become
    like flames of fire." *Psalm 104:4*

⁸But God said this about his Son:

"God, your throne will last forever
    and ever.
  You will rule your kingdom with
    fairness.
⁹You love what is right and hate evil.
  So God has chosen you to rule
    those with you.
  Your God has given you much joy."

Psalm 45:6-7

¹⁰God also says,

"Lord, in the beginning you made
    the earth.
  And your hands made the skies.
¹¹They will be destroyed, but you will
    remain.
  They will all wear out like clothes.
¹²You will fold them like a coat.
  And, like clothes, you will change
    them.
  But you never change.
  And your life will never end."

Psalm 102:25-27

¹³And God never said this to an angel:

"Sit by me at my right side
  until I put your enemies under your
    control."*n* *Psalm 110:1*

¹⁴All the angels are spirits who serve God and are sent to help those who will receive salvation.

Our Salvation Is Great

2 So we must be more careful to follow what we were taught. Then we will not be pulled away from the truth. ²The teaching that God spoke through angels was shown to be true. And anyone who did not follow it or obey it received the punishment he earned. ³The salvation that was given to us is

---

*n***"Let . . . him."** These words are found in Deuteronomy 32:43 in the Septuagint, the Greek version of the Old Testament, and in a Hebrew copy among the Dead Sea Scrolls.
*n***until . . . control** Literally, "until I make your enemies a footstool for your feet."

very great. So surely we also will be punished if we live as if this salvation were not important. It was the Lord himself who first told about this salvation. And those who heard him proved to us that this salvation is true. [4]God also proved it by using wonders, great signs, and many kinds of miracles.[d] And he proved it by giving people gifts through the Holy Spirit,[d] just as he wanted.

Christ Became like Men

[5]God did not choose angels to be the rulers of the new world that was coming. It is that future world we have been talking about. [6]It is written somewhere in the Scriptures,[d]

"Why is man important to you?
Why do you take care of the son of man?[n]
[7]For a short time you made him
lower than the angels.
But you crowned him with glory
and honor.
[8] You put all things under his control."

Psalm 8:4-6

If God put everything under his control, there was nothing left that he did not rule. But we do not yet see him ruling over everything. [9]But we see Jesus! For a short time he was made lower than the angels. But now we see him wearing a crown of glory and honor because he suffered and died. Because of God's grace, he died for everyone.

[10]God is the One who made all things. And all things are for his glory. God wanted to have many sons share his glory. So God made perfect the One who leads people to salvation. He made Jesus a perfect Savior through Jesus' suffering.

[11]Jesus, who makes people holy, and those who are made holy are from the same family. So he is not ashamed to call them his brothers. [12]He says,

"Then, I will tell my fellow Israelites
about you.

I will praise you when your people
meet to worship you."

Psalm 22:22

[13]He also says,

"I will trust in God."   *Isaiah 8:17*
And he also says,
"I am here. And with me are the
children that God has given
me."   *Isaiah 8:18*

[14]These children are people with physical bodies. So Jesus himself became like them and had the same experiences they have. He did this so that, by dying, he could destroy the one who has the power of death. That one is the devil. [15]Jesus became like men and died so that he could free them. They were like slaves all their lives because of their fear of death. [16]Clearly, it is not angels that Jesus helps, but the people who are from Abraham.[n] [17]For this reason Jesus had to be made like his brothers in every way. He became like men so that he could be their merciful and faithful high priest in service to God. Then Jesus could bring forgiveness for their sins. [18]And now he can help those who are tempted. He is able to help because he himself suffered and was tempted.

Jesus Is Greater than Moses

3 So all of you, holy brothers, should think about Jesus. You were all called by God. God sent Jesus to us, and he is the high priest of our faith. [2]And Jesus was faithful to God as Moses was. Moses did everything God wanted him to do in God's family. [3]A man who is the head of a family receives more honor than others in the family. It is the same with Jesus. Jesus should have more honor than Moses. [4]Every family has its head, but God is the head of everything. [5]Moses was faithful in God's family as a servant. He told what God would say in the future. [6]But Christ is faithful as a Son who is the head of God's family. And we are God's family

---

[n]**son of man**   This can mean any, but the name "Son of Man" is often used to mean Jesus. When Jesus became a man, he showed what God planned for all people to be.

[n]**Abraham**   Most respected ancestor of the Jews. Every Jew hoped to see Abraham.

if we hold on to our faith and are proud of the great hope we have.

We Must Continue to Follow God

[7]So it is as the Holy Spirit[d] says:
"Today listen to what he says.
[8]   Do not be stubborn as in the past
      when you turned against God.
There you tested God in the desert.
[9]   For 40 years in the desert your
            ancestors saw the things I did.
   But they tested me and my
            patience.
[10]I was angry with them.
   I said, 'They are not loyal to me.
   They have not understood my
            ways.'
[11]So I was angry and made a promise.
   'They will never enter my land of
            rest.'"[n]   *Psalm 95:7-11*

[12]So brothers, be careful that none of you has an evil, unbelieving heart. This will stop you from following the living God. [13]But encourage each other every day. Do this while it is "today."[n] Help each other so that none of you will become hardened because of sin and its tricks. [14]We all share in Christ. This is true if we keep till the end the sure faith we had in the beginning. [15]This is what the Scripture[d] says:

"-Today listen to what he says.
Do not be stubborn as in the past
   when you turned against God."
                                   Psalm 95:7-8

[16]Who heard God's voice and was against him? It was all those people Moses led out of Egypt. [17]And whom was God angry with for 40 years? He was angry with those who sinned, who died in the desert. [18]And whom was God talking to when he promised that they would never enter and have his rest? He was talking to those who did not obey him. [19]So we see that they were not allowed to enter and have God's rest because they did not believe.

4 Now God has left us that promise that we may enter and have his rest. Let us be very careful, then, so that none of you will fail to get that rest. [2]The Good News[d] was preached to us just as it was to them. But the teaching they heard did not help them. They heard it but did not accept it with faith. [3]We who have believed are able to enter and have God's rest. As God has said,

"So I was angry and made a promise.
   'They will never enter my land of
            rest.'"   *Psalm 95:11*

The Bible
HEBREWS 4:12-13

Kids love sword fights. Some kids can make swords out of almost anything–sticks, brooms, rulers, pencils, you name it. Playing with those kinds of swords is fun. No one is trying to hurt anyone. When the Bible was written, however, armies used swords in battle. Swords were sharp. They would cut and hurt people.

These verses say that the Bible is like a sword. No, it won't cut anyone. It is a spiritual weapon. God uses it to open us up to his truth. He wants us to use it to get rid of ungodly thoughts and attitudes. Fortunately, God also uses his sword to heal us.

Learn to use this sword. And use it carefully. It will help you win life's battles.

---

[n]**rest**   A place of rest God promised to give his people.
[n]**"today"**   This word is taken from verse 7. It means that it is important to do these things now.

But God's work was finished from the time he made the world. [4]Somewhere in the Scriptures[d] he talked about the seventh day of the week: "And on the seventh day God rested from all his work."[n] [5]And again in the Scripture God said, "They will never enter my land of rest."

[6]It is still true that some people will enter and have God's rest. But those who first heard the way to be saved did not enter. They did not enter because they did not obey. [7]So God planned another day, called "today." He spoke about that day through David a long time later. It is the same Scripture used before:

"Today listen to what he says.
    Do not be stubborn."   *Psalm 95:7-8*
[8]We know that Joshua[n] did not lead the people into that rest. We know this because God spoke later about another day. [9]This shows that the seventh-day rest[n] for God's people is still coming. [10]For anyone who enters and has God's rest will rest from his work as God did. [11]So let us try as hard as we can to enter God's rest. We must try hard so that no one will be lost by following the example of those who refused to obey.

[12]God's word is alive and working. It is sharper than a sword sharpened on both sides. It cuts all the way into us, where the soul and the spirit are joined. It cuts to the center of our joints and our bones. And God's word judges the thoughts and feelings in our hearts. [13]Nothing in all the world can be hidden from God. Everything is clear and lies open before him. And to him we must explain the way we have lived.

Jesus Is Our High Priest

[14]We have a great high priest who has gone into heaven. He is Jesus the Son of God. So let us hold on to the faith we have. [15]For our high priest is able to understand our weaknesses. When

Temptation
HEBREWS 4:14-16

"**N**ot guilty!"

That's the good news for us when temptation strikes. We don't have to feel guilty just because we are tempted. Being tempted is not wrong. These verses say that Jesus himself was "tempted in every way that we are, but he did not sin." That means that it is possible to be tempted and yet not do anything wrong, so we don't have to feel guilty. That's great news!

Guilt can be a warning sign from God that something is wrong. It may be a warning that we are off his perfect path. But it is possible to *feel* guilty even when we haven't done anything wrong. Remember, if Jesus was tempted without sinning, then it is not a sin for us to be tempted.

So relax. God says if you don't sin, you are *not guilty.*

To learn more about temptation, zoom to page 1505.

To learn more about temptation, zoom to page 1505.

[n]**"And . . . work."** Quotation from Genesis 2:2.
[n]**Joshua** After Moses died, Joshua became leader of the Jewish people. Joshua led them into the land that God promised to give them.
[n]**seventh-day rest** Literally, "sabbath rest," meaning a sharing in the rest that God began after he created the world.

he lived on earth, he was tempted in every way that we are, but he did not sin. [16]Let us, then, feel free to come before God's throne. Here there is grace. And we can receive mercy and grace to help us when we need it.

5 Every high priest is chosen from among men. He is given the work of going before God for them. He must offer gifts and sacrifices for sins. [2]He himself is weak. So he is able to be gentle with those who do not understand and who are doing wrong things. [3]Because he is weak the high priest must offer sacrifices for his own sins. And then he offers sacrifices for the sins of the people.

[4]To be a high priest is an honor. But no one chooses himself for this work. He must be called by God as Aaron[n] was. [5]So also Christ did not choose himself to have the honor of being a high priest. But God chose him. God said to him,

"You are my Son;

today I have become your Father."

Psalm 2:7

[6]And in another Scripture[d] God says,

"You are a priest forever,

a priest like Melchizedek.""[n]

Psalm 110:4

[7]While Jesus lived on earth, he prayed to God and asked God for help. He prayed with loud cries and tears to the One who could save him from death. And his prayer was heard because he left it all up to God. [8]Even though Jesus was the Son of God, he learned to obey by what he suffered. [9]And he became our perfect high priest. He gives eternal salvation to all who obey him. [10]And God made Jesus high priest, a priest like Melchizedek.

Warning Against Falling Away

[11]We have much to say about this. But it is hard to explain because you are so slow to understand. [12]You have had enough time so that by now you should be teachers. But you need someone to teach you again the first lessons of God's message. You still need the teaching that is like milk. You are not ready for solid food. [13]Anyone who lives on milk is still a baby. He knows nothing about

Faith and How It Works
HEBREWS 6:12

While people hope for different things in life, Christians are hoping for the most incredible thing of all—heaven. Life on earth can be difficult. We work hard, we cry because sad things happen, and we get angry with bad people. But God promises that in heaven "there will be no more death, sadness, crying, or pain, because all the old ways are gone" (Revelation 21:4).

This verse in Hebrews is not talking about the hope that you will get a good grade in a class at school or that you will get a special present for Christmas. You don't know for sure about the class or the gift, but you *do* know for sure about heaven. You hope for it because you don't see it yet, but if you are a Christian, you can know for sure that you will be there with Jesus.

Thank God that your faith is not a "maybe"—it's for sure!

To find out more about faith and how it works, fly to page 1498.

To find out more about faith and how it works, fly to page 1498.

[n]**Aaron** Aaron was the first Jewish high priest. He was Moses' brother.
[n]**Melchizedek** A priest and king who lived in the time of Abraham. (Read Genesis 14:17-24.)

right teaching. [14]But solid food is for those who are grown up. They have practiced in order to know the difference between good and evil.

6 So let us go on to grown-up teaching. Let us not go back over the beginning lessons we learned about Christ. We should not start over again with teaching about turning from acts that lead to death and about believing in God. [2]We should not return to the

[7]Some people are like land that gets plenty of rain. The land produces a good crop for those who work it, and it receives God's blessings. [8]Other people are like land that grows thorns and weeds and is worthless. It is in danger of being cursed by God. It will be destroyed by fire.

[9]Dear friends, we are saying this to

Helping Others
HEBREWS 6:10

"**T**hank you!" "Gracias!" "Merci!" "Danke!" "Obrigado!"

That's how people express their gratitude in English, Spanish, French, German, and Portuguese. Any way you say it, it's wonderful to hear those words: Thank you!

Sometimes people forget to say thank you when they should. Maybe you worked very hard or went out of your way to help someone, and that person didn't even say a word of thanks. Or maybe your efforts at being helpful went totally unnoticed. Either way, it's pretty disappointing.

This verse gives us some encouragement. Even when no one else notices the helpful things we do, God does. And he never forgets. It is hard to imagine what "thank you" would sound like in God's own language, but it would probably be the happiest sound we've ever heard. Keep helping others, and some day, you will!

---

teaching of baptisms,[n] of laying on of hands,[n] of the raising of the dead and eternal judgment. [3]And we will go on to grown-up teaching if God allows.

[4]Some people cannot be brought back again to a changed life. They were once in God's light. They enjoyed heaven's gift, and they shared in the Holy Spirit.[d] [5]They found out how good God's word is, and they received the powers of his new world. [6]And then they fell away from Christ! It is not possible to keep on bringing them back to a changed life again. For they are nailing the Son of God to a cross again and are shaming him in front of others.

you. But we really expect better things from you that will lead to your salvation. [10]God is fair. He will not forget the work you did and the love you showed for him by helping his people. And he will remember that you are still helping them. [11]We want each of you to go on with the same hard work all your lives. Then you will surely get what you hope for. [12]We do not want you to become lazy. Be like those who have faith and patience. They will receive what God has promised.

[13]God made a promise to Abraham. And as there is no one greater than God, he used himself when he swore to

---

[n]**baptisms** The word here may refer to Christian baptism, or it may refer to the Jewish ceremonial washings.

[n]**laying . . . hands** Putting the hands on people showed that they were being given some special work or some spiritual gift or blessing.

Abraham. [14]He said, "I will surely bless you and give you many descendants."[n] [15]Abraham waited patiently for this to happen. And he received what God promised.

[16]People always use the name of someone greater than themselves when they swear. The oath proves that what they say is true. And this ends all arguing about what they say. [17]God wanted to prove that his promise was true. He wanted to prove this to those who would get what he promised. He wanted them to understand clearly that his purposes never change. So God proved his promise by also making an oath. [18]These two things cannot change. God cannot lie when he makes a promise, and he cannot lie when he makes an oath. These things encourage us who came to God for safety. They give us strength to hold on to the hope we have been given. [19]We have this hope as an anchor for the soul, sure and strong. It enters behind the curtain in the Most Holy Place in heaven. [20]Jesus has gone in there ahead of us and for us. He has become the high priest forever, a priest like Melchizedek."[n]

The Priest Melchizedek

7 Melchizedek[n] was the king of Salem and a priest for the Most High God. He met Abraham when Abraham was coming back after defeating the kings. When they met, Melchizedek blessed Abraham. [2]And Abraham gave Melchizedek a tenth of everything he had brought back from the battle. First, Melchizedek's name means "king of goodness." Also, he is king of Salem, which means "king of peace." [3]No one knows who Melchizedek's father or mother was.[n] No one knows where he came from. And no one knows when he was born or when he died. Melchizedek is like the Son of God; he continues being a priest forever.

Good Kings and Bad Kings

MELCHIZEDEK • HEBREWS 7:1

Melchizedek's story first appears in chapter 14 of Genesis. After Abram won a great victory, Melchizedek, the king of Salem, brought bread and wine to him. Melchizedek was a priest of God, and he blessed Abraham. In return, Abraham gave Melchizedek a tenth of everything he won in the battle.

Melchizedek is called a good king for many reasons. First, his name means "king of righteousness." Second, Melchizedek honored God at a time when hardly anyone believed in him. Third, Melchizedek reminded Abram that God was responsible for his victory. Abram showed respect to Melchizedek by giving him part of his wealth. Finally, Melchizedek reminds us of Jesus. In the same way that Melchizedek served Abram, Jesus serves us. He takes away our sin and gives us God's blessings.

Do you give thanks to God for all you have? Do you share what you have with others? Remember Abram's meeting with Melchizedek when you feel like being selfish.

---

[n]**"I . . . descendants."** Quotation from Genesis 22:17.
[n]**Melchizedek** A priest and king who lived in the time of Abraham. (Read Genesis 14:17-24.)
[n]**No . . . was** Literally, "Melchizedek was without father, without mother, without genealogy."

[4]You can see that Melchizedek was very great. Abraham, the great father, gave Melchizedek a tenth of everything that Abraham won in battle. [5]Now the law says that those in the tribe[d] of Levi who become priests must get a tenth from the people. The priests collect it from their own people, even though the priests and the people are both from the family of Abraham. [6]Melchizedek was not from the tribe of Levi. But he got a tenth from Abraham. And he blessed Abraham, the man who had God's promises. [7]And everyone knows that the more important person blesses the less important person. [8]Those priests get a tenth, but they are only men who live and then die. But Melchizedek, who got a tenth from Abraham, continues living, as the Scripture[d] says. [9]It is Levi who gets a tenth from the people. But we might even say that when Abraham paid Melchizedek a tenth, then Levi also paid it. [10]Levi was not yet born. But Levi was in the body of his ancestor Abraham when Melchizedek met Abraham.

[11]The people were given the law[n] based on a system of priests from the tribe of Levi. But they could not be made spiritually perfect through that system of priests. So there was a need for another priest to come. I mean a priest like Melchizedek, not Aaron. [12]And when a different kind of priest comes, the law must be changed, too. [13]We are saying these things about Christ. He belonged to a different tribe. No one from that tribe ever served as a priest at the altar. [14]It is clear that our Lord came from the tribe of Judah. And Moses said nothing about priests belonging to that tribe.

Jesus Is like Melchizedek

[15]And this becomes even more clear. We see that another priest comes, who is like Melchizedek.[n] [16]He was not made a priest by human rules and laws. He became a priest through the power of his life, which continues forever. [17]In the Scriptures,[d] this is said about him:

> "You are a priest forever,
> a priest like Melchizedek."

Psalm 110:4

[18]The old rule is now set aside because it was weak and useless. [19]The law of Moses could not make anything perfect. But now a better hope has been given to us. And with this hope we can come near to God.

[20]Also, it is important that God made an oath when he made Jesus high priest. When the others became priests, there was no oath. [21]But Christ became a priest with God's oath. God said:

> "The Lord has made a promise
> and will not change his mind.
> 'You are a priest forever.'"

Psalm 110:4

[22]So this means that Jesus is the guarantee of a better agreement[n] from God to his people.

[23]Also, when one of the other priests died, he could not continue being a priest. So there were many priests. [24]But Jesus lives forever. He will never stop serving as priest. [25]So he is always able to save those who come to God through him. He can do this, because he always lives, ready to help those who come before God.

[26]So Jesus is the kind of high priest that we need. He is holy; he has no sin in him. He is pure and not influenced by sinners. And he is raised above the heavens. [27]He is not like the other priests. They had to offer sacrifices every day, first for their own sins, and then for the sins of the people. But Christ does not need to do that. He offered his sacrifice only once and for all time. Christ offered himself! [28]The law chooses high priests who are men with all their weaknesses. But the word of God's oath came later than the law.

---

[n]**The . . . law**   This refers to the people of Israel who were given the law of Moses.
[n]**Melchizedek**   A priest and king who lived in the time of Abraham. (Read Genesis 14:17-24.)
[n]**agreement**   God gives a contract or agreement to his people. For the Jews, this agreement was the law of Moses. But now God has given a better agreement to his people through Christ.

It made God's Son to be the high priest. And that Son has been made perfect forever.

Jesus Is Our High Priest

8 Here is the point of what we are saying: We do have a high priest who sits on the right side of God's throne in heaven. [2]Our high priest serves in the Most Holy Place. He serves in the true place of worship that was made by God, not by men.

[3]Every high priest has the work of offering gifts and sacrifices to God. So our high priest must also offer something to God. [4]If our high priest were now living on earth, he would not be a priest. I say this because there are already priests here who follow the law by offering gifts to God. [5]The work that they do as priests is only a dim copy of what is in heaven. For when Moses was ready to build the Holy Tent,[d] God warned him: "Be very careful to make everything by the plan I showed you on the mountain."[n] [6]But the priestly work that has been given to Jesus is much greater than the work that was given to the other priests. In the same way, the new agreement that Jesus brought from God to his people is much greater than the old one. And the new agreement is based on promises of better things.

[7]If there was nothing wrong with the first agreement,[n] there would be no need for a second agreement. [8]But God found something wrong with his people. He says:

"The time is coming, says the Lord,
 when I will make a new
  agreement.
It will be with the people of Israel
 and the people of Judah.
[9]It will not be like the agreement
 I made with their ancestors.
That was when I took them by
 the hand
 to bring them out of Egypt.
But they broke that agreement,
and I turned away from them, says
 the Lord.
[10]In the future I will make this
 agreement
with the people of Israel, says
 the Lord.
I will put my teachings in their minds.
And I will write them on their
 hearts.
I will be their God,
 and they will be my people.
[11]People will no longer have to teach
 their neighbors and relatives to
 know the Lord.
This is because all will know me,
 from the least to the most
 important.
[12]I will forgive them for the wicked
 things they did.
I will not remember their sins
 anymore."   *Jeremiah 31:31-34*

[13]God called this a new agreement, so he has made the first agreement old. And anything that is old and worn out is ready to disappear.

Worship Under the Old Agreement

9 The first agreement[n] had rules for worship. And it had a man-made place for worship. [2]The Holy Tent[d] was set up for this. The first area in the Tent was called the Holy Place. In it were the lamp and the table with the bread that was made holy for God. [3]Behind the second curtain was a room called the Most Holy Place. [4]In it was a golden altar for burning incense.[d] Also there was the Holy Box[d] that held the old agreement. The Holy Box was covered with gold. Inside this Holy Box was a golden jar of manna[d] and Aaron's rod—the rod that once grew leaves. Also in it were the stone tablets of the old agreement. [5]Above the Holy Box were the creatures with wings that showed God's glory. The wings of the creatures reached over the lid. But we cannot tell everything about these things now.

---

[n]**"Be . . . mountain."**   Quotation from Exodus 25:40.
[n]**first agreement**   The contract God gave the Jewish people when he gave them the law of Moses.

[6]Everything in the Tent was made ready in this way. Then the priests went into the first room every day to do their worship. [7]But only the high priest could go into the second room, and he did that only once a year. He could never enter the inner room without taking blood with him. He offered that blood to God for himself and for the people's sins. These were sins people did without knowing that they were sinning. [8]The Holy Spirit[d] uses this to show that the way into the Most Holy Place was not open. This was while the system of the old Holy Tent was still being used. [9]This is an example for the present time. It shows that the gifts and sacrifices offered cannot make the worshiper perfect in his heart. [10]These gifts and sacrifices were only about food and drink and special washings. They were rules for the body, to be followed until the time of God's new way.

Worship Under the New Agreement

[11]But Christ has come as the high priest of the good things we now have. The tent he entered is greater and more perfect. It is not made by men. It does not belong to this world. [12]Christ entered the Most Holy Place only once—and for all time. He did not take with him the blood of goats and calves. His sacrifice was his own blood. He entered the Most Holy Place and set us free from sin forever. [13]The blood of goats and bulls and the ashes of a cow are sprinkled on the people who are unclean[d] and this makes their bodies clean again.

[14]How much more is done by the blood of Christ. He offered himself through the eternal Spirit[n] as a perfect sacrifice to God. His blood will make our hearts clean from useless acts. We are made pure so that we may serve the living God.

[15]So Christ brings a new agreement from God to his people. Those who are called by God can now receive the blessings that God has promised. These blessings will last forever. They can have those things because Christ died so that the people who lived under the first agreement could be set free from sin.

[16]When there is a will,[n] it must be proven that the man who wrote that will is dead. [17]A will means nothing while the man is alive. It can be used only after he dies. [18]This is why even the first agreement could not begin without blood to show death. [19]First, Moses told all the people every command in the law. Next he took the blood of calves and mixed it with water. Then he used red wool and a branch of the hyssop plant to sprinkle the blood and water on the book of the law and on all the people. [20]He said, "This is the blood which begins the agreement that God commanded you to obey."[n] [21]In the same way, Moses sprinkled the blood on the Holy Tent[d] and over all the things used in worship. [22]The law says that almost everything must be made clean by blood. And sins cannot be forgiven without blood to show death.

Christ's Death Takes Away Sins

[23]So the copies of the real things in heaven had to be made clean[d] by animal sacrifices. But the real things in heaven need much better sacrifices. [24]For Christ did not go into the Most Holy Place made by men. It is only a copy of the real one. He went into heaven itself. He is there now before God to help us. [25]The high priest enters the Most Holy Place once every year. He takes with him blood that is not his own blood. But Christ did not go into

---

[n]**Spirit**   This refers to the Holy Spirit; to Christ's own spirit; or to the spiritual and eternal nature of his sacrifice.

[n]**will**   A legal document that shows how a person's money and property are to be distributed at the time of his death. This is the same word in Greek as "agreement" in verse 15.

[n]**"This . . . obey."**   Quotation from Exodus 24:8.

heaven to offer himself many times.
26Then he would have had to suffer many times since the world was made. But Christ came only once and for all time. He came at just the right time to take away all sin by sacrificing himself. 27Everyone must die once. After a person dies, he is judged. 28So Christ was offered as a sacrifice one time to take away the sins of many people. And he will come a second time, but not to offer himself for sin. He will come again to bring salvation to those who are waiting for him.

10 The law is only an unclear picture of the good things coming in the future. It is not a perfect picture of the real things. The people under the law offered the same sacrifices every year. These sacrifices can never make perfect those who come near to worship God. 2If the law could make them perfect, the sacrifices would have already stopped. The worshipers would be made clean, and they would no longer feel guilty for their sins. 3These sacrifices remind them of their sins every year, 4because it is not possible for the blood of bulls and goats to take away sins.

5So when Christ came into the world, he said:
"You do not want sacrifices and
　　offerings.
　But you have prepared a body for
　　me.
6You do not ask for burnt offerings
　and offerings to take away sins.
7Then I said, 'Look, I have come.
　It is written about me in the book.
　My God, I have come to do what
　　you want.'" *Psalm 40:6-8*
8In this Scripture*d* he first said, "You do not want sacrifices and offerings. You do not ask for burnt offerings and offerings to take away sins." (These are all sacrifices that the law commands.) 9Then he said, "Here I am. I have come to do what you want." So God ends the first system of sacrifices so that he can set up the new system. 10Jesus Christ

did what God wanted him to do. And because of this, we are made holy through the sacrifice of his body. Christ made this sacrifice only once, and for all time.

11Every day the priests stand and do their religious service. Again and again they offer the same sacrifices. But those sacrifices can never take away sins. 12But Christ offered one sacrifice for sins, and it is good forever. Then he sat down at the right side of God. 13And now Christ waits there for his enemies to be put under his power. 14With one sacrifice he made perfect forever those who are being made holy.

15The Holy Spirit*d* also tells us about this. First he says:
16"In the future I will make this
　　agreement*n*
　with the people of Israel, says
　　the Lord.
I will put my teachings in their hearts.
　And I will write them on their
　　minds." *Jeremiah 31:33*
17Then he says:
"Their sins and the evil things they
　　do—
　I will not remember anymore."
　　　　　　　　　Jeremiah 31:34
18And when these have been forgiven, there is no more need for a sacrifice for sins.

Continue to Trust God

19So, brothers, we are completely free to enter the Most Holy Place. We can do this without fear because of the blood of Jesus' death. 20We can enter through a new way that Jesus opened for us. It is a living way. It leads through the curtain—Christ's body. 21And we have a great priest over God's house. 22So let us come near to God with a sincere heart and a sure faith. We have been cleansed and made free from feelings of guilt. And our bodies have been washed with pure water. 23Let us hold firmly to the hope that we have confessed. We can trust God to do what he promised.

---

*n***agreement** God gives a contract or agreement to his people. For the Jews, this agreement was the law of Moses. But now God has given a better agreement to his people through Christ.

[24]Let us think about each other and help each other to show love and do good deeds. [25]You should not stay away from the church meetings, as some are doing. But you should meet together and encourage each other. Do this even more as you see the Day[n] coming.

[26]If we decide to go on sinning after we have learned the truth, there is no longer any sacrifice for sins. [27]There is nothing but fear in waiting for the judgment and the angry fire that will destroy all those who live against God. [28]Any person who refused to obey the law of Moses was found guilty from the proof given by two or three witnesses. He was put to death without mercy. [29]So what do you think should be done to a person who does not respect the Son of God? He looks at the blood of the agreement, the blood that made him holy, as no different from other men's blood. He insults the Spirit[d] of God's grace. Surely he should have a much worse punishment. [30]We know that God said, "I will punish those who do wrong. I will repay them."[n] And he also said, "The Lord will judge his people."[n] [31]It is a terrible thing to fall into the hands of the living God.

[32]Remember those days in the past when you first learned the truth. You had a hard struggle with many sufferings, but you continued strong. [33]Sometimes you were hurt and persecuted before crowds of people. And sometimes you shared with those who were being treated that way. [34]You helped the prisoners. And you even had joy when all that you owned was taken from you. You were joyful because you knew that you had something better and more lasting.

[35]So do not lose the courage that you had in the past. It has a great reward. [36]You must hold on, so you can do what God wants and receive what he has promised. [37]For in a very short time,

"The One who is coming will come.
 He will not be late.
[38]The person who is right with me
 will have life because of his faith.
But if he turns back with fear,
 I will not be pleased with him."

Habakkuk 2:3-4

[39]But we are not those who turn back and are lost. We are people who have faith and are saved.

> Faith means being sure of the things we hope for. And faith means knowing that something is real even if we do not see it.
> • Hebrews 11:1

Faith

11 Faith means being sure of the things we hope for. And faith means knowing that something is real even if we do not see it. [2]People who lived in the past became famous because of faith.

[3]It is by faith we understand that the whole world was made by God's command. This means that what we see was made by something that cannot be seen.

[4]It was by faith that Abel offered God a better sacrifice than Cain did. God said he was pleased with the gifts Abel offered. So God called Abel a good man because of his faith. Abel died, but through his faith he is still speaking.

[5]It was by faith that Enoch was taken to heaven. He never died. He could not be found, because God had taken him away. Before he was taken, the Scripture[d] says that he was a man who truly pleased God. [6]Without faith no one can please God. Anyone who comes to God must believe that he is real and that he rewards those who truly want to find him.

⁷It was by faith Noah heard God's warnings about things that he could not yet see. He obeyed God and built a large boat to save his family. By his faith, Noah showed that the world was wrong. And he became one of those who are made right with God through faith.

almost dead. But from him came as many descendants as there are stars in the sky. They are as many as the grains of sand on the seashore that cannot be counted.

¹³All these great men died in faith.

Faith and How It Works
HEBREWS 11:1

When you get ready to go on a vacation, do you get really excited? Vacations are fun because they are adventures; some things you already know will happen (you may know that you will set up the tent at the campsite), and some things will be surprises (a raccoon may steal some of your food).

Living as a Christian is also an adventure. Some things you already know (how much God loves you and his promise to guide you); some things will be surprises (the way God will protect you or the great new Christian friends you will make). You know that God will always do what is best for you.

That is what faith means: you can be certain of what you hope for, even when you can't see it and don't know what it will be like. When you have faith in God, your whole life is an adventure!

To find out more about faith and how it works, fly to page 1499.

⁸It was by faith Abraham obeyed God's call to go to another place that God promised to give him. He left his own country, not knowing where he was to go. ⁹It was by faith that he lived in the country God promised to give him. He lived there like a visitor who did not belong. He lived in tents with Isaac and Jacob, who had received that same promise from God. ¹⁰Abraham was waiting for the city*ⁿ* that has real foundations—the city planned and built by God.

¹¹He was too old to have children, and Sarah was not able to have children. It was by faith that Abraham was made able to become a father. Abraham trusted God to do what he had promised. ¹²This man was so old that he was

They did not get the things that God promised his people. But they saw them coming far in the future and were glad. They said that they were like visitors and strangers on earth. ¹⁴When people say such things, then they show that they are looking for a country that will be their own country. ¹⁵If they had been thinking about that country they had left, they could have gone back. ¹⁶But those men were waiting for a better country—a heavenly country. So God is not ashamed to be called their God. For he has prepared a city for them.

¹⁷It was by faith that Abraham offered his son Isaac as a sacrifice. God made the promises to Abraham. But God tested him. And Abraham was ready to offer his own son as a sacrifice. ¹⁸God

ⁿcity The spiritual "city" where God's people live with him. Also called "the heavenly Jerusalem." (See Hebrews 12:22.)

had said, "The descendants I promised you will be from Isaac."[n] [19]Abraham believed that God could raise the dead. And really, it was as if Abraham got Isaac back from death.

"**Y**ou know, kids, people talk about faith all the time. But what do they really mean? The faith the Bible talks about is a certain kind of faith. *That's* the faith God wants us to have. Check out Hebrews 11:1-40."

[20]It was by faith that Isaac blessed the future of Jacob and Esau. [21]It was by faith that Jacob blessed each one of Joseph's sons. He did this while he was dying. Then he worshiped as he leaned on the top of his walking stick.

[22]It was by faith that Joseph spoke about the Israelites leaving Egypt while he was dying. He told them what to do with his body.

[23]It was by faith that Moses' parents hid him for three months after he was born. They saw that Moses was a beautiful baby. And they were not afraid to disobey the king's order.

[24]It was by faith that Moses, when he grew up, refused to be called the son of the king of Egypt's daughter. [25]He chose to suffer with God's people instead of enjoying sin for a short time. [26]He thought that it was better to suffer for the Christ[d] than to have all the treasures of Egypt. He was looking only for God's reward. [27]It was by faith that Moses left Egypt. He was not afraid of the king's anger. Moses continued strong as if he could see the God that no one can see. [28]It was by faith that Moses prepared the Passover[d] and spread the blood on the doors. It was spread so that the one who brings death would not kill the firstborn[d] sons of Israel.

[29]It was by faith that the people crossed the Red Sea as if it were dry land. The Egyptians also tried to do it, but they were drowned.

Faith and How It Works
HEBREWS 11:32-34

All of this chapter (Hebrews 11) tells about people who had great faith in God. All of these people made some mistakes in their lives or sinned against God. Not one of them was perfect, yet God used them because of their faith. Some of these people experienced great victories or amazing escapes because they believed in God's power. Others were persecuted because they believed in God. Whether they lived or died, all of them were winners because they believed in God and trusted him no matter what happened, through good times and bad.

That's genuine faith—trusting in God through whatever happens in life. Is your faith genuine? Trust God when things are going good and when you are having tough times too.

To find out more about faith and how it works, fly to page 1508.

[n]"The descendants . . . Isaac."   Quotation from Genesis 21:12.

³⁰It was by faith that the walls of Jericho fell. They fell after the people had marched around the walls of Jericho for seven days.

³¹It was by faith that Rahab, the prostitute,[d] welcomed the spies and was not killed with those who refused to obey God.

³²Do I need to give more examples? I do not have time to tell you about Gideon, Barak, Samson, Jephthah, David, Samuel, and the prophets.[d] ³³Through their faith they defeated kingdoms. They did what was right and received what God promised. They shut the mouths of lions, ³⁴stopped great fires and were saved from being killed with swords. They were weak, and yet were made strong. They were powerful in battle and defeated other armies. ³⁵Women received their dead relatives raised back to life. Others were tortured and refused to accept their freedom. They did this so that they could be raised from death to a better life. ³⁶Some were laughed at and beaten. Others were tied and put into prison. ³⁷They were killed with stones and they were cut in half. They were killed with swords. Some wore the skins of sheep and goats. They were poor, abused, and treated badly. ³⁸The world was not good enough for them! They wandered in deserts and mountains, living in caves and holes in the earth.

³⁹All these people are known for their faith. But none of them received what God had promised. ⁴⁰God planned to give us something better. Then they would be made perfect, but only together with us.

Follow Jesus' Example

12 So we have many people of faith around us. Their lives tell us what faith means. So let us run the race that is before us and never give up. We should remove from our lives anything that would get in the way. And we should remove the sin that so easily catches us. ²Let us look only to Jesus. He is the one who began our faith, and he makes our faith perfect. Jesus suffered death on the cross. But he accepted the shame of the cross as if it were nothing. He did this because of the joy that God put before him. And now he is sitting at the right side of

God's Children
HEBREWS 12:7

What would you do if your parents told you they would never discipline you again? Throw a party? What if you:

... painted your brother's fingernails while he slept, and nobody noticed.

... made a trampoline out of your bed springs, and everyone ignored you.

... created a pitcher's mound out of the garden, and nothing happened.

Pretty soon you might begin to wonder if anyone cared about you at all. The truth is that caring parents do notice when we do wrong. So does our loving heavenly father. He disciplines us when we disobey him because we are his kids, and he cares for us.

God's discipline is a good sign that you are his child. When bad things happen, God is teaching you. It shows he cares for you.

To learn more about God's children, zoom to page 1513.

God's throne. [3]Think about Jesus. He held on patiently while sinful men were doing evil things against him. Look at Jesus' example so that you will not get tired and stop trying.

God Is like a Father

[4]You are struggling against sin, but your struggles have not yet caused you to be killed. [5]You have forgotten his encouraging words for his sons:

"My son, don't think the Lord's
    discipline of you is worth
    nothing.
And don't stop trying when the
    Lord corrects you.
[6]The Lord corrects those he loves.
And he punishes everyone he
    accepts as his child."

Proverbs 3:11-12

[7]So accept your sufferings as if they were a father's punishment. God does these things to you as a father punishing his sons. All sons are punished by their fathers. [8]If you are never punished (and every son must be punished), you are not true children and not really sons. [9]We have all had fathers here on earth who punished us. And we respected our fathers. So it is even more important that we accept punishment from the Father of our spirits. If we do this, we will have life. [10]Our fathers on earth punished us for a short time. They punished us the way they thought was best. But God punishes us to help us, so that we can become holy as he is. [11]We do not enjoy punishment. Being punished is painful. But later, after we have learned from being punished, we have peace, because we start living in the right way.

Be Careful How You Live

[12]You have become weak. So make yourselves strong again. [13]Live in the right way so that you will be saved and your weakness will not cause you to be lost.

[14]Try to live in peace with all people. And try to live lives free from sin. If anyone's life is not holy, he will never see the Lord. [15]Be careful that no one fails to get God's grace. Be careful that no one becomes like a bitter weed growing among you. A person like that can ruin all of you. [16]Be careful that no one takes part in sexual sin. And be careful that no person is like Esau and never thinks about God. Esau was the oldest son, and he would have received everything from his father. But Esau sold all that for a single meal. [17]You remember that after Esau did this, he wanted to get his father's blessing. He wanted this blessing so much that he cried. But his father refused to give him the blessing, because Esau could find no way to change what he had done.

[18]You have not come to a mountain that can be touched and that is burning with fire. You have not come to darkness, sadness and storms. [19]You have not come to the noise of a trumpet or to the sound of a voice. When the people of Israel heard the voice, they begged not to have to hear another word. [20]They did not want to hear the command: "If anything, even an animal, touches the mountain, it must be put to death with stones."[n] [21]What they saw was so terrible that Moses said, "I am shaking with fear."[n]

[22]But you have not come to that kind of place. The new place you have come to is Mount Zion.[n] You have come to the city of the living God, the heavenly Jerusalem. You have come to thousands of angels gathered together with joy. [23]You have come to the meeting of God's firstborn[n] children. Their names are written in heaven. You have come to God, the judge of all people. And

---

[n]**"If . . . stones."** Quotation from Exodus 19:12-13.
[n]**"I . . . fear."** Quotation from Deuteronomy 9:19.
[n]**Mount Zion** Another name for Jerusalem, here meaning the spiritual city of God's people.
[n]**firstborn** The first son born in a Jewish family was given the most important place in the family and received special blessings. All of God's children are like that.

you have come to the spirits of good people who have been made perfect. 24You have come to Jesus, the One who brought the new agreement from God to his people. You have come to the sprinkled blood[n] that has a better message than the blood of Abel.[n]

25So be careful and do not refuse to listen when God speaks. They refused to listen to him when he warned them on earth. And they did not escape. Now God is warning us from heaven. So it will be worse for us if we refuse to listen to him. 26When he spoke before, his voice shook the earth. But now he has promised, "Once again I will shake not only the earth but also the heavens."[n] 27The words "once again" clearly show us that everything that was made will be destroyed. These are the things that can be shaken. And only the things that cannot be shaken will remain.

28So let us be thankful because we have a kingdom that cannot be shaken. We should worship God in a way that pleases him. So let us worship him with respect and fear, 29because our God is like a fire that burns things up.

13 Keep on loving each other as brothers in Christ. 2Remember to welcome strangers into your homes. Some people have done this and have welcomed angels without knowing it. 3Do not forget those who are in prison. Remember them as if you were in prison with them. Remember those who are suffering as if you were suffering with them.

4Marriage should be honored by everyone. Husband and wife should keep their marriage pure. God will judge guilty those who take part in sexual sins. 5Keep your lives free from the love of money. And be satisfied with what you have. God has said,

"I will never leave you;
I will never forget you."

Deuteronomy 31:6

6So we can feel sure and say,

"I will not be afraid because the
    Lord is my helper.
People can't do anything to me."

Psalm 118:6

7Remember your leaders. They taught God's message to you. Remember how they lived and died, and copy their faith. 8Jesus Christ is the same yesterday, today, and forever.

Jesus Christ is the same yesterday, today, and forever.
• Hebrews 13:8

9Do not let all kinds of strange teachings lead you into the wrong way. Your hearts should be strengthened by God's grace, not by obeying rules about foods. Obeying such rules does not help anyone.

10We have a sacrifice. But the priests who serve in the Holy Tent[d] cannot eat from it. 11The high priest carries the blood of animals into the Most Holy Place. There he offers this blood for sins. But the bodies of the animals are burned outside the camp. 12So Jesus also suffered outside the city. He died to make his people holy with his own blood. 13So let us go to Jesus outside the camp. We should accept the same shame that Jesus had.

14Here on earth we do not have a city that lasts forever. But we are looking for the city that we will have in the future. 15So through Jesus let us always offer our sacrifice to God. This sacrifice is our praise, coming from lips that speak his name. 16Do not forget to do good to others. And share with them what you have. These are the sacrifices that please God.

17Obey your leaders and be under

---

[n]**sprinkled blood** The blood of Jesus' death.
[n]**Abel** The son of Adam and Eve, who was killed by his brother Cain (Genesis 4:8).
[n]**"Once . . . heavens."** Quotation from Haggai 2:6,21.

their authority. These men are watching you because they are responsible for your souls. Obey them so that they will do this work with joy, not sadness. It will not help you to make their work hard.

¹⁸Continue praying for us. We feel sure about what we are doing, because we always want to do the right thing. ¹⁹And I beg you to pray that God will send me back to you soon.

²⁰⁻²¹I pray that the God of peace will give you every good thing you need so that you can do what he wants. God is the One who raised from death our Lord Jesus, the Great Shepherd of the sheep. God raised him because of the blood of his death. His blood began the agreement that God made with his people. And this agreement is eternal. I pray that God, through Christ, will do in us what pleases him. And to Jesus Christ be glory forever and ever. Amen.

²²My brothers, I beg you to listen patiently to this message I have written to encourage you. This letter is not very long. ²³I want you to know that our brother Timothy has been let out of prison. If he arrives soon, we will both come to see you.

²⁴Greet all your leaders and all of God's people. Those from Italy send greetings to you.

²⁵God's grace be with you all.

JAMES

How to Live As a Christian

1 From James, a servant of God and of the Lord Jesus Christ. To all of God's people who are scattered everywhere in the world:

Greetings.

God, you must believe. Do not doubt God. Anyone who doubts is like a wave in the sea. The wind blows the wave up and down. 7-8He who doubts is thinking two different things at the same time. He cannot decide about anything he does. A person like that should not think that he will receive anything from the Lord.

Unsung Heroes

JAMES • JAMES 1:1

James was one of Jesus' half-brothers (his mother was Mary and his father was Joseph; Jesus' mother was Mary, but his father was God). James didn't believe in Jesus at first, but later he did. He became the leader of the church in Jerusalem. Many Christians had been Jews, but they didn't know that people who were not Jews (called Gentiles) could also believe in Jesus. When some Gentiles became Christians, James taught the church that everyone who believes in Jesus should be welcome and that all Christians should love one another. (You can read about this in Acts 15.)

Now there are Christians all over the world! And God wants us all to love each other.

Faith and Wisdom

2My brothers, you will have many kinds of troubles. But when these things happen, you should be very happy. 3You know that these things are testing your faith. And this will give you patience. 4Let your patience show itself perfectly in what you do. Then you will be perfect and complete. You will have everything you need. 5But if any of you needs wisdom, you should ask God for it. God is generous. He enjoys giving to all people, so God will give you wisdom. 6But when you ask

True Riches

9If a believer is poor, he should be proud because God has made him

"**S**ometimes my little sister Jessie shows me she's growing up because she tries to be patient when I tease her! There's some good stuff to learn in James 1:2-8."

spiritually rich. [10]If he is rich, he should be proud because God has shown him that he is spiritually poor. The rich person will die like a wild flower in the grass. [11]The sun rises and becomes hotter and hotter. The heat makes the plants very dry, and the flower falls off. The flower was beautiful, but now it is dead. It is the same with a rich person. While he is still taking care of his business, he will die.

Temptation Is Not from God

[12]When a person is tempted and still continues strong, he should be happy. After he has proved his faith, God will reward him with life forever. God promised this to all people who love him. [13]When someone is being tempted, he should not say, "God is tempting me." Evil cannot tempt God, and God himself does not tempt anyone. [14]It is the evil that a person wants that tempts him. His own evil desire leads him away and holds him. [15]This desire causes sin. Then the sin grows and brings death.

[16]My dear brothers, do not be fooled about this. [17]Every good action and every perfect gift is from God. These good gifts come down from the Creator of the sun, moon, and stars. God does not change like their shifting shadows.

[18]God decided to give us life through the word of truth. He wanted us to be the most important of all the things he made.

Listening and Obeying

[19]My dear brothers, always be willing to listen and slow to speak. Do not become angry easily. [20]Anger will not help you live a good life as God wants. [21]So put out of your life every evil thing and every kind of wrong you do. Don't be proud but accept God's teaching that is planted in your hearts. This teaching can save your souls.

[22]Do what God's teaching says; do not just listen and do nothing. When you only sit and listen, you are fooling yourselves. [23]A person who hears God's teaching and does nothing is like a man looking in a mirror. [24]He sees his face, then goes away and quickly forgets what he looked like. [25]But the truly happy person is the one who carefully studies God's perfect law that makes people free. He continues to study it. He listens to God's teaching and does not forget what he heard. Then he obeys what God's teaching says. When he does this, it makes him happy.

Temptation
JAMES 1:13

"If God didn't want me to steal those apples off Mr. Smith's trees, he wouldn't let them grow over the fence where I could reach them."

We love to make excuses or blame others for our wrong actions! We are experts at getting out of admitting that we have made a mistake. Sometimes it even works, and we succeed in making someone else (like a brother or sister) look guilty. This verse takes away one excuse. We can never, ever blame God for making us do something wrong, because he wouldn't do that. We can even call on him to keep us out of situations where we will be tempted to sin.

When you are in a place or situation where you feel like you are going to go against God's laws, pray and ask God to get you out of there. He will hear you and give you a way out. All you have to do is ask.

Whit's Wisdom: Living Your Faith • James 2

We talk about faith all the time at Whit's End. The kids and I agree that faith is a lot like play time—it's more important to do it than to just talk about it. Having faith and talking about faith aren't the same thing. We want to talk about faith so we can walk and live by faith afterwards.

We are interested in learning and living a particular kind of faith—Christian faith. There are all sorts of faiths out there. And we have to have *some* faith to get through every day. Last week I had to have faith that Dylan's tree house wouldn't fall out of the tree if I climbed up there. If you're sitting in a chair right now, you have faith that it will hold you. You didn't have to think about it—you just believed it! You can see that faith is what I think on the inside and what I do on the outside. It has two important parts.

So, what is Christian faith? Well, one clue is right in the name. Can you see it? *Christ*ian faith. Christian faith starts with Christ—believing that he is our Savior. Read James 2:14-20 to see that God wants our faith in him to be something other people know about.

I like to tell the kids in Odyssey that Christian faith is *who* we know, *who* we trust, and *how* we live. We know Christ, we trust God, and we live for him. Sometimes we just have to trust. Like trusting that Jesus has a special place for us in heaven. Or trusting that God still cares when something bad happens to us. But every day we have many opportunities to obey God and to do what he tells us to do. We're trusting Christ by obeying him. Are you trusting Jesus today?

Related passages: Matthew 25:34-46; 1 Peter 1:5-9

Teacher/Parent Hint: One simple illustration of the outward/inward aspects of faith and trust can be shown with some thread, a piece of rope, and a short board. Announce to the kids that you plan to put up a swing. It's going in a big tree, so they can all swing really high! Tell them to help you decide whether to use the rope or the thread to hang the swing. Challenge them by asking, "I thought you had faith, why don't we use the thread? It will be cheaper." Explain that trust is only as dependable as the trustworthiness of what or who it's resting on.

The True Way to Worship God

26A person might think he is religious. But if he says things he should not say, then he is just fooling himself. His "religion" is worth nothing. 27Religion that God accepts is this: caring for orphans or widows who need help; and keeping yourself free from the world's evil influence. This is the kind of religion that God accepts as pure and good.

Love All People

2 My dear brothers, you are believers in our glorious Lord Jesus Christ. So never think that some people are more important than others. 2Suppose someone comes into your church meeting wearing very nice clothes and a gold ring. At the same time a poor man comes in wearing old, dirty clothes. 3You show special attention to the one wearing nice clothes. You say, "Please, sit here in this good seat." But you say to the poor man, "Stand over there," or "Sit on the floor by my feet!" [4]What are you doing? You are making some people more important than others. With evil thoughts you are deciding which person is better.

[5]Listen, my dear brothers! God chose the poor in the world to be rich with faith. He chose them to receive the kingdom God promised to people who love him. [6]But you show no respect to the poor man. And you know that it is the rich who are always trying to control your lives. And they are the ones who take you to court. [7]They are the ones who say bad things against Jesus, who owns you.

[8]One law rules over all other laws. This royal law is found in the Scriptures:[d] "Love your neighbor as you love yourself."[n] If you obey this law, then you are doing right. [9]But if you are treating one person as if he were more important than another, then you are sinning. That royal law proves that you are guilty of breaking God's law. [10]A person might follow all of God's law. But if he fails to obey even one command, he is guilty of breaking all the commands in that law. [11]God said, "You must not be guilty of adultery."[dn] The same God also said, "You must not murder anyone."[n] So if you do not take part in adultery, but you murder someone, then you are guilty of breaking all of God's law. [12]You will be judged by the law that makes people free. You should remember this in everything you say and do. [13]Yes, you must show mercy to others, or God will not show mercy to you when he judges you. But the person who shows mercy can stand without fear when he is judged.

Faith and Good Works

[14]My brothers, if someone says he has faith, but does nothing, his faith is worth nothing. Can faith like that save him? [15]A brother or sister in Christ might need clothes or might need food. [16]And you say to him, "God be with you! I hope you stay warm and get plenty to eat." You say this, but you do not give that person the things he needs. Unless you help him, your words are worth nothing. [17]It is the same with faith. If faith does nothing, then that faith is dead, because it is alone.

[18]Someone might say, "You have faith, but I do things. Show me your faith! Your faith does nothing. I will show you my faith by the things I do." [19]You believe there is one God. Good! But the demons[d] believe that, too! And they shake with fear.

[20]You foolish person! Must you be shown that faith that does nothing is worth nothing? [21]Abraham is our father. He was made right with God by the things he did. He offered his son Isaac to God on the altar. [22]So you see that Abraham's faith and the things he did worked together. His faith was made perfect by what he did. [23]This shows the full meaning of the Scripture[d] that says: "Abraham believed God, and God accepted Abraham's faith, and that faith made him right with God."[n] And Abraham was called "God's friend."[n] [24]So you see that a person is made right with God by the things he does. He cannot be made right by faith only.

[25]Another example is Rahab, who was a prostitute.[d] But she was made right with God by something she did: She helped the spies for God's people. She welcomed them into her home and helped them escape by a different road.

[26]A person's body that does not have a spirit is dead. It is the same with faith. Faith that does nothing is dead!

---

[n]**"Love . . . yourself."** Quotation from Leviticus 19:18.
[n]**"You . . . adultery."** Quotation from Exodus 20:14 and Deuteronomy 5:18.
[n]**"You . . . anyone."** Quotation from Exodus 20:13 and Deuteronomy 5:17.
[n]**"Abraham . . . God."** Quotation from Genesis 15:6.
[n]**"God's friend."** These words about Abraham are found in 2 Chronicles 20:7 and Isaiah 41:8.

Controlling the Things We Say

3 My brothers, not many of you should become teachers. You know that we who teach will be judged more strictly than others. ²We all make many mistakes. If there were a person who never said anything wrong, he would be perfect. He would be able to control his whole body, too. ³We put bits into and evil. It is full of poison that can kill. ⁹We use our tongues to praise our Lord and Father, but then we curse people. And God made them like himself. ¹⁰Praises and curses come from the same mouth! My brothers, this should not happen. ¹¹Do good and bad

Faith and How It Works
JAMES 2:26

Suppose you bought a radio. You looked at it and put it on your dresser, but you never plugged it in to listen to it. Even though you had a radio, it was as good as broken because it didn't do what it was supposed to do—play radio stations.

Suppose you believed in Jesus as your Savior, but you never read your Bible, prayed, helped other people, or lived any differently than you did before you believed in him. Even though Jesus may still be your Savior, your faith is as good as "broken" because it isn't doing what it is supposed to do—serve God.

What can you do to show that your faith is alive and working? How can you serve God?

To find out more about faith and how it works, fly to page 1512.

the mouths of horses to make them obey us. We can control their whole bodies. ⁴It is the same with ships. A ship is very big, and it is pushed by strong winds. But a very small rudder controls that big ship. The man who controls the rudder decides where the ship will go. The ship goes where the man wants. ⁵It is the same with the tongue. It is a small part of the body, but it brags about doing great things.

A big forest fire can be started with only a little flame. ⁶And the tongue is like a fire. It is a whole world of evil among the parts of our bodies. The tongue spreads its evil through the whole body. It starts a fire that influences all of life. The tongue gets this fire from hell. ⁷People can tame every kind of wild animal, bird, reptile, and fish, and they have tamed them. ⁸But no one can tame the tongue. It is wild water flow from the same spring? ¹²My brothers, can a fig tree make olives? Can a grapevine make figs? No! And a well full of salty water cannot give good water.

True Wisdom

¹³Is there anyone among you who is truly wise and understanding? Then he should show his wisdom by living right. He should do good things without being proud. A wise person does not brag. ¹⁴But if you are selfish and have bitter jealousy in your hearts, you have no reason to brag. Your bragging is a lie that hides the truth. ¹⁵That kind of "wisdom" does not come from God. That "wisdom" comes from the world. It is not spiritual. It is from the devil. ¹⁶Where there is jealousy and selfishness, there will be confusion and every kind of evil. ¹⁷But the wisdom that comes from God

is like this: First, it is pure. Then it is also peaceful, gentle, and easy to please. This wisdom is always ready to help those who are troubled and to do good for others. This wisdom is always fair and honest. [18]When people work for peace in a peaceful way, they receive the good result of their right-living.

Give Yourselves to God

4 Do you know where your fights and arguments come from? They come from the selfish desires that make war says, "The Spirit[d] that God made to live in us wants us for himself alone."[n] [6]But God gives us even more grace, as the Scripture says,

> "God is against the proud,
>   but he gives grace to the humble."
>
> *Proverbs 3:34*

[7]So give yourselves to God. Stand against the devil, and the devil will run away from you. [8]Come near to God, and

---

Humility
JAMES 4:6

When you choose people to be on your team, whom do you pick? You probably choose the best players. After all, you want good players on your side when you're trying to win.

God chooses sides, too, but he doesn't always choose the best people or the ones with the most talent or ability. How does God decide who is on his team and who is not? Here it says that one of the things God considers is whether a person is *proud* or *humble*. God is "against the proud," but he "gives grace to the humble." In other words, God looks for true humility in a person. If he sees it, he is pleased. If he does not, he is displeased.

This should help you decide whether you are the kind of person God wants on his team or not. Wouldn't you like to be on *the* winning side? Then be *humble*.

To learn more about humility, zoom to page 1518

---

inside you. [2]You want things, but you do not have them. So you are ready to kill and are jealous of other people. But you still cannot get what you want. So you argue and fight. You do not get what you want because you do not ask God. [3]Or when you ask, you do not receive because the reason you ask is wrong. You want things only so that you can use them for your own pleasures.

[4]So, you people are not loyal to God! You should know that loving the world is the same as hating God. So if a person wants to be a friend of the world, he makes himself God's enemy. [5]Do you think the Scripture[d] means nothing? It

God will come near to you. You are sinners. So clean sin out of your lives. You are trying to follow God and the world at the same time. Make your thinking pure. [9]Be sad, cry, and weep! Change your laughter into crying.

> So give yourselves to God. Stand against the devil, and the devil will run away from you.
> • James 4:7

---

[n]**"The Spirit . . . alone."**   These words may be from Exodus 20:5.

Change your joy into sadness. [10]Don't be too proud before the Lord, and he will make you great.

You Are Not the Judge

[11]Brothers, do not say bad things about each other. If you say bad things about your brother in Christ or judge him, then you are saying bad things about the law he follows. You are also judging the law he follows. And when you are judging the law, you are not a follower of the law. You have become a judge! [12]God is the only One who makes laws, and he is the only Judge. He is the only One who can save and destroy. So it is not right for you to judge your neighbor.

Let God Plan Your Life

[13]Some of you say, "Today or tomorrow we will go to some city. We will stay there a year, do business, and make money." [14]But you do not know what will happen tomorrow! Your life is like a mist. You can see it for a short time, but then it goes away. [15]So you should say, "If the Lord wants, we will live and do this or that." [16]But now you are proud and you brag. All of this bragging is wrong. [17]And when a person knows the right thing to do, but does not do it, then he is sinning.

A Warning to the Rich

5 You rich people, listen! Cry and be very sad because of the trouble that will come to you. [2]Your riches will rot, and your clothes will be eaten by moths. [3]Your gold and silver will rust, and rust will be a proof that you were wrong. It will eat your bodies like fire. You saved your treasure for the last days. [4]Men worked in your fields, but you did not pay them. They harvested your crops and are crying out against you. Now the Lord of heaven's armies has heard their cries. [5]Your life on earth was full of rich living. You pleased yourselves with everything you wanted. You made yourselves fat,

like an animal ready to be killed. [6]You showed no mercy to the innocent man. You murdered him. He cannot stand against you.

Be Patient

[7]Brothers, be patient until the Lord comes again. A farmer is patient. He waits for his valuable crop to grow from the earth. He waits patiently for it to receive the first rain and the last rain. [8]You, too, must be patient. Do not give up hope. The Lord is coming soon. [9]Brothers, do not complain against each other. If you do not stop complaining, you will be judged guilty. And the Judge is ready to come! [10]Brothers, follow the example of the prophets[d] who spoke for the Lord. They suffered many hard things, but they were patient. [11]We say they are happy because they were able to do this. You have heard about Job's patience. You know that after all his trouble, the Lord helped him. This shows that the Lord is full of mercy and is kind.

Be Careful What You Say

[12]My brothers, it is very important that you not use an oath when you make a promise. Don't use the name of heaven, earth, or anything else to prove what you say. When you mean yes, say only "yes." When you mean no, say only "no." Do this so that you will not be judged guilty.

The Power of Prayer

[13]If one of you is having troubles, he should pray. If one of you is happy, he should sing praises. [14]If one of you is sick, he should call the church's elders.[d] The elders should pour oil on him[n] in the name of the Lord and pray for him. [15]And the prayer that is said with faith will make the sick person well. The Lord will heal him. And if he has sinned, God will forgive him. [16]Confess your sins to each other and pray for each other. Do this so that God can heal

---

[n]**pour oil on him**   Oil was used like medicine, so that is probably how the believers used it.

you. When a good man prays, great things happen. [17]Elijah was a man just like us. He prayed that it would not rain. And it did not rain on the land for three and a half years! [18]Then Elijah prayed again. And the rain came down from the sky, and the land grew crops again.

Saving a Soul

[19]My brothers, one of you may wander away from the truth. And someone may help him come back. [20]Remember this: Anyone who brings a sinner back from the wrong way will save that sinner's soul from death. By doing this, that person will cause many sins to be forgiven.

1 PETER

*Encouragement
for Suffering Christians*

1 From Peter, an apostle[d] of Jesus Christ.

To God's chosen people who are away from their homes. You are scattered all around the countries of Pontus, Galatia, Cappadocia, Asia, and Bithynia. [2]God planned long ago to choose you by making you his holy people. Making you holy is the Spirit's[d] work. God wanted you to obey him and to be made clean by the blood of the death of Jesus Christ. Grace and peace be yours more and more.

A Living Hope

[3]Praise be to the God and Father of our Lord Jesus Christ. God has great mercy, and because of his mercy he gave us a new life. He gave us a living hope because Jesus Christ rose from death. [4]Now we hope for the blessings God has for his children. These blessings are kept for you in heaven. They cannot be destroyed or be spoiled or lose their beauty. [5]God's power protects you through your faith, and it keeps you safe until your salvation comes. That salvation is ready to be given to you at the end of time. [6]This makes you very happy. But now for a short time different kinds of troubles may make you sad. [7]These troubles come to prove that your faith is pure. This purity of faith is worth more than gold. Gold can be proved to be pure by fire, but gold will ruin. But the purity of your faith will bring you praise and glory and honor when Jesus Christ comes again. [8]You have not seen Christ, but still you love him. You cannot see him now, but you believe in him. You are filled with a joy that cannot be explained. And that joy is full of glory. [9]Your faith has a goal, to save your souls. And you are receiving that goal— your salvation.

Faith and How It Works
1 PETER 1:7

Life is filled with ups and downs, happy times and sad times. Having faith in God doesn't mean that life will always be easy and happy. You will still have the good times and bad times, but there will be a difference if you have faith. God wants to help your faith grow stronger, so that no matter what happens your faith will become like pure gold.

Peter compared faith to gold because gold is made pure by being heated in a fire—all the bad materials are burned away. Peter explained that bad times in life can be like the fire and can make your faith as perfect as pure gold. When you have a sad or difficult time, trust God to help you through it. As you trust him, he will help your faith become like pure gold!

[10]The prophets[d] searched carefully and tried to learn about this salvation. They spoke about the grace that was coming to you. [11]The Spirit[d] of Christ was in the prophets. And the Spirit was telling about the sufferings that would happen to Christ and about the glory that would come after those

again. [14]In the past you did not understand, so you did the evil things you wanted. But now you are children of God who obey. So do not live as you lived in the past. [15]But be holy in all that you do, just as God is holy. God is

God's Children
1 PETER 1:14

What do you think would be the hardest thing for a football player to get used to if he began playing soccer? For one thing, it might take some practice to remember not to slam the other team's players to the ground! It's a new game, and he would have to play with new rules.

God's children play by different rules, too—God's rules. They want to obey him and follow his rules. People who are not God's children play by their own rules and do whatever they want to do. You were like that, too, before you became his child.

As God's child, now you are different. So don't go back to your old ways and your own rules. Think about how it would be if the football player suddenly started playing by the rules of football in the middle of a soccer game! What a disaster! Playing by God's rules is the only way to play.

To learn more about God's children, *zoom to page 1525.*

sufferings. The prophets tried to learn about what the Spirit was showing them. They tried to learn when those things would happen and what the world would be like at that time. [12]It was shown to them that their service was not for themselves. It was for you. They were serving you when they told about the truths you have now heard. The men who preached the Good News[d] to you told you those things. They did it with the help of the Holy Spirit that was sent from heaven. These are truths that even the angels want very much to know about.

A Call to Holy Living

[13]So prepare your minds for service and have self-control. All your hope should be for the gift of grace that will be yours when Jesus Christ comes

the One who called you. [16]It is written in the Scriptures:[d] "You must be holy, because I am holy."[n]

[17]You pray to God and call him Father. And this Father judges each man's work equally. So while you are here on earth, you should live with respect for God. [18]You know that in the past you were living in a worthless way. You got that way of living from the people who lived before you. But you were saved from that useless life. You were bought, but not with something that ruins like gold or silver. [19]You were bought with the precious blood of the death of Christ, who was like a pure and perfect lamb. [20]Christ was chosen before the world was made. But he was shown to the world in these last times for you. [21]You believe in God through Christ. God raised Christ from

[n]**"You must be . . . holy."**   Quotation from Leviticus 11:45; 19:2; 20:7.

death and gave him glory. So your faith and your hope are in God.

²²Now you have made yourselves pure by obeying the truth. Now you can have true love for your brothers. So love each other deeply with all your heart.

how good the Lord is.

⁴The Lord Jesus is the "stone"ⁿ that lives. The people of the world did not want this stone. But he was the stone

Staying Away from Selfishness
1 PETER 1:22

What do you do when you're hungry? *You eat.* What do you do when you're tired? *You rest.* How about when you're sad? *You cry.* When you have needs for food, for rest, or for tears, you meet them as soon as possible.

But what about when someone else is hungry, or tired, or sad? Are you as concerned about that person's needs? Most of us would have to say, "No." We are much more concerned about meeting our own needs than helping anyone else. That's part of our sinful nature—we are selfish.

Peter, however, tells us that we are to love each other "deeply," with all our hearts. That means caring about the needs of other Christians as much as we care about ourselves. That may sound difficult, but remember that it is how God cares for you. Ask God to help you care for others like he does.

²³You have been born again. This new life did not come from something that dies, but from something that cannot die. You were born again through God's living message that continues forever. ²⁴The Scripture says,

"All people are like the grass.
   And all their strength is like the
      flowers of the field.
The grass dies and the flowers fall.
²⁵But the word of the Lord will live
      forever."   *Isaiah 40:6-8*
And this is the word that was preached to you.

Jesus Is the Living Stone

2 So then, get rid of all evil and all lying. Do not be a hypocrite.ᵈ Do not be jealous or speak evil of others. Put all these things out of your life. ²As newborn babies want milk, you should want the pure and simple teaching. By it you can grow up and be saved. ³For you have already examined and seen

God chose. To God he was worth much. So come to him. ⁵You also are like living stones. Let yourselves be used to build a spiritual temple—to be holy priests who offer spiritual sacrifices to God. He will accept those sacrifices through Jesus Christ. ⁶The Scriptureᵈ says:

"I will put a stone in the ground in
      Jerusalem.
Everything will be built on this
      important and precious rock.
Anyone who trusts in him
   will never be disappointed."
                        Isaiah 28:16

"**T**he Bible says that Jesus is a kind of stone. Can you find what kind of stone he is and why he's called that? Check out 1 Peter 2:1-8."

ⁿ"**stone**" The most important stone in God's spiritual temple or house (his people).

[7]This stone is worth much to you who believe. But to the people who do not believe, he is

"the stone that the builders did not want.

It has become the cornerstone."[d]

Psalm 118:22

[8]To people who do not believe, he is

"a stone that causes people to stumble.

It is a rock that makes them fall."

Isaiah 8:14

They stumble because they do not obey what God says. This is what God planned to happen to them.

[9]But you are chosen people. You are the King's priests. You are a holy nation. You are a nation that belongs to God alone. God chose you to tell about the wonderful things he has done. He called you out of darkness into his wonderful light. [10]At one time you were not God's people. But now you are his people. In the past you had never received mercy. But now you have received God's mercy.

Live for God

[11]Dear friends, you are like visitors and strangers in this world. So I beg you to stay away from the evil things your bodies want to do. These things fight against your soul. [12]People who do not believe are living all around you. They might say that you are doing wrong. So live good lives. Then they will see the good things you do, and they will give glory to God on the day when Christ comes again.

Obey Every Human Authority

[13]Obey the people who have authority in this world. Do this for the Lord. Obey the king, who is the highest authority. [14]And obey the leaders who are sent by the king. They are sent to punish those who do wrong and to praise those who do right. [15]So when you do good, you stop foolish people from saying stupid things about you. This is what God wants. [16]Live as free men. But do not use your freedom as an excuse to do evil. Live as servants of God. [17]Show respect for all people. Love the brothers and sisters of God's family. Respect God. Honor the king.

Follow Christ's Example

[18]Slaves, accept the authority of your masters. Do this with all respect. You should obey masters who are good and kind, and you should obey masters who are bad. [19]A person might have to suffer even when he has done nothing wrong. But if he thinks of God and bears the pain, this pleases God. [20]If you

Get Ready, Get Set, Grow!
1 PETER 2:2

When you were just a baby, your mother fed you milk. You couldn't chew because you didn't have any teeth and your body wasn't ready for solid food.

When you first believed in Jesus, you learned about who he is and what he did for you. Peter tells new Christians to be like tiny babies who want milk. You should want to know more and more about Jesus, but it will still be "pure and simple teaching." You don't need to worry about understanding everything in the Bible. Some things are difficult and you will want to learn about them later. Everything that you learn now will help you with the more difficult lessons later.

So listen closely at church and in family devotions. What you learn will help you grow!

are punished for doing wrong, there is no reason to praise you for bearing punishment. But if you suffer for doing good, and you are patient, then that pleases God. 21That is what you were called to do. Christ suffered for you. He gave you an example to follow. So you should do as he did. 22"He did no sin.

He never lied."   *Isaiah 53:9*

23People insulted Christ, but he did not insult them in return. Christ suffered, but he did not threaten. He let God take care of him. God is the One who judges rightly. 24Christ carried our sins in his body on the cross. He did this so that we would stop living for sin and start living for what is right. And we are healed because of his wounds. 25You were like sheep that went the wrong way. But now you have come back to the Shepherd and Protector of your souls.

Wives and Husbands

3 In the same way, you wives should accept the authority of your husbands. Then, if some husbands have not obeyed God's teaching, they will be persuaded to believe. You will not need to say a word to them. They will be persuaded by the way their wives live. 2Your husbands will see the pure lives that you live with your respect for God. 3It is not fancy hair, gold jewelry, or fine clothes that should make you beautiful. 4No, your beauty should come from within you—the beauty of a gentle and quiet spirit. This beauty will never disappear, and it is worth very much to God. 5It was the same with the holy women who lived long ago and followed God. They made themselves beautiful in this way. They accepted the authority of their husbands. 6Sarah obeyed Abraham, her husband, and called him her master. And you women are true children of Sarah if you always do what is right and are not afraid.

7In the same way, you husbands should live with your wives in an understanding way. You should show respect to them. They are weaker than you. But God gives them the same blessing that he gives you—the grace that gives true life. Do this so that nothing will stop your prayers.

Suffering for Doing Right

8Finally, all of you should live together in peace. Try to understand each other. Love each other as brothers. Be kind and humble. 9Do not do wrong to a person to pay him back for doing wrong to you. Or do not insult someone to pay him back for insulting you. But ask God to bless that person. Do this, because you yourselves were called to receive a blessing. 10The Scripture*d* says,

"A person must do these things
    to enjoy life and have many, happy
       days.
He must not say evil things.
    He must not tell lies.
11He must stop doing evil and do good.
    He must look for peace and work
       for it.
12The Lord sees the good people.
    He listens to their prayers.
But the Lord is against
    those who do evil."   *Psalm 34:12-16*

13If you are always trying to do good, no one can really hurt you. 14But you may suffer for doing right. Even if that happens, you are blessed.

"Don't be afraid of the things they
       fear.
Do not dread those things.
15But respect Christ as the holy Lord
    in your hearts."   *Isaiah 8:12-13*

Always be ready to answer everyone who asks you to explain about the hope you have. 16But answer in a gentle way and with respect. Always feel that you are doing right. Then, those who speak evil of your good life in Christ will be made ashamed. 17It is better to suffer for doing good than for doing wrong. Yes, it is better, if that is what God wants. 18Christ himself died for you. And that one death paid for your sins. He was not guilty, but he died for those who are guilty. He did this to bring you all to God. His body was killed, but he was made alive in the spirit. [19]And in the spirit he went and preached to the spirits in prison. [20]These were the spirits who refused to obey God long ago in the time of Noah. God was waiting patiently for them while Noah was building the boat. Only a few people—eight in all—were saved by water. [21]That water is like baptism that now saves you—not the washing of dirt from the body, but the promise made to God from a good heart. And this is because Jesus Christ was raised from death. [22]Now Jesus has gone into heaven and is at God's right side. He rules over angels, authorities, and powers.

Changed Lives

4 Christ suffered while he was in his body. So you should strengthen yourselves with the same way of thinking Christ had. The person who has suffered in his body is finished with sin. [2]Strengthen yourselves so that you will live your lives here on earth doing what God wants, not doing the evil things that people want. [3]In the past you wasted too much time doing what the non-believers like to do. You were guilty of sexual sins and had evil desires. You were getting drunk, you had wild and drunken parties, and you did wrong by worshiping idols. [4]Non-believers think it is strange that you do not do the many wild and wasteful things that they do. And so they insult you. [5]But they will have to explain about what they have done. They must explain to God who is ready to judge the living and the dead. [6]The Good News[d] was preached to those who are now dead. By their dying, they were judged like all men. But the Good News was preached to them so that they could live in the spirit as God lives.

Use God's Gifts Wisely

[7]The time is near when all things will end. So keep your minds clear, and control yourselves. Then you will be able to pray. [8]Most importantly, love each other deeply. Love has a way of not looking at others' sins. [9]Open your homes to each other, without complaining. [10]Each of you received a spiritual gift. God has shown you his grace in giving you different gifts. And you are like servants who are responsible for using God's gifts. So be good servants and use your gifts to serve each other. [11]Anyone who speaks should speak words from God. The person who serves should serve with the strength that God gives. You should do these things so that in everything God will be praised through Jesus Christ. Power and glory belong to him forever and ever. Amen.

Suffering as a Christian

[12]My friends, do not be surprised at the painful things you are now suffering. These things are testing your faith. So do not think that something strange is happening to you. [13]But you should be happy that you are sharing in Christ's sufferings. You will be happy and full of joy when Christ comes again in glory. [14]When people insult you because you follow Christ, then you are blessed. You are blessed because the glorious Spirit,[d] the Spirit of God, is with you. [15]Do not suffer for murder, theft, or any other crime, nor because you trouble other people. [16]But if you suffer because you are a Christian, then do not be ashamed. You should praise God because you wear that name. [17]It is time for judgment to begin, and it will begin with God's family. If that judging begins with us, what will happen to those people who do not obey the Good News[d] of God?

[18]"It is very hard for a good person to
       be saved.
    Then the wicked person and
       the sinner will surely be lost!"[n]

[19]So then those who suffer as God wants them to should trust their souls to him. God is the One who made them, and they can trust him. So they should continue to do what is right.

---

[n]**"It . . . lost!"** Quotation from Proverbs 11:31 in the Septuagint, the Greek version of the Old Testament.

The Flock of God

5 Now I have something to say to the elders[d] in your group. I am also an elder. I myself have seen Christ's sufferings. And I will share in the glory that will be shown to us. I beg you to ²take care of God's flock, his people, that you are responsible for. Watch over it because you want to, not because you are forced to do it. That is how God wants it. Do it because you are happy to serve, not because you want money. ³Do not be like a ruler over people you are responsible for. Be good examples to them. ⁴Then when Christ, the Head Shepherd, comes, you will get a crown. This crown will be glorious, and it will never lose its beauty.

⁵In the same way, younger men should be willing to be under older men. And all of you should be very humble with each other.

"God is against the proud,
    but he gives grace to the humble."

Proverbs 3:34

⁶So be humble under God's powerful hand. Then he will lift you up when the right time comes. ⁷Give all your worries to him, because he cares for you.

⁸Control yourselves and be careful! The devil is your enemy. And he goes around like a roaring lion looking for someone to eat. ⁹Refuse to give in to the devil. Stand strong in your faith. You know that your Christian brothers and sisters all over the world are having the same sufferings you have.

¹⁰Yes, you will suffer for a short time. But after that, God will make everything right. He will make you strong. He will support you and keep you from falling. He is the God who gives all grace. He called you to share in his glory in Christ. That glory will continue forever. ¹¹All power is his forever and ever. Amen.

Final Greetings

¹²I wrote this short letter with the help of Silas. I know that he is a faithful brother in Christ. I wrote to comfort and encourage you. I wanted to tell you that this is the true grace of God. Stand strong in that grace.

¹³The church in Babylon sends you greetings. They were chosen the same as you. Mark, my son in Christ, also greets you. ¹⁴Give each other a kiss of Christian love when you meet.

Peace to all of you who are in Christ.

Humility
1 PETER 5:5-6

If you have been reading the other Imagination Station notes about *humility* (if not, now would be a good time to read through some of them), you have probably learned that it is good to be humble. Just about everyone would agree with that. The hard part comes when you have to actually do it. You can't just agree to *be* humble; you have to *act* and *behave* humbly. And doing that often involves giving in to someone else, like your parents or your teachers. Uh-oh! Being humble just got more difficult!

It *is* tough sometimes to obey our parents, teachers, coaches and other adults. But here we read that a humble person submits to older people and is gentle and nice to everyone.

If you act that way, you *are* a humble person. And God is happy with you!

2 PETER

Correcting
False Teachings

1 From Simon Peter, a servant and apostle[d] of Jesus Christ.

To you who have received a faith as valuable as ours. You received that faith because our God and Savior Jesus Christ is fair and does what is right.

[2]Grace and peace be given to you more and more. You will have grace and peace because you truly know God and Jesus our Lord.

God Has Given Us Blessings

[3]Jesus has the power of God. His power has given us everything we need to live and to serve God. We have these things because we know him. Jesus called us by his glory and goodness. [4]Through his glory and goodness, he gave us the very great and rich gifts he promised us. With those gifts you can share in being like God. And so the world will not ruin you with its evil desires.

"Kids, did you know that the Bible talks about addition? In 2 Peter 1:3-9, how many things can you find that the Bible tells you to add to your life?"

[5]Because you have these blessings, you should try as much as you can to add these things to your lives: to your faith, add goodness; and to your goodness, add knowledge; [6]and to your knowledge, add self-control; and to your self-control, add the ability to hold on; and to your ability to hold on,

add service for God; [7]and to your service for God, add kindness for your brothers and sisters in Christ; and to this kindness, add love. [8]If all these things are in you and are growing, they will help you never to be useless. They will help your knowledge of our Lord Jesus Christ make your lives better. [9]But if anyone does not have these things, he cannot see clearly. He is blind. He has forgotten that he was made clean from his past sins.

[10]My brothers, God called you and chose you to be his. Try hard to show that you really are God's chosen people. If you do all these things, you will never fall. [11]And you will be given a very great welcome into the kingdom of our Lord and Savior Jesus Christ. That kingdom continues forever.

[12]You know these things, and you are very strong in the truth. But I will always help you to remember these things. [13]I think it is right for me to help you remember while I am still living here on earth. [14]I know that I must soon leave this body. Our Lord Jesus Christ has shown me that. [15]I will try the best I can to help you remember these things always. I want you to be able to remember them even after I am gone.

We Saw Christ's Glory

[16]We have told you about the powerful coming of our Lord Jesus Christ. What we told you were not just smart stories that someone invented. But we saw the greatness of Jesus with our own eyes. [17]Jesus heard the voice of God, the Greatest Glory. That was when Jesus received honor and glory from God the Father. The voice said, "This

is my Son, and I love him. I am very pleased with him." [18]We heard that voice. It came from heaven while we were with Jesus on the holy mountain.

[19]This makes us more sure about the message the prophets[d] gave. And it is good for you to follow closely what they said. Their message is like a light shining in a dark place. That light shines until the day begins and the morning star rises in your hearts. [20]Most of all, you must understand this: No prophecy in the Scriptures[d] ever comes from the prophet's own interpretation. [21]No prophecy ever came from what a man wanted to say. But men led by the Holy Spirit[d] spoke words from God.

False Teachers

2 There used to be false prophets[d] among God's people, just as there are now. And you will have some false teachers in your group. They will secretly teach things that are wrong— teachings that will cause people to be lost. They will even refuse to accept the Master, Jesus, who bought their freedom. And so they will quickly destroy themselves. [2]Many will follow their evil ways and say evil things about the Way of truth. [3]Those false teachers only want your money. So they will use you by telling you what is not true. But God has already judged them guilty. And they will not escape the One who will destroy them.

[4]When angels sinned, God did not let them go free without punishment. God sent them to hell and put them in caves of darkness. They are being held there to be judged. [5]And God punished the evil people who lived long ago. He brought a flood to the world that was full of people who were against him. But God saved Noah and seven other people with him. Noah was a man who preached about being right with God. [6]And God also punished the evil cities of Sodom and Gomorrah.[n] He burned those cities until there was nothing left but ashes. He made those cities an example to show what will happen to those who are against God. [7]But God saved Lot from those cities. Lot, a good man, was troubled because of the dirty lives of evil people. [8](Lot was a good man, but he lived with evil people every day. His good heart was hurt by the evil things that he saw and heard.) [9]And so the Lord knows how to save those who serve him. He will save them when troubles come. And the Lord will hold evil people and punish them, while waiting for the Judgment Day. [10]That punishment is especially for those who live by doing the evil things their sinful selves want, and for those who hate the Lord's authority.

These false teachers do anything they want and brag about it. They are not afraid to say bad things about the glorious angels. [11]The angels are much stronger and more powerful than false teachers. But even the angels do not accuse them with insults before the Lord. [12]But these men say bad things about what they do not understand. They are like animals that act without thinking. These animals are born to be caught and killed. And, like wild animals, these false teachers will be destroyed. [13]They have caused many people to suffer; so they themselves will suffer. That is their pay for what they have done. They take pleasure in doing evil things openly. So they are like dirty spots and stains among you. They bring shame to you in the meals that you eat together. [14]Every time they look at a woman they want her. Their desire for sin is never satisfied. They lead weak people into the trap of sin. They have taught their hearts to be selfish. God will punish them. [15]These false teachers left the right road and lost their way. They followed the way that Balaam went. Balaam was the son of Beor, who loved being paid for doing wrong. [16]But a donkey told Balaam that he was sinning. And the donkey is an animal that cannot talk. But the donkey spoke with a man's

[n]**Sodom and Gomorrah** Two cities God destroyed because the people were so evil.

voice and stopped the prophet's crazy thinking.

[17]Those false teachers are like rivers that have no water. They are like clouds blown by a storm. A place in the blackest darkness has been kept for them. [18]They brag with words that mean nothing. By their evil desires they lead people into the trap of sin. They lead away people who are just beginning to escape from other people who live in error. [19]They promise them freedom, but they themselves are not free. They are slaves of things that will be destroyed. For a person is a slave of anything that controls him. [20]They were made free from the evil in the world by knowing our Lord and Savior Jesus Christ. But if they return to evil things and those things control them, then it is worse for them than it was before. [21]Yes, it would be better for them to have never known the right way. That would be better than to know the right way and then to turn away from the holy teaching that was given to them. [22]What they did is like this true saying: "A dog eats what it throws up."[n] And, "After a pig is washed, it goes back and rolls in the mud."

Jesus Will Come Again

3 My friends, this is the second letter I have written to you. I wrote both letters to you to help your honest minds remember something. [2]I want you to remember the words that the holy prophets[d] spoke in the past. And remember the command that our Lord and Savior gave us through your apostles.[d] [3]It is important for you to understand what will happen in the last days. People will laugh at you. They will live doing the evil things they want to do. [4]They will say, "Jesus promised to come again. Where is he? Our fathers have died. But the world continues the way it has been since it was made." [5]But they do not want to remember what happened long ago. God spoke and made heaven and earth. He made the earth from water and with water. [6]Then the world was flooded and destroyed with water. [7]And that same word of God is keeping heaven and earth that we have now. They are being kept to be destroyed by fire. They are being kept for the Judgment Day and the destruction of all who are against God.

[8]But do not forget this one thing, dear friends: To the Lord one day is as a thousand years, and a thousand years is as one day. [9]The Lord is not slow in doing what he promised—the way some people understand slowness. But God is being patient with you. He does not want anyone to be lost. He wants everyone to change his heart and life.

[10]But the day the Lord comes again will be a surprise, like a thief. The skies will disappear with a loud noise. Everything in the skies will be destroyed by fire. And the earth and everything in it will be burned up.[n] [11]In that way everything will be destroyed. So what kind of people should you be? You should live holy lives and serve God. [12]You should wait for the day of God and look forward to its coming. When that day comes, the skies will be destroyed with fire, and everything in the skies will melt with heat. [13]But God made a promise to us. And we are waiting for what he promised—a new heaven and a new earth where goodness lives.

[14]Dear friends, we are waiting for this to happen. So try as hard as you can to be without sin and without fault. Try to be at peace with God. [15]Remember that we are saved because our Lord is patient. Our dear brother Paul told you the same thing when he wrote to you with the wisdom that God gave him. [16]Paul writes about this in all his letters. Sometimes there are things in Paul's letters that are hard to understand. And some people explain these things falsely. They are ignorant and weak in faith. They also falsely explain the other

---

[n]**"A dog . . . up."**   Quotation from Proverbs 26:11.

[n]**will be burned up**   Many Greek copies say, "will be found." One copy says, "will disappear."

Scriptures.[d] But they are destroying themselves by doing that.

[17]Dear friends, you already know about this. So be careful. Do not let those evil people lead you away by the wrong they do. Be careful so that you will not fall from your strong faith. [18]But grow in the grace and knowledge of our Lord and Savior Jesus Christ. Glory be to him now and forever! Amen.

1 JOHN

Love
One Another

1 We write you now about something that has always existed.
We have heard.
We have seen with our own eyes.
We have watched,
and we have touched with our hands.
We write to you about the Word[n] that gives life. [2]He who gives life was shown to us. We saw him, and we can give proof about it. And now we tell you that he has life that continues forever. The one who gives this life was with God the Father. God showed him to us. [3]Now we tell you what we have seen and heard because we want you to have fellowship with us. The fellowship we share together is with God the Father and his Son, Jesus Christ. [4]We write this to you so that you can be full of joy with us.

God Forgives Our Sins

[5]Here is the message we have heard from God and now tell to you: God is light,[n] and in him there is no darkness at all. [6]So if we say that we have fellowship with God, but we continue living in darkness, then we are liars. We do not follow the truth. [7]God is in the light. We should live in the light, too. If we live in the light, we share fellowship with each other. And when we live in the light, the blood of the death of Jesus, God's Son, is making us clean from every sin.

[8]If we say that we have no sin, we are fooling ourselves, and the truth is not in us. [9]But if we confess our sins, he will forgive our sins. We can trust God. He does what is right. He will make us clean from all the wrongs we have

---

Sin
1 JOHN 1:9

Wouldn't it be great to know that you were forgiven for every wrong you've ever done? Every wrong thought, word, or action?

Good news! First John 1:9 says that you can be forgiven, totally. All you have to do is admit your sins to God and ask for his forgiveness. You can be forgiven. All you have to do is ask.

Is there sin in your life that you need to talk to God about? Don't wait. Confess it to him. Ask him to forgive you and take that sin out of your life. He will.

---

[n]**Word** The Greek word is "logos," meaning any kind of communication. It could be translated "message." Here, it means Christ. Christ was the way God told people about himself.
[n]**light** This word is used to show what God is like. It means goodness or truth.

> But if we confess our sins, he will forgive our sins. We can trust God. He does what is right. He will make us clean from all the wrongs we have done.
> • 1 John 1:9

done. ¹⁰If we say that we have not sinned, then we make God a liar. We do not accept God's true teaching.

Jesus Is Our Helper

2 My dear children, I write this letter to you so that you will not sin. But if anyone does sin, we have Jesus Christ to help us. He is the Righteous One. He defends us before God the Father. ²Jesus is the way our sins are taken away. And Jesus is the way that all people can have their sins taken away, too.

³If we obey what God has told us to do, then we are sure that we truly know God. ⁴If someone says, "I know God!" but does not obey God's commands, then he is a liar. The truth is not in him. ⁵But if someone obeys God's teaching, then God's love has truly arrived at its goal in him. This is how we know that we are following God: ⁶Whoever says that God lives in him must live as Jesus lived.

The Command to Love Others

⁷My dear friends, I am not writing a new command to you. It is the same command you have had since the beginning. It is the teaching you have already heard. ⁸But I am writing a new command to you. This command is true; you can see its truth in Jesus and in yourselves. The darkness is passing away, and the true light is already shining.

⁹Someone says, "I am in the light."ⁿ But if he hates his brother, he is still in the darkness. ¹⁰Whoever loves his brother lives in the light, and there is nothing in him that will cause him to do wrong. ¹¹But whoever hates his brother is in darkness. He lives in darkness and does not know where he is going. The darkness has made him blind.

¹²I write to you, dear children, because your sins are forgiven through Christ.

Honesty
1 JOHN 2:4

What would you think about a boy who said he could throw a curve ball, but never did it? Or a girl who said she could play the piano, but you never heard her play it? You would probably have some doubts that they could do what they said.

The same is true of a person who claims to be a Christian but never does what God says to do. Anyone can *say,* "I'm a Christian" or "I love the Lord." A trained parrot could say those words. But according to this verse, the proof of being a Christian is obeying God. That person can be considered honest and is honestly following Jesus.

It is important that we go to church, read our Bible, and say our prayers. But the *real* test of our Christian faith is whether we do what God says in the Bible. Then we have *the truth* in us.

ⁿ**light** This word is used to show what God is like. It means goodness or truth.

¹³I write to you, fathers,
   because you know the One who
      existed from the beginning.
I write to you, young men,
   because you have defeated the
      Evil One.
¹⁴I write to you, children,
   because you know the Father.
I write to you, fathers,
   because you know the One who
      existed from the beginning.
I write to you, young men,
   because you are strong;
   the word of God lives in you,
   and you have defeated the Evil One.

¹⁵Do not love the world or the things in the world. If anyone loves the world, the love of the Father is not in him. ¹⁶These are the evil things in the world: wanting things to please our sinful selves, wanting the sinful things we see, being too proud of the things we have. But none of those things comes from the Father. All of them come from the world. ¹⁷The world is passing away. And everything that people want in the world is passing away. But the person who does what God wants lives forever.

Reject the Enemies of Christ

¹⁸My dear children, the end is near! You have heard that the Enemy of Christ[d] is coming. And now many enemies of Christ are already here. So we know that the end is near. ¹⁹Those enemies of Christ were in our group. But they left us. They did not really belong with us. If they were really part of our group, then they would have stayed with us. But they left. This shows that none of them really belonged with us.

²⁰You have the gift[n] that the Holy One gave you. So you all know the truth. ²¹Why do I write to you? Do I write because you do not know the truth? No, I write this letter because you do know the truth. And you know that no lie comes from the truth.

²²So who is the liar? It is the person who says Jesus is not the Christ. A person who says Jesus is not the Christ is the enemy of Christ. He does not believe in the Father or in his Son. ²³If anyone does not believe in the Son, he does not have the Father. But whoever accepts the Son has the Father, too.

²⁴Be sure that you continue to follow the teaching that you heard from the beginning. If you continue in that teaching, you will stay in the Son and in the Father. ²⁵And this is what the Son promised to us—life forever.

²⁶I am writing this letter about those people who are trying to lead you the wrong way. ²⁷Christ gave you a special

God's Children
1 JOHN 3:1

Adopted children have very special stories. They were not born into the families that raise them. Instead they were chosen by their adoptive parents. Then they became just as loved and as much a part of the family as if they were born into it.

To become a child of God, the Bible says people are "born" and "adopted." God loves us so much that when we believe in Jesus and accept him as our Savior, we become his children. Not everyone is a child of God. Each person must choose to trust in Christ.

To learn more about God's children, zoom to page 1530.

ⁿ**gift** This might mean the Holy Spirit. Or it might mean teaching or truth as in verse 24.

gift. You still have this gift in you. So you do not need any other teacher. The gift he gave you teaches you about everything. This gift is true, not false. So continue to live in Christ, as his gift taught you.

28Yes, my dear children, live in him. If we do this, we can be without fear on the day when Christ comes back. We will not need to hide and be ashamed when he comes. 29You know that Christ is righteous. So you know that all who do what is right are God's children.

We Are God's Children

3 The Father has loved us so much! He loved us so much that we are

God's law. Yes, sinning is the same as living against God's law. 5You know that Christ came to take away sins. There is no sin in Christ. 6So the person who lives in Christ does not go on sinning. If he goes on sinning, he has never really understood Christ and has never known him.

7Dear children, do not let any person lead you the wrong way. Christ is righteous. To be like Christ, a person must do what is right. 8The devil has been sinning since the beginning. Anyone who continues to sin belongs to the devil. The Son of God came for this purpose: to destroy the devil's work.

9When God makes someone his child, that person does not go on sinning. The new life God gave that person

People Who Made Mistakes

CAIN • 1 JOHN 3:12

After Adam and Eve sinned, God wanted the people to make sacrifices in order to find forgiveness for their sins. To make a sacrifice, they had to kill an animal and burn it on a fire. Abel, who was a shepherd, made his sacrifice to God by offering one of his sheep. Cain was a farmer. He thought he could bring vegetables to God as his sacrifice instead of an animal. God was not pleased with Cain's offering because it was not what he asked.

Today, people still try to please God by their own efforts. Rather than believing in Jesus as their Savior, they think they can get to heaven just by being good. These people have made the same mistake Cain made, because they are not doing what God told them to do.

We need to do what God asks.

called children of God. And we really are his children. But the people in the world do not understand that we are God's children, because they have not known him. 2Dear friends, now we are children of God. We have not yet been shown what we will be in the future. But we know that when Christ comes again, we will be like him. We will see him as he really is. 3Christ is pure. And every person who has this hope in Christ keeps himself pure like Christ.

4When a person sins, he breaks

stays in him. So he is not able to go on sinning, because he has become a child of God. 10So we can see who God's children are and who the devil's children are. Those who do not do what is right are not children of God. And anyone who does not love his brother is not a child of God.

We Must Love Each Other

11This is the teaching you have heard from the beginning: We must love each other. 12Do not be like Cain who belonged to the Evil One. Cain killed his brother. He killed his brother because the things Cain did were evil, and the things his brother did were good.

¹³Brothers, do not be surprised when

hearts make us feel guilty, we can still have peace before God. God is greater than our hearts, and he knows everything.

Friendships
1 JOHN 4:8, 20-21

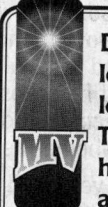

It's pretty easy to say we love God when it doesn't cost us much. We can show up at church on Sunday morning and put some of our parents' money in the offering plate without too much trouble. But God knows whether we love him by the way we treat the people around us.

The Bible says that people who say they love God but don't love their own brother or sister are liars!

Unfortunately, it is sometimes more difficult to love the people we are close to than complete strangers! Living day in and day out with the same people does cause problems. But God thinks these relationships are important. He wants us to show our love for him by being kind to our family members and friends.

the people of this world hate you. ¹⁴We know that we have left death and have come into life. We know this because we love our brothers in Christ. Whoever does not love is still in death. ¹⁵Everyone who hates his brother is a murderer.″ And you know that no murderer has eternal life in him. ¹⁶This is how we know what real love is: Jesus gave his life for us. So we should give our lives for our brothers. ¹⁷Suppose a believer is rich enough to have all that he needs. He sees his brother in Christ who is poor and does not have what he needs. What if the believer does not help the poor brother? Then the believer does not have God's love in his heart. ¹⁸My children, our love should not be only words and talk. Our love must be true love. And we should show that love by what we do.

¹⁹⁻²⁰This is the way we know that we belong to the way of truth. When our

²¹My dear friends, if we do not feel that we are doing wrong, we can be without fear when we come to God. ²²And God gives us the things we ask for. We receive these things because we obey God's commands, and we do what pleases him. ²³This is what God commands: that we believe in his Son, Jesus Christ, and that we love each other, just as he commanded. ²⁴The person who obeys God's commands lives in God. And God lives in him. How

> Dear friends, we should love each other, because love comes from God. The person who loves has become God's child and knows God.
> • 1 John 4:7

″**Everyone . . . murderer.** If a person hates his brother in Christ, then in his mind he has killed his brother. Jesus taught about this sin to his followers (Matthew 5:21-26).

"**M**ost people have heard that God is love. The Bible does say that. But notice in 1 John 4:7-21 what else the Bible talks about when it says that God is love."

do we know that God lives in us? We know because of the Spirit[d] whom God gave us.

Warning Against False Teachers

4 My dear friends, many false prophets[d] are in the world now. So do not believe every spirit. But test the spirits to see if they are from God. [2]This is how you can know God's Spirit:[d] One spirit says, "I believe that Jesus is the Christ who came to earth and became a man." That Spirit is from God. [3]Another spirit refuses to say this about Jesus. That spirit is not from God but is the spirit of the Enemy of Christ. You have heard that the Enemy of Christ is coming. And now he is already in the world.

[4]My dear children, you belong to God. So you have defeated them because God's Spirit, who is in you, is greater than the devil, who is in the world. [5]And they belong to the world. What they say is from the world, and the world listens to them. [6]But we are from God, and those who know God listen to us. But those who are not from God do not listen to us. That is how we know the Spirit that is true and the spirit that is false.

Love Comes from God

[7]Dear friends, we should love each other, because love comes from God. The person who loves has become God's child and knows God. [8]Whoever does not love does not know God, because God is love. [9]This is how God showed his love to us: He sent his only Son into the world to give us life through him. [10]True love is God's love for us, not our love for God. God sent his Son to be the way to take away our sins.

[11]That is how much God loved us, dear friends! So we also must love each other. [12]No one has ever seen God. But if we love each other, God lives in us. If we love each other, God's love has reached its goal. It is made perfect in us.

[13]We know that we live in God and

God's Love for Us
1 JOHN 4:9-10

How would feel about someone who said he really, *really* wanted to be your friend, but he would never do anything for you? You ask him to spend time with you, and he says no. Or you ask if you can ride his bike, and he grabs it and rides away. Or you ask her if you can see her doll collection, and she says, "Maybe later." You would probably begin to doubt whether he or she really wanted to be friends at all.

But if that person said yes to all those things and was always willing to help you no matter what the cost—that's a real friend. That person *proves* his friendship for you by his actions. That's what God has done for us in sending Jesus to take away our sins. Even though it cost the life of his son, God was willing to do that for us. That's a *real* friend!

God lives in us. We know this because God gave us his Spirit.[d] [14]We have seen that the Father sent his Son to be the Savior of the world. That is what we teach. [15]If someone says, "I believe that Jesus is the Son of God," then God lives in him. And he lives in God. [16]And so we know the love that God has for us, and we trust that love.

God is love. Whoever lives in love

Faith in the Son of God

5 Everyone who believes that Jesus is the Christ[d] is God's child. The person who loves the Father also loves the Father's children. [2]How do we know that we love God's children? We know

What God Is Like
1 JOHN 4:16

There are times in every Christian's life when he or she is not living the way God wants. It may come through in big ways, like disobeying parents, getting in trouble at school, or even breaking the law. Or it may be in less noticeable ways, like having a bad attitude or whining and complaining all the time. When those times come, we may not want to take our problems to God. He is holy, and we are not. He knows everything, and that includes all the bad things we have done, said, and thought. God is just, and we are afraid he may give us what we deserve—and that's the last thing we want.

When those times come, remember: God *is* holy, he *does* know everything, and he *is* just. But he is also *loving*. In fact, 1 John 4:16 says that God is *love*. Because of that, we don't have to be afraid to go to him and get things right with him.

lives in God, and God lives in him. [17]If God's love is made perfect in us, then we can be without fear on the day God judges us. We will be without fear, because in this world we are like him. [18]Where God's love is, there is no fear, because God's perfect love takes away fear. It is punishment that makes a person fear. So love is not made perfect in the person who has fear.

[19]We love because God first loved us. [20]If someone says, "I love God," but hates his brother, he is a liar. He can see his brother, but he hates him. So he cannot love God, whom he has never seen. [21]And God gave us this command: Whoever loves God must also love his brother.

because we love God and we obey his commands. [3]Loving God means obeying his commands. And God's commands are not too hard for us. [4]Everyone who is a child of God has the power to win against the world. It is our faith that wins the victory against the world. [5]So the one who wins against the world is the person who believes that Jesus is the Son of God.

[6]Jesus Christ is the One who came with water[n] and with blood.[n] He did not come by water only. He came by both water and blood. And the Spirit[d] says that this is true. The Spirit is the truth. [7]So there are three witnesses that tell us about Jesus: [8]the Spirit, the water, and the blood. These three witnesses

[n]**water** This probably means the water of Jesus' baptism.
[n]**blood** This probably means the blood of Jesus' death.

agree. [9]We believe people when they say something is true. But what God says is more important. And he has told us the truth about his own Son. [10]Anyone who believes in the Son of God has the truth that God told us. Anyone who does not believe makes God a liar. He does not believe what God told us about his Son. [11]This is what God told us: God has given us eternal life, and this life is in his Son. [12]Whoever has the Son has life. But the person who does not have the Son of God does not have life.

We Have Eternal Life Now

[13]I write this letter to you who believe in the Son of God. I write so that you will know that you have eternal life now. [14]We can come to God with no doubts. This means that when we ask God for things (and those things agree with what God wants for us), then God cares about what we say. [15]God listens to us every time we ask him. So we know that he gives us the things that we ask from him.

[16]Suppose someone sees his brother in Christ sinning (sin that does not lead to eternal death). That person should pray for his brother who is sinning. Then God will give the brother life. I am talking about people whose sin does not lead to eternal death. There is sin that leads to death. I do not mean that a person should pray about that sin. [17]Doing wrong is always sin. But there is sin that does not lead to eternal death.

[18]We know that anyone who is God's child does not continue to sin. The Son of God keeps him safe, and the Evil One cannot hurt him. [19]We know that we belong to God. But the Evil One controls the whole world. [20]And we know that the Son of God has come and has given us understanding. Now we can know God, the One who is true. And our lives are in that true God and in his Son, Jesus Christ. He is the true God, and he is eternal life. [21]So, dear children, keep yourselves away from false gods.

God's Children
1 JOHN 5:1

Brothers and sisters have a special pact. Some kids talk about it and some kids don't, but all of them have it. The pact is this: I may not always like you, but I love you. You are my *family*.

Haven't you ever gotten mad when someone started picking on your brother? Or didn't you get upset the last time someone called your sister a name? Being in the same family brings us together. We don't just love our parents—we love our brothers and sisters too.

God's children are all part of God's family. God is their father, and they are all brothers and sisters. And that's why God tells us to love one another. We should treat each other just like brothers and sisters, because that's what we are.

God has other children besides you. Remember the pact!

2 JOHN

Do Not Help
False Teachers

¹From the Elder.*

To the chosen lady* and to her children:

I love all of you in the truth.* Also, all those who know the truth love you. ²We love you because of the truth—the truth that lives in us and will be with us forever.

³Grace, mercy, and peace will be with us from God the Father and from his Son, Jesus Christ. And may we have these blessings in truth and love.

⁴I was very happy to learn about some of your children. I am happy that they are following the way of truth, as the Father commanded us. ⁵And now, dear lady, I tell you: We should all love each other. This is not a new command. It is the same command we have had from the beginning. ⁶And loving means living the way he commanded us to live. And God's command is this: that you live a life of love. You have heard this command from the beginning.

⁷Many false teachers are in the world now. They refuse to say that Jesus Christ came to earth and became a man. Anyone who refuses to say this is a false teacher and an enemy of Christ. ⁸Be careful! Do not lose the reward that you have worked for. Be careful, so that you will receive your full reward.

⁹A person must continue to follow only the teaching of Christ. If he goes beyond Christ's teaching, then he does not have God. But if he continues following the teaching of Christ, then he has both the Father and the Son. ¹⁰If someone comes to you, but does not bring this teaching, then do not accept him into your house. Do not welcome him. ¹¹If you accept him, you are helping him with his evil work.

¹²I have much to say to you, but I do not want to use paper and ink. Instead, I hope to come visit you. Then we can be together and talk. That will make us very happy. ¹³The children of your chosen sister* send you their love.

---

*Elder   This is probably John the apostle. "Elder" means an older man. It can also mean a special leader in the church (as in Titus 1:5).

*lady   This might mean a woman. Or, in this letter, it might mean a church. If it is a church, then "her children" would be the people of the church.

*truth   The truth or "Good News" about Jesus Christ that joins all believers together.

*sister   Sister of the "lady" in verse 1. This might be another woman or another church.

3 JOHN

Help Christians Who Teach Truth

¹From the Elder.ⁿ

To my dear friend Gaius whom I love in the truth:ⁿ

²My dear friend, I know your soul is doing well. I pray that you are doing fine in every way and that your health is good. ³Some brothers in Christ came and told me about the truth in your life. They said that you are following the way of truth. This made me very happy. ⁴It always gives me the greatest joy when I hear that my children are following the way of truth.

⁵My dear friend, it is good that you continue to help the brothers. You are helping those that you do not even know! ⁶These brothers told the church about the love you have. Please help them to continue their trip. Help them in a way that will please God. ⁷They started out on their trip to serve Christ. They did not accept any help from those who are not believers. ⁸So we should help these brothers. And when we do, we share in their work for the truth.

⁹I wrote a letter to the church. But Diotrephes will not listen to what we say. He always wants to be their leader. ¹⁰When I come, I will talk about what Diotrephes is doing. He lies and says evil things about us. But that is not all he does. He refuses to help those who are working to serve Christ. He also stops those who want to help the brothers and puts them out of the church.

¹¹My dear friend, do not follow what is bad; follow what is good. He who does what is good is from God. But he who does evil has never known God.

¹²Everyone says good things about Demetrius. And the truth agrees with what they say. Also, we say good about him. And you know that what we say is true.

¹³I have many things I want to tell you, but I do not want to use pen and ink. ¹⁴I hope to visit you soon. Then we can be together and talk. ¹⁵Peace to you. The friends here with me send their love. Please give our love to each one of the friends there.

ⁿ**Elder** This is probably John the apostle. "Elder" means an older man. It can also mean a special leader in the church (as Titus 1:5).

ⁿ**truth** The truth or "Good News" about Jesus Christ that joins all believers together.

JUDE
Warnings About False Teachers

[1] From Jude, a servant of Jesus Christ and a brother of James.

To all who have been called by God. God the Father loves you, and you have been kept safe in Jesus Christ.

[2] All mercy, peace, and love be yours.

God Will Punish Sinners

[3] Dear friends, I wanted very much to write to you about the salvation we all share together. But I felt the need to write to you about something else: I want to encourage you to fight hard for the faith that God gave his holy people. God gave this faith once, and it is good for all time. [4] Some people have secretly entered your group. They have already been judged guilty for the things they are doing. Long ago the prophets[d] wrote about these people. They are against God. They have used the grace of our God in the wrong way—to do sinful things. They refuse to accept Jesus Christ, our only Master and Lord.

[5] I want to remind you of some things that you already know: Remember that the Lord saved his people by bringing them out of the land of Egypt. But later the Lord destroyed all those who did not believe. [6] And remember the angels who had power but did not keep it. They left their own home. So the Lord has kept these angels in darkness. They are bound with everlasting chains, to be judged on the great day. [7] Also remember the cities of Sodom and Gomorrah[n] and the other towns around them. They acted as the angels who did not obey God. Their towns were full of sexual sin and men having sexual relations with men. They suffer the punishment of eternal fire, as an example for all to see.

[8] It is the same with these people who have entered your group. They are guided by dreams. They make themselves dirty with sin. They reject God's authority and say bad things against the glorious angels. [9] Not even the archangel[n] Michael did this. He argued with the devil about who would have the body of Moses. Michael did not dare to accuse the devil with insults. He said, "The Lord punish you." [10] But these people say bad things about what they do not understand. They do understand some things. But they understand them not by thinking, but by feeling, the way dumb animals understand things. And these are the very things that destroy them. [11] It will be bad for them. They have followed the way that Cain went. To make money, they have given themselves to doing the wrong that Balaam did. They have fought against God as Korah did. And like Korah, they will be destroyed. [12] They are like dirty spots in the special meals you share together. They eat with you and have no fear. They take care of only themselves. They are clouds without rain. The wind blows them around. They are trees that have no fruit when it is time and are pulled out of the ground. So they are dead two times. [13] They are like wild waves in the sea. These people do shameful things in the same way waves make foam. They are like stars that wander in the sky. A place in the blackest darkness has been kept for them forever.

---

[n] **Sodom and Gomorrah** Two cities God destroyed because they were so evil.
[n] **archangel** The leader among God's angels or messengers.

[14]Enoch, the seventh descendant[d] from Adam, said this about these people: "Look, the Lord is coming with thousands and thousands of his holy angels. [15]The Lord will judge every person. He is coming to judge everyone and to punish all who are against God. He will punish them for all the evil they have done against him. And he will punish the sinners who are against God. He will punish them for all the evil things they have said against him."

[16]These people always complain and blame others. They always do the evil things they want to do. They brag about themselves. The only reason they say good things about other people is to get what they want.

A Warning and Things to Do

[17]Dear friends, remember what the apostles[d] of our Lord Jesus Christ said before. [18]They said to you, "In the last times there will be people who laugh about God. They will do only what they want to do—things that are against God." [19]These are the people who divide you. They do only what their sinful selves want. They do not have the Spirit.[d]

[20]But dear friends, use your most holy faith to build yourselves up strong. Pray with the Holy Spirit. [21]Keep yourselves in God's love. Wait for the Lord Jesus Christ with his mercy to give you life forever.

[22]Show mercy to people who have doubts. [23]Save them. Take them out of the fire. Show mercy mixed with fear to others. Hate even their clothes which are dirty from sin.

Praise God

[24]God is strong and can help you not to fall. He can bring you before his glory without any wrong in you and give you great joy. [25]He is the only God. He is the One who saves us. To him be glory, greatness, power, and authority through Jesus Christ our Lord for all time past, now, and forever. Amen.

REVELATION

*Christ Will Win
over Evil*

John Tells About This Book

1 This is the revelation[n] of Jesus Christ. God gave this revelation to Jesus, to show his servants what must soon happen. And Jesus sent his angel to show it to his servant John. [2]John has told everything that he has seen. It is the truth that Jesus Christ told him; it is the message from God. [3]The one who reads the words of God's message is happy. And the people who hear this message and do what is written in it are happy. The time is near when all of this will happen.

Jesus' Message to the Churches

[4]From John,

To the seven churches in the country of Asia:

Grace and peace to you from the One who is and was and is coming, and from the seven spirits before his throne, [5]and from Jesus Christ. Jesus is the faithful witness. He is first among those raised from death. He is the ruler of the kings of the earth.

He is the One who loves us. And he is the One who made us free from our sins with the blood of his death. [6]He made us to be a kingdom of priests who serve God his Father. To Jesus Christ be glory and power forever and ever! Amen.

[7]Look, Jesus is coming with the clouds! Everyone will see him, even those who stabbed him. And all peoples of the earth will cry loudly because of him. Yes, this will happen! Amen.

[8]The Lord God says, "I am the Alpha and the Omega.[n] I am the One who is and was and is coming. I am the All-Powerful."

[9]I am John, and I am your brother in Christ. We are together in Jesus, and we share in these things: in suffering, in the kingdom, and in patience. I was on the island of Patmos[n] because I had preached God's message and the truth about Jesus. [10]On the Lord's day the Spirit[d] took control of me. I heard a loud voice behind me that sounded like a trumpet. [11]The voice said, "Write what you see and send that book to the seven churches: to Ephesus, Smyrna, Pergamum, Thyatira, Sardis, Philadelphia, and Laodicea."

> "**D**o you have any idea what Jesus looks like today? There's a word-picture in Revelation 1:12-16. Check it out."

[12]I turned to see who was talking to me. When I turned, I saw seven golden lampstands. [13]I saw someone among the lampstands who was "like a Son of Man."[n] He was dressed in a long robe. He had a gold band around his chest. [14]His head and hair were white like

[n]**revelation** A making known of truth that has been hidden.
[n]**Alpha and the Omega** The first and last letters in the Greek alphabet. This means "the beginning and the end."
[n]**Patmos** A small island in the Aegean Sea, near the coast of Asia Minor (modern Turkey).
[n]**"like ... Man"** "Son of Man" is a name Jesus called himself. It showed he was God's Son, but he was also a man. See dictionary.

wool, as white as snow. His eyes were like flames of fire. ¹⁵His feet were like bronze that glows hot in a furnace. His voice was like the noise of flooding water. ¹⁶He held seven stars in his right hand. A sharp two-edged sword came out of his mouth. He looked like the sun shining at its brightest time.

"The One who holds the seven stars in his right hand and walks among the seven golden lampstands says this to you. ²I know what you do. You work hard, and you never give up. I know that you do not accept evil people. You have tested those who say that they are apostles[d] but really are not. You found that they are liars. ³You continue to serve me. You have suffered troubles for my name, and you have not given up.

People Who Spoke God's Words

JOHN • REVELATION 1:1-9

John had been one of Jesus' disciples. He served God for many years, teaching people about God's love and how they could be saved from their sins. About sixty years after Jesus returned to heaven, Jesus' followers had told the gospel across much of the world. This made some of the government officials angry. They sent John to an island called Patmos. That was like being in prison. But while he was on the island, God showed him about what the end of the world will be like and how God will take all his people to heaven to be with him forever.

Some day this prophecy will come true because God's words always come true. When Jesus comes again, will you be ready to meet him?

¹⁷When I saw him, I fell down at his feet like a dead man. He put his right hand on me and said, "Do not be afraid! I am the First and the Last. ¹⁸I am the One who lives. I was dead, but look: I am alive forever and ever! And I hold the keys of death and where the dead are. ¹⁹So write the things you see, what is now and what will happen later. ²⁰Here is the hidden meaning of the seven stars that you saw in my right hand and the seven golden lampstands that you saw: The seven lampstands are the seven churches. The seven stars are the angels of the seven churches.

To the Church in Ephesus

2 "Write this to the angel of the church in Ephesus:

⁴"But I have this against you: You have left the love you had in the beginning. ⁵So remember where you were before you fell. Change your hearts and do what you did at first. If you do not change, I will come to you. I will take away your lampstand from its place. ⁶But there is something you do that is right: You hate what the Nicolaitans[n] do, as much as I.

⁷"Every person who has ears should listen to what the Spirit[d] says to the churches. To him who wins the victory I will give the right to eat the fruit from the tree of life. This tree is in the garden of God.

To the Church in Smyrna

⁸"Write this to the angel of the church in Smyrna:

ⁿNicolaitans   This is the name of a religious group that followed false beliefs and ideas.

"The One who is the First and the Last says this to you. He is the One who died and came to life again. [9]I know your troubles. I know that you are poor, but really you are rich! I know the bad things that some people say about you. They say they are Jews, but they are not true Jews. They are a synagogue[d] that belongs to Satan. [10]Do not be afraid of what will happen to you. I tell you, the devil will put some of you in prison to test you. You will suffer for ten days. But be faithful, even if you have to die. If you are faithful, I will give you the crown of life.

[11]"Everyone who has ears should listen to what the Spirit[d] says to the churches. He who wins the victory will not be hurt by the second death.

To the Church in Pergamum

[12]"Write this to the angel of the church in Pergamum:

"The One who has the sharp two-edged sword says this to you. [13]I know where you live. You live where Satan has his throne. But you are true to me. You did not refuse to tell about your faith in me even during the time of Antipas. Antipas was my faithful witness who was killed in your city. Your city is where Satan lives.

[14]"But I have a few things against you: You have some there who follow the teaching of Balaam. Balaam taught Balak how to cause the people of Israel to sin. They sinned by eating food offered to idols and by taking part in sexual sins. [15]You also have some who follow the teaching of the Nicolaitans.[n] [16]So change your hearts and lives! If you do not, I will come to you quickly and fight against them with the sword that comes out of my mouth.

[17]"Everyone who has ears should listen to what the Spirit[d] says to the churches!

"I will give the hidden manna[d] to everyone who wins the victory. I will also give him a white stone with a new name written on it. No one knows this new name except the one who receives it.

To the Church in Thyatira

[18]"Write this to the angel of the church in Thyatira:

"The Son of God is saying these things. He is the One who has eyes that blaze like fire and feet like shining bronze. He says this to you: [19]I know what you do. I know about your love, your faith, your service, and your patience. I know that you are doing more now than you did at first. [20]But I have this against you: You let that woman Jezebel do what she wants. She says that she is a prophetess.[d] But she is leading my people away with her teaching. Jezebel leads them to take part in sexual sins and to eat food that is offered to idols. [21]I have given her time to change her heart and turn away from her sin. But she does not want to change. [22]And so I will throw her on a bed of suffering. And all those who take part in adultery[d] with her will suffer greatly. I will do this now if they do not turn away from the wrongs she does. [23]I will also kill her followers. Then all the churches will know that I am the One who knows what people feel and think. And I will repay each of you for what you have done.

[24]"But others of you in Thyatira have not followed her teaching. You have not learned what some call Satan's deep secrets. This is what I say to you: I will not put any other load on you. [25]Only continue the way you are until I come.

[26]"I will give power to everyone who wins the victory and continues to the end to do what I want. I will give him power over the nations:
[27]'You will make them obey you
    by punishing them with an
    iron rod.
You will break them into pieces
    like pottery.'   *Psalm 2:9*
[28]This is the same power I received from my Father. I will also give him the

---

[n]**Nicolaitans**   This is the name of a religious group that followed false beliefs and ideas.

morning star. [29]Everyone who has ears should listen to what the Spirit[d] says to the churches.

To the Church in Sardis

3 "Write this to the angel of the church in Sardis:

"The One who has the seven spirits and the seven stars says this to you. I know what you do. People say that you are alive, but really you are dead. [2]Wake up! Make yourselves stronger while you still have something left and before it dies completely. I have found that what you are doing is not good enough for my God. [3]So do not forget what you have received and heard. Obey it. Change your hearts and lives! You must wake up, or I will come to you and surprise you like a thief. And you will not know when I will come. [4]But you have a few there in Sardis who have kept themselves clean. They will walk with me. They will wear white clothes, because they are worthy. [5]He who wins the victory will be dressed in white clothes like them. I will not take away his name from the book of life. I will say that he belongs to me before my Father and before his angels. [6]Everyone who has ears should listen to what the Spirit[d] says to the churches.

To the Church in Philadelphia

[7]"Write this to the angel of the church in Philadelphia:

"The One who is holy and true says this to you. He holds the key of David. When he opens something, it cannot be closed. And when he closes something, it cannot be opened. [8]I know what you do. I have put an open door before you, and no one can close it. I know that you have a little strength. But you were followed my teaching. And you were not afraid to speak my name. [9]Listen! There is a synagogue[d] that belongs to Satan. Those in this synagogue say they are Jews, but they are liars. They are not true Jews. I will make them come before you and bow at your feet. They will know that I have loved you. [10]You have followed my teaching about not giving up. So I will keep you from the time of trouble that will come to the whole world. This trouble will test those who live on earth.

[11]"I am coming soon. Continue the way you are now. Then no one will take away your crown. [12]I will make the one who wins the victory a pillar in the temple of my God. He will never have to leave it. I will write on him the name of my God and the name of the city of my God. This city is the new Jerusalem.[n] It comes down out of heaven from my God. I will also write on him my new name. [13]Every person who has ears should listen to what the Spirit[d] says to the churches.

To the Church in Laodicea

[14]"Write this to the angel of the church in Laodicea:

"The Amen[n] is the One who is the faithful and true witness. He is the ruler of all that God has made. He says this to you: [15]I know what you do. You are not hot or cold. I wish that you were hot or cold! [16]But you are only warm—not hot, not cold. So I am ready to spit you out of my mouth. [17]You say you are rich. You think you have become wealthy and do not need anything. But you do not know that you are really miserable, pitiful, poor, blind, and naked. [18]I advise you to buy gold from me—gold made pure in fire. Then you can be truly rich. Buy from me clothes that are white. Then you can cover your shameful nakedness. Buy from me medicine to put on your eyes. Then you can truly see.

[19]"I correct and punish those whom I love. So be eager to do right. Change your hearts and lives. [20]Here I am! I stand at the door and knock. If anyone hears my voice and opens the door, I will come in and eat with him. And he will eat with me.

[n]**Jerusalem**   This name is used to mean the spiritual city God built for his people.
[n]**Amen**   Used here as a name for Jesus, it means to agree fully that something is true.

[21]"He who wins the victory will sit with me on my throne. It was the same with me. I won the victory and sat down with my Father on his throne. [22]Everyone who has ears should listen to what the Spirit[d] says to the churches."

John Sees Heaven

4 After this I looked, and there before me was an open door in heaven. And I heard the same voice that spoke to me before. It was the voice that sounded like a trumpet. The voice said, "Come up here, and I will show you what must happen after this." [2]Then the Spirit[d] took control of me. There before me was a throne in heaven. Someone was sitting on the throne. [3]The One who sat on the throne looked like precious stones, like jasper and carnelian. All around the throne was a rainbow the color of an emerald. [4]Around the throne there were 24 other thrones. There were 24 elders[n] sitting on the 24 thrones. The elders were dressed in white, and they had golden crowns on their heads. [5]Lightning flashes and noises of thunder came from the throne. Before the throne there were seven lamps burning. These lamps are the seven spirits of God. [6]Also before the throne there was something that looked like a sea of glass. It was clear like crystal.

Around the throne, on each side, there were four living things. These living things had eyes all over them, in front and in back. [7]The first living thing was like a lion. The second was like a calf. The third had a face like a man. The fourth was like a flying eagle. [8]Each of these four living things had six wings. The living things were covered all over with eyes, inside and out. Day and night they never stop saying:

"Holy, holy, holy is the Lord God
   All-Powerful.
He was, he is, and he is coming."

[9]These living things give glory and honor and thanks to the One who sits on the throne. He is the One who lives forever and ever. And every time the living things do this, [10]the 24 elders bow down before the One who sits on the throne. The elders worship him who lives forever and ever. They put their crowns down before the throne and say:

[11]"Our Lord and God! You are worthy
   to receive glory and honor
     and power.
You made all things.
   Everything existed and was made
   because you wanted it."

5 Then I saw a scroll in the right hand of the One sitting on the throne. The scroll had writing on both sides. It was kept closed with seven seals. [2]And I saw a powerful angel. He called in a loud voice, "Who is worthy to break the seals and open the scroll?"

Animals in the Bible

LIONS • REVELATION 5:5

What animal is the king of the beasts? If you said a lion, you are correct! In the Bible, lions are associated with kings and greatness. They reminded people of power and success. When Solomon was king, he had lion statues around his throne (1 Kings 10:19-20).

The Lord Jesus is called the Lion of Judah because he is the King of kings and the ruler of God's kingdom. Is he your king?

---

[n]**24 elders** Elder means "older." Here the elders probably represent God's people.

³But there was no one in heaven or on earth or under the earth who could open the scroll or look inside it. ⁴I cried and cried because there was no one who was worthy to open the scroll or look inside. ⁵But one of the elders said to me, "Do not cry! The Lion[n] from the tribe[d] of Judah has won the victory. He is David's descendant.[d] He is able to open the scroll and its seven seals."

"You are worthy to take the scroll
and to open its seals,
because you were killed;
and with the blood of your death
you bought men for God
from every tribe, language, people,
and nation.
¹⁰You made them to be a kingdom of
priests for our God.

Prayer
REVELATION 5:8

Have you ever wondered how God sees our prayers? Does he treat them as a bother? "Oh no, there's that Smith kid asking for a baby brother again." Or, "Hey, that's Mrs. Harris calling. I haven't heard from her since the last time she was in trouble."

According to this verse, nothing could be further from the truth. Here our prayers are described as "golden bowls full of incense." That's a picture of something super valuable and very pleasant—golden bowls filled with sweet smells. That's how God sees our prayers!

When you need to pray, don't worry that God is going to be annoyed with you or that he will think your prayers as bothersome. He is a good father. And, like all good fathers, he loves to spend time with his children. He loves to hear what is in their hearts, no matter how small it might seem. Our prayers mean so much to him that he treats them like "golden bowls full of incense"!

---

⁶Then I saw a Lamb standing in the center of the throne with the four living things around it. The elders were also around the Lamb. The Lamb looked as if he had been killed. He had seven horns and seven eyes. These are the seven spirits of God that were sent into all the world. ⁷The Lamb came and took the scroll from the right hand of the One sitting on the throne. ⁸After he took the scroll, the four living things and the 24 elders bowed down before the Lamb. Each one of them had a harp. Also, they were holding golden bowls full of incense.[d] These bowls of incense are the prayers of God's holy people. ⁹And they all sang a new song to the Lamb:

And they will rule on the earth."
¹¹Then I looked, and I heard the voices of many angels. The angels were around the throne, the four living things, and the elders. There were thousands and thousands of angels— there were 10,000 times 10,000. ¹²The angels said in a loud voice:
"The Lamb who was killed is worthy
to receive power, wealth, wisdom
and strength,
honor, glory, and praise!"
¹³Then I heard every living thing in heaven and on earth and under the earth and in the sea. I heard every thing in all these places, saying:
"All praise and honor and glory and
power

[n]**Lion** Here refers to Christ.

forever and ever
to the One who sits on the throne
and to the Lamb!"

[14]The four living things said, "Amen!" And the elders bowed down and worshiped.

6 Then I watched while the Lamb opened the first of the seven seals. I heard one of the four living things speak with a voice like thunder. It said, "Come!" [2]I looked and there before me was a white horse. The rider on the horse held a bow, and he was given a crown. And he rode out, defeating the enemy. He rode out to win the victory.

[3]The Lamb opened the second seal. Then I heard the second living thing say, "Come!" [4]Then another horse came out. This was a red horse. Its rider was given power to take away peace from the earth. He was given power to make people kill each other. And he was given a big sword.

[5]The Lamb opened the third seal. Then I heard the third living thing say, "Come!" I looked, and there before me was a black horse. Its rider held a pair of scales in his hand. [6]Then I heard something that sounded like a voice. It came from where the four living things were. The voice said, "A quart of wheat for a day's pay. And three quarts of barley for a day's pay. And do not damage the olive oil and wine!"

[7]The Lamb opened the fourth seal. Then I heard the voice of the fourth living thing say, "Come!" [8]I looked, and there before me was a pale horse. Its rider was named death. Hades[n] was following close behind him. They were given power over a fourth of the earth. They were given power to kill people by war, by starving them, by disease, and by the wild animals of the earth.

[9]The Lamb opened the fifth seal. Then I saw some souls under the altar. They were the souls of those who had been killed because they were faithful to God's message and to the truth they had received. [10]These souls shouted in a loud voice, "Holy and true Lord, how long until you judge the people of the earth and punish them for killing us?" [11]Then each one of these souls was given a white robe. They were told to wait a short time longer. There were still some of their brothers in the service of Christ who must be killed as they were. They were told to wait until all of this killing was finished.

[12]Then I watched while the Lamb opened the sixth seal. There was a great earthquake. The sun became black like rough black cloth. The full moon became red like blood. [13]The stars in the sky fell to the earth like figs falling from a fig tree when the wind blows. [14]The sky disappeared. It was rolled up like a scroll. And every mountain and island was moved from its place.

[15]Then all people hid in caves and behind the rocks on the mountains. There were the kings of the earth, the rulers, the generals, the rich people and the powerful people. Everyone, slave and free, hid himself. [16]They called to the mountains and the rocks, "Fall on us. Hide us from the face of the One who sits on the throne. Hide us from the anger of the Lamb! [17]The great day for their anger has come. Who can stand against it?"

The 144,000 People of Israel

7 After this I saw four angels standing at the four corners of the earth. The angels were holding the four winds of the earth. They were stopping the wind from blowing on the land or on the sea or on any tree. [2]Then I saw another angel coming from the east. This angel had the seal of the living God. He called out in a loud voice to the four angels. These were the four angels that God had given power to harm the earth and the sea. He said to the four angels, [3]"Do not harm the land or the sea or the trees before we put the sign on the people who serve our God. We must put the sign on their foreheads." [4]Then I heard how many people were marked

---

[n]**Hades** The unseen world where the dead are.

with the sign. There were 144,000. They were from every tribe[d] of the people of Israel.

[5]From the tribe of Judah 12,000 were marked with the sign,

from the tribe of Reuben 12,000,
from the tribe of Gad 12,000,
[6]from the tribe of Asher 12,000,
from the tribe of Naphtali 12,000,
from the tribe of Manasseh 12,000,
[7]from the tribe of Simeon 12,000,
from the tribe of Levi 12,000,
from the tribe of Issachar 12,000,
[8]from the tribe of Zebulun 12,000,
from the tribe of Joseph 12,000,
from the tribe of Benjamin 12,000.

and before the Lamb. They wore white robes and had palm branches in their hands. [10]They were shouting in a loud voice, "Salvation belongs to our God, who sits on the throne, and to the Lamb." [11]The elders[n] and the four living things were there. All the angels were standing around them and the throne. The angels bowed down on their faces before the throne and worshiped God. [12]They were saying, "Amen! Praise, glory, wisdom, thanks, honor, power, and strength belong to our God forever and ever. Amen!"

[13]Then one of the elders asked me, "Who are these people in white robes? Where did they come from?"

[14]I answered, "You know who they are, sir."

Visiting Angels
REVELATION 7:11-12

Many angels are mentioned in this book of the Bible. They carry out God's commands and judgments against sin in the world. God has promised us that if we follow him, we will be with him forever in heaven. One day life on this earth will end, and God will create a new heaven and a new earth. We don't know when this will happen or what it will be like, but we can trust God that it will be wonderful for us.

The book of Revelation describes all of God's angels singing praises and worshiping God. We will not become angels when we get to heaven. Instead, God promises that we will have new bodies that will last forever. We will never get sick. The angels sing about God because they have been with him. Some day we will be with God too, and we will sing and worship him because of all he has done for us. Won't that be wonderful!

The Great Crowd

[9]Then I looked, and there was a great number of people. There were so many people that no one could count them. They were from every nation, tribe,[d] people, and language of the earth. They were all standing before the throne

And the elder said, "These are the people who have come out of the great suffering. They have washed their robes[n] with the blood of the Lamb. Now they are clean and white. [15]And they are before the throne of God. They worship God day and night in his temple. And the One who sits on the

---

[n]**elders** Elder means "older." Here the elders probably represent God's people.
[n]**washed their robes** This means they believed in Jesus so that their sins could be forgiven by Christ's blood.

throne will protect them. [16]Those people will never be hungry again. They will never be thirsty again. The sun will not hurt them. No heat will burn them. [17]For the Lamb at the center of the throne will be their shepherd. He will lead them to springs of water that give life. And God will wipe away every tear from their eyes."

The Seventh Seal

8 The Lamb opened the seventh seal. Then there was silence in heaven for about half an hour. [2]And I saw the seven angels who stand before God. They were given seven trumpets.

[3]Another angel came and stood at the altar. This angel had a golden pan for incense.[d] The angel was given much incense to offer with the prayers of all God's holy people. The angel put this offering on the golden altar before the throne. [4]The smoke from the incense went up from the angel's hand to God. It went up with the prayers of God's people. [5]Then the angel filled the incense pan with fire from the altar and threw it on the earth. There were flashes of lightning, thunder and loud noises, and an earthquake.

The Seven Angels and Trumpets

[6]Then the seven angels who had the seven trumpets prepared to blow them.

[7]The first angel blew his trumpet. Then hail and fire mixed with blood was poured down on the earth. And a third of the earth and all the green grass and a third of the trees were burned up.

[8]The second angel blew his trumpet. Then something that looked like a big mountain burning with fire was thrown into the sea. And a third of the sea became blood. [9]And a third of the living things in the sea died, and a third of the ships were destroyed.

[10]The third angel blew his trumpet. Then a large star, burning like a torch, fell from the sky. It fell on a third of the rivers and on the springs of water. [11]The name of the star is Wormwood.[n] And a third of all the water became bitter. Many people died from drinking the water that was bitter.

[12]The fourth angel blew his trumpet. Then a third of the sun and a third of the moon and a third of the stars were hit. So a third of them became dark. A third of the day was without light.

[13]While I watched, I heard an eagle that was flying high in the air. The eagle said with a loud voice, "Trouble! Trouble! Trouble for those who live on the earth! The trouble will begin with the sounds of the trumpets that the other three angels are about to blow."

9 Then the fifth angel blew his trumpet. And I saw a star fall from the sky to the earth. The star was given the key to the deep hole that leads down to the bottomless pit. [2]Then it opened the bottomless pit. Smoke came up from the hole like smoke from a big furnace. The sun and sky became dark because of the smoke from the hole. [3]Then locusts[d] came down to the earth out of the smoke. They were given the power to sting like scorpions.[n] [4]They were told not to harm the grass on the earth or any plant or tree. They could harm only the people who did not have the sign of God on their foreheads. [5]These locusts were given the power to cause pain to the people for five months. But they were not given the power to kill anyone. And the pain they felt was like the pain that a scorpion gives when it stings a person. [6]During those days people will look for a way to die, but they will not find it. They will want to die, but death will run away from them.

[7]The locusts looked like horses prepared for battle. On their heads they wore things that looked like crowns of gold. Their faces looked like human faces. [8]Their hair was like women's hair, and their teeth were like lions' teeth. [9]Their chests looked like iron

---

[n]**Wormwood**   Name of a very bitter plant, used here to give the idea of bitter sorrow.

[n]**scorpions**   A scorpion is an insect that stings with a bad poison.

breastplates. The sound their wings made was like the noise of many horses and chariots hurrying into battle. [10]The locusts had tails with stingers like scorpions. The power they had to hurt people for five months was in their tails. [11]The locusts had a king who was the angel of the bottomless pit. His name in the Hebrew language is Abaddon. In the Greek language his name is Apollyon."

[12]The first great trouble is past. There are still two other great troubles that will come.

[13]The sixth angel blew his trumpet. Then I heard a voice coming from the horns on the golden altar that is before God. [14]The voice said to the sixth angel who had the trumpet, "Free the four angels who are tied at the great river Euphrates." [15]These four angels had been kept ready for this hour and day and month and year. They were freed to kill a third of all people on the earth. [16]I heard how many troops on horses were in their army. There were 200,000,000.

[17]In my vision I saw the horses and their riders. They looked like this: They had breastplates that were fiery red, dark blue, and yellow like sulfur. The heads of the horses looked like heads of lions. The horses had fire, smoke, and sulfur coming out of their mouths. [18]A third of all the people on earth were killed by these three terrible things coming out of the horses' mouths: the fire, the smoke, and the sulfur. [19]The horses' power was in their mouths and also in their tails. Their tails were like snakes that have heads to bite and hurt people.

[20]The other people on the earth were not killed by these terrible things. But they still did not change their hearts and turn away from what they had made with their own hands. They did not stop worshiping demons[d] and idols made of gold, silver, bronze, stone, and wood—things that cannot see or hear or walk. [21]These people did not change their hearts and turn away from murder or evil magic, from their sexual sins or stealing.

The Angel and the Little Scroll

10 Then I saw another powerful angel coming down from heaven. He was dressed in a cloud and had a rainbow around his head. His face was like the sun, and his legs were like poles of fire. [2]The angel was holding a small scroll open in his hand. He put his right foot on the sea and his left foot on the land. [3]He shouted loudly like the roaring of a lion. When he shouted, the voices of seven thunders spoke. [4]The seven thunders spoke, and I started to write. But then I heard a voice from heaven. The voice said, "Do not write what the seven thunders said. Keep these things secret."

[5]Then the angel I saw standing on the sea and on the land raised his right hand to heaven. [6]He made a promise by the power of the One who lives forever and ever. He is the One who made the skies and all that is in them. He made the earth and all that is in it, and he made the sea and all that is in it. The angel said, "There will be no more waiting! [7]In the days when the seventh angel is ready to blow his trumpet, God's secret plan will be finished. This plan is the Good News[d] God told to his servants, the prophets."[d]

[8]Then I heard the same voice from heaven again. The voice said to me, "Go and take the open scroll that is in the angel's hand. This is the angel that is standing on the sea and on the land."

[9]So I went to the angel and asked him to give me the little scroll. He said to me, "Take the scroll and eat it. It will be sour in your stomach. But in your mouth it will be sweet as honey." [10]So I took the little scroll from the angel's hand and I ate it. In my mouth it tasted sweet as honey. But after I ate it, it was sour in my stomach. [11]Then I was told, "You must prophesy[d] again about many peoples, nations, languages, and kings."

"**Abaddon, Apollyon** Both names mean "Destroyer."

The Two Witnesses

11 Then I was given a measuring stick like a rod. I was told, "Go and measure the temple[n] of God and the altar, and count the number of people worshiping there. [2]But do not measure the yard outside the temple. Leave it alone. It has been given to the people who are not Jews. They will walk on the holy city for 42 months. [3]And I will give power to my two witnesses to prophesy[d] for 1,260 days. They will be dressed in rough cloth to show how sad they are."

[4]These two witnesses are the two olive trees and the two lampstands that stand before the Lord of the earth. [5]If anyone tries to hurt the witnesses, fire comes from their mouths and kills their enemies. Anyone who tries to hurt them will die like this. [6]These witnesses have the power to stop the sky from raining during the time they are prophesying. They have power to make the waters become blood. They have power to send every kind of trouble to the earth. They can do this as many times as they want.

[7]When the two witnesses have finished telling their message, the beast will fight against them. This is the beast that comes up from the bottomless pit. He will defeat them and kill them. [8]The bodies of the two witnesses will lie in the street of the great city. This city is named Sodom[n] and Egypt. These names for the city have a special meaning. It is the city where the Lord was killed. [9]Men from every race of people, tribe,[d] language, and nation will look at the bodies of the two witnesses for three and a half days. They will refuse to bury them. [10]People who live on the earth will be happy because these two are dead. They will have parties and send each other gifts. They will do these things because these two prophets brought much suffering to those who live on the earth.

[11]But after three and a half days, God put the breath of life into the two prophets again. They stood on their feet. Everyone who saw them was filled with fear. [12]Then the two prophets heard a loud voice from heaven say, "Come up here!" And they went up into heaven in a cloud. Their enemies watched them go.

[13]At that same time there was a great earthquake. A tenth of the city was destroyed. And 7,000 people were killed in the earthquake. Those who did not die were very afraid. They gave glory to the God of heaven.

[14]The second great trouble is finished. The third great trouble is coming soon.

The Seventh Trumpet

[15]Then the seventh angel blew his trumpet. And there were loud voices in heaven. The voices said:

"The power to rule the world
now belongs to our Lord and his
Christ.[d]
And he will rule forever and ever."

[16]Then the 24 elders[n] bowed down on their faces and worshiped God. These are the elders who sit on their thrones before God. [17]They said:

"We give thanks to you, Lord God
All-Powerful.
You are the One who is and who
was.
We thank you because you have
used your great power
and have begun to rule!
[18]The people of the world were angry;
but now is the time for your anger.
Now is the time for the dead to be
judged.
It is time to reward your servants
the prophets[d]
and to reward your holy people,
all who respect you, great and small.
It is time to destroy those who
destroy the earth!"

---

[n]**temple** God's house—the place where God's people worship and serve him. Here, John sees it pictured as the special building in Jerusalem where God commanded the Jews to worship him.
[n]**Sodom** City that God destroyed because the people were so evil.
[n]**24 elders** Elder means "older." Here the elders probably represent God's people.

[19]Then God's temple[n] in heaven was opened. The Holy Box[d] that holds the agreement that God gave to his people could be seen in his temple. Then there were flashes of lightning, noises, thunder, an earthquake, and a great hailstorm.

The Woman and the Dragon

12 And then a great wonder appeared in heaven: There was a woman who was clothed with the sun. The moon was under her feet. She had a crown of 12 stars on her head. [2]The woman was pregnant. She cried out with pain because she was about to give birth. [3]Then another wonder appeared in heaven: There was a giant red dragon. He had seven heads with seven crowns on each head. He also had ten horns. [4]The dragon's tail swept a third of the stars out of the sky and threw them down to the earth. The dragon stood in front of the woman who was ready to give birth to a baby. He wanted to eat the woman's baby as soon as it was born. [5]The woman gave birth to a son. He will rule all the nations with an iron scepter.[d] But her child was taken up to God and to his throne. [6]The woman ran away into the desert to a place God prepared for her. There she would be taken care of for 1,260 days.

[7]Then there was a war in heaven. Michael[n] and his angels fought against the dragon. The dragon and his angels fought back. [8]But the dragon was not strong enough. He and his angels lost their place in heaven. [9]He was thrown down out of heaven. (The giant dragon is that old snake called the devil or Satan. He leads the whole world the wrong way.) The dragon with his angels was thrown down to the earth.

[10]Then I heard a loud voice in heaven say:

"The salvation and the power and the kingdom of our God
and the authority of his Christ[d]
have now come.
They have come because the
accuser of our brothers
has been thrown out.
He has accused our brothers
day and night before
our God.
[11]And our brothers defeated him
by the blood of the Lamb's
death
and by the truth they preached.
They did not love their lives so
much
that they were afraid of death.
[12]So be happy, you heavens
and all who live there!
But it will be terrible for the earth
and the sea,
because the devil has come down
to you!
He is filled with anger.
He knows that he does not have
much time."

[13]The dragon saw that he had been thrown down to the earth. So he hunted down the woman who had given birth to the son. [14]But the woman was given the two wings of a great eagle. Then she could fly to the place that was prepared for her in the desert. There she would be taken care of for three and a half years. There she would be away from the snake. [15]Then the snake poured water out of its mouth like a river. He poured the water toward the woman, so that the flood would carry her away. [16]But the earth helped her. The earth opened its mouth and swallowed the river that came from the mouth of the dragon. [17]Then the dragon was very angry at the woman. He went off to make war against all her other children. Her children are those who obey God's commands and have the truth that Jesus taught.

[18]And the dragon stood on the seashore.

---

[n]**temple** God's house—the place where God's people worship and serve him. John sees the heavenly temple pictured to be like the Temple of God's people in the Old Testament.
[n]**Michael** The archangel—leader among God's angels or messengers (Jude 9).

The Two Beasts

13 Then I saw a beast coming up out of the sea. It had ten horns and seven heads. There was a crown on each horn. A name against God was written on each head. [2]This beast looked like a leopard, with feet like a bear's feet. He had a mouth like a lion's mouth. The dragon gave the beast all of his power and his throne and great authority. [3]One of the heads of the beast looked as if it had been wounded and killed. But this death wound was healed. The whole world was amazed and followed the beast. [4]People worshiped the dragon because he had given his power to the beast. And they also worshiped the beast. They asked, "Who is as powerful as the beast? Who can make war against him?"

[5]The beast was allowed to say proud words and words against God. He was allowed to use his power for 42 months. [6]He used his mouth to speak against God. He spoke against God's name, against the place where God lives, and against all those who live in heaven. [7]He was given power to make war against God's holy people and to defeat them. He was given power over every tribe,[d] people, language, and nation. [8]All who live on earth will worship the beast. These are all the people since the beginning of the world whose names are not written in the Lamb's book of life. The Lamb is the One who was killed.

[9]If anyone has ears, he should listen:
[10]If anyone is to be a prisoner,
    then he will be a prisoner.
If anyone is to be killed with the
        sword,
    then he will be killed with the
        sword.
This means that God's holy people must have patience and faith.

[11]Then I saw another beast coming up out of the earth. He had two horns like a lamb, but he talked like a dragon. [12]This beast stands before the first beast and uses the same power that the first beast has. He uses this power to make everyone living on earth worship the first beast. The first beast was the one that had the death wound that was healed. [13]The second one does great miracles.[d] He even makes fire come down from heaven to earth while people are watching. [14]This second beast fools those who live on earth. He fools them by the miracles he has been given the power to do. He does these miracles to serve the first beast. The second beast ordered people to make an idol to honor the first beast. This was the one that was wounded by the sword but did not die. [15]The second beast was given power to give life to the idol of the first one. Then the idol could speak and order all who did not worship it to be killed. [16]The second animal also forced all people, small and great, rich and poor, free and slave, to have a mark on their right hand or on their forehead. [17]No one could buy or sell without this mark. This mark is the name of the beast or the number of his name. [18]Whoever has understanding can find the meaning of the number. This requires wisdom. This number is the number of a man. His number is 666.

The Song of the Saved

14 Then I looked, and there before me was the Lamb. He was standing on Mount Zion.[n] There were 144,000 people with him. They all had his name and his Father's name written on their foreheads. [2]And I heard a sound from heaven like the noise of flooding water and like the sound of loud thunder. The sound I heard was like people playing harps. [3]And they sang a new song before the throne and before the four living things and the elders.[n] The only ones who could learn the new song were the 144,000 who had been saved from the earth. No one else could learn the song. [4]These 144,000 are the ones who did not do sinful things with women. They kept themselves pure. They follow the Lamb every place he goes. These 144,000 were saved from among the people of the earth. They are the first people to be offered to God and the Lamb. [5]They were not guilty of telling lies. They are without fault.

The Three Angels

[6]Then I saw another angel flying high in the air. The angel had the eternal Good News[d] to preach to those who live on earth—to every nation, tribe,[d] language, and people. [7]The angel said in a loud voice, "Fear God and give him praise. The time has come for God to judge all people. Worship God. He made the heavens, the earth, the sea, and the springs of water."

[8]Then the second angel followed the first angel and said, "She is destroyed! The great city of Babylon is destroyed! She made all the nations drink the wine of her adultery[d] and of God's anger."

[9]A third angel followed the first two angels. This third angel said in a loud voice: "It will be bad for the person who worships the beast and his idol and gets the beast's mark on the forehead or on the hand. [10]He will drink the wine of God's anger. This wine is prepared with all its strength in the cup of God's anger. He will be put in pain with burning sulfur before the holy angels and the Lamb. [11]And the smoke from their burning pain will rise forever and ever. There will be no rest, day or night, for those who worship the beast and his idol or who get the mark of his name." [12]This means that God's holy people must be patient. They must obey God's commands and keep their faith in Jesus.

[13]Then I heard a voice from heaven. It said, "Write this: From now on, the dead who were in the Lord when they died are happy."

The Spirit[d] says, "Yes, that is true. They will rest from their hard work. The reward of all they have done stays with them."

The Earth Is Harvested

[14]I looked and there before me was a white cloud. Sitting on the white cloud was One who looked like a Son of Man.[n] He had a gold crown on his head and a sharp sickle[n] in his hand. [15]Then another angel came out of the temple. This angel called to the One who was sitting on the cloud, "Take your sickle and gather from the earth. The time to harvest has come. The fruit of the earth is ripe." [16]So the One that was sitting on the cloud swung his sickle over the earth. And the earth was harvested.

[17]Then another angel came out of the temple in heaven. This angel also had a sharp sickle. [18]And then another angel came from the altar. This angel has power over the fire. This angel called to the angel with the sharp sickle. He said, "Take your sharp sickle and gather the bunches of grapes from the earth's vine. The earth's grapes are ripe." [19]The angel swung his sickle over the earth. He gathered the earth's grapes and threw them into the great winepress[d] of God's anger. [20]The grapes were crushed in the winepress outside the city. And blood flowed out of the winepress. It rose as high as the heads of the horses for a distance of 200 miles.

The Last Troubles

15 Then I saw another wonder in heaven. It was great and amazing. There were seven angels bringing seven troubles. These are the last troubles, because after these troubles God's anger is finished.

[2]I saw what looked like a sea of glass mixed with fire. All of those who had

---

[n]**Son of Man**   "Son of Man" is a name Jesus called himself. It showed he was God's Son, but he was also a man. See dictionary.
[n]**sickle**   A farming tool with a curved blade. It was used to harvest grain.

won the victory over the beast and his idol and over the number of his name were standing by the sea. They had harps that God had given them. ³They sang the song of Moses, the servant of God, and the song of the Lamb:

"You do great and wonderful things,
Psalm 111:2
Lord God, the God of heaven's armies. *Amos 3:13*
Everything the Lord does is right and true, *Psalm 145:17*
King of the nations.
⁴Everyone will respect you, Lord.
Jeremiah 10:7
They will honor you.
Only you are holy.
All people will come and worship you. *Psalm 86:9,10*
This is because he is a faithful God who does no wrong.
He is right and fair."
Deuteronomy 32:4

⁵After this I saw the temple (the Tent*d* of the Agreement) in heaven. The temple was opened. ⁶And the seven angels bringing the seven troubles came out of the temple. They were dressed in clean, shining linen. They wore golden bands tied around their chests. ⁷Then one of the four living things gave seven golden bowls to the seven angels. The bowls were filled with the anger of God, who lives forever and ever. ⁸The temple was filled with smoke from the glory and the power of God. No one could enter the temple until the seven troubles of the seven angels were finished.

The Bowls of God's Anger

16 Then I heard a loud voice from the temple. The voice said to the seven angels, "Go and pour out the seven bowls of God's anger on the earth."

²The first angel left. He poured out his bowl on the land. Then ugly and painful sores came upon all those who had the mark of the beast and who worshiped his idol.

³The second angel poured out his bowl on the sea. Then the sea became blood like that of a dead man. Every living thing in the sea died.

⁴The third angel poured out his bowl on the rivers and the springs of water. And they became blood. ⁵Then I heard the angel of the waters say to God:

"Holy One, you are the One who is and who was.
You are right to decide to punish these evil people.
⁶They have spilled the blood of your holy people and your prophets.*d*
Now you have given them blood to drink as they deserve."
⁷And I heard the altar say:
"Yes, Lord God All-Powerful,
the way you punish evil people is right and fair."

⁸The fourth angel poured out his bowl on the sun. The sun was given power to burn the people with fire. ⁹They were burned by the great heat, and they cursed the name of God. God is the One who had control over these troubles. But the people refused to change their hearts and lives and give glory to God.

¹⁰The fifth angel poured out his bowl on the throne of the beast. And darkness covered the beast's kingdom. People bit their tongues because of the pain. ¹¹They cursed the God of heaven because of their pain and the sores they had. But they refused to change their hearts and turn away from the evil things they did.

¹²The sixth angel poured out his bowl on the great river Euphrates. The water in the river was dried up. This prepared the way for the kings from the east to come. ¹³Then I saw three evil spirits that looked like frogs. They came out of the mouth of the dragon, out of the mouth of the beast, and out of the mouth of the false prophet.*d* ¹⁴These evil spirits are the spirits of demons.*d* They have power to do miracles.*d* They go out to the kings of the whole world. They go out to gather the kings for battle on the great day of God All-Powerful.

[15]"Listen! I will come as a thief comes! Happy is the person who stays awake and keeps his clothes with him. Then he will not have to go without clothes and be ashamed because he is naked."

[16]Then the evil spirits gathered the kings together to the place that is called Armageddon[n]in the Hebrew language.

[17]The seventh angel poured out his bowl into the air. Then a loud voice came out of the temple from the throne. The voice said, "It is finished!" [18]Then there were flashes of lightning, noises, thunder, and a big earthquake. This was the worst earthquake that has ever happened since people have been on earth. [19]The great city split into three parts. The cities of the nations were destroyed. And God did not forget to punish Babylon the Great. He gave that city the cup filled with the wine of his terrible anger. [20]Every island disappeared, and there were no more mountains. [21]Giant hailstones fell on people from the sky. The hailstones weighed about 100 pounds each. People cursed God because of the hail. This trouble was a terrible thing.

The Woman on the Animal

17 One of the seven angels came and spoke to me. This was one of the angels that had the seven bowls. He said, "Come, and I will show you the punishment that will be given to the famous prostitute.[d] She is the one sitting over many waters. [2]The kings of the earth sinned sexually with her. And the people of the earth became drunk from the wine of her sexual sin."

[3]Then the angel carried me away by the Spirit[d] to the desert. There I saw a woman sitting on a red beast. He was covered with names against God written on him. He had seven heads and ten horns. [4]The woman was dressed in purple and red. She was shining with the gold, jewels, and pearls she was wearing. She had a golden cup in her

hand. This cup was filled with evil things and the uncleanness of her sexual sin. [5]She had a title written on her forehead. This title has a hidden meaning. This is what was written:

THE GREAT BABYLON
MOTHER OF PROSTITUTES
AND THE EVIL THINGS OF THE EARTH

[6]I saw that the woman was drunk. She was drunk with the blood of God's holy people. She was drunk with the blood of those who were killed because of their faith in Jesus.

When I saw the woman, I was fully amazed. [7]Then the angel said to me, "Why are you amazed? I will tell you the hidden meaning of this woman and the beast she rides—the one with seven heads and ten horns. [8]The beast that you saw was once alive. He is not alive now. But he will be alive and come up out of the bottomless pit and go away to be destroyed. The people who live on earth will be amazed when they see the beast. They will be amazed because he was once alive, is not alive now, but will come again. These are the people whose names have never been written in the book of life since the beginning of the world.

[9]"You need a wise mind to understand this. The seven heads on the beast are the seven hills where the woman sits. They are also seven kings. [10]Five of the kings have already died. One of the kings lives now. And the last king is coming. When he comes, he will stay only a short time. [11]The beast that was once alive but is not alive now is an eighth king. This eighth king also belongs to the first seven kings. And he will go away to be destroyed. [12]"The ten horns you saw are ten kings. These ten kings have not yet begun to rule. But they will receive power to rule with the beast for one hour. [13]All ten of these kings have the same purpose. And they will give their power and authority to the beast. [14]They will make war against the Lamb. But the Lamb will defeat them,

[n]**Armageddon** This word means "Hill of Megiddo," where many battles were fought long ago.

because he is Lord of lords and King of kings. He will defeat them with his chosen and faithful followers—the people that he has called."

[15] Then the angel said to me, "You saw the water where the prostitute sits. These waters are the many peoples, the different races, nations, and languages. [16] The beast and the ten horns you saw will hate the prostitute. They will take everything she has and leave her naked. They will eat her body and burn her with fire. [17] God made the ten horns want to carry out his purpose: They agreed to give the beast their power to rule. They will rule until what God has said is completed. [18] The woman you saw is the great city that rules over the kings of the earth."

Babylon Is Destroyed

18 Then I saw another angel coming down from heaven. This angel had great power. The angel's glory made the earth bright. [2] The angel shouted in a powerful voice:

"The great city of Babylon is
destroyed!
She has become a home for
demons.[d]
She has become a city for every
evil spirit,
a city for every unclean[d] and
hated bird.
[3] All the peoples of the earth have
drunk
the strong wine of her sexual sin.
The kings of the earth have sinned
sexually with her,
and the businessmen of the world
have grown rich from the
great wealth of her luxury."

[4] Then I heard another voice from heaven say:

"Come out of that city, my people,
so that you will not share in her
sins.
Then you will not receive the
terrible things that will happen
to her.
[5] The city's sins are piled up as high
as the sky.

God has not forgotten the wrongs
she has done.
[6] Give that city the same as she gave
to others.
Pay her back twice as much as
she did.
Prepare wine for her that is twice
as strong
as the wine she prepared for
others.
[7] She gave herself much glory and
rich living.
Give her that much suffering
and sadness.
She says to herself, 'I am a queen
sitting on my throne.
I am not a widow; I will never
be sad.'
[8] So these terrible things will come to
her in one day:
death, crying, and great hunger.
She will be destroyed by fire,
because the Lord God who judges
her is powerful."

[9] The kings of the earth who sinned sexually with her and shared her wealth will see the smoke from her burning. Then they will cry and weep because of her death. [10] They will be afraid of her suffering and stand far away. They will say:

"Terrible! How terrible, great city,
powerful city of Babylon!
Your punishment has come in one
hour!"

[11] And the businessmen of the earth will cry and weep for her. They will be sad because now there is no one to buy the things they sell. [12] They sell gold, silver, jewels, pearls, fine linen cloth, purple cloth, silk, and red cloth. They sell all kinds of citron wood and all kinds of things made from ivory, expensive wood, bronze, iron, and marble. [13] They also sell cinnamon, spice, incense,[d] myrrh,[d] frankincense,[d] wine, and olive oil; fine flour, wheat, cattle, sheep, horses, and carriages. They sell the bodies and souls of men.

[14] They will say,

"Babylon, the good things you
wanted are gone from you.

All your rich and fancy things have
disappeared.
You will never have them again."
¹⁵The businessmen will be afraid of
her suffering and stand far away from
her. These are the men who became
rich from selling those things to her.
The men will cry and be sad. ¹⁶They
will say:
"Terrible! How terrible for the great
city!
She was dressed in fine linen,
purple and red cloth.
She was shining with gold, jewels,
and pearls!
¹⁷All these riches have been
destroyed in one hour!"
Every sea captain, all those who travel on ships, the sailors, and all the people who earn money from the sea stood
far away from Babylon. ¹⁸They saw the
smoke from her burning. They said
loudly, "There was never a city like
this great city!" ¹⁹They threw dust on
their heads and cried to show how sad
they were. They said:
"Terrible! How terrible for the
great city!
All the people who had ships on
the sea
became rich because of her
wealth!
But she has been destroyed in
one hour!
²⁰Be happy because of this, heaven!
Be happy, God's holy people and
apostles[d] and prophets![d]
God has punished her because of
what she did to you."
²¹Then a powerful angel picked up a
stone like a large stone for grinding
grain. The angel threw the stone into
the sea and said:
"That is how the great city of
Babylon will be thrown down.
The city will never be found again.
²²The music of people playing harps
and other instruments, flutes
and trumpets,
will never be heard in you again.

No workman doing any job
will ever be found in you again.
The sound of grinding grain
will never be heard in you again.
²³The light of a lamp
will never shine in you again.
The voices of a bridegroom
and bride
will never be heard in you again.
Your businessmen were the world's
great men.
All the nations were tricked by
your magic.
²⁴She is guilty of the death
of the prophets and God's holy
people
and of all who have been killed
on earth."

People in Heaven Praise God

19 After this I heard what sounded
like a great many people in heav-
en. They were saying:
"Hallelujah![n]
Salvation, glory, and power belong
to our God.
²   His judgments are true and right.
Our God has punished the
prostitute.[d]
She is the one who made the earth
evil with her sexual sin.
God has punished the prostitute to
pay her for the death of his
servants."
³Again they said:
"Hallelujah!
She is burning, and her smoke will
rise forever and ever."
⁴Then the 24 elders[n] and the four
living things bowed down. They worshiped God, who sits on the throne.
They said:
"Amen, Hallelujah!"
⁵Then a voice came from the throne:
"Praise our God, all you who serve
him!
Praise our God, all you who honor
him, both small and great!"
⁶Then I heard what sounded like a
great many people. It sounded like the

noise of flooding water and like loud thunder. The people were saying:
"Hallelujah!

Our Lord God rules. He is the All-Powerful.
[7]Let us rejoice and be happy and give God glory!

Give God glory, because the wedding of the Lamb has come.
And the Lamb's bride has made herself ready.
[8]Fine linen was given to the bride for her to wear.

The linen was bright and clean."
(The fine linen means the good things done by God's holy people.)

[9]Then the angel said to me, "Write this: Those who are invited to the wedding meal of the Lamb are happy!" Then the angel said, "These are the true words of God."

[10]Then I bowed down at the angel's feet to worship him. But he said to me, "Do not worship me! I am a servant like you and your brothers who have the truth of Jesus. Worship God! Because the truth about Jesus is the spirit that gives all prophecy."[d]

The Rider on the White Horse

[11]Then I saw heaven open. There before me was a white horse. The rider on the horse is called Faithful and True. He is right when he judges and makes war. [12]His eyes are like burning fire, and on his head are many crowns. He has a name written on him, but he is the only one who knows the name. No other person knows the name. [13]He is dressed in a robe dipped in blood. His name is the Word of God. [14]The armies of heaven were following him on white horses. They were dressed in fine linen, white and clean. [15]A sharp sword comes out of the rider's mouth. He will use this sword to defeat the nations. He will rule them with a scepter[d] of iron. He will crush out the wine in the winepress[d] of the terrible anger of God All-Powerful. [16]On his robe and on his leg was written this name: "KING OF KINGS AND LORD OF LORDS."

[17]Then I saw an angel standing in the sun. The angel called with a loud voice to all the birds flying in the sky, "Come together for the great feast of God. [18]Come together so that you can eat the bodies of kings and generals and famous men. Come to eat the bodies of the horses and their riders and the bodies of all people—free, slave, small, and great."

[19]Then I saw the beast and the kings of the earth. Their armies were gathered together to make war against the rider on the horse and his army. [20]But the beast was captured and with him the false prophet.[d] This false prophet was the one who did the miracles[d] for the beast. The false prophet had used these miracles to trick those who had the mark of the beast and worshiped his idol. The false prophet and the beast were thrown alive into the lake of fire that burns with sulfur. [21]Their armies were killed with the sword that came out of the mouth of the rider on the horse. All the birds ate the bodies until they were full.

The 1,000 Years

20 I saw an angel coming down from heaven. He had the key to the bottomless pit. He also held a large chain in his hand. [2]The angel grabbed the dragon, that old snake who is the devil. The angel tied him up for 1,000 years. [3]Then he threw him into the bottomless pit and closed it and locked it over him. The angel did this so that he could not trick the people of the earth anymore until the 1,000 years were ended. After 1,000 years he must be set free for a short time.

[4]Then I saw some thrones and people sitting on them. They had been given the power to judge. And I saw the souls of those who had been killed because they were faithful to the truth of Jesus and the message from God. They had not worshiped the beast or his idol. They had not received the mark of the beast on their foreheads or on their hands. They came back to

life and ruled with Christ for 1,000 years. [5] (The others that were dead did not live again until the 1,000 years were ended.) This is the first raising of the dead. [6] Blessed and holy are those who share in this first raising of the dead. The second death has no power over them. They will be priests for God and for Christ. They will rule with him for 1,000 years.

[7] When the 1,000 years are over, Satan will be set free from his prison. [8] He will go out to trick the nations in all the earth—Gog and Magog. Satan will gather them for battle. There will be so many people that they will be like sand on the seashore. [9] And Satan's army marched across the earth and gathered around the camp of God's people and the city that God loves. But fire came down from heaven and burned them up. [10] And Satan, who tricked them, was thrown into the lake of burning sulfur with the beast and the false prophet.[d] There they will be punished day and night forever and ever.

People of the World Are Judged

[11] Then I saw a great white throne and the One who was sitting on it. Earth and sky ran away from him and disappeared. [12] And I saw the dead, great and small, standing before the throne. And the book of life was opened. There were also other books opened. The dead were judged by what they had done, which was written in the books. [13] The sea gave up the dead who were in it. Death and Hades[n] gave up the dead who were in them. Each person was judged by what he had done. [14] And Death and Hades were thrown into the lake of fire. This lake of fire is the second death. [15] And if anyone's name was not found written in the book of life, he was thrown into the lake of fire.

The New Jerusalem

21 Then I saw a new heaven and a new earth. The first heaven and the first earth had disappeared. Now there was no sea. [2] And I saw the holy city coming down out of heaven from God. This holy city is the new Jerusalem.[n] It was prepared like a bride dressed for her husband. [3] I heard a loud voice from the throne. The voice said, "Now God's home is with men. He will live with them, and they will be his people. God himself will be with them and will be their God. [4] He will wipe away every tear from their eyes. There will be no more death, sadness, crying, or pain. All the old ways are gone."

[5] The One who was sitting on the throne said, "Look! I am making everything new!" Then he said, "Write this, because these words are true and can be trusted."

[6] The One on the throne said to me: "It is finished! I am the Alpha and the Omega,[n] the Beginning and the End. I will give free water from the spring of the water of life to anyone who is thirsty. [7] Anyone who wins the victory will receive this. And I will be his God, and he will be my son. [8] But those who are cowards, who refuse to believe, who do evil things, who kill, who sin sexually, who do evil magic, who worship idols, and who tell lies—all these will have a place in the lake of burning sulfur. This is the second death."

[9] One of the seven angels came to me. This was one of the angels who had the seven bowls full of the seven last troubles. He said, "Come with me. I will show you the bride, the wife of the Lamb." [10] The angel carried me away by the Spirit[d] to a very large and high mountain. He showed me the holy city, Jerusalem. It was coming down out of heaven from God. [11] It was shining with the glory of God. It was shining bright like a very expensive

[n]**Hades** Where the dead are.
[n]**new Jerusalem** The spiritual city where God's people live with him.
[n]**Alpha and the Omega** The first and last letters in the Greek alphabet. This means "the beginning and the end."

jewel, like a jasper. It was clear as crystal. [12]The city had a great high wall with 12 gates. There were 12 angels at the gates. On each gate was written the name of 1 of the 12 tribes[d] of Israel. [13]There were three gates on the east, three on the north, three on the south, and three on the west. [14]The walls of the city were built on 12 foundation stones. On the stones were written the names of the 12 apostles[d] of the Lamb.

[15]The angel who talked with me had a measuring rod made of gold. He had this rod to measure the city, its gates, and its wall. [16]The city was built in a square. Its length was equal to its width. The angel measured the city with the rod. The city was 12,000 stadia[n] long, 12,000 stadia wide, and 12,000 stadia high. [17]The angel also measured the wall. It was 144 cubits[n] high, by man's measurement. That was the measurement the angel was using. [18]The wall was made of jasper. The city was made of pure gold, as pure as glass. [19]The foundation stones of the city walls had every kind of jewel in them. The first cornerstone was jasper, the second was sapphire, the third was chalcedony, the fourth was emerald, [20]the fifth was onyx, the sixth was carnelian, the seventh was chrysolite, the eighth was beryl, the ninth was topaz, the tenth was chrysoprase, the eleventh was jacinth, and the twelfth was amethyst. [21]The 12 gates were 12 pearls. Each gate was made from a single pearl. The street of the city was made of pure gold. The gold was clear as glass.

[22]I did not see a temple in the city. The Lord God All-Powerful and the Lamb are the city's temple. [23]The city does not need the sun or the moon to shine on it. The glory of God is its light, and the Lamb is the city's lamp. [24]By its light the people of the world will walk. The kings of the earth will bring their glory into it. [25]The city's gates will never be shut on any day, because there is no night there. [26]The greatness and the honor of the nations will be brought into it. [27]Nothing unclean[d] will ever enter the city. No one who does shameful things or tells lies will ever go into it. Only those whose names are written in the Lamb's book of life will enter the city.

"**K**ids, this may be the end of the Bible, but it talks about the beginning of eternal life! I don't want you to miss that. Keep reading and obeying God's Word. If you need more reasons, read Revelation 22:1-14."

22 Then the angel showed me the river of the water of life. The river was shining like crystal. It flows from the throne of God and of the Lamb [2]down the middle of the street of the city. The tree of life was on each side of the river. It produces fruit 12 times a year, once each month. The leaves of the tree are for the healing of all people. [3]Nothing that God judges guilty will be in that city. The throne of God and of the Lamb will be there. And God's servants will worship him. [4]They will see his face, and his name will be written on their foreheads. [5]There will never be night again. They will not need the light of a lamp or the light of the sun. The Lord God will give them light. And they will rule like kings forever and ever.

[6]The angel said to me, "These words are true and can be trusted. The Lord is the God of the spirits of the prophets.[d] He sent his angel to show his servants the things that must happen soon."

[7]"Listen! I am coming soon! He who obeys the words of prophecy in this book will be happy."

---

[n]**stadia** One stadion was a distance of about 200 yards. It was one-eighth of a Roman mile.
[n]**cubits** A cubit is about half a yard, the length from the elbow to the tip of the little finger.

⁸I am John. I am the one who heard and saw these things. When I heard and saw them, I bowed down to worship at the feet of the angel who showed these things to me. ⁹But the angel said to me, "Do not worship me! I am a servant like you and your brothers the prophets. I am a servant like all those who obey the words in this book. Worship God!"

¹⁰Then the angel told me, "Do not keep secret the words of prophecy in this book. The time is near for all this to happen. ¹¹Whoever is doing evil, let him continue to do evil. Whoever is unclean, let him continue to be unclean. Whoever is doing right, let him continue to do right. Whoever is holy, let him continue to be holy."

¹²"Listen! I am coming soon! I will bring rewards with me. I will repay each one for what he has done. ¹³I am the Alpha and the Omega,ⁿ the First and the Last, the Beginning and the End.

¹⁴"Those who wash their robesⁿ will be blessed. They will have the right to eat the fruit from the tree of life. They may go through the gates into the city.

¹⁵Outside the city are the evil people, those who do evil magic, who sin sexually, who murder, who worship idols, and who love lies and tell lies.

¹⁶"I, Jesus, have sent my angel to tell you these things for the churches. I am the descendantᵈ from the family of David. I am the bright morning star."

¹⁷The Spiritᵈ and the bride say, "Come!" Everyone who hears this should also say, "Come!" If anyone is thirsty, let him come; whoever wishes it may have the water of life as a free gift.

¹⁸I warn everyone who hears the words of the prophecy of this book: If anyone adds anything to these words, God will give him the troubles written about in this book. ¹⁹And if anyone takes away from the words of this book of prophecy, God will take away his share of the tree of life and of the holy city, which are written about in this book.

²⁰Jesus is the One who says that these things are true. Now he says, "Yes, I am coming soon."

Amen. Come, Lord Jesus!

²¹The grace of the Lord Jesus be with all. Amen.

ⁿ**Alpha and the Omega** The first and last letters in the Greek alphabet. This means "the beginning and the end."

ⁿ**wash their robes** This means they believed in Jesus so that their sins could be forgiven by Christ's blood.

MEMORY VERSES

OLD TESTAMENT

Verse	Date Memorized	Verse	Date Memorized
Genesis 1:27, p. 3		Proverbs 3:5-6, p. 744	
Joshua 1:9, p. 257		Proverbs 12:1, p. 753	
1 Samuel 12:24, p. 338		Proverbs 13:1, p. 755	
1 Chronicles 16:29, p. 503		Proverbs 16:20, p. 760	
Job 36:26, p. 637		Proverbs 18:24, p. 763	
Psalm 1:6, p. 645		Proverbs 23:22, p. 769	
Psalm 23:1-3, p. 659		Isaiah 40:8, p. 844	
Psalm 27:1, p. 661		Isaiah 53:6, p. 854	
Psalm 40:8, p. 670		Micah 6:8, p. 1088	
Psalm 111:10, p. 719		Nahum 1:7, p. 1091	

NEW TESTAMENT

Verse	Date Memorized	Verse	Date Memorized
Matthew 6:24, p. 1134		Romans 12:10, p. 1391	
Matthew 6:33, p. 1135		1 Corinthians 6:19-20, p. 1402	
Matthew 7:7-8, p. 1135		1 Corinthians 10:13, p. 1406	
Matthew 7:24, p. 1136		Galatians 1:10, p. 1430	
Luke 1:37, p. 1219		Galatians 5:22-23, p. 1436	
John 1:1, p. 1272		Ephesians 2:8-9, p. 1440	
John 3:16, p. 1278		Ephesians 4:32, p. 1443	
John 14:6, p. 1302		Philippians 2:3-4, p. 1449	
Acts 1:8, p. 1315		Philippians 4:13, p. 1454	
Acts 5:29, p. 1324		Colossians 3:20, p. 1459	
Romans 3:23, p. 1376		Hebrews 11:1, p. 1497	
Romans 5:8, p. 1378		Hebrews 13:8, p. 1502	
Romans 6:23, p. 1381		James 4:7, p. 1509	
Romans 8:28, p. 1384		1 John 1:9, p. 1524	
Romans 12:1-2, p. 1391		1 John 4:7-8, p. 1527	

INDEX

709; Matthew 6:7, p. 1134; Matthew 26:36-41, p. 1174; Mark 1:35, p. 1182; Luke 6:27-28, p. 1230; Luke 11:5-13, p. 1242; Ephesians 6:18, p. 1447; Philippians 4:6, p. 1453; Revelation 5:8, p. 1540

13—The Bible

2 Chronicles 17:9, p. 535; 2 Chronicles 34:14-21, p. 558; Psalm 119:97-100, p. 725; Psalm 119:105, p. 726; Matthew 5:18, p. 1130; Luke 8:4-15, p. 1234; John 8:31-32, p. 1289; Acts 17:10-12, p. 1350; 2 Timothy 3:16-17, p. 1478; Hebrews 4:12-13, p. 1488

14—Staying Away from Selfishness

Genesis 25:29-34, p. 36; 2 Kings 5:20-27, p. 449; 2 Kings 7:3-9, p. 452; Proverbs 28:22, p. 775; Matthew 20:20-23, p. 1161; Mark 8:34-35, p. 1198; John 3:30, p. 1278; Acts 2:44-45, p. 1318; 1 Peter 1:22, p. 1514

15—Character

Genesis 6:9, p. 9; 1 Samuel 16:7, p. 344; 1 Chronicles 21:8, p. 507; Psalm 25:21, p. 660; Proverbs 17:17, p. 761; Matthew 5:48, p. 1133; Matthew 25:14-46, p. 1171; Romans 5:3-4, p. 1378; 1 Corinthians 13:2-7, p. 1411; Galatians 5:22-23, p. 1435

16—God's Children

Genesis 12:1-3, p. 16; Genesis 17:1-8, p. 23; Matthew 12:50, p. 1148; Luke 20:36, p. 1262; Ephesians 5:1, p. 1445; Philippians 2:15, p. 1451; Hebrews 12:7, p. 1500; 1 Peter 1:14, p. 1513; 1 John 3:1, p. 1525; 1 John 5:1, p. 1530

17—Witnessing

Exodus 4:10-13, p. 80; Joshua 22:34, p. 283; Proverbs 29:25, p. 776; Jeremiah 20:7-9, p. 909; Jonah 3:1-5, p. 1080; Matthew 5:14-15, p. 1129; Matthew 28:18-20, p. 1179; Mark 5:18-20, p. 1189; Acts 1:8, p. 1315; Acts 17:32-34, p. 1351

18—Thankfulness

1 Chronicles 16:8, p. 502; Psalm 100:4, p. 707; Psalm 106:1, p. 714; Psalm 107:8, p. 716; Daniel 6:10, p. 1038; Luke 17:11-19, p. 1256; 1 Corinthians 15:57, p. 1416; 2 Corinthians 9:11-12, p. 1424; Ephesians 1:16, p. 1438; 1 Thessalonians 5:18, p. 1464

19—Faith

Habakkuk 2:4, p. 1096; Luke 17:5-6, p. 1253; John 1:12, p. 1272; Romans 10:17, p. 1388; Galatians 2:16, p. 1431; Hebrews 6:12, p. 1490; Hebrews 11:1, p. 1498; Hebrews 11:32-34, p. 1499; James 2:26, p. 1508; 1 Peter 1:7, p. 1512

20—Growing

Deuteronomy 5:1, p. 221; Isaiah 27:2-6, p. 829; Hosea 14:9, p. 1061; Luke 2:51-52, p. 1223; Ephesians 4:15-16, p. 1443; Philippians 1:6, p. 1448; Colossians 2:6-7, p. 1456; 1 Timothy 4:6, p. 1470; 2 Timothy 2:15, p. 1477; 1 Peter 2:2, p. 1515

Strata-Flyer Reference Chains

1—Children Who Saw God at Work

Isaac (Genesis 22:2-13), p. 31; Joseph (Genesis 37:18-28), p. 54; Samuel (1 Samuel 3:1-10), p. 329; David (1 Samuel 17:1-50), p. 346; Naaman's Slave (2 Kings 5:1-5), p. 448; Joash (2 Chronicles 23:1-11), p. 542; Jairus's Daughter (Mark 5:35-43), p. 1191; The Boy in the Crowd (John 6:2-13), p. 1283; Eutychus (Acts 20:7-12), p. 1355

2—People Who Made Mistakes

Adam and Eve (Genesis 3), p. 4; Lot (Genesis 13), p. 17; Moses (Numbers 20:1-13), p. 194; King Saul (1 Samuel 28), p. 362; Peter (John 18:25-27), p. 1308; Ananias and Sapphira (Acts 5:1-11), p. 1323; Simon the Sorcerer (Acts 8:9-25), p. 1329; Demas (2 Timothy 4:10), p. 1479; Cain (1 John 3:12), p. 1526

3—Boats with Precious Cargo

Genesis 6:11-2210; Exodus 2:1-4, p. 75; Jonah 1, p. 1078; Matthew 8:23-27, p. 1139; Matthew 14:22-33, p. 1152; Mark 4:1, p. 1186; Luke 5:1-11, p. 1228; Acts 27:27-41, p. 1367

4—Plans That Backfired

Tower of Babel (Genesis 11:1-9), p. 15; Joseph's Brothers (Genesis 45), p. 65; King Balak and Balaam (Numbers 22), p. 197; Ahab (1 Kings 16:29—17:1), p. 427; Jezebel (1 Kings 21), p. 435; Haman (Esther 7), p. 600; Herod the

Great (Matthew 3), p. 1125; Judas (Mark 14), p. 1209; Herod Agrippa (Acts 12), p. 1337

5—Miracles from God

Judges 6:36-40, p. 297; 1 Kings 18:16-46, p. 430; 2 Kings 4:1-7, p. 444; Matthew 15:29-39, p. 1153; Mark 2:1-12, p. 1183; Mark 4:33-41, p. 1188; Luke 17:11-19, p. 1255; John 6:16-21, p. 1284; John 21:1-14, p. 1312; Acts 9:36-42, p. 1332

6—Amazing Events That Showed God's Power

Genesis 9:8-17, p. 12; Genesis 19:24-29, p. 27; Exodus 10:21-29, p. 88; Exodus 14:21-22, p. 93; Joshua 10:12-14, p. 267; 2 Kings 2:11, p. 442; 2 Kings 20:9-11, p. 472; Matthew 2:1-2, p. 1123; Mark 11:12-21, p. 1204; Acts 1:10-11, p. 1316

7—Heroes Who Trusted God

Abraham (Genesis 14:13-17), p. 19; Joshua (Joshua 1:6-11), p. 256; Rahab (Joshua 2:8-15), p. 258; Deborah (Judges 4:4-10), p. 291; Gideon (Judges 7:19-22), p. 298; Samson (Judges 16:23-30), p. 312; Jonathan (1 Samuel 14:1-23), p. 340; Abigail (1 Samuel 25:23-28), p. 359; Esther (Esther 4:15-16), p. 598; Mary (Luke 1:26-38), p. 1219

8—Animals in the Bible

Frogs (Exodus 8:1-15), p. 84; Eagles (Deuteronomy 32:11), p. 251; Sheep (Psalm 23)658; Donkeys (Psalm 32:9), p. 664; Badgers (Proverbs 30:24-26), p. 778; Camels (Zechariah 14:15), p. 1115; Birds (Matthew 6:26-27), p. 1135; Doves (Matthew 10:16), p. 1142; Snakes (Acts 28:1-6), p. 1369; Lions (Revelation 5:5), p. 1539

9—People Who Depended on God

Abraham (Genesis 13:14-18), p. 18; Caleb (Numbers 13:26-30), p. 185; Joshua (Joshua 3:5-17), p. 259; Hezekiah (2 Kings 19:14-19), p. 471; Zerubbabel (Ezra 6:15-18), p. 568; Nehemiah (Nehemiah 2:1-9), p. 577; Shadrach, Meshach, and Abednego (Daniel 3:16-27), p. 1032; Roman Officer (Matthew 8:8-12), p. 1138; A Sick Woman (Mark 5:25-34), p. 1190; Cornelius (Acts 10:1-8), p. 1334

10—Unsung Heroes

Ezra (Ezra 7:8-10), p. 570; Mordecai (Esther 2:5-7), p. 595; Baruch (Jeremiah 36), p. 933; Ebed-melech (Jeremiah 38:6-13)936; Joseph of Arimathea (Mark 15:42-46), p. 1214; Rhoda (Acts 12:13-14), p. 1339; Philippian Jailer (Acts 16:25-34), p. 1348; Paul's Nephew (Acts 23:12-22), p. 1361; Julius (Acts 27:42-44), p. 1368; James (James 1), p. 1504

11—Touring Bible Lands

Canaan (Genesis 15:18), p. 21; Egypt (Exodus 1:1), p. 74; Jerusalem (2 Samuel 5:6-7), p. 372; Ninevah (2 Kings 17:1-6), p. 466; Babylon (2 Kings 25:1-21), p. 480; Bethlehem (Micah 5:2), p. 1086; Lake Galilee (Mark 7:31), p. 1195; Antioch (Acts 11:26), p. 1336; The Mediterranean Sea (Acts 13:4), p. 1340; Rome (Acts 28:14), p. 1370

12—Visiting Angels

Genesis 16:7-10, p. 22; 1 Kings 19:5-7, p. 432; Daniel 6:22, p. 1039; Daniel 10:4-12, p. 1045; Matthew 1:20-21, p. 1122; Luke 1:5-19, p. 1217; Luke 2:9-14, p. 1221; Luke 24:4-8, p. 1270; Acts 12:7-10, p. 1338; Revelation 7:11-12, p. 1542

13—Words to Know: Old Testament

Well (Genesis 24:11), p. 33; Cloak (Genesis 37:3), p. 52; Walking Stick (Exodus 4:1-4), p. 79; Passover (Exodus 12:6-11), p. 89; Tent (Exodus 18:7), p. 99; Priest (Exodus 28:1), p. 110; Idol (Exodus 32:1-6), p. 117; Ark of the Agreement (Exodus 37:1), p. 125; Holy Tent (Exodus 40:34), p. 130; Temple (2 Chronicles 3:13-14), p. 521

14—Jobs in the Bible

Cup Bearer (Genesis 40:13), p. 58; Weaver (Exodus 28:31-39), p. 112; Craftsman (Exodus 31:1-11), p. 116; Shepherd (1 Samuel 16:11), p. 345; Musician (1 Chronicles 6:31-46), p. 489; Potter (Jeremiah 18:1-4), p. 907; Fisherman (Matthew 4:18), p. 1126; Tax Collector (Mark 2:13-17), p. 1184; Tanner (Acts 9:43), p. 1333; Tentmaker (Acts 18:3), p. 1352

15—Brothers and Sisters

Cain and Abel (Genesis 4:1-12), p. 8;

Esau and Jacob (Genesis 33), p. 48; Joseph and His Brothers (Genesis 37:4-20), p. 53; Nadab and Abihu (Leviticus 10), p. 141; Moses, Aaron, and Miriam (Numbers 12), p. 184; Adonijah and Solomon (1 Kings 1:5-30), p. 400; James and John (Mark 10:35-40), p. 1202; Peter and Andrew (John 1:41), p. 1273; Jesus and James (John 7:1-5), p. 1286; Mary, Martha, and Lazarus (John 11:1-6), p. 1294

16—People Who Got Away

Lot (Genesis 19:15-29), p. 26; Jacob (Genesis 27:41-44), p. 39; Moses (Exodus 2:11-15), p. 76; Ehud (Judges 3:15-26), p. 290; Jotham (Judges 9:1-21), p. 301; David (1 Samuel 19:13), p. 351; The Aramean Army (2 Kings 6:8-23), p. 450; Saul (Acts 9:20-25), p. 1331; Paul (2 Corinthians 11), p. 1426; Onesimus (Philemon 12), p. 1485

17—People Who Spoke God's Words

David (2 Samuel 22), p. 393; Elisha (2 Kings 2:9), p. 441; Isaiah (Isaiah 6:8), p. 807; Jeremiah (Lamentations 2:11), p. 964; Ezekiel (Ezekiel 3:10-11), p. 972; Daniel (Daniel 2:17-28), p. 1030; Haggai (Haggai 1:5), p. 1103; John the Baptist (Mark 1:4-8), p. 1180; John (Revelation 1:1-9), p. 1536

18—Women Who Trusted God

Rebekah (Genesis 24:15-21), p. 34; Deborah (Judges 5:31), p. 292; Naomi (Ruth 1:8), p. 320; Ruth (Ruth 2:11-12), p. 322; Hannah (1 Samuel 1:9-11), p. 325; Anna (Luke 2:36), p. 1222; Mary (John 12:1-3), p. 1297; Lydia (Acts 16:14), p. 1345; Phoebe (Romans 16:1), p. 1395; Lois and Eunice (2 Timothy 1:5), p. 1475

19—Words to Know: New Testament

Sabbath (Matthew 12:1-14), p. 1146; Sadducees (Matthew 22:23), p. 1165; Pharisees (Mark 7:1), p. 1194; Cross (Mark 15:21-24), p. 1213; Tomb (Mark 16:1-5), p. 1215; Parable (Luke 15:3-7), p. 1249; Leprosy (Luke 17:11-14), p. 1254; Disciple/Apostle (Acts 1:2), p. 1314; Synagogue (Acts 17:1-2), p. 1349; Roman Soldiers (Acts 22:22-29), p. 1360

20—Good Kings and Bad Kings

Saul (1 Samuel 15:17-26), p. 343; Solomon (1 Kings 11:1-13), p. 417; Rehoboam (1 Kings 12:1-17), p. 420; Jehoshaphat (2 Chronicles 19:1-3), p. 537; Hezekiah (2 Chronicles 31:20-21), p. 553; Manasseh (2 Chronicles 33:12-13), p. 556; David (Psalm 51), p. 676; Cyrus (Isaiah 44:28), p. 854; Nebuchadnezzar (Daniel 4:28-33), p. 1035; The Herod Family (Luke 23:6-12), p. 1267; Melchizedek (Hebrews 7:1), p. 1492

Whit's Wisdom Bible References

Theme	Reference	Page
Creation	Genesis 1 and 2	1
Complaining and Asking	Exodus 17	97
The Ten Commandments	Deuteronomy 5	223
Parents Need God	2 Kings 5	447
Patience and Suffering	Job 40-42	641
Wisdom	Proverbs 2	743
Responsibility	Jeremiah 1	
The Beatitudes	Matthew 5	
A Solid Foundation	Matthew 7:24-29	
Money and Possessions	Luke 18:18-27	
Eternal Life	John 3	
Singing to God	Acts 16:16-34	
The Body of Christ	1 Corinthians 12:12-27	
The Source of Faith	Colossians 2:6-7	
Growing in Faith	1 Timothy 4:12	
Living Your Faith	James 2	

DICTIONARY

A

Aaron (AIR-ohn) was the older brother of Moses. He often spoke for Moses. Only men from Aaron's family could be priests. (Exodus 4-40; Numbers 1-25)

Abba (AB-uh) was a child's word for "father" in the Aramaic language. Early Christians used this word in speaking to God. This shows how close we can feel to him. (Mark 14:36; Romans 8:15; Galatians 4:6)

Abib (ah-BEEB) means "young ears of grain." It is the first month of the Jewish calendar and about the same time of year as our March or April. It is also called Nisan. (Exodus 13:4; 34:18; Deuteronomy 16:1)

Abraham (AY-brah-ham) was the most respected man in the Jewish nation. The Jewish people called him "father Abraham." He was known for his great faith. (Genesis 12-25; John 8:39; Romans 4:1, 16; Hebrews 11:11-12)

Adam (AD-um) means "out of the earth." He was the first man God created. He was made from the dust of the ground. (Genesis 1-4; 1 Corinthians 15:45)

adultery (ah-DUL-ter-ee) is breaking a marriage promise by having sexual relations with someone other than your husband or wife. (Exodus 20:14; Mark 10:11, 12; John 8:3-5)

agreement (uh-GREE-ment) is a contract or promise. It is sometimes called a covenant. God made agreements with his people. One agreement was the "law of Moses." God has given a new agreement to his people through Christ in the New Testament. Hebrews 8-10 explains the differences between the two agreements. (Genesis 9:9-17; Hebrews 9:15-22)

Agrippa (uh-GRIP-pah) See "Herod Agrippa II."

alabaster (AL-a-bas-ter) is a light-colored stone with streaks or stripes through it. Perfume was often kept in beautiful containers made of alabaster. (Matthew 26:7; Luke 7:37)

alamoth (AL-a-moth) was probably a musical word. It may mean "like a flute" or "high-pitched." (Psalm 46)

aloes (AL-ohs) were oils from the sweet-smelling sap of certain trees. They were used for perfume, medicine and to prepare bodies for burial. (Numbers 24:6; John 19:39)

altar (ALL-ter) was a place where sacrifices, gifts or prayers were offered to God. Altars were sometimes made of dirt, grass or rocks piled up in the shape of a table on which the gift could be placed. (Genesis 8:20; 22:9; 1 Kings 18:30-35; Matthew 5:23-24; James 2:21)

amen (AY-MEN or AH-MEN) is a Hebrew word for "that is right." A person says "amen" to show he agrees with what has been said. (1 Chronicles 16:36; Nehemiah 5:13; 8:6; Psalm 106:48; 1 Corinthians 14:16; Revelation 7:11, 12)

Anak/Anakites (A-nak/AN-uh-kites) The Anakites were named for their ancestor Anak. They were a group of people who lived in Canaan when the Israelites arrived. They were known as large, mean, fighting people. (Numbers 13:22, 28, 33; Deuteronomy 1:28; 2:10-11; 9:2; Joshua 11:21-22)

Andrew (AN-droo) was a fisherman and the brother of the apostle Peter. Andrew was also one of the 12 apostles of Jesus. (Mark 1:16-18; 3:14-19; John 1:40-44; Acts 1:13)

angel (AIN-jel) is a Greek word that means "messenger." Angels are heavenly beings. They can sometimes look like people. God used angels to help his people and to announce important events. (Genesis 21:17; 22:11-15; Matthew 25:41; Luke 2:8-15; Hebrews 1:14; 12:22; 13:2; 2 Peter 2:4)

Annas (An-us) was a high priest of the Jews during Jesus' lifetime. He served as the high priest in Jerusalem from A.D. 7 to 14. (Luke 3:2; John 18:12-23; Acts 4:6) See also "priest."

apostle (uh-POS-'l) is a Greek word that means "someone who is sent off." Jesus gave the name to the 12 men he chose as his special followers. He sent them to tell the good news about him to the whole world. Later, after Judas killed himself, Matthias became an apostle. Paul was also called an apostle. (Matthew 10:1-4; Mark 3:14-19; Acts 1:2-26; 1 Corinthians 15:8-10)

Aquila (AK-wi-lah) was a Jewish Christian from the city of Rome. He and his wife Priscilla (or Prisca) worked as tentmakers and traveled with Paul. When they were at home in Rome or working in Ephesus, the Christians worshiped in their home. (Acts 18:2-3, 18, 26; Romans 16:3-5; 1 Corinthians 16:19)

Aramaic (AIR-uh-MAY-ik) was the language of the people in the nation of Aram. The Jewish people in the country of Palestine started speaking Aramaic when they were taken as slaves by the Babylonian people. Jesus probably spoke Aramaic. (2 Kings 18:26-28; John 19:20)

ark, Noah's In this Bible it is called Noah's boat. (Genesis 6:13, 14; 1 Peter 3:20)

Ark of the Covenant See "Box of the Agreement with the Lord."

Asherah (ah-SHIR-ah) was the name of a false goddess of the people of Canaan. She was thought to be the wife of the false god Baal. (Judges 3:7; 1 Kings 15:13; 2 Kings 21:7; 2 Chronicles 15:16)

Ashtoreth (ASH-toh-reth) was the name of a false goddess of the Canaanites. (Judges 2:13; 1 Samuel 7:3; 12:10; 1 Kings 11:5, 33)

Augustus Caesar (aw-GUS-tus SEE-zer) or Caesar Augustus was the first

Roman emperor. He was the ruler when Jesus was born. He was a nephew to the famous Julius Caesar. (Luke 2:1, 2)

B

Baal was a false god of the Canaanites. (1 Kings 18:17-40; Jeremiah 11:13)

Babylonians (bab-e-LONE-e-unz) were the people from Babylonia. This was a land east of Israel. Their largest city was Babylon. When Nebuchadnezzar was their king, they took many of the people of Judah to Babylonia as captives. The Babylonians were sometimes called Chaldeans. (2 Kings 25:4-26; 2 Chronicles 36; Daniel 1-4)

balm was an oil from a plant used as a medicine to comfort and heal sore skin. (Genesis 37:25; Jeremiah 51:8)

Baptist (BAP-tist) means "someone who baptizes." John, a relative of Jesus, was called this because he baptized many people. (Matthew 3:11)

baptize (BAP-tize) is from a Greek word that in New Testament times meant to dip or immerse. Baptism as practiced by Christians was in water. Baptism reminds us of Jesus' death, burial and rising to live again. It shows our death to sin and our being raised to new life with Christ. (Acts 2:38, 41; 8:36-39; 10:47; 16:15, 33; 18:8; Romans 6:3, 4)

Barabbas (bah-RAB-us) means "son of a father." He was a robber who had murdered someone in Jerusalem. He was in jail when Jesus was on trial. It was the time of year when a criminal would be freed from prison. The people cried out to have Barabbas freed and Jesus killed on the cross. Pilate, the Roman governor, did as they demanded. (Matthew 27:16-26; Mark 15:6-11)

Barnabas (BAR-nah-bus) means "one who encourages." The apostles gave this name to Joseph because he helped others. Barnabas, who was from Cyprus, often traveled with Paul to teach about Jesus. The journeys of Barnabas with Paul are told in Acts 13-15. (Acts 4:36-37; 11:22-26)

Bartholomew (bar-THOL-oh-mew) was one of the 12 apostles of Jesus. He may also have been called Nathanael. (Matthew 10:2-3; Luke 6:13-15; John 1:43-50)

beatitude (bee-A-ti-tyood) means "blessed" or "happy." This name is often used for Jesus' teaching in Matthew 5:3-12 and Luke 6:20-22. In these verses Jesus described a blessed or happy person.

Beelzebul (bee-EL-ze-bull), also spelled Beelzebub, came from the name Baal-Zebub. This was the name of the false god of the Philistines. In the New Testament, Beelzebul is a name sometimes used for the devil. (Matthew 12:24; Mark 3:22, 23)

Bel was a false god of the Babylonians. (Jeremiah 50:2)

believers (be-LEE-vers) is a word used in the New Testament to describe the followers of Jesus. (Acts 2:41-47; 5:14)

Bethlehem (BETH-le-hem) means "house of bread." It is a small town five miles from Jerusalem in the country of Judea. It was the hometown of King David in the Old Testament. Jesus was born there. (1 Samuel 16:4; Matthew 2:1; Luke 2:15-18)

Bible (BY-bul) means "the book." The Bible is a group of books and letters that Christians accept as the word of God. It is divided into two parts. The Old Testament contains 39 books, and the New Testament contains 27 books. See also "Scriptures."

blasphemy (BLAS-feh-mee) is saying things against God. Jesus was often accused of blasphemy because he said he was the Son of God. The people who accused him did not understand that he really was God's Son. (Matthew 9:3; 26:65; John 10:36)

blessing (BLES-ing) is a good gift from God to his people. (Luke 6:28; 24:50, 51; Acts 3:26; Hebrews 6:7; 1 Peter 3:9)

Box of the Agreement with the Lord *or* **Holy Box** is often called Ark of the Covenant. It was a special box made of acacia wood and gold. Gold creatures with wings covered the top. Inside were the stone tablets where the Ten Commandments were written. Later, a pot of manna and Aaron's walking stick were also put into the Box. It was to remind the people of Israel of God's promise to be with them. In this Bible it is also called the Holy Box or the Holy Box of God. (Exodus 25:10-22; 26:34; Joshua 3:1-17; 2 Chronicles 35:3; Hebrews 9:4)

bread that shows we are in God's presence is also called Bread of the Presence, or showbread. It was a group of 12 loaves of bread that were kept on the table in the Holy Tent and later in the Temple. This special bread reminded the people that they were always in God's presence. (Exodus 25:30; Leviticus 24:5-9; Luke 6:1-4)

C

Caesar (SEE-zer) was the name of a famous Roman family. In New Testament times it was used as the title of the Roman emperors. (Luke 2:1; 3:1; 20:22-25) See "Agustus Caesar."

Caiaphas (KAY-uh-fus) was the Jewish high priest from A.D. 18 to 36. He was one of those who planned to kill Jesus. (Matthew 26:57-68; John 11:49-53; 18:12-28)

calamus (KAH-lah-mus) is a sweet-tasting plant stalk probably like sugar cane. (Exodus 30:23; Jeremiah 6:20; Ezekiel 27:19)

capital is the top of a pillar. This top part of the pillar was usually decorated with beautiful carvings. (Amos 9:1; 1 Kings 7:16-20; 2 Kings 25:17)

cassia (CASH-ah) is a pleasant-smelling powder. Its odor is like that of the cinnamon plant. (Exodus 30:24; Psalm 45:8)

centurion (sin-TUR-ree-un) was a Roman army officer who commanded 100 soldiers. (Matthew 8:5; 7:12)

Cephas (SEE-fus) See "Peter."

chaff (CHAF) is the husk of a head of grain. Farmers must separate it from the good part of the grain. In Bible times they tossed the grain and chaff together into the air. Since the chaff is lighter, the wind blew it away and the good grain fell back to the threshing floor. (Job 21:18; Psalms 1:4; 35:5; Isaiah 29:5; 41:2) See "threshing floor."

chariot (CHAIR-e-ut) was a fast, two-wheeled cart usually pulled by two horses. It was used for battles, traveling and parades. (Genesis 46:29; Exodus 14:6; Acts 8:28-31)

Chemosh (KEE-mosh) was the name of a false god of the Moabites. (Numbers 21:29; Jeremiah 48:46)

Christ (KRYST) means "anointed (or chosen) one" in Greek. In Hebrew the word is "Messiah." Jesus is the Christ. He was chosen by God to save people from their sins. (Mark 8:29; 14:61-62; Luke 23:2; Acts 2:36; 17:3; 18:28)

Christian (KRIS-chun) means "belonging to Christ." Christ's followers are called Christians. (Acts 11:26; 26:28; 1 Peter 4:16)

church in the New Testament means a group of Christians. In those times the church often met in someone's home. (Matthew 16:18; Acts 2:47; 14:27; Romans 16:5)

circumcision (SIR-kum-SIH-zhun) This means to cut off the foreskin of the male sex organ. Each Jewish baby boy was circumcised on the eighth day after he was born. This act was done as a sign of the agreement God had made with his people, the Jews. Because of this, the Jewish people sometimes are called "the circumcision" and non-Jews are called "the uncircumcision." (Leviticus 12:3; John 7:22; Acts 7:8)

clean is used to describe the state of a person, animal or action that is pleasing to God. God called some animals clean and said they could be eaten. People who had not touched or eaten anything God said was unclean were called clean. Or, if they did not have a disease that made them unclean, they were called clean. They could live and serve God normally. (Genesis 7:2; Leviticus 20:25; Deuteronomy 14:3-20) See "unclean."

Cleansing, Day of is also called the Day of Atonement. It was the most special day of the year for the Israelites. No one worked or ate on that day. This was the one day of the year when the high priest could go into the Most Holy Place. Animals were sacrificed for the sins of the people. This was a sign to the people that they were cleansed from their sins for a year. Jews still celebrate this day today. It is called Yom Kippur. (Leviticus 16:1-34; 25:9)

confess (kun-FES) means to admit that something is true. The New Testament teaches a believer to confess that Jesus is the Son of God. Christians are also told to confess their sins, to admit that they have done wrong. (Romans 10:9, 10; Philippians 2:11; 1 John 1:9)

coral (KOR-al) is a type of limestone that forms in the ocean. Coral is usually a rich red or deep pink color. It is used to make jewelry. (Job 28:18; Ezekiel 27:16)

cornerstone This was the most important stone at a corner in the base of a building. The cornerstone had to be perfect so the building's walls would be straight. The other stones were fitted against the cornerstone. Jesus is called the cornerstone of the new law. (Joshua 6:26; Job 38:6; Ephesians 2:20)

council (KOWN-s'l), or meeting, was the highest Jewish court in the days of Jesus. Its proper name was the "Sanhedrin." The men of the council sat in a half circle to hear the people who came to speak to them. The trials of Jesus and Stephen were held in front of this council. (Matthew 26:57-68; Acts 6:13-15)

covenant (KUV-eh-nant) See "agreement."

cross refers to a cruel way of killing criminals in New Testament times. The person was tied or nailed to two rough beams of wood nailed together in the shape of an "x" or a "t." Then, he was left hanging in a public place to die. Jesus was killed by the Roman soldiers this way. In the New Testament the word "cross" is often used to remind us that Christ's death on the cross was God's way of saving us from our sins. (John 19:17-31; 1 Corinthians 1:18-25; Galatians 6:12; Ephesians 2:15-16)

cud An animal that chews the cud chews its food and swallows it. Then it chews it a second time. (Leviticus 11:3)

D

Dagon (DAY-gon) was one of the false gods of the Philistines. (Judges 16:23; 1 Samuel 5:2-7; 1 Chronicles 10:10)

Daniel (DAN-yel) was a Hebrew captive taken to Babylon as a young man. He told Nebuchadnezzar what his dream meant. God also made him able to tell Belshazzar what the strange handwriting on the wall meant. When he was about 80 years old, Daniel was put in the lions' den by King Darius. But God saved him. (Daniel 1-6)

David (DAY-vid) was Israel's greatest king. Jesus is called the "Son of David" because he was born to members of David's family. (1 Samuel 1:16-31; Luke 1:69; 2:4; 18:38; Acts 2:29-31; 13:22)

deacon (DEE-kun) is a Greek word meaning "servant." Deacons are people chosen to serve the church in special ways. The men named in Acts 6:1-6 may have been the first deacons. Deacons are described in 1 Timothy 3:8-13.

Dead Sea is a large lake at the south end of the Jordan River. The Jordan and several small streams flow into it. But it has no outlet. And it is so salty that nothing lives in it. It is about 50 miles long and 10 miles wide. In Bible days it was often called the Salt Sea, the Eastern Sea or the Sea of the Arabah. (Genesis 14:3; Numbers 34:3-12; Joshua 3:16)

demon (DEE-mun) was an evil spirit from the devil. Sometimes a demon lived in a person. But Jesus has more power than demons and could make them come out of people. (Deuteronomy 32:17; Psalm 106:37; Matthew 12:22; Luke 8:26-39)

descendants (de-SIN-dants) are family members who are born to a person and his children. They would include grandchildren, great-grandchildren, great-great-grandchildren and so on. (Genesis 12:7; Leviticus 21:21; Romans 4:18)

devil (DEV-'l) means "one who accuses." In the New Testament, the devil is often called Satan or Beelzebul. He is a spirit and the enemy of God and man. (Matthew 4:1-11; John 13:2; Ephesians 4:27; 6:10-17) See "Beelzebul."

disciple (dih-SYE-p'l) See "follower."

E

Edom (E-dum) means "red." Edom was also called Esau, the older son of Isaac. The land where Esau's descendants lived was named Edom. It was south of the Dead Sea. Seir is another name for the land of Edom. (Genesis 25:30; 36:8; 2 Samuel 8:14; Psalm 137:7; Ezekiel 25:12-14; Obadiah 10-14)

elder (EL-der) means "older." In the Old Testament this Bible uses elders, older leaders, to describe a special group of men who led God's people. In the New Testament elders are appointed leaders in the church. (Numbers 11:16; Acts 20:17-38; 1 Timothy 3:1-7; 1 Peter 5:1-4)

Elijah (e-LIE-juh) was a man who spoke for God in the Old Testament. He was a prophet about 800 years before Jesus was born. (1 Kings 17-21; 2 Kings 1-2; Matthew 16:14; 17:3-4; 27:47; Luke 1:17; James 5:17)

ephod (EF-ahd) See "vest, holy."

epistle (e-PIS-'l) is a Greek word meaning "letter." Many books of the New Testament were actually letters written to Christians in various cities. Some of these letters are Ephesians, Galatians, Romans, 1 and 2 Corinthians, Philippians and Colossians. (Colossians 4:16; 1 Thessalonians 5:27; 2 Thessalonians 3:17; 2 Peter 3:16)

Esau (E-saw) See "Edom."

eternal life (e-TER-nul LIFE) is the new kind of life promised to those who follow Jesus. It is living with a new help from God. It is also life that will never end. (John 3:16; 4:14; Galatians 2:20; 1 John 5:11-15)

eunuch (YOU-nuk) is a man who cannot have sexual relations. In the Bible eunuchs were often high officers in royal palaces or armies. (2 Kings 9:32; Esther 2:3; Isaiah 56:3-5; Acts 8:26-40)

Eutychus (YOU-ti-cus) means "lucky." Eutychus was a young man in the city of Troas. As he was sitting in an upstairs window listening to Paul preach, he went to sleep. He fell out of the window and died. But Paul, by God's power, brought him back to life. (Acts 20:7-12)

Ezra (EZ-ra) was the leader of a group of Israelites who were allowed to return to Jerusalem from Babylon. He taught them to worship and serve God correctly. (Ezra 7-10; Nehemiah 8-9)

F

faith (FAYTH) is belief and trust. People who have great faith in God do what he says to do, even when they do not understand why. They do it because they believe in him and trust him. Faith in Jesus means believing he is the Son of God and trusting in him. (2 Chronicles 20:20; Isaiah 7:9; Habakkuk 2:4; Matthew 8:10; Luke 8:24, 25; Romans 4:16-22; 5:1,2; Ephesians 4:13; Hebrews 11)

fasting (FAST-ing) means giving up food for a while. People sometimes fast during a special time of prayer and worship to God. Jesus fasted for 40 days before he began preaching. It was also done to show sadness. (2 Samuel 12:16-22; Ezra 8:23; Matthew 4:1-11; 6:16-18; 9:14-15; Acts 12:2-3; 14:23)

feast (FEEST) is a special meal and celebration for a certain purpose. There were many different feasts in Bible times.

Feast of Dedication was an eight-day celebration for the Jewish people. It was a way of being thankful that the Temple had been cleansed again. This was done in 164 B.C. after the Greeks had spoiled and ruined it. Today the celebration is called Hanukkah. (John 10:22)

Feast of Harvest See "Feast of Weeks."

Feast of Shelters is also called the Feast of Booths or Feast of Tabernacles. The people gathered fruit and lived in tentlike shelters for a week. This feast reminded them of how God had taken care of them when the Israelites left Egypt and lived in tents in the wilderness. (Exodus 23:14-17; Deuteronomy 16:13-17)

Feast of Unleavened Bread was also called Passover. It was held to remember how God helped the Israelites in Egypt. He saved them from the one that brings death that passed over their families. And God led them out of slavery. For seven days they ate bread made without yeast and did only certain types of work. (Exodus 12:14-20; Numbers 28:16-25; Deuteronomy 16:1-8) See "Passover Feast."

Feast of Weeks was also called Pentecost, the Feast of Harvest and the Day of Firstfruits. It was held seven weeks and one day after Passover. This was a feast of thanksgiving for the summer harvest. (Exodus 34:22; Leviticus 23:15-22; Numbers 28:26-31; Deuteronomy 16:9-12; Acts 2) See "Pentecost."

Felix (FEE-lix) was the Roman governor of Judea from A.D. 52 to 54. He was a cruel ruler. He kept the apostle Paul in prison for two years to please the Jews who hated Jesus and Paul. His full name was Marcus Antonius Felix. (Acts 23:24-24:27)

fellowship (FEL-o-ship) is sharing friendship and love with others. Christians have a very special fellowship with God and his people. (Acts 2:42; 1 John 1:3-7)

Festus (FES-tus) was the governor of Judea after Felix. His full name was Porcius (POR-shus) Festus. He allowed Paul to go to Rome to be tried by Caesar. (Acts 24:27-25:27; 26:24-32)

firstborn (FIRST-born) is the oldest child in a family. The son born first to a Jewish family received a double share of his father's wealth. Then he became the leader of the family when his father died. The Israelite people were called God's firstborn because he gave them special privileges. Jesus was also called God's firstborn son. He is now ruling over all creation. (Genesis 35:23; Exodus 4:22; Psalm 89:27; Romans 8:29; Colossians 1:18; Hebrews 1:6)

firstfruits (FIRST-fruits) were the first and best crops and animals the Israelites raised. They were to give these to God. This showed that they knew everything really belonged to God. (Exodus 34:22-26; Leviticus 23:9-21; Numbers 28:26; Deuteronomy 18:4)

flax (FLAKS) is a plant used to make clothing and ropes. The inside of the plant was combed and spun into thread. Then it was woven into cloth. (Exodus 9:31; Joshua 2:6; Proverbs 31:13; Isaiah 19:9)

follower (FAHL-o-wer) is a person who is learning from someone. Jesus' followers are those who believe and obey his teaching. Another word for "follower" is "disciple." During his ministry, Jesus chose 12 special followers and made them his apostles. (Matthew 15:32-39; John 19:38; Acts 6:1-7; 11:26)

forgiveness (for-GIV-ness) means to be pardoned and not punished for a wrong thing done. A sinner who is sorry for his sin and stops doing that sin will be forgiven when he comes to God. That person will not be punished. Christians are also to forgive others for wrong things done to them. (Genesis 50:17; Psalms 19:12; 32:1-5; 51:1-17; Matthew 6:12-15; 9:2-8; 18:21, 22; Acts 8:22; Romans 4:7; 1 John 1:9)

frankincense (FRANK-in-senz) is a very expensive, sweet-smelling perfume. It comes from inside the terebinth tree that grows in the country of Arabia. Some wise men gave frankincense to Jesus when he was born. (Exodus 30:34; Matthew 2:11; Revelation 18:13)

G

Gabriel (GAY-bree-el) is God's angel who announced that John the Baptist and Jesus would be born. (Luke 1:11-20, 26-35)

Galilee (GAL-i-lee) was the country between the Jordan River and the Mediterranean Sea. It had lots of water and trees, and the land was good for growing grains like wheat and barley. Jesus grew up in the city of Nazareth in Galilee and, so, was often called "the Galilean." (Matthew 4:23-25; 21:11; John 2:1-2; 7:1, 9, 41)

Galilee, Lake (GAL-i-lee) is also called the "Sea of Galilee." It is really a lake 13 miles long and about 8 miles wide. Storms often come up very quickly on this lake. Jesus spent much time around Lake Galilee. (Matthew 4:18-22; 8:23-27; 14:22-36; John 6:1-2, 16-21)

gazelle (gah-ZEL) is an animal of the antelope family. It is known for its beauty and speed. It is usually about two feet tall and three feet long. (Deuteronomy 12:15, 22; 2 Samuel 2:18; Proverbs 6:5)

Gentiles (JEN-tiles) means "nations." The Jewish people called anyone who was not Jewish a Gentile. They thought all non-Jewish people were enemies. The Good News of Jesus is for all people, both Jewish and non-Jewish people. (Acts 10:44-48; 11:18; 13:46-48; Romans 1:5; 11:11-13; Ephesians 3:6-8)

Gethsemane (geth-SEM-uh-nee) was a garden of olive trees just outside Jerusalem. It was at the bottom of the Mount of Olives. The night before Jesus was killed, he prayed in this garden. Jesus was there when Judas brought the soldiers to arrest him. (Matthew 26:36-50; Mark 14:32)

gittith (GIT-tith) is probably a musical word and may be a kind of musical instrument. (Psalms 8; 81; 84)

God is the One who made the world and everything in it. He is a spirit and does not have a body as man does. But people can know what God is like because he sent Jesus into the world to show them. God hates evil, but he loves his people so much that he let his Son die for them. God is the wisest and most powerful being in the universe. He has always been alive, and he will always be alive. He is love.

Christians are called "children of God" because they have been given a spirit like God. (Genesis 1:1; Psalm 139:7-12; Isaiah 44:6; Matthew 5:9; John 4:24; 14:9; Romans 1:18; 5:8-11; 8:16; 11:36; Hebrews 1:1-4; 1 John 4:7-12)

Golgotha (GOL-guh-thuh) is an Aramaic word meaning "skull." The Latin word for it is "Calvary." This is the hill where Jesus was killed on the cross by the Roman soldiers. It may have been called "the place of the skull" because many people died there. Or it may have been called that because the hill looks like a giant skull. (Matthew 27:32-35; Mark 15:22-24; John 19:17, 18)

Good News is also called the gospel. In the New Testament, the Good News is that Jesus died for us on the cross, was buried in a tomb and came back to life. Because he did these things for us, we can be saved. That is good news. (Mark 1:1; Acts 20:24; Colossians 1:21-23; 2 Timothy 1:10) See "gospel."

gospel (GOS-p'l) means "good news." It refers to Jesus' life, death and rising to live again. The first four books of the New Testament are called the gospels because they tell the good news of what Jesus has done for us. (Philippians 1:5, 7, 12; 2 Thessalonians 1:8) See "Good News."

grace is God's kindness and love shown to us, even though we do not deserve them. Part of God's grace is his forgiveness. He forgives us for the wrong things we do. He even let Jesus take the punishment for our sins. (John 1:14; Acts 15:11; Romans 5:1, 2, 8; 1 Corinthians 15:10; 2 Corinthians 6:1, 2; Ephesians 2:4, 5, 8; Titus 3:3-7; Hebrews 4:16)

Greek is the language of the people of Greece. The New Testament was first written in the Greek language. Also, a person from the country of Greece is called a Greek. (John 19:20; Acts 14:1; 16:1, 3; 21:37; Colossians 3:11)

H

Hades (HAY-deez) is where the dead,

both good and bad, are. (Acts 2:27, 31; Revelation 1:18)

heart in the Bible usually means the mind or feelings. It is not talking about the physical heart that pumps blood through the body. (Deuteronomy 30:10-17; Psalm 26:2; Proverbs 15:13-16; Mark 12:30; Luke 2:19; 6:45; 12:34; Acts 2:46)

heaven (HEV-'n) is the home of God. In the New Testament it is said to be a place where there is no pain, no crying, no sadness, no night and no death. Jesus showed us his love by leaving heaven and coming to earth to die on a cross. God's people will live in heaven with him forever. (John 3:13; 6:38-40; Acts 7:56; 2 Corinthians 5:1-10; 1 Peter 1:4; Revelation 21:4)

Hebrews (HEE-brooz) is another name for the Jewish people. The book of Hebrews is a letter written to Jewish Christians. (2 Corinthians 11:22; Philippians 3:5; Hebrews)

heir (AIR) is the person who is supposed to inherit what belongs to a relative. The heir usually receives these things when the relative dies. Because through Christ we can be adopted children of God, Christians are heirs of God's riches. (Genesis 15:3-4; 2 Samuel 14:7; Galatians 4:1)

hell is the home of the devil. It is the place of punishment forever for those who turn against God. Hell is described in the New Testament as a place of fire, pain, sorrow and sadness. (Matthew 23:33; 25:41; 2 Peter 2:4, 9; Revelation 20:14, 15; 21:8)

Herod (HEH-rud) was the name of four different rulers in the New Testament: **Herod I** (Herod the Great) was king of the country of Palestine from the year 40 B.C. until about 4 B.C. He tried to kill the baby Jesus because Jesus was called a "king." Herod thought Jesus was an earthly king and would take away his throne. (Matthew 2:1-16; Luke 1:5)

Herod Antipas was the son of Herod I. He had John the Baptist's head cut off. Later, Jesus was sent to this man for trial. He ruled from the year 4 B.C. to about A.D. 39. (Matthew 14:1; Mark 6:14; Luke 23:6)

Herod Agrippa I was the king of Palestine for about three years (A.D. 41-44). He was the grandson of Herod I. He had the apostle James killed and the apostle Peter arrested. He did it to please the Jews who hated Jesus' followers. Later, this man was eaten by worms and died because he let the people treat him like a god. (Acts 12:1-21)

Herod Agrippa II was king of Palestine from the year A.D. 48 to 93. He was the great-grandson to Herod I. He heard the apostle Paul speak. He sent Paul to Caesar for trial. (Acts 25;13, 26; 26:1-32)

higgaion (hig-GI-on) is probably a musical word. It seems to mean "to meditate." So it may mean a time to think quietly during a song. (Psalm 9:16)

high priest was the most important religious leader of the Jewish people. He was often as important as the king. Caiaphas was the high priest when Jesus was killed. Annas was another high priest at that time. (Matthew 26:3, 57; Acts 23:2-5)

holy (HO-lee) means pure, belong to and willing to serve God. God's people are called "holy people." (Exodus 3:5; 22:31; 31:13; 1 Corinthians 1:2; Ephesians 1:4; Philemon 4; 1 Peter 1:15, 16)

Holy Place This was a room in the Holy Tent and the Temple. The priests came to this room every day to burn candles and incense to the Lord. Each week fresh loaves of bread were placed on the table there. A curtain separated the Holy Place from the Most Holy Place. (Exodus 26:31-35; 31:11; Leviticus 6:30) See "bread that shows we are in God's presence."

Holy Spirit (HO-lee SPIH-rit) is one of the three persons of God. The other two persons are God the Father and God the Son (Jesus). The Holy Spirit helped the apostles do miracles. He

led men to write God's word. The Holy Spirit lives in Christians today. He is also called the Spirit of Christ, the Spirit of God, and the Comforter. (Genesis 1:2; John 3:5-8; 16:13; Acts 2:1-4; 5:32; Romans 5:5; 8:9-16; 2 Peter 1:20-21)

Holy Tent See "Meeting Tent."

hypocrite (HIP-oh-krit) comes from the word for an actor on a stage. In the Bible it is a person who acts as if he is good but isn't. (Matthew 6:2, 5, 16; 7:3-5; Luke 13:15-17)

I

idol (EYE-d'l) is a false god. The non-Jewish people often worshiped statues they made from wood, stone or metal. They worshiped these idols instead of the true God of heaven. (Leviticus 19:4; 2 Kings 17:12-17; Acts 7:40-43; 17:16-23; 1 Thessalonians 1:9)

incense (IN-senz) was a spice burned to make a sweet smell. This was done by the priests in the Meeting Tent and the Temple. A special altar was used to burn incense as worship to God. Since the smoke seemed to go up to God, this reminded people of prayer. (Exodus 30:1-10, 34-38; Psalm 141:2; Luke 1:9; Revelation 8:3-4)

Isaac (EYE-zak) means "laughter." He was the son of Abraham and Sarah. He was named Isaac because Sarah laughed when the angel told her she would have a baby. She thought she was too old. God tested Abraham by asking him to offer Isaac as a sacrifice on an altar. When God saw that Abraham would obey him, he saved Isaac's life. (Genesis 21-26; Mark 12:26; Hebrews 11:17-20)

Isaiah (i-ZAY-uh) was one of the great prophets of the Old Testament. He often gave God's message to King Hezekiah. (2 Kings 19-20; Isaiah 6-9; 53)

Israel (IZ-rah-el) is a Hebrew word that means "he who wrestles with God." When Jacob struggled with an angel at Bethel, God named him Israel. The 12 tribes of the Jewish nation were descendants of Jacob. They were called Israelites. (Exodus 3:16-18; Psalm 73:1; Luke 1:68; Acts 2:36; 5:33-36)

J

Jacob (JAY-cub) was one of the sons of Isaac. He was the father of the 12 tribes of God's chosen people. He had 12 sons, and each son was the head of a tribe. (Genesis 25-36; Matthew 1:2; 8:11; John 4:6)

Jacob's Portion (JAY-cubs POR-shun) is a name for God. It means that God cares for Jacob's people, the Israelites. (Jeremiah 10:16; 51:19)

James was the name of several men in the New Testament:

James, the son of Zebedee, was an apostle of Jesus and a brother of the apostle John. He was killed by Herod Agrippa I. (Matthew 10:2; Mark 10:35, 41; Acts 12:2)

James, the son of Alphaeus, was also one of Jesus' apostles. He may have been a cousin to Jesus. (Matthew 10:3)

James, the brother of Jesus, was a respected leader in the church in Jerusalem. He probably wrote the book of James in the New Testament. (Matthew 13:55; John 7:5; Acts 12:17; 21:18; Galatians 1:19)

Jeremiah (jer-eh-MY-ah) was a prophet who warned the people of Judah. He told them they were disobeying God and would be punished. He had a very difficult life, but he stayed faithful to God. He lived to see Jerusalem destroyed and the people taken to Babylon. (2 Chronicles 35:25; 36:21-22; Jeremiah 1-2; 20:1-6; 28:5; 36-40)

Jericho (JEHR-ih-ko) is the oldest city in the world. God caused the walls of Jericho to fall down when the Israelites did what God told them. This was their first victory in the promised land. Jericho was rebuilt and destroyed several times. In New Testament times Herod rebuilt it a mile away from where it had been. Here Jesus healed blind Bartimaeus and met Zacchaeus. Jericho is called "the city of palm

trees" because a spring there makes it an oasis in the desert. (Joshua 2; 6; 1 Kings 16:34; Nehemiah 3:2; Mark 10:46-52; Luke 19:1-10)

Jerusalem (jeh-ROO-suh-lem) is sometimes called "Zion" or the "City of David." It was the greatest city of the country of Palestine. It was the center of the Jewish religion because the Temple was there. Jesus was killed on the cross near Jerusalem. The city was destroyed by the Roman army in the year A.D. 70. Later, it was rebuilt in the same place by the Moslems and is a great city today in the Middle East. (2 Samuel 5:5-6; 2 Chronicles 36:14, 19; Ezra 1:1-11; Luke 2:22-45; 13:34; 24:13, 18, 33, 47, 49; Acts 2:5, 14) See "Zion."

Jesus (JEE-zus) means "savior." He is the Son of God. He was born to Mary, a young Jewish woman. Mary was told by the angel Gabriel that she would have a baby boy. She was to name him "Jesus" because he would save his people from their sins. He is also called "Christ" and "Messiah." He lived a perfect life and never sinned. But he was killed by Roman soldiers on a cross near Jerusalem. Then, he came back to life and now lives in heaven with his father, God. He is one of the three persons of God. The other two persons are God the Father and God the Holy Spirit. (Matthew 1:21; Luke 2:21; 3:23; John 20:19; Acts 1:19, 36; 4:10; Philippians 2:10-11) See "Christ" and "Messiah."

Jesus was a common name among the Jewish people, so there were other less important men in the New Testament named Jesus, too. (Colossians 4:11)

Jew (JOO) at first means someone from the tribe of Judah. Judah was one of Jacob's 12 sons and the head of one of the 12 tribes of Israel. Later, the word meant any person in any of the 12 tribes (Hebrews 1-13). A person who is not Jewish is called a Gentile or non-Jew. Jesus was Jewish. (Ezra 4:12; Matthew 2:2; 28:11-15; Acts 2:5; Romans 1:16; 10:12)

John was the name of several men in the New Testament:

John, the apostle, was one of the sons of Zebedee. He and his brother James were fishermen. He wrote the Gospel of John, the books of 1, 2 and 3 John and probably Revelation. He is sometimes referred to as "the one Jesus loved." John, Peter and James were Jesus' closest friends. (Mark 1:19-20; 9:2; 14:33-34; Acts 3:1-11; Revelation 1:1-4, 9)

John the Baptist was Jesus' relative and the son of Elizabeth and Zechariah the priest. He lived in the desert and ate locusts and wild honey. He preached that the Savior, Jesus, was coming soon. Jesus came to John the Baptist to be baptized in the Jordan River. Herod Antipas had John killed by cutting off his head. (Matthew 3:1-17; 11:11-13; 14:3-12; Luke 1:13-17)

John Mark See Mark.

Jordan (JOR-d'n) is the only large river in the country of Palestine. It runs about 75 miles from Mount Hermon to the Dead Sea. It also makes two lakes—Lake Huleh and Lake Galilee. Jesus was baptized in the Jordan River near the city of Jericho. (Joshua 3:11-17; 2 Kings 5:10, 14; Matthew 3:5-17)

Joseph was the name of several men in the Bible.

Joseph, the son of Jacob, was one of the 12 sons of Israel. His jealous brothers sold him into slavery in Egypt. He became a great leader. When his brothers came to Egypt for food, he forgave them. Later he brought them, their families, and his father to Egypt. His two sons, Ephraim and Manasseh, each started a tribe. (Genesis 37-50; Exodus 1:5-8; 13:19; Acts 7:10-14)

Joseph of Nazareth was the husband of Mary, Jesus' mother. He was a carpenter. He may have died when Jesus was a young man because he is not mentioned after Jesus' childhood. The New Testament says he was "a good man." (Matthew 1:18-24; 2:13-23)

Joseph of Arimathea took the body of Jesus down from the cross and buried it in a tomb he had dug for himself. He was a member of the Jewish religious court called the Sanhedrin. He was probably a Christian. (Matthew 27:57-60; Mark 15:43-46)

Jubilee (JOO-bih-lee) was a Jewish celebration that took place every fifty years. Israelites were to do three things: (1) give the soil a rest and not farm, (2) free Israelite slaves and (3) return land and houses to the first owners or their children. (Leviticus 25)

Judas Iscariot (JOO-dus is-CARE-ee-ut) was the apostle who turned against Jesus and handed him over to the Roman soldiers to be killed. For this he was paid only 30 pieces of silver, the price of a slave. Later, Judas killed himself. (Matthew 26:47-50; 27:3-5; John 13:26-30)

Jude (JOOD) was possibly a brother of Jesus and James. In Jesus' early ministry, Jude did not believe Jesus was the Son of God. Later, he believed and became a leader in Christ's church. He wrote the book of Jude in the New Testament. (John 7:5; Jude)

Judea (joo-DEE-uh) was the land of the Jewish people. It was a district in the country of Palestine. Both Jerusalem and Bethlehem were cities in Judea. John the Baptist began his preaching in the desert of Judea. (Matthew 2:1; Luke 1:5; 2:4; Acts 1:8)

judges (JUJ-es) were the leaders of Israel before Israel had kings. A judge decided who was guilty in court, led the army in battle and was in charge of the government, like a governor. Israel had 15 judges in all. (Judges 2:16-19; 1 Samuel 7:15-17)

Judgment Day (JUJ-ment DAY) is the day Christ will judge all people. He will take his followers to live with him forever in heaven. Those who have followed the devil will be sent to live with him in hell forever. (Matthew 11:20-24; Hebrews 9:27, 28; 2 Peter 2:9, 10; 3:7)

L

lamb (LAM) is an animal that the Jews often offered as a sacrifice (gift) to God. Since Jesus died as a sacrifice for us, he is called the Lamb of God that takes away the sins of the world. (Genesis 4:4; 22:7; Exodus 12:3-13; John 1:29, 36; 1 Corinthians 5:7)

Lazarus (LAZ-uh-rus) was the name of two men in the New Testament: **Lazarus of Bethany** was a brother to Mary and Martha. He was also a very dear friend of Jesus. When he died, Jesus brought him back to life. (John 11:1-45; 12:1-11)
Lazarus, the beggar, was the name of a person in a story Jesus told his followers. (Luke 16:19-31)

leprosy (LEH-prah-see) is a name for some bad skin diseases. A person with leprosy was called a leper and had to live outside the city. When people came by, the lepers had to warn them by crying out, "Unclean! Unclean!" (Leviticus 13:45-46; 2 Kings 5:1-27; 2 Chronicles 26:19-23; Matthew 8:1-3; Luke 17:11-19)

Leviathan (lee-VI-ah-than) was the name for a sea monster. Some people think it was a crocodile. (Job 3:8; 41:1; Psalm 74:14; Isaiah 27:1)

Levites (LEE-vites) were descendants of Levi, one of Jacob's sons. The priests all came from this tribe. But not all Levites were priests. Those who were not priests worked in the Meeting Tent or Temple in other ways. (Exodus 32:25-29; Numbers 1:47-53; 8:5-26; Deuteronomy 10:8-9; 18:1-8; 1 Kings 12:31; Luke 10:32)

lid on the Holy Box is also called the mercy seat. This was the beautiful gold lid on the Box of the Agreement. It had a gold creature with wings on each end of it. This Holy Box was kept in the Most Holy Place of the Meeting Tent and later in the Temple. (Exodus 25:17-22; 26:34; Leviticus 16:2, 14-16; Hebrews 9:5)

locust (LO-cust) is an insect that looks like a grasshopper. Locusts travel in large groups. They eat crops and other green plants. Locusts were sometimes eaten as food. (Exodus 10:4-19; Deuteronomy 28:38-42; Joel 1:4; Matthew 3:4)

lord means "master" or one who is in control. Jesus is called Lord because he rules over all the world and universe. Christians let Jesus be the Lord of their lives. (Acts 2:36; 21:12-14; Romans 10:9; 1 Corinthians 6:11; Colossians 3:17-24)

Lord's Prayer is the name often given to the model prayer Jesus taught his followers. (Matthew 6:9-13; Luke 11:1-4)

Lord's Supper is the meal Jesus' followers eat to remember how he died for them. The bread reminds us of his body. The fruit of the vine reminds us of his blood. The Lord's Supper also shows that Jesus came back to life and now lives in heaven with God. (Matthew 26:26-30; Luke 22:14-20; 1 Corinthians 10:17; 11:23-32)

lots were sticks, stones or pieces of bone thrown like dice to decide something. Often God controlled the result of the lots to let the people know what he wanted them to do. (Numbers 26:55-56; Proverbs 18:18; Jonah 1:7; Luke 1:9; 23:34; Acts 1:26)

Luke was a non-Jewish doctor who often traveled with the apostle Paul. He was a very educated man. He wrote the books of Luke and Acts in the New Testament. Luke tells many acts of Jesus that are not told in the other three gospels. (Colossians 4:14; 2 Timothy 4:11)

lyre (LIRE) is a musical instrument with strings. It is similar to a harp, but smaller. (2 Samuel 6:5; 1 Chronicles 15:16-28; Psalms 33:2; 144:9; 150:3)

M

mahalath (mah-HAY-lath), or mahalath leannoth, was probably a musical word. It may have been the name of a tune, or it may mean to dance and shout. (Psalms 53; 88).

manna (MAN-ah) means "what is it?" It was the white, sweet-tasting food God gave the people of Israel in the wilderness. It appeared on the ground during the night so they could gather it in the morning. (Exodus 16:13-35; Numbers 11:7-9; Joshua 5:12; Hebrews 9:4)

Marduk (MAR-dook) was a false god of the Babylonians. (Jeremiah 50:2)

Mark, sometimes called John Mark, was a cousin to Barnabas. Mark traveled with Paul and Barnabas on part of their first missionary journey. He also wrote the Gospel of Mark. Christians met in the home of Mark's mother, Mary, to pray for Peter to be freed from prison. (Acts 12:12, 25; 13:5, 13; 15:36-41; Colossians 4:10; 2 Timothy 4:11)

Martha (MAR-thuh) was the sister of Mary and Lazarus. They lived in the village of Bethany, which is very near Jerusalem. Jesus often stayed in their home when he was in that area. Martha and her brother and sister loved Jesus very much. (Luke 10:38-41; John 11:1-39; 12:12)

martyr (MAR-ter) is a Greek word that means "witness." Being a witness means telling what you know about something. Later, martyr came to mean a person who was killed for being a witness. Stephen was the first Christian martyr. He was killed because he told people that Jesus is the Son of God. It is believed that all the apostles, except one, were martyrs for being witnesses about Jesus. (Acts 7:54-60; 12:2; 22:20; Revelation 2:13)

Mary is the name of several women in the New Testament:

Mary, the mother of Jesus, was a Jewish woman whom God chose to give birth to his only Son. This was a great honor and blessing from God. She married a man named Joseph. Mary stood at the foot of the cross when Jesus was killed. (Matthew 1:18-25; Luke 1:27-45; John 19:25-27)

Mary Magdalene was from the town of Magdala. She was a follower of Jesus. She watched the men put Jesus' body in the tomb. She was the first person to see Jesus after he came back to life. (Matthew 27:56, 61; Mark 15:40, 47; 16:1, 9; John 20:1-18)

Mary of Bethany was the sister of Martha and Lazarus. She was a dear friend of Jesus. Mary sat at Jesus' feet and listened to him teach. One time she poured some expensive perfume on his feet and dried them with her hair. (Luke 10:39-42)

maskil (MAS-kil) is probably a description of the kind of song that some of the Psalms were. It appears with 13 of the Psalms. (Psalms 32; 42; 44; 45)

Matthew (MATH-you), also called Levi, was a tax collector. He was one of Jesus' 12 apostles. He wrote the Gospel of Matthew. (Matthew 9:9-10; 10:3)

medium (MEED-ee-um) means "go-between." This is a person who tries to help living people talk to the spirits of dead people. (Leviticus 19:31; Deuteronomy 18:11; 1 Samuel 28:3-9; 2 Kings 23:24; Isaiah 8:19-20)

Meeting Tent is often called the Tabernacle or Holy Tent. This was the special tent where the Israelites worshiped God. It was used from the time they left Egypt until Solomon built the Temple in Jerusalem. This tent was kept in the middle of their camp to remind them that God was always with them. (Exodus 25-27; 39:32-40:36; Numbers 8; 2 Chronicles 1:3-13; 5:5)

Melchizedek (mel-KIZ-ih-dek) means "king of righteousness." He was a priest and king who worshiped God in the time of Abraham. Jesus is now the Christian's king and high priest. In this way, Jesus is a priest and a king like Melchizedek. (Genesis 14:17-24; Hebrews 5:4-10; 7:1-17)

mercy (MUR-see) is kindness and forgiveness. God had mercy on us. He sent his only Son, Jesus, to die on the cross for our sins. We, too, are taught to have mercy on other people. God says he will be as merciful to us as we are to others. (Genesis 43:14; 2 Samuel 24:14; Matthew 5:7; Romans 11:32; James 2:13; 5:11; 1 Peter 2:10)

mercy seat See "lid on the Holy Box."

Messiah (muh-SYE-uh) is a Hebrew word for "anointed one" or "one chosen by God." The Greek word for Messiah is "Christ." Christians believe that Jesus is the Messiah or Christ. (John 1:41; 4:25)

miktam (MIK-tam) is probably a description of what kind of song some of the Psalms were. It may mean that it is a sad song or a song about danger. (Psalms 16; 56-60)

mildew (MIL-doo) is a growth that appears on things that have been damp for a long time. (Leviticus 13:47-59; 14:33-54)

minister (MIN-i-ster) means "servant." It also means one who lives serving God and others. Christians are taught to minister to each other and to non-Christians. (Romans 15:16)

miracle (MEER-ih-k'l) is a Latin word that means "wonderful thing." It is a great event that can be done only by God's help. Miracles are special signs to show God's power. In the Old Testament God used miracles to rescue his people. Jesus did miracles to prove that he was God's Son. The Bible tells us of many miracles. The sick were healed, the blind were given sight, the crippled were able to walk and people could speak languages they had never studied. Sometimes people were even brought back to life after they had died. The best miracle was Jesus' coming back to life after he was killed on the cross. (Nehemiah 9:17; Psalm 77:11, 14; Matthew 28:5-7; Luke 23:8; John 2:1-11; 3:2; 20:30-31; Acts 4:16-22; 8:13)

Molech (MO-lek) was a false god of the Canaanite people. Those who worshiped Molech often sacrificed their own children to him by burning them on altars. (Leviticus 18:21; 20:1-5; 2 Kings 23:10; Jeremiah 32:35)

mortar (MORE-tar) It can be a stone bowl where grain is ground into flour by pounding. Manna was ground this way. (See Numbers 11:8; Proverbs 27:22.)

Mortar is also the sticky material that holds bricks together. It was often made of mud or clay. (Genesis 11:3; Exodus 1:14; Isaiah 41:25)

Moses (MO-zez) in Hebrew means "saved from the water." Moses led God's people out of the land of Egypt where they had been slaves for 400 years. Moses wrote the first five books of the Old Testament. On Mount Sinai God gave to Moses the law for the Israelite people. It is called "the law of Moses." (Exodus 2-40; Numbers 1-26; Deuteronomy 27-34; John 1:17, 45; 3:14; Hebrews 11:23-24; Revelation 15:3)

Most Holy Place was the inner and most special room in the Meeting Tent and the Temple. The Box of the Agreement was kept here. Only the high priest could come into this room, and he could enter only once a year. This was when he sprinkled blood on the lid of the Holy Box to remind the people that their sins needed to be forgiven. (Exodus 26:33, 34; Leviticus 16:2-20; 1 Kings 6:16-35; Hebrews 9:3-25)

Mount of Olives is a hill covered with olive trees near Jerusalem. The garden of Gethsemane is on one side of the Mount of Olives. Jesus was praying there when the Roman soldiers came to arrest him. Some of the same olive trees that were in the garden when Jesus was on earth may still be there today. (2 Samuel 15:30; Luke 22:39-52; Acts 1:12)

Mount Zion (ZI-on) at first meant one of the hills on which Jerusalem was built. Later Zion became another name for the whole city of Jerusalem. In the New Testament, Zion is also used as a name for heaven. (Psalms 48:2, 11; 74:2; 78:68; Obadiah 17; Hebrews 12:22)

myrrh (MUR) was a sweet-smelling liquid taken from certain trees and shrubs. It was used as a perfume and as a pain reliever. It was one of the gifts the wise men gave Jesus when he was born. (Genesis 37:25; 43:11; Proverbs 7:17; Matthew 2:11; Mark 15:23; John 19:39)

N

nard was an expensive perfume. It cost so much because it had to be imported from India. (Song of Solomon 4:13; Mark 14:3; John 12:3)

Nazarene (NAZ-uh-reen) is a person from the town of Nazareth. Jesus grew up in Nazareth and was called a Nazarene. Sometimes Christians also were called Nazarenes, since they followed Jesus. (Matthew 2:23; Acts 24:5)

Nazirite (NAZ-e-rite) was a Jewish person who made a special promise to God. He was to serve God by following special rules. Samson and Samuel were Nazirites. (Numbers 6:1-21; Judges 13:7; 16:17)

Nebo (NEE-boh) **1.**-The name of a Babylonian god. He was thought to be the god of writing and the son of Bel. (See Isaiah 46:1.) **2.**-Nebo was also the name of the mountain where Moses died, as well as a town nearby. (Numbers 32:3; Deuteronomy 34:1; Isaiah 15:2)

Nehemiah (nee-uh-MY-uh) was a servant of King Artaxerxes I of Persia. He got permission to take a group of Jewish people back to Jerusalem to rebuild its walls. Nehemiah was such a good leader that they finished the job even though they had many difficulties. (Nehemiah 1-12)

Nephilim (NEF-eh-lim) were a group of people who were famous for being large and strong. The ten spies who were afraid to enter Canaan had seen the Nephilim who lived there. (Genesis 6:4; Numbers 13:33)

New Moon was a Jewish feast held on the first day of the month. It was celebrated with animal sacrifices and the blowing of trumpets. It was a way for the Israelites to dedicate the month to the Lord. (Numbers 10:10; 28:14; 1 Samuel 20:5, 24; Psalm 81:3; Ezekiel 46:3-6; Colossians 2:16)

Noah (NO-uh) and his family were the only people of their time who served God. So God told them about the great flood that was coming. They built a large boat (often called an ark) about 450 feet long. Noah's family and every kind of animal were saved to start the world all over again. (Genesis 6-9; 1 Peter 3:20)

P

parable (PARE-uh-b'l) is a story that teaches a lesson by comparing two things. Jesus often used parables to teach the people. Some examples of parables can be found in Mark 12:1-12, Luke 10:29-37 and Luke 15:1-31.

Passover Feast (PASS-o-ver FEEST) was an important holy day for the Jewish people in the spring of each year. They ate a special meal on this day to remind them that God had freed them from being slaves in Egypt. Jesus was killed at Passover time. (Exodus 12:27; Numbers 9; Joshua 5:10; Matthew 26:2, 17-19)

Paul is the Roman name for "Saul." Saul was Jewish, born in the city of Tarsus. He studied under Gamaliel, a famous teacher of God's law. At first, Paul tried to destroy Christ's church by putting Christians in jail and killing them. But Jesus appeared to him and changed his life completely. He was then called Paul. And he became an apostle and a great servant of God. He traveled to many countries, teaching about Jesus. Paul wrote many of the books of the New Testament as letters to Christians in different cities, such as Romans, Colossians and Corinthians. (Acts 7:58-60; 9:1-31; Philippians 3:5-7)

Pentecost (PEN-tee-cost) means "fifty." Pentecost was a Jewish feast day celebrating the summer harvest. It took place 50 days after the Passover Feast. The apostles began telling the Good News on Pentecost after Jesus died. (Acts 2; 20:16; 1 Corinthians 16:8)

persecute (PUR-seh-cute) means to hurt people. Christians in the New Testament times were often persecuted. Saul persecuted Christians by dragging them from their homes, putting them in jail and killing them. (Matthew 5:11, 12; Acts 8:1-4; Galatians 6:12; 1 Peter 3:13-15)

Peter (PEE-ter) was a fisherman. He and his brother, Andrew, were the first two apostles Jesus chose. He was first named Simon, but Jesus changed his name to Cephas, which means "rock" in Aramaic. In Greek the name is Peter. Peter, James and John were Jesus' closest friends. Peter was the first to tell the Good News of Jesus to the non-Jewish people. Later in his life Peter wrote the New Testament books of 1 and 2 Peter. He probably died as a martyr for Christ. (Matthew 14:25-33; 16:13-18; Mark 14:27-39; Luke 22:54-62; John 20:1-6; Acts 3:1-26; 10:1-48)

pharaoh (FAY-row) was the title given to the kings of Egypt. The word first meant "great house," meaning the palace where the king lived. Later it became the title of the king who lived in the great house. Pharaoh is also called "king of Egypt." (Genesis 40-47; Exodus 1-14; 2 Kings 23:29)

Pharisees (FARE-uh-seez) means "the separate people." They were a Jewish religious group who followed the religious laws and customs very strictly. Jesus often spoke against the Pharisees for their religious teachings and traditions. Many of the Pharisees did not like Jesus because he did not follow all of their rules. (Matthew 5:20; 23:23-36; Mark 7:1-13; Luke 18:9-14)

Philip (FIL-ip) was the name of several men in the New Testament:

Philip, the apostle, was from the city of Bethsaida and was a friend of Peter and Andrew. He brought Nathanael to Jesus. (Matthew 10:2-3; John 1:43-48; 12:21; 14:8-9)

Philip, the evangelist, was a Greek-speaking Jewish Christian. He was one of the seven men chosen to serve in the church in Jerusalem. Later, he preached the Good News in many places. (Acts 6:1-6; 8:5-40; 21:8-9)

Philip, the tetrarch (ruler), was the son of Herod I and Cleopatra. He built the city of Caesarea Philippi. (Luke 3:1)

Philistines (FIL-ih-steens) were Israel's enemies for many years. They had five strong cities near the Mediterranean Sea: Ashdod, Ashkelon, Ekron, Gath and Gaza. They worshiped several false gods. They were finally defeated by the Egyptians. (Judges 15-16; 1 Samuel 4:1-10; 6-7; 17-18; 1 Chronicles 18:1)

plumb line (PLUM LINE) is a string with a rock or other weight on one end. People used it to see if a wall was straight. The plumb line was sometimes used to mean that God was checking to see if his people were living right. This is just as they checked to see if a wall was built right. (2 Kings 21:13; Amos 7:7-8)

pomegranate (PAHM-gran-it) is a red fruit about the size of an apple. It has many seeds. Each seed has a pocket of sweet juice around it. (Exodus 28:33; 39:24; Numbers 13:23; Deuteronomy 8:8; 1 Samuel 14:2)

Pontius Pilate (PON-shus PIE-lut) means "armed with a spear." Pilate was the Roman governor of Judea from A.D. 26 to 36. The Jewish leaders who wanted Jesus killed brought him to Pilate. He did not find Jesus guilty of any crime. But Pilate allowed Jesus to be crucified because he was afraid of the people. (Luke 13:1; 23:1-52; Acts 3:13; 4:27; 1 Timothy 6:13)

Preparation Day (prep-a-RAY-shun DAY) was the day before the Sabbath day. On that day the Jews prepared or got everything ready for the Sabbath. (Luke 23:54; John 19:14, 31)

Priest (PREEST) in the Old Testament was a servant of God who worked in the Meeting Tent or Temple. Priests helped the people offer their gifts and sacrifices to God. Jesus is the Christian's high priest. He brings man and God together. Because of this all Christians are now priests. (Leviticus 21-22; Hebrews 7:26-28; 1 Peter 2:5, 9; Revelation 1:5, 6) See "high Priest"

Priscilla (prih-SIL-uh) See "Aquila."

prophecy (PRAH-feh-see) means "message." It is God speaking through chosen people called prophets. The Old Testament has many prophecies about the Savior who was to come into the world. Jesus was the answer to these prophecies. (Ezekiel 12:26-28; 2 Peter 1:20-21; Revelation 22:18-19) See "prophet."

prophesy (PRAH-fes-sy) is to speak a prophecy. See "prophecy."

prophet (PRAH-fet) means "messenger" or one who speaks for someone else. With God's help, a prophet was able to tell the people God's message correctly. Sometimes prophets told what would happen in the future. A woman who spoke God's message was called a prophetess (2 Kings 22:14; Luke 2:36). Several books of the Old Testament were written by prophets, including Jeremiah, Amos, Jonah and Micah. (2 Kings 6:12-16; 17:12-13; Matthew 2:5-6; Luke 16:29-31; 24:25-27; Romans 1:2; 1 Corinthians 12:28-29; 1 Peter 1:10-12)

prophetess See "prophet."

prostitute (PRAH-sti-toot) is a person who sells his or her body for sexual relations with someone to whom he or she is not married. This is a sin. In the Old Testament God's people often worshiped other gods. God said this was acting like a prostitute. (Genesis 38:15; Exodus 34:15-16; Proverbs 23:27; Jeremiah 3:1-6; Hosea 3:3; 1 Corinthians 6:15)

proverbs (PRAH-verbs) are wise sayings. They are usually short so they can be easily remembered. The Old Testament book of Proverbs contains many wise sayings. They tell how to live a good and happy life. (book of Proverbs)

psalm (SAHM) means "song." The book of Psalms is like a songbook. The Jews sang many of these psalms, particularly at special times. There are many musical directions in the Psalms, such as the tune or the instruments to be used. (book of Psalms)

Q

Queen Goddess is another name for Ishtar, a goddess of the Babylonians. During Jeremiah's time some of the Israelites worshiped her. (Jeremiah 7:18; 44:17-25)

R

Rahab (RAY-hab) was the name of a make-believe dragon. In a well-known story, Rahab looked strong but was defeated. Egypt was sometimes called Rahab to show that it would be defeated as Rahab was. (See Job 9:13; 26:12; Psalms 87:4; 89:10; Isaiah 30:7; 51:9.)

Rahab was also the name of a woman in Jericho. She hid the Israelite spies and helped them escape. (Joshua 2:1-3; 6:17-25; Matthew 1:5; Hebrews 11:31; James 2:25)

Rapha (RAY-fa) was a leader of a group of people in Canaan. They may have been giants. The descendants of Rapha are called Rephaites. (Genesis 14:5; Deuteronomy 2:11; 2 Samuel 21:16-22)

Red Sea is sometimes called the Sea of Reeds. It is a large body of water between Africa and Arabia. At the northern end it has two parts, one on each side of the Sinai Peninsula. God used a miracle to divide these waters on the northern end on the west side. Then the Israelites could walk across on dry land and escape from Egypt. (Exodus 13:17-15:22; Joshua 2:10; 4:23; Psalm 106:7-22)

repent (ree-PENT) means being sorry for doing something wrong and not continuing to do that wrong thing. To repent is to "change your heart and life." (2 Chronicles 32:26; Matthew 3:2; 4:17; Mark 1:15; Luke 15:7, 10; Acts 2:38; 3:19)

Raphaites See "Rapha."

resurrection (REZ-uh-REK-shun) is a dead person's coming back to life. In the New Testament several people came back to life with God's help. Some of them were Lazarus (John 11:38-45), Tabitha (Acts 9:36-42), the widow's son in the town of Nain (Luke 7:11-17), and Eutychus (Acts 20:8-12). Jesus, the Son of God, came back to life after being dead three days. This was the most important resurrection. *His resurrection from* death means we can be saved and live in heaven forever. (Matthew 28:1-10; 1 Corinthians 15; 1 Peter 3:21, 22)

revelation (rev-uh-LAY-shun) means to show plainly something that has been hidden. The last book in the New Testament is called the Revelation to John. God showed the apostle John what to write to Christians to give them hope and faith even though they were being persecuted. (2 Corinthians 12:1; Revelation 1:1-3)

Rock is often used as a name for God. A large rock is strong and a good place to hide. God is strong and protects us from our enemies. (Genesis 49:24; Deuteronomy 32:4, 15, 18, 30; 2 Samuel 22:32, 47; Psalm 18:2, 31, 46)

S

Sabbath (SAB-uth) means "rest." It was the seventh day of the Jewish week, their day of worship to God. The Jewish people were not allowed to work on this day. Some Jewish leaders became angry with Jesus because he healed people on the Sabbath. They thought this was breaking the Old Testament law of the Sabbath. (Exodus 16:23-30; 20:8-11; Matthew 12:9-14; Luke 6:1-11; Acts 18:4; Colossians 2:16-17)

Sadducees (SAD-you-seez) were a Jewish religious group. They were rich and important men. They believed that only the first five books of the Old Testament were true. They did not believe in angels or life after death (resurrection). The Sadducees lost their power and importance after Jerusalem was destroyed by the Romans about the year A.D. 70. (Matthew 22:23-33; Acts 4:1-2; 5:17-18; 23:6-9)

safety, city of is sometimes called City of Refuge. In Bible times, someone who had accidentally killed another person could go to a city of safety for protection. As long as the

person was in a city of safety, the dead person's relative could not punish him. There were six cities of safety. (Numbers 35:6-34; Joshua 20)

saffron (SAF-ron) is a purple flower. Parts of it are used as a spice. (Song of Solomon 4:14)

saint is another word for Christian. God has set Christians apart to serve him. They live to please God and be like him—pure and holy. (Acts 9:13, 32, 41; 26:10; Romans 1:7; 1 Corinthians 1:2; Ephesians 1:1)

Samaritan (suh-MEHR-ih-t'n) was a person from the area of Samaria in Palestine. Samaria was between Galilee and Judea. These people were only part Jewish, so the Jewish people did not accept them. They even hated the Samaritans. But Jesus showed love and concern for the Samaritans. One story that Jesus told is known as the story of "the good Samaritan." (Luke 10:30-37; John 4:1-42)

Samuel (SAM-you-el) was the last judge in Israel. God used him to choose both Saul and David as kings. (1 Samuel 1-3; 7-16)

Sanhedrin (san-HEE-drin) See "council."

Satan (SAY-t'n) in Hebrew means "enemy." It is a name for the devil, the enemy of God and man. (1 Chronicles 21:1; Job 1:6-9; Matthew 4:10; Luke 10:18-19; Acts 5:3; 26:18)

Saul (SAWL) In the Old Testament Saul the son of Kish was the first king of Israel. (See 1 Samuel 9-31.) Saul in the New Testament was a man whose name was changed to Paul. See "Paul."

savior (SAVE-yor) is someone who saves people from danger. The name Jesus means "savior." Jesus is the Savior of the people of this world. His life, death and resurrection made it possible for people to be saved from death and punishment for their sins. (Luke 2:11; John 4:42; Ephesians 5:23; Philippians 3:20; Titus 1:4; 1 John 4:14)

scepter (SEP-tur) is a wand or a rod that the king holds. It is a sign of his power. Some are long and thin. Others are short and flat like a paddle. Some of them are highly decorated with gold. (Esther 4:11; 5:2; 8:4; Psalm 2:9)

scribe is a Hebrew word that means to write, to count and to put in order. In New Testament times scribes were men who wrote copies of the Scriptures. They were very careful when they copied the words of God. To be sure they had not made a mistake in copying, they would count the number of letters on each line they wrote. Scribes were educated, and some of them served as secretaries, royal assistants and teachers. (Nehemiah 8:1; Jeremiah 36:26; Matthew 7:29; 15:1-9, 23:1-36; Luke 22:2)

Scriptures (SCRIP-churs) means "writings." They are the special writings of God's word for man. When the word Scriptures is used in the New Testament, it usually means the Old Testament. Later, it came to mean the whole Bible. (Daniel 9:2; Luke 24:27, 32, 45; Acts 8:32-35; 17:2, 11; 2 Timothy 3:16; 2 Peter 1:20; 3:16) See "Bible."

scroll is a long roll of paper used for writing. In Bible times books were written on scrolls. These scrolls were rolled up from each end to the middle. They were made of papyrus (a plant), or parchment (an animal skin). Some scrolls were as long as 35 feet. (Numbers 5:23; Isaiah 8:1; Jeremiah 36; Luke 4:17-20; 2 Timothy 4:13; Revelation 5:1-5)

Sea of Galilee See "Galilee, Lake."

seal was a tool with a design or picture carved on it. Kings pressed this seal into wax that would be placed on important papers to close them. It was like a person's signature. If the seal was broken, it showed that someone else had looked at the papers. A seal also showed who owned something. Sometimes these seals were worn as rings. (1 Kings 21:8; Esther 8:8; 2 Corinthians 1:22) See "signet ring."

seer was another name for prophet. (1 Samuel 9:9) See "prophet."

Selah (SEE-lah) is probably a musical direction and is used in the Psalms. It may mean to pause. The word was not intended to be spoken when reading the Psalm. (Psalms 3; 4; 9; 24)

sheminith (SHEM-e-nith) means "on the eighth." It is probably a musical word in the Psalms that means an octave. It may mean to use an instrument with eight strings. (1 Chronicles 15:21; Psalms 6; 12)

shepherd (SHEP-'rd) is a person who cares for and protects sheep. A shepherd loves his sheep and gives them food and water. He guides them to a quiet place to rest. He protects the sheep from wolves and other wild animals. A good shepherd will even die trying to protect his sheep. Jesus is called the Good Shepherd because he loves and cares for his followers who are often called sheep. Jesus was willing to die for his followers to save them. (Psalm 23; Mark 6:34; John 10:1-30; 1 Peter 2:25; 5:4)

shiggaion/shigionoth (shi-GY-on/shi-gi-O-noth) could be musical words meaning a sad song. (Psalm 7; Habakkuk 3:1)

signet ring (SIG-net ring) was a ring worn by a king or other important person. It had his seal on it. He would stamp things with this ring to show that he owned them. The stamp was like a signature. (Genesis 41:42; Esther 3:10; 8:2-10; Daniel 6:17) See "seal."

Silas (SY-lus) is sometimes called Silvanus. He was a teacher in the church in Jerusalem who often traveled with Paul. He became one of Paul's most trusted helpers. He may have written down some of Peter's and Paul's letters for them. (Acts 15:22, 30-17:16; 18:5; 1 Thessalonians 1:1; 1 Peter 5:12)

Simeon (SIM-ee-un) Simeon is a name that means "God has heard." He was one of the 12 sons of Israel. (See Genesis 29:33; 35:23.)

Another Simeon was a godly man who lived in Jerusalem. When he saw the baby Jesus in the Temple, he knew that this child would save his people from their sins. He held the baby Jesus in his arms and said a prayer of thanks to God. (Luke 2:25-35)

Simon (SY-mun), sometimes called Simeon, is a name that means "God has heard." The apostle Peter was first named Simon.

Simon of Cyrene carried the cross of Jesus to the hill of Calvary. (Matthew 27:32)

Simon, the magician, tried to buy the power of the Holy Spirit to do miracles. (Acts 8:9-24)

Simon, the Zealot, was one of the 12 apostles. (Matthew 10:4)

Simon, the brother of Jesus (Matthew 13:55)

sin is a word, thought or act against the law of God. Sin is doing something God said not to do, or it could be not doing something he said to do. Jesus came to save us from being punished for our sins. (Psalm 32:2; Romans 3:23; 5:12; 1 Corinthians 15:3; Galatians 1:4; Hebrews 4:15, 16; 1 John 1:8-10; 2:1, 2)

Solomon (SOL-o-mon) was a son of David. He took his father's place as king. He was famous for his wisdom and for building the Temple in Jerusalem. (1 Kings 1-11; 2 Chronicles 1-11)

Solomon's Porch (SOL-o-mon's PORCH) was a covered courtyard on the east side of the Temple. People gathered here to sell animals and exchange money. Others met to discuss the Law of Moses. (1 Kings 7:6; John 10:23; Acts 3:11; 5:12)

Son of David was a name the Jewish people used for the Christ who was to save the world. This was because the Savior was to come from the family of King David. Jesus was the "Son of David." (Matthew 9:27; 20:30; 21:9)

Son of Man was a name Jesus called himself. It showed that he was God's Son, but he was also a man. This title for Jesus comes from "one who looked like a human being" in Daniel 7:13-14. There Daniel prophesies about Jesus. (Matthew 24:30; 26:64;

Mark 13:26; 14:62; Luke 21:27; 22:69)

sorcery (SOR-sir-ee) means trying to put magical spells on people or harming them by some kind of magic. The Bible warns against doing this. (Leviticus 19:26; Deuteronomy 18:14; 2 Kings 17:17)

soul (SOLE) is what makes a person alive. Sometimes the Bible writers used words like heart and soul to mean a person's whole being or the person himself. (Deuteronomy 4:29; Psalm 108:1; Matthew 10:28)

Spirit See "Holy Spirit."

spirit (SPIH-rit) is the part of man that was made to be like God because God is spirit. The New Testament also talks about evil spirits. (Isaiah 26:9; John 4:23, 24; James 2:24-26) See "demons," "Holy Spirit" and "soul."

Stephen (STEE-ven) was one of the seven men chosen to serve the church in Jerusalem. The New Testament says he was a man who had much faith. He was able to do miracles. Stephen was the first martyr for Christ. He was killed by people throwing stones at him because he taught that Jesus was the Son of God. (Acts 6:5-15; 7:54-60; 22:20)

synagogue (SIN-uh-gog) is a Greek word that means "a meeting." By the first century, the Jewish people met in synagogues to read and study the Scriptures. The building was also used as a court of religious law and as a school. Both Jesus and Paul often went to the Jewish synagogues to teach and discuss the Scriptures. (Matthew 4:23; Luke 4:16-17; Acts 15:21; 17:1, 10)

Syria (SEER-ee-uh) is a Hebrew word that means "plain." In New Testament times it was the area north of Galilee and east of the Mediterranean Sea. Damascus was its capital city. In Old Testament times, this country was called Aram. (1 Kings 11:25; 2 Kings 5:1; Matthew 4:24; 15:23)

T

tabernacle (TAB-er-NAK-'l)   See "Meeting Tent."

tambourine (tam-buh-REEN) is a musical instrument that is beaten to keep rhythm. (Exodus 15:20; 1 Samuel 18:6; Psalm 81:2)

tax collector was a Jew hired by the Romans to collect taxes. Most people did not like tax collectors because they worked for the Romans and often cheated people. The apostle Matthew was a tax collector before he became an apostle. Zacchaeus was also a tax collector. (Matthew 9:10, 11; 10:3; Luke 5:27; 19:1-8)

temple (TEM-p'l) is a building where people worship their gods. God told the Jewish people to worship him at the Temple in Jerusalem. This Temple had been built by King Solomon. It stood for almost 400 years. The Babylonians destroyed it when they conquered Judea. Zerubbabel rebuilt the Temple 70 years later. It stood for more than 500 years. Herod started to remodel it in Jesus' time. The remodeling went on for 70 years and was never finished. The Romans destroyed the Temple in a war with the Jewish people. (See 2 Chronicles 2-7; Ezra 3:10-12; Mark 11:15-17; Acts 7:47; 19:27.)

The New Testament also speaks of a Christian's body as a temple. That is because God's Spirit lives in the Christian. (See Acts 7:48; 19:27; 1 Corinthians 6:19.)

temptation (temp-TAY-shun) is the devil's trying to get us to do something wrong. God has promised to help us when we are tempted, so we can choose to do the right thing. (Matthew 4:1-11; 1 Corinthians 10:13; Hebrews 2:18; 4:15, 16; James 1:12-14)

Tent See "Meeting Tent."

testament (TES-tuh-ment) See "agreement."

Thaddaeus (THAD-ee-us) was one of the 12 apostles. Little else is known about him. (Matthew 10:3; Mark 3:18)

Thomas (TOM-us), or Didymus, is a name that means "twin." He was one of Jesus' 12 apostles. His courage and love for Jesus are shown in John 11:16. Sometimes people call him "doubting Thomas." The other apostles told him Jesus had been raised from death. But Thomas did not believe it until he saw Jesus himself. (John 14:5-7; 20:24-29; 21:2)

threshing floor was a place where farmers separated grain from chaff. This was done by beating the stalks on the hard ground. Then they would throw it in the air and let the wind blow the chaff away. (Genesis 50:10; Judges 6:11; 2 Samuel 24:16-24) See "chaff."

Thummim (THUM-im) The Urim and Thummim were something attached to the holy vest of the high priest. They may have been gems. They were used in some way to find out what God wanted the Israelites to do. (Exodus 28:30; Leviticus 8:8; Deuteronomy 33:8)

Tiberius Caesar (tie-BEER-ee-u SEE-zur) was the Roman emperor during the last half of Jesus' life. He ruled from A.D. 14 to 37. The city of Tiberias was named for him. (Luke 3:1)

Timothy (TIM-oh-thee) means "one who honors God." Timothy was a close friend and helper of the apostle Paul. He was the son of a Greek father and Jewish Christian mother. His mother Eunice and his grandmother Lois taught him the Scriptures. Paul wrote two letters, called 1 and 2 Timothy, to him. (Acts 16:1-3; 17:13-16; 1 Corinthians 4:17; 1 Thessalonians 3:1-6; 2 Timothy 1:2-5)

tithe (TIETH) means "tenth." In the Old Testament the Jewish people were told to give one-tenth of what they earned to God. (Leviticus 27:30-32; Malachi 3:8; Luke 11:42; 18:12)

Titus (TIE-tus) was a trusted friend and helper of the apostle Paul. He often traveled with or for Paul. Paul wrote the book of Titus to him while Titus was on the island of Crete. (2 Corinthians 2:13; 7:6-7, 13-15; 8:6, 16, 23; Titus 1:4-5)

tomb (TOOM) is a place where a dead person's body is buried. Some tombs were underground. More often, in biblical times they were dug out of the side of a huge rock or mountain. A large stone was then rolled in front of the tomb to seal it. (Genesis 50:5; Luke 23:53-55; 24:1, 2; John 20;1-9; 11:38-41)

transfiguration (tranz-fig-you-RAY-shun) means "to change." Jesus was transfigured in front of Peter, James and John. Jesus had taken them up on a mountain with him. There his face and clothes began to shine brightly. God spoke to the apostles. He said that Jesus is his Son and that they should obey only him. (Matthew 17:1-9)

tribe was all the descendants of a certain person. The 12 tribes of Israel were the descendants of the 12 sons of Jacob, who was later named Israel. (Genesis 49:28; Joshua 3:12; 7:14)

U

uncircumcised See "circumcision."

unclean is used to describe the state of a person, animal or action that was not pleasing to God. In the Old Testament God said certain animals were unclean. They were not to be eaten. If a person disobeyed this (or some other rule about being clean), that person was called unclean. He could not serve God until he was made clean again. (Genesis 7:2; Leviticus 11-15; Romans 14:14) See "clean."

unleavened bread (un-LEV-'nd bread) is bread made without yeast. This kind of bread is like a flat, thin cracker because it does not rise when it is baked. God told the Jews to use unleavened bread for the Passover Feast. (Exodus 12:20; Matthew 26:17-29; Mark 14:12-25)

Unleavened Bread, Day of was the first day of the Feast of Unleavened Bread or Passover. (Luke 22:7)

Urim (YOUR-im) See "Thummim."

V

vest, holy is often called the "ephod." This was a special type of clothing for e priests in the Old Testament. The holy vest for the high priest had gold and gems on it. The Urim and Thummim were attached to the holy vest. (Exodus 25; 28; 39) See "Thummim."

virgin (VUR-jin) is a woman or girl who has not had sexual relations. (Genesis 24:16; Deuteronomy 22:15-28; Isaiah 7:14; Matthew 1:23; Luke 1:34)

vision (VIZ-zhun) is like a dream. A vision may come to a person when he is awake or asleep. God used visions to tell people what he wanted them to do, to teach them something or to let them know something that was going to happen. Peter had a vision of a sheet filled with animals. (Genesis 15:1; Daniel 2:19; Acts 9:10-12; 10:3-19; 11:5; 16:9-10; 18:9)

W

winepress was a pit where grapes were mashed to get the juice out. People stepped on the grapes. The juice ran out into another container. The winepress is sometimes used to describe how God will punish people. When they sinned terribly, God would allow enemy armies to defeat them as if they were grapes crushed in a winepress. (Deuteronomy 15:14; Judges 6:11; Lamentations 1:15)

wise men, or "magi," was a name for men who studied the stars. Some wise men followed a star from the East and brought gifts to Jesus when he was born. (Matthew 2:1-12)

witchcraft means using the power of the devil to do magic. (Deuteronomy 18:10; 2 Chronicles 33:6; Galatians 5:20)

witness (WIT-ness) is someone who tells what he has seen or what he knows. The apostles were witnesses for Christ because they told people that Jesus is the Son of God. (Acts 1:8, 22; 2:32; 22:14, 15)

woman, slave is also called a concubine. She was a woman who may have been captured by a man during a war. Or he may have bought her as a slave. She was like a second-class wife whose main purpose was to have children for him. (Genesis 36:12; 2 Chronicles 11:21)

word in the Bible often means God's message to us in the Scriptures. (1 Peter 1:24, 25; 1 John 2:14) Jesus is called the "Word" because he shows us what God is like. (John 1:1-5, 14)

Y

yoke is a wooden frame that fits on the necks of animals to hold them together while working. Two oxen were often yoked together to pull a farmer's plow. The word yoke is also used to mean the work a person is to do. (Deuteronomy 21:3; 2 Chronicles 10:4-11; Matthew 11:29)

Z

Zealots (ZEL-ots) were a group of Jewish men who were also called "Enthusiasts." They hated the Romans for controlling their home country and planned to force them out. Simon, the apostle, was a Zealot. (Luke 6:15; Acts 1:13)

Zion (ZY-on) was a hill inside the city of Jerusalem. Later, the name Zion, or Sion, was used to mean all of Jerusalem. In the New Testament, Mount Zion is sometimes even used as a name for heaven. (Hebrews 12:22; Revelation 14:1)

For further information about
Adventures in Odyssey contact:

Focus on the Family
8605 Explorer Drive
Colorado Springs, Colorado
80920

or

Word Publishing
1501 LBJ Freeway
Suite 650
Dallas, Texas
75234

Editorial consultation and development provided by
Livingstone Corporation.

*Art direction, design, typesetting, digital
color and production services provided by*
Koechel Peterson and Associates, Inc.

Illustration services provided by
Marietta Mason Illustration.

Illustrations by
Paul Fricke

Digital Colorization by
Koechel Peterson and Associates, Inc.